TENNESSEE WILLIAMS

TENNESSEE WILLIAMS

PLAYS 1957–1980

Edited by
Mel Gussow
Kenneth Holditch

THE LIBRARY OF AMERICA

Published in the United States by Library of America.
Visit our website at www.loa.org.

Published by arrangement with New Directions Publishing Corporation, New York, Publisher of the plays of Tennessee Williams, and The University of the South, copyright proprietor of the works of Tennessee Williams. For copyrights, see page 990.

This paper exceeds the requirements of ANSI/NISO Z39.48–1992 (Permanence of Paper).

Distributed to the trade in the United States
by Penguin Random House Inc.
and in Canada by Penguin Random House Canada Ltd.

Library of Congress Catalog Number: 00–030190
For cataloging information, see end of Notes.
ISBN 978–1–883011–87–1
ISBN 1–883011–87–6

Seventh Printing
The Library of America—120

Manufactured in the United States of America

Tennessee Williams: Plays 1957–1980
is kept in print in honor of

DARLENE MARCOS SHILEY

by a grant from

The Shiley Foundation

to the Guardians of American Letters Fund,
established by Library of America
to ensure that every volume in the series
will be permanently available.

Contents

ORPHEUS DESCENDING

For Marion Black Vaccaro

THE PAST, THE PRESENT AND THE PERHAPS

ONE icy bright winter morning in the last week of 1940, my brave representative, Audrey Wood, and I were crossing the Common in Boston, from an undistinguished hotel on one side to the grandeur of the Ritz-Carlton on the other. We had just read the morning notices of *Battle of Angels*, which had opened at the Wilbur the evening before. As we crossed the Common there was a series of loud reports like gunfire from the street that we were approaching, and one of us said, "My God, they're shooting at us!"

We were still laughing, a bit hysterically, as we entered the Ritz-Carlton suite in which the big brass of the Theatre Guild and director Margaret Webster were waiting for us with that special air of gentle gravity that hangs over the demise of a play so much like the atmosphere that hangs over a home from which a living soul has been snatched by the Reaper.

Not present was little Miriam Hopkins, who was understandably shattered and cloistered after the events of the evening before, in which a simulated on-stage fire had erupted clouds of smoke so realistically over both stage and auditorium that a lot of Theatre Guild first-nighters had fled choking from the Wilbur before the choking star took her bows, which were about the quickest and most distracted that I have seen in a theatre.

It was not that morning that I was informed that the show must close. That morning I was only told that the play must be cut to the bone. I came with a rewrite of the final scene and I remember saying, heroically, "I will crawl on my belly through brimstone if you will substitute this!" The response was gently evasive. It was a few mornings later that I received the *coup de grace*, the announcement that the play would close at the completion of its run in Boston. On that occasion I made an equally dramatic statement, on a note of anguish. "You don't seem to see that I put my heart into this play!"

It was Miss Webster who answered with a remark I have never forgotten and yet never heeded. She said, "You must not wear your heart on your sleeve for daws to peck at!"

Someone else said, "At least you are not out of pocket." I don't think I had any answer for that one, any more than I had anything in my pocket to be out of.

Well, in the end, when the Boston run was finished, I was given a check for $200 and told to get off somewhere and rewrite the play. I squandered half of this subsidy on the first of four operations performed on a cataracted left eye, and the other half took me to Key West for the rewrite. It was a long rewrite. In fact, it is still going on, though the two hundred bucks are long gone.

Why have I stuck so stubbornly to this play? For seventeen years, in fact? Well, nothing is more precious to anybody than the emotional record of his youth, and you will find the trail of my sleeve-worn heart in this completed play that I now call *Orpheus Descending*. On its surface it was and still is the tale of a wild-spirited boy who wanders into a conventional community of the South and creates the commotion of a fox in a chicken coop.

But beneath that now familiar surface it is a play about unanswered questions that haunt the hearts of people and the difference between continuing to ask them, a difference represented by the four major protagonists of the play, and the acceptance of prescribed answers that are not answers at all, but expedient adaptations or surrender to a state of quandary.

Battle was actually my fifth long play, but the first to be given a professional production. Two of the others, *Candles to the Sun* and *Fugitive Kind*, were produced by a brilliant, but semiprofessional group called The Mummers of St. Louis. A third one, called *Spring Storm*, was written for the late Prof. E. C. Mabie's seminar in playwriting at the University of Iowa, and I read it aloud, appropriately in the spring.

When I had finished reading, the good professor's eyes had a glassy look as though he had drifted into a state of trance. There was a long and all but unendurable silence. Everyone seemed more or less embarrassed. At last the professor pushed back his chair, thus dismissing the seminar, and remarked casually and kindly, "Well, we all have to paint our nudes!" And this is the only reference that I can remember anyone making to the play. That is, in the playwriting class, but I do remember that the late Lemuel Ayers, who was a graduate student at

Iowa that year, read it and gave me sufficient praise for its dialogue and atmosphere to reverse my decision to give up the theatre in favor of my other occupation of waiting on tables, or more precisely, handing out trays in the cafeteria of the State Hospital.

Then there was Chicago for a while and a desperate effort to get on the W.P.A. Writers' Project, which didn't succeed, for my work lacked "social content" or "protest" and I couldn't prove that my family was destitute and I still had, in those days, a touch of refinement in my social behavior which made me seem frivolous and decadent to the conscientiously rough-hewn pillars of the Chicago Project.

And so I drifted back to St. Louis, again, and wrote my fourth long play which was the best of the lot. It was called *Not About Nightingales* and it concerned prison life, and I have never written anything since then that could compete with it in violence and horror, for it was based on something that actually occurred along about that time, the literal roasting-alive of a group of intransigent convicts sent for correction to a hot room called "The Klondike."

I submitted it to The Mummers of St. Louis and they were eager to perform it but they had come to the end of their economic tether and had to disband at this point.

Then there was New Orleans and another effort, while waiting on tables in a restaurant where meals cost only two-bits, to get on a Writers' Project or the Theatre Project, again unsuccessful.

And then there was a wild and wonderful trip to California with a young clarinet player. We ran out of gas in El Paso, also out of cash, and it seemed for days that we would never go farther, but my grandmother was an "easy touch" and I got a letter with a $10 bill stitched neatly to one of the pages, and we continued westward.

In the Los Angeles area, in the summer of 1939, I worked for a while at Clark's Bootery in Culver City, within sight of the M-G-M studio and I lived on a pigeon ranch, and I rode between the two, a distance of ten miles, on a secondhand bicycle that I bought for $5.

Then a most wonderful thing happened. While in New Orleans I had heard about a play contest being conducted by the Group Theatre of New York. I submitted all four of the long plays I have mentioned that preceded *Battle of Angels*, plus a group of one-acts called *American Blues*. One fine day I received, when I returned to the ranch on my bike, a telegram saying that I had won a special award of $100 for the one-acts, and it was signed by Harold Clurman, Molly Day Thacher, who is the present Mrs. Elia Kazan, and that fine writer, Irwin Shaw, the judges of the contest.

I retired from Clark's Bootery and from picking squabs at the pigeon ranch. And the clarinet player and I hopped on our bicycles and rode all the way down to Tiajuana and back as far as Laguna Beach, where we obtained, rent free, a small cabin on a small ranch in return for taking care of the poultry.

We lived all that summer on the $100 from the Group Theatre and I think it was the happiest summer of my life. All the days were pure gold, the nights were starry, and I looked so young, or carefree, that they would sometimes refuse to sell me a drink because I did not appear to have reached 21. But toward the end of the summer, maybe only because it was the end of the summer as well as the end of the $100, the clarinet player became very moody and disappeared without warning into the San Bernardino Mountains to commune with his soul in solitude, and there was nothing left in the cabin in the canyon but a bag of dried peas.

I lived on stolen eggs and avocados and dried peas for a week, and also on a faint hope stirred by a letter from a lady in New York whose name was Audrey Wood, who had taken hold of all those plays that I had submitted to the Group Theatre contest, and told me that it might be possible to get me one of the Rockefeller Fellowships, or grants, of $1,000 which were being passed out to gifted young writers at that time. And I began to write *Battle of Angels*, a lyrical play about memories and the loneliness of them. Although my beloved grandmother was living on the pension of a retired minister (I believe it was only $85 a month in those days), and her meager earnings as a piano instructor, she once again stitched some bills to a page of a letter, and I took a bus to St. Louis. *Battle of Angels* was finished late that fall and sent to Miss Wood.

One day the phone rang and, in a terrified tone, my mother

told me that it was long distance, for me. The voice was Audrey Wood's. Mother waited, shakily, in the doorway. When I hung up I said, quietly, "Rockefeller has given me a $1,000 grant and they want me to come to New York." For the first time since I had known her, my mother burst into tears. "I am so happy," she said. It was all she could say.

And so you see it is a very old play that *Orpheus Descending* has come out of, but a play is never an old one until you quit working on it and I have never quit working on this one, not even now. It never went into the trunk, it always stayed on the work bench, and I am not presenting it now because I have run out of ideas or material for completely new work. I am offering it this season because I honestly believe that it is finally finished. About 75 per cent of it is new writing, but what is much more important, I believe that I have now finally managed to say in it what I wanted to say, and I feel that it now has in it a sort of emotional bridge between those early years described in this article and my present state of existence as a playwright.

So much for the past and present. The future is called "perhaps," which is the only possible thing to call the future. And the important thing is not to allow that to scare you.

Tennessee Williams

ACT ONE

PROLOGUE

SCENE: *The set represents in nonrealistic fashion a general dry-goods store and part of a connecting "confectionery" in a small Southern town. The ceiling is high and the upper walls are dark, as if streaked with moisture and cobwebbed. A great dusty window upstage offers a view of disturbing emptiness that fades into late dusk. The action of the play occurs during a rainy season, late winter and early spring, and sometimes the window turns opaque but glistening silver with sheets of rain. "TORRANCE MERCANTILE STORE" is lettered on the window in gilt of old-fashioned design.*

Merchandise is represented very sparsely and it is not realistic. Bolts of pepperel and percale stand upright on large spools, the black skeleton of a dressmaker's dummy stands meaninglessly against a thin white column, and there is a motionless ceiling fan with strips of flypaper hanging from it.

There are stairs that lead to a landing and disappear above it, and on the landing there is a sinister-looking artificial palm tree in a greenish-brown jardiniere.

But the confectionery, which is seen partly through a wide arched door, is shadowy and poetic as some inner dimension of the play.

Another, much smaller, playing area is a tiny bedroom alcove which is usually masked by an Oriental drapery which is worn dim but bears the formal design of a gold tree with scarlet fruit and fantastic birds.

At the rise of the curtain two youngish middle-aged women, Dolly and Beulah, are laying out a buffet supper on a pair of pink-and-gray-veined marble-topped tables with gracefully curved black-iron legs, brought into the main area from the confectionery. They are wives of small planters and tastelessly overdressed in a somewhat bizarre fashion.

A train whistles in the distance and dogs bark in response from various points and distances. The women pause in their occupations at the tables and rush to the archway, crying out harshly.

DOLLY: Pee Wee!

BEULAH: Dawg!

DOLLY: Cannonball is comin' into th' depot!

BEULAH: You all git down to th' depot an' meet that train!

(*Their husbands slouch through, heavy, red-faced men in clothes that are too tight for them or too loose, and mud-stained boots.*)

PEE WEE: I fed that one-armed bandit a hunnerd nickels an' it coughed up five.

DOG: Must have hed indigestion.

PEE WEE: I'm gonna speak to Jabe about them slots. (*They go out and a motor starts and pauses.*)

DOLLY: I guess Jabe Torrance has got more to worry about than the slot machines and pinball games in that confectionery.

BEULAH: You're not tellin' a lie. I wint to see Dr. Johnny about Dawg's condition. Dawg's got sugar in his urine again, an' as I was leavin' I ast him what was the facks about Jabe Torrance's operation in Mimphis. Well—

DOLLY: What'd he tell you, Beulah?

BEULAH: He said the worse thing a doctor ever can say.

DOLLY: What's that, Beulah?

BEULAH: Nothin' a-tall, not a spoken word did he utter! He just looked at me with those big dark eyes of his and shook his haid like this!

DOLLY (*with doleful satisfaction*): I guess he signed Jabe Torrance's death warrant with just that single silent motion of his haid.

BEULAH: That's exactly what passed through my mind. I understand that they cut him open— (*Pauses to taste something on the table.*)

DOLLY:—An' sewed him right back up!—that's what I heard . . .

BEULAH: I didn't know these olives had seeds in them!

DOLLY: You thought they was stuffed?

BEULAH: Uh-huh. Where's the Temple sisters?

DOLLY: Where d'you think?

BEULAH: Snoopin' aroun' upstairs. If Lady catches 'em at it she'll give those two old maids a touch of her tongue! She's not a Dago for nothin''!

DOLLY: Ha, ha, no! You spoke a true word, honey . . . (*Looks out door as car passes*) Well, I was surprised when I wint up myself!

BEULAH: You wint up you'self?

DOLLY: I did and so did you because I seen you, Beulah.

BEULAH: I never said that I didn't. Curiosity is a human instinct.

DOLLY: They got two separate bedrooms which are not even connectin'. At opposite ends of the hall, and everything is so dingy an' dark up there. Y'know what it seemed like to me? A county jail! I swear to goodness it didn't seem to me like a place for white people to live in!—that's the truth . . .

BEULAH (*darkly*): Well, I wasn't surprised. Jabe Torrance bought that woman.

DOLLY: Bought her?

BEULAH: Yais, he bought her, when she was a girl of eighteen! He bought her and bought her cheap because she'd been thrown over and her heart was broken by that— (*Jerks head toward a passing car, then continues:*) —that Cutrere boy. . . . *Oh*, what a— *Mmmm*, what a—*beautiful* thing he was. . . . And those two met like you struck two stones together and made a fire!—yes—fire . . .

DOLLY: What?

BEULAH: *Fire!*—Ha . . . (*Strikes another match and lights one of the candelabra. Mandolin begins to fade in. The following monologue should be treated frankly as exposition, spoken to audience, almost directly, with a force that commands attention. Dolly does not remain in the playing area, and after the first few sentences, there is no longer any pretense of a duologue.*)

—Well, that was a long time ago, before you and Dog moved into Two River County. Although you must have heard of it. Lady's father was a Wop from the old country and when he first come here with a mandolin and a monkey that wore a little green velvet suit, ha ha.

—He picked up dimes and quarters in the saloons—this was before Prohibition. . . .

—People just called him The Wop, nobody knew his name, just called him 'The Wop,' ha ha ha. . . .

DOLLY (*Off, vaguely*): Anh-hannnh. . . .

(*Beulah switches in the chair and fixes the audience with her eyes, leaning slightly forward to compel their attention. Her voice is rich with nostalgia, and at a sign of restlessness, she rises and comes straight out to the proscenium, like a pitchman. This monologue should set the nonrealistic key for the whole production.*)

BEULAH: Oh, my law, well, that was Lady's daddy! Then come prohibition an' first thing ennyone knew, The Wop had took to bootleggin' like a duck to water! He picked up a piece of land cheap, it was on the no'th shore of Moon Lake which used to be the old channel of the river and people thought some day the river might swing back that way, and so he got it cheap. . . . (*Moves her chair up closer to proscenium.*) He planted an orchard on it; he covered the whole no'th shore of the lake with grapevines and fruit trees, and then he built little arbors, little white wooden arbors with tables and benches to drink in and carry on in, ha ha! And in the spring and the summer, young couples would come out there, like me and Pee Wee, we used to go out there, an' court up a storm, ha ha, just court up a—storm! Ha ha!—The county was dry in those days, I don't mean dry like now, why, now you just walk a couple of feet off the highway and whistle three times like a jaybird and a nigger pops out of a bush with a bottle of corn!

DOLLY: Ain't that the truth? Ha ha.

BEULAH: But in those days the county was dry for true, I mean bone dry except for The Wop's wine garden. So we'd go out to The Wop's an' drink that Dago red wine an' cut up an' carry on an' raise such cane in those arbors! Why, I remember one Sunday old Doctor Tooker, Methodist minister then, he bust a blood vessel denouncing The Wop in the pulpit!

DOLLY: Lawd have mercy!

BEULAH: Yes, ma'am!—Each of those white wooden arbors had a lamp in it, and one by one, here and there, the lamps would go out as the couples begun to make love . . .

DOLLY: *Oh*—oh . . .

BEULAH: What strange noises you could hear if you listened, calls, cries, whispers, moans—giggles. . . . (*Her voice is soft with recollection*)—And then, one by one, the lamps would be lighted again, and The Wop and his daughter would sing and play Dago songs. . . . (*Bring up mandolin: voice under* 'Dicitencello Vuoi.') But sometimes The Wop would look around for his daughter, and all of a sudden Lady wouldn't be there!

DOLLY: Where would she be?

BEULAH: She'd be with David Cutrere.

DOLLY: Awwwwww—ha ha . . .

BEULAH:—Carol Cutrere's big brother, Lady and him would disappear in the orchard and old Papa Romano, The Wop, would holler, "Lady, Lady!"—no answer whatsoever, no matter how long he called and no matter how loud. . . .

DOLLY: Well, I guess it's hard to shout back, "Here I am, Papa," when where you are is in the arms of your lover!

BEULAH: Well, that spring, no, it was late that summer . . . (*Dolly retires again from the playing area.*)—Papa Romano made a bad mistake. He sold liquor to niggers. The Mystic Crew took action.—They rode out there, one night, with gallons of coal oil—it was a real dry summer—and set that place on fire!—They burned the whole thing up, vines, arbors, fruit trees.—Pee Wee and me, we stood on the dance pavilion across the lake and watched that fire spring up. Inside of tin minutes the whole nawth shore of the lake was a mass of flames, a regular sea of flames, and all the way over the lake we could hear Lady's papa shouting, "Fire, fire, fire!"—as if it was necessary to let people know, and the whole sky lit up with it, as red as Guinea red wine!—Ha ha ha ha. . . . Not a fire engine, not a single engine pulled out of a station that night in Two River County!—The poor old fellow, The Wop, he took a blanket and run up into the orchard to fight the fire singlehanded—*and* burned *alive*. . . . Uh-huh! *burned alive*. . . .

(*Mandolin stops short. Dolly has returned to the table to have her coffee.*)

You know what I sometimes wonder?

DOLLY: No. What do you wonder?

BEULAH: I wonder sometimes if Lady has any suspicion that her husband, Jabe Torrance, was the leader of the Mystic

Crew the night they burned up her father in his wine garden on Moon Lake?

DOLLY: Beulah Binnings, you make my blood run cold with such a thought! How could she live in marriage twenty years with a man if she knew he'd burned her father up in his wine garden?

(*Dog bays in distance.*)

BEULAH: She could live with him in hate. People can live together in hate for a long time, Dolly. Notice their passion for money. I've always noticed when couples don't love each other they develop a passion for money. Haven't you seen that happen? Of course you have. Now there's not many couples that stay devoted forever. Why, some git so they just barely tolerate each other's existence. Isn't that true?

DOLLY: You couldn't of spoken a truer word if you read it out loud from the Bible!

BEULAH: Barely tolerate each other's existence, and some don't even do that. You know, Dolly Hamma, I don't think half as many married min have committed suicide in this county as the Coroner says has done so!

DOLLY (*with voluptuous appreciation of Beulah's wit*): You think it's their wives that give them the deep six, honey?

BEULAH: I don't think so, I know so. Why there's couples that loathe and despise the sight, smell and sound of each other before that round-trip honeymoon ticket is punched at both ends, Dolly.

DOLLY: I hate to admit it but I can't deny it.

BEULAH: But they hang on together.

DOLLY: Yes, they hang on together.

BEULAH: Year after year after year, accumulating property and money, building up wealth and respect and position in the towns they live in and the counties and cities and the churches they go to, belonging to the clubs and so on and so forth and not a soul but them knowin' they have to go wash their hands after touching something the other one just put down! ha ha ha ha ha!—

DOLLY: Beulah, that's an evil laugh of yours, that laugh of yours is evil!

BEULAH (*louder*): Ha ha ha ha ha!—But you know it's the truth.

DOLLY: Yes, she's tellin' the truth! (*Nods to audience.*)

BEULAH: Then one of them—gits—*cincer* or has a—*stroke* or somethin'?—The other one—

DOLLY:—Hauls in the loot?

BEULAH: That's right, hauls in the loot! Oh, my, then you should see how him or her blossoms out. New house, new car, new clothes. Some of 'em even change to a different church!—If it's a widow, she goes with a younger man, and if it's a widower, he starts courtin' some chick, ha ha ha ha ha!

And so I said, I said to Lady this morning before she left for Mamphis to bring Jabe home, I said, "Lady, I don't suppose you're going to reopen the confectionery till Jabe is completely recovered from his operation." She said, "It can't wait for anything that might take that much time." Those are her exact words. It can't wait for anything that might take that much time. Too much is invested in it. It's going to be done over, redecorated, and opened on schedule the Saturday before Easter this spring!—Why?—Because—she knows Jabe is dying and she wants to clean up quick!

DOLLY: An awful thought. But a true one. Most awful thoughts are.

(*They are startled by sudden light laughter from the dim upstage area. The light changes on the stage to mark a division.*)

SCENE ONE

The women turn to see Carol Cutrere in the archway between the store and the confectionery. She is past thirty and, lacking prettiness, she has an odd, fugitive beauty which is stressed, almost to the point of fantasy, by a style of makeup with which a dancer named Valli has lately made such an impression in the bohemian centers of France and Italy, the face and lips powdered white and the eyes outlined and exaggerated with black pencil and the lids tinted blue. Her family name is the oldest and most distinguished in the country.

BEULAH: Somebody don't seem to know that the store is closed.

DOLLY: Beulah?

BEULAH: What?

DOLLY: Can you understand how anybody would deliberately make themselves look fantastic as that?

BEULAH: Some people have to show off, it's a passion with them, anything on earth to get attention.

DOLLY: I sure wouldn't care for that kind of attention. Not me. I wouldn't desire it. . . .

(*During these lines, just loud enough for her to hear them, Carol has crossed to the pay-phone and deposited a coin.*)

CAROL: I want Tulane 0370 in New Orleans. What? Oh. Hold on a minute.

(*Eva Temple is descending the stairs, slowly, as if awed by Carol's appearance. Carol rings open the cashbox and removes some coins; returns to deposit coins in phone.*)

BEULAH: She helped herself to money out of the cashbox.

(*Eva passes Carol like a timid child skirting a lion cage.*)

CAROL: Hello, Sister.

EVA: I'm Eva.

CAROL: Hello, Eva.

EVA: Hello . . . (*Then in a loud whisper to Beulah and Dolly:*) She took money out of the cashbox.

DOLLY: Oh, she can do as she pleases, she's a Cutrere!

BEULAH: Shoot . . .

EVA: What is she doin' barefooted?

BEULAH: The last time she was arrested on the highway, they say that she was naked under her coat.

CAROL (*to operator*): I'm waiting. (*Then to women:*)—I caught the heel of my slipper in that rotten boardwalk out there and it broke right off. (*Raises slippers in hand.*) They say if you break the heel of your slipper in the morning it means you'll meet the love of your life before dark. But it was already dark when I broke the heel of my slipper. Maybe that means I'll meet the love of my life before daybreak. (*The *quality of her voice is curiously clear and childlike. Sister Temple appears on stair landing bearing an old waffle iron.*)

SISTER: Wasn't that them?

EVA: No, it was Carol Cutrere!

CAROL (*at phone*): Just keep on ringing, please, he's probably drunk.

(*Sister crosses by her as Eva did.*)

Sometimes it takes quite a while to get through the living-room furniture. . . .

SISTER:—She a *sight*?

EVA: Uh-huh!

CAROL: Bertie?—Carol!—Hi, doll! Did you trip over something? I heard a crash. Well, I'm leaving right now, I'm already on the highway and everything's fixed, I've got my allowance back on condition that I remain forever away from Two River County! I had to blackmail them a little. I came to dinner with my eyes made up and my little black sequin jacket and Betsy Boo, my brother's wife, said, "Carol, you going out to a fancy dress ball?" I said, "Oh, no, I'm just going jooking tonight up and down the Dixie Highway between here and Memphis like I used to when I lived here." Why, honey, she flew so fast you couldn't see her passing and came back in with the ink still wet on the check! And this will be done once a month as long as I stay away from Two River County. . . . (*Laughs gaily.*)—How's Jackie? Bless his heart, give him a sweet kiss for me! Oh, honey, I'm driving straight through, not even stopping for pickups unless you need one! I'll meet you in the Starlite Lounge before it closes, or if I'm irresistibly delayed, I'll certainly join you for coffee at the Morning Call before the all-night places have closed for the day . . . —I—Bertie? Bertie? (*Laughs uncertainly and hangs up.*)—let's see, now. . . . (*Removes a revolver from her trench-coat pocket and crosses to fill it with cartridges back of counter.*)

EVA: What she looking for?

SISTER: Ask her.

EVA (*advancing*): What're you looking for, Carol?

CAROL: Cartridges for my revolver.

DOLLY: She don't have a license to carry a pistol.

BEULAH: She don't have a license to drive a car.

CAROL: When I stop for someone I want to be sure it's someone I want to stop for.

DOLLY: Sheriff Talbott ought to know about this when he gits back from the depot.

CAROL: Tell him, ladies. I've already given him notice that if he ever attempts to stop me again on the highway, I'll shoot it out with him. . . .

BEULAH: When anybody has trouble with the law—

(*Her sentence is interrupted by a panicky scream from Eva, immediately repeated by Sister. The Temple Sisters scramble upstairs to the landing. Dolly also cries out and turns, covering her face. A Negro Conjure Man has entered the store. His tattered garments are fantastically bedizened with many talismans and good-luck charms of shell and bone and feather. His blue-black skin is daubed with cryptic signs in white paint.*)

DOLLY: Git him out, git him out, he's going to mark my baby!

BEULAH: Oh, shoot, Dolly. . . .

(*Dolly has now fled after the Temple Sisters, to the landing of the stairs. The Conjure Man advances with a soft, rapid, toothless mumble of words that sound like wind in dry grass. He is holding out something in his shaking hand.*)

It's just that old crazy conjure man from Blue Mountain. He cain't mark your baby.

(*Phrase of primitive music or percussion as Negro moves into light. Beulah follows Dolly to landing.*)

CAROL (*very high and clear voice*): Come here, Uncle, and let me see what you've got there. Oh, it's a bone of some kind. No, I don't want to touch it, it isn't clean yet, there's still some flesh clinging to it.

(*Women make sounds of revulsion.*)

Yes, I know it's the breastbone of a bird but it's still tainted with corruption. Leave it a long time on a bare rock in the rain and the sun till every sign of corruption is burned and washed away from it, and then it will be a good charm, a white charm, but now it's a black charm, Uncle. So take it away and do what I told you with it. . . .

(*The Negro makes a ducking obeisance and shuffles slowly back to the door.*)

Hey, Uncle Pleasant, give us the Choctaw cry.

(*Negro stops in confectionery.*)

He's part Choctaw, he knows the Choctaw cry.

SISTER TEMPLE: Don't let him holler in *here*!

CAROL: Come on, Uncle Pleasant, *you* know it!

(*She takes off her coat and sits on the R. window sill. She starts the cry herself. The Negro throws back his head and completes it: a series of barking sounds that rise to a high sustained note of wild intensity. The women on the landing retreat further upstairs. Just then, as though the cry had brought him, Val enters the store. He is a young man, about 30, who has a kind of wild beauty about him that the cry would suggest. He does not wear Levi's or a T-shirt, he has on a pair of dark serge pants, glazed from long wear and not excessively tight-fitting. His remarkable garment is a snakeskin jacket, mottled white, black and gray. He carries a guitar which is covered with inscriptions.*)

CAROL (*looking at the young man*): Thanks, Uncle . . .

BEULAH: *Hey, old man, you! Choctaw! Conjure man! Nigguh! Will you go out-a this sto'? So we can come back down stairs?*

(*Carol hands Negro a dollar; he goes out right cackling. Val holds the door open for Vee Talbott, a heavy, vague woman in her forties. She does primitive oil paintings and carries one into the store, saying:*)

VEE: I got m'skirt caught in th' door of the Chevrolet an' I'm afraid I tore it.

(*The women descend into store: laconic greetings, interest focused on Val.*)

Is it dark in here or am I losin' my eyesight? I been painting all day, finished a picture in a ten-hour stretch, just stopped a few minutes fo' coffee and went back to it again while I had a clear vision. I think I got it this time. But I'm so exhausted I could drop in my tracks. There's nothing more exhausting than that kind of work on earth, it's not so much that it tires your body out, but it leaves you drained inside. Y'know what I mean? Inside? Like you was burned out by something? Well! Still!—You feel you've accomplished something when you're through with it, sometimes you feel—*elevated!* How are you, Dolly?

DOLLY: All right, Mrs. Talbott.

VEE: That's good. How are *you*, Beulah?

BEULAH: Oh, I'm all right, I reckon.

VEE: Still can't make out much. Who is that there? (*Indicates Carol's figure by the window. A significant silence greets this question. Vee, suddenly:*)

Oh! I thought her folks had got her out of the county . . .

(*Carol utters a very light, slightly rueful laugh, her eyes drifting back to Val as she moves back into confectionery.*)

Jabe and Lady back yet?

DOLLY: Pee Wee an' Dawg have gone to the depot to meet 'em.

VEE: Aw. Well, I'm just in time. I brought my new picture with me, the paint isn't dry on it yet. I thought that Lady might want to hang it up in Jabe's room while he's convalescin' from the operation, cause after a close shave with death, people like to be reminded of spiritual things. Huh? Yes! This is the Holy Ghost ascending. . . .

DOLLY (*looking at canvas*): You didn't put a head on it.

VEE: The head was a blaze of light, that's all I saw in my vision.

DOLLY: Who's the young man with yuh?

VEE: Aw, excuse me, I'm too worn out to have manners. This is Mr. Valentine Xavier, Mrs. Hamma and Mrs.— I'm sorry, Beulah. I never *can* get y' last *name*!

BEULAH: I fo'give you. My name is Beulah Binnings.

VAL: What shall I do with this here?

VEE: Oh, that bowl of sherbet. I thought that Jabe might need something light an' digestible so I brought a bowl of sherbet.

DOLLY: What flavor is it?

VEE: Pineapple.

DOLLY: Oh, goody, I love pineapple. Better put it in the icebox before it starts to melt.

BEULAH (*looking under napkin that covers bowl*): I'm afraid you're lockin' th' stable after the horse is gone.

DOLLY: Aw, is it melted already?

BEULAH: Reduced to juice.

VEE: Aw, shoot. Well, put it on ice anyhow, it might thicken up.

(*Women are still watching Val.*)

Where's the icebox?

BEULAH: In the confectionery.

VEE: I thought that Lady had closed the confectionery.

BEULAH: Yes, but the Frigidaire's still there.

(*Val goes out R. through confectionery.*)

VEE: Mr. Xavier is a stranger in our midst. His car broke down in that storm last night and I let him sleep in the lockup. He's lookin' for work and I thought I'd introduce him to Lady an' Jabe because if Jabe can't work they're going to need somebody to help out in th' store.

BEULAH: That's a good idea.

DOLLY: Uh-huh.

BEULAH: Well, come on in, you all, it don't look like they're comin' straight home from the depot anyhow.

DOLLY: Maybe that wasn't the Cannonball Express.

BEULAH: Or maybe they stopped off fo' Pee Wee to buy some liquor.

DOLLY: Yeah . . . at Ruby Lightfoot's.

(*They move past Carol and out of sight. Carol has risen. Now she crosses into the main store area, watching Val with the candid curiosity of one child observing another. He pays no attention but concentrates on his belt buckle which he is repairing with a pocketknife.*)

CAROL: What're you fixing?

VAL: Belt buckle.

CAROL: Boys like you are always fixing something. Could you fix my slipper?

VAL: What's wrong with your slipper?

CAROL: Why are you pretending not to remember me?

VAL: It's hard to remember someone you never met.

CAROL: Then why'd you look so startled when you saw me?

VAL: Did I?

CAROL: I thought for a moment you'd run back out the door.

VAL: The sight of a woman can make me walk in a hurry but I don't think it's ever made me run.—You're standing in my light.

CAROL (*moving aside slightly*): Oh, excuse me. Better?

VAL: Thanks. . . .

CAROL: Are you afraid I'll snitch?

VAL: Do what?

CAROL: Snitch? I wouldn't; I'm not a snitch. But I can prove that I know you if I have to. It was New Year's Eve in New Orleans.

VAL: I need a small pair of pliers. . . .

CAROL: You had on that jacket and a snake ring with a ruby eye.

VAL: I never had a snake ring with a ruby eye.

CAROL: A snake ring with an emerald eye?

VAL: I never had a snake ring with any kind of an eye. . . . (*Begins to whistle softly, his face averted.*)

CAROL (*smiling gently*): Then maybe it was a dragon ring with an emerald eye or a diamond or a ruby eye. You told us that it was a gift from a lady osteopath that you'd met somewhere in your travels and that any time you were broke you'd wire this lady osteopath collect, and no matter how far you were or how long it was since you'd seen her, she'd send you a money order for twenty-five dollars with the same sweet message each time. "I love you. When will you come back?" And to prove the story, not that it was difficult to believe it, you took the latest of these sweet messages from your wallet for us to see. . . . (*She throws back her head with soft laughter. He looks away still further and busies himself with the belt buckle.*)—We followed you through five places before we made contact with you and I was the one that made contact. I went up to the bar where you were standing and touched your jacket and said, "What stuff is this made of?" and when you said it was snakeskin, I said, "I wish you'd told me before I touched it." And you said something not nice. You said, "Maybe that will learn you to hold back your hands." I was drunk by that time which was after midnight. Do you remember what I said to you? I said, "What on earth can you do on this earth but catch at whatever comes near you, with both your hands, until your fingers are broken?" I'd never said that before, or even consciously thought it, but afterwards it seemed like the truest thing that my lips had ever spoken, what on earth can you do but catch at whatever comes near you with both your hands until your fingers are broken. . . . You gave me a quick, sober look. I think you nodded slightly, and then you picked up your guitar and began to sing. After singing you passed the kitty. Whenever paper money was dropped in the kitty you blew a whistle. My cousin Bertie and I dropped in five dollars, you blew the whistle five times and then sat down at our table for a drink, Schenley's with Seven Up. You showed us all those signatures on your guitar. . . . Any correction so far?

VAL: Why are you so anxious to prove I know you?

CAROL: Because I want to know you better and better! I'd like to go out jooking with you tonight.

VAL: What's jooking?

CAROL: Oh, don't you know what that is? That's where you get in a car and drink a little and drive a little and stop and dance a little to a juke box and then you drink a little more and drive a little more and stop and dance a little more to a juke box and then you stop dancing and you just drink and drive and then you stop driving and just drink, and then, finally, you stop drinking. . . .

VAL:—What do you do, then?

CAROL: That depends on the weather and who you're jooking with. If it's a clear night you spread a blanket among the memorial stones on Cypress Hill, which is the local bone orchard, but if it's not a fair night, and this one certainly isn't, why, usually then you go to the Idlewild cabins between here and Sunset on the Dixie Highway. . . .

VAL:—That's about what I figured. But I don't go that route. Heavy drinking and smoking the weed and shacking with strangers is okay for kids in their twenties but this is my thirtieth birthday and I'm all through with that route. (*Looks up with dark eyes.*) I'm not young any more.

CAROL: You're young at thirty—I hope so! I'm twenty-nine!

VAL: Naw, you're not young at thirty if you've been on a Goddam party since you were fifteen!

(*Picks up his guitar and sings and plays "Heavenly Grass." Carol has taken a pint of bourbon from her trench-coat pocket and she passes it to him.*)

CAROL: Thanks. That's lovely. Many happy returns of your birthday, Snakeskin.

(*She is very close to him. Vee enters and says sharply:*)

VEE: Mr. Xavier don't drink.

CAROL: Oh, ex-cuse *me*!

VEE: And if you behaved yourself better your father would not be paralyzed in bed!

(*Sound of car out front. Women come running with various cries. Lady enters, nodding to the women, and holding the door open for her husband and the men following him. She greets the women in almost toneless murmurs, as if too tired to speak. She could be any age between thirty-five and forty-five, in appearance, but her figure is youthful. Her face taut. She is a woman who met with emotional disaster in her girlhood; verges on hysteria under strain. Her voice is often shrill and her body tense. But when in repose, a girlish softness emerges again and she looks ten years younger.*)

LADY: Come in, Jabe. We've got a reception committee here to meet us. They've set up a buffet supper.

(*Jabe enters. A gaunt, wolfish man, gray and yellow. The women chatter idiotically.*)

BEULAH: Well, look who's here!

DOLLY: Well, *Jabe*!

BEULAH: I don't think he's been sick. I think he's been to Miami. Look at that wonderful color in his face!

DOLLY: I never seen him look better in my life!

BEULAH: Who does he think he's foolin'? Ha ha ha!—not *me*!

JABE: Whew, Jesus—I'm mighty—tired. . . .

(*An uncomfortable silence, everyone staring greedily at the dying man with his tense, wolfish smile and nervous cough.*)

PEE WEE: Well, Jabe, we been feedin' lots of nickels to those one-arm bandits in there.

DOG: An' that pinball machine is hotter'n a pistol.

PEE WEE: Ha ha.

(*Eva Temple appears on stairs and screams for her sister.*)

EVA: Sistuh! Sistuh! Sistuh! Cousin Jabe's here!

(*A loud clatter upstairs and shrieks.*)

JABE: Jesus. . . .

(*Eva rushing at him—stops short and bursts into tears.*)

LADY: Oh, cut that out, Eva Temple!—What were you doin' upstairs?

EVA: I can't help it, it's so good to see him, it's so wonderful to see our cousin again, oh, Jabe, *blessed*!

SISTER: Where's Jabe, where's precious Jabe? Where's our precious cousin?

EVA: Right here, Sister!

SISTER: Well, bless your old sweet life, and lookit the color he's got in his face, will you?

BEULAH: I just told him he looks like he's been to Miami and got a Florida suntan, haha ha!

(*The preceding speeches are very rapid, all overlapping.*)

JABE: I ain't been out in no sun an' if you all will excuse me I'm gonna do my celebratin' upstairs in bed because I'm kind of—worn out. (*Goes creakily to foot of steps while Eva and Sister sob into their handkerchiefs behind him.*)—I see they's been some changes made here. Uh-huh. Uh-huh. How come the shoe department's back here now? (*Instant hostility as if habitual between them.*)

LADY: We always had a problem with light in this store.

JABE: So you put the shoe department further away from the window? That's sensible. A very intelligent solution to the problem, Lady.

LADY: Jabe, you know I told you we got a fluorescent tube coming to put back here.

JABE: Uh-huh. Uh-huh. Well. Tomorrow I'll get me some niggers to help me move the shoe department back front.

LADY: You do whatever you want to, it's your store.

JABE: Uh-huh. Uh-huh. I'm glad you reminded me of it.

(*Lady turns sharply away. He starts up stairs. Pee Wee and Dog follow him up. The women huddle and whisper in the store. Lady sinks wearily into chair at table.*)

BEULAH: That man will never come down those stairs again!

DOLLY: Never in this world, honey.

BEULAH: He has th' death sweat on him! Did you notice that death sweat on him?

DOLLY: An' yellow as butter, just as yellow as—

(*Sister sobs.*)

EVA: Sister, Sister!

BEULAH (*crossing to Lady*): Lady, I don't suppose you feel much like talking about it right now but Dog and me are so worried.

DOLLY: Pee Wee and me are worried sick about it.

LADY:—About what?

BEULAH: Jabe's operation in Memphis. Was it successful?

DOLLY: Wasn't it successful?

(*Lady stares at them blindly. The women, except Carol, close avidly about her, tense with morbid interest.*)

SISTER: Was it too late for surgical interference?

EVA: Wasn't it successful?

(*A loud, measured knock begins on the floor above.*)

BEULAH: Somebody told us it had gone past the knife.

DOLLY: We do hope it ain't hopeless.

EVA: We hope and pray it ain't hopeless.

(*All their faces wear faint, unconscious smiles. Lady looks from face to face; then utters a slight, startled laugh and springs up from the table and crosses to the stairs.*)

LADY (*as if in flight*): Excuse me, I have to go up, Jabe's knocking for me. (*Lady goes upstairs. The women gaze after her.*)

CAROL (*suddenly and clearly, in the silence*): Speaking of knocks, I have a knock in my engine. It goes knock, knock, and I say who's there. I don't know whether I'm in communication with some dead ancestor or the motor's about to drop out and leave me stranded in the dead of night on the Dixie Highway. Do you have any knowledge of mechanics? I'm sure you do. Would you be sweet and take a short drive with me? So you could hear that knock?

VAL: I don't have time.

CAROL: What have you got to do?

VAL: I'm waiting to see about a job in this store.

CAROL: I'm offering you a job.

VAL: I want a job that pays.

CAROL: I expect to pay you.

(*Women whisper loudly in the background.*)

VAL: Maybe sometime tomorrow.

CAROL: I can't stay here overnight; I'm not allowed to stay overnight in this county.

(*Whispers rise. The word "corrupt" is distinguished.*)

(*Without turning, smiling very brightly:*) What are they saying about me? Can you hear what those women are saying about me?

VAL:—Play it cool. . . .

CAROL: I don't like playing it cool! What are they saying about me? That I'm corrupt?

VAL: If you don't want to be talked about, why do you make up like that, why do you—

CAROL: *To show off!*

VAL: What?

CAROL: *I'm an exhibitionist!* I want to be noticed, seen, heard, felt! I want them to know I'm alive! Don't you want them to know you're alive?

VAL: I want to live and I don't care if they know I'm alive or not.

CAROL: Then why do you play a guitar?

VAL: Why do you make a Goddam show of yourself?

CAROL: That's right, for the same reason.

VAL: We don't go the same route. . . . (*He keeps moving away from her; she continually follows him. Her speech is compulsive.*)

CAROL: I used to be what they call a Christ-bitten reformer. You know what that is?—A kind of benign exhibitionist. . . . I delivered stump speeches, wrote letters of protest about the gradual massacre of the colored majority in the county. I thought it was wrong for pellagra and slow starvation to cut them down when the cotton crop failed from army worm or boll weevil or too much rain in summer. I wanted to, tried to, put up free clinics, I squandered the money my mother left me on it. And when that Willie McGee thing came along—he was sent to the chair for having improper relations with a white whore— (*Her voice is like a passionate incantation.*) I made a fuss about it. I put on a potato sack and set out for the capitol on foot. This was in winter. I walked barefoot in this burlap sack to deliver a personal protest to the Governor of the State. Oh, I suppose it was partly exhibitionism on my part, but it wasn't completely exhibitionism; there was something else in it, too. You know how far I got? Six miles out of town—hooted, jeered at, even spit on!—every step of the way—and then arrested! Guess what for? Lewd vagrancy! Uh-huh, that was the charge, "lewd vagrancy," because they said that potato sack I had on was not a respectable garment. . . . Well, all that was a pretty long time ago, and now I'm not a reformer any more. I'm just a "lewd vagrant." And I'm showing the "S.O.B.S." how lewd a "lewd vagrant" can be if she puts her whole heart in it like I do mine! All right. I've told you my story, the story of an exhibitionist. Now I want you to do something for me. Take me out to Cypress Hill in my car. And we'll hear the dead people talk. They do talk there. They chatter together like birds on Cypress Hill, but all they say is one word and that one word is "live," they say "Live, live, live, live, live!" It's all they've learned, it's the only advice they can give.—Just live. . . . (*She opens the door.*) Simple!—a very simple instruction. . . .

(*Goes out. Women's voices rise from the steady, indistinct murmur, like hissing geese.*)

WOMEN'S VOICES:—No, not liquor! Dope!
—Something not normal all right!
—Her father and brother were warned by the Vigilantes to keep her out of this county.
—She's absolutely degraded!
—Yes, corrupt!
—Corrupt! (Etc., etc.)

(*As if repelled by their hissing voices, Val suddenly picks up his guitar and goes out of the store as—Vee Talbott appears on the landing and calls down to him.*)

VEE: Mr. Xavier! Where is Mr. Xavier?
BEULAH: Gone, honey.
DOLLY: You might as well face it, Vee. This is one candidate for salvation that you have lost to the opposition.
BEULAH: He's gone off to Cypress Hill with the Cutrere girl.
VEE (*descending*):—If some of you older women in Two River County would set a better example there'd be more decent young people!
BEULAH: What was that remark?
VEE: I mean that people who give drinkin' parties an' get so drunk they don't know which is their husband and which is somebody else's and people who serve on the altar guild and still play cards on Sundays—
BEULAH: Just stop right there! Now I've discovered the source of that dirty gossip!
VEE: I'm only repeating what I've been told by others. I never been to these parties!
BEULAH: No, and you never will! You're a public kill-joy, a professional hypocrite!
VEE: I try to build up characters! You and your drinkin' parties are only concerned with tearin' characters down! I'm goin' upstairs, I'm goin' back upstairs! (*Rushes upstairs.*)
BEULAH: Well, I'm glad I said what I said to that woman. I've got no earthly patience with that sort of hypocriticism. Dolly, let's put this perishable stuff in the Frigidaire and leave here. I've never been so thoroughly disgusted!

DOLLY: Oh, my Lawd. (*Pauses at stairs and shouts:*) *PEE WEE!* (*Goes off with the dishes.*)

SISTER: Both of those wimmen are as common as dirt.

EVA: Dolly's folks in Blue Mountain are nothin' at all but the poorest kind of white trash. Why, Lollie Tucker told me the old man sits on the porch with his shoes off drinkin' beer out of a bucket!—Let's take these flowers with us to put on the altar.

SISTER: Yes, we can give Jabe credit in the parish notes.

EVA: I'm going to take these olive-nut sandwiches, too. They'll come in handy for the Bishop Adjutant's tea.

(*Dolly and Beulah cross through.*)

DOLLY: We still have time to make the second show.

BEULAH (*shouting*): Dog!

DOLLY: Pee Wee! (*They rush out of store.*)

EVA: Sits on the porch with his shoes off?

SISTER: Drinkin' beer out of a bucket! (*They go out with umbrellas, etc. Men descend stairs.*)

SHERIFF TALBOTT: Well, it looks to me like Jabe will more than likely go under before the cotton comes up.

PEE WEE: He never looked good.

DOG: Naw, but now he looks worse.

(*They cross to door.*)

SHERIFF: Vee!

VEE (*from landing*): Hush that bawling. I had to speak to Lady about that boy and I couldn't speak to her in front of Jabe because he thinks he's gonna be able to go back to work himself.

SHERIFF: Well, move along, quit foolin'.

VEE: I think I ought to wait till that boy gits back.

SHERIFF: I'm sick of you making a goddam fool of yourself over every stray bastard that wanders into this county.

(*Car horn honks loudly. Vee follows her husband out. Sound of cars driving off. Dogs bay in distance as lights dim to indicate short passage of time.*)

SCENE TWO

A couple of hours later that night. Through the great window the landscape is faintly luminous under a scudding moonlit sky. Outside a girl's laughter, Carol's, rings out high and clear and is followed by the sound of a motor, rapidly going off.

Val enters the store before the car sound quite fades out and while a dog is still barking at it somewhere along the highway. He says "Christ" under his breath, goes to the buffet table and scrubs lipstick stain off his mouth and face with a paper napkin, picks up his guitar which he had left on a counter.

Footsteps descending: Lady appears on the landing in a flannel robe, shivering in the cold air; she snaps her fingers impatiently for the old dog, Bella, who comes limping down beside her. She doesn't see Val, seated on the shadowy counter, and she goes directly to the phone near the stairs. Her manner is desperate, her voice harsh and shrill.

LADY: Ge' me the drugstore, will you? I know the drugstore's closed, this is Mrs. Torrance, my store's closed, too, but I got a sick man here, just back from the hospital, yeah, yeah, an emergency, wake up Mr. Dubinsky, keep ringing till he answers, it's an emergency! (*Pause: she mutters under her breath:*) —*Porca la miseria!*—I wish I was dead, dead, dead. . . .

VAL (*quietly*): No, you don't, Lady.

(*She gasps, turning and seeing him, without leaving the phone, she rings the cashbox open and snatches out something.*)

LADY: What're you doin' here? You know this store is closed!

VAL: I seen a light was still on and the door was open so I come back to—

LADY: You see what I got in my hand? (*Raises revolver above level of counter.*)

VAL: You going to shoot me?

LADY: You better believe it if you don't get out of here, mister!

VAL: That's all right, Lady, I just come back to pick up my guitar.

LADY: To pick up your guitar?

(*He lifts it gravely.*)

—Huh. . . .

VAL: Miss Talbott brought me here. I was here when you got back from Memphis, don't you remember?

LADY:—Aw. Aw, yeah. . . . You been here all this time?

VAL: No. I went out and come back.

LADY (*into the phone*): I told you to keep ringing till he answers! Go on, keep ringing, keep ringing! (*Then to Val:*) You went out and come back?

VAL: Yeah.

LADY: What for?

VAL: You know that girl that was here?

LADY: Carol Cutrere?

VAL: She said she had car trouble and could I fix it.

LADY:—Did you fix it?

VAL: She didn't have no car trouble, that wasn't her trouble, oh, she had trouble, all right, but *that* wasn't it. . . .

LADY: What was her trouble?

VAL: She made a mistake about me.

LADY: What mistake?

VAL: She thought I had a sign "Male at Stud" hung on me.

LADY: She thought you—? (*Into phone suddenly:*) Oh, Mr. Dubinsky, I'm sorry to wake you up but I just brought my husband back from the Memphis hospital and I left my box of luminal tablets in the— I got to have some! I ain't slep' for three nights, I'm going to pieces, you hear me, I'm going to pieces, I ain't slept in three nights, I got to have some tonight. Now you look here, if you want to keep my trade, you send me over some tablets. Then bring them yourself, God damn it, excuse my French! Because I'm going to pieces right this minute! (*Hangs up violently.*) —*Mannage la miseria!*—Christ. . . . I'm shivering!—It's cold as a Goddam ice-plant in this store, I don't know why, it never seems to hold heat, the ceiling's too high or something, it don't hold heat at all.—Now what do you want? I got to go upstairs.

VAL: Here. Put this on you.

(*He removes his jacket and hands it to her. She doesn't take it at once, stares at him questioningly and then slowly takes the jacket in her hands and examines it, running her fingers curiously over the snakeskin.*)

LADY: What is this stuff this thing's made of? It looks like it was snakeskin.

VAL: Yeah, well, that's what it is.

LADY: What're you doing with a snakeskin jacket?

VAL: It's a sort of a trademark; people call me Snakeskin.

LADY: Who calls you Snakeskin?

VAL: Oh, in the bars, the sort of places I work in—but I've quit that. I'm through with that stuff now. . . .

LADY: You're a—entertainer?

VAL: I sing and play the guitar.

LADY:—Aw? (*She puts the jacket on as if to explore it.*) It feels warm all right.

VAL: It's warm from my body, I guess. . . .

LADY: You must be a warm-blooded boy. . . .

VAL: That's right. . . .

LADY: Well, what in God's name are you lookin' for around here?

VAL:—Work.

LADY: Boys like you don't work.

VAL: What d'you mean by boys like me?

LADY: Ones that play th' guitar and go around talkin' about how warm they are. . . .

VAL: That happens t' be the truth. My temperature's always a couple degrees above normal the same as a dog's, it's normal for me the same as it is for a dog, that's the truth. . . .

LADY:—Huh!

VAL: You don't believe me?

LADY: I have no reason to doubt you, but what about it?

VAL:—Why—nothing. . . .

(*Lady laughs softly and suddenly; Val smiles slowly and warmly.*)

LADY: You're a peculiar somebody all right, you sure are! How did you get around here?

VAL: I was driving through here last night and an axle broke on my car, that stopped me here, and I went to the county jail for a place to sleep out of the rain. Mizz Talbott took me in and give me a cot in the lockup and said if I hung around till you got back that you might give me a job in the store to help out since your husband was tooken sick.

LADY:—Uh-huh. Well—she was wrong about that. . . . If I took on help here it would have to be local help, I couldn't hire no stranger with a—snakeskin jacket and a guitar . . . and that runs a temperature as high as a dog's! (*Throws back her head in another soft, sudden laugh and starts to take off the jacket.*)

VAL: Keep it on.

LADY: No, I got to go up now and you had better be going . . .

VAL: I got nowhere to go.

LADY: Well, everyone's got a problem and that's yours.

VAL:—What nationality are you?

LADY: Why do you ask me that?

VAL: You seem to be like a foreigner.

LADY: I'm the daughter of a Wop bootlegger burned to death in his orchard!—Take your jacket. . . .

VAL: What was that you said about your father?

LADY: Why?

VAL:—A "Wop bootlegger"?

LADY:—They burned him to death in his orchard! What about it? The story's well known around here.

(*Jabe knocks on ceiling.*)

I got to go up, I'm being called for.

(*She turns out light over counter and at the same moment he begins to sing softly with his guitar: "Heavenly Grass." He suddenly stops short and says abruptly:*)

VAL: I do electric repairs.

(*Lady stares at him softly.*)

I can do all kinds of odd jobs. Lady, I'm thirty today and I'm through with the life that I've been leading. (*Pause. Dog bays in distance.*) I lived in corruption but I'm not corrupted. Here is why. (*Picks up his guitar.*) My life's companion! It washes me clean like water when anything unclean has touched me. . . . (*Plays softly, with a slow smile.*)

LADY: What's all that writing on it?
VAL: Autographs of musicians I run into here and there.
LADY: Can I see it?
VAL: Turn on that light above you.

(*She switches on green-shaded bulb over counter. Val holds the instrument tenderly between them as if it were a child; his voice is soft, intimate, tender.*)

See this name? Leadbelly?
LADY: Leadbelly?
VAL: Greatest man ever lived on the twelve-string guitar! Played it so good he broke the stone heart of a Texas governor with it and won himself a pardon out of jail. . . . And see this name Oliver? King Oliver? That name is immortal, Lady. Greatest man since Gabriel on a horn. . . .
LADY: What's this name?
VAL: Oh. That name? That name is also immortal. The name Bessie Smith is written in the stars!—Jim Crow killed her, John Barleycorn and Jim Crow killed Bessie Smith but that's another story. . . . See this name here? That's another immortal!
LADY: Fats Waller? Is his name written in the stars, too?
VAL: Yes, his name is written in the stars, too. . . .

(*Her voice is also intimate and soft: a spell of softness between them, their bodies almost touching, only divided by the guitar.*)

LADY: You had any sales experience?
VAL: All my life I been selling something to someone.
LADY: So's everybody. You got any character reference on you?
VAL: I have this—letter.

(*Removes a worn, folded letter from a wallet, dropping a lot of snapshots and cards of various kinds on the floor. He passes the letter to her gravely and crouches to collect the dropped articles while she peruses the character reference.*)

LADY (*reading slowly aloud*): "This boy worked for me three months in my auto repair shop and is a real hard worker and is good and honest but is a peculiar talker and that is the reason I got to let him go but would like to—(*Holds letter closer to light.*)—would like to—keep him. Yours truly."

(*Val stares at her gravely, blinking a little.*)

Huh!—Some reference!

VAL:—Is that what it says?

LADY: Didn't you know what it said?

VAL: No.—The man sealed the envelope on it.

LADY: Well, that's not the sort of character reference that will do you much good, boy.

VAL: Naw. I guess it ain't.

LADY:—However. . . .

VAL:—What?

LADY: What people say about you don't mean much. Can you read shoe sizes?

VAL: I guess so.

LADY: What does 75 David mean?

(*Val stares at her, shakes head slowly.*)

75 means seven and one half long and David mean "D" wide. You know how to make change?

VAL: Yeah, I could make change in a store.

LADY: Change for better or worse? Ha ha!—Well— (*Pause.*) Well—you see that other room there, through that arch there? That's the confectionery; it's closed now but it's going to be reopened in a short while and I'm going to compete for the night life in this county, the after-the-movies trade. I'm going to serve setups in there and I'm going to redecorate. I got it all planned. (*She is talking eagerly now, as if to herself.*) Artificial branches of fruit trees in flower on the walls and ceilings!—It's going to be like an orchard in the spring!—My father, he had an orchard on Moon Lake. He made a wine garden of it. We had fifteen little white arbors with tables in them and they were covered with—grapevines and—we sold Dago red wine an' bootleg whiskey and beer.—They burned it up! My father was burned up in it. . . .

(*Jabe knocks above more loudly and a hoarse voice shouts*

"Lady!" Figure appears at the door and calls: "Mrs. Torrance?")

Oh, that's the sandman with my sleeping tablets. (*Crosses to door.*) Thanks, Mr. Dubinsky, sorry I had to disturb you, sorry I—

(*Man mutters something and goes. She closes the door.*)

Well, go to hell, then, old bastard. . . . (*Returns with package.*) —You ever have trouble sleeping?

VAL: I can sleep or not sleep as long or short as I want to.

LADY: Is that right?

VAL: I can sleep on a concrete floor or go without sleeping, without even feeling sleepy, for forty-eight hours. And I can hold my breath three minutes without blacking out; I made ten dollars betting I could do it and I did it! And I can go a whole day without passing water.

LADY (*startled*): Is *that* a *fact*?

VAL (*very simply as if he'd made an ordinary remark*): That's a fact. I served time on a chain gang for vagrancy once and they tied me to a post all day and I stood there all day without passing water to show the sons of bitches that I could do it.

LADY:—I see what that auto repair man was talking about when he said this boy is a peculiar talker! Well—what else can you do? Tell me some more about your self-control!

VAL (*grinning*): Well, they say that a woman can burn a man down. But I can burn down a woman.

LADY: Which woman?

VAL: Any two-footed woman.

LADY (*throws back her head in sudden friendly laughter as he grins at her with the simple candor of a child*):—Well, there's lots of two-footed women round here that might be willin' to test the truth of that statement.

VAL: I'm saying I could. I'm not saying I would.

LADY: Don't worry, boy. I'm one two-footed woman that you don't have to convince of your perfect controls.

VAL: No, I'm done with all that.

LADY: What's the matter? Have they tired you out?

VAL: I'm not tired. I'm disgusted.

LADY: Aw, you're disgusted, huh?

VAL: I'm telling you, Lady, there's people bought and sold in this world like carcasses of hogs in butcher shops!

LADY: You ain't tellin' me nothin' I don't know.

VAL: You might think there's many and many kinds of people in this world but, Lady, there's just two kinds of people, the ones that are bought and the buyers! No!—there's one other kind . . .

LADY: What kind's that?

VAL: The kind that's never been branded.

LADY: You will be, man.

VAL: They got to catch me first.

LADY: Well, then, you better not settle down in this county.

VAL: You know they's a kind of bird that don't have legs so it can't light on nothing but has to stay all its life on its wings in the sky? That's true. I seen one once, it had died and fallen to earth and it was light-blue colored and its body was tiny as your little finger, that's the truth, it had a body as tiny as your little finger and so light on the palm of your hand it didn't weigh more than a feather, but its wings spread out this wide but they was transparent, the color of the sky and you could see through them. That's what they call protection coloring. Camouflage, they call it. You can't tell those birds from the sky and that's why the hawks don't catch them, don't see them up there in the high blue sky near the sun!

LADY: How about in gray weather?

VAL: They fly so high in gray weather the Goddam hawks would get dizzy. But those little birds, they don't have no legs at all and they live their whole lives on the wing, and they sleep on the wind, that's how they sleep at night, they just spread their wings and go to sleep on the wind like other birds fold their wings and go to sleep on a tree. . . . (*Music fades in.*) —They sleep on the wind and . . . (*His eyes grow soft and vague and he lifts his guitar and accompanies the very faint music.*)—never light on this earth but one time when they die!

LADY:—I'd like to be one of those birds.

VAL: So'd I like to be one of those birds; they's lots of people would like to be one of those birds and never be—corrupted!

LADY: If one of those birds ever dies and falls on the ground and you happen to find it, I wish you would show it to me because I think maybe you just imagine there is a bird of that kind in existence. Because I don't think nothing living has ever been that free, not even nearly. Show me one of them birds and I'll say, Yes, God's made one perfect creature!—I sure would give this mercantile store and every bit of stock in it to be that tiny bird the color of the sky . . . for one night to sleep on the wind and—float!—around under th'—stars . . .

(*Jabe knocks on floor. Lady's eyes return to Val.*)

—Because I sleep with a son of a bitch who bought me at a fire sale, and not in fifteen years have I had a single good dream, not one—oh!—*Shit* . . . I don't know why I'm—telling a stranger—this. . . . (*She rings the cashbox open.*) Take this dollar and go eat at the Al-Nite on the highway and come back here in the morning and I'll put you to work. I'll break you in clerking here and when the new confectionery opens, well, maybe I can use you in there.—That door locks when you close it!—But let's get one thing straight.

VAL: What thing?

LADY: I'm not interested in your perfect functions, in fact you don't interest me no more than the air that you stand in. If that's understood we'll have a good working relation, but otherwise trouble!—Of course I know you're crazy, but they's lots of crazier people than you are still running loose and some of them in high positions, too. Just remember. No monkey business with me. Now go. Go eat, you're hungry.

VAL: Mind if I leave this here? My life's companion? (*He means his guitar.*)

LADY: Leave it here if you want to.

VAL: Thanks, Lady.

LADY: Don't mention it.

(*He crosses toward the door as a dog barks with passionate clarity in the distance. He turns to smile back at her and says:*)

VAL: I don't know nothing about you except you're nice but you are just about the nicest person that I have ever run into! And I'm going to be steady and honest and hard-working to please you and any time you have any more trouble sleeping, I know how to fix that for you. A lady osteopath taught me how to make little adjustments in the neck and spine that give you sound, natural sleep. Well, g'night, now.

(*He goes out. Count five. Then she throws back her head and laughs as lightly and gaily as a young girl. Then she turns and wonderingly picks up and runs her hands tenderly over his guitar as the curtain falls.*)

ACT TWO

SCENE ONE

The store, afternoon, a few weeks later. The table and chair are back in the confectionery. Lady is hanging up the phone. Val is standing just outside the door. He turns and enters. Outside on the highway a mule team is laboring to pull a big truck back on the icy pavement. A Negro's voice shouts: "Hyyyyyyyyy-up."

VAL (*moving to R. window*): One a them big Diamond T trucks an' trailors gone off the highway last night and a six mule team is tryin' t' pull it back on. . . . (*He looks out window.*)

LADY (*coming from behind to R. of counter*): Mister, we just now gotten a big fat complaint about you from a woman that says if she wasn't a widow her husband would come in here and beat the tar out of you.

VAL (*taking a step toward her*): Yeah?—Is this a small pink-headed woman?

LADY: *Pin*-headed woman did you say?

VAL: Naw, I said, "Pink!"—A little pink-haired woman, in a checkered coat with pearl buttons this big on it.

LADY: I talked to her on the phone. She didn't go into such details about her appearance but she did say you got familiar. I said, "How? by his talk or behavior?" And she said, "Both!"—Now I was afraid of this when I warned you last week, "No monkey business here, boy!"

VAL: This little pink-headed woman bought a valentine from me and all I said is my *name* is Valentine to her. Few minutes later a small colored boy come in and delivered the valentine to me with something wrote on it an' I believe I still got it. . . . (*Finds and shows it to Lady who goes to him. Lady reads it, and tears it fiercely to pieces. He lights a cigarette.*)

LADY: Signed it with a lipstick kiss? You didn't show up for this date?

VAL: No, ma'am. That's why she complained. (*Throws match on floor.*)

LADY: Pick that match up off the floor.

VAL: Are you bucking for sergeant, or something?

(*He throws match out the door with elaborate care. Her eyes follow his back. Val returns lazily toward her.*)

LADY: Did you walk around in front of her that way?

VAL (*at counter*): What way?

LADY: Slew-foot, slew-foot!

(*He regards her closely with good-humored perplexity.*)

Did you stand in front of her like that? That close? In that, that—*position*?

VAL: What position?

LADY: Ev'rything you do is suggestive!

VAL: Suggestive of what?

LADY: Of what you said you was through with—somethin'—*Oh, shoot, you know what I mean.*—Why'd 'ya think I give you a plain, dark business suit to work in?

VAL (*sadly*): Un-hun. . . . (*Sighs and removes his blue jacket.*)

LADY: Now what're you takin' that off for?

VAL: I'm giving the suit back to you. I'll change my pants in the closet. (*Gives her the jacket and crosses into alcove.*)

LADY: Hey! I'm sorry! You hear me? I didn't sleep well last night. Hey! I said I'm sorry! You hear me? (*She enters alcove and returns immediately with Val's guitar and crosses to D.R. He follows.*)

VAL: Le' me have my guitar, Lady. You find too many faults with me and I tried to do good.

LADY: I told you I'm sorry. You want me to get down and lick the dust off your shoes?

VAL: Just give me back my guitar.

LADY: I ain't dissatisfied with you. I'm pleased with you, sincerely!

VAL: You sure don't show it.

LADY: My nerves are all shot to pieces. (*Extends hand to him.*) Shake.

VAL: You mean I ain't fired, so I don't have to quit?

(*They shake hands like two men. She hands him guitar—then silence falls between them.*)

LADY: You see, we don't know each other, we're, we're—just gettin'—acquainted.

VAL: That's right, like a couple of animals sniffin' around each other. . . .

(*The image embarrasses her. He crosses to counter, leans over and puts guitar behind it.*)

LADY: Well, not exactly like that, but—!

VAL: We don't know each other. How do people get to know each other? I used to think they did it by touch.

LADY: By what?

VAL: By touch, by touchin' each other.

LADY (*moving up and sitting on shoe-fitting chair which has been moved to R. window*): Oh, you mean by close—contact!

VAL: But later it seemed like that made them more strangers than ever, uhh, huh, more strangers than ever. . . .

LADY: Then how d'you think they get to know each other?

VAL (*sitting on counter*): Well, in answer to your last question, I would say this: Nobody ever gets to know *no body*! We're all of us sentenced to solitary confinement inside our own skins, for life! You understand me, Lady?—I'm tellin' you it's the truth, we got to face it, we're under a lifelong sentence to solitary confinement inside our own lonely skins for as long as we live on this earth!

LADY (*rising and crossing to him*): Oh, no, I'm not a big optimist but I cannot agree with something as sad as that statement!

(*They are sweetly grave as two children; the store is somewhat dusky. She sits in chair R. of counter.*)

VAL: *Listen!*—When I was a kid on Witches Bayou? After my folks all scattered away like loose chicken's feathers blown around by the wind?—I stayed there alone on the bayou, hunted and trapped out of season and hid from the law!—*Listen!*—All that time, all that lonely time, I felt I was—waiting for something!

LADY: What for?

VAL: What does anyone wait for? For something to happen, for anything to happen, to make things make more sense. . . . It's hard to remember what that feeling was like because I've lost it now, but I was waiting for something like if you ask a question you wait for someone to answer, but you ask the wrong question or you ask the wrong person and the answer don't come.

Does everything stop because you don't get the answer? No, it goes right on as if the answer was given, day comes after day and night comes after night, and you're still waiting for someone to answer the question and going right on as if the question was answered. And then—well—then. . . .

LADY: Then what?

VAL: You get the make-believe answer.

LADY: What answer is that?

VAL: Don't pretend you don't know because you do!

LADY:—Love?

VAL (*placing hand on her shoulder*): That's the make-believe answer. It's fooled many a fool besides you an' me, that's the God's truth, Lady, and you had better believe it.

(*Lady looks reflectively at Val and he goes on speaking and sits on stool below counter.*)

—I met a girl on the bayou when I was fourteen. I'd had a feeling that day that if I just kept poling the boat down the bayou a little bit further I would come bang into whatever it was I'd been so long expecting!

LADY: Was she the answer, this girl that you met on the bayou?

VAL: She made me think that she was.

LADY: How did she do that?

VAL: By coming out on the dogtrot of a cabin as naked as I was in that flat-bottom boat! She stood there a while with the daylight burning around her as bright as heaven as far as I could see. You seen the inside of a shell, how white that is, pearly white? Her naked skin was like that.—Oh, God, I remember a bird flown out of the moss and its wings made a shadow on her, and then it sung a single, high clear note, and as if she was waiting for that as a kind of a signal to catch me, she turned and smiled, and walked on back in the cabin. . . .

LADY: You followed?

VAL: Yes, I followed, I followed, like a bird's tail follows a bird, I followed!

I thought that she give me the answer to the question, I'd been waiting for, but afterwards I wasn't sure that was it, but from that time the question wasn't much plainer than the answer and—

LADY:—What?

VAL: At fifteen I left Witches Bayou. When the dog died I sold my boat and the gun. . . . I went to New Orleans in this snakeskin jacket. . . . It didn't take long for me to learn the score.

LADY: What did you learn?

VAL: I learned that I had something to sell besides snakeskins and other wild things' skins I caught on the bayou. I was corrupted! That's the answer. . . .

LADY: Naw, that ain't the answer!

VAL: Okay, *you* tell me the answer!

LADY: I don't know the answer, I just know corruption ain't the answer. I know that much. If I thought that was the answer I'd take Jabe's pistol or his morphine tablets and—

(*A woman bursts into store.*)

WOMAN: I got to use your pay-phone!

LADY: Go ahead. Help yourself.

(*Woman crosses to phone, deposits coin. Lady crosses to confectionery. To Val:*)

Get me a coke from the cooler.

(*Val crosses and goes out R. During the intense activity among the choral women, Lady and Val seem bemused as if they were thinking back over their talk before. For the past minute or two a car horn has been heard blowing repeatedly in the near distance.*)

WOMAN (*at phone*): Cutrere place, get me the Cutrere place, will yuh? David Cutrere or his wife, whichever comes to the phone!

(*Beulah rushes in from the street to R.C.*)

BEULAH: Lady, Lady, where's Lady! Carol Cutrere is—!
WOMAN: Quiet, please! I am callin' her brother about her!

(*Lady sits at table in confectionery.*)

(*At phone:*) Who's this I'm talking to? Good! I'm calling about your sister, Carol Cutrere. She is blowing her car horn at the Red Crown station, she is blowing and blowing her car horn at the Red Crown station because my husband give the station attendants instructions not to service her car, and she is blowing and blowing and blowing on her horn, drawing a big crowd there and, Mr. Cutrere, I thought that you and your father had agreed to keep that girl out of Two River County for good, that's what we all understood around here.

(*Car horn.*)

BEULAH (*Listening with excited approval*): Good! Good! Tell him that if—

(*Dolly enters.*)

DOLLY: She's gotten out of the car and—
BEULAH: *Shhh!*

WOMAN: Well, I just wanted to let you know she's back here in town makin' another disturbance and my husband's on the phone now at the Red Crown station—

(*Dolly goes outside and looks off.*)

trying to get the Sheriff, so if she gits picked up again by th' law, you can't say I didn't warn you, Mr. Cutrere.

(*Car horn.*)

DOLLY (*coming back in*): *Oh, good! Good!*
BEULAH: Where is she, where's she gone now?
WOMAN: You better be quick about it. Yes, I do. I sympathize with you and your father and with Mrs. Cutrere, but Carol cannot demand service at our station, we just refuse to wait on her, she's not— Hello? Hello? (*She jiggles phone violently.*)
BEULAH: What's he doin'? Comin' to pick her up?
DOLLY: Call the Sheriff's office!

(*Beulah goes outside again. Val comes back with a bottle of Coca-Cola—hands it to Lady and leans on juke box.*)

(*Going out to Beulah*) What's goin' on now?
BEULAH (*outside*): Look, look, they're pushing her out of the station driveway.

(*They forget Lady in this new excitement. Ad libs continual. The short woman from the station charges back out of the store.*)

DOLLY: Where is Carol?
BEULAH: Going into the White Star Pharmacy!

(*Dolly rushes back in to the phone.*)

BEULAH (*crossing to Lady*): Lady, I want you to give me your word that if that Cutrere girl comes in here, you won't wait on her! You hear me?
LADY: No.
BEULAH:—What? Will you refuse to wait on her?
LADY: I can't refuse to wait on anyone in this store.
BEULAH: Well, I'd like to know why you can't.
DOLLY: Shhh! I'm on the phone!

BEULAH: Who you phonin' Dolly?

DOLLY: That White Star Pharmacy! I want to make sure that Mr. Dubinsky refuses to wait on that girl! (*Having found and deposited coin*) I want the White Far Starmacy. I mean the—(*Stamps foot*)—White Star Pharmacy!—I'm so upset my tongue's twisted!

(*Lady hands coke to Val. Beulah is at the window.*)

I'm getting a busy signal. Has she come out yet?

BEULAH: No, she's still in the White Star!

DOLLY: Maybe they're not waiting on her.

BEULAH: Dubinsky'd wait on a purple-bottom baboon if it put a dime on th' counter an' pointed at something!

DOLLY: I know she sat at a table in the Blue Bird Café half'n hour last time she was here and the waitresses never came near her!

BEULAH: That's different. They're not foreigners there!

(*Dolly crosses to counter.*)

You can't ostracize a person out of this county unless everybody cooperates. Lady just told me that she was going to wait on her if she comes here.

DOLLY: Lady wouldn't do that.

BEULAH: *Ask* her! She told *me* she would!

LADY (*rising and turning at once to the women and shouting at them*): Oh, for God's sake, no! I'm not going to refuse to wait on her because you all don't like her! Besides I'm delighted that wild girl is givin' her brother so much trouble! (*After this outburst she goes back of the counter.*)

DOLLY (*at phone*): Hush! Mr. Dubinsky! This is Dolly Hamma, Mr. "Dog" Hamma's wife!

(*Carol quietly enters the front door.*)

I want to ask you, is Carol Cutrere in your drugstore?

BEULAH (*warningly*): Dolly!

CAROL: No. She isn't.

DOLLY:—What?

CAROL: She's here.

(*Beulah goes into confectionery. Carol moves toward Val to D.R.C.*)

DOLLY:—Aw!—Never mind, Mr. Dubinsky, I— (*Hangs up furiously and crosses to door.*)

(*A silence in which they all stare at the girl from various positions about the store. She has been on the road all night in an open car: her hair is blown wild, her face flushed and eyes bright with fever. Her manner in the scene is that of a wild animal at bay, desperate but fearless.*)

LADY (*finally and quietly*): Hello, Carol.
CAROL: Hello, Lady.
LADY (*defiantly cordial*): I thought that you were in New Orleans, Carol.
CAROL: Yes, I was. Last night.
LADY: Well, you got back fast.
CAROL: I drove all night.
LADY: In that storm?
CAROL: The wind took the top off my car but I didn't stop.

(*She watches Val steadily; he steadily ignores her; turns away and puts bottles of Coca-Cola on a table.*)

LADY (*with growing impatience*): Is something wrong at home, is someone sick?
CAROL (*absently*): No. No, not that I know of, I wouldn't know if there was, they—may I sit down?
LADY: Why, sure.
CAROL (*crossing to chair at counter and sitting*):—They pay me to stay away so I wouldn't know. . . .

(*Silence. Val walks deliberately past her and goes into alcove.*)

—I think I have a fever, I feel like I'm catching pneumonia, everything's so far away. . . .

(*Silence again except for the faint, hissing whispers of Beulah and Dolly at the back of the store.*)

LADY (*with a touch of exasperation*): Is there something you want?
CAROL: Everything seems miles away. . . .
LADY: Carol, I said is there anything you want here?
CAROL: Excuse me!—yes. . . .
LADY: Yes, what?

CAROL: Don't bother now. I'll wait.

(*Val comes out of alcove with the blue jacket on.*)

LADY: Wait for what, what are you waiting for! You don't have to wait for nothing, just say what you want and if I got it in stock I'll give it to you!

(*Phone rings once.*)

CAROL (*vaguely*):—Thank you—no. . . .

LADY (*to Val*): Get that phone, Val.

(*Dolly crosses and hisses something inaudible to Beulah.*)

BEULAH (*rising*): I just want to wait here to see if she does or she don't.

DOLLY: She just said she would!

BEULAH: Just the same, I'm gonna wait!!

VAL (*at phone*): Yes, sir, she is.—I'll tell her. (*Hangs up and speaks to Lady:*) Her brother's heard she's here and he's coming to pick her up.

LADY: *David Cutrere is not coming in this store!*

DOLLY: Aw-aw!

BEULAH: David Cutrere used to be her lover.

DOLLY: I remember you told me.

LADY (*wheels about suddenly toward the women*): Beulah! Dolly! Why're you back there hissing together like geese? (*Coming from behind counter to R.C.*) Why don't you go to th'—Blue Bird and—have some hot coffee—talk there!

BEULAH: It looks like we're getting what they call the bum's rush.

DOLLY: I never stay where I'm not wanted and when I'm not wanted somewhere I never come back!

(*They cross out and slam door.*)

LADY (*after a pause*): What did you come here for?

CAROL: To deliver a message.

LADY: To me?

CAROL: No.

LADY: Then who?

(*Carol stares at Lady gravely a moment, then turns slowly to look at Val.*)

—Him?—Him?

(*Carol nods slowly and slightly.*)

OK, then, give him the message, deliver the message to him.

CAROL: It's a private message. Could I speak to him alone, please?

(*Lady gets a shawl from a hook.*)

LADY: Oh, for God's sake! Your brother's plantation is ten minutes from here in that sky-blue Cadillac his rich wife give him. Now look, he's on his way here but I won't let him come in, I don't even want his hand to touch the door-handle. I know your message, this boy knows your message, there's nothing private about it. But I tell you, that this boy's not for sale in my store!—Now—I'm going out to watch for the sky-blue Cadillac on the highway. When I see it, I'm going to throw this door open and holler and when I holler, I want you out of this door like a shot from a pistol!—that fast! Understand?

(NOTE: *Above scene is overextended. This can be remedied by a very lively performance. It might also help to indicate a division between the Lady-Val scene and the group scene that follows.*)

(*Lady slams door behind her. The loud noise of the door-slam increases the silence that follows. Val's oblivious attitude is not exactly hostile, but deliberate. There's a kind of purity in it; also a kind of refusal to concern himself with a problem that isn't his own. He holds his guitar with a specially tender concentration, and strikes a soft chord on it. The girl stares at Val; he whistles a note and tightens a guitar string to the pitch of the whistle, not looking at the girl. Since this scene is followed by the emotional scene between Lady and David, it should be keyed somewhat lower than written; it's important that Val should not seem brutal in his attitude toward Carol; there should be an air between them of two lonely children.*)

VAL (*in a soft, preoccupied tone*): You told the lady I work for that you had a message for me. Is that right, Miss? Have you got a message for me?

CAROL (*she rises, moves a few steps toward him, hesitantly. Val whistles, plucks guitar string, changes pitch*): You've spilt some ashes on your new blue suit.

VAL: Is that the message?

CAROL (*moves away a step*): No. No, that was just an excuse to touch you. The message is—

VAL: What?

(*Music fades in—guitar.*)

CAROL:—I'd love to hold something the way you hold your guitar, that's how I'd love to hold something, with such—*tender protection!* I'd love to hold *you* that way, with that same—*tender protection!* (*Her hand has fallen onto his knee, which he has drawn up to rest a foot on the counter stool.*) —*Because you hang the moon for me!*

VAL (*he speaks to her, not roughly but in a tone that holds a long history that began with a romantic acceptance of such declarations as she has just made to him, and that turned gradually to his present distrust. He puts guitar down and goes to her*): Who're you tryin' t' fool beside you'self? You couldn't stand the weight of a man's body on you. (*He casually picks up her wrist and pushes the sleeve back from it.*) What's this here? A human wrist with a bone? It feels like a twig I could snap with two fingers. . . . (*Gently, negligently, pushes collar of her trench coat back from her bare throat and shoulders. Runs a finger along her neck tracing a vein.*) Little girl, you're transparent, I can see the veins in you. A man's weight on you would break you like a bundle of sticks. . . .

(*Music fades out.*)

CAROL (*gazes at him, startled by his perception*): Isn't it funny! You've hit on the truth about me. The act of lovemaking is almost unbearably painful, and yet, of course, I do bear it, because to be not alone, even for a few moments, is worth the pain and the danger. It's dangerous for me because I'm not built for childbearing.

VAL: Well, then, fly away, little bird, fly away before you—get broke. (*He turns back to his guitar.*)

CAROL: Why do you dislike me?

VAL (*turning back*): I never dislike nobody till they interfere with me.

CAROL: How have I interfered with you? Did I snitch when I saw my cousin's watch on you?

VAL (*beginning to remove his watch*):—You won't take my word for a true thing I told you. I'm thirty years old and I'm done with the crowd you run with and the places you run to. The Club Rendezvous, the Starlite Lounge, the Music Bar, and all the night places. Here—(*Offers watch*)—take this Rolex Chronometer that tells the time of the day and the day of the week and the month and all the crazy moon's phases. I never stole nothing before. When I stole that I known it was time for me to get off the party, so take it back, now, to Bertie. . . . (*He takes her hand and tries to force the watch into her fist. There is a little struggle, he can't open her fist. She is crying, but staring fiercely into his eyes. He draws a hissing breath and hurls watch violently across the floor.*)

—That's my message to you and the pack you run with!

CAROL (*flinging coat away*): *I RUN WITH NOBODY!*—I hoped I could run with you. . . . (*Music stops short.*) You're in danger here, Snakeskin. You've taken off the jacket that said: "I'm wild, I'm alone!" and put on the nice blue uniform of a convict! . . . Last night I woke up thinking about you again. I drove all night to bring you this warning of danger. . . . (*Her trembling hand covers her lips.*)—The message I came here to give you was a warning of danger! I hoped you'd hear me and let me take you away before it's—too late.

(*Door bursts open. Lady rushes inside, crying out:*)

LADY: *Your brother's coming, go out! He can't come in!*

(*Carol picks up coat and goes into confectionery, sobbing. Val crosses toward door.*)

Lock that door! Don't let him come in my store!

(*Carol sinks sobbing at table. Lady runs up to the landing of the stairs as David Cutrere enters the store. He is a tall man in hunter's clothes. He is hardly less handsome now than he was in his youth but something has gone: his power is that of a captive who rules over other captives. His face, his eyes, have something of the same desperate, unnatural hardness that Lady meets the world with.*)

DAVID: Carol?

VAL: She's in there. (*He nods toward the dim confectionery into which the girl has retreated.*)

DAVID (*crossing*): Carol!

(*She rises and advances a few steps into the lighted area of the stage.*)

You broke the agreement.

(*Carol nods slightly, staring at Val.*)

(*Harshly:*) All right. I'll drive you back. Where's your coat?

(*Carol murmurs something inaudible, staring at Val.*)

Where is her coat, where is my sister's coat?

(*Val crosses below and picks up the coat that Carol has dropped on the floor and hands it to David. He throws it roughly about Carol's shoulders and propels her forcefully toward the store entrance. Val moves away to D.R.*)

LADY (*suddenly and sharply*): *Wait, please!*

(*David looks up at the landing; stands frozen as Lady rushes down the stairs.*)

DAVID (*softly, hoarsely*): How—*are* you, Lady?

LADY (*turning to Val*): Val, go out.

DAVID (*to Carol*): Carol, will you wait for me in my car?

(*He opens the door for his sister; she glances back at Val with desolation in her eyes. Val crosses quickly through the confectionery. Sound of door closing in there. Carol nods slightly as if in sad response to some painful question and goes out of the store. Pause.*)

LADY: I told you once to never come in this store.

DAVID: I came for my sister. . . . (*He turns as if to go.*)

LADY: No, wait!

DAVID: I don't dare leave my sister alone on the road.

LADY: I have something to tell you I never told you before. (*She crosses to him. David turns back to her, then moves away to D.R.C.*) —I—carried your child in my body the summer you quit me.

(*Silence.*)

DAVID:—I—didn't know.

LADY: No, no, I didn't write you no letter about it; I was proud then; I had pride. But I had your child in my body the summer you quit me, that summer they burned my father in his wine garden, and you, you washed your hands clean of any connection with a Dago bootlegger's daughter and—(*Her breathless voice momentarily falters and she makes a fierce gesture as she struggles to speak.*)—took that—society girl that—restored your homeplace and give you such—(*Catches breath.*)—wellborn children. . . .

DAVID:—I—didn't know.

LADY: Well, now you do know, you know now. I carried your child in my body the summer you quit me but I had it cut out of my body, and they cut my heart out with it!

DAVID:—I—didn't know.

LADY: I wanted death after that, but death don't come when you *want* it, it comes when you don't want it! I wanted death, then, but I took the next best thing. *You* sold *yourself. I* sold *my* self. *You* was bought. *I* was bought. You made whores of us both!

DAVID:—I—didn't know. . . .

(*Mandolin, barely audible,* "Dicitincello Voie.")

LADY: But that's all a long time ago. Some reason I drove by there a few nights ago; the shore of the lake where my father had his wine garden? You remember? You remember the wine garden of my father?

(*David stares at her. She turns away.*)

No, you don't? You don't remember it even?

DAVID:—Lady, I don't—remember—anything else. . . .

LADY: The mandolin of my father, the songs that I sang with my father in my father's wine garden?

DAVID: Yes, I don't remember anything else. . . .

LADY: *Core Ingrata! Come Le Rose!* And we disappeared and

he would call, *"Lady? Lady?"* (*Turns to him.*) *How could I answer him with two tongues in my mouth!* (*A sharp hissing intake of breath, eyes opened wide, hand clapped over her mouth as if what she said was unendurable to her. He turns instantly, sharply away.*)

(*Music stops short. Jabe begins to knock for her on the floor above. She crosses to stairs, stops, turns.*)

I hold hard feelings!—Don't ever come here again. If your wild sister comes here, send somebody else for her, not you, not you. Because I hope never to feel this knife again in me. (*Her hand is on her chest; she breathes with difficulty.*)

(*He turns away from her; starts toward the door. She takes a step toward him.*)

And don't pity me neither. I haven't gone down so terribly far in the world. I got a going concern in this mercantile store, in there's the confectionery which'll reopen this spring, it's being done over to make it the place that all the young people will come to, it's going to be like—

(*He touches the door, pauses with his back to her.*)

—the wine garden of my father, those wine-drinking nights when you had something better than anything you've had since!

DAVID: Lady— *That's*—

LADY:—*What?*

DAVID:—*True!* (*Opens door.*)

LADY: Go now. I just wanted to tell you my life ain't over.

(*He goes out as Jabe continues knocking. She stands, stunned, motionless till Val quietly re-enters the store. She becomes aware of his return rather slowly; then she murmurs:*)

I made a fool of myself. . . .

VAL: What?

(*She crosses to stairs.*)

LADY: *I made a fool of myself!*

(*She goes up the stairs with effort as the lights change slowly to mark a division of scenes.*)

SCENE TWO

Sunset of that day. Val is alone in the store, as if preparing to go. The sunset is fiery. A large woman opens the door and stands there looking dazed. It is Vee Talbott.

VAL (*turning*): Hello, Mrs. Talbott.

VEE: Something's gone wrong with my eyes. I can't see nothing.

VAL (*going to her*): Here, let me help you. You probably drove up here with that setting sun in your face. (*Leading her to shoe-fitting chair at R. window.*) There now. Set down right here.

VEE: Thank you—so—much. . . .

VAL: I haven't seen you since that night you brought me here to ask for this job.

VEE: Has the minister called on you yet? Reverend Tooker? I made him promise he would. I told him you were new around here and weren't affiliated to any church yet. I want you to go to ours.

VAL:—That's—mighty kind of you.

VEE: The Church of the Resurrection, it's Episcopal.

VAL: Uh, huh.

VEE: Unwrap that picture, please.

VAL: Sure. (*He tears paper off canvas.*)

VEE: It's the Church of the Resurrection. I give it a sort of imaginative treatment. You know, Jabe and Lady have never darkened a church door. I thought it ought to be hung where Jabe could look at it, it might help to bring that poor dying man to Jesus. . . .

(*Val places it against chair R. of counter and crouches before the canvas, studying it long and seriously. Vee coughs nervously, gets up, bends to look at the canvas, sits uncertainly back down. Val smiles at her warmly, then back to the canvas.*)

VAL (*at last*): What's this here in the picture?

VEE: The steeple.

VAL: Aw.—Is the church steeple red?

VEE: Why—no, but—

VAL: Why'd you paint it red, then?

VEE: Oh, well, you see, I—(*Laughs nervously, childlike in her growing excitement.*)—I just, just *felt* it that way! I paint a thing how I feel it instead of always the way it actually is. Appearances are misleading, nothing is what it looks like to the eyes. You got to have—*vision—to see!*

VAL:—Yes. Vision. Vision!—to see. . . . (*Rises, nodding gravely, emphatically.*)

VEE: I paint from vision. They call me a visionary.

VAL: Oh.

VEE (*with shy pride*): That's what the New Orleans and Memphis newspaper people admire so much in my work. They call it a primitive style, the work of a visionary. One of my pictures is hung on the exhibition in Audubon Park museum and they have asked for others. I can't turn them out fast enough!—I have to wait for—visions, no, I—I can't paint without—visions . . . I couldn't *live* without visions!

VAL: Have you always had visions?

VEE: No, just since I was born, I— (*Stops short, startled by the absurdity of her answer. Both laugh suddenly, then she rushes on, her great bosom heaving with curious excitement, twisting in her chair, gesturing with clenched hands.*) I was born, I was born with a caul! A sort of thing like a veil, a thin, thin sort of a web was over my eyes. They call that a caul. It's a sign that you're going to have visions, and I did, I had them! (*Pauses for breath; light fades.*) —When I was little my baby sister died. Just one day old, she died. They had to baptize her at midnight to save her soul.

VAL: Uh-huh. (*He sits opposite her, smiling, attentive.*)

VEE: The minister came at midnight, and after the baptism service, he handed the bowl of holy water to me and told me, "Be sure to empty this out on the ground!" —I didn't. I was scared to go out at midnight, with, with—death! in the—house and—I sneaked into the kitchen; I emptied the holy water into the kitchen sink—thunder struck!—the kitchen sink turned black, the kitchen sink turned absolutely black!

(*Sheriff Talbott enters the front door.*)

TALBOTT: Mama! What're you doin'?

VEE: Talkin'.

TALBOTT: I'm gonna see Jabe a minute, you go out and wait in th' car. (*He goes up. She rises slowly, picks up canvas and moves to counter.*)

VEE:—Oh, I—tell you!—since I got into this painting, my whole outlook is different. I can't explain how it is, the difference to me.

VAL: You don't have to explain. I know what you mean. Before you started to paint, it didn't make sense.

VEE:—What—what didn't?

VAL: Existence!

VEE (*slowly and softly*): No—no, it didn't . . . existence didn't make sense. . . . (*She places canvas on guitar on counter and sits in chair.*)

VAL (*rising and crossing to her*): You lived in Two River County, the wife of the county Sheriff. You saw awful things take place.

VEE: Awful! Things!

VAL: Beatings!

VEE: Yes!

VAL: Lynchings!

VEE: Yes!

VAL: Runaway convicts torn to pieces by hounds!

(*This is the first time she could express this horror.*)

VEE: *Chain-gang dogs!*

VAL: Yeah?

VEE: Tear fugitives!

VAL: Yeah?

VEE:—to *pieces.* . . .

(*She had half risen: now sinks back faintly. Val looks beyond her in the dim store, his light eyes have a dark gaze. It may be that his speech is too articulate: counteract this effect by groping, hesitations.*)

VAL (*moving away a step*): But violence ain't quick always. Sometimes it's slow. Some tornadoes are slow. Corruption —rots men's hearts and—rot is slow. . . .

VEE:—How do you—?

VAL: Know? I been a witness, I know!

VEE: *I* been a witness! *I* know!

VAL: We seen these things from seats down front at the show. (*He crouches before her and touches her hands in her lap. Her breath shudders.*) And so you begun to paint your visions. Without no plan, no training, you started to paint as if God touched your fingers. (*He lifts her hands slowly, gently from her soft lap.*) You made some beauty out of this dark country with these two, soft, woman hands. . . .

(*Talbott appears on the stair landing, looks down, silent.*) Yeah, you made some beauty! (*Strangely, gently, he lifts her hands to his mouth. She gasps. Talbott calls out:*)

TALBOTT: *Hey!*

(*Vee springs up, gasping.*)

(*Descending*) *Cut this crap!*

(*Val moves away to R.C.*)

(*To Vee:*) Go out. Wait in the car. (*He stares at Val till Vee lumbers out as if dazed. After a while:*)

Jabe Torrance told me to take a good look at you. (*Crosses to Val.*) Well, now, I've taken that look. (*Nods shortly. Goes out of store. The store is now very dim. As door closes on Talbott, Val picks up painting; he goes behind counter and places it on a shelf, then picks up his guitar and sits on counter. Lights go down to mark a division as he sings and plays "Heavenly Grass."*)

SCENE THREE

As Val finishes the song, Lady descends the stair. He rises and turns on a green-shaded light bulb.

VAL (*to Lady*): You been up there a long time.

LADY:—I gave him morphine. He must be out of his mind. He says such awful things to me. He says I want him to die.

VAL: You sure you don't?

LADY: I don't want no one to die. Death's terrible, Val.

(*Pause. She wanders to the front window R. He takes his guitar and crosses to the door.*) You gotta go now?

VAL: I'm late.

LADY: Late for what? You got a date with somebody?

VAL:—No. . . .

LADY: Then stay a while. Play something. I'm all unstrung. . . .

(*He crosses back and leans against counter; the guitar is barely audible, under the speeches.*)

I made a terrible fool of myself down here today with—

VAL:—That girl's brother?

LADY: Yes, I—threw away——pride. . . .

VAL: His sister said she'd come here to give me a warning. I wonder what of?

LADY (*sitting in shoe-fitting chair*):—I said things to him I should of been too proud to say. . . .

(*Both are pursuing their own reflections; guitar continues softly.*)

VAL: Once or twice lately I've woke up with a fast heart, shouting something, and had to pick up my guitar to calm myself down. . . . Somehow or other I can't get used to this place, I don't feel safe in this place, but I—want to stay. . . . (*Stops short; sound of wild baying.*)

LADY: The chain-gang dogs are chasing some runaway convict. . . .

VAL: *Run boy! Run fast, brother! If they catch you, you never will run again! That's*—(*He has thrust his guitar under his arm on this line and crossed to the door.*)—for sure. . . . (*The baying of the dogs changes, becomes almost a single savage note.*) —Uh-huh—the dogs've got him. . . . (*Pause.*) They're tearing him to pieces! (*Pause. Baying continues. A shot is fired. The baying dies out. He stops with his hand on the door; glances back at her; nods; draws the door open. The wind sings loud in the dusk.*)

LADY: *Wait!*

VAL:—Huh?

LADY:—Where do you stay?

VAL:—When?

LADY: Nights.

VAL: I stay at the Wildwood cabins on the highway.

LADY: You like it there?

VAL: Uh-huh.

LADY:—Why?

VAL: I got a comfortable bed, a two-burner stove, a shower and icebox there.

LADY: You want to save money?

VAL: I never could in my life.

LADY: You could if you stayed on the place.

VAL: What place?

LADY: This place.

VAL: Whereabouts on this place?

LADY (*pointing to alcove*): Back of that curtain.

VAL:—Where they try on clothes?

LADY: There's a cot there. A nurse slept on it when Jabe had his first operation, and there's a washroom down here and I'll get a plumber to put in a hot an' cold shower! I'll—fix it up nice for you. . . . (*She rises, crosses to foot of stairs. Pause. He lets the door shut, staring at her.*)

VAL (*moving D.C.*):—I—don't like to be—obligated.

LADY: There wouldn't be no obligation, you'd do me a favor. I'd feel safer at night with somebody on the place. I would; it would cost you nothing! And you could save up that money you spend on the cabin. How much? Ten a week? Why, two or three months from now you'd—save enough money to— (*Makes a wide gesture with a short laugh as if startled.*) Go on! Take a look at it! See if it don't suit you!—All right. . . .

(*But he doesn't move; he appears reflective.*)

LADY (*shivering, hugging herself*): Where does heat go in this building?

VAL (*reflectively*):—Heat rises. . . .

LADY: You with your dog's temperature, don't feel cold, do you? I do! I turn blue with it!

VAL:—Yeah. . . .

(*The wait is unendurable to Lady.*)

LADY: *Well, aren't you going to look at it, the room back there, and see if it suits you or not?!*

VAL:—I'll go and take a look at it. . . .

(*He crosses to the alcove and disappears behind the curtain. A light goes on behind it, making its bizarre pattern translucent: a gold tree with scarlet fruit and white birds in it, formally designed. Truck roars; lights sweep the frosted window. Lady gasps aloud; takes out a pint bottle and a glass from under the counter, setting them down with a crash that makes her utter a startled exclamation: then a startled laugh. She pours a drink and sits in chair R. of counter. The lights turn off behind the alcove curtain and Val comes back out. She sits stiffly without looking at him as he crosses back lazily, goes behind counter, puts guitar down. His manner is gently sad as if he had met with a familiar, expected disappointment. He sits down quietly on edge of counter and takes the pint bottle and pours himself a shot of the liquor with a reflective sigh. Boards creak loudly, contracting with the cold. Lady's voice is harsh and sudden, demanding:*)

LADY: *Well, is it okay or—what!*

VAL: I never been in a position where I could turn down something I got for nothing in my life. I like that picture in there. That's a famous picture, that "September Morn" picture you got on the wall in there. Ha ha! I might have trouble sleeping in a room with that picture. I might keep turning the light on to take another look at it! The way she's cold in that water and sort of crouched over in it, holding her body like that, that—might—ha ha!—sort of keep me awake. . . .

LADY: Aw, you with your dog's temperature and your control of all functions, it would take more than a picture to keep you awake!

VAL: I was just kidding.

LADY: I was just kidding too.

VAL: But you know how a single man is. He don't come home every night with just his shadow.

(*Pause. She takes a drink.*)

LADY: You bring girls home nights to the Wildwood cabins, do you?

VAL: I ain't so far. But I would like to feel free to. That old life is what I'm used to. I always worked nights in cities and if you work nights in cities you live in a different city from those that work days.

LADY: Yes. I know, I—imagine. . . .

VAL: The ones that work days in cities and the ones that work nights in cities, they live in different cities. The cities have the same name but they are different cities. As different as night and day. There's something wild in the country that only the night people know. . . .

LADY: Yeah, I know!

VAL: I'm thirty years old!—but sudden changes don't work, it takes—

LADY:—Time—yes. . . .

(*Slight pause which she finds disconcerting. He slides off counter and moves around below it.*)

VAL: You been good to me, Lady.—Why d'you want me to stay here?

LADY (*defensively*): I told you why.

VAL: For company nights?

LADY: Yeah, to, to!—*guard the store*, nights!

VAL: To be a night watchman?

LADY: Yeah, to be a night *watchman.*

VAL: You feel nervous alone here?

LADY: Naturally now!—Jabe sleeps with a pistol next to him but if somebody broke in the store, he couldn't git up and all I could do is holler!—Who'd *hear* me? They got a telephone girl on the night shift with—sleepin' sickness, I think! Anyhow, why're you so suspicious? You look at me like you thought I was *plottin'*.—Kind people *exist*: Even me! (*She sits up rigid in chair, lips and eyes tight closed, drawing in a loud breath which comes from a tension both personal and vicarious.*)

VAL: I understand, Lady, but. . . . Why're you sitting up so stiff in that chair?

LADY: Ha! (*Sharp laugh; she leans back in chair.*)

VAL: You're still unrelaxed.

LADY: I know.

VAL: Relax. (*Moving around close to her.*) I'm going to show you some tricks I learned from a lady osteopath that took me in, too.

LADY: What tricks?

VAL: How to manipulate joints and bones in a way that makes you feel like a loose piece of string. (*Moves behind her chair. She watches him.*) Do you trust me or don't you?

LADY: Yeah, I trust you completely, but—

VAL: Well then, lean forward a little and raise your arms up and turn sideways in the chair.

(*She follows these instructions.*)

Drop your head. (*He manipulates her head and neck.*) Now the spine, Lady. (*He places his knee against the small of her backbone and she utters a sharp, startled laugh as he draws her backbone hard against his kneecap.*)

LADY: Ha, ha!—That makes a sound like, like, like!—boards contracting with cold in the building, ha, ha!

(*He relaxes.*)

VAL: Better?

LADY: Oh, yes!—much . . . thanks. . . .

VAL (*stroking her neck*): Your skin is like silk. You're light skinned to be Italian.

LADY: Most people in this country think Italian people are dark. Some are but not all are! Some of them are fair . . . very fair. . . . My father's people were dark but my mother's people were fair. Ha ha!

(*The laughter is senseless. He smiles understandingly at her as she chatters to cover confusion. He turns away, then goes above and sits on counter close to her.*)

My mother's mother's sister—come here from Monte Cassino, to die, with relations!—but I think people always die alone . . . with or without relations. I was a little girl then and I remember it took her such a long, long time to die we almost forgot her.—And she was so quiet . . . in a corner. . . . And I remember asking her one time, Zia Teresa, how does it feel to die?—Only a little girl would ask such a question, ha ha! Oh, and I remember her answer. She said—"It's a lonely feeling."

I think she wished she had stayed in Italy and died in a place that she knew. . . . (*Looks at him directly for the first time since mentioning the alcove.*) Well, there is a washroom, and I'll get the plumber to put in a hot and cold shower! Well— (*Rises, retreats awkwardly from the chair. His interest seems to have wandered from her.*) I'll go up and get some clean linen and make up that bed in there.

(*She turns and walks rapidly, almost running, to stairs. He appears lost in some private reflection but as soon as she has disappeared above the landing, he says something under his breath and crosses directly to the cashbox. He coughs loudly to cover the sound of ringing it open; scoops out a fistful of bills and coughs again to cover the sound of slamming drawer shut. Picks up his guitar and goes out the front door of store. Lady returns downstairs, laden with linen. The outer darkness moans through the door left open. She crosses to the door and a little outside it, peering both ways down the dark road. Then she comes in furiously, with an Italian curse, shutting the door with her foot or shoulder, and throws the linen down on counter. She crosses abruptly to cashbox, rings it open and discovers theft. Slams drawer violently shut.*)

Thief! Thief!

(*Turns to phone, lifts receiver. Holds it a moment, then slams it back into place. Wanders desolately back to the door, opens it and stands staring out into the starless night as the scene dims out. Music: blues—guitar.*)

SCENE FOUR

Late that night. Val enters the store, a little unsteadily, with his guitar; goes to the cashbox and rings it open. He counts some bills off a big wad and returns them to the cashbox and the larger wad to the pocket of his snakeskin jacket. Sudden footsteps above; light spills onto stair landing. He quickly moves away from the cashbox as Lady appears on the landing in a white sateen robe; she carries a flashlight.

LADY: Who's that?

(*Music fades out.*)

VAL:—Me.

(*She turns the flashlight on his figure.*)

LADY: Oh, my God, how you scared me!
VAL: You didn't expect me?
LADY: How'd I know it was you I heard come in?
VAL: I thought you give me a room here.
LADY: You left without letting me know if you took it or not. (*She is descending the stairs into store, flashlight still on him.*)
VAL: Catch me turning down something I get for nothing.
LADY: Well, you might have said something so I'd expect you or not.
VAL: I thought you took it for granted.
LADY: I don't take nothing for granted.

(*He starts back to the alcove.*)

Wait!—I'm coming downstairs. . . . (*She descends with the flashlight beam on his face.*)
VAL: You're blinding me with that flashlight.

(*He laughs. She keeps the flashlight on him. He starts back again toward the alcove.*)

LADY: The bed's not made because I didn't expect you.
VAL: That's all right.
LADY: I brought the linen downstairs and you'd cut out.
VAL:—Yeah, well—

(*She picks up linen on counter.*)

Give me that stuff. I can make up my own rack. Tomorrow you'll have to get yourself a new clerk. (*Takes it from her and goes again toward alcove.*) I had a lucky night. (*Exhibits a wad of bills.*)
LADY: *Hey!*

(*He stops near the curtain. She goes and turns on green-shaded bulb over cashbox.*)

—*Did you just open this cashbox?*
VAL:—Why you ask that?
LADY: I thought I heard it ring open a minute ago, that's why I come down here.

VAL:—In your—white satin—kimona?

LADY: *Did you just open the cashbox?!*

VAL:—I wonder who did if I didn't. . . .

LADY: Nobody did if you didn't, but somebody did! (*Opens cashbox and hurriedly counts money. She is trembling violently.*)

VAL: How come you didn't lock the cash up in the safe this evening, Lady?

LADY: Sometimes I forget to.

VAL: That's careless.

LADY:—Why'd you open the cashbox when you come in?

VAL: I opened it twice this evening, once before I went out and again when I come back. I borrowed some money and put it back in the box an' got all this left over! (*Shows her the wad of bills.*) I beat a blackjack dealer five times straight. With this much loot I can retire for the season. . . . (*He returns money to pocket.*)

LADY: *Chicken-feed!*—I'm sorry for you.

VAL: You're sorry for me?

LADY: I'm sorry for you because nobody can help you. I was touched by your—strangeness, your strange talk.—That thing about birds with no feet so they have to sleep on the wind?—I said to myself, "This boy is a bird with no feet so he has to sleep on the wind," and that softened my fool Dago heart and I wanted to help you. . . . Fool, me!—I got what I should of expected. You robbed me while I was upstairs to get sheets to make up your bed!

(*He starts out toward the door.*)

I guess I'm a fool to even feel disappointed.

VAL (*stopping C. and dropping linen on counter*): You're disappointed in me. I was disappointed in you.

LADY (*coming from behind counter*):—How did I disappoint you?

VAL: There wasn't no cot behind that curtain before. You put it back there for a purpose.

LADY: It was back there!—folded behind the mirror.

VAL: It wasn't back of no mirror when you told me three times to go and—

LADY (*cutting in*): I left that money in the cashbox on purpose, to find out if I could trust you.

VAL: You got back th' . . .

LADY: No, no, no, I can't trust you, now I know I can't trust you, I got to trust anybody or I don't want him.

VAL: That's OK, I don't expect no character reference from you.

LADY: I'll give you a character reference. I'd say this boy's a peculiar talker! But I wouldn't say a real hard worker or honest. I'd say a peculiar slew-footer that sweet talks you while he's got his hand in the cashbox.

VAL: I took out less than you owed me.

LADY: Don't mix up the issue. I see through you, mister!

VAL: I see through you, Lady.

LADY: What d'you see through me?

VAL: You sure you want me to tell?

LADY: I'd love for you to.

VAL:—A not so young and not so satisfied woman, that hired a man off the highway to do double duty without paying overtime for it. . . . I mean a store clerk days and a stud nights, and—

LADY: God, no! You—! (*She raises her hand as if to strike at him.*) Oh, God no . . . you cheap little— (*Invectives fail her so she uses her fists, hammering at him with them. He seizes her wrists. She struggles a few moments more, then collapses, in chair, sobbing. He lets go of her gently.*)

VAL: It's natural. You felt—lonely. . . .

(*She sobs brokenly against the counter.*)

LADY: Why did you come back here?

VAL: To put back the money I took so you wouldn't remember me as not honest or grateful— (*He picks up his guitar and starts to the door nodding gravely. She catches her breath; rushes to intercept him, spreading her arms like a crossbar over the door.*)

LADY: NO, NO, DON'T GO . . . I NEED YOU!!!

(*He faces her for five beats. The true passion of her outcry touches him then, and he turns about and crosses to the alcove. . . . As he draws the curtain across it he looks back at her.*)

TO LIVE. . . . TO GO ON LIVING!!!

(*Music fades in—"Lady's Love Song"—guitar. He closes the curtain and turns on the light behind it, making it translucent. Through an opening in the alcove entrance, we see him sitting down with his guitar. Lady picks up the linen and crosses to the alcove like a spellbound child. Just outside it she stops, frozen with uncertainty, a conflict of feelings, but then he begins to whisper the words of a song so tenderly that she is able to draw the curtain open and enter the alcove. He looks up gravely at her from his guitar. She closes the curtain behind her. Its bizarre design, a gold tree with white birds and scarlet fruit in it, is softly translucent with the bulb lighted behind it. The guitar continues softly for a few moments; stops; the stage darkens till only the curtain of the alcove is clearly visible.*)

Curtain

ACT THREE

SCENE ONE

An early morning. The Saturday before Easter. The sleeping alcove is lighted. Val is smoking, half dressed, on the edge of the cot. Lady comes running, panting downstairs, her hair loose, in dressing robe and slippers and calls out in a panicky, shrill whisper.

LADY: Val! Val, he's comin' downstairs!
VAL (*hoarse with sleep*): Who's—what?
LADY: Jabe!
VAL: Jabe?
LADY: I swear he is, he's coming downstairs!
VAL: What of it?
LADY: Jesus, will you get up and put some clothes on? The damned nurse told him that he could come down in the store to check over the stock! You want him to catch you half dressed on that bed there?

VAL: Don't he know I sleep here?
LADY: Nobody knows you sleep here but you and me.

(*Voices above.*)

Oh, God!—they've started.
NURSE: Don't hurry now. Take one step at a time.

(*Footsteps on stairs, slow, shuffling. The professional, nasal cheer of a nurse's voice.*)

LADY (*panicky*): Get your shirt on! Come out!
NURSE: That's right. One step at a time, one step at a time, lean on my shoulder and take one step at a time.

(*Val rises, still dazed from sleep. Lady gasps and sweeps the curtain across the alcove just a moment before the descending figures enter the sight-lines on the landing. Lady breathes like an exhausted runner as she backs away from the alcove and assumes a forced smile. Jabe and the nurse, Miss Porter, appear on the landing of the stairs and at the same moment scudding clouds expose the sun. A narrow window on the landing admits a brilliant shaft of light upon the pair. They have a bizarre and awful appearance, the tall man, his rusty black suit hanging on him like an empty sack, his eyes burning malignantly from his yellow face, leaning on a stumpy little woman with bright pink or orange hair, clad all in starched white, with a voice that purrs with the faintly contemptuous cheer and sweetness of those hired to care for the dying.*)

NURSE: Aw, now, just look at that, that nice bright sun comin' out.
LADY: Miss Porter? It's—it's cold down here!
JABE: What's she say?
NURSE: She says it's cold down here.
LADY: The—the—the air's not warm enough yet, the air's not heated!
NURSE: He's determined to come right down, Mrs. Torrance.
LADY: I know but—
NURSE: Wild horses couldn't hold him a minute longer.
JABE (*exhausted*):—Let's—rest here a minute. . . .
LADY (*eagerly*): Yes! Rest there a minute!

NURSE: Okay. We'll rest here a minute. . . .

(*They sit down side by side on a bench under the artificial palm tree in the shaft of light. Jabe glares into the light like a fierce dying old beast. There are sounds from the alcove. To cover them up, Lady keeps making startled, laughing sounds in her throat, half laughing, half panting, chafing her hands together at the foot of the stairs, and coughing falsely.*)

JABE: Lady, what's wrong? Why are you so excited?
LADY: It seems like a miracle to me.
JABE: What seems like a miracle to you?
LADY: You coming downstairs.
JABE: You never thought I would come downstairs again?
LADY: Not this quick! Not as quick as this, Jabe! Did you think he would pick up as quick as this, Miss Porter?

(*Jabe rises.*)

NURSE: Ready?
JABE: Ready.
NURSE: He's doing fine, knock wood.
LADY: Yes, knock wood, knock wood!

(*Drums counter loudly with her knuckles. Val steps silently from behind the alcove curtain as the Nurse and Jabe resume their slow, shuffling descent of the stairs.*)

(*Moving back to D.R.C.*) You got to be careful not to overdo. You don't want another setback. Ain't that right, Miss Porter?
NURSE: Well, it's my policy to mobilize the patient.
LADY (*to Val in a shrill whisper*): Coffee's boiling, take the Goddamn coffee pot off the burner! (*She gives Val a panicky signal to go in the alcove.*)
JABE: Who're you talking to, Lady?
LADY: To—to—to Val, the clerk! I told him to—get you a—chair!
JABE: Who's that?
LADY: Val, Val, the clerk, you know Val!
JABE: Not yet. I'm anxious to meet him. Where is he?
LADY: Right here, right here, here's Val!

(*Val returns from the alcove.*)

JABE: He's here bright and early.
LADY: The early bird catches the worm!
JABE: That's right. Where is the worm?
LADY (*loudly*): Ha ha!
NURSE: Careful! One step at a time, Mr. Torrance.
LADY: Saturday before Easter's our biggest sales-day of the year, I mean second biggest, but sometimes it's even bigger than Christmas Eve! So I told Val to get here a half hour early.

(*Jabe misses his step and stumbles to foot of stairs. Lady screams. Nurse rushes down to him. Val advances and raises the man to his feet.*)

VAL: Here. Here.
LADY: Oh, my God.
NURSE: Oh, oh!
JABE: I'm all right.
NURSE: Are you sure?
LADY: Are you sure?
JABE: Let me go! (*He staggers to lean against counter, panting, glaring, with a malignant smile.*)
LADY: Oh, my God. Oh, my—God. . . .
JABE: This is the boy that works here?
LADY: Yes, this is the clerk I hired to help us out, Jabe.
JABE: How is he doing?
LADY: Fine, fine.
JABE: He's mighty good-looking. Do women give him much trouble?
LADY: When school lets out the high-school girls are thick as flies in this store!
JABE: How about older women? Don't he attract older women? The older ones are the buyers, they got the money. They sweat it out of their husbands and throw it away! What's your salary, boy, how much do I pay you?
LADY: Twenty-two fifty a week.
JABE: You're getting him cheap.
VAL: I get—commissions.
JABE: Commissions?

VAL: Yes. One percent of all sales.
JABE: Oh? Oh? I didn't know about that.
LADY: I knew he would bring in trade and he brings it in.
JABE: I bet.
LADY: Val, get Jabe a chair, he ought to sit down.
JABE: No, I don't want to sit down. I want to take a look at the new confectionery.
LADY: Oh, yes, yes! Take a look at it! Val, Val, turn on the lights in the confectionery! I want Jabe to see the way I done it over! I'm—real—*proud*!

(*Val crosses and switches on light in confectionery. The bulbs in the arches and the juke box light up.*)

Go in and look at it, Jabe. I am real proud of it!

(*He stares at Lady a moment; then shuffles slowly into the spectral radiance of the confectionery. Lady moves D.C. At the same time a calliope becomes faintly audible and slowly but steadily builds. Miss Porter goes with the patient, holding his elbow.*)

VAL (*returning to Lady*): He looks like death.
LADY (*moving away from him*): *Hush!*

(*Val goes up above counter and stands in the shadows.*)

NURSE: Well, isn't this artistic.
JABE: Yeh. Artistic as hell.
NURSE: I never seen anything like it before.
JABE: Nobody else did either.
NURSE (*coming back to U.R.C.*): Who done these decorations?
LADY (*defiantly*): I did them, all by myself!
NURSE: What do you know. It sure is something artistic.

(*Calliope is now up loud.*)

JABE (*coming back to D.R.*): Is there a circus or carnival in the county?
LADY: What?
JABE: That sounds like a circus calliope on the highway.
LADY: That's no circus calliope. It's advertising the gala opening of the Torrance Confectionery tonight!

JABE: Doing what did you say?

LADY: It's announcing the opening of our confectionery, it's going all over Glorious Hill this morning and all over Sunset and Lyon this afternoon. Hurry on here so you can see it go by the store. (*She rushes excitedly to open the front door as the ragtime music of the calliope approaches.*)

JABE: I married a live one, Miss Porter. How much does that damn thing cost me?

LADY: You'll be surprised how little. (*She is talking with an hysterical vivacity now.*) I hired it for a song!

JABE: How much of a song did you hire it for?

LADY (*closing door*): Next to nothing, seven-fifty an hour! And it covers three towns in Two River County!

(*Calliope fades out.*)

JABE (*with a muted ferocity*): Miss Porter, I married a live one! Didn't I marry a live one? (*Switches off lights in confectionery*) Her daddy "The Wop" was just as much of a live one till he burned up.

(*Lady gasps as if struck.*)

(*With a slow, ugly grin:*) He had a wine garden on the north shore of Moon Lake. The new confectionery sort of reminds me of it. But he made a mistake, he made a bad mistake, one time, selling liquor to niggers. We burned him out. We burned him out, house and orchard and vines and "The Wop" was burned up trying to fight the fire. (*He turns.*) I think I better go up.

LADY:—Did you say "WE"?

JABE:—I have a kind of a cramp. . . .

NURSE (*taking his arm*): Well, let's go up.

JABE:—Yes, I better go up. . . .

(*They cross to stairs. Calliope fades in.*)

LADY (*almost shouting as she moves D.C.*): Jabe, did you say "WE" did it, did you say "WE" did it?

JABE (*at foot of stairs, stops, turns*): Yes, I said *"We"* did it. You heard me, Lady.

NURSE: One step at a time, one step at a time, take it easy.

(*They ascend gradually to the landing and above. The calliope passes directly before the store and a clown is seen, or heard, shouting through megaphone.*)

CLOWN: Don't forget tonight, folks, the gala opening of the Torrance Confectionery, free drinks and free favors, don't forget it, the gala opening of the confectionery.

(*Fade. Jabe and the Nurse disappear above the landing. Calliope gradually fades. A hoarse cry above. The Nurse runs back downstairs, exclaiming:*)

NURSE: He's bleeding, he's having a hemm'rhage! (*Runs to phone.*) Dr. Buchanan's office! (*Turns again to Lady.*) Your husband is having a hemm'rhage!

(*Calliope is loud still. Lady appears not to hear. She speaks to Val:*)

LADY: Did you hear what he said? He said "We" did it, "WE" burned—house—vines—orchard—"The Wop" burned fighting the fire. . . .

(*The scene dims out; calliope fades out.*)

SCENE TWO

Sunset of the same day. At rise Val is alone. He is standing stock-still down center stage, almost beneath the proscenium, in the tense, frozen attitude of a wild animal listening to something that warns it of danger, his head turned as if he were looking off stage left, out over the house, frowning slightly, attentively. After a moment he mutters something sharply, and his body relaxes; he takes out a cigarette and crosses to the store entrance, opens the door and stands looking out. It has been raining steadily and will rain again in a while, but right now it is clearing: the sun breaks through, suddenly, with great brilliance; and almost at the same instant, at some distance, a woman cries out a great hoarse cry of terror and exaltation; the cry is repeated as she comes running nearer.

Vee Talbott appears through the window as if blind and demented, stiff, groping gestures, shielding her eyes with one arm as she feels along the store window for the entrance, gasping for breath. Val steps aside, taking hold of her arm to guide her into the store. For a few moments she leans weakly, blindly panting for breath against the oval glass of the door, then calls out.

VEE: I'm—*struck blind!*

VAL: You can't see?

VEE:—No! Nothing. . . .

VAL (*assisting her to stool below counter*): Set down here, Mrs. Talbott.

VEE:—Where?

VAL (*pushing her gently*): Here.

(*Vee sinks moaning onto stool.*)

What hurt your eyes, Mrs. Talbott, what happened to your eyes?

VEE (*drawing a long, deep breath*): The vision I waited and prayed for all my life long!

VAL: You had a vision?

VEE: I saw the eyes of my Saviour!—They struck me blind. (*Leans forward, clasping her eyes in anguish.*) Ohhhh, they burned out my eyes!

VAL: Lean back.

VEE: Eyeballs burn like fire. . . .

VAL (*going off R.*): I'll get you something cold to put on your eyes.

VEE: I knew a vision was coming, oh, I had many signs!

VAL (*in confectionery*): It must be a terrible shock to have a vision. . . . (*He speaks gravely, gently, scooping chipped ice from the soft-drink cooler and wrapping it in his handkerchief.*)

VEE (*with the naïveté of a child, as Val comes back to her*): I *thought* I would see my Saviour on the day of His passion, which was yesterday, Good Friday, that's when I expected to see Him. But I was mistaken, I was—disappointed. Yesterday passed and nothing, nothing much happened but—today—

(*Val places handkerchief over her eyes.*)

—this afternoon, somehow I pulled myself together and walked outdoors and started to go to pray in the empty church and meditate on the Rising of Christ tomorrow. Along the road as I walked, thinking about the mysteries of Easter, veils!—(*She makes a long shuddering word out of "veils."*)—seemed to drop off my eyes! Light, oh, light! I never have seen such brilliance! It *PRICKED* my eyeballs like *NEEDLES*!

VAL:—Light?

VEE: Yes, yes, light. YOU know, you know we live in light and shadow, that's, that's what we *live* in, a world of—*light* and—*shadow*. . . .

VAL: Yes. In light and shadow. (*He nods with complete understanding and agreement. They are like two children who have found life's meaning, simply and quietly, along a country road.*)

VEE: A world of light and shadow is what we live in, and—it's—confusing. . . .

(*A man is peering in at store window.*)

VAL: Yeah, they—*do* get—*mixed*. . . .

VEE: Well, and then—(*Hesitates to recapture her vision.*)—I heard this clap of thunder! Sky!—Split open!—And there in the split-open sky, I saw, I tell you, I *saw* the TWO HUGE BLAZING EYES OF JESUS CHRIST RISEN!—Not crucified but Risen! I mean Crucified and *then* RISEN!—The blazing eyes of Christ Risen! And then a great— (*Raises both arms and makes a great sweeping motion to describe an apocalyptic disturbance of the atmosphere.*) —His hand!—*Invisible!*—I didn't *see* his hand!—But it *touched* me—*here!* (*She seizes Val's hand and presses it to her great heaving bosom.*)

TALBOTT (*appearing R. in confectionery, furiously*): VEE!

(*She starts up, throwing the compress from her eyes. Utters a sharp gasp and staggers backward with terror and blasted ecstacy and dismay and belief, all confused in her look.*)

VEE: You!

TALBOTT: VEE!

VEE: *You!*

TALBOTT (*advancing*): VEE!

VEE (*making two syllables of the word "eyes"*):—The Ey—es! (*She collapses, forward, falls to her knees, her arms thrown about Val. He seizes her to lift her. Two or three men are peering in at the store window.*)

TALBOTT (*pushing Val away*): Let go of her, don't put your hands on my wife! (*He seizes her roughly and hauls her to the door. Val moves up to help Vee.*) Don't move. (*At door, to Val:*) I'm coming back.

VAL: I'm not goin' nowhere.

TALBOTT (*to Dog, as he goes off L. with Vee*): Dog, go in there with that boy.

VOICE (*outside*): Sheriff caught him messin' with his wife.

(*Repeat: Another Voice at a distance. "Dog" Hamma enters and stands silently beside the door while there is a continued murmur of excited voices on the street. The following scene should be underplayed, played almost casually, like the performance of some familiar ritual.*)

VAL: What do you want?

(*Dog says nothing but removes from his pocket and opens a spring-blade knife and moves to D.R. Pee Wee enters. Through the open door—voices.*)

VOICES (*outside*):—Son of a low-down bitch foolin' with—
—That's right, ought to be—
—Cut the son of a—

VAL: What do you—?

(*Pee Wee closes the door and silently stands beside it, opening a spring-blade knife. Val looks from one to the other.*)

—It's six o'clock. Store's closed.

(*Men chuckle like dry leaves rattling. Val crosses toward the door; is confronted by Talbott; stops short.*)

TALBOTT: Boy, I said stay here.

VAL: I'm not—goin' nowhere. . . .

TALBOTT: Stand back under that light.

VAL: Which light?

TALBOTT: That light.

(*Points. Val goes behind counter.*)

I want to look at you while I run through some photos of men wanted.

VAL: I'm not wanted.

TALBOTT: A good-looking boy like you is always wanted.

(*Men chuckle. Val stands in hot light under green-shaded bulb. Talbott shuffles through photos he has removed from his pocket.*)

—How tall are you, boy?

VAL: Never measured.

TALBOTT: How much do you weigh?

VAL: Never weighed.

TALBOTT: Got any scars or marks of identification on your face or body?

VAL: No, sir.

TALBOTT: Open your shirt.

VAL: What for? (*He doesn't.*)

TALBOTT: Open his shirt for him, Dog.

(*Dog steps quickly forward and rips shirt open to waist. Val starts forward; men point knives; he draws back.*)

That's right, stay there, boy. What did you do before?

(*Pee Wee sits on stairs.*)

VAL: Before—what?

TALBOTT: Before you come here?

VAL:—Traveled and—played. . . .

TALBOTT: Played?

DOG (*advancing to C.*): What?

PEE WEE: With wimmen?

(*Dog laughs.*)

VAL: No. Played guitar—and sang. . . .

(*Val touches guitar on counter.*)

TALBOTT: Let me see that guitar.

VAL: Look at it. But don't touch it. I don't let nobody but musicians touch it.

(*Men come close.*)

DOG: What're you smiling for, boy?

PEE WEE: He ain't smiling, his mouth's just twitching like a dead chicken's foot.

(*They laugh.*)

TALBOTT: What is all that writing on the guitar?

VAL:—Names. . . .

TALBOTT: What of?

VAL: Autographs of musicians dead and living.

(*Men read aloud the names printed on the guitar: Bessie Smith, Leadbelly, Woody Guthrie, Jelly Roll Morton, etc. They bend close to it, keeping the open knife blades pointed at Val's body; Dog touches neck of the guitar, draws it toward him. Val suddenly springs, with catlike agility, onto the counter. He runs along it, kicking at their hands as they catch at his legs. The Nurse runs down to the landing.*)

MISS PORTER: *What's going on?*

TALBOTT (*at the same time*): *Stop that!*

(*Jabe calls hoarsely above.*)

MISS PORTER (*excitedly, all in one breath, as Jabe calls*): Where's Mrs. Torrance? I got a very sick man up there and his wife's disappeared.

(*Jabe calls out again.*)

I been on a whole lot of cases but never seen one where a wife showed no concern for a—

(*Jabe cries out again. Her voice fades out as she returns above.*)

TALBOTT (*overlapping Nurse's speech*): Dog! Pee Wee! You all stand back from that counter. Dog, why don't you an' Pee Wee go up an' see Jabe. Leave me straighten this boy out, go on, go on up.

PEE WEE: C'mon, Dawg. . . .

(*They go up. Val remains panting on counter.*)

TALBOTT (*sits in shoe chair at R. window. In Talbott's manner there is a curious, half-abashed gentleness, when alone with the boy, as if he recognized the purity in him and was, truly, for the moment, ashamed of the sadism implicit in the occurrence*): Awright, boy. Git on down off th' counter, I ain't gonna touch y'r guitar.

(*Val jumps off counter.*)

But I'm gonna tell you something. They's a certain county I know of which has a big sign at the county line that says, "Nigger, don't let the sun go down on you in this county." That's all it says, it don't threaten nothing, it just says, "Nigger, don't let the sun go down on you in this county!" (*Chuckles hoarsely. Rises and takes a step toward Val.*)

Well, son! You ain't a nigger and this is not that county, but, son, I want you to just imagine that you seen a sign that said to you: "Boy, don't let the sun rise on you in this county." I said "rise," not "go down" because it's too close to sunset for you to git packed an' move on before that. But I think if you value that instrument in your hands as much as you seem to, you'll simplify my job by not allowing the sun tomorrow to rise on you in this county. 'S that understood, now, boy?

(*Val stares at him, expressionless, panting.*)

(*Crossing to door*) I *hope* so. I don't like *violence.* (*He looks back and nods at Val from the door. Then goes outside in the fiery afterglow of the sunset. Dogs bark in the distance. Music fades in: "Dog Howl Blues"—minor—guitar. Pause in which Val remains motionless, cradling guitar in his arms. Then Val's faraway, troubled look is resolved in a slight, abrupt nod of his head. He sweeps back the alcove curtain and enters the alcove and closes the curtain behind him. Lights dim down to indicate a division of scenes.*)

SCENE THREE

Half an hour later. The lighting is less realistic than in the previous scenes of the play. The interior of the store is so dim that only the vertical lines of the pillars and such selected items as the palm tree on the stair landing and the ghostly paper vineyard of the confectionery are plainly visible. The view through the great front window has virtually become the background of the action: A singing wind sweeps clouds before the moon so that the witch-like country brightens and dims and brightens again. The Marshall's hounds are restless: their baying is heard now and then. A lamp outside the door sometimes catches a figure that moves past with mysterious urgency, calling out softly and raising an arm to beckon, like a shade in the under kingdom.

At rise, or when the stage is lighted again, it is empty but footsteps are descending the stairs as Dolly and Beulah rush into the store and call out, in soft shouts:

DOLLY: Dawg?

BEULAH: Pee Wee?

EVA TEMPLE (*appearing on landing and calling down softly in the superior tone of a privileged attendant in a sick-chamber*): Please don't shout!—Mr. Binnings and Mr. Hamma (*Names of the two husbands*) are upstairs sitting with Jabe. . . . (*She continues her descent. Then Eva Temple appears, sobbing, on landing.*)

—Come down carefully, Sister.

SISTER: Help me, I'm all to pieces. . . .

(*Eva ignores this request and faces the two women.*)

BEULAH: Has the bleedin' quit yit?

EVA: The hemorrhage seems to have stopped. Sister, Sister, pull yourself together, we all have to face these things sometime in life.

DOLLY: Has he sunk into a coma?

EVA: No. Cousin Jabe is conscious. Nurse Porter says his pulse is remarkably strong for a man that lost so much blood. Of course he's had a transfusion.

SISTER: Two of 'em.

EVA (*crossing to Dolly*): Yais, an' they put him on glucose. His strength came back like magic.

BEULAH: She up there?

EVA: *Who?*

BEULAH: Lady!

EVA: No! When last reported she had just stepped into the Glorious Hill Beauty Parlor.

BEULAH: You don't mean it.

EVA: Ask Sister!

SISTER: She's planning to go ahead with—!

EVA:—The gala opening of the confectionery. Switch on the lights in there, Sister.

(*Sister crosses and switches on lights and moves off R. The decorated confectionery is lighted. Dolly and Beulah exclaim in awed voices.*)

—Of course it's not normal behavior; it's downright lunacy, but still that's no excuse for it! And when she called up at five, about one hour ago, it wasn't to ask about Jabe, oh, no, she didn't mention his name. She asked if Ruby Lightfoot had delivered a case of Seagram's. Yais, she just shouted that question and hung up the phone, before I could— (*She crosses and goes off R.*)

BEULAH (*going into confectionery*): *Oh, I understand, now! Now I see what she's up to!* Electric moon, cut-out silver-paper stars and artificial vines? Why, it's her father's wine garden on Moon Lake she's turned this room into!

DOLLY (*suddenly as she sits in shoe chair*): *Here she comes, here she comes!*

(*The Temple Sisters retreat from view in confectionery as Lady enters the store. She wears a hooded rain-cape and carries a large paper shopping bag and paper carton box.*)

LADY: Go on, ladies, don't stop, my ears are burning!

BEULAH (*coming in to U.R.C.*):—Lady, oh, Lady, Lady. . . .

LADY: Why d'you speak my name in that pitiful voice? Hanh? (*Throws back hood of cape, her eyes blazing, and places bag and box on counter.*) *Val? Val!* Where is that boy that works here?

(*Dolly shakes her head.*)

I guess he's havin' a T-bone steak with French fries and coleslaw fo' ninety-five cents at the Blue Bird. . . .

(*Sounds in confectionery.*)

Who's in the confectionery, is that you, Val?

(*Temple Sisters emerge and stalk past her.*)

Going, girls?

(*They go out of store.*)

Yes, gone! (*She laughs and throws off rain-cape, onto counter, revealing a low-cut gown, triple strand of pearls and a purple satin-ribboned corsage.*)

BEULAH (*sadly*): How long have I known you, Lady?

LADY (*going behind counter, unpacks paper hats and whistles*): A long time, Beulah. I think you remember when my people come here on a banana boat from Palermo, Sicily, by way of Caracas, Venezuela, yes, with a grind-organ and a monkey my papa had bought in Venezuela. I was not much bigger than the monkey, ha ha! You remember the monkey? The man that sold Papa the monkey said it was a very young monkey, but he was a liar, it was a very old monkey, it was on its last legs, ha ha ha! But it was a well-dressed monkey. (*Coming around to R. of counter*) It had a green velvet suit and a little red cap that it tipped and a tambourine that it passed around for money, ha ha ha. . . . The grind-organ played and the monkey danced in the sun, ha ha!—*"O Sole Mio, Da Da Da daaa . . . !"* (*Sits in chair at counter*) —One day, the monkey danced too much in the sun and it was a very old monkey and it dropped dead. . . . My Papa, he turned to the people, he made them a bow and he said, "The show is over, the monkey is dead." Ha ha!

(*Slight pause. Then Dolly pipes up venomously:*)

DOLLY: Ain't it wonderful Lady can be so brave?

BEULAH: Yaiss, wonderful! Hanh. . . .

LADY: For me the show is not over, the monkey is not dead yet! (*Then suddenly:*) *Val, is that you, Val?*

(*Someone has entered the confectionery door, out of sight, and the draught of air has set the wind-chimes tinkling wildly. Lady rushes forward but stops short as Carol appears. She wears a trench coat and a white sailor's cap with a turned-*

down brim, inscribed with the name of a vessel and a date, past or future, memory or anticipation.)

DOLLY: Well, here's your first customer, Lady.
LADY (*going behind counter*):—Carol, that room ain't open.
CAROL: There's a big sign outside that says "Open Tonite!"
LADY: It ain't open to you.
CAROL: I have to stay here a while. They stopped my car, you see, I don't have a license; my license has been revoked and I have to find someone to drive me across the river.
LADY: You can call a taxi.
CAROL: I heard that the boy that works for you is leaving tonight and I—
LADY: *Who said he's leaving?*
CAROL (*crossing to counter*): Sheriff Talbott. The County Marshall suggested I get him to drive me over the river since he'd be crossing it too.
LADY: You got some mighty wrong information!
CAROL: Where is he? I don't see him?
LADY: Why d'you keep coming back here bothering that boy? He's not interested in you! Why would he be leaving here tonight?

(*Door opens off as she comes from behind counter.*)

Val, is that you, Val?

(*Conjure Man enters through confectionery, mumbling rapidly, holding out something. Beulah and Dolly take flight out the door with cries of revulsion.*)

No conjure stuff, go away!

(*He starts to withdraw.*)

CAROL (*crossing to U.R.C.*): Uncle! The Choctaw cry! I'll give you a dollar for it.

(*Lady turns away with a gasp, with a gesture of refusal. The Negro nods, then throws back his turkey neck and utters a series of sharp barking sounds that rise to a sustained cry of great intensity and wildness. The cry produces a violent reaction in the building. Beulah and Dolly run out of the store. Lady does not move but she catches her breath. Dog and Pee

Wee run down the stairs with ad libs and hustle the Negro out of the store, ignoring Lady, as their wives call: "Pee Wee!" and "Dawg!" outside on the walk. Val sweeps back the alcove curtain and appears as if the cry were his cue. Above, in the sick room, hoarse, outraged shouts that subside with exhaustion. Carol crosses downstage and speaks to the audience and to herself:)

CAROL: Something is still wild in the country! This country used to be wild, the men and women were wild and there was a wild sort of sweetness in their hearts, for each other, but now it's sick with neon, it's broken out sick, with neon, like most other places. . . . I'll wait outside in my car. It's the fastest thing on wheels in Two River County!

(*She goes out of the store R. Lady stares at Val with great asking eyes, a hand to her throat.*)

LADY (*with false boldness*): Well, ain't you going with her?

VAL: I'm going with no one I didn't come here with. And I come here with no one.

LADY: Then get into your white jacket. I need your services in that room there tonight.

(*Val regards her steadily for several beats.*)

(*Clapping her hands together twice*) Move, move, stop goofing! The Delta Brilliant lets out in half'n hour and they'll be driving up here. You got to shave ice for the setups!

VAL (*as if he thought she'd gone crazy*): "Shave ice for the setups"? (*He moves up to counter.*)

LADY: Yes, an' call Ruby Lightfoot, tell her I need me a dozen more half-pints of Seagram's. They all call for Seven-and-Sevens. You know how t' sell bottle goods under a counter? It's OK. We're gonna git paid for protection. (*Gasps, touching her diaphragm*) But one thing you gotta watch out for is sellin' to minors. Don't serve liquor to minors. Ask for his driver's license if they's any doubt. Anybody born earlier than—let's see, twenty-one from—oh, I'll figure it later. Hey! Move! Move! Stop goofing!

VAL (*placing guitar on counter*):—You're the one that's goofing, not me, Lady.

LADY: Move, I said, *move!*

VAL: What kick are you on, are you on a benny kick, Lady? 'Ve you washed down a couple of bennies with a pot of black coffee t' make you come on strong for th' three o'clock show? (*His mockery is gentle, almost tender, but he has already made a departure; he is back in the all-night bars with the B-girls and raffish entertainers. He stands at counter as she rushes about. As she crosses between the two rooms, he reaches out to catch hold of her bare arm and he pulls her to him and grips her arms.*)

LADY: Hey!

VAL: Will you quit thrashin' around like a hooked catfish?

LADY: Go git in y'r white jacket an'—

VAL: Sit down. I want to talk to you.

LADY: I don't have time.

VAL: I got to reason with you.

LADY: It's not possible to.

VAL: You can't open a night-place here this night.

LADY: You bet your sweet life I'm *going* to!

VAL: Not *me,* not *my* sweet life!

LADY: I'm betting *my* life on it! Sweet or *not* sweet, I'm—

VAL: Yours is yours, mine is mine. . . . (*He releases her with a sad shrug.*)

LADY: You don't get the point, huh? There's a man up there that set fire to my father's wine garden and I lost my life in it, yeah, I lost my life in it, *three* lives was lost in it, two *born* lives and *one—not.* . . . I was made to commit a *murder* by him up there! (*Has frozen momentarily*) —I want that man to see the wine garden come open again when he's dying! I want him to hear it coming open again here tonight! While he's dying. It's necessary, no power on earth can stop it. Hell, I don't even want it, it's just necessary, it's just something's got to be done to square things away, to, to, to—be *not defeated! You get me? Just to be not defeated!* Ah, oh, I won't be defeated, not again, in my life! (*Embraces him*) Thank you for staying here with me!—God bless you for it. . . . Now please go and get in your white jacket . . .

(*Val looks at her as if he were trying to decide between a natural sensibility of heart and what his life's taught him since he left Witches' Bayou. Then he sighs again, with the same slight, sad shrug, and crosses into alcove to put on a jacket and remove from under his cot a canvas-wrapped package of his belongings. Lady takes paper hats and carnival stuff from counter, crosses into confectionery and puts them on the tables, then starts back but stops short as she sees Val come out of alcove with his snakeskin jacket and luggage.*)

LADY: That's not your white jacket, that's that snakeskin jacket you had on when you come here.

VAL: I come and I go in this jacket.

LADY: *Go,* did you say?

VAL: Yes, ma'am, I did, I said go. All that stays to be settled is a little matter of wages.

(*The dreaded thing's happened to her. This is what they call "the moment of truth" in the bull ring, when the matador goes in over the horns of the bull to plant the mortal swordthrust.*)

LADY:—So you're—cutting out, are you?

VAL: My gear's all packed. I'm catchin' the southbound bus.

LADY: Uh-huh, in a pig's eye. You're not conning me, mister. She's waiting for you outside in her high-powered car and you're—

(*Sudden footsteps on stairs. They break apart, Val puts suitcase down, drawing back into shadow, as Nurse Porter appears on the stair landing.*)

NURSE PORTER: Miss Torrance, are you down there?

LADY (*crossing to foot of stairs*): Yeah. I'm here. I'm back.

NURSE PORTER: Can I talk to you up here about Mr. Torrance?

LADY (*shouting to Nurse*): I'll be up in a minute. (*Door closes above. Lady turns to Val:*) OK, now, mister. You're scared about something, ain't you?

VAL: I been threatened with violence if I stay here.

LADY: I got paid for protection in this county, plenty paid for it, and it covers you too.

VAL: No, ma'am. My time is up here.

LADY: Y' say that like you'd served a sentence in jail.

VAL: I got in deeper than I meant to, Lady.

LADY: Yeah, and how about me?

VAL (*going to her*): I would of cut out before you got back to the store, but I wanted to tell you something I never told no one before. (*Places hand on her shoulder.*) I feel a true love for you, Lady! (*He kisses her.*) I'll wait for you out of this county, just name the time and the . . .

LADY (*moving back*): Oh, don't talk about love, not to me. It's easy to say "Love, Love!" with fast and free transportation waiting right out the door for you!

VAL: D'you remember some things I told you about me the night we met here?

LADY (*crossing to R.C.*): Yeah, many things. Yeah, temperature of a dog. And some bird, oh, yeah, without legs so it had to sleep on the wind!

VAL (*through her speech*): Naw, not that; not that.

LADY: And how you could burn down a woman? I said "Bull!" I take that back. You can! You can burn down a woman and stamp on her ashes to make sure the fire is put out!

VAL: I mean what I said about gettin' away from . . .

LADY: How long've you held this first steady job in your life?

VAL: Too long, too long!

LADY: Four months and five days, mister. All right! How much pay have you took?

VAL: I told you to keep out all but—

LADY: Y'r living expenses. I can give you the figures to a dime. Eighty-five bucks, no, ninety! Chicken-feed, mister! Y'know how much you got coming? IF you get it? I don't need paper to figure, I got it all in my head. You got five hundred and eighty-six bucks coming to you, not, not chicken-feed, that. But, mister. (*Gasps for breath*) —If you try to walk out on me, now, tonight, without notice!— You're going to get just nothing! A great big zero. . . .

(*Somebody hollers at door off R.: "Hey! You open?" She rushes toward it shouting, "CLOSED! CLOSED! GO AWAY!"— Val crosses to the cashbox. She turns back toward him, gasps:*)

Now you watch your next move and I'll watch mine. You open that cashbox and I swear I'll throw open that door and holler, clerk's robbing the store!

VAL:—Lady?

LADY (*fiercely*): Hanh?

VAL:—Nothing, you've—

LADY:—Hanh?

VAL: Blown your stack. I will go without pay.

LADY (*coming to* C.): Then you ain't understood me! With or without pay, you're staying!

VAL: I've got my gear. (*Picks up suitcase. She rushes to seize his guitar.*)

LADY: Then I'll go up and git mine! And take this with me, just t'make sure you wait till I'm— (*She moves back to R.C. He puts suitcase down.*)

VAL (*advancing toward her*): Lady, what're you—?

LADY (*entreating with guitar raised*): *Don't—!*

VAL:—Doing with—

LADY:—*Don't!*

VAL:—my guitar!

LADY: *Holding it for security while I—*

VAL: Lady, you been a lunatic since this morning!

LADY: Longer, longer than morning! I'm going to keep hold of your "life companion" while I pack! I am! I am goin' to pack an' go, if you go, where you go!

(*He makes a move toward her. She crosses below and around to counter.*)

You didn't think so, you actually didn't think so? What was I going to do, in your opinion? What, in your opinion, would I be doing? Stay on here in a store full of bottles and boxes while you go far, while you go fast and far, without me having your—forwarding address!—even?

VAL: I'll—give you a forwarding address. . . .

LADY: Thanks, oh, thanks! Would I take your forwarding address back of that curtain? "Oh, dear forwarding address, hold me, kiss me, be faithful!" (*Utters grotesque, stifled cry; presses fist to mouth.*)

(*He advances cautiously, hand stretched toward the guitar. She retreats above to U.R.C., biting lip, eyes flaring. Jabe knocks above.*)

Stay back! You want me to smash it!

VAL (*D.C.*): He's—knocking for you. . . .

LADY: I know! Death's knocking for me! Don't you think I hear him, knock, knock, knock? It sounds like what it is! Bones knocking bones. . . . Ask me how it felt to be coupled with death up there, and I can tell you. My skin crawled when he touched me. But I endured it. I guess my heart knew that somebody must be coming to take me out of this hell! You did. You came. Now look at me! I'm alive once more! (*Convulsive sobbing controlled: continues more calmly and harshly:*)

—*I won't wither in dark!* Got that through your skull? Now. Listen! Everything in this rotten store is yours, not just your pay, but everything Death's scraped together down here!—but Death has got to die before we can go. . . . You got that memorized, now?—Then get into your white jacket!—*Tonight is the gala opening*—(*Rushes through confectionery.*)—*of the confectionery*—

(*Val runs and seizes her arm holding guitar. She breaks violently free.*)

Smash me against a rock and I'll smash your guitar! I will, if you—

(*Rapid footsteps on stairs.*)

Oh, Miss Porter!

(*She motions Val back. He retreats into alcove. Lady puts guitar down beside juke-box. Miss Porter is descending the stairs.*)

NURSE PORTER (*descending watchfully*): You been out a long time.

LADY (*moving U.R.C.*): Yeah, well, I had lots of— (*Her voice expires breathlessly. She stares fiercely, blindly, into the other's hard face.*)

NURSE PORTER:—Of what?

LADY: Things to—things to—take care of. . . . (*Draws a deep, shuddering breath, clenched fist to her bosom.*)

NURSE PORTER: Didn't I hear you shouting to someone just now?

LADY:—Uh-huh. Some drunk tourist made a fuss because I wouldn't sell him no—liquor. . . .

NURSE (*crossing to the door*): Oh. Mr. Torrance is sleeping under medication.

LADY: That's good. (*She sits in shoe-fitting chair.*)

NURSE: I gave him a hypo at five.

LADY:—Don't all that morphine weaken the heart, Miss Porter?

NURSE: Gradually, yes.

LADY: How long does it usually take for them to let go?

NURSE: It varies according to the age of the patient and the condition his heart's in. Why?

LADY: Miss Porter, don't people sort of help them let go?

NURSE: How do you mean, Mrs. Torrance?

LADY: Shorten their suffering for them?

NURSE: Oh, I see what you mean. (*Snaps her purse shut.*) —I see what you mean, Mrs. Torrance. But killing is killing, regardless of circumstances.

LADY: Nobody said killing.

NURSE: You said "shorten their suffering."

LADY: Yes, like merciful people shorten an animal's suffering when he's . . .

NURSE: A human being is not the same as an animal, Mrs. Torrance. And I don't hold with what they call—

LADY (*overlapping*): *Don't give me a sermon,* Miss Porter I just wanted to know if—

NURSE (*overlapping*): I'm not giving a sermon. I just answered your question. If you want to get somebody to shorten your husband's life—

LADY (*jumping up; overlapping*): Why, how dare you say that I—

NURSE: I'll be back at ten-thirty.

LADY: Don't!

NURSE: What?

LADY (*crossing behind counter*): Don't come back at ten-thirty, don't come back.

NURSE: I'm always discharged by the doctors on my cases.

LADY: This time you're being discharged by the patient's wife.

NURSE: That's something we'll have to discuss with Dr. Buchanan.

LADY: I'll call him myself about it. I don't like you. I don't think you belong in the nursing profession, you have cold eyes; I think you like to watch pain!

NURSE: I know why you don't like my eyes. (*Snaps purse shut.*) You don't like my eyes because you know they see clear.

LADY: Why are you staring at *me*?

NURSE: I'm not staring at you, I'm staring at the curtain. There's something burning in there, smoke's coming out! (*Starts toward alcove.*) Oh.

LADY: Oh, no, you don't. (*Seizes her arm.*)

NURSE (*pushes her roughly aside and crosses to the curtain. Val rises from cot, opens the curtain and faces her coolly*): Oh, excuse me! (*She turns to Lady.*) —The moment I looked at you when I was called on this case last Friday morning I knew that you were pregnant.

(*Lady gasps.*)

I also knew the moment I looked at your husband it wasn't by him. (*She stalks to the door. Lady suddenly cries out:*)

LADY: Thank you for telling me what I hoped for is true.

MISS PORTER: You don't seem to have any shame.

LADY (*exalted*): No. I don't have shame. I have—*great*—*joy!*

MISS PORTER (*venomously*): Then why don't you get the calliope and the clown to make the announcement?

LADY: You do it for me, save me the money! Make the announcement, all over!

(*Nurse goes out. Val crosses swiftly to the door and locks it. Then he advances toward her, saying:*)

VAL: Is it true what she said?

(*Lady moves as if stunned to the counter; the stunned look gradually turns to a look of wonder. On the counter is a heap of silver and gold paper hats and trumpets for the gala opening of the confectionery.*)

VAL (*in a hoarse whisper*): Is it true or not true, what that woman told you?

LADY: You sound like a scared little boy.

VAL: She's gone out to tell.

(*Pause.*)

LADY: You gotta go now—it's dangerous for you to stay here. . . . Take your pay out of the cashbox, you can go. Go, go, take the keys to my car, cross the river into some other county. You've done what you came here to do. . . .

VAL:—It's true then, it's—?

LADY (*sitting in chair of counter*): True as God's word! I have life in my body, this dead tree, my body, has burst in flower! You've given me life, you can go!

(*He crouches down gravely opposite her, gently takes hold of her knotted fingers and draws them to his lips, breathing on them as if to warm them. She sits bolt upright, tense, blind as a clairvoyant.*)

VAL:—Why didn't you tell me before?

LADY:—When a woman's been childless as long as I've been childless, it's hard to believe that you're still able to bear!—We used to have a little fig tree between the house and the orchard. It never bore any fruit, they said it was barren. Time went by it, spring after useless spring, and it almost started to—die. . . . Then one day I discovered a small green fig on the tree they said wouldn't bear! (*She is clasping a gilt paper horn.*) I ran through the orchard. I ran through the wine garden shouting, "Oh, Father, it's going to bear, the fig tree is going to bear!"—It seemed such a wonderful thing, after those ten barren springs, for the little fig tree to bear, it called for a celebration—I ran to a closet, I opened a box that we kept Christmas ornaments in!—I took them out, glass bells, glass birds, tinsel, icicles, stars. . . . And I hung the little tree with them, I decorated the fig tree with glass bells and glass birds, and silver icicles and stars, because it won the battle and it would bear! (*Rises, ecstatic*) Unpack the box! Unpack the box with the Christmas ornaments in it, put them on me, glass bells and glass birds and stars and tinsel and snow! (*In a sort of delirium she thrusts the conical gilt paper hat on her head and runs to the foot of the stairs with the paper horn. She blows the horn over and over, grotesquely mounting the stairs, as Val tries to stop her. She breaks away from him and runs up to the landing, blowing the paper horn and crying out:*) I've won, I've won, Mr. Death, I'm going to bear! (*Then suddenly she falters, catches her breath in a shocked gasp and awkwardly retreats to the stairs. Then turns screaming and runs back down them, her cries dying out as she arrives at the floor level. She retreats haltingly as a blind person, a hand stretched out to Val, as slow, clumping footsteps and hoarse breathing are heard on the stairs. She moans:*)—Oh, God, oh—God. . . .

(*Jabe appears on the landing, by the artificial palm tree in its dully lustrous green jardiniere, a stained purple robe hangs loosely about his wasted yellowed frame. He is death's self, and malignancy, as he peers, crouching, down into the store's dimness to discover his quarry.*)

JABE: Buzzards! Buzzards! (*Clutching the trunk of the false palm tree, he raises the other hand holding a revolver and fires down into the store. Lady screams and rushes to cover Val's motionless figure with hers. Jabe scrambles down a few steps and fires again and the bullet strikes her, expelling her breath in a great "Hah!" He fires again; the great "Hah!" is repeated. She turns to face him, still covering Val with her body, her face with all the passions and secrets of life and death in it now, her fierce eyes blazing, knowing, defying and accepting. But the revolver is empty; it clicks impotently and Jabe hurls it toward them; he descends and passes them, shouting out hoarsely:*) I'll have you burned! I burned her father and I'll have you burned! (*He opens the door and rushes out onto the road, shouting hoarsely:*) The clerk is robbing the store, he shot my wife, the clerk is robbing the store, he killed my wife!

VAL:—Did it—?

LADY:—Yes!—it did. . . .

(*A curious, almost formal, dignity appears in them both. She turns to him with the sort of smile that people offer in apology for an awkward speech, and he looks back at her gravely, raising one hand as if to stay her. But she shakes her head slightly and points to the ghostly radiance of her make-believe orchard and she begins to move a little unsteadily toward it. Music.*

Lady enters the confectionery and looks about it as people look for the last time at a loved place they are deserting.)

The show is over. The monkey is dead . . .

(*Music rises to cover whatever sound Death makes in the confectionery. It halts abruptly. Figures appear through the great front window of the store, pocket-lamps stare through the glass and someone begins to force the front door open. Val cries out:*)

VAL: Which way!

(*He turns and runs through the dim radiance of the confectionery, out of our sight. Something slams. Something cracks open. Men are in the store and the dark is full of hoarse, shouting voices.*)

VOICES OF MEN (*shouting*):—Keep to the walls! He's armed!
—Upstairs, Dog!
—Jack, the confectionery!

(*Wild cry back of store.*)

Got him. GOT HIM!
—They got him!
—Rope, git rope!
—Git rope from th' hardware section!
—I got something better than rope!
—What've you got?
—What's that, what's he got?
—A BLOWTORCH!
—Christ. . . .

(*A momentary hush.*)

—Come on, what in hell are we waiting for?
—Hold on a minute, I wanta see if it works!
—Wait, Wait!
—LOOK here!

(*A jet of blue flame stabs the dark. It flickers on Carol's figure in the confectionery. The men cry out together in hoarse passion crouching toward the fierce blue jet of fire, their faces lit by it like the faces of demons.*)

—Christ!
—It works!

(*They rush out. Confused shouting behind. Motors start. Fade quickly. There is almost silence, a dog bays in the distance. Then—the Conjure Man appears with a bundle of garments which he examines, dropping them all except the snakeskin jacket, which he holds up with a toothless mumble of excitement.*)

CAROL (*quietly, gently*): What have you got there, Uncle? Come here and let me see.

(*He crosses to her.*)

Oh yes, his snakeskin jacket. I'll give you a gold ring for it.

(*She slowly twists ring off her finger. Somewhere there is a cry of anguish. She listens attentively till it fades out, then nods with understanding.*)

—Wild things leave skins behind them, they leave clean skins and teeth and white bones behind them, and these are tokens passed from one to another, so that the fugitive kind can always follow their kind. . . .

(*The cry is repeated more terribly than before. It expires again. She draws the jacket about her as if she were cold, nods to the old Negro, handing him the ring. Then she crosses toward the door, pausing halfway as Sheriff Talbott enters with his pocket-lamp.*)

SHERIFF: Don't no one move, don't move!

(*She crosses directly past him as if she no longer saw him, and out the door. He shouts furiously:*)

Stay here!

(*Her laughter rings outside. He follows the girl, shouting:*)

Stop! Stop!

(*Silence. The Negro looks up with a secret smile as the curtain falls slowly.*)

SUDDENLY LAST SUMMER

To Anne Meacham

SCENE ONE

The set may be as unrealistic as the decor of a dramatic ballet. It represents part of a mansion of Victorian Gothic style in the Garden District of New Orleans on a late afternoon, between late summer and early fall. The interior is blended with a fantastic garden which is more like a tropical jungle, or forest, in the prehistoric age of giant fern-forests when living creatures had flippers turning to limbs and scales to skin. The colors of this jungle-garden are violent, especially since it is steaming with heat after rain. There are massive tree-flowers that suggest organs of a body, torn out, still glistening with undried blood; there are harsh cries and sibilant hissings and thrashing sounds in the garden as if it were inhabited by beasts, serpents and birds, all of savage nature. . . .

The jungle tumult continues a few moments after the curtain rises; then subsides into relative quiet, which is occasionally broken by a new outburst.

A lady enters with the assistance of a silver-knobbed cane. She has light orange or pink hair and wears a lavender lace dress, and over her withered bosom is pinned a starfish of diamonds.

She is followed by a young blond Doctor, all in white, glacially brilliant, very, very good-looking, and the old lady's manner and eloquence indicate her undeliberate response to his icy charm.

MRS. VENABLE: Yes, this was Sebastian's garden. The Latin names of the plants were printed on tags attached to them but the print's fading out. Those ones there—(*She draws a deep breath*)—are the oldest plants on earth, survivors from the age of the giant fern-forests. Of course in this semi-tropical climate—(*She takes another deep breath*)—some of the rarest plants, such as the Venus flytrap—you know what this is, Doctor? The Venus flytrap?

DOCTOR: An insectivorous plant?

MRS. VENABLE: Yes, it feeds on insects. It has to be kept under glass from early fall to late spring and when it went under glass, my son, Sebastian, had to provide it with fruit flies flown in at great expense from a Florida laboratory that used fruit flies for experiments in genetics. Well, I can't do that, Doctor. (*She takes a deep breath.*) I can't, I just can't do it! It's not the expense but the—

DOCTOR: Effort.

MRS. VENABLE: Yes. So goodbye, Venus flytrap!—like so much else . . . Whew! . . . (*She draws breath.*) —I don't know why, but—! I already feel I can lean on your shoulder, Doctor—Cu?—Cu?

DOCTOR: Cu-kro-wicz. It's a Polish word that means sugar, so let's make it simple and call me Doctor Sugar.

(*He returns her smile.*)

MRS. VENABLE: Well, now, Doctor Sugar, you've seen Sebastian's garden.

(*They are advancing slowly to the patio area.*)

DOCTOR: It's like a well-groomed jungle. . . .

MRS. VENABLE: That's how he meant it to be, nothing was accidental, everything was planned and designed in Sebastian's life and his—(*She dabs her forehead with her handkerchief which she had taken from her reticule*)—work!

DOCTOR: What was your son's work, Mrs. Venable?—besides this garden?

MRS. VENABLE: As many times as I've had to answer that question! D'you know it still shocks me a little?—to realize that Sebastian Venable the poet is still unknown outside of a small coterie of friends, including his mother.

DOCTOR: Oh.

MRS. VENABLE: You see, strictly speaking, his *life* was his occupation.

DOCTOR: I see.

MRS. VENABLE: No, you *don't* see, yet, but before I'm through, you will.—Sebastian was a poet! That's what I meant when I said his life was his work because the work of a poet is the life of a poet and—vice versa, the life of a poet is the work of a poet, I mean you can't separate them, I mean—well, for instance, a salesman's work is one thing and his life is another—or can be. The same thing's true of—doctor, lawyer, merchant, *thief!*—But a poet's life is his work and his work is his life in a special sense because—oh, I've already talked myself breathless and dizzy.

(*The Doctor offers his arm.*)

Thank you.

DOCTOR: Mrs. Venable, did your doctor okay this thing?

MRS. VENABLE (*breathless*): What thing?

DOCTOR: Your meeting this girl that you think is responsible for your son's death?

MRS. VENABLE: I've waited months to face her because I couldn't get to St. Mary's to face her—I've had her brought here to my house. I won't collapse! She'll collapse! I mean her lies will collapse—not my truth—not the truth. . . . *Forward march, Doctor Sugar!*

(*He conducts her slowly to the patio.*)

Ah, we've *made* it, *ha ha!* I didn't know that I was so weak on my pins! Sit down, Doctor. I'm not afraid of using every last ounce and inch of my little, left-over strength in doing just what I'm doing. I'm devoting all that's left of my life, Doctor, to the defense of a dead poet's reputation. Sebastian had no public name as a poet, he didn't want one, he refused to have one. He *dreaded, abhorred!*—false values that come from being publicly known, from fame, from personal—exploitation. . . . Oh, he'd say to me: "Violet? Mother?—You're going to outlive me!!"

DOCTOR: What made him think that?

MRS. VENABLE: Poets are always clairvoyant!—And he had rheumatic fever when he was fifteen and it affected a heart-valve and he wouldn't stay off horses and out of water and so forth. . . . "Violet? Mother? You're going to live longer than me, and then, when I'm gone, it will be yours, in your hands, to do whatever you please with!"—Meaning, of course, his future recognition!—That he *did* want, he wanted it after his death when it couldn't disturb him; then he did want to offer his work to the world. All right. Have I made my point, Doctor? Well, here is my son's work, Doctor, here's his life going *on*!

(*She lifts a thin gilt-edged volume from the patio table as if elevating the Host before the altar. Its gold leaf and lettering catch the afternoon sun. It says* Poem of Summer. *Her face suddenly has a different look, the look of a visionary, an exalted* religieuse. *At the same instant a bird sings clearly and purely in the garden and the old lady seems to be almost young for a moment.*)

DOCTOR (*reading the title*): *Poem of Summer*?

MRS. VENABLE: *Poem of Summer*, and the date of the summer, there are twenty-five of them, he wrote one poem a year which he printed himself on an eighteenth-century hand-press at his—atelier in the—French—Quarter—so no one but he could see it. . . .

(*She seems dizzy for a moment.*)

DOCTOR: He wrote one poem a year?

MRS. VENABLE: One for each summer that we traveled together. The other nine months of the year were really only a preparation.

DOCTOR: Nine months?

MRS. VENABLE: The length of a pregnancy, yes. . . .

DOCTOR: The poem was hard to deliver?

MRS. VENABLE: Yes, even with me! *Without* me, *impossible*, Doctor!—he wrote no poem last summer.

DOCTOR: He died last summer?

MRS. VENABLE: Without me he died last summer, that was his last summer's poem.

(*She staggers; he assists her toward a chair. She catches her breath with difficulty.*)

One long-ago summer—now, why am I thinking of this?—my son, Sebastian, said, "Mother?—Listen to this!"—He read me Herman Melville's description of the Encantadas, the Galapagos Islands. Quote—take five and twenty heaps of cinders dumped here and there in an outside city lot. Imagine some of them magnified into mountains, and the vacant lot, the sea. And you'll have a fit idea of the general aspect of the Encantadas, the Enchanted Isles—extinct volcanos, looking much as the world at large might look—after a last conflagration—end quote. He read me that description and said that we had to go there. And so we did go there that summer on a chartered boat, a four-masted schooner, as close as possible to the sort of a boat that Melville must have sailed on. . . . We saw the Encantadas, but on the Encantadas we saw something Melville *hadn't* written about. We saw the great sea-turtles crawl up out of the sea for their annual egg-laying. . . . Once a year the female of the sea-turtle crawls up out of the equatorial sea onto the blazing sand-beach of a volcanic island to dig a pit in the sand and deposit her eggs there. It's a long and dreadful thing, the depositing of the eggs in the sand-pits, and when it's finished the exhausted female turtle crawls back to the sea half-dead. She never sees her off-spring, but we did. Sebastian knew exactly when the sea-turtle eggs would be hatched out and we returned in time for it. . . .

DOCTOR: You went back to the—?

MRS. VENABLE: Terrible Encantadas, those heaps of extinct volcanos, in time to witness the hatching of the sea-turtles and their desperate flight to the sea!

(*There is a sound of harsh bird-cries in the air. She looks up.*)

—The narrow beach, the color of caviar, was all in motion! But the sky was in motion, too. . . .

DOCTOR: The sky was in motion, too?

MRS. VENABLE:—Full of flesh-eating birds and the noise of the birds, the horrible savage cries of the—

DOCTOR: Carnivorous birds?

MRS. VENABLE: Over the narrow black beach of the Encantadas as the just hatched sea-turtles scrambled out of the sand-pits and started their race to the sea. . . .

DOCTOR: Race to the sea?

MRS. VENABLE: To escape the flesh-eating birds that made the sky almost as black as the beach!

(*She gazes up again: we hear the wild, ravenous, harsh cries of the birds. The sound comes in rhythmic waves like a savage chant.*)

And the sand all alive, all alive, as the hatched sea-turtles made their dash for the sea, while the birds hovered and swooped to attack and hovered and—swooped to attack! They were diving down on the hatched sea-turtles, turning them over to expose their soft undersides, tearing the undersides open and rending and eating their flesh. Sebastian guessed that possibly only a hundredth of one per cent of their number would escape to the sea. . . .

DOCTOR: What was it about this that fascinated your son?

MRS. VENABLE: My son was looking for— (*She stops short with a slight gasp.*) —Let's just say he was interested in sea-turtles!

DOCTOR: That isn't what you started to say.

MRS. VENABLE: I stopped myself just in time.

DOCTOR: Say what you started to say.

MRS. VENABLE: I started to say that my son was looking for God and I stopped myself because I thought you'd think 'Oh, a pretentious young crackpot!'—which Sebastian was *not*!

DOCTOR: Mrs. Venable, doctors look for God, too.

MRS. VENABLE: Oh?

DOCTOR: I think they have to look harder for him than priests since they don't have the help of such well-known guide-books and well-organized expeditions as the priests have with their scriptures and—churches. . . .

MRS. VENABLE: You mean they go on a solitary safari like a poet?

DOCTOR: Yes. Some do. I do.

MRS. VENABLE: I believe, I *believe* you! (*She laughs, startled.*)

DOCTOR: Let me tell you something—the first operation I performed at Lion's View.—You can imagine how anxious and nervous I was about the outcome.

MRS. VENABLE: Yes.

DOCTOR: The patient was a young girl regarded as hopeless and put in the Drum—

MRS. VENABLE: Yes.

DOCTOR: The name for the violent ward at Lion's View because it looks like the inside of a drum with very bright lights burning all day and all night.—So the attendants can see any change of expression or movement among the inmates in time to grab them if they're about to attack. After the operation I stayed with the girl, as if I'd delivered a child that might stop breathing.—When they finally wheeled her out of surgery, I still stayed with her. I walked along by the rolling table holding onto her hand—with my heart in my throat. . . .

(*We hear faint music.*)

—It was a nice afternoon, as fair as this one. And the moment we wheeled her outside, she whispered something, she whispered: "Oh, how blue the sky is!"—And I felt proud, I felt proud and relieved, because up till then her speech, everything that she'd babbled, was a torrent of obscenities!

MRS. VENABLE: Yes, well, now, I can tell you without any hesitation that my son *was* looking for God, I mean for a clear image of him. He spent that whole blazing equatorial day in the crow's-nest of the schooner watching this thing on the beach till it was too dark to see it, and when he came down the rigging he said "Well, now I've seen Him!," and he meant God.—And for several weeks after that he had a fever, he was delirious with it.—

(*The Encantadas music then fades in again, briefly, at a lower level, a whisper.*)

DOCTOR: I can see how he *might* be, I think he *would* be disturbed if he thought he'd seen God's image, an equation of God, in that spectacle you watched in the Encantadas: creatures of the air hovering over and swooping down to devour creatures of the sea that had had the bad luck to be hatched on land and weren't able to scramble back into the sea fast enough to escape that massacre you witnessed, yes, I can see how such a spectacle could be equated with a good deal of—*experience, existence!*—but not with *God*! Can *you*?

MRS. VENABLE: Dr. Sugar, I'm a reasonably loyal member of the Protestant Episcopal Church, but I understood what he meant.

DOCTOR: Did he mean we must rise above God?

MRS. VENABLE: He meant that God shows a savage face to people and shouts some fierce things at them, it's all we see or hear of Him. Isn't it all we ever really see and hear of Him, now?—Nobody seems to know why. . . .

(*Music fades out again.*)

Shall I go on from there?

DOCTOR: Yes, do.

MRS. VENABLE: Well, next?—India—China—

(*Miss Foxhill appears with the medicine. Mrs. Venable sees her.*)

FOXHILL: Mrs. Venable.

MRS. VENABLE: Oh, God—elixir of—. (*She takes the glass.*) Isn't it kind of the drugstore to keep me alive. Where was I, Doctor?

DOCTOR: In the Himalayas.

MRS. VENABLE: Oh yes, that long-ago summer. . . . In the Himalayas he almost entered a Buddhist monastery, had gone so far as to shave his head and eat just rice out of a wood bowl on a grass mat. He'd promised those sly Buddhist monks that he would give up the world and himself and all his worldly possessions to their mendicant order.—Well, I cabled his father, "For God's sake notify bank to freeze Sebastian's accounts!"—I got back this cable from my late husband's lawyer: "Mr. Venable critically ill Stop Wants you Stop Needs you Stop Immediate return advised most strongly. Stop. Cable time of arrival. . . ."

DOCTOR: Did you go back to your husband?

MRS. VENABLE: I made the hardest decision of my life. I stayed with my son. I got him through that crisis too. In less than a month he got up off the filthy grass mat and threw the rice bowl away—and booked us into Shepheard's Hotel in Cairo and the Ritz in Paris—. And from then on, oh, we—still lived in a—world of light and shadow. . . .

(*She turns vaguely with empty glass. He rises and takes it from her.*)

But the shadow was almost as luminous as the light.

DOCTOR: Don't you want to sit down now?

MRS. VENABLE: Yes, indeed I do, before I fall down.

(*He assists her into wheelchair.*)

—Are your hind-legs still on you?

DOCTOR (*still concerned over her agitation*):—My what? Oh—hind legs!—Yes . . .

MRS. VENABLE: Well, then you're not a donkey, you're certainly not a donkey because I've been talking the hind-legs off a donkey—several donkeys. . . . But I had to make it clear to you that the world lost a great deal too when I lost my son last summer. . . . You would have liked my son, he would have been charmed by you. My son, Sebastian, was not a family snob or a money snob but he was a snob, all right. He was a snob about personal charm in people, he insisted upon good looks in people around him, and, oh, he had a perfect little court of young and beautiful people around him always, wherever he was, here in New *Orleans* or New York or on the Riviera or in Paris and Venice, he always had a little entourage of the beautiful and the talented and the young!

DOCTOR: Your son was young, Mrs. Venable?

MRS. VENABLE: Both of us were young, and stayed young, Doctor.

DOCTOR: Could I see a photograph of your son, Mrs. Venable?

MRS. VENABLE: Yes, indeed you could, Doctor. I'm glad that you asked to see one. I'm going to show you not one photograph but two. Here. Here is my son, Sebastian, in a Renaissance pageboy's costume at a masked ball in Cannes. Here is my son, Sebastian, in the same costume at a masked ball in Venice. These two pictures were taken twenty years apart. Now which is the older one, Doctor?

DOCTOR: This photograph looks older.

MRS. VENABLE: The photograph looks older but not the subject. It takes character to refuse to grow old, Doctor—successfully to refuse to. It calls for discipline, abstention. One cocktail before dinner, not two, four, six—a single lean chop and lime juice on a salad in restaurants famed for rich dishes.

(*Foxhill comes from the house.*)

FOXHILL: Mrs. Venable, Miss Holly's mother and brother are—

(*Simultaneously Mrs. Holly and George appear in the window.*)

GEORGE: Hi, Aunt Vi!

MRS. HOLLY: Violet dear, we're here.

FOXHILL: They're here.

MRS. VENABLE: Wait upstairs in my upstairs living room for me.

(*To Miss Foxhill:*)

Get them upstairs. I don't want them at that window during this talk.

(*To the Doctor:*)

Let's get away from the window.

(*He wheels her to stage center.*)

DOCTOR: Mrs. Venable? Did your son have a—well—what kind of a *personal*, well, *private* life did—

MRS. VENABLE: That's a question I wanted you to ask me.

DOCTOR: Why?

MRS. VENABLE: I haven't heard the girl's story except indirectly in a watered-down version, being too ill to go to hear it directly, but I've gathered enough to know that it's a hideous attack on my son's moral character which, being dead, he can't defend himself from. I have to be the defender. Now. Sit down. Listen to me . . .

(*The Doctor sits.*)

. . . before you hear whatever you're going to hear from the girl when she gets here. My son, Sebastian, was chaste. Not c-h-a-s-e-d! Oh, he was chased in that way of spelling it, too, we had to be very fleet-footed I can tell you, with his looks and his charm, to keep ahead of pursuers, every kind of pursuer!—I mean he was c-h-a-s-t-e!—Chaste. . . .

DOCTOR: I understood what you meant, Mrs. Venable.

MRS. VENABLE: And you *believe* me, don't you?

DOCTOR: Yes, but—

MRS. VENABLE: But *what*?

DOCTOR: Chastity at—what age was your son last summer?

MRS. VENABLE: *Forty*, maybe. We really didn't count birthdays. . . .

DOCTOR: He lived a celibate life?

MRS. VENABLE: As strictly as if he'd *vowed* to! This sounds like vanity, Doctor, but really I was actually the only one in his life that satisfied the demands he made of people. Time after time my son would let people go, dismiss them!—because their, their, their!—*attitude* toward him was—

DOCTOR: Not as pure as—

MRS. VENABLE: My son, Sebastian, demanded! We were a famous couple. People didn't speak of Sebastian and his mother or Mrs. Venable and her son, they said "Sebastian and Violet, Violet and Sebastian are staying at the Lido, they're at the Ritz in Madrid. Sebastian and Violet, Violet and Sebastian have taken a house at Biarritz for the season," and every appearance, every time we appeared, attention was centered on *us!—everyone else! Eclipsed!* Vanity? Ohhhh, no, Doctor, you can't call it that—

DOCTOR: I didn't call it that.

MRS. VENABLE:—It wasn't *folie de grandeur*, it was grandeur.

DOCTOR: I see.

MRS. VENABLE: An attitude toward life that's hardly been known in the world since the great Renaissance princes were crowded out of their palaces and gardens by successful shopkeepers!

DOCTOR: I see.

MRS. VENABLE: Most people's lives—what are they but trails of debris, each day more debris, more debris, long, long trails of debris with nothing to clean it all up but, finally, death. . . .

(*We hear lyric music.*)

My son, Sebastian, and I constructed our days, each day, we would—carve out each day of our lives like a piece of sculpture.—Yes, we left behind us a trail of days like a gallery of sculpture! But, last summer—

(*Pause: the music continues.*)

I can't forgive him for it, not even now that he's paid for it with his life!—he let in this—*vandal!* This—

DOCTOR: The girl that—?

MRS. VENABLE: That you're going to meet here this afternoon! Yes. He admitted this vandal and with her tongue for a hatchet she's gone about smashing our legend, the memory of—

DOCTOR: Mrs. Venable, what do you think is her reason?

MRS. VENABLE: Lunatics don't have reason!

DOCTOR: I mean what do you think is her—motive?

MRS. VENABLE: What a question!—We put the bread in her mouth and the clothes on her back. People that like you for that or even forgive you for it are, are—*hen's teeth*, Doctor. The role of the benefactor is worse than thankless, it's the role of a victim, Doctor, a sacrificial victim, yes, they want your blood, Doctor, they want your blood on the altar steps of their *outraged, outrageous* egos!

DOCTOR: Oh. You mean she resented the—

MRS. VENABLE: Loathed!—They can't shut her up at St. Mary's.

DOCTOR: I thought she'd been there for months.

MRS. VENABLE: I mean keep her *still* there. She *babbles!* They couldn't shut her up in Cabeza de Lobo or at the clinic in Paris—she babbled, babbled!—smashing my son's reputation.—On the Berengaria bringing her back to the States she broke out of the stateroom and babbled, babbled; even at the airport when she was flown down here, she babbled a bit of her story before they could whisk her into an ambulance to St. Mary's. This is a reticule, Doctor. (*She raises a cloth bag.*) A catch-all, carry-all bag for an elderly lady which I turned into last summer. . . . Will you open it for me, my hands are stiff, and fish out some cigarettes and a cigarette holder.

(*He does.*)

DOCTOR: I don't have matches.

MRS. VENABLE: I think there's a table-lighter on the table.

DOCTOR: Yes, there is.

(*He lights it, it flames up high.*)

My Lord, what a torch!

MRS. VENABLE (*with a sudden, sweet smile*): "So shines a good deed in a naughty world," Doctor—Sugar. . . .

(*Pause. A bird sings sweetly in the garden.*)

DOCTOR: Mrs. Venable?

MRS. VENABLE: Yes?

DOCTOR: In your letter last week you made some reference to a, to a—fund of some kind, an endowment fund of—

MRS. VENABLE: I wrote you that my lawyers and bankers and certified public accountants were setting up the Sebastian Venable Memorial Foundation to subsidize the work of young people like you that are pushing out the frontiers of art and science but have a financial problem. You have a financial problem, don't you, Doctor?

DOCTOR: Yes, we do have that problem. My work is such a *new* and *radical* thing that people in charge of state funds are naturally a little scared of it and keep us on a small budget, so small that—. We need a separate ward for my patients, I need trained assistants, I'd like to marry a girl I can't afford to marry!—But there's also the problem of getting right patients, not just—criminal psychopaths that the State turns over to us for my operation!—because it's—well—risky. . . . I don't want to turn you against my work at Lion's View but I have to be honest with you. There is a good deal of risk in my operation. Whenever you enter the brain with a foreign object . . .

MRS. VENABLE: Yes.

DOCTOR:—Even a needle-thin knife . .

MRS. VENABLE: Yes.

DOCTOR:—In a skilled surgeon's fingers . . .

MRS. VENABLE: Yes.

DOCTOR:—There is a good deal of risk involved in—the operation. . . .

MRS. VENABLE: You said that it pacifies them, it quiets them down, it suddenly makes them peaceful.

DOCTOR: Yes. It does that, that much we already know, but—

MRS. VENABLE: What?

DOCTOR: Well, it will be ten years before we can tell if the immediate benefits of the operation will be lasting or—passing or even if there'd still be—and this is what haunts me about it!—any possibility, afterwards, of—reconstructing a—totally sound person, it may be that the person will always be limited afterwards, relieved of acute disturbances but—*limited*, Mrs. Venable. . . .

MRS. VENABLE: Oh, but what a blessing to them, Doctor, to be just peaceful, to be just suddenly—peaceful. . . .

(*A bird sings sweetly in the garden.*)

After all that horror, after those nightmares: just to be able to lift up their eyes and see—(*She looks up and raises a hand to indicate the sky*)—a sky not as black with savage, devouring birds as the sky that we saw in the Encantadas, Doctor.

DOCTOR:—Mrs. Venable? I can't guarantee that a lobotomy would stop her—*babbling!!*

MRS. VENABLE: That may be, maybe not, but after the operation, who would *believe* her, Doctor?

(*Pause: faint jungle music.*)

DOCTOR (*quietly*): My God. (*Pause.*) —Mrs. Venable, suppose after meeting the girl and observing the girl and hearing this story she babbles—I still shouldn't feel that her condition's—intractable enough! to justify the risks of—suppose I shouldn't feel that non-surgical treatment such as insulin shock and electric shock and—

MRS. VENABLE: SHE'S HAD ALL THAT AT SAINT MARY'S!! Nothing else is left for her.

DOCTOR: But if I disagreed with you? (*Pause.*)

MRS. VENABLE: That's just part of a question: finish the question, Doctor.

DOCTOR: Would you still be interested in my work at Lion's View? I mean would the Sebastian Venable Memorial Foundation still be interested in it?

MRS. VENABLE: Aren't we always more interested in a thing that concerns us personally, Doctor?

DOCTOR: Mrs. Venable!!

(*Catharine Holly appears between the lace window curtains.*)

You're such an innocent person that it doesn't occur to you, it obviously hasn't even occurred to you that anybody less innocent than you are could possibly interpret this offer of a subsidy as—well, as sort of a *bribe*?

MRS. VENABLE (*laughs, throwing her head back*): Name it that —I don't care—. There's just two things to remember. She's a destroyer. My son was a *creator*!—Now if my honesty's shocked you—pick up your little black bag without the subsidy in it, and run away from this garden!—

Nobody's heard our conversation but you and I, Doctor Sugar. . . .

(*Miss Foxhill comes out of the house and calls.*)

MISS FOXHILL: Mrs. Venable?
MRS. VENABLE: What is it, what do you want, Miss Foxhill?
MISS FOXHILL: Mrs. Venable? Miss Holly is here, with—

(*Mrs. Venable sees Catharine at the window.*)

MRS. VENABLE: Oh, my God. There she is, in the window!—I told you I didn't want her to enter my house again, I told you to meet them at the door and lead them around the side of the house to the garden and you didn't listen. I'm not ready to face her. I have to have my five o'clock cocktail first, to fortify me. Take my chair inside. Doctor? Are you still here? I thought you'd run out of the garden. I'm going back through the garden to the other entrance. Doctor? Sugar? You may stay in the garden if you wish to or run out of the garden if you wish to or go in this way if you wish to or do anything that you wish to but I'm going to have my five o'clock daiquiri, *frozen!*—before I face her. . . .

(*All during this she has been sailing very slowly off through the garden like a stately vessel at sea with a fair wind in her sails, a pirate's frigate or a treasure-laden galleon. The young Doctor stares at Catharine framed by the lace window curtains. Sister Felicity appears beside her and draws her away from the window. Music: an ominous fanfare. Sister Felicity holds the door open for Catharine as the Doctor starts quickly forward. He starts to pick up his bag but doesn't. Catharine rushes out, they almost collide with each other.*)

CATHARINE: *Excuse me.*
DOCTOR: *I'm sorry. . . .*

(*She looks after him as he goes into the house.*)

SISTER FELICITY: Sit down and be still till your family come outside.

Dim Out

SCENE TWO

Catharine removes a cigarette from a lacquered box on the table and lights it. The following quick, cadenced lines are accompanied by quick, dancelike movement, almost formal, as the Sister in her sweeping white habit, which should be starched to make a crackling sound, pursues the girl about the white wicker patio table and among the wicker chairs: this can be accompanied by quick music.

SISTER: What did you take out of that box on the table?
CATHARINE: Just a cigarette, Sister.
SISTER: Put it back in the box.
CATHARINE: Too late, it's already lighted.
SISTER: Give it here.
CATHARINE: Oh, please, let me smoke, Sister!
SISTER: Give it here.
CATHARINE: *Please*, Sister Felicity.
SISTER: Catharine, give it here. You know that you're not allowed to smoke at Saint Mary's.
CATHARINE: We're not at Saint Mary's, this is an afternoon out.
SISTER: You're still in my charge. I can't permit you to smoke because the last time you smoked you dropped a lighted cigarette on your dress and started a fire.
CATHARINE: Oh, I did not start a fire. I just burned a hole in my skirt because I was half unconscious under medication. (*She is now back of a white wicker chair.*)
SISTER (*overlapping her*): Catharine, give it here.
CATHARINE: Don't be such a bully!
SISTER: Disobedience has to be paid for later.
CATHARINE: All right, I'll pay for it later.
SISTER (*overlapping*): Give me that cigarette or I'll make a report that'll put you right back on the violent ward, if you don't. (*She claps her hands twice and holds one hand out across the table.*)
CATHARINE (*overlapping*): I'm not being violent, Sister.
SISTER (*overlapping*): Give me that cigarette, I'm holding my hand out for it!
CATHARINE: All right, take it, here, take it!

(*She thrusts the lighted end of the cigarette into the palm of the Sister's hand. The Sister cries out and sucks her burned hand.*)

SISTER: *You burned me with it!*

CATHARINE: I'm sorry, I didn't mean to.

SISTER (*shocked, hurt*): You deliberately burned me!

CATHARINE (*overlapping*): You said give it to you and so I gave it to you.

SISTER (*overlapping*): You stuck the lighted end of that cigarette in my hand!

CATHARINE (*overlapping*): I'm *sick*, I'm *sick!*—of being *bossed* and *bullied!*

SISTER (*commandingly*): *Sit down!*

(*Catharine sits down stiffly in a white wicker chair on forestage, facing the audience. The Sister resumes sucking the burned palm of her hand. Ten beats. Then from inside the house the whirr of a mechanical mixer.*)

CATHARINE: There goes the Waring Mixer, Aunt Violet's about to have her five o'clock frozen daiquiri, you could set a watch by it! (*She almost laughs. Then she draws a deep, shuddering breath and leans back in her chair, but her hands remain clenched on the white wicker arms.*) —We're in Sebastian's garden. *My God, I can still cry!*

SISTER: Did you have any medication before you went out?

CATHARINE: No. I didn't have any. Will you give me some, Sister?

SISTER (*almost gently*): I can't. I wasn't told to. However, I think the doctor will give you something.

CATHARINE: The young blond man I bumped into?

SISTER: Yes. The young doctor's a specialist from another hospital.

CATHARINE: What hospital?

SISTER: A word to the wise is sufficient. . . .

(*The Doctor has appeared in the window.*)

CATHARINE (*rising abruptly*): I knew I was being watched, he's in the window, staring out at me!

SISTER: Sit down and be still. Your family's coming outside.

CATHARINE (*overlapping*): LION'S VIEW, IS IT! DOCTOR?

(*She has advanced toward the bay window. The Doctor draws back, letting the misty white gauze curtains down to obscure him.*)

SISTER (*rising with a restraining gesture which is almost pitying*): Sit down, dear.

CATHARINE: IS IT LION'S VIEW? DOCTOR?!

SISTER: Be still. . . .

CATHARINE: WHEN CAN I STOP RUNNING DOWN THAT STEEP WHITE STREET IN CABEZA DE LOBO?

SISTER: Catharine, dear, sit down.

CATHARINE: I loved him, Sister! Why wouldn't he let me save him? I tried to hold onto his hand but he struck me away and ran, ran, ran in the wrong direction, Sister!

SISTER: Catharine, dear—be still.

(*The Sister sneezes.*)

CATHARINE: Bless you, Sister. (*She says this absently, still watching the window.*)

SISTER: Thank you.

CATHARINE: The Doctor's still at the window but he's too blond to hide behind window curtains, he catches the light, he shines through them. (*She turns from the window.*) —We were *going* to blonds, blonds were next on the menu.

SISTER: Be still now. Quiet, dear.

CATHARINE: Cousin Sebastian said he was famished for blonds, he was fed up with the dark ones and was famished for blonds. All the travel brochures he picked up were advertisements of the blond northern countries. I think he'd already booked us to—Copenhagen or—Stockholm.—Fed up with dark ones, famished for light ones: that's how he talked about people, as if they were—items on a menu.—"That one's delicious-looking, that one is appetizing," or "that one is *not* appetizing"—I think because he was really nearly half-starved from living on pills and salads. . . .

SISTER: *Stop it!*—Catharine, be still.

CATHARINE: He liked me and so I loved him. . . . (*She cries a little again.*) If he'd kept hold of my hand I could have saved him!—Sebastian suddenly said to me last summer: "Let's fly north, little bird—I want to walk under those radiant, cold northern lights—I've never *seen* the aurora borealis!"—Somebody said once or wrote, once: "We're all of us children in a vast kindergarten trying to spell God's name with the wrong alphabet blocks!"

MRS. HOLLY (*offstage*): *Sister?*

(*The Sister rises.*)

CATHARINE (*rising*): I think it's *me* they're calling, they call *me* "Sister," Sister!

SCENE THREE

The Sister resumes her seat impassively as the girl's mother and younger brother appear from the garden. The mother, Mrs. Holly, is a fatuous Southern lady who requires no other description. The brother, George, is typically good-looking, he has the best "looks" of the family, tall and elegant of figure. They enter.

MRS. HOLLY: Catharine, dear! Catharine—

(*They embrace tentatively.*)

Well, well! Doesn't she look fine, George?

GEORGE: Uh huh.

CATHARINE: They send you to the beauty parlor whenever you're going to have a family visit. Other times you look awful, you can't have a compact or lipstick or anything made out of metal because they're afraid you'll swallow it.

MRS. HOLLY (*giving a tinkly little laugh*): I think she looks just splendid, don't you, George?

GEORGE: Can't we talk to her without the nun for a minute?

MRS. HOLLY: Yes, I'm sure it's all right to. Sister?

CATHARINE: Excuse me, Sister Felicity, this is my mother, Mrs. Holly, and my brother, George.

SISTER: How do you do.

GEORGE: How d'ya do.

CATHARINE: This is Sister Felicity. . . .

MRS. HOLLY: We're so happy that Catharine's at Saint Mary's! So very grateful for all you're doing for her.

SISTER (*sadly, mechanically*): We do the best we can for her, Mrs. Holly.

MRS. HOLLY: I'm sure you do. Yes, well—I wonder if you would mind if we had a little private chat with our Cathie?

SISTER: I'm not supposed to let her out of my sight.

MRS. HOLLY: It's just for a minute. You can sit in the hall or the garden and we'll call you right back here the minute the private part of the little talk is over.

(*Sister Felicity withdraws with an uncertain nod and a swish of starched fabric.*)

GEORGE (*to Catharine*): *Jesus! What are you up to? Huh? Sister? Are you trying to RUIN us?!*

MRS. HOLLY: GAWGE! WILL YOU BE QUIET. You're upsetting your sister!

(*He jumps up and stalks off a little, rapping his knee with his zipper-covered tennis racket.*)

CATHARINE: How elegant George looks.

MRS. HOLLY: George inherited Cousin Sebastian's wardrobe but everything else is in probate! Did you know that? That everything else is in probate and Violet can keep it in probate just as long as she wants to?

CATHARINE: Where is Aunt Violet?

MRS. HOLLY: *George, come back here!*

(*He does, sulkily.*)

Violet's on her way down.

GEORGE: Yeah. Aunt Violet has an elevator now.

MRS. HOLLY: Yais, she has, she's had an elevator installed where the back stairs were, and, Sister, it's the cutest little thing you ever did see! It's paneled in Chinese lacquer, black an' gold Chinese lacquer, with lovely bird-pictures on it. But there's only room for two people at a time in it. George and I came down on foot.—I think she's havin' her frozen daiquiri now, she still has a frozen daiquiri promptly at five o'clock ev'ry afternoon in the world . . . in warm weather. . . . Sister, the horrible death of Sebastian just about *killed* her!—She's now slightly better . . . but it's a question of time.—Dear, you know, I'm sure that you understand, why we haven't been out to see you at Saint Mary's. They said you were too disturbed, and a family visit might disturb you more. But I want you to know that nobody, absolutely nobody in the city, knows a thing about what you've been through. Have they, George? Not a thing. Not a soul even knows that you've come back from Europe. When people enquire, when they question us about you, we just say that you've stayed abroad to study something or other. (*She catches her breath.*) Now. Sister?—I want you to please be *very* careful what you say to your Aunt Violet about what happened to Sebastian in Cabeza de Lobo.

CATHARINE: What do you want me to say about what—?

MRS. HOLLY: Just don't repeat that same fantastic story! For my sake and George's sake, the sake of your brother and mother, don't repeat that horrible story again! Not to Violet! Will you?

CATHARINE: Then I am going to have to tell Aunt Violet what happened to her son in Cabeza de Lobo?

MRS. HOLLY: Honey, that's why you're here. She has *INSISTED* on hearing it straight from YOU!

GEORGE: You were the only witness to it, Cathie.

CATHARINE: No, there were others. That *ran.*

MRS. HOLLY: Oh, Sister, you've just had a little sort of a—*nightmare* about it! Now, listen to me, will you, Sister? Sebastian has left, has BEQUEATHED!—to you an' Gawge in his *will*—

GEORGE (*religiously*): *To each of us, fifty grand, each!*—AFTER! TAXES!—GET IT?

CATHARINE: Oh, yes, but if they give me an injection—I won't have any choice but to tell exactly what happened in Cabeza de Lobo last summer. Don't you see? I won't have any choice but to tell the truth. It makes you tell the truth because it shuts something off that might make you able not to and *everything* comes out, decent or *not* decent, you have no control, but always, always the truth!

MRS. HOLLY: Catharine, darling. I don't know the full story, but surely you're not too sick in your *head* to know in your *heart* that the story you've been telling is just—too—

GEORGE (*cutting in*): Cathie, Cathie, you got to forget that story! Can'tcha? For *your* fifty grand?

MRS. HOLLY: Because if Aunt Vi contests the will, and we know she'll contest it, she'll keep it in the courts forever!—We'll be—

GEORGE: It's in PROBATE NOW! And'll never get out of probate until you drop that story—we can't afford to hire lawyers good enough to contest it! So if you don't stop telling that crazy story, we won't have a pot to—cook *greens* in!

(*He turns away with a fierce grimace and a sharp, abrupt wave of his hand, as if slapping down something. Catharine stares at his tall back for a moment and laughs wildly.*)

MRS. HOLLY: Catharine, don't laugh like that, it scares me, Catharine.

(*Jungle birds scream in the garden.*)

GEORGE (*turning his back on his sister*): Cathie, the money is all tied up.

(*He stoops over sofa, hands on flannel knees, speaking directly into Catharine's face as if she were hard of hearing. She raises a hand to touch his cheek affectionately; he seizes the hand and removes it but holds it tight.*)

If Aunt Vi decided to contest Sebastian's will that leaves us all of this cash?!—Am I coming through to you?

CATHARINE: Yes, little brother, you are.

GEORGE: You see, Mama, she's crazy like a coyote!

(*He gives her a quick cold kiss*)

We won't get a single damn penny, honest t' God we won't! So you've just GOT to stop tellin' that story about what you say happened to Cousin Sebastian in Cabeza de Lobo, even if it's what it *couldn't* be, TRUE!—You got to drop it, Sister, you can't tell such a story to civilized people in a civilized up-to-date country!

MRS. HOLLY: Cathie, why, why, why!—did you invent such a tale?

CATHARINE: But, Mother, I DIDN'T invent it. I know it's a hideous story but it's a true story of our time and the world we live in and what did truly happen to Cousin Sebastian in Cabeza de Lobo. . . .

GEORGE: Oh, then you are going to tell it. Mama, she *IS* going to tell it! Right to Aunt Vi, and lose us a hundred thousand!—Cathie? You are a BITCH!

MRS. HOLLY: GAWGE!

GEORGE: I repeat it, a bitch! She isn't crazy, Mama, she's no more crazy than I am, she's just, just—PERVERSE! Was ALWAYS!—perverse. . . .

(*Catharine turns away and breaks into quiet sobbing.*)

MRS. HOLLY: Gawge, Gawge, apologize to Sister, this is no way for you to talk to your sister. You come right back over here and tell your sweet little sister you're sorry you spoke like that to her!

GEORGE (*turning back to Catharine*): I'm sorry, Cathie, but you know we NEED that money! Mama and me, we—Cathie? I got *ambitions*! And, Cathie, I'm YOUNG!—I *want* things, I *need* them, Cathie! So will you please think about ME? Us?

MISS FOXHILL (*offstage*): Mrs. Holly? Mrs. Holly?

MRS. HOLLY: Somebody's callin' fo' me. Catharine, Gawge put it very badly but you know that it's TRUE! WE DO HAVE TO GET WHAT SEBASTIAN HAS LEFT US IN HIS WILL, DEAREST! AND YOU WON'T LET US DOWN? PROMISE? YOU WON'T? LET US DOWN?

GEORGE (*fiercely shouting*): HERE COMES AUNT VI! Mama, Cathie, Aunt Violet's—here is Aunt Vi!

SCENE FOUR

Mrs. Venable enters downstage area. Entrance music.

MRS. HOLLY: *Cathie! Here's Aunt Vi!*

MRS. VENABLE: She sees me and I see her. That's all that's necessary. Miss Foxhill, put my chair in this corner. Crank the back up a little.

(*Miss Foxhill does this business.*)

More. More. Not that much!—Let it back down a little. All right. Now, then. I'll have my frozen daiquiri, now. . . . Do any of you want coffee?

GEORGE: I'd like a chocolate malt.

MRS. HOLLY: Gawge!

MRS. VENABLE: This isn't a drugstore.

MRS. HOLLY: Oh, Gawge is just being Gawge.

MRS. VENABLE: That's what I *thought* he was being!

(*An uncomfortable silence falls. Miss Foxhill creeps out like a burglar. She speaks in a breathless whisper, presenting a card-board folder toward Mrs. Venable.*)

MISS FOXHILL: Here's the portfolio marked Cabeza de Lobo. It has all your correspondence with the police there and the American consul.

MRS. VENABLE: I asked for the *English transcript*! It's in a separate—

MISS FOXHILL: Separate, yes, here it is!

MRS. VENABLE: Oh . . .

MISS FOXHILL: And here's the report of the private investigators and here's the report of—

MRS. VENABLE: Yes, yes, yes! Where's the doctor?

MISS FOXHILL: On the phone in the library!

MRS. VENABLE: Why does he choose such a moment to make a phone-call?

MISS FOXHILL: He didn't make a phone-call, he received a phone-call from—

MRS. VENABLE: Miss Foxhill, why are you talking to me like a burglar!?

(*Miss Foxhill giggles a little desperately.*)

CATHARINE: Aunt Violet, she's frightened.—Can I move? Can I get up and move around till it starts?

MRS. HOLLY: Cathie, Cathie, dear, did Gawge tell you that he received bids from every good fraternity on the Tulane campus and went Phi Delt because Paul Junior did?

MRS. VENABLE: I see that he had the natural tact and good taste to come here this afternoon outfitted from head to foot in clothes that belonged to my son!

GEORGE: You gave 'em to me, Aunt Vi.

MRS. VENABLE: I didn't know you'd parade them in front of me, George.

MRS. HOLLY (*quickly*): Gawge, tell Aunt Violet how grateful you are for—

GEORGE: I found a little Jew tailor on Britannia Street that makes alterations so good you'd never guess that they weren't cut *out* for me to *begin* with!

MRS. HOLLY: *AND* so reasonable!—Luckily, since it seems that Sebastian's wonderful, wonderful bequest to Gawge an' Cathie is going to be tied up a while!?

GEORGE: Aunt Vi? About the will?

(*Mrs. Holly coughs.*)

I was just wondering if we can't figure out some way to, to—

MRS. HOLLY: Gawge means to EXPEDITE it! To get through the red tape quicker?

MRS. VENABLE: I understand his meaning. Foxhill, get the Doctor.

(*She has risen with her cane and hobbled to the door.*)

MISS FOXHILL (*exits calling*): Doctor!

MRS. HOLLY: Gawge, no more about money.

GEORGE: How do we know we'll ever see her again?

(*Catharine gasps and rises; she moves downstage, followed quickly by Sister Felicity.*)

SISTER (*mechanically*): What's wrong, dear?

CATHARINE: I think I'm just dreaming this, it doesn't seem real!

(*Miss Foxhill comes back out, saying:*)

FOXHILL: He had to answer an urgent call from Lion's View.

(*Slight, tense pause.*)

MRS. HOLLY: Violet! *Not* Lion's View!

(*Sister Felicity had started conducting Catharine back to the patio; she stops her, now.*)

SISTER: Wait, dear.

CATHARINE: What for? I know what's coming.

MRS. VENABLE (*at same time*): Why? are you all prepared to put out a thousand a month plus extra charges for treatments to keep the girl at St. Mary's?

MRS. HOLLY: Cathie? Cathie, dear?

(*Catharine has returned with the Sister.*)

Tell Aunt Violet how grateful you are for her makin' it possible for you to rest an' recuperate at such a sweet, sweet place as St. Mary's!

CATHARINE: No place for lunatics is a sweet, sweet place.

MRS. HOLLY: But the food's good there. Isn't the food good there?

CATHARINE: Just give me written permission not to eat fried grits. I had yard privileges till I refused to eat fried grits.

SISTER: She lost yard privileges because she couldn't be trusted in the yard without constant supervision or even with it because she'd run to the fence and make signs to cars on the highway.

CATHARINE: Yes, I did, I did that because I've been trying for weeks to get a message out of that "sweet, sweet place."

MRS. HOLLY: What message, dear?

CATHARINE: I got panicky, Mother.

MRS. HOLLY: Sister, I don't understand.

GEORGE: What're you scared of, Sister?

CATHARINE: What they might do to me now, after they've done all the rest!—That man in the window's a specialist from Lion's View! We get newspapers. I know what they're . . .

(*The Doctor comes out.*)

MRS. VENABLE: Why, Doctor, I thought you'd left us with just that little black bag to remember you by!

DOCTOR: Oh, no. Don't you remember our talk? I had to answer a call about a patient that—

MRS. VENABLE: This is Dr. Cukrowicz. He says it means "sugar" and we can call him "Sugar"—

(*George laughs.*)

He's a specialist from Lion's View.

CATHARINE (*cutting in*): WHAT DOES HE SPECIALIZE IN?

MRS. VENABLE: Something new. When other treatments have failed.

(*Pause. The jungle clamor comes up and subsides again.*)

CATHARINE: *Do you want to bore a hole in my skull and turn a knife in my brain?* Everything else was done to me!

(*Mrs. Holly sobs. George raps his knee with the tennis racket.*)

You'd have to have my mother's permission for that.

MRS. VENABLE: I'm paying to keep you in a private asylum.

CATHARINE: You're not my legal guardian.

MRS. VENABLE: Your mother's dependent on me. All of you are!—Financially. . . .

CATHARINE: I think the situation is—clear to me, now. . . .

MRS. VENABLE: Good! In that case. . . .

DOCTOR: I think a quiet atmosphere will get us the best results.

MRS. VENABLE: I don't know what you mean by a quiet atmosphere. She shouted, I didn't.

DOCTOR: Mrs. Venable, let's try to keep things on a quiet level, now. Your niece seems to be disturbed.

MRS. VENABLE: She has every reason to be. She took my son from me, and then she—

CATHARINE: Aunt Violet, you're not being fair.

MRS. VENABLE: Oh, aren't I?

CATHARINE (*to the others*): She's not being fair.

(*Then back to Mrs. Venable:*)

Aunt Violet, you know why Sebastian asked me to travel with him.

MRS. VENABLE: Yes, I *do* know why!

CATHARINE: You weren't able to travel. You'd had a— (*She stops short.*)

MRS. VENABLE: Go on! *What* had I had? Are you afraid to say it in front of the Doctor? She meant that I had a stroke.—I DID NOT HAVE A STROKE!—I had a slight aneurism. You know what that is, Doctor? A little vascular convulsion! Not a hemorrhage, just a little convulsion of a blood-vessel.

I had it when I discovered that she was trying to take my son away from me. Then I had it. It gave a little temporary—muscular—contraction.—To one side of my face. . . . (*She crosses back into main acting area.*) These people are not blood-relatives of mine, they're my dead husband's relations. I always detested these people, my dead husband's sister and—her two worthless children. But I did more than my duty to keep their heads above water. To please my son, whose weakness was being excessively softhearted, I went to the expense and humiliation, yes, public humiliation, of giving this girl a debut which was a fiasco. Nobody liked her when I brought her out. Oh, she had some kind of—notoriety! She had a sharp tongue that some people mistook for wit. A habit of laughing in the faces of decent people which would infuriate them, and also reflected adversely on me and Sebastian, too. But, he, Sebastian, was amused by this girl. While I was disgusted, sickened. And halfway through the season, she was dropped off the party lists, yes, dropped off the lists in spite of my position. Why? Because she'd lost her head over a young married man, made a scandalous scene at a Mardi Gras ball, in the middle of the ballroom. Then everybody dropped her like a hot—rock, but— (*She loses her breath.*) My son, Sebastian, still felt sorry for her and took her with him last summer instead of me. . . .

CATHARINE (*springing up with a cry*): I can't change truth, I'm not God! I'm not even sure that He could, I don't think God can change truth! How can I change the story of what happened to her son in Cabeza de Lobo?

MRS. VENABLE (*at the same time*): She was in love with my son!

CATHARINE (*overlapping*): Let me go back to Saint Mary's. Sister Felicity, let's go back to Saint—

MRS. VENABLE (*overlapping*): Oh, no! That's not where you'll go!

CATHARINE (*overlapping*): All right, *Lion's View* but don't ask me to—

MRS. VENABLE (*overlapping*): You *know* that you were!

CATHARINE (*overlapping*): That I was *what,* Aunt Violet?

MRS. VENABLE (*overlapping*): Don't call me "Aunt," you're the niece of my dead husband, not me!

MRS. HOLLY (*overlapping*): Catharine, Catharine, don't upset your— Doctor? Oh, Doctor!

(*But the Doctor is calmly observing the scene, with detachment. The jungle garden is loud with the sounds of its feathered and scaled inhabitants.*)

CATHARINE: I don't want to, I didn't want to come here! I know what she thinks, she thinks I murdered her son, she thinks that I was responsible for his death.

MRS. VENABLE: That's right. I told him when he told me that he was going with you in my place last summer that I'd never see him again and I never did. And only you know why!

CATHARINE: Oh, my God, I—

(*She rushes out toward garden, followed immediately by the Sister.*)

SISTER: Miss Catharine, Miss Catharine—

DOCTOR (*overlapping*): Mrs. Venable?

SISTER (*overlapping*): Miss Catharine?

DOCTOR (*overlapping*): Mrs. Venable?

MRS. VENABLE: What?

DOCTOR: I'd like to be left alone with Miss Catharine for a few minutes.

MRS. HOLLY: George, talk to her, George.

(*George crouches appealingly before the old lady's chair, peering close into her face, a hand on her knee.*)

GEORGE: Aunt Vi? Cathie can't go to Lion's View. Everyone in the Garden District would know you'd put your niece in a state asylum, Aunt Vi.

MRS. VENABLE: Foxhill!

GEORGE: What do you want, Aunt Vi?

MRS. VENABLE: Let go of my chair. Foxhill? Get me away from these people!

GEORGE: Aunt Vi, listen, think of the talk it—

MRS. VENABLE: I can't get up! Push me, push me away!

GEORGE (*rising but holding chair*): I'll push her, Miss Foxhill.

MRS. VENABLE: Let go of my chair or—

MISS FOXHILL: Mr. Holly, I—

GEORGE: I got to talk to her.

(*He pushes her chair downstage.*)

MRS. VENABLE: Foxhill!
MISS FOXHILL: Mr. Holly, she doesn't want you to push her.
GEORGE: I know what I'm doing, leave me alone with Aunt Vi!
MRS. VENABLE: Let go me or I'll *strike* you!
GEORGE: Oh, Aunt Vi!
MRS. VENABLE: Foxhill!
MRS. HOLLY: George—
GEORGE: Aunt Vi?

(*She strikes at him with her cane. He releases the chair and Miss Foxhill pushes her off. He trots after her a few steps, then he returns to Mrs. Holly, who is sobbing into a handkerchief. He sighs, and sits down beside her, taking her hand. The scene fades as light is brought up on Catharine and the Sister in the garden. The Doctor comes up to them. Mrs. Holly stretches her arms out to George, sobbing, and he crouches before her chair and rests his head in her lap. She strokes his head. During this: the Sister has stood beside Catharine, holding onto her arm.*)

CATHARINE: You don't have to hold onto me. I can't run away.
DOCTOR: Miss Catharine?
CATHARINE: What?
DOCTOR: Your aunt is a very sick woman. She had a stroke last spring?
CATHARINE: Yes, she did, but she'll never admit it. . . .
DOCTOR: You have to understand why.
CATHARINE: I do, I understand why. I didn't want to come here.
DOCTOR: Miss Catharine, do you hate her?
CATHARINE: I don't understand what hate is. How can you hate anybody and still be sane? You see, I still think I'm sane!
DOCTOR: You think she did have a stroke?
CATHARINE: She had a slight stroke in April. It just affected one side, the left side, of her face . . . but it was disfiguring, and after that, Sebastian couldn't use her.

DOCTOR: Use her? Did you say use her?

(*The sounds of the jungle garden are not loud but ominous.*)

CATHARINE: Yes, we all use each other and that's what we think of as love, and not being able to use each other is what's—*hate*. . . .

DOCTOR: Do you hate her, Miss Catharine?

CATHARINE: Didn't you ask me that, once? And didn't I say that I didn't understand hate. A ship struck an iceberg at sea—everyone sinking—

DOCTOR: Go on, Miss Catharine!

CATHARINE: But that's no reason for everyone drowning for hating everyone drowning! Is it, Doctor?

DOCTOR: Tell me: what was your feeling for your cousin Sebastian?

CATHARINE: He liked me and so I loved him.

DOCTOR: In what way did you love him?

CATHARINE: The only way he'd accept:—a sort of motherly way. I tried to save him, Doctor.

DOCTOR: From what? Save him from what?

CATHARINE: Completing!—a sort of!—*image!*—he had of himself as a sort of!—*sacrifice* to a!—*terrible* sort of a—

DOCTOR:—God?

CATHARINE: Yes, a—*cruel* one, Doctor!

DOCTOR: How did you feel about that?

CATHARINE: Doctor, my feelings are the sort of feelings that you have in a dream. . . .

DOCTOR: Your life doesn't seem real to you?

CATHARINE: Suddenly last winter I began to write my journal in the third person.

(*He grasps her elbow and leads her out upon forestage. At the same time Miss Foxhill wheels Mrs. Venable off, Mrs. Holly weeps into a handkerchief and George rises and shrugs and turns his back to the audience.*)

DOCTOR: Something happened last winter?

CATHARINE: At a Mardi Gras ball some—some boy that took me to it got too drunk to stand up! (*A short, mirthless note of laughter.*) I wanted to go home. My coat was in the cloakroom, they couldn't find the check for it in his pockets. I said, "Oh, hell, let it go!"—I started out for a taxi. Somebody took my arm and said, "I'll drive you home." He took off his coat as we left the hotel and put it over my shoulders, and then I looked at him and—I don't think I'd ever even seen him before then, really!—He took me home in his car but took me another place first. We stopped near the Duelling Oaks at the end of Esplanade Street. . . . Stopped!—I said, "What for?"—He didn't answer, just struck a match in the car to light a cigarette in the car and I looked at him in the car and I knew "what for"!—I think I got out of the car before he got out of the car, and we walked through the wet grass to the great misty oaks as if somebody was calling us for help there!

(*Pause. The subdued, toneless bird-cries in the garden turn to a single bird-song.*)

DOCTOR: After that?

CATHARINE: I lost him.—He took me home and said an awful thing to me. "We'd better forget it," he said, "my wife's expecting a child and—." —I just entered the house and sat there thinking a little and then I suddenly called a taxi and went right back to the Roosevelt Hotel ballroom. The ball was still going on. I thought I'd gone back to pick up my borrowed coat but that wasn't what I'd gone back for. I'd gone back to make a scene on the floor of the ballroom, yes, I didn't stop at the cloakroom to pick up Aunt Violet's old mink stole, no, I rushed right into the ballroom and spotted him on the floor and ran up to him and beat him as hard as I could in the face and chest with my fists till—Cousin Sebastian took me away.—After that, the next morning, I started writing my diary in the third person, singular, such as "She's still living this morning," meaning that *I* was. . . . —"WHAT'S NEXT FOR HER? GOD KNOWS!"—I couldn't go out any more.—However one morning my Cousin Sebastian came in my bedroom and said: "Get up!"—Well . . . if you're still alive after dying, well then, you're obedient, Doctor.—I got up. He took me downtown to a place for passport photos. Said: "Mother can't go abroad with me this summer. You're going to go with me this summer instead of Mother."—If you don't believe me, read my journal of Paris!—"She woke up at daybreak this morning, had her coffee and dressed and took a brief walk—"

DOCTOR: *Who* did?

CATHARINE: *She* did. *I* did—from the Hotel Plaza Athénée to the Place de l'Étoile as if pursued by a pack of Siberian wolves! (*She laughs her tired, helpless laugh.*)—Went right through all stop signs—couldn't wait for green signals.—"Where did she think she was going? Back to the Duelling Oaks?"—Everything chilly and dim but his hot, ravenous mouth! on—

DOCTOR: Miss Catharine, let me give you something.

(*The others go out, leaving Catharine and the Doctor onstage.*)

CATHARINE: Do I have to have the injection again, this time? What am I going to be stuck with this time, Doctor? I don't care. I've been stuck so often that if you connected me with a garden hose I'd make a good sprinkler.

DOCTOR (*preparing needle*): Please take off your jacket.

(*She does. The Doctor gives her an injection.*)

CATHARINE: I didn't feel it.

DOCTOR: That's good. Now sit down.

(*She sits down.*)

CATHARINE: Shall I start counting backwards from a hundred?

DOCTOR: Do you like counting backwards?

CATHARINE: Love it! Just love it! One hundred! Ninety-nine! Ninety-eight! Ninety-seven. Ninety-six. Ninety—five—. Oh! —I already feel it! How funny!

DOCTOR: That's right. Close your eyes for a minute.

(*He moves his chair closer to hers. Half a minute passes.*)

Miss Catharine? I want you to give me something.

CATHARINE: Name it and it's yours, Doctor Sugar.

DOCTOR: Give me all your resistance.

CATHARINE: Resistance to what?

DOCTOR: The truth. Which you're going to tell me.

CATHARINE: The truth's the one thing I have never resisted!

DOCTOR: Sometimes people just think they don't resist it, but still do.

CATHARINE: They say it's at the bottom of a bottomless well, you know:

DOCTOR: Relax.

CATHARINE: Truth.

DOCTOR: Don't talk.

CATHARINE: Where was I, now? At ninety?

DOCTOR: You don't have to count backwards.

CATHARINE: At ninety something?

DOCTOR: You can open your eyes.

CATHARINE: Oh, I do feel funny!

(*Silence, pause.*)

You know what I think you're doing? I think you're trying to hypnotize me. Aren't you? You're looking so straight at me and doing something to me with your eyes and your—eyes. . . . Is that what you're doing to me?

DOCTOR: Is that what you *feel* I'm doing?

CATHARINE: Yes! I feel so peculiar. And it's not just the drug.

DOCTOR: Give me all your resistance. See. I'm holding my hand out. I want you to put yours in mine and give me all your resistance. Pass all of your resistance out of your hand to mine.

CATHARINE: Here's my hand. But there's no resistance in it.

DOCTOR: You are totally passive.

CATHARINE: Yes, I am.

DOCTOR: You will do what I ask.

CATHARINE: Yes, I will try.

DOCTOR: You will tell the true story.

CATHARINE: Yes, I will.

DOCTOR: The absolutely true story. No lies, nothing not spoken. Everything told, exactly.

CATHARINE: Everything. Exactly. Because I'll have to. Can I—can I stand up?

DOCTOR: Yes, but be careful. You might feel a little bit dizzy.

(*She struggles to rise, then falls back.*)

CATHARINE: I can't get up! Tell me to. Then I think I could do it.

DOCTOR: Stand up.

(*She rises unsteadily.*)

CATHARINE: How funny! Now I can! Oh, I do feel dizzy! Help me, I'm—

(*He rushes to support her.*)

—about to fall over. . . .

(*He holds her. She looks out vaguely toward the brilliant, steaming garden. Looks back at him. Suddenly sways toward him, against him.*)

DOCTOR: You see, you lost your balance.

CATHARINE: No, I didn't. I did what I wanted to do without you telling me to.

(*She holds him tight against her.*)

Let me! Let! Let! Let me! Let me, let me, oh, let me. . . .

(*She crushes her mouth to his violently. He tries to disengage himself. She presses her lips to his fiercely, clutching his body against her. Her brother George enters.*)

Please hold me! I've been so lonely. It's lonelier than death, if I've gone mad, it's lonelier than death!

GEORGE (*shocked, disgusted*): *Cathie!*—you've got a hell of a nerve.

(*She falls back, panting, covers her face, runs a few paces and grabs the back of a chair. Mrs. Holly enters.*)

MRS. HOLLY: What's the matter, George? Is Catharine ill?

GEORGE: No.

DOCTOR: Miss Catharine had an injection that made her a little unsteady.

MRS. HOLLY: What did he say about Catharine?

(*Catharine has gone out into the dazzling jungle of the garden.*)

SISTER (*returning*): She's gone into the garden.

DOCTOR: That's all right, she'll come back when I call her.

SISTER: It may be all right for you. You're not responsible for her.

(*Mrs. Venable has re-entered.*)

MRS. VENABLE: Call her now!

DOCTOR: Miss Catharine! Come back.

(*To the Sister:*)

Bring her back, please, Sister!

(*Catharine enters quietly, a little unsteady.*)

Now, Miss Catharine, you're going to tell the true story.

CATHARINE: Where do I start the story?

DOCTOR: Wherever you think it started.

CATHARINE: I think it started the day he was born in this house.

MRS. VENABLE: Ha! You see!

GEORGE: Cathie.

DOCTOR: Let's start later than that. (*Pause.*) Shall we begin with last summer?

CATHARINE: Oh. Last summer.

DOCTOR: Yes. Last summer.

(*There is a long pause. The raucous sounds in the garden fade into a bird-song which is clear and sweet. Mrs. Holly coughs. Mrs. Venable stirs impatiently. George crosses downstage to catch Catharine's eye as he lights a cigarette.*)

CATHARINE: Could I—?

MRS. VENABLE: Keep that boy away from her!

GEORGE: She wants to smoke, Aunt Vi.

CATHARINE: Something helps in the—hands. . . .

SISTER: Unh unh!

DOCTOR: It's all right, Sister. (*He lights her cigarette.*) About last summer: how did it begin?

CATHARINE: It began with his kindness and the six days at sea that took me so far away from the—Duelling Oaks that I forgot them, nearly. He was affectionate with me, so sweet and attentive to me, that some people took us for a honeymoon couple until they noticed that we had—separate staterooms, and—then in Paris, he took me to Patou and Schiaparelli's—*this* is from Schiaparelli's! (*Like a child, she indicates her suit.*) —bought me so many new clothes that I gave away my old ones to make room for my new ones in my new luggage to—travel. . . . I turned into a peacock! Of course, so was *he* one, too. . . .

GEORGE: *Ha Ha!*

MRS. VENABLE: Shh!

CATHARINE: But then I made the mistake of responding too much to his kindness, of taking hold of his hand before he'd take hold of mine, of holding onto his arm and leaning on his shoulder, of appreciating his kindness more than he wanted me to, and, suddenly, last summer, he began to be restless, and—oh!

DOCTOR: Go on.

CATHARINE: The Blue Jay notebook!

DOCTOR: Did you say notebook?

MRS. VENABLE: I know what she means by that, she's talking about the school composition book with a Blue Jay trademark that Sebastian used for making notes and revisions on his "Poem of Summer." It went with him everywhere that he went, in his jacket pocket, even his dinner jacket. I have the one that he had with him last summer. *Foxhill! The Blue Jay notebook!*

(*Miss Foxhill rushes in with a gasp.*)

It came with his personal effects shipped back from Cabeza de Lobo.

DOCTOR: I don't quite get the connection between new clothes and so forth and the Blue Jay notebook.

MRS. VENABLE: I HAVE IT!—Doctor, tell her I've found it.

(*Miss Foxhill hears this as she comes back out of house: gasps with relief, retires.*)

DOCTOR: With all these interruptions it's going to be awfully hard to—

MRS. VENABLE: This is important. I don't know why she mentioned the Blue Jay notebook but I want you to see it. Here it is, here! (*She holds up a notebook and leafs swiftly through the pages.*) Title? "Poem of Summer," and the date of the summer—1935. After that: *what? Blank pages, blank pages,* nothing but *nothing!*—last summer. . . .

DOCTOR: What's that got to do with—?

MRS. VENABLE: His destruction? I'll tell you. A poet's vocation is something that rests on something as thin and fine as the web of a spider, Doctor. That's all that holds him *over*!—out of destruction. . . . Few, very few are able to do it alone! Great help is needed! I *did* give it! She *didn't.*

CATHARINE: She's right about that. I failed him. I wasn't able to keep the web from—breaking. . . . I saw it breaking but couldn't save or—repair it!

MRS. VENABLE: There now, the truth's coming out. We had an agreement between us, a sort of contract or covenant between us which he broke last summer when he broke away from me and took her with him, not me! When he was frightened and I knew when and what of, because his hands would shake and his eyes looked in, not out, I'd reach across a table and touch his hands and say not a word, just look, and touch his hands with my hand until his hands stopped shaking and his eyes looked out, not in, and in the morning, the poem would be continued. *Continued until it was finished!*

(*The following ten speeches are said very rapidly, overlapping.*)

CATHARINE: I—couldn't!

MRS. VENABLE: *Naturally* not! He was *mine*! I *knew* how to help him, I *could*! You didn't, you couldn't!

DOCTOR: These interruptions—

MRS. VENABLE: I would say "You *will*" and he *would*, I—!

CATHARINE: Yes, you see, I failed him! And so, last summer, we went to Cabeza de Lobo, we flew down there from where he gave up writing his poem last summer. . . .

MRS. VENABLE: Because he'd broken our—

CATHARINE: Yes! Yes, something had broken, that string of pearls that old mothers hold their sons by like a—sort of a—sort of—*umbilical* cord, *long—after* . . .

MRS. VENABLE: She means that I held him back from—

DOCTOR: *Please!*

MRS. VENABLE: *Destruction!*

CATHARINE: All I know is that suddenly, last summer, he wasn't young any more, and we went to Cabeza de Lobo, and he suddenly switched from the evenings to the beach. . . .

DOCTOR: From evenings? To beach?

CATHARINE: I mean from the evenings to the afternoons and from the fa—fash—

(*Silence: Mrs. Holly draws a long, long painful breath. George stirs impatiently.*)

DOCTOR: Fashionable! Is that the word you—?

CATHARINE: Yes. Suddenly, last summer Cousin Sebastian changed to the afternoons and the beach.

DOCTOR: What beach?

CATHARINE: In Cabeza de Lobo there is a beach that's named for Sebastian's name saint, it's known as La Playa San Sebastian, and that's where we started spending all afternoon, every day.

DOCTOR: What kind of beach was it?

CATHARINE: It was a big city beach near the harbor.

DOCTOR: It was a big public beach?

CATHARINE: Yes, public.

MRS. VENABLE: It's little statements like that that give her away.

(*The Doctor rises and crosses to Mrs. Venable without breaking his concentration on Catharine.*)

After all I've told you about his fastidiousness, can you accept such a statement?

DOCTOR: You mustn't interrupt her.

MRS. VENABLE (*overlapping him*): That Sebastian would go every day to some dirty free public beach near a harbor? A man that had to go out a mile in a boat to find water fit to swim in?

DOCTOR: Mrs. Venable, no matter what she says you have to let her say it without any more interruptions or this interview will be useless.

MRS. VENABLE: I won't speak again. I'll keep still, if it kills me.

CATHARINE: I don't want to go on. . . .

DOCTOR: Go on with the story. Every afternoon last summer your Cousin Sebastian and you went out to this free public beach?

CATHARINE: No, it wasn't the free one, the free one was right next to it, there was a fence between the free beach and the one that we went to that charged a small charge of admission.

DOCTOR: Yes, and what did you do there?

(*He still stands beside Mrs. Venable and the light gradually changes as the girl gets deeper into her story: the light concentrates on Catharine, the other figures sink into shadow.*)

Did anything happen there that disturbed you about it?

CATHARINE: Yes!

DOCTOR: What?

CATHARINE: He bought me a swim-suit I didn't want to wear. I laughed. I said, "I can't wear that, it's a scandal to the jay-birds!"

DOCTOR: What did you mean by that? That the suit was immodest?

CATHARINE: My God, yes! It was a one-piece suit made of white lisle, the water made it transparent! (*She laughs sadly at the memory of it.*) —I didn't want to swim in it, but he'd grab my hand and drag me into the water, all the way in, and I'd come out looking naked!

DOCTOR: Why did he do that? Did you understand why?

CATHARINE:—Yes! To attract!—Attention.

DOCTOR: He wanted you to attract attention, did he, because he felt you were moody? Lonely? He wanted to shock you out of your depression last summer?

CATHARINE: Don't you understand? I was PROCURING for him!

(*Mrs. Venable's gasp is like the sound that a great hooked fish might make.*)

She used to do it, *too.*

(*Mrs. Venable cries out.*)

Not consciously! She didn't *know* that she was procuring for him in the smart, the fashionable places they used to go to before last summer! Sebastian was shy with people. She wasn't. Neither was I. We both did the same thing for him, made contacts for him, but she did it in nice places and in decent ways and I had to do it the way that I just told you!—Sebastian was lonely, Doctor, and the empty Blue Jay notebook got bigger and bigger, so big it was big and empty as that big empty blue sea and sky. . . . I knew what I was doing. I came out in the French Quarter years before I came out in the Garden District. . . .

MRS. HOLLY: Oh, Cathie! Sister . . .

DOCTOR: Hush!

CATHARINE: And before long, when the weather got warmer and the beach so crowded, he didn't need me any more for that purpose. The ones on the free beach began to climb over the fence or swim around it, bands of homeless young people that lived on the free beach like scavenger dogs, hungry children. . . . So now he let me wear a decent dark suit. I'd go to a faraway empty end of the beach, write postcards and letters and keep up my—third-person journal till it was—five o'clock and time to meet him outside the bathhouses, on the street. . . . He would come out, *followed.*

DOCTOR: Who would follow him out?

CATHARINE: The homeless, hungry young people that had climbed over the fence from the free beach that they lived on. He'd pass out tips among them as if they'd all—shined his shoes or called taxis for him. . . . Each day the crowd was bigger, noisier, greedier!—Sebastian began to be frightened.—At last we stopped going out there. . . .

DOCTOR: And then? After that? After you quit going out to the public beach?

CATHARINE: Then one day, a few days after we stopped going out to the beach—it was one of those white blazing days in Cabeza de Lobo, not a blazing hot *blue* one but a blazing hot *white* one.

DOCTOR: Yes?

CATHARINE: We had a late lunch at one of those open-air restaurants on the sea there.—Sebastian was white as the weather. He had on a spotless white silk Shantung suit and a white silk tie and a white panama and white shoes, white

—white lizard skin—pumps! He—(*She throws back her head in a startled laugh at the recollection*)—kept touching his face and his throat here and there with a white silk handkerchief and popping little white pills in his mouth, and I knew he was having a bad time with his heart and was frightened about it and that was the reason we hadn't gone out to the beach. . . .

(*During the monologue the lights have changed, the surrounding area has dimmed out and a hot white spot is focused on Catharine.*)

"I think we ought to go north," he kept saying, "I think we've done Cabeza de Lobo, I think we've done it, don't you?" *I* thought we'd done it!—but I had learned it was better not to seem to have an opinion because if I did, well, Sebastian, well, you know Sebastian, he always preferred to do what no one else wanted to do, and I always tried to give the impression that I was agreeing reluctantly to his wishes . . . it was a—game. . . .

SISTER: She's dropped her cigarette.

DOCTOR: I've got it, Sister.

(*There are whispers, various movements in the penumbra. The Doctor fills a glass for her from the cocktail shaker.*)

CATHARINE: Where was I? Oh, yes, that five o'clock lunch at one of those fish-places along the harbor of Cabeza de Lobo, it was between the city and the sea, and there were naked children along the beach which was fenced off with barbed wire from the restaurant and we had our table less than a yard from the barbed wire fence that held the beggars at bay. . . . There were naked children along the beach, a band of frightfully thin and dark naked children that looked like a flock of plucked birds, and they would come darting up to the barbed wire fence as if blown there by the wind, the hot white wind from the sea, all crying out, *"Pan, pan, pan!"*

DOCTOR (*quietly*): What's *pan*?

CATHARINE: The word for bread, and they made gobbling noises with their little black mouths, stuffing their little back fists to their mouths and making those gobbling noises, with frightful grins!—Of course we were sorry that we had come to this place but it was too late to go. . . .

DOCTOR (*quietly*): Why was it "too late to go"?

CATHARINE: I told you Cousin Sebastian wasn't well. He was popping those little white pills in his mouth. I think he had popped in so many of them that they had made him feel weak. . . . His, his!—eyes looked—dazed, but he said: "Don't look at those little monsters. Beggars are a social disease in this country. If you look at them, you get sick of the country, it spoils the whole country for you. . . ."

DOCTOR: Go on.

CATHARINE: I'm going on. I have to wait now and then till it gets clearer. Under the drug it has to be a vision, or nothing comes. . . .

DOCTOR: All right?

CATHARINE: Always when I was with him I did what he told me. I didn't look at the band of naked children, not even when the waiters drove them away from the barbed wire fence with sticks!—Rushing out through a wicket gate like an assault party in war!—and beating them screaming away from the barbed wire fence with the sticks. . . . Then! (*Pause.*)

DOCTOR: Go on, Miss Catherine, what comes next in the vision?

CATHARINE: The, the the!—band of children began to—serenade us. . . .

DOCTOR: Do what?

CATHARINE: Play for us! On instruments! Make music!—if you could call it music. . . .

DOCTOR: Oh?

CATHARINE: Their, their—instruments were—instruments of percussion!—Do you know what I mean?

DOCTOR (*making a note*): Yes. Instruments of percussion such as—*drums*?

CATHARINE: I stole glances at them when Cousin Sebastian wasn't looking, and as well as I could make out in the white blaze of the sand-beach, the instruments were tin cans strung together.

DOCTOR (*slowly, writing*): *Tin—cans—strung—together.*

CATHARINE: *And, and, and, and—and!—bits of metal,* other bits of metal that had been flattened out, made into—

DOCTOR: What?

CATHARINE: *Cymbals!* You know? *Cymbals?*

DOCTOR: Yes. Brass plates hit together.

CATHARINE: That's right, Doctor.—Tin cans flattened out and clashed together!—Cymbals. . . .

DOCTOR: Yes. I understand. What's after that, in the vision?

CATHARINE (*rapidly, panting a little*): And others had paper bags, bags made out of—coarse paper!—with something on a string inside the bags which they pulled up and down, back and forth, to make a sort of a—

DOCTOR: Sort of a—?

CATHARINE: Noise like—

DOCTOR: Noise like?

CATHARINE (*rising stiffly from chair*): Ooompa! Oompa! Oooooompa!

DOCTOR: Ahhh . . . a sound like a *tuba?*

CATHARINE: That's right!—they made a sound like a tuba. . . .

DOCTOR: Oompa, oompa, oompa, like a tuba.

(*He is making a note of the description.*)

CATHARINE: Oompa, oompa, oompa, like a—

(*Short pause.*)

DOCTOR:—Tuba. . . .

CATHARINE: All during lunch they stayed at a—a fairly *close—distance.* . . .

DOCTOR: Go on with the vision, Miss Catharine.

CATHARINE (*striding about the table*): *Oh, I'm going on, nothing could stop it now!!*

DOCTOR: Your Cousin Sebastian was *entertained* by this—*concert?*

CATHARINE: I think he was *terrified* of it!

DOCTOR: Why was he terrified of it?

CATHARINE: I think he recognized some of the musicians, some of the boys, between childhood and—older. . . .

DOCTOR: What did he do? Did he do anything about it, Miss Catharine?—Did he complain to the manager about it?

CATHARINE: *What* manager? *God?* Oh, *no*!—The manager of the fish-place on the beach? Haha!—No!—You don't understand my cousin!

DOCTOR: What do you mean?

CATHARINE: *He!—accepted!—all!*—as—how!—things!—are! —And thought nobody had any right to complain or interfere in any way whatsoever, and even though he knew that what was awful was awful, that what was wrong was wrong, and my Cousin Sebastian was certainly never sure that anything was wrong!—He thought it unfitting to ever take any action about anything whatsoever!—except to go on doing as something in him directed. . . .

DOCTOR: What did something in him direct him to do?—I mean on this occasion in Cabeza de Lobo.

CATHARINE: After the salad, before they brought the coffee, he suddenly pushed himself away from the table, and said, "They've got to stop that! Waiter, make them stop that. I'm not a well man, I have a heart condition, it's making me sick!"—This was the first time that Cousin Sebastian had ever attempted to correct a human situation!—I think perhaps that *that* was his—fatal error. . . . It was then that the waiters, all eight or ten of them, charged out of the barbed wire wicket gate and beat the little musicians away with clubs and skillets and anything hard that they could snatch from the kitchen!—Cousin Sebastian left the table. He stalked out of the restaurant after throwing a handful of paper money on the table and he fled from the place. I followed. It was all white outside. White hot, a blazing white hot, hot blazing white, at five o'clock in the afternoon in the city of—Cabeza de Lobo. It looked as if—

DOCTOR: It looked as if?

CATHARINE: As if a huge white bone had caught on fire in the sky and blazed so bright it was white and turned the sky and everything under the sky white with it!

DOCTOR:—White . . .

CATHARINE: Yes—white . . .

DOCTOR: You followed your Cousin Sebastian out of the restaurant onto the hot white street?

CATHARINE: Running up and down hill. . . .

DOCTOR: You ran up and down hill?

CATHARINE: No, no! *Didn't!*—move either *way!*—at first, we were—

(*During this recitation there are various sound effects. The percussive sounds described are very softly employed.*)

I rarely made any suggestion but *this* time I *did*. . . .

DOCTOR: What did you suggest?

CATHARINE: Cousin Sebastian seemed to be paralyzed near the entrance of the café, so I said, "Let's go." I remember that it was a very wide and steep white street, and I said, "Cousin Sebastian, down that way is the waterfront and we are more likely to find a taxi near there. . . . Or why don't we go back in?—and have them *call* us a taxi! Oh, let's do! Let's do *that*, that's better!" And he said, "*Mad*, are you *mad*? Go back in that filthy place? Never! That gang of kids shouted vile things about me to the waiters!" "Oh," I said, "then let's go down toward the docks, down there at the bottom of the hill, let's not try to climb the hill in this dreadful heat." And Cousin Sebastian shouted, "Please shut up, let me handle this situation, will you? I want to handle this thing." And he started up the steep street with a hand stuck in his jacket where I knew he was having a pain in his chest from his palpitations. . . . But he walked faster and faster, in panic, but the faster he walked the louder and closer it got!

DOCTOR: What got louder?

CATHARINE: The music.

DOCTOR: The music again.

CATHARINE: The oompa-oompa of the—following band.—They'd somehow gotten through the barbed wire and out on the street, and they were following, following!—up the blazing white street. The band of naked children pursued us up the steep white street in the sun that was like a great white bone of a giant beast that had caught on fire in the sky!—Sebastian started to run and they all screamed at once and seemed to fly in the air, they outran him so quickly. I screamed. I heard Sebastian scream, he screamed just once before this flock of black plucked little birds that pursued him and overtook him halfway up the white hill.

DOCTOR: And you, Miss Catharine, what did *you* do, then?

CATHARINE: Ran!

DOCTOR: Ran where?

CATHARINE: Down! Oh, I ran down, the easier direction to run was down, down, down, down!—The hot, white, blazing street, screaming out "Help" all the way, till—

DOCTOR: What?

CATHARINE:—Waiters, police, and others—ran out of buildings and rushed back up the hill with me. When we got back to where my Cousin Sebastian had disappeared in the flock of featherless little black sparrows, he—he was lying naked as they had been naked against a white wall, and this you won't believe, nobody *has* believed it, nobody *could* believe it, nobody, nobody on earth could possibly believe it, and I don't *blame* them!—They had *devoured* parts of him.

(*Mrs. Venable cries out softly.*)

Torn or cut parts of him away with their hands or knives or maybe those jagged tin cans they made music with, they had torn bits of him away and stuffed them into those gobbling fierce little empty black mouths of theirs. There wasn't a sound any more, there was nothing to see but Sebastian, what was left of him, that looked like a big white-paper-wrapped bunch of red roses had been *torn, thrown, crushed!*—against that blazing white wall. . . .

(*Mrs. Venable springs with amazing power from her wheelchair, stumbles erratically but swiftly toward the girl and tries to strike her with her cane. The Doctor snatches it from her and catches her as she is about to fall. She gasps hoarsely several times as he leads her toward the exit.*)

MRS. VENABLE (*offstage*): *Lion's View! State asylum, cut this hideous story out of her brain!*

(*Mrs. Holly sobs and crosses to George, who turns away from her, saying:*)

GEORGE: Mom, I'll quit school, I'll get a job, I'll—

MRS. HOLLY: Hush son! Doctor, can't you say something?

(*Pause. The Doctor comes downstage. Catharine wanders out into the garden followed by the Sister.*)

DOCTOR (*after a while, reflectively, into space*): I think we ought at least to consider the possibility that the girl's story could be true. . . .

The End

SWEET BIRD OF YOUTH

Relentless caper for all those who step
The legend of their youth into the noon
HART CRANE

To Cheryl Crawford

FOREWORD*

When I came to my writing desk on a recent morning, I found lying on my desk top an unmailed letter that I had written. I began reading it and found this sentence: "We are all civilized people, which means that we are all savages at heart but observing a few amenities of civilized behavior." Then I went on to say: "I am afraid that I observe fewer of these amenities than you do. Reason? My back is to the wall and has been to the wall for so long that the pressure of my back on the wall has started to crumble the plaster that covers the bricks and mortar."

Isn't it odd that I said the wall was giving way, not my back? I think so. Pursuing this course of free association, I suddenly remembered a dinner date I once had with a distinguished colleague. During the course of this dinner, rather close to the end of it, he broke a long, mournful silence by lifting to me his sympathetic gaze and saying to me, sweetly, "Tennessee, don't you feel that you are blocked as a writer?"

I didn't stop to think of an answer; it came immediately off my tongue without any pause for planning. I said, "Oh, yes, I've always been blocked as a writer but my desire to write has been so strong that it has always broken down the block and gone past it."

Nothing untrue comes off the tongue that quickly. It is planned speeches that contain lies or dissimulations, not what you blurt out so spontaneously in one instant.

It was literally true. At the age of fourteen I discovered writing as an escape from a world of reality in which I felt acutely uncomfortable. It immediately became my place of retreat, my cave, my refuge. From what? From being called a sissy by the neighborhood kids, and Miss Nancy by my father, because I would rather read books in my grandfather's large and classical library than play marbles and baseball and other normal kid games, a result of a severe childhood illness and of excessive attachment to the female members of my family, who had coaxed me back into life.

*Written prior to the Broadway opening of *Sweet Bird of Youth* and published in the *New York Times* on Sunday, March 8, 1959.

I think no more than a week after I started writing I ran into the first block. It's hard to describe it in a way that will be understandable to anyone who is not a neurotic. I will try. All my life I have been haunted by the obsession that to desire a thing or to love a thing intensely is to place yourself in a vulnerable position, to be a possible, if not a probable, loser of what you most want. Let's leave it like that. That block has always been there and always will be, and my chance of getting, or achieving, anything that I long for will always be gravely reduced by the interminable existence of that block.

I described it once in a poem called "The Marvelous Children."

"He, the demon, set up barricades of gold and purple tinfoil, labeled Fear (and other august titles), which they, the children, would leap lightly over, always tossing backwards their wild laughter."

But having, always, to contend with this adversary of fear, which was sometimes terror, gave me a certain tendency toward an atmosphere of hysteria and violence in my writing, an atmosphere that has existed in it since the beginning.

In my first published work, for which I received the big sum of thirty-five dollars, a story published in the July or August issue of Weird Tales in the year 1928, I drew upon a paragraph in the ancient histories of Herodotus to create a story of how the Egyptian queen, Nitocris, invited all of her enemies to a lavish banquet in a subterranean hall on the shores of the Nile, and how, at the height of this banquet, she excused herself from the table and opened sluice gates admitting the waters of the Nile into the locked banquet hall, drowning her unloved guests like so many rats.

I was sixteen when I wrote this story, but already a confirmed writer, having entered upon this vocation at the age of fourteen, and, if you're well acquainted with my writings since then, I don't have to tell you that it set the keynote for most of the work that has followed.

My first four plays, two of them performed in St. Louis, were correspondingly violent or more so. My first play professionally produced and aimed at Broadway was *Battle of Angels* and it was about as violent as you can get on the stage.

During the nineteen years since then I have only produced five plays that are *not* violent: *The Glass Menagerie*, *You Touched Me*, *Summer and Smoke*, *The Rose Tattoo* and, recently in Florida, a serious comedy called *Period of Adjustment*, which is still being worked on.

What surprises me is the degree to which both critics and audience have accepted this barrage of violence. I think I was surprised, most of all, by the acceptance and praise of *Suddenly Last Summer*. When it was done off Broadway, I thought I would be critically tarred and feathered and ridden on a fence rail out of the New York theatre, with no future haven except in translation for theatres abroad, who might mistakenly construe my work as a castigation of American morals, not understanding that I write about violence in American life only because I am not so well acquainted with the society of other countries.

Last year I thought it might help me as a writer to undertake psychoanalysis and so I did. The analyst, being acquainted with my work and recognizing the psychic wounds expressed in it, asked me, soon after we started, "Why are you so full of hate, anger and envy?"

Hate was the word I contested. After much discussion and argument, we decided that "hate" was just a provisional term and that we would only use it till we had discovered the more precise term. But unfortunately I got restless and started hopping back and forth between the analyst's couch and some Caribbean beaches. I think before we called it quits I had persuaded the doctor that hate was not the right word, that there was some other thing, some other word for it, which we had not yet uncovered, and we left it like that.

Anger, oh yes! And envy, yes! But not hate. I think that hate is a thing, a feeling, that can only exist where there is no understanding. Significantly, good physicians never have it. They never hate their patients, no matter how hateful their patients may seem to be, with their relentless, maniacal concentration on their own tortured egos.

Since I am a member of the human race, when I attack its behavior toward fellow members I am obviously including myself in the attack, unless I regard myself as not human but superior to humanity. I don't. In fact, I can't expose a human weakness on the stage unless I know it through having it myself. I have exposed a good many human weaknesses and brutalities and consequently I have them.

I don't even think that I am more conscious of mine than any of you are of yours. Guilt is universal. I mean a strong sense of guilt. If there exists any area in which a man can rise above his moral condition, imposed upon him at birth and long before birth, by the nature of his breed, then I think it is only a willingness to know it, to face its existence in him, and I think that at least below the conscious level, we all face it. Hence guilty feelings, and hence defiant aggressions, and hence the deep dark of despair that haunts our dreams, our creative work, and makes us distrust each other.

Enough of these philosophical abstractions, for now. To get back to writing for the theatre, if there is any truth in the Aristotelian idea that violence is purged by its poetic representation on a stage, then it may be that my cycle of violent plays have had a moral justification after all. I know that I have felt it. I have always felt a release from the sense of meaninglessness and death when a work of tragic intention has seemed to me to have achieved that intention, even if only approximately, nearly.

I would say that there is something much bigger in life and death than we have become aware of (or adequately recorded) in our living and dying. And, further, to compound this shameless romanticism, I would say that our serious theatre is a search for that something that is not yet successful but is still going on.

Synopsis of Scenes

ACT ONE

SCENE ONE: A bedroom in the Royal Palms Hotel, somewhere on the Gulf Coast.

SCENE TWO: The same. Later.

ACT TWO

SCENE ONE: The terrace of Boss Finley's house in St. Cloud.

SCENE TWO: The cocktail lounge and Palm Garden of the Royal Palms Hotel.

ACT THREE

The bedroom again.

TIME: Modern, an Easter Sunday, from late morning till late night.

SETTING AND "SPECIAL EFFECTS": The stage is backed by a cyclorama that should give a poetic unity of mood to the several specific settings. There are nonrealistic projections on this "cyc," the most important and constant being a grove of royal palm trees. There is nearly always a wind among these very tall palm trees, sometimes loud, sometimes just a whisper, and sometimes it blends into a thematic music which will be identified, when it occurs, as "The Lament."

During the daytime scenes the cyclorama projection is a poetic abstraction of semitropical sea and sky in fair spring weather. At night it is the palm garden with its branches among the stars.

The specific settings should be treated as freely and sparingly as the sets for *Cat on a Hot Tin Roof* or *Summer and Smoke*. They'll be described as you come to them in the script.

ACT ONE

SCENE ONE

A bedroom of an old-fashioned but still fashionable hotel somewhere along the Gulf Coast in a town called St. Cloud. I think of it as resembling one of those "Grand Hotels" around Sorrento or Monte Carlo, set in a palm garden. The style is vaguely "Moorish." The principal set-piece is a great double bed which should be raked toward the audience. In a sort of Moorish corner backed by shuttered windows, is a wicker tabouret and two wicker stools, over which is suspended a Moorish lamp on a brass chain. The windows are floor length and they open out upon a gallery. There is also a practical door frame, opening onto a corridor: the walls are only suggested.

On the great bed are two figures, a sleeping woman, and a young man awake, sitting up, in the trousers of white silk pajamas. The sleeping woman's face is partly covered by an eyeless black satin domino to protect her from morning glare. She breathes and tosses on the bed as if in the grip of a nightmare. The young man is lighting his first cigarette of the day.

Outside the windows there is heard the soft, urgent cries of birds, the sound of their wings. Then a colored waiter, Fly, appears at door on the corridor, bearing coffee-service for two. He knocks. Chance rises, pauses a moment at a mirror in the fourth wall to run a comb through his slightly thinning blond hair before he crosses to open the door.

CHANCE: Aw, good, put it in there.

FLY: Yes, suh.

CHANCE: Give me the Bromo first. You better mix it for me, I'm—

FLY: Hands kind of shaky this mawnin'?

CHANCE (*shuddering after the Bromo*): Open the shutters a little. Hey, I said a little, not much, not that much!

(*As the shutters are opened we see him clearly for the first time: he's in his late twenties and his face looks slightly older than that; you might describe it as a "ravaged young face" and yet it is still exceptionally good-looking. His body shows no decline, yet it's the kind of a body that white silk pajamas are, or ought to be, made for. A church bell tolls, and from another church, nearer, a choir starts singing The Alleluia Chorus. It draws him to the window, and as he crosses, he says:*)

I didn't know it was—Sunday.

FLY: Yes, suh, it's *Easter* Sunday.

CHANCE (*leans out a moment, hands gripping the shutters*): Uh-huh. . . .

FLY: That's the Episcopal Church they're singin' in. The bell's from the Catholic Church.

CHANCE: I'll put your tip on the check.

FLY: Thank you, Mr. Wayne.

CHANCE (*as Fly starts for the door*): Hey. How did you know my name?

FLY: I waited tables in the Grand Ballroom when you used to come to the dances on Saturday nights, with that real pretty girl you used to dance so good with, Mr. Boss Finley's daughter?

CHANCE: I'm increasing your tip to five dollars in return for a favor which is not to remember that you have recognized me or anything else at all. Your name is Fly—Shoo, Fly. Close the door with no noise.

VOICE OUTSIDE: Just a minute.

CHANCE: Who's that?

VOICE OUTSIDE: George Scudder.

(*Slight pause. Fly exits.*)

CHANCE: How did you know I was here?

(*George Scudder enters: a coolly nice-looking, business-like young man who might be the head of the Junior Chamber of Commerce but is actually a young doctor, about thirty-six or -seven.*)

SCUDDER: The assistant manager that checked you in here last night phoned me this morning that you'd come back to St. Cloud.

CHANCE: So you came right over to welcome me home?

SCUDDER: Your lady friend sounds like she's coming out of ether.

CHANCE: The Princess had a rough night.

SCUDDER: You've latched onto a Princess? (*mockingly*) Gee.

CHANCE: She's traveling incognito.

SCUDDER: Golly, I should think she would, if she's checking in hotels with *you*.

CHANCE: George, you're the only man I know that still says "gee," "golly," and "gosh."

SCUDDER: Well, I'm not the sophisticated type, Chance.

CHANCE: That's for sure. Want some coffee?

SCUDDER: Nope. Just came for a talk. A quick one.

CHANCE: Okay. Start talking, man.

SCUDDER: Why've you come back to St. Cloud?

CHANCE: I've still got a mother and a girl in St. Cloud. How's Heavenly, George?

SCUDDER: We'll get around to that later. (*He glances at his watch.*) I've got to be in surgery at the hospital in twenty-five minutes.

CHANCE: You operate now, do you?

SCUDDER (*opening doctor's bag*): I'm chief-of-staff there now.

CHANCE: Man, you've got it made.

SCUDDER: Why have you come back?

CHANCE: I heard that my mother was sick.

SCUDDER: But you said, "How's Heavenly," not "How's my mother," Chance. (*Chance sips coffee.*) Your mother died a couple of weeks ago. . . .

(*Chance slowly turns his back on the man and crosses to the window. Shadows of birds sweep the blind. He lowers it a little before he turns back to Scudder.*)

CHANCE: Why wasn't I notified?

SCUDDER: You were. A wire was sent you three days before she died at the last address she had for you which was General Delivery, Los Angeles. We got no answer from that and another wire was sent you after she died, the same day of her death and we got no response from that either. Here's the Church Record. The church took up a collection for her hospital and funeral expenses. She was buried nicely in your family plot and the church has also given her a very nice headstone. I'm giving you these details in spite of the fact that I know and everyone here in town knows that you had no interest in her, less than people who knew her only slightly, such as myself.

CHANCE: How did she go?

SCUDDER: She had a long illness, Chance. You know about that.

CHANCE: Yes. She was sick when I left here the last time.

SCUDDER: She was sick at heart as well as sick in her body at that time, Chance. But people were very good to her, especially people who knew her in church, and the Reverend Walker was with her at the end.

(*Chance sits down on the bed. He puts out his unfinished cigarette and immediately lights another. His voice becomes thin and strained.*)

CHANCE: She never had any luck.

SCUDDER: Luck? Well, that's all over with now. If you want to know anything more about that, you can get in touch with Reverend Walker about it, although I'm afraid he won't be likely to show much cordiality to you.

CHANCE: She's gone. Why talk about it?

SCUDDER: I hope you haven't forgotten the letter I wrote you soon after you last left town.

CHANCE: No. I got no letter.

SCUDDER: I wrote you in care of an address your mother gave me about a very important private matter.

CHANCE: I've been moving a lot.

SCUDDER: I didn't even mention names in the letter.

CHANCE: What was the letter about?

SCUDDER: Sit over here so I don't have to talk loud about this. Come over here. I can't talk loud about this. (*Scudder indicates the chair by the tabouret. Chance crosses and rests a foot on the chair.*) In this letter I just told you that a certain girl we know had to go through an awful experience, a tragic ordeal, because of past contact with you. I told you that I was only giving you this information so that you would know better than to come back to St. Cloud, but you didn't know better.

CHANCE: I told you I got no letter. Don't tell me about a letter, I didn't get any letter.

SCUDDER: I'm telling you what I told you in this letter.

CHANCE: All right. Tell me what you told me, don't—don't talk to me like a club, a chamber of something. What did you tell me? What ordeal? What girl? Heavenly? Heavenly? George?

SCUDDER: I see it's not going to be possible to talk about this quietly and so I . . .

CHANCE (*rising to block Scudder's way*): Heavenly? What ordeal?

SCUDDER: We will not mention names. Chance, I rushed over here this morning as soon as I heard you were back in St. Cloud, before the girl's father and brother could hear that you were back in St. Cloud, to stop you from trying to get in touch with the girl and to get out of here. That is absolutely all I have to say to you in this room at this moment. . . . But I hope I have said it in a way to impress you with the vital urgency of it, so you will leave. . . .

CHANCE: Jesus! If something's happened to Heavenly, will you please tell me—what?

SCUDDER: I said no names. We are not alone in this room. Now when I go downstairs now, I'll speak to Dan Hatcher, assistant manager here . . . he told me you'd checked in here . . . and tell him you want to check out, so you'd better get Sleeping Beauty and yourself ready to travel, and I suggest that you keep on traveling till you've crossed the State line. . . .

CHANCE: You're not going to leave this room till you've explained to me what you've been hinting at about my girl in St. Cloud.

SCUDDER: There's a lot more to this which we feel ought not to be talked about to anyone, least of all to you, since you have turned into a criminal degenerate, the only right term for you, but, Chance, I think I ought to remind you that once long ago the father of this girl wrote out a prescription for you, a sort of medical prescription, which is castration. You'd better think about that, that would deprive you of all you've got to get by on. (*He moves toward the steps.*)

CHANCE: I'm used to that threat. I'm not going to leave St. Cloud without my girl.

SCUDDER (*on the steps*): You don't have a girl in St. Cloud. Heavenly and I are going to be married next month. (*He leaves abruptly.*)

(*Chance, shaken by what he has heard, turns and picks up phone, and kneels on the floor.*)

CHANCE: Hello? St. Cloud 525. Hello, Aunt Nonnie? This is Chance, yes Chance. I'm staying at the Royal Palms and I . . . what's the matter, has something happened to Heavenly? Why can't you talk now? George Scudder was here and . . . Aunt Nonnie? Aunt Nonnie?

(*The other end hangs up. The sleeping woman suddenly cries out in her sleep. Chance drops the phone on its cradle and runs to the bed.*)

CHANCE (*bending over her as she struggles out of a nightmare*): Princess! Princess! Hey, *Princess Kos*! (*He removes her eye-mask; she sits up gasping and staring wild-eyed about her.*)

PRINCESS: Who are you? Help!

CHANCE (*on the bed*): Hush now. . . .

PRINCESS: Oh . . . I . . . had . . . a *terrible* dream.

CHANCE: It's all right. Chance's with you.

PRINCESS: Who?

CHANCE: Me.

PRINCESS: I don't know who you are!

CHANCE: You'll remember soon, Princess.

PRINCESS: I don't know, I don't know. . . .

CHANCE: It'll come back to you soon. What are you reachin' for, honey?

PRINCESS: Oxygen! Mask!

CHANCE: Why? Do you feel short-winded?

PRINCESS: Yes! I have . . . air . . . shortage!

CHANCE (*looking for the correct piece of luggage*): Which bag is your oxygen in? I can't remember which bag we packed it in. Aw, yeah, the crocodile case, the one with the combination lock. Wasn't the first number zero . . . (*He comes back to the bed and reaches for a bag under its far side.*)

PRINCESS (*as if with her dying breath*): Zero, zero. Two zeros to the right and then back around to . . .

CHANCE: Zero, three zeros, two of them to the right and the last one to the left. . . .

PRINCESS: Hurry! I can't breathe, I'm dying!

CHANCE: I'm getting it, Princess.

PRINCESS: HURRY!

CHANCE: Here we are, I've got it. . . .

(*He has extracted from case a small oxygen cylinder and mask. He fits the inhalator over her nose and mouth. She falls back on the pillow. He places the other pillow under her head. After a moment, her panicky breath subsiding, she growls at him.*)

PRINCESS: Why in hell did you lock it up in that case?

CHANCE (*standing at the head of the bed*): You said to put all your valuables in that case.

PRINCESS: I meant my jewelry, and you know it, you, bastard!

CHANCE: Princess, I didn't think you'd have these attacks any more. I thought that having me with you to protect you would stop these attacks of panic, I . . .

PRINCESS: Give me a pill.

CHANCE: Which pill?

PRINCESS: A pink one, a pinkie, and vodka . . .

(*He puts the tank on the floor, and goes over to the trunk. The phone rings. Chance gives the Princess a pill, picks up the vodka bottle and goes to the phone. He sits down with the bottle between his knees.*)

CHANCE (*pouring a drink, phone held between shoulder and ear*): Hello? Oh, hello, Mr. Hatcher——Oh? But Mr. Hatcher, when we checked in here last night we weren't told that, and Miss Alexandra Del Lago . . .

PRINCESS (*shouting*): *Don't use my name!*

CHANCE: . . . is suffering from exhaustion, she's not at all well, Mr. Hatcher, and certainly not in any condition to travel. . . . I'm sure you don't want to take the responsibility for what might happen to Miss Del Lago . . .

PRINCESS (*shouting again*): *Don't use my name!*

CHANCE: . . . if she attempted to leave here today in the condition she's in . . . do you?

PRINCESS: *Hang up!* (*He does. He comes over with his drink and the bottle to the Princess.*) I want to forget everything, I want to forget who I am. . . .

CHANCE (*handing her the drink*): He said that . . .

PRINCESS (*drinking*): Please shut up, I'm *forgetting*!

CHANCE (*taking the glass from her*): Okay, go on forget. There's nothing better than that, I wish I could do it. . . .

PRINCESS: I can, I will. I'm forgetting . . . I'm forgetting. . . .

(*She lies down. Chance moves to the foot of the bed, where he seems to be struck with an idea. He puts the bottle down on the floor, runs to the chaise and picks up a tape recorder. Taking it back to the bed, he places the recorder on the floor. As he plugs it in, he coughs.*)

What's going on?

CHANCE: Looking for my toothbrush.

PRINCESS (*throwing the oxygen mask on the bed*): Will you please take that away.

CHANCE: Sure you've had enough of it?

PRINCESS (*laughs breathlessly*): Yes, for God's sake, take it away. I must look hideous in it.

CHANCE (*taking the mask*): No, no, you just look exotic, like a Princess from Mars or a big magnified insect.

PRINCESS: Thank you, check the cylinder please.

CHANCE: For what?

PRINCESS: Check the air left in it; there's a gauge on the cylinder that gives the pressure. . . .

CHANCE: You're still breathing like a quarter horse that's been run a full mile. Are you sure you don't want a doctor?

PRINCESS: No, for God's sake . . . no!

CHANCE: Why are you so scared of doctors?

PRINCESS (*hoarsely, quickly*): I don't need them. What happened is nothing at all. It happens frequently to me. Something disturbs me . . . adrenalin's pumped in my blood and I get short-winded, that's all, that's all there is to it . . . I woke up, I didn't know where I was or who I was with, I got panicky . . . adrenalin was released and I got short-winded. . . .

CHANCE: Are you okay now, Princess? Huh? (*He kneels on the bed, and helps straighten up the pillows.*)

PRINCESS: Not quite yet, but I will be. I will be.

CHANCE: You're full of complexes, plump lady.

PRINCESS: What did you call me?

CHANCE: Plump lady.

PRINCESS: Why do you call me that? Have I let go of my figure?

CHANCE: You put on a good deal of weight after that disappointment you had last month.

PRINCESS (*hitting him with a small pillow*): What disappointment? I don't remember any.

CHANCE: Can you control your memory like that?

PRINCESS: Yes. I've had to learn to. What is this place, a hospital? And you, what are you, a male nurse?

CHANCE: I take care of you but I'm not your nurse.

PRINCESS: But you're employed by me, aren't you? For some purpose or other?

CHANCE: I'm not on salary with you.

PRINCESS: What are you on? Just expenses?

CHANCE: Yep. You're footing the bills.

PRINCESS: I see. Yes, I see.

CHANCE: Why're you rubbing your eyes?

PRINCESS: My vision's so cloudy! Don't I wear glasses, don't I have any glasses?

CHANCE: You had a little accident with your glasses.

PRINCESS: What was that?

CHANCE: You fell on your face with them on.

PRINCESS: Were they completely demolished?

CHANCE: One lens cracked.

PRINCESS: Well, please give me the remnants. I don't mind waking up in an intimate situation with someone, but I like to see who it's with, so I can make whatever adjustment seems called for. . . .

CHANCE (*rises and goes to the trunk, where he lights cigarette*): You know what I look like.

PRINCESS: No, I don't.

CHANCE: You did.

PRINCESS: I tell you I don't remember, it's all gone away!

CHANCE: I don't believe in amnesia.

PRINCESS: Neither do I. But you have to believe a thing that happens to you.

CHANCE: Where did I put your glasses?

PRINCESS: Don't ask me. You say I fell on them. If I was in that condition I wouldn't be likely to know where anything is I had with me. What happened last night?

(*He has picked them up but not given them to her.*)

CHANCE: You knocked yourself out.

PRINCESS: Did we sleep here together?

CHANCE: Yes, but I didn't molest you.

PRINCESS: Should I thank you for that, or accuse you of cheating? (*She laughs sadly.*)

CHANCE: I like you, you're a nice monster.

PRINCESS: Your voice sounds young. Are you young?

CHANCE: My age is twenty-nine years.

PRINCESS: That's young for anyone but an Arab. Are you very good-looking?

CHANCE: I used to be the best-looking boy in this town.

PRINCESS: How large is the town?

CHANCE: Fair-sized.

PRINCESS: Well, I like a good mystery novel, I read them to put me to sleep and if they don't put me to sleep, they're good; but this one's a little too good for comfort. I wish you would find me my glasses. . . .

(*He reaches over headboard to hand the glasses to her. She puts them on and looks him over. Then she motions him to come nearer and touches his bare chest with her finger tips.*)

Well, I may have done better, but God knows I've done worse.

CHANCE: What are you doing now, Princess?

PRINCESS: The tactile approach.

CHANCE: You do that like you were feeling a piece of goods to see if it was genuine silk or phony. . . .

PRINCESS: It feels like silk. Genuine! This much I do remember, that I like bodies to be hairless, silky-smooth gold!

CHANCE: Do I meet these requirements?

PRINCESS: You seem to meet those requirements. But I still have a feeling that something is not satisfied in the relation between us.

CHANCE (*moving away from her*): You've had your experiences, I've had mine. You can't expect everything to be settled at once. . . . Two different experiences of two different people. Naturally there's some things that have to be settled between them before there's any absolute agreement.

PRINCESS (*throwing the glasses on the bed*): Take that splintered lens out before it gets in my eye.

CHANCE (*obeying this instruction by knocking the glasses sharply on the bed table*): You like to give orders, don't you?

PRINCESS: It's something I seem to be used to.

CHANCE: How would you like to *take* them? To be a slave?

PRINCESS: What time is it?

CHANCE: My watch is in hock somewhere. Why don't you look at yours?

PRINCESS: Where's mine?

(*He reaches lazily over to the table, and hands it to her.*)

CHANCE: It's stopped, at five past seven.

PRINCESS: Surely it's later than that, or earlier, that's no hour when I'm . . .

CHANCE: Platinum, is it?

PRINCESS: No, it's only white gold. I never travel with anything very expensive.

CHANCE: Why? Do you get robbed much? Huh? Do you get "rolled" often?

PRINCESS: Get what?

CHANCE: "Rolled." Isn't that expression in your vocabulary?

PRINCESS: Give me the phone.

CHANCE: For what?

PRINCESS: I said give me the phone.

CHANCE: I know. And I said for what?

PRINCESS: I want to enquire where I am and who is with me?

CHANCE: Take it easy.

PRINCESS: Will you give me the phone?

CHANCE: Relax. You're getting short-winded again. . . . (*He takes hold of her shoulders.*)

PRINCESS: Please let go of me.

CHANCE: Don't you feel secure with me? Lean back. Lean back against me.

PRINCESS: Lean back?

CHANCE: This way, this way. There . . .

(*He pulls her into his arms: She rests in them, panting a little like a trapped rabbit.*)

PRINCESS: It gives you an awful trapped feeling this, this memory block. . . . I feel as if someone I loved had died lately, and I don't want to remember who it could be.

CHANCE: Do you remember your name?

PRINCESS: Yes, I do.

CHANCE: What's your name?

PRINCESS: I think there's some reason why I prefer not to tell you.

CHANCE: Well, I happen to know it. You registered under a phony name in Palm Beach but I discovered your real one. And you admitted it to me.

PRINCESS: I'm the Princess Kosmonopolis.

CHANCE: Yes, and you used to be known as . . .

PRINCESS (*sits up sharply*): No, stop . . . will you let me do it? Quietly, in my own way? The last place I remember . . .

CHANCE: What's the last place you remember?

PRINCESS: A town with the crazy name of Tallahassee.

CHANCE: Yeah. We drove through there. That's where I reminded you that today would be Sunday and we ought to lay in a supply of liquor to get us through it without us being dehydrated too severely, and so we stopped there but it was a college town and we had some trouble locating a package store, open. . . .

PRINCESS: But we did, did we?

CHANCE (*getting up for the bottle and pouring her a drink*): Oh, sure, we bought three bottles of Vodka. You curled up in the back seat with one of those bottles and when I looked back you were blotto. I intended to stay on the old Spanish Trail straight through to Texas, where you had some oil wells to look at. I didn't stop here . . . I was stopped.

PRINCESS: What by, a cop? Or . . .

CHANCE: No. No cop, but I was arrested by something.

PRINCESS: My car. Where is my car?

CHANCE (*handling her the drink*): In the hotel parking lot, Princess.

PRINCESS: Oh, then, this is a hotel?

CHANCE: It's the elegant old Royal Palms Hotel in the town of St. Cloud.

(*Gulls fly past window, shadows sweeping the blind: they cry out with soft urgency.*)

PRINCESS: Those pigeons out there sound hoarse. They sound like gulls to me. Of course, they could be pigeons with laryngitis.

(*Chance glances at her with his flickering smile and laughs softly.*)

Will you help me please? I'm about to get up.

CHANCE: What do you want? I'll get it.

PRINCESS: I want to go to the window.

CHANCE: What for?

PRINCESS: To look out of it.

CHANCE: I can describe the view to you.

PRINCESS: I'm not sure I'd trust your description. WELL?

CHANCE: Okay, *oopsa-daisy.*

PRINCESS: My God! I said help me up, not . . . toss me onto the carpet! (*Sways dizzily a moment, clutching bed. Then draws a breath and crosses to the window.*)

(*Pauses as she gazes out, squinting into noon's brilliance.*)

CHANCE: Well, what do you see? Give me your description of the view, Princess?

PRINCESS (*faces the audience*): I see a palm garden.

CHANCE: And a four-lane highway just past it.

PRINCESS (*squinting and shielding her eyes*): Yes, I see that and a strip of beach with some bathers and then, an infinite stretch of nothing but water and . . . (*She cries out softly and turns away from the window.*)

CHANCE: What? . . .

PRINCESS: Oh God, I remember the thing I wanted not to. The goddam end of my life! (*She draws a deep shuddering breath.*)

CHANCE (*running to her aid*): What's the matter?

PRINCESS: Help me back to bed. Oh God, no wonder I didn't want to remember, I was no fool!

(*He assists her to the bed. There is an unmistakable sympathy in his manner, however shallow.*)

CHANCE: Oxygen?

PRINCESS (*draws another deep shuddering breath*): No! Where's the stuff? Did you leave it in the car?

CHANCE: Oh, the stuff? Under the mattress. (*Moving to the other side of the bed, he pulls out a small pouch.*)

PRINCESS: A stupid place to put it.

CHANCE (*sits at the foot of the bed*): What's wrong with under the mattress?

PRINCESS (*sits up on the edge of the bed*): There's such a thing as chambermaids in the world, they make up beds, they come across lumps in a mattress.

CHANCE: This isn't pot. What is it?

PRINCESS: Wouldn't that be pretty? A year in jail in one of those model prisons for distinguished addicts. What is it? Don't you know what it is, you beautiful, stupid young man? It's hashish, Moroccan, the finest.

CHANCE: Oh, hash! How'd you get it through customs when you came back for your come-back?

PRINCESS: I didn't get it through customs. The ship's doctor gave me injections while this stuff was winging over the ocean to a shifty young gentleman who thought he could blackmail me for it. (*She puts on her slippers with a vigorous gesture.*)

CHANCE: Couldn't he?

PRINCESS: Of course not. I called his bluff.

CHANCE: You took injections coming over?

PRINCESS: With my neuritis? I had to. Come on give it to me.

CHANCE: Don't you want it packed right?

PRINCESS: You talk too much. You ask too many questions. I need something quick. (*She rises.*)

CHANCE: I'm a new hand at this.

PRINCESS: I'm sure, or you wouldn't discuss it in a hotel room. . . .

(*She turns to the audience, and intermittently changes the focus of her attention.*)

For years they all told me that it was ridiculous of me to feel that I couldn't go back to the screen or the stage as a middle-aged woman. They told me I was an artist, not just a star whose career depended on youth. But I knew in my heart that the legend of Alexandra del Lago couldn't be separated from an appearance of youth. . . .

There's no more valuable knowledge than knowing the right time to go. I knew it. I went at the right time to go. RETIRED! Where to? To what? To that dead planet the moon. . . .

There's nowhere else to retire to when you retire from an art because, believe it or not, I really was once an artist. So I retired to the moon, but the atmosphere of the moon doesn't have any oxygen in it. I began to feel breathless, in that withered, withering country, of time coming after time not meant to come after, and so I discovered . . . Haven't you fixed it yet?

(*Chance rises and goes to her with a cigarette he has been preparing.*)

Discovered this!

And other practices like it, to put to sleep the tiger that raged in my nerves. . . . Why the unsatisfied tiger? In the nerves jungle? Why is anything, anywhere, unsatisfied, and raging? . . .

Ask somebody's good doctor. But don't believe his answer because it isn't . . . the answer . . . if I had just been old but you see, I wasn't old. . . .

I just wasn't young, not young, young. I just wasn't young anymore. . . .

CHANCE: Nobody's young anymore. . . .

PRINCESS: But you see, I couldn't get old with that tiger still in me raging.

CHANCE: Nobody can get old. . . .

PRINCESS: Stars in retirement sometimes give acting lessons. Or take up painting, paint flowers on pots, or landscapes. I could have painted the landscape of the endless, withering country in which I wandered like a lost nomad. If I could paint deserts and nomads, if I could paint . . . hahaha. . . .

CHANCE: SH-Sh-sh-

PRINCESS: Sorry!

CHANCE: Smoke.

PRINCESS: Yes, smoke! And then the young lovers. . . .

CHANCE: Me?

PRINCESS: You? Yes, finally you. But you come after the come-back. Ha . . . Ha . . . The glorious come-back, when I turned fool and came back. . . . The screen's a very clear mirror. There's a thing called a close-up. The camera advances and you stand still and your head, your face, is caught in the frame of the picture with a light blazing on it and all your terrible history screams while you smile. . . .

CHANCE: How do you know? Maybe it wasn't a failure, maybe you were just scared, just chicken, Princess . . . ha-ha-ha. . . .

PRINCESS: Not a failure . . . after that close-up they gasped. . . . People gasped. . . . I heard them whisper, their shocked whispers. Is that her? Is that her? Her? . . . I made the mistake of wearing a very elaborate gown to the *première,* a gown with a train that had to be gathered up as I rose from my seat and began the interminable retreat from the city of flames, up, up, up the unbearably long theatre aisle, gasping for breath and still clutching up the regal white train of my gown, all the way up the forever . . . length of the aisle, and behind me some small unknown man grabbing at me, saying, stay, stay! At last the top of the aisle, I turned and struck him, then let the train fall, forgot it, and tried to run down the marble stairs, tripped of course, fell and, rolled, rolled, like a sailor's drunk whore to the bottom . . . hands, merciful hands without faces, assisted me to get up. After that? Flight, just flight, not interrupted until I woke up this morning. . . . Oh God it's gone out. . . .

CHANCE: Let me fix you another. Huh? Shall I fix you another?

PRINCESS: Let me finish yours. You can't retire with the outcrying heart of an artist still crying out, in your body, in your nerves, in your what? Heart? Oh, no that's gone, that's . . .

CHANCE (*He goes to her, takes the cigarette out of her hand and gives her a fresh one.*) Here, I've fixed you another one . . . Princess, I've fixed you another. . . . (*He sits on the floor, leaning against the foot of the bed.*)

PRINCESS: Well, sooner or later, at some point in your life, the thing that you lived for is lost or abandoned, and then . . . you die, or find something else. This is my something else. . . . (*She approaches the bed.*) And ordinarily I take the most fantastic precautions against . . . detection. . . . (*She sits on the bed, then lies down on her back, her head over the foot, near his.*) I cannot imagine what possessed me to let you know. Knowing so little about you as I seem to know.

CHANCE: I must've inspired a good deal of confidence in you.

PRINCESS: If that's the case, I've gone crazy. Now tell me something. What is that body of water, that sea, out past the palm garden and four-lane highway? I ask you because I remember now that we turned west from the sea when we went onto that highway called the Old Spanish Trail.

CHANCE: We've come back to the sea.

PRINCESS: What sea?

CHANCE: The Gulf.

PRINCESS: The Gulf?

CHANCE: The Gulf of misunderstanding between me and you. . . .

PRINCESS: We don't understand each other? And lie here smoking this stuff?

CHANCE: Princess, don't forget that this stuff is yours, that you provided me with it.

PRINCESS: What are you trying to prove? (*Church bells toll.*) Sundays go on a long time.

CHANCE: You don't deny it was yours.

PRINCESS: What's mine?

CHANCE: You brought it into the country, you smuggled it through customs into the U.S.A. and you had a fair supply of it at that hotel in Palm Beach and were asked to check out before you were ready to do so, because its aroma drifted into the corridor one breezy night.

PRINCESS: What are you trying to prove?

CHANCE: You don't deny that you introduced me to it?

PRINCESS: Boy, I doubt very much that I have any vice that I'd need to introduce to you. . . .

CHANCE: Don't call me "boy."

PRINCESS: Why not?

CHANCE: It sounds condescending. And all my vices were caught from other people.

PRINCESS: What are you trying to prove? My memory's come back now. Excessively clearly. It was this mutual practice that brought us together. When you came in my cabana to give me one of those papaya cream rubs, you sniffed, you grinned and said you'd like a stick too.

CHANCE: That's right. I knew the smell of it.

PRINCESS: What are you trying to prove?

CHANCE: You asked me four or five times what I'm trying to prove, the answer is nothing. I'm just making sure that your memory's cleared up now. You do remember me coming in your cabana to give you those papaya cream rubs?

PRINCESS: Of course I do, Carl!

CHANCE: My name is not Carl. It's Chance.

PRINCESS: You called yourself Carl.

CHANCE: I always carry an extra name in my pocket.

PRINCESS: You're not a criminal, are you?

CHANCE: No ma'am, not me. You're the one that's committed a federal offense.

(*She stares at him a moment, and then goes to the door leading to the hall, looks out and listens.*)

What did you do that for?

PRINCESS (*closing the door*): To see if someone was planted outside the door.

CHANCE: You still don't trust me?

PRINCESS: Someone that gives me a false name?

CHANCE: You registered under a phony one in Palm Beach.

PRINCESS: Yes, to avoid getting any reports or condolences on the disaster I ran from. (*She crosses to the window. There is a pause followed by "The Lament."*) And so we've not arrived at any agreement?

CHANCE: No ma'am, not a complete one.

(*She turns her back to the window and gazes at him from there.*)

PRINCESS: What's the gimmick? The hitch?

CHANCE: The usual one.

PRINCESS: What's that?

CHANCE: Doesn't somebody always hold out for something?

PRINCESS: Are you holding out for something?

CHANCE: Uh-huh. . . .

PRINCESS: What?

CHANCE: You said that you had a large block of stock, more than half ownership in a sort of a second-rate Hollywood Studio, and could put me under contract. I doubted your word about that. You're not like any phony I've met before, but phonies come in all types and sizes. So I held out, even after we locked your cabana door for the papaya cream rubs. . . . You wired for some contract papers we signed. It was notarized and witnessed by three strangers found in a bar.

PRINCESS: Then why did you hold out, still?

CHANCE: I didn't have much faith in it. You know, you can buy those things for six bits in novelty stores. I've been conned and tricked too often to put much faith in anything that could still be phony.

PRINCESS: You're wise. However, I have the impression that there's been a certain amount of intimacy between us.

CHANCE: A certain amount. No more. I wanted to hold your interest.

PRINCESS: Well, you miscalculated. My interest always increases with satisfaction.

CHANCE: Then you're unusual in that respect, too.

PRINCESS: In all respects I'm not common.

CHANCE: But I guess the contract we signed is full of loopholes?

PRINCESS: Truthfully, yes, it is. I can get out of it if I wanted to. And so can the studio. Do you have any talent?

CHANCE: For what?

PRINCESS: Acting, baby, ACTING!

CHANCE: I'm not as positive of it as I once was. I've had more chances than I could count on my fingers, and made the grade almost, but not quite, every time. Something always blocks me. . . .

PRINCESS: What? What? Do you *know*? (*He rises. The lamentation is heard very faintly.*) *Fear?*

CHANCE: No not fear, but terror . . . otherwise would I be your goddam caretaker, hauling you across the country? Picking you up when you fall? Well would I? Except for that block, by anything less than a star?

PRINCESS: CARL!

CHANCE: Chance. . . . Chance Wayne. You're stoned.

PRINCESS: Chance, come back to your youth. Put off this false, ugly hardness and . . .

CHANCE: And be took in by every con-merchant I meet?

PRINCESS: I'm not a phony, believe me.

CHANCE: Well, then, what is it you want? Come on say it, Princess.

PRINCESS: Chance, come here. (*He smiles but doesn't move.*) Come here and let's comfort each other a little. (*He crouches by the bed; she encircles him with her bare arms.*)

CHANCE: Princess! Do you know something? All this conversation has been recorded on tape?

PRINCESS: What are you talking about?

CHANCE: Listen. I'll play it back to you. (*He uncovers the tape recorder; approaches her with the earpiece.*)

PRINCESS: How did you get that thing?

CHANCE: You bought it for me in Palm Beach. I said that I wanted it to improve my diction. . . .

(*He presses the "play" button on the recorder. The following in the left column can either be on a public address system, or can be cut.*)

(PLAYBACK)

PRINCESS: What is it? Don't you know what it is? You stupid, beautiful young man. It's hashish, Moroccan, the finest.

CHANCE: Oh, hash? How'd you get it through customs when you came back for your "come-back"?

PRINCESS: I didn't get it through customs. The ship's doctor. . . .

PRINCESS: What a smart cookie you are.

CHANCE: How does it feel to be over a great big barrel?

(*He snaps off the recorder and picks up the reels.*)

PRINCESS: This is blackmail is it? Where's my mink stole?

CHANCE: Not stolen.

(*He tosses it to her contemptuously from a chair.*)

PRINCESS: Where is my jewel case?

CHANCE (*picks it up off the floor and throws it on the bed*): Here.

PRINCESS (*opens it up and starts to put on some jewelry*): Every piece is insured and described in detail. Lloyd's in London.

CHANCE: *Who's* a smart cookie, Princess? You want your purse now so you can count your money?

PRINCESS: I don't carry currency with me, just travelers' checks.

CHANCE: I noted that fact already. But I got a fountain pen you can sign them with.

PRINCESS: Ho, Ho!

CHANCE: "Ho, ho!" What an insincere laugh, if that's how you fake a laugh, no wonder you didn't make good in your come-back picture. . . .

PRINCESS: Are you serious about this attempt to blackmail me?

CHANCE: You'd better believe it. Your trade's turned dirt on you, Princess. You understand that language?

PRINCESS: The language of the gutter is understood anywhere that anyone ever fell in it.

CHANCE: Aw, then you *do* understand.

PRINCESS: And if I shouldn't comply with this order of yours?

CHANCE: You still got a name, you're still a personage, Princess. You wouldn't want "Confidential" or "Whisper" or "Hush-Hush" or the narcotics department of the F.B.I. to get hold of one of these tape-records, would you? And I'm going to make lots of copies. Huh? Princess?

PRINCESS: You are trembling and sweating . . . you see this part doesn't suit you, you just don't play it well, Chance. . . . (*Chance puts the reels in a suitcase.*) I hate to think of what kind of desperation has made you try to intimidate me, ME? ALEXANDRA DEL LAGO? with that ridiculous threat. Why it's so silly, it's touching, downright endearing, it makes me feel close to you, Chance.

You were well born, weren't you? Born of good Southern stock, in a genteel tradition, with just one disadvantage, a laurel wreath on your forehead, given too early, without enough effort to earn it . . . where's your scrapbook,

Chance? (*He crosses to the bed, takes a travelers' checkbook out of her purse, and extends it to her.*) Where's your book full of little theatre notices and stills that show you in the background of . . .

CHANCE: Here! Here! Start signing . . . or . . .

PRINCESS (*pointing to the bathroom*): Or WHAT? Go take a shower under cold water. I don't like hot sweaty bodies in a tropical climate. Oh, you, I do want and will accept, still . . . under certain conditions which I will make very clear to you.

CHANCE: Here. (*Throws the checkbook toward the bed.*)

PRINCESS: Put this away. And your leaky fountain pen. . . . When monster meets monster, one monster has to give way, AND IT WILL NEVER BE ME. I'm an older hand at it . . . with much more natural aptitude at it than you have. . . . Now then, you put the cart a little in front of the horse. Signed checks are payment, delivery comes first. Certainly I can afford it, I could deduct you, as my caretaker, Chance, remember that I was a star before big taxes . . . and had a husband who was a great merchant prince. He taught me to deal with money. . . . Now, Chance, please pay close attention while I tell you the very special conditions under which I will keep you in my employment . . . after this miscalculation. . . .

Forget the legend that I was and the ruin of that legend.

Whether or not I do have a disease of the heart that places an early terminal date on my life, no mention of that, no reference to it ever. No mention of death, never, never a word on that odious subject. I've been accused of having a death wish but I think it's life that I wish for, terribly, shamelessly, on any terms whatsoever.

When I say now, the answer must not be later. I have only one way to forget these things I don't want to remember and that's through the act of love-making. That's the only dependable distraction so when I say now, because I need that distraction, it has to be now, not later.

(*She crosses to the bed: He rises from the opposite side of the bed and goes to the window: She gazes at his back as he looks out the window. Pause: Lamentation.*)

(*Princess, finally, softly.*)

Chance, I need that distraction. It's time for me to find out if you're able to give it to me. You mustn't hang onto your silly little idea that you can increase your value by turning away and looking out a window when somebody wants you. . . . I want you. . . . I say now and I mean now, then and not until then will I call downstairs and tell the hotel cashier that I'm sending a young man down with some travelers' checks to cash for me. . . .

CHANCE (*turning slowly from the window*): Aren't you ashamed, a little?

PRINCESS: Of course I am. Aren't you?

CHANCE: More than a little. . . .

PRINCESS: Close the shutters, draw the curtain across them.

(*He obeys these commands.*)

Now get a little sweet music on the radio and come here to me and make me almost believe that we're a pair of young lovers without any shame.

SCENE TWO

As the curtain rises, the Princess has a fountain pen in hand and is signing checks. Chance, now wearing dark slacks, socks and shoes of the fashionable loafer type, is putting on his shirt and speaks as the curtain opens.

CHANCE: Keep on writing, has the pen gone dry?

PRINCESS: I started at the back of the book where the big ones are.

CHANCE: Yes, but you stopped too soon.

PRINCESS: All right, one more from the front of the book as a token of some satisfaction. I said some, not complete.

CHANCE (*picking up the phone*): Operator— Give me the cashier please.

PRINCESS: What are you doing that for?

CHANCE: You have to tell the cashier you're sending me down with some travelers' checks to cash for you.

PRINCESS: Have to? Did you say have to?

CHANCE: Cashier? Just a moment. The Princess Kosmonopolis. (*He thrusts the phone at her.*)

PRINCESS (*into the phone*): Who is this? But I don't want the cashier. My watch has stopped and I want to know the right time . . . five after three? Thank you . . . he says it's five after three. (*She hangs up and smiles at Chance.*) I'm not ready to be left alone in this room. Now let's not fight any more over little points like that, let's save our strength for the big ones. I'll have the checks cashed for you as soon as I've put on my face. I just don't want to be left alone in this place till I've put on the face that I face the world with, baby. Maybe after we get to know each other, we won't fight over little points any more, the struggle will stop, maybe we won't even fight over big points, baby. Will you open the shutters a little bit please? (*He doesn't seem to hear her. The lament is heard.*) I won't be able to see my face in the mirror. . . . Open the shutters, I won't be able to see my face in the mirror.

CHANCE: Do you want to?

PRINCESS (*pointing*): Unfortunately I have to! Open the shutters!

(*He does. He remains by the open shutters, looking out as the lament in the air continues.*)

CHANCE:—I was born in this town. I was born in St. Cloud.

PRINCESS: That's a good way to begin to tell your life story. Tell me your life story. I'm interested in it, I really would like to know it. Let's make it your audition, a sort of screen test for you. I can watch you in the mirror while I put my face on. And tell me your life story, and if you hold my attention with your life story, I'll know you have talent, I'll wire my studio on the Coast that I'm still alive and I'm on my way to the Coast with a young man named Chance Wayne that I think is cut out to be a great young star.

CHANCE (*moving out on the forestage*): Here is the town I was born in, and lived in till ten years ago, in St. Cloud. I was a twelve-pound baby, normal and healthy, but with some kind of quantity "X" in my blood, a wish or a need to be different. . . . The kids that I grew up with are mostly still here and what they call "settled down," gone into business, married and bringing up children, the little crowd I was in with, that I used to be the star of, was the snobset, the ones with the big names and money. I didn't have either . . . (*The Princess utters a soft laugh in her dimmed-out area.*) What I had was . . . (*The Princess half turns, brush poised in a faint, dusty beam of light.*)

PRINCESS: BEAUTY! Say it! Say it! What you had was beauty! I had it! I say it, with pride, no matter how sad, being gone, now.

CHANCE: Yes, well . . . the others . . . (*The Princess resumes brushing hair and the sudden cold beam of light on her goes out again.*) . . . are all now members of the young social set here. The girls are young matrons, bridge-players, and the boys belong to the Junior Chamber of Commerce and some of them, clubs in New Orleans such as Rex and Comus and ride on the Mardi Gras floats. Wonderful? No boring . . . I wanted, expected, intended to get, something better . . . Yes, and I did, I got it. I did things that fat-headed gang never dreamed of. Hell when they were still freshmen at Tulane or LSU or Ole Miss, I sang in the chorus of the biggest show in New York, in "Oklahoma," and had pictures in LIFE in a cowboy outfit, tossin' a ten-gallon hat in the air! YIP . . . EEEEEE! Ha-ha. . . . And at the same time pursued my other vocation. . . .

Maybe the only one I was truly meant for, love-making . . . slept in the social register of New York! Millionaires' widows and wives and debutante daughters of such famous names as Vanderbrook and Masters and Halloway and Connaught, names mentioned daily in columns, whose credit cards are their faces. . . . And . . .

PRINCESS: What did they pay you?

CHANCE: I gave people more than I took. Middle-aged people I gave back a feeling of youth. Lonely girls? Understanding, appreciation! An absolutely convincing show of affection. Sad people, lost people? Something light and uplifting! Eccentrics? Tolerance, even odd things they long for. . . .

But always just at the point when I might get something back that would solve my own need, which was great, to rise to their level, the memory of my girl would pull me back home to her . . . and when I came home for those visits, man oh man how that town buzzed with excitement. I'm telling you, it would blaze with it, and then that thing in Korea came along. I was about to be sucked into the Army so I went into the Navy, because a sailor's uniform suited me better, the uniform was all that suited me, though. . . .

PRINCESS: Ah-ha!

CHANCE (*mocking her*): Ah-ha. I wasn't able to stand the goddam routine, discipline. . . .

I kept thinking, this stops everything. I was twenty-three, that was the peak of my youth and I knew my youth wouldn't last long. By the time I got out, Christ knows, I might be nearly thirty! Who would remember Chance Wayne? In a life like mine, you just can't stop, you know, can't take time out between steps, you've got to keep going right on up from one thing to the other, once you drop out, it leaves you and goes on without you and you're washed up.

PRINCESS: I don't think I know what you're talking about.

CHANCE: I'm talking about the parade. THE parade! The parade! the boys that go places that's the parade I'm talking about, not a parade of swabbies on a wet deck. And so I ran my comb through my hair one morning and noticed that eight or ten hairs had come out, a warning signal of a future baldness. My hair was still thick. But would it be five years from now, or even three? When the war would be over, that scared me, that speculation. I started to have bad dreams. Nightmares and cold sweats at night, and I had palpitations, and on my leaves I got drunk and woke up in strange places with faces on the next pillow I had never seen before. My eyes had a wild look in them in the mirror. . . . I got the idea I wouldn't live through the war, that I wouldn't come back, that all the excitement and glory of being Chance Wayne would go up in smoke at the moment of contact between my brain and a bit of hot steel that happened to be in the air at the same time and place that my head was . . . that thought didn't comfort me any. Imagine a whole lifetime of dreams and ambitions and hopes dissolving away in one instant, being blacked out like some arithmetic problem washed off a blackboard by a wet sponge, just by some little accident like a bullet, not even aimed at you but just shot off in space, and so I cracked up, my nerves did. I got a medical discharge out of the service and I came home in civvies, then it was when I noticed how different it was, the town and the people in it. Polite? Yes, but not cordial. No headlines in the papers, just an item that measured one inch at the bottom of page five saying that Chance Wayne, the son of Mrs. Emily Wayne of North Front Street had received an honorable discharge from the Navy as the result of illness and was home to recover . . . that was when Heavenly became more important to me than anything else. . . .

PRINCESS: Is Heavenly a girl's name?

CHANCE: Heavenly is the name of my girl in St. Cloud.

PRINCESS: Is Heavenly why we stopped here?

CHANCE: What other reason for stopping here can you think of?

PRINCESS: So . . . I'm being used. Why not? Even a dead race horse is used to make glue. Is she pretty?

CHANCE (*handing Princess a snapshot*): This is a flashlight photo I took of her, nude, one night on Diamond Key, which is a little sandbar about half a mile off shore which is under water at high tide. This was taken with the tide coming in. The water is just beginning to lap over her body like it desired her like I did and still do and will always, always. (*Chance takes back the snapshot.*) Heavenly was her name. You can see that it fits her. This was her at fifteen.

PRINCESS: Did you have her that early?

CHANCE: I was just two years older, we had each other that early.

PRINCESS: Sheer luck!

CHANCE: Princess, the great difference between people in this world is not between the rich and the poor or the good and the evil, the biggest of all differences in this world is between the ones that had or have pleasure in love and those that haven't and hadn't any pleasure in love, but just watched it with envy, sick envy. The spectators and the performers. I don't mean just ordinary pleasure or the kind you can buy, I mean great pleasure, and nothing that's happened to me or to Heavenly since can cancel out the many long nights without sleep when we gave each other such pleasure in love as very few people can look back on in their lives . . .

PRINCESS: No question, go on with your story.

CHANCE: Each time I came back to St. Cloud I had her love to come back to. . . .

PRINCESS: Something permanent in a world of change?

CHANCE: Yes, after each disappointment, each failure at something, I'd come back to her like going to a hospital. . . .

PRINCESS: She put cool bandages on your wounds? Why didn't you marry this Heavenly little physician?

CHANCE: Didn't I tell you that Heavenly is the daughter of Boss Finley, the biggest political wheel in this part of the country? Well, if I didn't I made a serious omission.

PRINCESS: He disapproved?

CHANCE: He figured his daughter rated someone a hundred, a thousand percent better than me, Chance Wayne. . . . The last time I came back here, she phoned me from the drugstore and told me to swim out to Diamond Key, that she would meet me there. I waited a long time, till almost sunset, and the tide started coming in before I heard the put-put of an outboard motor boat coming out to the sandbar. The sun was behind her, I squinted. She had on a silky wet tank suit and fans of water and mist made rainbows about her . . . she stood up in the boat as if she was water-skiing, shouting things at me an' circling around the sandbar, around and around it!

PRINCESS: She didn't come to the sandbar?

CHANCE: No, just circled around it, shouting things at me. I'd swim toward the boat, I would just about reach it and she'd race it away, throwing up misty rainbows, disappearing in rainbows and then circled back and shouting things at me again. . . .

PRINCESS: What things?

CHANCE: Things like, "Chance go away," "Don't come back to St. Cloud." "Chance, you're a liar." "Chance, I'm sick of your lies!" "My father's right about you!" "Chance, you're no good any more." "Chance, stay away from St. Cloud." The last time around the sandbar she shouted nothing, just waved good-by and turned the boat back to shore.

PRINCESS: Is that the end of the story?

CHANCE: Princess, the end of the story is up to you. You want to help me?

PRINCESS: I want to help you. Believe me, not everybody wants to hurt everybody. I don't want to hurt you, can you believe me?

CHANCE: I can if you prove it to me.

PRINCESS: How can I prove it to you?

CHANCE: I have something in mind.

PRINCESS: Yes, what?

CHANCE: Okay I'll give you a quick outline of this project I have in mind. Soon as I've talked to my girl and shown her my contract, we go on, you and me. Not far, just to New Orleans, Princess. But no more hiding away, we check in at the Hotel Roosevelt there as Alexandra Del Lago and Chance Wayne. Right away the newspapers call you and give a press conference. . . .

PRINCESS: Oh?

CHANCE: Yes! The idea briefly, a local contest of talent to find a pair of young people to star as unknowns in a picture you're planning to make to show your faith in YOUTH, Princess. You stage this contest, you invite other judges, but your decision decides it!

PRINCESS: And you and . . . ?

CHANCE: Yes, Heavenly and I win it. We get her out of St. Cloud, we go to the West Coast together.

PRINCESS: And me?

CHANCE: You?

PRINCESS: Have you forgotten, for instance, that any public attention is what I least want in the world?

CHANCE: What better way can you think of to show the public that you're a person with bigger than personal interest?

PRINCESS: Oh, yes, yes, but not true.

CHANCE: You could pretend it was true.

PRINCESS: If I didn't despise pretending!

CHANCE: I understand. Time does it. Hardens people. Time and the world that you've lived in.

PRINCESS: Which you want for yourself. Isn't that what you want? (*She looks at him then goes to the phone.*) (*in phone*) Cashier?

Hello Cashier? This is the Princess Kosmonopolis speaking. I'm sending down a young man to cash some travelers' checks for me. (*She hangs up.*)

CHANCE: And I want to borrow your Cadillac for a while. . . .

PRINCESS: What for, Chance?

CHANCE (*posturing*): I'm pretentious. I want to be seen in your car on the streets of St. Cloud. Drive all around town in it, blowing those long silver trumpets and dressed in the fine clothes you bought me. . . . Can I?

PRINCESS: Chance, you're a lost little boy that I really would like to help find himself.

CHANCE: I passed the screen test!

PRINCESS: Come here, kiss me, I love you. (*She faces the audience.*) Did I say that? Did I mean it? (*Then to Chance with arms outstretched.*) What a child you are. . . . Come here. . . . (*He ducks under her arms, and escapes to the chair.*)

CHANCE: I want this big display. Big phony display in your Cadillac around town. And a wad a dough to flash in their faces and the fine clothes you've bought me, on me.

PRINCESS: Did I buy you fine clothes?

CHANCE (*picking up his jacket from the chair*): The finest. When you stopped being lonely because of my company at that Palm Beach Hotel, you bought me the finest. That's the deal for tonight, to toot those silver horns and drive slowly around in the Cadillac convertible so everybody that thought I was washed up will see me. And I have taken my false or true contract to flash in the faces of various people that called me washed up. All right that's the deal. Tomorrow you'll get the car back and what's left of your money. Tonight's all that counts.

PRINCESS: How do you know that as soon as you walk out of this room I won't call the police?

CHANCE: You wouldn't do that, Princess. (*He puts on his jacket.*) You'll find the car in back of the hotel parking lot, and the left-over dough will be in the glove compartment of the car.

PRINCESS: Where will you be?

CHANCE: With my girl, or nowhere.

PRINCESS: Chance Wayne! This was not necessary, all this. I'm not a phony and I wanted to be your friend.

CHANCE: Go back to sleep. As far as I know you're not a bad person, but you just got into bad company on this occasion.

PRINCESS: I am your friend and I'm not a phony. (*Chance turns and goes to the steps.*) When will I see you?

CHANCE (*at the top of the steps*): I don't know—maybe never.

PRINCESS: Never is a long time, Chance, I'll wait.

(*She throws him a kiss.*)

CHANCE: So long.

(*The Princess stands looking after him as the lights dim and the curtain closes.*)

ACT TWO

SCENE ONE

The terrace of Boss Finley's house, which is a frame house of Victorian Gothic design, suggested by a door frame at the right and a single white column. As in the other scenes, there are no walls, the action occurring against the sky and sea cyclorama.

The Gulf is suggested by the brightness and the gulls crying as in Act One. There is only essential porch furniture, Victorian wicker but painted bone white. The men should also be wearing white or off-white suits: the tableau is all blue and white, as strict as a canvas of Georgia O'Keeffe's.

At the rise of the curtain, Boss Finley is standing in the center and George Scudder nearby.

BOSS FINLEY: Chance Wayne had my daughter when she was fifteen.

SCUDDER: That young.

BOSS: When she was fifteen he had her. Know how I know? Some flashlight photos were made of her, naked, on Diamond Key.

SCUDDER: By Chance Wayne?

BOSS: My little girl was fifteen, barely out of her childhood when— (*calling offstage*) Charles—

(*Charles enters.*)

BOSS: Call Miss Heavenly—

CHARLES (*concurrently*): Miss Heavenly. Miss Heavenly. Your daddy wants to see you.

(*Charles leaves.*)

BOSS (*to Scudder*): By Chance Wayne? Who the hell else do you reckon? I seen them. He had them developed by some studio in Pass Christian that made more copies of them than Chance Wayne ordered and these photos were circulated. I seen them. That was when I first warned the son-of-a-bitch to git and out of St. Cloud. But he's back in St. Cloud right now. I tell you—

SCUDDER: Boss, let me make a suggestion. Call off this rally, I mean your appearance at it, and take it easy tonight. Go out on your boat, you and Heavenly take a short cruise on the Starfish. . . .

BOSS: I'm not about to start sparing myself. Oh, I know, I'll have me a coronary and go like that. But not because Chance Wayne had the unbelievable gall to come back to St. Cloud. (*calling offstage*) Tom Junior!

TOM JUNIOR (*offstage*): Yes, sir!

BOSS: Has he checked out yet?

TOM JUNIOR (*entering*): Hatcher says he called their room at the Royal Palms, and Chance Wayne answered the phone, and Hatcher says . . .

BOSS: Hatcher says,—who's Hatcher?

TOM JUNIOR: Dan Hatcher.

BOSS: I hate to expose my ignorance like this but the name Dan Hatcher has no more meaning to me than the name of Hatcher, which is none whatsoever.

SCUDDER (*quietly, deferentially*): Hatcher, Dan Hatcher, is the assistant manager of the Royal Palms Hotel, and the man that informed me this morning that Chance Wayne was back in St. Cloud.

BOSS: Is this Hatcher a talker, or can he keep his mouth shut?

SCUDDER: I think I impressed him how important it is to handle this thing discreetly.

BOSS: Discreetly, like you handled that operation you done on my daughter, so discreetly that a hillbilly heckler is shouting me questions about it wherever I speak?

SCUDDER: I went to fantastic lengths to preserve the secrecy of that operation.

TOM JUNIOR: When Papa's upset he hits out at anyone near him.

BOSS: I just want to know—Has Wayne left?

TOM JUNIOR: Hatcher says that Chance Wayne told him that this old movie star that he's latched on to . . .

SCUDDER: Alexandra Del Lago.

TOM JUNIOR: She's not well enough to travel.

BOSS: Okay, you're a doctor, remove her to a hospital. Call an ambulance and haul her out of the Royal Palms Hotel.

SCUDDER: Without her consent?

BOSS: Say she's got something contagious, typhoid, bubonic plague. Haul her out and slap a quarantine on her hospital door. That way you can separate them. We can remove Chance Wayne from St. Cloud as soon as this Miss Del Lago is removed from Chance Wayne.

SCUDDER: I'm not so sure that's the right way to go about it.

BOSS: Okay, you think of a way. My daughter's no whore, but she had a whore's operation after the last time he had her. I don't want him passin' another night in St. Cloud. Tom Junior.

TOM JUNIOR: Yes, sir.

BOSS: I want him gone by tomorrow—tomorrow commences at midnight.

TOM JUNIOR: I know what to do, Papa. Can I use the boat?

BOSS: Don't ask me, don't tell me nothin'—

TOM JUNIOR: Can I have *The Starfish* tonight?

BOSS: I don't want to know how, just go about it. Where's your sister?

(*Charles appears on the gallery, points out Heavenly lying on the beach to Boss and exits.*)

TOM JUNIOR: She's lyin' out on the beach like a dead body washed up on it.

BOSS (*calling*): Heavenly!

TOM JUNIOR: Gawge, I want you with me on this boat trip tonight, Gawge.

BOSS (*calling*): Heavenly!

SCUDDER: I know what you mean, Tom Junior, but I couldn't be involved in it. I can't even know about it.

BOSS (*calling again*): Heavenly!

TOM JUNIOR: Okay, don't be involved in it. There's a pretty fair doctor that lost his license for helping a girl out of trouble, and he won't be so goddam finicky about doing this absolutely just thing.

SCUDDER: I don't question the moral justification, which is complete without question. . . .

TOM JUNIOR: Yeah, complete without question.

SCUDDER: But I am a reputable doctor, I haven't lost my license. I'm chief of staff at the great hospital put up by your father. . . .

TOM JUNIOR: I said, don't know about it.

SCUDDER: No, sir, I won't know about it . . . (*Boss starts to cough.*) I can't afford to, and neither can your father. . . . (*Scudder goes to gallery writing prescription.*)

BOSS: Heavenly! Come up here, sugar. (*to Scudder*) What's that you're writing?

SCUDDER: Prescription for that cough.

BOSS: Tear it up, throw it away. I've hawked and spit all my life, and I'll be hawking and spitting in the hereafter. You all can count on that.

(*Auto horn is heard.*)

TOM JUNIOR (*leaps up on the gallery and starts to leave*): Papa, he's drivin' back by.

BOSS: Tom Junior.

(*Tom Junior stops.*)

TOM JUNIOR: Is Chance Wayne insane?

SCUDDER: Is a criminal degenerate sane or insane is a question that lots of law courts haven't been able to settle.

BOSS: Take it to the Supreme Court, they'll hand you down a decision on that question. They'll tell you a handsome young criminal degenerate like Chance Wayne is the mental and moral equal of any white man in the country.

TOM JUNIOR: He's stopped at the foot of the drive.
BOSS: Don't move, don't move, Tom Junior.
TOM JUNIOR: I'm not movin', Papa.
CHANCE (*offstage*): Aunt Nonnie! Hey, Aunt Nonnie!
BOSS: What's he shouting?
TOM JUNIOR: He's shouting at Aunt Nonnie.
BOSS: Where is she?
TOM JUNIOR: Runnin' up the drive like a dog-track rabbit.
BOSS: He ain't followin', is he?
TOM JUNIOR: Nope. He's drove away.

(*Aunt Nonnie appears before the veranda, terribly flustered, rooting in her purse for something, apparently blind to the men on the veranda.*)

BOSS: Whatcha lookin' for, Nonnie?
NONNIE (*stopping short*): Oh—I didn't notice you, Tom. I was looking for my *door*-key.
BOSS: Door's open, Nonnie, it's wide open, like a church door.
NONNIE (*laughing*): Oh, ha, ha . . .
BOSS: Why didn't you answer that good-lookin' boy in the Cadillac car that shouted at you, Nonnie?
NONNIE: Oh. I hoped you hadn't seen him. (*Draws a deep breath and comes on to the terrace, closing her white purse.*) That was Chance Wayne. He's back in St. Cloud, he's at the Royal Palms, he's—
BOSS: Why did you snub him like that? After all these years of devotion?
NONNIE: I went to the Royal Palms to warn him not to stay here but—
BOSS: He was out showing off in that big white Cadillac with the trumpet horns on it.
NONNIE: I left a message for him, I—
TOM JUNIOR: What was the message, Aunt Nonnie? Love and kisses?
NONNIE: Just get out of St. Cloud right away, Chance.
TOM JUNIOR: He's gonna git out, but not in that fish-tail Caddy.
NONNIE (*to Tom Junior*): I hope you don't mean violence—(*turning to Boss*) does he, Tom? Violence don't solve

problems. It never solves young people's problems. If you will leave it to me, I'll get him out of St. Cloud. I can, I will, I promise. I don't think Heavenly knows he's back in St. Cloud. Tom, you know, Heavenly says it wasn't Chance that— She says it wasn't Chance.

BOSS: You're like your dead sister, Nonnie, gullible as my wife was. You don't know a lie if you bump into it on a street in the daytime. Now go out there and tell Heavenly I want to see her.

NONNIE: Tom, she's not well enough to—

BOSS: Nonnie, you got a whole lot to answer for.

NONNIE: Have I?

BOSS: Yes, you sure have, Nonnie. You favored Chance Wayne, encouraged, aided and abetted him in his corruption of Heavenly over a long, long time. You go get her. You sure do have a lot to answer for. You got a helluva lot to answer for.

NONNIE: I remember when Chance was the finest, nicest, sweetest boy in St. Cloud, and he stayed that way till you, till you—

BOSS: Go get her, go get her! (*She leaves by the far side of the terrace. After a moment her voice is heard calling, "Heavenly? Heavenly?"*) It's a curious thing, a mighty peculiar thing, how often a man that rises to high public office is drug back down by every soul he harbors under his roof. He harbors them under his roof, and they pull the roof down on him. Every last living one of them.

TOM JUNIOR: Does that include me, Papa?

BOSS: If the shoe fits, put it on you.

TOM JUNIOR: How does that shoe fit me?

BOSS: If it pinches your foot, just slit it down the sides a little—it'll feel comfortable on you.

TOM JUNIOR: Papa, you are UNJUST.

BOSS: What do you want credit for?

TOM JUNIOR: I have devoted the past year to organizin' the "Youth for Tom Finley" clubs.

BOSS: I'm carryin' Tom Finley Junior on my ticket.

TOM JUNIOR: You're lucky to have me on it.

BOSS: How do you figure I'm lucky to have you on it?

TOM JUNIOR: I got more newspaper coverage in the last six months than . . .

BOSS: Once for drunk drivin', once for a stag party you thrown in Capitol City that cost me five thousand dollars to hush it up!

TOM JUNIOR: You are so unjust, it . . .

BOSS: And everyone knows you had to be drove through school like a blazeface mule pullin' a plow uphill: flunked out of college with grades that only a moron would have an excuse for.

TOM JUNIOR: I got re-admitted to college.

BOSS: At my insistence. By fake examinations, answers provided beforehand, stuck in your fancy pockets. And your promiscuity. Why, these Youth for Tom Finley clubs are practically nothin' but gangs of juvenile delinquents, wearin' badges with my name and my photograph on them.

TOM JUNIOR: How about your well known promiscuity, Papa? How about your Miss Lucy?

BOSS: Who is Miss Lucy?

TOM JUNIOR (*laughing so hard he staggers*): Who is Miss Lucy? You don't even know who she is, this woman you keep in a fifty-dollar a day hotel suite at the Royal Palms, Papa?

BOSS: What're you talkin' about?

TOM JUNIOR: That rides down the Gulf Stream Highway with a motorcycle escort blowin' their sirens like the Queen of Sheba was going into New Orleans for the day. To use her charge accounts there. And you ask who's Miss Lucy? She don't even talk good of you. She says you're too old for a lover.

BOSS: That is a goddam lie. Who says Miss Lucy says that?

TOM JUNIOR: She wrote it with lipstick on the ladies' room mirror at the Royal Palms.

BOSS: Wrote what?

TOM JUNIOR: I'll quote it to you exactly. "Boss Finley," she wrote, "is too old to cut the mustard."

(*Pause: the two stags, the old and the young one, face each other, panting. Scudder has discreetly withdrawn to a far end of porch.*)

BOSS: I don't believe this story!

TOM JUNIOR: Don't believe it.

BOSS: I will check on it, however.

TOM JUNIOR: I already checked on it. Papa, why don't you get rid of her, huh, Papa?

(*Boss Finley turns away, wounded, baffled: stares out at the audience with his old, bloodshot eyes as if he thought that someone out there had shouted a question at him which he didn't quite hear.*)

BOSS: Mind your own goddam business. A man with a mission, which he holds sacred, and on the strength of which he rises to high public office—crucified in this way, publicly, by his own offspring. (*Heavenly has entered on the gallery.*) Ah, here she is, here's my little girl. (*stopping Heavenly*) You stay here, honey. I think you all had better leave me alone with Heavenly now, huh—yeah. . . . (*Tom Junior and Scudder exit.*) Now, honey, you stay here. I want to have a talk with you.

HEAVENLY: Papa, I can't talk now.

BOSS: It's necessary.

HEAVENLY: I can't, I can't talk now.

BOSS: All right, don't talk, just listen.

(*But she doesn't want to listen, starts away: He would have restrained her forcibly if an old colored manservant, Charles, had not, at that moment, come out on the porch. He carries a stick, a hat, a package, wrapped as a present. Puts them on a table.*)

CHARLES: It's five o'clock, Mister Finley.

BOSS: Huh? Oh—thanks . . .

(*Charles turns on a coach lamp by the door. This marks a formal division in the scene. The light change is not realistic; the light doesn't seem to come from the coach lamp but from a spectral radiance in the sky, flooding the terrace.*)

(*The sea wind sings. Heavenly lifts her face to it. Later that night may be stormy, but now there is just a quickness and freshness coming in from the Gulf. Heavenly is always looking that way, toward the Gulf, so that the light from Point Lookout catches her face with its repeated soft stroke of clarity.*)

(*In her father, a sudden dignity is revived. Looking at his very beautiful daughter, he becomes almost stately. He ap-*

proaches her, soon as the colored man returns inside, like an aged courtier comes deferentially up to a Crown Princess or Infanta. It's important not to think of his attitude toward her in the terms of crudely conscious incestuous feeling, but just in the natural terms of almost any aging father's feeling for a beautiful young daughter who reminds him of a dead wife that he desired intensely when she was the age of his daughter.)

(*At this point there might be a phrase of stately, Mozartian music, suggesting a court dance. The flagged terrace may suggest the parquet floor of a ballroom and the two players' movements may suggest the stately, formal movements of a court dance of that time; but if this effect is used, it should be just a suggestion. The change toward "stylization" ought to be held in check.*)

BOSS: You're still a beautiful girl.

HEAVENLY: Am I, Papa?

BOSS: Of course you are. Lookin' at you nobody could guess that—

HEAVENLY (*laughs*): The embalmers must have done a good job on me, Papa. . . .

BOSS: You got to quit talkin' like that. (*then, seeing Charles*) Will you get back in the house! (*Phone rings.*)

CHARLES: Yes, sir, I was just—

BOSS: Go on in! If that phone call is for me, I'm in only to the governor of the state and the president of the Tidewater Oil Corporation.

CHARLES (*offstage*): It's for Miss Heavenly again.

BOSS: Say she ain't in.

CHARLES: Sorry, she ain't in.

(*Heavenly has moved upstage to the low parapet or sea wall that separates the courtyard and lawn from the beach. It is early dusk. The coach lamp has cast a strange light on the setting which is neo-romantic: Heavenly stops by an ornamental urn containing a tall fern that the salty Gulf wind has stripped nearly bare. The Boss follows her, baffled.*)

BOSS: Honey, you say and do things in the presence of people as if you had no regard of the fact that people have ears to hear you and tongues to repeat what they hear. And so you become a issue.

HEAVENLY: Become what, Papa?

BOSS: A issue, a issue, subject of talk, of scandal—which can defeat the mission that—

HEAVENLY: Don't give me your "Voice of God" speech. Papa, there was a time when you could have saved me, by letting me marry a boy that was still young and clean, but instead you drove him away, drove him out of St. Cloud. And when he came back, you took me out of St. Cloud, and tried to force me to marry a fifty-year-old money bag that you wanted something out of—

BOSS: Now, honey—

HEAVENLY:—and then another, another, all of them ones that you wanted something out of. I'd gone, so Chance went away. Tried to compete, make himself big as these big-shots you wanted to use me for a bond with. He went. He tried. The right doors wouldn't open, and so he went in the wrong ones, and— Papa, you married for love, why wouldn't you let me do it, while I was alive, inside, and the boy still clean, still decent?

BOSS: Are you reproaching me for—?

HEAVENLY (*shouting*): Yes, I am, Papa, I am. You married for love, but you wouldn't let me do it, and even though you'd done it, you broke Mama's heart, Miss Lucy had been your mistress—

BOSS: Who is Miss Lucy?

HEAVENLY: Oh, Papa, she was your mistress long before Mama died. And Mama was just a front for you. Can I go in now, Papa? Can I go in now?

BOSS: No, no, not till I'm through with you. What a terrible, terrible thing for my baby to say . . . (*He takes her in his arms.*) Tomorrow, tomorrow morning, when the big after-Easter sales commence in the stores—I'm gonna send you in town with a motorcycle escort, straight to the Maison Blanche. When you arrive at the store, I want you to go directly up to the office of Mr. Harvey C. Petrie and tell him to give you unlimited credit there. Then go down and outfit yourself as if you was—buyin' a trousseau to marry the Prince of Monaco. . . . Purchase a full wardrobe, includin' furs. Keep 'em in storage until winter. Gown? Three, four, five, the most lavish. Slippers? Hell, pairs and pairs of 'em. Not one hat—but a dozen. I made a pile of dough on a deal involvin' the sale of rights to oil under water here lately, and baby, I want you to buy a piece of jewelry. Now about that, you better tell Harvey to call me. Or better still, maybe Miss Lucy had better help you select it. She's wise as a backhouse rat when it comes to a stone,—that's for sure. . . . Now where'd I buy that clip that I give your mama? D'you remember the clip I bought your mama? Last thing I give your mama before she died . . . I knowed she was dyin' when I bought her that clip, and I bought that clip for fifteen thousand dollars mainly to make her think she was going to get well. . . . When I pinned it on her on the nightgown she was wearing, that poor thing started crying. She said, for God's sake, Boss, what does a dying woman want with such a big diamond? I said to her, honey, look at the price tag on it. What does the price tag say? See them five figures, that one and that five and them three aughts on there? Now, honey, make sense, I told her. If you was dying, if there was any chance of it, would I invest fifteen grand in a diamond clip to pin on the neck of a shroud? Ha, haha. That made the old lady laugh. And she sat up as bright as a little bird in that bed with the diamond clip on, receiving callers all day, and laughing and chatting with them, with that diamond clip on inside and she died before midnight, with that diamond clip on her. And not till the very last minute did she believe that the diamonds wasn't a proof that she wasn't dying. (*He moves to terrace, takes off robe and starts to put on tuxedo coat.*)

HEAVENLY: Did you bury her with it?

BOSS: Bury her with it? Hell, no. I took it back to the jewelry store in the morning.

HEAVENLY: Then it didn't cost you fifteen grand after all.

BOSS: Hell, did I care what it cost me? I'm not a small man. I wouldn't have cared one hoot if it cost me a million . . . if at that time I had that kind of loot in my pockets. It would have been worth that money to see that one little smile your mama bird give me at noon of the day she was dying.

HEAVENLY: I guess that shows, demonstrates very clearly, that you have got a pretty big heart after all.

BOSS: Who doubts it then? Who? Who ever? (*He laughs.*)

(*Heavenly starts to laugh and then screams hysterically. She starts going toward the house.*)

(*Boss throws down his cane and grabs her.*)

Just a minute, Missy. Stop it. Stop it. Listen to me, I'm gonna tell you something. Last week in New Bethesda, when I was speaking on the threat of desegregation to white women's chastity in the South, some heckler in the crowd shouted out, "Hey, Boss Finley, how about your daughter? How about that operation you had done on your daughter at the Thomas J. Finley hospital in St. Cloud? Did she put on black in mourning for her appendix?" Same heckler, same question when I spoke in the Coliseum at the state capitol.

HEAVENLY: What was your answer to him?

BOSS: He was removed from the hall at both places and roughed up a little outside it.

HEAVENLY: Papa, you have got an illusion of power.

BOSS: I have power, which is not an illusion.

HEAVENLY: Papa, I'm sorry my operation has brought this embarrassment on you, but can you imagine it, Papa? I felt worse than embarrassed when I found out that Dr. George Scudder's knife had cut the youth out of my body, made me an old childless woman. Dry, cold, empty, like an old woman. I feel as if I ought to rattle like a dead dried-up vine when the Gulf Wind blows, but, Papa—I won't embarrass you any more. I've made up my mind about something. If they'll let me, accept me, I'm going into a convent.

BOSS (*shouting*): You ain't going into no convent. This state is a Protestant region and a daughter in a convent would politically ruin me. Oh, I know, you took your mama's religion because in your heart you always wished to defy me. Now, tonight, I'm addressing the Youth for Tom Finley clubs in the ballroom of the Royal Palms Hotel. My speech is going out over a national TV network, and Missy, you're going to march in the ballroom on my arm. You're going to be wearing the stainless white of a virgin, with a Youth for Tom Finley button on one shoulder and a corsage of lilies on the other. You're going to be on the speaker's platform with me, you on one side of me and Tom Junior on the other, to scotch these rumors about your corruption. And you're gonna wear a proud happy smile on your face, you're gonna stare straight out at the crowd in the ballroom with pride and joy in your eyes. Lookin' at you, all in white like a virgin, nobody would dare to speak or believe the ugly stories about you. I'm relying a great deal on this campaign to bring in young voters for the crusade I'm leading. I'm all that stands between the South and the black days of Reconstruction. And you and Tom Junior are going to stand there beside me in the grand crystal ballroom, as shining examples of white Southern youth—in danger.

HEAVENLY (*defiant*): Papa, I'm not going to do it.

BOSS: I didn't say would you, I said you would, and you will.

HEAVENLY: Suppose I still say I won't.

BOSS: Then you won't, that's all. If you won't, you won't. But there would be consequences you might not like. (*Phone rings.*) Chance Wayne is back in St. Cloud.

CHARLES (*offstage*): Mr. Finley's residence. Miss Heavenly? Sorry, she's not in.

BOSS: I'm going to remove him, he's going to be removed from St. Cloud. How do you want him to leave, in that white Cadillac he's riding around in, or in the scow that totes the garbage out to the dumping place in the Gulf?

HEAVENLY: You wouldn't dare!

BOSS: You want to take a chance on it?

CHARLES (*enters*): That call was for you again, Miss Heavenly.

BOSS: A lot of people approve of taking violent action against corrupters. And on all of them that want to adulterate the pure white blood of the South. Hell, when I was fifteen, I come down barefoot out of the red clay hills as if the Voice of God called me. Which it did, I believe. I firmly believe He called me. And nothing, nobody, nowhere is gonna stop me, never. . . . (*He motions to Charles for gift. Charles hands it to him.*) Thank you, Charles. I'm gonna pay me an early call on Miss Lucy.

(A sad, uncertain note has come into his voice on this final line. He turns and plods wearily, doggedly off at left.)

The Curtain Falls

(House remains dark for short intermission.)

SCENE TWO

A corner of cocktail lounge and of outside gallery of the Royal Palms Hotel. This corresponds in style to the bedroom set: Victorian with Moorish influence. Royal palms are projected on the cyclorama which is deep violet with dusk. There are Moorish arches between gallery and interior: over the single table, inside, is suspended the same lamp, stained glass and ornately wrought metal, that hung in the bedroom. Perhaps on the gallery there is a low stone balustrade that supports, where steps descend into the garden, an electric light standard with five branches and pear-shaped globes of a dim pearly luster. Somewhere out of the sight-lines an entertainer plays a piano or novachord.

The interior table is occupied by two couples that represent society in St. Cloud. They are contemporaries of Chance's. Behind the bar is Stuff who feels the dignity of his recent advancement from drugstore soda-fountain to the Royal Palms cocktail lounge: he has on a white mess-jacket, a scarlet cummerbund and light blue trousers, flatteringly close-fitted. Chance Wayne was once barman here: Stuff moves with an indolent male grace that he may have unconsciously remembered admiring in Chance.

Boss Finley's mistress, Miss Lucy, enters the cocktail lounge dressed in a ball gown elaborately ruffled and very bouffant like an antebellum Southern belle's. A single blonde curl is arranged to switch girlishly at one side of her sharp little terrier face. She is outraged over something and her glare is concentrated on Stuff who "plays it cool" behind the bar.

STUFF: Ev'nin', Miss Lucy.

MISS LUCY: I wasn't allowed to sit at the banquet table. No. I was put at a little side table, with a couple of state legislators an' wives. (*She sweeps behind the bar in a proprietary fashion.*) Where's your Grant's twelve-year-old? Hey! Do you have a big mouth? I used to remember a kid that jerked sodas at Walgreen's that had a big mouth. . . . Put some ice in this. . . . Is yours big, huh? I want to tell you something.

STUFF: What's the matter with your finger?

(*She catches him by his scarlet cummerbund.*)

MISS LUCY: I'm going to tell you just now. The boss came over to me with a big candy Easter egg for me. The top of the egg unscrewed. He told me to unscrew it. So I unscrewed it. Inside was a little blue velvet jewel box, no not little, a big one, as big as somebody's mouth, too.

STUFF: Whose mouth?

MISS LUCY: The mouth of somebody who's not a hundred miles from here.

STUFF (*going off at the left*): I got to set my chairs. (*Stuff re-enters at once carrying two chairs. Sets them at tables while Miss Lucy talks.*)

MISS LUCY: I open the jewel box an' start to remove the great big diamond clip in it. I just got my fingers on it, and start to remove it and the old son of a bitch slams the lid of the box on my fingers. One fingernail is still blue. And the boss says to me, "Now go downstairs to the cocktail lounge and go in the ladies' room and describe this diamond clip with lipstick on the ladies' room mirror down there. Hanh?—" and he put the jewel box in his pocket and slammed the door so hard goin' out of my suite that a picture fell off the wall.

STUFF (*setting the chairs at the table*): Miss Lucy, you are the one that said, "I wish you would see what's written with lipstick on the ladies' room mirror" las' Saturday night.

MISS LUCY: To you! Because I thought I could trust you.

STUFF: Other people were here an' all of them heard it.

MISS LUCY: Nobody but you at the bar belonged to the Youth for Boss Finley Club.

(*Both stop short. They've noticed a tall man who has entered the cocktail lounge. He has the length and leanness and luminous pallor of a face that El Greco gave to his saints. He has a small bandage near the hairline. His clothes are country.*)

Hey, you.

HECKLER: Evenin', ma'am.

MISS LUCY: You with the Hillbilly Ramblers? You with the band?

HECKLER: I'm a hillbilly, but I'm not with no band.

(*He notices Miss Lucy's steady, interested stare. Stuff leaves with a tray of drinks.*)

MISS LUCY: What do you want here?

HECKLER: I come to hear Boss Finley talk. (*His voice is clear but strained. He rubs his large Adam's apple as he speaks.*)

MISS LUCY: You can't get in the ballroom without a jacket and a tie on. . . . I know who you are. You're the heckler, aren't you?

HECKLER: I don't heckle. I just ask questions, one question or two or three questions, depending on how much time it takes them to grab me and throw me out of the hall.

MISS LUCY: Those questions are loaded questions. You gonna repeat them tonight?

HECKLER: Yes, ma'am, if I can get in the ballroom, and make myself heard.

MISS LUCY: What's wrong with your voice?

HECKLER: When I shouted my questions in New Bethesda last week I got hit in the Adam's apple with the butt of a pistol, and that affected my voice. It still ain't good, but it's better. (*Starts to go.*)

MISS LUCY (*goes to back of bar, where she gets jacket, the kind kept in places with dress regulations, and throws it to Heckler*): Wait. Here, put this on. The Boss's talking on a national TV hookup tonight. There's a tie in the pocket. You sit perfectly still at the bar till the Boss starts speaking. Keep your face back of this *Evening Banner.* O.K.?

HECKLER (*opening the paper in front of his face*): I thank you.

MISS LUCY: I thank you, too, and I wish you more luck than you're likely to have.

(*Stuff re-enters and goes to back of the bar.*)

FLY (*entering on the gallery*): Paging Chance Wayne. (*auto horn offstage*) Mr. Chance Wayne, please. Paging Chance Wayne. (*He leaves.*)

MISS LUCY (*to Stuff who has re-entered*): Is Chance Wayne back in St. Cloud?

STUFF: You remember Alexandra Del Lago?

MISS LUCY: I guess I do. I was president of her local fan club. Why?

CHANCE (*offstage*): Hey, Boy, park that car up front and don't wrinkle them fenders.

STUFF: She and Chance Wayne checked in here last night.

MISS LUCY: Well I'll be a dawg's mother. I'm going to look into that. (*Lucy exits.*)

CHANCE (*entering and crossing to the bar*): Hey, Stuff! (*He takes a cocktail off the bar and sips it.*)

STUFF: Put that down. This ain't no cocktail party.

CHANCE: Man, don't you know . . . phew . . . nobody drinks gin martinis with olives. Everybody drinks vodka martinis with lemon twist nowadays, except the squares in St. Cloud. When I had your job, when I was the barman here at the Royal Palms, I created that uniform you've got on. . . . I copied it from an outfit Vic Mature wore in a Foreign Legion picture, and I looked better in it than he did, and almost as good in it as you do, ha, ha. . . .

AUNT NONNIE (*who has entered at the right*): Chance. Chance . . .

CHANCE: Aunt Nonnie! (*to Stuff*) Hey, I want a tablecloth on that table, and a bucket of champagne . . . Mumm's Cordon Rouge. . . .

AUNT NONNIE: You come out here.

CHANCE: But, I just ordered champagne in here. (*Suddenly his effusive manner collapses, as she stares at him gravely.*)

AUNT NONNIE: I can't be seen talking to you. . . .

(*She leads him to one side of the stage. A light change has occurred which has made it a royal palm grove with a bench. They cross to it solemnly. Stuff busies himself at the bar, which is barely lit. After a moment he exits with a few drinks to main body of the cocktail lounge off left. Bar music. Quiereme Mucho.*)

CHANCE (*following her*): Why?

AUNT NONNIE: I've got just one thing to tell you, Chance, get out of St. Cloud.

CHANCE: Why does everybody treat me like a low criminal in the town I was born in?

AUNT NONNIE: Ask yourself that question, ask your conscience that question.

CHANCE: What question?

AUNT NONNIE: You know, and I know you know . . .

CHANCE: Know what?

AUNT NONNIE: I'm not going to talk about it. I just can't talk about it. Your head and your tongue run wild. You can't be trusted. We have to live in St. Cloud. . . . Oh, Chance, why have you changed like you've changed? Why do you live on nothing but wild dreams now, and have no address where anybody can reach you in time to—reach you?

CHANCE: Wild dreams! Yes. Isn't life a wild dream? I never heard a better description of it. . . . (*He takes a pill and a swallow from a flask.*)

AUNT NONNIE: What did you just take, Chance? You took something out of your pocket and washed it down with liquor.

CHANCE: Yes, I took a wild dream and—washed it down with another wild dream, Aunt Nonnie, that's my life now. . . .

AUNT NONNIE: Why, son?

CHANCE: Oh, Aunt Nonnie, for God's sake, have you forgotten what was expected of me?

AUNT NONNIE: People that loved you expected just one thing of you—sweetness and honesty and . . .

(*Stuff leaves with tray.*)

CHANCE (*kneeling at her side*): No, not after the brilliant beginning I made. Why, at seventeen, I put on, directed, and played the leading role in "The Valiant," that one-act play that won the state drama contest. Heavenly played in it with me, and have you forgotten? You went with us as the girls' chaperone to the national contest held in . . .

AUNT NONNIE: Son, of course I remember.

CHANCE: In the parlor car? How we sang together?

AUNT NONNIE: You were in love even then.

CHANCE: God, yes, we were in love! (*He sings softly*)

"If you like-a me, like I like-a you,
And we like-a both the same"

TOGETHER:

"I'd like-a say, this very day,
I'd like-a change your name."

(*Chance laughs softly, wildly, in the cool light of the palm grove. Aunt Nonnie rises abruptly. Chance catches her hands.*)

AUNT NONNIE: You—*Do*—Take unfair advantage. . . .

CHANCE: Aunt Nonnie, we didn't win that lousy national contest, we just placed second.

AUNT NONNIE: Chance, you didn't place second. You got honorable mention. Fourth place, except it was just called honorable mention.

CHANCE: Just honorable mention. But in a national contest, honorable mention means something. . . . We would have won it, but I blew my lines. Yes, I that put on and produced the damn thing, couldn't even hear the damn lines being hissed at me by that fat girl with the book in the wings. (*He buries his face in his hands.*)

AUNT NONNIE: I loved you for that, son, and so did Heavenly, too.

CHANCE: It was on the way home in the train that she and I—

AUNT NONNIE (*with a flurry of feeling*): I know, I—I—

CHANCE (*rising*): I bribed the Pullman Conductor to let us use for an hour a vacant compartment on that sad, home-going train—

AUNT NONNIE: I know, I—I—

CHANCE: Gave him five dollars, but that wasn't enough, and so I gave him my wrist watch, and my collar pin and tie clip and signet ring and my suit, that I'd bought on credit to go to the contest. First suit I'd ever put on that cost more than thirty dollars.

AUNT NONNIE: Don't go back over that.

CHANCE:—To buy the first hour of love that we had together. When she undressed, I saw that her body was just then, barely, beginning to be a woman's and . . .

AUNT NONNIE: Stop, Chance.

CHANCE: I said, oh, Heavenly, no, but she said yes, and I cried in her arms that night, and didn't know that what I was crying for was—youth, that would go.

AUNT NONNIE: It was from that time on, you've changed.

CHANCE: I swore in my heart that I'd never again come in second in any contest, especially not now that Heavenly was my— Aunt Nonnie, look at this contract. (*He snatches out papers and lights lighter.*)

AUNT NONNIE: I don't want to see false papers.

CHANCE: These are genuine papers. Look at the notary's seal and the signatures of the three witnesses on them. Aunt Nonnie, do you know who I'm with? I'm with Alexandra Del Lago, the Princess Kosmonopolis is my—

AUNT NONNIE: Is your what?

CHANCE: Patroness! Agent! Producer! She hasn't been seen much lately, but still has influence, power, and money—money that can open all doors. That I've knocked at all these years till my knuckles are bloody.

AUNT NONNIE: Chance, even now, if you came back here simply saying, "I couldn't remember the lines, I lost the contest, I—failed," but you've come back here again with—

CHANCE: Will you just listen one minute more? Aunt Nonnie, here is the plan. A local-contest-of-Beauty.

AUNT NONNIE: Oh, Chance.

CHANCE: A local contest of talent that she will win.

AUNT NONNIE: Who?

CHANCE: Heavenly.

AUNT NONNIE: No, Chance. She's not young now, she's faded, she's . . .

CHANCE: Nothing goes that quick, not even youth.

AUNT NONNIE: Yes, it does.

CHANCE: It will come back like magic. Soon as I . . .

AUNT NONNIE: For what? For a fake contest?

CHANCE: For love. The moment I hold her.

AUNT NONNIE: Chance.

CHANCE: It's not going to be a local thing, Aunt Nonnie. It's going to get national coverage. The Princess Kosmonopolis's best friend is that sob sister, Sally Powers. Even you know Sally Powers. Most powerful movie columnist in the world. Whose name is law in the motion . . .

AUNT NONNIE: Chance, lower your voice.

CHANCE: I want people to hear me.

AUNT NONNIE: No, you don't, no you don't. Because if your voice gets to Boss Finley, you'll be in great danger, Chance.

CHANCE: I go back to Heavenly, or I don't. I live or die. There's nothing in between for me.

AUNT NONNIE: What you want to go back to is your clean, unashamed youth. And you can't.

CHANCE: You still don't believe me, Aunt Nonnie?

AUNT NONNIE: No, I don't. Please go. Go away from here, Chance.

CHANCE: Please.

AUNT NONNIE: No, no, go away!

CHANCE: Where to? Where can I go? This is the home of my heart. Don't make me homeless.

AUNT NONNIE: Oh, Chance.

CHANCE: Aunt Nonnie. Please.

AUNT NONNIE (*rises and starts to go*): I'll write to you. Send me an address. I'll write to you.

(*She exits through bar. Stuff enters and moves to bar.*)

CHANCE: Aunt Nonnie . . .

(*She's gone.*)

(*Chance removes a pint bottle of vodka from his pocket and something else which he washes down with the vodka. He stands back as two couples come up the steps and cross the gallery into the bar: they sit at a table. Chance takes a deep breath. Fly enters lighted area inside, singing out "Paging Mr. Chance Wayne, pagin' Mr. Chance Wayne."—Turns about smartly and goes back out through lobby. The name has stirred a commotion at the bar and table visible inside.*)

EDNA: Did you hear *that*? Is *Chance Wayne* back in St. Cloud?

(*Chance draws a deep breath. Then, he stalks back into the main part of the cocktail lounge like a matador entering a bull ring.*)

VIOLET: My God, yes—there he is.

(*Chance reads Fly's message.*)

CHANCE (*to Fly*): Not now, later, later.

(*The entertainer off left begins to play a piano . . . The "evening" in the cocktail lounge is just beginning.*)

(*Fly leaves through the gallery.*)

Well! Same old place, same old gang. Time doesn't pass in St. Cloud. (*To Bud and Scotty*) Hi!

BUD: How are you . . .

CHANCE (*shouting offstage*): (*Fly enters and stands on terrace*) Hey, Jackie . . . (*Piano stops. Chance crosses over to the table that holds the foursome.*) . . . remember my song? Do you —remember my song? . . . You see, he remembers my song. (*The entertainer swings into "It's a Big Wide Wonderful World."*) Now I feel at home. In my home town . . . Come on, everybody—sing!

(*This token of apparent acceptance reassures him. The foursome at the table on stage studiously ignore him. He sings:*)

"When you're in love you're a master
Of all you survey, you're a gay Santa Claus.
There's a great big star-spangled sky up above you,
When you're in love you're a hero . . ."

Come on! Sing, ev'rybody!

(*In the old days they did; now they don't. He goes on, singing a bit; then his voice dies out on a note of embarrassment. Somebody at the bar whispers something and another laughs. Chance chuckles uneasily and says:*)

What's wrong here? The place is dead.

STUFF: You been away too long, Chance.

CHANCE: Is that the trouble?

STUFF: That's all. . . .

(*Jackie, off, finishes with an arpeggio. The piano lid slams. There is a curious hush in the bar. Chance looks at the table. Violet whispers something to Bud. Both girls rise abruptly and cross out of the bar.*)

BUD (*yelling at Stuff*): Check, Stuff.

CHANCE (*with exaggerated surprise*): Well, *Bud and Scotty.* I didn't see you at all. Wasn't that Violet and Edna at your table? (*He sits at the table between Bud and Scotty.*)

SCOTTY: I guess they didn't recognize you, Chance.

BUD: Violet did.

SCOTTY: Did Violet?

BUD: She said, "My God, Chance Wayne."

SCOTTY: That's recognition and profanity, too.

CHANCE: I don't mind. I've been snubbed by experts, and I've done some snubbing myself. . . . Hey! (*Miss Lucy has entered at left. Chance sees her and goes toward her.*)—Is that Miss Lucy or is that Scarlett O'Hara?

MISS LUCY: Hello there, Chance Wayne. Somebody said that you were back in St. Cloud, but I didn't believe them. I said I'd have to see it with my own eyes before . . . Usually there's an item in the paper, in Gwen Phillips's column saying "St. Cloud youth home on visit is slated to play featured role in important new picture," and me being a movie fan I'm always thrilled by it. . . . (*She ruffles his hair.*)

CHANCE: Never do that to a man with thinning hair. (*Chance's smile is unflinching; it gets harder and brighter.*)

MISS LUCY: Is your hair thinning, baby? Maybe that's the difference I noticed in your appearance. Don't go 'way till I get back with my drink. . . .

(*She goes to back of bar to mix herself a drink. Meanwhile, Chance combs his hair.*)

SCOTTY (*to Chance*): Don't throw away those golden hairs you combed out, Chance. Save 'em and send 'em each in letters to your fan clubs.

BUD: Does Chance Wayne have a fan club?

SCOTTY: The most patient one in the world. They've been waiting years for him to show up on the screen for more than five seconds in a crowd scene.

MISS LUCY (*returning to the table*): Y'know this boy Chance Wayne used to be so attractive I couldn't stand it. But now I can, almost stand it. Every Sunday in summer I used to drive out to the municipal beach and watch him dive off the high tower. I'd take binoculars with me when he put on those free divin' exhibitions. You still dive, Chance? Or have you given that up?

CHANCE (*uneasily*): I did some diving last Sunday.

MISS LUCY: Good, as ever?

CHANCE: I was a little off form, but the crowd didn't notice. I can still get away with a double back somersault and a—

MISS LUCY: Where was this, in Palm Beach, Florida, Chance?

(*Hatcher enters.*)

CHANCE (*stiffening*): Why Palm Beach? Why there?

MISS LUCY: Who was it said they seen you last month in Palm Beach? Oh yes, Hatcher—that you had a job as a beach-boy at some big hotel there?

HATCHER (*stops at steps of the terrace, then leaves across the gallery*): Yeah, that's what I heard.

CHANCE: Had a job—as a beach-boy?

STUFF: Rubbing oil into big fat millionaires.

CHANCE: What joker thought up that one? (*His laugh is a little too loud.*)

SCOTTY: You ought to get their names and sue them for slander.

CHANCE: I long ago gave up tracking down sources of rumors about me. Of course, it's flattering, it's gratifying to know that you're still being talked about in your old home town, even if what they say is completely fantastic. Hahaha.

(*Entertainer returns, sweeps into "Quiereme Mucho."*)

MISS LUCY: Baby, you've changed in some way, but I can't put my finger on it. You all see a change in him, or has he just gotten older? (*She sits down next to Chance.*)

CHANCE (*quickly*): To change is to live, Miss Lucy, to live is to change, and not to change is to die. You know that, don't you? It used to scare me sometimes. I'm not scared of it now. Are you scared of it, Miss Lucy? Does it scare you?

(*Behind Chance's back one of the girls has appeared and signaled the boys to join them outside. Scotty nods and holds up two fingers to mean they'll come in a couple of minutes. The girl goes back out with an angry head-toss.*)

SCOTTY: Chance, did you know Boss Finley was holding a Youth for Tom Finley rally upstairs tonight?

CHANCE: I saw the announcements of it all over town.

BUD: He's going to state his position on that emasculation business that's stirred up such a mess in the state. Had you heard about that?

CHANCE: No.

SCOTTY: He must have been up in some earth satellite if he hasn't heard about that.

CHANCE: No, just out of St. Cloud.

SCOTTY: Well, they picked out a nigger at random and castrated the bastard to show they mean business about white women's protection in this state.

BUD: Some people think they went too far about it. There's been a whole lot of Northern agitation all over the country.

SCOTTY: The Boss is going to state his own position about that thing before the Youth for Boss Finley Rally upstairs in the Crystal Ballroom.

CHANCE: Aw. Tonight?

STUFF: Yeah, t'night.

BUD: They say that Heavenly Finley and Tom Junior are going to be standing on the platform with him.

PAGEBOY (*entering*): Paging Chance Wayne. Paging . . .

(*He is stopped short by Edna.*)

CHANCE: I *doubt* that story, somehow I *doubt* that story.

SCOTTY: You doubt they cut that nigger?

CHANCE: Oh, no, that I don't doubt. You know what that is, don't you? Sex-envy is what that is, and the revenge for sex-envy which is a widespread disease that I have run into personally too often for me to doubt its existence or any manifestation. (*The group push back their chairs, snubbing him. Chance takes the message from the Pageboy, reads it and throws it on the floor.*) Hey, Stuff— What d'ya have to do, stand on your head to get a drink around here?— Later, tell her.—Miss Lucy, can you get that Walgreen's soda jerk to give me a shot of vodka on the rocks? (*She snaps her fingers at Stuff. He shrugs and sloshes some vodka onto ice.*)

MISS LUCY: Chance? You're too loud, baby.

CHANCE: Not loud enough, Miss Lucy. No. What I meant that I doubt is that Heavenly Finley, that only I know in St. Cloud, would stoop to stand on a platform next to her father while he explains and excuses on TV this random emasculation of a young Nigra caught on a street after midnight. (*Chance is speaking with an almost incoherent excitement, one knee resting on the seat of his chair, swaying the chair back and forth. The Heckler lowers his newspaper from his face; a slow fierce smile spreads over his face as he leans forward with tensed throat muscles to catch Chance's burst of oratory.*) No! That's what I do not believe. If I believed it, oh, I'd give you a diving exhibition. I'd dive off municipal pier and swim straight out to Diamond Key and past it, and keep on swimming till sharks and barracuda took me for live bait, brother. (*His chair topples over backward, and he sprawls to the floor. The Heckler springs up to catch him. Miss Lucy springs up too, and sweeps between Chance and the Heckler, pushing the Heckler back with a quick, warning look or gesture. Nobody notices the Heckler. Chance scrambles back to his feet, flushed, laughing. Bud and Scotty outlaugh him. Chance picks up his chair and continues. The laughter stops.*) Because I have come back to St. Cloud to take her out of St. Cloud. Where I'll take her is not to a place anywhere except to her place in my heart. (*He has removed a pink capsule from his pocket, quickly and furtively, and drunk it down with his vodka.*)

BUD: Chance, what did you swallow just now?

CHANCE: Some hundred-proof vodka.

BUD: You washed something down with it that you took out of your pocket.

SCOTTY: It looked like a little pink pill.

CHANCE: Oh, ha ha. Yes, I washed down a goof-ball. You want one? I got a bunch of them. I always carry them with me. When you're not having fun, it makes you have it. When you're having fun, it makes you have more of it. Have one and see.

SCOTTY: Don't that damage the brain?

CHANCE: No, the contrary. It stimulates the brain cells.

SCOTTY: Don't it make your eyes look different, Chance?

MISS LUCY: Maybe that's what I noticed. (*as if wishing to change the subject*) Chance, I wish you'd settle an argument for me.

CHANCE: What argument, Miss Lucy?

MISS LUCY: About who you're traveling with. I heard you checked in here with a famous old movie star.

(*They all stare at him. . . . In a way he now has what he wants. He's the center of attraction: everybody is looking at him, even though with hostility, suspicion and a cruel sense of sport.*)

CHANCE: Miss Lucy I'm traveling with the vice-president and major stockholder of the film studio which just signed me.

MISS LUCY: Wasn't she once in the movies and very well known?

CHANCE: She was and still is and never will cease to be an important, a legendary figure in the picture industry, here and all over the world, and I am now under personal contract to her.

MISS LUCY: What's her name, Chance?

CHANCE: She doesn't want her name known. Like all great figures, world-known, she doesn't want or need and refuses to have the wrong type of attention. Privacy is a luxury to great stars. Don't ask me her name. I respect her too much to speak her name at this table. I'm obligated to her because she has shown faith in me. It took a long hard time to find that sort of faith in my talent that this woman has shown me. And I refuse to betray it at this table. (*His voice rises; he is already "high."*)

MISS LUCY: Baby, why are you sweating and your hands shaking so? You're not sick, are you?

CHANCE: Sick? Who's sick? I'm the least sick one you know.

MISS LUCY: Well, baby, you know you oughtn't to stay in St. Cloud. Y'know that, don't you? I couldn't believe my ears when I heard you were back here. (*to the two boys*) Could you all believe he was back here?

SCOTTY: What did you come back for?

CHANCE: I wish you would give me one reason why I shouldn't come back to visit the grave of my mother and pick out a monument for her, and share my happiness with a girl that I've loved many years. It's her, Heavenly Finley, that I've fought my way up for, and now that I've made it, the glory will be hers, too. And I've just about persuaded the powers to be to let her appear with me in a picture I'm signed for. Because I . . .

BUD: What is the name of this picture?

CHANCE: . . . Name of it? "Youth!"

BUD: Just "Youth?"

CHANCE: Isn't that a great title for a picture introducing young talent? You all look doubtful. If you don't believe me, well, look. Look at this contract. (*Removes it from his pocket.*)

SCOTTY: You carry the contract with you?

CHANCE: I happen to have it in this jacket pocket.

MISS LUCY: Leaving, Scotty? (*Scotty has risen from the table.*)

SCOTTY: It's getting too deep at this table.

BUD: The girls are waiting.

CHANCE (*quickly*): Gee, Bud, that's a clean set of rags you're wearing, but let me give you a tip for your tailor. A guy of medium stature looks better with natural shoulders, the padding cuts down your height, it broadens your figure and gives you a sort of squat look.

BUD: Thanks, Chance.

SCOTTY: You got any helpful hints for my tailor, Chance?

CHANCE: Scotty, there's no tailor on earth that can disguise a sedentary occupation.

MISS LUCY: Chance, baby . . .

CHANCE: You still work down at the bank? You sit on your can all day countin' century notes and once every week they let you slip one in your pockets? That's a fine set-up, Scotty, if you're satisfied with it but it's starting to give you a little pot and a can.

VIOLET (*appears in the door, angry*): Bud! Scotty! Come on.

SCOTTY: I don't get by on my looks, but I drive my own car. It isn't a Caddy, but it's my own car. And if my own mother died, I'd bury her myself; I wouldn't let a church take up a collection to do it.

VIOLET (*impatiently*): Scotty, if you all don't come now I'm going home in a taxi.

(The two boys follow her into the Palm Garden. There they can be seen giving their wives cab money, and indicating they are staying.)

CHANCE: The squares have left us, Miss Lucy.

MISS LUCY: Yeah.

CHANCE: Well . . . I didn't come back here to fight with old friends of mine. . . . Well, it's quarter past seven.

MISS LUCY: Is it?

(There are a number of men, now, sitting around in the darker corners of the bar, looking at him. They are not ominous in their attitudes. They are simply waiting for something, for the meeting to start upstairs, for something. . . . Miss Lucy stares at Chance and the men, then again at Chance, nearsightedly, her head cocked like a puzzled terrier's. Chance is discomfited.)

CHANCE: Yep . . . How is that Hickory Hollow for steaks? Is it still the best place in town for a steak?

STUFF (*answering the phone at the bar*): Yeah, it's him. He's here. (*Looks at Chance ever so briefly, hangs up.*)

MISS LUCY: Baby, I'll go to the checkroom and pick up my wrap and call for my car and I'll drive you out to the airport. They've got an air-taxi out there, a whirly-bird taxi, a helicopter, you know, that'll hop you to New Orleans in fifteen minutes.

CHANCE: I'm not leaving St. Cloud. What did I say to make you think I was?

MISS LUCY: I thought you had sense enough to know that you'd better.

CHANCE: Miss Lucy, you've been drinking, it's gone to your sweet little head.

MISS LUCY: Think it over while I'm getting my wrap. You still got a friend in St. Cloud.

CHANCE: I still have a girl in St. Cloud, and I'm not leaving without her.

PAGEBOY (*offstage*): Paging Chance Wayne, Mr. Chance Wayne, please.

PRINCESS (*entering with Pageboy*): Louder, young man, louder . . . Oh, never mind, here he is!

(*But Chance has already rushed out onto the gallery. The Princess looks as if she had thrown on her clothes to escape a building on fire. Her blue-sequined gown is unzipped, or partially zipped, her hair is disheveled, her eyes have a dazed, drugged brightness; she is holding up the eyeglasses with the broken lens, shakily, hanging onto her mink stole with the other hand; her movements are unsteady.*)

MISS LUCY: I know who you are. Alexandra Del Lago.

(*Loud whispering. A pause.*)

PRINCESS (*on the step to the gallery*): What? Chance!

MISS LUCY: Honey, let me fix that zipper for you. Hold still just a second. Honey, let me take you upstairs. You mustn't be seen down here in this condition. . . .

(*Chance suddenly rushes in from the gallery: he conducts the Princess outside: she is on the verge of panic. The Princess rushes half down the steps to the palm garden: leans panting on the stone balustrade under the ornamental light standard with its five great pearls of light. The interior is dimmed as Chance comes out behind her.*)

PRINCESS: Chance! Chance! Chance! Chance!

CHANCE (*softly*): If you'd stayed upstairs that wouldn't have happened to you.

PRINCESS: I did, I stayed.

CHANCE: I told you to wait.

PRINCESS: I waited.

CHANCE: Didn't I tell you to wait till I got back?

PRINCESS: I did, I waited forever, I waited forever for you. Then finally I heard those long sad silver trumpets blowing through the palm garden and then—Chance, the most wonderful thing has happened to me. Will you listen to me? Will you let me tell you?

MISS LUCY (*to the group at the bar*): Shhh!

PRINCESS: Chance, when I saw you driving under the window with your head held high, with that terrible stiff-necked pride of the defeated which I know so well; I knew that your come-back had been a failure like mine. And I felt something in my heart for you. That's a miracle, Chance. That's the wonderful thing that happened to me. I felt something for someone besides myself. That means my heart's still alive, at least some part of it is, not all of my heart is dead yet. Part's alive still. . . . Chance, please listen to me. I'm ashamed of this morning. I'll never degrade you again, I'll never degrade myself, you and me, again by —I wasn't always this monster. Once I wasn't this monster. And what I felt in my heart when I saw you returning, defeated, to this palm garden, Chance, gave me hope that I could stop being a monster. Chance, you've got to help me stop being the monster that I was this morning, and you can do it, can help me. I won't be ungrateful for it. I almost died this morning, suffocated in a panic. But even through my panic, I saw your kindness. I saw a true kindness in you that you have almost destroyed, but that's still there, a little. . . .

CHANCE: What kind thing did I do?

PRINCESS: You gave my oxygen to me.

CHANCE: Anyone would do that.

PRINCESS: It could have taken you longer to give it to me.

CHANCE: I'm not that kind of monster.

PRINCESS: You're no kind of monster. You're just—

CHANCE: What?

PRINCESS: Lost in the beanstalk country, the ogre's country at the top of the beanstalk, the country of the flesh-hungry, blood-thirsty ogre—

(*Suddenly a voice is heard from off.*)

VOICE: Wayne?

(*The call is distinct but not loud. Chance hears it, but doesn't turn toward it; he freezes momentarily, like a stag scenting hunters. Among the people gathered inside in the cocktail lounge we see the speaker, Dan Hatcher. In appearance, dress and manner he is the apotheosis of the assistant hotel manager, about Chance's age, thin, blond-haired, trim blond mustache, suave, boyish, betraying an instinct for murder only by the ruby-glass studs in his matching cuff links and tie clip.*)

HATCHER: Wayne!

(*He steps forward a little and at the same instant Tom Junior and Scotty appear behind him, just in view. Scotty strikes a match for Tom Junior's cigarette as they wait there. Chance suddenly gives the Princess his complete and tender attention, putting an arm around her and turning her toward the Moorish arch to the bar entrance.*)

CHANCE (*loudly*): I'll get you a drink, and then I'll take you upstairs. You're not well enough to stay down here.

HATCHER (*crossing quickly to the foot of the stairs*): Wayne!

(*The call is too loud to ignore: Chance half turns and calls back.*)

CHANCE: Who's that?

HATCHER: Step down here a minute!

CHANCE: Oh, *Hatcher*! I'll be right with you.

PRINCESS: Chance, don't leave me alone.

(*At this moment the arrival of Boss Finley is heralded by the sirens of several squad cars. The forestage is suddenly brightened from off Left, presumably the floodlights of the cars arriving at the entrance to the hotel. This is the signal the men at the bar have been waiting for. Everybody rushes off Left. In the hot light all alone on stage is Chance; behind him, is the Princess. And the Heckler is at the bar. The entertainer plays a feverish tango. Now, off Left, Boss Finley can be heard, his public personality very much "on." Amid the flash of flash bulbs we hear off:*)

BOSS (*off*): Hahaha! Little Bit, smile! Go on, smile for the birdie! Ain't she Heavenly, ain't that the right name for her!

HEAVENLY (*off*): Papa, I want to go in!

(*At this instant she runs in—to face Chance. . . . The Heckler rises. For a long instant, Chance and Heavenly stand there: he on the steps leading to the Palm Garden and gallery; she in the cocktail lounge. They simply look at each other . . . the Heckler between them. Then the Boss comes in and seizes her by the arm. . . . And there he is facing the Heckler and Chance both. . . . For a split second he faces them, half lifts his cane to strike at them, but doesn't strike . . . then pulls Heavenly back off Left stage . . . where the photographing and interviews proceed during what follows. Chance has seen that Heavenly is going to go on the platform with her father. . . . He stands there stunned. . . .)*

PRINCESS: Chance! Chance? (*He turns to her blindly.*) Call the car and let's go. Everything's packed, even the . . . tape recorder with my shameless voice on it. . . .

(*The Heckler has returned to his position at the bar. Now Hatcher and Scotty and a couple of other of the boys have come out. . . . The Princess sees them and is silent. . . . She's never been in anything like this before. . . .*)

HATCHER: Wayne, step down here, will you.
CHANCE: What for, what do you want?
HATCHER: Come down here, I'll tell you.
CHANCE: You come up here and tell me.
TOM JUNIOR: Come on, you chicken-gut bastard.
CHANCE: Why, hello, Tom Junior. Why are you hiding down there?
TOM JUNIOR: You're hiding, not me, chicken-gut.
CHANCE: You're in the dark, not me.
HATCHER: Tom Junior wants to talk to you privately down here.
CHANCE: He can talk to me privately up here.
TOM JUNIOR: Hatcher, tell him I'll talk to him in the washroom on the mezzanine floor.
CHANCE: I don't hold conversations with people in washrooms. . . .

(*Tom Junior infuriated, starts to rush forward. Men restrain him.*)

What is all this anyhow? It's fantastic. You all having a little conference there? I used to leave places when I was told to. Not now. That time's over. Now I leave when I'm ready. Hear that, Tom Junior? Give your father that message. This is my town. I was born in St. Cloud, not him. He was just called here. He was just called down from the hills to preach hate. I was born here to make love. Tell him about that difference between him and me, and ask him which he thinks has more right to stay here. . . . (*He gets no answer from the huddled little group which is restraining Tom Junior from perpetrating murder right there in the cocktail lounge.*

After all, that would be a bad incident to precede the Boss's all-South-wide TV appearance . . . and they all know it. Chance, at the same time, continues to taunt them.) Tom, Tom Junior! What do you want me for? To pay me back for the ball game and picture show money I gave you when you were cutting your father's yard grass for a dollar on Saturday? Thank me for the times I gave you my motorcycle and got you a girl to ride the buddy seat with you?

Come here! I'll give you the keys to my Caddy. I'll give you the price of any whore in St. Cloud. You still got credit with me because you're Heavenly's brother.

TOM JUNIOR (*almost bursting free*): Don't say the name of my sister!

CHANCE: I said the name of my girl!

TOM JUNIOR (*breaking away from the group*): I'm all right, I'm all right. Leave us alone, will you. I don't want Chance to feel that he's outnumbered. (*He herds them out.*) O.K.? Come on down here.

PRINCESS (*trying to restrain Chance*): No, Chance, don't.

TOM JUNIOR: Excuse yourself from the lady and come on down here. Don't be scared to. I just want to talk to you quietly. Just talk. Quiet talk.

CHANCE: Tom Junior, I know that since the last time I was here something has happened to Heavenly and I—

TOM JUNIOR: Don't—speak the name of my sister. Just leave her name off your tongue—

CHANCE: Just tell me what happened to her.

TOM JUNIOR: Keep your ruttin' voice down.

CHANCE: I know I've done many wrong things in my life, many more than I can name or number, but I swear I never hurt Heavenly in my life.

TOM JUNIOR: You mean to say my sister was had by somebody else—diseased by somebody else the last time you were in St. Cloud? . . . I know, it's possible, it's barely possible that you didn't know what you done to my little sister the last time you come to St. Cloud. You remember that time when you came home broke? My sister had to pick up your tabs in restaurants and bars, and had to cover bad checks you wrote on banks where you had no accounts. Until you met this rich bitch, Minnie, the Texas one with the yacht, and started spending week ends on her yacht, and coming back Mondays with money from Minnie to go on with my sister. I mean, you'd sleep with Minnie, that slept with any goddam gigolo bastard she could pick up on Bourbon Street or the docks, and then you would go on sleeping again with my sister. And sometime, during that time, you got something besides your gigolo fee from Minnie and passed it onto my sister, my little sister that had hardly even heard of a thing like that, and didn't know what it was till it had gone on too long and—

CHANCE: I left town before I found out I—

(*The lamentation music is heard.*)

TOM JUNIOR: You found out! Did you tell my little sister?

CHANCE: I thought if something was wrong she'd write me or call me—

TOM JUNIOR: How could she write you or call you, there're no addresses, no phone numbers in gutters. I'm itching to kill you—here, on this spot! . . . My little sister, Heavenly, didn't know about the diseases and operations of whores, till she had to be cleaned and cured—I mean spayed like a dawg by Dr. George Scudder's knife. That's right—by the knife! . . . And tonight—if you stay here tonight, if you're here after this rally, you're gonna get the knife, too. You know? The knife? That's all. Now go on back to the lady, I'm going back to my father. (*Tom Junior exits.*)

PRINCESS (*as Chance returns to her*): Chance, for God's sake, let's go now . . .

(*The Lament is in the air. It blends with the wind-blown sound of the palms.*)

All day I've kept hearing a sort of lament that drifts through the air of this place. It says, "Lost, lost, never to be found again." Palm gardens by the sea and olive groves on Mediterranean islands all have that lament drifting through them. "Lost, lost". . . . The isle of Cyprus, Monte Carlo, San Remo, Torremolenos, Tangiers. They're all places of exile from whatever we loved. Dark glasses, wide-brimmed hats and whispers, "Is that her?" Shocked whispers. . . . Oh, Chance, believe me, after failure comes flight. Nothing ever comes after failure but flight. Face it. Call the car, have them bring down the luggage and let's go on along the Old Spanish Trail. (*She tries to hold him.*)

CHANCE: Keep your grabbing hands off me.

(*Marchers offstage start to sing "Bonnie Blue Flag."*)

PRINCESS: There's no one but me to hold you back from destruction in this place.

CHANCE: I don't want to be held.

PRINCESS: Don't leave me. If you do I'll turn into the monster again. I'll be the first lady of the Beanstalk Country.

CHANCE: Go back to the room.

PRINCESS: I'm going nowhere alone. I can't.

CHANCE (*in desperation*): Wheel chair! (*Marchers enter from the left, Tom Junior and Boss with them.*) Wheel chair! Stuff, get the lady a wheel chair! She's having another attack!

(*Stuff and a Bellboy catch at her . . . but she pushes Chance away and stares at him reproachfully. . . . The Bellboy takes her by the arm. She accepts this anonymous arm and exits. Chance and the Heckler are alone on stage.*)

CHANCE (*as if reassuring, comforting somebody besides himself*): It's all right, I'm alone now, nobody's hanging onto me.

(*He is panting. Loosens his tie and collar. Band in the Crystal Ballroom, muted, strikes up a lively but lyrically distorted variation of some such popular tune as the Liechtensteiner Polka. Chance turns toward the sound. Then, from Left stage, comes a drum majorette, bearing a gold and purple silk banner inscribed, "Youth For Tom Finley," prancing and followed by Boss Finley, Heavenly and Tom Junior, with a tight grip on her arm, as if he were conducting her to a death chamber.*)

TOM JUNIOR: Papa? Papa! Will you tell Sister to march?

BOSS FINLEY: Little Bit, you hold your haid up *high* when we march into that ballroom. (*Music up high . . . They march up the steps and onto the gallery in the rear . . . then start across it. The Boss calling out:*) Now march! (*And they disappear up the stairs.*)

VOICE (*offstage*): Now let us pray. (*There is a prayer mumbled by many voices.*)

MISS LUCY (*who has remained behind*): You still want to try it?

HECKLER: I'm going to take a shot at it. How's my voice?

MISS LUCY: Better.

HECKLER: I better wait here till he starts talkin', huh?

MISS LUCY: Wait till they turn down the chandeliers in the ballroom. . . . Why don't you switch to a question that won't hurt his daughter?

HECKLER: I don't want to hurt his daughter. But he's going to hold her up as the fair white virgin exposed to black lust in the South, and that's his build-up, his lead into his Voice of God speech.

MISS LUCY: He honestly believes it.

HECKLER: I don't believe it. I believe that the silence of God, the absolute speechlessness of Him is a long, long and awful thing that the whole world is lost because of. I think it's yet to be broken to any man, living or any yet lived on earth,—no exceptions, and least of all Boss Finley.

(*Stuff enters, goes to table, starts to wipe it. The chandelier lights go down.*)

MISS LUCY (*with admiration*): It takes a hillbilly to cut down a hillbilly. . . . (*to Stuff*) Turn on the television, baby.

VOICE (*offstage*): I give you the beloved Thomas J. Finley.

(*Stuff makes a gesture as if to turn on the TV, which we play in the fourth wall. A wavering beam of light, flickering, narrow, intense, comes from the balcony rail. Stuff moves his head so that he's in it, looking into it. . . . Chance walks slowly downstage, his head also in the narrow flickering beam of light. As he walks downstage, there suddenly appears on the big TV screen, which is the whole back wall of the stage, the image of Boss Finley. His arm is around Heavenly and he is speaking. . . . When Chance sees the Boss's arm around Heavenly, he makes a noise in his throat like a hard fist hit him low. . . . Now the sound, which always follows the picture by an instant, comes on . . . loud.*)

BOSS (*on TV screen*): Thank you, my friends, neighbors, kinfolk, fellow Americans. . . . I have told you before, but I will tell you again. I got a mission that I hold sacred to perform in the Southland. . . . When I was fifteen I came down barefooted out of the red clay hills. . . . Why? Because the Voice of God called me to execute this mission.

MISS LUCY (*to Stuff*): He's too loud.

HECKLER: Listen!

BOSS: And what is this mission? I have told you before but I will tell you again. To shield from pollution a blood that I think is not only sacred to me, but sacred to Him.

(*Upstage we see the Heckler step up the last steps and make a gesture as if he were throwing doors open. . . . He advances into the hall, out of our sight.*)

MISS LUCY: Turn it down, Stuff.

STUFF (*motioning to her*): Shh!

BOSS: Who is the colored man's best friend in the South? That's right . . .

MISS LUCY: Stuff, turn down the volume.

BOSS: It's me, Tom Finley. So recognized by both races.

STUFF (*shouting*): He's speaking the word. Pour it on!

BOSS: However—I can't and will not accept, tolerate, condone this threat of a blood pollution.

(*Miss Lucy turns down the volume of the TV set.*)

BOSS: As you all know I had no part in a certain operation on a young black gentleman. I call that incident a deplorable thing. That is the one thing about which I am in total agreement with the Northern radical press. It was a deplorable thing. However . . . I understand the emotions that lay behind it. The passion to protect by this violent emotion something that we hold sacred: our purity of our own blood! But I had no part in, and I did

CHANCE: Christ! What lies. What a liar!

MISS LUCY: Wait! . . . Chance, you can still go. I can still help you, baby.

CHANCE (*putting hands on Miss Lucy's shoulders*): Thanks, but no thank you, Miss Lucy. Tonight, God help me, somehow, I don't know how, but somehow I'll take her out of St. Cloud. I'll wake her up in my arms, and I'll give her life back to her. Yes, somehow, God help me, somehow!

not condone the operation performed on the unfortunate colored gentleman caught prowling the midnight streets of our Capitol City. . . .

(*Stuff turns up volume of TV set.*)

HECKLER (*as voice on the TV*): Hey, Boss Finley! (*The TV camera swings to show him at the back of the hall.*) How about your daughter's operation? How about that operation your daughter had done on her at the Thomas J. Finley hospital here in St. Cloud? Did she put on black in mourning for her appendix? . . .

(*We hear a gasp, as if the Heckler had been hit.*)

(*Picture: Heavenly horrified. Sounds of a disturbance. Then the doors at the top of stairs up Left burst open and the Heckler tumbles down. . . . The picture changes to Boss Finley. He is trying to dominate the disturbance in the hall.*)

BOSS: Will you repeat that question. Have that man step forward. I will answer his question. Where is he? Have that man step forward, I will answer his question. . . . Last Friday . . . Last Friday, Good Friday. I said last Friday, Good Friday . . . Quiet, may I have your attention please. . . . Last Friday, Good Friday, I seen a horrible thing on the campus of our great State University, which I built for the State. A hideous straw-stuffed effigy of myself, Tom Finley, was hung and set fire to in the main quadrangle of the college. This outrage was inspired . . . inspired by the Northern radical press. However, that was Good Friday. Today is Easter. I saw that was Good Friday. Today is Easter Sunday and I am in St. Cloud.

(*During this a gruesome, not-lighted, silent struggle has been going on. The Heckler defended himself, but finally has been overwhelmed and rather systematically beaten. . . . The tight intense follow spot beam stayed on Chance. If he had any impulse to go to the Heckler's aid, he'd be discouraged by Stuff and another man who stand behind him, watching him. . . . At the height of the beating, there are bursts of great applause. . . . At a point during it, Heavenly is suddenly escorted down the stairs, sobbing, and collapses. . . .)*

Curtain

ACT THREE

A while later that night: the hotel bedroom. The shutters in the Moorish Corner are thrown open on the Palm Garden: scattered sounds of disturbance are still heard: something burns in the Palm Garden: an effigy, an emblem? Flickering light from it falls on the Princess. Over the interior scene, the constant serene projection of royal palms, branched among stars.

PRINCESS (*pacing with the phone*): Operator! What's happened to my driver?

(*Chance enters on the gallery, sees someone approaching on other side—quickly pulls back and stands in shadows on the gallery.*)

You told me you'd get me a driver. . . . Why can't you get me a driver when you said that you would? Somebody in this hotel can surely get me somebody to drive me at any price asked!—out of this infernal . . .

(*She turns suddenly as Dan Hatcher knocks at the corridor door. Behind him appear Tom Junior, Bud and Scotty, sweaty, disheveled from the riot in the Palm Garden.*)

Who's that?

SCOTTY: She ain't gonna open, break it in.

PRINCESS (*dropping phone*): What do you want?

HATCHER: Miss Del Lago . . .

BUD: Don't answer till she opens.

PRINCESS: Who's out there! What do you want?

SCOTTY (*to shaky Hatcher*): Tell her you want her out of the goddamn room.

HATCHER (*with forced note of authority*): Shut up. Let me handle this . . . Miss Del Lago, your check-out time was three-thirty P.M., and it's now after midnight. . . . I'm sorry but you can't hold this room any longer.

PRINCESS (*throwing open the door*): What did you say? Will you repeat what you said! (*Her imperious voice, jewels, furs and commanding presence abash them for a moment.*)

HATCHER: Miss Del Lago . . .

TOM JUNIOR (*recovering quickest*): This is Mr. Hatcher, assistant manager here. You checked in last night with a character not wanted here, and we been informed he's stayin' in your room with you. We brought Mr. Hatcher up here to remind you that the check-out time is long past and—

PRINCESS (*powerfully*): My check-out time at any hotel in the world is *when I want to check out*. . . .

TOM JUNIOR: This ain't any hotel in the world.

PRINCESS (*making no room for entrance*): Also, I don't talk to assistant managers of hotels when I have complaints to make about discourtesies to me, which I do most certainly have to make about my experiences here. I don't even talk to managers of hotels, I talk to owners of them. Directly to hotel owners about discourtesies to me. (*Picks up satin sheets on bed.*) These sheets are mine, they go with me. And I have never suffered such dreadful discourtesies to me at any hotel at any time or place anywhere in the world. Now I have found out the name of this hotel owner. This is a chain hotel under the ownership of a personal friend of mine whose guest I have been in foreign capitals such as . . . (*Tom Junior has pushed past her into the room.*) What in hell is he doing in my room?

TOM JUNIOR: Where is Chance Wayne?

PRINCESS: Is that what you've come here for? You can go away then. He hasn't been in this room since he left this morning.

TOM JUNIOR: Scotty, check the bathroom. . . . (*He checks a closet, stoops to peer under the bed. Scotty goes off at right.*) Like I told you before, we know you're Alexandra Del Lago traveling with a degenerate that I'm sure you don't know. That's why you can't stay in St. Cloud, especially after this ruckus that we— (*Scotty re-enters from the bathroom and indicates to Tom Junior that Chance is not there.*) —Now if you need any help in getting out of St. Cloud, I'll be—

PRINCESS (*cutting in*): Yes. I want a driver. Someone to drive my car. I want to leave here. I'm desperate to leave here. I'm not able to drive. I have to be driven away!

TOM JUNIOR: Scotty, you and Hatcher wait outside while I explain something to her. . . . (*They go and wait outside the door, on the left end of the gallery.*) I'm gonna git you a driver, Miss Del Lago. I'll git you a state trooper, half a dozen state troopers if I can't get you no driver. O.K.? Some time come back to our town n' see us, hear? We'll lay out a red carpet for you. O.K.? G'night, Miss Del Lago.

(*They disappear down the hall, which is then dimmed out. Chance now turns from where he's been waiting at the other end of the corridor and slowly, cautiously, approaches the entrance to the room. Wind sweeps the Palm Garden; it seems to dissolve the walks; the rest of the play is acted against the night sky. The shuttered doors on the veranda open and Chance enters the room. He has gone a good deal further across the border of reason since we last saw him. The Princess isn't aware of his entrance until he slams the shuttered doors. She turns, startled, to face him.*)

PRINCESS: Chance!

CHANCE: You had some company here.

PRINCESS: Some men were here looking for you. They told me I wasn't welcome in this hotel and this town because I had come here with "a criminal degenerate." I asked them to get me a driver so I can go.

CHANCE: I'm your driver. I'm still your driver, Princess.

PRINCESS: You couldn't drive through the palm garden.

CHANCE: I'll be all right in a minute.

PRINCESS: It takes more than a minute, Chance, will you listen to me? Can you listen to me? I listened to you this morning, with understanding and pity, I did, I listened with pity to your story this morning. I felt something in my heart for you which I thought I couldn't feel. I remembered young men who were what you are or what you're hoping to be. I saw them all clearly, all clearly, eyes, voices, smiles, bodies clearly. But their names wouldn't come back to me. I couldn't get their names back without digging into old programs of plays that I starred in at twenty in which they said, "Madam, the Count's waiting for you," or—Chance? They almost made it. Oh, oh, Franz! Yes, Franz . . . what? Albertzart. Franz Albertzart, oh God, God, Franz Albertzart . . . I had to fire him. He held me too tight in the waltz scene, his anxious fingers left bruises once so violent, they, they dislocated a disc in my spine, and—

CHANCE: I'm waiting for you to shut up.

PRINCESS: I saw him in Monte Carlo not too long ago. He was with a woman of seventy, and his eyes looked older than hers. She held him, she led him by an invisible chain through Grand Hotel . . . lobbies and casinos and bars like a blind, dying lap dog; he wasn't much older than you are now. Not long after that he drove his Alfa-Romeo or Ferrari off the Grand Corniche—accidentally?—Broke his skull like an eggshell. I wonder what they found in it? Old, despaired-of ambitions, little treacheries, possibly even little attempts at blackmail that didn't quite come off, and whatever traces are left of really great charm and sweetness. Chance, Franz Albertzart is Chance Wayne. Will you please try to face it so we can go on together?

CHANCE (*pulls away from her*): Are you through? Have you finished?

PRINCESS: You didn't listen, did you?

CHANCE (*picking up the phone*): I didn't have to. I told you that story this morning—I'm not going to drive off nothing and crack my head like an eggshell.

PRINCESS: No, because you can't drive.

CHANCE: Operator? Long distance.

PRINCESS: You would drive into a palm tree. Franz Albertzart . . .

CHANCE: Where's your address book, your book of telephone numbers?

PRINCESS: I don't know what you think that you are up to, but it's no good. The only hope for you now is to let me lead you by that invisible loving steel chain through Carltons and Ritzes and Grand Hotels and—

CHANCE: Don't you know, I'd die first? I would rather die first . . . (*into phone*) Operator? This is an urgent person-to-person call from Miss Alexandra Del Lago to Miss Sally Powers in Beverly Hills, California. . . .

PRINCESS: Oh, no! . . . Chance!

CHANCE: Miss Sally Powers, the Hollywood columnist, yes, Sally Powers. Yes, well get information. I'll wait, I'll wait. . . .

PRINCESS: Her number is Coldwater five-nine thousand. . . . (*Her hand goes to her mouth—but too late.*)

CHANCE: In Beverly Hills, California, Coldwater five-nine thousand.

(*The Princess moves out onto forestage; surrounding areas dim till nothing is clear behind her but the palm garden.*)

PRINCESS: Why did I give him the number? Well, why not, after all, I'd have to know sooner or later . . . I started to call several times, picked up the phone, put it down again. Well, let him do it for me. Something's happened. I'm breathing freely and deeply as if the panic was over. Maybe it's over. He's doing the dreadful thing for me, asking the answer for me. He doesn't exist for me now except as somebody making this awful call for me, asking the answer for me. The light's on me. He's almost invisible now. What does that mean? Does it mean that I still wasn't ready to be washed up, counted out?

CHANCE: All right, call Chasen's. Try to reach her at Chasen's.

PRINCESS: Well, one thing's sure. It's only this call I care for. I seem to be standing in light with everything else dimmed out. He's in the dimmed out background as if he'd never left the obscurity he was born in. I've taken the light again as a crown on my head to which I am suited by something in the cells of my blood and body from the time of my birth. It's mine, I was born to own it, as he was born to make this phone call for me to Sally Powers, dear faithful custodian of my outlived legend. (*Phone rings in distance.*) The legend that I've outlived. . . . Monsters don't die early; they hang on long. Awfully long. Their vanity's infinite, almost as infinite as their disgust with themselves. . . . (*Phone rings louder: it brings the stage light back up on the hotel bedroom. She turns to Chance and the play returns to a more realistic level.*) The phone's still ringing.

CHANCE: They gave me another number. . . .

PRINCESS: If she isn't there, give my name and ask them where I can reach her.

CHANCE: Princess?

PRINCESS: What?

CHANCE: I have a personal reason for making this phone call.

PRINCESS: I'm quite certain of that.

CHANCE (*into phone*): I'm calling for Alexandra Del Lago. She wants to speak to Miss Sally Powers— Oh, is there any number where the Princess could reach her?

PRINCESS: It will be a good sign if they give you a number.

CHANCE: Oh?—Good, I'll call that number . . . Operator? Try another number for Miss Sally Powers. It's Canyon seven-five thousand . . . Say it's urgent, it's Princess Kosmonopolis . . .

PRINCESS: Alexandra Del Lago.

CHANCE: Alexandra Del Lago is calling Miss Powers.

PRINCESS (*to herself*): Oxygen, please, a little. . . .

CHANCE: Is that you, Miss Powers? This is Chance Wayne talking . . . I'm calling for the Princess Kosmonopolis, she wants to speak to you. She'll come to the phone in a minute. . . .

PRINCESS: I can't. . . . Say I've . . .

CHANCE (*stretching phone cord*): This is as far as I can stretch the cord, Princess, you've got to meet it halfway.

(*Princess hesitates; then advances to the extended phone.*)

PRINCESS (*in a low, strident whisper*): Sally? Sally? Is it really you, Sally? Yes, it's me, Alexandra. It's what's left of me, Sally. Oh, yes, I was there, but I only stayed a few minutes. Soon as they started laughing in the wrong places, I fled up the aisle and into the street screaming Taxi—and never stopped running till now. No, I've talked to nobody, heard nothing, read nothing . . . just wanted—dark . . . What? You're just being kind.

CHANCE (*as if to himself*): Tell her that you've discovered a pair of new stars. Two of them.

PRINCESS: One moment, Sally, I'm—breathless!

CHANCE (*gripping her arm*): And lay it on thick. Tell her to break it tomorrow in her column, in all of her columns, and in her radio talks . . . that you've discovered a pair of young people who are the stars of tomorrow!

PRINCESS (*to Chance*): Go into the bathroom. Stick your head under cold water. . . . Sally . . . Do you really think so? You're not just being nice, Sally, because of old times—Grown, did you say? My talent? In what way, Sally? More depth? More what, did you say? More power!—well, Sally, God bless you, dear Sally.

CHANCE: Cut the chatter. Talk about me and *HEAVENLY*!

PRINCESS: No, of course I didn't read the reviews. I told you I flew, I flew. I flew as fast and fast as I could. Oh. Oh? Oh . . . How very sweet of you, Sally. I don't even care if you're not altogether sincere in that statement, Sally. I think you know what the past fifteen years have been like, because I do have the—"out-crying heart of an—artist." Excuse me, Sally, I'm crying, and I don't have any Kleenex. Excuse me, Sally, I'm crying. . . .

CHANCE (*hissing behind her*): Hey. Talk about me! (*She kicks Chance's leg.*)

PRINCESS: What's that, Sally? Do you really believe so? Who? For what part? Oh, my God! . . . Oxygen, oxygen, quick!

CHANCE (*seizing her by the hair and hissing*): Me! Me!—You bitch!

PRINCESS: Sally? I'm too overwhelmed. Can I call you back later? Sally, I'll call back later. . . . (*She drops phone in a daze of rapture.*) My picture has broken box-office records. In New York and L. A.!

CHANCE: Call her back, get her on the phone.

PRINCESS: Broken box-office records. The greatest comeback in the history of the industry, that's what she calls it. . . .

CHANCE: You didn't mention me to her.

PRINCESS (*to herself*): I can't appear, not yet. I'll need a week in a clinic, then a week or ten days at the Morning Star Ranch at Vegas. I'd better get Ackermann down there for a series of shots before I go on to the Coast. . . .

CHANCE (*at phone*): Come back here, call her again.

PRINCESS: I'll leave the car in New Orleans and go on by plane to, to, to—Tucson. I'd better get Strauss working on publicity for me. I'd better be sure my tracks are covered up well these last few weeks in—hell!—

CHANCE: Here. Here, get her back on this phone.

PRINCESS: Do what?

CHANCE: Talk about me and talk about Heavenly to her.

PRINCESS: Talk about a beach-boy I picked up for pleasure, distraction from panic? Now? When the nightmare is over? Involve my name, which is Alexandra Del Lago with the record of a— You've just been using me. Using me. When I needed you downstairs you shouted, "Get her a wheel chair!" Well, I didn't need a wheel chair, I came up alone, as always. I climbed back alone up the beanstalk to the ogre's country where I live, now, alone. Chance, you've gone past something you couldn't afford to go past; your time, your youth, you've passed it. It's all you had, and you've had it.

CHANCE: Who in hell's talking! Look. (*He turns her forcibly to the mirror.*) Look in that mirror. What do you see in that mirror?

PRINCESS: I see—Alexandra Del Lago, artist and star! Now it's your turn, you look and what do you see?

CHANCE: I see—Chance Wayne. . . .

PRINCESS: The face of a Franz Albertzart, a face that tomorrow's sun will touch without mercy. Of course, you were crowned with laurel in the beginning, your gold hair was wreathed with laurel, but the gold is thinning and the laurel has withered. Face it—pitiful monster. (*She touches the crown of his head.*) . . . Of course, I know I'm one too. But one with a difference. Do you know what that difference is? No, you don't know. I'll tell you. We are two monsters, but with this difference between us. Out of the passion and torment of my existence I have created a thing that I can unveil, a sculpture, almost heroic, that I can unveil, which is true. But you? You've come back to the town you were born in, to a girl that won't see you because you put such rot in her body she had to be gutted and hung on a butcher's hook, like a chicken dressed for Sunday. . . . (*He wheels about to strike at her but his raised fist changes its course and strikes down at his own belly and he bends double with a sick cry. Palm Garden wind: whisper of The Lament.*) Yes, and her brother who was one of my callers, threatens the same thing for you: castration, if you stay here.

CHANCE: That can't be done to me twice. You did that to me this morning, here on this bed, where I had the honor, where I had the great honor . . .

(*Windy sound rises: They move away from each other, he to the bed, she close to her portable dressing table.*)

PRINCESS: Age does the same thing to a woman. . . . (*Scrapes pearls and pillboxes off table top into handbag.*) Well . . .

(*All at once her power is exhausted, her fury gone. Something uncertain appears in her face and voice betraying the fact which she probably suddenly knows, that her future course is not a progression of triumphs. She still maintains a grand air as she snatches up her platinum mink stole and tosses it about her: it slides immediately off her shoulders; she doesn't seem to notice. He picks the stole up for her, puts it about her shoulders. She grunts disdainfully, her back to him; then resolution falters; she turns to face him with great, dark eyes that are fearful, lonely, and tender.*)

PRINCESS: I am going, now, on my way. (*He nods slightly, loosening the Windsor-knot of his knitted black silk tie. Her eyes stay on him.*) Well, are you leaving or staying?

CHANCE: Staying.

PRINCESS: You can't stay here. I'll take you to the next town.

CHANCE: Thanks but no thank you, Princess.

PRINCESS (*seizing his arm*): Come on, you've got to leave with me. My name is connected with you, we checked in here together. Whatever happens to you, my name will be dragged in with it.

CHANCE: Whatever happens to me's already happened.

PRINCESS: What are you trying to prove?

CHANCE: Something's got to mean something, don't it, Princess? I mean like your life means nothing, except that you never could make it, always almost, never quite? Well, something's still got to mean something.

PRINCESS: I'll send a boy up for my luggage. You'd better come down with my luggage.

CHANCE: I'm not part of your luggage.

PRINCESS: What else can you be?

CHANCE: Nothing . . . but not part of your luggage.

(NOTE: *in this area it is very important that Chance's attitude should be self-recognition but* not *self-pity—a sort of deathbed dignity and honesty apparent in it. In both Chance and the Princess, we should return to the huddling-together of the lost, but not with sentiment, which is false, but with whatever is truthful in the moments when people share doom, face firing squads together. Because the Princess is really equally doomed. She can't turn back the clock any more than can Chance, and the clock is equally relentless to them both. For the Princess: a little, very temporary, return to, recapture of, the spurious glory. The report from Sally Powers may be and probably is a factually accurate report: but to indicate she is going on to further triumph would be to falsify her future. She makes this instinctive admission to herself when she sits down by Chance on the bed, facing the audience. Both are faced with castration, and in her heart she knows it. They sit side by side on the bed like two passengers on a train sharing a bench.*)

PRINCESS: Chance, we've got to go on.

CHANCE: Go on to where? I couldn't go past my youth, but I've gone past it.

(*The Lament fades in, continues through the scene to the last curtain.*)

PRINCESS: You're still young, Chance.

CHANCE: Princess, the age of some people can only be calculated by the level of—level of—rot in them. And by that measure I'm ancient.

PRINCESS: What am I?—I know, I'm dead, as old Egypt . . . Isn't it funny? We're still sitting here together, side by side in this room, like we were occupying the same bench on a train—going on together . . . Look. That little donkey's marching around and around to draw water out of a well. . . . (*She points off at something as if outside a train window.*) Look, a shepherd boy's leading a flock.—What an old country, timeless.—Look—

(*The sound of a clock ticking is heard, louder and louder.*)

CHANCE: No, listen. I didn't know there was a clock in this room.

PRINCESS: I guess there's a clock in every room people live in. . . .

CHANCE: It goes tick-tick, it's quieter than your heart-beat, but it's slow dynamite, a gradual explosion, blasting the world we lived in to burnt-out pieces. . . . Time—who could beat it, who could defeat it ever? Maybe some saints and heroes, but not Chance Wayne. I lived on something, that—time?

PRINCESS: Yes, time.

CHANCE: . . . Gnaws away, like a rat gnaws off its own foot caught in a trap, and then, with its foot gnawed off and the rat set free, couldn't run, couldn't go, bled and died. . . .

(*The clock ticking fades away.*)

TOM JUNIOR (*offstage left*): Miss Del Lago . . .

PRINCESS: I think they're calling our—station. . . .

TOM JUNIOR (*still offstage*): Miss Del Lago, I have got a driver for you.

(*A trooper enters and waits on gallery.*)

(*With a sort of tired grace, she rises from the bed, one hand lingering on her seat-companion's shoulder as she moves a little unsteadily to the door. When she opens it, she is confronted by Tom Junior.*)

PRINCESS: Come on, Chance, we're going to change trains at this station. . . . So, come on, we've got to go on. . . . Chance, please. . . .

(*Chance shakes his head and the Princess gives up. She weaves out of sight with the trooper down the corridor.*)

(*Tom Junior enters from steps, pauses and then gives a low whistle to Scotty, Bud, and third man who enter and stand waiting. Tom Junior comes down bedroom steps and stands on bottom step.*)

CHANCE (*rising and advancing to the forestage*): I don't ask for your pity, but just for your understanding—not even that—no. Just for your recognition of me in you, and the enemy, time, in us all.

(*The curtain closes.*)

The End

PERIOD OF ADJUSTMENT

High Point Over a Cavern

A Serious Comedy

To the director and the cast

The Scene

The action of the play takes place in Ralph Bates' home, Memphis, Tennessee. The time is Christmas Eve.

ACT ONE

The set is the interior and entrance of a "cute" little Spanish-type suburban bungalow. Two rooms are visible onstage, the living room with its small dining alcove and the bedroom. There are doors to the kitchen and bath. A bit of the stucco exterior surrounds the entrance, downstage right or left. A Christmas wreath is on the door, while above the door is an ornamental porch light, or coach lantern, with amber glass or possibly glass in several colors. The fireplace in the fourth wall of the set is represented by a flickering red light. Of course the living room contains a TV set with its back to the audience, its face to a big sofa that opens into a bed. The dog is a cocker spaniel. There's a rather large Christmas tree, decorated, with a child's toys under it and a woman's fur coat in an open box, but no child and no woman. Ralph Bates, a boyish-looking man in his middle thirties, is approaching the TV set, facing upstage, with a can of beer and opener.

TV COMMERCIAL: Millions of Americans each day are discovering the difference between this new miracle product and the old horse-and-buggy type of cleanser which made washday a torture to Mom and left her too tired at sundown to light up the house with the sunshine of her smile.

RALPH: *No snow!*

(*He hoists himself onto a very high bar stool facing the TV.*)

TV COMMERCIAL: So don't let unnecessary fatigue cast a shadow over your household, especially not at this—

(*He leaps off the stool and crouches to change the channel. He gets snatches of several dramatic and musical offerings, settles for a chorus of "White Christmas," sighs, picks up a poker and stabs at the flickering ruddy light in the fourth wall. It comes up brighter. He crouches to fan the fire with an antique bellows: the fire brightens. He sighs again, hoists himself back onto the brass-studded red-leather-topped stool, which has evidently been removed from the "cute" little bar, which is upstage. For theatrical purpose, this stool is about half a foot higher than any other sitting-surface on the stage. Whenever*

Ralph assumes a seat on this stool he is like a judge mounting his judicial bench, except he's not pompous or bewigged about it. He is detached, considering, thinking, and over his face comes that characteristic look of a gentle gravity which is the heart of Ralph. Perhaps his pose should suggest Rodin's "Thinker." Ralph is one of those rare people that have the capacity of heart to truly care, and care deeply, about other people.

(*A car horn, urgent, is heard out front, offstage, Ralph slides off the stool and rushes out the front door; he stands under the amber coach lantern. It's snowing, the snowflakes are projected on his figure, tiny, obliquely falling particles of shadow. There's a muffled shout from the car that's stopped below the terrace of the bungalow.*)

RALPH (*shouting back*): *Hey, there, drive her up under th' carport!*

GEORGE (*Texas voice*): Whacha say, boy?

RALPH: PUT 'ER UNDER THE CARPORT!

GEORGE: Wheels won't catch, too steep!

RALPH: Back her all the way out and then shoot 'er up in first!

ISABEL'S VOICE (*high-pitched with strain*): Will you please let me out first, George!

(*There is the sound of a car door. Ralph ducks back in, grinning, and seizes a carton of rice.*)

RALPH: Yeah, come on in, little lady.

(*Isabel appears before the house, small and white-faced with fatigue, eyes dark-circled, manner dazed and uncertain. She wears a cheap navy-blue cloth coat, carries a shiny new patent-leather purse, has on red wool mittens. Ralph pelts her with rice. She ducks the bombardment with a laugh that's more like a sob.*)

ISABEL: Oh, no, please! I never want to see rice again in my life, not uncooked anyhow. . . . That fire looks wonderful to me. I'm Isabel Crane, Mr. Bates.

(*She removes a red mitten and extends her hand.*)

RALPH: I thought you'd married that boy.

(*Both speak in deep Southern voices; hers is distinctly Texan.*)

ISABEL: I mean Mrs. George Haverstick.

(*She says her new name with a hint of grimness.*)

RALPH (*still in the door*): Wait'll I put m'shoes on, I'll come out!

(*This shout is unheard.*)

ISABEL: You have a sweet little house.

RALPH (*with a touch of amiable grimness*): Yeah, we sure do. Wheels cain't git any traction, 'stoo damn steep.

(*He shouts down.*)

LOCK IT UP, LEAVE IT OUT FRONT!—I guess he's gonna do that, yep, that's what he's doin', uh-huh, that's what he's doin. . . .

ISABEL: Does it snow often in Memphis?

RALPH: No, no, rarely, rarely.

(*He gives her a glance. Ralph has a sometimes disconcerting way of seeming either oblivious to a person he's with or regarding the person with a sudden intense concentration, as if he'd just noticed something startling or puzzling about them. But this is a mannerism that the actor should use with restraint.*)

ISABEL: It was snowing all the way down here; it's my first acquaintance with snow except for one little flurry of snow in Saint Louis the day befo' Thanksgivin' day, this is my first real acquaintance with, with—with a real *snow*. . . . What *is* he doing down there?

RALPH: He's unloadin' th' car.

ISABEL: I just want my small zipper bag. Will you please call down to him that's all I want of my things?

RALPH (*shouting*): Leave all that stuff till later. Ha ha. I didn't know you could get all that in a car.

ISABEL: Surely he isn't removing our wedding presents! Is he *insane*, Mr. Bates?

(*She goes to the door.*)

George! Just my small zipper bag, not everything in the car! Oh, Lord.

(*She retreats into the room.*)

He must think we're going to *live* here for the rest of our *lives*! He didn't even warn you all we were coming.

RALPH: He called me up from West Memphis.

ISABEL: Yes, just across the river.

RALPH: What is that car, a Caddy?

ISABEL: It's a fifty-two Cadillac with a mileage close to a hundred and twenty thousand. It ought to be retired with an old-age pension, Mr. Bates.

RALPH (*at the door*): It looks like one of them funeral limousines.

ISABEL (*wryly*): Mr. Bates, you have hit the nail on the head with the head of the hammer. That is just what it was. It's piled up a hundred and twenty thousand miles between Burkemeyer's Mortuary and various graveyards serving Greater Saint Louis. JAWGE, CAN YOU HEAR ME, JAWGE? Excuse me, Mr. Bates.

(*She slips past him onto the terrace again.*)

JAWGE, JUST MY SMALL ZIPPER BAG.

(*Indistinct shout from below. She turns back in.*)

I give up, Mr. Bates.

(*She ducks under his arm to enter the house again and stands behind Ralph in the doorway.*)

RALPH (*still chuckling at the door*): What's he want with a funeral limousine? On a honeymoon trip?

ISABEL: I asked him that same question and got a very odd answer. He said there's no better credit card in the world than driving up at a bank door in a Cadillac limousine.

(*She tries to laugh.*)

Oh, I don't know, I—love Spanish-type architecture, Spanish mission-type houses, I—don't think you ought to stand in that door with just that light shirt on you, this is a—such a—*sweet* house. . . .

(*She seems close to tears. Something in her tone catches his attention and he comes in, closing the door.*)

RALPH: Ha, ha, well, how's it going? Is the marriage in orbit?

ISABEL (*tries to laugh at this, too*): Oh! Will you please do me a favor? Don't encourage him, please don't invite him to spend the night here, Mr. Bates! I'm thinking of your wife, because last night—in Cape Girardeau, Missouri?—he thought it would be very nice to look up an old war buddy he had there, too. He sincerely thought so, and possibly the war buddy thought so, too, but NOT the wife! Oh, no, not *that* lady, no! They'd hardly got through their first beer cans with—remembrances of Korea, when that bright little woman began to direct us to a highway motel which she said was only a hop, skip and jump from their house but turned out to be almost across the state line into—Arkansas? Yaias, Arkansas. I think I can take this off, now!

(*She removes a red woolen muffler. He takes it from her and she murmurs "Thanks."*)

What is holding him up? Why is he—? Mr. Bates, I did tell him that this is one night of the year when you just don't intrude on another young married couple.

RALPH: Aw, come off that, little lady! Why, I been beggin' that boy ever since we got out of the service to come to Memphis. He had to git married to make it. Why, every time I'd git drunk, I'd call that boy on the phone to say "Git to hell down here, you old Texas jack rabbit!" And I'd just about given up hope he'd ever show!

ISABEL: Is he still fooling with luggage?

(*There is a noise outside. Ralph goes to the open door.*)

RALPH: *Hey!*

ISABEL: *What?*

RALPH: Ha ha ha! He put these bags at the door and run back down to the car.

ISABEL: *What* did he—?

RALPH: Gone back down for more luggage. I'll take these in.

ISABEL (*as the bags are brought in*): Those are *my* pieces of luggage! All but the small zipper bag which is all that I wanted!

RALPH (*calling out the open door*): *Hey!*

ISABEL: *What?*

RALPH: *Hey, boy!* He's gotten back in the car an' driven *off,* ha ha!

ISABEL (*rushing to the door*): *Driven? Off?* Did you say? My heavens. You're right, he's *gone*! Mr. Bates, he's *deposited me on your hands and driven away.*

(*She is stunned.*)

Oh, *how funny*! Isn't this *funny*!

(*Laughs wildly, close to sobbing.*)

It's no *surprise* to me, though! All the way down here from Cape Girardeau, where we stopped for our wedding night, Mr. Bates, I had a feeling that the first chance he got to, he would abandon me somewhere!

RALPH: Aw, now, take it easy!

ISABEL: That's what he's done! Put me and my bags in your hands and run away.

RALPH: Aw, now, no! The old boy wouldn't do that, ha ha, for Chrissakes. He just remembered something he had to, had to—go and get at a—drugstore.

ISABEL: If that was the case wouldn't he mention it to me?

RALPH: Aw now, I known that boy a long time and he's always been sort of way out, but never way out that far!

ISABEL: Where is your wife? Where's Mrs. Bates, Mr. Bates?

RALPH: Oh, she's not here, right now.

ISABEL: I'm SUCH A FOOL!

(*She giggles a little hysterically.*)

Oh, I'm such a *fool*! . . . Why didn't I know better, can you answer me that? . . . I hope the news of our approach didn't drive your wife away on Christmas eve, Mr. Bates. . . .

RALPH: No, honey.

ISABEL: He brought up everything but the little blue zipper bag which is all I asked faw! . . . It had my, all my, it had my—*night* things in it. . . .

RALPH: Just let me get you a drink. I'm sorry I don't have any egg nog. But I can make a wonderful hot buttered rum. How about a little hot buttered rum?

ISABEL: Thank you, no, I don't drink. . . .
RALPH: It's never too late to begin to.
ISABEL: No, I don't want liquor.
RALPH: Coffee? Want some hot coffee?
ISABEL: Where is your wife, Mr. Bates?
RALPH: Oh, she's—not here now, I'll tell you about that later.
ISABEL: She will be outraged. This is one night of the year when you don't want outside disturbances—on your hands. . . .
RALPH: I think I know what to give you.
ISABEL: I did expect it but yet I didn't expect it!—I mean it occurred to me, the possibility of it, but I thought I was just being morbid.
RALPH: Aw, now, I know that boy. We been through two wars together, took basic training together and officer's training together. He wouldn't ditch you like that unless he's gone crazy.
ISABEL: George Haverstick is a very sick man, Mr. Bates. He was a patient in neurological at Barnes Hospital in Saint Louis, that's how I met him. I was a student nurse there.

(*She is talking quickly, shrilly. She has a prim, severe manner that disguises her prettiness.*)

RALPH: Yeah? What was wrong with him in the hospital, honey?
ISABEL: If we see him again, if he ever comes back to this house, you will *see* what's wrong. *He shakes!* Sometimes it's just barely noticeable, just a constant, slight tremor, you know, a sort of—vibration, like a—like an electric vibration in his muscles or nerves?
RALPH: Aw. That old tremor has come back on him, huh? He had that thing in Korea.
ISABEL: How bad did he have it in Korea, Mr. Bates?
RALPH: You know—like a heavy drinker—except he didn't drink heavy.
ISABEL: It's like he had Parkinson's disease but he doesn't have it.

(*She speaks like an outraged spinster, which is quite incongruous to her pretty, childlike appearance.*)

RALPH: What in hell is it then?

ISABEL: THAT is a MYSTERY! He shakes, that's all. He just shakes. Sometimes you'd think that he was shaking to pieces. . . . Was that a car out front?

(*She goes to the window.*)

No! I've caught a head cold, darn it.

(*Blows her nose.*)

When I met Mr. George Haverstick— Excuse me, you're watching TV!

RALPH (*turning off set*): Naw, I'm not watchin' TV.

ISABEL: I'm so wound up, sitting in silence all day beside my—silent bridegroom, I can't seem to stop talking now, although I—hardly know you. Yes. I met him at Barnes Hospital, the biggest one in Saint Louis, where I was taking my training as a nurse, he had gone in Barnes instead of the Veterans Hospital because in the Veterans Hospital they couldn't discover any physical cause of this tremor and he thought they just said there wasn't any physical cause in order to avoid having to pay him a physical disability—compensation! I had him as a patient at Barnes Hospital, on the night shift. My, did he keep me running! The little buzzer was never out of his hand. Couldn't sleep under any kind of sedation less than enough to knock an elephant out!—Well, that's where I met George, I was very touched by him, honestly, very, very touched by the boy! I thought he sincerely loved me. . . . Yes, I *have* caught a head cold, or am I crying? I guess it's fatigue—exhaustion.

RALPH: You're just going through a period of adjustment.

ISABEL: Of course at Barnes he got the same diagnosis, or lack of diagnosis, that he'd gotten at the Vets Hospital in Korea and Texas and elsewhere, no physical basis for the tremor, perfect physical health, suggested—psychiatry to him! He blew the roof off! You'd think they'd accused him of beating up his grandmother, at least, if not worse! I swear! Mr. Bates, I still have sympathy for him, but it wasn't fair of him not to let me know he'd quit his job at the airfield till after our marriage. He gave me that information after the wedding, right after the wedding he told me, right on the bridge, Eads Bridge between Saint Louis and East Saint Louis, he said, "Little Bit? Take a good look at Saint Louie because it may be your last one!" I'm quoting him exactly, those were his words. I don't know why I didn't say drive me right back. . . . Isn't it strange that I didn't say turn around on the other side of this bridge and drive me right back? I gave up student nursing at a great hospital to marry a man not honest enough to let me know he'd given up his job till an hour after the wedding!

RALPH: George is a high-strung boy. But they don't make them any better.

ISABEL: A man's opinion of a man! If they don't make them any better than George Haverstick they ought to stop production!

(*Ralph throws back his head, laughing heartily.*)

No, I mean it, if they don't make them better than a man that would abandon his bride in less than—how many hours?—on the doorstep of a war buddy and drive on without her or any apology to her, if that's the best they make them, I say *don't make them!*

(*There is a pause. She has crouched before the fire again, holding her hands out to the flickering glow.*)

Did George tell you on the phone that he's quit his job?

RALPH (*pouring brandy*): What job did he quit, honey?

ISABEL: He was a ground mechanic at Lambert's airfield in Saint Louis. I had lost my job too, I hadn't quit, no, I was politely dismissed. My first day in surgery?—I *fainted!*—when the doctor made the incision and I saw the blood, I keeled over . . .

RALPH: That's understandable, honey.

ISABEL: Not in a nurse, not in a girl that had set her heart on nursing, that—how long has he been gone?

RALPH: Just a few minutes, honey. Xmas Eve traffic is heavy and George being George, he may have stopped at a bar on his way back here. . . . You'd been going steady how long?

ISABEL: Ever since his discharge from Barnes Hopsital. Isn't this suburb called High Point?

RALPH: Yes. High Point over a cavern.

ISABEL: His place was in High Point, too. Another suburb called High Point, spelled Hi dash Point—hyphenated.

RALPH: I guess all fair-sized American cities have got a suburb called High Point, hyphenated or not, but this is the only one I know of that's built on a cavern.

ISABEL (*without really listening to him*): Cavern?

(*She laughs faintly as if it were a weak joke.*)

Well, I said, George, on the bridge, we're not driving down to Florida in that case. We're going to find you a job; we're going from city to city until you find a new job and I don't care if we cross the Rio Grande, we're not going to stop until you find one! Did I or didn't I make the right decision? In your opinion, Mr. Bates.

RALPH: Well. How did he react to it?

ISABEL: Stopped talking and started shaking! So violently I was scared he would drive that funeral car off the road! Ever since then it's been hell! And I am—

(*She springs up from the fireplace chair.*)

—not exactly the spirit of Christmas, am I?

(*She goes to the window to look out; sees nothing but windy snow. There is a low rumble. A picture falls off the wall.*)

What was that?

RALPH: Oh, nothing. The ground just settled a little. We get that all the time here because this suburb, High Point, is built over a great big underground cavern and is sinking into it gradually, an inch or two inches a year. It would cost three thousand dollars to stabilize the foundation of this house even temporarily! But it's not publicly known and we homeowners and the promoters of the project have got together to keep it a secret till we have sold out, in alphabetical order, at a loss but not a complete sacrifice. Collusion, connivance. Disgusting but necessary.

(*She doesn't hear this, murmurs "What?" as she crosses back to the window at the sound of a car going by.*)

ISABEL: It's funny, I had a hunch he was going to leave me somewhere.

(*She laughs sadly, forlornly, and lets the white window curtains fall together.*)

RALPH: Why don't you take off your coat and sit back down by the fire? That coat keeps the heat off you, honey. That boy's comin' back.

ISABEL: Thank you.

(*She removes her coat.*)

RALPH (*observing with solemn appreciation the perfect neatness of her small body*): I'm *sure* that boy's coming back. I am now *positive* of it! That's a cute little suit you're wearing. Were you married in that?

ISABEL: Yes, I was married in this traveling suit. Appropriately.

RALPH: You couldn't have looked any prettier in white satin.

(*Ralph is at the bar preparing a snifter of brandy for her. Now he puts a match to it and as it flares up blue, she cries out a little.*)

ISABEL: What is, what are you—?

RALPH: Something to warm up your insides, little lady.

ISABEL: Well, isn't that sweet of you? Will it burn if I touch it?

RALPH: Naw, naw, naw, take it, take it.

ISABEL: Beautiful. Let me hold it to warm my hands first, before I—

(*He puts the snifter glass of blue-flaming brandy in her hands and they return to the fireplace.*)

I'm not a drinker, I don't think doctors or nurses have any right to be, but I guess *now*—I'm *out* of the nursing profession! *So* . . . What a sweet little bar. What a sweet little house. And such a sweet Christmas tree.

RALPH: Yeah. Everything's sweet here. I married a homely girl, honey, but I tried to love her.

(*Isabel doesn't really hear this remark.*)

ISABEL: I hope your wife didn't take your little boy out because we were coming.

RALPH: I sure did make an effort to love that woman. I almost stopped realizing that she was homely.

ISABEL: So he didn't actually tell you he was going to a drugstore, Mr. Bates?

RALPH (*uncomfortably*): He didn't say so. I just figured he was.

ISABEL: I—well, he's abandoned me here.

RALPH: How long've you known George?

ISABEL: I'm afraid I married a stranger.

RALPH: Everybody does that.

ISABEL: Where did you say your wife was?

RALPH: My wife has quit me.

ISABEL: No! You're joking, aren't you?

RALPH: She walked out on me this evening when I let her know I'd quit my job.

ISABEL (*beginning to listen to him*): Surely it's just temporary, Mr. Bates.

RALPH: Nope. Don't think so. I quit my job and so my wife quit me.

ISABEL: I don't think a woman leaves a man as nice as you, Mr. Bates, for such a reason as that.

RALPH: Marriage is an economic arrangement in many ways, let's face it, honey. Also, the situation between us was complicated by the fact that I worked for her father. But that's another story. That's a long other story and you got your mind on George.

ISABEL: I think my pride has been hurt.

RALPH: I told you he's coming back and I'm just as sure of it as I'm sure Dorothea isn't. Or if she does, that she'll find me waiting for her. Ohhhhh, nooooo! I'm cutting out of this High Point over a Cavern on the first military transport I can catch out of Memphis.

ISABEL (*vaguely*): You don't mean that, Mr. Bates, you're talking through your hat, out of hurt feelings, hurt pride.

(*She opens the front door and stands looking out as forlornly as a lost child. She really does have a remarkably cute little figure and Ralph takes slow, continual and rather wistful stock of it with his eyes.*)

RALPH: I got what I had comin' to me, that I admit, for maryin' a girl that didn't attract me.

(*He comes up behind her at the door.*)

ISABEL: Did you say didn't attract you?

RALPH: Naw, she didn't attract me in the beginning. She's one year older'n me and I'm no chicken. But I guess I'm not the only man that would marry the only daughter of an old millionaire with diabetes and gallstones and one kidney. Am I?

ISABEL: It's nice out here.

RALPH: But I'm telling you I'm convinced there is no greater assurance of longevity in this world than one kidney, gall-stones an' diabetes! That old man has been cheating the undertaker for yea many years. Seems to thrive on one kid-ney and . . .

(*He tosses the beer can down the terrace.*)

Oh, they live on anything—nothing!

ISABEL: Do you always throw beer cans on your front lawn, Mr. Bates?

RALPH: Never before in my life. I sure enjoyed it. George is gonna be shocked when he sees me. I sacrificed my youth to—

ISABEL: What?

RALPH: Yep, it's nice out here. I mean, nicer than in there.

ISABEL: You sacrificed your youth?

RALPH: Oh, that. Yeah! I'll tell you more about that unless it bores you.

ISABEL: No.

RALPH: She had fallen into the hands of a psychiatrist when I married this girl. This psychiatrist was charging her father fifty dollars a session to treat her for a condition that he di-agnosed as "psychological frigidity." She would shiver vio-lently every time she came within touching distance of a possible boy friend. Well—I think the psychiatrist misun-derstood her shivers.

ISABEL: She might have shivered because of—

RALPH: That's what I *mean*! Why, the night I met her, I heard a noise like castanets at a distance. I thought some Spanish dancers were about to come on! Ha ha! Then I no-ticed her teeth—she had buck teeth at that time which were later extracted!—were chattering together and her whole body was uncontrollably shaking!

ISABEL: We both married into the shakes! But Mr. Bates, I don't think it's very nice of you to ridicule the appearance of your wife.

RALPH: Oh, I'm not!

ISABEL: You WERE!

RALPH: At my suggestion she had the buck teeth extracted. It was like kissing a rock pile before the extractions! I swear!

ISABEL: Now, Mr. Bates.

RALPH: This snow almost feels warm as white ashes out of a—chimney.

ISABEL: Excuse me. I'll get my—sweater.

(*She goes in. He remains on the little paved terrace. When she comes out again in her cardigan, he goes on talking as if there'd been no interruption.*)

RALPH: Yep, her old man was payin' this head-shrinker fifty dollars per session for this condition he diagnosed as "psychological frigidity." I cured her of that completely almost overnight. But at thirty-seven, my age, you ain't middle-aged but you're in the shadow of it and it's a spooky shadow. I mean, when you look at *late* middle-aged couples like the McGillicuddys, my absent wife's parents . . .

ISABEL: Mr. Bates, don't you think I should go downtown and take a hotel room? Even if George comes back, he ought not to find me here like a checked package waiting for him to return with the claim check. Because if you give up your pride, what are you left with, really?

(*She turns and goes back inside. He follows her in. Immediately after they enter, a Negro Girl appears on the terrace.*)

Don't you agree, Mr. Bates?

(*The Girl rings the doorbell.*)

RALPH: *Here he is now. You see?*

(*Isabel, who had sunk onto a hassock before the fireplace, now rises tensely as Ralph calls out:*)

COME ON IN, LOVER BOY! THAT DOOR AIN'T LOCKED!

(*Ralph opens the door.*)

Oh . . . What can I do fo' you, Susie?

(*Susie comes into the room with a sheepish grin.*)

SUSIE: 'Scuse me for comin' to the front door, Mr. Bates, but that snow's wet and I got a hole in muh shoe!

RALPH: You alone?

SUSIE: Yes, suh.

RALPH: They sent you for somethin'?

SUSIE: Yes, suh, they sent me faw th' chile's Santie Claus.

RALPH: Aw, they did, huh? Well, you go right back an' tell the McGillicuddys that "the chile's Santie Claus" is stayin' right here till the chile comes over for it, because I bought it, not them, and I am at least *half* responsible for the "chile's" existence, *also*. Tell them the chile did not come into the world without a father and it's about time for the chile to acknowledge that fact and for them to acknowledge that fact and— How did you git here, Susie?

SUSIE: Charlie brought me.

RALPH: Who's Charlie?

SUSIE: Charlie's they new *showfer*, Mr. Bates.

RALPH: Aw. Well, tell my wife and her folks, the McGillicuddys, that I won't be here tomorrow but "the chile's Santie Claus" will be here under the tree and say that I said Merry Christmas. Can you remember all that?

SUSIE: Yes, suh. (*She turns and shouts through the door:*) Charlie! Don't come up, I'm comin' right down, Charlie!

(*The sound of a Cadillac motor starting is heard below the terrace as Susie leaves. Ralph looks out of the open door till the car is gone, then slams it shut.*)

RALPH: Dig that, will yuh! Sent a colored girl over to collect the kid's Christmas! This is typical of the Stuart McGillicuddys. I'd like to have seen Mr. Stuart McGillicuddy, the look on his face, when that Western Union messenger give him my message of resignation this afternoon and he was at last exposed to my true opinions of him!

ISABEL: You should have let her take the child's Christmas to it.

RALPH: They'll be over. Don't worry. And—I will be waiting for them with both barrels, man—will I blast 'em! Think of the psychiatrist fees that I saved her fat-head father! I even made her think that she was attractive, and over a five-year period got one pay raise when she give birth to my son which she has turned to a sissy.

(*Isabel hasn't listened to his speech.*)

ISABEL: I thought that was George at the door. . . .
RALPH: That's life for you.
ISABEL: What?
RALPH: I said isn't that life for you!
ISABEL: *What* is life for us *all*?

(*She sighs.*)

My philosophy professor at the Baptist college I went to, he said one day, "We are all of us born, live and die in the shadow of a giant question mark that refers to three questions: Where do we *come* from? *Why? And where, oh where, are we going!*"
RALPH: When did you say you got married?
ISABEL: Yesterday. Yesterday morning.
RALPH: That lately? Well, he'll be back before you can say—Joe Blow.

(*He appreciates her neat figure again.*)

ISABEL: What?
RALPH: Nothing.
ISABEL: Well!
RALPH: D'you like Christmas music?
ISABEL: Everything but "White Christmas."

(*As she extends her palms to the imaginary fireplace, Ralph is standing a little behind her, still looking her up and down with solemn appreciation.*)

RALPH: Aw, y' don't like "White Christmas"?
ISABEL: The radio in that car is practically the only thing in it that *works*! We had it on all the time.

(*She gives a little tired laugh.*)

Conversation was impossible, even if there had been a desire to talk! It kept playing "White Christmas" because it was snowing I guess all the way down here, yesterday and—today. . . .

RALPH: A radio in a funeral limousine?

ISABEL: I guess they just played it on the way back from the graveyard. Anyway, once I reached over and turned the volume down. He didn't say anything, he just reached over and turned the volume back up. Isn't it funny how a little thing like that can be so insulting to you? Then I started crying and still haven't stopped! I pretended to be looking out the car window till it got dark.

RALPH: You're just going through a little period of adjustment to each other.

ISABEL: What do you do with a bride left on your doorstep, Mr. Bates?

RALPH: Well, I, *ha ha!*—never *had* that experience!

ISABEL: Before? Well, now you're faced with it, I hope you know how to handle it. You know why I know he's left me? He only took in my bags, he left his own in the car, he brought in all of mine except my little blue zipper overnight bag, *that* he kept for some reason. Perhaps he intends to pick up another female companion who could use its contents.

RALPH: Little lady, you're in a bad state of nerves.

ISABEL: Have you ever been so tired that you don't know what you're doing or saying?

RALPH: Yes. Often.

ISABEL: That's my condition, so make allowances for it. Yes, indeed, that *sure* is a mighty *far* drugstore. . . .

(*She wanders back to the window, and parts the curtain to peer out.*)

RALPH: He seems gone twice as long because you're thinking about it.

ISABEL: I don't know why I should care except for my overnight bag with my toilet articles in it.

RALPH (*obliquely investigating*): Where did you spend last night?

ISABEL (*vaguely*): Where did we spend last night?

RALPH: Yeah. Where did you stop for the night?

ISABEL (*rubbing her forehead and sighing with perplexity*): In a, in a—oh, a tourist camp called the—Old Man River Motel? Yes, the Old Man River Motel.

RALPH: That's a mistake. The first night ought to be spent in a real fine place regardless of what it cost you. It's so important to get off on the right foot.

(*He has freshened his drink and come around to the front of the bar. She has gone back to the window at the sound of a car.*)

If you get off on the wrong foot, it can take a long time to correct it.

(*She nods in slow confirmation of this opinion.*)

Um-hmmm. Walls are built up between people a hell of a damn sight faster than—broken down. . . . Y'want me to give you my word that he's coming back? I will, I'll give you my word. Hey.

(*He snaps his fingers.*)

Had he brought me a Christmas present? If not, *that's* what he's doing. *That* explains where he went to.

(*There is a pause. She sits sadly by the fireplace.*)

What went wrong last night?

ISABEL: Let's not talk about that.

RALPH: I don't mean to pry into such a private, intimate thing, but—

ISABEL: No, let's don't! I'll just put it this way and perhaps you will understand me. In spite of my being a student nurse, till discharged—my experience has been limited, Mr. Bates. Perhaps it's because I grew up in a small town, an only child, too protected. I wasn't allowed to date till my last year at High and then my father insisted on meeting the boys I went out with and laid down pretty strict rules, such as when to bring me home from parties and so forth. If he smelled liquor on the breath of a boy? At the door? That boy would not enter the door! And that little rule ruled out a goodly number.

RALPH: I bet it did. They should've ate peanuts befo' they called for you, honey.

(*He chuckles; reflectively poking at the fire.*)

That's what we done at the Sisters of Mercy Orphans' Home in Mobile.

ISABEL (*touched*): Oh. Were you an *orphan*, Mr. Bates?

RALPH: Yes, I had that advantage.

(*He slides off the high stool again to poke at the fire. She picks up the antique bellows and fans the flames, crouching beside him.*)

ISABEL: So you were an orphan! People that grow up orphans, don't they value love more?

RALPH: Well, let's put it this way. They get it less easy. To get it, they have to give it: so, yeah, they do value it more.

(*He slides back onto the bar stool. She crouches at the fireplace to fan the fire with the bellows; the flickering light brightens their shy, tender faces.*)

ISABEL: But it's also an advantage to have a parent like my daddy.

(*She's again close to tears.*)

Very strict but devoted. Opposed me going into the nursing profession but I had my heart set on it, I thought I had a vocation, I saw myself as a Florence Nightingale nurse. A lamp in her hand? Establishin' clinics in the—upper Amazon country. . . .

(*She laughs a little ruefully.*)

Yais, I had heroic daydreams about myself as a dedicated young nurse working side by side with a—

(*She pauses shyly.*)

RALPH: With a dedicated young doctor?

ISABEL: No, the doctor would be older, well, not too old, but—older. I saw myself passing among the pallets, you know, the straw mats, administering to the plague victims in the jungle, exposing myself to contagion. . . .

(*She exhibits a bit of humor here.*)

RALPH: *Catchin'* it?

ISABEL: Yais, contractin' it eventually *m'self.* . . .
RALPH: What were the symptoms of it?
ISABEL: A slight blemish appearing on the—hands?

(*She gives him a darting smile.*)

RALPH (*joining in the fantasy with her*): Which you'd wear gloves to conceal?
ISABEL: Yais, rubber gloves all the time.
RALPH: A crusty-lookin' blemish or more like a fungus?

(*They laugh together.*)

ISABEL: I don't think I—yais, I did, I imagined it being like *scaa-ales*! Like silver fish scales appearing on my hainds and then progressing gradually to the wrists and *fo'*-arms. . . .
RALPH: And the young doctor discovering you were concealing this condition?
ISABEL: The *youngish middle-aged* doctor, Mr. Bates! Yais, discovering I had contracted the plague myself and then a big scene in which she says, Oh, no, you mustn't touch me but he seizes her passionately in his arms, of course, and—exposes himself to contagion.

(*Ralph chuckles heartily getting off stool to poke at the fire again. She joins him on the floor to fan the flames with the bellows.*)

ISABEL: And love is stronger than death. You get the picture?
RALPH: Yep, I've seen the picture.
ISABEL: We've had a good laugh together. You're a magician, Ralph, to make me laugh tonight in my present situation. George and I never laugh, we never laugh together. Oh, he makes JOKES, YAIS!But we never have a really genuine laugh together and that's a bad sign, I think, because I don't think a married couple can go through life without laughs together any more than they can without tears.
RALPH: Nope.

(*He removes his shoes.*)

Take your slippers off, honey.
ISABEL: I have the funniest sensation in the back of my head, like—

RALPH: Like a tight rope was coming unknotted?
ISABEL: Exactly! Like a tight rope was being unknotted!

(*He removes her slippers and puts them on the hearth, crosses into the bedroom and comes out with a pair of fluffy pink bedroom slippers. He crouches beside her and feels the sole of her stocking.*)

RALPH: Yep, damp. Take those damp stockings off.
ISABEL (*unconsciously following the suggestion*): Does George have a sense of humor? In your opinion? Has he got the ability to laugh at himself and at life and at—human situations? Outside of off-color jokes? In your opinon, Mr. Bates?
RALPH (*taking the damp stockings from her and hanging them over the footlights*): Yes. We had some good laughs together, me an'—"Gawge," ha ha. . . .
ISABEL: We never had any together.
RALPH: That's the solemnity of romantic love, little lady, I mean like Romeo and Juliet was not exactly a joke book, ha ha ha.
ISABEL: "The solemnity of romantic love"!—I wouldn't expect an old war buddy of George's to use an expression like that.
RALPH: Lemme put these on your feet, little lady.

(*She sighs and extends her feet and he slips the soft fleecy pink slippers on them.*)

But you know something? I'm gonna tell you something which isn't out of the joke books either. You got a wonderful boy in your hands, on your hands, they don't make them any better than him and I mean it.

(*He does.*)

ISABEL: I appreciate your loyalty to an old war buddy.
RALPH: Naw, naw, it's not just that.
ISABEL: But if they don't make them any better than George Haverstick, they ought to stop making them, they ought to *cease producing*!

(*She utters a sort of wild, sad laugh which stops as abruptly as it started. Suddenly she observes the bedroom slippers on her feet.*)

What's these, where did they come from?

RALPH: Honey, I just put them on you. Didn't you know?

ISABEL: No!—How strange!—I didn't, I wasn't at all aware of it. . . .

(*They are both a little embarrassed.*)

Where is your wife, Mr. Bates?

RALPH: Honey, I told you she quit me and went home to her folks.

ISABEL: Oh, excuse me, I remember. You told me. . . .

(*Suddenly the blazing logs make a sharp cracking noise; a spark apparently has spit out of the grate onto Isabel's skirt. She gasps and springs up, retreating from the fireplace, and Ralph jumps off the bar stool to brush at her skirt. Under the material of the Angora wool skirt is the equal and warmer softness of her young body. Ralph is abruptly embarrassed, coughs, turns back to the fireplace and picks up copper tongs to shift the position of crackling logs.*

(*This is a moment between them that must be done just right to avoid misinterpretation. Ralph would never make a play for the bride of a buddy. What should come out of the moment is not a suggestion that he will or might but that Dotty's body never felt that way. He remembers bodies that did. What comes out of Isabel's reaction is a warm understanding of his warm understanding; just that, nothing more, at all.*)

ISABEL: Thank you. This Angora wool is, is—highly inflammable stuff, at least I would—think it—might be. . . .

RALPH: Yeah, and I don't want "Gawge" to come back here and find, a toasted marshmallow bride . . . by my fireplace.

(*They sit down rather self-consciously, Ralph on the high stool, Isabel on the low hassock.*)

ISABEL: Yais . . .

RALPH: Huh?

ISABEL: Daddy opposed me going into nursing so much that he didn't speak to me, wouldn't even look at me for a whole week before I took off for Saint Louie.

RALPH: Aw? Tch!

ISABEL: However, at the last moment, just before the train pulled out of the depot, he came stalking up the platform to the coach window with a gift package and an envelope. The package contained flannel nighties and the envelope had in it a list of moral instructions in the form of prayers such as: "O Heavenly Father, give thy weak daughter strength to—

(*She giggles.*)

"—resist the—"

(*She covers her mouth with a hand to suppress a spasm of laughter.*)

Oh, my Lord. Well, you would have to know Daddy to appreciate the—

RALPH: Honey, I reckon I know your daddy. That's what I meant about the orphan's advantage, honey.

(*They laugh together.*)

ISABEL: We sure do have some good laughs together, Mr. Bates. Now where did I get *these*?

(*She means the bedroom slippers.*)

These aren't mine, where did, how did—? *Oh—yes,* you—

(*They resume their grave contemplation of the fire.*)

"Heavenly Father, give thy weak daughter the strength of will to resist the lusts of men. Amen."

(*Ralph chuckles sadly.*)

And I was never tempted to, *not* to, resist them, till—George. . . .

RALPH: Did George arouse a—?

ISABEL: I don't suppose another man could see George the way I see him: SAW him. So *handsome*? And so *afflicted*? So afflicted and—*handsome*? With that mysterious *tremor*? With those SHAKES?

RALPH: How did "Gawge" come on?

ISABEL: Huh? Oh. No. I don't mean he came on like a—

RALPH: Bull? Exactly?

ISABEL: No, no, no, no. It was very strange, very—strange. . . .

RALPH: What?

ISABEL: He always wanted us to go out on double dates or with a whole bunch of—others. And when we were alone? Together? There was a—funny, oh, a very *odd*—sort of—*timidity!*—between us. . . . And that, of course is what touched me; oh, that—*touched* me. . . .

(*There is a pause in the talk. Ralph descends from his high perch and passes behind her low hassock with a smile behind her back which is a recognition of the truth of her romantic commitment to George. This is also in the slight, tender pat that he gives to the honey-colored crown of her head.*)

And so although I had many strong opportunities to give in to my "weakness" on, on—weekend dates with young interns and doctors at Barnes?—I was never tempted to do so. But with George—

RALPH: You did? Give in?

ISABEL: Mr. Bates, George Haverstick married a virgin, and I can't say for sure that it was my strength of will and not *his* that—deserves the credit. . . .

(*Ralph returns to fireplace with beer.*)

RALPH: Yeah, well. Now I'm going to tell you something about that boy that might surprise you after your experience last night at the Old Man River Motel.

(*He opens a beer can.*)

He always bluffs about his ferocious treatment of women, believe me! To hear him talk you'd think he spared them no pity! However, I happen to know he didn't come on as strong with those dolls in Tokyo and Hong Kong and Korea as he liked to pretend to. Because I heard from those dolls. . . . He'd just sit up there on a pillow and drink that rice wine with them and teach them *English*! Then come downstairs from there, hitching his belt and shouting, *"Oh, man! Oh, brother!"*—like he' laid 'em to waste.

ISABEL: That was not his behavior in the Old Man River Motel. Last night.

RALPH: What went wrong in the Old Man River Motel?

ISABEL: Too many men think that girls in the nursing profession must be—*shock*proof. I'm not, I wasn't—last night. . . .

RALPH: Oh. Was he drunk?

ISABEL: He'd been drinking all day in that heaterless retired funeral hack in a snowstorm to keep himself warm. Since I don't drink, I just had to endure it. Then. We stopped at the Old Man River Motel, as dreary a place as you could find on this earth! The electric heater in our cabin lit up but gave off no heat! Oh, *George* was comfortable there! Threw off his clothes and sat down in front of the heater as if I were not even present.

RALPH: Aw.

ISABEL: Continuing drinking!

RALPH: Aw.

ISABEL: Then began the courtship, and, oh, what a courtship it was, such tenderness, romance! I finally screamed. I locked myself in the bathroom and didn't come out till he had gotten to bed and then I—slept in a chair. . . .

RALPH: You wouldn't—

ISABEL: Mr. Bates, I just couldn't! The atmosphere just wasn't right. And he—

(*She covers her face.*)

—I can't tell you more about it just now except that it was a nightmare, him in the bed, pretending to be asleep, and me in the chair pretending to be asleep too and both of us knowing the other one *wasn't* asleep and, and, and— I can't tell you more about it right now, I just can't tell more than I've told you about it, I—

(*Her sobs become violent and there is a pause.*)

RALPH: Hey! Let me kiss the bride! Huh? Can I kiss the bride?

ISABEL: You're very kind, Mr. Bates. I'm sure you were more understanding with your wife when you were going through this—

RALPH:—period of adjustment? Yeah. That's all it is, it's just a little—period of adjustment.

(*He bestows a kiss on her tear-stained cheek and a pat on her head. She squeezes his hand and sinks down again before the fireplace.*)

ISABEL: It isn't as if I'd given him to believe that I was *experienced*! I made it clear that I *wasn't*. He knows my background and we'd talked at great *length* about my—inhibitions which I know are—*inhibitions*, but—which an understanding husband wouldn't expect his bride to overcome at *once*, in a tourist cabin, after a *long—silent—ride!* —in a *funeral hack* in a *snowstorm* with the *heater not working* in a *shocked! condition!*—having just been told that—we were *both* unemployed, and—

RALPH: Little Bit, Little Bit—you had a sleepless night in that motel—why don't you put in a little sack time now. You need it, honey. Take Dotty's bed in there and think about nothing till morning.

ISABEL: You mean you know, now, that George is not coming back?

RALPH: No. I mean that Dotty's not coming back.

ISABEL: I don't think you ever thought that he would come back for me any more than I did.

RALPH: Take Dotty's bed, get some sleep on that foam-rubber mattress while I sit here and watch the Late Late Show on TV.

ISABEL: But, Mister Bates, if your wife does come back here I wouldn't want her to find a stranger in your bedroom.

RALPH: Honey, finding a stranger in a bedroom is far from being the biggest surprise of a lifetime. So you go on in there and lock the door.

ISABEL: Thank you, Mister Bates.

(*She enters bedroom.*)

I'm only locking the door because of the slight possibility that Mister George Haverstick the fourth might come back drunk and try to repeat the comedy and tragedy of last night. I hope you realize that.

RALPH: Oh, sure. Good night, sleep tight, honey.

(*She locks the bedroom door as Ralph returns to the fireplace.*)

RALPH (*to himself and the audience*): What a bitch of a Christmas.

Curtain

ACT TWO

No time lapse.

Isabel jumps up as a car is heard stopping out front. She looks wildly at Ralph, who gives her a nod and a smile as he crosses to the front door. Snow blows into the living room as he goes out and shouts:

RALPH: HEY!

(*Isabel catches her breath, waiting.*)

Ha ha!

(*Isabel expels her breath and sits down. Ralph, shouting through snow:*)

Your wife thought she was deserted!
GEORGE (*from a distance*): *Hey!*

(*Isabel springs up and rushes to a mirror to wipe away tears.*
(*A car door is heard slamming in front of the house. Isabel sits down. She immediately rises, rubbing her hands together, and then sits down again. Then she springs up and starts toward the bedroom. Stops short as*
(*George enters.*)

I'm the son of a camel, ha ha! My mother was a camel with two humps, a double hump—dromedary! Ha ha ha!

(*George and Ralph catch each other in a big, rocking hug. Isabel stares, ignored, as the male greetings continue.*)

RALPH: *You ole son of a tail gun!*
GEORGE: *How'sa young squirrel? Ha ha!*
RALPH: *How'sa Texas jack rabbit?*

(*There is a sudden, incongruous stillness. They stare, all three of them, Isabel at George, George and Ralph at each other. George is suddenly embarrassed and says:*)

GEORGE: Well, I see yuh still got yuh dawg.
RALPH: Yeah, m' wife's folks are cat lovers.
GEORGE: You'll get your wife back tomorrow.
RALPH: Hell, I don't want her back.
GEORGE: Y'don't want 'er back?
RALPH: That's right.
GEORGE: Hell, in that case, you won't be able to beat 'er off with a stick, ha ha!

(*His laugh expires as he catches Isabel's outraged look.*)

Won't be able to beat her away from the door with a stick t'morrow. . . .

(*They stare at each other brightly, with little chuckles, a constant series of little chuckles. Isabel feels ignored.*)

ISABEL: I doubt that Mr. Bates means it.
GEORGE: Didn't you all have a kid of some kind? I don't remember if it was a boy or a girl.
ISABEL: The toys under the tree might give you a clue as to that.
RALPH: Yeah, it's a boy, I guess. Drink?
GEORGE: You bet.

(*George goes to the bar and starts mixing drinks.*)

ISABEL: How old is your little boy?
RALPH: Three years old and she's awready made him a sissy.
GEORGE: They'll do it ev'ry time, man.

(*He keeps chuckling, as does Ralph.*)

RALPH: I didn't want this kind of a dawg, either. I wanted a Doberman pinscher, a dawg with some guts, not a whiner! But she wanted a poodle and this flop-eared sad sack of a spaniel was a compromise which turned out to be worse'n a poodle, ha, ha. . . .
GEORGE: I'll bet yuh dollars to doughnuts your wife and kid'll be back here tomorrow.

RALPH (*in his slow drawl*): They won't find me here if they do. I'm all packed to go. I would of been gone when you called but I'm waitin' t' git a call from a boy about t' git married. I want him to come over here an' make a cash offer on all this household stuff since I spent too much on Christmas and won't be around to collect my unemployment.

GEORGE: Come along with us. We got a big car out there an' we're as free as a breeze. Ain't that right, Little Bit?

ISABEL: Don't ask me what's right. I don't know! I *do* know, though, that couples with children don't separate at Christmas, and, George, let your friend work out his problems himself. You don't know the situation and don't have any right to interfere in it. And now will you please go get my little blue zipper bag for me? *Please?*

RALPH (*to George, as if she hadn't spoken*): Naw, I'm just going out to the army airfield a couple miles down the highway and catch the first plane going west.

GEORGE: We'll talk about that.

ISABEL: *George!*

GEORGE: Aw, HERE! I forgot to give you your present! After drivin' almost back into Memphis to find a liquor store open.

(*He extends a gift-wrapped magnum of champagne.*)

RALPH: Lover Jesus, champagne?

GEORGE: Imported and already cold.

RALPH (*glancing briefly at Isabel*): Didn't I tell you that he was buyin' me something? She thought you'd deserted her, boy.

ISABEL: *All right, I'll get it myself! I'll go out and get it out of the car myself!*

(*She rushes out into snow, leaving the door open.*

(*George closes the door without apparently noticing her exit.*)

GEORGE: Boy, you an' me have got a lot to talk over.

RALPH: We sure got lots of territory to cover.

GEORGE: So your goddam marriage has cracked up on yuh, has it?

RALPH: How's yours goin'? So far?

GEORGE: We'll talk about it *later*. Discuss it *thoroughly*! *Later!*
RALPH: Y'got married yestiddy mawnin'?
GEORGE: Yeah.
RALPH: How was last night?
GEORGE: We'll talk about *that* later, too.

(*Isabel rushes into the room in outrage, panting.*)

ISABEL: *I* can't break the lock on that *car*!
GEORGE: Little Bit, I didn't know that you wuh bawn in a barn.

(*He means she left the door open again.*)

ISABEL: I didn't know a lot about you, either!

(*George closes door.*)

Mr. Bates! Mr. Bates!

(*He turns toward her with a vague smile.*)

The gentleman I married refuses to get my zipper bag out of the car or unlock the car so I can get it myself.

(*The phone rings. Ralph picks it up.*)

RALPH (*in a slow, hoarse drawl, at the phone*): Aw, hi, Smokey. I'm glad you got my message. Look. I quit Regal Dairy Products and I'm flyin' out of here late tonight or early tomorrow morning and I thought maybe you might like to look over some of my stuff here, the household equipment, and make me a cash offer for it. I'll take less in cash than a check since I'm not gonna stop at the Coast, I'm flying straight through to Hong Kong so it would be difficult for me to cash yuh check an' of course I expect to make a sacrifice on the stuff here. Hey! Would you like a beaver-skin coat, sheared beaver-skin coat for Gertrude? Aw. I'd let you have it for a, for a—third off! Aw. Well, anyhow, come over right away, Smokey, and make me an offer in cash on as much of this household stuff as you figure that you could use when you git married. O.K.?

(*He hangs up.*)

GEORGE: Hong Kong?
RALPH: Yeah.

GEORGE: Well, how about that! Back to Miss Lotus Blossom in the Pavilion of Joys?

RALPH: I never had it so good. At least not *since.*

ISABEL (*acidly*): Mr. Bates, your character has changed since my gypsy husband appeared! He seems to have had an immediate influence on you, and not a good one. May I wash up in your bathroom?

(*They both look at her with slight, enigmatic smiles.*)

RALPH: What's that, honey?

ISABEL: Will you let me use your bathroom?

RALPH: Aw, sure, honey. I'm sorry you—

GEORGE: Now what's the matter with her?

(*He turns to Isabel.*)

Now what's the matter with you?

ISABEL: May I talk to you alone? In another room?

RALPH: You all go in the bedroom and straighten things out.

(*Ralph goes out into the snow flurry. George leads Isabel into next room.*)

GEORGE: Now what's the matter with you?

ISABEL: Is this a sample of how I'm going to be treated?

GEORGE: What do you mean? How have I treated you, huh?

ISABEL: I might as well not be present! For all the attention I have been paid since you and your buddy had this tender reunion!

GEORGE: Aren't you being a little unreasonable, honey?

ISABEL: I don't think so. George? If you are unhappy, our marriage can still be annulled. Y'know that, don't you?

GEORGE: You want to get *out* of it, do you?

(*Ralph comes back in with her traveling case. He sets it down and goes to the kitchenette.*)

ISABEL: I don't think it's really very unreasonable of me to want to be treated as if I LIVED! EXISTED!

GEORGE: Will you quit actin' like a spoiled little bitch? I want to tell you something. You're the first woman that ever put me down! Sleepin' las' night in a chair? What kind of basis is that for a happy marriage?

ISABEL: You had to get drunk on a highway! In a heaterless funeral car, after informing me you had just quit your job! Blasting my eardrums, afterward, with a car radio you wouldn't let me turn down. How was I supposed to react to such kindness? Women are human beings and I am not an exception to that rule, I assure you! I HATED YOU LAST NIGHT AFTER YOU HAD BEEN HATING ME AND TORTURING ME ALL DAY LONG!

(*Ralph comes back into the front room.*)

GEORGE: Torturing you, did you say? WHY DON'T YOU SIMMER DOWN! We ain't ALONE here, y'know!

RALPH (*quietly, from the living room*): You all are just goin' through a perfectly usual little period of adjustment. That's all it is, I told her—

GEORGE: Aw! You all have been talking?

ISABEL: What did you think we'd been doing while you were gone in that instrument of torture you have for a car?

GEORGE: You've got to simmer down to a lower boiling point, baby.

RALPH (*entering the bedroom*): Just goin' through a period of adjustment. . . .

ISABEL: Adjustment to what, Mr. Bates? Humiliation? For the rest of my life? Well, I won't have it! I don't want such an "adjustment." I want to— May I—

(*She sobs.*)

—freshen up a little bit in your bathroom before we drive downtown? To check in at a hotel?

RALPH: Sure you can.

GEORGE: I ain't goin' downtown—or checkin' in no hotel.

(*He goes back into the living room.*)

ISABEL: YOU may do as you *please*! *I'm* checking in a hotel.

RALPH (*offering her a glass*): You never finished your drink.

ISABEL: I don't care to, thanks. Too many people think that liquor solves problems, all problems. I think all it does is *confuse* them!

RALPH: I would say that it—*obfuscates* them a little, but—

ISABEL: Does *what* to them, Mr. Bates?

RALPH: I work crossword puzzles. I—ha ha!—pick up a lot of long words. Obfuscates means obscures. And problems need obfuscation now and then, honey. I don't mean total or permanent obfuscation, I just mean *temporary* obfuscation, that's all.

(*He is touched by the girl and he is standing close to her, still holding the glass out toward her. He has a fine, simple sweetness and gentleness when he's not "bugged" by people.*)

D'ya always say *Mister* to men?

ISABEL: Yes, I do till I know them. I had an old-fashioned upbringing and I can't say I regret it. Yes.

(*She is still peering out the door at her new husband.*)

RALPH: I wish you would say Ralph to me like you *know* me, honey. You got a tension between you, and tensions obfuscate love. Why don't you get that cross look off your face and give him a loving expression? Obfuscate his problems with a sweet smile on your face and—

ISABEL: YOU do that! I'm not in a mood to "obfuscate" his problems. Mr. Bates, I think he'd do better to face them like I'm facing mine, such as the problem of having married a man that seems to dislike me after one day of marriage.

RALPH: Finish this drink and obfuscate that problem because it doesn't exist.

(*He closes the bedroom door. As he comes back to Isabel with the glass, George reopens the door between the two rooms, glares in for a moment and switches the overhead light on, then goes back into the parlor. Ralph smiles tolerantly at this show of distrust which is not justified.*)

ISABEL: You have a sweet little bedroom, Mr. Bates.

RALPH: I married a *sweet, homely* woman. Almost started to *like* her. I can like *anybody*, but—

ISABEL: Mr. Bates? Ralph? This house has a *sweetness* about it!

RALPH: You don't think it's "tacky?"

ISABEL: No. I think it's—sweet!

RALPH: We got it cheap because this section of town is built right over a cavern.

ISABEL (*without listening*): What?

RALPH: This High Point suburb is built over an underground cavern and is gradually sinking down in it. You see those cracks in the walls?

ISABEL: Oh. . . .

(*She hasn't listened to him or looked.*)

Oh! My little blue bag. May I have it?

RALPH (*through the door*): She wants a little blue bag.

GEORGE: *Here, give it to her, goddam it!*

(*He tosses the bag into the bedroom. Isabel screams. Ralph catches the bag.*)

Now whatcha screamin' faw?

ISABEL: Thank heaven Mr. Bates is such a good catch. All my colognes and perfumes are in that bag, including a twenty-five dollar bottle of Vol-de-nuit. Mr. Bates, will it be necessary for me to phone the hotel?

GEORGE: Didn't you hear what I said?

ISABEL: Mr. Bates! Would you mind phoning some clean, inexpensive hotel to hold a room for us tonight?

GEORGE: I said I'm not gonna check in a hotel tonight!

ISABEL: Reserve a *single* room, please!

RALPH: Sure, sure, honey, I'll do that. Now you just rest an' fresh up an'— Come on, George, let her alone here now, so she can rest an' calm down.

(*He leads George back into the parlor.*)

GEORGE: Look at my hands! Willya look at my hands?

RALPH: What about your hands?

GEORGE: Remember that tremor? Which I had in Korea? Those shakes? Which started in Korea?

RALPH: Aw is it come back on yuh?

GEORGE: Are you blind, man?

RALPH: Yeah. How's your drink?

GEORGE: She in the bathroom yet?

RALPH: Naw, she's still in the bedroom.

GEORGE: Wait'll she gits in the bathroom so we can talk.

RALPH: What's your drink, ole son?

GEORGE: Beer's fine. Jesus!

RALPH (*at the bar*): Rough?

GEORGE: Just wait'll she gits in the bathroom so I can tell you about last night.
RALPH: Here.

(*He hands him a beer.*)

GEORGE (*at the bedroom door*): She's still sittin' there bawling on that bed. Step outside a minute.

(*He goes to the front door and out onto the tiny paved porch. The interior dims as Ralph follows him out. For a while they just stand drinking beer with the snow shadows swarming about them.*)

RALPH: Chilly.
GEORGE: I don't feel chilly.
RALPH: *I* do.

(*He pauses.*)

You're not for that little lady in that damn silly little sissy mess of a bedroom!
GEORGE: What's wrong with the bedroom, it looked like a nice little bedroom.
RALPH: A bedroom is just as nice as whoever sleeps in it with you.
GEORGE: I missed that. What was that, now?

(*He rests an arm on Ralph's shoulders.*)

RALPH: How would you like ev'ry time you wint t'bed with your wife, you had to imagine on the bed in the dark that it wasn't her on it with you, in the dark with you, but any one of a list of a thousand or so lovely lays? I done a despicable thing. I married a girl that had no attraction for me excepting I felt sorry for her and her old man's money! I got what I should have gotten: nothing! Just a goddam desk job at Regal Dairy Products, one of her daddy's business operations in Memphis, at eighty-five lousy rutten dollars a week! With my background? In the Air Force?
GEORGE: Man an air record will cut you no ice on the ground. All it leaves you is a—mysterious tremor. Come on back in. I'm freezing to death out here. I'll git her into that bathroom so we can talk.

(*He tosses the beer cans into yard.*)

RALPH: Don't y'know better'n to throw beer cans in a man's front yard?

(*He says this vaguely, glumly, as he follows George back into the cottage and shuts the door behind them. George goes to bedroom.*)

GEORGE (*entering*): Little Bit, you told me you couldn't wait to get under a good hot shower. There's a good shower in that bathroom. Why don't you go and get under that good hot shower?

ISABEL: I have a lot to think over, George.

GEORGE: Think it over under a good shower in that bedroom, will you? I want to take a bath, too.

ISABEL (*suddenly turning to face him from the bed*): George, I feel so lonely!

GEORGE: Yeah, and whose fault is that?

ISABEL: I don't know why I suddenly felt so lonely!

(*She sobs again. He regards her coolly from the door.*)

GEORGE: Little Bit, go in the bathroom and take your shower, so I can go take mine, or do you want us to go in and take one together?

(*She rises with a sigh and goes to bathroom door.*)

Naw, I didn't think so.

(*She enters the bathroom. He waits till the shower starts, then returns to the front room.*)

There now, she's in!

(*He shakes both fists in the air with a grimace of torment.*)

Look! I got to get rid of that girl. I got to get rid of her quick. Jesus, you got to help me. I can't stay with that girl.

RALPH: Man, you're married to her.

GEORGE: You're married to one! Where's yours? You son of a tail gun! Don't tell me I'm married to her when we ain't exchanged five remarks with each other since we drove out of Cape Girardeau where she refused to—has she come out of the bathroom? No!—Even *undress*! But huddled up in a chair all night in a blanket, crying? Because she had the misfortune to be my wife?

RALPH: I wouldn't count on it.

GEORGE: On what?

RALPH: Her thinking it's such a misfortune.

GEORGE: I described to you how we passed the night, last night!

RALPH: Is this girl a virgin?

GEORGE: She is a *cast-iron* virgin! And's going to stay one! Determined!

RALPH: I wouldn't count on that.

GEORGE: I would. I count on it. First thing I do tomorrow is pack her onto a plane back to Saint Louie.

RALPH: You must have done something to shock her.

GEORGE: That's the truth, I tried to sleep with her.

RALPH: Maybe you handled the little lady too rough.

GEORGE: Now don't talk to me like a wise old man of the mountain about how to deal with a woman. Who was it had to make dates for who at Big Springs and who was it even had to make arrangements for you with those Toyko dolls?

RALPH: That's not women, that's gash.

GEORGE: Gash are women.

RALPH: They are used women. You've got a unused woman and got to approach her as one.

GEORGE: She's gonna stay unused as far as I am concerned.

(*He stoops by the Christmas tree.*)

Now what the hell is this thing?

(*He has crouched among the toys under the tree.*)

RALPH: Rocket launcher. Miniature of the rocket-launchin' pad at Cape Canaveral.

GEORGE: No snow! How's it work?

RALPH: Gimme the countdown. I'll show you.

GEORGE: Ten. Nine. Eight. Seven. Six. Five. Four. Three. Two. OWW!

(*The rocket has fired in his face.*)

RALPH: Ain't you got sense enough to stand clear of a rocket launcher? Ha ha! Last week, just last week, I caught the little bugger playin' with a rag doll. Well. I snatched that doll away from him an' pitched it into the fireplace. He tried to pull it out an' burned his hand! Dotty called me a monster! The child screamed "I hate you!" an' kicked my shins black an' blue! But I'll be damned if any son of Ralph Bates will grow up playin' with dolls. Why, I'll bet you he rides this hawss side-saddle! Naw, a sissy tendency in a boy's got to be nipped in the bud, otherwise the bud will blossom.

GEORGE: I would prefer to have a little girl.

(*He says this wistfully, still rubbing his bruised forehead.*)

Little girls prefer Daddy. Female instinct comes out early in them.

RALPH: I wanted a boy but I'm not sure I got one. However, I got him a real red-blooded boy's Christmas, at no small expense for a man in my income bracket!

(*Isabel comes out of the bathroom.*)

I like the kid, I mean I—sure would suffer worse than he would if the neighborhood gang called him "Sissy!" I'm tolerant. By nature. But if I git partial custody of the kid, even one month in summer, I will correct the sissy tendency in him. Because in this world you got to be what your physical sex is or correct it in Denmark. I mean we got a *man's* world coming up, man! Technical! Terrific! And it's gotta be *fearless*! *Terrific!*

ISABEL: Mr. Bates.

GEORGE (*on his way to the door*): Whadaya want?

ISABEL: I called for Mistuh Bates.

GEORGE: Mistuh Bates, Mrs. Haverstick is anxious to talk to you, suh.

ISABEL: I just want to know if you have called the hotel.

RALPH (*entering*): Sure, sure, honey. Don't worry about a thing. Everything's gonna be fine.

ISABEL (*she is in a silk robe*): Thanks, Ralph. You've been awf'ly kind to me. Oh! I helped myself to a little Pepto-Bismol I found in your sweet little bathroom.

RALPH: Aw, that pink stuff? Take it all. I never touch it. It's Dorothea's. She used to get acid stomach.

ISABEL: It's very soothing.

(*George crosses to the bedroom door, head cocked, somewhat suspicious.*)

RALPH: Well, I cured her of that. I doubt that she's hit that Pepto-Bismol bottle once in the last five years.

ISABEL: I rarely suffer from an upset stomach. Rarely as snow in Memphis!

(*She laughs lightly.*)

But the human stomach is an emotional barometer with some people. Some get headaches, others get upset stomachs.

RALPH: Some even git diarrhea.

ISABEL: The combination of nervous strain and— Oh! What's this?

(*She picks up a gorgeously robed statue of the infant Jesus.*)

RALPH: Aw, that.

(*He moves farther into the bedroom. George moves closer to the door.*)

That's the infant of Prague. Prague, Czechoslovakia?

ISABEL: Oh?

RALPH: It was discovered there in the ruins of an old monastery. It has miraculous properties.

ISABEL: Does it?

RALPH: They say that it does. Whoever gives you the Infant of Prague gives you a piece of money to put underneath it for luck. Her father presented this infant to Dorothea so the piece of money was *naturally one penny.* It's s'posed to give you prosperity if you're not prosperous and a child if you're childless. It give us a child but the money is yet to come in, the money's just been goin' out. However, I don't blame the Infant of Prague for that, because—

ISABEL: Mr. Bates? Ralph? You know, very often people can be absolutely blind, stupid, and helpless about their own problems and still have a keen intuition about the problems of others?

RALPH: Yeah?

ISABEL: There is such a tender atmosphere in this sweet little house, especially this little bedroom, you can almost—

touch it, feel it! I mean you can *breathe* the tender atmosphere in it!

RALPH (*in a slow, sad drawl*): The color scheme in this bedroom is battleship gray. And will you notice the cute inscriptions on the twin beds? "His" on this one, "Hers" on that one? The linen's marked his and hers, too. Well. The space between the two beds was no-man's land for a while. Her psychological frigidity was like a, like a—artillery barrage!—between his and hers. I didn't try to break through it the first few nights. Nope. I said to myself, "Let *her* make the first move."

ISABEL: *Did* she?

RALPH: What do *you* think?

ISABEL: I think she *did*.

RALPH: *Right you are!*

(*He gives her a little congratulatory pat on the shoulder.*)

GEORGE: What's this heart-to-heart talk goin' on in here?

RALPH (*chuckling*): Come on out of here, boy. I got something to tell you.

(*He leads George out.*)

GEORGE: What were you up to in there?

RALPH (*whispering loudly*): Go in there, quick, before she gets dressed, you fool!

GEORGE: I'll be damned if I will!

RALPH: I'll turn the TV on loud.

ISABEL (*calling out*): I'll be dressed in a jiffy!

RALPH: Go ON! You just got a jiffy!

GEORGE: Yeah, and I've got some pride, too. She put me down last night, first woman ever to put me down in—

RALPH: I know, you told me, GO IN! Lock the door and—

GEORGE: YOU go in! That's what you WANT to do! I never had a girl yet that you didn't want to take over. This time you're welcome. GO IN! GO BACK IN AND BREATHE THE TENDER ATMOSPHERE OF THAT—

RALPH: Gawge? Hey— You're *shakin'*, man, you're shakin' to pieces! What kind of a son of a bitch d'you take me faw?

GEORGE: The kind which you are, which you always have been!

RALPH: She is right about you. You are not well, son. . . .

GEORGE: Where d'ya git this "son" stuff! Don't call me "son."

RALPH: Then grow up, will yuh! What's your drink? Same?

GEORGE: Same . . .

RALPH: You're shakin' because you want to go in that bedroom. Go IN! Take the bottle in with you! I'll sit here and watch TV till—

(*Isabel has put on her traveling suit. She comes into the living room.*)

—Too late *now*!

ISABEL (*in a sweet Texas drawl*): Mr. Bates? Ralph? It breaks my heart to see all those lovely child's toys under the tree and the little boy not here to have his Christmas.

RALPH: He's with his mother.

ISABEL: I know, but his Christmas is here.

RALPH: He's a Mama's boy. He's better off with his Mama.

ISABEL: How are *you* feeling, now, George?

(*George grunts and turns to the bar.*
(*Isabel makes a despairing gesture to Ralph.*
(*George wheels about abruptly, suspecting some dumb-play.*
(*Isabel laughs lightly and then sighs deeply.*)

GEORGE: I thought you'd set your heart on a single hotel room tonight.

ISABEL: George, you're shaking worse than I've even seen you.

GEORGE: That's, that's not your problem, that's—*my* problem, not *yours*!

RALPH (*to Isabel*): Honey? Come here a minute.

(*He whispers something to her.*)

ISABEL: Oh, no. No! Mr. Bates, you are confusing the function of a wife with that of a— I feel sorry, I feel very sorry for you not-so-young young men who've depended for love, for tenderness in your lives, on the sort of women available near army camps, in occupied territories! Mr. Bates? Ralph?

RALPH: Just take his hand and lead him into the—

ISABEL: RALPH! NO! BELIEVE ME!
RALPH: All right. . . .

(*There is a pause.*)

ISABEL: Ralph, why did you quit YOUR job? Did you get the shakes, too?
GEORGE: Don't get bitchy with him.
ISABEL: I WASN'T BEING BITCHY!
RALPH: She wasn't being bitchy. She asked a logical question.
ISABEL: Just a question!
GEORGE: Can't you mind your own business for a change? You got fired too, don't forget! All three of us here is jobless!
ISABEL: I am not forgetting.

(*Primly, with dignity.*)

I am not forgetting a thing, and I have a lot to remember.
GEORGE: Good. I hope you remember it. *Memorize* it!

(*He is getting tight.*)

ISABEL (*sniffling a little*): I think I caught cold in that car.
GEORGE: Hell, you were born with a cold—
ISABEL: *Stop that!*
GEORGE: In your damn little—
ISABEL: MR. BATES, MAKE HIM STOP!
RALPH: Let him blow off some steam.
(*Overlapping barely intelligible*)
GEORGE: Incurable cold! You didn't catch it from me.
ISABEL: I wish you had shown this side of your nature before, just a hint, just a clue, so I'd have known what I was in for.
GEORGE: What hint did you give *me*? What clue did *I* have to *your* nature?
ISABEL: Did I disguise my nature?
GEORGE: You sure in hell did.
ISABEL: In what *way*, tell me, please!
GEORGE: You didn't put the freeze on me at Barnes Hospital!

(*To Ralph.*)

She was nurse at Barnes when I went there for those tests? To find out the cause of my shakes? She was my night nurse at Barnes.

ISABEL: Oh, stop! Don't be so crude! How can you be so crude?

GEORGE: She was my night nurse at Barnes and gave me alcohol rubdowns at bedtime.

ISABEL: That was my job. I had to.

GEORGE: Hell, she stroked and petted me with her hands like she had on a pair of silk gloves.

ISABEL: This is insufferable. I am going downtown.

(*She covers her face, sobbing.*)

Just give me carfare downtown.

GEORGE: You remember those dolls with silk gloves on their hands in Tokyo, Ralph? Hell, she could of given them Jap dolls lessons!

ISABEL: I DID NOT TOUCH YOUR BODY EXCEPT AS A NURSE HIRED TO DO IT! YOU KNOW I DIDN'T! I DID NOT TOUCH YOUR BIG OLD LECHEROUS BODY.

GEORGE: How'd you give me a rubdown without touching my body? Huh? How could you give me rubdowns without touching my body? Huh?

ISABEL: Please, please, make him be still. Mr. Bates? You believe me? He's making out I seduced him while I was his nurse.

GEORGE: I didn't say that. Don't say I said that. I didn't say that. I said you had soft little fingers and you knew what you were doing. She'd say, "Turn over." I couldn't turn over. I had to stay on my stomach. I was embarrassed not to.

ISABEL: Ah—I feel nauseated. What filth you have in your mind!

RALPH: Honey? Little lady? Come over and sit here with me. All this will all straighten out. It's going to be all straightened out.

(*George pours himself a drink. The glass slips out of his shaking fingers.*)

GEORGE: *Worse than ever, worse than ever before!* How could I have kept that job? A ground mechanic with hands that can't hold tools?

ISABEL: Go take your tranquillizers. They're in my zipper bag.

GEORGE: Oh, Jesus.

RALPH (*picking up the dropped glass*): See, honey? That boy isn't well. Make some allowances for him. You're both nice kids, both of you, wonderful people. And very good-looking people. I'm afraid you're doomed to be happy for a long time together, soon as this little period of adjustment that you're going through right now passes over.

(*George holds his violently shaking hands in front of him, staring at them fiercely.*

(*He goes to the bedroom.*)

ISABEL: May I call my father, collect?

RALPH: Don't call home, now. Why upset the old people on Christmas Eve?

ISABEL: I'll just say I miss them and want to come home for Christmas.

RALPH: They'll know something's wrong if you go home without your brand-new husband.

ISABEL: Husband! What husband? That man who describes me as a Tokyo whore? Implies that I seduced him in a hospital because I was required to give him alcohol rubdowns at night?

RALPH: All he meant was you excited him, honey.

ISABEL: I assure you that was *not* my intention! I am naturally gentle, I am gentle by nature, and if my touch on his big lecherous body created—*sexual fantasies* in his *mind*!—that's hardly *my* fault, is it?

GEORGE (*returning*): I am sorry that I upset you.

ISABEL: Will you tell him the truth?

GEORGE: Sure I will. What about?

ISABEL: Did I deliberately excite you in Barnes Hospital?

GEORGE: No. I never said that.

ISABEL: Anybody that heard you would get that impression.

GEORGE: You didn't deliberately do it, you just did it because I was horny for you, that's all, that's all, that's—all. . . .

(*He slumps in a chair with a long, despairing sigh.*

(*There is a silent pause.*)

ISABEL: I don't blame you alone, George. I blame myself, too. Not for deliberate sexual provocation, but for not realizing before our marriage yesterday that we were—opposite types.

GEORGE (*sadly*): Yes, opposite types. . . .

ISABEL: *I want to talk to my father!*

GEORGE: Talk to him. Call him. I'll pay Ralph the charges.

ISABEL: May I?

RALPH: Sure, honey, call your folks and wish 'em a Merry Christmas.

ISABEL: Thank you. I will if I can stop crying.

RALPH: George? This little girl needs you. Go on, be nice to her, boy.

GEORGE: I need somebody, too. She hasn't got the incurable shakes, *I* have, *I* got 'em! Was *she* nice to *me*? *Last night?*

ISABEL (*tearfully*): Operator? I want to call long distance, Sweetwater, Texas. Oh-seven-oh-three. No, anybody that answers. It will be Daddy, Mama can't get out of—

(*She sobs.*)

—bed!

(*Ralph makes a sign to George to go over and sit by her. George disregards the suggestion.*)

RALPH: You better hang up and let them call you back. Long distance is very busy on Christmas Eve. Everyone callin' the home folks.

ISABEL: I just hope I stop crying! I don't want Daddy to hear me.

(*She pauses.*)

Poor ole thing. So sweet and faithful to Mama, bedridden with arthritis for seven years, now . . . Hello? What? Oh. You'll call me back when you complete the connection, will you, because it's very important, it's really very urgent. . . .

(*She hangs up. There is silence.*)

RALPH (*finally*): One bad night in a rutten highway motel and you all are acting like born enemies toward each other!

GEORGE: Don't upset her, she's going to talk to her daddy. And tell him she's married to a stinker.

ISABEL: No, I'm not. I'm going to tell him that I am blissfully happy, married to the kindest man in the world, the second kindest, the kindest man next to my daddy!

GEORGE: Thanks.

ISABEL: Waits hand and foot on Mama, bedridden with arthritis.

GEORGE: You told Ralph about that.

ISABEL: And has held down a job in a pharmacy all these years. . . .

GEORGE: Wonderful. I didn't expect to marry a girl in love with her father.

ISABEL: George Haverstick, you are truly a monster!

(*The phone rings.*
(*She snatches it up.*)

What?—DAD! OH, PRECIOUS DADDY!

(*She bursts into violent tears.*)

Can't talk, can't talk, can't talk, can't talk, *can't—talk!*

RALPH: Honey, gi' me the phone!

(*She surrenders it to him.*)

Hello? Hi, Pop, merry Christmas. No, this isn't George, this is a buddy of his. Isabel wants to talk to you to tell you how happy she is, but she just broke up with emotion. You know how it is, don't you, Pop? Newlyweds? They're naturally full of emotion. They got to go through a little period of adjustment between them.——Fine, yes, she's fine. She'll talk to you soon as she blows her nose. Hey, honey? Your daddy wants to talk to you.

(*She takes the phone, then bursts into violent sobbing again, covering her mouth and handing the phone back to Ralph.*)

Pop? I'll have to talk for her. She's all shook up.

(*He forces the phone back into Isabel's hand.*)

ISABEL (*choked*): Dad?

(*She bawls again, covering the mouthpiece. Ralph takes the phone back from her.*)

RALPH: Pop? Just talk to her, Pop. She's too shook up to talk back.

(*He forces the phone into her hands again.*)

ISABEL: Dad? How are you, Daddy? Are you? That's wonderful, Daddy. Oh, I'm fine, too. I got married yesterday. Yesterday . . . How is Mom? Just the same? Daddy? I may be seeing you soon. Yes. You know I gave up my nursing job at Barnes when I married and so I have lots of free time and I might just suddenly pop in on you—*tomorrow!* ——I love you and miss you so much! Good-by, Merry Christmas, Daddy!

(*She hangs up blindly and goes over to the Christmas tree.*)

I think it's awful your little boy's missing his Christmas. Such a wonderful Christmas. A choo-choo train with depot and tunnel, cowboy outfit, chemical set and a set of alphabet blocks. . . .

GEORGE: He knows what he got for his kid, you don't have to tell him.

(*There is a pause.*)

ISABEL: Well, now, I feel better, after talking to Daddy.

GEORGE: Does it make you feel uplifted, spiritually?

ISABEL: I feel less lonely. That's all.

GEORGE: I wonder if it would have that effect on me if I called my daddy or mama in Amarillo? That's in Texas, too. Maybe I'd feel less lonely. Huh, Little Bit?

(*She starts out.*)

Just wait a minute. I want to tell you something. In my thirty-four years I've been with a fair share of women and you are the first, you are the first of the lot, that has found me repulsive.

ISABEL: I don't find you "repulsive," not even your vanity, George, silly but not repulsive.

RALPH: Hey, now, you all quit this.

GEORGE: Can you stand there and tell me you find me attractive?

ISABEL: I'm afraid I can't, at this moment.

GEORGE: Well, goddam it, what in hell did you marry me faw?

ISABEL: Mr. Bates, your animal is standing by the door as as if it wants out. Shall I let it out for you?

RALPH: You two are just goin' through this adjustment period that all young couples go through.

ISABEL: Such a sweet animal! What is this animal's name?

GEORGE: The animal is a dog.

ISABEL: I know it's a dog.

GEORGE: Then why don't you call it a dog!

RALPH: Better put 'er lead on 'er. Her name is Bess.

ISABEL: Shall we take a walk, Bessie? Huh? A nice little run in the snow. See! She does want out. Oh! My coat. . . .

RALPH: Here, put on this one, honey.

(*He takes the beaver coat out of the Christmas box under the tree.*)

ISABEL: Oh, what beautiful sheared beaver! It's your wife's Christmas present?

RALPH: It was but it ain't no more.

ISABEL: How soft! Now I know that you love her. You couldn't feel the softness of this fur and not know it was bought as a present for someone you love.

RALPH: Put it on. It's yours. A wedding present to you.

ISABEL: Oh, no I—

RALPH: WILL YOU PLEASE PUT IT ON YUH?

ISABEL: I guess the snow won't hurt it. Come on, Bessie, that's a good lady, come on. . . .

(*She goes out.*)

GEORGE: I know of *two* animals that want out and one of them ain't no dawg!

ISABEL (*returning*): I heard you say that!

GEORGE: Well, good.

ISABEL: If you want out of our marriage, a divorce isn't necessary. We can just get an annulment! So maybe last night was fortunate after all!

(*She stares at him a moment and then goes back out with the dog. As they leave, the dog is barking at something outside.*

(*George comes up beside Ralph and rests an affectionate arm on his shoulders.*

(*The tempo now becomes very fast.*)

RALPH: You old Texas jack rabbit!

GEORGE: You tail-gunner son of a— How you feel?
RALPH: I feel fine!

(*They chuckle shyly together. Then:*
(*They catch each other in an affectionate bear hug.*)

GEORGE: How much money you got?
RALPH: Why?
GEORGE: Remember how we talked about going into something together when we got out of the service? Well, we're out of the service. How much money do you think you can raise?
RALPH: What are *your* assets, Buddy?
GEORGE: I've saved five hundred dollars and can get a thousand for that '52 Caddy.
RALPH: You can't go into no business on as little as that.
GEORGE: You're selling out this house and everything in it, ain't you?
RALPH: I'd have to split it with Dorothea, I reckon.
GEORGE: Look. Let's cut out tomorrow. Let's go to Texas together. We can swing the financing to pick up a piece of ranchland near San Antone and raise us a herd of fine cattle.
RALPH: Why San Antone?
GEORGE: I said near it. It's a beautiful town. A winding river goes through it.
RALPH: Uh-huh. You mentioned "swing the financing." How did you—visualize—that?
GEORGE: Noticed my car out there?
RALPH: That funeral limousine?
GEORGE: We cut out of here tomorrow bright and early and drive straight through to West Texas. In West Texas we git us a colored boy, put a showfer's cap on him an' set him back of the wheel. He drives us up in front of the biggest San Antone bank and there we demand an immediate interview with the president of it. My folks staked out West Texas. The name of the first George Haverstick in West Texas is engraved on the memorial tablet to the Alamo heroes in San Antone! I'm not snowin' you, man! An' they's no better credit card in West Texas than an ancestor's name on that memorial tablet. We will arrive at lunch time an'—invite

this bank executive to lunch at the San Antone country club to which I can git us a guest card an' befo' we're in sight of the golf links the financing deal will be swung!

RALPH: Man, a bank president has rode in a awful lot of funeral processions. It's almost one of his main professional duties. He's rode in too many funeral limousines not to know when he's in one. And ain't you afraid that he might, well—notice your shakes?

GEORGE: This little tremor would disappear completely the moment I crossed into Texas!

RALPH: I hope so, man, permanently and completely, but—

GEORGE: Go on. Tear down the project!

RALPH: There's no Ralph Bates, first, second, third, fourth or fifth on that memorial tablet to those—Alamo heroes.

GEORGE: Haven't you blazoned your name in the memory of two wars?

RALPH: Who remembers two wars? Or even one, after some years. There's a great public amnesia about a former war hero.

(*He goes reflectively to the front door.*)

GEORGE: Where you goin'?

RALPH: I'm goin' out to think in this cool night air.

(*He exits onto the paved terrace, switching off the interior lights. George follows gravely. Ralph stoops to light up a string of colored bulbs that cover the arched entrance to carport.*

(*It casts a dim rainbow glow on the terrace. Shadowy flakes of snow drift through it.*)

Why San Antone? Why cattle? Why not electric equipment?

GEORGE: I know San Antone and cattle!

RALPH: And I know electric equipment.

GEORGE: Yes, you can turn on a set of little Christmas tree lights.

RALPH: I don't want to be your ranch hand!

GEORGE: We'd buy in *equal.*

RALPH: How? One minute you say you'll liquidate all your assets that only appear to be an old funeral car, the next you say we'll drive a bank president out in this funeral car, and you want me to put up all that I realize on the sale of this property here? Your sense of equity is very unequal, and shit-fire anyhow, even if I sell this property, by remote control, from Hong Kong, and Dotty's folks would sure in hell block the transaction—well, look at the cracks in this stucco, y'know how they got there? This Goddam High Point suburb—*listen!*—happens to be built over a great big underground cavern into which it is *sinking*!

GEORGE: *Sinking?*

RALPH: I'm not snowing you, man, this whole community here is gradually sinking, inch by inch by year, into this subterranean cavern and the property owners and the real-estate promoters are in collusion to keep this secret about it: so we can sell out to the next bunch of suckers: DISGUSTING!

GEORGE: Built over a—

RALPH: *Cavern: yes!—a big subterranean cavern*, but so is *your* project, not to mention your *marriage. Cattle!—Cattle?*

GEORGE: The Texas Longhorn isn't just cattle, it's a—dignified beast.

RALPH: Did you say Texas Longhorn? Son, the Texas Longhorn is not only dignified, it is *obsolete.*

GEORGE: Historical, yeah, like the Haversticks of West Texas.

RALPH: The Haversticks of West Texas are not yet obsolete, are they?

GEORGE: I am the last one of 'em an' the prospects of another don't look bright at this moment. But the Texas Longhorn—

(*He exhales.*)

—compared to modern beef cattle such as your Hereford or your Black Angus—it has no carcass value.

RALPH: Well, in that case, why don't you *breed* the Black Angus or the—

GEORGE: I anticipated that question.

RALPH: I hope you're prepared with some answer. . . .

GEORGE (*draws on cigarette and flips it away*): Le' me put it this way. How would you like to breed a herd of noble cattle, a herd that stood for the frontier days of this country! —an' ride to the depot one mawnin' in your station wagon, the name of your ranch stamped on it, to watch these great, dignified beasts being herded onto a string of flatcars, penned in and hauled off to K City packin' houses, Chicago slaughterhouses, the shockin' atrocities which cannot even be thought about without a shudder!—an' wave 'em good-by as if they was off for a mother-lovin' church picnic?

RALPH: It's it's a—heart-breakin' pitcher!

(*He chuckles.*)

But I do love a good steak, ha ha! A prime-cut sirloin, however— What would you want to breed this noble herd for? For *kicks*, for—?

GEORGE: *You* got TV in there, ain't you? Turn on your TV any late afternoon or early evenin' and what do you get—beside the commercials, I mean? A goddam Western, on film. Y'know what I see, outside the camera range? A big painted sign that says: "Haverstick-Bates Ranch"—or "Bates-Haverstick," you can have top billing!—"The Last Stand of the Texas Longhorn, a Dignified Beast! We breed cattle for TV Westerns." We breed us some buffalo, too. The buffalo is also a dignified beast, almost extinct, only thirty thousand head of the buffalo left in this land. We'll increase that number by a sizable fraction. Hell, we could double that number befo' we—

RALPH: Hang up our boots an' saddles under the—dignified sky of West Texas?

GEORGE (*with feeling*): There *is* dignity in that sky! There's dignity in the agrarian, the pastoral—way of—existence! A dignity too long lost out of the—American dream—

(*He is shaking a good deal with emotion.*)

—as it used to be in the West Texas–Haverstick days. . . .

RALPH: But I want to be dignified, too.

GEORGE: Human dignity's what I'm—

RALPH: I don't want to be caught short by a Texas Longhorn while crossing a pasture one mawnin' in West Texas! Ha ha ha. Naw, I don't want to catch me an ass full of Texas Longhorns before I can jump a fence rail out of that West Texas pasture. I—

GEORGE: SHUT UP! WILL YUH? YOU TV WATCHIN', CANNED-BEER DRINKIN', SPANISH-SUBURBAN-STUCCO-TYPE SON OF— Y'KNOW I THINK BEER IS DOPED? DOPED? I THINK THEY DOPE IT TO CREATE A NATIONAL TOLERANCE OF THE TV COMMERCIAL! No— No— I'm sorry I come through Memphis. . . .

(*He moves away, sadly.*)

I cherished a memory of you—

(*Carolers are heard from a distance.*)

—idolized an old picture of which I was suddenly faced with a, with a—*goddam travesty* of it!—When you opened the door and I was confronted with a—DEFEATED! MIDDLE-AGED! NEGATIVE! LOST!—poor bastard . . .

RALPH: What do you think I saw when I opened that door? A ghostly apparition!

GEORGE: ME?

RALPH: A young man I used to know with an old man's affliction: the palsy!

GEORGE: Thanks!—I appreciate that.

(*Next door the Carolers sing: "God Rest Ye Merry, Gentlemen, May Nothing Ye Dismay!"*)

Oh, man, oh brother, I sure do appreciate that!

(*He sits down quickly, shaking fiercely, in a metal porch chair, turning it away from Ralph to face the audience. Ralph is immediately and truly contrite.*)

Yeah. In addition to those other changes I mentioned in you, you've now exposed another which is the worst of the bunch. You've turned *vicious*!

RALPH: Aw, now—

GEORGE: Yeah, yeah, bitter and vicious! To ridicule an affliction like *mine*, like *this*, is vicious, *vicious*!

(*He holds up his shaky hand. Ralph reaches his hand out to take it but doesn't. Instead he drops his hand on George's shoulder.*)

Take that mother-grabbin' hand off my shoulder or I'll break it off you!

RALPH: You ridiculed *my* afflictions.
GEORGE: What afflictions?
RALPH: My life has been an affliction.

(*He says this without self-pity, simply as a matter of fact.*)

GEORGE: Now don't make me cry into this can of Budweiser with that sad, sad story of your childhood in that home for illegitimate orphans.
RALPH: *Foundlings!* Home. I was not illegitimate.
GEORGE: Foundlings are illegitimate.
RALPH: Not—*necessarily—always* . . .

(*He says this with a humility that might be touching to anyone less absorbed in his own problems than George. Ralph looks up at the drift of snow from the dark.*)

No, I meant to live a life in a Spanish-type stucco cottage in a—high point over a cavern, that is an affliction for someone that wanted and dreamed of—*oh, I wish I could be the first man in a moon rocket!* No, not the moon, but Mars, Venus! Hell, I'd like to be transported and transplanted to colonize and fertilize, to be the Adam on a—star in a different *galaxy*, yeah, that far away even!—it's wonderful knowing that such a thing is no longer inconceivable, huh?
GEORGE: You're talking out of character. You're a dedicated conformist, the most earthbound earth man on earth.
RALPH: If you think that about me, you never known me.
GEORGE (*starts off the terrace*): I'm going walking, alone!

(*He stops abruptly.*)

Naw, if she sees me walking, she'll think I'm out looking for her.
RALPH: Goddam it, why don't you? Intercept her and don't say a word, just stick your hand inside that beaver-skin coat I give her and apply a little soft pressure to her—solar plexus—putting your other arm around her waist, and bring her back here, gently. . . .
GEORGE: That's what *you* want to do. Go on, *you* intercept her! And bring her back here gently!
RALPH: O.K., I *would* like to do it. But do you think I'd *do* it?

GEORGE: Can you honestly say you wouldn't put the make on her if you thought she'd give in?

RALPH: Nope! I wouldn't do it. And if you don't believe me, git back in that funeral hack and drive to West Texas in it, you—*legitimate* bastard.

GEORGE: Nope, I don't think you would. You're too much of a square.

RALPH: *There's her! There she is!*

GEORGE: Where?

RALPH: Corner. Why's she turning around? She must be lost, go get her. Look. She's joining the carolers!

GEORGE: Good, let her stay with them, and sing! Carols!

RALPH: Naw, I better go get her.

GEORGE: Go and get your *own* wife: leave mine alone!

(*Ralph puts his arm around George's shoulder.*)

And I told you to keep your rutten hand off my shoulder.

RALPH: Break it off me.

GEORGE: What I mean is, the point is—you *chose* your afflictions! Married into them. Mine I didn't choose! It just come on me, mysteriously: my shakes. You wouldn't even be interested in the awful implications of an affliction like mine.

(*He holds up his shaking hand.*)

RALPH: Sure, I'm interested in it, but—

GEORGE: S'pose it never lets up? This thing they can't treat or even find the cause of! S'pose I shake all my life like, like — dice in a crap shooter's fist?—Huh?—I mean at all moments of tension, all times of crisis, I shake! . . . Huh? And there's other aspects to it beside the career side. It could affect my love life. Huh? I could start shaking so hard when I started to make out with a girl that I couldn't do it. You know? Couldn't make the scene with her. . . .

(*There is a slight pause.*)

RALPH: Aw. Was that it?

GEORGE: Was what what?

RALPH: Was that the trouble at the Old Man River Motel, last night, you were scared of impotence with her? Was that the problem?

GEORGE: I don't have that problem. I *never* had that problem.
RALPH: No?
GEORGE: *No!*

(*Tense pause.*)

WHY? Do *you* have that problem?
RALPH: Sometimes. I wasn't excited enough by Dotty to satisfy her, sometimes. . . .
GEORGE: The thought of her old man's money couldn't always excite you?
RALPH: Nope, it couldn't always, that's the truth.

(*He switches off the lights, senselessly, and switches them back on again.*)

Poor ole Dotty. She's got so she always wants it and when I can't give it to her I feel guilty, guilty. . . .

(*He turns the Christmas lights off again, turns them back on again.*)

GEORGE: Well, you know *me.* An Eveready battery, built-in in me.
RALPH (*turning to him with a slow, gentle smile*): Yeah, I understand, son.
GEORGE: *Don't be so damned understanding!*
RALPH: Well, there she goes—Mrs. George Haverstick the Fifth. Look. She's going up to the wrong Spanish-type stucco cottage, there's five almost identical ones in this block.
GEORGE: Don't your dawg know where it lives?
RALPH: Aw, it's a dignified beast. A constant Frigidaire pointer. Points at the Westinghouse Frij an' whines for a handout whenever you enter the kitchen. Knows everyone on the block an' pays calls like a new preacher wherever he thinks—

(*Whistles at dog*)

—he might be offered a—

(*Whistles*)

—handout.

(*Voices down the block, hearty, drunken.*)

You better go git your wife. That Spanish-type stucco cottage is occupied by a bachelor decorator and you know how they destroy wimmen. . . . He is running a sort of a unofficial USO at his house. Service men congregate there.

GEORGE: HAH!

(*He is amused by the picture.*)

RALPH: I got to climb back in a back window because you shut this door and I had put the catch on it.

(*He crosses out the door to the carport as George gazes gravely off.*

(*The Carolers are closer. They go into "God Rest Ye Merry, Gentlemen" again.*

(*George is not inclined to be merry. He glares into the starless air.*

(*In the bedroom, a windowpane is smashed and Ralph's arm reaches through, his fingers groping for the window latch. He finds it, gets the window up and clambers through with some muttered invectives against the hostility of the inanimate objects of the world. As soon as he enters the interior, light and sound inside are brought up. Oddly enough, a TV Western is in progress, approaching the climax of an Indian attack or a cattle stampede. It catches Ralph's attention. He turns gravely to the TV set, for the moment forgetting George outside. Gunfire subsides and the dialogue is brought up loud:*)

DIALOGUE

—Save your ammunition, they'll come back.

—HOW LONG HAVE WE GOT?

—Till sundown. They'll hit us again after dark.

—Let's make a run for it now!

—We'll have to abandon the wagons if we make a run for it. The Rio Grande is at least five miles south of here.

—Mount the women, one woman behind each man on the hawses, unhitch the hawses! Then stampede the cattle. That'll give us a cover while we make our break.

—What is our chances, you think?

—You want a *honest* answer or a *comforting* answer?

—Give me the honest answer.

—The comforting answer would have been fifty-fifty: I'll leave you to imagine the honest answer.

—Rosemary? Come here, a minute. Take this pistol. There's five shots in it. Save the fifth shot for yourself. Now git on this hawss behind me.

—Oh, Buck! I'm so scared!

—*Git up!* O.K. sweetheart?

—Yes!

—Hold onto me tight. Dusty, when I count ten, start the cattle stampede.

(*He starts counting, slowly.*)

GEORGE (*to himself as he paces the terrace*): Now I don't even want her. If she asked me for it, I wouldn't give it to her, the way I feel now.

(*Sneezes.*)

Catchin' a cold out here! What's he doing in there, the motherless bastard? BATES! REMEMBER ME?

RALPH (*opening the door*): I thought you'd gone faw your wife.

(*Ralph chuckles and holds the front door open as George withdraws his head from the window and reappears a moment later on the terrace.*

(*Ralph lets him in.*)

GEORGE: Will you look at that? A Western on Christmas eve, even! It's a goddam NATIONAL OBSESSIONAL.

RALPH: Yep, a national homesickness in the American heart for the old wild frontiers with the yelping redskins and the covered wagons on fire and—

GEORGE: Will you look at those miserable shorthorn cattle! Those cows, in this corny Western?

(*They both face the TV. There is a pause.*)

RALPH: Yep—an undignified beast. Man? Buddy? I don't have too much confidence in the project of the Dignified West Texas Longhorn Ranch, even now, but I will go along with you. Don't ask me why. I couldn't tell you why, but I will go along with you. Want to shake on it, Buddy?

GEORGE: That champagne ought to be cold now, let's break out that champagne now.

RALPH: It'll be still colder when you've picked up your wife.

GEORGE: I told you my policy, don't interfere with it, huh?

RALPH: Women are vulnerable creatures.

GEORGE: So's a man.

RALPH (*crosses to the kitchenette door*): I'll open up the champagne while you pick up your wife.

GEORGE: Ralpho? Man?

RALPH: Huh?

GEORGE: Now I know why I come here. You're a *decent! square!*

(*The kitchen door swings closed on them; Carolers are singing out front. After a moment Isabel appears before the house with the dog.*

(*A Lady Caroler appears on the terrace with a collection plate.*)

ISABEL: Oh—I'm afraid I don't have any money to give you, but—

(*She knocks at the door.*)

Wait!—till they answer the door, I—

(*Raucous voices are heard within.*)

—Some people regard the celebration of the birthday of Jesus as a, as a—sort of a—occasion, excuse for!—just getting drunk and—*disgusting!* I'll probably have to go round the back to get in. . . .

(*Great howls of hilarity have been coming from the back of the cottage, drowning out Isabel's efforts to draw attention to the front door.*)

I'm very sorry, I just don't have any money.

(*The Caroler accepts this in good grace and leaves.*

(*Isabel goes around through the carport. A few seconds later George, in a state of Wild West exuberance, comes charging out of the kitchen with the champagne bottle, shouting:*)

GEORGE: POWDER RIVER, POWWWWW-der RIV-errrr!—a mile wide and—

RALPH: TWO INCHES DEEP!

(*He follows him out as Isabel's head appears through the open window in the dim bedroom: she lifts the dog through and hoists herself over the sill.*)

GEORGE: Git me a pitcher with ice and two cans of that Ballantine's ale and I will make us BLACK VELVET!

RALPH: Huh?

GEORGE: Man, you know Black Velvet!

(*He is back in the kitchen.*)

I made it that time in Hong Kong when we had those girls from the—

(*Ralph has gone in behind him. The door swings shut as Isabel picks up the bedside phone in the bedroom.*)

ISABEL: Operator? I want a cab right away, it's an *emergency, yaiss*!

(*Slight pause.*)

Yellow Cab? Checkered! Well, please send a cab right away to— Oh, my goodness, I can't tell you the address, oh, I'll—I'll find out the address and I'll call you right back, right away. . . .

(*She hangs up with a little stricken cry, followed by convulsive sobs that she stifles forcibly. On the bed, in the pink-shaded lamplight, she looks like a little girl making a first discovery of life's sorrow. Instinctively she reaches out for the Infant of Prague; at the same time, the Carolers start singing below the terrace: "I Wonder as I Wander." This is a sentimental moment, but not "sticky."*)

Little Boy Jesus, so lonesome on your birthday. I know how you feel, *exactly!*—

(*She clasps the infant to her breast, tenderly.*)

—just exactly, because I feel the same way. . . .

Dim Out

INTERMISSION

ACT THREE

No time lapse.

The men return with an open, foaming bottle of champagne, and pass it back and forth between them before the fireplace, not noticing that the dog has returned or suspecting Isabel's presence in the bedroom.

GEORGE: I put them in five categories. Those that worship it, those that love it, those that just like it, those that don't like it, those that just tolerate it, those that *don't* tolerate it, those that can't stand it, and, finally, those that not only can't stand it but want to cut it off you.

RALPH (*following him with glasses, chuckling*): That's more than five categories.

GEORGE: How many did I name?

RALPH: I don't know. I lost count.

GEORGE: Well, you know what I mean. And I have married into that last category. What scares me is that she has had hospital training and is probably able to do a pretty good cutting job. You know what I mean?

RALPH: Ha ha, yeah. Wel-l-l. . . .

(*He sets the glasses down and takes the bottle from George. The little parlor is flickering with firelight.*)

GEORGE: Which class did you marry into? Into the same category?

RALPH: No. She got to like it. More than I did even.

GEORGE: Now you're braggin'.

RALPH: Love is a very difficult—occupation. You got to work at it, man. It ain't a thing every Tom, Dick and Harry has got a true aptitude for. Y'know what I mean? Not every Tom, Dick or Harry understands how to use it. It's not a—offensive weapon. It shouldn't be used like one. Too many guys, they use it like a offensive weapon to beat down a woman with. All right. That rouses resistance. Because a woman has pride, even a woman has pride and resents being raped, and most love-making is rape with these self-regarded—experts! That come downstairs yelling, "Oh, man, Oh, brother," and hitching their belts up like they'd accomplished something.

GEORGE (*getting the allusion and resentful*): You mean me?

RALPH: Naw, naw, will yuh listen a minute? I've got ideas on this subject.

GEORGE: A self-regarded expert!

RALPH: You know Goddam right I'm an expert. I know I never had your good looks but made out better.

GEORGE: One man's opinion!

RALPH: Look! Lissen! You got to use—TENDERNESS!—with it, not roughness like raping, snatch-and-grab roughness but true tenderness with it or—

GEORGE: O.K., build yourself up! If that's what you need to!

RALPH: Naw, now, lissen! You know I know what I'm sayin'!

GEORGE: Sure, self-regarded expert!

(*They are both pretty high now.*)

RALPH: I know what went wrong last night at that Cape Girardeau motel as well as if I had seen it all on TV!

GEORGE: What went wrong is that I found myself hitched up with a woman in the "cut-it-off" category!

(*Isabel is listening to all this in the bedroom. She stands up and sits down, stands up and sits down, barely able to keep from shouting something.*)

RALPH: Aw, naw, aw, naw. I will tell you what happened. Drink your champagne. What happened, man, is this! You didn't appreciate the natural need for using some tenderness with it. Lacking confidence with it, you wanted to hit her, smash her, clobber her with it. You've got violence in you! That's what made you such a good fighter pilot, the best there was! Sexual violence, that's what gives you the shakes, that's what makes you unstable. That's what made you just sit on the straw mats with the Tokyo dolls, drinking sake with them, teaching them English till it was time to come downstairs and holler, "Oh, man, oh, brother" like you had laid them to waste!

(*There is a slight pause. George is sweating, flushed.*)

GEORGE: Who in hell ever told you I—

RALPH: I heard it directly from them. You just sat up there drinkin' sake with 'em an' teachin' 'em English, and then you'd come down shouting, "Oh, man, oh, brother!" like you had laid 'em to waste.

GEORGE: Which of them told you this story?

RALPH: *Which* of them? ALL! EV'RY ONE!

(*They pause. Isabel sits down on the bed again, raises her hands to either side of her face, slowly shaking her head with a gradual comprehension.*)

GEORGE: Man, at this moment I'd like to bust your face in!

RALPH: I'm tryin' to help you. Don't you know that I am tryin' t' help you?

(*A pause. They look away from each other in solemn reverie for some moments. Isabel rises again from the bed but still doesn't move. After some moments she sits back down. She is crying now.*)

RALPH (*continuing gently*): You have got this problem.

GEORGE: In Tokyo I never told you—

RALPH: What?

GEORGE: I was choosy. I had a girl on the side. I mean a nice one. One that I wanted to keep to myself, strictly. I didn't want to expose her to a bunch of—

RALPH: Aw, now, man, you don't have to start fabricating some kind of a *Sayonara* fantasy like this!

GEORGE: How about Big Springs, Texas?

RALPH: What about Big Springs, Texas, besides being boring, I mean, what *else* about it?

GEORGE: Plenty. I fixed you up there. You never got nowhere in Big Springs, Texas, till I opened it up for you.

RALPH: Baby, don't be sore.

GEORGE: Sore, I'm not sore. You've done your damndest to make me feel like a phony, but I'm not sore. *You're* sore. Not *me*. *I'm* not sore.

RALPH: You sure are shaking.

GEORGE: Yeah, well, I got this tremor. . . . Jesus, my goddam voice is got the shakes too! But you know it's the truth, in Big Springs, Texas, we had the best damn time you ever had in your life, and I broke the ice there, for you.

RALPH: I don't deny that women naturally like you. Everybody likes you! Don't you know that? People never lowrate you! Don't you know that? I like you. That's for sure. But I hate to see you shaking because of—

GEORGE (*cutting in*): Look! We're both free now. Like two birds. You're gonna cut out of this High Point over a Cavern. And we'll buy us a piece of ranchland near San Antone and both of us—

RALPH: Yeah, yeah, let's go back to what we wuh tawkin' about. *Tenderness.* With a *woman.*

GEORGE: I don't want to hear a goddam lecture from you about such a thing as that when here you are, night before Christmas, with just a cocker spaniel and presents under a tree, with no one to *take* them from you!

RALPH (*abruptly*): *Hey!*

GEORGE: *Huh?*

RALPH: Th' *dawg* is back. How *come?*

GEORGE: The dawg come *back*, tha's all. . . .

(*Isabel comes out of the bedroom in coat and hat.*)

ISABEL: Yes, I brought the dog back.

(*A pause, rather long.*)

RALPH: We, uh, we—saw you going up to the wrong—Spanish-type cottage. . . .

ISABEL: I haven't discovered the *right* one, Mr. Bates.

RALPH: I ain't discovered it either.

GEORGE: What kept you so long in the wrong one?

ISABEL: They invited me in and made me sit down to a lovely buffet supper while they looked up the High Point Bates in the phone book.

(*She pauses.*)

I heard your very enlightening conversation from the bedroom. You're a pair of small boys. Boasting, bragging, showing off to each other. . . . I want to call a cab. I'm going downtown, George.

(*He crosses unsteadily to the phone, lifts it and hands it to her with an effort at stateliness.*)

Thank you.

(*To Ralph*)

Do you know the cab number?

GEORGE: Whacha want, yellow, checkered or what? I'll git it for yuh!

RALPH: Put down th' phone.

ISABEL: I'll get one.

(*She dials the operator.*)

GEORGE: Leave her alone. Let her go downtown. She's free to.

(*Ralph takes the phone from her and puts it back in the cradle.*)

ISABEL: Do I have to walk?

(*She goes to the door, opens it and starts out.*)

There's a car in front of your house, Mr. Bates.

RALPH (*rising with sudden energy and rushing to the door*): YEP! IT'S HER OLD MAN'S CAR! Dorothea's papa, my ex-boss!

ISABEL: Perhaps he'll be kind enough to—

RALPH: Go back in, little lady! Stay in the bedroom till I git through this! Then I'll drive you downtown if you're still determined to go.

(*He has drawn her back in the house.*)

SET DOWN, GEORGE! For Chrissakes. Little lady, will you please wait in the bedroom till I get through this hassle with her old man?

ISABEL: It's all so ridiculous. Yes, all right, I will, but please don't forget your promise to take me downtown right afterwards, Mr. Bates!

(*She returns to the bedroom with dignity. Mr. and Mrs. McGillicuddy appear before the house.*
(*They are a pair of old bulls.*)

MRS. MCGILLICUDDY: The first thing to discuss is their joint savings account.

(*Mr. McGillicuddy hammers the knocker on the door.*)

I wish you'd listened to me an' brought your lawyer.

MR. MCGILLICUDDY: I can handle that boy. You keep your mouth out of it. Just collect the silver and china and let me handle the talk.

(*He knocks again, violently, dislodging the Christmas wreath attached to the knocker. Mrs. McGillicuddy picks it up.*)

Now what are you gonna do with that Christmas wreath? You gonna crown him with it?

(*Ralph opens the door.*)

RALPH: Well, Mr. and Mrs. *Mac*!

MR. MCGILLICUDDY (*handing him the wreath*): This come off your knocker.

RALPH: Ha, ha, what a surprise!

MRS. MCGILLICUDDY: We've come to pick up some things of Dorothea's.

RALPH: That's O.K. Take out anything that's hers, but don't touch nothing that belongs to us both.

MRS. MCGILLICUDDY: We've come with a list of things that belong exclusively to Dorothea!

MR. MCGILLICUDDY: Is it true that you called up Emory Sparks at the place you quit your job at and asked him to come over here tonight and make you a cash-on-the-barrel offer for everything in this house?

RALPH: Nope.

MR. MCGILLICUDDY: Then how come Emory's fiancée called up Dorothea to give her that information?

MRS. MCGILLICUDDY (*impatiently*): Come on in here, Susie.

(*Susie is the colored maid. She enters with a large laundry basket.*)

Is that the biggest basket you could find?

SUSIE: Yes, ma'am, it's the laundry basket.

MRS. MCGILLICUDDY: It isn't the large one. You'll have to make several trips up and down those slippery front steps with that little basket.

MR. MCGILLICUDDY: Haven't you got any ice-cream salt?

RALPH: You want to make some ice cream?

MR. MCGILLICUDDY: Susie, before you go down those steps with my daughter's china, you'd better collect some clinkers out of the furnace in the basement.

RALPH: How is she going to get clinkers out of an oil-burning furnace?

MR. MCGILLICUDDY: Oh, that's right. You burn oil. I forgot about that. Well, Susie, you better tote the basket of china down the terrace. Don't try to make the steps with it.

RALPH: She's not takin' no china out of this house.

MR. MCGILLICUDDY: You're not going to sell a goddam thing of my daughter's in this house!

RALPH: All I done was call up Emory Sparks because he's about to get married and invited him over to take a look at this place because I've got to unload it and I can't wait a couple of months to—

MR. MCGILLICUDDY: Now, hold on a minute, war hero!

RALPH: I don't like the way you always call me war hero!

MR. MCGILLICUDDY: *Why?* Ain't that what you *were*?

GEORGE: You're goddam right he was! I flown over seventy bombing missions with this boy in Korea and before that in the—

MR. MCGILLICUDDY: Yes, yes, yes, I know it backwards and forwards, and I know who you are. You are Haverstick, ain't you?

GEORGE: Yeah, you got my name right.

MR. MCGILLICUDDY: Well, Haverstick, the war's over and you two bombers are grounded. Now, Susie, go in the kitchen and get that Mixmaster and that new Rotisserie out in the basket while I collect the silver in that sideboard in there.

RALPH: Susie, don't go in my kitchen. You want to be arrested for trespassing, Susie?

MRS. MCGILLICUDDY: Stuart, you'd better call that policeman in here.

RALPH: NO KIDDING!

MRS. MCGILLICUDDY: We anticipated that you'd make trouble.

RALPH: How does Dorothea feel about you all doing this?

MR. MCGILLICUDDY (*at the door*): OFFICER!—He's coming.

RALPH: How does Dotty feel? What is her attitude toward this kind of—

(*He is trembling. His voice chokes. George rises and puts a hand on Ralph's shoulder as a young Police Officer enters looking embarrassed.*)

MR. MCGILLICUDDY: You know the situation, Lieutenant. We have to remove my daughter's valuables from the house because we've been tipped off this man here, Ralph Bates, is intending to make a quick cash sale of everything in the house and skip out of Memphis tomorrow.

RALPH: THAT'S A GODDAM LIE! WHO TOLD YOU THAT?

MRS. MCGILLICUDDY: Emory Sparks' fiancée is Dorothea's good friend! That's how we got the warning. She called to enquire if Dorothea was serious about this matter. How did Dotty feel, how did she FEEL? I'll tell you! SICK AT HER STOMACH! VIOLENTLY SICK AT HER STOMACH.

RALPH: I should think so, goddam it. I should THINK so! She's got many a fault she got from you two, but, hell, she'd never agree to a piece of cheapness like this any more'n she'd believe that story about me callin'—

MR. MCGILLICUDDY: How could there be any possible doubt about it when Emory Sparks' fiancée—

RALPH: Will you allow me to speak? I did call Emory Sparks and told him my wife had quit me because I had quit my job, and I merely suggested that he come over and kind of look over the stuff here and see if any of all this goddam electric equipment and so forth would be of any use to him since it isn't to me and since I got to have some financial—

(*He becomes suddenly speechless and breathless. George embraces his shoulder.*)

GEORGE: Now, now, son, this is going to work out. Don't blow a gasket over it.

RALPH: I think you folks had better consider some legal angles of what you're up to here.

MR. MCGILLICUDDY (*puffing, red in the face*): Aw, there's no legal angle about it that I don't know, and if there was, I could cope with that, too. I'm prepared to cope with that trouble. You got no goddam position in this town but what I give you!

RALPH: *Oh!* Uh-huh—

(*Mrs. McGillicuddy has gone to the bedroom and discovered Isabel in it.*)

MRS. MCGILLICUDDY: *Stuart, they have a woman in Dotty's bedroom!*

RALPH: George's wife is in there.

MRS. MCGILLICUDDY: How long have you been planning this?

(*She knocks on the bedroom door.*)

Can I come in?

ISABEL: Yes, please.

(*Mrs. McGillicuddy enters the bedroom.*)

MRS. MCGILLICUDDY (*coldly*): I've come to pick up some things that belong to my daughter.

ISABEL: I told my husband we'd dropped in at the wrong time.

MRS. MCGILLICUDDY: May I ask who you are?

ISABEL: I'm Mrs. George Haverstick. You probably saw my husband in the front room.

MRS. MCGILLICUDDY: Your husband's an old friend of Ralph's, one of his wartime buddies?

ISABEL: Yes, he is, Mrs.— I didn't get your name.

MRS. MCGILLICUDDY: All I can say is "Watch out," if he's an old friend of Ralph's!

ISABEL: Why?

MRS. MCGILLICUDDY: Birds of a feather, that's all.

(*Mrs. McGillicuddy opens the closet and starts piling clothes on the bed. In the living room, Mr. McGillicuddy takes a seat in silence.*)

ISABEL: Are you sure you're doing the right thing?

MRS. MCGILLICUDDY (*calling out the door*): Susie!

SUSIE (*entering*): Yes, ma'am?

MRS. MCGILLICUDDY: Take these clothes of Miss Dotty's out to the car.

(*Susie carries out the clothes.*)

ISABEL: I think young people should be given a chance to work things out by themselves.

MRS. MCGILLICUDDY: You have no idea at all of the situation. And I'm sure you have your own problems if you have married a friend of my daughter's husband. Is he living on his war record like Ralph Bates is?

ISABEL: He has a distinguished war record and a nervous disability that was a result of seventy-two flying missions in Korea and, and—more than twice that many in—

MRS. MCGILLICUDDY: *I'm sick of hearing about past glories! Susie!*

(*Susie comes in again.*)

Now pick up all Dotty's shoes on the floor of that closet, put 'em in the bottom of the basket, put some paper over them, and then pile her little undies on top of the paper.—Then! If you still have room in the basket, collect some of the china out of the sideboard and cupboards. Be very careful with that. Don't try to carry too much at one time, Susie. That walk and those steps are a hazard.

(*There has been a prolonged silence in the front room during the scene above, which they have been listening to.*)

MR. MCGILLICUDDY (*at last*): Well, you seem to be living the life of Riley. French champagne. Who was the little girl I saw come out and go back in?

RALPH: Mrs. George Haverstick.

MR. MCGILLICUDDY: That means as much to me as if you said she was a lady from Mars.

RALPH: There's no reason why it should mean anything to you. I just answered your question.

MR. MCGILLICUDDY: Why do you feel so superior to me?

RALPH: Aw. Did you notice that?

MR. MCGILLICUDDY: From the first time I met you. You have always acted very superior to me for some unknown reason.

I'd like to know what it is. You were employed by me till you quit your job today.

RALPH: Does that mean I had to feel inferior to you, Mac?

MR. MCGILLICUDDY: You've started calling me "Mac"?

RALPH: I'm not employed by you, now.

MR. MCGILLICUDDY: If there was a war you could be a war hero again, but in a cold war I don't see how you're going to be such a hero. A cold-war hero, ha ha, is not such a hero, at least not in the newspapers.

(*Gathering confidence*)

Huh? Why don't you answer my question?

RALPH: Which, Mac?

MR. MCGILLICUDDY: Why you feel so rutten superior to me.

RALPH: Can I consider that question? For a minute?

MR. MCGILLICUDDY: Yeah, consider it, will you? I fail to see anything *special* about you, war hero!

(*He lights a cigar with jerky motions. The two younger men stare at his red, puffy face with intolerant smiles.*)

GEORGE: Let me answer for him. He feels superior to you because you're a big male cow, a spiritual male cow.

RALPH: Shut up, George. Well, Mr. Mac? Let me ask you a question. Why did you ask me to marry your daughter?

MR. MCGILLICUDDY: DID WHAT? I NEVER! Done any such thing and—

(*Mrs. McGillicuddy snorts indignantly from the open bedroom door.*)

RALPH: You mean to say you've forgotten that you suggested to me that I marry Dotty?

(*Mrs. McGillicuddy advances from the bedroom door, bearing a French porcelain clock.*)

MR. MCGILLICUDDY: I never forgotten a thing in my adult life, but I never have any such recollections as that. I do remember a conversation I held with you soon after you started to work at Regal Dairy Products an' come to my office to quit because you said you weren't gittin' paid well enough an' th' work was monotonous to you.

RALPH: That's right. Five years ago this winter.

MR. MCGILLICUDDY: I gave you a fatherly talk. I told you monotony was a part of life. And I said I had an eye on you, which I did at that time.

RALPH: How about the rest of the conversation? In which you said that Dotty was your only child, that you had no son, and Dotty was int'rested in me and if Dotty got married her husband would be the heir to your throne as owner of Regal Dairy an' its subsidiaries such as Royal Ice Cream and Monarch Cheese, huh?

MRS. MCGILLICUDDY: HANH!

RALPH: An' you hadn't long for this world because of acute diabetes and so forth and—

MRS. MCGILLICUDDY: HANH!

RALPH: And I would be shot right into your shoes when you departed this world? Well, you sure in hell lingered!

MRS. MCGILLICUDDY: ARE YOU GOING TO STAND THERE LISTENING TO THIS, STUART? I'M NOT!

MR. MCGILLICUDDY: Be still, Mama. I can talk for myself. I did discuss these things with you but how did you arrive at the idea I asked you to marry my daughter?

MRS. MCGILLICUDDY: HANH!

(*George goes to look out the window as if the scene had ceased to amuse him.*)

RALPH: What other way could it be interpreted, Mac?

(*He is no longer angry.*)

MR. MCGILLICUDDY: I offered you a splendid chance in the world which you spit on by your disrespect, your superior—!

RALPH: I respect Dorothea. Always did and still do.

MR. MCGILLICUDDY: I'm talkin' about your attitude to me.

RALPH: I know you are. That's all that you care about, not about Dorothea. You don't love Dotty. She let you down by having psychological problems that you brought on her, that you an' Mrs. Mac gave her by pushing her socially past her social endowments.

MRS. MCGILLICUDDY: WHAT DO YOU MEAN BY THAT?

RALPH: Dotty was never cut out to boost your social position in this city. Which you expected her to. You made her feel inferior all her life.

MRS. MCGILLICUDDY: *Me? Me?*

RALPH: Both of yuh. I respected her, though, and sincerely liked her and I married Dotty. Give me credit for that, and provided her with an—offspring. Maybe not much of an offspring, but an offspring, a male one, at least it started a male one. I can't help it if she's turnin' him into a sissy, I—

MRS. MCGILLICUDDY: MY GOD, STUART, HOW LONG ARE YOU GONNA STAND THERE AND LISTEN TO THIS WITHOUT—

MR. MCGILLICUDDY: *Mama, I told you to keep your mouth outa this!*

RALPH: Yeah, but I MARRIED your baby. Give me credit for that. And provided her with an—offspring!

MRS. MCGILLICUDDY: What does he mean by that? That *he* had the baby, not Dotty?

MR. MCGILLICUDDY: Mama, I told you to keep your mouth out of this.

MRS. MCGILLICUDDY: He talks like he thought he did Dotty a FAVOR!

RALPH: Now, listen. I don't want to be forced into saying unkind things about Dotty. But you all know damn well that Dotty was half a year older than me when I married that girl and if I hadn't you would have been stuck with a lonely, unmarried daughter for the rest of your lives!

MRS. MCGILLICUDDY: *Oh*, my—GOD!

MR. MCGILLICUDDY: Let him talk. I want to hear all, all, all! he has to say about Dotty.

RALPH: You're *going* to hear it, if you stay in my house! I put up a five-year battle between our marriage and your goddam hold on her! You just wouldn't release her!—although I doubt that you wanted her always unmarried.

MRS. MCGILLICUDDY: WHAT MAKES YOU THINK SHE WOULD HAVE STAYED UNMARRIED?

RALPH: The indications, past history, when I met her—

MRS. MCGILLICUDDY: This is too sickening. I can't stand it, Stuart?

MR. MCGILLICUDDY: A bum like you?

RALPH: Don't call *me* a bum!

MR. MCGILLICUDDY: What in hell else *are* you? I give you your job which you quit today without warning! Carried you in it despite your indifference to it for—for—for—five—

RALPH: Wait! Like I said. I still respect your daughter, don't want to say anything not kind about her, but let's face facts. Who else but a sucker like me, Ralph Bates, would have married a girl with no looks, a plain, homely girl that probably no one but me had ever felt anything but just—SORRY FOR!

MRS. MCGILLICUDDY: OH GOD! STUART, ARE YOU GOING TO STAND THERE AND LET HIM GO ON WITH THAT TALK?

RALPH: HOW IN HELL DO YOU FIGURE HE'S GOING TO STOP ME?

MRS. MCGILLICUDDY: OFFICER! CAN'T YOU GET THIS MAN OUT OF HERE?

OFFICER: No, ma'am. I can't arrest him.

RALPH: ARREST ME FOR WHAT, MRS. MAC?

GEORGE: That's right, arrest him for what?

MRS. MCGILLICUDDY: Stuart? Take out the silver. I don't know where Susie is. We should have come here with your lawyer as well as this—*remarkably—incompetent—policeman!*

MR. MCGILLICUDDY: Susie took out the silver.

GEORGE: Naw, she didn't. I got the goddam silver. I'm sitting on it!

(*He sits on silver, then rises and stuffs it under sofa pillow, having been discomfited by the forks.*)

MR. MCGILLICUDDY: I guess I'll have to call the Chief of Police, who's a lodge brother of mine, and get a little more police co-operation than we have gotten so far.

OFFICER: O.K., you do that, Mister.

MR. MCGILLICUDDY: He'll call you to the phone and give you exact instructions.

OFFICER: That's all right. If he gives 'em, I'll take 'em.

(*Mrs. McGillicuddy has charged back into the bedroom to collect more things.*)

RALPH: Mr. McGillicuddy, you are the worst thing any person can be: mean-minded, small-hearted, and CHEAP! Outstandingly and notoriously cheap! It was almost two months before I could *kiss* Dorothea, sincerely, after meeting her father! That's no crap. It wasn't the homeliness that threw me, it was the association she had in my mind with *you*! It wasn't till I found out she despised you as much as I did that I was able to make real love to Dotty.

MR. MCGILLICUDDY: My daughter is *crazy* about me!

RALPH: You're crazy if you *think* so!

(*Mrs. McGillicuddy comes out of the bedroom.*)

MRS. MCGILLICUDDY: All right. All of Dotty's clothes have been taken out. I think we may as well leave now.

MR. MCGILLICUDDY: How about the TV? Which I gave Dotty *last* Christmas?

RALPH: You want the TV? O.K.! Here's the TV!

(*He shoves it to the door and pulls the door open.*)

Take the TV out of here—an' git out with it!

MRS. MCGILLICUDDY: What is that under the tree? It looks like a new fur coat!

RALPH: That's right. A seven-hundred-and-forty-five-dollar sheared-beaver coat that I'd bought for Dotty for Christmas!—but which I have just now presented to Mrs. George Haverstick as her weddin' present.

MR. MCGILLICUDDY: The hell you have! How did you git hold of seven hundred and—

RALPH: From my savings account.

MR. MCGILLICUDDY: That was a *joint* account!

MRS. MCGILLICUDDY: STUART! TAKE THAT COAT! GO ON, PICK UP THAT COAT!

RALPH: By God, if he touches that coat, I'll smash him into next week, and I never hit an old man before in my life.

MRS. MCGILLICUDDY: OFFICER! PICK UP THAT COAT!

RALPH: I'll hit any man that tries to pick up that coat!

OFFICER (*putting down the phone, which he has been talking into quietly*): I talked to my chief. He gave me my instructions. He says not to take any action that might result in publicity, because of Mr. Bates having been a very well-known war hero.

MR. MCGILLICUDDY: Come on, Mama. I'll just have to refer this whole disgusting business to my lawyer tomorrow, put it all in his hands and get the necessary papers to protect our baby.

MRS. MCGILLICUDDY: I just want to say one thing more! Ralph Bates, don't you think for a moment that you are going to escape financial responsibility for the support of your child! Now come on, Stuart!—Isn't it pitiful? All that little boy's Christmas under the tree?

RALPH: Send him over tomorrow to pick it all up. That can go out of the house, the little boy's Christmas can go. . . .

(*They all leave. Isabel enters from bedroom.*)

ISABEL: Mr. Bates! I don't believe that this is what your wife wanted. I'll also bet you that she is outside in that car and if you would just stick your head out the window and call her, she would come running in here.

(*Dorothea comes onto the paved terrace and knocks at the door. Ralph does not move. She knocks again, harder and longer. He starts to rise, sits down again.*)

George, let his wife in the house.

GEORGE: Let's just keep out of this. I reckon he knows what he's doing.

(*A car honks. A Woman's Voice is heard.*)

WOMAN (*off*): Dorothea! Come back! We'll get the police!

DOROTHEA (*calling at the door*): Ralph? Ralph? It's Dotty! I want the child's Christmas things!

RALPH: HE'LL GET THEM HERE OR NOWHERE!

DOROTHEA: *I'm not going to leave here without the child's Christmas things!*—Ralph.

RALPH: *Let him come here alone tomorrow morning.*

DOROTHEA: *You can't do that to a child.*—Ralph!

(*The car honks again, long and loud.*)

RALPH (*shouting back*): Put the kid in a taxi in the morning and I'll let him in to collect his Christmas presents!

MRS. MCGILLICUDDY (*appearing behind Dorothea*): Dorothea! I will not let you humiliate yourself like this! Come away from that door!

DOROTHEA: Mama, stay in the car!

WOMAN: Your father won't wait any longer. He's started the car. He's determined to get the police.

DOROTHEA: RALPH! (*She has removed the door key from her bag.*) I'M COMING IN!

WOMAN: *Dotty, where is your pride!*

(*Dorothea enters and slams the door. The Woman rushes off, crying "Stuart!"*

(*Dorothea stares at Ralph from the door. He gazes stubbornly at the opposite wall.*)

DOROTHEA: I could tell you'd been drinkin' by your voice. Who are these people you've got staying in the house.

RALPH: Talk about the police! I could get you all arrested for illegal entry!

DOROTHEA: This is your liquor speaking, not you, Ralph.

RALPH: You have abandoned me. You got no right by law to come back into this house and make insulting remarks about my friends.

DOROTHEA: Ralph? Ralph? I know I acted—impetuously this mawnin'. . . .

RALPH: Naw, I think you made the correct decision. You realized that you had tied yourself down to a square peg in a round hole that had now popped out of the hole and consequently would be of no further use to you. You were perfectly satisfied for me to remain at that rutten little desk job, tyrannized over by inferior men, for as long as my—heart kept beating.

DOROTHEA: No, Ralph. I wasn't. MY aim for you was your aim. Independence! A business of your own!

RALPH: Not when you were *faced* with it.

DOROTHEA: You sprung it on me at the wrong moment, Ralph. Our savings account is at a very low ebb.

RALPH: Our savings account is all gone, little woman. It went on Christmas, all of it.

(*He pokes at the fire. There is a pause. The fire crackles and flickers.*)

DOROTHEA: *Mama* says you—bought me a *fur coat* for Christmas.

RALPH: Yeah, she took a look at it. Enquired the price. Wanted to take it off with her.

DOROTHEA: You wouldn't have bought me such a beautiful coat if you didn't still care for me, Ralph. You know that, don't you?

RALPH: I made a decision affecting my whole future life. I know it was a big step, but I had the courage to make it.

DOROTHEA: I've always admired your courage.

RALPH: Hah!—I break the news. You walked right out on me, Dotty, takin' my son that you've turned into a sissy. He won't want these boys' toys under that tree. What he'll want is a doll and a—*tea* set.

DOROTHEA: All of these things are a little too old for Ralph Junior but he'll be delighted with them just the same, Ralph.

(*She takes off her cloth coat.*)

I'm going to try on that wonderful-looking beaver.

RALPH: It's not going out of the house, off you or on you, Dotty.

(*She puts on the beaver-skin coat.*)

DOROTHEA: Oh, how lovely, how lovely! Ralph, it *does* prove you love me!

RALPH: It cleaned out our savings account.

DOROTHEA: Both of us have been guilty of impetuous actions. You must've been awfully lonely, inviting a pair of strangers to occupy our bedroom on Christmas Eve.

RALPH: George Haverstick is not any stranger to me. We both of us died in two wars, repeatedly died in two wars and were buried in suburbs named High Point, but his was hyphenated. H-i-hyphen-Point. Mine was spelled out but was built on a cavern for the daughter and grandchild of Mr. and Mrs. Stuart McGillicuddy. Oh, I told him something which I should have told you five years ago, Dorothea. I married you without love. I married you for—

DOROTHEA: Ralph? Please don't!

RALPH: I married you for your stingy-fisted old papa's promise to—

DOROTHEA: *Ralphie! Don't! I know!*

RALPH:—to make me his Heir Apparent! Assurances, lies! Even broad hints that he would soon kick off!

DOROTHEA: Ralph?

(*She puts her hand over his mouth, beseechingly.*)

Don't you know I know that?

RALPH: Why, you accept it? If you—

DOROTHEA: I was so—

(*She covers her face.*)

RALPH: Cut it out, have some pride!

DOROTHEA: I *do*!

RALPH: In *what*?

DOROTHEA: In *you*!

RALPH: Oh, for the love of— In me? Why, I'm telling you I'm nothin' better'n a goddam—

DOROTHEA: I know, don't tell me again. I always knew it.—I had my nose done over and my front teeth extracted to look better for you, Ralphie!

RALPH: "Ralphie!" *Shoot* . . .

(*Isabel raps discreetly at the bedroom door.*)

Huh? What is it?

ISABEL: I've made some coffee.

DOROTHEA: I *did* improve my appearance, didn't I, Ralph? It was extremely painful.

RALPH: Don't claim you done it for me! Every woman wants to improve on nature any way that she can. Yes! Of course you look better! You think you've won a *argument*?

DOROTHEA: *Me? What* argument? *No!* I've come back *crawling*!—not even embarrassed to do so!

(*Isabel comes in from the kitchenette with coffee.*)

Oh, Hello. I didn't know you were—

ISABEL: Mrs. Bates. I'm Isabel Haverstick. I took the liberty of making some coffee in your sweet little kitchen. Mrs. Bates, can I give you some coffee?

DOROTHEA: Thanks, that's awfully sweet of you, Mrs. Haverstick. It's nice of you and your husband to drop in on Ralph, but the situation between Ralph and me has changed. I guess I don't have to explain it. You see I've come home. We only have one bedroom and Ralph and I have an awful lot to talk over.

ISABEL: I understand perfectly. George and I are going to go right downtown.

DOROTHEA (*softening*): You don't have to do that. This sofa lets out to a bed and it's actually more comfortable than the beds in the bedroom. I know, because other times when we've had a falling out, less serious than this time, I have—occupied it.

(*With a little, soft, sad, embarrassed laugh.*)

Of course, I usually called Ralph in before mawnin'. . . .

ISABEL: Oh, but this is no time for strangers to be here with you!

DOROTHEA (*now really warming*): You all stay here! I insist! It's really not easy to get a hotel room downtown with so many folks coming into town for Christmas.

ISABEL: Well, if you're sure, if you're absolutely certain our presence wouldn't be inconvenient at all?—I do love this room. The fire is still burning bright!—and the Christmas tree is so—pretty.

DOROTHEA: I'll tell my mother and father, they're still outside in the car, to drive home and then we'll all have coffee together!

(*She rushes out in her beaver coat.*)

ISABEL: I like her! She's really nice!

RALPH: She came back for the fur coat.

ISABEL: I think she came back for you.

RALPH: She walked out on me this morning because I had liberated myself from a slave's situation!—and she took the kid with her.

ISABEL: You're just going through a—period of adjustment.

RALPH: We've been married six years.

ISABEL: But all that time you've been under terrible strain, hating what you were doing, and maybe taking it out on your wife, Ralph Bates.

(*Dorothea returns.*)

DOROTHEA: All right. I sent them home, much against their objections. I just slammed the car door on them.

RALPH: They comin' back with the police?

DOROTHEA: No. You know they were bluffing.

ISABEL: I think you two should have your coffee alone in your own little bedroom. We'll all get acquainted tomorrow.

DOROTHEA: Ralph?

RALPH (*sadly*): I don't know. We're living over a cavern. . . .

(*He follows Dorothea into the bedroom. It remains dimly lighted.*)

DOROTHEA: But Mama's took all my things! I forgot to ask them back from her. I'll just have to sleep jay-bird since she took even my nighties.

RALPH: Yes, she was fast and thorough, but didn't get out with that seven-hundred-buck beaver coat.

DOROTHEA: I like your friends. But the girl looks terribly nervous. Well-bred, however, and the boy is certainly very good-looking!

RALPH: Thanks.

(*The bedroom dims out as Dorothea enters the bathroom. A silence has fallen between the pair in the living room.*)

ISABEL: Coffee, George?

GEORGE: No, thanks.

ISABEL: Moods change quickly, don't they?

GEORGE: Basic attitudes don't.

ISABEL: Yes, but it takes a long time to form basic attitudes and to know what they are, and meantime you just have to act according to moods.

GEORGE: Is that what you are acting according to, now?

ISABEL: I'm not acting according to anything at all now, I—

(*She sits on a hassock before the fireplace.*)

I don't think she came back just for the coat. Do you?

GEORGE: It's not my business. I don't have any opinion. If that was her reason, Ralph Bates will soon find it out.

ISABEL: Yes . . .

DOROTHEA (*at the door*): Excuse me, may I come in?

ISABEL: Oh, please.

DOROTHEA (*entering*): Mama took all my *things*! Have you got an extra nightie that I could borrow?

ISABEL: Of course I have.

DOROTHEA: I forgot to take anything back. . . .

(*Isabel opens her overnight bag and extends a gossamer nightgown to Dorothea.*)

Oh! How exquisite! No!—that's your honeymoon nightie. Just give me any old plain one!

ISABEL: Really, I have two of them, exactly alike. Please take it!

DOROTHEA: Are you sure?

ISABEL: I'm positive. You take it!

(*She holds up another.*)

See? The same thing exactly, just a different color. I gave you the blue one and kept the pink one for me.

DOROTHEA: Oh. Well, thank you so much.

ISABEL: If you'd prefer the pink one—?

DOROTHEA: I'm delighted with the blue one! Well, g'night, you folks. Sweet dreams.

(*She returns to the dark bedroom. Ralph is prone and motionless on the bed. A tiny light spills from the bathroom door. Dorothea enters the bathroom and closes the door so the bedroom turns pitch-black.*)

GEORGE (*grimly*): D'ya want me to go outside while you undress?

ISABEL: No, I, I—I'm just going to take off my *suit*. I—I, I have a *slip* on, I—

(*She gives him a quick, scared look. The removal of her suit is almost panickily self-conscious and awkward.*)

GEORGE: Well. Ralph and I have decided to—

ISABEL (*fearfully*): *What?*

GEORGE (*finishes his drink, then goes on*): Ralph and I have decided to go in the cattle business, near San Antone.

ISABEL: Who is going to finance it?

(*She has turned out the lamp.*)

GEORGE: We think we can work it out. We have to be smart, and lucky. Just smart and lucky.

(*Isabel drops her skirt to her feet and stands before the flickering fireplace in a slip that the light makes transparent.*)

ISABEL: We all have to be smart and lucky. Or unlucky and silly.

(*Dorothea comes out of the bathroom. Light from the bathroom brightens the bedroom, where Ralph is slowly undressing.*)

RALPH: All right, you're back. But a lot has been discussed and decided on since you cut out of here, Dotty.
DOROTHEA (*picks up something on the dresser*): Good! What?
RALPH: Please don't rub that Vick's Vap-O-Rub on your chest.
DOROTHEA: I'm *not*! This is Hind's honey-almond cream for my *hands*!
RALPH: Aw.

(*She starts taking off her shoes.*
(*In the living room:*)

GEORGE: What're you up to?
ISABEL: Up to?
GEORGE: Standin' in front of that fire with that transparent thing on you. You must know it's transparent.
ISABEL: I honestly didn't even think about that.

(*Isabel crouches by the fire, holding her delicate hands out to its faint, flickering glow.*
(*In the bedroom:*)

RALPH: All right. Here it is. George and me are going to cash in every bit of collateral we possess, including the beaverskin coat and his fifty-two Caddy to buy a piece of ranchland near San Antone.
DOROTHEA: Oh. What are you planning to do on this—
RALPH:—ranch? Breed cattle. Texas Longhorns.

(*A pause.*)

DOROTHEA: I like animals, Ralph.
RALPH: Cocker spaniels.

DOROTHEA: No, I like horses, too. I took equitation at Sophie Newcomb's. I even learned how to post.

RALPH: Uh-huh.

DOROTHEA: For a little ole Texas girl she sure does have some mighty French taste in nighties!

RALPH: I don't imagine she suffers from psychological frigidity.

DOROTHEA: Honey, I never suffered from that. Did you believe I really suffered from that?

RALPH: When your father proposed to me—

DOROTHEA: Ralph, don't say things like that! Don't, don't humiliate me!

RALPH: Honey, I—

DOROTHEA: PLEASE don't humiliate me by—

RALPH: HONEY!

(*He goes up to her at the dressing table. Sobbing, she presses her head against him.*)

You KNOW I respect you, honey.

ISABEL (*in the other room*): What an awful, frightening thing it is!

GEORGE: What?

ISABEL: Two people living together, two, two—different worlds!—attempting—existence—together!

(*In the bedroom:*)

RALPH: Honey, will you stop?

DOROTHEA: Respect me, respect me, is that all you can give me when I've loved you so much that sometimes I shake all over at the sight or touch of you? Still? Now? Always?

RALPH: The human heart would never pass the drunk test.

DOROTHEA: Huh?

RALPH: If you took the human heart out of the human body and put a pair of legs on it and told it to walk a straight line, it couldn't do it. It never could pass the drunk test.

DOROTHEA: I love you, baby. And I love animals, too. Hawses, spaniels, longhorns!

RALPH: The Texas longhorn is a—dignified beast.

DOROTHEA: You say that like you thought it was TOO GOOD FOR ME!

RALPH: How do I know that you didn't just come back here for that sheared beaver coat?

(*Living room:*)

ISABEL: I hope they're getting things ironed out between them.
GEORGE: Why?
ISABEL: They need each other. That's why.
GEORGE: Let's mind our own business, huh?

(*Bedroom:*)

DOROTHEA: You'll just have to WONDER! And WONDER!

(*Living room:*)

GEORGE: It's a parallel situation. They're going through a period of adjustment just like us.

(*Bedroom:*)

RALPH: All my life, huh?
DOROTHEA: And I'll have to wonder, too, if you love me, Ralph. There's an awful lot of wondering between people.
RALPH: Come on. Turn out the light. Let's go to bed-ville, baby.
DOROTHEA (*turning out the light*): His or hers?
RALPH: In West Texas we'll get a big one called OURS!

(*In the living room, George has turned on TV and a chorus is singing "White Christmas."*)

GEORGE: Aw. You hate "White Christmas."

(*He turns it down.*)

ISABEL: I don't hate it now, baby.

(*He turns it back up, but softly.*)

DOROTHEA: I'm lookin' *forward* to it. I always wanted a big one, OURS!
RALPH: There's more dignity in it.
DOROTHEA: *Yes!*

(*She giggles breathlessly in the dark.*)

ISABEL (*in the living room*): I think they've talked things over and are working things out.

(*Bedroom:*)

RALPH: Yes. It makes it easy to know if—I mean, you don't have to wonder if—

(*Dorothea giggles in the dark.*)

That long, long, dangerous walk between "His" and "Hers" can be accomplished, or not. . . .

(*Living room:*)

ISABEL: I didn't know until now that the shakes are catching! Why do you keep standing up and sitting back down like a big old jack-in-the-box?

(*A low rumble is heard. It builds. Something falls off a shelf in the kitchenette. Crockery rattles together.*)

WHAT'S THIS!?

GEORGE: Aw, nothin', nothin'.

RALPH (*entering the doorway*): Well, she jus' slipped again!

DOROTHEA (*appearing behind him*): Did you all feel that tremor?

ISABEL: Yes, it felt like an earthquake.

DOROTHEA: We get those little tremors all the time because it seems that this suburb is built over a huge underground cavern and is sinking into it, bit by bit. That's the secret of how we could afford to buy this nice little home of ours at such a knockdown price.

ISABEL: It isn't likely to fall in the cavern *tonight*?

DOROTHEA: No. They say it's going to be gradual, about half an inch every year. Do you all mind if I turn on the light a second to see if there's any new cracks?

ISABEL: No, I'll—put on my robe.

(*She does. The room is lighted.*)

DOROTHEA: Yais! Ralph? A *new* one! This one is a jim-dandy, all the way 'cross the ceiling! See it, honey? All the way 'cross the ceiling. Well—

(*A pause.*)

We will leave you alone now. I still feel badly about you having to sleep on that folding contraption.

RALPH: Anything I can do? Anything I can—

DOROTHEA: Ralph! Leave them alone. Merry Christmas!

(*She shuts the door.*

(*Pause. Isabel stands before fireplace in the fourth wall.*

(*Pause.*)

GEORGE: Isabel? Little Bit? Marriage is a big step for a man to take, especially when he's—nervous. I'm pretty—nervous.

ISABEL: I know.

GEORGE: For a man with the shakes, especially, it's a—big step to take, it's—

ISABEL: I know what you're trying to tell me.

GEORGE (*taking seat on high stool near fire*): Do you, honey?

(*He looks up at her quickly, then down.*)

ISABEL: Of course I do. I expect all men are a little bit nervous about the same thing.

GEORGE: What?

ISABEL: About how they'll be at love-making.

GEORGE: Yeah, well, they don't have the shakes. I mean, not all the others have got a nervous tremor like I've got.

ISABEL: Inside or outside, they've all got a nervous tremor of some kind, sweetheart. The world is a big hospital, and I am a nurse in it, George. The world world's a big hospital, a big neurological ward and I am a student nurse in it. I guess that's still my job!—I love this fire. It feels so good on my skin through this little pink slip. I'm glad she left me the *pink* nightie, tonight.

GEORGE (*huskily*): Yeah, I'm glad she did, too.

(*Isabel retires to slip into her nightgown.*)

I wish I had that—little electric buzzer I—had at—Barnes. . . .

ISABEL: You don't need a buzzer. I'm not way down at the end of a corridor, baby. If you call me, I'll hear you.

(*She returns and hugs her knees, sitting before the fireplace. He rests his head on his cupped hands. She begins to sing softly:*)

"Now the boat goes round the bend,
Good-by, my lover, good-by,
It's loaded down with boys and men,
Good-by, my lover, good-by!"

RALPH (*in the dark other room*): She's singin'!

(*Pause.*)

DOROTHEA: Papa said you told him that I was—homely! Did you say that, Ralph? That I was homely?

RALPH: Dotty, you used to be homely but you improved in appearance.

DOROTHEA: You never told me you thought I was homely, Ralph.

RALPH: I just meant you had a off-beat kind of face, honey, but—the rest of you is attractive.

DOROTHEA (*giggles*): I always knew *I* was homely but you were good enough lookin' to make *up* for it! Baby—

(*Isabel is singing again, a little forlornly, by the fireplace.*)

ISABEL:

"Bye low, my baby! Bye low, my baby!
Bye low, my baby! Good-by, my lover, good-by!"

(*George whistles softly.*)

Was that for me?

GEORGE: Come here!

ISABEL: No, you come here. It's very nice by the fire.

(*In the other room, as the curtain begins to fall:*)

DOROTHEA: Careful, let me do it!—It isn't mine!

(*She means the borrowed nightgown.*

(*In the front room, George has risen from the bed and is crossing to the fireplace as:*)

The Curtain Falls

THE NIGHT OF THE IGUANA

And so, as kinsmen met a night,
We talked between the rooms,
Until the moss had reached our lips,
And covered up our names.

EMILY DICKINSON

The play takes place in the summer of 1940 in a rather rustic and very Bohemian hotel, the Costa Verde, which, as its name implies, sits on a jungle-covered hilltop overlooking the "caleta," or "morning beach" of Puerto Barrio in Mexico. But this is decidedly not the Puerto Barrio of today. At that time—twenty years ago—the west coast of Mexico had not yet become the Las Vegas and Miami Beach of Mexico. The villages were still predominantly primitive Indian villages, and the still-water morning beach of Puerto Barrio and the rain forests above it were among the world's wildest and loveliest populated places.

The setting for the play is the wide verandah of the hotel. This roofed verandah, enclosed by a railing, runs around all four sides of the somewhat dilapidated, tropical-style frame structure, but on the stage we see only the front and one side. Below the verandah, which is slightly raised above the stage level, are shrubs with vivid trumpet-shaped flowers and a few cactus plants, while at the sides we see the foliage of the encroaching jungle. A tall coconut palm slants upward at one side, its trunk notched for a climber to chop down coconuts for rum-cocos. In the back wall of the verandah are the doors of a line of small cubicle bedrooms which are screened with mosquito-net curtains. For the night scenes they are lighted from within, so that each cubicle appears as a little interior stage, the curtains giving a misty effect to their dim inside lighting. A path which goes down through the rain forest to the highway and the beach, its opening masked by foliage, leads off from one side of the verandah. A canvas hammock is strung from posts on the verandah and there are a few old wicker rockers and rattan lounging chairs at one side.

ACT ONE

As the curtain rises, there are sounds of a party of excited female tourists arriving by bus on the road down the hill below the Costa Verde Hotel. Mrs. Maxine Faulk, the proprietor of the hotel, comes around the turn of the verandah. She is a stout, swarthy woman in her middle forties—affable and rapaciously lusty. She is wearing a pair of levis and a blouse that is half unbuttoned. She is followed by Pedro, a Mexican of about twenty—slim and attractive. He is an employee in the hotel and also her casual lover. Pedro is stuffing his shirt under the belt of his pants and sweating as if he had been working hard in the sun. Mrs. Faulk looks down the hill and is pleased by the sight of someone coming up from the tourist bus below.

MAXINE (*calling out*): Shannon! (*A man's voice from below answers:* "Hi!") Hah! (*Maxine always laughs with a single harsh, loud bark, opening her mouth like a seal expecting a fish to be thrown to it.*) My spies told me that you were back under the border! (*to Pedro*) Anda, hombre, anda!

(*Maxine's delight expands and vibrates in her as Shannon labors up the hill to the hotel. He does not appear on the jungle path for a minute or two after the shouting between them starts.*)

MAXINE: Hah! My spies told me you went through Saltillo last week with a busload of women—a whole busload of females, all females, hah! How many you laid so far? Hah!

SHANNON (*from below, panting*): Great Caesar's ghost . . . stop . . . shouting!

MAXINE: No wonder your ass is draggin', hah!

SHANNON: Tell the kid to help me up with this bag.

MAXINE (*shouting directions*): Pedro! Anda—la maléta. Pancho, no seas flojo! Va y trae el equipaje del señor.

(*Pancho, another young Mexican, comes around the verandah and trots down the jungle path. Pedro has climbed up a coconut tree with a machete and is chopping down nuts for rum-cocos.*)

SHANNON (*shouting, below*): Fred? Hey, Fred!

MAXINE (*with a momentary gravity*): Fred can't hear you, Shannon. (*She goes over and picks up a coconut, shaking it against her ear to see if it has milk in it.*)

SHANNON (*still below*): Where is Fred—gone fishing?

(*Maxine lops the end off a coconut with the machete, as Pancho trots up to the verandah with Shannon's bag—a beat-up Gladstone covered with travel stickers from all over the world. Then Shannon appears, in a crumpled white linen suit. He is panting, sweating and wild-eyed. About thirty-five, Shannon is "black Irish." His nervous state is terribly apparent; he is a young man who has cracked up before and is going to crack up again—perhaps repeatedly.*)

MAXINE: Well! Lemme look at you!

SHANNON: Don't look at me, get dressed!

MAXINE: Gee, you look like you had it!

SHANNON: You look like you been having it, too. Get dressed!

MAXINE: Hell, I'm dressed. I never dress in September. Don't you know I never dress in September?

SHANNON: Well, just, just—button your shirt up.

MAXINE: How long you been off it, Shannon?

SHANNON: Off what?

MAXINE: The wagon . . .

SHANNON: Hell, I'm dizzy with fever. Hundred and three this morning in Cuernavaca.

MAXINE: Watcha got wrong with you?

SHANNON: Fever . . . fever . . . Where's Fred?

MAXINE: Dead.

SHANNON: Did you say *dead*?

MAXINE: That's what I said. Fred is dead.

SHANNON: How?

MAXINE: Less'n two weeks ago, Fred cut his hand on a fish-hook, it got infected, infection got in his blood stream, and he was dead inside of forty-eight hours. (*to Pancho*) Vete!

SHANNON: Holy smoke. . . .

MAXINE: I can't quite realize it yet. . . .

SHANNON: You don't seem—inconsolable about it.

MAXINE: Fred was an old man, baby. Ten years older'n me. We hadn't had sex together in. . . .

SHANNON: What's that got to do with it?

MAXINE: Lie down and have a rum-coco.

SHANNON: No, no. I want a cold beer. If I start drinking rum-cocos now I won't stop drinking rum-cocos. So Fred is dead? I looked forward to lying in this hammock and talking to Fred.

MAXINE: Well Fred's not talking now, Shannon. A diabetic gets a blood infection, he goes like that without a decent hospital in less'n a week. (*A bus horn is heard blowing from below.*) Why don't your busload of women come on up here? They're blowing the bus horn down there.

SHANNON: Let 'em blow it, blow it. . . . (*He sways a little.*) I got a fever. (*He goes to the top of the path, divides the flowering bushes and shouts down the hill to the bus.*) Hank! Hank! Get them out of the bus and bring 'em up here! Tell 'em the rates are OK. Tell 'em the . . . (*His voice gives out, and he stumbles back to the verandah, where he sinks down onto the low steps, panting.*) Absolutely the worst party I've ever been out with in ten years of conducting tours. For God's sake, help me with 'em because I can't go on. I got to rest here a while. (*She gives him a cold beer.*) Thanks. Look and see if they're getting out of the bus. (*She crosses to the masking foliage and separates it to look down the hill.*) Are they getting out of the bus or are they staying in it, the stingy—daughters of—bitches. . . . Schoolteachers at a Baptist Female College in Blowing Rock, Texas. Eleven, eleven of them.

MAXINE: A football squad of old maids.

SHANNON: Yeah, and I'm the football. Are they out of the bus?

MAXINE: One's gotten out—she's going into the bushes.

SHANNON: Well, I've got the ignition key to the bus in my pocket—this pocket—so they can't continue without me unless they walk.

MAXINE: They're still blowin' that horn.

SHANNON: Fantastic. I can't lose this party. Blake Tours has put me on probation because I had a bad party last month that tried to get me sacked and I am now on probation with Blake Tours. If I lose this party I'll be sacked for sure . . . Ah, my God, are they still all in the bus? (*He *heaves himself off the steps and staggers back to the path, dividing the foliage to look down it, then shouts.*) Hank! Get them out of the busssss! Bring them up heeee-re!

HANK'S VOICE (*from below*): They wanta go back in toooooowwww-n.

SHANNON: They *can't* go back in tooowwwwn!—Whew—Five years ago this summer I was conducting round-the-world tours for Cook's. Exclusive groups of retired Wall Street financiers. We traveled in fleets of Pierce Arrows and Hispano Suizas.—Are they getting out of the bus?

MAXINE: You're going to pieces, are you?

SHANNON: No! Gone! Gone! (*He rises and shouts down the hill again.*) Hank! come up here! Come on up here a minute! I wanta talk to you about this situation!—Incredible, fantastic . . . (*He drops back on the steps, his head falling into his hands.*)

MAXINE: They're not getting out of the bus.—Shannon . . . you're not in a nervous condition to cope with this party, Shannon, so let them go and you stay.

SHANNON: You know my situation: I lose this job, what's next? There's nothing lower than Blake Tours, Maxine honey.—Are they getting out of the bus? Are they getting out of it now?

MAXINE: Man's comin' up the hill.

SHANNON: Aw. Hank. You gotta help me with him.

MAXINE: I'll give him a rum-coco.

(*Hank comes grinning onto the verandah.*)

HANK: Shannon, them ladies are not gonna come up here, so you better come on back to the bus.

SHANNON: Fantastic.—I'm not going down to the bus and I've got the ignition key to the bus in my pocket. It's going to stay in my pocket for the next three days.

HANK: You can't get away with that, Shannon. Hell, they'll walk back to town if you don't give up the bus key.

SHANNON: They'd drop like flies from sunstrokes on that road. . . . Fantastic, absolutely fantastic . . . (*Panting and sweating, he drops a hand on Hank's shoulder.*) Hank, I want your co-operation. Can I have it? Because when you're out with a difficult party like this, the tour conductor—me—and the guide—you—have got to stick together to control the situations as they come up against us. It's a test of strength between two men, in this case, and a busload of old wet *hens*! You know that, don't you?

HANK: Well. . . . (*He chuckles.*) There's this kid that's crying on the back seat all the time, and that's what's rucked up the deal. Hell, I don't know if you did or you didn't, but they all think that you did 'cause the kid keeps crying.

SHANNON: *Hank? Look!* I don't care what they think. A tour conducted by T. Lawrence Shannon is in his charge, completely—where to go, when to go, every detail of it. Otherwise I resign. So go on back down there and get them out of that bus before they suffocate in it. Haul them out by force if necessary and herd them up here. Hear me? Don't give me any argument about it. Mrs. Faulk, honey? Give him a menu, give him one of your sample menus to show the ladies. She's got a Chinaman cook here, you won't believe the menu. The cook's from Shanghai, handled the kitchen at an exclusive club there. I got him here for her, and he's a bug, a fanatic about—whew!—continental cuisine . . . can even make beef Strogonoff and thermidor dishes. Mrs. Faulk, honey? Hand him one of those —whew!—one of those fantastic sample menus. (*Maxine chuckles, as if perpetrating a practical joke, as she hands him a sheet of paper.*) Thanks. Now, here. Go on back down there and show them this fantastic menu. Describe the view from the hill, and . . . (*Hank accepts the menu with a chuckling shake of the head.*) And have a cold Carta Blanca and. . . .

HANK: You better go down with me.

SHANNON: I can't leave this verandah for at least forty-eight hours. *What in blazes is this?* A little animated cartoon by Hieronymus Bosch?

(*The German family which is staying at the hotel, the Fahrenkopfs, their daughter and son-in-law, suddenly make a startling, dreamlike entrance upon the scene. They troop around the verandah, then turn down into the jungle path. They are all dressed in the minimal concession to decency and all are pink and gold like baroque cupids in various sizes—*

Rubensesque, splendidly physical. The bride, Hilda, walks astride a big inflated rubber horse which has an ecstatic smile and great winking eyes. She shouts "Horsey, horsey, giddap!" *as she waddles astride it, followed by her Wagnerian-tenor bridegroom, Wolfgang, and her father, Herr Fahrenkopf, a tank manufacturer from Frankfurt. He is carrying a portable shortwave radio, which is tuned in to the crackle and guttural voices of a German broadcast reporting the Battle of Britain. Frau Fahrenkopf, bursting with rich, healthy fat and carrying a basket of food for a picnic at the beach, brings up the rear. They begin to sing a Nazi marching song.*)

SHANNON: Aw—Nazis. How come there's so many of them down here lately?

MAXINE: Mexico's the front door to South America—and the back door to the States, that's why.

SHANNON: Aw, and you're setting yourself up here as a receptionist at both doors, now that Fred's dead? (*Maxine comes over and sits down on him in the hammock.*) Get off my pelvis before you crack it. If you want to crack something, crack some ice for my forehead. (*She removes a chunk of ice from her glass and massages his forehead with it.*)—Ah, God. . . .

MAXINE (*chuckling*): Ha, so you took the young chick and the old hens are squawking about it, Shannon?

SHANNON: The kid asked for it, no kidding, but she's seventeen—less, a month less'n seventeen. So it's serious, it's very serious, because the kid is not just emotionally precocious, she's a musical prodigy, too.

MAXINE: What's that got to do with it?

SHANNON: Here's what it's got to do with it, she's traveling under the wing, the military escort, of this, this—butch vocal teacher who organizes little community sings in the bus. Ah, God! I'm surprised they're not singing now, they must've already suffocated. Or they'd be singing some morale-boosting number like "She's a Jolly Good Fellow" or "Pop Goes the Weasel."—Oh, God. . . . (*Maxine chuckles up and down the scale.*) And each night after supper, after the complaints about the supper and the check-up on the checks by the math instructor, and the vomiting of the supper by several ladies, who have inspected the kitchen—then the kid, the canary, will give a vocal recital. She opens her mouth and out flies Carrie Jacobs Bond or Ethelbert Nevin. I mean after a day of one indescribable torment after another, such as three blowouts, and a leaking radiator in Tierra Caliente. . . . (*He sits up slowly in the hammock as these recollections gather force.*) And an evening climb up sierras, through torrents of rain, around hairpin turns over gorges and chasms measureless to man, and with a thermos-jug under the driver's seat which the Baptist College ladies think is filled with icewater but which I know is filled with iced tequila—I mean after such a day has finally come to a close, the musical prodigy, Miss Charlotte Goodall, right after supper, before there's a chance to escape, will give a heartbreaking and earsplitting rendition of Carrie Jacobs Bond's "End of a Perfect Day"—with absolutely no humor. . . .

MAXINE: Hah!

SHANNON: Yeah, "Hah!" Last night—no, night before last, the bus burned out its brake linings in Chilpancingo. This town has a hotel . . . this hotel has a piano, which hasn't been tuned since they shot Maximilian. This Texas songbird opens her mouth and out flies "I Love You Truly," and it flies straight at *me*, with *gestures*, all right at *me*, till her chaperone, this Diesel-driven vocal instructor of hers, slams the piano lid down and hauls her out of the mess hall. But as she's hauled out Miss Bird-Girl opens her mouth and out flies, "Larry, Larry, I love you, I love you truly!" That night, when I went to my room, I found that I had a roommate.

MAXINE: The musical prodigy had moved in with you?

SHANNON: The *spook* had moved in with me. In that hot room with one bed, the width of an ironing board and about as hard, the spook was up there on it, sweating, stinking, grinning up at me.

MAXINE: Aw, the spook. (*She chuckles.*) So you've got the spook with you again.

SHANNON: That's right, he's the only passenger that got off the bus with me, honey.

MAXINE: Is he here now?

SHANNON: Not far.

MAXINE: On the verandah?

SHANNON: He might be on the other side of the verandah. Oh, he's around somewhere, but he's like the Sioux Indians in the Wild West fiction, he doesn't attack before sundown, he's an after-sundown shadow. . . .

(*Shannon wriggles out of the hammock as the bus horn gives one last, long protesting blast.*)

MAXINE:

I have a little shadow
That goes in and out with me,
And what can be the use of him
Is more than I can see.

He's very, very like me,
From his heels up to his head,
And he always hops before me
When I hop into my bed.

SHANNON: That's the truth. He sure hops in the bed with me.

MAXINE: When you're sleeping alone, or . . . ?

SHANNON: I haven't slept in three nights.

MAXINE: Aw, you will tonight, baby.

(*The bus horn sounds again. Shannon rises and squints down the hill at the bus.*)

SHANNON: How long's it take to sweat the faculty of a Baptist Female College out of a bus that's parked in the sun when it's a hundred degrees in the shade?

MAXINE: They're staggering out of it now.

SHANNON: Yeah, I've won *this* round, I reckon. What're they doing down there, can you see?

MAXINE: They're crowding around your pal Hank.

SHANNON: Tearing him to pieces?

MAXINE: One of them's slapped him, he's ducked back into the bus, and she is starting up here.

SHANNON: Oh, Great Caesar's ghost, it's the butch vocal teacher.

MISS FELLOWES (*in a strident voice, from below*): Shannon! Shannon!

SHANNON: For God's sake, help me with her.

MAXINE: You know I'll help you, baby, but why don't you lay off the young ones and cultivate an interest in normal grown-up women?

MISS FELLOWES (*her voice coming nearer*): Shannon!

SHANNON (*shouting down the hill*): Come on up, Miss Fellowes, everything's fixed. (*to Maxine*) Oh, God, here she comes chargin' up the hill like a bull elephant on a rampage!

(*Miss Fellowes thrashes through the foliage at the top of the jungle path.*)

SHANNON: Miss Fellowes, never do that! Not at high noon in a tropical country in summer. Never charge up a hill like you were leading a troop of cavalry attacking an almost impregnable. . . .

MISS FELLOWES (*panting and furious*): I don't want advice or instructions, I want the *bus key*!

SHANNON: Mrs. Faulk, this is Miss Judith Fellowes.

MISS FELLOWES: Is this man making a deal with you?

MAXINE: I don't know what you—

MISS FELLOWES: Is this man getting a *kickback* out of you?

MAXINE: Nobody gets any kickback out of me. I turn away more people than—

MISS FELLOWES (*cutting in*): This isn't the Ambos Mundos. It says in the brochure that in Puerto Barrio we stay at the Ambos Mundos in the heart of the city.

SHANNON: Yes, on the plaza—tell her about the plaza.

MAXINE: What about the plaza?

SHANNON: It's hot, noisy, stinking, swarming with flies. Pariah dogs dying in the—

MISS FELLOWES: How is this place better?

SHANNON: The view from this verandah is equal and I think better than the view from Victoria Peak in Hong Kong, the view from the roof-terrace of the Sultan's palace in—

MISS FELLOWES (*cutting in*): I want the view of a clean bed, a bathroom with plumbing that works, and food that is eatable and digestible and not contaminated by filthy—

SHANNON: *Miss Fellowes!*

MISS FELLOWES: Take your hand off my arm.

SHANNON: Look at this sample menu. The cook is a Chinese imported from Shanghai by *me*! Sent here by *me*, year before last, in nineteen thirty-eight. He was the chef at the Royal Colonial Club in—

MISS FELLOWES (*cutting in*): You got a telephone here?

MAXINE: Sure, in the office.

MISS FELLOWES: I want to use it— I'll call collect. Where's the office?

MAXINE (*to Pancho*): Llevala al telefono!

(*With Pancho showing her the way, Miss Fellowes stalks off around the verandah to the office. Shannon falls back, sighing desperately, against the verandah wall.*)

MAXINE: Hah!

SHANNON: Why did you have to . . . ?

MAXINE: Huh?

SHANNON: Come out looking like this! For you it's funny but for me it's. . . .

MAXINE: This is how I *look*. What's wrong with how I *look*?

SHANNON: I told you to button your shirt. Are you so proud of your boobs that you won't button your shirt up?—Go in the office and see if she's calling Blake Tours to get me fired.

MAXINE: She better not unless she pays for the call.

(*She goes around the turn of the verandah.*

(*Miss Hannah Jelkes appears below the verandah steps and stops short as Shannon turns to the wall, pounding his fist against it with a sobbing sound in his throat.*)

HANNAH: Excuse me.

(*Shannon looks down at her, dazed. Hannah is remarkable-looking—ethereal, almost ghostly. She suggests a Gothic cathedral image of a medieval saint, but animated. She could be thirty, she could be forty: she is totally feminine and yet androgynous-looking—almost timeless. She is wearing a cotton print dress and has a bag slung on a strap over her shoulder.*)

HANNAH: Is this the Costa Verde Hotel?

SHANNON (*suddenly pacified by her appearance*): Yes. Yes, it is.

HANNAH: Are you . . . you're not, the hotel manager, are you?

SHANNON: No. She'll be right back.

HANNAH: Thank you. Do you have any idea if they have two vacancies here? One for myself and one for my grandfather who's waiting in a taxi down there on the road. I didn't want to bring him up the hill—till I'd made sure they have rooms for us first.

SHANNON: Well, there's plenty of room here out-of-season—like now.

HANNAH: Good! Wonderful! I'll get him out of the taxi.

SHANNON: Need any help?

HANNAH: No, thank you. We'll make it all right.

(*She gives him a pleasant nod and goes back off down the path through the rain forest. A coconut plops to the ground; a parrot screams at a distance. Shannon drops into the hammock and stretches out. Then Maxine reappears.*)

SHANNON: How about the call? Did she make a phone call?

MAXINE: She called a judge in Texas—Blowing Rock, Texas. Collect.

SHANNON: She's trying to get me fired and she is also trying to pin on me a rape charge, a charge of statutory rape.

MAXINE: What's "statutory rape"? I've never known what that was.

SHANNON: That's when a man is seduced by a girl under twenty. (*She chuckles.*) It's not funny, Maxine honey.

MAXINE: Why do you want the young ones—or think that you do?

SHANNON: I don't want any, any—regardless of age.

MAXINE: Then why do you take them, Shannon? (*He swallows but does not answer.*)—Huh, Shannon.

SHANNON: People need human contact, Maxine honey.

MAXINE: What size shoe do you wear?

SHANNON: I don't get the point of that question.

MAXINE: These shoes are shot and if I remember correctly, you travel with only one pair. Fred's estate included one good pair of shoes and your feet look about his size.

SHANNON: I loved ole Fred but I don't want to fill his shoes, honey.

(*She has removed Shannon's beat-up, English-made oxfords.*)

MAXINE: Your socks are shot. Fred's socks would fit you, too, Shannon. (*She opens his collar.*) Aw-aw, I see you got on your gold cross. That's a bad sign, it means you're thinkin' again about goin' back to the Church.

SHANNON: This is my last tour, Maxine. I wrote my old Bishop this morning a complete confession and a complete capitulation.

(*She takes a letter from his damp shirt pocket.*)

MAXINE: If this is the letter, baby, you've sweated through it, so the old bugger couldn't read it even if you mailed it to him this time.

(*She has started around the verandah, and goes off as Hank reappears up the hill-path, mopping his face. Shannon's relaxed position in the hammock aggravates Hank sorely.*)

HANK: Will you get your ass out of that hammock?

SHANNON: No, I will not.

HANK: Shannon, git out of that hammock! (*He kicks at Shannon's hips in the hammock.*)

SHANNON: Hank, if you can't function under rough circumstances, you are in the wrong racket, man. I gave you instructions, the instructions were simple. I said get them out of the bus and. . . .

(*Maxine comes back with a kettle of water, a towel and other shaving equipment.*)

HANK: Out of the hammock, Shannon! (*He kicks Shannon again, harder.*)

SHANNON (*warningly*): That's enough, Hank. A little familiarity goes a long way, but not as far as you're going. (*Maxine starts lathering his face.*) What's this, what are you . . . ?

MAXINE: Haven't you ever had a shave-and-haircut by a lady barber?

HANK: The kid has gone into hysterics.

MAXINE: Hold still, Shannon.

SHANNON: Hank, hysteria is a natural phenomenon, the common denominator of the female nature. It's the big female weapon, and the test of a man is his ability to cope with it, and I can't believe you can't. If I believed that you couldn't, I would not be able—

MAXINE: Hold still!

SHANNON: I'm holding still. (*to Hank*) No, I wouldn't be able to take you out with me again. So go on back down there and—

HANK: You want me to go back down there and tell them you're getting a shave up here in a hammock?

MAXINE: Tell them that Reverend Larry is going back to the Church so they can go back to the Female College in Texas.

HANK: I want another beer.

MAXINE: Help yourself, piggly-wiggly, the cooler's in my office right around there. (*She points around the corner of the verandah.*)

SHANNON (*as Hank goes off*): It's horrible how you got to bluff and keep bluffing even when hollering "Help!" is all you're up to, Maxine. *You cut me!*

MAXINE: You didn't hold still.

SHANNON: Just trim the beard a little.

MAXINE: I know. Baby, tonight we'll go night-swimming, whether it storms or not.

SHANNON: Ah, God. . . .

MAXINE: The Mexican kids are wonderful night-swimmers. . . . Hah, when I found 'em they were taking the two-hundred-foot dives off the Quebrada, but the Quebrada Hotel kicked 'em out for being over-attentive to the lady guests there. That's how I got hold of them.

SHANNON: Maxine, you're bigger than life and twice as unnatural, honey.

MAXINE: No one's bigger than life-size, Shannon, or even ever that big, except maybe Fred. (*She shouts* "Fred?" *and gets a faint answering echo from an adjoining hill.*) Little Sir Echo is all that answers for him now, Shannon, but. . . . (*She pats some bay rum on his face.*) Dear old Fred was always a mystery to me. He was so patient and tolerant with me that it was insulting to me. A man and a woman have got to challenge each other, y'know what I mean. I mean I hired those diving-boys from the Quebrada six months before Fred died, and did he care? Did he give a damn when

I started night-swimming with them? No. He'd go night-*fishing*, all night, and when I got up the next day, he'd be preparing to go out fishing again, but he just caught the fish and threw them back in the sea.

(*Hank returns and sits drinking his beer on the steps.*)

SHANNON: The mystery of old Fred was simple. He was just cool and decent, that's all the mystery of him. . . . Get your pair of night-swimmers to grab my ladies' luggage out of the bus before the vocal-teacher gets off the phone and stops them.

MAXINE (*shouting*): Pedro! Pancho! Muchachos! Trae las maletas al anejo! Pronto! (*The Mexican boys start down the path. Maxine sits in the hammock beside Shannon.*) You I'll put in Fred's old room, next to me.

SHANNON: You want me in his socks and his shoes and in his room next to *you*? (*He stares at her with a shocked surmise of her intentions toward him, then flops back down in the hammock with an incredulous laugh.*) Oh no, honey. I've just been hanging on till I could get in this hammock on this verandah over the rain forest and the still-water beach, that's all that can pull me through this last tour in a condition to go back to my . . . original . . . vocation.

MAXINE: Hah, you still have some rational moments when you face the fact that churchgoers don't go to church to hear atheistical sermons.

SHANNON: Goddamit, I never preached an atheistical sermon in a church in my life, and. . . .

(*Miss Fellowes has charged out of the office and rounds the verandah to bear down on Shannon and Maxine, who jumps up out of the hammock.*)

MISS FELLOWES: I've completed my call, which I made collect to Texas.

(*Maxine shrugs, going by her around the verandah. Miss Fellowes runs across the verandah.*)

SHANNON (*sitting up in the hammock*): Excuse me, Miss Fellowes, for not getting out of this hammock, but I . . .

Miss Fellowes? Please sit down a minute, I want to confess something to you.

MISS FELLOWES: *That* ought to be int'restin'! *What?*

SHANNON: Just that—well, like everyone else, at some point or other in life, my life has cracked up on me.

MISS FELLOWES: How does that compensate *us*?

SHANNON: I don't think I know what you mean by *compensate*, Miss Fellowes. (*He props himself up and gazes at her with the gentlest bewilderment, calculated to melt a heart of stone.*) I mean I've just confessed to you that I'm at the end of my rope, and you say, "How does that compensate *us*?" Please, Miss Fellowes. Don't make me feel that any adult human being puts personal compensation before the dreadful, bare fact of a man at the end of his rope who still has to try to go on, to continue, as if he'd never been better or stronger in his whole existence. No, don't do that, it would. . . .

MISS FELLOWES: It would *what*?

SHANNON: Shake if not shatter everything left of my faith in essential . . . human . . . *goodness*!

MAXINE (*returning, with a pair of socks*): Hah!

MISS FELLOWES: Can you sit there, I mean lie there—yeah, I mean *lie* there . . . ! and talk to me about—

MAXINE: Hah!

MISS FELLOWES: "Essential human goodness"? Why, just plain human decency is beyond your imagination, Shannon, so lie there, lie there and *lie* there, we're *going*!

SHANNON (*rising from the hammock*): Miss Fellowes, I thought that I was conducting this party, not you.

MISS FELLOWES: You? You just now *admitted* you're incompetent, as well as. . . .

MAXINE: Hah.

SHANNON: Maxine, will you—

MISS FELLOWES (*cutting in with cold, righteous fury*): *Shannon*, we girls have worked and slaved all year at Baptist Female College for this Mexican tour, and the tour is a cheat!

SHANNON (*to himself*): Fantastic!

MISS FELLOWES: Yes, *cheat*! You haven't stuck to the schedule and you haven't stuck to the itinerary advertised in the brochure which Blake Tours put out. Now either Blake

Tours is cheating us or you are cheating Blake Tours, and I'm putting wheels in motion—I don't care *what* it costs me—I'm. . . .

SHANNON: Oh, Miss Fellowes, isn't it just as plain to you as it is to me that your hysterical insults, which are not at all easy for any born and bred gentleman to accept, are not . . . *motivated*, *provoked* by . . . anything as *trivial* as the, the . . . the motivations that you're, you're . . . *ascribing* them to? Now can't we talk about the *real*, *true* cause of. . . .

MISS FELLOWES: Cause of *what*?

(*Charlotte Goodall appears at the top of the hill.*)

SHANNON:—Cause of your *rage* Miss Fellowes, your—

MISS FELLOWES: *Charlotte!* Stay down the hill in the *bus*!

CHARLOTTE: Judy, they're—

MISS FELLOWES: *Obey me! Down!*

(*Charlotte retreats from view like a well-trained dog. Miss Fellowes charges back to Shannon who has gotten out of the hammock. He places a conciliatory hand on her arm.*)

MISS FELLOWES: *Take your hand off my arm!*

MAXINE: Hah!

SHANNON: *Fantastic.* Miss Fellowes, please! No more shouting? Please? Now I really must ask you to let this party of ladies come up here and judge the accommodations for themselves and compare them with what they saw passing through town. Miss Fellowes, there is such a thing as charm and beauty in some places, as much as there's nothing but dull, ugly imitation of highway motels in Texas and—

(*Miss Fellowes charges over to the path to see if Charlotte has obeyed her. Shannon follows, still propitiatory. Maxine says* "Hah," *but she gives him an affectionate little pat as he goes by her. He pushes her hand away as he continues his appeal to Miss Fellowes.*)

MISS FELLOWES: I've taken a look at those rooms and they'd make a room at the "Y" look like a suite at the Ritz.

SHANNON: Miss Fellowes, I am employed by Blake Tours and so I'm not in a position to tell you quite frankly what mistakes they've made in their advertising brochure. They just don't know Mexico. I do. I know it as well as I know five out of all six continents on the—

MISS FELLOWES: *Continent! Mexico?* You never even studied geography if you—

SHANNON: My degree from Sewanee is *Doctor* of *Divinity*, but for the past ten years geography's been my *specialty*, Miss Fellowes, honey! Name any tourist agency I haven't worked for! You couldn't! I'm only, now, with Blake Tours because I—

MISS FELLOWES: Because you *what*? Couldn't keep your hands off innocent, under-age girls in your—

SHANNON: Now, Miss Fellowes. . . . (*He touches her arm again.*)

MISS FELLOWES: Take your hand off my arm!

SHANNON: For days I've known you were furious and unhappy, but—

MISS FELLOWES: *Oh!* You think it's just *me* that's unhappy! Hauled in that stifling bus over the byways, off the highways, shook up and bumped up so you could get your rake-off, is that what you—

SHANNON: What I know is, all I know is, that you are the *leader* of the *insurrection*!

MISS FELLOWES: All of the girls in this party have dysentery!

SHANNON: That you can't hold me to blame for.

MISS FELLOWES: I *do* hold you to blame for it.

SHANNON: Before we entered Mexico, at New Laredo, Texas, I called you ladies together in the depot on the Texas side of the border and I passed out mimeographed sheets of instructions on what to eat and what *not* to eat, what to drink, what *not* to drink in the—

MISS FELLOWES: It's not *what* we ate but *where* we ate that gave us dysentery!

SHANNON (*shaking his head like a metronome*): It is not dysentery.

MISS FELLOWES: The result of eating in places that would be condemned by the Board of Health in—

SHANNON: Now wait a minute—

MISS FELLOWES: For disregarding all rules of sanitation.

SHANNON: It is not dysentery, it is not amoebic, it's nothing at all but—

MAXINE: Montezuma's Revenge! That's what we call it.

SHANNON: I even passed out pills. I passed out bottles of Enteroviaform because I knew that some of you ladies would rather be victims of Montezuma's Revenge than spend cinco centavos on bottled water in stations.

MISS FELLOWES: You sold those pills at a profit of fifty cents per bottle.

MAXINE: Hah-hah! (*She knocks off the end of a coconut with the machete, preparing a rum-coco.*)

SHANNON: Now fun is fun, Miss Fellowes, but an accusation like that—

MISS FELLOWES: I *priced* them in *pharmacies*, because I suspected that—

SHANNON: Miss Fellowes, I am a gentleman, and as a gentleman I can't be insulted like this. I mean I can't accept insults of that kind even from a member of a tour that I am conducting. And, Miss Fellowes, I think you might also remember, you might try to remember, that you're speaking to an ordained minister of the Church.

MISS FELLOWES: *De*-frocked! But still trying to pass himself off as a minister!

MAXINE: How about a rum-coco? We give a complimentary rum-coco to all our guests here. (*Her offer is apparently unheard. She shrugs and drinks the rum-coco herself.*)

SHANNON:—Miss Fellowes? In every party there is always one individual that's discontented, that is not satisfied with all I do to make the tour more . . . unique—to make it different from the ordinary, to give it a personal thing, the Shannon touch.

MISS FELLOWES: The gyp touch, the touch of a defrocked minister.

SHANNON: Miss Fellowes, don't, don't, don't . . . do what . . . you're doing! (*He is on the verge of hysteria, he makes some incoherent sounds, gesticulates with clenched fists, then stumbles wildly across the verandah and leans panting for breath against a post.*) Don't! Break! *Human! Pride!*

VOICE FROM DOWN THE HILL (*a very Texan accent*): Judy? They're taking our luggage!

MISS FELLOWES (*shouting down the hill*): Girls! Girls! Don't let those boys touch your luggage. Don't let them bring your luggage in this dump!

GIRL'S VOICE (*from below*): Judy! We can't stop them!

MAXINE: Those kids don't understand English.

MISS FELLOWES (*wild with rage*): Will you please tell those boys to take that luggage back down to the bus? (*She calls to the party below again.*) Girls! Hold onto your luggage, don't let them take it away! We're going to drive back to A-cap-ul-co! *You hear?*

GIRL'S VOICE: Judy, they want a swim, first!

MISS FELLOWES: I'll be right back. (*She rushes off, shouting at the Mexican boys.*) You! Boys! Muchachos! *You carry that luggage back down!*

(*The voices continue, fading. Shannon moves brokenly across the verandah. Maxine shakes her head.*)

MAXINE: Shannon, give 'em the bus key and let 'em go.

SHANNON: And me do what?

MAXINE: Stay here.

SHANNON: In Fred's old bedroom—yeah, in Fred's old bedroom.

MAXINE: You could do worse.

SHANNON: Could I? Well, then, I'll do worse, I'll . . . do worse.

MAXINE: Aw now, baby.

SHANNON: If I could do worse, I'll do worse. . . . (*He grips the section of railing by the verandah steps and stares with wide, lost eyes. His chest heaves like a spent runner's and he is bathed in sweat.*)

MAXINE: Give me that ignition key. I'll take it down to the driver while you bathe and rest and have a rum-coco, baby.

(*Shannon simply shakes his head slightly. Harsh bird cries sound in the rain forest. Voices are heard on the path.*)

HANNAH: Nonno, you've lost your sun glasses.

NONNO: No. Took them off. No sun.

(*Hannah appears at the top of the path, pushing her grandfather, Nonno, in a wheelchair. He is a very old man but has *a powerful voice for his age and always seems to be shouting something of importance. Nonno is a poet and a showman. There is a good kind of pride and he has it, carrying it like a banner wherever he goes. He is immaculately dressed—a linen suit, white as his thick poet's hair; a black string tie; and he is holding a black cane with a gold crook.*)

NONNO: Which way is the sea?

HANNAH: Right down below the hill, Nonno. (*He turns in the wheelchair and raises a hand to shield his eyes.*) We can't see it from here. (*The old man is deaf, and she shouts to make him hear.*)

NONNO: I can feel it and smell it. (*A murmur of wind sweeps through the rain forest.*) It's the cradle of life. (*He is shouting, too.*) Life began in the sea.

MAXINE: These two with your party?

SHANNON: No.

MAXINE: They look like a pair of loonies.

SHANNON: Shut up.

(*Shannon looks at Hannah and Nonno steadily, with a relief of tension almost like that of someone going under hypnosis. The old man still squints down the path, blindly, but Hannah is facing the verandah with a proud person's hope of acceptance when it is desperately needed.*)

HANNAH: How do you do.

MAXINE: Hello.

HANNAH: Have you ever tried pushing a gentleman in a wheelchair uphill through a rain forest?

MAXINE: Nope, and I wouldn't even try it *downhill.*

HANNAH: Well, now that we've made it, I don't regret the effort. What a view for a painter! (*She looks about her, panting, digging into her shoulder-bag for a handkerchief, aware that her face is flushed and sweating.*) They told me in town that this was the ideal place for a painter, and they weren't —*whew*—exaggerating!

SHANNON: You've got a scratch on your forehead.

HANNAH: Oh, is that what I felt.

SHANNON: Better put iodine on it.

HANNAH: Yes, I'll attend to that—*whew*—later, thank you.

MAXINE: Anything I can do for you?

HANNAH: I'm looking for the manager of the hotel.
MAXINE: Me—speaking.
HANNAH: Oh, *you're* the manager, *good*! How do you do, I'm Hannah Jelkes, Mrs. . . .
MAXINE: Faulk, Maxine Faulk. What can I do for you folks? (*Her tone indicates no desire to do anything for them.*)
HANNAH (*turning quickly to her grandfather*): Nonno, the manager is a *lady* from the *States.*

(*Nonno lifts a branch of wild orchids from his lap, ceremonially, with the instinctive gallantry of his kind.*)

NONNO (*shouting*): Give the lady these—botanical curiosities! —you picked on the way up.
HANNAH: I believe they're wild orchids, isn't that what they are?
SHANNON: Laelia tibicina.
HANNAH: Oh!
NONNO: But tell her, Hannah, tell her to keep them in the icebox till after dark, they draw bees in the sun! (*He rubs a sting on his chin with a rueful chuckle.*)
MAXINE: Are you all looking for rooms here?
HANNAH: Yes, we are, but we've come without reservations.
MAXINE: Well, honey, the Costa Verde is closed in September —except for a few special guests, so. . . .
SHANNON: They're special guests, for God's sake.
MAXINE: I thought you said they didn't come with your party.
HANNAH: Please let us be special guests.
MAXINE: *Watch out!*

(*Nonno has started struggling out of the wheelchair. Shannon rushes over to keep him from falling. Hannah has started toward him, too, then seeing that Shannon has caught him, she turns back to Maxine.*)

HANNAH: In twenty-five years of travel this is the first time we've ever arrived at a place without advance reservations.
MAXINE: Honey, that old man ought to be in a hospital.
HANNAH: Oh, no, no, he just sprained his ankle a little in Taxco this morning. He just needs a good night's rest, he'll be on his feet tomorrow. His recuperative powers are absolutely amazing for someone who is ninety-seven years *young*.

SHANNON: Easy, Grampa. Hang on. (*He is supporting the old man up to the verandah.*) Two steps. One! Two! Now you've made it, Grampa.

(*Nonno keeps chuckling breathlessly as Shannon gets him onto the verandah and into a wicker rocker.*)

HANNAH (*breaking in quickly*): I can't tell you how much I appreciate your taking us in here now. It's—providential.

MAXINE: Well, I can't send that old man back down the hill—right now—but like I told you the Costa Verde's practically closed in September. I just take in a few folks as a special accommodation and we operate on a special basis this month.

NONNO (*cutting in abruptly and loudly*): Hannah, tell the lady that my perambulator is temporary. I will soon be ready to crawl and then to toddle and before long I will be leaping around here like an—old—mountain—goat, ha-ha-ha-ha. . . .

HANNAH: Yes, I explained that, Grandfather.

NONNO: I don't like being on wheels.

HANNAH: Yes, my grandfather feels that the decline of the western world began with the invention of the wheel. (*She laughs heartily, but Maxine's look is unresponsive.*)

NONNO: And tell the manager . . . the, uh, lady . . . that I know some hotels don't want to take dogs, cats or monkeys and some don't even solicit the patronage of infants in their late nineties who arrive in perambulators with flowers instead of rattles . . . (*He chuckles with a sort of fearful, slightly mad quality. Hannah perhaps has the impulse to clap a hand over his mouth at this moment but must stand there smiling and smiling and smiling.*) . . . and a brandy flask instead of a teething ring, but tell her that these, uh, concessions to man's seventh age are only temporary, and. . . .

HANNAH: Nonno, I told her the wheelchair's because of a sprained ankle, Nonno!

SHANNON (*to himself*): Fantastic.

NONNO: And after my siesta, I'll wheel it back down the hill, I'll kick it back down the hill, right into the sea, and tell her. . . .

HANNAH: Yes? What, Nonno? (*She has stopped smiling now. Her tone and her look are frankly desperate.*) What shall I tell her now, Nonno?

NONNO: Tell her that if she'll forgive my disgraceful longevity and this . . . temporary decrepitude . . . I will present her with the last signed . . . compitty [*he means* "copy"] of my first volume of verse, published in . . . when, Hannah?

HANNAH (*hopelessly*): The day that President Ulysses S. Grant was inaugurated, Nonno.

NONNO: *Morning Trumpet!* Where is it—you have it, give it to her right now.

HANNAH: Later, a little later! (*Then she turns to Maxine and Shannon.*) My grandfather is the poet Jonathan Coffin. He is ninety-seven years *young* and will be ninety-eight years *young* the fifth of next month, October.

MAXINE: Old folks are remarkable, yep. The office phone's ringing—excuse me, I'll be right back. (*She goes around the verandah.*)

NONNO: Did I talk too much?

HANNAH (*quietly, to Shannon*): I'm afraid that he did. I don't think she's going to take us.

SHANNON: She'll take you. Don't worry about it.

HANNAH: Nobody would take us in town, and if we don't get in here, I would have to wheel him back down through the rain forest, and then *what*, then *where*? There would just be the road, and no direction to move in, except out to sea—and I doubt that we could make it divide before us.

SHANNON: That won't be necessary. I have a little influence with the patrona.

HANNAH: Oh, then, do use it, please. Her eyes said *no* in big blue capital letters.

(*Shannon pours some water from a pitcher on the verandah and hands it to the old man.*)

NONNO: What is this—libation?

SHANNON: Some icewater, Grampa.

HANNAH: Oh, that's kind of you. Thank you. I'd better give him a couple of salt tablets to wash down with it. (*Briskly she removes a bottle from her shoulder-bag.*) Won't you have some? I see you're perspiring, too. You have to be careful not to become dehydrated in the hot seasons under the Tropic of Cancer.

SHANNON (*pouring another glass of water*): Are you a little *financially* dehydrated, too?

HANNAH: That's right. Bone-dry, and I think the patrona suspects it. It's a logical assumption, since I pushed him up here myself, and the patrona has the look of a very logical woman. I am sure she knows that we couldn't afford to hire the taxi driver to help us up here.

MAXINE (*calling from the back*): Pancho?

HANNAH: A woman's practicality when she's managing something is harder than a man's for another woman to cope with, so if you have influence with her, please do use it. Please try to convince her that my grandfather will be on his feet tomorrow, if not tonight, and with any luck whatsoever, the money situation will be solved just as quickly. Oh, here she comes back, do help us!

(*Involuntarily, Hannah seizes hold of Shannon's wrist as Maxine stalks back onto the verandah, still shouting for Pancho. The Mexican boy reappears, sucking a juicy peeled mango—its juice running down his chin onto his throat.*)

MAXINE: Pancho, run down to the beach and tell Herr Fahrenkopf that the German Embassy's waiting on the phone for him. (*Pancho stares at her blankly until she repeats the order in Spanish.*) Dile a Herr Fahrenkopf que la embajada alemana lo llama al telefono. Corre, corre! (*Pancho starts indolently down the path, still sucking noisily on the mango.*) I said *run*! Corre, corre! (*He goes into a leisurely loping pace and disappears through the foliage.*)

HANNAH: What graceful people they are!

MAXINE: Yeah, they're graceful like cats, and just as dependable, too.

HANNAH: Shall we, uh, . . . *register* now?

MAXINE: You all can register later but I'll have to collect six dollars from you first if you want to put your names in the pot for supper. That's how I've got to operate here out of season.

HANNAH: Six? Dollars?

MAXINE: Yeah, three each. In season we operate on the continental plan but out of season like this we change to the modified American plan.

HANNAH: Oh, what is the, uh . . . modification of it? (*She gives Shannon a quick glance of appeal as she stalls for time, but his attention has turned inward as the bus horn blows down the hill.*)

MAXINE: Just two meals are included instead of all three.

HANNAH (*moving closer to Shannon and raising her voice*): Breakfast and dinner?

MAXINE: A continental breakfast and a cold lunch.

SHANNON (*aside*): Yeah, very cold—cracked ice—if you crack it yourself.

HANNAH (*reflectively*): Not dinner.

MAXINE: No! Not dinner.

HANNAH: Oh, I see, uh, but . . . we, uh, operate on a special basis ourselves. I'd better explain it to you.

MAXINE: How do you mean "operate,"—on what "basis"?

HANNAH: Here's our card. I think you may have heard of us. (*She presents the card to Maxine.*) We've had a good many write-ups. My grandfather is the oldest living and practicing poet. *And* he gives recitations. I . . . paint . . . water colors and I'm a "quick sketch artist." We travel together. We pay our way as we go by my grandfather's recitations and the sale of my water colors and quick character sketches in charcoal or pastel.

SHANNON (*to himself*): I have fever.

HANNAH: I usually pass among the tables at lunch and dinner in a hotel. I wear an artist's smock—picturesquely dabbed with paint—wide Byronic collar and flowing silk tie. I don't push myself on people. I just display my work and smile at them sweetly and if they invite me to do so sit down to make a quick character sketch in pastel or charcoal. If not? Smile sweetly and go on.

SHANNON: What does Grandpa do?

HANNAH: We pass among the tables together slowly. I introduce him as the world's oldest living and practicing poet. If invited, he gives a recitation of a poem. Unfortunately all of his poems were written a long time ago. But do you know, he has started a new poem?

For the first time in twenty years he's started another poem!

SHANNON: Hasn't finished it yet?

HANNAH: He still has inspiration, but his power of concentration has weakened a little, of course.

MAXINE: Right now he's not concentrating.

SHANNON: Grandpa's catchin' forty winks. Grampa? Let's hit the sack.

MAXINE: Now wait a minute. I'm going to call a taxi for these folks to take them back to town.

HANNAH: Please don't do that. We tried every hotel in town and they wouldn't take us. I'm afraid I have to place myself at your . . . mercy.

(*With infinite gentleness Shannon has roused the old man and is leading him into one of the cubicles back of the verandah. Distant cries of bathers are heard from the beach. The afternoon light is fading very fast now as the sun has dropped behind an island hilltop out to sea.*)

MAXINE: Looks like you're in for one night. Just one.

HANNAH: Thank you.

MAXINE: The old man's in number 4. You take 3. Where's your luggage—no luggage?

HANNAH: I hid it behind some palmettos at the foot of the path.

SHANNON (*shouting to Pancho*): Bring up her luggage. Tu, flojo . . . las maletas . . . baja las palmas. Vamos! (*The Mexican boys rush down the path.*) Maxine honey, would you cash a postdated check for me?

MAXINE (*shrewdly*): Yeah—mañana, maybe.

SHANNON: Thanks—generosity is the cornerstone of your nature.

(*Maxine utters her one-note bark of a laugh as she marches around the corner of the verandah.*)

HANNAH: I'm dreadfully afraid my grandfather had a slight stroke in those high passes through the sierras. (*She says this with the coolness of someone saying that it may rain before nightfall. An instant later, a long, long sigh of wind sweeps the hillside. The bathers are heard shouting below.*)

SHANNON: Very old people get these little "cerebral accidents," as they call them. They're not regular strokes, they're just little cerebral . . . incidents. The symptoms clear up so quickly that sometimes the old people don't even know they've had them.

(*They exchange this quiet talk without looking at each other. The Mexican boys crash back through the bushes at the top of the path, bearing some pieces of ancient luggage fantastically plastered with hotel and travel stickers indicating a vast range of wandering. The boys deposit the luggage near the steps.*)

SHANNON: How many times have you been around the world?

HANNAH: Almost as many times as the world's been around the sun, and I feel as if I had gone the whole way on foot.

SHANNON (*picking up her luggage*): What's your cell number?

HANNAH (*smiling faintly*): I believe she said it was cell number 3.

SHANNON: She probably gave you the one with the leaky roof. (*He carries the bags into the cubicle. Maxine is visible to the audience only as she appears outside the door to her office on the wing of the verandah.*) But you won't find out till it rains and then it'll be too late to do much about it but swim out of it. (*Hannah laughs wanly. Her fatigue is now very plain. Shannon comes back out with her luggage.*) Yep, she gave you the one with the leaky roof so you take mine and. . . .

HANNAH: Oh, no, no, Mr. Shannon, I'll find a dry spot if it rains.

MAXINE (*from around the corner of the verandah*): Shannon!

(*A bit of pantomime occurs between Hannah and Shannon. He wants to put her luggage in cubicle number 5. She catches hold of his arm, indicating by gesture toward the back that it is necessary to avoid displeasing the proprietor. Maxine shouts his name louder. Shannon surrenders to Hannah's pleading and puts her luggage back in the leaky cubicle number 3.*)

HANNAH: Thank you so much, Mr. Shannon. (*She disappears behind the mosquito netting. Maxine advances to the verandah angle as Shannon starts toward his own cubicle.*)

MAXINE (*mimicking Hannah's voice*): "Thank you so much, Mr. Shannon."

SHANNON: Don't be bitchy. Some people say thank you sincerely. (*He goes past her and down the steps from the end of the verandah.*) I'm going down for a swim now.

MAXINE: The water's blood temperature this time of day.

SHANNON: Yeah, well, I have a fever so it'll seem cooler to me. (*He crosses rapidly to the jungle path leading to the beach.*)

MAXINE (*following him*): Wait for me, I'll. . . .

(*She means she will go down with him, but he ignores her call and disappears into the foliage. Maxine shrugs angrily and goes back onto the verandah. She faces out, gripping the railing tightly and glaring into the blaze of the sunset as if it were a personal enemy. Then the ocean breathes a long cooling breath up the hill, as Nonno's voice is heard from his cubicle.*)

NONNO:

How calmly does the orange branch
Observe the sky begin to blanch,
Without a cry, without a prayer,
With no expression of despair. . . .

(*And from a beach cantina in the distance a marimba band is heard playing a popular song of that summer of 1940, "Palabras de Mujer"—which means "Words of Women."*)

Slow Dim Out and Slow Curtain

ACT TWO

Several hours later: near sunset.

The scene is bathed in a deep golden, almost coppery light; the heavy tropical foliage gleams with wetness from a recent rain.

Maxine comes around the turn of the verandah. To the formalities of evening she has made the concession of changing from levis to clean white cotton pants, and from a blue work shirt to a pink one. She is about to set up the folding cardtables for the evening meal which is served on the verandah. All the while she is talking, she is setting up tables, etc.

MAXINE: Miss Jelkes?

(*Hannah lifts the mosquito net over the door of cubicle number 3.*)

HANNAH: Yes, Mrs. Faulk?

MAXINE: Can I speak to you while I set up these tables for supper?

HANNAH: Of course, you may. I wanted to speak to you, too. (*She comes out. She is now wearing her artist's smock.*)

MAXINE: Good.

HANNAH: I just wanted to ask you if there's a tub-bath Grandfather could use. A shower is fine for me—I prefer a shower to a tub—but for my grandfather there is some danger of falling down in a shower and at his age, although he says he is made out of India rubber, a broken hipbone would be a very serious matter, so I. . . .

MAXINE: What I wanted to say is I called up the Casa de Huéspedes about you and your Grampa, and I can get you in there.

HANNAH: Oh, but we don't want to *move*!

MAXINE: The Costa Verde isn't the right place for you. Y'see, we cater to folks that like to rough it a little, and—well, frankly, we cater to younger people.

(*Hannah has started unfolding a cardtable.*)

HANNAH: Oh yes . . . uh . . . well . . . the, uh, Casa de Huéspedes, that means a, uh, sort of a rooming house, Mrs. Faulk?

MAXINE: Boarding house. They feed you, they'll even feed you on credit.

HANNAH: Where is it located?

MAXINE: It has a central location. You could get a doctor there quick if the old man took sick on you. You got to think about that.

HANNAH: Yes, I—(*She nods gravely, more to herself than Maxine.*)—I *have* thought about that, but. . . .

MAXINE: What are you doing?

HANNAH: Making myself useful.

MAXINE: Don't do that. I don't accept help from guests here.

(*Hannah hesitates, but goes on setting the tables.*)

HANNAH: Oh, please, let me. Knife and fork on one side, spoon on the . . . ? (*Her voice dies out.*)

MAXINE: Just put the plates on the napkins so they don't blow away.

HANNAH: Yes, it is getting breezy on the verandah. (*She continues setting the table.*)

MAXINE: Hurricane winds are already hitting up coast.

HANNAH: We've been through several typhoons in the Orient. Sometimes *outside* disturbances like that are an almost welcome distraction from *inside* disturbances, aren't they? (*This is said almost to herself. She finishes putting the plates on the paper napkins.*) When do you want us to leave here, Mrs. Faulk?

MAXINE: The boys'll move you in my station wagon tomorrow—no charge for the service.

HANNAH: That is very kind of you. (*Maxine starts away.*) Mrs. Faulk?

MAXINE (*turning back to her with obvious reluctance*): Huh?

HANNAH: Do you know jade?

MAXINE: Jade?

HANNAH: Yes.

MAXINE: Why?

HANNAH: I have a small but interesting collection of jade pieces. I asked if you know jade because in jade it's the craftsmanship, the carving of the jade, that's most important about it. (*She has removed a jade ornament from her blouse.*) This one, for instance—a miracle of carving. Tiny as it is, it has two figures carved on it—the legendary Prince Ahk and Princess Angh, and a heron flying above them. The artist that carved it probably received for this miraculously delicate workmanship, well, I would say perhaps the price of a month's supply of rice for his family, but the merchant who employed him sold it, I would guess, for at least three hundred pounds sterling to an English lady who got tired of it and gave it to me, perhaps because I painted her not as she was at that time but as I could see she must have looked in her youth. Can you see the carving?

MAXINE: Yeah, honey, but I'm not operating a hock shop here, I'm trying to run a hotel.

HANNAH: I know, but couldn't you just accept it as security for a few days' stay here?

MAXINE: You're completely broke, are you?

HANNAH: Yes, we are—completely.

MAXINE: You say that like you're proud of it.

HANNAH: I'm not proud of it or ashamed of it either. It just happens to be what's happened to us, which has never happened before in all our travels.

MAXINE (*grudgingly*): You're telling the truth, I reckon, but I told you the truth, too, when I told you, when you came here, that I had just lost my husband and he'd left me in such a financial hole that if living didn't mean more to me than money, I'd might as well have been dropped in the ocean with him.

HANNAH: Ocean?

MAXINE (*peacefully philosophical about it*): I carried out his burial instructions exactly. Yep, my husband, Fred Faulk, was the greatest game fisherman on the West Coast of Mexico—he'd racked up unbeatable records in sailfish, tarpon, kingfish, barracuda—and on his deathbed, last week, he requested to be dropped in the sea, yeah, right out there in that bay, not even sewed up in canvas, just in his fisherman outfit. So now old Freddie the Fisherman is feeding the fish—fishes' revenge on old Freddie. How about that, I ask you?

HANNAH (*regarding Maxine sharply*): I doubt that he regrets it.

MAXINE: I do. It gives me the shivers.

(*She is distracted by the German party singing a marching song on the path up from the beach. Shannon appears at the top of the path, a wet beachrobe clinging to him. Maxine's whole concentration shifts abruptly to him. She freezes and blazes with it like an exposed power line. For a moment the "hot light" is concentrated on her tense, furious figure. Hannah provides a visual counterpoint. She clenches her eyes shut for a moment, and when they open, it is on a look of stoical despair of the refuge she has unsuccessfully fought for. Then Shannon approaches the verandah and the scene is his.*)

SHANNON: Here they come up, your conquerors of the world, Maxine honey, singing "Horst Wessel." (*He chuckles fiercely, and starts toward the verandah steps.*)

MAXINE: Shannon, wash that sand off you before you come on the verandah.

(*The Germans are heard singing the "Horst Wessel" marching song. Soon they appear, trooping up from the beach like an animated canvas by Rubens. They are all nearly nude, pinked and bronzed by the sun. The women have decked themselves with garlands of pale green seaweed, glistening wet, and the Munich-opera bridegroom is blowing on a great conch shell. His father-in-law, the tank manufacturer, has his portable radio, which is still transmitting a shortwave broadcast about the Battle of Britain, now at its climax.*)

HILDA (*capering, astride her rubber horse*): Horsey, horsey, horsey!

HERR FAHRENKOPF (*ecstatically*): London is burning, the heart of London's on fire! (*Wolfgang turns a handspring onto the verandah and walks on his hands a few paces, then tumbles over with a great whoop. Maxine laughs delightedly with the Germans.*) Beer, beer, beer!

FRAU FAHRENKOPF: Tonight champagne!

(*The euphoric horseplay and shouting continue as they gambol around the turn of the verandah. Shannon has come onto the porch. Maxine's laughter dies out a little sadly, with envy.*)

SHANNON: You're turning this place into the Mexican Berchtesgaden, Maxine honey?

MAXINE: I told you to wash that sand off. (*Shouts for beer from the Germans draw her around the verandah corner.*)

HANNAH: Mr. Shannon, do you happen to know the Casa de Huéspedes, or anything about it, I mean? (*Shannon stares at her somewhat blankly.*) We are, uh, thinking of . . . *moving* there tomorrow. Do you, uh, recommend it?

SHANNON: I recommend it along with the Black Hole of Calcutta and the Siberian salt mines.

HANNAH (*nodding reflectively*): I suspected as much. Mr. Shannon, in your touring party, do you think there might be anyone interested in my water colors? Or in my character sketches?

SHANNON: I doubt it. I doubt that they're corny enough to please my ladies. *Oh-oh! Great Caesar's ghost.* . . .

(*This exclamation is prompted by the shrill, approaching call of his name. Charlotte appears from the rear, coming from the hotel annex, and rushes like a teen-age Medea toward the verandah. Shannon ducks into his cubicle, slamming the door so quickly that a corner of the mosquito netting is caught and sticks out, flirtatiously. Charlotte rushes onto the verandah.*)

CHARLOTTE: *Larry!*

HANNAH: Are you looking for someone, dear?

CHARLOTTE: Yeah, the man conducting our tour, Larry Shannon.

HANNAH: Oh, Mr. Shannon. I think he went down to the beach.

CHARLOTTE: I just now saw him coming up from the beach. (*She is tense and trembling, and her eyes keep darting up and down the verandah.*)

HANNAH: Oh. Well. . . . But. . . .

CHARLOTTE: Larry? Larry! (*Her shouts startle the rain-forest birds into a clamorous moment.*)

HANNAH: Would you like to leave a message for him, dear?

CHARLOTTE: No. I'm staying right here till he comes out of wherever he's hiding.

HANNAH: Why don't you just sit down, dear. I'm an artist, a painter. I was just sorting out my water colors and sketches in this portfolio, and look what I've come across. (*She selects a sketch and holds it up.*)

SHANNON (*from inside his cubicle*): Oh, God!

CHARLOTTE (*darting to the cubicle*): Larry, let me in there!

(*She beats on the door of the cubicle as Herr Fahrenkopf comes around the verandah with his portable radio. He is bug-eyed with excitement over the news broadcast in German.*)

HANNAH: Guten abend.

(*Herr Fahrenkopf jerks his head with a toothy grin, raising a hand for silence. Hannah nods agreeably and approaches him with her portfolio of drawings. He maintains the grin as she displays one picture after another. Hannah is uncertain whether the grin is for the pictures or the news broadcast. He stares at the pictures, jerking his head from time to time. It is rather like the pantomine of showing lantern slides.*)

CHARLOTTE (*suddenly crying out again*): Larry, open this door and let me in! I know you're in there, Larry!

HERR FAHRENKOPF: Silence, please, for one moment! This is a recording of Der Führer addressing the Reichstag just . . . (*He glances at his wristwatch.*) . . . eight hours ago, today, transmitted by Deutsches Nachrichtenbüro to Mexico City. Please! Quiet, bitte!

(*A human voice like a mad dog's bark emerges from the static momentarily. Charlotte goes on pounding on Shannon's door. Hannah suggests in pantomime that they go to the back verandah, but Herr Fahrenkopf despairs of hearing the broadcast. As he rises to leave, the light catches his polished glasses so that he appears for a moment to have electric light bulbs in his forehead. Then he ducks his head in a genial little bow and goes out beyond the verandah, where he performs some muscle-flexing movements of a formalized nature, like the preliminary stances of Japanese Suma wrestlers.*)

HANNAH: May I show you my work on the other verandah?

(*Hannah had started to follow Herr Fahrenkopf with her portfolio, but the sketches fall out, and she stops to gather them from the floor with the sad, preoccupied air of a lonely child picking flowers.*

(*Shannon's head slowly, furtively, appears through the window of his cubicle. He draws quickly back as Charlotte darts that way, stepping on Hannah's spilt sketches. Hannah utters a soft cry of protest, which is drowned by Charlotte's renewed clamor.*)

CHARLOTTE: Larry, Larry, Judy's looking for me. Let me come in, Larry, before she finds me here!

SHANNON: You can't come in. Stop shouting and I'll come out.

CHARLOTTE: All right, come out.

SHANNON: Stand back from the door so I *can*.

(*She moves a little aside and he emerges from his cubicle like a man entering a place of execution. He leans against the wall, mopping the sweat off his face with a handkerchief.*)

SHANNON: How does Miss Fellowes know what happened that night? Did you tell her?

CHARLOTTE: I didn't tell her, she guessed.

SHANNON: Guessing isn't knowing. If she is just guessing, that means she doesn't know—I mean if you're not lying, if you didn't tell her.

(*Hannah has finished picking up her drawings and moves quietly over to the far side of the verandah.*)

CHARLOTTE: Don't talk to me like that.

SHANNON: Don't complicate my life now, please, for God's sake, don't complicate my life now.

CHARLOTTE: Why have you changed like this?

SHANNON: I have a fever. Don't complicate my . . . fever.

CHARLOTTE: You act like you hated me now.

SHANNON: You're going to get me kicked out of Blake Tours, Charlotte.

CHARLOTTE: Judy is, not me.

SHANNON: Why did you sing "I Love You Truly" at me?

CHARLOTTE: Because I do love you truly!

SHANNON: Honey girl, don't you know that nothing worse could happen to a girl in your, your . . . unstable condition . . . than to get emotionally mixed up with a man in my unstable condition, huh?

CHARLOTTE: No, no, no, I—

SHANNON (*cutting through*): Two unstable conditions can set a whole world on fire, can blow it up, past repair, and that is just as true between two people as it's true between. . . .

CHARLOTTE: All I know is you've got to marry me, Larry, after what happened between us in Mexico City!

SHANNON: A man in my condition can't marry, it isn't decent or legal. He's lucky if he can even hold onto his job. (*He keeps catching hold of her hands and plucking them off his shoulders.*) I'm almost out of my mind, can't you see that, honey?

CHARLOTTE: I don't believe you don't love me.

SHANNON: Honey, it's almost impossible for anybody to believe they're not loved by someone they believe they love, but, honey, I love *nobody*. I'm like that, it isn't my fault. When I brought you home that night I told you goodnight in the hall, just kissed you on the cheek like the little girl that you are, but the instant I opened my door, you rushed into my room and I couldn't get you out of it, not even when I, oh God, tried to scare you out of it by, oh God, don't you remember?

(*Miss Fellowes' voice is heard from back of the hotel calling,* "Charlotte!")

CHARLOTTE: Yes, I remember that after making love to me, you hit me, Larry, you struck me in the face, and you twisted my arm to make me kneel on the floor and pray with you for forgiveness.

SHANNON: I do that, I do that always when I, when . . . I don't have a dime left in my nervous emotional bank account—I can't write a check on it, now.

CHARLOTTE: Larry, let me help you!

MISS FELLOWES (*approaching*): Charlotte, Charlotte, Charlie!

CHARLOTTE: Help me and let me help you!

SHANNON: The helpless can't help the helpless!

CHARLOTTE: Let me in, Judy's coming!

SHANNON: Let me go. Go away!

(*He thrusts her violently back and rushes into his cubicle, slamming and bolting the door—though the gauze netting is left sticking out. As Miss Fellowes charges onto the verandah, Charlotte runs into the next cubicle, and Hannah moves over from where she has been watching and meets her in the center.*)

MISS FELLOWES: Shannon, Shannon! Where are you?

HANNAH: I think Mr. Shannon has gone down to the beach.

MISS FELLOWES: Was Charlotte Goodall with him? A young blonde girl in our party—was she with him?

HANNAH: No, nobody was with him, he was completely alone.

MISS FELLOWES: I heard a door slam.

HANNAH: That was mine.

MISS FELLOWES (*pointing to the door with the gauze sticking out*): Is this yours?

HANNAH: Yes, mine. I rushed out to catch the sunset.

(*At this moment Miss Fellowes hears Charlotte sobbing in Hannah's cubicle. She throws the door open.*)

MISS FELLOWES: Charlotte! Come out of there, Charlie! (*She has seized Charlotte by the wrist.*) What's your word worth—nothing? You promised you'd stay away from him! (*Charlotte frees her arm, sobbing bitterly. Miss Fellowes seizes her again, tighter, and starts dragging her away.*) I have talked to your father about this man by long distance and he's getting out a warrant for his arrest, if he dare try coming back to the States after this!

CHARLOTTE: I don't care.

MISS FELLOWES: I do! I'm responsible for you.

CHARLOTTE: I don't want to go back to Texas!

MISS FELLOWES: Yes, you do! And you will!

(*She takes Charlotte firmly by the arm and drags her away behind the hotel. Hannah comes out of her cubicle, where she had gone when Miss Fellowes pulled Charlotte out of it.*)

SHANNON (*from his cubicle*): Ah, God. . . .

(*Hannah crosses to his cubicle and knocks by the door.*)

HANNAH: The coast is clear now, Mr. Shannon.

(*Shannon does not answer or appear. She sets down her portfolio to pick up Nonno's white linen suit, which she had pressed and hung on the verandah. She crosses to his cubicle with it, and calls in.*)

HANNAH: Nonno? It's almost time for supper! There's going to be a lovely, stormy sunset in a few minutes.

NONNO (*from within*): Coming!

HANNAH: So is Christmas, Nonno.

NONNO: So is the Fourth of July!

HANNAH: We're past the Fourth of July. Hallowe'en comes next and then Thanksgiving. I hope you'll come forth sooner. (*She lifts the gauze net over his cubicle door.*) Here's your suit, I've pressed it. (*She enters the cubicle.*)

NONNO: It's mighty dark in here, Hannah.

HANNAH: I'll turn the light on for you.

(*Shannon comes out of his cubicle, like the survivor of a plane crash, bringing out with him several pieces of his clerical garb. The black heavy silk bib is loosely fastened about his panting, sweating chest. He hangs over it a heavy gold cross with an amethyst center and attempts to fasten on a starched round collar. Now Hannah comes back out of Nonno's cubicle, adjusting the flowing silk tie which goes with her "artist" costume. For a moment they both face front, adjusting their two outfits. They are like two actors in a play which is about to fold on the road, preparing gravely for a performance which may be the last one.*)

HANNAH (*glancing at Shannon*): Are you planning to conduct church services of some kind here tonight, Mr. Shannon?

SHANNON: Goddamit, please help me with this! (*He means the round collar.*)

HANNAH (*crossing behind him*): If you're not going to conduct a church service, why get into that uncomfortable outfit?

SHANNON: Because I've been accused of being defrocked and of lying about it, that's why. I want to show the ladies that I'm still a clocked—*frocked!*—minister of the. . . .

HANNAH: Isn't that lovely gold cross enough to convince the ladies?

SHANNON: No, they know I redeemed it from a Mexico City pawnshop, and they suspect that that's where I got it in the first place.

HANNAH: Hold still just a minute. (*She is behind him, trying to fasten the collar.*) There now, let's hope it stays on. The button hole is so frayed I'm afraid that it won't hold the button. (*Her fear is instantly confirmed: the button pops out.*)

SHANNON: Where'd it go?

HANNAH: Here, right under. . . .

(*She picks it up. Shannon rips the collar off, crumples it and hurls it off the verandah. Then he falls into the hammock, panting and twisting. Hannah quietly opens her sketch pad and begins to sketch him. He doesn't at first notice what she is doing.*)

HANNAH (*as she sketches*): How long have you been inactive in the, uh, Church, Mr. Shannon?

SHANNON: What's that got to do with the price of rice in China?

HANNAH (*gently*): Nothing.

SHANNON: What's it got to do with the price of coffee beans in Brazil?

HANNAH: I retract the question. With apologies.

SHANNON: To answer your question politely, I have been inactive in the Church for all but one year since I was ordained a minister of the Church.

HANNAH (*sketching rapidly and moving forward a bit to see his face better*): Well, that's quite a sabbatical, Mr. Shannon.

SHANNON: Yeah, that's . . . quite a . . . sabbatical.

(*Nonno's voice is heard from his cubicle repeating a line of poetry several times.*)

SHANNON: Is your grandfather talking to himself in there?

HANNAH: No, he composes out loud. He has to commit his lines to memory because he can't see to write them or read them.

SHANNON: Sounds like he's stuck on one line.

HANNAH: Yes. I'm afraid his memory is failing. Memory failure is his greatest dread. (*She says this almost coolly, as if it didn't matter.*)

SHANNON: Are you drawing me?

HANNAH: Trying to. You're a very difficult subject. When the Mexican painter Siqueiros did his portrait of the American poet Hart Crane he had to paint him with closed eyes because he couldn't paint his eyes open—there was too much suffering in them and he couldn't paint it.

SHANNON: Sorry, but I'm not going to close my eyes for you. I'm hypnotizing myself—at least trying to—by looking at the light on the orange tree . . . leaves.

HANNAH: That's all right. I can paint your eyes open.

SHANNON: I had one parish one year and then I wasn't defrocked but I was . . . locked out of my church.

HANNAH: Oh . . . Why did they lock you out of it?

SHANNON: Fornication and heresy . . . in the same week.

HANNAH (*sketching rapidly*): What were the circumstances of the . . . uh . . . first offense?

SHANNON: Yeah, the fornication came first, preceded the heresy by several days. A very young Sunday-school teacher asked to see me privately in my study. A pretty little thing—no chance in the world—only child, and both of her parents were spinsters, almost identical spinsters wearing clothes of the opposite sexes. Fooling some of the people some of the time but not me—none of the time. . . . (*He is pacing the verandah with gathering agitation, and the all-inclusive mockery that his guilt produces.*) Well, she declared herself to me—wildly.

HANNAH: A declaration of love?

SHANNON: Don't make *fun* of me, honey!

HANNAH: I wasn't.

SHANNON: The natural, or unnatural, attraction of one . . . lunatic for . . . another . . . that's all it was. I was the goddamnedest prig in those days that even you could imagine. I said, let's kneel down together and pray and we did, we knelt down, but all of a sudden the kneeling position turned to a reclining position on the rug of my study and . . . When we got up? I struck her. Yes, I did, I struck her in the face and called her a damned little tramp. So she ran home. I heard the next day she'd cut herself with her father's straightblade razor. Yeah, the paternal spinster shaved.

HANNAH: Fatally?

SHANNON: Just broke the skin surface enough to bleed a little, but it made a scandal.

HANNAH: Yes, I can imagine that it . . . provoked some comment.

SHANNON: That it did, it did that. (*He pauses a moment in his fierce pacing as if the recollection still appalled him.*) So the next Sunday when I climbed into the pulpit and looked down over all of those smug, disapproving, accusing faces uplifted, I had an impulse to shake them—so I shook them. I had a prepared sermon—meek, apologetic—I threw it away, tossed it into the chancel. Look here, I said, I shouted, I'm tired of conducting services in praise and worship of a senile delinquent—yeah, that's what I said, I shouted! All your Western theologies, the whole mythology of them, are based on the concept of God as a *senile delinquent* and, by God, I will not and cannot continue to conduct services in praise and worship of this, this . . . this. . . .

HANNAH (*quietly*): Senile delinquent?

SHANNON: Yeah, this angry, petulant old man. I mean he's represented like a bad-tempered childish old, old, sick, peevish man—I mean like the sort of old man in a nursing home that's putting together a jigsaw puzzle and can't put it together and gets furious at it and kicks over the table. Yes, I tell you they *do* that, all our theologies do it—accuse God of being a cruel, senile delinquent, blaming the world and brutally punishing all he created for his own faults in construction, and then, ha-ha, yeah—a thunderstorm broke that Sunday. . . .

HANNAH: You mean *outside* the church?

SHANNON: Yep, it was wilder than I was! And out they slithered, they slithered out of their pews to their shiny black cockroach sedans, ha-ha, and I shouted after them, hell, I even followed them halfway out of the church, shouting after them as they. . . . (*He stops with a gasp for breath.*)

HANNAH: Slithered out?

SHANNON: I shouted after them, go on, go home and close your house windows, all your windows and doors, against the truth about God!

HANNAH: Oh, my heavens. Which is just what they did—poor things.

SHANNON: Miss Jelkes honey, Pleasant Valley, Virginia, was an exclusive suburb of a large city and these poor things were not poor—materially speaking.

HANNAH (*smiling a bit*): What was the, uh, upshot of it?

SHANNON: Upshot of it? Well, I wasn't defrocked. I was just locked out of the church in Pleasant Valley, Virginia, and put in a nice little private asylum to recuperate from a complete nervous breakdown as they preferred to regard it, and then, and then I . . . I entered my present line—tours of God's world conducted by a minister of God with a cross and a round collar to prove it. Collecting evidence!

HANNAH: Evidence of what, Mr. Shannon?

SHANNON (*a touch shyly now*): My personal idea of God, not as a senile delinquent, but as a. . . .

HANNAH: Incomplete sentence.

SHANNON: It's going to storm tonight—a terrific electric storm. Then you will see the Reverend T. Lawrence Shannon's conception of God Almighty paying a visit to the world he created. I want to go back to the Church and preach the gospel of God as Lightning and Thunder . . . and also stray dogs vivisected and . . . and . . . and. . . . (*He points out suddenly toward the sea.*) That's him! There he is now! (*He is pointing out at a blaze, a majestic apocalypse of gold light, shafting the sky as the sun drops into the Pacific.*) His oblivious majesty—and *here I am* on this . . . dilapidated verandah of a cheap hotel, out of season, in a country caught and destroyed in its flesh and corrupted in its spirit by its gold-hungry Conquistadors that bore the flag of the Inquisition along with the Cross of Christ. Yes . . . and. . . . (*There is a pause.*)

HANNAH: Mr. Shannon . . . ?

SHANNON: Yes . . . ?

HANNAH (*smiling a little*): I have a strong feeling you will go back to the Church with this evidence you've been collecting, but when you do and it's a black Sunday morning, look out over the congregation, over the smug, complacent faces for a few old, very old faces, looking up at you, as you begin your sermon, with eyes like a piercing cry for something to still look up to, something to still believe in. And then I think you'll not shout what you say you shouted that black Sunday in Pleasant Valley, Virginia. I think you will throw away the violent, furious sermon, you'll toss *it* into the chancel, and talk about . . . no, maybe talk about . . . nothing . . . just. . . .

SHANNON: What?

HANNAH: Lead them beside still waters because you know how badly they need the still waters, Mr. Shannon.

(*There is a moment of silence between them.*)

SHANNON: Lemme see that thing. (*He seizes the sketch pad from her and is visibly impressed by what he sees. There is another moment which is prolonged to Hannah's embarrassment.*)

HANNAH: Where did you say the patrona put your party of ladies?

SHANNON: She had her . . . Mexican concubines put their luggage in the annex.

HANNAH: Where is the annex?

SHANNON: Right down the hill back of here, but all of my ladies except the teen-age Medea and the older Medea have gone out in a glass-bottomed boat to observe the . . . submarine marvels.

HANNAH: Well, when they come back to the annex they're going to observe my water colors with some marvelous submarine prices marked on the mattings.

SHANNON: By God, you're a hustler, aren't you, you're a fantastic cool hustler.

HANNAH: Yes, like *you*, Mr. Shannon. (*She gently removes her sketch pad from his grasp.*) Oh, Mr. Shannon, if Nonno, Grandfather, comes out of his cell number 4 before I get back, will you please look out for him for me? I won't be longer than three shakes of a lively sheep's tail. (*She snatches up her portfolio and goes briskly off the verandah.*)

SHANNON: Fantastic, absolutely fantastic.

(*There is a windy sound in the rain forest and a flicker of gold light like a silent scattering of gold coins on the verandah; then the sound of shouting voices. The Mexican boys appear with a wildly agitated creature—a captive iguana tied up in a shirt. They crouch down by the cactus clumps that are growing below the verandah and hitch the iguana to a post with a piece of rope. Maxine is attracted by the commotion and appears on the verandah above them.*)

PEDRO: Tenemos fiesta!*

PANCHO: Comeremos bien.

PEDRO: Damela, damela! Yo la ataré.

PANCHO: *Yo* la cojí—*yo* la ataré!

PEDRO: Lo que vas a *hacer* es dejarla escapar.

MAXINE: Ammarla fuerte! Ole, ole! No la dejes escapar. Dejala moverse! (*to Shannon*) They caught an iguana.

SHANNON: I've noticed they did that, Maxine.

(*She is holding her drink deliberately close to him. The Germans have heard the commotion and crowd onto the verandah. Frau Fahrenkopf rushes over to Maxine.*)

*We're going to have a feast! / We'll eat good. / Give it to me! I'll tie it up. / *I* caught it—*I'll* tie it up! / You'll only let it get away. / Tie it up tight! Ole, ole! Don't let it get away. Give it enough room!

FRAU FAHRENKOPF: What is this? What's going on? A snake? Did they catch a snake?

MAXINE: No. *Lizard.*

FRAU FAHRENKOPF (*with exaggerated revulsion*): *Ouuu . . . lizard!* (*She strikes a grotesque attitude of terror as if she were threatened by Jack the Ripper.*)

SHANNON (*to Maxine*): You like iguana meat, don't you?

FRAU FAHRENKOPF: Eat? *Eat?* A big *lizard*?

MAXINE: Yep, they're mighty good eating—taste like white meat of chicken.

(*Frau Fahrenkopf rushes back to her family. They talk excitedly in German about the iguana.*)

SHANNON: If you mean Mexican chicken, that's no recommendation. Mexican chickens are scavengers and they taste like what they scavenge.

MAXINE: Naw, I mean Texas chicken.

SHANNON (*dreamily*): Texas . . . chicken. . . .

(*He paces restlessly down the verandah. Maxine divides her attention between his tall, lean figure, that seems incapable of stillness, and the wriggling bodies of the Mexican boys lying on their stomachs half under the verandah—as if she were mentally comparing two opposite attractions to her simple, sensual nature. Shannon turns at the end of the verandah and sees her eyes fixed on him.*)

SHANNON: What is the sex of this iguana, Maxine?

MAXINE: Hah, who cares about the sex of an iguana . . . (*He passes close by her.*) . . . except another . . . iguana?

SHANNON: Haven't you heard the limerick about iguanas? (*He removes her drink from her hand and it seems as if he might drink it, but he only sniffs it, with an expression of repugnance. She chuckles.*)

There was a young gaucho named Bruno
Who said about love, This I do know:
Women are fine, and sheep are divine,
But iguanas are—*Numero Uno!*

(*On* "Numero Uno" *Shannon empties Maxine's drink over the railing, deliberately onto the humped, wriggling posterior of Pedro, who springs up with angry protests.*)

PEDRO: Me cágo . . . hijo de la . . .
SHANNON: Qué? Qué?
MAXINE: Véte!

(*Shannon laughs viciously. The iguana escapes and both boys rush shouting after it. One of them dives on it and recaptures it at the edge of the jungle.*)

PANCHO: La iguana se escapé.
MAXINE: Cojela, cojela! La cojíste? Si no la cojes, te morderá el culo. La cojíste?
PEDRO: La cojí.*

(*The boys wriggle back under the verandah with the iguana.*)

MAXINE (*returning to Shannon*): I thought you were gonna break down and take a drink, Reverend.
SHANNON: Just the odor of liquor makes me feel nauseated.
MAXINE: You couldn't smell it if you got it *in* you. (*She touches his sweating forehead. He brushes her hand off like an insect.*) Hah! (*She crosses over to the liquor cart, and he looks after her with a sadistic grin.*)
SHANNON: Maxine honey, whoever told you that you look good in tight pants was not a sincere friend of yours.

(*He turns away. At the same instant, a crash and a hoarse, startled outcry are heard from Nonno's cubicle.*)

MAXINE: I knew it, I *knew* it! The old man's took a fall!

(*Shannon rushes into the cubicle, followed by Maxine.*

(*The light has been gradually, steadily dimming during the incident of the iguana's escape. There is, in effect, a division of scenes here, though it is accomplished without a blackout or curtain. As Shannon and Maxine enter Nonno's cubicle, Herr Fahrenkopf appears on the now twilit verandah. He turns on an outsize light fixture that is suspended from overhead, a full pearly-moon of a light globe that gives an unearthly luster to the scene. The great pearly globe is decorated by night insects, large but gossamer moths that have*

*The iguana's escaped. / Get it, get it! Have you got it? If you don't, it'll bite your behind. Have you got it? / He's got it.

immolated themselves on its surface: the light through their wings gives them an opalescent color, a touch of fantasy.

(*Now Shannon leads the old poet out of his cubicle, onto the facing verandah. The old man is impeccably dressed in snow-white linen with a black string tie. His leonine mane of hair gleams like silver as he passes under the globe.*)

NONNO: No bones broke, I'm made out of India rubber!

SHANNON: A traveler-born falls down many times in his travels.

NONNO: Hannah? (*His vision and other senses have so far deteriorated that he thinks he is being led out by Hannah.*) I'm pretty sure I'm going to finish it here.

SHANNON (*shouting, gently*): I've got the same feeling, Grampa.

(*Maxine follows them out of the cubicle.*)

NONNO: I've never been surer of anything in my life.

SHANNON (*gently and wryly*): I've never been surer of anything in mine either.

(*Herr Fahrenkopf has been listening with an expression of entrancement to his portable radio, held close to his ear, the sound unrealistically low. Now he turns it off and makes an excited speech.*)

HERR FAHRENKOPF: The London fires have spread all the way from the heart of London to the Channel coast! Goering, Field Marshall Goering, calls it "the new phase of conquest!" *Super-firebombs! Each night!*

(*Nonno catches only the excited tone of this announcement and interprets it as a request for a recitation. He strikes the floor with his cane, throws back his silver-maned head and begins the delivery in a grand, declamatory style.*)

NONNO:

Youth must be wanton, youth must be quick,
Dance to the candle while lasteth the wick,
Youth must be foolish and. . . .

(*Nonno falters on the line, a look of confusion and fear on his face. The Germans are amused. Wolfgang goes up to Nonno and shouts into his face.*)

WOLFGANG: Sir? What is your age? How old?

(*Hannah, who has just returned to the verandah, rushes up to her grandfather and answers for him.*)

HANNAH: He is ninety-seven years *young*!
HERR FAHRENKOPF: How old?
HANNAH: Ninety-seven—almost a *century young*!

(*Herr Fahrenkopf repeats this information to his beaming wife and Hilda in German.*)

NONNO (*cutting in on the Germans*):
Youth must be foolish and mirthful and blind,
Gaze not before and glance not behind,
Mark not. . . .

(*He falters again.*)

HANNAH (*prompting him, holding tightly onto his arm*):
Mark not the shadow that darkens the way—

(*They recite the next lines together.*)

Regret not the glitter of any lost day,
But laugh with no reason except the red wine,
For youth must be youthful and foolish and blind!

(*The Germans are loudly amused. Wolfgang applauds directly in the old poet's face. Nonno makes a little unsteady bow, leaning forward precariously on his cane. Shannon takes a firm hold of his arm as Hannah turns to the Germans, opening her portfolio of sketches and addressing Wolfgang.*)

HANNAH: Am I right in thinking you are on your honeymoon? (*There is no response, and she repeats the question in German while Frau Fahrenkopf laughs and nods vehemently.*) Habe ich recht dass Sie auf Ihrer Hochzeitsreise sind? Was für eine hübsche junge Braut! Ich mache Pastell-Skizzen . . . darf ich, würden Sie mir erlauben . . . ? Wurden Sie, bitte . . . bitte. . . .

(*Herr Fahrenkopf bursts into a Nazi marching song and leads his party to the champagne bucket on the table at the left. Shannon has steered Nonno to the other table.*)

NONNO (*exhilarated*): Hannah! What was the *take*?

HANNAH (*embarrassed*): Grandfather, sit down, please stop shouting!

NONNO: Hah? Did they cross your palm with silver or paper, Hannah?

HANNAH (*almost desperately*): Nonno! No more shouting! Sit down at the table. It's time to *eat*!

SHANNON: Chow time, Grampa.

NONNO (*confused but still shouting*): How much did they come across with?

HANNAH: Nonno! *Please!*

NONNO: Did they, did you . . . sell 'em a . . . water color?

HANNAH: No sale, Grandfather!

MAXINE: Hah!

(*Hannah turns to Shannon, her usual composure shattered, or nearly so.*)

HANNAH: He won't sit down or stop shouting.

NONNO (*blinking and beaming with the grotesque suggestion of an old coquette*): Hah? How rich did we strike it, Hannah?

SHANNON: *You* sit down, Miss Jelkes. (*He says it with gentle authority, to which she yields. He takes hold of the old man's forearm and places in his hand a crumpled Mexican bill.*) Sir? Sir? (*He is shouting.*) Five! Dollars! I'm putting it in your pocket.

HANNAH: We can't accept . . . gratuities, Mr. Shannon.

SHANNON: Hell, I gave him five pesos.

NONNO: Mighty good for one poem!

SHANNON: Sir? Sir? The *pecuniary rewards* of a *poem* are *grossly inferior* to its *merits, always!*

(*He is being fiercely, almost mockingly tender with the old man—a thing we are when the pathos of the old, the ancient, the dying is such a wound to our own* [*savagely beleaguered*] *nerves and sensibilities that this outside demand on us is beyond our collateral, our emotional reserve. This is as true of Hannah as it is of Shannon, of course. They have both overdrawn their reserves at this point of the encounter between them.*)

NONNO: Hah? Yes. . . . (*He is worn out now, but still shouting.*) We're going to clean up in this place!

SHANNON: You bet you're going to clean up here!

(*Maxine utters her one-note bark of a laugh. Shannon throws a hard roll at her. She wanders amiably back toward the German table.*)

NONNO (*tottering, panting, hanging onto Shannon's arm, thinking it is Hannah's*): Is the, the . . . diningroom . . . *crowded?* (*He looks blindly about with wild surmise.*)

SHANNON: Yep, it's filled to capacity! There's a big crowd at the door! (*His voice doesn't penetrate the old man's deafness.*)

NONNO: If there's a cocktail lounge, Hannah, we ought to . . . work that . . . first. Strike while the iron is hot, ho, ho, while it's hot. . . . (*This is like a delirium—only as strong a woman as Hannah could remain outwardly impassive.*)

HANNAH: He thinks you're me, Mr. Shannon. Help him into a chair. Please stay with him a minute, I. . . .

(*She moves away from the table and breathes as if she has just been dragged up half-drowned from the sea. Shannon eases the old man into a chair. Almost at once Nonno's feverish vitality collapses and he starts drifting back toward half sleep.*)

SHANNON (*crossing to Hannah*): What're you breathing like that for?

HANNAH: Some people take a drink, some take a pill. I just take a few deep breaths.

SHANNON: You're making too much out of this. It's a natural thing in a man as old as Grampa.

HANNAH: I know, I know. He's had more than one of these little "cerebral accidents" as you call them, and all in the last few months. He was amazing till lately. I had to show his passport to prove that he was the oldest living and practicing poet on earth. We did well, we made expenses and *more*! But . . . when I saw he was failing, I tried to persuade him to go back to Nantucket, but he conducts our tours. He said, "No, *Mexico*!" So here we are on this windy hilltop like a pair of scarecrows. . . . The bus from Mexico City broke down at an altitude of 15,000 feet above sea level. That's when I think the latest cerebral incident happened. It isn't so much the loss of hearing and sight but the . . . dimming out of the mind that I can't bear, because until lately, just lately, his mind was amazingly clear. But yesterday? In Taxco? I spent nearly all we had left on the wheelchair for him and still he insisted that we go on with the trip till we got to the sea, the . . . cradle of life as he calls it. . . . (*She suddenly notices Nonno, sunk in his chair as if lifeless. She draws a sharp breath, and goes quietly to him.*)

SHANNON (*to the Mexican boys*): Servicio! Aqui! (*The force of his order proves effective: they serve the fish course.*)

HANNAH: What a kind man you are. I don't know how to thank you, Mr. Shannon. I'm going to wake him up now. Nonno! (*She claps her hands quietly at his ear. The old man rouses with a confused, breathless chuckle.*) Nonno, linen napkins. (*She removes a napkin from the pocket of her smock.*) I always carry one with me, you see, in case we run into paper napkins as sometimes happens, you see. . . .

NONNO: Wonderful place here. . . . I hope it is à la carte, Hannah, I want a very light supper so I won't get sleepy. I'm going to work after supper. I'm going to finish it here.

HANNAH: Nonno? We've made a friend here. Nonno, this is the Reverend Mr. Shannon.

NONNO (*struggling out of his confusion*): Reverend?

HANNAH (*shouting to him*): Mr. Shannon's an Episcopal clergyman, Nonno.

NONNO: A man of God?

HANNAH: A man of God, on vacation.

NONNO: Hannah, tell him I'm too old to baptize and too young to bury but on the market for marriage to a rich widow, fat, fair and forty.

(*Nonno is delighted by all of his own little jokes. One can see him exchanging these pleasantries with the rocking-chair brigades of summer hotels at the turn of the century—and with professors' wives at little colleges in New England. But now it has become somewhat grotesque in a touching way, this desire to please, this playful manner, these venerable jokes. Shannon goes along with it. The old man touches something in him which is outside of his concern with himself. This part of the scene, which is played in a "scherzo" mood, has an accompanying windy obligato on the hilltop—all through it we hear the wind from the sea gradually rising, sweeping up the hill through the rain forest, and there are fitful glimmers of lightning in the sky.*)

NONNO: But very few ladies ever go past forty if you believe 'em, ho, ho! Ask him to . . . give the blessing. Mexican food needs blessing.

SHANNON: Sir, you give the blessing. I'll be right with you. (*He has broken one of his shoe laces.*)

NONNO: Tell him I will oblige him on one condition.

SHANNON: What condition, sir?

NONNO: That you'll keep my daughter company when I retire after dinner. I go to bed with the chickens and get up with the roosters, ho, ho! So you're a man of God. A benedict or a bachelor?

SHANNON: Bachelor, sir. No sane and civilized woman would have me, Mr. Coffin.

NONNO: What did he say, Hannah?

HANNAH (*embarrassed*): Nonno, give the blessing.

NONNO (*not hearing this*): I call her my daughter, but she's my daughter's daughter. We've been in charge of each other since she lost both her parents in the very first automobile crash on the island of Nantucket.

HANNAH: Nonno, give the blessing.

NONNO: She isn't a modern flapper, she isn't modern and she —doesn't flap, but she was brought up to be a wonderful wife and mother. But . . . I'm a selfish old man so I've kept her all to myself.

HANNAH (*shouting into his ear*): Nonno, Nonno, the blessing!

NONNO (*rising with an effort*): Yes, the blessing. Bless this food to our use, and ourselves to Thy service. Amen. (*He totters back into his chair.*)

SHANNON: Amen.

(*Nonno's mind starts drifting, his head drooping forward. He murmurs to himself.*)

SHANNON: How good is the old man's poetry?

HANNAH: My grandfather was a fairly well-known minor poet before the First World War and for a little while after.

SHANNON: In the minor league, huh?

HANNAH: Yes, a minor league poet with a major league spirit. I'm proud to be his granddaughter. . . . (*She draws a pack of cigarettes from her pocket, then replaces it immediately without taking a cigarette.*)

NONNO (*very confused*): Hannah, it's too hot for . . . hot cereals this . . . morning. . . . (*He shakes his head several times with a rueful chuckle.*)

HANNAH: He's not quite back, you see, he thinks it's morning. (*She says this as if making an embarrassing admission, with a quick, frightened smile at Shannon.)*

SHANNON: Fantastic—*fantastic.*

HANNAH: That word "fantastic" seems to be your favorite word, Mr. Shannon.

SHANNON (*looking out gloomily from the verandah*): Yeah, well, you know we—live on two levels, Miss Jelkes, the realistic level and the fantastic level, and which is the real one, really. . . .

HANNAH: I would say both, Mr. Shannon.

SHANNON: But when you live on the fantastic level as I have lately but have got to operate on the realistic level, that's when you're spooked, that's the spook. . . . (*This is said as if it were a private reflection.*) I thought I'd shake the spook here but conditions have changed here. I didn't know the patrona had turned to a widow, a sort of bright widow spider. (*He chuckles almost like Nonno.*)

(*Maxine has pushed one of those gay little brass-and-glass liquor carts around the corner of the verandah. It is laden with an ice bucket, coconuts and a variety of liquors. She hums gaily to herself as she pushes the cart close to the table.*)

MAXINE: Cocktails, anybody?

HANNAH: No, thank you, Mrs. Faulk, I don't think we care for any.

SHANNON: People don't drink cocktails between the fish and the entrée, Maxine honey.

MAXINE: Grampa needs a toddy to wake him up. Old folks need a toddy to pick 'em up. (*She shouts into the old man's ear.*) Grampa! How about a toddy? (*Her hips are thrust out at Shannon.*)

SHANNON: Maxine, your ass—excuse me, Miss Jelkes—your hips, Maxine, are too fat for this verandah.

MAXINE: Hah! Mexicans like 'em, if I can judge by the pokes and pinches I get in the busses to town. And so do the Germans. Ev'ry time I go near Herr Fahrenkopf he gives me a pinch or a goose.

SHANNON: Then go near him again for another goose.

MAXINE: Hah! I'm mixing Grampa a Manhattan with two cherries in it so he'll live through dinner.

SHANNON: Go on back to your Nazis, I'll mix the Manhattan for him. (*He goes to the liquor cart.*)

MAXINE (*to Hannah*): How about you, honey, a little soda with lime juice?

HANNAH: Nothing for me, thank you.

SHANNON: Don't make nervous people more nervous, Maxine.

MAXINE: You better let me mix that toddy for Grampa, you're making a mess of it, Shannon.

(*With a snort of fury, he thrusts the liquor cart like a battering ram at her belly. Some of the bottles fall off it; she thrusts it right back at him.*)

HANNAH: Mrs. Faulk, Mr. Shannon, this is childish, please stop it!

(*The Germans are attracted by the disturbance. They cluster around, laughing delightedly. Shannon and Maxine seize opposite ends of the rolling liquor cart and thrust it toward each other, both grinning fiercely as gladiators in mortal combat. The Germans shriek with laughter and chatter in German.*)

HANNAH: Mr. Shannon, stop it! (*She appeals to the Germans.*) *Bitte!* Nehmen Sie die Spirituosen weg. Bitte, nehmen Sie sie weg.

(*Shannon has wrested the cart from Maxine and pushed it at the Germans. They scream delightedly. The cart crashes into the wall of the verandah. Shannon leaps down the steps and runs into the foliage. Birds scream in the rain forest. Then sudden quiet returns to the verandah as the Germans go back to their own table.*)

MAXINE: Crazy, black Irish protestant son of a . . . protestant!

HANNAH: Mrs. Faulk, he's putting up a struggle not to drink.

MAXINE: Don't interfere. You're an interfering woman.

HANNAH: Mr. Shannon is dangerously . . . disturbed.

MAXINE: I know how to handle him, honey—you just met him today. Here's Grampa's Manhattan cocktail with two cherries in it.

HANNAH: Please don't call him Grampa.

MAXINE: Shannon calls him Grampa.

HANNAH (*taking the drink*): He doesn't make it sound condescending, but you *do*. My grandfather is a gentleman in the true sense of the word, he is a *gentle man*.

MAXINE: What are you?

HANNAH: I am his granddaughter.

MAXINE: Is that all you are?

HANNAH: I think it's enough to be.

MAXINE: Yeah, but you're also a deadbeat, using that dying old man for a front to get in places without the cash to pay even one day in advance. Why, you're dragging him around with you like Mexican beggars carry around a sick baby to put the touch on the tourists.

HANNAH: I told you I had no money.

MAXINE: Yes, and I told you that I was a widow—recent. In such a financial hole they might as well have buried me with my husband.

(*Shannon reappears from the jungle foliage but remains unnoticed by Hannah and Maxine.*)

HANNAH (*with forced calm*): Tomorrow morning, at daybreak, I will go in town. I will set up my easel in the plaza and peddle my water colors and sketch tourists. I am not a weak person, my failure here isn't typical of me.

MAXINE: I'm not a weak person either.

HANNAH: No. By no means, no. Your strength is awe-inspiring.

MAXINE: You're goddam right about that, but how do you think you'll get to Acapulco without the cabfare or even the busfare there?

HANNAH: I will go on shanks' mare, Mrs. Faulk—islanders are good walkers. And if you doubt my word for it, if you really think I came here as a deadbeat, then I will put my grandfather back in his wheelchair and push him back down this hill to the road and all the way back into town.

MAXINE: Ten miles, with a storm coming up?

HANNAH: Yes, I would—I will. (*She is dominating Maxine in this exchange. Both stand beside the table. Nonno's head is drooping back into sleep.*)

MAXINE: I wouldn't let you.

HANNAH: But you've made it clear that you don't want us to stay here for one night even.

MAXINE: The storm would blow that old man out of his wheelchair like a dead leaf.

HANNAH: He would prefer that to staying where he's not welcome, and I would prefer it for him, and for myself, Mrs. Faulk. (*She turns to the Mexican boys.*) Where is his wheelchair? Where is my grandfather's wheelchair?

(*This exchange has roused the old man. He struggles up from his chair, confused, strikes the floor with his cane and starts declaiming a poem.*)

NONNO:

Love's an old remembered song
A drunken fiddler plays,
Stumbling crazily along
Crooked alleyways.

When his heart is mad with music
He will play the—

HANNAH: Nonno, not now, Nonno! He thought someone asked for a poem. (*She gets him back into the chair. Hannah and Maxine are still unaware of Shannon.*)

MAXINE: Calm down, honey.

HANNAH: I'm perfectly calm, Mrs. Faulk.

MAXINE: I'm *not.* That's the trouble.

HANNAH: I understand that, Mrs. Faulk. You lost your husband just lately. I think you probably miss him more than you know.

MAXINE: No, the trouble is Shannon.

HANNAH: You mean his nervous state and his . . . ?

MAXINE: No, I just mean Shannon. I want you to lay off him, honey. You're not for Shannon and Shannon isn't for you.

HANNAH: Mrs. Faulk, I'm a New England spinster who is pushing forty.

MAXINE: I got the vibrations between you—I'm very good at catching vibrations between people—and there sure was a vibration between you and Shannon the moment you got here. That, just that, believe me, nothing but that has made this . . . misunderstanding between us. So if you just don't mess with Shannon, you and your Grampa can stay on here as long as you want to, honey.

HANNAH: Oh, Mrs. Faulk, do I look like a *vamp*?

MAXINE: They come in all types. I've had all types of them here.

(*Shannon comes over to the table.*)

SHANNON: Maxine, I told you don't make nervous people more nervous, but you wouldn't listen.

MAXINE: What you need is a drink.

SHANNON: Let me decide about that.

HANNAH: Won't you sit down with us, Mr. Shannon, and eat something? Please. You'll feel better.

SHANNON: I'm not hungry right now.

HANNAH: Well, just sit down with us, won't you?

(*Shannon sits down with Hannah.*)

MAXINE (*warningly to Hannah*): O.K. O.K. . . .

NONNO (*rousing a bit and mumbling*): Wonderful . . . wonderful place here.

(*Maxine retires from the table and wheels the liquor cart over to the German party.*)

SHANNON: Would you have gone through with it?

HANNAH: Haven't you ever played poker, Mr. Shannon?

SHANNON: You mean you were bluffing?

HANNAH: Let's say I was drawing to an inside straight. (*The wind rises and sweeps up the hill like a great waking sigh from the ocean.*) It *is* going to storm. I hope your ladies aren't still out in that, that . . . glass-bottomed boat, observing the, uh, submarine . . . marvels.

SHANNON: That's because you don't know these ladies. However, they're back from the boat trip. They're down at the cantina, dancing together to the jukebox and hatching new plots to get me kicked out of Blake Tours.

HANNAH: What would you do if you. . . .

SHANNON: Got the sack? Go back to the Church or take the long swim to China. (*Hannah removes a crumpled pack of cigarettes from her pocket. She discovers only two left in the pack and decides to save them for later. She returns the pack to her pocket.*) May I have one of your cigarettes, Miss Jelkes? (*She offers him the pack. He takes it from her and crumples it and throws it off the verandah.*) Never smoke those, they're made out of tobacco from cigarette stubs that beggars pick up off sidewalks and out of gutters in Mexico City. (*He produces a tin of English cigarettes.*) Have these—Benson and Hedges, imported, in an airtight tin, my luxury in my life.

HANNAH: Why—thank you, I will, since you have thrown mine away.

SHANNON: I'm going to tell you something about yourself. You are a lady, a *real* one and a *great* one.

HANNAH: What have I done to merit that compliment from you?

SHANNON: It isn't a compliment, it's just a report on what I've noticed about you at a time when it's hard for me to notice anything outside myself. You took out those Mexican cigarettes, you found you just had two left, you can't afford to buy a new pack of even that cheap brand, so you put them away for later. Right?

HANNAH: Mercilessly accurate, Mr. Shannon.

SHANNON: But when I asked you for one, you offered it to me without a sign of reluctance.

HANNAH: Aren't you making a big point out of a small matter?

SHANNON: Just the opposite, honey, I'm making a small point out of a very large matter. (*Shannon has put a cigarette in his lips but has no matches. Hannah has some and she lights his cigarette for him.*) How'd you learn how to light a match in the wind?

HANNAH: Oh, I've learned lots of useful little things like that. I wish I'd learned some *big* ones.

SHANNON: Such as what?

HANNAH: How to help you, Mr. Shannon. . . .

SHANNON: Now I know why I came here!

HANNAH: To meet someone who can light a match in the wind?

SHANNON (*looking down at the table, his voice choking*): To meet someone who wants to *help me*, Miss Jelkes. . . . (*He makes a quick, embarrassed turn in the chair, as if to avoid her seeing that he has tears in his eyes. She regards him steadily and tenderly, as she would her grandfather.*)

HANNAH: Has it been so long since anyone has wanted to help you, or have you just. . . .

SHANNON: Have I—what?

HANNAH: Just been so much involved with a struggle in yourself that you haven't noticed when people have wanted to help you, the little they can? I know people torture each other many times like devils, but sometimes they do see and know each other, you know, and then, if they're decent, they do want to help each other all that they can. Now will you please help *me*? Take care of Nonno while I remove my water colors from the annex verandah because the storm is coming up by leaps and bounds now.

(*He gives a quick, jerky nod, dropping his face briefly into the cup of his hands. She murmurs* "Thank you" *and springs up, starting along the verandah. Halfway across, as the storm closes in upon the hilltop with a thunderclap and a sound of rain coming, Hannah turns to look back at the table. Shannon has risen and gone around the table to Nonno.*)

SHANNON: Grampa? Nonno? Let's get up before the rain hits us, Grampa.

NONNO: What? What?

(*Shannon gets the old man out of his chair and shepherds him to the back of the verandah as Hannah rushes toward the annex. The Mexican boys hastily clear the table, fold it up and lean it against the wall. Shannon and Nonno turn and face toward the storm, like brave men facing a firing squad. Maxine is excitedly giving orders to the boys.*)

MAXINE: Pronto, pronto, muchachos! Pronto, pronto!* Llevaros todas las cosas! Pronto, pronto! Recoje los platos! Apurate con el mantel!

*Hurry, hurry, boys! Pick everything up! Get the plates! Hurry with the table cloth! / We *are* hurrying! / Let the storm wash the plates!

PEDRO: Nos estamos dando prisa!
PANCHO: Que el chubasco lave los platos!

(*The German party look on the storm as a Wagnerian climax. They rise from their table as the boys come to clear it, and start singing exultantly. The storm, with its white convulsions of light, is like a giant white bird attacking the hilltop of the Costa Verde. Hannah reappears with her water colors clutched against her chest.*)

SHANNON: Got them?
HANNAH: Yes, just in time. Here is your God, Mr. Shannon.
SHANNON (*quietly*): Yes, I see him, I hear him, I know him. And if he doesn't know that I know him, let him strike me dead with a bolt of his lightning.

(*He moves away from the wall to the edge of the verandah as a fine silver sheet of rain descends off the sloping roof, catching the light and dimming the figures behind it. Now everything is silver, delicately lustrous. Shannon extends his hands under the rainfall, turning them in it as if to cool them. Then he cups them to catch the water in his palms and bathes his forehead with it. The rainfall increases. The sound of the marimba band at the beach cantina is brought up the hill by the wind. Shannon lowers his hands from his burning forehead and stretches them out through the rain's silver sheet as if he were reaching for something outside and beyond himself. Then nothing is visible but these reaching-out hands. A pure white flash of lightning reveals Hannah and Nonno against the wall, behind Shannon, and the electric globe suspended from the roof goes out, the power extinguished by the storm. A clear shaft of light stays on Shannon's reaching-out hands till the stage curtain has fallen, slowly.*)*

Intermission

**Note:* In staging, the plastic elements should be restrained so that they don't take precedence over the more important human values. It should not seem like an "effect curtain." The faint, windy music of the marimba band from the cantina should continue as the house-lights are brought up for the intermission.

ACT THREE

The verandah, several hours later. Cubicles number 3, 4, and 5 are dimly lighted within. We see Hannah in number 3, and Nonno in number 4. Shannon, who has taken off his shirt, is seated at a table on the verandah, writing a letter to his Bishop. All but this table have been folded and stacked against the wall and Maxine is putting the hammock back up which had been taken down for dinner. The electric power is still off and the cubicles are lighted by oil lamps. The sky has cleared completely, the moon is making for full and it bathes the scene in an almost garish silver which is intensified by the wetness from the recent rainstorm. Everything is drenched—there are pools of silver here and there on the floor of the verandah. At one side a smudge-pot is burning to repel the mosquitoes, which are particularly vicious after a tropical downpour when the wind is exhausted.

Shannon is working feverishly on the letter to the Bishop, now and then slapping at a mosquito on his bare torso. He is shiny with perspiration, still breathing like a spent runner, muttering to himself as he writes and sometimes suddenly drawing a loud deep breath and simultaneously throwing back his head to stare up wildly at the night sky. Hannah is seated on a straight-back chair behind the mosquito netting in her cubicle—very straight herself, holding a small book in her hands but looking steadily over it at Shannon, like a guardian angel. Her hair has been let down. Nonno can be seen in his cubicle rocking back and forth on the edge of the narrow bed as he goes over and over the lines of his first new poem in "twenty-some years"—which he knows is his last one.

Now and then the sound of distant music drifts up from the beach cantina.

MAXINE: Workin' on your sermon for next Sunday, Rev'rend?

SHANNON: I'm writing a very important letter, Maxine. (*He means don't disturb me.*)

MAXINE: Who to, Shannon?

SHANNON: The Dean of the Divinity School at Sewanee. (*Maxine repeats* "Sewanee" *to herself, tolerantly.*) Yes, and I'd appreciate it very much, Maxine honey, if you'd get Pedro or Pancho to drive into town with it tonight so it will go out first thing in the morning.

MAXINE: The kids took off in the station wagon already—for some cold beers and hot whores at the cantina.

SHANNON: "Fred's dead"—he's lucky. . . .

MAXINE: Don't misunderstand me about Fred, baby. I miss him, but we'd not only stopped sleeping together, we'd stopped talking together except in grunts—no quarrels, no misunderstandings, but if we exchanged two grunts in the course of a day, it was a long conversation we'd had that day between us.

SHANNON: Fred knew when I was spooked—wouldn't have to tell him. He'd just look at me and say, "Well, Shannon, you're spooked."

MAXINE: Yeah, well, Fred and me'd reached the point of just grunting.

SHANNON: Maybe he thought you'd turned into a pig, Maxine.

MAXINE: Hah! You know damn well that Fred respected me, Shannon, like I did Fred. We just, well, you know . . . age difference. . . .

SHANNON: Well, you've got Pedro and Pancho.

MAXINE: Employees. They don't respect me enough. When you let employees get too free with you, personally, they stop respecting you, Shannon. And it's, well, it's . . . humiliating—not to be . . . respected.

SHANNON: Then take more bus trips to town for the Mexican pokes and the pinches, or get Herr Fahrenkopf to "respect" you, honey.

MAXINE: Hah! You kill me. I been thinking lately of selling out here and going back to the States, to Texas, and operating a tourist camp outside some live town like Houston or Dallas, on a highway, and renting out cabins to business executives wanting a comfortable little intimate little place to give a little after-hours dictation to their cute little secretaries that can't type or write shorthand. Complimentary rum-cocos—bathrooms with bidets. I'll introduce the bidet to the States.

SHANNON: Does everything have to wind up on that level with you, Maxine?

MAXINE: Yes and no, baby. I know the difference between loving someone and just sleeping with someone—even I know about that. (*He starts to rise.*) We've both reached a point where we've got to settle for something that works for us in our lives—even if it isn't on the highest kind of level.

SHANNON: I don't want to rot.

MAXINE: You wouldn't. I wouldn't let you! I know your psychological history. I remember one of your conversations on this verandah with Fred. You was explaining to him how your problems first started. You told him that Mama, your Mama, used to send you to bed before you was ready to sleep—so you practiced the little boy's vice, you amused yourself with yourself. And once she caught you at it and whaled your backside with the back side of a hairbrush because she said she had to punish you for it because it made God mad as much as it did Mama, and she had to punish you for it so God wouldn't punish you for it harder than she would.

SHANNON: I was talking to Fred.

MAXINE: Yeah, but I heard it, all of it. You said you loved God and Mama and so you quit it to please them, but it was your secret pleasure and you harbored a secret resentment against Mama and God for making you give it up. And so you got back at God by preaching atheistical sermons and you got back at Mama by starting to lay young girls.

SHANNON: I have never delivered an atheistical sermon, and never would or could when I go back to the Church.

MAXINE: You're not going back to no Church. Did you mention the charge of statutory rape to the Divinity Dean?

SHANNON (*thrusting his chair back so vehemently that it topples over*): Why don't you *let up* on me? You haven't let up on me since I got here this morning! *Let up on me!* Will you please *let up* on me?

MAXINE (*smiling serenely into his rage*): Aw baby. . . .

SHANNON: What do you mean by "aw baby"? What do you want out of me, Maxine honey?

MAXINE: Just to do this. (*She runs her fingers through his hair. He thrusts her hand away.*)

SHANNON: Ah, God. (*Words fail him. He shakes his head with a slight, helpless laugh and goes down the steps from the verandah.*)

MAXINE: The Chinaman in the kitchen says, "No sweat." . . . "No sweat." He says that's all his philosophy. All the Chinese philosophy in three words, "Mei yoo guanchi"—which is Chinese for "No sweat." . . . With your record and a charge of statutory rape hanging over you in Texas, how could you go to a church except to the Holy Rollers with some lively young female rollers and a bushel of hay on the church floor?

SHANNON: I'll drive into town in the bus to post this letter tonight. (*He has started toward the path. There are sounds below. He divides the masking foliage with his hands and looks down the hill.*)

MAXINE (*descending the steps from the verandah*): Watch out for the spook, he's out there.

SHANNON: My ladies are up to something. They're all down there on the road, around the bus.

MAXINE: They're running out on you, Shannon.

(*She comes up beside him. He draws back and she looks down the hill. The light in number 3 cubicle comes on and Hannah rises from the little table that she had cleared for letter-writing. She removes her Kabuki robe from a hook and puts it on as an actor puts on a costume in his dressing room. Nonno's cubicle is also lighted dimly. He sits on the edge of his cot, rocking slightly back and forth, uttering an indistinguishable mumble of lines from his poem.*)

MAXINE: Yeah. There's a little fat man down there that looks like Jake Latta to me. Yep, that's Jake, that's Latta. I reckon Blake Tours has sent him here to take over your party, Shannon. (*Shannon looks out over the jungle and lights a cigarette with jerky fingers.*) Well, let him do it. No sweat! He's coming up here now. Want me to handle it for you?

SHANNON: I'll handle it for myself. You keep out of it, please.

(*He speaks with a desperate composure. Hannah stands just behind the curtain of her cubicle, motionless as a painted figure, during the scene that follows. Jake Latta comes puffing up the verandah steps, beaming genially.*)

LATTA: Hi there, Larry.

SHANNON: Hello, Jake. (*He folds his letter into an envelope.*) Mrs. Faulk honey, this goes air special.
MAXINE: First you'd better address it.
SHANNON: Oh!

(*Shannon laughs and snatches the letter back, fumbling in his pocket for an address book, his fingers shaking uncontrollably. Latta winks at Maxine. She smiles tolerantly.*)

LATTA: How's our boy doin', Maxine?
MAXINE: He'd feel better if I could get him to take a drink.
LATTA: Can't you get a drink down him?
MAXINE: Nope, not even a rum-coco.
LATTA: Let's have a rum-coco, Larry.
SHANNON: You have a rum-coco, Jake. I have a party of ladies to take care of. And I've discovered that situations come up in this business that call for cold, sober judgment. How about you? Haven't you ever made that discovery, Jake? What're you doing here? Are you here with a party?
LATTA: I'm here to pick up your party, Larry boy.
SHANNON: That's interesting! On whose authority, Jake?
LATTA: Blake Tours wired me in Cuernavaca to pick up your party here and put them together with mine cause you'd had this little nervous upset of yours and. . . .
SHANNON: Show me the wire! Huh?
LATTA: The bus driver says you took the ignition key to the bus.
SHANNON: That's right. I have the ignition key to the bus and I have this party and neither the bus or the party will pull out of here till I say so.
LATTA: Larry, you're a sick boy. Don't give me trouble.
SHANNON: What jail did they bail you out of, you fat zero?
LATTA: Let's have the bus key, Larry.
SHANNON: Where did they dig you up? You've got no party in Cuernavaca, you haven't been out with a party since 'thirty-seven.
LATTA: Just give me the bus key, Larry.
SHANNON: In a pig's—snout!—like yours!
LATTA: Where is the reverend's bedroom, Mrs. Faulk?
SHANNON: The bus key is in my pocket. (*He slaps his pants pocket fiercely.*) Here, right here, in my pocket! Want it? Try and get it, Fatso!

LATTA: What language for a reverend to use, Mrs. Faulk. . . .

SHANNON (*holding up the key*): See it? (*He thrusts it back into his pocket.*) Now go back wherever you crawled from. My party of ladies is staying here three more days because several of them are in no condition to travel and neither—neither am I.

LATTA: They're getting in the bus now.

SHANNON: How are you going to start it?

LATTA: Larry, don't make me call the bus driver up here to hold you down while I get that key away from you. You want to see the wire from Blake Tours? Here. (*He produces the wire.*) Read it.

SHANNON: You sent that wire to yourself.

LATTA: From Houston?

SHANNON: You had it sent you from Houston. What's that prove? Why, Blake Tours was nothing, *nothing!*—till they got me. You think they'd let me go?—Ho, ho! Latta, it's caught up with you, Latta, all the whores and tequila have hit your brain now, Latta. (*Latta shouts down the hill for the bus driver.*) Don't you realize what I mean to Blake Tours? Haven't you seen the brochure in which they mention, they brag, that special parties are conducted by the Reverend T. Lawrence Shannon, D.D., noted world traveler, lecturer, son of a minister and grandson of a bishop, and the direct descendant of two colonial governors? (*Miss Fellowes appears at the verandah steps.*) Miss Fellowes has read the brochure, she's memorized the brochure. She knows what it says about me.

MISS FELLOWES (*to Latta*): Have you got the bus key?

LATTA: Bus driver's going to get it away from him, lady. (*He lights a cigar with dirty, shaky fingers.*)

SHANNON: Ha-ha-ha-ha-ha! (*His laughter shakes him back against the verandah wall.*)

LATTA: He's gone. (*He touches his forehead.*)

SHANNON: Why, those ladies . . . have had . . . some of them, most of them if not all of them . . . for the first time in their lives the advantage of contact, social contact, with a gentleman born and bred, whom under no other circumstances they could have possibly met . . . let alone be given the chance to insult and accuse and. . . .

MISS FELLOWES: Shannon! The girls are in the bus and we want to go now, so give up that key. Now!

(*Hank, the bus driver, appears at the top of the path, whistling casually: he is not noticed at first.*)

SHANNON: If I didn't have a decent sense of responsibility to these parties I take out, I would gladly turn over your party —because I don't like your party—to this degenerate here, this Jake Latta of the gutter-rat Lattas. Yes, I would—I would surrender the bus key in my pocket, even to Latta, but I am not that irresponsible, no, I'm not, to the parties that I take out, regardless of the party's treatment of me. I still feel responsible for them till I get them back wherever I picked them up. (*Hank comes onto the verandah.*) Hi, Hank. Are you friend or foe?

HANK: Larry, I got to get that ignition key now so we can get moving down there.

SHANNON: Oh! Then *foe!* I'm disappointed, Hank. I thought you were friend, not foe. (*Hank puts a wrestler's armlock on Shannon and Latta removes the bus key from his pocket. Hannah raises a hand to her eyes.*) O.K., O.K., you've got the bus key. By force. I feel exonerated now of all responsibility. Take the bus and the ladies in it and go. Hey, Jake, did you know they had lesbians in Texas—without the dikes the plains of Texas would be engulfed by the Gulf. (*He nods his head violently toward Miss Fellowes, who springs forward and slaps him.*) Thank you, Miss Fellowes. Latta, hold on a minute. I will not be stranded here. I've had unusual expenses on this trip. Right now I don't have my fare back to Houston or even to Mexico City. Now if there's any truth in your statement that Blake Tours have really authorized you to take over my party, then I am sure they have . . . (*He draws a breath, almost gasping.*) . . . I'm sure they must have given you something in the . . . the nature of . . . *severance* pay? Or at least enough to get me back to the States?

LATTA: I got no money for you.

SHANNON: I hate to question your word, but. . . .

LATTA: We'll drive you back to Mexico City. You can sit up front with the driver.

SHANNON: *You* would do that, Latta. *I'd* find it *humiliating*. Now! Give me my severance pay!

LATTA: Blake Tours is having to refund those ladies half the price of the tour. That's your severance pay. And Miss Fellowes tells me you got plenty of money out of this young girl you seduced in. . . .

SHANNON: Miss Fellowes, did you really make such a . . . ?

MISS FELLOWES: When Charlotte returned that night, she'd cashed two traveler's checks.

SHANNON: After I had spent all my own cash.

MISS FELLOWES: On what? Whores in the filthy places you took her through?

SHANNON: Miss Charlotte cashed two ten-dollar traveler's checks because I had spent all the cash I had on me. And I've never had to, I've certainly never desired to, have relations with whores.

MISS FELLOWES: You took her through ghastly places, such as. . . .

SHANNON: I showed her what she wanted me to show her. Ask her! I showed her San Juan de Letran, I showed her Tenampa and some other places not listed in the Blake Tours brochure. I showed her more than the floating gardens at Xochimilco, Maximilian's Palace, and the mad Empress Carlotta's little homesick chapel, Our Lady of Guadalupe, the monument to Juarez, the relics of the Aztec civilization, the sword of Cortez, the headdress of Montezuma. I showed her what she told me she wanted to see. Where is she? Where is Miss . . . oh, down there with the ladies. (*He leans over the rail and shouts down.*) Charlotte! Charlotte! (*Miss Fellowes seizes his arm and thrusts him away from the verandah rail.*)

MISS FELLOWES: Don't you dare!

SHANNON: Dare what?

MISS FELLOWES: Call her, speak to her, go near her, you, you . . . *filthy!*

(*Maxine reappears at the corner of the verandah, with the ceremonial rapidity of a cuckoo bursting from a clock to announce the hour. She just stands there with an incongruous grin, her big eyes unblinking, as if they were painted on her round beaming face. Hannah holds a gold-lacquered Japanese fan motionless but open in one hand; the other hand touches the netting at the cubicle door as if she were checking an impulse to rush to Shannon's defense. Her attitude has the style of a Kabuki dancer's pose. Shannon's manner becomes courtly again.*)

SHANNON: Oh, all right, I won't. I only wanted her to confirm my story that I took her out that night at her request, not at my . . . suggestion. All that I did was offer my services to her when *she* told *me* she'd like to see things not listed in the brochure, not usually witnessed by ordinary tourists such as. . . .

MISS FELLOWES: Your hotel bedroom? Later? That too? She came back *flea*-bitten!

SHANNON: Oh, now, don't exaggerate, please. Nobody ever got any fleas off Shannon.

MISS FELLOWES: Her clothes had to be fumigated!

SHANNON: I understand your annoyance, but you are going too far when you try to make out that I gave Charlotte fleas. I don't deny that. . . .

MISS FELLOWES: Wait till they get my *report*!

SHANNON: I don't deny that it's possible to get fleabites on a tour of inspection of what lies under the public surface of cities, off the grand boulevards, away from the nightclubs, even away from Diego Rivera's murals, but. . . .

MISS FELLOWES: Oh, preach that in a pulpit, Reverend Shannon *de*-frocked!

SHANNON (*ominously*): You've said that once too often. (*He seizes her arm.*) This time before witnesses. Miss Jelkes? Miss Jelkes!

(*Hannah opens the curtain of her cubicle.*)

HANNAH: Yes, Mr. Shannon, what is it?

SHANNON: You heard what this. . . .

MISS FELLOWES: Shannon! Take your hand off my arm!

SHANNON: Miss Jelkes, just tell me, did you hear what she . . . (*His voice stops oddly with a choked sobbing sound. He runs at the wall and pounds it with his fists.*)

MISS FELLOWES: I spent this entire afternoon and over twenty dollars checking up on this impostor, with long-distance phone calls.

HANNAH: Not impostor—you mustn't say things like that.

MISS FELLOWES: You were locked out of your church!—for atheism and seducing of girls!

SHANNON (*turning about*): In front of God and witnesses, you are lying, lying!

LATTA: Miss Fellowes, I want you to know that Blake Tours was deceived about this character's background and Blake Tours will see that he is blacklisted from now on at every travel agency in the States.

SHANNON: How about Africa, Asia, Australia? The whole world, Latta, God's world, has been the range of my travels. I haven't stuck to the schedules of the brochures and I've always allowed the ones that were willing to see, to *see*!—the underworlds of all places, and if they had hearts to be touched, feelings to feel with, I gave them a priceless chance to feel and be touched. And none will ever forget it, none of them, ever, never! (*The passion of his speech imposes a little stillness.*)

LATTA: Go on, lie back in your hammock, that's all you're good for, Shannon. (*He goes to the top of the path and shouts down the hill.*) O.K., let's get cracking. Get that luggage strapped on top of the bus, we're moving! (*He starts down the hill with Miss Fellowes.*)

NONNO (*incongruously, from his cubicle*):

How calmly does the orange branch
Observe the sky begin to blanch. . . .

(*Shannon sucks in his breath with an abrupt, fierce sound. He rushes off the verandah and down the path toward the road. Hannah calls after him, with a restraining gesture. Maxine appears on the verandah. Then a great commotion commences below the hill, with shrieks of outrage and squeals of shocked laughter.*)

MAXINE (*rushing to the path*): Shannon! Shannon! Get back up here, get back up here. Pedro, Pancho, traerme a Shannon. Que está haciendo allí? Oh, my God! Stop him, for God's sake, somebody stop him!

(*Shannon returns, panting and spent. He is followed by Maxine.*)

MAXINE: Shannon, go in your room and stay there until that party's gone.

SHANNON: Don't give me orders.

MAXINE: You do what I tell you to do or I'll have you removed —you know where.

SHANNON: Don't push me, don't pull at me, Maxine.

MAXINE: All right, do as I say.

SHANNON: Shannon obeys only Shannon.

MAXINE: You'll sing a different tune if they put you where they put you in 'thirty-six. Remember 'thirty-six, Shannon?

SHANNON: O.K., Maxine, just . . . let me breathe alone, please. I won't go but I will lie in the . . . hammock.

MAXINE: Go into Fred's room where I can watch you.

SHANNON: Later, Maxine, not yet.

MAXINE: Why do you always come here to crack up, Shannon?

SHANNON: It's the hammock, Maxine, the hammock by the rain forest.

MAXINE: Shannon, go in your room and stay there until I get back. Oh, my God, the money. They haven't paid the mother-grabbin' bill. I got to go back down there and collect their goddam bill before they. . . . Pancho, vijilalo, entiendes? (*She rushes back down the hill, shouting* "Hey! Just a minute down there!")

SHANNON: What did I do? (*He shakes his head, stunned.*) I don't know what I did.

(*Hannah opens the screen of her cubicle but doesn't come out. She is softly lighted so that she looks, again, like a medieval sculpture of a saint. Her pale gold hair catches the soft light. She has let it down and still holds the silver-backed brush with which she was brushing it.*)

SHANNON: God almighty, I . . . what did I do? I don't know what I did. (*He turns to the Mexican boys who have come back up the path.*) Que hice? Que hice?

(*There is breathless, spasmodic laughter from the boys as Pancho informs him that he pissed on the ladies' luggage.*)

PANCHO: Tú measte en las maletas de las señoras!

(*Shannon tries to laugh with the boys, while they bend double with amusement. Shannon's laughter dies out in little choked spasms. Down the hill, Maxine's voice is raised in angry altercation with Jake Latta. Miss Fellowes' voice is lifted and then there is a general rhubarb to which is added the roar of the bus motor.*)

SHANNON: There go my ladies, ha, ha! There go my . . . (*He turns about to meet Hannah's grave, compassionate gaze. He tries to laugh again. She shakes her head with a slight restraining gesture and drops the curtain so that her softly luminous figure is seen as through a mist.*) . . . ladies, the last of my—ha, ha!—ladies. (*He bends far over the verandah rail, then straightens violently and with an animal outcry begins to pull at the chain suspending the gold cross about his neck. Pancho watches indifferently as the chain cuts the back of Shannon's neck. Hannah rushes out to him.*)

HANNAH: Mr. Shannon, stop that! You're cutting yourself doing that. That isn't necessary, so stop it! (*to Pancho:*) Agarrale las manos! (*Pancho makes a halfhearted effort to comply, but Shannon kicks at him and goes on with the furious self-laceration.*) Shannon, let me do it, let me take it off you. Can I take it off you? (*He drops his arms. She struggles with the clasp of the chain but her fingers are too shaky to work it.*)

SHANNON: No, no, it won't come off, I'll have to break it off me.

HANNAH: No, no, wait—I've got it. (*She has now removed it.*)

SHANNON: Thanks. Keep it. Goodbye! (*He starts toward the path down to the beach.*)

HANNAH: Where are you going? What are you going to do?

SHANNON: I'm going swimming. I'm going to swim out to China!

HANNAH: No, no, not tonight, Shannon! Tomorrow . . . tomorrow, Shannon!

(*But he divides the trumpet-flowered bushes and passes through them. Hannah rushes after him, screaming for* "Mrs. Faulk." *Maxine can be heard shouting for the Mexican boys.*)

MAXINE: Muchachos, cojerlo! Atarlo! Está loco. Traerlo acqui. Catch him, he's crazy. Bring him back and tie him up!

(*In a few moments Shannon is hauled back through the bushes and onto the verandah by Maxine and the boys. They rope him into the hammock. His struggle is probably not much of a real struggle—histrionics mostly. But Hannah stands wringing her hands by the steps as Shannon, gasping for breath, is tied up.*)

HANNAH: The ropes are too tight on his chest!

MAXINE: No, they're not. He's acting, acting. He likes it! I know this black Irish bastard like nobody ever knowed him, so you keep out of it, honey. He cracks up like this so regular that you can set a calendar by it. Every eighteen months he does it, and twice he's done it here and I've had to pay for his medical care. Now I'm going to call in town to get a doctor to come out here and give him a knockout injection, and if he's not better tomorrow he's going into the Casa de Locos again like he did the last time he cracked up on me!

(*There is a moment of silence.*)

SHANNON: Miss Jelkes?

HANNAH: Yes.

SHANNON: Where are you?

HANNAH: I'm right here behind you. Can I do anything for you?

SHANNON: Sit here where I can see you. Don't stop talking. I have to fight this panic.

(*There is a pause. She moves a chair beside his hammock. The Germans troop up from the beach. They are delighted by the drama that Shannon has provided. In their scanty swimsuits they parade onto the verandah and gather about Shannon's captive figure as if they were looking at a funny animal in a zoo. Their talk is in German except when they speak directly to Shannon or Hannah. Their heavily handsome figures gleam with oily wetness and they keep chuckling lubriciously.*)

HANNAH: Please! Will you be so kind as to leave him alone?

(*They pretend not to understand her. Frau Fahrenkopf bends over Shannon in his hammock and speaks to him loudly and slowly in English.*)

FRAU FAHRENKOPF: Is this true you make pee-pee all over the suitcases of the ladies from Texas? Hah? Hah? You run down there to the bus and right in front of the ladies you pees all over the luggage of the ladies from Texas?

(*Hannah's indignant protest is drowned in the Rabelaisian laughter of the Germans.*)

HERR FAHRENKOPF: Thees is vunderbar, vunderbar! Hah? Thees is a *epic gesture*! Hah? Thees is the way to demonstrate to ladies that you are a American *gentleman*! Hah?

(*He turns to the others and makes a ribald comment. The two women shriek with amusement, Hilda falling back into the arms of Wolfgang, who catches her with his hands over her almost nude breasts.*)

HANNAH (*calling out*): Mrs. Faulk! Mrs. Faulk! (*She rushes to the verandah angle as Maxine appears there.*) Will you please ask these people to leave him alone. They're tormenting him like an animal in a trap.

(*The Germans are already trooping around the verandah, laughing and capering gaily.*)

SHANNON (*suddenly, in a great shout*): Regression to infantilism, ha, ha, regression to infantilism . . . The infantile protest, ha, ha, ha, the infantile expression of rage at Mama and rage at God and rage at the goddam crib, and rage at the everything, rage at the . . . everything. . . . Regression to infantilism. . . .

(*Now all have left but Hannah and Shannon.*)

SHANNON: Untie me.
HANNAH: Not yet.
SHANNON: I can't stand being tied up.
HANNAH: You'll have to stand it a while.
SHANNON: It makes me panicky.
HANNAH: I know.
SHANNON: A man can die of panic.
HANNAH: Not if he enjoys it as much as you, Mr. Shannon.

(*She goes into her cubicle directly behind his hammock. The cubicle is lighted and we see her removing a small teapot and a tin of tea from her suitcase on the cot, then a little alcohol burner. She comes back out with these articles.*)

SHANNON: What did you mean by that insulting remark?

HANNAH: What remark, Mr. Shannon?

SHANNON: That I enjoy it.

HANNAH: Oh . . . that.

SHANNON: Yes. That.

HANNAH: That wasn't meant as an insult, just an observation. I don't judge people, I draw them. That's all I do, just draw them, but in order to draw them I have to observe them, don't I?

SHANNON: And you've observed, you think you've observed, that I like being tied in this hammock, trussed up in it like a hog being hauled off to the slaughter house, Miss Jelkes.

HANNAH: Who wouldn't like to suffer and atone for the sins of himself and the world if it could be done in a hammock with ropes instead of nails, on a hill that's so much lovelier than Golgotha, the Place of the Skull, Mr. Shannon? There's something almost voluptuous in the way that you twist and groan in that hammock—no nails, no blood, no death. Isn't that a comparatively comfortable, almost voluptuous kind of crucifixion to suffer for the guilt of the world, Mr. Shannon?

(*She strikes a match to light the alcohol burner. A pure blue jet of flame springs up to cast a flickering, rather unearthly glow on their section of the verandah. The glow is delicately refracted by the subtle, faded colors of her robe—a robe given to her by a Kabuki actor who posed for her in Japan.*)

SHANNON: Why have you turned against me all of a sudden, when I need you the most?

HANNAH: I haven't turned against you at all, Mr. Shannon. I'm just attempting to give you a character sketch of yourself, in words instead of pastel crayons or charcoal.

SHANNON: You're certainly suddenly very sure of some New England spinsterish attitudes that I didn't know you had in you. I thought that you were an *emancipated* Puritan, Miss Jelkes.

HANNAH: Who is . . . ever . . . completely?

SHANNON: I thought you were sexless but you've suddenly turned into a woman. Know how I know that? Because you, not me—not me—are taking pleasure in my tied-up condition. All women, whether they face it or not, want to see a man in a tied-up situation. They work at it all their lives, to get a man in a tied-up situation. Their lives are fulfilled, they're satisfied at last, when they get a man, or as many men as they can, in the tied-up situation. (*Hannah leaves the alcohol burner and teapot and moves to the railing where she grips a verandah post and draws a few deep breaths.*) You don't like this observation of you? The shoe's too tight for comfort when it's on your own foot, Miss Jelkes? Some deep breaths again—feeling panic?

HANNAH (*recovering and returning to the burner*): I'd like to untie you right now, but let me wait till you've passed through your present disturbance. You're still indulging yourself in your . . . your Passion Play performance. I can't help observing this self-indulgence in you.

SHANNON: What rotten indulgence?

HANNAH: Well, your busload of ladies from the female college in Texas. I don't like those ladies any more than you do, but after all, they did save up all year to make this Mexican tour, to stay in stuffy hotels and eat the food they're used to. They want to be at home away from home, but you . . . you indulged yourself, Mr. Shannon. You did conduct the tour as if it was just for you, for your own pleasure.

SHANNON: Hell, what pleasure—going through hell all the way?

HANNAH: Yes, but comforted, now and then, weren't you, by the little musical prodigy under the wing of the college vocal instructor?

SHANNON: Funny, ha-ha funny! Nantucket spinsters have their wry humor, don't they?

HANNAH: Yes, they do. They have to.

SHANNON (*becoming progressively quieter under the cool influence of her voice behind him*): I can't see what you're up to, Miss Jelkes honey, but I'd almost swear you're making a pot of tea over there.

HANNAH: That is just what I'm doing.

SHANNON: Does this strike you as the right time for a tea party?

HANNAH: This isn't plain tea, this is poppyseed tea.

SHANNON: Are you a slave to the poppy?

HANNAH: It's a mild, sedative drink that helps you get through nights that are hard for you to get through and I'm making it for my grandfather and myself as well as for you, Mr. Shannon. Because, for all three of us, this won't be an easy night to get through. Can't you hear him in his cell number 4, mumbling over and over and over the lines of his new poem? It's like a blind man climbing a staircase that goes to nowhere, that just falls off into space, and I hate to say what it is. . . . (*She draws a few deep breaths behind him.*)

SHANNON: Put some hemlock in his poppyseed tea tonight so he won't wake up tomorrow for the removal to the Casa de Huéspedes. Do that act of mercy. Put in the hemlock and I will consecrate it, turn it to God's blood. Hell, if you'll get me out of this hammock I'll serve it to him myself, I'll be your accomplice in this act of mercy. I'll say, "Take and drink this, the blood of our—"

HANNAH: Stop it! Stop being childishly cruel! I can't stand for a person that I respect to talk and behave like a small, cruel boy, Mr. Shannon.

SHANNON: What've you found to respect in me, Miss . . . Thin-Standing-Up-Female-Buddha?

HANNAH: I respect a person that has had to fight and howl for his decency and his—

SHANNON: *What* decency?

HANNAH: Yes, for his decency and his bit of goodness, much more than I respect the lucky ones that just had theirs handed out to them at birth and never afterwards snatched away from them by . . . unbearable . . . torments, I. . . .

SHANNON: You *respect* me?

HANNAH: I do.

SHANNON: But you just said that I'm taking pleasure in a . . . voluptuous crucifixion without nails. A . . . what? . . . painless atonement for the—

HANNAH (*cutting in*): Yes, but I think—

SHANNON: Untie me!

HANNAH: Soon, soon. Be patient.

SHANNON: Now!

HANNAH: Not quite yet, Mr. Shannon. Not till I'm reasonably sure that you won't swim out to China, because, you see, I think you think of the . . . "the long swim to China" as another painless atonement. I mean I don't think you think you'd be intercepted by sharks and barracudas before you got far past the barrier reef. And I'm afraid you *would be*. It's as simple as that, if that is simple.

SHANNON: What's simple?

HANNAH: Nothing, except for simpletons, Mr. Shannon.

SHANNON: Do you believe in people being tied up?

HANNAH: Only when they might take the long swim to China.

SHANNON: All right, Miss Thin-Standing-Up-Female-Buddha, just light a Benson & Hedges cigarette for me and put it in my mouth and take it out when you hear me choking on it—if that doesn't seem to you like another bit of voluptuous self-crucifixion.

HANNAH (*looking about the verandah*): I will, but . . . where did I put them?

SHANNON: I have a pack of my own in my pocket.

HANNAH: Which pocket?

SHANNON: I don't know which pocket, you'll have to frisk me for it. (*She pats his jacket pocket.*)

HANNAH: They're not in your coat-pocket.

SHANNON: Then look for them in my pants' pockets.

(*She hesitates to put her hand in his pants' pockets, for a moment. Hannah has always had a sort of fastidiousness, a reluctance, toward intimate physical contact. But after the momentary fastidious hesitation, she puts her hands in his pants' pocket and draws out the cigarette pack.*)

SHANNON: Now light it for me and put it in my mouth.

(*She complies with these directions. Almost at once he chokes and the cigarette is expelled.*)

HANNAH: You've dropped it on you—where is it?

SHANNON (*twisting and lunging about in the hammock*): It's under me, under me, burning. Untie me, for God's sake, will you—it's burning me through my pants!

HANNAH: Raise your hips so I can—

SHANNON: I can't, the ropes are too tight. Untie me, untieeeee meeeeee!

HANNAH: I've found it, I've got it!

(*But Shannon's shout has brought Maxine out of her office. She rushes onto the verandah and sits on Shannon's legs.*)

MAXINE: Now hear this, you crazy black Irish mick, you! You Protestant black Irish looney, I've called up Lopez, Doc Lopez. Remember him—the man in the dirty white jacket that come here the last time you cracked up here? And hauled you off to the Casa de Locos? Where they threw you into that cell with nothing in it but a bucket and straw and a water pipe? That you crawled up the water pipe? And dropped head-down on the floor and got a concussion? Yeah, and I told him you were back here to crack up again and if you didn't quiet down here tonight you should be hauled out in the morning.

SHANNON (*cutting in, with the honking sound of a panicky goose*): Off, off, off, off, off!

HANNAH: Oh, Mrs. Faulk, Mr. Shannon won't quiet down till he's left alone in the hammock.

MAXINE: Then why don't *you* leave him alone?

HANNAH: I'm not sitting on him and he . . . has to be cared for by someone.

MAXINE: And the someone is *you*?

HANNAH: A long time ago, Mrs. Faulk, I had experience with someone in Mr. Shannon's condition, so I know how necessary it is to let them be quiet for a while.

MAXINE: He wasn't quiet, he was shouting.

HANNAH: He will quiet down again. I'm preparing a sedative tea for him, Mrs. Faulk.

MAXINE: Yeah, I see. Put it out. Nobody cooks here but the Chinaman in the kitchen.

HANNAH: This is just a little alcohol burner, a spirit lamp, Mrs. Faulk.

MAXINE: I know what it is. It goes out! (*She blows out the flame under the burner.*)

SHANNON: Maxine honey? (*He speaks quietly now.*) Stop persecuting this lady. You can't intimidate her. A bitch is no match for a lady except in a brass bed, honey, and sometimes not even there.

(*The Germans are heard shouting for beer—a case of it to take down to the beach.*)

WOLFGANG: Eine Kiste Carta Blanca.

FRAU FAHRENKOPF: Wir haben genug gehabt . . . vielleicht nicht.

HERR FAHRENKOPF: Nein! Niemals genug.

HILDA: Mutter du bist dick . . . aber wir sind es nicht.

SHANNON: Maxine, you're neglecting your duties as a beer-hall waitress. (*His tone is deceptively gentle.*) They want a case of Carta Blanca to carry down to the beach, so give it to 'em . . . and tonight, when the moon's gone down, if you'll let me out of this hammock, I'll try to imagine you as a . . . as a nymph in her teens.

MAXINE: A fat lot of good you'd be in your present condition.

SHANNON: Don't be a sexual snob at your age, honey.

MAXINE: Hah! (*But the unflattering offer has pleased her realistically modest soul, so she goes back to the Germans.*)

SHANNON: Now let me try a bit of your poppyseed tea, Miss Jelkes.

HANNAH: I ran out of sugar, but I had some ginger, some sugared ginger. (*She pours a cup of tea and sips it.*) Oh, it's not well brewed yet, but try to drink some now and the— (*She lights the burner again.*)—the second cup will be better. (*She crouches by the hammock and presses the cup to his lips. He raises his head to sip it, but he gags and chokes.*)

SHANNON: *Caesar's ghost!*—it could be chased by the witches' brew from Macbeth.

HANNAH: Yes, I know, it's still bitter.

(*The Germans appear on the wing of the verandah and go trooping down to the beach, for a beer festival and a moonlight swim. Even in the relative dark they have a luminous color, an almost phosphorescent pink and gold color of skin. They carry with them a case of Carta Blanca beer and the fantastically painted rubber horse. On their faces are smiles of euphoria as they move like a dream-image, starting to sing a marching song as they go.*)

SHANNON: Fiends out of hell with the . . . voices of . . . angels.

HANNAH: Yes, they call it "the logic of contradictions," Mr. Shannon.

SHANNON (*lunging suddenly forward and undoing the loosened ropes*): Out! Free! Unassisted!

HANNAH: Yes, I never doubted that you could get loose, Mr. Shannon.

SHANNON: Thanks for your help, anyhow.

HANNAH: Where are you going?

(*He has crossed to the liquor cart.*)

SHANNON: Not far. To the liquor cart to make myself a rum-coco.

HANNAH: Oh. . . .

SHANNON (*at the liquor cart*): Coconut? Check. Machete? Check. Rum? Double check! Ice? The ice-bucket's empty. O.K., it's a night for warm drinks. Miss Jelkes? Would you care to have your complimentary rum-coco?

HANNAH: No thank you, Mr. Shannon.

SHANNON: You don't mind me having mine?

HANNAH: Not at all, Mr. Shannon.

SHANNON: You don't disapprove of this weakness, this self-indulgence?

HANNAH: Liquor isn't your problem, Mr. Shannon.

SHANNON: What is my problem, Mr. Jelkes?

HANNAH: The oldest one in the world—the need to believe in something or in someone—almost anyone—almost anything . . . something.

SHANNON: Your voice sounds hopeless about it.

HANNAH: No, I'm not hopeless about it. In fact, I've discovered something to believe in.

SHANNON: Something like . . . God?

HANNAH: No.

SHANNON: What?

HANNAH: Broken gates between people so they can reach each other, even if it's just for one night only.

SHANNON: One night stands, huh?

HANNAH: One night . . . communication between them on a verandah outside their . . . separate cubicles, Mr. Shannon.

SHANNON: You don't mean physically, do you?

HANNAH: No.

SHANNON: I didn't think so. Then what?

HANNAH: A little understanding exchanged between them, a wanting to help each other through nights like this.

SHANNON: Who was the someone you told the widow you'd helped long ago to get through a crack-up like this one I'm going through?

HANNAH: Oh . . . that. Myself.

SHANNON: You?

HANNAH: Yes. I can help you because I've been through what you are going through now. I had something like your spook—I just had a different name for him. I called him the blue devil, and . . . oh . . . we had quite a battle, quite a contest between us.

SHANNON: Which you obviously won.

HANNAH: I couldn't afford to lose.

SHANNON: How'd you beat your blue devil?

HANNAH: I showed him that I could endure him and I made him respect my endurance.

SHANNON: How?

HANNAH: Just by, just by . . . enduring. Endurance is something that spooks and blue devils respect. And they respect all the tricks that panicky people use to outlast and outwit their panic.

SHANNON: Like poppyseed tea?

HANNAH: Poppyseed tea or rum-cocos or just a few deep breaths. Anything, everything, that we take to give them the slip, and so to keep on going.

SHANNON: To where?

HANNAH: To somewhere like this, perhaps. This verandah over the rain forest and the still-water beach, after long, difficult travels. And I don't mean just travels about the world, the earth's surface. I mean . . . subterranean travels, the . . . the journeys that the spooked and bedevilled people are forced to take through the . . . the *unlighted* sides of their natures.

SHANNON: Don't tell me you have a dark side to your nature.

(*He says this sardonically.*)

HANNAH: I'm sure I don't have to tell a man as experienced and knowledgeable as you, Mr. Shannon, that everything has its shadowy side?

(*She glances up at him and observes that she doesn't have his attention. He is gazing tensely at something off the verandah. It is the kind of abstraction, not vague but fiercely concentrated, that occurs in madness. She turns to look where he's looking. She closes her eyes for a moment and draws a deep breath, then goes on speaking in a voice like a hypnotist's, as if the words didn't matter, since he is not listening to her so much as to the tone and the cadence of her voice.*)

HANNAH: Everything in the whole solar system has a shadowy side to it except the sun itself—the sun is the single exception. You're not listening, are you?

SHANNON (*as if replying to her*): The spook is in the rain forest. (*He suddenly hurls his coconut shell with great violence off the verandah, creating a commotion among the jungle birds.*) Good shot—it caught him right on the kisser and his teeth flew out like popcorn from a popper.

HANNAH: Has he gone off—to the dentist?

SHANNON: He's retreated a little way away for a little while, but when I buzz for my breakfast tomorrow, he'll bring it in to me with a grin that'll curdle the milk in the coffee and he'll stink like a . . . a gringo drunk in a Mexican jail who's slept all night in his vomit.

HANNAH: If you wake up before I'm out, I'll bring your coffee in to you . . . if you call me.

SHANNON (*His attention returns to her*): No, you'll be gone, God help me.

HANNAH: Maybe and maybe not. I might think of something tomorrow to placate the widow.

SHANNON: The widow's implacable, honey.

HANNAH: I think I'll think of something because I have to. I can't let Nonno be moved to the Casa de Huéspedes, Mr. Shannon. Not any more than I could let you take the long swim out to China. You know that. Not if I can prevent it, and when I have to be resourceful, I can be very resourceful.

SHANNON: How'd you get over your crack-up?

HANNAH: I never cracked up, I couldn't afford to. Of course, I nearly did once. I was young once, Mr. Shannon, but I was one of those people who can be young without really having their youth, and not to have your youth when you are young is naturally very disturbing. But I was lucky. My work, this occupational therapy that I gave myself—painting and doing quick character sketches—made me look out of myself, not in, and gradually, at the far end of the tunnel that I was struggling out of I began to see this faint, very faint gray light—the light of the world outside me—and I kept climbing toward it. I had to.

SHANNON: Did it stay a gray light?

HANNAH: No, no, it turned white.

SHANNON: Only white, never gold?

HANNAH: No, it stayed only white, but white is a very good light to see at the end of a long black tunnel you thought would be neverending, that only God or Death could put a stop to, especially when you . . . since I was . . . far from sure about God.

SHANNON: You're still unsure about him?

HANNAH: Not as unsure as I was. You see, in my profession I have to look hard and close at human faces in order to catch something in them before they get restless and call out, "Waiter, the check, we're leaving." Of course sometimes, a few times, I just see blobs of wet dough that pass for human faces, with bits of jelly for eyes. Then I cue in Nonno to give a recitation, because I can't draw such faces. But those aren't the usual faces, I don't think they're even real. Most times I *do* see something, and I can catch it—I *can*, like I caught something in your face when I sketched you this afternoon with your eyes open. Are you still listening to me? (*He crouches beside her chair, looking up at her intently.*) In Shanghai, Shannon, there is a place that's called the House for the Dying—the old and penniless dying, whose younger, penniless living children and grandchildren take them there for them to get through with their dying on pallets, on straw mats. The first time I went there it shocked me, I ran away from it. But I came back later and I saw that their children and grandchildren and the custodians of the place had put little comforts beside their death-pallets, little flowers and opium candies and religious emblems. That made me able to stay to draw their dying faces. Sometimes only their eyes were still alive, but, Mr. Shannon, those eyes of the penniless dying with those last little comforts beside them, I tell you, Mr. Shannon, those eyes looked up with their last dim life left in them as clear as the stars in the Southern Cross, Mr. Shannon. And now . . . now I am going to say something to you that will sound like something that only the spinster granddaughter of a minor romantic poet is likely to say. . . . Nothing I've ever seen has seemed as beautiful to me, not even the view from this verandah between the sky and the still-water beach, and lately . . . lately my grandfather's eyes have looked up at me like that. . . . (*She rises abruptly and crosses to the front of the verandah.*) Tell me, what is that sound I keep hearing down there?

SHANNON: There's a marimba band at the cantina on the beach.

HANNAH: I don't mean that, I mean that scraping, scuffling sound that I keep hearing under the verandah.

SHANNON: Oh, that. The Mexican boys that work here have caught an iguana and tied it up under the verandah, hitched it to a post, and naturally of course it's trying to scramble away. But it's got to the end of its rope, and get any further it cannot. Ha-ha—that's it. (*He quotes from Nonno's poem:* "And still the orange," etc.) Do you have any life of your own—besides your water colors and sketches and your travels with Grampa?

HANNAH: We make a home for each other, my grandfather and I. Do you know what I mean by a home? I don't mean a regular home. I mean I don't mean what other people mean when they speak of a home, because I don't regard a home as a . . . well, as a place, a building . . . a house . . . of wood, bricks, stone. I think of a home as being a thing that two people have between them in which each can . . . well, nest—rest—live in, emotionally speaking. Does that make any sense to you, Mr. Shannon?

SHANNON: Yeah, complete. But. . . .

HANNAH: Another incomplete sentence.

SHANNON: We better leave it that way. I might've said something to hurt you.

HANNAH: I'm not thin skinned, Mr. Shannon.

SHANNON: No, well, then, I'll say it. . . . (*He moves to the liquor cart.*) When a bird builds a nest to rest in and live in, it doesn't build it in a . . . a falling-down tree.

HANNAH: I'm not a bird, Mr. Shannon.

SHANNON: I was making an analogy, Miss Jelkes.

HANNAH: I thought you were making yourself another rum-coco, Mr. Shannon.

SHANNON: Both. When a bird builds a nest, it builds it with an eye for the . . . the relative permanence of the location, and also for the purpose of mating and propagating its species.

HANNAH: I still say that I'm not a bird, Mr. Shannon, I'm a human being and when a member of that fantastic species builds a nest in the heart of another, the question of permanence isn't the first or even the last thing that's considered . . . necessarily? . . . always? Nonno and I have been continually reminded of the impermanence of things lately. We go back to a hotel where we've been many times before and it isn't there any more. It's been demolished and there's one of those glassy, brassy new ones. Or if the old one's still there, the manager or the Maitre D who always welcomed us back so cordially before has been replaced by someone new who looks at us with suspicion.

SHANNON: Yeah, but you still had each other.

HANNAH: Yes. We did.

SHANNON: But when the old gentleman goes?

HANNAH: Yes?

SHANNON: What will you do? Stop?

HANNAH: Stop or go on . . . probably go on.

SHANNON: Alone? Checking into hotels alone, eating alone at tables for one in a corner, the tables waiters call aces.

HANNAH: Thank you for your sympathy, Mr. Shannon, but in my profession I'm obliged to make quick contacts with strangers who turn to friends very quickly.

SHANNON: Customers aren't friends.

HANNAH: They turn to friends, if they're friendly.

SHANNON: Yeah, but how will it seem to be traveling alone after so many years of traveling with. . . .

HANNAH: I will know how it feels when I feel it—and don't say alone as if nobody had ever gone on alone. For instance, you.

SHANNON: I've always traveled with trainloads, planeloads and busloads of tourists.

HANNAH: That doesn't mean you're still not really alone.

SHANNON: I never fail to make an intimate connection with someone in my parties.

HANNAH: Yes, the youngest young lady, and I was on the verandah this afternoon when the latest of these young ladies gave a demonstration of how lonely the intimate connection has always been for you. The episode in the cold, inhuman hotel room, Mr. Shannon, for which you despise the lady almost as much as you despise yourself. Afterwards you are so polite to the lady that I'm sure it must chill her to the bone, the scrupulous little attentions that you pay her in return for your little enjoyment of her. The gentleman-of-Virginia act that you put on for her, your noblesse oblige treatment of her . . . Oh no, Mr. Shannon, don't kid yourself that you ever travel with someone. You have always traveled alone except for your spook, as you call it. He's your traveling companion. Nothing, nobody else has traveled with you.

SHANNON: Thank you for your sympathy, Miss Jelkes.

HANNAH: You're welcome, Mr. Shannon. And now I think I had better warm up the poppyseed tea for Nonno. Only a good night's sleep could make it possible for him to go on from here tomorrow.

SHANNON: Yes, well, if the conversation is over—I think I'll go down for a swim now.

HANNAH: To China?

SHANNON: No, not to China, just to the little island out here with the sleepy bar on it . . . called the Cantina Serena.

HANNAH: Why?

SHANNON: Because I'm not a nice drunk and I was about to ask you a not nice question.

HANNAH: Ask it. There's no set limit on questions here tonight.

SHANNON: And no set limit on answers?

HANNAH: None I can think of between you and me, Mr. Shannon.

SHANNON: That I will take you up on.

HANNAH: Do.

SHANNON: It's a bargain.

HANNAH: Only do lie back down in the hammock and drink a full cup of the poppyseed tea this time. It's warmer now and the sugared ginger will make it easier to get down.

SHANNON: All right. The question is this: have you never had in your life any kind of a lovelife? (*Hannah stiffens for a moment.*) I thought you said there was no limit set on questions.

HANNAH: We'll make a bargain—I will answer your question *after* you've had a full cup of the poppyseed tea so you'll be able to get the good night's sleep you need, too. It's fairly warm now and the sugared ginger's made it much more—(*She sips the cup.*)—palatable.

SHANNON: You think I'm going to drift into dreamland so you can welch on the bargain? (*He accepts the cup from her.*)

HANNAH: I'm not a welcher on bargains. Drink it all. All. *All!*

SHANNON (*with a disgusted grimace as he drains the cup*): *Great* Caesar's *ghost.* (*He tosses the cup off the verandah and falls into the hammock, chuckling.*) The oriental idea of a Mickey Finn, huh? Sit down where I can see you, Miss Jelkes honey. (*She sits down in a straight-back chair, some distance from the hammock.*) Where I can *see* you! I don't have an x-ray eye in the back of my head, Miss Jelkes. (*She moves the chair alongside the hammock.*) Further, further, up further. (*She complies.*) There now. Answer the question now, Miss Jelkes honey.

HANNAH: Would you mind repeating the question.

SHANNON (*slowly, with emphasis*): Have you never had in all of your life and your travels any experience, any encounter, with what Larry-the-crackpot Shannon thinks of as a lovelife?

HANNAH: There are . . . worse things than chastity, Mr. Shannon.

SHANNON: Yeah, lunacy and death are both a little worse, *maybe!* But chastity isn't a thing that a beautiful woman or an attractive man falls into like a booby trap or an over-grown gopher hole, is it? (*There is a pause.*) I still think you are welching on the bargain and I. . . . (*He starts out of the hammock.*)

HANNAH: Mr. Shannon, this night is just as hard for me to get through as it is for you to get through. But it's you that are welching on the bargain, you're not staying in the hammock. Lie back down in the hammock. Now. Yes. Yes, I have had two experiences, well, encounters, with. . . .

SHANNON: *Two*, did you say?

HANNAH: Yes, I said two. And I wasn't exaggerating and don't you say "fantastic" before I've told you both stories. When I was sixteen, your favorite age, Mr. Shannon, each Saturday afternoon my grandfather Nonno would give me thirty cents, my allowance, my pay for my secretarial and housekeeping duties. Twenty-five cents for admission to the Saturday matinee at the Nantucket movie theatre and five cents extra for a bag of popcorn, Mr. Shannon. I'd sit at the almost empty back of the movie theatre so that the popcorn munching wouldn't disturb the other movie patrons. Well . . . one afternoon a young man sat down beside me and pushed his . . . knee against mine and . . . I moved over two seats but he moved over beside me and continued this . . . pressure! I jumped up and screamed, Mr. Shannon. He was arrested for molesting a minor.

SHANNON: Is he still in the Nantucket jail?

HANNAH: No. I got him out. I told the police that it was a Clara Bow picture—it *was* a Clara Bow picture—and I was just overexcited.

SHANNON: Fantastic.

HANNAH: Yes, very! The second experience is much more recent, only two years ago, when Nonno and I were operating at the Raffles Hotel in Singapore, and doing very well there, making expenses and more. One evening in the Palm Court of the Raffles we met this middle-aged, sort of nondescript Australian salesman. You know—plump, bald-spotted, with a bad attempt at speaking with an upper-class accent and terribly overfriendly. He was alone and looked lonely. Grandfather said him a poem and I did a quick character sketch that was shamelessly flattering of him. He paid me more than my usual asking price and gave my grandfather five Malayan dollars, yes, and he even purchased one of my water colors. Then it was Nonno's bedtime. The Aussie salesman asked me out in a sampan with him. Well, he'd been so generous . . . I accepted. I did, I accepted. Grandfather went up to bed and I went out in the sampan with this ladies' underwear salesman. I noticed that he became more and more. . . .

SHANNON: What?

HANNAH: Well . . . *agitated* . . . as the afterglow of the sunset faded out on the water. (*She laughs with a delicate sadness.*) Well, finally, eventually, he leaned toward me . . . we were vis-à-vis in the sampan . . . and he looked intensely, passionately into my eyes. (*She laughs again.*) And he said to me: "Miss Jelkes? Will you do me a favor? Will you do something for me?" "What?" said I. "Well," said he, "if I turn my back, if I look the other way, will you take off some piece of your clothes and let me hold it, just hold it?"

SHANNON: Fantastic!

HANNAH: Then he said, "It will just take a few seconds." "Just a few seconds for what?" I asked him. (*She gives the same laugh again.*) He didn't say for what, but. . . .

SHANNON: His satisfaction?

HANNAH: Yes.

SHANNON: What did you do—in a situation like that?

HANNAH: I . . . gratified his request, I did! And he kept his promise. He did keep his back turned till I said ready and threw him . . . the part of my clothes.

SHANNON: What did he do with it?

HANNAH: He didn't move, except to seize the article he'd requested. I looked the other way while his satisfaction took place.

SHANNON: Watch out for commercial travelers in the Far East. Is that the moral, Miss Jelkes honey?

HANNAH: Oh, no, the moral is oriental. Accept whatever situation you cannot improve.

SHANNON: "When it's inevitable, lean back and enjoy it" is that it?

HANNAH: He'd bought a water color. The incident was embarrassing, not violent. I left and returned unmolested. Oh, and the funniest part of all is that when we got back to the Raffles Hotel, he took the piece of apparel out of his pocket like a bashful boy producing an apple for his schoolteacher and tried to slip it into my hand in the elevator. I wouldn't accept it. I whispered, "Oh, please keep it, Mr. Willoughby!" He'd paid the asking price for my water color and somehow the little experience had been rather touching, I mean it was so *lonely*, out there in the sampan with violet streaks in the sky and this little middle-aged Australian making sounds like he was dying of asthma! And the planet Venus coming serenely out of a fair-weather cloud, over the Straits of Malacca. . . .

SHANNON: And that experience . . . you call that a. . . .

HANNAH: A love experience? Yes. I do call it one.

(*He regards her with incredulity, peering into her face so closely that she is embarrassed and becomes defensive.*)

SHANNON: That, that . . . sad, dirty little episode, you call it a . . . ?

HANNAH (*cutting in sharply*): Sad it certainly was—for the odd little man—but why do you call it "dirty"?

SHANNON: How did you feel when you went into your bedroom?

HANNAH: Confused, I . . . a little confused, I suppose. . . . I'd known about loneliness—but not that degree or . . . depth of it.

SHANNON: You mean it didn't *disgust* you?

HANNAH: Nothing human disgusts me unless it's unkind, violent. And I told you how gentle he was—apologetic, shy, and really very, well, *delicate* about it. However, I do grant you it was on the rather fantastic level.

SHANNON: You're. . . .

HANNAH: I am *what*? "Fantastic"?

(*While they have been talking, Nonno's voice has been heard now and then, mumbling, from his cubicle. Suddenly it becomes loud and clear.*)

NONNO:

And finally the broken stem,
The plummeting to earth and then. . . .

(*His voice subsides to its mumble. Shannon, standing behind Hannah, places his hand on her throat.*)

HANNAH: What is that for? Are you about to strangle me, Mr. Shannon?

SHANNON: You can't stand to be touched?

HANNAH: Save it for the widow. It isn't for me.

SHANNON: Yes, you're right. (*He removes his hand.*) I could do it with Mrs. Faulk, the inconsolable widow, but I couldn't with you.

HANNAH (*dryly and lightly*): Spinster's loss, widow's gain, Mr. Shannon.

SHANNON: Or widow's loss, spinster's gain. Anyhow it sounds like some old parlor game in a Virginia or Nantucket Island parlor. But . . . I wonder something. . . .

HANNAH: What do you wonder?

SHANNON: If we couldn't . . . *travel* together, I mean just *travel* together?

HANNAH: Could we? In your opinion?

SHANNON: Why not, I don't see why not.

HANNAH: I think the impracticality of the idea will appear much clearer to you in the morning, Mr. Shannon. (*She folds her dimly gold-lacquered fan and rises from her chair.*) Morning can always be counted on to bring us back to a more realistic level. . . . Good night, Mr. Shannon. I have to pack before I'm too tired to.

SHANNON: Don't leave me out here alone yet.

HANNAH: I have to pack now so I can get up at daybreak and try my luck in the plaza.

SHANNON: You won't sell a water color or sketch in that blazing hot plaza tomorrow. Miss Jelkes honey, I don't think you're operating on the realistic level.

HANNAH: Would I be if I thought we could travel together?

SHANNON: I still don't see why we couldn't.

HANNAH: Mr. Shannon, you're not well enough to travel anywhere with anybody right now. Does that sound cruel of me?

SHANNON: You mean that I'm stuck here for good? Winding up with the . . . inconsolable widow?

HANNAH: We all wind up with something or with someone, and if it's someone instead of just something, we're lucky, perhaps . . . unusually lucky. (*She starts to enter her cubicle, then turns to him again in the doorway.*) Oh, and tomorrow. . . . (*She touches her forehead as if a little confused as well as exhausted.*)

SHANNON: What about tomorrow?

HANNAH (*with difficulty*): I think it might be better, tomorrow, if we avoid showing any particular interest in each other, because Mrs. Faulk is a morbidly jealous woman.

SHANNON: *Is* she?

HANNAH: Yes, she seems to have misunderstood our . . . sympathetic interest in each other. So I think we'd better avoid any more long talks on the verandah. I mean till she's thoroughly reassured it might be better if we just say good morning or good night to each other.

SHANNON: We don't even have to say that.

HANNAH: I will, but you don't have to answer.

SHANNON (*savagely*): How about wall-tappings between us by way of communication? You know, like convicts in separate cells communicate with each other by tapping on the walls of the cells? One tap: I'm here. Two taps: are you there? Three taps: yes, I am. Four taps: that's good, we're together. *Christ!* . . . Here, take this. (*He snatches the gold cross from his pocket.*) Take my gold cross and hock it, it's 22-carat gold.

HANNAH: What do you, what are you . . . ?

SHANNON: There's a fine amethyst in it, it'll pay your travel expenses back to the States.

HANNAH: Mr. Shannon, you're making no sense at all now.

SHANNON: Neither are you, Miss Jelkes talking about tomorrow, and. . . .

HANNAH: All I was saying was. . . .

SHANNON: You won't *be* here tomorrow! Had you forgotten you won't be here tomorrow?

HANNAH (*with a slight, shocked laugh*): Yes, I *had*, I'd *forgotten!*

SHANNON: The widow wants you out and out you'll go, even if you sell your water colors like hotcakes to the pariah dogs in the plaza. (*He stares at her, shaking his head hopelessly.*)

HANNAH: I suppose you're right, Mr. Shannon. I must be too tired to think or I've contracted your fever. . . . It had actually slipped my mind for a moment that—

NONNO (*abruptly, from his cubicle*): Hannah!

HANNAH (*rushing to his door*): Yes, what is it, Nonno? (*He doesn't hear her and repeats her name louder.*) Here I am, I'm here.

NONNO: Don't come in yet, but stay where I can call you.

HANNAH: Yes, I'll *hear* you, Nonno. (*She turns toward Shannon, drawing a deep breath.*)

SHANNON: Listen, if you don't take this gold cross that I never want on me again, I'm going to pitch it off the verandah at the spook in the rain forest. (*He raises an arm to throw it, but she catches his arm to restrain him.*)

HANNAH: All right, Mr. Shannon, I'll take it, I'll hold it for you.

SHANNON: Hock it, honey, you've got to.

HANNAH: Well, if I do, I'll mail the pawn ticket to you so you can redeem it, because you'll want it again, when you've gotten over your fever. (*She moves blindly down the verandah and starts to enter the wrong cubicle.*)

SHANNON: That isn't your cell, you went past it. (*His voice is gentle again.*)

HANNAH: I did, I'm sorry. I've never been this tired in all my life. (*She turns to face him again. He stares into her face. She looks blindly out, past him.*) *Never!* (*There is a slight pause.*) What did you say is making that constant, dry, scuffling sound beneath the verandah?

SHANNON: I told you.

HANNAH: I didn't hear you.

SHANNON: I'll get my flashlight, I'll show you. (*He lurches rapidly into his cubicle and back out with a flashlight.*) It's an iguana. I'll show you. . . . See? The iguana? At the end of its rope? Trying to go on past the end of its goddam rope? Like *you*! Like *me*! Like Grampa with his last poem!

(*In the pause which follows singing is heard from the beach.*)

HANNAH: What is a—what—iguana?

SHANNON: It's a kind of lizard—a big one, a giant one. The Mexican kids caught it and tied it up.

HANNAH: Why did they tie it up?

SHANNON: Because that's what they do. They tie them up and fatten them up and then eat them up, when they're ready for eating. They're a delicacy. Taste like white meat of chicken. At least the Mexicans think so. And also the kids, the Mexican kids, have a lot of fun with them, poking out their eyes with sticks and burning their tails with matches. You know? Fun? Like that?

HANNAH: Mr. Shannon, please go down and cut it loose!

SHANNON: I can't do that.

HANNAH: Why can't you?

SHANNON: Mrs. Faulk wants to eat it. I've got to please Mrs. Faulk, I am at her mercy. I am at her disposal.

HANNAH: I don't understand. I mean I don't understand how anyone could eat a big lizard.

SHANNON: Don't be so critical. If you got hungry enough you'd eat it too. You'd be surprised what people will eat if hungry. There's a lot of hungry people still in the world. Many have died of starvation, but a lot are still living and hungry, believe you me, if you will take my word for it. Why, when I was conducting a party of—*ladies*?—yes, ladies . . . through a country that shall be nameless but in this world, we were passing by rubberneck bus along a tropical coast when we saw a great mound of . . . well, the smell was unpleasant. One of my ladies said, "Oh, Larry, what is that?" My name being Lawrence, the most familiar ladies sometimes call me Larry. I didn't use the four letter word for what the great mound was. I didn't think it was necessary to say it. Then she noticed, and I noticed too, a pair of very old natives of this nameless country, practically naked except for a few filthy rags, creeping and crawling about this mound of . . . and . . . occasionally stopping to pick something out of it, and pop it into their mouths. What? Bits of undigested . . . food particles, Miss Jelkes. (*There is silence for a moment. She makes a gagging sound in her throat and rushes the length of the verandah to the wooden steps and disappears for a while. Shannon continues, to himself and the moon.*) Now why did I tell her that? Because it's true? That's no reason to tell her, because it's true. Yeah. Because it's true was a good reason not to tell her. Except . . . I think I first *faced* it in that nameless country. The gradual, rapid, natural, unnatural—predestined, accidental—cracking up and going to pieces of young Mr. T. Lawrence Shannon, yes, still *young* Mr. T. Lawrence Shannon, by which rapid-slow process . . . his final tour of ladies through tropical countries. . . . Why did I say "tropical"? Hell! Yes! It's always been tropical countries I took ladies through. Does that, does that—huh?—signify something, I wonder? Maybe. Fast decay is a thing of hot climates, steamy, hot, wet climates, and I run back to them like a. . . . Incomplete sentence. . . . Always seducing a lady or two, or three or four or five ladies in the party, but really ravaging her first by pointing out to her the—what?—horrors? Yes, horrors!—of the tropical country being conducted a tour through. My . . . brain's going out now, like a failing —power. . . . So I stay here, I reckon, and live off la patrona for the rest of my life. Well, she's old enough to predecease me. She could check out of here first, and I imagine that after a couple of years of having to satisfy her I might be prepared for the shock of her passing on. . . . Cruelty . . . pity. What is it? . . . Don't know, all I know is. . . .

HANNAH (*from below the verandah*): You're talking to yourself.

SHANNON: No. To you. I knew you could hear me out there, but not being able to see you I could say it easier, you know . . . ?

NONNO:

A chronicle no longer gold,
A bargaining with mist and mould. . . .

HANNAH (*coming back onto the verandah*): I took a closer look at the iguana down there.

SHANNON: You did? How did you like it? Charming? Attractive?

HANNAH: No, it's not an attractive creature. Nevertheless I think it should be cut loose.

SHANNON: Iguanas have been known to bite their tails off when they're tied up by their tails.

HANNAH: This one is tied by its throat. It can't bite its own head off to escape from the end of the rope, Mr. Shannon. Can you look at me and tell me truthfully that you don't know it's able to feel pain and panic?

SHANNON: You mean it's one of God's creatures?

HANNAH: If you want to put it that way, yes, it is. Mr. Shannon, will you please cut it loose, set it free? Because if you don't, I will.

SHANNON: Can you look at *me* and tell *me* truthfully that this reptilian creature, tied up down there, doesn't mostly disturb you because of its parallel situation to your Grampa's dying-out effort to finish one last poem, Miss Jelkes?

HANNAH: Yes, I. . . .

SHANNON: Never mind completing that sentence. We'll play God tonight like kids play house with old broken crates and boxes. All right? Now Shannon is going to go down there with his machete and cut the damn lizard loose so it can run back to its bushes because God won't do it and we are going to play God here.

HANNAH: I knew you'd do that. And I thank you.

(*Shannon goes down the two steps from the verandah with the machete. He crouches beside the cactus that hides the iguana and cuts the rope with a quick, hard stroke of the machete. He turns to look after its flight, as the low, excited mumble in cubicle 3 grows louder. Then Nonno's voice turns to a sudden shout.*)

NONNO: *Hannah! Hannah!* (*She rushes to him, as he wheels himself out of his cubicle onto the verandah.*)

HANNAH: Grandfather! What is it?

NONNO: I! believe! it! is! *finished!* Quick, before I forget it—pencil, paper! Quick! please! Ready?

HANNAH: Yes. All ready, grandfather.

NONNO (*in a loud, exalted voice*):

How calmly does the orange branch
Observe the sky begin to blanch
Without a cry, without a prayer,
With no betrayal of despair.

Sometime while night obscures the tree
The zenith of its life will be
Gone past forever, and from thence
A second history will commence.

A chronicle no longer gold,
A bargaining with mist and mould,
And finally the broken stem
The plummeting to earth; and then

An intercourse not well designed
For beings of a golden kind
Whose native green must arch above
The earth's obscene, corrupting love.

And still the ripe fruit and the branch
Observe the sky begin to blanch
Without a cry, without a prayer,
With no betrayal of despair.

O Courage, could you not as well
Select a second place to dwell,
Not only in that golden tree
But in the frightened heart of me?

Have you got it?

HANNAH: Yes!

NONNO: All of it?

HANNAH: Every word of it.

NONNO: It is *finished*?

HANNAH: Yes.

NONNO: Oh! God! Finally finished?

HANNAH: Yes, finally finished. (*She is crying. The singing voices flow up from the beach.*)

NONNO: After waiting so long!

HANNAH: Yes, we waited so long.

NONNO: And it's good! It is *good*?

HANNAH: It's—it's. . . .

NONNO: What?

HANNAH: Beautiful, grandfather! (*She springs up, a fist to her mouth.*) Oh, grandfather, I am so happy for you. Thank you for writing such a lovely poem! It was worth the long wait. Can you sleep now, grandfather?

NONNO: You'll have it typewritten tomorrow?

HANNAH: Yes, I'll have it typed up and send it off to *Harper's*.

NONNO: Hah? I didn't hear that, Hannah.

HANNAH (*shouting*): I'll have it typed up tomorrow, and mail it to *Harper's* tomorrow! They've been waiting for it a long time, too! You know!

NONNO: Yes, I'd like to pray now.

HANNAH: Good night. Sleep now, Grandfather. You've finished your loveliest poem.

NONNO (*faintly, drifting off*): Yes, thanks and praise . . .

(*Maxine comes around the front of the verandah, followed by Pedro playing a harmonica softly. She is prepared for a night swim, a vividly striped towel thrown over her shoulders. It is apparent that the night's progress has mellowed her spirit: her face wears a faint smile which is suggestive of those cool, impersonal, all-comprehending smiles on the carved heads of Egyptian or Oriental dieties. Bearing a rum-coco, she approaches the hammock, discovers it empty, the ropes on the floor, and calls softly to Pedro.*)

MAXINE: Shannon ha escapado! (*Pedro goes on playing dreamily. She throws back her head and shouts.*) SHANNON! (*The call is echoed by the hill beyond. Pedro advances a few steps and points under the verandah.*)

PEDRO: Miré. Allé hasta Shannon.

(*Shannon comes into view from below the verandah, the severed rope and machete dangling from his hands.*)

MAXINE: What are you doing down there, Shannon?

SHANNON: I cut loose one of God's creatures at the end of the rope.

(*Hannah, who has stood motionless with closed eyes behind the wicker chair, goes quietly toward the cubicles and out of the moon's glare.*)

MAXINE (*tolerantly*): What'd you do that for, Shannon.

SHANNON: So that one of God's creatures could scramble home safe and free. . . . A little act of grace, Maxine.

MAXINE (*smiling a bit more definitely*): C'mon up here, Shannon. I want to talk to you.

SHANNON (*starting to climb onto the verandah, as Maxine rattles the ice in the coconut shell*): What d'ya want to talk about, Widow Faulk?

MAXINE: Let's go down and swim in that liquid moonlight.

SHANNON: Where did you pick up that poetic expression?

(*Maxine glances back at Pedro and dismisses him with,* "Vamos." *He leaves with a shrug, the harmonica fading out.*)

MAXINE: Shannon, I want you to stay with me.

SHANNON (*taking the rum-coco from her*): You want a drinking companion?

MAXINE: No, I just want you to stay here, because I'm alone here now and I need somebody to help me manage the place.

(*Hannah strikes a match for a cigarette.*)

SHANNON (*looking toward her*): I want to remember that face. I won't see it again.

MAXINE: Let's go down to the beach.

SHANNON: I can make it down the hill, but not back up.

MAXINE: I'll get you back up the hill. (*They have started off now, toward the path down through the rain forest.*) I've got five more years, maybe ten, to make this place attractive to the male clientele, the middle-aged ones at least. And you can take care of the women that are with them. That's what you can do, you know that, Shannon.

(*He chuckles happily. They are now on the path, Maxine half leading half supporting him. Their voices fade as Hannah goes into Nonno's cubicle and comes back with a shawl, her cigarette left inside. She pauses between the door and the wicker chair and speaks to herself and the sky.*)

HANNAH: Oh, God, can't we stop now? Finally? Please let us. It's so quiet here, now.

(*She starts to put the shawl about Nonno, but at the same moment his head drops to the side. With a soft intake of breath, she extends a hand before his mouth to see if he is still breathing. He isn't. In a panicky moment, she looks right and left for someone to call to. There's no one. Then she bends to press her head to the crown of Nonno's and the curtain starts to descend.*)

The End

NAZI MARCHING SONG

Heute wollen wir ein Liedlein singen,
Trinken wollen wir den kuehlen Wein;
Und die Glaeser sollen dazu klingen,
Denn es muss, es muss geschieden sein.

Gib' mir deine Hand,
Deine weisse Hand,
Leb'wohl, mein Schatz, leb'wohl, mein Schatz
Lebe wohl, lebe wohl,
Denn wir fahren. Boom! Boom!
Denn wir fahren. Boom! Boom!
Denn wir fahren gegen Engelland. Boom! Boom!

Let's sing a little song today,
And drink some cool wine;
The glasses should be ringing
Since we must, we must part.

Give me your hand,
Your white hand,
Farewell, my love, farewell,
Farewell, farewell,
Since we're going—
Since we're going—
Since we're going against England.

THE ECCENTRICITIES OF A NIGHTINGALE

CHARACTERS

ALMA WINEMILLER
THE REVEREND WINEMILLER, her father
MRS. WINEMILLER, her mother
JOHN BUCHANAN, JR.
MRS. BUCHANAN, his mother
ROGER DOREMUS
VERNON
MRS. BASSETT
ROSEMARY
A TRAVELING SALESMAN

SCENES

ACT ONE

THE FEELING OF A SINGER

SCENE 1 The Fountain
SCENE 2 The Rectory
SCENE 3 The same

ACT TWO

THE TENDERNESS OF A MOTHER

SCENE 1 The Buchanan House
SCENE 2 The Rectory
SCENE 3 Dr. Buchanan's Office
SCENE 4 The Rectory

ACT THREE

A CAVALIER'S PLUME

SCENE 1 The Fountain
SCENE 2 A Small Hotel

EPILOGUE: The Fountain

The entire action of the play takes place in Glorious Hill, Mississippi. The time is shortly before the First World War.

AUTHOR'S NOTE

Aside from the characters having the same names and the locale remaining the same, I think *The Eccentricities of a Nightingale* is a substantially different play from *Summer and Smoke*, and I prefer it. It is less conventional and melodramatic. I wrote it in Rome one summer and brought it with me to London the fall that *Summer and Smoke* was about to be produced there. But I arrived with it too late. The original version of the play was already in rehearsal.

This radically different version of the play has never been produced on Broadway. I hope that its publication in this volume may lead to its production and that the production may confirm my feeling that it is a better work than the play from which it derived.

ACT ONE

The Feeling of a Singer

SCENE ONE

It is the evening of July 4th of a year shortly before the First World War.

The exterior set is part of a public square in the small Southern town of Glorious Hill, Mississippi. Two stone steps ascend, at the rear, to a public fountain which is in the form of a stone angel (Eternity), in a gracefully crouching position with wings lifted and hands held together in front to form a cup from which water flows. Near the fountain is a small bench. Framing the set above are mossy branches. Behind is a sky with stars beginning to appear.

Before and for a few minutes after the curtain rises, a somewhat-better-than-typical church soprano is heard singing a semi-secular song such as "O That We Two Were Maying."

The Reverend and Mrs. Winemiller, an Episcopal clergyman and his wife, in their early sixties, are on the bench. Sitting on the steps to the fountain is John Buchanan.

The song ends, there is a burst of applause, and while it continues, Miss Alma Winemiller enters from the right. At the same moment a rocket explodes in the sky, casting a momentary white radiance beneath it.

ALMA (*excitedly calling to her parents*): The first sky-rocket! Oh, look at it burst into a million stars!

(*There is a long-drawn "Ahhh" from unseen spectators. After the brief glare the stage seems very dark. Barely visible figures, laughing, chattering, sweep about the fountain like a sudden passage of birds. Alma cries out as if frightened.*)

ALMA: Oh, I'm blinded, I can't see a *thing*! Father, Father, where *are* you?

(*A child imitates her mockingly.*)

REV. WINEMILLER: Here we are, Alma, we're down here on the bench.

ALMA: Oh . . . (*She rushes breathlessly down to them.*)

(*The stage lightens again. Alma is dressed in pale yellow and carries a parasol to match.*)

ALMA: The words flew out of my mind. I sang the same verse twice. Was it noticeable? Please open my bag for me, Father. My fingers are frozen stiff. I want my handkerchief. My face and my throat are drenched with perspiration. Was that— Oh, I'm talking too loudly! (*She lowers her voice to a shrill whisper.*) *Is that John Buchanan up there by the fountain?* I rushed right by him but I think he spoke! Don't look now, he'll know we're talking about him. But I think it is!

REV. WINEMILLER: Suppose it is! What of it? Sit down, Alma.

ALMA: Oh, the Gulf wind is blowing, what a relief! . . . Yes . . . yes, that *is* John Buchanan. . . . (*Her voice quivers over the name. Her father hands her the handkerchief.*) Oh, thank you, Father. Yesssss—that's John Buchanan, he's been home for a week but hasn't called or dropped over . . . I wonder *why*! Don't you think it's *peculiar*?

REV. WINEMILLER: Why "peculiar"?

(*A stout dowager in black lace and pearls approaches John Buchanan and takes his arm.*)

ALMA: His mother stands guard over him like an old dragon! Look at her, keeping time to the music with her lorgnette, one arm hooked through John's, terrified that someone will snatch him from her!

REV. WINEMILLER: Alma, sit still for a minute. Just sit here quietly and listen to the music until you get back a little composure.

ALMA (*in a shrill rapid whisper, staring straight out*): She'll pretend not to see me. I remember the last time John came home from college, no, the time before last, two, two summers ago, while he was still at Johns Hopkins, I was sitting on the front porch one evening. I nodded to him as he went by the house and he lifted his hat and started to come up to me to say hello. Do you know what she did? She immediately stuck her head out of their window and shouted to him, literally shouted to him as if the house had caught fire, "John! John! Come here right this minute! Your father wants you *immediately* in his office!"

REV. WINEMILLER: Do you want them to overhear you?

ALMA: Oh, they're not *there* any more, she's dragged him out of danger!

REV. WINEMILLER: Mrs. Buchanan is always friendly and I don't think it's reasonable of you to blame her for his failure to pay you as much attention as you would like. Now where is your mother gone?

MRS. WINEMILLER (*wistfully, at a distance*): *Where is the ice cream man?*

ALMA: Mother, there *isn't* any ice cream man!

REV. WINEMILLER: I'll have to take her right home. She's on her bad behavior.

ALMA: Has she been talking about the Musée Mécanique?

REV. WINEMILLER: Babbling about it to everybody we meet!

ALMA: Let her go home. She can get home by herself. It's good for her. Oh, I see where she's headed, she's going across the Square to the White Star Pharmacy to treat herself to an ice cream sundae.

REV. WINEMILLER: What a terrible cross to have to bear!

ALMA: The only thing to do with a cross is *bear* it, Father.

REV. WINEMILLER: The failure of a vocation is a terrible thing, and it's all the more terrible when you're not responsible for the failure yourself, when it's the result of a vicious impulse to destroy in some other person.

ALMA: Mother isn't responsible for her condition. You know that.

REV. WINEMILLER: Your mother has *chosen* to be the way she is. She isn't out of her mind. It's all deliberate. One week after our marriage a look came into her eyes, a certain look, a look I can't describe to you, a sort of a cold and secretly spiteful look as if I, who loved her, who was *devoted* to her, had done her some, some—*injury!*—that couldn't be—*mentioned. . . .*

ALMA: I think there are women who feel that way about marriage.

REV. WINEMILLER: They ought not to marry.

ALMA: I know, but they do, they *do*! They are the *ones* that marry! The ones that could bring to marriage the sort of almost—*transcendental! tenderness* that it calls for—what do they do? Teach school! Teach singing! Make a life out of little accomplishments. Father . . . *Look! Mrs. Buchanan is making another entrance!*

(*The dowager approaches her son again.*)

ALMA: She looks so sweet and soft, but under the black lace and pearls is something harder and colder than the stuff that stone angel is made of! And something runs in her veins that's warm and sympathetic as—mineral water! She's come to take her son home. He's too exposed in this place. He might meet a girl without money! A girl who was able to give him nothing but love!

REV. WINEMILLER: Alma, you're talking wildly. I don't like this kind of talk!

ALMA: Oh, yes, oh, yes. She told Miss Preston, who works at the public library, that she was determined that John should make the right kind of marriage for a young doctor to make, a girl with beauty and wealth and social position somewhere in the East!—the Orient where the sun rises! *Ha ha ha!*

(*Mrs. Buchanan calls "John? John? John?" with idiotic persistence, like a bird.*)

REV. WINEMILLER: Alma, I think you had better come home with me, you're not yourself. You're talking almost as wildly as your mother. . . .

ALMA: I'm sorry, Father. Singing in public always leaves me feeling overexcited. You go, you go on home, I'll be all right in a moment or two. I have to wait for Roger. . . .

REV. WINEMILLER: I'm not sure I like you being seen so much and associated in people's minds with that, that—well—that rather *peculiar* young man. . . .

ALMA: You make me think of that story about the Quakers. One Quaker met another Quaker and he said, "Everybody is mad in this world but thee and me, and thou art a little peculiar!" *Ha ha ha!*

REV. WINEMILLER: Why do you laugh like that?

ALMA: Like what, Father?

REV. WINEMILLER: You throw your head back so far it's a wonder you don't break your neck!—Ah, me . . . Hmmm . . . (*He strolls away with a slight parting nod.*)

(*A sky-rocket goes off. There is a long "Ahhh!" from the crowd.*)

(*In dumb play, John's mother tries to lead him from the square, but he protests. Somebody calls her. She reluctantly goes, passing in front of Miss Alma.*)

ALMA (*overbrightly*): Good evening, Mrs. Buchanan.

MRS. BUCHANAN: Why, Miss Alma! I want to congratulate you. I heard you sing and I've never heard anyone sing with quite so much . . . *feeling!* No wonder they call you "the Nightingale of the Delta."

ALMA: It's sweet of you to fib so, I sang so badly.

MRS. BUCHANAN: You're just being modest! (*She simpers, as she goes off.*)

(*Alma had risen from the bench. She now sits down again and closes her eyes, unfolding a fan suspended about her throat.*)

(*John glances down at her, then notices an unexploded fire-cracker. He picks it up, lights it, and tosses it under the bench. It goes off and Alma springs up with a sharp outcry. He laughs and descends the steps and comes over to the bench.*)

JOHN: Hello, Miss Alma.

ALMA: Johnny Buchanan, did you throw that firecracker?

JOHN: Ha ha!

ALMA: It scared me out of my wits! Why, I'm still breathless.

JOHN: Ha ha!

ALMA: Ha ha ha! I think I needed a little shock like that to get me over the shock of my fiasco—on the bandstand!

JOHN: I heard you sing. I liked it.

ALMA: Ha ha ha ha ha! You liked both verses of it? I sang *one twice*! Ha ha ha . . .

JOHN: It was good enough to sing three or four times more.

ALMA: *Chivalry!* Chivalry still survives in the Southern states!

JOHN: Mind if I sit down with you?

ALMA: Oh, please, please *do!* There's room enough for us both. Neither of us is terribly large—in *diameter!* Ha ha ha!

(*He sits down. There is an awkward pause.*)

JOHN: You sang with so much feeling, Miss Alma.

ALMA: The feeling was panic!

JOHN: It sounded O.K. to me.

ALMA: Oh, I can't hear myself sing, I just feel my throat and tongue working and my heart beating fast!—a *hammer* . . .

JOHN: Do you have palpitations when you sing?

ALMA: Sometimes I'm surprised that I don't just drop dead!

JOHN: Then maybe you shouldn't.

ALMA: Oh, afterwards I feel I've done something, and that's a different feeling from what one feels—most times. . . .

JOHN: You seem to be still shaking?

ALMA: That firecracker was a shock to my whole nervous system! Ha ha ha!

JOHN: I'm sorry. I had no idea that you were so nervous.

ALMA: Nobody has a right to be so nervous! You're—you're home for the holidays, are you? I mean home for the rest of the summer?

JOHN: I've finished medical school. But I'm connected with a hospital now, doing laboratory work.

ALMA: Oh, in *what*, how *thrilling*! How thrilling that sounds, in *what*?—Uh?

JOHN: Bacteriology.

ALMA: *That's*—(*She gasps.*)—that's something to do with, with, with a—*microscope*?—Uh?

JOHN: Sometimes you have to look through a microscope.

ALMA: I looked through a telescope once, at Oxford, Mississippi, at the state university when Father delivered the baccalaureate address there one spring. But I've never, never looked through a *microscope*! Tell me, what do you see, I mean, what is it like, through a microscope, if that question makes any sense?—Uh?

JOHN (*slowly*): Well—you see pretty much the same thing that you see through a telescope.

ALMA: Ohhhh?

JOHN: A—a cosmos, a—microcosmos!—part anarchy and—part order. . . .

(*Music is heard again.*)

ALMA: Part anarchy and part order! Oh, the *poetry* of science, the *incredible* poetry of it! Ha ha ha!

JOHN (*vaguely*): Yes . . .

ALMA: Part anarchy and part order—the footprints of God!—Uh?

JOHN: His footprints, maybe, yes . . . but not—God!

ALMA: Isn't it strange? He never really, *really*—exposes Himself! Here and there is a footprint, but even the footprints are not very easy to follow! No, you can't follow. In fact you don't even know which way they're pointing. . . . Ha ha ha!

JOHN: How did we get started on that subject?

ALMA: Heaven knows, but we did!—So you're home for a while! I bet your mother's delighted, she's so crazy about you, constantly singing your praises, tells me you graduated magna cum laude from Johns Hopkins last summer! What are your—future plans?

JOHN: I'm leaving tomorrow.

ALMA: Oh, tomorrow? So soon! As soon as all that?!

JOHN: Just got a wire from an old teacher of mine who's fighting bugs in Cuba.

ALMA: Fighting bugs! In Cuba?

JOHN: Yes. Bugs in Cuba. *Fever* bugs.

ALMA: Ohhhh, fever!—Ha ha ha . . .

JOHN: There's a little epidemic down there with some unusual—aspects, he says. And I've always wanted to visit a Latin country. (*He spreads his knees.*)

ALMA: Oh, those Latins. All they do is dream in the sun, dream, dream in the sun and indulge their senses!

JOHN (*smiling suddenly*): Well, I've heard that cantinas are better than saloons, and they tell me that señoritas are—caviar among females!

ALMA: Be careful you don't get caught. They say that the tropics are a perfect quagmire. People go there and never are *heard* of again!

JOHN: Well, it couldn't be hotter than here, that's one sure thing.

ALMA: Oh, my, isn't it dreadful? Summer isn't the pleasantest time of year to renew your acquaintance with Glorious Hill, Mississippi.—The Gulf wind has failed us this year. It usually cools the nights off, but it has failed us this year.

JOHN: Driving along the river cools you off.

ALMA: How heavenly that sounds, driving along the river to cool off!

JOHN: Does it sound good to you?

ALMA: Almost too good to believe!

JOHN: Why don't we take a drive.

ALMA: What a *divine suggestion*! (*She springs up. But Mrs. Buchanan enters quickly.*)

MRS. BUCHANAN: *John! John, darling!*

JOHN: What is it, Mother?

MRS. BUCHANAN: Your father and I have been searching the whole Square for you!—Excuse us, Miss Alma!

ALMA: Certainly, Mrs. Buchanan. (*She closes her eyes for a moment with a look of infinite desolation.*)

MRS. BUCHANAN (*continuing as she grabs hold of John's arm*): Your father's received a call from Mrs. Arbuckle, but I insist that he must go right to bed; he's about to collapse from exhaustion, and there's absolutely no reason why you can't go and give that woman—please excuse us, Miss Alma!—(*She is dragging him away.*)—the morphine injection, that's all that can be done. . . .

JOHN (*calling back*): Goodbye, Miss Alma.

ALMA: Goodbye! Goodbye! (*She sinks back down on the bench.*)

(*A sky-rocket goes up. The crowd cries "Ahhh!"*)

(*Roger Doremus, a young man with the little excitements of a sparrow, rushes on with his French horn in a case.*)

ROGER: How did it go, my solo on the French horn?

ALMA: I'm!—please get me some water, water, from the fountain, I—I—

ROGER: You're not feeling well?

ALMA: I have to take one of my tablets but my mouth is so dry that I can't swallow the tablet. (*She leans back, touching her throat as Roger crosses anxiously to the fountain.*)

(*The scene dims out.*)

SCENE TWO

The Rectory interior on Christmas Eve of the following winter. During the interval the soprano sings a traditional Christmas carol, one not too familiar.

Like all the sets, the Rectory interior is barely suggested, by window and door frames and a few essential properties.

The Reverend and Mrs. Winemiller are seated on either side of a small round clawfoot table that supports a cut-glass bowl of eggnog with cups. Rev. Winemiller faces the fireplace, which is in the fourth wall and is indicated by a flickering red glow. (Every interior in the play has a fireplace indicated in this way in the same position.) Evidently the fire gives little warmth, for the minister has a lady's lavender woolen shawl wrapped about his hunched shoulders.

Mrs. Winemiller is never quite silent, although her interior monologue is never loud enough to be intelligible. She sounds like a small running brook or a swarm of bees and her face changes expression as her interior world falls under light and shadow.

Miss Alma is a little outside the lighted area as the scene begins and her responses to Rev. Winemiller's singsong elegiac ruminations come out of the shadow where the window frame is located. In this frame is a small candle.

REV. WINEMILLER (*as if continuing*): Actually we have about the same number of communicants we've had for the past ten years, but church attendance has dropped off about, hmmm, twenty per cent.

ALMA: Just remember what old Doctor Hoctor announced to his congregation one year, he said to his congregation, "We haven't had any additions to the congregation this year but we've had a number of valuable subtractions."

REV. WINEMILLER: In the old days before they had the church pension fund ministers stayed in the pulpit as long as they were able to crawl up the chancel.

ALMA: Yes, poor old Doctor Hoctor, he hung on forever! Much longer than his congregation. They say it finally dwindled down to just a pair of old ladies, one widow and one spinster who hated each other so fiercely that one would sit in the front pew and the other so far in the rear that old Doctor Hoctor, who had lost his sight but still had a little hearing, was never quite certain whether she was there or not except when she had the hiccoughs. Ha ha!

REV. WINEMILLER: A man must know when he's outlived his term of usefulness and let go. I'm going to retire next year. . . .

ALMA: But, Father, you won't come into the pension for five more years! What will we live on, what I make teaching singing?

REV. WINEMILLER: The Bishop has hinted to me that if I don't feel able to continue, it might be arranged for me to come into my pension a little bit sooner than I'm due to get it.

ALMA: Ah? (*She suddenly turns out a lamp and rushes back to the window.*) I have never seen anything so ridiculous! Mrs. Buchanan has put on a Santie Claus outfit and is going out their front walk with a sack of presents. I wonder if—John's with her. Yes!—Perhaps they'll . . . Oh, we must get Mother upstairs! They'll come here first, I should think, since we're next door. Yes, they are, they're going to come here first! Mother! Mother! Go upstairs and I'll bring you a piece of fruitcake! Mother? A piece of—! Oh . . . No . . . They're *not* going to come here first. They're crossing the street. (*In a tone of desolation*) They've crossed the street, yes, they've—crossed—the street. . . . You don't suppose they'll—*overlook* us this year?

REV. WINEMILLER: You're constantly at that window spying on the Buchanans.

ALMA: *Spy*ing on the Buchanans? What a notion!

REV. WINEMILLER: You come in the parlor, turn out the lamp, gravitate to that window as if you had to stand by that window to breathe.

ALMA: Why, Father, I've been looking at the snow. I just happened to notice Mrs. Buchanan in her Santie Claus outfit coming out of the . . .

REV. WINEMILLER: The house is surrounded by snow on all four sides and all four sides of the house have windows in them through which you could look at the snow if it is only the snow that holds such a fascination over you.

ALMA: It does, it *does* fascinate me, why, it's the first snow that's fallen on Glorious Hill in more than a hundred years, and when it started falling, they closed all the stores on Front Street and every office in town, even the bank. And all came out, just like overgrown boys, and had snow fights on the street!—Roger Doremus told me . . . No. I don't believe they're going to come here at all. They've gone in the other direction down the block. . . . (*She pours a cup of eggnog, sips it with one hand extended toward the glow of the fireplace.*) The snow reminds me of an old proverb. "Before you love, you must learn how to walk over snow—and leave no footprint. . . ."

(*A carol is heard at some distance.*)

The Methodist carolers have already gone out. I must get . . .

REV. WINEMILLER: Alma. Sit down for a moment. There's something I want to talk to you about.

ALMA (*apprehensively*): I have to get ready to go out with the carolers, Father.

REV. WINEMILLER: They're not going out until half-past eight.

ALMA: That's almost now.

REV. WINEMILLER: Then let them start without you. This is more important.

ALMA: That means it's something unpleasant?

REV. WINEMILLER: Yes, extremely unpleasant and that's why it's important. Alma, I've had one heavy cross to bear. (*He nods toward Mrs. Winemiller.*) One almost insufferable cross. A minister isn't complete without a family, he needs his wife and his family to make a—a social bond—with the parish!

ALMA: Father, I do all I can. More than I have the strength for. I have my vocal pupils. I sing at weddings, I sing at funerals, I swear there's nothing I don't sing at except the conception of infants!

REV. WINEMILLER: Alma, I won't endure that kind—!

ALMA: Excuse me, Father, but you know it's true. And I serve on the Altar Guild and I teach the primary class at Sunday school. I made all their little costumes for the Christmas pageant, their angel wings and dresses, and you know what thanks I got for that! Mrs. Peacock cried out that the costumes were inflammable! Inflammable, she screamed! Exactly as if she thought it was my secret hope, my intention, to burn the children up at the Christmas pageant! No, she said, those costumes are inflammable, if they wear those costumes they can't march in with candles! (*She gasps.*)— And so the candles weren't lighted. They marched in holding little stumps of wax!—holding little dirty stumps of wax! The absurdity of it, as if a wind had blown all the candles out—the whole effect I'd worked so hard to create was destroyed by that woman, and I had to bite my tongue because I couldn't answer, I knew that *you* wouldn't want me to answer back. Oh, I've had to bite my tongue so much it's a wonder I have one left!

REV. WINEMILLER: Please, more calmly, Alma. You're going to swallow your tongue from overexcitement some day, not bite it off from holding back indignation! I asked you to please sit down. Alma— Because of the circumstances, I mean your mother's condition, pitiable, and the never, never outlived notoriety of your Aunt Albertine and the Musée Mécanique . . .

ALMA: Why can't we forget something that happened fifteen years ago?

REV. WINEMILLER: Because other people remember!

ALMA: *I'm* not going to elope with a Mr. Otto Schwarzkopf!

REV. WINEMILLER: We must discuss this quietly.

ALMA: Discuss what quietly? *What!*

REV. WINEMILLER: Alma, someone, Alma—someone, Alma, who is—deeply devoted to you—who has your interests—very much at heart—almost as fond of you as her own daughter!

ALMA: Oh, this is Mrs. Peacock—my bête noire!

REV. WINEMILLER: She was deeply, deeply distressed over something that happened lately. It seems that she overheard someone giving an imitation of you at a young people's party. . . .

ALMA: An imitation? An imitation, Father? Of what? Of what? Of *me*!

REV. WINEMILLER: Yes, of you.

ALMA (*gasping*): What was it they imitated? What did they imitate about me, Father?

REV. WINEMILLER: The point is, Alma—

ALMA: No, please tell me, I want to, I *have* to be told, I must—know . . .

REV. WINEMILLER: What they imitated was your singing, I think, at a wedding.

ALMA: My voice? They imitated my voice?

REV. WINEMILLER: Not your voice but your gestures and facial expressions . . .

ALMA: Ohhh . . . This leaves me quite speechless!

REV. WINEMILLER: You're inclined to—dramatize your songs a—bit too much! You, you get carried away by the, the emotion of it! That's why you choke sometimes and get hoarse when you're singing and Mrs. Peacock says that sometimes you weep!

ALMA: That's not true. It's true that I feel the emotion of a song. Even an ordinary little song like "The Voice That Breathed O'er Eden" or "O Promise Me" or "Because"—why, even commonplace little songs like "I Love You Truly," they have a sincere emotion and a singer must feel it, and when you feel it, you *show* it! A singer's face and hands are part of a singer's *equipment*! Why, even a singer's heart is part of her equipment! That's what they taught me at the Conservatory!

REV. WINEMILLER: I'm sometimes sorry you went to the Conservatory.

ALMA (*in a stricken voice*): All right! I'll give up singing . . . *everything!*

REV. WINEMILLER: The thing for you to give up is your affectations, Alma, your little put-on mannerisms that make you seem—well—slightly *peculiar* to people! It isn't just your singing I'm talking about. In ordinary conversations you get carried away by your emotions or something, I don't know what, and neither does anyone else. You, you, you—*gild the lily!*—You—express yourself in—fantastic highflown—phrases! Your hands fly about you like a pair of wild birds! You, you get out of breath, you—stammer, you—laugh hysterically and clutch at your throat! Now please remember. I wouldn't mention these things if I didn't know that they were just mannerisms, things that you could control, that you can correct! Otherwise I wouldn't mention them to you. Because I can see that you are upset, but you can correct them. All you have to do is *concentrate*. When you're talking, just watch yourself, keep an eye on your hands, and when you're singing, put them in *one* position and *keep* them there. Like *this*!

ALMA: Make a steeple?—No, I'd rather not sing. . . .

REV. WINEMILLER: You're taking altogether the wrong attitude about this.

ALMA: I'll, I'll just give up my—social efforts, Father—all of them!

REV. WINEMILLER: The thing for you to give up is this little band of eccentrics, this collection of misfits that you've gathered about you which you call your club, the ones you say will be meeting *here* next Monday!

ALMA: What a cruel thing to say about a group of sweet and serious people that get together because of—interests in common—cultural interests—who want to create something—vital—in this town!

REV. WINEMILLER: These young people are not the sort of young people that it's an advantage to be identified with! And one thing more—

ALMA: What else, Father?

REV. WINEMILLER: Is it true that you go to the Square with a sack of crumbs?

ALMA: What, what, what?

REV. WINEMILLER: Is it true that you go every day to the Square with a sack of crumbs which you throw to the birds?

ALMA: I scatter breadcrumbs in the Square for the starving birds. *That's* true!

REV. WINEMILLER: Have you thought how it might look to people?

ALMA: I thought it only concerned myself and the birds.

REV. WINEMILLER: Little things like that, an accumulation of them, Alma, little habits, little, little mannerisms, little—peculiarities of behavior—they are what get people known, eventually, as—*eccentrics!* And eccentric people are not happy, they are not happy people, Alma. Eccentrics are—what are you doing?

ALMA (*breathlessly*): I can't open the box, I can't open the box, I can't open the box!

REV. WINEMILLER: Your amytal tablets?

ALMA: I can't open the box!

REV. WINEMILLER: Give it to me.—Hysteria was the beginning of your mother's condition.

ALMA: *I can't breathe!* (*She rushes out.*)

REV. WINEMILLER: Alma! Don't leave the house till you get your mother upstairs! (*She has run out. He turns to his wife and shouts in her ear.*) Grace! This is Christmas Eve and we are going to have callers! You must go up to your bedroom and I will bring you up a piece of fruitcake!

MRS. WINEMILLER (*rousing slightly*): No, oh, no, not till you give me the letter, you've hidden it from me, Albertine's last letter! It's got the new address of the Musée Mécanique!

(*The "Valse Musette" fades in.*)

REV. WINEMILLER (*after a pause*): Grace, listen to me. Albertine has been dead for fifteen years. She and her paramour both died in a fire fifteen years ago, when Mr. Schwarzkopf set fire to the Musée Mécanique.

MRS. WINEMILLER: Oh, I remember the address, Seven Pearl Street!—I must keep that in my mind, that's the new address of the Musée Mécanique, it's Seven Pearl Street—or was it—Seventeen Pearl Street?

(*The doorbell rings.*)

REV. WINEMILLER: *There, there now, visitors!* And look at yourself, how you look! Go upstairs *quickly, quickly!* (*He claps his hands violently together.*)

MRS. WINEMILLER: Yes . . .

(*She makes a confused turn. He leads her out of the lighted area.*)

(*The scene dims out.*)

SCENE THREE

A few minutes later. John and his mother and the Reverend Winemiller are seated in the Rectory parlor. Mrs. Buchanan is ludicrously attired as a female Santa Claus with the incongruous addition of a lorgnon on a silver chain.

She is spotted first before the light comes up on the others.

MRS. BUCHANAN: The children say to me, You're not Santie Claus, Santie Claus has whiskers, and I say, No, I'm Santie Claus's *wife*! They're so surprised!

REV. WINEMILLER: I know they must be delighted.

MRS. BUCHANAN: Tickled to death! Having a wife gives him such a respectability! And how has Grace been lately?

REV. WINEMILLER: A—uh—little disturbed.

MRS. BUCHANAN: All the excitement in the air, don't you think? Mrs. Santie Claus has something for her, but if she's a little disturbed, we'll just put it under the tree. Is that Miss Alma? Oh, it *is*. How *lovely*!

(*Alma's high-pitched laughter is heard. John rises from a hassock before the fireplace.*)

ALMA: *Joyeux Noel!* Ha ha!

MRS. BUCHANAN: How pretty you look, Miss Alma! I was afraid we'd miss you.

ALMA: I sang one carol and my throat felt scratchy. The combined church choirs are doing Handel's Messiah. (*She gasps.*) Such dreadful demands on the voice! That's Thursday. No, no, Friday, Friday evening, in the high school—goodness, I *am* getting hoarse!—auditorium!

MRS. BUCHANAN: Let John give you a gargle.

ALMA: Nasty gargles. . . . I hate them! The voice is such a delicate instrument. When was the last time I saw you? Last—last . . . ?

JOHN: Fourth of July. The band concert in the Square.

ALMA: Oh!—oh, dear, the recollection of that . . . !

JOHN: I heard you sing.

ALMA: Goodness, yes, I still shudder. The same verse twice!

JOHN: Ha ha! And I threw a firecracker at you!

ALMA: Goodness, yes, you *did*! Ha ha! That was so naughty of you! You always did as a boy, I mean as a little boy, you always threw—firecrackers! Ha ha!—into the Rectory lawn! No Fourth of July was complete without— (*She gasps.*)

JOHN: Ha ha! That's right. I had to keep up the tradition.

ALMA (*gasping*): That's right, that's right, you had to keep up the tradition! Let me give you some—oh, where is it?—eggnog!

JOHN: We've already been served.

ALMA: Have you? Why, yes, I'm *blind*! I have snow in my eyelashes. It makes rainbows in the light! What an adventure, just imagine, the first snow that's fallen on Glorious Hill in—how many years? Almost a century. Before it began to snow it rained for two days. Suddenly the temperature fell. The rain froze on the trees, on the lawns, on the bushes and hedges, on the roofs, the steeples, the telephone wires. . . . (*She pauses to gasp for breath.*)

REV. WINEMILLER: Alma, sit down so John can sit down.

ALMA: Yes, forgive me!—Till the whole town was literally sheathed in ice!—And when the sun rose that morning . . . you can't imagine how *dazzling*! It made you suddenly *see* how dull things *usually* are—the trees, oh, the trees, like huge crystal chandeliers!—turned upside down!

MRS. BUCHANAN: It's just like fairyland.

ALMA: Exactly like fairyland.

JOHN: I wish I had five cents for every time someone has said that.

MRS. BUCHANAN: Little John has been north so long it's made him a cynic.

ALMA: Have you lost patience with our romantic clichés?

MRS. BUCHANAN: Little John, Little John, I can see that your shoes are still damp!—We call him Little John and his father we call *Big* John although Little John is almost twice as tall as Big John is!

ALMA: How tall is Little John?

MRS. BUCHANAN: As tall as Jack's beanstalk!

ALMA: I don't think it's fair for a boy to have such curls!

MRS. BUCHANAN: As a boy he was so indifferent to the ladies! But those days are all gone now. Every morning cards and letters this high, to the junior Doctor Buchanan in green pink and lavender ink with all the odors of springtime!

ALMA: What a success he's going to have as a doctor.

MRS. BUCHANAN: His waiting room will be large as a railroad station.

ALMA: At least that large and probably with an annex.

MRS. BUCHANAN: But his love is bugs! He's specializing in something I can't even pronounce.

ALMA: *Bacteriology!* He told me last Fourth of July.

MRS. BUCHANAN (*turning to Rev. Winemiller*): Graduated magna cum laude from Johns Hopkins with the highest marks in the history of the college. Already—think of it—seven fine offers from staffs of various hospitals in the East, and one in California!

ALMA (*gasping*): All the gifts of the gods were showered on him!

MRS. BUCHANAN (*to Rev. Winemiller*): I wanted to have five sons but I only had one. But if I had had fifteen I don't think it would have been reasonable to expect that one of the lot would have turned out *quite* so *fine*!

ALMA: Your mother is proud as a peacock.

MRS. BUCHANAN: Don't you think it's excusable in a mother?

ALMA: Not only excusable but . . . Your cup is empty, John, do let me—fill it!

MRS. BUCHANAN: Don't make him tipsy! John, your shoes *are* damp, I can tell by just looking at them! (*Declining eggnog*) Oh, no, no more for me, I have to climb down some more chimneys!—That sounds like Grace!

(*Mrs. Winemiller is heard descending the stairs, imitating Alma's shrill laugh.*)

REV. WINEMILLER (*anxiously*): Alma, I think your mother is—

ALMA (*gasping*): Oh, excuse me!—I'll see what Mother wants.

(*She rushes out. Mrs. Buchanan touches the minister's arm.*)

MRS. BUCHANAN: Oh, such a tragedy, such a terrible cross for you to bear! Little John, I think we had better go, now, the reindeers must be getting restless.

(*John sneezes. She throws her hands up in terror.*)

I knew it, I knew it, I *knew* it! You *have* caught cold!

JOHN: *Oh, for God's sake!*

MRS. BUCHANAN: *John!*

(*John sneezes again.*)

That settles it, you're going straight home to bed!

(*Mrs. Winemiller rushes into the parlor. Alma follows her.*)

ALMA: Father, Mother *insists* on remaining downstairs. She says that she wasn't ready to go to bed.

MRS. WINEMILLER (*excitedly*): I have found my letter with the address on it. It's Seven Pearl Street in New Orleans. That's where Albertine is with Mr. Schwarzkopf and the Musée Mécanique. Oh, such a lot of news in it!

REV. WINEMILLER: Yes, I am sure. But let's not discuss the news now.

MRS. WINEMILLER (*to Mrs. Buchanan*): Have *you* ever been to the Musée Mécanique?

MRS. BUCHANAN: Long ago, Grace, long ago I—had that pleasure. . . . (*She touches her lips nervously with her lorgnon.*)

MRS. WINEMILLER: Then you know what it is? It's a collection of mechanical marvels, invented and operated by my sister's—husband!—Mr. Otto Schwarzkopf! Mechanical marvels, all of them, but, then, you know, when everything's run by mechanics it takes a mechanical genius to keep them in good condition all of the time and sometimes poor Mr. Schwarzkopf is not in condition to keep them all—in—condition. . . .

MRS. BUCHANAN: Well, this is a mechanical age we live in. . . .

ALMA: Mother, Mrs. Buchanan has brought her son with her and we are so eager to hear about his work and his—studies at—Johns Hopkins!

JOHN: Oh, let's hear about the Museum, Miss Alma.

MRS. WINEMILLER: Yes! That's what I'm telling you about, the Museum!—of mechanical marvels. Do you know what they are? Well, let me tell you. There's the mechanical man that plays the flute. There's the mechanical drummer—oh, such a sweet little boy all made out of tin that shines like a brand new dollar! Boom, boom, boom, beats the drum. Toot, toot, toot, goes the flute. And the mechanical soldier waves his flag, waves it, waves it, and waves it! Ha ha ha!—And oh! *Oh!*—the loveliest thing of all—the mechanical bird-girl! Yes, the mechanical bird-girl is almost the biggest mechanical triumph since the Eiffel Tower, according to people who know. She's made of sterling silver! Every three minutes, right on the dot, a little mechanical bird pops out of her mouth and sings three beautiful notes, as clear as—a bell!

REV. WINEMILLER: Grace, Mrs. Buchanan remembers all of that.

MRS. WINEMILLER: The young man *doesn't*! I don't believe he's seen the Musée Mécanique.

JOHN: No, I've never. It sounds very exciting!

MRS. WINEMILLER: Well, lately, I personally think they have made a mistake. I think it was a mistake to buy the *big snake*!

JOHN: A mechanical snake?

MRS. WINEMILLER: Oh no, a real one, a live one, a boa constrictor. Some meddlesome maddie told them "Big snakes pay good."—So Mr. Schwarzkopf, who is not a practical man, a genius without any business sense whatsoever—mortgaged the whole Museum to pay for this great big snake!—So far, so good!—But! The snake was used to living in a warm climate. It was winter. New Orleans *can* be cold!—The snake seemed chilly, it became *very stupid*, and so they gave it a *blanket*!—Well!—Now in this letter I've just received today—Albertine tells me a *terrible* thing has happened!

JOHN: What did the big snake do?

MRS. WINEMILLER: Nothing!—JUST *swallowed* his *blanket*!

JOHN: I thought you were going to say it swallowed Mr. Schwarzkopf.

MRS. BUCHANAN: Oh, now, Little John, *hush*, you bad boy, you! (*She touches her lips with the lorgnon.*)

MRS. WINEMILLER: Swallowed its blanket!

JOHN: Did the blanket disagree with it?

MRS. WINEMILLER: Disagree with it? I should say it did! What can a stomach, even the stomach of a boa constrictor, do with a heavy blanket?

JOHN: What did they do about the—situation?

MRS. WINEMILLER: Everything they could think of—which wasn't *much* . . . Veterinarians, experts from the—zoo!—Nobody could suggest anything to . . . Finally they sent a telegram to the man who had sold them the snake. "The big snake has swallowed his blanket! What shall we do?"—He'd told them big snakes pay good, but *dead* snakes—what do they pay?—They pay what the little boy shot at! —Well!—Do you know what the man that sold the snake to them wired back?—"All you can do is get on your knees and pray!" That's what he replied.

MRS. BUCHANAN: Oh, now, really! How cruel!
JOHN: Ha ha ha!
ALMA (*desperately*): Mother, I think you—
JOHN: And did they pray for the snake?
MRS. WINEMILLER: They prayed for the big investment!—They should have stuck to mechanics in the—Museum—but somebody told them that big snakes pay good. . . .
ALMA: Mother, it's past your bedtime. You go up to bed and I will bring you a slice of delicious fruitcake. Won't that be nice?
MRS. WINEMILLER: Yes!—if you really bring it. (*She starts hurriedly off, then turns and waves to the company.*) Merry Christmas!
REV. WINEMILLER: She is—well, as you see . . . she's . . .
MRS. BUCHANAN: Yes! A little disturbed right now. All the excitement of the holiday season. Little John, we must be running along, don't you think? Big John's waiting for us.
JOHN: I've just persuaded Miss Alma to sing us something.
MRS. BUCHANAN: Oh! (*insincerely*) How nice!

(*Alma is at the piano.*)

ALMA: Would you care for something profane or sacred?
JOHN: Oh, something profane, by all means!
REV. WINEMILLER (*weakly*): I think I will try a little of this eggnog. . . .

(*Miss Alma sings. It is not necessary for the actress to have a very good voice. If she has no singing voice at all, the song can be dubbed, the piano placed so her back or her profile will be to the audience.*)

ALMA (*singing*):

From the land of the sky-blue water,
They brought a captive maid,
Her eyes are lit with lightning,
Her heart is not afraid!

I stole to her tent at dawning.
I wooed her with my flute!
She is sick for the sky-blue water.
The captive maid is mute. . . .

MRS. BUCHANAN (*interrupting the song*): Oh, how lovely, how lovely, one of my favorite pieces, and such a beautiful voice! —Before I forget it, Mrs. Santie Claus has some gifts to put under your tree. . . .—Where *is* your Christmas tree?

ALMA: Oh, this year we put it up in Father's study!

(*Rev. Winemiller leads Mrs. Buchanan offstage. Alma and John remain by the piano.*)

ALMA: My hands are so stiff from the cold I could hardly touch the right keys. . . .

JOHN: Shall we sit by the fire?

ALMA: Oh, yes, that's a good suggestion . . . an excellent suggestion!

JOHN: You sing very well, Miss Alma.

ALMA: Thank you—thank you . . . (*Pause. She clears her throat.*)

JOHN: Don't they call you "the Nightingale of the Delta"?

ALMA: Sarcastically, perhaps!

(*She has drawn up a hassock to the imagined fireplace. He sits on the floor with his palms extended toward the flickering red glow.*)

I have a lyric soprano. Not strong enough to make a career of singing but just about right for the church and for social occasions and I—teach singing!—But let's—let's talk about you—your—your—life and your—plans! Such a wonderful profession, being a doctor! Most of us lead such empty, useless lives! But a doctor!—Oh!—With his wonderful ability to relieve—human suffering, of which there is always—so—much! (*Her tongue runs away with her.*) I don't think it's just a profession, it's a *vocation*! I think it's something to which some people are just—*appointed by God*! (*She claps her hands together and rolls her eyes.*) Yes, just divinely appointed!—Some of us have no choice but to lead a useless existence—endure for the sake of endurance—but a young doctor, you!—with *surgeon's fingers*!

(*She has sprung up to fill his cup with eggnog. The silver ladle slips from her fingers. She utters a startled cry.*)

Ouuu!—Oh, look what I've done! I've dropped the spoon in the bowl and it is completely submerged! What can I fish it out with, oh, what can I fish it out with?

JOHN: Do you mind if I use my surgeon's fingers?

ALMA: *Ohhhhh—pleeeeeeeease!—do*—ha ha ha! (*She gasps.*)

JOHN: Well—that was not such a delicate operation. . . .

ALMA: Now you must have a napkin to wipe those fingers!

JOHN: My handkerchief will do!

ALMA: No, no, no, no, no, not that beautiful handkerchief with your monogram on it!—probably given you by someone who loves you for—Christmas. . . .

(*She picks up a napkin, grabs his hand, and wipes his fingers with tremulous care.*)

I guess you're totally "booked up," as they say, for the short time you'll be home from your laboratory?

JOHN (*gently*): Just about all.

ALMA: There's a group of young people with interests in common meeting here at the Rectory Monday. Monday evening. I know you'd like them *so* much!—Wouldn't you be able to—drop over? For just a *while*?

JOHN: What sort of interests do they have in common?

ALMA: Oh!—vaguely—*cultural*, I guess. . . . We write things, we read things aloud, we—criticize and—discuss!

JOHN: At what time does it start, this—meeting?

ALMA: Oh, *early*—at eight!

JOHN: I'll—try to make it.

ALMA: Don't say *try* as if it required some Herculean effort. All you have to do is cross the yard.—We serve refreshments, both liquid and solid!

JOHN: Reserve me a seat by the punchbowl.

ALMA (*her voice nearly failing with emotion*): That gives me a splendid idea. I *will* serve punch. Fruit punch with claret in it.—Do you like claret?

JOHN: Oh yes. I'm crazy about it.

ALMA: We *start* so early. We *finish* early, too! You'll have time for something exciting later. Your evenings are long ones, I know that!—I'll tell you *how* I know!—Your *room* is—opposite *mine*. . . .

JOHN: How do you know?

ALMA: Your light—shines in my *window*! ha ha ha!

JOHN: At two or three in the morning?

ALMA: Or *three* or *four*!—in the morning! ha ha!

JOHN: It—wakes you up? (*He smiles warmly. She glances away.*)

ALMA: Ha ha—yes . . .

JOHN: You should have let me know, you should have—complained about it.

ALMA: Complained?—Goodness, no—why *should* I?

JOHN: Well, if it . . .

ALMA: Oh, it . . .

JOHN: It doesn't?

ALMA (*very flustered*): *What?*

JOHN: Wake you up? Disturb your sleep?

ALMA: Oh, no, I'm—awake, already. . . .

JOHN: You must not sleep very well, or maybe you're getting home from late parties, too!

ALMA: The first supposition, I'm afraid, is the right one.

JOHN: I'll give you a prescription for sleeping tablets.

ALMA: Oh no. You misunderstood me. I *finally* sleep, I, I, I—wasn't complaining.

(*He suddenly takes her hand.*)

JOHN: What is the matter?

ALMA: What is the matter? I don't understand that question.

JOHN: Yes, you do. What is the matter, Miss Alma?

(*Mrs. Winemiller has appeared at the edge of the lighted area in her nightgown. She suddenly announces—*)

MRS. WINEMILLER: *Alma has fallen in love with that tall boy!*

ALMA (*springing up*): Mother! What do you want downstairs?

MRS. WINEMILLER: That piece of fruitcake you said you would bring up to me.

ALMA: Go back to your bedroom. I will bring it up.

MRS. WINEMILLER: Now?

ALMA: Yes. Yes, now. Right now!

(*She steals a frightened glance at John, touches her throat as the stage dims out and the returning voices of Mrs. Buchanan and Rev. Winemiller fade in.*)

(*Fade out.*)

ACT TWO

The Tenderness of a Mother

SCENE ONE

The Buchanans'. We see John in pajamas seated on the floor, smoking before the fireplace; nothing else.

His mother, Mrs. Buchanan, enters the lighted area in her lace negligee.

MRS. BUCHANAN: Son?

JOHN: Yes, Mother?

MRS. BUCHANAN: You mustn't misunderstand me about Miss Alma. Naturally I feel sorry for her, too. But, precious, precious! In every Southern town there's a girl or two like that. People feel sorry for them, they're kind to them, but, darling, they keep at a distance, they don't get involved with them. Especially not in a sentimental way.

JOHN: I don't know what you mean about Miss Alma. She's a little bit—quaint, she's very excitable, but—there's nothing *wrong* with her.

MRS. BUCHANAN: Precious, can't you see? Miss Alma is an *eccentric*!

JOHN: You mean she isn't like all the other girls in Glorious Hill?

MRS. BUCHANAN: There's always at least one like her in every Southern town, sometimes, like Miss Alma, rather sweet, sometimes even gifted, and I think that Miss Alma *does* have a rather appealing voice when she doesn't become too carried away by her singing. Sometimes, but not often, pretty. I have seen Miss Alma when she was almost pretty. But never, never *quite*.

JOHN: There are moments when she has beauty.

MRS. BUCHANAN: Those moments haven't occurred when *I* looked at her! Such a wide mouth she has, like the mouth of a clown! And she distorts her face with all those false expressions. However, Miss Alma's looks are beside the point.

JOHN: Her, her eyes are fascinating!

MRS. BUCHANAN: Goodness, yes, disturbing!

JOHN: No, quite lovely, I think. They're never the same for two seconds. The light keeps changing in them like, like—a running stream of clear water. . . .

MRS. BUCHANAN: They have a demented look!

JOHN: She's not demented, Mother.

MRS. BUCHANAN: *Ha!* You should see her in the Square when she feeds the birds.

(*John laughs a little.*)

Talks to them, calls them! "Here, birds, here, birds, here, birdies!" Holding out her hand with some scraps of bread!—huh!—Son, your hair is still damp. It's lucky that Mother peeped in. Now let me rub those curls dry.—My boy's such a handsome boy, and I'm so proud of him! I can see his future so clearly, such a wonderful future! I can see the girl that he will marry! A girl with every advantage, nothing less will do!

JOHN: A girl with money?

MRS. BUCHANAN: Everything, everything! Intelligence, beauty, charm, background—yes! Wealth, wealth, too! It's not to be sneezed at, money, especially in the wife of a young doctor. It takes a while for a doctor to get established, and I want you to take your time and not make any mistakes and go a long, long, long, long way!—further, much further than your dear father, although he hasn't done badly. . . . Yes, Mother can see her future daughter-in-law!—Healthy! Normal! Pretty!

JOHN: A girl like all the others?

MRS. BUCHANAN: Superior to the others!

JOHN: And sort of smug about it?

MRS. BUCHANAN: Oh, people have to be slightly smug sometimes. A little bit snobbish, even. People who have a position have to hold it, and my future daughter-in-law, my coming daughter—she'll have the sort of poise that only comes with the very best of breeding and all the advantages that the best background can give her.

JOHN: She won't be tiresome, will she?

MRS. BUCHANAN: Heavens, no! How could she?

JOHN: I've met some debutantes in Baltimore that found, somehow, a way of being tiresome. . . .

MRS. BUCHANAN: Just wait till you meet the right one! I have already met her, in my dreams! Oh, son, how she will adore you!

JOHN: More than she does herself?

MRS. BUCHANAN: She'll worship the ground you walk on.

JOHN: And her babies, how will they be?

MRS. BUCHANAN: Healthy! Normal!

JOHN: Not little pink and white pigs? With ribbons around their tails?

MRS. BUCHANAN: Ho-ho-ho-ho-ho! Your babies, my son's babies, pigs?! Oh, precious! I see them, I know them, I feel their dear little bodies in my arms! My adorable little grandchildren. Little pink things for the girl. Little blue things for the boy. A nursery full of their funny little toys. Mother Goose illustrations on the wallpaper, and their own wee little table where they sit with their bibs and their silver spoons, just so high, yes, and their own little chairs, their tiny straight back chairs and their wee little rockers, ho, ho, ho!—And on the lawn, on the enormous, grassy, shady lawn of the—Georgian, yes, *Georgian* mansion, not Greek revival, I'm tired of Greek revival!—will be their swing, their shallow pool for goldfish, their miniature train, their pony—oh, no, not a pony, no, no, not a pony!—I knew a little girl, once, that fell off a pony and landed on her head! *Goodness, she grew up to be almost as odd as Miss Alma!*

(*At this point a dim spot of light appears on Miss Alma standing raptly before a window frame at the other side of the stage. A strain of music is heard.*)

JOHN: Miss Alma has asked me over next Monday night!

MRS. BUCHANAN: Oh, I knew it, trying to rope you in!

JOHN: She says there's to be a club meeting at the Rectory. A little group of young people with interests in common.

MRS. BUCHANAN: Oh, yes, I know, I know what they have in common, the freaks of the town! Every Southern town has them and probably every Northern town has them, too. A certain little group that don't fit in with the others, sort of outcast people that have, or imagine they have, little talents for this thing or that thing or the other—over which they make a big fuss among themselves in order to bolster up their poor little, hurt little egos! They band together, they meet at each other's houses once a week, and make believe they're disliked and not wanted at other places because they're special, superior—gifted! . . . Now your curls are all dry! But let me feel your footsies, I want to make sure the footsies are dry, too, I bet anything they're not, I bet they're damp! Let Mother feel them! (*He extends his bare feet.*) Ho, ho, ho, ho! What enormous little footsies!

JOHN (*as she rubs them with towel*): You know, Mama, I never dreamed that you could be such an old tiger. Tigress, I mean.

MRS. BUCHANAN: Every mother's a tiger when her son's future happiness is threatened.

JOHN: I'm not in love with Miss Alma, if that's what you're scared of. I just *respect* her. . . .

MRS. BUCHANAN: For what?

JOHN: I'm not quite sure what it is, but it's something she has, a sort of—*gallantry*, maybe. . . .

MRS. BUCHANAN: Admire her for her good qualities and I am sure she must have some, but *do not get involved*! Don't go to the little club meeting. Make an excuse and don't go. Write a sweet little note explaining that you had forgotten another engagement. Or let Mother do it. Mother can do it sweetly. There won't be any hurt feelings. . . . Now give me that cigarette. I won't leave you to smoke it in bed. That's how fires start. I don't want us all burned up like the Musée Mécanique!

JOHN: Oh, did the Museum burn?

MRS. BUCHANAN: Heavens, yes, that's a story, but it's too long for bedtime. (*She bends to kiss him fondly, with a lingering caress.*) Good night, my precious! Sleep tight!

(*She turns out the light as she leaves. The dim spot remains on Miss Alma a moment longer. . . .*)

ALMA: Oh, my love, my love, your light is out, now—I can sleep!

SCENE TWO

The following Monday evening. The little group is meeting in the Rectory parlor. An animated discussion is in progress.

VERNON: I think it's a question of whether or not we have a serious purpose. I was under the impression that we *had* a serious purpose, but of course, if we *don't* have a serious purpose—

ALMA: Of course we *do* have a serious purpose, but I don't see why that means we have to publish a—manifesto about it!

ROGER: What's wrong with a manifesto?

VERNON: Even if nobody reads the manifesto, it—*crystallizes!* —our purpose, in our own minds.

ALMA: Oh, but to say that we—have such lofty ambitions.

ROGER: But, Miss Alma, *you* are the one who said we were going to make Glorious Hill the *Athens of the Delta*!

ALMA: Yes, but in the manifesto it says the Athens of the whole *South*, and besides an ambition, a hope of that kind, doesn't have to be—published! In a way to publish it—destroys it!—a little. . . .

MRS. BASSETT: The manifesto is beautiful, *perfectly* beautiful, it made me *cry*!

VERNON (*who composed it*): Thank you, Nancy.

ROGER: Boys and girls, the meeting is called to order. Miss Alma will read us the minutes of the last meeting.

MRS. BASSETT: Oh, let's skip the minutes! Who cares what happened last time? Let's concentrate on the present and the future! That's a widow's philosophy!

(*The doorbell rings. Alma drops her papers.*)

Butter-fingers!

ALMA (*breathlessly*): Did I—hear the bell—ring?

(*The bell rings again.*)

Yes!—it did! (*She starts to pick up the papers; they slip again.*)

MRS. BASSETT: Miss Alma, I don't think I've ever seen you quite so nervous!

ALMA: I forgot to mention it!—I . . . invited a . . . guest!—someone just home for the holidays—young Doctor

Buchanan, the old doctor's son, you know!—he—lives next door!—and he . . .

VERNON: I thought we had all agreed not to have outsiders unless we took a vote on them beforehand!

ALMA: It was presumptuous of me, but I'm sure you'll forgive me when you meet him!

(*She flies out. They all exchange excited looks and whispers as she is heard offstage admitting John to the hall.*)

ROSEMARY: I don't care who he is, if a group *is* a group there must be something a *little* exclusive about it!—otherwise it . . .

MRS. BASSETT: *Listen!* Why, she is *hysterical* about him!

(*Miss Alma's excited voice is heard and her breathless laughter offstage racing.*)

ALMA: Well, well, well, our guest of honor has finally made his appearance!

JOHN: Sorry I'm late.

ALMA: Oh, you're not *very* late.

JOHN: Dad's laid up. I have to call on his patients.

ALMA: Oh, is your father *not well*?

JOHN: Just a slight touch of grippe.

ALMA: There's so much going around.

JOHN: These delta houses aren't built for cold weather.

ALMA: Indeed they aren't! The Rectory's made out of paper, I believe.

(*All of this is said offstage, in the hall.*)

ROSEMARY: Her voice has gone up *two octaves*!

MRS. BASSETT: Obviously *infatuated* with him!

ROSEMARY: Oh, my *stars*!

MRS. BASSETT: The last time I was here—the lunatic mother made a sudden entrance!

VERNON: *Shhhh!—girls!*

(*Alma enters with John. He is embarrassed by the curious intensity of her manner and the greedily curious glances of the group.*)

ALMA: Everybody!—this is Doctor John Buchanan, *Junior*!

JOHN: Hello, everybody. I'm sorry if I interrupted the meeting.

MRS. BASSETT: Nothing was interrupted. We'd decided to skip the minutes.

ALMA: Mrs. Bassett says it's a widow's philosophy to skip the minutes. And so we are skipping the minutes—ha, ha, ha! I hope everybody is comfortable?

ROSEMARY: I'm just as cold as Greenland's icy mountains!

ALMA: Rosemary, you always are chilly, even in warm weather. I think you must be thin-blooded!—Here. Take this shawl!

ROSEMARY: No thank you, not a shawl!—at least not a gray woolen shawl, I'm not *that* old yet, that I have to be wrapped in a gray shawl.

ALMA: *Excuse* me, *do forgive* me!—John, I'll put you on this loveseat, next to me.—Well, now we are completely assembled!

MRS. BASSETT: Vernon has his verse play with him tonight!

ALMA (*uneasily*): Is that right, Vernon?

(*He has a huge manuscript in his lap which he solemnly elevates.*)

Oh, I *see* that you have.

ROSEMARY: I thought that I was supposed to read my paper on William Blake at the meeting.

ALMA: Well, obviously we can't have both at once. That would be an embarrassment of riches!—Now why don't we save the verse play, which appears to be rather long, till some more comfortable evening. I think it's too important to hear under any but ideal circumstances, in warmer weather, with—with *music!*—planned to go with it. . . .

ROGER: Yes, let's hear Rosemary's paper on William Blake!

MRS. BASSETT: No, no, no, those dead poets can keep!—Vernon's alive and he's got his verse play with him; he's brought it three times! And each time been disappointed.

VERNON: I am not disappointed not to read my verse play, *that* isn't the point at all, *but*—

ALMA: Shall we take a standing vote on the question?

ROGER: Yes, let's do.

ALMA: Good, good, perfect, let's do! A standing vote. All in favor of postponing the verse play till the next meeting, stand up!

(*Rosemary is late in rising.*)

ROSEMARY: Is this a vote?

(*As she starts to rise Mrs. Bassett jerks her arm.*)

ROGER: Now, Mrs. Bassett, no rough tactics, please!
ALMA: So we'll save the verse play and begin the New Year with it!

(*Rosemary puts on her glasses and rises portentously.*)

ROSEMARY: The poet—William Blake!
MRS. BASSETT: Insane, insane, that man was a mad fanatic!

(*She squints her eyes tight shut and thrusts her thumbs into her ears. The reactions range from indignant to conciliatory.*)

ROGER: Now, Mrs. Bassett!
MRS. BASSETT: This is a free country. I can speak my opinion. And I have *read up* on him. Go on, Rosemary. I wasn't criticizing your paper.

(*But Rosemary sits down, hurt.*)

ALMA: Mrs. Bassett is only joking, Rosemary.
ROSEMARY: No, I don't want to read it if she feels that strongly about it.
MRS. BASSETT: Not a bit, don't be silly! I just don't see why we should encourage the writings of people like that who have already gone into a drunkard's grave!
VARIOUS VOICES (*exclaiming*): Did he? I never heard that about him. Is that true?
ALMA: Mrs. Bassett is mistaken about that. Mrs. Bassett, you have confused Blake with someone else.
MRS. BASSETT (*positively*): Oh, no, don't tell me. I've read up on him and know what I'm talking about. He traveled around with that Frenchman who took a shot at him and landed them both in jail! Brussels, Brussels!
ROGER (*gaily*): Brussels sprouts!
MRS. BASSETT: That's where it happened, fired a gun at him in a drunken stupor, and later one of them died of T.B. in the gutter! All right. I'm finished. I won't say anything more. Go on with your paper, Rosemary. There's nothing like contact with culture!

(*Alma gets up.*)

ALMA: Before Rosemary reads her paper on Blake, I think it would be a good idea, since some of us aren't acquainted with his work, to preface the critical and biographical comments with a reading of one of his loveliest lyric poems.
ROSEMARY: I'm not going to read anything at all! Not I!
ALMA: Then let me read it then. (*She takes a paper from Rosemary.*) . . . This is called "Love's Secret."

(*She clears her throat and waits for a hush to settle. Rosemary looks stonily at the carpet. Mrs. Bassett looks at the ceiling. John coughs.*)

Never seek to tell thy love,
Love that never told can be;
For the gentle wind doth move
Silently, invisibly.

I told my love, I told my love,
I told him all my heart.
Trembling, cold, in ghastly fear
Did my love depart.

No sooner had he gone from me
Than a stranger passing by,
Silently, invisibly,
Took him with a sigh!

(*There are various effusions and enthusiastic applause.*)

MRS. BASSETT: Honey, you're right. That isn't the man I meant. I was thinking about the one who wrote about the "bought red lips." Who was it that wrote about the "bought red lips"?
ALMA: You're thinking about a poem by Ernest Dowson.

(*The bell rings.*)

MRS. BASSETT: Ohhhhh, the doorbell *again*!
MRS. WINEMILLER (*above*): Alma, Alma!

(*Alma crosses the stage and goes out.*)

ROSEMARY: Aren't you all cold? I'm just freezing to death! I've never been in a house as cold as this!

ALMA (*in the hall*): Why, Mrs. Buchanan! How sweet of you to—drop over. . . .

MRS. BUCHANAN: I can't stay, Alma. I just came to fetch my Little John home.

ALMA: Fetch—John!?

MRS. BUCHANAN: His father's just received an urgent call from old Mrs. Arbuckle's house. The poor woman is in a dreadful pain. John? John, darling? I hate to drag you away but your father can't budge from the house!

ALMA: Mrs. Buchanan, do you know everybody?

MRS. BUCHANAN: Why, yes, I think so.—John? Come, dear! I'm so sorry . . .

(*It is obvious that she is delivering a cool snub to the gathering. There are various embarrassed murmurs as John makes his departure. Miss Alma appears quite stricken.*)

ALMA (*after the departure*): Shall we go on with the reading?

ROSEMARY: "The Poet, William Blake, was born in the year of our Lord, 1757. . . ."

(*Mrs. Winemiller cries out and bursts into the room half in and out of her clothes.*)

MRS. WINEMILLER: Alma, Alma, I've got to go to New Orleans right away, immediately, Alma, by the midnight train. They've closed the Museum, confiscated the marvels! Mr. Schwarzkopf is almost out of his mind. He's going to burn the place up, he's going to set it on fire—before the auction—Monday!

ALMA: *Oh, Mother!* (*She makes a helpless gesture; then bursts into tears and runs out of the room, followed by Mrs. Winemiller.*)

MRS. BASSETT: I think we'd all better go—poor Miss Alma!

ROGER: I move that the meeting adjourn.

VERNON: I second the motion!

MRS. BASSETT: *Poor* Miss Alma! But I knew it was a mistake to have us meet here. (*Sotto voce*) *Nobody* comes to the Rectory any more!—this *always* happens . . . the *mother!*—invariably makes a scene of some kind. . . .

(*They trail off.*)

ROSEMARY (*slowly, wonderingly, as she follows them off*): I don't understand!—What happened?

(*Fade out.*)

SCENE THREE

Later that night.

The interior of the doctor's office is suggested by a chart of anatomy, a black leather divan and an oak desk and chair behind it.

A buzzer sounds in the dark.

VOICES MURMUR ABOVE:

—John?

—Hannh?

—The bell's ringing in the office. You'd better answer it or it will wake up your father.

—All right, Mama.

(*A panicky knocking begins. John enters in pajamas and robe, carrying a book. There are sounds of releasing a lock. Lights go up as Miss Alma enters. She has thrown on a coat over a nightgown, her hair is in disorder, and her appearance very distracted. She is having "an attack."*)

JOHN: Why, it's you, Miss Alma!

ALMA (*panting*): Your father, please.

JOHN: Is something the matter?

ALMA: I have to see your father.

JOHN: Won't I do?

ALMA: No, I think not. Please call your father.

JOHN: Big John's asleep, he's not well.

ALMA: I'm having an attack, I've got to see him!

JOHN: It's after two, Miss Alma.

ALMA: I know the time, I know what time it is! Do you think I'd run over here at two in the morning if I weren't terribly ill?

JOHN: I don't think you would be able to run over here at two in the morning if you *were* terribly ill. Now sit down here. (*He leads her to the divan.*) And stop swallowing air.

ALMA: Swallowing what?

JOHN: Air. You swallow air when you get overexcited. It presses against your heart and starts it pounding. That frightens you more. You swallow more air and get more palpitations and before you know it you're in a state of panic like this. Now you lean back. No, no, lean all the way back and just breathe slowly and deeply. You're not going to suffocate and your heart's going to keep on beating. Look at your fingers, shame on you! You've got them clenched like you're getting ready to hit me. Are you going to hit me? Let those fingers loosen up, now.

ALMA: I can't, I can't, I'm too . . .

JOHN: You couldn't sleep?

ALMA: I couldn't sleep.

JOHN: You felt walled in, the room started getting smaller?

ALMA: I felt—walled in—suffocated!

JOHN: You started hearing your heart as if somebody had stuffed it in the pillow?

ALMA: Yes, like a drum in the pillow.

JOHN: A natural thing. But it scared you. (*He hands her a small glass of brandy.*) Toss this down.

(*He places a hand behind her, raising her shoulders from the divan.*)

ALMA: What is it?

JOHN: Shot of brandy.

ALMA: Oh, that's a stimulant, I need something to calm me.

JOHN: This will calm you.

ALMA: Your father gives me—

JOHN: Let's try this to begin with.

ALMA: He gives me some little white tablets dissolved in—

JOHN: Get this down.

(*She sips and chokes.*)

ALMA: Oh!

JOHN: Went down the wrong way?

ALMA: The muscles of my throat are paralyzed!

JOHN: Undo those fists, undo them, loosen those fingers. (*He presses her hands between his.*)

ALMA: I'm sorry I—woke you up. . . .

JOHN: I was reading in bed. A physicist named Albert Einstein. I'm going to turn this light out.

ALMA: *Oh, no!*

JOHN: Why not? Are you afraid of the dark?

ALMA: Yes . . .

JOHN: It won't be very dark. I'm going to open these shutters and you can look at the stars while I tell you what I was reading.

(*He turns off the lamp on the desk. Crossing to the window frame, he makes a motion of opening shutters. A dim blue radiance floods the stage.*)

I was reading that time is one side of the four-dimensional continuum that we exist in. I was reading that space is curved. It turns back on itself instead of going on indefinitely like we used to believe, and it's hanging adrift in something that's even less than space; it's hanging like a soap-bubble in something less than space. . . .

ALMA: Where is the . . . ?

JOHN: Brandy? Right here . . . Throat muscles still paralyzed?

ALMA: No, I—think I can—get it down, now. . . .

JOHN: There's nothing wrong with your heart but a little functional disturbance, but I'll check it for you. Unbutton your gown.

ALMA: Unbutton? . . .

JOHN: Just the top of your gown.

ALMA: Hadn't I better come back in the morning when your father is . . . ?

JOHN: Sure. If you'd rather.

ALMA: I—my fingers are . . .

JOHN: Fingers won't work?

ALMA: They are just as if frozen!

JOHN (*kneeling beside her*): Let me. (*He leans over her, unbuttoning the gown.*) Little pearl buttons . . . (*Stethoscope to her chest*) Breathe.—Now out . . . Breathe . . . Now out . . . (*Finally he rises.*) Um-hmmmm.

ALMA: What do you hear in my heart?

JOHN: Just a little voice saying, "Miss Alma is lonesome."

(*She springs up angrily.*)

ALMA: If your idea of helping a patient is to ridicule and insult—

JOHN: My idea of helping you is to tell you the truth.

ALMA (*snatching up her cloak*): Oh, how wise and superior you are! John Buchanan, Junior, graduate of Johns Hopkins, magna cum laude!—Brilliant, yes, as the branches after the ice storm, and just as cold and inhuman! Oh, you put us in our place tonight, my, my little collection of—eccentrics, my club of—fellow misfits! You sat among us like a lord of the earth, the only handsome one there, the one superior one! And oh, how we all devoured you with our eyes, you were like holy bread being broken among us.—But snatched away! Fetched home by your mother with that lame excuse, that invention about Mrs. Arbuckle's turn for the worse. I called the Arbuckles.—Better, much better, they told me, no doctor was called! Oh I suppose you're right to despise us, my little company of the faded and frightened and different and odd and lonely. You don't belong to that club but I hold an office in it! (*She laughs harshly.*)

JOHN: Hush, Miss Alma, you'll wake up the house!

ALMA: Wake up my wealthy neighbors? Oh, no, I mustn't. Everything in this house is *comme il faut.*

(*A clock strikes offstage.*)

Even the clock makes music when it strikes, a dainty little music. Hear it, hear it? It sounds like the voice of your mother, saying, "John? John, darling? We must go home now!" (*She laughs convulsively, then chokes, and seizes the brandy glass.*) And when you marry, you'll marry some Northern beauty. She will have no eccentricities but the eccentricity of beauty and perfect calm. Her hands will have such repose, such perfect repose when she speaks. They won't fly about her like wild birds, oh, no, she'll hold them together, press the little pink tips of her fingers together, making a—steeple—or fold them sweetly and gravely in her lap! She'll only move them when she lifts a tea cup—they won't reach above her when she cries out in the night! Suddenly, desperately—fly up, fly up in the night!—reaching for something—nothing!—clutching at—space. . . .

JOHN: Please! Miss Alma! You are—exhausting yourself. . . .

ALMA: No, the bride will have beauty! (*Her voice is now a shrill whisper; she leans far toward him across the desk.*) The bride will have beauty, beauty! Admirable family background, no lunacy in it, no skeletons in the closet—no Aunt Albertine and Mr. Otto Schwarzkopf, no Musée Mécanique with a shady past!—No, no, nothing morbid, nothing peculiar, nothing eccentric! No—deviations!—But everything perfect and regular as the—tick of that—clock!

MRS. BUCHANAN'S VOICE (*above*): John! John, darling! What on earth is the matter down there?

JOHN (*at the door*): Nothing. Go to sleep, Mother.

MRS. BUCHANAN'S VOICE: Is someone badly hurt?

JOHN: Yes, Mother. Hurt. But not badly. Go back to sleep.

(*He closes the door.*)

Now. You see? You are gasping for breath again. Lie down, lie down. . . .

ALMA: I am not afraid any more and I don't care to lie down.

JOHN: Perhaps, after all, that outburst did you some good.

ALMA: Yes—Yes— (*Then suddenly*) *I'm so ashamed of myself!*

JOHN: You should be proud of yourself. You know, you know, it's surprising how few people there are that dare in this world to say what is in their hearts.

ALMA: I had no right—to talk to you like that. . . .

JOHN: I was—stupid, I—hurt you. . . .

ALMA: No. I hurt myself! I exposed myself. Father is frightened of me and he's right. On the surface I'm still the Episcopal minister's daughter but there's something else that's—

JOHN: Yes, something else! What is it?

ALMA (*slowly shaking her head*): Something—else that's—frantic!

JOHN: A doppelgänger?

ALMA (*nodding slowly*): A—doppelgänger!

JOHN: Fighting for its life in the prison of a little conventional world full of walls and . . .

ALMA: What was it you said about space when you turned the light out?

JOHN: Space, I said, is curved.

ALMA: Then even space is a prison!—not—infinite. . . .

JOHN: A very large prison, even large enough for you to feel free in, Miss Alma. (*He takes her hand and blows his breath on her fingers.*) Are your fingers still frozen?

(*She leans against the desk, turning her face to the audience, closing her eyes.*)

ALMA: Your breath!—is . . . *warm.* . . .

JOHN: Yours, too. Your breath is warm.

ALMA: All human breath is warm—so pitifully! So pitifully warm and soft as children's fingers. . . . (*She turns her face to him and takes his face between the fingers of both her hands.*) The brandy worked very quickly. You know what I feel like now. I feel like a water-lily on a—Chinese lagoon. . . . I will sleep, perhaps. But—I won't see you —again. . . .

JOHN: I'm leaving next Monday.

ALMA: Monday . . .

JOHN: Aren't there any more meetings we could—go to?

ALMA: You don't like meetings.

JOHN: The only meetings I like are between two people.

ALMA: We are two people, we've met—did you like our meeting?

(*John nods, smiling.*)

Then meet me again!

JOHN: I'll take you to see Mary Pickford at the Delta Brilliant tomorrow.

(*Alma throws back her head with a gasping laugh, checks it quickly. She retreats with a slight gasp as Mrs. Buchanan enters in a lace negligee.*)

MRS. BUCHANAN (*with acid sweetness*): Oh, the patient's Miss *Alma*!

ALMA: Yes. Miss Alma's the patient. Forgive me for disturbing you. Good night. (*She turns quickly but with a fleeting glance at John, who grins by the door.*) Au revoir! (*She goes out.*)

MRS. BUCHANAN: And what was the matter with *her*?!

JOHN: Palpitations, Mother. (*He turns out the office light.*) *Haven't* you ever had them?

MRS. BUCHANAN: *Had* them? *Yes*!—But *controlled* them!

(*He laughs gaily on the stairs. She follows with an outraged "Huh!"*)

(*Dim out.*)

SCENE FOUR

The next night, New Year's Eve. Roger and Miss Alma are in the Rectory parlor with a magic lantern.

ROGER: Is it in focus, Miss Alma?
ALMA (*absently*): Yes.

(*The image is completely blurred.*)

ROGER: Are you sure it's in focus?
ALMA (*in a sad whisper*): Yes, perfectly in focus.
ROGER (*rising from behind the lantern*): What is it a picture of?
ALMA (*faintly*): What, Roger?
ROGER: I said, "What is it a picture of?"
ALMA: Why, I can't tell, it seems to be out of focus. . . .
ROGER: You just now said that it was in perfect focus.
ALMA: Excuse me, Roger. My wits are woolgathering.
ROGER: I will turn off the lantern and put the slides away. (*He does so.*) Now let's turn the sofa to face the window so we won't have to twist our necks to gaze at the house next door.—You were expecting him tonight?
ALMA: He'd asked me to go to the movies.
ROGER: Then why did you ask me to bring my magic lantern?
ALMA: Some people called for him at seven. He left the house. I think he'd forgotten he asked me to go to the movies. I just couldn't sit here alone waiting to see if he had, or if he'd remember. I just couldn't bear it!
ROGER: How late is he now?
ALMA: Twenty, no, twenty-five minutes!
ROGER: I think I would go and give him up then.
ALMA: I have, almost. I almost wish I was dead!
ROGER: People who bark up wrong trees . . .
ALMA: Sometimes the only tree you want to bark up is the wrong one. . . . Don't you know that?

ROGER: Miss Alma, we're fond of each other. We get along well together. We have interests in common. Companionship is something.

ALMA: Something, but not enough. I want more than that.—*I see him!*—No . . . No, that isn't him. . . . You and I, we have no desire for each other. They intimated to you at the bank that you'd be advanced more rapidly if you were married. But, Roger, I want more than that. . . . Even if all I get in the end is a button—like Aunt Albertine. . . .

ROGER: A button?

ALMA: You've heard her story?

ROGER: I've heard your mother make some allusions to it, but nothing very—coherent. . . .

ALMA: She grew up, like me, in the shadow of the church. Until one Sunday a strange man came to the service and dropped a ten-dollar bill in the collection plate! —Of course he was immediately invited to dinner at the Rectory. . . . At dinner he sat next to my Aunt Albertine—the next day she bought a plumed hat and the following Wednesday he took her away from the Rectory forever. . . . He'd been married twice already, without a divorce, but bigamy was the least of his delinquencies, and obviously Aunt Albertine found living in sin preferable to life in the Rectory.—Mr. Schwarzkopf was a mechanical genius. They traveled about the South with a sort of show called the Musée Mécanique. I'm sure you've heard Mother speak of it—a collection of mechanical marvels that Mr. Schwarzkopf had created. Among them was a mechanical bird-girl. She was his masterpiece. Every five minutes a tin bird flew out of her mouth and whistled three times, clear as a bell, and flew back in again. She smiled and nodded, lifted her arms as if to embrace a lover. Mr. Schwarzkopf was enchanted by his bird-girl. Everything else was neglected. . . . He'd suddenly get out of bed in the night and go downstairs to wind her up and sit in front of her, drinking, until she seemed alive to him. . . . Then one winter they made a dreadful mistake. They mortgaged the whole Museum to buy a boa constrictor because somebody had told them "Big snakes pay good"—well, this one didn't, it swallowed a blanket and died. . . . You may have heard Mother speak of it. But not of the fire. She refuses to believe in the fire.

ROGER: There was a fire?

ALMA: Oh, yes. Creditors took the Museum and locked Mr. Schwarzkopf out. There was to be an auction of the mechanical marvels but the night before the auction Mr. Schwarzkopf broke into the Museum and set it on fire. Albertine rushed into the burning building and caught Mr. Schwarzkopf by the sleeve of his coat but he broke away from her. When they dragged her out, she was dying, but still holding onto a button she'd torn from his sleeve. "Some people," she said, "don't even die empty-handed!"

ROGER: What did she mean by that?

ALMA: The button, of course . . . all that was left of her darling Mr. Schwarzkopf!

(*The bell rings. She seems paralyzed for a moment, then gasps and rushes out of the lighted area. A moment later her voice is heard.*)

I'd almost given you up!

(*Dim out.*)

ACT THREE

A Cavalier's Plume

SCENE ONE

That night, after the movies, before the angel of the fountain.

ALMA: May we stop here for a moment?

JOHN: You're not cold?

ALMA: No.

(*A silence.*)

JOHN: You've been very quiet, Miss Alma.

ALMA: I always say too much or say too little. The few young men I've gone out with have found me . . . I've only gone out with three at all seriously—and with each one there was a desert between us.

JOHN: What do you mean by a desert?

ALMA: Oh, wide, wide stretches of uninhabitable ground. I'd try to talk, he'd try to talk. Oh, we'd talk quite a lot—but then it would be—exhausted—the talk, the effort. I'd twist the ring on my finger, so hard sometimes it would cut my finger. He'd look at his watch as if he had never seen a watch before. . . . And we would both know that the useless undertaking had come to a close. At the door— (*She turns slowly to the fountain.*) At the door he would say, "I'll call you." "I'll call you" meant goodbye! (*She laughs a little.*)

JOHN (*gently*): Would you care much?

ALMA: Not—not about them. . . .

JOHN: Then about what would you care?

(*Far away nonrealistic baying of a hound. "Valse des Regrets" by Brahms fades in softly.*)

ALMA: They only mattered as shadows of some failure that would come later.

JOHN: What failure?

ALMA: A failure such as—tonight. . . .

JOHN: Tonight is a failure?

ALMA: I think it will be a failure. Look. My ring has cut my finger. No! I shall have to be honest! I can't play any kind of a game! Do you remember what Mother said when she burst into the room? "Alma has fallen in love with that tall boy!" It's true. I had. But longer ago than that. I remember the long afternoons of our childhood when I had to stay indoors and practice my music. I heard your playmates calling you, Johnny, Johnny! Oh, how it used to go through me just to hear your name called. I ran to the window to watch you jump the porch railing, stood at a distance halfway down the block only to keep in sight of your torn red sweater racing about the vacant lot you played in. "Johnny, Johnny!"—It had begun that early, this affliction of love, and it's never let go of me since, but kept on growing and growing. I've lived next door to you all the days of my life, a weak and divided person, lived in your shadow, no, I mean in your brightness which made a shadow I lived in, but lived in adoring awe of your radiance, your strength . . . your singleness. Now Father tells me that I am becoming known as an eccentric. People think me affected, laugh at me, imitate me at parties! I'm marked to be different, it's stamped on me in big letters so people can read from a distance: "This Person Is Strange." . . . Well, I may be eccentric but not so eccentric that I don't have the ordinary human need for love. I have that need, and I must satisfy it, in whatever way my good or bad fortune will make possible for me. . . . One time in the movies I sat next to a strange man. I didn't look at his face, but after a while I felt the pressure of his knee against mine. I thought it might be accidental. I moved aside. But then it began again. I didn't look at him. I sprang from my seat. I rushed out of the theater. I wonder sometimes. If I had dared to look at his face in the queer flickering white light that comes from the screen, and it had been like yours, at *all* like yours, even the *faintest resemblance*—Would I have sprung from my seat, or would I have *stayed*?

JOHN: A dangerous speculation for a minister's daughter!

ALMA: Very dangerous indeed! But not as dangerous as what I did tonight. Didn't you feel it? Didn't you feel the pressure of my—knee?—Tonight?—In the movies?

(*The audience may laugh at this question. Take a count of ten. Perhaps John crosses slowly to drink at the fountain.*)

I have embarrassed you.

JOHN (*gently*): Yes.

ALMA: I told you I had to be honest. Now you take me home. You may take me back to the house between your house and the Episcopal church, you may take me back there, now, unless—unless . . .

JOHN: Unless what, Miss Alma?

ALMA: Unless, unless—by the most unlikely chance in the world you wanted to take me somewhere else!

JOHN: Where is—"somewhere else"?

ALMA: Anywhere that two people could be alone.

JOHN: Oh . . .

ALMA: I told you I had to be honest.

JOHN: We are alone in the Square.

ALMA: I was thinking of—

JOHN: A room?

ALMA: A—little room with—a fireplace . . .

JOHN: One of those rooms that people engage for an hour? A bottle of wine in a bucket of ice—brrr! No!—No ice—No, one of those red wines in straw-covered bottles from Italy. I think they call it—Chianti. . . .

ALMA: Just—four walls and a—fireplace . . .

JOHN: I'm glad you include a fireplace. That might be necessary to take the chill off, Miss Alma.

ALMA: Are there—are there such places?

JOHN: Yes. There have been such places since the beginning of time. Little rooms that seem empty even when you are in them but have sad little tokens of people that occupied them before you, a sprinkle of light pink powder on the dresser, a hairpin on the carpet—a few withered rose petals —in the wastebasket of course an empty pint bottle of some inexpensive whisky. Yes. There is such a place in Glorious Hill—even . . .

ALMA: Do you—know where to find it?

JOHN: I could find it blindfolded.

ALMA: You've been to it often?

JOHN: I grew up in this town. Yes. I remember the place. It wasn't attractive, Miss Alma, you wouldn't like it.

ALMA: I would like it with you.

JOHN: You might think that you would until you got there and then discover you didn't. The first time I went there was with one of those anonymous young ladies who get off the Cannonball Express at midnight and stand aimlessly around the entrance to the waiting room at the depot with one small suitcase like a small dog close to their slippers—that first time I went there because *she* knew of the place. . . . I made an excuse to slip away from the room, and I ran like a rabbit, ha ha, I ran like a rabbit!—I left a white linen jacket over a chair with a wallet containing eight dollars. Later, much later, I believe a year later, yes, the following summer—I went back there again, and the grinning old colored porter handed me the white jacket. "A young lady left it for you, Mistuh Johnny, one time last summer," he told me. The wallet was still in the pocket, and in the wallet was a note from the lady. "Baby, I took five dollars to get me to Memphis."—Ha ha ha—signed "Alice" . . .

ALMA: Alice . . .

JOHN: Yes. Alice. She had a small nose with freckles which is probably still leading her into trouble as straight as a good bird-dog will point at a partridge! Ha ha ha!—No, Miss Alma, you wouldn't care for the place, and besides it's New Year's Eve and it will be crowded, there, and after all, you're not unknown in this town, you're the Nightingale of the Delta! Oh, they wouldn't be people you'd run into at church, but . . .

ALMA: John, I want to go there. I want to be in a small room with you at midnight when the bells ring!

JOHN: You're quite sure that you want to?

ALMA: Do you see any shadow of doubt in my eyes?

JOHN: No— No, not in your eyes—but of course you know that it might turn out badly.

(*She nods her head slowly and gravely. He grips her gloved hands.*)

It would be an experiment that might fail so miserably that it would have been much better not to have tried it. Because—well—"propinquity," as you call it—just propinquity—sometimes isn't enough. Oh, I wouldn't run out of the room like a rabbit and leave my jacket over the back of the chair! I'm a *big* boy, now! But you know, Miss Alma—or *do* you know?—that regardless of how it was, whether or not the experiment went well or very badly—you must know that I couldn't—couldn't—

ALMA: Go on with it? Yes. I know that.

JOHN: There are many practical reasons.

ALMA: And many impractical reasons. I know all of that!

JOHN: The most important one is the one I'd rather not say, but I guess you know what it is.

ALMA: I know that you don't love me.

JOHN: No. No, I'm not in love with you.

ALMA: I wasn't counting on that tonight or ever.

JOHN: God. Yes, God. You talk as straight as a man and you look right into my eyes and say you're expecting *nothing*?!

ALMA: I'm looking into your eyes but I'm not saying that. I expect a great deal. But for tonight only. Afterwards, nothing, nothing! Nothing at all.

JOHN: Afterwards would come quickly in a room that you rent for an hour.

ALMA: An hour is the lifetime of some creatures.

JOHN: Generations of some creatures can be fitted into an hour, the sort of creatures I see through my microscope. But you're not one of those creatures. You're a complex being. You have that mysterious something, as thin as smoke, that makes the difference between the human and all other beings! An hour isn't a lifetime for you, Miss Alma.

ALMA: Give me the hour, and I'll make a lifetime of it.

JOHN (*smiling a little*): For you, Miss Alma, the name of the stone angel is barely long enough and nothing less than that *could* be!

ALMA: What is the answer, John?

JOHN: Excuse me a minute. I will find a taxi.

ALMA: *Leave something with me to guarantee your return!*

(*Her laughter rings out high and clear, not like a woman's: more like the cry of a bird. He half turns as if startled; then grins wryly, raises an arm, and shouts: "Taxi!"*)

(*The scene dims out.*)

(*A soprano sings: "I Love You" by Grieg, during the change of scene.*)

SCENE TWO

A short while later that night. The skeletal set is a bedroom in a small hotel of the sort that is called, sometimes, a "house of convenience": a place where rooms are let out for periods as brief as an hour. Next door is a night resort. We hear a mechanical piano playing ragtime.

A Negro porter enters and prepares the room for occupants waiting outside. He sets whisky and two glasses on a small round table by the bed. The long shadows of the waiting couple, still outside, are thrown across the lighted area, until the porter withdraws. Then John and Alma enter the lighted area; they stand silent on the edge of it for a moment like timid bathers at the edge of cold water.

JOHN: The room is cold.
ALMA: Will—will—will the fire light?
JOHN: That remains to be seen. . . .
ALMA: Try it, try to light it!

(*He still pauses.*)

What are you waiting for, John?
JOHN: For you to think . . .
ALMA: Think about what?
JOHN: If you really want to go on with this—adventure. . . .
ALMA: My answer is yes! What's yours?

(*Another long pause.*)

JOHN (*finally*): This room reminds me of a hospital room. Even a folding white screen of the sort they put around patients about to expire.
ALMA: Rooms of this kind, are they always like this?
JOHN: You think I've had a vast experience with them?
ALMA: I'm sure you must have had some.
JOHN: Actually, probably not much more than *you've* had.

(*She crosses to the table by the bed.*)

ALMA: Oh, look, I've found a withered rose petal and a sprinkle of powder!
JOHN: That takes the curse off a little.
ALMA: Turn out the light. Let's see how it looks with the light out.

(*He switches off the bare bulb.*)

JOHN: You know what it looks like now? It looks like a cave in Capri that's called the Blue Grotto!
ALMA: Put a match to the fire.

JOHN (*crouching before the fireplace*): The logs are damp.
ALMA: There's paper underneath them.
JOHN: It's damp, too.
ALMA: But try!
JOHN: I shall try, Miss Alma.—But you know I told you this could turn out badly.
ALMA: Yes, I know. You warned me.

(*He strikes a match. A flickering red glow falls upon their figures as he draws the match back from the fire.*)

There, there now, it's *burning*!
JOHN: Temporarily . . .
ALMA: Let's pray it will keep! . . . Put paper on it, put more paper on.
JOHN: I have none!
ALMA: There must be some. Quick, quick, it's expiring! Ring for the boy, ring for the boy! We must have a fire to take the chill off the room!
JOHN: Are you sure that a fire would take the chill off the room?

(*She suddenly seizes her hat and tears off the plume, starts to cast the plume into the fireplace. He seizes her hand.*)

Miss Alma!
ALMA: This plume will burn!
JOHN: *Don't!*
ALMA: This plume will burn! Something has to be sacrificed to a fire.
JOHN (*still gripping her hand that holds the plume*): Miss Alma. Miss Alma. The fire has gone out and nothing will revive it. Take my word for it, nothing!

(*Music is heard very faintly.*)

It never was much of a fire, it never really got started, and now it's out. . . . Sometimes things say things for people. Things that people find too painful or too embarrassing to say, a thing will say it, a thing will say it for them so they don't have to say it. . . . The fire is out, it's gone out, and you feel how the room is now, it's deathly chill. There's no use in staying in it.

(*She turns on the light, walks a few steps from him, twisting her ring. There is a pause.*)

You are twisting your ring. (*He catches hold of her hand again and holds it still.*)

ALMA: How gently a failure can happen! The way that some people die, lightly, unconsciously, losing themselves with their breath. . . .

JOHN: Why—why call it a failure?

ALMA: Why call a spade a spade? I have to be honest. If I had had beauty and desirability and the grace of a woman, it would not have been necessary for me to be honest. My eccentricities—made it necessary. . . .

JOHN: I think your honesty is the plume on your hat. And you ought to wear it proudly.

ALMA: Proudly or not proudly, I shall wear it. Now I must put it back on. Where is my hat?—Oh.—Here—the plume is restored to its place!

(*Downstairs a hoarse whisky contralto starts singing "Hello, my honey, hello, my baby, hello, my ragtime doll!"*)

Who is—what is . . . Oh!—a party—downstairs . . .

JOHN: This is—a honky-tonk.

ALMA: *Yes!* Perhaps I shall get to know it a great deal better!

JOHN: The plume on your hat is lovely, it almost sweeps the ceiling!

ALMA: You *flatterer*! (*She smiles at him with harshness, almost mockery.*)

JOHN: *Don't!*—we have to still like each other!—Don't be *harsh.*

ALMA:

> If I wore a tall hat in a sunny room,
> I would sweep the ceiling with a cavalier's plume—
> If I wore a frock coat on a polished stair,
> I would charm a grande dame with my gallant air.
> If I wore a . . .

I don't remember the rest of it. Do you?

JOHN:

> If I wore a gold sword on a white verandah,
> I would shock a simple heart with my heartless candor!

ALMA: Yes, that's how it goes. . . .

(*The music dies out. All over town the church bells begin to ring in various tones, some urgent, some melancholy, some tender, and horns are blown and things exploded or rattled.*)

There. There it is, the New Year! I hope it will be all that you want it to be! (*She says this with a sudden warm sincerity, smiling directly into his face.*) What a strange way we've spent New Year's Eve! Going to a Mary Pickford picture at the Delta Brilliant, having a long conversation in a cold square, and coming to a strange and bare little room like a hospital room where a fire wouldn't burn, in spite of our invocations!—But now—it's another year. . . . Another stretch of time to be discovered and entered and explored, and who knows what we'll find in it? Perhaps the coming true of our most improbable dreams!—I'm not ashamed of tonight! I think that you and I have been honest together, even though we failed!

(*Something changes between them. He reaches above him, turns out the light bulb. Almost invisibly at first a flickering red glow comes from the fireplace. She has lowered the veil attached to her plumed hat. He turns it gently back from her face.*)

ALMA: What are you doing that for?

JOHN: So that I won't get your veil in my mouth when I kiss you. (*He does.*)

(*Alma turns her face to the audience. The stage has darkened but a flickering red glow now falls across their figures. The fire has miraculously revived itself, a phoenix.*)

ALMA: I don't dare to believe it, but look, oh, look, look, John! (*She points at the fireplace from which the glow springs.*) Where did the fire come from?

JOHN: No one has ever been able to answer that question!

(*The red glow brightens.*)

(*The scene dims gradually out.*)

EPILOGUE

The Square, before the stone angel. A Fourth of July night an indefinite time later. Another soprano is singing.

A young traveling salesman approaches the bench on which Alma is seated. Band music is heard.

ALMA: How did you like her voice?

SALESMAN: She sang all right.

ALMA: Her face was blank. She didn't seem to know what to do with her hands. And I didn't think she sang with any emotion. A singer's face and her hands and even her heart are part of her equipment and ought to be used expressively when she sings. That girl is one of my former vocal pupils—I used to teach singing here—and so I feel that I have a right to be critical. I used to sing at public occasions like this. I don't any more.

SALESMAN: Why don't you any more?

ALMA: I'm not asked any more.

SALESMAN: Why's that?

(*Alma shrugs slightly and unfolds her fan. The salesman coughs a little.*)

ALMA: You're a stranger in town?

SALESMAN: I'm a traveling salesman.

ALMA: Ahhhh. A salesman who travels. You're younger than most of them are, and not so fat.

SALESMAN: I'm—uh—just starting out. . . .

ALMA: Oh.—The pyrotechnical display is late in starting.

SALESMAN: What—what did you say?

ALMA: The fireworks, I said. I said they ought to be starting. —I don't suppose you're familiar with this town. This town is Glorious Hill, Mississippi, population five thousand souls and an equal number of bodies.

SALESMAN: Ha ha! An equal number of bodies, that's good, ha ha!

ALMA: Isn't it? My name is Alma. Alma is Spanish for soul. Usted habla Español, señor?

SALESMAN: Un poquito. Usted habla Español, señorita?

ALMA: Tambien! Un poquito.

SALESMAN: Sometimes un poquito is plenty!

ALMA: Yes, indeed, and we have to be grateful for it. Sit down and I'll point out a few of our historical landmarks to you. Directly across the Square is the county courthouse: slaves were sold on the steps before the abolition of slavery in the South; now gray old men with nothing better to do sit on them all day. Over there is the Roman Catholic Church, a small unimpressive building, this being a Protestant town. And there—

(*She points in another direction.*)

—There is the Episcopal church. My father was rector of it before his death. It has an unusual steeple.

(*Her voice is rising in volume and tempo. One or two indistinct figures pause behind the stone bench, whispering, laughing at her. She turns about abruptly, imitating the laughter with a rather frightening boldness: the figures withdraw. She continues.*)

Yes, instead of a cross on top of the steeple, it has an enormous gilded hand with its index finger pointing straight up, accusingly, at—heaven. . . . (*She holds her hand up to demonstrate.*)

(*The young salesman laughs uneasily and glances back of him as other figures appear in silhouette behind them.*)

Are you looking at the angel of the fountain? It's the loveliest thing in Glorious Hill. The angel's name is Eternity. The name is carved in the stone block at the base of the statue, but it's not visible in this light, you'd have to read it with your fingers as if you were blind. . . . Straight ahead but not visible, either, is another part of town: it's concealed by the respectable front of the Square: it's called Tiger Town, it's the part of town that a traveling salesman might be interested in. Are you interested in it?

SALESMAN: What's it got to offer?

ALMA: Saloons, penny arcades, and rooms that can be rented for one hour, which is a short space of time for human beings, but there are living—organisms—only visible through a microscope—that live and die and are succeeded by several generations in an hour, or less than an hour, even. . . .

Oh!—There goes the first sky-rocket! Look at it burst into a million stars!

(*A long-drawn "Ahhh" from the unseen crowd in the Square as a rocket explodes above it and casts a dim gold radiance on Alma's upturned face. She closes her eyes very tightly for a moment, then rises, smiling down at the young salesman.*)

Now would you like to go to Tiger Town? The part of town back of the courthouse?

SALESMAN (*rising, nervously grinning*): Sure, why not, let's go!

ALMA: Good, go ahead, get a taxi, it's better if I follow a little behind you. . . .

SALESMAN: Don't get lost, don't lose me!

(*The salesman starts off jauntily as the band strikes up "The Santiago Waltz."*)

ALMA: Oh, no, I'm not going to lose you before I've lost you!

(*He is out of the lighted area.*)

(*Another rocket explodes, much lower and brighter: The angel, Eternity, is clearly revealed for a moment or two. Alma gives it a little parting salute as she follows after the young salesman, touching the plume on her hat as if to see if it were still there.*)

(*The radiance of the sky-rocket fades out; the scene is dimmed out with it.*)

The End

THE MILK TRAIN DOESN'T STOP HERE ANYMORE

"Consume my heart away; sick with desire
And fastened to a dying animal
It knows not what it is; and gather me
Into the artifice of eternity."

—FROM *Sailing to Byzantium*
BY WILLIAM BUTLER YEATS

AUTHOR'S NOTES

Sometimes theatrical effects and devices such as those I have adopted in the third (and I hope final) version of this play are ascribed to affectation or "artiness," so it may be helpful for me to explain a bit of my intention in the use of these effects and devices, and let the play's production justify or condemn them.

I have added to the cast a pair of stage assistants that function in a way that's between the Kabuki Theatre of Japan and the chorus of Greek theatre. My excuse, or reason, is that I think the play will come off better the further it is removed from conventional theatre, since it's been rightly described as an allegory and as a "sophisticated fairy tale."

Stage assistants in Japanese Kabuki are a theatrical expedient. They work on stage during the performance, shifting set pieces, placing and removing properties and furniture. Now and then in this play they have lines to speak, very short ones that serve as cues to the principal performers. . . . They should be regarded, therefore, as members of the cast. They sometimes take a balletic part in the action of the play. They should be dressed in black, very simply, to represent invisibility to the other players. The other players should never appear to see them, even when they speak or take part in the action, except when they appear "in costume."

THE SETTING *represents the library and bedroom of the white villa, downstage, and the bedrooms of the pink and blue villinos: most importantly, the terrace of the white villa, I think, should extend the whole width of the proscenium, with a small apron for a white iron bench, a step down from the terrace.*

Separations between interior and exterior should not be clearly defined except by lighting. When a single interior is being used, the other interior areas should be masked by light, folding screens, painted to blend with the cyclorama, that is, in sea-and-sky colors: they should be set in place and removed by the stage assistants. The cyclorama and these folding screens represent, preferably in a semi-abstract style, the mountain-sea-sky of Italy's Divina Costiera *in summer.*

Since the villas are, naturally, much farther apart than they can appear on the stage, the director could adopt a convention of having actors, who are to go from one villa to another, make their exits into the wings. They would wait till the stage assistants have removed the screens that mask the next interior to be used, and then come back out and enter that area.

August, 1963.

THE PLAYERS

MRS. GOFORTH
CHRISTOPHER FLANDERS
BLACKIE
THE WITCH OF CAPRI
RUDY, a watchman
GIULIO
SIMONETTA
TWO STAGE ASSISTANTS
(Sometimes appearing in costume for small parts)
MEMBERS OF THE KITCHEN STAFF

PROLOGUE

At the rise of the curtain, the Stage Assistants are on stage. All the interior areas are masked by their individual screens. The light of the cyclorama suggests early dawn.

ONE: Daybreak: flag-raising ceremony on Mrs. Goforth's mountain.

TWO: Above the oldest sea in the Western world.

ONE: Banner.

(*Two hands it to him. Two places the staff in a socket near the right wings and attaches the flag to it. A fan in the wings whips it out as it is being raised, so that the audience can see the device on it clearly.*)

ONE: The device on the banner is a golden griffin.

TWO: A mythological monster, half lion, and half eagle.

ONE: And completely human.

TWO: Yes, wholly and completely human, that's true.

ONE: We are also a device.

TWO: A theatrical device of ancient and oriental origin.

ONE: With occidental variations, however.

TOGETHER: We are Stage Assistants. We move the screens that mask the interior playing areas of the stage presentation.

ONE: We fetch and carry.

TWO: Furniture and props.

ONE: To make the presentation—the play or masque or pageant—move more gracefully, quickly through the course of the two final days of Mrs. Goforth's existence.

MRS. GOFORTH'S VOICE (*offstage; half sleeping*): Ahhhhhhhh, Meeeeeeeee . . .

(*There is heard the sound of distant church bells.*)

ONE: The actors will not seem to hear us except when we're in costume.

TWO: They will never see us, except when we're in costume.

ONE: Sometimes we will give them cues for speech and participate in the action.

MRS. GOFORTH'S VOICE (*off stage*): Ahhhhhhh, Ahhhhhh, Ahhhhhh . . .

(*One and Two show no reaction to this human cry.*)

MRS. GOFORTH'S VOICE (*off stage; more wakefully*): Another day, Oh, Christ, Oh, Mother of Christ!

(*There is silence, a pause, as the cyclorama's lighting indicates the progress of the day toward the meridian.*)

ONE *and* TWO (*together*): Our hearts are invisible, too.

(*The fan that whipped out the flag bearing the personal emblem, the griffin, of Mrs. Goforth, dies down and the flag subsides with it, and will not whip out again till the flag-lowering ceremony which will take place during the last three lines of the play.*

(*Now it is noon. Electric buzzers sound from various points on the stage. The Stage Assistants cross rapidly up center and remove a screen, the middle panel of which is topped by Mrs. Goforth's heraldic device, the gold griffin. The library of the white villa is unmasked and the play begins.*)

SCENE ONE

Mrs. Goforth and her secretary, Blackie, are on stage.

MRS. GOFORTH: I made my greatest mistake when I put a fast car in his hands, that red demon sports car, his fighting cock, I called it, which he drove insanely, recklessly, between my estate and the Casino at Monte Carlo, so recklessly that the Police Commissioner of Monaco came personally to ask me. Correction, *beg* me. Correction, *implore* me!—To insist that he go with me in the Rolls with a chauffeur at the wheel, as a protection of his life and of the lives of others.—M. le Commissionaire, I said, for me there are no others.—I know, Madame, he said, but for the others there are others.—Then I confessed to the Commissioner of Police that over this young poet with Romanov blood in his veins, I had no more control than my hands had over the sea-wind or the storms of the sea. At night he had flying dreams, he would thrash his arms like wings, and once his hand, on which he wore a signet ring with the heavy Romanov crest, struck me in the mouth and drew blood. After *that, necessarily*—twin beds . . .

BLACKIE: Mrs. Goforth, excuse me, but the last thing I have typed up is—oh, here it is.—"My first two husbands were ugly as apes and my third one resembled an ostrich."—Now if this passage you're dictating to me comes in direct sequence it will sound as if you had put the fast car in the hands of the ostrich.

(*There is a long, tempestuous pause.*)

MRS. GOFORTH: Aren't you the sly one, oh, you're sly as ten flies when you want to give me the needle, aren't you, Miss Blackie? My first three marriages were into Dun and Bradstreet's and the Social Register, both!—My first husband, Harlon Goforth, whose name I still carry after three later marriages—that dignified financier, *tycoon!*—was a man that Presidents put next to their wives at banquets in the White House, and you sit there smoking in my face, when you know I've been told to quit smoking, and you make a joke of my work with a dead-pan expression on your Vassar-girl face, in your Vassar-girl voice, and *I will not tolerate it!*—You know goddamn well I'm talking about my *fourth* husband, the *last* one, the one I married for love, who plunged off the Grande Corniche between Monte Carlo and—died that night in my arms in a clinic at Nice: and my heart died with him! Forever! (*Her voice breaks.*)

BLACKIE: I'm sorry, Mrs. Goforth. (*Puts out cigarette.*) I'm no writer but I do think in writing there has to be some kind of logical—sequence, continuity—between one bit and the next bit, and the last thing you dictated to me—

MRS. GOFORTH: Was it something I put on the tape-recorder in my bedroom after I'd been given one of those injections that upset my balance at night?

BLACKIE: I took it off your bedroom tape this morning.

MRS. GOFORTH: Always check those night recordings with me before we begin to work the following morning. We're working against time, Blackie. Remember, try to remember, I've got two deadlines to meet, my New York publishers and my London publishers, both, have my memoirs on their Fall List. I said fall. It's already late in August. Now do you see why there's no time for goofing, or must I draw you a picture of autumn leaves falling?

BLACKIE: Mrs. Goforth, I think those publishers' deadlines are unrealistic, not to say cruel, and as for me, I not only have to function as a secretary but as an *editor*, I have to *collate* the material you dictate to me and I'm not being sly or cruel, I'm just being *honest* with you when I tell you—

MRS. GOFORTH (*cutting in*): All cruel people describe themselves as paragons of frankness!

BLACKIE: I think we'd better stop now.

MRS. GOFORTH: *I* think we'd better go *on*, now!

BLACKIE: Mrs. Goforth, the Police Commissioner of Monaco was right when he told you that there were "others." I am one of those "others." I've had no sleep, scarcely any at all and—

MRS. GOFORTH: *You've* had no sleep? What about me, how much sleep do *I* get?

BLACKIE: You sleep till noon or after!

MRS. GOFORTH: Under sedation, with nightmares!

BLACKIE: Your broker is on the phone . . .

(*The Stage Assistants have entered with phone.*)

MRS. GOFORTH (*immediately brightening*): Chuck, baby, how're we doing? Ah-huh, glamour stocks still slipping? Don't hold on to 'em, dump them before they drop under what I bought 'em at, baby. We'll start buying back when they hit the basement level.—Don't give me an argument, Sell! *Sell! Hell!*—It's building into a crash! So, baby, I'm hitting the silk! High, low, jack and the game! Ho ho!

(*She bangs down the phone, exhilarated, and it is removed by one of the Stage Assistants. The other Assistant has rushed to the stage-right wings, and he now appears in a white doctor's jacket. This is one of the costumes that make the Assistants seen and heard by the other actors.*)

ASSISTANT (*as Dr. Lullo*): *Buon giorno!*

MRS. GOFORTH: What's he wheeling in here that looks like a baby-buggy for a baby from Mars?

(*He is pushing a "mock-up" of a portable X-ray machine.*)

BLACKIE: It's something your doctor in Rome, Dr.—what? Rengucci?—had sent up here to spare you the trouble of interrupting your work to take a new set of pictures to show what progress there is in the healing of the lesion, the lung abscess, that—

MRS. GOFORTH: Oh, so you're having private consultations with that quack in Rome?

BLACKIE: Just routine calls that he told me to make sure to spare you the trouble of—

MRS. GOFORTH: Spare me no trouble, just spare me your goddamn *presumptions!*

DR. LULLO: *Forse più tardi, forse un po' più tardi?*

MRS. GOFORTH: Will you get your sneaky grin out of here? *Va, va. Presto!*

(*He retires quickly from the lighted area. Mrs. Goforth advances both fearfully and threateningly upon the medical apparatus.*)

My outside is public, but my insides are private, and the Rome quack was hired by my bitch daughter that wants to hang black crepe on me. Wants to know if I'm going, and when I'll go. Doesn't know that if and when I do go, she gets one dollar, the rest goes to a—a *cultural foundation!*—named for *me*! Blackie, wheel this thing off the terrace, to the cliff-side of the mountain and shove it over!

BLACKIE: Mrs. Goforth, you mustn't ask me to do ridiculous things.

MRS. GOFORTH: I don't do ridiculous things and don't ask anyone else to do 'em for me. But if you think it's ridiculous of me to show my opinion of Rengucci's presumption and— *Look, watch this! Here we go, perambulator from Mars. Out, down, go!*

(*She thrusts it violently onto the forestage, where it is seized by the Stage Assistants and rushed into the wings. She crosses onto the forestage, leaning forward to watch its fall off the cliff. After a couple of moments, we hear a muted crash that signifies its destruction on the rocky beach under the mountain. Then she straightens, dizzily, with a fierce laugh, and staggers back toward the library area, where Blackie, meanwhile, has closed her notebook and rushed off stage. Heart-beat sounds *are heard amplified, as Mrs. Goforth moves distractedly about the library area, calling out breathlessly for Blackie. She presses several buttons on the "intercom" box on the desk: electric buzzers sound from here and there on the stage but no one responds: She washes down a pill with a swig of brandy. The heart-beat sounds subside as her agitation passes. She sinks into the desk chair.*)

Ahhh . . .

(*She activates her tape-recorder and speaks into it with a voice that is plaintively childlike.*)

Blackie, the boss is sorry she took her nerves out on you. It's those night injections I take for my—neuralgia—neuritis—bursitis. The pick-up pills and the quiet-down pills: nerves shot . . .

(*A sea wave booms under the mountain.*)

Oh, God, Blackie, I'm *scared*! You know what I'm scared of? Possibly, maybe, the Boss is—dying this summer! On the *Divina Costiera*, under that, that—angry old lion, the sun, and the—insincere sympathy of the— (*Her mood suddenly reverses again.*) No, no, no, I don't want her goddamn sympathy, I'll take that slobbery stuff off the tape and— *Begin! Continue! Dictation!* (*She rises, paces the forestage with a portable "mike."*)

(*A phrase of lyrical music is heard. She stops short, lifting a jeweled hand as if to say "Listen!" Then suddenly the accretion of years is broken through. The stage dims out except for her follow-spot on the forestage.*)

"Cloudy symbols of a—high romance . . ." Who said that, where is that from? Check tomorrow, Blackie, in the *Book of Familiar Quotations* . . . Begin, continue dictation.

(*A pause, while she paces back and forth.*)

The love of true understanding isn't something a man brings up the road to you every day or once in a blue moon, even. But it was brought to me once, almost too late but not quite. . . .

The hard shell of my heart, the calcium deposits grown around it, could still be cracked, broken through, and my last husband broke through it, and I was brought back to life and almost back to—what?—Youth. . . .

The nights, the nights, especially the first one I spent with Alex! The way that a lover undresses, removes his clothes the first night you spend together, is a clue, a definite clue, to your whole future relationship with him, you know. Alex unclothed himself *unconsciously gracefully,* as if before no one in a—room made of windows, and then, unclothed—*correction:* clothed in a god's perfection, his naked body!—he went from window to window, all the way round the bedroom, drawing the curtains together so that daybreak beginning wouldn't wake us early from the sleep after love, which is a heavenly sleep that shouldn't be broken early. Then came to rest in a god's perfection beside me: reached up to turn off the light: I reached up and turned it *back on!*

(*At this point, Mrs. Goforth's watchdogs* (lupos) *set up a great clamor on the inland side of the mountain. A Man shouts. Woman Servants scream in Italian. Somebody calls, "Rudy, Rudy!" Mrs. Goforth is very annoyed by this disruption of her tender recollections: she presses various buttons on the intercom box on her desk.*)

MRS. GOFORTH (*shouting over the dogs*): *Che succede! Che fa, Cretini! Stronzi!* (*etc.*)

(*The savage barking continues but diminishes a little in volume as a Young Man, who has just been assaulted by dogs, limps and stumbles onto the terrace. He bears a heavy white sack over his shoulder, looking back as if to make sure he's no longer pursued. Blackie appears behind him, panting, looking as if she'd also been roughed up by the dogs.*)

BLACKIE (*to the Young Man*): Places go mad, it's catching, people catch it! (*She draws a breath.*) There's a doctor up here, I'll get him for you.

CHRIS: Can I see Mrs. Goforth?

BLACKIE: Sit down somewhere. I'll see if she can see you, and I'll—

(*The Young Man, Chris, limps out upon the forestage, sinks onto a white iron bench. A wave crashes below the mountain. He looks blankly out at the audience for a moment, then shakes his head and utters a desperate-sounding laugh. Blackie rushes into the library area.*)

Mrs. Goforth, I can't stand this sort of thing!

MRS. GOFORTH: *What?*

BLACKIE: Those dogs of Rudy's, those wolves, attacked a young man just now.

MRS. GOFORTH: What young man, doing what?

BLACKIE: He was climbing the mountain to see you!

MRS. GOFORTH: Who is he, what does he want?

BLACKIE: I didn't stop to ask that. I had to drive the dogs off to keep him from being torn to pieces before I—asked him questions. Look! (*She shows Mrs. Goforth a laceration on her thigh, just over the knee.*) The others just watched and screamed like children at a circus!

MRS. GOFORTH: Sit down, have a brandy. A place like this is always protected by dogs.

(*There is the sound of another wave crashing.*)

CHRIS: *Boom.* (*He discovers that his leather pants, lederhosen, have been split down his thigh.*)

BLACKIE: That gangster's bodyguard, Rudy, just stood there and watched!

MRS. GOFORTH: Blackie, this estate contains things appraised by Lloyd's at over two million pounds sterling, besides my jewels and summer furs, and that's why it has to be guarded against trespassers, uninvited intruders. Have you had your anti-tetanus shot, or—whatever they call it?

BLACKIE: Yes, I'm all right but he isn't. (*She presses a button on the intercom box.*)

MRS. GOFORTH: Who're you calling?

BLACKIE: I'm calling Dr. Lullo.

MRS. GOFORTH: Stop that, leave that to me! Do you think I want to be sued by this trespasser? Get away from my desk. I'm going to buzz Rudy. (*She presses another button.*) Rudy, *dove* Rudy? *Io lo voglio in libreria, subito, presto! Capito?*

(*The Young Man staggers to his feet and calls: "Mrs. Goforth!" Mrs. Goforth picks up a pair of binoculars and gazes out at the terrace. Blackie stares at her with consternation.*)

CHRIS: Mrs. Goforth?

(*Rudy, the watchman, in semi-military costume, appears on the terrace.*)

RUDY: Shut up, stop that shouting. (*He enters the library area.*)

MRS. GOFORTH: Aw. Rudy. What happened, what's the report?

RUDY: I caught this man out there climbing up here from the highway.

BLACKIE: He set the dogs on him.

MRS. GOFORTH: That's what the dogs are here for. Rudy, what's the sign say on the gate on the highway?

RUDY: "Private Property."

MRS. GOFORTH: Just "Private Property," not "Beware of Dogs"?

RUDY: There's nothing about dogs down there.

MRS. GOFORTH: Well, for Chrissake, put up "Beware of Dogs," too. Put it up right away. If this man sues me, I've got to prove *there was a "Beware of Dogs"* sign.

BLACKIE: How can you prove what's not true?

MRS. GOFORTH (*to Rudy*): Go on, hurry it up!

(*Rudy leaves.*)

MRS. GOFORTH (*to Blackie*): Now pull yourself together. What a day! It's too much for me, I'll have to go back to bed. . . .

(*Giulio, the gardener's son, a boy of seventeen, appears on the terrace.*)

GIULIO (*to the Young Man, who is applying an antiseptic to his lacerations*): *Come va? Meglio?*

CHRIS: *Si, meglio, grazie.* Do you understand English?

GIULIO: Yes, English.

CHRIS: Good. Would you please tell Mrs. Goforth that Mr. Christopher Flanders is here to see her, and— Oh, give her this book, there's a letter in it, and—ask her if I may see her, don't—don't mention the dogs, just say I—I want very much to see her, if she's willing to see me. . . .

(*During this exchange on the forestage, Mrs. Goforth has picked up a pair of binoculars. Giulio knocks at the screen that represents the door between the terrace and the library.*)

MRS. GOFORTH: Come in, come in, *avanti!*

(*The Boy enters, excitedly.*)

GIULIO: Man bring this up road.

MRS. GOFORTH (*gingerly accepting the book in her hand*): Young man that dogs bite bring this—(*squints at book*)—to me?

GIULIO: This, this, brings! Up mountains!

(*She turns the book and squints at a photograph of the author.*)

MRS. GOFORTH: Man resemble this photo?

(*Blackie is still quietly weeping at the desk.*)

GIULIO: *Non capisco.*

MRS. GOFORTH: Man!—*Uomo!*—resemble, look like—this photo?

GIULIO: Yes, this man. This man that dogs bite on mountain. (*Points out excitedly toward the Young Man on the bench.*)

MRS. GOFORTH: Well, go back out—*vada fuori e dica*—Blackie! Tell him to go back out there and say that I am very upset over the accident with the dogs, but that I would like to know why he came here without invitation, and that I am not responsible for anybody that comes here without invitation!

BLACKIE (*strongly, as she rises*): No, I will not. I will not give a man nearly killed by dogs such an inhuman message.

MRS. GOFORTH: He hasn't been seriously hurt, he's standing up now. Listen he's shouting my name.

(*The Young Man has called, "Mrs. Goforth?" in a hoarse, panting voice. His shirt and one leg of his lederhosen have been nearly stripped off him. He has the opposite appearance to that which is ordinarily encountered in poets as they are popularly imagined. His appearance is rough and weathered;*

his eyes wild, haggard. He has the look of a powerful, battered, but still undefeated, fighter.)

CHRIS: *Mrs. Goforth!*

(*His call is almost imperious. A wave crashes under the mountain: Chris closes his eyes, opens them, crosses to the lounge chair on the terrace and throws himself down in it, dropping a large canvas sack on the terrace tiles. The excited, distant barking of the dogs has now died out. Female voices are still heard exclaiming at a distance, in Italian.*)

MRS. GOFORTH (*looking again through her binoculars*): Pull yourself together. The continent has been overrun by beatniks lately, I've been besieged by them, Blackie. Writers that don't write, painters that don't paint. A bunch of free-loaders, Blackie. They come over here on a Jugoslavian freighter with about a hundred dollars in travelers' checks and the summer addresses of everybody they think they can free-load on. That's why I'm not so sympathetic to them. Look, I made it, I got it because I made it, but they'll never work for a living as long as there is a name on their sucker list, Blackie. Now cut the hysterics now, and go out there and—

BLACKIE: *What?*

MRS. GOFORTH: Interrogate him for me!

BLACKIE: Interrogate? A badly injured young man?

MRS. GOFORTH: Trespasser! Get that straight in case he tries to sue me. (*She continues inspecting him through the binoculars.*) Hmm, he's not bad-looking, in a wild sort of way, but I'm afraid he's a beatnik. He has a beard and looks like he hasn't seen water for bathing purposes in a couple of weeks.

BLACKIE: You would, too, if a pack of wild dogs had attacked you.

MRS. GOFORTH: *Watchdogs, lupos,* defending private property: get that straight. He has on lederhosen. Hmm.—The first time I saw Alex, in the Bavarian Alps, he had on lederhosen and the right legs for 'em, too. And it's odd, it's a coincidence that I was dictating some recollections of Alex, who was a poet, when this young—*trespasser*—got here. Now if the sweat and the filthy appearance just come from the dogs' attack on him, I mean from *meeting* the dogs, you can tell by the smell of him while you're talking to him.

BLACKIE: You want me to go out and smell him? I'm not a dog, Mrs. Goforth.

MRS. GOFORTH: You don't have to be a dog to smell a beatnik. Sometimes they smell to high heaven because not washing is almost a religion with 'em. Why, last summer one of those ones you see in *Life* and *Look*, came up here. I had to talk to him with a handkerchief held to my nose. It was a short conversation and the last one between us.

(*Chris staggers up from the lounge chair and shouts: "Mrs. Goforth."*)

MRS. GOFORTH: What impudence, going on shouting at me like that!

BLACKIE: I think the least you could do is go out there yourself and show some decent concern over the dogs' attack on him.

MRS. GOFORTH: I'm not going to see him till I've checked with my lawyers about my liability, if any. So be a good scout, a nice Brownie den-mother, and go out there and—

BLACKIE: *Interrogate* him?

MRS. GOFORTH: Ask him politely what he wants here, why he came to see me without invitation, and if you get the right answers, put him in the pink villino. And I'll see him later, after my siesta. He might be O.K. for a while, and I could use some male companionship up here since all I've got is you and Generalissimo Rudy for company this summer. I do need male company, Blackie, that's what I need to be me, the old Sissy Goforth, high, low, jack and the game!

BLACKIE: I'll go see if he's seriously hurt.

(*She crosses out, to the terrace, and approaches Chris limping about the forestage.*)

BLACKIE (*to Chris*): How are you, are you all right, now?

CHRIS: Not all right, but better. Could I see Mrs. Goforth?

BLACKIE: Not yet, not right now, but she told me to put you in the little pink guest house, if you can—walk a little. It's a little way down the mountain.

CHRIS: Well, thank God, and— (*He tries to lift his sack and stumbles under its weight.*) Mrs. Goforth, of course . . .

BLACKIE (*calling*): *Giulio! Vieni qui!*

(*Giulio comes on to the terrace.*)

BLACKIE: *Porta questo sacco al villino rosa.*

GIULIO (*lifting sack*): *Pesante!—Dio . . .*

BLACKIE: *Tu sei pesante nella testa!* (*Then to Chris*) You can bathe and rest till Mrs. Goforth feels better and is ready to see you.

CHRIS: Oh.—Thanks . . .

(*He follows her off the terrace. The Stage Assistants fold and remove the screen masking a bed upstage. The bed is small but rococo, and all pink. The Stage Assistants return downstage with the screen and wait near Mrs. Goforth, who is still watching the terrace scene through her binoculars.*)

MRS. GOFORTH (*to herself*): Ah, God . . . (*Raises a hand unconsciously to a pain in her chest.*)

(*The Stage Assistants unfold the screen before her, as the library area is dimmed out.*)

SCENE TWO

The area representing the pink villino is lighted: the light is warm gold afternoon light and striated as if coming through half-open shutters. A cupid is lowered over the bed by a wire: there are smaller cupids on the four posts of the bed. Blackie, Chris, and Giulio enter the narrow lighted area, the young poet limping. Giulio bears the canvas sack with difficulty, muttering "Pesante!"

BLACKIE: Here you are, this is it. Now!

CHRIS: What?

BLACKIE: How are your legs? Mrs. Goforth keeps a doctor on the place, a resident physician, and I think he ought to come here and do a proper job on those dog-bites.

CHRIS: They're not that bad, really.

BLACKIE: Have you had shots?
CHRIS: Shots?
BLACKIE: For tetanus?
CHRIS: Yes, yes, sometime or other. I'm actually just—tired out.
BLACKIE: Giulio, see if the water's running in the bathroom. I'm sure you want to bathe before you rest, Mr. Flanders. Oh, oh, no covers on the bed.
CHRIS: Don't bother about covers on it.
BLACKIE: I think, I have an idea, you're going to sleep a good while, and you might as well sleep comfortably. Giulio. Covers for bed.
GIULIO: *Dove?*
BLACKIE: *Cerca nell' armadio del bagno.*

(*Giulio goes out. Chris sits down on the foot of the narrow bed. His head falls forward.*)

Mr. Flanders! (*He pulls himself up.*) Please try to stay awake till the bed's made up and you've bathed.
CHRIS: Your name is—? (*He rises, unsteadily.*)
BLACKIE: Frances Black, called Blackie.
CHRIS: How do you do. Mine's Flanders, Christopher Flanders.

(*Giulio enters.*)

GIULIO: *Non c'è acqua.*
BLACKIE: Well, tell your papa to turn the water on.

(*Giulio tosses some pink silk sheets on the bed and runs back out.*)

I hope you don't mind camphor, the smell of camphor.

(*He shakes his head slightly, holding onto a bed post.*)

The water ought to be running in a minute.
CHRIS: I hope there's a shower. A tub wouldn't be safe for me. I don't think even drowning would wake me up.
BLACKIE: I'll wait here till you've bathed.
CHRIS: It's wonderful here after—yesterday in—Naples . . .
BLACKIE: Would you please get on the other side of the bed and help me spread these sheets?

(*He staggers around the bed. They make it up.*)

CHRIS: You—

BLACKIE: What?

CHRIS: I wondered if you're related to Mrs. Goforth or if you're—

BLACKIE: Not related. I'm working for Mrs. Goforth: secretarial work. She's writing a sort of—all right, you can sit down, now—she's writing her memoirs and I'm helping her with it, the little, as best I—can. . . .

(*He sinks back onto the bed and drops his head in his hands.*)

Mr. Flanders, the water's turned on, now.

CHRIS (*staggering up*): Oh. Good. Thank you. This way? (*Starts off.*)

BLACKIE: I'll fill the tub for you. Do you want warm or cold water, or—

CHRIS: Cold, please. Let me do it.

BLACKIE: No, just stay on your feet till it's ready for you.

(*She passes him and goes off. There is the sound of running water. He sits exhaustedly on the bed and sways. His forehead strikes the newel-post which is topped by a cupid. The room is full of painted and carved cupids. He looks up at the cupid on the post, shakes his head with a sad, wry grimace, drops his head in his hands, and slumps over again. Blackie returns from the bathroom with a towel-robe. She claps her hands.*)

BLACKIE: I told you to stay on your feet.

CHRIS (*struggling up*): Sorry. What is—I almost said "Where am I?"

BLACKIE: Here's a towel-robe for you. You'd better just duck in and out.

CHRIS (*crossing to door and looking back at her from the threshold*): Is this called the Cupid Room?

BLACKIE: I don't know if it's called that but it should be.

CHRIS (*starting to leave but on threshold*): What a remarkable bathtub, it's almost the size of a deck pool on a steamship.

BLACKIE (*dryly*): Yes, Mrs. Goforth thinks a bathtub should be built for at least two people.

CHRIS (*entering*): She must have been to Japan.

BLACKIE: Yes. She probably owns it.

(*Chris enters the bathroom: There is a splash, a loud gasp.*)

BLACKIE: Oh, I should have warned you, it's mountain spring water.

CHRIS: Does it come from a glacier?

(*Blackie picks up the cords of his rucksack to drag it away from the bedside. She finds it startlingly heavy. She kneels beside it to loosen the drawstrings, draws out a silvery section of some metalwork. She rises guiltily as Chris reappears in the towel-robe.*)

BLACKIE: You're—shivering.

CHRIS: For exercise. Shivering's good exercise.

BLACKIE: I don't think you need any more exercise for a while. How did you get this sack of yours up the mountain?

CHRIS: Carried it—from Genoa.

BLACKIE: I could hardly drag it away from the bed.

CHRIS: Yes, it's heavy with metal. I work in metal, now. I construct mobiles, but it's not the mobiles that are heavy, it's the metalsmith tools.

BLACKIE: You, uh—sell—mobiles, do you?

CHRIS: No, mostly give 'em away. Of course I—

BLACKIE: What?

CHRIS: Some things aren't made to be sold. Oh, you sell them, but they're not made for that, not for selling, they're made for—

BLACKIE: Making them?

CHRIS: Is there something buzzing in the room or is the buzz in my head? Oh, a wasp. It'll fly back out the shutter. Is this a cigarette box? (*Opens box on small bedside table.*) Empty.

BLACKIE: Have a *Nazionale.* (*She offers him the pack.*)

CHRIS: Thank you.

BLACKIE: I'll leave the pack here, I have more in my room.— Your hair's not dry, it's still wet. (*He shakes his head like a spaniel.*) Dry it with the towel and get right into bed. I have to get back to work now. I work here, I do secretarial work and I—

CHRIS: Don't go right away.

BLACKIE: You need to rest, right away.

CHRIS: The ice water woke me up.

BLACKIE: Just temporarily, maybe.

CHRIS: I'll rest much better if I know a bit more, such as— Did Mrs. Goforth remember who I was?

BLACKIE: I don't know about that but she liked your looks, if that's any comfort to you.

CHRIS: I didn't see her. She saw me?

BLACKIE: She inspected you through a pair of military field-glasses before she had me take you to the pink villa with the—king-size bathtub, the pink silk sheets, and the cupids.

CHRIS: Do they, uh—signify something?

BLACKIE: Everything signifies something. I'll—I'll shut the shutters and you get into bed. (*She turns away from him.*)

CHRIS (*sitting on the bed*): What is the program for me when I awake?

BLACKIE (*with her back still toward him*): Don't you make out your own programs?

CHRIS: Not when I'm visiting people. I try to adapt myself as well as I can to their programs, when I'm—visiting people.

BLACKIE: Is that much of the time?

CHRIS: Yes, that's—*most* of the time. . . .

BLACKIE: Well, I think you're in for a while, if you play your cards right. You do want to be in, don't you? After hauling that sack all the way from Genoa and up this mountain to Mrs. Goforth? Or have the pink silk sheets and the cupids scared you, worse than the dogs you ran into?

CHRIS: You have a sharp tongue, Blackie.

BLACKIE: I'm sorry but I was mistaken when I thought I had strong nerves. They're finished for today if not for the season, for—years. . . . (*She starts away.*)

CHRIS: Have a cigarette with me. (*He extends the pack to her.*)

BLACKIE: You want to get some more information from me?

CHRIS: I'd sleep better if I knew a bit more.

BLACKIE: I wouldn't be too sure of *that.*

CHRIS: I've heard, I've been told, that Mrs. Goforth hasn't been well lately.

(*Blackie laughs as if startled.*)

CHRIS: She's lucky to have you with her.

BLACKIE: Why?

CHRIS: I can see you're—sympathetic and understanding about Mrs. Goforth's—condition, but—not sentimental about it. Aren't I right about that?

BLACKIE: I'm not understanding about it, and I'm afraid I've stopped being sympathetic. Mrs. Goforth is a dying monster. (*Rises.*) *Sorry, I'm talking too much!*

CHRIS: No, not enough. Go on.

BLACKIE: Why do you want to hear it?

CHRIS: I've climbed a mountain and fought off a wolf pack to see her.

BLACKIE: *Why?*

CHRIS: No where else to go, now.

BLACKIE: Well, that's an honest admission.

CHRIS: Let's stick to honest admissions.

BLACKIE (*sitting back down by the bed*): All right. I'll give you something to sleep on. You'll probably wish I hadn't but here it is. She eats nothing but pills: around the clock. And at night she has nightmares in spite of morphine injections. I rarely sleep a night through without an electric buzzer by my bed waking me up. I tried ignoring the buzzer, but found out that if I did she'd come stumbling out of her bedroom, onto the terrace, raving into a microphone that's connected to a tape-recorder, stumbling about and raving her—

CHRIS: Raving?

BLACKIE: Yes, her demented memoirs, her memories of her career as a great international beauty which she thinks she still is. I'm here, employed here, to—take down and type up these—

CHRIS: Memories?

BLACKIE: That's enough for you now. Don't you think so?

CHRIS: She doesn't know she's—

BLACKIE: Dying? Oh, no! Won't face it! Apparently never thought that her—legendary—existence—could go on less than forever! Insists she's only suffering from neuralgia, neuritis, allergies, and bursitis! Well? Can you still sleep? After this—bedtime story?

CHRIS: Blackie, I've had a good bit of experience with old dying ladies, scared to death of dying, ladies with lives like Mrs. Goforth's behind them, which they won't think are over, and I've discovered it's possible to give them, at least to offer them, something closer to what they need than what they think they still want. Yes. . . . Would you please throw me the strings of my sack, Blackie?

(*She tosses the strings to the bedside. He hauls the rucksack over, leans out of the bed to open it: removes a mobile.*)

Give her this for me, Blackie. It took me six months to make it. It has a name, a title. It's called "The Earth Is a Wheel in a Great Big Gambling Casino."

(*Music is heard playing softly.*)

BLACKIE:—"The Earth Is—"?

CHRIS: ". . . a Wheel in a Great Big Gambling Casino." I made it on hinges, it has to be unfolded before it's hung up. I think you'd better hang it up before you show it to her, if you don't mind, and in a place where it will turn in the wind, so it will make a—more impressive—impression. . . . And this is for you, this book. (*He hands a book to her.*)

BLACKIE: Poems?

CHRIS: It's a verse-adaptation I made of the writings of a Swami, a great Hindu teacher, my—teacher. Oh. One thing more. I'd like to make a phone call to a friend, an invalid lady, in Sicily—Taormina, a mountain above Taormina.—Would Mrs. Goforth object if I—?

BLACKIE: Not if she doesn't know. What's the number?

(*He gives her the number in Italian and is told that it will not go through for some time.*)

There'll be a delay. Is it very important?

CHRIS: Yes, it is. She's dying. Blackie? You're the kindest person I've met in a long, long time. . . .

BLACKIE (*Drawing a sheet over him*): This sort of thing is just automatic in women.

CHRIS: Only in some of them, Blackie. (*His eyes fall shut.*)

BLACKIE: You're falling asleep.

CHRIS: Yes, automatic—like kindness in some women. . . . (*He drops his cigarette and she picks it up and crosses to the phone.*)

BLACKIE (*Into the phone*): Mariella? Bring a tray of food up to the pink villa. Better make it cold things. The guest's asleep and won't wake up for hours. (*She hangs up, looks at Chris and exits with book.*)

(*Lights dim on this area and a spot of light immediately picks up Mrs. Goforth on the terrace. The Stage Assistants have set a screen before this area and light is brought up on the forestage which represents the terrace of the white villa. The Stage Assistants remove a wide screen and we see Mrs. Goforth with two servants, Giulio and Simonetta. Mrs. Goforth is preparing to take a sun bath on the terrace. Her appearance is bizarre. She has on a silk robe covered with the signs of the zodiac, and harlequin sunglasses with purple lenses.*)

MRS. GOFORTH (*in her very "pidgin" Italian*): Table here. *Capito? Tabolo.* (*Points.*) *Qui.* On *tabolo*, I want—What are you grinning at?

GIULIO (*very Neapolitan*): *Niente, niente ma scusa!* (*He places table by chaise.*)

SIMONETTA (*giggling*): *Tabolo.*

MRS. GOFORTH: On *tabolo voglio—una bottiglia d'acqua minerale, San Pellegrino, capite, molto ghiacciata: capite?*

(*Simonetta giggles behind her hand at Giulio's antic deference to the Signora. Mrs. Goforth glares suspiciously from one to the other, turning from side to side like a bull wondering which way to charge. Blackie enters the terrace area with the mobile, folded.*)

Che stronzi! Both of 'em.

BLACKIE: You mustn't call them that, it has an insulting meaning.

MRS. GOFORTH: I know what it means and that's what I mean it to mean. Generalissimo Rudy says they sleep together and carry on together some nights right here on my terrace.

BLACKIE: They're from Naples, and—

MRS. GOFORTH: What's that got to do with it?

BLACKIE:—and Generalissimo Rudy wants the girl for himself, so he—

MRS. GOFORTH: *Will you please tell them what I want on the table by this chaise. Here?*

BLACKIE: What do you want on the table?

MRS. GOFORTH: I—want a cold bottle of *acqua minerale*, cigarettes, matches, my Bain-Soleil, my codeine and empirin tablets, a shot of cognac on the rocks, the Paris *Herald-Tribune*, the Rome *Daily American*, the Wall Street *Journal*, the London *Times* and *Express*, the— Hey, what did you do with the—

BLACKIE: The visitor?

MRS. GOFORTH: The beatnik trespasser, yes, and what the hell have you got there that rattles like a string of boxcars crossing a railyard switch?

BLACKIE: The young man's in the pink villa, where you told me to put him. This is something he gave me for me to give you. It seems he constructs mobiles.

MRS. GOFORTH: Mobiles? Constructs?

BLACKIE: Yes, those metal decorations. He gives them titles. This one's called "The Earth Is a Wheel in a Great Big Gambling Casino."

MRS. GOFORTH: Is it a present—or something he hopes he can sell me?

BLACKIE: It's a present. He wanted me to suspend it before you saw it, but since you've already seen it—shall I hang it up somewhere?

MRS. GOFORTH: No, just put it down somewhere and help me up. The sun is making me dizzy. I don't know why I came out here. What am I doing out here?

BLACKIE: I was going to remind you that Dr. Rengucci warned you not to expose yourself to the sun, till the chest abscess, the lesion, has healed completely.

MRS. GOFORTH: *I don't have a chest abscess!*—Stop putting bad mouth on me! Open the door, I'm going in the library. . . .

(*The Stage Assistants rush out and remove the screen masking that area as Mrs. Goforth starts toward it, lifting a hand like a Roman Empress saluting the populace.*)

MRS. GOFORTH (*as she enters the library area*): What did he have to say?

BLACKIE: The—?

MRS. GOFORTH: *Trespasser*, what did he have to say?

BLACKIE: About what?

MRS. GOFORTH: *Me.*

BLACKIE: He wondered if you remembered him or not.

MRS. GOFORTH: Oh, I might have met him somewhere, sometime or other, when I was still meeting people, interested in it, before they all seemed like the same person over and over and I got tired of the person.

BLACKIE: This young man won't seem like the same person to you.

MRS. GOFORTH: That remains to be— Blackie, y'know what I need to shake off this, this—depression, what would do me more good this summer than all the shots and pills in the pharmaceutical kingdom? I need me a lover.

BLACKIE: What do you mean by "a lover"?

MRS. GOFORTH: I mean a lover! What do *you* mean by a lover, or is that word outside your Vassar vocabulary?

BLACKIE: I've only had one lover, my husband Charles, and I lost Charles last spring.

MRS. GOFORTH: What beats me is how you could have a husband named Charles and not call him Charlie. I mean the fact that you called him Charles and not Charlie describes your whole relationship with him, don't it?

BLACKIE (*flaring*): *Stop about my husband!*

MRS. GOFORTH: The dead are dead and the living are living!

BLACKIE: Not so, I'm not dead but not living!

MRS. GOFORTH: Giulio! (*He has entered the library area with the mineral water.*) *Va al villino rosa e portami qui* the sack—*il sacco!—dell' ospite là.*

BLACKIE: Oh, no, you mustn't do that, that's too undignified of you!

(*Giulio goes out to perform this errand.*)

MRS. GOFORTH: Take care of your own dignity and lemme take care of mine. It's a perfectly natural, legitimate thing to do, to go through the luggage of a trespasser on your place for—possible—weapons, and so forth. . . . (*She sits at the desk.*) Pencil, notebook, dictation.

(*Blackie pays no attention to these demands, but lights a cigarette behind Mrs. Goforth's back as she begins dictating.*)

—Season of '24, costume ball at Cannes. Never mind the style, now. Polish up later. . . .

—Went as Lady Godiva. All of me, gilded, my whole body painted gold, except for—green velvet fig leaf. Breasts? Famous breasts? Nude, nude completely!

—Astride a white horse, led into the ballroom by a young nigger. Correction. A Nubian—slave-boy. Appearance created a riot. Men clutched at my legs, trying to dismount me so they could *mount* me. Maddest party ever, ever imaginable in those days of mad parties. This set the record for madness.—In '29, so much ended, but not for me. I smelt the crash coming, animal instinct—very valuable asset. Put everything into absolutely indestructible utilities such as—Tel. and Tel., *electric power.* . . .

(*Giulio enters with the rucksack.*)

GIULIO: *Ecco, il sacco!* (*Drops it before Mrs. Goforth with a crash that makes her gasp.*)

BLACKIE: May I be excused? I don't want to take part in this.

MRS. GOFORTH: Stay here. You heard that noise, that wasn't just clothes, that was metal.

BLACKIE: Yes, I suppose he's come here to seize the mountain by force of arms.

MRS. GOFORTH (*to Giulio*): Giulio, open, *aprite*!

(*Giulio opens the sack and the inspection begins.*)

BLACKIE: I told you he made mobiles. The sack's full of metalsmith's tools.

MRS. GOFORTH: He hauled this stuff up the mountain?

BLACKIE: It didn't fly up.

MRS. GOFORTH: He must have the back of a dray horse. Tell this idiot to hold the sack upside down and empty it all on the floor, he's taking things out like it was a Christmas stocking.

BLACKIE: I'll do it. He'd break everything. (*She carefully empties the contents of the sack onto the floor.*)

MRS. GOFORTH: See if he's got any travelers' checks and how much they amount to.

BLACKIE (*ignoring this order and picking up a book*): He offered me this book, I forgot to take it.

MRS. GOFORTH (*glaring at the book through her glasses*): *Meanings Known and Unknown.* It sounds like something religious.

BLACKIE: He says it's a verse-adaptation he did of a—

MRS. GOFORTH: Swami Something. See if you can locate the little book they always carry with names and addresses in it. Sometimes it gives you a clue to their backgrounds and—inclinations. Here. This is it. (*Snatches up an address book.*)—Christ, Lady Emerald Fowler, she's been in hell for ten years.—Christabel Smithers, that name rings a long-ago church bell for a dead bitch, too. Mary Cole, *dead!* Laurie Emerson, *dead!* Is he a graveyard sexton? My God, where's his passport?

BLACKIE (*picking it up*): Here.

MRS. GOFORTH: Date of birth: 1928. Hmmm, no chicken, Blackie. How old's that make him?

BLACKIE:—Thirty-five.

(*She lights a cigarette. Mrs. Goforth snatches the cigarette from Blackie's hand. She sets it on the desk and in a moment starts smoking it herself.*)

MRS. GOFORTH: No travelers' checks whatsoever. Did he have some cash on him?

BLACKIE: I don't know, I neglected to frisk him.

MRS. GOFORTH: Did you get him to bathe?

BLACKIE: Yes.

MRS. GOFORTH: How'd he look in the bathtub?

BLACKIE: I'm afraid I can't give you any report on that.

MRS. GOFORTH: Where's his clothes? No clothes, *niente vestiti in sacco?*

GIULIO (*produces one shirt, laundered but not ironed*): *Ecco una camicia, una bella camicia!*

MRS. GOFORTH: One shirt!

BLACKIE: He probably had to check some of his luggage somewhere, in order to get up the—goatpath . . . and the clothes he had on were demolished by Rudy's dogs.

MRS. GOFORTH: Well, put a robe in his room. I know—the Samurai warrior's robe that Alex wore at breakfast. We always wore robes at breakfast in case we wanted to go back to bed right after. . . .

(*A Stage Assistant enters with an ancient Japanese robe, with a belt and sword attached.*)

BLACKIE: Did he keep the sword on him at breakfast?

MRS. GOFORTH: Yes, he did and sometimes he'd draw it out of the scabbard and poke me with it. Ho ho. Tickle me with the point of it, ho ho ho ho!

BLACKIE: You weren't afraid he'd—accidentally—?

MRS. GOFORTH: Sure, and it was exciting. I had me a little revolver. I'd draw a bead on him sometimes and I'd say, you are too beautiful to live, and so you have to die, now, tonight—tomorrow—

(*The Stage Assistant hands the robe to Blackie, who accepts it without a glance at him.*)

—put the robe in the pink villino, and then call the Witch of Capri.

BLACKIE: Which witch?

MRS. GOFORTH: The one that wired me last month: "Are you still living?" Tell her I am. And get her over for dinner, tell her it's *urgentissimo*! Everything's *urgentissimo* here this summer. . . .

(*Phone buzzes on desk. As Blackie starts off, Mrs. Goforth answers the phone.*)

Pronto, pronto, chi parla?—Taormina? Sicilia?—I've placed no call to that place. (*She slams down the phone.*) —Hmmm, the summer is coming to life! I'm coming back to life with it!

(*She presses buttons on her intercom system. Electric buzzers sound from various points on the stage as the Stage Assistants cover the library area with the griffin-crested screen.*)

The Scene Dims Out.

SCENE THREE

That evening. The setting is the terrace of the white villa and a small section of Mrs. Goforth's bedroom, upstage left. In this scene, the Stage Assistants may double as Butlers, with or without white jackets. At the curtain's rise, the two screens are lighted, one masking the small dinner table on the forestage, the other Mrs. Goforth; a Stage Assistant stands beside each screen so that they can be removed simultaneously when a chord provides the signal. The middle panel of Mrs. Goforth's screen is topped by a gold-winged griffin to signify that she is "in residence" behind it.

MRS. GOFORTH'S VOICE (*asthmatically*): *Simonetta, la roba.*

(*Simonetta rushes behind the screen with an elaborate Oriental costume.*)

Attenzione, goddamn it, *questa roba molto, molto valore. Va bene. Adesso, parruca!**

SIMONETTA (*emerging from the screen*): *A parruca bionda?*

MRS. GOFORTH: *Nera, nera!*

(*There is heard a reedy chord as on a harmonium. The screens are whisked away. In the stage-left area, we see Mrs. Goforth in the Oriental robe, on the forestage, Rudy in his semi-military outfit pouring himself a drink, and a small section of balustrade on which is a copper brazier, flickering with blue flame. Blackie enters, stage right, with a napkin and silver and sets a third place at the table, Rudy hovers behind her.*)

BLACKIE: Stop breathing down my neck.

MRS. GOFORTH: *Ecco!*

(*She puts on a black Kabuki wig with fantastic ornaments stuck in it. Her appearance is gorgeously bizarre. As she moves, out upon the forestage, there is Oriental music.*)

Well, no comment, Blackie?

BLACKIE: The Witch of Capri has just gotten out of the boat and is getting into the funicular.

*Wig.

MRS. GOFORTH: You kill me, Blackie, you do, you literally kill me. I come out here in this fantastic costume and all you say is the Witch of Capri has landed.

BLACKIE: I told you how fantastic it was when you wore it last week-end, when that Italian screen star didn't show up for dinner, so I didn't think it would be necessary to tell you again, but what I do want to tell you is that I wish you'd explain to Rudy that I find him resistible, and when I say resistible I'm putting it as politely as I know how.

MRS. GOFORTH: What's Rudy doing to you?

BLACKIE: Standing behind me, and—

MRS. GOFORTH: You want him in front of you, Blackie?

BLACKIE: I want him off the terrace while I'm on it.

MRS. GOFORTH: Rudy, you'd better go check my bedroom safe. These rocks I've put on tonight are so hot they're radioactive. (*to Blackie*) Guess what I'm worth on the hoof in this regalia?

BLACKIE: I'm no good at guessing the value of—

MRS. GOFORTH: I can't stand anything false. Even my kidney stones, if I had kidney stones, would be genuine diamonds fit for a Queen's crown, Blackie.

(*Blackie lights a cigarette. Mrs. Goforth takes the cigarette from her.*)

A witch and a bitch always dress up for each other, because otherwise the witch would upstage the bitch, or the bitch would upstage the witch, and the result would be havoc.

BLACKIE: Fine feathers flying in all directions?

MRS. GOFORTH: That's right. The Witch has a fairly large collection of rocks herself, but no important pieces. (*She crosses, smoking, to the table.*) Hey. The table's set for three. Are you having dinner with us?

BLACKIE: Not this evening, thanks, I have to catch up on my typing.

MRS. GOFORTH: Then who's this third place set for?

BLACKIE: The young man in the pink villa, I thought he'd be dining with you.

MRS. GOFORTH: That was presumptuous of you. He's having no meals with me till I know more about him. The Witch of Capri can give me the low-down on him. In fact, the only reason I asked the Witch to dinner was to get the lowdown on this mountain climber.

THE WITCH (*at a distance*): Yoo-hoo!

MRS. GOFORTH: Yooo-hooo! She won't be here more than a minute before she makes some disparaging comment on my appearance. Codeine, empirin, brandy, before she gets here. She takes a morbid interest in the health of her friends because her own's on the downgrade.

THE WITCH (*nearer*): Yoo-hoo!

MRS. GOFORTH: Yooo-hooo! Here she comes, here comes the Witch.

(*The Witch of Capri, the Marchesa Constance Ridgeway-Condotti, appears on the terrace. She looks like a creature out of a sophisticated fairy tale, her costume like something that might have been designed for Fata Morgana. Her dress is gray chiffon, paneled, and on her blue-tinted head she wears a cone-shaped hat studded with pearls, the peak of it draped with the material of her dress. Her expressive, claw-like hands are aglitter with gems. At the sight of Mrs. Goforth, she halts dramatically, opening her eyes very wide for a moment, as if confronted by a frightening apparition, then she utters a dramatic little cry and extends her arms in a counterfeit gesture of pity.*)

THE WITCH: *Sissy! Love!*

MRS. GOFORTH: Connie . . .

(*They embrace ritually and coolly, then stand back from each other with sizing-up stares.*)

THE WITCH: Sissy, don't tell me we're having a Chinese dinner.

MRS. GOFORTH: This isn't a Chinese robe, it's a Kabuki dancer's, a Japanese national treasure that Simon Willingham bought me on our reconciliation trip to Japan. It's only some centuries old. I had to sneak it through customs—Japanese customs—by wearing it tucked up under a chinchilla coat. Y'know I studied Kabuki, and got to be very good at it. I was a guest artist once at a thing for typhoon relief, and I can still do it, you see.

(*She opens her lacquered fan and executes some Kabuki dance movements, humming weirdly. The effect has a sort of grotesque beauty, but she is suddenly dizzy and staggers against the table. The Witch utters a shrill cry; Blackie rushes to catch her and support the table. Mrs. Goforth tries to laugh it off.*)

Ha, ha, too much codeine, I took a little codeine for my neuralgia before you got here.

THE WITCH: Well, I'm suffering, too. We're suffering together. Will you look at my arm. (*She draws up her flowing sleeve to expose a bandaged forearm.*) The sea is full of Medusas.

MRS. GOFORTH: Full of what?

THE WITCH: Medusas, you know, those jellyfish that sting. The Latins call them Medusas, and one of them got me this morning, a giant one, at the *Piccola Marina.* I want a martini. . . . I've got to stay slightly drunk to bear the pain. (*She tosses her parasol to Blackie and advances to the liquor cart.*) Sissy, your view is a *meraviglia, veramente una meraviglia!* (*She drains a martini that Blackie pours her, then swings full circle and dizzily returns to a chair at the table.*) Do we have to eat?—I'm so full of canapés from Mona's cocktail do . . .

MRS. GOFORTH: Oh, is that what you're full of? We're having a very light supper, because the smell of food after codeine nauseates me, Connie.

BLACKIE: Mrs. Goforth, shouldn't I take something to your house guest since he's not dining with you?

MRS. GOFORTH: No, meaning no, but you can leave us now, Blackie. Oh, excuse me, this is my secretary, Miss Black. Blackie, this is—what's your latest name, Connie?

THE WITCH: I mailed you my wedding invitation the spring before last spring to some hospital in Boston, the Leahey Clinic, and never received a word of acknowledgment from you.

MRS. GOFORTH: Oh, weddings and funerals're things you show up at or you don't according to where you are and—

(*She rings bell for service: the Stage Assistants appear with white towels over their forearms or colored mess-jackets. Note: Although they sometimes take part in the action of the play, the characters in the play never appear to notice the Stage Assistants.*)

—*other* circumstances: Have a gull's egg, Connie.

THE WITCH: No, thank you, I can't stand gulls.

MRS. GOFORTH: Well, eating their eggs cuts down on their population.

THE WITCH: What is this monster of the deep?

MRS. GOFORTH: *Dentice, dentice freddo.*

THE WITCH: It has a horrid expression on its face.

MRS. GOFORTH: Don't look at it, just eat it.

THE WITCH: Couldn't possibly, thank you.

MRS. GOFORTH: Are you still living on blood transfusions, Connie? That's not good, it turns you into a vampire, a *pipistrella*, ha, ha. . . . Your neck's getting too thin, Connie. Is it true that you had that sheep embryo—plantation in—Switzerland? I heard so. I don't approve of it. It keys you up for a while and then you collapse, completely. The human system can't stand too much stimulation after —sixty. . . .

THE WITCH: What did they find out at the Leahey Clinic, Sissy?

MRS. GOFORTH: Oh, *that*, that was just a little—routine check-up. . . .

THE WITCH: When you called me today I was so relieved I could die: shouted "Hallelujah" silently, to myself. I'd heard such distressing rumors about you lately, Sissy.

MRS. GOFORTH: Rumors? Hell, what rumors?

THE WITCH (*crossing to the bar cart for a refill*): I can't tell you the rumors that have been circulating about you since your house party last month. The ones you brought over from Capri came back to Capri with stories that I love you too much to repeat.

MRS. GOFORTH: Repeat them, Connie, repeat them.

THE WITCH: Are you sure you feel well enough to take them? (*She returns to her chair.*) Well—they said you were, well, that you seemed to be off your rocker. They said you spent the whole night shouting over loudspeakers so nobody could sleep, and that what you shouted was not to be *believed!*

MRS. GOFORTH: Oh, how *nice* of them, Connie. Capri's

turned into a nest of vipers, Connie—and the sea is full of Medusas? Mmm. The Medusas are spawned by the bitches. You want to know the truth behind this gossip? Or would you rather believe a pack of malicious inventions?

THE WITCH: You know I love you, Sissy. What's the truth?

MRS. GOFORTH: Not that.—I'll tell you the truth. (*She rises and indicates the intercom speaker.*) I'm writing my memoirs this summer. I've got the whole place wired for sound, a sort of very elaborate intercom or walkie-talkie system, so I can dictate to my secretary, Blackie. I buzz my secretary any time of the day and night and continue dictating to her. That's the truth, the true story. (*She goes over to The Witch.*)

THE WITCH (*taking her hand*): I'm so glad you told me, Sissy, love!

MRS. GOFORTH: Has it ever struck you, Connie, that life is all memory, except for the one present moment that goes by you so quick you hardly catch it going? It's really all memory, Connie, except for each passing moment. What I just now said to you is a memory now—recollection. Uh-hummm . . . (*She paces the terrace.*) —I'm up now. When I was at the table is a memory, now. (*She arrives at the edge of lighted area downstage right, and turns.*) —when I turned at the other end of the terrace is a memory, now. . . .

(*The Witch gets up and goes toward her.*)

Practically everything is a memory to me, now, so I'm writing my memoirs. . . . (*She points up.*) Shooting star: it's shot:—a memory now. Four husbands, all memory now. All lovers, all memory now.

THE WITCH: So you're writing your memoirs.

MRS. GOFORTH: Devoting all of me to it, and all of my time. . . . At noon today, I was dictating to Blackie on a tape-recorder: the beautiful part of my life, my love with Alex, my final marriage. Alex . . .

THE WITCH (*going to the bar cart*): Oh, the young Russian dancer from the Diaghilev troupe?

MRS. GOFORTH (*returning to her chair*): Oh, God, no, I never married a dancer. Slept with a couple but never married a one. They're too narcissistic for me; they love only mirrors.

Nope, Alex was a young poet with a spirit that was as beautiful as his body, the only one I married that wasn't rich as Croesus. Alex made love without mirrors. He used my eyes for his mirrors. The only husband I've had, of the six I've had, that I could make love to with a bright light burning over the bed. Hundred-watt bulbs overhead! To see, while we loved. . . .

THE WITCH (*going back to the table with the pitcher of martinis*): Are you dictating this. Over a loudspeaker?

MRS. GOFORTH: Ah, God—Alex . . .

THE WITCH: Are you in pain? Do you have a pain in your chest?

MRS. GOFORTH: Why?

THE WITCH: You keep touching your chest.

MRS. GOFORTH: Emotion. I've been very emotional all day. . . . At noon today, a young poet came up the goatpath from the highway just as I was in the emotional—throes—of dictating my memories of young Alex. . . .

THE WITCH (*draining her martini*): Ah-ha.

MRS. GOFORTH: He came up the goatpath from the Amalfi Drive wearing lederhosen like Alex was wearing the first time I set eyes on him.

THE WITCH (*starting to pour another martini*): Ahh-ha!

MRS. GOFORTH (*snatching the pitcher from The Witch and placing it on the floor*): Do you want to hear this story?

THE WITCH: Liquor improves my concentration. Go on. You've met a new poet. What was the name of this poet?

MRS. GOFORTH: His name was on the book.

THE WITCH: Yes, sometimes they do put the author's name on a book.

MRS. GOFORTH (*unamused*): Sanders? No. Manders? No.

THE WITCH: Flanders. Christopher Flanders. (*Makes large eyes.*) Is he still in circulation?

MRS. GOFORTH: I don't know if he's in circulation or not but I do know he came up here to see me and not by the boat and funicular, he—

THE WITCH (*moving toward Mrs. Goforth*): Well, God help you, Sissy.

MRS. GOFORTH: Why, is something wrong with him?

THE WITCH: Not if you're not superstitious. Are you superstitious?

MRS. GOFORTH: What's superstition got to do with—

THE WITCH: I've got to have a wee drop of brandy on this! (*She crosses over to the bar cart.*) This is really uncanny!

MRS. GOFORTH: *Well, come out with it, what?*

THE WITCH (*selecting the brandy bottle*): I think I'd rather not tell you.

MRS. GOFORTH (*commandingly*): *What?*

THE WITCH: Promise me not to be frightened?

MRS. GOFORTH: When've I ever been frightened? Of what? Not even that stiletto you've got for a tongue can scare me! (*She downs her own martini at a gulp.*) So what's the—

THE WITCH: Chris, poor Chris Flanders, he has the bad habit of coming to call on a lady just a step or two ahead of the undertaker. (*She sits down.*) Last summer, at Portofino, he stayed with some Texas oil people, and at supper one night that wicked old Duke of Parma, you know the one that we call the Parma Violet, he emptied a champagne bottle on Christopher's head and he said, "I christen thee, Christopher Flanders, the Angel of Death." The name has stuck to him, Sissy. Why, some people in our age bracket, we're senior citizens, Sissy, would set their dogs on him if he entered their grounds, but since you're not superstitious— Why isn't he dining here with us?

MRS. GOFORTH: I wanted some information about him before I—

THE WITCH: Let him stay here?

MRS. GOFORTH: He's here on probation. (*She rings for Giulio, and then crosses center.*) I put him in the pink villa where he's been sleeping since noon, when he climbed up a goat-path to see me.

THE WITCH (*following Mrs. Goforth*): I hope he's not playing his sleeping trick on you, Sissy.

MRS. GOFORTH: Trick? Sleeping?

THE WITCH: Yes, last summer when he was with that Portofino couple from Texas, they were thrown into panic when they heard his nickname, "Angel of Death," and told him that night to check out in the morning. Well, that night, he swallowed some sleeping pills that night, Sissy, but of course he took the precaution of leaving an early morning call so he could be found and revived before the pills could—

(*Mrs. Goforth abruptly begins to leave.*)

Where're you going, Sissy?

MRS. GOFORTH: Follow me to the pink villa, hurry, hurry, I better make sure he's not playing that trick on me.

(*She rushes off. The Witch laughs wickedly as she follows. The Stage Assistants immediately set a screen before this acting area and the light dims. Then they remove a screen upstage, and we see Chris asleep in the pink villa. A lullaby, perhaps the Brahms one is heard. Mrs. Goforth and The Witch appear just on the edge of the small lighted area.*)

MRS. GOFORTH: Everything's pink in this villa, so it's called the pink villa.

THE WITCH: I see. That's logical, Sissy. Hmmm. There he is, sleeping.

MRS. GOFORTH (*in a shrill whisper as they draw closer to the bed*): Can you tell if he's—?

(*The Witch removes her slippers, creeps to the bedside and touches his wrist.*)

—Well?

THE WITCH: Hush! (*She slips back to Mrs. Goforth.*) You're lucky, Sissy. His pulse seems normal, he's sleeping normally, and he has a good color. (*She slips back to the bed, and bends her face to his.*) Let me see if there's liquor on his breath. No. It's sweet as a baby's.

MRS. GOFORTH: Don't go to bed with him!

THE WITCH: No, that's your privilege, Sissy.

MRS. GOFORTH (*moving downstage from the lighted area in a follow-spot*): Come out here.

THE WITCH (*reluctantly following*): You must have met him before.

MRS. GOFORTH: Oh, somewhere, sometime, when I was still meeting people, before they all seemed like the same person over and over, and I got tired of the—person.

THE WITCH: You know his story, don't you?

(*The Stage Assistants place a section of balustrade, at an angle, beside them, and a copper brazier with the blue flame in it. The flame flickers eerily on The Witch's face as she tells *what she knows of Chris. Music plays against her stylized recitation.*)

Sally Ferguson found him at a ski lodge in Nevada where he was working as a ski instructor.

MRS. GOFORTH: A poet, a ski instructor?

THE WITCH: Everything about him was like that, a contradiction. He taught Sally skiing at this Nevada lodge where Sally was trying to prove she was a generation younger than she was, and thought she could get away with it. Well, she should have stuck to the gentle slopes, since her bones had gone dry, but one day she took the ski lift to the top of the mountain, drank a hot buttered rum, and took off like a wild thing, a crazy bird, down the mountain, slammed into a tree, and broke her hip bone. Well, Christopher Flanders carried her back to the ski lodge. We all thought she was done for, but Chris worked a miracle on her that lasted for quite a while. He got her back on her pins after they'd pinned her broken hip together with steel pins. They traveled together, to and from Europe together, but then one time in rough weather, on the promenade deck of one of the *Queen* ships, the *Mary*, he suddenly let go of her, she took a spill and her old hip bone broke again, too badly for steel pins to pin her back together again, and Sally gave up her travels except from one room to another, on a rolling couch pushed by Chris. We all advised her to let Chris go, like Chris had let go of her on the promenade deck of the *Mary*. Would she? Never! She called him "my saint," "my angel," till the day she died. And her children contested her will, so that Chris got nothing, just his poems published, dedicated to Sally. The book won a prize of some kind, and *Vogue* and *Harper's Bazaar* played it up big with lovely photos of Chris looking like what she called him, an angel, a saint. . . .

MRS. GOFORTH: Did he sleep with that old Ferguson bitch? Or was he just her Death Angel?

(*The phone rings on the bedside table: the area has remained softly lighted. Chris starts up, drops back, feigning sleep, as Mrs. Goforth rushes to the phone and snatches it up.*

—*Pronto, dica.*— Taormina, Sicily? No, *sbagliato!*

(*Mrs. Goforth looks with angry suspicion at Chris, who murmurs as if in sleep. She notices the food tray by the bed, and snatches it up, then returns to The Witch, downstage.*)

He's already making long-distance calls on the phone and look at this! He's had them bring him a food tray, and I am going to remove it, I can't stand guests, especially not invited, that act like they're in a hotel, charging calls and calling for room service. Come on, I'm turning out the lights.

THE WITCH: My slippers.

(*She slips back to the bed and picks up her slippers, lingering over Chris. Suddenly she bends to kiss him on the mouth. He rolls over quickly, shielding his lower face with an arm and uttering a grunt of distaste.*

Possum!

(*The lights dim in the area, as The Witch moves downstage. Mrs. Goforth has disappeared.*)

Siss? Sissy! Yoo-hoo!

MRS. GOFORTH (*from a distance*): Yoo-hoo!

THE WITCH (*following*): Yoooooooo-hooooooooo . . .

(*The Stage Assistants replace the screen that masked the pink villa bed. Then they fold and remove the screen before Blackie's bed in the blue villa. The area remains dark until a faint dawn light appears on the cyclorama. Then Blackie's bed is lighted, and we see her seated on it, brushing her dark hair with a silver-backed brush.*)

The Scene Dims Out.

SCENE FOUR

It is later that night. The terrace of the white villa. The Watchman, Rudy, sweeps the audience with the beam of his flashlight. We hear a long, anguished "Ahhhh" from behind the screen masking Mrs. Goforth's bed. Rudy, as if he heard the outcry, turns the flashlight momentarily on the screen behind which it comes. He chuckles, sways drunkenly, then suddenly turns the light beam on Chris who has entered quietly from the wings, stage right.

CHRIS (*shielding his eyes from the flashlight*): Oh. Hello.
RUDY: You still prowling around here?
CHRIS (*agreeably*): No, I'm— Well, yes, I'm— (*His smile fades as Rudy moves in closer.*) I just now woke up hungry. I didn't want to disturb anybody, so I—
RUDY: You just now woke up, huh?
CHRIS: Yes, I—
RUDY: Where'd you just now wake up?
CHRIS: In the, uh, guest house, the—
RUDY: Looking for the dogs again, are you? (*He whistles the dogs awake. They set up a clamor far away.*)
CHRIS: I told you I just now woke up hungry. I came out to see if—
RUDY (*moving still closer and cutting in*): Aw, you woke up *hungry*?
CHRIS: Yes. Famished.
RUDY: How about this, how'd you like to eat this, something like this, huh?

(*He thrusts his stick hard into Chris's stomach. Chris expells his breath in a "hah."*)

'Sthat feel good on your belly? Want some more of that, huh? huh?

(*He drives the stick again into Chris's stomach, so hard that Chris bends over, unable to speak. Blackie rushes onto the terrace in a dressing gown, her hair loose.*)

BLACKIE: *Rudy! What's going on here?*

(*The dogs, roused, are barking, still at a distance.*)

This young man is a guest of Mrs. Goforth. He's staying in the pink villa. Are you all right, Mr. Flanders?

(*Chris can't speak. He leans on a section of balustrade, bent over, making a retching sound.*)

Rudy, get off the terrace!—you drunk gorilla!

RUDY (*grinning*): He's got the dry heaves, Blackie. He woke up hungry and he's got the dry heaves.
CHRIS: *Can't—catch—breath!*

(*From her bed behind the griffin-crested screen, Mrs. Goforth cries out in her sleep, a long, anguished "Ahhhhhh!" The dogs' barking subsides gradually. The "Ahhhhh" is repeated and a faint light appears behind her screen. Blackie turns on Rudy, fiercely.*)

BLACKIE: I said get off the terrace, now get off it.
RUDY: You shoulda told me you—
BLACKIE: Off it, off the terrace!
RUDY (*overlapping Blackie's speech*): You got yourself a boy friend up here, Blackie! You should've let me know that.
BLACKIE: Mr. Flanders, I'll take you back to your place.
CHRIS (*gasping*): Is there—anywhere closer—I could catch my breath?

(*She stands protectively near him as Rudy goes off the terrace, laughing.*

(*The Stage Assistants rush out to remove a screen masking Blackie's bed in the blue villa, indicating "Blackie's bedroom." Chris straightens slowly, still gasping. The Stage Assistants leave. Then Chris and Blackie cross to her villino, represented only by a narrow blue-sheeted bed with a stand beside it that supports an intercom box.*)

BLACKIE: Now tell me just what happened so I can give a report to Mrs. Goforth tomorrow.
CHRIS: The truth is I was looking for something to eat. I've had no food for five days, Blackie, except some oranges that I picked on the road. And you know what the acid, the citric acid in oranges, does to an empty stomach, so I—I woke up feeling as if I had a—a bushel of burning sawdust in my stomach, and I—
BLACKIE: I had food sent to your room. You didn't find it?
CHRIS: No. God, no!
BLACKIE: Then the cook didn't send it, or it was taken out while you were sleeping, and I'm afraid you'll have to wait till morning for something to eat. You see, the only kitchen

is in Mrs. Goforth's villa. It's locked up like a bank vault till Mrs. Goforth wakes up and has it opened.

CHRIS: How long is it till morning?

BLACKIE: Oh, my—watch has stopped. I'm a watch-winding person, but I forgot to wind it.

(*The sky has lightened a little and there is the sound of church bells at a distance.*)

CHRIS: The church-bells are waking up on the other mountains.

BLACKIE: Yes, it's, it must be near morning, but morning doesn't begin on Mrs. Goforth's mountain till she sleeps off her drugs and starts pressing buttons for the sun to come up. So—

CHRIS: What?

(*The intercom box comes alive with a shrill electric buzz.*)

BLACKIE: Oh, God, she's awake, buzzing for me!

CHRIS: Oh, then, could you ask her to open the kitchen? A glass of milk, just some milk, is all I—

BLACKIE: Mrs. Goforth isn't buzzing for morning, she's buzzing for me to take dictation and, oh, God, I don't think I can do it. I haven't slept tonight and I just couldn't take it right now, I—

CHRIS: Let me take it for you.

BLACKIE: No. I'll have to answer myself, or she'll come stumbling, raving out, and might fall off the cliff.

(*She presses a button on the intercom box.*)

Mrs. Goforth? Mrs. Goforth?

(*The Stage Assistants remove the screen masking Mrs. Goforth's bed, upstage left. We see her through the gauze curtains enclosing the bed. She pulls a cord, opening the curtains, and speaks hoarsely into a microphone.*)

MRS. GOFORTH: *Blackie? It's night, late night!*

BLACKIE: Yes, it's late, Mrs. Goforth.

MRS. GOFORTH: Don't answer: this is dictation. Don't interrupt me, this is clear as a vision. The death of Harlon Goforth, just now—clearly—remembered, clear as a vision.

It's night, late night, without sleep. He's crushing me under the awful weight of his body. Then suddenly he stops trying to make love to me. He says, "Flora, I have a pain in my head, a terrible pain in my head." And silently, to myself, I say, "Thank God," but out loud I say something else: "Tablets, you want your tablets?" He answers with the groan of—I reach up and turn on the light, and I see—death in his eyes! I see, I know. He has death in his eyes, and something worse in them, terror. I see terror in his eyes. I see it, I feel it, myself, and I get out of the bed, I get out of the bed as if escaping from quicksand! I don't look at him again, I move away from the bed. . . .

(*She rises from the bed, the microphone gripped in her hand.*

I move away from death, terror! I don't look back, I go straight to the door, the door onto the terrace!

(*She moves downstage with the microphone.*)

It's closed, I tear it open, I leave him alone with his death, his—

BLACKIE: She's out of bed, she's going out on the—

(*She rushes into the wings. The light dims on the blue villa bed.*)

MRS. GOFORTH (*dropping the microphone as she moves out on white villa terrace*): I've gone out, now, I'm outside, I'm on the terrace, twenty-five stories over the high, high city of Goforth. I see lights blazing under the high, high terrace but not a light blazing as bright as the blaze of terror that I saw in his eyes!

(*She staggers to the edge of the forestage.*)

Wind, cold wind, clean, clean! Release! Relief! Escape from—

(*She reaches the edges of the orchestra pit. A wave crashes loudly below.*)

I'm lost, blind, dying! I don't know where I—

BLACKIE (*rushing out behind her*): Mrs. Goforth! Don't move! You're at the edge of the cliff!

MRS. GOFORTH (*stopping, her hands over her eyes*): *Blackie!* (*She sways. Blackie rushes forward to catch her.*) *Blackie, don't leave me alone!*

(*The stage is blacked out.*)

Intermission.

SCENE FIVE

The scene is the terrace of the white villa the following morning. Mrs. Goforth is standing on the terrace while dictating to Blackie, who sits at a small table. Above the table and about the balustrade are cascades of bougainvillaea. Coins of gold light, reflected from the sea far below, flicker upon the playing area, which is backed by fair sky. There has been a long, reflective pause in the dictation. Mrs. Goforth stands glaring somberly out at the sea.

MRS. GOFORTH: Blackie, I want to begin this chapter on a more serious note.

(*She moves around to the right of the table. Then continues emphatically and loudly.*)

Meaning of life!

BLACKIE: Dictation?

MRS. GOFORTH: Not yet, wait, don't rush me. (*Repeats in a softer tone.*) Meaning of life . . .

(*Chris appears at the far end of the terrace. He wears the Samurai robe. Blackie sees him, but Mrs. Goforth doesn't. Blackie indicates by gesture that he should not approach yet.*)

Yes, I feel this chapter ought to begin with a serious comment on the meaning of life, because y'know, sooner or later, a person's obliged to face it.

BLACKIE: Dictating now, Mrs. Goforth?

MRS. GOFORTH: No, no, thinking—reflecting, I'll raise my hand when I begin the dictation. (*She raises a jeweled hand to demonstrate the signal that she will use.*)

BLACKIE: Begin now?

(*Chris smiles at her tone of voice. Blackie shrugs and closes her notebook, rises quietly, and goes up to Chris, who lights her cigarette.*)

MRS. GOFORTH: One time at Flora's Folly, which was the name of the sixteenth-century coach house, renovated, near Paris where I had my salon, my literary evenings, I brought up the question, "What is the meaning of life?" And do you know they treated it like a joke? Ha ha, very funny, Sissy can't be serious!—but she *was*, she *was*. . . .

CHRIS: I think she's started dictating. Is there something to eat?

BLACKIE: Black coffee and saccharine tablets.

CHRIS: That's *all*?!

BLACKIE: Soon as I get a chance, I'll raid the kitchen for you.

MRS. GOFORTH (*almost plaintively*): Why is it considered ridiculous, bad taste, *mauvais gout*, to seriously consider and discuss the possible meaning of life, and only stylish to assume it's just—what?

(*The Stage Assistants have come out of the wings.*)

ONE: Charade. Game.

TWO (*tossing a spangled ball to his partner*): Pastime.

ONE (*tossing the ball back*): Flora's Folly.

TWO (*tossing the ball back*): Accident of atoms.

ONE (*returning ball*): Resulting from indiscriminate copulation.

(*Blackie throws her cigarette away and returns to her former position. The Stage Assistants withdraw.*)

MRS. GOFORTH: I've often wondered, but I've wondered *more* lately . . . meaning of *life*.

(*The Stage Assistants reappear with a small table and two chairs. They wait in the wings for a moment before placing them. They then retire.*)

Sometimes I think, I suspect, that everything that we do is a way of—*not* thinking about it. Meaning of life, and meaning of death, too. . . . *What in hell are we doing?* (*She raises her jeweled hand.*) Just going from one goddamn frantic distraction to another, till finally one too many goddamn frantic distractions leads to disaster, and blackout? Eclipse of, total of sun?

(*She keeps staring out from the terrace, her head turning slowly right and left, into the swimming gold light below her, murmuring to herself, nodding a little, then shaking her head a little. Her small jeweled hands appear to be groping blindly for something. She coughs from time to time.*)

There's a fog coming in. See it over there, that fog coming in?

BLACKIE: No. It's perfectly clear in all directions this morning.

MRS. GOFORTH: When I woke up this morning, I said to myself—

BLACKIE: Dictation?

MRS. GOFORTH: Shut up! I said to myself, "Oh, God, not morning again, oh, no, no, I can't bear it." But I *did*, I bore it. You really don't see that mist coming in out there?

BLACKIE (*closing her notebook*): Mrs. Goforth, the young man in the pink villa, Mr. Flanders, is waiting out here to see you. He has on the Samurai robe you gave him to wear while his clothes are being repaired, and it's very becoming to him.

MRS. GOFORTH: Call him over.

BLACKIE: Mr. Flanders!

MRS. GOFORTH: Hey, Samurai! *Banzai!*

(*Approaching, Chris ducks under a brilliant cascade of bougainvillaea vine.*)

BLACKIE: You certainly had a long sleep.

CHRIS: Did I ever!

MRS. GOFORTH (*sitting*): Did he ever, ho ho. He slept round the clock, but still has romantic shadows under his eyes! There was a chorus girl in the Follies—I used to be in the Follies, before my first marriage—when she'd show up with circles under her eyes, she'd say, "The blackbirds kissed me last night," meaning she's been too busy to sleep that night, ho ho. . . .

CHRIS: I was busy sleeping, just sleeping. (*He bends over her hand.*)

MRS. GOFORTH: No, no, none of that stuff. Old Georgia swamp-bitches don't go in for hand kissing but—*setzen Sie doon*, and— Are you coming out here for battle with that sword on?

CHRIS (*sitting*): Oh. No, but—I ran into a pack of wild dogs on the mountain, yesterday, when I climbed up here.

MRS. GOFORTH: Yes, I heard about your little misunderstanding with the dogs. You don't seem much the worse for it. You're lucky they didn't get at— (*grins wickedly*) your *face.*

CHRIS: I'm sorry if it disturbed you, but their bite was worse than their bark.

MRS. GOFORTH: The Italians call them *lupos* which means wolves. These watchdogs, they're necessary for the protection of estates like this, but—didn't you notice the "Private Property" sign in English and Italian, and the "Beware of Dogs" sign when you started up that goatpath from the highway?

CHRIS: I don't think I noticed a reference to dogs, no. I don't remember any mention of dogs, in English or Italian.

BLACKIE (*quickly*): Naturally not, the "Beware of Dogs" sign was put up *after* Mr. Flanders' "little misunderstanding with the dogs."

MRS. GOFORTH: Blackie, that is not so.

BLACKIE: Yes, it *is* so, I heard you ordering the sign put up after, just after the—

MRS. GOFORTH (*trembling with fury*): Blackie! You have *work* to do, don't you?

BLACKIE: I've never taken a job that called for collusion in—falsehood!

MRS. GOFORTH (*mocking her*): Oh, what virtue, what high moral character, Blackie.

CHRIS (*cutting in quickly*): Mrs. Goforth, Miss Black, I obviously *did* enter and trespass on private property at my own risk.

MRS. GOFORTH: If that statement's typed up—Blackie, type it up—would you be willing to sign it, Mr. Flanders?

CHRIS: Certainly, yes, of course, but let me write it up in my own handwriting and sign it right now. I'd hate for you to think I'd—

BLACKIE: He was attacked again last night.

MRS. GOFORTH: Again, by dogs?

BLACKIE: Not by dogs, by a dog. Your watchman, Rudy, attacked him because he woke up hungry and came outside to—

MRS. GOFORTH (*rising*): *Blackie, get off the terrace!*

BLACKIE: I want to get off this mountain gone mad with your madness! I try to help you, I try to feel sorry for you because you're—

MRS. GOFORTH: What? What am I?

CHRIS: Please. (*He tears a page out of Blackie's notebook and speaks to her quietly.*) It's all right. Go in.

MRS. GOFORTH: What did you say to that woman?

CHRIS: I said you're very upset, I said you're trembling.

MRS. GOFORTH: *I've been up here surrounded by traitors all summer!* (*She staggers.*) Ahhhhh!

(*Chris helps her into her chair.*)

God! God . . .

CHRIS: Now. (*He scribbles rapidly on the sheet of paper.*) Here. "I, Christopher Flanders, entered a gate marked 'Private' at my own risk and am solely responsible for a—misunderstanding with—dogs." Witnesses? Of the signature?

MRS. GOFORTH: Can you unscrew this bottle? (*She has been trying to open her codeine bottle.*)

CHRIS (*taking it from her and removing the cap*): One?

MRS. GOFORTH: Two.— Thank you.—Brandy on that— (*She indicates liquor cart.*)

CHRIS: Courvoisier?

MRS. GOFORTH: Rémy-Martin.—Thank you.

CHRIS: Welcome. (*He resumes his seat and smiles at her warmly.*) Let me hold that glass for you.

(*She has spilled some of the brandy, her hand is shaking so violently.*)

MRS. GOFORTH: Thank you.—Ahh . . . (*She draws a deep breath, recovering herself.*) You have nice teeth. Are they capped?

(*Chris shakes his head, smiling.*)

Well, you got beautiful teeth. In that respect nature's been favorable to you.

CHRIS: Thank you.

MRS. GOFORTH: Don't thank me, thank your dentist. (*She puts on lipstick, dabbing her nostrils with a bit of disposable tissue.*)

CHRIS: I've never been to a dentist—honestly not.

MRS. GOFORTH: Well, then, thank the Lord for the calcium that you got from your mother's milk. Well, I have a pretty wonderful set of teeth myself. In fact, my teeth are so good people think they are false. But look, look here! (*She takes her large incisors between thumb and forefinger to demonstrate the firmness of their attachment.*) See? Not even a bridge. In my whole mouth I've had exactly three fillings which are still there, put in there ten years ago! See them? (*She opens her mouth wide.*) This tooth here was slightly chipped when my daughter's third baby struck me in the mouth with the butt of a water pistol at Murray Bay. I told my daughter that girl would turn into a problem child, and it sure as hell did.—A little pocket-size bitch, getting bigger! I'm allergic to bitches. Although some people regard me as one myself . . . Sometimes *with* some justification. Want some coffee, Mr. Trojan Horse Guest?

CHRIS: Thanks, yes. Why do you call me that, a Trojan Horse Guest?

MRS. GOFORTH: Because you've arrived here without invitation, like the Trojan Horse got into Troy.

(*She rises shakily to pour him a cup of coffee from a silver urn on the smaller, upstage table. While her back is turned, Chris quietly crumples the sheet from Blackie's notebook and throws it into the orchestra pit.*)

CHRIS: Don't you remember our meeting and conversation at the Ballet Ball, some years ago, quite a few, when you asked me to come here whenever I was in Europe?

MRS. GOFORTH: Passports expire and so do invitations. They've got to be renewed every couple of years.

CHRIS: Has my invitation expired?

MRS. GOFORTH: Coffee. We'll see about that, that remains to be seen. Don't you smoke with your coffee?

CHRIS: Usually, but I—

(*He indicates he has no cigarettes. Mrs. Goforth smiles knowingly and opens a cigarette box on the table.*)

How does it feel, Mrs. Goforth, to be a legend in your own lifetime?

MRS. GOFORTH (*pleased*): If that's a serious question, I'll give it a serious answer. A legend in my own lifetime, yes, I reckon I am. Well, I had certain advantages, endowments to start with: a face people naturally noticed and a figure that was not just sensational, but very durable, too. Some women my age, or younger, 've got breasts that look like a couple of mules hangin' their heads over the top rail of a fence. (*Touches her bosom.*) This is natural, not padded, not supported, and nothing's ever been lifted. Hell, I was born between a swamp and the wrong side of the tracks in One Street, Georgia, but not even that could stop me in my tracks, wrong side or right side, or no side. Hit show-biz at fifteen when a carnival show, I mean the manager of it, saw me and dug me on that *one street* in One Street, Georgia. I was billed at the Dixie Doxy, was just supposed to move my anatomy, but was smart enough to keep my tongue moving, too, and the verbal comments I made on my anatomical motions while in motion were a public delight. So I breezed through show-biz like a tornado, rising from one-week "gigs" in the sticks to star billing in the Follies while still in m'teens, ho ho . . . and I was still in my teens when I married Harlon Goforth, a marriage into the Social Register and Dun and Bradstreet's, both. Was barely out of my teens when I became his widow. Scared to make out a will, he died intestate, so everything went to me.

CHRIS: Marvelous. Amazing.

MRS. GOFORTH: That's right. All my life was and still is, except here, lately I'm a little run down, like a race horse that's been entered in just one race too many, even for me. . . . How do *you* feel about being a legend in your own lifetime? Huh?

CHRIS: Oh, *me*! I don't feel like a—mythological—griffin with gold wings, but this strong fresh wind's reviving me like I'd had a—terrific breakfast!

MRS. GOFORTH: Griffin, what's a griffin?

CHRIS: A force in life that's almost stronger than death. (*He springs up and turns to the booming sea.*) The sea's full of white race horses today. May I—would you mind if I—suggested a program for us? A picnic on the beach, rest on the rocks in the sun till nearly sundown, then we'd come back up here revitalized for whatever the lovely evening had to offer?

MRS. GOFORTH: What do you think it would have to offer?

CHRIS: Dinner on the terrace with the sea still booming? How is that for a program? Say, with music, a couple of tarantella dancers brought up from the village, and—

(*Rudy appears on the terrace.*)

RUDY: Mrs. Goforth, I've taken care of that for you. They're going—on the way out.

MRS. GOFORTH: No trouble?

RUDY: Oh, yeah, sure, they want to see the Signora.

MRS. GOFORTH: No, no, no. I won't see them!

(*But "they" are appearing upstage: the members of her kitchen staff, who have been discharged.*)

Here they come, hold them back!

(*She staggers up, turns her back on them. They cry out to her in Italian. Rudy rushes upstage and herds them violently off. A wave crashes.*)

CHRIS (*quietly*): Boom. What was their—?

MRS. GOFORTH: What?

CHRIS:—transgression?

MRS. GOFORTH: They'd been robbing me blind. He caught them at it. We had—an inventory and discovered that—they'd been robbing me blind like I was—blind. . . .

CHRIS (*his back to her, speaking as if to himself*): When a wave breaks down there, it looks as delicate as a white lace fan, but I bet if it hit you, it would knock you against the rocks and break your bones. . . .

MRS. GOFORTH: What?

CHRIS: I said it's so wonderful here, after yesterday in Naples. . . .

MRS. GOFORTH: What was wrong with yesterday in Naples? Were you picked up for vagrancy in Naples?

CHRIS: I wasn't picked up for anything in Naples.

MRS. GOFORTH: That's worse than being picked up for vagrancy, baby.

(*She chuckles. He grins agreeably.*)

CHRIS: Mrs. Goforth, I'm going to tell you the truth.

MRS. GOFORTH: The truth is all you could tell me that I'd believe—so tell me the truth, Mr. Flanders.

CHRIS: I'll go back a little further than Naples, Mrs. Goforth. I'd drawn out all my savings to come over here this summer on a Jugoslavian freighter that landed at Genoa.

MRS. GOFORTH: You're leading up to financial troubles, aren't you?

CHRIS: Not so much that as—something harder, much harder, for me to deal with, a state of— Well, let me put it this way. Everybody has a sense of *reality* of some kind or other, some kind of sense of things being real or not real in his, his—particular—world. . . .

MRS. GOFORTH: I know what you mean. Go on.

CHRIS: I've lost it lately, this sense of reality in my particular world. We don't all live in the same world, you know, Mrs. Goforth. Oh, we all see the same things—sea, sun, sky, human faces and inhuman faces, but—they're different in *here!* (*Touches his forehead.*) And one person's sense of reality can be another person's sense of—well, of madness!—chaos!—and, and—

MRS. GOFORTH: Go on. I'm still with you.

CHRIS: And when one person's sense of reality, or loss of sense of reality, disturbs another one's sense of reality— I know how mixed up this—

MRS. GOFORTH: Not a bit, clear as a bell, so keep on, y'haven't lost my attention.

CHRIS: Being able to talk: wonderful! When one person's sense of reality seems too—disturbingly different from another person's, uh—

MRS. GOFORTH: Sense of reality. Continue.

CHRIS: Well, he's—avoided! Not welcome! It's—*that simple. . . .* And—yesterday in Naples, I suddenly realized that I was in that situation. (*He turns to the booming sea and says "Boom."*) I found out that I was now a—*leper!*

MRS. GOFORTH: Leopard?

CHRIS: *Leper!*—Boom!

(*She ignores the "boom."*)

Yes, you see, they hang labels, tags of false identification on people that disturb their own sense of reality too much, like the bells that used to be hung on the necks of—lepers!—Boom!

The lady I'd come over to visit, who lives in a castle on the top of Ravello, sent me a wire to Naples. I walked to Naples on foot to pick it up, and picked it up at American Express in Naples, and what it said was: "Not yet, not ready for you, dear—Angel of—Death. . . ."

(*She regards him a bit uncomfortably. He smiles very warmly at her; she relaxes.*)

MRS. GOFORTH: Ridiculous!

CHRIS: Yes, and inconvenient since I'd—

MRS. GOFORTH: Invested all your remaining capital in this standing invitation that had stopped standing, collapsed, ho, ho, ho!

CHRIS:—Yes . . .

MRS. GOFORTH: Who's this bitch at Ravello?

CHRIS: I'd rather forget her name, now.

MRS. GOFORTH: But you see you young people, well, you *reasonably* young people who used to be younger, you get in the habit of being sort of—professional house guests, and as you get a bit older, and who doesn't get a bit older, some more than just a *bit* older, you're still professional house guests, and—

CHRIS: Yes?

MRS. GOFORTH: Oh, you have charm, all of you, you still have your good looks and charm and you all do something creative, such as writing but not writing, and painting but not painting, and that goes fine for a time but—

CHRIS: You've made your point, Mrs. Goforth.

MRS. GOFORTH: No, not yet, quite yet. Your case is special. You've gotten a special nickname, "dear Angel of Death." And it's lucky for you I couldn't be less superstitious, deliberately walk under ladders, think a black cat's as lucky as a white cat, am only against the human cats of this world, of which there's no small number. So! What're you looking around for, Angel of Death, as they call you?

CHRIS: I would love to have some buttered toast with my coffee.

MRS. GOFORTH: Oh, no toast with *my* coffee, buttered, unbuttered—no toast. For breakfast I have only black coffee. Anything solid takes the edge off my energy, and it's the time after breakfast when I do my best work.

CHRIS: What are you working on?

MRS. GOFORTH: My memories, my memoirs, night and day, to meet the publisher's deadlines. The pressure has brought on a sort of nervous breakdown, and I'm enjoying every minute of it because it has taken the form of making me absolutely frank and honest with people. No more pretenses, although I was always frank and honest with people, comparatively. But now much more so. No more pretenses at all . . .

CHRIS: It's wonderful.

MRS. GOFORTH: What?

CHRIS: That you and I have happened to meet at just this time, because I have reached the same point in my life as you say you have come to in yours.

MRS. GOFORTH (*suspiciously*): What? Which? Point?

CHRIS: The point you mentioned, the point of no more pretenses.

MRS. GOFORTH: You say you've reached that point, too?

(*Chris nods, smiling warmly.*)

Hmmmm.

(*The sound is skeptical and so is the look she gives him.*)

CHRIS: It's *true*, I *have*, Mrs. Goforth.

MRS. GOFORTH: I don't mean to call you a liar or even a phantasist, but I don't see how you could afford to arrive at the point of no more pretenses, Chris.

CHRIS: I probably couldn't afford to arrive at that point any more than I could afford to travel this summer.

MRS. GOFORTH: Hmmm. I see. But you traveled?

CHRIS: Yes, mostly on foot, Mrs. Goforth—since—Genoa.

MRS. GOFORTH (*rising and walking near the balustrade*): One of the reasons I took this place here is because it's supposed to be inaccessible except from the sea. Between here and the highway there's just a goatpath, hardly possible to get down, and I thought impossible to get up. Hmm. Yes. Well. But you got yourself up.

CHRIS (*pouring the last of the coffee*): I had to. I had to get up it.

MRS. GOFORTH (*turning back to him and sitting*): Let's play the truth game. Do you know the truth game?

CHRIS: Yes, but I don't like it. I've always made excuses to get out of it when it's played at parties because I think the truth is too delicate and, well, *dangerous* a thing to be played with at parties, Mrs. Goforth. It's nitroglycerin, it has to be handled with the—the carefulest care, or somebody hurts somebody and gets hurt back and the party turns to a—devastating explosion, people crying, people screaming, people even fighting and throwing things at each other. I've seen it happen, and there's no truth in it—that's true.

MRS. GOFORTH: But you say you've reached the same point that I have this summer, the point of no more pretenses, so why can't we play the truth game together, huh, Chris?

CHRIS: Why don't we put it off till—say, after—supper?

MRS. GOFORTH: You play it better on a full stomach, do you?

CHRIS: Yes, you have to be physically fortified for it as well as—morally fortified for it.

MRS. GOFORTH: And you'd like to stay for supper? You don't have any other engagement for supper?

CHRIS: I have no engagements of any kind now, Mrs. Goforth.

MRS. GOFORTH: Well, I don't know about supper. Sometimes I don't want any.

CHRIS: How about after—?

MRS. GOFORTH:—What?

CHRIS: After lunch?

MRS. GOFORTH: Oh, sometimes I don't have lunch, either.

CHRIS: You're not on a healthful regime. You know, the spirit has to live in the body, and so you have to keep the body in a state of repair because it's the home of the—spirit. . . .

MRS. GOFORTH: Hmmm. Are you talking about your spirit and body, or mine?

CHRIS: Yours.

MRS. GOFORTH: One long-ago meeting between us, and you expect me to believe you care more about my spirit and body than your own, Mr. Flanders?

CHRIS: Mrs. Goforth, some people, some people, most of them, get panicky when they're not cared for by somebody, but I get panicky when I have no one to care for.

MRS. GOFORTH: Oh, you seem to be setting yourself up as a—as a saint of some kind. . . .

CHRIS: All I said is I need somebody to care for. I don't say that— (*He has finished his coffee and he crosses to the warmer for more.*) I'm playing the truth game with you. Caring for somebody gives me the sense of being—sheltered, protected. . . .

MRS. GOFORTH: "Sheltered, protected" from what?

CHRIS (*standing above her*): *Unreality!—lostness?* Have you ever seen how two little animals sleep together, a pair of kittens or puppies? All day they seem so secure in the house of their master, but at night, when they sleep, they don't seem sure of their owner's true care for them. Then they draw close together, they curl up against each other, and now and then, if you watch them, you notice they nudge each other a little with their heads or their paws, exchange little signals between them. The signals mean: we're not in danger . . . sleep: we're close: it's safe here. Their owner's house is never a sure protection, a reliable shelter. Everything going on in it is mysterious to them, and no matter how hard they try to please, how do they know if they please? They hear so many sounds, voices, and see so many things they can't comprehend! Oh, it's ever so much better than the petshop window, but what's become of their mother?—who warmed them and sheltered them and fed them until they were snatched away from her, for no reason they know. We're all of us living in a house we're not used to . . . a house full of—voices, noises, objects, strange shadows, light that's even stranger— We can't understand. We bark and jump around and try to—be—*pleasingly playful* in this big mysterious house but—in our hearts we're all very frightened of it. Don't you think so? Then it gets to be dark. We're left alone with each other. We have to creep close to each other and give those gentle little nudges with our paws and our muzzles before we can slip into—sleep and—rest for the next day's—playtime . . . and the next day's mysteries.

(*He lights a cigarette for her. The Witch enters dramatically on the terrace.*)

THE WITCH: The next day's mysteries! *Ecco, sono qui.*

MRS. GOFORTH (*with unconcealed displeasure*): My Lord, are you still here?

THE WITCH (*as if amazed*): Christopher! Flanders!

CHRIS: How do you do, Mrs.— Oh, I started to say Mrs. Ridgeway but that isn't it, now, is it?

THE WITCH: What a back number you are!

CHRIS (*drawing away from her*): Yes.

MRS. GOFORTH: How'd you miss your return trip to Capri last night? I thought you'd gone back there last night. I had the boatman waiting up for you last night.

THE WITCH: Oh, last *night!* What confusion! (*She puts down her hat and follows Chris.*) When was the last time I saw you?

MRS. GOFORTH: If *you* don't know, why should he?

THE WITCH: Oh, at the wedding banquet those Texas oil people gave me in Portofino, oh, yes, you were staying with them, and so depressed over the loss of—

CHRIS (*cutting in*): *Yes.* (*He moves toward the balustrade.*)

THE WITCH: You'd taken such beautiful care of that poor old ridiculous woman, but couldn't save her, and, oh, the old Duke of Parma did such a wicked thing to you, poured champagne on your head and—called you—what did he call you?

MRS. GOFORTH: Let him forget it, Connie.

(*The Witch gives her a glance and moves up to Chris.*)

THE WITCH: Something else awful happened and you were involved in some way but I can't remember the details.

CHRIS: Yes, it's better forgotten, Mrs. Goforth is right. Some of the details are much better forgotten if you'll let me—forget them. . . .

(*Mrs. Goforth rises and starts to go inside.*)

THE WITCH: Are you leaving us, Sissy?

MRS. GOFORTH: I'm going to phone the boat house t'make sure there's a boat ready for your trip back to Capri, because I know you want back there as soon as possible, Connie. (*She goes into the library.*)

THE WITCH (*going to the table*): Chris, you're not intending to *stay* here!?

CHRIS: Yes, if I'm invited: I would like to.

THE WITCH: Don't you know, can't you tell? Poor Sissy's going, she's gone. The shock I got last night when I—I had to drink myself blind!—when I saw her condition! (*She comes closer to him.*) You don't want to be stuck with a person in her appalling condition. You're young, have fun. Oh, Chris, you've been foolish too long. The years you devoted to that old Ferguson bitch, and what did you get?

CHRIS (*lighting a cigarette*): Get?

THE WITCH: Yes, get? She *had* you, you were *had!—left* you? *Nothing!*—I bet, or why would you be here?

CHRIS: Please don't make me be rude. We don't understand each other, which is natural, but don't make me say things to you that I don't want to say.

THE WITCH: What can you say to me that I haven't heard said?

CHRIS: Have you heard this said to your face about you: that you're the heart of a world that has no heart, the heartless world you live in—has anyone said that to you, Mrs. Ridgeway?

THE WITCH: Condotti, Marchesa Ridgeway-Condotti, Mr. Death Angel Flanders.

CHRIS: Yes, we both have new titles.

THE WITCH (*throwing back her head*): Sally! Laurie! Sissy! It's time for death, old girls, beddy-bye! (*Less shrilly.*) Beddy-bye, old girls, the Death Angel's coming, no dreams . . .

CHRIS: I'm sorry you forced me to say what I feel about you.

THE WITCH: Oh, that. My heart pumps blood that isn't my own blood, it's the blood of anonymous blood donors. And as for the world I live in, you know it as well as I know it. Come to Capri, it's a mountain, too.

CHRIS (*moving away*): You're not afraid of the nickname I've been given?

THE WITCH: No, I think it's a joke that you take seriously, Chris. You've gotten too solemn. (*She follows him.*) Let me take that curse off you. Come to Capri and I'll give you a party, decorated with your mobiles, and—

MRS. GOFORTH (*to Blackie*): *See? She's out there putting the make on—*

(*Blackie leaves as Mrs. Goforth comes from the library toward the terrace.*)

THE WITCH (*to Chris*): You're pale, you look anemic, you look famished, you need someone to put you back in the picture, the social swim. Capri?

(*Mrs. Goforth, on the terrace, advances behind Chris and The Witch.*)

MRS. GOFORTH: What picture? What swim? Capri?

THE WITCH: It's marvelous there this season.

MRS. GOFORTH: The sea is full of Medusas. Didn't you tell me the sea is full of Medusas, and a giant one got you?

THE WITCH (*crossing to her*): Oh, they'll wash out, they'll be washed out by tomorrow.

MRS. GOFORTH: When are *you* going to wash out? I thought you'd washed out last night. I've ordered a boat to take you back to Capri.

THE WITCH: I can't go back to Capri in a dinner gown before sundown. (*She sits at the table and stares at Chris.*)

MRS. GOFORTH: Well, try my hot sulphur baths, or just look the place over, it's worth it. It's worth looking over. Me, I'm about to start work, so I can't talk to you right now. (*She gets The Witch's hat and brings it to her.*) I'm right on the edge of breaking through here today, I'm on a strict discipline, Connie, as I explained last night to you, and— (*She coughs, falls into her chair.*)

THE WITCH: Sissy, I don't like that cough.

MRS. GOFORTH: Hell, do you think I like it? Neuralgia, nerves, overwork, but I'm going to beat it, it isn't going to beat *me*, or it'll be the first thing that ever *did* beat me!

THE WITCH (*rising and going to her*): Be brave, Sissy.

MRS. GOFORTH: Leave me alone, go, Connie, it'll do you in, too. (*She fumbles for a tissue.*)

THE WITCH (*looking wide-eyed at Chris and moving close to him*): Watch out for each other!—Chris, give her the Swami's book you translated. *Ciao!* (*She throws him a kiss and moves off, calling back.*) *Questo è veramente una meraviglia . . . Ciao, arrivederci. . . . Amici!*

(*The Witch goes out of the lighted area and down the goat-path. Chris goes to the table and sits, looking about.*)

MRS. GOFORTH: What are you looking for now?

CHRIS: I was just looking for the cream and sugar.

MRS. GOFORTH: Never touch it. Y'want a saccharine tablet?

CHRIS: Oh, no, thanks, I—don't like the chemical taste.

MRS. GOFORTH (*coming to the table*): Well, it's black coffee or else, I'm afraid, Mr. What?—Chris!

CHRIS: You have *three* villas here?

MRS. GOFORTH: One villa and two villinos. Villino means a small villa. I also have a little grass hut, very Polynesian—(*moving in front of the table*)—down on my private beach too. I have a special use for it, and a funny name for it, too.

CHRIS: Oh?

MRS. GOFORTH: Yes, I call it "the Oubliette." Ever heard of an oubliette?

CHRIS: A place where people are put to be forgotten?

MRS. GOFORTH: That's right, Chris. You've had some education along that line. (*She returns to where he sits.*)

CHRIS: Yes, quite a lot, Mrs. Goforth, especially lately.

MRS. GOFORTH: As for the use of it, well, I've been plagued by imposters lately, the last few summers. The continent has been overrun by imposters of celebrities, writers, actors, and so forth. I mean they arrive and say, like "I am Truman Capote." Well, they look a bit like him so you are taken in by the announcement, "I am Truman Capote," and you receive him cordially only to find out later it isn't the true

Truman Capote, it's the false Truman Capote. Last summer I had the false Truman Capote, and the year before that I had the false Mary McCarthy. That's before I took to checking the passports of sudden visitors. Well—(*She moves to the opposite chair and sits facing him.*) as far as I know they're still down there in that little grass hut on the beach, where undesirables are transferred to, when the villas are overcrowded. The Oubliette. A medieval institution that I think, personally, was discarded too soon. It was a dungeon, where people were put for keeps to be forgotten. You say you know about it?

(*Chris stares straight at her, not answering by word or gesture. His look is gentle, troubled.*)

So that's what I call my little grass shack on the beach, I call it "the Oubliette" from the French verb "*oublier*" which means to forget, to forget, to put away and—

CHRIS:—forget. . . .

MRS. GOFORTH: And I do really forget 'em. Maybe you think I'm joking but it's the truth. Can't stand to be made a Patsy. Understand what I mean?

(*He nods.*)

This is nothing personal. You came with your book—(*picks up his book of poetry*) with a photograph of you on it, which still looks like you just, well, ten years younger, but still unmistakably you. You're not the false Chris Flanders, I'm sure about that.

CHRIS: Thank you. I try not to be.

MRS. GOFORTH: However, I don't keep up with the new personalities in the world of art like I used to. Too much a waste of vital energy, Chris. Of course you're not exactly a new personality in it: would you say so?

(*Chris smiles and shakes his head slightly.*)

You're almost a veteran in it. I said a veteran, I didn't say a "has been"— (*She sneezes violently.*) I'm allergic to something around here. I haven't found out just what, but when I do, oh, brother, watch it go!

CHRIS (*rising and bringing her a clean tissue*): I hope it isn't the bougainvillaea vines.

MRS. GOFORTH: No, it isn't the bougainvillaea, but I'm having an allergy specialist flown down here from Rome to check me with every goddamn plant and animal on the place, and whatever it is has to go.

CHRIS: Have you tried breathing sea water?

MRS. GOFORTH: Oh, you want to drown me?

CHRIS (*returning to his chair and sitting*): Ha ha, no. I meant have you tried snuffing it up in your nostrils to irrigate your nasal passages, Mrs. Goforth, it's sometimes a very effective treatment for—

MRS. GOFORTH: Aside from this allergy and a little neuralgia, sometimes more than a little, I'm a healthy woman. Know how I've kept in shape, my body, the way it still is?

CHRIS: Exercise?

MRS. GOFORTH: Yes! In bed! Plenty of it, still going on! . . . But there's this worship of youth in the States, this Whistler's Mother complex, you know what I mean, this idea that at a certain age a woman ought to resign herself to being a sweet old thing in a rocker. Well, last week-end, a man, a *young* man, came in my bedroom and it wasn't too easy to get him out of it. I had to be very firm about it.

(*Blackie appears on the terrace with a plate of food for Chris. Mrs. Goforth rises.*)

What've you got there, Blackie?

BLACKIE: Mr. Flanders' breakfast. I'm sure he would like some.

MRS. GOFORTH: Aw, now, isn't that thoughtful. Put it down there.

(*As Blackie starts to put it down on the table, Mrs. Goforth indicates the serving table.*

I said down there. And get me my menthol inhaler and Kleenex. I have run out.

(*Blackie sets the plate on the serving table and retires from the lighted area.*

Simonetta!

(*Mrs. Goforth rings and hands the tray to Simonetta as she enters.*)

Take this away. I can't stand the smell of food now.

(*Simonetta goes out.*)

CHRIS (*who has moved toward the serving table and stands stunned*): Mrs. Goforth, I feel that I have, I must have disturbed you, annoyed you—disturbed you because I— (*He crosses back to the table.*)

MRS. GOFORTH: Don't reach for a cigarette till I offer you one.

CHRIS: May I have one, Mrs. Goforth?

MRS. GOFORTH: Take one. Be my Trojan Horse Guest. Wait.

(*She moves beside him.*)

Kiss me for it.

(*Chris doesn't move.*)

Kiss me for it, I told you.

CHRIS (*putting the cigarette away*): Mrs. Goforth, there are moments for kisses and moments not for kisses.

MRS. GOFORTH: This is a "not for kiss" moment?

(*He turns away, and she follows and takes his arm.*)

I've shocked *you* by my ferocity, have I? Sometimes I shock myself by it.

(*They move together toward the balustrade.*)

Look: a coin has two sides. On one side is an eagle, but on the other side is—something else. . . .

CHRIS: Yes, something else, usually some elderly potentate's profile.

(*She laughs appreciatively at his riposte and touches his shoulder. He moves a step away from her.*)

MRS. GOFORTH: Why didn't you grab the plate and run off with it?

CHRIS: Like a dog grabs a bone?

MRS. GOFORTH: Sure! Why not? It might've pleased me to see you show some fight.

CHRIS: I can fight if I have to, but the fighting style of dogs is not my style.

MRS. GOFORTH: *Grab, fight, or go hungry!* Nothing else works.

CHRIS: How is it possible for a woman of your reputation as a patron of arts and artists, to live up here, with all this beauty about you, and yet be—

MRS. GOFORTH: A bitch, a swamp-bitch, a devil? Oh, I see it, the view, but it makes me feel ugly this summer for some reason or other—bitchy, a female devil.

CHRIS: You'd like the view to be ugly to make you feel superior to it?

MRS. GOFORTH (*turning to him*): Why don't we sing that old church hymn:

"From Greenland's icy mountains to India's coral Isle
Everything is beautiful . . ."

CHRIS: "Man alone is vile."

MRS. GOFORTH: Hmm. Devils can be driven out of the heart by the touch of a hand on a hand, or a mouth on a mouth. Because, like Alex said once, "Evil isn't a person: evil is a thing that comes sneaky-snaking into the heart of a person, and takes it over: a mean intruder, a *squatter*!"

CHRIS: May I touch your hand, please?

MRS. GOFORTH (*as he does*): Your hand's turned cold. I've shocked the warm blood out of it. Let me rub it back in.

CHRIS: Your hand's cold, too, Mrs. Goforth.

MRS. GOFORTH: Oh, that's just—nervous tension, never mind that. I'll tell you something, Chris, you came here at a time unusually favorable to you. Now we're going to talk turkey. At least *I'm* going to talk turkey. You can talk ducks and geese, but I am going to talk turkey, cold turkey. You've come here at a time when I'm restless, bored, and shocked by the news of deaths of three friends in the States, one, two, three, like firecrackers going off, right together almost, like rat-a-tat-tat blindfolded against the wall.—Well, you see I— (*She moves down to the lower terrace.*) I had a bad scare last winter. I was visiting relatives I'd set up on a grand estate on Long Island when some little psychosomatic symptom gave me a scare. They made a big deal of it, had me removed by a seaplane to the East River where they had an ambulance waiting for me, and whisked me off to a— Know what I said when I was advised to go under the knife the next day? Ha, I'll tell you, ha ha!—Called my law firm and dictated a letter cutting them off with one dollar apiece in my will. . . .

CHRIS (*who has come down to her*): Mrs. Goforth, are you still afraid of— (*He hesitates.*)

MRS. GOFORTH: Death—never even think of it. (*She takes his arm and they move down to a bench, and sit.*)

CHRIS: Death is one moment, and life is so many of them.

MRS. GOFORTH: A million billion of them, if you think in terms of a lifetime as rich as mine's been, Chris.

CHRIS: Yes, life is something, death's nothing. . . .

MRS. GOFORTH: Nothing, nothing, but nothing. I've had to refer to many deaths in my memoirs. Oh, I don't think I'm immortal—I still go to sleep every night wondering if I'll—wake up the next day . . . (*Coughs and gasps for breath.*) —face that angry old lion.

CHRIS: Angry old—?

MRS. GOFORTH:—lion!

CHRIS: The sun? You think it's angry?

MRS. GOFORTH: Naturally, of course—looking down on—? Well, you know what it looks down on. . . .

CHRIS: It seems to accept and understand things today. . . .

MRS. GOFORTH: It's just a big fire-ball that toughens the skin, including the skin of the heart.

CHRIS: How lovely the evenings must be here—when the fishing boats go out on the Gulf of Salerno with their little lamps shining.

MRS. GOFORTH: Well, they call this coast the *Divina Costiera.* That means the divine coast, you know.

CHRIS: Yes, I know. I suppose . . .

MRS. GOFORTH: You suppose what?

CHRIS: I suppose you dine on the terrace about the time the fishing boats go out with their little lamps and the stars come out of the—

MRS. GOFORTH: Firmament. Call it the firmament, not the sky, it's much more classy to call it the firmament, baby. How about spring? You write about spring and live in it, you write about love in the spring, haven't you written love-poems for susceptible—patrons?—Well! How many books of poems have you come out with?

CHRIS: Just the one that I brought you.

MRS. GOFORTH: You mean you burnt out as a poet?

CHRIS:—Pardon?

MRS. GOFORTH: You mean you burnt out as a poet?

(*Chris laughs uncomfortably.*)

Why're you laughing? I didn't say anything funny.

CHRIS: I didn't know I was laughing. Excuse me, Mrs. Goforth. But you are very—direct.

MRS. GOFORTH: Is that shocking?

CHRIS: No. No, not really. In fact I like that about you.

MRS. GOFORTH: But you give that little embarrassed laugh, like I'd made you uncomfortable.

CHRIS: My nerves are—

MRS. GOFORTH: Gone through like your list of suckers. (*Mrs. Goforth sneezes and gets up to look for another tissue.*)

CHRIS (*standing*): Mrs. Goforth—if you want me to go—

MRS. GOFORTH: That depends.

CHRIS: What does it depend on?

MRS. GOFORTH: Frankly, I'm very lonely up here this summer.

CHRIS: I can understand that.

MRS. GOFORTH: Now, you're not stupid. You're attractive to me. You know that you are. You've deliberately set out to be attractive to me, and you are. So don't be a free-loader.

(*Chris doesn't speak for a moment.*)

CHRIS (*gently*): Mrs. Goforth, I think you've been exposed to the wrong kind of people and—

MRS. GOFORTH (*cutting in*): I'm sick of moral blackmail! You know what that is. People imposing on you by the old, old trick of making you feel it would be unkind of you not to permit them to do it. In their hearts they despise you. So much they can't quite hide it. It pops out in sudden little remarks and looks they give you. Busting with malice—because you have what they haven't. You know what some writer called that? "A robust conscience, and the Viking spirit in life!"

CHRIS (*going back on the terrace*): Oh? Is that what he called it?

MRS. GOFORTH (*following*): He called it that, and I have it! I give away nothing, I sell and I buy in my life, and I've always wound up with a profit, one way or another. You came up that hill from the highway with an old book of poems that you got published ten years ago, by playing on the terrible, desperate loneliness of a rich old broken-hipped woman, who, all she could do, was pretend that someone still loved her. . . .

CHRIS: You're talking about Mrs. Ferguson.

MRS. GOFORTH: Yes, I am.

CHRIS (*moving away from her*): I made her walk again. She published my poems.

MRS. GOFORTH: How long after she published your poems did you let go of her arm so she fell on the deck of a steamship and her hip broke again?

CHRIS: I didn't let her go. She broke away from me—

(*Mrs. Goforth laughs uproariously*)

—if you'll allow me to make a minor correction in the story. We were walking very slowly about the promenade deck of the *Queen Mary*, eight summers ago, more than a year after my poems were published. A young man called to her from a deck chair that we'd just passed, and she wheeled around and broke away from my hand, and slipped and fell, and her hip was broken again. Of course some malicious "friends" blamed me, but—I wouldn't leave her.

MRS. GOFORTH: No? She was still your meal-ticket?

CHRIS: Not at all.

MRS. GOFORTH: Who *was*?

CHRIS (*sitting*): I was fashionable, then.

MRS. GOFORTH: Do you sit down while a lady is standing?

CHRIS (*springing up with a rather ferocious smile*): Sorry, won't you sit down!

(*His tone is so commanding, abruptly, that she does sit down in the chair he jerks out for her.*)

May I tell you something about yourself? It may seem presumptuous of me to tell you this, but I'm going to tell you this: you're suffering more than you need to.

MRS. GOFORTH: I am—

CHRIS (*cutting through her protest*): You're suffering from the worst of all human maladies, of all afflictions, and I don't mean one of the body, I mean the thing people feel when they go from room to room for no reason, and then they go back from room to room for no reason, and then they go *out* for no reason and come back *in* for no reason—

MRS. GOFORTH: You mean I'm alone here, don't you?

(*Chris takes hold of her hand. She snatches it away from him.*)

I'm *working* up here this summer, *working*! *Ever heard of it?*

(*A Stage Assistant appears in the wings as if she had shouted for him. He hands her a letter.*)

This morning's mail brought me this! My London publisher's letter! "Darling Flora: Your book of memoirs, *Facts and a Figure*, will, in my opinion, rank with and possibly—"

(*She squints, unable to decipher the letter further. Chris removes it from her trembling, jeweled hand, and completes the reading.*)

CHRIS: "—rank with and possibly even out-rank the great Marcel Proust's *Remembrance of Things Past* as a social documentation of two continents in three decades. . . ."

MRS. GOFORTH: Well?

CHRIS: A letter like this should fall on a higher mountain.

MRS. GOFORTH: Huh?

CHRIS: A letter like this should be delivered above the snow line of an Alpine peak because it's snow, a snow job.

(*She snatches it back from him.*)

MRS. GOFORTH (*raging*): For you, a blond beatnik, coming from Naples on foot up a goddamn goatpath, wearing at this table a Japanese robe because dogs tore your britches, I think your presumption is not excusable, Mister! It lacks the excuse of much youth, you're not young enough for your moxey. This publisher's not a lover. A lover might snow me, but this man's a business associate, and they don't snow you, not *me*, not *Sissy Goforth*! They don't snow me—*snow me!* They don't get up that early in the morning—

(*Her agitation somehow touches him. His smile turns warm again.*)

—that they could— (*coughs*) snow me. . . .

(*The Stage Assistants lean, whispering together, as they retire from the stage.*)

CHRIS: Of course, without having your publisher's advantage of knowing *Facts and a Figure*—

MRS. GOFORTH: Nothing, not a word of it!

CHRIS: No, not a word, but what I was going to say was that I think you need *companionship*, not just employees about you, up here, but— How often do you see old friends or new friends this summer, Mrs. Goforth? Often or not so often?

MRS. GOFORTH: Hell, all I have to do is pick up a phone to crowd this mountain with—

CHRIS: Crowds? Is it that easy this summer? You're proud. You don't want to ask people up here that might not come, because they're pleasure-seekers, frantic choosers of silly little distractions, and—and—

MRS. GOFORTH: "and—and" *what?*

CHRIS: Your condition, the terrible strain of your work, makes you seem—eccentric, disturbing!— To those sea-level, those lower-than-sea-level, people. . . .

MRS. GOFORTH: *Get to whatever you're leading up to, will you!*

CHRIS: I notice you have trouble reading. I've been told I have a good reading voice.

MRS. GOFORTH: Most human voices are very monotonous to me. Besides, I'm more interested in producing literature this summer than having it read to me.

CHRIS: Mmm—but you do need some agreeable companionship.

MRS. GOFORTH: Right you are about *that*, but how do I know your idea of agreeable companionship is the same as mine? You purr at me like a cat, now, but a cat will purr at you one minute and scratch your eyes out the next.

(*He leans back, smiling, working the sword up and down in its scabbard.*)

I think you better take off that old sword belt.

CHRIS: There're no buttons on the robe, so without the belt on it—

MRS. GOFORTH: Take it off you!

CHRIS: The *robe*?

MRS. GOFORTH: The *sword* belt. You grin and fiddle with the hilt—the sword—like you had—evil—intentions.

CHRIS: Oh. You suspect I'm a possible assassin?

MRS. GOFORTH: *Take it off, give it here!*

CHRIS: All right. Formal surrender, *unconditional . . . nearly.* (*He takes the sword belt off and hands it to her.*)

MRS. GOFORTH: *O.K., Robert E. Lee! At Appomattox . . .*

(*She hurls the sword belt to the terrace tiles behind her. A Stage Assistant darts out of the wings to remove it. The other Assistant laughs off stage.*)

CHRIS: Now what can I use for a sash to keep things proper?

MRS. GOFORTH: See if this goes around you, if being proper's so important to you.

(*She hands him a brilliant scarf she has been wearing about her throat. He turns upstage to tie the scarf about him. A phone is heard ringing, off stage. Blackie appears from behind the library screen.*)

MRS. GOFORTH (*to Blackie*): Who's calling? My broker again, with the closing quotations?

BLACKIE: The call's for *Mr. Flanders.*

CHRIS: *Me*, for *me*? But who could know I'm up here!

MRS. GOFORTH: Cut the bull. You got a call up here last night. Business is picking up for you.

CHRIS: This is—mystifying!

BLACKIE: The phone's in the library.

CHRIS: Excuse me.

(*He goes quickly behind the library screen. Mrs. Goforth crosses toward it but remains, listening, outside it.*)

CHRIS (*behind screen*): *Pronto, pronto.* Madelyn!—How are you, how's your dear mother?—Oh, my God!—I meant to come straight down there but—was it, uh, what they call peaceful? (*Pause.*) Oh, I'm so glad, I prayed so hard that it *would* be! And I'm so relieved that it *was.* I did so long to be with you but had to stop on the way. And you? Will you be all right? Yes, I know, *expected*, but still I could be some use in making the necessary arrangements? I'm at Flora Goforth's place, but if you could send a car to pick me up I could— Oh?—Oh?—Well, Madelyn, all I can say is *accept* it.—Bless you, goodbye. *Accept* it.

(*Mrs. Goforth is shaken. She moves to the table as if she had received a personal shock. Chris comes back out. At the same moment, church bells ring in a village below the mountain.*)

CHRIS:—Church bells? In the village?

MRS. GOFORTH: Yes, appropriate, aren't they? Ringing right on a dead cue . . .

CHRIS: I just received news that's—*shocked* me. . . .

MRS. GOFORTH: Another name you have to scratch off the list?

CHRIS: Did you say "list"?

MRS. GOFORTH (*smiling at him cunningly, fiercely*): I went to a spiritualist once. She said to me, "I hear many dead voices calling, 'Flora, Flora.' " I knew she was a fake, then, since all my close friends call me Sissy. I said, "Tell them to mind their own business, play their gold harps and mind their own harp-playing. Sissy Goforth's not ready to go forth yet and won't go forth till she's ready. . . ."

(*Chris extends a hand to her. The bells stop ringing.*)

What are you reaching out for?

CHRIS: Your hand, if I may, Mrs. Goforth. (*He has taken hold of it.*)

MRS. GOFORTH: Hold it but don't squeeze it. The rings cut my fingers.

CHRIS: I'm glad we've talked so frankly, so quickly today. The conversation we had at the ball at the Waldorf in 1950 was a long conversation but not as deep as this one.

MRS. GOFORTH: Who said anything deep? I don't say anything deep in a conversation, not this summer, I save it for my memoirs. Did you say anything deep, in your opinion? If you did, it escaped me, escaped my notice completely. Oh, you've known Swanees. Excuse me, Swamis. You've been exposed to the—intellectual scene, and it's rubbed off on you a little, but only skin-deep, as deep as your little blond beard. . . .

CHRIS: Perhaps I used the wrong word.

(*She places a cigarette in her mouth and waits for him to light it. He turns deliberately away from her, and places a foot on the low balustrade, facing seaward.*)

This "wine-dark sea," it's the oldest sea in the world. . . . Know what I see down there?

MRS. GOFORTH: The sea.

CHRIS: Yes, and a fleet of Roman triremes, those galleys with three banks of oars, rowed by slaves, commanded by commanders headed for conquests. Out for loot. *Boom!* Out for conquering, pillaging, and collecting more slaves. *Boom!* Here's where the whole show started, it's the oldest sea in the Western world, Mrs. Goforth, this sea called the Mediterranean Sea, which means the middle of the earth, was the cradle, of life, not the grave, but the cradle of pagan and Christian—civilizations, this sea, and its connecting river, that old water snake, the Nile.

MRS. GOFORTH: I've been on the Nile. No message. Couple of winters ago I stayed at the Mena House, that hotel under the pyramids. I could see the pyramids, those big-big calcified fools-caps from my breakfast balcony. No message. Rode up to 'em on a camel so I could say I'd done the whole bit.

CHRIS: No message?

MRS. GOFORTH: No message, except you can get seasick on a camel. Yep, you can get mighty seasick on the hump of a camel. Went inside those old king-size tombstones.

CHRIS: No message inside them, either?

MRS. GOFORTH: No message, except the Pharaohs and their families had the idiotic idea they were going to wake up hungry and thirsty and so provided themselves with breakfasts which had gone very stale and dry, and the Pharaohs and families were still sound asleep, ho ho. . . .

(*He still has his back to her. She is obviously annoyed by his loss of attention.*)

And if you look this way, you'll notice I've got a cigarette in my mouth and I'm waiting for you to light it. Didn't that old Sally Ferguson bitch teach you to light a cigarette for a lady?

CHRIS (*facing her*): She wasn't a bitch, unless all old dying ladies are bitches. She was dying, and scared to death of dying, which made her a little—eccentric . . .

(*He has picked up Mrs. Goforth's diamond-studded lighter. He lights her cigarette but doesn't return the lighter to the table. He tosses it in the palm of his hand.*)

MRS. GOFORTH: Thanks. Now put it down.

(*He sits down, smiling, on the low balustrade. There has occurred a marked change in his surface attitude toward her: the deferential air has gone completely.*)

I meant my Bulgari lighter, not your—*backside!*

(*He studies the lighter as if to calculate its value. There is a pause.*)

If you don't put that lighter back down on the table, I'm going to call for Rudy! You know Rudy. You've made his acquaintance, I think.

CHRIS: If I don't put it down on the table but in my pocket, and if I were to run down the goatpath with it—how fast can Rudy run?

MRS. GOFORTH: How fast can *you* run? Could you outrun the dogs? Yesterday you didn't outrun the dogs.

CHRIS: That was—uphill, on the other side of your mountain. I think I could get down this side, yes, by the—funicular, I could operate it.

MRS. GOFORTH: Can you outrun a bullet?

CHRIS: Oh, would you have Rudy shoot at me for this lighter?

MRS. GOFORTH: You bet I would. That's a very valuable lighter.

(*Chris laughs and tosses the lighter on the table.*)

CHRIS: Hmmm. On a parapet over the Western world's oldest sea, the lady that owns it had a gangster—

MRS. GOFORTH: The bodyguard of a syndicate gangster!

CHRIS: Yes, the lady that owns it had her bodyguard shoot down a—what?—burnt-out poet who had confiscated a diamond-studded lighter because he was unfed and hungry. He'd been on a five-day fast for—nonsecular reasons, and it had upset his reason.

(*Mrs. Goforth rings the bell on the table. Chris seizes her hand and wrests the bell away from it. She rises from the table and shouts: "Rudy!"*)

CHRIS (*louder than she*): Rudy!

MRS. GOFORTH: You couldn't get away with it!

CHRIS: Oh, yes, I could, if I wanted. (*He tosses the bell back on the table with a mocking grin.*)

MRS. GOFORTH: What a peculiar—puzzlesome young man you are! You came out here like a dandy, kissed my hand, and now you're coming on like a young hood all of a sudden, and I don't like the change, it makes me nervous with you, and now I don't know if I want you around here or not, or if I'm—not superstitious. See? You've made me shaky.

CHRIS: You didn't know I was teasing?

MRS. GOFORTH: No. You're too good at it.

CHRIS (*looking seaward*): I see it, your oubliette on the beach, it looks attractive to me.

MRS. GOFORTH: Help me into my bedroom. (*She tries to rise but falls back into the chair.*) It's time for my siesta.

CHRIS: Could I stay there, a while?

MRS. GOFORTH: Later maybe. Not now. I need to rest.

CHRIS: I meant the grass hut on the beach, not your bedroom.

MRS. GOFORTH: Be still, she's coming back out, my secretary, and I'm not sure I trust her.

CHRIS: Do you trust anybody?

MRS. GOFORTH: Nobody human, just dogs. All except poodles, I never trusted a poodle. . . .

(*Blackie comes onto the terrace.*)

In again, out again, Finnegan! What's it *this* time, Blackie?

BLACKIE: Is it true you've discharged the kitchen staff again, Mrs. Goforth?

MRS. GOFORTH: Yes, it's true. . . . Haven't you heard about the inventory?

BLACKIE: What inventory, inventory of what?

MRS. GOFORTH: I had an intuition that things were disappearing and had Rudy check my list of fabulous china, my Sèvres, Limoges, Lowestoff, against what was still on the mountain. Half of it gone, decimated! And my Medici silver, banquet silver used by the Medicis hundreds of years ago, *gone*!—That's what the inventory disclosed!

BLACKIE: Mrs. Goforth, is it possible you don't remember—

MRS. GOFORTH: *What?*

BLACKIE: You had it removed to a storage house in Naples, in an armored truck.

MRS. GOFORTH: *Me?*

BLACKIE: *You!*

MRS. GOFORTH: *Not true!*

BLACKIE: Mrs. Goforth, when people are very ill and taking drugs for it, they get confused, their memories are confused, they get delusions.

MRS. GOFORTH: *This mountain has been systematically pillaged!*—That's what the inventory—

BLACKIE: An inventory made by the bodyguard of a syndicate gangster?

MRS. GOFORTH: How dare you suggest— *I have a guest at the table!*

BLACKIE: *I will always dare to say what I know to be true!*

MRS. GOFORTH: *Go in, find my checkbook and write out a check for yourself for whatever's coming to you, and bring it out here and I'll sign it for cash, at the Naples branch of my bank! You wanted out, now you got it, so take it! Take it!*

BLACKIE: *Gladly! Gladly!*

MRS. GOFORTH: Mutually *gladly! Go in!*

(*Blackie starts to go. Mrs. Goforth's shouting has brought on a coughing spasm. She covers her mouth with her hands and rushes, in a crouched position, toward the upstage area of the library.*)

CHRIS:—*Boom* . . .

BLACKIE: *Release!*

CHRIS (*pointing at the terrace pavement*): Blackie? Look!—Blood, she's bleeding. . . .

MRS. GOFORTH'S VOICE (*Off stage, hoarsely*): *Dottore, chiama il dottore! Giulio, Simonetta!*

CHRIS: You'd better go in there with her.

BLACKIE: I can't yet. They'll get the doctor for her. (*She moves downstage, gasping.*) You see, she's made me *inhuman!*

(*Simonetta explodes onto the forestage.*)

SIMONETTA: *Signorina, la Signora é molto, molto malata!*

BLACKIE (*going toward her*): *Dov'è la Signora, in camera da letto?*

SIMONETTA: *No, nella biblioteca, con il dottore!* (*She sits on a bench and sobs hysterically.*)

BLACKIE: Well, I'd better go in there.

CHRIS: What shall I do? Anything?

BLACKIE: Yes, stay here, don't go. (*Then, to Simonetta, who is now crying theatrically*) *Ferma questa—commedia.*

(*Simonetta stops crying, and begins straightening up the table.*)

(*To Chris*) Call the hospital in Rome, Salvatore Mundi, and ask for Dr. Rengucci. Tell him what's happening here and a nurse is needed at once. Then come in there, the library, and we'll—

(*Giulio rushes out onto the forestage.*)

GIULIO: *La Signora Goforth vuol' vedere il Signore, presto, molto presto!*

BLACKIE (*to Chris*): She's calling for *you.* I'd better go in first. Make the call and then come to the library.

(*She goes out one way, Chris the other.*)

GIULIO (*to Simonetta*): She's dying?

SIMONETTA: No one's been paid this week. Who will pay us if she dies today?

GIULIO: *Guarda!*

(*He shows her a gold bracelet. Simonetta snatches at it. Giulio pockets it with a grin, and starts off as she follows.*)

The Scene Dims Out.

SCENE SIX

Later the same day, toward sundown. The interiors of the white villa are screened and the terrace is lighted more coolly. Blackie is seated at the downstage table, jotting in a notebook memoranda of things to be done before leaving. The Stage Assistants stand by the flagstaff ready to lower the banner of Mrs. Goforth.

ONE: Cable her daughter that the old bitch is dying.
TWO: The banner of the griffin is about to be lowered.
BLACKIE (*as if translating their speech into a polite paraphrase*): Cable Mrs. Goforth's daughter at Point Goforth, Long Island, that her mother is not expected to survive the night, and I'm waiting for—immediate—instructions.
ONE: Fireworks tonight at Point Goforth, Long Island.
TWO: A champagne fountain.
ONE *and* TWO (*together*): Death: celebration.
BLACKIE: Call police in Amalfi to guard the library safe till Rudy has gone.
ONE: Rudy's root-a-toot-tooting through that safe right now.
TWO: He's disappointed to discover that the old bitch still has on her most important jewels.
ONE: And she's still conscious—fiercely!
BLACKIE: Contact mortuary. Amalfi.
TWO: That Blackie's a cool one.

(*Chris comes onto the terrace, now wearing his repaired lederhosen and a washed, but unironed, white shirt.*)

CHRIS: Blackie?
BLACKIE (*glancing up*): Oh. I'm making out a list of things to do before leaving.
CHRIS: You're not leaving right away, are you?

BLACKIE: Soon as I get instructions from her daughter.

CHRIS: I called the Rome doctor and told him what had happened. He said he's expected it sooner, and there's nothing more to be done that can't be done by the doctor on the place.

BLACKIE: The little doctor, Lullo, has given her a strong shot of adrenalin which was a mistake, I think. She won't go to bed, keeps pressing electric buzzers for Simonetta who's run away, and she's put on all her rings so they won't be stolen. She's more afraid of being robbed of her jewelry than her life. What time would it be in the States?

CHRIS: What time is it here?

BLACKIE: Sundown, nearly.

CHRIS: About seven-thirty here would make it—about two-thirty there.

BLACKIE: Maybe a phone call would get through before a cable.

(*She rises. One of the Stage Assistants brings a phone from the table by the chaise lounge, a little upstage. Blackie takes the phone.*)

Try her daughter's husband at Goforth, Faller and Rush, Incorporated, Plaza 1-9000, while I—

(*She gives Chris the phone, and pours herself a brandy. Rudy comes out with a strongbox from the safe.*)

Who's that? Oh! *You!* What are you taking out?

RUDY: Just what I was told to take out.

BLACKIE: Well, take it out, but don't forget that everything's been listed.

RUDY: I don't forget nothing, Blackie. (*He goes off.*)

STAGE ASSISTANT ONE (*removing the crested screen*): Her bedroom in the white villa.

TWO: The griffin is staring at death, and trying to outstare it.

(*We see Mrs. Goforth seated. She wears a majestic ermine-trimmed robe to which she has pinned her "most important jewels," and rings blaze on her fingers that clench the chair arms.*)

ONE: Her eyes are bright as her diamonds.

TWO: Until she starts bleeding again, she'll give no ground to any real or suspected adversary. . . .

ONE: And *then*?

(*During this exchange between the Assistants, who now back into the wings on their soundless shoes, Blackie has made several other notations. Without looking up at Chris, she asks him:*)

BLACKIE: You're still very hungry, aren't you?

CHRIS: Yes, very.

BLACKIE: The new kitchen staff has arrived. I've put a bottle of milk in your rucksack, and your rucksack is in the library. You'd better just have the milk now. We'll have dinner later together.

CHRIS: Blackie, I've seen her grass hut on the beach, her oubliette, as she calls it. And—I wonder how long I could stay down there before I'd be discovered and—evicted?

BLACKIE: Long as you want to. Indefinitely, I guess. But how would you live down there with the villas all closed?

CHRIS: Oh, on—*frutti di mare:* shellfish. And I'd make a spear for spear-fishing.

BLACKIE: There's no fresh water down there, just the sea water.

CHRIS: I know how to make fresh water out of sea water.

BLACKIE: Why would you want to stay down there?

CHRIS (*as a wave crashes under the mountain*): Boom! I'd like to make a mobile. I'd call it "Boom." The sea and the sky are turning the same color, dissolving into each other. Wine-dark sea and wine-dark sky. In a little while the little fishing boats with their lamps for night fishing will make the sea look like the night sky turned upside down, and you and I will have a sort of valedictory dinner on the terrace.

BLACKIE: Yes, it sounds very peaceful. . . .

(*The bedroom of the white villa is now brightened. Mrs. Goforth staggers from her chair, knocking it over. The Stage Assistants dart out to snatch the small chair and move it farther away, as she leans on a bed post, gasping. Then she draws herself up, advances to the chair's new position a little farther back. She reaches out for it. The Assistants pull it farther. She staggers dizzily after it. The Assistants exchange inquiring looks. They silently agree to allow her the chair and they back out of the area. She sits down with a cry of fury and resumes her fierce contest with death. A reserve of power, triggered by the adrenalin, begins to reanimate her. She rises and drags the chair to a small boudoir table and calls out:*)

MRS. GOFORTH: *Chris? Chris?*

BLACKIE: That's her, she's calling for you. Can you stand to go in there?

CHRIS: Sure I can—it's a professional duty.

(*As he turns upstage, the Stage Assistants remove the screen masking the library. He enters that area. One of the Stage Assistants turns the screen perpendicular to the proscenium so that it represents a wall division between bedroom and library. They retire.*)

Boom! Mrs. Goforth?

MRS. GOFORTH: Oh, you've finally got here. Stay out there, don't come in here right away. The doctor gave me a shot that's made me a little dizzy, I'll call you in—in a minute. . . . (*She staggers up from the chair, knocking it over.*)

CHRIS: Are you all right, Mrs. Goforth? (*He discovers his sack, removes and opens the milk bottle.*)

MRS. GOFORTH: Just a little unsteady after the shot, the doctor said. The bleeding was from a little blood vessel at the back of my throat. But he thinks I ought to lay off the work for a while, just wind up this volume and save the rest for—sequels. . . .

(*Chris opens the milk bottle and sips the milk as if it were sacramental wine.*)

Don't you think that's better, since it's such a strain on me?

CHRIS: Yes, I do, I think it's a—(*drinks milk*)—a wise decision. . . . (*He catches some drops of milk that have run down his chin, licks them almost reverently off the palm of his hand.*)

MRS. GOFORTH (*entering the library*): All that work, the pressure, was burning me up, it was literally burning me up like a house on fire.

CHRIS (*assisting her to the desk chair*): Yes, we—all live in a house on fire, no fire department to call; no way out, just the upstairs window to look out of while the fire burns the house down with us trapped, locked in it.

MRS. GOFORTH: What do you mean by—what windows?

CHRIS (*touching his forehead*): These upstairs windows, not wide enough to crawl out of, just wide enough to lean out of and look out of, and—look and look and look, till we're almost nothing but looking, nothing, almost, but *vision*. . . .

MRS. GOFORTH: Hmmm.—Yes. It isn't as cool out here as it was in my bedroom and this robe I've put on is too heavy. So come on in. We can talk in my bedroom. (*She retires behind the bedroom screen.*)

MRS. GOFORTH'S VOICE (*from behind her screen*): Talking between rooms is a strain on the ears and the vocal cords—so come in, now: I'm ready.

(*He crosses to the screens, stops short.*)

CHRIS: Oh. Sorry. (*He turns away from the screens.*) I'll wait till you've—

MRS. GOFORTH'S VOICE: Modesty? *Modesty*? I wouldn't expect you to suffer from modesty, Chris. I never was bothered with silliness of that kind. If you've got a figure that's pleasing to look at, why be selfish with it?

CHRIS: Yes, it *was* a pleasure, Mrs. Goforth.

MRS. GOFORTH'S VOICE: Then why'd you retreat, back away? In my bedroom, in here, I almost never, if ever, wear a stitch of clothes in summer. I like to feel cool air on my bare skin in summer. Don't you like that? Cool air and cool water on the bare skin in summer's the nicest thing about summer. Huh? Don't you think so, too?

CHRIS: I've found my duffel bag. It wandered in here, for some reason.

MRS. GOFORTH'S VOICE: I had it brought there so I could get your passport for the local police. They want a look at the passport of anyone just arrived.

CHRIS: I see.

MRS. GOFORTH'S VOICE: You'll get it back when you go, you know, there's no hurry, is there?

CHRIS: I'm not sure about that. (*Finds passport.*) Anyway, it's already been returned.

MRS. GOFORTH: We've just been getting acquainted. The preliminaries of a friendship, or any kind of relationship, are the most difficult part, and our talk on the terrace was just a—preliminary.

CHRIS (*wryly, so low that she cannot hear*): Sometimes the preliminaries are rougher than the main bout. (*He is rearranging articles in the rucksack.*)

MRS. GOFORTH: I didn't catch that. What was that?

CHRIS (*to himself*): I didn't mean you to catch it.

MRS. GOFORTH: Stop mumbling and fussing with that metal stuff in the sack. The fussing drowns out the mumbling. D'ya want me to break another blood vessel in my throat talking to you from here?

CHRIS: Are you dressed now, Mrs. Goforth?

MRS. GOFORTH: Hell, I told you I'm never dressed in my bedroom.

CHRIS: You said "rarely if ever"—not "never." (*He sighs and crosses to the door again.*) You have a beautiful body, Mrs. Goforth. It's a privilege to be permitted to admire it. It makes me think of one of those great fountain figures in Scandinavian countries.

MRS. GOFORTH: Yeah, well, baby, a fountain figure is a stone figure and my body isn't a stone figure, although it's been sculpted by several world-famous sculptors, it's still a flesh and blood figure. And don't think it's been easy to keep it the way it still is. I'm going to lie down and rest now on this cool bed. Mmmm, these sheets are so cool—come on in. Why are you standing there paralyzed in that door?

CHRIS: I'm—silent on a peak in—Darien. . . . (*Turns away from the door.*) I came here hoping to be your friend, Mrs. Goforth, but—

MRS. GOFORTH'S VOICE: You said "but" something, but what?

CHRIS: I wouldn't have come here unless I thought I was able to serve some purpose or other, in return for a temporary refuge, a place to rest and work in, where I could get back that sense of reality I've been losing lately, as I tried to explain on the terrace, but— (*He has removed the large mobile under her desk. He climbs on the desk to attach the mobile to the chandelier above it.*) You knew I was hungry but it was "black coffee or else."

MRS. GOFORTH: Is that why you won't come in here?

CHRIS: It would just be embarrassing for us both if I did. (*He jumps off the desk.*)

MRS. GOFORTH: *What's that, what're you doing?*

CHRIS: I hung up a gift I brought you, a mobile called "The Earth Is a Wheel in a Great Big Gambling Casino." And now I think I should leave, I have a long way to go.

MRS. GOFORTH: Just a minute. I'm coming back out there to see this mobile of yours. (*She comes from behind the screen, pulling the regal white robe about her.*) Well, where is it?

CHRIS: Right over your head.

(*She looks up, staggering against the desk.*)

MRS. GOFORTH: It doesn't move, doesn't go.

CHRIS: It will, when it's caught by the wind.

(*The mobile begins to turn, casting faint flickers of light.*)

There now, the winds caught it, it's turning. (*He picks up his canvas sack, preparing to leave.*)

MRS. GOFORTH: (*picking up the phone, suddenly*): *Kitchen, cucina, cucina!—Cucina? Un momento!* (*She thrusts the phone toward Chris.*) Tell the cook what you would like for supper.

CHRIS: Anything, Mrs. Goforth.

MRS. GOFORTH (*into the phone*): O.K.— *Cucina? Senta— Pranzo questa sera.—Pastina in brodo, per cominciare. Capish?—Si!—Poi, una grande pesca, si, si, una grandissima pesca, anche—carne freddo, si, si, carne freddo— Roast Beef, Bif, Beeeeeef!* (*Gasps, catches her breath.*) *Prosciutto, legumi, tutti, tutti legumi. Capito? Poi, un' insalata verde. No, Mista! Insalata mista, Mista!* They don't know their own language. . . . *Poi, dolce, zuppa inglese, frutta, formaggio, tutte formaggio, e vino, vino, bianco e rosso, una bottiglia di Soave e una bottiglia di—* (*gasps for breath again.*) *Valpolicella. Hanh?—Va bene. . . .* (*hangs up.*) This new cook sounds like a—Mau-mau. . . . She'll probably serve us long pig with—shrunk heads on toothpicks stuck in it. . . . (*She tries to laugh, but coughs.*) Now, then, you see, you're not just going to be fed, you're going to be wined and dined in high style tonight on the terrace. But meanwhile, we're going to enjoy a long siesta together in the cool of my bedroom which is full of historical treasures, including myself! (*She crosses to the bedroom doors, beckons him commandingly. He doesn't move.*) Well?!

CHRIS: I'm afraid I came here too late to accept these— invitations.

MRS. GOFORTH: Who else has invited you somewhere?

CHRIS: I've passed the point where I wait for invitations, but I think I'll be welcomed by the elderly spinster lady whose mother died in Taormina today.

MRS. GOFORTH: Not if she's heard your nickname. And Sicily's an island. How'll you get there, can you walk on water?

CHRIS: Your discharged secretary gave me a bottle of milk with some ten thousand lire notes attached to it with a— rubber band. So—goodbye, Mrs. Goforth. (*He bends to hoist his rucksack over his shoulder.*)

MRS. GOFORTH: Mr. Flanders, you have the distinction, the dubious distinction, of being the first man that wouldn't come into my bedroom when invited to enter.

CHRIS: I'm sorry.

MRS. GOFORTH: Man bring this up road, huh? (*She has snatched up his book of poems.*)

CHRIS: No, I—

MRS. GOFORTH: What else? Your book of poems, your calling card? Y'must be running short of 'em. Here take it back! (*She hurls it at his feet.*) I haven't read it but I can imagine the contents. *Facile sentiment!* To be good a poem's got to be tough and to write a good, tough poem you've got to cut your teeth on the marrow bone of this world. I think you're still cutting your milk teeth, Mr. Flanders.

CHRIS: I know you better than you know me. I admire you, admire you so much I almost like you, *almost.* I think if that old Greek explorer, Pytheas, hadn't beat you to it by centuries, you would've sailed up through the Gates of Hercules to map out the Western world, and you would have sailed up farther and mapped it out better than he did. No storm could've driven you back or changed your course. Oh, no, you're nobody's fool, but you're a fool, Mrs. Goforth, if you don't know that finally, sooner or later, you need somebody or something to mean God to you, even if it's a cow on the streets of Bombay, or carved rock on the Easter Islands or—

MRS. GOFORTH: You came here to bring me *God*, did you?

CHRIS: I didn't say God, I said someone or something to—

MRS. GOFORTH: I heard what you said, you said *God*. My eyes are out of focus but not my ears! Well, *bring* Him, I'm ready to lay out a red carpet for Him, but how do you bring Him? Whistle? Ring a bell for Him? (*She snatches a bell off her desk and rings it fiercely.*) Huh? How? What? (*She staggers back against the desk, gasping.*)

CHRIS: I've failed, I've disappointed some people in what they wanted or thought they wanted from me, Mrs. Goforth, but sometimes, once in a while, I've given them what they needed even if they didn't know what it was. I brought it up the road to them, and that's how I got the name that's made me unwelcome this summer.

STAGE ASSISTANT ONE: Tell her about the first time!

STAGE ASSISTANTS (*together*): Tell her, tell her, the first time!

(*They draw back to the wings. Music begins to be heard softly*).

CHRIS:—I was at Mrs. Ferguson's mountain above Palm Springs, the first time. I wasn't used to her world of elegant bitches and dandies. . . . Early one morning I went down the mountain and across the desert on a walking trip to a village in Baja California, where a great Hindu teacher had gathered a group of pupils, disciples, about him. Along the road I passed a rest home that looked like a grand hotel, and just a little farther along, I came to an inlet, an estuary of the ocean, and I stopped for a swim off the beach that was completely deserted. Swam out in the cool water till my head felt cool as the water, then turned and swam back in, but the beach wasn't deserted completely any more. There was a very old gentleman on it. He called "Help!" to me, as if he was in the water drowning, and I was on the shore. I swam in and asked him how I could help him and he said this, he said: "Help me out there! I can't make it alone, I've gone past pain I can bear." I could see it was true. He was elegantly dressed but emaciated, cadaverous. I gave him the help he wanted, I led him out in the water, it wasn't easy. Once he started to panic; I had to hold onto him tight as a lover till he got back his courage and said, "All right." The tide took him as light as a leaf. But just before I did that, and this is the oddest thing, he took out his wallet and thrust all the money in it into my hand. Here take this, he said to me. And I—

MRS. GOFORTH: Took it, did you, you took it?

CHRIS: The sea had no use for his money. The fish in the sea had no use for it, either, so I took it and went on where I was going.

MRS. GOFORTH: How much were you paid for this—service?

CHRIS: It was a very special difficult service. I was well paid for it.

MRS. GOFORTH: Did you tell the old Hindu, the Swami, when you got to his place, that you'd killed an old man on the way and—

CHRIS: I told him that I had helped a dying old man to get through it.

MRS. GOFORTH: What did he say about that?

CHRIS (*reflectively*): What did he say?—He said, "You've found your vocation," and he smiled. It was a beautiful smile in spite of showing bare gums, and—he held out his hand for the money. The hand was beautiful, too, in spite of being dry skin, pulled tight as a glove, over bones.

MRS. GOFORTH: Did you give him the money?

CHRIS: Yes, they needed the money. I didn't. I gave it to them.

MRS. GOFORTH: I *bet* you did.

CHRIS: I *did.*

MRS. GOFORTH: Did he say thank you for it?

CHRIS: I don't know if he did. You see, they— No, I guess you don't see. They had a belief in believing that too much is said, when feeling, quiet feelings—enough—says more. . . .

And he had a gift for gesture. You couldn't believe how a hand that shriveled and splotched could make such a beautiful gesture of holding out the hand to be helped up from the ground. It made me, so quickly, peaceful. That was important to me, that sudden feeling of quiet, because I'd come there, all the way down there, with the—the spectre of lunacy at my heels all the way— He said: "Stay."—We sat about a fire on the beach that night: Nobody said anything.

MRS. GOFORTH: No message, he didn't have any message?

CHRIS: Yes, that night it was silence, it was the meaning of silence.

MRS. GOFORTH: Silence? Meaning?

CHRIS: Acceptance.

MRS. GOFORTH: What of?

CHRIS: Oh, many things, everything, nearly. Such as how to live and to die in a way that's more dignified than most of us know how to do it. And of how not to be frightened of not knowing what isn't meant to be known, acceptance of not knowing *anything* but the moment of still existing, until we stop existing—and acceptance of that moment, too.

MRS. GOFORTH: How do you know he wasn't just an old faker?

CHRIS: How do you know that I'm not just a young one?

MRS. GOFORTH: I don't. You *are* what they call you!

CHRIS (*taking hold of her hand*): As much as *anyone* is what anyone calls him.

MRS. GOFORTH: A butcher is called a butcher, and that's what he is. A baker is called a baker, and he's a baker. A—

CHRIS: Whatever they're called, they're men, and being *men*, they're not known by themselves or anyone else.

MRS. GOFORTH (*presses a button that shrills on the stage*): Rudy? Rudy!

CHRIS: Your bodyguard's gone, Mrs. Goforth.

(*She goes on pressing the button.*)

He left with the contents of your strongbox, your safe.

MRS. GOFORTH:—I've got on me all my important jewels, and if Rudy's gone, I want you to go, too. Go on to your next appointment. You've tired me, you've done me in. This day has been the most awful day of my life. . . .

CHRIS: I know. That's why you need me here a while longer.

(*He places his arm about her.*)

MRS. GOFORTH: *Don't, don't.* You—*scare* me!

CHRIS: Let me take you into your bedroom, now, and put you to bed, Mrs. Goforth.

MRS. GOFORTH: *No, no,* GO. *Let me* GO!!

(*He releases her and picks up his canvas sack.*)

Hey!

(*He pauses with his back to her.*)

Did somebody tell you I was dying this summer? Yes, isn't that why you came here, because you imagined that I'd be ripe for a soft touch because I'm dying this summer? Come on, for once in your life be honestly frank, be frankly honest with someone! You've been tipped off that old Flora Goforth is about to go forth this summer.

CHRIS: Yes, that's why I came here.

MRS. GOFORTH: Well, I've escorted four husbands to the eternal threshold, and come back alone without them, just with the loot of *three* of them, and, ah, God, it was like I was building a shell of bone round my heart with their goddamn loot, their loot the material for it— It's my turn, now, to go forth, and I've got no choice but to do it. But I'll do it alone. I don't want to be escorted. I want to go forth alone. But you, you counted on touching my heart because you'd heard I was dying, and old dying people are your specialty, your vocation. But you miscalculated with this one. This milk train doesn't stop here anymore. I'll give you some practical advice. Go back to Naples. Walk along Santa Lucia, the bay-front. Yesterday, there, they smelt the smell of no money, and treated you like a used, discarded used person. It'll be different this time. You'll probably run into some Americans at a sidewalk table along there, a party that's in for some shopping from the islands. If you're lucky, they'll ask you to sit down with them and say, "Won't you have something, Chris?"—Well, *have* something, Chris! and if you play your cards right, they might invite you to go back to an island with them. Your best bet is strangers, I guess. Don't work on the young ones or anybody attractive. They're not ripe to be taken. And not the old ones, either, they've been taken too often.

Work on the middle-aged drunks, that's who to work on, Chris, work on them. Sometimes the old milk train still comes to a temporary stop at their crazy station, so concentrate on the middle-aged drunks in Naples.

CHRIS: This isn't the time for such—practical advice. . . .

(*She makes a gasping sound and presses a tissue to her mouth, turning away.*)

MRS. GOFORTH (*facing front*):— A paper rose . . . (*The tissue is dyed red with blood.*) Before you go, help me into my bedroom, I can't make it alone. . . .

(*He conducts her to the screen between the two rooms as the Stage Assistants advance from the wings to remove it.*)

—It's full of historical treasures. The chandelier, if the dealer that sold it to me wasn't a liar, used to hang in Versailles, and the bed, if he wasn't lying, was the bed of Countess Walewska, Napoleon's Polish mistress. It's a famous old bed, for a famous old body. . . .

(*The Stage Assistants remove the screen masking the bed.*)

CHRIS: Yes, it looks like the catafalque of an Empress. (*He lifts her onto the bed, and draws a cover over her.*)

MRS. GOFORTH: *Don't leave me alone till—*

CHRIS: I never leave till the end.

(*She blindly stretches out her jeweled hand. He takes it.*)

MRS. GOFORTH:—*Not so tight, the—*

CHRIS: I know, the rings cut your fingers.

(*He draws a ring off a finger. She gasps. He draws off another. She gasps again.*)

MRS. GOFORTH: Be here, when I wake up.

(*The Stage Assistants place before her bed the screen with the gold-winged griffin on the middle panel. Light dims out on that area, and is brought up on the turning mobile. Music seems to come from the turning mobile that casts very delicate gleams of light on the stage. Blackie appears on the forestage as the Stage Assistants bring out a dinner table and rapidly set two places. Then they cross to the flagstaff by the right wings and begin slowly to lower the flag.*)

ONE: Flag-lowering ceremony on the late Mrs. Goforth's mountain.

TWO: Bugle?

(*A muted bugle is heard from a distance.*)

That's not Taps, that's Reveille.

ONE: It's Reveille always, Taps never, for the gold griffin.

TWO: One more obvious statement is one too many. (*He snaps his fingers.*) Let's go.

(*They go out with the folded banner. Chris comes from behind the bedroom screen, onto the terrace where Blackie sits coolly waiting. She rises and pours wine into a medieval goblet as she speaks to Chris.*)

BLACKIE:—Is it—is she—?

(*Chris nods as he moves out onto the forestage.*)

Was it what they call "peaceful"?

(*Chris nods again.*)

With all that fierce life in her?

CHRIS: You always wonder afterwards where it's gone, so far, so quickly. You feel it must be still around somewhere, in the air. But there's no sign of it.

BLACKIE: Did she say anything to you before she—?

CHRIS: She said to me: "Be here when I wake up." After I'd taken her hand and stripped the rings off her fingers.

BLACKIE: What did you do with—?

CHRIS (*giving her a quick look that might suggest an understandable shrewdness*): Under her pillow like a Pharaoh's breakfast waiting for the Pharaoh to wake up hungry. . . .

(*Blackie comes up beside him on the forestage and offers him the wine goblet. A wave is heard breaking under the mountain.*)

BLACKIE: The sea is saying the name of your next mobile.

CHRIS: *Boom!*

BLACKIE: What does it mean?

CHRIS: It says "Boom" and that's what it means. No translation, no explanation, just "Boom." (*He drinks from the goblet and passes it back to her.*)

The Curtain Falls Slowly.

THE MUTILATED

PRODUCTION NOTE

The sets are as delicate as Japanese line drawings; they should be so abstract, so spidery, with the exception of Trinket Dugan's bedroom, that the audience will accept the nonrealistic style of the play.

The first set represents The Silver Dollar Hotel on South Rampart Street in New Orleans with the front wall lifted except for a doorframe to the lobby which contains only the desk and switchboard, stage left, a spring-ruptured old sofa, and a Christmas tree which has shed nearly bare of its needles. A few steps curve behind the back wall of the lobby indicating stairway to the floors above. The name of the hotel appears in pale blue neon above the skeleton structure a few moments after the curtain has risen on it.

The verses that appear preceding the play, after various scenes, and at the end of the play will be set to music and sung (probably *a cappella*) as "rounds" by a band of carollers. This band should comprise all the characters in the play and they will be signaled by a pitch pipe. Trinket and Celeste should sing in Trinket's room or as they descend the exterior stairs to the forestage.

SCENE ONE

The Silver Dollar Hotel on South Rampart Street—the old French Quarter in New Orleans. At the desk is seated the night clerk, Bernie, in a swivel chair that leans way back, permitting him to rest his feet on the low counter. He's reading a comic book. If the switchboard buzzes, he can make a connection with very slight change of position. There is a spindling outside staircase of gray wood to a landing on a level above. For some reason, possibly because it used to be a private frame residence, this stair-landing only has access to one room. This favored room is Trinket Dugan's. As the curtain rises, we hear the carollers sing the first verses of the carol.

CAROLLERS:

I think the strange, the crazed, the queer
Will have their holiday this year
And for a while, A little while,
There will be pity for the wild.
A miracle, A miracle!
A sanctuary for the wild.

I think the mutilated will
Be touched by hands that nearly heal,
At night the agonized will feel
A comfort that is nearly real.
A miracle, a miracle!
A comfort that is nearly real.

The constant star of wanderers
Will light the forest where they fall
And they will see and they will hear
A radiance, A distant call.
A miracle, a miracle!
A vision and a distant call.

At last for each someone may come
And even though he may not stay,
It may be softer where he was,
It may be sweeter where he lay.
A miracle, a miracle!
Stones may soften where he lay.

(*The carollers finish and disperse. Celeste and her brother, Henry, appear before the hotel. Celeste is a short, plump little woman with a large bosom of which she is excessively proud, wearing low-cut dresses by night and day. She has hennaed hair with bangs and her muskrat jacket was discovered one lucky day in the window of a thrift shop. She has a passion for satins because they fit close and catch light, and pearls cannot be big enough to suit her. She has a very large purse, for shoplifting. Her age is fifty; her spirit, unconquerable.*)

CELESTE: Come on in with me, Henry.

HENRY: No.

CELESTE: Aw, just for a minute. I want you to meet the nice boy on the desk nights. (*She says this with eager cordiality which is rebuffed by her undertaker-brother.*)

HENRY: Look. (*He has produced a notebook and a Waterman pen which he received for Christmas when he was a child of ten.*) I'm gonna write down the address of the Rainbow Bakery for you and the name of the man to talk to when you get down there.

CELESTE: Oh, good, do that, Henry, dear! (*She squeezes his stiff arm against her.*) A girl never had a sweeter brother than you! Y'know that, Henry? How much I appreciate it?

HENRY: I know from experience how much good this'll do. You got no more idea of earning an honest living than flying to the moon.

CELESTE: I'm gonna surprise you, Henry.

HENRY: You got any decent clothes to go to work in?

CELESTE: Blood is thicker than water, ain't it, Henry?

HENRY: I'm not talkin' about blood. I asked if you got a suitable thing to wear to the bakery Monday after New Year's.

CELESTE: I know where I can pick up some real sweet little housedresses, for less than five dollars each and I'll pay you back out of my first week's wages, Henry.

HENRY: You think I'm fool enough to advance you cash for housedresses when right this minute you are staring over my shoulder at the bar on the corner? Now put this address in that suitcase you carry around like a purse. Hell. The size of that old purse would mark you as a shoplifter even if every store in town didn't already know you as one. (*He hands her the bakery address.*)

CELESTE: Don't have my "specs." What's it say?

HENRY: It says 820 Carondelet. That's on a corner, at Carondelet and Dauphine.

CELESTE: Rainbow Bakery, Carondelet and Dauphine, bright and early the first Monday after New Year's. Bless you, Henry, you old sweet thing, you!

HENRY: I'll see if the cook has some old white uniforms for you. You got to wear white in a bakery, I reckon. Well. . . . Oh, what name shall I tell this man when I phone him you're coming?

CELESTE: What name, why my own name of course, Celeste Delacroix Griffin! I'm not ashamed to work in a bakery, Henry, I don't have false pride about it.

HENRY: You don't have pride true or false about anything ever. That's not the point. The point is I don't want you using my name any more. Not there nor anywhere else. I got children growing up here. I don't want you using our name. So give me a madeup name for me to give Mr. Noonan.

CELESTE: —Oh! —Well, give him the name—Agnes Jones. . . .

HENRY: OK. Agnes Jones. (*He starts off abruptly, then stops at the exit and calls back to her.*) —I'll also tell Mr. Noonan that ten a week from your salary gets held back for me till I recover the full amount that it cost me to get you out of the jug.

CELESTE (*calling after him*): See you for Xmas dinner tomorrow, Henry?

HENRY: I never want to see you again in my life, so bum your Xmas dinner off somebody else!

CELESTE: Henry, you don't mean that.

HENRY (*shouting back from a distance*): Yes, I do!

CELESTE: —Yes, he does. Yes, I guess he does. . . . (*A cold wind whines: she raises her hands to her bosom, crossing her arms.*) Well, this time last year, on Xmas eve, Trinket Dugan and I were in her bedroom upstairs. (*On this cue, Trinket Dugan's bedroom is lighted at a low level and we see Trinket in a Japanese kimono, pale rose-colored, seated on the edge of a small, peeling-white, iron bed, holding a schoolchild's notebook on her lap, biting a pencil, about to make an entry in her diary. Her victrola is playing very softly by the bed. A gallon jug of California Tokay is on a tiny table: the wine catches the light with a delicate, jewel-like glow.*)

TRINKET (*aloud*): Dear Diary! Dear Diary! —I have nothing to say. . . . (*She closes the book with a sigh and pours a glass of Tokay.*)

CELESTE: She's up in her room right now, and five will get you fifty, if I had five, that she's got herself a gallon jug of California Tokay. She's a terrible wino: can afford gin, drinks wine. . . . Well. She's rich and selfish. Purse-proud. But mutilated, oh, yes, ha ha, she's a mutilated woman. I know it, I'm the only one who knows it. —That's my ace-in-the-hole. I'm going up there now by these side stairs and offer the peace pipe to her, I'll tell her on the evening of Christ's birthday even a pair of old bitches like Trinket and Celeste should bury the hatchet, forget all past wounds that either's given the other, and drink a toast to the birth of the Babe in the Manger with a sweet golden wine, with Tokay. . . . (*The sound of drunk sailors singing is heard.*) Just a minute! —Business before pleasure. (*Bruno and Slim go by: she opens her mangy old fur to display her bosom but they pass right by, singing, as if she were invisible although she almost straddles the walk.*) Blind drunk! —Otherwise they would have noticed my bosom. Hell, even the sergeant on the desk when I checked out of the pokey took a good look at my bosom, didn't fail to observe it. Well, I'm mighty lucky to still be so firm-breasted when many women past forty or even thirty have boobs like a couple of mules hanging their heads over the top rail of a fence. (*She starts up the outside staircase but is distracted again by a street noise.*)

VOICE: *Bird-Girl, see the Bird-Girl, fifty cents, four bits to see the Bird-Girl!*

CELESTE: Oh-oh, oh-oh, Maxie and the Bird-Girl. (*She chuckles evilly.*) I can make out there if I play my cards right, he's gonna gather a crowd right on this corner, ah-*HAH*!

VOICE (*strident, approaching*): See the Bird-Girl, two bits to see the Bird-Girl!

CELESTE: *OH*-oh! —Dropped the price! (*A fat man, Maxie, appears before the hotel with a cloaked and hooded companion who moves with a shuffling, pigeon-toed gait.*) Hi, Maxie! Merry Xmas, Bird-Girl!

MAXIE (*viciously, to Celeste*): Git lost, yuh bum! —See the Bird-Girl, two bits to see the Bird-Girl uncovered, unmasked, the world's greatest freak attraction! (*A few drifters pause on the walk. A drunk staggers out of the Silver Dollar Hotel, digging in his pocket for a quarter.*)

CELESTE (*seeing the drunk is a live one*): Shoot, that's no Bird-Girl, I know her personally. That's Rampart Street Rose with chicken feathers glued to her. It's a painful, dangerous thing, I know from experience, Mister. (*She turns to the Bird-Girl again.*) Hey, Rose, how much does Maxie pay you, how much is he payin' you, Rosie? (*Maxie raises a threatening hand over his head. The Bird-Girl makes angry bird noises.*) Maxie? Maxie? (*She rushes up close to him.*) I ain't gonna expose you, just give me five dollars, Maxie. I just got out of the pokey, gimme five bucks, will yuh? For a Xmas bottle? Huh, Maxie? To keep my mouth shut, Maxie?

VERY FAST OVERLAPPED

MAXIE: I'll shut your fat mouth for you, for less'n five dollars!

CELESTE: Don't raise your hand at me, Maxie!

MAXIE: Go on, go on, get lost!

CELESTE: Why, I was the Bird-Girl myself! Have you forgotten I was the Bird-Girl myself? Got two-degree burns when you put that hot glue on me?

MAXIE: You want trouble? You want trouble, you want?

BIRD-GIRL: *Awk awk awk!*

CELESTE: No, I want two dollars and twenty cents to buy a half gallon of California Tokay.

(*A cop enters. The Bird-Girl whistles and croaks wildly as she flaps off.*)

COP: Break it up.

MAXIE: She's scared th' Bird-Girl away!

BIRD-GIRL (*offstage*): AWK AWK AWK!

MAXIE (*running after her*): Bird-Girl, hey, Bird-Girl! (*He whistles shrilly. The wind howls.*)

CELESTE (*picking up a loose feather*): Poor Rosie, she lost some feathers, ah, well that's life for you, tch, tch! If she was a bird, the humane society would be interested in her situation but since she's a human being, they couldn't care less. (*She turns to the Cop*): How about that? I mean the irony of it? (*The wind whines coldly.*)

COP: Where you live?

CELESTE: My address? Here, right here! Hotel Silver Dollar.

COP: Get off the street. . . .

CELESTE: Aw, now really!

COP: I know you from night court, go in and stay off the street. (*He moves on. Another sailor appears: Celeste opens her coat, hopefully displaying her bosom.*)

CELESTE: Hello, there, Merry Christmas!

SAILOR (*shoving past her*): Get lost. (*Her vivacious smile fades: she closes her coat like a book with a sad ending.*)

CELESTE: —I am. . . . (*She means lost.*) —When you're lost in this world you're lost and not found, the lost-and-found department is just the lost department, but I'm going in that lobby like I've just come back from the biggest social event of the Goddam season, no shit. . . . (*She starts to the door but freezes just outside it.*) Well, I'll count five and then enter. One. —Two. —Three. —Four. —Four and one-half. —Four and three-quarters. . . . (*Trinket starts a loud lively record on her victrola: four-four tempo—"Santiago Waltz."*) Hmm. Sounds like she's trying to boost her morale up there. I used to boost her morale. I'd say to her every day, forget your mutilation, it's not the end of the world for you or the world. Hell, I'd say, we all have our mutilations, some from birth, some from long before birth, and some from later in life, and some stay with us forever. Well, there's nothing like a week in the pokey to bring out the philosopher in you, but in me it's brought out the chicken in me, too. Scared to enter the lobby of a flea-bag. Four and seven-eighths. —No. Nope. —I need to be morally fortified before I count to five and face that lobby. . . . (*She turns to the outside staircase.*) —What'll I say to her? Well, I'll think of something when I— (*She goes on up to the landing and knocks at the outside door of Trinket's room.*)

TRINKET: Who's knocking at my door?

CELESTE: Me, Celeste, let's bury the hatchet for Christmas.

TRINKET: —We can't bury the hatchet. We hit each other too hard, and now it's too late to forget it.

CELESTE: Think of the wonderful times we had together!

TRINKET: They weren't wonderful times. We bummed around town together, I took you to breakfast, I took you to lunch, I took you to dinner. I took you to the movies. In return for all those favors, I just got envy, resentment, and sly insinuations that if I didn't go on sucking up to you, just for company in my time of despair, you'd give away my secret.

CELESTE: That's not true. No soul knows about your mutilation but me.

TRINKET: You kept reminding me of it. That no soul knew about my mutilation except Celeste. Why would you do that if you didn't mean to threaten me with exposure?

CELESTE: People don't trust each other. I was afraid you'd suddenly get tired of me, bored with me! Trinket? Let me in! I'm scared to pass through the lobby.

TRINKET: —They've checked you out, you've lost your room here, Celeste.

CELESTE: That's what I was afraid of: I suspected! —I see you're drinking Tokay. Let me in for a drink, it will give me the courage to face my situation in the lobby.

TRINKET: Celeste, we're through with each other. You know why. Remember the night you wanted to eat at Commander's Palace in the Garden District? I wanted to eat Chinese. . . . (*She starts addressing the audience instead of Celeste.*) I wanted some Moo Goo Gai Pan at the Chinese place on Dauphine Street. Oh, no, she said, no. If you want to eat boiled rats, go eat Chinese. —I wouldn't dream of it, I told her. Of course I knew two things: she couldn't afford a hamburger at the White Castle, and Moo Goo Gai Pan is made from water chestnuts, snow peas, and breast of chicken, one of the world's most famous and delicate dishes. I turned away from her and walked on without her toward the Chinaman's place. Pretty soon, in fact in less than a minute, I heard the rat-tat-tat of her high heels in pursuit. She caught my elbow. I faced her, her face was *livid* with *hate*. "Who knows except me about your mutilation? Have

I ever exposed you?!" "Let me go, go, go, go," I said, "let me go! Go to Commander's Palace," I said, "or Galatoire's and feast yourself on any dish you crave with imported wine, but go, go, go, let me go, I'm eating Chinese: I want to and I do what I want to!" —Know what she said, then, to me? *"Eat Chinese, you mutilated monster!"* —Well, that didn't improve our friendship. That terminated our friendship. Can you blame me? To taunt an old friend because of a mutilation in order to get a free meal in the place she wanted? (*Celeste resumes pounding at the stair-landing door.*) Go, go, go, go away, it's too late to bury the hatchet!

CELESTE: No, no!

TRINKET: Go, go!

CELESTE: Let me just pass through the room. People are kind at Christmas!

TRINKET: You just want to get in here because you can see this wine and you're a wino!

CELESTE: Me, a wino?

TRINKET: A notorious wino!

CELESTE: You call *me* a wino, sitting in there with your big economy jug of California Tokay, so big you can hardly carry it half a block down Rampart, you being too cheap to have it delivered to you? Ho-ho! (*She rattles the doorknob.*)

TRINKET (*springing up wildly*): Go, go, go, go away, you merciless monster, before I call downstairs to get the police!

CELESTE: You fink, you freak! I'll get even with you, oh, will I ever get even with you, Trinket Dugan! Alias Agnes Jones! (*She rushes back downstairs and into the lobby with an air of bravado. Bernie, the night clerk, has his feet still propped on the desk and the comic book in his lap. Celeste is bold as brass.*) Hi, Bernie, Merry Xmas! Guess what's happened!

BERNIE: Yeah, you got sprung for Christmas.

CELESTE: Got what, Bernie, what, baby?

BERNIE: They let you out of the pokey for Xmas, did they?

CELESTE: Bernie, Bernie, you're lost in the comic-book world, God bless you and let me kiss you, you big sexy thing you, I could jump over this desk and just gobble you up. Oh, baby, let's have a quickie right now, in a vacant room.

BERNIE: —I got a message for you.

CELESTE: Boy, oh, baby, have I got a message for *you*!

BERNIE: Yeah, I bet, but the message I got for you is your stuff's locked up, and is gonna be held in storage till you've paid up your bill here.

CELESTE: —I don't understand this message.

BERNIE: Repeat it to yourself a couple of times and maybe you'll understand it.

CELESTE: You said my stuff—locked up? My personal belongings, no, I don't get this message, it's such a peculiar message that I could repeat it over and over and still be mystified by it.

BERNIE (*making switchboard connections*): Aw, come off it, everyone knows that knows you that you've been in the House of Detention, because you got caught shoplifting at Goodman's department store Monday. You're coming down fast in the world, you used to shoplift at the Canal Street stores and—

CELESTE: What a lie, who said so?

BERNIE: It come out in the papers. *Picayune*, *Item* and *States*.

CELESTE: Show me the item so I can call my lawyer.

BERNIE: I don't save clippings, press clippings, for kleptos, sister.

CELESTE: It was a false accusation to begin with. My brother, Henry Delacroix Griffin, set them straight and also has got me a job, that's the news, the message, I rushed in here to let you be first to know of it.

BERNIE: It's about time you quit hustling, not because you think so but because the guys you hustle for the price of a bottle or a couple of drinks have eyes to see you with, sister, and what they see is a wino, long in the tooth.

CELESTE: Is this any way to talk to a girl at Xmas?

BERNIE (*with an amiable grin*): Aw, no, face it, you can't make it, Celeste, can't even get away with a little shoplifting at Christmas.

CELESTE (*grandly*): Give me the key to my room, I don't want to stay in this lobby.

BERNIE: You don't have a room here no more. You been checked out and your stuff locked up in the basement by order of Katz.

CELESTE: Katz wouldn't do this to me. When did he do this to me?

BERNIE: When it come out in the papers that a lady identifying herself as Miss Agnes Jones had been arrested shoplifting.

CELESTE: —Agnes Jones is who? Not me!—sounds like a made-up name. My name is Celeste Delacroix Griffin.

BERNIE: Yeah, but we were tipped off that you give a made-up name when the cops picked you up and it's Agnes Jones.

CELESTE: —Who told you such a false story?

BERNIE: Trinket, your old friend, Trinket, saw the newspaper item about your shoplifting rap and said, "Agnes Jones? It's Celeste!"

CELESTE: Me? Agnes Jones? Not me! Agnes Jones is the name she gave at Mercy Hospital when she— I never spoke of it before. She used the name Agnes Jones for her secret operation. (*There is a pause: contemplation.*) I got to go upstairs, I got to go to the little girls' room a minute.

BERNIE: Use the toilet down here.

CELESTE: Get crabs for Christmas? I don't want crabs for Christmas. You use it if you want to be infested with crabs but I'm going to the upstairs john. (*She crosses to the stairs off the lobby and goes up. Bernie answers a switchboard call.*)

BERNIE: Silver Dollar Hotel. —No, gone. —I said GONE. —People *go*! —Checked out of here and left no forwardin' address. Sorry, Merry Christmas. . . . (*The switchboard rings again as Bernie is plugging out. He answers this second ring.*)

TRINKET (*at the phone in her room*): Bernie, is she down there? I mean Celeste.

BERNIE: She's not in the lobby right now.

TRINKET: Good! Then I can come down. I don't want to run into her. (*Bernie plugs out. He unpeels a candy bar and starts munching on it slowly with lazy enjoyment. Celeste returns to the desk with an oddly accomplished smile, more than a mere visit to the "loo" would account for.*)

CELESTE (*excitedly malicious*): —I see there's been a Christmas celebration. Was it organized by Trinket Dugan? Did she put on her Santie Claus suit and ring a cowbell under that sorry tree? I never seen a worse-decorated tree, broken ornaments on it and needles already shedding, it sure looks sad. —Sample bottles of cheap perfume for the ladies and dime-store ties for the gents? Ha ha! Christmas is something you got to do big or don't do it. (*There is a pause.*

Bernie munches his candy bar. Celeste hugs her bosom as if she were still on the chilly street. She watches him munching slowly at his candy bar as he reads a book of cartoons.) Whatcha eatin', Bernie, a candy bar? (*Bernie barely grunts.*) What kind of candy bar is it? O Henry? Baby Ruth? (*Picking up the candy wrapper.*) Aw. A Mr. Goodbar. I never have had one of them. I'm a Hershey milk-chocolate girl. The only thing better than a Hershey milk-chocolate bar is a Hershey almond bar, Bernie. They used to come in the fifty-cent size, when I was in convent school. A girlfriend of mine and me would buy us that fifty-cent bar and eat away on it all afternoon. —Dibs on the last bite, Bernie. Huh? Dibs on the last bite, Bernie? They give me the cold-turkey treatment in the pokey, and that, that—treatment, it—it leaves you with an awful craving for sweets . . . —My mouth is watering, Bernie!

BERNIE: —Yeh, well, swallow or spit. . . . (*He finishes the bar and leans back in his swivel chair, eyes falling shut.*)

CELESTE: —In summer the chocolate sticks to the candy wrapper but in the winter, the wrapper comes off clean . . . (*She licks a tiny bit of chocolate off the candy wrapper.*) —It sure comes off clean in winter. . . .

BERNIE (*sleepily*): Why don't you give up?

CELESTE: Give up, did you say? An easy piece of advice to give but not to follow. (*She moves back to the ruptured sofa under the Christmas tree, removes from the tree a garland of popcorn, and munches it as she speaks.*) Give up? My life? Oh, no. I still have longings, and as long as you have longings, satisfaction is possible. Appetites? —Satisfaction's always possible, Bernie. Cravings? Such as a craving for sweets or liquor or love? Satisfaction is still possible, Bernie, and on a give-and-take basis. Why, just today a man was talking to me. He didn't look in my eyes. He kept his eyes on my breasts. At last I laughed, I said, "Touch 'em, they won't break, they're not soap bubbles and they're not a padded brassiere." —Bernie? —Bernie! —How would you like a quickie in my old room? It wouldn't be the first time, would it, Bernie?

BERNIE: Give up.

CELESTE (*sitting back down*): —Give up is something I never even think of. I'll go on—not to the Rainbow Bakery after

New Year's, that's not for me. —I'm too imaginative to fool with bread. Bread is something that has to be broken in kindness, in friendship or understanding as it was broken among the Apostles at Our Lord's Last Supper. Gee, the cold-turkey treatment sure does leave you hungry and with such a craving for sweets that if I was employed right now at the Rainbow Bakery, the doughnuts and pastry and fruit-cakes, cream puffs and—last year Trinket Dugan had some little fancy cornucopias full of hard candy on the tree, now just stale popcorn. —Katz is a long man to wait for. . . . When do you think he'll— (*Trinket enters the lobby by the interior stairway, she is wild-eyed, shaken. Celeste has snatched up an old copy of the Saturday Evening Post; she has raised it to cover her face but is peeking over the top of the dirty cover.*)

BERNIE (*making a switchboard connection*): Silver Dollar.

TRINKET (*faintly*): Bernie?

CELESTE (*giggling*): —What a funny cartoon! You can't beat the cartoons in the *Saturday Evening Post*!

BERNIE (*into the phone*): No such party here. Nope, no such party. (*He unplugs.*)

TRINKET (*louder*): Bernie! May I speak to you, please?

BERNIE: Sure. What?

TRINKET: Come outside for a moment. This is private, Bernie.

BERNIE: I can't leave the switchboard, Miss Dugan.

TRINKET: I think you'd better. This is a serious matter. I can't speak to you about it in front of that woman.

CELESTE: What a funny cartoon, it's a scream, ho ho ho!

TRINKET: This is something that may call for legal action.

CELESTE (*turning a page*): Here's another funny one, ho ho ho!

TRINKET: On several occasions I found signs that my bed-room had been entered while I was out. Not by the hall door but by the outside entrance, from the stairs outside. The lock wasn't broken. It was entered by someone who held a key to that entrance. Only one person did. Consequently I knew who'd been coming in. Still I re-frained from reporting it to the police: out of pity, Bernie, I made no report, no complaint, although the sneak had been drinking up my wine and picking up money that I deliberately left on the bureau, out of pity. This is a person, Bernie, that I have befriended over a long, long period. You might say supported, even. Bernie, you know that I could afford to stay at a first-class hotel but I've stayed here out of loyalty and friendship. I dressed that Christmas tree. I bought a gift for everyone registered here and put them under the tree. To all employees I passed out a five-dollar gold piece. I pity transients at Christmas. This hotel is full of derelicts, Bernie, lost, lonely, homeless at Christmas. (*Her voice is high and shaky.*) Heaven knows what secret sorrows they carry with them! And very few care!

CELESTE (*throwing down the magazine*): Bernie, get her some music to go with that speech!

TRINKET (*her voice rising*): I've been lucky, financially. I'm not boasting about it. I feel humbly grateful about it. My daddy left me three oil wells in West Texas; one is bone-dry right now, one comes in now and then but the number three well is a gusher, it's a continual gusher. Now, Bernie. I'm not purse-proud. See this? (*She removes a large wad of paper money from her purse.*) —I never walk out of the Silver Dollar Hotel without a wad of money that you could choke a horse with. That's not what I do with it, though. I have a horde of friends in financial trouble. As long as they're loyal to me, I'm devoted to them. I give out gifts called loans, expecting no repayment, except in friendship, Bernie. Bernie, go up to the stair landing and see what some vicious person has scratched on the wall up there. It has to come off right away.

BERNIE: Something's written up there?

TRINKET: No, not written, scratched, I said, scratched, probably with a nail file.

BERNIE: Well, I'll go take a look.

TRINKET (*breathlessly*): Yes, please do, thank you, Bernie. (*He goes up the few steps that curve behind the back wall of the lobby.*)

CELESTE (*in a fierce whisper*): I told you I'd get even. This is just the beginning.

TRINKET: Yes, I knew who did it.

CELESTE: I spent every day for years, for years!

TRINKET: Living off me!

CELESTE: Cheering you up, getting you out of depression, distracting you from your mutilation, you know it! (*Bernie comes back to the lobby.*)

BERNIE: Miss Dugan, I seen it but I don't know how to remove it because it's scratched in the wall.

TRINKET: Cover it with something, with a, with a—with a "no smoking" sign.

BERNIE: The only sign we got's a "no loitering" sign in the downstairs washroom and it wouldn't make sense on the landing.

TRINKET: Cover it up with this calendar. (*She points to a pictorial calendar over the desk.*)

BERNIE: I don't have no thumbtacks here.

TRINKET: Use adhesive tape, then.

BERNIE: Don't have that neither.

TRINKET (*putting money in his hands*): Run to the drugstore next door and get some adhesive tape, fast as you can. Nobody must go up or down those stairs till that vicious lie about me is covered up. Hurry. Otherwise the Silver Dollar Hotel will lose its only good tipper. And for New Year's I'm planning to pass out presents again!

BERNIE: OK, OK.

TRINKET: I'll watch the switchboard for you. (*Bernie goes out. There is a dead silence in lobby. Trinket speaks without looking at Celeste.*) If I were you, I wouldn't sit there much longer.

CELESTE: The calendar won't stay up.

TRINKET: If it doesn't, I'll know who's taken it down and I'll take action.

CELESTE: What action?

TRINKET: *Action!*

CELESTE: How do you know it won't appear other places? There's other places, it might break out like a plague.

TRINKET: Yes, in the House of Detention! Print it on the walls in the House of Detention, cover the prison walls with it!

BERNIE (*returning*): Got it.

TRINKET: Here's the calendar: *hurry!* (*Bernie goes up the short curving flight of steps and disappears behind the back wall of the lobby. The two women are silent.*)

CELESTE (*rising from sofa*): How much a discount do you get on a Xmas tree from last year? I'm covered with needles off it. (*She brushes herself elaborately.*)

TRINKET: I would like for you to return me the key to my outside entrance. I'd be much obliged if you hand it back to me right now so I won't have to put a padlock and a burglar alarm on that door.

CELESTE: I thrown it away long ago.

TRINKET: You know I know that's a lie, and let me warn you that if tonight I discover any evidence that you've been in my room while I'm out, you'll find yourself right back in the House of Detention, yes, right back there tonight.

CELESTE: Tonight I'll be at my brother's for eggnog and fruitcake. Huey P. Long will be there. I love the Kingfish and he seems to find me amusing.

TRINKET: Who *doesn't* find you *absurd*!

CELESTE: Uh-huh, well, I won't be alone with a continual gusher of jealousy in my heart, tonight and all other nights, forever and ever, Amen. (*Bernie returns to the lobby.*)

BERNIE: OK, I got it covered.

CELESTE: So long, Agnes Jones. (*She exits to the street.*)

TRINKET (*to Bernie*): You don't believe it, do you? That vicious lie about me?

BERNIE: Hell, Miss Dugan, I got my own business to mind.

TRINKET: —I—*can't imagine! Impossible to imagine*—malice like *that*! (*The lobby dims out as she goes out to the street and the carollers sing.*)

SCENE TWO

On the forestage is a bench in Jackson Park. Behind it, on the scrim, is a projection of the equestrian statue of Andrew Jackson. Trinket enters and sits on the bench, stiffly.

TRINKET: It's going to take me a little while to recover from that shock. I'm still shivering from it. Yes, I felt close to panic, but now I'll get hold of myself. —Why do I care so much? There's nothing shameful, nothing criminal about an affliction, a—mutilation. . . . (*She shakily lights a cigarette.*) I am *not* Agnes Jones, I am Trinket Dugan, and *I have absolutely no intention of giving up, not a bit in the world, wouldn't dare to or—care to!* —Tonight I'll drive out Agnes Jones, I'll do it right now. How? I'll walk around this bench and when I've walked around it, Agnes Jones will be out of me and never get back in! (*She springs up. The sudden action makes her dizzy: she falls back onto the bench and gasps for breath. Then she rises and starts a slow march about the bench.*) Out, Agnes Jones, out, Agnes Jones, out Agnes Jones. (*She has returned to the front of the bench.*) There, now. It's such a clear, frosty night, I can see my breath in the air and, yes, I'm calming down now. I knew I would and I am. (*She sways a bit and falls back onto the bench. Now she speaks in a different voice: harsh with anger and self-contempt.*) —In the afternoons, old people with nothing else to do come here and stay and stay till the sun is fading away. When they leave here, I come here. I'm the night bench-sitter of Jackson Square. The gates are closed at midnight. It's nearly midnight. My hands are still shaky. It's time for me to go to the Cafe Boheme and have my absinthe frappé at a corner table with an empty chair across from me. Overtipping as if it was necessary to apologize for sitting alone at a table meant for two. *Two!* In life there *has* to be two! —The old winter voice of Agnes Jones is still in me. I said OUT, Agnes Jones, out, out, out and stay out! Once more around the bench. (*She marches around the bench again.*) —But of course I do have to prepare myself for the possibility that Celeste will be in the Cafe Boheme tonight, and when I come in, is likely to make a vicious remark of some kind. Oh, I'd—sink through the floor, I'd never be able to enter the place again! —OUT, AGNES JONES! (*She arrives in front of the bench.*) —Such a clear, frosty night. Andrew Jackson is all wet, shiny green like he'd rode up out of the sea. Oh, with so much beauty around me, yes, still, even now, why should I have room in me for the ugly, cowardly voice of Agnes Jones. Too much solitude can be corrected, yes, it *must* be corrected. I will correct solitude by—what? —Why not enter the Cafe Boheme tonight like a gladiator, shouting:

"Here I am, the mutilated Trinket Dugan alias—Agnes Jones!" No! Impossible! Couldn't! Not necessary! She can't prove the mutilation unless I expose it to someone. Oh, but not daring to expose the mutilation has made me go without love for three years now, and it's the lack of what I need most that makes me speak to myself with the bitter-old, winter-cold voice of—Agnes Jones: LOVE! —a hand on my *breast. . . .* (*She makes a sound like a hooked fish would make if it could make a sound. She rises, then sits back down: she gives way not to despair but to some inner convulsion which makes her produce these dreadful soft cries. They are accompanied by abrupt, indecisive movements to rise or reach out or— Gradually they subside: she pulls herself together.*) No. No more negative thoughts. Tonight I'll give myself the Christmas gift of a lover, yes, I'll find him tonight and he will be—beautiful! Perfect! —Perhaps he'll be kind, even, so kind I can tell him about my—mutilation. (*She acts out the admission.*) "There's something I feel I should tell you before I—before we—" COULDN'T—get the words out! —Oh, but I'll think of something, if I find him tonight, if that miracle happens tonight at the Cafe Boheme!

VOICE (*offstage*): Gates closing!

TRINKET: Gates closing, must go. . . .

(*She leaves as the bench is dimmed out. The carollers enter.*)

CAROLLERS:

The lost will find a public place
Where their names are not unknown
And there, oh, there an act of grace
May lift the weight of stone on stone.
A miracle, a miracle!
The finding of a love unknown.

Oh, but to love they need to know
How to walk upon fresh snow
And leave no footprint where they go,
Walking on new-fallen snow.
A miracle, a miracle!
No footprint on new-fallen snow.

The wounded and the fugitive,
The solitary ones will know
Somewhere a place that's set apart
A place of stillness cool as snow.
A miracle, a miracle!
A place that quiets the outraged heart.

It may be in a public park
That has a bench that's set apart,
And not by daylight, after dark,
With winter mist upon the park.
A miracle, a miracle!
A mist that veils a winter park.

SCENE THREE

The park bench is removed and the scene becomes the interior of the Cafe Boheme. The bar is shaped like a horseshoe; inside is standing Tiger, the proprietor, who was formerly a boxer and a seaman and who is now in his fifties. About the bar are several patrons. The sound of an ambulance is now receding into the distance. Trinket Dugan appears in the lighted area.

TRINKET: Merry Christmas! (*She gets no response. Has Celeste been there, talking against her? She is uncertain whether to stay in the bar, but where else is there to go? Nowhere. She slips quietly, then, to a solitary table, beside the bar. . . . There is a slight pause.*)

WOMAN AT BAR: I can't believe it! Can you? Alive and laughing one second, dead the next!

PIOUS QUEEN (*at the bar*): He told a very sacrilegious story.

TIGER: Hell, don't you think that God has a sense of humor? Ted just laughed a little too loud and bust a blood vessel. Maybe God laughed too.

WOMAN AT BAR: And "bust a blood vessel" too?

TIGER: —It wasn't a bad way to go.

TRINKET (*sitting up straight and stiff and calling out shrilly*): WHO DIED? DID SOMEBODY DIE?

TIGER: Yeah, somebody died, so he died. Somebody always dies, don't he? What yours, Trinket? Name your drinks, everybody, it's all on the house in memory of the deceased. (*They murmur their drinks. Trinket calls out hers as loudly as if she was furious over something: a hand has risen to her mutilated bosom.*)

TRINKET: Absinthe frappé, please, Tiger! (*The old electric piano is started again: it plays another ragtime tune or medley, starting with "Under the Bamboo Tree," as two sailors enter. One is short, named Bruno, one tall, called Slim. Everyone turns to glance at them: it's the tall one they look at, because he shines like a star. Suddenly, Trinket calls shrilly.*) "Tiger, Tiger, burning bright!" —I need my absinthe frappé!

SLIM: Is this the place?

BRUNO: Yeh, yeh, this is the place.

SLIM: Where is he?

BRUNO: What're you shouting about?

SLIM: Why should I whisper, what's there to whisper about?

BRUNO: Don't make you'self conspicuous in this place.

SLIM: Why? Is they somethin' wrong with it?

BRUNO: No. They's nothin' wrong with it except it's special. You notice how quiet people are?

SLIM: Yeah. The place is spooky. Why's a place so quiet on Xmas Eve?

BRUNO: Sit down at the bar.

SLIM: Where's your rich friend, is he here or not here? I want to go if he ain't.

BRUNO: We are ten minutes early.

TIGER: Boys, you can't stay here. This place is off limits to the Navy.

BRUNO: We're just lookin' for someone.

TIGER: Who're you lookin' for, Mac?

BRUNO: —A—a—fellow I met on my last liberty here.

TIGER: What's his name?

BRUNO: His name was Ted.

TIGER: If you mean Ted Dinwiddie, Ted Dinwiddie is dead.

BRUNO: No kidding.

SLIM: Jesus, come on, let's go. I knew somebody had died here.

WOMAN AT BAR: He died here tonight. Screamed and fell off that barstool an hour ago.

PIOUS QUEEN: This one, right next to me.

WOMAN: Th' coroner said he was probably already dead when he hit the floor. . . .

TRINKET (*rising and crossing to the bar*): That is no way to break the news of a death!

SLIM: He died and he's dead, let's go.

BRUNO: Hell, I need a drink first.

TRINKET: The news of a death is shocking to anyone living and it ought to be broken more gently.

BRUNO: Gimme a C.C. and Seven.

TIGER: I told you, you're off limits here.

PIOUS QUEEN (*rising from the barstool*): Boys, boys, I have a room next door and I can provide you both with civilian outfits. In civvies, you know, you can go anywhere in town.

TRINKET: Your clothes wouldn't fit these boys. I have a better suggestion. (*She grips Bruno's elbows.*) Get your buddy outside, I'll wait by the door. (*She goes out of the bar. The electric piano starts up and the voices fade as Trinket departs. She waits tensely on the forestage, then suddenly runs back into the bar, calling out—*) Shore Police are coming!

SLIM: I got no liberty pass.

TIGER: Go out the back way.

BRUNO: I got a liberty pass, I'll go out front. Slim, you go in the "head." (*The light on the bar area dims out as the sailors run in separate directions. Bruno, the short sailor, comes out and stands beside Trinket.*)

TRINKET: Here they come. (*She means the Shore Police: she advances to intercept them as the lights dim out.*) Merry Christmas, boys.

SCENE FOUR

As the scrim closes and lights come up on forestage, the Shore Police ignore Trinket and ask to see Bruno's liberty pass which he produces very slowly.

TRINKET: —He's got his pass: he is my little brother, we are just standing here discussing where to go next.

SHORE POLICE: Yeah, well, don't go in here, this place is off limits.

TRINKET: Oh, we're not going in that bar, we're going to the—the cathedral for the midnight candlelight service. Aren't we, Buddy?

BRUNO: Yes, ma'am. —Sister. (*The Shore Police "case" the bar; they look offstage and then depart.*)

TRINKET: —That's that. Now get your buddy.

BRUNO: I don't wanna insult you, but we're not out looking for whores.

TRINKET: Oh, I'm not insulted, I'm—flattered, but you couldn't be more mistaken. Here, looky here. (*She opens her purse and produces a roll of large bills.*) —See this roll of greenbacks? You could choke a horse with it, if you wanted to choke a horse, but who wants to choke a horse. So money isn't my problem, my problem is not economic, my problem is— (*She raises a trembling hand to her left breast.*)

BRUNO: Is what?

TRINKET: —Human, a human problem. Only one person knows it besides myself. Only one other person in the world knows about it but me.

BRUNO: What's your problem?

TRINKET: This other person who knows it was a person I trusted, but now, just tonight, she betrayed me: in such a horrible way, she— (*She clenches a gloved fist in the air.*)

BRUNO: Are you scared to tell me this problem?

TRINKET: It's a thing, it's a thing, a— (*She can't force herself to confess it.*)

BRUNO (*chuckling*): Everything is a thing.

TRINKET: This is a thing that—

BRUNO: You got a nice little body—have you ever done it outdoors?

TRINKET: What? No!

BRUNO: I've done it outdoors in the Quarter. You just slip between two buildings, out of the light, and it's just as private as it would be in your room.

TRINKET: You're talking about alley cats, and you don't understand: I'm attracted to your friend, I'm waiting out here for him. Get him out of the bar before the wolves snatch him away.

BRUNO: Him? Slim? He's ignorant like a baby. I'm experienced at it.

TRINKET: Slim, his name's Slim?

BRUNO: Forget him.

TRINKET (*calling out*): Slim! Slim! (*Bruno makes another effort to put his hand under her cape. She cries out in panic.*) Stop it! I'm mutilated! (*At this exact moment Celeste's loud, drunken voice is heard.*)

CELESTE: Jingle bells, jingle bells, jingle bells, jingle—bells—jingle—bells. . . . (*It seems to be all she remembers of the song.*)

TRINKET: Oh, God, it's her, it's Celeste, stand in front of me, hide me! (*She clutches Bruno by the lapels of his pea jacket and draws them about her, pressing her face to his chest as Celeste appears and stalks across the forestage, still tonelessly singing.*)

CELESTE: Jingle bells, jingle bells, jingle bells, jingle bells, jingle all the—jingle all the—*wayyyyy*! (*On the word "wayyyyy," she arrives at the lamp post and turns front, opening her coat, her eyes very wide in a farcically lascivious way. She must be trying to attract the attention of someone across the street. Then she resumes the hoarse, toneless chant and stalks off.*)

TRINKET: —Ahhh, God, has she gone? That awful demented creature goes singing at night through the Quarter to catch the attention of near- and far-sighted drunks, and when they hear her in the Cafe Boheme, they all laugh, they all say, "There goes old Madame Goat." Did she see me, she didn't see me, did she? If she'd seen me, she would have shouted a criminal slander about me for which I would have her locked up. Now! Quick! Find your buddy! It's him that I want for Christmas! (*She moves a few steps from Bruno, so that the rest of the speech will seem addressed to herself, rhapsodically.*) Tall, crowned with gold that's so gold it's like his head had caught fire, and I know, I remember the kind of skin that goes with flame-colored hair, it's like snow, it's like sunlight on snow, I remember, I know! (*Slim appears with Celeste, entering from the left. She is stoutly supporting his tall, wobbly frame. Trinket cries out—*) Oh, God, he's been snagged by an old wino, get him away from her, quick! That woman's criminal, a shoplifter, a convicted klepto, evicted, takes old men up alleys for the price of a drink!

CELESTE: *I heard that remark, Agnes Jones!* (*She squares off like a bull about to charge. There should be flashes of bluish-white light on the stage as if an acetylene torch, a soundless one, was drilling the street, throwing fantastically long, tall shadows over the street-fronts. Inside the bar, the electric piano plays a* paso-doble.)

TRINKET: Just out of jail, less than an hour ago, I swear, I swear! Get him away from her quick, quick! She is infested with vermin, lice, LICE!

CELESTE: *I heard that remark!* (*She stamps like a bull pawing the earth before charging.*)

BRUNO: Slim? Hey, Slim! (*But Bruno doesn't approach Celeste who stands guarding Slim.*)

TRINKET (*in a transport, an ecstasy of fury*): Don't just *call* him, go *GET* him!

CELESTE: *Try.* He's felt my *bosom*! He's felt my *breasts*, *both* of them!

TRINKET (*wildly*): *Shut up, for God's sake, be still!* (*Celeste spits at her from a distance.*) SHE SPITS! —Where's the toad? Wherever a witch spits it produces a *toad*! (*Bruno is amused, now, chuckling drunkenly. Slim rests against the proscenium, with a weak, vague grin.*)

SLIM: Cat-fight.

BRUNO: C'mon, this one here's got money.

SLIM: Aw, frig 'em all.

TRINKET: Oh, I—have a *warning* for you! Celeste? Let me give you this warning! I have engaged the biggest lawyer in town, a criminal lawyer, that never loses a case and I will spare no expense, *no expense*!—to have you committed to the State Hospital for the CRIMINAL INSANE! —Bread and water, not wine! That's what you'll— (*Celeste suddenly charges forward and snatches Trinket's purse from her.*) *Thief, thief, stop thief!* (*With an Indian war whoop, Celeste has dashed offstage. Slim slides slowly down the proscenium edge till he sits against it. There is a change of light and music. The electric piano goes into a number such as "Please Don't Talk About Me When I'm Gone."*) Hah! She snatched an empty purse! I had my money out, look, here, in my hand! (*She holds up her roll of bills.)* —Now, hurry, catch us a taxi before I die on this corner! (*Bruno is getting Slim onto his feet, with soothing, affectionate murmurs as the carollers assemble on the forestage and sing.*)

CAROLLERS:

For dreamers there will be a night
That seems more radiant than day,
And they'll forget, forget they must,
That light's a thing that will not stay.
A miracle, a miracle!
We dream forever and a day.

Now round about and in and out
We will turn and we will shout.
Round about and in and out
Again we turn, again we shout.
A miracle, a miracle!
A magic game that children play.

(*The forestage dims out as the carollers disperse.*)

SCENE FIVE

Trinket's bedroom is lighted, as she comes up the outside stairs with Slim, who is leaning heavily on her.

TRINKET: Well, here we are: Did you think we'd ever make it?

SLIM: Yeh, I thought we'd make it.

TRINKET: I wasn't so sure. I mean that we'd make it together. But here we are, together. This is my—little home. . . .

SLIM: Not much to it.

TRINKET: No, there's not much to it, but it's—familiar, it's—home. I lived here before my father's good luck in the oil-fields and I became so attached to this room that I stay on and on. You know, you can love a room you live in like a person you live with, if you live with a person. I don't. I live alone here. I have the advantage of a private, outside entrance, and that's an important advantage, especially if I, when you—have a guest with you at night. I don't, you, uh, don't—always want to have to go through the hotel lobby which I'd have to do at any big hotel with—

SLIM: —With house dicks in it?

TRINKET: With anyone, everyone in it.

SLIM (*suspiciously*): Hmmmm.

TRINKET: You're so tall you make the ceiling seem low. Take off your coat and sit down.

SLIM: Not till I make up my mind if I want to stay here or not.

TRINKET (*nervously*): Oh.

SLIM: "Oh." I can take care of myself in this situation or any Goddam situation that that wop Bruno's ever gotten me into. Las' week-en' he innerduced me to a rich ole freak that had a two-story apartment at the Crescent Hotel. I looked around and I was alone with this freak. I said to the freak, "Something's not natural here," an' the freak said to me: "I'm your slave! I'm your slaaaa-ve!" —I said "OK, slave, show me the color of your money!"

TRINKET (*sadly*): Oh.

SLIM: What do you mean by "oh"?

TRINKET: I just mean oh.

SLIM (*broodingly*): Oh. Then the rich freak says, "Master, I am your slave. My money is green as lettuce and as good as gold." I said, "Slave, forget the description, lemme see it. —Show me the color of your money!"

TRINKET: —Are you speaking to me, or—?

SLIM: I'm telling you something that happened las' week-en' which cost me home leave for Chris'mas. This character, this freak, fell down on her knees an' said: "You hit me, oh, boo, hoo, you hit me." I hadn't touched this freak. But then I got the idea. The freak wanted me to hit her. "OK, slave, get up." The freak got up and I shoved her into a gold frame mirror so hard it cracked the glass. "Now, slave, I don't wanna hear a description of your money, I wanta see it." —What're you messing aroun' with over there?

TRINKET: Me?

SLIM: You.

TRINKET: I'm boiling some water to make you some instant coffee. (*She comes from behind an ornamental screen or hanging.*)

SLIM: Are you having a heart attack?

TRINKET: Oh, no! Why? Why?

SLIM: You keep a hand over your chest. (*He reaches out to pull her hand away. She gasps and retreats.*)

TRINKET: *No, no, no, no, no!* (*In panic, to divert him, she snatches a photograph from the dresser.*) Look at this! Would you recognize me? In this newspaper photo I am standing between the Mayor and the president of the International Trade Mart. Then, at that time, I was in the field of public relations, I was called the Texas Tornado. I planned and organized the funeral of Mr. Depression, yes, I had the idea of burying Mr. Depression, holding an exact imitation of a funeral for him. All civic leaders backed me. There was a parade, I mean a funeral procession—*no, no, no, no*! (*He has stretched his hand out again to remove her hand from her chest.*) —For, for Mr. Depression! (*It should be apparent that this was the climax of her life.*)

SLIM: There's something not natural here.

TRINKET: Oh? No! —Mr. Depression was carried along Canal Street and up Saint Charles with big paper lilies on his twelve-foot coffin and there was a band playing a funeral march and I led the band, I walked in front of it dressed like a widow sobbing in a black veil. (*He reaches again for her hand still clasped in panic to her chest.*) *No, no, no, no, no!* —It went, the procession went, all the way to Audubon Park: and then can you guess what happened? (*Slim, weaving, pays no attention to this.*) —It rained like rain had never fallen before upon the earth! Cats, dogs, crocodiles—ZEBRAS! The procession broke up, band quit, everything dissolved, dispersed in the cloudburst! —Kettle's whistling. . . . (*She rushes back of the screen or hanging.*)

SLIM: Morbid!

TRINKET (*rushing back out*): Here, but let it cool first before you— (*He takes the cup and empties it on the floor.*) —Oh, you spilt it, I'll— (*She rushes back of the screen and back out with a towel, mops up the spilt coffee.*) —Now I'm no longer in public relations at all, it seems like another life in another world to me. It's hard to imagine the energy, confidence, drive I had when I first hit this town. Personalities go through such radical changes when something happens to change the course of their lives. Don't they? Haven't you noticed? (*There is a pause between them. Celeste appears before the hotel. She has two purses: Trinket's and hers. She stands at the foot of the outside stairs to Trinket's room and stamps her foot twice.*)

SLIM: There's somethin' Goddam wrong here, peculiar, not natural, morbid.

TRINKET: —I don't know what it could be except that you won't sit down and you won't take coffee. —Is it something about me? I'm a simple, ordinary person, and you're my guest and I'm your friend, not your slave. I've always maintained that this city is hard on the unformed characters of young people that come here, especially if they, oh, now, please sit down! Do! I'd be so happy!

SLIM: I don't sit down and stay down in any morbid place till I know if I want to stay in it. Be my slave. And show me the lettuce color of your money. —Good as—gold. . . . (*Celeste remains at the foot of the stairs. She stamps her foot twice more.*)

TRINKET (*in a shamed voice.*): It's green as lettuce and it's—good as my father's continual gusher in Texas. . . . (*Celeste stamps her feet twice more and tosses Trinket's purse onto the sidewalk. She stamps on the purse.*)

CELESTE (*in a strange chanting voice, separating each syllable*):

Sa-rah Bern-hardt had one leg.
The oth-er was a wood-en peg.
But good she did, yep, she did good,
Clump-ing on a STUMP OF WOOD!

(*She throws back her head and laughs at the sky.*)

TRINKET: It's a pity so many people choose the night of Our Savior's birth to behave in such a— (*Celeste kicks Trinket's purse into the orchestra pit as a policeman comes on.*)

POLICEMAN: Move along.

CELESTE: That's just what I'm doing. (*She goes off one way, the policeman the other.*)

SLIM: What've you got to drink here?

TRINKET: You don't want more to drink, Slim.

SLIM: Don' argue with me or I'll throw you across a room an'—

TRINKET: Oh, Slim, you don't mean that. You only say that because I'm afraid your friend has led you into the wrong kind of company, Slim. Oh, your hair is red gold, red gold, your skin is like—sunlight on snow. . . .

SLIM: Liquor! Out with it! Quick, before I—

TRINKET: I have nothing but wine here.

SLIM: Produce it, out with it, quick, before I—break you a—mirror!

TRINKET: No one can frighten me, Slim, but— (*She pours a glass of wine from her crystal decanter.*) —here!

SLIM: You take a drink of it, first, I'm takin' no chances.

TRINKET: Why, thank you, I will, I can use it. (*She sips the wine, then offers the glass to him.*)

SLIM: Pour me a clean other glass. I don't wanna drink outa yours an' catch somethin' morbid.

TRINKET: You mustn't talk like that to me, even though you don't mean it. Do you know how long it's been since a man has been in this room? Several years. And it seemed like a lifetime—a *death* time. (*Celeste marches into sight again, stops at the foot of the stairs, and stamps her foot twice as if about to commence the formal parade of a palace guard.*)

SLIM (*falling onto the bed*): I'm paralyzed here in a morbid—situation. . . .

(*Celeste opens her huge purse and removes a key: then she mounts the stairs, saying "Clump!" with each step. Trinket gasps and rushes to bolt the outside door. Celeste tries the door with her key: no luck: then she throws back her head like a dog yowling at the moon and she cries out—*)

CELESTE: Agnes—*JOOOOOO—OOOOOnes!*

TRINKET: Yes, it's the whore that snatched my purse on the street! (*She gasps and turns out the light as if that would protect her from Celeste's maniacal siege.*)

CELESTE: You'll find your empty purse outside in the gutter where I kicked it, you FINK! It's got your rosary in it an' your father's picture standin' next to his GUSHER! You better come out an' get it before the trash-man sweeps it into a sewer!

TRINKET: Celeste, go back to the House of Detention and ask for medical help there. You are out of your mind, howling like a mad dog on my stairs!

CELESTE: You told Bernie and Katz I'd been to jail, you fink.

TRINKET: You scratched a hideous lie on the stairs about me!

CELESTE: I scratched the truth about you! You got two mutilations, not one! The worse mutilation you've got is a crime of the Christian commandments, STINGINESS, CHEAPNESS, PURSE PRIDE! Your rosary's in the gutter with your GUSHER! Goddam, you got me thrown out, out, out! (*She stamps her foot with each "out."*) And everything that I owned locked up in a basement!

TRINKET: You know what you did, I don't have to remind you, and now go back down the stairs before I— I have the phone in my hand! (*She has picked up the telephone.*)

CELESTE: FINK, MUTILATED FINK!

TRINKET (*into the telephone*): BERNIE! (*Celeste runs down the stairs. At the bottom, she stops and looks up sobbing at the sky, weeping like a lost child. There is a pause, a silence. Celeste approaches the orchestra pit, stoops, her hand extended. The purse is handed back to her from below. She returns sobbing to the bottom of the outside staircase; she removes the rosary from Trinket's purse and begins to "tell her beads," sobbing.*) I believe she—

SLIM: —I'd a-been home for Christmas an' not broke Mom's heart if I hadn' gone AWOL las' week-en' but 'stead of home I'm paralyzed here in a morbid situation with a morbid hooker an' Goddam Bruno's gone where?

TRINKET (*at the telephone*): Bernie? Trinket! (*Bernie is lighted dimly at the switchboard in the lobby.*) —Be a doll, Bernie, and fetch me two hamburgers from the White Castle and a big carton of black coffee, and hurry back with it. This is a five-dollar tip night for you, Bernie. (*Celeste stands shivering in a blue spotlight at the foot of the outside stairs.*)

CELESTE: Anyhow, I'm not mutilated. She is. (*Bernie walks past her to the White Castle.*) Bernie? —Sweetheart? (*He ignores her as he goes. Slim falls back onto the bed, Trinket unties his shoes.*)

SLIM (*falling asleep*): Morbid, unnatural—slave. . . .

TRINKET: Oh, please stay awake with me!

SLIM: Ah-gah-wah. . . . (*He rolls away from her and begins to snore.*)

TRINKET: —Well, anyhow, I have somebody here with me. Celeste's alone but I'm not, I'm not alone but she is.

CELESTE (*sinking onto the bottom step of the outside stairs*): No, I'm not mutilated. She is. (*Trinket switches on the radio: it's soundless.*)

TRINKET: —The candlelight service is over. —The Holy Infant has been born in the manger. Now He's under the starry blue robe of His Mother. His blind, sweet hands are fumbling to find her breast. Now He's found it. His sweet, hungry lips are at her rose-petal nipple. —Oh, such *wanting* things lips are, and such *giving* things, breasts! (*The carollers have quietly assembled before the hotel. As the bedroom scene dims out, they begin to sing.*)

CAROLLERS:

I think for some uncertain reason
Mercy will be shown this season
To the wayward and deformed,
To the lonely and misfit.
A miracle! a miracle!
The homeless will be housed and warmed.

SINGLE CAROLLER (*stepping out of the group*):

I think they will be housed and warmed
And fed and comforted a while.
And still not yet, not for a while
The guileful word, the practiced smile.

CAROLLERS:

A miracle! a miracle!
The dark held back a little while.

(*They disperse.*)

SCENE SIX

Daylight comes. Celeste is on the sofa under the Christmas tree, snoring and sighing, her huge purse in her lap. Then Trinket's bedroom is lighted. She is in a kimono, seated on the bed. Slim enters from the hall.

TRINKET: Good morning. I thought you'd gone. (*He grunts disdainfully and turns away from her to comb his hair.*)

SLIM: —You got some free publicity on the bathroom wall down the hall there. It says if you don't mind sex with a mutilated woman, knock at room #307, which is this room number.

TRINKET: Oh. —How horrible of someone. I think I know who it is, the monster that did it.

SLIM: —Where's my wallet?

TRINKET: I *know* I know who did it, the monster last night.

SLIM: You're talking about one thing, I'm talking about another. You being mutilated is your own business except it's a stinking trick to take a fellow to bed without letting him know he's going to bed with someone mutilated. (*She begins to gasp "Ah," first very softly, then building to a scream. He claps his hand over her mouth as Bruno rushes into the room. Slim releases Trinket.*) Hey, Bruno, this Goddam lunatic rolled me! (*Trinket plunges toward the open wall of the room. The sailors drag her back. She writhes grotesquely in their grasp, then collapses to the floor.*) She's got my wallet with eighty-six dollars!

BRUNO: Have you got rocks in your head?

SLIM: I got no rocks in my head, she's got my wallet.

BRUNO: Lady, are you okay? (*Trinket moans, crouching by the bed. Bruno hisses at Slim.*) You lack decent human feelings! —You lack— (*He picks up Trinket and puts her on the bed.*) Are you all right? Are you all right? Huh, Miss?

TRINKET (*faintly*): —Yeah. . . .

BRUNO (*to Trinket*): Are you sure you're all right?

TRINKET: Get him out of here, will you?

BRUNO (*to Slim*): Come out in the hall, rock-head.

SLIM: I got no rocks in my head, she's got my wallet, that mutilated whore has got my wallet, hid somewhere in this fly-trap!

BRUNO: That woman ain't got your wallet, you gave your wallet to me to hold for you, rock-head.

SLIM: I'll count the money left in it. (*They have started to leave.*)

BRUNO: This is the last time I go out on liberty with you, never again, never under any conditions, no time, ever!

(*During this, Trinket has been slowly lifting a trembling hand to her breast.*)

TRINKET: —Ahhhh! (*She opens her diary.*) —Dear Diary, the pain's come back.

(*The singers enter from the wings. The pitch pipe is blown but no one sings. They're waiting for someone. He enters from the upstage door of the hotel lobby, in a black cowboy's suit, with diamond-like brilliants outlining his shirt pockets, belt, holster and the edge of his wide-brimmed hat. The pitch pipe is blown again.*)

CAROLLERS:

I think—

(*There is a long pause: the pitch pipe is blown.*)

I think—

(*Long pause: the leader blows long and hard on the pitch pipe.*)

I think—

(*The leader hurls his pitch pipe to the floor. Then the black-clad cowboy, Jack In Black, steps forward and sings alone with a hand on his holster.*)

JACK IN BLACK:

I think the ones with measured time
Before the tolling of the bell
Will meet a friend and tell their friend
That nothing's wrong, that all goes well.

CAROLLERS:

A miracle, a miracle!
Nothing's wrong and all goes well.

JACK IN BLACK:

They'll say it once and once again
Until they say it to themselves,
And nearly think it may be true,
No early tolling of the bell.

CAROLLERS:

A miracle, a miracle!
Nothing's wrong, all is well!

SCENE SEVEN

Later that day: it is silver dusk; there is a murmur of rain. Trinket is dimly lighted in her bedroom: Bernie is back at the switchboard. Celeste is still on the sofa.

TRINKET (*at the telephone*): Is she still down there, Bernie?

BERNIE: Her? (*He leans forward in his swivel chair to look.*) —Yeah. . . .

TRINKET: What's she doing, Bernie?

BERNIE: Nothin'. Sittin'.

TRINKET: She can't sit down there forever, or can she, Bernie?

BERNIE: No. Katz don't like it. He told me to git her out and I said then git me a stick of dynamite, will yuh.

TRINKET: —I have been thinking things over this afternoon, Bernie, and Celeste is not a mentally grown-up person. She's mentally retarded. You know that, Bernie? Irresponsible. Childish. She doesn't examine her actions, she can't distinguish between a right and wrong thing, she acts impulsively, Bernie, like children do. You know how children act. Impulsively, thoughtlessly, Bernie? Her shoplifting, for instance, is the act of a child. She sees a thing, she wants it, she picks it up. Like a child picks a flower. . . .

CELESTE (*rousing slightly*): What's she sayin' about me?

TRINKET: Bernie, you can't hold malice against a child for bad actions. No matter how much it hurts you, you know the limitations and you forgive. —Bernie, tell her to come on up to my room and have a glass of wine with me. I want to bury the hatchet.

CELESTE (*rising heavily*): What's she saying, huh, Bernie?

BERNIE: Excuse me, Miss Dugan. (*He turns to Celeste.*) You got a invitation. Miss Dugan wants you to have a glass of wine upstairs with her.

CELESTE: —Never! —I still have pride!

BERNIE: Yeah, she's comin', Miss Dugan.

CELESTE: Never! I'd sooner die!

BERNIE: G'bye, Miss Dugan. (*He hangs up and leans back again with his comic book.*)

CELESTE (*She draws her ratty fur coat about her and stalks outside. There is no hesitation. She goes straight up the outside stairs to Trinket's. Hearing her approaching footsteps, Trinket unlocks the outside door. Celeste enters with an air of dignity.*) I just come up here to tell you my friendship isn't for sale. (*But her eyes gravitate to a cut-glass decanter of Tokay on the table. She stops speaking, her eyes gleam and jaws hang ajar. . . .*)

TRINKET: —It must be raining out there. Your coat looks wet. Let me hang it up by the heater to dry.

CELESTE: Aw, yeah. Thanks. (*Her eyes glitter, fastened on the California Tokay.*)

TRINKET: Sit down, dear. Would you like a glass of Tokay?

CELESTE: Aw, yeah! Thanks!

TRINKET: Help yourself, please. I filled the cut-glass decanter. There's more in the jug.

CELESTE: Where's the jug?

TRINKET: It's right under the table.

CELESTE: Aw, yeah—thanks!

TRINKET: —Well, it seems like old times.

CELESTE: You used to keep those little sweet biscuits, you know, the—

TRINKET: The vanilla cream wafers? Nabiscos?

CELESTE: Yes, yes, Nabiscos!

TRINKET: It's possible I still have some.

CELESTE (*half rising with excitement*): You kept them in a tin box, a round—

TRINKET: Yes, in this round tin box. Let's see if there's any left in it.

TRINKET: Why, yes!

CELESTE: Aw! Good! It's hard to beat a Nabisco vanilla wafer in the way of a sweet cake or cookie.

TRINKET (*with a little shuddering cry of horror*): There's a dead cockroach in the box!

CELESTE: Now, now, now, now, it's just a dead bug in a box, give me the box, I'll get rid of the bug! (*Celeste picks the bug out of the box.*)

TRINKET: Not in the room, out the door!

CELESTE: OK, OK, out the door! (*She tosses the bug out the door and immediately starts munching a wafer.*)

TRINKET (*sadly, imploringly*): Oh, Celeste! You mustn't eat after a cockroach, you can't eat after a cockroach! Don't, please, eat after a cockroach!

CELESTE: Honey, in the best restaurants people eat after cockroaches! Hey! Let's bum around town tomorrow! Huh? Huh? Yeah, we'll bum around town and have lunch together at Arnaud's. Oysters Rockefeller? Yeah, yeah, to begin with! Then a shrimp bisque and—

TRINKET: TODAY I FOUND!

CELESTE: —What? You said you found something today?

TRINKET: Today I found! —A *scorpion* in my bed. . . .

CELESTE: —Is that a insect? Forget it. —Well, then, after Arnaud's—a movie? An afternoon at the movies with a large size Hershey, a big Hershey almond bar, huh? Then home together. Trinket, we got to pick up the thread of our old lives together. It's essential, necessary, we got to! —And go on and on and on and on, like it was! —Because we were happy together before we hurt each other and all that's finished, we won't hurt each other again as long as we live, will we, dear? Uh-uh! —Music? A little radio music?

TRINKET: —I think we ought to go out after while to hear the boys' choir sing at the cathedral. The Christmas afternoon Mass.

CELESTE: M'clothes are too wet to go out again tonight, Trinket. Get the boys' choir on the radio, honey.

TRINKET: The cathedral service is peaceful.

CELESTE: Well, light a candle and let the boys' choir sing on the radio, dear.

TRINKET: No, it's not the same thing. Christ is present, Christ and Our Lady are present in the cathedral, but here. . . . (*A drunken sailor stumbles up the steps. Hearing their voices, he stops, tries the door and knocks.*)

CELESTE: —Somebody's at the door, Trinket . . . (*Her voice is already slurred by the Tokay.*)

TRINKET: —The hotel is full of drunk sailors on leave. Don't let him in, he'll drink the wine up on us.

CELESTE: I'll just peek out.

TRINKET: No, don't *you*, let *me*. I won't admit a drunk sailor after last night. (*She peeks out but the sailor has stumbled back off. She shuts the door.*) —Nobody.

CELESTE: But you opened the door for someone that knocked and how do you know that that someone didn't come in?

TRINKET: Make sense, please. How could he? Where would he be? We'd see anybody that entered.

CELESTE: Not necessarily, Trinket. I've always believed in invisibility. I've always had faith in invisi-*bee*-able *presence*! (*She rises and faces the audience with a mysterious air.*)

TRINKET (*skeptically*): Oh, Celeste, I—

CELESTE: Not so loud.

TRINKET: I remember when you used to see colored aureoles around people's heads, and—

CELESTE: Not aureoles, *auras.*

TRINKET: Yes, auras, different-colored auras and you'd tell their fortunes and characters by the color of the aura. You said mine was purple.

CELESTE: Stop talking. Be still. Act naturally. Give the presence a chance to manifest itself. It will. It's still in the room. Have a little wine, dear. (*She refills their glasses. Jack In Black enters the lobby from the upstage opening. He lounges, smiling, in the downstage entrance. A distant bell starts tolling. Celeste's voice and manner become even more mysterious.*) There was an elderly sister at Sacred Heart Convent School that received invisible presences, and once she told me that if I was ever cut off and forgotten by the blood of my blood and was homeless alone in the world, I would receive the invisible presence of Our Lady in a room I was in. She said that I would smell roses. I smell roses. She said I would smell candles burning. I smell burning candles. She said I would smell incense. I smell incense. I would hear a bell ringing. I hear a bell ringing. (*More singers appear from the wings.*) —I feel it, yes, I feel it, I know it! Our Lady's in the room with us. She entered the room invisible when you opened the door. You opened the door of your heart and Our Lady came in! (*She falls to her knees.*) MARY? MARY? OUR LADY? (*Then, in a loud whisper*): Trinket, kneel beside me! (*Trinket hesitates only a moment, then kneels beside Celeste. There has been a gradual change of light in the room: it now seems to be coming through stained glass windows—a subjective phenomenon of the trance falling over the women. Celeste stretches out a hand as if feeling for the invisible presence. She suddenly cries out and draws back her hand as if it had touched the presence.*)

TRINKET: *What, what?*

CELESTE (*sobbing and rocking on her knees*): I touched Her robe, I touched the robe of Our Lady!

TRINKET: *Where is it, where is the robe of Our Lady?*

CELESTE: *Here!* (*She seizes Trinket's hand and draws it forward.*)

TRINKET (*fallen into the trance*): *Here?*

CELESTE: *Yes, there! Kiss the robe of Our Lady!* (*Both women stretch their hands out and draw them back to their mouths as if kissing the robe.*)

TRINKET (*crying out wildly*): *The pain in my breast is gone!*

CELESTE: *A miracle!*

TRINKET: *Finally!*

CELESTE & TRINKET (*Together*): *Finally, oh, finally!*

JACK IN BLACK (*singing alone*):

And finally, oh, finally
The tolling of a ghostly bell
Cries out farewell, to flesh farewell,
Farewell to flesh, to flesh farewell!

OTHER SINGERS (*with him*):

A miracle, a miracle!
The tolling of a ghostly bell.

(*Celeste and Trinket begin to sing with them*):

SINGERS (*without soloist*):

The tolling of a ghostly bell
Will gather us from where we fell,
And, oh, so lightly will we rise
With so much wonder in our eyes!
A miracle, a miracle!
The light of wonder in our eyes.

(*Jack In Black crosses through them, smiling and lifting his hat.*)

But that's a dream, for dream we must
That we're made not of mortal dust.
There's Jack, there's Jack, there's Jack In Black!

JACK IN BLACK:

Expect me, but not yet, not yet!

CHORUS:

A miracle, a miracle!
He's smiling and it means not yet.

(*The bell stops tolling.*)

JACK IN BLACK (*singing alone*):

I'm Jack In Black who stacks the deck,
Who loads the dice and tricks the wheel.
The bell has stopped because I smile.
It means forget me for a while.

CHORUS:

A miracle, a miracle!
Forget him for a little while.

(*Jack In Black moves his lifted hat from left to right in the style of a matador dedicating his fight to the audience.*)

The Curtain Falls

KINGDOM OF EARTH

(*The Seven Descents of Myrtle*)

SCENE ONE

At rise of the curtain, the stage set, uninhabited, has the mood of a blues song whose subject is loneliness. It is the back of a Mississippi Delta farmhouse, a story and a half high, its walls gray against a sky the same color. On either side of it stand growths of cane, half the height of the house, rattling in a moaning wind. Continually through these sounds is heard the low, insistent murmur of vast waters in flood or near it. This back wall of the house, except for a doorway, is represented by a scrim that will lift when the house is entered. Then the interior will be exposed: a kitchen to the right, a mysterious little "parlor" to the left, a narrow, dark hall between them: a flight of stairs to an upper hall and a low, slant-ceilinged bedroom to the left. The right side of the upper half-story is never used in the play and is always masked. It is a difficult set that requires the inventions of a very gifted designer. A few moments after the curtain rises, a car is heard approaching and stopping close by.

MAN'S VOICE: Hey, Chicken! Chicken!

(*There is a whine of wind. Then the one being called appears from offstage. He is a young man (30 or 35) in rubber hip boots covered with river slick. He seems a suitable antagonist to a flooding river.*)

WOMAN'S VOICE: We're clearin' out of our place.
CHICKEN: I see.
MAN'S VOICE: We're goin' up to Sunset. That's over the crest of the river.
CHICKEN: That's radio talk. I pay no attention to it.
WOMAN'S VOICE: Sorry we don't have room for you in our car.
CHICKEN: Never mind that. I wouldn't go if I had my own car to go in.

(*He is staring straight out as if the voices came from the back of the theatre. Dull lightning flickers about the gray place.*)

—So don't worry about it.
WOMAN'S VOICE (*turned openly malicious*): I ain't worried about it, it's your worry, Chicken, but we got word that ole man Sikes might dynamite his south bank levee tonight to

save his nawth bank levee, and if he does, this place of yours will be under at least ten foot of water, you know that.

CHICKEN (*raising his voice*): I'd sooner be caught in my house by ten foot of water than caught in the mud on a road between here an' Sunset an' drown like kittens tied in a sack with rocks an' thrown in the river, cause anyhow in this house which is stood out five floods there's something I can climb onto, I can climb on the roof and set on the roof with the chickens till the water goes down. I done that before and can do it again, why, that's how I got my name Chicken, they named me Chicken because I set on the roof with the chickens one time this place was flooded.

WOMAN'S VOICE (*spitefully*): A person could git awful hungry on a roof befo' the water wint down.

CHICKEN: Shit, if I got hungry I'd bite the haid off one of the other chickens and drink its blood.

MAN'S VOICE: I seen a man do that in a freak show once.

WOMAN'S VOICE: Chicken looks like he could do it, an' enjoy it. G'bye, Chicken. Daddy, le's go, we're cold.

(*Motor roars and splutters; the tires spin in the muck.*)

CHICKEN: Seems like you're stuck already. Sorry I don't have room fo' you in the house.

WOMAN'S VOICE: Sorry we don't have room fo' *you* in the car.

(*Tires catch*)

MAN'S VOICE: *Here we go!*

(*The sound of the car and bawling children fade out and we hear the muted warning of the river. The cane stalks make a sad rattling noise in the whining wind. Chicken enters kitchen and strikes a match; lights an oil lamp and warms his hands on its chimney as the glass gets hot. The flame makes grotesque shadows on his dark face. He is a strange-looking young man but also remarkably good-looking with his very light eyes, darker-than-olive skin, and the power and male grace of his body. After his hands are warmed up on the lamp chimney, he crosses with lamp to stove but on the way is distracted by a nude girl's body in a calendar picture, tacked directly over a disordered army cot pushed against kitchen wall. He turns the lamp up higher to see the picture more clearly, one hand at the same time falling involuntarily down his body. But he mutters sharply, "Nah!" and then goes on to the stove and cupboard. He starts preparing himself a pot of coffee, from time to time repeating the Woman's mocking shout, "Sorry we don't have room for you in the car." After some moments he abruptly freezes, cocking his head like an animal at a warning sound. He listens for several beats before the audience can hear what he hears—the sound of an approaching motor. As the sound gets close to the house, he blows out the lamp and leans over it, as if glaring out a dim window in the open wall of the set. Then mutters sharply to himself—)*

CHICKEN: *Him!*

(*Motor stops nearby and a Woman's Voice is heard crying out something. Chicken grunts, astonished.*)

—Him and a *woman*!

(*He sets the lamp down quickly and runs to lock the door between the narrow, dark hall and the kitchen. Myrtle and Lot appear downstage left, by the back door of the house. Neither is a person that could avoid curious attention. Myrtle is a rather fleshy young woman, amiably loud-voiced. She is wearing a pink turtle-neck sweater and tight checkered slacks. Her blond-dyed hair is tied up in a wet silk scarf, magenta-colored. Her appearance suggests an imitation of a Hollywood glamor-girl which doesn't succeed as a good imitation. Lot comes on behind her, bearing two suitcases with great difficulty. He is a frail, delicately—you might say exotically—pretty youth of about twenty. He is ten years younger than Myrtle, and his frailty makes him look even younger. Myrtle dominates him in an amiable way.*)

MYRTLE: This here ain't the front door of the house.

LOT (*panting*): No. Back.

MYRTLE: Well, then, you just march yourself around to the front door, then, cause I'm not about to enter my new home for th' first time by th' back door, No, Siree, I'm not!

(*Has already started around house, brushing through the canebrake.*)

I don't expect you to carry me over the threshold like you ought to but at least you don't have to take me in the back door.

(*Her complaint is affable, gay; she is enormously relieved that the dreadful journey is over safely. Myrtle is a good-natured thing—almost ridiculously so. She has nothing else to meet the world with but good nature. . . . Her vigorous voice fades under the whine of wind. Lot draws a deep, difficult breath and attempts to follow her vigorous lead but can't make it: He staggers coughing against the rain-washed gray wall of the house, dropping his damp, cardboard suitcase. He leans panting against the wet frame wall as Myrtle calls to him from out front, above wind.*)

Hey, Lot, come awn!

(*Inside the dim kitchen, at a safe distance from the dusty windowpane in the imaginary fourth wall, Chicken is leaning stiffly over to look out and listen, like a crouched animal. He is muttering barely audibly to himself. After about ten beats, Myrtle stops waiting out front and comes charging back around the side of the house, imitating the howl of the wind.*)

Woooo! Woooo! That wind is penetratin'! Sharp as a butcher's knife! What's holdin' you up back here?

LOT: No—breath—left . . .

(*She rushes up to him—an avalanche of motherly concern.*)

MYRTLE: Aw, baby, love!

LOT: Shouldn't have tried to carry—luggage . . .

(*He raises his pale, lost eyes to the fading-out sky above Myrtle's look of concern.*)

MYRTLE: Well, I swan!

LOT (*breathlessly, with a touch of disdain*): —What is swan, why swan?

MYRTLE: You'll have to ask my dead Granny, she always said "I swan."

LOT (*lowering his gaze to Myrtle*): To prove she wasn't a goose?

(*He bends, stiffly, to pick up a suitcase but Myrtle snatches it from him.*)

MYRTLE: You come on and stop leaning against those cold, wet boards and let's get into our house! (*She has the suitcase and is trying the back door, saying—*) This door is locked.

LOT: No. Just stuck, always sticks in wet weather.

(*She pulls, the door gives violently and she almost tumbles off the back steps. She recovers, laughing, and hauls the suitcase inside, heading straight up the dark, narrow hall.*)

LOT (*behind her*): Where are you going?

MYRTLE: I'm goin' straight to the parlor. I want the parlor to be my first impression of my new home. Is this the door to the parlor?

LOT: Uh-huh.

MYRTLE: It's stuck, too. (*It gives before her weight.*) *There now!*

LOT: Go in.

MYRTLE: You go in and light the lights in that parlor so I can see it.

LOT (*pressing the switch*): —The lights don't light.

MYRTLE: How come they don't light, baby?

LOT: Sometimes— (*He draws a deep breath.*) —when the river is flooding some places, the electric current that makes the lights light— (*He is talking to her as if she were mentally deficient. He draws another deep breath that wheezes in his throat.*) —is temporarily interrupted, Myrtle.

MYRTLE: How long is temporarily?

LOT: Oh, it comes back on when the— (*deep breath*) —water goes down. These drapes are velvet drapes—neglected lately.

(*He opens them as gently as if they had feeling. Fading gray light enters the parlor.*)

MYRTLE: —Well, this is an elegant parlor, an elegant little parlor.

LOT: My mother did all she could to give some quality to the place but my father— (*deep breath*) —was not just indifferent to the effort she made but opposed it. He was a man that liked to sit in a kitchen and wouldn't let Mother build a dining room onto the house. When he died, howling like a wild beast, Mother was free to transform this place or tear it down to the ground, but life was cruel to Mother. It gave her no time to carry out her plans.

MYRTLE: —She—?
LOT: Outlived my father by shortly less than one year.
MYRTLE: —Sad . . .
LOT: —Yes. —Tragic.
MYRTLE: —Hmmm. A parlor with gold chairs is—like a dream!
LOT: The chandelier is crystal but the pendants are dusty, they've got to be all taken down, one by one, dipped in hot, soapy water. Then rinsed in a bowl of clear water, then dried off with soft tissue paper and hung back up.

(*Chicken grins savagely in the kitchen.*)

Mother and I used to do it, she never allowed the colored girl to touch a thing in this parlor or even come in it. Beautiful things can only be safely cared for by people that know and love them. The day before she died, do you know what she did?

(*Myrtle shakes her head, staring curiously at her exotic young husband.*)

—She climbed a ladder in here and removed each crystal pendant from the little brass hook it hung on, passed it down to me, to be soaped and rinsed and dried, and then replaced on its little brass hook. "Son," she said to me, "help me down off this ladder, I don't know why I'm so tired."

MYRTLE: Baby, you got a mother complex, as they call it, and I'm gonna make you forget it. You hear me?
LOT: You've got a voice that no one in a room with you could help but hear when you speak.
MYRTLE: That's awright. When I speak I want to be heard. Now, baby, this mother complex, I'm gonna get that out of you, Lot, cause I'm not just your wife, I'm also your mother, and I'm not daid, I'm livin'. A-course I don't mean I'm gonna replace her in your heart, but—

(*She draws up one of the little gilded chairs close to the one on which he is seated.*)

LOT: Don't sit on mother's gold chairs. They break too easy.
MYRTLE: You are sittin' on one.
LOT: I'm lighter than you.

MYRTLE: Well! I stand corrected! —Mr. Skin and Bones! —Do I have to stay on my feet in this parlor or can I sit on the sofa?

LOT: Yes, sit on the sofa. (*Slight pause. His head droops forward and his violet-lidded eyes close.*) —The little animal has to make a home of its own. . . .

MYRTLE: I didn't catch that remark.

LOT: —What?

MYRTLE: You said something about an animal.

LOT: I'm too tired to know what I'm saying.

MYRTLE: Are you too tired to hear what *I'm* saying?

LOT: What are you saying?

MYRTLE: I'm saying that all my electric equipment is sitting out there under the leaky roof of your car.

LOT: —Oh. —Yes . . .

MYRTLE: Didn' you tell me you had niggers here working fo' you?

LOT: There's a house girl named Clara and her unmarried husband.

MYRTLE: How do you call this unmarried couple of niggers when you want something done?

LOT: You— (*deep breath*) —have to step outside and ring a bell for 'em.

MYRTLE: Where is this bell you ring for 'em?

LOT: The bell is— (*deep breath*) —in the kitchen.

MYRTLE: Well, kitchen here I come!

(*During the above, Chicken had opened the kitchen door to hear the talk in the parlor. Now he closes and locks the door silently.*)

The unmarried nigra couple're gonna step pretty lively fo' Mrs. Lot Ravenstock.

(*She charges to the kitchen door behind which Chicken is lurking. Lot sways and falls off the chair; staggers to the sofa. Myrtle finds the door locked, rattles the knob and calls out*—)

Who is in there? Who is in this kitchen? —Somebody's in there!

(*She presses her ear to the door. Chicken breathes loudly as if he'd been fighting. Myrtle rattles the knob again and a key falls to the floor inside the kitchen. Myrtle is startled and subdued: she returns to the parlor as if a little frightened.*)

—If that's a dawg in there, why don't it bark?

LOT: —Dawg?

MYRTLE: That kitchen door was locked or it was stuck mighty tight. And I swear I heard something breathing right behind it, like a big dawg was in there. Then I rattled the knob and I heard a key fall to the floor. Will you wake up an' lissen t'what I tell you?

LOT (*hoarse whisper*): I thought he was hiding in there.

MYRTLE: Who? What?

LOT: —Chicken. . . .

MYRTLE: Chicken? Hiding? A chicken, you say, is hiding in the kitchen? What are you tawkin about! —No chicken breathes that loud that I ever met!

LOT: Myrtle, when I say "Chicken" I don't mean the kind of chicken with feathers, I mean my half brother Chicken who runs this place for me.

MYRTLE: I'll be switched! This is a piece of news!

LOT: Keep your voice down, please. I got some things to tell you about the situation on this place.

MYRTLE: —Maybe you should've told me about it before?

LOT: Yes, maybe. But anyhow . . . now . . .

MYRTLE: You are making me nervous. You mean your brother is hiding in that kitchen while we are sitting in here half frozen?

LOT: Cain't you talk quiet?

MYRTLE: Not when I am upset. If he is in there, why don't you call him out?

LOT: He'll come out after while. The sight of a woman talking in this house must have give him a little something to think about in that kitchen, is what I figure.

MYRTLE: Well, all I can say is—*"Well!"*

LOT: —That's what I figure.

MYRTLE: And that's why you're shaking all over, not cause it's cold.

LOT: I'm shaking because I am cold with no fire anywhere in this house except in the kitchen. And it's locked up. With him in it.

MYRTLE: This makes about as much sense as a Chinese crossword puzzle to me, but maybe that long, wet ride has injured my brain. Can you explain to me why this half brother of yours would be hiding in the kitchen when we come home, pretending not to be here or—God knows what?!

LOT: Everything can't be explained to you all at once here, Myrtle. Will you try to remember something? Will you just try to get something in your haid?

MYRTLE: What?

LOT: This place is mine. You are my wife. You are now the lady of the house. Is that understood?

MYRTLE: Then why—?

LOT: Sh! Will you? Please? Keep your voice down to something under a shout?

MYRTLE: But—

LOT: Will you? Will you PLEASE?

(*Pause*)

MYRTLE: Awright. (*Sniffs*) Now I got the shivers, too. —If he's in the kitchen, why don't he come out?

LOT: Oh, he'll come out, after he's had three or four drinks in there to work up his nerve.

MYRTLE: You mean he's bashful?

LOT: He's strange by nature, and not accepted around here.

MYRTLE: I think we ought to go call him, it would be more natural to.

LOT: He won't come out till he's ready. Be patient. Do you like sherry wine?

MYRTLE: I don't think I ever had any.

LOT: Some of Miss Lottie's sherry's still left in this ole cut-glass decanter.

MYRTLE (*absently*): Aw. Good. Good. . . .

LOT (*in his thin, breathless voice*): This is Bohemian glass, these here wineglasses are.

MYRTLE: —What dya know. . . .

LOT: Ev'ry afternoon about this time, Miss Lottie would take a glass of this Spanish sherry with a raw egg in it to keep her strength up. It would always revive her, even when she was down to eighty-two pounds, her afternoon sherry and eggs, she called it her sherry flip, would pick her right up and she'd be bright an' lively.

MYRTLE: —Imagine me thinkin' that that was a dawg in there! Yeah, I thought that huffing I heard in there was a big old dawg in the kitchen, locked up in there. I didn't—Ha Ha!—suspect that it was—Ha Ha!—your—*brother*. . . .

(*He begins to cough: the cough shakes him like a dead leaf, and he leans panting against the wall staring at Myrtle with pale, stricken eyes. She gathers him close in her arms. . . .*)

Why, baby! Precious love! —That's an *awful* cough! —I wonder if you could be comin' down with th' flu?

LOT: —Lissen! —He's movin' now!

(*Chicken's frozen attitude by the door was released by the sound of Lot's paroxysm of coughing: He crosses to a cupboard, takes out a jug and takes a long, long drink.*)

—A place with no woman sure does all go to pieces.

MYRTLE: Well, now they's a woman here.

LOT: That's right: we'll make some changes.

MYRTLE: You bet we will. And bright and early tomorrow, the first thing we do after breakfast, we'll, we'll, we'll! —We'll get out that ole stepladder and wash those whatcha-ma-call-ems and make them shine like the chandelier in Loew's State on Main Street in Memphis! And we will—oh, we'll do a whole lot of things as soon as this weather clears up. And soon it's going to be summer. You know that, Sugar? It's going to be summer real soon and—a small animal needs a place of its own.

LOT: Yeah, it'll be summer, the afternoons'll be long, the damp'll dry out of the walls and—

MYRTLE: I'M GONNA MAKE YOU REST! And build you up. You hear me? I'm gonna make you recover your lost strength, baby. —You and me are gonna have us a baby, and if it's a boy, we're going to call it Lot and if it's a girl we're gonna name her Lottie.

LOT (*his eyes falling shut*): If beds could talk what stories they could tell. . . .

MYRTLE: Baby, last night don't count. You was too nervous. I'll tell you something I know that might surprise you. A man is twice as nervous as a woman and you are twice as nervous as a man.

LOT: Do you mean I'm not a man?

MYRTLE: I mean you're a man but superior to a man. (*Hugs him to her and sings—*)

> "Cuddle up a little closer, baby mine.
> Cuddle up and say you'll be my clinging vine!"

Mmmm, Sugar! Last night you touched the deepest chord in my nature which is the maternal chord in me. T'night I'm gonna cradle you in my arms, probably won't sleep, just watch you sleepin' an' hold you all night long, and it'll be better than sleep. Do you know, do you realize what a beautiful thing you are?

LOT: I realize that I resemble my mother.

MYRTLE: To me you resemble just *you*. The first, the most, the *only* refined man in my life. Skin, eyes, hair any girl would be jealous of. A mouth like a flower. Kiss me! (*He submits to a kiss.*) Mmmm. I could kiss you forever!

LOT: I wouldn't be able to breathe.

MYRTLE: You're refined and elegant as this parlor.

LOT: I want you to promise me something. If Chicken asks you, and when he gets drunk he will ask you—

MYRTLE: Chicken will ask me nothing that I won't answer in aces and spades.

LOT: There's something you mustn't answer if he asks you.

MYRTLE: What thing is that, baby?

LOT: If I'm a—

MYRTLE: If you're a what?

LOT: Strong lover. —Tell him I satisfy you.

MYRTLE: Oh, now, baby, there'd be no lie about that. Y'know, they's a lot more to this sex business than two people jumpin' up an' down on each other's eggs. You know that or you *ought* to.

LOT: I'm going to satisfy you when I get my strength back, and meanwhile—make out like I do. Completely. Already. I mean when talking to Chicken.

MYRTLE: Aw, Chicken again, a man that huffs like a dawg an' hides in the kitchen, do you think I'd talk about us to him, about our love with each other? All I want from that man is that he opens the kitchen door so I can go in there and grab hold of that bell and ring the clapper off it for that girl that works here, that Clara. I'll make her step, all right, and step quick, too. The first thing she's gotta do is haul in all that electric equipment settin' in the car, before it gits damp an' rusts on me.

LOT: Myrtle, I told you that when there's danger of flood, the colored help on a place cut out for high ground. —Till the danger's over.

MYRTLE: Then what're we doin' on low ground instid of high ground?

LOT: To protect our property from possible flood damage. This is your house, your home. Aren't you concerned with protecting it for us?

MYRTLE: My house, my home! I never known, I never even suspected, how much havin' property of my own could mean to me till all of a sudden I have some. House, home, land, a little dream of a parlor, elegant as you, refined as you are.

(*During this talk, Chicken has his ear pressed to the kitchen door, fiercely muttering phrases from the talk.*)

LOT: —Chicken calls me a sissy.

MYRTLE: Well, he better not call you no sissy when Myrtle's around. I'll fix his wagon up good, I mean I WILL!

LOT: SHH! —Myrtle, you've got an uncontrollable voice. He's listening to us. —You think you could handle Chicken?

MYRTLE: Want to make a bet on it? I've yet to meet the man that I couldn't handle.

LOT: You ain't met Chicken.

MYRTLE: I'm gonna meet him!—whin he comes outa that kitchen. . . .

LOT: He will, soon, now. It's gettin' dark outside and I heard him set the jug down on the kitchen table.

MYRTLE: Awright, I'm *ready* for him, anytime he comes out, I'm ready to meet him and one thing I want to git straight. Who's going to be running this place, me or this Chicken?

LOT: This place is mine. You're my wife.

MYRTLE: That's what I wanted to know. Then I'm in charge here.

LOT: You're taking the place of Miss Lottie. She ran the house and you'll run it.

MYRTLE: Good. Then that's understood.

LOT: It better be understood. Cause Chicken is not my brother, we're just half brothers and the place went to me. It's mine.

MYRTLE: Did you have diff'rent daddies?

LOT: No, we had diff'rent mothers. *Very* diff'rent mothers!

(*Chicken snorts like a wild horse*)

He's coming out now!

(*Chicken emerges slowly from the kitchen and starts up the dark, narrow hall.*)

MYRTLE: Yes. I hear him coming. Let's go meet him.

LOT: No. Wait here. Sit tight. And remember that you're the lady of the house.

(*Chicken pauses, listening in the dim hall.*)

MYRTLE: It don't seem natural to me.

(*Lot removes an ivory cigarette holder from a coat pocket, puts a cigarette in it and lights it. His hands are shaky.*)

(*nervously*) —A parlor with gold chairs is like a dream!

LOT: —A woman in the house is like a dream.

MYRTLE: —I must be hearing things.

LOT: What did you hear?

MYRTLE: I, I—thought I heard footsteps in the hall.

LOT: Human or animal footsteps?

(*Chicken opens the parlor door.*)

Aw. —Hello, Chicken. Don't come in the parlor till you take off those muddy boots.

(*Chicken disregards this instruction: enters the parlor. Myrtle rises nervously but Lot remains seated, smiling icily through a cloud of cigarette smoke.*)

CHICKEN: They turn you loose from the hospital?

LOT: I wasn't locked in it. A hospital ain't a jail. I was dismissed.

CHICKEN: Couldn't do nothing more for you?

LOT: I was dismissed as cured.

CHICKEN: I see. And who is this woman?

LOT: You mean who is this lady. This lady is my wife. Myrtle, this is Chicken. Chicken, this is Myrtle.

CHICKEN: Why did you all come back here?

LOT: Wanted to is the reason.

CHICKEN: With this flood? In the county?

LOT: That's right. I wanted to see that my mother's things are taken out of the parlor before the downstairs is flooded.

CHICKEN: What good'll that do if the upstairs is flooded, too?

MYRTLE: Oh, my God, the flood won't go *that* high, will it?

CHICKEN: You don't know much about floods.

MYRTLE: All I know is I'm scared to death of deep water.

CHICKEN: Then how come you drove back here through that high water you must've hit south of Sunset?

MYRTLE: I begged Lot to turn back but he was bound an' determined to git us home, I couldn't stop him, he was determined to make it.

CHICKEN: Wanta know something? This time tomorrow, both floors of this house will be full of floodwater.

(*Myrtle draws a long, noisy breath of dismay and terror.*)

The river gauge is thirty-two foot of water at Friar's Point and the crest is still above Memphis. And I just got word from those sons of bitches, Potters, that ole man Sikes is about to blow up the south end of his levee to save the rest of it, he's planning to dynamite it tonight and you—come home just in time for it.

MYRTLE: Lot, baby, I think we ought to turn right around and drive back.

LOT: No. We're home. We're not gonna leave here. Chicken's just tryin' to scare us. Why don't you leave, Chicken, if you're scared of the flood?

CHICKEN: I ain't about to leave here. You know we got this agreement. Have you forgotten about the agreement we signed between us?

LOT: That was before I got married. Now I am.

CHICKEN (*to Myrtle*): Are you his nurse?

MYRTLE: Why, no, I'm Mrs. Lot Ravenstock and have been Mrs. Lot Ravenstock since yesterday mawnin.

CHICKEN: I know of invalid men to marry their nurses, or anyhow live with 'em like they was married.

MYRTLE: We're married, and I wasn't a nurse. Y'know, I don't think I ever seen so little resemblance between two brothers.

CHICKEN: We're half brothers.

LOT: Chicken's much darker complected. Don't you notice?

MYRTLE: There's so little light in the room.

CHICKEN: I work out in the fields and Lot just lays in bed.

LOT: —I'd like some hot coffee, now.

CHICKEN: Coffee's in the kitchen. (*He returns to the kitchen.*)

MYRTLE: Git up, Lot. Come along.

LOT (*remaining on sofa*): How does he impress you?

MYRTLE: I wouldn't call that man a pleasant surprise, and I don't understand why you never mentioned him to me so I'd be a little prepared, but—

LOT: Don't let him scare you.

MYRTLE: I'm not scared of that man, or any man livin'! No, sir!

CHICKEN (*at kitchen door*): Decided y'don't want coffee?

MYRTLE: Be right there.

LOT (*staggering up from the sofa*): If he sees he can bluff an' bully you, that's what he'll do, so remember—we're two against one in this house and the house is ours.

(*They go hand in hand to the kitchen. Chicken sets tin cups on the table.*)

—Myrtle an' I'll have our coffee in china cups.

CHICKEN: The china cups all broke.

LOT: You broke Mother's china cups?

MYRTLE: Lot, baby, china breaks, nobody breaks it on purpose unless there's a fight. This is— I like our kitchen. All but that nakid girl's pitcher on the wall there. I could do without that.

CHICKEN: Jealous of her?

MYRTLE: I think it's pitiful of a strong, grown man like you to pleasure yourself like a kid with that kind of pitcher. I don't have to ask if you're a bachelor now.

CHICKEN: Lot an' me are bachelors, both of us.
MYRTLE: You're a bachelor but my baby ain't.
CHICKEN: Your baby's more of a bachelor than me.
MYRTLE: I'm here to prove he ain't.
CHICKEN: Hmm. I didn't catch your name.
MYRTLE: My maiden name was Myrtle Kane, but now it's legally changed to Mrs. Lot Ravenstock.
CHICKEN: How long've you been Lot's nurse?
MYRTLE: I am nobody's nurse. To repeat that statement.
LOT: We've been married two days, almost.
MYRTLE: My girl-friend, Georgia, said I was robbin' the cradle, you know, cradle snatchin'.

(*No response to her laugh.*)

And I had always boasted that I was too practical-minded for love at first sight but practicality flew out the window whin this boy come in. —I want you to know it turned my bones to water!
LOT: Chicken, we'll have some coffee.
CHICKEN: Pour some out of the coffeepot on the stove.

(*He stares steadily at Myrtle.*)

So you're in the—nursin' profession?
LOT: Myrtle was in show business.
MYRTLE: Why do you keep askin' if I'm a nurse? Oh, I once did a little of what they call practical nursing, took care of a feeble person till he died on me, out of kindness—sympathy. . . .

(*She is pouring coffee into three tin cups.*)

Is everyone's name in the pot? The coffee's still hot.
CHICKEN: Yeah. Show business, huh?
MYRTLE: I've hed all kinds of employment in my life. Respectable employment.

(*She laughs genially and gives Chicken a playful little slap on the shoulder.*)

Oh, in my life I've taken the sweets with the sours, and it's been smooth as silk in my experience and other times rough as a cob. Yais, I've known both in my time. However, I've kept my haid above water, that I can say for myself, and I've rowed my own boat, too. Never had to depend on another soul. No, sir. I've pulled my own weight in this world. Here is my right hand to God, if you don't believe me, and nothing, nobody, never has made me bitter. No sir! What all have I done? I'll tell you all that I've done in my life, and that's a-plenty, yes, siree, a-plenty.

LOT: Myrtle?

MYRTLE: Huh? What, baby?

LOT: I think it's time to bring in that carload of electric equipment.

MYRTLE: Your brother 'n' me'll do that, don't worry about it. Your brother wants to know what all I've done in my life, and I'm gonna tell him. You might find it int'restin', too.

LOT: Yes, I might, if I hadn't already heard it.

(*He sinks into a chair and his eyes fall shut. His eyelids are violet. He sways a little as if he might fall from the chair.*)

MYRTLE: I'll just hit the high spots, baby. Whin I was fifteen I worked as operator of a Photo-matic machine on the beach at Galveston, Texas. I been—you won't believe this but it's true as I'm standin' here before you!—I been the headless woman in a carnival show. All a fake, done with mirrors! Sat in a chair and pretended to have no haid, it was done with mirrors! But completely convincin'!

LOT: Myrtle, skip to show business.

MYRTLE: Baby, that was show business, my first experience in it and it's where my heart still belongs.

CHICKEN: —What is she talkin' about?

LOT (*as if asleep*): Myrtle was in show business.

CHICKEN: Hunh?

LOT (*rousing a bit*): Show him that picture of "The Four Hot Shots from Mobile."

MYRTLE: Oh, that ole snap, that ole publicity still, I wonder if I still got it.

LOT: You showed it to me a minute after we met.

MYRTLE: I'll see if I still got it on me.

LOT: You put it back in your handbag.

MYRTLE: Pandora's box!

CHICKEN: Whose box?

MYRTLE (*a bit nervously*): Cups refilled with coffee. Now let me lead a parade back into that elegant little parlor and I'll show you and tell you about the Four Hot Shots from Mobile. Come along, follow me, boys. . . .

(*She has put the tin cups of coffee on a plate: marches into the parlor and sets the plate down on a table before the couch. Lot and Chicken are still in the kitchen.*)

CHICKEN: Only a lunatic would marry you and you sure have found the right party.
LOT: Is the black bird of jealousy eating at your heart, Chicken?
MYRTLE: Boys, I've found the pitcher of the Four Hot Shots from Mobile and I'm waiting to show it to you.
CHICKEN: She wants you to get up out of the chair and go in Miss Lottie's parlor if you can.
LOT: Sure I can. Without trouble.

(*He gets up and falls to his knees. Chicken laughs and sets him on his feet.*)

CHICKEN: Able to walk or do you have to be carried?
LOT: The long trip made my dizzy.
MYRTLE: *Boys!*
CHICKEN: I bet there's a buzzard circlin' over the house, since you got here.

(*He turns away from Lot and goes to the parlor. Lot leans on the kitchen table a moment. Then gathers a bit of strength and follows into the parlor. Myrtle has had no trouble at all in finding the "publicity still." She gazes at the photograph with a beguilement that it has never failed to give her. Chicken enters the parlor. She turns to him with a warm smile, extending the photo to him. Chicken takes it from her and regards it with considerable interest. Consciously or not, he drops one of his large, dusky hands over his crotch, which is emphasized, pushed out, by his hip boots.*)

MYRTLE: Well, there you are, here we are!

(*Lot sits carefully down on one of the "little gold chairs."*)

Here we are outside the Dew Drop Inn—in the live town of Tallahassee, F-L-A! It's in color, you see.

CHICKEN: Yes, I can see color. Where's these hot shots now, gone back to Mobile?

MYRTLE: —You ast me a sad question, where's them girls. You know somethin'? (*She is sincerely distressed.*)

CHICKEN: I know lots of things but I won't know *that* till you tell me.

MYRTLE (*blows her nose and dabs at her eyes*): From right to left. This tall redhead they called The Statuesque Beauty. (*Chicken grunts—but with interest.*) —her mutilated corpse was found under a trestle three years ago this Spring. (*Chicken grunts again.*) Don't that break your heart?

CHICKEN: No.

MYRTLE: Some one, some pervert I reckon, had cut her up with a knife, writ up in all the papers, you must've heard about it. I'm telling you it just about broke my heart, she was full of vim, vigor and vitality. And *fun*? The Statuesque Beauty was a continual circus.

CHICKEN: Unh. Circus quit now.

MYRTLE: This one next to her, sweet thing, still in her teens, billed as The Gulf Coast Blaze—a victim of a illegal operation.

CHICKEN: Daid?

MYRTLE (*blowing her nose again*): Not livin', brother, bless her old sweet soul. And this one next to her, billed as The Texas Explosion, somehow I feel that her end was saddest of all. Devoured a full bottle of sleeping pills one night in a Wichita, Kansas hotel.

CHICKEN: Suicide, huh?

MYRTLE: Well, brother, you don't devour a full bottle of sleeping pills with much expectation of getting up early tomorrow. Oh, and this one, my God, The Midnight Stawm! —She wint on drugs. Y'see, all of us four girls lived in the same little frame house t' share expenses, y'know, and, well, one night I happened to be passin' down th' hall outside the bedroom of The Midnight Stawm. I smelt a strong smell of incense. I knocked at The Midnight Stawm's door and this strange voice called out "Who's there?" "Me, Myrtle." "Aw, you, come in." So in I wint, and she was sittin' there smokin' this thin cigarette with incense burnin' beside her. "What're you smokin'? "I'm smokin' grass," she answered, "have a stick with me, Myrtle." But instink tole me not to.

LOT: I'm tired, let's go up now.

MYRTLE (*hugging him to her*): Rest on Myrtle, baby, and lemme finish the story. At that time, in Mobile, I was totally ignorant thin of things like that, but I had a suspicion that something had gone wrong with The Midnight Stawm.

CHICKEN: Aw?

MYRTLE: She'd took the first step to what she finally come to. So we other girls an' me, we talked it over and regretfully hed to ask The Midnight Stawm to give up her room there with us. Painful, very. But we didn't want the house raided. We were clean-livin' girls, as you'd hope to find in show business. —Here is me, The Petite Personality Kid that had all the luck in that outfit, and even her luck come mighty close to petering out once or twice, but character saved me.

CHICKEN: You are The Petite Personality Kid?

MYRTLE: That's how they billed me, brother.

CHICKEN: Built you?

MYRTLE: No, no, billed, not built. It's a term in show business meaning the name by which you're introduced to the public.

CHICKEN: You been introduced to the public?

MYRTLE: Yes, many times, many places. (*Returns snapshot to patent-leather purse.*)

CHICKEN: —How did the public like it? (*He gives her a slow, wolfish grin, his eyes appraising her body.*) —Did they yell "take it off" or did they yell "keep it on?"

(*Myrtle laughs heartily but with a note of uncertainty.*)

LOT: Myrtle has a personality that the public responds to.

CHICKEN: Aw?

LOT: She received an ovation on TV. I saw it, I heard it. I was there to audition as— (*draws a long, painful breath*) —MC for a—"Tonight in Memphis" show. . . .

CHICKEN: Did the public respond to you, too?

LOT: —I—was—interviewed, and— (*He shrugs slightly and puts a cigarette in an ivory holder.*)

CHICKEN: After this interview, you thought you'd do better back here? With a stripper to nurse you?

MYRTLE: Now, I don't like that, that's a little uncalled for!
CHICKEN: Did I say something wrong?
LOT: You said something wrong and offensive.
MYRTLE: It's my personality that I sell to the public—mainly.
CHICKEN: Yes, I bet. You kick with the right leg, you kick with the left leg, and between your legs you make your living?
MYRTLE: —Some remarks I deliberately don't hear!
LOT: Chicken, now that I'm home, in *my* home, on *my* land, with *my* wife, filthy talk has got to stop around here, I don't care if it means us getting along without you.
CHICKEN: Aw, you want me to go, now.
MYRTLE: Lot baby didn't mean that!
CHICKEN: What did "Lot baby" mean?
MYRTLE: All he means was we're sittin' here in this elegant little parlor under a crystal glass chandelier and Lot feels and I feel, too, that we should all talk and act like gentlemen an'—ladies!
LOT: I want to go up to bed, while I still have strength to.
CHICKEN: Your nurse'll carry you up.
MYRTLE: Lot, show your brother we're married, let him see the license.

(*Lot produces a paper.*)

CHICKEN: Shit, you can buy those things for two bits in a novelty store to show in a motel where you brought a woman to lay.
MYRTLE: This marriage license is genuine and if you doubt my word for it, call up the TV station in Memphis where we were married.
LOT: Myrtle and I were married on television yesterday morning.
CHICKEN: That statement makes no more sense than if you told me you licked TB and've got the strength of a mule team.
MYRTLE: Want to hear the whole story?
CHICKEN: I like to hear a good joke.
MYRTLE: Brother, this is no joke!
LOT: Let me lie down on this sofa.
MYRTLE: Lie down, baby, and rest your head in my lap while I tell your brother what happened to me in Memphis two days ago.

(*Lot reclines on the sofa with his head in Myrtle's lap. As she tells her story, she strokes his forehead and hair.*)

To start at the beginning, my luck had run out, you know luck does that sometimes, it peters out on you no matter how hard you try and decent and clean you live and close you are to your Saviour. Trials come in a lifetime and you got to face and accept them till the wheel of fortune turns again your way.

CHICKEN: Make this story short.

MYRTLE: Awright, day before yestiddy I happened to be on the street in Memphis for no particular reason and I seen this long line of people, all wimmen, and I said to myself these people are waiting for something, and if that many people are standing in line for something, it must be good.

CHICKEN: Uh-huh. Get on with the story.

MYRTLE: Well, I fell in the line-up with these other ladies and suddenly, all at once, this little Jewish type man come bolting out and hollered, "Ladies, the studio's full, no more admissions today." Everybody went "Awwwww," disappointed, but I said, "Mister, I don't know what this is but I want in on this thing, I been standing here two hours and I want in on this thing, whatever it is!" —I had him by the arm. He give me a funny look, he must've seen something in me, and he said, "Girlie, you just watch where I go and follow me fast as you can without attracting attention." He sort of whispered this to me out of the side of his mouth. So I stepped out of the line. I seen him bustling into a little alleyway back of the TV studio. I followed him around there and in a fire-escape door, and you know where I found myself? On a TV stage! And there I was, right there, right smack in the middle of a TV show, and this nice little plump little man, he had me by the elbow with such a tight grip I don't think a greased alligator could of got loose, and the first I known, d'ya know what I was doin'?

CHICKEN: Hustlin' a fast buck or two?

MYRTLE: I was standin' in front of a mike with cameras and lights on me, telling my story, broadcasting my woes to the world. I started to cry and everyone started to laugh, the studio rocked with 'em laughing. Why, when I was in show business as The Personality Kid, if I'd ever rocked a club like I rocked that TV public, I would, I bet you, hed hed my name in white lights on Broadway, that's the truth, I would of!

CHICKEN: Come to the point of the story if there is one.

MYRTLE: I sobbed and cried and it made me mad that they laughed. Y'know how mad it makes you to pour your heart out at someone an' have him mock you? Well, then I cut loose, I let 'em have it, I hollered out "What's so funny?" And then this little man that had ushered me in the back way, he whispered something to the MC of the show, and to my shock and astonishment a moment later I was led up to and set down on a golden throne and a big gold jewelled crown was set on my haid and the MC shouted to the audience, all applauding, "Hail to the Queen! All hail!" (*She makes a grand gesture.*) "All hail to thee, Queen of the Day!"

LOT: Myrtle, condense the story.

MYRTLE (*oblivious to his suggestion*): WELL! —I'm telling you, brother, I could have dropped through that stage floor to the boiler-room in the basement, whin I realized, that accidentally, just out of the blue, that I hed been chosen, selected as queen for nothing more or less than pouring out my heart to a room full of strangers.

LOT: I was there in that room.

MYRTLE: Yais, that's right, my blessed baby was there. Now then. I was given two choices, to be the "Hollywood-Queen-for-a-Day" or the "Take-Life-Easy Queen."

CHICKEN: This is a bitch of a story.

MYRTLE: Yais, ain't it! Now the "Hollywood-Queen-for-a-Day" is sent to Hollywood, first class on a plane, provided with a sport ensemble for daytime and a formal for night and has her hair styled by the hair stylist for the stars, and she spends eight hours hobnobbing with screen celebrities in famous places. On the other hand, the "Take-Life-Easy Queen" gets a small fortune in electric household equipment. Well, like ev'ry girl in show business, and many out of it, too, Hollywood was my dream, but—

LOT: Tell him why you switched and how we got married on a national hook-up.

MYRTLE: That's what I'm working up to.

CHICKEN: You're working up to it slowly.

MYRTLE: Give me patience, you want to know how this happened!

CHICKEN: Not if it takes till midnight.

MYRTLE: I'm leading up to the climax which is the climax of my life. I hed naturally chosen to be the Hollywood-Queen-for-a-Day and the ceremony was just about finished when somebody touches my arm. I turn around, still in my robe and crown, and there was my precious baby, completely unknown to me then. Gold-haired, soft-voiced, appealing. It was love-at-first-sight, immediate as a surprise, bang, right between my eyes. "Can I have your autograph, please?" is what he said to me. In that instant the love bug hit me, cupid's arrow shot a bull's eye in my heart. We made a date. On this date he said the love bug had bit him too, love-at-first-sight for us both. I phoned the TV studio and told 'em what had happened and I was going to git married and for that reason could I switch to being the Take-It-Easy-Life-Queen with all that electric equipment to start out with. There was no objection but there was a suggestion. "How would you and your husband-to-be like to be married on TV? In a lace bride's gown with a bouquet of lilies?"

LOT: That's the story. Yesterday we were married on TV.

CHICKEN: You acted out a make-believe marriage to fool the public, huh?

MYRTLE: If it wasn't a genuine marriage it sure fooled us.

LOT: It was a genuine marriage performed by a famous revivalist preacher.

MYRTLE: No more disagreeable talk. Back to the kitchen fo' the bell!

(*She rushes back to the kitchen and snatches up a cowbell on the table. Returns to parlor with it.*)

Is this the bell you ring fo' th' unmarried colored couple?

(*Chicken turns to give her a slow, blank look.*)

I am goin' out an' ring this bell and they are gonna bring in my 'lectric equipment before it rusts on me. I got a, I got a—'lectric washer, two of 'em, one fo' clo'se and one for dishes, I got a, I got a—'lectric home permanent set, 'lectric heater an' blanket an' a table model radio-TV set, so many 'lectric appliances we hardly had room enough for 'em in the car. You'll see whin that unmarried couple hauls them in here t' be dried off, an' connected.

CHICKEN: Yeah, I'll see. Go out an' ring the bell. Ring it loud and long, they don't hear good from a distance.

(*Myrtle goes out on the back steps and rings the bell while Chicken and Lot stare silently at each other. She rings the bell loud and long but the only response is moaning wind and a dull flicker of lightning.*)

LOT (*finally speaking*): Well, I guess I surprised you.

CHICKEN: You got a bigger surprise comin' to you.

LOT: What do you mean by that?

CHICKEN: If I said what I mean by it, it wouldn't be as big a surprise to you, would it?

(*Myrtle returns.*)

MYRTLE: I rang an' rang an' got no answer out there.

CHICKEN: Don't let that bother you much. I don't think you all could git it on the roof whin the floodwater fills the house.

LOT: Stop talking about a flood to scare my wife.

MYRTLE: I don't and I can't believe a man would stay in this house if he really thought it was going to be flooded, so I'm not a-tall scared. Now who's going to help me bring in my prizes in the car?

CHICKEN: Your TV husband will do that.

LOT: Chicken will bring it in.

CHICKEN: Oh, no, Chicken won't.

MYRTLE: Thank you both very kindly. I'll bring in what I can carry without your help.

(*She goes out and off.*)

LOT: Help her with it. If you still work on the place.

CHICKEN: I will like shit.

LOT: Let's make an effort to forget what's past and work out a—decent—future.

CHICKEN: There's no future for you. I talked to your doctor before I made out that paper. You remember that agreement between us, witnessed, signed, notarized, giving the place to me when you take the one-way trip to the kingdom of heaven? I never have that paper out of my wallet in here. (*He taps the pocket of his leather jacket.*) —I was curious to know how long I might have to wait. I got your Memphis doctor on the phone to ask about the condition of your lungs. One's gone, he told me, and the other one's going. Limit: six months. Now passed.

(*Myrtle rushes back into the house with a load of portable electric equipment.*)

MYRTLE: I carried in what I can carry and will get some help to bring the heavy stuff in.

(*She enters the parlor: the men ignore her. She sets the electric stuff down, as if she'd forgotten it, observing the tension between the two men. Sad, dull lightning quivers about the house.*)

CHICKEN: Didn't you tell this woman how you bleed?

MYRTLE: Bleed, Lot, baby? Bleed?

CHICKEN: Yeah, Lot baby bleeds. He bleeds like a chicken with its head chopped off. I'm Chicken, he's headless Chicken. Yes, he bleeds, he bleeds. But no, he don't have TB: He just makes a blood donation to Red Cross, only Red Cross is not quick enough to catch it in a—bucket. . . .

(*Lot suddenly springs forward, striking fiercely at Chicken. Chicken pushes him almost gently to the floor. Lot crawls groaning to his feet and staggers into hall and starts to drag himself up the steep, dark, narrow steps.*)

MYRTLE: I don't understand! What is it?

CHICKEN (*mimicking her*): "I don't understand! What is it?"

MYRTLE (*backing up steps*): You scare me!

CHICKEN: "You scare me!"

MYRTLE (*running up a few more steps*): I'm going up with Lot!

CHICKEN: "I'm going up with Lot!"

(*She draws a gasping breath and scrambles up the narrow steps to the bedroom door that Lot has entered. Myrtle comes up behind him and clings to his arm.*)

MYRTLE: I never been so terrified in my life!

LOT (*sadly, reflectively, his eyes searching the dim sky*): Chicken says my doctor said—I'm dying!

MYRTLE: He mocked everything I said, he just stood there and mocked everything I said!

LOT: Can you imagine that? I'm going to die!

MYRTLE: Oh, let's go back, let's drive right back to Memphis!

LOT: —We can't, Myrtle.

MYRTLE: Why can't we? Why can't we drive back?

LOT: I'm going to die, that's why. . . .

(*He glances at her with a soft, surprised, rueful laugh. The scene dims out.*)

Intermission.

SCENE TWO

The upstairs bedroom is lighted by an oil lamp. Late dusk surrounds the house, the "apple green dusk" of an evening clearing after rain which has just stopped. Water is heard running busily along tin gutters, down a spout and into a big mossy barrel beside the back door. Bullfrogs and possibly some crickets are making their forlorn and desultory comments, desultory as the forlorn talk in the bedroom where Myrtle is washing out some things at the rose-bud-printed washbowl and where Lot is in a rocker facing the audience at an angle; the chair is one of those wicker rockers that they have, or used to have, on verandahs of old-fashioned summer hotels in the South. And Lot's fair head, delicately pretty as a girl's, leans against a souvenir pillow from Biloxi. The pillow is made of green satin, the same as the counterpane on the brass bed. The aura of its former feminine occupant, Lot's mother, still persists in this bedroom: a lady who liked violets and lace and mother-of-pearl and decorative fringes on things. . . . Lot is smoking with his long ivory holder; Myrtle is wringing out some nylons as the curtain rises. She glances, from time to time, at her bridegroom as an uneasy scientist might glance at a test tube whose contents had turned an unexpected color. . . . All during this scene between Lot and Myrtle, Chicken is seen in the very dim-lit kitchen, carving something into the kitchen table with a switch-blade knife—on his face a wolfish grin.

MYRTLE: I wish I knew what was going on back of that long ivory cigarette holder and that Mona Lisa smile.

LOT: I got them both from my mother.

MYRTLE: Yes, well, regardless of where you got 'em, they baffle me. We been up here about two hours, I reckon, and all you've said to me is, "I'm dyin', Myrtle." When a couple has been married for twenty or thirty years it's natural for them to fall into long-drawn silences between them because they've talked themselves out, but you and me have been married for less than two days.

LOT: Why didn't you say something to me? I would've answered.

MYRTLE: Thanks. That's a comforting piece of news. —I didn't speak till you lit a cigarette because I thought you'd fallen asleep in that rocker.

LOT: No. I was sitting here thinking.

MYRTLE: I was standin' here thinkin', too, while I washed my nylons and undies.

LOT: Tell me your thoughts, Myrtle.

MYRTLE: I'll tell you one of 'em. Do you think you played fair and square with me when you brought me down here without a word of warning about that man, that animal, down there?

LOT: I thought it was better not to mention Chicken.

MYRTLE: Better for who? For you!

LOT: Yes, for me. You might not've come down here and I couldn't come down here alone.

MYRTLE: Selfishness in your nature isn't a thing to brag of.

LOT: No. I wasn't bragging.

MYRTLE: Every car, truck, wagon, crowds of people on foot headed the opposite way, and you wouldn't turn back! Can you give me a reasonable reason for that?

LOT: —I guess—

MYRTLE: What do you guess?

LOT: I guess I thought in my heart what Chicken told me and wanted to die in this bedroom where I was born. Yes, selfish as hell, but when people are desperate, Myrtle, they only think of themselves.

MYRTLE: Some people. Not all.

LOT: Some people—including me. —Don't hate me for it.

MYRTLE: Whin I love I don't hate.

LOT: You don't have a complex nature. —What time is it, Myrtle?

MYRTLE: My watch don't run. I just wear it now as a bracelet.

LOT: You wound it too tight and broke the springs?

MYRTLE: No, no, baby. Last Fourth of July I wint to a Shriners' picnic on a lake and a couple of drunk Shriners thought it was very funny to throw me in a lake with my watch on, so the works rusted.

LOT: What you should've done to prevent the works from rusting was to take it directly to a jewellers' shop and have the works removed and soaked in oil over-night.

MYRTLE (*sadly*): I should of done many things in my life which I neglected t'do, and not soaking my watch in oil is not the most important I can think of.

LOT: You mean what you regret most is getting married to a—a impotent one-lung sissy who's got one foot in the grave and's about to step in with the other.

MYRTLE: You're putting words in my mouth that I wouldn't speak to anybody I love!

(*She has removed her slacks and is getting into a sheer blouse sprinkled with tiny brilliants and a velveteen skirt.*)

LOT: What're you dressing up for?

MYRTLE: I never keep on slacks after six p.m.

LOT: That outfit you're getting into looks like a costume.

MYRTLE: Baby, all of my dresses are made over from costumes.

LOT (*slowly with little pauses for breath*): This particular one wasn't made over enough to prevent it from still looking like a costume.

MYRTLE: That could be so or not so, but I think it's a sweet little outfit.

LOT: One girl's opinion.

MYRTLE: Yais, an' trusted by her—with your permission.

LOT: I'm not in a position to give or not give permission.

MYRTLE: Lot? Baby? When people are under the weather, it often has the effeck of makin' 'em too critical or sarcastic.

LOT: My mother subscribed to *Vogue* and we both read it. I know the secret of dressing well is to dress in a way that's appropriate to the occasion.

MYRTLE: What occasion is this? Can you tell me?

LOT: It could be the end of the world, but even then—that almost ankle-length imitation velvet skirt might not be appropriate to it.

MYRTLE: This ain't the end of the world, God help me, Jesus, and this skirt is washable velvet.

LOT: There is no such thing as real velvet that's washable, Myrtle.

MYRTLE: Well, I swan, you talk like a dressmaker, Baby.

LOT: My mother, Miss Lottie, had a sense of style that a Paris designer might envy.

MYRTLE: If you talk about her much more, you'll turn me aginst her, Lot.

LOT: —That wouldn't matter. She doesn't exist any more. . . .

MYRTLE: All this style thet she hed, wasn't it wasted down here?

LOT: No, strangely no. In spite of my father who had the taste of a hawg, who ate with his hands and wiped them on his trousers, my mother, Miss Lottie, was socially accepted by sev'ral families with standing in Two River County.

MYRTLE: With so much style, accepted instid of refused, why did she marry this hawg?

LOT: That's a question I can no more answer than if you asked me why God made little green apples.

MYRTLE (*opening closet door in the back wall of the bedroom*): I see, UH-HUH, well, tomorrow, baby, you or me or both of us is gonna clear your mother's clothes outa this closet so I don't have to live out of a suitcase.

LOT: —I'm sorry, but tomorrow—

(*He doesn't complete the sentence. Myrtle's attention is diverted by the loud sound of Chicken pushing his chair back from the kitchen table. He gets up and starts chopping potatoes into a hot skillet, dousing them with grease out of a can on the stove, and tossing into the skillet some strips of bacon. During the bedroom dialogue, he will pick out the fried bacon and eat it, all of it, and wipe his fingers on the seat of his pants. Lot coughs, rackingly. Myrtle feels his forehead.*)

MYRTLE: That's a mean cough you got there, and I don't need a thermometer to tell me you're runnin' a fever, Baby. Yes, Sir, burnin' up with it!

LOT (*gasping*): Fever is—the body's protection—reaction—to the enemy in it—any kind of—infection. . . .

MYRTLE: Sometimes you talk over my head. —I love you, precious baby, I love you and I'm here to protect and care for you, always! (*She presses her head to his.*)

LOT: Love me but don't smother me with it, Myrtle.

MYRTLE: —What a mean thing to say!

LOT: I didn't mean it that way. I meant I have trouble breathing and when you crouch over me like that, it makes it harder for me to draw my breath, that's all.

(*He puts another cigarette in the ivory holder. She snatches the holder away from him.*)

—Give that holder back to me!

MYRTLE: The last thing you need is to smoke!

LOT: It makes no difference now!

MYRTLE: It does to me!

LOT: If you don't return my holder, I'll smoke without it and nobody's going to stop me—at the end of the world. . . .

MYRTLE: Here! Take it back and drive a nail in your coffin but don't talk to me about the end of the world, I haven't come to it yet and don't intend to!

LOT: Thank you, Myrtle.

MYRTLE: Never talk that way to your wife that loves you, my precious blond-headed baby.

LOT: —I'm no more blond than you are. —My hair is bleached.

MYRTLE (*shocked*): Did you say your hair is—bleached?

LOT: As bleached as yours. But I do a better job on my hair than you do on yours because my mother taught me. Ev'ry morning of the world, and if I'm alive tomorrow I'll do it again, I get up, brush my teeth and obey the calls of nature, and the next thing I do, in the hospital or out, is put a wad of cotton on the tip of an orange stick and dip it into a bottle and rub the roots of my hair so it never shows dark, and I don't use peroxide, I use a special formula which my mother invented and passed on to me. She said with blue eyes and fair skin, I'd look best as a blond, the same as she did. . . .

MYRTLE (*aghast*): Well, I'll be switched. . . .

LOT: Now you're disillusioned with your young husband?

MYRTLE: —I thought at least I had married a natural blond.

LOT: Don't let it throw you and don't imagine you have married a fairy.

MYRTLE: Such an idea would never— (*leaves the statement in air*)

LOT: You've married someone to whom no kind of sex relation was ever as important as fighting sickness and trying with his mother to make, to create, a little elegance in a corner of the earth we lived in that wasn't favorable to it.

MYRTLE: —I—

LOT: —You what?

MYRTLE: —Understand. And I'm going to devote myself to you like a religion, mystery as you are, back of that ivory holder and Mona Lisa smile.

(*Pause. Chicken turns up the lamp in the kitchen and blows on the inscription he has carved into the kitchen table, grins at it. Then carries the lamp to the back wall of the kitchen and peers at the photo-in-color of a nude girl, tacked to the wall. —After a moment, he crosses into the hall and calls out—*)

CHICKEN: Hey, up there, Myrtle, Mrs. Lot Ravenstock. Ain't you all getting hungry for something besides each other?

MYRTLE: Should I answer that man?

LOT: Answer him if you're hungry.

MYRTLE (*calling down from the upper hall*): Lot needs feeding and I could eat something, too.

CHICKEN: Come on down, then.

MYRTLE: All right, thank you, I will.

CHICKEN (*lowering his voice*): Come down in a show costume and put on a show.

(*Myrtle kisses Lot on the forehead as Chicken returns to the kitchen.*)

MYRTLE: Oh, child, you're hot as fire! They say feed a cold and starve a fever, but you got both.
LOT: I'm hungry for nothing.
MYRTLE: You're hungry for love, and you're gonna have supper with it.
LOT: At the same time, with no appetite for either?
MYRTLE: When the sun comes out like a bright new five dollar gold piece, your appetite for both will come out with it.
LOT: All of a sudden the days in this place are long and hot an' yellow and—time gets lost. . . . (*His eyes fall shut.*)
MYRTLE: I oughtn't to go down there after the way he mocked me but I smell fried potatoes which is something I cain't resist.
LOT: If you didn't smell fried potatoes you'd smell chicken. . . .
MYRTLE: What?
LOT: Nothing. Go down in your washable velvet and eat for us both.
MYRTLE: I want to say one thing more before I face that creature in the kitchen. You're precious to me, you're beautiful to me, I love you with all my heart, and if you don't feel good now, you're gonna feel wonderful later and you believe it. Believe it?
LOT (*with closed eyes and an enigmatic smile*): Yes, I do, completely.
MYRTLE: You sure better. Here goes! —To what I don't know. . . .

(*She goes down the hall steps as if approaching a jungle.*)

MYRTLE (*entering the kitchen*): Hi. —Hello. —How are you?

(*He ignores all three salutations.*)

Y'know what I thought I smelt down here?
CHICKEN: Me? Chicken?
MYRTLE: Ha, ha, no. I thought I smelt French fries down here.

CHICKEN: There's potatoes down here but there's nothing French about 'em.

MYRTLE: Bacon with 'em?

CHICKEN: You come down too late for the bacon.

MYRTLE: Oh, did I miss out on it?

CHICKEN: You sure missed out on the bacon but there's some bacon grease in the skillet with the potatoes.

MYRTLE: Bacon grease gives potatoes a wonderful flavor. (*She looks about nervously.*) —Memphis is famous for its French fries.

CHICKEN: 'Sthat what it's famous for?

MYRTLE: Yais. —I worked last winter at a place called the French Fried Heaven.

(*Chicken grunts at this information.*)

—Put on ten pounds. —The way they cooked French fries, they put the potatoes in a wire basket and put the wire basket in deep fat.

CHICKEN: The fried potatoes here come out of a skillet.

MYRTLE: Oh, I didn' expeck you t'have a wire basket here. —In the country. I'll, uh, help myself an' then take a plate up to Lot.

(*As she fills a plate with potatoes, Chicken turns the lamp up.*)

Where do you keep the silver?

CHICKEN: You mean knife an' fork?

MYRTLE: Just a fork. I don't need a knife for potatoes.

(*Chicken grunts.*)

Still hot.

CHICKEN: Who?

MYRTLE: I meant the potatoes.

CHICKEN: Aw. I misunnerstood you.

MYRTLE: —Here's the silver. It needs t'be polished. That colored girl Clara don't make herself very useful, I'll have to talk to her.

CHICKEN (*rising*): Take this chair, this is a good chair for you.

MYRTLE: I don't want to take your chair. You stay where you are.

CHICKEN: No, you take this chair, I've warmed it up for you and I'm going back out for another look at the levee.
MYRTLE: Right away?

(*He is pulling on his hip boots.*)

CHICKEN: I'll stay a while if you want me in here with you.
MYRTLE: This is a perfeck time for us to get better acquainted, don't you think so?

(*She avoids his grinning look and sits gingerly down at the kitchen table.*)

CHICKEN: You don' have enough light.
MYRTLE: Yais, enough, I kin see.
CHICKEN (*pushing oil lamp toward her*): Don't strain your eyesight an' go blind before time to.
MYRTLE (*noticing the knife with which he'd been carving something onto the table*): —Is, uh, this, uh, this switch-blade knife your knife?
CHICKEN: —Is it your or Lot's knife?
MYRTLE: We don't, I don't, he don't—carry a switch-blade knife.

(*Tries to laugh; coughs.*)

CHICKEN: Then I reckon it'd be a safe bet that it's mine.
MYRTLE: Will you please put it away? I never could stand the sight of a big switch-blade knife like that fo' some—reason. . . .
CHICKEN: Why's that?
MYRTLE: —It, it— (*Shakes her head, tremulously.*) —Just, just —makes me uncomf'table always.
CHICKEN: —Reminds you of the end of one of the Mobile Hot Shots?
MYRTLE: —Yais. —No.
CHICKEN: Yais and no are two opposite answers. Maybe you mean maybe. (*He laughs and folds the switch-blade knife and puts it in his pocket.*)
MYRTLE: Maybe I ought to fill another plate fo' Lot an' eat with him upstairs. A sick person is lonesome.
CHICKEN: Eat a little with me befo' you go up. I need some company, too. (*He empties the rest of the potatoes in another plate and starts eating them.*)

MYRTLE (*in a strained voice*): —I think I'll move this lamp a little your way.

(*She shoves it toward his seat at the table. He shoves it back toward hers.*)

A, uh, growin' boy or a—single, unmarried man, specially one in the country, allows his mind to dwell on an' give too much attention to—

CHICKEN: —To what? In your opinion?

MYRTLE: —You know what I'm talkin' about.

CHICKEN: I don't have no idea, not a bit.

MYRTLE: Well, I'll tell you, as if it was necessary. A single man in the country might amuse hisself by cutting a—indecent word and a indecent picture in a kitchen table.

CHICKEN: What brought that up, that subjeck?

MYRTLE: They's no point in me pretendin' I didn't notice these fresh wood-shavings on this table and what's been cut in the wood. I want to say just this. A thing like this's understandable in a, uh, growin' boy in the country but you're past that. You ought to be beyond that. An' you ought to know it's insulting to a clean-livin' woman who is not int'rested or attracted to—indecent things in her life.

CHICKEN: I'm glad you unnerstand that a single man in the country has got to amuse hisself.

MYRTLE: I said a growin' boy in the country, not a—adult—man with a—nawmul—mind.

CHICKEN: Aw. I misunnerstood you. You're not eatin' those good home-fried potatoes. You only like French-fried potatoes?

MYRTLE: —I've said what I hed t'say an' now, if you will excuse me, I'll take this plate up to Lot. (*She rises with plate.*)

CHICKEN: Lemme hold the lamp at the foot of the steps an' watch an' admire your hips as you climb up.

(*She hurries into the hall and he follows with the lamp. She stumbles on the steps and drops the plate.*)

Spilt 'em? On the steps?

MYRTLE: I could of got upstairs with them better without your—watching! Would you be good enough to put a, put some—

CHICKEN: If you mean more potatoes you're outa luck. They's nothin' but grease in th' skillet.

(*They face each other a silent moment. Then Chicken laughs and scrapes the spilt potatoes off the steps back onto the tin plate.*)

Here you are. He'll never know you spilt 'em unless you tell him—

MYRTLE: *I'd* know I spilt 'em an' wouldn't dream of—of not infawmin' my husban' exactly of all that wint on down here. Good night!

CHICKEN: Hurry back down agin, sister! Enjoyed your company down here! Hurry back down.

(*She stumbles rapidly up the steps with the tin plate. As she enters the bedroom, Chicken returns to the kitchen, sets the lamp down by carving and inscription and grins savagely at them. Then he blows out the lamp.*)

SCENE THREE

Immediately afterwards, upstairs. Lot is in the chair, eyes shut.

MYRTLE: Lot? Are you asleep?

LOT: No. No, I'm awake.

MYRTLE: Can you eat a little?

LOT: No. I don't want food.

MYRTLE: I got to tell you something. Something awful. I am still shaking all over. Feel how cold my hand is. Well. I come down in the kitchen. I said I smelled some bacon. He said I come down too slow. The bacon was gone. But I could have some potatoes. So I hed some potatoes. I had to swallow my pride because I was dyin' of hunger not having nothing to eat since that ham sandwich we hed on the road this mawnin. Well. I helped myself to potatoes and then I set down at the table. I started to try to make some polite conversation. Not that I wanted to talk to that son of a bitch but because I knowed that people living together under one roof have got to make some effort to get along.

Well. I notice a pocket knife and some fresh wood shavings in the middle of the table. Well. That was peculiar but I said nothing about it. Then I noticed he kept turning the lamp up. Each time a little bit higher. Then all at once I noticed. I seen the reason. *That man is a lunatic!* You know what he had done? He had cut out a disgusting picture in the table, in the wood of the table, right in front of my plate, a disgusting word and a disgusting pitcher. I!—I started to choke! When I seen it. I sprung up from the table. He says, "What is the matter with you, Myrtle?" Just as innocent-like as you could imagine! Well. I didn't admit that I had seen a damn thing on that table. I just said, "I better take Lot up some food."

LOT (*mysteriously smiling*): What was the picture of? A man or a woman?

MYRTLE: Both!

LOT: Both?

MYRTLE: Yes, both.

LOT: Doing what?

MYRTLE: Can't you imagine what? With his dirty mind?

(*Lot laughs and coughs.*)

You think it's funny?

LOT: I think everything's funny. In this world. I even think it's funny I'm going to die.

MYRTLE: It may surprise you a little but I'm going to tell you what *I* am planning to do. I'm planning to get on the phone and call to THE POlice.

LOT: How are you going to do that?

MYRTLE: He's got into his hip boots. He's going back out on that levee and soon as he goes I'm going to call the police.

LOT: You think they'll come.

MYRTLE: I reckon they will when I tell them he's out of his mind and I am your wife and afraid to stay in the house with him over this night!

LOT: Nobody will come. Nobody will answer the phone.

MYRTLE: Why do you say they won't come?

LOT: Have you forgotten this county is half under water, and the crest of the flood is still coming?

MYRTLE: I keep forgetting that fact because it's like a bad dream I don't believe. And anyhow. Decent people have got to be protected, flood or no flood, yes, come hell or high water.

LOT: —There he goes.

MYRTLE: Who? Chicken?

LOT: Who else is here but you and me and Chicken?

MYRTLE: Well! I'm going down there and try to phone the police.

LOT: See if you can get hold of his wallet.

MYRTLE: What for?

LOT: He's got a paper in it he made me sign. It leaves the place to him if I should die.

MYRTLE: And me? What about me! Left with nothing?

LOT: I don't know if the paper will still be good or not good if I die with a widow.

MYRTLE: —How could I git this paper?

LOT: How well can you hold liquor?

MYRTLE: I guess that question has a point but I don't see it.

LOT: I wondered if you could drink with a man till he passes out but you don't. Chicken's been drinking down there. I've heard him clump the liquor jug on the kitchen table every few minutes or so since we came upstairs, and he was probably drinking a good while before we got here.

MYRTLE: I guess you're drivin' at something but I don't know what.

LOT: Chicken always has on him, in his wallet, that legal paper that leaves this place to him when I go.

MYRTLE: I don't understand what—

LOT: Let me tell you this without interruption, Myrtle, and try to listen to me. Get Chicken drunk but don't get drunk yourself and when he passes out, get this legal paper out of his wallet, tear it to bits and pieces and burn 'em up. Then, as my wife, when I die, this place will be yours, go to you. —Valuable property.

MYRTLE: I don't know how to pretend to not drink but—

LOT: This paper in Lot's wallet—he sleeps on a cot in the kitchen—he keeps this wallet containin' this paper under his pillow like it was sacred to him. Which it is. Sacred. Is my head too vague to explain this?

MYRTLE: You've explained it, but it sounds like a risky suggestion, he's such a bull of a man, and—

LOT: Don't you want this place, all your own, when I go?

MYRTLE: Risky. Suppose he—?

LOT: Anything worth having and doing in this world is risky. So go down and use your charms on him and drink but out of your drink take little sips like a bird while he sloshes down his till he falls on his cot, passed out, and you take out his wallet and out of his wallet take that legal paper and destroy it. Own this place. It would haunt me in my grave and my mother in hers if this place went to Chicken. That paper gone, you'll own a good piece of property and you can run him off it, marry again, and be happy.

MYRTLE: How do I know if—?

LOT: Here's your chance to own something.

MYRTLE: —Is this the reason you married me, baby, an' brought me down here?

LOT: I married and brought you down here to own a place of your own an' be a lady.

MYRTLE: —Well—I'll give it a try. Hmmm. I wasn't called the Petite Personality Kid for nothing.

LOT: Hear him? Coming back in the kitchen?

MYRTLE: Yais, down I go, wish me luck. God knows I'm gonna need it.

LOT: I wish you luck and my mother does, too.

(*Myrtle picks up the oil lamp and starts to the door.*)

Do you have to remove the lamp and leave me gasping in dark?

MYRTLE: Don't I have to light myself down the stairs?

LOT: Go ahead, take it. The moon's out like the bleary eye of a drunkard.

MYRTLE: 'Sthere anything I can do for you 'fore I go down?

LOT: Nothing. Go down. Get the paper.

(*She exits from the bedroom with the lamp. The bedroom is completely dimmed out except for a faint and fitful streak of moonlight on Lot in the rocker.*)

SCENE FOUR

Immediately following, Myrtle descends the stairs with the lamp and the laundry. Hearing her, Chicken returns to the kitchen table and turns up the lamp.

MYRTLE: —I thought you'd gone out of the house.

CHICKEN: —What would I go out for? That wet electric equipment that's gonna git wetter?

MYRTLE: —I'm afraid I let my nerves get the better of me. Let's forget it. I, uh, come down to tell you I'm worried sick about Lot. He has trouble drawing his breath.

CHICKEN: It's hard to draw breath without lungs.

MYRTLE: He won't stop smoking. And says it's the end of the world. I simply couldn't stand it a minute longer without a—drink. Have you got some liquor down here?

CHICKEN: They don't sell me bottle liquor in this county but I can git it by the jug from a—ole colored man that brews a pretty good brew.

MYRTLE: Is, uh, that the jug there?

CHICKEN: Yep, and it ain't drained yet. I'll give you a drink. —I treat you pretty nice, don't I? For a single man in the country?

MYRTLE: We just—haven't yet got used to each other. And this has been a day an' a night that would make any girl nervous with or without nerves in her.

CHICKEN: I guess you want a stiff drink, a pretty stiff one.

MYRTLE: Oh, uh, for me, just average. You have one with me, let's drink together an' git better acquainted. —Oh. This wash. I noticed you have a clothes line in the kitchen. Do you object if I hang up my undies to dry?

CHICKEN: Hang 'em up. (*She daintily hangs up some rayon panties and a brassiere.*) They'll dry out good in the flood.

MYRTLE: Do me a favor and stop reminding me of this—possible flood.

CHICKEN: It's not a possible flood, this flood is certain.

MYRTLE: Let's not—talk about it. I like drinking from a tin cup, I like the metal taste you git from it.

CHICKEN: —Why do you make that whistling noise when you breathe?

MYRTLE: I am choked up with asthma.

CHICKEN: Aw, you got as'ma.

MYRTLE: Oh, no, I haven't got asthma, it's got me. I got that allergy thing. You know about it—I wint to a Memphis doctor who give me the allergy tests and guess what he found out, he found out I was living with a cat and had a allergy to it. Yes, I had a cat I was real, real fond of, cat named Fluffy. Well, they discovered this cat, she had a allergy to me. I had to git rid of Fluffy, it was her or me. First I give her a great big head of a catfish, which was her favorite food. Like the last supper of the condemned. Then chloroformed her. Poor Fluffy. I was so attached to her and her to me. —I wept a bucket full of tears that night! Whew. (*rises*) From the way I suffer from my asthma tonight, I'm willing to bet that there's a cat somewhere on this place.

CHICKEN: I got a cat.

MYRTLE: That explains it.

CHICKEN: I brought her in for company tonight.

(*Lifts a cat in his lap. Myrtle knew the cat was there but pretends to be surprised.*)

MYRTLE: Oh, no wonder I am choking with asthma, git that cat out of here, for heaven's sake, please!

CHICKEN: *Here, Kitty.* (*He lazily seizes cat and pulls up a trap door near the kitchen table and drops cat through it. She drops with a howl and a splash below. He drops the trap door shut.*)

MYRTLE: Why, that cellar is flooded! I heard a splash!

CHICKEN: You said you wanted her out.

MYRTLE: Out the door, not *drowned*!

(*She raises trap door and cries "Kitty!" He nudges her stooping figure with his knee. She screams and rolls on the floor.*)

Oh, my God, you tried to push me in! You tried to drown me!

CHICKEN: Ha ha ha!

MYRTLE: Oh, my God, my God, you tried to drown me!

CHICKEN: Ha ha ha ha ha ha ha!

LOT (*calling weakly above*): *Myrtle, Myrtle!*

CHICKEN: Your lover is calling for you.

MYRTLE (*crawling away on the floor*): Close!—Close that trap door!

CHICKEN: Aw, come on, knock it off! Nobody's going to drown you—Myrtle Turtle!

MYRTLE: You wanted to drown me like you drowned that cat!

CHICKEN: That cat ain't drowned. She swum on top of the wood-pile. —Same as you'd do if I put you down there with her.

MYRTLE: —I—cain't—swim!

CHICKEN: —Can you do anything? —Outside of bed?

MYRTLE: Chicken, please shut that trap door.

(*He kicks it shut.*)

Oh, my heart! How you scared me! (*Gasps and rises weakly.*) Please, I—give me a shot of that—whiskey. . . .

CHICKEN: Go on. Pour you' self one.

MYRTLE (*breathlessly laughing*): I'm afraid to git up! I swear to goodness I am!

CHICKEN: Aw, now, knock it off. I was just fooling a little.

MYRTLE (*cautiously crossing to table*): Where is—where is a cup. My heart is—still beating!

CHICKEN: Shit, if your heart wasn' beatin' you'd be daid!

MYRTLE: Not like this! It's beatin' like a hammer!

CHICKEN: You remember that song?

MYRTLE (*nervously*): Which—which song?

CHICKEN:

"My heart beat like a ham-mer!
Your arms—wound around me tight!
And stars—fell on Alabama—last—night!"

MYRTLE: Yes, I do, I remember.—Do you remember this one? This one's another old-timer!

"Is it true what they say about Dixie?
Is a dream by that stream so sublime?
Do they laugh, do they love
Like they say in ev'ry song!
—If it's true—that's where *I—be—long*!"

CHICKEN: Ha ha ha ha ha! That one goes back a long way. Yes, siree, Bob, that's a real old-timer!

MYRTLE: And how about this one? Oh, this one is a—

LOT: Myr-*tlllllle*!

MYRTLE: Coming, honey, coming in just a minute!— (*Fearfully as he approaches the table toward her.*)

—Oh, this is fun, this—*singing*—I—love a song-fest, I love a—community—singing! Almost more than anything I can think of.

CHICKEN: Go on and sing! What song?

MYRTLE: —Wait till I—get my drink down! (*She walks in back of table with her whiskey in a tin cup.*)

CHICKEN: Wettin' your whistle, first?

MYRTLE: That's right, wetting my whistle!

CHICKEN: You almost wet something else when I pushed you toward that trap door! Huh, Myrtle? —*Ha ha ha ha ha!*

MYRTLE (*faintly and mirthlessly*): Ha ha ha . . .

CHICKEN: Awright, now, what song was you going to sing for me, next on the program of old-time fav'rites?

MYRTLE: I wish that I had my little ukulele! My—dear ole uke!

CHICKEN: How 'bout a guitar, will that do?

MYRTLE (*with air of delight*): Oh, hev you got a guitar!

CHICKEN: Yeah. Here. (*Removes guitar from back of closet door and hands it to her.*)

MYRTLE: This is a *man*size instrument!

CHICKEN: Don't you like a man-size instrument?

MYRTLE: I'm just wondering if I—

CHICKEN: Oh, I bet you can play it!

MYRTLE: We'll find out if I can.

CHICKEN: Sure you can. What's the number? I'll sing along with you!

MYRTLE: I love the old-time numbers. Don't you love them?

CHICKEN: The old-time tunes are the best.

MYRTLE: Here's one I can pick out with a—few—chords. . . . (*She is almost too breathless to sing.*)

"They's a long, long trail a-windin'
Into the land of my dreams!
Where the nightingale is—"

(*He moves toward the trap door. Her voice dies out in panic.*)

CHICKEN: Whacha stop for?

MYRTLE: You was going to sing with me.

CHICKEN: Sing it through once by you'self so I'll get the words.

MYRTLE: You mean you don't know the words to that old number? I thought everyone does. That song dates back a long ways, it dates back to World War One.

CHICKEN: Then how come you know it? You don't date back that far.

MYRTLE: It's one of those songs that—

CHICKEN: What?

MYRTLE: Never go out of—fashion. —Do me a favor, Chicken. Don't stand there by that trap-door to the cellar. It makes me too nervous to sing. Sit over here by me.

CHICKEN: Aw, you ain't nervous, you just think you're nervous.

MYRTLE: I'm nervous enough to scream.

CHICKEN: Don't scream. Sing! Sing some other old song.

MYRTLE: Like, uh—what?

CHICKEN: How about something religious?

MYRTLE: You really want something religious?

CHICKEN: Yeah, yeah, something from church, something out of the Hymn-book.

MYRTLE: Funny I—know lots of church songs but—can't think of any right now, ha ha! Ain't that funny? Wait a minute! Wait a minute! One's comin' back to me now. Oh, yes. Oh, yes, I got one, ha ha, I got one now! (*Assumes a rapt, grotesquely stiff smile, throws her head back and croons with her eyes half closed.*)

"My feet took a walk in heavenly grass.
All day while the sky shone clear as glass.
My feet took a walk in heavenly grass,
All night while the lonesome stars rolled past.
Then my feet come down to walk on earth,
And my mother cried when she give me birth.
Now my feet walk far and my feet walk fast,
But they still got an itch for heavenly grass.
But they still got an itch for heavenly grass."

CHICKEN: You're gettin' hoarse, Myrtle.

MYRTLE: I thought you was gonna sing with me.

CHICKEN: I don't sing good enough to.

MYRTLE: You got a *good* voice. You know, you always expect a big man is going to sing baritone or bass but they usually sing tenor? You got a sweet tenor voice. Ain't I silly? Gaspin' for breath like this!

CHICKEN: It's that cat allergy thing, you got that allergy thing!

MYRTLE: No, no, it's not cats, it's—!

CHICKEN: It's what? What, Myrtle?

MYRTLE: *Nerves!* A nervous condition!

CHICKEN: You're worried about that cat, that's what's your trouble. I think you're a member of that society, that human humane society, maybe the president of it (*He is pulling on his rubber hip boots.*)

MYRTLE: What's you getting into those rubber boots for?

CHICKEN: I'm going down in the basement to fetch that cat.

MYRTLE: Oh, she's done for, she's gone, now.

CHICKEN: No, she ain't. Come on, let's find that cat. You're worried about her, so let's go down in the basement an' find that cat.

MYRTLE (*backing away from him*): You—*you* do that—if it's possible for you to do.

(*He jerks the trap door open. Myrtle screams and hurls the guitar away as she rushes into the hall and scrambles up the stairs, screaming repeatedly. Chicken howls with laughter; then leaps abruptly into the basement with a splash, calling "pussy, pussy, pussy?" The cat yowls and Chicken laughs. He leaps back up from the trap door, still laughing, with the cat in his hand. He is still laughing and holding the cat as the stage dims out.*)

Intermission.

SCENE FIVE

Immediately following. The bedroom is lighted and, at a much lower level, so are the back steps of the house where Chicken sits with his cat. The parlor is now masked by an opaque transparency. Lot remains in the wicker chair in the bedroom. He is still smoking with his mother's ivory holder and wearing now her white silk wrapper. His "Mona Lisa" smile is more sardonic and the violet shadows about his eyes are deeper. Myrtle stands, panting, in the doorway.

LOT: —From the singing and other commotions I heard down there, I don't need to ask you if you got the paper. —Did you? No, you didn't.

MYRTLE: You listen here! Enough is enough and more than enough is too much!

LOT: You didn't get much liquor down him. —Did you?

MYRTLE: That man, that animal down there, could drink a liquor store dry and walk straight to another!

LOT: I thought you told me there wasn't a man on earth that you weren't able to manage. Well. If that statement was accurate, then either Chicken isn't a man or he isn't on earth. And I think he is both.

MYRTLE: Don't be sarcastic with *me.*

LOT: Don't shout so he can hear you. Can you speak without shouting?

MYRTLE: I said don't be sarcastic with me. I'm not in a mood to take it after what I went through in the kitchen with your so-called brother.

LOT: My opposite type. I hate that man with a passion.

MYRTLE: I'm terrified of him. Is there a key to this door to lock him out?

LOT: No. I hate and despise him with such a passion that if this place or anything on this place became his property—

MYRTLE: S'pose he comes up here and drags me down?

LOT: Neither mother or me could rest in peace in Old Gray Cemetery.

MYRTLE: I'm not in a cemetery. What about me?

LOT: What about you except you—

MYRTLE: There's not just you, there's me. The selfish streak in your nature is wide as the river—flooding!

LOT: Have you ever owned much of anything in your life?

MYRTLE: Yais! My self-respeck an' decency as a woman!

LOT: In addition to that, marvelous as it is, would you like to own and possess entirely as your own a place that's worth much more than it gives appearance of being?

MYRTLE: —Worth what? In cash?

LOT: Over fifty thousand and could increase well-managed. . . . (*Long pause*) —Well? Attractive to you or not?

MYRTLE: I've never owned a stone I could call my own.

LOT: —A pitiful confession, but now's your chance if you want it.

(*A pause as Myrtle reflects.*)

MYRTLE: —Sugar? Baby? Why don't you get in bed instead of sitting at a window in a light silk wrapper?

LOT: I breathe better sitting up in a chair—and can look at the sky.

MYRTLE: The sky's clouded over.

LOT: Once in a while the moon comes out of those fast-moving clouds, and it—says things to me in the soft voice of my mother. . . .

MYRTLE: I wish you would get in bed and let me hold you and love you.

LOT: You don't have to hold me to love me.

MYRTLE: You're shivering. Lemme put something heavier around you like a blanket.

LOT: No, no, don't. I don't want to be smothered.

MYRTLE: Chicken's out of the kitchen, so I am going back in it and fill a hot-water bottle for you an' git you in this bed if you like it or not.

LOT: There's not any hot-water bottle.

MYRTLE: I never travel without one. It's in my traveling case.

LOT: I should've known.

MYRTLE: What?

LOT: —Nothing, and not much of that either.

MYRTLE: That seems to be what you know, but I am going back down there and get hold of that paper, how I don't know, but somehow. And I'm going down there in my show costume as the Personality Kid. (*She changes quickly into the costume.*)

LOT: I think what attracts you back down there is nothing made of rubber and nothing made of paper, whether you face it or not.

MYRTLE: Your fever's gone to your haid, if you think that.

LOT: I don't just think it, I know it. —I won't see daylight again.

MYRTLE: I can pick you up and carry you to the bed and that's what I'm gonna do when I've filled my hot-water bottle.

LOT: Anybody with arms could pick me up—if they wanted to force me against my will.

MYRTLE: Is it against your will to be loved and made well?

LOT: —No. —If you can't make him pass out to get that paper, knock him out with a hammer that's in the drawer of the kitchen table and don't come up here again without that paper. You get that paper and you can pick me up and carry me to the bed with no resistance and I'll—rest in your arms. . . .

MYRTLE: I got to take this lamp to get down the stairs in my—shaky condition.

LOT: Take it. I get enough light from the sky.

(*She goes back into the hall and starts down the steps. She is halfway down them with the lamp when Chicken slams open the back door and enters the lower hall.*)

MYRTLE (*terrified gasp*): HAH! (*She drops the oil lamp on the stairs; it goes out.*)

CHICKEN: Trying to start a fire? Burn your place down? Before it goes under water?

MYRTLE: —I thought—

CHICKEN: Don't strain your brain thinkin'.

MYRTLE: Lot's—Lot's havin' a chill. Terrible. I want to fill up a hot-water bottle for him. Kin I come down?

CHICKEN: Why do you ask to come downstairs in your house?

MYRTLE: I don't possess this house or anything in it except what I brought here with me.

CHICKEN: All that electric equipment to make life easy for you?

(*He laughs and enters the kitchen. Myrtle stops in the downstairs hall and speaks tremulously*—)

MYRTLE: Please do me a favor before I come in the kitchen.

CHICKEN: Such as what? (*He turns up the kitchen lamp.*)

MYRTLE: Of course I know you wuh teasing me with that trap door open, but would you please push the table over it now.

CHICKEN: It ain't open now.

MYRTLE: Open or shut, I couldn't be comf'table in the kitchen unless that table was over that trap-door.

CHICKEN: (*pushing the table with his foot*): You're Mistress of the House, the Lady in it. Whatever you tell me to do I'm obliged t'do it.

(*Myrtle moves nervously to the kitchen threshold.*)

MYRTLE: I'm just a visitor here, but would you push the table over the trap-door a little bit further than that? Please?

CHICKEN: Why, sure, Mrs. Lot Ravenstock. A hired hand on a place always does what pleases the lady and the boss-man. (*He shoves the table further with his foot.*)

—How's that now, does that suit you?

MYRTLE: (*entering the kitchen*): Yes, thank you, fine, perfeck. I feel much more easy.

CHICKEN: You're a city lady and I'm a country boy with common habits. I hope you'll excuse me for them.

MYRTLE: I've been teased in my life. I had two older brothers, Jack and Jim, that teased me nearly to death. Y'see, my curls were long then. And they would pull them and yell "Ding-dong." Oh, it never hurt much but it always scared me. Holler? Oh, would I holler! Sometimes it wouldn't be necessary for them to pull my curls, they could just say "Ding-Dong" and I'd scream fit to kill and blaze a trail to the house, so you see I'm used to teasing, but so much has happened in the last few hours I feel un-strung. —A little.

CHICKEN: You're walking around like you wuh lookin' fo' something.

MYRTLE: A kettle to boil water in. So I can fill a hot-water bottle in my traveling case.

(*She removes the hot-water bottle from the beat-up case and wanders distractedly about the kitchen.*)

CHICKEN: Why don'tcha put the hot-water bottle down while you look for the kettle so you'll have both your hands free?

MYRTLE: Ha! —What's the matter with me? I sure don't seem to have my head on my—!

(*Chicken rises, setting the cat on the floor.*)

That cat didn't drown in the cellar?

CHICKEN: Shit, no. You can't drown a cat unless you put her in a sack full of rocks. She swum on top of th' woodpile. Didn't you, pussy? (*He hands a kettle to her.*)

MYRTLE: Thanks. (*She sets the kettle on the stove.*)

CHICKEN: —Is that how you do it?

MYRTLE: —Huh?

CHICKEN: —You git the kettle hot first and thin put th' water in it?

MYRTLE: Ha ha! Ain't that *somethin*? Shows how upset I am! I put that empty kettle on the stove without water in it!

CHICKEN: Gimme th' kettle. I'll git you some water in it from the rain barrel out there.

(*Crosses to the door with the kettle and descends to the rain barrel. She follows to the door.*)

MYRTLE: They say rain water's the purest water there is.

CHICKEN: Is that what they say? Well, nothin's too pure for Lot.

MYRTLE: —Not that it matters in a hot-water bottle. . . .

CHICKEN: Yeah, well . . .

(*Hands her the dripping kettle. She returns inside. He watches her back as she moves to the stove and gives a slight wolf whistle. She gets the kettle on the stove with a bang that makes her give a startled laugh.*)

What's the joke? (*She goes on laughing, helplessly.*) Let me in on the joke, it must be a good one.

MYRTLE: I just, just!—*got—hysterics!* (*Continues giggling.*)

CHICKEN: They's two ways to stop hysterics in a woman. One way is to give her a slap in the face and the other way is to lay her. Sometimes you got to do both.

MYRTLE: Oh, I'm all right now. I come out of hysterics as quick as I go in them. —How come a handsome young man like you is still single?

CHICKEN: —I'm dark-complected.

MYRTLE: What of it?

CHICKEN: They's not been a woman on this place, not since Miss Lottie died, but the colored girl Clara and she's took to the hills to get away from the flood.

MYRTLE: You mention this flood like it didn't scare you a bit.

CHICKEN: Floods make the land richer.
MYRTLE: What good does that do if you drown?
CHICKEN: I'm not gonna drown. —Are you?
MYRTLE: Lord God Jesus, I pray to my Saviour I won't!
CHICKEN: You'd do better praying to Chicken.
MYRTLE: I'm counting on your protection.
CHICKEN: You better not count on that.
MYRTLE: That's what I'm counting on, Chicken.
CHICKEN: Count on nothing. Set down.
MYRTLE: I prefer to stay on my feet a while if—
CHICKEN: If what?
MYRTLE: —If you don't object.
CHICKEN: Shit, I don't mind if you stand on your head if you want to! But look. I got this old auto cushion I'll put on this here chair and'll make you a nice soft seat. I know a woman don't like a hard seat, does she? Well, here's a real soft cushion for you to sit on while we talk.
MYRTLE: —Thanks! (*She seats herself tensely on the edge of the auto cushion.*)
CHICKEN (*with a slow, wolfish grin*): Now you got *three* cushions?
MYRTLE: —*Three?* —*OH!* —*Ha ha!* —yaissss—three . . .

(*Loud silence in the kitchen.*)

CHICKEN: You feel comf'table?
MYRTLE: Yaiss! Yes, very! Are you?
CHICKEN: I always make myself comfortable as I can.
MYRTLE: Why not? You should! —a man should . . .
CHICKEN: —Should what?
MYRTLE: —Why—uh—make himself as comf'table as he—can . . .
CHICKEN: —How about you? Are you comf'table, too? On those three soft cushions?
MYRTLE: Yes, I told you I was. I'm just a little worried about my husband. I had no idea, I simply had no notion at all that he was in such a bad condition as this. I mean I . . . I just didn't have an idea . . .
CHICKEN: It's like you bought a used car that turned out to be a lemon.

MYRTLE: Oh, that's not how I look at it. That boy has touched the deepest chord in my nature. I mean I . . . (*She suddenly sobs.*)

CHICKEN: Quit that. I want to talk to you.

MYRTLE: Yes, talk!

CHICKEN: I guess you know the setup.

MYRTLE (*struggling for composure*): The what?

CHICKEN: The setup. Do you know it?

MYRTLE (*with a weak attempt at levity*): The only setup I know of is in a dry state they'll serve you a setup for liquor but not the liquor. You got to bring that with you.

CHICKEN: —If I was your lawyer I would advise you not to try to be funny.

MYRTLE: Can't we—joke a little?

CHICKEN: I'd advise you aginst it.

MYRTLE: Awright, I'll take that advice, but, Chicken, do you know that all the electric equipment I won as the Take-Life-Easy Queen is still in that car with a leakin' top bein' rained on?

CHICKEN: Fawgit that stuff. It can't be saved from flood-water. Can you concentrate on the legal setup if I explain it to you, or do you think it's something that don't concern you?

MYRTLE: I'm—anxious to know the—setup. Is the kettle boilin', is that water hot yet?

CHICKEN: Fawgit th' kettle. The fire is low in the stove.

MYRTLE: But I told Lot I'd—

CHICKEN: You don't seem t'want to know about the setup.

MYRTLE: Oh, that's not true, I do!

CHICKEN: I'll explain it to you.

MYRTLE: Yais, wonderful, do that! Whatever concerns this place an' my future life on it is impawtent t' me to understand an' t'know.

CHICKEN: Lot an' me are half brothers. Has that sunk into your haid yet?

MYRTLE: Oh, yes, that I do know. It come out in the, the—conversation we hed when we—first met, this—day.

CHICKEN: That's right. You got that straight. Maybe you know the rest of it.

MYRTLE: Lemme pour you some liquor while you explain the setup.

(*She tries to lift the jug off the table but her hands are too weak and shaky.*)

CHICKEN: Cain't lift the jug, you're so nervous about the setup. Open your mouth and I'll pour some liquor down *you.*

MYRTLE: Thanks, I thank you. I couldn't git through this night without liquor in me. Could you?

CHICKEN: Mouth open.

(*She opens her mouth a little: He presses the mouth of the jug to it. The liquor runs down her chin and neck.*)

MYRTLE: Oh, it's stainin' my dress!

CHICKEN: You wouldn't swallow the liquor, drooled it out.

MYRTLE: I wasn't actually thirsty. You drink some. I like to see a man drink.

CHICKEN: What I am going to do is tell you about the setup, all of it. The rest that you might now know.

MYRTLE: What is the rest of the setup?

CHICKEN: Daddy got Lot in marriage but not me. You're lookin' at what is called a wood's-colt. (*He perches himself on the table and the light is hot on him.*) Whin I was ten years old he married this little blond haided woman that worked in a beauty shop in Clarksdale. Are you list'nin' or still too nervous to lissen?

MYRTLE: I'm list'nin' close. All ears.

CHICKEN: I wouldn't say that about you but I'd advise you to lissen close as you're able to me. This little lady that worked in the beauty parlor in Clarksdale was named Miss Lottie, so when Lot was bawn, he got the name of Lot. Legal; bawn in marriage. Not a wood's-colt. Me—wood's-colt. You know what a wood's-colt is?

MYRTLE: No, I don't know that I know. All I know is you look—

CHICKEN: —Dark-complected?

MYRTLE: Foreign. —Foreign?

CHICKEN: My son of a bitch of a daddy got me offen a dark-complected woman he lived with in Alabama. —What about it?

MYRTLE: Why—nothing!

(*Slight pause.*)

Ain't you drinkin' no more? This awful night?

CHICKEN: Why're you so anxious for me to drink more?

MYRTLE: I don't like drinking alone. It makes me lonesome.

CHICKEN: I can drink you under this kitchen table, tonight.

MYRTLE: I'd rather stay on my feet with the flood you say's coming.

CHICKEN: You'd rather drown standing up?

MYRTLE: Don't talk about drowning. You wouldn't let that happen.

CHICKEN: —Let's get back to the setup. —Lot's mother, Miss Lottie, she thought she was surely going to bury my daddy. Hell, he was sixty when he married Miss Lottie.

MYRTLE: Is that what you mean by the setup?

CHICKEN: Just shut up and listen. —She'd no sooner got married to him that she begun to cheat on him with a good-looking young Greek fellow that had a fruit store in town. Why, ev'ry afternoon, Miss Lottie would say to daddy, "Daddy, I think I will drive in town to buy some fruit to make us a nice fruit salad." And when she got to the store, the store man would let her in and lock the door and she'd stay in for two hours and come out with four or five peaches like it had took her them two hours to pick out that small bag of peaches.

MYRTLE: Why didn't you tell your daddy?

CHICKEN: If I had told him, he'd've told her I told him, and she would of got me thrown outa here in minutes! —Well, she did bury my daddy and the place was hers but she didn't have long to hold it. The Greek sold out his fruit store, quit Miss Lottie, and left. —He just left town but Miss Lottie left the world.

MYRTLE: Daid. Yes. Lot told me. —Tragic.

CHICKEN: Well, she lived long enough to throw me off the place. Called me in her little parlor one day and fired me like a field hand. "Chicken," she said, "I think it's just about time for you to clear off this place and make your own way in the world." I said, "Well, gimme what's comin' to me." —What she give me amounted to just about the pay that a field hand gets for a week's work. It got me down the state to Meridian where I worked in a sawmill till. . . . And then this happened—Miss Lottie couldn't go on without trips to that fruit store so she quit eating, quit sleeping—quit breathing. And one month after she died, Lot started dying. One lung gone and one going, but trying to run this place. Didn't take long for him to find out he couldn't, so I begun to hear from him. He sent for me to come back and operate this place for him, sent for me twice by letter and a third time by wire. First and only wire *I* ever got in my life. Chicken, come back, was the message, I will make a deal with you. —Well, I'm no fool.

MYRTLE: No, no, you're no fool.

CHICKEN: I said, "All right, but I'm going to name the deal, and here's the deal." I said, "If you want me to run this place for you, well, here's the deal. Whin you are through with TB!—it goes to me. . . ."

MYRTLE: TB?

CHICKEN: You ain't paying attention to what I tell you. Not TB. The place, this *place*!

MYRTLE: —Oh! —So that's the setup.

CHICKEN: Yes, Ma'am, that is the setup.

MYRTLE: Oh. Uh-huh. I see. . . .

CHICKEN: You don't look happy about it!

MYRTLE: Don't I? Well, now, after all, you can't expect me to be overjoyed about it. I mean, after all, I'm human. And—

CHICKEN: And what?

MYRTLE: —Nothin, nothin but—

CHICKEN: But what?

MYRTLE: —If Lot dies I'm his widow and—

CHICKEN: That's just exactly the point that I'm coming to later, that's just the little situation we're tryin to git straightened out right now in this kitchen before the floodwater comes. I got a decision to make.

MYRTLE: What decision?

CHICKEN: A big one. A big one for you and me both. —Have you ever climbed on a roof?

MYRTLE: Me? Climbed on a roof? No. Not that I can remember. It don't seem—likely. . . . Why? Why do you ask me if I ever climbed on a roof?

CHICKEN: If you can't climb on a roof Lot won't have a widow when the floodwater comes. Now do you understand why I asked you that question? —Yeah. I can see that you do. So now to go on with what —What's the matt—? Why are you getting up?

(*Myrtle has risen stiffly from the chair with a look of slow and dreadful comprehension. Her breathing is audible and rapid.*)

—Your breath is whistling again. You want the cat out of here?

MYRTLE: *No, no, no, no, no, no, no!*

CHICKEN: I can put her back in the cellar if she is giving you as'ma.

MYRTLE: No, no, no, I'm all right, I'm—*fine*, I'm—all right. . . .

CHICKEN: Then why don't you stay in your seat? Ain't that auto cushion comfortable to sit on?

MYRTLE: Sure, it's—fine!

(*She remains standing, her eyes wide and bright but not focussed. He rises deliberately and picks up the auto cushion, examines it and dusts it and puts it back down again.*)

CHICKEN: You women have got a lot of heat in you. That cushion is warm from your body. Why don't you sit down while I finish explaining the setup?

MYRTLE: Oh, it's all clear now. I understand the setup and I want you to know, here is my right hand to God, that everything you told me is okay as far as I am concerned. I got no designs on nothing. You know it's funny how quickly the human mind changes! Ain't it queer how quick it changes? I had my heart set on a quiet, happy married life. Now what I want most in the world is to return to show business! —that's what I'm going to do, I'm going to cut out all fats and sweets and fried foods and get back my shape and go straight back to show business. It keeps you alive. It keeps you trim. It keeps you alert. It's the business for me. Absolutely no other can compare with it for keeping you healthy and active. —Now I think I can fill that hot-water bottle and take it up to that poor child I married . . . —*God please pity us both!*

(*She starts toward the stove but he seizes her wrist.*)

CHICKEN: I want you to stay sitting here till I've finished talking to you. You going to do that?

MYRTLE: —Why—sure!

CHICKEN: Good. Take a shot of this liquor. It might be good for your as'ma.

MYRTLE: Why, thanks! (*The tin cup shakes: She lifts it with both hands to her lips.*) —thanks. . . .

CHICKEN: So I said to him. I said to my half brother, "Lot, I want this place when you're gone. I been on this place all my life and I want to stay on this place all my life till I die. I was here before you come to it and I want to be here when you go. Is that understood? Is that understood, now, clearly?"

MYRTLE: Yes, yes, clearly, clearly . . .

CHICKEN: Good. So the place goes to Chicken, the place and everything on it goes to Chicken when you die.

MYRTLE: *Me? Die?*

CHICKEN: *Lot!*

MYRTLE: —Oh . . .

CHICKEN: Yes! "OH!"—we got to get things straightened out. . . .

MYRTLE: I told you I—

CHICKEN: Has anyone ever told you you talk too much? If I had married a woman with such a loose mouth, I'd put a stopper in it. "All right," I said. "All right. That's the agreement and I want it on paper, so let's put it on paper. Otherwise I don't stay." He said, "Stay, stay, we'll put it on paper," so we put it on paper. Had it drawn up, legal. Notary seal. Witnesses' names put on it. Signed in their presence! Now! (*Removes wallet and unfolds from about it a thick rubber band.*) I got this paper to prove it. The paper we drawn up between us with a notary seal and names of witnesses on it.

(*She stretches out her hand as he produces the paper from his wallet.*)

Oh, no. Someone's got itchy fingers. —Look but don't touch! —Understand? I never let this paper out of my hands. I sleep with this paper underneath my pillow and when I wake up in the mawning, you know what I find? I find my hand clutching my wallet with this paper in it. Even in my sleep I protect this paper! I guard it with my life and my soul and my body. Because it gives me this place when my half brother is gone! So now you see.

MYRTLE: Oh, yes, now I see.

CHICKEN: You ain't even looking at it. Look at this paper, will you? (*He shakes it in front of her.*) Does it look legal to you? You see this notary seal and names of witnesses on it? You see Lot's signature on it and my signature on it?

MYRTLE: Yes, yes!

CHICKEN: You want more light so you can see it more clearly? (*He turns up the lamp.*) There now, you can see it clearly!

MYRTLE: —It, it—sure looks—legal.

CHICKEN: —Yeah, but—you never can tell. . . .

MYRTLE: —What?

CHICKEN: A smart Jew lawyer might find some loopholes in it or make some if some wasn't there! —'specially if there was a widow surviving. . . . —I guess you think that I'm hard. Well, I got to be hard. A man and his life both got to be equally hard. Made out of the same hard thing. Man, rock. Life, rock. Otherwise one will break and the one that breaks won't be life. The one that breaks is the soft one and that's never life. If one is the soft one, the soft one that breaks will be man, not life, no, no, not life! —that's rock . . . yep—rock! Solid rock. . . . —Now then if you're satisfied that this is a legal paper I'll put it away.

MYRTLE: Of course I can see it is legal.

CHICKEN: But law is tricky. I never figured that Lot was going to git married. I certainly never thought he'd leave a widow. So I am faced with this important decision. Whether or not to haul you up on the roof when the house is flooded. Because if I do, then Lot will have a widow and this thing here might not be worth the paper it's typewritten on. You see what I mean about it? You see why I got to think this whole thing out step by step as careful as possible, do you? —Naw, I never thought he would leave a widow. You see? You see how easy it is to git buggered up? Law is a tricky thing. I never would of dreamed that son of a bitch would marry and leave a widow. And maybe now that changes the situation. Maybe now this agreement will not hold up in a court of law.

MYRTLE: I wouldn't—worry about it.

CHICKEN: Naw, you wouldn't worry about it. Why would you worry about it? You'd git the place, not Chicken!

MYRTLE: I, I, I—don't want this place! What would I do with this place?

CHICKEN: Want it or not you'd git it if bein his widow makes this paper—

MYRTLE (*rising stiffly*): Look, Chicken!

CHICKEN: —makes this paper not good!

MYRTLE: Chicken, Chicken, look here!

CHICKEN: That's what he figured. Son of a bitch thought he'd screw me by leaving a widow. But one thing he didn't count on was the house being flooded and him and his widow both—

MYRTLE: Oh, now, look here, Chicken!

CHICKEN: Him and his widow both!

MYRTLE: Chicken!

CHICKEN: —drowned in it!—unless I haul his widow up on the roof.

MYRTLE: *Chicken, I—can't catch my breath!* I got a bad asthma attack, it's that—

CHICKEN: Huh?

MYRTLE (*gasping*): Allergy thing, that—

CHICKEN: You want the cat out of here?

MYRTLE: Not, not, not in the—cellar but—

CHICKEN: Come on, pussy. You go set in the parlor.

(*He lifts the cat and crosses into the hall with her, shoves her into the parlor and kicks the door shut. Myrtle stands gasping like a fish out of water, leaning for support against table.*)

MYRTLE: Chicken, this, this, this joke is gone on too long. I, I. We, we.

CHICKEN: Take a good breath. Then talk.

MYRTLE: I'm trying to catch one! —Lot an' me, we—ain't—married!

CHICKEN: You an Lot ain't married?

MYRTLE: No, a-course not! Are you kiddin? (*She tries to laugh.*)

You didn't *believe* that, did you? Ha ha! I'm surprised at you for being so, so—gullible! Ha ha!—ha—ha . . . —Why, me and that boy are no more married than the man in the moon!

CHICKEN: He showed me a license.

MYRTLE: Yeah, but you said yourself you can buy those things for two bits at a novelty store to git you a hotel room to lay a woman!

CHICKEN: And the "Just Married" sign and the old shoes tied to the car?

MYRTLE: A joke, can't you take a joke? Ha ha!

CHICKEN: This is no jokin' matter.

MYRTLE: Well, it was just a joke, Chicken, it was all just a joke, Ha ha!

(*Her laugh is hollow: it expires in a gasp.*)

CHICKEN: Yeah. Well. *Maybe.*

MYRTLE: They's no maybe about it. I ought to know I'm not married!

CHICKEN: No?

MYRTLE: No! Look, whin I take that step, a step as serious in my life as marriage would be, I wouldn't take it with a—TB case! You want to know something? You want to know something, Chicken?

CHICKEN: Yeah, I want to know something.

MYRTLE: That poor boy bleaches his hair, not only has TB but bleaches his hair. Look, now, seriously! Do you imagine that I'd give up a career in show business to marry a, a, to marry a, to, to, to marry a—

CHICKEN: —What's wrong now?

MYRTLE (*with a grimace*): Throat's! Stopped!

CHICKEN: Choked on lies!

MYRTLE: No! No!

CHICKEN: That's what you done, you choked you'self on lies!

MYRTLE: Now, Chicken.

CHICKEN: "Now, Chicken."

MYRTLE: Oh, don't mock me, please!

CHICKEN: I think I better take a new look at that paper. Go up and git me that paper.

MYRTLE: Which, which paper?

CHICKEN: This license you say you got from a novelty store.

MYRTLE: Lot's, Lot's got it, he's got it! I, I don't have it, Lot's got it!

CHICKEN: Jesus. I never seen anybody in such a condition as you seem to be in.

MYRTLE: I told you about how scared I am of— (*She turns away, gasping as if drowning.*) —water! (*Gasps twice and clutches chair back.*) —Ever since I was baptized by a preacher that held me under—too *long*. . . .

CHICKEN: I'm not going to hold you under. Shit. It wouldn't be necessary to hold you under. If you can't climb on the roof when the house is flooded, and I don't reckon you can. It wouldn't be necessary to hold you under. Unless you float like a cork. Do you float like a cork?

MYRTLE: Oh, God, Chicken, why don't you take my word? I'm not Lot's widow, I mean I won't be his widow if he dies, cause we ain't married.

CHICKEN: Go up an git that paper.

MYRTLE: —Whin?

CHICKEN: Now.

MYRTLE: Wait till I catch my breath.

CHICKEN: Git the paper now and catch your breath later.

MYRTLE: I can't climb stairs without breath. And Lot's water's boiling, the kettle is boiling, I'll fill his hot-water bottle.

CHICKEN: All right. Fill his hot-water bottle and git that paper and bring it down here so I can give it a careful examination.

MYRTLE: Help me. I can't—do—this!

(*She drops the hot-water bottle. Chicken picks it up and fills it by the stove.*)

CHICKEN: Now go up and give him his hot-water bottle and git that marriage license while you're up there.

(*She starts upstairs.*)

CHICKEN (*to her back*): Hurry.

MYRTLE: I'm goin' fast as I can, unable to breathe!

CHICKEN: You're breathin'.

(*She opens the bedroom door and calls softly.*)

MYRTLE: Lot? Lot, baby? Are you asleep, Lot, baby?

(*Light falls on him: He looks like a Far Eastern idol. He doesn't answer except by rocking his wicker chair in the pool of moonlight.*)

How are you, now, Lot, baby?

LOT: You know how I am: still breathing. Have you got Chicken drunk yet?

MYRTLE: I don't think he's gonna get drunk, liquor don't seem to affect him.

LOT: Then you won't get the paper and he'll get the place.

MYRTLE: —Well . . .

LOT: You sound resigned to it, Myrtle.

MYRTLE: —If this house is flooded, both floors, could *you* get me up on the roof?

LOT: Aw. Chicken has offered to get you up on the roof.

MYRTLE: You brought me here and put me at his mercy, don't forget that.

LOT: I thought you could handle Chicken.

MYRTLE: You gave me no warning.

CHICKEN (*impatiently, below stairs*): *Hey! Come on!*

LOT: What's he want? Just your company down there?

MYRTLE: I got your hot-water bottle. Here's your hot-water bottle.

LOT: My chill's gone now. I'm burning up with fever. What I need's an ice pack.

MYRTLE: Honey, you know there ain't no ice in this house.

LOT: What were you doing down there with Chicken?

MYRTLE: I was waitin' for the kettle to boil so I could fill up this hot-water bottle which you don't want no more.

LOT: You know something?

MYRTLE: Huh?

LOT: I think you're a whore.

MYRTLE (*sadly, almost gently*): Lot, baby, that is the most cruel thing that anybody has ever said to me in my entire life. Here is my right hand to God! After all that I have suffered to stay on the straight and narrow, to be called a whore by my just married husband.

LOT: I said it looks like I married a prostitute and brought her home for Chicken.

MYRTLE: I know, I know what you said, you don't have to repeat it. The strange thing about this is, *I*, I haven't blamed *you*! *You* are blaming *me*!

(*Dialogue overlaps.*)

LOT: I married a whore and . . .

MYRTLE: Here I'm standing, here, full of TB germs because you . . .

LOT: . . . brought her back here to Chicken.

MYRTLE: . . . lied! Lied to me! And have bleached hair and—

LOT: Goddam whore an' brought her back here to Chicken for him to lay while I die up here in this rocker, you *common*-trash!

MYRTLE: God! —How mean people are! —I'm going downstairs after that.

LOT: Sure, and it makes how many times you gone down them!? To Chicken?

MYRTLE: This time is the last time. I'm not going to come back up. Not till you call me up and apologize to me and maybe not even then. No, not even then—maybe. . . .

(*Starts out: Turns back and roots in his coat pocket: coat hangs on hook on wall.*)

LOT: What are you doing? What did you take from my coat?

MYRTLE: Our marriage license! Your half brother wants to look at it to see if it's real.

(*She starts out again: Lot begins to laugh softly as she closes the door. She pushes it open again and says*—)

—What are you laughing at?

LOT: At life! —I think it's funny.

MYRTLE: —I think it's like a bad dream. . . .

LOT: —A bad dream can be funny!

MYRTLE: —I guess it can. At that. . . . (*Closes door rather softly. Chicken waits in the hall. She descends.*)

SCENE SIX

(*Myrtle enters kitchen.*)

MYRTLE: Here it is, this is it. (*Hands him the license.*) You can see it's no good.

CHICKEN: —It's got signatures on it.

MYRTLE: Sure, they put signatures on 'em to make 'em look real, but—

CHICKEN: This looks like a genuine license to me.

MYRTLE: I give you my right hand to God! —That thing is fake!

CHICKEN: Don't give me your right hand to God. I don't want it and He don't want it neither. Nobody wants your right or left hand to nothing. However, I'll keep this thing. I'll put it with my legal agreement with Lot. (*He folds the license into his wallet and studies her somberly.*) Are you able to write?

MYRTLE: Why, uh—yais!

CHICKEN: I don't mean just your name.

MYRTLE: No! Yais, I mean yais! —I been through four grades of school.

CHICKEN: Take a seat at this table. I'm gonna give you a little test in writing. (*He tears a sheet from a writing tablet and sets it before her with a pen and an ink bottle.*) You say you are able to write, and I am able to read. You see this pin an' paper I set befo' you?

MYRTLE: Yais! Perfectly! Plainly!

CHICKEN: Do you write standing up?

MYRTLE: Yais! No, I mean no! (*She scrambles into the chair.*)

CHICKEN: Now take this pin and write out on this paper what I tell you to write.

MYRTLE: What do you—?

CHICKEN: Shut up. I'm gonna dictate to you a letter that you will write an' sign and this letter will be to me.

MYRTLE: Why should I write you a letter when, when—you're right here?

CHICKEN: You'll understand why when you write it and write it out plain enough so anybody can read it.

MYRTLE: —My hand is—

CHICKEN: What?

MYRTLE: Shakin'!

CHICKEN: Control it.

MYRTLE: It's hard to control it with my nerves so unstrung.

CHICKEN: Which hand do you write with, with the left or the right?

MYRTLE: Oh, with the right, I'm right-handed.

CHICKEN: Well, give me that shaky right hand.

MYRTLE: What do you want with my hand?

CHICKEN: Stop it shakin'. (*He takes hold of her hand in both of his.*)

MYRTLE: What big hands you got, Chicken.

CHICKEN: Feel the calluses on 'em? I got those calluses on my hands from a life of hard work on this fuckin' place, worked on it like a nigger and got nothin' for it but bed and board and the bed was a cot in the kitchen and the board was no better than slops in the trough of a sow. However, things do change, they do gradually change, you just got to wait and be patient till the time comes to strike and then strike hard. (*He is rubbing her hand between his.*) Now it's comin', that time. This place is gonna be mine when the house is flooded an' I won't be unhappy sittin' on the roof of it till the flood goes down.

MYRTLE: No. Me neither. I'll be—pleased and—relieved!

CHICKEN: You mean if you are still in the land of the livin'.

MYRTLE: Don't make my hand shake again.

CHICKEN: I guess you think that I'm hard.

MYRTLE: I don't think a man should be soft.

CHICKEN: You know what life is made out of?

MYRTLE: Evil, I think it's evil.

CHICKEN: I think that life just plain don't care for the weak. Or the soft. A man and his life. Like I said, a man and his life both got to be made out of the same stuff or one or the other will break and the one that breaks won't be life. Now then. Your hand ain't shakin.

MYRTLE: No. My hand has stopped shaking because . . .

CHICKEN: —What?

MYRTLE: I know in my heart that you don't hate Myrtle.

CHICKEN: I hate nobody and I love nobody. Now pick up that pin, hold it steady, and write down what I tell you.

(*She picks up the pen, grips it.*)

Dip it in the ink, it don't write dry.

(*She wets the pen.*)

Ready?

MYRTLE: Ready, my hand is steady.

CHICKEN: I got to be careful how I word this thing, it's too important for me to bugger it up.

MYRTLE: Let's make two copies of it, one for, for—practice and the other—final.

CHICKEN: Won't be necessary. I got it now. Now write down what I tell you in big letters or print. "Me, Mrs. Lot Ravenstock, if I had a claim on this place called Raven Roost or anything on this place give up and deny all claims when my husband is dead. Because this place goes to Chicken. I known about this setup before my TV marriage and the paper which Chicken holds with notary seal, two names of witnesses on it, still holds good. I declare this. The place and all on it will be Chicken's, all Chicken's, when Lot Ravenstock dies and also if I die too because of river in flood, a natural act of God."

MYRTLE (*who has been scribbling frantically*): "All Chicken's when Lot dies."

CHICKEN: Now put in the punctuation and dot all the i's an' cross all the t's an' sign your name plain at the bottom.

MYRTLE: Yais, Yais, I did, I already did that, Chicken.

CHICKEN: Give it here. (*He takes the paper from her.*) Huh. I bet they never give you no spelling or handwriting prize when you went to school, but anyhow it's possible to read it if the question comes up in case of you being alive when the flood goes down. There's still one question, though. Where's the witnesses and the notary seal so this would hold up in court?

MYRTLE: Oh, we could get them later, we—!

CHICKEN: You wrote this thing because you're scared of drowning. How do I know you wouldn't back out of it when the flood's over with?

MYRTLE: I swear I wouldn't.

CHICKEN: Well, anyhow it's something, and something's better than nothing. It's worth putting in my wallet with Lot's witnessed letter and the true or false license.

MYRTLE: Chicken, trust my word. I've given you my word and never gone back on my word in all my life.

CHICKEN: I'm not counting on your word, but something else about you.

MYRTLE: What? Else? About me?

CHICKEN: —You're weak.

MYRTLE: I've always been weak compared to men, to a man. I think that's natural, don't you?

(*They have been sitting in chairs on opposite sides of the small, square kitchen table, chairs angled toward the audience. Now Chicken rises and moves close to her.*)

CHICKEN: Look me straight in the eyes and answer a question.

MYRTLE: What? Question?

CHICKEN: Can you kiss and like kissin' a man that's been accused of having some black blood in him?

MYRTLE: No! Yes! It would make no diff'rence to me.

CHICKEN: Let's try it out. Put your arms about me an' give me a kiss on the mouth. Mouth open.

(*She complies nervously, gingerly to this request. During the kiss, he puts a hand on her hips.*)

CHICKEN (*releasing her*): —Well? How did it feel? Disgusting?

MYRTLE: No, not a bit. I was pleased an' relieved that you wanted to kiss me, Chicken.

CHICKEN: That kiss was just a beginning. You know that. Does that please and relieve you?

MYRTLE: I'm a warm-natured woman. You might say passionate, even. A Memphis doctor prescribed me a bottle of pills to keep down the heat of my nature, but those pills are worthless. Have no effect, I'm through with them. —Don't you know I would never back down on that letter you dictated to me? Not if I could, never would!

CHICKEN: No, I reckon you wouldn't.

(*Chicken hoists himself onto the kitchen table, directly in front of her, legs spread wide.*)

MYRTLE: Wouldn't you be more comf'tble in a chair?

CHICKEN: I wouldn' be as close to you. —I'm right in front of you now.

MYRTLE: That's a—high—table. I have to strain my neck to look in your face.

CHICKEN (*with a slow, savage grin*): —You don't have to look in my face, my face ain't all they is to me. . . .

(*She begins suddenly to cry like a child.*)

Why're you cryin' fo' something you want an' can have?

(*He snatches up the lamp and blows it out. The kitchen is blacked out: an opaque scrim falls over its open wall. The light brightens in the bedroom where Lot sits in the wicker rocker; the moonlight on him brightens, fades, and brightens again.*)

LOT: Lamp's gone out in the kitchen and I don't hear a sound. —What I've done is deliver a woman to Chicken, brought home a whore for Chicken that he don't have to pay. —A present from the dying.

The Scene Dims Out.

SCENE SEVEN

The lights come up as Chicken lights the lamp on the table. He is still perched on the table and Myrtle is still on a chair so close to the table that she's between his boots, and she looks as if she had undergone an experience of exceptional nature and magnitude.

CHICKEN: Let there be light. That's what they say that God said on the first day of creation.

(*Slight pause as he fastens the clasp of his belt.*)

MYRTLE: Chicken, I want you to know that—

CHICKEN: What do you want me to know that I don't know?

MYRTLE: That that's the first time I've gone that far with a man, no matter how strongly attracted.

CHICKEN: You mean on the first date?

MYRTLE: I mean practickly never.

CHICKEN: Maybe when instink is powerful enough, then practice is not necessary. But in my opinion, them little white tablets you take to keep your nature down you oughta send back to the Memphis doctor an' demand a refund on whatever they cost you.

MYRTLE: It's possible that the tablets are meant for ordinary attraction but not for terrific attraction.

CHICKEN: Like a levee holds back a river up till a point where the pressure is too strong for it?

MYRTLE: Yes, like that. Exackly.

(*She rises from her chair and makes a weak-kneed effort to climb on the table.*)

CHICKEN: What're you doin'?

MYRTLE: Tryin' to climb up beside you an' lean on your shoulder.

CHICKEN: Naw, naw, stay in your chair a while longer. I don't like to touch or be touched by a woman right after havin' such close relations with her.

MYRTLE (*returning to her chair, humbly*): Are you disgusted with her?

CHICKEN: Just not int'rested in her.

MYRTLE: How long does that feelin' last?

CHICKEN: Sometimes five or tin minutes.

MYRTLE: Minutes kin seem like hours whin the attraction's terrific.

CHICKEN: —I wonder something about you.

MYRTLE (*nervously*): Wh—what do you wonder?

CHICKEN: If the attraction would still be terrific if I was to tell you the talk an' suspicion about me are based on fact.

MYRTLE: —What, uh, talk an' suspicion?

CHICKEN: That I got colored blood in me.

(*Note: Myrtle has the typical southern lower-class dread and awe of Negroes.*)

MYRTLE: Oh, I, why, I—I know they's no truth in that.

CHICKEN (*grinning at her savagely*): How do you know they isn't?

MYRTLE: Lot would of *tole* me.

CHICKEN: I come near to killin' him once fo' sayin' I had colored blood an' Lot hasn't forgotten; he's not so dumb he don't know that if he told you, I'd know.

MYRTLE: Thin why would you tell me thet you—

CHICKEN: I thought you oughta know after havin' such close relations.

(*Shaken and awed by the disclosure, she rises from her chair and pulls it back from the table.*)

CHICKEN: Why'd you do that, Mrs. Lot Ravenstock?

MYRTLE: —Why'd I do what did I do, I—

CHICKEN: You moved your chair back from the table like a monster was on it.

MYRTLE: You wuh swingin' your boots with mud on 'em stainin' my blouse, an'—

CHICKEN: Your blouse was awready stained. Has to be washed in floodwater.

MYRTLE: Chicken, fo' God's sake, don't mention a possible flood to a girl scared as I am of water.

CHICKEN: Move your chair back where it was.

MYRTLE: I don't know where it was.

CHICKEN: Then what do you know? Nothin'?

(*Myrtle moves her chair back to approximately its former position.*)

MYRTLE: Was it here?

CHICKEN: About. Now lissen to me. My mother had colored blood in her. She wasn't black but she wasn't white neither, and that's why I'm dark complected with freckled eyes an' live the life of a dawg that nobody owns and owns nothing. Ask any dawg on a road or a street, any dawg, any road, any street, if that ain't th' fuckin' truth which is made me suspicioned around here. So. Are you cryin' agin?

MYRTLE: —With, with—nervous—sympathy fo' you.

CHICKEN: Keep it, shove it, forget it. I don't want it. When you want sympathy, then is when you're in trouble. Up to your ass, up to your tits, up to your eyebrows in it, ask any dawg in the street, includin' you'self.

MYRTLE: Please don't talk thet way to me. (*She moves her chair back a little, still sniffling.*)

CHICKEN (*broodingly*): One night last winter, for instance, I come up to this girl at the Dixie Star, a night-place on the highway. This girl I come up to politely was known as Desperate Dotty because she put out for men right and left and up the center an' down it.

MYRTLE: —No self-respeck?

CHICKEN: No self-respeck an' no white tablets from the quack in Memphis, but I was so horny that night my balls were achin', so I come up to this girl when the man she was with fell outa their booth to th' floor an' laid there belchin' an' snorin'. I spoke to this girl politely. "Hello, how are you, Miss Bows, terrible weather," and so forth. Then lowered my voice an' leaned on th' table toward her, an' said "Miss Bows, this man you're with here t'night cain't do you no good, any dawg on th' road can tell you that, so why not step over his laigs an' sit in a clean booth with me, I got almost a full pint of Four Roses on me." —What did I git fo' this polite invitation?

MYRTLE (*still sniffling*): I don't, I should, I—

CHICKEN: I'll tell you what I got. She give me a quick, mean look an' said, "Nigger, stay in your place." That's it. That's how it is with me an' wimmen around here. Talk, suspicion, insult. An' when Miss Lottie, Lot's mother, dismissed me off this place, she said to me, "Chicken, I don't want my son to be known as half brother to a nigra." Wonderful, huh? Yeah, great. I'll tell you what her son does to amuse himself here. He gits in his dead mother's clothes—panties, brassiere, slippers, dress, an' a wig he made out of cornsilk. Ask any dawg in the street!

MYRTLE: —Oh, I—wouldn't ask any dawg a, a, a—thing like thet, I—

CHICKEN: Comes downstairs lookin' jus' like her an' sits in her parlor, talkin' to himself in the same voice as hers. OK? —Well, I'm back here, now, alone, suspicioned, despised.

MYRTLE: —I, uh—

CHICKEN: Oh, if I walk in town, I can go to the movies an' sit in th' white section an' watch a female actriss messin' around in a wrapper that you can almost see through. Shit,

I've seen kids play with themselves at The Delta Brilliant an' I don't blame 'em. The movie industry is run by ole men with hot pants, you can ask any dawg in the street if that's not true. Pool hall, I can go to the pool hall, but nobody's anxious to git me in a game with 'em. Can go to the highway night-place, an' sit by myself, left out of the conversation, talked about in whispers. So what I do, practickly everything, I do by myself, you can ask any dawg that.

MYRTLE: You should, I would—pay no attention, rise above talk an' suspicion you know ain't true.

CHICKEN: I just now told you it was. Oh, but naw. You don't wanta believe it after the close relation we had between us, naw, your folks in Mobile wuh so ignorant an' low class they filtered your mind with the idea that you'd be ruined like poisoned by havin' a close relation to someone with colored blood. So? Yais, so. I know.

MYRTLE: I was just, just simply—I was surprised for a—minute, which is over with now.

CHICKEN: You're still holdin' onto th' arms of that chair with your haid leant back like you was about to be electrocuted.

MYRTLE: I been through a good deal t'day, more than some girls go through in their whole lifetimes.

CHICKEN: Like the Four Hot Shots from Mobile?

(*He gets off the table and moves to the back door which is the only solid enclosure of the set—the rest is created by lighting.*)

MYRTLE (*rising fearfully*): Where are you goin'?

CHICKEN: The river's louder. I'm goin' to look at the levee.

MYRTLE: What good does it do to look at it?

CHICKEN: I can tell if the levee will hold the crest or not.

MYRTLE: Don't—

(*He goes off.*)

—leave me alone here. . . .

(*The bedroom upstairs is lighted by the moon. Lot is struggling out of the wicker rocker, knocking it over. He staggers to a closet and with his back to the audience, throws off the silk wrapper. He steps quickly into a gauzy white dress and sets a blond wig on his head. He turns around again, gasps, staggers to the foot of the brass bed and clings to its bars. Then he slides down them to a kneeling position.*)

LOT: —Will—make it—Miss Lottie! And order them both off the place!

(*The moon is obscured again and the bedroom returns to dark, a scrim descending over its front. During this, Myrtle has stood at the open kitchen door. Now Chicken returns, hip boots covered with wet mud as when we first saw him.*)

MYRTLE: I thought you'd never git back here.
CHICKEN: You thought wrong, Missy.

(*He sits on the table again.*)

MYRTLE: —Those five or tin minutes are over with, now, ain't they?
CHICKEN: Cain't you see the clock?
MYRTLE: A clock is mechanical but a man is human.
CHICKEN: Sometimes you say a true thing.
MYRTLE: I pride myself on that, and another thing I pride myself on is noticin' an' appreciatin' a man's appearance. More, much more, than most girls I look at a man with appreciation. Physical. I notice such things about him as a strong figure in fine proportion. Mouth? Full. Teeth? White. Glist'nin'. Why, you look like a man that could hold back the flood of a river!
CHICKEN: No man can hold back a flood but some can live through one.
MYRTLE: —With a—with a woman?
CHICKEN: Uh-huh, even with a woman. —How'd you like to stay on here after Lot's gone?
MYRTLE: —Lit's not put it like thet.
CHICKEN: What other way would you put it?
MYRTLE: No, I don't know what other way I could put it. And I know thet ev'ry girl in the world has a dream in her heart that's sweeter an' more precicious to her than any other.
CHICKEN: What's that dream in her heart?
MYRTLE: That dream is settl'n' down somewhere, sometime, with a man to who she's very strongly attracted.

CHICKEN: Think it over an' I'll think it over, too. You're not a match fo' the pitcher tacked on the wall, but—

MYRTLE: No, no, but I—know!

CHICKEN: Yais, I'd say you know, an' if it's necessary to climb on the roof tonight, I'll git you up the ladder in the hall upstairs with a blanket in case we need more'n each other to keep us warm.

MYRTLE: What'd we eat up there if we had to stay up there long?

CHICKEN: The chickens'll fly up there, and if a helly-copter don't come over to pick us up, we'll drink some warm chicken blood to keep us goin'.

MYRTLE: Oh, I couldn't do that!

CHICKEN: What people have to do they always do. —So ev'rything understood now?

MYRTLE: I think we've come to a perfeck understandin'.

CHICKEN: Good. Let's have a drink on it. (*He pours liquor into two tin cups.*) —Have you ever been what they call saved?

MYRTLE: Why, yais, I have, I have been saved by you.

CHICKEN: What I was speakin' of is *religious* salvation.

(*He removes her importunate hand from his shoulder and resumes his seat on the table. The lamp light concentrates on him hotly during the monologue, the expression of his credo, that follows. Myrtle is a shadowy presence.*)

MYRTLE: Oh, *religious* salvation.

CHICKEN: That's right.

MYRTLE: Well, I'm not a steady churchgoer, I wake up so tired on Sundays, y'see, but when I'm perplexed or worried over something, I always appeal to my Saviour and, knock on wood, He has never let me down.

(*The bright light is now fixed on Chicken.*)

CHICKEN: Hmm. Uh-huh. —I reckon you'd never guess from me, the way I am now, that I was what they call saved by this preacher Gypsy Smith when he come through here last Spring. But I sure in hell was, I was what they call saved, but it didn't last much longer than a cold in the head. Hmmm. And talking about salvation, I think there's a good deal of truth in the statement, the saying, that either you're saved or you ain't, and the best thing to do is find out which and stick to it. Because with human beings, and I'm a human being and you are, too, what counts most is—

(*Myrtle perches herself beside him on the table and leans against him.*)

With human beings, the ones I known in my life, what counts most is personal satisfaction, and God knows you'll never get that by denying yourself what you want most in the world, by straining and struggling for what they call salvation when it's something you're just not cut out for. That preacher, that salvation preacher last spring, he claimed that we had to put up a terrible struggle against our lustful body. And I did for a while. Y'know, these preachers all think we got lustful bodies and that's one thing I know they're right about. Huh?

MYRTLE: Oh, yes. They're right about that. They're not mistaken.

CHICKEN: And they also believe that we have spiritual gates, and they preach about how you should haul down those spiritual gates on your lustful body. Well. Those are two opposite things and one of 'em's got to be stronger if they're in the same body. One's got to win and one lose. Well, I tried to haul down my spiritual gates for a while but I seemed to be reaching up for something that wasn't in me. You can't haul down your spiritual gates if you don't have any in you. I think that's the case in my case. I was just created without them. And either you're saved or you ain't, you can be or never will be, and I think you're a hell of a lot better off putting all hope of salvation out of your mind completely than to put up a long, painful struggle that's bound to be useless. Sooner or later, you're going to backslide, and that's that. Hmm? What do you think?

MYRTLE: In my case, I never had that experience, being saved, not even for a short while, but I do say prayers, anyhow, to God and to human beings.

CHICKEN: What do you pray for?

MYRTLE: I pray for protection, and right now I feel like that prayer is going to be answered. Go on talking in that deep voice of yours. I don't just hear it. It, it—it gives me a sensation in my ears and goes all through my body, it, it—it *vibrates* in me. I don't even hear the river!

CHICKEN (*with a touch of tolerant contempt*): Mmm, mmm-hmmm. What you're saying is you're anxious to please me in order to git on the roof whin the house is flooded.

MYRTLE (*very nervously*): Oh, no, that, that—that's already been settled.

CHICKEN: Things can be settled one way and then unsettled another.

MYRTLE: You wouldn't back out on it now after givin' your word, you couldn't, you're too good a man! God love you, Chicken!

CHICKEN: This house ain't built out of rock or brick or—cement. This is an old wood house. Oh, I'll git you up on the roof whin the levee collapses. But that's no guarantee that the crest of a flood of a river as big as this might not uproot this house like a weed and wash and toss it down and around till not a board or a shingle stuck together.

MYRTLE: Don't, don't—scare me out of my life!

CHICKEN (*sloshing liquor from the jug into their tin cups*): I'll tell you how I look at life in my life, or in any man's life. There's nothing in the world, in this whole kingdom of earth, that can compare with one thing, and that one thing is what's able to happen between a man and a woman, just that thing, nothing more, is perfect. The rest is crap, all of the rest is almost nothing but crap. Just that one thing's good, and if you never had nothing else but that, no property, no success in the world, but still had *that*, why, then I say this life would still be worth something, and you better believe it. Yes, you could come home to a house like a shack, in blazing heat, and look for water and find not a drop to drink, and look for food and find not a single crumb of it. But if on the bed you seen you a woman waiting, maybe not very young or good-looking even, and she looked up at you and said to you "Daddy, I want it," why, then I say you got a square deal out of life, and whoever don't think so has just not had the right woman. That's how I look at it, that's how I see it now, in this kingdom of earth.

(Lot appears like an apparition in the pool of cool light at the stair-top. He has put on the gauzy white dress to conjure an image of his mother in summer. As he stands above the stairs he puts on a translucent, wide "picture hat;" the crown is trimmed with faded flowers. The effect is both bizarre and beautiful. There is a phrase of music like a muted trumpet playing a blues song. Then Lot starts his descent of the stairs. With each step his gasping for breath is louder, but his agony is transfigured by the sexless passion of the transvestite. He has a fixed smile which is almost ecstatic. Chicken leaps off the kitchen table and goes to the kitchen door. He seems impressed but not surprised. Myrtle is terrified.)

MYRTLE: Chicken, Oh, God, stop him!
CHICKEN: What faw?
MYRTLE: Take him back up!
CHICKEN: Naw, naw, let him be in Miss Lottie's parlor.

(At the foot of the stairs, Lot turns blindly towards the parlor. His gasping breath is now like a death rattle. Even in death he has the ecstasy of a transvestite. As he staggers into the bizarre little parlor, the room is lighted with a delicate rose light. There he stands swaying for a few moments; then sinks into one of the little gold chairs, facing the window. Myrtle is panicky but not Chicken. Lot, in his transfiguration, stares blindly. He is even smiling as if on a social occasion. He holds onto his garden hat, holding it by the crown, as if a wind might blow it away. He is swaying back and forth. Chicken's attitude is impassive.)

—You're dressed fo' summer t'night.

(Lot is past hearing any remark. He rises from the chair, sways, seems to bow to an applauding audience, then crumples to the floor. Chicken doesn't enter the parlor until Lot's death agony is finished. Only then does he enter and sits gingerly on one of the gilt chairs for a moment. Then, almost tenderly, he moves the lifeless body to the sofa. Myrtle, in a state of mental shock, has retreated to the kitchen and opened the icebox as if it were a place of refuge.)

MYRTLE: Aigs. Bacon. Slab of it. New potatoes.

(*She removes these reassuring items from the iceless box. An egg or two splatters on the floor. She makes a few more rapid, irresolute turns.*)

Pan? —Pan! —Knife? —Knife!

(*She heads for the wall where these utensils are hanging and discovers her arms are full. Then she rushes back to deposit the foodstuff on the table. Entirely unnoticed by her, an egg or two more splatters on the floor. Then she rushes back to remove the utensils from their hooks.*)

In no condition to—got to!

(*She then instructs herself as if she were a pupil in a very primary cooking class.*)

Slice bacon in pan with knife. —Stove? —Burnin'!

(*Her words are interspersed with slight, breathless sobs. Chicken has stood over the summer gauze apparition of his half brother without a word or gesture. Now he turns out the chandelier and moves with dark satisfaction down the short hall to the kitchen area. He looks about him appraisingly, a man who has come into possessions fiercely desired. Myrtle's back is to him and when he speaks she catches her breath loudly.*)

CHICKEN: Makin' supper?
MYRTLE: What I'm doin' I don't know what I'm doin', I—
CHICKEN: You're doin' a sensible thing since it might be sev'ral days before we have a hot meal again.
MYRTLE (*turning to face him*): Chicken, as Christian people—
CHICKEN: What about Christian people, something or nothing?
MYRTLE: We got to call in a doctor.
CHICKEN: If there was a doctor that hadn't hauled his ass out of Two River County, there's nothin' he could do here but clean up a mess of aigs you dropt on the floor.
MYRTLE: —Lot is—?
CHICKEN: Isn't.
MYRTLE: —God have mercy on my—
CHICKEN: What?

MYRTLE: —The potatoes will be home-fried.

CHICKEN: That's right. Fried in my home. You couldn't peel 'em?

MYRTLE: Cut my finger!

CHICKEN: A nervous woman has a rough time in this world.

(*He stares at her broodingly for a couple of moments as she sucks her cut finger.*)

I don't reckon that, no, I reckon you couldn't.

MYRTLE: Couldn't? What?

CHICKEN: Produce me a son. Produce a child for me, could you? I've always wanted a child from an all-white woman.

MYRTLE: —I want t' be perfeckly frank with you on that subjeck.

CHICKEN: I could tell if you lied on that subjeck or any other.

(*He holds the lamp toward her still panicky face.*)

MYRTLE: I got five adopted children.

CHICKEN: You adopted five children?

MYRTLE: No, what I mean is, Chicken, I hed five children that hed t' be adopted because I wasn' financially able to give these children the care an' attention—an' care a infant child's got t' have, an' so I hed t' hev 'em adopted, all by families with yearly incomes no less 'n two thousan' dollars. Oh, it broke my heart five times. All five was red-headed like me an' cute as a bug.

CHICKEN: I don't want a child that looks like a bug.

MYRTLE: Oh, that's just a, you know, a—expression.

(*He replaces the lamp on the table.*)

No, sir. The deepest chord in my nature is the— Don't that river sound louder? Or am I just more scared to death of it?

CHICKEN: The flood crest is close to here now. (*He starts outside.*)

MYRTLE (*wildly*): *Don't leave me alone here!*

CHICKEN: I'm goin' out th' door for a minute. Sit down. Peel the home-fried potatoes. —I want to look at my land. (*He goes out and moves forward, his face exultant.*)

—Sing it out, frogs an' crickets, Chicken is king!

(*Myrtle has come out behind him. There is a great booming sound.*)

Up! Quick!

(*He says this as the curtain is descending.*)

End.

SMALL CRAFT WARNINGS

TO BILL BARNES:
YOU SAID TO GO ON, AND I WENT.

TOO PERSONAL?*

THE greatest danger, professionally, of becoming the subject of so many "write-ups" and personal appearances on TV and lecture platforms is that the materials of your life, which are, in the case of all organic writing, the materials of your work, are sort of telegraphed in to those who see you and to those who read about you. So, when you get to the serious organization of this material into your work, people (meaning audiences and critics—all but the few most tolerant whom you naturally regard as the best) have a sort of *déjà vu* or *déjà entendu* reaction to these materials which you have submitted to the cathartic process of your "sullen craft and art."

You may justifiably wonder why a man of my years in his profession, recognizing this hazard, has yet been willing to expose himself (with a frequency which seems almost symptomatic of clinical exhibitionism) to all of these interviews and the fewer, but equally personal, exposures on platform and "the tube."

I can offer you at least two reasons for this phenomenon. One is probably something with which you will immediately empathize. When one has passed through an extensive period of that excess of privacy which is imposed upon a person drifting almost willfullly out of contact with the world, anticipating that final seclusion of the nonbeing, there comes upon him, when that period wears itself out and he is still alive, an almost insatiable hunger for recognition of the fact that he is, indeed, still alive, both as man and artist. That's reason number one. The other is rather comical, I'm afraid. You get a devastatingly bad write-up, and you feel that you are washed up for good. Then some magazine editor gets through to you on that phone in the studio of your tropical retreat, the phone that you never pick up till it's rung so persistently that you assume that your secretary and house guests have been immobilized by nerve gas or something of that nature, and this editor speaks to you as sympathetically

*This was meant to be submitted to *The New York Times* as a preopening piece, but they chose to interview me instead.—T.W.

as the family doctor to a child stricken with a perforated appendix and tells you that he is as shocked as you were by the tasteless exposé-type of interview which appeared about you in a recent issue of some other mag. And then, of course, you forget about work, and you rage yourself into a slather over the iniquities and duplicities of the "interviewer" referred to. You say, "Why, that creature was so drunk he didn't know what street I lived on, and the guy that set me up for him laced my martini with sodium pentothal, and all I remember about this occasion is that my head came off my shoulders and hit the ceiling and I heard myself babbling away like an hysteric and I hadn't the slightest notion that he had a concealed tape recorder with him, and later he offered to play bridge with me that night, and he came over again with the tape recorder in some orifice of his body, I presume, and you know I do not see well and you know I like to hold forth to apparently amiable listeners, and I just assume that when they say 'I am interested only in your work,' that that's what they mean."

Now the editor has you on the hook.

"That's exactly my reaction to the revolting piece and how about letting us do a piece to correct it?"

You grasp at this offer like a drowning rat climbs on to anything that will float it. So you get another write-up. Then after this write-up, which is usually more colorful and better written than the one before, but equally nonserious, if not downright clownish, you feel that it is a life-or-death matter, professionally, with a new play opening somewhere, to correct the hilarious misquotes and exaggerations which embellished the second write-up, and so you go on to others and others. Now at last you have poured out, compulsively and perhaps fatally, all the recent content of your experience which should have been held in reserve for its proper place, which is in the work you're doing every morning (which, in my case, is the writing I do every morning).

Is it or is it not right or wrong for a playwright to put his persona into his work?

My answer is: "What else can he do?"—I mean the very root-necessity of all creative work is to express those things most involved in his experience. Otherwise, is the work, however well executed, not a manufactured, a synthetic thing? I've said, perhaps repeatedly, that I have two major classifications for writing: that which is organic and that which is not. And this opinion still holds.

Now let me attempt to entertain you once more with an anecdote.

Long ago, in the early forties, I attended a very posh party given by the Theatre Guild. I was comfortably and happily seated at a small table with my dear friend Miss Jo Healy, who was receptionist at the Guild in those days, when a lady with eyes that blazed with some nameless frenzy rushed up to me like a guided missile and seized me by the arm and shrieked to me, "You've got to meet Miss Ferber, she's dying to meet you."

Now in those days I was at least pliable, and so I permitted myself to be hauled over to a large table at which were seated a number of Diamond T trucks disguised as ladies.

"Oh, Miss Ferber," shrieked my unknown pilot, "this is Tennessee Williams."

Miss Ferber gazed slowly up and delivered this annihilating one-liner:

"The best I can manage is a mild 'Yippee.' "

"Madam," I said, "I can't even manage that."

Now everyone knows, who is cognizant of the world of letters, that Miss Edna Ferber was a creature of mammoth productivity and success. She was good at doing her thing; her novel and picture sales are fairly astronomical, I would guess.

I bring her up because she represents to me the classic, the archetypal, example of a writer whose work is impersonal, at least upon any recognizable level. I cannot see her in the oil fields of Texas with Rock Hudson and the late James Dean. Nor can I see her in any of her other impressive epics. I see her only as a lady who chose to put down a writer who was then young and vulnerable with such a gratuitously malicious one-liner. I mean without provocation, since I had literally been dragged to the steps of her throne.

So far I have spoken only in defense of the personal kind of writing. Now I assure you that I know it can be overdone. It is the responsibility of the writer to put his experience as a being into work that refines it and elevates it and that makes of it an essence that a wide audience can somehow manage to feel in themselves: "This is true."

In all human experience, there are parallels which permit common understanding in the telling and hearing, and it is the frightening responsibility of an artist to make what is directly or allusively close to his own being communicable and understandable, however disturbingly, to the hearts and minds of all whom he addresses.

T.W.
MARCH 26, 1972

Act I: A bar along the Southern California Coast

Act II: An hour or two later

ACT I

The curtain rises. The sound of ocean wind is heard. The stage is lighted at a very low level.

The scene is a somewhat nonrealistic evocation of a bar on the beach-front in one of those coastal towns between Los Angeles and San Diego. It attracts a group of regular patrons who are nearly all so well known to each other that it is like a community club, and most of these regulars spend the whole evening there. Ideally, the walls of the bar, on all three sides, should have the effect of fog rolling in from the ocean. A blue neon outside the door says: "Monk's Place." The bar runs diagonally from upstage to down; over it is suspended a large varnished sailfish, whose gaping bill and goggle-eyes give it a constant look of amazement. There are about three tables, with red-checked tablecloths. Stage right there is a juke box, and in the wall at right are doors to the ladies' and gents' lavatories. A flight of stairs ascends to the bar-owner's living quarters. The stairs should be masked above the first few steps.

The bar interior is dimly, evenly lit at rise. At some time in the course of the play, when a character disengages himself from the group to speak as if to himself, the light in the bar should dim, and a special spot should illuminate each actor as he speaks.

Monk is behind the bar serving Doc. Monk, the bar-owner, and Doc, who lost his license for heavy drinking but still practices more or less clandestinely, are middle-aged.

At a downstage table sits Violet, at her feet a battered suitcase fastened with a rope. Her eyes are too large for her face, and they are usually moist: her appearance suggests a derelict kind of existence; still, she has about her a pale, bizarre sort of beauty. As Leona Dawson later puts it, she's like a water plant.

MONK (*to Doc*): Notice? (*He nods his head.*) Over there?

(*Doc emerges from introspection to glance the way indicated by Monk. They both gaze at Violet.*)

VIOLET (*singing a bit, self-conscious under their scrutiny*):

The wheel of fortune
Keeps turning around . . .

(*She can't remember past this.*)

DOC (*voice filtered through booze*): Oh, yes, she's a noticeable thing. She has a sort of not-quite-with-it appearance. Amorphous, that's the word. Something more like a possibility than a completed creature.

MONK: What I mean is the *suitcase. With* her.

DOC: Oh, yes, the suitcase. Does she think she's in the waiting room of a depot?

MONK: I think she thinks she's moved in here.

DOC: Oh. That's a possible problem for you there.

MONK: You're Goddam right. I'm running a tavern that's licensed to dispense spirits, not a pad for vagrants. You see, they see those stairs. They know I live up there.

DOC: Yep, they see those stairs to the living quarters above, and it hits them dimly that you might need the solace of their companionship up there some nights when they find it convenient to offer it to you, and I don't need to tell you that this solace of companionship is not the least expensive item on the shelves of the fucking supermarket a man of my age has to spend what's left of his life in. Oh, that solace, that comfort of companionship is on the shelves of the market even for me, but I tell you, the price is inflated on it. I had me one last summer. Remember that plump little Chicano woman used to come in here with me some nights last summer? A little wet-leg woman, nice boobs on her and a national monument for an ass? Well, she came to me for medical attention.

(*Monk laughs heartily at this.*

(*Bill enters the bar; he comes up to it with an overrelaxed amiability like a loser putting up a bold front: by definition, a "stud"—but what are definitions?*

(*Monk mechanically produces Bill's can of Miller's but doesn't open it for him.*)

She had worms, diet of rotten beef tacos, I reckon, or tamales or something. I diagnosed it correctly. I gave her the little bottle and the wooden spoon and I said to her, "Bring me in a sample of your stool for lab analysis." She didn't know what I meant. Language barrier. I finally said, "Señorita, bring a little piece of your shit in the bottle tomorrow." (*He and Monk laugh heartily.*)

(*Bill is worried over the fact his beer can is not opened and served.*)

VIOLET: Hey, Bill . . .

DOC: Some beginning of some romance. Dewormed the lady and laid her in place of payment. Jesus, what a love story. I had her all summer, but in September she met a good-looking young pimp who made her critical of me. She called me a dirty old man, so I let her go.

BILL: Hey, Monk. About that beer.

MONK (*ignoring Bill*): I don't remember you coming in here with a woman.

DOC: We always sat at a back table arguing over the fair expense of her ass.

BILL: Jesus, Monk, how big a tab has Leona run up here!? For Chrissake! (*He leans across the bar and snatches the can of Miller's from Monk's hand. Monk had ignored him only half deliberately and is annoyed by the grab.*)

MONK: Look, I don't run Leona's tab through a computer, since I know she's good for it. If you want the can opened, give it back here. (*He opens the can.*) Now if it was your tab, not hers, I'd worry, but since it's hers, not yours, I don't. OK? No offense, no complaint, just . . .

VIOLET: Bill?

BILL: I could tell you some things.

MONK: Why don't you tell 'em to Violet, she's called you three times.

BILL (*glancing at her*): Hi, Vi.

VIOLET: I had an awful experience today with Mr. Menzies at the amusement arcade. (*Sobbing sound*) Oh, I don't know what to do. Min broke in. Last night. Menzies said I . . . Come over here so I can tell you. Oh, and bring me a beer and a pepperoni, I'm famished. Lonesome and famished.

BILL: You want me to solve both those situations for you?

VIOLET: Yes, please.

BILL (*to Monk*): Another Miller's and a coupla Slim Jims.

MONK: Yep, I got that message. Have you left Leona?

VIOLET: Bill, where's Leona?

BILL: Crying into a stew in her Goddam trailer.

(*Monk opens another beer, and Bill ambles over to Violet with the pepperonis and beer and the smile he meets the world with. It is a hustler's smile, the smile of a professional stud—now aging a bit but still with considerable memorabilia of his young charm.*)

VIOLET: Thanks, Bill . . .

(*Monk is toying with a radio which is over the bar.*)

RADIO VOICE: Heavy seas from Point Conception south to the Mexican border, fog continuing till tomorrow noon, extreme caution should be observed on all highways along this section of the coastline.

MONK (*ironically, turning off radio*): Small craft warnings, Doc.

DOC: That's right, Monk, and you're running a place of refuge for vulnerable human vessels, and . . .

VIOLET (*closer to Bill*): Have you left Leona? For good?

BILL: Just till she gets her knickers out of that twist. She had this brother, a faggot that played the fiddle in church, and whenever she's drunk, she starts to cry up a storm about this little fag that she admitted was arrested for loitering in the Greyhound bus station men's room, and if I say, "Well, he was asking for it," she throws something at me.

VIOLET (*leaning amorously toward him*): A man like you.

BILL: A man like me?

VIOLET: A bull of a man like you. You got arms on you big as the sides of a ham. (*She strokes his bare arm.*)

BILL: That ain't all I got big.

VIOLET: You mean what I think?

BILL: If you can't see you can feel.

(*She reaches under the table, and it is obvious that she is feeling him.*)

A man likes appreciation. Now I got a letter this week from a female guv'ment employee in Sacramento who's a Reagan supporter.

VIOLET: Huh?

BILL: Shit. She ain't seen me since '65 but remembers me clearly and wants me back on her aquabed with her, and if you've slept in an aquabed it don't matter who's in it with you.

(*The door bursts open. Leona enters like a small bull making his charge into the ring. Leona, a large, ungainly woman, is wearing white clam-digger slacks and a woolly pink sweater. On her head of dyed corkscrew curls is a sailor's hat which she occasionally whips off her head to slap something with—the bar, a tabletop, somebody's back—to emphasize a point. There are abrupt changes of position at the downstage table at her entrance, but she notices only Bill there.*)

LEONA: YOUUUUU . . . MOTHER! I was talkin' to you from the stove and you weren't there!

(*Bill chuckles and winks.*)

Three hours I spent shopping for and preparing a . . . memorial dinner while you watched TV.

BILL: Stew and veg.

LEONA (*lyrically, as a pop-poem*): Lamb stew with garden fresh vegetables from the Farmer's Market, seasoned with bay leaves, and rosemary and thyme.

BILL: Stew.

LEONA: I'd set up a little banquet table in that trailer tonight, my grandmother's silver and Irish lace tablecloth, my crystal candlesticks with the vine leaves filigreed on 'em in silver which I'd polished, all spit-polished for this memorial dinner, set the candles on either side of my single rose vase containing a single talisman rose just opened, a table like a photo from *House and Garden*. I talk from the stove to no one. I open the fridge to get out the jellied bouillon, madrilene, topped with . . . "Okayyyy, ready." I come in and I'm received by the TV set and the trailer door hanging open, and in the confusion I knock over and break my cut-glass decanter of Burgundy, imported.

BILL: I went out for a bottle. You'd kilt a fifth of Imp. She was crying in the stew to save on salt.

LEONA: Without word or a note on the table. You went! Why? For what?

VIOLET: Leona, Bill's not happy tonight, so let him be.

LEONA: Two people's not happy and one of 'em with *reason*! Is that your suitcase with you? Are you thrown out, evicted? A lady of the street? Oh, my God, here's a good one I heard at the shop today about a pair of street-ladies in Dublin. One enters a pub, elegant but pissed, and she says to the barman, "Two gins for two ladies." He observes her condition and says, "Where is the other lady?" "The other lady," she says, "is in the gutter, resting." (*Only she is amused by the story.*) Oh, well, I thought it was funny. (*Leona sits at table with Violet and Bill.*) Violet, dear, will you look at your nails?

VIOLET: I know, the enamel's chipping.

LEONA: Yes! Exposing the dirt.

(*Violet drops her hands under the table.*)

Oh, my God, forget it, forget the whole enchilada. Not worth a thought.

(*No response.*)

Excuse me a moment. I'm going to press one button three times on that multiselector, and Violet, here's an orange stick for your nails . . . Don't be depressed. A sure cure for depression is the ax.

VIOLET: I'm not depressed.

LEONA (*laughing*): Then you must not be conscious. (*She crosses to the juke box.*) I hope nobody objects to the number I play. It's going to be played here repeatedly tonight, appreciated or not. (*She bends over the juke box to find the desired number, which she herself contributed to the "Classicals" on the box.*) Rock? No! Popular? No! Classicals—yes! Number? Number? Which?

VIOLET: Tell her I'm not depressed.

(*Violet's hand has dropped under the table. It is apparent that she is reaching for Bill.*)

BILL: *She's* depressed . . . and depressing. (*Leans back luxuriously in chair. A look to Leona. He speaks with emphasis, rather than volume.*) . . . Not bad, huh? A definite . . . personal . . . asset?

(*Monk turns up radio. Gets static.*)

LEONA: Do you have to turn that on when I'm . . .

(*At this precise moment she is caught by the change in attitudes at the downstage table. Her eyes widen; her hands clench; she takes a couple of paces toward the table and crouches a bit to peer under it. Then quick as a shot:*)

YOUUU . . . CUNT!

(*She charges.*

(*Violet screams and springs up, overturning her chair.*)

MONK: Hold her!

(*Bill's massive frame obstructs Leona, not only her motion but her view of Violet. Bill is holding her by both shoulders, grinning into her face.*

(*The following lines overlap.*)

LEONA: OFF HANDS!
MONK: Nope, nope, nope, nope, nope!
LEONA: McCorkle, DON' YOU . . . !
MONK: Keep her at that table!

(*During this Monk has crossed from behind the bar.*

(*Violet has turned about dizzily, then fled into the ladies'.*

(*Leona stamps on Bill's foot. He yells, falls back an instant, releasing her. As she rushes forward, he gives her a hard slap on the butt; she turns to give him battle, and is caught from behind by Monk. She kicks at Monk's shin, and gives Bill a wallop in the face with her cap.*)

BILL (*rubbing his eyes*): Goddam, she . . .
MONK: I'm havin' no violence here! Never! None! From no one!

(*A sudden hush falls: a sudden moment of stillness in a corrida.*)

LEONA (*incredulously, profoundly, hurtly, right into Bill's face*): YOU! Let *her*! In front of ME? . . . in PUBLIC! . . . In a BAR!
BILL: What the fuck of it! You hit me right in the eyes with . . .
LEONA (*makes a big-theater turn and shouts*): Where *IS* she? Where's she gone? (*Receiving no answer—there is still no

sound from Violet's place of refuge—she suddenly rushes for the stairs.)

MONK: Nobody's up my stairs! Come down those . . .

(*Violet's lamentation begins.*)

LEONA: Aw! She's gone to the LADIES'! Change the name on that door.

MONK: I'm operating a place for gents and ladies. (*He is panting a bit.*)

LEONA: Gents and . . . what?

MONK: Ladies.

LEONA: Aw, now, Monk. I thought you run a clean place but don't come on with . . . her? Lady? Him? Gent? (*She points toward the ladies' room and then toward Bill.*) There's limits to . . .

MONK: Yes. Stay away from . . .

(*Leona had started toward the ladies'. Monk blocks her. She throws her head back and utters an apocalyptic outcry. It's like the outcry of all human protest.*)

No more disturbance of . . .

LEONA (*drawing herself up heroically as she confronts Monk almost nose-to-nose*): LET ME SET YOU STRAIGHT ABOUT WHAT'S A LADY! A lady's a woman, with respect for herself and for relations of others! HER? IN THERE? WAILING? RESPECT FOR? . . . She's got no respect for herself and that is the single respect in which she's correct to! No one could blame her for that! (*She has resumed her pacing and slapping at things with sailor's cap.*) What could she possibly find to respect in herself? She lives like an animal in a room with no bath that's directly over the amusement arcade at the foot of the pier, yeah, right over the billiards, the pinball games, and the bowling alleys at the amusement arcade, it's bang, bang, bang, loud as a TV western all day and all night, and then bang, bang again at eight A.M. It would drive a sane person crazy but she couldn't care less. She don't have a closet, she didn't have a bureau so she hangs her dresses on a piece of rope that hangs across a corner between two nails, and her other possessions she keeps on the floor in boxes.

BILL: What business is it of yours?

LEONA: None, not a Goddam bit! When she was sick? I went there to bring her a chicken. I asked her, where is your silver? She didn't have any silver, not a fork, spoon, or knife, hell, not even a plate, but she ate the chicken, aw, yeah, she ate the chicken like a dog would eat it, she picked it up in her paws and gnawed at it just like a dog. Who came to see if she was living or dead? ME! ONLY! I got her a bureau, I got her a knife, fork, and spoon, I got her china, I got her a change of bed linen for her broken-down cot, and ev'ry day after work I come by that Goddam rathole with a bottle of hot beef bouillon or a chicken or meatloaf to see what she needed and bring it, and then one time I come by there to see what she needed and bring it. The bitch wasn't there. I thought my God she's died or they put her away. I run downstairs, and I heard her screaming with joy in the amusement arcade. She was having herself a ball with a shipload of drunk sailor boys; she hardly had time to speak to me.

BILL: Maybe she'd gotten sick of you. That's a possible reason.

LEONA: It's a possible reason I was sick of her, too, but I'd thought that the bitch was dying of malnutrition, and I thought she was human, and a human life is worth saving or what the shit *is* worth saving. But is she human? She's just a parasite creature, not even made out of flesh but out of wet biscuit dough, she always looks like the bones are dissolving in her.

BILL (*banging his beer bottle on the table*): DO YOU THINK I BELONG TO YOU? I BELONG TO MYSELF, I JUST BELONG TO MYSELF.

LEONA: Aw, you pitiful piece of . . . worthless . . . conceit! (*She addresses the bar.*) . . . Never done a lick of work in his life . . . He has a name for his thing. He calls it Junior. He says he takes care of Junior and Junior takes care of him. How long is that gonna last? How long does he figure Junior is going to continue to provide for him, huh? HUH! . . . Forever or *less* than forever? . . . Thinks the sun rises and sets between his legs and that's the reason I put him in my trailer, feed him, give him beer-money, pretend I don't notice there's five or ten bucks less in my pocketbook in the morning than my pocketbook had in it when I fell to sleep, night before.

BILL: Go out on the beach and tell that to the sea gulls, they'd be more int'rested in it.

VIOLET (*shrilly, from the ladies' room*): Help me, help me, somebody, somebody call the po-liiiiice!

LEONA: Is she howling out the ladies' room window?

VIOLET: How long do I have to stay in here before you get the police?

LEONA: If that fink is howling out the ladies' room window, I'm going out back and throw a brick in at her.

MONK: Leona, now cool it, Leona.

LEONA: I'll pay the damage, I'll pay the hospital expenses.

MONK: Leona, why don't you play your violin number on the box and settle down at a table and . . .

LEONA: When I been insulted by someone, I don't settle down at a table, or nowhere, NOWHERE!

(*Violet sobs and wails as Steve comes into the bar. Steve is wearing a floral-patterned sports shirt under a tan jacket and the greasy white trousers of a short-order cook.*)

STEVE: Is that Violet in there?

LEONA: Who else do you think would be howling out the ladies' room window but her, and you better keep out of this, this is between her and me.

STEVE: What happened? Did you hit Violet?

LEONA: You're Goddam right I busted that filthy bitch in the kisser, and when she comes out of the ladies', if she ever comes out, I'm gonna bust her in the kisser again, and kiss my ass, I'm just the one that can do it! MONK! DRINK! BOURBON SWEET!

MONK: Leona, you're on a mean drunk, and I don't serve liquor to no one on a mean drunk.

LEONA: Well, you can kiss it, too, you monkey-faced mother. (*She slaps the bar top with her sailor hat.*)

STEVE: Hey, did you hit Violet?

(*Bill laughs at this anticlimactic question.*)

LEONA: Have you gone deaf, have you got wax in your ears, can't you hear her howling in there? Did I hit Violet? The answer is yes, and I'm not through with her yet. (*Leona approaches the door of the ladies' room.*) COME ON OUT OF THERE, VIOLET, OR I'LL BREAK IN THE DOOR! (*She bangs her fist on the door, then slaps it contemptuously with her cap, and resumes her pacing.*)

(*Bill keeps grinning and chuckling.*)

STEVE: Why did she hit Violet?

LEONA: Why don't you ask *me* why?

STEVE: Why did you hit Violet?

LEONA: I hit Violet because she acted indecent with that son of a bitch I been supporting for six months in my trailer.

STEVE: What do you mean "indecent"?

LEONA: Jesus, don't you know her habits? Are you unconscious ev'ry night in this bar and in her rathole over the amusement arcade? I mean she acted indecent with her dirty paws under the table. I came in here tonight and saw her hands on the table. The red enamel had nearly all chipped off the nails and the fingernails, black, I mean *black*, like she'd spend every day for a month without washing her hands after making mud-pies with filthy motherless kids, and I thought to myself, it's awful, the degradation a woman can sink down into without respect for herself, so I said to her, Violet, will you look at your hands, will you look at your fingernails, Violet?

STEVE: Is that why you hit Violet?

LEONA: Goddam it, NO! Will you listen? I told her to look at her nails and she said, oh, the enamel is peeling, I know. I mean the dirtiness of the nails was not a thing she could notice, just the chipped red enamel.

STEVE: Is that why you hit Violet?

LEONA: Shit, will you shut up till I tell you why I hit her? I wouldn't hit her just for being unclean, unsanitary. I wouldn't hit her for nothing that affected just her. And now, if you'll pay attention, I'm going to tell you exactly why I did hit her. I got up from the table to play "Souvenir."

STEVE: What is she talking about? What are you talking about?

LEONA: When I come back to the table her hands had disappeared off it. I thought to myself, I'm sorry, I made her ashamed of her hands and she's hiding them now.

STEVE: Is that why you hit Violet?

LEONA: Why do you come in a bar when you're already drunk? No! Listen! It wasn't embarrassment over her filthy nails that had made her take her hands off the table top, it was her old habit, as filthy as her nails. The reason her pitiful hands had disappeared off the table was because under the table she was acting indecent with her hands in the lap of that ape that moved himself into my trailer and tonight will move himself out as fast as he moved himself in. And now do you know why I hit her? If you had balls, which it doesn't look like you do, you would've hit her yourself instead of making me do it.

STEVE: I wasn't there when it happened, but that's the reason you hit her?

LEONA: Yeah, now the reason has got through the fog in your head, which is thick as the fog on the beach.

(*Violet wails from the ladies' room.*)

STEVE: I'm not married to Violet, I never was or will be. I just wanted to know who hit her and why you hit her.

LEONA (*slapping at him with her cap*): Annhh!

STEVE: Don't slap at me with that cap. What do I have to do with what she done or she does?

LEONA: No responsibility? No affection? No pity? You stand there hearing her wailing in the ladies' and deny there's any connection between you? Well, now I feel sorry for her. I regret that I hit her. She can come back out now and I won't hit her again. I see her life, the awfulness of her hands reaching out under a table, automatically creeping under a table into the lap of anything with a thing that she can catch hold of. Let her out of the ladies', I'll never hit her again. I feel too much pity for her, but I'm going out for a minute to breathe some clean air and to get me a drink where a barman's willing to serve me, and then I'll come back to pay up whatever I owe here and say good-bye to the sailfish, hooked and shellacked and strung up like a flag over . . . over . . . lesser, much lesser . . . creatures that never, ever sailed an inch in their . . . lives . . .

(*The pauses at the end of this speech are due to a shift of her attention toward a young man and a boy who have entered the bar. Her eyes have followed them as they walked past her to a table in the front.*

(*She continues speaking, but now as if to herself.*)

. . . When I leave here tonight, none of you will ever see me again. I'm going to stop by the shop, let myself in with my passkey and collect my own equipment, which is enough to open a shop of my own, write a good-bye note to Flo, she isn't a bad old bitch, I doubled her trade since I been there, she's going to miss me, poor Flo, then leave my passkey and cut back to my trailer and pack like lightning and move on to . . .

BILL: . . . Where?

LEONA: Where I go next. You won't know, but you'll know I went fast.

(*Now she forgets her stated intention of going out of the bar and crosses to the table taken by the young man and the boy.*

(*The boy, Bobby, wears faded jeans and a sweatshirt on the back of which is lettered "Iowa to Mexico." The young man, Quentin, is dressed effetely in a yachting jacket, maroon linen slacks, and a silk neck-scarf. Despite this costume, he has a quality of sexlessness, not effeminacy. Some years ago, he must have been remarkably handsome. Now his face seems to have been burned thin by a fever that is not of the flesh.*)

LEONA (*suddenly very amiable*): Hi, boys!

QUENTIN: Oh. Hello. Good Evening.

BOBBY (*with shy friendliness*): Hello.

(*Bill is grinning and chuckling. Violet's weeping in the ladies' room no longer seems to interest anyone in the bar.*)

LEONA (*to Bobby*): How's the corn growing out there where the tall corn grows?

BOBBY: Oh, it's still growing tall.

LEONA: Good for the corn. What town or city are you from in Iowa?

BOBBY: Goldenfield. It's close to Dubuque.

LEONA: Dubuque, no shoot? I could recite the telephone book of Dubuque, but excuse me a minute, I want to play a selection on the number selector, and I'll come right back to discuss Dubuque with you. Huh? (*She moves as if totally pacified to the juke box and removes some coins from a pocket. They fall to the floor. She starts to bend over to pick them up, then decides not to bother, gives them a slight kick, gets a dollar bill out of a pocket, calling out:*) Monk, gimme change for a buck. (*Leona crosses to Monk at bar, waving a dollar bill.*)

QUENTIN: Barman? . . . Barman? . . . What's necessary to get the barman's attention here, I wonder.

(*Leona crosses back to juke box, stage right. Bobby hands Leona the change he's picked up off the floor. She looks for a number on the juke box.*)

MONK: I heard you. You've come in the wrong place. You're looking for the Jungle Bar, half a mile up the beach.

QUENTIN: Does that mean you'd rather not serve us?

MONK: Let me see the kid's draft card.

BOBBY: I just want a Coke.

QUENTIN: He wants a plain Coca-Cola, I'd like a vodka and tonic.

(*Leona lights up the juke box with a coin and selects a violin number, "Souvenir." A look of ineffable sweetness appears on her face, at the first note of music.*)

BILL: Y' can't insult 'em, there's no way to bring 'em down except to beat 'em and roll 'em.

(*The bar starts to dim, and a special spot comes up on Bill. The violin music on the juke box plays softly under.*)

I noticed him stop at the door before he come in. He was about to go right back out when he caught sight of me. Then he decided to stay. A piss-elegant one like that is asking for it. After a while, say about fifteen minutes, I'll go in the gents' and he'll follow me in there for a look at Junior.

Then I'll have him hooked. He'll ask me to meet him outside by his car or at the White Castle. It'll be a short wait and I don't think I'll have t'do more than scare him a little. I don't like beating 'em up. They can't help the way they are. Who can? Not me. Left home at fifteen, and like Leona says, I've never done a lick of work in my life and I never plan to, not as long as Junior keeps batting on the home team, but my time with Leona's run out. She means to pull out of here and I mean to stay . . .

(*The bar is relighted. Leona is still at the juke box. She is leaning against the juke box, listening intently to the music.*)

MONK (*rapping at the ladies'*): Violet, you can come out, now, she's playing that violin number.

(*Bill and Steve laugh. The bar starts to dim, and a special spot comes up on Steve. The violin number still plays under.*)

STEVE: I guess Violet's a pig, all right, and I ought to be ashamed to go around with her. But a man unmarried, forty-seven years old, employed as a short-order cook at a salary he can barely get by on alone, he can't be choosy. Nope, he has to be satisfied with the Goddam scraps in this world, and Violet's one of those scraps. She's a pitiful scrap, but . . . (*He shrugs sadly and lifts the beer bottle to his mouth.*) . . . something's better than nothing and I had nothing before I took up with her. She gave me a clap once and tried to tell me I got it off a toilet seat. I asked the doctor, is it possible to get a clap off a public toilet seat, and he said, yes, you can get it that way but you *don't*. (*He grins sadly and drinks again, wobbling slightly.*) . . . Oh, my life, my miserable, cheap life! It's like a bone thrown to a dog! I'm the dog, she's the bone. Hell, I know her habits. She's always down there in that amusement arcade when I go to pick her up, she's down there as close as she can get to some Navy kid, playing a pinball game, and one hand is out of sight. Hustling? I reckon that's it. I know I don't provide for her, just buy her a few beers here, and a hot dog on the way home. But, Bill, why's he let her mess around with him? One night he was braggin' about the size of his tool, he said all he had to do to make a living was wear tight pants on the street. Life! . . . Throw it to a dog. I'm not a dog, I don't want it. I think I'll sit at the bar and pay no attention to her when she comes out . . .

(*The light in the bar comes up to normal level as the spot fades out. After a moment, Violet comes out of the ladies' room slowly, with a piteous expression. She is dabbing her nostrils with a bit of toilet tissue. Her lips are pursed in sorrow so that she is like travesty of a female saint under torture. She gasps and draws back a little at the sight of Leona; then, discreetly sobbing, she edges onto a bar stool, and Monk gives her a beer. Steve glares at her. She avoids looking at him. Bill grins and chuckles at his table. Leona ignores the fact that Violet has emerged from her retreat. She goes on pacing the bar, but is enthralled by the music.*)

LEONA: My God, what an instrument, it's like a thing in your heart, it's a thing that's sad but better than being happy, in a . . . crazy drunk way . . .

VIOLET (*piteously*): I don't know if I can drink, I feel sick at my stomach.

LEONA: Aw, shit, Violet. Who do you think you're kidding? You'll drink whatever is put in the reach of your paws. (*She slaps herself on the thigh with the sailor cap and laughs.*)

VIOLET: I do feel sick at my stomach.

LEONA: You're lucky you're sick at your stomach because your stomach can vomit, but when you're sick at your heart, that's when it's awful, because your heart can't vomit the memories of your lifetime. I wish my heart could vomit, I wish my heart could throw up the heartbreaks of my lifetime, my days in a beauty shop and my nights in a trailer. It wouldn't surprise me at all if I drove up to Sausalito alone this night. With no one . . .

(*She glances at Bill, who grins and chuckles. Violet sobs piteously again. Leona gives Violet a fairly hard slap on the shoulders with her sailor's cap. Violet cries out in affected terror.*)

Shuddup, I'm not gonna hit you. Steve, take her off that bar stool and put her at a table, she's on a crying jag and it makes me sick.

STEVE (*to Violet*): Come off it, Violet. Sit over here at a table, before you fall off the bar stool.

LEONA: She hasn't got a mark on her, not a mark, but she acts like I'd nearly kilt her, and turns to a weeping willow. But as for that ape that I put up in my trailer, I took him in because a life in a trailer, going from place to place any way the wind blows you, gets to be lonely, sometimes. But that's a mistake I'll not make again . . . knock wood! (*Knocks table top.*)

STEVE (*wishing to smooth troubled waters*): Know what that means, to knock wood? It means to touch the wood of the true cross, Leona. (*He peers gravely and nearsightedly into Leona's face.*)

LEONA: Yeh, for luck, you need it.

MONK (*to Violet at bar*): That's mine! Here's yours. (*She has reached out for Monk's drink.*)

STEVE: Violet, get off that stool and sit at a table.

LEONA: You got to move her. She's got to be moved.

(*Steve accepts this necessity. He supports Violet's frail, liquid figure to a table upstage, but her long, thin arm snakes out to remove Monk's drink from the bar top as she goes.*

(*The phone rings, and Monk lifts it.*)

MONK: Monk's Place . . . Doc, it's for you.

DOC (*crossing to the end of the bar*): Thanks, Monk.

MONK: The old Doc's worked up a pretty good practice for a man in retirement.

LEONA: Retirement your ass, he was kicked out of the medical profession for performing operations when he was so loaded he couldn't tell the appendix from the gizzard.

MONK: Leona, go sit at your table.

LEONA: You want responsibility for a human life, do you?

MONK: Bill, I think she's ready to go home now.

LEONA: I'll go home when I'm ready and I'll do it alone.

BILL: I seen a circus with a polar bear in it that rode a three-wheel bicycle. That's what you make me think of tonight.

LEONA: You want to know something, McCorkle? I could beat the shit out of you.

BILL: Set down somewhere and shut up.

LEONA: I got a suggestion for you. Take this cab fare . . . (*She throws a handful of silver on the table.*) . . . And go get your stuff out of my trailer. Clear it all out, because when I go home tonight and find any stuff of yours there, I'll pitch it out of the trailer and bolt the door on you. I'm just in the right mood to do it.

BILL: Don't break my heart.

LEONA: What heart? We been in my trailer together for six months and you contributed nothing.

BILL: Shit, for six months I satisfied you in your trailer!

LEONA: You never satisfied nothing but my mother complex. Never mind, forget it, it's forgotten. Just do this. Take this quarter and punch number K-6 three times on the juke box.

BILL: Nobody wants to hear that violin number again.

LEONA: I do, I'm somebody. My brother, my young brother, played it as good if not better than Heifetz on that box. Y'know, I look at you and I ask myself a question. How does it feel to've never had anything beautiful in your life and not even know you've missed it? (*She crosses toward the juke box.*) Walking home with you some night, I've said, Bill, look at the sky, will you look at that sky? You never looked up, just grunted. In your life you've had no experiation . . . experience! Appreciation! . . . of the beauty of God in the sky, so what is your life but a bottle of, can of, glass of . . . one, two, three! (*She has punched the violin selection three times.*)

MONK: The Doc's still on the phone.

LEONA: "Souvenir" is a soft number.

(*The violin number starts to play again on the juke box.*)

DOC (*returning to the bar*): I've got to deliver a baby. Shot of brandy.

LEONA (*returning to Bill's table*): It wouldn't be sad if you didn't know what you missed by coming into this world and going out of it some day without ever having a sense of, experience of and memory of, a beautiful thing in your life such as I have in mine when I remember the violin of and the face of my young brother . . .

BILL: You told me your brother was a fruit.

LEONA: I told you privately something you're repeating in public with words as cheap as yourself. My brother who played this number had pernicious anemia from the age of thirteen and any fool knows a disease, a condition, like that would make any boy too weak to go with a woman, but he was so full of love he had to give it to someone like his music. And in my work, my profession as a beautician, I never seen skin or hair or eyes that could touch my brother's. His hair was a natural blond as soft as silk and his eyes were two pieces of heaven in a human face, and he played on the violin like he was making love to it. I cry! I cry! . . . No, I don't, I *don't* cry! . . . I'm proud that I've had something beautiful to remember as long as I live in my lifetime . . .

(*Violet sniffles softly.*)

When they passed around the plate for the offering at church, they'd have him play in the choir stall and he played and he looked like an angel, standing under the light through the stained glass window. Um-hummm. (*Her expression is rapt.*) . . . And people, even the tightwads, would drop paper money in the plates when he played. Yes, always before the service, I'd give him a shampoo-rinse so that his silky hair, the silkiest hair I've ever known on a human head in my lifetime as a beautician, would look like an angel's halo, touched with heavenly light. Why, people cried like I'm crying and the preacher was still choked up when he delivered the sermon. "Angels of Light," that was it, the number he played that Easter . . . (*She sings a phrase of the song.*) Emotions of people can be worse than people but sometimes better than people, yes, superior to them, and Haley had that gift of making people's emotions uplifted, superior to them! But he got weaker and weaker and thinner and thinner till one Sunday he collapsed in the choir stall, and after that he failed fast, just faded out of this world. Anemia—pernicious . . .

VIOLET (*sobbing*): Anemia, that's what I've got!

LEONA: Don't compare yourself to him, how dare you compare yourself to him. He was too beautiful to live and so he died. Otherwise we'd be living together in my trailer. I'd train him to be a beautician, to bring out the homeliness in . . . I mean the, I mean the . . . (*She is confused for a moment. She lurches into a bar stool and knocks it over.*) I mean I'd train my young brother to lay his hands on the heads of the homely and lonely and bring some beauty out in them, at least for one night or one day or at least for an hour. We'd have our own shop, maybe two of 'em, and I wouldn't give you . . . (*She directs herself to Bill.*) . . . the time of the day, the time of the night, the time of the morning or afternoon, the sight of you never would have entered my sight to make me feel pity for you, no, noooo! (*She bends over Bill's table, resting her spread palms on it, to talk directly into his face.*) The companionship and the violin of my brother would be all I had any need for in my lifetime till my death-time! Remember this, Bill, if your brain can remember. Everyone needs! One beautiful thing! In the course of a lifetime! To save the heart from colluption!

BILL: What is "colluption," fat lady?

LEONA: *CORRUPTION!* . . . Without one beautiful thing in the course of a lifetime, it's all a death-time. A woman turns to a slob that lives with a slob, and life is disgusting to her and she's disgusting to life, and I'm just the one to . . .

BILL (*cutting in*): If you'd rather live with a fruit . . .

LEONA: *Don't say it! Don't say it!* (*She seizes hold of a chair and raises it mightily over her head. Violet screams. Leona hurls the chair to the floor.*) Shit, he's not worth the price of a broken chair! (*Suddenly she bursts into laughter that is prodigious as her anger or even more, it's like an unleashed element of nature. Several patrons of the bar, involuntarily, laugh with her. Abruptly as it started, the laughter stops short. There is total silence except for the ocean sound outside.*)

VIOLET: Steve, love, get me a hot dog with chili and onion, huh? Or maybe a Whopper.

STEVE: Oh, now you want a Whopper, a king-size burger, now, huh? Always got your hand out for something.

VIOLET: That's a cruel injustice. (*Sobs.*)

STEVE: Stop it!

VIOLET: I'm in paiii-in!

LEONA: Look at her, not a mark on her, but says she's in pain and wants a hot dog with everything on it, and I heard on

TV that the Food Administration found insect and rodent parts in some hot dogs sold lately. (*She has been stalking the bar.*) Let her have him for supper! (*Indicates Bill.*)

DOC (*rising from his bar stool*): Well, I better be going. Somebody's about to be born at Treasure Island.

LEONA: That's my trailer court where I keep my trailer. A baby's about to be born there?

BILL: Naw, not a baby, a full-grown adult's about to be born there, and that's why the Doc had t'brace himself with a coupla shots of brandy.

DOC (*turning about on his bar stool, glass in hand*): You can't make jokes about birth and you can't make jokes about death. They're miracles, holy miracles, both, yes, that's what both of them are, even though, now, they're usually surrounded by . . . expedients that seem to take away the dignity of them. Birth? Rubber gloves, boiled water, forceps, surgical shears. And death? . . . The wheeze of an oxygen tank, the jab of a hypodermic needle to put out the panic light in the dying-out eyes, tubes in the arms and the kidneys, absorbent cotton inserted in the rectum to hold back the bowels discharged when the . . . the *being stops.* (*During this speech the bar dims, and a special spot comes up on Doc.*) . . . It's hard to see back of this cloud of . . . irreverent . . . paraphernalia. But behind them both are the holy mysteries of . . . birth and . . . death . . . They're dark as the face of a black man, yes, that's right, a Negro, yes. I've always figured that God is a black man with no light on his face, He moves in the dark like a black man, a Negro miner in the pit of a lightless coal mine, obscured completely by the . . . irrelevancies and irreverencies of public worship . . . standing to sing, kneeling to pray, sitting to hear the banalities of a preacher . . . Monk, did I give you my . . . ?

(*As light comes up in bar, the spot fades out.*)

MONK: Bag? Yeah, here. (*Monk hands a medical kit across the bar.*)

LEONA: I want to know, is nobody going to stop him from going out, in his condition, to deliver a baby? I want to know quick, or I'll stop him myself!

DOC: Thanks. And I'll have a shot of brandy to wash down a Benzedrine tablet to steady my hands.

LEONA: NOBODY, HUH?

DOC: Tonight, as I drove down Canyon Road, I noticed a clear bright star in the sky, and it was right over that trailer court, Treasure Island, where I'm going to deliver a baby. So now I know: I'm going to deliver a new Messiah tonight.

LEONA: The hell you are, you criminal, murdering quack, leggo of that bag!

(*Leona rushes Doc and snatches his bag. She starts toward the door but is blocked by one of the men; starts in another direction and is blocked again. She is then warily approached from three or four sides by Monk, Doc, Bill, and Steve as trainers approaching an angry "big cat."*

(*All ad-lib during this, and in the lines that follow, Monk, Leona, and Doc speak almost simultaneously, while Steve keeps up a continual placating repetition of "Violet says" and "Have a beer with us, Leona."*

(*The effect should almost suggest a quartet in opera: several voices blended but each pursuing its separate plaint.*)

MONK: Don't let her out with . . .

DOC: My bag! The instruments in that bag . . .

MONK: Steve, Bill, hold her, I can't with my . . .

DOC: Are worth and insured for . . . over two thousand! If you damage the contents of that bag . . . I'll sue you for their value and for slander!

(*Leona sits on Doc's bag at center table.*)

LEONA: I'll surrender this bag to you in a courtroom only!

DOC: Very expensive, very, very expensive.

STEVE: Look, she's sitting on Doc's bag. Violet says she's, Leona, Violet wants to, listen, listen, listen Leona, set down and have a beer with us! Violet says she . . .

VIOLET: Not at this table, no, no, I'm scared of Leona, she . . .

STEVE: Violet, shuddup. Leona? Violet's offered you to a . . . drink! Have a drink with us, Leona.

LEONA: I'll stay sitting on it till some action is taken to stop this man from illegal . . .

(*Bill squirts a mouthful of beer at her, and she immediately leaps up to strike at him fiercely with the sailor's cap. In that instant Monk seizes the bag from the chair and tosses it to Doc, who rushes out the door with it.*)

All of you are responsible! . . . If he murders a baby tonight and the baby's mother! Is life worth nothing in here? I'm going out. I am going to make a phone call.

(*Bill makes a move to stop her.*)

Don't you *dare* to! Try to!

MONK: Who're you going to call?

STEVE: Who's she going to call?

LEONA (*to Monk*): That's my business, strictly. I'm not gonna use your phone. (*She charges out the door, and the door is again left open on the sound of surf.*)

MONK: What's she up to?

STEVE: What's she up to, Bill?

BILL (*grinning and shrugging*): I know what she's up to. She's gonna call the office at Treasure Island and tell 'em the Doc's comin' out there to deliver a baby.

MONK: Well, stop her, go stop her!

STEVE: Yeh, you better stop her.

BILL (*indifferently*): She's disappeared in the fog.

MONK: She can get the Doc into serious trouble, and his condition's no better than mine is . . .

BILL: Shit, they know her too well to pay any attention to her call.

MONK: I hate to eighty-six anyone out of my place; I never have done that in the six years I've run it, but I swear to God, I . . . have to avoid . . . disturbance.

VIOLET (*plaintively*): Last week she gave me a perm and a rinse for nothing, and then tonight she turns on me, threatens to kill me.

BILL: Aw, she blows hot and cold, dependin' on whichever way her liquor hits her.

VIOLET: She's got two natures in her. Sometimes she couldn't be nicer. A minute later she . . .

MONK (*at the telephone*): Shut up a minute. Treasure Island? This is Monk speaking from Monk's Place . . . Yeah. Now. If you get a phone call out there from Leona Dawson, you know her, she's got a trailer out there, don't listen to her; she's on a crazy mean drunk, out to make trouble for a capable doctor who's been called by someone out there, an emergency call. So I thought I'd warn you, thank you. (*Monk hangs up the telephone.*)

(*Violet comes downstage, and the light is focused on her.*)

VIOLET: It's perfectly true that I have a room over the amusement arcade facing the pier. But it wasn't like Leona describes it. It took me a while to get it in shipshape condition because I was not a well girl when I moved in there, but I got it clean and attractive. It wasn't luxurious but it was clean and attractive and had an atmosphere to it. I don't see anything wrong with living upstairs from the amusement arcade, facing the pier. I don't have a bath or a toilet but I keep myself clean with a sponge bath at the washbasin and use the toilet in the amusement arcade. Anyhow it was a temporary arrangement, that's all it was, a temporary arrangement . . .

(*Leona returns to the bar. Bill rises quickly and walks over to the bar.*)

LEONA: One, two, button my shoe, three, four, shut the door, five, six, pick up sticks . . . (*No one speaks.*) . . . Silence, absolute silence. Am I being ostracized? (*She goes to the table of Quentin and Bobby.*) Well, boys, what went wrong?

QUENTIN: I'm afraid I don't know what you mean.

LEONA: Sure you know what I mean. You're not talking to each other, you don't even look at each other. There's some kind of tension between you. What is it? Is it guilt feelings? Embarrassment with guilt feelings?

BOBBY: I still don't know what you mean, but, uh . . .

LEONA: "But, uh" what?

QUENTIN: Don't you think you're being a little presumptuous?

LEONA: Naw, I know the gay scene. I learned it from my kid brother. He came out early, younger than this boy here. I know the gay scene and I know the language of it and I know how full it is of sickness and sadness; it's so full of sadness and sickness, I could almost be glad that my little brother died before he had time to be infected with all that sadness and sickness in the heart of a gay boy. This kid from Iowa, here, reminds me a little of how my brother was, and you, you remind me of how he might have become if he'd lived.

QUENTIN: Yes, you should be relieved he's dead, then.

(*She flops awkwardly into a chair at the table.*)

QUENTIN (*testily*): Excuse me, won't you sit down?

LEONA: D'ya think I'm still standing up?

QUENTIN: Perhaps we took your table.

LEONA: I don't have any table. I'm moving about tonight like an animal in a zoo because tonight is the night of the death-day of my brother and . . . Look, the barman won't serve me, he thinks I'm on a mean drunk, so do me a favor, order a double bourbon and pretend it's for you. Do that, I'll love you for it, and of course I'll pay you for it.

QUENTIN (*calling out*): Barman? I'd like a double bourbon.

MONK: If it's for the lady, I can't serve you.

(*Bill laughs heartily at the next table.*)

QUENTIN: It isn't for the lady, it's for me.

LEONA: How do you like that shit? (*She shrugs.*) Now what went wrong between you before you come in here, you can tell me and maybe I can advise you. I'm practically what they call a faggot's moll.

QUENTIN: Oh. Are you?

LEONA: Yes, I am. I always locate at least one gay bar in whatever city I'm in. I live in a home on wheels, I live in a trailer, so I been quite a few places. And have a few more to go. Now nobody's listening to us, they're involved in their own situations. What went wrong?

QUENTIN: Nothing, exactly. I just made a mistake, and he did, too.

LEONA: Oh. Mistakes. How did you make these mistakes? Nobody's listening, tell me.

QUENTIN: I passed him riding his bicycle up Canyon Road and I stopped my car and reversed it till I was right by his bike and I . . . spoke to him.

LEONA: What did you say to him?

BOBBY: Do you have to talk about it?

QUENTIN: Why not? I said: "Did you really ride that bike all the way from Iowa to the Pacific Coast," and he grinned and said, yes, he'd done that. And I said: "You must be tired?" and he said he was and I said: "Put your bike in the back seat of my car and come home with me for dinner."

LEONA: What went wrong? At dinner? You didn't *give* him the dinner?

QUENTIN: No, I gave him drinks, first, because I thought that after he'd had dinner, he might say: "Thank you, good night."

BOBBY: Let's shut up about that. I had dinner after.

LEONA: After what?

QUENTIN: After . . .

BOBBY: I guess to you people who live here it's just an old thing you're used to, I mean the ocean out there, the Pacific, it's not an *experience* to you any more like it is to me. You say it's the Pacific, but me, I say THE PACIFIC!

QUENTIN: Well, everything is in "caps" at your age, Bobby.

LEONA (*to Quentin*): Do you work for the movies?

QUENTIN: Naturally, what else?

LEONA: Act in them, you're an actor?

QUENTIN: No. Script writer.

LEONA (*vaguely*): Aw, you write movies, huh?

QUENTIN: Mostly rewrite. Adapt. Oh, I had a bit of a set-back when they found me too literate for my first assignment . . . converting an epic into a vehicle for the producer's doxy, a grammar school dropout. But the industry is using me now to make blue movies bluer with . . . you know, touches of special . . . erotica . . . lovely.

(*Leona laughs.*)

LEONA: Name?

QUENTIN: Quentin . . . Miss? (*He rises.*)

LEONA: Leona. Dawson. And he's?

QUENTIN: Bobby.

LEONA: Bobby, come back to the party. I want you back here, love. Resume your seat. (*Resting a hand on the boy's stiff shoulder*) . . . You're a literary gent with the suede shitkickers and a brass-button blazer and a . . . (*Flicks his scarf.*)

BILL (*leering from bar*): Ask him if he's got change for a three-dollar bill.

QUENTIN: Yes, if you have the bill.

LEONA: Ignore the peasants. I don't think that monkey-faced mother will serve us that bourbon . . . I never left his bar without leaving a dollar tip on the table, and this is what thanks I get for it, just because it's the death-day of my brother and I showed a little human emotion about it. Now what's the trouble between you and this kid from Iowa where the tall corn blows, I mean grows?

QUENTIN: I only go for straight trade. But this boy . . . look at him! Would you guess he was gay? . . . I didn't, I thought he was straight. But I had an unpleasant surprise when he responded to my hand on his knee by putting his hand on mine.

BOBBY: I don't dig the word "*gay.*" To me they mean nothing, those words.

LEONA: Aw, you've got plenty of time to learn the meanings of words and cynical attitudes. Why he's got eyes like my brother's! Have you paid him?

QUENTIN: For disappointment?

LEONA: Don't be a mean-minded mother. Give him a five, a ten. If you picked up what you don't want, it's your mistake and pay for it.

BOBBY: I don't want money from him. I thought he was nice, I liked him.

LEONA: Your mistake, too. (*She turns to Quentin.*) Gimme your wallet.

(*Quentin hands her his wallet.*)

BOBBY: He's disappointed. I don't want anything from him.

LEONA: Don't be a fool. Fools aren't respected, you fool. (*She removes a bill from the wallet and stuffs it in the pocket of Bobby's shirt. Bobby starts to return it.*) OK, I'll hold it for you till he cuts out of here to make another pickup and remind me to give it back to you when he goes. He wants to pay you, it's part of his sad routine. It's like doing penance . . . penitence.

BILL (*loudly*): Monk, where's the head?

MONK: None of that here, Bill.

QUENTIN (*with a twist of a smile toward Bill*): Pity.

LEONA (*turning to Quentin*): Do you like being alone except for vicious pickups? The kind you go for? If I understood you correctly? . . . Christ, you have terrible eyes, the expression in them! What are you looking at?

QUENTIN: The fish over the bar . . .

LEONA: You're changing the subject.

QUENTIN: No, I'm not, not a bit . . . Now suppose some night I woke up and I found that fantastic fish . . . what is it?

LEONA: Sailfish. What about it?

QUENTIN: Suppose I woke up some midnight and found that peculiar thing swimming around in my bedroom? Up the Canyon?

LEONA: In a fish bowl? Aquarium?

QUENTIN: No, not in a bowl or aquarium: free, unconfined.

LEONA: Impossible.

QUENTIN: Granted. It's impossible. But suppose it occurred just the same, as so many impossible things *do* occur just the same. Suppose I woke up and discovered it there, swimming round and round in the darkness over my bed, with a faint phosphorescent glow in its big goggle-eyes and its gorgeously iridescent fins and tail making a swishing sound as it circles around and about and around and about right over my head in my bed.

LEONA: Hah!

QUENTIN: Now suppose this admittedly preposterous thing did occur. What do you think I would say?

LEONA: To the fish?

QUENTIN: To myself and the fish.

LEONA: . . . I'll be raped by an ape if I can imagine what a person would say in a situation like that.

QUENTIN: I'll tell you what I would say, I would say: "Oh, well . . ."

LEONA: . . . Just "Oh, well"?

QUENTIN: "Oh, well" is all I would say before I went back to sleep.

LEONA: What I would say is: "Get the hell out of here, you goggle-eyed monstrosity of a mother," that's what I'd say to it.

MONK: Leona, let's lighten it up.

QUENTIN: You don't see the point of my story?

LEONA: Nope.

QUENTIN (*to Bobby*): Do *you* see the point of my story?

(*Bobby shakes his head.*)

Well, maybe I don't either.

LEONA: Then why'd you tell it?

QUENTIN: What is the thing that you mustn't lose in this world before you're ready to leave it? The one thing you mustn't lose ever?

LEONA: . . . Love?

(*Quentin laughs.*)

BOBBY: Interest?

QUENTIN: That's closer, much closer. Yes, that's almost it. The word that I had in mind is surprise, though. The capacity for being surprised. I've lost the capacity for being surprised, so completely lost it, that if I woke up in my bedroom late some night and saw that fantastic fish swimming right over my head, I wouldn't be really surprised.

LEONA: You mean you'd think you were dreaming?

QUENTIN: Oh, no. Wide awake. But not really surprised. (*The special spot concentrates on him. The bar dims, but an eerie glow should remain on the sailfish over the bar.*) There's a coarseness, a deadening coarseness, in the experience of most homosexuals. The experiences are quick, and hard, and brutal, and the pattern of them is practically unchanging. Their act of love is like the jabbing of a hypodermic needle to which they're addicted but which is more and more empty of real interest and surprise. This lack of variation and surprise in their . . . "love life" . . . (*He smiles harshly.*) . . . spreads into other areas of . . . "sensibility?" (*He smiles again.*) . . . Yes, once, quite a long while ago, I was often startled by the sense of being alive, of being *myself, living!* Present on earth, in the flesh, yes, for some completely mysterious reason, a single, separate, intensely conscious being, *myself: living!* . . . Whenever I would feel this . . . *feeling*, this . . . shock of . . . what? . . . self-realization? . . . I would be stunned, I would be thunder-struck by it. And by the existence of everything that exists, I'd be lightning-struck with astonishment . . . it would do more than astound me, it would give me a feeling of panic, the sudden sense of . . . I suppose it was like an epileptic seizure, except that I didn't fall to the ground in convulsions; no, I'd be more apt to try to lose myself in a crowd on a street until the seizure was finished . . . They were dangerous seizures. One time I drove into the mountains and smashed the car into a tree, and I'm not sure if I *meant* to do that, or . . . In a forest you'll sometimes see a giant tree, several hundred years old, that's scarred, that's blazed by lightning, and the wound is almost obscured by the obstinately still living and growing bark. I wonder if such a tree has learned the same lesson that I have, not to feel astonishment any more but just go on, continue for two or three hundred years more? . . . This boy I picked up tonight, the kid from the tall corn country, still has the capacity for being surprised by what he sees, hears and feels in this kingdom of earth. All the way up the canyon to my place, he kept saying, *I can't believe it, I'm here, I've come to the Pacific, the world's greatest ocean!* . . . as if nobody, Magellan or Balboa or even the Indians had ever seen it before him; yes, like he'd discovered this ocean, the largest on earth, and so now, because he'd found it himself, it existed, now, for the first time, never before . . . And this excitement of his reminded me of my having lost the ability to say: "My God!" instead of just: "Oh, well." I've asked all the questions, shouted them at deaf heaven, till I was hoarse in the voice box and blue in the face, and gotten no answer, not the whisper of one, nothing at all, you see, but the sun coming up each morning and going down that night, and the galaxies of the night sky trooping onstage like chorines, robot chorines: one, two, three, kick, one two, three, kick . . . Repeat any question too often and what do you get, what's given? . . . A big carved rock by the desert, a . . . monumental symbol of worn-out passion and bewilderment in you, a stupid stone paralyzed sphinx that knows no answers that you don't but comes on like the oracle of all time, waiting on her belly to give out some outcries of universal wisdom, and if she woke up some midnight at the edge of the desert and saw that fantastic fish swimming over her head . . . y'know what she'd say, too? She'd say: "Oh, well" . . . and go back to sleep for another five thousand years. (*He turns back; and the bar is relighted. He returns to the table and adjusts his neck-scarf as he speaks to Bobby.*) . . . Your bicycle's still in my car. Shall I put it on the sidewalk?

BOBBY: I'll go get it.

QUENTIN: No. You will find it here, by the door. (*Desires no further exposure to Bobby.*)

LEONA (*to Bobby*): Stay here awhile . . . Set down. He wants to escape.

BOBBY: From me? (*Meaning "Why?"*)

LEONA (*visibly enchanted by Bobby, whom she associates with her lost brother*): Maybe more from himself. Stay here awhile.

BOBBY: . . . It's . . . late for the road. (*But he may resume his seat here.*)

LEONA: On a bike, yeh, too late, with the dreaded fog people out. Y'know, I got a suggestion. It's sudden but it's terrific. (*She leans across the table, urgently.*) Put your bike in my trailer. It's got two bunks.

BOBBY: Thank you but . . .

LEONA: It wouldn't cost you nothing and we'd be company for each other. My trailer's not ordinary, it's a Fonda deluxe, stereo with two speakers, color TV with an eight-inch screen, touchamatic, and baby, you don't look well fed. I'm a hell of a cook, could qualify as a pro in that line, too.

BILL (*to Steve*): What a desperate pitch. I was the wrong sex. She wants a fruit in her stinkin' trailer.

LEONA: Nothing stunk in my trailer but what's out now . . . He can't understand a person wanting to give protection to another, it's past his little reception. (*To Bobby*) Why're you staring out into space with visibility zero?

BOBBY (*slowly, with a growing ardor*): I've got a lot of important things to think over alone, new things. I feel new vibes, vibrations, I've got to sort out alone.

LEONA: Mexico's a dangerous country for you, and there's lonely stretches of road . . . (*She's thinking of herself, too.*)
BOBBY (*firmly but warmly to her*): Yes . . . I need that, now.
LEONA: Baby, are you scared I'd put the make on you?

(*Bill grunts contemptuously but with the knowledge that he is now truly evicted.*)

I don't, like they say, come on heavy . . . never, not with . . . (*She lightly touches Bobby's hand on the table.*) *This* is my touch! Is it *heavy*?

(*Bobby rises. Quentin is seen dimly, setting the bicycle at the door.*)

BOBBY: That man didn't come on heavy. (*Looking out at Quentin.*) His hand on my knee was just a human touch and it seemed natural to me to return it.
LEONA: Baby, his hand had . . . ambitions . . . And, oh, my God, you've got the skin and hair of my brother and even almost the eyes!
BILL: Can he play the fiddle?
BOBBY: In Goldenfield, Iowa, there was a man like that, ran a flower shop with a back room, decorated Chinese, with incense and naked pictures, which he invited boys into. I heard about it. Well, things like that aren't tolerated for long in towns like Goldenfield. There's suspicion and talk and then public outrage and action, and he had to leave so quick he didn't clear out the shop. (*The bar lights have faded out, and the special spot illuminates Bobby.*) A bunch of us entered one night. The drying-up flowers rattled in the wind and the wind-chimes tinkled and the . . . naked pictures were just . . . pathetic, y'know. Except for a sketch of Michelangelo's David. I don't think anyone noticed me snatch it off the wall and stuff it into my pocket. Dreams . . . images . . . nights . . . On the plains of Nebraska I passed a night with a group of runaway kids my age and it got cold after sunset. A lovely wild young girl invited me under a blanket with just a smile, and then a boy, me between, and both of them kept saying "love," one of 'em in one ear and one in the other, till I didn't know which was which "love" in which ear or which . . .

touch . . . The plain was high and the night air . . . exhilarating and the touches not heavy . . . The man with the hangup has set my bike by the door. (*Extends his hand to Leona. The bar is relighted.*) It's been a pleasure to meet a lady like you. Oh, I've got a lot of new adventures, experiences, to think over alone on my speed iron. I think I'll drive all night, I don't feel tired. (*Bobby smiles as he opens the door and nods good-bye to Monk's Place.*)

LEONA: Hey, Iowa to Mexico, the money . . . here's the money! (*She rushes to the door, but Bobby is gone with his bicycle.*)

BILL: He don't want a lousy five bucks, he wants everything in the wallet. He'll roll the faggot and hop back on his bike looking sweet and innocent as her brother fiddling in church.

(*Leona rushes out, calling.*)

STEVE: The Coast is overrun with 'em, they come running out here like animals out of a brushfire.

MONK (*as he goes to each table, collecting the empty cans and bottles, emptying ash trays on a large serving tray*): I've got no moral objections to them as a part of humanity, but I don't encourage them here. One comes in, others follow. First thing you know you're operating what they call a gay bar and it sounds like a bird cage, they're standing three deep at the bar and lining up at the men's room. Business is terrific for a few months. Then in comes the law. The place is raided, the boys hauled off in the wagon, and your place is padlocked. And then a cop or gangster pays you a social visit, big smile, all buddy-buddy. You had a good thing going, a real swinging place, he tells you, but you needed protection. He offers you protection and you buy it. The place is reopened and business is terrific a few months more. And then? It's raided again, and the next time it's reopened, you pay out of your nose, your ears, and your ass. Who wants it? I don't want it. I want a small steady place that I can handle alone, that brings in a small, steady profit. No buddy-buddy association with gangsters and the police. I want to know the people that come in my place so well I can serve them their brand of liquor or beer before they name it, soon as they come in the door. And all their personal problems, I want to know that, too.

(*Violet begins to hum softly, swaying to and fro like a water plant.*

(*When Monk finishes cleaning off the tables, he returns behind the bar. The bar lights dim, and his special spot comes up.*)

I'm fond of, I've got an affection for, a sincere interest in my regular customers here. They send me post cards from wherever they go and tell me what's new in their lives and I am interested in it. Just last month one of them I hadn't seen in about five years, he died in Mexico City and I was notified of the death and that he'd willed me all he owned in the world, his personal effects and a two-hundred-fifty-dollar savings account in a bank. A thing like that is beautiful as music. These things, these people, take the place of a family in my life. I love to come down those steps from my room to open the place for the evening, and when I've closed for the night, I love climbing back up those steps with my can of Ballantine's ale, and the stories, the jokes, the confidences and confessions I've heard that night, it makes me feel not alone . . . I've had heart attacks, and I'd be a liar to say they didn't scare me and don't still scare me. I'll die some night up those steps, I'll die in the night alone, and I hope it don't wake me up, that I just slip away, quietly.

(*Leona has returned. The light in the bar comes up but remains at a low level.*)

LEONA: . . . Is there a steam engine in here? Did somebody drive in here on a steam engine while I was out?

MONK (*returning from his meditation*): . . . Did what?

LEONA: I hear something going huff-huff like an old locomotive pulling into a station. (*She is referring to a sound like a panting dog. It comes from Bill at the unlighted table where Violet is seated between him and Steve.*) . . . Oh, well, my home is on wheels . . . Bourbon sweet, Monk.

MONK: Leona, you don't need another.

LEONA: Monk, it's after midnight, my brother's death-day is over, I'll be all right, don't worry. (*She goes to the bar.*) . . . It was selfish of me to wish he was still alive.

(*A pin-spot of light picks up Violet's tear-stained and tranced face at the otherwise dark table.*)

. . . She's got some form of religion in her hands . . .

Curtain

ACT II

An hour later. "Group singing" is in progress at the table stage right. Leona is not participating. She is sitting moodily at the bar facing front.

VIOLET: "I don't want to set the world on fii-yuh."
STEVE: "I don't want to set the world on fii-yuh."
VIOLET: I like old numbers best. Here's an oldie that I learned from my mother. (*She rises and assumes a sentimental look.*)

"Lay me where sweet flowers blos-som,
Where the dainty lily blows
Where the pinks and violets min-gle,
Lay me underneath the rose."

LEONA: Shit. Y'don't need a rose to lay her, you could lay her under a cactus and she wouldn't notice the diff-rence.

(*Bill crosses to the bar for a beer.*)

I guess you don't think I'm serious about it, hitting the highway tonight.

(*Bill shrugs and crosses to a downstage table.*)

Well, I am, I'm serious about it. (*She sits at his table.*) An experienced expert beautician can always get work anywhere.

BILL: Your own appearance is a bad advertisement for your line of work.

LEONA: I don't care how I look as long as I'm clean and decent . . . and *self-supporting*. When I haul into a new town, I just look through the yellow pages of the telephone directory and pick out a beauty shop that's close to my trailer camp. I go to the shop and offer to work a couple of days for nothing, and after that couple of days I'm in like Flynn, and on my own terms, which is fifty per cent of charges for all I do, and my tips, of course, too. They like my work and they like my personality, my approach to customers. I keep them laughing.

BILL: You keep me laughing, too.

LEONA: . . . Of course, there's things about you I'll remember with pleasure, such as waking up sometimes in the night and looking over the edge of the upper bunk to see you asleep in the lower. (*Bill leaves the table. She raises her voice to address the bar-at-large.*) Yeah, he slept in the lower 'cause when he'd passed out or nearly, it would of taken a derrick to haul him into the upper bunk. So I gave him the lower bunk and took the upper myself.

BILL: As if you never pass out. Is that the idea you're selling?

LEONA: When I pass out I wake up in a chair or on the floor, oh, no, the floor was good enough for me in your opinion, and sometimes you stepped on me even, yeah, like I was a rug or a bug, because your nature is selfish. You think because you've lived off one woman after another woman after eight or ten women you're something superior, special. Well, you're special but not superior, baby. I'm going to worry about you after I've gone and I'm sure as hell leaving tonight, fog or no fog on the highway, but I'll worry about you because you refuse to grow up and that's a mistake that you make, because you can only refuse to grow up for a limited period in your lifetime and get by with it . . . I *loved* you! . . . I'm not going to cry. It's only being so tired that makes me cry.

(*Violet starts weeping for her.*)

VIOLET: Bill, get up and tell Leona good-bye. She's a lonely girl without a soul in the world.

LEONA: I've got the world in the world, and McCorkle don't have to make the effort to get himself or any part of him up, it's easier to stay down. And as for being lonely, listen, ducks, that applies to every mother's son and daughter of us alive, we were given warning of that before we were born almost, and yet . . . When I come to a new place, it takes me two or three weeks, that's all it takes me, to find somebody to live with in my home on wheels and to find a night spot to hang out in. Those first two or three weeks are rough, sometimes I wish I'd stayed where I was before, but I know from experience that I'll find somebody and locate a night spot to booze in, and get acquainted with . . . friends . . . (*The light has focused on her. She moves downstage with her hands in her pockets, her face and voice very grave as if she were less confident that things will be as she says.*) And then, all at once, something wonderful happens. All the past disappointments in people I left behind me, just disappear, evaporate from my mind, and I just remember the good things, such as their sleeping faces, and . . . Life! Life! I never just said, "Oh, well," I've always said "Life!" to life, like a song to God, too, because I've lived in my lifetime and not been afraid of . . . changes . . . (*She goes back to the bar.*) . . . However, y'see, I've got this pride in my nature. When I live with a person I love and care for in my life, I expect his respect, and when I see I've lost it, I GO, GO! . . . So a home on wheels is the only right home for me.

(*Violet starts toward Leona.*)

What is she doing here?

(*Violet has weaved to the bar.*)

Hey! What are *you* doing here?

VIOLET: You're the best friend I ever had, the best friend I . . . (*She sways and sobs like a* religieuse *in the grip of a vision.*)

LEONA: What's that, what're you saying?

(*Violet sobs.*)

She can't talk. What was she saying?

VIOLET: . . . BEST . . . !

LEONA: WHAT?

VIOLET: . . . *Friend!*

LEONA: I'd go further than that, I'd be willing to bet I'm the *only* friend that you've had, and the next time you come down sick nobody will bring you nothing, no chicken, no hot beef bouillon, no chinaware, no silver, and no interest and concern about your condition, and you'll die in your rattrap with no human voice, just bang, bang, bang from the bowling alley and billiards. And when you die you should feel a relief from the conditions you lived in. Now I'm leaving you two suffering, bleeding hearts together, I'm going to sit at the bar. I had a Italian boy friend that taught me a saying, *"Meglior solo que mal accompanota,"* which means that you're better alone than in the company of a bad companion.

(*She starts to the bar, as Doc enters.*)

Back already, huh? It didn't take you much time to deliver the baby. Or did you bury the baby? Or did you bury the mother? Or did you bury them both, the mother and baby?

DOC (*to Monk*): Can you shut up this woman?

LEONA: Nobody can shut up this woman. Quack, quack, quack, Doctor Duck, quack, quack, quack, quack, quack!

DOC: I'M A LICENSED PHYSICIAN!

LEONA: SHOW *me your license. I'll shut up when I see it!*

DOC: A doctor's license to practice isn't the size of a drunken driver's license, you don't put it in a wallet, you hang it on the wall of your office.

LEONA: Here is your office! Which wall is your license hung on? Beside the sailfish or where? Where is your license to practice hung up, in the gents', with other filthy scribbles?!

MONK: Leona, you said your brother's death-day was over and I thought you meant you were . . .

LEONA: THOUGHT I MEANT I WAS *WHAT*?

MONK: You were ready to cool it. BILL! . . . Take Leona home, now.

LEONA: Christ, do you think I'd let him come near me?! Or near my trailer?! Tonight?! (*She slaps the bar several times with her sailor cap, turning to the right and left as if to ward off assailants, her great bosom heaving, a jungle-look in her eyes.*)

VIOLET: Steve, if we don't go now the King-burger stand will shut on us, and I've had nothing but liquids on my stomach all day. So I need a Whopper tonight.

(*Bill laughs.*)

STEVE: You'll get a hot dog with chili and everything on the way home. Get me . . . get me . . . get me. Grab and grope. You disgrace me! . . . your habits.

VIOLET: You're underdeveloped and you blame me.

LEONA (*looking out*): Yes . . . (*She slaps something with her cap.*) *Yes!*

VIOLET: What did she mean by that? Another sarcastic crack?

LEONA: When I say "yes" it is not sarcastic . . . It means a decision to act.

MONK: The place is closing so will everybody get themselves together now, please.

VIOLET: I do have to have something solid. Too much liquids and not enough solids in the system upsets the whole system. Ask the Doc if it don't. Doc, don't it upset the system, liquids without solids? All day long?

(*Doc has been sunk in profoundly dark and private reflections. He emerges momentarily to reply to Violet's direct question.*)

DOC: If that's a professional question to a doctor whose office is here . . . (*A certain ferocity is boiling in him and directed mostly at himself.*) My fee is . . . another brandy. (*He turns away with a short, disgusted laugh.*)

MONK: Something wrong, Doc?

(*Violet has crossed to Bill, as a child seeking protection.*)

DOC: Why, no, what could be wrong? But a need to put more liquid in my system . . .

LEONA (*convulsively turning about*): Yes . . . *yes!* (*This no longer relates to anything but her private decision.*)

BILL (*to himself*): I'm not about to spend the night on the beach . . .

VIOLET (*leaning toward Bill*): I am not neither, so why don't we check in somewhere? Us, two, together?

STEVE: I heard that.

LEONA: Yes . . . *yes!*

MONK: I said the place is closing.

VIOLET: Let's go together, us three, and talk things over at the King-burger stand.

STEVE: Being a cook I know the quality of those giant hamburgers called Whoppers, and they're fit only for dog food.

VIOLET: I think we better leave, now. (*Extends her delicate hands to both men.*) Steve? Bill? (*They all rise unsteadily and prepare to leave.*) Bill, you know I feel so protected now. (*Violet, Steve, and Bill start out.*)

LEONA (*stomping the floor with a powerful foot*): Y' WANT YOUR ASS IN A SLING? BEFORE YOU'RE LAID UNDER THAT ROSE?

VIOLET (*shepherded past Leona by Steve and Bill*): If we don't see you again, good luck wherever you're going.

(*They go out the door.*)

LEONA (*rushing after them*): That's what she wants, she wants her ass in a sling!

(*She rushes out the door. A moment or two later, as Monk looks out, and above the boom of the surf, Violet's histrionically shrill outcries are heard. This is followed by an offstage quarrel between Leona and a night watchman on the beach. Their overlapping, ad-lib dialogue continues in varying intensity as background to the business on stage: "If you don't settle down and come along peaceful-like, I'm going to call the wagon! . . ." "Do that, I just dare you to do it—go on, I just dare you to call the wagon! I want to ride in a wagon—it's got wheels, hasn't it—I'll ride any Goddam thing on wheels! . . ." "Oh, no—listen, lady, what's your name anyhow? . . ." "I'm just the one to do it! . . . I tell you my name? I'm going to tell you my name? What's your name?* I *want your name! Oh boy, do I want your name! . . ." "Listen, please, come on, now, let's take this thing easy . . ." "I've been drinking in this bar, and it's not the first time you . . ." "Let's go! You raise hell every night! . . ." "Every night! This isn't the first time—I've been meaning to report you! Yes, I'm going to report you! Yes, how's that for a switch? . . ." "I'm just trying to do my duty! . . ." "I live in a home on wheels, and every night you try to molest me when

I come home! . . ." "No! You're wrong—you're always in there drinking and raising hell and . . ." "Yeah, but you let criminals go free, right? . . ." "No, I don't! . . ." "People can't walk in the street, murdering, robbing, thieving, and all I do is have a few Goddam drinks, just because it's my brother's death-day, so I was showing a little human emotion —take your hands off me! . . ." "Come on now! . . ." "Don't you put your hands on a lady like me! . . ." "No, I'm not! . . ." "I'm a Goddam lady! That's what I am, and you just lay off! . . ." "I've had enough of this! . . ." "Every night I come out here, you're looking for free drinks, that's what's the matter with you! . . ." "I've never had a drink in my life, lady! . . ." "You never had a drink in your life! . . ." "No, I haven't, I've . . ." "Show me your identification, that's what I want to see! . . ." "I'm just trying to do my duty . . ." "Look here, old man . . ." "I don't know why I have to put up with an old dame like you this way . . ." "Oh!—Oh!—Why you Goddam son of a! . . ." "Now! . . ." "Don't you talk to me like that . . ." "I'm not talking to you, I'm telling you to come over here and let me get you to the telephone here! . . ." "You've been harassing that man Monk! . . ." "I'm not harassing anybody! . . ." "You're not harassing anybody? . . ." "You come over to this Monk's Place every night and raise hell, the whole damn bunch of you, and a poor man like me trying to earn a few dollars and make a living for his old woman and . . ." "Let me see your identification! What precinct are you from? . . ." "Oh, yeah . . ." "Go on, I want that identification, and I want that uniform off you, and that badge . . ." "You won't do anything of the sort! . . ." "Oh, yeah . . ." "Yes, I'm doing my job, what I'm doing is legal! . . ." "I happen to have more influence up at that station than you . . . Goddam pig! . . ." "I haven't done nothing to you, I'm just trying to do my job . . ." "Do your job? . . ." "Yes, and you're giving me a lot of hard time! . . ." "There's raping and thieving and criminals and robbers walking the streets, breaking store fronts, breaking into every bar . . ." "Well, that's not my—listen, lady! I'm just the night watchman around this beach here. I'm just on the beach nights, I don't have anything to do with what's going on somewhere else in the city, just on this beach! . . ."

"You don't know what's going on on the beach . . ." "I know what's going on on the beach, and it's you and that crowd drinking every night, raising hell! . . ." "We're not raising hell every night! . . ." "If I was your husband, golly, I—I—by God I would take care of you, I wouldn't put up with your likes, you and that crowd drinking every night! . . ." "I like that uniform you've got on you, and I'm gonna have it! . . ." "Why do you have to pick on a little man like me for? . . ." "I've seen you sneaking around, Peeping Tom, that's what you are! . . ." "No, that's not so! . . ." "I've seen you sneaking around looking in ladies' windows . . ." "That's not true! I'm just trying to do my duty! I keep telling you . . ." "Yeah, peeping in windows . . ." "No! . . ." "Watching people undress . . ." "No! You . . ." "I've seen you, you lascivious old man! . . ." "I've seen you taking these young men over to your trailer court and making studs out of them! . . ." "Yeah!—Yeah!—Yeah! Men, that's what I take to my trailer! I wouldn't take a palsied old man like you! . . ." "You know damn well I wasn't trying to get you to . . . ! I was trying to get you to this telephone box, where I was going to! . . ." "You will not be able to, old man! . . ." "Listen, Miss, I asked you to give me your identification! You give me your identification so I can tell who you are! . . ." "I want your *identification! I've seen you, I've seen you sneaking around the trailer court, I've seen you looking in windows . . ." "Oh, that's a lie! I never did a thing like that in all my life, I go to church. I'm a good Christian man! . . ." "Oh yeah! Yeah! Yeah! . . ." "I could take you in if I were younger, I wouldn't* have *to call the highway patrol, but I'm going to do that right now! . . ." "Listen, Holy Willie! I've seen your likes in church before! I wouldn't trust you with a . . ." "A little church wouldn't do you any harm neither! . . ." "Old man . . . Yeah! Yeah! . . ." "I've seen you with those young studs! . . ." "Doesn't that make you excited? . . ." "No, by God, it doesn't! . . ." "Is that your problem? . . ." "No, I don't have none! You're the one with the hang-ups and problems—*you *are a problem! You hang out here all night in that damn Monk's Place! . . ." "I've got my own man, I don't have to worry about any other man, I got my own man in my trailer! . . ." "Anyone want to spend the night with you, he must be a pig then, he must be*

some kind of pig living with you! . . ." "Fat old bag of wind, don't you talk to me! . . ." "Look, I'm tired of talking to you, by God, I've put up with you all I'm going to! I told you I was going to call the highway patrol! . . ." "I've seen the way you look at me when you . . ." "That's a lie!—I never . . ." "Yeah! Yeah! . . ." "I—I . . ." "I've seen you skulking around in the dark, looking in windows! . . ." "I don't need your kind! I've got a good woman at home, and she takes care of me, she takes good care of me! If I can get this job done and you'll just settle down and be quiet, we wouldn't have all this noise! . . ." "Does your wife know about the girls you go out with? . . ." "You're trying to incriminate me! . . ." "Does she know about that? . . ." "I know what you're trying to do . . ." "I've seen you . . ." "Trying to get me in trouble! Trying to get me to lose my job here! . . ." "I know what you holy boys are like! . . ." "Why don't you go back in there and raise some more hell with those young studs? . . ." "I ain't doing that neither . . ." "If you'd be quiet! . . ." "Stop harassing! . . ." "I ain't harassing nothing! . . ." "Every time you want a drink, yes? . . ." "I don't, I don't . . .")

MONK (*to Doc*): Goddam, she's left her suitcase.

DOC (*musing darkly*): . . . Done what?

MONK: She's left that bag in here, which means she's coming back.

DOC: Aw, yeah, a guarantee of it, she's going to provide you with the solace of her companionship up those stairs to the living quarters. (*He faces out from the bar.*) Y'know, that narrow flight of stairs is like the uterine passage to life, and I'd say that strange, that amorphous-looking creature is expecting to enter the world up the uterine passage to your living quarters above. (*He rises, chuckling darkly.*) Is the toilet repaired in the gents' room?

MONK (*listening to noises outside*): Yeh, plumber fixed it today.

(*Doc sighs and lumbers heavily the way pointed by the chalk-white hand signed "GENTS" off stage right.*

(*Monk crosses to the door to assess the disturbance outside. Bill rushes into the bar.*)

BILL: For Chrissake, get an ambulance with a strait jacket for her.

MONK: You mean you can't hold her, you stupid prick?

BILL: No man can hold that woman when she goes ape. Gimme a dime, I'm gonna call the Star of the Sea psycho ward.

MONK: Don't put a hand on that phone.

(*Violet now rushes in the door. She continues her histrionic outcries.*)

VIOLET: They're callin' the wagon for her, she's like a wild thing out there, lock the door, don't let her at me. Hide me, help me! Please! (*She rushes toward the stairs.*)

MONK: Stay down those stairs, pick up your luggage, I'll . . . I'll . . . call a taxi for you.

VIOLET: Steve done nothin' to . . . nothin' . . . Just run!

(*Altercation rises outside. Violet rushes into the ladies'. Monk closes the door and bolts it. Doc returns from the gents', putting on his jacket. His pant cuffs are wet.*)

DOC: The toilet still overflows.

(*Steve calls at the locked door.*)

STEVE: Vi'let? Monk?

(*Monk admits him. Steve enters with a confused look about, two dripping hot dogs in his hand.*)

STEVE: Vi'let, is Vi'let, did Vi'let get back in here?

MONK: Yeh, she's back in the ladies'. (*Monk closes door.*)

STEVE (*shuffling rapidly to the ladies'*): Vi'let? Vi'let? Hear me?

MONK: No. She don't.

STEVE: Vi'let, the King-burger's closed. So I couldn't get a Whopper . . . I got you two dogs, with chili and sauerkraut. You can come out now, Leona's getting arrested. Violet screamed for help to a cop that hates and hassles me ev'ry time I go home.

MONK: Those dogs you're holding are dripping on the floor.

DOC: Committing a nuisance . . .

STEVE: Vi'let, the dogs'll turn cold, the chili's dripping off 'em. You can't stay all night in a toilet, Vi'let.

VIOLET (*from the ladies'*): I can, I will, go away.

STEVE: She says she's gonna stay all night in a toilet. Wow . . . I mean . . . wow. (*Starts eating one of the hot dogs with a slurping sound.*)

MONK: If she's called the law here I want her to shut up in there.

STEVE: Vi'let, shut up in there. Come out for your dog.

VIOLET: Take your dog away and leave me alone. You give me no protection and no support a'tall.

(*Doc utters a laugh that is dark with an ultimate recognition of human absurdity and his own self-loathing.*)

MONK (*touching his chest*): . . . Doc? . . . Have a nightcap with me.

DOC: Thanks, Monk, I could use one.

MONK (*leaning back in chair and tapping his upper abdomen*): Angina or gastritis, prob'ly both.

DOC: In that location, it's gas.

MONK: What happened at Treasure Island?

DOC (*sipping his "shot"*): Tell you when I . . . get this . . . down.

BILL: Time . . . runs out with one and you go to another. Got a call from a woman guv'ment employee in Sacramento. She's got a co-op in a high-rise condominium, lives so high on the hog with payoffs an' all she can't see ground beneath her.

MONK: Why're you shouting, at who?

BILL: Nobody's ever thrown McCorkle out.

MONK: Unusual and not expected things can happen.

(*Leona is heard from off stage: "Okay, you make your phone call, and I'll make mine."*)

So, Doc, how'd it go at the trailer camp?

(*He and Doc are seated in profile at the downstage table. Steve and Bill are silhouetted at the edge of the lighted area.*)

DOC: The birth of the baby was at least three months premature, so it was born dead, of course, and just beginning to look like a human baby . . . The man living with the woman in the trailer said, "Don't let her see it, get it out of the trailer." I agreed with the man that she shouldn't see it, so I put this fetus in a shoe box . . . (*He speaks with difficulty, as if compelled to.*) The trailer was right by the beach, the tide was coming in with heavy surf, so I put the shoe box . . . and contents . . . where the tide would take it.

MONK: . . . Are you sure that was legal?

DOC: Christ, no, it wasn't legal . . . I'd barely set the box down when the man came out shouting for me. The woman had started to hemorrhage. When I went back in the trailer, she was bleeding to death. The man hollered at me, "Do something, can't you do something for her!"

MONK: . . . Could you?

DOC: . . . I could have told the man to call an ambulance for her, but I thought of the probable consequences to me, and while I thought about that, the woman died. She was a small woman, but not small enough to fit in a shoe box, so I . . . I gave the man a fifty-dollar bill that I'd received today for performing an abortion. I gave it to him in return for his promise not to remember my name . . . (*He reaches for the bottle. His hand shakes so that he can't refill his shotglass. Monk fills it for him.*) . . . You see, I can't make out certificates of death, since I have no legal right any more to practice medicine, Monk.

MONK: . . . In the light of what happened, there's something I'd better tell you, Doc. Soon as you left here to deliver that baby, Leona ran out of the bar to make a phone call to the office at Treasure Island, warning them that you were on your way out there to deliver a baby. So, Doc, you may be in trouble . . . If you stay here . . .

DOC: I'll take a Benzedrine tablet and pack and . . .

MONK: Hit the road before morning.

DOC: I'll hit the road tonight.

MONK: Don't let it hit you. (*Stands to shake.*) G'bye, Doc. Keep in touch.

DOC: G'bye, Monk. Thanks for all and the warning.

MONK: Take care, Doc.

STEVE: Yeh, Doc, you got to take care. Bye, Doc.

BILL: No sweat, Doc, g'bye.

(*Doc exits.*)

MONK: That old son of a bitch's paid his dues . . .

(*Altercation rises outside once more: "I'm gonna slap the cuffs on you! . . ." "That does it, let go of me, you fink, you pig!" Approach of a squad car siren is heard at a distance.*)

Yep, coming the law!

BILL: I don't want in on this.

STEVE: Not me neither.

(*They rush out. Squad car screeches to a stop. Leona appears at the door, shouting and pounding.*)

LEONA: MONK! THE PADDY WAGON IS SINGING MY SONG!

(*Monk lets her in and locks the door.*)

MONK: Go upstairs. Can you make it?

(*She clambers up the steps, slips, nearly falls.*
(*Policeman knocks at the door. Monk admits him.*)

Hi, Tony.

TONY: Hi, Monk. What's this about a fight going on here, Monk?

MONK: Fight? Not here. It's been very peaceful tonight. The bar is closed. I'm sitting here having a nightcap with . . .

TONY: Who's that bawling back there?

MONK (*pouring a drink for Tony*): Some dame disappointed in love, the usual thing. Try this and if it suits you, take the bottle.

TONY (*He drinks.*): . . . O.K. Good.

MONK: Take the bottle. Drop in more often. I miss you.

TONY: Thanks, g'night. (*He goes out.*)

MONK: Coast is clear, Leona. (*As Monk puts another bottle on the table, Leona comes awkwardly back down the stairs.*)

LEONA: Monk? Thanks, Monk. (*She and Monk sit at the table. Violet comes out of the ladies' room.*)

VIOLET: Steve? . . . Bill? (*She sees Leona at the table and starts to retreat.*)

LEONA: Aw, hell, Violet. Come over and sit down with us, we're having a nightcap, all of us, my brother's death-day is over.

VIOLET: Why does everyone hate me? (*She sits at the table: drinks are poured from the bottle. Violet hitches her chair close *to Monk's. In a few moments she will deliberately drop a matchbook under the table, bend to retrieve it, and the hand on Monk's side will not return to the table surface.*)

LEONA: Nobody hates you, Violet. It would be a compliment to you if they did.

VIOLET: I'd hate to think that I'd come between you and Bill.

LEONA: Don't torture yourself with an awful thought like that. Two people living together is something you don't understand, and since you don't understand it you don't respect it, but, Violet, this being our last conversation, I want to advise something to you. I think you need medical help in the mental department and I think this because you remind me of a . . . of a . . . of a plant of some kind . . .

VIOLET: Because my name is Violet?

LEONA: No, I wasn't thinking of violets, I was thinking of water plants, yeah, plants that don't grow in the ground but float on water. With you everything is such a . . . such a . . . well, you know what I mean, don't you?

VIOLET: Temporary arrangement?

LEONA: Yes, you could put it that way. Do you know how you got into that place upstairs from the amusement arcade?

VIOLET: . . . How?

LEONA: Yes, *how* or *why* or *when*?

VIOLET: . . . Why, I . . . (*She obviously is uncertain on all three points.*)

LEONA: Take your time. And *think*. How, why, when?

VIOLET: Why, I was . . . in L.A., and . . .

LEONA: Are you sure you were in L.A.? Are you sure about even that? Or is everything foggy to you, is your mind in a cloud?

VIOLET: Yes, I was . . .

LEONA: I said take your time, don't push it. Can you come out of the fog?

MONK: Leona, take it easy, we all know Violet's got problems.

LEONA: Her problems are mental problems and I want her to face them, now, in our last conversation. Violet? Can you come out of the fog and tell us how, when, and why you're living out of a suitcase upstairs from the amusement arcade, can you just . . .

MONK: (*cutting in*): She's left the amusement arcade, she left it tonight, she came here with her suitcase.

LEONA: Yeah, she's a water plant, with roots in water, drifting the way it takes her.

(*Violet weeps.*)

And she cries too easy, the water works are back on. I'll give her some music to cry to before I go back to my home on wheels and get it cracking up the Old Spanish Trail. (*She rises from the table.*)

MONK: Not tonight, Leona. You have to sleep off your liquor before you get on the highway in this fog.

LEONA: That's what you think, not what I think, Monk. My time's run out in this place. (*She has walked to the juke box and started the violin piece.*) . . . How, when, and why, and her only answer is tears. Couldn't say how, couldn't say when, couldn't say why. And I don't think she's sure where she was before she come here, any more sure than she is where she'll go when she leaves here. She don't dare remember and she don't dare look forward, neither. Her mind floats on a cloud and her body floats on water. And her dirty fingernail hands reach out to hold onto something she hopes can hold her together. (*She starts back toward the table, stops; the bar dims and light is focused on her.*) . . . Oh, my God, she's at it again, she got a hand under the table. (*Leona laughs sadly.*) Well, I guess she can't help it. It's sad, though. It's a pitiful thing to have to reach under a table to find some reason to live. You know, she's worshipping her idea of God Almighty in her personal church. Why the hell should I care she done it to a nowhere person that I put up in my trailer for a few months? I wish that kid from I-oh-a with eyes like my lost brother had been willing to travel with me, but I guess I scared him. What I think I'll do is turn back to a faggot's moll when I haul up to Sausalito or San Francisco. You always find one in the gay bars that needs a big sister with him, to camp with and laugh and cry with, and I hope I'll find one soon . . . it scares me to be alone in my home on wheels built for two . . . (*She turns as the bar is lighted and goes back to the table.*) Monk, HEY, MONK! What's my tab here t'night?

MONK: Forget it, don't think about it, go home and sleep, Leona. (*He and Violet appear to be in a state of trance together.*)

LEONA: I'm not going to sleep and I never leave debts behind me. This twenty ought to do it. (*She places a bill on the table.*)

MONK: Uh-huh, sure, keep in touch . . .

LEONA: Tell Bill he'll find his effects in the trailer-court office, and when he's hustled himself a new meal ticket, he'd better try and respect her, at least in public. . . . Well . . . (*She extends her hand slightly. Monk and Violet are sitting with closed eyes.*) . . . I guess I've already gone.

VIOLET: G'bye, Leona.

MONK: G'bye . . .

LEONA: "Meglior solo," huh, ducks? (*Leona lets herself out of the bar.*)

MONK: . . . G'bye, Leona.

VIOLET: . . . Monk?

MONK (*correctly suspecting her intent*): You want your suitcase, it's . . .

VIOLET: I don't mean my suitcase, nothing valuable's in it but my . . . undies and . . .

MONK: Then what've you got in mind?

VIOLET: . . . In *what*?

MONK: Sorry. No offense meant. But there's taverns licensed for rooms, and taverns licensed for liquor and food and liquor, and I am a tavern only licensed for . . .

VIOLET (*overlapping with a tone and gesture of such ultimate supplication that it would break the heart of a stone*): I just meant . . . let's go upstairs. Huh? Monk? (*Monk stares at her reflectively for a while, considering all the potential complications of her taking up semi- or permanent residence up there.*) Why're you looking at me that way? I just want a temporary, a night, a . . .

MONK: . . . Yeah, go on up and make yourself at home. Take a shower up there while I lock up the bar.

VIOLET: God love you, Monk, like me. (*She crosses, with a touch of "labyrinthitis," to the stairs and mounts two steps.*) Monk! . . . I'm scared of these stairs, they're almost steep as a ladder. I better take off my slippers. Take my slippers off for me. (*There is a tone in her voice that implies she has *already "moved in" . . . She holds out one leg from the steps, then the other. Monk removes her slippers and she goes on up, calling down to him:*) Bring up some beer, sweetheart.

MONK: Yeh, I'll bring some beer up. Don't forget your shower. (*Alone in the bar, Monk crosses downstage.*) I'm going to stay down here till I hear that shower running, I am not going up there till she's took a shower. (*He sniffs the ratty slipper.*) Dirty, worn-out slipper still being worn, sour-smelling with sweat from being worn too long, but still set by the bed to be worn again the next day, walked on here and there on—pointless—errands till the sole's worn through, and even then not thrown away, just padded with cardboard till the cardboard's worn through and still not thrown away, still put on to walk on till it's . . . past all repair . . . (*He has been, during this, turning out lamps in the bar.*) Hey, Violet, will you for Chrissake take a . . . (*This shouted appeal breaks off with a disgusted laugh. He drops the slipper, then grins sadly.*) She probably thinks she'd dissolve in water. I shouldn't of let her stay here. Well, I won't touch her, I'll have no contact with her, maybe I won't even go up there tonight. (*He crosses to open the door. We hear the boom of the ocean outside.*) I always leave the door open for a few minutes to clear the smoke and liquor smell out of the place, the human odors, and to hear the ocean. Y'know, it sounds different this late than it does with the crowd on the beach-front. It has a private sound to it, a sound that's just for itself and for me. (*Monk switches off the blue neon sign. It goes dark outside. He closes door.*)

(*Sound of water running above. He slowly looks toward the sound.*)

That ain't rain.

(*Tired from the hectic night, maybe feeling a stitch of pain in his heart [but he's used to that], Monk starts to the stairs. In the spill of light beneath them, he glances up with a slow smile, wry, but not bitter. A smile that's old too early, but it grows a bit warmer as he starts up the stairs.*)

Curtain

NOTES AFTER THE SECOND INVITED AUDIENCE:
(And a Troubled Sleep.)

THE play has drifted out of focus: I was almost inclined to think, "My God, this is a play about groping!"

The production of this play, and I think the play itself, deserves something better than that. The designer, the lighting and sound men, have caught perfectly the mood, the poetry, the ambience of the play.

But unfortunately in performance that lyricism—which is, as always, what I must chiefly rely upon as a playwright—is not being fully explored and utilized. At this moment, I must make a number of exceptions which will be made privately: I would say, however, to all the cast that at last night's performance the only parts that were totally and beautifully realized were those of "Doc," "Steve," "Quentin," and "Bobby."

We have now arrived at a point where we must approach this undertaking with the same seriousness—and I do not mean ponderousness but the opposite of ponderousness—that I had buried somewhere in me, beneath the liquor and the drugs that made my life a death-time in the late sixties; a sort of lyric appeal to my remnant of life to somehow redeem and save me—not from life's end, which can't be revealed through any court of appeals, but from a sinking into shadow and eclipse of so much of everything that had made my life meaningful to me.

I am sorry to return to a self-concerned note. Believe me, my concern is now much broader than self-concern, and in this particular instance, the case of this play and its players and its producers and its artists—which all of you certainly are (I doubt that you can believe how much I care for each of you as a person, and with the truest and purest kind of caring)—I would set down as an axiom that a playwright should never direct his work unassisted by someone who shares his concept but is better able to implement it through discipline.

The word "discipline" is not a pretty word to bring up at this point, and yet it must be. I am too old a hand at the abuse of self-discipline to fail to recognize a failure of self-discipline when I see it so nakedly on a stage before audiences.

The clinical name for this failure to discipline the self to achieve its goal is "the impulse toward self-destruction," which is the opposite and dark side of the will to create and to flower.

Self-transcendence, as well as self-discipline, is now in order. Each of us must put aside as best we can his and her personal stake in this adventure, this play, in order to serve its true creation as a whole. Ensemble and entity must take precedence, now, over that Mae West line to her manager, "How did the lady come on tonight?"—the wonderful bitch did not expect to receive a negative response, and she never got one, but it's a pity he didn't catch her act in the "Breckinridge" comeback. Or speak up about it.

Now to specifics about *Small Craft Warnings*:

I know that our designer, Fred Voelpel, will move that sailfish about a foot and a half out from the wall of the bar and have it suspended over the bar directly, with always just a bit of a light on its astonished expression. This will not upstage but will just provide a muted but persistent key to the tender irony which is the keynote to the still-possible success of this play.

Right now what troubles me most—in the way of specific staging and writing—is that, as physical climaxes to both acts, we have such closely corresponding chase-scenes of Violet by Leona. Of course this could be solved by returning to the opening of *Confessional* and starting the play with Violet wailing in the ladies' room and Leona pacing about in the middle of a tirade. This would eliminate one chase scene. However, it would also eliminate the establishment of place, situation, and identification of characters. And, incidentally, it would finally persuade me that I am no longer able to write a Goddam thing for the American theatre.

The other option—which I hope we can take—is to sharply differentiate the second chase scene from the first. I love the return of Steve and Bill, but I don't like the total absence of a "rhubarb" on the beach until the squad car siren is heard. I think something better than this can somehow be managed for us. I think that Leona has been in furious altercation with a cop or watchman on the beach-front all this time, and the sound of it should "bleed under" like the lights "bleed under" Doc's big monologue. But let us be aware it is going on out there, although—for the uses of a really not literal or naturalistic play—it is faded under the monologue till that has scored for us and is then brought up again a few beats preceding Leona's rush back into the bar, because the beach cop has finally had to call the wagon for her.

For a while, let Leona ad-lib the altercation outside at a level set by the director—and meanwhile, I will write it. Let's say, for the moment, it goes something like this:

LEONA: Okay, do that! I just dare you to do that! Call the wagon! I'm willing to ride in a wagon! It's got wheels, I'll ride in any Goddam thing on wheels, I'm just the one to do it! Okay? Want to call the wagon out here for me? What are you waiting for? Me to go? Oh, no, I'm not going yet. Take your hand off my arm, you fuckin' pig! Don't put your hand on the arm of a lady! (*Sound of a slap: then Bill rushes back in to make his phone call.*)

I think that there can be an interior of bar "hold" for this loud outside altercation between Leona and the beach cop right after Monk calls Doc over to the table: he can do this before Bill and Steve enter. And there can be a dramatic tension in Doc's unreadiness to tell of the disasters at Treasure Island for the time that Leona's off-stage rhubarb with the beach cop is heard. At the end of the Doc's story and just after his exit, Leona's voice can be heard again, continuing her rhubarb with the beach cop: "All right, I'm waiting, I am standing here waiting till that wagon gets here"—then the siren begins:

LEONA: That does it, let go of me, you fink, you pig!" (*Having struggled free of the beach cop's clasp on her arm, she now charges back into the bar, crying out:*) MONK! THE PADDY-WAGON IS SINGING MY SONG!

And let us please have "singing," not "playing."

Other specifics:

I think I've already gotten across to you the necessity of building up those elements in the play not concerned with the groin and the groping so that the audiences will recognize that this is not a sordid piece of writing. Now I think—with the exception of "Steve"—everybody in the cast—except "Monk" and "Doc"—is giving us a Bowery drunk bit, and that's not where the play's at. We don't want to sit out there looking at "vulnerable human vessels" that can touch us with their individual hearts, each at a time of crisis that compells it to cry out.

Finally, unless there's a sudden upsurge of energies and of selective focus, I think we need a later opening than is now scheduled.* I have always opposed an Easter Sunday opening for very personal but understandable reasons. Now I oppose it for reasons that seem almost desperately practical. The play strikes me as inviting disaster unless it is given time to pull itself together from its present state—and I gravely doubt that four more days are enough. It seems to me that the book has to be studied till there is no longer any groping after lines. Till mugging is not substituted for the delivery of the right ones.

I have always suspected that actors regard playwrights as hostile beings, and this has always made me shy around them. I hope you prove me wrong, since we are all sitting together in this small craft and have been warned by two audiences that the sea is very rough.

However, at this moment I prefer the *Marseillaise* to "extreme unction."

Corággio!

T.W.

*Sunday, April 2, 1972.

OUT CRY

"A garden enclosed is my sister . . ."
Song of Solomon, 4:6

DEDICATED TO THE LADY MARIA ST. JUST

A DISPENSABLE FOREWORD

HAVING the necessary arrogance to assume that a failed production of a play is not necessarily a failed play, I have prepared this new version for publication and subsequent reappearance on other stages.

Here it is, the play, subject to your appraisal upon the printed page, under the distinguished imprimatur of my most loyal advocate in the world of letters, the publishing house of New Directions.

And as for my depression over the failed production, I think it is temporary, a nervous phenomenon responsive to the treatment of a long ocean voyage with an "outside cabin" —slowly West by way of East, a time to get it together, all of it, the memoirs, the new play, and myself.

Hopefully or *Deo volente*, as my grandfather used to say when setting out on a journey in his nineties, the cry is still *en avant.*

T.W.

1973

SYNOPSIS OF SCENES

Before and after the performance: an evening in an unspecified locality.

During the performance: a nice afternoon in a deep Southern town called New Bethesda. Images may be projected on the stage backdrop: they should have a subjective quality, changing subtly with the mood of the play.

PART ONE

Before the performance.

At curtain rise, Felice stands motionless as a hunted creature at the sound of pursuers. He is on the platform of a raked stage, a notebook hanging open from his downstage hand. There should be, at a low level, a number of mechanical sounds suggesting an inhuman quality to the (half underground) vault of a foreign theater at which he has recently arrived. He is staring from the raked platform (on which a fragmentary set has been assembled) at a huge, dark statue upstage, a work of great power and darkly subjective meaning. Something about it, its monolithic presence and its suggestion of things anguished and perverse (in his own nature?) rivet his attention, which is shocked and fearful.

Almost immediately he starts to move toward it, at first slowly and cautiously. The mechanical sounds might increase slightly in volume and tempo as he approaches the upstage edge of the platform. Then he leaps off to the pediment of the sculpture that towers over him and begins a fierce, demonic effort to push it away. It is too heavy to be moved by a man alone. He shouts for assistance.

FELICE: *Is someone, anyone, back here to help me move this—please? I can't alone!* (*There is an echo of his "alone."*) This place has an echo-only answering voice. (*A door slams off stage*) Is that you Fox? Fox! (*There is an echo of his "Fox."*) Impossible! Where did it begin, where, when? (*He runs his hands through his hair.*) This feeling of confusion began when—I can't think where. My God I've tried to conceal it, this confusion, but it's pretty obvious, now that I've shown some evidence of it . . .

(*He has taken some cushions out of an old wicker box in which "props" are carried. His speech is breathless; sometimes ironic, sometimes savage.*)

FELICE (*exhibiting the articles mentioned*): Scratch pad and pencil! (*He kneels, panting, among the cushions.*) The setting isn't Morocco, the cushions just arrived without the sofa! (*He draws a deep breath to compose himself.*) Act One, Scene

One. At rise of curtain I am discovered on stage alone, yes, necessarily alone since she never enters on cue and never in a condition that I can predict anymore.

CLARE (*in a strangulated cry, at a distance*): Felice?

FELICE: I know what that cry means: she's rising reluctantly to the surface of consciousness, I—understand her—reluctance, but sometimes patience—gets impatient, you know . . . Cockroach! (*He sucks in his breath with disgust.*) —A humanizing touch! I think I read somewhere that cockroaches are immune to radiation and so are destined to be among the last organic survivors of—the great "Amen" . . .

CLARE (*same distance, a little clearer*): Felice?

FELICE (*shouting*): *Pla-ces!* —Fear . . . (*He has glanced upstage and at the "chained monster."*) *Fear!* —The fierce little man with the drum inside the rib-cage. —Compared to fear grown to panic that has no limit—short of consciousness blowing out and not reviving again—no other emotion a living, feeling creature is able to have, not even love or hate, is comparable in—what? —Force? —Magnitude? —Too rhetorical, that, work over later . . . —Of course you realize that I'm trying to catch you and hold you with an opening monologue that has to be extended through several—rather arbitrary—transitions, only related in a general way to— (*He gestures toward the statue with eyes shut tight.*)

CLARE (*slightly closer*): Where!

FELICE (*flips a page of the pad without otherwise relating to it*): —There is the love and the—substitutions, the surrogate attachments, doomed to brief duration, no matter how—necessary . . . —You can't, you must never catch hold of and cry out to a person, loved or needed as deeply as if loved— "Take care of me, I'm frightened, don't know the next step!" The one so loved and needed would hold you in contempt of human law and resisting arrest. In the heart of this person—him-her—is a little automatic sound apparatus, and it whispers to this person: "Demand! Blackmail! Despicable! Reject it!" —And so the next morning you have to make your own coffee, your own phone calls, and go alone to the doctor to say: "I'm afraid I'm dying."

CLARE (*in the wings*): Felice!

FELICE: Clare! (*He tosses away the scratch pad and pencil.*)

CLARE (*appearing, lighted dimly*): Nobody called me.

FELICE: I yelled my head off.

CLARE: Oh. —Decapitated? —Sorry! —How much time have we got?

FELICE (*to the audience, rising*): Imagine the curtain is down. (*He comes downstage and peeks through the imaginary curtain.*) They're coming in. It's nearly curtain time.

CLARE: Where is everybody?

FELICE: Everybody is somewhere, Clare. —What I have to do now is keep her from getting too panicky to give a good performance in this state theater of a state unknown, but she's not easy to fool, in spite of her—condition.

(*Clare enters, falteringly, blindly: almost at once she encounters the huge statue and utters a terrified outcry.*)

(*Felice drops an article removed from the prop basket.*)

CLARE: *Whose—monstrous aberration—is this?!*

FELICE: *I honestly don't know but it's there and it can't be moved!*

CLARE: It—dominates, it towers over the stage, what play on earth could be performed under this? Not even *Medea* or —*Oedipus Rex!* And— *"Can't be moved,"* did you say?

FELICE (*helplessly*): It—won't be lighted.

CLARE: *If anything is lighted the light will catch it.*

FELICE: *Will you quit shouting with an audience out there?*

CLARE: *You* are shouting.

FELICE: Will you, please, will you—!

CLARE: Will I what?

FELICE: Your chronic hysteria's cracking my nerves, Clare, I—

CLARE: What about my nerves? —I'm also a vertebrate with a nervous system that's been subjected to shock after shock till— (*She stumbles and cries out again.*)

FELICE: CARE! —ful.

CLARE: Felice, that chained monster's *obscene!*

FELICE: I made the same observation, I tried to move it, I couldn't, I called for assistance, I got none, so now we have to forget it. And by now you surely must have noticed that on these long, long tours we run always into certain—*unalterable circumstances* that we just have to—*ignore!*

CLARE (*abruptly controlling her shock*): Yes, I've—noticed that, too, on these long, long tours—unalterable circumstances, "Pox vobiscum," P-O-X—rhymes with Fox. . . —What I'm going to do in my leisure time from now on—while waiting for custom inspectors to, to confiscate things, and so forth, is—

FELICE: Will you please—? *Migraine!*—no codeine left! (*He is clasping his head.*)

CLARE: Is make out a list, un—unabridged—compendium of these—unexpected and—*unalterable—circumstance*, I'll—see you later. . .

(*She starts a slow, unsteady progress downstage, alongside the acting platform: her eyes have an unnatural, feverish brightness.*)

I forget—*unalterable circumstance*, but— Remember the time that destitute old—painter—invited us to tea on the—Viale—something—somewhere and when we arrived—the concierge said, suspiciously, "Oh, him, huh, five flights up, not worth it!" —Five flights up, not worth it! —No, not exactly worth it, the old, old painter was seated in *rigor mortis* before a totally blank canvas, teakettle boiled dry on the—burner—under a skylight—that sort of light through a dirty winter skylight is—*unalterable—circumstance*—but there is no skylight here, I haven't noticed a window— Is this theater under the ground? Is this the subterranean—pleasure-dome of—Kabla—Kubla—Koon?

(*During this speech, Felice has stood transfixed with dismay at her condition, motionless, an astrological chart in his hand.*)

—Sacred river must be—frozen over— (*She collides with something: a startled cry.*) *Felice!*

FELICE: Clare! —Hush!

CLARE: Will you please help me through this nightmare of debris? Why, it's like the surface of a sea where some great ship's gone under, spewing up wreckage!

FELICE: Parasol?

CLARE: Did you say "parasol"? I thought you said "parasol" —a dreadful thought. . .

FELICE: I'm checking props.

CLARE: Props, parasol—I don't want to think what I'm thinking.

FELICE: Strike a match and watch your step back there.

CLARE: Too late for watching my step, since I was conceived and delivered and fell into this—profession? —I will move not a step more till you remember that you are—the remnant of a gentleman *and* my brother— I will stand here motionless as that monster until you—

FELICE: Gloves!—hat. . .

CLARE: I said—

FELICE: Wait one minute, a moment. —You know, I can't tell your highs from your lows any more, Clare.

CLARE: I can't either, it's all one endless—continuum of—endurance. . .

FELICE (*cutting through*): Bowl of soapwater but only one spool.

CLARE (*moving downstage*): After last season's disasters we should have taken a rest on some quiet Riviera instead of touring these primitive faraway places.

FELICE: Clare, you couldn't stop any more than I could.

CLARE: I couldn't unless you stopped with me. (*She sits on the prop basket, stage left.*)

FELICE: We had to go on together. No alternative ever.

CLARE: I suppose when two people have lived together and worked together for such an—incalculably long time—it's natural to feel panicky as I felt when I recovered consciousness in that—travesty of a dressing room back there. You know what woke me up? A squeaky noise and a flapping about of wings up toward the invisible ceiling. I said to myself: "It's a bat," but I wasn't scared—I wasn't even surprised.

(*They both laugh, sadly and lightly.*)

That dressing room is a sight to behold, it's a filthy refrigerator, but I was so exhausted I fell right asleep in a broken-back chair.

FELICE: I'm glad you got some sleep.

CLARE: I'm still half asleep and my voice is going. Listen! My voice is practically gone!

FELICE (*still arranging props*): Phone on piano top.—You never come on stage just before curtain time, without giving me the comforting bit of news that your voice is gone and you'll have to perform in pantomime tonight.

CLARE: It always seems to be true.

FELICE: But somehow never is.

CLARE: I try my best to understand your nervous anxieties. Why don't you try to understand mine a little?

FELICE: I do, but you have so many of them, you know. Will you come on the set, I have new business to give you.

CLARE: And *I* some to give *you.* I want you to look at me on stage, stop avoiding my eyes, I can't act with you when you won't look in my eyes like you really saw me.

FELICE: Clare, I'd continue to see you if I were stone-blind, Clare.

CLARE (*moving toward the proscenium*): Let me have a peek at *them.*

FELICE (*drawing her back*): No! Don't!

CLARE: Why not?

FELICE: When you look at an audience before a performance, you play self-consciously, you don't get lost in the play.

CLARE: Why are we talking to each other like this, like tonight was the end of the world and we're blaming each other for it?

FELICE: You've been resting, I haven't. I'm dead-beat, I'll probably dry up several times tonight.

CLARE: You nearly always tell me your memory's gone when the curtain's about to go up.

FELICE: It always seems to be true.

CLARE: But somehow never is. (*In a frightened voice*) You have on father's astrology shirt.

FELICE (*impatiently*): Yes, I'm already in costume.

CLARE: For *The Two-Character Play*?

FELICE: The other play is canceled.

CLARE: I have to be informed when a performance is canceled, or else I won't perform. Those stairs, those stairs aren't the stairs for *The Two-Character Play.*

FELICE: So far, only parts of the set have arrived.

CLARE: These stairs go nowhere, they stop in space.

FELICE: I have placed your gloves and parasol up there. Climb some steps and I'll say you've gone upstairs.

CLARE: Are you serious? About playing it that way?

FELICE: Desperately.

CLARE: Where is the sofa?

FELICE: It didn't arrive. We'll have to use cushions, Moroccan style.

CLARE: Are you going to throw new speeches at me tonight?

FELICE: Tonight, I feel there'll be a lot of improvisation, but if we're both lost in the play, the bits of improvisation won't matter at all, in fact they may make the play better.

CLARE: I like to know what I'm playing and especially how a play ends. *The Two-Character Play* never had an ending.

FELICE: When the curtain is up and the lights are on, you'll fly like a bird through the play, and if you dry up—use it.

CLARE: Felice, do you have a fever?

FELICE: No. Do you?

CLARE: I'm on fire with panic.

(*She starts toward the proscenium again, to peek out at the audience. He seizes her arm and drags her back.*)

You looked out. Why can't I?

FELICE: You know how bad it is for you.

CLARE: Well, just let me ask you one question. One little question only.

FELICE: All right, ask me, but don't depend on getting much of an answer.

CLARE: Can you tell me how long were we on the way here? It seemed everlasting to me. All those frontiers, I didn't know the world had so many frontiers. And God help me, Felice, I honestly don't remember where we got on the train. Do you?

FELICE: Certainly. Of course.

CLARE: Then where, tell me where?

FELICE: Oh, Clare, don't! Don't, don't question me now, save all questions till after the performance.

CLARE: Is it all right if I make a comment on your appearance?

FELICE: Yes. What?

CLARE: You have lovely hair but there's much too much of it. Why, it's almost as long as mine.

FELICE: I don't think Felice is a man who could force himself to go to a barber often.

CLARE: The part of Felice is not the only part that you play. *The Two-Character Play* is certainly the most unusual play in the repertory, but it isn't the one and only we perform.

FELICE: From now on, it might be.

CLARE: Wouldn't *that* please the company! What would they be doing?

FELICE: I don't have any idea or a particle of interest.

CLARE: Oh! How regal! (*She pauses.*) Is this tour nearly over?

FELICE: It could end tonight if we don't give a brilliant performance.

CLARE: ALL I remember about this last trip—I must've had a fever—is that it would be light and then it would be dark and then it would be light or half light again and then dark again, and the country changed from prairies to mountains and then back to prairies again and then back to mountains, and my watch froze to death, and I tell you honestly I don't have any idea or any suspicion of where we are now except we seem to be in a huge mausoleum of a theater somewhere that seems like nowhere.

(*There is a guttural mumbling of voices from the "house." Felice pounds the stage floor again.*)

FELICE: After the performance, Clare, I'll answer any question you can think of, but I'm not going to hold up the curtain to answer a single one now.

CLARE: Felice, do you think I am not your equal?

FELICE: You're not my equal. You're my superior, Clare.

CLARE: I'm your superior in only one respect. I'm more realistic than you are, and I insist on knowing why no one is here but us two.

FELICE: Do you hear mumbling and growling?

CLARE: Yes, it sounds like a house full of furious unfed apes, but let's get back to my question. Where's everybody? (*She searches for a cigarette.*) Cigarette shortage.

(*She lights a cigarette with shaky fingers. Felice pounds the stage three times.*)

I said where *is* everybody? And I *insist* on an answer.

FELICE: You *insist* on an answer? You're sure you *do* want an answer?

CLARE: I do want an answer, right now.

FELICE: All right, you win, Clare, but I think you'll wish you'd lost. (*He takes a paper from his pocket.*) Here. Look at this.

CLARE: Telegram? You know I'm blind without my reading glasses. Here, strike a lucifer for me.

FELICE: Shortage of matches. (*He strikes a match and hands the telegram to her.*)

CLARE (*reading aloud, slowly*): "Your sister and you are—*insane!*"

FELICE: Signed—"The Company." Charming?

CLARE: "We have all borrowed money to return to—" (*The match goes out. She turns to the piano and strikes a note.*) Well, as they say—

FELICE: What?

CLARE: That sort of wraps things up.

FELICE: The whole company's left us, there is no staff except for two inscrutable stagehands who came in without a word and put up this piece of the set and helped me hang the lights before they—

CLARE: Deserted us, too?

FELICE: I tried to make them talk but they wouldn't or couldn't. They were silent as executioners, wouldn't look at me, even, just put up the door and the curtains and then weren't there any more.

CLARE: Would you recognize them again if they came back?

FELICE: You're the one that recognizes stagehands. I smile and shake hands with them but never remember their names.

CLARE: You're always so absorbed in your work, Felice, that you hardly recognize me—I understand that, but naturally a new company wouldn't, they'd be offended by it and go into a huddle and come to the conclusion that you were a bit *dérangé*, not just an eccentric artist but *un peu dérangé*. And you'd fallen into a habit of shouting out at rehearsals, "Mad, I'm going mad!" So finally they took your word for it, Felice.

FELICE: When you read the telegram did it say that *I* was insane, me, just *me*?

CLARE: Oh, Felice, no, no, it said: "You and your sister." But Felice, you know that artists put so much into their work, that they've got very little left over for acting like other people, their behavior is bound to seem peculiar . . . even freakish. Doesn't that seem logical to you?

FELICE: The company had been with us, except for a death now and then, or a commitment to an asylum now and then, for—

CLARE: How long?

FELICE: A considerable length of time.

CLARE: A considerable length of time is not a very precise statement of exactly how much time.

FELICE (*pounding the stage floor again*): Then *you* tell me how long!

CLARE: I've always left time up to you. (*She pauses.*) Didn't I get you a new piece of fur for the collar on that coat?

FELICE: Yes, but I preferred my mangy sable.

CLARE: Well, never mind that—what are we going to do? Something or nothing whatsoever at all?

FELICE: Only the dead can do nothing at all and get away with it, Clare.

CLARE: Yes, they do get away with it pretty nicely.

FELICE: But we're alive.

CLARE: Yes, unperished and relatively imperishable?

FELICE: The living have to do something.

CLARE: What is it going to be, in your opinion? Has anything occurred to you, or are you still waiting for a last-moment inspiration?

FELICE: We're going to do *The Two-Character Play* as we've never done it before.

CLARE: Impossible.

FELICE: Necessary.

CLARE: Some necessary things are impossible.

FELICE: And some impossible things are necessary.

CLARE: What an argument!

FELICE: No argument—decision.

CLARE: One-sided. Felice Devoto commanding, but you can't be a commander without someone to command. I won't be commanded since I know what would happen. Chaos of improvisation, new speeches thrown at me like stones, as if I'd been condemned to be stoned to death. Would you like to play with me in absolute panic and in total confusion?

Maybe you would, but you won't. No, thank you, Felice. This isn't the first time I've had to save you from self-destruction which would destroy me, too.

FELICE: We'll toss some new speeches back and forth at each other.

CLARE: Not I, said the fly. Felice, if we attempted to give a performance tonight, it would prove it was true.

FELICE: Prove what was true?

CLARE: What the company called us—insane. I'm going back to my dressing room and put on my coat and go to the hotel and sleep and sleep and—

FELICE: Clare, you have your coat on.

(*There is a pause. Clare strikes a chord on the piano.*)

CLARE: Do you have your brandy flask on you?

FELICE: For after the performance, not before.

CLARE: There can't be a performance.

FELICE: What is there going to be?

CLARE: An announcement by Mr. Fox that the company and the stagehands and the sets have yet to arrive here and so the performance is canceled.

FELICE (*gently and firmly*): No. There'll be a performance of *The Two-Character Play.* (*He takes a silver flask from his pocket and offers it to her.*)

CLARE (*drinking from flask*): Do you think—do you think they really do think we're insane, or were they just being bitchy because the long tour has been such a long disappointment?

FELICE: Since they've quit, I see no reason to think about what they think.

CLARE: You don't find it—disturbing? Well, I do, I find it very disturbing, because I—

FELICE: Let's discuss it after the performance.

CLARE: That witch Florence said to me on the train: "Do you and your brother always go into a trance before a performance?"

FELICE: I'm afraid you're a little confused, since that witch Florence wasn't with us this season. (*Felice goes into the wings.*)

CLARE: Even with the lights on it's cold to the bone, bone cold, and in *The Two-Character Play* we can't keep our coats on, we've got to take off our coats and make the audience and ourselves feel it's a summer day in the South.

(*She coughs. He takes off his coat, holds his hand out to take hers. She gives him her hand with a pleading look.*)

FELICE (*patiently*): I don't want your hand. I want your coat.

CLARE: I'm not going to take off my coat in this big, filthy icebox. If you're able to give a performance, do your pantomime for them.

(*Felice tears off Clare's coat. She cries out. He throws their coats behind the sofa; then thumps the stage again with the stick.*)

Felice, try to understand what that telegram did to me. I can't play tonight, not *The Two-Character Play*—why, I can't remember a line.

FELICE: You will when it starts, and we'll get through it somehow.

CLARE: You think you're being brave, but you're just being desperate and irrational. Felice, believe me, I'm not lying, I can't, I couldn't go through it!

FELICE: Clare, you're going to play Clare.

CLARE: I am going back to my dressing room, and you are going to announce the performance is canceled because of impossible circumstances.

FELICE: I am going out right now and announce the change of program, and when I come back, you will be here, on stage.

CLARE: Don't count on that. Sometimes I make decisions and stick to them.

FELICE: Feel my forehead! Sweating!

CLARE: Because you have fever.

FELICE: I'm sweating because it's a hot summer day in the South.

CLARE: —Somebody, a doctor, once told me that I had unusual courage and so did you. I said: "Oh, no, my brother and I are terrified of our shadows!" And he said: "I know that, and that's exactly why I admire your courage so much." What kind of sense does that make? Felice? I'll make the announcement in English, Spanish, and French.

I'll make a lovely announcement that sometimes things just make it impossible to give a performance and I'll, I'll—I'll crouch before them with my hand held out for pity.

(*She falls to her knees. He clasps her shoulders, tenderly.*)

FELICE: The telegram was shocking, but we're both over that now. Now all we have to do is remember that if we're not artists, we're nothing. And play *The Two-Character Play* the best we've ever played it no matter what our condition of panic may be.

CLARE (*raising her hands to his head*): Your hair's grown so long you look hermaphroditic.

FELICE: Yes? Do I? Good. Thank you. (*He thumps the stage floor with the stick and throws it behind the sofa.*)

CLARE: *Bonne chance!* I'll see you later!

(*Disregarding this threat, Felice advances to the proscenium.*)

FELICE (*to the audience*): Good evening, ladies and gentlemen. I want you to know that my sister and I feel deeply honored to take our own small part in this enormously important idea and program of, of—cultural exchange. Of course there have been some, a number of, unexpected difficulties, but being artists of the theater we have been long prepared for working under unexpected conditions. This evening my sister and I are going to perform alone, since the rest of our company has been delayed by, uh, transportation difficulties due to the eccentricities of the weather bird, perhaps I should say the perversities of the weather bird. (*He laughs hollowly.*) However, it so happens that our favorite play in our repertory is a play for two characters, which is logically entitled *The Two-Character Play.* (*He gives the same hollow laugh, followed by a cough.*) This evening we had expected—

CLARE: Poor Felice, he's dried up. (*She puts on her coat.*)

FELICE: This play, this evening, we will now perform for you, and we hope that you will forgive the technical difficulties and problems due to the delay of our company's arrival—unavoidable— (*He bows and steps back into the setting, then speaks commandingly.*) Clare! Places! I'm going to start the play.

CLARE: You'll find me in my dressing room with the weather bird. Oh, Felice, please! *Don't* humiliate yourself!

FELICE: It's *you* that want to disgrace us! Our performance must continue. No escape!

CLARE: If you start *The Two-Character Play* it will be a one-character play, and I'll know the company's telegram is the truth.

(*Felice disappears into the wings. Clare starts blindly off the stage, then stops by the giant's statue and leans her head against its pedestal. There is the sound of curtains opening. The violet dusk of the stage that surrounds the interior set turns lighter, and strange inhuman mocking laughter is heard. At the sound of the laughter, Clare turns quickly about and defiantly faces the house. Felice returns from the wings.*)

FELICE: Clare! Please!

(*The mocking laughter builds. Clare throws off her coat as if accepting a challenge.*)

CLARE (*to Felice*): Do I enter first or do you?

FELICE: Tonight you go in first.

(*Clare returns to the interior set, goes to the piano and strikes a treble note. Felice enters.*)

Your place is by the phone.

CLARE: Yes, by the phone.

FELICE: The performance commences.

(*Clare goes to the phone.*)

FELICE: Who are you calling, Clare? (*She seems not to hear him.*) *Clare! Who are you calling?*

CLARE: —Not a soul still existing in the world gone away . . .

FELICE: Then why are you holding the phone?

CLARE: I just picked it up to see if it's still connected.

FELICE: Is it?

CLARE: It hums in my ear. Doesn't that mean it's connected?

FELICE: The telephone company would send us a notice before they turned off the phone.

CLARE (*vaguely and sadly*): Sometimes notices aren't—noticed.

FELICE: The house is—

CLARE: Still occupied but they might have the idea it wasn't, since it's not lighted at night and no one still comes and goes.

FELICE: We would have received a notice if one was sent.

CLARE: We can't count on that.

FELICE: We mustn't start counting things that can't be counted on, Clare.

CLARE: We must trust in things—

FELICE: Continuing as they've—

CLARE: Continued?

FELICE: Yes, as they've continued, for such a long time that they seem—

CLARE: Dependable to us.

FELICE: Permanently dependable, yes, but we were—

CLARE: Shocked when the—

FELICE: Lights refused to turn on, and it was lucky the moon was so nearly full that, with the window shades raised, it lighted the downstairs rooms.

CLARE: But we collided with things in the upstairs hall.

FELICE: Now we could find our way around in it blind.

CLARE: We can, we do. Without even touching the walls.

FELICE: It's a small house and we've lived in it always.

CLARE: You say that I was indulging in a bit of somnambulism last night.

FELICE: Clare, you had a restless night.

CLARE: You did, too.

FELICE: In a small house when—

CLARE: One of the occupants has a restless night—

FELICE: It keeps the other awake.

CLARE (*crying out*): *Why do I have to sleep in that death chamber?*

FELICE (*controlled*): We agreed that their room was just a room now. Everything about them's been removed.

CLARE: Except Father's voice in the walls and his eyes in the ceiling so that I can't shut mine. —That night of the accident night, you ran to the foot of the stairs but not a step further, you blocked the steps, I had to force my way past you to the room where—Mother opened the door as if I'd knocked like a visitor not—expected.

FELICE: Stop repeating, repeating!

CLARE: No sign of recognizing me at the door, no greeting, a look of surprise, very slight, till she opened her mouth on a soundless fountain of blood, and Father behind her saw and received me quietly, too, oh, it was a quiet reception that I received at the door, quiet, polite, just a little surprised till the dreadful torrent and Father said, "Not yet, Clare," just as quietly, gently to me as *that*, before they went separate ways, she to the door of the bathroom where she fell and he to the window where he fired again looking out at—*out* . . .

(*Felice strikes his fist on piano keys.*)

And you tell me it isn't their room any more, that it belongs to me now, inherited without effort not to remember what you never entered so have no memory of?

FELICE: I said: "LET IT REST!"

CLARE: Not in that room at night? Who passed that death sentence on me?

FELICE (*with forced quiet*): You weren't in that room last night, you came to the door of mine.

CLARE (*fearfully*): To ask for—a—cigarette . . .

FELICE: We've had no cigarettes since—

CLARE: Is it improper for me not to stay in one place? All night? Alone?

FELICE: You didn't stay in one place, you wandered about the house, upstairs and down as if you were searching for something.

CLARE: Exploring the premises, yes.

FELICE: With a fine-tooth comb. —Did you find it?

CLARE: No, but I came across something, this old memento, this token of— (*She lifts her hand to show a ring.*)

FELICE: What?

CLARE: This ring with my birthstone, the opal called a fire opal.

FELICE: You haven't worn it for so long that I thought it was lost.

(*Evanescent music fades in.*)

CLARE: Mother told me that opals were unlucky.

FELICE: Frigid women are given to little fears and superstitions, and—

CLARE: Opals do have a sinister reputation. And it was a gift from Father.

FELICE: That was enough to prejudice her against it.

CLARE: Sleepless people love rummaging. I look through pockets that I know are empty. I found this ring in the pocket of an old mildewed corduroy coat which I'd forgotten I'd ever owned and didn't care if the stone was unlucky or not.

FELICE: Nothing could be unlucky that's so lovely, Clare. (*He turns it on her finger, a sort of love-making.*)

(*The music stops.*)

CLARE (*Striking the piano key*): Didn't you say that you went out today?

FELICE: Yes, you saw me come in.

CLARE: I didn't see you go out.

FELICE: When you see somebody come in you know he's been out.

CLARE (*skeptically*): How far outside did you go? Past the sunflowers, or—?

FELICE: I went out to the gate, and do you know what I noticed?

CLARE: Something that scared you back in?

FELICE: No, what I saw didn't scare me, but it, it—startled me, though. It was—

CLARE: What?

FELICE: Clare.

CLARE: What?

FELICE (*stage whisper*): You know *The Two-Character Play.*

CLARE (*in a loud stage whisper*): The telegram is still on the set.

FELICE: Clare, there wasn't, there isn't a telegram in *The Two-Character Play.*

CLARE: Then take it off the sofa where I can see it. When you see a thing, you can't think it doesn't exist.

(*He picks up the telegram, crumples it, throwing it out the window.*)

FELICE: There now, it never existed, it was just a moment of panic.

CLARE: What a convenient way to dispose of a panicky moment!

FELICE: Dismissed completely, like that! And now I'll tell you what I saw in the yard when I went out.

CLARE: Yes, do that! Do, please.

FELICE: I saw a sunflower out there that's grown as tall as the house.

CLARE: Felice, you know that's not so!

FELICE: Go out and see for yourself.

(*She tries to laugh.*)

Or just look outside the window, it's in the front yard, on this side.

CLARE: *Front* yard? (*He nods but averts his face with a slight smile.*) Now I know you're fooling.

FELICE: Oh, no, you don't or you'd go look out the window. It shot up quick as Jack's beanstalk, and it's so gold, so brilliant that it—seems to be shouting sensational things about us. Tourists will be attracted?

CLARE: Why are you—?

FELICE: Botanists, you know botanists, they'll flock to New Bethesda to marvel at this marvel, photograph it for the—*National Geographic*, this marvel of nature. This two-headed sunflower taller than a two-story house which is still inhabited by a—recluse brother and sister who never go out any more . . .

CLARE: It's such a long afternoon . . .

FELICE: It's summer, which is our season, but after the afternoon, we have to remember that there are unexpected collisions in an unlighted house, and not always only with —furniture and—walls . . .

CLARE: Call it the poem of two and dark as—

FELICE: Our blood?

CLARE: Yes, why don't you say it? Abnormality! —Say it! And point at me!

FELICE: At myself, first.

CLARE: Now—let's close the child's eyes and—light candles . . .

FELICE: There's no such line in the script.

CLARE (*smiling brightly*): *Tant pire, che peccato*, meaning "too bad."

(*An abrupt change in style of performance occurs at this point, as if they were startled out of a dream.*)

FELICE: —Clare, somebody is knocking. Why don't you go to the door? Don't you hear them knocking?

CLARE: Who?

FELICE: I can't see through the door.

CLARE: I don't hear any knocking. (*He drums the table with his knuckles.*) Oh, yes, now I do, but— (*He drums the table again.*) They're very insistent, aren't they?

FELICE: Go see who's there.

CLARE: I can't imagine. I'm not properly dressed, I'm not fit to be seen.

FELICE: You're perfectly dressed and look unusually well, but me, I don't have a tie on, and this old shirt of Father's, I've sweated through it.

CLARE: That's excusable on a—hot afternoon. You, you let them in and say you'll call me down if it'd be they want to see *me*.

FELICE: Christ, have you reached the point where you're scared to answer the door?

CLARE: Reached and— (*She starts up the spiral stairs that stop in space.*) —The knocking's stopped. —I think they've gone away. —No! Look! They're slipping a slip of paper under the door!

(*They stare fearfully at the doorsill, the supposed piece of paper.*)

FELICE: —They've left.

CLARE: Yes, pick up the—

(*He crosses to the door and makes the gesture of picking up a card: frowns at it, breath audible.*)

FELICE: "Citizens—Relief."

CLARE: —I've never heard of such a thing in my life. Have you ever heard of Citizens Relief?

FELICE: No, I think it's wise to be cautious about things you've never—

CLARE: Heard of. It might be a trick of some kind, an excuse to—

FELICE: Intrude on our—

CLARE: Privacy, yes. Shall we destroy the card or keep it in case of a desperate situation?

FELICE: That's not a thing we seem to have to wait for, is it?

CLARE: Oh, but all the questions we'd have to—

FELICE: —Answer . . .

CLARE: Yes, there'd be interviews and questionnaires to fill out and—

FELICE: Organizations are such—

CLARE: *Cold!*

FELICE: Yes, impersonal things.

CLARE: I'll put the card under grandmother's wedding picture, just in case a desperate situation—

FELICE: Increases in desperation—

CLARE: *Anyway, here it is,* at least we—know where it is. Now I—suppose we have to prepare for—public action against us, since they know we're—still here.

FELICE: What action, such as what?

CLARE: —Removal by force of—eviction?

FELICE: You do ask for trouble by—having notions like that.

CLARE: I don't know what to do next! (*She turns about distractedly, hands clasped together.*)

FELICE: I do, I know.

CLARE: Sit there and stare at that threadbare rose in the carpet till it withers?

(*He has sunk onto the sofa, chin in hands, staring at the carpet.*)

FELICE: And you? What are you doing but clasping your hands together as if in prayer?

CLARE: Nothing unless it's something to pace about the house in a maze of amazement, upstairs, downstairs, day and night, in and out. *Out!* Oh, Felice, I want to go out, today I want to go out, I want to walk on the street—like a favorite of nature in public view without—shame . . .

FELICE: —Oh? —You want to go out calling?

CLAIRE: Yes, out calling!

FELICE: Go out!

CLAIRE: *Alone?* —Not *alone*!

FELICE: Ladies go calling alone on such nice afternoons.

CLARE: You come out calling with me.

FELICE: I can't, I have to stay here.

CLARE: For what?

FELICE: —To guard the house against—

CLARE: What?

FELICE: *Curious—trespassers!* Somebody has to stay on the premises and it has to be me, but you go out calling, Clare. You must have known when you got up this morning that the day would be different for you, not a stay-at-home day, of which there've been so many, but a day for going out calling, smiling, talking. You've washed your hair, it's yellow as corn silk, you've pinned it up nicely, you have on your dressed-up dress that you washed to go out in today, and you have the face of an angel, Clare, you match the fair weather, so carry out your impulse, go out calling. You know what you could do? Everywhere you went calling you could say, "Oh, do you know how idiotic I am? I went out without cigarettes!" And they'd offer you one at each place, and you could slip them into your purse, save them till you got home, and we could smoke them here, Clare. So! Go! (*He opens the door for her.*)

CLARE: Why have you opened the door?

FELICE: For you to go out calling.

CLARE: Oh, how thoughtful, yes, very gentlemanly of you to open the door for me to go outside without parasol or gloves, but not very imaginative of you to imagine that I'd go out alone.

(*They stand a moment staring at each other near the open door; her hands and lips tremble; the slight smile, mocking and tender, twists his mouth.*)

—Suppose I came home alone, and in front of the house there was a collection of people around an ambulance or police car or both? We've had that happen before. People are attracted by a sudden disturbance in a house that seemed vacant. No. I won't go out alone. (*She slams the door shut.*) My legs wouldn't hold me up, and as for smiling and talking, I think I'd have on my face the grimace of a doll and my hair would stick to the sweat on my forehead. Oh, I'd hardly sit down for this friendly call on—what friends?—before I—staggered back up, that is, if, if—the colored girl had been allowed to admit me.

FELICE: It was your idea. You shouted "Out!" not me.

CLARE: I'd never dream of going out without you in your—disturbed—*condition.*

FELICE: And *you* in *yours.*

CLARE: Me, calling, a fire engine shrieks, a revolver—bang—discharges! Would I sit there continuing with the smile and the talk? (*She is sobbing a little: her trembling hand stretches toward him.*) No, I'd spring up, run, run, and my heart would stop on the street!

FELICE (*his smile fading out*): I never believed you'd go calling.

CLARE: Right you were about that if you thought alone—but calling? Yes, I'll do that! Phone-calling is calling! (*She rushes to the telephone and snatches up the receiver.*)

FELICE: Calling, who are you—? *Careful!*

CLARE (*into phone*): Operator, the Reverend Mr. Wiley! Urgent, very, please hurry!

(*Felice tries to wrest the phone from her grasp: for a moment they struggle for it.*)

FELICE: Clare!

CLARE: Reverend Wiley, this is Clare Devoto, yes, you remember, the daughter of the— (*Then to Felice*) You have to let me go on or he'll think I'm—

FELICE: What are you! Out of your—!

CLARE (*into phone again*): Excuse me, Reverend Wiley, there was—an interruption. My brother and I still live in our parents' home after, after the—terrible accident in the house which was reported so maliciously falsely in *The Press-Scimitar.* Father did *not* kill Mother and himself but— The house was, was—broken into by some—

FELICE: Favorite of nature?

CLARE: Housebreaker who murdered our parents, but I think *we* are suspected! Oh, it's hard to stay on here, but we do, we're still here, but such a terrible thing has been going on and on. My brother Felice and I are surrounded by so much suspicion and malice that we almost never, we hardly ever, dare to go out of the house. In the nighttime people stop and linger on the sidewalk and whisper charges, anomalous letters of obscenities are sent us, and *The Press-Scimitar*—sly allusions to us as the deranged children of a father who was a false mystic and, Reverend Wiley, our father was a man who had true psychic, mystical powers, granted only to an Aries whose element is cardinal fire. (*She is sobbing now.*) Oh, I can't tell you how horrifying it's been, why, the neighbor's child has a slingshot and bombards the house with rocks, we heard his *parents* give the slingshot to him and *tell* him to— Ha! *Another rock struck just now!*

(*She drops the phone in panic. He picks it up.*)

FELICE: Mr. Wiley, my sister has a fever.

CLARE: No.

FELICE: She's not herself today, forget what, excuse and— (*He hangs up, wipes sweat off his forehead with trembling hand.*) Wonderful, that does it! Our one chance is privacy, and you babble away to a man who'll think it is his Christian duty to have us *confined* in—

(*She gasps and stumbles to the piano. She strikes a treble note repeatedly on the piano. He snatches her hand from the keyboard and slams the lid down.*)

Clare!

CLARE: You shouldn't have spoken that word! *"Confined!"* That word is not in the—

FELICE: Oh. A prohibited word. When a word can't be used, when it's prohibited, its silence increases its size. It gets larger and larger till it's so enormous that no house can hold it.

CLARE: Then say the word, over and over, you perverse monster, you—!

(*Felice turns away.*)

Scared to? Afraid of a—?

FELICE: I won't do lunatic things. I have to try to pretend there's some sanity here.

CLARE: Oh, is that what you're trying? I thought you were trying to go as far as possible without going past all limits.

(*He turns to face her, furiously. She smiles and forms the word "confined" with her lips; then she says it with a whisper. He snatches up a sofa pillow.*)

Confined, confined!

(*He thrusts the pillow over her mouth, holding her by the shoulder. She struggles as if suffocating. Suddenly she stops struggling and looks out toward the audience. She then speaks in a quiet and flat tone. Completely real.*)

Felice! There is a gunman out there. A man with a gun pointed at me.

FELICE: Clare! Please. (*Felice stares at her helplessly for a few moments, then turns to the audience and says:*) I am afraid there will have to be an interval of about ten minutes while my sister recovers. You see, she is not at all well tonight.

(*Very quietly and gently he leads her off stage. The house-lights go on.*)

An Interval of Ten Minutes

PART TWO

As the houselights dim Felice and Clare enter hurriedly to the side of the stage outside the set.

We see Felice forcibly drawing Clare back onto the set as the curtain rises: both are panting, and there is evidence of struggle between them during the interval. (*He points to a bowl by the window.*)

FELICE (*her wrist still firmly in his grip*): What is that?—what is it doing here?

CLARE (*defiantly lifting her face to his*): It's equipment for the amusement of children on hot summer afternoons. Have you forgotten how we blew soap bubbles on the back steps those long—

FELICE: On the back steps, yes, but don't remember that we ever blew soap bubbles here in the parlor.

CLARE: Yesterday you said, "There's nothing to do, there's nothing at all to do," kept saying it, wouldn't quit. All right. Here's soap-bubble equipment. Look! Look! I haven't forgotten how! (*She blows a bubble.*)

FELICE: —Beautiful but—they break.

CLARE: You try, it's your turn now.

(*Felice stares at her for a moment: then breaks into [desperate?] laughter.*)

What has struck you so funny?

FELICE: Madness has a funny side to it, Clare. —And we can't turn back into children in public view.

CLARE: That's my line, not yours.

FELICE (*continues to laugh the same way: then suddenly is quite sober*): —I haven't told you something you'll have to know.

CLARE: You're jumping a page.

(*Felice stares at her blankly.*)

CLARE (*solicitous*): —Have you dried up, Felice? (*She leads him to the cushions as if he were senseless: gently pushes him.*) Lean back, breathe quietly, I'll take it— From where?

(*Slight pause.*)

FELICE: When Father gave up his—

CLARE: —When father gave up his equipment, his psychic readings and astrological predictions, a few days before the *un, inexplicable*—accident!—in the house— Well, he didn't give them up, exactly.

FELICE: No, not exactly by choice.

CLARE: Mother had locked up his equipment.

FELICE: Except for this worn-out shirt of his I have on, which bears the signs of the zodiac on it, and his rising sign, and a chart of the sky as it was on the hour before daybreak of the day of his nativity here in New Bethesda!

CLARE: You know, he seemed to—accept. At least he said nothing. Not even when she spoke of State Haven to him. "Yes, I can see your mind is going again. Check yourself into State Haven for a long rest—voluntarily, or I'll—" He didn't answer these threats. He became very quiet. Except when she ordered him to cut down our sacred flowers in front of the house, and said if he didn't do it she would.

FELICE: Yes, Mother, Regina, made several threats of emasculation to—

CLARE: "You cut them down or I will." (*She continues in a different voice.*) "Do that if you dare."

FELICE: And she didn't. And he—

CLARE: Was restlessly quiet. Sat almost continually where you're sitting and stared at that threadbare rose in the carpet's center and it seemed to smolder, yes, that rose seemed to smolder like his eyes and yours, and when a carpet catches fire in a wooden house, the house will catch fire too. Felice, I swear that this is a house made of wood and that rose is smoldering, now! And cloth and wood are two inflammable things. Your eyes make three!

FELICE: No, four! I'm not a one-eyed Cyclops! And adding your eyes makes six!

(*She strikes a sharp note on the piano. He glares at her furiously, but she strikes the note again, louder.*)

—Line!

CLARE: Didn't you tell me you'd thought of something we have to do today?

FELICE: —Yes, it's something we can't put off any longer.

CLARE: The letter of protest to the—

FELICE: No, no, letters of protest are barely even opened, no, what we *must* do today is go out of the house.

CLARE: To some particular place, or—

FELICE: To Grossman's Market.

CLARE: There?!

FELICE: Yes, *there*!

CLARE: We tried that before and turned back.

FELICE: We didn't have a strong enough reason, and it wasn't such a favorable afternoon.

CLARE: This afternoon is—?

FELICE: Much more favorable. And I simply know that it's necessary for us to go to Grossman's Market today since—I've kept this from you, but sometimes the postman still comes through the barricade of sunflowers and that he did some days ago with a notification that no more—

CLARE: —Deliveries?

FELICE: Will be delivered to the steps of—

CLARE: I knew. Payment for costlies has been long—overdue.

FELICE: So out we do have to go to Grossman's Market, directly to Mr. Grossman, and speak personally to him.

CLARE: What would we speak about to him, if we found him?

FELICE: He has an office.

CLARE: His office! Where's his office? Probably tucked away in some never-discovered corner of that shadowy labyrinth of a—

FELICE: We'll ask a clerk to tell us, to take us, to—

CLARE: If the clerk saw us, he'd pretend that he didn't.

FELICE: Not if we enter with some air of assurance and, and—importance about us, as if some unexpected, some, some—providential thing had occurred in our—

CLARE: An air of importance? To nature? And to Grossman's?

FELICE: We're going to enter Grossman's Market today like a pair of—

CLARE: Prosperous, paying customers?

FELICE: Yes, with excellent credit! We'll speak, first, to a clerk and say to him: "Please show us into the office of Mr. Grossman." We are going to go into his office, we are going to tell him convincingly that in spite of all spite and, and—contrary—accusations—Father's insurance policy will be paid to us on, say, the first of next month, yes, on September the first.

CLARE: But we know that it won't be, on the first or last day of any month of the year!

FELICE: We have to say that it *will* be!

CLARE: I don't think, I'm not so sure that—

FELICE: Don't think, don't be sure. You have a resistance to all positive actions.

CLARE: It's *I* that do the little there's still to be done here.

(*They have crossed downstage to opposite sides of the interior set: face out.*)

CLARE (*at a fast pace*): But we've been informed by the—

FELICE (*at a fast pace*): Acme Insurance Company.

CLARE (*at a fast pace*): Yes, they notified us, that courtesy they did offer, and I'm sure that Grossman knows it—doesn't he know everything?—that the insurance money is —what's the word? Confiscated?

FELICE (*at a fast pace*): Forfeited.

CLARE (*at a fast pace*): Yes, the payment of the insurance policy is forfeited in the—what is the word?

FELICE (*at a fast pace*): Event.

CLARE (*at a fast pace*): Yes, in the event of a man— (*She stops, pressing her fist to her mouth.*)

FELICE (*at a fast pace*): In the event of a man killing his wife, then himself, and—

CLARE: Forgetting his children.

FELICE: —That's what's called a legal technicality . . .

(*They turn to each other.*)

CLARE: What do you know about anything legal, Felice? I'm not impressed by your pose of—

FELICE: I know there are situations in which legal technicalities have to be, to be disregarded in the interests of human, human—

CLARE: I'm afraid you underesteem the, the huge inhumanelessness of a company called *the Acme*. Why, they wrote only three sentences to us in reply to the twelve-page appeal that we wrote and rewrote for a week.

FELICE: It was a mistake to appeal, we should have demanded.

CLARE: And you should have taken the letter to the post office instead of putting it on the mailbox for the ancient postman or for the wind to collect it.

FELICE: I put a rock on the note to the postman on the letter to the—*Will you stop driving me mad?—The Acme* wouldn't have answered with even three sentences if they hadn't received the twelve-page appeal—and— When terrible accidents happen, details get confused. Like you got confused the accident night? Ran downstairs and phoned a dead doctor, summoned him from a ten-year stay in Old Gray.

CLARE: Who could tell the dead from the living that night?

FELICE: But couldn't remember our address? Told his widow to send him to the house behind the sunflowers? Yes, details do get confused.

CLARE: Not when publicly published.

FELICE: Forgotten, forgotten! Publicly. Now, will you listen to me?

CLARE: Your voice is coming out of your voice box clearly.

FELICE: We must say that what we saw, there was only us to see, and what we saw was Mother with the revolver, first killing Father and then herself and—

CLARE: A simple lie is one thing, but the absolute opposite of the truth is another.

FELICE (*wildly*): *What's the truth in pieces of metal exploding from the hand of a man driven mad by—!*

CLARE: What you suggest is that we confront Mr. Conrad Grossman, that favorite of nature, in this possible office of his—would there be chairs in it for us to sit down in, or would we have to stand at attention facing the, the—firing squad of his glittering, bifocaled eyes? While we stammered out this fabrication which you propose that we—

FELICE (*mockingly*): We could look an inch over his eyes or an inch under his eyes and talk to him very fast, very, very, very—

CLARE: Together?

FELICE: Each of us would have to confirm the statements of the—

CLARE: Other.

FELICE: And keep smiling and saying "Isn't it *wonderful*?" to him.

CLARE: Isn't what *"wonderful"* to him?

FELICE: That, that *Acme* has at, at—last conceded that—

CLARE: Hmmm. Yes, a plan, a plot, but I think this plot, this plan is something we ought to sleep on and carry out early tomorrow, not late today.

FELICE: Today you have on the dress I call your fair-weather matching.

CLARE: Yes, repaired it and washed it in Ivory. The blouse has worn thin. Oh, I'm afraid it's . . . indecent.

FELICE: It's fetching.

CLARE: What did you call it?

FELICE: Fetching, it's very fetching.

CLARE: Fetching what? Oh, fetching new credit at Grossman's?

FELICE: And when you face Mr. Grossman, it wouldn't hurt to give him a fetching smile. Well? Well? Do we do it or forget it?

CLARE: Sometimes our fear is . . .

FELICE: Our private badge of . . .

CLARE: Courage . . .

FELICE: Right! The door is open. Are we going out?

(*Pause. She backs away from him a step.*)

CLARE: See if there are people on the street.

FELICE: Of course there are, there are always people on streets, that's what streets are made for, for people on them.

CLARE: I meant those boys. You know, those vicious boys that—

FELICE: Oh, yes. You stopped on the walk and shouted "Stop!" to the boys. Covered your ears with your hands and shouted "Stop, stop!" They stopped and they crossed the street. I said: "For God's sake, what did you think they were doing? Why did you shout 'Stop' at them?"

CLARE: You heard them, too. You were right beside me.

FELICE: I was right beside you and I heard nothing but ordinary boys' talk.

(*She rushes downstage to one side of the interior set. He goes out to the opposite side. They face out.*

(*Lightning pace, often overlapping: the effect of a Mass recited in a church containing a time bomb about to explode.*)

CLARE (*overlapping*): They were staring and grinning at me and spelling out a—

FELICE (*overlapping*): You said they were spelling out an obscene word at you.

CLARE (*overlapping*): Yes, an obscene word, the same obscene word that somebody scrawled on our back fence.

FELICE (*overlapping*): Yes, you told me that too. I looked at the back fence and nothing was scrawled on it, Clare.

CLARE (*overlapping*): If you heard nothing the last time we went out, why wouldn't you go on alone to the grocery store? Why did you run back with me to the house?

FELICE (*overlapping*): You were panicky. I was scared what you might do.

CLARE (*overlapping*): What did you think I might do?

FELICE (*overlapping*): What Father and Mother did when—

CLARE (*overlapping*): Stop here, we can't go on!

FELICE (*overlapping*): Go on!

CLARE (*overlapping*): Line!

FELICE (*overlapping*): A few days ago you—

CLARE: No, you, you, not I! I can't sleep at night in a house where a revolver is hidden. Tell me where you hid it. We'll smash it, destroy it together—line!

FELICE: I took the cartridges out when I put it away.

CLARE: What good's that do when you know where the cartridges are?

FELICE: I removed them from the revolver, and put them away, where I've deliberately forgotten and won't remember.

CLARE: "Deliberately forgotten!" Worthless! In a dream you'll remember. Felice, there's death in the house and you know where it's waiting.

FELICE: —Do you prefer locked doors of separate buildings?

CLARE: You've been obsessed with locked doors since your stay at State Haven!

FELICE: Yes, I have the advantage of having experienced, once, the comforts, the security, the humanizing influence of—

CLARE: Locked doors!

FELICE: At State Haven!

CLARE: I'm sorry but you'd allowed yourself to lose contact with anything that seemed real.

FELICE: Seemed and real don't fit.

CLARE: Stopped speaking!

FELICE: Had nothing to speak of.

CLARE: Stared without recognition!

FELICE: With nothing to recognize!

CLARE: In a little house filled with familiar—?

FELICE: Nothing can blind you more than the familiar twisted into—

CLARE: I was here, too, and saw nothing familiar twisted into—

FELICE: Oh, I don't think you knew where you were any more, you—

CLARE: Knew enough to get out of bed in the morning instead of crouching under covers all day.

FELICE (*rushes to stairs and starts up them*): Was that a sign of clearer—

CLARE: It was a sign of ability to go on with—

FELICE (*on stairs*): Customary habits!

CLARE: An appearance of—

FELICE (*beside himself, from top of stairs*): Fuck appearance!

CLARE: Hush! —You've hidden the revolver, give it up. I'll take it down to the cellar and smash it with the wood chopper. And then be able to sleep again in this house.

FELICE (*descending the steps to Clare; exhausted, tender*): —People don't know, sometimes, what keeps them awake . . . (*He starts the tape. The pace slows from exhaustion.*)

CLARE: The need to search for—

FELICE: The contents of empty pockets?

CLARE: Not always empty! Sometimes there's a birthstone in them that isn't lucky!

(*Pause: they stare, panting, at each other.*
(*Very slowly, with lost eyes, he closes the door—nearly.*)

FELICE: —You have the face of an angel—I could no more ever, no matter how much you begged me, fire a revolver at you than any impossible, unimaginable thing. Not even to lead you outside a door that can't be closed completely without its locking itself till the end of—

(*She turns to face him.*)

—I haven't completely closed it, it isn't finally closed . . . Clare, don't you know that you haven't an enemy in the world except yourself?

CLARE: —To be your own enemy is to have against you the worst, the most relentless, enemy of all.

FELICE: That I don't need to be told. Clare, the door's still open.

CLARE (*with a slight, sad smile*): Yes, a little, enough to admit the talk of—

FELICE: Are we going out, now, or giving up all but one possible thing?

CLARE: —We're—going out, now. There never really was any question about it, you know.

FELICE: Good. At last you admit it.

(*Pause*)

CLARE (*assuming a different air*): But you're not properly dressed. For this auspicious occasion I want you to look your best. Close the door a moment.

FELICE: If it were closed, it might never open again.

CLARE: I'm just—just going upstairs to fetch your fair-weather jacket and a tie to go with it. (*She turns upstage.*) Oh, but no stairs going off!

FELICE: The set's incomplete.

CLARE: I know, I knew, you told me. I have gone upstairs and you are alone in the parlor. (*She goes up the spiral stairs.*)

FELICE: Yes, I am alone in the parlor with the front door open. —I hear voices from the street, the calls and laughter of demons. "Loonies, loonie, loonies, looo-nies!" —I—shut the door, remembering what I'd said.

CLARE: You said that it might never be opened again. (*She turns abruptly downstage.*) Oh, there you *are*!

FELICE: Yes. Of course, *waiting* for you.

CLARE: I wasn't long, was I?

FELICE: —No, but I wondered if you would actually come back down.

CLARE: Here I am, and here is your jacket, and here is your tie. (*She holds out empty hands.*)

FELICE: The articles are invisible.

CLARE (*with a mocking smile*): Put on your invisible jacket and your invisible tie.

FELICE: —I go through the motions of—

CLARE: Ah, now, what a difference! Run a comb through your hair!

FELICE: —Where is—?

CLARE: The inside jacket pocket. I put it there.

FELICE: —Oh? —Yes—thanks . . . (*He makes the gesture of removing a comb from his invisible jacket.*)

CLARE: Oh, let *me* do it! (*She arranges his hair with her fingers.*)

FELICE: That's enough. That will do.
CLARE: Hold still just one moment longer.
FELICE: No, no, that's enough, Clare.
CLARE: Yes, well, now you look like a gentleman with excellent credit at every store in the town of New Bethesda!
FELICE: Hmmm . . .
CLARE: The door is shut—why did you shut the door?
FELICE: —The wind was blowing dust in.
CLARE: There is no wind at all.
FELICE: There *was*, so I—
CLARE: Shut the door. Will you be able to open it again?
FELICE: —Yes. Of course. (*He starts the tape recorder again. Then, after a hesitant moment, he draws the door open.*)
CLARE: —What are you waiting for?
FELICE: For you to go out.
CLARE: You go first. I'll follow.
FELICE: —How do I know you would?
CLARE: When a thing has been settled, I don't back out.
FELICE: That may be, but you are going out first.
CLARE: Will you come out right behind me or will you bolt the door on me and—

(*He seizes her hand and draws her forcibly to the door. She gasps.*)

FELICE: Out!
CLARE: See if—!
FELICE: There are no boys on the street! Stop this foolishness. Afternoons aren't everlasting you know.
CLARE: May I set my hat straight, *please?* (*She turns to a little dusty gilt-framed oval mirror to put the old straw hat on her head; it should have a touch of pathos but not be ludicrous.*)
FELICE: I thought you hated that hat.
CLARE: I certainly don't regard it as the most stylish piece of headgear in New Bethesda, but—I don't intend to make a call without a hat on my head. (*She removes the sprig of artificial cornflowers from the silk hatband and tries it in another position.*) Well, it just doesn't—

(*Felice snatches the hat off her head and tosses it on the stairs: then thrusts her through the door. She cries out a little as if dashed in cold water. He shuts the door behind them, takes her hand and leads her a few steps forward.*)

FELICE: Are you going to go on shaking like that?

CLARE: I will if you go on pushing me around.

FELICE: It's a—

CLARE: What?

FELICE: —Nice afternoon.

CLARE (*tensely*): Yes!

FELICE: You couldn't ask for a nicer afternoon, if afternoons could be asked for.

CLARE: I—have no complaints about it.

(*Slight pause*)

FELICE: I don't know what we're waiting here for. Do you? (*She makes a sudden startled turn.*)

CLARE: Slingshot in the—!

FELICE: No, no, no!

CLARE: Something moved in—

FELICE: A kangaroo! Jumped!

(*Clare tries to laugh.*)

We're waiting here like it was a bus stop back of the sunflowers. And it's only a block and a half from here to Grossman's Market. So let's get a move on, slingshots, kangaroos, or—anything you can dream of. The sooner we get started the sooner we'll return with credit established again and livables and—necessities of persistence—three bags full!—including cigarettes . . .

CLARE: We mustn't—seem too greedy—all at once . . .

FELICE: Once we've assured Mr. Grossman that Acme will pay, there'll be no limit.

CLARE: You couldn't ask for a nicer afternoon, but—I think my suggestion was better.

FELICE: What was your suggestion?

CLARE: That *you* go to Grossman's Market and talk to Mr. Grossman.

FELICE: Alone? Without you?

CLARE: Yes, without me. I don't know why, but I'm shaking, I can't control it. It would make a bad impression on Mr. Grossman.

FELICE: You're not going to back out now. I won't allow you.

CLARE: Felice, while you're gone, I could, could, could—make a phone call to "Citizens Relief," you know, those people we wouldn't let in the house. I could tell them to come right over, and answer all their questions, and we would receive their relief even if Mr. Grossman doesn't believe the story.

FELICE: Clare, quit stalling. Let's go now.

CLARE: —I left something in the house.

FELICE: What?

CLARE: I left my—my—

FELICE: You see, you don't know what you left, so it can't be important.

CLARE: Oh, it is, it's very—it's the—cotton I put in my nose when I have a nosebleed, and I feel like I might have one almost any minute. The *lime dust*!

(*She turns quickly to the door but he blocks her, stretching his arms across the doorway. She utters a soft cry and runs around to the window. He reaches the window before she can climb in.*)

FELICE: You're not going to climb in that window!

CLARE: I am! Let me, I have to! I have a pain in my heart!

FELICE: Don't make me drag you by force to Grossman's Market!

CLARE: The moment I get back in I'll call the people from "Citizens Relief"!

FELICE: *Liar! Liar, and coward!*

CLARE: Oh, Felice, I—

(*She runs back to the door. He remains by the window. She enters the interior set and stares out at him, hands clasped tightly together. He steps over the low window sill, and they face each other silently for a moment.*)

FELICE: If we're not able to walk one block and a half to Grossman's Market, we're not able to live in this house or anywhere else but in two separate closed wards at State Haven. So now listen to me, Clare. Either you come back out and go through the program at Grossman's, or I will leave here and never come back here again, and you'll stay on here alone.

CLARE: You know what I'd do if I was left here alone.

FELICE: Yes, I know what she'd do, so I seize her arm and shout into her face: "Out again, the front door!" I try to drag her to it.

CLARE: I catch hold of something, cling to it! Cling to it for dear life!

FELICE: Cling to it!

CLARE: It's not on the set, the newel post of the stairs. I wrap both arms about it and he can't tear me loose.

FELICE: Stay here, stay here alone! When I go out of this house I'll never come back. I'll go and go! Away, away!

CLARE: I'll wait!

FELICE: For *what*?

CLARE: For *you*!

FELICE: That will be a long wait, a longer wait than you imagine. I'm leaving you now. *Good-bye!* (*He steps out over the low sill of the window.*)

CLARE (*calling out after him*): Don't stay long! Hurry back!

FELICE: Hah. (*He comes forward and speaks pantingly to the audience.*) The audience is supposed to imagine that the front of the house, where I am standing now, is shielded by sunflowers, too, but that was impractical as it would cut off the view. I stand here—move not a step further. Impossible without her. No, I can't leave her alone. I feel so exposed, so cold. And behind me I feel the house. It seems to be breathing a faint, warm breath on my back. I feel it the way you feel a loved person standing close behind you. Yes, I'm already defeated. The house is so old, so faded, so warm that, yes, it seems to be breathing. It seems to be whispering to me: "You can't go away. Give up. Come in and stay." Such a *gentle* command! What do I do? Naturally, I obey. (*He turns and enters by the door.*) I come back into the house, very quietly. I don't look at my sister.

CLARE: We're ashamed to look at each other. We're ashamed of having retreated—surrendered so quickly.

FELICE: There is a pause, a silence, our eyes avoiding each other's.

CLARE: Guiltily.

FELICE: No rock hits the house. No insults and obscenities are shouted.

CLARE: The afternoon light.

FELICE: Yes, the afternoon light is unbelievably golden on—

CLARE: The furniture which is so much older than we are—

FELICE: I realize, now, that the house has turned into a prison.

CLARE: I know it's a prison, too, but it's one that isn't strange to us.

(*For the first time since he re-entered the house, they look directly at each other, slowly, with difficulty.*)

FELICE: I don't lift my arms, not willingly. —They are lifted and they extend as if they weren't a part of me. —I don't know what I feel except a sense of—danger and—longing.

CLARE: I—have no—breath.

(*She takes several faltering steps toward him: then rushes into his extended arms: there is a convulsive embrace—like two lovers meeting after a long separation. Her lips are whispering against his face—inaudible words.*)

FELICE: Not—possible, the—stairs don't go upstairs, the steps—stop in—space!

CLARE: There's nothing, then, but—

(*Very gently, he thrusts her away from him: her eyes turn away from him too.*)

FELICE: "A garden enclosed is my sister . . ."

CLARE: What did I do with the card from Citizens Relief?

FELICE: You put it under—

CLARE: Oh. Grandmother's wedding picture. (*She lifts the picture and looks at it yearningly for a moment.*) A coronet of pearls, a hand lifting the veil from her radiant face.

FELICE: Clare, we've seen that picture all our lives. It's the card under the picture you picked the picture up for.

CLARE: To get the office number.

FELICE: Of Citizens Relief. It might close early you know.

CLARE: I'm going to call them at once.

FELICE: Make it just a simple dignified appeal for—necessary—assistance.

CLARE: Simple, dignified, yes.

(*She has crossed to the phone but her hand stops short of the receiver. He picks it up and thrusts it into her hand. She lifts it to her ear.*)

It makes no sound. I feel like screaming "Help, help!"

FELICE: —Is it—?

CLARE (*hanging up the receiver*): Sometimes a phone will go dead temporarily, just for a little while, and come back to life, you know.

FELICE: Yes, I know. Of course.

CLARE: —So we stay here and wait till it's connected again?

FELICE: We might have to wait till after the Relief Office closes. It might be a better idea to ask the people next door if we can use their phone since something's gone wrong with ours.

CLARE: That's right. Why don't you do that?

FELICE: *You* do that. It's the sort of thing you could do better. Look! (*He points at window.*) The woman next door is taking some clothes off her washline. Call her through the window.

(*Clare catches her breath. Then rushes to the window and calls out in a stifled voice:*)

CLARE: Please, may I, please, may we—!

FELICE: Not loud enough, call louder.

CLARE (*turning from the window*): —Did you really imagine that I could call and beg for "Citizens Relief" in front of those malicious people next door, on their phone, in their presence? Why, they gave their son a slingshot to stone the house! Whenever they catch a glimpse of us through a window, they grin like death.

(*Slight pause.*)

FELICE: You asked me what people did when they had nothing at all left to do.

CLARE: I asked you no such thing. (*After a moment, she dips a spool in the soapy water.*)

FELICE: Instead of calling the woman next door through the parlor window, you blow soap bubbles through it. Did you blow the soap bubbles out the window as an appeal to the world? They are lovely as your birthstone. They rise through the fading afternoon light. But they are a sign of surrender, and we know it. —And now I touch her hand lightly, which is a signal that I am about to speak a new line in *The Two-Character Play.* (*He touches her hand.*) Clare, didn't you tell me that yesterday or last night or today you found, you came across, a box of cartridges for Father's revolver?

CLARE: No! No, I—

FELICE: Clare, you say "yes," not "no." And then I pick up the property of the play which she's always hated and dreaded, so much that she refuses to remember that it exists in the play.

CLARE: I've said it's—*unnecessary.*

(*Felice has picked up a revolver from under the sheet music on the piano top.*)

Has it *always* been there?

FELICE: The revolver and the box of cartridges that you found last night have never been anywhere else, not in any performance of the play. Now I remove the blank cartridges and insert the real ones as calmly as if I were removing dead flowers from a vase and putting in fresh ones. Yes, as calmly as—

(*But his fingers are shaking so that the revolver falls to the floor. Clare gasps, then laughs breathlessly.*)

Stop it!

(*Clare covers her mouth with her hands.*)

Now I— (*He pauses.*)

CLARE: Have you forgotten what you do next? Too bad. I don't remember.

FELICE: I haven't forgotten what I do next. I put the revolver in the center of the little table across which we had discussed the attitude of nature toward its creatures that are regarded as *unnatural* creatures, and then I— (*After placing the revolver on the table, he pauses.*)

CLARE: What do you do next?

FELICE: Yes, I put on the tape and then I—I pick up my spool and dip it in the water and blow a soap bubble out the parlor window without the slightest concern about what neighbors may think. Of course, sometimes the soap bubble bursts before it rises, but this time please imagine you see it rising through gold light, above the gold sunflower heads. Now I turn to my sister who has the face of an angel and say to her: "Look! Do you see?" (*He mimes the action of blowing soap bubbles.*)

CLARE: Yes, I do, it's lovely and you made it . . . and it still hasn't broken.

FELICE: Sometimes we do still see the same things at the same time.

CLARE: Yes, and we would till locked in separate buildings and marched out at different hours, you by bullet-eyed guards and me by bullet-eyed matrons. (*She strikes a note on the piano.*) Oh, what a long, long, way we've traveled together, too long, now, for separation. Yes, all the way back to sunflowers and soap bubbles, and there's no turning back on the road even if the road's backward, and backward.

(*The tape machine misses and plays the music at triple tempo, which rises to a sound like a kind of shriek.*

(*Clare removes her white cotton gloves, glances at her brother's tranced face: he stares past her blindly. She draws a breath: then crosses to the machine and stops its playing.*

(*A couple of beats: silence.*)

—Well, that's that. (*She crosses to pick up her cloak.*) Put on your coat, Felice, I'm putting on mine, and I'll remove this —bewitching bit of millinery from my corn-silk head now. (*She takes off her hat, fiercely snatching the sprig of cornflowers from its band and tossing it to the floor.*)

FELICE (*blankly*): What?

CLARE: Felice, come out of the play! The house is completely empty.

FELICE: Walked? Out? All?

CLARE: Yes, yes, were you unconscious? One stood up down front with a grunt and the others all followed suit and shuffled out—en masse! And I'm glad the torture is over!

FELICE: *It—wasn't—your play!*

(*She brings him his coat.*)

CLARE: No, but you *wrote* it for me. Have I expressed my appreciation enough? (*She throws his coat about him and tries to button it.*)

FELICE: Don't! —Don't put things on me I can put on myself! This is not State Haven!

CLARE: —Only three smokables left. Soooo!—they've broken our rice bowl. —Smoke?

(*She hands him a cigarette. He looks out blindly.*)

Here! —And now call Fox. See if there's cash enough to get us out of this place to somewhere further south of the —Arctic Circle.

(*There is a pause. Felice is afraid to call Fox, who may be gone.*)

Well, for God's sake, call him!

FELICE (*calling into the house*): Fox! —*Fox!*

CLARE: Faithful Fox is silent as the proverbial—

FELICE: *Fox!*

CLARE: *Fox, Fox, Fox!*

TOGETHER: *Fox!*

(*There is an echo from their call.*)

CLARE: I'll tell you an unpleasant thought that's entered my head. Fox has absconded with the box-office receipts.

FELICE: Well, we'll track him down.

CLARE: I don't feel like fox hunting.

FELICE: Then what do you feel like?

CLARE (*lying down on the cushions*): Like falling into bed at the nearest hotel and sleeping the next thousand years.

FELICE: Well, go get your things.

CLARE: Get what things?

FELICE: Your purse, your handbag for instance.

CLARE: I don't have one to get.

FELICE: You've lost it again?

CLARE: I told you days ago that my bag had disappeared and it hasn't returned. What have you got in your wallet?

FELICE: Phone numbers and addresses of people mostly forgotten.

CLARE: Did we start with no money or just arrive here with no money?

FELICE: Things have kept disappearing. Isn't that how it was?

CLARE: Don't ask me how anything was, or is, or will be.

FELICE: When you make remarks of that kind, other people take them literally.

CLARE: This still seems like a performance of *The Two-Character Play*. The worst thing that's disappeared in our lives—I'll tell you what it is. Not the company, not Fox, not brandy in your flask, not successes that give confidence to go on—no, none of that. The worst thing that's disappeared in our lives is being aware of what's going on in our lives. We don't dare talk about, it's like a secret that we're conspiring to keep from each other, even though each of us knows that the other one knows it. (*She strikes a piano key.*) Felice, about the play. *The Two-Character Play.* I wonder sometimes if it isn't a little too personal, too special, for most audiences. Maybe—

FELICE: What do you mean by "too special"?

CLARE: Too personal, that's all, such as using our own names in it, and—

FELICE: At the first reading of it, you made a hypocritical remark. You said: "Why, it's like new wine, it has to be properly aged, so don't let's include it in this season's repertory."

CLARE: I said no such thing but I can tell you who did. It was poor old Gwendolyn Forbes that said that, and that's not all she said. She also said *The Two-Character Play* is a tour de force, it's more like an exercise in performance by two star performers, than like a play, a real play.

FELICE: There was never anyone by that name—what name did you say?—in the company.

CLARE: Felice, there was hardly a soul in the company whose name you could remember. The person I'm talking about is the one that burned to death in that hotel fire in—wherever it was—in some place—

FELICE: Oh. Her. She had a passion for incineration. Burned to death in a hotel fire and then had herself cremated.

CLARE: People burned to death don't have themselves cremated. We're both too tired to make sense. Call a limousine to pick us up and take us to a hotel.

(*Felice sits on the piano stool.*)

Felice, you're as tired as I am. Help me get up. My legs are gone.

(*He rises to help her but topples onto the cushions.*)

Thank you. Will we ever get up. We're sitting here panting for breath like a couple of dogs. Last cigarette, unless you have some.

FELICE: No. (*He lights her cigarette.*)

CLARE: We'll share it. Felice, is it possible that *The Two-Character Play* never had an ending? (*She passes the cigarette to him.*)

FELICE: Even if we were what the company called us in the telegram, we'd never attempt to perform a play that had no end to it, Clare.

CLARE: Then tell me how it ends, because I honestly can't remember a bit of it past the point where we stopped tonight.

FELICE: *The Two-Character Play* doesn't have a conventional ending.

CLARE: I don't mind that, that's fine, but what's the unconventional ending? Or can't you remember any better than I can?

(*He hands her the cigarette.*)

It never seems to end but just to stop, and it always seems to stop just short of something of a disturbing nature when you say: "The performance is over."

FELICE: It's possible for a play to have no ending in the usual sense of an ending, in order to make a point about nothing really ending.

CLARE: I didn't know you believed in the everlasting.

FELICE: That's not what I meant at all.

CLARE: I don't think you know what you meant. Things do end, they do actually have to.

FELICE: Well— (*Rising*) Up! Hotel! Grand entrance! We'll face everything tomorrow.

CLARE: Just before the performance you told me that Fox the foxy hasn't made us hotel reservations here, wherever here is!

FELICE: The one hotel in town is directly across the street from the theater, and we'll enter in such grand style that we'll need no reservations.

(*He crosses hurriedly into the wings and she starts to follow, but her exhaustion stops her at the upstage edge of the platform, facing the statue.*)

CLARE (*to the statue*): —Unalterable—circumstance—unaltered . . .

(*Offstage, frantic sounds begin to be heard, running footsteps, fists pounding and feet kicking at metal: muffled cries faintly echoed. This should continue at a varying pitch during Clare's solitary presence on the stage and should sometimes catch her attention.*

(*She slowly turns about to face downstage in a spot of light.*)

Well, he lost his argument about the impossible being necessary tonight. I think the impossible and the necessary pass each other on streets without recognition, could sit side by side without sign of the slightest acquaintance before or now or—ever . . .

(*Metallic crash, off stage.*)

Felice! —Well, it wasn't always all lost. —There were nights of—triumph, ovations—times of public honor! Memorable —celebrations— Crossing the Tiber in an open carriage, over that bridge of stone angels, when, suddenly, a hailstorm stung our faces and hands with little flowers of ice that made us sing and sing! (*She sings a snatch of "Come le rose" or "Dicitencello Vuoie." Stops, hearing distant shouts.*) *Felice?* —Oh, and that night in the wine garden on the Danube, the lights of a river boat, Russian soldiers singing in chorus! (*She sings a verse of the Russian Gypsy song "Coachman, don't whip the horses, I have no where to hurry to, I have no one to love"*—(*words in Russian*). *More pounding and shouting, muted.*) Felice! —"Your sister and you—insane, and so—" "Do you always go into a trance before a performance?" —"Yes, and after one, too." —Long dead now, many—gone . . . Felice, Felice!—when he finds that I am not following him as I've done all my life, he won't be coming back here with glad tidings, or a corsage of violets to pin on my—

(*She touches the lapel of her coat as Felice returns. He seems not to see her at first: he's breathless and stunned.*)

Well? —Have we met with some *new*—unalterable circumstance now?

(*He collapses among the cushions.*)

—Yes, I can see there's been another disaster. Let's put the props back into the old prop basket while we—prepare . . . (*She gathers up all but one cushion on which he has fallen and throws them into the battered wicker basket.*) Aren't you going to speak to me? Ever? Again?

FELICE: Clare, I'm afraid we may have to stay here a while.

CLARE: In this frozen country?

FELICE: I meant here in the theater.

CLARE: Oh!

FELICE: Yes, you see the front and back doors are locked from the outside, and as you know this building is windowless as a casket.

CLARE: Does this mean we have to stay here freezing till they open the building in the morning?

FELICE: Clare, there's no guarantee they'll open up the building in the morning or even in the evening or any morning or even after that.

CLARE: Out! Out! Out! (*Crazed with panic, she whirls about and snatches up the "play" phone. She realizes what it is and drops it as if it had scorched her hand.*)

FELICE: Hysteria won't help, Clare.

CLARE: The, the backstage phone?

FELICE: Disconnected as the phone in the play was.

CLARE: I think that this is some sort of dramatic metaphor that you are trying to catch me in, but I refuse to be caught!

FELICE: Even if it were possible to, would I want to?

CLARE: Obviously you accept this, it was your play and this is the end you want!

FELICE: Clare, I want no end but—

CLARE: —But?

FELICE: There seems to be no choice but—

CLARE: To march between the chaplain and warden conducting us to the execution chamber without resistance?

FELICE: The sentence was passed such a long time ago that the dread of execution is worn out. Fear *does* have a limit.

Contrary to my—opening—monologue, even fear has a limit . . .

CLARE (*tonelessly*): Monologue? —Opening?

FELICE (*with a passion of something—self-derision? despair?—but with a passion*): *I'd started a new play. —I would have been too tired to finish it, though.*

CLARE (*again abstracted*): —Oh . . .

FELICE (*with the same bitter force*): Just this evening, before you entered, I composed the opening monologue of a play that's—*closed! Unopened* . . . (*He throws his head back in a [silent?] self-mocking laugh—make sure it's not self-pity.*) You could put it *this* way. Fear is limited by the ability of a person to care any more.

CLARE: For anything but—

(*She clasps his head against her. A hollow metallic sound is heard.*)

I hear.

FELICE: This empty vault is full of echoes and echoes and echoes. The heat has been turned off and metal contracts with cold.

CLARE: That's a lovely elegiac note in your voice! Are you paralyzed there? Yes, you, but not me, I am not paralyzed, I am going to find the way out. (*She makes aborted moves in several directions, terrified of the dark that surrounds the dimming area of the stage: at each rush stops short with sharply arrested gestures.*) *Human Out Cry!*

FELICE: Give it up, Clare, give it up, it's useless. There are punctuation marks in life and it's time to admit that they include periods—one of which is final . . .

CLARE: Who do you think you're addressing? You're talking to your insanely practical sister, not to violet-haired Drama Club Ladies, digesting—*vol-au-vent* and *pêche-Melba*. —Felice, please! It's cold. It's not like the cold anywhere on the planet Earth, it's like the cold at the far, the further, the go-no-more last edge of space . . . So it's a prison, this last theater of yours.

FELICE: Yes, it would seem to be one.

CLARE: I've always suspected that theaters are prisons for players . . .

(*The sound of distant explosions*)

Listen! Gunfire! Bombardment!

FELICE: Or holiday firecrackers blocks away . . .

(*The sound of distant gunfire.*)

Clare, you're not frightened, are you?

CLARE: I'm too tired to be frightened, at least not yet. That's strange, you know, because I've always had such a dread of being locked up, caught, confined in a place—it's the greatest dread of my life. No, what I feel right now is bone-tired and bone-cold. Otherwise I'd get up and see for myself if these awful mysteries you've reported to me are exactly as you've reported.

FELICE: Do you think I've just imagined them, dreamed them, Clare?

(*He goes out the door of the interior set. Clare becomes panicky.*)

CLARE: Felice! Where are you going?

FELICE: To get the telegram from the company. (*He returns with it and smoothes it out on the table. He looks at it as if he had just received it.*)

CLARE: You have a dark thought in your head and I think I know what it is.

FELICE: Sometimes we have the same thoughts at the same time.

CLARE: It's getting colder and colder, moment by moment.

FELICE: During the performance—

CLARE: Yes, such as it was or wasn't—

FELICE: It was cold even with the lights on us, but I was so lost in the play that it seemed warm as summer.

CLARE: You're suggesting that—

FELICE: We must go back into the play.

CLARE: But with the stage so dim—

FELICE: If we can imagine summer, we can imagine more light.

CLARE: When we're lost in the play.

FELICE: Yes, completely lost in *The Two-Character Play.*

CLARE: We could try it, we could give it a try.

FELICE: Other alternatives lacking.

CLARE: Could we keep on our coats?

FELICE: Oh, we could, I suppose, but I think the feeling of summer with sunflowers and soap bubbles would come more easily to us if we took our coats off.

CLARE: All right. Do we stop where we stopped tonight or do we look for the ending?

FELICE: Don't worry about the ending, it'll come to us, Clare. I think you'll find it wherever you hid it.

CLARE: Wherever *you* hid it, not me. (*She catches her breath, suddenly, and raises a hand to her mouth.*)

FELICE: Is something wrong?

CLARE: No!—no—

(*He helps her remove her coat. As he removes his, she hugs her shoulders against the cold. He takes the revolver off the table.*)

FELICE: The properties of the play are the properties of our lives. Where would you like me to hide it?

CLARE: Under a sofa pillow?

FELICE: Yes, I guess that will do.

(*He places the revolver under the pillow. Clare starts the tape.*)

CLARE: And we'll find the end of the play?

FELICE: By the time we come to the end, we'll be so lost in the play that—

CLARE: The end will simply happen.

FELICE: Yes, just happen.

CLARE: Where shall we start, at the top of the play, the phone bit?

FELICE: Yes, take your place by the phone. The performance commences.

CLARE: When a performance works out inevitably, it works out well. (*She lifts the telephone.*)

FELICE: Who are you calling, Clare?

CLARE: Not a soul existing in the world gone away.

FELICE (*very fast*): Then why did you pick up the phone?

CLARE: To see if it's still connected.

FELICE: We would have been notified if—

CLARE: It's a mistake to depend on—notification. Especially when a house looks vacant at night. (*She hangs up the phone.*)

FELICE: Night, what a restless night.

CLARE: Wasn't it, though?

FELICE: I didn't sleep at all well and neither did you. I heard you wandering about the house as if you were looking for something.

CLARE: Yes, I was and I found it. (*She pauses.*) Are you lost in the play?

FELICE: Yes, it's a warm August day.

CLARE (*raising a hand, tenderly, to his head*): I'm sure Acme and Mr. Grossman will believe our story. We can believe it ourselves, and then livables, and necessities of persistence will be delivered through the barricade of—

FELICE: Go straight to the tall sunflowers.

CLARE: Quick as that?

FELICE: That quick!

CLARE: Felice, look out the window. There's a giant sunflower out there that's grown as tall as the house.

(*He draws a long breath, then leans out the window.*)

FELICE: *Oh, yes, I see it. Its color's so brilliant that it seems to be shouting!*

CLARE: Keep your eyes on it a minute, it's a sight to be seen.

(*She crosses to the sofa: lifts the pillow beneath which the revolver is concealed: gasps and drops the pillow back: looks toward Felice.*)

FELICE: Hurry, it won't hold!

(*She crosses to him and touches his hand.*)

CLARE: —Magic is a habit.

(*They look slowly up at the sunflower projections.*)

FELICE: —Magic is the habit of our existence . . .

(*The lights fade, and they accept its fading, as a death, somehow transcended.*)

Curtain

VIEUX CARRÉ

INSCRIBED TO KEITH HACK

TIME: The period between winter 1938 and spring 1939.

PLACE: A rooming house, No. 722 Toulouse Street, in the French Quarter of New Orleans.

THE SETTING OF THE PLAY: The stage seems bare. Various playing areas may be distinguished by sketchy partitions and doorframes. In the barrenness there should be a poetic evocation of all the cheap rooming houses of the world. This one is in the Vieux Carré of New Orleans, where it remains standing, at 722 Toulouse Street, now converted to an art gallery. I will describe the building as it was when I rented an attic room in the late thirties, not as it will be designed, or realized for the stage.

It is a three-story building. There are a pair of alcoves, facing Toulouse Street. These alcove cubicles are separated by plywood, which provides a minimal separation (spatially) between the writer (myself those many years ago) and an older painter, a terribly wasted man, dying of tuberculosis, but fiercely denying this circumstance to himself.

A curved staircase ascends from the rear of a dark narrow passageway from the street entrance to the kitchen area. From there it ascends to the third floor, or gabled attic with its mansard roof.

A narrow hall separates the gabled cubicles from the studio (with skylight) which is occupied by Jane and Tye.

Obviously the elevations of these acting areas can be only suggested by a few shallow steps: a realistic setting is impossible, and the solution lies mainly in very skillful lighting and minimal furnishings.

PART ONE

SCENE ONE

WRITER (*spotlighted downstage*): Once this house was alive, it was occupied once. In my recollection, it still is, but by shadowy occupants like ghosts. Now they enter the lighter areas of my memory.

(*Fade in dimly visible characters of the play, turning about in a stylized manner. The spotlight fades on the writer and is brought up on Mrs. Wire, who assumes her active character in the play.*)

MRS. WIRE: Nursie! Nursie—where's my pillows?

(*Nursie is spotlighted on a slightly higher level, looking up fearfully at something. She screams.*)

Hey, what the hell is going on in there!

NURSIE (*running down in a sort of football crouch*): A bat, a bat's in the kitchen!

MRS. WIRE: Bat? I never seen a bat nowhere on these premises, Nursie.

NURSIE: Why, Mizz Wire, I swear it was a bull bat up there in the kitchen. You tell me no bats, why, they's a pack of bats that hang upside down from that ole banana tree in the courtyard from dark till daybreak, when they all scream at once and fly up like a—explosion of—damned souls out of a graveyard.

MRS. WIRE: If such a thing was true—

NURSIE: As God's word is true!

MRS. WIRE: I repeat, if such a thing was true—which it isn't—an' you go tawkin' about it with you big black mouth, why it could ruin the reputation of this rooming house which is the only respectable rooming house in the Quarter. Now where's my pillows, Nursie?

NURSIE (sotto voce *as she arranges the pallet*): Shit . . .

MRS. WIRE: What you say?

NURSIE: I said shoot . . . faw shit. You'd see they're on the cot if you had a light bulb in this hall. (*She is making up the cot.*) What you got against light? First thing God said on the first day of creation was, "Let there be light."

MRS. WIRE: You hear him say that?

NURSIE: You never read the scriptures.

MRS. WIRE: Why should I bother to read 'em with you quotin' 'em to me like a female preacher. Book say this, say that, makes me sick of the book. Where's my flashlight, Nursie?

NURSIE: 'Sunder the pillows. (*She stumbles on a heavy knapsack.*) Lawd! What that there?

MRS. WIRE: Some crazy young man come here wantin' a room. I told him I had no vacancies for Bourbon Street bums. He dropped that sack on the floor and said he'd pick it up tomorrow, which he won't unless he pays fifty cents for storage . . .

NURSIE: It's got something written on it that shines in the dark.

MRS. WIRE: "Sky"—say that's his name. Carry it on upstairs with you, Nursie.

NURSIE: Mizz Wire, I cain't hardly get myself up them steps no more, you know that.

MRS. WIRE: Shoot.

NURSIE: Mizz Wire, I think I oughta inform you I'm thinkin' of retirin'.

MRS. WIRE: *Retirin'* to what, Nursie? The banana tree in the courtyard with the bats you got in your head?

NURSIE: They's lots of folks my age, black an' white, that's called bag people. They just wander round with paper bags that hold ev'rything they possess or they can collect. Nights they sleep on doorsteps: spend days on boxes on corners of Canal Street with a tin cup. They get along: they live—long as intended to by the Lord.

MRS. WIRE: Yor place is with me, Nursie.

NURSIE: I can't please you no more. You keep callin' Nursie, Nursie, do this, do that, with all these stairs in the house and my failin' eyesight. No Ma'am, it's time for me to retire.

(*She crosses upstage. The kitchen area is dimly lighted. Nursie sits at the table with a cup of chicory coffee, eyes large and ominously dark as the continent of her race.*

(*A spot of light picks up the writer dimly at the entrance to the hall.*)

MRS. WIRE: Who? Who?

WRITER: It's—

MRS. WIRE: *You* . . .

WRITER: Mrs. Wire, you're blinding me with that light. (*He shields his left eye with a hand.*)

MRS. WIRE (*switching off the light*): Git upstairs, boy. We'll talk in the mawnin' about your future plans.

WRITER: I have no plans for the future, Mrs. Wire.

MRS. WIRE: That's a situation you'd better correct right quick.

(*The writer, too, collides with the bizarre, colorfully decorated knapsack.*)

WRITER: What's—?

MRS. WIRE: Carry that sack upstairs with you. Nursie refused to.

(*With an effort the writer shoulders the sack and mounts a step or two to the kitchen level.*)

WRITER: Mrs. Wire told me to carry this sack up here.

NURSIE: Just put it somewhere it won't trip me up.

WRITER: Sky? Sky?

NURSIE: She say that's his name. Whose name? I think her mind is goin' on her again. Lately she calls out, "Timmy, Timmy," or she carries on conversations with her dead husband, Horace . . .

WRITER: A name—Sky? (*To himself:*) Shines like a prediction.

(*He drops the knapsack at the edge of the kitchen light and wanders musingly back to the table. Nursie automatically pours him a cup of chicory.*

(*Again the area serving as the entrance passage is lighted, and the sound of a key scraping at a resistant lock is heard.*)

MRS. WIRE (*starting up from her cot*): Who? Who?

(*Jane enters exhaustedly.*)

JANE: Why, Mrs. Wire, you scared me! (*She has an elegance about her and a vulnerability.*)

MRS. WIRE: Miss Sparks, what're you doin' out so late on the streets of the Quarter?

JANE: Mrs. Wire, according to the luminous dial on my watch, it is only ten after twelve.

MRS. WIRE: When I give you a room here . . .

JANE: Gave me? I thought rented . . .

MRS. WIRE (*cutting through*): I told you a single girl was expected in at midnight.

JANE: I'm afraid I didn't take that too seriously. Not since I lived with my parents in New Rochelle, New York, before I went to college, have I been told to be in at a certain hour, and even then I had my own key and disregarded the order more often than not. However! I *am* going to tell you why and where I've gone tonight. I have gone to the all-night drugstore, Waterbury's, on Canal Street, to buy a spray can of Black Flag, which is an insect repellent. I took a cab there tonight and made this purchase because, Mrs. Wire, when I opened the window without a screen in my room, a cockroach, a *flying* cockroach, flew right into my face and was followed by a squadron of others. *Well!* I do *not* have an Oriental, a Buddhistic tolerance for certain insects, least of all a cockroach and even less a flying one. Oh, I've learned to live reluctantly with the ordinary pedestrian kind of cockroach, but to have one fly directly into my face almost gave me convulsions! Now as for the window without a screen, if a screen has not been put in that window by tomorrow, I will buy one for it myself and deduct the cost from next month's rent. (*She goes past Mrs. Wire toward the steps.*)

MRS. WIRE: Hold on a minute, young lady. When you took your room here, you gave your name as Miss Sparks. Now is that young fellow that's living up there with you Mr. Sparks, and if so why did you register as Miss instead of Mrs.?

JANE: I'm sure you've known for some time that I'm sharing my room with a young man, whose name is not Mr. Sparks, whose name is Tye McCool. And if that offends your moral scruples—well—sometimes it offends mine, too.

MRS. WIRE: If I had not been a young lady myself once! Oh yes, once, yaiss! I'd have evicted, both, so fast you'd think that . . .

JANE: No, I've stopped thinking. Just let things happen to me.

(*Jane is now at the stairs and starts up them weakly. Mrs. Wire grunts despairingly and falls back to her cot. Jane enters the kitchen.*)

NURSIE: Why, hello, Miss Sparks.

JANE: Good evening, Nursie—why is Mrs. Wire sleeping in the entrance hall?

NURSIE: Lawd, that woman, she got the idea that 722 Toulouse Street is the address of a jailhouse. And she's the keeper—have some hot chick'ry with me?

JANE: Do you know I still don't know what chicory is? A beverage of some kind?

NURSIE: Why chicory's South'n style coffee.

JANE: Oh, well, thank you, maybe I could try a bit of it to get me up that flight of stairs . . .

(*She sits at the table. Below, the door has opened a third time. The painter called Nightingale stands in the doorway with a pickup.*)

MRS. WIRE: Who? Ah!

NIGHTINGALE (*voice rising*): Well, cousin, uh, Jake . . .

PICKUP (*uneasily*): Blake.

NIGHTINGALE: Yes, we do have a lot of family news to exchange. Come on in. We'll talk a bit more in my room.

MRS. WIRE: In a pig's snout you will!

NIGHTINGALE: Why, Mrs. Wire! (*He chuckles, coughs.*) Are you sleeping in the hall now?

MRS. WIRE: I'm keeping watch on the comings and goings at night of tenants in my house.

NIGHTINGALE: Oh, yes, I know your aversion to visitors at night, but this is my first cousin. I just bumped into him at Gray Goose bus station. He is here for one day only, so I have taken the license of inviting him in for a little family talk since we'll have no other chance.

MRS. WIRE: If you had half the cousins you claim to have, you'd belong to the biggest family since Adam's.

PICKUP: Thanks, but I got to move on. Been nice seeing you—cousin . . .

NIGHTINGALE: Wait—here—take this five. Go to the America Hotel on Exchange Alley just off Canal Street, and I will drop in at noon tomorrow—cousin . . . (*He starts to cough.*)

PICKUP: Thanks, I'll see ya, cousin.

MRS. WIRE: Hah, cousin.

(*Nightingale coughs and spits near her cot.*)

Don't you spit by my bed!

NIGHTINGALE: Fuck off, you old witch!

MR. WIRE: What did you say to me?

NIGHTINGALE: Nothing not said to and about you before! (*He mounts the steps.*)

MRS. WIRE: Nursie! Nursie! (*Receiving no response she lowers herself with a groan onto the cot.*)

NIGHTINGALE (*starting up the stairs*): Midnight staircase—still in—your (*coughs*) fatal position . . . (*He climbs slowly up.*)

(*The writer, Jane, and Nursie are in the kitchen. The crones enter, wild-eyed and panting with greasy paper bags. The kitchen area is lighted.*)

MARY MAUDE: Nursie? Miss Carrie and I ordered a little more dinner this evening than we could eat, so we had the waiter put the remains of the, the—

MISS CARRIE (*her wild eyes very wild*): The steak "Diane," I had the steak Diane and Mary Maude had the chicken "bonne femme." But our eyes were a little bigger than our stomachs.

MARY MAUDE: The sight of too much on a table can kill your appetite! But this food is too good to waste.

MISS CARRIE: And we don't have ice to preserve it in our room, so would you kindly put it in Mrs. Wire's icebox, Nursie.

NURSIE: The last time I done that Miss Wire raised Cain about it, had me throw it right out. She said it didn' smell good.

JANE: I have an icebox in which I'd be glad to keep it for you ladies.

MARY MAUDE: Oh, that's very kind of you!

WRITER (*rising from the kitchen table*): Let me carry it up.

(*He picks up the greasy bags and starts upstairs. Miss Carrie's asthmatic respiration has steadily increased. She staggers with a breathless laugh.*)

MARY MAUDE: Oh, Miss Carrie, you better get right to bed. She's having another attack of her awful asthma. Our room gets no sun, and the walls are so damp, so—dark . . .

(*They totter out of the light together.*)

NURSIE (*averting her face from the bag with a sniff of repugnance*): They didn't go to no restaurant. They been to the garbage pail on the walk outside, don't bother with it, it's spoiled (*pointing upstage*), just put it over there, I'll throw it out.

JANE: I wonder if they'd be offended if I bought them a sack of groceries at Solari's tomorrow.

NURSIE: Offend 'em did you say?

JANE: I meant their pride.

NURSIE: Honey, they gone as far past pride as they gone past mistaking a buzzard for a bluebird.

(*She chuckles. Tye appears. Jane pretends not to notice.*)

JANE: I'm afraid pride's an easy thing to go past sometimes. I am living—I am sharing my studio with a, an addicted—delinquent, a barker at a—stripshow joint. (*She has pretended to ignore Tye's disheveled, drugged, but vulnerably boyish appearance at the edge of the light.*)

TYE (*in a slurred voice*): You wouldn't be tawkin' about—nobody—present . . .

JANE: Why, hello, Tye. How'd you get back so early? How'd you get back at all, in this—condition?

TYE: Honey! If I didn't have my arms full of—packages.

JANE: The less you say out loud about the hot merchandise you've been accumulating here . . .

TYE: Babe, you're asking for a— (*He doubles his fist.*)

JANE: Which I'd return with a kick in the balls! (*She gasps.*) My Lord, did I say that?

MRS. WIRE: What's that shoutin' about?

(*Jane breaks into tears. She falls back into the chair and buries her head in her arms.*)

TYE: Hey, love, come here, I knocked off work early to be with you—do you think I'd really hit you?

JANE: I don't know . . .

TYE: Come to—bed . . .
JANE: Don't lean on me.

(*They cross out of the light. The writer looks after them wistfully as the light dims out.*)

SCENE TWO

The writer has undressed and is in bed. Nightingale coughs—a fiendish, racking cough. He is hacking and spitting up bloody phlegm. He enters his cubicle.

Then across the makeshift partition in the writer's cubicle, unlighted except by a faint glow in its alcove window, another sound commences—a sound of dry and desperate sobbing which sounds as though nothing in the world could ever appease the wound from which it comes: loneliness, inborn and inbred to the bone.

Slowly, as his coughing fit subsides, Nightingale, the quick-sketch artist, turns his head in profile to the sound of the sobbing. Then the writer, across the partition, is dimly lighted, too. He is also sitting up on his cot, staring at the partition between his cell and Nightingale's.

Nightingale clears his throat loudly and sings hoarsely and softly a pop song of the era such as "If I Didn't Care" or "Paper Doll." Slowly the audience of one whom he is serenading succeeds in completely stifling the dry sobbing with a pillow. Nightingale's voice rises a bit as he gets up and lights a cigarette; then he goes toward the upstage limit of the dim stage lighting and makes the gesture of opening a door.

He moves into the other gable room of the attic and stands, silent, for several beats of the song as the writer slowly, reluctantly, turns on his cot to face him.

NIGHTINGALE: . . . I want to ask you something.
WRITER: Huh?
NIGHTINGALE: The word "landlady" as applied to Mrs. Wire and to all landladies that I've encountered in my life—isn't it the biggest one-word contradiction in the English language? (*The writer is embarrassed by Nightingale's intrusion and steady scrutiny.*) She owns the land, yes, but is the witch a lady? Mind if I switch on your light?

WRITER: The bulb's burned out.

NIGHTINGALE (*chuckles and coughs*): She hasn't replaced a burnt-out light bulb in this attic since I moved here last spring. I have to provide my own light bulbs by unscrewing them from the gentleman's lavatory at the City of the Two Parrots, where I ply my trade. Temporarily, you know. Doing portraits in pastel of the tourist clientele. (*His voice is curiously soft and intimate, more as if he were speaking of personal matters.*)

Of course I . . . (*He coughs and clears his throat.*) . . . *have no shame about it*, no guilt at all, since what I do there is a travesty of my talent, I mean a prostitution of it, I mean, painting these tourists at the Two Parrots, which are actually two very noisy macaws. Oh, they have a nice patio there, you know, palm trees and azaleas when in season, but the cuisine and the service . . . abominable. The menu sometimes includes cockroaches . . . (There are a lot of great eating places in New Orleans, like Galatoire's, Antoine's, Arnaud's in the Vieux Carré and . . . Commander's Palace and Plantation House in the Garden District . . . lovely old mansions, you know, converted to restaurants with a gracious style . . . haunted by dead residents, of course, but with charm . . .)

(*This monologue is like a soothing incantation, interspersed with hoarseness and coughing.*)

Like many writers, I know you're a writer, you're a young man of very few spoken words, compared to my garrulity.

WRITER: Yes, I . . .

NIGHTINGALE: So far, kid, you're practically . . . monosyllabic.

WRITER: I . . . don't feel well . . . tonight.

NIGHTINGALE: That's why I intruded. You have a candle on that box beside your cot.

WRITER: Yes, but no matches.

NIGHTINGALE: I have matches, I'll light it. Talk is easier . . . (*He strikes the match and advances to the writer's bedside.*) . . . between two people visible to each other, if . . . not too sharply . . . (*He lights the candle.*) Once I put up for a night in a flophouse without doors, and a gentleman entered my cubicle without invitation, came straight to my cot and struck a match, leaned over me peering directly into my face . . . and then said, "No," and walked out . . . as if he assumed that I would have said, "Yes." (*He laughs and coughs.*)

(*Pause*)

You're not a man of few words but a boy of no words. I'll just sit on the cot if you don't object.

WRITER: . . . I, uh . . . do need sleep.

NIGHTINGALE: You need some company first. I know the sound of loneliness: heard it through the partition. (*He has sat on the cot. The writer huddles away to the wall, acutely embarrassed.*) . . . Trying not to, but crying . . . why try not to? Think it's unmanly? Crying is a release for man or woman . . .

WRITER: I was taught not to cry because it's . . . humiliating . . .

NIGHTINGALE: You're a victim of conventional teaching, which you'd better forget. What were you crying about? Some particular sorrow or . . . for the human condition.

WRITER: Some . . . particular sorrow. My closest relative died last month.

NIGHTINGALE: Your mother?

WRITER: The mother of my mother, Grand. She died after a long illness just before I left home, and at night I remember . . .

NIGHTINGALE (*giving a comforting pat*): Well, losses must be accepted and survived. How strange it is that we've occupied these adjoining rooms for about three weeks now and have just barely said hello to each other when passing on the stairs. You have interesting eyes.

WRITER: In what way do you mean?

NIGHTINGALE: Isn't the pupil of the left one a little bit lighter?

WRITER: . . . I'm afraid I'm . . . developing a—cataract in that eye.

NIGHTINGALE: That's not possible for a kid.

WRITER: I am twenty-eight.

NIGHTINGALE: What I meant is, your face is still youthful as your vulnerable nature, they go—together. Of course, I'd see an oculist if you suspect there's a cataract.

WRITER: I plan to when I . . . if I . . . can ever afford to . . . the vision in that eye's getting cloudy.

NIGHTINGALE: Don't wait till you can afford to. Go straight away and don't receive the bill.

WRITER: I couldn't do that.

NIGHTINGALE: Don't be so honest in this dishonest world. (*He pauses and coughs.*) Shit, the witch don't sleep in her bedroom you know.

WRITER: Yes, I noticed she is sleeping on a cot in the hall now.

NIGHTINGALE: When I came in now she sprang up and hollered out, "Who?" And I answer her with a hoot owl imitation, "Hoo, Hooo, Hooooo." Why, the lady is all three furies in one. A single man needs visitors at night. Necessary as bread, as blood in the body. Why, there's a saying, "Better to live with your worst enemy than to live alone."

WRITER: Yes, loneliness is an—affliction.

NIGHTINGALE: Well, now you have a friend here.

WRITER (*dryly*): Thanks.

NIGHTINGALE: Of course we're in a madhouse. I wouldn't tolerate the conditions here if the season wasn't so slow that—my financial condition is difficult right now. I don't like insults and *la vie solitaire*—with bedbugs bleeding me like leeches . . . but now we know each other, the plywood partition between us has been dissolved, no more just hellos. So tonight you were crying in here alone. What of it? Don't we all? Have a cigarette.

WRITER: Thanks.

(*Nightingale holds the candle out.*)

I won't smoke it now, I'll save it till morning. I like a cigarette when I sit down to work.

(*Nightingale's steady scrutiny embarrasses him. They fall silent. After several beats, the writer resumes.*)

There's—a lot of human material—in the Quarter for a writer . . .

NIGHTINGALE: I used to hear you typing. Where's your typewriter?

WRITER: I, uh, hocked it.

NIGHTINGALE: That's what I figured. Wha'd you get for it?

WRITER: Ten dollars. It was a secondhand Underwood portable. I'm worried about just how I'll redeem it. (*He is increasingly embarrassed.*)

NIGHTINGALE: Excuse my cusiosity, I mean concern. It's sympathetic . . . Smoke a cigarette now and have another for mawnin'. You're not managing right. Need advice and . . . company in this sad ole house. I'm happy to give both if accepted.

WRITER: . . . I appreciate . . . both.

NIGHTINGALE: You don't seem experienced yet . . . kid, are you . . . excuse my blunt approach . . . but are you . . . ? (*He completes the question by placing a shaky hand on the writer's crumpled, sheet-covered body.*)

WRITER (*in a stifled voice*): Oh . . . I'm not sure I know . . . I . . .

NIGHTINGALE: Ain't come out completely, as we put it?

WRITER: Completely, no, just one—experience.

NIGHTINGALE: Tell me about that one experience.

WRITER: I'm not sure I want to discuss it.

NIGHTINGALE: That's no way to begin a confidential friendship.

WRITER: . . . Well, New Year's Eve, I was entertained by a married couple I had a letter of introduction to when I came down here, the . . . man's a painter, does popular bayou pictures displayed in shop windows in the Quarter, his name is . . .

NIGHTINGALE: Oh, I know him. He's got a good thing going, commercially speaking, tourists buy them calendar illustrations in dreamy rainbow colors that never existed but in the head of a hack like him.

WRITER: . . . The, uh, atmosphere is . . . effective.

NIGHTINGALE: Oh, they sell to people that don't know paint from art. Maybe you've never seen artistic paintings. (*His voice shakes with feverish pride.*) I could do it, in fact I've done good painting, serious work. But I got to live, and you can't live on good painting until you're dead, or nearly.

So, I make it, temporarily, as a quick sketch artist. I flatter old bitches by makin' 'em ten pounds lighter and ten years younger and with some touches of—decent humanity in their eyes that God forgot to put there, or they've decided to dispense with, not always easy. But what is? So—you had an experience with the bayou painter? I didn't know he was, oh, inclined to boys, this is killing?

WRITER (*slowly with embarrassment*): It wasn't with Mr. Block, it was with a . . . paratrooper.

NIGHTINGALE: Aha, a paratrooper dropped out of the sky for you, huh? You have such nice smooth skin . . . Would you like a bit of white port? I keep a half pint by my bed to wash down my sandman special when this touch of flu and the bedbugs keep me awake. Just a mo', I'll fetch it, we'll have a nightcap—now that we're acquainted! (*He goes out rapidly, coughing, then rushes back in with the bottle.*)

The witch has removed the glass, we'll have to drink from the bottle. I'll wash my pill down now, the rest is yours. (*He pops a capsule into his mouth and gulps from the bottle, immediately coughing and gagging. He extends the bottle to the writer.*)

(*Pause. The writer half extends his hand toward the bottle, then draws it back and shakes his head.*)

Oh yes, flu is contagious, how stupid of me, I'm sorry.

WRITER: Never mind, I don't care much for liquor.

NIGHTINGALE: Where you from?

WRITER: . . . St. Louis.

NIGHTINGALE: Christ, do people live there?

WRITER: It has a good art museum and a fine symphony orchestra and . . .

NIGHTINGALE: No decent gay life at all?

WRITER: You mean . . .

NIGHTINGALE: You know what I mean. I mean like the . . . paratrooper.

WRITER: Oh. No. There could be but . . . living at home . . .

NIGHTINGALE: Tell me, how did it go with the paratrooper who descended on you at Block's?

WRITER: Well at midnight we went out on the gallery and he, the paratrooper, was out on the lower gallery with a party of older men, antique dealers, they were all singing "Auld Lang Syne."

NIGHTINGALE: How imaginative and *appropriate* to them.

WRITER: —I noticed him down there and he noticed me.

NIGHTINGALE: Noticing him?

WRITER: . . . Yes. He grinned, and hollered to come down; he took me into the lower apartment. It was vacant, the others still on the gallery, you see I . . . couldn't understand his presence among the . . .

NIGHTINGALE: Screaming old faggots at that antique dealer's. Well, they're rich and they buy boys, but that's a scene that you haven't learned yet. So. What happened downstairs?

WRITER: He took me into a bedroom; he told me I looked pale and wouldn't I like a sunlamp treatment. I thought he meant my face so I—agreed—

NIGHTINGALE: Jesus, you've got to be joking.

WRITER: I was shaking violently like I was a victim of—St. Vitus's Dance, you know, when he said, "Undress"!

NIGHTINGALE: But you did.

WRITER: Yes. He helped me. And I stretched out on the bed under the sunlamp and suddenly he—

NIGHTINGALE: . . . turned it off and did you?

WRITER: Yes, that's what happened. I think that he was shocked by my reaction.

NIGHTINGALE: You did *him* or—?

WRITER: . . . I told him that I . . . loved . . . him. I'd been drinking.

NIGHTINGALE: Love can happen like that. For one night only.

WRITER: He said, he laughed and said, "Forget it. I'm flying out tomorrow for training base."

NIGHTINGALE: He said to you, "Forget it," but you didn't forget it.

WRITER: No . . . I don't even have his address and I've forgotten his name . . .

NIGHTINGALE: Still, I think you loved him.

WRITER: . . . Yes. I . . . I'd like to see some of your serious paintings sometime.

NIGHTINGALE: Yeah. You will. Soon. When I get them canvases shipped down from Baton Rouge next week. But meanwhile . . . (*His hand is sliding down the sheet.*) How about this?

WRITER (*with gathering panic*): . . . I think I'd better get some sleep now. I didn't mean to tell you all that. Good-night, I'm going to sleep.

NIGHTINGALE (*urgently*): This would help you.

WRITER: I need to sleep nights—to work.

NIGHTINGALE: You are alone in the world, and I am, too. Listen. Rain!

(*They are silent. The sound of rain is heard on the roof.*)

Look. I'll give you two things for sleep. First, this. (*He draws back the sheet. The light dims.*) And then one of these pills I call my sandman special.

WRITER: I don't . . .

NIGHTINGALE: Shh, walls have ears! Lie back and imagine the paratrooper.

(*The dim light goes completely out. A passage of blues piano is heard. It is an hour later. There is a spotlight on the writer as narrator, smoking at the foot of the cot, the sheet drawn about him like a toga.*)

WRITER: When I was alone in the room, the visitor having retreated beyond the plywood partition between his cubicle and mine, which was chalk white that turned ash-gray at night, not just he but everything visible was gone except for the lighter gray of the alcove with its window over Toulouse Street. An apparition came to me with the hypnotic effect of the painter's sandman special. It was in the form of an elderly female saint, of course. She materialized soundlessly. Her eyes fixed on me with a gentle questioning look which I came to remember as having belonged to my grandmother during her sieges of illness, when I used to go to her room and sit by her bed and want, so much, to say something or to put my hand over hers, but could do neither, knowing that if I did, I'd betray my feelings with tears that would trouble her more than her illness . . . Now it was she who stood next to my bed for a while. And as I drifted toward sleep, I wondered if she'd witnessed the encounter between the painter and me and what her attitude was toward such—perversions? Of longing?

(*The sound of stifled coughing is heard across the plywood partition.*)

Nothing about her gave me any sign. The weightless hands clasping each other so loosely, the cool and believing gray eyes in the faint pearly face were as immobile as statuary. I felt that she neither blamed nor approved the encounter. No. Wait. She . . . seemed to lift one hand very, very slightly before my eyes closed with sleep. An almost invisible gesture of . . . forgiveness? . . . through understanding? . . . Before she dissolved into sleep . . .

SCENE THREE

Tye is in a seminarcotized state on the bed in Jane's room. Jane is in the hall burdened with paper sacks of groceries; the writer appears behind her.

JANE (*brightly*): Good morning.

WRITER (*shyly*): Oh, good morning.

JANE: Such a difficult operation, opening a purse with one hand.

WRITER: Let me hold the sacks for you.

JANE: Oh, thanks; now then, come in, put the sacks on one of those chairs. Over the weekend we run out of everything. Ice isn't delivered on Sundays: milk spoils. Everything of a perishable kind has got to be replaced. Oh, don't go out. Have you had a coffee?

WRITER (*looking at Tye*): I was about to but . . .

JANE: Stay and have some with me. Sorry it's instant, can you stand instant coffee?

WRITER: I beg your pardon?

JANE: Don't mind him, when his eyes are half open it doesn't mean he is conscious.

TYE: Bullshit, you picked up a kid on the street?

JANE (*suppressing anger*): This is the young man from across the hall— I'm Jane Sparks, my friend is Tye McCool, and you are—

WRITER (*pretending to observe a chess board to cover his embarrassment*): What a beautiful chess board!

JANE: Oh, that, yes!

WRITER: Ivory and ebony? Figures?

JANE: The white squares are mother-of-pearl. Do you play chess?

WRITER: Used to. You play together, you and Mr.— McCool?

TYE: Aw, yeh, we play together but not chess. (*He rubs his crotch. Jane and the writer nervously study the chess board.*)

JANE: I play alone, a solitary game, to keep in practice in case I meet a partner.

WRITER: Look. Black is in check.

JANE: My imaginary opponent. I choose sides you see, although I play for both.

WRITER: I'd be happy to—I mean sometimes when you—

TYE (*touching the saucepan on the burner*): OW!

JANE: I set it to boil before I went to the store.

(*Jane sets a cup and doughnuts on the table.*)

TYE: Hey, kid, why don't you take your cup across the hall to your own room?

JANE: Because I've just now—you heard me—invited him to have it here in this room with me.

TYE: I didn't invite him in, and I want you to git something straight: I live here. And if I live in a place I got equal rights in this place, and it just so happens I don't entertain no stranger to look at me undressed.

WRITER (*gulping down his coffee*): Please. Uh, please, I think I'd rather go in my room because I, I've got some work to do there. I always work immediately after my coffee.

JANE: I will not have this young grifter who has established squatter's rights here telling me that I can't enjoy a little society in a place where—frankly I am frantic with loneliness!

(*The writer does not know what to do. Tye suddenly grins. He pulls out a chair for the writer at the table as if it were for a lady.*)

TYE: Have a seat kid, you like one lump or two? Where's the cat? Can I invite the goddam cat to breakfast?

JANE: Tye, you said you were pleased with the robe I gave you for your birthday, but you never wear it.

TYE: I don't dress for breakfast.

JANE: Putting on a silk robe isn't dressing.

(*She removes the robe from a hook and throws it about Tye's shoulders. Automatically he circles her hips with an arm.*)

TYE: Mmm. Good. Feels good.

JANE (*shyly disengaging herself from his embrace*): It ought to. Shantung silk.

TYE: I didn't mean the robe, babe.

JANE: Tye, behave yourself. (*She turns to the writer.*) I've cherished the hope that by introducing Tye to certain little improvements in wearing apparel and language, I may gradually, despite his resistance—

TYE: Ain't that lovely? That classy langwidge she uses?

JANE: Inspire him to—seek out some higher level of employment. (*Ignoring Tye, she speaks.*) I heard that you are a writer?

WRITER: I, uh—write, but—

JANE: What form of writing? I mean fiction or poetry or . . .

TYE: Faggots, they all do something artistic, all of 'em.

JANE (*quickly*): Do you know, I find myself drinking twice as much coffee here as I did in New York. For me the climate here is debilitating. Perhaps because of the dampness and the, and the—very low altitude, really there's no altitude at all, it's slightly under sea level. Have another cup with me?

(*The writer doesn't answer: Jane prepares two more cups of the instant coffee. Tye is staring steadily, challengingly at the writer, who appears to be hypnotized.*)

Of course, Manhattan hasn't much altitude either. But I grew up in the Adirondacks really. We lived on high ground, good elevation.

TYE: I met one of 'em once by accident on the street. You see. I was out of a job, and he came up to me on a corner in the Quarter an' invited me to his place for supper with him. I seen right off what he was an' what he wanted, but I didn't have the price of a poor boy sandwich so I accepted, I went. The place was all Japanese-like, everything very artistic. He said to me, "Cross over that little bridge that crosses my little lake which I made myself and sit on the bench under my willow tree while I make supper for us and bathe an' change my clo'se. I won't be long." So I crossed over the bridge over the lake, and I stretched out under the weepin' willow tree: fell right asleep. I was woke up by what looked like a female but was him in drag. "Supper ready," he—she—said. Then this freak, put her hand on my—I said, "It's gonna cost you more than supper . . . ."

JANE: Tye.

TYE: Huh, baby?

JANE: You will *not* continue that story.

TYE: It's a damn good story. What's your objection to it? I ain't got to the part that's really funny. (*He speaks to the writer, who is crossing out of the light.*) Don't you like the story?

(*The writer exits.*)

JANE: Why did you do that?

TYE: Do what?

JANE: You know what, and the boy knew what you meant by it. Why did you want to hurt him with the implication that he was in a class with a common, a predatory transvestite?

TYE: Look Jane . . . You say you was brought up on high ground, good elevation, but you come in here, you bring in here and expose me to a little queer, and . . .

JANE: Does everyone with civilized behavior, good manners, seem to be a queer to you?

TYE: . . . Was it good manners the way he looked at me, Babe?

JANE (*voice rising*): Was it good manners for you to stand in front of him rubbing your—groin the way you did?

TYE: I wanted you to notice his reaction.

JANE: He was just embarrassed.

TYE: You got a lot to learn about life in the Quarter.

JANE: I think that he's a serious person that I can talk to, and I need some one to talk to!

(*Pause*)

TYE: You can't talk to *me* huh?

JANE: With you working all night at a Bourbon Street strip-joint, and sleeping nearly all day? Involving yourself with all the underworld elements of this corrupt city . . .

TYE: 'Sthat all I do? Just that? I never pleasure you, babe?

(*Fade in piano blues. She draws a breath and moves as if half asleep behind Tye's chair.*)

JANE: Yes, you—pleasure me, Tye.

TYE: I try to do my best to, Babe. Sometimes I wonder why a girl—

JANE: Not a girl, Tye. A woman.

TYE: —How did—why did—you get yourself mixed up with me?

JANE: A sudden change of circumstances removed me from—how shall I put it so you'd understand?

TYE: Just—say.

JANE: What I'd thought was myself. So I quit my former connections, I came down here to— (*She stops short.*) Well, to make an adjustment to— (*Pause*) We met by chance on Royal Street when a deluge of rain backed me into a doorway? Didn't know you were behind me until you put your hand on my hip and I turned to say, "Stop that!" but didn't because you were something I'd never encountered before—faintly innocent—boy's eyes. Smiling. Said to myself, "Why not, with nothing to lose!" Of course you pleasure me, Tye! —I'd been alone so long . . .

(*She touches his throat with trembling fingers. He leans sensually back against her. She runs her hand down his chest.*)

Silk on silk is—lovely . . . regardless of the danger.

(*As the light on this area dims, typing begins offstage. The dim-out is completed.*)

SCENE FOUR

A lighted area represents Mrs. Wire's kitchen, in which she is preparing a big pot of gumbo despite the hour, which is midnight. She could be mistaken for a witch from Macbeth *in vaguely modern but not new costume.*

The writer's footsteps catch her attention. He appears at the edge of the light in all that remains of his wardrobe: riding boots and britches, a faded red flannel shirt.

MRS. WIRE: Who, who? —Aw, you, dressed up like a jockey in a donkey race!

WRITER: —My, uh, clothes are at the cleaners.

MRS. WIRE: Do they clean clothes at the pawnshop, yeah, I reckon they do clean clothes not redeemed. Oh. Don't go upstairs. Your room is forfeited, too.

WRITER: . . . You mean I'm . . . ?

MRS. WIRE: A loser, boy, possibly you could git a cot at the Salvation Army.

WRITER (*averting his eyes*): May I sit down a moment?

MRS. WIRE: Why, for what?

WRITER: Eviction presents . . . a problem.

MRS. WIRE: I thought you was gittin' on the WPA Writers' Project? That's what you tole me when I inquired about your prospects for employment, you said, "Oh, I've applied for work on the WPA for writers."

WRITER: I couldn't prove that my father was destitute, and the fact he contributes nothing to my support seemed—immaterial to them.

MRS. WIRE: Why're you shifty-eyed? I never seen a more shifty-eyed boy.

WRITER: I, uh, have had a little eye trouble, lately.

MRS. WIRE: You're gettin' a cataract on your left eye, boy, face it! —Cataracts don't usually hit at your age.

WRITER: I've noticed a lot of things have hit me—prematurely . . .

MRS. WIRE (*stirring gumbo*): Hungry? I bet. I eat at irregular hours. I suddenly got a notion to cook up a gumbo, and when I do, the smell of it is an attraction, draws company in the kitchen. Oh ho—*footsteps fast. Here comes the ladies.*

WRITER: Mrs. Wire, those old ladies are starving, dying of malnutrition.

(*Miss Carrie and Mary Maude appear at the edge of the lighted area with queer, high-pitched laughter or some bizarre relation to laughter.*)

MRS. WIRE: Set back down there, boy. (*Pause.*) Why, Mizz Wayne an' Miss Carrie, you girls still up at this hour!

MISS CARRIE: We heard you moving about and wondered if we could . . .

MARY MAUDE: Be of some assistance.

MRS. WIRE: Shoot, Mrs. Wayne, do you imagine that rusty ole saucepan of yours is invisible to me? Why, I know when I put this gumbo on the stove and lit the fire, it would smoke you ladies out of your locked room. What do you all do in that locked room so much?

MARY MAUDE: We keep ourselves occupied.

MISS CARRIE: We are compiling a cookbook which we hope to have published. A Creole cookbook, recipes we remember from our childhood.

MRS. WIRE: A recipe is a poor substitute for food.

MARY MAUDE (*with a slight breathless pause*): We ought to go out more regularly for meals but our . . . our light bulbs have burned out, so we can't distinguish night from day anymore. Only shadows come in.

MISS CARRIE: Sshh! (*Pause.*) Y'know, I turned down an invitation to dinner this evening at my cousin Mathilde Devereau Pathet's in the Garden District.

MRS. WIRE: Objected to the menu?

MISS CARRIE: No, but you know, very rich people are so inconsiderate sometimes. With four limousines and drivers at their constant disposal, they wouldn't send one to fetch me.

MRS. WIRE: Four? Limousines? Four drivers?

(*A delicate, evanescent music steals in as the scene acquires a touch of the bizarre. At moments the players seem bewildered as if caught in a dream.*)

MISS CARRIE: Oh, yes, four, four . . . spanking new Cadillacs with uniformed chauffeurs!

MRS. WIRE: Now, that's very impressive.

MISS CARRIE: They call Mr. Pathet the "Southern Planter."

MRS. WIRE: Has a plantation, in the Garden District?

MISS CARRIE (*gasping*): Oh, no, no, no, no. He's a mortician, most prominent mortician, buries all the best families in the parish.

MRS. WIRE: And poor relations, too? I hope.

MARY MAUDE: Miss Carrie goes into a family vault when she goes.

MRS. WIRE: When?

MARY MAUDE: Yes, above ground: has a vault reserved in . . .

MISS CARRIE: Let's not speak of that! . . . now.

MRS. WIRE: Why not speak of that? You got to consider the advantage of this connection. Because of the expenses of "The Inevitable" someday, soon, specially with your asthma? No light? And bad nutrition?

MISS CARRIE: The dampness of the old walls in the Quarter—you know how they hold damp. This city is actually eight feet below sea level. Niggers are buried under the ground, and their caskets fill immediately with water.

MRS. WIRE: But I reckon your family vault is above this nigger water level?

MISS CARRIE: Oh, yes, above water level, in fact, I'll be on top of my great-great-uncle, Jean Pierre Devereau, the third.

(*The writer laughs a bit, involuntarily. The ladies glare at him.*)

Mrs. Wire, who is this . . . transient? Young man?

MARY MAUDE: We did understand that this was a guesthouse, not a . . . refuge for delinquents.

MISS CARRIE (*turning her back on the writer*): They do set an exquisite table at the Pathets, with excellent food, but it's not appetizing, you know, to be conducted on a tour of inspection of the business display room, you know, the latest model of caskets on display, and that's what René Pathet does, invariably escorts me, proud as a peacock, through the coffin display rooms before . . . we sit down to dinner. And all through dinner, he discusses his latest clients and . . . those expected shortly.

MRS. WIRE: Maybe he wants you to pick out your casket cause he's noticed your asthma from damp walls in the Quarter.

MISS CARRIE: I do, of course, understand that business is business with him, a night and day occupation.

MRS. WIRE: You know, I always spit in a pot of gumbo to give it special flavor, like a bootblack spits on a shoe. (*She pretends to spit in the pot. The crones try to laugh.*) Now help yourself, fill your saucepan full, and I'll loan you a couple of spoons, but let it cool a while, don't blister your gums . . . (*Handing them spoons*) . . . and Mrs. Wayne, I'll be watching the mailbox for Buster's army paycheck.

MARY MAUDE: That boy has never let me down, he's the most devoted son a mother could hope for.

MRS. WIRE: Yais, if she had no hope.

MARY MAUDE: I got a postcard from him . . .

MRS. WIRE: A postcard can't be cashed.

MARY MAUDE (*diverting Mrs. Wire's attention, she hopes, as Miss Carrie ladles out gumbo*): Of course, I wasn't prepared for the circumstance that struck me when I discovered that Mr. Wayne had not kept up his insurance payments, *that* I was not prepared for, that it was *lapsed*.

MRS. WIRE (*amused*): I bet you wasn't prepared for a little surprise like that.

MARY MAUDE: No, not for that nor for the discovery that secretly for years he'd been providing cash and real estate to that little redheaded doxy he'd kept in Bay St. Louie.

MISS CARRIE: Owwwww!

(*Mrs. Wire whirls about, and Miss Carrie is forced to swallow the scalding mouthful.*)

MRS. WIRE: I bet that mouthful scorched your throat, Miss Carrie. Didn't I tell you to wait?

MARY MAUDE: Carrie, give me that saucepan before you spill it, your hand's so shaky. Thank you, Mrs. Wire. Carrie, thank Mrs. Wire for her being so concerned always about our—circumstances here. Now let's go and see what can be done for that throat. (*They move toward the stairs but do not exit.*)

MRS. WIRE: Cut it, if all else fails.

(*Something crashes on the stairs. All turn that way. Tye appears dimly, bearing two heavy cartons; he speaks to the writer, who is nearest to him.*)

TYE: Hey, you, boy?

WRITER: —Me?

TYE: Yeh, yeh, you, I dropped one of these packages on th' steps, so goddam dark I dropped it. And I'd appreciate it if you'd pick it up fo' me an' help me git it upstairs.
WRITER: I'll be—glad to try to . . .

(*Tye focuses dimly on Miss Carrie. He blinks several times in disbelief.*)

TYE: Am I . . . in the right place?
MRS. WIRE (*shouting*): Not in your present condition. Go on back out. Sleep it off in the gutter.
MISS CARRIE (*to Mrs. Wire*): Tragic for such a nice-looking young man to return to his wife in that condition at night.
MRS. WIRE: Practically every night.

(*Miss Carrie and Mary Maude exit.*

(*Tye has almost miraculously managed to collect his dropped packages, and he staggers to stage right where the lower steps to the attic are dimly seen. The writer follows.*)

TYE (*stumbling back against the writer*): Can you make it? Can you make it, kid?

(*They slowly mount the steps. The lighted kitchen is dimmed out. There is a brief pause. A soft light is cast on the attic hall.*)

TYE: Now, kid, can you locate my room key in my pocket?
WRITER: Which, uh—pocket?
TYE: Pan's pocket.
WRITER: Left pocket or—
TYE: —Head—spinnin'—money in hip pocket, key in—right—lef' side. Shit—key befo' I—fall . . .

(*The writer's hand starts to enter a pocket when Tye collapses, spilling the boxes on the floor and sprawling across them.*)

WRITER: You're right outside my cubbyhole. I suggest you rest in there before you—wake up your wife . . .
TYE: M'ole lady, she chews my ass off if I come home this ways . . . (*He struggles heroically to near standing position as the writer guides him into his cubicle.*) . . . This—bed?

(*There is a soft, ghostly laugh from the adjoining cubicle. A match strikes briefly.*)

WRITER: Swing your legs other way, that way's the pillow—would you, uh, like your wet shoes off?

TYE: Shoes? Yes, but nothin' else. Once I—passed out on—Bourbon Street—late night—in a dark doorway—woke up—this guy, was takin' liberties with me and I don't go for that stuff—

WRITER: I don't take advantages of that kind, I am—going back downstairs, if you're comfortable now . . .

TYE: I said to this guy, "Okay, if you wanto blow me, you can pay me one hunnerd dollars—before, not after."

(*Tye's voice dies out. Nightingale becomes visible, rising stealthily in his cubicle and slipping on a robe, as Tye begins to snore.*

(*The attic lights dim out. The lights on the kitchen come up as the writer re-enters.*)

MRS. WIRE: Got that bum to bed? Set down, son. Ha! Notice I called you, son. Where do you go nights?

WRITER: Oh, I walk, I take long solitary walks. Sometimes I . . . I . . .

MRS. WIRE: Sometimes you what? You can say it's none of my business, but I, well, I have a sort of a, well you could say I have a sort of a—maternal—concern. You see, I do have a son that I never see no more, but I worry about him so I reckon it's natural for me to worry about you a little. And get things straight in my head about you—you've changed since you've been in this house. You know that?

WRITER: Yes, I know that.

MRS. WIRE: This I'll tell you, when you first come to my door, I swear I seen and I recognized a young gentleman in you—shy. Shaky, but . . .

WRITER: Panicky! Yes! Gentleman? My folks say so. I wonder.

(*The light narrows and focuses on the writer alone; the speech becomes an interior reflection.*)

I've noticed I do have some troublesome little scruples in my nature that may cause difficulties in my . . . (*He rises and rests his foot on the chair.*) . . . negotiated—truce with—life. Oh—there's a price for things, that's something I've learned in the Vieux Carré. For everything that you purchase in this marketplace you pay out of *here*! (*He thumps his chest.*) And the cash which is the stuff you use in your work can be overdrawn, depleted, like a reservoir going dry in a long season of drought . . .

(*The scene is resumed on a realistic level with a change in the lighting.*)

MRS. WIRE (*passing a bowl of gumbo to the writer*): Here, son, have some gumbo. Let it cool a while. I just pretended to spit in it, you know.

WRITER: I know.

MRS. WIRE: I make the best gumbo, I do the best Creole cookin' in Louisiana. It's God's truth, and now I'll tell you what I'm plannin' to do while your gumbo's coolin'. I'll tell you because it involves a way you could pay your room and board here.

WRITER: Oh?

MRS. WIRE: Uh huh, I'm plannin' to open a lunchroom.

WRITER: On the premises? Here?

MRS. WIRE: On the premises, in my bedroom, which I'm gonna convert into a small dinin' room. So I'm gonna git printed up some bus'ness cards. At twelve noon ev'ry day except Sundays you can hit the streets with these little bus'ness cards announcin' that lunch is bein' served for twenty-five cents, a cheaper lunch than you could git in a greasy spoon on Chartres . . . and no better cooking in the Garden District or the Vieux Carré.

WRITER: Meals for a quarter in the Quarter.

MRS. WIRE: Hey! That's the slogan! I'll print it on those cards that you'll pass out.

WRITER (*dreamily*): Wonderful gumbo.

MRS. WIRE: Why this "Meals for a quarter in the Quarter" is going to put me back in the black, yeah! Boy! . . . (*She throws him the key to his attic rooms. The lights dim out briefly.*)

TYE'S VOICE: Hey! Whatcha doin'? Git yuh fuckin' hands off me!

(*The writer appears dimly in the attic hall outside his room. He stops.*)

NIGHTINGALE'S VOICE: I thought that I was visiting a friend.

TYE'S VOICE: 'S that how you visit a friend, unzippin' his pants an' pullin' out his dick?

NIGHTINGALE'S VOICE: I assure you it was a mistake of—identity . . .

TYE (*becoming visible on the side of the bed in the writer's cubicle*): This ain't my room. Where is my ole lady? Hey, *hey, Jane*!

WRITER: You collapsed in the hall outside your door so I helped you in here.

TYE: Both of you git this straight. No goddam faggot messes with me, never! For less'n a hundred dollars!

(*Jane becomes visible in the hall before this line.*)

A hunnerd dollars, yes, maybe, but not a dime less.

NIGHTINGALE (*emerging from the cubicle in his robe*): I am afraid that you have priced yourself out of the market.

JANE: Tye, come out of there.

TYE: I been interfered with cause you'd locked me out.

WRITER: Miss, uh, Sparks, I didn't touch your friend except to, to . . . offer him my bed till you let him in.

JANE: *Tye, stand up—if you can stand! Stand. Walk.*

(*Tye stumbles against her, and she cries out as she is pushed against the wall.*)

TYE'S VOICE: Locked out, bolted outa my room, to be—molested.

JANE: I heard you name a price, with you everything has a price. Thanks, good night.

(*During this exchange Nightingale in his purple robe has leaned, smoking with a somewhat sardonic look, against the partition between the two cubicles. The writer reappears.*)

NIGHTINGALE: Back so quick? —*Tant pis* . . .

WRITER: I think if I were you, I'd go in your own room and get to bed.

(*The writer enters his cubicle. Nightingale's face slowly turns to a mask of sorrow past expression. There is music. Nightingale puts out his cigarette and enters his cubicle.*

(Jane undresses Tye. The writer undresses. Nightingale sits on his cot. Tye and Jane begin to make love. Downstairs, Nursie mops the floor, singing to herself. The writer moves slowly to his bed and places his hand on the warm sheets that Tye has left. The light dims.

(There is a passage of time.)

SCENE FIVE

The attic rooms are dimly lit. Nightingale is adjusting a neckerchief about his wasted throat. He enters the writer's cubicle without knocking.

NIGHTINGALE: May I intrude once more? It's embarrassing—this incident. Not of any importance, nothing worth a second thought. (*He coughs.*) Oh Christ. You know my mattress is full of bedbugs. Last night I smashed one at least the size of my thumbnail, it left a big blood spot on the pillow. (*He coughs and gasps for breath.*) I showed it to the colored woman that the witch calls Nursie, and Nursie told her about it, and she came charging up here and demanded that I exhibit the bug, which I naturally . . . (*A note of uncertainty and fear enters his voice.*)

WRITER: . . . removed from the pillow.

NIGHTINGALE: Who in hell wouldn't remove the remains of a squashed bedbug from his pillow? Nobody I'd want social or any acquaintance with . . . she even . . . intimated that I coughed up the blood, as if I had . . . (*coughs*) consumption.

WRITER (*stripped to his shorts and about to go to bed*): I think with that persistent cough of yours you should get more rest.

NIGHTINGALE: Restlessness. Insomnia. I can't imagine a worse affliction, and I've suffered from it nearly all my life. I consulted a doctor about it once, and he said, "You don't sleep because it reminds you of death." A ludicrous assumption—the only true regret I'd have over leaving this world is that I'd leave so much of my serious work unfinished.

WRITER (*holding the bedsheet up to his chin*): Do show me your serious work.

NIGHTINGALE: I know why you're taking this tone.

WRITER: I am not taking any tone.

NIGHTINGALE: Oh yes you are, you're very annoyed with me because my restlessness, my loneliness, made me so indiscreet as to—offer my attentions to that stupid but—physically appealing young man you'd put on that cot with the idea of reserving him for yourself. And so I do think your tone is a bit hypocritical, don't you?

WRITER: All right, I do admit I find him attractive, too, but I did *not* make a pass at him.

NIGHTINGALE: I heard him warn you.

WRITER: I simply removed his wet shoes.

NIGHTINGALE: Little man, you are sensual, but I, I—am rapacious.

WRITER: And I am tired.

NIGHTINGALE: Too tired to return my visits? Not very appreciative of you, but lack of appreciation is something I've come to expect and almost to accept as if God—the alleged—had stamped on me a sign at birth—"This man will offer himself and not be accepted, not by anyone ever!"

WRITER: Please don't light that candle.

NIGHTINGALE: I shall, the candle is lit.

WRITER: I do wish that you'd return to your side of the wall —well, now I am taking a tone, but it's . . . . justified. Now do please get out, get out, I mean it, when I blow out the candle I want to be alone.

NIGHTINGALE: You know, you're going to grow into a selfish, callous man. Returning no visits, reciprocating no . . . caring.

WRITER: . . . Why do you predict that?

NIGHTINGALE: That little opacity on your left eye pupil could mean a like thing happening to your heart. (*He sits on the cot.*)

WRITER: You have to protect your heart.

NIGHTINGALE: With a shell of calcium? Would that improve your work?

WRITER: You talk like you have a fever, I . . .

NIGHTINGALE: I have a fever you'd be lucky to catch, a fever to hold and be held! (*He throws off his tattered silk robe.*) Hold me! Please, please hold me.

WRITER: I'm afraid I'm tired, I need to sleep and . . . I don't want to catch your cold.

(*Slowly with dignity, Nightingale rises from the cot and puts his silk robe on.*)

NIGHTINGALE: And I don't want to catch yours, which is a cold in the heart, that's a hell of a lot more fatal to a boy with literary pretensions.

(*This releases in the writer a cold rage which he has never felt before. He springs up and glares at Nightingale, who is coughing.*)

WRITER (*in a voice quick and hard as a knife*): I think there has been some deterioration in your condition and you ought to face it! A man has got to face everything sometime and call it by its true name, not to try to escape it by—cowardly!—evasion—go have your lungs x-rayed and don't receive the doctor's bill when it's sent! But go there quick, have the disease stated clearly! Don't, don't call it a cold anymore or a touch of the flu!

NIGHTINGALE (*turning with a gasp*): You've gone mad, you've gone out of your mind here, you little one-eyed bitch! (*He coughs again and staggers out of the light.*)

MRS. WIRE'S VOICE: I heard you from the kitchen, boy! Was he molesting you in here? I heard him. Was he molesting you in here? Speak up! You watch out, I'll get the goods on you yet!

NIGHTINGALE'S VOICE: The persecution continues.

SCENE SIX

Daylight appears in the alcove window—daylight tinged with rain. The room of Jane and Tye is lighted. Tye is sprawled, apparently sleeping, in shorts on the studio bed. Jane has just completed a fashion design. She stares at it with disgust, then crumples it and throws it to the floor with a sob of frustration.

JANE: Yes? Who's there?

WRITER: Uh, me, from across the hall, I brought in a letter for you—it was getting rained on.

JANE: Oh, one moment, please. (*She throws a robe over her panties and bra and opens the door.*) A letter for me?

WRITER: The mail gets wet when it rains since the lid's come off the mailbox.

(*His look irresistibly takes in the figure of Tye. Jane tears the letter open and gasps softly. She looks slowly up, with a stunned expression, at the young writer.*)

JANE: Would you care for some coffee?

WRITER: Thanks, no, I just take it in the morning.

JANE: Then please have a drink with me. I need a drink. Please, please come in. (*Jane is speaking hysterically but abruptly controls it.*) Excuse me—would you pour the drinks—I can't. I . . .

WRITER (*crossing to the cabinet*): Will you have . . .

JANE: Bourbon. Three fingers.

WRITER: With?

JANE: Nothing, nothing.

(*The writer glances again at Tye as he pours the bourbon.*)

Nothing . . . (*The writer crosses to her with the drink.*) Nothing. And you?

WRITER: Nothing, thanks. I have to retype the manuscripts soaked in the rain.

JANE: *Manuscripts*, you said? Oh, yes, you're a writer. I knew, it just slipped my mind. The manuscripts were returned? Does that mean rejection? —Rejection is always so painful.

WRITER (*with shy pride*): This time instead of a printed slip there was this personal signed note . . .

JANE: Encouraging—that. Oh, my glass is weeping—an Italian expression. Would you play barman again? Please? (*She doesn't know where to put the letter, which he keeps glancing at.*)

WRITER: Yes, I am encouraged. He says, "This one doesn't quite make it but try us again." *Story* magazine—they print William Saroyan, you know!

JANE: It takes a good while to get established in a creative field.

WRITER: And meanwhile you've got to survive.

JANE: I was lucky, but the luck didn't hold. (*She is taking little sips of the straight bourbon.*)

WRITER: You're—upset by that—letter? I noticed it came from—isn't Ochsner's a clinic?

JANE: Yes, actually. I am, I was. It concerns a relative rather—critically ill there.

WRITER: Someone close to you?

JANE: Yes. Quite close, although lately I hardly recognize the lady at all anymore . . .

(*Tye stirs on the bed; the writer irresistibly glances at him.*)

Pull the sheet over him. I think he unconsciously displays himself like that as if posing for a painter of sensual inclinations. Wasted on me. I just illustrate fashions for ladies.

TYE (*stirring*): Beret? Beret?

(*The writer starts off, pausing at the edge of the light.*)

WRITER: Jane, what was the letter, wasn't it about you?

JANE: Let's just say it was a sort of a personal, signed rejection slip, too.

(*The writer exits with a backward glance.*)

TYE: Where's Beret, where's the goddam cat?

(*Jane is fiercely tearing the letter to bits. The lights dim out.*)

SCENE SEVEN

A dim light comes up on the writer, stage front, as narrator.

WRITER: The basement of the building had been leased by Mrs. Wire to a fashionable youngish photographer, one T. Hamilton Biggs, a very effete man he was, who had somehow acquired a perfect Oxford accent in Baton Rouge, Louisiana. He made a good living in New Orleans out of artfully lighted photos of debutantes and society matrons in the Garden District, but for his personal amusement—he also photographed, more realistically, some of the many young drifters to be found along the streets of the Vieux Carré.

(*The lights go up on the kitchen. Mrs. Wire is seen at the stove, which bears steaming pots of water.*)

MRS. WIRE (*to the writer*): Aw, it's you sneakin' in at two A.M. like a thief.

WRITER: Yes, uh, good night.

MRS. WIRE: Hold on, don't go up yet. He's at it again down there, he's throwin' one of his orgies, and this'll be the last one he throws down there. By God an' by Jesus, the society folk in this city may tolerate vice but not me. Take one of them pots off the stove.

WRITER: You're, uh . . . cooking at this hour?

MRS. WIRE: Not cooking . . . I'm boiling water! I take this pot and you take the other one, we'll pour this water through the hole in this kitchen floor, which is directly over that studio of his!

WRITER: Mrs. Wire, I can't be involved in . . .

MRS. WIRE: Boy, you're employed by me, you're fed and housed here, and you do like I tell you or you'll go on the street. (*She lifts a great kettle off the stove.*) Take that pot off the stove! (*She empties the steaming water on the floor. Almost instant screams are heard below.*) Hahh, down there, what's the disturbance over?!

WRITER: Mrs. Wire, that man has taken out a peace warrant against you, you know that.

MRS. WIRE: Git out of my way, you shifty-eyed little— (*With demonical energy she seizes the other pot and empties it onto the floor, and the screams continue. She looks and runs to the proscenium as if peering out a window.*) Two of 'em run out naked. Got two of you, I'm not done with you yet! . . . you perverts!

WRITER: Mrs. Wire, he'll call the police.

MRS. WIRE: Let him, just let him, my nephew is a lieutenant on the police force! But these Quarter police, why anybody can buy 'em, and that Biggs, he's got big money. Best we be quiet, sit tight. Act real casual-like. If they git in that door, you seen a, you seen a—

WRITER: What?

MRS. WIRE: A drunk spillin' water in here.

WRITER: . . . that much water?

MRS. WIRE: *Hush up!* One contradictory word out of you and I'll brain you with this saucepan here.

(*Nightingale enters in his robe.*)

NIGHTINGALE: May I inquire what this bedlam is about? (*He pants for breath.*) I had just finally managed to . . . (*He gasps.*) This hellish disturbance . . .

MRS. WIRE: May you inquire, yeah, you may inquire. Look. Here's the story! You're in a doped-up condition. Drunk and doped-up you staggered against the stove and accidentally knocked a kettle of boiling water off it. Now that's the story you'll tell in payment of back rent and your habits! . . . disgracing my house!

NIGHTINGALE (*to writer*): *What* is she talking about?

MRS. WIRE: And *you . . . one eye*! (*She turns to the writer.*) You say you witnesses it, you back up the story, you heah?

WRITER (*grinning*): Mrs. Wire, the story wouldn't . . . hold water.

MRS. WIRE: I said accidental. In his condition who'd doubt it?

NIGHTINGALE: Hoo, hoo, hoo!

MRS. WIRE: That night court buzzard on the bench, he'd throw the book at me for no reason but the fight that I've put up against the corruption and evil that this Quarter is built on! All I'm asking is . . .

(*Abruptly Miss Carrie and Mary Maude in outrageous negligees burst into the kitchen. At the sight of them, Mrs. Wire starts to scream wordlessly as a peacock at a pitch that stuns the writer but not Nightingale and the crones. Just as abruptly she falls silent and flops into a chair.*)

MISS CARRIE: Oh, Mrs. Wire!

MARY MAUDE: We thought the house had caught fire!

NIGHTINGALE (*loftily*): . . . What a remarkable . . . *tableau vivant* . . . The paddy wagon's approaching. Means night court, you know.

WRITER: . . . I think I'll . . . go to bed now . . .

MRS. WIRE: Like shoot you will!

(*Jane appears, stage right, in a robe. She speaks to the writer, who is nearest to her.*)

JANE: Can you tell me what is going on down here?

WRITER: Miss Sparks, why don't you stay in your room right now?

JANE: Why?

WRITER: There's been a terrible incident down here, I think the police are coming.

(*Mary Maude screams, wringing her hands.*)

MARY MAUDE: Police!

MISS CARRIE: Oh, Mary Maude, this is not time for hysterics. You're not involved, nor am I! We simply came in to see what the disturbance was about.

JANE (*to the writer*): Was Tye here? Was Tye involved in this . . .

WRITER (*in a low voice to Jane*): Nobody was involved but Mrs. Wire. She poured boiling water through a hole in the floor.

MRS. WIRE (*like a field marshal*): Everybody in here stay here and sit tight till the facts are reported.

(*Nursie enters with black majesty. She is humming a church hymn softly, "He walks with me and he talks with me." She remains at the edge of the action, calm as if unaware.*)

I meant ev'ry goddam one of you except Nursie. Nursie! Don't stand there singin' gospel, barefoot, in that old dirty nightgown!

WRITER (*to Jane*): She wants us to support a totally false story.

MRS. WIRE: I tell you—the Vieux Carré is the new Babylon destroyed by evil in Scriptures!!

JANE: It's like a dream . . .

NIGHTINGALE: The photographer downstairs belongs to the Chateau family, one of the finest and most important families in the Garden District.

MRS. WIRE: Oh, do you write the social register now?

NIGHTINGALE: I know he is New Orleans's most prominent society photographer!

MRS. WIRE: I know he's the city's most notorious *per*vert and is occupying space in my building!

MISS CARRIE: Mary Maude and I can't afford the notoriety of a thing like this.

(*Mary Maud cries out and leans against the table.*)

MARY MAUDE: Mrs. Wire, Miss Carrie and I have—positions to maintain!

JANE: Mrs. Wire, surely there's no need for these ladies to be involved in this.

MRS. WIRE: Deadbeats, all, all! Will stay right here and—

JANE: Do what?

MRS. WIRE: —testify to what happened!

NIGHTINGALE: She wishes you all to corroborate her lie! That I, that I! Oh, yes, I'm appointed to assume responsibility for—

PHOTOGRAPHER (*off stage*): Right up there! Burns like this could disfigure me for life!

(*Mrs. Wire rushes to slam and bolt the door.*)

MISS CARRIE (*to Mary Maude*): Honey? Can you move now?

MRS. WIRE: No, she cain't, she stays—which applies to you all!

PHOTOGRAPHER: The fact that she is insane and allowed to remain at large . . . doesn't excuse it.

(*A patrolman bangs at the door.*)

MRS. WIRE: Shh! Nobody make a sound!

PHOTOGRAPHER: Not only she but her tenants; why, the place is a psycho ward.

(*More banging is heard.*)

MRS. WIRE: What's this banging about?

PATROLMAN: Open this door.

PHOTOGRAPHER: One of my guests was the nephew of the District Attorney!

PATROLMAN: Open or I'll force it.

PHOTOGRAPHER: Break it in! Kick it open!

MRS. WIRE (*galvanized*): You ain't comin' in here, you got no warrant to enter, you filthy—morphodite, you!

WRITER: Mrs. Wire, you said not to make a sound.

MRS. WIRE: Make no sound when they're breakin' in my house, you one-eye Jack? (*The banging continues.*) What's the meaning of this, wakin' me up at two A.M. in the mawnin'?

PHOTOGRAPHER: Scalded! Five guests, including two art models!

MRS. WIRE (*overlapping*): You broken the terms of your lease, and it's now broke. I rented you that downstair space for legitimate business, you turned it into a—continual awgy!

PATROLMAN: Open that door, ma'am, people have been seriously injured.

MRS. WIRE: That's no concern of mine! I open no door till I phone my nephew, a lieutenant on the police force, Jim Flynn, who knows the situation I've put up with here, and then we'll see who calls the law on who!

WRITER: I hear more police sirens comin'.

(*The pounding and shouting continue. A patrolman forces entry, followed by another. All during the bit just preceding, Miss Carie and Mary Maude have clung together, their terrified whispers maintaining a low-pitched threnody to the shouting and banging. Now as the two patrolmen enter, their hysteria erupts in shrill screams. The screams are so intense that the patrolmen's attention is directed upon them.*)

PATROLMAN I: Christ! Is this a fuckin' madhouse?

(*Still clinging together, the emaciated crones sink to their knees as if at the feet of an implacable deity.*)

MRS. WIRE (*inspired*): Officers, remove these demented, old horrors. Why, you know what they done? Poured water on the floor of my kitchen, boiling water!

NIGHTINGALE: She's lying. These unfortunate old ladies just came in, they thought the house was on fire.

PHOTOGRAPHER: This woman is the notorious Mrs. Wire, and it was she who screamed out the window. Why, these old women should be hospitalized, naturally, but it's her, her! (*He points at Mrs. Wire from the door.*) that poured the scalding water into my studio, and screamed with delight when my art models and guests ran naked into the street!

MRS. WIRE: There, now, AWGY CONFESSED!!

PATROLMAN I: All out to the wagon!

(*The scene is dimmed out fast. A spot comes up on the writer in the witness box at night court.*)

OLD JUDGE'S VOICE: Let's not have no more beatin' aroun' the bush in this court, young fellow. The question is plain. You're under oath to give an honest answer. Now for the last time, at risk of being held in contempt of court, "Did you or did you not see the proprietor of the rooming house . . ."

MRS. WIRE'S VOICE (*shrilly*): Restaurant and roomin' house respectfully run!

(*The judge pounds his gavel.*)

OLD JUDGE'S VOICE: Defendant will keep silent during the witness' testimony. To repeat the question: "Did you or did you not see this lady here pour boiling water through the floor of her kitchen down into the studio of Mr. T. Hamilton Biggs?"

WRITER (*swallows, then in a low voice*): I, uh . . . think it's unlikely . . . a lady would do such a thing.

OLD JUDGE'S VOICE: Speak up so I can heah you! What's that you said?

WRITER: . . . I said I thought it very unlikely a lady would do such a thing.

(*Laughter is heard in the night court. The judge gavels, then pronounces the verdict.*)

OLD JUDGE'S VOICE: This court finds the defendant, Mrs. Hortense Wire, guilty as charged and imposes a fine of fifty dollars plus damages and releases her on probation in the custody of her nephew, Police Lieutenant James Flynn of New Orleans Parish, for a period of . . .

(*His voice fades out as does the scene. A spotlight comes up on Mrs. Wire in a flannel robe, drinking at the kitchen table. The writer appears hesitantly at the edge of the kitchen light.*)

MRS. WIRE (*without turning*): I know you're standing there, but I don't wanta see you. It sure does surprise me that you'd dare to enter this house again after double-crossing me in court tonight.

WRITER: —I—just came back to pick up my things.

MRS. WIRE: You ain't gonna remove nothing from this place till you paid off what you owe me.

WRITER: You know I'm—destitute.

MRS. WIRE: You get tips from the customers.

WRITER: Nickels and dimes. (*Pause. The sound of rain is heard.*) —Mrs. Wire? (*She turns slowly to look at him.*) Do you think I really intended to lose you that case? Other witnesses had testified I was in the kitchen when you poured those kettles of water through the floor. And the judge knew I could see with at least one eye. I was on the witness stand under oath, couldn't perjure myself. I did try not to answer directly. I *didn't* answer directly. All I said was—

MRS. WIRE: You said what lost me the case, goddam it! Did you expect that old buzzard on the bench to mistake me for a lady, my hair in curlers, me wearin' the late, long ago Mr. Wire's old ragged bathrobe. Shoot! All of you witnesses betrayed me in night court because you live off me an' can't forgive me for it.

WRITER: —I guess you want me to go . . .

MRS. WIRE: To where would you go? How far could you get on your nickels and dimes? You're shiverin' like a wet dog. Set down. Have a drink with me befo' you go up to bed.

WRITER: You mean I can stay? (*She nods slightly. He sits down at the kitchen table, she pours him a drink.*) I don't think I ever saw you drink before, Mrs. Wire.

MRS. WIRE: I only touch this bottle, which also belonged to the late Mr. Wire, before he descended to hell between two crooked lawyers, I touch it only when forced to by such a shocking experience as I had tonight, the discovery that I was completely alone in the world, a solitary ole woman cared for by no one. You know, I heard some doctor say on the radio that people die of loneliness, specially at my age. They do. Die of it, it kills 'em. Oh, that's not the cause that's put on the death warrant, but that's the *true* cause. I tell you, there's so much loneliness in this house that you can hear it. Set still and you can hear it: a sort of awful—soft—groaning in all the walls.

WRITER: All I hear is rain on the roof.

MRS. WIRE: You're still too young to hear it, but I hear it and I feel it, too, like a—ache in ev'ry bone of my body. It makes me want to scream, but I got to keep still. A landlady ain't permitted to scream. It would disturb the tenants. But some time I will, I'll scream, I'll scream loud enough to bring the roof down on us all.

WRITER: This house is full of people?

MRS. WIRE: People I let rooms to. Less than strangers to me.

WRITER: There's—me. I'm not.

MRS. WIRE: You—just endure my company 'cause you're employed here, boy.

WRITER: Miss Sparks isn't employed here.

MRS. WIRE: That woman is close to no one but the bum she keeps here. I'll show you. (*She rises and knocks her chair over, then bawls out as if to Tye.*) More boxes! Take 'em out an' stay out with 'em, sleep it off on the streets!

(*Jane rises in her dim spot of light. She crosses to the door.*)

JANE (*offstage*): Tye! Tye! I thought I heard Tye down there.

MRS. WIRE: Miss Sparks—don't you know that bum don't quit work till daybreak and rarely shows here before noon?

JANE: Sorry. Excuse me.

WRITER (*his speech slurred by drink*): God, but I was ignorant when I came here! This place has been a— I ought to pay you—tuition . . .

MRS. WIRE: One drink has made you drunk, boy. Go up to bed. We're goin' on tomorrow like nothing happened. (*He rises and crosses unsteadily from the kitchen light.*) Be careful on the steps.

WRITER (*pausing to look back at her*): Good night, Mrs. Wire. (*He disappears.*)

MRS. WIRE: —It's true, people die of it . . .

(*On the hall stairs the writer meets Nightingale, who speaks before the writer enters his own cubicle.*)

NIGHTINGALE (*imitating the writer's testimony in night court*): "I, uh, think it's unlikely a lady would do such a thing." (*He coughs.*) —A statement belonging in a glossary of deathless quotations. (*He coughs again.*) —Completely convinced me you really do have a future in the—literary—profession.

(*The light builds on Mrs. Wire, and she rises from the kitchen table and utters a piercing cry. Nursie appears.*)

NURSIE: Mizz Wire, what on earth is it? A bat?

MRS. WIRE: I just felt like screaming, and so I screamed! That's all . . .

(*The lights dim out.*)

Interval

PART TWO

SCENE EIGHT

A spotlight focuses on the writer working at his dilapidated typewriter in his gabled room in the attic.

WRITER: Instinct, it must have been (*He starts typing.*) directed me here, to the Vieux Carré of New Orleans, down country as a—river flows no plan. I couldn't have consciously, deliberately, selected a better place than here to discover—to encounter—my true nature. *Exposition! Shit!*

(*He springs up and kicks at the worn, wobbly table. A lean, gangling young man, whose charming but irresponsible nature is apparent in his genial grin, appears at the entrance of the writer's cubicle.*)

SKY: Having trouble?

WRITER: Even the typewriter objected to those goddamn lines. The ribbon stuck, won't reverse.

SKY: Let me look at it. (*He enters the cubicle.*) Oh, my name is Schuyler but they call me Sky.

WRITER: The owner of the knapsack with "SKY" printed on it, that was—that was deposited here last winter sometime?

SKY (*working on the typewriter*): Right. Landlady won't surrender it to me for less than twenty-five bucks, which is more than I can pay. Yeah, you see—I'm a fugitive from—from legal wedlock in Tampa, Florida, with the prettiest little bitsy piece of it you ever did see. There, now, the ribbon's reversing, it slipped out of the slots like I slipped out of matrimony in Tampa—couldn't you see that?

WRITER: I don't think there's a room in this building where you could be certain it was night or day, and I've . . .
SKY: Something wrong with that eye.
WRITER: Operation. For a cataract. Just waiting till it heals.—Are you staying here?
SKY: Just for a day or two while I look into spots for a jazz musician in the Quarter.
WRITER: There's several jazz combos just around the corner on Bourbon Street.
SKY: Yeah, I know, but they're black and not anxious to work with a honky. So, I'll probably drive on West.
WRITER: How far West?
SKY: The Coast. Is there a toilet up here? I gotta piss. Downstairs john's occupied.
WRITER: I know a girl across the hall with a bathroom, but she's probably sleeping.
SKY: With the angels wetting the roof, would it matter if I did, too?
WRITER: Go ahead.

(*Sky leaps onto the alcove and pisses upstage out of the window.*)

Why'd you decide not to marry?
SKY: Suddenly realized I wasn't ready to settle. The girl, she had a passion for pink, but she extended it out of bounds in the love nest she'd picked out for us. Pink, pink, pink. So I cut out before daybreak.
WRITER: Without a word to the girl?
SKY: A note, "Not ready. Be back." Wonder if she believed it, or if I did. That was Christmas week. I asked permission to leave my knapsack here with the landlady, overnight. She said, "For fifty cents." Extortionary, but I accepted the deal. However was unavoidably detained like they say. Returned last night for my gear and goddam, this landlady here refuses to surrender it to me except for twenty-five bucks. Crazy witch!

(*Mrs. Wire is at the cubicle entrance.*)

MRS. WIRE: What's he doin' up there?
SKY: Admiring the view.

MRS. WIRE: You was urinating out of the window! Jailbird! You ain't been in a hospital four months, you been in the House of Detention for resistin' arrest and assaultin' an officer of the law. I know. You admire the view in the bathroom. I don't allow no trashy behavior here. (*She turns to the writer.*) Why ain't you on the streets with those business cards?

WRITER: Because I'm at the last paragraph of a story.

MRS. WIRE: Knock it off this minute! Why, the streets are swarming this Sunday with the Azalea Festival trade.

WRITER: The time I give to "Meals for a Quarter in the Quarter" has begun to exceed the time originally agreed on, Mrs. Wire.

MRS. WIRE: It's decent, healthy work that can keep you off bad habits, bad company that I know you been drifting into.

WRITER: How would you know anything outside of this moldy, old—

MRS. WIRE: Don't talk that way about this—*historical* old building. Why, 722 Toulouse Street is one of the oldest buildings in the Vieux Carré, and the courtyard, why, that courtyard out there is on the tourist list of attractions!

WRITER: The tourists don't hear you shoutin' orders and insults to your, your—prisoners here!

MRS. WIRE: Two worthless dependents on me, that pair of scavenger crones that creep about after dark.

(*Nightingale coughs in his cubicle. Mrs. Wire raises her voice.*)

And I got that TB case spitting contagion wherever he goes, leaves a track of blood behind him like a chicken that's had it's head chopped off.

NIGHTINGALE: 'sa goddam libelous lie!

MRS. WIRE (*crossing to the entrance of the adjoining cubicle*): Been discharged from the Two Parrots, they told you to fold up your easel and git out!

NIGHTINGALE (*hoarsely*): I'm making notes on these lies, and my friend, the writer, is witness to them!

MRS. WIRE: You is been discharged from the Two Parrots. It's God's truth, I got it from the cashier!

(*Sky chuckles, fascinated. He sits on the edge of the table or cot, taking a cigarette and offering one to the writer. Their casual friendly talk is contrapuntal to the violent altercation in progress outside.*)

She told me they had to scrub the pavement around your easel with a bucket of lye each night, that customers had left without payin' because you'd hawked an' spit by their tables!

NIGHTINGALE: Bucket of lies, not lye, that's what she told you!

MRS. WIRE: They only kept you there out of human pity!

NIGHTINGALE: Pity!

MRS. WIRE: Yais, pity! But finally pity and patience was exhausted, it run out there and it's run out here! Unlock that door! NURSIE!

NURSIE (*off stage*): Now what?

MRS. WIRE: Bring up my keys! Mr. Nightingale's locked himself in! You're gonna find you'self mighty quicker than you expected in a charity ward on your way to a pauper's grave!

WRITER: Mrs. Wire, be easy on him . . .

MRS. WIRE: You ain't heard what he calls me? Why, things he's said to me I hate to repeat. He's called me a fuckin' ole witch, yes, because I stop him from bringin' pickups in here at midnight that might stick a knife in the heart of anyone in the buildin' after they done it to him.

NIGHTINGALE (*in a wheezing voice as he drops onto the cot in his cubicle*): It's you that'll get a knife stuck in you, between your—dried up old—dugs . . .

WRITER (sotto voce, *near tears*): Be easy on him, he's dying.

MRS. WIRE: Not here. He's defamed this place as infested with bedbugs to try to explain away the blood he coughs on his pillow.

WRITER: That's—his last defense against—

MRS. WIRE: The truth, there's no defense against truth. Ev'rything in that room is contaminated, has got to be removed to the incinerator an' burned. Start with the mattress, Nursie!

(*Nursie has entered the lighted area with a bunch of musty keys.*)

NIGHTINGALE: I warn you, if you attempt to enter my room, I'll strike you down with this easel!

MRS. WIRE: You do that, just try, the effort of the exertion would finish you right here! Oh, shoot, here's the master key, opens all doors!

NIGHTINGALE: At your own risk— I'll brain you, you bitch.

MRS. WIRE: Go on in there, Nursie!

NURSIE: Aw, no, not me! I told you I would never go in that room!

MRS. WIRE: We're coming in!

NIGHTINGALE: WATCH OUT!

(*He is backed into the alcove, the easel held over his head like a crucifix to exorcise a demon. A spasm of coughing wracks him. He bends double, dropping the easel, collapses to his knees, and then falls flat upon the floor.*)

NURSIE (*awed*): Is he daid, Mizz Wire?

MRS. WIRE: Don't touch him. Leave him there until the coroner gets here.

NIGHTINGALE (*gasping*): Coroner, your ass—I'll outlive you.

MRS. WIRE: If I dropped dead this second! Nursie, haul out that filthy mattress of his, pour kerosene on it.

NURSIE: Wouldn't touch that mattress with a pole . . .

MRS. WIRE: And burn it. Git a nigger to help you haul everything in here out, it's all contaminated. Why, this whole place could be quarantined!

NURSIE: Furniture?

MRS. WIRE: All! Then wash off your hands in alcohol to prevent infection, Nursie.

NURSIE: Mizz Wire, the courtyard is full of them Azalea Festival ladies that paid admission to enter! You want me to smoke 'em out?

MRS. WIRE: Collect the stuff you can move.

NURSIE: Move where?

MRS. WIRE: Pile it under the banana tree in the courtyard, cover it with tarpaulin, we can burn it later.

NIGHTINGALE: If anyone lays a hand on my personal effects, I'll (*His voice chokes with sobs.*) —I will be back in the Two Parrots tonight. I wasn't fired. I was given a leave of absence till I recovered from . . . asthma . . .

MRS. WIRE (*with an abrupt compassion*): Mr. Nightingale.

NIGHTINGALE: Rossignol!—of the Baton Rouge Rossignols, as any dog could tell you . . .

MRS. WIRE: I won't consult a dawg on this subject. However, the place for you is not here but in the charity ward at St. Vincent's. Rest there till I've made arrangements to remove you.

SKY: The altercation's subsided.

WRITER (*to Sky, who has begun to play his clarinet*): What kind of horn is that?

(*Mrs. Wire appears at the entrance to the writer's cubicle. Sky plays entrance music—"Ta-ta-taaaa!"*)

SKY: It's not a horn, kid, horns are brass. A clarinet's a woodwind instrument, not a horn.

MRS. WIRE: Yais, now about you all.

SKY: Never mind about us. We're leaving for the West Coast.

(*Mrs. Wire and the writer are equally stunned in opposite ways.*)

MRS. WIRE: —What's he mean, son? You're leavin' with this jailbird?

WRITER: —I—

MRS. WIRE: You won't if I can prevent it, and I know how. In my register book, when you signed in here, you wrote St. Louis. We got your home address, street and number. I'm gonna inform your folks of the vicious ways and companions you been slipping into. They's a shockin' diff'rence between your looks an' manners since when you arrived here an' now, mockin' me with that grin an' that shifty-eyed indifference, evidence you're setting out on a future life of corruption. Address and phone number, I'll write, I'll phone! —You're not leavin' here with a piece of trash *like* that that pissed out the window! —Son, son, don't do it! (*She covers her face, unraveled with emotion. Exchanging a look with Sky, the writer places an arm gingerly about her shoulder.*) You know I've sort of adopted you like the son took away from me by the late Mr. Wire and a—and a crooked lawyer, they got me declared to be—mentally incompetent.

WRITER: Mrs. Wire, I didn't escape from one mother to look for another.

(*Nursie returns, huffing, to the lighted area.*)

NURSIE: Mizz Wire, those tourists ladies, I can't control them, they're pickin' the azaleas off the bushes, and—

MRS. WIRE: That's what I told you to stay in the courtyard to stop.

NURSIE: Oh, I try, but one of 'em jus' called me a impudent ole nigger, and I won't take it. I come here to tell you I QUIT!

MRS. WIRE: AGAIN! COME BACK OUT THERE WITH ME! (*She turns to the writer.*) We'll continue this later. (*She exits with Nursie.*)

WRITER (*to Sky*): —Were you serious about the West Coast offer?

SKY: You're welcome to come along with me. I don't like to travel a long distance like that by myself.

WRITER: How do you travel?

SKY: I've got a beat-up old '32 Ford across the street with a little oil and about half a tank of gas in it. If you want to go, we could share the expense. Have you got any cash?

WRITER: I guess I've accumulated a capital of about thirty-five dollars.

SKY: We'll siphon gas on the way.

WRITER: Siphon?

SKY: I travel with a little rubber tube, and at night I unscrew the top of somebody's gas tank and suck the gas out through the tube and spit it into a bucket and empty it into my car. Is it a deal?

WRITER (*with suppressed excitement*): How would we live on the road?

SKY (*rolling a cigarette with obvious practice*): We'd have to exercise our wits. And our personal charm. And, well, if that don't suffice, I have a blanket in the car, and there's plenty of wide open spaces between here and the Coast. (*He pauses for a beat.*) Scared? Of the undertaking?

WRITER (*smiling slowly*): No—the Coast—starting when?

SKY: Why not this evening? The landlady won't admit me to the house again, but I'll call you. Just keep your window open. I'll blow my clarinet in the courtyard. Let's say about six.

(*The conversation may continue in undertones as the area is dimmed out.*)

SCENE NINE

The lights come up on Jane's studio area. The shuttered doors to the windows overlooking the courtyard below are ajar. Jane is trying to rouse Tye from an unnaturally deep sleep. It is evident that she has been engaged in packing her effects and his.

JANE: Tye, Tye, oh—Christ . . .

(*He drops a bare arm off the disordered bed and moans slightly. She bends over to examine a needle mark on his arm.*)

TYE: —Wh—?

(*Jane crosses to the sink and wets a towel, then returns to slap Tye's face with it. He begins to wake slowly.*)

Some men would beat a chick up for less'n that, y'know.

JANE: All right, get out of bed and beat me up, but get *up*.

TYE (*stroking a promontory beneath the bed sheet*): —Can't you see I *am* up?

JANE: I don't mean that kind of up, and don't bring strip show lewdness in here this—Sunday afternoon.

TYE: Babe, don't mention the show to me t'day.

JANE: I'd like to remind you that when we first stumbled into this—crazy—co-habitation, you promised me you'd quit the show in a week.

TYE: For what? Tight as work is for a dude with five grades of school and no skill training from the Mississippi sticks?

JANE: You could find something less—publicly embarrassing, like a—filling station attendant.

TYE: Ha!

JANE: But of course your choice of employment is no concern of mine now.

TYE: Why not, Babe?

JANE: I'm not "Babe" and not "Chick"!

TYE: You say you're not my chick?

JANE: I say I'm nobody's chick.

TYE: Any chick who shacks with me's my chick.

JANE: This is my place. You just—moved in and stayed.

TYE: I paid the rent this month.

JANE: Half of it, for the first time, my savings being as close to exhaustion as me.

(*There is the sound of a funky piano and a voice on the Bourbon Street corner: "I've stayed around and played around this old town too long." Jane's mood softens under its influence.*)

Lord, I don't know how I managed to haul you to bed.

TYE: Hey, you put me to bed last night?

JANE: It was much too much exertion for someone in my—condition.

TYE (*focusing on her more closely*): —Honey, are you pregnant?

JANE: No, Lord, now who'd be fool enough to get pregnant by a Bourbon Street strip show barker?

TYE: When a chick talks about her condition, don't it mean she's pregnant?

JANE: All female conditions are not pregnancy, Tye. (*She staggers, then finishes her coffee.*) Mine is that of a desperate young woman living with a young bum employed by gangsters and using her place as a depository for hot merchandise. Well, they're all packed. You're packed too.

TYE: —Come to bed.

JANE: No, thank you. Your face is smeared with lipstick; also other parts of you. I didn't know lip rouge ever covered so much—territory.

TYE: I honestly don't remember a fuckin' thing after midnight.

JANE: That I do believe. Now have some coffee, I've warmed it. It isn't instant, it's percolated.

TYE: Who's birthday is it?

JANE: It's percolated in honor of our day of parting.

TYE: Aw, be sweet, Babe, please come back to bed. I need comfort, not coffee.

JANE: You broke a promise to me.

TYE: Which?

JANE: Among the many? You used a needle last night. I saw the mark of it on you.

TYE: No shit. Where?

JANE (*returning to the bedside*): There, right there on your— (*He circles her with his arm and pulls her onto the bed.*) I've been betrayed by a—sensual streak in my nature. Susceptibility to touch. And you have skin like a child. I'd gladly support you if I believed you'd—if I had the means to and the time to. Time. Means. Luck. Things that expire, run out. And all at once you're stranded.

TYE: Jane you—lie down with me and hold me.

JANE: I'm afraid, Tye, we'll just have to hold each other in our memories from now on.

TYE (*childishly*): Don't talk that way. I never had a rougher night in my life. Do I have to think and remember?

JANE: Tye, we've had a long spell of dreaming, but now we suddenly have to.

TYE: Got any aspirin, Babe?

JANE: You're past aspirin, Tye. I think you've gone past all legal—analgesics.

TYE: You say words to me I've never heard before.

JANE: Tye, I've been forced to make an urgent phone call to someone I never wanted to call.

TYE: Call?

JANE: And then I packed your personal belongings and all that lot you've been holding here. Exertion of packing nearly blacked me out. Trembling, sweating—had to bathe and change.

TYE: Babe?

JANE: You're vacating the premises, "Babe." It's *afternoon.*

TYE: Look, if you're knocked up, have the kid. I'm against abortion.

JANE: On moral principles?

TYE: Have the kid, Babe. I'd pull myself together for a kid.

JANE: You didn't for me.

TYE: A baby would be a livin' thing between us, with both our blood.

JANE: Never mind.

(*Voices in the courtyard are heard.*)

NURSIE: Any donations t'keep the cou'tyard up, just drop it in my apron as you go out, ladies! . . .

JANE: Those tourists down there in the courtyard! If I'd known when I took this room it was over a tourist attraction—

TYE: It's the Festival, Babe. It ain't always Festival . . . Gimme my cigarettes, ought to be some left in a pocket.

JANE (*throwing his pants and a fancy sport shirt on the bed*): Here, your clothes, get in them.

TYE (*putting on his shorts*): Not yet. It's Sunday, Babe . . . Where's Beret? I like Beret to be here when I wake up.

JANE: Not even a cat will wait ten, twelve hours for you to sleep off whatever you shot last night. How did a girl well educated and reasonably well brought up get involved in this . . . Oh, I'm talking to myself.

TYE: I hear you, Babe, and I see you.

JANE: Then . . . get up and dressed.

TYE: It's not dark yet, Babe. Y'know I never get dressed till after dark on Sundays.

JANE: Today has to be an exception. I'm . . . expecting a caller, very important to me.

TYE: Fashion designer?

JANE: No. Buyer . . . to look at my illustrations. They're no good, I'm no good. I just had a flair, not a talent, and the flair flared out, I'm . . . finished. These sketches are evidence of it! (*She starts tearing fashion sketches off the wall.*) Look at me! Bangles, jangles! All taste gone! (*She tears off her costume jewelry.*)

TYE: Babe, you're in no shape to meet a buyer.

JANE (*slowly and bitterly*): He's no buyer of anything but me.

TYE: —Buyer of *you*? Look. You said that you were expecting a buyer to look at your drawin's here.

JANE: I know what I said, I said a buyer to look at my illustrations, but what I said was a lie. Among other things, many other undreamed of before, you've taught me to practice deception.

VOICES OFFSTAGE: Edwina, Edwina, come see this dream of a little courtyard. Oh, my, yaiss, like a dream.

JANE: I know what I said, but let's say, Tye, that I experienced last week a somewhat less than triumphant encounter with the buyer of fashion illustrations at *Vogue Moderne*. In fact, it left me too shattered to carry my portfolio home without a shot of Metaxas brandy at the Blue Lantern, which was on the street level of the building. It was there that I met a gentleman from Brazil. He had observed my entrance, the Brazilian, and apparently took me for a hooker, sprang up with surprising agility for a gentleman of his corpulence, hauled me to his table, and introduced me to his *camaradas*, "Señorita, this is Señor and Señor and Señor," declared me, *"Bonita muy, muy, bonita"*—tried to press a hundred-dollar bill in my hand. Well, some atavistic bit of propriety surfaced and I, like a fool, rejected it—but did accept his business card, just in case— This morning, Tye, I called him. "Senorita Bonita of the Blue Lantern awaits you, top floor of seven-two-two Toulouse," that was the invitation that I phoned in to the message desk— He must have received it by now at the Hotel Royal Orleans, where the Presidential Suite somehow contains him.

TYE: Who're you talkin' about?

JANE: My expected caller, a responsible businessman from Brazil. Sincerely interested in my bankrupt state . . .

TYE: Forget it, come back to bed and I'll undress you, Babe, you need rest.

JANE: The bed bit is finished between us. You're moving out today.

(*He slowly stumbles up, crosses to the table, and gulps coffee, then grasps her arm and draws her to bed.*)

No, no, no, no, no, no!

TYE: Yes, yes, yes, yes, yes!

(*He throws her onto the bed and starts to strip her; she resists; he prevails. As the lights very gradually dim, a Negro singer-pianist at a nearby bar fades in, "Fly a-way! Sweet Kentucky baby-bay, fly, away . . ."*)

MRS. WIRE (*from a few steps below the writer*): What's paralyzed you there? Son?

WRITER: Miss Sparks is crying.

(*Mrs. Wire appears behind the writer in the lighted spot.*)

MRS. WIRE: That woman's moanin' in there don't mean she's in pain. Son, I got a suspicion you never had close relations with wimmen in your life.

JANE: Ohhh!

WRITER: I never heard sounds like that.

(*Jane utters a wild cry. It impresses even Mrs. Wire.*)

TYE'S VOICE: Babe, I don't wanna force you . . .

JANE'S VOICE: Plee-ase! I'm not a thing, I'm not-a-thing!

MRS. WIRE (*shouting*): You all quit that loud fornication in there!

TYE'S VOICE (*shouting back*): Get the fuck downstairs, goddam ole witch!

MRS. WIRE: Howlin' insults at me in my own house, won't tolerate it! (*She bursts into the room.*) Never seen such a disgustin' exhibition!

(*Tye starts to rise from the bed. Jane clings desperately to him.*)

JANE: As! You see!—Mrs. Wire!—Everything is!—packed, he's—moving—today . . .

TYE: The rent is paid in full! So get the fuck outa here!

JANE: Tye, please.

MRS. WIRE: What's in them boxes?

TYE: None of your—

JANE: Our personal—belongings, Mrs. Wire.

MRS. WIRE: That I doubt! The contents of these boxes will be inspected before removed from this place and in the presence of my nephew on the police force!

(*Tye charges toward Mrs. Wire.*)

Don't you expose yourself naykid in my presence! Nursie!

JANE: Mrs. Wire, for once I do agree with you! Can you get him out, please, please get him out!

MRS. WIRE (*averting her face with an air of shocked propriety*): Dress at once and—

NURSIE: Mizz Wire, I got the hospital on the phone.

MRS. WIRE: They sendin' an ambulance for Nightingale?

NURSIE: Soon's they got a bed for him, but they want you to call 'em back and—

MRS. WIRE: St. Vincent's is run by taxpayers' money, I'll remind 'em of that. (*She crosses off stage. Tye slams the door.*)

(*Jane is sobbing on the bed.*)

TYE: Now, Babe.
JANE: If you approach this bed—
TYE: Just want to comfort you, honey. Can't we just rest together? Can't we? Rest and comfort each other?

(*The area dims as the black pianist sings "Kentucky Baby."*)

MRS. WIRE: Cut out that obscene talking up there, I'm on the phone. Emergency call is from here at 722 Toulouse. Christ Almighty, you drive me to profane language. You mean to admit you don't know the location of the most historical street in the Vieux Carré? You're not talking to no . . . no nobody, but a personage. Responsible. Reputable. Known to the authorities on the list of attractions. God damn it, you twist my tongue up with your . . . Nursie! Nursie! Will you talk to this incompetent . . . Nursie! Nursie!

(*Nursie appears.*)

Got some idiot on the phone at the hospital. Will you inform this idiot who I am in the Quarter. Phone. Talk.

(*Nursie takes the phone.*)

NURSIE: Stairs . . . took my breath . . .
MRS. WIRE (*snatching back the phone*): Now I want you to know, this here Nightingale case . . . I don't lack sympathy for the dying or the hopelessly inflicted . . . (*She kicks at Nursie beside here.*) Git! But I've got responsibilities to my tenants. Valuable paying tenants, distinguished society ladies, will quit my premises this day, I swear they will, if this Nightingale remains. Why, the State Board of Health will clap a suit on me unless . . . at once . . . ambulance. When? At what time? Don't say approximate to me. Emergency means immediate. Not when you drag your arse around to it. And just you remember I'm a taxpayer . . . No, no, you not me. I pay, you collect. Now get the ambulance here immediately, 722 Toulouse, with a stretcher

with straps, the Nightingale is violent with fever. (*She slams down the phone.*) Shit!

NURSIE: My guess is they're going to remove you, too.

(*Mrs. Wire leans on Nursie.*)

SCENE TEN

There is a spotlight on the writer, stage front, as narrator.

WRITER: That Sunday I served my last meal for a quarter in the Quarter, then I returned to the attic. From Nightingale's cage there was silence so complete I thought, "He's dead." Then he cried out softly—

NIGHTINGALE: Christ, how long do I have to go on like this?

WRITER: Then, for the first time, I returned his visits. (*He makes the gesture of knocking at Nightingale's door.*) —Mr. Rossignol . . .

(*There is a sound of staggering and wheezing. Nightingale opens the door; the writer catches him as he nearly falls and assists him back to his cot.*)

—You shouldn't try to dress.

NIGHTINGALE: Got to—escape! She wants to commit me to a charnel house on false charges . . .

WRITER: It's raining out.

NIGHTINGALE: A Rossignol will not be hauled away to a charity hospital.

WRITER: Let me call a private doctor. He wouldn't allow them to move you in your—condition . . .

NIGHTINGALE: My faith's in Christ—not doctors . . .

WRITER: Lie down.

NIGHTINGALE: Can't breathe lying—down . . .

WRITER: I've brought you this pillow. I'll put it back of your head. (*He places the pillow gently in back of Nightingale.*) Two plilows help you breathe.

NIGHTINGALE (*leaning weakly back*): Ah—thanks—better . . . Sit down.

(*A dim light comes up on the studio area as Tye lights a joint, sitting on the table.*)

WRITER: Theren' nowhere to sit.

NIGHTINGALE: You mean nowhere not contaminated? (*The writer sits.*) —*God's got to give me time for serious work!* Even God has moral obligations, don't He? —Well, *don't* He?

WRITER: I think that morals are a human invention that He ignores as successfully as we do.

NIGHTINGALE: Christ, that's evil, that is infidel talk. (*He crosses himself.*) I'm a Cath'lic believer. A priest would say that you have fallen from Grace, boy.

WRITER: What's that you're holding?

NIGHTINGALE: Articles left me by my sainted mother. Her tortoise-shell comb with a mother-of-pearl handle and her silver framed mirror.

(*He sits up with difficulty and starts combing his hair before the mirror as if preparing for a social appearance.*)

Precious heirlooms, been in the Rossignol family three generations. I look pale from confinement with asthma. Bottom of box is—toiletries, cosmetics—please!

WRITER: You're planning to make a public appearance, intending to go on the streets with this—advanced case of asthma?

NIGHTINGALE: Would you kindly hand me my Max Factor, my makeup kit?!

WRITER: I have a friend who wears cosmetics at night—they dissolve in the rain.

NIGHTINGALE: If necessary, I'll go into *Sanctuary*!

(*The writer utters a startled, helpless laugh; he shakes with it and leans against the stippled wall.*)

Joke, is it, is it a joke?! Foxes have holes, but the Son of Man hath nowhere to hide His head!

WRITER: Don't you know you're delirious with fever?

NIGHTINGALE: You used to be kind—gentle. In less than four months you've turned your back on that side of your nature, turned rock-hard as the world.

WRITER: I had to survive in the world. Now where's your pills for sleep, you need to rest.

NIGHTINGALE: On the chair by the bed.

(*Pause.*)

WRITER (*softly*): Maybe this time you ought to take more than one.

NIGHTINGALE: Why, you're suggesting suicide to me which is a cardinal sin, would put me in unhallowed ground in—potter's field. I believe in God the Father, God the Son, and God the Holy Ghost . . . you've turned into a killer?

WRITER (*compulsively, with difficulty*): Stop calling it asthma —the flu, a bad cold. Face the facts, deal with them. (*He opens the pillbox.*) Press tab to open, push down, unscrew the top. Here it is where you can reach it.

NIGHTINGALE: —Boy with soft skin and stone heart . . .

(*Pause. The writer blows the candle out and takes Nightingale's hand.*)

WRITER: Hear the rain, let the rain talk to you, I can't.

NIGHTINGALE: Light the candle.

WRITER: The candle's not necessary. You've got an alcove, too, with a window and bench. Keep your eyes on it, she might come in here before you fall asleep.

(*A strain of music is heard. The angel enters from her dark passage and seats herself, just visible faintly, on Nightingale's alcove bench.*)

Do you see her in the alcove?

NIGHTINGALE: Who?

WRITER: Do you feel a comforting presence?

NIGHTINGALE: None.

WRITER: Remember my mother's mother? Grand?

NIGHTINGALE: I don't receive apparitions. They're only seen by the mad.

(*The writer returns to his cubicle and continues as narrator.*)

WRITER: In my own cubicle, I wasn't sure if Grand had entered with me or not. I couldn't distinguish her from a— diffusion of light through the low running clouds. I thought I saw her, but her image was much fainter than it had ever been before, and I suspected that it would fade more and more as the storm of my father's blood obliterated the tenderness of Grand's. I began to pack my belongings. I was about to make a panicky departure to nowhere I could imagine . . . The West Coast? With Sky?

(*He is throwing things into a cardboard suitcase. Nursie appears at the edge of his light with a coffee tray.*)

NURSIE: Mizz Wire knows you're packin' to leave an' she tole me to bring you up this hot coffee and cold biscuits.

WRITER: Thank her. Thank you both.

NURSIE: She says don't make no mistakes.

WRITER (*harshly*): None, never?

NURSIE: None if you can help, and I agree with her about that. She's phoned your folks about you. They're coming down here tomorrow.

WRITER: If she's not bluffing . . .

NURSIE: She ain't bluffin', I heard her on the phone myself. Mizz Wire is gettin' you confused with her son Timmy. Her mind is slippin' again. Been through that before. Can't do it again.

WRITER: We all have our confusions . . . (*He gulps down the coffee as Nursie crosses out of the light.*)

NURSIE (*singing softly*): "My home is on Jordan."

WRITER: Then I started to write. I worked the longest I'd ever worked in my life, nearly all that Sunday. I wrote about Jane and Tye, I could hear them across the narrow hall. —Writers are shameless spies . . .

SCENE ELEVEN

The studio light builds. Jane is sobbing on the bed. Tye is rolling a joint, seated on the table. The clearing sky has faded toward early blue dusk. Tye regards Jane with a puzzled look. Faintly we hear the black singer-pianist. "Bye, bye, blues. Don't cry blues," etc.

TYE: Want a hit, Babe? (*She ignores the question.*) How long have I been asleep? Christ, what are you crying about. Didn't I just give you one helluva Sunday afternoon ball, and you're cryin' about it like your mother died.

JANE: You forced me, you little—pig, you did, you forced me.

TYE: You wanted it.

JANE: I didn't.

TYE: Sure you did. (*Jane is dressing again.*) Honey, you got shadows under your eyes.

JANE: Blackbirds kissed me last night. Isn't that what they say about shadows under the eyes, that blackbirds kissed her last night. The Brazilian must have been blind drunk when he took a fancy to me in the Blue Lantern, mistook me for a hundred-dollar girl. —Tye, I'm not a whore! I'm the Northern equivalent of a lady, fallen, yes, but a lady, not a whore.

TYE: Whores get paid for it, Babe. I never had to.

JANE: You little—prick—! Now I'm talkin' your jive, how do you like it? Does she talk like that when she's smearing you with lipstick, when you ball her, which I know you do, repeatedly, between shows.

TYE: —Who're you talkin' about?

JANE: That headliner at the strip show, the Champagne Girl.

TYE (*gravely*): She's—not with the show no more.

JANE: The headliner's quit the show?

TYE: Yeah, honey, the Champagne Girl is dead an' so she's not in the show.

JANE: You mean—not such a hot attraction any more?

TYE: Don't be funny about it, it ain't funny.

JANE: You mean she's actually—

TYE: Yes. Ackshally. Dead. Real dead, about as dead as dead, which is totally dead— So now you know why I needed a needle to get me through last night.

JANE: —Well, of course that's—

TYE: You was jealous of her . . . (*Jane looks away.*) I never touched the Champagne Girl. She was strictly the property of the Man. Nobody else dared t' touch her.

JANE: The Man—what man?

TYE: The Man—no other name known by— Well—he wasted her.

JANE: —Killed her?—Why?

TYE: Cause she quit sleeping with him. She was offered a deal on the West Coast, Babe. The Man said, "No." The Champagne Girl said, "Yes." So the Man . . . you don't say no to the Man—so if she's going to the West Coast it'll be packed in ice—

(*Voices are heard from the courtyard.*)

TOURIST 1: My slippers are wet through.

(*Piano music is heard.*)

TOUTIST 2: What's next on the tour, or is it nearly finished?

TYE: When the Man is annoyed by something, he piles his lupos in the back seat of his bulletproof limo and he let's 'em loose on the source of his annoyance.

JANE: —Lupos?

TYE: Lupos are those big black dawgs that're used for attack. The Man has three of 'em, and when he patrols his territory at night, they sit in the back seat of his Lincoln, set up there, mouths wide open on their dagger teeth and their black eyes rollin' like dice in a nigger crapshooter's hands. And night before last, Jesus! he let 'em into the Champagne Girl's apartment, and they—well, they ate her. Gnawed her tits off her ribs, gnawed her sweet little ass off. Of course the story is that the Champagne Girl entertained a pervert who killed her and ate her like that, but it's pretty well known it was them lupos that devoured that girl, under those ceiling mirrors and crystal chandeliers in her all white satin bedroom.—Yep—gone—the headliner— Y'know what you say when the Man wastes somebody? You got to say that he or she has "Gone to Spain." So they tole me last night, when people ask you where's the Champagne Girl, answer 'em that the Champagne Girl's gone to Spain. —Sweet kid from Pascagoula.

JANE: Please don't—continue—the story.

TYE: All champagne colored without face or body makeup on her, light gold like pale champagne and not a line, not a pore to be seen on her body! Was she meant for dawg food? I said, was she meant for dawg food? Those lupos ate that kid like she was their—last—supper . . .

JANE (*who has now managed to get round the table*): Tye, Tye, open the shutters!

TYE: Why? You goin' out naked?

JANE: I'm going to vomit and die—in clean air . . . (*She has moved slowly upstage to the gallery with its closed shutters, moving from one piece of furniture to another for support. Now she opens the shutter doors and staggers out onto the gallery, and the tourist ladies' voices are raised in thrilled shock and dismay.*)

TOURIST 1: Look at that!

TOURIST 2: What at?

TOURIST 1: There's a whore at the gallery window! Practically naked!

(*All gallery speeches should overlap.*)

JANE (*wildly*): Out, out, out, out, out!

NURSIE: Miss, Miss Sparks! These are Festival ladies who've paid admission.

JANE: Can't endure any more! Please, please, I'm sick!

TYE: Fawgit it, Babe, come back in.

JANE: It isn't real, it couldn't be—

(*The writer shakes his head with a sad smile.*)

But it was—it is . . . like a dream . . .

TYE: What did you say, Babe?

JANE: Close the gallery door—please?

TYE: Sure, Babe. (*He shuts the door on the voices below.*)

JANE: And—the hall door—bolt it. Why do you bring home nightmare stories to me?!

TYE (*gently*): Babe, you brought up the subject, you asked me about the Champagne Girl, I wasn't planning to tell you. Chair?

JANE: Bed.

TYE: Grass?

JANE: —Coffee.

TYE: Cold.

JANE: —Cold—coffee.

(*Tye pours her a cup and puts it in her trembling hand. He holds the hand and lifts the cup to her lips, standing behind her. He lets his hand fall to her breasts; she sobs and removes the hand.*

(*The singer-pianist is heard again.*)

JANE: . . . Why do you want to stay on here?

TYE: Here's where you are, Babe.

JANE (*shaking her head*): No more. I . . . have to dress . . . (*She dresses awkwardly, frantically. He watches in silence.*)

You have to get dressed, too. I told you I was expecting a very important visitor. Tye, the situation's turned impossible on us, face it.

TYE: You're not walkin' out on me.

JANE: Who have I got to appeal to except God, whose phone's disconnected, or this . . . providential . . . protector.

TYE: From the banana republic, a greaseball. And you'd quit me for that?

JANE: You've got to be mature and understanding. At least for once, now dress. The Brazilian is past due . . . I realized your defects, but you touched me like nobody else in my life had ever before or ever could again. But, Tye, I counted on you to grow up, and you refused to. I took you for someone gentle caught in violence and degradation that he'd escape from . . .

TYE: Whatever you took me for, I took you for honest, for decent, for . . .

JANE: Don't be so . . . "Decent"? You ridiculous little . . . sorry, no. Let's not go into . . . abuse . . . Tye? When we went into this it wasn't with any long-term thing in mind. That's him on the steps. Go in the bathroom quiet!

TYE: You go in the bathroom quiet. I'll explain without words.

(*She thrusts his clothes at him. He throws them savagely about the stage.*)

. . . Well?

(*There is a sound on the stairs.*)

Sounds like the footsteps of a responsible man.

(*Tye opens the door. We see hospital interns with a stretcher. Jane stares out. The interns pass again with Nightingale's dying body on the stretcher. The writer is with them. Jane gasps and covers her face with her arm. The writer turns to her.*)

WRITER: It's just—they're removing the painter.

JANE: —*Just!*

TYE: No Brazilian, no buyer?

JANE: No. No sale . . .

WRITER (*standing in the open doorway*): It was getting dim in the room.

TYE: It's almost getting dark.

WRITER: They didn't talk. He smoked his reefer. He looked at her steady in the room getting dark and said . . .

TYE: I see you clear.

WRITER: She turned her face away. He walked around that way and looked at her from that side. She turned her face the other way. She was crying without a sound, and a black man was playing piano at the Four Deuces round the corner, an oldie, right for the atmosphere . . . something like . . .

(*The piano fades in, "Seem like Old Times." Tye begins to sing softly with the piano.*)

JANE: *Don't.*

(*Tye stops the soft singing but continues to stare at Jane.*)

DON'T.

(*Pause.*)

TYE: Jane. You've gotten sort of—skinny. How much weight you lost?

JANE: I . . . don't know . . .

TYE: Sometimes you walk a block and can't go no further.

(*Pause.*)

JANE: I guess I'm a yellow-cab girl. With limousine aspirations.

TYE: Cut the smart talk, Babe. Let's level.

(*Pause. She extends her hand.*)

Want a hit? Well?

(*Jane nods and take a hit off his cigarette.*)

Huh?

JANE: Well, after all, why not, if you're interested in it. It hasn't been just lately I've lost weight and energy but for more than a year in New York. Some—blood thing—progressing rather fast at my age . . . I think I had a remission when I met you.

A definite remission . . . here . . . like the world stopped and turned backward, or like it entered another universe—

months! (*She moves convulsively; Tye grips her shoulders.*) . . . Then . . . it . . . I . . .

TYE: Us?

JANE: No, no, that unnatural tiredness started in again. I went to Ochsners. Don't you remember when the doctor's letter was delivered? No, I guess you don't, being half conscious all the time. It was from Ochsners. It informed me that my blood count had changed for the worse. It was close to . . . collapse . . . (*Pause.*) . . . Those are the clinical details. Are you satisfied with them? Have you any more questions to ask?

(*She stares at him; he averts his face. She moves around him to look at his face; he averts it again. She claps it between her hands and compels him to look at her. He looks down. A scratching sound is heard at the shutter doors.*)

JANE: That's Beret, let her in. Isn't it nice how cats go away and come back and—you don't have to worry about them. So unlike human beings.

(*Tye opens the door. He opens a can of cat food and sets it on the floor, then crosses to his clothes, collecting them from the floor.*)

TYE (*gently*): Jane, it's getting dark and I—I better get dressed now.

JANE (*with a touch of harshness*): Yes, dress—dress . . . (*But he is lost in reflection, lighting a joint. She snatches it from his lips.*)
And leave me alone as always in a room that smells, that reeks of marijuana!

SCENE TWELVE

WRITER (*as narrator*): She was watching him with an unspoken question in her eyes, a little resentful now.

MRS. WIRE'S VOICE (*from off stage, curiously altered*): Why are those stairs so dark?

(*The light in the studio area is dimmed to half during the brief scene that follows. The writer rises and stands apprehen-*

sively alert as Mrs. Wire becomes visible in a yellowed silk robe with torn lace, a reliquary garment. Her hair is loose, her steps unsteady, her eyes hallucinated.)

WRITER (*crossing from the studio, dismayed*): Is that you, Mrs. Wire?

MRS. WIRE: Now, Timmy, Timmy, you mustn't cry every time Daddy gets home from the road and naturally wants to be in bed just with Mommy. It's Daddy's privilege, Mommy's —obligation. You'll understand when you're older—you see, Daddy finds Mommy attractive.

WRITER (*backing away from the cubicle entrance*): Mrs. Wire, you're dreaming.

MRS. WIRE: Things between grownups in love and marriage can't be told to a child. (*She sits on the writer's cot.*) Now lie down and Mommy will sing you a little sleepy-time song. (*She is staring into space. He moves to the cubicle entrance; the candle is turned over and snuffed out.*)

MRS. WIRE: "Rock-a-bye, baby, in a tree top, If the wind blows, the cradle will rock . . ."

WRITER: Mrs. Wire, I'm not Timothy, I'm not Tim, I'm not Timmy. (*He touches her.*)

MRS. WIRE: Dear child given to me of love . . .

WRITER: Mrs. Wire, I'm not your child. I am nobody's child. Was maybe, but not now. I've grown into a man, about to take his first step out of this waiting station into the world.

MRS. WIRE: Mummy knows you're scared sleeping alone in the dark. But the Lord gave us dark for sleep, and Daddy don't like to find you took his rightful place . . .

WRITER: Mrs. Wire, I'm no relation to you, none but a tenant that earned his keep a while . . . Nursie! Nursie!

NURSIE (*approaching*): She gone up there? (*Nursie appears.*) She gets these spells, goes back in time. I think it musta been all that Azalea Festival excitement done it.

MRS. WIRE: "If the bough breaks, the cradle will fall . . ."

NURSIE (*at the cubicle entrance*): Mizz Wire, it's Nursie. I'll take you back downstairs.

MRS. WIRE (*rousing a bit*): It all seemed so real. —I even remember lovemaking . . .

NURSIE: Get up, Mizz Wire, come down with Nursie.

MRS. WIRE (*accepting Nursie's support*): Now I'm—old.

(*They withdraw from the light.*)

MRS. WIRE'S VOICE: Ahhhhhhhh . . . Ahhhhhhhh . . . Ahhhh . . . Ahhhhh . . .

(*This expression of despair is lost in the murmur of the wind. The writer sinks onto his cot; the angel of the alcove appears in the dusk.*)

WRITER: Grand! (*She lifts her hand in a valedictory gesture.*) I guess angels warn you to leave a place by leaving before you.

(*The light dims in the cubicle as the writer begins to pack and builds back up in the studio. The writer returns to the edge of the studio light.*)

JANE: You said you were going to get dressed and go back to your place of employment and resume the pitch for the ladies.

TYE: What did you say, Babe?

(*He has finished dressing and is now at the mirror, absorbed in combing his hair. Jane utters a soft, involuntary laugh.*)

JANE: A hundred dollars, the price, and worth it, certainly worth it. I must be much in your debt, way over my means to pay off!

TYE: Well, I ain't paid to make a bad appearance at work. (*He puts on a sport shirt with girls in grass skirts printed on it.*)

JANE: I hate that shirt.

TYE: I know you think it's tacky. Well, I'm tacky, and it's the only clean one I got.

JANE: It isn't clean, not really. And does it express much grief over the Champagne Girl's violent departure to Spain?

TYE: Do you have to hit me with that? What reason . . . ?

JANE: I've really got no reason to hit a goddamn soul but myself that lacked pride to keep my secrets. You know I shouldn't have told you about my—intentions, I should have just slipped away. The Brazilian was far from attractive but —my circumstances required some drastic—compromises.

TYE (*crouching beside her*): You're talking no sense, Jane. The Brazilian's out of the picture; those steps on the stairs were steps of hospital workers coming to take a—pick a dying fruit outa the place.

JANE: *Do you think I expect you back here again?* You'll say yes, assure me now as if forever—but—reconsider—the moment of impulse . . .

TYE: Cut some slack for me, Babe. We all gotta cut some slack for each other in this fucking world. Lissen. You don't have to sweat it.

JANE: Give me another remission; one that lasts!

TYE: Gotta go now, it's late, after dark and I'm dressed.

JANE: Well, zip your fly up unless you're now in the show. (*She rises and zips up his fly, touches his face and throat with trembling fingers.*)

TYE: Jane, we got love between us! Don't ya know that?

JANE (*not harshly*): Lovely old word, love, it's travelled a long way, Tye.

TYE: And still's a long way to go. Hate to leave you alone, but—

JANE: I'm not alone. I've got Beret. An animal is a comforting presence sometimes. I wonder if they'd admit her to St. Vincent's?

TYE: St. Vincent's?

JANE: That charity hospital where they took the painter called Nightingale.

TYE: You ain't going there, honey.

JANE: It strikes me as being a likely destination.

TYE: Why?

JANE: I watched you dress. I didn't exist for you. Nothing existed for you but your image in the mirror. Understandably so. (*With her last strength she draws herself up.*)

TYE: What's understandable, Jane? —You got a fever? (*He rises, too, and stretches out a hand to touch her forehead. She knocks it away.*)

JANE: What's understandable is that your present convenience is about to become an encumbrance. An invalid, of no use, financial or sexual. Sickness is repellent, Tye, demands more care and gives less and less in return. The person you loved —assuming that you *did* love when she was still useful—is now, is now absorbed in preparing herself for oblivion as you were absorbed in your—your image in the—mirror!

TYE (*frightened by her vehemence*): Hey, Jane!

(*Again she strikes away his extended hand.*)

JANE: Readies herself for it as you do for the street! (*She continues as to herself.*) —Withdraws into another dimension. Is indifferent to you except as—caretaker! Is less aware of you than of— (*Panting, she looks up slowly through the skylight.*) —sky that's visible to her from her bed under the skylight—at night, these—filmy white clouds, they move, they drift over the roofs of the Vieux Carré so close that if you have fever you feel as if you could touch them, and bits would come off on your fingers, soft as—cotton candy—

TYE: Rest, Babe. I'll be back early. I'll get Smokey to take over for me at midnight, and I'll come back with tamales and a bottle of vino! (*He crosses out of the light. She rushes to the door.*)

JANE: *No, no, not before daybreak and with a new needle mark on your arm.* Beret? Beret!

(*She staggers wildly out of the light, calling the cat again and again.*)

WRITER: I lifted her from the floor where she'd fallen . . .

(*Various voices are heard exclaiming around the house.*

(*The writer reappears in the studio area supporting Jane, who appears half conscious.*)

Jane? Jane?

JANE: —My cat, I scared it away . . .

NURSIE (*offstage*): What is goin' on up there?

WRITER: She was frightened by something.

JANE: I lost my cat, that's all. —They don't understand . . . (*The writer places her on the bed.*) Alone. I'm alone.

WRITER: She'll be back. Jane didn't seem to hear me. She was looking up at the skylight.

JANE: It isn't blue any more, it's suddenly turned quite dark.

WRITER: It was dark as the question in her eyes. (*The blues piano fades in.*)

JANE: It's black as the piano man playing around the corner.

WRITER: It must be after six. What's the time now?

JANE: Time? What? Oh. Time. My sight is blurred. (*She shows him her wristwatch.*) Can't make out the luminous dial, can you?

WRITER: It says five of twelve.

JANE: An improbable hour. Must have run down.

WRITER: I'll take it off. To wind it. (*He puts the watch to his ear.*) I'm afraid it's broken.

JANE (*vaguely*): I hadn't noticed. —Lately—I tell time by the sky.

WRITER: His name was Sky.

JANE: Tye . . .

WRITER: No, not Tye. Sky was the name of someone who offered me a ride West.

JANE: —I've had fever all day. Did you ask me a question?

WRITER: I said I'd planned a trip to the West Coast with this young vagrant, a musician.

JANE: Young vagrants are irresponsible. I'm not at all surprised—he let you down? Well. I have travel plans, too.

WRITER: With Tye?

JANE: No, I was going alone, not with Tye. What are you doing there?

WRITER: Setting up the chess board. Want to play?

JANE: Oh, yes, you said you play. I'd have a partner for once. But my concentration's—I warn you—it's likely to be—impaired.

WRITER: Want to play white or black?

JANE: You choose.

(*The piano fades in. Jane looks about in a confused way.*)

WRITER: Black. In honor of the musician around the corner.

JANE: —He's playing something appropriate to the occasion as if I'd phoned in a request. How's it go, so familiar?

WRITER:

"Makes no difference how things break,
I'll still get by somehow
I'm not sorry, cause it makes no difference now."

JANE: Each of us abandoned to the other. You know this is almost our first private conversation. (*She nearly falls to the floor. He catches her and supports her to the chair at the upstage side of the table.*) Shall we play, let's do. With no distractions at all. (*She seems unable to move; she has a frozen attitude.*)

(*There is a distant sustained high note from Sky's clarinet. They both hear it. Jane tries to distract the writer's attention from the sound and continues quickly with feverish animation. The sound of the clarinet becomes more urgent.*)

Vagrants, I can tell you about them. From experience. Incorirgibly delinquent. Purposeless. Addictive. Grab at you for support when support's what *you* need—gone? Whistling down the last flight, such a lively popular tune. Well, I have travel plans, but in the company of no charming young vagrant. Love Mediterranean countries but somehow missed Spain. I plan to go. Now! Madrid, to visit the Prado, most celebrated museum of all. Admire the Goyas, El Grecos. Hire a car to cross the—gold plains of Toledo.

WRITER: Jane, you don't have to make up stories, I heard your talk with Tye—all of it.

JANE: Then you must have heard his leaving. How his steps picked up speed on the second flight down—started whistling . . .

WRITER: He always whistles down stairs—it's habitual to him—you mustn't attach a special meaning to it.

(*The clarinet music is closer; the sound penetrates the shut windows.*)

JANE: At night the Quarter's so full of jazz music, so many entertainers. Isn't it now your move?

WRITER (*embarrassed*): It's your move, Jane.

JANE (*relinguishing her game*): No yours—your vagrant musician is late but you're not forgotten.

WRITER: I'll call down, ask him to wait till midnight when Tye said he'll be back.

JANE: With tamales and vino to celebrate— (*She staggers to the window, shatters a pane of glass, and shouts.*) —Your friend's coming right down, just picking up his luggage!

(*She leans against the wall, panting, her bleeding hand behind her.*)

Now go, quick. He might not wait, you'd regret it.

WRITER: Can't I do something for you?

JANE: Pour me three fingers of bourbon.

(*She has returned to the table. He pours the shot.*)

Now hurry, hurry. I know that Tye will be back early tonight.

WRITER: Yes, of course he will . . . (*He crosses from the studio light.*)

JANE (*smiling somewhat bitterly*): Naturally, yes, how could I possibly doubt it. With tamales and vino . . . (*She uncloses her fist; the blood is running from palm to wrist. The writer picks up a cardboard laundry box and the typewriter case.*)

WRITER: As I left, I glanced in Jane's door. She seemed to be or was pretending to be—absorbed in her solitary chess game. I went down the second flight and on the cot in the dark passageway was— (*He calls out.*) Beret?

(*For the first time the cat is visible, white and fluffy as a piece of cloud. Nursie looms dimly behind him, a dark solemn fact, lamplit.*)

NURSIE: It's the cat Miss Sparks come runnin' after.

WRITER: Take it to her, Nursie. She's alone up there.

MRS. WIRE: Now watch out, boy. Be careful of the future. It's a long ways for the young. Some makes it and others git lost.

WRITER: I know . . . (*He turns to the audience.*) I stood by the door uncertainly for a moment or two. I must have been frightened of it . . .

MRS. WIRE: Can you see the door?

WRITER: Yes—but to open it is a desperate undertaking . . . !

(*He does, hesitantly. Transparencies close from either wing. Dim spots of light touch each character of the play in a characteristic position.*

(*As he first draws the door open, he is forced back a few steps by a cacophony of sound: the waiting storm of his future—mechanical racking cries of pain and pleasure, snatches of song. It fades out. Again there is the urgent call of the clarinet. He crosses to the open door.*)

They're disappearing behind me. Going. People you've known in places do that: they go when you go. The earth seems to swallow them up, the walls absorb them like moisture, remain with you only as ghosts; their voices are echoes, fading but remembered.

(*The clarinet calls again. He turns for a moment at the door.*)

This house is empty now.

The End

A LOVELY SUNDAY FOR CREVE COEUR

SCENE ONE

It is late on a Sunday morning, early June, in St. Louis.

The interior is what was called an efficiency apartment in the period of this play, the middle or late thirties. It is in the West End of St. Louis. Attempts to give the apartment brightness and cheer have gone brilliantly and disastrously wrong, and this wrongness is emphasized by the fiercely yellow glare of light through the oversize windows which look out upon vistas of surrounding apartment buildings, vistas that suggest the paintings of Ben Shahn: the dried-blood horror of lower middle-class American urban neighborhoods. The second thing which assails our senses is a combination of counting and panting from the bedroom, to the left, where a marginally youthful but attractive woman, Dorothea, is taking "setting-up exercises" with fearful effort.

SOUND: Ninety-one, *ha!* —ninety-two, *ha!* —ninety-three, *ha!* —ninety-four, *ha!*

This breathless counting continues till one hundred is achieved with a great gasp of deliverance. At some point during the counting, a rather short, plumpish woman, early middle-aged, has entered from the opposite doorway with a copy of the big Sunday St. Louis Post-Dispatch.

The phone rings just as Bodey, who is hard-of-hearing, sits down on a sofa in the middle of the room. Bodey, absorbed in the paper, ignores the ringing phone, but it has caused Dorothea to gasp with emotion so strong that she is physically frozen except for her voice. She catches hold of something for a moment, as if reeling in a storm, then plunges to the bedroom door and rushes out into the living room with a dramatic door-bang.

DOROTHEA: WHY DIDN'T YOU GET THAT PHONE?

BODEY (*rising and going to the kitchenette at the right*): Where, where, what, what phone?

DOROTHEA: Is there more than one phone here? Are there several other phones I haven't discovered as yet?

BODEY: —Dotty, I think these setting-up exercises get you overexcited, emotional, I mean.

DOROTHEA (*continuing*): That phone was ringing and I told you when I woke up that I was expecting a phone call from Ralph Ellis who told me he had something very important to tell me and would phone me today before noon.

BODEY: Sure, he had something to tell you but he didn't.

DOROTHEA: Bodey, you are not hearing, or comprehending, what I'm saying at all. Your face is a dead giveaway. I said Ralph Ellis—you've heard me speak of Ralph?

BODEY: Oh, yes, Ralph, you speak continuously of him, that name Ralph Ellis is one I got fixed in my head so I could never forget it.

DOROTHEA: Oh, you mean I'm not permitted to mention the name Ralph Ellis to you?

BODEY (*preparing fried chicken in the kitchenette*): Dotty, when two girls are sharing a small apartment, naturally each of the girls should feel perfectly free to speak of whatever concerns her. I don't think it's possible for two girls sharing a small apartment *not* to speak of whatever concerns her whenever—whatever—*concerns* her, but, Dotty, I know that I'm not your older sister. However, if I was, I would have a suspicion that you have got a crush on this Ralph Ellis, and as an older sister, I'd feel obliged to advise you to, well, look before you leap in that direction. I mean just don't put all your eggs in one basket till you are one hundred percent convinced that the basket is the right one, that's all I mean. . . . Well, this is a lovely Sunday for a picnic at Creve Coeur. . . . Didn't you notice out at Creve Coeur last Sunday how Buddy's slimmed down round the middle?

DOROTHEA: No, I didn't.

BODEY: Huh?

DOROTHEA: Notice.

BODEY: Well, it was noticeable, Dotty.

DOROTHEA: Bodey, why should I be interested in whatever fractional—fluctuations—occur in your twin brother's waistline—as if it was the Wall Street market and I was a heavy investor?

BODEY: You mean you don't care if Buddy shapes up or not?

DOROTHEA: Shapes up for what?

BODEY: Nacherly for you, Dotty.

DOROTHEA: Does he regard me as an athletic event, the high jump or pole vault? Please, please, Bodey, convince him his shape does not concern me at all.

BODEY: Buddy don't discuss his work with me often, but lately he said his boss at Anheuser-Busch has got an eye on him.

DOROTHEA: How could his boss ignore such a sizeable object? —Bodey, what are you up to in that cute little kitchenette?

BODEY: Honey, I stopped by Piggly-Wiggly's yesterday noon when I got off the streetcar on the way home from the office, and I picked up three beautiful fryers, you know, nice and plump fryers.

DOROTHEA: I'd better remain out here till Ralph calls back, so I can catch it myself. (*She lies on the purple carpet and begins another series of formalized exercises.*)

BODEY: The fryers are sizzling so loud I didn't catch that, Dotty. You know, now that the office lets out at noon Saturday, it's easier to lay in supplies for Sunday. I think that Roosevelt did something for the country when he got us half Saturdays off because it used to be that by the time I got off the streetcar from International Shoe, Piggly-Wiggly's on the corner would be closed, but now it's still wide open. So I went in Piggly-Wiggly's, I went to the meat department and I said to the nice old man, Mr. Butts, the butcher, "Mr. Butts, have you got any real nice fryers?" —"You bet your life!" he said, "I must of been expectin' you to drop in. Feel these nice plump fryers." Mr. Butts always lets me feel his meat. The feel of a piece of meat is the way to test it, but there's very few modern butchers will allow you to feel it. It's the German in me. I got to feel the meat to know it's good. A piece of meat can look good over the counter but to know for sure I always want to feel it. Mr. Butts, being German, he understands that, always says to me, "Feel it, go on, feel it." So I felt the fryers. "Don't they feel good and fresh?" I said, "Yes, Mr. Butts, but will they keep till tomorrow?" "Haven't you got any ice in your icebox?" he asked me. I said to him, "I hope so, but ice goes fast in hot weather. I told the girl that shares my apartment with me to put up the card for a twenty-five pound lump of ice but sometimes she forgets to." Well, thank goodness, this time you didn't forget to. You always got so much on your mind in the morning, civics and—other things at the high school. —What are you laughin' at, Dotty? (*She turns around to glance at Dorothea who is covering her mouth to stifle breathless sounds of laughter.*)

DOROTHEA: Honestly, Bodey, I think you missed your calling. You should be in Congress to deliver a filibuster. I never knew it was possible to talk at such length about ice and a butcher.

BODEY: Well, Dotty, you know we agreed when you moved in here with me that I would take care of the shopping. We've kept good books on expenses. Haven't we kept good books? We've never had any argument over expense or disagreements between us over what I should shop for.—OW!

DOROTHEA: Now what?

BODEY: The skillet spit at me. Some hot grease flew in my face. I'll put bakin' soda on it.

DOROTHEA: So you are really and truly frying chickens in this terrible heat?

BODEY: And boiling eggs, I'm going to make deviled eggs, too. Dotty, what is it? You sound hysterical, Dotty!

DOROTHEA (*half strangled with laughter*): Which came first, fried chicken or deviled eggs? —I swear to goodness, you do the funniest things. Honestly, Bodey, you are a source of continual astonishment and amusement to me. Now, Bodey, please suspend this culinary frenzy until the phone rings again so you can hear it this time before it stops ringing for me.

BODEY: Dotty, I was right here and that phone was not ringin'. I give you my word that phone was not makin' a sound. It was quiet as a mouse.

DOROTHEA: Why, it was ringing its head off!

BODEY: Dotty, about some things everyone is mistaken, and this is something you are mistaken about. I think your exercises give you a ringing noise in your head. I think they're too strenuous for you, 'specially on Sunday, a day of rest, recreation . . .

DOROTHEA: We are both entitled to separate opinions, Bodey, but I assure you I do not suffer from ringing in my head.

That phone was RINGING. And why you did not hear it is simply because you don't have your hearing aid on!

(*The shouting is congruent with the fiercely bright colors of the interior.*)

BODEY: I honestly ain't that deaf. I swear I ain't that deaf, Dotty. The ear specialist says I just got this little calcification, this calcium in my—eardrums. But I do hear a telephone ring, a sharp, loud sound like that, I hear it, I hear it clearly.

DOROTHEA: Well, let's hope Ralph won't imagine I'm out and will call back in a while. But do put your hearing aid in. I don't share your confidence in your hearing a phone ring or a dynamite blast without it, and anyway, Bodey, you must adjust to it, you must get used to it, and after a while, when you're accustomed to it, you won't feel complete without it.

BODEY: —Yes, well— This is the best Sunday yet for a picnic at Creve Coeur . . .

DOROTHEA: That we'll talk about later. Just put your hearing aid in before I continue with my exercises. Put it in right now so I can see you.

BODEY: You still ain't finished with those exercises?

DOROTHEA: I've done one hundred bends and I did my floor exercises. I just have these bust development exercises and my swivels and— BODEY! PUT YOUR HEARING AID IN!

BODEY: I hear you, honey, I will. I'll put it on right now.

(*She comes into the living room from the kitchenette and picks up the hearing aid and several large artificial flowers from a table. She hastily moves the newspaper from the sofa to a chair behind her, then inserts the device in an ear with an agonized look.*)

DOROTHEA: It can't be that difficult to insert it. Why, from your expression, you could be performing major surgery on yourself! . . . without anesthesia . . .

BODEY: I'm just—not used to it yet. (*She covers the defective ear with an artificial chrysanthemum.*)

DOROTHEA (*in the doorway*): You keep reminding yourself of it by covering it up with those enormous artificial flowers.

Now if you feel you have to do that, why don't you pick out a flower that's suitable to the season? Chrysanthemums are for autumn and this is June.

BODEY: Yes. June. How about this poppy?

DOROTHEA: Well, frankly, dear, that big poppy is tacky.

BODEY: —The tiger lily?

DOROTHEA (*despairing*): Yes, the tiger lily! Of course, Bodey, the truth of the matter is that your idea of concealing your hearing aid with a big artificial flower is ever so slightly fantastic.

BODEY: —Everybody is sensitive about something . . .

DOROTHEA: But complexes, obsessions must not be cultivated. Well. Back to my exercises. Be sure not to miss the phone. Ralph is going to call me any minute now. (*She starts to close the bedroom door.*)

BODEY: Dotty?

DOROTHEA: Yes?

BODEY: Dotty, I'm gonna ask Buddy to go to Creve Coeur with us again today for the picnic. That's okay with you, huh?

DOROTHEA (*pausing in the doorway*): Bodey, Buddy is your brother and I fully understand your attachment to him. He's got many fine things about him. A really solid character and all that. But, Bodey, I think it's unfair to Buddy for you to go on attempting to bring us together because—well, everyone has a type she is attracted to and in the case of Buddy, no matter how much—I appreciate his sterling qualities and all, he simply isn't— (*She has gone into the bedroom and started swiveling her hips.*)

BODEY: Isn't what, Dotty?

DOROTHEA: A type that I can respond to. You know what I mean. In a romantic fashion, honey. And to me—romance is—essential.

BODEY: Oh—but—well, there's other things to consider besides—romance . . .

DOROTHEA (*swiveling her hips as she talks*): Bodey, can you honestly feel that Buddy and I are exactly right for each other? Somehow I suspect that Buddy would do better looking about for a steady, German-type girl in South St. Louis—a girl to drink beer with and eat Wiener schnitzel and get fat along with him, not a girl—well, a girl already romantically—pour me a little more coffee? —Thanks. —Why do you keep forgetting the understanding between me and Mr. Ellis? Is that fair to Buddy? To build up his hopes for an inevitable letdown?

(*Dorothea stops her swivels and returns to the living room to get the coffee Bodey has poured for her.*)

BODEY: This Mr. T. Ralph Ellis, well . . .
DOROTHEA: Well, *what*?
BODEY: Nothing except . . .
DOROTHEA: *What?*
BODEY: He might not be as reliable as Buddy—in the long run.
DOROTHEA: What is "the long run," honey?
BODEY: The long run is—*life*.
DOROTHEA: Oh, so that is the long run, the long run is life! With Buddy? Well, then give me the short run, I'm sorry, but I'll take the short run, much less exhausting in the heat of the day and the night!
BODEY: Dotty, I tell you, Dotty, in the long run or the short run I'd place my bet on Buddy, not on a—fly-by-night sort of proposition like this, this—romantic idea you got about a man that mostly you see wrote up in—society pages . . .
DOROTHEA: *That is your misconception!* —Of something about which you are in total ignorance, because I rarely step out of the civics classroom at Blewett without seeing Ralph Ellis a few steps down the corridor, pretending to take a drink at the water cooler on my floor which is two floors up from his office!
BODEY: Not really taking a drink but just pretending? Not a good sign, Dotty—pretending . . .
DOROTHEA: What I mean is—we have to arrange secret little encounters of this sort to avoid gossip at Blewett.
BODEY: —Well—
DOROTHEA: *WHAT*?
BODEY: I never trusted pretending.
DOROTHEA: Then why the paper flowers over the hearing aid, dear?
BODEY: That's—just—a little—sensitivity, there . . .

DOROTHEA: Look, you've got to live with it so take off the concealment, the paper tiger lily, and turn the hearing aid up or I will be obliged to finish my hip swivels out here to catch Ralph's telephone call.

BODEY (*as she is turning up the hearing aid, it makes a shrill sound*): See? See?

DOROTHEA: I think you mean hear, hear! —Turn it down just a bit, find the right level for it!

BODEY: Yes, yes, I— (*She fumbles with the hearing aid, dislodging the paper flower.*)

DOROTHEA: For heaven's sake, let me adjust it for you! (*She rushes over to Bodey and fiddles with the hearing aid.*) Now! —Not shrieking. —But can you hear me? I said can you hear me! At this level!?

BODEY: Yes. Where's my tiger lily?

DOROTHEA: Dropped on the fierce purple carpet. Here. (*She picks it up and hands it to Bodey.*) What's wrong with you?

BODEY: I'm—upset. Over this maybe—dangerous—trust you've got in Ralph Ellis's—intentions . . .

DOROTHEA (*dreamily, eyes going soft*): I don't like discussing an intimate thing like this but—the last time I went out in Ralph Ellis's Reo, that new sedan he's got called the Flying Cloud . . .

BODEY: Cloud? Flying?

DOROTHEA (*raising her voice to a shout*): The Reo is advertised as "The Flying Cloud."

BODEY: Oh. Yes. He'd be attracted to that.

DOROTHEA: It was pouring down rain and Art Hill was deserted, no other cars on it but Ralph and I in his Reo. The windows curtained with rain that glistened in the lamplight.

BODEY: Dotty, I hope you're not leading up to something that shouldn't of happened in this Flying Cloud on Art Hill. It really scares me, Dotty . . .

DOROTHEA: Frankly, I was a little frightened myself because—we've never had this kind of discussion before, it's rather—difficult for me but you must understand. I've always drawn a strict line with a man till this occasion.

BODEY: Dotty, do you mean—?

DOROTHEA: It was so magical to me, the windows curtained with rain, the soft look in his eyes, the warmth of his breath that's always scented with clove, his fingers touching so gently as he—

BODEY: Dotty, I don't think I want to know any more about this—experience on Art Hill because, because—I got a suspicion, Dotty, that you didn't hold the line with him.

DOROTHEA: The line just—didn't exist when he parked the car and turned and looked at me and I turned and looked at him. Our eyes, our eyes—

BODEY: Your eyes?

DOROTHEA: Burned the line out of existence, like it had never existed!

BODEY: —I'm not gonna tell this to Buddy!

DOROTHEA: You know, I wasn't aware until then that the Reo was equipped with adjustable seats.

BODEY: Seats that—?

DOROTHEA: Adjusted to pressure, yes, reclined beneath me when he pushed a lever.

BODEY (*distracted from the phonebook which she had begun to leaf through*): —How far did this seat recline beneath you, Dotty?

DOROTHEA: Horizontally, nearly. So gradually though that I didn't know till later, later. Later, not then—the earth was whirling beneath me and the sky was spinning above.

BODEY: Oh-ho, he got you drunk, did he, with a flask of liquor in that Flying Cloud on—

DOROTHEA: Drunk on a single Pink Lady?

BODEY: Pink?

DOROTHEA: Lady. —The mildest sort of cocktail! Made with sloe gin and grenadine.

BODEY: The gin was slow, maybe, but that man is a fast one, seducing a girl with adjustable seats and a flask of liquor in that Flying Cloud on—

DOROTHEA: Not a flask, a cocktail, and not in the Reo but in a small private club called The Onyx, a club so exclusive he had to present an engraved card at the entrance.

BODEY: Oh yes, I know such places!

DOROTHEA: How would you know such places?

BODEY: I seen one at the movies and so did you, at the West End Lyric, the last time you was all broke up from expectin' a call from this Ellis which never came in, so we seen Roy D'Arcy take poor Janet Gaynor to one of them—private clubs to—!

(*Bodey has not found the Blewett number in the phonebook. She dials the operator.*)

Blewett, Blewett, get me the high school named Blewett.

DOROTHEA: Bodey, what are you doing at the phone which I begged you not to use till Ralph has called?

BODEY: Reporting him to Blewett!

DOROTHEA: Bodey, that takes the cake, reporting on the principal of Blewett to Blewett that's closed on Sundays. What a remarkable—

BODEY (*darting about*): Paper, pen!

DOROTHEA: Now what?

BODEY: A written report to the Board of Education of St. Louis. I tell you, that Board will be interested in all details of how that principal of the school system got you lying down drunk and defenseless in his Flying Cloud in a storm on Art Hill, every advantage taken with Valentino sheik tricks on a innocent teacher of civics just up from Memphis.

DOROTHEA: YOU WILL NOT—

BODEY: DON'T TELL ME NOT!

DOROTHEA: LIBEL THE REPUTATION OF A MAN THAT I LOVE, GAVE MYSELF TO NOT JUST FREELY BUT WITH ABANDON, WITH JOY!

BODEY (*aloud as she writes*): Board of Education of St. Louis, Missouri. I think you should know that your principal at Blewett used his position to take disgusting advantage of a young teacher employed there by him for that purpose. I know, I got the facts, including the date and—

(*Dorothea snatches up and crumples the letter.*)

My letter, you tore up my—!

DOROTHEA: Bodey, if you had written and mailed that letter, do you know what you'd have obliged me to do? I would be morally obliged to go personally down to the Board of Education and tell them an *opposite* story which happens to be the *true* one: that I *desired* Ralph Ellis, possibly even more than he did me!

(*Bodey huffs and puffs wordlessly till she can speak.*)

BODEY: —Well, God help you, Dotty. —But I give you my word I won't repeat this to Buddy.

DOROTHEA: How does it concern Buddy?

BODEY: It concerns Buddy and me because Buddy's got deep feelings and respect for you, Dotty. He would respect you too much to cross the proper line before you had stood up together in the First Lutheran Church on South Grand.

DOROTHEA: *Now* you *admit* it!

BODEY: It's you that's makin' admissions of a terrible kind that might shock Buddy out of his serious intentions.

DOROTHEA: You are admitting that—

(*As she had threatened, Dorothea has begun doing her hip swivels in the living room, but now she stops and stares indignantly at Bodey.*)

—you've been deliberately planning and plotting to marry me off to your twin brother so that my life would be just one long Creve Coeur picnic, interspersed with knockwurst, sauerkraut—hot potato salad dinners. —Would I be asked to prepare them? Even in summer? I know what you Germans regard as the limits, the boundaries of a woman's life—*Kirche, Küche, und Kinder*—while being asphyxiated gradually by cheap cigars. I'm sorry but the life I design for myself is not along those lines or in those limits. My life must include romance. Without romance in my life, I could no more live than I could without breath. I've got to find a partner in life, or my life will have no meaning. But what I must have and finally do have is an affair of the heart, two hearts, a true consummated romance—yes consummated, I'm not ashamed! (*She gasps and sways.*)

BODEY: Dotty, Dotty, set down and catch your breath!

DOROTHEA: In this breathless efficiency apartment? —I've got to have space in my life.

BODEY: —Did I tell you that Buddy has made a down payment on a Buick?

DOROTHEA: No, you didn't and why should you, as it does not concern— Oh, my God, Blessed Savior!

BODEY: Dotty, what Dotty? D'you want your, your whatamacallit tablets?

DOROTHEA: Mebaral? No, I have not collapsed yet, but you've just about driven me to it.

BODEY: Take a breather, take a seventh inning stretch while I—

DOROTHEA: Bodey, this room is GLARING; it's not cheerful but GLARING!

BODEY: Stretch out on the sofa and look up, the ceiling is white!

DOROTHEA: I don't know why I'm so out of breath today.

BODEY: Don't do no more exercises. You drink too much coffee an' Cokes. That's stimulants for a girl high-strung like you. With a nervous heart condition.

DOROTHEA: It's functional—not nervous.

BODEY: Lie down a minute.

DOROTHEA: I will rest a little—but not because you say so. (*Between gasps she sinks into a chair.*) You're very bossy—and very inquisitive, too.

BODEY: I'm older'n you, and I got your interests at heart.

DOROTHEA: Whew!

BODEY: Think how cool it will be on the open-air streetcar to Creve Coeur.

DOROTHEA: You must have had your hearing aid off when I said I had other plans.

BODEY: Buddy, I been telling Buddy to cut down on his beer, and Buddy is listening to me. He's cut down to eight a day—from a dozen and will cut down more . . .

DOROTHEA: Bodey, could you stop talking about Buddy this hot Sunday morning? It's not a suitable subject for hot weather. I know brother-sister relationships are deep, but it's not just the beer, it's the almost total lack of interests in common, no topics of conversations, of—of mutual—interest.

BODEY: They could develop. I know Buddy just feels embarrassed. He hasn't opened up yet. Give him time and he will.

DOROTHEA: Bodey, this discussion is embarrassingly pointless in view of the fact that I'm already committed to Ralph Ellis. I still have to do my hip swivels . . .

(*Sipping coffee as she goes, Dorothea returns to the bedroom and resumes her exercises.*)

BODEY (*rushing to the phone*): Olive 2697, Olive 2697! Buddy? Me! *Grosser Gott!* I can't talk now, but you absolutely got to go to Creve Coeur with us this Sunday. —Dress good! Don't smoke cigars! And laugh at her witty remarks. —Well, they *are*, they're witty! She teaches *civics.*

(*The doorbell rings*).

Now be at the Creve Coeur station at 1:30, huh? —Please!—Somebody's at the door, I can't talk now. (*Leaving the phone off the hook, she rushes to the door and opens it.*) Oh. Hello.

HELENA: Good morning.

BODEY: Are you a friend of Dotty's?

(*A stylishly dressed woman with the eyes of a predatory bird appears.*)

HELENA: Of Dorothea's? —Yes.

BODEY: Well, then come on in. Any friend of Dotty's is a friend of mine.

HELENA: Is that so?

BODEY (*discomfited*): Yes, I—got grease on my hand. I was fryin' up some chickens for a picnic.

HELENA: —Well! This is a surprise! (*She makes several turns in a mechanical, rigid fashion, eyes staring.*)

BODEY: Excuse me, I should of—interduced myself.

HELENA: You are Miss Bodenheifer.

BODEY: Hafer, not heifer. (*She laughs nervously.*) Heifer meaning a cow.

HELENA: No conscious association whatsoever. (*She advances forward a step.*) So this is Schlogger Haven?

BODEY: Oh, Schlogger Haven, that's just a joke of Dotty's. The landlord's name is Schlogger, that's all—that's all . . .

HELENA: Dorothea was joking, was she?

BODEY: Yeh, she jokes a lot, full of humor. We have lots of laughs. (*Bodey extends her hand.*)

HELENA: I can imagine you might, Miss Bodenheifer.

BODEY: You can forget the Miss. —Everyone at the office calls me Bodey.

HELENA: But we are not at the office—we are here in Schlogger Haven. (*She continues enigmatically.*) Hmmm . . . I've never ventured this side of Blewett before.

BODEY: Never gone downtown?

HELENA: I do nearly all my shopping in the West End, so naturally it amazed me to discover street after street without a shade tree on it, and the glare, the glare, and the heat refracted by all the brick, concrete, asphalt—was so overpowering that I nearly collapsed. I think I must be afflicted with a combination of photo- and heliophobia, both.

BODEY (*unconsciously retreating a step as if fearing contagion*): I never heard of neither—but you got *both*?

HELENA: An exceptional sensitivity to both heat and strong light.

BODEY: Aw.

HELENA: Yes. Now would you please let Dorothea know I'm here to see her?

BODEY: Does Dotty expect you, Miss, uh—

HELENA: Helena Brookmire, no, she doesn't expect me, but a very urgent business matter has obliged me to drop by this early.

BODEY: She won't have no one in there with her. She's exercising.

HELENA: But Dorothea and I are well acquainted.

BODEY: Well acquainted or not acquainted at all, makes no difference. I think that modern girls emphasize too much these advertised treatments and keep their weight down too much for their health.

HELENA: The preservation of youth requires some sacrifices.

(*She continues to stare about her, blinking her birdlike eyes as if dazzled.*)

BODEY: —I guess you and Dotty teach together at Blewett High?

HELENA: —Separately.

BODEY: You mean you're not at Blewett where Dotty teaches civics?

HELENA (*as if addressing a backward child*): I teach there, too. When I said separately, I meant we teach separate classes.

BODEY: Oh, naturally, yes. (*She tries to laugh.*) I been to high school.

HELENA: Have you?

BODEY: Yes. I know that two teachers don't teach in the same class at the same time, on two different subjects.

HELENA (*opening her eyes very wide*): Wouldn't *that* be peculiar.

BODEY: Yes. That would be peculiar.

HELENA (*chuckling unpleasantly*): It might create some confusion among the students.

BODEY: Yes, I reckon it would.

HELENA: Especially if the subjects were as different as civics and the history of *art.*

(*Bodey attempts to laugh again; Helena imitates the laugh almost exactly.*)

(*Pause*)

This *is*, it really *is*!

BODEY: Is *what*?

HELENA: The most remarkable room that I've ever stepped into! Especially the combination of colors! Such a *vivid* contrast! May I sit down?

BODEY: Yeh, yeh, excuse me, I'm not myself today. It's the heat and the—

HELENA: Colors? —The vivid contrast of colors? (*She removes a pair of round, white-rimmed dark glasses from her purse and puts them on.*) Did Dorothea assist you, Miss Bodenheifer, in decorating this room?

BODEY: No, when Dotty moved in, it was just like it is now.

HELENA: Then you are solely responsible for this inspired selection of colors?

(*There is a loud sputter of hot fat from the kitchenette.*)

BODEY: Excuse me a moment, I got to turn over the fryers in the skillet.

HELENA: Don't let me interrupt your preparations for a picnic.

BODEY: Didn't catch that. I don't hear good sometimes.

HELENA: Oh?

BODEY: You see, I got this calcium deposit in my ears . . . and they advised me to have an operation, but it's very expensive for me and sometimes it don't work.

PHONE VOICE: Booow-deeee!

(*Helena notices but doesn't comment on the unhooked phone.*)

HELENA: I would advise you against it. I had an elderly acquaintance who had this calcification problem and she had a hole bored in her skull to correct it. The operation is called fenestration—it involves a good deal of danger and whether or not it was successful could not be determined since she never recovered consciousness.

BODEY: Never recovered?

HELENA: Consciousness.

BODEY: Yeh, well, I think maybe I'd better learn to live with it.

PHONE VOICE (*shouting again*): Bodeyyyyy—Bodeyyyy—

BODEY: What's that?

HELENA: I was wondering, too. Very strange barking sounds are coming out of the phone.

BODEY (*laughing*): Oh, God, I left it unhooked. (*She snatches it up.*) Buddy, sorry, somebody just dropped in, forgot you was still on the line. Buddy, call me back in a few minutes, huh, Buddy, it's, uh, very important. (*She hangs up the phone.*) That was my brother. Buddy. He says he drunk two beers and made him a liverwurst sandwich before I got back to the phone. Thank God he is so good-natured. . . . He and me are going out on a picnic at Creve Coeur with Dotty this afternoon. My brother is very interested in Dotty.

HELENA: Interested? Romantically?

BODEY: Oh, yes, Buddy's a very serious person.

HELENA (*rising*): —I am very impressed!

BODEY: By what, what by?

HELENA (*with disguised fury*): The ingenuity with which you've fitted yourself into this limited space. Every inch seems to be utilized by some appliance or—*decoration*? (*She picks up a large painted china frog.*) —A frahg?

BODEY: Yes, frawg.

HELENA: So realistically colored and designed you'd almost expect it to croak. —Oh, and you have a canary . . . stuffed!

BODEY: Little Hilda . . . she lived ten years. That's the limit for a canary.

HELENA: Limit of longevity for the species?

BODEY: She broke it by three months.

HELENA: Establishing a record. It's quite heroic, enduring more than ten years in such confinement. What tenacity to existence some creatures do have!

BODEY: I got so attached to it, I took it to a, a—

HELENA: Taxidermist.

BODEY: Excuse me a moment. (*She rushes to the stove in the alcove.*) OW! —Got burnt again.

HELENA (*following curiously*): You were burnt before?

(*Bodey profusely powders her arms with baking soda. Helena backs away.*)

Miss Bodenheifer, *please!* You've sprinkled my clothes with that powder!

BODEY: Sorry, I didn't mean to.

HELENA: Intentional or not, I'm afraid you have! May I have a clothes brush?

BODEY: Look at that, I spilt it on the carpet. (*She rushes to fetch a broom.*)

HELENA: Miss Bodenheifer, I WOULD LIKE A CLOTHES BRUSH, IF YOU HAVE A *CLOTHES* BRUSH! Not a broom. I am not a carpet.

BODEY: AW. SURE. Dotty's got a clothes brush. Oh. Help yourself to some coffee. (*She drops the broom and enters the bedroom.*)

(*Through the open door, Dorothea can be heard counting as she swivels.*)

DOROTHEA'S VOICE: Sixty, *ha!* Sixty-one, *ha!* (*She continues counting but stops when she notices Bodey.*) —The PHONE? Is it the PHONE?

BODEY: Clothes brush. (*Bodey closes the bedroom door and begins opening and shutting drawers as she looks for the clothes brush.*)

DOROTHEA: DON'T, DON'T, DON'T—slam a drawer shut like that! I feel like screaming!

(*Helena opens a closet in the kitchenette; a box falls out.*)

HELENA: The hazards of this place almost equal the horrors.

DOROTHEA (*in the bedroom*): I asked you if the phone rang.

BODEY: No, no, the doorbell.

HELENA (*who has moved to the icebox*): Ah. Ice, mostly melted, what squalor!

(*This dual scene must be carefully timed.*)

DOROTHEA: I presume it's Miss Gluck from upstairs in boudoir cap and wrapper. Bodey, get her out as quickly as possible. The sight of that woman destroys me for the whole day.

HELENA (*still in the kitchenette*): This remnant of ice will not survive in this steaming glass of coffee.

(*A knock at the door is heard.*)

What's that?

(*Sophie Gluck opens the front door and sticks her head in. At the sight of Helena, she withdraws in alarm.*)

Another tenant. *Demented!*

(*Helena moves to the door and slams and bolts it with such force that Sophie, outside, utters a soft cry of confused panic.*)

BODEY: Don't do no more calisthenics if it affecks you this way.

DOROTHEA: Just, just—knock at the door when Miss Gluck has gone back upstairs, that's my—whew!—only—request . . .

BODEY: —Yes, well . . .

DOROTHEA: No coffee, no crullers or she—will stay—down here—forever—ha!

(*The phone rings; Helena picks it up. Bodey emerges from the bedroom with a whisk broom, closing the door behind her. Helena is at the phone.*)

HELENA: Oh, she seems engaged for the moment . . .

BODEY: Aw, the phone! Is it that principal, Ellis?

HELENA (*aside from the phone*): I'm afraid not. It seems to be Dorothea's other admirer—*quel embarras de richesses* . . .

BODEY (*rushing to the phone*): Must be Buddy. —Buddy? Well? —Yeh, good, what suit you got on? Well, take it off.

It don't look good on you, Buddy. Put on the striped suit, Buddy an' the polka dot tie, and, Buddy, if you smoke a cigar at Creve Coeur, excuse yourself and smoke it in the bushes.

HELENA: This is—

BODEY: That's right, 'bye.

HELENA: —absolutely bizarre! You found a clothes brush? That's not a clothes brush. It's a whisk broom. Sorry. It doesn't look clean.

BODEY: Sorry. My nerves.

HELENA (*taking it and brushing herself delicately here and there*): What was that counting I heard? Is Dorothea counting something in there?

BODEY: She's counting her swivels in there.

HELENA: Swivels of what?

BODEY: Hip swivels, that's what. She's counting. Every morning she does one hundred bends and one hundred set-ups and one hundred hip swivels.

HELENA: Regardless of weather?

BODEY: That's right, regardless of weather.

HELENA: And regardless of— Hmmm . . .

(*Bodey senses a touch of malice implicit in this unfinished sentence.*)

BODEY: —What else, huh?

HELENA: Dorothea has always impressed me as an emotionally fragile type of person who might collapse, just suddenly collapse, when confronted with the disappointing facts of a situation about which she'd allowed herself to have—romantic illusions.

(*It is now Bodey's turn to say, "Hmmm . . ."*)

—No matter how—well, I hate to say foolish but even intelligent girls can make mistakes of this nature . . . of course we all felt she was attaching too much importance to—

BODEY: "We all" is who?

HELENA: Our little group at Blewett.

BODEY: Yeh, there's always a gossipy little group, even down at International Shoe where I work there is a gossipy little group that feels superior to the rest of us. Well, personally,

I don't want in with this gossipy little group because the gossip is malicious. Oh, they call it being concerned, but it's not the right kind of concern, naw, I'd hate for that gossipy little group to feel concerned about me, don't want that and don't need it.

HELENA: Understandably, yaiss. I will return this whisk broom to Dorothea.

BODEY: No, no, just return it to me.

HELENA: I have to speak to her and in order to do that I'll have to enter that room. So if you'll excuse me I'll—

(*She starts toward the bedroom. Bodey snatches the whisk broom from her with a force that makes Helena gasp.*)

BODEY: Miss Brooksit, you're a visitor here but the visit was not expected. Now you excuse me but I got to say you sort of act like this apartment was yours.

HELENA: —What a dismaying idea! I mean I—

BODEY: And excuse me or don't excuse me but I got a very strong feeling that you got something in mind. All right, your mind is your mind, what's in it is yours but keep it to yourself, huh?

HELENA (*cutting in*): Miss Bodenheifer, you seem to be implying something that's a mystery to me.

BODEY: You know what I mean and I know what I mean so where's the mystery, huh?

DOROTHEA (*calling from the bedroom*): Is somebody out there, Bodey?

BODEY: Just Sophie Gluck.

DOROTHEA: Oh, Lord!

HELENA: What was that you called me?

BODEY: I told Dotty that you was Miss Gluck from upstairs.

HELENA: —Gluck?

BODEY: Yeah, Miss Gluck is a lady upstairs that comes downstairs to visit.

HELENA: She comes down to see Dorothea?

BODEY: No, no, more to see me, and to drink coffee. She lost her mother, an' she's got a depression so bad she can't make coffee, so I save her a cup, keep her a cup in the pot. You know for a single girl to lose a mother is a terrible thing. What else can you do? She oughta be down. Weekdays she comes down at seven. Well, this is Sunday.

HELENA: Yes. This is Sunday.

BODEY: Sundays she comes down for coffee and a cruller at ten.

HELENA: Cruller? What is a cruller?

BODEY: Aw. You call it a doughnut, but me, bein' German, was raised to call it a cruller.

HELENA: Oh. A cruller is a doughnut but you call it a cruller. Now if you'll excuse me a moment, I will go in there and relieve Dorothea of the mistaken impression that I am Miss Gluck from upstairs who has come down for her coffee and —cruller.

BODEY: Oh, no, don't interrupt her calisthenics.

(*Helena ignores this admonition and opens the bedroom door.*)

DOROTHEA: Why, Helena Brookmire! —What a surprise. I—I—look a—*mess!*

HELENA: I heard this counting and gasping. Inquired what was going on. Your friend Miss—what?

DOROTHEA: You've met Miss Bodenhafer?

HELENA: Yes, she received me very cordially. We've dispensed with introductions. She says any friend of yours is a friend of hers and wants me to call her Bodey as they do at the office. Excuse me, Miss Bodenheifer, I must have a bit of private conversation—

(*Helena closes the bedroom door, shutting out Bodey.*)

DOROTHEA: Well, I wasn't expecting a visitor today, obviously not this early. You see, I—never receive a visitor here. . . . Is there something too urgent to hold off till Monday, Helena?

HELENA: Have our negotiations with the realty firm of Orthwein and Muller slipped your flighty mind?

DOROTHEA: Oh, the real estate people, but surely on Sunday—

HELENA: Mr. Orthwein called Cousin Dee-Dee last night and she called me this morning that now the news has leaked out and there's competitive bidding for the apartment on Westmoreland Place and the deal must be settled at once.

DOROTHEA: You mean by—?
HELENA: Immediate payment, yes, to pin it down.
DOROTHEA: *Today? Sunday?*
HELENA: The sanctity of a Sunday must sometimes be profaned by business transactions.

(*Bodey has now entered.*)

DOROTHEA: Helena, if you'll just have some coffee and wait in the living room, I will come out as soon as I've showered and dressed.
BODEY: Yeh, yeh, do that. You're embarrassing Dotty, so come back out and—

(*Bodey almost drags Helena out of the bedroom, kicking the bedroom door shut.*)

HELENA: Gracious!
BODEY: Yes, gracious, here! Set down, I'll get you some coffee.
HELENA (*with a sharp laugh*): She said, "I look a mess," and I couldn't contradict her.
BODEY: Here! Your coffee! Your cruller!
HELENA (*haughtily*): I don't care for the cruller, as you call it. Pastries are not included in my diet. However—I'd like a clean napkin. You've splashed coffee everywhere.
BODEY: Sure, we got plenty of napkins. You name it, we got it. (*She thrusts a paper napkin at Helena like a challenge.*)
HELENA: This paper napkin is stained. Would you please give me—
BODEY: Take 'em all. You stained that napkin yourself. (*She thrusts the entire pile of napkins at Helena.*)
HELENA: You shoved the cup at me so roughly the coffee splashed.

(*Helena fastidiously wipes the tabletop. There is a rap at the door.*)

BODEY: Aw, that's Sophie Gluck.
HELENA: I don't care to meet Miss Gluck.
BODEY: Will you set down so I can let in Sophie Gluck?
HELENA: So if you're going to admit her, I will take refuge again in Dorothea's bedroom. . . . There is another matter I've come here to . . .

BODEY (*seizing Helena's arm as she crosses toward the bedroom*): I know what you're up to! —JUST A MINUTE, *BITTE*, SOPHIE! I can guess the other matter you just can't hold your tongue about, but you're gonna hold it. It's not gonna be mentioned to cloud over the day and spoil the Creve Coeur picnic for Dotty, Buddy, an' me! — COMIN', SOPHIE! (*Then, to Helena, fiercely.*) YOU SET BACK DOWN!

(*During this altercation, Dorothea has been standing in the bedroom paralyzed with embarrassment and dismay. Now she calls sweetly through the door, opened a crack.*)

DOROTHEA: Bodey, Bodey, what *is* going on out there? How could a phone be heard above that shouting? Oh, My Blessed Savior, I was bawn on a Sunday, and I am convinced that I shall die on a Sunday! Could you please tell me what is the cause of the nerve-shattering altercations going on out there?

HELENA: Dorothea, Miss Bodenheifer's about to receive Miss Gluck.

DOROTHEA: Oh, no, oh no, Bodey, entertain her upstairs! I'm not in shape for another visit today, especially not—Bodey!

BODEY: Sophie, Sophie, you had me worried about you.

HELENA: I'm afraid, Dorothea, your request has fallen upon a calcified eardrum.

BODEY: You come downstairs so late.

MISS GLUCK: *Sie hat die Tür in mein Kopf zugeschlagen!*

BODEY (*to Helena*): You done that to Sophie!

HELENA: An unknown creature of demented appearance entering like a sneak thief!

BODEY: My best friend in the building!

HELENA: What a pitiful admission!

BODEY: You come here uninvited, not by Dotty or me, since I never heard of you, but got the nerve to call my best friend in the building . . .

MISS GLUCK: *Diese Frau ist ein Spion.*

BODEY: What did you call her?

HELENA: I called that woman demented. What I would call you is intolerably offensive.

MISS GLUCK: *Verstehen Sie?* Spy. *Vom Irrenhaus.*

BODEY: We live here, you don't. See the difference?

HELENA: Thank God for the difference. *Vive la différence.*

DOROTHEA (*coming just inside the living room*): Helena, Bodey.

HELENA: Be calm Dorothea—don't get overexcited.

MISS GLUCK: *Zwei Jahre.* Two years.

DOROTHEA: Why is she coming at me like this?

MISS GLUCK: State asylum.

BODEY: You come here to scrounge money outta Dotty which she ain't got.

MISS GLUCK: *Sie ist hier—mich noch einmal—im Irrenhaus zu bringen.* To take back to hospital.

HELENA: Aside from the total inaccuracy of your assumption and the insulting manner in which you express it—. As you very well know, Dorothea and I are both employed at Blewett. We are both on salary there! And I have not come here to involve myself in your social group but to rescue my colleague from it.

BODEY: Awright, you put it your way, it adds up to the same thing. You want money from Dotty which she ain't got to give you. Dotty is broke, flat broke, and she's been on a big buying spree, so big that just last night I had to loan her the price of a medium bottle of Golden Glow Shampoo, and not only that, I had to go purchase it for her because she come home exhausted. Dotty was too exhausted to walk to the drugstore. Well, me, I was tired, too, after my work at International Shoe and shopping, but out I hoofed it to Liggett's and forked out the forty-nine cents for the medium size Golden Glow from my own pockets, money I set aside for incidentals at the Creve Coeur picnic. There's always—

HELENA (*cutting in*): Miss Bodenheifer, you certainly have a gift for the felicitous phrase such as "out you hoofed it to Liggett's," sorry, sorry, but it does evoke an image.

BODEY: I know what you mean by "hoof it" since you keep repeating "heifer" for "hafer." I'm not too dumb like which you regard me to know why you're struck so funny by "hoof it."

HELENA: You said you "hoofed it," not me.

BODEY: You keep saying "heifer" for "hafer." Me, I'm a sensitive person with feelings I feel, but sensitive to you I am not. Insults from you bounce off me. I just want you to know that you come here shaking your tin cup at the wrong door.

(*As a soft but vibrant counterpoint to this exchange, Sophie, sobbing and rolling her eyes like a* religieuse *in a state of sorrowful vision, continues her slow shuffle toward Dorothea as she repeats in German an account of her violent ejection by Helena.*)

DOROTHEA (*breathlessly*): Bodey, what is she saying? Translate and explain to her I have no knowledge of German.

HELENA: Babbling, just lunatic babbling!

BODEY: One minute, one minute, Dotty. I got to explain to this woman she's wasting her time here and yours—and had the moxie to slam Sophie out of the door.

HELENA: Miss Bodenheifer, it's useless to attempt to intimidate me. . . . I would like the use of your phone for a moment. Then—

DOROTHEA: No calls on the phone!

BODEY: Dotty don't want this phone used; she's expecting a call to come in, but there is a pay phone at Liggett's three blocks east on West Pine and Pearl.

HELENA: Drugstores are shut on Sundays!

DOROTHEA: Quiet! Listen! All! This thing's getting out of hand!

HELENA: I want only to call a taxi for myself and for Dorothea. She's trapped here and should be removed at once. You may not know that just two weeks after she came to Blewett she collapsed on the staircase, and the staff doctor examined her and discovered that Dorothea's afflicted with neuro-circulatory asthenia.

(*Dorothea has disappeared behind the sofa. Miss Gluck is looking down at her with lamentations.*)

MISS GLUCK: BODEY.

BODEY: Moment, Sophie.

MISS GLUCK: Dotty, Dotty . . .

HELENA: What is she saying? Where's Dorothea?

BODEY: Dotty?

MISS GLUCK: *Hier, auf dem Fussboden. Ist fallen.*

HELENA: This Gluck creature has thrown Dorothea onto the floor.

BODEY: *Gott im—! Wo ist*—Dotty?

HELENA: The Gluck has flung her to the floor behind the sofa!

BODEY: Dotty!

HELENA: Dorothea, I'm calling us a cab. Is she conscious?

DOROTHEA: Mebaral—tablet—quick!

BODEY: Mebarals, where?

(*Sophie wails loudly.*)

DOROTHEA: My pocketbook!

BODEY: Hold on now, slowly, slowly—

DOROTHEA: Mebaral! Tablets!

HELENA: My physician told me those tablets are only prescribed for persons with—extreme nervous tension and asthenia.

BODEY: Will you goddam shut up? —Dotty, you just need to—

HELENA: What she needs is to stop these strenuous exercises and avoid all future confrontations with that lunatic from upstairs!

BODEY: Dotty, let me lift you.

DOROTHEA: Oh, oh, noooo, I—can't, I—I am *paralyzed, Bodey!*

BODEY: HEY, YOU BROOKS-IT, TAKE DOTTY'S OTHER ARM. HELP ME CARRY HER TO HER BED WILL YUH?

(*Sophie is moaning through clenched fists.*)

HELENA: All right, all right, but then I shall call my physician!

(*Dorothea is carried into the bedroom and deposited on the bed. Sophie props pillows behind her.*)

DOROTHEA: Meb—my meb . . .

BODEY: Tablets. Bathroom. In your pocketbook.

(*Bodey rushes into the bathroom, then out with a small bottle. Dorothea raises a hand weakly and Bodey drops tablets in it.*)

Dotty, don't swallow, that's three tablets!

DOROTHEA: My sherry to wash it down with—

BODEY: Dotty, take out the *two extra tablets*, Dotty!

HELENA: Sherry? Did she say sherry? Where is it?

DOROTHEA: There, there.

BODEY: Dotty, open your mouth, I got to take out those extras!

HELENA: No glass, you must drink from the bottle.

BODEY: NO! NOOOO!

HELENA: STOP CLUTCHING AT ME!

(*Miss Gluck utters a terrified wail. Dorothea drinks from the bottle and falls back onto the pillows with a gasp.*)

BODEY (*so angry she speaks half in German*): You *Schwein*, you bitch! *Alte böse Katze.* (*She then goes on in English.*) You washed three tablets down Dotty!

DOROTHEA: Now will you BOTH get out so I can breathe!

HELENA: The door's obstructed by Gluck.

BODEY: Sophie, go out, Sophie, go out of here with me for coffee and crullers!

(*Sobbing, Sophie retreats. Bodey grabs a strong hold of Helena's wrist.*)

HELENA: Let go of my wrist. Oh, my God, you have broken. . . . I heard a bone snap in my—!

BODEY: WALK! OUT! MOVE IT! . . .

HELENA (*turning quickly about and retreating behind the sofa*): Miss Bodenheifer, you are a one-woman demonstration of the aptness of the term "Huns" for Germans. . . . And, incidentally, what you broke was not my wrist but my Cartier wristwatch, a birthday present from my Cousin Dee-Dee; you shattered the crystal, and you've broken the minute hand and bent the two others. I am afraid the repair bill will cost you considerably more than keeping Dorothea in Golden Glow Shampoo.

BODEY: It's all right, Sophie, set down right here and I'll. . . . Coffee's still hot for you. Have a coupla crullers. Blow your nose on this napkin and—

(*Helena laughs tonelessly.*)

What's funny, is something funny? You never been depressed, no sorrows in your life ever, yeh, and you call yourself a human.

HELENA: Really, this is fantastic as the—color scheme of this room or the—view through the windows.

(*In the bedroom, Dorothea has staggered from the bed and stumbled to the floor.*)

DOROTHEA: Bodey.
HELENA: Dorothea.
BODEY (*calling through*): Dotty.
HELENA: You really must let me check on her condition.
DOROTHEA (*in the bedroom*): Don't forget . . . phone call.
BODEY: No, Dotty.
DOROTHEA (*faintly, clinging to something*): Tell Miss Brookmire I've retired for the day.
HELENA: *What?*
BODEY: She's not coming out. She's not coming out till you leave here—

(*Bodey bolts the bedroom door.*)

HELENA: I beg to differ. She *will* and I'll sit here till she does!

(*Miss Gluck has taken a bite of a cruller, dunked in coffee, and begins to blubber, the coffee-soaked cruller dribbling down her chin.*)

BODEY: Look, you upset Sophie!
MISS GLUCK: *Eine—Woche vor—Sonntag—meine Mutter—*
BODEY (*comfortingly*): *Ich weiss,* Sophie, *ich weiss.*
MISS GLUCK: *Gestorben!*
BODEY: But she went *sudden*, huh, Sophie? (*She crouches beside Miss Gluck, removing the dribblings of cruller and coffee from her mouth and chin.*)
HELENA: I don't understand the language, and the scene appears to be private.
BODEY: Yeh, keep out of it. (*She turns to Miss Gluck.*) —Your mother, she didn't hang on like the doctor thought she would, Sophie. Now, face it, it was better sudden, no big hospital bill, just went and is waiting for you in Heaven.
HELENA: With open arms, I presume, and with coffee and crullers.
BODEY: So, Sophie, just be grateful that she went quick with no pain.

MISS GLUCK (*grotesquely tragic*): *Nein, nein, sie hat geschrien!* I woke up runnin'!

BODEY: To her bed, you reached it and she was dead. Just one scream, it was over—wasn't that a mercy?

(*Helena laughs.*)

Sophie, honey, this woman here's not sympathetic. She laughs at sorrow, so maybe you better take the coffee, the cruller—here's another—upstairs, Sophie, and when we get back from the Creve Coeur picnic, I will bring you beautiful flowers, *schöne Blume*. Then I'll come up and sing to you in German—I will sing you to sleep.

(*Miss Gluck slowly rises with coffee and crullers. Bodey conducts her gently to the door.*)

MISS GLUCK (*crying out*): *Ich bin allein, allein! In der Welt, freundlos!*

BODEY: No, no, Sophie, that is negative thinking.

MISS GLUCK: *Ich habe niemand in der Welt!*

BODEY: Sophie, God is with you, I'm with you. Your mother, all your relations are waiting for you in Heaven!

(*Shepherding Miss Gluck into the hall, Bodey repeats this assurance in German.*)

HELENA: Sometimes despair is just being realistic, the only logical thing for certain persons to *feel*. (*She addresses herself with a certain seriousness, now.*) Loss. Despair. I've faced them and actually they have—fortified and protected, not overcome me at all . . .

BODEY (*in the hall with Miss Gluck*): Okay? *Verstehst du*, Sophie?

HELENA (*still ruminating privately*): The weak. The strong. Only important division between living creatures. (*She nods birdlike affirmation.*)

(*Miss Gluck remains visible in the hall, afraid to return upstairs.*)

MISS GLUCK: *Allein, allein.*

(*There is a change in the light. Helena moves a small chair downstage and delivers the following to herself.*)

HELENA: *Allein, allein* means alone, alone. (*A frightened look appears in her eyes.*) Last week I dined alone, alone three nights in a row. There's nothing lonelier than a woman dining alone, and although I loathe preparing food for myself, I cannot bear the humiliation of occupying a restaurant table for one. Dining *au solitaire*! But I would rather starve than reduce my social standards by accepting dinner invitations from that middle-aged gaggle of preposterously vulgar old maids that wants to suck me into their group despite my total abhorrence of all they stand for. Loneliness in the company of five intellectually destitute spinsters is simply loneliness multiplied by five . . .

(*There is a crash in the hallway.*)

DOROTHEA (*from the bedroom*): Is it the phone?

HELENA: Another visit so soon? Miss Bodenheifer, your bereaved friend from upstairs is favoring you with another visit.

MISS GLUCK (*wildly*): *Mein Zimmer is gespukt, gespukt!*

HELENA: "Spooked, spooked"?

BODEY: Sophie, your apartment isn't haunted.

HELENA: Perhaps if you went up with her, it would despook the apartment.

BODEY: Aw, no, I got to stay down and keep a sharp eye on *you*.

HELENA: Which means that she will remain here?

BODEY: Long as she pleases to. What's it to you? She got nothin' contagious. You can't catch heartbreak if you have got no heart.

HELENA: May I suggest that you put her in the back yard in the sun. I think that woman's complexion could stand a touch of color.

BODEY: I am puttin' her nowhere she don't want to be. How about you settin' in the back yard? Some natural color would do your face good for a change.

(*Sensing the hostile "vibes," Miss Gluck moans, swaying a little.*)

HELENA: Miss Bodenheifer, I will not dignify your insults with response or attention!

(*Miss Gluck moans louder.*)

Aren't you able to see that this Miss Gluck is mental? Distressing to hear and to look at! . . . Be that as it may, I shall wait.

BODEY: Sitting? Tight as a tombstone? Huh?

HELENA: I can assure you that for me to remain in this place is at least as unpleasant to me as to you. (*She cries out to Dorothea who is still in the bedroom.*) Dorothea? Dorothea? Can you hear me?

DOROTHEA (*clinging to something in the bedroom*): See you—Blewett—t'morrow . . .

HELENA: No, no, at once, Dorothea, the situation out here is dreadful beyond endurance.

(*Abruptly, Miss Gluck cries out, clutching her abdomen.*)

BODEY: Sophie, what is it, Sophie?

MISS GLUCK: *Heisser Kaffee gibt mir immer Krampf und Durchfall.*

(*This episode in the play must be handled carefully to avoid excessive scatology but keep the humor.*)

BODEY: You got the runs? *Zum Badezimmer*? Sophie's got to go to the bathroom, Dotty.

DOROTHEA: Hasn't she got one upstairs?

BODEY: After hot coffee, it gives her diarrhea!

DOROTHEA: Must she have it down here?

MISS GLUCK (*in German*): *KANN NICHT WARTEN!*

BODEY: She can't wait, here, bathroom, Sophie! *Badezimmer!*

(*Miss Gluck rushes through the bedroom into the bathroom.*)

DOROTHEA: What a scene for Helena to report at Blewett. Miss Gluck, turn on both water faucets full force.

BODEY: Sophie, *beide Wasser rennen.*

DOROTHEA: Bodey, while I am here don't serve her hot coffee again since it results in these—crises!

BODEY: Dotty, you know that Sophie's got this problem.

DOROTHEA: Then send her coffee upstairs.

BODEY: Dotty, you know she needs companionship, Dotty.

DOROTHEA: That I cannot provide her with just now!

(*Bodey returns to the living room.*)

HELENA: How did Dorothea react to Miss Gluck's sudden indisposition?

BODEY: Dotty's a girl that understands human afflictions.

(*There is a crash in the bathroom.*)

DOROTHEA: Phone, Ralph's call—has he—did he?

BODEY: Phone, Dotty? No, no phone.

HELENA: I wouldn't expect—

BODEY (*to Helena*): Watch it!

HELENA: Watch what, Miss Bodenheifer? What is it you want me to watch?

BODEY: That mouth of yours, the tongue in it, with such a tongue in a mouth you could dig your grave with like a shovel!

HELENA (*her laughter tinkling like ice in a glass*): —The syntax of that sentence was rather confusing. You know, I suspect that English is not your native language but one that you've not quite adequately adopted.

BODEY: I was born on South Grand, a block from Tower Grove Park in this city of St. Louis!

HELENA: Ah, the German section. Your parents were German speaking?

BODEY: I learned plenty English at school, had eight grades of school and a year of business college.

HELENA: I see, I see, forgive me. (*She turns to a window, possibly in the "fourth wall."*) Is a visitor permitted to look out the window?

BODEY: A visitor like you's permitted to jump out it.

HELENA (*laughing indulgently*): With so many restrictions placed on one's speech and actions—

(*Bodey turns up her hearing aid so high that it screeches shrilly.*)

DOROTHEA: Is it the phone?

HELENA: Please. Is it controllable, that electric hearing device?

BODEY: What did you say?

(*The screeching continues.*)

HELENA: Ow . . . ow . . .

(*Bodey finally manages to turn down the hearing aid.*)

DOROTHEA: Oh please bring a mop, Bodey. Water's streaming under—the bathroom door. Miss Gluck's flooded the bathroom.

BODEY: What? Bring?

HELENA: *Mop, mop!*

(*Helena moves toward the bedroom door but Bodey shoves her back.*)

BODEY: Stay! Put! Stay put!

(*Bodey grabs a mop from the closet and then rushes into the bedroom.*)

DOROTHEA: See? Water? Flooding?

BODEY: You told her to turn on both faucets. SOPHIE! *Halte das Wasser ab*, Sophie! (*Bodey opens the bathroom door and thrusts in the mop.*) Here, *das Wust, das Wust*, Sophie!

DOROTHEA (*to herself*): This is incredible to me, I simply do not believe it! (*She then speaks to Bodey who has started back toward the living room.*) May I detain you a moment? The truth has finally struck me. Ralph's calls have been intercepted. He has been repeatedly calling me on that phone, and you have been just as repeatedly lying to me that he hasn't.

BODEY: LYING TO—?

DOROTHEA: YES, LYING! (*She stumbles to the door of the bedroom.*) Helena, will *you* please watch that phone for me now?

HELENA (*crossing to the bedroom door*): I'm afraid, Dorothea, that a watched phone never rings!

(*Bodey emerges from the bedroom. She and Helena return to the living room while Dorothea retreats to the bed, shutting the door behind her.*)

What a view through this window, totally devoid of—why, no, a living creature, a pigeon! Capable of flight but perched for a moment in this absolute desolation . . .

Interval

SCENE TWO

The scene is the same as before. The spotlight focuses on the left-hand, "bedroom" portion of the stage where Dorothea, seated at her vanity table and mellowed by her mebaral and sherry "cocktail," soliloquizes.

DOROTHEA (*taking a large swallow of sherry*): Best years of my youth thrown away, wasted on poor Hathaway James. (*She removes his picture from the vanity table and with closed eyes thrusts it out of sight.*) Shouldn't say wasted but so unwisely devoted. Not even sure it was love. Unconsummated love, is it really love? More likely just a reverence for his talent—precocious achievements . . . musical prodigy. Scholarship to Juilliard, performed a concerto with the Nashville Symphony at fifteen. (*She sips more sherry.*) But those dreadful embarrassing evenings on Aunt Belle's front porch in Memphis! He'd say: "Turn out the light, it's attracting insects." I'd switch it out. He'd grab me so tight it would take my breath away, and invariably I'd feel plunging, plunging against me that—that—frantic part of him . . . then he'd release me at once and collapse on the porch swing, breathing hoarsely. With the corner gas lamp shining through the wisteria vines, it was impossible not to notice the wet stain spreading on his light flannel trousers. . . . Miss Gluck, MOP IN!!

(*Miss Gluck, who has timidly opened the bathroom door and begun to emerge, with the mop, into the bedroom, hastily retreats from sight.*)

Such afflictions—visited on the gifted. . . . Finally worked up the courage to discuss the—Hathaway's—problem with the family doctor, delicately but clearly as I could. "Honey, this Hathaway fellow's afflicted with something clinically known as—chronic case of—premature ejaculation—must have a large laundry bill. . . ." "Is it curable, Doctor?" —"Maybe with great patience, honey, but remember you're only young once, don't gamble on it, relinquish him to his interest in music, let him go."

(*Miss Gluck's mop protrudes from the bathroom again.*)

MISS GLUCK, I SAID MOP IN. REMAIN IN BATHROOM WITH WET MOP TILL MOP UP COMPLETED. MERCIFUL HEAVENS.

(*Helena and Bodey are now seen in the living room.*)

HELENA: Is Dorothea attempting a conversation with Miss Gluck in there?

BODEY: No, no just to herself—you gave her the sherry on top of mebaral tablets.

HELENA: She talks to herself? That isn't a practice that I would encourage her in.

BODEY: She don't need no encouragement in it, and as for you, I got an idea you'd encourage nobody in nothing.

DOROTHEA (*in the bedroom*): After Hathaway James, there was nothing left for me but—CIVICS.

HELENA (*who has moved to the bedroom door the better to hear Dorothea's "confessions"*): This is not to B. B.!

BODEY: Stop listening at the door. Go back to your pigeon watching.

HELENA: How long is this apt to continue?

DOROTHEA: Oh, God, thank you that Ralph Ellis has no such affliction—is healthily aggressive.

HELENA: I have a luncheon engagement in La Due at two!

BODEY: Well, go keep it! On time!

HELENA: My business with Dorothea must take precedence over anything else! (*Helena pauses to watch with amused suspicion as Bodey "attacks" the Sunday* Post-Dispatch *which she has picked up from the chair.*) What is that you're doing, Miss Bodenheifer?

BODEY: Tearing a certain item out of the paper.

HELENA: A ludicrous thing to do since the news will be all over Blewett High School tomorrow.

BODEY: Never mind tomorrow. There's ways and ways to break a piece of news like that to a girl with a heart like Dotty. You wouldn't know about that, no, you'd do it right now—malicious! —You got eyes like a bird and I don't mean a songbird.

HELENA: Oh, is that *so*?
BODEY: Yeh, yeh, that's so, I know!

(*Pause. Bodey, who has torn out about half of the top page of one section, puts the rest of the paper on the sofa, and takes the section from which the piece has been torn with her as she crosses to the kitchenette, crumpling and throwing the torn piece into the wastebasket on her way.*)

HELENA: Miss Bodenheifer.
BODEY (*from the kitchenette*): Hafer!
HELENA: I have no wish to offend you, but surely you're able to see that for Dorothea to stay in these circumstances must be extremely embarrassing to her at least.
BODEY: Aw, you think Dotty's embarrassed here, do you?

(*Bodey has begun to line a shoebox with the section of newspaper she took with her. During the following exchange with Helena, Bodey packs the fried chicken and other picnic fare in the shoebox.*)

HELENA: She has hinted it's almost intolerable to her. The visitations of this Gluck person who has rushed to the bathroom, this nightmare of clashing colors, the purple carpet, orange drapes at the windows looking out at that view of brick and concrete and asphalt, lamp shades with violent yellow daisies on them, and wallpaper with roses exploding like bombshells, why it would give her a breakdown! It's giving me claustrophobia briefly as I have been here. Why, this is not a place for a civilized person to possibly exist in!
BODEY: What's so civilized about you, Miss Brooks-it? Stylish, yes, civilized, no, unless a hawk or a buzzard is a civilized creature. Now you see, you got a tongue in your mouth, but I got one in mine, too.
HELENA: You are being hysterical and offensive!
BODEY: You ain't heard nothing compared to what you'll hear if you continue to try to offer all this concern you feel about Dotty to Dotty in this apartment.
HELENA: Dorothea Gallaway and I keep nothing from each other and naturally I intend, as soon as she has recovered, to prepare her for what she can hardly avoid facing sooner or later and I—

BODEY (*cutting in*): I don't want heartbreak for Dotty. For Dotty I want a—life.

HELENA: A life of—?

BODEY: A life, a *life*—

HELENA: You mean as opposed to a death?

BODEY: Don't get smart with me. I got your number the moment you come in that door like a well-dressed snake.

HELENA: So far you have compared me to a snake and a bird. Please decide which—since the archaeopteryx, the only known combination of bird and snake, is long extinct!

BODEY: Yes, well, you talk with a kind of a hiss. Awright, you just hiss away but not in this room which you think ain't a civilized room. Okay, it's too cheerful for you but for me and Dotty it's fine. And this afternoon, at the picnic at Creve Coeur Lake, I will tell Dotty, gentle, in my own way, if it's necessary to tell her, that this unprincipled man has just been using her. But Buddy, my brother Buddy, if in some ways he don't suit her like he is now, I will see he quits beer, I will see he cuts out his cigars, I will see he continues to take off five pounds a week. And by Dotty and Buddy there will be children—children! —I will never have none, myself, no! But Dotty and Buddy will have beautiful kiddies. Me? Nieces—nephews. . . . —Now you! I've wrapped up the picnic. It's nice and cool at Creve Coeur Lake and the ride on the open-air streetcar is lickety-split through green country and there's flowers you can pull off the bushes you pass. It's a fine excursion. Dotty will forget not gettin' that phone call. We'll stay out till it's close to dark and the fireflies—fly. I will slip away and Buddy will be alone with her on the lake shore. He will smoke no smelly cigar. He will just respectfully hold her hand and say—"I love you, Dotty. Please be mine," not meanin' a girl in a car parked up on Art Hill but—for the long run of life.

HELENA: —Can Dorothea be really attached to your brother? Is it a mutual attraction?

BODEY: Dotty will settle for Buddy. She's got a few reservations about him so far, but at Creve Coeur she'll suddenly recognize the—wonderful side of his nature.

HELENA: Miss Bodenheifer, Dorothea is not intending to remain in this tasteless apartment. Hasn't she informed you that she is planning to share a lovely apartment with me? The upstairs of a duplex on Westmoreland Place?

BODEY: Stylish? Civilized, huh? And too expensive for you to swing it alone, so you want to rope Dotty in, rope her into a place that far from Blewett? Share expenses? You prob'ly mean pay most.

HELENA: To move from such an unsuitable environment must naturally involve some expense.

(*Miss Gluck falls out of the bathroom onto Dorothea's bed.*)

DOROTHEA: MISS GLUCK! CAREFUL! Bodey, Bodey, Sophie Gluck's collapsed on my bed in a cloud of steam!

HELENA: Has Miss Gluck broken a steam pipe?

(*Bodey rushes from the kitchenette into the bedroom.*)

BODEY (*to Helena*): You stay out.

(*Dorothea emerges from the bedroom. She closes the door and leans against it briefly, closing her eyes as if dizzy or faint.*)

HELENA: At last.

DOROTHEA: I'm so mortified.

HELENA: Are you feeling better?

DOROTHEA: Sundays are always different—

HELENA: This one exceptionally so.

DOROTHEA: I don't know why but—I don't quite understand why I am so—agitated. Something happened last week, just a few evenings ago that—

HELENA: Yes? What?

DOROTHEA: Nothing that I'm—something I can't discuss with you. I was and still am expecting a very important phone call—

HELENA: May I ask you from whom?

DOROTHEA: No, please.

HELENA: Then may I hazard a guess that the expected call not received was from a young gentleman who cuts a quite spectacular figure in the country club set but somehow became involved in the educational system?

DOROTHEA: If you don't mind, Helena, I'd much prefer not to discuss anything of a—private nature right now.

HELENA: Yes, I understand, dear. And since you've located that chair, why don't you seat yourself in it?

DOROTHEA: Oh, yes, excuse me. (*She sits down, weakly, her hand lifted to her throat.*) The happenings here today are still a bit confused in my head. I was doing my exercises before you dropped by.

HELENA: And for quite a while after.

DOROTHEA: I was about to—no, I'd taken my shower. I was about to get dressed.

HELENA: But the Gluck intervened. Such discipline! Well! I've had the privilege of an extended meeting with Miss Bodenheifer— (*She lowers her voice.*) She seemed completely surprised when I mentioned that you were moving to Westmoreland Place.

DOROTHEA: Oh, you told her. —I'm glad. —I'm such a coward, I couldn't.

HELENA: Well, I broke the news to her.

DOROTHEA: I—just hadn't the heart to.

(*Miss Gluck advances from the bedroom with a dripping wet mop and a dazed look.*)

HELENA (*to Dorothea*): Can't you see she's already found a replacement?

DOROTHEA: Oh, no, there's a limit even to Bodey's endurance! Miss Gluck, would you please return that wet mop to the kitchen and wring it out. *Küche*—mop—Sophie.

HELENA: Appears to be catatonic.

DOROTHEA (*as she goes into the bedroom to get Bodey*): Excuse me.

(*Bodey enters from the bedroom and takes Miss Gluck, with mop, into the kitchenette.*)

BODEY (*singing nervously in the kitchenette*): "I'm just breezing along with the breeze, pleasing to live, and living to please!"

(*Dorothea returns to the living room.*)

DOROTHEA: How did Bodey take the news I was moving?

HELENA: "That far from *Blewett*!" she said as if it were transcontinental.

DOROTHEA: Well, it is a bit far, compared to this location.

HELENA: Surely you wouldn't compare it to *this* location.

DOROTHEA: Oh, no, Westmoreland Place is a—fashionable address, incomparable in that respect, but it is quite a distance. Of course, just a block from Delmar Boulevard and the Olive Street car-line, that would let me off at—what point closest to Blewett?

HELENA: Dorothea, forget transportation, that problem. We're going by automobile.

DOROTHEA: By—what automobile do you—?

HELENA: I have a lovely surprise for you, dear.

DOROTHEA: Someone is going to drive us?

HELENA: Yes, I will be the chauffeur and you the passenger, dear. You see, my wealthy cousin Dee-Dee, who lives in La Due, has replaced her foreign-made car, an Hispano-Suiza, no less, practically brand-new, with a Pierce Arrow limousine and has offered to sell us the Hispano for just a song! Immediately, as soon as she made me this offer, I applied for a driver's license.

(*A moment of shocked silence is interrupted by a short squawk from Bodey's hearing aid.*)

BODEY (*advancing quickly from the kitchenette*): Limazine? What limazine? With a show-fer?

HELENA: Miss Bodenheifer, how does this concern you?

BODEY: Who's gonna foot the bill for it, that's how!

HELENA: My cousin Dee-Dee in La Due will accept payment on time.

BODEY: Whose time and how much?

HELENA: *Negligible! A rich cousin!* —Oh, my Lord, I've always heard that Germans—

BODEY: Lay off Germans!

HELENA: Have this excessive concern with money matters.

BODEY: *Whose* money?

HELENA: Practicality can be a stupefying—

MISS GLUCK: Bodey?

HELENA: —virtue, if it *is* one.

MISS GLUCK: *Ich kann nicht*—go up.

HELENA: Go up just one step to the kitchen! Please, Dorothea, can't we—have a private discussion, briefly?

MISS GLUCK: *Das Schlafzimmer is gespukt!*

HELENA: Because you see, Dorothea, as I told you, I do have to make a payment on the Westmoreland Place apartment early tomorrow, and so must collect your half of it today.

DOROTHEA: —My half would amount to—?

HELENA: Seventy.

DOROTHEA: Ohhh! —Would the real estate people accept a—postdated check?

HELENA: Reluctantly—very.

DOROTHEA: You see, I had unusually heavy expenses this week—clothes, lingerie, a suitcase . . .

HELENA: Sounds as if you'd been purchasing a trousseau. —Miss Bodenhafer says that her brother, "Buddy," is seriously interested in you. How selfish of you to keep it such a secret!—even from me!

DOROTHEA: Oh, my heavens, has Miss Bodenhafer—how fantastic!

HELENA: Yes, she is a bit, to put it politely.

DOROTHEA: I meant has she given you the preposterous impression that I am interested in her brother? Oh, my Lord, what a fantastic visit you've had! Believe me, the circumstances aren't always so—chaotic. Well! *Il n'y a rien à faire.* When I tell you that she calls her brother Buddy and that he is her *twin*! (*She throws up her arms.*)

HELENA: Identical?

DOROTHEA: Except for gender, alike as two peas in a pod. You're not so gullible, Helena, that you could really imagine for a moment that I'd—you know me better than that!

HELENA: Sometimes when a girl is on the rebound from a disappointing infatuation, she will leap without looking into the most improbable sort of—liaison—

DOROTHEA: Maybe some girls, but certainly not I. And what makes you think that I'm the victim of a "disappointing infatuation," Helena?

HELENA: Sometimes a thing will seem like the end of the world, and yet the world continues.

DOROTHEA: I personally feel that my world is just beginning. . . . Excuse me for a moment. I'll get my checkbook. . . .

(*Dorothea goes into the bedroom. Miss Gluck wanders back into the living room from the kitchenette, wringing her hands and sobbing.*)

HELENA: MISS BODENHEIFER!

BODEY: Don't bother to tell me good-bye.

HELENA: I am not yet leaving.

BODEY: And it ain't necessary to shake the walls when you call me, I got my hearing aid on.

HELENA: Would you be so kind as to confine Miss Gluck to that charming little kitchen while I'm completing my business with Dorothea?

(*Bodey crosses toward Miss Gluck.*)

BODEY: Sophie, come in here with me. You like a deviled egg don't you? And a nice fried drumstick when your—digestion is better? Just stay in here with me.

(*Bodey leads Miss Gluck back to the kitchenette, then turns to Helena.*)

I can catch every word that you say to Dotty in there, and you better be careful the conversation don't take the wrong turn!

MISS GLUCK (*half in German*): *Ich kann nicht* liven opstairs no more, *nimmer, nimmer—kann nicht*—can't go!

BODEY: You know what, Sophie? You better change apartments. There's a brand-new vacancy. See—right over there, the fifth floor. It's bright and cheerful—I used to go up there sometimes—it's a sublet, furnished, everything in cheerful colors. I'll speak to Mr. Schlogger, no, no, to *Mrs.* Schlogger, she makes better terms. Him, bein' paralyzed, he's got to accept 'em, y'know.

MISS GLUCK: I think— (*She sobs.*) —Missus Schlogger don't like me.

BODEY: That's—*impossible*, Sophie. I think she just had a little misunderstanding with your— (*She stops herself.*)

MISS GLUCK: *Meine Mutter, ja—*

BODEY: Sophie, speak of the Schloggers, she's wheeling that old *Halunke* out on their fire escape.

(*The Schloggers are heard from offstage.*)

MR. SCHLOGGER'S VOICE: I didn't say *out* in the sun.
MRS. SCHLOGGER'S VOICE: You said out, so you're out.
BODEY (*shouting out the window*): Oh, my *Gott*, Missus Schlogger, a stranger that didn't know you would think you meant to push him offa the landin'. Haul him back in, you better. Watch his cane, he's about to hit you with it. Amazin' the strength he's still got in his good arm.
MRS. SCHLOGGER'S VOICE: Now you want back in?

(*Helena rises to watch this episode on the fire escape.*)

MR. SCHLOGGER'S VOICE: Not in the kitchen with you.
HELENA (*to herself but rather loudly*). Schloggers, so those are Schloggers.
BODEY (*to Miss Gluck*): She's got him back in. I'm gonna speak to her right now. —HEY MISSUS SCHLOGGER, YOU KNOW MISS GLUCK? AW, SURE YOU REMEMBER SOPHIE UPSTAIRS IN 4-F? SHE LOST HER MOTHER LAST SUNDAY. Sophie, come here, stick your head out, Sophie. NOW YOU REMEMBER HER, DON'T YOU?
MRS. SCHLOGGER'S VOICE: *Ja, ja.*
BODEY: *JA, JA*, SURE YOU REMEMBER! MRS. SCHLOGGER, POOR SOPHIE CAN'T LIVE ALONE IN 4-F WHERE SHE LOST HER MOTHER. SHE NEEDS A NEW APARTMENT THAT'S BRIGHT AND CHEERFUL TO GET HER OUT OF DEPRESSION. HOW ABOUT THE VACANCY ON THE FIFTH FLOOR FOR SOPHIE. WE GOT TO LOOK OUT FOR EACH OTHER IN TIMES OF SORROW. *VERSTEHEN SIE?*
MRS. SCHLOGGER'S VOICE: I don't know.
BODEY: GIVE SOPHIE THAT VACANCY UP THERE. THEN TERMS I'LL DISCUSS WITH YOU. (*She draws Miss Gluck back from the window.*) Sophie, I think that done it, and that apartment on five is bright and cheerful like here. And you're not gonna be lonely. We got three chairs at this table, and we can work out an arrangement so you can eat here with us, more economical that way. It's no good cooking for one, cookin' and eatin' alone is—lonely after—

(*Helena resumes her seat as Bodey and Miss Gluck return to the kitchenette.*)

HELENA (*with obscure meaning*): Yes— (*She draws a long breath and calls out.*) Dorothea, can't you locate your checkbook in there?

(*Dorothea returns from the bedroom wearing a girlish summer print dress and looking quite pretty.*)

DOROTHEA: I was just slipping into a dress. Now, then, here it is, my checkbook.

HELENA: Good. Where did you buy that new dress?

DOROTHEA: Why, at Scruggs-Vandervoort.

HELENA: Let me remove the price tag. (*As she removes the tag, she looks at it and assumes an amused and slightly superior air.*) Oh, my dear. I must teach you where to find the best values in clothes. In La Due there is a little French boutique, not expensive but excellent taste. I think a woman looks best when she dresses without the illusion she's still a girl in her teens. Don't you?

DOROTHEA (*stung*): —My half will be—how much did you say?

HELENA: To be exact, $82.50.

DOROTHEA: My goodness, that will take a good bite out of my savings. Helena, I thought you mentioned a lower amount. Didn't you say it would be seventy?

HELENA: Yes, I'd forgotten—utilities, dear. Now, we don't want to move into a place with the phone turned off, the lights off. Utilities must be *on*, wouldn't you say?

DOROTHEA: —Yes. —Of course, I don't think I'll be dependent on my savings much longer, and a duplex on Westmoreland Place— (*She writes out a check.*) —*is* a—quite a—worthwhile—investment . . .

HELENA: I should think it would strike you as one after confinement with Miss Bodenhafer in this nightmare of colors.

DOROTHEA: Oh. —Yes. —Excuse me . . . (*She extends the check slightly.*)

HELENA: —Are you holding it out for the ink to dry on it?

DOROTHEA: —Sorry. —Here. (*She crosses to Helena and hands the check to her.*)

(*Helena puts on her glasses to examine the check carefully. She then folds it, puts it into her purse, and snaps the purse shut.*)

HELENA: Well, that's that. I hate financial dealings but they do have to be dealt with. Don't they?

DOROTHEA: Yes, they seem to . . .

HELENA: Require it. —Oh, contract.

DOROTHEA: Contract? For the apartment?

HELENA: Oh, no, a book on contract bridge, the bidding system and so forth. You do play bridge a little? I asked you once before and you said you did sometimes.

DOROTHEA: Here?

HELENA: Naturally not here. But on Westmoreland Place I hope you'll join in the twice-weekly games. You remember Joan Goode?

DOROTHEA: Yes, vaguely. Why?

HELENA: We were partners in duplicate bridge, which we usually played, worked out our own set of bidding conventions. But now Joan's gone to Wellesley for her Master's degree in, of all things, the pre-Ptolemaic dynasties of Egypt.

DOROTHEA: Did she do that? I didn't know what she did.

HELENA: You were only very casually—

DOROTHEA: Acquainted.

HELENA: My cousin Dee-Dee from La Due takes part whenever her social calendar permits her to. She often sends over dainty little sandwiches, watercress, tomato, sherbets from Zeller's in the summer. And a nicely uniformed maid to serve. Well, now we're converting from auction to contract, which is more complicated but stimulates the mind. —Dorothea, you have an abstracted look. Are you troubled over something?

DOROTHEA: Are these parties mixed?

HELENA: "Mixed" in what manner?

DOROTHEA: I mean would I invite Ralph?

HELENA: I have a feeling that Mr. T. Ralph Ellis might not be able to spare the time this summer. And anyway, professional women do need social occasions without the—male intrusion . . .

DOROTHEA (*with spirit*): I've never thought of the presence of men as being an intrusion.

HELENA: Dorothea, that's just a lingering symptom of your Southern belle complex.

DOROTHEA: In order to be completely honest with you, Helena, I think I ought to tell you—I probably won't be able to share expenses with you in Westmoreland Place for very long, Helena!

HELENA: Oh, is that so? Is that why you've given me the postdated check which you could cancel tomorrow?

DOROTHEA: You know I wouldn't do that, but—

HELENA: Yes, but—you could and possibly you would. . . . Look before you, there stands the specter that confronts you . . .

DOROTHEA: Miss??

HELENA: Gluck, the perennial, the irremediable, Miss Gluck! You probably think me superficial to value as much as I do, cousin Dee-Dee of La Due, contract bridge, possession of an elegant foreign car. Dorothea, only such things can protect us from a future of descent into the Gluck abyss of surrender to the bottom level of squalor. Look at it and tell me honestly that you can afford not to provide yourself with the Westmoreland Place apartment . . . its elevation, its style, its kind of *éclat*.

(*Miss Gluck, who has come out of the kitchenette and moved downstage during Helena's speech, throws a glass of water in Helena's face.*)

DOROTHEA: Bodey, RESTRAIN HER, RESTRAIN MISS GLUCK, SHE'S TURNED VIOLENT.

BODEY: Sophie, no, no. I didn't say you done wrong. I think you done right. I don't think you did enough.

HELENA: Violence does exist in the vegetable kingdom, you see! It doesn't terrify me since I shall soon be safely out of its range. . . . Just let me draw two good deep breaths and I'll be myself again. (*She does so.*) That did it. . . . I'm back in my skin. Oh, Dorothea, we must, must advance in appearances. You don't seem to know how vastly important it is, the move to Westmoreland Place, particularly now at this time when you must escape from reminders of, specters of, that alternative there! Surrender without conditions . . .

DOROTHEA: Sorry. I am a little abstracted. Helena, you sound as if you haven't even suspected that Ralph and I have been dating . . .

HELENA: Seriously?

DOROTHEA: Well, now that I've mentioned it to you, yes, quite. You see, I don't intend to devote the rest of my life to teaching civics at Blewett. I dream, I've always dreamed, of a marriage someday, and I think you should know that it might become a reality this summer.

HELENA: With whom?

DOROTHEA: Why, naturally with the person whom I love. And obviously loves me.

HELENA: T? RALPH? ELLIS?

(*Bodey, still in the kitchenette, nervously sings "Me and My Shadow."*)

DOROTHEA: I thought I'd made that clear, thought I'd made everything clear.

HELENA: Oh, Dorothea, my dear. I hope and pray that you haven't allowed him to take advantage of your—generous nature.

DOROTHEA: Miss Bodenhafer has the same apprehension.

HELENA: That is the one and only respect in which your friend, Miss Bodenhafer, and I have something in common.

DOROTHEA: Poor Miss Bodenhafer is terribly naïve for a girl approaching forty.

HELENA: Miss Bodenhafer is not approaching forty. She has encountered forty and continued past it, undaunted.

DOROTHEA: I don't believe she's the sort of girl who would conceal her age.

HELENA (*laughing like a cawing crow*): Dorothea, no girl could tell me she's under forty and still be singing a song of that vintage. Why, she knows every word of it, including—what do they call it? The introductory verse? Why is she cracking hard-boiled eggs in there?

DOROTHEA: She's making deviled eggs for a picnic lunch.

HELENA: Oh. In Forest Park.

DOROTHEA: No, at Creve Coeur.

HELENA: Oh, at Creve Coeur, that amusement park on a lake, of which Miss Bodenheifer gave such a lyrical account. Would you like a Lucky?

DOROTHEA: No. Thank you. My father smoked Chesterfields. Do you know Creve Coeur?

HELENA: Heard of it. Only. You go out, just the two of you?

DOROTHEA: No, her brother, Buddy, usually goes with us on these excursions. They say they've been going out there since they were children, Bodey and Buddy. They still ride the Ferris wheel, you know, and there's a sort of loop-the-loop that takes you down to the lake shore. Seats much too narrow sometimes. You see, it's become embarrassing to me lately, the brother you know . . .

HELENA: Who doesn't interest you?

DOROTHEA: Heavens, no, it's—pathetic. I don't want to hurt Bodey's feelings, but the infatuation is hardly a mutual thing and it never could be, of course, since I am—well, involved with—

HELENA: The dashing, the irresistible new principal at Blewett.

(*Bodey sings.*)

DOROTHEA: —I'd rather not talk about that—prematurely, you know. Ralph feels it's not quite proper for a principal to be involved with a teacher. He's—a very, very scrupulous young man.

HELENA: Oh? Is that the impression he gives you? I'm rather surprised he's given you that impression.

DOROTHEA: I don't see why. Is it just because he's young and attractive with breeding, background? Frequently mentioned in the social columns? Therefore beyond involvement with a person of my ignominious position.

HELENA: Personally, I'd avoid him like a—snakebite!

(*Bodey, in the kitchenette, sings "I'm Just Breezing along with the Breeze" again.*)

Another one of her oldies! The prospect of this picnic at Creve Coeur seems to make her absolutely euphoric.

DOROTHEA: I'm afraid that they're the high points in her life. Sad . . . Helena, I'm very puzzled by your attitude toward

Ralph Ellis. Why on earth would a girl want to avoid a charming young man like Ralph?

HELENA: Perhaps you'll understand a little later.

(*Dorothea glances at her watch and the silent phone.*)

DOROTHEA (*raising her voice*): Bodey, please not quite so loud in there! Miss Brookmire and I are holding a conversation in here, you know. (*She turns back to Helena and continues the conversation with an abrupt vehemence.*) —Helena, that woman wants to absorb my life like a blotter, and I'm not an ink splash! I'm sorry you had to meet her. I'm awfully—embarrassed, believe me.

HELENA: I don't regret it at all. I found her most amusing. Even the Gluck!

DOROTHEA (*resuming with the same intensity*): Bodey wants me to follow the same, same old routine that she follows day in and day out and I—feel sympathy for the loneliness of the girl, but we have nothing, nothing, but *nothing* at all, in common. (*She interrupts herself.*) Shall we have some coffee?

HELENA: Yes, please. I do love iced coffee, but perhaps the ice is depleted.

BODEY (*from the kitchenette*): She knows darn well she used the last piece.

HELENA: Is it still warm?

(*Dorothea has risen and gone into the kitchenette where she pours two cups of coffee.*)

DOROTHEA: It never cools off in this electric percolator, runs out, but never cools off. Do you take cream?

HELENA: No, thank you.

DOROTHEA (*bringing the coffee into the living room*): Bodey does make very good coffee. I think she was born and raised in a kitchen and will probably die in a kitchen if ever she does break her routine that way.

(*Bodey crosses to the kitchen table with Dorothea's purse and hat which she has collected from the living room while Helena and Dorothea sip their coffee.*)

BODEY: Dotty, remember, Buddy is waiting for us at the Creve Coeur station, we mustn't let him think we've stood him up.

DOROTHEA (*sighing*): Excuse me, Helena, there really has been a terrible problem with communication today. (*She crosses to Bodey and adjusts her hearing aid for her.*) Can you hear me clearly, now at last?

BODEY: You got something to tell me?

DOROTHEA: Something I've told you already, frequently, loudly, and clearly, but which you simply will not admit because of your hostility toward Ralph Ellis. I'm waiting here to receive an important call from him, and I am not going anywhere till it's come through.

BODEY: Dotty. It's past noon and he still hasn't called.

DOROTHEA: On Saturday evenings he's out late at social affairs and consequently sleeps late on Sundays.

BODEY: This late?

HELENA: Miss Bodenhafer doesn't know how the privileged classes live.

BODEY: No, I guess not, we're ignorant of the history of art, but Buddy and me, we've got a life going on, you understand, we got a life . . .

DOROTHEA: Bodey, you know I'm sorry to disappoint your plans for the Creve Coeur picnic, but you must realize by now—after our conversation before Miss Brookmire dropped in—that I can't allow this well-meant design of yours to get me involved with your brother to go any further. So that even if I were *not* expecting this important phone call, I would not go to Creve Coeur with you and your brother this afternoon—or ever! It wouldn't be fair to your brother to, to—lead him on that way . . .

BODEY: Well, I did fry up three chickens and I boiled a dozen eggs, but, well, that's—

HELENA: Life for you, Miss Bodenhafer. We've got to face it.

BODEY: But I really was hoping—expecting—

(*Tears appear in Bodey's large, childlike eyes.*)

HELENA: Dorothea, I believe she's beginning to weep over this. Say something comforting to her.

DOROTHEA: Bodey? Bodey? This afternoon you must break the news to your brother that—much as I appreciate his attentions—I am seriously involved with someone else, and I think you can do this without hurting his feelings. Let him have some beer first and a—cigar. . . . And about this superabundance of chicken and deviled eggs, Bodey, why don't you call some girl who works in your office and get her to go to Creve Coeur and enjoy the picnic with you this afternoon?

BODEY: Buddy and I, we—don't have fun with—strangers . . .

DOROTHEA: Now, how can you call them strangers when you've been working in the same office with these girls at International Shoe for—how many years? Almost twenty? Strangers? Still?

BODEY: —Not all of 'em have been there long as me . . . (*She blows her nose.*)

DOROTHEA: Oh, some of them must have, surely, unless the death rate in the office is higher than—a cat's back.

(*Dorothea smiles half-apologetically at Helena. Helena stifles a malicious chuckle.*)

BODEY: —You see, Dotty, Buddy and me feel so at home with you now.

DOROTHEA: Bodey, we knew that I was here just for a while because it's so close to Blewett. Please don't make me feel *guilty*. I have no reason to, do I?

BODEY: —No, no, Dotty—but don't worry about it. Buddy and me, we are both—big eaters, and if there's somethin' left over, there's always cute little children around Creve Coeur that we could share with, Dotty, so—

DOROTHEA: Yes, there must be. Do that. Let's not prolong this discussion. I see it's painful to you.

BODEY: —Do you? No. It's—you I'm thinking of, Dotty. —Now if for some reason you should change your mind, here is the schedule of the open-air streetcars to Creve Coeur.

HELENA: Yellowing with antiquity. Is it legible still?

BODEY: We'll still be hoping that you might decide to join us, you know that, Dotty.

DOROTHEA: Yes, of course—I know that. Now why don't you finish packing and start out to the station?

BODEY: —Yes. —But remember how welcome you would be if—shoes. (*She starts into the bedroom to put on her shoes.*) I still have my slippers on.

DOROTHEA (*to Helena after Bodey has gone into the bedroom*): So! You've got the postdated check. I will move to Westmoreland Place with you July first, although I'll have to stretch quite a bit to make ends meet in such an expensive apartment.

HELENA: Think of the advantages. A fashionable address, two bedrooms, a baby grand in the front room and—

DOROTHEA: Yes, I know. It would be a very good place to entertain Ralph.

HELENA: I trust that entertaining Ralph is not your only motive in making this move to Westmoreland Place.

DOROTHEA: Not the only, but the principal one.

HELENA (*leaning forward slowly, eyes widening*): Oh, my dear Dorothea! I have the very odd feeling that I saw the name Ralph Ellis in the newspaper. In the society section.

DOROTHEA: In the society section?

HELENA: I think so, yes. I'm sure so.

(*Rising tensely, Dorothea locates the Sunday paper which Bodey had left on the sofa, in some disarray, after removing the "certain item"—the society page. She hurriedly looks through the various sections trying to find the society news.*)

DOROTHEA: Bodey? —BOOO-DEYY!

BODEY: What, Dotty?

DOROTHEA: Where is the society page of the *Post-Dispatch*?

BODEY: —Oh . . .

DOROTHEA: What does "oh" mean? It's disappeared from the paper and I'd like to know where.

BODEY: Dotty, I—

DOROTHEA: What's wrong with you? Why are you upset? I just want to know if you've seen the society page of the Sunday paper?

BODEY: —Why, I—used it to wrap fried chicken up with, honey.

DOROTHEA (*to Helena*): The only part of the paper in which I have any interest. She takes it and wraps fried chicken in it before I get up in the morning! You see what I mean? Do you understand now? (*She turns back to Bodey.*) Please remove the fried chicken from the society page and *let me have it!*

BODEY: —Honey, the chicken makes the paper so greasy that—

DOROTHEA: *I will unwrap it myself!* (*She charges into the kitchenette, unwraps the chicken, and folds out the section of pages.*) —A section has been torn out of it? Why? What for?

BODEY: Is it? I—

DOROTHEA: Nobody possibly could have done it but you. What did you do with the torn out piece of the paper?

BODEY: —I— (*She shakes her head helplessly.*)

DOROTHEA: Here it is! —Crumpled and tossed in the wastebasket!—What for, I wonder? (*She snatches up the crumpled paper from the wastebasket and straightens it, using both palms to press it hard against the kitchen table so as to flatten it. She holds up the torn-out section of the paper so the audience can see a large photograph of a young woman, good looking in a plain fashion, wearing a hard smile of triumph, then she reads aloud in a hoarse, stricken voice.*) Mr. and Mrs. James Finley announce the engagement of their daughter, Miss Constance Finley, to Mr.—T. Ralph Ellis, principal of—

(*Pause. There is much stage business. Dorothea is stunned for some moments but then comes to violent life and action. She picks up the picnic shoebox, thrusts it fiercely into Bodey's hands, opens the door for her but rushes back to pick up Bodey's small black straw hat trimmed with paper daisies, then opens the door for Bodey again with a violent gesture meaning, "Go quick!" Bodey goes. In the hall we hear various articles falling from Bodey's hold and a small, panting gasp. Then there is silence. Helena gets up with a mechanical air of sympathy.*)

HELENA: That woman is sly all right but not as sly as she's stupid. She might have guessed you'd want the society page and notice Mr. Ellis's engagement had been torn out. Anyhow, the news would have reached you at the school tomorrow. Of course I can't understand how you could be taken in by whatever little attentions you may have received from Ralph Ellis.

DOROTHEA: —"Little—attentions?" I assure you they were not—"little attentions," they were—

HELENA: Little attentions which you magnified in your imagination. Well, now, let us dismiss the matter, which has dismissed itself! Dorothea, about the postdated check, I'm not sure the real estate agents would be satisfied with that.

Now surely, Dorothea, surely you have relatives who could help you with a down payment in cash?

DOROTHEA: —Helena, I'm not interested in Westmoreland Place. —Now.

HELENA: What!

DOROTHEA: I've—abandoned that idea. I've decided not to move.

HELENA (*aghast*): —Do you realize what a shockingly irresponsible thing you are doing? Don't you realize that you are placing me in a very unfair position? You led me to believe I could count on your sharing the expense of the place, and now, at the last moment, when I have no time to get hold of someone else, you suddenly—pull out. It's really irresponsible of you. It's a really very irresponsible thing to do.

DOROTHEA: —I'm afraid we wouldn't have really gotten along together. I'm not uncomfortable here. It's only two blocks from the school and—I won't be needing a place I can't afford to entertain—anyone now.—I think I would like to be alone.

HELENA: All I can say is, the only thing I can say is—

DOROTHEA: Don't say it, just, just—leave me alone, now, Helena.

HELENA: Well, that I shall do. You may be right, we wouldn't have gotten along. Perhaps Miss Bodenheifer and her twin brother are much more on your social and cultural level than I'd hoped. And of course there's always the charm of Miss Gluck from upstairs.

DOROTHEA: The prospect of that is not as dismaying to me, Helena, as the little card parties and teas you'd had in mind for us on Westmoreland Place . . .

HELENA: *Chacun à son goût.*

DOROTHEA: Yes, yes.

HELENA (*at the door*): There is rarely a graceful way to say good-bye. (*She exits.*)

(*Pause. Dorothea shuts her eyes very tight and raises a clenched hand in the air, nodding her head several times as if affirming an unhappy suspicion regarding the way of the world. This gesture suffices to discharge her sense of defeat. Now she springs up determinedly and goes to the phone.*

(*While waiting for a connection, she notices Miss Gluck seated disconsolately in a corner of the kitchenette.*)

DOROTHEA: Now Miss Gluck, now Sophie, we must pull ourselves together and go on. Go on, we must just go on, that's all that life seems to offer and—demand. (*She turns her attention to the phone.*) Hello, operator, can you get me information, please? —Hello? Information? Can you get me the number of the little station at the end of the Delmar car-line where you catch the, the—open streetcar that goes out to Creve Coeur Lake? —Thank you.

MISS GLUCK (*speaking English with difficulty and a heavy German accent*): Please don't leave me alone. I can't go up!

DOROTHEA (*her attention still occupied with the phone*): Creve Coeur car-line station? Look. On the platform in a few minutes will be a plumpish little woman with a big artificial flower over one ear and a stoutish man with her, probably with a cigar. I have to get an important message to them. Tell them that Dotty called and has decided to go to Creve Coeur with them after all so will they please wait. You'll have to shout to the woman because she's—*deaf* . . .

(*For some reason the word "deaf" chokes her and she begins to sob as she hangs up the phone. Miss Gluck rises, sobbing louder.*)

No, no, Sophie, come here. (*Impulsively she draws Miss Gluck into her arms.*) I know, Sophie, I know, crying is a release, but it—inflames the eyes.

(*She takes Miss Gluck to the armchair and seats her there. Then she goes to the kitchenette, gets a cup of coffee and a cruller, and brings them to Sophie.*)

Make yourself comfortable, Sophie.

(*She goes to the bedroom, gets a pair of gloves, then returns and crosses to the kitchen table to collect her hat and pocketbook. She goes to the door, opens it, and says . . .*)

We'll be back before dark.

The Lights Dim Out

CHRONOLOGY

NOTE ON THE TEXTS

NOTES

Chronology

1911 Born March 26 in Columbus, Mississippi, the second child of Edwina Estelle Dakin Williams and Cornelius Coffin Williams, and christened Thomas Lanier Williams III. (Grandfather Thomas Lanier Williams II was an unsuccessful candidate for governor of Tennessee who later served as state railroad commissioner. Father, born 1879 in Knoxville and known as "C.C.," served in the Spanish-American War, worked for a telephone company as a regional manager, and then became a traveling salesman for a Knoxville men's clothing company. Mother, born 1884 in Marysville, Ohio, moved between Ohio and Tennessee before her family settled in Mississippi in 1901. Parents married in 1907; their first child, Rose, was born in 1909.) Lives with mother, sister, and grandparents in the rectory of St. Paul's Church, where grandfather Walter Dakin, an Episcopal priest, serves as minister; father is usually away from home on business.

1913 Family moves to Nashville when grandfather becomes rector of the Church of the Advent.

1914 Father takes new job as traveling salesman for a St. Louis shoe company, and continues to be away from family most of the time.

1915 Family returns to Mississippi when grandfather becomes rector in Canton and then Clarksdale, town in the Mississippi Delta. Williams is read to by grandparents and mother and listens to animal stories told by "Ozzie," his African-American nurse.

1916 Develops diphtheria during summer, followed by Bright's disease, which leaves him confined to his house and unable to walk for a year and a half. Mother reads to him from Dickens and Shakespeare.

1918 Father moves family in July to St. Louis, where he has taken a job as a branch manager with the International

Shoe Company. Williams enters Eugene Field Elementary School in September. Intimidated by his father, who calls him "Miss Nancy" because of his sensitivity and shyness.

1919 Brother Walter Dakin Williams, called Dakin, born February 21. Tension increases between his parents.

1920 Williams is sent to Clarksdale to stay with his grandparents when his mother becomes ill.

1922 Father is promoted to sales manager and moves family into better apartment. Williams enters Stix School, where he becomes friends with Hazel Kramer.

1924 Family moves into another apartment. Williams enters Ben Blewett Junior High School and begins writing on a secondhand typewriter given to him by his mother. Short story "Isolated" is printed in the school newspaper in November.

1925 Poem "Demon Smoke" appears in school yearbook. Family spends August in Elkmont, Tennessee, in the Smoky Mountains, where Williams learns to swim. Father's drinking becomes chronic problem. Rose, growing increasingly disturbed and rebellious, is sent to All Saints College in Vicksburg, Mississippi. Friendship with Hazel Kramer continues.

1926 Mother has hysterectomy. Williams enters Soldan High School in January. Family moves in June to apartment in University City just west of St. Louis. Williams enters University City High School.

1927 Wins $5 as third prize from *Smart Set* for writing an answer to the question "Can a good wife be a good sport?" Wins a prize for reviewing the film *Stella Dallas.*

1928 Short story "The Vengeance of Nitocris" published in *Weird Tales.* Rose begins to show signs of a deepening depression. Williams goes with his grandfather Dakin to New York, where they see *Show Boat* on Broadway, then sails to Europe with grandfather and a church group from Mississippi for a tour of the Continent. Visits France, Italy, Switzerland, Germany, the Netherlands, and England.

1929 Graduates from high school and enters the University of Missouri at Columbia, intending to study journalism. Pledges Alpha Tau Omega fraternity at his father's insistence. Becomes good friends with Esmeralda Mayes, who is also a poet.

1930 Writes one-act play *Beauty Is the Word*, for a modern drama class he is auditing. Submits it to the Dramatic Arts Club contest and wins honorable mention, the first freshman to be so honored.

1931 Works as typist at International Shoe Company during the summer. Enrolls in the University of Missouri School of Journalism at Columbia.

1932 Completes third year of college, but because he has failed ROTC, father makes him leave school and work as a clerk at the shoe company. Votes for Socialist candidate Norman Thomas for president.

1933 Continues writing and has poems accepted for publication in various journals. Short story "Stella for Star" awarded first prize in the St. Louis Writers' Guild contest.

1935 Suffers collapse from exhaustion in January and is hospitalized. Father allows him to leave the shoe company and spend the summer in Memphis with his Dakin grandparents. Writes *Cairo! Shanghai! Bombay!*, which is produced by an amateur company in Memphis, Williams' first play to be staged. Begins reading the stories of Anton Chekhov. Returns to St. Louis in the fall and audits courses at Washington University.

1936 Admitted to Washington University and writes plays *The Magic Tower* and *Candles to the Sun* for the Mummers, a St. Louis drama group. Becomes friendly with a group of young poets, including Clark Mills McBurney, who introduces him to the work of Hart Crane. Publishes poetry in the university magazine. Deeply moved by seeing Alla Nazimova in a touring company of Ibsen's *Ghosts.*

1937 *Candles to the Sun* is performed by the Mummers in St. Louis in March. Rose is committed to a psychiatric ward in St. Louis, then moved to a Catholic convalescent home, where she is diagnosed as having dementia praecox (schizophrenia). In the summer she is transferred to the state hospital at Farmington, Missouri, and given insulin shock treatment. Supported by the Rev. and Mrs. Dakin, Williams studies playwriting at the University of Iowa under well-known professors E. C. Mabie and E. P. Conkle. Works on a "living newspaper" drama. *The Fugitive Kind* is produced by the Mummers. Completes a draft of *Spring Storm* late in the year.

1938 Submits *Spring Storm* in March to his playwriting class at the University of Iowa, but it is not well received. Awarded B.A. degree in English by the University of Iowa. Spends summer and fall in St. Louis and submits *Spring Storm* to the Mummers, but they do not produce it. Begins writing *Not About Nightingales* in September after reading newspaper account of inmates suffocated in a steam room in a Pennsylvania prison. The St. Louis Poets' Workshop, which McBurney and William Jay Smith had established, continues to meet in the Williams home. Uses name "Tennessee Williams" for the first time on entry form for Group Theatre play contest. Goes to New Orleans in late December for the first of many stays there and is shocked by the lifestyle in the French Quarter. Soon makes friends, and becomes accustomed to and embraces the free-wheeling attitude of Quarterites.

1939 Moves January 1 to 722 Toulouse in the French Quarter, where he remains several weeks, supporting himself briefly as a waiter. Meets artists and writers, including Lyle Saxon and Roark Bradford, and attempts to secure a position with the Federal Writers' Project. Submits *Fugitive Kind* to the Project and continues work on *Not About Nightingales.* Leaves for California on February 20 with James Parrott, a musician who becomes a close friend. Wins $100 from the Group Theatre in March for one-act play collection. Engages Audrey Wood as his agent after she contacts him; she places "The Field of Blue Children" with *Story* magazine, his first publication using the name "Tennessee." Visits Frieda Lawrence in New Mexico because of his devotion to D. H. Lawrence's work. Returns to St. Louis in December, where he learns that he has been awarded a $1,000 grant from the Rockefeller Foundation.

1940 Moves to New York and enrolls in John Gassner's modern drama course at the New School for Social Research. Becomes friends with Donald Windham and Gilbert Maxwell. Lives for a while in Provincetown, Massachusetts, where he meets and falls in love with Kip Kiernan, a dancer. The Theatre Guild opens *Battle of Angels*, directed by Margaret Webster, in Boston on December 30. Becomes friends with Paul Bigelow, who works for the Guild.

1941 *Battle of Angels* closes January 11. Receives draft deferment because of his poor eyesight. Stays briefly in St. Louis, Miami, and Key West, where he meets Marion Vaccaro, who will become one of his best friends. Receives $500 advance from the Theatre Guild to rewrite *Battle of Angels*. Returns to New York and submits the revised play, which is rejected by the Guild. Hume Cronyn takes an option on one-act plays. Spends part of the summer in Provincetown. Returns to New Orleans in September and in November goes to St. Louis, where his grandmother Dakin is ill. Takes a job as a cashier at a New Orleans restaurant in December. Completes draft of a long play, *Stairs to the Roof.*

1942 Stays with friends in New York in January, working on several plays and taking a variety of odd jobs. One-act plays anthologized in *American Scenes* and *Best One-Act Plays.* Collaborates with Donald Windham on a play, *You Touched Me!*, based on a D. H. Lawrence story. Spends part of the summer in Macon, Georgia, with Paul Bigelow, and in Jacksonville, Florida, where he operates a teletype for the U.S. Engineers Office. Returns to New York, where he stays with friends and continues work on *You Touched Me!* In Texas, meets Margo Jones, a leader in the regional theater movement. Meets James Laughlin, publisher of New Directions, in December; he becomes a close friend.

1943 Rose, still confined in a mental institution, undergoes a bilateral prefrontal lobotomy in January. Williams lives in a Brooklyn hotel, then moves to the YMCA. Works briefly as elevator operator, movie theater usher, and bellhop. Returns to St. Louis, where he works on a dramatic adaptation of his story "Portrait of a Girl in

Glass" called "The Gentleman Caller." In May, at the instigation of his agent Audrey Wood, goes to Hollywood to write for MGM at $250 a week. Works on a variety of scripts, including ones for Lana Turner and Margaret O'Brien, and his own "The Gentleman Caller," but is not successful as a screenwriter. Directed by Guthrie McClintic, *You Touched Me!* opens October 13 in Cleveland, Ohio, and is later staged in Pasadena, California.

1944 Grandmother Rose Dakin dies in January in St. Louis, where he is visiting. Kip Kiernan dies from brain tumor in March. Receives a $1,000 grant from Academy of Arts and Letters and goes to Provincetown, where he rewrites "The Gentleman Caller" as a stage play. In September James Laughlin publishes 26 of his poems in *Five Young American Poets* (from this point on, New Directions will publish most of Williams' books). During rehearsals for *The Glass Menagerie*, the new title of "The Gentleman Caller," returns to St. Louis and there is interviewed by a local drama critic, William Inge, an aspiring dramatist himself. *The Glass Menagerie* opens in Chicago on December 26, with Laurette Taylor as Amanda Wingfield. The play receives excellent reviews from drama critics Claudia Cassidy and Ashton Stevens, who write about it repeatedly and are instrumental in making it a hit in Chicago.

1945 *The Glass Menagerie* opens on Broadway on March 31 to generally favorable reviews. Critics have high praise for Laurette Taylor, but some, including George Jean Nathan, have reservations about the play. Two weeks after its opening, it wins the New York Drama Critics Circle Award. Success of the play relieves Williams from the financial troubles that have burdened him; he assigns half of the royalties to his mother. Following eye surgery, goes to Mexico to work on a play called "The Moth," then renamed "Blanche's Chair in the Moon," and later "The Poker Night." New Directions publishes *27 Wagons Full of Cotton and Other One-Act Plays.* Remains in Mexico until August, when he visits Margo Jones in Dallas, then goes to Boston for rehearsals of *You Touched Me!* It debuts in New York on September 25 to generally poor reviews, and closes after 109 performances.

1946 Settles in the French Quarter in New Orleans with Pancho Rodriguez y Gonzales, whom he had met in New Mexico. Writes *Ten Blocks on the Camino Real.* Travels with Rodriguez in May to Taos, where he suffers a severe attack of diverticulitis that requires surgery. Goes to Nantucket for the summer and writes an appreciative letter to Carson McCullers, who soon joins him on the island and shares a house with him and Rodriguez for the summer, beginning an enduring friendship. Meets dramatist Thornton Wilder on Nantucket. Moves in the fall to St. Peter Street in New Orleans and works on two plays, "The Poker Night" and "Chart of Anatomy." Learns of the death of Laurette Taylor. Grandfather Dakin comes to New Orleans to stay with Williams and Rodriguez.

1947 In January, Hume Cronyn produces three Williams plays, including *Portrait of a Madonna*, starring Jessica Tandy, in Los Angeles. Williams travels with Rodriguez and grandfather Dakin to Key West, where actress Miriam Hopkins has a party for them. Sends finished version of "The Poker Night," soon renamed *A Streetcar Named Desire*, to Audrey Wood in March. Meets Irene Selznick, who will produce the play, in Charleston, South Carolina. Settles with Rodriguez in Provincetown, where he meets Frank Merlo. Rodriguez is enraged and they soon end their often tempestuous relationship. Dallas production of "Chart of Anatomy," retitled *Summer and Smoke*, opens July 8. Goes to Los Angeles for a month and sees Jessica Tandy in *Portrait of a Madonna*; she is cast as Blanche in *Streetcar*. Goes to Dallas to see Margo Jones's production of *Summer and Smoke.* Marlon Brando comes to Provincetown in August to read and is cast as Stanley. *A Streetcar Named Desire*, directed by Elia Kazan and starring Tandy, Brando, and Kim Hunter, opens December 3 in New York. Williams leaves for Europe at the end of the year.

1948 Parents separate. *A Streetcar Named Desire* is awarded the Pulitzer Prize and the Drama Critics Circle Award. Williams stays in London, Paris, and Rome, where he meets Truman Capote and Gore Vidal and becomes involved with a young Italian named Salvatore. In England, visits Helen Hayes, who is in rehearsal for *The Glass Menagerie*; meets John Gielgud, Noël Coward, Laurence

Olivier, and Vivien Leigh. Becomes friends with Maria Britneva (later Lady Maria St. Just). Returns to Paris, where he meets Jean Cocteau, who wants to stage a French production of *Streetcar*. In July, his mother and brother come to London for the British opening of *The Glass Menagerie*. Returns to U.S. in September on the *Queen Mary* with Truman Capote. *One Arm and Other Stories* is published by New Directions. *Summer and Smoke*, directed by Margo Jones, opens in New York. In October Frank Merlo moves in with him, beginning the longest intimate relationship of his life. Starts work on a preliminary draft of *Sweet Bird of Youth*. Arranges for Rose to receive half the royalties from *Summer and Smoke*. Visits Paul and Jane Bowles in Tangier in December with Frank Merlo.

1949 Arranges for Rose to be transferred from the state hospital to a private sanitarium in Connecticut. Travels in January with Merlo to Italy, where they take an apartment, and later to Sicily, where they meet Merlo's family. Begins work on the novel *The Roman Spring of Mrs. Stone*. Starts to rely heavily on drugs. In March, travels with Merlo, Capote, and Jack Dunphy to Ischia. Argues frequently with Capote and others. Goes to London in April and visits with Laurence Olivier, director of the London production of *Streetcar*, and Vivien Leigh, who will star as Blanche. Returns with Merlo to New York in September, then goes to Hollywood to advise on the script of the film version of *The Glass Menagerie*. Moves with Merlo and grandfather Dakin to Key West in November. Begins work on *The Rose Tattoo*. New York production of *Streetcar* closes after two years, the longest run of any of his plays on Broadway.

1950 Goes to New York for the openings of Inge's *Come Back, Little Sheba* and Carson McCullers' stage adaptation of *The Member of the Wedding*. Returns to Key West and works on *The Rose Tattoo*, which he dedicates to Merlo. Attends a limited New York run of *Streetcar* starring Uta Hagen and Anthony Quinn and at the end of May sails with Merlo and Jane Smith to Europe. In Paris endeavors to persuade Anna Magnani to star in the stage production of *The Rose Tattoo* but she declines, feeling that she does not speak English well enough. With Merlo, again visits

Sicily, where he hopes to learn local dialect for use in *Tattoo.* They settle for a time in Rome, visit Vienna, then return to the U.S. Buys a house on Duncan Street in Key West that he had previously rented. *The Rose Tattoo* has its off-Broadway premiere in Chicago in December.

1951 *The Rose Tattoo*, starring Maureen Stapleton and Eli Wallach and produced by Cheryl Crawford, opens February 3 on Broadway and later wins Tony Award as best play. Transfers Rose to Stony Lodge, clinic near Ossining, New York, where she will spend most of the rest of her life; visits her often and on occasion takes her to visit Carson McCullers in Nyack or to shop in New York. Begins work on revision of *Battle of Angels* that will become *Orpheus Descending.* Travels with Merlo to England, Italy, Spain, Germany, and to Sweden and Denmark for the premieres of *The Rose Tattoo.* Grows increasingly dependent on alcohol and drugs. Goes to London for premiere of the play, then returns to the U.S. Elia Kazan's film of *A Streetcar Named Desire*, with Marlon Brando as Stanley and Vivien Leigh as Blanche, is released.

1952 Visits New Orleans, then goes to Key West, where he revises *Ten Blocks on the Camino Real* and a screenplay that will ultimately become *Baby Doll.* Goes to New York to see José Quintero's successful revival of *Summer and Smoke* in New York in April at Circle in the Square with Geraldine Page; is moved by the direction and acting. Elected to the National Institute of Arts and Letters. Spends summer in Europe with Merlo, with whom his relations are increasingly strained. Frequently sees Anna Magnani, Carson McCullers, and her husband, Reeves McCullers. Returns to Key West.

1953 *Camino Real* opens in New York March 19 after previews in New Haven and Philadelphia, and is not well received. William, depressed by the reviews and attacks from Walter Winchell and Ed Sullivan, returns to Key West to revise *Camino Real* for publication by New Directions. Works on *Cat on a Hot Tin Roof.* Directs Donald Windham's *The Starless Air* at the Playhouse Theatre in Houston. Argues with Windham about the play and their friendship is strained. Visits his grandfather at the Gayoso Hotel in Memphis, where the Reverend Dakin is living.

Travels extensively in Europe with Merlo and Paul Bowles in the summer. Begins work on a short story, "Man Bring This Up Road," that will ultimately become *The Milk Train Doesn't Stop Here Anymore.* Goes with Paul Bowles to Tangier in the fall. Returns to New York with Merlo in October, then goes to New Orleans, with grandfather Dakin, and spends the rest of the year there.

1954 Spends early months of the year in Key West working on *Cat on a Hot Tin Roof.* Continues work on screenplay, now called "Hide and Seek," that will become *Baby Doll.* Gives poetry reading with Carson McCullers in New York in May. Goes with Merlo a month later to Rome, where they join Maria Britneva and travel to Spain. Drinks heavily and takes increasing amounts of drugs. Returns to U.S. in September with Merlo and Anna Magnani for the filming of *The Rose Tattoo* in Key West. Continues work on revision of *Battle of Angels. Hard Candy*, his second collection of short stories, is published. Grandfather Dakin suffers a stroke in St. Louis.

1955 After some difficulty, Williams and agent Audrey Wood choose Elia Kazan to direct *Cat on a Hot Tin Roof.* Disagrees with Kazan on the ending of the play but eventually revises third act following Kazan's recommendation. Goes to New Orleans in mid-January to direct *27 Wagons Full of Cotton* and opera based on *Lord Byron's Love Letter* at Tulane University. Attends rehearsals of *Cat on a Hot Tin Roof* in New York. Grandfather Dakin dies February 14 in St. Louis at age 97. *Cat on a Hot Tin Roof*, starring Burl Ives, Barbara Bel Geddes, and Ben Gazzara, opens on Broadway March 24 with the revised third act and is a critical triumph. Subsequently wins the Drama Critics Circle award and the Pulitzer Prize. Film of *The Rose Tattoo* is released. Returns to Key West in April with Carson McCullers; they work together, then go to Havana briefly. In June goes again to Europe for the summer. Learns in July that Margo Jones has died. Suffering from writer's block, Williams continues to rely on drink and drugs. Attends Stockholm opening of the Swedish *Cat on a Hot Tin Roof* and visits his friend Lilla von Saher. Returns to New York to work on the screenplay of *Baby Doll*, and also works on "The Enemy: Time," which will become *Sweet Bird of Youth.*

1956 Goes with Maria Britneva and Marion Vaccaro to Miami, where Tallulah Bankhead is starring in a revival of *Streetcar*; his dissatisfaction with her performance is publicized and Williams apologizes to an angry Bankhead. *Sweet Bird of Youth*, directed by George Keathley, opens in Miami on April 16. Williams goes to Rome alone as the tension between him and Merlo increases. In November, *The Glass Menagerie* is revived in New York starring Helen Hayes as Amanda. The film *Baby Doll*, directed by Elia Kazan and starring Carroll Baker and Eli Wallach, is released; it is denounced by Cardinal Spellman, and condemned by the Catholic Legion of Decency and other groups. Goes to Key West with his mother. First collection of poetry, *In the Winter of Cities*, is published.

1957 Travels to New York for revisions and rehearsals of *Orpheus Descending*. Directed by Harold Clurman, the play opens on Broadway on March 21 and closes after two months; its negative reviews worsen Williams' depression. Father dies March 27, and Williams attends funeral in Knoxville with his brother Dakin. In June begins psychotherapy with Dr. Lawrence S. Kubie, a Freudian analyst, who, according to Williams, urges him to quit writing and to live as a heterosexual. Spends the summer in New York, visiting friends and often going to Stony Lodge to see Rose. Works on *Suddenly Last Summer*.

1958 On January 7 *Garden District*, consisting of *Suddenly Last Summer* and *Something Unspoken*, premieres Off Broadway in New York to favorable reviews. Returns to Key West to work on *Sweet Bird of Youth*. Ends his analysis with Dr. Kubie in March and leaves again for Europe. *Cat on a Hot Tin Roof* opens in London and in August the film version, directed by Richard Brooks and starring Elizabeth Taylor, Paul Newman, and Burl Ives, is released. Returns to Florida in the fall, and collaborates with Meade Roberts on script for film of *Orpheus Descending*, which is retitled *The Fugitive Kind*. Continues work on *Sweet Bird of Youth* and *Period of Adjustment*, which opens on December 29 for a brief run at the Coconut Grove Playhouse.

1959 Goes to New York in February for rehearsals of *Sweet Bird of Youth*. Directed by Elia Kazan and starring Geraldine

Page and Paul Newman, it opens on Broadway March 10. Depressed by critical response to the play, Williams leaves New York for Miami and then goes with Marion Vaccaro to Havana, where he meets Fidel Castro, an admirer of Williams' work. Returns with Vaccaro to Key West for a few weeks and in May flies with her to London for the English premiere of *Orpheus Descending*. Returns to New York in June for rehearsals of *The Fugitive Kind*. In July attends a Chicago production of *Suddenly Last Summer* with Diana Barrymore. After the play closes, returns to Havana with Vaccaro and Barrymore. Leaves in August on three-month around-the-world trip. Film of *Suddenly Last Summer*, directed by Joseph L. Mankiewicz and starring Katharine Hepburn, Elizabeth Taylor, and Montgomery Clift, is released.

1960 Settles with Merlo in Key West to work on *The Night of the Iguana* and *Period of Adjustment*. In June goes with his mother, brother Dakin, and Dakin's wife, Joyce, to Los Angeles, where they meet Elvis Presley and Mae West. Returns to Key West to work. Relations with Merlo, who shows signs of illness, are strained. *The Fugitive Kind*, film version of *Orpheus Descending*, directed by Sidney Lumet and starring Marlon Brando and Anna Magnani, is released. *The Night of the Iguana* is staged at Coconut Grove in August. *Period of Adjustment* opens on Broadway.

1961 Works in Key West on revisions of *The Night of the Iguana*. Goes with Vaccaro in January to Europe. In Rome they meet Donald Windham and Sandy Campbell, then settle in Taormina, Sicily, where he works on the play. Returns to Key West in the autumn, depressed by what he sees as his waning career and more and more dependent on liquor and pills. During previews in Detroit, Williams is hospitalized after his dog bites him. After previews in several other cities, *The Night of the Iguana*, starring Bette Davis, Margaret Leighton, and Patrick O'Neal, opens in New York on December 28.

1962 *The Night of the Iguana* wins Drama Critics Circle Award as best play. Buys a multi-story townhouse in the French Quarter in New Orleans, using income from film versions of his plays. Made lifetime member of the American Academy of Arts and Letters. Lucy Freeman collaborates with Williams' mother on her memoir, *Remember Me to Tom*. The Spoleto Festival of the Two Worlds in Italy premieres a version of *The Milk Train Doesn't Stop Here Anymore*. Poet Frederick Nicklaus, who has moved in with Williams and Merlo in Key West, accompanies him to Italy. Contacted in London by Audrey Wood, who informs him that Merlo is very ill, he flies back to the U.S.

1963 *Milk Train* moves to New York January 16 and runs for only two months. Merlo is diagnosed with lung cancer and goes to Key West, then back to New York to stay with Williams and Nicklaus. Williams begins revisions of *Milk Train* in preparation for a revival. Merlo dies in September. After the funeral, Williams and Nicklaus fly to Mexico where *Night of the Iguana* is being filmed by John Huston, with a cast including Ava Gardner, Deborah Kerr, and Richard Burton. Williams begins a period of depression and heavy dependence on drugs that he will call his "Stoned Age."

1964 Revival of *Milk Train*, starring Tallulah Bankhead, Tab Hunter, Ruth Ford, and Marion Seldes opens January 1 and closes after three days. Goes to Jamaica and then to Key West, where Nicklaus leaves him in March. Back in New York, he begins seeing a new analyst and becomes a patient of Dr. Max Jacobson, who provides him with amphetamines and barbiturates in pill and injection form. Writes *Slapstick Tragedy*, consisting of two short plays, *The Gnädiges Fräulein* and *The Mutilated*. Realizing that he should not be alone, given his reliance on alcohol and drugs, he hires the first of a series of paid companions, William Glavin, to move in with him and travel with him. Film of *The Night of the Iguana* released.

1965 *The Glass Menagerie* revived with Maureen Stapleton as Amanda. *Milk Train* is revived again in San Francisco and is positively received. Goes to St. Louis to visit his mother, who has begun to suffer from delusions. Continues work on *Slapstick Tragedy*, other plays, and short stories. *The Eccentricities of a Nightingale*, a revision of *Summer and Smoke*, is published.

1966 *Slapstick Tragedy*, starring Zoe Caldwell, Margaret Leighton, and Kate Reid opens in New York in January and runs for only four days. Williams issues a public statement condemning America's involvement in Vietnam. Reliance on drugs grows, abetted by Dr. Jacobson, and his mental state becomes progressively unstable. Works on the film script of *Milk Train*, then goes with Glavin and Lester Persky, who will produce it, to London. Film of *This Property Is Condemned*, loosely based on his one-act play, is released.

1967 Goes with Glavin to Virgin Islands where parts of "Goforth!" (soon retitled *Boom!*), based on *Milk Train*, are being filmed. Travels in the summer with Glavin to Europe, visiting Sardinia where *Boom!* is now being filmed by director Joseph Losey with a cast including Elizabeth Taylor, Richard Burton, and Noël Coward. Friends such as Audrey Wood and Elia Kazan are increasingly concerned by his dependence on drugs and his mental state. Carson McCullers dies September 29 following a massive stroke. *The Knightly Quest: A Novella and Four Short Stories* is published by New Directions. Attends the world premiere of *The Two-Character Play* in London in December with Audrey Wood.

1968 Production of *Kingdom of Earth* with Harry Guardino, Estelle Parsons, and Brian Bedford premieres in February in Philadelphia and then opens in New York on March 27 under the direction of José Quintero and retitled *The Seven Descents of Myrtle.* It runs only a month. *Boom!* is released to unfavorable reviews. Friend Lilla van Saher dies. Works on revision of *The Two-Character Play* and on a new play, *In the Bar of a Tokyo Hotel.* At the end of the year, suffering increasingly from paranoid symptoms exacerbated by drug use, goes with Glavin to Key West.

1969 Dakin, at Audrey Wood's suggestion, goes to Key West to check on Williams, who has grown confused and disoriented. Dakin arranges for him to be received into the Roman Catholic church on January 10, although Williams will later deny that the conversion was authentic. In the spring, assumes direction of the New York production of *In the Bar of a Tokyo Hotel*, which opens May 11 in New York and is widely condemned by critics.

Receives National Institute of Arts and Letters gold medal and an honorary doctorate from the University of Missouri at Columbia. In June, flies with actress Anne Meacham to Tokyo where they meet writer Yukio Mishima and see part of the Japanese production of *Streetcar*. Returns to Key West, where Glavin joins him, then goes to San Francisco again and to New Orleans to see Pancho Rodriguez. Becomes progressively more dependent on drugs and increasingly paranoid. In September Dakin convinces him to enter Barnes Hospital in St. Louis, where he is placed in the mental ward. Suffers seizures and two heart attacks related to withdrawal from drugs. Recovers sufficiently to return to Key West in December.

1970 Goes to New York in January for revival of *Camino Real*. Discusses his homosexuality in a television interview with David Frost. Marion Black Vaccaro dies in April. At the end of summer, travels with Oliver Evans to New Orleans and then to Hawaii, Hong Kong, Thailand, and Japan, where he meets with Yukio Mishima shortly before Mishima commits ritual suicide. *Dragon Country: A Book of Plays* is published.

1971 Attends rehearsals in Chicago of production of *Out Cry* (a revised version of *The Two-Character Play*), starring Donald Madden and Eileen Herlie. Resumes use of drugs and, in a fit of anger, dismisses his agent, Audrey Wood, who is replaced by Bill Barnes. Revises and expands *Confessional* into full-length play *Small Craft Warnings*. New Directions begins publication of the multi-volume set, *The Theatre of Tennessee Williams*. Speaks out against American involvement in the Vietnam War at a rally at the Cathedral of St. John the Divine in New York in December.

1972 Moves into an apartment in the New Orleans townhouse he had bought in 1962. *Small Craft Warnings* opens in Philadelphia in February and in New York in April. Awarded honorary degree by Purdue University. Appears in *Small Craft Warnings* as the character Doc in an attempt to boost ticket sales. Spends fall and winter in New York, Key West, and New Orleans. Completes first draft of *Memoirs*, using title "Flee, Flee This Sad Hotel." Attends the Venice Film Festival in August as a juror.

Robert Carroll becomes his companion-secretary and travels with him.

1973 *Out Cry*, with Michael York and Cara Duff-MacCormick, opens in New York March 1 and closes after twelve performances. Visits Los Angeles for a new staging of *Streetcar* and meets with Canadian television producer Harry Rasky, who has made a documentary film about him. Travels with Carroll to the Far East and then to Rome. In May Jane Bowles dies and in June William Inge commits suicide. Travels to Rome and then to Tangier to visit Paul Bowles. Works on *The Red Devil Battery Sign*. Saddened in September by the death of Anna Magnani. Awarded the first Centennial Medal of the Cathedral of St. John the Divine. Williams and Robert Carroll separate for a while.

1974 Travels extensively and visits Rose often. Works on *The Red Devil Battery Sign*. Goes to London in March for a revival of *Streetcar* with Claire Bloom. While in England, stays with Lady Maria St. Just (formerly Maria Britneva). In July *Cat on a Hot Tin Roof* is revived in New York with Elizabeth Ashley and Keir Dullea. Short story collection *Eight Mortal Ladies Possessed* is published.

1975 Receives National Arts Club's gold medal for literature in February and is given the key to the city of New York. Works on *This Is (An Entertainment)*. Second novel, *Moise and the World of Reason*, is published in May. In June, *The Red Devil Battery Sign* with Claire Bloom and Anthony Quinn opens in Boston and closes in 10 days. A successful revival of *Sweet Bird of Youth* opens in Boston and then moves to New York; there are also revivals of *Summer and Smoke* and of *The Glass Menagerie* in New York. *Memoirs* is published.

1976 *This Is (An Entertainment)* premieres in January in San Francisco, where Williams meets Lyle Leverich, whom he later selects as his biographer. Harry Rasky's documentary film *Tennessee Williams's South* appears on television. A series of young men alternate with Robert Carroll as paid companions. Returns in October to San Francisco for Leverich's production of *The Two-Character Play*. *The Eccentricities of a Nightingale* premieres in Buffalo, New

York, then moves to New York City November 23. *The Night of the Iguana* is revived in London. Inducted into the American Academy of Arts and Letters in December.

1977 *Vieux Carré* opens in May on Broadway and closes after only five performances. Goes to London in June for the premiere of *The Red Devil Battery Sign*. Second volume of poetry, *Androgyne, Mon Amour*, is published. Develops cataract on his right eye. Works on adapting the *Baby Doll* screenplay into a play, *Tiger Tail*, and writing the play *Creve Coeur*.

1978 *Tiger Tail* debuts in Atlanta but closes quickly. Returns to New Orleans for a public appearance in which he reads his poetry and fiction. The Spoleto Festival in Charleston, South Carolina, stages *Creve Coeur* (later retitled *A Lovely Sunday for Creve Coeur*). *Vieux Carré* is revived in London in August with Sylvia Miles. Mitch Douglas succeeds Bill Barnes as Williams' agent. Publishes collection of essays, *Where I Live*. Travels extensively before taking an apartment at Manhattan Plaza in New York. Brings Rose to New York for the holidays.

1979 *A Lovely Sunday for Creve Coeur* opens in New York on January 1 for a brief run. After his gardener in Key West is murdered, Williams discovers that the man had stolen manuscripts, other papers, and photographs. Works on revisions of *The Milk Train Doesn't Stop Here Anymore* and *Clothes for a Summer Hotel*. Brings Rose to Key West to live in a cottage near him, under the care of a cousin, but the arrangement proves unsatisfactory. *Kirche, Kuchen, und Kinder* opens in New York in September. In December Williams receives Kennedy Center Honors from President Jimmy Carter.

1980 In January *Will Mr. Merriwether Return from Memphis?* premieres in Key West at the opening of the Tennessee Williams Performing Arts Center. *Clothes for a Summer Hotel*, directed by José Quintero and starring Geraldine Page and Kenneth Haigh, opens in Washington, then Chicago, and in New York on March 26, his birthday, which Mayor Ed Koch declares Tennessee Williams Day; it is to be his last play on Broadway during his lifetime. Mother dies on June 1 at age 95. Travels in Europe in

June and July with artist Henry Faulkner. Works at Goodman Theatre in Chicago on three one-act plays. Appointed Distinguished Writer in Residence at the University of British Columbia in Vancouver, but does not remain for the full term. The triad of short plays, collectively called *Tennessee Laughs*, is presented at the Goodman Theatre. Spends holiday season in Key West, where he arranges for Rose to be returned to the nursing home in Ossining, New York.

1981 Works on *A House Not Meant to Stand* at Goodman. The Goodman has a party to celebrate his seventieth birthday, after which *A House Not Meant to Stand* opens. In April, former agent Audrey Wood suffers a stroke that leaves her in a coma. In the summer, works on his version of Chekhov's *The Sea Gull*, which will become *The Notebook of Trigorin*, and on *Something Cloudy, Something Clear*. The latter opens August 24 for a limited run by the Jean Cocteau Repertory, the last of his plays to debut in New York during his lifetime. In the fall, two old friends, poet Oliver Evans and artist Henry Faulkner, die. Along with Harold Pinter, he is awarded the Common Wealth Award of $11,000. Luis Sanjurjo replaces Mitch Douglas as his agent.

1982 Works in Key West on a revision of *A House Not Meant to Stand*. Travels to New York in February to receive the city's medallion of honor. *Something Cloudy, Something Clear* is revived in February by the Jean Cocteau Repertory. Goes to Chicago to discuss staging of the revised and expanded *A House Not Meant to Stand*, which opens in April for a limited run. Receives an honorary doctorate from Harvard in June. Attends staging of several of his plays at the Williamstown Theater Festival in Williamstown, Massachusetts. Works in Key West on a screenplay, then travels with Jane Smith to London and Sicily, where he works on a new play, *The Lingering Hour*. Makes last public appearance in November at the 92nd Street Y in New York. Hospitalized in Key West in December suffering from drug toxicity.

1983 In January, visits Jane Smith in New York, returns to Key West, then goes to New Orleans to arrange the sale of his townhouse. Flies to Taormina in February for a final brief visit before returning to New York. Dies on February 24; the cause of death may have been the result of an overdose of Seconal or from asphyxia caused by choking on a plastic cap of the type used on bottles of nasal spray or eyedrops. Funeral services are held at the St. Louis Cathedral on March 5; Williams is buried next to his mother in the Calvary Cemetery in St. Louis.

Note on the Texts

This volume contains 13 plays by Tennessee Williams that were first produced and published between 1957 and 1980. The texts printed here are taken from the first editions of the plays in book form.

Because Williams habitually revised his works, most of his plays exist in multiple versions. Williams revised many of them after initial book publication for editions published by Dramatists Play Service (intended for use by actors and directors), for subsequent American and English book editions, and for the collected edition *The Theatre of Tennessee Williams*, published by New Directions.

The Dramatists Play Service editions of the plays are meant chiefly to aid in staging and omit prefaces and commentary that are part of the texts of the book editions.

Williams revised the book editions of several of his plays relatively soon after their first publication. For the second printing of the first American edition of *Suddenly Last Summer*, published in 1959, Williams omitted several lines of dialogue included in the first printing; for the English edition of *The Milk Train Doesn't Stop Here Anymore*, published in 1965, Williams inserted a passage that does not appear in American editions of the play and made several other changes. Williams' revisions, however, are not always retained in subsequent editions of the plays, which sometimes revert to the texts of the first editions. In certain instances, Williams' revisions cause inconsistencies within a play, and occasionally he deleted or altered potentially objectionable material.

In 1971, New Directions published the first three volumes of *The Theatre of Tennessee Williams*, a collected edition of Williams' plays. Three additional volumes of this eight-volume series were published during Williams' lifetime and incorporated substantial changes in several plays. For example, the version of *Battle of Angels* printed in *The Theatre of Tennessee Williams* incorporates passages from Williams' play *Orpheus Descending*, and the version of *Kingdom of Earth (The Seven Descents of Myrtle)* is a shortened version of the play as first published.

The texts of the first book editions have been chosen for inclusion in the present volume because they are the versions of the plays Williams published for general readers immediately following the plays' composition.

Orpheus Descending is a rewritten version of Williams' play *Battle of Angels*, first staged in 1940 and published in *Pharos* in 1945. Williams completed his revisions for *Orpheus Descending* shortly before the play opened in New York on March 21, 1957, in a production directed by Harold Clurman. The Prologue was omitted in this production but was included when the play was collected in *Orpheus Descending, with Battle of Angels*, published by New Directions on February 5, 1958. The preface, "The Past, the Present and the Perhaps," first appeared in *The New York Times* on March 17, 1957, as "Tennessee Williams on the Past, the Present and the Perhaps."

For the Dramatists Play Service edition of *Orpheus Descending*, published in 1959, Williams changed the order of some of the material in the play. The version of *Battle of Angels* that was included in Volume 1 (1971) of *The Theatre of Tennessee Williams* combines passages from *Battle of Angels* and *Orpheus Descending*; the text of *Orpheus Descending* in Volume 2 of *The Theatre of Tennessee Williams* follows that of the 1958 New Directions edition. The text printed here is taken from the 1958 New Directions edition of *Orpheus Descending, with Battle of Angels.*

By November 1957, had Williams completed the version of *Suddenly Last Summer* that was staged, along with the one-act play "Something Unspoken," as *Garden District* in a production, directed by Herbert Machiz, that opened in New York on January 7, 1958. New Directions published the book version of *Suddenly Last Summer* on April 23, 1958. The Dramatists Play Service edition published in 1969 does not differ significantly from the first New Directions edition.

Williams revised *Suddenly Last Summer* for the 1959 second printing of the New Directions edition, omitting dialogue from Scene One about the Doctor's operations at Lion's View and Sebastian Venable's vision in the Encantadas. The text of *Suddenly Last Summer* included in *Garden District* (London: Secker & Warburg, 1959), follows that of the first printing of the 1958 New Directions edition, as does the version of the play that appears in Volume 3 (1971) of *The Theatre of Tennessee Williams.* The text printed here is taken from the 1958 New Directions first printing of *Suddenly Last Summer.*

Sweet Bird of Youth is derived from "The Big Time Operators," an unfinished play Williams wrote in 1948, and the story "Two on a Party," written in 1951 and 1952, in which a young man travels with an older woman from New Orleans to West Palm Beach. Williams then incorporated some of this material in "The Enemy: Time," a one-act play published in *The Theatre* in March 1959. Williams had sent a draft of "The Enemy: Time" in January 1956 to George Keathley, manager of the Studio M Playhouse in Coral Gables, Florida, who then offered to stage the play in the spring of that year. Williams revised the play, now titled *Sweet Bird of Youth*, in February and March for its April 16, 1956, opening, and continued to work on it after Keathley's production closed. In March 1958, Williams told Audrey Wood, his agent, that he had finished a new draft to submit to Cheryl Crawford; by the fall, Crawford had agreed to stage a production in New York, and Elia Kazan was hired as its director. In November 1958 Williams sent his most recent draft to Kazan, who responded in a letter with comments and suggestions. Williams continued to revise the play during rehearsals in February 1959. After a trial run in Philadelphia, *Sweet Bird of Youth* opened in New York on March 10, 1959. A version of the play appeared in *Esquire* the following month.

The New Directions edition of *Sweet Bird of Youth* was published on November 24, 1959. Its preface had appeared, as "Williams' Wells of Violence," in *The New York Times* on March 8, 1959. The New Directions version of the play differs significantly from the *Esquire* text; among other changes, Williams removed a scene from Act II and altered several passages in Act III. The acting edition published by Dramatists Play Service in 1962 makes further changes and includes an alternate ending after the end of Act III. Both the English edition, published in 1961 by Secker & Warburg, and the version published in Volume 4 (1972) of *The Theatre of Tennessee Williams* follow the 1959 New Directions edition of *Sweet Bird of Youth*. The text printed here is taken from the 1959 New Directions edition.

Williams completed the first draft of *Period of Adjustment* in the fall of 1958. In December 1958 Williams directed a version of the play, billed as a work in progress, at the Coconut Grove Theatre in Florida, and he continued to work on it during 1959 and 1960. Cheryl Crawford announced a Broadway production and named George Roy Hill as director in April 1960. *Period of Adjustment* opened in New York on November 10, 1960, and New Directions published the book version on November 14, 1960. The working script that Williams had subsequently revised during rehearsals for the New York opening was published in *Esquire* in December 1960.

Changes were made in the text of *Period of Adjustment* in the second printing of the first edition because New Directions was concerned that the specificity of the setting might expose the firm to a libel suit. The setting of the play was changed from "Memphis" to "a mid-southern city," and several, though not all, references to

"Memphis" were changed to "Dixon." Williams made further revisions for the Dramatists Play Service edition published in 1961. The English edition, published by Secker & Warburg in 1961, does not differ significantly from the first printing of the 1959 New Directions edition. The version that appears in Volume 4 (1972) of *The Theatre of Tennessee Williams* follows the second printing of the first New Directions edition but alters a reference to Memphis that was not changed in earlier editions. The text of *Period of Adjustment* printed here is taken from the 1959 New Directions edition, first printing.

The Night of the Iguana was first performed as a one-act play in Spoleto, Italy, on July 2, 1959, in a production directed by Frank Corsaro. (A short story with the same title, completed in 1948 and collected by Williams in *One Arm and Other Stories* in 1954, is remotely related to the play.) Over the next two years, *The Night of the Iguana* became a full-length play, and it was staged in two different versions by Corsaro in fall 1959 and summer 1960. Williams continued to expand and revise the play for the New York production by the Actors Studio, also directed by Corsaro, that opened on December 28, 1961. The working script that Williams had subsequently revised during rehearsals for the December opening was published in *Esquire* in February 1962. The book version of *The Night of the Iguana* was published by New Directions on February 28, 1962. The acting edition published by Dramatists Play Service the following year is a shortened version of the play. Neither the English edition published by Secker & Warburg in 1963 nor the version included in Volume 4 (1972) of *The Theatre of Tennessee Williams* was revised by Williams; the texts of those editions follow that of the 1962 New Directions first edition. The text printed here is taken from the 1962 New Directions edition of *The Night of the Iguana.*

The Eccentricities of a Nightingale is a rewritten version of Williams' play *Summer and Smoke*, first staged in 1948. Williams revised *Summer and Smoke* heavily in 1952, hoping to have his changes incorporated into a London revival of the play, but these revisions were not finished in time for the London production and were not used in subsequent revivals of *Summer and Smoke.* It appears that many of these revisions were incorporated into *The Eccentricities of a Nightingale.* Williams finished working on the play by 1964, and it was published, in *The Eccentricities of a Nightingale and Summer and Smoke*, by New Directions on February 12, 1965. This version of the play was included in Volume 2 (1971) of *The Theatre of Tennessee Williams.* The first Dramatists Play Service edition was published in

1977 and reflects changes made by Williams for the play's first stage production in 1976. The text printed here is taken from the 1965 New Directions *The Eccentricities of a Nightingale and Summer and Smoke.*

In 1958, Williams began working on a series of dialogues based on his story "Man Bring This Up Road," written in 1953 and collected in Williams' *The Knightly Quest* in 1967. By 1962 these dialogues were incorporated into a short play, *The Milk Train Doesn't Stop Here Anymore*, which was staged in July 1962 at the Festival of Two Worlds in Spoleto, Italy. Rehearsals began later that year for another production, directed by Herbert Machiz, that opened in New York on January 10, 1963, and closed after 69 performances. Williams continued to revise and expand the play for a revival staged in Aberdeen, Virginia, in September 1963 and then wrote new scenes for the second New York production, directed by Tony Richardson, which opened on January 1, 1964.

New Directions published the book version of *The Milk Train Doesn't Stop Here Anymore* on June 9, 1964. While the book was in production, Williams discovered that lines from the second scene had been accidentally transposed to the end of the first scene. The error was corrected in some copies of the first printing and in subsequent printings. For the English edition, published by Secker & Warburg in September 1964, Williams added a short passage in Scene 5 and made other changes, mostly to stage directions. Williams did not revise the play for the Dramatists Play Service edition published in 1964 or for the version that appears in Volume 5 (1976) of *The Theatre of Tennessee Williams.* The texts of these editions follow the corrected version of the first New Directions edition. The corrected first printing of the 1964 New Directions edition of *The Milk Train Doesn't Stop Here Anymore* is the text printed here.

Williams completed a draft of *The Mutilated* by the end of 1964. A production of the play, paired with *The Gnädiges Fräulein* under the title *Slapstick Tragedy*, was scheduled for early 1965, but this production was canceled because of insufficient funding. A new production of *Slapstick Tragedy*, to be directed by Alan Schneider, was announced later that year, and a version of the play was published in *Esquire* in August 1965. Williams revised *The Mutilated* while *Slapstick Tragedy* was in rehearsal in early 1966 in New York; the production opened on February 22, 1966. *The Mutilated* was published by Dramatists Play Service in 1967, then revised for inclusion in *Dragon Country: A Book of Plays*, which was published by New Directions on March 30, 1970. Williams did not revise *The Mutilated* after its publication in *Dragon Country.* The text of *The Mutilated* printed here is taken from the 1970 New Directions edition of *Dragon Country: A Book of Plays.*

Kingdom of Earth originated in the short story "The Kingdom of Earth," first published in 1954 by New Directions in a limited edition of Williams' collection *Hard Candy.* The story was adapted for a one-act play that was published in *Esquire* in February 1967; later that year, David Merrick agreed to stage a full-length version of *Kingdom of Earth.* After a trial run in Philadelphia, the play opened in New York on March 27, 1968, in a production directed by José Quintero; for the New York production, Williams changed the title to *The Seven Descents of Myrtle.* New Directions published the book version, *Kingdom of Earth (The Seven Descents of Myrtle)*, on October 31, 1968. Williams made minor revisions in the play for the acting edition, which was published by Dramatists Play Service the following year. The version that is included in Volume 5 (1976) of *The Theatre of Tennessee Williams* is shorter than the New Directions and the Dramatists Play Service versions, because Williams hoped that a shortened version of the play would be revived. The text printed here is taken from the 1968 New Directions edition of *Kingdom of Earth (The Seven Descents of Myrtle).*

Small Craft Warnings is an expanded version of *Confessional*, a one-act play published in *Dragon Country: A Book of Plays* in 1970. The favorable reception of William Hunt's 1971 production of *Confessional* prompted Bill Barnes, Williams' agent, to contact three New York producers about staging a full-length version. After a New York production was announced, Williams worked on revising and expanding the play during late 1971 and early 1972. Now titled *Small Craft Warnings*, the play went into rehearsal in early 1972 with Hunt as the director. Hunt quit the production while in rehearsal and was replaced at first by Williams, then by Richard Altman. *Small Craft Warnings* opened in New York on April 2, 1972. New Directions published the book version on November 15, 1972. Williams did not revise *Small Craft Warnings* for the English edition published in 1973 by Secker & Warburg or for its inclusion in Volume 5 (1976) of *The Theatre of Tennessee Williams.* The text printed here is taken from the 1972 New Directions edition.

Out Cry is a rewritten version of *The Two-Character Play*, a play Williams began writing in 1966. *The Two-Character Play* was first staged in 1967 in a production directed by James Rosse-Evans and was published in a limited edition by New Directions in 1969. Williams then wrote a new version of the play, using the title *Out Cry*, which was staged in July 1971 in a production directed by George Keathley and was published by New Directions on October 24, 1973. The text printed here is taken from the 1973 New Directions edition, the only edition of *Out Cry* to be published during Williams' lifetime. (Williams later extensively revised the play, again using the title *The Two-Character Play*; this version, which was staged in March 1973 and published by New Directions in 1975, is a distinct work significantly different from both *Out Cry* and the version of *The Two-Character Play* published in 1969.)

Williams began working on *Vieux Carré* in 1976, although some of the play was drawn from plays and stories that Williams had written earlier. A New York production of the play, directed by Arthur Alan Seidelman, was in rehearsal in early 1977. Although Williams did not attend rehearsals for the first New York production, he did send revisions from his hotel in New York to Seidelman and the cast. *Vieux Carré* opened in New York in March 1977 and was revived the following year in two English productions, both directed by Keith Hack. The book version was published by New Directions on June 25, 1979. This was the only edition of *Vieux Carré* published during Williams' lifetime, and is the source of the text printed here.

Williams wrote a one-act play, "Creve Coeur," in San Francisco in 1976. He read the play in 1977 to Craig Anderson, director of the Hudson Theatre Guild in New York, who agreed to stage a production. Williams expanded and revised "Creve Coeur" for a June 1978 production, directed by Keith Hack, at the Spoleto Festival in Charleston, S.C.; then he continued to work on the play for its New York production, changing its title to *A Lovely Sunday for Creve Coeur*. Final revisions were completed while the New York production was in rehearsal in late 1978. *A Lovely Sunday for Creve Coeur*, directed by Keith Hack, opened on January 1, 1979. The book version was published by New Directions on April 30, 1980. Some of the characters and dialogue of *A Lovely Sunday for Creve Coeur* appear in *All Gaul Is Divided*, a screenplay that was published posthumously in *Stopped Rocking and Other Screenplays* (New York: New Directions, 1984). In a 1979 note to *All Gaul Is Divided*, Williams wrote, "I would guess that the 'teleplay' was written almost twenty years before I wrote the play, *A Lovely Sunday for Creve Coeur* . . . The most remarkable thing about the teleplay is that I had *totally* forgotten its existence when I wrote *Creve Coeur* in San Francisco about three years ago." The 1980 New Directions edition of *A Lovely Sunday for Creve Coeur* is the only version of the play published during Williams' lifetime and is the source of the text printed here.

This volume presents the texts of the original printings chosen for inclusion here, but it does not attempt to reproduce features of their typographic design. The texts are presented without change, except for the correction of typographical errors. Spelling, punctuation, and capitalization are often expressive features and are not altered, even when inconsistent or irregular. The following is a list of typographical errors corrected, cited by page and line number: 10.17, an; 31.24, lady; 158.2, *Allelulia*; 187.26, *O'Keefe's*; 199.29, dare?; 201.26, Hanh?—; 221.35, Torremolenas; 261.9, —resist the—; 261.32, Jawge; 262.14, An; 282.10, [ ] May; 303.14, *He*; 317.6, Why'; 320.26, ot; 332.26, rum-coco; 346.13, susspected; 399.8, *Hanna's*; 404.19, our—; 413.4, built; 426.17, 'hasta; 427.7, *Hannnah*; 448.11, how; 451.15, operate; 516.14, you *you*; 517.5, breats; 529.27, She; 552.34, been—; 556.23, look; 564.32, lighter.; 574.4, embarrasing; 574.30, *legumi*; 579.24, wth; 589.39, *shilly*; 592.2, Galatoires; 647.17, Day!; 648.24, lillies; 668.16, ukelele; 695.15, and'; 696.14, weather, and so forth."; 710.9, penathol; 751.26, *Violets*; 753.18, Doc; 755.27, *precint*; 812.24, sister...; 813.28, glimpe; 829.32, soto; 856.2, S'; 878.10, *it's*; 880.4, Babe,; 884.20, charnal; 909.18, Jut; 957.22, *daises*.

ACKNOWLEDGMENTS

The plays in this volume are published by arrangement with New Directions Publishing Corporation, New York, Publisher of the plays of Tennessee Williams, and with The University of the South, copyright proprietor of the works of Tennessee Williams.

Notes

In the notes below, the reference numbers denote page and line of this volume. No note is made for material included in standard desk-reference books such as Webster's *Collegiate*, *Biographical*, and *Geographical* dictionaries. Biblical quotations are keyed to the King James Version. Quotations from Shakespeare are keyed to *The Riverside Shakespeare*, ed. G. Blakemore Evans (Boston: Houghton Mifflin, 1974). Cast lists and production information are taken from the first book editions of the plays, except for *The Eccentricities of a Nightingale* and *The Mutilated*, where they are taken from Dramatists Play Service editions, and *The Milk Train Doesn't Stop Here Anymore*, where they are taken from Volume 5 of *The Theatre of Tennessee Williams* (New York: New Directions, 1976). For further biographical information than is contained in the Chronology, see Albert J. Devlin (ed.), *Conversations with Tennessee Williams* (Jackson: University Press of Mississippi, 1986); Ronald Hayman, *Tennessee Williams: Everyone Else Is an Audience* (New Haven: Yale University Press, 1993); Lyle Leverich, *Tom: The Unknown Tennessee Williams* (New York: W.W. Norton & Company, 1995); Harry Rasky, *Tennessee Williams: A Portrait in Laughter and Lamentation* (New York: Dodd, 1986); Donald Spoto, *The Kindness of Strangers: The Life of Tennessee Williams* (Boston: Little, Brown and Company, 1985); Dakin Williams and Shepherd Mead, *Tennessee Williams: An Intimate Biography* (New York: Arbor House, 1983); Edwina Dakin Williams as told to Lucy Freeman, *Remember Me to Tom* (New York: Putnam, 1963); Donald Windham (ed.), *Tennessee Williams' Letters to Donald Windham 1940–1965* (New York: Holt, Rinehart & Winston, 1977).

ORPHEUS DESCENDING

1.1 *Orpheus Descending*] *Orpheus Descending* was presented at the Martin Beck Theatre in New York on March 21, 1957, by the Producers Theatre. It was directed by Harold Clurman; the stage set was designed by Boris Aronson, the costumes by Lucinda Ballard, and the lighting by Feder. The cast was as follows: DOLLY HAMMA: Elizabeth Eustis; BEULAH BINNINGS: Jane Rose; PEE WEE BINNINGS: Warren Kemmerling; DOG HAMMA: David Clarke; CAROL CUTRERE: Lois Smith; EVA TEMPLE: Nell Harrison; SISTER TEMPLE: Mary Farrell; UNCLE PLEASANT: John Marriott; VAL XAVIER: Cliff Robertson; VEE TALBOT: Joanna Roos; LADY TORRANCE: Maureen Stapleton;

JABE TORRANCE: Crahan Denton; SHERIFF TALBOTT: R. G. Armstrong; MR. DUBINSKY: Beau Tilden; WOMAN: Janice Mars; DAVID CUTRERE: Robert Webber; NURSE PORTER: Virgilia Chew; FIRST MAN: Albert Henderson; SECOND MAN: Charles Tyner.

3.37–38 "You must not . . . peck at!"] Cf. *Othello*, I.i.64.

5.7 W.P.A. Writers' Project] Federal program under the Works Progress Administration to provide work for authors during the Depression.

13.18–19 Mystic Crew] Williams' name for the Ku Klux Klan.

15.33 *Valli*] Movie actress Alida Valli (b. 1921).

17.30 Morning Call] For more than a hundred years a coffee stand in the French Market of New Orleans.

24.7 *"Heavenly Grass."*] Williams' poem, collected in *In the Winter of Cities* (1956), was set to music by Paul Bowles.

28.15 Willie McGee] Willie McGee was convicted in 1949 of raping Willamette Hawkins, a white woman, and sentenced to death. The U.S. Supreme Court refused to review McGee's case and despite international protests he was electrocuted in Laurel, Mississippi, on May 8, 1951.

62.20 "September Morn"] Painting (1912) by French salon artist Paul Emile Chabas (1869–1937); it was widely reproduced, and was banned in some American cities.

SUDDENLY LAST SUMMER

99.1 *Suddenly Last Summer*] *Suddenly Last Summer*, with *Something Unspoken*, were presented together under the collective title of *Garden District* at the York Theatre on First Avenue in New York on January 7, 1958, by John C. Wilson and Warner Le Roy. It was directed by Herbert Machiz; the scenery was designed by Robert Soule and the costumes by Stanley Simmons. Lighting was by Lee Watson and the incidental music was by Ned Rorem. *Cast of Characters*: MRS. VENABLE: Hortense Alden; DR. CUKROWICZ: Robert Lansing; MISS FOXHILL: Donna Cameron; MRS. HOLLY: Eleanor Phelps; GEORGE HOLLY: Alan Mixon; CATHERINE HOLLY: Anne Meacham; SISTER FELICITY: Nanom-Kiam.

112.32–33 "So shines . . . world,"] Shakespeare, *The Merchant of Venice*, V.i.91.

SWEET BIRD OF YOUTH

149.1 *Sweet Bird of Youth*] *Sweet Bird of Youth* was presented at the Martin Beck Theatre in New York on March 10, 1959, by Cheryl Crawford. It was directed by Elia Kazan; the scenery and lighting were by Jo Mielziner, the costumes by Anna Hill Johnstone, and the music by Paul Bowles;

production stage manager, David Pardoll. The cast was as follows: CHANCE WAYNE: Paul Newman; THE PRINCESS KOSMONOPOLIS: Geraldine Page; FLY: Milton J. Williams; MAID: Patricia Ripley; GEORGE SCUDDER: Logan Ramsey; HATCHER: John Napier; BOSS FINLEY: Sidney Blackmer; TOM JUNIOR: Rip Torn; AUNT NONNIE: Martine Bartlett; HEAVENLY FINLEY: Diana Hyland; CHARLES: Earl Sydnor; STUFF: Bruce Dern; MISS LUCY: Madeleine Sherwood; THE HECKLER: Charles Tyner; VIOLET: Monica May; EDNA: Hilda Brawner; SCOTTY: Charles McDaniel; BUD: Jim Jeter; MEN IN BAR: Duke Farley, Ron Harper, Kenneth Blake; PAGE: Glenn Stensel.

149.2–4 *Relentless caper . . .* CRANE] "Legend" (1925), lines 22–23.

200.16 *novachord.*] A six-octave electronic keyboard.

203.22 Vic Mature] Movie actor Victor Mature (1915–99); his films included *Samson and Delilah* (1949) and *Zarak* (1956).

205.2–6 "If you like-a me . . . change your name."] From "Under the Bamboo Tree" (1902) by Robert Cole and J. Rosamond Johnson.

222.5 *"Bonnie Blue Flag."*] "The Bonnie Blue Flag" (1861) by Mrs. Annie Chambers-Ketchum and Harry MacCarthy, a popular song of the Confederacy during the Civil War.

PERIOD OF ADJUSTMENT

237.1 *Period of Adjustment*] *Period of Adjustment* was presented at the Helen Hayes Theatre in New York on November 10, 1960, by Cheryl Crawford. It was directed by George Roy Hill; the scenery and lighting were by Jo Mielziner and the costumes by Partricia Zipprodt; production stage manager, William Chambers. The cast, in order of appearance, was as follows: RALPH BATES: James Daly; ISABEL HAVERSTICK: Barbara Baxley; GEORGE HAVERSTICK: Robert Webber; SUSIE: Helen Martin; LADY CAROLER: Esther Benson; MRS. MCGILLICUDDY: Nancy R. Pollock; MR. MCGILLICUDDY: Lester Mack; THE POLICE OFFICER: Charles McDaniel; DOROTHY BATES: Rosemary Murphy.

301.31 *Sayonara*] James A. Michener novel (1954) of American soldiers in occupied Japan; it was filmed in 1955 with Marlon Brando and Red Buttons.

322.2 Sophie Newcomb's.] Women's college in New Orleans.

326.1–4 "Now the boat . . . good-by!"] From "Goodbye, My Lover, Goodbye," popular English song of the 19th century.

THE NIGHT OF THE IGUANA

327.1 *The Night of the Iguana*] *The Night of the Iguana* was presented at the Royale Theatre in New York on December 28, 1961, by Charles Bowden, in association with Violla Rubber. It was directed by Frank Corsaro; the scenery was designed by Oliver Smith; lighting by Jean Rosenthal; costumes by Noel Taylor; audio effects by Edward Beyer. The cast, in order of appearance, was as follows: MAXINE FAULK: Bette Davis; PEDRO: James Farentino; PANCHO: Christopher Jones; REVEREND SHANNON: Patrick O'Neal; HANK: Theseus George; HERR FAHRENKOPF: Heinz Hohenwald; FRAU FAHRENKOPF: Lucy Landau; WOLFGANG: Bruce Glover; HILDA: Laryssa Lauret; JUDITH FELLOWES: Patricia Roe; HANNAH JELKES: Margaret Leighton; CHARLOTTE GOODALL: Lane Bradbury; JONATHAN COFFIN (NONNO): Alan Webb; JAKE LATTA: Louis Guss.

327.2–6 *And so* . . . DICKINSOn] "I died for Beauty—but was scarce," stanza 3.

329.30–31 Anda . . . del señor.] Go—the suitcase. Pancho, don't be lazy! Go and get the gentleman's luggage.

335.3–4 Carrie Jacobs Bond or Ethelbert Nevin.] Bond (1862–1946), songwriter whose works included "A Perfect Day" and "God Remembers When the World Forgets"; Nevin (1862–1901), songwriter whose works included "Little Boy Blue" and "Mighty Lak' a Rose."

336.10–17 I have . . . my bed.] Cf. Robert Louis Stevenson, "My Shadow," in *A Child's Garden of Verses* (1885).

338.9 Llevala al telefono!] Show her to the telephone!

356.17–20 How . . . despair] Adaptation of a poem, "How Still the Lemon on the Branch," one of several Williams wrote in Mexico in 1940.

359.38 "Horst Wessel."] Nazi party song that became the second national anthem of the Third Reich.

360.24 Berchtesgaden,] Adolf Hitler's Bavarian mountain villa.

375.27–31 Habe . . . bitte. . . .] Am I right in thinking that you are on your honeymoon? What a pretty young bride! I'm making pastel sketches . . . may I, will you permit me . . . ? Would you, please . . . please . . .

381.28–29 *Bitte!* . . . weg.] Please! Take the liquor away. Please, take it away.

398.23–24 vijilalo, entiendes?] Keep an eye on things, understand?

399.19 Agarrale las manos!] Grab his hands!

407.5–9 Eine . . . nicht.] A case of Carta Blanca. / We've had enough . . . maybe not. / No! Never enough. / You're fat, mother . . . but we're not.

THE ECCENTRICITIES OF A NIGHTINGALE

429.1 *The Eccentricities of a Nightingale*] *The Eccentricities of a Nightingale* was presented by Gloria Hope Sher, in association with Neal Du Brock, at the Morosco Theatre, in New York City, on November 23, 1976. It was directed by Edwin Sherin; the scenery was designed by William Ritman; costumes were designed by Theoni V. Aldredge; lighting was by Marc B. Weiss; and the original music was by Charles Gross. The cast, in order of appearance, was as follows: ALMA WINEMILLER: Betsy Palmer; THE REV. WINEMILLER: Sheppard Strudwick; MRS. WINEMILLER: Grace Carney; MRS. BUCHANAN: Nan Martin; JOHN BUCHANAN, JR.: David Selby; ROGER DOREMUS: Peter Blaxill; MRS. BASSETT: Jen Jones; ROSEMARY: Patricia Guinan; VERNON: W. P. Dremak; TRAVELING SALESMAN: Thomas Stechschulte.

464.29–30 that Frenchman . . . Brussels!] During a drunken quarrel in Brussels in July 1873, Paul Verlaine fired a shot at Arthur Rimbaud, wounding him in the arm.

465.28 "bought red lips."] Cf. Ernest Dowson, "Non Sum Qualis Eram Bonae Sub Regno Cynarae," line 9: "Surely the kisses of her bought red mouth were sweet."

THE MILK TRAIN DOESN'T STOP HERE ANYMORE

489.1 *The Milk Train Doesn't Stop Here Anymore*] *The Milk Train Doesn't Stop Here Anymore* was presented at the Brooks Atkinson Theatre in New York on January 1, 1964, by David Merrick, with Neil Hartley as associate producer and Kermit Kegley as stage manager. Directed by Tony Richardson, the set design was by Rouben Ter-Artunian, the music by Ned Rorem, the lighting by Martin Aronstein, and the hair styles by Michel Kazan. The cast included the following: MRS. GOFORTH: Tallulah Bankhead; CHRISTOPER FLANDERS: Tab Hunter; BLACKIE: Marian Seldes; RUDY: Ralph Roberts; THE WITCH OF CAPRI: Ruth Ford; STAGE ASSISTANTS: Bobby Dean Hooks, Konrad Matthaei.

An earlier version of *The Milk Train Doesn't Stop Here Anymore* was staged for the first time anywhere at the Festival of Two Worlds in Spoleto, Italy, on July 11, 1962. It reopened in New York on January 10, 1963, produced by Roger L. Stevens and directed by Herbert Machiz, with scenery and lightning by Jo Mielziner, costumes supervision by Fred Voelpel from sketches by Peter Hall, and music by Paul Bowles. The cast included Hermione Baddeley (Flora Goforth), Ann Williams (Francis Black), Clyde Ventura (Giulio), Paul Roebling (Chris Flanders), Maria Tucci (Angelina), Bruce Gibson (Rudy), and Mildred Dunnock (Vera Ridgeway Condotti).

499.12 *Forse . . . tardi?*] Maybe later, maybe a little later?

500.28 "Cloudy . . . romance] Cf. John Keats, "When I have fears that I may cease to be."

507.3–7 *Giulio! . . . testa!*] Giulio! Come here! / Take this bag to the pink villa. / Heavy!—God . . . / Your head is heavy!

508.14 *Cerca . . . bagno.*] Look in the bathroom cupboard.

522.15 *Fata Morgana.*] Morgan Le Fay, in Arthurian legend.

524.13–14 *pipistrella,*] Bat.

548.13 *Ecco, sono qui.*] Here they are.

555.15–16 "From Greenland's . . . vile."] Cf. "Missionary Hymn" (1819) by Reginald Heber.

567.19 *Ferma questa—commedia.*] Finish this—comedy.

573.31 silent . . . Darien. . . .] Cf. John Keats, "On First Looking Into Chapman's Homer."

THE MUTILATED

583.1 *The Mutilated*] *The Mutilated* was first presented, as part of a double bill entitled *Slapstick Tragedy*, by Charles Bowden and Lester Persky in association with Sidney Lanier, at the Longacre Theatre, in New York City, on February 22, 1966. It was directed by Alan Schneider; the scenery was designed by Ming Cho Lee; the costumes designed by Noel Taylor; music was composed and selected by Lee Hoiby; and the lighting was by Martin Aronstein. Production was in association with Frenman Productions, Ltd. The cast, in order of appearance, was as follows: CELESTE: Kate Reid; HENRY: Ralph Waite; TRINKET: Margaret Leighton; SLIM: James Olson; BRUNO: Ralph Waite; MAXIE: David Sabin; BIRD GIRL: Renee Orin; COP: Jordan Charney; BERNIE: Tom Aldredge; WOMAN AT BAR: Adelle Rasey; PIOUS QUEEN: Dan Bly; TIGER: Henry Oliver; SHORE POLICE: Hank Brunjes.

603.12–13 "Tiger, Tiger, burning bright!"] Cf. William Blake's "The Tiger," line 1.

607.8 paso-doble.] March-time music of Latin American origin.

KINGDOM OF EARTH

623.1 *Kingdom of Earth (The Seven Descents of Myrtle)*] *Kingdom of Earth (The Seven Descents of Myrtle)* was presented at the Ethel Barrymore Theatre in New York on March 27, 1968, by David Merrick. It was directed by José Quintero; the scenery and lighting by Jo Mielziner; costumes by Jane Greenwood. The cast, in order of appearance, was as follows: CHICKEN: Harry Guardino; MYRTLE: Estelle Parsons; LOT: Brian Bedford.

699.35 Gypsy Smith] Rodney "Gypsy" Smith (1860–1947), British-born evangelist.

SMALL CRAFT WARNINGS

707.1 *Small Craft Warnings*] *Small Craft Warnings* was presented at the Truck and Warehouse Theatre in New York on April 2, 1972, by Ecco Productions, Robert Currie, Mario de Maria, William Orton. It was directed by Richard Altman; the scenery and costumes were by Fred Voelpel, lighting by John Gleason; production stage manager, Robert Currie. The cast was as follows: VIOLET: Cherry Davis; DOC: David Hooks; MONK: Gene Fanning; BILL MCCORKLE: Brad Sullivan; LEONA DAWSON: Helena Carroll; STEVE: William Hickey; QUENTIN: Alan Mixon; BOBBY: David Huffman; TONY, THE COP: John David Kees.

709.10–11 *déjà entendu*] Already heard.

709.12 "sullen craft and art."] Cf. Dylan Thomas, "In My Craft or Sullen Art."

711.30–31 oil fields . . . James Dean.] Reference to the 1955 movie version of Edna Ferber's *Giant*, starring Rock Hudson and James Dean.

719.34 Imp.] Imperial, a brand of whisky.

764.14 "Meglior solo,"] Better alone.

764.37 *"labyrinthitis,"*] An inflammation of the inner ear resulting in vertigo.

767.12–13 "Breckinridge" comeback.] At age 78 Mae West returned to the screen in *Myra Breckinridge* (1970), based on Gore Vidal's novel.

767.26 *Confessional*] An early version of *Small Craft Warnings*, published in *Dragon Country* (1970).

OUT CRY

771.1 *Out Cry*] *Out Cry* opened at the Lyceum Theatre in New York on March 1, 1973, produced by David Merrick Arts Foundation and Kennedy Center Productions, Inc., and directed by Peter Glenville. The lighting and stage design were by Jo Mielziner, the costumes by Sandy Cole, with Alan Hall as stage manager. The cast was as follows: FELICE: Michael York; CLARE: Cara Duff-MacCormick. An earlier version of *Out Cry* was presented in Chicago on July 8, 1971, at the Ivanhoe Theatre. It was produced and directed by George Keathley, with Donald Madden and Eileen Herlie in the principal roles. A still earlier version, under the title of *The Two-Character Play*, was offered at the Hampstead Theatre Club.

778.3 "Pox vobiscum,"] Parody of "pax vobiscum" (peace be unto you).

VIEUX CARRÉ

825.1 *Vieux Carré*] The Nottingham Playhouse Production of *Vieux Carré* was presented at The Playhouse Theatre, Nottingham, on May 16, 1978, and at the Piccadilly Theatre, London, on August 9, 1978. It was directed by Keith Hack; stage design was by Voytek, lighting by Francis Reid, costumes by Maria Björnson, and music by Jeremy Nicholas; company stage manager, James Gill. The cast in order of appearance was as follows: MRS. WIRE: Sylvia Miles; NURSIE: Nadia Cattouse; THE WRITER: Karl Johnson; JANE: Di Trevis; NIGHTINGALE: Richard Kane; MARY MAUDE: Betty Hardy; MISS CARRIE: Judith Fellows; TYE: Jonathan Kent; PHOTOGRAPHER: Robin McDonald; SKY: Jack Elliott.

849.16–17 WPA Writers' Project?] See note 5.7.

856.31 *Tant pis . . .*] So much the worse.

864.20 *"He walks with me and he talks with me."*] "In the Garden," hymn composed in 1913 by C. Austin Miles (1868–1946).

885.29–30 Foxes have holes . . . head!] Cf. Matthew 8:20, Luke 9:58.

A LOVELY SUNDAY FOR CREVE COEUR

903.1 *A Lovely Sunday for Creve Coeur*] The New York premiere of *A Lovely Sunday for Creve Coeur* took place at the Hudson Guild Theatre on January 1, 1979. It was directed by Keith Hack; set design by John Conklin; lighting design by Craig Miller; costume design by Linda Fisher; producing director, Craig Anderson. The cast in order of appearance was as follows: DOROTHEA: Shirley Knight; BODEY: Peg Murray; HELENA: Charlotte Moore; MISS GLUCK: Jane Lowry.

914.1 Roy D'Arcy take poor Janet Gaynor] Roy D'Arcy (1894–1969), character actor who specialized in playing lecherous villains; Janet Gaynor (1906–84), star of *Seventh Heaven* (1927) and *Street Angel* (1928).

915.22 *Kirche, Küche, und Kinder*] Church, kitchen, and children.

927.26 *Sie . . . zugeschlagen!*] She slammed the door in my face!

927.39 *Vom Irrenhaus.*] From the insane asylum.

931.11 *Alte böse Katze.*] Vicious old cat.

932.22–24 *Eine . . . Gestorben!*] A—week ago—Sunday—my mother—/ I know, Sophie, I know./ Died!

933.1 *Nein . . . geschrien!*] No, no, she screamed!

933.14–15 *Ich . . . freundlos!*] I am alone, alone! Without a friend in the world!

933.17 *Ich . . . Welt!*] I have no one in the world!

935.16–17 *Heisser . . . Durchfall.*] Hot coffee always gives me cramps and diarrhea.

935.25 *KANN NICHT WARTEN!*] Can't wait!

937.14 *Halte das Wasser ab,*] Turn the water off.

937.15 *das Wust,*] The mess.

945.1 *Das Schlafzimmer ist gespukt!*] The bedroom is haunted!

945.23 *Il n'y a rien à faire.*] There's nothing to be done.

946.36 *Halunke*] Rascal.

Library of Congress Cataloging-in-Publication Data

Williams, Tennessee, 1911–1983.
[Plays. Selections]
Plays / Tennessee Williams.
p. cm. —(The Library of America 119–120)
Selection and notes by Mel Gussow and Kenneth Holditch.
Contents [v. 1] Plays 1937–1955: Spring storm. Not about nightingales. Battle of angels. I rise in flame, cried the phoenix. From 27 wagons full of cotton (1946) . . . . The glass menagerie. A streetcar named Desire. Summer and smoke. The rose tattoo. Camino Real. From 27 Wagons full of cotton (1953) . . . . Cat on a hot tin roof—[v. 2] Plays 1957–1980: Orpheus descending. Suddenly last summer. Sweet bird of youth. Period of adjustment. The night of the iguana. The eccentricities of a nightingale. The milk train doesn't stop here anymore. The mutilated. Kingdom of earth (The seven descents of Myrtle). Small craft warnings. Out cry. Vieux Carré. A lovely Sunday for Creve Coeur.
ISBN 1–883011–86–8 (v. I : alk. paper)—ISBN 1–883011–87–6 (v. 2 : alk. paper)
I. Gussow, Mel. II. Holditch, Kenneth. III. Title. IV. Series.
PS3545.I5365 A6 2000
812'.54—dc21 00-030190

THE LIBRARY OF AMERICA SERIES

Library of America fosters appreciation of America's literary heritage by publishing, and keeping permanently in print, authoritative editions of America's best and most significant writing. An independent nonprofit organization, it was founded in 1979 with seed funding from the National Endowment for the Humanities and the Ford Foundation.

1. Herman Melville: Typee, Omoo, Mardi
2. Nathaniel Hawthorne: Tales & Sketches
3. Walt Whitman: Poetry & Prose
4. Harriet Beecher Stowe: Three Novels
5. Mark Twain: Mississippi Writings
6. Jack London: Novels & Stories
7. Jack London: Novels & Social Writings
8. William Dean Howells: Novels 1875–1886
9. Herman Melville: Redburn, White-Jacket, Moby-Dick
10. Nathaniel Hawthorne: Collected Novels

11 & 12. Francis Parkman: France and England in North America

13. Henry James: Novels 1871–1880
14. Henry Adams: Novels, Mont Saint Michel, The Education
15. Ralph Waldo Emerson: Essays & Lectures
16. Washington Irving: History, Tales & Sketches
17. Thomas Jefferson: Writings
18. Stephen Crane: Prose & Poetry
19. Edgar Allan Poe: Poetry & Tales
20. Edgar Allan Poe: Essays & Reviews
21. Mark Twain: The Innocents Abroad, Roughing It

22 & 23. Henry James: Literary Criticism

24. Herman Melville: Pierre, Israel Potter, The Confidence-Man, Tales & Billy Budd
25. William Faulkner: Novels 1930–1935

26 & 27. James Fenimore Cooper: The Leatherstocking Tales

28. Henry David Thoreau: A Week, Walden, The Maine Woods, Cape Cod
29. Henry James: Novels 1881–1886
30. Edith Wharton: Novels

31 & 32. Henry Adams: History of the U.S. during the Administrations of Jefferson & Madison

33. Frank Norris: Novels & Essays
34. W.E.B. Du Bois: Writings
35. Willa Cather: Early Novels & Stories
36. Theodore Dreiser: Sister Carrie, Jennie Gerhardt, Twelve Men
37. Benjamin Franklin: Writings (2 vols.)
38. William James: Writings 1902–1910
39. Flannery O'Connor: Collected Works

40, 41, & 42. Eugene O'Neill: Complete Plays

43. Henry James: Novels 1886–1890
44. William Dean Howells: Novels 1886–1888

45 & 46. Abraham Lincoln: Speeches & Writings

47. Edith Wharton: Novellas & Other Writings
48. William Faulkner: Novels 1936–1940
49. Willa Cather: Later Novels
50. Ulysses S. Grant: Memoirs & Selected Letters
51. William Tecumseh Sherman: Memoirs
52. Washington Irving: Bracebridge Hall, Tales of a Traveller, The Alhambra
53. Francis Parkman: The Oregon Trail, The Conspiracy of Pontiac
54. James Fenimore Cooper: Sea Tales

55 & 56. Richard Wright: Works

57. Willa Cather: Stories, Poems, & Other Writings
58. William James: Writings 1878–1899
59. Sinclair Lewis: Main Street & Babbitt

60 & 61. Mark Twain: Collected Tales, Sketches, Speeches, & Essays

62 & 63. The Debate on the Constitution

64 & 65. Henry James: Collected Travel Writings

66 & 67. American Poetry: The Nineteenth Century

68. Frederick Douglass: Autobiographies
69. Sarah Orne Jewett: Novels & Stories
70. Ralph Waldo Emerson: Collected Poems & Translations
71. Mark Twain: Historical Romances
72. John Steinbeck: Novels & Stories 1932–1937
73. William Faulkner: Novels 1942–1954

74 & 75. Zora Neale Hurston: Novels, Stories, & Other Writings

76. Thomas Paine: Collected Writings

77 & 78. Reporting World War II: American Journalism

79 & 80. Raymond Chandler: Novels, Stories, & Other Writings

81. Robert Frost: Collected Poems, Prose, & Plays
82 & 83. Henry James: Complete Stories 1892–1910
84. William Bartram: Travels & Other Writings
85. John Dos Passos: U.S.A.
86. John Steinbeck: The Grapes of Wrath & Other Writings 1936–1941
87, 88, & 89. Vladimir Nabokov: Novels & Other Writings
90. James Thurber: Writings & Drawings
91. George Washington: Writings
92. John Muir: Nature Writings
93. Nathanael West: Novels & Other Writings
94 & 95. Crime Novels: American Noir of the 1930s, 40s, & 50s
96. Wallace Stevens: Collected Poetry & Prose
97. James Baldwin: Early Novels & Stories
98. James Baldwin: Collected Essays
99 & 100. Gertrude Stein: Writings
101 & 102. Eudora Welty: Novels, Stories, & Other Writings
103. Charles Brockden Brown: Three Gothic Novels
104 & 105. Reporting Vietnam: American Journalism
106 & 107. Henry James: Complete Stories 1874–1891
108. American Sermons
109. James Madison: Writings
110. Dashiell Hammett: Complete Novels
111. Henry James: Complete Stories 1864–1874
112. William Faulkner: Novels 1957–1962
113. John James Audubon: Writings & Drawings
114. Slave Narratives
115 & 116. American Poetry: The Twentieth Century
117. F. Scott Fitzgerald: Novels & Stories 1920–1922
118. Henry Wadsworth Longfellow: Poems & Other Writings
119 & 120. Tennessee Williams: Collected Plays
121 & 122. Edith Wharton: Collected Stories
123. The American Revolution: Writings from the War of Independence
124. Henry David Thoreau: Collected Essays & Poems
125. Dashiell Hammett: Crime Stories & Other Writings
126 & 127. Dawn Powell: Novels
128. Carson McCullers: Complete Novels
129. Alexander Hamilton: Writings
130. Mark Twain: The Gilded Age & Later Novels
131. Charles W. Chesnutt: Stories, Novels, & Essays
132. John Steinbeck: Novels 1942–1952
133. Sinclair Lewis: Arrowsmith, Elmer Gantry, Dodsworth
134 & 135. Paul Bowles: Novels, Stories, & Other Writings
136. Kate Chopin: Complete Novels & Stories
137 & 138. Reporting Civil Rights: American Journalism
139. Henry James: Novels 1896–1899
140. Theodore Dreiser: An American Tragedy
141. Saul Bellow: Novels 1944–1953
142. John Dos Passos: Novels 1920–1925
143. John Dos Passos: Travel Books & Other Writings
144. Ezra Pound: Poems & Translations
145. James Weldon Johnson: Writings
146. Washington Irving: Three Western Narratives
147. Alexis de Tocqueville: Democracy in America
148. James T. Farrell: Studs Lonigan Trilogy
149, 150, & 151. Isaac Bashevis Singer: Collected Stories
152. Kaufman & Co.: Broadway Comedies
153. Theodore Roosevelt: Rough Riders, An Autobiography
154. Theodore Roosevelt: Letters & Speeches
155. H. P. Lovecraft: Tales
156. Louisa May Alcott: Little Women, Little Men, Jo's Boys
157. Philip Roth: Novels & Stories 1959–1962
158. Philip Roth: Novels 1967–1972
159. James Agee: Let Us Now Praise Famous Men, A Death in the Family, Shorter Fiction
160. James Agee: Film Writing & Selected Journalism
161. Richard Henry Dana Jr.: Two Years Before the Mast & Other Voyages
162. Henry James: Novels 1901–1902
163. Arthur Miller: Plays 1944–1961
164. William Faulkner: Novels 1926–1929
165. Philip Roth: Novels 1973–1977
166 & 167. American Speeches: Political Oratory
168. Hart Crane: Complete Poems & Selected Letters

169. Saul Bellow: Novels 1956–1964
170. John Steinbeck: Travels with Charley & Later Novels
171. Capt. John Smith: Writings with Other Narratives
172. Thornton Wilder: Collected Plays & Writings on Theater
173. Philip K. Dick: Four Novels of the 1960s
174. Jack Kerouac: Road Novels 1957–1960
175. Philip Roth: Zuckerman Bound
176 & 177. Edmund Wilson: Literary Essays & Reviews
178. American Poetry: The 17th & 18th Centuries
179. William Maxwell: Early Novels & Stories
180. Elizabeth Bishop: Poems, Prose, & Letters
181. A. J. Liebling: World War II Writings
182. American Earth: Environmental Writing Since Thoreau
183. Philip K. Dick: Five Novels of the 1960s & 70s
184. William Maxwell: Later Novels & Stories
185. Philip Roth: Novels & Other Narratives 1986–1991
186. Katherine Anne Porter: Collected Stories & Other Writings
187. John Ashbery: Collected Poems 1956–1987
188 & 189. John Cheever: Complete Novels & Collected Stories
190. Lafcadio Hearn: American Writings
191. A. J. Liebling: The Sweet Science & Other Writings
192. The Lincoln Anthology
193. Philip K. Dick: VALIS & Later Novels
194. Thornton Wilder: The Bridge of San Luis Rey & Other Novels 1926–1948
195. Raymond Carver: Collected Stories
196 & 197. American Fantastic Tales
198. John Marshall: Writings
199. The Mark Twain Anthology
200. Mark Twain: A Tramp Abroad, Following the Equator, Other Travels
201 & 202. Ralph Waldo Emerson: Selected Journals
203. The American Stage: Writing on Theater
204. Shirley Jackson: Novels & Stories
205. Philip Roth: Novels 1993–1995
206 & 207. H. L. Mencken: Prejudices
208. John Kenneth Galbraith: The Affluent Society & Other Writings 1952–1967
209. Saul Bellow: Novels 1970–1982
210 & 211. Lynd Ward: Six Novels in Woodcuts
212. The Civil War: The First Year
213 & 214. John Adams: Revolutionary Writings
215. Henry James: Novels 1903–1911
216. Kurt Vonnegut: Novels & Stories 1963–1973
217 & 218. Harlem Renaissance Novels
219. Ambrose Bierce: The Devil's Dictionary, Tales, & Memoirs
220. Philip Roth: The American Trilogy 1997–2000
221. The Civil War: The Second Year
222. Barbara W. Tuchman: The Guns of August, The Proud Tower
223. Arthur Miller: Plays 1964–1982
224. Thornton Wilder: The Eighth Day, Theophilus North, Autobiographical Writings
225. David Goodis: Five Noir Novels of the 1940s & 50s
226. Kurt Vonnegut: Novels & Stories 1950–1962
227 & 228. American Science Fiction: Nine Novels of the 1950s
229 & 230. Laura Ingalls Wilder: The Little House Books
231. Jack Kerouac: Collected Poems
232. The War of 1812
233. American Antislavery Writings
234. The Civil War: The Third Year
235. Sherwood Anderson: Collected Stories
236. Philip Roth: Novels 2001–2007
237. Philip Roth: Nemeses
238. Aldo Leopold: A Sand County Almanac & Other Writings
239. May Swenson: Collected Poems
240 & 241. W. S. Merwin: Collected Poems
242 & 243. John Updike: Collected Stories
244. Ring Lardner: Stories & Other Writings
245. Jonathan Edwards: Writings from the Great Awakening
246. Susan Sontag: Essays of the 1960s & 70s
247. William Wells Brown: Clotel & Other Writings
248 & 249. Bernard Malamud: Novels & Stories of the 1940s, 50s, & 60s
250. The Civil War: The Final Year
251. Shakespeare in America

252. Kurt Vonnegut: Novels 1976–1985
253 & 254. American Musicals 1927–1969
255. Elmore Leonard: Four Novels of the 1970s
256. Louisa May Alcott: Work, Eight Cousins, Rose in Bloom, Stories & Other Writings
257. H. L. Mencken: The Days Trilogy
258. Virgil Thomson: Music Chronicles 1940–1954
259. Art in America 1945–1970
260. Saul Bellow: Novels 1984–2000
261. Arthur Miller: Plays 1987–2004
262. Jack Kerouac: Visions of Cody, Visions of Gerard, Big Sur
263. Reinhold Niebuhr: Major Works on Religion & Politics
264. Ross Macdonald: Four Novels of the 1950s
265 & 266. The American Revolution: Writings from the Pamphlet Debate
267. Elmore Leonard: Four Novels of the 1980s
268 & 269. Women Crime Writers: Suspense Novels of the 1940s & 50s
270. Frederick Law Olmsted: Writings on Landscape, Culture, & Society
271. Edith Wharton: Four Novels of the 1920s
272. James Baldwin: Later Novels
273. Kurt Vonnegut: Novels 1987–1997
274. Henry James: Autobiographies
275. Abigail Adams: Letters
276. John Adams: Writings from the New Nation 1784–1826
277. Virgil Thomson: The State of Music & Other Writings
278. War No More: American Antiwar & Peace Writing
279. Ross Macdonald: Three Novels of the Early 1960s
280. Elmore Leonard: Four Later Novels
281. Ursula K. Le Guin: The Complete Orsinia
282. John O'Hara: Stories
283. The Unknown Kerouac: Rare, Unpublished & Newly Translated Writings
284. Albert Murray: Collected Essays & Memoirs
285 & 286. Loren Eiseley: Collected Essays on Evolution, Nature, & the Cosmos
287. Carson McCullers: Stories, Plays & Other Writings
288. Jane Bowles: Collected Writings
289. World War I and America: Told by the Americans Who Lived It
290 & 291. Mary McCarthy: The Complete Fiction
292. Susan Sontag: Later Essays
293 & 294. John Quincy Adams: Diaries
295. Ross Macdonald: Four Later Novels
296 & 297. Ursula K. Le Guin: The Hainish Novels & Stories
298 & 299. Peter Taylor: The Complete Stories
300. Philip Roth: Why Write? Collected Nonfiction 1960–2014
301. John Ashbery: Collected Poems 1991–2000
302. Wendell Berry: Port William Novels & Stories: The Civil War to World War II
303. Reconstruction: Voices from America's First Great Struggle for Racial Equality
304. Albert Murray: Collected Novels & Poems
305 & 306. Norman Mailer: The Sixties
307. Rachel Carson: Silent Spring & Other Writings on the Environment
308. Elmore Leonard: Westerns
309 & 310. Madeleine L'Engle: The Kairos Novels
311. John Updike: Novels 1959–1965
312. James Fenimore Cooper: Two Novels of the American Revolution
313. John O'Hara: Four Novels of the 1930s
314. Ann Petry: The Street, The Narrows
315. Ursula K. Le Guin: Always Coming Home
316 & 317. Wendell Berry: Collected Essays
318. Cornelius Ryan: The Longest Day, A Bridge Too Far
319. Booth Tarkington: Novels & Stories
320. Herman Melville: Complete Poems
321 & 322. American Science Fiction: Eight Classic Novels of the 1960s
323. Frances Hodgson Burnett: The Secret Garden, A Little Princess, Little Lord Fauntleroy
324. Jean Stafford: Complete Novels
325. Joan Didion: The 1960s & 70s
326. John Updike: Novels 1968–1975
327. Constance Fenimore Woolson: Collected Stories
328. Robert Stone: Dog Soldiers, Flag for Sunrise, Outerbridge Reach
329. Jonathan Schell: The Fate of the Earth, The Abolition, The Unconquerable World
330. Richard Hofstadter: Anti-Intellectualism in American Life, The Paranoid Style in American Politics, Uncollected Essays 1956–1965

*This book is set in 10 point Linotron Galliard,
a face designed for photocomposition by Matthew Carter
and based on the sixteenth-century face Granjon. The paper is acid-free
lightweight opaque that will not turn yellow or brittle with age.
The binding is sewn, which allows the book to open easily and lie flat.
The binding board is covered in Brillianta, a woven rayon cloth
made by Van Heek–Scholco Textielfabrieken, Holland.
Composition by The Clarinda Company.
Printing by Sheridan Grand Rapids, Grand Rapids, MI.
Binding by Dekker Bookbinding, Wyoming, MI.
Designed by Bruce Campbell.*

TENNESSEE WILLIAMS

Tennessee Williams

PLAYS 1937–1955

Editors
Mel Gussow
Kenneth Holditch

THE LIBRARY OF AMERICA

Published by arrangement with New Directions Publishing Corporation, New York, Publisher of the plays of Tennessee Williams, and The University of the South, copyright proprietor of the works of Tennessee Williams. For copyrights, see page 1036.

The paper used in this publication meets the minimum requirements of the American National Standard for Information Sciences—Permanence of Paper for Printed Library Materials, ANSI Z39.48—1984.

Distributed to the trade in the United States
by Penguin Group (USA) Inc.
and in Canada by Penguin Books Canada Ltd.

Library of Congress Catalog Number: 00–030190
For cataloging information, see end of Notes.
ISBN: 978–1–883011–86–4
ISBN: 1–883011–86–8

Sixth Printing
The Library of America—119

Manufactured in the United States of America

Tennessee Williams' *Plays 1937–1955*
is kept in print in memory of

RICHARD SANTINO
(1946–1994)

by a gift from

Richard Poirier

to the Guardians of American Letters Fund,
established by The Library of America
to ensure that every volume in the series
will be permanently available.

Contents

SPRING STORM

PLACE: Port Tyler, a small Mississippi town on the Mississippi River

TIME: Spring, 1937

ACT ONE: A high bluff overlooking the Mississippi River on a spring afternoon

ACT TWO:

Scene One: The Critchfield home, the afternoon of Friday, the same week

Scene Two: Same, that evening

Scene Three: Same, three in the morning

ACT THREE:

Scene One: Lawn of the Lamphrey residence, the next evening (Saturday), a party is in full swing

Scene Two: The Port Tyler Carnegie Public Library, the same evening

Scene Three: The Critchfield home, late afternoon toward evening of the next day (Sunday)

ACT ONE

SCENE ONE

The house lights go down. Children's voices are heard singing "Here We Go Round the Mulberry Bush," interspersed with laughter and shouting.

The curtain rises to reveal a high, windy bluff over the Mississippi River. It is called Lover's Leap. On its verge are two old trees whose leafless branches have been grotesquely twisted by the winds. At first the scene has a mellow quality, the sky flooded with deep amber light from the sunset. But as it progresses, it changes to one of stormy violence to form a dramatic contrast between Heavenly's scene and Hertha's. The atmospheric change is caused by the approach of the spring storm which breaks at the scene's culmination.

Dick is discovered alone on the bluff. He is a good-looking boy, say about twenty-three or four, tall and athletic in build, with a fund of restless energy and imagination which prevents him from fitting into the conventional social pattern. Out of ten such men, or maybe a hundred, one becomes an Abraham Lincoln or a Clarence Darrow, and the rest live out their lives in frustrated rebellion. Maybe Dick will be the chosen one or maybe he'll just be one of the ninety-nine: that will depend upon future accidents of life which his author will not pretend to foresee.

The singing continues from below, then fades out in scattered shouting.

Heavenly enters. The important thing about Heavenly is that she is physically attractive. She has the natural and yet highly-developed charm that is characteristic of girls of pure southern stock. She is frankly sensuous without being coarse, fiery-tempered and yet disarmingly sweet. Her nature is confusing to herself and to all who know her. She wears a white skirt and sweater with a bright-colored scarf.

HEAVENLY: Dick! What are you doing up here?

DICK: Watchin' the rivuh. She's risen plenty since mawnin'. See how she's pushed up Wild Hoss Crick up there no'th o' Sutters? Ole man Sutter's gonna go to bed some night in the state o' Mississippi and wake up in Arkansaw. That is, if he's lucky. If he isn't lucky he's gonna wake up a hell of a lot fu'ther south'n *any* state in the Union. Now if they'd just put that breakwater ha'f a mile fu'ther—

HEAVENLY (*exasperated*): Dick!

DICK: Yeah?

HEAVENLY: Why do you walk off by yourself like this, honey? It looks peculiuh to people.

DICK: Does it?

HEAVENLY: Of cou'se it does!

DICK: I'm sorry. I stuck it out as long's I could. But those guessin' games got my goat—lissen to that! I used my five words in one sentence beginnin' with 'g'—games got my goat! No, that's just four.

HEAVENLY: That's remarkable, honey—you're a remarkable man, but I wish you'd pay some attention to what I'm sayin!

DICK: What're you sayin?

HEAVENLY: I'm sayin it looks peculiuh to people when you come up here by yourself and leave me down there.

DICK: Well, why don't you come up here, too?

HEAVENLY: Because I can't. It's impolite, Dick.

DICK: Aw, politeness! Bein' a damn hypocrite, that's politeness!—Me, I don't truck with politeness, I do like I please!

HEAVENLY: Dick, you're tryin' to aggravate me!

DICK (*laughing*): Sure I'm tryin to aggravate you. Honey, I like to aggravate you.

HEAVENLY: I know you do. You take the greatest delight in getting me aggravated.

DICK: Sure I do. Cause when you get aggravated you're just as cute as a nine-tailed catawampus— Lookit that nigger down there in a flatboat tryin' to pull into shore. Bet he don't make it! Lookit by God! He's lost an oar!

HEAVENLY: Never mind that nigger. You come on down to the picnic.

DICK: Guessin' game over yet?

HEAVENLY: An hour ago.

DICK: I hope so. There's some things a grown man in his right senses can't put up with an' one of 'em's havin' some ole maid ask him what she's thinkin' of that's red, white, an' blue and begins with 'f'— I felt like sayin' "Your fanny!"

HEAVENLY: Dick!

DICK (*grinning slowly*): She wouldn't have understood. She would have said, "No, suh! My name is Agnes!"—That's her now comin' up the hill with that balmy sky-rider.

HEAVENLY: Shh, Dick!—That's Miss Peabody an' Reverend Hooker!

(*These two appear from below, a conventional, affable Episcopal clergyman and a coquettish spinster bubbling with animation.*)

AGNES: I told her it was strongly reminiscent of something I'd seen in the *Atlantic Monthly.* Not that I'm accusing you of plagiarism, I said, but when there is such a startling similarity—

DR. HOOKER (*ignoring her prattle, heartily*): Well, Richard, my boy, why aren't you down there participating in some of the big athletic events?

(*Everybody speaks simultaneously—confused chatter with a background of singing.*)

AGNES: Of course there was nothing I could do about it. Her parents were furious—

HEAVENLY: Hello, Dr. Hooker.

DR. HOOKER: How are you dear? If I remember correctly this young man of yours was quite a power on the high school football team back in—when did you graduate, Richard?

RICHARD: Thirty-two.

DR. HOOKER: Your laurels are still green, my lad, your laurels are still green—glorious sunset, Heavenly, glorious.

AGNES: Dr. Hooker, look at those clouds!

DR. HOOKER: And how does it happen your mother isn't with us this afternoon?

AGNES: Those clouds, Dr. Hooker.

HEAVENLY: Mother was very skeptical about the weather.

DR. HOOKER: Yes, storm clouds— "Swear not by the inconstant—April! Her moods are various—"

AGNES: Yes, but, Dr. Hooker—

HEAVENLY: I hope the picnic's a financial success.

AGNES: Yes but—

DR. HOOKER: Oh, indeed, yes. Richard, we're going to have the cake sale.

AGNES: Yes, but from the purely esthetic point of—

DICK (*indifferently*): Yeah?

DR. HOOKER: Purely esthetic, yes!

AGNES: Such a beautiful cumulus formation in all my life!

DR. HOOKER: I presume you'll wish to make a bid for the young lady's culinary masterpiece! (*He laughs.*)

VOICE BELOW: Dr. Hooker!

AGNES: Oh, they're calling you Dr. Hooker!

DR. HOOKER: Coming! Coming!

AGNES (*following him off*): It's the potato race, they're going to have the potato race! Wait for me, wait for Dr. Hookuh!

(*Exeunt. Dick has turned his back to the others and is still looking out from the bluff.*)

HEAVENLY (*slipping her arm through his*): Still watching the river?

DICK: Sure. (*Dick turns around and moves back up to look at the river.*)

HEAVENLY: Can't I compete with the river?

DICK: Not right now.

HEAVENLY: Why not?

DICK: It's goin' somewhere.

HEAVENLY: Oh! So'm I. (*She starts off. He grabs her arm.*)

DICK: No, you're a woman. Women never go anywhere unless a man makes 'em. Don't you know what's the real diff'rence between the sexes?

HEAVENLY: Yes, I mean, no. I don't want to hear any dirty jokes.

DICK: This isn't dirty, this is scientific. Set down an' I'll tell you. The real diff'rence is that a man knows that legs're made to move on but a woman thinks they're just for wearin' silk stockin's.

HEAVENLY: You're crazy. I haven't got any stockings on mine.

DICK: Naw. But as Agnes would say they're "purely exthetic!" Ornamental—ain't that what she means?

HEAVENLY: Why shouldn't they be?

DICK: That's right. Why shouldn't they be?

HEAVENLY: You'd be the first to complain if they weren't.

DICK: Sure— But don't you get restless sometimes. Don't that river-wind ever slap you in the face an' say, "Git movin', yuh damn l'il goober digger, git movin'!"?

HEAVENLY: No.

DICK: It does me.

HEAVENLY: You're gettin' one of your restless spells?

DICK: I'd like to follow that river down there—find out where she's goin'.

HEAVENLY: I know where it's goin' an' I'm not anxious to follow. Gulf of Mexico's the scummiest body of water I ever refused to put my feet in. Crawdads an' stingarees an'—

DICK: Aw, is 'at where it's goin? I thought it was goin' further'n that. I thought it was goin' way on out to th' Caribbean an' then some. I didn't think it would stop till it got clear round th' Straits o' Magellan!

HEAVENLY: What is this? A geography lesson?

DICK: Naw. It hasn't got a damn thing to do with geography.

HEAVENLY: Oh. You're speaking symbolically about the Gypsy in you or something. Every spring you get restless like this and talk about goin' off places.

DICK: Time I got started.

HEAVENLY: You mean it's time you stopped. It's gettin damned monotonous.—Even way back in grade school you had spells like this. Used to make me play hooky so we could watch the trains coming in.

(*Pause. The children are playing another singing game. Their voices float up with a melancholy sweetness.*)

DICK: That was fun, huh?

HEAVENLY: Not for me. I was terribly bored.

DICK: Then what did you tag along for?

HEAVENLY: Because I was crazy about you just like I am now. I was always secretly hoping that you'd get romantic and try to kiss me or something, but you never did. You were never interested in anything but trains, trains! I tried everything I could to distract you, even hid behind cotton bales to make you look for me, but it never did any good.

DICK: Was that why you kept hiding from me?

HEAVENLY: I'd been reading *The Sheik*—I wanted to be pursued an' captured an' made a slave to passion!

DICK: On a station platform?

HEAVENLY: Anywhere. I was very romantic in those days.

DICK: Sort of precocious for thirteen.

HEAVENLY: But you weren't a damn bit. It was two years before you finally kissed me.

DICK: An' then you didn't like it.

HEAVENLY: Not the first time. It was an awful anticlimax to what I'd expected. (*She kisses him, he suddenly draws her against him with real passion.*) —Mmmm. Your technique has improved a little since then. (*She wipes the lipstick off his mouth.*)

DICK: So's yours.

HEAVENLY: I couldn't have been so bad even then. I made you stop looking at trains.

DICK: Yes, you did that.

HEAVENLY: And now I've made you stop watchin' the rivuh—haven't I?

DICK: Not quite.

HEAVENLY: Liuh!

DICK: I still like to watch things goin' places.

HEAVENLY: My idea of goin' places is to make a success of things where you are.

DICK: Sure. Provided you're in the right place.

(*He rises and stretches. The singing has ended. An excited woman's voice—*)

MRS. ASBURY (*off-stage*): Ronald! Oh, Ron-*ald*! (*She appears, a dumpy little matron in slacks.*) Oh Heavenly! Have you seen my child? Hertha Neilson's getting ready to tell the children one of her charming little fairy stories, and I don't want Ronald to miss it.

HEAVENLY: Sorry but I haven't seen him.

DICK: Is he a short fat kid with buck teeth wearin' glasses?

MRS. ASBURY (*outraged*): Why, no!! —I mean—uh— (*She tries to laugh.*) That's not a very flattering description! Which way did he go?

DICK: Down that-away. Tow'd the Devil's Icebox.

MRS. ASBURY: The Devil's—? Oh, Heavens! (*She goes off shrieking her son's name.*)

HEAVENLY: You should've offuhed to help her find him.

DICK: Hell. She needs to run some a' the lard off that carcass of hers.

HEAVENLY: Dick!—Dick, you know we've got to have some kind of social position when we get married, and we can't without bein' nice to people like Mrs. Asbury.

DICK: That's what I'm scahed of.

HEAVENLY: You mean you're scahed of marriage?

DICK: You remembuh that high-school play we acted in? Honey?

HEAVENLY: *Satuhday's Children*?

DICK: Yeah, there was one swell line in that play.

HEAVENLY: What's that?

DICK: Marriage is last year's love affair.

HEAVENLY: Oh! You don't want marriage!

DICK: Not the kind that ties ropes around people. (*He goes to the edge of the bluff.*) Listen to those whistles blowin'. They're gettin' out now. Pretty soon they'll be settlin' down in their overstuffed chairs t' look at the evenin' papers. Gettin' the news of the day. Who went to Mrs. Smith's afternoon tea. What happened in Czechoslovakia at eleven A.M. Who's runnin' for gov'nor in the state of Arkansas. Ain't that somethin' for you, you bastards, you poor beer guzzlers. Tomorrow you'll wake up at half past six with alarm clocks janglin' like hell's own beautiful bells in your ears. The little woman will get her fat shanks out of bed an' put on the coffee to boil. At a quarter past seven you'll kiss her good-bye, you'll give her a cold eggy smack on the kisser. She'll tell you to remember your overshoes. Or to stop at the West End butcher's for a pound o' calves' liver. Don't forget, Papa. Papa, for God's sake don't forget to bring home that thirty cents worth of calves' liver. That's good, that's sweet of you, Papa. —Bye-bye! (*He turns slowly back to Heavenly.*) And they call that *livin'* down there. I got another word for it, Heavenly, and it don't commence with an "l"!

(*Mrs. Asbury's voice is heard calling Ronald. Dick continues, mocking.*)

"Ronald, oh, Ron-*ald*!"—don't fall an' break your fat little neck! —Christ, Heavenly, I want to get away from that sort of stuff down there. That's what I mean when I say I want to go places!

HEAVENLY: I know. You talk just as though I didn't exist.

DICK: Oh, I know you exist.

HEAVENLY: No you don't. You think I'm completely out of the picture. But I'm not. I think I'm pretty much involved in your plans for the future whether you know it or not.

DICK: I haven't got any plans for the future.

HEAVENLY: Yes, you have. I've got some for you.

DICK: Yeah?

HEAVENLY: I was talking to Dad last night. He says Mr. Kramer's willing to put you on at his office as soon as buying picks up.

DICK: Tell your Dad I'm much obliged but I don't want a job in Mr. Kramer's office or anybody else's. I don't want a white-collar job.

HEAVENLY: You prefer to work around a drugstore?

DICK: No, I prefer to get the hell out of here.

HEAVENLY: You want to go on the bum?

DICK: I want to do something worthwhile.

HEAVENLY: What is worthwhile in your opinion?

DICK: I don't know. Maybe if I did some traveling I'd find out.

HEAVENLY: All right. Let's take a round-the-world cruise.

DICK: I'd rather take a cattleboat to South America. (*He quickly rationalizes his impulse.*) There's lots of business opportunities down there. I could get into radio or engineering or—

HEAVENLY: Oh. Don't let me stop you!

DICK: Don't worry, it's just a pipe dream.

HEAVENLY: Worry? Not me! I guess you think I'd be sitting at home knitting socks till you came back with a long white beard to reward my patience. No, not me! "Faithful unto death" isn't the sort of thing I want carved on my tombstone.

(*Enter Susan Lamphrey, a fat girl of Heavenly's age.*)

SUSAN: Heavenly, you missed it!

HEAVENLY: Missed what?

SUSAN: The auction! Guess who bought your cake?

HEAVENLY: Who bought it?

SUSAN: Arthur Shannon. Paid eighty dollars for it.

HEAVENLY: You're foolin'!

SUSAN: I hope to fall dead if I am. I nearly did anow. And he came with that girl who works at the library. Hertha Neilson. I wonder how *she* felt?—Hello, Richard. Goodness, you are the exclusive Mr. Somebody! I didn't even know you'd come to the picnic! Oh, what I wanted to ask you—before I forget—I'm givin' a little lawn party in honor of Arthur Shannon this Saturday evenin' an' want you to come, Heavenly—an' bring along Dick!

HEAVENLY: Thanks. We'll come.

SUSAN: I've got to rush down there an' help pack things up. Bye-bye! (*She rushes off.*)

DICK: You can count me out.

HEAVENLY: Dick.

DICK: You know I don't mix with those kind of people.

HEAVENLY: All right. Don't put yourself out. I'll go with Arthur Shannon. He deserves some reward, anyway, for payin' eighty dollars for that little coconut cake! (*Dick turns his back.*) Saturday Arthuh will take me to the Lamphrey's lawn party.

DICK: Is he?

HEAVENLY: Yes. And Sunday evenin' we're going to the Country Club for supper. (*There is a tense pause.*) An' on the way home he'll ask me to marry him.

DICK: —Will he?

HEAVENLY: Yes! I know how to work those things.

DICK: Yes. You're very clever.

HEAVENLY (*bursting out*): And you, you can take that river barge down to New Orleans an' ship out on a cattleboat if you want to. You can go clear down to the Straits of whatever-you-call-it 's far's I'm concerned! If you're restless, if you want to get rid of me so bad, don't think I'm gonna stand in your way! (*She turns away, sobbing convulsively.*)

DICK (*slowly*): You know that's not true. You can't make me jealous about that little milk-fed millionaire's brat. Suckin' a sugar-tit all his life. I remember him in grade school before he went off to Europe. God, what a sissy! His chauffeur brought him to school an' called for him afterwards an' at recess he used to sit in a corner of the play yard readin' *The Wizard of Oz.* Remember how we used to serenade him when he drove up to school in his limousine?

Artie, Smartie, went to a party!
What did he go for? To play with his dolly!

HEAVENLY: Oh, you're disgusting!

DICK: You used to sing it yourself. I guess that's what gave him the nervous breakdown so he had to quit school an' be shipped abroad. He was kind of stuck on you even then, wasn't he? We used to kid you about the way he kept hangin' around you.

HEAVENLY: With Arthur Shannon's prospects he can afford to have some faults.

DICK: Meaning I can't?

HEAVENLY: Exactly! Meaning just that. I've given up plenty of chances for you. In hopes you'd turn over a new leaf an' amount to something. Now I see that you never will. Arthur Shannon's going to ask me to marry him, and I'm going to do it.

DICK: You won't.

HEAVENLY: You just think I won't.

(*He grabs her shoulders.*)

Let go of me, damn you!

(*She strikes him across the face. He draws back. They stand facing each other in the deepening dusk.—From below them comes the sound of the closing hymns at the church picnic—*

Now the day is over
Night is drawing nigh,
Shadows of the evening
Steal across the sky.

The soft poignant quality of the hymn penetrates their mood and softens them both. Heavenly turns away, crying. Dick comes to her and embraces her gently. His voice is very low—)

DICK: Listen Heavenly! Honey, listen! You don't mean none of those things you just said. Why you couldn't shake me off anymore than you could your own skin. An' I couldn't either.—I've had my talk out. I'm always blowin' off my damn fool head about somethin'. But that's all over.

Understan'? You and me, we'll get married this summer! Yeah. We'll have one a them June weddin's you see written up in sassiety columns with everything white an' sweet smellin' an' candles an' lilies an' yards an' yards of white lace for you to walk down like a queen with that new pipe organ playin' "I Love You Truly." An' me, I'll take that job of Mr. Kramer's!

HEAVENLY: Dick!

DICK: Sure . . . See those lights goin' on down there? One of them'll be ours! A little one off at the side—

(*He laughs gently. The closing hymn ends. There are sounds of general departure. Mrs. Lamphrey appears calling, "Ethel!"*)

MRS. LAMPHREY: Heavenly. Have you seen Mrs. Asbury? She's going home in our car.

HEAVENLY: She's gone after Ronald. He's exploring the Devil's Icebox.

MRS. LAMPHREY: Oh, that boy. Everybody's leaving; it looks so threatening!

HEAVENLY: Dick. Won't you hunt them up for Mrs. Lamphrey? I can't imagine what's keeping them so long.

MRS. LAMPHREY: Oh, I'd be so much obliged, Mr. Miles. (*She turns to Heavenly as Dick goes off.*) Richard is such a nice boy. I don't blame you, Heavenly.

HEAVENLY: For what?

MRS. LAMPHREY: For finding him irresistible. He has that—that sort of—primitive masculinity that's enough to make a girl lose her head!

HEAVENLY: Oh, I think I've kept mine.

MRS. LAMPHREY (*archly*): Oh, do you? Good heavens, the storm's going to break any minute. And here comes Arthur Shannon with that Neilson girl. (*Calling.*) Arthur, did you ever see such a sky?

(*Arthur enters, followed by Hertha. He is a good-looking esthetic young man, about twenty-four. He wears white flannels, a sports coat, and a scarf about his throat. Hertha is thin and dark, about twenty-eight. Without money or social position, she has to depend upon a feverish animation and cleverness to make her place among people. She has an original mind with a distinct gift for creative work. She is probably the most sensitive and intelligent person in Port Tyler, Mississippi. Much of the dialogue following is simultaneous.*)

ARTHUR: Marvelous, isn't it? We're coming up to a better view. (*To Heavenly.*) Hello!

MRS. LAMPHREY (*to Hertha*): Oh, Miss Neilson, I enjoyed your little story so much. It was charming. Did you make it up yourself? Goodness! What wind! What wind!

HEAVENLY: Oh, is that my cake Arthur? It was sweet of you to buy it.

MRS. LAMPHREY: Heavenly! Hadn't we better go down? This wind is terrific.

HEAVENLY: I would have taken more pains if I thought it was going to bring such a big price. What is it Mrs. Lamphrey?

MRS. LAMPHREY: Don't you think we'd better go down?

ARTHUR: You won't forget about our dinner Sunday?

HEAVENLY: Oh, no. Yes, Mrs. Lamphrey! I'm coming.

MRS. LAMPHREY (*calling back to Hertha*): Oh, Miss Neilson. Would you please remind your mother about those alterations to Susan's little pink blouse?

(*Hertha says nothing. Heavenly and Mrs. Lamphrey exeunt.*)

ARTHUR: Tired?

HERTHA: A little.

ARTHUR: It's your own fault. You would keep on climbing.

HERTHA: I wanted to reach the top.

ARTHUR: Well, now you're there.

HERTHA (*panting*): Not quite. I'm going to save the rest till later. I'm going to wait till it's just the right color and then I'm going to go up the rest of the way—and then you'll probably hear me shouting "hello" to God!

ARTHUR: It *is* nice up here.

HERTHA: Lovely. I hate living on a flat surface. It's bad for you, Arthur.

ARTHUR: Is it?

HERTHA: Yes, you don't know how bad it is till you get up on a high place like this and see how your spirit expands.

ARTHUR: Is your spirit expanding?

HERTHA: Enormously, enormously! Don't you see how it's filling up the whole sky?

ARTHUR: Oh, is that your spirit?
HERTHA (*laughing*): Yes!
ARTHUR: Congratulations! I haven't seen such a pyrotechnical display since July 14th, at Versailles!

(*Dick returns followed by the straggling Asburys.*)

RONALD: Aw, hell, Ma—
MRS. ASBURY: What did you say, Ronald?
RONALD: Nothing.
MRS. ASBURY: I'm afraid your father will be very angry when he hears about this. (*To Dick.*) Oh, Mr. Miles. I'm so grateful to you.—I hope you haven't lost Heavenly!
DICK: I reckon she's gone on with the others.

(*Exeunt all three.*)

HERTHA: We seem to be the sole survivors.
ARTHUR: Yes, thank heavens. I get so bored with those people.
HERTHA: Why do you bother with them?
ARTHUR: Have to. It's in the line of duty. I'm being groomed for the Planter's State Bank, so I have to make myself agreeable to depositors.
HERTHA (*seating herself on the hillside*): Oh.
ARTHUR (*sitting beside her*): Why do *you* bother with them?
HERTHA: I sort of—*belong* to them!
ARTHUR: How do you mean?
HERTHA: The Storybook Lady's a public institution.
ARTHUR: What?
HERTHA: The Storybook Lady—that's me! Every Tuesday, Thursday, and Saturday mornings, ten o'clock at the Carnegie Public Library. Have you ever heard what happened to the dark-haired princess in the magic tower when the handsome young prince went out to look for adventure? (*They both laugh.*) Oh, I don't mind that part of it. I like to make-believe as much as any of the kids. It's the old women that I can't stand, the ones like Mrs. Lamphrey who're so afraid that you'll forget your mother's a seamstress and your father's a night watchman at the lumberyard who gets notoriously drunk every Saturday night! —Oh, they're very sweet to me, call me darling and send me flowers when I'm sick, but they take every precaution

to see that I don't forget my social limitations— Did you hear Mrs. Lamphrey remind me about Susan's little pink blouse? Size forty-eight?—Know why she did that? She's worried you didn't know that mother took in sewing. She's worried about you and me—she thinks I'm trying to captivate you or something! (*She laughs.*) Of course things like that are only *amusing*, that's all!

(*Pause. Arthur lights a cigarette.*)

ARTHUR: You ought to get away from this place.

HERTHA: How could I?

ARTHUR: I don't know but there must be some way. You've got lots of talent and you're wasting it here.

HERTHA: So are you, wasting yours—at the Planter's State Bank.

ARTHUR (*lightly but with bitterness*): No, I'm not wasting anything. In literature I'm one of those tragic "not quites"!

HERTHA: That's silly. You're terribly young still.

ARTHUR: I know my limitations. I haven't got it in me to be anything but a good amateur, I know that. You see, my poetry, it isn't a terrific volcanic eruption— No—it's just a little bonfire of dry leaves and dead branches. (*He laughs harshly.*) This morning I received an invitation to join the Junior Chamber of Commerce.

HERTHA (*pausing*): Of course you refused?

ARTHUR: No. Accepted.

HERTHA: Arthur!

ARTHUR: Why not? Father was tickled pink—slapped me on the back three times and told me I was going places!

HERTHA: Did he tell you what places you were going?

ARTHUR: No. (*He laughs.*) There's no necessity for being explicit about such things—going places is just going places.

HERTHA: I see. (*Pause.*) Sometimes I wonder if anybody's ever gone anyplace—or do we always just go back to where we started?—I guess there's something significant about the fact that the world is round and all of the planets are round and all of them are going round and round the sun! (*She laughs.*) The whole damned universe seems to be laid out on a more or less elliptical plan. (*She rises.*) But I can't get used to it, Arthur. I can't adjust myself to it like you're doing— (*She gropes for words.*) —You see I can't get over the idea that it might be possible for somebody—sometime—somewhere—to follow a straight line upwards and get some place that nobody's ever been yet! (*Pause.*)

ARTHUR (*looking up at her with a slight smile*): You mean to Paradise, don't you?

HERTHA: You're laughing at me. You think it's foolish.

ARTHUR (*slowly*): I know what you mean. But I don't believe in it. I think it's just one of those romantic fallacies that everybody gets knocked out of him in the course of time. —Where are you going?

HERTHA: I'm going on up the rest of the way.

ARTHUR: To see God?

HERTHA: Yes. (*Arthur laughs.*) Don't you think I'll find him up there?

ARTHUR: Oh, you might! And then you *might* just find the other side of the hill!

HERTHA: Coming?

ARTHUR: No! I hate steep places. They make me feel like falling.

HERTHA: I love them. They make me feel like flying!

(*She climbs slowly up the hillside, Arthur remaining below. When she reaches the top, she stands there silently, silhouetted between the two dead trees. It has grown almost dark except for the magenta streaks of color in the fading sunset. The wind is beginning to rise, and there is a fitful glimmer of lightning.*)

ARTHUR: Well, have you found Him? (*Pause.*)

HERTHA: Yes!

ARTHUR: What does he have to say?

HERTHA: Oh, he doesn't say anything, he doesn't use any words—just a lot of beautiful gestures which I can't understand.

ARTHUR: What does he look like? The fatherly type?

HERTHA: No!—He's a very vague sort of person. He reminds me a little bit of an old Irishman who used to get drunk with my father on Saturday nights.

ARTHUR (*laughing*): Yes?

HERTHA: An awfully funny old fellow— He never said much but he had a beautiful smile—especially when he was playing pinochle.

(*Arthur laughs.*)

You should come up and look at the river! It's marvelous! It's like a big yellow sea! (*Pause.*)

(*Arthur rises.*)

ARTHUR: That wind's too cold!
HERTHA: I like the taste of it.
ARTHUR: What does it taste like?
HERTHA: The outer edge of space. It's got the cold flavor of stars in it.
ARTHUR: That's the pine trees! You'd better come down and get into my trench coat, Miss Neilson.
HERTHA: I want to stay up here. I'm never coming down.
ARTHUR: Do I have to come up there and get you?
HERTHA: Yes, if you want me!

(*Arthur joins her above. The wind rises and blows Hertha's hair loose. They both point at things in the distance, talking and laughing, but the wind drowns their voices. Suddenly Hertha points upwards with a loud cry.*)

Wild geese!

(*If possible a faint honking should be heard as the geese pass over.*)

ARTHUR: Yes.
HERTHA: They're going up north to the lakes.—Why don't they take me with them?
ARTHUR: You're not a wild goose.
HERTHA: But I could be one—I could be anything that flies!

(*The wind roars about them.*)

ARTHUR: We'd better get down from here before we're blown down.
HERTHA: Not yet!
ARTHUR: Yes. Right now!

(*He jumps to the lower level, catches her waist and lifts her down with him. They descend to a lower level and seat themselves on the rocks. Arthur wraps his coat carefully about her. She looks at him silently—the wind falls.*)

HERTHA: Maybe the storm's blown over.

ARTHUR: No. This is just the traditional hush before it gets started.

HERTHA: If it storms let's stay up here! I love spring storms!

ARTHUR: If you caught your death of cold the kiddies would blame it on me—they'd say that I killed their Storybook Lady.

HERTHA: I'd like to die in a storm!

ARTHUR: Why would you?

HERTHA: I don't know. I think it's a good way of dying—Paul Cezanne died from painting in a storm.

ARTHUR: Did he?

HERTHA: Yes. I think that's the noblest death I ever heard of.

ARTHUR (*rising with a laugh*): Hertha! You're getting morbid —we'd better go back down.

HERTHA: Give me a few more minutes!

ARTHUR: Gosh. (*She sits back down.*) You sound like Mme. Du Barry at the foot of the guillotine.

HERTHA: Did she say that? Poor thing. I know just how she felt— She had her head chopped off and tomorrow I'll be back at the Carnegie Public Library!

ARTHUR: You're terribly dissatisfied with things, aren't you?

HERTHA: Why wouldn't I be?

ARTHUR (*carefully*): I wonder if it isn't because—

HERTHA: Because what?

ARTHUR: I knew a girl in London when I was going to school over there and she was terribly dissatisfied with things, too. We had a love affair.

HERTHA: Oh.

ARTHUR: It was her first experience and mine, too. It did us both good. We were both slightly crazy before it happened, and afterwards we were perfectly sane.

HERTHA: Why did you tell me that?

ARTHUR (*uncomfortably*): I don't know exactly.

HERTHA: Did you think that my case corresponded to hers?

ARTHUR: No.

HERTHA: Did you suppose that fornication was the straight line upwards that I'd been trying to find?

ARTHUR: I didn't think I was putting it quite that crudely.

HERTHA: I'm sorry. You were trying to be very delicate about it.

ARTHUR: It just popped out.

HERTHA: I see

ARTHUR: We talk about things so frankly in Europe. I forgot that your southern puritanism might rise up in arms at anything too boldly stated.

HERTHA: I'm not offended. No I want to thank you for being so honest with me, Arthur.—How did this idyllic affair of yours turn out?

ARTHUR: The way you'd expect. We were both disappointed to find out that the world didn't burst into a million glittering stars simply because a man and a woman shared the same bed. But we got over that. She was very practical about it. She said it was in the interest of science or something, and the next summer she married a young M.P.

HERTHA: So now you're in mourning for her?

ARTHUR: No. Not for her.

HERTHA: For somebody else?

ARTHUR: Yes. A funny thing happened to me. I've just described one of those vicious circles that you were complaining about. I've come back to something that I went away from.

HERTHA: What's that?

ARTHUR: The girl in the white skirt.

HERTHA: Heavenly Critchfield?

ARTHUR: Yes.

HERTHA: What do you mean?

ARTHUR: I loved her a long time ago. When we were in grade school.

HERTHA: That long ago?

ARTHUR: Yes. It doesn't sound possible, but it's true. I was terribly shy and one day she laughed at me. After that I couldn't go back to school anymore. They had to send me to Europe.

HERTHA: Because she laughed at you?

ARTHUR: Yes. I thought I'd forgotten about it. But now I'm beginning to see she's been in me all the time, laughing at me—and everything that I've done since then has been a sort of desperate effort to—to—

HERTHA: To compensate for her laughing at you?

ARTHUR: Yes, that's it!

HERTHA: But now that you *do* understand it, you ought to be able to get away from it.

ARTHUR: That's the funny thing. I can't. I don't think I'll be able to get away from it until I've possessed her.

HERTHA: And made her stop laughing!

ARTHUR: Yes—yes, made her stop laughing.

HERTHA: And to do that you think you will have to possess her?

ARTHUR: Yes. Or somebody else!!

HERTHA: Somebody else.

ARTHUR: Who could make me stop thinking about her.

HERTHA: Do you think that anyone could?

ARTHUR: I don't know. . . .

HERTHA: Neither do I. . . . (*She rises.*) When did we start being serious?

ARTHUR: I don't know.

HERTHA: We shouldn't be. This isn't the serious season. It's the season for green things and frivolity and—

ARTHUR (*trying to catch her mood*): And catching colds in the head.

HERTHA: Yes, the modern twist! The whimsical anticlimax! (*She jumps up to the second level.*)

ARTHUR: Where are you going?

HERTHA (*pointing gaily*): You see those two old trees up there? I used to call them the two weird sisters—they look like they're putting a curse on the town!

(*The wind rises again with great force. There is lightning and a rumble of thunder.*)

ARTHUR: Hertha. Come down from there! It's starting to rain—the storm's breaking!

(*She waves to him gaily from the summit.*)

HERTHA: Look, Arthur! There's three of us now! We're putting a curse on the town. (*She laughs wildly.*)

(*Lightning outlines her figure between the two dead trees. There is a crescendo of wind and thunder—*)

Curtain

ACT TWO

SCENE ONE

The curtain rises on the living room of the Critchfield home. We leave the practical arrangement of this room to the scene designer with these suggestions:

It is furnished in good taste with the impediment of very limited funds and a passion for antiques that are not too well-preserved. Nevertheless the room has charm. It should have a pastel spring-like quality which should be accomplished by the use of light wallpaper with a floral pattern and a pleasing combination of pastel shades in the furnishings. Mrs. Critchfield is a foolish woman, but she has made a conscientious study of the women's fashion and home magazines.

There are a few essential features: a sofa with a table lamp on a table directly beside it; a large military-equestrian portrait of a Civil War hero hung prominently on the wall, preferably in a position that seems to command the whole room; a pair of French doors with white or cream curtains; a big chair with a floor lamp beside it; a bookcase or "secretary" and a radio cabinet.

As the scene opens, Aunt Lila is seated in her rocker close to the radio. It is important that this rocker should squeak audibly when in motion. Aunt Lila is a spinster with humor and charm. She shows evidence of having been beautiful in her youth and is by no means a conventional old maid. The doorbell sounds.

MESSENGER BOY (*offstage*): Cutrere's.
MRS. CRITCHFIELD (*in the hall*): Flowers? How lovely!

(*The door is closed. After a few moments, Mrs. Critchfield enters with a light blue vase of talisman roses which she sets down on the radio cabinet. Mrs. Critchfield is a woman with large hips, pearl eardrops, and pince-nez. Walking she always leans slightly forward from her hips like a kangaroo. Her mobile hands and quick jerky movements serve to emphasize this resemblance. She has a loud "cultured" voice and a manner that seems to be derived from a long career of presiding over women's clubs. On her breast are pinned emblems of the D.A.R. and D.O.C. She is always subconsciously aware of Colonel Wayne's presence in her domestic sphere and many times during the play we catch her glancing at his portrait as a source of continual moral support.*)

MRS. CRITCHFIELD (*bustling into the room*): A dozen roses from Cutrere's!

LILA: That Shannon boy send 'em?

MRS. CRITCHFIELD (*arranging*): Of course!

LILA: What did you do with the old ones?

MRS. CRITCHFIELD: Threw them out.

LILA: When I was a girl I used to save the petals and make sachets.

MRS. CRITCHFIELD: Heavenly isn't quite that sentimental. (*She plumps down on the sofa with her sewing and a copy of* Vogue) Where is Heavenly?

LILA: Out.

MRS. CRITCHFIELD: I knew that much.

LILA: Well, that's all I can tell you.

MRS. CRITCHFIELD: Lila, what is that you're working on?

LILA: Some goods I got at Power's spring sale. It looked like a good buy so I bought it.

MRS. CRITCHFIELD: Your dividend come in from the compress stock?

LILA: It did.

MRS. CRITCHFIELD: My dear! Don't you think you might spend it a little more judiciously?

LILA: It's mine. I can spend it the way I want to.

MRS. CRITCHFIELD: Of course you can, my dear! But you might think of better ways than buying goods that will make you look like a holiday at the races.

LILA: This is for Heavenly to wear to Susan Lamphrey's lawn party.

MRS. CRITCHFIELD: Oh, now, that's sweet of you, Lila. But Heavenly's going to wear her white organdy.

LILA: What organdy?

MRS. CRITCHFIELD: Why, the one she wore at her high school commencement.

LILA: Land of Goshen. You can think of more ways to cheat the moths.

MRS. CRITCHFIELD: The material's perfectly good. I'm making it over by this new pattern in *Vogue*. (*She hands Lila the magazine.*) Princess sleeves with a little circular cape effect round the shoulders.

LILA: April's too early for organdy.

MRS. CRITCHFIELD: Not necessarily.—Everybody will be wearing summer formals.

LILA: Who said so?

MRS. CRITCHFIELD: Mrs. Lamphrey said so herself.

LILA: She just wants Heavenly to come looking peculiar so that fat Susan of hers won't show up so bad in comparison.

MRS. CRITCHFIELD: Now Lila. Why do you always attribute such awful motives to people?

LILA: Because I know 'em.

MRS. CRITCHFIELD: Know them nothing. You practically never go out of the house anymore. All you know is what Agnes Peabody tells you over the phone.

LILA: She tells me enough.

MRS. CRITCHFIELD: Yes, I'll have to admit she keeps well-informed.

LILA: Yes, speaking of information, she told me this morning that Mary Louise Shumaker's expecting another.

MRS. CRITCHFIELD: When?

LILA: Next October. I bet you Mary Louise hasn't found it out herself yet.—You'd think that Agnes was taking mail orders for the stork the way she scoops the town on things like that.

MRS. CRITCHFIELD: Lila, dear, can you see to thread this needle? I'm so nervous I can't hold it still.—Well, if I don't get finished I suppose she could wear her blue knitted suit.

LILA: That would be more sensible. April really is too early for organdy.

MRS. CRITCHFIELD: Everything's early this spring. (*She takes the needle.*) Thank you, dear. The crepe myrtle's been out a week.

LILA: What's that got to do with it?

MRS. CRITCHFIELD: I always start wearing white when the crepe myrtle's out. The boys are wearing white flannels. I saw Arthur Shannon in the public library this morning wearing white flannel pants and white shoes and a white sweater.

LILA: Trust him to do the outlandish!

MRS. CRITCHFIELD: I said to him, "My, my but you're all in white this morning!"

LILA: What did he say?

MRS. CRITCHFIELD: He said, "Yes, it's good cricket weather!" (*She bites off the end of the thread.*)

LILA: Cricket! What is cricket anyhow?

MRS. CRITCHFIELD: A game they play at Oxford. Terribly stylish.

LILA: Somehow I can't picture that boy playing anything more strenuous than checkers, and even then he'd probably have his chauffeur or valet or something to push 'em around for him.

MRS. CRITCHFIELD: Lila, dear, I want to ask you as a special favor to me to please desist from making those sarcastic remarks about Arthur Shannon and his parents, especially when Heavenly's around.

LILA: Why, I scarcely mention the Shannons! I haven't for twenty years! But why should I anyhow?

MRS. CRITCHFIELD: I'm hoping they'll make a match of it.

LILA: Heavenly and Arthur Shannon?

MRS. CRITCHFIELD: Yes. Do you have any objections?

LILA: —No. But I think Heavenly has.

MRS. CRITCHFIELD: Not if she's got any sense. Lila, you surely don't want her to make your mistake.

LILA: Which mistake do you mean?

MRS. CRITCHFIELD: Everybody expected you to make a brilliant marriage when you were a girl, but you spoiled all your chances by being a sentimental fool. You had a dozen good chances that you simply threw to the wind.

LILA: There was only one that I wanted.

MRS. CRITCHFIELD: You could have had *him*. You could have been sitting up there right now in the biggest house in town.

LILA: Yes, if I'd wanted to hold him against his will.

MRS. CRITCHFIELD: Let's not discuss that affair. It's one of those things that are better forgotten, especially when there's a young girl in the house.

LILA: You brought it up. I didn't. Don't think I'm turned against the boy on account of his father. If anything I'm holding *that* in his favor. I've still got lots of respect for Gale Shannon. The point I'm making is simply that Heavenly's been going with Richard Miles too long to switch to another.

MRS. CRITCHFIELD (*looking at her sharply*): What do you mean?

LILA: Nothing but what I said.

MRS. CRITCHFIELD (*uneasily after a pause*): I'm afraid there's been some gossip about Heavenly and that Miles boy. Mrs. Lamphrey said something right funny at the D.A.R. board meeting. She said she was glad that Susan hadn't centered her affections too definitely on any one boy, and she gave me the most pointed look, as if it had some special application to me or to Heavenly.

LILA: Centered her affections! That's good. The only thing that girl has ever centered is fat in the wrong places.

MRS. CRITCHFIELD: Lila!

LILA: Well, it's the truth.

MRS. CRITCHFIELD: It's painfully obvious that people are beginning to talk. And you can't altogether blame them. Heavenly is sometimes terribly indiscreet.

LILA: Is she?

MRS. CRITCHFIELD: You know that she is. And the Miles boy doesn't have a nice reputation. Didn't even get through high school and he's never been known to hold a job for more than two months at a time. One of these congenital loafers, that's what he is. Is that the kind of boy I want my daughter's name to be associated with? No, it is not!

LILA: I'm not saying that I approve of Dick Miles either. But love is something it's a mistake to interfere with.

MRS. CRITCHFIELD: Love!—If I were a girl I'd be thrilled by Arthur's attentions. He's got looks, money, social position —everything!

LILA: Except a backbone.

MRS. CRITCHFIELD: You're prejudiced against him, you're holding a grudge.

LILA: I'm holding no grudge. Arthur bores the girl to death sitting here reading poetry to her and talking about—

MRS. CRITCHFIELD: Is there anything wrong with having intellectual interests?

LILA: Not if they're reasonably unobtrusive. Oh, he's nice enough I suppose. But I wouldn't put too much stock in him as a prospective son-in-law.

MRS. CRITCHFIELD: Didn't he pay eighty dollars for Heavenly's cake at that church affair?

LILA: He doesn't know eighty dollars from eighty cents. Agnes Peabody says he's taken a notion to that librarian, Hertha What's-her-name, that went to the picnic with him.

MRS. CRITCHFIELD: Hertha Neilson? That girl's peculiar!

LILA: Is she?

MRS. CRITCHFIELD: Yes! She paints very odd pictures.—Wears her hair in braids like a schoolgirl and she's easily twenty-eight or thirty.

LILA: Anything else wrong with her?

MRS. CRITCHFIELD: Indeed there is. Her father's a drunkard and her mother takes in sewing.—You can imagine the Shannons allowing their son to get himself mixed up with that kind of trash.

LILA: Well, they're both artistic and Heavenly isn't.

MRS. CRITCHFIELD: Heavenly is quite artistic. Those teacups she painted in the eighth grade. Absolutely remarkable! What's happened to them?

LILA: Don't you remember? You gave them to Ozzie.

MRS. CRITCHFIELD: I didn't.—She must have acquired them in her usual way.—Arthur is just being nice to the Neilson girl because of her pitiful circumstances.

(*The phone rings. Mrs. Critchfield rushes into the hall and can be heard answering phone in her flute-like company voice.*)

Mr. Critchfield's residence— No. Heavenly is not in at the moment. Who's calling, please? Oh! (*Her tone becomes icy.*) No, she's out and I hardly believe she'll be in the rest of the evening. (*She hangs up with a bang and re-enters living room.*)

LILA: Richard Miles?

MRS. CRITCHFIELD: Yes.—Disgusting!

LILA: You shouldn't have cut him off so short!

MRS. CRITCHFIELD: Why shouldn't I? I'm sick and tired of that boy monopolizing Heavenly's time. (*She speaks from the window.*) There she comes up the walk now without any hat on and the rain just pouring. (*She crosses to the hall.*) I guess she thinks we haven't got worries enough without— Heavenly!

(*Mrs. Critchfield exits. Lila turns on the radio.*)

ANNOUNCER'S VOICE: —And for his first selection, your old friend and neighbor would like to read you a little poem by Sara Teasdale which seems especially appropriate to a rainy spring afternoon—

(*A recitation with organ background follows.*)

When I am dead and over me bright April
Shakes out her rain-drenched hair
Though you should lean above me broken-hearted
I shall not care

I shall have peace as leafy trees are peaceful
When rain bends down the bough
And I shall be more silent and cold-hearted
Than you are now!

(*Mrs. Critchfield re-enters near the close of the poem.*)

MRS. CRITCHFIELD (*referring to some act of Heavenly's*) Insolence! What is that sob-stuff you're listening to?

LILA: The Village Rhymester.

MRS. CRITCHFIELD: Please use the earphones! (*She switches off the radio.*) Sentimentality is something that turns my stomach.

(*Aunt Lila quietly adjusts earphones and turns the radio back on. During the dialogue between Heavenly and Mrs.

Critchfield, Aunt Lila is seen dissolving into tears as she listens to this, her favorite program—she dabs her eyes and her nostrils and looks dreamily at the ceiling—she finally blows her nose—it is evident that the Village Rhymester is giving his audience a thorough workout. Heavenly enters immediately after Mrs. Critchfield's speech directly above. Mrs. Critchfield continues.)

What do you mean by running upstairs when I ask you a question?

HEAVENLY: Did you want me to stand there dripping rain all over the carpet?

MRS. CRITCHFIELD: Where have you been—the drugstore?

HEAVENLY: Yes.

MRS. CRITCHFIELD: What for?

HEAVENLY: A Coke.

MRS. CRITCHFIELD: We've got bottled Cokes in the basement.

HEAVENLY: I like fountain Cokes, Mother.

MRS. CRITCHFIELD: What was that package you were trying to hide in your slicker?

HEAVENLY: I wasn't hiding it, I was trying to keep it dry.

MRS. CRITCHFIELD: What was it?

HEAVENLY: Perfume.

MRS. CRITCHFIELD: Perfume!

HEAVENLY: One ounce of *Quelques Fleurs.* I didn't have a drop left.

MRS. CRITCHFIELD: Did you charge it?

HEAVENLY: Of course I charged it, Mother.

MRS. CRITCHFIELD: Well, I suppose I shall have to have that account discontinued.

HEAVENLY: Suit yourself about that.

MRS. CRITCHFIELD: You don't seem to realize the financial condition this family's in.

HEAVENLY: Don't I?

MRS. CRITCHFIELD: No. For a girl of your age you show remarkably little sense about our account at Mungers. When I was twenty-two, I was married and keeping house. And believe me, I learned the value of every cent.

HEAVENLY: Yes, Mother.—Did anyone call?

MRS. CRITCHFIELD: Arthur called.

HEAVENLY: Who else?

(*Mrs. Critchfield says nothing.*)

I was expecting a call from Dick.

MRS. CRITCHFIELD: Didn't you see him at the drugstore?

HEAVENLY: No. He was out.

MRS. CRITCHFIELD: Imagine! A delivery boy.

HEAVENLY: He's not a delivery boy. He's assistant pharmacist.

MRS. CRITCHFIELD: Soda jerker.

LILA: Dick has never jerked a soda in his life. Besides, it's only a temporary job—Mr. Kramer's promised him something.

MRS. CRITCHFIELD: Did your father do that?

HEAVENLY: Yes.

MRS. CRITCHFIELD: Your father will just get himself in bad with Mr. Kramer. That Miles boy will never be able to hold a job.

HEAVENLY: He's going to hold this one.

MRS. CRITCHFIELD: You have a dinner engagement with Arthur, you know.

HEAVENLY: Yes, I know. Sunday night.

MRS. CRITCHFIELD: I think you should wear your blue knitted suit. It's really more stylish than ever. (*Heavenly rises.*) Where are you going?

HEAVENLY: I'm going to phone Dick.

MRS. CRITCHFIELD: Listen, Heavenly—

HEAVENLY: What?

MRS. CRITCHFIELD: If you let a chance like this slip through your fingers—

HEAVENLY: What chance are you talking about?

MRS. CRITCHFIELD: Arthur Shannon.

HEAVENLY (*smiling wryly*): Oh. (*She starts to leave.*)

MRS. CRITCHFIELD: Heavenly, come back here. I want to talk to you—you can call that boy later.

AUNT LILA (*huskily as she removes earphones*): "—But only God can make a tree!" (*She rises and dabs her eyes.*) Shall I make tea for anyone else? Heavenly? Esmeralda?

HEAVENLY: No, thanks, Aunty.

MRS. CRITCHFIELD: No.

(*Lila goes out, still under emotional spell of the Village Rhymester.*)

MRS. CRITCHFIELD (*after a short, uncomfortable pause*): How have you been feeling, dear?

HEAVENLY: Perfectly well, Mother.

MRS. CRITCHFIELD: I believe you've fallen off some.

HEAVENLY: Is that what you wanted to talk about?

MRS. CRITCHFIELD: No, it is not. When you assume that defensive attitude toward your mother, it makes it very difficult for her to discuss things with you. (*Heavenly lights a cigarette.*) You're smoking too much, Heavenly. It makes you nervous and cross and discolors your teeth.—Now what I wanted to say is—

HEAVENLY: Arthur Shannon?

MRS. CRITCHFIELD: Yes.

HEAVENLY: Please don't. (*She rises abruptly and crosses to the French window.*)

(*During this following speech, Mrs. Critchfield should acquire a certain dignity and force. She is talking about something she feels keenly which is the very core of her existence.*)

MRS. CRITCHFIELD: Don't you think that having the finest blood in America imposes on you some obligations? I'm sure that you do. It's a question of self-respect. But it's also a question of something deeper than that. Maybe I'm being old-fashioned. Hanging on to something that's lost its meaning. I know that some people say so. But they're people who never had anything worth hanging onto. You're not one of them, Heavenly. A girl whose name is listed under five or six different headings in Zella Armstrong's *Notable Families* and every other good southern genealogy couldn't help but feel it her sacred duty to live up to the best that's in her. The Waynes, the Critchfields, the Tylers, the Hallidays, and the Brookes. You've got them in you, Heavenly. You can't get them out. And they're going to fight you to the last wall if you try to mix their blood with ditchwater!

HEAVENLY (*turning furiously*): What do you mean?

MRS. CRITCHFIELD (*breathing heavily*): I mean that Arthur Shannon comes from your kind of people and the other one doesn't. You're not going to throw him over for a boy whose people are so low, so common that—!

HEAVENLY (*screaming*): Stop it! I won't listen to it!

MRS. CRITCHFIELD: You sit right back down there, young lady, and wait till I'm finished! There are certain practical considerations that I don't like to mention. You know what they are. The Shannons are the wealthiest family in the Delta. They own fifteen thousand acres of land and Gale Shannon's President of the Planter's State Bank. I know that sounds cheap and crude and mercenary, and I could hardly force myself to say it. But I had to. You forced me to, Heavenly.—Your father's health is uncertain. I was talking to Dr. Gray about his last examination and it seems it was not as favorable as it might have been.

HEAVENLY: Nobody pays any attention to Dr. Gray.

MRS. CRITCHFIELD: No? He brought us into the world. He's been our family physician for nearly sixty years.

HEAVENLY: He's in his dotage.

MRS. CRITCHFIELD: Very well, just ignore my warnings.—Some day you'll have a sad awakening, young lady.

HEAVENLY: Oh, mother, I know, I know!

MRS. CRITCHFIELD: You *don't* know. But under the circumstances I think it best you *should*.

HEAVENLY: Know what?

MRS. CRITCHFIELD: Dr. Gray intimated that your father does not have much longer to live.

(*A pause: Heavenly is slightly stunned.*)

HEAVENLY: I don't believe it.

MRS. CRITCHFIELD: I've kept this from you all. I've borne it alone— Your father's hypertensive condition has been aggravated by business worries. It's taken a serious turn. And if something should happen on top of everything else—

HEAVENLY: You mean if Dick and I should get married?

MRS. CRITCHFIELD: Yes! Precisely! Would you be willing to sign your father's death warrant? And mine, too? Do you know that we haven't managed to put by a single dollar since the stock crash, and now with this business recession— Our account's been cut off at Mungers— It's not at all unlikely that we'll have to go on relief next winter.

HEAVENLY (*in a quiet strained voice*): If you want me to marry Arthur Shannon, you might as well know right now that it isn't possible.

MRS. CRITCHFIELD: What do you mean?

HEAVENLY: I mean it isn't possible. (*She averts her face.*)

(*A pause while this penetrates Mrs. Critchfield's shocked brain.*)

MRS. CRITCHFIELD (*gasping*): Heavenly! (*Then she speaks slowly.*) Has there been—? Have you—?

HEAVENLY: Yes. I *have*. That's the answer.

(*A strangling sound comes from Mrs. Critchfield's throat. Her suffering is too acute to be ludicrous—she looks desperately about the room, her antiques, her heirlooms, even Colonel Wayne's portrait, fail to support her in this moment. Heavenly lights a cigarette.*)

MRS. CRITCHFIELD (*choked*): You dare to come into this house, in my presence and make that shameful confession?!

HEAVENLY (*with some of Colonel Wayne's courage*): You asked for it and I'm not ashamed. We love each other. God knows that's not as immoral as what you want me to do! And I'm not going to do it.

MRS. CRITCHFIELD: I—I feel sick.—No, it isn't the truth, you've made this up, it's a lie!

HEAVENLY: It's not a lie, mother.

MRS. CRITCHFIELD (*because she can't face it.*): It's got to be! Don't you understand? It's got to be— (*She sinks weakly on the sofa and looks at Colonel Wayne's portrait.*) You're never going to see him again.

HEAVENLY: Didn't you hear what I told you? We already belong to each other.

MRS. CRITCHFIELD: No. Not one more word! Or I'll report the whole thing to your father, even if it kills him.—So it *is* true. But I suppose it isn't too late?!

HEAVENLY: What do you mean?

MRS. CRITCHFIELD (*anxiously*): Nothing's happened! You haven't gotten yourself in trouble, have you?!

HEAVENLY (*turning away in distaste*): No.

MRS. CRITCHFIELD: Then it *isn't* too late. It can still be covered up.

HEAVENLY: Covered up?

MRS. CRITCHFIELD: Yes. You can leave town for awhile. Visit Aunt Clara down in Biloxi, in a month or two you'll—

HEAVENLY: I'm not going to give Dick up.

MRS. CRITCHFIELD: You've got to.

HEAVENLY: I can't. I'm not going to be an old maid.

MRS. CRITCHFIELD: You don't have to be an old maid.

HEAVENLY: Oh. You think Arthur Shannon would be willing to take me secondhand?

MRS. CRITCHFIELD: Does Arthur know?

HEAVENLY: I'd tell him.

MRS. CRITCHFIELD: No, you couldn't. You wouldn't have to. There's precious few girls that get married nowadays without having had one or two love affairs in the past.

HEAVENLY: Maybe not. But I've got a sense of decency.

MRS. CRITCHFIELD: *You* talk about *decency*!

HEAVENLY: Yes, I do.

MRS. CRITCHFIELD: You don't know what the word means.

HEAVENLY: It's you that don't know what it means. It's you that wants to make a prostitute of me.

MRS. CRITCHFIELD: Shut up! You dare to stand in front of me and say things like that. I don't know why I should let you kill me, you mean, despicable girl!

HEAVENLY: I haven't done anything terribly wrong. Dick and I loved each other—so much that—whatever happened it really wasn't our fault.

MRS. CRITCHFIELD: How long has it been going on?

HEAVENLY: For a year. Ever since last spring. I couldn't help it. I don't know how to explain. He lost his job at the planing mill and he was going to leave town—he was feeling so discouraged and restless and all—I couldn't bear it—I couldn't give him up—

MRS. CRITCHFIELD: And so to hold him you—

HEAVENLY: Yes. To hold him.

MRS. CRITCHFIELD: Without any shame you come to me and say that?

HEAVENLY: Yes. Without any shame.

MRS. CRITCHFIELD: You horrible, shameless, ungrateful girl!

HEAVENLY: Yes. (*She turns to leave.*)

MRS. CRITCHFIELD: Heavenly! (*Then with real feeling.*) Oh, my poor, poor daughter! (*She breaks down sobbing.*)

HEAVENLY (*slightly moved*): I'm sorry mother. (*Pause.*)

MRS. CRITCHFIELD (*sobbing*): When you were a little girl and did something wrong—I used to make you come in here and apologize to Colonel Wayne's portrait—don't you remember, Heavenly?

HEAVENLY: Yes.

MRS. CRITCHFIELD: That was because I wanted you to understand the responsibility of having fine blood in you. Heavenly—I want you to do that now. I want you to stand here in front of your great-grandfather's picture and beg his forgiveness for the first disgrace that's ever come to his name.

HEAVENLY (*stiffening*): I won't do it.

MRS. CRITCHFIELD: You've got to. Your family's all you've got left, you poor girl. If you don't respect that you've got nothing.—You come here and tell Colonel Wayne you're sorry for those awful things you talked about in his presence— *Heavenly!*

HEAVENLY (*dully*): Yes. (*She walks stiffly up to the portrait, stands before it, sobbing—then suddenly blurts out.*) Aw, go back to Gettysburg you big palooka!

(*She runs out of the room sobbing.*)

Curtain

SCENE TWO

Dinner has just been concluded. Mr. Critchfield slouches into the living room, thoughtfully manipulating a toothpick. He removes his coat and shoes and loosens his tie; he flops wearily into the big chair under the floor lamp and unfolds his evening paper to the market reports. As Lila enters, he mechanically extends a section of the paper to her with a muffled grunt.

LILA: No thanks, Oliver. I misplaced my glasses. (*She settles into her usual place by radio and picks up her sewing.*) How's cotton?

OLIVER: Off two points on the Memphis curb. One at New Orleans.

LILA (*glancing at him*): Well, did you go to the clinic today?

OLIVER: Huh?—Yes. I went.

LILA: What did they tell you?

OLIVER (*sheepishly*): Nothing wrong with my heart. Just gas on the stomach.

LILA (*relieved*): I knew it! I get palpitations myself when I eat too many starchy things. Nervous stomach's the curse of the Critchfields. Alf struggled against it for years, so did Cousin Rachel.

(*From the dining room across the hall Mrs. Critchfield's strident voice is heard directing the colored servant.*)

MRS. CRITCHFIELD: Hurry up, get this table cleared off. I want the place to look decent in case Mr. Shannon comes in. No, no, you've been in the house twenty years and you still don't know where the percolator sits! No, take the dishes, take the dishes, I'll take care of the silver! Ozzie, be careful. Don't try to carry three things off at once, here, you let me—

(*There is a startled outcry from Ozzie and a crash of broken china. Mrs. Critchfield screams in agony.*)

MRS. CRITCHFIELD: Oh, my good— *Ooooh!*

LILA (*with fatalistic calm*): She broke another piece of the Havilland.

MRS. CRITCHFIELD: Get out of here, you trifling nigger, get on back to the kitchen.

OZZIE: Yes'm, Mizz Critchfield.

LILA (*calling*): What happened in there?

MRS. CRITCHFIELD: She broke another piece of the Havilland.

LILA (*sotto voce*): It's no wonder. The way she devils that girl would drive a saint to distraction. (*She rubs her forearms.*) It's chilly, I've got goose pimples— (*She takes a few more stitches.*) Somebody must be walking over my grave . . .

(*Mrs. Critchfield charges into the front room. She stands stage center, her eyes shooting Olympian bolts at her husband's *oblivious figure. She suddenly swoops down on him like a predatory hawk and snatches the newspaper from his hands.*)

MRS. CRITCHFIELD: Yes, to you it's a matter of complete indifference!

OLIVER: What the Sam Hill—!

MRS. CRITCHFIELD: No, Oliver, I shouldn't annoy you! I should go right on bearing the whole intolerable burden just as I've done the past twenty-three or four years.

LILA: Why don't you let him digest his dinner?

MRS. CRITCHFIELD: There are some things more important than digestion.

LILA: That's a matter of opinion.

MRS. CRITCHFIELD: You probably wouldn't think so. But I'm not willing nor able to bury my head in the sand like an ostrich when my daughter's whole future is at stake!

OLIVER: What's the matter with Heavenly?

MRS. CRITCHFIELD: It's high time you asked that question. Oliver, I've deliberately shouldered the whole thing myself because of your disinclination to accept any responsibility and also because of your health—

LILA: Stop carping on Oliver's health.—He's gone through the Memphis clinic this morning, and there's not a thing wrong with him except nervous stomach.

MRS. CRITCHFIELD: Oh! Well. Is this true?

(*Oliver clears his throat uneasily.*)

You didn't mention it to me? You didn't think it was necessary to relieve my mind of all the anxiety I've had to suffer because of your constant complaints?

LILA: I guess he wanted to break it to you gently. (*She switches on the radio.*)

MRS. CRITCHFIELD: But from what Dr. Gray said—

LILA: Dr. Gray said nothing. He never says anything except, "How's your bowels!"

MRS. CRITCHFIELD: Please! Will you turn that radio off?—There's something I've got to discuss seriously with Oliver, something that— (*Her voice breaks.*)

LILA (*rising*): Mind if I take the comics? (*She winks at him and crosses offstage.*)

MRS. CRITCHFIELD (*with extreme acidity as Lila closes the door*): It is sometimes difficult to believe that your sister comes of a genteel family. I suppose Heavenly's lack of principles is not entirely her fault.

OLIVER: If you mean she's a Critchfield, Ezzie, that's nothing to her discredit.—Whatever the girl has done or hasn't, I'm pretty sure it can't be as serious as your hysteria would make a person suppose.

MRS. CRITCHFIELD: Oh, no, it's nothing serious when a girl is being talked about by the whole town!

OLIVER (*a little anxious*): Talked about, eh? I should consider it much more serious if she wasn't being talked about. (*There is a pause while he goes about filling his pipe.*)

MRS. CRITCHFIELD: Leave that pipe alone and listen to what I'm saying!—You've adopted that humorous tone too often in dealing with your child's problems.—This time it won't do.

OLIVER: All right, Esmeralda! When you've told me the cause of Heavenly's disgrace I'll be in a much better position to adopt a suitable tone of voice. What's she done this time?

MRS. CRITCHFIELD: For quite a while I've heard rumors—little insinuations—about Heavenly and that trifling boy she's been going with.

OLIVER: Richard Miles?

MRS. CRITCHFIELD: Yes! I chose to ignore it because I thought my daughter was above such things. Well, now I've discovered that I was mistaken.

OLIVER: Discovered what?

MRS. CRITCHFIELD: This afternoon right here in this room she came to me with the horrible, disgusting confession that— Oh. I don't know how I've managed to keep my senses.

OLIVER (*alarmed*): What in tarnation are you driving at? What confession? Esmeralda!

(*The sound of a car stopping is heard.*)

MRS. CRITCHFIELD (*in a sudden flurry*): Get those things out of here, those papers, your coat, your shoes! It's Arthur Shannon!—We'll finish this talk upstairs!

OLIVER: Good Lord!

(*He belches and rubs his stomach. He crosses the room. Mrs. Critchfield hastily snatches up various articles, arranges sofa pillows and changes the position of her antique chair. She switches on the little museum light over Colonel Wayne's portrait and then rushes out. Arthur enters first. His manner is markedly different from the first scene. His continental poise is lost, and he is awkward as an adolescent. He goes to the radio on which the roses are placed. Heavenly enters.*)

HEAVENLY (*removing her hat*): Lord, I'm glad to get this off! Arthur, I have a marvelous idea for a new spring hat. I'm going to pin a couple of roses on Aunt Lila's purple silk parasol. (*She crosses to Arthur.*) Oh, aren't they lovely! How did you know that talisman roses are my favorite flowers?

ARTHUR: Are they? I thought all girls preferred orchids.

HEAVENLY: I hate orchids.

ARTHUR: Hate them! Why?

HEAVENLY: Oh, I've seen 'em at debuts in Memphis and the girls that wear 'em are always those money-snobs who give you a look that peels the gilt off your slippers and puts ten years on your formal.

ARTHUR: Possibly if you wore one yourself you might overcome that aversion.

HEAVENLY: Yes. Possibly. Orchids are seen around here about as often as Haley's Comet. Gosh, me with an orchid! I wouldn't know what to do with it! I'd probably go parading up and down Front Street, holding it over my head and singing "The Star-spangled Banner"! (*She seats herself on the sofa.*)

ARTHUR: Or you might wear it to Lamphrey's tomorrow night.

HEAVENLY (*springing up breathlessly*): Ahthuh!

ARTHUR: It was just an impulse. They weren't available at Mr. Cutrere's so I ordered one from Memphis.

HEAVENLY: You dahling! (*She hugs him.*) I'm—I'm completely flabbergasted! I'm so excited I could bust!

ARTHUR: I guess I should've surprised you with it, but when you said you hated orchids I was afraid you might be really allergic to them or something and so I—

HEAVENLY: Oh, no—no! I *love* orchids, I'm *crazy* about them! Gosh, me with an orchid! From Memphis? Won't that create a sensation! Oh, I can just see it in the society column—"Miss Heavenly Critchfield lived up to her name last night in a divine white creation with a regal orchid pinned to her shoulder!"

ARTHUR: What's a "divine white creation"?

HEAVENLY: Oh, that's my white organdy— Mrs. Dowd, the society reporter, thinks it's divine because it's so damned everlasting. I graduated in it about five years ago, and it's been getting more divine ever since till now it's about fit to be worn as a nightshirt by Jesus! Wait a minute, will you? (*She flies out of the room and is heard on the stairs*—) Mothuh! Aunt Lila! What do you think?

(*The upstairs door slams on her exuberant voice. Arthur goes hastily to the mantle mirror where he adjusts his tie and combs his hair; in a moment, Heavenly re-enters with two Coke bottles.*)

Mothuh was just tickled silly and so was Aunt Lila. I thought maybe I could get a new pahty dress to go with it but nothing doing. I've got to wear God's nightie. You'll have a Coke with me, won't you? (*She exits through the rear door.*)

ARTHUR: A what?

HEAVENLY (*from offstage*): A Coca-Cola. Don't you know? It's a new kind of drink.

ARTHUR: No, thank you.

HEAVENLY (*re-entering*): Why not?

ARTHUR: I never touch stimulants after six-thirty, especially when I'm not sleeping well.

HEAVENLY (*drinking rapidly from the bottle*): Haven't you been sleeping well?

ARTHUR: No. Not lately.

HEAVENLY: Oh, that's a shame. (*She returns to sofa, finishes one bottle and starts on the second.*) What shall we talk about?

ARTHUR (*uncomfortably*): Well, I—don't know!

HEAVENLY (*giggling*): You know what mother said to me before we went out? She said, "Heavenly, you must try to choose intelligent subjects of conversation so that Arthuh won't get bored!" What do you think of that, Arthur? (*She takes another long gulp.*)

ARTHUR: I think it was quite unnecessary.

HEAVENLY: Yes. So do I. Because I really don't know any intelligent subjects of conversation. (*She laughs.*) I asked Mothuh what she meant and she said, "Oh, books and things!" I said, "Well, I know what books are but what's things?" And that made her furious, she turned as red as a lobster, and Aunt Lila and I both nearly died laughing—She called me an ignoramus! Which is perfectly true . . .

ARTHUR: I don't think it is.

HEAVENLY: Ah! That's terribly chivalrous of you. (*She finishes the second bottle, then leans back on the sofa.*) I feel like music tonight. Music and dancing. I hope we'll have fun at the Lamphrey's, don't you?

ARTHUR: Yes.

(*There is a constrained pause.*)

HEAVENLY: What are you thinking about?

ARTHUR: Pardon?

HEAVENLY: I said what are you thinking about.

ARTHUR (*very uncomfortable*): Oh—things.

HEAVENLY (*with a slightly derisive smile*): Books and things?

ARTHUR: No.

HEAVENLY: Just books?

ARTHUR: No.

HEAVENLY: Oh! Just *things.* That's nice. I wish I could think about things.

ARTHUR: Can't you? (*Heavenly shakes her head.*) Why not? (*Heavenly shrugs.*)

HEAVENLY: It's a wasted effort. It's a lot easier just to feel things and it's a lot more fun.

ARTHUR: Feeling some things isn't fun.

HEAVENLY: No, of cou'se not. But thinking about them doesn't help them any.

ARTHUR: Seems to me we're getting a little metaphysical here.

HEAVENLY (*wide-eyed*): What's that?

ARTHUR: Metaphysical?

HEAVENLY: Yes.

ARTHUR: It's sort of— dealing with insubstantial matters.

HEAVENLY: Oh. Like books and things. (*She laughs.*)

ARTHUR: I always have a rather uncomfortable feeling when you laugh that way.

HEAVENLY: Why?

ARTHUR: I suppose you'd call it a sort of—atavistic emotion.

HEAVENLY: A what?

ARTHUR (*confused*): Nothing.

HEAVENLY: Oh—nothing. (*She smiles almost mockingly and lowers her eyes.*) Look. It's a bunny-rabbit. (*She has twisted her white handkerchief into the semblance of a long-eared rabbit's head.*) It's wiggling its ears at you. It says "Shame on Ahthuh fo' usin' such long words!" (*She laughs.*) It says, "If I went to school at Oxfo'd I'd be sma't too an' use big words, but I'm just a dumb little bunny that doesn't know anything but how to wiggle its ears an' eat grass!" (*Slowly, dreamily she shakes the handkerchief out—she smiles sadly and shakes her head.*) Poor bunny! He's all disappeared —he's just a little white hankie now. But he still smells nice. (*She lifts it delicately to her nostrils, glancing provocatively at Arthur from under her dark lashes.*) He smells like dead rose leaves. Mmmm. Aunt Lila makes your talisman roses into sachets when they're withered an' puts 'em in our handkerchief boxes—gives 'em such a sad, sweet smell. (*She smiles.*) Like old maids' memories, that's what it reminds me of! (*She sniffs the cloth delicately once more, and then smooths it thoughtfully on her lap. Suddenly she raises her face to Arthur's with a look of startling intensity.*) *I'd rather die than be an old maid!* (*Pause for emphasis.*)

ARTHUR: Surely that's not a possibility!

HEAVENLY (*intensely*): Oh, yes it is. All the boys go No'th or East to make a livin' unless they've got plantations. And that leaves a lot of girls sitting out on the front porch waitin' fo' the afte'noon mail. Sometimes it stops comin'. And they're still sitting out there on the swing in their best white dresses, smilin' so hard it's a wonder they don't crack their faces—so people across the street won't know what's happened! "Isn't it marvelous weather? The sky's so perfectly blue! Mother and I put up six quarts of blackberry jam last night!"—*Oh, God!*— (*She rises quickly and walks over to the French window.*) That's why girls like me act so silly, Ahthuh, like music an' dancing instead of books and things, because we're scared inside, so scared it makes us feel sick at the stomach—

ARTHUR: Scared of what?

HEAVENLY: Of sitting out there forever on the front porch in our best dresses!

ARTHUR: That's quite understandable in the case of some girls.

HEAVENLY: But not in mine?

ARTHUR: Certainly not.

HEAVENLY: Thanks. But you don't know.

ARTHUR: Know what?

HEAVENLY: I made a mistake.

ARTHUR: In what way?

HEAVENLY: I—I loved the wrong boy.

ARTHUR: Oh.—You still do?

HEAVENLY: Yes. And now—

ARTHUR: Now?

HEAVENLY (*desperate fear showing in her face*): Now he's trying to break away—he wants to work on the river! He'd like to get rid of me now!

ARTHUR: Has he said so?

HEAVENLY: No, but I can feel it coming. (*She smiles bitterly.*) Oh, my! (*She turns to the window, parts the curtains, and looks out with her back to Arthur. He looks at her, troubled, confused, his hands clenched.*) —I don't know why I should bother you with all this! (*She laughs.*) It's not your affair! (*She turns slowly back to him.*) It's starting to rain again—it makes such a sleepy sound I can hardly keep my eyes open. . . . (*She has returned to the sofa, draws her feet under her, and leans back provocatively. She looks at Arthur from under her lashes with a very slight smile.*) I hope that Mothuh doesn't come in. I'm not in what you would call a very ladylike position. However I'm too comfortable to care. (*She allows one arm to slip languidly from the sofa, fingers trailing the floor.*)

ARTHUR (*clears his throat and rises*): Heavenly, I—

HEAVENLY: What?

(*He has started toward her and then, as if frightened, draws back. He mechanically removes a small book from his pocket.*)

ARTHUR: I wanted to give you this.

HEAVENLY: What is it?

ARTHUR: A book of modern verse.

HEAVENLY (*in a tone of final despair*): Oh.

ARTHUR: It's an autographed first edition of Humphrey Hardcastle.

HEAVENLY: Oh.

ARTHUR: There's just a short passage I marked last night.

HEAVENLY: Oh.

ARTHUR (*fumbling in an agony of embarrassment through the pages*): Here it is.

HEAVENLY (*sadly*): Please commence the reading.

ARTHUR: It's called "Apostrophe to a Dead Lover!"

HEAVENLY: It sounds so't of spooky.

(*Arthur springs up violently and flings the book to the floor.*)

HEAVENLY: What's the matter?

ARTHUR (*choked*): Nothing! I don't know. I'm in a state of confusion! (*He crosses the room a few steps.*) I guess you think I'm a pretty queer sort of person. I am. I was brought up in a school for problem children, I've never had any normal relations with people. I want what I'm afraid of and I'm afraid of what I want so that I'm like a storm inside that can't break loose! Do you see?

HEAVENLY: No, not quite. (*She smiles at his back.*)

ARTHUR (*sharply*): Why are you laughing at me?

HEAVENLY: I wasn't.

ARTHUR: You were—I could see you in the mirror!

HEAVENLY: I was only smiling a little.

ARTHUR: You smile like that a great deal. You used to smile that way when I knew you in grade school.

HEAVENLY: Can you remember me that long ago?

ARTHUR: Yes. Very clearly. Especially the way that you smiled.

HEAVENLY: I didn't know my smile was that hard to forget.

ARTHUR: Ordinarily it might not be. But I was sensitive.

HEAVENLY: You mean you thought I was making fun of you?

ARTHUR: I knew that you were.

HEAVENLY: I don't remember.

ARTHUR: Don't you remember that afternoon when a bunch of them cornered me in the recess yard and kept yelling "sissy" at me until I cried? You stood there laughing at me. I never forgot that afternoon. That was something I never got over. It wasn't the boys yelling sissy that hurt me so much. It was you—you standing there laughing at me the way you were laughing a minute ago when I caught your face in the mirror. That laugh, that was why I couldn't go back to school anymore—so they had to send me to Europe and say that I'd had a nervous breakdown.

HEAVENLY: You mean that was all on my account?

ARTHUR: Yes. On account of you.

HEAVENLY: Then I should think you would hate me.

ARTHUR: I did. I hated you.

HEAVENLY: You still do? Now?

ARTHUR: Yes. You don't get over things like that. When I saw you again this spring for the first time in thirteen years it was exactly the same. It started all over again.

HEAVENLY: You mean that afternoon at your mother's reception?

ARTHUR: Yes. When I came downstairs and saw you standing in the hall looking up at me with that politely contemptuous smile of yours—it was the same exactly—all you needed was a white hair ribbon and a handful of jacks!

HEAVENLY: You turned and went back upstairs.

ARTHUR: You must've been awfully amused.

HEAVENLY: I was. At Mothuh's disappointment.

ARTHUR: The next morning I called Cutrere's. Had them send you a dozen roses without any name.

HEAVENLY: What did you do that for?

ARTHUR: I don't know. Everything that I've done since then has been done by compulsion. If you only knew the heroic effort it took for me to ask you to the country club that first time.

HEAVENLY: Your voice sounded funny over the phone.

ARTHUR: I had butterflies in my throat. At lunch I kept dropping the silver.

HEAVENLY: I thought you were sick.

ARTHUR: I was.

HEAVENLY: But if I made you so miserable why did you want to be with me?

ARTHUR: You don't know much about psychology.

HEAVENLY: No.

ARTHUR: The reason I hated you was that I loved you.

HEAVENLY: *Loved* me?

ARTHUR: Yes.

HEAVENLY: I don't see how that's possible. You couldn't love anybody that you hated.

ARTHUR: Oh, yes, you could. Very easily. Strindberg says "It's called love-hatred and it hails from the pit!"

HEAVENLY: I don't know anything about Strindberg, but it doesn't sound practical to me. How could you be in love at that age?

ARTHUR: Thirteen's old enough. Of course, there wasn't anything consciously sexual about it.

HEAVENLY: I should hope not.

ARTHUR: I think you can love more at that age than any time afterwards. At least it's the hardest to get over.

HEAVENLY: But you *have* gotten over it *now*?

ARTHUR: Of course I haven't.

HEAVENLY: You mean you still—?

ARTHUR: Yes. More than ever.

HEAVENLY (*crossing to the sofa*): I don't believe you. What you want is to have your revenge. Once you got me you wouldn't want me anymore. You'd leave me cold.

ARTHUR: No!

HEAVENLY: Yes, that's it. Whether you know it or not that's how it would be. No. Thanks! I'd rather take a chance on Dick. At least he's honest. It's none of your psychological business—we're really in love!

ARTHUR: Heavenly— (*He moves uncertainly toward her.*)

HEAVENLY: You'd better go now. I've got another engagement.

ARTHUR: Who with? Richard Miles?

HEAVENLY: Yes.

ARTHUR (*with childish cruelty*): I've heard about you and him.

HEAVENLY (*stiffening*): Have you?

ARTHUR: Yes. People have told me.

HEAVENLY: Who's told you what? That long-nosed mother of yours?

ARTHUR: You don't have to insult my mother.

HEAVENLY: I don't like having people gossip about my business.

ARTHUR: My mother's never mentioned your name.

HEAVENLY: Oh, hasn't she? I've heard different.

ARTHUR: You've heard that she gossips about you?

HEAVENLY: Yes. (*Her voice breaks.*) They all do.

ARTHUR: If he was the right kind he wouldn't expose you to that sort of thing. He'd respect you too much.

HEAVENLY: He didn't seduce me if that's what you mean. He didn't have to. I wanted him as much as he wanted me.

ARTHUR (*pausing*): We're being childish, both of us. Deliberately hurting each other. It doesn't matter about you and that boy. I've had an affair myself with a girl in London.

HEAVENLY: One of those intellectual affairs?

ARTHUR: No. Quite the opposite.

HEAVENLY: That's sort of hard to imagine.

ARTHUR: Why is it hard to imagine?

HEAVENLY (*smiling cruelly*): Why? I can't explain why.

ARTHUR: STOP IT! (*He raises his hands to his ears, then lowers them slowly.*) Don't smile at me that way!

HEAVENLY: Why did you cover your ears?

ARTHUR: I could hear them—yelling sissy at me—in the yard . . .

HEAVENLY: Oh.

MRS. CRITCHFIELD (*in the hall*): Heavenly, dear!

HEAVENLY (*sotto voce*): It's Mother. Please go now. She'll keep us forever and I've got to meet Dick.

(*Arthur doesn't move.*)

Will you please go?

MRS. CRITCHFIELD (*appearing in the hall with pitcher of lemonade*): Heavenly, I'm going to drop these glasses! Ahthuh, how are you? Mmmm. (*She purrs dotingly as she extends her hand.*) I thought you young people might enjoy a little refreshment. It's just lemonade. (*She giggles foolishly and then notices the empty Coca-Cola bottles.*) Oh, dear, you've already had drinks?

HEAVENLY: I had a Coke. Ahthuh didn't want any.

MRS. CRITCHFIELD: Of course Ahthuh didn't. He's got too much sense to poison himself with that stuff. I've heard it's habit-forming. (*She sets down the pitcher.*). Heavenly, there's a little plate of Aunt Lila's gingerbread cookies on the kitchen table. And you might bring in a few napkins, dear.

HEAVENLY: Yes, mother. (*She crosses quickly out of the room.*)

MRS. CRITCHFIELD (*sitting with a benign purr*): How is Mrs. Shannon?

ARTHUR (*also sitting*): Quite well, thank you.

MRS. CRITCHFIELD: That's good!—Mmmm—I suppose she must have told you about the honor that she received last week?

ARTHUR: An honor?

MRS. CRITCHFIELD: Oh, my *yes*—yes, *indeed*! She was elected Vice-Regent of the D.A. *Ahhh!* I was so pleased when her papers went through. We need women of your mother's caliber so badly in our patriotic societies. I happen to be serving as Regent this year. I've served twice before in that capacity and once as Advisory Regent and once as Sergeant-at-Arms! Mmmm. Club-work is so absorbing. It makes one neglect other things. Such as books. What do you think of the works of James Fenimore Cooper?

ARTHUR (*absently*): Pardon?

MRS. CRITCHFIELD: James Fenimore Cooper—what do you think of his works?

ARTHUR: Oh, yes—yes, indeed!

MRS. CRITCHFIELD (*brightly*): Do you? I wondered if you did!

ARTHUR: Yes. . . .

MRS. CRITCHFIELD: Yes. . . .

(*There is a constrained silence. Mrs. Critchfield clears her throat and looks uneasily toward the rear door.*)

MRS. CRITCHFIELD: Pardon me a moment. I think Heavenly must be having some trouble in the kitchen.

(*Arthur rises as she goes out.*)

MRS. CRITCHFIELD (*from offstage*): Heavenly, dear! Where *are* you, dear?

(*A terrible silence. She is heard running upstairs calling her daughter's name above. Arthur stands waiting in nervous *misery till Mrs. Critchfield re-enters the room. She is completely unstrung by Heavenly's shocking flight, but with the invincible spirit of Colonel Wayne she resolves to carry it off as bravely as she is able, giving Arthur her most brilliant smile, a little tremulous at the corners.*)

Oh, dear, I'm afraid that Heavenly won't be able to come back in. The poor child is just prostrated and so I told her to go right on up to her bed and let me give you her excuses, Arthur. She didn't want to but when I saw how ill she was looking I—I just insisted! I told her that I was sure you would excuse her since she was feeling so badly.

ARTHUR (*embarrassed*): Certainly, I—I'm dreadfully sorry. (*He moves toward the door.*) I hope it's nothing serious.

MRS. CRITCHFIELD: Oh, no, nothing serious, Arthur. She has such a nervous stomach, poor child. We call it the curse of the Critchfields.

ARTHUR: Oh. Please give her my sympathy. And tell her I hope she'll be well enough to go to the lawn party tomorrow.

MRS. CRITCHFIELD: Oh, she will! Arthur, I'm sure she will. Her nerves are just a little unstrung you know. She needs rest—I'll tell her that you excused her, Arthur.

ARTHUR: Thank you, Mrs. Critchfield.—Good night.

(*Arthur turns and goes into the hall. Mrs. Critchfield follows him.*)

MRS. CRITCHFIELD: Good night, Arthur. Give your mother my love. Tell her I do hope she'll be at the meeting tomorrow. Good night, Arthur. Good night—

(*The door is heard closing. Mrs. Critchfield comes slowly back into the living room with the brilliant, artificial smile still set on her face, her hand still raised in a parting gesture. The hand slowly falls and clasps her bosom. She simpers foolishly to herself, then gazes helplessly about the room. She lifts her hands to her lips with a breathless gasp, then her face puckers grotesquely and she begins to cry like a child as*—)

The Curtain Falls.

SCENE THREE

It is later that night. The stage is dark. Moonlight shines intermittently through the French window. Heavenly enters from the hall in pajamas. She walks slowly up to Colonel Wayne's portrait and speaks to it in a low voice.

HEAVENLY: Colonel Wayne! I'm sorry for what I said. I didn't mean it. I want you to forgive me! Please excuse me for disgracing your name!—If that's what I've done. I don't want to disgrace it—not any more than I have to. You know that as well as I do, Colonel Wayne! So please don't blame me too much! . . . I'm in an awful fix. I don't know what to do! . . . So why don't you come down off your horse and tell me instead of lookin' so big and important up there?

(*A light goes on in the hall. Mr. Critchfield enters in his dressing robe.*)

MR. CRITCHFIELD: Who's in there? Chicken?

HEAVENLY: Yes.

MR. CRITCHFIELD: What are you doing down here at three o'clock in the morning? I thought I heard you talking to somebody.

HEAVENLY: I was.

MR. CRITCHFIELD: Who was it? Who did you have in here at this hour? (*He turns on a table lamp.*)

HEAVENLY: Colonel Wayne.

MR. CRITCHFIELD: What?

HEAVENLY: Colonel Wayne! I was apologizing to him.

MR. CRITCHFIELD: Good Lord! (*He smiles a little.*) It's a long time since I heard you do that.

HEAVENLY: It's a long time since I told him to go back to Gettysburg.

MR. CRITCHFIELD: Did you?

HEAVENLY: Yes. Mother and I had a fight this afternoon. Didn't she tell you?

MR. CRITCHFIELD: Yes. We had a long talk tonight.

HEAVENLY: About—me?

MR. CRITCHFIELD: Yes. About you.

HEAVENLY: Dad, I— What's that you're drinking?

MR. CRITCHFIELD: Whiskey and soda. For my nerves.

HEAVENLY: I'd like to have one, too.

MR. CRITCHFIELD: Well—Heavenly, I—

HEAVENLY: Where is it? Behind the flour bin?

MR. CRITCHFIELD: You're psychic. (*She goes out to the kitchen; he calls to her.*) The soda's in the Frigidaire.

HEAVENLY (*calling*): Yes, I know. (*In a moment she returns with a drink.*) You know, Daddy, this is the first drink we've ever had together.

MR. CRITCHFIELD: Yes, so it is. (*She sits on the sofa beside him.*)

HEAVENLY: It's stopped raining. The moon is coming out. (*She draws up her feet and leans against him.*) Daddy, are you very worried about me?

MR. CRITCHFIELD: Naturally I'm a little disturbed. But I'm not going to cross-examine you about your love affairs. I guess your mother's done plenty of that.

HEAVENLY: Everything's going to turn out all right. Dick's going to work for Mr. Kramer, and we're going to get married this summer. So there's nothing to worry about.

MR. CRITCHFIELD (*ruefully shaking his head*): Chicken, chicken! Are you absolutely sure that you aren't talking through your little spring bonnet?

HEAVENLY (*hiding her face on his shoulder*): No! I'm not!

MR. CRITCHFIELD (*stroking her head*): Not even a little bit?

HEAVENLY (*abruptly straightening*): Daddy! (*She looks at him with desperate pleading.*) Why is everything so crazy, so mixed up!? Why can't people be happy together? Why can't they want the same things, instead of—fighting and torturing and—hating each other—even when they're in love?!!

(*Mr. Critchfield gazes sadly, reflectively at the glittering ice in his glass.*)

MR. CRITCHFIELD: I guess those things are sort of natural phenomena. Like these spring storms we've been having. They do lots of damage. Bust the levees, wash out the bridges, destroy property and even kill people. What for? I don't know. (*He drains his glass and puts it on the table.*) I s'pose they're just the natural necessary parts of the changing season. . . . I'm getting sleepy.

HEAVENLY: Me, too. Let's tell Colonel Wayne good night!

(*Mr. Critchfield switches off the table lamp.*)

MR. CRITCHFIELD (*with grave humor*): Honey, the Colonel and I haven't been on speakin' terms for about twenty years!

(*He puts his arm about her as they go out.*)

Slow lights down—end of Act Two

ACT THREE

SCENE ONE

This scene should follow the dramaturgic pattern of Act One, starting lightly and rising through an emotional crescendo that culminates in the fight between Dick and Arthur and the outbreak of the storm.

The scene is the Lamphrey's lawn party. We are shown a secluded corner of the big lawn—a summer house or an arbor. Japanese lanterns are strung overhead and the set is backed by a trellis covered with flowering vines. In a prominent place is a small fountain with a little statue of Eros. Beside it is a stone bench, and at the right a punch stand with a cut-glass bowl and cups. For a touch of humor, the white-coated Negro servant is asleep, seated directly beneath the statue of Eros. The stringed orchestra from Memphis is playing. It stops—there is laughter and applause. In a moment Mrs. Lamphrey and three chaperones appear from the right.

MRS. DOWD: What do they call it? The Bag?

MRS. BUFORD: No, the Shag! I think it's horrid, don't you?

MRS. DOWD: I fail to see anything graceful about it. Now the old-fashioned cakewalk required some real skill in dancing—

MRS. LAMPHREY: Jackson! Wake up!

JACKSON: Yes'm, Mizz Lamphrey! Did I miss de contes'?

MRS. LAMPHREY: Yes, it's just over.

JACKSON: Doggone.

MRS. LAMPHREY: Pour the ladies some punch.

MRS. BUFORD: Oh, your moonvines are out.

MRS. LAMPHREY: Yes, everything's early this spring.

MRS. DOWD: So early.

MRS. ADAMS: Even Heavenly Critchfield's white organdy has come out a little earlier than usual this year.

MRS. BUFORD: It's fortunate that Esmeralda's so clever with the needle.

MRS. ADAMS: I don't believe they've bought a stitch of new clothes in five years.

MRS. BUFORD: What *are* their circumstances?

MRS. ADAMS: Desperate! Walter's been forced to discontinue their account.

MRS. BUFORD: Goodness!

MRS. LAMPHREY: They've been blacklisted for years by the Merchants' Credit Association.—It's a miracle to me how they're able to keep going. Mrs. Dowd— (*She offers her a glass.*)

MRS. DOWD: Thank you.

MRS. BUFORD: I pity Esmeralda but I've got no sympathy for Heavenly Critchfield.

MRS. ADAMS: She made a disgusting exhibition of herself.

MRS. LAMPHREY: Extremely!—Jackson, don't fill the glasses so full, they splash over.

MRS. ADAMS: Kicking up her skirts like a carnival dancer!

MRS. DOWD: Of course she's quite young—

MRS. ADAMS: Young nothing! She's twenty-three or four.

MRS. DOWD: And with such a fine old family as the Waynes and the Critchfields—

MRS. ADAMS: She'll be ostracized, mark my word! Not a decent boy in town'll be seen with her. She'll end up sitting on a front porch.

MRS. BUFORD: Or going with drummers!

MRS. DOWD: Well, at present the Shannon boy seems to be quite devoted.

MRS. LAMPHREY: I wonder how Mrs. Shannon feels about that?

MRS. ADAMS: Strongly opposed, of course. (*Sotto voce.*) Have you heard what Tom Newby told his mother this morning about what he saw at Moon Lake?

MRS. LAMPHREY: Goodness, no! What?

MRS. ADAMS: Heavenly and the Miles boy were seen coming out of a tourist cabin—

MRS. LAMPHREY: Tourist cabin!

MRS. ADAMS: Yes, at about two o'clock this morning!

MRS. LAMPHREY: Why didn't you tell me before? Oh, my Lord!

MRS. DOWD: I think it's unfair to repeat that kind of gossip.

MRS. ADAMS: It's been substantiated. And of course I've thought right along—

MRS. LAMPHREY: Oh, I did, *too.* But after *this*!

MRS. ADAMS: I think some definite measures should be taken to express our feelings. After all she's associating with our sons and daughters.

MRS. LAMPHREY: Oh, my goodness, yes! Susan has very little to do with her but *still*—

MRS. ADAMS: I've warned Henry.

MRS. BUFORD: Annabelle and John Dudley dropped her in high school. They say she's so uppity and independent that—

MRS. DOWD: Mrs. Lamphrey!

MRS. LAMPHREY: Yes?

MRS. DOWD: Such delicious punch!

MRS. ADAMS: Oh, yes, isn't it though? Are those rain clouds?

MRS. LAMPHREY: If it does rain, we'll simply move the pahty indoors.

MRS. BUFORD: Look! She's coming across the lawn with your son.

MRS. ADAMS (*alarmed*): Henry?

MRS. LAMPHREY: And Arthur Shannon!

MRS. BUFORD: I wouldn't be surprised if—

MRS. LAMPHREY: Shhh!

(*Heavenly enters with Arthur and Henry. The men are in tuxedos. Heavenly is a radiant dream-like vision in her white organdy under the soft-colored lanterns and with the background of poignant string music. She is bearing a frosted, candle-lit cake which she has just won at the dance.*)

HEAVENLY: Oh, I'm still out of breath! Hank, did you get the cake knife?

HENRY: You bet.

HEAVENLY: Thanks. Hello. (*To the ladies in general.*) Can't I offer you a slice, Mrs. Lamphrey? Mrs. Adams—Mrs. Buford—Mrs. Dowd?

(*They decline, Mrs. Dowd politely, but the others with noticeable coolness.*)

Hank, will you?

HENRY: You bet.

MRS. ADAMS (*quickly*): Henry, will you please get me my shawl from the house?

MRS. LAMPHREY: There's a wind coming up. I should have known better than to give an outdoor party at this time of year.

MRS. BUFORD: Such peculiar weather! Torrential rains and days like midsummer! I wonder if the levee's in danger?

MRS. ADAMS: It is north of here. We've moved all our furniture upstairs and the quarters have simply cleared out. (*She turns to her son who has not moved.*) —Henry! Right away, dear!—Mrs. Buford, I want you to meet those Tupelo girls, they're lovely, so nice and *refined*!

(*Mrs. Adams, Mrs. Buford and Mrs. Lamphrey go out right.*)

MRS. DOWD (*to Heavenly*): Congratulations, dear. I enjoyed your dancing so much and your little white dress is divine. I'm going to make a special note of it in my column tomorrow! (*She kisses Heavenly quickly and goes out.*)

HEAVENLY: I don't know which I'd rather be, snubbed or pitied. (*To Jackson.*) Jackson, have you got anything in the punch?

JACKSON: No, Ma'am, Mizz Lamphrey gib me obstructions not to put in a drap.

HEAVENLY: Not even for the gentlemen?

JACKSON: Well, Mr. Lamphrey, he sez, I should keep dis bottle hid unduh de napkin case some ob de *olduh* gennulmens ast for it an'—

HEAVENLY: Give it here!

JACKSON: An' den I was to gib em a small amount an'—

HEAVENLY: Let me have it!

JACKSON: An' no more!

HEAVENLY (*wresting it from him*): I'll do the mixing myself, you might give me too much. Arthur? Oh, I forgot—you never take stimulants after six-thirty.

ARTHUR: Tonight I'll make an exception.

HEAVENLY: Marvelous!—Jackson, if you snitch on me I'll get Dick Miles to skin you alive!—Well, that's *quite* an exception! Are you planning to do some desperate deed tonight?

MRS. LAMPHREY (*offstage*): Jackson!

JACKSON: Yes'm, Mizz Lamphrey?

MRS. LAMPHREY (*appearing, nervous*): Jackson, you'll have to help clear off the table. I'm afraid it's going to rain before long and I want you to get all the linen and silver inside. Heavenly, dear, we'll leave you in chahge of the punch! (*Mrs. Lamphrey exits with Jackson.*)

(*There is a constrained silence between Heavenly and Arthur. He stands by the fountain with his back to her. She seats herself on the stone bench—suddenly laughs.*)

ARTHUR: What are you laughing at?

HEAVENLY: Oh, nothing.—I didn't think I'd ever see you after last night.

ARTHUR: Neither did I.

HEAVENLY: It was sweet of you to fo'give me. In fact it was noble.

ARTHUR: Being noble is one of my worst afflictions.

HEAVENLY: I don't think so.—I know my behavior is awful.

ARTHUR: The worst thing about your behavior is its complete inconsistency.

HEAVENLY: Yes?

ARTHUR: Last night you expressed a desperate fear of being left on a porch swing. And yet right afterwards you do things that are perfectly calculated to bring that about!

HEAVENLY: I know, I know! I'm a fool!—*Look!*

ARTHUR: What?

HEAVENLY (*softly*): It's the first lightnin' bug!

(*Pause. Music is heard.*)

HEAVENLY: Wonder what makes 'em go off and on like that? —Did you take any science courses at Oxfo'd? I took geology my third yeah at high.

ARTHUR (*coldly*): Did you really?

HEAVENLY: Yes. We used to go out on field expeditions they called 'em, collectin' fossils an' things.

ARTHUR: That must've been nice!

HEAVENLY: Yes, an' just think!—Someday we'll be fossils, too. They'll dig us up an' say, "Gosh what long legs that girl had!"—or "Didn't he have nice ears!" —An' that's all they'll know about us, I suppose.

ARTHUR: I suppose so.

HEAVENLY: It won't matter who we got married to or whether we lived to be old or died young. They won't care; it won't make any difference to them. We'll just be little marks on a piece of rock. Or maybe not even that much.—Does it make you feel sad?

ARTHUR: No.—Are you trying to make conversation?

HEAVENLY: Um-hmm.

ARTHUR: What for?

HEAVENLY: It's part of my social training.

ARTHUR: You needn't.

HEAVENLY: You're still mad about last night. I thought you accepted my apologies over the phone.

ARTHUR: I knew you were lying over the phone.

HEAVENLY: You mean about my nervous indigestion?

ARTHUR: Yes, your mother came back to me with that same ridiculous story after calling your name all over the house.

HEAVENLY: Mother's a terrible fool sometimes.

ARTHUR: I felt sorry for her. I could understand your wanting to hurt me—because after all you've done that repeatedly in the past—but it did surprise me a little that you'd be willing to cause your mother such embarrassment.

HEAVENLY: You said I was cruel before.

ARTHUR: I said unconsciously cruel. But what you did last night was on purpose.

HEAVENLY: It really wasn't on purpose. You made me so mad, what you said about Dick an' me, that when mother sent me out for the napkins—well I just kept going till I'd gotten six blocks from the house. An' then it was too late to go back so I went to meet Dick an' he took me out to Moon Lake.

ARTHUR (*coldly*): Oh.

HEAVENLY: But I didn't have any fun. I kept thinking about what I'd done all the time an' I really did feel sorry, Ahthuh. I wasn't lyin' when I told you that over the phone. —Now do you fo'give me?

ARTHUR: I don't think it particularly matters whether I forgive you or not.

HEAVENLY: I think it does. I think I should like you an awful lot if you'd just be a little more human.

ARTHUR: What is being human?

HEAVENLY: You see you don't even know!

(*Henry enters.*)

HENRY: Heavenly, can I speak to you about something?

HEAVENLY: Sure you can, honey.

HENRY: I mean alone, Heavenly.

ARTHUR: Excuse me. (*He exits stage left.*)

HEAVENLY: Gosh, Hank, you look awful serious, honey! What's wrong?

HENRY: I thought you oughta know that Tom Newby's been talking about you to people. He told his mother and she's gone an' told Mizz Lamphrey an' Mizz Lamphrey's told Fanny and—and—

HEAVENLY: Told what?

HENRY: Tom Newby said—he said he saw you an' Dick Miles comin' out of a tourist cabin last night.

HEAVENLY: Oh.

HENRY: At Moon Lake, he said, and it was two o'clock in the morning! Of cou'se I know he's lyin' but—

HEAVENLY: What if it's true? (*She speaks violently.*) Whose business is it anyhow? What right have they got to—!

HENRY: I know but some of the old ladies, I heard 'em talking when I brought Mother's shawl— Mrs. Adams, she said she thought you ought to be—ostracized! What's that?

HEAVENLY: Ostracized? Did she say that?

HENRY: Yes. Is that what they did to that—you know—that girl across the Sunflower River?

HEAVENLY: No. Honey, you run back to the dance.

HENRY: That stinkin' polecat, Newby, I'm gonna push his face in! But I thought you oughta know first.

HEAVENLY: Thanks, honey.

HENRY (*blurting this out*): Heavenly, you're—you're beautiful! I wish that I was Dick Miles! (*He goes quickly out right.*)

(*Heavenly laughs wildly.*)

ARTHUR (*returning*): What's so hilariously funny?

HEAVENLY: He wished he was Dick Miles! Oh, God, it's beautiful, isn't it? (*Then she speaks furiously.*) I'm going to tell those bitches where to head in!

ARTHUR (*catching her wrist*): Heavenly!

HEAVENLY (*quietly after a moment*): Thanks. It's good you did that. Sometimes I don't think what I'm doing.

ARTHUR: You never do. You've got the instinct for self-destruction.

HEAVENLY: Is that what it is?

ARTHUR: Yes.

HEAVENLY: I probably got it from Colonel Wayne. You know he led the charge up Cemetery Hill.

ARTHUR: And you want to do the same thing?

HEAVENLY: If I have to.

ARTHUR: Right in the teeth of their guns with the odds all against you?

HEAVENLY: Why not? I wish I was ten years younger, I'd like to kick Tom Newby so hard he couldn't sit down for a month. I did that once about ten years ago and it's given me satisfaction ever since.

ARTHUR: What's he done?

HEAVENLY: Snitched on me, same as he did last time!

ARTHUR: About what?

HEAVENLY: Oh, you'll hear soon enough. The whole town will.—(*She continues, frightened.*) Mrs. Adams said I ought to be ostracized. Do you know what that means?

ARTHUR: Yes. It's what happens to rebels.

HEAVENLY: I don't give a damn.—It's the Pink Lady Waltz! Let's dance!

ARTHUR: No.

HEAVENLY: Why not?

ARTHUR: I'm not a good dancer.

HEAVENLY: You're good enough. Come on! (*She takes his arm.*)

ARTHUR: I'd rather not dance.

HEAVENLY: Oh, you're ashamed to dance with me? It might damage your good reputation.

ARTHUR: You know it's not that.

HEAVENLY: What is it then?

ARTHUR: I'm very uncomfortable when we're dancing together.

HEAVENLY: Why are you?

ARTHUR: Sometimes it hurts a man to be close to a woman—just so close and not any closer than that.

HEAVENLY: Oh! (*Pause.*) I wouldn't expect you to say a thing like that.

ARTHUR: Why not? Isn't that part of what you call being human?

HEAVENLY: Yes. That's why it surprised me so much.

(*There is a murmur of wind and a glimmer of lighting on the cyclorama.*)

Lightning. It's going to storm.

ARTHUR: Yes. I guess that's why the Little God's so excited. —He likes spring storms.

HEAVENLY: Does he?

ARTHUR: Yes. They've so much in common, you know. They're both so damn cruel—reckless and destructive!

HEAVENLY: Like me. Is that what you mean?

ARTHUR: Yes. I believe the Greeks were laughing when they made him the Little God. Eros is really the biggest god of them all. He's the one that's got thunderbolts!

HEAVENLY: What did you call him?

ARTHUR: Pardon me! I thought that you knew each other!—This is Eros, the Little God of Love, Miss Heavenly Critchfield!

HEAVENLY: How do you do? (*She laughs.*) I've always called him Cupid.

ARTHUR: Yes, that's the usual misconception. People think he's a cute, chubby little fellow with dimples and curly locks—but they're fooling themselves because he's really a monster!

HEAVENLY: Is he?

(*The scene plays very fast from here to Dick's entrance.*)

ARTHUR: Yes. Can't you feel him breathing fire in your face?

(*The wind rises. The orchestra is playing a fast waltz.*)

HEAVENLY: No. Not in mine.

ARTHUR: You're lucky, Miss Critchfield— Luckier than I.— What're you laughing at?

HEAVENLY: At you! You make such fancy speeches!

ARTHUR: You think I'm ludicrous, don't you?

HEAVENLY: No. I think you're a fake! (*Pause.*)

ARTHUR (*quietly*): A fake?

HEAVENLY: Yes, an absolute fake!

ARTHUR: You're right. I *am* a fake. I haven't got a real bone in my body.

HEAVENLY: I know you haven't.

ARTHUR: You know it surprises me sometimes to see that I even make a shadow in the light. It's a wonder the light doesn't shine right through me like it does through a cloud of dust in the road.

HEAVENLY: That's funny—I have the same feeling about you.

ARTHUR: I know that you do. (*He crosses to her.*) But just once I'd like to touch you and make you feel I'm alive.

HEAVENLY (*away*): What?

ARTHUR: Because then maybe I *would* be alive. You could give me back what you took away from me—that afternoon when you laughed at me in the recess yard!

HEAVENLY: What I took away from you? Then?

ARTHUR: Yes! You took away everything!

HEAVENLY: Arthur—

ARTHUR: After that I wasn't real anymore.

HEAVENLY: You're drunk.

ARTHUR: No, I was just the shadow of something and that's all I've been ever since.

HEAVENLY: What could I do about that?

ARTHUR: You could—you could *love* me—make me sure again I'm alive!

HEAVENLY: Oh, I see. (*She laughs.*) You mean what Henry meant when he said he wished that he was Dick Miles— Only you dress it up in prettier speeches, don't you? Here. Take the rest of the whiskey. Go cross the Sunflower River and get yourself one of those bright-skinned women they've got over there. They're marvelous at—at proving you're alive, if that's what you're worried about!

ARTHUR: You don't understand.

HEAVENLY: Oh, yes I do.

ARTHUR: I want you to marry me, Heavenly!

HEAVENLY: What?—You didn't say that! (*Pause.*)

ARTHUR: Will you? Will you, Heavenly?

HEAVENLY (*very softly*): I don't know. I don't see how I could.

ARTHUR: You couldn't love me?

HEAVENLY: How should I know? You've never even kissed me.

ARTHUR (*importunately*): May I? Will you let me?

HEAVENLY: Oh, you're so funny, Arthur! (*She laughs.*) I gave you every chance last night an' you started to read mode'n verse.

ARTHUR: I couldn't help it!—I've always run away from things that I wanted.

HEAVENLY: I don't know what to think, what to say! Everything's going so fast!—You know I can feel the earth moving! It's going a thousand miles a minute, it's spinning round and round!

ARTHUR: That's the wind!

HEAVENLY: I know, I know, but it's making me dizzy! (*She sinks down.*)

FANNY (*offstage*): Oh, Heavenly! Heavenly!

HEAVENLY: You see how fast it's going? We can't be still for a minute! (*She answers Fanny.*) Yes?

(*Fanny enters followed by Dick Miles.*)

FANNY: Oh, here you are, still having a *tête-à-tête* with the guest of honor!—There's another gentleman to see you!

HEAVENLY: Dick!

DICK: Scuse me for bustin' in, but I got something important to talk to you about.

HEAVENLY: How could you come here like this? You look like you've been having a mud-fight!

DICK: I have! I've been rasseling the river.

FANNY: Oh, we'll excuse your appearance. (*To Heavenly.*) We all know that Dick Miles is too big for social conventions.

DICK: That's right.

FANNY (*to Arthur*): Have you all met each othuh?

ARTHUR (*coldly*): I've had the pleasure quite some time ago.

DICK: Sure. (*He grins*) Do you still read *The Wizard of Oz*?

ARTHUR (*furiously*): No. Do you still enjoy taking advantage of your—your physical superiority? Do you still—

HEAVENLY: Arthur!

FANNY: Arthur, that's my favorite piece they're playing!

ARTHUR: Excuse me. (*He goes off with Fanny.*)

HEAVENLY: Now are you satisfied? You've made a beautiful scene!

DICK: Sorry. I had to see you. This is important, honey.

HEAVENLY: Important? You couldn't tell me tomorrow?

DICK: No. I'm not going to be here tomorrow.

HEAVENLY: —What?

DICK: We're leaving town.

HEAVENLY: We? —Thanks for telling me.

DICK: I mean it this time. Absolutely no doggin'. I been to Friar's Point—that's where I picked up this mud I got on me. (*He places his hands on her shoulders.*) Heavenly, I've got a job on the Government levee project.

HEAVENLY: No!

DICK: I've already signed the papers. I can show 'em to you.

HEAVENLY (*desperately*): No, Dick!

DICK: Huh?

HEAVENLY: You can't do a thing like that to me!

DICK: A thing like what?

HEAVENLY: You can't walk out on me, Dick!

DICK: I'm not walking out on you, honey. I'm takin' you with me.

HEAVENLY: Me? On a government levee project?

DICK: Sure, a man's allowed to be married.

HEAVENLY: Is he? I didn't know that. I thought those levee workers lived with niggers.

DICK: Heavenly—

HEAVENLY: That's what I heard. I heard they kept colored women in their shacks with them.

DICK (*disgustedly*): I knew you'd take it like that.

HEAVENLY: Dick, you've got a job here.

DICK: In the drugstore.

HEAVENLY: No. In Mr. Kramer's cotton office.

DICK: That's absolutely out. I won't take it.

HEAVENLY: Dad's made him promise. It's a sure thing.

DICK: No! I won't take it! (*He catches her shoulders.*) Honey, it takes a pair of boots and a flannel shirt to make me feel like a man. I'm sick of bath salts and spirits of ammonia. An' I wouldn't like cotton much better. Cotton's soft. It's fuzzy stuff that sticks to your fingers. I wouldn't like that. I want to get my hands on something hard and tough that fights back, like the river. When you're fighting a river you're fighting something your size. Don't you see? They've put out flood warnings up at Friar's Point. She's rose six feet since morning. Fifty-nine, that's flood stage, and God only knows when she'll stop. They're fighting like crazy to hold her back but she keeps on coming, big an' yellow an' daring 'em all to try an' make her stay put. She'll win this time maybe. Push right through their sandbags an' run 'em out of the county, tearin' down sharecroppers' houses an' drownin' the stock. If the people are lucky they'll climb on top of their roofs an' we'll take 'em off in boats. But some of 'em won't be lucky. Ole Mammies with breakbone fever ain't good at roof climbing. The river'll catch 'em at night an' they won't have a chance. But maybe next time we'll win. We'll catch her an' tame her an' make her stay in her place. That's a big job, honey, the kind of job that I want! (*Pause.*)

HEAVENLY: More than you want me? That much?

DICK: I want you and the job both.

HEAVENLY: You can't have both. I can't live like that, in a shack on the river— You can't ask me to.

DICK: Well, that's what I'm asking. You'll have to go with me or—

HEAVENLY: Oh, it's an ultimatum.

DICK: You can call it that.

HEAVENLY: In other words you're tired of me, you've had enough!

DICK: Come off your high horse!

HEAVENLY: I've still got some pride, some self-respect!

DICK: You've still got your ancestry, your marvelous ancestry! You can't forget about that!

HEAVENLY: I can't forget that I'm decent!

DICK: But you can forget Moon Lake last night, or yesterday up on the hill? You can forget those things in about twenty minutes and throw it up to me that I'm not good enough for you?

HEAVENLY: It's you that's forgetting, not me. Every spring it's the same. You get a spell like this an' later you come to your senses.

DICK: You got around me last spring. Made me stay.

HEAVENLY: Don't you remember *how* I made you stay?

DICK: Yes, I remember how.

HEAVENLY: It wasn't easy for me to do that. I thought it meant something.

DICK: It did.

HEAVENLY: Not to you or you wouldn't be throwing me over.

DICK: Honey, I'm *not* throwing you over.

HEAVENLY: You are. You're throwing me over—you want me to be like Agnes Peabody next door—a front porch girl! She sits on the front porch in her best dress and the men walk by in the evening and tip their hats and keep right on walking. People remember how she went out all the time with a boy that's left town. Now she just sits on the front porch waiting!—waiting for nothing, getting to be an old maid!—That's what you want to happen to me!

DICK: No, honey, you know better than that.

HEAVENLY: How should I know any better?

DICK: I asked you to go with me.

HEAVENLY: Yes, you asked me to go with you! And you knew damn well that I couldn't!

DICK: I knew you loved me. I mean I thought I knew you loved me.

HEAVENLY: Oh. And now you think different. You think that I've done what I've done because I'm just naturally rotten. Is that what you think?

DICK: No. Let it go.

HEAVENLY: I won't. We'll have this out now.

DICK: All right. You can do what you please but I'm goin'.

HEAVENLY (*her voice breaking*): Then it's all finished then. You can go, you don't have to come back. I'd rather sit out on a front porch the rest of my life than ever see you again. —But I won't be sitting on the front porch! I'll take Arthur! He told me he wanted me just now, before you came butting in!

DICK: Heavenly!—

HEAVENLY: Go away!

DICK: You don't want me to! Lissen, Heavenly!
HEAVENLY: No!
DICK: Have you ever spent a night on the river, honey?
HEAVENLY: Let go of me!

(*He forces her down on the bench and holds her against him.*)

DICK: Have you ever spent a night on a river barge, honey? That clean wet smell of the woods and maybe a hole in the roof you can see the stars through? Katydids hummin' an' bullfrogs off in the shallows. That dark warm smell of the water real close an' the sound that it makes that's so quiet it's sca'cely a sound, just a big, big blackness movin' around you, an' up on the deck a nigger pickin' a fiddle an' singin' an ole river song, an' that lazy soft rise an' fall of the water under the boat an' the lightnin' bugs blinkin' way off over there on the flat cotton fields or down in the cypress break an' that wild coon laughter all of a sudden comin' up out of the dark where they're makin' love on the levee—like cryin' almost—an' then not a thing anymore but that slow slappin'-slap of the water . . .
HEAVENLY: Dick—
DICK: I've spent nights like that on the river! By myself or with a bunch of fellows—but never with a girl I loved!
HEAVENLY (*breaking away*): Dick, it's impossible!

(*The wind has risen. They have to shout above it.*)

DICK (*trying to kiss her again*): No, it isn't!
HEAVENLY: Stop it!
DICK (*slowly*): You mean you won't go?
HEAVENLY (*brokenly*): You know that I couldn't stand it.
DICK: You could if you loved me.
HEAVENLY: If I loved you, if I loved you!—All that you think of is self, self, self!
DICK: It's you that don't think of anything but self!
HEAVENLY: Oh, Dick! Don't say any more tonight, please don't!
DICK: I got nothing more to say.
HEAVENLY: They're all going in the house, it's going to storm.—I can't stay out here any longer, Dick.
DICK: I'm not keeping you.

HEAVENLY (*catching his arm*): Oh, Dick—don't, don't! *Please* don't!

(*Arthur enters right.*)

ARTHUR (*drunkenly*): Heavenly, where are you, Heavenly?

DICK: What do *you* want?

ARTHUR: I want to take her inside!

DICK: You take her nowhere, Sonny. She's going with me.

HEAVENLY: Dick, don't make another scene!

ARTHUR: Why don't you leave her alone? You can't marry her, all you can do is make her talked about. (*He's in a drunken rage.*) You know what they say about the two of you—do you know?

HEAVENLY (*screaming*): Arthur! Go 'way! Go back to the house!

ARTHUR: They say she's your mistress! They say—

(*Dick knocks him down—then jerks him up, shakes him, and flings him down again—Heavenly tries to stop him.*)

HEAVENLY: Dick! You'll kill him—he's drunk!

DICK: —I didn't hurt him.

HEAVENLY (*bends over Arthur*): You did.

DICK: All right. You stay here with him. Wrap him up in tissue paper and send him back to Mama with my regards!

(*He starts off.*)

HEAVENLY (*rising*): Dick!—

DICK: Good-bye!

HEAVENLY: Call me tomorrow! You'll call me, won't you?

DICK: Good-bye, Heavenly! (*He exits.*)

(*She runs after him a short distance, calling his name wildly. She stops, sobbing aloud. As the storm breaks, she turns and runs toward the house.*

(The Japanese lanterns flicker and sway in the wind. The cable that supports them snaps and they are blown tumbling across the stage. There is the sound of branches thrashing, a cacophony of noises from the suddenly disrupted lawn party, and, through it all, expressing the frenzied spirit of the scene, are heard the distant strains of the waltz, fast and feverishly

gay. There is a crash of thunder.—Arthur rises, staggering. He goes over to the statue of Eros. He stands unsteadily before it, laughing louder and louder as the storm's fury increases— There is a vivid flash of lightning and then complete darkness.)

The Curtain Falls

SCENE TWO

The scene is the Carnegie Public Library of Port Tyler. The set is furnished with a yellow oak desk, a table, a chair, and a newspaper and magazine rack. A green-shaded bulb is suspended over the librarian's desk and a small lamp rests on the table. Against the back wall or on the bulletin board are travel posters of "Beautiful Switzerland" and "Romantic Italy." A sign on the desk says "Quiet Please" In the middle of the back wall is an opaque glass-paned door marked "Stacks." Hertha is seated at the desk in a prim gray smock and glasses. She looks tired and strained. Enter Mrs. Kramer, a prim-looking matron.

MRS. KRAMER (*marching to the desk*): I found this book in my daughter's bedroom!

HERTHA: Yes?

MRS. KRAMER: I don't think books like this should be exposed on the shelves.

HERTHA: It happens to be a private copy of my own.

MRS. KRAMER: Well, how did she get it?

HERTHA: She saw me reading it and asked to read it herself.

MRS. KRAMER: Oh. It may be fit reading for an older person, but Dorothea's sixteen. So far I've managed to keep her mind entirely free of—of sordid things such as—

HERTHA: This book? There's nothing sordid about this book, Mrs. Kramer—nothing whatsoever!

MRS. KRAMER: Oh, isn't there? I always consult Reverend Hooker about my child's reading matter— When I showed him this book he turned directly to this passage and asked me if it was the sort of thing I wanted my child's mind infected with—here it is— (*She reads a verse of love poetry.*)

What lips my lips have kissed, and where and why,
I have forgotten, and what arms have lain
Under my head till morning—

HERTHA (*snatching the book*): You can't read it like that, Mrs. Kramer!

MRS. KRAMER: No?

HERTHA (*repeating the passage with feeling*):

What lips my lips have kissed, and where and why,
I have forgotten, and what arms have lain
Under my head till morning; but the rain
Is full of ghosts tonight, that tap and sigh
Upon the glass and listen for reply:

And in my heart there stirs a quiet pain
For unremembered lads that not again
Will turn to me at midnight with a cry.

(*She fixes her eyes on Mrs. Kramer and recites the rest of the poem from memory.*)

Thus in the winter stands the lonely tree,
Nor knows what birds have vanished one by one,
Yet knows its boughs more silent than before:
I cannot say what loves have come and gone;
I only know that summer sang in me
A little while, that in me sings no more.

Now don't you like it better?

MRS. KRAMER: No. I think it's outrageous. Next time Dorothea wants a book, please give her one of the Alcott series.

HERTHA: Isn't Dorothea rather old for the Alcott series?

MRS. KRAMER (*furiously*): She's not too old for innocence, thank heavens, and she's not too young for common sense— Good night, Miss Neilson. (*She marches out.*)

(*Hertha opens the book— Music comes through the opened windows from the Lamphrey's party. Hertha closes the book, rises quickly and shuts the window. She returns slowly to the desk. After a moment, Miss Schlagmann comes out of the door marked "Stacks."*)

MISS SCHLAGMANN: Oh, it's so close in here. Why did you close that window?

HERTHA: It's going to storm.

MISS SCHLAGMANN: We might as well leave it open till it rains in. (*She goes over and raises the window. Music enters again and there is the glimmer of lightning outside.*) Listen! You can hear the music from the Lamphrey's lawn party!

HERTHA: Yes.

MISS SCHLAGMANN: They've got Japanese lanterns strung all over the place.—It looks like fairyland.

HERTHA: Yes.

MISS SCHLAGMANN: Oh, dear—young people have such a good time, don't they? How would you like to go to the movies with me next Saturday night, Hertha?

HERTHA: Thank you, but—

MISS SCHLAGMANN: It'll be my treat this time!—They have that Tyrone Power picture. And they always have the Tarzan serial.

HERTHA: Do they?

MISS SCHLAGMANN (*laughing sharply*): They're so absurd! But they *are* exciting! At the end of the last one he and the girl were locked in a dungeon with lions!— (*She laughs.*) But I suppose they'll manage to get out somehow.

HERTHA: Yes. (*She smiles slightly.*)

MISS SCHLAGMANN: They're obliged to get out. That's only the sixteenth chapter and there's supposed to be thirty-two— If they killed 'em off now they wouldn't have anything to put in the other sixteen.

HERTHA: No. Not unless they had a very elaborate funeral.

MISS SCHLAGMANN: You don't like the movies?

HERTHA: Sometimes. I liked that last one of Greta Garbo's.

MISS SCHLAGMANN: Her things are always so morbid or sordid or something!

HERTHA (*laughing*): That's twice this evening that I've been accused of having sordid predilections.

MISS SCHLAGMANN (*starting back to the "Stacks," she pauses at the desk*): Here's something *I* like—jonquils!—They're so fresh looking! (*She sniffs them delicately, then exits through the rear door.*)

(*Hertha reopens the book of poems. The muted strains of the Strauss waltz from the Lamphrey's are heard. Suddenly she throws down the book. She rushes to the window and slams it shut. She raises one hand to her lips in an almost terrified gesture, then touches her forehead and returns slowly to the desk. She clears her throat and straightens things on the desk with a furious but aimless haste— A young couple enters—Mabel and Ralph.*)

MABEL: It would have to rain.
RALPH: Jeez, what a wind's comin' up.
MABEL: I'm scared sick a' storms. Specially when it thunders. Ralph! (*She clings to him.*)
RALPH: Aw, honey, thunder can't hurtcha.
MABEL (*giggling*): She's lookin' at us.
RALPH: What do we care, huh?
HERTHA (*rising and approaching them stiffly*): This room is for reading purposes only.
RALPH: What're we doin'?
HERTHA: You're creating a disturbance.
RALPH: A disturbance, huh?
HERTHA: Yes!
RALPH: Can't we even carry on a little conversation in here?
HERTHA: Conversation, yes, but not disorderly behavior.
MABEL (*rising indignantly*): He's my fiancé!—Ralph, let's get out of this place! (*She crosses to the door.*) I'd rather get pneumonia than be bawled out by that cranky old maid!

(*As they go out Ralph laughs rudely. Hertha stands erect till they have gone—then suddenly covers her face— She quickly lowers her hands as the inner door opens and Miss Schlagmann comes back out with an armful of books.*)

MISS SCHLAGMANN: I thought I heard some loud talk in here.
HERTHA: That boy and girl were in here again. The ones that were necking in here last week.
MISS SCHLAGMANN: Oh!
HERTHA: I asked them to please be quiet and they were horribly rude to me.

MISS SCHLAGMANN: I'm going to speak to Mr. Gillam. She works there, at the hosiery counter. I think—being a vestryman of St. George's—he'd like to know how one of his salesgirls spends her free time, making a public show of herself and her common affairs.

HERTHA: No. Don't.—He might discharge her.

MISS SCHLAGMANN: He should.

HERTHA: No. It wasn't anything at all. I haven't been feeling well and they made me nervous.—They called me a—

MISS SCHLAGMANN: Called you what?

HERTHA (*averting her face*): A—cranky old maid.

MISS SCHLAGMANN (*furious*): Well, what preposterous—!

HERTHA: No, they were right! That's what I am now!

MISS SCHLAGMANN (*shocked*): Hertha! What's wrong with you child?

HERTHA (*crossing behind the desk*): Nothing. I'm nervous.

MISS SCHLAGMANN: I'm going to report this to Mr. Gillam.

HERTHA: Please don't. (*She takes a handkerchief from a drawer and turns her back.*)

MISS SCHLAGMANN: Hertha, I'm afraid you're getting run down again this spring. You'd better take a week off.

HERTHA: I'm all right. It's just nervousness. (*She turns and sits down rigidly at the desk.*) —Maybe I'm losing my mind.

MISS SCHLAGMANN: Don't be absurd!

HERTHA: Lots of girls do at my age. Twenty-eight. Lots of them get *dementia praecox* at about that age, especially when they're not married. I've read about it. They get morbid and everything excites them and they think they're being persecuted by people. I'm getting like that.

MISS SCHLAGMANN: You are not! (*She speaks gently.*) I know what's wrong with you, Hertha. It's that Shannon boy— Isn't it now?

HERTHA (*with effort*): —Yes.

MISS SCHLAGMANN: I knew that was it. You took him too seriously. I could have told you right at the start he wouldn't do anything but make you unhappy. I had him spotted. Attractive and intelligent and all that but selfish right to the core. One of these spoiled millionaire's children. They're all the same way. They think the whole earth was created for their entertainment. (*She returns several books to a shelf.*) You get him out of your mind.

HERTHA: I can't. (*She looks almost wildly about the room.*) He's the first man that ever looked at me twice. And I can't stop thinking about him. Even at night. I haven't been sleeping.

MISS SCHLAGMANN: I know you haven't. You need a change of scene.

HERTHA: Oh, no, I can't stop working!

MISS SCHLAGMANN: You can if it's necessary to stop a nervous breakdown.

HERTHA: It wouldn't help. I've got to keep busy. You see when I'm not busy I— (*She presses her hands to her temples.*) Why doesn't God have a little mercy on people like me? You go to church, Miss Schlagmann, you teach Sunday school. You ought to know. Why doesn't God have a little mercy on people like me? Ask Him that the next time you go to St. George's. Tell Him He shouldn't give homely girls the same feelings that He gives the pretty ones. Tell Him that. Tell Him it isn't fair to let the homely girls fall in love with men that don't care!

(*Miss Schlagmann makes a gesture of shocked pity; she bites her lips and fumbles at the silver cross suspended over her flat bosom.*)

MISS SCHLAGMANN (*hesitantly*): Hertha, I wish you would go with me to some of the Lenten services next week at St. George's. It's going to be Holy Week. Our Lord's Passion, you know.—Don't you suppose He went through moments like these that you're going through—when He suffered and doubted and—prepared His soul for climbing up that hill and being nailed on a cross between two thieves!

HERTHA (*slowly*): Well, if He did, He ought to know what it's like and He ought to have some pity! I can't go on living much longer in this kind of vacuum. It isn't fair to make me, it isn't fair!

MISS SCHLAGMANN: Lots of things aren't fair, but we've got to put up with them just the same. That's life.

HERTHA (*fiercely*): I'm tired of hearing people say, "That's life!"

MISS SCHLAGMANN: I know. I've been through the same thing. It's a sort of an emotional crisis that all of us have to go through that don't get married and haven't the courage for anything else. After a while it gets better. You find out that you can put those feelings into other things.

HERTHA (*bitterly*): Yes. Sublimation. Choir singing and raising petunias. I don't want that.

MISS SCHLAGMANN: Hertha!

HERTHA: There ought to be something else! (*She speaks almost to herself.*) A straight line upwards to someplace nobody's ever been yet. I told him that and he laughed, Arthur did. He said I meant 'Paradise'—but I didn't. I don't know what I meant.—Why doesn't your fashionable Episcopal minister at St. George's try to figure that out instead of worrying about how he's going to finance the new pipe organ?

MISS SCHLAGMANN: Don't talk like that!

HERTHA: I know, I know. I ought to keep my mouth shut. That's what's expected of me. But I can't anymore. I'm sick of it.

(*Agnes Peabody enters.*)

MISS SCHLAGMANN: It's Agnes Peabody. You'd better go in the back room.

HERTHA (*turning to the shelves*): No. I'll be all right.

(*Miss Peabody closes the door and shakes her umbrella and comes briskly up to the desk.*)

MISS PEABODY: I know it's closing time, Birdie, but I've just got to see the new *Vogue*. I bought some of that silk print at Gillam's. They had the most marvelous sale, and—

MISS SCHLAGMANN: The new *Vogue*'s out.

MISS PEABODY (*disappointed*): Oh, is it?

MISS SCHLAGMANN: Yes. Mrs. Critchfield has it. She's using one of those patterns, too.

MISS PEABODY: Oh. Something for Heavenly, I guess. Hmmmm. I guess she's planning to sew on a trousseau this spring.

MISS SCHLAGMANN: Trousseau?

MISS PEABODY: Yes. Haven't you heard? (*Glances sharply at Hertha's back.*) I hope I'm not letting the cat out of the bag. That Arthur Shannon created such an excitement when he came back to town— I'm afraid there'll be quite a few disappointed young ladies when they make the announcement! (*She giggles shrilly.*) Did you ever see such a rain? Forty-eight hours without a let up. But that's April for you. OHH! I have a run in my stocking! Hello, Hertha.

HERTHA (*barely turning*): Good evening.

MISS PEABODY (*simpering*): You were so quiet I didn't know you were there. I've got to be running. I'm going to Memphis tomorrow. Did you see the *Commercial-Appeal*? Fifty percent reduction on furs at Hess and Williamson! Isn't that marvelous? That's where I got the muskrat cape I'm wearing with my brown tweed suit. Oh, heavens it's nearly nine! You'll save the new *Vogue* for me? —Good night!

MISS SCHLAGMANN: Good night.

MISS PEABODY (*with marvelous gaiety*): Good night, Hertha!

(*She laughs and snatches up her umbrella and darts out the door. All of her actions have that brilliant, exaggerated animation which is characteristic of some southern spinsters. Miss Schlagmann glances uneasily at Hertha's back. Hertha slowly raises another book and places it on the shelf. As she does so the clock strikes nine in a slow, gentle tone.*)

MISS SCHLAGMANN: We're half an hour late. Hertha, you go on home, you don't need to wait for me.

HERTHA (*turning slowly*): No. I'll wait till you're ready.

MISS SCHLAGMANN: All right! We'll stop in Greenbaum's and have a hot chocolate! It will help you sleep.

HERTHA (*dully*): Yes.

(*Miss Schlagmann retires to the back room and closes the door. Hertha sits down mechanically at the desk and stares in front of her. Her face has a dead expressionless look. After a moment, the outer door is pushed open and Arthur enters—he is drunk, disheveled, his flannel coat and trousers bedraggled with rain and his hair hanging over his forehead. He leans against the door and grins satirically at Hertha.*)

ARTHUR: Good evening, Miss Neilson!

HERTHA: Arthur! (*She touches her hair.*) I wasn't expecting you. You didn't call last night. (*She notices his strange appearance.*) Arthur, what's wrong with you, Arthur?

ARTHUR (*laughing*): Excuse my experience!—I've come here to show you that southern chivalry is still in flower.

HERTHA: I'm afraid you've been drinking.

ARTHUR: She's afraid I've been drinking.—You put it so tactfully, Miss Neilson. Yes, I'm drunk. You ought to try it sometime yourself. It's exciting. Makes everything look different. Even you, Miss Neilson, you look almost human tonight!

HERTHA: What have you done this for? Arthur, why have you gotten yourself in such a condition?

ARTHUR: Haven't you ever seen a drunk man before? Sure you have. Your father, the Terrible Swede, as they call him. He comes home polluted on Saturday nights, so I hear. Makes a big scene, throws things, calls you names. So what are you getting so puritanical for?

HERTHA (*stiffening*): Is that amusing to you? Are you laughing because of that?

ARTHUR (*a bit ashamed*): Sure. Everything's funny tonight. (*He rubs his forehead confusedly.*) Excuse me. Heavenly gave me some liquor and told me to go out and get drunk—so I did.

HERTHA: Heavenly Critchfield—?

ARTHUR: Yes. I told her that I was in love with her, and she said that I should go out and get drunk because that was the only thing that would do me any good. So I got drunk. It's the first time I ever got drunk in my life and it was swell. Till I started thinking about her again making love to Dick Miles.

HERTHA: Arthur! I'm sorry, I— (*She extends her hand towards him in a slight, pitying gesture.*)

ARTHUR: I can forget all that with you, can't I? You're a girl, too. You could make love as well as she could. But not with Dick Miles. With me. (*He moves toward her. Hertha steps back.*) What are you backing away for? Are you scared? That's flattering. Nobody's ever been scared of me before. I was like you, Hertha. I hid behind books all the time because they used to call me a sissy when I was a kid in school. I never got over that. Not till tonight when I got drunk. God! I never knew it could be so good to get drunk and feel like a man inside. Literature and the arts. Stravinsky, Beethoven, Brahms. Concerts, matinees, recitals —what's all that? If I told you you'd blush. You don't like that kind of language. Sure, I sat through all of that stuff and thought it was great. Got my stuff published in those little magazines with the big cultural movements. Art for art's sake. Give America back to the Indians. I thought I was being highbrow. Intellectual. The hell with that stuff. Dick Miles's got the right idea. He was the one that she gave herself to, not me, not me. The one that got drunk and had himself a good time, he was the one that got Heavenly, and me with my intellectual pretensions, my fancy education, and my father's money—what did I get? Pushed in the face! Thrown over for a boy that clerks in a drugstore because he knows how to make love and I don't! Well now I can, too. I can get drunk and act like the rest of them. How about it, Miss Neilson? Why don't you come out from behind those tortoise-shell glasses of yours? (*He reaches across the table and plucks them off.*)

HERTHA: Arthur, please go home. (*She crosses in front of the desk.*) Don't touch me!

ARTHUR (*laughing*): Don't touch you? Yes. That's it—purity! The Carnegie Vestal! (*He crosses toward her.*)

HERTHA: No! Don't touch me!

ARTHUR: Why not? It would do you some good. You with your books, your anthologies, your metaphysical poets. William Blake and John Donne. They're dead, Hertha. All your lovers are dead and bound up in books. They can't touch you. They can't make love to you tonight. They've been in the ground too long. Don't you know that? (*He turns out the suspended light above.*) This is life and you're scared of it. You've never come up against it before. You haven't found it in any of your alphabetical files. It's taken you by surprise, Hertha, the way it took me when I came back from Europe and saw Heavenly Critchfield again, laughing at me the way that she used to. It hurts you. It's big and awful and crazy and makes you want to run and hide from it. But you can't, Hertha. Hiding doesn't do any good. (*He catches one of her hands which she holds before her in a defensive gesture.*) You've got little hands—they're little candle-wax hands.

HERTHA (*faintly*): Let go of me, Arthur.

ARTHUR: No. I won't let go.

HERTHA: Please do.

ARTHUR: No.

HERTHA: If you don't I'll have to call Miss Schlagmann.

ARTHUR: Go ahead. Call her.—Haven't you ever been kissed? No. Only in books. By William Blake and John Donne. "Go, and catch a falling star,/Get with child a mandrake root."—Those are your lovers but they've got cold lips. They've been in the ground so long not even April can make them warm, again, Hertha. But I'm not cold. Heavenly thinks I am but she's mistaken. The whiskey's made me warm for a change. I'm hot inside. If I touched you with my lips you'd think you'd been scorched by fire. You'd crumple up like a little white moth that's flown into the candle flame, Hertha. That's what you'd do. (*He pulls her against him.*)

HERTHA (*breathlessly*): No, no, please let me go.

(*He kisses her. She struggles and then is limp in his arms. After a moment he thrusts her away from him. There is a long pause. The stunned expression recedes from her face and she moves a step toward him.*)

You kissed me, Arthur. (*She touches her lips wonderingly.*)

ARTHUR (*hoarsely*): Excuse me. I was drunk. (*He averts his face in distaste.*)

HERTHA: You kissed me.—It isn't Heavenly Critchfield you're in love with, it's me! Isn't it, Arthur? It's me! (*She smiles raptly like a child.*)

(*Arthur is shocked out of his drunkenness and repelled by his own action and by Hertha's unexpected reaction to it.*)

ARTHUR (*in confusion*): I didn't know what I was doing. I'm sorry. (*He goes back a few steps.*) I'd better be going.

HERTHA (*blind with inner brightness*): Arthur! Now I can tell you!—I love you! I love you. So much that I've nearly gone mad! Oh, God, why didn't you know, why didn't you know? (*Slowly she extends her hand toward the shaded light on the table.*) Arthur! Take me out of here, Arthur, some place where we can be together. (*She turns the light off.*)

ARTHUR (*moving away from her*): No, I don't want you Hertha.

HERTHA: Arthur!

ARTHUR: Don't you understand? I don't want you! (*Pause.*) I didn't know you were like that. I thought you were different.

HERTHA (*agonized*): Arthur!

ARTHUR: You—you *disgust* me!

(*His shadow can be seen moving uncertainly toward the door —it closes and he is gone. A wild cry breaks from Hertha's lips and she falls to her knees. After a moment Miss Schlagmann comes out of the stacks, running.*)

MISS SCHLAGMANN: Hertha! What's happened, child? (*She turns the light on.*)

HERTHA (*vaguely*): There was a man. He scared me. I fainted —please get me some water.

MISS SCHLAGMANN: Hertha! I'll call the police!

HERTHA: No, no! Nothing happened! (*She sobs like a child.*) I want to go home, I want to go home!

MISS SCHLAGMANN: Hertha, poor Hertha!—I'll get you a glass of water!

(*She rushes into the other room. With a choked cry Hertha darts out the front door. When Miss Schlagmann returns with the glass of water, she has disappeared.*)

Hertha! Where are you child? Good heavens, she's gone!

(*Miss Schlagmann rushes out the front door and can be heard calling Hertha's name several times. She returns, frustrated —still holding glass of water. She continues, vaguely.*)

She's gone. . . .

(*She looks helplessly at the glass of water and then slowly, mechanically, pours it into the bowl of yellow jonquils on the desk—*)

Slow Curtain

SCENE THREE

It is the next evening in the Critchfield living room. Aunt Lila is sewing in her rocker. Heavenly enters slowly in a white cellophane rain cape.

LILA: Still raining?

HEAVENLY (*looking stunned*): Oh. Yes.

LILA: What's the matter with you?

HEAVENLY: He's gone.

LILA: Richard?

HEAVENLY: Yes.

LILA: Left town, you mean?

HEAVENLY: Yes.—I don't want to talk about it.

LILA: Don't be so tragic. Sit down here and let's get this thing straightened out.

HEAVENLY: Some things can't be straightened out, Auntie.

LILA: I've never known anything yet didn't straighten itself out if you gave it time enough.

HEAVENLY: Time! Yes! A couple of centuries—

LILA: That's how it looks when you're young.

HEAVENLY (*suddenly angry*): You don't know how it feels!

LILA: Yes, I do know! And I know it's hard to be young! Almost as hard as it is to be old! Sometimes it's even harder because when you're old—you get so you appreciate a good cup of coffee! But the young ones, the kids like you, they think the sun won't rise tomorrow unless they get what they want.

HEAVENLY (*coming down a bit from her anger and despair*): Have you got a cigarette?

LILA (*brightly*): A whole pack of 'em. My dividend came in from the compress stock!

HEAVENLY: Thanks.

LILA: By the way, I'm making you a new dress out of some goods I bought at Power's.

HEAVENLY: Thanks, Auntie.

LILA: It's got a lot of red in it. Your mother thinks it's tacky. But I always say that spring's a damn good excuse for wearing bright colors.

HEAVENLY: It's no use, Auntie. I don't feel like being bucked up. (*Her voice catches.*)

LILA: That's right. Go on and do a little crying—and then go upstairs and get dressed for your dinner date.

HEAVENLY (*sobbing.*): Do you think I'm going out?

LILA: Of course you are. You aren't the sort of girl that gives up going to parties. I was, and look where it got me. (*She offers Heavenly a light.*) Here. Smoke your cigarette. Cigarettes were made for moments like these. Girls didn't smoke 'em back in the days when I had my big romantic catastrophes. I used to go out in the hayloft and stuff my mouth full of straw which wasn't nearly so nice. They had rats in the hayloft. I remember once when I was right on the point of deciding to kill myself when one of those big gray monsters trotted over my ankle and gave me such a fit of the shudders that I completely forgot about my broken heart.

HEAVENLY (*rising impatiently*): Oh, I haven't got any broken heart.

LILA: No. They're out of style. Where's he gone to?

HEAVENLY: To work on the levee. That was his big ambition, that's what he wanted to do. He said it took a flannel shirt and pair of boots to make him feel like a man.—He wanted me to go with him. Me! Live like a nigger on a lousy river barge. He expected me to do that.

LILA: Doesn't he give you credit for having a lick of sense?

HEAVENLY: Oh, I don't know. I might do it if he hadn't been so casual about it. He didn't call me all day so I went down to the drugstore, and the soda jerk told me he'd quit his job and gone to Friar's Point and left a note for me in an empty Alka-Seltzer bottle.

LILA: Huh! What did the note say?

HEAVENLY: If I wanted him, I could meet him in Friar's Point tonight. And get married.

LILA: You wouldn't do a fool thing like that.

HEAVENLY: I don't know.

LILA: He's the restless kind. He's never stuck at anything very long.

HEAVENLY: No, he goes from one thing to another.

LILA: One of these drifters.

HEAVENLY: It isn't just that. He isn't satisfied with the things that other people are satisfied with.

LILA: No. You can't blame him for that. But that isn't a very good reason for marrying him. He wanted to get away from the drugstore and the town. Maybe he'd be wanting to get away from you next.

HEAVENLY: I know. I can't be sure.

LILA: You could never be sure.

HEAVENLY: If I thought I could hold him I'd take a chance on the rest. I'd live like a nigger for him on a lousy river barge. I'd even do that, if I thought he wouldn't decide in the end that I was just another thing that he wanted to break away from.

LILA: When they've got the itch in them shoes there's nothing but six feet of dirt can ever make 'em stay put.

HEAVENLY: Tell me what to do.

LILA: You've got a date with Arthur Shannon tonight. Go upstairs and get dressed for it.

HEAVENLY: No!

LILA: I know that sounds like an awful anticlimax to a broken heart or whatever you call it nowadays, but so was the rat that ran over my ankle in the hayloft, and it was the rat that brought me back to my senses and made me see what a sentimental fool I was being! You're better off than I was. You've got another to fall back on.

HEAVENLY: Arthur? I don't think I could ever care much for him.

LILA: Why not?

HEAVENLY: He doesn't seem quite human. All he does is talk and talk.

LILA: He'll get over that.

HEAVENLY: Oh, God, I don't know what to do!

VOICE OF MESSENGER BOY: Cutrere's!

MRS. CRITCHFIELD: Flowers? How lovely! (*She enters with an open box.*) Look at this! Just look! It's talisman roses! Heavenly! Arthur's sent you a corsage! To wear to the Country Club tonight.

HEAVENLY: Oh, I know, I know.

MRS. CRITCHFIELD (*turning to Lila*): What's the matter with her? What's she crying about?

LILA: Richard Miles left town.

MRS. CRITCHFIELD: Well. Good riddance! I told you how much you could depend on a boy of that kind.— (*She decides to take no further notice of Heavenly's grief.*) Look at this! Did you ever see anything more exquisite? (*She holds the corsage up to Heavenly's shoulder.*) It's going to look lovely on your blue knitted suit.

HEAVENLY (*pushing the corsage aside*): Let go of me! Leave me alone!

MRS. CRITCHFIELD: Well, that's gratitude for you!

LILA: Leave her alone, Esmeralda.

MRS. CRITCHFIELD: Oh, I know that you were fond of him, Heavenly, but I can't help feeling that his leaving town's the most fortunate thing that *could* have happened.

HEAVENLY: Fond of him. (*She laughs wildly.*) I was crazy about him. You ought to know that.

MRS. CRITCHFIELD: I won't hear any more about that disgusting business.

HEAVENLY (*practically shouting*): Crazy about him, do you hear?

MRS. CRITCHFIELD: That horrible—

LILA: Esmeralda!

HEAVENLY: Do you think I'm going to give him up?

MRS. CRITCHFIELD: Of course you're going to give him up. You're going to forget all about him.

HEAVENLY: I won't!

MRS. CRITCHFIELD: You're going to be sensible now.

HEAVENLY: That's what you think!

MRS. CRITCHFIELD: You're going upstairs and get dressed!

HEAVENLY: I'm going upstairs and pack my grip!

MRS. CRITCHFIELD: Do what?

HEAVENLY: I'm going to Friar's Point. Dick's going to meet me there. We're going to get married!

MRS. CRITCHFIELD (*aghast*): No!

HEAVENLY: Yes. By a colored preacher. And we're going to live on a river barge.

MRS. CRITCHFIELD: You wouldn't dare—!

HEAVENLY: I thought you'd know by now how much I'd dare to do. Didn't I open your eyes when I told you what had been going on between him and me? Yes, an affair! The gossips were right this time, you can chalk it up in their favor. But I'm not as immoral as you are, I'm not as indecent as you want to make me. I'm not going to give myself to one man and then go marry another that I don't even like. No, hell, no! I'm gonna take the nine o'clock train to Friar's Point and marry Dick and you can't stop me! (*She flies out of the room.*)

MRS. CRITCHFIELD (*she is nearly prostrate*): Oh! Call her father!

LILA: No. Leave this to me, Esmeralda.

MRS. CRITCHFIELD: Get Oliver this instant! We've got to stop her!

LILA: Now don't go all to pieces. Is it true what she said about her and the boy having had an affair?

MRS. CRITCHFIELD (*choked*): Yes, it's true.

LILA: When did she tell you?

MRS. CRITCHFIELD: Don't stand there and ask me questions!

LILA: If it's true then maybe she'd better go and marry the boy.

MRS. CRITCHFIELD: No! I'd never permit it! She can marry Arthur Shannon.

LILA: Does he know about her and Richard?

MRS. CRITCHFIELD: No, of course he doesn't. Do you think we want it published in all the papers?

LILA: Why didn't you get Oliver to go and see the boy and get it straightened out?

MRS. CRITCHFIELD: Oliver would have shot him! Wouldn't that have created a nice scandal!

LILA: Oliver wouldn't have done any such thing.

MRS. CRITCHFIELD: Then you don't think family honor means anything to your brother?

LILA: Family honor hasn't got anything to do with normal young people's emotions.

MRS. CRITCHFIELD: Normal! Emotions. It's easy to see what side of the family she gets her indecency from.

LILA: Indecency nothing! She's human that's all. Maybe a little too human. And if she gets that from the Critchfields I'm not ashamed of it.

MRS. CRITCHFIELD: No! You're all shameless.

LILA: Maybe so, but that's beside the point. Did Heavenly tell you anything else?

MRS. CRITCHFIELD: No. There haven't been any serious consequences.

LILA: Well, I'm going upstairs.

MRS. CRITCHFIELD (*desperately hopeful*): You're going to talk her out of it?

LILA: I'm not going to talk her in or out of anything. I'm going to help her decide for herself.

MRS. CRITCHFIELD: Lila!

LILA: It's the only thing to do.

MRS. CRITCHFIELD: I understand your attitude. You're doing this because you hate the Shannons.

LILA: I don't hate the Shannons. (*She goes out.*)

MRS. CRITCHFIELD (*shouting after her*): Yes, you do. You're holding a grudge! (*The doorbell rings.*) Oh, that's Arthur.

(*She pulls herself desperately together and scurries about the shabby room putting things straight. Her actions show a pathetic inability to rise above trivialities, even in a time of crisis. She switches on the light above Colonel Wayne's portrait; then she rushes into the hall and can be heard admitting Arthur in her best social manner. She ushers him into the living room talking a mile a minute to cover up her nervousness. This should be played for comedy but not farce.*)

Oh, my dear boy, it's started raining again! Your lovely white panama hat, did it get very damp? (*She enters the room followed by Arthur whose manner is very constrained.*) Oh, I think it was such a dreadful shame about last night. Susan Lamphrey'd been planning that lawn party for weeks and then the rains came along and spoiled all the nice preparations. But that's April for you! I suppose they just had to move everything indoors. Fortunately they have a very spacious downstairs—

ARTHUR (*politely disinterested*): Oh, they have.

MRS. CRITCHFIELD: Yes, that's the mahvelous thing about those old ante-bellum houses, they knew absolutely *nothing* about the economy of space. It's awfully hard to keep them warm in winter but in spring and summer I think they're simply delightful.

ARTHUR: Yes. Yes, I suppose so.

MRS. CRITCHFIELD: Oh, I often wish we hadn't given up the old Wayne plantation. The house was nearly two hundred years old. It was the most historic place in the Delta. That's Colonel Wayne's picture there on the wall.

ARTHUR: Oh, is it?

MRS. CRITCHFIELD: Yes. He led the charge up Cemetery Hill. If we'd won the war he would've been president of the Confederacy. He was a great friend of Jefferson Davis. Upstairs we have the very bed that Mr. Davis slept in when he visited our plantation. It's in Heavenly's room.

ARTHUR: Oh, is it?

MRS. CRITCHFIELD: Yes, that chair is hers, too. Mr. Critchfield's always nagging me to have things upholstered, but you know I just can't bear to change them when they're so rich in tradition and all. Sometime I'm going to have you look through our family papers, Arthur. Writers are always so interested in things like that. With your literary gifts I'm quite sure you could write some things up for me. For instance that very dramatic little episode that took place on Colonel Wayne's plantation the second year of the war when it was rumored that Sherman had crossed the border—

(*A loud crash is heard upstairs.*)

Oh, heavens, what's that? (*She pauses nervously, recovers and smiles.*) Heavenly must be romping with the dog! What were we talking about? Oh, yes of course, books! I have a cousin who writes them. Had one published. I forget just what the name of it was. (*Another loud noise is heard above.*) Oh, yes, *The Stroke of Doom*, that was it! A mystery novel based on the most remarkable coincidence that actually took place. (*The noise continues.*) Seems to me the setting was somewhere in Europe. Or was it Africa? Oh, no, it was Australia! And just think, Cousin Alfred was an invalid—he'd never been out of Mississippi in all his life! He got his information, every bit of it, out of the *Encyclopedia Britannica*.

HEAVENLY'S VOICE (*upstairs*): I won't, I tell you, I won't.

(*A door slams violently.*)

MRS. CRITCHFIELD (*in extreme agitation*): Perhaps I'd better go up and tell Heavenly that you're here— If you'll excuse me for just a moment.

ARTHUR (*rising*): Certainly, Mrs. Critchfield.

(*Mrs. Critchfield rushes out. Arthur looks keenly distressed and puzzled. After a brief interval Aunt Lila enters.*)

LILA: Good evening, young man.

ARTHUR: Oh, good evening, Miss Critchfield.

(*Lila adjusts her glasses and looks at him sharply; she touches her forehead with a handkerchief.*)

LILA: Eau de cologne—it's very refreshing when you've been through a nervous ordeal! (*She smiles.*) I've been trying to talk some sense into my niece's head. You probably wondered about that racket up there. Sit down and I'll tell you.

ARTHUR: Uh—thanks.

LILA: I haven't had much chance to get acquainted with Gale Shannon's boy. Tell me about yourself. What are you going to do, what are you planning to be? A young nincompoop all your life? (*She laughs kindly.*) No, you look too much like your father for that. I used to go out with Gale Shannon when I was a girl. He threw me over for your mother, God bless him, but he's still aces with me. (*Then she continues quite seriously and gently.*) Are you in love with Heavenly?

ARTHUR (*rising gravely*): Yes, Ma'am. I do have that misfortune.

LILA: Misfortune? I wouldn't say that!

ARTHUR: Neither would I, Ma'am, if I thought I had a chance in the world.

LILA: I think you have got a chance if you take it. But it's absolutely your last.

ARTHUR: Yes, Ma'am? What's that?

LILA: She's planning to run off with a young jackanapes that's gone to work on the river.

ARTHUR: Richard Miles?

LILA: Yes. There's nothing wrong with that boy and there's nothing wrong with Heavenly, but the two of 'em can't team together, they'd never run the same way— So if you're sure you love her and you want her there's just one thing for you to do.

ARTHUR: What's that?

LILA: Grab her and don't let her go!

ARTHUR: Grab her?

LILA: Certainly. The main reason Nature's provided you with arms, is so you can grab what you want, and by the Eternal, young man, if you don't grab things in this world you don't have a coon's chance of ever getting 'em. Do you think a drink would do you any good?

ARTHUR: Yes, Ma'am, I think it might.

LILA (*producing a bottle from the bookcase*): Take a swig of this. It's Oliver's.

ARTHUR (*taking the bottle*): That's funny.

LILA: What?

ARTHUR: Nothing much. Just a little coincidence.

LILA: Take a good one. She'll be flying down those steps in a minute—pretendin' like she's going to the Country Club. But she isn't. I know what she's got up her sleeve. She's going to ask you to drive her over to Friar's Point where that boy's gone. Don't do it. Just grab her and make her stay here. And make her like it. Heavenly's no angel, in fact she's a regular little hussy. I think she likes you better'n you think if you treat her like she needs to be treated— Here she's coming! Let me get out of here quick!

(*Aunt Lila flies out the rear door as Heavenly enters. Her eyes have a hectic brilliance. She is like some beautiful wild animal at the point of flight.*)

ARTHUR (*starting forward*): Heavenly—

HEAVENLY: What?

ARTHUR: I thought you weren't going to the Country Club.

HEAVENLY: How did you know? Did Auntie tell you?

ARTHUR (*tensely*): I thought you were going to Friar's Point—

HEAVENLY: Shhh! Mother doesn't know. So be quiet till we get outside. (*She crosses to him.*) I want you to do me a big favor, Arthur. I want you to drive me over to Friar's Point tonight— Will you?

ARTHUR: Heavenly, I— Heavenly. (*He suddenly grabs her in his arms.*)
HEAVENLY (*struggling*): What do you think you're doing?

(*Arthur kisses her wildly. She struggles to free herself, strikes at him with her fists, but he doesn't release her.*)

Stop, Arthur. You're hurting me! Don't!

(*He slightly relaxes his grip. She continues aghast.*)

You must be out of your senses, Arthur Shannon!
ARTHUR: Yes, I'm crazy. (*He kisses her again.*)
HEAVENLY: Don't Arthur. I won't stand for this!
ARTHUR: You won't?
HEAVENLY: No, I *won't.*

(*Arthur kisses her repeatedly: on the lips, throat, shoulders. Heavenly gasps for breath, stops resisting. She leans passively against him. There is a long pause.*)

ARTHUR (*in a soft anxious voice*): Heavenly, have I—hurt you, Heavenly?
HEAVENLY: No, I— I guess it doesn't matter. (*She smiles slightly.*) I really didn't think you were capable of doing anything like this.
ARTHUR: I didn't mean to do it. I was—out of my senses. (*He starts to release her.*)
HEAVENLY: No, don't let go of me. Don't let me go.
ARTHUR: You don't want me to?
HEAVENLY: No. I want to rest like this for awhile. I'm so tired. I was going to do something crazy Arthur. Going someplace where I wasn't wanted. But now I guess I don't have to. Maybe this is the answer.
ARTHUR: Heavenly, what do you mean?
HEAVENLY: I don't know yet. Give me a cigarette, please. (*He does.*) Thanks. I'll take a few drags and then I'll be able to tell you.

(*She sinks on the sofa and leans back.*)

ARTHUR: I'm sorry, Heavenly. I can't tell you how I despise myself.
HEAVENLY: Sorry, for what?

ARTHUR: For acting like an animal.

HEAVENLY: Needn't be sorry for that. That's the first thing you've done to convince me that you're a human being. I didn't think you were alive till just now. I thought you were just a sort of walking dictionary or something. I didn't think you could use your lips for anything but putting long words together. And now—well, I'm glad to find out that I was mistaken!

ARTHUR: What were you going to Friar's Point for?

HEAVENLY: I was going to marry Dick. He's gone there. We've been in love for a long time, ever since sophomore cotillion at high school about seven years ago. And you can't expect people to go on loving each other all that time without something happenin' between them.

ARTHUR: You don't need to—

HEAVENLY: Repeat the horrible confession? That's what mother called it. I told her the other day about Dick and me, but she was still anxious for me to give him up and take you. She approves of you, Arthur, and she thinks dishonesty's the best policy in love affairs— She didn't want me to tell you the awful truth.

ARTHUR: I'm glad that you did.

HEAVENLY: Why? Does it make it easier for you to forget me?

ARTHUR: No. I'd never try to do that.

HEAVENLY: Then do you still want me? Even secondhand?

ARTHUR: Yes. Anyway I can have you.

HEAVENLY: All right. (*She puts out her cigarette.*) It's all settled. Instead of marrying Dick and living on a lousy river barge, I'm going to marry Arthur Shannon and live in the biggest house in town!

ARTHUR: Heavenly, is that how you feel about it?

HEAVENLY (*gently*): No, not really—if you hadn't made love to me I would have gone to Friar's Point.

ARTHUR: But you aren't going now?

HEAVENLY: No, I'm not going now. Can you reach the light? (*He extinguishes the table lamp.*) Thanks. It's so much nicer in the dark, especially when there's rain and lightnin' outside. (*He sits beside her.*) What kind of talcum powder do you use? I like the smell of it. (*She leans on his shoulder.*) Mmmm. I like your flannel coat sleeve too. It feels nice. It's astonishing how many nice things I've found out about you, Arthur Shannon, in the last few minutes.—For God's sake, don't start talking!—When you're making love to a girl you should always be quiet because there aren't any words that are good enough to say what you mean anyhow . . .

(*The phone rings in the hall. Heavenly continues, a slight catch in her voice.*)

That's Dick calling from Friar's Point to find out whether or not I'm coming.

ARTHUR: Don't get up. Don't answer it.
HEAVENLY: Why not?
ARTHUR: Because if you do you'll never come back.
HEAVENLY: All right. I'll stay here with you. I won't move.

(*Aunt Lila can be heard answering the phone in the hall. Her voice comes indistinctly through the closed door. After a few moments she opens it and stands in the doorway. She turns on the light.*)

LILA (*with constraint*): I beg your pardon.
HEAVENLY (*laughing*): Auntie, don't be so formal. You know I've been kissed before.
LILA: I wasn't thinking of that.
HEAVENLY: Oh. What were you thinking of?
LILA: Someone just called.
HEAVENLY: For me?
LILA: No.
HEAVENLY (*sharply*): Don't be so mysterious, Auntie! What's happened?

(*Lila turns slowly to Arthur.*)

LILA: Arthur. You haven't heard about Hertha Neilson?
ARTHUR (*anxiously*): Heard *what* about her?
LILA (*after a slight pause*): She was killed last night. They found her body in the freight yards.

(*Arthur is stunned.*)

HEAVENLY: The freight yards!
LILA: Yes. It wasn't identified till an hour ago.

HEAVENLY (*looking at Arthur*): Auntie, why did you have to come in here and tell him like this?

LILA: Because that isn't all. Miss Schlagmann told me that Hertha Neilson and a young man had a violent scene of some kind in the library before it happened.

HEAVENLY: What young man? What did Miss Schlagmann say what man it was?

LILA: She didn't see him and Hertha Neilson didn't say. But maybe Arthur could tell you.

HEAVENLY: No. Leave Arthur alone. Whatever happened I'm sure it wasn't his fault.

LILA: Maybe not. But I think he ought to be prepared for what people are likely to say.

HEAVENLY: What can they say? Everybody knows the poor girl was out of her mind.

(*Arthur rises slowly and goes blindly across the room toward the French doors. Lightning glimmers through them.*)

Arthur, I know it's dreadful. But it wasn't your fault. (*She turns to Lila.*) Auntie, what are you standing there for? Please get out!

LILA: I think Arthur ought to leave now.

HEAVENLY: No. Why should he?

ARTHUR: She's right. I'll have to go.

HEAVENLY: Please, Auntie! Get out!

(*Lila exits.*)

Tell me, Arthur—was it you?

ARTHUR: Yes.

HEAVENLY: What happened?

ARTHUR: I took your advice, I got drunk. After I left you and your lover at the party, I got drunk, but I didn't go across the Sunflower like you suggested. I went to the library instead.

HEAVENLY: What happened? You'd better tell me.

ARTHUR: Oh, God. I can't. The freight yards.

HEAVENLY: Don't think about that.

ARTHUR (*verging on hysteria*): I wonder how many boxcars there were last night? Sometimes they're terribly long. Once I counted fifty-seven.

HEAVENLY: Don't, Arthur! Hold on to yourself!

ARTHUR: No wonder she was dead when they found her. Not identified till just now. How did they ever find out? Because she wasn't down at the library this morning? The Storybook Lady—the dark-haired princess in the Magic Tower. And I called her—The Carnegie Vestal—I called her that. And kissed her. And then she came alive in my arms and begged me to take her. Because she was like I was, lonely and hungry, and I—I lost my desire. I told her that she was disgusting—

HEAVENLY: You didn't do that!

ARTHUR: Yes.

HEAVENLY: That was cruel.

ARTHUR: Yes. And after that she screamed. And I ran out the door and all I could hear for blocks and blocks was that screaming. And then it was quiet. Nothing but rain on my face. I was glad that I'd gotten away. And then a funny thing happened. (*He turns slowly toward Heavenly.*) I came to an alley. It was in back of your house. It was filled with the fresh smell of roses. I went sort of crazy. Covered my face with those flowers and whispered your name. (*He turns away.*) And I guess about that time Hertha was standing out in the freight yards with the rain on her face, too—and the engine's light in her eyes, screaming— We were driving that engine last night, Heavenly, you and me.

HEAVENLY: No.

ARTHUR: We were inside those boxcars, we were the ones that killed her.

HEAVENLY: No. Arthur. You couldn't help it that you loved me instead of her.

ARTHUR: Loved you—yes—I told her that. She climbed up the hill and stood between the two dead trees and said she was one of them now. I was too full of myself to know what she meant or to care.

HEAVENLY: That's natural. We're all of us full of ourselves. (*She kisses him.*)

ARTHUR: How can you stand to do that?

HEAVENLY: Because I want to. It's funny how I feel toward you now. So much diff'rent. (*She clings to him.*) You've done me a favor tonight. You've taught me something very important about the nature of love. It's our bodies we love with mostly. When you kissed me just now, I could have believed it was him, Dick— It gave me the same sensation, exactly the same— You've made me love you, Arthur.

ARTHUR: How can you talk about *us* after what's happened?

HEAVENLY: Because I was bo'n twice as old as you are an' you'll never catch up.

(*She goes over to the sofa and switches off the small light above Colonel Wayne's portrait. Her voice is low.*)

Come over here and be quiet.

ARTHUR: No. Your aunt was right. I've got to leave here.

HEAVENLY: Why should you leave?

ARTHUR: Don't you see why? There'll be an investigation and they'll find things out. I'll be disgraced. I'll have to leave town.

HEAVENLY: You're afraid of people?

ARTHUR: Not so much as I'm afraid of myself. I've committed murder and I can't stay here at the scene of the crime. It would hound me.

HEAVENLY: Then take me away with you. I don't want to stay here either.

ARTHUR: I can't take you with me. I've got to be off by myself for awhile. With strangers, Heavenly. They're—they're a sort of—catharsis. Like cold water on your face and hands. They make you feel clean. Whenever I touched you now it would be like dipping my hands in her blood.

HEAVENLY: Arthur. Don't say that.

ARTHUR: It would.—I'm sorry, Heavenly. I'll come back later if you still want me.

HEAVENLY: No. If you leave me now I'll hate you. I'll never want to see you again.

ARTHUR: Maybe that would be a good thing. (*He moves toward the hall.*)

HEAVENLY (*desperately*): You're a coward. You're running away.

ARTHUR (*dully*): Yes. That's a habit of mine.

HEAVENLY: You can't leave me now! (*She follows him to the hall door.*)

ARTHUR: Good-bye, Heavenly.

HEAVENLY (*wildly*): You can't say that, too! *Arthur!*

(*The door is heard closing. Heavenly is in bewildered agony.*)

Oh—

(*Heavenly wanders back to the middle of the room, her eyes dull and exhausted. After a moment Lila comes quietly in.*)

LILA: He's gone?
HEAVENLY: Yes. They've both gone.
LILA: Are you going to Richard?
HEAVENLY: No, he doesn't want me either. He's got what he wanted. But maybe someday he'll want me again. Or maybe Arthur will. I don't know. I'll have to wait and see.

(*She moves slowly toward the hall.*)

LILA: Where are you going?

(*Heavenly turns in the doorway and stares vacantly into space.*)

HEAVENLY: I'm going out and sit on the front porch till one of them comes back.

Curtain

NOT ABOUT NIGHTINGALES

This play is dedicated to the memory
of Clarence Darrow, The Great Defender,
whose mental frontiers were the
four corners of the sky.

OPENING

The action takes place in a large American prison during the summer of 1938. The conditions which the play presents are those of no particular prison but a composite picture of many.

LOUD-SPEAKER: Yeah, this is the Lorelei excursion steamer, All-day trip around Sandy Point. Leave 8 A.M., return at Midnight. Sight-seeing, dancing, entertainment with Lorelei Lou and her eight Lorelights! Got your ticket, lady? Got your ticket? Okay, that's all. We're shoving off now. Now we're leaving the boat dock, folks. We're out in the harbor. Magnificent skyline of the city against the early morning sunlight. It's still a little misty around the tops of the big towers downtown. Hear those bells ringing? That's St. Patrick's Cathedral. Finest chimes in America. It's eight o'clock sharp. Sun's bright as a dollar, swell day, bright, warm, makes you mighty proud to be alive, yes, Ma'am! There it is! You can see it now, folks. That's the Island. Sort of misty still. See them big stone walls. Dynamite-proof, escape-proof! Thirty-five hundred men in there, folks, and lots of 'em 'll never get out! Boy, oh, boy, I wonder how it feels t' be locked up in a place like that till doomsday? Oh, oh!! There goes the band, folks! Dancing on the Upper Deck! Dancing, folks! Lorelei Lou and her eight Lorelights! Dancing on the Upper Deck—dancing!—Dancing!—Dancing . . . (*Fade.*)

(*Flash forward to end of play. Light fades except for a spot on Eva, clutching Jim's shoes.*)

LOUD-SPEAKER: Aw, there it is! You can see it now, folks. That's the Island! Sort of misty tonight. You'd see it better if there was a moon. Those walls are dynamite-proof, escape-proof— Thirty-five hundred men in there—some won't get out till Doomsday.—There's the band!—Dancing on the Upper Deck, folks! Lorelei Lou and her eight Lorelights! Dancing—dancing—dancing . . . (*Fade.*)

(*Music comes up. The shoes fall from Eva's hands, and she covers her face.*)

Blackout

ACT ONE

EPISODE ONE

Announcer: "Miss Crane Applies for a Job"

A spot lights the bench outside the Warden's office where Mrs. Bristol is sitting. Mrs. B is a worn matron in black, holding a napkin-covered basket on her lap. Eva enters the spot from the right and sits on the bench, nervously. She grips her pocketbook tensely and stares straight ahead.

MRS. B: Your hat!
EVA: My hat?
MRS. B: Yes, look!
EVA: Oh, dear!
MRS. B: Here.
EVA: Thanks!

(*Mrs. Bristol removes a spot from Eva's hat with tissue paper from her basket.*)

MRS. B: It's those pigeons, the little rascals!
EVA: Yes, they're much too casual about such things.
MRS. B: It's such a nice hat, too.
EVA: Oh, it's quite old. (*She puts the hat back on and drops her purse.*)
MRS. B: You're nervous.
EVA: So nervous I could scream!
MRS. B: Is it your husband?
EVA: Who?
MRS. B: That you're coming to see about?
EVA: Oh, no. No I'm coming to see about a job.
MRS. B: A job? Here?
EVA: Yes, here. I've heard there's a vacancy.
MRS. B: But wouldn't you find it an awfully depressing sort of place to work in?
EVA: I don't think so. It's not an ordinary prison.
MRS. B: Isn't it?
EVA: No, it's supposed to be a model institution.
MRS. B: A model institution!

EVA: Yes, everything's done scientifically they say. They've got experts—in psychology and sociology and things like that, you know!

MRS. B: Well!

EVA: The old idea used to be punishment of crime but nowadays it's—social rehabilitation!

MRS. B: Now just imagine! How did you come to know?

EVA: I read all about it in the *Sunday Supplement*!

(*Jim passes across the spot.*)

EVA (*jumping up*): May I see the Warden?

JIM: Sorry. He's not back yet. (*He crosses into the door of the office.*)

EVA: Oh.

MRS. B: I've got a son in here. He used to be a sailor. Jack's his name.

EVA: A sailor?

MRS. B: Yes, he was one of Uncle Sam's Navy-boys. Till he got in trouble with some kind of woman.

EVA: What a shame!

MRS. B: Yes, wasn't it though—the common slut!—Excuse me but that's what she was. My Scott! (*She clutches her bosom.*)

EVA: What?

MRS. B: I've got the most awful palpitations!

EVA (*jumping up*): You're sick? Let me get you some water!

MRS. B: No, thanks, dear. I'll just take one of my phenobarbital tablets, and I'll be all right in a jiffy. (*Stage business.*) I've been under such a strain lately with Jack on my mind all the time.

EVA: You shouldn't be worried. My landlady's brother-in-law is one of the guards—it was through him that I heard about this vacancy—and he says they have less serious trouble here than any penitentiary in the country. Mr. Whalen, the Warden, is very highly respected.

MRS. B: Well, I do hope you're right for Jack's sake. But I haven't gotten much comfort out of his letters. Especially the last one. It was that one which upset me so. It wasn't at all like those long marvelous letters that he used to write me when he was at sea. It was scribbled in such a bad hand

and—well—it sounded sort of—*feverish* to me!—What is Klondike?

EVA: Klondike? Part of Alaska!

MRS. B: That's what I thought. But in Jack's letter he said he'd been sent down there and it was as hot as—well, I won't say it!

EVA: Possibly it's one of those colonization schemes.

MRS. B: No, I don't think so. In fact I'm positive it isn't. He said they wouldn't let him write me about it if they knew, so he was sneakin' the letter out by one of the boys.

EVA: How long does he have to stay here?

MRS. B: Five years!

EVA: Oh, that's not so long.

MRS. B: It seems like forever to me.

EVA: He'll probably come out a better and stronger boy than before he went in.

MRS. B: Oh no. They couldn't make a better and stronger boy than Jack was. I don't understand all about it, but I know one thing—whatever happened it wasn't my boy's fault!—And that's what I'm going to say to the Warden soon as I get in to see him—I've been waiting here two days—he never has time!

EVA (*rising*): I can't stand waiting. It makes me too nervous. I'm going right in and make that young fellow tell me when Mr. Whalen will be here.

MRS. B: Yes, do! Tell him how long I've been waiting! And ask him if Jack—

(*Eva has already entered office—Mrs. B sinks slowly down, clutching her bosom.*)

Oh, dear . . .

(*The spot moves from the bench to the interior of the office.*)

EVA (*at the door*): I beg your pardon.

JIM (*giving her a long look*): For what?

EVA: For intruding like this. But I couldn't sit still any longer. When can I see Mr. Whalen?

JIM: What about?

EVA: A job.

(*Jim is filing papers in a cabinet. He continues all the while.*)

JIM: He's out right now. Inspecting the grounds.

EVA: Oh. Will it take him long?

JIM: That depends on how much grounds he feels like inspecting.

EVA: Oh.

JIM: Sometimes inspecting the grounds doesn't mean inspecting the grounds. (*He gives her a brief smile.*)

EVA: Doesn't it?

JIM: No. (*He crumples a paper.*) Sometimes it's an idiomatic expression for having a couple of beers in the back room at Tony's which is a sort of unofficial clubhouse for the prison staff— Would you like to sit down?

EVA: About how long do you suppose I'd have to wait?

JIM: It's a hot afternoon. He might do a lot of ground-inspection and then again he might not. His actions are pretty unpredictable. That's a good word.

EVA: What?

JIM: Unpredictable. Anything with five syllables is a good word.

EVA: You like long words?

JIM: They're my stock-in-trade. I'm supposed to use a lot of 'em to impress you with my erudition. There's another one right there!

EVA: Erudition?

JIM: Yes, only four but it's unusual. I get 'em all out of this big book.

EVA: Dictionary?

JIM: *Webster's Unabridged.* (*He slams the file cabinet shut and leans against it.*) Y'see I'm one of the exhibition pieces.

EVA: Are you really?

JIM: I'm supposed to tell you that when I came in here I was just an ordinary grifter. But look at me now. I'm reading Spengler's *Decline of the West* and I'm editor of the prison monthly. Ask me what is an archaeopteryx.

EVA: What is it?

JIM: An extinct species of reptile-bird. Here's our latest issue.

EVA (*more and more confused*): Of—what?

JIM: *The Archaeopteryx.* Our monthly publication.

EVA: Why do you call it that?

JIM: It sounds impressive. Do you know what an amaranth is?

EVA: No. What is it?

JIM: A flower that never dies. (*He lifts a book.*) I came across it in here. One of the classical poets compares it to love. What's your opinion of that.

EVA: Well, I—what's yours?

JIM: I wouldn't know. I started my present career at the age of sixteen.

EVA: That early.

JIM: Yes, the usual case of bad influences. And at that age of course—love is something you dream about and blush when you look at yourself in the mirror next morning! (*He laughs. Eva looks away in slight confusion.*) Say, d'you know that song?

EVA: What song?

JIM (*giving a sour imitation*): "Ah, tis love and love alone the world is seeking!" A guy sang it in chapel last night— Is that on the level?

EVA: Well, I—not exactly.

JIM: You're inclined to admit a few qualifications?

EVA: Yes. For instance what I'm seeking is a job. And a new pair of stockings.

JIM: Those look good to me.

EVA: They're worn to shreds!

JIM: Well, perhaps I'm prejudiced.

(*Eva clears her throat. Jim clears his.*)

EVA (*picking up the newspaper*): "Prison: the door to Opportunity!"

JIM: Yes, that's one of my best editorials. It's been reproduced all over the country—I got ten years of copper for writing that.

EVA: Copper?

JIM: Not what they make pennies out of. In here copper means good time. Time off your sentence for good behavior. I've got about ten years of copper stashed away in the files and most of it's for extolling the inspirational quality of prison life—

(*Mrs. Bristol enters timidly, clutching her basket.*)

JIM: Hello.

MRS. B: How do you do. Is Mr. Whalen in yet?

JIM: No, he's still out inspecting the grounds.

MRS. B: Oh, I do so want to see him this afternoon. I'm—I'm Jack Bristol's mother.

JIM: Sailor Jack?

MRS. B (*advancing a few steps*): Yes—yes! You—know him?

JIM: Slightly.

MRS. B (*struggling to speak*): How is my boy?

JIM: Sorry. I'm not allowed to give out information.

MRS. B: Oh.

JIM: You'd better talk to Mr. Whalen tomorrow morning.

MRS. B: What time, please?

JIM: Ten o'clock.

MRS. B: Ten o'clock. Could you give him these now? (*She places the basket carefully on the table.*) I'm afraid they'll get stale if they're kept any longer. They're for my boy. (*She turns slowly and goes out.*)

EVA: Couldn't you tell her something to relieve her mind?

JIM: Not about Sailor Jack!

EVA: Why not?

JIM: He's gone—stir bugs.

EVA: You mean?

JIM (*touching his forehead*): Cracked up in here. It's sort of an occupational disease among convicts.

EVA: But they said in the *Sunday Supplement*—

JIM: I know. They interviewed me and the Warden.

EVA: You didn't tell them the truth?

JIM: What is it that Plato said about truth? Truth is—truth is— Funny I can't remember! Was it the *Sunday Supplement* that gave you the idea of getting a job in here?

EVA: That and my landlady. Her brother-in-law is Mr. McBurney, one of the prison guards.

JIM: Mac's a pretty good screw.

EVA: What?

JIM: That means a guard in here. Here's one of our sample menus. It shows what a connie gets to eat every day. You can see that it compares quite favorably with the bill-of-fare at any well-known boarding school. Everything's done scientifically here. We have an expert dietitian. Weighs everything by calories. Units of body heat— Hello, Mr. Whalen!

(*Whalen enters. He is a powerful man, rather stout, but with coarse good looks.*)

WARDEN: Hello, hello there! (*He removes his coat and tosses it to Jim.*) Breezy day, hot breezy day! (*He winks at Jim, then belches.*) Too much ground-inspection! (*He loosens his collar and tie.*) Excuse me, lady, I'm going to do a striptease! Yep, it's a mighty wind—feels like it comes out of an oven! Reminds me of those—(*He wipes his forehead.*)—those beautiful golden-brown biscuits my mother used to bake! What's this? (*He removes the cover from the basket.*) Speak of biscuits and what turns up but a nice batch of homemade cookies! Have one, young lady—Jimmy boy!

(*Jim takes two.*)

Uh-h, you've got an awful big paw, Jimmy! (*He laughs.*) Show the new Arky-what's-it to Miss *Daily News*—or is it the *Morning Star*? Have a chair! I'll be right with you—(*He vanishes for a moment into the inner room.*) Sweat, sweat, sweat's all I do these hot breezy days!

JIM (*sotto voce*): He thinks you're a newspaper woman.

WARDEN (*emerging*): Turn on that fan. Well, now, let's see—

EVA: To begin with I'm not—

WARDEN: You've probably come here to question me about that ex-convict's story in that damned yellow sheet down there in Wilkes County— That stuff about getting pellagra in here— Jimmy, hand me that sample menu!

JIM: She's not a reporter.

WARDEN: Aw.—What *is* your business, young lady?

EVA (*in breathless haste*): I understand that there's a vacancy here. Mr. McBurney, my landlady's brother-in-law, told her that you were needing a new stenographer, and I'm sure that I can qualify for the position. I'm a college graduate, Mr. Whalen. I've had three years of business experience—references with me—but, oh—I've—I've had such abominable luck these last six months—the last place I worked—the business recession set in—they had to cut down on their salesforce—they gave me a wonderful letter— I've got it with me— (*She opens her purse and spills its contents on the floor.*) Oh, goodness! I've—broken my glasses!

WARDEN: (*coldly*): Yeah?

EVA (*rising slowly*): Could you give me a job?—Please, I'm—terribly nervous, I—if I don't get a job soon I'll—

WARDEN: What? Go off the deep end?

EVA: Yes, something like that! (*She smiles desperately.*)

WARDEN: Well, Miss—uh—

EVA (*eagerly*): Crane! Eva Crane!

WARDEN: They call that window the "Quick Way Out"! It's the only one in the house without bars. I don't need bars. It's right over the bay. So if it's suicide you got in mind that window is at your disposal. No, Miss Crane. Next time you apply for a job don't pull a sob story. What your business executive is interested in is your potential value, not your—your personal misfortunes! (*He takes a cigar.*)

EVA (*turning away*): I see. Then I—

WARDEN: Hold on a minute.

EVA: Yes?

WARDEN (*biting and spitting out the end of the cigar*): There's just one prerequisite for a job in this office. Jimmy will explain that to you.

EVA (*turning to Jim*): Yes?

JIM: The ability to keep your mouth shut except when you're given specific instructions to speak!

WARDEN: Think you could do that?

EVA: Yes.

JIM: The motorboat leaves the dock at seven forty-five in the morning.

EVA: Thanks— Yes, *thanks!* (*She turns quickly and goes out, blind with joy.*)

WARDEN: What do you think of her, Jimmy boy? Okay, huh?

JIM: Yes, Sir.

WARDEN: Yes, Siree! Dizzy as hell— But she's got a shape on her that would knock the bricks out of a Federal Pen! (*He erupts in sudden booming laughter.*)

Dim Out

EPISODE TWO

Announcer: "Sailor Jack."

Musical theme up: "Auprès de ma Blonde." Fade.

There is a spot on a cell. Electric lights from the corridor throw the shadow of bars across floor. The cell is empty except for the figure of Sailor Jack, slumped on a stool with the shadow of bars thrown across him. His face has the vacant look of the schizophrenic, and he is mumbling inaudibly to himself. His voice rises—

SAILOR JACK: Where? Port Said!—And not one of 'em but woulda done it 'emselves if they'd 'ad ha'f a chance. (*He begins to sing hoarsely.*)

Auprès de ma blonde
Il fait bon, fait bon, fait bon!
Auprès de ma blonde
qu'il fait bon dormir!

No chance for advancement, huh? What would you say if I told you that I was Admiral of the whole bitchin' navy? (*He laughs.*)

Je donnerai Versailles,
Paris et Saint Denis—

(*Sounds are heard: a shrill whistle in hall and the shuffle of feet: the door of the cell clangs open and Joe, Butch, and the Queen enter.*)

SCHULTZ: Lights out in five minutes.

BUTCH: Ahh, yuh fruit, go toot yuh goddam horn outa here. Mus' think they runnin' a stinkin' sweatshop, this workin' overtime stuff. Git yuh task done or come back after supper. Goddam machine got stuck. Delib'rate sabotage, he calls it. I'd like to sabotage his guts. (*To Queen.*): What happened to you this mornin'?

QUEEN (*in a high tenor voice*): I got an awful pain in the back of my neck and flipped out. When I come to I was in the hospital. They was stickin' a needle in my arm— Say! What does plus four mean?

JOE: Christ! It means—

BUTCH: Pocket yuh marbles!

QUEEN: Naw. Is it bad?

JOE: We're in swell sassiety, Butch. A lunatic an' a case of the syph!

QUEEN: The syph?

(*A whistle is heard: the lights dim in the corridor.*)

QUEEN: Naw! (*He tries to laugh.*) It don't mean that!

SAILOR: *Auprès de ma blonde*
Il fait bon, fait bon, fait bon!
Auprès de ma blonde—

SCHULTZ: Cut the cackle in there! It's after lights.

BUTCH: God damn it, can't you see he's blown his top?

JOE: Yeah, get him out of here!

SCHULTZ: He's putting on an act.

SAILOR: *Je donnerai Versailles,*
Paris et Saint Denis—

SCHULTZ: You take another trip to Klondike, Sailor, it won't be on a round-trip ticket!

BUTCH: It's Klondike that got him like this. He's been ravin' ever since you brung him upstairs. You must've cooked the brains out of him down there, Schultz.

SAILOR: *La Tour d'Eiffel aussi!*

SCHULTZ (*rapping the bars*): Dummy up, the lot of you! One more squawk an' I'll call the strong-arm squad!

QUEEN: Mr. Schultz!

SCHULTZ: Yeah?

QUEEN: What does plus four mean?

(*Schultz laughs and moves off.*)

BUTCH: If I wasn't scared of losin' all my copper I'd reach through and grab that bastard. I'd rattle them pea-pod brains of his 'n roll 'em out on the floor like a pair of dice. The trouble is in here you gotta pick your man. If I rubbed out a screw I'd never git a chance at the boss.—What time is it?

JOE: Ten-thirty.

BUTCH: Mac comes on duty now.

JOE: You think he'll take the Sailor out?

BUTCH: I'll tell him to.

QUEEN: Naw. It's nothin' that serious or they woulda kept me in the hospital. It's just indigestion. That's what I told 'em, I said the food is no good. It don't set good on my stomach. Spaghetti, spaghetti, spaghetti! I said I'm sicka spaghetti!

SAILOR: *Auprès de ma blonde*
Il fait bon, fait bon, fait bon!
Auprès de ma blonde
qu'il fait bon dormir!

(*Butch clips him with a fist.*)

JOE: What did you do that for?

BUTCH: You wanta tangle with the strong-arm squadron on account of him?

(*A whistle is heard: doors clang.*)

They're changin' now. (*He goes to the bars.*) Who's 'at? McBurney?

MAC: What do you want, Butch?

BUTCH: For Chrissakes git this kid outta here.

MAC: Which kid?

BUTCH: Sailor Jack. He's been stir-bugs since they brung him upstairs a week ago Tuesday.

MAC (*at the door*): What's he doing?

BUTCH: He's out right now. I had to conk him one.

MAC: What did they tell you about roughin' up the boys?

BUTCH: Roughin'? ME? Lissen!—Ask Joe, ask anybody, ask the Canary—the kid had blown his top—Schultz was gonna call the strong-arm squad an' have us all thrown in Klondike cause he wouldn't quit singin' them dirty French songs! Ain't that right, Joe?

JOE: Sure, Mac.

(*Whistle.*)

MAC: Where's his stuff?

BUTCH: Here. I got it tied up nice.

MAC: Well, it's no put-in of mine. He should've done his task in the shop.
BUTCH: He done his task pretty good.
JOE: That boy worked hard.
MAC: Not hard enough to suit the Boss.

(*Enter guards.*)

Awright, git him outta here. Put him in isolation tonight an' have him looked after tomorrow.
QUEEN: Mr. McBurney, what does plus four mean? Mr. McBurney—

(*Mac goes out with guards carrying Sailor. Bird calls are heard in the hall.*)

VOICE (*in hall*): Goodnight, Mac.
MAC: G'night, Jim.
BUTCH: Who's 'at? Allison?
JOE: Yeah. It's the Canary.
SAILOR (*from down the hall*): *"Auprès de ma blonde Il fait bon, fait bon, fait bon!"*

(*The sound fades.*)

BUTCH: Hey, Canary! Allison!

(*The spot shifts to include Allison's cell.*)

JIM: What do you want, Butch? (*He is shown removing his shirt and shoes.*)
BUTCH: Next time you're in a huddle with the boss tell him the Angels in Hall C have put another black mark on his name for Sailor Jack.
JIM: I'll tell him that.
BUTCH: Tell him some day we're going to appoint a special committee of one to come down there an' settle up the score.—You hear me, Stool?
JIM: I hear you.
BUTCH: Just think—I used to be cell-mates with him. I lie awake at night regrettin' all the times I had a chance to split his guts—but didn't!
JOE: Why didn'tcha?

BUTCH: That was before he started workin' for the boss. But now he's number three on the Angel's Records. First Whalen, then Schultz, and then the Stool! You hear that, Stool?

JIM: Yes, I hear you, Butch. (*He rolls and lights a cigarette.*)

BUTCH: That's good. I'm glad you do.

JIM: I know you're glad.

JOE: What's he say?

BUTCH: He says he knows I'm glad.

JOE: He oughta know. Wonder he don't go stir-bugs, too. Nobody have nothin' to do with him but Ollie.

BUTCH: He'll blow his top sometime, if I don't git him first. You hear that, Stool? I said you'll blow your top sometime like Sailor Jack—I'm lookin' forward to it.

JOE: What's he say?

BUTCH: Nothin'. He's smokin' in there.

JOE: We oughta tip 'em off.

BUTCH: Naw, I never ratted on nobody. Not even that Stool.

QUEEN: Allison! Hey! Jim! What does plus four mean?

JIM: Who's got plus four?

QUEEN: I have. What does it mean, Jim?

JIM: It means your physical condition is four points above perfect.

QUEEN (*relieved*): Aw. These bastards had me worried.

BUTCH (*climbing on a stool by the window*): Foghorns. It's thick as soup outside— Lissen!

JOE: What?

BUTCH: Excursion steamer.

JOE: Which one?

BUTCH: The Lorelei.

JOE: Lookit them lights on her, will yuh. Red, white, green, yellow!

BUTCH: Hear that orchester?

JOE: What're they playin'?

BUTCH: "Roses a Picardy!"

JOE: That's an old one.

BUTCH: It come up the year I got sent up. Why, I remember dancin' to that piece. At the Princess Ballroom. With Goldie. She requested that number ev'ry time I took her out on the floor. We danced there the night they pinched me. On the way out—right at the turn-stile—them six bulls met me—six of 'em—that's how many it took—they had the wagon waitin' at the curb.

JOE: Last time it was four bulls. You're gettin' less conservative, Butch.

BUTCH: "Roses a Picardy." I'd like to dance that number one more time. With Goldie.

JOE: Maybe it was her that put the finger on you.

BUTCH: Naw. Not Goldie. I bet that girl's still holdin' the torch for me.

JOE: Keep your illusions, Butch, if they're a comfort to yuh. But I bet if Goldie was still holdin' all the torches that she's held before an' after you got put in the stir she'd throw more light across the water than a third-alarm fire!

QUEEN: Where's my manicure set?

BUTCH: I wonder if a guy is any good at sixty?

JOE: What do you mean?

BUTCH: You know. With women.

JOE: I guess it depends on the guy.

BUTCH: I'll still be good. But twenty years is a lot of time to wait.

QUEEN: Has anybody seen my manicure set?

BUTCH: You know there's a window in Boss Whalen's office from which a guy could jump right into the Bay.

JOE: Yeah. The Quick Way Out.

BUTCH: I was thinkin' that it would be a good way to kill two birds with a stone. Rub him out an' jump through that window for the getaway. Providin' you could swim. But me I can't swim a goddam stroke. I wish that I'd learned how before I come in here.

JOE: Wouldn't do you no good. Nobody's ever swum it yet.

BUTCH: I'd like to try.—They say some people swim instinctive like a duck.

JOE: You'd take a chance on that?

BUTCH: Naw. I'm scared a water.

QUEEN (*excitedly*): I put it here last night. Butch, did you see it?

BUTCH: What?

QUEEN: My manicure set.

BUTCH: It's gone out wit' the slop-bucket.

QUEEN: What did you do that for?

BUTCH: It stunk up the place. Smelt like rotten bananas— What's this on Sailor Jack's bunk?

JOE: A package a letters from his ole lady.

BUTCH: Aw.

JOE: She said she was comin' from Wisconsin to see him in the last one.

QUEEN: All my life I've been persecuted by people because I'm refined.

BUTCH: Somebody oughta told her how the Sailor is.

JOE: Well, she'll find out.

QUEEN: Because I'm sensitive I been persecuted all my life!

BUTCH: Yeah, she'll find out.

QUEEN: Sometimes I wish I was dead. Oh, Lord, Lord, Lord! I wish I was dead!

(*Musical theme up. Fade.*)

Blackout

EPISODE THREE

Announcer: "The Prognosis"

A spot comes up on the Warden's office. He's looking at a racing form-sheet when Eva Crane, his secretary, enters.

WARDEN (*lifting the phone and dialing*): How's the track, Bert? Fast? Okay. I want twenty bucks on Windy Blue to show. (*He hangs up.*) Anybody outside?

EVA: Yes. That woman.

WARDEN: What woman?

EVA: The one from Wisconsin. She's still waiting—

WARDEN: I told you I— (*Sailor Jack's mother has quietly entered. She carries a neatly wrapped bundle in brown paper— she smiles diffidently at the Warden.*)

MRS. B: I beg your pardon, I—I took the liberty of coming in. I hope you won't mind. You see I'm Jack Bristol's mother and I've been wanting to have a talk with you so long about—about my boy!

WARDEN: Set down. I'm pretty short on time.

MRS. B: I won't take much. To begin with, Mr. Whalen, I never felt the jury did exactly right in giving Jack three years. But that's done now. I've got to look to the future.

WARDEN: Yes, the future—that's right.

MRS. B: I haven't heard from Jack lately. He'd been writing me once a week till just lately.

WARDEN: Lots of boys get careless about their correspondence.

MRS. B: For two years not a week passed without a letter. Then suddenly just a month ago they stopped coming. Naturally I felt rather anxious.

WARDEN: Jim!

JIM: Yes, sir?

WARDEN: Check on a boy named Bristol.

MRS. B: Thank you, I—I came all the way from Wisconsin.

WARDEN: Long trip, huh? Wisconsin's where they make all that fine cheese.

MRS. B: Yes, we're very proud of our dairy products up there. (*She looks anxiously after Jim who has gone slowly to the file-case as though stalling for time.*)

WARDEN: They manufacture the best cheese this side of Switzerland. Yes, Siree!

MRS. B: Jack's last letter was strange. I—I have it with me. It's not at all like Jack. He wasn't transferred to any other prison, was he? Because he kept complaining all through his letter about how terribly hot it was in a place called Klondike. His penmanship has always been quite irregular but this was so bad I could scarcely read it at all—I thought possibly he wasn't well when he wrote it—feverish, you know—he's very subject to colds especially this time of year. I—I brought this wool comforter with me. For Jack. I know it's not easy, Mr. Whalen, to make exceptions in an institution like this. But in Jack's case where there are so many, *many* considerations—so much that I regret *myself* when I look back at things— Mistakes that I made—

WARDEN: Mistakes, yes, we all make mistakes.

MRS. B: Such *grave* mistakes, Mr. Whalen. Our household was not an altogether happy one, you see. Jack's father—well, he was a Methodist minister and his views naturally differed quite a bit from most young boys'—

WARDEN (*with a cynical smile.*): A preacher's son?

MRS. B: Yes! But there was a disagreement among the congregation not long ago and my husband was forced to retire.

WARDEN (*impatiently*): I see. I'm very busy, I— (*To Jim.*): Have you found that card?

JIM (*stalling*): Not yet.

MRS. B: He was so—so uncompromising, even with poor Jack. So Jack left home. Of course it was against my wishes but— (*She opens her bag and produces sheaf of letters.*) Oh, those long marvelous letters that he wrote! If you would only read them you'd see for yourself what an exceptional boy Jack was. Port Said, Marseilles, Cairo, Shanghai, Bombay! "Oh, mother, it's so big, so terribly, terribly big," he kept on writing. As though he'd tried to squeeze it in his heart until the bigness of it made this heart crack open! Look! These envelopes! You see they're packed so full that he could hardly close them! Pictures of places, too! Elephants in India. They're used like packhorses, he said, for common labor. Little Chinese junkets have square sails. They scoot about like dragonflies on top of the water. The bay at Rangoon. Here's where the sun comes up like thunder, he wrote on the back of this one! Kipling, you know— I wrote him constantly—"Jack, there's no advancement in it. A sailor's always a sailor. Get out of it, son. Get into the Civil Service!" He wrote me back—"I kept the middle watch last night. You see more stars down here than in the northern water. The Southern Cross is right above me now, but won't be long—because our course is changing—" I stopped opposing then, I thought that anything he loved as much as that would surely keep him safe. And then he didn't write a while—until this came. I still can't understand it! He mentioned a girl— He said it wasn't his fault, I know that it wasn't—If I could convince you of that—!

WARDEN: It's no use ma'am! You might as well be talking to the moon. He's had his chance.

MRS. B: But in Jack's case—!

WARDEN: I know, I know. I've heard all that before. Jim, have you found that card?

JIM (*coming slowly forward with a card from files*): You'd better look at it yourself.

WARDEN: Read it, read it! We running a social service bureau?

(*Jim looks uncertainly at Mrs. Bristol who raises a clenched hand to her breast.*)

MRS. B (*softly*): If anything's gone wrong I'd like to know.

JIM (*reading huskily*): "Jack Bristol. Larceny. Convicted May, 1936. Sentenced three years." (*Looks up.*) He slacked his work. Spent three days in Klondike.

WARDEN (*sharply*): Is that on the card?

JIM: No, but I wanted to explain to this lady what happened.

MRS. B: (*rising slowly*): What happened?

JIM: You see, ma'am—

WARDEN (*sharply*): Read what's on the card, that's all!

JIM: "Came up before the lunacy commission, May 1938, transferred to the psychopathic ward. Violent. Delusions. Prognosis—Dementia Praecox"—

(*Pause.*)

MRS. B: That isn't—Jack—my boy!

WARDEN: Now see here—I— (*He motions to Jim to get her out.*) I know how you feel about this. I got all the sympathy in the world for you women that come in here, but this is a penal institution and we simply can't be taking time out from our routine business for things like this.

MRS. B: My boy, Jack, my boy! Not what you said! Anything but that! Say he's dead, say you killed him, killed him! But don't tell me that. I know, I know. I know how it was in here. He wrote me letters. The food not decent. I tried to send him food—he didn't get it—no, even that you took from him. That place you sent him three days. Klondike. I know— You tortured him there, that's what you did, you tortured him until you drove him— (*She turns slowly to

Jim.) —Crazy? Is that what you said?—Oh, my precious Jesus, oh, my God! (*She breaks down, sobbing wildly.*)

WARDEN: Get that woman out!

(*Jim assists her to the door.*)

Whew! (*He lights a cigar and picks up the form-sheet.*)

Blackout

EPISODE FOUR

Announcer: "Conversations at Midnight!"

The spot lights the two cells with a partition between. Ollie kneels praying by his bunk. Butch lounges, covertly smoking, on a bench along the wall. The others sit on their bunks.

OLLIE (*in an audible whisper*): Oh, Lawd, de proteckter an preserbation ob all, remebuh dis nigguh. Remebuh his wife Susie an his six chillun, Rachel, Rebekah, Solomon, Moses, Ecclesiastics an' Deuteronomy Jackson. You look out fo' dem while Ise in jail. An ah'd git out fo de cole weathuh sets in cause Susie's gonna have another baby, Lawd, an' she can't git aroun't' gatherin' kindlin' wood. God bless my ole woman an' daddy an' Presiden' Roosevelt an' de W.P.A. in Jesus Chris' name—Amen. (*He rises stiffly.*)

BUTCH (*grinning*): Hey, Ollie, yuh better have 'em reverse the charges on that one!

OLLIE: It don' cos' nothin'.

BUTCH: It ain't worth nothin'.

OLLIE: De Lawd remembuhs who remembuhs Him.

BUTCH: Hawshit!

(*Ollie sits dejectedly on the edge of his bunk. There are derisive whistles and bird-calls in the hall as Jim enters.*)

JIM: Whatsamatter, Ollie?

OLLIE (*jerking his thumb at Butch's cell*): He says there ain't no God.

JIM: How's he know?

OLLIE: That's what I say.

(*Jim removes his shirt and swabs sweat off his face and chest with it, then pitches it into the corner. He picks up a naked art magazine and fans himself with it.*)

OLLIE: You think they is, don't you, Jim?

JIM: Somebody upstairs?—I dunno. I guess I'm what they call an agnostic.

OLLIE: You mean a Piscopalian?

JIM: Yeah. Rub my back for me, Ollie. I'm tired.

OLLIE: Awright. Liniment aw bacon grease?

JIM: Gimme the liniment.

BUTCH: Haven't you started seein' 'em yet, Canary?

JIM (*as Ollie starts to rub*): Gawd, it burns good.

BUTCH: Them little blue devils, they're the first symptom.

JIM: It makes the air feel cool.

BUTCH: They crawl in through the bars an' sit on the end of yuh bunk an' make faces at yuh.

JIM: Rub harder on the left shoulder.

BUTCH: Yuh'd better start sleepin' with one eye open, Canary. Can yuh do that?

JIM: Never tried it, Butch.—Ah, that's good.

BUTCH: Well, yuh better, cause if they catch you off guard, Canary, they'll climb down yuh throat an' tie knots in yuh gizzard! (*He laughs delightedly at the prospect.*)

JIM: That's good, ah that's—swell.

OLLIE: How'd you get them purple scars, Jim?

JIM: From Dr. Jones.

OLLIE: Who's Dr. Jones?

BUTCH: Dr. Jones is the guy that gave Canary his singin' lessons! Remembuh when I found out that you'd grown feathers?

JIM (*to Ollie*): That's enough. Thanks. (*He produces cigarettes.*) Have one?

OLLIE: Thanks, Jim.

BUTCH: It's lucky for you that I was interrupted—or you'd be readin' books witcha fingers instead of yer eyes! It's listed on th' record as unfinished business, to be took care of at some future date— I figure that ev'ry dog has his day an' mine's comin' pretty soon now.

OLLIE: Don't pay him no mind.

JIM: Naw. There's a wall between him an' me.

BUTCH: You bet there is. Or you'd be a dead Canary. There'd be yellow feathers floating all over Hall C!

JIM (*exhaling smoke as he speaks—à la Jules Garfield*): There's a wall like that around ev'ry man in here an' outside of here, Ollie.

OLLIE: Outside? Naw!

JIM: Sure there is. Ev'ry man living is walking around in a cage. He carries it with him wherever he goes and don't let it go till he's dead. Then the walls come to pieces and he stops being lonesome—

(*Butch grins delightedly and nudges Joe; he describes a circle with his finger and points at Jim's cell. They both crouch grinning, listening, on the bench by the wall.*)

—Cause he's part of something bigger than him.

OLLIE: Bigger than him?

JIM: Yes.

OLLIE: What's that?

JIM (*blowing an enormous smoke ring and piercing it with his finger*): The Universe!

(*Butch erupts in hoarse derisive laughter.*)

JIM (*ignoring Butch's outburst*): But, sometimes, I think, Ollie, a guy don't have to wait till he's dead to get outside of his cage.

OLLIE: Yuh mean he should bump himself off?

JIM: No. A guy can use his brain two ways. He can make it a wall to shut him in from the world or a great big door to let him out. (*He continues musingly.*) Intellectual emancipation!

OLLIE: Huh?

(*Butch gives a long whistle.*)

OLLIE: What's that?

JIM: Couple of words I came across in a book.

OLLIE: Sound like big words.

JIM: They *are* big words. So big that the *world* hangs on 'em. They can tell us what to read, what to say, what to do—

But they can't tell us what to *think*! And as long as man can think as he pleases he's never exactly locked up anywhere. He can think himself outside of all their walls and boundaries and make the world his place to live in— It's a swell feeling, Ollie, when you've done that. It's like being alone on the top of a mountain at night with nothing around you but stars. Only you're not alone, though, cause you know that you're part of everything living and everything living is part of you. Then you get an idea of what God is. Not Mr. Santie Claus, Ollie, dropping answers to prayers down chimneys—

OLLIE: Naw?

JIM: No, not that. But something big and terrible as night is, and yet—

OLLIE: Huh?

JIM: And yet—as soft as a woman. Y'see what I mean?

BUTCH: I see whatcha mean—it's kind of a—*balmy* feeling! (*Butch and Joe laugh. Jim looks resentfully at wall.*)

JIM: You guys don't get what I'm talking about.

OLLIE (*musingly*): Naw, but I do. Thinkin's like prayin', excep' that prayin' yuh feel like yuh've got some one on the other end a th' line . . .

JIM (*smiling*): Yeah.

(*The spot fades on Jim's cell and focuses on Butch's.*)

QUEEN: Be quiet, you *all.* I'm sick. I need my sleep. (*He mutters to himself.*)

(*A searchlight from river shines on the window.*)

JOE: Where's that light from?

BUTCH (*at the window*): Anudder boat load a goddam jitterbugs. Dey're trowin th' glims on us. Whaddaya think this is? Th' Municipal Zoo or something? Go to hell, yuh sons-a-bitches, yuh lousy—

SCHULTZ (*rapping at the bars with a stick*): After lights in there!

BUTCH: Someday it's gonna be permanuntly 'after lights' for that old screw.

JOE (*twisting on bed*): Oooooo!

BUTCH: Bellyache?

JOE: Yeah, from them stinkin' meatballs. By God I'm gonna quit eatin' if they don't start puttin' in more digestable food.

BUTCH (*reflectively*): Quit eating, huh?—I think yuh got something there.

JOE: Oooooo—*Christ!* (*He draws his knees up to his chin.*)

BUTCH: You ever heard of a hunger-strike, Joe?

JOE: Uh.

BUTCH: Sometimes it works. Gits in the papers. Starts investigations. They git better food.

JOE: *Oooooo!* We'd git—*uh!—Klondike!*

BUTCH: Klondike won't hold thirty-five hundred men.

JOE: No. But Hall C would go first on account of our reputation.

BUTCH: Okay. We'll beat Klondike.

JOE: You talk too big sometimes. You ever been in Klondike?

BUTCH: Yeah. Once.

JOE: What's it like?

BUTCH: It's a little suburb of hell.

JOE: That's what I thought.

BUTCH: They got radiators all aroun' the walls an' there ain't no windows.

JOE: Christ Almighty!

BUTCH: Steam hisses outa the valves like this. (*He imitates the sound.*) Till it gits so thick you can't see nothing around you. It's like breathin' fire in yer lungs. The floor is so hot you can't stand on it, but there's no place else to stand—

JOE: How do yuh live?

BUTCH: There's an air hole about this size at the bottom of the wall. But when there's a bunch in Klondike they git panicky an' fight over the air hole an' the ones that ain't strong don't make it.

JOE: It kills 'em?

BUTCH: Sure. Unless the Boss takes 'em out. And when you beat Klondike you beat everything they've got to offer in here. It's their Ace of Spades!

QUEEN (*rising sleepily on his bunk*): What's that about Klondike, Butch?

JOE: Nothing. He's talking in his sleep.

QUEEN: I dreamed about Klondike one night.

JOE: Did ja?

QUEEN: Sure. That was the night I woke up screaming. Remember?

JOE: Sure. I remember.—Oooooo! Uhhhhhh! Ahhhhhh! Jesus! (*He springs out of bed and crouches on the floor, clasping his stomach.*)

Blackout

EPISODE FIVE

Announcer: "Band Music!"

Theme up: Tchaikovsky, "1812 Overture," 2nd Theme. Fade.

A spot comes up on the office. Jim is settled comfortably in a chair by the window, writing. Eva enters.

EVA (*brightly*): Good morning.

JIM: Hi.

EVA (*removing her hat, etc.*): I believe you spend more time here than the boss does.

JIM: I like it here. Especially when I'm alone.

EVA: Oh—well, excuse my intrusion.

JIM: I don't mean you. You don't bother me. (*His immediate tension at her entrance belies this.*)

EVA: Thanks.

JIM (*watching her as she removes the cover from the machine*): As a matter of fact it's a rare and enviable privilege for a connie to get close to a member of the opposite sex.

EVA: Really?

JIM: Yes. Really and truly. I have to blink my eyes a couple of times to be sure you're not just one of them—visual and auditory hallucinations—that some fellows develop in stir.

EVA (*inserting a form-sheet in the typewriter*): Wasn't there a girl working here before me?

JIM: There was. But she wasn't nearly such a strain upon one's—credulity.

EVA: How do you mean?

JIM: She was sort of a cow.

EVA: Oh.

JIM: Whalen's wife's second cousin. But he's a remarkable man.

EVA (*whose typing obscured the last phrase*): He is or she is?

JIM: They both were. (*He laughs.*) Now you know why I'm called the Canary. I talk too much.

EVA: No. In what way?

JIM (*thumbing toward the inner room*): He had her in there the first week.

EVA: What's in there?

JIM: He goes in there to relax after ground-inspection. She would go in there with him.—She died of an operation and Whalen bought his wife a mink coat. How do you like your new job?

EVA: Well!—Not so good now.

JIM: There's some features of life on the grounds that aren't mentioned in the *Sunday Supplement.*

EVA: Yes. I didn't sleep last night.

JIM: No?

EVA: From thinking about that boy's mother.

JIM: You'll get used to things like that.

EVA: I don't want to get used to them.

JIM: Why don't you quit, then?

EVA: Say! You don't know much about the unemployment situation.

JIM: No. I got here before the Depression.

EVA: You're lucky.

JIM: Think so?

EVA: There was a case in the paper where a man busted a plate-glass window so he could go to jail and get something to eat.

JIM: I bet he regretted it afterwards. Especially if he came here.

EVA: I don't know. The sample menu's okay.

JIM: Huh! We spill that stuff on everybody comes in the office to cover up what's actually going on.

EVA (*removing the form-sheet*): What's that?

JIM: Starvation.

EVA: You're crazy!

JIM: Sure I am, crazy as a bedbug! But I've still got sense enough to recognize beans an' hamburger an' spaghetti—when I see them six or seven times a week in slightly variegated combinations! You wonder why we make such a fuss about eating? Well, I'll tell you why. It's because eating's all we got. We got nothing else, no women to sleep with, no hammers, no shovels, no papers to write on, no automobiles, no golf—nothin' to do but eat—so eating's important to us. And when they make that so darned monotonous that you feel like puking at the sight of it—then they're putting the match to a keg of powder! (*He lights his cigarette.*) Ask me what is a pyrotechnical display!

EVA: I think I know.

JIM: You'll know better if you stick around. We're going to have the loveliest Fourth o'July you ever laid eyes on. Only it's going to come, maybe in the middle of August. Y'see I've got my ear to the ground—in here and in Hall C—This place, lady, is the practical equivalent of Mt. Vesuvius. Maybe a hundred years from now little woolly white lambs will be grazing peacefully on the slopes of an extinct volcano. But down at the bottom tourist guides will be pointing out the bones of people who didn't get out of Pompeii!

EVA: Too bad you won't be one of the guides. You make such good speeches.

JIM: Okay. Be funny about it.

(*The sound of a brass band playing a martial air in the assembly hall is heard.*)

EVA (*her face brightening*): Band music!

JIM: Yes. They're practicing for the Commissioner's banquet.

EVA (*rising*): Sounds very gay!

JIM: Uh-huh. If you believed in brass bands you'd think the millennium was going to arrive at exactly 6 A.M. tomorrow.

EVA (*facing him with desperate gaiety*): Why not? Maybe it will!—A brass band can sell me *anything*, Jim!

JIM: Can it sell you this? (*He catches her against him in a hard impulsive embrace.*)

EVA (*breaking away*): Yes, it could even sell me that! (*Then she laughs.*)—But not in the Warden's office! (*She goes quickly back to her typing— Jim stands motionless looking at her back—his arms raised slowly—the hands clench into fists—they vibrate, outstretched, with a terrific intensity—then slowly fall to his sides. Eva whistles gaily to the band music.*)

Dim Out

EPISODE SIX

Announcer: "Mister Olympics!"

A spot comes up on the cell. Men have just returned from supper.

JOE: Did you eat yours?
BUTCH: Eat that stuff? Naw. It made me sick to look at it.
JOE: Spaghetti four times a week!
BUTCH: That's nutten. I useta work in a spaghetti factory.
QUEEN: Really?
BUTCH: Yeah. I remember one time the spaghetti machines got out of control. We couldn't stop 'em. The whole place was full of spaghetti. It was spaghetti ev'rywhere, oozin' out of the floor an' the walls, an' the ceilin', spaghetti, spaghetti, blockin' up the windows an' the doors, a big suffocatin' mass of spaghetti.
QUEEN: Please!
BUTCH: So I says to the foreman, "For Chrissakes, how we gonna git outa this place wit' all this spaghetti sloppin' aroun' ev'rywhere?"—An' the boss says, "Boys—there's only one way to git out of here now!"—"How's that?" I ast him.—"Here!" he says—an' he han's me a big knife an' fork—"Yuh got to *EAT* yuh way out!"
QUEEN: Oh, for the love of nasturtiums!

(*The steel doors clang.*)

VOICE: Hello, new boy! (*Other greetings are given.*)
BUTCH: They're bringin' a new boy in.

(*Schultz stops in front of the cell with Swifty.*)

SCHULTZ: Here's yer boudoir, Sonny.

SWIFTY: Here?

SCHULTZ: Yeah. Here. (*He shoves him roughly in and slams the door.*)

SWIFTY: What did he do that for? Shove me! I was going in, wasn't I?

JOE: Sure you was going in. He just wanted to help you.

SWIFTY: I don't like being pushed around like that.

JOE: I'd complain to the Governor.

SWIFTY (*pausing as he looks about*): I've got an appeal coming before the Governor.

JOE: Have you now?

SWIFTY: Yes, I didn't get a fair trial. I was railroaded up here. My lawyer said so.

JOE: Your lawyer said so.

SWIFTY: Yes, he said— Hey, do we all stay in here together like this? Jeez, it's too small!

JOE: What's that your lawyer said?

SWIFTY: He said— What's that? A cockroach! Gosh—I don't like being cooped up like this!

JOE: What did your lawyer say?

SWIFTY: He said for me to sit tight. He'd have me out of here in two weeks, a month at the most.

JOE: A month at the most! What do you think of that, Butch?

BUTCH: I think it's a lot of what they use shovels to clean off the stable floor! (*He rises.*)—That's your new bunk, new boy. Get up there an' lissen to what I tell yuh.—Go on!

SWIFTY: Quit shoving!

BUTCH: Huh?

SWIFTY: I told you I don't like being pushed around!

BUTCH (*exhibiting his fists*): When you talk back to me you're talking back to this!—Now git up there an' pay attention to what I say.

SWIFTY: Why should I take orders from you? You're not one of the officials around here.

BUTCH: Ain't I?

SWIFTY: No!

BUTCH: Lissen, buddy. In Spain, it's Mussolini.

JOE: You mean Italy it's Mussolini.

BUTCH: I mean wherever there's wops! An' in Germany it's that monkey wit' the trick mustache!—But in here it's

Butch O'Fallon! And Butch O'Fallon is me! So now that we've been properly introduced I would like to repeat my polite invitation to remove your butt from my bunk an' git up in your own! (*Butch jerks Swifty up by the collar and hoists him by the seat of his pants to the upper bunk.*) What's yuh name?

SWIFTY: Jeremy Trout.

BUTCH: This yuh first stretch?

SWIFTY: Yes. What of it?

BUTCH: What's yuh rap?

SWIFTY: I was indicted for—stealing—money.

BUTCH: What from?

SWIFTY: Cash register in a chain store. I was cashier. But I didn't do it. I was framed by a couple of clerks.

BUTCH: I believe you. You don't look like you'd have gumption enough to crack a till. How much you got?

SWIFTY: On me? Nothing. They even took my cigarettes.

BUTCH: I mean your stretch. How long?

SWIFTY: Judge Eggleston gave me five years. But my lawyer says—

BUTCH: You'll *do* five years.

SWIFTY: In here? Why, I'd go crazy locked in here that long!

BUTCH: Pocket yuh marbles!

SWIFTY: I—I feel sick. The air in here's no good.

BUTCH: No?

SWIFTY: It smells. It's making me sick at the stomach.

BUTCH: There's the slop bucket.

SWIFTY: No!

BUTCH: It ain't been emptied yet. That's your job. The new man always empties.

SWIFTY: No— (*He sinks into his bunk.*) —Five years? I couldn't stand being cooped up that long. I got to have space around me. I get restless. That's why I didn't like working in the chain store. Kept me behind a counter all day, felt like I was tied up there.—At high school I was a runner.

BUTCH: A runner, huh?

QUEEN: That's what I said to myself. He looks athletic.

SWIFTY: Yes. I held the 220 state record for three years.

BUTCH: Fancy that.

SWIFTY: I like anything that's moving, that don't stay put. It's not an ordinary thing with me, it's kind of an obsession. I like to kill distance. See a straight track—get to the other end of it first, before anyone else— That's what I was made for—running—look at my legs!

JOE: Pips, huh?

SWIFTY: That's from training. If this hadn't happened I'd be on my way to the Olympics right now. I could still have a chance at the New York eliminations if my lawyer can spring me before the fifteenth. (*He flexes his legs.*) —But look at that! Getting loose already!—If I could get permission to run around the yard a few times—say, before breakfast or supper—why, I could keep in pretty good shape even in here. Even if I had to stay in here a year—that way I could keep in condition!

JOE: He'll go like Sailor Jack.

BUTCH: Pocket yuh marbles!—Buddy, I ain't sentimental—but I feel sorry for you.

SWIFTY: Why? Don't you think he'll let me?

BUTCH: Naw.

SWIFTY: Why not?

BUTCH: Because you're a con.

SWIFTY: But a con's a human being. He's got to be treated like one.

BUTCH: A con ain't a human being. A con's a con. (*The lights fade on the others and concentrate on Butch.*) He's stuck in here and the world's forgot him. As far as the world is concerned he don't exist anymore. What happens to him in here—them people outside don't know, they don't care. He's entrusted to the care of the State. The State? Hell! The State turns him over to a guy called a Warden and a bunch of other guys called guards. Who're they? Men who like to boss other men. Maybe they could've been truck-drivers or street cleaners or circus clowns. But they didn't wanta be none a them. Why? Cause they've got a natural instinck for swinging a shelailee! They like to crack heads, make sausage out of human flesh! And so they get to be guards. That sounds like 'gods'—which ain't so much a coincidence either, because the only diff'rence between 'guards' an' 'gods' is that 'guards' has an 'r' in it an' the 'r' stands for 'rat'!—That's what a guard is accordin' to my definition—'A rat who thinks that he's GOD!'—You better not forget that. Because, Sonny, you're not in high school no more. You ain't in the chain store, you're not at the Olympics— That's Part One of your education. Part Two is stay away from stool pigeons. Hey, Canary!—He ain't in yet but we got a little songbird in the next cage who sings real sweetly sometimes for the boss.—So don't be buddies wit him. Give 'im a cigarette, Joe.

JOE: Here, mister Olympics.

BUTCH: Keep it covered.—How's yuh stomach now?

SWIFTY: Some better.

BUTCH: Hungry?

SWIFTY: No.

BUTCH: That's good. Because we might quit eating.

QUEEN: Quit eating?

BUTCH: Yep. I been thinkin' over what we talked about las' night, Joe, an' I'm just about sold on it.

JOE: I'm still on the fence about that.

BUTCH: There ain't any fence to be on, Joe. When I say hunger strike in here it's going to be hunger strike.

QUEEN: Hunger strike!

SWIFTY: What's that?

BUTCH: Pocket yuh marbles. The Canary's comin' to roost.

(*Derisive whistles are heard in the hall.*)

Help me off wit' these shoes, Queenie. That's right. Here, hang up my shirt. Joe—

JOE: What the hell?

BUTCH: You fold my pants up nice an' lay 'em over the chair.—Hello, moon. (*He stands in a shaft of moonlight through the barred window.*)

JOE: You're going like Sailor Jack, saying hello to the moon!

BUTCH: She's big an' yellow tonight. Y'know me an' God have got something in common, Joe.

JOE: Yeah, what's that?

BUTCH: A weakness for blondes!

Blackout

EPISODE SEVEN

Announcer: "A Rubber Duck for the Baby!"

A spot comes up on the Warden's office. The Boss is seated at his desk inflating a rubber duck.

WARDEN (*to Eva who lays papers on his desk*): Look at this.

EVA: Yes.

WARDEN: It's a rubber duck for the baby.

EVA: I didn't know you had one.

WARDEN: You bet I got one. Cutest little baby doll you ever set eyes on!

EVA: Boy or girl?

WARDEN: Girl! Wouldn't have nothing else. Will she be tickled when she sees this! (*Eva starts to leave.*) Wait! I'm gonna git her on the phone now! You wanta hear this, Eva? (*He dials.*) Hello, Mama? How's tricks? Yeah? Well, put the baby on, will yuh? (*To Eva*): Now lissen to this! Puddikins? Popsy dust wanted to know if oo was bein' a dood little durl! Oo are? Dat's dood. Popsy'd dot somefin fo dood little durls! No. Not a stick-candies. Oo see when Popsy dets home, 'es oo will! Bye-bye now! Bye-bye!— (*He hangs up with a chuckle.*) Cute 's the dickens—looks just like Shirley Temple—don't she though? (*He shows a picture to Eva.*)

EVA: Yes, there is a resemblance.

(*Jim enters.*)

WARDEN (*heartily*): Hello, Jimmy boy! What's new?

JIM: Nothing new. Just the same old complaints about food. Only they're getting louder all the time, Boss.

WARDEN: What do they want? Caviar? Cream puffs? Charlotte Russes? Do they want us to have printed menus so they can order their meals *à la carte*? Stick these medical reports in the file case, Eva.

JIM: If you look those reports over you'll see there was seven cases of ptomaine poisoning after the Wednesday night supper. Those meatballs were worse on the stomach than they were on the nose!

WARDEN: What do you mean? They weren't good?

JIM: I think they were meant for the buzzards out at the zoo. Got mixed up at the market or something and came over here by mistake.

WARDEN: Look here, Jim. You're talking too uppity. Showing off for Miss Crane, I guess—'s at it?

JIM: No, Sir. If I didn't give you my honest opinion what good would I be?

WARDEN (*slowly, studying Jim's face*): Okay. Yeah, you're a good boy, Jim.

JIM: Thanks.

WARDEN (*leaning back*): I like you, Jim. Why? Cause you got a face that looks like it was cut outa rock. Turn sideways, Jim— Eva?

EVA (*at the files*): Yes, Sir?

WARDEN: Ever seen a cleaner-cut profile than that? Like it was carved in stone, huh? Them jaws, the nose, the mouth? I tried to break that when Jim first come in here. Never did. It stayed like it is—stone face! Never got it to change, not even when I give him fifty stripes with a rubber hose ev'ry morning for fourteen days.—Remember that, Jim?

JIM (*his face barely tightening*): Yes, Sir.

WARDEN: When I seen I couldn't break him I said to myself, "Hey, Bert, here's a man you could use!" So I did. Jim's a trusty, now, a stool pigeon—Canary Jim—that's what the other cons all call him. Ain't that so, Jim?

JIM: Yes, Sir.

WARDEN: Keeps me posted on conditions among the men. He don't come gum-shoeing, whispering like the other stool pigeons I got in here—he comes straight out and says what he thinks!—That's what makes him valuable to me!—But the men don't like him. They hate your guts, don't they, Jim?

JIM: Yes, Sir. (*He speaks in almost a whisper.*)

WARDEN: Jim's on my side, all right. I couldn't break him so I made him useful. Take off your shirt, Jim—show Eva your back.

JIM: Yes, Sir. (*He obeys with curious, machine-like precision. Diagonally across his shoulder down to the waist are long scars which ten years could not obliterate.*)

WARDEN: See them scars, Eva? He got them ten years ago. Pretty sight he was then. Raw meat. The skin hung down from his back like pieces of red tissue paper! The flesh was all pulpy, beat up, the blood squirted out like juice from a ripe tomato ev'ry time I brung the whip down on him. "Had enough, Jim? Ready to go back to that embossing machine?"—"Naw," says Jim,—"Not till it's fixed!"—He defied me like that for fourteen days.—I seen I'd either have to kill him or I'd have to admit that he had me licked.—I says to him, "Jim, you win! You don't go back to that embossing machine, you stay right here in the office an' work for me because you're a man that's made out of stuff that I like!" Stone face! Huh, Jim?

JIM: Yes, Sir. (*The papers have already slipped from Eva's hands. She utters a slight breathless cry and grips the edge of the desk.*)

WARDEN: Thunderation! What's wrong?

JIM: I think she's fainting. (*He catches Eva.*)

WARDEN: Let go of that girl—get your shirt on and get out.—Tell the boys in Hall C I'm tired a complaints about food.—Well, young lady?

EVA: I'm all right now.

WARDEN: Awright, I've got her.—Get your shirt back on, Jim—I want you to have a little talk with Butch O'Fallon tonight.—Tell him I'm tired a complaints in Hall C, and if he wants trouble I'm the baby that can dish it out!—Go on, get on out!

JIM: Yes, Sir. (*He exits slowly.*)

WARDEN (*to Eva who has sunk in her chair*): Well, young lady?

EVA: I'm all right now.

WARDEN: Sorry. I didn't mean to make it that strong. Jim's a good boy, but it don't hurt to remind him once in a while of his old friend Dr. Jones.

(*Eva averts her face.*)

You think I'm brutal, dontcha? You got to realize the position I'm in. I got thirty-five hundred men here, men that would knife their own mothers for the price of a beer. It takes a mighty firm hand.—Yes, Siree! (*He picks up the rubber duck—inflates it some more.*) Cute, huh?—She'll make a fuss over this!

Dim Out

EPISODE EIGHT

Announcer: "Explosion!"

The spot comes up on the cell. We should feel a definite increase of tension over the preceding cell scenes. Butch paces restlessly. The others sit sullenly on their bunks, the Queen with an old movie magazine, Swifty anxiously flexing his legs.

JOE (*entering from the hall and removing the jacket*): Save your shoe leather.

BUTCH: What for?

JOE: You might want to eat it tonight instead of cold beans.

BUTCH: Beans, huh?

SWIFTY (*with a letter*): It's from my lawyer.

QUEEN: What's he say, honey?

SWIFTY: He says for me to sit tight.

QUEEN: Goodness!—My nails are in awful condition.

SWIFTY: Sit tight! What does he think I've been doing since I got here? Sit tight—sit tight! Don't he know I've got to be moving around?

BUTCH: Take it easy, Mister Olympics!—Who toleja cold beans?

JOE: Boy that works in the kitchen.

SWIFTY: I don't trust that lawyer. This time he says six months.

QUEEN: I don't trust no man, honey. No further'n I could kick Grant's Tomb with a fractured toe! (*He giggles.*)

BUTCH: He oughta know.

SWIFTY: My lawyer?

BUTCH: Your lawyer! Naw—the kitchen boy.

JOE: Maybe our friend the Canary forgot to spill.

BUTCH: He'd never forget to spill anything.

JOE: Then maybe the Boss don't care how we feel about cold beans for supper.

BUTCH: He wants to call our hand.

JOE: Sure. He's got an ace in the hole.—Klondike!

BUTCH: We've got one, too.

JOE: Hunger strike?

BUTCH: You named it, Brother.

JOE: Two guys can't hold the ace of spades.

BUTCH: Once I sat in a game where that was the situation.

JOE: How didja solve it?

BUTCH (*producing his razor*): Wit' this.

JOE: You better quit flashin' that thing.

BUTCH: Ev'rybody knows I got tough whiskers. (*He laughs and replaces razor in his belt.*) "Fawchun's always hid-ing—/ I looked ev'rywhere!"

(*Bird calls are heard from the hall.*)

Here it comes, it's th' Canary. (*He gives a shrill whistle.*) Hello, Canary. How's them solo flights you been makin? You know—out there on the mountain tops wit' nothing around ja but the stars? (*He and Joe laugh.*)

OLLIE (*from next cell*): Don't pay 'em no mind, Jim.

JIM: Never mind about that. I got something to tell you.

BUTCH: Tell us about Goldilocks and the bears.

JOE: I like Goody-Two-Shoes.

JIM: Come outside for a minute.

BUTCH: You wanta fight?

JIM: No, I wanta talk.

BUTCH: You allus wanta talk, that's your trouble. If you got something to spill come in here.

JIM: I know what happened last time I got in a cage with you, Butch.

BUTCH: I'm glad I made that good an impression.

JIM: Are you coming out?

BUTCH: Naw. Are you coming in?

JIM: Yeah. I will. Soon as they douse the glims.

QUEEN: Better not, honey. Butch has got tough whiskers.

JIM: Yeah, I know what he cuts 'em with.

BUTCH: Why dontcha spill it, then?

JIM: I never deliberately ratted on nobody, Butch.

(*A whistle sounds. The lights dim.*)

Okay. I'm coming in now. (*He unlocks the cell and enters.*)

QUEEN: Now, Butch—

JOE: Watch, yourself. It's not worth getting jerked to Jesus for.

BUTCH: Naw, Canary, my respect for you is increased two hundred percent. I never thought you'd have what it takes to step inside here.

JIM: It's like what I was telling Ollie last night. We've all got walls around ourselves, Butch, that we can't see through—that's why we make so many mistakes about each other. Have a smoke?

BUTCH: Naw. Just say what you got to say and then take a double powder. I don't wanta lose control.

JIM: I know what you've got in mind.

BUTCH: What?

JIM: Hunger strike.

BUTCH: What of it?

JIM: I don't recommend it, Butch.

BUTCH: Did Whalen tell you to say that?

JIM: Naw, this is on the level, Butch.

BUTCH: Yeah, about as level as the Adirondacks.

JIM: I'll admit I've made myself useful to him. But I haven't forgotten two weeks we spent in the Hole together, and those visits he paid every morning to inquire about our health. He was even more solicitous about mine than yours, Butch. Things like that can make a common bond between men that nothing afterwards can ever—

BUTCH: Come to the point!

JIM: All right. I'm coming up for parole next month.

BUTCH (*rising*): You are, huh?

JIM: There's a chance I might get it. And if I do I'm going to justify my reputation as a brilliant vocalist, Butch. I'm going to sing so loud and so high that the echo will knock these walls down! I know plenty from working in the office. I know all the pet grafts. I know all about the intimidation of employees and torture of convicts; I know about the Hole, about the water cure, about the overcoat—about Klondike!—And I know about the kind of food—or slop, rather!—that we been eating! You wait a month! That's all! When I get through Whalen will be where he belongs—in the psychopathic ward with Sailor Jack! And I promise you things will change in here—look—here's an article about the Industrial Reformatory in Chillicothe!—that's the kind of a place this'll be!

BUTCH (*throwing the paper aside*): I don't want no articles!—Allison, you're full of shit.

JOE: Take it easy, Butch. (*To Jim.*) So you don't want us to go on hunger strike?

JIM: No. It won't do any good. The Boss'll throw the bunch of you in Klondike. Do yourself a favor. Work with me. We can case this jug. But not if we keep on going opposite ways.—Give me your hand on it, Butch.

BUTCH: Fuck you!

JIM: It's no dice, huh? What do you say, Joe? Swifty?

BUTCH: They say what I say! Now git out before I lose my last ounce a restriction!

JIM: Okay. (*He goes out.*)

JOE: Maybe he *was* on the level.

BUTCH: He will be on the level when he's laid out straight under ground. (*He slaps Swifty's rump.*) Git up! It's supper time!

SWIFTY (*his face buried in the pillow*): Leave me alone. I'm sick. I'm not hungry.

BUTCH: You're coming along anyhow. We need you to help make some noise in case the kitchen boy was right about supper.

JOE: Noise?

BUTCH: Yep, *plenty* of noise!

(*The bell rings in the hall.*)

BUTCH: Come along, youse! (*He shoves Queen and jerks Swifty to his feet.*) Hell's bells are ringin'! Come on, boys! Before them biscuits git cold! T-bone steaks for supper! Smothered in mushrooms! Come and git it!

(*A whistle is heard and the lights dim out. Theme up: "1812 Overture." Fade.*)

Blackout

EPISODE NINE

Announcer: "Hunger Strike!"

A spot comes up on the office. Eva enters.

WARDEN: Had your supper?

EVA: Yes.

WARDEN (*watching her as she crosses downstage*): Hate to keep you overtime like this—but with the boys in Hall C kicking up such a rumpus, we got to have all our books in perfect shape—just in case the professional snoopers git on our tails about something!

EVA: Yes Sir. (*She removes the cover from the typewriter.*)

WARDEN (*watching her closely*): Hope working nights don't interfere too much with your social life.

EVA (*tiredly*): I don't have any social life right now.

WARDEN: How come?

EVA: I've been so busy job hunting since I moved here that I haven't had much time to cultivate friends.

WARDEN: No boyfriends, huh?

EVA: Oh, I have a few that I correspond with.

WARDEN: Yeah, but there's a limit to what can be put in an envelope, huh?

EVA: I suppose there is.—Mr. Whalen, there seem to be quite a number of bad discrepancies in the commissary report.

WARDEN: You mean it don't add up right?

EVA: I failed to account for about six hundred dollars.

(*The Warden whistles.*)

What shall I do about it?

WARDEN: I'll git Jim to check it over with you. You know a lot can be done about things like that by a little manipulation of figures. Jim'll explain that to you.

EVA: I see.

WARDEN: How long have you been working here?

EVA: Two weeks.

WARDEN: Gin'rally I git shut of a girl in less time'n that if she don't measure up to the job.

EVA (*tensely*): I hope that I've shown my efficiency.

WARDEN: Aw, efficiency! I don't look for efficiency in my girls.

EVA: What do you look for, Mr. Whalen?

WARDEN: Personality! You're in a position where you got to meet the public. Big men politically come in this office—you give 'em a smile, they feel good—what do they care about the tax-payers' money?—Those boobs that go aroun' checkin' over accounts, where did this nickel go, what's done with that dime—jitney bums, I call 'em!—No, Siree, I got no respect for a man that wants a job where he's got to make note of ev'ry red copper that happens to slip through his hands!—Well—policy, that's what I'm after!—Being political about certain matters, it don't hurt *ever*, yuh see?

EVA: Yes, I think so.

WARDEN (*pausing*): What color's that blouse you got on?

EVA (*nervously sensing his approach*): Chartreuse.

WARDEN (*half-extending his hand*): It's right Frenchy-looking.

EVA: Thank you. (*She types rapidly.*)

WARDEN (*opening the inner door and coughing uncertainly*): Look here.

EVA: Yes?

WARDEN: Why don't you drop that formality stuff? (*He crosses to her.*) How do I look to you? Unromantic? Not so much like one of the movie stars?—Well, it might surprise you to know how well I go over with some of the girls! (*He seats himself on corner of the desk.*)—I had a date not so long ago—girl works over at the Cattle and Grain Market—'bout your age, build, ev'rything—(*He licks his lips.*)—When I got through loving her up she says to me—"Do it again, Papa do it again!"—(*He roars with laughter and slaps the desk.*)—Why? Because she *loved* it, that why! (*He rises and goes to the inner door.*) You ever been in here?

EVA: No.

WARDEN (*heartily*): Come on in. I wanta show you how nice I got it fixed up.

EVA: No.

WARDEN: Why not?

EVA (*rising stiffly*): You're married, Mr. Whalen. I'm not that kind of girl.

WARDEN: Aw, that act's been off the stage for years!

EVA: It's not an act, Mr. Whalen!

WARDEN: Naw, neither was *Uncle Tom's Cabin* when little Eva goes up to heaven in Act III on a bunch of steel wires! (*He slams the inner door angrily, then laughs.*) You're okay, sister. You keep right on pitching in there.

EVA: Now that you know me better, do I still have a job?

WARDEN: Why, you betcha life you still got a job! (*He laughs and grips her in a fumbling embrace which she rigidly endures. Jim enters.*)

JIM: Excuse me.

WARDEN (*still laughing*): Come on in, Jimmy boy. Want you to check over this commissary report with Miss Crane. She says there's a few—what you call 'em? Discrepancies! You know how to fix that up!

JIM: Yes, Sir.

WARDEN: How's things in Hall C? Pretty quiet?

JIM: Too quiet.

WARDEN: How's that?

JIM: When they make a noise you know what's going on.

WARDEN: They're scared to let a peep out since I put that bunch in the Hole.

JIM: I don't think so. I got an idea they might quit eating tonight.

WARDEN: Quit eating? You mean—*hunger strike*? (*The word scares him a little.*)

JIM: Yes. They're tired of spaghetti.

WARDEN: Maybe a change of climate would improve their appetites!

JIM: Klondike?

WARDEN: Yeah.

JIM: Klondike won't hold thirty-five hundred men.

WARDEN: It would hold Hall C.

JIM: Yes, but Butch is in Hall C.

WARDEN: What of it?

JIM: He's got a lot of influence with the men.

WARDEN: He's a troublemaker an' I'm gonna sweat it out of him.

JIM: I wouldn't try that, Boss. Hunger makes men pretty desperate and if you tortured them on top of that there's no telling what might happen.

WARDEN: Hunger strike's something I won't put up with in here. Creates a sensation all over the country. Then what? Cranks of ev'ry description start bitching about the brutal treatment of those goddamn mugs that would knife their own mothers for the price of a beer!

JIM: The easiest way to avoid it would be to improve the food.

WARDEN: Avoid it, hell. I'll bust it to pieces! Wait'll they see that gang we've got in the Hole—if that don't make sufficient impression I'll give 'em the heat! (*He leaves the office.*)

JIM: The man's a lunatic. Ask him who he is, he'd say, "Benito Mussolini!"

EVA: You're right about him. I suspected it last week when he made you show me those scars on your back. Just now—before you came in—he convinced me of it.

JIM: What happened?

EVA: He wanted me to go in that room with him.

JIM: You didn't?

EVA: No. I was sure he'd fire me but he only laughed and squeezed my arm— Look!

JIM: What?

EVA: I've got a blue mark on my arm where he pinched me.

JIM: When he was a boy I bet he got lots of fun drowning kittens and pulling the wings off butterflies.—Were you scared?

EVA: Terribly scared—and at the same time—something else.

JIM: What?

EVA: If I told you, you'd be disgusted with me.

JIM: Attracted?

EVA: Yes, in a way. I knew that if he touched me I wouldn't be able to move.

JIM: In the pulps they call it fascinated horror.

EVA: Yes. Or a horrible fascination.

JIM: So you're convinced it's no place for a lady?

EVA: I'm not going to quit. Not yet.

JIM: No? If you wait for a third alarm it might be too late.

EVA: I'm going to stay. I've got a favorite nightmare, Jim, about finding myself alone in a big empty house. And knowing that something or somebody was hidden behind one of the doors, waiting to grab me— But instead of running out of the house I always go searching through it; opening all of the closed doors— Even when I come to the last one, I don't stop, Jim—I open that one, too.

JIM: And what do you find?

EVA: I don't know. I always wake up just then.

JIM: So you're going to try the same thing here?

EVA: Something like that.

JIM: I guarantee you won't be disappointed. Gimme the commissary report— No, take that sheet out, we'll start over again— See how much spaghetti we can make out of a Packard Six. Ten pounds of sodium fluoride. No, you better make it sixteen.

EVA: Sixteen pounds of sodium fluoride.

JIM: Sixteen pounds of—sodium fluoride.

EVA: You just gave me that.

JIM: Aw. Twenty bushels of—

EVA: Jim.

JIM: Yeah?

EVA: Why don't you ever open the door *you're* hiding behind?

JIM: What makes you think I'm hiding behind anything?

EVA: Your eyes, the way your hands shake sometimes.

JIM: Oh. That.

EVA: It would help to let go. I mean with the right person.

JIM: Who is that right person?

EVA: Me.

JIM: How do I know?

EVA: Because I tell you.

JIM: Lots of people tell lots of things and most of them are lies.

EVA: I'm not lying, Jim—I want you to trust me.

JIM: Okay.

EVA: Then tell me—what is it?

JIM: What?

EVA: Your hands—why do they shake like this?

JIM: I thought I gave you a clear demonstration once.

EVA: When?

JIM: That morning we heard the band music.

EVA: You mean it's—repression.

JIM: That's it. Something that's locked up and keeps getting more and more all the time. There's lots of men in here with fingers that shake like this. It's power. Outside it runs dynamos, lights up big cities. But in here the power's all gone to waste. It just feeds on itself, gets bigger, does nothing. Till something sets it off like a match does a keg of powder—and then you got an explosion!

EVA: Explosions are such a—waste—of power!

JIM: Yeah. But what's the alternative here?

EVA: Your writing!

JIM: Editorials for *The Archaeopteryx*?

EVA: No! You've got next month to think of, Jim.

JIM: Next month is still on the lap of the gods. Which is a complimentary way of referring to the Board of Pardons and Paroles.

EVA: I don't know why, but I feel so sure of it, Jim. These ten years of—of waiting— They've made you stronger than other men are— You've stored up so much in you that when you get it out, there's nothing could stand in your way— You'll push down all the ordinary walls and walk right over them, Jim— People will say, "Who is this man? Where did he come from?"—and I'll smile proudly because I'll know.—He's a man from another country, I'll say— He's a giant— He's got lightning in his right hand and thunder in his left— But I'll know— I'll know secrets about you—all the sweet, strange things that only a woman can know—and I can tell you— (*Whalen enters.*) How many pounds was that—of sodium fluoride?

JIM: Sixteen.

WARDEN: How you getting along with that report?

JIM: We haven't done much yet. We got to talking.

WARDEN: About what?

JIM: Fireworks.

WARDEN: Very appropriate. Schultz is bringing the Hole gang up for inspection. Get them chairs out of the way.

JIM: Yes, Sir.

WARDEN: You stand over by the window and look sharp! Eva—you wanta stay in here or go in the next room?

EVA: I'll stay.

(*A buzzer sounds.*)

WARDEN: Okay. March 'em in! (*A file of haggard, ghostly figures shuffles into the room, their eyes blinking against the light, barely able to stand—some with heads bloody, others with clotted, shredded shirts. The Warden whistles.*)

SCHULTZ: Stand up against that wall!

WARDEN: Nice-lookin' bunch. Oughta make quite an impression when they go back to Hall C! (*To Swifty*): How long have you been in the hole, Son?

(*Swifty cannot speak. His lips move and he staggers forward with a pleading gesture. The Warden raises the "billy" and continues.*)

Stand back there! Why don't you speak?

JIM: He can't talk.

WARDEN: Dumb?

EVA: No. Sick. He's had five days in a strait jacket.

WARDEN: I think he needs five more.

(*Swiftly falls to his knees.*)

JIM: I think Swifty's had enough, boss.

WARDEN: Who asked you?

JIM: Nobody.

WARDEN: Just volunteered the information?

JIM: Yes, Sir.

WARDEN: Maybe you'd like to take his place down there?

JIM: No, Sir.

WARDEN: Then you'd better cut the cackle. Ollie?

OLLIE (*faintly*): Yes, Sir.

WARDEN: You look kind of all in.

OLLIE (*his voice shaking*): I is, suh. I neahly checked out las' night. Boss, ah didn' think ad'd live t' see day!

WARDEN: Think another night would just about fix you up?

OLLIE: Couldn't make it, Boss.

WARDEN: What do you think, Schultz?

SCHULTZ: I think another night would do that boy a world of good, Mr. Whalen.

OLLIE (*wildly*): Please, God, Boss, ah cain't make it! Ah cain't *make* it!

WARDEN: Two nights!—One extra for squawking!

OLLIE: Oh, Laws, a mussy, please, oh, Jesus, please, a mussy— (*He continues this prayer in a sort of chant as they are led out the door.*)

WARDEN: Get 'em out! I'll check 'em over again tomorrow morning.

(*They shuffle out slowly, Ollie chanting his prayer. Jim follows.*)

Ever heard such a squawk?

(*Eva sinks wearily into a chair.*)

You going to flip out again?

EVA: No. I'm all right. They looked so awful it made me a little sick.

WARDEN: Sure they looked awful. Maybe they'll appreciate good treatment after this— I'll wager there'll be no more kick about food.

(*From the hall comes the sound of a disturbance—Jim enters.*)

WARDEN: What's going on out there?

JIM: Ollie just—

WARDEN: Took a dive?

JIM: Yes. Butted his head against a wall and broke it.

WARDEN: Head or wall?

JIM: Head.

WARDEN: All right. Cart him over to the sick-house.

JIM: Not the sick-house.

WARDEN: Dead?

JIM: Yes.

WARDEN: Why dontcha watch out? You coulda prevented that— Give Eva one of them cards— Naw, outa the top drawer. Fill that out. Name— What was that smoke's name?

JIM: Oliver. Oliver Jackson.

WARDEN: Special friend of yours?

JIM: All of the men liked Ollie.

WARDEN: Huh. How old?

JIM: Twenty-six.

WARDEN: Color—black! Sentence—

JIM: Three years.

WARDEN: Charge?

JIM (*slowly*): Stole a crate of canned goods off a truck to feed his family.

WARDEN: Larceny!—Cause of death?—What's his Wasserman?

JIM: Negative.

WARDEN: Hmmm. Put this down, Eva. Stomach Ulcers. Severe hemorrhages.

JIM: That's what you gave the boy last week.

WARDEN: Well, make it a bad cold—complications—pneumonia!

(*The sounds of yammering begin to penetrate the office.*)

(*The Warden is unnerved for a moment but continues.*) What's that?

JIM: They're making a noise.

WARDEN (*instinctively seizing his whip*): Where's it from? Hall C?

JIM: Naw. Halls A, B, C, D, E, and F!

WARDEN (*shakily*): What are they bitching about now?

JIM: They must have heard about Ollie. They like him pretty good.

WARDEN: Aw— (*He looks frightened.*) —Schultz! (*He seizes the phone.*) Schultz? How's the pipes in Klondike? Git them radiators tested an' ready for action.

(*There is a sudden complete darkness on stage.*)

WHISPERS (*gradually rising in volume and pitch*): Somebody got hurt downstairs— Who was it?—Ollie!—Ollie?—Yeah, they killed Ollie—Ollie's dead.—They killed Ollie—Ollie's dead— They KILLED OLLIE—THEY KILLED OLLIE —OLLIE'S DEAD!

(*A spot comes up on the cell. Butch is bending to the wall. He suddenly rises.*)

BUTCH: Ollie's dead— THEY KILLED OLLIE! (*He shouts through the bars.*)

CHORUS: Ollie's dead! They killed Ollie!

JOE: What are we going to do about it?

BUTCH: Quit eating! (*He shouts through the bars*) QUIT EATING!

CHORUS: Quit eating! Quit eating!

(*Blackout.*)

WHISPERS: What does Butch say?—Butch says quit eating—hunger strike?—Yeah, hunger strike!—Butch says HUNGER STRIKE!—Hunger strike—quit eating—Quit eating —HUNGER STRIKE!

VOICE: The men in Hall C have quit eating!
SECOND VOICE: Hunger strike in Hall C!
NEWSBOY: *Morning Star!* Paper! *Morning Star!* Paper! Read about the big hunger strike!
WOMAN'S VOICE: It is reported that some of the men in the state prison have gone on a hunger strike!

(*The click of a telegraph is heard.*)

VOICE: Associated Press Bulletin— Hunger strike at Monroe City Penitentiary! Men rebel against monotonous diet!
VOICE: United Press!
VOICE: Columbia Broadcasting System!
VOICE: Commissioners promise an investigation of alleged starvation in state penitentiary!
VOICE: Warden denies hunger strike!
VOICE: Hunger strike reported!
VOICE: Hunger strike denied!
VOICE: Hunger strike! HUNGER STRIKE!

(*Traffic noises, sirens, bells are heard. Theme up: "1812 Overture" theme reprise. Blackout. Fade.*)

End of Act One

ACT TWO

EPISODE ONE

Announcer: "Not About Nightingales!"

A spot comes up on the office. The hunger strike has been in effect for several days and a tense, electric atmosphere prevails as everyone waits for the inevitable explosion when nerves are stretched beyond the point of endurance. Eva is seated alone as the scene opens. Her movements are jittery. The phone rings.

EVA: Warden's office. *The Morning Star*? No, Mr. Whalen is not seeing any reporters. No, there is no serious trouble. No, you can't get on the Island without a special permit from Mr. Whalen. The rule has been in effect for about six days. No, not on account of a hunger strike! Yes, good-bye.

(*During this the Chaplain has entered. Eva is startled, then continues.*)

Oh!

CHAPLAIN: Nervous, young lady?

EVA: Terribly—terribly!

CHAPLAIN: I don't blame you. So am I. This thing has got to be stopped before something serious happens.

EVA: Oh, if it only could be!

CHAPLAIN: That's what I want to see Mr. Whalen about. It does no good trying to suppress all news of what's going on. We might as well face the music—and do something constructive to put a stop to it!

EVA: Yes. Something constructive.

CHAPLAIN: But in the meantime—couldn't you take a little vacation?

EVA: You think there's real—danger?

CHAPLAIN: Certainly there's danger. And it's aggravated by the fact that Mr. Whalen apparently won't recognize it. I wish that I could reason with that man, but— Well— (*He glances at his watch.*) —I'll visit some boys in the hospital and be back here for a talk with the Boss in about twenty minutes.

EVA: All right.

(*Jim enters.*)

CHAPLAIN: Hello, Jim. How are things upstairs?

JIM (*showing a bloody arm in a torn sleeve*): That's the answer!

EVA (*springing up*): Jim!

JIM (*laughing grimly*): I walked too close to one of the cages.

CHAPLAIN: Who did that?

JIM (*slowly shaking his head*): I don't know.

CHAPLAIN (*patting his back*): You've had ten bad years, Jim. I hope next month will be the end of it for you.

JIM: Thanks, Reverend. (*The Chaplain goes out.*)

EVA: Jim, I'll—I'll fix that up for you.

(*He sits down by desk.*)

JIM: They gave me this stuff to put on it down at the sick-house. They were sore as hell because I wouldn't tell them who done it.

EVA (*painting his arm and applying a bandage*): You shouldn't stay up there. It's not safe for you.

JIM: No place is safe in here. Aren't you finally convinced of that?

EVA: Why are you so anxious to get rid of me?

JIM: You know a lot you could tell.

EVA: Yes. I suppose I do.

JIM: Why don't you then?

EVA: I want to stay here a while longer. Maybe next month I'll go—we'll both go then.

JIM: They've been on a hunger strike six days and the Warden only gave them seven. Tonight may be the deadline. Tomorrow night at the latest.

EVA: Then what?

JIM: The boiler room is in perfect condition. The pipes have been reinforced.

EVA: I can't imagine anything as brutal as that—I don't believe it!

JIM: Well—I ought to spill it myself—but if I did it would cost my ticket-of-leave!—It's funny.

EVA: What?

JIM: Nothing has quite so much value as the skin our own guts are wrapped in. (*He takes a book and sits down at the window.*)

(*Eva resumes typing. Jim suddenly tears a page out and throws it on the floor in disgust.*)

Christ!

EVA: What did you do that for?

JIM: I didn't like it.

EVA: What was it?

JIM: A little piece of verbal embroidery by a guy named Keats.

EVA: What's wrong with it?

JIM: It's sissy stuff—"Ode to a Nightingale!" Don't those literary punks know there's something more important to write about than that? They ought to spend a few years in stir before they select their subjects!

EVA: Why don't you show them, then?
JIM: I'd give my right arm for the chance.
EVA: You have the chance!
JIM: Not in here I don't. If I wrote what I wanted to write, I'd stay in here till Klondike becomes an ice-plant!—But maybe next month—
EVA: Yes. Next month—
JIM: Maybe then I'll start writing—but not about nightingales!
EVA: John Keats didn't have a very good time of it, Jim.
JIM: No?
EVA: No. He died at the age of twenty-six.
JIM: Smothered himself in lilies, I guess.
EVA: No. He wanted to live. Terribly. He was like you, he had a lot of things he wanted to say but no chance to say them. He wrote another poem, Jim. A poem you'd like. Give me the book—here it is! (*She reads the sonnet "When I have fears that I may cease to be"*):

> When I have fears that I may cease to be
> Before my pen has gleaned my teeming brain,
> Before high pilèd books, in charactry,
> Hold like rich garners the full-ripened grain;
> When I behold, upon the night's starred face,
> Huge cloudy symbols of high romance,
> And think that I may never live to trace
> Their shadows, with the magic hand of chance;
> And when I feel, fair creature of an hour!
> That I shall never look upon thee more,
> Never have relish in the faery power
> Of unreflecting love!—then on the shore
> Of the wide world I stand alone, and think
> Till Love and Fame to nothingness do sink.

You see he was like you, Jim. He got out of his prison by looking at the stars. He wrote about beauty as a form of escape.
JIM: Escape, huh? That's not my kind of escape.
EVA: What is your form of escape?
JIM: Blowing things wide open!
EVA: Destruction, you mean?

JIM: Yes! Destruction!

EVA: I'm sorry to hear you say that.

JIM: Would you rather hear me warbling about nightingales?

EVA: No. But there are other things.

JIM: For instance?

EVA: There must be some things you love.

JIM: Love?

EVA: Yes.

JIM: Love is something nasty that's done in dark corners around this place.

EVA: I'm sorry you're so bitter.

JIM: Why should you be sorry about anything except the possible loss of your job?

EVA: Why should I? Because I like you, Jim.

JIM: Even after—after the last time we were in here together?

EVA: More than ever.

JIM: When you've been without women as long as I have, there's something mythological about them. You can't believe they're real, not even when you place your hands on them like this and—

EVA: Jim! (*She breaks away as Whalen enters.*)

WARDEN: What's the matter Jim?

JIM: Why?

WARDEN: You got a funny look on your face.

JIM: I'm just concentrating.

WARDEN: On what?

JIM: The new *Archaeopteryx.*

WARDEN: Aw, what are you going to write about, Jim?

JIM (*quietly*): Not about—nightingales.

WARDEN: Huh? (*Absently fiddles with his papers.*) Aw, Jim—

JIM: Yes, Sir?

WARDEN: You might want to drop a word to the boys on hunger strike about the radiator test we made in Klondike. We got the temperature up to 150 degrees— You might mention that. You know a word to the wise is sufficient.

JIM: I'm afraid there's not much wisdom in Hall C. Good night.

(*Jim goes out. The Chaplain enters.*)

WARDEN (*lighting cigar*): What do yuh want, Reverend?

CHAPLAIN: I want to talk to you about the death of Oliver Jackson.

WARDEN: What about it?

CHAPLAIN: I think it could have been avoided.

WARDEN: Sure it could. Nobody made that fool nigger take a dive.

CHAPLAIN: He was goaded to desperation.

WARDEN: Oh, you think so?

CHAPLAIN: There have been too many suicides, several drownings, hangings, so-called accidents, since I've been here. Now it appears that we're in danger of having a mass suicide in Hall C. The men have gone on hunger strike which I think is fully justified by the quality of food they've been getting.

WARDEN: Aw. Now I'm beginning to suspect who's responsible for the wild stories that have been leaking out to the public about things here. I'm afraid you're what the boys call a—stool pigeon, Reverend.

CHAPLAIN: I'm a conscientious steward of Christ, and as such I protest against the inhuman treatment of convicts in this prison!

WARDEN (*jumping up*): Who's running this prison, you or me?

CHAPLAIN: Mr. Whalen, the universe is like a set of blocks. The kind you had in kindergarten. A little one that fits into a big one, a bigger one over that, till you get on up to the very biggest of them all that fits on top of all the rest—

WARDEN: Yes?

CHAPLAIN: Yes, and that biggest block is the one I'm representing—the Kingdom of God. (*He rises with dignity.*)

WARDEN: Well, I'm afraid your work here has begun to interfere with your—your higher duties—I want you to climb up there on top of that great big block you're talkin' about an' stay up there. That's your place. You leave me alone down here on the little block— There's your notice, Reverend— You're free to go now.

CHAPLAIN: I could leave here gladly if it wasn't for what I have to take with me.

WARDEN: You're taking nothing with you but the clothes on your back.

CHAPLAIN: I'm taking much more than that.

WARDEN: Aw. Maybe I'd better have you frisked on the way out.

CHAPLAIN: You could strip me naked and I'd still have these.

WARDEN: These what?

CHAPLAIN: Memories—shadows—ghosts!

WARDEN: Ahhhh? (*He lifts phone.*) Git me Atwater 2770.

CHAPLAIN: Things I've seen that I can't forget. Men, tortured, twisted, driven mad. Death's the least of it. It's the *life* in here that's going to stay with me like an incurable sickness. And by God, Whalen, that's not profanity—by God, I won't rest easy till I've seen these walls torn down, stone by stone, and others put up in their place that let the air in! Good night!— (*He goes out quickly.*)

WARDEN: Hello. Reverend? This is Warden Whalen. Our chaplain's just resigned. I want you to come over and talk to me—might be a steady job in it for you. Yes, Siree! You be over here in time for Sunday service— (*He hangs up.*) Memories, shadows, ghosts! What a screwball! (*He pours himself a drink.*)

Dim Out

EPISODE TWO

Announcer: "Sunday Morning in Hall C!"

A spot comes up on the cell. Joe, Queen, and Swifty are reading sections of a Sunday paper. From down the corridor comes Butch's voice—

BUTCH (*approaching*): "I'm forever BLOW-ing BUB-BLES!" (*He enters the cell with a straight razor, towel, and soap.*) Who gave you that paper?

JOE: Allison. The Canary.

BUTCH: Git it out of here!

JOE: What for?

BUTCH: It's contaminated.

JOE: Aw, take a look at t' comics.

BUTCH: Naw, gimme 'at pitcher section. Hey! Look at 'is!

JOE: What?

BUTCH: "A bow-ket of buds!"

JOE: Yeah. They're comin' out in sassiety.

BUTCH: "Miss Hortense Maxine Schultz, daughter of Mr. and Mrs. Max W. Schultz, 79 Willow Drive, will make her bow to society early this Fall. She is one of a group of young women who traveled through Europe this summer with Mrs. J. Mortimer Finchwell—"

JOE: So what?

BUTCH: "On her fadder's side Miss Schultz is directly descendant from William th' Conq'ror an' on her mudders from Ponce de Leon, Sir Isaac Newton an' George Washington's Aunt!"

JOE: Gosh, de're pikers! Why don't they throw in Benito Mussolini for good measure?

BUTCH: "Her grandfather was duh late Benjamin F. Schultz, President and founder of th' Shultz Bottling Works."

JOE: Lotsa mazooma, huh?

BUTCH: "In addition to her many udder accomplishments—!" Hey, listen to this!

JOE: Huh?

BUTCH: Down here at th' bottom they come right out an' admit that she ain't even human!

JOE: How's that?

BUTCH: It says here "In addition to her many udder accomplishments, Miss Schultz is an excellent *horse*-woman!"

JOE: Hell, you could tell that by lookin' at her pitcher.

Blackout

EPISODE THREE

Announcer: "Mr. Whalen Interviews the New Chaplain!"

A spot comes up on the office. Whalen and the Reverend Hooker have just returned from Sunday dinner. The Reverend Hooker is a nervous, precise little man with a prodigious anxiety to please.

WARDEN: I got you up here on pretty short notice. You see me an' the old chaplain had a little disagreement last night, which resulted in him handing in his resignation right off the bat!—He made one fatal mistake, Reverend— He kind of forgot who was in charge of this institution.

REVEREND: I don't think I shall make that error, Mr. Whalen.

WARDEN: Naw, neither do I. First time I seen you I said to myself "Here's a man who looks like he could adjust himself to conditions."

REVEREND: I pride myself on being—adjustable!

WARDEN: Good. You'll find that's an asset around this place, a definite asset. What's your idea of the universe, Reverend?

REVEREND: I beg your pardon?

WARDEN: Suppose you give me a little word-picture of how you conceive of this great mysterious— (*He makes a sweeping gesture.*)

REVEREND: Cosmos?

WARDEN: Yes! In which we humans are little fluttering motes, so to speak. (*He makes a derisive fluttering gesture with hands.*)

REVEREND: Well—uh—of course there's the orthodox conception of the universe as consisting of three elements—

WARDEN: Yep?

REVEREND: Heaven, earth and the— uh—regions below.

WARDEN: We call that Klondike in here.

REVEREND: I beg your pardon?

WARDEN: Skip it, Reverend.

REVEREND: Hmmm. Of course there is some question as to the *material* existence of those—uh—nether regions—

WARDEN: There's no doubt about 'em here. Naw, Sir. But what I wanted to know, Reverend, is if you've got any theories about a set of blocks—with you occupying the one on top and me way down at the bottom—that's what got the last preacher in trouble with me.

REVEREND: Blocks? Oh, dear, no! That strikes me as rather—elementary to say the least!

WARDEN: Yeah, kindergarten stuff. Well, you'll do, Reverend. (*He glances at his ponderous gold watch.*) We got about five minutes till church takes up. Are you good at makin' up extemporaneous speeches?

REVEREND: Oh, yes, indeed, yes, indeed! I think I may safely say that I have never lacked words for any occasion, Mr. Whalen.

WARDEN: Well, your job depends on this one. I haven't got time to go into details, Reverend. But I want you to touch on three particular subjects. I don't care how you bring 'em in, just so you *do* and so you give 'em the right emphasis!

REVEREND: Three subjects!

WARDEN: Yes, Siree. You mark 'em down, Reverend—food!

REVEREND: Food?

WARDEN: That's the first one. Then—heat!

REVEREND: Heat?

WARDEN: Yep. And then—Klondike! (*A bell sounds.*) There goes the bell. I'm two minutes slow. Remember, now, food, heat, and Klondike!

REVEREND: What was the last one? Klondike? You mean—uh—missionary work in the far north? Among the Eskimos? I'm afraid the association of ideas is going to be a little difficult for me to grasp, Mr. Whalen—but—

(*Dim out; a spot comes up on the Reverend Hooker behind a small lectern.*)

REVEREND: Yes—uh—very good afternoon to you all. (*He clears his throat: then beams at the convicts.*) I hope that you enjoyed your dinner as much as I did mine—

VOICE: Hamburgers and spaghetti! (*There is a chorus of booing. A warning whistle sounds, then silence.*)

REVEREND: Food is such a familiar blessing that—uh we sometimes forget to be properly grateful for it. But when I read about the horrible conditions in famine-stricken portions of Europe and Asia—tch, tch!—I feel that I am indeed very fortunate to have a full stomach!

(*Booing is heard; someone whistles.*)

When one thinks of food—uh—one also thinks by a natural association of ideas—about—uh—the marvelous blessing of—uh— *Heat!* Heat—uh—that makes food possible—wonderful *heat!* Heat of all kinds! The heat of the sun that warms the earth's atmosphere and permits the growth of the vegetables and the grains and the—uh—fruits—uh—

the heat of the—uh—body—uh— (*He wipes his forehead.*) heat, universal heat— At this time of the year some of us find heat oppressive—uh—but that is ungrateful of us, extremely ungrateful—

(*There is a slow stomping of feet.*)

(*The preacher continues, raising his voice.*) For all living matter depends on the presence of heat—northward and southward from the Equator to the twin poles—even to far Alaska—even in *Klondike*—

(*The stomping grows louder.*)

What would Klondike be without heat? A frozen wasteland! (*He scrubs his forehead and glances nervously about.*) In Klondike our brave missionaries, risking their lives among savage tribes of war—painted Indians—

(*A hymnal is hurled: there is furious stomping.*)

Goodness!—As I was saying—in Klondike—!

(*He is bombarded with hymnals. A whistle blows; there is shouting; a siren sounds. Dim out. A mocking jazz interlude plays. A spot comes up on the office. The Reverend rushes in clasping his handkerchief to his forehead.*)

REVEREND: Oh, mercy upon us!

WARDEN (*at the phone*): Schultz? All guards on duty! Find out who conked the Reverend with that song book. Whew! I give you my word, Reverend, I wasn't expecting no such a reaction as this! It come as a complete surprise!

REVEREND: Ohhhh! I'm afraid I shall have to receive some medical attention.

WARDEN: Yeah, well, I want you to take this fin, Reverend.

REVEREND: And the nervous shock, you know! Tch, Tch!

WARDEN: Yeah? Well—

REVEREND: Terrific, terrific! A shocking experience!

WARDEN: Here's another two bucks.

(*Theme up: jazz*)

Blackout

EPISODE FOUR

Announcer: "Zero Hour!"

A spot comes up on the warden's office. Eva is typing nervously. Jim enters. His chronic tension has now risen to the point of breaking. Even his movements are stiff like those of a mechanical man: his eyes are smoldering.

EVA (*jumping up as he enters*): Jim, you're not—?
JIM: Naw, I'm not locked up in Hall C.
EVA: I hadn't seen you. I was afraid—
JIM: You must have forgotten what a special value there is attached to my hide.
EVA: You look awfully tired, Jim.
JIM: Yes. How do *you* sleep at night?
EVA: Not well lately.
JIM: How do you sleep at all knowing what you know and keeping still?
EVA: What else can I do but keep still?
JIM: You could talk. You could tell the State Humane Society that thirty-five hundred animals are being starved to death and threatened with torture.
EVA: And lose my job?
JIM: Aw. Excuse me for being so impractical.
EVA: You don't understand. I was out of work six months before I got this job.
JIM: You told me that.
EVA: I got down to my last dime. Once a man followed along the street and I stood still, waiting for him to catch up with me. Yes, I'd gotten down that low, I was going to ask him for money—
JIM: Did you?
EVA: No. At the last moment I couldn't. I went hungry instead.

(*Jim looks at her.*)

Now you want me to go back to that? Times haven't improved. Now maybe I'd have more courage, or less decency, or maybe I'd be hungrier than I was before.

JIM: You'd better hold on to your job, Miss Crane—even if it does mean participating in a massacre!

EVA: It's not that bad.

JIM: It's going to be that bad. I'm going to talk myself now. Even if it means giving up my chance of parole.

EVA: No, you can't do that. Wait a while and see how things turn out.

JIM: This is the zero hour. Whalen has given instructions to put Hall C in Klondike tonight if they don't eat supper.

EVA: I know. I heard him.

(*Jim lifts the telephone receiver*)

What are you going to do?

JIM: Blow the lid off this stinking hole!

EVA (*grabbing the phone*): No, Jim! I'll do it, myself! I'll talk!

JIM: When?

EVA (*lowering her voice*): Now. Tonight. I'll visit the newspaper on my way home.

JIM: You will, huh?

EVA: Yes!

JIM: No. Wait till tomorrow. We'll have more definite evidence then. With Hall C in Klondike.

(*Whalen enters.*)

WARDEN: Well, Jim. What do the boys in Hall C think about the change in climate that I've arranged for them?

JIM: They haven't heard yet. Wilson is going to tell them when he brings the men up from the Hole.

WARDEN: They'll be eating supper tonight.

JIM: What have they got for supper?

WARDEN: The old perennial favorites, hamburger and spaghetti. I'm not going to mollycoddle those bastards.—Excuse me, Eva.

JIM: I don't think they'll eat.

WARDEN: You don't, huh? Well, I do! Eva—

EVA (*who has gotten her hat*): Yes, Sir?

WARDEN: I'll want you back after supper. We've got to have things in perfect order in case the snoopers get busy.

EVA: All right.

WARDEN: You'd better catch the ferry at seven-fifteen.

EVA: Yes, Sir. (*She exits.*)
JIM: About my parole, Mr. Whalen—
WARDEN: Yes? What about it?
JIM: It's coming up next month.
WARDEN (*grunting*): Humph.
JIM: I guess it pretty much hangs on your decision.
WARDEN: You've got a lot of brass.
JIM: Why do you say that?
WARDEN: Bothering me about your goddamn parole at a time like this!
JIM: It's important to me. I've been in here ten years and I've got ten years of copper. I'm due for a ticket-of-leave.
WARDEN: You'll get a ticket to Klondike if you got any more to say on that subject!
JIM (*starting forward*): By God, I—
WARDEN: What?
JIM (*with desperate control*): Nothing.
WARDEN (*uneasily*): I'm going out for supper. Be back about eight or eight-thirty. You watch things here.
JIM: Yes, Sir.

(*Whalen exits. Jim covers his face, strangling a sob.*)

Blackout

EPISODE FIVE

Musical theme up: "I'm Forever Blowing Bubbles."

Announcer: "Hall C!" Musical theme fade.

A spot comes up on the cell. The dialogue is fairly light, but an undercurrent of desperation should be felt.

BUTCH (*hoarsely*): "I'm forever blow-ing BUBBLES!"
JOE: Quit croakin' that corny number. Why dontcha learn something new?
BUTCH: That was new last I heard it.
JOE: Before you got in stir?

BUTCH: It had just come out.
JOE: It's had time to grow whiskers since then.
BUTCH: It was Goldie's fav'rite.
JOE: I thought you said she liked *Dardanella.*
BUTCH: She liked that one, too.
JOE: What's become of her?
BUTCH: How should I know? She quit writing ten years ago.
JOE: Christ. She's probably died of the syph by now.
BUTCH: Naw, not Goldie.
QUEEN: I wish I was dead. I used to have nice fingernails. Look at 'em now. My teeth was nice, too. I had nice hair. Now when I look at myself I wish I was dead.
BUTCH: "Faw'chun's always hi-ding! I looked ev'ry where!"

(*A mimic down the hall echoes the refrain.*)

BUTCH (*jumping to the bars*): Who was that? You, Krause?—Anytime I want you small-time grifters to muscle in on my singin' I'll send you a special request.
QUEEN: Yes, I wish I was dead. I hope that I starve to death. And I will. I can feel myself dying already.
BUTCH: "They fly so high, nearly reach the sky—" They used to turn out the light on that number. There was a sort of silver glass ball at the top of the ceilin' that would turn round and round an' throw little rainbow-colored reflections all over the floor an' the walls— God, it was lovely!
QUEEN (*rising*): Honest to God, I can't hold out much longer, Butch!
BUTCH: Naw?
QUEEN: Naw, I got a weak constitution. I was in a nervous run-down condition before I got sent up here. Hell, it was a bum rap. I didn't sell any weeds. I used to smoke 'em but I never sold any!—Persecution, all my life, persecution! Now maybe they'll kill me down there in Klondike, I'll never git out, never—never git out!
BUTCH: Dummy up!
QUEEN: You ever been in Klondike, Joe?
JOE: Naw. Butch has.
QUEEN: What's it like, Butch?
BUTCH (*rising slowly and going to stage front*): "Then like my dreams they fade an' die—"

QUEEN: They say it ain't the heat so much.

JOE: What is it? The humidity?

QUEEN: Naw, you can't breathe good. It's kind of—suffocating! (*He fingers his collar.*)

BUTCH: Fortune's always hiding—I looked ev'rywhere! I'm forever blow-ing BUBBLES! (*He stops short.*)

(*A door clangs—the men rise simultaneously, tense. There is the sound of a wracking cough and delirious sobbing.*)

(*Butch continues softly.*) They're bringin' 'em up from the Hole.

SCHULTZ: Gwan, git a move on, it ain't no funeral march yet awhile!

(*The dull shuffling of feet is heard accompanied by coughing, sobbing. The heads of the men in the cells move slowly from left to right, mouths open, as though watching some awful procession.*)

Halt! Face your cells!—You, too, Shapiro, do I have to speak Yiddish to make you understand?

(*A low yammering commences. Butch seizes his tin cup and holds it poised. A whistle sounds; the cell door opens.*)

March in! Git in there, Trout—Shapiro!

(*Swifty stumbles into the cell, unshaven, ghastly, sobbing.*)

Awright! Take a good look at 'em. An' remember this! The Hole is just a small dose compared to Klondike! Klondike's the big medicine and the Boss is all set to pour it out in double doses for any of you wise bastards that don't feel like eating supper tonight!

VOICE (*slowly and emphatically*): Where's Ollie?

ANOTHER (*staccato*): Yeah, where's Ollie?

CHORUS: Where's Ollie, where's Ollie, what did you do with Ollie?

(*Slight pause.*)

SCHULTZ: Who's responsible if some fool nigger takes a notion to butt his own brains out? (*There is a slight whine of fear in his voice.*)

(*Butch suddenly hammers the cell bar with his cup. Yammering commences. During the preceding speeches, from the point of his entrance, Swifty has stood dazed; then he sags slowly to his knees beside the bunk. The Queen comforts him awkwardly. Joe and Butch stand with attention fixed on Schultz. A whistle sounds. The yammering subsides a little.*)

(*Schultz, standing directly outside the open cell door, continues*): You see this here thermometer? (*He extracts a large one from his pocket.*) See that little red mark there? That says Blood Heat. Now see this one up here twenty degrees more? It says Fever Heat. You think it's going to stop there? Not a chance! It's going to keep right on rising till it busts clean out of the top of the little doojigit! It's going to break all records. It's going to be the biggest heat wave in history. Now if you don't think I'm a good weather prophet, just one of you finicky lads leave a little spaghetti on his plate tonight an' see what happens!

VOICE: Spaghetti?

(*There is complete tense silence for a moment.*)

SCHULTZ: Yeah, spaghetti!

BUTCH: Spaghetti, huh?—We ain't gonna eat it tonight or no other time—not till Whalen cuts out the graft and feeds us something besides hog-slop!

SCHULTZ: Is 'at what you want me to tell him?

BUTCH: Yeah, tell him that, an' if he don't like it—

(*Yammering; a whistle; the door clangs shut; the yammering subsides.*)

VOICE: Klondike?

ANOTHER: Tonight?

ANOTHER: Yeah, if we don't eat!

VOICE: Klondike? No?

ANOTHER: Not if we go to Klondike!

VOICE (*shrill and despairing*): We can't make it!!

(*A wracking cough and delirious sobbing are heard. Mex prays in a hoarse strangled voice.*)

MEX: *Santa María—Madre de Dios*—etc.

(*Butch advances to the bars and raps commandingly.*)

VOICE: It's Butch!

ANOTHER: What does Butch say?

MEX: *Jésus—muerto por nuestros pecados!*

BUTCH: Cut the cackle all of yuz! That goes for you too, Mex. You got plenty of time for talking to Jesus when you git there! Lissen here now!—Anybody in Hall C that eats is gonna pay for his supper in Kangaroo Court. I'll assess the maximum fine, you know what!—You're scared of Klondike? I say let 'em throw us in Klondike!—Maybe some of you weak sisters will be melted down to grease-chunks. But not all twenty-five of us! Some of us are gonna beat Klondike! And Klondike's dere las' trump card, when you got that licked, you've licked everything they've got to offer in here! You got 'em over the barrel for good! So then what happens? They come up to us and they say, "You win! What is it you want?" We say, "Boss Whalen is out! Git us a new Warden! Git us decent livin' conditions! No more overcrowdin', no more bunkin' up wit' contajus dis-easus; fresh air in the cell-blocks, fumigation, an' most of all—WE WANT SOME FOOD THAT'S FIT TO PUT IN OUR BELLIES! (*Applause.*) No more hamburger an' spaghetti an' beans, and beans an' hamburger an' spaghetti till you feel like the whole fucking world was made of nothin' else but hamburger an' beans an' spaghetti—(*Applause.*)—Maybe when we git through housecleaning this place'll be like the Industrial Reformatory they got at Chillicothe! A place where guys are learnt how to make a livin' after they git outa stir! Where they teach 'em trades an' improve their ejication! Not just lock 'em up in dirty holes an' hope to God they'll die so as to save the State some money!! (*Fierce yammering.*) Tonight we go to Klondike!—Dere's three compartments! One of 'em's little hell, one of 'em's middle-sized hell an' one of 'em's BIG HELL!—You know which one Butch O'Fallon is gonna be in!—So if I ain't yellow, boys, don't you be neither! That's all I got to say.

VOICE: Okay, Butch.

ANOTHER: We're witcha!

CHORUS: We'll beat Klondike!—You bet we'll bet it!—Put Whalen over a barrel— (*There is nervous laughter and applause.*)

(*Their voices die abruptly under a shadow of fear.*)

MEX (*chanting*): *Muerto—por nuestros pecados—rojo—de sangre es—el Sol!*

Blackout

EPISODE SIX

Announcer: "Definition of Life!"

A spot comes up on the office. Jim, facing downstage, leans against the desk, smoking. Eva enters.

EVA: Hello, Jim.
JIM: Yeah.
EVA: Nice out. A little bit cooler.—What's wrong with you?
JIM (*grinning wryly*): Ask me what life is, Eva.

(*Eva looks at him and crosses downstage.*)

Ask me what it is and I'll tell you.
EVA (*removing her hat*): No, darling.
JIM: Why not?
EVA: It smells like a bad epigram.
JIM (*tossing away his cigarette*): It's a gradual process of dying, that's what it is!
EVA: Worse than I expected.
JIM: That's what it is in here. Maybe it's something else on your side of the fence. I'd like to find out, but I guess I won't have the chance!
EVA (*seriously*): Your parole?

(*Jim strikes a match, watches it burn.*)

Turned down?
JIM: Not yet but it will be. I was talking about it to Whalen.

EVA: Oh. You shouldn't have mentioned it now when he's all steamed up about the hunger strike.

JIM: I didn't mean to. It just popped somehow. I'm getting out of control—Butch named me for the right kind of bird. Canaries never get out of their cages, do they, Eva?

EVA: Jim! Don't be a fool.

JIM: Naw, they die in 'em—singin' sweetly till doomsday! God damn!

EVA (*brushing her hat*): Speaking of birds—I wish the pigeons would be a little more careful! Don't you think it's a nice hat, Jim?

JIM (*without looking*): Yes, colossal.

EVA: I bought it on the way home. I felt sort of gay and irresponsible—knowing tomorrow was the last day, I suppose! Jim! (*She catches his arm: he averts his face.*)

JIM (*his fear visible*): If I get turned down again this time, I'll never get another chance.

EVA: Why not?

JIM: Because I'll blow-up!—Crack to pieces! I'm drawn as tight as I can get right now!

EVA: Don't be a damn fool, Jim.

JIM: You know what it's been like. Hated like poison for ten years by everybody but him. Working for him and all the time hating him so that it made me sick at the guts to look at him even! Ten years of being his stooge. Jimmy boy, do this, do that! Yes, Sir. Yes, Mr. Whalen!—My hands aching to catch that beefy red neck of his and choke the breath out of it! That's one reason why they shake so much—and here's another. Standing here at this window, looking out, seeing the streets, the buildings, the traffic moving, the lights going off and on, and me being pent up here, in these walls, locked in 'em so tight it's like I was buried under the earth in a coffin with a glass lid that I could see the world through! While I felt the worms crawling inside me . . .

EVA: No. Don't be a fool. (*She crosses upstage to the window.*) It's nice out. Gotten cooler.

JIM: You said that before.

EVA (*smiling desperately*): Well, it's still true. There's a carnival on South Bay. I ran in like a kid and took a ride on the zebra!

JIM: Yes?

EVA: There's two seats on the zebra, Jim. One in front, one in back— Next month we'll ride him together!

JIM (*suddenly breaking*): Eva! Eva! (*He covers his face.*)

EVA (*running to him*): I love you!

(*Pause.*)

JIM (*his voice choking*): What is this place? What's it for? Why, why! The judges say guilty. But what is guilty? What does that word mean, anyhow? It's funny, but I don't know. (*He picks up the dictionary.*) Look it up in *Webster's Dictionary.* What's it say? "Responsible for the commission of crime." But why responsible? What's responsible mean? Who's ever been given a choice? When they mix up all the little molecules we're made out of, do they ask each one politely which he will be—rich man, poor man, beggar man, thief? God, no! It's all accidental. And yet the Judge says, "Jim, you're guilty!" (*He tosses the dictionary to the floor.*) This book's no good anymore. We need a new one with a brand new set of definitions.

EVA: Don't say any more—I won't let you! (*She kisses him.*)

JIM: How did this happen between you and me?

EVA: I don't know.

JIM: It's the dirtiest trick they've played on us yet.

EVA: Don't say that!

JIM: We can't have each other. We never can, Eva.

EVA: We can!

JIM: Where?

EVA: Somewhere.

JIM: How?

EVA: I don't know how.

JIM: Neither do I.

EVA: But next month—

JIM: There won't be any next month!

EVA: There will, oh, there will, there must be!

JIM: Why?—Why?

EVA: Because I love you so much that it's got to happen the way I want it to happen!

JIM: Why do you love me?

EVA: Why is anything on earth? I don't know why.

JIM: Neither do I—

(*They cling together in tortured ecstasy. Blackout. The lights come up as the phone rings.*)

JIM: Yes? I'll tell him. (*He hangs up.*)
EVA: What is it?
JIM: Schultz. They won't eat.
EVA: What's he going to do?
JIM: He's already got his instructions from Whalen. They'll be in Klondike at seven.
EVA (*pausing*): I won't be down here tomorrow.
JIM: No?
EVA: I'll be in the newspaper offices. And at City Hall. Any place where people will listen!
JIM: You think they'll listen anywhere, Eva?
EVA: I'll make them listen!
JIM: And afterwards what will you do? With no job?
EVA: I'll only have to wait three weeks. And then I'll be *your* responsibility, Jim!
JIM: I hope to God you're right.
EVA: I am! I know I am!

(*Whalen enters.*)

WARDEN: Hello! Still here, Jim?
JIM: Yes, Sir. Schultz called. They wouldn't eat supper.
WARDEN: Well—he's got his instructions.
JIM: Yes, he said that he had.
WARDEN (*scribbling on a piece of paper*): Take this down to the switchboard and have it posted there and sent to all stations.
JIM: Does this mean—?
WARDEN: Never mind what it means. Just take it down there. And step lively!
JIM: Yes, Sir.

(*Jim goes out.*)

WARDEN (*to Eva*): Back on the job, huh?
EVA: Yes.
WARDEN (*belching and removing his coat*): I should have told you to bring some things with you.

EVA: What things?

WARDEN: Your little silk nightie and stuff.

EVA: What do you mean?

WARDEN: Quarantine! A bad epidemic's broken out! Twenty-five cases are going to be running a pretty high fever tonight so I've put this place under quarantine restrictions —nobody's gonna leave the grounds till the epidemic is over.

EVA: I can't stay here.

WARDEN (*busy with papers*): Sure you can. My wife'll fix a room for you. You'll be very comfortable here.

EVA: No, I won't do it.

WARDEN: You've got no choice in the matter.

EVA: Haven't I?

WARDEN: Naw, I'm not running a risk on any outside interference while this trouble is going on. It's my business, I'm going to keep it my business. So just as a routine precaution I've ordered the boats to take no passengers on or off the island without my special permission.

EVA: I think you're exceeding your authority.

WARDEN: Naw, you're wrong there. Times of emergency I can do what I damn please. Say—what are you worried about?

EVA (*frightened*): I—

WARDEN: I know. It's a nervous strain we've all been under these last few days. I got gas on the stomach myself. Here. (*He pours a shot of whiskey.*)

EVA: No, you've been drinking too much. I'm afraid it's affected your sense of judgment. You ought to know you can't get away with a thing like this!

WARDEN: Hey, now—look here!

EVA (*excitedly*): I'm not a prisoner—I'm free to go and do as I please—you can't stop me!

WARDEN: Look here, now!

(*She grasps the phone.*)

EVA: Riverside 3854 W! Riverside 3–8— (*She realizes the phone is cut off.*)

WARDEN: No out-going calls can get through. You're wasting your time.

EVA: Then I—I *am* a prisoner here!

WARDEN: You're temporarily detained on the island—might as well make the best of it! (*He pours another drink.*)

EVA: Oh!

WARDEN: Here, now, what's wrong with you?

EVA: I don't know why, but I'm terribly frightened.

WARDEN (*soothingly*): You've gone and worked yourself up. There's nothing for you to be nervous about.

EVA: You! I'm afraid of you! (*She backs away from him.*)

WARDEN: Me? Why should you be scared of me?

EVA: I am, though. I'm scared to death of you. You've got to let me go, I can't stay with you any longer, Mr. Whalen.

WARDEN: Now, now.

EVA: No, don't touch me! Please don't.

WARDEN: You're hysterical, Eva.

EVA: Yes!

WARDEN (*purring*): My wife gets spells like that, too—that "don't touch me" stuff!

EVA (*retreating*): Yes!

WARDEN: I know a good treatment for it that always works. There, now little girl you just take it easy. Relax. You're all worked up over nothing. You're stiff, see? Your nerves and your muscles are all drawn up real tight.

EVA: Yes . . . (*She has nearly collapsed with nervous exhaustion—his purring voice has a hypnotic effect.*)

WARDEN: Mmm. Now when my wife gets like this, I—I rub my fingers along her throat—real, real gently—till all the stiffness goes out . . .

EVA (*her eyes falling shut*): Yes . . .

WARDEN (*gazes at her lasciviously*): . . . and then I—

(*Eva sighs as though asleep.*)

WARDEN: Eva?—Eva? (*He rises and opens the inner door, then hesitates—*)

(*The phone rings.*)

For Chrissakes, what is it now? Yeah? What? I'm coming right down there now!— (*He hangs up—purring drunkenly.*) You wait, li'l girl, I'll be right back in here! Yes, Siree . . . (*He fumbles into his coat and goes out.*)

(*Eva gasps as the door slams shut—she slowly rises. The outer door opens— Eva screams— Jim enters.*)

EVA: Jim! Jim!

(*Jim catches her in his arms.*)

Get me out of here, oh, please, *please*, get me out of here! (*She sobs wildly.*)

JIM: Hold on to yourself! (*He shakes her.*) Hold on to yourself!

EVA: I'm trying to, Jim.

JIM: Take a deep breath. Here—at the window.

EVA: Yes!

JIM: See those lights over there?

EVA: Yes!

JIM: That's the Lorelei on her way out. Be real quiet and you can hear the music. (*She leans against him—faint music is heard.*) Better now?

EVA: Yes. Thanks, Jim.

JIM: What happened? Just tell me real quietly and don't get excited about it.

EVA: He told me I—I'm a prisoner here! I can't leave! I don't know why, but it made me terribly frightened all of a sudden. His eyes, the way he looked at me, Jim—I had a feeling that something awful was going to happen—

JIM: Easy, now!

EVA: Yes. I guess I'm an awful sissy.

JIM: No, you've got more guts than me.

EVA: He—he came real close to me—and his voice—sort of put me to sleep.

JIM: Did he—?

EVA: No! He only opened that door. And then a bell rang—I could hear it like it was a thousand miles off!

JIM: A bell?

EVA: They called him upstairs, I guess. He left the room and I—I would have jumped out the window if you hadn't come just then!

JIM: There's nothing but water out there.

EVA: I didn't care. I just wanted to get away somehow.

JIM: You'll get away.

EVA: With you, Jim? You'll take me?

JIM: Yes. In a while. Don't you feel the walls shaking? They can't hold up much longer. There's too much boiling inside them—hate, torture, madness, fury! They'll blow wide open in a little while and we'll be loose!

EVA: I want to be with you when that happens! I want you to hold me like this—so that when the walls start falling I won't be crushed down under them, Jim.

JIM: We'll be together.

EVA: Where?

JIM: Meet me tonight in the southwest corner of the yard.

EVA: Will we be safe there?

JIM (*in a whisper*): It's dark. Nobody could see us.

Blackout—End of Act Two

ACT THREE

EPISODE ONE

Announcer: "Morning of August 15!"

A spot comes up on the office. The warden is at the phone. During the following episodes the theater is filled almost constantly with the soft hiss of live steam from the radiators—

WARDEN: Schultz? How hot is it down there now? 125? What's the matter? Git it up to 130! You got Butch O'Fallon in No. 3 aintcha? Okay, give No. 3 135 and don't let up on it till you git instructions from me. Hey! Got them windows in the hall shut? Good. Keep 'em shut an' let 'em squawk their goddamn heads off!

(*Blackout. A spot comes up on Klondike. The torture cell is seen through a scrim to give a misty or steam-clouded effect to the atmosphere. The men are sprawled on the floor, breathing heavily, their shirts off, skin shiny with sweat. A ceiling light glares relentlessly down on them. The walls are bare and glistening wet. Along them are radiators from which rise hissing clouds of live steam.*)

JOE (*coughing*): W'at time is it?

BUTCH: How in hell would I know?

SWIFTY (*whimpering*): Water—water.

JOE: I wonder if we been in here all night.

BUTCH: Sure we have. I can see daylight through the hole.

JOE: How long was you in that time?

BUTCH: Thirty-six hours.

JOE: Christ!

BUTCH: Yeah. And we've just done about eight.

SWIFTY: Water!

BUTCH: Hey! Y'know what—what the old maid said to the burglar when she—she found him trying to jimmy th' lock on th'—

JOE: Yeah. (*He coughs.*)

QUEEN: Swifty's sick. I am, too. Why don't somebody come here?

BUTCH: Aw, you heard that one?

JOE: Yeah. A long time ago, Butch. (*He coughs.*)

BUTCH: You oughta know some new ones.

JOE: Naw. Not any new ones, Butch.

BUTCH: Then tell some old ones, goddamn it!! Dontcha all lie there like you was ready to be laid under! Let's have some life in this party— Sing! Sing! You know some good songs, Queenie, you got a voice! C'mon you sons-of-guns! Put some pep in it! Sing it out, sing it out loud, boys! (*He sings wildly, hoarsely.*)

> Pack up your troubles in yuhr ole kit bag an'
> Smile, smile, smile!

(*The others join in feebly*—)

Sing it out! Goddamit, sing it out loud!

> What's the use of worrying
> It never was worthwhile!

(*Joe tries to sing—he is suddenly bent double in a paroxysm of coughing.*)

SWIFTY (*in a loud anguished cry*): Water! Water! Water! (*He sobs.*)

(*There is a loud shrill hiss of steam from the radiators as more pressure is turned on.*)

QUEEN (*in frantic horror*): *They're givin' us more!* Oh, my God, why don't they stop now! Why don't they let us out! Oh, Jesus, Jesus, please, please, please! (*He sobs wildly and falls on the floor.*)

SWIFTY (*weakly*): Water—water . . .

BUTCH: Yeah. They're givin' us more heat. Sure, they're givin' us more heat. Dontcha know you're in Klondike? Aw, w'at's a use, yer crybabies. Yuh wanta go on suckin' a sugar-tit all yer life? Gwan, sing it out—

I'm forever blowing BUBBLES!
Pretty bubbles in the—AIR!

SHAPIRO: There is nothing to be done about it, nothing at all. I come of a people that are used to suffer. It is not a new thing. I have it in my blood to suffer persecution, misery, starvation, death.

SWIFTY: Water.

SHAPIRO (*mumbles in Yiddish, then*): My head is full, full. Aching in here. Broken already, perhaps. Rose? Rose? You know the property on South Maple Street—it's all in your name, my darling—be careful—don't make bad investments—

JOE (*coughing*): Lemme at the air hole.

QUEEN: You're hoggin' it!

JOE: Cantcha see I'm choking to death? (*He coughs.*)

(*The steam hisses louder.*)

BUTCH (*rising*): We got to systematize this business. Quit fightin' over the air hole. The only air that's fit to breathe is comin' through there. We gotta take turns breathin' it. We done sixteen hours about. Maybe we'll do ten more, twenty more, thirty more.

JOE: Christ!

QUEEN: We can't make it!

BUTCH: We can if we organize. Keep close to the floor. Stay in a circle round the wall. Each guy take his turn. Fifteen seconds. Maybe later ten seconds or five seconds. I do the counting. And when a guy flips out—he's finished—he's through—push him outa the line— This ain't a first-aid station—this is Klondike—and by God—some of us are gonna beat it—Okay? Okay, Joe?

JOE: Yeah.

BUTCH: Well, git started then.

SWIFTY: Water!

BUTCH: Push the kid up here first.

(*They shove Swifty's inert body to the air hole.*)

Breathe! Breathe! Breathe, goddamn you, breathe! (*He jerks Swifty up by the collar—stares at his face.*) Naw, it's no use. I guess he's beating a cinder track around the stars now!

QUEEN: He ain't dead! Not yet! He's unconscious, Butch! Give him a chance!

BUTCH (*inexorably*): Push him outa the line. (*As the lights dim . . .*) Okay—Shapiro—Joe—

(*Theme up: "I'm Forever Blowing Bubbles." Fade.*)

Dim Out

EPISODE TWO

Announcer: "Evening of August 15!"

A spot comes up on the office. Whalen is at the phone.

WARDEN: You heard 'em what? Singin! Well, give 'em something to sing about! 140? Git it up to 145 in Butch's compartment! You bet I want 'em left in there all night. Naw, keep the windows shut. Water? Let 'em make their own water!

(*Blackout. A spot comes up on Klondike. Swifty lies dead in center, a shirt over his face. The voices are hoarse, breathing more labored. Joe coughs wrackingly. The radiators hiss loudly.*)

BUTCH: Here comes more! Keep down! Keep down!

(*Queen sobs wildly. Shapiro mumbles in Yiddish.*)

Joe! Look! I got it with me! (*He extracts a razor from his belt.*)

JOE: That's one way out.

BUTCH: Maybe the boss will come down here to look us over.

JOE (*coughing*): Naw, he wouldn't.

BUTCH: Maybe Schultz will. Or the Canary. (*He rises.*) Schultz! Schultz! Naw, it's no dice, he's too yellow to stick his puss in here! But if he does ever—

(*A whistle sounds.*)

Hear that? It's the lock-up bell! We've done twenty-four hours, Joe. We only got twelve more to go!

JOE: How d'you know how long it will be?

BUTCH: They don't want to kill us!

JOE: Why don't they? (*He coughs.*)—Your turn, Butch.

BUTCH: Yeah, git moving, Queenie!

QUEEN: Naw! Lemme breathe!

(*Butch tears him away from air hole. Shapiro shouts something in Yiddish. Queen continues rising and staggering.*)

I got to get out of here! Lemme out, lemme out! (*He pounds at the wall, then staggers blindly towards the radiators.*)

BUTCH: Stay away from the radiators!

(*Queen staggers directly into the cloud of steam—screams—falls to the floor.*)

He's scalded himself.

(*Queen screams and sobs.*)

Stop it! Goddamn yuh— (*He grasps Queen's collar and cracks his head against floor.*) There now!

JOE: Butch—you killed him.

BUTCH: Somebody shoulda done him that favor a long time ago.

(*Shapiro mumbles in Yiddish.*)

You heard that one about—the niggers in church? "—Rastus, she says— Naw, he says—Mandy—Mandy how long does the Preacher—"

(*Dim out. A spot comes up on the office. Whalen is on the phone.*)

WARDEN: Schultz? How hot is it down there now in Butch's compartment? 150? Good! Keep it there till I give you further instructions— I'll be in my office till about midnight and if anything comes up—

(*Fade out. A spot comes up on Klondike. Shapiro, Queen, and Swifty are dead and lie in the center. Butch and Joe, gasping, crouch together by the air hole.*)

JOE: Butch—
BUTCH: Yeah.
JOE: Y'know that razor—
BUTCH: What about it?
JOE: Use it on me! Quick! I wanta get done with this!
BUTCH: Keep hold of yourself, Joe. You can make it.
JOE: Naw, I can't, Butch. I'm chokin' t' death. I can't stand it.
BUTCH: Breathe!
JOE: There ain't no air coming in now, Butch.
BUTCH: There's air—breathe it, Joe.
JOE: Naw . . .

(*Butch raises his face and shakes him.*)

BUTCH (*hoarsely*): Goddamn yuh, don't chicken out! Stay with me, Joe! We can beat Klondike!

(*Joe laughs deliriously. Butch continues, springing up.*)

Turn off them fucking radiators!! Turn the heat off, goddamn yuh, turn it off! (*He staggers toward the radiators.*) Stop it, y'hear me? Quit that SSSS! SSSS! (*He imitates the hissing sound.*) I'll turn yuh off, yuh suns-a-bitches! (*He springs on the radiators and grapples with them as though with a human adversary—he tries to throttle steam with his hands—he's scalded—screams with agony—backs away, his face contorted, wringing his hands.*) SSSSS! SSSSS! SSSSS! (*He is crazily imitating their noise.*)

JOE: Christ, Butch, it ain't no good that way. You've blown your top. What's the percentage? (*Butch staggers back to the air hole.*)

BUTCH: Joe! Hey, Joe! Swifty! You, Queen! Shapiro! (*He tugs at one of the bodies.*) Let's sing! Let's all sing something! Sing it out! Loud!

For-tune's always hid-ing!

Why don't you bastards sing something! Come on—sing! Sing!

I looked ev'rywhere—!

(*The lights dim as the music completes the final lines of "Bubbles."*)

Dim Out

EPISODE THREE

Announcer: "The Southwest Corner of the Yard!"

Dark stage and complete silence for several moments. Then—

EVA: Jim!
JIM: Here!
EVA: I'm late. I couldn't help it.
JIM: Shhh!
EVA (*lowering her voice*): His wife's not on the Island. She left this afternoon. I can't stay there in that place with him, Jim, I can't do it!
JIM: Shhh. Don't talk.
EVA: What am I going to do, Jim? What am I going to do?
JIM: *Don't talk!* It's not safe. They might hear us. Eva—

(*Pause. The beam of a searchlight moves over them.*)

EVA: Jim! They're moving the light!
JIM: Shhh! Keep it down!

(*The light disappears.*)

EVA: Oh. Thank God.
JIM: Now!
EVA: You've never even said that you loved me.
JIM: I love you. Now!
EVA: Oh, Jim—Jim! (*A longer pause.*)
JIM: The light again!

(*It circles lower this time and pauses directly above them.*)

Christ! Keep down low!
EVA: Jim!
JIM: Crawl! No, that way! Quick!

(*The light suddenly moves down and shines full upon Eva's face. Eva screams. A siren sounds. Blackout. A spot comes up on the office. Jim and Eva are there with a Guard. Whalen enters.*)

WARDEN: What *is* this?
GUARD: It looks like the Canary's turned into a lovebird, Mr. Whalen.
WARDEN: Aw!
GUARD: I heard a noise in the southwest corner of the yard. Sounded like a girl's voice. I dropped the light on—there they was!
WARDEN: Aw! Doing what?
GUARD: Well, they weren't picking daisies.
WARDEN: Aw! (*To Eva.*): You a while ago. Got hysterical in here. Objected because there wasn't no chaperone in the house. Then you run out there like a bitch in heat and—
JIM (*starting forward*): Stop it!
WARDEN: Aw!
JIM: It's easy to say things like that when you've got a gun stuck in my back.
WARDEN: Put the gun down. (*He takes a rubber hose from the hall.*) It's disillusioning what happens when you put too much confidence in the wrong people. Take your coat off.
EVA: No, you can't do that to him. I won't stand for it. It wasn't his fault. I asked him to meet me out there. Because I was scared. Scared of you! Scared of this awful place

you've got us locked up in! And now you let us out! You let us both out of here now! Before I scream! I'll let the whole world know what's going on here!

WARDEN: Take hold of that girl!

JIM (*springing toward them*): Let her go!

(*Whalen flails at Jim with the hose. Jim staggers to the floor, covering his face. Eva screams and struggles.*)

WARDEN: Take him out of here!

GUARD: Where to?

WARDEN: Klondike! Throw him in there with Butch O'Fallon! They're real good friends! (*He laughs.*)

(*The guard goes out dragging Jim.*)

Well, Eva—

(*Eva turns her face sharply away.*)

I'm sorry about this whole thing. I mean it sincerely. What I just said—forget that! You probably don't stop to realize what a strain I've been under. It's not easy to be the head of an institution like this. I've handled it like I would handle anything else. The best I knew how. Sometimes—I'm telling you the truth, girl—I've been so sick at heart at things I've had to do and see done—that it hurt me to look into my own little girl's face and hear her call me—Daddy! (*He pours himself a drink.*) Here. You take one, too. (*He is breathing heavily and for the moment is perfectly in earnest.*) Maybe it's done something to me in here. (*He touches his head.*) Sometimes I don't feel quite the same anymore. Awful, awful! Men down there now being subjected to awful torture! But what can I do about it? I got to keep discipline—dealing with criminals—there's no other way—Take your drink.

EVA: Thank you. (*She takes it.*)

WARDEN: There's two ways I could look at this. It could be a serious business. By your own confession you—you remember what you said, you—had Jim meet you out in the yard— Now I'm inclined to be broad-minded about such things—these discrepancies in the commissary report—

(*He shrugs and smiles.*)—things like that—serious sometimes—at least they can look that way—

EVA: What do you mean, Mr. Whalen? You mean you would—try to accuse me of—!

WARDEN: No, no, no! (*He smiles engagingly.*) Not unless you forced me to.

EVA: What do you want?

WARDEN: What does any man want? What did Jim want, what did you give him?—Sympathy!

EVA: Oh.

WARDEN: That way it could be very simple. We're all of us nervous, strained, overwrought!—Sympathy! All of us need it!

EVA: Oh. What will you do to Jim now?

WARDEN: Well—

EVA: I love him! You probably don't understand how it happened between us— He's coming up for parole next month.

WARDEN: Yes, I have the letter in my desk now.

EVA: What letter?

WARDEN: Recommending Jim's—release! Of course after this—

EVA: You won't send it?

WARDEN: Well—

EVA: Suppose I—I did sympathize—as you say—and—and kept my mouth shut and anything else that you want! Would you send the letter? Would Jim get his parole?

WARDEN (*smiling*): Why not? (*He laughs gently.*) You see how easy it is to straighten things out!

EVA: Now? Would you send it now?

WARDEN: Now? It's—pretty late now—

EVA: The mailboat leaves at eleven-forty-five. You could have it sent over by that. Don't worry. I won't back out. I'm not afraid of you now. I like you—I'd like to show you how much!

(*The Warden removes the letter from the drawer and rings the bell. A guard enters.*)

WARDEN: Put this in the mail.

GUARD: Yes, Sir. (*He goes out.*)

WARDEN: My head aches, aches all the time—my wife's left me—the little girl, too— (*He opens the inner door.*) We're all of us nervous and tired, overwrought! Aren't we? Yes— (*He ushers Eva in as the light fades.*)

Dim Out

EPISODE FOUR

Announcer: "The Showdown"

A spot comes up on Klondike. Butch lies by the air hole. The bodies of the others are heaped in the center—Butch is apparently unconscious. Voices are heard in the hall. Butch slowly raises his head, becomes tense.

SCHULTZ (*as the door opens*): —makin' love to the Boss's secretary out in the yard—fancy that!

(*Butch rolls over quickly and feigns unconsciousness.*)

Whew! What a stink! Hey—Chick! C'mere! Steam's s' goddamn thick I can't see nothin'. Gimme that flash—

CHICK: Looks t' me like—Jeez! They're *stiffs*!

SCHULTZ: Stiffs! Y'mean—

CHICK: Roasted! Roasted alive! God Almighty! I didn't know nothin' like this was going on in here.

SCHULTZ: Shut up! How many are there?

(*During this Butch has slowly risen and poised himself for attack.*)

Gimme the flash! Shapiro, Joe—Swifty—The Queen—Where's Butch?

BUTCH (*springing*): Here! Here! (*He clutches Schultz by the throat.*)

(*Jim attacks Chick. A shot is fired; Jim wrests the revolver from the guard.*)

JIM: Toss your mittens!

BUTCH (*slowly releasing Schultz*): Aw! You! The Canary!

SCHULTZ (*uncertainly*): Good work, Jim!

JIM: I mean you, Schultz! Reach high! Butch—get them keys off him!

BUTCH (*slowly grinning*): Aw—*aw!* (*He snatches the keys.*)

SCHULTZ: What is this?

JIM: Butch—let the boys out! We're going upstairs!

BUTCH: Yeah!

SCHULTZ: You'll get the hot seat for this! Every mother's bastard of you will! What are you going to do, Jim?

JIM: Get into something comfortable, Schultz! You're going to SWEAT!

(*Jim backs out and slams the door. Schultz rushes to it, pounds and screams. Blackout. The stage is dark for a moment. There is the long wail of a siren. A spot comes up in the Warden's office. Whalen steps out of the inner room—he listens, tense with alarm.—The office door is thrown open—Jim enters.*)

WARDEN: Jim!

JIM (*his clothes torn and bloody from the earlier beating*): Yeah! Sometimes even hell breaks open and the damned get loose!

WARDEN: What's happened—downstairs? (*He edges back—pushes a buzzer.*)

JIM: No use pushing that. There's nobody on the other end of it.

WARDEN: They've broken out of—Klondike?

JIM: Yes. All of 'em but four. Four didn't break out cause they're dead—but they sent their regards to you, Boss, they want to be remembered!

WARDEN: How did you get that? (*He points to the revolver.*)

JIM: Raided the munitions!

WARDEN: What happened to Schultz?

JIM: He got in trouble downstairs, he's locked in Klondike, keeping the dead boys company down there— The other screws are locked up in the cellblock. Stand outa the way. (*He removes a revolver from the desk.*) Where's the girl?

WARDEN: She—left.

JIM: You're sure of that.

WARDEN: Yes— Why?

JIM: This ain't a safe place to be right now.

WARDEN: Look here, Jim—

JIM: What's the matter? You don't look good.

WARDEN: I'll make a deal with you—where are the—boys?

JIM (*jerking his thumb toward the door*): Waiting out there at the gate. I wanted to make sure the girl wasn't here before I let 'em come in.

WARDEN: Naw! You can't do that!

JIM: Sure. I'm the reception committee. I've got the keys.

(*Men are heard shouting outside. Eva appears at the inner door.*)

JIM: Eva!

EVA: Jim, don't do it, Jim! It's no use— He's written a letter asking for your parole, he sent it already!

WARDEN: Yes, Jim. I done it just now, because she—

JIM: Because she—what? (*He looks at them both.*) Aw! Get back inside there, Eva.

(*The boss starts to follow. Jim jerks him back.*)

Naw, you stay out here!

EVA: Jim! (*He forces her inside and locks the door.*)

WARDEN: Jim, you wouldn't give up your parole for the chair?

JIM: Sure. It's worth it. I haven't forgotten.

WARDEN: Forgotten—what?

JIM: Twenty-one days in the Hole. Dr. Jones.

WARDEN (*following him to door*): Afterwards I was your friend!

JIM: I wasn't yours!

WARDEN (*nearly screaming*): I was good to you afterwards, Jim!

JIM: I still had your signature on my back! Now we've got a new whipping-boss waiting out there—Butch O'Fallon!

WARDEN: Naw! Jim! Jim!

(*Jim has gone out—the roar of the men rises as doors are opened. The Warden gasps and darts behind the desk— Men enter like a pack of wolves and circle about the walls.*)

BUTCH (*lunging through*): Where is he?

WARDEN: Butch!

BUTCH (*his eyes blinded*): There! I've caught the smell of him now!

(*The two rulers face each other for the first time. Outside there is scattered gunfire, and a flickering light is thrown through the windows like the reflection of flames.*)

It's been you an' me a long time—you in here—me out there— But now it's—together at last— It's a pleasure, pig face, to make your acquaintance!

WARDEN: Look here now, boys—O'Fallon—Jim—I'll make a deal with you all— You've got to remember now—I've got the United States army in back of me!

BUTCH (*laughing and coming toward him*): You've got that wall in back of you— Where's the Doctor?

CONVICT: Here! (*He snatches the rubber hose from the wall and hands it to Butch.*)

BUTCH: Yeah!

WARDEN: Naw! Think of the consequences! Don't be fools!

(*Butch strikes him with the hose.*)

WARDEN (*cowering to the floor*): Stop! I'm a family man! I've got a wife! A daughter! A little—*girrrrl!* (*The final word turns into a scream of anguish as Butch crouches over him with the whip beating him with demoniacal fury till he is senseless.*)

(*The siren of an approaching boat is heard.*)

CONVICT: What is it?

ANOTHER: Gunboat!

ANOTHER: Troopers!

ANOTHER: They're landing!

ANOTHER: Douse the glims!

(*The room is plunged into total darkness except for the weird flickering of flame shadows on the walls— Men begin a panicky exodus from the room.*)

VOICES: Git down there— Fight 'em off— Troopers!—Not a chance— No chance anyhow!—You wanta go back to Klondike?—Fight!—Sure, fight!—We got nothing to lose!

(*Names are shouted—gates clang—machine gun fire is heard.*)

(*The noise becomes remote and dream-like—the room is almost quiet except for the distant, sad wail of the siren which continues endlessly* [*like the voice of damnation at the palace gates*].)

JIM: What have you done to him?

BUTCH: Thrown his blubbering carcass out the window.

JIM: Into the water?

BUTCH: Yeah. Straight down.

JIM: Butch—we've got a chance that way.

BUTCH: Swim for it? Naw, not me. I don't know how to swim. Besides it's half a mile to shore and rough as hell.

JIM: What will you do?

BUTCH: Stay here and fight it out.

JIM: I think I'll take my chances with the water.

BUTCH (*slowly extending his hand*): Good luck, I had you figured wrong.

JIM: Thanks.

BUTCH (*pulling off ring*): Here. There used to be a girl named Goldie at the Paradise Dance Hall on Brook Street west of the Ferry. If you should ever meet her, give her this— And tell her that I—kept it—all this time.

JIM: Sure, Butch—I will if I make—

BUTCH (*going to the door*): So long.

(*Rapid gunfire and distant shouting heard outside. Jim unlocks the inner door.*)

JIM: Eva.

(*Eva comes out slowly—she falls sobbing on his shoulder.*)

JIM: Don't cry!

EVA: No. I won't. There'd be no use in that. Jim, you were right about the pyrotechnical display!

JIM: Stand back from the window!

EVA (*hysterically gay*): It's lovely, isn't it, Jim!

JIM: Yes, lovely as hell!

EVA: What did they do to him?—Whalen?

JIM (*thumb to window*): The fish will have indigestion.

EVA: Jim! Have you thought what you'll get for this?
JIM: Nothing. They won't have a chance.
EVA: What are you going to do?

(*Sound cue: faint music.*)

JIM: There's water out that window. I can swim.
EVA: No, Jim, there's not a chance that way.
JIM: A chance? What's that? I never heard of it! (*On this speech he slowly approaches the window over the sea.*) Hear that? That music! It's—
EVA: The Lorelei!
JIM: The Lorelei— (*He tears off his coat.*) Now I retract those unkind things I said!
EVA: What will you do?
JIM: Swim out and catch a ride!
EVA: You couldn't, Jim— They'd bring you back— They wouldn't let you go!
JIM: They'll never see me.
EVA: Why?
JIM: Don't ask me why! There'll be a rope or something hanging over the side. Or if she doesn't ride too high I'll grab the rail! How! Don't ask me how! Now is the time for unexpected things, for miracles, for wild adventures like the storybooks!
EVA: Oh, Jim, there's not a chance that way!
JIM: Almost a chance! I've heard of people winning on a long shot. And if I don't— At least I'll be outside!
EVA: Oh, Jim I would have liked to live with you outside. We might have found a place where searchlights couldn't point their fingers at us when we kissed. I would have given you so much you've never had. Quick love is hard. It gives so little pleasure. We should have had long nights together with no walls. Or no *stone* walls— I know the place! A tourist camp beside a highway, Jim, with all night long the great trucks rumbling by—but only making shadows through the blinds! I'd touch the stone you're made of, Jim, and make you warm, so warm, so terribly warm your love would burn a scar upon my body that no length of time could heal!—Oh, Jim. If we could meet like that, at some appointed time, some place decided

now, where we could love in secret and be warm, protected, not afraid of things— We could forget all this as something dreamed!—Where shall it be? When, Jim? Tell me before you go!

JIM: Quick! It's almost close enough! Get that shoe off!

EVA (*pulling off his shoes*): Yes Jim! But tell me where?

JIM (*climbing to the sill*): Watch the personal columns!

EVA: Jim!—Good-bye! (*He plunges from the window.*) — Good-bye . . .

(*Music from the Lorelei swells. Flame-shadows brighten on the walls. Shouting and footsteps are heard. Troopers rush in.*)

ONE (*switching on light.*): A girl—

TWO: The Warden's Secretary!

THREE (*crossing to her*): You're all right, sister. (*To others*): She's dazed, can't talk— Get her a drink, somebody.

ONE: What's that she's got?

THREE: A pair of—shoes!

ONE: Whose are they? What's she doing with them?

EVA (*facing the window with a faint smile*): I picked them up somewhere. I can't remember.

(*Light fades except for a spot on Eva, clutching Jim's shoes. Music from the Lorelei rises to a crescendo as a string of colored lights slides past the window. Dim out.*)

LOUD-SPEAKER: Aw there, it is! Y'can see it now, folks. That's the Island! Sort of misty tonight on account of the moon's gone under. Them walls are *escape-proof*, folks. Thirty-five hundred men locked in there an' some of them gonna stay there till Doomsday—(*Music.*)—Ah, music again! Dancing on the upper deck, folks, dancing,— dancing . . .

(*Musical theme up.*)

The End

BATTLE OF ANGELS

PROLOGUE

THE SCENE: *A "mercantile" store in a very small and old-fashioned town in the Deep South. It has large windows facing a tired dirt road, across which is a gasoline pump, a broken down wagon and cotton fields which extend to a cypress brake and the levee. The windows are shielded from sunlight by a tin portico so that the interior is rather dusky. The ceiling is very high and has two or three ceiling fans and old-fashioned lighting fixtures. There are a good many vertical lines which contribute to a dramatic atmosphere in the setting. In the back wall of the store is a steep flight of stairs leading up to the living quarters above. Left of this stairway is an open arch revealing a further room, the store's confectionery department.*

At the time this Prologue takes place—a Sunday afternoon about a year after the culmination of the tragedy—the store is no longer being run as a store, but has been converted into a museum exhibiting souvenirs of the sensational events which had taken place there. Various articles connected with the tragedy are on display, such as the snakeskin jacket, which is suspended in a conspicuous position. All these articles are labeled with crude handlettered signs.

An ancient Negro, The Conjure Man, is dozing in a chair in the archway. There is an awesome dignity in his appearance, despite the grotesque touches of his costume. He is small and cadaverous, a wizard-like figure, with a double strand of bleached chicken or hawk bones strung about his neck, tiny bells sewn to the sleeves of his garments so that he makes a slight tinkling sound when he moves, and various other odd tokens or charms scattered about his garments, which he sells to the superstitious.

(*There is a knock at the door.*)

WOMAN'S VOICE: Uncle! Uncle! (*The old Negro starts up. He rises and shuffles leisurely across to the door, unbolts it and draws it open on the mellow afternoon sunlight. Eva and Blanch Temple step inside.*)

EVA: Goodness . . .

BLANCH: Gracious sakes alive! It takes you forever to move a couple of inches. Come on in, folks! This is the famous Torrance Mercantile Store of Two Rivers, Mississippi. (*They are followed by a pair of middle-aged tourists.*)

EVA: Some people think it's sort of commercial of us to turn it into what the newspapers refer to as a Tragic Museum—but after all . . .

BLANCH: There's nothing else we can do to pay the taxes. Nobody would use this building for any other purpose, knowing what all happened in here once.

EVA: Not that it's haunted, but . . .

BLANCH: It's full of shadows. Electric power's cut off. Needless expense.

EVA: Electric power was off at the time it happened.

BLANCH: The power always goes off when it rains real hard and that Good Friday was one of the heaviest rains we've had in Two Rivers County.

EVA: Miss Harkaway called it a cataclysm of nature.

BLANCH: She was that wonderful Memphis newspaper-woman who wrote it all up in the *Commercial Appeal.*

EVA: Everything's just as it was.

BLANCH: Except of course the merchandise was removed.

EVA: Nothing has been took out that had a connection.

BLANCH: Everything in the museum has a label on it. You all can just browse around and we'll explain everything.

EVA: How can they ask any questions, you talking so fast?

BLANCH: You get me all balled up with your interruptions! Now that over there is the famous Jesus picture!

EVA: Don't call it *that.*

BLANCH: That's what *everyone* calls it. He *was* good-looking.

EVA: I never noticed he was.

BLANCH: Don't be ridiculous. *Everyone* noticed he was.

EVA: Now that dress there is the dress that Myra was wearing. Beulah said to her, "What do they call that color?"

BLANCH: She smiled an' she said, "They call it ecstasy blue!" Then didn't Myra . . . ?

EVA: Myra went back upstairs. Jabe knocked on the ceiling. That was when Vee . . .

BLANCH: Never mind about that. We'll tell that later. There is the phone . . .

EVA: The receiver is still off the hook.

BLANCH: The cash-box drawer's still open.

EVA: The money has been removed.

BLANCH: (*regretfully*) There *wasn't* much.

EVA: Frightfully, frightfully *little*. We are the only surviving relations, of course.

BLANCH: (*She points to the floor.*) You see those stains?

EVA: They're fading out. We'll have to touch them up.

BLANCH: Across the floor? Toward the confectionery?

EVA: Let's go in there! (*She rushes eagerly forward.*) Uncle, the *lamp*!

BLANCH: You probably wonder why we put up with such a peculiar old man as the caretaker here. Well, it's like this . . .

EVA: He's part of the exhibition!

BLANCH: Don't call it that!

EVA: Oh, the memorial then! What's the difference? This Conjure Man, as they call him . . .

BLANCH: Comes from Blue Mountain. Myra gave him odd jobs.

EVA: He was on the place when everything happened that happened.

BLANCH: He claims he knows some things that he isn't telling.

EVA: He's kind of daft. Now this room here is the Torrance Confectionery. Myra had it all done over for spring.

BLANCH: Yes, re-decorated. Somebody made a remark how lovely it was. "Yes," said Myra, "It's supposed to resemble the orchard across from Moon Lake!" Notice those imitations . . .

EVA: Dogwood blossoms. And that big Japanese lantern. It's dingy now but you all can just imagine how lovely it was.

BLANCH: Miss Harkaway put it in such a beautiful way. The mercantile store, she said, was reality, harsh and drab, but Myra's confectionery . . .

EVA: That was where she kept her dreams. Uncle, turn up that lamp. I want these people to see the place where she kept her dreams. (*The lamp is turned up higher. The confectionery blooms into a nostalgic radiance, as dim and soft as memory itself.*) Remind me, Blanch, to sprinkle a little roach powder on this floor.

EVA: Let's go upstairs.

BLANCH: I think we've left out something.

EVA: You can talk so fast I didn't keep track of it all.

BLANCH: It's you with your interruptions that ball things up. Watch out for these stairs, they're terrible, terrible steep.

EVA: We can't be responsible for an accident on them.

BLANCH: Goodness sakes alive, *no!* These terrible taxes . . .

EVA: Keep us poor as church mice! (*They lead the way up the stairs.*)

BLANCH: You keep awake, Uncle.

EVA: If anyone else stops in, just ring the bell.

BLANCH: (*She opens the door on the landing.*) Now these are the living quarters.

EVA: Myra's bedroom's on the right an' Jabe's on the left. (*The light fades out as the door closes. The Conjure Man laughs to himself as the curtain falls.*)

ACT ONE

THE SCENE: *The same as for the Prologue, except that it is now a year earlier—in early February—and the store is in operation, stocked with merchandise. There are great bolts of pepperell and percale which stand upright on the counters. The black skeleton of a dressmaker's dummy stands meaninglessly in front of a thin white column. Along the wall at the left is the shoe department, with a ladder that slides along the shelves and two or three shoe-fitting chairs. Racks of dresses, marked "Spring Styles," line the right wall.*

Dolly and Beulah are arranging candles and setting a buffet table in the general store. They are wives of small planters, about thirty and over-dressed. Dolly's husband, Pee Wee, and the town sheriff are in the confectionery shooting pin-ball. A train whistles in the distance.

DOLLY: Pee Wee! That's the Cannonball!

PEE WEE: (*from the confectionery*) Okay, Mama! (*Pee Wee enters. He is a heavy man. His vest comes mid-way down the *white-shirted bulge of his belly; his laced boots are caked with mud.*) Ninety-five nickels an' no pay-off! What would you call that, Mama?

DOLLY: Outrageous! Not the machine, but you poor suckers that play it.

BEULAH: This meringue turned out real good.

SHERIFF: (*He enters from the confectionery, laughing.*) You got to mid-aisle it three times straight's the only way to crack that goddam pot.

PEE WEE: I'm gonna tell Jabe about it. Ninety-five nickels an' no pay-off. (*They go out.*)

DOLLY: I guess Jabe Torrance has got more to think about than that ole pin-ball game in the confectionery. Huh?

BEULAH: He ought to have. That meringue *is* nice and light. I put in two drops of almond. Yesterday I was talking to Dr. Bob. You know, young Dr. Bob?

DOLLY: Uh-huh. What did he say?

BEULAH: I ast him how Jabe was, what kind of condition he really seemed to be in. He's seen them X-ray pictures they took in the Memphis Hospital after the operation. Well . . .

DOLLY: What did he say, Beulah?

BEULAH: He said the worst that a doctor can ever say.

DOLLY: What's that?

BEULAH: Nothing at all, not a spoken word did he utter; he simply looked at me with those big dark eyes and shook his haid—like this!

DOLLY: (*She speaks with doleful optimism.*) I guess he signed Jabe Torrance's death-warrant with just that single motion of his haid.

BEULAH: Exackly what I thought. I understand that they cut him open . . .

DOLLY: An' sewed him right back up?

BEULAH: (*struggling to speak and strangling on an olive*) Mmm. Mmm. (*She points at her stuffed mouth.*) I didn't know these olives had seeds in them.

DOLLY: You thought they was stuffed?

BEULAH: Uh-huh.

DOLLY: Where's the Temple Sisters?

BEULAH: Snooping around upstairs.

DOLLY: Let Myra catch 'em at it, she'll lay 'em both out good. She never did invite nobody up there.

BEULAH: Well, I was surprised when I went up myself.

DOLLY: I know it.

BEULAH: Two separate bedrooms, too! Maybe it's just since Jabe's been sick.

DOLLY: Naw, it's permanent, honey. As a girl in Tupelo she certainly wasn't cold-blooded. We used to go double together me an' Pee Wee an' her and that Anderson boy. All of one spring we would go to the orchard across from Moon Lake ev'ry night. We was engaged, but they wasn't. Boll weevil and army-worm struck his cotton awful three times straight. He married into the Delta Planters' Bank and Myra married Jabe. Myra was Myra then. Since then she's just a woman that works in a mercantile store.

(*Cassandra Whiteside enters at the door on the right. She is dark and strikingly beautiful, of a type rather peculiar to the South—physically delicate with clear translucent skin and luminous eyes as though burnt thin by her intensity of feeling. With people she has a rather disdainful ease, not deliberate or conscious, but rooted in her class origin and the cynical candor with which she recognizes herself and the social contradictions and tragic falsity of the world she lives in. Sandra is the only woman of aristocratic extraction in the group. Her family is the oldest in this part of the Delta and was once the richest, but their plantation has dwindled with each successive generation. Sandra has been "going out" for ten years and is still unmarried, which is enough in itself to destroy a girl's reputation.*)

DOLLY: Sandra Whiteside! How are you?

SANDRA: Oh, I seem to be still living. God knows why. Where's Myra?

DOLLY: Gone to Memphis to bring Jabe back from the hospital.

BEULAH: The men folks just now went to the depot to meet them.

SANDRA: Oh. . . . I want some cartridges for this pistol of mine. (*She removes it from her bag.*) I thought I better carry one with me. I'm on the road so much you'd think I was making a political campaign tour, the number of places I've got to visit this weekend. Memphis, Jackson— Is this the hardware section? (*approaching the counter*) Aw, here's cartridges! (*She helps herself.*) Then on down to New Awleuns for the start of the carnival season. Tell Myra to charge these to me. I ought to buy an airplane. They say that you only crack up once in the air.

DOLLY: Well, you'd better stay out of airplanes, honey.

BEULAH: How many times have you cracked up on the highway?

SANDRA: Today was the seventh since New Year's.

DOLLY: No!

SANDRA: I fell asleep at the wheel an' ran into a fence.

BEULAH: Goodness!

DOLLY: Gracious!

BEULAH: Last week she had a collision with a mule.

DOLLY: My Lawd!

SANDRA: And just to show you the absolute lack of justice, the mule was killed and I was completely uninjured!

DOLLY: (*with false concern*) Darling, you'd better be careful!

SANDRA: Oh, I don't know. What else can you do when you live in Two River County but drive like hell! (*There is the sound of a car out in front.*)

BEULAH: 'S 'at them?

DOLLY: (*sarcastically*) Naw, it's the Sheriff's little fireside companion.

BEULAH: Vee Talbot! Who is that with her? A *man*! (*This word creates a visible stir among the three women.*)

DOLLY: Uh-huh! Yes, it is!

BEULAH: Who could it be I wonder?

DOLLY: I can't make out. Oh, my goodness! What an outfit he's got on! It looks like a snakeskin jacket.

BEULAH: *Wha-at?* Do you know him?

DOLLY: Naw, I don't know him a-tall. He looks like an absolute stranger. Poor Vee has got her skirt caught in the car door or something, it's hitched up over her knees and she's simply *frantic* about it! (*She utters a sharp laugh.*)

BEULAH: She's such a big clumsy thing. Who do you think the man is?

DOLLY: I told you I never have seen him, don't know him from Adam, darling. Maybe he's one of the Twelve Apostles that she's been painting on.

SANDRA: Is Vee painting the Twelve Apostles?

DOLLY: She's been painting them for twelve years, one each year. She says that she sees them in visions. But every one of them looks like some man around Two River County. She told Birdie Wilson that she was hoping she'd have a vision of Jesus next Passion Week so she could paint Him, too.

BEULAH: You better quit staring.

DOLLY: She's finally got her skirt loose. Oh, God, the hem's ripped out, it's trailing the ground! (*She laughs and crosses from the window.*)

(*Vee enters from the street. She is a heavy, middle-aged woman, about forty, whose personality, frustrated in its contact with externals, has turned deeply inward. She has found refuge in religion and primitive art and has become known as an eccentric. Although a religious fanatic, a mystic, she should not be made ridiculous. Her portrayal will contain certain incidents of humor, but not be devoid of all dignity or pathos. She wanders slowly about with a vague dreamy smile on her face. Her expression is often bewildered.*)

BEULAH: (*with loud, false cordiality*) Hello, Vee honey, how are you?

DOLLY: Hello, Vee.

VEE: (*faintly*) Hello. I got m' skirt caught in the lock of the Chevrolet door an' I think it's torn loose a little. I can't see behind me good. Does it look like it's torn to you? (*She peers awkwardly, ponderously, behind her at the hem which dangles across the floor, like a big heavy dog trying to catch its tail.*)

BEULAH: Just a little bit, honey.

DOLLY: Yes, it's scarcely noticeable even. (*She giggles.*)

VEE: I feel like something was dragging. Oh, it *has* been torn, the young man told me it wasn't!

DOLLY: Say, who is he?

VEE: I don't know who he is, but I think he's all right, though. He told me he'd been saved, doesn't smoke, doesn't drink. His parents are dead, both of them, but he's got an uncle who's a Catholic priest and he says that he stayed six years—I mean his uncle—in some leper colony on a South Sea Island without ever catching any sign of disease. Isn't that wonderful, though?

DOLLY: Huh.

BEULAH: What's he doing here?

VEE: Says he's exploring the world an' ev'rything in it.

DOLLY: Laudamighty!

VEE: He come to the lock-up las' night an' ast for a bed, but he couldn't stay in it, though, the bars made him nervous.

DOLLY: So what did you do with him then?

VEE: What do you mean? I was alone in the house so I give him a blanket, he went out to sleep in his car.

DOLLY: Sounds like a peculiar person.

BEULAH: Yeah.

VEE: Oh, no, he just isn't a type that you are used to seeing. I'm going to speak a good word for him to Myra, she said she might be needing some help around here. (*Val appears in the front door. He is about twenty-five years old. He has a fresh and primitive quality, a virile grace and freedom of body, and a strong physical appeal.*) Come right on in, Mr. Xavier.

VAL: What shall I do with this here?

VEE: Jus' give me the sherbet. I thought Mr. Torrance might need somethin' light an' digestible so I brought sherbet.

BEULAH: What flavuh is it? Pineapple?

VEE: Pineapple.

BEULAH: Oh, goody, I love pineapple. Don't you-all? (*She hands Vee the napkin-wrapped bowl.*)

VEE: Mr. Xavier, I was just telling these ladies about your uncle that went to live with the lepers. Some people are doubtful about the power of faith but there's an example I think should convince anybody.

BEULAH: Isn't it, though? Let's put this right in the frigidaire before it stahts t' melt.

DOLLY: (*She lifts the napkin.*) I'm afraid you're locking the stable after the hause is gone.

BEULAH: Wh-at? Is it melted awready?

DOLLY: Reduced to juice!

BEULAH: Oh foot!—Well, let's put it in anyhow, it might thicken up.

VEE: Where is the frigidaire?

BEULAH: It's in the confectionery. (*The three women go back through the archway. Sandra is left with Val. She laughs in her throat and leans provocatively back. Val stares at her with a touch of antagonism. This challenging silence continues for a marked pause. Then Sandra laughs again, somewhat louder.*)

VAL: (*sharply*) Is something amusing you, lady?

SANDRA: (*drawling*) Yes. Very much. I think it's that jacket you're wearing. What stuff is it made of?

VAL: Snakeskin.

SANDRA: (*with a disgusted grimace*) Ouuu!

VAL: I didn't ask your opinion.

SANDRA: I didn't express one, did I?

VAL: Yeah. You said "Ouuu!" (*He mocks her grimace.*)

SANDRA: You know what that was? It was fascinated revulsion. (*She goes into the confectionery and starts the juke box. It plays "Custro Vidas."*) Would you like to dance?

VAL: I don't know how to dance.

SANDRA: I'd love to teach you. We'll go out jooking some night.

VAL: Jooking? What's that?

SANDRA: That's where you get in a car and drink a little and drive a little and dance a little. Then you drink a little more and drive a little more and dance a little more. Then you stop dancing and just drink and drive. Then you stop driving and you just drink. And then, finally, you stop drinking.

VAL: Then what do you do?

SANDRA: That depends entirely on who you happen to be out jooking with. If you're out with me, and you're sufficiently attractive, you nearly always wind up on Cypress Hill.

VAL: What's that?

SANDRA: That's the graveyard, honey. It's situated, appropriately enough, on the highest point of land in Two River County, a beautiful windy bluff just west of the Sunflower River.

VAL: Why do you go out there?

SANDRA: Because dead people give such good advice.

VAL: What advice do they give?

SANDRA: Just one word—*live!* (*Beulah rushes in with a bowl of something.*)

BEULAH: You're going to stay fo' the pahty, Mr. . . . ?

VAL: Xavier.

BEULAH: I know some Seviers in Blue Mountain. Any relation?

VAL: Spelt with an "S" or an "X"?

BEULAH: An "S," I believe.

VAL: No relation.

BEULAH: (*sympathetically*) Awwww. (*She rushes back out.*)

SANDRA: I have a great aunt who's laid away on Cypress Hill. Her name was Cassandra, the same as mine is, so I always empty my bottles on her grave. She loved to drink. She finally got so she just lay on the bed and drank and drank all night and all day. They asked her if she didn't get tired of it. She said, "No, I never get bored. I have moving pictures on my ceiling. They go on all the time, continuous performance. I'm the main actress," she said, "and I do the most mah-velous things!" That was Cassandra the second. I'm the third. The first was a little Greek girl who slept in the shrine of Apollo. Her ears were snake-bitten, like mine, so that she could understand the secret language of the birds. You know what they told her, Snakeskin? They contradicted everything that she'd been told before. They said it was all stuff an' nonsense, a pack of lies. They advised her to drive her car as fast as she wanted to drive it, to dance like she wanted to dance. Get drunk, they said, raise hell at Moon Lake casina, do bumps an' wiggle your fanny! (*Vee Talbot enters; she stops short with an outraged look. Sandra laughs and extends a pack of cigarettes toward Val.*)

VEE: Mr. Xavier, don't smoke. (*She sets the potato chips down and goes out.*)

DOLLY: (*rushing through*) Mr. Xavier, if you're looking for work, you might drop in on my husband, Pee Wee Bland. He runs that cotton gin right over the road there.

BEULAH: The Marguerites! I smell them burning! (*She runs out.*)

SANDRA: How did you happen to come to this dark, wild river country of ours?

VAL: A broken axle stopped me here last night.

SANDRA: You'd better mend it quick and move along.

VAL: Why's that?

SANDRA: Why? Why? Don't you know what those women are suffering from? Sexual malnutrition! They look at you with eyes that scream "Eureka!" (*She laughs and saunters casually to the door. She raises her revolver and fires two shots into the sky.*)

VAL: For God's sake! (*The three women scream and come rushing back in. The Temple Sisters shriek upstairs and come scuttling down, Blanch losing her footing and sliding down the last three steps. There is babble and confusion.*)

DOLLY: What are you *doing*? Oh, God, in my condition! I . . .

BEULAH: Sandra, for the love of . . .

BLANCH: (*moaning*) I've broke my laig in two!

EVA: (*screaming*) She's broken her laig! (*Vee goes over to her.*)

DOLLY: Oh, she has *not*! Sandra, what on earth did you fire that damn thing faw?

SANDRA: (*She laughs and comes unsteadily back into the store.*) I took a pot shot at a buzzard!

BEULAH: A what? (*Sandra laughs wildly and looks at Val who crosses to her and takes the pistol roughly from her grasp. Myra enters. Myra is a slight, fair woman, about thirty-four years old. She is a woman who met emotional disaster in her girlhood and whose personality bears traces of the resulting trauma. Frequently sharp and suspicious, she verges on hysteria under slight strain. Her voice is often shrill and her body tense. But when in repose, a girlish softness emerges—evidence of her capacity for great tenderness.*)

MYRA: What in God's holy name has been going on here? Who fired those shots out the door? (*She sees Val with the revolver in his hand; she gasps and starts toward the door.*) You! (*They stare at each other for a brief moment.*)

VAL: (*slowly smiling*) No Ma'am, it wasn't me. It was this young lady here.

SANDRA: Yes, I fired it, darling.

MYRA: What at?

SANDRA: A bird of ill-omen was circling over the store.

MYRA: Yea? One of those imaginary things that people see in a certain condition. Hello, Beulah, Dolly. (*She flings off her hat.*) I'm evermore tired. I've never had such a trip. Jabe took a bad spell on the train. They carried him up the back way. How are yuh, Vee. Blanch Temple, what are you sitting on the floor faw?

EVA: She took a spill on the stairs when Sandra Whiteside fired the shots!

MYRA: On the stairs? You two were upstairs, were you?

EVA: Yes, we were straightening things up a little . . .

MYRA: (*quickly*) I see. An investigation?

EVA: Yes. I mean . . .

BLANCH: No, no, no! We wanted to see that ev'rything was in order. I've got such awful weak ankles, I'm always tripping and falling. An' I've got to march in church with the choir if I got to go on crutches. (*She rises painfully with Beulah's and Eva's assistance.*)

MYRA: Oh, look what you all have done, that beautiful table! Candles an' ev'rything sweet that goes to make a nice party! Some of your lovely floating-island, Beulah? Sweet! The spirit is willing but the flesh is completely exhausted. (*A Negro enters, crosses to Myra carrying a tower of pastel-colored hat-boxes and a big gay placard reading "Welcome Sweet Springtime."*) Oh, Joe, bring me those cards. Welcome sweet springtime! I've bought a pile of spring hats. (*She extricates one of the cards.*) This one here is the nicest—"In the spring, a young maid's fancy lightly turns to new chapeaux."

BEULAH: (*reading the rest of it*) "Mary Lou and Jane and Frances wear new hats to please their beaux!"

DOLLY: Oh, that's perfectly dahling. It seems so eahly, though, to think about spring.

EVA: I don't know. Somebody tole me that carps have been seen in Yazoo Pass. That always indicates that flood season's 'bout to start.

BLANCH: Myra . . . .

MYRA: Yes?

BLANCH: I don't suppose you feel like talkin' about it right now, but I do hope Jabe's operation was completely successful.

MYRA: No.

BLANCH: It wasn't? (*All the women stare greedily at Myra.*)

MYRA: No. It *wasn't.*

BLANCH: Oh!

EVA: My! My!

BEULAH: I'm so sorry to hear it.

DOLLY: If there's anything I can do . . . I—? (*Jabe is heard knocking on the ceiling from his room above. Myra's face becomes suddenly listless and tired.*)

EVA: What's that knocking upstairs?

MYRA: Jabe.

SHERIFF: Myra, Jabe wants you.

MYRA: Excuse me, I'll have to go up. (*She crosses wearily toward the stairs, her hat dangling from one hand, pauses before the "Welcome Sweet Springtime" sign, with its bluebirds, flutes and gilded scrolls and cherubim, gravely lifts it and places it in a higher position.*) Dolly, look at this hat! I think it must have been created just for you! (*She smiles and goes on upstairs.*)

SANDRA: (*who has engaged Val in low conversation since Myra's entrance*) Speaking of knocks, I've got one in my engine. A very mysterious noise. I can't decide whether I'm in communication with one of my dead ancestors or whether the carburetor or something is just about to drop out an' leave me stranded, probably at midnight in the middle of some lonesome black forest! (*She smiles at Val.*) I don't suppose you'd have any knowledge of mechanics?

VAL: I dunno. I might. (*Dolly is trying on the hat but is watchful of this exchange—also the other women who are opening hat-boxes.*)

SANDRA: Would you be willing to undertake a kind of exploratory operation on it?

VAL: Well, I might if it didn't take too long.

SANDRA: (*drawling*) Oh, with your expert knowledge it shouldn't take lo-ong at-all! (*Dolly giggles.*)

BEULAH: (*pointedly*) What are you laughin' at?

DOLLY: This hat! Isn't it the strangest thing?

BEULAH: Them things on the brim—what are they—carrots an' peas? I think they'd be much better *creamed*—with chicken croquettes! (*Val has slid slowly off the counter. He *moves past Sandra and the secret looks of the women, toward the door.*)

VEE: Mr. Xavier . . . (*She crosses as if to stop him but they have already disappeared.*) Oh. I was going to ask Myra if she would give him a job.

BEULAH: Well . . .

DOLLY: It looks like he's got one now!

EVA: What did she say? A knock . . . ?

BLANCH: In her engine! (*innocently*) Whatever that is.

DOLLY: (*with a peal of laughter*) Did you *evuh* see such a puh-faum-ance! *Nevuh* in all my . . .

BEULAH: Bawn days? *Neither* did I! You see how she looked at the boy? An' the tone of huh voice. Corrupt? Absolutely —de-*grad-ed*!

DOLLY: Hank says her father got drunk one time at the Elks an' told him that she was kicked out of both of those girls' schools. Had to send her out East where morals don't matter. She's got two degrees or something in *lit*-era-*chure.*

BEULAH: Six degrees of fever if you ask me!

VEE: (*who has been silently brooding over the situation*) I certainly hope she doesn't get him to drink.

DOLLY: Vee, honey, you might as well face it, this is one candidate fo' salvation that you have *lost* to the opposition!

VEE: I don't believe it. He told me that he'd been saved already. (*She fixes her resentment on Dolly.*) If some of the older women in Two River County would set a better example there'd be more justice in their talk about girls!

DOLLY: (*with asperity*) What do you mean by that remark?

VEE: I mean that people who give drinkin' pahties an' get so drunk they don't know which is *their husband* an' which is somebody elses' an' people who serve on the altar guild an' still play cards on Sundays . . .

DOLLY: Just stop right there! Now I've discovered the source of that dirty gossip!

VEE: I'm only repeating what I've been told by others! I certainly never have been entertained at such affairs as that!

DOLLY: No, an' you never will be, you're a public kill-joy, a professional hypocrite!

BEULAH: Dolly!

DOLLY: She spends her time re-fauming tramps that her husband puts in the *lock-up*! Brings them here in Myra's store an' tries to get them jobs here when God knows what kind of vicious ideas they've probably got in their heads!

VEE: I try to build up characters! You an' your drinkin' pahties are only concerned with tearin' characters down! I'm goin' upstairs with Myra. (*She goes out.*)

DOLLY: Well, you know what brought on that tantrum? She's jealous of Sandra Whiteside's running off with that strange boy. She hasn't lived as a natural wife for ten years or more (*to Eva*) so her husband has got to pick up with some bright-skinned nigger.

BEULAH: Oh, Dolly, you're awful. Sometimes I think you ought to wear a back-house on your haid instead of a hat.

DOLLY: I've got no earthly patience with that sort of hypocriticism. Beulah, let's put all this perishable stuff in the Frigidaire and get out of here. I've never been so thoroughly disgusted.

BEULAH: Oh, my Lawd! (*They go into the confectionery.*)

EVA: Both of those two women are as common as dirt.

BLANCH: Dolly's folks in Blue Mountain are nothin' at all but the poorest kind of white trash. Why, Lollie Tucker told me the old man sits on the porch with his shoes off drinkin' beer out of a bucket! Nobody wants these Marguerites. (*She goes to the hardware counter and gets her bag.*) Let's take 'em, huh?

EVA: (*looking at the flowers*) I was just wondering what we'd use to decorate the altar with tomorrow. The Bishop Adjutant's comin'. As far's I know nobody's offered flowers. We can give Myra credit in the Parish notes.

BLANCH: Put the olive-nut sandwiches in here with the Marguerites. Be careful you tote them so they won't get squashed.

EVA: They'll come in very nicely for the Bishop's tea. (*Dolly and Beulah re-enter from the confectionery.*)

DOLLY: We still have time to make the second show.

BEULAH: Dolly, you still have on that awful hat!

DOLLY: Oh, Lawd! (*She tosses it on the counter. Dolly and Beulah go out quickly together.*)

EVA: (*when they are out*) Sits on the po'ch with his shoes off?

BLANCH: Yes! Drinkin' *beer* from a *bucket*! (*Eva and Blanch go out. The Sheriff comes downstairs, grunting and puffing, followed by Pee Wee.*)

PEE WEE: Took one dose at noon. When that didn't work, I took a double one about five o'clock. Jabe sure looks bad.

SHERIFF: Looks no better 'n no worse 'n he always looked, but if what they say is correct, he'll more'n likely go under before the cotton comes up! See that there? (*He indicates his bandaged knuckle.*) Broke my knuckle! Never hit a buck-tooth nigger in the mouf! That's *the moral of it.* (*Pee Wee laughs.*) Oh, Vee! . . . Them fool wimmin got in a ruckus down here, I don't know what it's about. (*Vee comes downstairs.*)

VEE: Hush that bawling will yuh? I wanted to speak with Myra about that young man who needs work but I couldn't in front of Jabe. He thinks he's gonna be able to go back to work himself.

SHERIFF: Well, come awn here, quit foolin'!

VEE: I think I ought to wait 'till that young man gets back.

SHERIFF: Mama, you come awn. Aw else stay here, an' *walk* when you git ready. (*He strides out after Pee Wee. The car engine roars. Vee looks troubled and follows them slowly out. There is a slight pause. The Negro enters from the confectionery. He looks about him and laughs with a gentle, quiet laughter at something secret, opens the soft drink cooler and takes a coke out. He laughs again, softly, secretly, and goes out the front door of the store, leaving the door open. A hound bays in the distance. After a moment Val comes back in, and shuts the door behind him. He goes to the table, picks up a paper napkin and scrubs lipstick off his mouth. He settles himself on the counter. After a moment or two Myra comes downstairs bearing an oil lamp. She has on a cheap Japanese kimona of shiny black satin with large scarlet poppies on it. She appears to be very distraught and doesn't notice Val. She crosses directly to the phone and turns the crank.*)

MYRA: Get me the drug-store, please. Mr. Dubinsky? This is Myra Torrance. Were you asleep? I'm sorry. I'm in a bad situation. I left my luminal tablets in the Memphis hotel and I can't sleep without them. . . . I know your store's closed up. So's mine. I know the lights are out, they're out over here. But you don't need a thousand watt bulb to put a few luminal tablets in a little card-board box or paper bag. . . . Now look here, Mr. Dubinsky, if you want to keep my trade, you send your nigger right over with that box of tablets. Gone? Then bring 'em yourself! I'm absolutely desperate from lack of sleep. My nerves are all on edge. If I don't get a good sleep tonight, I'll go all to pieces. I've got a sick man to take care of. . . . Yes, I just brought him home from the Memphis hospital. The operation was not at all successful. Will you do that? I'll be very much obliged. Thank you, Mr. Dubinsky. Excuse me for speaking so sharply. Thank you, Mr. Dubinsky. I appreciate that, Mr. Dubinsky. Goodbye, Mr. Dubinsky. (*She hangs up the phone and leans exhaustedly against the wall.*) Oh, oh, oh, I wish I was dead—dead—dead.

VAL: (*quietly*) No, you don't Mrs. Torrance.

MYRA: My God! (*She gasps and clutches her wrapper about her throat.*)

VAL: I didn't mean to scare you.

MYRA: *What is this?* What are you still doing here? Who *are you*? My God, you got eyes that shine in the dark like a dog's. Get out or I'll call for the Sheriff!

VAL: Lady. . . .

MYRA: Well?

VAL: I've been to the Sheriff's already.

MYRA: Aw. Escaped from the lock-up?

VAL: Naw. The Sheriff's wife took me in there last night.

MYRA: She did, uh?

VAL: She give me a night's flop there but I didn't stay.

MYRA: Naw?

VAL: It made me uneasy being locked up. I got to have space around me.

MYRA: Look here, that's interesting, but this store's closed and I'll thank you to please get out. I've got a sick man upstairs that requires a lot of attention. If you're hungry. . . .

VAL: I'm not.

MYRA: There's lots of fancy stuff they put in the frigidaire, you might as well eat it, I can't.

VAL: No, thanks, but I'd be mighty obliged if you would give me a job.

MYRA: There's no work here.

VAL: Excuse the contradiction but there is. Mizz Talbot told me so.

MYRA: Vee Talbott? I'll thank her to let me decide such things for myself. I'm in the mercantile business, she's a painter of very peculiar pictures she calls the Apostles but look like men around town. She took you in, did she? Well!

VAL: Whatever it is you're suggesting is incorrect. I've met one bitch in this town but it wasn't her.

MYRA: (*furiously*) How—how—*dare* you say that!

VAL: It wasn't you neither, Ma'am! It was one that picked me up in here before you come in. Said she had engine trouble and would I fix it. She took me for a stud—and I slapped her face!

MYRA: You *what*?

VAL: I said I slapped her face. She wasn't a bad piece neither but I didn't like the way she went about it, like she was something special and I was trash!

MYRA: You . . . Cassandra Whiteside? *Slapped?* (*She bursts into wild laughter.*) I've never heard anything so beautiful in all my life! Have a drink and get out; I've got to go up.

VAL: (*stubbornly*) You'll need help here with your husband sick upstairs.

MYRA: You think so, uh? Well, if I do it'll have to be local help. I couldn't hire no stranger. 'Specially one that slapped the face of one of the richest girls in the Mississippi Delta. (*She laughs again.*) You had sales experience?

VAL: I've had all kinds of experience.

MYRA: That's not what I ast you. I ast you if you've had experience in the mercantile line. I want to know if you would be able to sell?

VAL: Sell?

MYRA: Yes!

VAL: Lots in hell to preachers!

MYRA: (*She utters again that sharp startled laugh, her fingers tightly clutching a magazine and nervously turning through it.*) I guess you got character ref'rence?

VAL: Sure.

MYRA: Where was the last place you worked?

VAL: Garage in Oakley.

MYRA: Tennessee?

VAL: Yeah.

MYRA: Grease-monkey, was you?

VAL: (*stiffly*) I wouldn't call myself that.

MYRA: Excuse me. Why did you quit that job?

VAL: If I told you, you'd think I was crazy.

MYRA: I think ev'rybody is crazy, including myself. Why did you quit it?

VAL: The place next door burnt down.

MYRA: What's that got to do with it?

VAL: I don't like fire. I dreamed about it three nights straight so I quit. I was burnt as a kid and ever since then it's been something I can't forget. (*He offers her a paper.*) Here's a letter he wrote.

MYRA: Who?

VAL: Garage manager.

MYRA: (*She reads aloud.*) "This here boy's peculiar but he sure does work real hard and he's honest as daylight." What does he mean "peculiar"?

VAL: Unusual is what he means.

MYRA: Why don't he say unusual?

VAL: He's not exactly an expert in the use of the language.

MYRA: Oh, but you are?

VAL: (*He removes a small book from his pocket.*) See this?

MYRA: Funk and Wagnall's Pocket Dictionary.

VAL: I carry that along with me wherever I go.

MYRA: What for?

VAL: You ever seen a coal-miner's cap? (*Myra shakes her head.*) I wore one once when I was mining in the Red Hills of Alabama. It had a little lamp in front so you could see what your pick was digging into. Well—I'm still digging.

MYRA: Digging?

VAL: I don't claim to know very much, but I am writing a *book.*

MYRA: Well—you don't have to spit in my face to convince me of it!

VAL: (*grinning*) Excuse me.

MYRA: What's your book about?

VAL: Life.

MYRA: Sorry but I can't use you.

VAL: Why not?

MYRA: Other people ain't as charitable as that garage-manager is. They wouldn't say "peculiar," they'd say "nuts!" Also your appearance is much against you.

VAL: What's wrong with that.

MYRA: I don't know exactly. If you're hungry, eat. But otherwise . . . (*She is interrupted by knocking on the ceiling.*) Otherwise . . . get out. I'm too bone-tired to carry on conversation.

VAL: If you'll excuse me for telling you so, you're just about the rudest talking woman I've ever met.

MYRA: Yes, I'm mean inside. You heard me cussing when I come downstairs? Inside I cuss like that all the time. I hate ev'rybody; I wish this town would be bombarded tomorrow and everyone daid. Because—

VAL: Because?

MYRA: I got to live in it when I'd rather be daid in it—an' buried. (*She takes a drink of wine.*) What I meant about your appearance is you're too good-looking. Can you read shoe sizes?

VAL: Yeah.

MYRA: What does 75 David mean? (*Val is stymied.*) You see how you lie? You lie like a dawg in summer! (*She laughs, not unkindly.*) 75 means 7½ in length and David means D wide. For flat-footed wimmin. You would either scare trade out of this store completely or else you'd bring it in so thick the floor would collapse. I can't decide which it would be.

VAL: I'd bring it in, lady.

MYRA: Gosh— (*There is a knock at the front door. Myra crosses to it.*) A new floor would be an awful expense! (*She opens the door and steps outside.*) Thank you Mr. Dubinsky. (*coming back in*) That was the Sand Man with my luminal tablets. Suppose you— (*She opens the box and places a tablet on her tongue, washing it down with wine.*)

VAL: Huh?

MYRA: Suppose you try to sell me a pair of white kid pumps out of that new stock there. Imagine me a customer hard to please and you the clerk. Go on . . . Naw, them over there is Red Goose shoes for kiddies. Them're men's shoes.

Growing girls', Misses'. Them on the end of the shelves are Women's; sizes range down from the top. (*He pulls out a pair.*) You call them kid? That's suede, young man; 'snot a pump, neither, 's a blucher oxford; I don't believe you've ever tried to sell a thing in your life. Go on, roll your hoop, you're worse than useless to me! (*as he moves slowly toward the door, Myra says softly*) Sure you're not hungry? You're walking kind of unsteady.

VAL: What's that to you? I've got dog's eyes—you don't like me!

MYRA: I didn't say that.

VAL: I can't read shoe sizes. I don't know suede from kid. You can't use me; I'm worse than useless! What does it matter whether I'm hungry or not? (*He shakes with fury.*)

MYRA: (*very softly, gently, with a slight mournful, tender shake of her head*) Lawd, child, come back in the mawning and I'll give you a job. (*She moves slowly over to the candles and blows them out. Val stares at her dumbly.*)

VAL: God, I—! Lady, you—!

MYRA: (*laughing a little*) God you an' lady me, huh. I think you are kind of exaggerating a little in both cases. (*They laugh. She blows out more of the candles leaving two lighted.*) You never have any trouble getting to sleep?

VAL: No. I know how to relax.

MYRA: How do you relax?

VAL: Imagine yourself a loose piece of string.

MYRA: A loose piece of string. That's lovely! I'm a loose piece of string. (*There is a knock on the ceiling.*)

VAL: What's that knocking upstairs?

MYRA: Jabe. (*She averts her face.*)

VAL: Who?

MYRA: My husband.

VAL: It scared me for a minute.

MYRA: Why?

VAL: Clump. Clump. Clump. Sounds like a skeleton walking around upstairs.

MYRA: Maybe you're gifted with too much imagination. (*She bends over to blow out the last candle.*)

VAL: Uh-huh. That's always been one of my biggest troubles. (*The candles gutter out. A dog is heard baying in the distance; the sound has a peculiar, passionate clarity.*)

MYRA: (*softly*) Hear that houn' dawg? . . . He's bayin' at th' moon. . . . Sky's cleared off? Yes, it's clean as a whistle. . . . Isn't that nice?

VAL: (*hoarsely*) Yes, Ma'am.

MYRA: Well. . . . (*It grows rapidly darker as they stand hesitantly apart, looking at each other. Myra turns slowly back toward the stairs.*) Well . . . The door locks itself when you slam it. Good night.

VAL: (*He speaks in a low, hoarse whisper.*) G'night. (*She starts up the stairs, slowly. He opens the door. Once more the dog is heard baying. They both stop short as though caught by the magic of the sound and face each other again from the stairway and the door. Val speaks again, still more hoarsely.*) G'night.

MYRA: (*in a whisper*) Good night.

Curtain

ACT TWO

SCENE I: *It is about a week later. Val is seated on the counter of the store leaning dreamily against a shelf. In his hand is a pencil and a shoe-box lid. He is raptly composing an idyllic passage in his book. The juke box is playing as he speaks aloud. Myra appears in the confectionery archway with a couple of boxes. She overhears his soliloquy and stops short to listen.*

VAL: Day used to come up slow through the long white curtains.

MYRA: Val! (*Val starts.*) Who are you talking to?

VAL: Myself, I suppose.

MYRA: Isn't that kind of peculiar, talking to yourself?

VAL: No, Ma'am. That's just a habit that lonesome people get into.

MYRA: Please don't do it when anyone's in the store. I don't want it spread around town that a lunatic's been employed here. That sunshine's *terrific*—you better let down the awnings. (*Val moves slowly from the counter.*) Slew-foot!

VAL: Huh?

MYRA: Slew-foot, slew-foot! You walk like you're on fly papers! Pick up your feet when you walk and get a *move* on! (*Val laughs and saunters leisurely out the door.*) Talks to himself, writing poems on shoe-boxes! What a mess. (*She stares through the window as Val lowers the awning. Three young girls follow Val as he comes back in.*)

A GIRL: Hello!

VAL: (*amiably*) Hello there.

THE GIRL: Jane wants to look at some kickies.

SECOND GIRL: (*She giggles.*) No—you do.

THIRD GIRL: I'd like to try on some. Can you dance in kickies?

VAL: Sure you can dance in kickies. Sit down there. Let's measure your little foot.

THE GIRL: (*She beats her to the chair.*) Me first, me first.

VAL: Okay. First come, first serve. (*He pulls her shoe off. She giggles spasmodically.*)

VAL: Five and one half, Bennie. (*He goes to the shelf.*)

THE GIRL: Isn't he *cute*?

SECOND GIRL: Say, do you dance?

THIRD GIRL: Would you like to go out jooking?

MYRA: Val! I'll wait on these girls. You take these empty boxes out of here. (*As soon as Val leaves, the girls giggle and run out of the store. Myra looks very annoyed as Eva Temple enters.*)

EVA: Mr. Xa-*vier*?

MYRA: (*sharply*) Our popular young shoe-clerk is in the basement. What do you want?

EVA: A pair of bedroom slippers.

MYRA: Sit down and I'll show you some.

EVA: I'll wait till Mr. Xavier comes back upstairs. He seems to understand my feet so well. How's Cousin Jabe this mawning?

MYRA: Just the same.

EVA: Dear me. (*Val reappears.*) Mr. Xa-*vier*!

VAL: How are you this mawning?

EVA: I seem to be comin' down with th' most abominable ear-ache.

MYRA: (*sympathetically*) Aww! Let me give you a little laudanum faw it.

EVA: No, thanks. I put some in already. I think Birdie Wilson was partially responsible faw it.

VAL: Why? Is ear-ache contagious?

EVA: No, but Birdie was singing right next to me at choir practice, which did it absolutely no good. (*She titters a little.*) What'm I sittin' here faw?

VAL: T' look at some shoes.

EVA: Aw. Well, I guess I might. Haven't you all noticed about Birdie? Her voice always cracks on that *Te Deum*. She can hit "A" pretty good but she always flats on "B." You'd think she'd have better sense than to even attempt to make "C" because it's completely out of her range, but I'll say this for Birdie, she's got the courage of her convictions.

VAL: These are the new wine shades.

EVA: Oh! Pretty! Yes, she goes right on up there and I'm telling you all, it's a perfect imitation of the Cannonball Express. (*She giggles.*) Oh, my goodness, these *pinch*!

VAL: Do they?

EVA: They certainly do. (*She giggles archly.*)

VAL: Well, let's try a David on that.

EVA: What's David?

VAL: Next size broader!

EVA: Oh, my goodness, no! There must be some mistake!

VAL: (*He climbs the shelf ladder.*) Don't you know what a broad foot's a sign of, Miss Temple? Imagination! And also of . . .

EVA: Of *what*? (*Cassandra Whiteside enters the front door.*)

MYRA: Hello, Sandra!

SANDRA: Hello, Myra. I just drove home from New Awleuns fo' the Delta Planters' Cotillion. And do you know I neglected to bring a single decent pair of evenin' slippers back with me.

MYRA: Oh, honey, we don't keep evenin' slippers in stock, we don't get any calls fo' them here.

SANDRA: (*She notices Val.*) I didn't suppose you would.

MYRA: Oh, wait! Val, reach me down that old Queen Quality box up there! (*Dolly and Beulah enter.*)

BEULAH: Well, it is exasperating to have your table broke up at the very last . . . *Sandra!*

DOLLY: Sandra Whiteside! I thought you were gonna stay in New Awleuns till after Mardi Gras.

SANDRA: I just drove home for the Delta Planters' Cotillion.

MYRA: (*wistfully*) How is Mardi Gras this yeah?

SANDRA: As mahvelously mad as usual. If I were refawming the world I'd make it last forever.

MYRA: I went to it once a long, long time ago. I remembuh they danced in the streets.

SANDRA: They do ev'rything in the streets!

MYRA: I was just fourteen, I had on my first long dress an' a marcel wave an' some perfume called "Baiser d'Amour" (that I bought at the Maison Blanche). Something wonderful happened.

SANDRA: What was it?

MYRA: A boy in a Pierrot suit.

SANDRA: How lovely! What did he do?

MYRA: Caught me around the waist, whirled me till I was dizzy—then kissed me and—*disappeared!*

SANDRA: Disappeared?

MYRA: Completely. In the crowd. The music stopped. I ran straight back to my room and lay on the bed an' stared an' stared at a big yellow spot on the ceiling.

SANDRA: Oh, my Lawd, how tragic.

MYRA: It *was.* (*She smiles.*) I still can feel it whenever the carnival's mentioned.

SANDRA: Your first heart-break!

MYRA: Uh-huh. (*She laughs.*)

VAL: (*He brings a shoe box.*) This one?

MYRA: Yes, that's it. (*to Sandra*) I hope you're not superstitious!

SANDRA: (*She lights a cigarette.*) Why?

MYRA: Because this box contains some silver and white satin slippers that were intended for Rosemary Wildberger . . .

DOLLY: Rosemary!

BEULAH: Wildberger!

MYRA: . . . to wear at her wedding exactly three years ago this Valentine's Day. (*She lifts one of the slippers.*) She had such a tiny foot.

BEULAH: Such a tiny, delicate girl. Rosemary . . .

DOLLY: Wildberger!

SANDRA: (*She laughs lightly.*) Well, what happened? Did she fall dead at the altar?

BEULAH: Oh, no.

DOLLY: Worse than that!

BEULAH: Much worse. The man stood her up.

MYRA: Where did Rosemary go, does anyone know?

BEULAH: Some people say she went crazy an' some people say she went to Cincinnati to study voice.

SANDRA: (*carelessly*) Which was it?

EVA: (*She pipes up resentfully, having been ignored.*) Neither. She went into Chinese missionary work.

DOLLY: (*sarcastically*) Trust Eva Temple to have complete information.

BEULAH: Oh, yes.

SANDRA: And these are the fabulous Rosemary's little silver and white wedding slippers. How lovely.

MYRA: I ordered 'em from St. Louis for her but, of course, I never had the heart to mention them to her parents after she disappeared. What size do you wear, honey?

SANDRA: Four, triple A.

MYRA: Gracious. These are four B. Val, see how they fit Miss Whiteside. (*She turns to Dolly.*) Oh, Dolly, I wanted you to see this; soon as I unpacked it I had a vision of you! (*She removes an outlandish red dress with brass trimming from the racks; it looks like a bareback rider's outfit.*)

DOLLY: (*She rushes to it.*) Oh, my God, ain't it lovely! But you know, honey, I won't be able to wear anything one piece this spring.

MYRA: Really?

DOLLY: Oh, for the usual reason. Y'know there's absolutely no justice in nature. I mean the way she ties some women down while others can run hog wild. Look at Myra, for instance. Not one kid an' me turning out the seventh.

MYRA: (*She averts her face.*) Bring your measurements—I'll order you some maternity garments from Memphis.

DOLLY: Measurements? Fifteen square yards. How long'll it take?

MYRA: Probably two or three weeks. (*Dolly shrieks and throws up her hands.*) Can't you wait that long?

DOLLY: I can, but my figure can't. (*Blanch Temple enters, and trips over the rubber mat at the door. She utters a shrill cry.*)

EVA: (*She jumps up.*) Blanch, that might have *thrown* you!

MYRA: Val, you must tack that down.

VAL: Get the nigger to do it.

BLANCH: My ankle is twisted. I can't even step on that foot.

EVA: Oh, my Lawd, she'll have to have it treated again. Cost us five or six dollars. I simply can't pay for these shoes.

MYRA: All right, you don't have to, Eva, we'll just call it square. Val! Wrap these up for Miss Temple. (*She turns to Sandra.*) How did they fit? (*Val picks up the shoes and goes to the cash register.*)

SANDRA: I couldn't wear them. Let me see a pair of plain, white pumps.

MYRA: Surely.

DOLLY: We must be goin', Beulah, bye, bye, you all. (*Dolly and Beulah go out.*)

BEULAH: (*Her voice is heard off stage.*) I just been thinkin'. Lulu Belle don't play contract at all. She just plays auction.

MYRA: Hurry back! (*She gets some other shoes down; sits on the stool; opens the box for Sandra.*)

BLANCH: (*She is peeking among the Valentines on the counter.*) Here's where she must've bought it 'cause here's another just like it.

VAL: What's that?

BLANCH: Somebody sent us a comic Valentine. It wasn't funny at all, it was simply malicious. Old Maids. There's no such thing as an old maid anymore.

EVA: No, they're bachelor girls.

VAL: (*He suppresses a smile.*) Here's your shoes, Miss Temple.

EVA: Oh, thanks, aw'fly. Miss DeQuincy was telling me you'd been to Yellowstone Park.

VAL: I've travelled all over, not only Yellowstone Park, but Yosemite, Gran' Canyon . . .

BLANCH: How marvelous. Why don't we get him to give us a little descriptive talk at our next auxiliary meeting?

EVA: Oh, would you do that, Mr. . . .

VAL: Xavier.

EVA: Mr. Xavier. You won't fo'get the meeting?

BLANCH: It's Saturday at four-fifteen.

MYRA: Val couldn't take the time off. We're too rushed on Saturday afternoon.

EVA: Aw, what a shame. I meant to ask you, how's Cousin Jabe?

MYRA: No better.
EVA: Aw. What exactly resulted from the operation in Memphis?
BLANCH: Is it true that . . .
EVA: It was too late for surgical interference?
MYRA: Yes, it is true.
BLANCH: Goodness gracious.
EVA: They cut him open and sewed him right back up?
MYRA: (*She turns away in distaste.*) Excuse me.
BLANCH: Eva.
EVA: What did I say?
BLANCH: Good-bye, Mr. Xavier. (*They go out.*)
SANDRA: Aren't they delightful. The little white doves of the Lord. (*with a sidelong glance at Val*) Do you suppose I'll get like that if I remain a virgin?
MYRA: Well, I don't believe I'd worry about it, Sandra. (*Jabe knocks overhead.*)
SANDRA: Ouuu! What's that noise?
MYRA: Jabe's knocking. (*Her face darkens.*)
SANDRA: Oh.
MYRA: I'll have to run up for a minute. (*She goes quickly upstairs.*)
SANDRA: (*She lights a cigarette, with a quizzical look at Val.*) I didn't come in here for evening slippers.
VAL: No. I figured you didn't.
SANDRA: I didn't come home for the Delta Planters' Cotillion. I came back here to see you. I haven't been able to get you off my mind. I woke up thinking about you last night in the Hotel Monteleone. I went downstairs to the bar at three o'clock in the morning. I thought I might forget if I got drunk. They must've poured my whiskey out of the wrong bottle, though. At half past three I was on the highway, headed back to Two Rivers—seventy, eighty, ninety miles an hour—scared that you'd be gone before I got here. What do you think about that?
VAL: I think you'd better go back to the Mardi Gras.
SANDRA: You don't like me very much, do you?
VAL: I want to keep this job. Every place I've gone to it's been some woman I finally had to leave on account of.
SANDRA: I believe that. You're the center of much discussion in Two River County—among the women. That snakeskin

jacket, those eyes; that special technique you use in fitting on shoes.

VAL: I don't use any special technique.

SANDRA: Maybe they just imagine that you do. I can understand why. You're beautiful, you're wild. I have a feeling we'll come together some night.

VAL: Yeah?

SANDRA: (*rhapsodically*) In the dark of the moon, beside a broken fence rail in some big rolling meadow. (*Val turns away.*) We won't even say hello.

VAL: Let's quit this!

SANDRA: This what?

VAL: Double talk.

SANDRA: All right. (*She removes her dark glasses and arches her body in a provocative pose. She speaks childishly.*) Why did you slap me, Val?

VAL: Because.

SANDRA: Just because?

VAL: I didn't want to be interfered with by you. You think I've got a sign "Male at Stud" hung on me?

SANDRA: Yes, I think you have. Nobody could possibly make a mistake about it.

VAL: You made a mistake about it. I'm not in your class. I'm the kind of fellow you get to wash your car or chop the cotton. That night you drove me up to Cypress Hill, I wasn't nothing to you. It was like you had hired me to give you a little amusement.

SANDRA: That's what you thought? You were wrong about that. I felt a resemblance between us.

VAL: There's none that I know of, lady.

SANDRA: You must be blind. You—savage. And me—aristocrat. Both of us things whose license has been revoked in the civilized world. Both of us equally damned and for the same good reason. Because we both want freedom. Of course, I knew you were really better than me. A whole lot better. I'm rotten. Neurotic. Our blood's gone bad from too much inter-breeding. They've set up the guillotine, not in the Place de Concorde, but here, inside our own bodies!

VAL: Double talk, smart double talk.

SANDRA: No. Look at my wrists. They're too thin. You could snap them like twigs. You can see through my skin. It's transparent like tissue paper. I'm lovely, aren't I? But I'm not any good. I wear dark glasses over my eyes because I've got secrets in them. Too much of something that makes me rather disgusting. Yes, you were right when you slapped me, Val. You should have killed me, before I kill myself. I will some day. I have an instinct for self-destruction. I'm running away from it all the time. Too fast. New Orleans, Vicksburg, Mobile. All over the God damn country with something after me every inch of the way! But the poison I've got in my blood isn't the kind that makes me fatal to kiss! Why don't you kiss me, Val? (*Val moves away from her but she follows him.*) Scaredy cat! Scaredy cat! (*Val catches his breath and starts to embrace her. She suddenly jabs him in the middle with her knee and bites his hand. She laughs wildly.*) There! There now! That's what I came back for! Nobody's ever slapped me and gotten away with it, Snakeskin! Goodbye! (*She runs out the door.*)

VAL: God damn little bitch! (*Myra appears on the stairway.*)

MYRA: What did she do?

VAL: She dared me to kiss her.

MYRA: Did you oblige her this time or did you slap her again?

VAL: I would've done it if she hadn't kicked me.

MYRA: Well, I'm glad that she kicked you. You can find some other place to do your carrying on.

VAL: I wasn't carrying on.

MYRA: You just admitted you would have if she'd let you. (*She goes to the shelves.*) Oh, lights of delirium, look where you put the kids!

VAL: You didn't say where to put them.

MYRA: In six days time I thought you might've caught on to where some things belong in this store.

VAL: Look here, if I was a mind reader, lady, I'd put up a tent on the commons and tell your fate by the stars at fifty cents a disaster!

MYRA: Disaster is right! I wish you'd use your noggin for something beside sweet looks at the women! Anybody with the brain of a new-born calf should know better'n to put a bunch of kids in here with—look at that, will you?

(*She tosses a box furiously to the floor.*) Those Queen Quality evening slippers stuck in here, too. Why don't you fill up the rest of the space with cigar boxes and candy bars? Why do you wanta show so little imagination that you don't put nothing but shoes in the Shoe Department? You're writing a book? Surely you can think of some fancy new ideas like hanging dresses from the ceiling fans!

VAL: Look here, Myra.

MYRA: Since when am I Myra to you? My name is Mrs. Torrance!

VAL: You call me Val.

MYRA: That's different. I'm the employer here, you work in my store!

VAL: You mean I *worked* in your goddam store! (*He tears off his white clerk's jacket and flings it to the floor. There is a shocked silence.*)

MYRA: I was going to give you your notice tonight, anyhow.

VAL: You don't have to give it to me, I've already took it.

MYRA: Well, you can't walk out in the middle of the day like this.

VAL: Why not? I'm no help to you.

MYRA: I didn't say that . . .

VAL: Oh, no? Actions speak louder than words, Mrs. Torrance! (*Myra looks at him, stunned, as he puts on his snakeskin jacket. A Negro huckster passes along the street singing his wares.*) You are a very difficult, hard-headed woman—and much as I wanted a job I got to admit that working for you is no pleasure. When you tell me to do things, how can I understand you, the way you talk?

MYRA: The way I talk?

VAL: You talk to the *wall*. You talk to the *ceiling*. You never talk straight to *me*! You never even look in my face when you say something to me! I just have to guess what you said 'cause you talk so fast an' hard an' keep your face turned away . . . I've had the feeling ever since I come here that everything I do has displeased you!

MYRA: (*She averts her face.*) I didn't mean to give you that impression. As a matter of fact I was pretty well satisfied with the way you were coming along.

VAL: You certainly kept your satisfaction a secret.

MYRA: I know, I know. I'm nervous, I'm cross, I'm jumpy. (*pathetically*) I thought that you understood my nervous condition and made some allowance for it!

VAL: Being nervous is no excuse for acting like a nine-tailed catawampus!

MYRA: What is a nine-tailed catawampus?

VAL: I don't know. But I sure would hate to meet one.

MYRA: (*She is hurt.*) Oh! (*She raises a handkerchief to her eyes.*) How should I act with you—you carrying on with people like Sandra Whiteside—right here in the store!

VAL: So that's why you flew off the handle.

MYRA: Not just that. You know why those high school girls keep flocking in here?

VAL: Sure. To buy spring shoes.

MYRA: Spring shoes nothing! They come in here for a *thrill!*

VAL: A *what*?

MYRA: A *thrill*. You know know what that is, don't you?

VAL: (*He laughs.*) Can I help it?

MYRA: Yes! You don't have to *give* them one.

VAL: How do I give them a thrill?

MYRA: Don't ask *me* how. You don't have to manipulate their knees to get shoes on them.

VAL: Manipulate their . . . I never *touch* their knees!

MYRA: I've got eyes in my head!

HUCKSTER: (*chanting out in the street*) Ahhhhh ahhhhh. Turnip greens, new potatoes, rutibagas. Ahhh-ahhh. Carrots, string beans, onions!

MYRA: Also your attitude is very suggestive.

VAL: Suggestive of what, Mrs. Torrance?

MYRA: Bedrooms, if you want to know.

VAL: Bedrooms!

MYRA: Yes!

VAL: That sure is peculiar. How do I do *that*?

MYRA: Everything that you do. The way you talk, the way you walk, every single motion of you. Slew-footing this way and that way like one of those awful, disgustin', carnival dancers! (*The huckster is heard calling further away. Val stares at Myra with a long troubled look.*)

MYRA: Quit looking at me like that! (*She sobs.*) I know how awful I look.

VAL: (*gently*) You don't look awful, Myra.

MYRA: Yes, I do—my hair all stringing down—my face always turns so red when I get worked up. (*She sobs and turns away.*)

VAL: (*very gently*) Myra—I mean, Mrs. Torrance. I wanted to keep this job. I was tired of moving around and being lonesome and only meeting with strangers. I wanted to feel like I belonged somewhere and lived like regular people. Instead of like a fox that's chased by hounds!

MYRA: Maybe I haven't understood you exactly.

VAL: No. You haven't.

MYRA: How could I though? You're still a stranger to me.

VAL: My name is Val Xavier.

MYRA: And mine is Myra Torrance. Now do you feel like you know me any better?

VAL: No.

MYRA: (*She is still sobbing a little.*) Well, I don't feel much better acquainted with *you*. Give me one of them tissue paper things. (*She blows her nose.*)

VAL: How do you get to know people? I used to think you did it by touching them with your hands. But later I found out that only made you more of a stranger than ever. Now I know that *nobody* ever gets to *know* anybody.

MYRA: Nobody ever gets to *know* anybody?

VAL: No. Don't you see how it is? We're all of us locked up tight inside our own bodies. Sentenced—you might say—to solitary confinement inside our own skins.

MYRA: (*She gives him a long, puzzled look.*) Is that something out of The Book?

VAL: (*grinning*) No. That goes into The Book.

MYRA: You're a queer one. A lot of people have dropped in off the road since I've been here, but nobody quite like you. I can't figure out what you *belong* to, exactly.

VAL: Me? Belong to? Nothing.

MYRA: Don't you have folks anywhere?

VAL: I used to.

MYRA: What become of them?

VAL: I lost track of 'em after they lost their land.

MYRA: They worked on shares?

VAL: No, not shares—but leavings, scraps, tid-bits! They never owned a single inch of the earth, but all their lives they gave to working on it. The land got poor, it wouldn't produce no more, and so my folks were thrown off it.

MYRA: Where did they go?

VAL: I don't know where. They were loose chicken feathers blown around by the wind.

MYRA: You didn't go with 'em?

VAL: No. No, I made up my mind about something and I've stuck to it ever since.

MYRA: What's that?

VAL: To live by myself. So when the others left, I stayed on Witches' Bayou. It was a good place to hide in. Big cypress trees all covered with long grey moss the sun couldn't hardly shine through. Not in chinks, though, not in squares but all spread out . . .

MYRA: Misty-like.

VAL: Yeah.

MYRA: How old were you? How did you live?

VAL: Fourteen. I lived like a fox. I hunted and fished but most of the time I was hungry. I guess it must've made me a little lightheaded, because I know I had some peculiar notions . . . I used to lay out naked in a flat-boat with the sun on me.

MYRA: What did you do that for?

VAL: I had a feeling that something *important* was going to come *in* to me.

MYRA: In? Through your skin?

VAL: Kind of. Most people don't expect nothing important to come *in* to them. They just expect to get up early—plow—rest—go turtle-eggin' an' then back to bed. They never look up at the sky, dark—or with stars—or blazing yellow with sunlight—and ask it "Why? why? why?"

MYRA: Did you ask it "Why"?

VAL: That was the first word I learned to spell out at school. And I expected some answer. I felt there was something secret that I would find out and then it would all make sense.

MYRA: How would you find it out?

VAL: It would come *in* to me. Through my eyes—see? Through my ears, through my skin. Like a net—see? If you don't spread it out, you won't catch nothing in it. But if you do, you *might.* Mine I used to spread it out, wide-open, those afternoons on the bayous—ears pricked, eyes peeled—watchin', waitin', listenin' for it to come!

MYRA: Did it ever?

VAL: No. Never quite. It would of though, if I hadn't gotten thrown off the track by the girl.

MYRA: There was a girl. What girl?

VAL: A girl I met on the bayou.

MYRA: Oh, what about her?

VAL: She was the first one, yeah. That day I was real excited. I had a feeling that if I just kept polin' on a little bit further I'd come bang on whatever it was I was after!

MYRA: And she was it?

VAL: (*violently*) Naw, she *wasn't*. But she made me *think* she was.

MYRA: How did she do that?

VAL: How? By standin' naked on the dog-trot, in the door of the cabin, without a stitch on.

MYRA: What was she like?

VAL: J'ya ever notice the inside of a shell? How white that is?

MYRA: She was young I suppose. Very young?

VAL: Her shape up here, it wasn't no bigger than this (*slightly cupping his palm*) I hadn't noticed before the special dif-f'rence in women.

MYRA: But you did then?

VAL: Yes, I did then.

MYRA: Was she . . . ?

VAL: What?

MYRA: More attractive than—anyone since?

VAL: She was—th' first.

MYRA: What did you do? What happened?

VAL: I poled th' boat up closer. An' she came out on the dog-trot an' stood there a while with the daylight burnin' around her as bright as heaven as far as I could see! Oh, God, I remember a bird flown out of the moss and its wings made a shadow on her! (*He bows his head.*) An' then it sang a single high clear note. An' as though she was waitin' for that as a kind of a signal—to *trap* me—she turned and smiled an' walked on back in the cabin!

MYRA: And you followed, of course? What was it like inside?

VAL: Inside it was—empty inside.

MYRA: It couldn't have been!

VAL: Well, maybe it wasn't, but all I remember's the bed.

MYRA: Only the bed?

VAL: Made out of cypress an' covered with heaps of moss.

MYRA: Doesn't sound nice.

VAL: Well, it was. She'd been lonesome.

MYRA: How did you know? Did she tell you?

VAL: She didn't have to. She had it carved in her body.

MYRA: Carved? Is lonesomeness carved in people's bodies? (*She unconsciously touches her own.*)

VAL: Kind of. Anyhow you can see it.

MYRA: Could you see it in anybody's?

VAL: Sure. You could see it. Or feel it.

MYRA: (*softly*) What did she say to you?

VAL: She couldn't talk much except in some cajun language. I taught her some words.

MYRA: Such as what?

VAL: Such as *love.*

MYRA: You taught her that?

VAL: It was then I thought I discovered what it was that I'd been hankerin' after all those times I used to go off on the bayou.

MYRA: You thought it was that? (*She turns to the shelves.*) You mean she answered "me"?

VAL: Her! Me! Us together! Then afterwards—afterwards I thought that wasn't it. I couldn't make up my mind. When I was with her, I quit thinking because I was satisfied with just that; that sweetness between us, them long afternoons on the moss. But when I'd left her, the satisfaction would leave me an' I'd be . . . like this. (*He clenches his fist.*) Right on the edge of something tremendous. It wasn't her. She was just a woman, not even a woman quite, and what I wanted was . . .

MYRA: Was *what*?

VAL: Christ I don't know. I gotta find out!

MYRA: I guess your love for her didn't amount to so much after all. What did you do after that?

VAL: I made some money cane-grindin', sold a bunch of 'gator an' diamond-back skins. And bought myself a jalopy. I took to moving around. I thought I might track it down, whatever it was I was after. It always kept one jump ahead of me. That went on for ten years. Then I settled down for a spell in Texas. Seemed like the restlessness had worn off and I might get connected with something. But things went wrong. Something happened.

MYRA: What?

VAL: Never mind what. But everything was different after that. I wasn't free anymore. I was followed by something I couldn't get off my mind. Till I came here . . .

MYRA: Well, now that you've come here and got a good job, you can live a regular life and forget all of that.

VAL: I don't forget as easy as you, Mrs. Torrance. You don't even remember that I've lost my job.

MYRA: You haven't lost your job.

VAL: I'm not fired, huh?

MYRA: (*She smiles and shakes her head.*) We both got a little upset but that's over.

VAL: God, I . . .

MYRA: God you and lady me? (*She laughs.*) What is this place, a funeral parlor. Let's have some lights, some music. Put something on the victrola.

VAL: What would you like?

MYRA: I like that Hawaiian number with the steel guitars.

VAL: Yeah, that one! (*He crosses to the confectionery and starts the music; then he comes back.*) Myra, you know the earth turns.

MYRA: Yes.

VAL: It's turning that way. East. And if a man turned West, no matter how fast, he'd still be going the other way, really, because the earth turns so much faster. It's no use to struggle, to try to move against it. You go the way the earth pulls you whether you want to or not. I don't want to touch you, Myra.

MYRA: No, I don't want you to.

VAL: It wouldn't be right for me to.

MYRA: (*half questioning*) On account of Jabe?

VAL: No, on account of you. You been good to me. I don't want nothing to hurt you. Let's shake hands with each other, huh?

MYRA: That's not necessary! (*Without knowing why, she is suddenly angry. She crosses to the foot of the stairs.*) Take off that horrible jacket and get back to work. I have to fix Jabe's lunch. (*He follows her to the stairs.*)

VAL: Why wouldn't you shake hands with me? You're not still afraid of me, are you? (*Myra starts quickly upstairs.*) Mrs. Torrance! Myra! (*Myra pauses a moment on the landing, looking down at him with nervous hesitation.*)

VAL: (*in an intense whisper*) Myra! (*She disappears through the door and slams it shut. Val stares in bewilderment.*)

Slow Curtain

SCENE II: *It is several hours later on the same day. The mellow afternoon sunlight is muted. There is the puff-puff of the cotton gin. Val stands in the confectionery archway with his back to the audience. He is staring intently up at a large Coca-Cola ad through the arch. In conjunction with the beverage, this ad forcefully expounds the charms of a "Petty Girl" in a one-piece lemon-yellow bathing suit. She and Val appear to be experiencing a long and silent spiritual communion. In his hand Val has a "coke." Slowly, dreamily, he elevates the bottle to his mouth. Outside, at some distance, a rooster crows longingly at the sun. A man enters the front door in boots and riding breeches, bearing a shot gun. He coughs twice to divert Val's attention from the seductive picture.*

VAL: (*turning*) Sorry I was dreaming. Beautiful afternoon, huh?

MAN: I'd like to see Mrs. Torrance.

VAL: She's gone upstairs with her husband. He's not so well.

MAN: Tell her that David Anderson is here.

VAL: Just press that buzzer on the counter and she'll be down.

ANDERSON: Thank you. (*Hesitantly he follows this suggestion. The buzzer is heard above. After a moment, the door on the landing opens and Myra appears. She descends a few steps. Then seeing Anderson, she stops short.*)

MYRA: (*sharply, involuntarily*) David! (*They exchange a long, wordless stare. Then Myra recovers herself and comes down.*)

MYRA: (*to Val*) Will you go to the drug store for me?

VAL: What do you want?

MYRA: Nothing. I mean some ice cream.

VAL: A pint of vanilla? (*Myra says nothing. Val looks curiously at them both and goes out.*)

MYRA: Well.

DAVID: How are you, Myra?

MYRA: Very well, thanks. How are you?

DAVID: (*staring at her*) All right. (*There is an awkward pause.*)

MYRA: You came in here once before and I ordered you out.

DAVID: That was six years ago.

MYRA: No. Eight.

DAVID: Right after your marriage.

MYRA: Not so long after yours.

DAVID: You can't hold a grudge that long.

MYRA: Oh yes I can. I think I can hold one forever. What do you want?

DAVID: Cartridges.

MYRA: You're going out shooting wild birds? I don't have to wish you luck. I haven't forgotten what a good marksman you were. Here's your cartridges. Is there anything else?

DAVID: It seems odd to see you in here, like this.

MYRA: Waiting on trade? Does that seem *common* to you?

DAVID: No. You never were practical, though. You were always such a . . .

MYRA: *Fool?* Yes! But I've changed since then.

DAVID: You haven't changed in appearance.

MYRA: Some women are like green things. They're kept on ice. I guess I'm one of that kind. You've changed a good deal. I wouldn't have known you at all except for your walk. You still move around like you were the lord of creation. I should think you might have found out by this time that your ten thousand acres don't make up the whole universe. Other people have got some property, too. I have this store, for instance. I don't have to *clerk* in it either. I *have* a clerk. (*Her voice trembles.*) I haven't come down so terribly far in the world.

DAVID: (*embarrassed*) Of course you haven't.

MYRA: No, I've gone *up*. And I'm going to go up still *higher.*

DAVID: I'm glad of that, Myra. People have told me about your husband's sickness. I . . .

MYRA: (*feverishly*) Yes. He's dying. After his death I'm planning to sell the store. Thirty or thirty-five thousand it ought to be worth. I'm planning to leave Two River and travel around. Florida, California, New York. I've been an object for pity for a little too long around here. "Poor Myra, she's hopeless, she's crushed!" That isn't exactly the truth and I'm tired of having it whispered behind my back. My life isn't over, my life is only *commencing*. A dollar ten for the cartridges, please.

DAVID: (*extending the money*) Here, Myra.

MYRA: Just put it down on the counter. Now get out. Don't ever come back here again.

DAVID: (*quietly*) All right, Myra. (*He goes slowly out. Myra looks after him. A rooster crows mournfully in the distance. Myra raises her hand to her lips. She looks stunned. Val enters. He grins at her.*)

VAL: Finished your talk?

MYRA: (*vaguely*) Yes, David.

VAL: David?

MYRA: (*starting*) Excuse me, I mean "Val." (*bitterly*) I made a fool of myself.

VAL: Huh?

MYRA: (*evasively*) That rooster always crows about sundown. Sounds like he's remembering something. (*Jabe knocks on the ceiling.*) I wonder if he is. (*She goes back upstairs. Val opens the ice cream, dips it out with his fingers. Vee Talbott enters, stops short in the doorway as though dazed. The rooster crows.*)

VAL: Oh, hello, Mrs. Talbott.

VEE: Something's gone wrong with my eyes. I can't see nothing.

VAL: Here, let me help you. You probably drove up here with that setting sun in your face.

VEE: What? Yes. That must be it.

VAL: There now. Sit down right here.

VEE: Oh, thank you so much.

VAL: I haven't seen you since that night you let me sleep in the lock-up.

VEE: Has the minister called on you yet? Reverend Tooker? I made him promise he would. I told him that you were new in the community and that you weren't affiliated with any church yet. I want you to visit ours.

VAL: Well, that's mighty gracious of you, Mrs. Talbott.

VEE: The Church of the Resurrection! Episcopal, you know. Some people, especially Catholics, think our church was founded by Henry the Eighth, that horrible, lecherous old man who had as many wives as a cat has lives! There's not a word of truth in it. We have direct Apostolic Succession through St. Paul, who converted the early Angles. Angles is what they called the original English.

VAL: Angles, huh?

VEE: Yes, Angles. Our church is sometimes known as the Anglican Church.

VAL: Well, now, that's right int'restin', Mrs. Talbott. What's that picture you got? Something to put on display?

VEE: I thought that Myra might put it up with the Easter decorations.

VAL: I tell you what. We'll put it on display in the confectionery. Myra is going to do it over for spring. What's this picture of?

VEE: The Church of the Resurrection!

VAL: I didn't recognize it.

VEE: Well, I give it a sort of imaginative treatment.

VAL: Aw. What's this?

VEE: The steeple.

VAL: Is the church steeple red?

VEE: Naw.

VAL: Why did you paint it red then?

VEE: I felt it that way. I always paint a thing the way that it strikes me instead of always the way that it actually is. That's why the New Awleuns artists took an in'rest in my work. They say that it shows a lot of imagination. Primitive is what they call it an' one of my pictures they've hung on *ex*-hibition in the Audubon Park museum! (*Her voice shakes with pride as she states this.*)

VAL: Aw. (*He crouches slowly in front of her with a faint smile.*) You need some new shoes.

VEE: Do I?

VAL: Yes. I'll sell you a pair of beautiful wine-colored slippers. (*He clambers quickly up the ladder and jerks out a box.*)

VEE: I don't know.

VAL: Come on. Sit down there. Give me your foot. (*He grasps it roughly and jerks the shoe off. He clasps her foot in both hands and rubs it.*) You got a bad circulation.

VEE: What?

VAL: Your feet are cold. Know why? These here elastic garters are too tight on you. Why don't you leave 'em off and roll your stockings like the other girls do?

VEE: Uh?

VAL: Skittish?

VEE: It's late; I got to be going!

VAL: With one shoe off and one shoe on? "Hey diddle, diddle, my son Tom!" Here, I'll put it back on for you. Just lean on my shoulder a minute!

VEE: No, I . . . (*She sways precariously.*)

VAL: Watch out. (*He clutches her about the thighs and looks up at her, grinning.*) *There* now! Got your balance?

VEE: (*She catches her breath sharply.*) Oh, I got to be going!

VAL: (*He jumps away from her, clambers up the ladder and places the picture on the shelf.*) How's that, Mrs. Talbott? Okay? (*Vee, still too startled to speak, turns vaguely and barges out of the door. Val looks after her, then suddenly breaks into light-hearted laughter. Myra comes back downstairs slowly with a tense, concentrated expression. Val smiles.*)

VAL: Myra, did you ever see a red church steeple?

MYRA: (*absently*) No.

VAL: (*chuckling*) Neither did I.

MYRA: Jabe's took a turn for the worse. I had to give him morphine.

VAL: So?

MYRA: He must be out of his mind; he says such awful things to me. Accuses me of wanting him to die.

VAL: Don't you?

MYRA: No! Death's terrible, Val. You're alive and everything's open and free, and you can go this way or that way, whichever direction you choose. And then all at once the doors start closing on you, the walls creep in, till finally there's just one way you can go—the dark way. Everything else is shut off.

VAL: Yes . . . (*then abruptly*) You got the sun at the back of your head. It brings the gold out in your hair!

MYRA: (*diverted*) Does it?

VAL: Yes, it looks pretty, Myra. (*They stand close together. She moves suddenly away with a slight, nervous smile.*)

MYRA: It's closing time.

VAL: Uh-huh. I'll put these back on the shelves. (*He picks up the wedding slippers.*) She had a small foot.

MYRA: Rosemary Wildberger?

VAL: Naw, Naw, that Whiteside bitch.

MYRA: I could wear these slippers.

VAL: They'd be too small.

MYRA: You want to bet? Try them on me.

VAL: (*laughing*) Okay! (*He slips the shoes on her feet.*) Pinch, don't they?

MYRA: No, they feel marvelous on me!

VAL: (*doubting*) Aw!

MYRA: They do! (*She looks down at them.*) Silver and white. Why isn't everything made out of silver and white?

VAL: Wouldn't be practical, Myra.

MYRA: Practical? What's that? I never heard of practical before. I wasn't cut out for the mercantile business, Val.

VAL: What was you cut out for? (*A derelict Negro, Loon, stops outside the door and begins to play his guitar in the fading warmth of the afternoon sun. At first the music is uncertain and sad; then it lifts suddenly into a gay waltz.*) What was you cut out for, Myra?

MYRA: (*She is enrapt with the music.*) Me cut out for? Silver and white! Music! Dancing! The orchard across from Moon Lake! You don't believe me, do you? Well, look at this. You know where I am? I'm on the Peabody Roof! I'm dancing to music! My dress is made out of mousseline de soie! Yes, with silver stars on it! And in my hair I've got lovely Cape Jasmine blossoms! I'm whirling; I'm dancing faster and faster! A Hollywood talent scout, a Broadway producer: "Isn't she lovely!" Photographers taking my pictures for the *Commercial Appeal* and for the *Times-Picayune*, for all the society columns and for the rotogravure! I'm surrounded by people. Autograph seekers, they want me to sign my name! But I keep on laughing and dancing and scattering stars and lovely Cape Jasmine blossoms! (*Her rhapsodic speech is suddenly interrupted by Jabe's furious knocking on the ceiling. Her elation is instantly crushed out. She stops dancing.*) I thought he had enough to go to sleep . . .

VAL: Why don't you give him enough to . . . ?

MYRA: Val! I'm a decent woman.

VAL: What's decent? I never heard of that word. I've written a book full of words but I never used that one. Why? Because it's disgusting. Decent is something that's scared like a little white rabbit. I'll give you a better word, Myra.

MYRA: What word is that? (*The guitar changes back to its original slow melody.*)

VAL: Love, Myra. The one I taught the little girl on the bayou.

MYRA: That's an old one.

VAL: You've never heard it before.

MYRA: You're wrong about that, my dear. I heard it mentioned quite often the spring before I got married.

VAL: Who was it mentioned by—Jabe?

MYRA: No! By a boy named David.

VAL: Oh. David.

MYRA: We used to go every night to the orchard across from Moon Lake. He used to say, "Love! Love! Love!" And so did I, and both of us meant it, I thought. But he quit me that summer for some aristocratic girl, a girl like Cassandra Whiteside! I seen a picture of them dancing together on the Peabody Roof in Memphis. Prominent planter's son and the debutante daughter of . . . Of course, after that, what I really wanted was death. But Jabe was the next best thing. A man who could take care of me, although there wasn't much talk about love between us.

VAL: No. There was nothing but hate.

MYRA: No!

VAL: Nothing but hate. Like the cancer, you wish you could kill him.

MYRA: Don't! You scare me. Don't talk that way. (*She crosses slowly to the door and Loon sings as the scene dims out.*)

SCENE III: *Immediately following without break in the music. As Loon stops playing Sheriff Talbott enters the store.*

SHERIFF: Hey, Loon! Didn't I see you on Front Street this mawnin' an' tell you to clear out of town?

LOON: I thought you was jokin', Cap'n.

SHERIFF: Well, you made a big mistake. We don't allow no unemployed white transients in this town an' I'll be dogged if I'm gonna put up with colored ones.

LOON: I ain't transient, Cap'n.

SHERIFF: Where you livin'?

LOON: Nowhere, right this minute. Slep' on the levee las' night.

SHERIFF: Where you workin'?

LOON: Nowhere, Cap'n. I'se dispossessed.

SHERIFF: Aw, you'se dispossessed! Where'd you pick up all that fancy langwidge? You mean that Mr. Henley got fed up with your no-'countness an' turned you offen his property?

LOON: He turned me off but not fo' no-'countness. I wukked hard.

SHERIFF: If you work hard, you oughta make the state a good road-hand. Come on, you're under arrest.

LOON: What fo', Cap'n.

SHERIFF: Vagrancy. Ten dollar fine or thirty days hard labor.

LOON: Cap'n Talbot, I likes nine-fifty of bein' able to pay that fine.

SHERIFF: Come along.

VAL: Just a minute. I owe this boy ten dollars on his guitar.

SHERIFF: Huh?

VAL: I just bought his musical instrument off him. Here's the money. (*Loon starts to turn it over to the Sheriff.*) Just a minute. Put that in your pocket. You can't fine a man for vagrancy when he's got ten dollars, can you, Sheriff? Not if I'm acquainted with the law.

SHERIFF: Huh?

VAL: He's also got a job. Hey, Loon, you drop back in tonight an' give me a *lesson* on this thing. Okay?

LOON: Yes, suh! Okay! (*He shuffles hurriedly out. The Sheriff stares hard and silently at Val. Val casually strums a chord on the guitar. Deputy Sheriff Pee Wee Bland wobbles ponderously into the doorway laughing heartily, having just delivered some witticism to the men on the porch. He notices the tension and beckons the others to enter. They have all been drinking.*)

MYRA: (*nervously*) Val, take these boxes . . .

SHERIFF: (*interrupting*) Just a minute. (*He catches Val's arm as Val starts to move past him. Val jerks his arm free. All this happens very rapidly.*) You beat the county out of a good road-hand.

VAL: I thought he might be better as a musician.

SHERIFF: Musician, hell! That worthless no'count nigger?

VAL: A man's not worthless because he's dispossessed.

PEE WEE: Hear, hear! *Dispossessed!*

FIRST MAN: Where'd he pick up that Nawthun radical lingo?

SECOND MAN: Who's he talkin' about?

FIRST MAN: That nigger, Loon.

SECOND MAN: Come down here to organize our niggers?

FIRST MAN: Make them bosses, huh? Us chop their cotton for 'em?

PEE WEE: It's talk like that that's back of all our colored tenant trouble. (*He wobbles up to Val.*) Dispossessed? Did you say *dispossessed*?

VAL: Yes, I *did*.

PEE WEE: How yuh figure a man can be dispossessed from somethin' that never was his'n.

VAL: The land belongs to the man that works the land!

PEE WEE: Hear, hear!

FIRST MAN: That's red talk!

SECOND MAN: Yeah, go back to Rooshuh!

FIRST MAN: Anybody don't like this guvement oughta go back to Rooshuh!

SECOND MAN: Pack 'em all off togethuh, Jews, and radicals, and niggers! Ship 'em all back to *Rooshuh*!

FIRST MAN: Back to Africa with 'em!

MYRA: (*frightened*) Sheriff, stop this disturbance! My husband is sick upstairs!

SHERIFF: Quiet down you boys!

PEE WEE: (*Very drunk and sententious, he talks like a Southern orator of the old school.*) Yeh, you all hush up. I'm talkin' to this young fellow. Now, looky here: a nigger works on a white man's property, don't he? White man houses him an' feeds him an' pays him livin' wages as long as he *produces*. But when he *don't*, it's like my daddy said, he's gotta be blasted out a th' ground like a *daid tree stump* befo' you can run a *plow* th'ough it! (*A third man enters; he is a huge lout.*)

THIRD MAN: What's this here?

FIRST MAN: Some red-neck peckerwood with a nawthun edjication's tellin' us how we oughta run our niggers!

MYRA: Sheriff, make them stop right now!

PEE WEE: That nigger, Loon, got dispossessed from nothin'. The land wasn't his.

VAL: No, nothin' was his. Nothin' but his own black skin and that was his damnation!

FIRST MAN: Listen to that!

SECOND MAN: The carpet-baggers are comin' back agin!

THIRD MAN: (*He goes up to Val.*) You know what I do when I see a snake?

VAL: No, what?

MYRA: Val!

THIRD MAN: I get me a good fork stick to pin it down with. Then I scotch it under the heel of my boot—I scotch its goddam yellow gizzards out!

SECOND MAN: Go *on*!

FIRST MAN: *Show* him, Pinkie.

MYRA: Sheriff! Please!

(*The Third Man spits at Val's shoe.*)

VAL: You spit on my shoe! Wipe it off! (*He spits again. Val knocks him down. The men close in about Val like a pack of hounds. There is a near riot for a few moments. Then the Sheriff disperses them.*)

SHERIFF: Come on, you all! Clear out! *Clear* out! Pee Wee, you're Deputy. Git these men out of here! (*The men are shoved out, grumbling.*)

MYRA: Those drunken stave-mill workers make nothing but trouble!

SHERIFF: (*to Val*) Who are you? What's your name?

VAL: Val Xavier.

MYRA: Val didn't mean anything; he's just a talker.

SHERIFF: Where do you come from?

VAL: Any number of places! (*He picks up the guitar again.*)

MYRA: Down state—Witches' Bayou.

SHERIFF: Let him answer for himself, Mizz Torrance.

MYRA: Well, don't snap questions at him like he was up on trial. I know everything about this boy.

SHERIFF: You do, huh?

MYRA: Yes, I do. He come to me with the highest recommendations.

SHERIFF: Who from?

MYRA: Friends, relatives. He likes to talk. He's done some writing, but he's no more a radical than you or me! I give you my trusted word on it.

SHERIFF: It ain't a question of doubtin' your word, Mizz Torrance.

MYRA: All right. Goodbye. I'm closin' up the store.

SHERIFF: Just one more question, please. What's your draft number, buddy? (*Val stares at him and strikes a chord on the guitar.*) *What's your draft number?*

MYRA: (*quickly*) Eight thousand an' something. Val, take those empty shoe-boxes out to the incinerator! (*Val goes out with the boxes.*)

SHERIFF: How do you happen to know his draft number?

MYRA: He happened to tell me this mawning. Is there anything else that I can do for you, Sheriff?

SHERIFF: Yes, ma'am. You can do yourself a favor an' get a new clerk. That impudent young peckerwood won't bring yuh nothin' but trouble. G'night. (*The Sheriff goes out. Myra leans exhaustedly against the door. Val re-enters slowly.*)

MYRA: Oh, Val, Val, Val, why didn't you keep your head. Why didn't you hold your tongue?

VAL: A man has got to stick up for his own kind of people.

MYRA: Your kind of people? That old colored beggar, Loon?

VAL: We're both of us dispossessed. Just give me my wages an' I'll be moving along.

MYRA: Where?

VAL: Where I was headed when I broke that axle. (*Myra stares at him speechlessly.*)

MYRA: Val, I don't want you to go.

VAL: I'd ruin your business for you.

MYRA: Never mind that.

VAL: Besides I'm under suspicion now, and it wouldn't be safe.

MYRA: Just wait. This'll all blow over.

VAL: No. There's something I didn't mention about me this mawning.

MYRA: What happened in Texas?

VAL: Yes. I'm *wanted*, Myra.

MYRA: Wanted You're *wanted*? (*Val gravely picks up the guitar, without looking at Myra, and strikes a slow chord on it.*) What are you *wanted* for, Val?

VAL: (*quietly, without looking up*) For rape.

MYRA: What?

VAL: Rape!

MYRA: Shhh! I don't believe it. That's something *nigguhs* are lynched for—not *you*, Val.

VAL: Yes, me. (*He strikes a chord on the guitar.*)

MYRA: When did it happen?

VAL: About two years ago.

MYRA: Who was the woman? (*Val punctuates his speech with strumming on the guitar which he never puts down till the end of the scene. He avoids Myra's eyes.*)

VAL: A woman from Waco, Texas. Wife of an oil-field superintendent. I boarded with them while I was working down there. A plain sort of woman; I never noticed her much. One night her husband got drunk. Passed out in the car. This woman from Waco come to my room that night. Well, I was drunk. What happened was accidental. Afterwards, I was disgusted with her and with me, I said to her, "Listen, I don't want nothing like this; I'm getting away!" "I'm goin' with yuh," she said. "Oh, no you're not," I told her, "I travel alone." She started to scream. She run to the phone and screamed that she'd been raped. I lost my head for a minute and struck her in the mouth. Then I left. I drove clean out of Texas before daybreak. But not long afterwards, though, I begun to see my name and my description in public buildings—"Wanted for Rape in Texas."

MYRA: You've changed your name.

VAL: Yes, but not my description.

MYRA: That's why you're quitting this job. You're scared she'll track you down?

VAL: Not just for that reason. I have another reason.

MYRA: What's that?

VAL: *You.* Like I told you this morning, I oughtn't to touch you, but I keep *wanting* to, Myra.

MYRA: Oh.

VAL: You don't get rid of something by holding it in. It gathers, it grows, it gets to be *enormous.*

MYRA: Yes.

VAL: You said this morning I touched the women too much when I tried shoes on them. Maybe I do. My hands—I'm afraid of my hands. I hold them in so hard the muscles ache. (*He strikes a chord sharply.*) You know what it's like? A herd of elephants, straining at a rope. How do I know the rope won't break sometime? With you or with somebody else?

MYRA: (*She goes slowly to the door.*) You don't have to leave on account of a reason like that. (*She touches her forehead.*) My head's still whirling from all that excitement in here. I don't seem able to *think.* The cotton gin bothers me, too. It makes a sound like your heart was pounding a lot too fast.

VAL: Mine does sometimes. (*strumming*)

MYRA: Everyone's does sometimes.

VAL: Your belt's untied in the back.

MYRA: Is it? Fix it for me.

VAL: (*Slowly he sets down the guitar on the counter. Crossing slowly to her, he touches her waist.*) You come way in at the middle.

MYRA: I haven't let go of my figure like some women do. I've kept it.

VAL: For what?

MYRA: What for? Maybe because I don't feel everything's done for me yet.

VAL: Why should you?

MYRA: Some women do about my age. They have babies.

VAL: You never?

MYRA: No. I lived in a state of—what do they call it?—artificial respiration. Something that pumps the breath in and out of your body when otherwise you'd be dead. Dead as a rock is, Val! (*She turns abruptly to him.*) Oh, Val, I don't want you to go. I'll make it all right. I'll fix things up so nobody's going to suspicion. I'll make up all kinds of stories if you'll stay here! Huh? Huh, Val?

VAL: (*hoarsely*) Myra. . . .

MYRA: Yes?

VAL: Let's—let's—go in the back room a minute. (*The cotton gin can be heard in the distance.*)

MYRA: That room's locked, Val.

VAL: Where's the key?

MYRA: I took it an' thrown it away.

VAL: What did you do that for?

MYRA: Because I known you would ask me to go in there sometime an' I was scared I might be weak enough to do it. So I took the key and I thrown it away so far I don't think you could find it. (*He releases her and goes quickly out through the confectionery. The gin seems to pump even louder. After a moment Val returns to the room.*)

VAL: (*in a hoarse whisper*) That lock was no good, Myra.

MYRA: You broke it open?

VAL: Yes.

MYRA: Christ! I was scared that you would. (*For a long moment they stare at each other, then rush together in a convulsive embrace.*)

Curtain

ACT THREE

THE SCENE: *The same, but the room in the rear through the arch has been re-decorated. The walls have been painted pale blue and have been copiously hung with imitation dogwood blossoms to achieve a striking effect of an orchard in full bloom. The room is almost subjective, a mood or a haunting memory beyond the drab actuality of the drygoods department. Its lighting fixtures have been covered with Japanese lanterns so that, when lighted, they give the room a soft, rosy glow. It is a rainy spring afternoon about two months after the preceding scene. The old-fashioned lights of the store cannot entirely dispel the silvery gloom. The Gothic features of the room are accentuated by this shadowy effect. Val is alone in the store. He is working on his book, the loose pages of which he keeps in a battered old tin box.*

He writes with a stub pencil which he chews reflectively; then scribbles with rapt expression. The juke-box is playing a number with steel guitars. He looks very simple and lonely, a little faun-like, seated on one of the low shoe-fitting stools, absorbed in his creative labor. There is a faint whisper of rain, and of wind. Myra enters from the street in a transparent white raincoat, very glowing and warm and happy. Val quickly stuffs the script back in the box and pushes it out of sight.

MYRA: Hello, hello, hello! What are you hiding from me? Is it the book? Ah, the mysterious book. I never was quite sure that it existed.

VAL: What d'ja think it was?

MYRA: Something you dreamed those afternoons on the bayou! Let me look at it.

VAL: No.

MYRA: Let me just hold it.

VAL: Don't be silly.

MYRA: Please! (*He surrenders the bundle of papers grudgingly.*) It's like holding a baby! Such a big book, too; so good an' solid.

VAL: It's got life in it, Myra. When people read it, they're going to be frightened. They'll say it's crazy because it tells the truth! Now, give it back to me, Myra. It's not finished yet.

MYRA: I wish that I had something to do with it, too. Wouldn't it make it kind of more legitimate like if it had two parents, Val? (*She laughs tenderly, and hands it back to him.*) I had a wonderful time this afternoon. After I got Jabe's new prescription, I drove over to Tunica to get my hair done. I knew it would be my last chance before Easter. How does it look, Val?

VAL: Swell.

MYRA: How're things going?

VAL: Slow. I haven't rung up a single cash-sale since noon.

MYRA: Rain, rain. You certainly kill our trade. I was stuck on th' road coming home for nearly an hour before I got pulled out. (*She takes off her raincape and puts on a bright smock.*) I kind of enjoyed it, though. The air was so fresh, an' when the bells started ringing . . .

VAL: What're they ringing for?

MYRA: Good Friday church service. Dr. Hector is preaching the Seven Last Words from the Cross. Just as they started to ring, a big white moth flew in the car window. Val, I hate most bugs, but this one I felt a kind of a sympathy for. He was terribly young.

VAL: How do you know he was young? Did you ask him his age?

MYRA: No, but he had that surprised, inexperienced look about him that young things have. It was easy to see he had just come from the cocoon, and was *sooo* disappointed. Of cou'se he expected th' world t' be bright an' gold, but what he found was a nasty, cold spring rain. His two long whiskers were covered with strings of pearls. He sat on the steering wheel an' shook them off. I asked him, "Why?" An' he said, "Don'tcha know? It's in bad taste to put on pearls before dark!"

VAL: You're talking foolishness, Myra.

MYRA: Am I? Fo'give me, da'ling. I'm in that kind of a humor. My God, you got eyes that shine in th' dark like a dawg's. (*She starts humming a tune.*) Remember that? Such a long time ago. Before Columbus discovered America even. Oh, beautiful fo' spacious skies, for amber fields of grain. . . . Greta Garbo is at the Delta Brilliant. . . . Fo' purple mountain majesties, above the fruited . . . Lemme up on that ladder. I want to be on a high, high place in the sun! What's these here?

VAL: Women's soft sole slippers. They just come in. (*Impulsively she gathers them up like an armful of plushy red flowers and tosses them into the air.*)

MYRA: (*ecstatically*) Wake me early, Mother, fo' I shall be Queen of the May!

VAL: For Chrissakes, Myra, what did'ja do that for?

MYRA: Oh, soft sole slippers. Women's soft sole slippers! They seem t' be so damned unnecessary!

VAL: What's the matter with you this afternoon?

MYRA: When people have dreams, unusually good dreams, they get up singing, they go to the beauty parlor, and act like fools all day! When serious-minded people who write big books say, "What's th' matter with you?" they simply smile an' say, "We have our secrets." (*Val opens the door.*) The rain's slacked up?

VAL: Yeah, a little.

MYRA: That's good. Maybe we'll have a nice bright Easter, Val. We'll go to church an' look so lovely the Lawd will have to fo'give us for all our sins!

VAL: (*in the doorway*) River's way up over flood-stage at Friar's Point Landing. They say sometimes this place is cut off by water.

MYRA: They say! They say! What of it? Ten thousand years from today we'll just be little tell-tale marks on the sides of rocks which people refer to as fossils. (*There is the sound of slow tolling bells across the wide, rainy fields.*) That's all will be left of our big tremendous adventures! (*She smiles with amazement at this thought.*) Teeny-weeny little pencil-scratches, things like pigeon tracks will be what's left of Myra—what's left of Val! Then old Mr. Important Scientific Professor will pick up his microscope—"Humph!" he'll say, "This girl had remarkable legs." Or, "Goodness, this young man lost a rib somewhere." That will be all they'll ever find out about us! Were we in love? Were we happy? Did white moths fly in our windows? How do they know? They can't tell. History isn't written about *little* people. All that little people ever get to be is marks on rocks called *fossils.*

VAL: Yes, unless they write books or something.

MYRA: Oh, yes, of course, unless they write books or something! Then they're remembered *always!* (*She jumps down from the ladder and hugs him tenderly against her.*) You will be, da'ling! Don't worry!

VAL: Sarcasm?

MYRA: No, not a bit! (*She laughs gently.*) You're such a wonderful, wonderful baby! When I'm a fossil, even if it makes Mr. Science Professor blush, I hope he discovers my scratches are all scrambled up with yours. (*She laughs gaily. A small Negro boy enters the store.*) Wipe yo' feet off, Sonny, don't track th' floor.

BOY: Yes, Ma'am.

MYRA: What do you want? Peanuts?

BOY: I wan' peanuts, but granny wan' a nickel's worth a snuff.

MYRA: Aw. Well, Granny's got to have her snuff, now, don't she? How is Granny feelin'?

BOY: She been laid up in bed with break-bone fever.

MYRA: Aw, now, that's a shame. You tell 'er Mizz Torrance say to get well quick, quick, quick, cause we can't do without 'er. (*A young Negro enters in overalls.*)

BOY: Yes, Ma'am.

NEGRO: Howdy, Mizz Torr'nce.

MYRA: Hello, Bennie. Val, give the little boy a bag full a goobers, will yuh? They're on th' house.

NEGRO: (*admiringly*) You sho' are gracious, Ma'am. I wunder if you would take my note for somethin'?

MYRA: Bennie, I've got enough notes from you to paper th' store with already. What do you want?

NEGRO: A little plug tobacco.

MYRA: Well, put your cross on this.

NEGRO: Thanks, Ma'am. (*The Negro boy comes back out with the peanuts and goes out the front door. There is a sound of shouting.*)

MYRA: Oh, they're shouting up over there at the big Lent meeting. Sounds like they might be hitting the sawdust trail.

NEGRO: Will be before sundown.

MYRA: How 'bout you, Bennie?

NEGRO: Me hit it? Naw, I guess I glories too much in the flesh for that. Good afternoon, Mizz Torrance.

MYRA: (*to the Negro*) Good afternoon. Where you takin' that load of sand-bags to?

NEGRO: Down river t' Mr. Sikeses.

MYRA: You think there's a chance the levee might go out?

NEGRO: Ah reckon not unless th' Lawd intends it to. G'by, Ma'am.

MYRA: Goodbye. (*The Negro starts the mules. His wagon wheels are heard.*) Val? (*There is no answer. She switches on the lights in the confectionery. Spring blooms with a soft radiance for an instant and then dies out as she releases the switch.*) Val! (*She turns smiling slightly, her lips moving as she whispers, excitedly, to herself. With a sudden, rapturous awareness she draws her hands up the front of her body and clasps them over her breasts.*) Oh . . . (*In the archway there is suspended a *string of Chinese glass pendants with a tiny gong. With an impulse of childish gaiety, she sets the pendants tinkling, softly, musically, in the store's greenish gloom and she laughs to herself with a child's quick, delicate laughter. While her back is turned, The Conjure Man glides noiselessly into the store. Now, for the first time, there is a low muttering of thunder. The lights in the confectionery flicker a little. Still unaware of The Conjure Man's presence, Myra shivers slightly and a bewildered, uncertain look appears on her face and she raises a hand to touch her cheek and her forehead. As though with a disturbing prescience of something unnatural, she turns about slowly and meets the Negro's gaze. She catches her breath in a sudden, sharp gasp. The Conjure Man smiles and makes a slight obeisance. He stretches out his small claw-like hand, in the hollow of which he is presenting some object.*)

MYRA: (*breathlessly*) What—what do you want? (*The Conjure man mumbles something which cannot be heard.*) What? No! No, I don't want it. (*then, smiling defiantly*) I don't need holy stones to bring me luck. (*The Conjure Man makes another slight bow, then starts to turn away.*) If you want to make an honest dollar, though, you can go out back and wash the Mississippi Delta off my car. You'll find a sponge, a bucket, and a bunch of old chamoises hanging in the garage. (*The Conjure Man mumbles some eager words of thanks and starts to the confectionery. Myra looks after him, troubled, not knowing why. In the archway he stops and looks back over his shoulder to meet her gaze. There is a moment of curiously tense stillness. Then he grins and makes another slight bow and disappears. There is the sound of low thunder again. The front door opens and Dolly comes in.*)

DOLLY: Has he gone?

MYRA: Who?

DOLLY: That *awful* lookin' ole darky.

MYRA: He's gone out back. Who is he?

DOLLY: They call him The Conjure Man—from Blue Mountain. When I first caught a sight of him out there, I swear to goodness I neahly had a conniption! I was scared to death that he would *mark* my *baby*! Which reminds me to ask you! Have those maternity garments got here yet?

MYRA: No, they haven't come yet.

DOLLY: What? I ordered 'em two months ago.

MYRA: I know, and I can't understand what's causin' the delay.

DOLLY: Neither can I. My God, what am I going to do?

MYRA: I'm sorry.

DOLLY: I guess I'll have to hang out a sign, "Excuse me people." (*Myra turns away in distaste. Beulah rushes in.*)

BEULAH: Excitement! Cassandra Whiteside's come in town drunk as a lord.

DOLLY: No.

BEULAH: I just seen her on Front Street. Wearin' a white satin evenin' dress. She's been in another wreck; the side of the car's bashed in.

DOLLY: I thought they revoked her license.

BEULAH: She's got her a nigger chauffeur. At least I *hope* he's a chauffeur.

DOLLY: Beulah.

BEULAH: Well, there has been a great deal of speculation about 'em that's not very pleasant. They say that she's been ostracized in Memphis, asked to leave sev'ral parties; and her father has actually received a warning note from the Klan.

DOLLY: Goodness. She'll be worse than ostracized if she keeps up at this rate.

BEULAH: Myra, what will you do if she comes in here and starts to make a disturbance?

MYRA: (*shortly*) Put her out.

BEULAH: You think you could? They say she fights like a tiger.

MYRA: (*as Val enters*) I think Val would be able to handle her for me.

VAL: (*He sets the boxes down.*) What did you call me for, Myra?

MYRA: (*confused*) Call you? Oh, yes, I—I can't remember just now.

BEULAH: That sounds extremely suspicious. (*She winks.*)

DOLLY: Don't it, though? Look, they're blushing.

BEULAH: Both of them. Oh, I think it's marvelous to see a man who can blush.

MYRA: (*with nervous haste*) Val, are those the new Keds?

VAL: No, women's rubbers.

MYRA: Just in time for the rain; how very lucky.

DOLLY: (*meaningfully*) How's Jabe?

MYRA: (*still confused*) Jabe?

DOLLY: Yes, your husband, honey. Jabe Torrance.

MYRA: Jabe's no better.

DOLLY: Ain't that turr'ble!

BEULAH: I don't guess you *could* look for much improvement.

MYRA: No. All we can do is try to relieve the pain. Val, bring up the rest of those boxes and stack them up there. (*Val is glad to get out.*)

DOLLY: Myra, that green is your color!

BEULAH: Don't it look sweet on her, though? I had my eye on that dress; it's the nices' thing you had in stock, Myra Torrance.

MYRA: It's more of a blue than a green.

BEULAH: What do they call it?

MYRA: (*with a slight, suppressed smile*) They call it "ecstasy blue."

DOLLY: I swan. (*She exchanges a significant look with Beulah.*)

BEULAH: But don't it become her, though? It brings the gold out in her hair.

DOLLY: *It does.*

MYRA: I just had it washed. That always brightens the color.

DOLLY: What with? Goldenfoam?

MYRA: No, with a few drops of lemon. That's all I use.

DOLLY: Honestly? Well, she's took on more *sparkle* this spring.

BEULAH: I think it's wonderful that you can be so brave.

MYRA: What do you mean?

BEULAH: Why, I mean about Jabe's condition.

MYRA: Oh, excuse me a minute. I gotta take Jabe his medicine. He's been so restless today. (*She goes back upstairs. Beulah looks at Dolly and giggles. Dolly looks at Beulah and giggles an octave higher. They both cover their mouths as the Temple sisters enter.*)

BLANCH: I want you to know . . .

EVA: Dr. Hector had just finished preaching the Seven Last Words from the Cross . . .

BLANCH: When who should we run into . . .

EVA: Yes! on Front Street.

BEULAH: Sandra Whiteside?

EVA AND BLANCH: Yes!

DOLLY: I know. We just been talking.

EVA: (*She catches her breath.*) Did you know she was just put out of the Cross Roads Inn?

BLANCH: Literally thrown out. They tried to get her father on the phone. Useless!

EVA: He's drunker than she is. We passed her just now up there on the Sunflower Bridge. She seemed to be having D.T.'s. What's that she was shouting, Blanch?

BLANCH: "Behold Cassandra! Shouting doom at the gates!"

EVA: Yes. An' some bright-skin nigger was in the car with her. It's really created a perfeckly terrible stir.

BLANCH: Imagine—on Good Friday!

EVA: Utterly shameless! Where's that nice-lookin' young man?

BLANCH: I got to return those shoes. I went to a very expensive obstetrician in Memphis. He said they'd ruined my feet. Why, Palm Sunday mawning I couldn't hardly march in church with the choir. (*She calls out.*) Mr. Xavier? Oh, they've closed the confectionery.

EVA: Yes. The noise was disturbing to Jabe.

BLANCH: She's had it re-decorated.

EVA: All done over. She says it's supposed to resemble the orchard across from Moon Lake. (*Vee enters. She wears black, nun-like garments for Good Friday, and her look is exalted.*) Vee! How are you, honey?

VEE: (*almost sobbing*) I've waited and prayed so long. Now it's finally come.

BEULAH: *What's* come?

VEE: The vision. I seen him early this mawning. I painted the picture.

BEULAH: Picture of what?

VEE: Of Jesus!

DOLLY: I thought you said you'd never paint the Lawd until you'd actually seen Him face to face.

VEE: (*simply*) I have. This mawning. On the way to church, by the cottonwood tree, where the road branches off toward the levee. I been on a fast since Ash Wednesday to clear my sight. Veils seemed to drop off my eyes. Light—light! I never have seen such brilliance. Like needles it was in my eyes; they actually ached when I stepped out in it.

BEULAH: In what?

VEE: The sun this mawning, before the Passion began.

DOLLY: Weakness from fasting. You're such an excitable nature.

VEE: No, no. I've had other signs. Look at my palms.

BEULAH: What about them?

VEE: Can't you see the red marks?

BEULAH: They do look so't of inflamed.

BLANCH: Ain't that remarkable, though?

BEULAH: What happened?

VEE: I been tormented. He took all the torment off me.

DOLLY: Tormented by what?

VEE: Evil thoughts. Those men in the lock-up, they write nasty words on the walls. At night I can see them. They keep coming up in my mind. He took that cross off me when he touched me.

BEULAH: Touched you?

DOLLY: Where? (*Vee lifts her hand reverently and touches her bosom.*) Aw. (*She giggles.*) He made a pass at you? (*She giggles.*) He made a pass at you?

BEULAH: Dolly, you're awful!

DOLLY: I couldn't help it; it just popped out of my mouth.

BEULAH: Vee, can't we see the picture?

BLANCH: Yes, let's see it.

VEE: I brung it here for Myra t' put on display. (*She starts to unwrap the canvas. There is the sound of an angry outburst and the simultaneous crash of glass on the floor above.*)

BEULAH: What's that? (*The women congregate quickly at the foot of the stairs in listening attitudes.*)

VEE: No, I've had other manifestations. (*at the right of Dolly*) When I was seven years old, my little sister, Rose, got typhoid fever.

MYRA: (*upstairs*) Jabe.

BEULAH: What's that?

DOLLY: Can you make it out?

MYRA: Jabe!

BEULAH: (*She goes to the foot of the steps.*) What's that shouting upstairs?

VEE: She hadn't been baptized yet an' the doctor said she was dyin'. So Reverend Dabney come over at midnight.

JABE: No, I won't take it.

MYRA: The doctor prescribed it for you. It helps the pain.

JABE: I know what you're trying to do. You're trying to kill me.

DOLLY: What?

BEULAH: What?

MYRA: You're out of your head.

DOLLY: What's that?

BLANCH: Sssh.

EVA: Sssh.

VEE: Afterwards, he give me the bowl of Holy water an' told me to empty it outside on the bare ground. But I didn't. I poured it out in the kitchen sink.

MYRA: Jabe, you don't know what you're saying. (*The door bangs open.*) I'll call for the doctor.

BLANCH: Delirious!

EVA: Yes, out of his haid!

VEE: (*slowly*) The kitchen sink turned *black. Black*—absolutely *black!* (*The door above is suddenly thrown open and Myra calls out wildly.*)

MYRA: Val! Val!

DOLLY: I'll get him for yuh, Myra! Mr. Xavier! (*There is great excitement. Val comes in.*)

VAL: What's the matter?

BLANCH: Oh, something's goin' on, I don't know what . . .

EVA: But it's awful! (*Myra appears above.*)

MYRA: *Val?*

VAL: Yeah?

MYRA: Phone Dr. Bob, and tell him to come right over! (*She slams the door.*)

EVA: Where's Dr. Bob?

BLANCH: Ain't he in Jackson Springs?

VAL: Howdy, Mizz Talbott.

EVA: I'm very much afraid the wires are down! (*As Val crosses in front of Vee, she slowly rises, following him with her eyes, her lower jaw sagging open slowly with a stricken expression.*)

VAL: (*He lifts the phone.*) Get me Jackson Springs. (*Vee utters a stifled cry. Val is struck by her shocked gaze.*) What's the matter, Mizz Talbott? (*into the phone*) Jackson Springs?

VEE: No, no!

DOLLY: What's the matter with Vee? She's white as goat's milk.

BEULAH: Seems to me like she's tooken some kind of a spell.

DOLLY: (*She grasps her shoulders roughly.*) Vee!

VEE: Le' me go! Leave me be!

BLANCH: That vision she had has probably got her wrought up.

EVA: Passion Week always upsets her. Get a wet cloth, somebody!

VAL: The wires are down.

BEULAH: Don't Myra keep some kind of a stimulant on the place?

VAL: There's some rum in the back. I'll get it.

VEE: (*She struggles up, panting.*) Naw, I can't stay, le' me go!

DOLLY: Nobody's holding you, honey.

VEE: (*Her eyes follow Val as he crosses to the confectionery.*) Where's he going to?

BEULAH: Get you a little something to pull you together. (*Dolly picks up the picture.*)

VEE: (*She cries out wildly.*) You take your hands off my picture! (*She wrests it from Dolly before she can see it.*)

BEULAH: Well!

VEE: It's not t' be touched by you, you foul-minded thing!

DOLLY: I thought that you brung it here to put on dis-*play.*

VEE: I never.

DOLLY: Just let me take one look!

VEE: No! (*Dolly makes a move toward the canvas. Beulah crosses to the right of the steps. Vee cries out and thrusts her away. Myra appears on the stairs.*)

MYRA: Oh, for God's sake, will you all please hush up? I've got to get in touch with Dr. Bob! (*Her hair is disarranged, and her dress torn open as though she had been in a struggle.*) Jabe's delirious. He wouldn't take the morphine. Did you hear him? He said I was trying to kill him! (*She picks up the receiver, jiggles it.*)

EVA: Val tried to phone.

BLANCH: They told him the wires were down.

MYRA: Then I'll just have to drive over.

BLANCH: Oh, but they say there's danger of the bridge collapsing.

MYRA: What else can I do?

EVA: Blanch, if you were married and your husband was desperately ill, wouldn't you take a chance on the bridge collapsing?

BLANCH: No, I certainly wouldn't. No, I certainly. . . . Oh, before you go, Myra—about these shoes . . .

MYRA: (*She snatches a raincoat from the closet.*) Oh, I'm distracted, I—Val, tell the nigger to put the chains on the tires!

VAL: I can't do six things at once. Miss Eva here wants some money back on a pair of shoes.

MYRA: Money back? What money? You got the shoes for nothing!

BLANCH: Oh, horrors, don't you remember how I tripped over that rubber mat an' practickly broke my ankle?

EVA: Two trips to the doctor it cost us!

BLANCH: Six dollars!

EVA: But we'll take five since Myra has been so . . .

MYRA: Thanks. Val, give the ladies five dollars out of the cash-box. Now if you'll excuse me . . .

BEULAH: Myra, if there's anything I can do.

DOLLY: Don't hesitate to call on me if they is. (*Myra has already disappeared through the confectionery.*)

BLANCH: Gracious . . .

EVA: Sakes alive! What excitement! Blanch, you go up an' sit with Cousin Jabe.

BLANCH: Oh, I couldn't. I'm having palpitations!

VEE: I . . . I . . . have to leave, too. (*She retreats toward the door.*)

DOLLY: Not without showin' the picture!

VEE: Dolly, get out of my way!

BEULAH: (*She snatches the picture held behind her back and tears the paper wrapping off. She gasps and shrieks with laughter.*) Mr. Xavier!

DOLLY: Mr. *Xavier*?

VAL: What?

BEULAH: Vee Talbott here has just conferred a wonderful honor on you.

DOLLY: Oh, so it *is*, I *suspected!*

BEULAH: You're going to sit at the head of the table with all of the Twelve Apostles sitting around'ja!

DOLLY: You even have a silver dish-pan sort of on top of your haid! (*They both shriek with laughter.*)

VEE: (*wildly*) No, no, no! Let go of my picture!

BEULAH: Ain't it a wonderful likeness?

DOLLY: From memory, too. Or did you pose for it, Val?

BEULAH: He didn't *have to.* She seen him in the cottonwood tree. The *lynching* tree, as they call it!

DOLLY: I hope that don't make you *nervous*, Val!

VEE: No! You're all of you cooking up something without no excuse!

DOLLY: No? No excuse? That's why you nearly collapsed when Mr. Xavier came up an' said hello to yuh!

BEULAH: Your spiritual nature an' all, what a big joke it is!

DOLLY: Carping at other people, criticizing their morals . . .

BEULAH: Stirring up all that card-playing rumpus here in the congregation.

DOLLY: Declaring in public that I wasn't fit to associate with because I had drinking parties.

BLANCH: Dolly!

EVA: Don't you all go on like this!

DOLLY: She's got to have her eyes opened, now, once an' for all. A vision of Jesus? No, but of Val Xavier, the shoe-clerk who sold 'er them shoes.

VAL: Mrs. Bland!

DOLLY: And where did she have this vision? Where? Under the cottonwood tree where the road turns off toward the levee. Exactly where time an' time again you see couples parked in cars with all of the shades pulled down! And what did he do? He stretched out his hand and *touched* yuh! (*She thrusts her hand against Vee's bosom. Vee cries aloud as though the hand were a knife thrust into her, and, turning awkwardly, runs out of the store.*)

VAL: You all better go or you'll get bogged down on th' road.

BLANCH: Dolly, you shouldn't have done that.

EVA: So unnecessary!

BEULAH: I don't know. She's always held herself so high.

DOLLY: Yes, superior to us all. I guess after this she won't have so much to say on the subjeck of bridge during Lent! Come on Beulah, let's go! Blanch, you an' Eva comin'?

BLANCH: Yes, just a minute! What happened to those old shoes? You see 'em, Mr. Xavier?

VAL: I thrown 'em in the trash-bin. You want 'em back?

BLANCH: Please.

EVA: We couldn't wear 'em, of course, but it's no use throwin' 'em away.

BLANCH: No. Wilful waste makes woeful want, they say. (*She giggles as they back skittishly out of the door.*) Don't you feel it? The atmosphere is simply charged with electric disturbance! (*Val is left alone. He picks up the canvas Vee left, places it on the counter and stares at it for several seconds. The Conjure Man comes back into the archway, gliding noiselessly as before. He stares inscrutably at Val's back. Val turns, as Myra had turned, with the same air of troubled presentiment, and catches the Negro's gaze. Unconsciously he raises his hands to draw his shirt closer about his throat as though the air had turned colder.*)

VAL: What—what do you want? (*The Conjure Man mumbles almost indistinguishably.*) Oh. Sure. You can stay back there all night, if it don't stop raining! (*The Conjure Man grins and bows, then extends his palm with the lucky token.*) Huh? Naw, naw, naw, I don't want it! Sorry but I don't truck with that conjure stuff. (*The Conjure Man bows once more and disappears as noiselessly as he came. There is a low muttering of thunder. Val looks uneasy. He takes off his working jacket. There is a wild burst of drunken laughter outside. The door is thrown open and Sandra enters, a flash of lightning behind her. Her hair hangs loose and she wears a rain-spattered, grass-stained white satin evening gown.*)

SANDRA: Behold Cassandra, shouting doom at the gates!

VAL: What do you want?

SANDRA: Oh. It's you. Snakeskin. Remember we're even now.

VAL: What do you want in here?

SANDRA: Protection. I'm in danger.

VAL: Danger of what?

SANDRA: Immolation at the hands of the outraged citizens of Two Rivers County. They've confiscated the nigger that drove my car and ordered me out of Two Rivers.

VAL: You must've given 'em some provocation.

SANDRA: Plenty of provocation. They say that I run around wild and stir up trouble—and neither parental nor civil law is able to restrain me. Why, only this afternoon I was on Cypress Hill with that bright-skinned nigger. They suspect me of having improper relations with him.

VAL: Did you?

SANDRA: No. I poured a libation of rum on my great-aunt's grave. But they don't believe me. The Vigilantes decided that I was persona non grata and warned me to leave before something bad happened to me. How about you?

VAL: Huh?

SANDRA: Why don't you come along with me? You an' me, we belong to the fugitive kind. We live on motion. Think of it, Val. Nothing but motion, motion, mile after mile, keeping up with the wind, or even faster! Doesn't that make you hungry for what you live on? (*Val shakes his head.*) Maybe we'll find something new, something never discovered. We'll stake out our claim before the others get to it. What do you say? (*Val turns away.*) Where's Myra?

VAL: She's gone to Jackson Springs to get a doctor.

SANDRA: Good! We're alone together.

VAL: What's good about it?

SANDRA: Why do you hate me, Val?

VAL: I don't want trouble.

SANDRA: Am I trouble?

VAL: Yeah. As fine a piece of trouble as ever I've seen.

SANDRA: Is Myra trouble?

VAL: Leave her out of it.

SANDRA: Don't you think I know what's going on?

VAL: What are you talking about?

SANDRA: I saw her in Tupelo this morning, having her hair fixed up! What radiance! What joy!

VAL: Shut up about Myra.

SANDRA: Oh, you'd better watch out. It isn't kiss and good-bye with a woman like that! She'll want to keep you forever. I'm not like that.

VAL: Aw, leave me alone. (*He takes his jacket from a hook.*)

SANDRA: Women will never leave you alone. Not as long as you wear that marvelous jacket.

VAL: I want to close up.

SANDRA: I'll go in a minute.

VAL: Make it *this* minute, will you? (*Sandra crosses to him. She loosens her red velvet cape and drops it to the floor at her feet. The white evening gown clings nakedly to her body.*)

VAL: Don't stand there in front of me like that!

SANDRA: Why not? I'm just looking at you. You know what I feel when I look at you, Val? Always the weight of your body bearing me down.

VAL: *Christ!*

SANDRA: You think I ought to be ashamed to say that? Well, I'm not. I think that passion is something to be proud of. It's the only one of the little alphabet blocks they give us to play with that seems to stand for anything of importance. Val . . . (*She touches his shoulder. He shoves her roughly away. The door opens and Myra enters.*)

MYRA: Oh!

SANDRA: (*casually*) Hello, there. I thought you'd gone for the doctor.

MYRA: I couldn't get over the river. The bridge is out. What are *you* doing here?

SANDRA: I came here to give you a warning.

MYRA: A warning? Warning of what?

SANDRA: They've passed a law against passion. Our license has been revoked. We have to give it up or else be ostracized by Memphis society. Jackson and Vicksburg, too. Whoever has too much passion, we're going to be burned like witches because we know too much.

MYRA: What are you talking about?

SANDRA: Damnation! You see my lips have been touched by prophetic fire.

MYRA: I think they've also been touched by too much liquor. The store is closed.

SANDRA: I want to talk to you, Myra.

MYRA: Come back in the morning.

SANDRA: What morning? There isn't going to be any.

MYRA: I think there is.

SANDRA: That's just a case of unwarranted optimism. I have it on the very best of authority that Time is all used up. There's no more time. Can't you see it? Feel it? (*with drunken exultation*) The atmosphere is pregnant with disaster! (*She laughs and suddenly clasps the palms of her hands to her ears.*) Now, I can even *hear* it!

VAL: What?

SANDRA: A battle in heaven. A battle of *angels* above us! And *thunder!* And *storm!* (*She laughs wildly.*)

MYRA: Sandra, I've had too much. I can't stand anything more. You go home now before I do something I shouldn't.

SANDRA: I believe you *would*. You'd fight like a *tiger* for him.

MYRA: Be careful, Sandra.

SANDRA: Yes, I can tell by looking at you in that mad dress with your eyes spitting fire like the Devil's, you've learned what I've learned, that there's nothing on earth you can do. No, nothing! But catch at whatever comes near you with both your hands, until your fingers are broken! (*Sandra flings herself upon Val and kisses him with abandon. Myra springs at her like a tiger and slaps her fiercely across the face.*)

MYRA: Leave him be, damn you, or I'll . . . (*Sandra whimpers and staggers to the counter. Her head lolls forward and the dark hair slides over her face; she slips to her knees on the floor.*) Take her upstairs to my room. When dogs go mad, they ought to be locked and chained. (*Val picks Sandra up and carries her up the stairs. The storm increases in violence; rain beats loud on the tin portico outside. There is a terribly loud thunder clap. Myra gasps. The electric current is disrupted and the lights dim out. Someone bangs at the door. Myra calls—*) The store's closed up!

MAN: It's me, Mrs. Torrance. Jim Talbott!

MYRA: Oh, Sheriff Talbott. (*She opens the door.*) Is something the matter?

SHERIFF: Yes. (*He enters, followed by a woman. There is something remarkably sinister about the woman's appearance. She is a hard, dyed blond in a dark suit. Her body is short and heavy but her face appears to have been burned thin by some consuming fever accentuated by the mask-like makeup she wears and the falsely glittering gems on her fingers which are knotted tight around her purse.*) This is Mrs. Regan from Waco, Texas.

WOMAN: Never mind about that. Where is the man that clerks here?

MYRA: Val?

WOMAN: Is that what he calls himself? In Waco he was known as Jonathan West.

MYRA: (*to the Sheriff*) What does this woman want here?

WOMAN: I want that man.

SHERIFF: That clerk of yours is wanted for rape in Texas.

MYRA: I'm sure you're mistaken.

WOMAN: Oh, no, I don't think I am. I've sent out descriptions of him to every town in the country. Canada, Mexico, even. The minute I got news of this shoe-clerk I hopped a plane out of Waco. I feel pretty sure that I've finally tracked him down. Where is he? Where does he keep himself?

MYRA: I don't know.

WOMAN: Surely you . . .

MYRA: I don't have any idea!

WOMAN: You—you *must*, Mrs. Torrance!

MYRA: *No!* No, I don't. Oh, yes, he—he drove into Memphis.

WOMAN: Two days before Easter? He suddenly drove into Memphis and left you without any help? That certainly does sound peculiar.

MYRA: I gave him his notice. He's gone.

WOMAN: I don't believe you.

MYRA: (*to the Sheriff*) This woman has got a pistol in her purse.

WOMAN: What if I have? You don't go hunting a dangerous animal down without any weapons. (*She suddenly starts forward.*) Wait! Look here! This picture! (*She crosses to Vee's portrait.*)

SHERIFF: It's one of my wife's.

WOMAN: Now I'm convinced. It's *him*. I'd recognize it hanging on the moon. Come along, Sheriff, we're wasting time with this woman. She's telling us lies to protect him. The place to look is them sporting houses on Front Street. (*She rushes from the store.*)

SHERIFF: Don't play with fire, Mrs. Torrance. (*He follows her out. Myra gasps and crosses to the door, bolting it shut. Val steps noiselessly out upon the upstairs landing and stares down at Myra. He descends a few steps with caution.*)

VAL: (*on the stairs*) Who was it?

MYRA: Sheriff Talbott.

VAL: (*descending two steps*) Who was the woman? (*Myra stares up at him dumbly.*) *Who was the woman with him?*

MYRA: Val, don't act so excited.

VAL: Oh. It was her then.

MYRA: Yes. The woman from Waco.

VAL: Christ! I heard her voice but I thought I must be dreaming. (*He suddenly catches his breath and darts down the stairs and toward the front door.*)

MYRA: Where do you think you're goin'?

VAL: *Out!*

MYRA: Don't be a fool. You can't leave now. Those drunken stave-mill workers are on the street.

VAL: They know, already? She's *told* 'em?

MYRA: Val, will you please . . .

VAL: Lock up that door!

MYRA: It's locked.

VAL: The door in the confectionery?

MYRA: That's locked, too.

VAL: What happened to the lights?

MYRA: Went out in the storm. I'll turn on a lamp . . .

VAL: No. *Don't!*

MYRA: In the confectionery. They can't see in.

VAL: What did you tell her?

MYRA: That you'd gone into Memphis.

VAL: Did she believe you?

MYRA: No.

VAL: Where did they go to look for me?

MYRA: Sporting houses on Front Street.

VAL: Yeah. She'd think of that. Oh, God, Myra, I've washed myself in melted snow on mountains trying to get the touch of her off my body. It's no good.

MYRA: Keep *hold* of yourself.

VAL: You can't understand what it is to be hounded by somebody's hate.

MYRA: I looked in her face. What I saw wasn't hate.

VAL: What was it then?

MYRA: A terrible, hopeless, twisted kind of *love.*

VAL: That's worse than hate.

MYRA: I *know.* (*She picks up a lamp.*) Dry as a bone. Give me the other one, Val. (*Val stares at nothing.*) Never mind, I'll get it. You're safe in here. They looked here once; they won't come back until morning.

VAL: *Safe?* She mentioned it in her description.

MYRA: Mentioned what?

VAL: Scars from burns on his legs. Afraid of fire. She'll have them *burn* me, Myra.

MYRA: Oh, Val, darling, don't act like a scared little boy.

VAL: I'm not so scared. I'm sick.

MYRA: I know how you feel.

VAL: Like something was crawling on me. Something that crawled up out of the basement of my brain. How did she look?

MYRA: A vicious, pitiful, artificial blond.

VAL: She had on black?

MYRA: Yes.

VAL: All loaded down with imitation diamonds. That's how I see her. Leaning against a wall and screaming, "You can't get away! Anywhere that yuh go I'll track yuh down!" And now she has— She's *here!*

MYRA: (*pityingly*) Oh, Val, stay there on the stairs. I'm going to fix you a drink. The rain has made the air colder. Don't you feel it?

VAL: No.

MYRA: I do. I seem to be shaking a little. I guess my blood's too thin. Of course, you'll have to get away from Two River.

VAL: Get away? Yes, if I'm lucky!

MYRA: Oh, you'll be lucky, darling. I was just thinking, thinking about *myself.* Val . . .

VAL: What?

MYRA: I haven't traveled much. I've never been west of the Mississippi. Never much east of it either. I think it's time I took a trip somewhere.

VAL: What are you talking about?

MYRA: I'm leaving here with you tonight!

VAL: No.

MYRA: Oh, yes, I *am.* I've *got* to. We'll run off *together* as soon as the storm slacks up.

VAL: (*He rises.*) Myra . . .

MYRA: Give me a nickel; I want to play the victrola.

VAL: Myra, you're . . .

MYRA: No. Never mind. I've got some change in my pocket. Wait just a minute. (*She goes to the juke box and starts the music.*)

VAL: Myra, you've got to . . .

MYRA: *Shhh!* (*She comes back in.*) When I was a girl, I was always expecting something tremendous to happen. Maybe not this time but next time. I used to dance all night, come home drunk at daybreak and tiptoe barefooted up the back stairs. The sky used to be so white in the early mornings. You know it's been a long time since I've even noticed what color the sky is at daybreak. Traveling on a lonely road all night in an open car I guess you'd notice such things. I'd enjoy that. I could point them out to you while you were driving the car. I'd say, "Look, Val, here's something to put in the book!" "What is it?" I'd say, "It's white!" "What is?" "The sky is!" "Oh," you'd say, "is it?" "Yes, I'd say, "it is, it is, it *is*!" And you would have to believe me! (*She clings to him; Val breaks away from her.*)

VAL: I got to go by myself. I couldn't take anyone with me.

MYRA: That's where you're mistaken. You're dreadfully mistaken if you think that I'm going to stay on here by myself in a store full of bottles and boxes while you go traipsing around through all the world's dark corners without me having a forwarding address even.

VAL: I'll give you a forwarding address.

MYRA: That's not enough. What could I do with a forwarding address, Val? Take it into the backroom with me at night? Oh, my darling, darling forwarding address! A wonderful companion *that* would be. So sweet. And satisfying!

VAL: Myra! Don't talk so loud!

MYRA: (*breathlessly*) Excuse me. I'll get your drink. (*She goes to the confectionery and comes back out with a bottle.*) How much do you want? Three fingers? What was I . . . ? Oh, Oh, yes, I wanted to tell you (*She pours the rum.*) we had a fig tree in the back of our yard that never bore any fruit. We thought that it never would. I'd always pitied it so because they said it was barren. But it surprised us one spring. I was the one that discovered the first little fig. Oh, my God, I was so excited. I ran in the house; I was screaming! "Daddy, daddy, it isn't barren, it isn't barren, daddy! The little fig tree . . ." I told him, "It's going to have figs this year!" It seemed such a marvelous thing, it needed a big celebration, so I took out Christmas ornaments. Yes, little colored glass bells and tinsel and artificial snow! (*She laughs breathlessly.*) And I put them all over the fig tree, there, in the middle of April, because it was going to bear fruit! Here, Val, step up to the bar and take your drink! (*Val crosses to her.*) Oh, darling, haven't we any Christmas ornaments to hang on me? (*Val stops short.*)

VAL: (*sharply*) What do you mean?

MYRA: I mean that I'm not barren. Not anymore!

VAL: You're making this up!

MYRA: No, Val! You see, being clever, Val, isn't enough when you're up against something as big as life is. Sure, you can make keys for a door. That's clever, Val, but somebody comes along and breaks the door down. That's life! And that's what happened to me. Oh, God, I knew that I wouldn't be barren when we went together that first time. I felt it already, stirring up inside me, beginning to live! The first little fig on the tree they said wouldn't bear! What a mistake they made! Here. Here's your drink. (*He stares at her dumbly.*) Take it! (*She thrusts it into his hand.*) So now you see we can't be separated! We're bound together, Val!

VAL: Bound? No! I'm not bound to nothing! Never could be, Myra!

MYRA: Oh, yes, you could!

VAL: What do you mean by that?

MYRA: In one respect I'm like that woman from Waco. I'll never let you get away from me, Val. I want you to understand that.

VAL: There's one thing you don't understand good, Myra.

MYRA: No? What's that?

VAL: I travel by myself. I don't take anything with me but my skin.

MYRA: Then I'm your skin. Skin yourself and you'll be rid of me!

VAL: Listen, Myra, there's one thing safe for me to do. Go back to New Mexico and live by myself.

MYRA: On the desert?

VAL: Yes.

MYRA: Would I make the desert crowded?

VAL: Yes, you would. You'd make it crowded, Myra.

MYRA: Oh, my God, I thought a desert was *big*.

VAL: It is big, Myra. It stretches clean out 'til tomorrow. Over here is the Labos mountains, and over there, that's Sangre de Cristo. And way up there, that's the sky! And there ain't nothing else in between, not you, not anybody, or nothing.

MYRA: I see.

VAL: Why, my God, it seems like sometimes when you're out there alone by yourself (not with nobody else!) that your brain is stretched out so far, it's pushing right up against the edges of the stars!

MYRA: Uh, huh! Maybe, that's what happened! (*She laughs harshly.*) That's why you act so peculiar; you scrambled your brains on the stars so you can't think straight!

VAL: Shut up, God damn you!

MYRA: Val! (*Rain falls in a gust on the tin portico. There is a silence between them.*)

VAL: I'm sorry, Myra.

MYRA: So what are you planning to do? Drive west by yourself?

VAL: Yes. (*He moves to the wall and takes his book out.*)

MYRA: You can't leave yet. Those stave-mill workers are still across the street.

VAL: In two or three more years she may forget . . .

MYRA: The woman from Waco?

VAL: Yes.

MYRA: I don't think so. I don't think she ever will.

VAL: Well, anyway, when I've finished this book I'm going to send for you.

MYRA: Are you? Why?

VAL: Because I do love you, Myra.

MYRA: Love? You're too selfish for love. You're just like a well full of water without any rope, without any bucket, without any tin cup even. God pity the fool that comes to you with a dry tongue!

VAL: I promise I'll send for you, Myra.

MYRA: Thanks. Thanks. And what'll I do in the meantime? Stay on here with our lucky little . . . What shall I call it? Myra's little Miracle from Heaven? (*She laughs wildly. Jabe knocks on the ceiling.*)

VAL: Jabe's knocking.

MYRA: Don't you think that I hear him? Knock, knock, knock! It sounds like bones, like death, and that's what it is. Ask me how it feels to be coupled with death up there. His face was always so thin, so yellow, so drawn. I swear to you, Val, his face on the pillow at night, it resembled a skull. He wore a night shirt like a shroud, and when he got up in the dark, you know what I said to myself? "It's walking," I said to myself, "the ghost is walking!" And I—I had to endure him! Ahh, my flesh always crawled when he touched me. Yes, but I stood it, though. I guess I knew in my heart that it wouldn't go on forever, the way I suppose the fig tree knew in spite of those ten useless springs it wouldn't be barren always. When you come in off the road and asked for a job, I said to myself "This is it, this is what you been waiting for, Myra!" So I said with my eyes, "Stay here, stay here, for the love of God, stay here." And you did, you stayed. And just about at that time, as though for that special purpose, he started dying upstairs, when I started coming to life. It was like a battle had gone on between us those ten years, and I, the living, had beaten, him the dead one, back to the grave he climbed out of! Oh, for a while I tried to fight myself but it was no use. It was like I was standing down there at the foot of the levee and watched it break and known it was no use running. I tried to get rid of the key but that didn't work. Since then all decency's left me, I've stood like a woman naked with nothing but love—love, love. (*She clings to him fiercely.*)

VAL: Let go of me, Myra. (*He shoves her roughly away.*) You're like the woman from Waco. The way you . . .

MYRA: (*slowly*) You know what I've done? I've smashed myself against a rock. (*She crosses to the door.*) If you try to leave here without me, I'll call for the Sheriff!

VAL: That's what she did.

MYRA: *I'll* do it, *too.* Strike me in the face so I can scream. (*She catches at him again, he breaks loose, she utters a choked cry. The door slams open on the landing. At this instant a flickering matchlight appears on the stairs and spills down them across the floor. Heavy dragging footsteps and hoarse breathing are heard.*)

MYRA: (*whispering*) Christ in Heaven, what's that? (*The ghastly, phantom-like effect of this entrance is dramatically underlined. Jabe's shadow precedes him down the stairs and his approach has the slow, clumping fatality of the traditional spook's. He is a living symbol of death, as Myra has described him. He wears a purple bathrobe which hangs shroud-like about his figure and his face is a virtual death-mask. Just as he appears in full-view in the stairwall, the match which he holds under his face flickers out and disappears from view, swallowed in darkness like a vanished apparition.*)

MYRA: (*horrified, incredulous*) *Jabe.*

JABE: (*hoarsely*) Yes, it's me! (*He strikes another match and this time his face wears a grotesque, grinning expression.*) I didn't have much luck at knocking on the floor.

MYRA: (*dazed*) I didn't hear you.

JABE: Naw?

MYRA: The storm made too much noise.

JABE: Aw, absorbed in the storm.

MYRA: Yes.

JABE: Lamp-light, huh?

MYRA: Yes, the lights went out when that awful lightning struck.

JABE: Your dress is torn open.

MYRA: You did that, Jabe, when I tried to give you morphine.

JABE: I thought you might give me too much.

MYRA: How did you get out of bed?

JABE: The usual way. Why? Does that seem remarkable to you?

MYRA: Yes. I didn't know you was able to.

JABE: You always been too optimistic about my condition. (*Myra gasps involuntarily with loathing. Jabe laughs hoarsely.*) I'm okay now. I'm not going to cash my checks in yet for a while. (*Val coughs uneasily and clears his throat.*)

MYRA: Jabe—Jabe, this is Val Xavier.

JABE: You don't need to introduce me. I know him; I'm payin' his wages. (*to Val*) Myra here seems to think I had a tumor on the brain and they cut the brain out an' left the tumor. (*He laughs again and Myra repeats her involuntary gasp of loathing.*) Gimme that lamp; I wanta look at the stock.

MYRA: Here. We finished straightening up.

JABE: Aw, is that what you was doing?

MYRA: Yes. Val couldn't go home in the storm so we took advantage of the extra time.

JABE: Uh-huh. (*He takes the candle and goes unsteadily toward the confectionery. He passes through the archway, the pale walls hung with artificial blossoms have an eery effect in candle-light. The confectionery has a misty, flickering unreal pallor like a region of death, and Jabe, in his long, dark robe, stands at the entrance like the very Prince of Darkness. He hesitates as though he senses that death-like quality himself.*) Hell. It looks like a goddam honky-tonk since you done it over! (*He moves resolutely on into the room.*)

MYRA: (*under her breath*) Oh, God, I can't stand it, Val. I'm going to scream! Say something to him. Don't stand there doing nothing!

VAL: What should I say to him?

MYRA: Oh, I don't know—anything! (*She speaks in a loud, false tone.*) It seems miraculous, don't it, to see him downstairs?

VAL: (*uncertainly*) Yes. (*Jabe laughs mockingly in the next room.*) (*very softly*) Death's in the orchard, Myra!

MYRA: Val.

JABE: How about a little pinball game? Would you like to play one, Mr. Whatsit?

MYRA: Answer him!

VAL: (*inaudibly*) No.

JABE: Huh? Can't you talk out loud in there?

VAL: (*shouting*) No! No!

MYRA: Shhh!

JABE: I think I'll shoot a few.

VAL: Give me my wages. Let me get out. (*Val moves towards the counter, but Myra blocks him.*)

MYRA: You can't leave me alone with him, would you?

JABE: Hot damn. I clicked on three.

MYRA: You couldn't be such a coward.

VAL: Let go of my arm.

JABE: Twenty-five hundred, Myra.

VAL: This place is shrinking; the walls are closing in!

JABE: Thirty-five. Forty-five.

MYRA: Give me time, darling. A little more time. (*Val tears loose.*)

JABE: Fifty!

MYRA: I swear to God, I won't let you.

JABE: Right down the middle aisle, twice straight.

VAL: Let go!

JABE: Sixty-five, seventy.

MYRA: You've got to stick with me, Val.

VAL: Don't have to do nothing. I'm going!

JABE: Buzzards! Buzzards!!!! I hear you croaking in there. You think you've got a corpse to feed on, but you ain't! I'm going to live, Myra (*Myra's hysteria is released. She laughs wildly and rushes to the doorway.*)

MYRA: Oh, no, you're not; no, you're not! You're going to die, Jabe. You're rotten with death already!

JABE: (*shouting*) Die, am I?

MYRA: Yes, and I'm glad, I'm *glad*, I'm planning a celebration! I'm going to wear Christmas ornaments in my hair! Why? Because I'm not barren. I've gotten death out of me and now I've taken life in! Yes, oh, yes, I've got *life* in me—in *here*! (*She clasps her hands over her stomach.*) Do you see what I've got my hands on? Well, that's where it *is*, you see! I'm way, way, way up *high*! And you can't drag me *down*! Not any more, *Mr. Death*! We're through with each other. (*She laughs in wild exultance; then suddenly covers her face and runs sobbing back to Val. She is terrified.*) Val! (*She clutches his arm. He breaks away and crosses toward the front door of the store.*)

VAL: It's finished! (*He goes to the cash register, rings it open. Jabe creeps in with the lantern, unseen by them, and steals towards the hardware counter.*)

MYRA: (*She screams at him wildly, completely distracted.*) What are you doing? You're robbing the store!

VAL: I'm taking my wages out.

MYRA: You're robbing the store; I won't let you! (*She rushes to the phone and shouts into it. Jabe is loading a revolver.*) Give me the Sheriff's house. The store's being robbed!

VAL: Go on, you little bitch.

MYRA: The store's being robbed, the clerk is robbing the store. He's running off with the money; you got to stop him! (*Jabe's face is livid with hatred and he holds the revolver which he levels carefully at Myra, holding the candle above him to give a light.*)

JABE: Buzzards! (*He fires. The first shot strikes Myra. She utters a smothered cry and clutches at the wall. Val springs at him and wrests the revolver from his grasp.*)

VAL: You shot her.

JABE: (*slowly, panting*) Naw. You shot her. Didn't'ja hear her shouting your name on the phone? She said you was robbing the store! They'll come here an' burn you for it! Buzzards! (*He turns slowly and staggers out the front door. His voice is heard shouting wildly against the wind. Val gasps, slams the door, and bolts it, the revolver still in his grasp. Myra moves out from the shadow of the wall with a slight, sobbing breath.*)

VAL: Myra! You're hurt!

MYRA: Yes.

VAL: How bad?

MYRA: I don't know. I don't feel nothing at all. It struck me here, where I would have carried the child. There's nothing but death in me now.

VAL: I'll call for the doctor!

MYRA: There's no way to get any doctor. Go on, look out for yourself, get away! I don't need anyone now . . . (*She staggers out from the wall.*) Isn't it funny that I should just now remember what happened to the fig tree? It was struck down in a storm, the very spring that I hung those ornaments on it. Why? Why? For what reason? Because some things are enemies of light and there is a battle between them in which some fall! (*The confectionery suddenly blooms into soft spring-like radiance as the electric current resumes.*) Oh, look! The lights have come on in the confectionery! (*She staggers through the archway.*) That's what I wanted! Not death, but David—the orchard across from Moon Lake! (*She advances a few more steps and disappears from sight. Her body is heard falling. Val crosses to the archway.*)

VAL: Myra! Myra! (*The lights flicker and go out. Now the clamor of the crowd is heard distantly. Under his breath.*) Fire! (*He looks frenziedly about him for a moment, then plunges out through the confectionery. A door opens at the top of the stairs and Sandra appears, aroused by the clamor. At first she descends the steps fearfully, then with a sort of exulta-*

tion, appearing like a priestess in her long, sculptural white dress. When she has reached the bottom of the stairs, the front door is opened and The Woman from Waco enters, the crowd crying out behind her and the pine torches glaring through the windows.)

WOMAN: (*to Sandra*) You—where is he?

SHERIFF: Watch out, Mrs. Regan! He's armed!

MRS. REGAN: So am I! Where is he?

SHERIFF: (*He advances not too bravely.*) Xavier! (*A flickering light appears in the confectionery.*)

MAN: In back!

VOICES: In the confectionery! Get him! Git him outta there! Kill him! Burn the son of a bitch! Burn him!

WOMAN FROM WACO: What are you waiting fo'? Scared—scared? (*She plunges toward the archway with drawn revolver. The Conjure Man suddenly appears bearing a lantern. The shocking apparitional effect of his entrance stuns them for a second. The woman from Waco stops short with a stifled cry.*)

VOICE: Christ! Who's that? The Conjure Man! The Conjure Man from Blue Mountain!

WOMAN: Git out of my way! Make him git outta my way!

SHERIFF: (*He steps up beside her.*) Where is Xavier, you niggah? (*Slowly, tremblingly, the Negro elevates something in his hand. He holds it above his head. There is a momentary hush as all eyes are centered upon this lividly mottled object, which, though inanimate, still keeps about it the hard, immaculate challenge of things untamed.*)

A VOICE: His jacket!

ANOTHER: *The Snakeskin Jacket!* (*The Woman from Waco screams and covers her face. A gong is struck and the stage is drowned in instant and utter blackness.*)

Curtain

EPILOGUE

THE SCENE: *After a few seconds the curtain is raised again, and we are returned to the Sunday afternoon a year later. The scene is the same as for The Prologue. The stage is empty and sinister with its testimony of past violence. Faintly, as from some distance, there comes the sound of chanting from a Negro church. The store itself is like a pillaged temple with the late afternoon sunlight thrown obliquely through the high Gothic windows in the wall at the left. The Conjure Man sits with immobile dignity upon his stool near the archway like The Spirit of the Dead Watching. The door at the top of the stairs opens and the Temple Sisters emerge with their customers.*

BLANCH: Watch out for these stairs; they're awful, awful steep! Eva, you better go first with the lamp.

EVA: (*She descends first.*) Uncle! Uncle!

BLANCH: He's deaf as a post! (*The Conjure Man rises.*)

EVA: Oh, there you are, Uncle. Bring us Cassandra's things from that shelf over there. (*The Conjure Man complies with slow dignity.*)

BLANCH: We only have two things that belonged to Cassandra Whiteside on display in the Museum.

EVA: (*She displays the articles.*) This pair of dark sun-glasses and this bright red cape.

BLANCH: Cassandra's body was never recovered from the Sunflower River.

EVA: Some people say that she didn't know the bridge was washed out.

BLANCH: But we know better, however. She deliberately drove her car into the river and drowned because she knew that *decent* people were done with her.

EVA: Absolutely. The Vigilantes had warned her to get out of town.

BLANCH: Now, Uncle, the *Snakeskin Jacket.*

EVA: He's already got it.

BLANCH: That is one article in the Museum that me an' Eva won't lay our bare hands on.

EVA: I don't know what, but it simply terrifies me.

BLANCH: Uncle, hold it up there in the archway like you did when you reported his capture. (*The Conjure Man unfolds the jacket which he had held in his lap and elevates it above his head as he did at the end of the preceding scene.*)

EVA: It's marvelous how fresh and clean it stays.

BLANCH: Other things get dusty. But not the jacket. What was it that Memphis newspaper-woman called it? "A souvenir of the jungle!"

EVA: "A shameless, flaunting symbol of the Beast Untamed!"

BLANCH: Put it down, Uncle. Uncle was washing the car in back of the store when the murderer tried to escape by that back door.

EVA: He fell right in the hands of the stave-mill workers.

BLANCH: They torn off his clothes an' thrown him into a car.

EVA: Drove him right down the road to the lynching tree . . .

BLANCH: That big cottonwood where the road turned off toward th' levee.

EVA: Exackly where Vee Talbott seen him that day in her vision.

BLANCH: We showed you the Jesus picture? That was the last thing she painted before she lost her mind.

EVA: Which makes five lives, as they said in one of the papers . . .

BLANCH: "Tied together in one fatal knot of passion."

EVA: Not counting the Woman from Waco, who disappeared.

BLANCH: Nobody knows what ever become of her. (*She crosses to the wall and takes something down.*)

EVA: (*with relish*) Oh, the blow-tawch!

BLANCH: It's not the original one but it's one just like it. Look! (*She presses a valve and a fierce blue jet of flame stabs into the dark atmosphere. A woman tourist utters a sharp, involuntary cry and sways slightly forward, covering her eyes.*)

WOMAN: Oliver, take me out! (*A man hastily assists her to the door.*)

BLANCH: (*to Eva*) They haven't paid yet!

EVA: *Fifty cents, please! That will be fifty cents!*

BLANCH: To keep up the museum!

EVA: Yes, to preserve the memorial—twenty-five cents each. (*They go out, following the tourists. The door remains open. Sunlight flows serenely, warmly, through it, a golden contradiction of all that is past. The Conjure Man glides toward the door. His face assumes a venomous, mocking look. He crouches forward, and spits out the open door with dry crackling laughter, then turns, and, unfolding the brilliant snakeskin jacket once more, he goes to the back wall and hangs it above his head in the shaft of sunlight through the door. He seems to make a slight obeisance before it. The religious chant from across the wide cotton fields now swells in exaltation as the curtain falls.)*

THE HISTORY OF A PLAY

(WITH PARENTHESES)

Battle of Angels was not my first play. I had previously written four others, long tragedies, innocent of structure. These earlier works were little more than preliminary exercises. Inept as the *Battle* is in certain respects, it was a huge advance over its predecessors, written before I knew what a proscenium arch is. Probably no man has ever written for the theatre with less foreknowledge of it. I had never been back-stage. I had not seen more than two or three professional productions: touring companies that passed through the South and Middle West. My conversion to the theatre arrived as mysteriously as those impulses that enter the flesh at puberty. Suddenly I found that I had a stage inside me: actors appeared out of nowhere; shaggy, undisciplined mummers trooped out of the shadowy wings and took the stage over. This cry of players had a gift for improvisation: they carried with them a greasy bundle of old scripts, crumpled and wadded into the bottom of the brass-bound trunk, beneath the tarnished helmets and rhinestone tiaras, the twisted candelabra and moth-eaten velvet capes and scarlet dominoes of traditional mummery. Now and then they would toss me a sheaf of papers like an old bone: only the title and theme were still apparent: the script illegible. "Write this over!" I was commanded. The work was mainly the actors' improvisations. But how I loved it!—this abuse of Cothurnus—is that her name? And the actors loved it, too. They could not wait for the lines to be set down. What thrilling disorder!

I took to the theatre with the impetus of compulsion. Writing since I was a child, I had begun to feel a frustrating lack of vitality in words alone. I wanted a plastic medium. I conceived things visually, in sound and color and movement. The writing of prose was just their description, not their essential being: or so I felt it to be. I was impatient of sentences. Tricks of style, polish, urbanity, all of those things that belong to the successful practitioner of letters seemed all the world removed from what I wanted and what I was writing for. The turbulent business of my nerves demanded something more animate than written language could be. It seemed to me that even the giants of literature, such as Chekhov, when writing narratives were only describing dramas. And they were altogether dependent upon the sensitivity of their readers. Nothing lived of what they had created unless the reader had the stage inside him, or the screen, on which their images could be visibly projected. However with a play, a play on a stage—let any fool come to it! It is there, it is really and truly there—whether the audience understands it or not! This may be a childish distinction: however, I felt it that way.

It seemed to me that all good writing is not just writing but is something organic. I say that as though it was a startling discovery of my own. Excuse me. But that is how it came to me, as a personal revelation. It should have come earlier, for I had been writing since twelve and was already wrapped up in literary style like the bandages of a mummy—and I am still struggling to break out of it. Lately the word "professional" has become odious to me because it seems removed from the flesh and blood business of my vocation. The best avenue away from professionalism in writing is really the stage, because the stage is ideally the most plastic, the most objective exercise for the writer. For me there was no other medium that was even relatively satisfactory. I am speaking for myself, not anyone else. If this sounds like a rejection of poetry—kick my face in! I don't mean any such thing. But poetry is also potentially a plastic medium. Nothing goes more naturally onto the ideal stage.

Later on I became sick and furious, unreasonably so, when I learned that people who feel as I do about the theatre cannot possess it. It doesn't belong to us. It belongs to Money. Then, after that, I felt more reasonably about it, for I saw that works for the ideal theatre can live on paper until the emancipated theatre is ready for them: just as a race of slaves can survive their period of bondage and eventually come into the sun as free individuals to realize their destiny. All that we really need is to believe, to work, and to survive with honesty. Virgo intacta.

That is Parenthesis One!

Battle of Angels was the first of these plays to release and purify the emotional storms of my earlier youth. The stage or setting of this drama was the country of my childhood. Onto it I projected the violent symbols of my adolescence. It was a synthesis of the two parts of my life already passed through. And so the history of the play begins anterior to the impulse to write it. It begins as far back as I remember, in the mysterious landscape of the Delta country, the smoky quality of light in the late afternoons when I, as a child, accompanied my grandfather, an Episcopal clergyman, on seemingly endless rounds of rural parishioners about such villages as Columbus, Canton, Clarksdale, and Lyons in Mississippi. Wherever my grandfather went, I tagged along. I remember a sympathetic old lady saying, "Tom looks tired," and my grandfather answering, "Tom is strong as an ox." It seems to me those afternoons were always spent in tremendously tall interiors to which memory gives a Gothic architecture, and that the light was always rather dustily golden. I remember a lady named Laura Young. She was dressed in checkered silk. She had a high, clear voice: a cataract of water. Something about her made me think of cherries and she was very beautiful. She was something cool and green in a sulphurous landscape. But there was a shadow upon her. There was something the matter with her. For that reason we called upon her more frequently than anyone else. She loved me. I adored her. She lived in a white house near an orchard and in an arch between two rooms were hung some pendants of glass that were a thousand colors. "That is a prism," she said. She lifted me and told me to shake them. When I did they made a delicate music.

This prism became a play.

When we stopped going there, I learned that the lady was dead. It was the death of a lady and the beginning of a personal myth. For this bright, misty lady was the beginning of Myra Torrance—even that long ago!

But these childish recollections provided me only with the country and with characters of phantom dimensions. I had to animate them with the turbulent stuff of later experience. The opportunity for this came after I had knocked about the States for five years, much as the character Val, with some such shadowy design as his mysterious "Book" as a fleeting objective. I retreated to the family home, which was then in Clayton, Missouri, and because I was stopped and temporarily worn out, it seemed like a final retreat. I hated Saint Louis, of which this town was the suburb—hated it quite unreasonably, associating it with certain personal disasters which had taken place there—so I immured myself in the attic of our home and wrote the tortured first draft of *Battle of Angels*, never at any time regarding it as more than a katharsis for myself. By this time, however, I had acquired from the distance a few contacts with the professional theatre. They were the Group Theatre and Audrey Wood, the agent. All of a sudden they worked a marvelous change in my situation. They had submitted earlier works of mine to the Rockefeller Foundation, which was at that time distributing fellowships of a thousand dollars each to promising playwrights. I received one of these about a week after completing *Battle of Angels* and so I came with the manuscript to New York and began to explore for the first time the world of the professional theatre.

The absurd though tragic dilemma of that little microcosmos is something that I am not at all prepared to write about. That the most exalted of the arts should have fallen into the receivership of business men and gamblers is a situation parallel in absurdity to the conduct of worship becoming the responsibility of a herd of water-buffalos. It is one of those things that a man of reason had rather not think about until the means of redemption is more apparent. That in spite of this situation small islands of idealism still remain in the American theatre is all the more miraculous and to be praised. Men and women of unquestionable integrity still operate in the American theatre, many in eminent positions. They only wait for the release of the money octopus to create out of their own high designs a theatre where truth can resume its exploration of our spiritual night. But as for the theatre as it now exists, I will only say that I feel a person desiring to write fine plays could make a much worse mistake than never visiting a Broadway playhouse.

By the end of this first season in New York my fellowship money had dangerously dwindled. I had already received enough disturbing impressions of the theatre capital to feel an impulse to travel. Summarily and with little enough warning to anybody concerned, I packed my property, mostly paper, and departed for Mexico. I had left behind me the first draft of *Battle of Angels.* The Theatre Guild, one of those small islands alluded to, had taken an option on it. No one, least of all myself, thought they would do more than finger it a little before passing it back to the tangent stream that poetic properties follow. When the monthly advances no longer reached me in Acapulco, where I was spending the summer, I assumed without any surprise that this release had already occurred. The fact that I had traveled too rapidly for mail to catch up with me was the true explanation, and the one I didn't think of. My life was an approximate paradise at this tropical port. I called it "La Vie Horizontale." I wrote in a hammock all morning, swam all afternoon in the warm waters of a landlocked bay, spent the evenings talking lazily to another American writer, Andrew Gun, and drinking rum-cocos on the verandah of hammocks. I would have been content to pursue this life for the rest of my days, but, toward the end of summer, too much Mexican grease or unwashed greens resulted in gastric disturbances in both myself and Mr. Gun. Mr. Gun was a war refugee from Tahiti and he had spent nearly all our evenings telling me about that island and a little French girl who was waiting for him there. Fearing to be immured there for the duration of the war due to the cancellation of passenger shipping, he had fled on the last boat out—now he regretted the action. He had learned of a means of returning and had covinced me that I also was a spiritual native of Tahiti. We were all set to go there, when shortly after we had again entered the States, I got hold of a copy of *The New York Times* and was startled to read in the dramatic columns that the Theatre Guild was doing *Battle of Angels* as their initial play of the season and that Miss Miriam Hopkins had already flown from Hollywood to take the starring role.

Well, I returned post-haste to New York and dived unwittingly into the little maelstrom my play had provoked. I was delighted with the selection of Miss Hopkins for the role of Myra, but I was alarmed that things had gone ahead so rapidly, that casting was already in progress when the script was really only a first draft. I knew that the ending of the play, as it then stood, was a melodramatic *tour-de-force.* Conceptually it was fine—the store was set afire and everything went up in the fiery purgation. Yes, very exciting. "A Wagnerian experience," as someone put it in the Guild office! "But how in hell are you going to stage it?" asked Margaret Webster, who had been engaged as director. This question and others were held in abeyance while the production went rocketing ahead. I realized that I had fooled these people. Because certain qualities in my writing had startled them, they took it for granted that I was an accomplished playwright and that some afternoon when I was not busy with interviews, casting, rehearsals, I would quietly withdraw for an hour or two and work out the dramaturgic problems as deftly as such things were done by men like Barry and Kaufmann and Behrmann. They had no idea how dazed and stymied I was by the rush of events into which my dreamy self was precipitated. Meantime Peggy Webster and I caught a plane to the Mississippi Delta. We spent two days down there, introducing Peggy to the South—visiting country stores and talking to Delta people. Peggy absorbed the South in twenty-four hours. It was a bit too much for her. She began to look a little punch-drunk, seeing just enough of this extraordinary country and its people to make them more mysterious than they were before. On a plane returning to New York, I recall a talk that we had. We had been reciting verse to each other, mostly lyrics of Shakespeare. I repeated the one containing the lines "Nothing of him that doth fade but doth suffer a sea-change into something rich and strange." "That," said Peggy, "is what they should say about *Battle of Angels.*"—"Perhaps," I answered, "but there are so many other things they may say about it."—Peggy assented gravely. Neither of us, however, had at this moment any intimation of the line of attack that really would be taken.

During all this time and the weeks that followed it had somehow occurred to none of us working on the production that we were dealing with a play that might be attacked on grounds of morality. If it was in the minds of others, certainly this suspicion was never communicated to me. Was I totally amoral? Was I too innocent or too evil—that I remained unprepared for what the audiences, censors and magistracy of

Boston were going to find in my play? I knew, of course, that I had written a play that touched upon human longings, about the sometimes conflicting desires of the flesh and the spirit. This struggle was thematic; implicit in the title of the play. Why had I never dreamed that such struggles could strike many people as filthy and seem to them unfit for articulation? Oh, if I had written a play full of licentious wiggling in filmy costumes, replete with allusions to the latrine, a play that was built about some titillating and vulgarly ribald predicament in a bedroom—why, then I would feel apprehensive about its moral valuation. However, it seemed to me that if *Battle of Angels* was nothing else, it was certainly clean, it was certainly idealistic. The very experience of writing it was like taking a bath in snow. Its purity seemed beyond question. But then—the dogma of the moral censor!—there again is something I cannot cope with and will have to pass over.

As rehearsals progressed it became more and more apparent that if nothing else needed fixing, the ending of the play certainly did. The store did not burn down convincingly nor were we, in the crucial parts of Cassandra and Val, able to find actors who seemed anything better than arbitrarily thrust into the parts. Three different leading men were unsuccessfully tried out in the five weeks of rehearsal before Wesley Addy was removed from *Twelfth Night* to play opposite Miss Hopkins. Though he did not have the physical quality the part demanded, Mr. Addy understood the play and certainly had talent enough to do a creative job. Miss Doris Dudley in the role of Cassandra was cruelly miscast. One of the most beautiful women in the theatre and also one of the sweetest, the terrifying demands of this part only increased her embarrassment. It was she who had to stand on the stairs of the burning store and lift the tragedy into a state of purgation with a set of lines—nowhere now present in the text—which she and all of us felt were quite impossible to integrate with the rest of the play as they seemed to come out of an altogether different script.

Toward the end of rehearsals, a series of frenzied conferences were held. Miss Hopkins, who played her part with heartbreaking beauty and something that only a woman of poetic understanding and deep experience could give—

whenever the confusion lifted sufficiently to give her a chance to do so—was now becoming definitely frightened. She looked to me for salvation. After all, I—poor captive thing—was the author. How it wrung my heart that I could do nothing for her! She had staked so much on this play. It was to mark her triumphal return to the stage, where her talent as a dramatic actress could operate without the bonds that bad screen vehicles had recently put on her. One could easily see why she regarded the production almost as a matter of life and death. Oh, if only my head would clear up a little—if I could only find some lucid interval in this dervish frenzy that was sweeping us all unprepared into Boston and disaster! But all the conferences only added to my feeling of impotence. Miss Hopkins' pleas and protestations—"For heaven's sake, do something, something!"—only made it more impossible for me to do anything at all. At last I went to Peggy and told her exactly how unable I was to cope with the emergency. "It is too late," I said, "I can't do anything more! If I could get away from all of you for a month—I could return with a new script. But that is not possible, so you will just have to take what there is and do what you can with it!"

"Very well," said Peggy, "the store will burn down! Now you stop worrying about it."

To insert another parenthesis: it seems to me that directly behind capital investment as a menace to good theatre is the fact that everything is done with such a machine-like haste. Five weeks is not long enough to prepare a complex play. Ideally it should have three months. Why wasn't that done with the Federal Theatre Project? Why didn't they put on one great play a season, instead of imitating the scrambling rush of Broadway? No wonder nearly all players have a tendency to chatter rather than speak on the stage! A play has become something like a feat of legerdemain. I will allow that rapid execution is the best policy with most Broadway plays, but when now and then something comes along that deserves a more leisurely gestation—why does it have to hop, skip and jump across the schedule as briskly as something that hinges upon the loss of a G-string or getting somebody's garter?

Answer: Money.

So after five weeks, only about three of which were conducted with a final cast, the company entrained for its opening engagement in the city of Boston. Only Miss Helburn and Mr. Langner appeared unshaken by any rumors of premonition. This I set down to their seniority, the fact that they had out-ridden so many previous storms. It was encouraging to observe their Olympian calm, but it made one all the more conscious of his own callow emotionalism.

In Boston we had but one night of rehearsal before we opened, in the Christmas season of 1940.

That night was about as black as any I'd experienced. Everything that had gone well, or passably well, at previous rehearsals went about as badly as possible. All the meaning seemed to have gone from the lines: nothing fitted together: the effect was kaleidoscopic. When it came time for the store to burn down—the little trickles of smoke under the wings, the flickering red lights, the bawling voices—against these had to be played the all-important scene that lifted the play to katharsis. Never had it seemed so impossible to combine the two actions. Either you heard only the mob's demonstration or you heard only the interior scene. Also it was suddenly discovered at this rehearsal that the musical score composed for the play could not be used. In my frank opinion, it was terrible. Miss Hopkins felt the same way about it. Almost tearfully she cried out, "How can I dance to that music?" No doubt it was a fine composition technically; but for the play, it was terrible. All of it went out, and at the last moment recorded selections were substituted: banal and make-shift they were but we were devoutly thankful—at least Miriam Hopkins and I—when the high-brow composition released its depressing grip. Suitable music could have done a great deal for the production, but this was really a solo composition—the sort of thing you would expect to hear at a modern dance recital where it could be accorded the proper deference.

I remember that Peggy jumped off the stage at one point and caught her ankle in a folding seat. She uttered a slight cry of pain—Miriam Hopkins screamed as if the sky had fallen—such was the state of our nerves.

I went home too exhausted to think or to sleep. Toward morning I wrote a new final scene. Dreadful it probably was!

Nobody paid any attention to it, but I remember saying dramatically that I would crawl on my belly through brimstone if they would only put off the opening and give me a few more days to contrive something else. Mr. Langner smiled at me fondly. A very kind man, he gave me what comfort and reassurance he could. Miss Helburn sent me a telegram—"Saint Michael and all Good Angels be with you!"—signed "Connecticut Updyke" (her married name, with the territorial appellation she had adapted in imitation of mine).

Opening night. Things started rolling peacefully enough. The elegant first night audience entered the theatre with an air of nobility and refinement which boded little of what was to come in our next three hours of communion with them. They looked on the first scenes with bland satisfaction. Gowned by Bergdorf-Goodman, Miss Hopkins was as radiantly beautiful as any of their debutante daughters. The character women upset the dowagers a little from time to time, but the general attitude toward the earthy humor they brought to the script was still indulgent. It was not till the action concerning Vee's visionary portrait of Val—not until that revelation—that the peculiar attitude which this audience brought to the theatre began to make itself seen, heard, and felt. Up and down the aisles the ladies and gentlemen began to converse with each other in sibilant whispers. Subdued hissings and clucking were punctuated now and then by the banging up of a seat and the regal swish of silken garments drawn hurriedly over projecting knees as here and there it became impossible for some spectator to countenance further infractions of standards.

The nature of this phenomenon, the fashionable first night audience, became shockingly plain to me all at once. What interests them is themselves, their dignity, their prestige and pretenses. What they want is a flattering mirror, a picture that does the opposite of Dorian Gray's, one that takes off all their blemishes in its reflection. After the play had closed a Brookline dowager wrote the Theatre Guild—I saw this letter—to say that when she went to the theatre she wanted to see cultivated people, people who talked, acted and dressed as she and her friends. Pictures of other *milieux* were not acceptable to her. I am afraid that she expressed a fairly widespread attitude among what is known as the "carriage trade" on which our theatre is still financially dependent. Hence the failure of the theatre really to explore the many levels of society except in the superficial and sensational way of *Tobacco Road* and its prototypes, which pleases the carriage trade inversely to polite drawing-room comedy by representing their social inferiors as laughable grotesques.

Returning to the performance. It was not until the point of the conflagration that the Boston audience was in a strategic position to vent its full displeasure. At the final dress-rehearsal there had not been enough smoke to make the fire convincing. Obviously this deficiency had been thoroughly impressed upon the gentlemen operating the smoke-pots, for on opening night when it came time for the store to burn down it was like the burning of Rome. Great sulphurous billows rolled chokingly onto the stage and coiled over the foot-lights. To an already antagonistic audience this was sufficient to excite something in the way of pandemonium. Outraged squawks, gabbling, spluttering spread through all the front rows of the theatre. Nothing that happened on the stage from then on was of any importance. Indeed the scene was nearly eclipsed by the fumes. Voices were lost in the banging up of seats as the front rows were evacuated.

When the curtain at last came down, as curtains eventually must, I had come to that point where one must laugh or go crazy. I laughed. There was little joy in it, but knowing I had to laugh, I found that I could. Miriam Hopkins accepted the same necessity. I see her coming out to face her audience. The stage is still full of smoke. Before her smiling face she is waving a small white hand, to clear the fumes away. She is coughing a little, apologetically touching her throat and chest. Their backs are turned to her, these elegant first-nighters, as they push up the aisles like heavy, heedless cattle. But she is still gallantly smiling and waving away the smoke with her delicate hand. The curtain bobs foolishly up and down to a patter of hands in the balcony that goes on after the lower floor is emptied.

The failure of a play!

The Boston reviewers tried to judge what they had seen as fairly and calmly as possible. In the reviewers there was none of the downright cruelty that the first-night audience had exhibited. Under the circumstances, the reviewers were as good as could be hoped for. Obviously that is not saying that they were good. References were made, however, to the reality of the atmosphere in the earlier scenes of the play and one lady reviewer went so far as to say that there were occasional lines of beauty in the script. Another reviewer made guarded allusions to good character touches in the lesser figures. There was an atmosphere of wariness and bated breath in all these printed reactions.

The magistracy of Boston did not step in till after the play had run for about a week. Then it was that the censors sat out front and demanded excision from the script of practically all that made it intelligible, let alone moving. Fortunately I had already left Boston at that time and did not take part in this really posthumous disturbance.

The play as you now read it was written many months later. Some day it will be done again. For that occasion I will probably prepare still another version, omitting the present prologue and epilogue. They were a defensive gesture which I wouldn't have made if it were not for the appalling memory of Boston. But I have never written a play that I thought was completed and I don't think I ever will. There is too much to say and not enough time to say it. Nor is there power enough. I am not a good writer. Sometimes I am a very bad writer indeed. There is hardly a successful writer in the field who cannot write circles around me and I am the first to admit it. But I think of writing as something more organic than words, something closer to being and action. I want to work more and more with a more plastic theatre than the one that I have so far. I have never for one moment doubted that there are people—millions!—to say things to. We come to each other, gradually, but with love. It is the short reach of my arms that hinders, not the length and multiplicity of theirs. With love and with honesty, the embrace is inevitable.

TENNESSEE WILLIAMS

Manhattan, March, 1944.

I RISE IN FLAME, CRIED THE PHŒNIX

The action of this play, which is imaginary, takes place in the French Riviera where D. H. Lawrence died.

Not long before Lawrence's death an exhibition of his paintings was held in London. Primitive in technique and boldly sensual in matter, this exhibition created a little tempest. The pictures were seized by the police and would have been burned if the authorities had not been restrained by an injunction. At this time Lawrence's great study of sexual passion, Lady Chatterly's Lover, *was likewise under the censor's ban, as much of his work had been in the past.*

Lawrence felt the mystery and power of sex, as the primal life urge, and was the lifelong adversary of those who wanted to keep the subject locked away in the cellars of prudery. Much of his work is chaotic and distorted by tangent obsessions, such as his insistence upon the woman's subservience to the male, but all in all his work is probably the greatest modern monument to the dark roots of creation.

—T. W.

New Orleans, September, 1941

A NOTE BY FRIEDA LAWRENCE

This book has a beautiful title. When I read this short play, I forgot that it was supposed to be Lawrence and me; it happens in that other world where creation takes place. The theme of it is the eternal antagonism and attraction between man and woman. This was between Lawrence and me too. But the greater reality was something else. I wish I could say in convincing words what it was—it is difficult. What was it? It was so different from the ordinary everyday being-in-love, that has its limits so very soon. It was life in its freedom, its limitless possibilities, that bound us together. In our poverty the whole world with everything in it was ours. It was living every moment, not only existing day by day. All that happened was a new experience. Because of the background of death, every happening was more vivid. Die we must, and no "Forest Lawn" can wipe death out.

Lawrence infused new meaning into the written word, by going deeper than the surface. We have had a lot of surface. We have become bored. Lawrence faced his own dying a death with clear courage, he lived it right through. When finally it was over for him and he lay dead on his bed, I felt a triumph in him. He was dead, but he had died with an unbroken spirit, he had lived in superb honesty and the pride of a man.

When I think of him now after all these years, it is as if a kind wind blew on my flame of life to make it burn brighter. He will do the same for others, if they give him a chance.

—Frieda Lawrence

The characters in this play are Lawrence, Frieda, and Bertha. The scene is at Vence, France, in the Alpes-Maritimes. It is late afternoon.

Lawrence is seated on a sunporch, the right wall of which is a window that faces the sun. A door in this wall opens out on the high seacliff. It is windy: the surf can be heard. Lawrence looks out that way. Behind him, on the left wall, woven in silver and scarlet and gold, is a large banner that bears the design of the Phœnix in a nest of flames—Lawrence's favorite symbol.

He sits quite still. His beard is fiercely red and his face is immobile, the color of baked clay with tints of purple in it. The hands that gripped the terrible stuff of life and made it plastic are folded on the black and white checked surface of an invalid's blanket. The long fingers of the Welsh coalminers, with their fine blond hairs and their knobby knuckles, made for rending the black heart out of the earth, are knotted together with a tightness that betrays the inner lack of repose. His slightly distended nostrils draw the breath in and out as tenderly as if it were an invisible silk thread that any unusual tension might snap in two. Born for contention, he is contending with something he can't get his hands on. He has to control his fury. And so he is seated motionless in the sunlight—wrapped in a checkered blanket and lavender wool shawl . . . The tiger in him is trapped, but not destroyed yet.

Frieda comes in, a large handsome woman of fifty, rather like a Valkyrie. She holds up a fancily wrapped little package.

LAWRENCE: (*without even turning his head*) What is it?
FRIEDA: Something left on the doorstep.
LAWRENCE: Give it here.
FRIEDA: The donor is anonymous. I only caught a glimpse of her through the window.
LAWRENCE: A woman?
FRIEDA: Yes . . .
LAWRENCE: Yes . . .

FRIEDA: Some breathless little spinster in a blue pea-jacket. She stuck it on the porch and scuttled back down the hill before I could answer the doorbell.

LAWRENCE: (*his voice rising, querulously shrill*) It's for me, isn't it?

FRIEDA: Ja, es ist für dich.

LAWRENCE: Well, give it here, damn you, you—!

FRIEDA: Tch! I thought that the sun had put you in a good humor.

LAWRENCE: It's put me in a vile humor. We've sat here making faces at each other the whole afternoon. I say to the sun, Make me well, you old bitch, give me strength, take hold of my hands and pull me up out of this chair! But the sun is a stingy Hausfrau. She goes about sweeping the steps and pretends not to hear me begging. Ah, well, I don't blame her. I never did care for beggars myself very much. A man shouldn't beg. A man should seize what he wants and tear it out of the hands of the adversary. And if he can't get it, if he can't tear it away, then he should let it go and give up and be contented with nothing. Look. (*He has unwrapped the package.*) A little jar of orange marmalade. (*He smiles with childish pleasure.*) This is the month of August put in a bottle.

FRIEDA: Ja! Sehr gut. You can have it for breakfast.

LAWRENCE: (*drawing tenderly on the fine gold thread*) Uh-huh. I can have it for breakfast as long as I live, huh, Frieda? It's just the right size for that.

FRIEDA: Shut up. (*She starts to take the jar from him. Quick as a cat, he snatches her wrist in a steel grip.*)

LAWRENCE: Leave go of it, damn you!

FRIEDA: (*laughing*) My God, but you still are strong!

LAWRENCE: You didn't think so?

FRIEDA: I had forgotten. You've been so gentle lately.

LAWRENCE: Thought you'd tamed me?

FRIEDA: Yes, but I should have known better. I should have suspected what you've been doing inside you, lapping that yellow cream up, you sly old fox, sucking the fierce red sun in your body all day and turning it into venom to spew in my face!

LAWRENCE: No . . . I've been making a trap. I've been making a shiny steel trap to catch you in, you vixen! Now break away if you can!

FRIEDA: (*grinning and wincing*) Oh, God, how you hurt!

LAWRENCE: (*slowly releasing her*) . . . Don't lie . . . You with that great life in you . . . Why did God give you so much and me so little? You could take my arm and snap it like a dry stick.

FRIEDA: No . . . You were always the stronger one. Big as I am, I never could beat you, could I?

LAWRENCE: (*with satisfaction*) No. You couldn't. (*His breath rasps hoarsely.*) Put the jar down on the sill.

FRIEDA: (*complying*) Ah, there's a card stuck on it. "From one of your devoted readers." And on the other side it says: "I worship you, Mr. Lawrence, because I know that only a god could know so much about Life!"

LAWRENCE: (*dryly*) In looking for God so unsuccessfully myself, it seems that I have accidentally managed to create one for an anonymous spinster in a blue pea-jacket. Upon the altar of her pagan deity she places a dainty jar of orange marmalade! What a *cynical* little woman she is! Only the little ones of the earth, who scuttle downhill like pebbles dislodged by the rain, are really capable of such monumental disbelief. They find their god and they give him marmalade. If I find mine . . . ever . . . If I found mine, I'd tear the heart out of my body and burn it before him.

FRIEDA: Your health is returning.

LAWRENCE: What makes you think so?

FRIEDA: You are getting so sentimental about yourself and so unappreciated and so misunderstood . . . You can't stand Jesus Christ because he beat you to it. Oh, how you would have loved to suffer the *original* crucifixion!

LAWRENCE: If only I had your throat between my fingers.

FRIEDA: (*crouching beside him*) Here is my throat . . . Now choke me.

LAWRENCE: (*gently touching her throat with the tips of his fingers*) Frieda . . . do you think I will ever get back to New Mexico?

FRIEDA: You will do what you want to do, Lawrence. There has never been any kind of resistance you couldn't jump over or crawl under or squeeze through.

LAWRENCE: Do you think I will ever get back on a strong white horse and go off like the wind across the glittering desert? I'm not a literary man, I'm tired of books. Nobody knows what an ugly joke it is that a life like mine should only come out in books.

FRIEDA: What else should it come out in?

LAWRENCE: In some kind of violent action. But all that I ever do is go packing around the world with women and manuscripts and a vile disposition. I pretend to be waging a war with bourgeois conceptions of morality, with prudery, with intellectuality, with all kinds of external forces that aren't external at all. What I'm fighting with really's the little old maid in myself, the breathless little spinster who scuttles back down the hill before God can answer the doorbell. Now I want to get back on the desert and try all over again to become a savage. I want to stand up on the Lobos and watch a rainstorm coming ten miles off like a silver-helmeted legion of marching giants. And that's what I'm going to do, damn you!

FRIEDA: Whoever said that you wouldn't?

LAWRENCE: You! . . You know that I won't. You know that the male savage part of me's dead and all that's left is the old pusillanimous squaw. Women have such a fine intuition of death. They smell it coming before it's started even. I think it's women that actually let death in. They whisper and beckon and slip it the dark latchkey from under their aprons . . . Don't they?

FRIEDA: No . . . It's women that pay the price of admission for life. And all of their lives they make of their arms a crossbar at the door that death wants to come in by. Men love death . . . Women don't. Men cut wounds in each other and women stop the bleeding.

LAWRENCE: Yes. By drinking the blood. Don't touch me so much! (*She releases his fingers.*) Your fingers, they make me feel weaker, they drain the strength out of my body.

FRIEDA: Oh, no, no, no, they put it back *in*, mein Liebchen.

LAWRENCE: I want you to promise me something. If I should die, Frieda . . . the moment I'm dying, please to leave me alone! . . Don't touch me, don't put your hands on me, and don't let anyone else . . . I have a nightmarish feeling that while I'm dying I'll be surrounded by women. They'll burst in the door and the windows the moment I lose the strength to push them away. They'll moan and they'll flutter like doves around the burnt-out Phœnix. They'll cover my face and my hands with filmy kisses and little trickling tears. Alma the nymphomaniac and the virginal Bertha—all of the under- and over-sexed women I've known, who think me the oracle of their messed-up libidos—they'll all return with their suffocating devotion. I don't want that. I want to die as a lonely old animal does. I want to die fiercely and cleanly with nothing but anger and fear and other hard things like that to deal with at the finish. You understand, Frieda? I've still got a bit of the male left in me and that's the part that I'm going to meet death with. When the last bleeding comes, and it *will* in a little while now, I won't be put into bed and huddled over by women. I won't stay in the house, Frieda. I'll open this door and go outside on the cliff. And I don't wish to be followed. That's the important point, Frieda. I'm going to do it alone. With the rocks and the water. Sunlight . . . starlight on me. No hands, no lips, no women! Nothing but . . . pitiless nature . . .

FRIEDA: I don't believe you. I don't think people want nothing but "pitiless nature" when they're . . .

LAWRENCE: Frieda! You mean you refuse?

FRIEDA: No. I consent absolutely.

LAWRENCE: You give me your promise?

FRIEDA: Ja doch! Ganz durch die Ewigkeit! Now think about something else. I'll go fix tea. (*She starts to go out.*)

LAWRENCE: (*suddenly noticing something*) Ah, my God.

FRIEDA: What's the matter?

LAWRENCE: Put the aquarium on the windowsill.

FRIEDA: Why?

LAWRENCE: So I can keep an eye on it. That detestable cat has attacked the goldfish again.

FRIEDA: How do you know?

LAWRENCE: How do I know? There used to be *four*, now there's *three*! *Beau Soleil!*

FRIEDA: She's gone outside.

LAWRENCE: To lick her chops, God damn her! Set the goldfish bowl on the windowsill.

FRIEDA: You can't keep them there in the sun. The sun will kill them.

LAWRENCE: (*furiously*) Don't answer me back, put 'em *there*!

FRIEDA: Wie du willst! (*She hastens to place the aquarium on the sill.*)

LAWRENCE: You know what I think? I think you *fed* her the fish. It's like you to do such a thing. You're both so fat, so rapacious, so viciously healthy and hungry!

FRIEDA: Such a fuss over a goldfish!

LAWRENCE: It isn't just a goldfish.

FRIEDA: What is it then?

LAWRENCE: Now that my strength's used up I can't help thinking how much of it's been thrown away in squabbling with you.

FRIEDA: (*suddenly covering her face*) Oh, Lawrence.

LAWRENCE: What are you doing? Crying? Stop it. I can't stand crying. It makes me worse.

FRIEDA: I think you *hate* me, Lawrence.

(*After a moment he shyly touches her arm.*)

LAWRENCE: Don't believe me . . . I love you. Ich liebe dich, Frieda. Put some rum in the tea. I'm getting much stronger, so why should I feel so weak?

FRIEDA: (*touching his forehead*) I wish you would go back to bed.

LAWRENCE: The bed's an old tarbaby. I'd get stuck. How do I know that I'd get loose again? Is my forehead hot? (*Frieda places her hand tenderly over his eyes. He recites in a childish treble:*)

> "Ladybug, ladybug, fly away home,
> thine house is on fire, thy children will burn!"

(*He smiles slightly.*) My mother used to sing that whenever she saw one . . . Simple . . . Most people are so damned complicated and yet there is nothing much to them.

FRIEDA: (*She starts out, then pauses before the banner.*) Ah, you old Phœnix . . . you brave and angry old bird in your nest of flames! I think you are just a little bit sentimental.

LAWRENCE: (*leaning suddenly forward*) Tea for three!

FRIEDA: Who is it?

LAWRENCE: Bertha! . . Back from London with news of the exhibition. (*He pulls himself out of the chair.*)

FRIEDA: What are you doing?

LAWRENCE: I'm going outside to meet her.

FRIEDA: Sit down, you fool! I'll meet her. And don't you dare to ask her to stay in this house . . . If you do, I'll leave! (*She goes out.*)

LAWRENCE: Cluck-cluck-cluck-cluck! . . You think I'm anxious to have more hens around me? (*He wriggles fretfully in the chair for a moment, then throws off the blanket and pushes himself to his feet. Stumbling with dizziness and breathing heavily, he moves to the inside rear door of the porch. He reaches it and pauses with a fit of coughing. He looks anxiously back toward the chair.*) No, no, damn you . . . I *won't!* (*He looks up at the Phœnix, straightens himself heroically and goes out.*)

(*After a few moments Frieda returns with Bertha, a small, sprightly person, an English gentlewoman with the quick voice and eyes of a child.*)

FRIEDA: My God, he's got up!

BERTHA: He shouldn't?

FRIEDA: Another hemorrhage will kill him. The least exertion is likely to bring one on. Lorenzo, where are you?

LAWRENCE: (*from the rear*) Quit clucking, you old wet hen. I'm fetching the tea.

BERTHA: Go back to him, make him stop!

FRIEDA: He wouldn't.

BERTHA: Does he want to die?

FRIEDA: Oh, no, no, no! He has no lungs and yet he goes on breathing. The heart's worn out and yet the heart keeps beating. It's awful to watch, this struggle. I wish he would stop, I wish that he'd give it up and just let go!

BERTHA: Frieda!

FRIEDA: His body's a house that's made out of tissuepaper and caught on fire. The walls are transparent, they're all lit up with the flame! When people are dying the spirit ought to go out, it ought to die out slowly before the flesh. You shouldn't be able to see it so terribly brightly consuming the walls that give it a place to inhabit!

BERTHA: I never have believed that Lorenzo could die. I don't think he will even now.

FRIEDA: But can he do it? Live without a body, I mean, be just a flame with nothing to feed itself on?

BERTHA: The Phœnix could do it.

FRIEDA: The Phœnix was legendary. Lorenzo's a man.

BERTHA: He's more than a man.

FRIEDA: I know you always thought so. But you're mistaken.

BERTHA: You'd never admit that Lorenzo was a god.

FRIEDA: Having slept with him . . . No, I wouldn't.

BERTHA: There's more to be known of a person than carnal knowledge.

FRIEDA: But carnal knowledge comes first.

BERTHA: I disagree with you.

FRIEDA: And also with Lawrence, then. He always insisted you couldn't know women until you had known their bodies.

BERTHA: Frieda, I think it is you who kept him so much in his body!

FRIEDA: Well, if I did he's got that to thank me for.

BERTHA: I'm not so sure it's something to be thankful for.

FRIEDA: What would you have done with him if ever you got your claws on him?

BERTHA: Claws? . . Frieda!

FRIEDA: You would have plucked him out of his body. Where would he be? . . In the air? Ah, your deep understanding and my stupidity always!

BERTHA: Frieda!

FRIEDA: You just don't know. The meaning of Lawrence escapes you. In all of his work he celebrates the body. How he despises the prudery of people that want to hide it!

BERTHA: Oh, Frieda, the same old quarrel!

FRIEDA: Yes, let's stop it. What's left of Lorenzo, let's not try to divide it!

BERTHA: What's left of Lorenzo is something that can't be divided!

FRIEDA: Sh! . . He's coming.

BERTHA: (*advancing a few steps to the door*) *Lorenzo!*

LAWRENCE: (*He is out of sight as he speaks.*) "Pussycat, pussycat, where have you been?"

BERTHA: (*gaily*) "I've been to London to look at the Queen!"

LAWRENCE: (*coming nearer*) "Pussycat, pussycat, what did you there?"

BERTHA: (*her voice catching slightly*) "I chased a little mouse . . . under a chair!"

(*Laughing, Lawrence appears in the doorway, pushing a small tea-cart. Bertha stares aghast.*)

LAWRENCE: Yes, I know . . . I know . . . I look an amateur's job of embalming, don't I?

BERTHA: (*bravely*) Lorenzo, you look very well.

LAWRENCE: It isn't rouge, it's the fever! I'm burning, burning, and still I never burn out. The doctors are all astonished. And disappointed. As for that expectant widow of mine, she's almost given up hope. (*Bertha moves to assist him with the table.*) Don't bother me. I can manage.

FRIEDA: He won't be still, he won't rest!

LAWRENCE: Cluck-cluck-cluck-cluck! You better watch out for the rooster, you old wet hen!

FRIEDA: A wonderful Chanticleer you make in that lavender shawl!

LAWRENCE: Who put it on me? *You*, you bitch! (*He flings it off.*) Rest was never any good for me, Brett.

BERTHA: Rest for a little while. Then we go sailing again!

LAWRENCE: We three go sailing again!

"Rub-a-dub-dub!
Three fools in a tub!
The Brett, the Frieda,
the old Fire-eater!"

BERTHA: (*tugging at his beard*) The old Fire-eater!

LAWRENCE: Watch out! Now I'll have to comb it. (*He takes out a little mirror and comb.*)

FRIEDA: So vain of his awful red whiskers!

LAWRENCE: (*combing*) She envies me my beard. All women resent men's whiskers. They can't stand anything, Brett, that distinguishes men from women.

FRIEDA: Quite the contrary. (*She pours the tea.*)

LAWRENCE: They take the male in their bodies . . . but only because they secretly hope that he won't be able to get back out again, that he'll be captured for good.

FRIEDA: What kind of talk for a maiden lady to hear!

LAWRENCE: There she goes again, Brett . . . obscene old creature! Gloating over your celibacy!

FRIEDA: Gloating over it? Never! I think how lucky she is that she doesn't have to be told a hundred times every day that a man is life and that woman is just a passive hunk of protoplasm.

LAWRENCE: I never said passive. I always said malignant. (*He puts the comb away and stares in the mirror.*) Ain't I the devil to look at?

FRIEDA: I tell you, Brett, his ideas of sex are becoming downright cosmic! When the sun comes up in the morning . . . you know what he says? No, I won't repeat it! And when the sun's going down . . . Oh, well, you will hear him yourself.

LAWRENCE: (*chuckling*) Yes, I always make the same remark. You'll hear me yourself in just a few more minutes . . . (*He puts the mirror away.*) Well, Brett!

BERTHA: Well, Lorenzo?

LAWRENCE: You haven't said anything yet.

BERTHA: Anything? About what?

LAWRENCE: What do you think that I sent you to London for?

BERTHA: To get me out of the way!

LAWRENCE: What else? . . Out with it, damn you! The show! How did they like my pictures?

BERTHA: Well . . .

FRIEDA: Go on, Brett, tell him the truth. The monster will not be satisfied till he hears it!

BERTHA: Well . . .

FRIEDA: The exhibition was a complete fiasco! Just as I said it would be!

LAWRENCE: You mean that they *liked* my pictures?

FRIEDA: *Liked* your pictures? They called your pictures *disgusting*!

LAWRENCE: Ah! . . *Success!* They said that I couldn't paint? That I draw like a child? They called my figures grotesque? Lumpy, obscene, misshapen, monstrous, deformed?

BERTHA: You must have seen the reviews, you've read them yourself!

LAWRENCE: Why? Am I quoting exactly?

FRIEDA: Yes, you are quoting exactly!

LAWRENCE: And what did the public think? And what of the people?

FRIEDA: The people laughed!

LAWRENCE: They laughed?

FRIEDA: Of course they laughed! Lorenzo, you're not a painter, you're a writer! Why, you can't even draw a straight line!

LAWRENCE: No! But I can draw a *crooked* line, Frieda. And that is the reason that I can put *life* in my pictures! How was the attendance? How many came to look?

BERTHA: After the disturbance, the entrance had to be roped off to hold back the crowds.

LAWRENCE: Disturbance? What disturbance?

FRIEDA: Just look. The monster's exulting!

LAWRENCE: Go on, tell me what happened!

BERTHA: A group of ladies' club members attempted to slash the picture of Adam and Eve.

(*Lawrence shakes with laughter.*)

FRIEDA: Lorenzo! Stop that!

BERTHA: That was what called the attention of the police.

LAWRENCE: The police? (*He rises.*) What did they do to my pictures? Burn them? *Destroy them?*

BERTHA: No. We got out an injunction to keep them from burning the pictures.

LAWRENCE: The pictures are safe?

BERTHA: The pictures are safe, Lorenzo.

FRIEDA: Sit down in that chair or I'll have to put you to bed!

(*She tries to push him down. He slaps her fiercely.*)

BERTHA: Lorenzo!

LAWRENCE: Vaunting her power, gloating over my weakness! Put me to bed? Just try it . . . I dare you to touch me!

FRIEDA: Lawrence, sit down in that chair or you'll start the bleeding again.

(*He stares at her for a moment and then obeys slowly.*)

LAWRENCE: (*weakly*) Give me back that shawl. The sun's getting weaker. The young blond god is beginning to be seduced by the harlot of darkness . . .

FRIEDA: Now he's going to make his classic remarks on the sunset. (*She puts the shawl about him.*)

LAWRENCE: Yes . . . the pictures . . . they weren't very good but they had a fierce life in them.

BERTHA: They had *you* in them. But why did you want to *paint*, Lorenzo?

LAWRENCE: Why did I want to write? Because I'm an artist . . . What is an artist? . . A man who loves life too intensely, a man who loves life till he hates her and has to strike out with his fist as I struck out at Frieda . . . To show her he knows her tricks, and he's still the master! (*The smoky yellow light is beginning to dim.*) Oh, Brett, oh, Frieda . . . I wanted to stretch out the long, sweet arms of my art and embrace the whole world! But it isn't enough to go out to the world with love. And so I doubled my fist and I struck and I struck. Words weren't enough . . . I had to have color, too. I took to paint and I painted the way that I wrote! Fiercely, without any shame! *This* is life, I told them, life is like *this*! Wonderful! Dark! Terrific! They banned my books and they wanted to burn my pictures! That's how it is . . . When first you look at the sun it strikes you blind. Life's . . . blinding . . . (*He stirs and leans forward.*) The sun's . . . going down. He's seduced by the harlot of darkness.

FRIEDA: Now he is going to say it . . . Stop up your ears!

LAWRENCE: Now she has got him, they're copulating together! The sun is exhausted, the harlot has taken his strength and now she will start to destroy him. She's eating him up . . . Oh, but he won't stay down. He'll climb back out of her belly and there will be light. In the end there will always be light . . . And I am the prophet of it! (*He rises with difficulty.*)

BERTHA: Lorenzo!

FRIEDA: Lawrence, be careful!

LAWRENCE: Shut up! Don't touch me! (*He staggers to the great window.*) In the end there is going to be light . . . light, light! (*His voice rises and he stretches his arms out like a Biblical prophet.*) Great light! . . Great, blinding, universal *light!* And *I* . . . I'm the *prophet* of it! (*He staggers and clutches his mouth.*)

FRIEDA: *Lawrence!*

BERTHA: (*terrified*) What *is* it?

FRIEDA: The *bleeding!*

BERTHA: *Lorenzo!* (*She tries to rush to him but Frieda clutches her arm.*)

LAWRENCE: Don't touch me, you women. I want to do it alone . . . Don't move till it's finished. (*Gradually, as though forced down to the earth by invisible arms, he begins to collapse, but still he clings to the wall and shuffles along it, gasping for breath, until he has reached the door. He opens the door.*) Don't follow. (*He goes out.*)

BERTHA: (*struggling fiercely with Frieda*) Let me go, let me go, I want to go to him.

FRIEDA: I promised "no women"!

BERTHA: You go!

FRIEDA: Nobody, nobody goes to him! Not you, not me, no woman!

BERTHA: He can't die alone, I won't let him! No human being would let him!

FRIEDA: (*agonized*) I will, I promised, I'll let him!

(*The wind blows open the door to the terrace. There is the sound of waves breaking. The silk banner of the Phœnix billows out from the wall. Bertha almost breaks away, but Frieda violently restrains her again. In the struggle the lamp is upset and goes out. Bertha cries* Monster! *and collapses sobbing to the floor. For a few moments, stillness: then faintly, as if from a distance, Lawrence's voice:*)

LAWRENCE: *Frieda!*

(*All in one instant Frieda thrusts the sobbing woman violently away from her and sweeps out upon the terrace like a great winged bird.*)

FRIEDA: (*wildly, with infinite tenderness*) Ich komm', Ich komm', mein Liebchen!

FROM

27 WAGONS FULL OF COTTON AND OTHER ONE-ACT PLAYS (1946)

27 Wagons Full of Cotton

A Mississippi Delta Comedy

'Now Eros shakes my soul, a wind on the mountain, falling on the oaks.'
SAPPHO

CHARACTERS

JAKE MEIGHAN, *a cotton-gin owner.*
FLORA MEIGHAN, *his wife.*
SILVA VICARRO, *superintendent of the Syndicate Plantation.*

All of the action takes place on the front porch of the Meighans' residence near Blue Mountain, Mississippi.

SCENE: *The front porch of the Meighans' cottage near Blue Mountain, Mississippi. The porch is narrow and rises into a single narrow gable. There are spindling white pillars on either side supporting the porch roof and a door of Gothic design and two Gothic windows on either side of it. The peaked door has an oval of richly stained glass, azure, crimson, emerald and gold. At the windows are fluffy white curtains gathered coquettishly in the middle by baby-blue satin bows. The effect is not unlike a doll's house.*

SCENE I

It is early evening and there is a faint rosy dusk in the sky. Shortly after the curtain rises, Jake Meighan, a fat man of sixty, scrambles out the front door and races around the corner of the house carrying a gallon can of coal-oil. A dog barks at him. A car is heard starting and receding rapidly in the distance. A moment later Flora calls from inside the house.

FLORA: Jake! I've lost m' white kid purse! (*closer to the door*) Jake? Look'n see 'f uh laid it on th' swing. (*There is a pause.*) Guess I could've left it in th' Chevy? (*She comes up to screen door.*) Jake. Look'n see if uh left it in th' Chevy. Jake? (*She steps outside in the fading rosy dusk. She switches on the porch light and stares about, slapping at gnats attracted by the light. Locusts provide the only answering voice. Flora gives a long nasal call.*) Ja-ay—a-a-ake! (*A cow moos in the distance with the same inflection. There is a muffled explosion somewhere about half a mile away. A strange flickering glow appears, the reflection of a burst of flame. Distant voices are heard exclaiming.*)

VOICES: (*shrill, cackling like hens*)
You heah that noise?
Yeah! Sound like a bomb went off!
Oh, look!
Why, it's a fire!
Where's it at? You tell?
Th' Syndicate Plantation!
Oh, my God! Let's go! (*A fire whistle sounds in the distance.*)
Henry! Start th' car! You all wanta go with us?
Yeah, we'll be right out!
Hurry, honey! (*A car can be heard starting up.*)
Be right there!
Well, hurry.

VOICE: (*just across the dirt road*) Missus Meighan?

FLORA: Ye-ah?

VOICE: Ahn't you goin' th' fire?

FLORA: I wish I could but Jake's gone off in th' Chevy.

VOICE: Come awn an' go with us, honey!

FLORA: Oh, I cain't an' leave th' house wide open! Jake's gone off with th' keys. What do you all think it is on fire?

VOICE: Th' Syndicate Plantation!

FLORA: Th' Syndicate Plan-*ta*-tion? (*The car starts off and recedes.*) Oh, my Go-od! (*She climbs laboriously back up on the porch and sits on the swing which faces the front. She speaks tragically to herself.*) Nobody! Nobody! Never! Never! Nobody! (*Locusts can be heard. A car is heard approaching and stopping at a distance back of house. After a moment Jake ambles casually up around the side of the house.*)

FLORA: (*in a petulant babyish tone*) *Well!*

JAKE: Whatsamatter, Baby?

FLORA: I never known a human being could be that mean an' thoughtless!

JAKE: Aw, now, that's a mighty broad statement fo' you to make, Mrs. Meighan. What's the complaint this time?

FLORA: Just flew out of the house without even sayin' a word!

JAKE: What's so bad about that?

FLORA: I told you I had a headache comin' on an' had to have a dope, there wassen a single bottle lef' in th' house, an' you said, Yeah, get into yuh things 'n' we'll drive in town right away! So I get into m' things an' I cain't find m' white kid purse. Then I remember I left it on th' front seat of th' Chevy. I come out here t' git it. Where are you? Gone off! Without a word! Then there's a big explosion! Feel my heart!

JAKE: Feel my baby's heart? (*He puts a hand on her huge bosom.*)

FLORA: Yeah, just you feel it, poundin' like a hammer! How'd I know what happened? You not here, just disappeared somewhere!

JAKE: (*sharply*) Shut up! (*He pushes her head roughly.*)

FLORA: Jake! What did you do that fo'?

JAKE: I don't like how you holler! Holler ev'ry thing you say!

FLORA: What's the matter with you?

JAKE: Nothing's the matter with me.

FLORA: Well, why did you go off?

JAKE: I didn' go off!

FLORA: You certainly *did* go off! Try an' tell me that you never went off when I just now seen an' heard you drivin' back in th' car? What uh you take me faw? No sense a-tall?

JAKE: If you got sense you keep your big mouth shut!

FLORA: Don't talk to me like that!

JAKE: Come on inside.

FLORA: I won't. Selfish an' inconsiderate, that's what you are! I told you at supper, There's not a bottle of Coca-Cola left on th' place. You said, Okay, right after supper we'll drive on over to th' White Star drugstore an' lay in a good supply. When I come out of th' house—

JAKE: (*He stands in front of her and grips her neck with both hands.*) Look here! Listen to what I tell you!

FLORA: *Jake!*

JAKE: Shhh! Just listen, Baby.

FLORA: Lemme go! G'damn you, le' go my throat!

JAKE: Jus' try an' concentrate on what I tell yuh!

FLORA: Tell me what?

JAKE: I ain't been off th' po'ch.

FLORA: Huh!

JAKE: I ain't been off th' front po'ch! Not since supper! Understand that, now?

FLORA: Jake, honey, you've gone out of you' mind!

JAKE: Maybe so. Never you mind. Just get that straight an' keep it in your haid. I ain't been off the porch of this house since supper.

FLORA: But you sure as God *was* off it! (*He twists her wrist.*) Ouuuu! Stop it, stop it, stop it!

JAKE: Where have I been since supper?

FLORA: Here, here! On th' porch! Fo' God's sake, quit that twistin'!

JAKE: Where have I been?

FLORA: Porch! Porch! Here!

JAKE: Doin' what?

FLORA: *Jake!*

JAKE: Doin' what?

FLORA: Lemme go! Christ, Jake! Let loose! Quit twisting, you'll break my wrist!

JAKE: (*laughing between his teeth*) Doin' what? What doin'? Since supper?

FLORA: (*crying out*) How in hell do I know!

JAKE: 'Cause you was right here with me, all the time, for every second! You an' me, sweetheart, was sittin' here together on th' swing, just swingin' back an' forth every minute since supper! You got that in your haid good now?

FLORA: (*whimpering*) Le'-go!

JAKE: Got it? In your haid good now?

FLORA: Yeh, yeh, yeh—leggo!

JAKE: What was I doin', then?

FLORA: Swinging! For Christ's sake—swingin'! (*He releases her. She whimpers and rubs her wrist but the impression is that the experience was not without pleasure for both parties. She groans and whimpers. He grips her loose curls in his hand and bends her head back. He plants a long wet kiss on her mouth.*)

FLORA: (*whimpering*) Mmmm-hmmmm! Mmmm! Mmmm!

JAKE: (*huskily*) Tha's my swee' baby girl.

FLORA: Mmmmm! Hurt! Hurt!
JAKE: Hurt?
FLORA: Mmmm! Hurt!
JAKE: Kiss?
FLORA: Mmmm!
JAKE: Good?
FLORA: Mmmm . . .
JAKE: Good! Make little room.
FLORA: Too hot!
JAKE: Go on, make little room.
FLORA: Mmmmm . . .
JAKE: Cross patch?
FLORA: Mmmmmm.
JAKE: Whose baby? Big? Sweet?
FLORA: Mmmmm! Hurt!
JAKE: Kiss! (*He lifts her wrist to his lips and makes gobbling sounds.*)
FLORA: (*giggling*) Stop! Silly! Mmmm!
JAKE: What would I do if you was a big piece of cake?
FLORA: Silly.
JAKE: Gobble! Gobble!
FLORA: Oh, you—
JAKE: What would I do if you was angel food cake? Big white piece with lots of nice thick icin'?
FLORA: (*giggling*) Quit!
JAKE: Gobble, gobble, gobble!
FLORA: (*squealing*) Jake!
JAKE: Huh?
FLORA: You *tick*-le!
JAKE: Answer little question!
FLORA: Wh-at?
JAKE: Where I been since supper?
FLORA: Off in the Chevy! (*He instantly seizes the wrist again. She shrieks.*)
JAKE: Where've I been since supper?
FLORA: Po'ch! Swing!
JAKE: Doin' what?
FLORA: *Swingin'!* Oh, Christ, Jake, let loose!
JAKE: Hurt?
FLORA: Mmmmm . . .

JAKE: Good?

FLORA: (*whimpering*) Mmmmm . . .

JAKE: Now you know where I been an' what I been doin' since supper?

FLORA: Yeah . . .

JAKE: Case anybody should ask?

FLORA: Who's going to ast?

JAKE: Never mind who's goin' t' ast, just you know the answers! Uh-huh?

FLORA: Uh-huh. (*lisping babyishly*) This is where you been. Settin' on th' swing since we had supper. Swingin'—back an' fo'th—back an' fo'th. . . . You didn' go off in th' Chevy. (*slowly*) An' you was awf'ly surprised w'en th' syndicate fire broke out! (*Jake slaps her.*) Jake!

JAKE: Everything you said is awright. But don't you get ideas.

FLORA: Ideas?

JAKE: A woman like you's not made to have ideas. Made to be hugged an' squeezed!

FLORA: (*babyishly*) Mmmm. . . .

JAKE: But not for ideas. So don't you have ideas. (*He rises.*) Go out an' get in th' Chevy.

FLORA: We goin to th' fire?

JAKE: No. We ain' goin' no fire. We goin' in town an' get us a case a dopes because we're hot an' thirsty.

FLORA: (*vaguely, as she rises*) I lost m' white—kid—purse . . .

JAKE: It's on the seat of th' Chevy whe' you left it.

FLORA: Whe' *you* goin'?

JAKE: I'm goin in t' th' toilet. I'll be right out. (*He goes inside, letting the screen door slam. Flora shuffles to the edge of the steps and stands there with a slight idiotic smile. She begins to descend, letting herself down each time with the same foot, like a child just learning to walk. She stops at the bottom of the steps and stares at the sky, vacantly and raptly, her fingers closing gently around the bruised wrist. Jake can be heard singing inside.*)

'My baby don' care fo' rings
or other expensive things—
My baby just cares—fo'—me!'

Curtain

SCENE II

It is just after noon. The sky is the color of the satin bows on the window curtains—a translucent, innocent blue. Heat devils are shimmering over the flat Delta country and the peaked white front of the house is like a shrill exclamation. Jake's gin is busy; heard like a steady pulse across the road. A delicate lint of cotton is drifting about in the atmosphere.

Jake appears, a large and purposeful man with arms like hams covered with a fuzz of fine blond hair. He is followed by Silva Vicarro who is the Superintendent of the Syndicate Plantation where the fire occurred last night. Vicarro is a rather small and wiry man of dark Latin looks and nature. He wears whipcord breeches, laced boots, and a white undershirt. He has a Roman Catholic medallion on a chain about his neck.

JAKE: (*with the good-natured condescension of a very large man for a small one*) Well, suh, all I got to say is you're a mighty lucky little fellow.

VICARRO: Lucky? In what way?

JAKE: That I can take on a job like this right now! Twenty-seven wagons full of cotton 's a pretty big piece of bus'ness, Mr. Vicarro. (*stopping at the steps*) *Baby!* (*He bites off a piece of tobacco plug.*) What's yuh firs' name?

VICARRO: Silva.

JAKE: How do you spell it?

VICARRO: S-I-L-V-A.

JAKE: Silva! Like a silver lining! Ev'ry cloud has got a silver lining. What does that come from? The Bible?

VICARRO: (*sitting on the steps*) No. The Mother Goose Book.

JAKE: Well, suh, you sure are lucky that I can do it. If I'd been busy like I was two weeks ago I would 've turned it down. *BABY! COME OUT HERE A MINUTE!* (*There is a vague response from inside.*)

VICARRO: Lucky. Very lucky. (*He lights a cigarette. Flora pushes open the screen door and comes out. She has on her watermelon pink silk dress and is clutching against her body the big white kid purse with her initials on it in big nickel plate.*)

JAKE: (*proudly*) Mr. Vicarro—I want you to meet Mrs. Meighan. Baby, this is a very down-at-the-mouth young fellow I want you to cheer up fo' me. He thinks he's out of luck because his cotton gin burnt down. He's got twenty-seven wagons full of cotton to be ginned out on a hurry-up order from his most impo'tant customers in Mobile. Well, suh, I said to him, Mr. Vicarro, you're to be congratulated —not because it burnt down, but because I happen to be in a situation to take the business over. Now you tell him just how lucky he is!

FLORA: (*nervously*) Well, I guess he don't see how it was lucky to have his gin burned down.

VICARRO: (*acidly*) No, ma'am.

JAKE: (*quickly*) Mr. Vicarro. Some fellows marry a girl when she's little an' tiny. They like a small figure. See? Then, when the girl gets comfo'tably settled down—what does she do? Puts on flesh—of cou'se!

FLORA: (*bashfully*) Jake!

JAKE: Now then! How do they react? Accept it as a matter of cou'se, as something which 'as been ordained by nature? Nope! No, suh, not a bit! They sta't to feeling abused. They think that fate must have a grudge against them because the little woman is not so little as she used to be. Because she's gone an' put on a matronly figure. Well, suh, that's at the root of a lot of domestic trouble. However, Mr. Vicarro, I never made that mistake. When I fell in love with this baby-doll I've got here, she was just the same size then that you see her today.

FLORA: (*crossing shyly to porch rail*) Jake . . .

JAKE: (*grinning*) A woman not large but tremendous! That's how I liked her—tremendous! I told her right off, when I slipped th' ring on her finger, one Satiddy night in a boathouse on Moon Lake—I said to her, Honey, if you take off one single pound of that body—I'm going to quit yuh! I'm going to quit yuh, I said, the minute I notice you've started to take off weight!

FLORA: Aw, Jake—please!

JAKE: I don't want nothing little, not in a woman. I'm not after nothing *petite*, as the Frenchmen call it. This is what I wanted—and what I *got!* Look at her, Mr. Vicarro. Look at her blush! (*He grips the back of Flora's neck and tries to turn her around.*)

FLORA: Aw, quit, Jake! Quit, will yuh?

JAKE: See what a doll she is? (*Flora turns suddenly and spanks him with the kid purse. He cackles and runs down the steps. At the corner of the house, he stops and turns.*) Baby, you keep Mr. Vicarro comfo'table while I'm ginnin' out that twenty-seven wagons full of cotton. Th' good-neighbor policy, Mr. Vicarro. You do me a good turn an' I'll do you a good one! Be see'n' yuh! So long, Baby! (*He walks away with an energetic stride.*)

VICARRO: The good-neighbor policy! (*He sits on the porch steps.*)

FLORA: (*sitting on the swing*) Izzen he out-*ray*-juss! (*She laughs foolishly and puts the purse in her lap. Vicarro stares gloomily across the dancing brilliance of the fields. His lip sticks out like a pouting child's. A rooster crows in the distance.*)

FLORA: I would'n' dare to expose myself like that.

VICARRO: Expose? To what?

FLORA: The sun. I take a terrible burn. I'll never forget the burn I took one time. It was on Moon Lake one Sunday before I was married. I never did like t' go fishin' but this young fellow, one of the Peterson boys, insisted that we go fishin'. Well, he didn't catch nothin' but jus' kep' fishin' an' fishin' an' I set there in th' boat with all that hot sun on me. I said, Stay under the willows. But he would'n' lissen to me, an' sure enough I took such an awful burn I had t' sleep on m' stummick th' nex' three nights.

VICARRO: (*absently*) What did you say? You got sun-burned?

FLORA: Yes. One time on Moon Lake.

VICARRO: That's too bad. You got over it all right?

FLORA: Oh, yes. Finally. Yes.

VICARRO: That must 've been pretty bad.

FLORA: I fell in the lake once, too. Also with one of the Peterson boys. On another fishing trip. That was a wild bunch of boys, those Peterson boys. I never went out with 'em but something happened which made me wish I hadn't. One time, sun-burned. One time, nearly drowned. One time—poison ivy! Well, lookin' back on it, now, we had a good deal of fun in spite of it, though.

VICARRO: The good-neighbor policy, huh? (*He slaps his boot with the riding crop. Then he rises from steps.*)

FLORA: You might as well come up on th' po'ch an' make you'self as comfo'table as you can.

VICARRO: Uh-huh.

FLORA: I'm not much good at—makin' conversation.

VICARRO: (*finally noticing her*) Now don't you bother to make conversation for my benefit, Mrs. Meighan. I'm the type that prefers a quiet understanding. (*Flora laughs uncertainly.*) One thing I always notice about you ladies . . .

FLORA: What's that, Mr. Vicarro?

VICARRO: You always have something in your hands—to hold onto. Now that kid purse . . .

FLORA: My purse?

VICARRO: You have no reason to keep that purse in your hands. You're certainly not afraid that I'm going to snatch it!

FLORA: Oh, God, no! I wassen afraid of that!

VICARRO: That wouldn't be the good-neighbor policy, would it? But you hold onto that purse because it gives you something to get a grip on. Isn't that right?

FLORA: Yes. I always like to have something in my hands.

VICARRO: Sure you do. You feel what a lot of uncertain things there are. Gins burn down. The volunteer fire department don't have decent equipment. Nothing is any protection. The afternoon sun is hot. It's no protection. The trees are back of the house. They're no protection. The goods that dress is made of—is no protection. So what do you do, Mrs. Meighan? You pick up the white kid purse. It's solid. It's sure. It's certain. It's something to hold *on* to. You get what I mean?

FLORA: Yeah. I think I do.

VICARRO: It gives you a feeling of being attached to something. The mother protects the baby? No, no, no—the baby protects the mother! From being lost and empty and having nothing but lifeless things in her hands! Maybe you think there isn't much connection!

FLORA: You'll have to excuse me from thinking. I'm too lazy.

VICARRO: What's your name, Mrs. Meighan?

FLORA: Flora.

VICARRO: Mine is Silva. Something not gold but—Silva!

FLORA: Like a silver dollar?

VICARRO: No, like a silver dime! It's an Italian name. I'm a native of New Orleans.

FLORA: Then it's not sun-burn. You're natcherally dark.

VICARRO: (*raising his undershirt from his belly*) Look at this!

FLORA: Mr. Vicarro!

VICARRO: Just as dark as my arm is!

FLORA: You don't have to show me! I'm not from Missouri!

VICARRO: (*grinning*) Excuse me.

FLORA: (*She laughs nervously.*) Whew! I'm sorry to say we don't have a coke in the house. We meant to get a case of cokes las' night, but what with all the excitement going on—

VICARRO: What excitement was that?

FLORA: Oh, the fire and all.

VICARRO: (*lighting a cigarette*) I shouldn't think you all would of been excited about the fire.

FLORA: A fire is always exciting. After a fire, dogs an' chickens don't sleep. I don't think our chickens got to sleep all night.

VICARRO: No?

FLORA: They cackled an' fussed an' flopped around on the roost—took on something awful! Myself, I couldn't sleep neither. I jus' lay there an' sweated all night long.

VICARRO: On account of th' fire?

FLORA: An' the heat an' mosquitoes. And I was mad at Jake.

VICARRO: Mad at Mr. Meighan? What about?

FLORA: Oh, he went off an' left me settin' here on this ole po'ch last night without a Coca-Cola on the place.

VICARRO: Went off an' left you, did he?

FLORA: Yep. Right after supper. An' when he got back the fire 'd already broke out an' instead of drivin' in to town like he said, he decided to go an' take a look at your burnt-down cotton gin. I got smoke in my eyes an' my nose an' throat. It hurt my sinus an' I was in such a wo'n out, nervous condition, it made me cry. I cried like a baby. Finally took two teaspoons of paregoric. Enough to put an elephant to sleep. But still I stayed awake an' heard them chickens carryin' on out there!

VICARRO: It sounds like you passed a very uncomfortable night.

FLORA: Sounds like? Well, it *was*.

VICARRO: So Mr. Meighan—you say—disappeared after supper? (*There is a pause while Flora looks at him blankly.*)

FLORA: Huh?

VICARRO: You say Mr. Meighan was out of the house for a while after supper? (*Something in his tone makes her aware of her indiscretion.*)

FLORA: Oh—uh—just for a moment.

VICARRO: Just for a moment, huh? How long a moment? (*He stares at her very hard.*)

FLORA: What are you driving at, Mr. Vicarro?

VICARRO: Driving at? Nothing.

FLORA: You're looking at me so funny.

VICARRO: He disappeared for a moment! Is that what he did? How long a moment did he disappear for? Can you remember, Mrs. Meighan?

FLORA: What difference does that make? What's it to you, anyhow?

VICARRO: Why should you mind me asking?

FLORA: You make this sound like I was on trial for something!

VICARRO: Don't you like to pretend like you're a witness?

FLORA: Witness of what, Mr. Vicarro?

VICARRO: Why—for instance—say—a case of arson!

FLORA: (*wetting her lips*) Case of—? What is—arson?

VICARRO: The willful destruction of property by fire. (*He slaps his boots sharply with the riding crop.*)

FLORA: (*startled*) Oh! (*She nervously fingers the purse.*) Well, now, don't you go and be getting any—funny ideas.

VICARRO: Ideas about what, Mrs. Meighan?

FLORA: My husband's disappearin'—after supper. I can explain that.

VICARRO: Can you?

FLORA: Sure I can.

VICARRO: Good! How do you explain it? (*He stares at her. She looks down.*) What's the matter? Can't you collect your thoughts, Mrs. Meighan?

FLORA: No, but—

VICARRO: Your mind's a blank on the subject?

FLORA: Look here, now— (*She squirms on the swing.*)

VICARRO: You find it impossible to remember just what your husband disappeared for after supper? You can't imagine what kind of errand it was that he went out on, can you?

FLORA: No! No, I can't!

VICARRO: But when he returned—let's see . . . The fire had just broken out at the Syndicate Plantation?

FLORA: Mr. Vicarro, I don't have the slightest idear what you could be driving at.

VICARRO: You're a very unsatisfactory witness, Mrs. Meighan.

FLORA: I never can think when people—stare straight at me.

VICARRO: Okay. I'll look away, then. (*He turns his back to her.*) Now does that improve your memory any? Now are you able to concentrate on the question?

FLORA: Huh . . .

VICARRO: No? You're not? (*He turns around again, grinning evilly.*) Well . . . shall we drop the subject?

FLORA: I sure do wish you would.

VICARRO: It's no use crying over a burnt-down gin. This world is built on the principle of tit for tat.

FLORA: What do you mean?

VICARRO: Nothing at all specific. Mind if I . . . ?

FLORA: What?

VICARRO: You want to move over a little an' make some room? (*Flora edges aside on the swing. He sits down with her.*) I like a swing. I've always liked to sit an' rock on a swing. Relaxes you . . . You relaxed?

FLORA: Sure.

VICARRO: No, you're not. Your nerves are all tied up.

FLORA: Well, you made me feel kind of nervous. All of them questions you ast me about the fire.

VICARRO: I didn' ask you questions about the fire. I only asked you about your husband's leaving the house after supper.

FLORA: I explained that to you.

VICARRO: Sure. That's right. You did. The good-neighbor policy. That was a lovely remark your husband made about the good-neighbor policy. I see what he means by that now.

FLORA: He was thinking about President Roosevelt's speech. We sat up an' lissened to it one night last week.

VICARRO: No, I think that he was talking about something closer to home, Mrs. Meighan. You do me a good turn and I'll do you one, that was the way that he put it. You have a piece of cotton on your face. Hold still—I'll pick it off. (*He delicately removes the lint.*) There now.

FLORA: (*nervously*) Thanks.

VICARRO: There's a lot of fine cotton lint floating round in the air.

FLORA: I know there is. It irritates my nose. I think it gets up in my sinus.

VICARRO: Well, you're a delicate woman.

FLORA: Delicate? Me? Oh, no. I'm too big for that.

VICARRO: Your size is part of your delicacy, Mrs. Meighan.

FLORA: How do you mean?

VICARRO: There's a lot of you, but every bit of you is delicate. Choice. Delectable, I might say.

FLORA: Huh?

VICARRO: I mean you're altogether lacking in any—coarseness. You're soft. Fine-fibered. And smooth.

FLORA: Our talk is certainly taking a personal turn.

VICARRO: Yes. You make me think of cotton.

FLORA: Huh?

VICARRO: Cotton!

FLORA: Well! Should I say thanks or something?

VICARRO: No, just smile, Mrs. Meighan. You have an attractive smile. Dimples!

FLORA: No . . .

VICARRO: Yes, you have! Smile, Mrs. Meighan! Come on—smile! (*Flora averts her face, smiling helplessly.*) There now. See? You've got them! (*He delicately touches one of the dimples.*)

FLORA: Please don't touch me. I don't like to be touched.

VICARRO: Then why do you giggle?

FLORA: Can't help it. You make me feel kind of hysterical, Mr. Vicarro. Mr. Vicarro—

VICARRO: Yes?

FLORA: I hope you don't think that Jake was mixed up in that fire. I swear to goodness he never left the front porch. I remember it perfeckly now. We just set here on the swing till the fire broke out and then we drove in town.

VICARRO: To celebrate?

FLORA: No, no, no.

VICARRO: Twenty-seven wagons full of cotton's a pretty big piece of business to fall in your lap like a gift from the gods, Mrs. Meighan.

FLORA: I thought you said that we would drop the subjeck.

VICARRO: You brought it up that time.

FLORA: Well, please don't try to mix me up any more. I swear to goodness the fire had already broke out when he got back.

VICARRO: That's not what you told me a moment ago.

FLORA: You got me all twisted up. We went in town. The fire broke out an' we didn't know about it.

VICARRO: I thought you said it irritated your sinus.

FLORA: Oh, my God, you sure put words in my mouth. Maybe I'd better make us some lemonade.

VICARRO: Don't go to the trouble.

FLORA: I'll go in an' fix it direckly, but right at this moment I'm too weak to get up. I don't know why, but I can't hardly hold my eyes open. They keep falling shut. . . . I think it's a little too crowded, two on a swing. Will you do me a favor an' set back down over there?

VICARRO: Why do you want me to move?

FLORA: It makes too much body heat when we're crowded together.

VICARRO: One body can borrow coolness from another.

FLORA: I always heard that bodies borrowed heat.

VICARRO: Not in this case. I'm cool.

FLORA: You don't seem like it to me.

VICARRO: I'm just as cool as a cucumber. If you don't believe it, touch me.

FLORA: Where?

VICARRO: Anywhere.

FLORA: (*rising with great effort*) Excuse me. I got to go in. (*He pulls her back down.*) What did you do that for?

VICARRO: I don't want to be deprived of your company yet.

FLORA: Mr. Vicarro, you're getting awf'ly familiar.

VICARRO: Haven't you got any fun-loving spirit about you?

FLORA: This isn't fun.

VICARRO: Then why do you giggle?

FLORA: I'm ticklish! Quit switching me, will yuh?

VICARRO: I'm just shooing the flies off.

FLORA: Leave 'em be, then, please. They don't hurt nothin'.

VICARRO: I think you like to be switched.

FLORA: I don't. I wish you'd quit.

VICARRO: You'd like to be switched harder.

FLORA: No, I wouldn't.

VICARRO: That blue mark on your wrist—
FLORA: What about it?
VICARRO: I've got a suspicion.
FLORA: Of what?
VICARRO: It was twisted. By your husband.
FLORA: You're crazy.
VICARRO: Yes, it was. And you liked it.
FLORA: I certainly didn't. Would you mind moving your arm?
VICARRO: Don't be so skittish.
FLORA: Awright. I'll get up then.
VICARRO: Go on.
FLORA: I feel so weak.
VICARRO: Dizzy?
FLORA: A little bit. Yeah. My head's spinning round. I wish you would stop the swing.
VICARRO: It's not swinging much.
FLORA: But even a little's too much.
VICARRO: You're a delicate woman. A pretty big woman, too.
FLORA: So is America. Big.
VICARRO: That's a funny remark.
FLORA: Yeah. I don't know why I made it. My head's so buzzy.
VICARRO: Fuzzy?
FLORA: Fuzzy an'—buzzy . . . Is something on my arm?
VICARRO: No.
FLORA: Then what 're you brushing?
VICARRO: Sweat off.
FLORA: Leave it alone.
VICARRO: Let me wipe it. (*He brushes her arm with a handkerchief.*)
FLORA: (*laughing weakly*) No, please, don't. It feels funny.
VICARRO: How does it feel?
FLORA: It tickles me. All up an' down. You cut it out now. If you don't cut it out I'm going to call.
VICARRO: Call who?
FLORA: I'm going to call that nigger. The nigger that's cutting the grass across the road.
VICARRO: Go on. Call, then.
FLORA: (*weakly*) Hey! Hey, boy!
VICARRO: Can't you call any louder?
FLORA: I feel so funny. What is the matter with me?

VICARRO: You're just relaxing. You're big. A big type of woman. I like you. Don't get so excited.

FLORA: I'm not, but you—

VICARRO: What am I doing?

FLORA: Suspicions. About my husband and ideas you have about me.

VICARRO: Such as what?

FLORA: He burnt your gin down. He didn't. And I'm not a big piece of cotton. (*She pulls herself up.*) I'm going inside.

VICARRO: (*rising*) I think that's a good idea.

FLORA: I said I was. Not you.

VICARRO: Why not me?

FLORA: Inside it might be crowded, with you an' me.

VICARRO: Three's a crowd. We're two.

FLORA: You stay out. Wait here.

VICARRO: What'll you do?

FLORA: I'll make us a pitcher of nice cold lemonade.

VICARRO: Okay. You go on in.

FLORA: What'll you do?

VICARRO: I'll follow.

FLORA: That's what I figured you might be aiming to do. We'll both stay out.

VICARRO: In the sun?

FLORA: We'll sit back down in th' shade. (*He blocks her.*) Don't stand in my way.

VICARRO: You're standing in mine.

FLORA: I'm dizzy.

VICARRO: You ought to lie down.

FLORA: How can I?

VICARRO: Go in.

FLORA: You'd follow me.

VICARRO: What if I did?

FLORA: I'm afraid.

VICARRO: You're starting to cry.

FLORA: I'm afraid!

VICARRO: What of?

FLORA: Of you.

VICARRO: I'm little.

FLORA: I'm dizzy. My knees are so weak they're like water. I've got to sit down.

VICARRO: Go in.
FLORA: I can't.
VICARRO: Why not?
FLORA: You'd follow.
VICARRO: Would that be so awful?
FLORA: You've got a mean look in your eyes and I don't like the whip. Honest to God he never. He didn't, I swear!
VICARRO: Do what?
FLORA: The fire . . .
VICARRO: Go on.
FLORA: Please don't!
VICARRO: Don't what?
FLORA: Put it down. The whip, please put it down. Leave it out here on the porch.
VICARRO: What are you scared of?
FLORA: You.
VICARRO: Go on. (*She turns helplessly and moves to the screen. He pulls it open.*)
FLORA: Don't follow. Please don't follow! (*She sways uncertainly. He presses his hand against her. She moves inside. He follows. The door is shut quietly. The gin pumps slowly and steadily across the road. From inside the house there is a wild and despairing cry. A door is slammed. The cry is repeated more faintly.*)

Curtain

Scene III

It is about nine o'clock the same evening. Although the sky behind the house is a dusky rose color, a full September moon of almost garish intensity gives the front of the house a ghostly brilliance. Dogs are howling like demons across the prostrate fields of the Delta.

The front porch of the Meighans is empty.

After a moment the screen door is pushed slowly open and Flora Meighan emerges gradually. Her appearance is ravaged. Her eyes have a vacant limpidity in the moonlight, her lips are slightly apart. She moves with her hands stretched gropingly before her till she has reached a pillar of the porch. There she stops and stands moaning a little. Her hair hangs loose and disordered. The upper part of her body is unclothed except for a torn pink band about her breasts. Dark streaks are visible on the bare shoulders and arms and there is a large discoloration along one cheek. A dark trickle, now congealed, descends from one corner of her mouth. These more apparent tokens she covers with one hand when Jake comes up on the porch. He is now heard approaching, singing to himself.

JAKE: By the light—by the light—by the light—Of the silvery mo-o-on! (*Instinctively Flora draws back into the sharply etched shadow from the porch roof. Jake is too tired and triumphant to notice her appearance.*) How's a baby? (*Flora utters a moaning grunt.*) Tired? Too tired t' talk? Well, that's how I feel. Too tired t' talk. Too goddam tired t' speak a friggin' word! (*He lets himself down on the steps, groaning and without giving Flora more than a glance.*) Twenty-seven wagons full of cotton. That's how much I've ginned since ten this mawnin'. A man-size job.

FLORA: (*huskily*) Uh-huh. . . . A man-size—job. . . .

JAKE: *Twen*-ty *sev*-en *wa*-gons *full* of *cot*-ton!

FLORA: (*senselessly repeating*) *Twen*-ty *sev*-en *wa*-gons *full* of *cot*-ton (*A dog howls. Flora utters a breathless laugh.*)

JAKE: What're you laughin' at, honey? Not at me, I hope.

FLORA: No. . . .

JAKE: That's good. The job that I've turned out is nothing to laugh at. I drove that pack of niggers like a mule-skinner. They don't have a brain in their bodies. All they got is bodies. You got to drive, drive, drive. I don't even see how niggers eat without somebody to tell them to put the food in their moufs! (*She laughs again, like water spilling out of her mouth.*) Huh! You got a laugh like a— Christ. A terrific day's work I finished.

FLORA: (*slowly*) I would'n' brag—about it. . . .

JAKE: I'm not braggin' about it, I'm just sayin' I done a big day's work, I'm all wo'n out an' I want a little appreciation, not cross speeches. Honey. . . .

FLORA: I'm not—(*She laughs again.*)—makin' cross speeches.

JAKE: To take on a big piece of work an' finish it up an' mention the fack that it's finished I wouldn't call braggin'.

FLORA: You're not the only one's—done a big day's—work.

JAKE: Who else that you know of? (*There is a pause.*)

FLORA: Maybe you think that I had an easy time. (*Her laughter spills out again.*)

JAKE: You're laughin' like you been on a goddam jag. (*Flora laughs.*) What did you get pissed on? Roach poison or citronella? I think I make it pretty easy for you, workin' like a mule-skinner so you can hire you a nigger to do the wash an' take the house-work on. An elephant woman who acks as frail as a kitten, that's the kind of a woman I got on m' hands.

FLORA: Sure. . . . (*She laughs.*) You make it easy!

JAKE: I've yet t' see you lift a little finger. Even gotten too lazy t' put you' things on. Round the house ha'f naked all th' time. Y' live in a cloud. All you can think of is "Give me a Coca-Cola!" Well, you better look out. They got a new bureau in the guvamint files. It's called U.W. Stands for Useless Wimmen. Tha's secret plans on foot t' have 'em shot! (*He laughs at his joke.*)

FLORA: Secret—plans—on foot?

JAKE: T' have 'em *shot.*

FLORA: That's good. I'm glad t' hear it. (*She laughs again.*)

JAKE: I come home tired an' you cain't wait t' peck at me. What 're you cross about now?

FLORA: I think it was a mistake.

JAKE: What was a mistake?

FLORA: Fo' you t' fool with th' Syndicate—Plantation. . . .

JAKE: I don't know about that. We wuh kind of up-against it, honey. Th' Syndicate buyin' up all th' lan' aroun' here an' turnin' the ole croppers off it without their wages—mighty near busted ev'ry mercantile store in Two Rivers County! An' then they build their own gin to gin their own cotton. It looked for a while like I was stuck up high an' dry. But when the gin burnt down an' Mr. Vicarro decided he'd better throw a little bus'ness my way—I'd say the situation was much improved!

FLORA: (*She laughs weakly.*) Then maybe you don't understand th' good-neighbor—policy.

JAKE: Don't understand it? Why, I'm the boy that invented it.

FLORA: Huh-huh! What an—*invention!* All I can say is—I hope you're satisfied now that you've ginned out—twenty-seven wagons full of—cotton.

JAKE: Vicarro was pretty well pleased w'en he dropped over.

FLORA: Yeah. He was—pretty well—pleased.

JAKE: How did you all get along?

FLORA: We got along jus' fine. Jus' fine an'—dandy.

JAKE: He didn't seem like a such a bad little guy. He takes a sensible attitude.

FLORA: (*laughing helplessly*) He—sure—does!

JAKE: I hope you made him comfo'table in the house?

FLORA: (*giggling*) I made him a pitcher—of nice cold—lemonade!

JAKE: With a little gin in it, huh? That's how you got pissed. A nice cool drink don't sound bad to me right now. Got any left?

FLORA: Not a bit, Mr. Meighan. We drank it *a-a-ll* up! (*She flops onto the swing.*)

JAKE: So you didn't have such a tiresome time after all?

FLORA: No. Not tiresome a bit. I had a nice conversation with Mistuh—Vicarro. . . .

JAKE: What did you all talk about?

FLORA: Th' good-neighbor policy.

JAKE: (*chuckling*) How does he feel about th' good-neighbor policy?

FLORA: Oh—(*She giggles.*)—He thinks it's a—good idea! He says—

JAKE: Huh? (*Flora laughs weakly.*) Says what?

FLORA: Says— (*She goes off into another spasm of laughter.*)

JAKE: What ever he said must've been a panic!

FLORA: He says—(*controlling her spasm*)—he don't think he'll build him a new cotton gin any more. He's gonna let you do a-a-lll his ginnin'—fo' him!

JAKE: I told you he'd take a sensible attitude.

FLORA: Yeah. Tomorrow he plans t' come back—with lots more cotton. Maybe another twenty-seven wagons.

JAKE: Yeah?

FLORA: An' while you're ginnin' it out—he'll have me entertain him with—nice lemonade! (*She has another fit of giggles.*)

JAKE: The more I hear about that lemonade the better I like it. Lemonade highballs, huh? Mr. Thomas Collins?

FLORA: I guess it's—gonna go on fo'—th' rest of th'—summer. . . .

JAKE: (*rising and stretching happily*) Well, it'll . . . it'll soon be fall. Cooler nights comin' on.

FLORA: I don't know that that will put a—stop to it—though. . . .

JAKE: (*obliviously*) The air feels cooler already. You shouldn't be settin' out here without you' shirt on, honey. A change in the air can give you a mighty bad cold.

FLORA: I couldn't stan' nothin' on me—nex' to my—skin.

JAKE: It ain't the heat that gives you all them hives, it's too much liquor. Grog-blossoms, that's what you got! I'm goin' inside to the toilet. When I come out— (*He opens the screen door and goes in.*)—We'll drive in town an' see what's at th' movies. You go hop in the Chevy! (*Flora laughs to herself. She slowly opens the huge kid purse and removes a wad of Kleenex. She touches herself tenderly here and there, giggling breathlessly.*)

FLORA: (*aloud*) I really oughtn' t' have a white kid purse. It's wadded full of—Kleenex—to make it big—like a baby! Big—in my arms—like a baby!

JAKE: (*from inside*) What did you say, Baby?

FLORA: (*dragging herself up by the chain of the swing*) I'm not—Baby. Mama! Ma! That's—me. . . . (*Cradling the big white purse in her arms, she advances slowly and tenderly to the edge of the porch. The moon shines full on her smiling and ravaged face. She begins to rock and sway gently, rocking the purse in her arms and crooning.*)

Rock-a-bye Baby—in uh tree-tops!
If a wind blows—a cradle will rock! (*She descends a step.*)
If a bough bends—a baby will fall! (*She descends another step.*)
Down will come Baby—cradle—an'—all! (*She laughs and stares raptly and vacantly up at the moon.*)

Curtain

*The Lady of Larkspur Lotion**

CHARACTERS

MRS. HARDWICKE-MOORE.
MRS. WIRE.
THE WRITER.

SCENE: *A wretchedly furnished room in the French Quarter of New Orleans. There are no windows, the room being a cubicle partitioned off from several others by imitation walls. A small slanting skylight admits the late and unencouraging day. There is a tall, black armoire, whose doors contain cracked mirrors, a swinging electric bulb, a black and graceless dresser, an awful picture of a Roman Saint and over the bed a coat-of-arms in a frame.*

Mrs. Hardwicke-Moore, a dyed-blonde woman of forty, is seated passively on the edge of the bed as though she could think of nothing better to do.

There is a rap at the door.

MRS. HARDWICKE-MOORE: (*in a sharp, affected tone*) Who is at the door, please?

MRS. WIRE: (*from outside, bluntly*) Me! (*Her face expressing a momentary panic, Mrs. Hardwicke-Moore rises stiffly.*)

MRS. HARDWICKE-MOORE: Oh. . . . Mrs. Wire. Come in. (*The landlady enters, a heavy, slovenly woman of fifty.*) I was just going to drop in your room to speak to you about something.

MRS. WIRE: Yeah? What about?

MRS. HARDWICKE-MOORE: (*humorously, but rather painfully smiling*) Mrs. Wire, I'm sorry to say that I just don't consider these cockroaches to be the most desirable kind of room-mates—do you?

MRS. WIRE: Cockroaches, huh?

MRS. HARDWICKE-MOORE: Yes. Precisely. Now I have had very little experience with cockroaches in my life but the

*Larkspur Lotion is a common treatment for body vermin.

few that I've seen before have been the pedestrian kind, the kind that *walk*. These, Mrs. Wire, appear to be *flying* cockroaches! I was shocked, in fact I was literally stunned, when one of them took off the floor and started to whiz through the air, around and around in a circle, just missing my face by barely a couple of inches. Mrs. Wire, I sat down on the edge of this bed and *wept*, I was just so shocked and disgusted! Imagine! Flying cockroaches, something I never dreamed to be in existence, whizzing around and around and around in front of my face! Why, Mrs. Wire, I want you to know—

MRS. WIRE: (*interrupting*) Flying cockroaches are nothing to be surprised at. They have them all over, even uptown they have them. But that ain't what I wanted to—

MRS. HARDWICKE-MOORE: (*interrupting*) That may be true, Mrs. Wire, but I may as well tell you that I have a horror of roaches, even the plain old-fashioned, pedestrian kind, and as for this type that flies—! If I'm going to stay on here these flying cockroaches have got to be gotten rid of and gotten rid of at *once!*

MRS. WIRE: Now how'm I going to stop them flying cockroaches from coming in through the windows? But that, however, is not what I—

MRS. HARDWICKE-MOORE: (*interrupting*) I don't know *how*, Mrs. Wire, but there certainly must be a method. All I know is they must be gotten rid of before I will sleep here one more night, Mrs. Wire. Why, if I woke up in the night and found one on my bed, I'd have a convulsion, I swear to goodness I'd simply *die* of convulsions!

MRS. WIRE: If you'll excuse me for sayin' so, Mrs. Hardshell-Moore, you're much more likely to die from over-drinkin' than cockroach convulsions! (*She seizes a bottle from the dresser.*) What's this here? Larkspur Lotion! *Well!*

MRS. HARDWICKE-MOORE: (*flushing*) I use it to take the old polish off my nails.

MRS. WIRE: Very fastidious, yes!

MRS. HARDWICKE-MOORE: What do you mean?

MRS. WIRE: There ain't an old house in the Quarter that don't have roaches.

MRS. HARDWICKE-MOORE: But not in such enormous quantities, do they? I tell you this place is actually crawling with them!

MRS. WIRE: It ain't as bad as all that. And by the way, you ain't yet paid me the rest of this week's rent. I don't want to get you off the subjeck of roaches, but, nevertheless, I want to colleck that money.

MRS. HARDWICKE-MOORE: I'll pay you the rest of the rent as soon as you've exterminated these roaches!

MRS. WIRE: You'll have to pay me the rent right away or get out.

MRS. HARDWICKE-MOORE: I intend to get out unless these *roaches* get out!

MRS. WIRE: Then get out then and quit just talking about it!

MRS. HARDWICKE-MOORE: You must be out of your mind, I can't get out right now!

MRS. WIRE: Then what did you mean about roaches?

MRS. HARDWICKE-MOORE: I meant what I said about roaches, they are not, in my opinion, the most desirable room-mates!

MRS. WIRE: Okay! Don't room with them! Pack your stuff and move where they don't have roaches!

MRS. HARDWICKE-MOORE: You mean that you *insist* upon having the roaches?

MRS. WIRE: No, I mean I insist upon having the rent you owe me.

MRS. HARDWICKE-MOORE: Right at the moment that is out of the question.

MRS. WIRE: Out of the question, is it?

MRS. HARDWICKE-MOORE: Yes, and I'll tell you why! The quarterly payments I receive from the man who is taking care of the rubber plantation have not been forwarded yet. I've been expecting them to come in for several weeks now but in the letter that I received this morning it seems there has been some little misunderstanding about the last year's taxes and—

MRS. WIRE: Oh, now stop it, I've heard enough of that goddam rubber plantation! The Brazilian rubber plantation! You think I've been in this business seventeen years without learning nothing about your kind of women?

MRS. HARDWICKE-MOORE: (*stiffly*) What is the implication in that remark?

MRS. WIRE: I suppose the men that you have in here nights come in to discuss the Brazilian rubber plantation?

MRS. HARDWICKE-MOORE: You must be crazy to say such a thing as that!

MRS. WIRE: I hear what I hear an' I know what's going on!

MRS. HARDWICKE-MOORE: I know you spy, I know you listen at doors!

MRS. WIRE: I never spy and I never listen at doors! The first thing a landlady in the French Quarter learns is not to *see* and not to *hear* but only collect your *money!* As long as that comes in—okay, I'm blind, I'm deaf, I'm dumb! But soon as it stops, I recover my hearing and also my sight and also the use of my voice. If necessary I go to the phone and call up the chief of police who happens to be an in-law of my sister's! I heard last night that argument over money.

MRS. HARDWICKE-MOORE: What argument? What money?

MRS. WIRE: He shouted so loud I had to shut the front window to keep the noise from carrying out on the streets! I heard no mention of any Brazilian plantation! But plenty of other things were plainly referred to in that little midnight conversation you had! Larkspur Lotion—to take the polish off nails! Am I in my infancy, am I? That's on a par with the wonderful *rubber* plantation! (*The door is thrown open. The Writer, wearing an ancient purple bathrobe, enters.*)

WRITER: Stop!

MRS. WIRE: *Oh!* It's *you!*

WRITER: Stop persecuting this woman!

MRS. WIRE: The second Mr. Shakespeare enters the scene!

WRITER: I heard your demon howling in my sleep!

MRS. WIRE: *Sleep?* Ho-*ho!* I think that what you *mean* is your *drunken stupor!*

WRITER: I rest because of my illness! Have I no right—

MRS. WIRE: (*interrupting*) Illness—*alcoholic!* Don't try to pull that beautiful wool over my eyes. I'm glad you come in now. Now I repeat for your benefit what I just said to this woman. I'm *done* with *dead beats!* Now is that plain to yuh? Completely fed-up with all you Quarter rats, half-breeds, drunkards, degenerates, who try to get by on promises, lies, delusions!

MRS. HARDWICKE-MOORE: (*covering her ears*) *Oh, please, please, please stop shrieking!* It's not necessary!

MRS. WIRE: (*turning on Mrs. Hardwicke-Moore*) You with your Brazilian rubber plantation. That coat-of-arms on the wall that you got from the junk-shop—the woman who sold it *told* me! One of the Hapsburgs! Yes! A titled lady! *The Lady of Larkspur Lotion! There's* your *title!* (*Mrs. Hardwicke-Moore cries out wildly and flings herself face down on the sagging bed.*)

WRITER: (*with a pitying gesture*) Stop badgering this unfortunate little woman! Is there no mercy left in the world anymore? What has become of compassion and understanding? Where have they all gone to? Where's God? Where's Christ? (*He leans trembling against the armoire.*) What if there *is* no Brazilian rubber plantation?

MRS. HARDWICKE-MOORE: (*sitting passionately erect*) I tell you there is, there *is!* (*Her throat is taut with conviction, her head thrown back.*)

WRITER: What if there *is* no rubber king in her life! There *ought* to be rubber kings in her life! Is she to be blamed because it is necessary for her to compensate for the cruel deficiencies of reality by the exercise of a little—what shall I say?—God-given—imagination?

MRS. HARDWICKE-MOORE: (*throwing herself face down on the bed once more*) No, no, no, no, it *isn't*—imagination!

MRS. WIRE: I'll ask you to please stop spitting me in the face those high-flown speeches! You with your 780-page masterpiece—right on a par with the Lady of Larkspur Lotion as far as the use of imagination's concerned!

WRITER: (*in a tired voice*) Ah, well, now, what if I am? Suppose there *is* no 780-page masterpiece in existence. (*He closes his eyes and touches his forehead.*) Supposing there is in existence no masterpiece whatsoever! What of that, Mrs. Wire? But only a few, a very few—vain scribblings—in my old trunk-bottom. . . . Suppose I wanted to be a great artist but lacked the force and the power! Suppose my books fell short of the final chapter, even my verses languished uncompleted! Suppose the curtains of my exalted fancy rose on magnificent dramas—but the house-lights darkened before the curtain fell! Suppose all of these unfortunate things are true! And suppose that I—stumbling from bar to bar, from drink to drink, till I sprawl at last on the lice-infested mattress of this brothel—suppose that I, to make this nightmare bearable for as long as I must continue to be the helpless protagonist of it—suppose that I ornament, illuminate—glorify it! With dreams and fictions and fancies! Such as the existence of a 780-page masterpiece—impending Broadway productions—marvelous volumes of verse in the hands of publishers only waiting for signatures to release them! Suppose that I live in this world of pitiful fiction! What satisfaction can it give you, good woman, to tear it to pieces, to crush it—call it a *lie?* I tell you this—now listen! There are no lies but the lies that are stuffed in the mouth by the hard-knuckled hand of need, the cold iron fist of necessity, Mrs. Wire! So I am a liar, yes! But your world is built on a lie, your world is a hideous fabrication of lies! Lies! Lies! . . . Now I'm tired and I've said my say and I have no money to give you so get away and leave this woman in peace! Leave her alone. Go on, get out, get away! (*He shoves her firmly out the door.*)

MRS. WIRE: (*shouting from the other side*) Tomorrow morning! Money or out you go! Both of you. Both together! 780-page masterpiece and Brazilian rubber plantation! *BALONEY!* (*Slowly the derelict Writer and the derelict woman turn to face each other. The daylight is waning grayly through the skylight. The Writer slowly and stiffly extends his arms in a gesture of helplessness.*)

MRS. HARDWICKE-MOORE: (*turning to avoid his look*) Roaches! Everywhere! Walls, ceiling, floor! The place is infested with them.

WRITER: (*gently*) I know. I suppose there weren't any roaches on the Brazilian rubber plantation.

MRS. HARDWICKE-MOORE: (*warming*) No, of course there weren't. Everything was immaculate always—always. *Immaculate!* The floors were so bright and clean they used to shine like—mirrors!

WRITER: I know. And the windows—I suppose they commanded a very lovely view!

MRS. HARDWICKE-MOORE: Indescribably lovely!

WRITER: How far was it from the Mediterranean?

MRS. HARDWICKE-MOORE: (*dimly*) The Mediterranean? Only a mile or two!

WRITER: On a very clear morning I daresay it was possible to distinguish the white chalk cliffs of Dover? . . . Across the channel?

MRS. HARDWICKE-MOORE: Yes—in very clear weather it *was.* (*The Writer silently passes her a pint bottle of whisky.*) Thank you, Mr.—?

WRITER: Chekhov! Anton Pavlovitch Chekhov!

MRS. HARDWICKE-MOORE: (*smiling with the remnants of coquetry*) Thank you, Mr.—Chekhov.

Curtain

The Last of My Solid Gold Watches

Ce ne peut être que la fin du monde, en avançant.
RIMBAUD

CHARACTERS

MR. CHARLIE COLTON.
A NEGRO, *a porter in the hotel.*
HARPER, *a traveling salesman.*

SCENE: *A hotel room in a Mississippi Delta town. The room has looked the same, with some deterioration, for thirty or forty years. The walls are mustard-colored. There are two windows with dull green blinds, torn slightly, a ceiling-fan, a white iron bed with a pink counterpane, a washstand with rose-buds painted on the pitcher and bowl, and on the wall a colored lithograph of blind-folded Hope with her broken lyre.*

The door opens and Mr. Charlie Colton comes in. He is a legendary character, seventy-eight years old but still "going strong." He is lavish of flesh, superbly massive and with a kingly dignity of bearing. Once he moved with a tidal ease and power. Now he puffs and rumbles; when no one is looking he clasps his hand to his chest and cocks his head to the warning heart inside him. His huge expanse of chest and belly is criss-crossed by multiple gold chains with various little fobs and trinkets suspended from them. On the back of his head is a derby and in his mouth a cigar. This is "Mistuh Charlie"—who sadly but proudly refers to himself as "the last of the Delta drummers." He is followed into the room by a Negro porter, as old as he is—thin and toothless and grizzled. He totes the long orange leather sample cases containing the shoes which Mr. Charlie is selling. He sets them down at the foot of the bed as Mr. Charlie fishes in his pocket for a quarter.

MR. CHARLIE: (*handing the coin to the Negro*) Hyunh!
NEGRO: (*breathlessly*) Thankyseh!

This play is inscribed to Mr. Sidney Greenstreet, for whom the principal character was hopefully conceived.

MR. CHARLIE: Huh! You're too old a darkey to tote them big heavy cases.

NEGRO: (*grinning sadly*) Don't say that, Mistuh Charlie.

MR. CHARLIE: I reckon you'll keep right at it until yuh drop some day.

NEGRO: That's right, Mistuh Charlie. (*Mr. Charlie fishes in his pocket for another quarter and tosses it to the Negro, who crouches and cackles as he receives it.*)

MR. CHARLIE: Hyunh!

NEGRO: Thankyseh, thankyseh!

MR. CHARLIE: Now set that fan in motion an' bring me in some ice-water by an' by!

NEGRO: De fan don' work, Mistuh Charlie.

MR. CHARLIE: Huh! Deterioration! Everything's going down-hill around here lately!

NEGRO: Yes, suh, dat's de troof, Mistuh Charlie, ev'ything's goin' down-hill.

MR. CHARLIE: Who all's registered here of my acquaintance? Any ole-timers in town?

NEGRO: Naw, suh, Mistuh Charlie.

MR. CHARLIE: "Naw-suh-Mistuh-Charlie" 's all I get any more! You mean to say I won't be able to scare up a poker-game?

NEGRO: (*chuckling sadly*) Mistuh Charlie, you's de bes' judge about dat!

MR. CHARLIE: Well, it's mighty slim pickin's these days. Ev'ry time I come in a town there's less of the old and more of the new and by God, nigguh, this new stand of cotton I see around the Delta's not worth pickin' off th' ground! Go down there an' tell that young fellow, Mr. Bob Harper, to drop up here for a drink!

NEGRO: (*withdrawing*) Yes, suh.

MR. CHARLIE: It looks like otherwise I'd be playin' solitaire!

(*The Negro closes the door. Mr. Charlie crosses to the window and raises the blind. The evening is turning faintly blue. He sighs and opens his valise to remove a quart of whisky and some decks of cards which he slaps down on the table. He pauses and clasps his hand over his chest.*)

MR. CHARLIE: (*ominously to himself*) Boom-boom-boom-boom-boom! Here comes th' parade! (*After some moments *there comes a rap at the door.*) Come awn in! (*Harper, a salesman of thirty-five, enters. He has never known the "great days of the road" and there is no vestige of grandeur in his manner. He is lean and sallow and has a book of colored comics stuffed in his coat pocket.*)

HARPER: How is the ole war-horse?

MR. CHARLIE: (*heartily*) Mighty fine an' dandy! How's the young squirrel?

HARPER: Okay.

MR. CHARLIE: That's the right answer! Step on in an' pour you'self a drink! Cigar?

HARPER: (*accepting both*) Thanks, Charlie.

MR. CHARLIE: (*staring at his back with distaste*) Why do you carry them comic sheets around with yuh?

HARPER: Gives me a couple of laughs ev'ry once and a while.

MR. CHARLIE: Poverty of imagination! (*Harper laughs a little resentfully.*) You can't tell me there's any real amusement in them things. (*He pulls it out of Harper's coat pocket.*) "Superman," "The Adventures of Tom Tyler!" Huh! None of it's half as fantastic as life itself! When you arrive at my age—which is seventy-eight—you have a perspective of time on earth that astounds you! Literally astounds you! Naw, you say it's not true, all of that couldn't have happened! And for what *reason?* Naw! You begin to wonder. . . . Well . . . You're with Schultz and Werner?

HARPER: That's right, Charlie.

MR. CHARLIE: That concern's comparatively a new one.

HARPER: I don't know about that. They been in th' bus'ness fo' goin' on twenty-five years now, Charlie.

MR. CHARLIE: Infancy! Infancy! You heard this one, Bob? A child in its infancy don't have half as much fun as adults—in their adultery! (*He roars with laughter. Harper grins. Mr. Charlie falls silent abruptly. He would have appreciated a more profound response. He remembers the time when a joke of his would precipitate a tornado. He fills up Harper's glass with whisky.*)

HARPER: Ain't you drinkin'?

MR. CHARLIE: Naw, suh. Quit!

HARPER: How come?

MR. CHARLIE: Stomach! Perforated!

HARPER: Ulcers? (*Mr. Charlie grunts. He bends with difficulty and heaves a sample case onto the bed.*) I had ulcers once.

MR. CHARLIE: *Ev'ry* drinkin' man has ulcers once. Some *twice.*

HARPER: You've fallen off some, ain't you?

MR. CHARLIE: (*opening the sample case*) Twenty-seven pounds I lost since August. (*Harper whistles. Mr. Charlie is fishing among his samples.*) Yay-*ep!* Twenty-seven pounds I lost since August. (*He pulls out an oxford which he regards disdainfully.*) Hmmm. . . . A waste of cow-hide! (*He throws it back in and continues fishing.*) A man of my age an' constitution, Bob—he oughtn't to carry so much of that—adipose tissue! It's— (*He straightens up, red in the face and puffing.*) —a terrible strain—on the *heart!* Hand me that other sample—over yonder. I wan' t' show you a little eyeful of queenly footwear in our new spring line! Some people say that the Cosmopolitan's not abreast of the times! That is an allegation which I deny and which I intend to disprove by the simple display of one little calf-skin slipper! (*opening up the second case*) Here we are, Son! (*fishing among the samples*) You knew ole "Marblehead" Langner in Friar's Point, Mississippi.

HARPER: Ole "Marblehead" Langner? Sure.

MR. CHARLIE: They found him dead in his bath-tub a week ago Satiddy night. *Here's* what I'm lookin' faw!

HARPER: "Marblehead"? Dead?

MR. CHARLIE: *Buried!* Had a Masonic funeral. I helped carry th' casket. Bob, I want you t' look at this Cuban-heel, shawl-tongue, perforated toe, calf-skin Misses' sport-oxford! (*He elevates it worshipfully.*) I want you to look at this shoe —and tell me what you think of it in plain language! (*Harper whistles and bugs his eyes.*) Ain't that a piece of *real* merchandise, you squirrel? Well, suh, I want you t' know—!

HARPER: Charlie, that certainly is a piece of merchandise there!

MR. CHARLIE: Bob, that piece of merchandise is only a small indication—of what our spring line consists of! You don't have to pick up a piece of merchandise like that—with I.S.C. branded on it!—and examine it with the microscope t' find out if it's quality stuff as well as quality *looks!* This ain't a shoe that Mrs. Jones of Hattiesburg, Mississippi, is going to throw back in your face a couple or three weeks later because it come to pieces like *card*-board in th' first *rain!* No, suh—I want you to know! We got some pretty fast-movers in our spring line—I'm layin' my samples out down there in th' lobby first thing in th' mornin'—I'll pack 'em up an' be gone out of town by *noon*— But by the Almighty Jehovah I bet you I'll have to *wire* the office to mail me a bunch of *brand*-new order-books at my next stopping-*off* place, Bob! *Hot* cakes! *That's* what I'm sellin'! (*He returns exhaustedly to the sample case and tosses the shoe back in, somewhat disheartened by Harper's vaguely benevolent contemplation of the brass light-fixture. He remembers a time when people's attention could be more securely riveted by talk. He slams the case shut and glances irritably at Harper who is staring very sadly at the brown carpet.*) Well, suh—(*He pours a shot of whisky.*) It was a mighty shocking piece of news I received this afternoon.

HARPER: (*blowing a smoke ring*) What piece of news was that?

MR. CHARLIE: The news about ole Gus Hamma—one of the old war-horses from *way* back, Bob. He and me an' this boy's daddy, C.C., used t' play poker ev'ry time we hit town together in this here self-same room! Well, suh, I want you t' know—

HARPER: (*screwing up his forehead*) I think I heard about that. Didn't he have a stroke or something a few months ago?

MR. CHARLIE: He *did*. An' partly *recovered.*

HARPER: Yeah? Last I heard he had t' be fed with a spoon.

MR. CHARLIE: (*quickly*) He did an' he partly recovered! He's been goin' round, y'know, in one of them chairs with a 'lectric motor on it. Goes chug-chug-chuggin' along th' road with th' butt of a cigar in his mouth. Well, suh, yestuddy in Blue Mountain, as I go out the Elks' Club door I pass him comin' in, bein' helped by th' nigguh—"Hello! Hiyuh, Gus!" That was at six-fifteen. Just half an hour later Carter Bowman stepped inside the hotel lobby where I was packin' up my sample cases an' give me the information that ole Gus Hamma had just now burnt himself to death in the Elks' Club lounge!

HARPER: (*involuntarily grinning*) What uh yuh talkin' about?

MR. CHARLIE: Yes, suh, the ole war-horse had fallen asleep with that nickel cigar in his mouth—set his clothes on fire—and burnt himself right up like a piece of paper!

HARPER: I don't believe yuh!

MR. CHARLIE: Now, why on earth would I be lyin' to yuh about a thing like that? He burnt himself right up like a piece of paper!

HARPER: Well, ain't that a bitch of a way for a man to go?

MR. CHARLIE: *One* way—*another* way—! (*gravely*) Maybe you don't *know* it—but all of us ole-timers, Bob, are disappearin' *fast!* We all gotta quit th' road one time or another. Me, I reckon I'm pretty nearly the last of th' Delta drummers!

HARPER: (*restively squirming and glancing at his watch*) The last—of th' Delta drummers! How long you been on th' road?

MR. CHARLIE: Fawty-six yeahs in Mahch!

HARPER: I don't believe yuh.

MR. CHARLIE: Why would I tell you a lie about something like that? No, suh, I want you t' know— I want you t' know— Hmmm. . . . I lost a mighty good customer this week.

HARPER: (*with total disinterest, adjusting the crotch of his trousers*) How's that, Charlie?

MR. CHARLIE: (*grimly*) Ole Ben Summers—Friar's Point, Mississippi . . . Fell over dead like a bolt of lightning had struck him just as he went to pour himself a drink at the Cotton Planters' Cotillion!

HARPER: Ain't that terrible, though! What was the trouble?

MR. CHARLIE: Mortality, that was the trouble! Some people think that millions now living are never going to *die.* I don't think that—I think it's a misapprehension not borne out by the facts! We go like flies when we come to the end of the summer . . . And who is going to prevent it? (*He becomes depressed.*) Who—is going—to prevent it! (*He nods gravely.*) The road is changed. The shoe industry is changed. These times are—revolution! (*He rises and moves to the window.*) I don't like the way that it looks. You can take it from me—the world that I used to know—the world that this boy's father used t' know—the world we belonged to, us old time war-horses!—is slipping and sliding away from under our shoes. Who is going to prevent it? The ALL LEATHER slogan don't sell shoes any more. The stuff that a shoe's made of is not what's going to sell it any more! No! STYLE! SMARTNESS! APPEARANCE! That's what counts with the modern shoe-purchaser, Bob! But try an' tell your style department that. Why, I remember the time when all I had to do was lay out my samples down there in the lobby. Open up my order-book an' write out orders until my fingers *ached!* A *sales*-talk was not *necessary.* A store was a place where people sold merchandise and to sell merchandise the retail-dealer had to obtain it from the wholesale manufacturer, Bob! Where they get merchandise now I do not pretend to know. But it don't look like they buy it from wholesale dealers! Out of the air—I guess it materializes! Or maybe stores don't *sell* stuff any more! Maybe I'm living in a world of illusion! I recognize that possibility, too!

HARPER: (*casually, removing the comic paper from his pocket*) Yep—yep. You must have witnessed some changes.

MR. CHARLIE: Changes? A mild expression. Young man—I have witnessed—a REVOLUTION! (*Harper has opened his comic paper but Mr. Charlie doesn't notice, for now his peroration is really addressed to himself.*) Yes, a *revolution!* The atmosphere that I *breathe* is not the same! Ah, well—I'm an old war-horse. (*He opens his coat and lifts the multiple golden chains from his vest. An amazing number of watches rise into view. Softly, proudly he speaks.*) Looky here, young fellow! You ever seen a man with this many watches? How did I *acquire* this many time-pieces? (*Harper has seen them before. He glances above the comic sheet with affected amazement.*) At every one of the annual sales conventions of the Cosmopolitan Shoe Company in St. Louis a seventeen-jewel, solid-gold, Swiss-movement Hamilton watch is presented to the ranking salesman of the year! Fifteen of those watches have been awarded to me! I think that represents something! I think that's *something* in the way of achievement! . . . Don't *you?*

HARPER: Yes, *siree!* You bet I *do,* Mistuh Charlie! (*He chuckles at a remark in the comic sheet. Mr. Charlie sticks out his *lips with a grunt of disgust and snatches the comic sheet from the young man's hands.*)

MR. CHARLIE: Young man—I'm talkin' to *you*, I'm talkin' for your *benefit.* And I expect the courtesy of your attention until I am through! I may be an old war-horse. I may have received—the last of my solid gold watches . . . But just the same—good manners are still a part of the road's tradition. And part of the *South's* tradition. Only a young peckerwood would look at the comics when old Charlie Colton is talking.

HARPER: (*taking another drink*) Excuse me, Charlie. I got a lot on my mind. I got some business to attend to directly.

MR. CHARLIE: And directly you shall attend to it! I just want you to know what I think of this new world of yours! I'm not one of those that go howling about a Communist being stuck in the White House now! I don't say that Washington's been took over by Reds! I don't say all of the wealth of the country is in the hands of the Jews! I like the Jews and I'm a friend to the niggers! I *do* say *this*—however. . . . The world I knew is gone—gone—gone with the wind! My pockets are full of watches which tell me that my time's just about over! (*A look of great trouble and bewilderment appears on his massive face. The rather noble tone of his speech slackens into a senile complaint.*) All of them—pigs that was slaughtered—carcasses dumped in the river! Farmers receivin' payment *not* t' grow wheat an' corn an' *not* t' plant cotton! All of these alphabet letters that's sprung up all about me! Meaning—unknown—to men of my generation! The rudeness—the lack of respect—the newspapers full of strange items! The terrible—fast—dark—rush of events in the world! Toward what and where and why! . . . I don't pretend to have any knowledge of now! I only say—and I say this very humbly—I don't understand—what's happened. . . . I'm one of them monsters you see reproduced in museums—out of the dark old ages—the giant *rep*-tiles, and the dino-whatever-you-call-ems. BUT—I *do* know *this!* And I state it without any shame! Initiative—self-reliance—independence of character! The old sterling qualities that distinguished one man from another—the clay from the potters—the potters from the clay—are— (*kneading the air with his hands*) How is it the old song goes? . . . Gone with the roses of *yesterday!* Yes—with the *wind!*

HARPER: (*whose boredom has increased by leaps and bounds*) You old-timers make one mistake. You only read one side of the vital statistics.

MR. CHARLIE: (*stung*) What do you mean by that?

HARPER: In the papers they print people *dead* in one corner and people *born* in the next and usually *one* just about levels *off* with the *other*.

MR. CHARLIE: Thank you for that information. I happen to be the godfather of several new infants in various points on the road. However, I think you have missed the whole point of what I was saying.

HARPER: I don't think so, Mr. Charlie.

MR. CHARLIE: Oh, yes, you have, young fellow. My point is this: the ALL-LEATHER slogan is not what sells any more—not in shoes and not in humanity, neither! The emphasis isn't on quality. Production, production, yes! But out of inferior goods! *Ersatz*—that's what they're making 'em out of!

HARPER: (*getting up*) That's your opinion because you belong to the past.

MR. CHARLIE: (*furiously*) A piece of impertinence, young man! I expect to be accorded a certain amount of respect by whipper-snappers like you!

HARPER: Hold on, Charlie.

MR. CHARLIE: I belong to—tradition. I am a *legend*. Known from one end of the Delta to the other. From the Peabody hotel in Memphis to Cat-Fish Row in Vicksburg. Mistuh Charlie—*Mistuh Charlie!* Who knows *you*? What do *you* represent? A line of goods of doubtful value, some kike concern in the East! Get out of my room! I'd rather play solitaire, than poker with men who're no more solid characters than the jacks in the deck! (*He opens the door for the young salesman who shrugs and steps out with alacrity. Then he slams the door shut and breathes heavily. The Negro enters with a pitcher of ice water.*)

NEGRO: (*grinning*) What you shoutin' about, Mistuh Charlie?

MR. CHARLIE: I lose my patience sometimes. Nigger—

NEGRO: Yes, suh?

MR. CHARLIE: You remember the way it used to be.

NEGRO: (*gently*) Yes, suh.

MR. CHARLIE: I used to come in town like a conquering hero! Why, my God, nigger—they all but laid red carpets at my feet! Isn't that so?

NEGRO: That's so, Mistuh Charlie.

MR. CHARLIE: This room was like a *throne*-room. My samples laid out over there on green velvet cloth! The ceiling-fan *going*—now *broken!* And over here—the wash-bowl an' pitcher removed and the table-top *loaded* with *liquor!* In and out from the time I arrived till the time I left, the men of the road who knew me, to whom I stood for things commanding respect! Poker—continuous! Shouting, laughing—hilarity! Where have they all gone to?

NEGRO: (*solemnly nodding*) The graveyard is crowded with folks we knew, Mistuh Charlie. It's mighty late in the day!

MR. CHARLIE: Huh! (*He crosses to the window.*) Nigguh, it ain't even late in the day any more— (*He throws up the blind.*) It's NIGHT! (*The space of the window is black.*)

NEGRO: (*softly, with a wise old smile*) Yes, suh . . . *Night*, Mistuh Charlie!

Curtain

Portrait of a Madonna

Respectfully dedicated to the talent and charm of Miss Lillian Gish.

CHARACTERS

MISS LUCRETIA COLLINS.
THE PORTER.
THE ELEVATOR BOY.
THE DOCTOR.
THE NURSE.
MR. ABRAMS.

SCENE: *The living room of a moderate-priced city apartment. The furnishings are old-fashioned and everything is in a state of neglect and disorder. There is a door in the back wall to a bedroom, and on the right to the outside hall.*

MISS COLLINS: Richard! (*The door bursts open and Miss Collins rushes out, distractedly. She is a middle-aged spinster, very slight and hunched of figure with a desiccated face that is flushed with excitement. Her hair is arranged in curls that would become a young girl and she wears a frilly negligee which might have come from an old hope chest of a period considerably earlier.*) No, no, no, no! I don't care if the whole church hears about it! (*She frenziedly snatches up the phone.*) Manager, I've got to speak to the manager! Hurry, oh, please hurry, there's a *man*—! (*wildly aside as if to an invisible figure*) Lost all respect, absolutely no respect! . . . Mr. Abrams? (*in a tense hushed voice*) I don't want any reporters to hear about this but something awful has been going on upstairs. Yes, this is Miss Collins' apartment on the top floor. I've refrained from making any complaint because of my connections with the church. I used to be assistant to the Sunday School superintendent and I once had the primary class. I helped them put on the Christmas pageant. I made the dress for the Virgin and Mother, made robes for the Wise Men. Yes, and now this has happened,

I'm not responsible for it, but night after night after night this man has been coming into my apartment and—indulging his senses! Do you understand? Not once but repeatedly, Mr. Abrams! I don't know whether he comes in the door or the window or up the fire-escape or whether there's some secret entrance they know about at the church, but he's here now, in my bedroom, and I can't force him to leave, I'll have to have some assistance! No, he isn't a thief, Mr. Abrams, he comes of a very fine family in Webb, Mississippi, but this woman has ruined his character, she's destroyed his respect for ladies! Mr. Abrams? Mr. Abrams! Oh, goodness! (*She slams up the receiver and looks distractedly about for a moment; then rushes back into the bedroom.*) *Richard!* (*The door slams shut. After a few moments an old porter enters in drab gray cover-alls. He looks about with a sorrowfully humorous curiosity, then timidly calls.*)

PORTER: Miss Collins? (*The elevator door slams open in hall and the Elevator Boy, wearing a uniform, comes in.*)

ELEVATOR BOY: Where is she?

PORTER: Gone in 'er bedroom.

ELEVATOR BOY: (*grinning*) She got him in there with her?

PORTER: Sounds like it. (*Miss Collins' voice can be heard faintly protesting with the mysterious intruder.*)

ELEVATOR BOY: What'd Abrams tell yuh to do?

PORTER: Stay here an' keep a watch on 'er till they git here.

ELEVATOR BOY: Jesus.

PORTER: Close 'at door.

ELEVATOR BOY: I gotta leave it open a little so I can hear the buzzer. Ain't this place a holy sight though?

PORTER: Don't look like it's had a good cleaning in fifteen or twenty years. I bet it ain't either. Abrams'll bust a blood-vessel when he takes a lookit them walls.

ELEVATOR BOY: How comes it's in this condition?

PORTER: She wouldn't let no one in.

ELEVATOR BOY: Not even the paper-hangers?

PORTER: Naw. Not even the plumbers. The plaster washed down in the bathroom underneath hers an' she admitted her plumbin' had been stopped up. Mr. Abrams had to let the plumber in with this here pass-key when she went out for a while.

ELEVATOR BOY: Holy Jeez. I wunner if she's got money stashed around here. A lotta freaks do stick away big sums of money in ole mattresses an' things.

PORTER: She ain't. She got a monthly pension check or something she always turned over to Mr. Abrams to dole it out to 'er. She tole him that Southern ladies was never brought up to manage finanshul affairs. Lately the checks quit comin'.

ELEVATOR BOY: Yeah?

PORTER: The pension give out or somethin'. Abrams says he got a contribution from the church to keep 'er on here without 'er knowin' about it. She's proud as a peacock's tail in spite of 'er awful appearance.

ELEVATOR BOY: Lissen to 'er in there!

PORTER: What's she sayin'?

ELEVATOR BOY: Apologizin' to him! For callin' the *police!*

PORTER: She thinks police 're comin'?

MISS COLLINS: (*from bedroom*) Stop it, it's got to stop!

ELEVATOR BOY: Fightin' to protect her honor again! What a commotion, no wunner folks are complainin'!

PORTER: (*lighting his pipe*) This here'll be the last time.

ELEVATOR BOY: She's goin' out, huh?

PORTER: (*blowing out the match*) Tonight.

ELEVATOR BOY: Where'll she go?

PORTER: (*slowly moving to the old gramophone*) She'll go to the state asylum.

ELEVATOR BOY: Holy G!

PORTER: Remember this ole number? (*He puts on a record of "I'm Forever Blowing Bubbles."*)

ELEVATOR BOY: Naw. When did that come out?

PORTER: Before your time, sonny boy. Machine needs oilin'. (*He takes out small oil-can and applies oil about the crank and other parts of gramophone.*)

ELEVATOR BOY: How long is the old girl been here?

PORTER: Abrams says she's been livin' here twenty-five, thirty years, since before he got to be manager even.

ELEVATOR BOY: Livin' alone all that time?

PORTER: She had an old mother died of an operation about fifteen years ago. Since then she ain't gone out of the place excep' on Sundays to church or Friday nights to some kind of religious meeting.

ELEVATOR BOY: Got an awful lot of ol' magazines piled aroun' here.

PORTER: She used to collect 'em. She'd go out in back and fish 'em out of the incinerator.

ELEVATOR BOY: What'n hell for?

PORTER: Mr. Abrams says she used to cut out the Campbell soup kids. Them red-tomato-headed kewpie dolls that go with the soup advertisements. You seen 'em, ain'tcha?

ELEVATOR BOY: Uh-huh.

PORTER: She made a collection of 'em. Filled a big lot of scrapbooks with them paper kiddies an' took 'em down to the Children's Hospitals on Xmas Eve an' Easter Sunday, exactly twicet a year. Sounds better, don't it? (*referring to gramophone, which resumes its faint, wheedling music*) Eliminated some a that crankin' noise . . .

ELEVATOR BOY: I didn't know that she'd been nuts *that* long.

PORTER: Who's nuts an' who ain't? If you ask me the world is populated with people that's just as peculiar as she is.

ELEVATOR BOY: Hell. She don't have brain *one.*

PORTER: There's important people in Europe got less'n she's got. Tonight they're takin' her off 'n' lockin' her up. They'd do a lot better to leave 'er go an' lock up some a them maniacs over there. She's harmless; they ain't. They kill millions of people an' go scot free!

ELEVATOR BOY: An ole woman like her is disgusting, though, imaginin' somebody's raped her.

PORTER: Pitiful, not disgusting. Watch out for them cigarette ashes.

ELEVATOR BOY: What's uh diff'rence? So much dust you can't see it. All a this here goes out in the morning, don't it?

PORTER: Uh-huh.

ELEVATOR BOY: I think I'll take a couple a those ole records as curiosities for my girl friend. She's got a portable in 'er bedroom, she says it's better with music!

PORTER: Leave 'em alone. She's still got 'er property rights.

ELEVATOR BOY: Aw, she's got all she wants with them dream-lovers of hers!

PORTER: *Hush up! (He makes a warning gesture as Miss Collins enters from bedroom. Her appearance is that of a ravaged woman. She leans exhaustedly in the doorway, hands clasped over her flat, virginal bosom.*)

MISS COLLINS: (*breathlessly*) Oh, Richard—Richard . . .

PORTER: (*coughing*) Miss—Collins.

ELEVATOR BOY: Hello, Miss Collins.

MISS COLLINS: (*just noticing the men*) Goodness! You've arrived already! Mother didn't tell me you were here! (*Self-consciously she touches her ridiculous corkscrew curls with the faded pink ribbon tied through them. Her manner becomes that of a slightly coquettish but prim little Southern belle.*) I must ask you gentlemen to excuse the terrible disorder.

PORTER: That's all right, Miss Collins.

MISS COLLINS: It's the maid's day off. Your No'thern girls receive such excellent domestic training, but in the South it was never considered essential for a girl to have anything but prettiness and charm! (*She laughs girlishly.*) Please do sit down. Is it too close? Would you like a window open?

PORTER: No, Miss Collins.

MISS COLLINS: (*advancing with delicate grace to the sofa*) Mother will bring in something cool after while. . . . Oh, my! (*She touches her forehead.*)

PORTER: (*kindly*) Is anything wrong, Miss Collins?

MISS COLLINS: Oh, no, no, thank you, nothing! My head is a little bit heavy. I'm always a little bit—malarial—this time of year! (*She sways dizzily as she starts to sink down on the sofa.*)

PORTER: (*helping her*) Careful there, Miss Collins.

MISS COLLINS: (*vaguely*) Yes, it is, I hadn't noticed before. (*She peers at them near-sightedly with a hesitant smile.*) You gentlemen have come from the church?

PORTER: No, ma'am. I'm Nick, the porter, Miss Collins, and this boy here is Frank that runs the elevator.

MISS COLLINS: (*stiffening a little*) Oh? . . . I don't understand.

PORTER: (*gently*) Mr. Abrams just asked me to drop in here an' see if you was getting along all right.

MISS COLLINS: Oh! Then he must have informed you of what's been going on in here!

PORTER: He mentioned some kind of—disturbance.

MISS COLLINS: Yes! Isn't it outrageous? But it mustn't go any further, you understand. I mean you mustn't repeat it to other people.

PORTER: No, I wouldn't say nothing.

MISS COLLINS: Not a word of it, please!

ELEVATOR BOY: Is the man still here, Miss Collins?

MISS COLLINS: Oh, no. No, he's gone now.

ELEVATOR BOY: How did he go, out the bedroom window, Miss Collins?

MISS COLLINS: (*vaguely*) Yes. . . .

ELEVATOR BOY: I seen a guy that could do that once. He crawled straight up the side of the building. They called him The Human Fly! Gosh, that's a wonderful publicity angle, Miss Collins—"Beautiful Young Society Lady Raped by The Human Fly!"

PORTER: (*nudging him sharply*) Git back in your cracker box!

MISS COLLINS: Publicity? No! It would be so humiliating! Mr. Abrams surely hasn't reported it to the papers!

PORTER: No, ma'am. Don't listen to this smarty pants.

MISS COLLINS: (*touching her curls*) Will pictures be taken, you think? There's one of him on the mantel.

ELEVATOR BOY: (*going to the mantel*) This one here, Miss Collins?

MISS COLLINS: Yes. Of the Sunday School faculty picnic. I had the little kindergarteners that year and he had the older boys. We rode in the cab of a railroad locomotive from Webb to Crystal Springs. (*She covers her ears with a girlish grimace and toss of her curls.*) Oh, how the steam-whistle blew! Blew! (*giggling*) *Blewwwww!* It frightened me so, he put his arm round my shoulders! But she was there, too, though she had no business being. She grabbed his hat and stuck it on the back of her head and they—they *rassled* for it, they actually *rassled* together! Everyone said it was *shameless!* Don't you think that it was?

PORTER: Yes, Miss Collins.

MISS COLLINS: That's the picture, the one in the silver frame up there on the mantel. We cooled the watermelon in the springs and afterwards played games. She hid somewhere and he took ages to find her. It got to be dark and he hadn't found her yet and everyone whispered and giggled about it and finally they came back together—her hangin' on to his arm like a common little strumpet—and Daisy Belle Huston shrieked out, "Look, everybody, the seat of Evelyn's skirt!" It was—covered with—grass-stains! Did you ever hear of anything as outrageous? It didn't faze her, though, she laughed like it was something very, very amusing! Rather *triumphant* she was!

ELEVATOR BOY: Which one is him, Miss Collins?

MISS COLLINS: The tall one in the blue shirt holding onto one of my curls. He loved to play with them.

ELEVATOR BOY: Quite a Romeo—1910 model, huh?

MISS COLLINS: (*vaguely*) Do you? It's nothing, really, but I like the lace on the collar. I said to Mother, "Even if I don't wear it, Mother, it will be *so* nice for my hope-chest!"

ELEVATOR BOY: How was he dressed tonight when he climbed into your balcony, Miss Collins?

MISS COLLINS: Pardon?

ELEVATOR BOY: Did he still wear that nifty little stick-candy-striped blue shirt with the celluloid collar?

MISS COLLINS: He hasn't changed.

ELEVATOR BOY: Oughta be easy to pick him up in that. What color pants did he wear?

MISS COLLINS: (*vaguely*) I don't remember.

ELEVATOR BOY: Maybe he didn't wear any. Shimmied out of 'em on the way up the wall! You could get him on grounds of indecent exposure, Miss Collins!

PORTER: (*grasping his arm*) Cut that or git back in your cage! Understand?

ELEVATOR BOY: (*snickering*) Take it easy. She don't hear a thing.

PORTER: Well, you keep a decent tongue or get to hell out. Miss Collins here is a lady. You understand that?

ELEVATOR BOY: Okay. She's Shoiley Temple.

PORTER: She's a *lady!*

ELEVATOR BOY: Yeah! (*He returns to the gramophone and looks through the records.*)

MISS COLLINS: I really shouldn't have created this disturbance. When the officers come I'll have to explain that to them. But you can understand my feelings, can't you?

PORTER: Sure, Miss Collins.

MISS COLLINS: When men take advantage of common white-trash women who smoke in public there is probably some excuse for it, but when it occurs to a lady who is single and always com-*pletely* above reproach in her moral behavior, there's really nothing to do but call for police protection! Unless of course the girl is fortunate enough to have a father and brothers who can take care of the matter privately without any scandal.

PORTER: Sure. That's right, Miss Collins.

MISS COLLINS: Of course it's bound to cause a great deal of very disagreeable talk. Especially 'round the *church!* Are you gentlemen Episcopalian?

PORTER: No, ma'am. Catholic, Miss Collins.

MISS COLLINS: Oh. Well, I suppose you know in England we're known as the English Catholic church. We have direct Apostolic succession through St. Paul who christened the Early Angles—which is what the original English people were called—and established the English branch of the Catholic church over there. So when you hear ignorant people claim that our church was founded by—by Henry the *Eighth*—that horrible, *lech*erous old man who had so many wives—as many as *Blue*-beard they say!—you can see how ridiculous it *is* and how thoroughly ob*nox*-ious to anybody who really *knows* and under*stands* Church *His*tory!

PORTER: (*comfortingly*) Sure, Miss Collins. Everybody knows that.

MISS COLLINS: I wish they *did*, but they need to be in*struc*ted! Before he died, my father was Rector at the Church of St. Michael and St. George at Glorious Hill, Mississippi. . . . I've literally grown up right in the very *shad*ow of the Episcopal church. At Pass Christian and Natchez, Biloxi, Gulfport, Port Gibson, Columbus and Glorious Hill! (*with gentle, bewildered sadness*) But you know I sometimes suspect that there has been some kind of spiritual schism in the modern church. These northern dioceses have completely departed from the good old church traditions. For instance our Rector at the Church of the Holy Communion has never darkened my door. It's a fashionable church and he's terribly busy, but even so you'd think he might have time to make a stranger in the congregation feel at home. But he doesn't though! Nobody seems to have the time any more. . . . (*She grows more excited as her mind sinks back into illusion.*) I ought not to mention this, but do you know they actually take a malicious de*light* over there at the Holy Communion—where I've recently transferred my letter—in what's been going on here at night in this apartment? *Yes!!* (*She laughs wildly and throws up her hands.*) They take a malicious de*LIGHT* in it!! (*She catches her breath and gropes vaguely about her wrapper.*)

PORTER: You lookin' for somethin', Miss Collins?

MISS COLLINS: My—handkerchief . . . (*She is blinking her eyes against tears.*)

PORTER: (*removing a rag from his pocket*) Here. Use this, Miss Collins. It's just a rag but it's clean, except along that edge where I wiped off the phonograph handle.

MISS COLLINS: Thanks. You gentlemen are very kind. Mother will bring in something cool after while. . . .

ELEVATOR BOY: (*placing a record on machine*) This one is got some kind of foreign title. (*The record begins to play Tschaikowsky's "None But the Lonely Heart."*)

MISS COLLINS: (*stuffing the rag daintily in her bosom*) Excuse me, please. Is the weather nice outside?

PORTER: (*huskily*) Yes, it's nice, Miss Collins.

MISS COLLINS: (*dreamily*) So wa'm for this time of year. I wore my little astrakhan cape to service but had to *carry* it *home*, as the weight of it actually seemed *oppres*sive to me. (*Her eyes fall shut.*) The sidewalks seem so dreadfully long in summer. . . .

ELEVATOR BOY: This ain't summer, Miss Collins.

MISS COLLINS: (*dreamily*) I used to think I'd never get to the end of that last block. And that's the block where all the trees went down in the big tornado. The walk is simply *glit*-tering with sunlight. (*pressing her eyelids*) Impossible to shade your face and I *do* perspire so freely! (*She touches her forehead daintily with the rag.*) Not a branch, not a leaf to give you a little protection! You simply *have* to en-*dure* it. Turn your hideous red face away from all the front-porches and walk as fast as you decently *can* till you get *by* them!

Oh, dear, dear Savior, sometimes you're not so lucky and you *meet* people and have to *smile!* You can't *avoid* them unless you cut *across* and that's so *ob*-vious, you know. . . . People would say you're pe*cul*iar. . . . His house is right in the middle of that awful leafless block, *their* house, his and *hers*, and they have an automobile and always get home early and sit on the porch and *watch* me walking by—Oh, Father in Heaven—with a ma*li*cious de*light!* (*She averts her face in remembered torture.*) She has such *penetrating* eyes, they look straight through me. She sees that terrible choking thing in my throat and the pain I have in *here*—(*touching her chest*)—and she points it out and laughs and whispers to him, "There she goes with her shiny big red nose, the poor old maid—that *loves* you!" (*She chokes and hides her face in the rag.*)

PORTER: Maybe you better forget all that, Miss Collins.

MISS COLLINS: Never, never forget it! Never, never! I left my parasol once—the one with long white fringe that belonged to Mother—I left it behind in the cloak-room at the church so I didn't have anything to cover my face with when I walked by, and I couldn't turn back either, with all those people behind me—giggling back of me, poking fun at my clothes! Oh, dear, dear! I had to walk straight forward—past the last elm tree and into that *merciless* sunlight. Oh! It beat down on me, *scorching* me! *Whips!* . . . Oh, Jesus! . . . Over my face and my body! . . . I tried to walk on fast but was dizzy and they kept closer behind me—! I stumbled, I nearly fell, and all of them burst out laughing! My face turned so *horribly* red, it got so red and wet, I knew how ugly it was in all that merciless glare—not a single shadow to hide in! And then—(*Her face contorts with fear.*)—their automobile drove up in front of their house, right where I had to pass by it, and *she* stepped out, in white, so fresh and easy, her stomach round with a baby, the first of the *six*. Oh, God! . . . And he stood smiling behind her, white and easy and cool, and they stood there waiting for me. *Waiting!* I had to keep on. What else could I do? I couldn't turn *back*, could I? *No!* I said dear *God*, strike me *dead!* He didn't, though. I put my head way down like I couldn't see them! You know what she did? She stretched out her hand to *stop* me! And *he*—he stepped up straight in front of me, *smiling*, blocking the walk with his terrible big white body! "*Lucretia*," he said, "Lucretia *Collins!*" I—I tried to speak but I couldn't, the breath went out of my body! I covered my face and—ran! . . . Ran! . . . *Ran!* (*beating the arm of the sofa*) Till I reached the end of the block—and the elm trees—*started* again. . . . Oh, Merciful Christ in Heaven, how *kind* they were! (*She leans back exhaustedly, her hand relaxed on sofa. She pauses and the music ends.*) I said to Mother, "Mother, we've got to leave town!" We *did* after that. And now after all these years he's finally remembered and come *back!* Moved away from that house and the woman and come *here*—I saw him in the back of the church one day. I wasn't sure—but it *was*. The night after that was the night that he first broke in—and indulged his senses with me. . . . He doesn't realize that I've changed, that I can't feel again the way that I used to feel, now that he's got six children by that Cincinnati girl—three in high-school already! Six! Think of that? Six children! I don't know what he'll say when he knows another one's coming! He'll probably blame *me* for it because a man always *does!* In spite of the fact that he *forced* me!

ELEVATOR BOY: (*grinning*) Did you say—a *baby*, Miss Collins?

MISS COLLINS: (*lowering her eyes but speaking with tenderness and pride*) Yes—I'm expecting a *child*.

ELEVATOR BOY: *Jeez!* (*He claps his hand over his mouth and turns away quickly.*)

MISS COLLINS: Even if it's not legitimate, I think it has a perfect right to its father's name—don't you?

PORTER: Yes. Sure, Miss Collins.

MISS COLLINS: A child is innocent and pure. No matter how it's conceived. And it must *not* be made to suffer! So I intend to dispose of the little property Cousin Ethel left me and give the child a private education where it won't come under the evil influence of the Christian church! I want to make sure that it doesn't grow up in the shadow of the cross and then have to walk along blocks that scorch you with terrible sunlight! (*The elevator buzzer sounds from the hall.*)

PORTER: Frank! Somebody wants to come up. (*The Elevator Boy goes out. The elevator door bangs shut. The Porter clears his throat.*) Yes, it'd be better—to go off some place else.

MISS COLLINS: If only I had the courage—but I don't. I've grown so used to it here, and people outside—it's always so *hard* to *face* them!

PORTER: Maybe you won't—have to face nobody, Miss Collins. (*The elevator door clangs open.*)

MISS COLLINS: (*rising fearfully*) Is someone coming—here?

PORTER: You just take it easy, Miss Collins.

MISS COLLINS: If that's the officers coming for Richard, tell them to go away. I've decided not to prosecute Mr. Martin. (*Mr. Abrams enters with the Doctor and the Nurse. The Elevator Boy gawks from the doorway. The Doctor is the weary, professional type, the Nurse hard and efficient. Mr. Abrams is a small, kindly person, sincerely troubled by the situation.*)

MISS COLLINS: (*shrinking back, her voice faltering*) I've decided not to—prosecute Mr. Martin . . .

DOCTOR: Miss Collins?

MR. ABRAMS: (*with attempted heartiness*) Yes, this is the lady you wanted to meet, Dr. White.

DOCTOR: Hmmm. (*briskly to the Nurse*) Go in her bedroom and get a few things together.

NURSE: Yes, sir. (*She goes quickly across to the bedroom.*)

MISS COLLINS: (*fearfully shrinking*) Things?

DOCTOR: Yes, Miss Tyler will help you pack up an overnight bag. (*smiling mechanically*) A strange place always seems more homelike the first few days when we have a few of our little personal articles around us.

MISS COLLINS: A strange—place?

DOCTOR: (*carelessly, making a memorandum*) Don't be disturbed, Miss Collins.

MISS COLLINS: I know! (*excitedly*) You've come from the Holy Communion to place me under arrest! On moral charges!

MR. ABRAMS: Oh, no, Miss Collins, you got the wrong idea. This is a doctor who—

DOCTOR: (*impatiently*) Now, now, you're just going away for a while till things get straightened out. (*He glances at his watch.*) Two-twenty-five! Miss Tyler?

NURSE: Coming!

MISS COLLINS: (*with slow and sad comprehension*) Oh. . . . I'm going away. . . .

MR. ABRAMS: She was always a lady, Doctor, such a perfect lady.

DOCTOR: Yes. No doubt.

MR. ABRAMS: It seems too bad!

MISS COLLINS: Let me—write him a note. A pencil? Please?

MR. ABRAMS: Here, Miss Collins. (*She takes the pencil and crouches over the table. The Nurse comes out with a hard, forced smile, carrying a suitcase.*)

DOCTOR: Ready, Miss Tyler?

NURSE: All ready, Dr. White. (*She goes up to Miss Collins.*) Come along, dear, we can tend to that later!

MR. ABRAMS: (*sharply*) Let her finish the note!

MISS COLLINS: (*straightening with a frightened smile*) It's—finished.

NURSE: All right, dear, come along. (*She propels her firmly toward the door.*)

MISS COLLINS: (*turning suddenly back*) Oh, Mr. Abrams!

MR. ABRAMS: Yes, Miss Collins?

MISS COLLINS: If he should come again—and find me gone—I'd rather you didn't tell him—about the baby. . . . I think its better for *me* to tell him *that.* (*gently smiling*) You know how men *are*, don't you?

MR. ABRAMS: Yes, Miss Collins.

PORTER: Goodbye, Miss Collins. (*The Nurse pulls firmly at her arm. She smiles over her shoulder with a slight apologetic gesture.*)

MISS COLLINS: Mother will bring in—something cool—after while . . . (*She disappears down the hall with the Nurse. The elevator door clangs shut with the metallic sound of a locked cage. The wires hum.*)

MR. ABRAMS: She wrote him a note.

PORTER: What did she write, Mr. Abrams?

MR. ABRAMS: "Dear—Richard. I'm going away for a while. But don't worry, I'll be back. I have a secret to tell you. Love—Lucretia." (*He coughs.*) We got to clear out this stuff an' pile it down in the basement till I find out where it goes.

PORTER: (*dully*) Tonight, Mr. Abrams?

MR. ABRAMS: (*roughly to hide his feeling*) No, no, not tonight, you old fool. Enough has happened tonight! (*then gently*) We can do it tomorrow. Turn out that bedroom light—and close the window. (*Music playing softly becomes audible as the men go out slowly, closing the door, and the light fades out.*)

Curtain

Auto-Da-Fé

A Tragedy in One Act

CHARACTERS

MME. DUVENET
ELOI,* *her son.*

SCENE: *The front porch of an old frame cottage in the Vieux Carré of New Orleans. There are palm or banana trees, one on either side of the porch steps: pots of geraniums and other vivid flowers along the low balustrade. There is an effect of sinister antiquity in the setting, even the flowers suggesting the richness of decay. Not far off on Bourbon Street the lurid procession of bars and hot-spots throws out distance-muted strains of the juke-organs and occasional shouts of laughter. Mme. Duvenet, a frail woman of sixty-seven, is rocking on the porch in the faint, sad glow of an August sunset. Eloi, her son, comes out the screen-door. He is a frail man in his late thirties, a gaunt, ascetic type with feverish dark eyes.*

Mother and son are both fanatics and their speech has something of the quality of poetic or religious incantation.

MME: DUVENET: Why did you speak so crossly to Miss Bordelon?

ELOI: (*standing against the column*) She gets on my nerves.

MME. DUVENET: You take a dislike to every boarder we get.

ELOI: She's not to be trusted. I think she goes in my room.

MME. DUVENET: What makes you think that?

ELOI: I've found some evidence of it.

MME. DUVENET: Well, I can assure you she doesn't go in your room.

ELOI: Somebody goes in my room and roots through my things.

*Pronounced Ell-wah. The part is created for Mr. John Abbott.

MME. DUVENET: Nobody ever touches a thing in your room.

ELOI: My room is my own. I don't want anyone in it.

MME. DUVENET: You know very well that I have to go in to clean it.

ELOI: I don't want it cleaned.

MME. DUVENET: You want the room to be filthy?

ELOI: Just don't go in it to clean it or anything else.

MME. DUVENET: How could you live in a room that was never cleaned?

ELOI: I'll clean it myself when cleaning is necessary.

MME. DUVENET: A person would think that you were concealing something.

ELOI: What would I have to conceal?

MME. DUVENET: Nothing that I can imagine. That's why it's so strange that you have such a strong objection to even your mother going into your room.

ELOI: Everyone wants a little privacy, Mother.

MME. DUVENET: (*stiffly*) Your privacy, Eloi, shall be regarded as sacred.

ELOI: Huh.

MME. DUVENET: I'll just allow the filth to accumulate there.

ELOI: (*sharply*) What do you mean by "the filth"?

MME. DUVENET: (*sadly*) The dust and disorder that you would rather live in than have your mother come in to clean it up.

ELOI: Your broom and your dust-pan wouldn't accomplish much. Even the air in this neighborhood is unclean.

MME. DUVENET: It is not as clean as it might be. I love clean window-curtains, I love white linen, I want immaculate, spotless things in a house.

ELOI: Then why don't we move to the new part of town where it's cleaner?

MME. DUVENET: The property in this block has lost all value. We couldn't sell our place for what it would cost us to put new paint on the walls.

ELOI: I don't understand you, Mother. You harp on purity, purity all the time, and yet you're willing to stay in the midst of corruption.

MME. DUVENET: I harp on nothing. I stay here because I have to. And as for corruption, I've never allowed it to touch me.

ELOI: It does, it does. We can't help breathing it here. It gets in our nostrils and even goes in our blood.

MME. DUVENET: I think you're the one that harps on things around here. You won't talk quietly. You always fly off on some tangent and raise your voice and get us all stirred up for no good reason.

ELOI: I've had about all that I can put up with, Mother.

MME. DUVENET: Then what do you want to do?

ELOI: Move, move. This asthma of mine, in a pure atmosphere uptown where the air is fresher, I know that I wouldn't have it nearly so often.

MME. DUVENET: I leave it entirely to you. If you can find someone to make an acceptable offer, I'm willing to move.

ELOI: You don't have the power to move or the will to break from anything that you're used to. You don't know how much we've been affected already!

MME. DUVENET: By what, Eloi?

ELOI: This fetid old swamp we live in, the Vieux Carré! Every imaginable kind of degeneracy springs up here, not at arm's length, even, but right in our presence!

MME. DUVENET: Now I think you're exaggerating a little.

ELOI: You read the papers, you hear people talk, you walk past open windows. You can't be entirely unconscious of what goes on! A woman was horribly mutilated last night. A man smashed a bottle and twisted the jagged end of it in her face.

MME. DUVENET: They bring such things on themselves by their loose behavior.

ELOI: Night after night there are crimes taking place in the parks.

MME. DUVENET: The parks aren't all in the Quarter.

ELOI: The parks aren't all in the Quarter but decadence is. This is the primary lesion, the—focal infection, the—chancre! In medical language, it spreads by—metastasis! It creeps through the capillaries and into the main blood vessels. From there it is spread all through the surrounding tissue! Finally nothing is left outside the decay!

MME. DUVENET: Eloi, you are being unnecessarily violent in your speech.

ELOI: I feel that strongly about it.

MME. DUVENET: You mustn't allow yourself to sound like a fanatic.

ELOI: You take no stand against it?

MME. DUVENET: You know the stand that I take.

ELOI: I know what ought to be done.

MME. DUVENET: There ought to be legislation to make for reforms.

ELOI: Not only reforms but action really drastic!

MME. DUVENET: I favor that, too, within all practical bounds.

ELOI: Practical, practical. You can't be practical, Mother, and wipe out evil! The town should be razed.

MME. DUVENET: You mean this old section torn down?

ELOI: Condemned and demolished!

MME. DUVENET: That's not a reasonable stand.

ELOI: It's the stand I take.

MME. DUVENET: Then I'm afraid you're not a reasonable person.

ELOI: I have good precedence for it.

MME. DUVENET: What do you mean?

ELOI: All through the Scriptures are cases of cities destroyed by the justice of fire when they got to be nests of foulness!

MME. DUVENET: Eloi, Eloi.

ELOI: Condemn it, I say, and purify it with fire!

MME. DUVENET: You're breathing hoarsely. That's what brings on asthma, over-excitement, not just breathing bad air!

ELOI: (*after a thoughtful pause*) I *am* breathing hoarsely.

MME. DUVENET: Sit down and try to relax.

ELOI: I can't any more.

MME. DUVENET: You'd better go in and take an amytal tablet.

ELOI: I don't want to get to depending too much on drugs. I'm not very well, I'm never well any more.

MME. DUVENET: You never will take the proper care of yourself.

ELOI: I can hardly remember the time when I really felt good.

MME. DUVENET: You've never been quite as strong as I'd like you to be.

ELOI: I seem to have chronic fatigue.

MME. DUVENET: The Duvenet trouble has always been mostly with nerves.

ELOI: Look! I had a sinus infection! You call that nerves?

MME. DUVENET: No, but—

ELOI: Look! This asthma, this choking, this suffocation I have, do you call that nerves?

MME. DUVENET: I never agreed with the doctor about that condition.

ELOI: You hate all doctors, you're rabid on the subject!

MME. DUVENET: I think all healing begins with faith in the spirit.

ELOI: How can I keep on going when I don't sleep?

MME. DUVENET: I think your insomnia's caused by eating at night.

ELOI: It soothes my stomach.

MME. DUVENET: Liquids would serve that purpose!

ELOI: Liquids don't satisfy me.

MME. DUVENET: Well, something digestible, then. A little hot cereal maybe with cocoa or Postum.

ELOI: All that kind of slop is nauseating to look at!

MME. DUVENET: I notice at night you won't keep the covers on you.

ELOI: I can't stand covers in summer.

MME. DUVENET: You've got to have something over your body at night.

ELOI: Oh, Lord, oh, Lord.

MME. DUVENET: Your body perspires and when it's exposed, you catch cold!

ELOI: You're rabid upon the subject of catching cold.

MME. DUVENET: Only because you're unusually prone to colds.

ELOI: (*with curious intensity*) It isn't a cold! It is a sinus infection!

MME. DUVENET: Sinus infection and all catarrhal conditions are caused by the same things as colds!

ELOI: At ten every morning, as regular as clock-work, a headache commences and doesn't let up till late in the afternoon.

MME. DUVENET: Nasal congestion is often the cause of headache.

ELOI: Nasal congestion has nothing to do with this one!

MME. DUVENET: How do you know?

ELOI: It isn't in that location!

MME. DUVENET: Where is it, then?

ELOI: It's here at the base of the skull. And it runs around here.

MME. DUVENET: Around where?

ELOI: Around here!

MME. DUVENET: (*touching his forehead*) Oh! There!

ELOI: No, no, are you blind? I said *here!*

MME. DUVENET: Oh, here!

ELOI: *Yes! Here!*

MME. DUVENET: Well, that could be eye-strain.

ELOI: When I've just changed my glasses?

MME. DUVENET: You read consistently in the wrong kind of light.

ELOI: You seem to think I'm a saboteur of myself.

MME. DUVENET: You actually are.

ELOI: You just don't know. (*darkly*) There's lots of things that you don't know about, Mother.

MME. DUVENET: I've never pretended nor wished to know a great deal. (*They fall into a silence, and Mme. Duvenet rocks slowly back and forth. The light is nearly gone. A distant juke-box can be heard playing "The New San Antonio Rose." She speaks, finally, in a gentle, liturgical tone.*) There are three simple rules I wish that you would observe. One: you should wear under-shirts whenever there's changeable weather! Two: don't sleep without covers, don't kick them off in the night! Three: chew your food, don't gulp it. Eat like a human being and not like a dog! In addition to those three very simple rules of common hygiene, all that you need is faith in spiritual healing! (*Eloi looks at her for a moment in weary desperation. Then he groans aloud and rises from the steps.*) Why that look, and the groan?

ELOI: (*intensely*) You—just—don't—*know!*

MME. DUVENET: Know what?

ELOI: Your world is so simple, you live in a fool's paradise!

MME. DUVENET: Do I indeed!

ELOI: Yes, Mother, you do indeed! I stand in your presence a stranger, a person unknown! I live in a house where nobody knows my name!

MME. DUVENET: You tire me, Eloi, when you become so excited!

ELOI: You just don't know. You rock on the porch and talk about clean white curtains! While I'm all flame, all burning, and no bell rings, nobody gives an alarm!

MME. DUVENET: What are you talking about?

ELOI: Intolerable burden! The conscience of all dirty men!

MME. DUVENET: I don't understand you.

ELOI: How can I speak any plainer?

MME. DUVENET: You go to confession!

ELOI: The priest is a cripple in skirts!

MME. DUVENET: How can you say that!

ELOI: Because I have seen his skirts and his crutches and heard his meaningless mumble through the wall!

MME. DUVENET: Don't speak like that in my presence!

ELOI: It's worn-out magic, it doesn't burn any more!

MME. DUVENET: Burn any more? Why should it!

ELOI: Because there needs to be burning!

MME. DUVENET: For what?

ELOI: (*leaning against the column*) For the sake of burning, for God, for the purification! Oh, God, oh, God. I can't go back in the house, and I can't stay out on the porch! I can't even breathe very freely, I don't know what is about to happen to me!

MME. DUVENET: You're going to bring on an attack. Sit down! Now tell me quietly and calmly what is the matter? What have you had on your mind for the last ten days?

ELOI: How do you know that I've had something on my mind?

MME. DUVENET: You've had something on your mind since a week ago Tuesday.

ELOI: Yes, that's true. I have. I didn't suppose you'd noticed . . .

MME. DUVENET: What happened at the post-office?

ELOI: How did you guess it was there?

MME. DUVENET: Because there is nothing at home to explain your condition.

ELOI: (*leaning back exhaustedly*) No.

MME. DUVENET: Then obviously it was something where you work.

ELOI: Yes . . .

MME. DUVENET: What was it, Eloi? (*Far down the street a tamale vendor cries out in his curiously rich haunting voice: "Re-ed ho-ot, re-ed ho-ot, re-e-ed!" He moves in the other direction and fades from hearing.*) What *was* it, Eloi?

ELOI: A letter.

MME. DUVENET: You got a letter from someone? And that upset you?

ELOI: I didn't get any letter.

MME. DUVENET: Then what did you mean by "a letter"?

ELOI: A letter came into my hands by accident, Mother.

MME. DUVENET: While you were sorting the mail?

ELOI: Yes.

MME. DUVENET: What was there about it to prey on your mind so much?

ELOI: The letter was mailed unsealed, and something fell out.

MME. DUVENET: Something fell out of the unsealed envelope?

ELOI: Yes!

MME. DUVENET: What was it fell out?

ELOI: A picture.

MME. DUVENET: A what?

ELOI: A picture!

MME. DUVENET: What kind of a picture? (*He does not answer. The juke-box starts playing again the same tune with its idiotic gaiety in the distance.*) Eloi, what kind of a picture fell out of the envelope?

ELOI: (*gently and sadly*) Miss Bordelon is standing in the hall and overhearing every word I say.

MME. DUVENET: (*turning sharply*) She's not in the hall.

ELOI: Her ear is clapped to the door!

MME. DUVENET: She's in her bedroom reading.

ELOI: Reading what?

MME. DUVENET: How do I know what she's reading? What difference does it make what she is reading!

ELOI: She keeps a journal of everything said in the house. I feel her taking short-hand notes at the table!

MME. DUVENET: Why, for what purpose, would she take short-hand notes on our conversation?

ELOI: Haven't you heard of hired investigators?

MME. DUVENET: Eloi, you're talking and saying such horrible things!

ELOI: (*gently*) I may be wrong. I may be wrong.

MME. DUVENET: Eloi, of course you're mistaken! Now go on and tell me what you started to say about the picture.

ELOI: A lewd photograph fell out of the envelope.

MME. DUVENET: A what?

ELOI: An indecent picture.

MME. DUVENET: Of whom?

ELOI: Of two naked figures.

MME. DUVENET: Oh! . . . That's all it was?

ELOI: You haven't looked at the picture.

MME. DUVENET: Was it so bad?

ELOI: It passes beyond all description!

MME. DUVENET: As bad as all that?

ELOI: No. Worse. I felt as though something exploded, blew up in my hands, and scalded my face with acid!

MME. DUVENET: Who sent this horrible photograph to you, Eloi?

ELOI: It wasn't to me.

MME. DUVENET: Who was it addressed to?

ELOI: One of those—opulent—antique dealers on—Royal . . .

MME. DUVENET: And who was the sender?

ELOI: A university student.

MME. DUVENET: Isn't the sender liable to prosecution?

ELOI: Of course. And to years in prison.

MME. DUVENET: I see no reason for clemency in such a case.

ELOI: Neither did I.

MME. DUVENET: Then what did you do about it?

ELOI: I haven't done anything yet.

MME. DUVENET: Eloi! You haven't reported it to the authorities yet?

ELOI: I haven't reported it to the authorities yet.

MME. DUVENET: I can't imagine one reason to hesitate!

ELOI: I couldn't proceed without some investigation.

MME. DUVENET: Investigation? Of what?

ELOI: Of all the circumstances around the case.

MME. DUVENET: What circumstances are there to think of but the fact that somebody used the mails for that purpose!

ELOI: The youth of the sender has something to do with the case.

MME. DUVENET: The sender was young?

ELOI: The sender was only nineteen.

MME. DUVENET: And are the sender's parents still alive?

ELOI: Both of them still living and in the city. The sender happens to be an only child.

MME. DUVENET: How do you know these facts about the sender?

ELOI: Because I've conducted a private investigation.

MME. DUVENET: How did you go about that?

ELOI: I called on the sender, I went to the dormitory. We talked in private and everything was discussed. The attitude taken was that I had come for money. That I was intending to hold the letter for blackmail.

MME. DUVENET: How perfectly awful.

ELOI: Of course I had to explain that I was a federal employee who had some obligation to his employers, and that it was really excessively fair on my part to even delay the action that ought to be taken.

MME. DUVENET: The action that has to be taken!

ELOI: And then the sender began to be ugly. Abusive. I can't repeat the charges, the evil suggestions! I ran from the room. I left my hat in the room. I couldn't even go back to pick it up!

MME. DUVENET: Eloi, Eloi. Oh, my dear Eloi. When did this happen, the interview with the sender?

ELOI: The interview was on Friday.

MME. DUVENET: Three days ago. And you haven't done anything yet?

ELOI: I thought and I thought and I couldn't take any action!

MME. DUVENET: Now it's too late.

ELOI: Why do you say it's too late?

MME. DUVENET: You've held the letter too long to take any action.

ELOI: Oh, no, I haven't. I'm not paralyzed any longer.

MME. DUVENET: But if you report on the letter now they will ask why you haven't reported on it sooner!

ELOI: I can explain the responsibility of it!

MME. DUVENET: No, no, it's much better not to do anything now!

ELOI: I've got to do something.

MME. DUVENET: You'd better destroy the letter.

ELOI: And let the offenders go scot free?

MME. DUVENET: What else can you do since you've hesitated so long!

ELOI: There's got to be punishment for it!

MME. DUVENET: Where is the letter?

ELOI: I have it here in my pocket.

MME. DUVENET: You have that thing on your person?

ELOI: My inside pocket.

MME. DUVENET: Oh, Eloi, how stupid, how foolish! Suppose something happened and something like that was found on you while you were unconscious and couldn't explain how you got it.

ELOI: Lower your voice! That woman is listening to us!

MME. DUVENET: Miss Bordelon? No!

ELOI: She is, she is. She's hired as investigator. She claps her ear to the wall when I talk in my sleep!

MME. DUVENET: Eloi, Eloi.

ELOI: They've hired her to spy, to poke and pry in the house!

MME. DUVENET: Who do you mean?

ELOI: The sender, the antique-dealer!

MME. DUVENET: You're talking so wildly you scare me. Eloi, you've got to destroy that letter at once!

ELOI: Destroy it?

MME. DUVENET: Yes!

ELOI: How?

MME. DUVENET: Burn it! (*Eloi rises unsteadily. For a third time the distant juke-organ begins to grind out "The New San Antonio Rose," with its polka rhythm and cries of insane exultation.*)

ELOI: (*faintly*) Yes, yes—burn it!

MME. DUVENET: Burn it this very instant!

ELOI: I'll take it inside to burn it.

MME. DUVENET: No, burn it right here in my presence.

ELOI: You can't look at it.

MME. DUVENET: My God, my God, I would pluck out my eyes before they would look at that picture!

ELOI: (*hoarsely*) I think it is better to go in the kitchen or basement.

MME. DUVENET: No, no, Eloi, burn it here! On the porch!

ELOI: Somebody might see.

MME. DUVENET: What of it?

ELOI: It might be thought that it was something of mine.

MME. DUVENET: Eloi, Eloi, take it out and burn it! Do you hear me? Burn it now! This instant!

ELOI: Turn your back. I'll take it out of my pocket.

MME. DUVENET: (*turning*) Have you matches, Eloi?

ELOI: (*sadly*) Yes, I have them, Mother.

MME. DUVENET: Very well, then. Burn the letter and burn the terrible picture. (*Eloi fumblingly removes some papers from his inside pocket. His hand is shaking so that the picture falls from his grasp to the porch-steps. Eloi groans as he stoops slowly to pick it up.*) Eloi! What is the matter?

ELOI: I—dropped the picture.

MME. DUVENET: Pick it up and set fire to it quickly!

ELOI: Yes . . . (*He strikes a match. His face is livid in the glow of the flame and as he stares at the slip of paper, his eyes seem to start from his head. He is breathing hoarsely. He draws the flame and the paper within one inch of each other but seems unable to move them any closer. All at once he utters a strangled cry and lets the match fall.*)

MME. DUVENET: (*turning*) Eloi, you've burned your fingers!

ELOI: Yes!

MME. DUVENET: Oh, come in the kitchen and let me put soda on it! (*Eloi turns and goes quickly into the house. She starts to follow.*) Go right in the kitchen! We'll put on baking soda! (*She reaches for the handle of the screen door. Eloi slips the latch into place. Madame Duvenet pulls the door and finds it locked.*) Eloi! (*He stares at her through the screen. A note of terror comes into her voice.*) Eloi! You've latched the door! What are you thinking of, Eloi? (*Eloi backs slowly away and out of sight.*) Eloi, Eloi! Come back here and open this door! (*A door slams inside the house, and the boarder's voice is raised in surprise and anger. Mme. Duvenet is now calling frantically.*) Eloi, Eloi! Why have you locked me out? What are you doing in there? Open the screen-door, please! (*Eloi's voice is raised violently. The woman inside cries out with fear. There is a metallic clatter as though a tin object were hurled against a wall. The woman screams; then there is a muffled explosion. Mme. Duvenet claws and beats at the screen door.*) *Eloi! Eloi!* Oh, answer me, Eloi! (*There is a sudden burst of fiery light from the interior of the cottage. It spills through the screen door and out upon the clawing, witch-like figure of the old woman. She screams in panic and turns dizzily about. With stiff, grotesque movements and gestures, she staggers down the porch-steps, and begins to shout hoarsely and despairingly.*) Fire! Fire! The house is on fire, on fire, the house is on fire!

Curtain

into the kitchen. The men rush forward and there is grappling and cursing. Something is overturned with a crash.)

BLANCHE (*shrilly*): My sister is going to have a baby!
MITCH: This is terrible.
BLANCHE: Lunacy, absolute lunacy!
MITCH: Get him in here, men.

(*Stanley is forced, pinioned by the two men, into the bedroom. He nearly throws them off. Then all at once he subsides and is limp in their grasp.*

(*They speak quietly and lovingly to him and he leans his face on one of their shoulders.*)

STELLA (*in a high, unnatural voice, out of sight*): I want to go away, I want to go away!
MITCH: Poker shouldn't be played in a house with women.

(*Blanche rushes into the bedroom*)

BLANCHE: I want my sister's clothes! We'll go to that woman's upstairs!
MITCH: Where is the clothes?
BLANCHE (*opening the closet*): I've got them! (*She rushes through to Stella*) Stella, Stella, precious! Dear, dear little sister, don't be afraid!

(*With her arms around Stella, Blanche guides her to the outside door and upstairs.*)

STANLEY (*dully*): What's the matter; what's happened?
MITCH: You just blew your top, Stan.
PABLO: He's okay, now.
STEVE: Sure, my boy's okay!
MITCH: Put him on the bed and get a wet towel.
PABLO: I think coffee would do him a world of good, now.
STANLEY (*thickly*): I want water.
MITCH: Put him under the shower!

(*The men talk quietly as they lead him to the bathroom.*)

STANLEY: Let the rut go of me, you sons of bitches!

(*Sounds of blows are heard. The water goes on full tilt.*)

STEVE: Let's get quick out of here!

(*They rush to the poker table and sweep up their winnings on their way out.*)

MITCH (*sadly but firmly*): Poker should not be played in a house with women.

(*The door closes on them and the place is still. The Negro entertainers in the bar around the corner play "Paper Doll" slow and blue. After a moment Stanley comes out of the bathroom dripping water and still in his clinging wet polka dot drawers.*)

STANLEY: Stella! (*There is a pause*) My baby doll's left me! (*He breaks into sobs. Then he goes to the phone and dials, still shuddering with sobs.*) Eunice? I want my baby! (*He waits a moment; then he hangs up and dials again*) Eunice! I'll keep on ringin' until I talk with my baby!

(*An indistinguishable shrill voice is heard. He hurls phone to floor. Dissonant brass and piano sounds as the rooms dim out to darkness and the outer walls appear in the night light. The "blue piano" plays for a brief interval.*

(*Finally, Stanley stumbles half-dressed out to the porch and down the wooden steps to the pavement before the building. There he throws back his head like a baying hound and bellows his wife's name: "Stella! Stella, sweetheart! Stella!"*)

STANLEY: Stell-*lahhhhh!*

EUNICE (*calling down from the door of her upper apartment*): Quit that howling out there an' go back to bed!

STANLEY: I want my baby down here. Stella, Stella!

EUNICE: She ain't comin' down so you quit! Or you'll git th' law on you!

STANLEY: Stella!

EUNICE: You can't beat on a woman an' then call 'er back! She won't come! And her goin' t' have a baby! . . . You stinker! You whelp of a Polack, you! I hope they do haul you in and turn the fire hose on you, same as the last time!

STANLEY (*humbly*): Eunice, I want my girl to come down with me!

EUNICE: Hah! (*She slams her door.*)

STANLEY (*with heaven-splitting violence*): *STELL-LAHHHHH!*

(The low-tone clarinet moans. The door upstairs opens again. Stella slips down the rickety stairs in her robe. Her eyes are glistening with tears and her hair loose about her throat and shoulders. They stare at each other. Then they come together with low, animal moans. He falls to his knees on the steps and presses his face to her belly, curving a little with maternity. Her eyes go blind with tenderness as she catches his head and raises him level with her. He snatches the screen door open and lifts her off her feet and bears her into the dark flat.

(Blanche comes out on the upper landing in her robe and slips fearfully down the steps.)

BLANCHE: Where is my little sister? Stella? Stella?

(She stops before the dark entrance of her sister's flat. Then catches her breath as if struck. She rushes down to the walk before the house. She looks right and left as if for a sanctuary.

(The music fades away. Mitch appears from around the corner.)

MITCH: Miss DuBois?

BLANCHE: Oh!

MITCH: All quiet on the Potomac now?

BLANCHE: She ran downstairs and went back in there with him.

MITCH: Sure she did.

BLANCHE: I'm terrified!

MITCH: Ho-ho! There's nothing to be scared of. They're crazy about each other.

BLANCHE: I'm not used to such—

MITCH: Naw, it's a shame this had to happen when you just got here. But don't take it serious.

BLANCHE: Violence! Is so—

MITCH: Set down on the steps and have a cigarette with me.

BLANCHE: I'm not properly dressed.

MITCH: That don't make no difference in the Quarter.

BLANCHE: Such a pretty silver case.

MITCH: I showed you the inscription, didn't I?

BLANCHE: Yes. (*During the pause, she looks up at the sky*) There's so much—so much confusion in the world . . . (*He coughs diffidently*) Thank you for being so kind! I need kindness now.

SCENE FOUR

It is early the following morning. There is a confusion of street cries like a choral chant.

Stella is lying down in the bedroom. Her face is serene in the early morning sunlight. One hand rests on her belly, rounding slightly with new maternity. From the other dangles a book of colored comics. Her eyes and lips have that almost narcotized tranquility that is in the faces of Eastern idols.

The table is sloppy with remains of breakfast and the debris of the preceding night, and Stanley's gaudy pyjamas lie across the threshold of the bathroom. The outside door is slightly ajar on a sky of summer brilliance.

Blanche appears at this door. She has spent a sleepless night and her appearance entirely contrasts with Stella's. She presses her knuckles nervously to her lips as she looks through the door, before entering.

BLANCHE: Stella?

STELLA (*stirring lazily*): Hmmh?

(*Blanche utters a moaning cry and runs into the bedroom, throwing herself down beside Stella in a rush of hysterical tenderness.*)

BLANCHE: Baby, my baby sister!

STELLA (*drawing away from her*): Blanche, what is the matter with you?

(*Blanche straightens up slowly and stands beside the bed looking down at her sister with knuckles pressed to her lips.*)

BLANCHE: He's left?

STELLA: Stan? Yes.

BLANCHE: Will he be back?

STELLA: He's gone to get the car greased. Why?

BLANCHE: Why! I've been half crazy, Stella! When I found out you'd been insane enough to come back in here after what happened—I started to rush in after you!

STELLA: I'm glad you didn't.

BLANCHE: What were you thinking of? (*Stella makes an indefinite gesture*) Answer me! What? What?

STELLA: Please, Blanche! Sit down and stop yelling.

BLANCHE: All right, Stella. I will repeat the question quietly now. How could you come back in this place last night? Why, you must have slept with him!

(*Stella gets up in a calm and leisurely way.*)

STELLA: Blanche, I'd forgotten how excitable you are. You're making much too much fuss about this.

BLANCHE: Am I?

STELLA: Yes, you are, Blanche. I know how it must have seemed to you and I'm awful sorry it had to happen, but it wasn't anything as serious as you seem to take it. In the first place, when men are drinking and playing poker anything can happen. It's always a powder-keg. He didn't know what he was doing. . . . He was as good as a lamb when I came back and he's really very, very ashamed of himself.

BLANCHE: And that—that makes it all right?

STELLA: No, it isn't all right for anybody to make such a terrible row, but—people do sometimes. Stanley's always smashed things. Why, on our wedding night—soon as we came in here—he snatched off one of my slippers and rushed about the place smashing the light-bulbs with it.

BLANCHE: He did—*what*?

STELLA: He smashed all the light-bulbs with the heel of my slipper! (*She laughs.*)

BLANCHE: And you—you *let* him? Didn't *run*, didn't *scream*?

STELLA: I was—sort of—thrilled by it. (*She waits for a moment*) Eunice and you had breakfast?

BLANCHE: Do you suppose I wanted any breakfast?

STELLA: There's some coffee left on the stove.

BLANCHE: You're so—matter of fact about it, Stella.

STELLA: What other can I be? He's taken the radio to get it fixed. It didn't land on the pavement so only one tube was smashed.

BLANCHE: And you are standing there smiling!

STELLA: What do you want me to do?

BLANCHE: Pull yourself together and face the facts.

STELLA: What are they, in your opinion?

BLANCHE: In my opinion? You're married to a madman!

STELLA: No!

BLANCHE: Yes, you are, your fix is worse than mine is! Only you're not being sensible about it. I'm going to *do* something. Get hold of myself and make myself a new life!

STELLA: Yes?

BLANCHE: But you've given in. And that isn't right, you're not old! You can get out.

STELLA (*slowly and emphatically*): I'm not in anything I want to get out of.

BLANCHE (*incredulously*): What—Stella?

STELLA: I said I am not in anything that I have a desire to get out of. Look at the mess in this room! And those empty bottles! They went through two cases last night! He promised this morning that he was going to quit having these poker parties, but you know how long such a promise is going to keep. Oh, well, it's his pleasure, like mine is movies and bridge. People have got to tolerate each other's habits, I guess.

BLANCHE: I don't understand you. (*Stella turns toward her*) I don't understand your indifference. Is this a Chinese philosophy you've—cultivated?

STELLA: Is what—what?

BLANCHE: This—shuffling about and mumbling—'One tube smashed—beer-bottles—mess in the kitchen!'—as if nothing out of the ordinary has happened! (*Stella laughs uncertainly and picking up the broom, twirls it in her hands.*)

BLANCHE: Are you deliberately shaking that thing in my face?

STELLA: No.

BLANCHE: Stop it. Let go of that broom. I won't have you cleaning up for him!

STELLA: Then who's going to do it? Are you?

BLANCHE: I? I!

STELLA: No, I didn't think so.

BLANCHE: Oh, let me think, if only my mind would function! We've got to get hold of some money, that's the way out!

STELLA: I guess that money is always nice to get hold of.

BLANCHE: Listen to me. I have an idea of some kind. (*Shakily she twists a cigarette into her holder*) Do you remember Shep Huntleigh? (*Stella shakes her head*) Of course you remember Shep Huntleigh. I went out with him at college and wore his pin for a while. Well—

STELLA: Well?

BLANCHE: I ran into him last winter. You know I went to Miami during the Christmas holidays?

STELLA: No.

BLANCHE: Well, I did. I took the trip as an investment, thinking I'd meet someone with a million dollars.

STELLA: Did you?

BLANCHE: Yes. I ran into Shep Huntleigh—I ran into him on Biscayne Boulevard, on Christmas Eve, about dusk . . . getting into his car—Cadillac convertible; must have been a block long!

STELLA: I should think it would have been—inconvenient in traffic!

BLANCHE: You've heard of oil-wells?

STELLA: Yes—remotely.

BLANCHE: He has them, all over Texas. Texas is literally spouting gold in his pockets.

STELLA: My, my.

BLANCHE: Y'know how indifferent I am to money. I think of money in terms of what it does for you. But he could do it, he could certainly do it!

STELLA: Do what, Blanche?

BLANCHE: Why—set us up in a—shop!

STELLA: What kind of a shop?

BLANCHE: Oh, a—shop of some kind! He could do it with half what his wife throws away at the races.

STELLA: He's married?

BLANCHE: Honey, would I be here if the man weren't married? (*Stella laughs a little. Blanche suddenly springs up and crosses to phone. She speaks shrilly*) How do I get Western Union?—Operator! Western Union!

STELLA: That's a dial phone, honey.

BLANCHE: I can't dial, I'm too—

STELLA: Just dial O.

BLANCHE: O?

STELLA: Yes, "O" for Operator! (*Blanche considers a moment; then she puts the phone down.*)

BLANCHE: Give me a pencil. Where is a slip of paper? I've got to write it down first—the message, I mean . . .

(*She goes to the dressing table, and grabs up a sheet of Kleenex and an eyebrow pencil for writing equipment.*)

Let me see now . . . (*She bites the pencil*) 'Darling Shep. Sister and I in desperate situation.'

STELLA: I beg your pardon!

BLANCHE: 'Sister and I in desperate situation. Will explain details later. Would you be interested in—?' (*She bites the pencil again*) 'Would you be—interested—in . . .' (*She smashes the pencil on the table and springs up*) You never get anywhere with direct appeals!

STELLA (*with a laugh*): Don't be so ridiculous, darling!

BLANCHE: But I'll think of something, I've *got* to think of—*some*thing! Don't, don't laugh at me, Stella! Please, please don't—I—I want you to look at the contents of my purse! Here's what's in it! (*She snatches her purse open*) Sixty-five measly cents in coin of the realm!

STELLA (*crossing to bureau*): Stanley doesn't give me a regular allowance, he likes to pay bills himself, but—this morning he gave me ten dollars to smooth things over. You take five of it, Blanche, and I'll keep the rest.

BLANCHE: Oh, no. No, Stella.

STELLA (*insisting*): I know how it helps your morale just having a little pocket-money on you.

BLANCHE: No, thank you—I'll take to the streets!

STELLA: Talk sense! How did you happen to get so low on funds?

BLANCHE: Money just goes—it goes places. (*She rubs her forehead*) Sometime today I've got to get hold of a bromo!

STELLA: I'll fix you one now.

BLANCHE: Not yet—I've got to keep thinking!

STELLA: I wish you'd just let things go, at least for a—while . . .

BLANCHE: Stella, I can't live with him! You can, he's your husband. But how could I stay here with him, after last night, with just those curtains between us?

STELLA: Blanche, you saw him at his worst last night.

BLANCHE: On the contrary, I saw him at his best! What such a man has to offer is animal force and he gave a wonderful exhibition of that! But the only way to live with such a man is to—go to bed with him! And that's your job—not mine!

STELLA: After you've rested a little, you'll see it's going to work out. You don't have to worry about anything while you're here. I mean—expenses . . .

BLANCHE: I have to plan for us both, to get us both—out!

STELLA: You take it for granted that I am in something that I want to get out of.

BLANCHE: I take it for granted that you still have sufficient memory of Belle Reve to find this place and these poker players impossible to live with.

STELLA: Well, you're taking entirely too much for granted.

BLANCHE: I can't believe you're in earnest.

STELLA: No?

BLANCHE: I understand how it happened—a little. You saw him in uniform, an officer, not here but—

STELLA: I'm not sure it would have made any difference where I saw him.

BLANCHE: Now don't say it was one of those mysterious electric things between people! If you do I'll laugh in your face.

STELLA: I am not going to say anything more at all about it!

BLANCHE: All right, then, don't!

STELLA: But there are things that happen between a man and a woman in the dark—that sort of make everything else seem—unimportant. (*Pause.*)

BLANCHE: What you are talking about is brutal desire—just—Desire!—the name of that rattle-trap street-car that bangs through the Quarter, up one old narrow street and down another . . .

STELLA: Haven't you ever ridden on that street-car?

BLANCHE: It brought me here.—Where I'm not wanted and where I'm ashamed to be . . .

STELLA: Then don't you think your superior attitude is a bit out of place?

BLANCHE: I am not being or feeling at all superior, Stella. Believe me I'm not! It's just this. This is how I look at it. A man like that is someone to go out with—once—twice—three times when the devil is in you. But live with? Have a child by?

STELLA: I have told you I love him.

BLANCHE: Then I *tremble* for you! I just—*tremble* for you. . . .

STELLA: I can't help your trembling if you insist on trembling!

(*There is a pause.*)

BLANCHE: May I—speak—*plainly*?

STELLA: Yes, do. Go ahead. As plainly as you want to.

(*Outside, a train approaches. They are silent till the noise subsides. They are both in the bedroom.*

(*Under cover of the train's noise Stanley enters from outside. He stands unseen by the women, holding some packages in his arms, and overhears their following conversation. He wears an undershirt and grease-stained seersucker pants.*)

BLANCHE: Well—if you'll forgive me—he's *common!*

STELLA: Why, yes, I suppose he is.

BLANCHE: Suppose! You can't have forgotten that much of our bringing up, Stella, that you just *suppose* that any part of a gentleman's in his nature! *Not one particle, no!* Oh, if he was just—*ordinary!* Just *plain*—but good and wholesome, but—*no.* There's something downright—*bestial*—about him! You're hating me saying this, aren't you?

STELLA (*coldly*): Go on and say it all, Blanche.

BLANCHE: He acts like an animal, has an animal's habits! Eats like one, moves like one, talks like one! There's even something—sub-human—something not quite to the stage of humanity yet! Yes, something—ape-like about him, like one of those pictures I've seen in—anthropological studies! Thousands and thousands of years have passed him right by, and there he is—Stanley Kowalski—survivor of the stone age! Bearing the raw meat home from the kill in the jungle! And you—*you* here—*waiting* for him! Maybe he'll strike you or maybe grunt and kiss you! That is, if kisses have been discovered yet! Night falls and the other apes gather! There in the front of the cave, all grunting like him, and swilling and gnawing and hulking! His poker night!—you call it—this party of apes! Somebody growls—some creature snatches at something—the fight is on! *God!* Maybe we are a long way from being made in God's image, but Stella—my sister—there has been *some* progress since then! Such things as art—as poetry and music—such kinds of new light have come into the world since then! In some kinds of people some tenderer feelings have had some little beginning! That we have got to make *grow!* And *cling* to, and hold as our flag! In this dark march toward whatever it is we're approaching. . . . *Don't—don't hang back with the brutes!*

(*Another train passes outside. Stanley hesitates, licking his lips. Then suddenly he turns stealthily about and withdraws through front door. The women are still unaware of his presence. When the train has passed he calls through the closed front door.*)

STANLEY: Hey! Hey, Stella!
STELLA (*who has listened gravely to Blanche*): Stanley!
BLANCHE: Stell, I—

(*But Stella has gone to the front door. Stanley enters casually with his packages.*)

STANLEY: Hiyuh, Stella. Blanche back?
STELLA: Yes, she's back.
STANLEY: Hiyuh, Blanche. (*He grins at her.*)
STELLA: You must've got under the car.
STANLEY: Them darn mechanics at Fritz's don't know their ass fr'm— *Hey!*

(*Stella has embraced him with both arms, fiercely, and full in the view of Blanche. He laughs and clasps her head to him. Over her head he grins through the curtains at Blanche.*

(*As the lights fade away, with a lingering brightness on their embrace, the music of the "blue piano" and trumpet and drums is heard.*)

SCENE FIVE

Blanche is seated in the bedroom fanning herself with a palm leaf as she reads over a just completed letter. Suddenly she bursts into a peal of laughter. Stella is dressing in the bedroom.

STELLA: What are you laughing at, honey?

BLANCHE: Myself, myself, for being such a liar! I'm writing a letter to Shep. (*She picks up the letter*) "Darling Shep. I am spending the summer on the wing, making flying visits here and there. And who knows, perhaps I shall take a sudden notion to *swoop* down on *Dallas!* How would you feel about that? Ha-ha! (*She laughs nervously and brightly, touching her throat as if actually talking to Shep*) Forewarned is forearmed, as they say!"—How does that sound?

STELLA: Uh-huh . . .

BLANCHE (*going on nervously*): "Most of my sister's friends go north in the summer but some have homes on the Gulf and there has been a continued round of entertainments, teas, cocktails, and luncheons—"

(*A disturbance is heard upstairs at the Hubbell's apartment.*)

STELLA (*crossing to the door*): Eunice seems to be having some trouble with Steve.

(*Eunice's voice shouts in terrible wrath.*)

EUNICE: I heard about you and that blonde!

STEVE: That's a damn lie!

EUNICE: You ain't pulling the wool over my eyes! I wouldn't mind if you'd stay down at the Four Deuces, but you always going up.

STEVE: Who ever seen me up?

EUNICE: I seen you chasing her 'round the balcony—I'm gonna call the vice squad!

STEVE: Don't you throw that at me!

EUNICE (*shrieking*): You hit me! I'm gonna call the police!

(*A clatter of aluminum striking a wall is heard, followed by a man's angry roar, shouts and overturned furniture. There is a crash; then a relative hush.*)

BLANCHE (*brightly*): Did he *kill* her?

(*Eunice appears on the steps in daemonic disorder.*)

STELLA: No! She's coming downstairs.

EUNICE: Call the police, I'm going to call the police! (*She rushes around the corner.*)

STELLA (*returning from the door*): Some of your sister's friends have stayed in the city.

(*They laugh lightly. Stanley comes around the corner in his green and scarlet silk bowling shirt. He trots up the steps and bangs into the kitchen. Blanche registers his entrance with nervous gestures.*)

STANLEY: What's a matter with Eun-uss?
STELLA: She and Steve had a row. Has she got the police?
STANLEY: Naw. She's gettin' a drink.
STELLA: That's much more practical!

(*Steve comes down nursing a bruise on his forehead and looks in the door.*)

STEVE: *She here?*
STANLEY: Naw, naw. At the Four Deuces.
STEVE: That rutting hunk! (*He looks around the corner a bit timidly, then turns with affected boldness and runs after her.*)
BLANCHE: I must jot that down in my notebook. Ha-ha! I'm compiling a notebook of quaint little words and phrases I've picked up here.
STANLEY: You won't pick up nothing here you ain't heard before.
BLANCHE: Can I count on that?
STANLEY: You can count on it up to five hundred.
BLANCHE: That's a mighty high number. (*He jerks open the bureau drawer, slams it shut and throws shoes in a corner. At each noise Blanche winces slightly. Finally she speaks*) What sign were you born under?
STANLEY (*while he is dressing*): Sign?
BLANCHE: Astrological sign. I bet you were born under Aries. Aries people are forceful and dynamic. They dote on noise! They love to bang things around! You must have had lots of banging around in the army and now that you're out, you make up for it by treating inanimate objects with such a fury!

(*Stella has been going in and out of closet during this scene. Now she pops her head out of the closet.*)

STELLA: Stanley was born just five minutes after Christmas.

BLANCHE: Capricorn—the Goat!

STANLEY: What sign were *you* born under?

BLANCHE: Oh, my birthday's next month, the fifteenth of September; that's under Virgo.

STANLEY: What's Virgo?

BLANCHE: Virgo is the Virgin.

STANLEY (*contemptuously*): *Hah!* (*He advances a little as he knots his tie*) Say, do you happen to know somebody named Shaw?

(*Her face expresses a faint shock. She reaches for the cologne bottle and dampens her handkerchief as she answers carefully.*)

BLANCHE: Why, everybody knows somebody named Shaw!

STANLEY: Well, this somebody named Shaw is under the impression he met you in Laurel, but I figure he must have got you mixed up with some other party because this other party is someone he met at a hotel called the Flamingo.

(*Blanche laughs breathlessly as she touches the cologne-dampened handkerchief to her temples.*)

BLANCHE: I'm afraid he does have me mixed up with this "other party." The Hotel Flamingo is not the sort of establishment I would dare to be seen in!

STANLEY: You know of it?

BLANCHE: Yes, I've seen it and smelled it.

STANLEY: You must've got pretty close if you could smell it.

BLANCHE: The odor of cheap perfume is penetrating.

STANLEY: That stuff you use is expensive?

BLANCHE: Twenty-five dollars an ounce! I'm nearly out. That's just a hint if you want to remember my birthday! (*She speaks lightly but her voice has a note of fear.*)

STANLEY: Shaw must've got you mixed up. He goes in and out of Laurel all the time so he can check on it and clear up any mistake.

(*He turns away and crosses to the portieres. Blanche closes her eyes as if faint. Her hand trembles as she lifts the handkerchief again to her forehead.*

(*Steve and Eunice come around corner. Steve's arm is around Eunice's shoulder and she is sobbing luxuriously and he is cooing love-words. There is a murmur of thunder as they go slowly upstairs in a tight embrace.*)

STANLEY (*to Stella*): I'll wait for you at the Four Deuces!
STELLA: Hey! Don't I rate one kiss?
STANLEY: Not in front of your sister.

(*He goes out. Blanche rises from her chair. She seems faint; looks about her with an expression of almost panic.*)

BLANCHE: Stella! What have you heard about me?
STELLA: Huh?
BLANCHE: What have people been telling you about me?
STELLA: Telling?
BLANCHE: You haven't heard any—unkind—gossip about me?
STELLA: Why, no, Blanche, of course not!
BLANCHE: Honey, there was—a good deal of talk in Laurel.
STELLA: About *you*, Blanche?
BLANCHE: I wasn't so good the last two years or so, after Belle Reve had started to slip through my fingers.
STELLA: All of us do things we—
BLANCHE: I never was hard or self-sufficient enough. When people are soft—soft people have got to court the favor of hard ones, Stella. Have got to be seductive—put on soft colors, the colors of butterfly wings, and glow—make a little—temporary magic just in order to pay for—one night's shelter! That's why I've been—not so awf'ly good lately. I've run for protection, Stella, from under one leaky roof to another leaky roof—because it was storm—all storm, and I was—caught in the center. . . . People don't see you—*men* don't—don't even admit your existence unless they are making love to you. And you've got to have your existence admitted by someone, if you're going to have someone's protection. And so the soft people have got to—shimmer and glow—put a—paper lantern over the light. . . . But I'm scared now—awf'ly scared. I don't know how much longer I can turn the trick. It isn't enough to be soft. You've got to be soft *and attractive*. And I—I'm fading now!

(*The afternoon has faded to dusk. Stella goes into the bedroom and turns on the light under the paper lantern. She holds a bottled soft drink in her hand.*)

BLANCHE: Have you been listening to me?

STELLA: I don't listen to you when you are being morbid! (*She advances with the bottled coke.*)

BLANCHE (*with abrupt change to gaiety*): Is that coke for me?

STELLA: Not for anyone else!

BLANCHE: Why, you precious thing, you! Is it just coke?

STELLA (*turning*): You mean you want a shot in it!

BLANCHE: Well, honey, a shot never does a coke any harm! Let me! You mustn't wait on me!

STELLA: I like to wait on you, Blanche. It makes it seem more like home. (*She goes into the kitchen, finds a glass and pours a shot of whiskey into it.*)

BLANCHE: I have to admit I love to be waited on . . .

(*She rushes into the bedroom. Stella goes to her with the glass. Blanche suddenly clutches Stella's free hand with a moaning sound and presses the hand to her lips. Stella is embarrassed by her show of emotion. Blanche speaks in a choked voice.*)

You're—you're—so *good* to me! And I—

STELLA: Blanche.

BLANCHE: I know, I won't! You hate me to talk sentimental! But honey, *believe* I feel things more than I *tell* you! I *won't* stay long! I won't, I *promise* I—

STELLA: Blanche!

BLANCHE (*hysterically*): I won't, I promise, *I'll* go! Go *soon!* I will *really!* I *won't* hang around until he—throws me out . . .

STELLA: Now will you stop talking foolish?

BLANCHE: Yes, honey. Watch how you pour—that fizzy stuff foams over!

(*Blanche laughs shrilly and grabs the glass, but her hand shakes so it almost slips from her grasp. Stella pours the coke into the glass. It foams over and spills. Blanche gives a piercing cry.*)

STELLA (*shocked by the cry*): Heavens!

BLANCHE: Right on my pretty white skirt!

STELLA: Oh . . . Use my hanky. Blot gently.

BLANCHE (*slowly recovering*): I know—gently—gently . . .

STELLA: Did it stain?

BLANCHE: Not a bit. Ha-ha! Isn't that lucky? (*She sits down shakily, taking a grateful drink. She holds the glass in both hands and continues to laugh a little.*)

STELLA: Why did you scream like that?

BLANCHE: I don't know why I screamed! (*continuing nervously*) Mitch—Mitch is coming at seven. I guess I am just feeling nervous about our relations. (*She begins to talk rapidly and breathlessly*) He hasn't gotten a thing but a goodnight kiss, that's all I have given him, Stella. I want his respect. And men don't want anything they get too easy. But on the other hand men lose interest quickly. Especially when the girl is over—thirty. They think a girl over thirty ought to—the vulgar term is—"put out." . . . And I—I'm not "putting out." Of course he—he doesn't know—I mean I haven't informed him—of my real age!

STELLA: Why are you sensitive about your age?

BLANCHE: Because of hard knocks my vanity's been given. What I mean is—he thinks I'm sort of—prim and proper, you know! (*She laughs out sharply*) I want to *deceive* him enough to make him—want me . . .

STELLA: Blanche, do you want *him*?

BLANCHE: I want to *rest!* I want to breathe quietly again! Yes—I *want* Mitch . . . *very badly!* Just think! If it happens! I can leave here and not be anyone's problem . . .

(*Stanley comes around the corner with a drink under his belt.*)

STANLEY (*bawling*): Hey, Steve! Hey, Eunice! Hey, Stella!

(*There are joyous calls from above. Trumpet and drums are heard from around the corner.*)

STELLA (*kissing Blanche impulsively*): It *will* happen!

BLANCHE (*doubtfully*): It will?

STELLA: It *will!* (*She goes across into the kitchen, looking back at Blanche.*) It will, honey, *it will.* . . . But don't take another drink! (*Her voice catches as she goes out the door to meet her husband.*

(*Blanche sinks faintly back in her chair with her drink. Eunice shrieks with laughter and runs down the steps. Steve bounds after her with goat-like screeches and chases her around corner. Stanley and Stella twine arms as they follow, laughing.*

(*Dusk settles deeper. The music from the Four Deuces is slow and blue.*)

BLANCHE: Ah, me, ah, me, ah, me . . .

(*Her eyes fall shut and the palm leaf fan drops from her fingers. She slaps her hand on the chair arm a couple of times; then she raises herself wearily to her feet and picks up the hand mirror. There is a little glimmer of lightning about the building.*

(*The Negro Woman, cackling hysterically, swaying drunkenly, comes around the corner from the Four Deuces. At the same time, a Young Man enters from the opposite direction. The Negro Woman snaps her fingers before his belt.*)

NEGRO WOMAN: Hey! Sugar!

(*She says something indistinguishable. The Young Man shakes his head violently and edges hastily up the steps. He rings the bell. Blanche puts down the mirror. The Negro Woman has wandered down the street.*)

BLANCHE: Come in.

(*The Young Man appears through the portieres. She regards him with interest.*)

BLANCHE: Well, well! What can I do for *you*?

YOUNG MAN: I'm collecting for *The Evening Star.*

BLANCHE: I didn't know that stars took up collections.

YOUNG MAN: It's the paper.

BLANCHE: I know, I was joking—feebly! Will you—have a drink?

YOUNG MAN: No, ma'am. No, thank you. I can't drink on the job.

BLANCHE: Oh, well, now, let's see. . . . No, I don't have a dime! I'm not the lady of the house. I'm her sister from Mississippi. I'm one of those poor relations you've heard about.

YOUNG MAN: That's all right. I'll drop by later. (*He starts to go out. She approaches a little.*)

BLANCHE: Hey! (*He turns back shyly. She puts a cigarette in a long holder*) Could you give me a light? (*She crosses toward him. They meet at the door between the two rooms.*)

YOUNG MAN: Sure. (*He takes out a lighter*) This doesn't always work.

BLANCHE: It's temperamental? (*It flares*) Ah!—thank you. (*He starts away again*) Hey! (*He turns again, still more uncertainly. She goes close to him*) Uh—what time is it?

YOUNG MAN: Fifteen of seven.

BLANCHE: That late, and still not dark! It just goes to show. . . . Do I seem intoxicated? (*The Young Man laughs uncomfortably*) I sure hope not because I'm expecting a caller bye and bye.

YOUNG MAN (*starting off*): Well, I—

BLANCHE: I bet you're going to college! And you work after school?

YOUNG MAN: That's right.

BLANCHE: What do you study?

YOUNG MAN: Pre-Med.

BLANCHE: Going to be a doctor! What's your name?

YOUNG MAN: Romano.

BLANCHE: Give me all three of them; I believe in numerology! (*She sways a little.*)

YOUNG MAN: Lucio Francesco Romano.

BLANCHE: My, my, my! I don't know what a numerologist would make out of that! (*The Young Man looks embarrassed*) Forgive me. (*She makes a gentle gesture*) I'm not a conventional person, and I'm so—restless today. . . . Don't you love these long, rainy afternoons in New Orleans when an hour isn't just an hour but a little piece of eternity dropped in our hands?—And who knows what to do with it!

(*In the ensuing pause, the "blue piano" is heard. It continues through the rest of this scene and the opening of the next. The young man clears his throat and looks yearningly at the door.*)

Young man! Young, young, young man! Has anyone ever told you that you look like a young Prince out of the Arabian Nights?

(*The Young Man laughs uncomfortably and stands like a bashful kid. Blanche speaks softly to him.*)

Well, you do, honey lamb! Come here. I want to kiss you, just once, softly and sweetly on your mouth!

(*Without waiting for him to accept, she crosses quickly to him and presses her lips to his.*)

Now run along, now, quickly! It would be nice to keep you, but I've got to be good—and keep my hands off children.

(*He stares at her a moment. She opens the door for him and blows a kiss at him as he goes down the steps with a dazed look. She stands there a little dreamily after he has disappeared. Then Mitch appears around the corner with a bunch of roses.*)

BLANCHE (*gaily*): Look who's coming! My Rosenkavalier! Bow to me first . . . now present them! *Ahhhh—Merciiii!*

(*She looks at him over them, coquettishly pressing them to her lips. He beams at her selfconsciously.*)

SCENE SIX

It is about two A.M. *on the same evening. The outer wall of the building is visible. Blanche and Mitch come in. The utter exhaustion which only a neurasthenic personality can know is evident in Blanche's voice and manner. Mitch is stolid but depressed. They have probably been out to the amusement park on Lake Pontchartrain, for Mitch is bearing, upside down, a plaster statuette of Mae West, the sort of prize won at shooting-galleries and carnival games of chance.*

BLANCHE (*stopping lifelessly at the steps*): Well—

(*Mitch laughs uneasily.*)

Well . . .

MITCH: I guess it must be pretty late—and you're tired.

BLANCHE: Even the hot tamale man has deserted the street, and he hangs on till the end. (*Mitch laughs uneasily again*) How will you get home?

MITCH: I'll walk over to Bourbon and catch an owl-car.

BLANCHE (*laughing grimly*): Is that street-car named Desire still grinding along the tracks at this hour?

MITCH (*heavily*): I'm afraid you haven't gotten much fun out of this evening, Blanche.

BLANCHE: I spoiled it for *you.*

MITCH: No, you didn't, but I felt all the time that I wasn't giving you much—entertainment.

BLANCHE: I simply couldn't rise to the occasion. That was all. I don't think I've ever tried so hard to be gay and made such a dismal mess of it. I get ten points for trying! —I *did* try.

MITCH: Why did you try if you didn't feel like it, Blanche?

BLANCHE: I was just obeying the law of nature.

MITCH: Which law is that?

BLANCHE: The one that says the lady must entertain the gentleman—or no dice! See if you can locate my door-key in this purse. When I'm so tired my fingers are all thumbs!

MITCH (*rooting in her purse*): This it?

BLANCHE: No, honey, that's the key to my trunk which I must soon be packing.

MITCH: You mean you are leaving here soon?

BLANCHE: I've outstayed my welcome.

MITCH: This it?

(*The music fades away.*)

BLANCHE: Eureka! Honey, you open the door while I take a last look at the sky. (*She leans on the porch rail. He opens the door and stands awkwardly behind her.*) I'm looking for the Pleiades, the Seven Sisters, but these girls are not out tonight. Oh, yes they are, there they are! God bless them! All in a bunch going home from their little bridge party. . . . Y' get the door open? Good boy! I guess you—want to go now . . .

(*He shuffles and coughs a little.*)

MITCH: Can I—uh—kiss you—goodnight?

BLANCHE: Why do you always ask me if you may?

MITCH: I don't know whether you want me to or not.

BLANCHE: Why should you be so doubtful?

MITCH: That night when we parked by the lake and I kissed you, you—

BLANCHE: Honey, it wasn't the kiss I objected to. I liked the kiss very much. It was the other little—familiarity—that I—felt obliged to—discourage. . . . I didn't resent it! Not a bit in the world! In fact, I was somewhat flattered that you—desired me! But, honey, you know as well as I do that a single girl, a girl alone in the world, has got to keep a firm hold on her emotions or she'll be lost!

MITCH (*solemnly*): Lost?

BLANCHE: I guess you are used to girls that like to be lost. The kind that get lost immediately, on the first date!

MITCH: I like you to be exactly the way that you are, because in all my—experience—I have never known anyone like you.

(*Blanche looks at him gravely; then she bursts into laughter and then claps a hand to her mouth.*)

MITCH: Are you laughing at me?

BLANCHE: No, honey. The lord and lady of the house have not yet returned, so come in. We'll have a night-cap. Let's leave the lights off. Shall we?

MITCH: You just—do what you want to.

(*Blanche precedes him into the kitchen. The outer wall of the building disappears and the interiors of the two rooms can be dimly seen.*)

BLANCHE (*remaining in the first room*): The other room's more comfortable—go on in. This crashing around in the dark is my search for some liquor.

MITCH: You want a drink?

BLANCHE: I want *you* to have a drink! You have been so anxious and solemn all evening, and so have I; we have both been anxious and solemn and now for these few last remaining moments of our lives together—I want to create—*joie de vivre!* I'm lighting a candle.

MITCH: That's good.

BLANCHE: We are going to be very Bohemian. We are going to pretend that we are sitting in a little artists' cafe on the Left Bank in Paris! (*She lights a candle stub and puts it in a bottle.*) *Je suis la Dame aux Camellias! Vous êtes—Armand!* Understand French?

MITCH (*heavily*): Naw. Naw, I—

BLANCHE: *Voulez-vous couchez avec moi ce soir? Vous ne comprenez pas? Ah, quelle dommage!*—I mean it's a damned good thing. . . . I've found some liquor! Just enough for two shots without any dividends, honey . . .

MITCH (*heavily*): That's—good.

(*She enters the bedroom with the drinks and the candle.*)

BLANCHE: Sit down! Why don't you take off your coat and loosen your collar?

MITCH: I better leave it on.

BLANCHE: No. I want you to be comfortable.

MITCH: I am ashamed of the way I perspire. My shirt is sticking to me.

BLANCHE: Perspiration is healthy. If people didn't perspire they would die in five minutes. (*She takes his coat from him*) This is a nice coat. What kind of material is it?

MITCH: They call that stuff alpaca.

BLANCHE: Oh. Alpaca.

MITCH: It's very light weight alpaca.

BLANCHE: Oh. Light weight alpaca.

MITCH: I don't like to wear a wash-coat even in summer because I sweat through it.

BLANCHE: Oh.

MITCH: And it don't look neat on me. A man with a heavy build has got to be careful of what he puts on him so he don't look too clumsy.

BLANCHE: You are not too heavy.

MITCH: You don't think I am?

BLANCHE: You are not the delicate type. You have a massive bone-structure and a very imposing physique.

MITCH: Thank you. Last Christmas I was given a membership to the New Orleans Athletic Club.

BLANCHE: Oh, good.

MITCH: It was the finest present I ever was given. I work out there with the weights and I swim and I keep myself fit. When I started there, I was getting soft in the belly but now my belly is hard. It is so hard now that a man can punch me in the belly and it don't hurt me. Punch me! Go on! See? (*She pokes lightly at him.*)

BLANCHE: Gracious. (*Her hand touches her chest.*)

MITCH: Guess how much I weigh, Blanche?

BLANCHE: Oh, I'd say in the vicinity of—one hundred and eighty?

MITCH: Guess again.

BLANCHE: Not that much?

MITCH: No. More.

BLANCHE: Well, you're a tall man and you can carry a good deal of weight without looking awkward.

MITCH: I weigh two hundred and seven pounds and I'm six feet one and one half inches tall in my bare feet—without shoes on. And that is what I weigh stripped.

BLANCHE: Oh, my goodness, me! It's awe-inspiring.

MITCH (*embarrassed*): My weight is not a very interesting subject to talk about. (*He hesitates for a moment*) What's yours?

BLANCHE: My weight?

MITCH: Yes.

BLANCHE: Guess!

MITCH: Let me lift you.

BLANCHE: Samson! Go on, lift me. (*He comes behind her and puts his hands on her waist and raises her lightly off the ground*) Well?

MITCH: You are light as a feather.

BLANCHE: Ha-ha! (*He lowers her but keeps his hands on her waist. Blanche speaks with an affectation of demureness*) You may release me now.

MITCH: Huh?

BLANCHE (*gaily*): I said unhand me, sir. (*He fumblingly embraces her. Her voice sounds gently reproving*) Now, Mitch. Just because Stanley and Stella aren't at home is no reason why you shouldn't behave like a gentleman.

MITCH: Just give me a slap whenever I step out of bounds.

BLANCHE: That won't be necessary. You're a natural gentleman, one of the very few that are left in the world. I don't want you to think that I am severe and old maid schoolteacherish or anything like that. It's just—well—

MITCH: Huh?

BLANCHE: I guess it is just that I have—old-fashioned ideals! (*She rolls her eyes, knowing he cannot see her face. Mitch goes to the front door. There is a considerable silence between them. Blanche sighs and Mitch coughs selfconsciously.*)

MITCH (*finally*): Where's Stanley and Stella tonight?

BLANCHE: They have gone out. With Mr. and Mrs. Hubbell upstairs.

MITCH: Where did they go?

BLANCHE: I think they were planning to go to a midnight preview at Loew's State.

MITCH: We should all go out together some night.

BLANCHE: No. That wouldn't be a good plan.

MITCH: Why not?

BLANCHE: You are an old friend of Stanley's?

MITCH: We was together in the Two-forty-first.

BLANCHE: I guess he talks to you frankly?

MITCH: Sure.

BLANCHE: Has he talked to you about me?

MITCH: Oh—not very much.

BLANCHE: The way you say that, I suspect that he has.

MITCH: No, he hasn't said much.

BLANCHE: But what he *has* said. What would you say his attitude toward me was?

MITCH: Why do you want to ask that?

BLANCHE: Well—

MITCH: Don't you get along with him?

BLANCHE: What do you think?

MITCH: I don't think he understands you.

BLANCHE: That is putting it mildly. If it weren't for Stella about to have a baby, I wouldn't be able to endure things here.

MITCH: He isn't—nice to you?

BLANCHE: He is insufferably rude. Goes out of his way to offend me.

MITCH: In what way, Blanche?

BLANCHE: Why, in every conceivable way.

MITCH: I'm surprised to hear that.

BLANCHE: Are you?

MITCH: Well, I—don't see how anybody could be rude to you.

BLANCHE: It's really a pretty frightful situation. You see, there's no privacy here. There's just these portieres between the two rooms at night. He stalks through the rooms in his underwear at night. And I have to ask him to close the bathroom door. That sort of commonness isn't necessary. You probably wonder why I don't move out. Well, I'll tell you frankly. A teacher's salary is barely sufficient for her living-expenses. I didn't save a penny last year and so I had to come here for the summer. That's why I have to put up with my sister's husband. And he has to put up with me, apparently so much against his wishes. . . . Surely he must have told you how much he hates me!

MITCH: I don't think he hates you.

BLANCHE: He hates me. Or why would he insult me? Of course there is such a thing as the hostility of—perhaps in some perverse kind of way he— No! To think of it makes me . . . (*She makes a gesture of revulsion. Then she finishes her drink. A pause follows.*)

MITCH: Blanche—

BLANCHE: Yes, honey?

MITCH: Can I ask you a question?

BLANCHE: Yes. What?

MITCH: How old are you?

(*She makes a nervous gesture.*)

BLANCHE: Why do you want to know?

MITCH: I talked to my mother about you and she said, "How old is Blanche?" And I wasn't able to tell her. (*There is another pause.*)

BLANCHE: You talked to your mother about me?

MITCH: Yes.

BLANCHE: Why?

MITCH: I told my mother how nice you were, and I liked you.

BLANCHE: Were you sincere about that?

MITCH: You know I was.

BLANCHE: Why did your mother want to know my age?

MITCH: Mother is sick.

BLANCHE: I'm sorry to hear it. Badly?

MITCH: She won't live long. Maybe just a few months.

BLANCHE: Oh.

MITCH: She worries because I'm not settled.

BLANCHE: Oh.

MITCH: She wants me to be settled down before she— (*His voice is hoarse and he clears his throat twice, shuffling nervously around with his hands in and out of his pockets.*)

BLANCHE: You love her very much, don't you?

MITCH: Yes.

BLANCHE: I think you have a great capacity for devotion. You will be lonely when she passes on, won't you? (*Mitch clears his throat and nods.*) I understand what that is.

MITCH: To be lonely?

BLANCHE: I loved someone, too, and the person I loved I lost.

MITCH: Dead? (*She crosses to the window and sits on the sill, looking out. She pours herself another drink.*) A man?

BLANCHE: He was a boy, just a boy, when I was a very young girl. When I was sixteen, I made the discovery—love. All at once and much, much too completely. It was like you suddenly turned a blinding light on something that had always been half in shadow, that's how it struck the world for me. But I was unlucky. Deluded. There was something different about the boy, a nervousness, a softness and tenderness which wasn't like a man's, although he wasn't the least bit effeminate looking—still—that thing was there. . . . He came to me for help. I didn't know that. I didn't find out anything till after our marriage when we'd run away and come back and all I knew was I'd failed him in some mysterious way and wasn't able to give the help he needed but couldn't speak of! He was in the quicksands and clutching at me—but I wasn't holding him out, I was slipping in with him! I didn't know that. I didn't know anything except I loved him unendurably but without being able to help him or help myself. Then I found out. In the worst of all possible ways. By coming suddenly into a room that I thought was empty—which wasn't empty, but had two people in it . . . the boy I had married and an older man who had been his friend for years . . .

(*A locomotive is heard approaching outside. She claps her hands to her ears and crouches over. The headlight of the locomotive glares into the room as it thunders past. As the noise recedes she straightens slowly and continues speaking.*)

Afterwards we pretended that nothing had been discovered. Yes, the three of us drove out to Moon Lake Casino, very drunk and laughing all the way.

(*Polka music sounds, in a minor key faint with distance.*)

We danced the Varsouviana! Suddenly in the middle of the dance the boy I had married broke away from me and ran out of the casino. A few moments later—a shot!

(*The Polka stops abruptly.*

(*Blanche rises stiffly. Then, the Polka resumes in a major key.*)

I ran out—all did!—all ran and gathered about the terrible thing at the edge of the lake! I couldn't get near for the crowding. Then somebody caught my arm. "Don't go any closer! Come back! You don't want to see!" See? See what! Then I heard voices say—Allan! Allan! The Grey boy! He'd stuck the revolver into his mouth, and fired—so that the back of his head had been—blown away!

(*She sways and covers her face.*)

It was because—on the dance-floor—unable to stop myself —I'd suddenly said—"I saw! I know! You disgust me . . ." And then the searchlight which had been turned on the world was turned off again and never for one moment since has there been any light that's stronger than this—kitchen—candle . . .

(*Mitch gets up awkwardly and moves toward her a little. The Polka music increases. Mitch stands beside her.*)

MITCH (*drawing her slowly into his arms*): You need somebody. And I need somebody, too. Could it be—you and me, Blanche?

(*She stares at him vacantly for a moment. Then with a soft cry huddles in his embrace. She makes a sobbing effort to speak but the words won't come. He kisses her forehead and her eyes and finally her lips. The Polka tune fades out. Her breath is drawn and released in long, grateful sobs.*)

BLANCHE: Sometimes—there's God—so quickly!

SCENE SEVEN

It is late afternoon in mid-September.

The portieres are open and a table is set for a birthday supper, with cake and flowers.

Stella is completing the decorations as Stanley comes in.

STANLEY: What's all this stuff for?

STELLA: Honey, it's Blanche's birthday.

STANLEY: She here?

STELLA: In the bathroom.

STANLEY (*mimicking*): "Washing out some things"?

STELLA: I reckon so.

STANLEY: How long she been in there?

STELLA: All afternoon.

STANLEY (*mimicking*): "Soaking in a hot tub"?

STELLA: Yes.

STANLEY: Temperature 100 on the nose, and she soaks herself in a hot tub.

STELLA: She says it cools her off for the evening.

STANLEY: And you run out an' get her cokes, I suppose? And serve 'em to Her Majesty in the tub? (*Stella shrugs*) Set down here a minute.

STELLA: Stanley, I've got things to do.

STANLEY: Set down! I've got th' dope on your big sister, Stella.

STELLA: Stanley, stop picking on Blanche.

STANLEY: That girl calls *me* common!

STELLA: Lately you been doing all you can think of to rub her the wrong way, Stanley, and Blanche is sensitive and you've got to realize that Blanche and I grew up under very different circumstances than you did.

STANLEY: So I been told. And told and told and told! You know she's been feeding us a pack of lies here?

STELLA: No, I don't, and—

STANLEY: Well, she has, however. But now the cat's out of the bag! I found out some things!

STELLA: What—things?

STANLEY: Things I already suspected. But now I got proof from the most reliable sources—which I have checked on!

(*Blanche is singing in the bathroom a saccharine popular ballad which is used contrapuntally with Stanley's speech.*)

STELLA (*to Stanley*): Lower your voice!

STANLEY: Some canary-bird, huh!

STELLA: Now please tell me quietly what you think you've found out about my sister.

STANLEY: Lie Number One: All this squeamishness she puts on! You should just know the line she's been feeding to Mitch. He thought she had never been more than kissed by a fellow! But Sister Blanche is no lily! Ha-ha! Some lily she is!

STELLA: What have you heard and who from?

STANLEY: Our supply-man down at the plant has been going through Laurel for years and he knows all about her and everybody else in the town of Laurel knows all about her. She is as famous in Laurel as if she was the President of the United States, only she is not respected by any party! This supply-man stops at a hotel called the Flamingo.

BLANCHE (*singing blithely*):

> "Say, it's only a paper moon, Sailing over a cardboard sea
> —But it wouldn't be make-believe If you believed in me!"

STELLA: What about the—Flamingo?

STANLEY: She stayed there, too.

STELLA: My sister lived at Belle Reve.

STANLEY: This is after the home-place had slipped through her lily-white fingers! She moved to the Flamingo! A second-class hotel which has the advantage of not interfering in the private social life of the personalities there! The Flamingo is used to all kinds of goings-on. But even the management of the Flamingo was impressed by Dame Blanche! In fact they was so impressed by Dame Blanche that they requested her to turn in her room-key—for permanently! This happened a couple of weeks before she showed here.

BLANCHE (*singing*):

"It's a Barnum and Bailey world, Just as phony as it can be—
But it wouldn't be make-believe If you believed in me!"

STELLA: What—contemptible—lies!

STANLEY: Sure, I can see how you would be upset by this. She pulled the wool over your eyes as much as Mitch's!

STELLA: It's pure invention! There's not a word of truth in it and if I were a man and this creature had dared to invent such things in my presence—

BLANCHE (*singing*):

"Without your love,
It's a honky-tonk parade!
Without your love,
It's a melody played In a penny arcade . . ."

STANLEY: Honey, I told you I thoroughly checked on these stories! Now wait till I'm finished. The trouble with Dame Blanche was that she couldn't put on her act any more in Laurel! They got wised up after two or three dates with her and then they quit, and she goes on to another, the same old line, same old act, same old hooey! But the town was too small for this to go on forever! And as time went by she became a town character. Regarded as not just different but downright loco—nuts.

(*Stella draws back.*)

And for the last year or two she has been washed up like poison. That's why she's here this summer, visiting royalty, putting on all this act—because she's practically told by the mayor to get out of town! Yes, did you know there was an army camp near Laurel and your sister's was one of the places called "Out-of-Bounds"?

BLANCHE:

"It's only a paper moon, Just as phony as it can be—
But it wouldn't be make-believe If you believed in me!"

STANLEY: Well, so much for her being such a refined and particular type of girl. Which brings us to Lie Number Two.

STELLA: I don't want to hear any more!

STANLEY: She's not going back to teach school! In fact I am willing to bet you that she never had no idea of returning to Laurel! She didn't resign temporarily from the high school because of her nerves! No, siree, Bob! She didn't. They kicked her out of that high school before the spring term ended—and I hate to tell you the reason that step was taken! A seventeen-year-old boy—she'd gotten mixed up with!

BLANCHE:

"It's a Barnum and Bailey world, Just as phony as it
can be—"

(*In the bathroom the water goes on loud; little breathless cries and peals of laughter are heard as if a child were frolicking in the tub.*)

STELLA: This is making me—sick!

STANLEY: The boy's dad learned about it and got in touch with the high school superintendent. Boy, oh, boy, I'd like to have been in that office when Dame Blanche was called on the carpet! I'd like to have seen her trying to squirm out of that one! But they had her on the hook good and proper that time and she knew that the jig was all up! They told her she better move on to some fresh territory. Yep, it was practickly a town ordinance passed against her!

(*The bathroom door is opened and Blanche thrusts her head out, holding a towel about her hair.*)

BLANCHE: Stella!

STELLA (*faintly*): Yes, Blanche?

BLANCHE: Give me another bath-towel to dry my hair with. I've just washed it.

STELLA: Yes, Blanche. (*She crosses in a dazed way from the kitchen to the bathroom door with a towel.*)

BLANCHE: What's the matter, honey?

STELLA: Matter? Why?

BLANCHE: You have such a strange expression on your face!

STELLA: Oh— (*She tries to laugh*) I guess I'm a little tired!

BLANCHE: Why don't you bathe, too, soon as I get out?

STANLEY (*calling from the kitchen*): How soon is that going to be?

BLANCHE: Not so terribly long! Possess your soul in patience!

STANLEY: It's not my soul, it's my kidneys I'm worried about!

(*Blanche slams the door. Stanley laughs harshly. Stella comes slowly back into the kitchen.*)

STANLEY: Well, what do you think of it?

STELLA: I don't believe all of those stories and I think your supply-man was mean and rotten to tell them. It's possible that some of the things he said are partly true. There are things about my sister I don't approve of—things that caused sorrow at home. She was always—flighty!

STANLEY: Flighty is some word for it!

STELLA: But when she was young, very young, she had an experience that—killed her illusions!

STANLEY: What experience was that?

STELLA: I mean her marriage, when she was—almost a child! She married a boy who wrote poetry. . . . He was extremely good-looking. I think Blanche didn't just love him but worshipped the ground he walked on! Adored him and thought him almost too fine to be human! But then she found out—

STANLEY: What?

STELLA: This beautiful and talented young man was a degenerate. Didn't your supply-man give you that information?

STANLEY: All we discussed was recent history. That must have been a pretty long time ago.

STELLA: Yes, it was—a pretty long time ago . . .

(*Stanley comes up and takes her by the shoulders rather gently. She gently withdraws from him. Automatically she starts sticking little pink candles in the birthday cake.*)

STANLEY: How many candles you putting in that cake?

STELLA: I'll stop at twenty-five.

STANLEY: Is company expected?

STELLA: We asked Mitch to come over for cake and ice-cream.

(*Stanley looks a little uncomfortable. He lights a cigarette from the one he has just finished.*)

STANLEY: I wouldn't be expecting Mitch over tonight.

(*Stella pauses in her occupation with candles and looks slowly around at Stanley.*)

STELLA: *Why?*

STANLEY: Mitch is a buddy of mine. We were in the same outfit together—Two-forty-first Engineers. We work in the same plant and now on the same bowling team. You think I could face him if—

STELLA: Stanley Kowalski, did you—did you repeat what that—?

STANLEY: You're goddam right I told him! I'd have that on my conscience the rest of my life if I knew all that stuff and let my best friend get caught!

STELLA: Is Mitch through with her?

STANLEY: Wouldn't you be if—?

STELLA: I said, *Is Mitch through with her?*

(*Blanche's voice is lifted again, serenely as a bell. She sings "But it wouldn't be make believe if you believed in me."*)

STANLEY: No, I don't think he's necessarily through with her—just wised up!

STELLA: Stanley, she thought Mitch was—going to—going to marry her. I was hoping so, too.

STANLEY: Well, he's not going to marry her. Maybe he *was*, but he's not going to jump in a tank with a school of sharks —now! (*He rises*) Blanche! Oh, Blanche! Can I please get in my bathroom? (*There is a pause.*)

BLANCHE: Yes, indeed, sir! Can you wait one second while I dry?

STANLEY: Having waited one hour I guess one second ought to pass in a hurry.

STELLA: And she hasn't got her job? Well, what will she do!

STANLEY: She's not stayin' here after Tuesday. You know that, don't you? Just to make sure I bought her ticket myself. A bus-ticket!

STELLA: In the first place, Blanche wouldn't go on a bus.

STANLEY: She'll go on a bus and like it.

STELLA: No, she won't, no, she won't, Stanley!

STANLEY: *She'll go!* Period. P.S. She'll go *Tuesday!*

STELLA (*slowly*): What'll—she—do? What on earth will she —*do!*

STANLEY: Her future is mapped out for her.
STELLA: What do you mean?

(*Blanche sings.*)

STANLEY: Hey, canary bird! Toots! Get *OUT* of the *BATHROOM!* Must I speak more plainly?

(*The bathroom door flies open and Blanche emerges with a gay peal of laughter, but as Stanley crosses past her, a frightened look appears in her face, almost a look of panic. He doesn't look at her but slams the bathroom door shut as he goes in.*)

BLANCHE (*snatching up a hair-brush*): Oh, I feel so good after my long, hot bath, I feel so good and cool and—rested!
STELLA (*sadly and doubtfully from the kitchen*): Do you, Blanche?
BLANCHE (*brushing her hair vigorously*): Yes, I do, so refreshed! (*She tinkles her highball glass.*) A hot bath and a long, cold drink always give me a brand new outlook on life! (*She looks through the portieres at Stella, standing between them, and slowly stops brushing*) Something has happened!—What is it?
STELLA (*turning away quickly*): Why, nothing has happened, Blanche.
BLANCHE: You're lying! Something has!

(*She stares fearfully at Stella, who pretends to be busy at the table. The distant piano goes into a hectic breakdown.*)

SCENE EIGHT

Three-quarters of an hour later.

The view through the big windows is fading gradually into a still-golden dusk. A torch of sunlight blazes on the side of a big water-tank or oil-drum across the empty lot toward the business district which is now pierced by pinpoints of lighted windows or windows reflecting the sunset.

The three people are completing a dismal birthday supper. Stanley looks sullen. Stella is embarrassed and sad.

Blanche has a tight, artificial smile on her drawn face. There is a fourth place at the table which is left vacant.

BLANCHE (*suddenly*): Stanley, tell us a joke, tell us a funny story to make us all laugh. I don't know what's the matter, we're all so solemn. Is it because I've been stood up by my beau?

(*Stella laughs feebly.*)

It's the first time in my entire experience with men, and I've had a good deal of all sorts, that I've actually been stood up by anybody! Ha-ha! I don't know how to take it. . . . Tell us a funny little story, Stanley! Something to help us out.

STANLEY: I didn't think you liked my stories, Blanche.

BLANCHE: I like them when they're amusing but not indecent.

STANLEY: I don't know any refined enough for your taste.

BLANCHE: Then let me tell one.

STELLA: Yes, you tell one, Blanche. You used to know lots of good stories.

(*The music fades.*)

BLANCHE: Let me see, now. . . . I must run through my repertoire! Oh, yes—I love parrot stories! Do you all like parrot stories? Well, this one's about the old maid and the parrot. This old maid, she had a parrot that cursed a blue streak and knew more vulgar expressions than Mr. Kowalski!

STANLEY: Huh.

BLANCHE: And the only way to hush the parrot up was to put the cover back on its cage so it would think it was night and go back to sleep. Well, one morning the old maid had just uncovered the parrot for the day—when who should she see coming up the front walk but the preacher! Well, she rushed back to the parrot and slipped the cover back on the cage and then she let in the preacher. And the parrot was perfectly still, just as quiet as a mouse, but just as she was asking the preacher how much sugar he wanted in his coffee—the parrot broke the silence with a loud—(*She whistles*)—and said—"God *damn*, but that was a short day!"

(*She throws back her head and laughs. Stella also makes an ineffectual effort to seem amused. Stanley pays no attention to the story but reaches way over the table to spear his fork into the remaining chop which he eats with his fingers.*)

BLANCHE: Apparently Mr. Kowalski was not amused.

STELLA: Mr. Kowalski is too busy making a pig of himself to think of anything else!

STANLEY: That's right, baby.

STELLA: Your face and your fingers are disgustingly greasy. Go and wash up and then help me clear the table.

(*He hurls a plate to the floor.*)

STANLEY: That's how I'll clear the table! (*He seizes her arm*) Don't ever talk that way to me! "Pig—Polack—disgusting—vulgar—greasy!"—them kind of words have been on your tongue and your sister's too much around here! What do you two think you are? A pair of queens? Remember what Huey Long said—"Every Man is a King!" And I am the king around here, so don't forget it! (*He hurls a cup and saucer to the floor*) My place is cleared! You want me to clear your places?

(*Stella begins to cry weakly. Stanley stalks out on the porch and lights a cigarette.*

(*The Negro entertainers around the corner are heard.*)

BLANCHE: What happened while I was bathing? What did he tell you, Stella?

STELLA: Nothing, nothing, nothing!

BLANCHE: I think he told you something about Mitch and me! You know why Mitch didn't come but you won't tell me! (*Stella shakes her head helplessly*) I'm going to call him!

STELLA: I wouldn't call him, Blanche.

BLANCHE: I am, I'm going to call him on the phone.

STELLA (*miserably*): I wish you wouldn't.

BLANCHE: I intend to be given some explanation from someone!

(*She rushes to the phone in the bedroom. Stella goes out on the porch and stares reproachfully at her husband. He grunts and turns away from her.*)

STELLA: I hope you're pleased with your doings. I never had so much trouble swallowing food in my life, looking at that girl's face and the empty chair! (*She cries quietly.*)

BLANCHE (*at the phone*): Hello. Mr. Mitchell, please. . . . Oh. . . . I would like to leave a number if I may. Magnolia 9047. And say it's important to call. . . . Yes, very important. . . . Thank you. (*She remains by the phone with a lost, frightened look.*)

(*Stanley turns slowly back toward his wife and takes her clumsily in his arms.*)

STANLEY: Stell, it's gonna be all right after she goes and after you've had the baby. It's gonna be all right again between you and me the way that it was. You remember that way that it was? Them nights we had together? God, honey, it's gonna be sweet when we can make noise in the night the way that we used to and get the colored lights going with nobody's sister behind the curtains to hear us!

(*Their upstairs neighbors are heard in bellowing laughter at something. Stanley chuckles.*)

Steve an' Eunice . . .

STELLA: Come on back in. (*She returns to the kitchen and starts lighting the candles on the white cake.*) Blanche?

BLANCHE: Yes. (*She returns from the bedroom to the table in the kitchen.*) Oh, those pretty, pretty little candles! Oh, don't burn them, Stella.

STELLA: I certainly will.

(*Stanley comes back in.*)

BLANCHE: You ought to save them for baby's birthdays. Oh, I hope candles are going to glow in his life and I hope that his eyes are going to be like candles, like two blue candles lighted in a white cake!

STANLEY (*sitting down*): What poetry!

BLANCHE: His Auntie knows candles aren't safe, that candles burn out in little boys' and girls' eyes, or wind blows them out and after that happens, electric light bulbs go on and you see too plainly . . . (*She pauses reflectively for a moment*) I shouldn't have called him.

STELLA: There's lots of things could have happened.

BLANCHE: There's no excuse for it, Stella. I don't have to put up with insults. I won't be taken for granted.

STANLEY: Goddamn, it's hot in here with the steam from the bathroom.

BLANCHE: I've said I was sorry three times. (*The piano fades out.*) I take hot baths for my nerves. Hydro-therapy, they call it. You healthy Polack, without a nerve in your body, of course you don't know what anxiety feels like!

STANLEY: I am not a Polack. People from Poland are Poles, not Polacks. But what I am is a one hundred percent American, born and raised in the greatest country on earth and proud as hell of it, so don't ever call me a Polack.

(*The phone rings. Blanche rises expectantly.*)

BLANCHE: Oh, that's for me, I'm sure.

STANLEY: *I'm* not sure. Keep your seat. (*He crosses leisurely to phone.*) H'lo. Aw, yeh, hello, Mac.

(*He leans against wall, staring insultingly in at Blanche. She sinks back in her chair with a frightened look. Stella leans over and touches her shoulder.*)

BLANCHE: Oh, keep your hands off me, Stella. What is the matter with you? Why do you look at me with that pitying look?

STANLEY (*bawling*): QUIET IN THERE!—We've got a noisy woman on the place.—Go on, Mac. At Riley's? No, I don't wanta bowl at Riley's. I had a little trouble with Riley last week. I'm the team-captain, ain't I? All right, then, we're not gonna bowl at Riley's, we're gonna bowl at the West Side or the Gala! All right, Mac. See you!

(*He hangs up and returns to the table. Blanche fiercely controls herself, drinking quickly from her tumbler of water. He doesn't look at her but reaches in a pocket. Then he speaks slowly and with false amiability.*)

Sister Blanche, I've got a little birthday remembrance for you.

BLANCHE: Oh, have you, Stanley? I wasn't expecting any, I—I don't know why Stella wants to observe my birthday! I'd much rather forget it—when you—reach twenty-seven! Well—age is a subject that you'd prefer to—ignore!

STANLEY: Twenty-seven?

BLANCHE (*quickly*): What is it? Is it for *me*?

(*He is holding a little envelope toward her.*)

STANLEY: Yes, I hope you like it!

BLANCHE: Why, why— Why, it's a—

STANLEY: Ticket! Back to Laurel! On the Greyhound! Tuesday!

(*The Varsouviana music steals in softly and continues playing. Stella rises abruptly and turns her back. Blanche tries to smile. Then she tries to laugh. Then she gives both up and springs from the table and runs into the next room. She clutches her throat and then runs into the bathroom. Coughing, gagging sounds are heard.*)

Well!

STELLA: You didn't need to do that.

STANLEY: Don't forget all that I took off her.

STELLA: You needn't have been so cruel to someone alone as she is.

STANLEY: Delicate piece she is.

STELLA: She is. She was. You didn't know Blanche as a girl. Nobody, nobody, was tender and trusting as she was. But people like you abused her, and forced her to change.

(*He crosses into the bedroom, ripping off his shirt, and changes into a brilliant silk bowling shirt. She follows him.*)

Do you think you're going bowling now?

STANLEY: Sure.

STELLA: You're not going bowling. (*She catches hold of his shirt*) Why did you do this to her?

STANLEY: I done nothing to no one. Let go of my shirt. You've torn it.

STELLA: I want to know why. Tell me why.

STANLEY: When we first met, me and you, you thought I was common. How right you was, baby. I was common as dirt. You showed me the snapshot of the place with the columns. I pulled you down off them columns and how you loved it, having them colored lights going! And wasn't we happy together, wasn't it all okay till she showed here?

(*Stella makes a slight movement. Her look goes suddenly inward as if some interior voice had called her name. She begins a slow, shuffling progress from the bedroom to the kitchen, leaning and resting on the back of the chair and then on the edge of a table with a blind look and listening expression. Stanley, finishing with his shirt, is unaware of her reaction.*)

And wasn't we happy together? Wasn't it all okay? Till she showed here. Hoity-toity, describing me as an ape. (*He suddenly notices the change in Stella*) Hey, what is it, Stel? (*He crosses to her.*)

STELLA (*quietly*): Take me to the hospital.

(*He is with her now, supporting her with his arm, murmuring indistinguishably as they go outside. The "Varsouviana" is heard, its music rising with sinister rapidity as the bathroom door opens slightly. Blanche comes out twisting a washcloth. She begins to whisper the words as the light fades slowly.*)

BLANCHE:

El pan de mais, el pan de mais,
El pan de mais sin sal.
El pan de mais, el pan de mais,
El pan de mais sin sal . . .

SCENE NINE

A while later that evening. Blanche is seated in a tense hunched position in a bedroom chair that she has recovered with diagonal green and white stripes. She has on her scarlet satin robe. On the table beside chair is a bottle of liquor and a glass. The rapid, feverish polka tune, the "Varsouviana," is heard. The music is in her mind; she is drinking to escape it and the sense of disaster closing in on her, and she seems to whisper the words of the song. An electric fan is turning back and forth across her.

Mitch comes around the corner in work clothes: blue denim shirt and pants. He is unshaven. He climbs the steps to the door and rings. Blanche is startled.

BLANCHE: Who is it, please?
MITCH (*hoarsely*): Me. Mitch.

(*The polka tune stops.*)

BLANCHE: Mitch!—Just a minute.

(*She rushes about frantically, hiding the bottle in a closet, crouching at the mirror and dabbing her face with cologne and powder. She is so excited that her breath is audible as she dashes about. At last she rushes to the door in the kitchen and lets him in.*)

Mitch!—Y'know, I really shouldn't let you in after the treatment I have received from you this evening! So utterly uncavalier! But hello, beautiful!

(*She offers him her lips. He ignores it and pushes past her into the flat. She looks fearfully after him as he stalks into the bedroom.*)

My, my, what a cold shoulder! And a face like a thunder-cloud! And such uncouth apparel! Why, you haven't even shaved! The unforgivable insult to a lady! But I forgive you. I forgive you because it's such a relief to see you. You've stopped that polka tune that I had caught in my head. Have you ever had anything caught in your head? Some words, a piece of music? That goes relentlessly on and on in your head? No, of course you haven't, you dumb angel-puss, you'd never get anything awful caught in your head!

(*He stares at her while she follows him while she talks. It is obvious that he has had a few drinks on the way over.*)

MITCH: Do we have to have that fan on?
BLANCHE: No!
MITCH: I don't like fans.
BLANCHE: Then let's turn it off, honey. I'm not partial to them!

(*She presses the switch and the fan nods slowly off. She clears her throat uneasily as Mitch plumps himself down on the bed in the bedroom and lights a cigarette.*)

I don't know what there is to drink. I—haven't investigated.

MITCH: I don't want Stan's liquor.

BLANCHE: It isn't Stan's. Everything here isn't Stan's. Some things on the premises are actually mine! How is your mother? Isn't your mother well?

MITCH: Why?

BLANCHE: Something's the matter tonight, but never mind. I won't cross-examine the witness. I'll just—(*She touches her forehead vaguely. The polka tune starts up again.*)—pretend I don't notice anything different about you! That—music again . . .

MITCH: What music?

BLANCHE: The "Varsouviana"! The polka tune they were playing when Allan— Wait!

(*A distant revolver shot is heard. Blanche seems relieved.*)

There now, the shot! It always stops after that.

(*The polka music dies out again.*)

Yes, now it's stopped.

MITCH: Are you boxed out of your mind?

BLANCHE: I'll go and see what I can find in the way of— (*She crosses into the closet, pretending to search for the bottle.*) Oh, by the way, excuse me for not being dressed. But I'd practically given you up! Had you forgotten your invitation to supper?

MITCH: I wasn't going to see you any more.

BLANCHE: Wait a minute. I can't hear what you're saying and you talk so little that when you do say something, I don't want to miss a single syllable of it. . . . What am I looking around here for? Oh, yes—liquor! We've had so much excitement around here this evening that I *am* boxed out of my mind! (*She pretends suddenly to find the bottle. He draws his foot up on the bed and stares at her contemptuously.*) Here's something. Southern Comfort! What is that, I wonder?

MITCH: If you don't know, it must belong to Stan.

BLANCHE: Take your foot off the bed. It has a light cover on it. Of course you boys don't notice things like that. I've done so much with this place since I've been here.

MITCH: I bet you have.

BLANCHE: You saw it before I came. Well, look at it now! This room is almost—dainty! I want to keep it that way. I wonder if this stuff ought to be mixed with something? Ummm, it's sweet, so sweet! It's terribly, terribly sweet! Why, it's a *liqueur*, I believe! Yes, that's what it *is*, a liqueur! (*Mitch grunts.*) I'm afraid you won't like it, but try it, and maybe you will.

MITCH: I told you already I don't want none of his liquor and I mean it. You ought to lay off his liquor. He says you been lapping it up all summer like a wild-cat!

BLANCHE: What a fantastic statement! Fantastic of him to say it, fantastic of you to repeat it! I won't descend to the level of such cheap accusations to answer them, even!

MITCH: Huh.

BLANCHE: What's in your mind? I see something in your eyes!

MITCH (*getting up*): It's dark in here.

BLANCHE: I like it dark. The dark is comforting to me.

MITCH: I don't think I ever seen you in the light. (*Blanche laughs breathlessly*) That's a fact!

BLANCHE: Is it?

MITCH: I've never seen you in the afternoon.

BLANCHE: Whose fault is that?

MITCH: You never want to go out in the afternoon.

BLANCHE: Why, Mitch, you're at the plant in the afternoon!

MITCH: Not Sunday afternoon. I've asked you to go out with me sometimes on Sundays but you always make an excuse. You never want to go out till after six and then it's always some place that's not lighted much.

BLANCHE: There is some obscure meaning in this but I fail to catch it.

MITCH: What it means is I've never had a real good look at you, Blanche.

BLANCHE: What are you leading up to?

MITCH: Let's turn the light on here.

BLANCHE (*fearfully*): Light? Which light? What for?

MITCH: This one with the paper thing on it. (*He tears the paper lantern off the light bulb. She utters a frightened gasp.*)

BLANCHE: What did you do that for?

MITCH: So I can take a look at you good and plain!

BLANCHE: Of course you don't really mean to be insulting!

MITCH: No, just realistic.

BLANCHE: I don't want realism.

MITCH: Naw, I guess not.

BLANCHE: I'll tell you what I want. Magic! (*Mitch laughs*) Yes, yes, magic! I try to give that to people. I misrepresent things to them. I don't tell truth, I tell what *ought* to be truth. And if that is sinful, then let me be damned for it!—*Don't turn the light on!*

(*Mitch crosses to the switch. He turns the light on and stares at her. She cries out and covers her face. He turns the light off again.*)

MITCH (*slowly and bitterly*): I don't mind you being older than what I thought. But all the rest of it—Christ! That pitch about your ideals being so old-fashioned and all the malarkey that you've dished out all summer. Oh, I knew you weren't sixteen any more. But I was a fool enough to believe you was straight.

BLANCHE: Who told you I wasn't—'straight'? My loving brother-in-law. And you believed him.

MITCH: I called him a liar at first. And then I checked on the story. First I asked our supply-man who travels through Laurel. And then I talked directly over long-distance to this merchant.

BLANCHE: Who is this merchant?

MITCH: Kiefaber.

BLANCHE: The merchant Kiefaber of Laurel! I know the man. He whistled at me. I put him in his place. So now for revenge he makes up stories about me.

MITCH: Three people, Kiefaber, Stanley and Shaw, swore to them!

BLANCHE: Rub-a-dub-dub, three men in a tub! And such a filthy tub!

MITCH: Didn't you stay at a hotel called The Flamingo?

BLANCHE: Flamingo? No! Tarantula was the name of it! I stayed at a hotel called The Tarantula Arms!

MITCH (*stupidly*): Tarantula?

BLANCHE: Yes, a big spider! That's where I brought my victims. (*She pours herself another drink*) Yes, I had many intimacies with strangers. After the death of Allan—intimacies with strangers was all I seemed able to fill my empty heart with. . . . I think it was panic, just panic, that drove me from one to another, hunting for some protection—here and there, in the most—unlikely places—even, at last, in a seventeen-year-old boy but—somebody wrote the superintendent about it—"This woman is morally unfit for her position!"

(*She throws back her head with convulsive, sobbing laughter. Then she repeats the statement, gasps, and drinks.*)

True? Yes, I suppose—unfit somehow—anyway. . . . So I came here. There was nowhere else I could go. I was played out. You know what played out is? My youth was suddenly gone up the water-spout, and—I met you. You said you needed somebody. Well, I needed somebody, too. I thanked God for you, because you seemed to be gentle—a cleft in the rock of the world that I could hide in! The poor man's Paradise—is a little peace. . . . But I guess I was asking, hoping—too much! Kiefaber, Stanley and Shaw have tied an old tin can to the tail of the kite.

(*There is a pause. Mitch stares at her dumbly.*)

MITCH: You lied to me, Blanche.
BLANCHE: Don't say I lied to you.
MITCH: Lies, lies, inside and out, all lies.
BLANCHE: Never inside, I didn't lie in my heart . . .

(*A Vendor comes around the corner. She is a blind Mexican woman in a dark shawl, carrying bunches of those gaudy tin flowers that lower class Mexicans display at funerals and other festive occasions. She is calling barely audibly. Her figure is only faintly visible outside the building.*)

MEXICAN WOMAN: *Flores. Flores. Flores para los muertos. Flores. Flores.*
BLANCHE: What? Oh! Somebody outside. . . . I—I lived in a house where dying old women remembered their dead men . . .
MEXICAN WOMAN: *Flores. Flores para los muertos . . .*

(*The polka tune fades in.*)

BLANCHE (*as if to herself*): Crumble and fade and—regrets—recriminations . . . 'If you'd done this, it wouldn't've cost me that!'

MEXICAN WOMAN: *Corones para los muertos. Corones . . .*

BLANCHE: Legacies! Huh. . . . And other things such as bloodstained pillow-slips—'Her linen needs changing'—'Yes Mother. But couldn't we get a colored girl to do it?' No, we couldn't of course. Everything gone but the—

MEXICAN WOMAN: *Flores.*

BLANCHE: Death—I used to sit here and she used to sit over there and death was as close as you are. . . . We didn't dare even admit we had ever heard of it!

MEXICAN WOMAN: *Flores para los muertos, flores—flores . . .*

BLANCHE: The opposite is desire. So do you wonder? How could you possibly wonder! Not far from Belle Reve, before we had lost Belle Reve, was a camp where they trained young soldiers. On Saturday nights they would go in town to get drunk—

MEXICAN WOMAN (*softly*): *Corones . . .*

BLANCHE: —and on the way back they would stagger onto my lawn and call—'Blanche! Blanche!'—The deaf old lady remaining suspected nothing. But sometimes I slipped outside to answer their calls. . . . Later the paddy-wagon would gather them up like daisies . . . the long way home . . .

(*The Mexican Woman turns slowly and drifts back off with her soft mournful cries. Blanche goes to the dresser and leans forward on it. After a moment, Mitch rises and follows her purposefully. The polka music fades away. He places his hands on her waist and tries to turn her about.*)

BLANCHE: What do you want?

MITCH (*fumbling to embrace her*): What I been missing all summer.

BLANCHE: Then marry me, Mitch!

MITCH: I don't think I want to marry you any more.

BLANCHE: No?

MITCH (*dropping his hands from her waist*): You're not clean enough to bring in the house with my mother.

BLANCHE: Go away, then. (*He stares at her*) Get out of here quick before I start screaming fire! (*Her throat is tightening with hysteria*) Get out of here quick before I start screaming fire.

(*He still remains staring. She suddenly rushes to the big window with its pale blue square of the soft summer light and cries wildly.*)

Fire! Fire! Fire!

(*With a startled gasp, Mitch turns and goes out the outer door, clatters awkwardly down the steps and around the corner of the building. Blanche staggers back from the window and falls to her knees. The distant piano is slow and blue.*)

SCENE TEN

It is a few hours later that night.

Blanche has been drinking fairly steadily since Mitch left. She has dragged her wardrobe trunk into the center of the bedroom. It hangs open with flowery dresses thrown across it. As the drinking and packing went on, a mood of hysterical exhilaration came into her and she has decked herself out in a somewhat soiled and crumpled white satin evening gown and a pair of scuffed silver slippers with brilliants set in their heels.

Now she is placing the rhinestone tiara on her head before the mirror of the dressing-table and murmuring excitedly as if to a group of spectral admirers.

BLANCHE: How about taking a swim, a moonlight swim at the old rock-quarry? If anyone's sober enough to drive a car! Ha-ha! Best way in the world to stop your head buzzing! Only you've got to be careful to dive where the deep pool is—if you hit a rock you don't come up till tomorrow . . .

(*Tremblingly she lifts the hand mirror for a closer inspection. She catches her breath and slams the mirror face down with such violence that the glass cracks. She moans a little and attempts to rise.*

(*Stanley appears around the corner of the building. He still has on the vivid green silk bowling shirt. As he rounds the corner the honky-tonk music is heard. It continues softly throughout the scene.*

(*He enters the kitchen, slamming the door. As he peers in at Blanche, he gives a low whistle. He has had a few drinks on the way and has brought some quart beer bottles home with him.*)

BLANCHE: How is my sister?

STANLEY: She is doing okay.

BLANCHE: And how is the baby?

STANLEY (*grinning amiably*): The baby won't come before morning so they told me to go home and get a little shut-eye.

BLANCHE: Does that mean we are to be alone in here?

STANLEY: Yep. Just me and you, Blanche. Unless you got somebody hid under the bed. What've you got on those fine feathers for?

BLANCHE: Oh, that's right. You left before my wire came.

STANLEY: You got a wire?

BLANCHE: I received a telegram from an old admirer of mine.

STANLEY: Anything good?

BLANCHE: I think so. An invitation.

STANLEY: What to? A fireman's ball?

BLANCHE (*throwing back her head*): A cruise of the Caribbean on a yacht!

STANLEY: Well, well. What do you know?

BLANCHE: I have never been so surprised in my life.

STANLEY: I guess not.

BLANCHE: It came like a bolt from the blue!

STANLEY: Who did you say it was from?

BLANCHE: An old beau of mine.

STANLEY: The one that give you the white fox-pieces?

BLANCHE: Mr. Shep Huntleigh. I wore his ATO pin my last year at college. I hadn't seen him again until last Christmas. I ran in to him on Biscayne Boulevard. Then—just now—this wire—inviting me on a cruise of the Caribbean! The problem is clothes. I tore into my trunk to see what I have that's suitable for the tropics!

STANLEY: And come up with that—gorgeous—diamond—tiara?

BLANCHE: This old relic? Ha-ha! It's only rhinestones.

STANLEY: Gosh. I thought it was Tiffany diamonds. (*He unbuttons his shirt.*)

BLANCHE: Well, anyhow, I shall be entertained in style.

STANLEY: Uh-huh. It goes to show, you never know what is coming.

BLANCHE: Just when I thought my luck had begun to fail me—

STANLEY: Into the picture pops this Miami millionaire.

BLANCHE: This man is not from Miami. This man is from Dallas.

STANLEY: This man is from Dallas?

BLANCHE: Yes, this man is from Dallas where gold spouts out of the ground!

STANLEY: Well, just so he's from somewhere! (*He starts removing his shirt.*)

BLANCHE: Close the curtains before you undress any further.

STANLEY (*amiably*): This is all I'm going to undress right now. (*He rips the sack off a quart beer-bottle*) Seen a bottle-opener?

(*She moves slowly toward the dresser, where she stands with her hands knotted together.*)

I used to have a cousin who could open a beer-bottle with his teeth. (*Pounding the bottle cap on the corner of table*) That was his only accomplishment, all he could do—he was just a human bottle-opener. And then one time, at a wedding party, he broke his front teeth off! After that he was so ashamed of himself he used t' sneak out of the house when company came . . .

(*The bottle cap pops off and a geyser of foam shoots up. Stanley laughs happily, holding up the bottle over his head.*)

Ha-ha! Rain from heaven! (*He extends the bottle toward her*) Shall we bury the hatchet and make it a loving-cup? Huh?

BLANCHE: No, thank you.

STANLEY: Well, it's a red letter night for us both. You having an oil-millionaire and me having a baby.

(*He goes to the bureau in the bedroom and crouches to remove something from the bottom drawer.*)

BLANCHE (*drawing back*): What are you doing in here?

STANLEY: Here's something I always break out on special occasions like this. The silk pyjamas I wore on my wedding night!

BLANCHE: Oh.

STANLEY: When the telephone rings and they say, "You've got a son!" I'll tear this off and wave it like a flag! (*He shakes out a brilliant pyjama coat*) I guess we are both entitled to put on the dog. (*He goes back to the kitchen with the coat over his arm.*)

BLANCHE: When I think of how divine it is going to be to have such a thing as privacy once more—I could weep with joy!

STANLEY: This millionaire from Dallas is not going to interfere with your privacy any?

BLANCHE: It won't be the sort of thing you have in mind. This man is a gentleman and he respects me. (*Improvising feverishly*) What he wants is my companionship. Having great wealth sometimes makes people lonely!

STANLEY: I wouldn't know about that.

BLANCHE: A cultivated woman, a woman of intelligence and breeding, can enrich a man's life—immeasurably! I have those things to offer, and this doesn't take them away. Physical beauty is passing. A transitory possession. But beauty of the mind and richness of the spirit and tenderness of the heart—and I have all of those things—aren't taken away, but grow! Increase with the years! How strange that I should be called a destitute woman! When I have all of these treasures locked in my heart. (*A choked sob comes from her*) I think of myself as a very, very rich woman! But I have been foolish—casting my pearls before swine!

STANLEY: Swine, huh?

BLANCHE: Yes, swine! Swine! And I'm thinking not only of you but of your friend, Mr. Mitchell. He came to see me tonight. He dared to come here in his work-clothes! And to repeat slander to me, vicious stories that he had gotten from you! I gave him his walking papers . . .

STANLEY: You did, huh?

BLANCHE: But then he came back. He returned with a box of roses to beg my forgiveness! He implored my forgiveness. But some things are not forgivable. Deliberate cruelty is not forgivable. It is the one unforgivable thing in my opinion and it is the one thing of which I have never, never been guilty. And so I told him, I said to him, "Thank you," but it was foolish of me to think that we could ever adapt ourselves to each other. Our ways of life are too different. Our attitudes and our backgrounds are incompatible. We have to be realistic about such things. So farewell, my friend! And let there be no hard feelings . . .

STANLEY: Was this before or after the telegram came from the Texas oil millionaire?

BLANCHE: What telegram? No! No, after! As a matter of fact, the wire came just as—

STANLEY: As a matter of fact there wasn't no wire at all!

BLANCHE: Oh, oh!

STANLEY: There isn't no millionaire! And Mitch didn't come back with roses 'cause I know where he is—

BLANCHE: Oh!

STANLEY: There isn't a goddam thing but imagination!

BLANCHE: Oh!

STANLEY: And lies and conceit and tricks!

BLANCHE: Oh!

STANLEY: And look at yourself! Take a look at yourself in that worn-out Mardi Gras outfit, rented for fifty cents from some rag-picker! And with the crazy crown on! What queen do you think you are?

BLANCHE: Oh—God . . .

STANLEY: I've been on to you from the start! Not once did you pull any wool over this boy's eyes! You come in here and sprinkle the place with powder and spray perfume and cover the light-bulb with a paper lantern, and lo and behold the place has turned into Egypt and you are the Queen of the Nile! Sitting on your throne and swilling down my liquor! I say—*Ha!—Ha!* Do you hear me? *Ha—ha—ha!* (*He walks into the bedroom.*)

BLANCHE: Don't come in here!

(*Lurid reflections appear on the walls around Blanche. The shadows are of a grotesque and menacing form. She catches her breath, crosses to the phone and jiggles the hook. Stanley goes into the bathroom and closes the door.*)

Operator, operator! Give me long-distance, please. . . . I want to get in touch with Mr. Shep Huntleigh of Dallas. He's so well-known he doesn't require any address. Just ask anybody who— Wait!!—No, I couldn't find it right now. . . . Please understand, I— No! No, wait! . . . One moment! Someone is— Nothing! Hold on, please!

(*She sets the phone down and crosses warily into the kitchen. The night is filled with inhuman voices like cries in a jungle.*

(*The shadows and lurid reflections move sinuously as flames along the wall spaces.*

(*Through the back wall of the rooms, which have become transparent, can be seen the sidewalk. A prostitute has rolled a drunkard. He pursues her along the walk, overtakes her and there is a struggle. A policeman's whistle breaks it up. The figures disappear.*

(*Some moments later the Negro Woman appears around the corner with a sequined bag which the prostitute had dropped on the walk. She is rooting excitedly through it.*

(*Blanche presses her knuckles to her lips and returns slowly to the phone. She speaks in a hoarse whisper.*)

BLANCHE: Operator! Operator! Never mind long-distance. Get Western Union. There isn't time to be— Western—Western Union!

(*She waits anxiously.*)

Western Union? Yes! I—want to—Take down this message! "In desperate, desperate circumstances! Help me! Caught in a trap. Caught in—" *Oh!*

(*The bathroom door is thrown open and Stanley comes out in the brilliant silk pyjamas. He grins at her as he knots the tasseled sash about his waist. She gasps and backs away from the phone. He stares at her for a count of ten. Then a clicking becomes audible from the telephone, steady and rasping.*)

STANLEY: You left th' phone off th' hook.

(*He crosses to it deliberately and sets it back on the hook. After he has replaced it, he stares at her again, his mouth slowly curving into a grin, as he waves between Blanche and the outer door.*

(*The barely audible "blue piano" begins to drum up louder. The sound of it turns into the roar of an approaching locomotive. Blanche crouches, pressing her fists to her ears until it has gone by.*)

BLANCHE (*finally straightening*): Let me—let me get by you!

STANLEY: Get by me? Sure. Go ahead. (*He moves back a pace in the doorway.*)

BLANCHE: You—you stand over there! (*She indicates a further position.*)

STANLEY (*grinning*): You got plenty of room to walk by me now.

BLANCHE: Not with you there! But I've got to get out somehow!

STANLEY: You think I'll interfere with you? Ha-ha!

(*The "blue piano" goes softly. She turns confusedly and makes a faint gesture. The inhuman jungle voices rise up. He takes a step toward her, biting his tongue which protrudes between his lips.*)

STANLEY (*softly*): Come to think of it—maybe you wouldn't be bad to—interfere with . . .

(*Blanche moves backward through the door into the bedroom.*)

BLANCHE: Stay back! Don't you come toward me another step or I'll—

STANLEY: What?

BLANCHE: Some awful thing will happen! It will!

STANLEY: What are you putting on now?

(*They are now both inside the bedroom.*)

BLANCHE: I warn you, don't, I'm in danger!

(*He takes another step. She smashes a bottle on the table and faces him, clutching the broken top.*)

STANLEY: What did you do that for?

BLANCHE: So I could twist the broken end in your face!

STANLEY: I bet you would do that!

BLANCHE: I would! I will if you—

STANLEY: Oh! So you want some rough-house! All right, let's have some rough-house!

(*He springs toward her, overturning the table. She cries out and strikes at him with the bottle top but he catches her wrist.*)

Tiger—tiger! Drop the bottle-top! Drop it! We've had this date with each other from the beginning!

(*She moans. The bottle-top falls. She sinks to her knees. He picks up her inert figure and carries her to the bed. The hot trumpet and drums from the Four Deuces sound loudly.*)

SCENE ELEVEN

It is some weeks later. Stella is packing Blanche's things. Sound of water can be heard running in the bathroom.

The portieres are partly open on the poker players—Stanley, Steve, Mitch and Pablo—who sit around the table in the kitchen. The atmosphere of the kitchen is now the same raw, lurid one of the disastrous poker night.

The building is framed by the sky of turquoise. Stella has been crying as she arranges the flowery dresses in the open trunk.

Eunice comes down the steps from her flat above and enters the kitchen. There is an outburst from the poker table.

STANLEY: Drew to an inside straight and made it, by God.

PABLO: *Maldita sea tu suerto!*

STANLEY: Put it in English, greaseball.

PABLO: I am cursing your rutting luck.

STANLEY (*prodigiously elated*): You know what luck is? Luck is believing you're lucky. Take at Salerno. I believed I was lucky. I figured that 4 out of 5 would not come through but I would . . . and I did. I put that down as a rule. To hold front position in this rat-race you've got to believe you are lucky.

MITCH: You . . . you . . . you. . . . Brag . . . brag . . . bull . . . bull.

(*Stella goes into the bedroom and starts folding a dress.*)

STANLEY: What's the matter with him?

EUNICE (*walking past the table*): I always did say that men are callous things with no feelings, but this does beat anything. Making pigs of yourselves. (*She comes through the portieres into the bedroom.*)

STANLEY: What's the matter with her?

STELLA: How is my baby?

EUNICE: Sleeping like a little angel. Brought you some grapes. (*She puts them on a stool and lowers her voice.*) Blanche?

STELLA: Bathing.

EUNICE: How is she?

STELLA: She wouldn't eat anything but asked for a drink.

EUNICE: What did you tell her?

STELLA: I—just told her that—we'd made arrangements for her to rest in the country. She's got it mixed in her mind with Shep Huntleigh.

(*Blanche opens the bathroom door slightly.*)

BLANCHE: Stella.

STELLA: Yes, Blanche?

BLANCHE: If anyone calls while I'm bathing take the number and tell them I'll call right back.

STELLA: Yes.

BLANCHE: That cool yellow silk—the bouclé. See if it's crushed. If it's not too crushed I'll wear it and on the lapel that silver and turquoise pin in the shape of a seahorse. You will find them in the heart-shaped box I keep my accessories in. And Stella . . . Try and locate a bunch of artificial violets in that box, too, to pin with the seahorse on the lapel of the jacket.

(*She closes the door. Stella turns to Eunice.*)

STELLA: I don't know if I did the right thing.

EUNICE: What else could you do?

STELLA: I couldn't believe her story and go on living with Stanley.

EUNICE: Don't ever believe it. Life has got to go on. No matter what happens, you've got to keep on going.

(*The bathroom door opens a little.*)

BLANCHE (*looking out*): Is the coast clear?
STELLA: Yes, Blanche. (*To Eunice*) Tell her how well she's looking.
BLANCHE: Please close the curtains before I come out.
STELLA: They're closed.
STANLEY: —How many for you?
PABLO: —Two.
STEVE: —Three.

(*Blanche appears in the amber light of the door. She has a tragic radiance in her red satin robe following the sculptural lines of her body. The "Varsouviana" rises audibly as Blanche enters the bedroom.*)

BLANCHE (*with faintly hysterical vivacity*): I have just washed my hair.
STELLA: Did you?
BLANCHE: I'm not sure I got the soap out.
EUNICE: Such fine hair!
BLANCHE: (*accepting the compliment*): It's a problem. Didn't I get a call?
STELLA: Who from, Blanche?
BLANCHE: Shep Huntleigh . . .
STELLA: Why, not yet, honey!
BLANCHE: How strange! I—

(*At the sound of Blanche's voice Mitch's arm supporting his cards has sagged and his gaze is dissolved into space. Stanley slaps him on the shoulder.*)

STANLEY: Hey, Mitch, come to!

(*The sound of this new voice shocks Blanche. She makes a shocked gesture, forming his name with her lips. Stella nods and looks quickly away. Blanche stands quite still for some moments—the silverbacked mirror in her hand and a look of sorrowful perplexity as though all human experience shows on her face. Blanche finally speaks but with sudden hysteria.*)

BLANCHE: What's going on here?

(*She turns from Stella to Eunice and back to Stella. Her rising voice penetrates the concentration of the game. Mitch ducks his head lower but Stanley shoves back his chair as if about to rise. Steve places a restraining hand on his arm.*)

BLANCHE (*continuing*): What's happened here? I want an explanation of what's happened here.

STELLA (*agonizingly*): Hush! Hush!

EUNICE: Hush! Hush! Honey.

STELLA: Please, Blanche.

BLANCHE: Why are you looking at me like that? Is something wrong with me?

EUNICE: You look wonderful, Blanche. Don't she look wonderful?

STELLA: Yes.

EUNICE: I understand you are going on a trip.

STELLA: Yes, Blanche *is*. She's going on a vacation.

EUNICE: I'm green with envy.

BLANCHE: Help me, help me get dressed!

STELLA (*handing her dress*): Is this what you—

BLANCHE: Yes, it will do! I'm anxious to get out of here—this place is a trap!

EUNICE: What a pretty blue jacket.

STELLA: It's lilac colored.

BLANCHE: You're both mistaken. It's Della Robbia blue. The blue of the robe in the old Madonna pictures. Are these grapes washed?

(*She fingers the bunch of grapes which Eunice had brought in.*)

EUNICE: Huh?

BLANCHE: Washed, I said. Are they washed?

EUNICE: They're from the French Market.

BLANCHE: That doesn't mean they've been washed. (*The cathedral bells chime*) Those cathedral bells—they're the only clean thing in the Quarter. Well, I'm going now. I'm ready to go.

EUNICE (*whispering*): She's going to walk out before they get here.

STELLA: Wait, Blanche.
BLANCHE: I don't want to pass in front of those men.
EUNICE: Then wait'll the game breaks up.
STELLA: Sit down and . . .

(*Blanche turns weakly, hesitantly about. She lets them push her into a chair.*)

BLANCHE: I can smell the sea air. The rest of my time I'm going to spend on the sea. And when I die, I'm going to die on the sea. You know what I shall die of? (*She plucks a grape*) I shall die of eating an unwashed grape one day out on the ocean. I will die—with my hand in the hand of some nice-looking ship's doctor, a very young one with a small blond mustache and a big silver watch. "Poor lady," they'll say, "the quinine did her no good. That unwashed grape has transported her soul to heaven." (*The cathedral chimes are heard*) And I'll be buried at sea sewn up in a clean white sack and dropped overboard—at noon—in the blaze of summer—and into an ocean as blue as (*Chimes again*) my first lover's eyes!

(*A Doctor and a Matron have appeared around the corner of the building and climbed the steps to the porch. The gravity of their profession is exaggerated—the unmistakable aura of the state institution with its cynical detachment. The Doctor rings the doorbell. The murmur of the game is interrupted.*)

EUNICE (*whispering to Stella*): That must be them.

(*Stella presses her fists to her lips.*)

BLANCHE (*rising slowly*): What is it?
EUNICE (*affectedly casual*): Excuse me while I see who's at the door.
STELLA: Yes.

(*Eunice goes into the kitchen.*)

BLANCHE (*tensely*): I wonder if it's for me.

(*A whispered colloquy takes place at the door.*)

EUNICE (*returning, brightly*): Someone is calling for Blanche.

BLANCHE: It *is* for me, then! (*She looks fearfully from one to the other and then to the portieres. The "Varsouviana" faintly plays*) Is it the gentleman I was expecting from Dallas?

EUNICE: I think it is, Blanche.

BLANCHE: I'm not quite ready.

STELLA: Ask him to wait outside.

BLANCHE: I . . .

(*Eunice goes back to the portieres. Drums sound very softly.*)

STELLA: Everything packed?

BLANCHE: My silver toilet articles are still out.

STELLA: Ah!

EUNICE (*returning*): They're waiting in front of the house.

BLANCHE: They! Who's "they"?

EUNICE: There's a lady with him.

BLANCHE: I cannot imagine who this "lady" could be! How is she dressed?

EUNICE: Just—just a sort of a—plain-tailored outfit.

BLANCHE: Possibly she's— (*Her voice dies out nervously.*)

STELLA: Shall we go, Blanche?

BLANCHE: Must we go through that room?

STELLA: I will go with you.

BLANCHE: How do I look?

STELLA: Lovely.

EUNICE (*echoing*): Lovely.

(*Blanche moves fearfully to the portieres. Eunice draws them open for her. Blanche goes into the kitchen.*)

BLANCHE (*to the men*): Please don't get up. I'm only passing through.

(*She crosses quickly to outside door. Stella and Eunice follow. The poker players stand awkwardly at the table—all except Mitch, who remains seated, looking down at the table. Blanche steps out on a small porch at the side of the door. She stops short and catches her breath.*)

DOCTOR: How do you do?

BLANCHE: You are not the gentleman I was expecting. (*She suddenly gasps and starts back up the steps. She stops by Stella, who stands just outside the door, and speaks in a frightening whisper*) That man isn't Shep Huntleigh.

(*The "Varsouviana" is playing distantly.*

(*Stella stares back at Blanche. Eunice is holding Stella's arm. There is a moment of silence—no sound but that of Stanley steadily shuffling the cards.*

(*Blanche catches her breath again and slips back into the flat. She enters the flat with a peculiar smile, her eyes wide and brilliant. As soon as her sister goes past her, Stella closes her eyes and clenches her hands. Eunice throws her arms comfortingly about her. Then she starts up to her flat. Blanche stops just inside the door. Mitch keeps staring down at his hands on the table, but the other men look at her curiously. At last she starts around the table toward the bedroom. As she does, Stanley suddenly pushes back his chair and rises as if to block her way. The Matron follows her into the flat.*)

STANLEY: Did you forget something?
BLANCHE (*shrilly*): Yes! Yes, I forgot something!

(*She rushes past him into the bedroom. Lurid reflections appear on the walls in odd, sinuous shapes. The "Varsouviana" is filtered into a weird distortion, accompanied by the cries and noises of the jungle. Blanche seizes the back of a chair as if to defend herself.*)

STANLEY: Doc, you better go in.
DOCTOR (*motioning to the Matron*): Nurse, bring her out.

(*The Matron advances on one side, Stanley on the other. Divested of all the softer properties of womanhood, the Matron is a peculiarly sinister figure in her severe dress. Her voice is bold and toneless as a firebell.*)

MATRON: Hello, Blanche.

(*The greeting is echoed and re-echoed by other mysterious voices behind the walls, as if reverberated through a canyon of rock.*)

STANLEY: She says that she forgot something.

(*The echo sounds in threatening whispers.*)

MATRON: That's all right.

STANLEY: What did you forget, Blanche?

BLANCHE: I— I—

MATRON: It don't matter. We can pick it up later.

STANLEY: Sure. We can send it along with the trunk.

BLANCHE (*retreating in panic*): I don't know you—I don't know you. I want to be—left alone—please!

MATRON: Now, Blanche!

ECHOES (*rising and falling*): Now, Blanche—now, Blanche—now, Blanche!

STANLEY: You left nothing here but spilt talcum and old empty perfume bottles—unless it's the paper lantern you want to take with you. You want the lantern?

(*He crosses to dressing table and seizes the paper lantern, tearing it off the light bulb, and extends it toward her. She cries out as if the lantern was herself. The Matron steps boldly toward her. She screams and tries to break past the Matron. All the men spring to their feet. Stella runs out to the porch, with Eunice following to comfort her, simultaneously with the confused voices of the men in the kitchen. Stella rushes into Eunice's embrace on the porch.*)

STELLA: Oh, my God, Eunice help me! Don't let them do that to her, don't let them hurt her! Oh, God, oh, please God, don't hurt her! What are they doing to her? What are they doing? (*She tries to break from Eunice's arms.*)

EUNICE: No, honey, no, no, honey. Stay here. Don't go back in there. Stay with me and don't look.

STELLA: What have I done to my sister? Oh, God, what have I done to my sister?

EUNICE: You done the right thing, the only thing you could do. She couldn't stay here; there wasn't no other place for her to go.

(*While Stella and Eunice are speaking on the porch the voices of the men in the kitchen overlap them.*)

STANLEY (*running in from the bedroom*): Hey! Hey! Doctor! Doctor, you better go in!

DOCTOR: Too bad, too bad. I always like to avoid it.

PABLO: This is a very bad thing.

STEVE: This is no way to do it. She should've been told.
PABLO: *Madre de Dios! Cosa mala, muy, muy mala!*

(*Mitch has started toward the bedroom. Stanley crosses to block him.*)

MITCH (*wildly*): You! You done this, all o' your God damn rutting with things you—
STANLEY: Quit the blubber! (*He pushes him aside.*)
MITCH: I'll kill you! (*He lunges and strikes at Stanley.*)
STANLEY: Hold this bone-headed cry-baby!
STEVE (*grasping Mitch*): Stop it, Mitch.
PABLO: Yeah, yeah, take it easy!

(*Mitch collapses at the table, sobbing.*

(*During the preceding scenes, the Matron catches hold of Blanche's arm and prevents her flight. Blanche turns wildly and scratches at the Matron. The heavy woman pinions her arms. Blanche cries out hoarsely and slips to her knees.*

MATRON: These fingernails have to be trimmed. (*The Doctor comes into the room and she looks at him.*) Jacket, Doctor?
DOCTOR: Not unless necessary.

(*He takes off his hat and now he becomes personalized. The unhuman quality goes. His voice is gentle and reassuring as he crosses to Blanche and crouches in front of her. As he speaks her name, her terror subsides a little. The lurid reflections fade from the walls, the inhuman cries and noises die out and her own hoarse crying is calmed.*)

DOCTOR: Miss DuBois.

(*She turns her face to him and stares at him with desperate pleading. He smiles; then he speaks to the Matron.*)

It won't be necessary.

BLANCHE (*faintly*): Ask her to let go of me.
DOCTOR (*to the Matron*): Let go.

(*The Matron releases her. Blanche extends her hands toward the Doctor. He draws her up gently and supports her with his arm and leads her through the portieres.*)

BLANCHE (*holding tight to his arm*): Whoever you are—I have always depended on the kindness of strangers.

(*The poker players stand back as Blanche and the Doctor cross the kitchen to the front door. She allows him to lead her as if she were blind. As they go out on the porch, Stella cries out her sister's name from where she is crouched a few steps up on the stairs.*)

STELLA: Blanche! Blanche, Blanche!

(*Blanche walks on without turning, followed by the Doctor and the Matron. They go around the corner of the building.*

(*Eunice descends to Stella and places the child in her arms. It is wrapped in a pale blue blanket. Stella accepts the child, sobbingly. Eunice continues downstairs and enters the kitchen where the men, except for Stanley, are returning silently to their places about the table. Stanley has gone out on the porch and stands at the foot of the steps looking at Stella.*)

STANLEY (*a bit uncertainly*): Stella?

(*She sobs with inhuman abandon. There is something luxurious in her complete surrender to crying now that her sister is gone.*)

STANLEY (*voluptuously, soothingly*): Now, honey. Now, love. Now, now, love. (*He kneels beside her and his fingers find the opening of her blouse*) Now, now, love. Now, love. . . .

(*The luxurious sobbing, the sensual murmur fade away under the swelling music of the "blue piano" and the muted trumpet.*)

STEVE: This game is seven-card stud.

Curtain

(LEGEND ON SCREEN: "THE OPENING OF A DOOR!")

(*Tom and Jim appear on the fire-escape steps and climb to landing. Hearing their approach, Laura rises with a panicky gesture. She retreats to the portieres.*)

(*The doorbell. Laura catches her breath and touches her throat. Low drums.*)

AMANDA: (*Calling*) Laura, sweetheart! The door!

(*Laura stares at it without moving.*)

JIM: I think we just beat the rain.
TOM: Uh-huh. (*He rings again, nervously. Jim whistles and fishes for a cigarette.*)
AMANDA: (*Very, very gaily*) Laura, that is your brother and Mr. O'Connor! Will you let them in, darling?

(*Laura crosses toward kitchenette door.*)

LAURA: (*Breathlessly*) Mother—you go to the door!

(*Amanda steps out of kitchenette and stares furiously at Laura. She points imperiously at the door.*)

LAURA: Please, please!
AMANDA: (*In a fierce whisper*) What is the matter with you, you silly thing?
LAURA: (*Desperately*) Please, you answer it, *please!*
AMANDA: I told you I wasn't going to humor you, Laura. Why have you chosen this moment to lose your mind?
LAURA: Please, please, please, you go!
AMANDA: You'll have to go to the door because I can't!
LAURA: (*Despairingly*) I can't either!
AMANDA: *Why?*
LAURA: I'm *sick!*
AMANDA: I'm sick, too—of your nonsense! Why can't you and your brother be normal people? Fantastic whims and behavior!

(*Tom gives a long ring.*)

Preposterous goings on! Can you give me one reason—(*Calls out lyrically*) COMING! JUST ONE SECOND!—why you should be afraid to open a door? Now you answer it, Laura!

LAURA: Oh, oh, oh . . . (*She returns through the portieres. Darts to the victrola and winds it frantically and turns it on.*)

AMANDA: Laura Wingfield, you march right to that door!

LAURA: Yes—yes, Mother! (*A faraway, scratchy rendition of "Dardanella" softens the air and gives her strength to move through it. She slips to the door and draws it cautiously open.*)

(*Tom enters with the caller, Jim O'Connor.*)

TOM: Laura, this is Jim. Jim, this is my sister, Laura.

JIM: (*Stepping inside*) I didn't know that Shakespeare had a sister!

LAURA: (*Retreating stiff and trembling from the door*) How—how do you do?

JIM: (*Heartily extending his hand*) Okay!

(*Laura touches it hesitantly with hers.*)

JIM: Your hand's *cold*, Laura!

LAURA: Yes, well—I've been playing the victrola. . . .

JIM: Must have been playing classical music on it! You ought to play a little hot swing music to warm you up!

LAURA: Excuse me—I haven't finished playing the victrola. . . . (*She turns awkwardly and hurries into the front room. She pauses a second by the victrola. Then catches her breath and darts through the portieres like a frightened deer.*)

JIM: (*Grinning*) What was the matter?

TOM: Oh—with Laura? Laura is—terribly shy.

JIM: Shy, huh? It's unusual to meet a shy girl nowadays. I don't believe you ever mentioned you had a sister.

TOM: Well, now you know. I have one. Here is the *Post Dispatch*. You want a piece of it?

JIM: Uh-huh.

TOM: What piece? The comics?

JIM: Sports! (*Glances at it*) Ole Dizzy Dean is on his bad behavior.

TOM: (*Disinterest*) Yeah? (*Lights cigarette and crosses back to fire-escape door.*)

JIM: Where are *you* going?

TOM: I'm going out on the terrace.

JIM: (*Goes after him*) You know, Shakespeare—I'm going to sell you a bill of goods!

TOM: What goods?

JIM: A course I'm taking.

TOM: Huh?

JIM: In public speaking! You and me, we're not the warehouse type.

TOM: Thanks—that's good news. But what has public speaking got to do with it?

JIM: It fits you for—executive positions!

TOM: Awww.

JIM: I tell you it's done a helluva lot for me.

(IMAGE: EXECUTIVE AT DESK.)

TOM: In what respect?

JIM: In every! Ask yourself what is the difference between you an' me and men in the office down front? Brains?—No!—Ability?—No! Then what? Just one little thing—

TOM: What is that one little thing?

JIM: Primarily it amounts to—social poise! Being able to square up to people and hold your own on any social level!

AMANDA: (*Off stage*) Tom?

TOM: Yes, Mother?

AMANDA: Is that you and Mr. O'Connor?

TOM: Yes, Mother.

AMANDA: Well, you just make yourselves comfortable in there.

TOM: Yes, Mother.

AMANDA: Ask Mr. O'Connor if he would like to wash his hands.

JIM: Aw, no—no—thank you—I took care of that at the warehouse. Tom—

TOM: Yes?

JIM: Mr. Mendoza was speaking to me about you.

TOM: Favorably?

JIM: What do you think?

TOM: Well—

JIM: You're going to be out of a job if you don't wake up.

TOM: I am waking up—

JIM: You show no signs.

TOM: The signs are interior.

(IMAGE ON SCREEN: THE SAILING VESSEL WITH JOLLY ROGER AGAIN.)

TOM: I'm planning to change. (*He leans over the rail speaking with quiet exhilaration. The incandescent marquees and signs of the first-run movie houses light his face from across the alley. He looks like a voyager*) I'm right at the point of committing myself to a future that doesn't include the warehouse and Mr. Mendoza or even a night-school course in public speaking.

JIM: What are you gassing about?

TOM: I'm tired of the movies.

JIM: Movies!

TOM: Yes, movies! Look at them— (*A wave toward the marvels of Grand Avenue*) All of those glamorous people—having adventures—hogging it all, gobbling the whole thing up! You know what happens? People go to the *movies* instead of *moving!* Hollywood characters are supposed to have all the adventures for everybody in America, while everybody in America sits in a dark room and watches them have them! Yes, until there's a war. That's when adventure becomes available to the masses! *Everyone's* dish, not only Gable's! Then the people in the dark room come out of the dark room to have some adventures themselves—Goody, goody!—It's our turn now, to go to the South Sea Island—to make a safari—to be exotic, far-off!—But I'm not patient. I don't want to wait till then. I'm tired of the *movies* and I am *about* to *move!*

JIM: (*Incredulously*) Move?

TOM: Yes.

JIM: When?

TOM: Soon!

JIM: Where? Where?

(THEME THREE MUSIC SEEMS TO ANSWER THE QUESTION, WHILE TOM THINKS IT OVER. HE SEARCHES AMONG HIS POCKETS.)

TOM: I'm starting to boil inside. I know I seem dreamy, but inside—well, I'm boiling!—Whenever I pick up a shoe, I shudder a little thinking how short life is and what I am doing!—Whatever that means, I know it doesn't mean shoes —except as something to wear on a traveler's feet! (*Finds paper*) Look—

JIM: What?

TOM: I'm a member.

JIM: (*Reading*) The Union of Merchant Seamen.

TOM: I paid my dues this month, instead of the light bill.

JIM: You will regret it when they turn the lights off.

TOM: I won't be here.

JIM: How about your mother?

TOM: I'm like my father. The bastard son of a bastard! See how he grins? And he's been absent going on sixteen years!

JIM: You're just talking, you drip. How does your mother feel about it?

TOM: Shhh!—Here comes Mother! Mother is not acquainted with my plans!

AMANDA: (*Enters portieres*) Where are you all?

TOM: On the terrace, Mother.

(*They start inside. She advances to them. Tom is distinctly shocked at her appearance. Even Jim blinks a little. He is making his first contact with girlish Southern vivacity and in spite of the night-school course in public speaking is somewhat thrown off the beam by the unexpected outlay of social charm.*)

(*Certain responses are attempted by Jim but are swept aside by Amanda's gay laughter and chatter. Tom is embarrassed but after the first shock Jim reacts very warmly. Grins and chuckles, is altogether won over.*)

(IMAGE: AMANDA AS A GIRL.)

AMANDA: (*Coyly smiling, shaking her girlish ringlets*) Well, well, well, so this is Mr. O'Connor. Introductions entirely unnecessary. I've heard so much about you from my boy. I finally said to him, Tom—good gracious!—why don't you bring this paragon to supper? I'd like to meet this nice young man at the warehouse!—Instead of just hearing him sing your praises so much!

I don't know why my son is so stand-offish—that's not Southern behavior!

Let's sit down and— I think we could stand a little more air in here! Tom, leave the door open. I felt a nice fresh breeze a moment ago. Where has it gone to?

Mmm, so warm already! And not quite summer, even. We're going to burn up when summer really gets started.

However, we're having—we're having a very light supper. I think light things are better fo' this time of year. The same as light clothes are. Light clothes an' light food are what warm weather calls fo'. You know our blood gets so thick during th' winter—it takes a while fo' us to *adjust* ou'selves!—when the season changes . . .

It's come so quick this year. I wasn't prepared. All of a sudden—heavens! Already summer!—I ran to the trunk an' pulled out this light dress— Terribly old! Historical almost! But feels so good—so good an' co-ol, y' know. . . .

TOM: Mother—

AMANDA: Yes, honey?

TOM: How about—supper?

AMANDA: Honey, you go ask Sister if supper is ready! You know that Sister is in full charge of supper!

Tell her you hungry boys are waiting for it. (*To Jim.*) Have you met Laura?

JIM: She—

AMANDA: Let you in? Oh, good, you've met already! It's rare for a girl as sweet an' pretty as Laura to be domestic! But Laura is, thank heavens, not only pretty but also very domestic. I'm not at all. I never was a bit. I never could make a thing but angel-food cake. Well, in the South we had so many servants. Gone, gone, gone. All vestige of gracious living! Gone completely! I wasn't prepared for what the future brought me. All of my gentlemen callers were sons of planters and so of course I assumed that I would be married to one and raise my family on a large piece of land with plenty of servants. But man proposes—and woman accepts the proposal!—To vary that old, old saying a little bit— I married no planter! I married a man who worked for the telephone company!—That gallantly smiling gentleman over there! (*Points to the picture*) A telephone man who—fell in love with long-distance!—Now he travels and I don't even know where!—But what am I going on for about my—tribulations?

Tell me yours—I hope you don't have any!

Tom?

TOM: (*Returning*) Yes, Mother?

AMANDA: Is supper nearly ready?

TOM: It looks to me like supper is on the table.

AMANDA: Let me look— (*She rises prettily and looks through portieres*) Oh, lovely!—But where is Sister?

TOM: Laura is not feeling well and she says that she thinks she'd better not come to the table.

AMANDA: What?—Nonsense!—Laura? Oh, Laura!

LAURA: (*Off stage, faintly*) Yes, Mother.

AMANDA: You really must come to the table. We won't be seated until you come to the table!

Come in, Mr. O'Connor. You sit over there, and I'll—

Laura? Laura Wingfield!

You're keeping us waiting, honey! We can't say grace until you come to the table!

(*The back door is pushed weakly open and Laura comes in. She is obviously quite faint, her lips trembling, her eyes wide and staring. She moves unsteadily toward the table.*)

(LEGEND: "TERROR!")

(*Outside a summer storm is coming abruptly. The white curtains billow inward at the windows and there is a sorrowful murmur and deep blue dusk.*)

(*Laura suddenly stumbles—she catches at a chair with a faint moan.*)

TOM: Laura!

AMANDA: Laura!

(*There is a clap of thunder.*)

(LEGEND: "AH!")

(*Despairingly*)

Why, Laura, you *are* sick, darling! Tom, help your sister into the living room, dear!

Sit in the living room, Laura—rest on the sofa.
Well!
(*To the gentleman caller.*) Standing over the hot stove made her ill!—I told her that it was just too warm this evening, but—

(*Tom comes back in. Laura is on the sofa.*)

Is Laura all right now?
TOM: Yes.
AMANDA: What *is* that? Rain? A nice cool rain has come up! (*She gives the gentleman caller a frightened look.*) I think we may—have grace—now . . . (*Tom looks at her stupidly.*) Tom, honey—you say grace!
TOM: Oh . . .
"For these and all thy mercies—" (*They bow their heads, Amanda stealing a nervous glance at Jim. In the living room Laura, stretched on the sofa, clenches her hand to her lips, to hold back a shuddering sob.*) God's Holy Name be praised—

THE SCENE DIMS OUT

SCENE VII

A Souvenir.

Half an hour later. Dinner is just being finished in the upstage area which is concealed by the drawn portieres.

As the curtain rises Laura is still huddled upon the sofa, her feet drawn under her, her head resting on a pale blue pillow, her eyes wide and mysteriously watchful. The new floor lamp with its shade of rose-colored silk gives a soft, becoming light to her face, bringing out the fragile, unearthly prettiness which usually escapes attention. There is a steady murmur of rain, but it is slackening and stops soon after the scene begins; the air outside becomes pale and luminous as the moon breaks out.

A moment after the curtain rises, the lights in both rooms flicker and go out.

JIM: Hey, there, Mr. Light Bulb!

(*Amanda laughs nervously.*)

(LEGEND: "SUSPENSION OF A PUBLIC SERVICE.")

AMANDA: Where was Moses when the lights went out? Ha-ha. Do you know the answer to that one, Mr. O'Connor?

JIM: No, Ma'am, what's the answer?

AMANDA: In the dark! (*Jim laughs appreciatively.*) Everybody sit still. I'll light the candles. Isn't it lucky we have them on the table? Where's a match? Which of you gentlemen can provide a match?

JIM: Here.

AMANDA: Thank you, sir.

JIM: Not at all, Ma'am!

AMANDA: I guess the fuse has burnt out. Mr. O'Connor, can you tell a burnt-out fuse? I know I can't and Tom is a total loss when it comes to mechanics.

(SOUND: GETTING UP: VOICES RECEDE A LITTLE TO KITCHENETTE.)

Oh, be careful you don't bump into something. We don't want our gentleman caller to break his neck. Now wouldn't that be a fine howdy-do?

JIM: Ha-ha! Where is the fuse-box?

AMANDA: Right here next to the stove. Can you see anything?

JIM: Just a minute.

AMANDA: Isn't electricity a mysterious thing? Wasn't it Benjamin Franklin who tied a key to a kite? We live in such a mysterious universe, don't we? Some people say that science clears up all the mysteries for us. In my opinion it only creates more!

Have you found it yet?

JIM: No, Ma'am. All these fuses look okay to me.

AMANDA: Tom!

TOM: Yes, Mother?

AMANDA: That light bill I gave you several days ago. The one I told you we got the notices about?

(LEGEND: "HA!")

TOM: Oh.—Yeah.

AMANDA: You didn't neglect to pay it by any chance?

TOM: Why, I—

AMANDA: Didn't! I might have known it!

JIM: Shakespeare probably wrote a poem on that light bill, Mrs. Wingfield.

AMANDA: I might have known better than to trust him with it! There's such a high price for negligence in this world!

JIM: Maybe the poem will win a ten-dollar prize.

AMANDA: We'll just have to spend the remainder of the evening in the nineteenth century, before Mr. Edison made the Mazda lamp!

JIM: Candlelight is my favorite kind of light.

AMANDA: That shows you're romantic! But that's no excuse for Tom.

Well, we got through dinner. Very considerate of them to let us get through dinner before they plunged us into everlasting darkness, wasn't it, Mr. O'Connor?

JIM: Ha-ha!

AMANDA: Tom, as a penalty for your carelessness you can help me with the dishes.

JIM: Let me give you a hand.

AMANDA: Indeed you will not!

JIM: I ought to be good for something.

AMANDA: Good for something? (*Her tone is rhapsodic.*) *You?* Why, Mr. O'Connor, nobody, *nobody's* given me this much entertainment in years—as you have!

JIM: Aw, now, Mrs. Wingfield!

AMANDA: I'm not exaggerating, not one bit! But Sister is all by her lonesome. You go keep her company in the parlor!

I'll give you this lovely old candelabrum that used to be on the altar at the church of the Heavenly Rest. It was melted a little out of shape when the church burnt down. Lightning struck it one spring. Gypsy Jones was holding a revival at the time and he intimated that the church was destroyed because the Episcopalians gave card parties.

JIM: Ha-ha.

AMANDA: And how about you coaxing Sister to drink a little wine? I think it would be good for her! Can you carry both at once?

JIM: Sure. I'm Superman!

AMANDA: Now, Thomas, get into this apron!

(*The door of kitchenette swings closed on Amanda's gay laughter; the flickering light approaches the portieres.*)

(*Laura sits up nervously as he enters. Her speech at first is low and breathless from the almost intolerable strain of being alone with a stranger.*)

(THE LEGEND: "I DON'T SUPPOSE YOU REMEMBER ME AT ALL!")

(*In her first speeches in this scene, before Jim's warmth overcomes her paralyzing shyness, Laura's voice is thin and breathless as though she has just run up a steep flight of stairs.*)

(*Jim's attitude is gently humorous. In playing this scene it should be stressed that while the incident is apparently unimportant, it is to Laura the climax of her secret life.*)

JIM: Hello, there, Laura.

LAURA: (*Faintly*) Hello. (*She clears her throat.*)

JIM: How are you feeling now? Better?

LAURA: Yes. Yes, thank you.

JIM: This is for you. A little dandelion wine. (*He extends it toward her with extravagant gallantry.*)

LAURA: Thank you.

JIM: Drink it—but don't get drunk! (*He laughs heartily. Laura takes the glass uncertainly; laughs shyly.*) Where shall I set the candles?

LAURA: Oh—oh, anywhere . . .

JIM: How about here on the floor? Any objections?

LAURA: No.

JIM: I'll spread a newspaper under to catch the drippings. I like to sit on the floor. Mind if I do?

LAURA: Oh, no.

JIM: Give me a pillow?

LAURA: What?

JIM: A pillow!

LAURA: Oh . . . (*Hands him one quickly.*)

JIM: How about you? Don't you like to sit on the floor?

LAURA: Oh—yes.

JIM: Why don't you, then?

LAURA: I—will.

JIM: Take a pillow! (*Laura does. Sits on the other side of the candelabrum. Jim crosses his legs and smiles engagingly at her*) I can't hardly see you sitting way over there.

LAURA: I can—see you.

JIM: I know, but that's not fair, I'm in the limelight. (*Laura moves her pillow closer*) Good! Now I can see you! Comfortable?

LAURA: Yes.

JIM: So am I. Comfortable as a cow! Will you have some gum?

LAURA: No, thank you.

JIM: I think that I will indulge, with your permission. (*Musingly unwraps it and holds it up*) Think of the fortune made by the guy that invented the first piece of chewing gum. Amazing, huh? The Wrigley Building is one of the sights of Chicago. —I saw it summer before last when I went up to the Century of Progress. Did you take in the Century of Progress?

LAURA: No, I didn't.

JIM: Well, it was quite a wonderful exposition. What impressed me most was the Hall of Science. Gives you an idea of what the future will be in America, even more wonderful than the present time is! (*Pause. Smiling at her*) Your brother tells me you're shy. Is that right, Laura?

LAURA: I—don't know.

JIM: I judge you to be an old-fashioned type of girl. Well, I think that's a pretty good type to be. Hope you don't think I'm being too personal—do you?

LAURA: (*Hastily, out of embarrassment*) I believe I *will* take a piece of gum, if you—don't mind. (*Clearing her throat*) Mr. O'Connor, have you—kept up with your singing?

JIM: Singing? Me?

LAURA: Yes. I remember what a beautiful voice you had.

JIM: When did you hear me sing?

(VOICE OFF STAGE IN THE PAUSE.)

VOICE: (*Off stage*)

O blow, ye winds, heigh-ho,
A-roving I will go!
I'm off to my love
With a boxing glove—
Ten thousand miles away!

JIM: You say you've heard me sing?

LAURA: Oh, yes! Yes, very often . . . I—don't suppose—you remember me—at all?

JIM: (*Smiling doubtfully*) You know I have an idea I've seen you before. I had that idea soon as you opened the door. It seemed almost like I was about to remember your name. But the name that I started to call you—wasn't a name! And so I stopped myself before I said it.

LAURA: Wasn't it—Blue Roses?

JIM: (*Springs up. Grinning*) Blue Roses!—My gosh, yes—Blue Roses! That's what I had on my tongue when you opened the door! Isn't it funny what tricks your memory plays? I didn't connect you with high school somehow or other. But that's where it was; it was high school. I didn't even know you were Shakespeare's sister! Gosh, I'm sorry.

LAURA: I didn't expect you to. You—barely knew me!

JIM: But we did have a speaking acquaintance, huh?

LAURA: Yes, we—spoke to each other.

JIM: When did you recognize me?

LAURA: Oh, right away!

JIM: Soon as I came in the door?

LAURA: When I heard your name I thought it was probably you. I knew that Tom used to know you a little in high school. So when you came in the door— Well, then I was—sure.

JIM: Why didn't you *say* something, then?

LAURA: (*Breathlessly*) I didn't know what to say, I was—too surprised!

JIM: For goodness' sakes! You know, this sure is funny!

LAURA: Yes! Yes, isn't it, though . . .

JIM: Didn't we have a class in something together?

LAURA: Yes, we did.

JIM: What class was that?

LAURA: It was—singing—Chorus!

JIM: Aw!

LAURA: I sat across the aisle from you in the Aud.

JIM: Aw.

LAURA: Mondays, Wednesdays and Fridays.

JIM: Now I remember—you always came in late.

LAURA: Yes, it was so hard for me, getting upstairs. I had that brace on my leg—it clumped so loud!

JIM: I never heard any clumping.

LAURA: (*Wincing at the recollection*) To me it sounded like—thunder!

JIM: Well, well, well, I never even noticed.

LAURA: And everybody was seated before I came in. I had to walk in front of all those people. My seat was in the back row. I had to go clumping all the way up the aisle with everyone watching!

JIM: You shouldn't have been self-conscious.

LAURA: I know, but I was. It was always such a relief when the singing started.

JIM: Aw, yes, I've placed you now! I used to call you Blue Roses. How was it that I got started calling you that?

LAURA: I was out of school a little while with pleurosis. When I came back you asked me what was the matter. I said I had pleurosis—you thought I said Blue Roses. That's what you always called me after that!

JIM: I hope you didn't mind.

LAURA: Oh, no—I liked it. You see, I wasn't acquainted with many—people. . . .

JIM: As I remember you sort of stuck by yourself.

LAURA: I—I—never have had much luck at—making friends.

JIM: I don't see why you wouldn't.

LAURA: Well, I—started out badly.

JIM: You mean being—

LAURA: Yes, it sort of—stood between me—

JIM: You shouldn't have let it!

LAURA: I know, but it did, and—

JIM: You were shy with people!

LAURA: I tried not to be but never could—

JIM: Overcome it?

LAURA: No, I—I never could!

JIM: I guess being shy is something you have to work out of kind of gradually.

LAURA: (*Sorrowfully*) Yes—I guess it—

JIM: Takes time!

LAURA: Yes—

JIM: People are not so dreadful when you know them. That's what you have to remember! And everybody has problems, not just you, but practically everybody has got some problems. You think of yourself as having the only problems, as being the only one who is disappointed. But just look around you and you will see lots of people as disappointed as you are. For instance, I hoped when I was going to high school that I would be further along at this time, six years later, than I am now— You remember that wonderful write-up I had in *The Torch*?

LAURA: Yes! (*She rises and crosses to table.*)

JIM: It said I was bound to succeed in anything I went into! (*Laura returns with the annual*) Holy Jeez! *The Torch!* (*He accepts it reverently. They smile across it with mutual wonder. Laura crouches beside him and they begin to turn through it. Laura's shyness is dissolving in his warmth.*)

LAURA: Here you are in *The Pirates of Penzance*!

JIM: (*Wistfully*) I sang the baritone lead in that operetta.

LAURA: (*Raptly*) So—*beautifully!*

JIM: (*Protesting*) Aw—

LAURA: Yes, yes—beautifully—beautifully!

JIM: You heard me?

LAURA: All three times!

JIM: No!

LAURA: Yes!

JIM: All three performances?

LAURA: (*Looking down*) Yes.

JIM: Why?

LAURA: I—wanted to ask you to—autograph my program.

JIM: Why didn't you ask me to?

LAURA: You were always surrounded by your own friends so much that I never had a chance to.

JIM: You should have just—

LAURA: Well, I—thought you might think I was—

JIM: Thought I might think you was—what?

LAURA: Oh—

JIM: (*With reflective relish*) I was beleaguered by females in those days.

LAURA: You were terribly popular!

JIM: Yeah—

LAURA: You had such a—friendly way—

JIM: I was spoiled in high school.

LAURA: Everybody—liked you!

JIM: Including you?

LAURA: I—yes, I—I did, too— (*She gently closes the book in her lap.*)

JIM: Well, well, well!—Give me that program, Laura. (*She hands it to him. He signs it with a flourish*) There you are—better late than never!

LAURA: Oh, I—what a—surprise!

JIM: My signature isn't worth very much right now. But some day—maybe—it will increase in value! Being disappointed is one thing and being discouraged is something else. I am disappointed but I am not discouraged. I'm twenty-three years old. How old are you?

LAURA: I'll be twenty-four in June.

JIM: That's not old age!

LAURA: No, but—

JIM: You finished high school?

LAURA: (*With difficulty*) I didn't go back.

JIM: You mean you dropped out?

LAURA: I made bad grades in my final examinations. (*She rises and replaces the book and the program. Her voice strained*) How is—Emily Meisenbach getting along?

JIM: Oh, that kraut-head!

LAURA: Why do you call her that?

JIM: That's what she was.

LAURA: You're not still—going with her?

JIM: I never see her.

LAURA: It said in the Personal Section that you were—engaged!

JIM: I know, but I wasn't impressed by that—propaganda!

LAURA: It wasn't—the truth?

JIM: Only in Emily's optimistic opinion!

LAURA: Oh—

(LEGEND: "WHAT HAVE YOU DONE SINCE HIGH SCHOOL?")

(*Jim lights a cigarette and leans indolently back on his elbows smiling at Laura with a warmth and charm which lights her inwardly with altar candles. She remains by the table and turns in her hands a piece of glass to cover her tumult.*)

JIM: (*After several reflective puffs on a cigarette*) What have you done since high school? (*She seems not to hear him*) Huh? (*Laura looks up*) I said what have you done since high school, Laura?

LAURA: Nothing much.

JIM: You must have been doing something these six long years.

LAURA: Yes.

JIM: Well, then, such as what?

LAURA: I took a business course at business college—

JIM: How did that work out?

LAURA: Well, not very—well—I had to drop out, it gave me—indigestion— (*Jim laughs gently.*)

JIM: What are you doing now?

LAURA: I don't do anything—much. Oh, please don't think I sit around doing nothing! My glass collection takes up a good deal of time. Glass is something you have to take good care of.

JIM: What did you say—about glass?

LAURA: Collection I said—I have one— (*She clears her throat and turns away again, acutely shy.*)

JIM: (*Abruptly*) You know what I judge to be the trouble with you? Inferiority complex! Know what that is? That's what they call it when someone low-rates himself! I understand it because I had it, too. Although my case was not so aggravated as yours seems to be. I had it until I took up public speaking, developed my voice, and learned that I had an aptitude for science. Before that time I never thought of myself as being outstanding in any way whatsoever!

Now I've never made a regular study of it, but I have a friend who says I can analyze people better than doctors that make a profession of it. I don't claim that to be necessarily true, but I can sure guess a person's psychology, Laura! (*Takes out his gum*) Excuse me, Laura. I always take it out when the flavor is gone. I'll use this scrap of paper to wrap it in. I know how it is to get it stuck on a shoe.

Yep—that's what I judge to be your principal trouble. A lack of confidence in yourself as a person. You don't have the proper amount of faith in yourself. I'm basing that fact on a number of your remarks and also on certain observations I've made. For instance that clumping you thought was so awful in high school. You say that you even dreaded to walk into class. You see what you did? You dropped out of school, you gave up an education because of a clump, which as far as I know was practically non-existent! A little physical defect is what you have. Hardly noticeable even! Magnified thousands of times by imagination!

You know what my strong advice to you is? Think of yourself as *superior* in some way!

LAURA: In what way would I think?

JIM: Why, man alive, Laura! Just look about you a little. What do you see? A world full of common people! All of 'em born and all of 'em going to die! Which of them has one-tenth of your good points! Or mine! Or anyone else's, as far as that goes— Gosh! Everybody excels in some one thing. Some in many! (*Unconsciously glances at himself in the mirror.*) All you've got to do is discover in *what!* Take me, for instance. (*He adjusts his tie at the mirror.*) My interest happens to lie in electro-dynamics. I'm taking a course in radio engineering at night school, Laura, on top of a fairly responsible job at the warehouse. I'm taking that course and studying public speaking.

LAURA: Ohhhh.

JIM: Because I believe in the future of television! (*Turning back to her.*) I wish to be ready to go up right along with it. Therefore I'm planning to get in on the ground floor. In fact I've already made the right connections and all that remains is for the industry itself to get under way! Full steam— (*His eyes are starry.*) *Knowledge*—Zzzzzp! *Money*—Zzzzzzp!—*Power!* That's the cycle democracy is built on! (*His attitude is convincingly dynamic. Laura stares at him, even her shyness eclipsed in her absolute wonder. He suddenly grins.*) I guess you think I think a lot of myself!

LAURA: No—o-o-o, I—

JIM: Now how about you? Isn't there something you take more interest in than anything else?

LAURA: Well, I do—as I said—have my—glass collection— (*A peal of girlish laughter from the kitchen.*)

JIM: I'm not right sure I know what you're talking about. What kind of glass is it?

LAURA: Little articles of it, they're ornaments mostly! Most of them are little animals made out of glass, the tiniest little animals in the world. Mother calls them a glass menagerie! Here's an example of one, if you'd like to see it! This one is one of the oldest. It's nearly thirteen.

(MUSIC: "THE GLASS MENAGERIE.")

(*He stretches out his hand.*)

Oh, be careful—if you breathe, it breaks!

JIM: I'd better not take it. I'm pretty clumsy with things.

LAURA: Go on, I trust you with him! (*Places it in his palm*) There now—you're holding him gently! Hold him over the light, he loves the light! You see how the light shines through him?

JIM: It sure does shine!

LAURA: I shouldn't be partial, but he is my favorite one.

JIM: What kind of a thing is this one supposed to be?

LAURA: Haven't you noticed the single horn on his forehead?

JIM: A unicorn, huh?

LAURA: Mmm-hmmm!

JIM: Unicorns, aren't they extinct in the modern world?

LAURA: I know!

JIM: Poor little fellow, he must feel sort of lonesome.

LAURA: (*Smiling*) Well, if he does he doesn't complain about it. He stays on a shelf with some horses that don't have horns and all of them seem to get along nicely together.

JIM: How do you know?

LAURA: (*Lightly*) I haven't heard any arguments among them!

JIM: (*Grinning*) No arguments, huh? Well, that's a pretty good sign! Where shall I set him?

LAURA: Put him on the table. They all like a change of scenery once in a while!

JIM: (*Stretching*) Well, well, well, well— Look how big my shadow is when I stretch!

LAURA: Oh, oh, yes—it stretches across the ceiling!

JIM: (*Crossing to door*) I think it's stopped raining. (*Opens fire-escape door*) Where does the music come from?

LAURA: From the Paradise Dance Hall across the alley.

JIM: How about cutting the rug a little, Miss Wingfield?

LAURA: Oh, I—

JIM: Or is your program filled up? Let me have a look at it. (*Grasps imaginary card*) Why, every dance is taken! I'll just have to scratch some out. (WALTZ MUSIC: "LA GOLONDRINA") Ahhh, a waltz! (*He executes some sweeping turns by himself then holds his arms toward Laura.*)

LAURA: (*Breathlessly*) I—can't dance!

JIM: There you go, that inferiority stuff!

LAURA: I've never danced in my life!

JIM: Come on, try!

LAURA: Oh, but I'd step on you!

JIM: I'm not made out of glass.

LAURA: How—how—how do we start?

JIM: Just leave it to me. You hold your arms out a little.

LAURA: Like this?

JIM: A little bit higher. Right. Now don't tighten up, that's that's the main thing about it—relax.

LAURA: (*Laughing breathlessly*) It's hard not to.

JIM: Okay.

LAURA: I'm afraid you can't budge me.

JIM: What do you bet I can't? (*He swings her into motion.*)

LAURA: Goodness, yes, you can!

JIM: Let yourself go, now, Laura, just let yourself go.

LAURA: I'm—

JIM: Come on!

LAURA: Trying!

JIM: Not so stiff— Easy does it!

LAURA: I know but I'm—

JIM: Loosen th' backbone! There now, that's a lot better.

LAURA: Am I?

JIM: Lots, lots better! (*He moves her about the room in a clumsy waltz.*)

LAURA: Oh, my!

JIM: Ha-ha!

LAURA: Oh, my goodness!

JIM: Ha-ha-ha! (*They suddenly bump into the table. Jim stops*) What did we hit on?

LAURA: Table.

JIM: Did something fall off it? I think—

LAURA: Yes.

JIM: I hope that it wasn't the little glass horse with the horn!

LAURA: Yes.

JIM: Aw, aw, aw. Is it broken?

LAURA: Now it is just like all the other horses.

JIM: It's lost its—

LAURA: Horn! It doesn't matter. Maybe it's a blessing in disguise.

JIM: You'll never forgive me. I bet that that was your favorite piece of glass.

LAURA: I don't have favorites much. It's no tragedy, Freckles. Glass breaks so easily. No matter how careful you are. The traffic jars the shelves and things fall off them.

JIM: Still I'm awfully sorry that I was the cause.

LAURA: (*Smiling*) I'll just imagine he had an operation. The horn was removed to make him feel less—freakish! (*They both laugh.*) Now he will feel more at home with the other horses, the ones that don't have horns . . .

JIM: Ha-ha, that's very funny! (*Suddenly serious.*) I'm glad to see that you have a sense of humor. You know—you're—well—very different! Surprisingly different from anyone else I know! (*His voice becomes soft and hesitant with a genuine feeling.*) Do you mind me telling you that? (*Laura is abashed beyond speech.*) I mean it in a nice way . . . (*Laura nods shyly, looking away.*) You make me feel sort of—I don't know how to put it! I'm usually pretty good at expressing things, but—This is something that I don't know how to say! (*Laura touches her throat and clears it—turns the broken unicorn in her hands.*) (*Even softer.*) Has anyone ever told you that you were pretty? (PAUSE: MUSIC.) (*Laura looks up slowly, with wonder, and shakes her head.*) Well, you are! In a very different way from anyone else. And all the nicer because of the difference, too. (*His voice becomes low and husky. Laura turns away, nearly faint with the novelty of her emotions.*) I wish that you were my sister. I'd teach you to have some confidence in yourself. The different people are not like other people, but being different is nothing to be ashamed of. Because other people are not such wonderful people. They're one hundred times one thousand. You're one times one! They walk all over the earth. You just stay here. They're common as—weeds, but—you—well, you're—*Blue Roses!*

(IMAGE ON SCREEN: BLUE ROSES.)

(MUSIC CHANGES.)

LAURA: But blue is wrong for—roses . . .
JIM: It's right for you!—You're—pretty!
LAURA: In what respect am I pretty?
JIM: In all respects—believe me! Your eyes—your hair—are pretty! Your hands are pretty! (*He catches hold of her hand.*) You think I'm making this up because I'm invited to dinner and have to be nice. Oh, I could do that! I could put on an act for you, Laura, and say lots of things without being very sincere. But this time I am. I'm talking to you sincerely. I happened to notice you had this inferiority complex that keeps you from feeling comfortable with people. Somebody needs to build your confidence up and make you proud instead of shy and turning away and—blushing— Somebody—ought to— Ought to—*kiss* you, Laura!

(*His hand slips slowly up her arm to her shoulder.*)

(MUSIC SWELLS TUMULTUOUSLY.)

(*He suddenly turns her about and kisses her on the lips.*)

(*When he releases her, Laura sinks on the sofa with a bright, dazed look.*)

(*Jim backs away and fishes in his pocket for a cigarette.*)

(LEGEND ON SCREEN: "SOUVENIR.")

Stumble-john!

(*He lights the cigarette, avoiding her look.*)

(*There is a peal of girlish laughter from Amanda in the kitchen.*)

(*Laura slowly raises and opens her hand. It still contains the little broken glass animal. She looks at it with a tender, bewildered expression.*)

Stumble-john! I shouldn't have done that— That was way off the beam. You don't smoke, do you?

(*She looks up, smiling, not hearing the question.*)

(*He sits beside her a little gingerly. She looks at him speechlessly—waiting.*)

(*He coughs decorously and moves a little farther aside as he considers the situation and senses her feelings, dimly, with perturbation.*)

(*Gently.*)

Would you—care for a—mint?

(*She doesn't seem to hear him but her look grows brighter even.*)

Peppermint—Life-Saver? My pocket's a regular drug store—wherever I go . . . (*He pops a mint in his mouth. Then gulps and decides to make a clean breast of it. He speaks slowly and gingerly.*) Laura, you know, if I had a sister like you, I'd do the same thing as Tom. I'd bring out fellows and—introduce her to them. The right type of boys of a type to—appreciate her. Only—well—he made a mistake about me. Maybe I've got no call to be saying this. That may not have been the idea in having me over. But what if it was? There's nothing wrong about that. The only trouble is that in my case—I'm not in a situation to—do the right thing. I can't take down your number and say I'll phone. I can't call up next week and—ask for a date. I thought I had better explain the situation in case you—misunderstood it and—hurt your feelings. . . .

(*Pause.*)

(*Slowly, very slowly, Laura's look changes, her eyes returning slowly from his to the ornament in her palm.*)

(*Amanda utters another gay laugh in the kitchen.*)

LAURA: (*Faintly*) You—won't—call again?

JIM: No, Laura, I can't. (*He rises from the sofa.*) As I was just explaining, I've—got strings on me. Laura, I've—been going steady! I go out all of the time with a girl named Betty. She's a home-girl like you, and Catholic, and Irish, and in a great many ways we—get along fine. I met her last summer on a moonlight boat trip up the river to Alton, on the *Majestic*. Well—right away from the start it was—love!

(LEGEND: LOVE!)

(*Laura sways slightly forward and grips the arm of the sofa. He fails to notice, now enrapt in his own comfortable being.*)

Being in love has made a new man of me!

(*Leaning stiffly forward, clutching the arm of the sofa, Laura struggles visibly with her storm. But Jim is oblivious, she is a long way off.*)

The power of love is really pretty tremendous! Love is something that—changes the whole world, Laura! (*The storm abates a little and Laura leans back. He notices her again.*) It happened that Betty's aunt took sick, she got a wire and had to go to Centralia. So Tom—when he asked me to dinner—I naturally just accepted the invitation, not knowing that you—that he—that I— (*He stops awkwardly.*) Huh—I'm a stumble-john! (*He flops back on the sofa.*)

(*The holy candles in the altar of Laura's face have been snuffed out. There is a look of almost infinite desolation.*)

(*Jim glances at her uneasily.*)

I wish that you would—say something. (*She bites her lip which was trembling and then bravely smiles. She opens her hand again on the broken glass ornament. Then she gently takes his hand and raises it level with her own. She carefully places the unicorn in the palm of his hand, then pushes his fingers closed upon it*) What are you—doing that for? You want me to have him?—Laura? (*She nods*) What for?

LAURA: A—souvenir . . .

(*She rises unsteadily and crouches beside the victrola to wind it up.*)

(LEGEND ON SCREEN: "THINGS HAVE A WAY OF TURNING OUT SO BADLY!")

(OR IMAGE: "GENTLEMAN CALLER WAVING GOOD-BYE!—GAILY.")

(*At this moment Amanda rushes brightly back in the front room. She bears a pitcher of fruit punch in an old-fashioned cut-glass pitcher and a plate of macaroons. The plate has a gold border and poppies painted on it.*)

AMANDA: Well, well, well! Isn't the air delightful after the shower? I've made you children a little liquid refreshment. (*Turns gaily to the gentleman caller*) Jim, do you know that song about lemonade?

"Lemonade, lemonade
Made in the shade and stirred with a spade—
Good enough for any old maid!"

JIM: (*Uneasily*) Ha-ha! No—I never heard it.

AMANDA: Why, Laura! You look so serious!

JIM: We were having a serious conversation.

AMANDA: Good! Now you're better acquainted!

JIM: (*Uncertainly*) Ha-ha! Yes.

AMANDA: You modern young people are much more serious-minded than my generation. I was so gay as a girl!

JIM: You haven't changed, Mrs. Wingfield.

AMANDA: Tonight I'm rejuvenated! The gaiety of the occasion, Mr. O'Connor! (*She tosses her head with a pearl of laughter. Spills lemonade.*) Oooo! I'm baptizing myself!

JIM: Here—let me—

AMANDA: (*Setting the pitcher down*) There now. I discovered we had some maraschino cherries. I dumped them in, juice and all!

JIM: You shouldn't have gone to that trouble, Mrs. Wingfield.

AMANDA: Trouble, trouble? Why, it was loads of fun! Didn't you hear me cutting up in the kitchen? I bet your ears were burning! I told Tom how outdone with him I was for keeping you to himself so long a time! He should have brought you over much, much sooner! Well, now that you've found your way, I want you to be a very frequent caller! Not just occasional but all the time.

Oh, we're going to have a lot of gay times together! I see them coming!

Mmm, just breathe that air! So fresh, and the moon's so pretty!

I'll skip back out—I know where my place is when young folks are having a—serious conversation!

JIM: Oh, don't go out, Mrs. Wingfield. The fact of the matter is I've got to be going.

AMANDA: Going, now? You're joking! Why, it's only the shank of the evening, Mr. O'Connor!

JIM: Well, you know how it is.

AMANDA: You mean you're a young workingman and have to keep workingmen's hours. We'll let you off early tonight. But only on the condition that next time you stay later.

What's the best night for you? Isn't Saturday night the best night for you workingmen?

JIM: I have a couple of time-clocks to punch, Mrs. Wingfield. One at morning, another one at night!

AMANDA: My, but you *are* ambitious! You work at night, too?

JIM: No, Ma'am, not work but—Betty! (*He crosses deliberately to pick up his hat. The band at the Paradise Dance Hall goes into a tender waltz.*)

AMANDA: Betty? Betty? Who's—Betty! (*There is an ominous cracking sound in the sky.*)

JIM: Oh, just a girl. The girl I go steady with! (*He smiles charmingly. The sky falls.*)

(LEGEND: "THE SKY FALLS.")

AMANDA: (*A long-drawn exhalation*) Ohhhh . . . Is it a serious romance, Mr. O'Connor?

JIM: We're going to be married the second Sunday in June.

AMANDA: Ohhhh—how nice! Tom didn't mention that you were engaged to be married.

JIM: The cat's not out of the bag at the warehouse yet. You know how they are. They call you Romeo and stuff like that. (*He stops at the oval mirror to put on his hat. He carefully shapes the brim and the crown to give a discreetly dashing effect.*) It's been a wonderful evening, Mrs. Wingfield. I guess this is what they mean by Southern hospitality.

AMANDA: It really wasn't anything at all.

JIM: I hope it don't seem like I'm rushing off. But I promised Betty I'd pick her up at the Wabash depot, an' by the time I get my jalopy down there her train'll be in. Some women are pretty upset if you keep 'em waiting.

AMANDA: Yes, I know— The tyranny of women! (*Extends her hand.*) Good-bye, Mr. O'Connor. I wish you luck—and happiness—and success! All three of them, and so does Laura!—Don't you, Laura?

LAURA: Yes!

JIM: (*Taking her hand*) Good-bye, Laura. I'm certainly going to treasure that souvenir. And don't you forget the good advice I gave you. (*Raises his voice to a cheery shout.*) So long, Shakespeare! Thanks again, ladies— Good night! (*He grins and ducks jauntily out.*)

(*Still bravely grimacing, Amanda closes the door on the gentleman caller. Then she turns back to the room with a puzzled expression. She and Laura don't dare to face each other. Laura crouches beside the victrola to wind it.*)

AMANDA: (*Faintly*) Things have a way of turning out so badly. I don't believe that I would play the victrola. Well, well— well— Our gentleman caller was engaged to be married! Tom!

TOM: (*From back*) Yes, Mother?

AMANDA: Come in here a minute. I want to tell you something awfully funny.

TOM: (*Enters with macaroon and a glass of the lemonade*) Has the gentleman caller gotten away already?

AMANDA: The gentleman caller has made an early departure. What a wonderful joke you played on us!

TOM: How do you mean?

AMANDA: You didn't mention that he was engaged to be married.

TOM: Jim? Engaged?

AMANDA: That's what he just informed us.

TOM: I'll be jiggered! I didn't know about that.

AMANDA: That seems very peculiar.

TOM: What's peculiar about it?

AMANDA: Didn't you call him your best friend down at the warehouse?

TOM: He is, but how did I know?

AMANDA: It seems extremely peculiar that you wouldn't know your best friend was going to be married!

TOM: The warehouse is where I work, not where I know things about people!

AMANDA: You don't know things anywhere! You live in a dream; you manufacture illusions! (*He crosses to door.*) Where are you going?

TOM: I'm going to the movies.

AMANDA: That's right, now that you've had us make such fools of ourselves. The effort, the preparations, all the expense! The new floor lamp, the rug, the clothes for Laura! All for what? To entertain some other girl's fiancé!

Go to the movies, go! Don't think about us, a mother deserted, an unmarried sister who's crippled and has no job! Don't let anything interfere with your selfish pleasure! Just go, go, go—to the movies!

TOM: All right, I will! The more you shout about my selfishness to me the quicker I'll go, and I won't go to the movies!

AMANDA: Go, then! Then go to the moon—you selfish dreamer!

(*Tom smashes his glass on the floor. He plunges out on the fire-escape, slamming the door. Laura screams—cut by door.*)

(*Dance-hall music up. Tom goes to the rail and grips it desperately, lifting his face in the chill white moonlight penetrating the narrow abyss of the alley.*)

(LEGEND ON SCREEN: "AND SO GOOD-BYE . . .")

(*Tom's closing speech is timed with the interior pantomime. The interior scene is played as though viewed through soundproof glass. Amanda appears to be making a comforting speech to Laura who is huddled upon the sofa. Now that we cannot hear the mother's speech, her silliness is gone and she has dignity and tragic beauty. Laura's dark hair hides her face until at the end of the speech she lifts it to smile at her mother. Amanda's gestures are slow and graceful, almost dance-like, as she comforts the daughter. At the end of her speech she glances a moment at the father's picture—then withdraws through the portieres. At close of Tom's speech, Laura blows out the candles, ending the play.*)

TOM: I didn't go to the moon, I went much further—for time is the longest distance between two places—

Not long after that I was fired for writing a poem on the lid of a shoe-box.

I left Saint Louis. I descended the steps of this fire-escape for a last time and followed, from then on, in my father's footsteps, attempting to find in motion what was lost in space—

I traveled around a great deal. The cities swept about me like dead leaves, leaves that were brightly colored but torn away from the branches.

I would have stopped, but I was pursued by something.

It always came upon me unawares, taking me altogether by surprise. Perhaps it was a familiar bit of music. Perhaps it was only a piece of transparent glass—

Perhaps I am walking along a street at night, in some strange city, before I have found companions. I pass the lighted window of a shop where perfume is sold. The window is filled with pieces of colored glass, tiny transparent bottles in delicate colors, like bits of a shattered rainbow.

Then all at once my sister touches my shoulder. I turn around and look into her eyes . . .

Oh, Laura, Laura, I tried to leave you behind me, but I am more faithful than I intended to be!

I reach for a cigarette, I cross the street, I run into the movies or a bar, I buy a drink, I speak to the nearest stranger—anything that can blow your candles out!

(*Laura bends over the candles.*)

—for nowadays the world is lit by lightning! Blow out your candles, Laura—and so good-bye. . . .

(*She blows the candles out.*)

THE SCENE DISSOLVES

A STREETCAR NAMED DESIRE

And so it was I entered the broken world
To trace the visionary company of love, its voice
An instant in the wind (I know not whither hurled)
But not for long to hold each desperate choice.

"The Broken Tower" by Hart Crane

THE CHARACTERS

BLANCHE
STELLA
STANLEY
MITCH
EUNICE
STEVE
PABLO
A NEGRO WOMAN
A DOCTOR
A NURSE
A YOUNG COLLECTOR
A MEXICAN WOMAN
A TAMALE VENDOR

SCENE ONE

The exterior of a two-story corner building on a street in New Orleans which is named Elysian Fields and runs between the L&N tracks and the river. The section is poor but, unlike corresponding sections in other American cities, it has a raffish charm. The houses are mostly white frame, weathered grey, with rickety outside stairs and galleries and quaintly ornamented gables. This building contains two flats, upstairs and down. Faded white stairs ascend to the entrances of both.

It is first dark of an evening early in May. The sky that shows around the dim white building is a peculiarly tender blue, almost a turquoise, which invests the scene with a kind of lyricism and gracefully attenuates the atmosphere of decay. You can almost feel the warm breath of the brown river beyond the river warehouses with their faint redolences of bananas and coffee. A corresponding air is evoked by the music of Negro entertainers at a barroom around the corner. In this part of New Orleans you are practically always just around the corner, or a few doors down the street, from a tinny piano being played with the infatuated fluency of brown fingers. This "Blue Piano" expresses the spirit of the life which goes on here.

Two women, one white and one colored, are taking the air on the steps of the building. The white woman is Eunice, who occupies the upstairs flat; the colored woman a neighbor, for New Orleans is a cosmopolitan city where there is a relatively warm and easy intermingling of races in the old part of town.

Above the music of the "Blue Piano" the voices of people on the street can be heard overlapping.

NEGRO WOMAN (*to Eunice*): . . . she says St. Barnabas would send out his dog to lick her and when he did she'd feel an icy cold wave all up an' down her. Well, that night when—

A MAN (*to a Sailor*): You keep right on going and you'll find it. You'll hear them tapping on the shutters.

SAILOR (*to Negro Woman and Eunice*): Where's the Four Deuces?

VENDOR: Red hot! Red hots!

NEGRO WOMAN: Don't waste your money in that clip joint!

SAILOR: I've got a date there.

VENDOR: Re-e-ed h-o-o-t!

NEGRO WOMAN: Don't let them sell you a Blue Moon cocktail or you won't go out on your own feet!

(*Two men come around the corner, Stanley Kowalski and Mitch. They are about twenty-eight or thirty years old, roughly dressed in blue denim work clothes. Stanley carries his bowling jacket and a red-stained package from a butcher's.*)

STANLEY (*to Mitch*): Well, what did he say?

MITCH: He said he'd give us even money.

STANLEY: Naw! We gotta have odds!

(*They stop at the foot of the steps.*)

STANLEY (*bellowing*): Hey, there! Stella, Baby!

(*Stella comes out on the first floor landing, a gentle young woman, about twenty-five, and of a background obviously quite different from her husband's.*)

STELLA (*mildly*): Don't holler at me like that. Hi, Mitch.

STANLEY: Catch!

STELLA: What?

STANLEY: Meat!

(*He heaves the package at her. She cries out in protest but manages to catch it: then she laughs breathlessly. Her husband and his companion have already started back around the corner.*)

STELLA (*calling after him*): Stanley! Where are you going?

STANLEY: Bowling!

STELLA: Can I come watch?

STANLEY: Come on. (*He goes out.*)

STELLA: Be over soon. (*To the white woman*) Hello, Eunice. How are you?

EUNICE: I'm all right. Tell Steve to get him a poor boy's sandwich 'cause nothing's left here.

(*They all laugh; the colored woman does not stop. Stella goes out.*)

COLORED WOMAN: What was that package he th'ew at 'er? (*She rises from steps, laughing louder.*)

EUNICE: You hush, now!
NEGRO WOMAN: Catch *what!*

(*She continues to laugh. Blanche comes around the corner, carrying a valise. She looks at a slip of paper, then at the building, then again at the slip and again at the building. Her expression is one of shocked disbelief. Her appearance is incongruous to this setting. She is daintily dressed in a white suit with a fluffy bodice, necklace and earrings of pearl, white gloves and hat, looking as if she were arriving at a summer tea or cocktail party in the garden district. She is about five years older than Stella. Her delicate beauty must avoid a strong light. There is something about her uncertain manner, as well as her white clothes, that suggests a moth.*)

EUNICE (*finally*): What's the matter, honey? Are you lost?
BLANCHE (*with faintly hysterical humor*): They told me to take a street-car named Desire, and then transfer to one called Cemeteries and ride six blocks and get off at—Elysian Fields!
EUNICE: That's where you are now.
BLANCHE: At Elysian Fields?
EUNICE: This here is Elysian Fields.
BLANCHE: They mustn't have—understood—what number I wanted . . .
EUNICE: What number you lookin' for?

(*Blanche wearily refers to the slip of paper.*)

BLANCHE: Six thirty-two.
EUNICE: You don't have to look no further.
BLANCHE (*uncomprehendingly*): I'm looking for my sister, Stella DuBois. I mean—Mrs. Stanley Kowalski.
EUNICE: That's the party.—You just did miss her, though.
BLANCHE: This—can this be—her home?
EUNICE: She's got the downstairs here and I got the up.
BLANCHE: Oh. She's—out?
EUNICE: You noticed that bowling alley around the corner?
BLANCHE: I'm—not sure I did.
EUNICE: Well, that's where she's at, watchin' her husband bowl. (*There is a pause*) You want to leave your suitcase here an' go find her?

BLANCHE: No.

NEGRO WOMAN: I'll go tell her you come.

BLANCHE: Thanks.

NEGRO WOMAN: You welcome. (*She goes out.*)

EUNICE: She wasn't expecting you?

BLANCHE: No. No, not tonight.

EUNICE: Well, why don't you just go in and make yourself at home till they get back.

BLANCHE: How could I—do that?

EUNICE: We own this place so I can let you in.

(*She gets up and opens the downstairs door. A light goes on behind the blind, turning it light blue. Blanche slowly follows her into the downstairs flat. The surrounding areas dim out as the interior is lighted.*

(*Two rooms can be seen, not too clearly defined. The one first entered is primarily a kitchen but contains a folding bed to be used by Blanche. The room beyond this is a bedroom. Off this room is a narrow door to a bathroom.*)

EUNICE (*defensively, noticing Blanche's look*): It's sort of messed up right now but when it's clean it's real sweet.

BLANCHE: Is it?

EUNICE: Uh-huh, I think so. So you're Stella's sister?

BLANCHE: Yes. (*Wanting to get rid of her*) Thanks for letting me in.

EUNICE: *Por nada*, as the Mexicans say, *por nada!* Stella spoke of you.

BLANCHE: Yes?

EUNICE: I think she said you taught school.

BLANCHE: Yes.

EUNICE: And you're from Mississippi, huh?

BLANCHE: Yes.

EUNICE: She showed me a picture of your home-place, the plantation.

BLANCHE: Belle Reve?

EUNICE: A great big place with white columns.

BLANCHE: Yes . . .

EUNICE: A place like that must be awful hard to keep up.

BLANCHE: If you will excuse me, I'm just about to drop.

EUNICE: Sure, honey. Why don't you set down?

BLANCHE: What I meant was I'd like to be left alone.
EUNICE (*offended*): Aw. I'll make myself scarce, in that case.
BLANCHE: I didn't mean to be rude, but—
EUNICE: I'll drop by the bowling alley an' hustle her up. (*She goes out the door.*)

(*Blanche sits in a chair very stiffly with her shoulders slightly hunched and her legs pressed close together and her hands tightly clutching her purse as if she were quite cold. After a while the blind look goes out of her eyes and she begins to look slowly around. A cat screeches. She catches her breath with a startled gesture. Suddenly she notices something in a half opened closet. She springs up and crosses to it, and removes a whiskey bottle. She pours a half tumbler of whiskey and tosses it down. She carefully replaces the bottle and washes out the tumbler at the sink. Then she resumes her seat in front of the table.*)

BLANCHE (*faintly to herself*): I've got to keep hold of myself!

(*Stella comes quickly around the corner of the building and runs to the door of the downstairs flat.*)

STELLA (*calling out joyfully*): *Blanche!*

(*For a moment they stare at each other. Then Blanche springs up and runs to her with a wild cry.*)

BLANCHE: Stella, oh, Stella, Stella! Stella for Star!

(*She begins to speak with feverish vivacity as if she feared for either of them to stop and think. They catch each other in a spasmodic embrace.*)

BLANCHE: Now, then, let me look at you. But don't you look at me, Stella, no, no, no, not till later, not till I've bathed and rested! And turn that over-light off! Turn that off! I won't be looked at in this merciless glare! (*Stella laughs and complies*) Come back here now! Oh, my baby! Stella! Stella for Star! (*She embraces her again*) I thought you would never come back to this horrible place! What am I saying? I didn't mean to say that. I meant to be nice about it and say—Oh, what a convenient location and such—Ha-a-ha! Precious lamb! You haven't said a *word* to me.

STELLA: You haven't given me a chance to, honey! (*She laughs, but her glance at Blanche is a little anxious.*)

BLANCHE: Well, now you talk. Open your pretty mouth and talk while I look around for some liquor! I know you must have some liquor on the place! Where could it be, I wonder? Oh, I spy, I spy!

(*She rushes to the closet and removes the bottle; she is shaking all over and panting for breath as she tries to laugh. The bottle nearly slips from her grasp.*)

STELLA (*noticing*): Blanche, you sit down and let me pour the drinks. I don't know what we've got to mix with. Maybe a coke's in the icebox. Look'n see, honey, while I'm—

BLANCHE: No coke, honey, not with my nerves tonight! Where—where—where is—?

STELLA: Stanley? Bowling! He loves it. They're having a—found some soda!—tournament . . .

BLANCHE: Just water, baby, to chase it! Now don't get worried, your sister hasn't turned into a drunkard, she's just all shaken up and hot and tired and dirty! You sit down, now, and explain this place to me! What are you doing in a place like this?

STELLA: Now, Blanche—

BLANCHE: Oh, I'm not going to be hypocritical, I'm going to be honestly critical about it! Never, never, never in my worst dreams could I picture— Only Poe! Only Mr. Edgar Allan Poe!—could do it justice! Out there I suppose is the ghoul-haunted woodland of Weir! (*She laughs.*)

STELLA: No, honey, those are the L&N tracks.

BLANCHE: No, now seriously, putting joking aside. Why didn't you tell me, why didn't you write me, honey, why didn't you let me know?

STELLA (*carefully, pouring herself a drink*): Tell you what, Blanche?

BLANCHE: Why, that you had to live in these conditions!

STELLA: Aren't you being a little intense about it? It's not that bad at all! New Orleans isn't like other cities.

BLANCHE: This has got nothing to do with New Orleans. You might as well say—forgive me, blessed baby! (*She suddenly stops short*) The subject is closed!

STELLA (*a little drily*): Thanks.

(*During the pause, Blanche stares at her. She smiles at Blanche.*)

BLANCHE (*looking down at her glass, which shakes in her hand*): You're all I've got in the world, and you're not glad to see me!

STELLA (*sincerely*): Why, Blanche, you know that's not true.

BLANCHE: No?—I'd forgotten how quiet you were.

STELLA: You never did give me a chance to say much, Blanche. So I just got in the habit of being quiet around you.

BLANCHE (*vaguely*): A good habit to get into . . . (*then, abruptly*) You haven't asked me how I happened to get away from the school before the spring term ended.

STELLA: Well, I thought you'd volunteer that information—if you wanted to tell me.

BLANCHE: You thought I'd been fired?

STELLA: No, I—thought you might have—resigned . . .

BLANCHE: I was so exhausted by all I'd been through my—nerves broke. (*Nervously tamping cigarette*) I was on the verge of—lunacy, almost! So Mr. Graves—Mr. Graves is the high school superintendent—he suggested I take a leave of absence. I couldn't put all of those details into the wire . . . (*She drinks quickly*) Oh, this buzzes right through me and feels so *good!*

STELLA: Won't you have another?

BLANCHE: No, one's my limit.

STELLA: Sure?

BLANCHE: You haven't said a word about my appearance.

STELLA: You look just fine.

BLANCHE: God love you for a liar! Daylight never exposed so total a ruin! But you—you've put on some weight, yes, you're just as plump as a little partridge! And it's so becoming to you!

STELLA: Now, Blanche—

BLANCHE: Yes, it is, it is or I wouldn't say it! You just have to watch around the hips a little. Stand up.

STELLA: Not now.

BLANCHE: You hear me? I said stand up! (*Stella complies reluctantly*) You messy child, you, you've spilt something on that pretty white lace collar! About your hair—you ought to have it cut in a feather bob with your dainty features. Stella, you have a maid, don't you?

STELLA: No. With only two rooms it's—

BLANCHE: What? *Two* rooms, did you say?

STELLA: This one and— (*She is embarrassed.*)

BLANCHE: The other one? (*She laughs sharply. There is an embarrassed silence*) How quiet you are, you're so peaceful. Look how you sit there with your little hands folded like a cherub in choir!

STELLA (*uncomfortably*): I never had anything like your energy, Blanche.

BLANCHE: Well, I never had your beautiful self-control. I am going to take just one little tiny nip more, sort of to put the stopper on, so to speak. . . . Then put the bottle away so I won't be tempted. (*She rises*) I want you to look at *my* figure! (*She turns around*) You know I haven't put on one ounce in ten years, Stella? I weigh what I weighed the summer you left Belle Reve. The summer Dad died and you left us . . .

STELLA (*a little wearily*): It's just incredible, Blanche, how well you're looking.

BLANCHE: You see I still have that awful vanity about my looks even now that my looks are slipping! (*She laughs nervously and glances at Stella for reassurance.*)

STELLA (*dutifully*): They haven't slipped one particle.

BLANCHE: After all I've been through? You think I believe that story? Blessed child! (*She touches her forehead shakily*) Stella, there's—only two rooms?

STELLA: And a bathroom.

BLANCHE: Oh, you do have a bathroom! First door to the right at the top of the stairs? (*They both laugh uncomfortably*) But, Stella, I don't see where you're going to put me!

STELLA: We're going to put you in here.

BLANCHE: What kind of bed's this—one of those collapsible things?

(*She sits on it.*)

STELLA: Does it feel all right?

BLANCHE (*dubiously*): Wonderful, honey. I don't like a bed that gives much. But there's no door between the two rooms, and Stanley—will it be decent?

STELLA: Stanley is Polish, you know.

BLANCHE: Oh, yes. They're something like Irish, aren't they?

STELLA: Well—

BLANCHE: Only not so—highbrow? (*They both laugh again in the same way*) I brought some nice clothes to meet all your lovely friends in.

STELLA: I'm afraid you won't think they are lovely.

BLANCHE: What are they like?

STELLA: They're Stanley's friends.

BLANCHE: Polacks?

STELLA: They're a mixed lot, Blanche.

BLANCHE: Heterogeneous—types?

STELLA: Oh, yes. Yes, types is right!

BLANCHE: Well—anyhow—I brought nice clothes and I'll wear them. I guess you're hoping I'll say I'll put up at a hotel, but I'm not going to put up at a hotel. I want to be *near* you, got to be *with* somebody, I *can't* be *alone!* Because—as you must have noticed—I'm—*not* very *well* . . . (*Her voice drops and her look is frightened.*)

STELLA: You seem a little bit nervous or overwrought or something.

BLANCHE: Will Stanley like me, or will I be just a visiting in-law, Stella? I couldn't stand that.

STELLA: You'll get along fine together, if you'll just try not to—well—compare him with men that we went out with at home.

BLANCHE: Is he so—different?

STELLA: Yes. A different species.

BLANCHE: In what way; what's he like?

STELLA: Oh, you can't describe someone you're in love with! Here's a picture of him! (*She hands a photograph to Blanche.*)

BLANCHE: An officer?

STELLA: A Master Sergeant in the Engineers' Corps. Those are decorations!

BLANCHE: He had those on when you met him?

STELLA: I assure you I wasn't just blinded by all the brass.

BLANCHE: That's not what I—

STELLA: But of course there were things to adjust myself to later on.

BLANCHE: Such as his civilian background! (*Stella laughs uncertainly*) How did he take it when you said I was coming?

STELLA: Oh, Stanley doesn't know yet.

BLANCHE (*frightened*): You—haven't told him?

STELLA: He's on the road a good deal.

BLANCHE: Oh. Travels?

STELLA: Yes.

BLANCHE: Good. I mean—isn't it?

STELLA (*half to herself*): I can hardly stand it when he is away for a night . . .

BLANCHE: Why, Stella!

STELLA: When he's away for a week I nearly go wild!

BLANCHE: Gracious!

STELLA: And when he comes back I cry on his lap like a baby . . .

(*She smiles to herself.*)

BLANCHE: I guess that is what is meant by being in love . . . (*Stella looks up with a radiant smile.*) Stella—

STELLA: What?

BLANCHE (*in an uneasy rush*): I haven't asked you the things you probably thought I was going to ask. And so I'll expect you to be understanding about what *I* have to tell *you.*

STELLA: What, Blanche? (*Her face turns anxious.*)

BLANCHE: Well, Stella—you're going to reproach me, I know that you're bound to reproach me—but before you do—take into consideration—you left! I stayed and struggled! You came to New Orleans and looked out for yourself! *I* stayed at *Belle Reve* and tried to hold it together! I'm not meaning this in any reproachful way, but *all* the burden descended on *my* shoulders.

STELLA: The best I could do was make my own living, Blanche.

(*Blanche begins to shake again with intensity.*)

BLANCHE: I know, I know. But you are the one that abandoned Belle Reve, not I! I stayed and fought for it, bled for it, almost died for it!

STELLA: Stop this hysterical outburst and tell me what's happened? What do you mean fought and bled? What kind of—

BLANCHE: I knew you would, Stella. I knew you would take this attitude about it!

STELLA: About—what?—please!

BLANCHE (*slowly*): The loss—the loss . . .

STELLA: Belle Reve? Lost, is it? No!

BLANCHE: Yes, Stella.

(*They stare at each other across the yellow-checked linoleum of the table. Blanche slowly nods her head and Stella looks slowly down at her hands folded on the table. The music of the "blue piano" grows louder. Blanche touches her handkerchief to her forehead.*)

STELLA: But how did it go? What happened?

BLANCHE (*springing up*): You're a fine one to ask me how it went!

STELLA: Blanche!

BLANCHE: You're a fine one to sit there *accusing me* of it!

STELLA: *Blanche!*

BLANCHE: I, I, *I* took the blows in my face and my body! All of those deaths! The long parade to the graveyard! Father, mother! Margaret, that dreadful way! So big with it, it couldn't be put in a coffin! But had to be burned like rubbish! You just came home in time for the funerals, Stella. And funerals are pretty compared to deaths. Funerals are quiet, but deaths—not always. Sometimes their breathing is hoarse, and sometimes it rattles, and sometimes they even cry out to you, "Don't let me go!" Even the old, sometimes, say, "Don't let me go." As if you were able to stop them! But funerals are quiet, with pretty flowers. And, oh, what gorgeous boxes they pack them away in! Unless you were there at the bed when they cried out, "Hold me!" you'd never suspect there was the struggle for breath and bleeding. You didn't dream, but I saw! *Saw! Saw!* And now you sit there telling me with your eyes that I let the place go! How in hell do you think all that sickness and dying was paid for? Death is expensive, Miss Stella! And old Cousin Jessie's right after Margaret's, hers! Why, the Grim Reaper had put up his tent on our doorstep! . . . Stella. Belle Reve was his headquarters! Honey—that's how it slipped through my fingers! Which of them left us a fortune? Which of them left a cent of insurance even? Only poor Jessie—one hundred to pay for her coffin. That was all, Stella! And I with my pitiful salary at the school. Yes, accuse me! Sit there and stare at me, thinking I let the place go! *I* let the place go? Where were *you!* In bed with your—Polack!

STELLA (*springing*): Blanche! You be still! That's enough! (*She starts out.*)

BLANCHE: Where are you going?

STELLA: I'm going into the bathroom to wash my face.

BLANCHE: Oh, Stella, Stella, you're crying!

STELLA: Does that surprise you?

(*Stella goes into the bathroom.*

(*Outside is the sound of men's voices. Stanley, Steve and Mitch cross to the foot of the steps.*)

STEVE: And the old lady is on her way to Mass and she's late and there's a cop standin' in front of th' church an' she comes runnin' up an' says, "Officer—is Mass out yet?" He looks her over and says, "No, Lady, y'r ass ain't out but y'r hat's on crooked!" (*They give a hoarse bellow of laughter.*)

STEVE: Playing poker tomorrow night?

STANLEY: Yeah—at Mitch's.

MITCH: Not at my place. My mother's still sick. (*He starts off.*)

STANLEY (*calling after him*): All right, we'll play at my place . . . but you bring the beer.

EUNICE (*hollering down from above*): Break it up down there! I made the spaghetti dish and ate it myself.

STEVE (*going upstairs*): I told you and phoned you we was playing. (*To the men*) Jax beer!

EUNICE: You never phoned me once.

STEVE: I told you at breakfast—and phoned you at lunch . . .

EUNICE: Well, never mind about that. You just get yourself home here once in a while.

STEVE: You want it in the papers?

(*More laughter and shouts of parting come from the men. Stanley throws the screen door of the kitchen open and comes in. He is of medium height, about five feet eight or nine, and strongly, compactly built. Animal joy in his being is implicit in all his movements and attitudes. Since earliest manhood the center of his life has been pleasure with women, the giving and taking of it, not with weak indulgence, dependently, but with the power and pride of a richly feathered male bird among hens. Branching out from this complete and satisfying center are all the auxiliary channels of his life, such as his heartiness with men, his appreciation of rough humor, his love of good drink and food and games, his car, his radio, everything that is his, that bears his emblem of the gaudy seed-bearer. He sizes women up at a glance, with sexual classifications, crude images flashing into his mind and determining the way he smiles at them.*)

BLANCHE (*drawing involuntarily back from his stare*): You must be Stanley. I'm Blanche.

STANLEY: Stella's sister?

BLANCHE: Yes.

STANLEY: H'lo. Where's the little woman?

BLANCHE: In the bathroom.

STANLEY: Oh. Didn't know you were coming in town.

BLANCHE: I—uh—

STANLEY: Where you from, Blanche?

BLANCHE: Why, I—live in Laurel.

(*He has crossed to the closet and removed the whiskey bottle.*)

STANLEY: In Laurel, huh? Oh, yeah. Yeah, in Laurel, that's right. Not in my territory. Liquor goes fast in hot weather. (*He holds the bottle to the light to observe its depletion.*) Have a shot?

BLANCHE: No, I—rarely touch it.

STANLEY: Some people rarely touch it, but it touches them often.

BLANCHE (*faintly*): Ha-ha.

STANLEY: My clothes're stickin' to me. Do you mind if I make myself comfortable? (*He starts to remove his shirt.*)

BLANCHE: Please, please do.

STANLEY: Be comfortable is my motto.

BLANCHE: It's mine, too. It's hard to stay looking fresh. I haven't washed or even powdered my face and—here you are!

STANLEY: You know you can catch cold sitting around in damp things, especially when you been exercising hard like bowling is. You're a teacher, aren't you?

BLANCHE: Yes.

STANLEY: What do you teach, Blanche?

BLANCHE: English.

STANLEY: I never was a very good English student. How long you here for, Blanche?

BLANCHE: I—don't know yet.

STANLEY: You going to shack up here?

BLANCHE: I thought I would if it's not inconvenient for you all.

STANLEY: Good.

BLANCHE: Traveling wears me out.

STANLEY: Well, take it easy.

(*A cat screeches near the window. Blanche springs up.*)

BLANCHE: What's that?

STANLEY: Cats . . . Hey, Stella!

STELLA (*faintly, from the bathroom*): Yes, Stanley.

STANLEY: Haven't fallen in, have you? (*He grins at Blanche. She tries unsuccessfully to smile back. There is a silence*) I'm afraid I'll strike you as being the unrefined type. Stella's spoke of you a good deal. You were married once, weren't you?

(*The music of the polka rises up, faint in the distance.*)

BLANCHE: Yes. When I was quite young.

STANLEY: What happened?

BLANCHE: The boy—the boy died. (*She sinks back down*) I'm afraid I'm—going to be sick!

(*Her head falls on her arms.*)

SCENE TWO

It is six o'clock the following evening. Blanche is bathing. Stella is completing her toilette. Blanche's dress, a flowered print, is laid out on Stella's bed.

Stanley enters the kitchen from outside, leaving the door open on the perpetual "blue piano" around the corner.

STANLEY: What's all this monkey doings?

STELLA: Oh, Stan! (*She jumps up and kisses him which he accepts with lordly composure*) I'm taking Blanche to Galatoire's for supper and then to a show, because it's your poker night.

STANLEY: How about my supper, huh? I'm not going to no Galatoire's for supper!

STELLA: I put you a cold plate on ice.

STANLEY: Well, isn't that just dandy!

STELLA: I'm going to try to keep Blanche out till the party breaks up because I don't know how she would take it. So we'll go to one of the little places in the Quarter afterwards and you'd better give me some money.

STANLEY: Where is she?

STELLA: She's soaking in a hot tub to quiet her nerves. She's terribly upset.

STANLEY: Over what?

STELLA: She's been through such an ordeal.

STANLEY: Yeah?

STELLA: Stan, we've—lost Belle Reve!

STANLEY: The place in the country?

STELLA: Yes.

STANLEY: How?

STELLA (*vaguely*): Oh, it had to be—sacrificed or something. (*There is a pause while Stanley considers. Stella is changing into her dress*) When she comes in be sure to say something nice about her appearance. And, oh! Don't mention the baby. I haven't said anything yet, I'm waiting until she gets in a quieter condition.

STANLEY (*ominously*): So?

STELLA: And try to understand her and be nice to her, Stan.

BLANCHE (*singing in the bathroom*):

"From the land of the sky blue water,
They brought a captive maid!"

STELLA: She wasn't expecting to find us in such a small place. You see I'd tried to gloss things over a little in my letters.

STANLEY: So?

STELLA: And admire her dress and tell her she's looking wonderful. That's important with Blanche. Her little weakness!

STANLEY: Yeah. I get the idea. Now let's skip back a little to where you said the country place was disposed of.

STELLA: Oh!—yes . . .

STANLEY: How about that? Let's have a few more details on that subjeck.

STELLA: It's best not to talk much about it until she's calmed down.

STANLEY: So that's the deal, huh? Sister Blanche cannot be annoyed with business details right now!

STELLA: You saw how she was last night.

STANLEY: Uh-hum, I saw how she was. Now let's have a gander at the bill of sale.

STELLA: I haven't seen any.

STANLEY: She didn't show you no papers, no deed of sale or nothing like that, huh?

STELLA: It seems like it wasn't sold.

STANLEY: Well, what in hell was it then, give away? To charity?

STELLA: Shhh! She'll hear you.

STANLEY: I don't care if she hears me. Let's see the papers!

STELLA: There weren't any papers, she didn't show any papers, I don't care about papers.

STANLEY: Have you ever heard of the Napoleonic code?

STELLA: No, Stanley, I haven't heard of the Napoleonic code and if I have, I don't see what it—

STANLEY: Let me enlighten you on a point or two, baby.

STELLA: Yes?

STANLEY: In the state of Louisiana we have the Napoleonic code according to which what belongs to the wife belongs to the husband and vice versa. For instance if I had a piece of property, or you had a piece of property—

STELLA: My head is swimming!

STANLEY: All right. I'll wait till she gets through soaking in a hot tub and then I'll inquire if *she* is acquainted with the Napoleonic code. It looks to me like you have been swindled, baby, and when you're swindled under the

Napoleonic code I'm swindled *too.* And I don't like to be *swindled.*

STELLA: There's plenty of time to ask her questions later but if you do now she'll go to pieces again. I don't understand what happened to Belle Reve but you don't know how ridiculous you are being when you suggest that my sister or I or anyone of our family could have perpetrated a swindle on anyone else.

STANLEY: Then where's the money if the place was sold?

STELLA: Not sold—*lost, lost!*

(*He stalks into bedroom, and she follows him.*)

Stanley!

(*He pulls open the wardrobe trunk standing in middle of room and jerks out an armful of dresses.*)

STANLEY: Open your eyes to this stuff! You think she got them out of a teacher's pay?

STELLA: Hush!

STANLEY: Look at these feathers and furs that she come here to preen herself in! What's this here? A solid-gold dress, I believe! And this one! What is these here? Fox-pieces! (*He blows on them*) Genuine fox fur-pieces, a half a mile long! Where are your fox-pieces, Stella? Bushy snow-white ones, no less! Where are your white fox-pieces?

STELLA: Those are inexpensive summer furs that Blanche has had a long time.

STANLEY: I got an acquaintance who deals in this sort of merchandise. I'll have him in here to appraise it. I'm willing to bet you there's thousands of dollars invested in this stuff here!

STELLA: Don't be such an idiot, Stanley!

(*He hurls the furs to the daybed. Then he jerks open small drawer in the trunk and pulls up a fist-full of costume jewelry.*)

STANLEY: And what have we here? The treasure chest of a pirate!

STELLA: Oh, Stanley!

STANLEY: Pearls! Ropes of them! What is this sister of yours, a deep-sea diver who brings up sunken treasures? Or is she the champion safe-cracker of all time! Bracelets of solid gold, too! Where are your pearls and gold bracelets?

STELLA: Shhh! Be still, Stanley!

STANLEY: And diamonds! A crown for an empress!

STELLA: A rhinestone tiara she wore to a costume hall.

STANLEY: What's rhinestone?

STELLA: Next door to glass.

STANLEY: Are you kidding? I have an acquaintance that works in a jewelry store. I'll have him in here to make an appraisal of this. Here's your plantation, or what was left of it, here!

STELLA: You have no idea how stupid and horrid you're being! Now close that trunk before she comes out of the bathroom!

(*He kicks the trunk partly closed and sits on the kitchen table.*)

STANLEY: The Kowalskis and the DuBois have different notions.

STELLA (*angrily*): Indeed they have, thank heavens!—*I'm* going outside. (*She snatches up her white hat and gloves and crosses to the outside door*) You come out with me while Blanche is getting dressed.

STANLEY: Since when do you give me orders?

STELLA: Are you going to stay here and insult her?

STANLEY: You're damn tootin' I'm going to stay here.

(*Stella goes out to the porch. Blanche comes out of the bathroom in a red satin robe.*)

BLANCHE (*airily*): Hello, Stanley! Here I am, all freshly bathed and scented, and feeling like a brand new human being!

(*He lights a cigarette.*)

STANLEY: That's good.

BLANCHE (*drawing the curtains at the windows*): Excuse me while I slip on my pretty new dress!

STANLEY: Go right ahead, Blanche.

(*She closes the drapes between the rooms.*)

BLANCHE: I understand there's to be a little card party to which we ladies are cordially *not* invited!

STANLEY (*ominously*): Yeah?

(*Blanche throws off her robe and slips into a flowered print dress.*)

BLANCHE: Where's Stella?

STANLEY: Out on the porch.

BLANCHE: I'm going to ask a favor of you in a moment.

STANLEY: What could that be, I wonder?

BLANCHE: Some buttons in back! You may enter!

(*He crosses through drapes with a smoldering look.*)

How do I look?

STANLEY: You look all right.

BLANCHE: Many thanks! Now the buttons!

STANLEY: I can't do nothing with them.

BLANCHE: You men with your big clumsy fingers. May I have a drag on your cig?

STANLEY: Have one for yourself.

BLANCHE: Why, thanks! . . . It looks like my trunk has exploded.

STANLEY: Me an' Stella were helping you unpack.

BLANCHE: Well, you certainly did a fast and thorough job of it!

STANLEY: It looks like you raided some stylish shops in Paris.

BLANCHE: Ha-ha! Yes—clothes are my passion!

STANLEY: What does it cost for a string of fur-pieces like that?

BLANCHE: Why, those were a tribute from an admirer of mine!

STANLEY: He must have had a lot of—admiration!

BLANCHE: Oh, in my youth I excited some admiration. But look at me now! (*She smiles at him radiantly*) Would you think it possible that I was once considered to be—attractive?

STANLEY: Your looks are okay.

BLANCHE: I was fishing for a compliment, Stanley.

STANLEY: I don't go in for that stuff.

BLANCHE: What—stuff?

STANLEY: Compliments to women about their looks. I never met a woman that didn't know if she was good-looking or not without being told, and some of them give themselves credit for more than they've got. I once went out with a doll who said to me, "I am the glamorous type, I am the glamorous type!" I said, "So what?"

BLANCHE: And what did she say then?

STANLEY: She didn't say nothing. That shut her up like a clam.

BLANCHE: Did it end the romance?

STANLEY: It ended the conversation—that was all. Some men are took in by this Hollywood glamor stuff and some men are not.

BLANCHE: I'm sure you belong in the second category.

STANLEY: That's right.

BLANCHE: I cannot imagine any witch of a woman casting a spell over you.

STANLEY: That's—right.

BLANCHE: You're simple, straightforward and honest, a little bit on the primitive side I should think. To interest you a woman would have to— (*She pauses with an indefinite gesture.*)

STANLEY (*slowly*): Lay . . . her cards on the table.

BLANCHE (*smiling*): Yes—yes—cards on the table. . . . Well, life is too full of evasions and ambiguities, I think. I like an artist who paints in strong, bold colors, primary colors. I don't like pinks and creams and I never cared for wishy-washy people. That was why, when you walked in here last night, I said to myself—"My sister has married a man!" —Of course that was all that I could tell about you.

STANLEY (*booming*): Now let's cut the re-bop!

BLANCHE (*pressing hands to her ears*): Ouuuuu!

STELLA (*calling from the steps*): Stanley! You come out here and let Blanche finish dressing!

BLANCHE: I'm through dressing, honey.

STELLA: Well, you come out, then.

STANLEY: Your sister and I are having a little talk.

BLANCHE (*lightly*): Honey, do me a favor. Run to the drug-store and get me a lemon-coke with plenty of chipped ice in it!—Will you do that for me, Sweetie?

STELLA (*uncertainly*): Yes. (*She goes around the corner of the building.*)

BLANCHE: The poor little thing was out there listening to us, and I have an idea she doesn't understand you as well as I do. . . . All right; now, Mr. Kowalski, let us proceed without any more double-talk. I'm ready to answer all questions. I've nothing to hide. What is it?

STANLEY: There is such a thing in this State of Louisiana as the Napoleonic code, according to which whatever belongs to my wife is also mine—and vice versa.

BLANCHE: My, but you have an impressive judicial air!

(*She sprays herself with her atomizer; then playfully sprays him with it. He seizes the atomizer and slams it down on the dresser. She throws back her head and laughs.*)

STANLEY: If I didn't know that you was my wife's sister I'd get ideas about you!

BLANCHE: Such as what!

STANLEY: Don't play so dumb. You know what!—Where's the papers?

BLANCHE: Papers?

STANLEY: Papers! That stuff people write on!

BLANCHE: Oh, papers, papers! Ha-ha! The first anniversary gift, all kinds of papers!

STANLEY: I'm talking of legal papers. Connected with the plantation.

BLANCHE: There *were* some papers.

STANLEY: You mean they're no longer existing?

BLANCHE: They probably are, somewhere.

STANLEY: But not in the trunk.

BLANCHE: Everything that I own is in that trunk.

STANLEY: Then why don't we have a look for them? (*He crosses to the trunk, shoves it roughly open and begins to open compartments.*)

BLANCHE: What in the name of heaven are you thinking of! What's in the back of that little boy's mind of yours? That I am absconding with something, attempting some kind of treachery on my sister?—Let me do that! It will be faster and simpler . . . (*She crosses to the trunk and takes out a box*) I keep my papers mostly in this tin box. (*She opens it.*)

STANLEY: What's them underneath? (*He indicates another sheaf of paper.*)

BLANCHE: These are love-letters, yellowing with antiquity, all from one boy. (*He snatches them up. She speaks fiercely*) Give those back to me!

STANLEY: I'll have a look at them first!
BLANCHE: The touch of your hands insults them!
STANLEY: Don't pull that stuff!

(*He rips off the ribbon and starts to examine them. Blanche snatches them from him, and they cascade to the floor.*)

BLANCHE: Now that you've touched them I'll burn them!
STANLEY (*staring, baffled*): What in hell are they?
BLANCHE (*on the floor gathering them up*): Poems a dead boy wrote. I hurt him the way that you would like to hurt me, but you can't! I'm not young and vulnerable any more. But my young husband was and I—never mind about that! Just give them back to me!
STANLEY: What do you mean by saying you'll have to burn them?
BLANCHE: I'm sorry, I must have lost my head for a moment. Everyone has something he won't let others touch because of their—intimate nature . . .

(*She now seems faint with exhaustion and she sits down with the strong box and puts on a pair of glasses and goes methodically through a large stack of papers.*)

Ambler & Ambler. Hmmmmm. . . . Crabtree. . . . More Ambler & Ambler.
STANLEY: What is Ambler & Ambler?
BLANCHE: A firm that made loans on the place.
STANLEY: Then it *was* lost on a mortgage?
BLANCHE (*touching her forehead*): That must've been what happened.
STANLEY: I don't want no ifs, ands or buts! What's all the rest of them papers?

(*She hands him the entire box. He carries it to the table and starts to examine the papers.*)

BLANCHE (*picking up a large envelope containing more papers*): There are thousands of papers, stretching back over hundreds of years, affecting Belle Reve as, piece by piece, our improvident grandfathers and father and uncles and brothers exchanged the land for their epic fornications—to put it plainly! (*She removes her glasses with an exhausted laugh*)

The four-letter word deprived us of our plantation, till finally all that was left—and Stella can verify that!—was the house itself and about twenty acres of ground, including a graveyard, to which now all but Stella and I have retreated. (*She pours the contents of the envelope on the table*) Here all of them are, all papers! I hereby endow you with them! Take them, peruse them—commit them to memory, even! I think it's wonderfully fitting that Belle Reve should finally be this bunch of old papers in your big, capable hands! . . . I wonder if Stella's come back with my lemon-coke . . . (*She leans back and closes her eyes.*)

STANLEY: I have a lawyer acquaintance who will study these out.

BLANCHE: Present them to him with a box of aspirin tablets.

STANLEY (*becoming somewhat sheepish*): You see, under the Napoleonic code—a man has to take an interest in his wife's affairs—especially now that she's going to have a baby.

(*Blanche opens her eyes. The "blue piano" sounds louder.*)

BLANCHE: Stella? Stella going to have a baby? (*dreamily*) I didn't know she was going to have a baby!

(*She gets up and crosses to the outside door. Stella appears around the corner with a carton from the drug-store.*

(*Stanley goes into the bedroom with the envelope and the box.*

(*The inner rooms fade to darkness and the outside wall of the house is visible. Blanche meets Stella at the foot of the steps to the sidewalk.*)

BLANCHE: Stella, Stella for Star! How lovely to have a baby! (*She embraces her sister. Stella returns the embrace with a convulsive sob. Blanche speaks softly*) Everything is all right; we thrashed it out. I feel a bit shaky, but I think I handled it nicely. I laughed and treated it all as a joke, called him a little boy and laughed—and flirted! Yes—I was flirting with your husband, Stella!

(*Steve and Pablo appear carrying a case of beer.*)

The guests are gathering for the poker party.

(*The two men pass between them, and with a short, curious stare at Blanche, they enter the house.*)

STELLA: I'm sorry he did that to you.

BLANCHE: He's just not the sort that goes for jasmine perfume! But maybe he's what we need to mix with our blood now that we've lost Belle Reve and have to go on without Belle Reve to protect us . . . How pretty the sky is! I ought to go there on a rocket that never comes down.

(*A tamale Vendor calls out as he rounds the corner.*)

VENDOR: Red hot! Red hots!

(*Blanche utters a sharp, frightened cry and shrinks away; then she laughs breathlessly again.*)

BLANCHE: Which way do we—go now—Stella?

VENDOR: Re-e-d ho-o-ot!

BLANCHE: The blind are—leading the blind!

(*They disappear around the corner, Blanche's desperate laughter ringing out once more.*

(*Then there is a bellowing laugh from the interior of the flat.*

(*Then the "blue piano" and the hot trumpet sound louder.*)

SCENE THREE

THE POKER NIGHT

There is a picture of Van Gogh's of a billiard-parlor at night. The kitchen now suggests that sort of lurid nocturnal brilliance, the raw colors of childhood's spectrum. Over the yellow linoleum of the kitchen table hangs an electric bulb with a vivid green glass shade. The poker players—Stanley, Steve, Mitch and Pablo—wear colored shirts, solid blues, a purple, a red-and-white check, a light green, and they are men at the peak of their physical manhood, as coarse and direct and powerful as the primary colors. There are vivid slices of watermelon on the table, whiskey bottles and glasses. The bedroom is relatively dim with only the light that spills between the portieres and through the wide window on the street.

For a moment, there is absorbed silence as a hand is dealt.

STEVE: Anything wild this deal?
PABLO: One-eyed jacks are wild.
STEVE: Give me two cards.
PABLO: You, Mitch?
MITCH: I'm out.
PABLO: One.
MITCH: Anyone want a shot?
STANLEY: Yeah. Me.
PABLO: Why don't somebody go to the Chinaman's and bring back a load of chop suey?
STANLEY: When I'm losing you want to eat! Ante up! Openers? Openers! Get y'r ass off the table, Mitch. Nothing belongs on a poker table but cards, chips and whiskey.

(*He lurches up and tosses some watermelon rinds to the floor.*)

MITCH: Kind of on your high horse, ain't you?
STANLEY: How many?
STEVE: Give me three.
STANLEY: One.
MITCH: I'm out again. I oughta go home pretty soon.
STANLEY: Shut up.
MITCH: I gotta sick mother. She don't go to sleep until I come in at night.
STANLEY: Then why don't you stay home with her?
MITCH: She says to go out, so I go, but I don't enjoy it. All the while I keep wondering how she is.
STANLEY: Aw, for the sake of Jesus, go home, then!
PABLO: What've you got?
STEVE: Spade flush.
MITCH: You all are married. But I'll be alone when she goes.—I'm going to the bathroom.
STANLEY: Hurry back and we'll fix you a sugar-tit.
MITCH: Aw, go rut. (*He crosses through the bedroom into the bathroom.*)
STEVE (*dealing a hand*): Seven card stud. (*Telling his joke as he deals*) This ole nigger is out in back of his house sittin' down th'owing corn to the chickens when all at once he hears a loud cackle and this young hen comes lickety split

around the side of the house with the rooster right behind her and gaining on her fast.

STANLEY (*impatient with the story*): Deal!

STEVE: But when the rooster catches sight of the nigger th'owing the corn he puts on the brakes and lets the hen get away and starts pecking corn. And the old nigger says, "Lord God, I hopes I never gits *that* hongry!"

(*Steve and Pablo laugh. The sisters appear around the corner of the building.*)

STELLA: The game is still going on.

BLANCHE: How do I look?

STELLA: Lovely, Blanche.

BLANCHE: I feel so hot and frazzled. Wait till I powder before you open the door. Do I look done in?

STELLA: Why no. You are as fresh as a daisy.

BLANCHE: One that's been picked a few days.

(*Stella opens the door and they enter.*)

STELLA: Well, well, well. I see you boys are still at it!

STANLEY: Where you been?

STELLA: Blanche and I took in a show. Blanche, this is Mr. Gonzales and Mr. Hubbell.

BLANCHE: Please don't get up.

STANLEY: Nobody's going to get up, so don't be worried.

STELLA: How much longer is this game going to continue?

STANLEY: Till we get ready to quit.

BLANCHE: Poker is so fascinating. Could I kibitz?

STANLEY: You could not. Why don't you women go up and sit with Eunice?

STELLA: Because it is nearly two-thirty. (*Blanche crosses into the bedroom and partially closes the portieres*) Couldn't you call it quits after one more hand?

(*A chair scrapes. Stanley gives a loud whack of his hand on her thigh.*)

STELLA (*sharply*): That's not fun, Stanley.

(*The men laugh. Stella goes into the bedroom.*)

STELLA: It makes me so mad when he does that in front of people.

BLANCHE: I think I will bathe.

STELLA: Again?

BLANCHE: My nerves are in knots. Is the bathroom occupied?

STELLA: I don't know.

(*Blanche knocks. Mitch opens the door and comes out, still wiping his hands on a towel.*)

BLANCHE: Oh!—good evening.

MITCH: Hello. (*He stares at her.*)

STELLA: Blanche, this is Harold Mitchell. My sister, Blanche DuBois.

MITCH (*with awkward courtesy*): How do you do, Miss DuBois.

STELLA: How is your mother now, Mitch?

MITCH: About the same, thanks. She appreciated your sending over that custard.—Excuse me, please.

(*He crosses slowly back into the kitchen, glancing back at Blanche and coughing a little shyly. He realizes he still has the towel in his hands and with an embarrassed laugh hands it to Stella. Blanche looks after him with a certain interest.*)

BLANCHE: That one seems—superior to the others.

STELLA: Yes, he is.

BLANCHE: I thought he had a sort of sensitive look.

STELLA: His mother is sick.

BLANCHE: Is he married?

STELLA: No.

BLANCHE: Is he a wolf?

STELLA: Why, Blanche! (*Blanche laughs.*) I don't think he would be.

BLANCHE: What does—what does he do?

(*She is unbuttoning her blouse.*)

STELLA: He's on the precision bench in the spare parts department. At the plant Stanley travels for.

BLANCHE: Is that something much?

STELLA: No. Stanley's the only one of his crowd that's likely to get anywhere.

BLANCHE: What makes you think Stanley will?

STELLA: Look at him.

BLANCHE: I've looked at him.

STELLA: Then you should know.

BLANCHE: I'm sorry, but I haven't noticed the stamp of genius even on Stanley's forehead.

(*She takes off the blouse and stands in her pink silk brassiere and white skirt in the light through the portieres. The game has continued in undertones.*)

STELLA: It isn't on his forehead and it isn't genius.

BLANCHE: Oh. Well, what is it, and where? I would like to know.

STELLA: It's a drive that he has. You're standing in the light, Blanche!

BLANCHE: Oh, am I!

(*She moves out of the yellow streak of light. Stella has removed her dress and put on a light blue satin kimona.*)

STELLA (*with girlish laughter*): You ought to see their wives.

BLANCHE (*laughingly*): I can imagine. Big, beefy things, I suppose.

STELLA: You know that one upstairs? (*More laughter*) One time (*laughing*) the plaster—(*laughing*) cracked—

STANLEY: You hens cut out that conversation in there!

STELLA: You can't hear us.

STANLEY: Well, you can hear me and I said to hush up!

STELLA: This is my house and I'll talk as much as I want to!

BLANCHE: Stella, don't start a row.

STELLA: He's half drunk!—I'll be out in a minute.

(*She goes into the bathroom. Blanche rises and crosses leisurely to a small white radio and turns it on.*)

STANLEY: Awright, Mitch, you in?

MITCH: What? Oh!—No, I'm out!

(*Blanche moves back into the streak of light. She raises her arms and stretches, as she moves indolently back to the chair.*

(*Rhumba music comes over the radio. Mitch rises at the table.*)

STANLEY: Who turned that on in there?
BLANCHE: I did. Do you mind?
STANLEY: Turn it off!
STEVE: Aw, let the girls have their music.
PABLO: Sure, that's good, leave it on!
STEVE: Sounds like Xavier Cugat!

(*Stanley jumps up and, crossing to the radio, turns it off. He stops short at the sight of Blanche in the chair. She returns his look without flinching. Then he sits again at the poker table.*

(*Two of the men have started arguing hotly.*)

STEVE: I didn't hear you name it.
PABLO: Didn't I name it, Mitch?
MITCH: I wasn't listenin'.
PABLO: What were you doing, then?
STANLEY: He was looking through them drapes. (*He jumps up and jerks roughly at curtains to close them*) Now deal the hand over again and let's play cards or quit. Some people get ants when they win.

(*Mitch rises as Stanley returns to his seat.*)

STANLEY (*yelling*): Sit down!
MITCH: I'm going to the "head." Deal me out.
PABLO: Sure he's got ants now. Seven five-dollar bills in his pants pocket folded up tight as spitballs.
STEVE: Tomorrow you'll see him at the cashier's window getting them changed into quarters.
STANLEY: And when he goes home he'll deposit them one by one in a piggy bank his mother give him for Christmas. (*Dealing*) This game is Spit in the Ocean.

(*Mitch laughs uncomfortably and continues through the portieres. He stops just inside.*)

BLANCHE (*softly*): Hello! The Little Boys' Room is busy right now.
MITCH: We've—been drinking beer.
BLANCHE: I hate beer.
MITCH: It's—a hot weather drink.
BLANCHE: Oh, I don't think so; it always makes me warmer. Have you got any cigs? (*She has slipped on the dark red satin wrapper.*)

MITCH: Sure.

BLANCHE: What kind are they?

MITCH: Luckies.

BLANCHE: Oh, good. What a pretty case. Silver?

MITCH: Yes. Yes; read the inscription.

BLANCHE: Oh, is there an inscription? I can't make it out. (*He strikes a match and moves closer*) Oh! (*reading with feigned difficulty*):

"And if God choose,
I shall but love thee better—after—death!"

Why, that's from my favorite sonnet by Mrs. Browning!

MITCH: You know it?

BLANCHE: Certainly I do!

MITCH: There's a story connected with that inscription.

BLANCHE: It sounds like a romance.

MITCH: A pretty sad one.

BLANCHE: Oh?

MITCH: The girl's dead now.

BLANCHE (*in a tone of deep sympathy*): *Oh!*

MITCH: She knew she was dying when she give me this. A very strange girl, very sweet—very!

BLANCHE: She must have been fond of you. Sick people have such deep, sincere attachments.

MITCH: That's right, they certainly do.

BLANCHE: Sorrow makes for sincerity, I think.

MITCH: It sure brings it out in people.

BLANCHE: The little there is belongs to people who have experienced some sorrow.

MITCH: I believe you are right about that.

BLANCHE: I'm positive that I am. Show me a person who hasn't known any sorrow and I'll show you a shuperficial—Listen to me! My tongue is a little—thick! You boys are responsible for it. The show let out at eleven and we couldn't come home on account of the poker game so we had to go somewhere and drink. I'm not accustomed to having more than one drink. Two is the limit—and *three!* (*She laughs*) Tonight I had three.

STANLEY: Mitch!

MITCH: Deal me out. I'm talking to Miss—

BLANCHE: DuBois.

MITCH: Miss DuBois?

BLANCHE: It's a French name. It means woods and Blanche means white, so the two together mean white woods. Like an orchard in spring! You can remember it by that.

MITCH: You're French?

BLANCHE: We are French by extraction. Our first American ancestors were French Huguenots.

MITCH: You are Stella's sister, are you not?

BLANCHE: Yes, Stella is my precious little sister. I call her little in spite of the fact she's somewhat older than I. Just slightly. Less than a year. Will you do something for me?

MITCH: Sure. What?

BLANCHE: I bought this adorable little colored paper lantern at a Chinese shop on Bourbon. Put it over the light bulb! Will you, please?

MITCH: Be glad to.

BLANCHE: I can't stand a naked light bulb, any more than I can a rude remark or a vulgar action.

MITCH (*adjusting the lantern*): I guess we strike you as being a pretty rough bunch.

BLANCHE: I'm very adaptable—to circumstances.

MITCH: Well, that's a good thing to be. You are visiting Stanley and Stella?

BLANCHE: Stella hasn't been so well lately, and I came down to help her for a while. She's very run down.

MITCH: You're not—?

BLANCHE: Married? No, no. I'm an old maid schoolteacher!

MITCH: You may teach school but you're certainly not an old maid.

BLANCHE: Thank you, sir! I appreciate your gallantry!

MITCH: So you are in the teaching profession?

BLANCHE: Yes. Ah, yes . . .

MITCH: Grade school or high school or—

STANLEY (*bellowing*): *Mitch!*

MITCH: *Coming!*

BLANCHE: Gracious, what lung-power! . . . I teach high school. In Laurel.

MITCH: What do you teach? What subject?

BLANCHE: Guess!

MITCH: I bet you teach art or music? (*Blanche laughs delicately*) Of course I could be wrong. You might teach arithmetic.

BLANCHE: Never arithmetic, sir; never arithmetic! (*with a laugh*) I don't even know my multiplication tables! No, I have the misfortune of being an English instructor. I attempt to instill a bunch of bobby-soxers and drug-store Romeos with reverence for Hawthorne and Whitman and Poe!

MITCH: I guess that some of them are more interested in other things.

BLANCHE: How very right you are! Their literary heritage is not what most of them treasure above all else! But they're sweet things! And in the spring, it's touching to notice them making their first discovery of love! As if nobody had ever known it before!

(*The bathroom door opens and Stella comes out. Blanche continues talking to Mitch.*)

Oh! Have you finished? Wait—I'll turn on the radio.

(*She turns the knobs on the radio and it begins to play "Wien, Wien, nur du allein." Blanche waltzes to the music with romantic gestures. Mitch is delighted and moves in awkward imitation like a dancing bear.*

(*Stanley stalks fiercely through the portieres into the bedroom. He crosses to the small white radio and snatches it off the table. With a shouted oath, he tosses the instrument out the window.*)

STELLA: *Drunk—drunk—animal thing, you!* (*She rushes through to the poker table*) All of you—please go home! If any of you have one spark of decency in you—

BLANCHE (*wildly*): Stella, watch out, he's—

(*Stanley charges after Stella.*)

MEN (*feebly*): Take it easy, Stanley. Easy, fellow.—Let's all—

STELLA: You lay your hands on me and I'll—

(*She backs out of sight. He advances and disappears. There is the sound of a blow. Stella cries out. Blanche screams and runs *into the kitchen. The men rush forward and there is grappling and cursing. Something is overturned with a crash.*)

BLANCHE (*shrilly*): My sister is going to have a baby!
MITCH: This is terrible.
BLANCHE: Lunacy, absolute lunacy!
MITCH: Get him in here, men.

(*Stanley is forced, pinioned by the two men, into the bedroom. He nearly throws them off. Then all at once he subsides and is limp in their grasp.*

(*They speak quietly and lovingly to him and he leans his face on one of their shoulders.*)

STELLA (*in a high, unnatural voice, out of sight*): I want to go away, I want to go away!
MITCH: Poker shouldn't be played in a house with women.

(*Blanche rushes into the bedroom*)

BLANCHE: I want my sister's clothes! We'll go to that woman's upstairs!
MITCH: Where is the clothes?
BLANCHE (*opening the closet*): I've got them! (*She rushes through to Stella*) Stella, Stella, precious! Dear, dear little sister, don't be afraid!

(*With her arms around Stella, Blanche guides her to the outside door and upstairs.*)

STANLEY (*dully*): What's the matter; what's happened?
MITCH: You just blew your top, Stan.
PABLO: He's okay, now.
STEVE: Sure, my boy's okay!
MITCH: Put him on the bed and get a wet towel.
PABLO: I think coffee would do him a world of good, now.
STANLEY (*thickly*): I want water.
MITCH: Put him under the shower!

(*The men talk quietly as they lead him to the bathroom.*)

STANLEY: Let the rut go of me, you sons of bitches!

(*Sounds of blows are heard. The water goes on full tilt.*)

STEVE: Let's get quick out of here!

(*They rush to the poker table and sweep up their winnings on their way out.*)

MITCH (*sadly but firmly*): Poker should not be played in a house with women.

(*The door closes on them and the place is still. The Negro entertainers in the bar around the corner play "Paper Doll" slow and blue. After a moment Stanley comes out of the bathroom dripping water and still in his clinging wet polka dot drawers.*)

STANLEY: Stella! (*There is a pause*) My baby doll's left me! (*He breaks into sobs. Then he goes to the phone and dials, still shuddering with sobs.*) Eunice? I want my baby! (*He waits a moment; then he hangs up and dials again*) Eunice! I'll keep on ringin' until I talk with my baby!

(*An indistinguishable shrill voice is heard. He hurls phone to floor. Dissonant brass and piano sounds as the rooms dim out to darkness and the outer walls appear in the night light. The "blue piano" plays for a brief interval.*

(*Finally, Stanley stumbles half-dressed out to the porch and down the wooden steps to the pavement before the building. There he throws back his head like a baying hound and bellows his wife's name: "Stella! Stella, sweetheart! Stella!"*)

STANLEY: Stell-*lahhhhh!*

EUNICE (*calling down from the door of her upper apartment*): Quit that howling out there an' go back to bed!

STANLEY: I want my baby down here. Stella, Stella!

EUNICE: She ain't comin' down so you quit! Or you'll git th' law on you!

STANLEY: Stella!

EUNICE: You can't beat on a woman an' then call 'er back! She won't come! And her goin' t' have a baby! . . . You stinker! You whelp of a Polack, you! I hope they do haul you in and turn the fire hose on you, same as the last time!

STANLEY (*humbly*): Eunice, I want my girl to come down with me!

EUNICE: Hah! (*She slams her door.*)

STANLEY (*with heaven-splitting violence*): *STELL-LAHHHHH!*

(*The low-tone clarinet moans. The door upstairs opens again. Stella slips down the rickety stairs in her robe. Her eyes are glistening with tears and her hair loose about her throat and shoulders. They stare at each other. Then they come together with low, animal moans. He falls to his knees on the steps and presses his face to her belly, curving a little with maternity. Her eyes go blind with tenderness as she catches his head and raises him level with her. He snatches the screen door open and lifts her off her feet and bears her into the dark flat.*

(*Blanche comes out on the upper landing in her robe and slips fearfully down the steps.*)

BLANCHE: Where is my little sister? Stella? Stella?

(*She stops before the dark entrance of her sister's flat. Then catches her breath as if struck. She rushes down to the walk before the house. She looks right and left as if for a sanctuary.*

(*The music fades away. Mitch appears from around the corner.*)

MITCH: Miss DuBois?

BLANCHE: Oh!

MITCH: All quiet on the Potomac now?

BLANCHE: She ran downstairs and went back in there with him.

MITCH: Sure she did.

BLANCHE: I'm terrified!

MITCH: Ho-ho! There's nothing to be scared of. They're crazy about each other.

BLANCHE: I'm not used to such—

MITCH: Naw, it's a shame this had to happen when you just got here. But don't take it serious.

BLANCHE: Violence! Is so—

MITCH: Set down on the steps and have a cigarette with me.

BLANCHE: I'm not properly dressed.

MITCH: That don't make no difference in the Quarter.

BLANCHE: Such a pretty silver case.

MITCH: I showed you the inscription, didn't I?

BLANCHE: Yes. (*During the pause, she looks up at the sky*) There's so much—so much confusion in the world . . . (*He coughs diffidently*) Thank you for being so kind! I need kindness now.

SCENE FOUR

It is early the following morning. There is a confusion of street cries like a choral chant.

Stella is lying down in the bedroom. Her face is serene in the early morning sunlight. One hand rests on her belly, rounding slightly with new maternity. From the other dangles a book of colored comics. Her eyes and lips have that almost narcotized tranquility that is in the faces of Eastern idols.

The table is sloppy with remains of breakfast and the debris of the preceding night, and Stanley's gaudy pyjamas lie across the threshold of the bathroom. The outside door is slightly ajar on a sky of summer brilliance.

Blanche appears at this door. She has spent a sleepless night and her appearance entirely contrasts with Stella's. She presses her knuckles nervously to her lips as she looks through the door, before entering.

BLANCHE: Stella?
STELLA (*stirring lazily*): Hmmh?

(*Blanche utters a moaning cry and runs into the bedroom, throwing herself down beside Stella in a rush of hysterical tenderness.*)

BLANCHE: Baby, my baby sister!
STELLA (*drawing away from her*): Blanche, what is the matter with you?

(*Blanche straightens up slowly and stands beside the bed looking down at her sister with knuckles pressed to her lips.*)

BLANCHE: He's left?
STELLA: Stan? Yes.
BLANCHE: Will he be back?
STELLA: He's gone to get the car greased. Why?
BLANCHE: Why! I've been half crazy, Stella! When I found out you'd been insane enough to come back in here after what happened—I started to rush in after you!
STELLA: I'm glad you didn't.
BLANCHE: What were you thinking of? (*Stella makes an indefinite gesture*) Answer me! What? What?

STELLA: Please, Blanche! Sit down and stop yelling.

BLANCHE: All right, Stella. I will repeat the question quietly now. How could you come back in this place last night? Why, you must have slept with him!

(*Stella gets up in a calm and leisurely way.*)

STELLA: Blanche, I'd forgotten how excitable you are. You're making much too much fuss about this.

BLANCHE: Am I?

STELLA: Yes, you are, Blanche. I know how it must have seemed to you and I'm awful sorry it had to happen, but it wasn't anything as serious as you seem to take it. In the first place, when men are drinking and playing poker anything can happen. It's always a powder-keg. He didn't know what he was doing. . . . He was as good as a lamb when I came back and he's really very, very ashamed of himself.

BLANCHE: And that—that makes it all right?

STELLA: No, it isn't all right for anybody to make such a terrible row, but—people do sometimes. Stanley's always smashed things. Why, on our wedding night—soon as we came in here—he snatched off one of my slippers and rushed about the place smashing the light-bulbs with it.

BLANCHE: He did—*what*?

STELLA: He smashed all the light-bulbs with the heel of my slipper! (*She laughs.*)

BLANCHE: And you—you *let* him? Didn't *run*, didn't *scream*?

STELLA: I was—sort of—thrilled by it. (*She waits for a moment*) Eunice and you had breakfast?

BLANCHE: Do you suppose I wanted any breakfast?

STELLA: There's some coffee left on the stove.

BLANCHE: You're so—matter of fact about it, Stella.

STELLA: What other can I be? He's taken the radio to get it fixed. It didn't land on the pavement so only one tube was smashed.

BLANCHE: And you are standing there smiling!

STELLA: What do you want me to do?

BLANCHE: Pull yourself together and face the facts.

STELLA: What are they, in your opinion?

BLANCHE: In my opinion? You're married to a madman!

STELLA: No!

BLANCHE: Yes, you are, your fix is worse than mine is! Only you're not being sensible about it. I'm going to *do* something. Get hold of myself and make myself a new life!

STELLA: Yes?

BLANCHE: But you've given in. And that isn't right, you're not old! You can get out.

STELLA (*slowly and emphatically*): I'm not in anything I want to get out of.

BLANCHE (*incredulously*): What—Stella?

STELLA: I said I am not in anything that I have a desire to get out of. Look at the mess in this room! And those empty bottles! They went through two cases last night! He promised this morning that he was going to quit having these poker parties, but you know how long such a promise is going to keep. Oh, well, it's his pleasure, like mine is movies and bridge. People have got to tolerate each other's habits, I guess.

BLANCHE: I don't understand you. (*Stella turns toward her*) I don't understand your indifference. Is this a Chinese philosophy you've—cultivated?

STELLA: Is what—what?

BLANCHE: This—shuffling about and mumbling—'One tube smashed—beer-bottles—mess in the kitchen!'—as if nothing out of the ordinary has happened! (*Stella laughs uncertainly and picking up the broom, twirls it in her hands.*)

BLANCHE: Are you deliberately shaking that thing in my face?

STELLA: No.

BLANCHE: Stop it. Let go of that broom. I won't have you cleaning up for him!

STELLA: Then who's going to do it? Are you?

BLANCHE: I? I!

STELLA: No, I didn't think so.

BLANCHE: Oh, let me think, if only my mind would function! We've got to get hold of some money, that's the way out!

STELLA: I guess that money is always nice to get hold of.

BLANCHE: Listen to me. I have an idea of some kind. (*Shakily she twists a cigarette into her holder*) Do you remember Shep Huntleigh? (*Stella shakes her head*) Of course you remember Shep Huntleigh. I went out with him at college and wore his pin for a while. Well—

STELLA: Well?

BLANCHE: I ran into him last winter. You know I went to Miami during the Christmas holidays?

STELLA: No.

BLANCHE: Well, I did. I took the trip as an investment, thinking I'd meet someone with a million dollars.

STELLA: Did you?

BLANCHE: Yes. I ran into Shep Huntleigh—I ran into him on Biscayne Boulevard, on Christmas Eve, about dusk . . . getting into his car—Cadillac convertible; must have been a block long!

STELLA: I should think it would have been—inconvenient in traffic!

BLANCHE: You've heard of oil-wells?

STELLA: Yes—remotely.

BLANCHE: He has them, all over Texas. Texas is literally spouting gold in his pockets.

STELLA: My, my.

BLANCHE: Y'know how indifferent I am to money. I think of money in terms of what it does for you. But he could do it, he could certainly do it!

STELLA: Do what, Blanche?

BLANCHE: Why—set us up in a—shop!

STELLA: What kind of a shop?

BLANCHE: Oh, a—shop of some kind! He could do it with half what his wife throws away at the races.

STELLA: He's married?

BLANCHE: Honey, would I be here if the man weren't married? (*Stella laughs a little. Blanche suddenly springs up and crosses to phone. She speaks shrilly*) How do I get Western Union?—Operator! Western Union!

STELLA: That's a dial phone, honey.

BLANCHE: I can't dial, I'm too—

STELLA: Just dial O.

BLANCHE: O?

STELLA: Yes, "O" for Operator! (*Blanche considers a moment; then she puts the phone down.*)

BLANCHE: Give me a pencil. Where is a slip of paper? I've got to write it down first—the message, I mean . . .

(*She goes to the dressing table, and grabs up a sheet of Kleenex and an eyebrow pencil for writing equipment.*)

Let me see now . . . (*She bites the pencil*) 'Darling Shep. Sister and I in desperate situation.'

STELLA: I beg your pardon!

BLANCHE: 'Sister and I in desperate situation. Will explain details later. Would you be interested in—?' (*She bites the pencil again*) 'Would you be—interested—in . . .' (*She smashes the pencil on the table and springs up*) You never get anywhere with direct appeals!

STELLA (*with a laugh*): Don't be so ridiculous, darling!

BLANCHE: But I'll think of something, I've *got* to think of—*some*thing! Don't, don't laugh at me, Stella! Please, please don't—I—I want you to look at the contents of my purse! Here's what's in it! (*She snatches her purse open*) Sixty-five measly cents in coin of the realm!

STELLA (*crossing to bureau*): Stanley doesn't give me a regular allowance, he likes to pay bills himself, but—this morning he gave me ten dollars to smooth things over. You take five of it, Blanche, and I'll keep the rest.

BLANCHE: Oh, no. No, Stella.

STELLA (*insisting*): I know how it helps your morale just having a little pocket-money on you.

BLANCHE: No, thank you—I'll take to the streets!

STELLA: Talk sense! How did you happen to get so low on funds?

BLANCHE: Money just goes—it goes places. (*She rubs her forehead*) Sometime today I've got to get hold of a bromo!

STELLA: I'll fix you one now.

BLANCHE: Not yet—I've got to keep thinking!

STELLA: I wish you'd just let things go, at least for a—while . . .

BLANCHE: Stella, I can't live with him! You can, he's your husband. But how could I stay here with him, after last night, with just those curtains between us?

STELLA: Blanche, you saw him at his worst last night.

BLANCHE: On the contrary, I saw him at his best! What such a man has to offer is animal force and he gave a wonderful exhibition of that! But the only way to live with such a man is to—go to bed with him! And that's your job—not mine!

STELLA: After you've rested a little, you'll see it's going to work out. You don't have to worry about anything while you're here. I mean—expenses . . .

BLANCHE: I have to plan for us both, to get us both—out!

STELLA: You take it for granted that I am in something that I want to get out of.

BLANCHE: I take it for granted that you still have sufficient memory of Belle Reve to find this place and these poker players impossible to live with.

STELLA: Well, you're taking entirely too much for granted.

BLANCHE: I can't believe you're in earnest.

STELLA: No?

BLANCHE: I understand how it happened—a little. You saw him in uniform, an officer, not here but—

STELLA: I'm not sure it would have made any difference where I saw him.

BLANCHE: Now don't say it was one of those mysterious electric things between people! If you do I'll laugh in your face.

STELLA: I am not going to say anything more at all about it!

BLANCHE: All right, then, don't!

STELLA: But there are things that happen between a man and a woman in the dark—that sort of make everything else seem—unimportant. (*Pause.*)

BLANCHE: What you are talking about is brutal desire—just—Desire!—the name of that rattle-trap street-car that bangs through the Quarter, up one old narrow street and down another . . .

STELLA: Haven't you ever ridden on that street-car?

BLANCHE: It brought me here.—Where I'm not wanted and where I'm ashamed to be . . .

STELLA: Then don't you think your superior attitude is a bit out of place?

BLANCHE: I am not being or feeling at all superior, Stella. Believe me I'm not! It's just this. This is how I look at it. A man like that is someone to go out with—once—twice—three times when the devil is in you. But live with? Have a child by?

STELLA: I have told you I love him.

BLANCHE: Then I *tremble* for you! I just—*tremble* for you. . . .

STELLA: I can't help your trembling if you insist on trembling!

(*There is a pause.*)

BLANCHE: May I—speak—*plainly*?

STELLA: Yes, do. Go ahead. As plainly as you want to.

(*Outside, a train approaches. They are silent till the noise subsides. They are both in the bedroom.*

(*Under cover of the train's noise Stanley enters from outside. He stands unseen by the women, holding some packages in his arms, and overhears their following conversation. He wears an undershirt and grease-stained seersucker pants.*)

BLANCHE: Well—if you'll forgive me—he's *common!*

STELLA: Why, yes, I suppose he is.

BLANCHE: Suppose! You can't have forgotten that much of our bringing up, Stella, that you just *suppose* that any part of a gentleman's in his nature! *Not one particle, no!* Oh, if he was just—*ordinary!* Just *plain*—but good and wholesome, but—*no.* There's something downright—*bestial*—about him! You're hating me saying this, aren't you?

STELLA (*coldly*): Go on and say it all, Blanche.

BLANCHE: He acts like an animal, has an animal's habits! Eats like one, moves like one, talks like one! There's even something—sub-human—something not quite to the stage of humanity yet! Yes, something—ape-like about him, like one of those pictures I've seen in—anthropological studies! Thousands and thousands of years have passed him right by, and there he is—Stanley Kowalski—survivor of the stone age! Bearing the raw meat home from the kill in the jungle! And you—*you* here—*waiting* for him! Maybe he'll strike you or maybe grunt and kiss you! That is, if kisses have been discovered yet! Night falls and the other apes gather! There in the front of the cave, all grunting like him, and swilling and gnawing and hulking! His poker night!—you call it—this party of apes! Somebody growls—some creature snatches at something—the fight is on! *God!* Maybe we are a long way from being made in God's image, but Stella—my sister—there has been *some* progress since then! Such things as art—as poetry and music—such kinds of new light have come into the world since then! In some kinds of people some tenderer feelings have had some little beginning! That we have got to make *grow!* And *cling* to, and hold as our flag! In this dark march toward whatever it is we're approaching. . . . *Don't—don't hang back with the brutes!*

(*Another train passes outside. Stanley hesitates, licking his lips. Then suddenly he turns stealthily about and withdraws through front door. The women are still unaware of his presence. When the train has passed he calls through the closed front door.*)

STANLEY: Hey! Hey, Stella!
STELLA (*who has listened gravely to Blanche*): Stanley!
BLANCHE: Stell, I—

(*But Stella has gone to the front door. Stanley enters casually with his packages.*)

STANLEY: Hiyuh, Stella. Blanche back?
STELLA: Yes, she's back.
STANLEY: Hiyuh, Blanche. (*He grins at her.*)
STELLA: You must've got under the car.
STANLEY: Them darn mechanics at Fritz's don't know their ass fr'm— *Hey!*

(*Stella has embraced him with both arms, fiercely, and full in the view of Blanche. He laughs and clasps her head to him. Over her head he grins through the curtains at Blanche.*

(*As the lights fade away, with a lingering brightness on their embrace, the music of the "blue piano" and trumpet and drums is heard.*)

SCENE FIVE

Blanche is seated in the bedroom fanning herself with a palm leaf as she reads over a just completed letter. Suddenly she bursts into a peal of laughter. Stella is dressing in the bedroom.

STELLA: What are you laughing at, honey?

BLANCHE: Myself, myself, for being such a liar! I'm writing a letter to Shep. (*She picks up the letter*) "Darling Shep. I am spending the summer on the wing, making flying visits here and there. And who knows, perhaps I shall take a sudden notion to *swoop* down on *Dallas!* How would you feel about that? Ha-ha! (*She laughs nervously and brightly, touching her throat as if actually talking to Shep*) Forewarned is forearmed, as they say!"—How does that sound?

STELLA: Uh-huh . . .

BLANCHE (*going on nervously*): "Most of my sister's friends go north in the summer but some have homes on the Gulf and there has been a continued round of entertainments, teas, cocktails, and luncheons—"

(*A disturbance is heard upstairs at the Hubbell's apartment.*)

STELLA (*crossing to the door*): Eunice seems to be having some trouble with Steve.

(*Eunice's voice shouts in terrible wrath.*)

EUNICE: I heard about you and that blonde!

STEVE: That's a damn lie!

EUNICE: You ain't pulling the wool over my eyes! I wouldn't mind if you'd stay down at the Four Deuces, but you always going up.

STEVE: Who ever seen me up?

EUNICE: I seen you chasing her 'round the balcony—I'm gonna call the vice squad!

STEVE: Don't you throw that at me!

EUNICE (*shrieking*): You hit me! I'm gonna call the police!

(*A clatter of aluminum striking a wall is heard, followed by a man's angry roar, shouts and overturned furniture. There is a crash; then a relative hush.*)

BLANCHE (*brightly*): Did he *kill* her?

(*Eunice appears on the steps in daemonic disorder.*)

STELLA: No! She's coming downstairs.

EUNICE: Call the police, I'm going to call the police! (*She rushes around the corner.*)

STELLA (*returning from the door*): Some of your sister's friends have stayed in the city.

(*They laugh lightly. Stanley comes around the corner in his green and scarlet silk bowling shirt. He trots up the steps and bangs into the kitchen. Blanche registers his entrance with nervous gestures.*)

STANLEY: What's a matter with Eun-uss?
STELLA: She and Steve had a row. Has she got the police?
STANLEY: Naw. She's gettin' a drink.
STELLA: That's much more practical!

(*Steve comes down nursing a bruise on his forehead and looks in the door.*)

STEVE: *She here?*
STANLEY: Naw, naw. At the Four Deuces.
STEVE: That rutting hunk! (*He looks around the corner a bit timidly, then turns with affected boldness and runs after her.*)
BLANCHE: I must jot that down in my notebook. Ha-ha! I'm compiling a notebook of quaint little words and phrases I've picked up here.
STANLEY: You won't pick up nothing here you ain't heard before.
BLANCHE: Can I count on that?
STANLEY: You can count on it up to five hundred.
BLANCHE: That's a mighty high number. (*He jerks open the bureau drawer, slams it shut and throws shoes in a corner. At each noise Blanche winces slightly. Finally she speaks*) What sign were you born under?
STANLEY (*while he is dressing*): Sign?
BLANCHE: Astrological sign. I bet you were born under Aries. Aries people are forceful and dynamic. They dote on noise! They love to bang things around! You must have had lots of banging around in the army and now that you're out, you make up for it by treating inanimate objects with such a fury!

(*Stella has been going in and out of closet during this scene. Now she pops her head out of the closet.*)

STELLA: Stanley was born just five minutes after Christmas.

BLANCHE: Capricorn—the Goat!

STANLEY: What sign were *you* born under?

BLANCHE: Oh, my birthday's next month, the fifteenth of September; that's under Virgo.

STANLEY: What's Virgo?

BLANCHE: Virgo is the Virgin.

STANLEY (*contemptuously*): *Hah!* (*He advances a little as he knots his tie*) Say, do you happen to know somebody named Shaw?

(*Her face expresses a faint shock. She reaches for the cologne bottle and dampens her handkerchief as she answers carefully.*)

BLANCHE: Why, everybody knows somebody named Shaw!

STANLEY: Well, this somebody named Shaw is under the impression he met you in Laurel, but I figure he must have got you mixed up with some other party because this other party is someone he met at a hotel called the Flamingo.

(*Blanche laughs breathlessly as she touches the cologne-dampened handkerchief to her temples.*)

BLANCHE: I'm afraid he does have me mixed up with this "other party." The Hotel Flamingo is not the sort of establishment I would dare to be seen in!

STANLEY: You know of it?

BLANCHE: Yes, I've seen it and smelled it.

STANLEY: You must've got pretty close if you could smell it.

BLANCHE: The odor of cheap perfume is penetrating.

STANLEY: That stuff you use is expensive?

BLANCHE: Twenty-five dollars an ounce! I'm nearly out. That's just a hint if you want to remember my birthday! (*She speaks lightly but her voice has a note of fear.*)

STANLEY: Shaw must've got you mixed up. He goes in and out of Laurel all the time so he can check on it and clear up any mistake.

(*He turns away and crosses to the portieres. Blanche closes her eyes as if faint. Her hand trembles as she lifts the handkerchief again to her forehead.*

(*Steve and Eunice come around corner. Steve's arm is around Eunice's shoulder and she is sobbing luxuriously and *he is cooing love-words. There is a murmur of thunder as they go slowly upstairs in a tight embrace.*)

STANLEY (*to Stella*): I'll wait for you at the Four Deuces!
STELLA: Hey! Don't I rate one kiss?
STANLEY: Not in front of your sister.

(*He goes out. Blanche rises from her chair. She seems faint; looks about her with an expression of almost panic.*)

BLANCHE: Stella! What have you heard about me?
STELLA: Huh?
BLANCHE: What have people been telling you about me?
STELLA: Telling?
BLANCHE: You haven't heard any—unkind—gossip about me?
STELLA: Why, no, Blanche, of course not!
BLANCHE: Honey, there was—a good deal of talk in Laurel.
STELLA: About *you*, Blanche?
BLANCHE: I wasn't so good the last two years or so, after Belle Reve had started to slip through my fingers.
STELLA: All of us do things we—
BLANCHE: I never was hard or self-sufficient enough. When people are soft—soft people have got to court the favor of hard ones, Stella. Have got to be seductive—put on soft colors, the colors of butterfly wings, and glow—make a little—temporary magic just in order to pay for—one night's shelter! That's why I've been—not so awf'ly good lately. I've run for protection, Stella, from under one leaky roof to another leaky roof—because it was storm—all storm, and I was—caught in the center. . . . People don't see you—*men* don't—don't even admit your existence unless they are making love to you. And you've got to have your existence admitted by someone, if you're going to have someone's protection. And so the soft people have got to—shimmer and glow—put a—paper lantern over the light. . . . But I'm scared now—awf'ly scared. I don't know how much longer I can turn the trick. It isn't enough to be soft. You've got to be soft *and attractive*. And I—I'm fading now!

(*The afternoon has faded to dusk. Stella goes into the bedroom and turns on the light under the paper lantern. She holds a bottled soft drink in her hand.*)

BLANCHE: Have you been listening to me?

STELLA: I don't listen to you when you are being morbid! (*She advances with the bottled coke.*)

BLANCHE (*with abrupt change to gaiety*): Is that coke for me?

STELLA: Not for anyone else!

BLANCHE: Why, you precious thing, you! Is it just coke?

STELLA (*turning*): You mean you want a shot in it!

BLANCHE: Well, honey, a shot never does a coke any harm! Let me! You mustn't wait on me!

STELLA: I like to wait on you, Blanche. It makes it seem more like home. (*She goes into the kitchen, finds a glass and pours a shot of whiskey into it.*)

BLANCHE: I have to admit I love to be waited on . . .

(*She rushes into the bedroom. Stella goes to her with the glass. Blanche suddenly clutches Stella's free hand with a moaning sound and presses the hand to her lips. Stella is embarrassed by her show of emotion. Blanche speaks in a choked voice.*)

You're—you're—so *good* to me! And I—

STELLA: Blanche.

BLANCHE: I know, I won't! You hate me to talk sentimental! But honey, *believe* I feel things more than I *tell* you! I *won't* stay long! I won't, I *promise* I—

STELLA: Blanche!

BLANCHE (*hysterically*): I won't, I promise, *I'll* go! Go *soon!* I will *really!* I *won't* hang around until he—throws me out . . .

STELLA: Now will you stop talking foolish?

BLANCHE: Yes, honey. Watch how you pour—that fizzy stuff foams over!

(*Blanche laughs shrilly and grabs the glass, but her hand shakes so it almost slips from her grasp. Stella pours the coke into the glass. It foams over and spills. Blanche gives a piercing cry.*)

STELLA (*shocked by the cry*): Heavens!

BLANCHE: Right on my pretty white skirt!

STELLA: Oh . . . Use my hanky. Blot gently.

BLANCHE (*slowly recovering*): I know—gently—gently . . .

STELLA: Did it stain?

BLANCHE: Not a bit. Ha-ha! Isn't that lucky? (*She sits down shakily, taking a grateful drink. She holds the glass in both hands and continues to laugh a little.*)

STELLA: Why did you scream like that?

BLANCHE: I don't know why I screamed! (*continuing nervously*) Mitch—Mitch is coming at seven. I guess I am just feeling nervous about our relations. (*She begins to talk rapidly and breathlessly*) He hasn't gotten a thing but a goodnight kiss, that's all I have given him, Stella. I want his respect. And men don't want anything they get too easy. But on the other hand men lose interest quickly. Especially when the girl is over—thirty. They think a girl over thirty ought to—the vulgar term is—"put out." . . . And I—I'm not "putting out." Of course he—he doesn't know—I mean I haven't informed him—of my real age!

STELLA: Why are you sensitive about your age?

BLANCHE: Because of hard knocks my vanity's been given. What I mean is—he thinks I'm sort of—prim and proper, you know! (*She laughs out sharply*) I want to *deceive* him enough to make him—want me . . .

STELLA: Blanche, do you want *him*?

BLANCHE: I want to *rest!* I want to breathe quietly again! Yes—I *want* Mitch . . . *very badly!* Just think! If it happens! I can leave here and not be anyone's problem . . .

(*Stanley comes around the corner with a drink under his belt.*)

STANLEY (*bawling*): Hey, Steve! Hey, Eunice! Hey, Stella!

(*There are joyous calls from above. Trumpet and drums are heard from around the corner.*)

STELLA (*kissing Blanche impulsively*): It *will* happen!

BLANCHE (*doubtfully*): It will?

STELLA: It *will!* (*She goes across into the kitchen, looking back at Blanche.*) It will, honey, *it will.* . . . But don't take another drink! (*Her voice catches as she goes out the door to meet her husband.*

(*Blanche sinks faintly back in her chair with her drink. Eunice shrieks with laughter and runs down the steps. Steve bounds after her with goat-like screeches and chases her *around corner. Stanley and Stella twine arms as they follow, laughing.*

(*Dusk settles deeper. The music from the Four Deuces is slow and blue.*)

BLANCHE: Ah, me, ah, me, ah, me . . .

(*Her eyes fall shut and the palm leaf fan drops from her fingers. She slaps her hand on the chair arm a couple of times; then she raises herself wearily to her feet and picks up the hand mirror. There is a little glimmer of lightning about the building.*

(*The Negro Woman, cackling hysterically, swaying drunkenly, comes around the corner from the Four Deuces. At the same time, a Young Man enters from the opposite direction. The Negro Woman snaps her fingers before his belt.*)

NEGRO WOMAN: Hey! Sugar!

(*She says something indistinguishable. The Young Man shakes his head violently and edges hastily up the steps. He rings the bell. Blanche puts down the mirror. The Negro Woman has wandered down the street.*)

BLANCHE: Come in.

(*The Young Man appears through the portieres. She regards him with interest.*)

BLANCHE: Well, well! What can I do for *you*?

YOUNG MAN: I'm collecting for *The Evening Star.*

BLANCHE: I didn't know that stars took up collections.

YOUNG MAN: It's the paper.

BLANCHE: I know, I was joking—feebly! Will you—have a drink?

YOUNG MAN: No, ma'am. No, thank you. I can't drink on the job.

BLANCHE: Oh, well, now, let's see. . . . No, I don't have a dime! I'm not the lady of the house. I'm her sister from Mississippi. I'm one of those poor relations you've heard about.

YOUNG MAN: That's all right. I'll drop by later. (*He starts to go out. She approaches a little.*)

BLANCHE: Hey! (*He turns back shyly. She puts a cigarette in a long holder*) Could you give me a light? (*She crosses toward him. They meet at the door between the two rooms.*)

YOUNG MAN: Sure. (*He takes out a lighter*) This doesn't always work.

BLANCHE: It's temperamental? (*It flares*) Ah!—thank you. (*He starts away again*) Hey! (*He turns again, still more uncertainly. She goes close to him*) Uh—what time is it?

YOUNG MAN: Fifteen of seven.

BLANCHE: That late, and still not dark! It just goes to show. . . . Do I seem intoxicated? (*The Young Man laughs uncomfortably*) I sure hope not because I'm expecting a caller bye and bye.

YOUNG MAN (*starting off*): Well, I—

BLANCHE: I bet you're going to college! And you work after school?

YOUNG MAN: That's right.

BLANCHE: What do you study?

YOUNG MAN: Pre-Med.

BLANCHE: Going to be a doctor! What's your name?

YOUNG MAN: Romano.

BLANCHE: Give me all three of them; I believe in numerology! (*She sways a little.*)

YOUNG MAN: Lucio Francesco Romano.

BLANCHE: My, my, my! I don't know what a numerologist would make out of that! (*The Young Man looks embarrassed*) Forgive me. (*She makes a gentle gesture*) I'm not a conventional person, and I'm so—restless today. . . . Don't you love these long, rainy afternoons in New Orleans when an hour isn't just an hour but a little piece of eternity dropped in our hands?—And who knows what to do with it!

(*In the ensuing pause, the "blue piano" is heard. It continues through the rest of this scene and the opening of the next. The young man clears his throat and looks yearningly at the door.*)

Young man! Young, young, young man! Has anyone ever told you that you look like a young Prince out of the Arabian Nights?

(*The Young Man laughs uncomfortably and stands like a bashful kid. Blanche speaks softly to him.*)

Well, you do, honey lamb! Come here. I want to kiss you, just once, softly and sweetly on your mouth!

(*Without waiting for him to accept, she crosses quickly to him and presses her lips to his.*)

Now run along, now, quickly! It would be nice to keep you, but I've got to be good—and keep my hands off children.

(*He stares at her a moment. She opens the door for him and blows a kiss at him as he goes down the steps with a dazed look. She stands there a little dreamily after he has disappeared. Then Mitch appears around the corner with a bunch of roses.*)

BLANCHE (*gaily*): Look who's coming! My Rosenkavalier! Bow to me first . . . now present them! *Ahhhh—Merciiii!*

(*She looks at him over them, coquettishly pressing them to her lips. He beams at her selfconsciously.*)

SCENE SIX

It is about two A.M. *on the same evening. The outer wall of the building is visible. Blanche and Mitch come in. The utter exhaustion which only a neurasthenic personality can know is evident in Blanche's voice and manner. Mitch is stolid but depressed. They have probably been out to the amusement park on Lake Pontchartrain, for Mitch is bearing, upside down, a plaster statuette of Mae West, the sort of prize won at shooting-galleries and carnival games of chance.*

BLANCHE (*stopping lifelessly at the steps*): Well—

(*Mitch laughs uneasily.*)

Well . . .

MITCH: I guess it must be pretty late—and you're tired.

BLANCHE: Even the hot tamale man has deserted the street, and he hangs on till the end. (*Mitch laughs uneasily again*) How will you get home?

MITCH: I'll walk over to Bourbon and catch an owl-car.

BLANCHE (*laughing grimly*): Is that street-car named Desire still grinding along the tracks at this hour?

MITCH (*heavily*): I'm afraid you haven't gotten much fun out of this evening, Blanche.

BLANCHE: I spoiled it for *you.*

MITCH: No, you didn't, but I felt all the time that I wasn't giving you much—entertainment.

BLANCHE: I simply couldn't rise to the occasion. That was all. I don't think I've ever tried so hard to be gay and made such a dismal mess of it. I get ten points for trying! —I *did* try.

MITCH: Why did you try if you didn't feel like it, Blanche?

BLANCHE: I was just obeying the law of nature.

MITCH: Which law is that?

BLANCHE: The one that says the lady must entertain the gentleman—or no dice! See if you can locate my door-key in this purse. When I'm so tired my fingers are all thumbs!

MITCH (*rooting in her purse*): This it?

BLANCHE: No, honey, that's the key to my trunk which I must soon be packing.

MITCH: You mean you are leaving here soon?

BLANCHE: I've outstayed my welcome.

MITCH: This it?

(*The music fades away.*)

BLANCHE: Eureka! Honey, you open the door while I take a last look at the sky. (*She leans on the porch rail. He opens the door and stands awkwardly behind her.*) I'm looking for the Pleiades, the Seven Sisters, but these girls are not out tonight. Oh, yes they are, there they are! God bless them! All in a bunch going home from their little bridge party. . . . Y' get the door open? Good boy! I guess you—want to go now . . .

(*He shuffles and coughs a little.*)

MITCH: Can I—uh—kiss you—goodnight?

BLANCHE: Why do you always ask me if you may?

MITCH: I don't know whether you want me to or not.

BLANCHE: Why should you be so doubtful?

MITCH: That night when we parked by the lake and I kissed you, you—

BLANCHE: Honey, it wasn't the kiss I objected to. I liked the kiss very much. It was the other little—familiarity—that I—felt obliged to—discourage. . . . I didn't resent it! Not a bit in the world! In fact, I was somewhat flattered that you—desired me! But, honey, you know as well as I do that a single girl, a girl alone in the world, has got to keep a firm hold on her emotions or she'll be lost!

MITCH (*solemnly*): Lost?

BLANCHE: I guess you are used to girls that like to be lost. The kind that get lost immediately, on the first date!

MITCH: I like you to be exactly the way that you are, because in all my—experience—I have never known anyone like you.

(*Blanche looks at him gravely; then she bursts into laughter and then claps a hand to her mouth.*)

MITCH: Are you laughing at me?

BLANCHE: No, honey. The lord and lady of the house have not yet returned, so come in. We'll have a night-cap. Let's leave the lights off. Shall we?

MITCH: You just—do what you want to.

(*Blanche precedes him into the kitchen. The outer wall of the building disappears and the interiors of the two rooms can be dimly seen.*)

BLANCHE (*remaining in the first room*): The other room's more comfortable—go on in. This crashing around in the dark is my search for some liquor.

MITCH: You want a drink?

BLANCHE: I want *you* to have a drink! You have been so anxious and solemn all evening, and so have I; we have both been anxious and solemn and now for these few last remaining moments of our lives together—I want to create—*joie de vivre!* I'm lighting a candle.

MITCH: That's good.

BLANCHE: We are going to be very Bohemian. We are going to pretend that we are sitting in a little artists' cafe on the Left Bank in Paris! (*She lights a candle stub and puts it in a bottle.*) *Je suis la Dame aux Camellias! Vous êtes—Armand!* Understand French?

MITCH (*heavily*): Naw. Naw, I—

BLANCHE: *Voulez-vous couchez avec moi ce soir? Vous ne comprenez pas? Ah, quelle dommage!*—I mean it's a damned good thing. . . . I've found some liquor! Just enough for two shots without any dividends, honey . . .

MITCH (*heavily*): That's—good.

(*She enters the bedroom with the drinks and the candle.*)

BLANCHE: Sit down! Why don't you take off your coat and loosen your collar?

MITCH: I better leave it on.

BLANCHE: No. I want you to be comfortable.

MITCH: I am ashamed of the way I perspire. My shirt is sticking to me.

BLANCHE: Perspiration is healthy. If people didn't perspire they would die in five minutes. (*She takes his coat from him*) This is a nice coat. What kind of material is it?

MITCH: They call that stuff alpaca.

BLANCHE: Oh. Alpaca.

MITCH: It's very light weight alpaca.

BLANCHE: Oh. Light weight alpaca.

MITCH: I don't like to wear a wash-coat even in summer because I sweat through it.

BLANCHE: Oh.

MITCH: And it don't look neat on me. A man with a heavy build has got to be careful of what he puts on him so he don't look too clumsy.

BLANCHE: You are not too heavy.

MITCH: You don't think I am?

BLANCHE: You are not the delicate type. You have a massive bone-structure and a very imposing physique.

MITCH: Thank you. Last Christmas I was given a membership to the New Orleans Athletic Club.

BLANCHE: Oh, good.

MITCH: It was the finest present I ever was given. I work out there with the weights and I swim and I keep myself fit. When I started there, I was getting soft in the belly but now my belly is hard. It is so hard now that a man can punch me in the belly and it don't hurt me. Punch me! Go on! See? (*She pokes lightly at him.*)

BLANCHE: Gracious. (*Her hand touches her chest.*)

MITCH: Guess how much I weigh, Blanche?

BLANCHE: Oh, I'd say in the vicinity of—one hundred and eighty?

MITCH: Guess again.

BLANCHE: Not that much?

MITCH: No. More.

BLANCHE: Well, you're a tall man and you can carry a good deal of weight without looking awkward.

MITCH: I weigh two hundred and seven pounds and I'm six feet one and one half inches tall in my bare feet—without shoes on. And that is what I weigh stripped.

BLANCHE: Oh, my goodness, me! It's awe-inspiring.

MITCH (*embarrassed*): My weight is not a very interesting subject to talk about. (*He hesitates for a moment*) What's yours?

BLANCHE: My weight?

MITCH: Yes.

BLANCHE: Guess!

MITCH: Let me lift you.

BLANCHE: Samson! Go on, lift me. (*He comes behind her and puts his hands on her waist and raises her lightly off the ground*) Well?

MITCH: You are light as a feather.

BLANCHE: Ha-ha! (*He lowers her but keeps his hands on her waist. Blanche speaks with an affectation of demureness*) You may release me now.

MITCH: Huh?

BLANCHE (*gaily*): I said unhand me, sir. (*He fumblingly embraces her. Her voice sounds gently reproving*) Now, Mitch. Just because Stanley and Stella aren't at home is no reason why you shouldn't behave like a gentleman.

MITCH: Just give me a slap whenever I step out of bounds.

BLANCHE: That won't be necessary. You're a natural gentleman, one of the very few that are left in the world. I don't want you to think that I am severe and old maid schoolteacherish or anything like that. It's just—well—

MITCH: Huh?

BLANCHE: I guess it is just that I have—old-fashioned ideals! (*She rolls her eyes, knowing he cannot see her face. Mitch goes to the front door. There is a considerable silence between them. Blanche sighs and Mitch coughs selfconsciously.*)

MITCH (*finally*): Where's Stanley and Stella tonight?

BLANCHE: They have gone out. With Mr. and Mrs. Hubbell upstairs.

MITCH: Where did they go?

BLANCHE: I think they were planning to go to a midnight preview at Loew's State.

MITCH: We should all go out together some night.

BLANCHE: No. That wouldn't be a good plan.

MITCH: Why not?

BLANCHE: You are an old friend of Stanley's?

MITCH: We was together in the Two-forty-first.

BLANCHE: I guess he talks to you frankly?

MITCH: Sure.

BLANCHE: Has he talked to you about me?

MITCH: Oh—not very much.

BLANCHE: The way you say that, I suspect that he has.

MITCH: No, he hasn't said much.

BLANCHE: But what he *has* said. What would you say his attitude toward me was?

MITCH: Why do you want to ask that?

BLANCHE: Well—

MITCH: Don't you get along with him?

BLANCHE: What do you think?

MITCH: I don't think he understands you.

BLANCHE: That is putting it mildly. If it weren't for Stella about to have a baby, I wouldn't be able to endure things here.

MITCH: He isn't—nice to you?

BLANCHE: He is insufferably rude. Goes out of his way to offend me.

MITCH: In what way, Blanche?

BLANCHE: Why, in every conceivable way.

MITCH: I'm surprised to hear that.

BLANCHE: Are you?

MITCH: Well, I—don't see how anybody could be rude to you.

BLANCHE: It's really a pretty frightful situation. You see, there's no privacy here. There's just these portieres between the two rooms at night. He stalks through the rooms in his underwear at night. And I have to ask him to close the bathroom door. That sort of commonness isn't necessary. You probably wonder why I don't move out. Well, I'll tell you frankly. A teacher's salary is barely sufficient for her living-expenses. I didn't save a penny last year and so I had to come here for the summer. That's why I have to put up with my sister's husband. And he has to put up with me, apparently so much against his wishes. . . . Surely he must have told you how much he hates me!

MITCH: I don't think he hates you.

BLANCHE: He hates me. Or why would he insult me? Of course there is such a thing as the hostility of—perhaps in some perverse kind of way he— No! To think of it makes me . . . (*She makes a gesture of revulsion. Then she finishes her drink. A pause follows.*)

MITCH: Blanche—

BLANCHE: Yes, honey?

MITCH: Can I ask you a question?

BLANCHE: Yes. What?

MITCH: How old are you?

(*She makes a nervous gesture.*)

BLANCHE: Why do you want to know?

MITCH: I talked to my mother about you and she said, "How old is Blanche?" And I wasn't able to tell her. (*There is another pause.*)

BLANCHE: You talked to your mother about me?

MITCH: Yes.

BLANCHE: Why?

MITCH: I told my mother how nice you were, and I liked you.

BLANCHE: Were you sincere about that?

MITCH: You know I was.

BLANCHE: Why did your mother want to know my age?

MITCH: Mother is sick.

BLANCHE: I'm sorry to hear it. Badly?

MITCH: She won't live long. Maybe just a few months.

BLANCHE: Oh.

MITCH: She worries because I'm not settled.

BLANCHE: Oh.

MITCH: She wants me to be settled down before she— (*His voice is hoarse and he clears his throat twice, shuffling nervously around with his hands in and out of his pockets.*)

BLANCHE: You love her very much, don't you?

MITCH: Yes.

BLANCHE: I think you have a great capacity for devotion. You will be lonely when she passes on, won't you? (*Mitch clears his throat and nods.*) I understand what that is.

MITCH: To be lonely?

BLANCHE: I loved someone, too, and the person I loved I lost.

MITCH: Dead? (*She crosses to the window and sits on the sill, looking out. She pours herself another drink.*) A man?

BLANCHE: He was a boy, just a boy, when I was a very young girl. When I was sixteen, I made the discovery—love. All at once and much, much too completely. It was like you suddenly turned a blinding light on something that had always been half in shadow, that's how it struck the world for me. But I was unlucky. Deluded. There was something different about the boy, a nervousness, a softness and tenderness which wasn't like a man's, although he wasn't the least bit effeminate looking—still—that thing was there. . . . He came to me for help. I didn't know that. I didn't find out anything till after our marriage when we'd run away and come back and all I knew was I'd failed him in some mysterious way and wasn't able to give the help he needed but couldn't speak of! He was in the quicksands and clutching at me—but I wasn't holding him out, I was slipping in with him! I didn't know that. I didn't know anything except I loved him unendurably but without being able to help him or help myself. Then I found out. In the worst of all possible ways. By coming suddenly into a room that I thought was empty—which wasn't empty, but had two people in it . . . the boy I had married and an older man who had been his friend for years . . .

(*A locomotive is heard approaching outside. She claps her hands to her ears and crouches over. The headlight of the locomotive glares into the room as it thunders past. As the noise recedes she straightens slowly and continues speaking.*)

Afterwards we pretended that nothing had been discovered. Yes, the three of us drove out to Moon Lake Casino, very drunk and laughing all the way.

(*Polka music sounds, in a minor key faint with distance.*)

We danced the Varsouviana! Suddenly in the middle of the dance the boy I had married broke away from me and ran out of the casino. A few moments later—a shot!

(*The Polka stops abruptly.*

(*Blanche rises stiffly. Then, the Polka resumes in a major key.*)

I ran out—all did!—all ran and gathered about the terrible thing at the edge of the lake! I couldn't get near for the crowding. Then somebody caught my arm. "Don't go any closer! Come back! You don't want to see!" See? See what! Then I heard voices say—Allan! Allan! The Grey boy! He'd stuck the revolver into his mouth, and fired—so that the back of his head had been—blown away!

(*She sways and covers her face.*)

It was because—on the dance-floor—unable to stop myself —I'd suddenly said—"I saw! I know! You disgust me . . ." And then the searchlight which had been turned on the world was turned off again and never for one moment since has there been any light that's stronger than this—kitchen—candle . . .

(*Mitch gets up awkwardly and moves toward her a little. The Polka music increases. Mitch stands beside her.*)

MITCH (*drawing her slowly into his arms*): You need somebody. And I need somebody, too. Could it be—you and me, Blanche?

(*She stares at him vacantly for a moment. Then with a soft cry huddles in his embrace. She makes a sobbing effort to speak but the words won't come. He kisses her forehead and her eyes and finally her lips. The Polka tune fades out. Her breath is drawn and released in long, grateful sobs.*)

BLANCHE: Sometimes—there's God—so quickly!

SCENE SEVEN

It is late afternoon in mid-September.

The portieres are open and a table is set for a birthday supper, with cake and flowers.

Stella is completing the decorations as Stanley comes in.

STANLEY: What's all this stuff for?

STELLA: Honey, it's Blanche's birthday.

STANLEY: She here?

STELLA: In the bathroom.

STANLEY (*mimicking*): "Washing out some things"?

STELLA: I reckon so.

STANLEY: How long she been in there?

STELLA: All afternoon.

STANLEY (*mimicking*): "Soaking in a hot tub"?

STELLA: Yes.

STANLEY: Temperature 100 on the nose, and she soaks herself in a hot tub.

STELLA: She says it cools her off for the evening.

STANLEY: And you run out an' get her cokes, I suppose? And serve 'em to Her Majesty in the tub? (*Stella shrugs*) Set down here a minute.

STELLA: Stanley, I've got things to do.

STANLEY: Set down! I've got th' dope on your big sister, Stella.

STELLA: Stanley, stop picking on Blanche.

STANLEY: That girl calls *me* common!

STELLA: Lately you been doing all you can think of to rub her the wrong way, Stanley, and Blanche is sensitive and you've got to realize that Blanche and I grew up under very different circumstances than you did.

STANLEY: So I been told. And told and told and told! You know she's been feeding us a pack of lies here?

STELLA: No, I don't, and—

STANLEY: Well, she has, however. But now the cat's out of the bag! I found out some things!

STELLA: What—things?

STANLEY: Things I already suspected. But now I got proof from the most reliable sources—which I have checked on!

(*Blanche is singing in the bathroom a saccharine popular ballad which is used contrapuntally with Stanley's speech.*)

STELLA (*to Stanley*): Lower your voice!

STANLEY: Some canary-bird, huh!

STELLA: Now please tell me quietly what you think you've found out about my sister.

STANLEY: Lie Number One: All this squeamishness she puts on! You should just know the line she's been feeding to Mitch. He thought she had never been more than kissed by a fellow! But Sister Blanche is no lily! Ha-ha! Some lily she is!

STELLA: What have you heard and who from?

STANLEY: Our supply-man down at the plant has been going through Laurel for years and he knows all about her and everybody else in the town of Laurel knows all about her. She is as famous in Laurel as if she was the President of the United States, only she is not respected by any party! This supply-man stops at a hotel called the Flamingo.

BLANCHE (*singing blithely*):

"Say, it's only a paper moon, Sailing over a cardboard sea
—But it wouldn't be make-believe If you believed in me!"

STELLA: What about the—Flamingo?

STANLEY: She stayed there, too.

STELLA: My sister lived at Belle Reve.

STANLEY: This is after the home-place had slipped through her lily-white fingers! She moved to the Flamingo! A second-class hotel which has the advantage of not interfering in the private social life of the personalities there! The Flamingo is used to all kinds of goings-on. But even the management of the Flamingo was impressed by Dame Blanche! In fact they was so impressed by Dame Blanche that they requested her to turn in her room-key—for permanently! This happened a couple of weeks before she showed here.

BLANCHE (*singing*):

"It's a Barnum and Bailey world, Just as phony as it can be—
But it wouldn't be make-believe If you believed in me!"

STELLA: What—contemptible—lies!

STANLEY: Sure, I can see how you would be upset by this. She pulled the wool over your eyes as much as Mitch's!

STELLA: It's pure invention! There's not a word of truth in it and if I were a man and this creature had dared to invent such things in my presence—

BLANCHE (*singing*):

"Without your love,
It's a honky-tonk parade!
Without your love,
It's a melody played In a penny arcade . . ."

STANLEY: Honey, I told you I thoroughly checked on these stories! Now wait till I'm finished. The trouble with Dame Blanche was that she couldn't put on her act any more in Laurel! They got wised up after two or three dates with her and then they quit, and she goes on to another, the same old line, same old act, same old hooey! But the town was too small for this to go on forever! And as time went by she became a town character. Regarded as not just different but downright loco—nuts.

(*Stella draws back.*)

And for the last year or two she has been washed up like poison. That's why she's here this summer, visiting royalty, putting on all this act—because she's practically told by the mayor to get out of town! Yes, did you know there was an army camp near Laurel and your sister's was one of the places called "Out-of-Bounds"?

BLANCHE:

"It's only a paper moon, Just as phony as it can be—
But it wouldn't be make-believe If you believed in me!"

STANLEY: Well, so much for her being such a refined and particular type of girl. Which brings us to Lie Number Two.

STELLA: I don't want to hear any more!

STANLEY: She's not going back to teach school! In fact I am willing to bet you that she never had no idea of returning to Laurel! She didn't resign temporarily from the high school because of her nerves! No, siree, Bob! She didn't. They kicked her out of that high school before the spring term ended—and I hate to tell you the reason that step was taken! A seventeen-year-old boy—she'd gotten mixed up with!

BLANCHE:

"It's a Barnum and Bailey world, Just as phony as it
can be—"

(*In the bathroom the water goes on loud; little breathless cries and peals of laughter are heard as if a child were frolicking in the tub.*)

STELLA: This is making me—sick!

STANLEY: The boy's dad learned about it and got in touch with the high school superintendent. Boy, oh, boy, I'd like to have been in that office when Dame Blanche was called on the carpet! I'd like to have seen her trying to squirm out of that one! But they had her on the hook good and proper that time and she knew that the jig was all up! They told her she better move on to some fresh territory. Yep, it was practickly a town ordinance passed against her!

(*The bathroom door is opened and Blanche thrusts her head out, holding a towel about her hair.*)

BLANCHE: Stella!

STELLA (*faintly*): Yes, Blanche?

BLANCHE: Give me another bath-towel to dry my hair with. I've just washed it.

STELLA: Yes, Blanche. (*She crosses in a dazed way from the kitchen to the bathroom door with a towel.*)

BLANCHE: What's the matter, honey?

STELLA: Matter? Why?

BLANCHE: You have such a strange expression on your face!

STELLA: Oh— (*She tries to laugh*) I guess I'm a little tired!

BLANCHE: Why don't you bathe, too, soon as I get out?

STANLEY (*calling from the kitchen*): How soon is that going to be?

BLANCHE: Not so terribly long! Possess your soul in patience!

STANLEY: It's not my soul, it's my kidneys I'm worried about!

(*Blanche slams the door. Stanley laughs harshly. Stella comes slowly back into the kitchen.*)

STANLEY: Well, what do you think of it?

STELLA: I don't believe all of those stories and I think your supply-man was mean and rotten to tell them. It's possible that some of the things he said are partly true. There are things about my sister I don't approve of—things that caused sorrow at home. She was always—flighty!

STANLEY: Flighty is some word for it!

STELLA: But when she was young, very young, she had an experience that—killed her illusions!

STANLEY: What experience was that?

STELLA: I mean her marriage, when she was—almost a child! She married a boy who wrote poetry. . . . He was extremely good-looking. I think Blanche didn't just love him but worshipped the ground he walked on! Adored him and thought him almost too fine to be human! But then she found out—

STANLEY: What?

STELLA: This beautiful and talented young man was a degenerate. Didn't your supply-man give you that information?

STANLEY: All we discussed was recent history. That must have been a pretty long time ago.

STELLA: Yes, it was—a pretty long time ago . . .

(*Stanley comes up and takes her by the shoulders rather gently. She gently withdraws from him. Automatically she starts sticking little pink candles in the birthday cake.*)

STANLEY: How many candles you putting in that cake?

STELLA: I'll stop at twenty-five.

STANLEY: Is company expected?

STELLA: We asked Mitch to come over for cake and ice-cream.

(*Stanley looks a little uncomfortable. He lights a cigarette from the one he has just finished.*)

STANLEY: I wouldn't be expecting Mitch over tonight.

(*Stella pauses in her occupation with candles and looks slowly around at Stanley.*)

STELLA: *Why?*

STANLEY: Mitch is a buddy of mine. We were in the same outfit together—Two-forty-first Engineers. We work in the same plant and now on the same bowling team. You think I could face him if—

STELLA: Stanley Kowalski, did you—did you repeat what that—?

STANLEY: You're goddam right I told him! I'd have that on my conscience the rest of my life if I knew all that stuff and let my best friend get caught!

STELLA: Is Mitch through with her?

STANLEY: Wouldn't you be if—?

STELLA: I said, *Is Mitch through with her?*

(*Blanche's voice is lifted again, serenely as a bell. She sings "But it wouldn't be make believe if you believed in me."*)

STANLEY: No, I don't think he's necessarily through with her—just wised up!

STELLA: Stanley, she thought Mitch was—going to—going to marry her. I was hoping so, too.

STANLEY: Well, he's not going to marry her. Maybe he *was*, but he's not going to jump in a tank with a school of sharks—now! (*He rises*) Blanche! Oh, Blanche! Can I please get in my bathroom? (*There is a pause.*)

BLANCHE: Yes, indeed, sir! Can you wait one second while I dry?

STANLEY: Having waited one hour I guess one second ought to pass in a hurry.

STELLA: And she hasn't got her job? Well, what will she do!

STANLEY: She's not stayin' here after Tuesday. You know that, don't you? Just to make sure I bought her ticket myself. A bus-ticket!

STELLA: In the first place, Blanche wouldn't go on a bus.

STANLEY: She'll go on a bus and like it.

STELLA: No, she won't, no, she won't, Stanley!

STANLEY: *She'll go!* Period. P.S. She'll go *Tuesday!*

STELLA (*slowly*): What'll—she—do? What on earth will she—*do!*

STANLEY: Her future is mapped out for her.
STELLA: What do you mean?

(*Blanche sings.*)

STANLEY: Hey, canary bird! Toots! Get *OUT* of the *BATHROOM!* Must I speak more plainly?

(*The bathroom door flies open and Blanche emerges with a gay peal of laughter, but as Stanley crosses past her, a frightened look appears in her face, almost a look of panic. He doesn't look at her but slams the bathroom door shut as he goes in.*)

BLANCHE (*snatching up a hair-brush*): Oh, I feel so good after my long, hot bath, I feel so good and cool and—rested!
STELLA (*sadly and doubtfully from the kitchen*): Do you, Blanche?
BLANCHE (*brushing her hair vigorously*): Yes, I do, so refreshed! (*She tinkles her highball glass.*) A hot bath and a long, cold drink always give me a brand new outlook on life! (*She looks through the portieres at Stella, standing between them, and slowly stops brushing*) Something has happened!—What is it?
STELLA (*turning away quickly*): Why, nothing has happened, Blanche.
BLANCHE: You're lying! Something has!

(*She stares fearfully at Stella, who pretends to be busy at the table. The distant piano goes into a hectic breakdown.*)

SCENE EIGHT

Three-quarters of an hour later.

The view through the big windows is fading gradually into a still-golden dusk. A torch of sunlight blazes on the side of a big water-tank or oil-drum across the empty lot toward the business district which is now pierced by pinpoints of lighted windows or windows reflecting the sunset.

The three people are completing a dismal birthday supper. Stanley looks sullen. Stella is embarrassed and sad.

Blanche has a tight, artificial smile on her drawn face. There is a fourth place at the table which is left vacant.

BLANCHE (*suddenly*): Stanley, tell us a joke, tell us a funny story to make us all laugh. I don't know what's the matter, we're all so solemn. Is it because I've been stood up by my beau?

(*Stella laughs feebly.*)

It's the first time in my entire experience with men, and I've had a good deal of all sorts, that I've actually been stood up by anybody! Ha-ha! I don't know how to take it. . . . Tell us a funny little story, Stanley! Something to help us out.

STANLEY: I didn't think you liked my stories, Blanche.

BLANCHE: I like them when they're amusing but not indecent.

STANLEY: I don't know any refined enough for your taste.

BLANCHE: Then let me tell one.

STELLA: Yes, you tell one, Blanche. You used to know lots of good stories.

(*The music fades.*)

BLANCHE: Let me see, now. . . . I must run through my repertoire! Oh, yes—I love parrot stories! Do you all like parrot stories? Well, this one's about the old maid and the parrot. This old maid, she had a parrot that cursed a blue streak and knew more vulgar expressions than Mr. Kowalski!

STANLEY: Huh.

BLANCHE: And the only way to hush the parrot up was to put the cover back on its cage so it would think it was night and go back to sleep. Well, one morning the old maid had just uncovered the parrot for the day—when who should she see coming up the front walk but the preacher! Well, she rushed back to the parrot and slipped the cover back on the cage and then she let in the preacher. And the parrot was perfectly still, just as quiet as a mouse, but just as she was asking the preacher how much sugar he wanted in his coffee—the parrot broke the silence with a loud—(*She whistles*)—and said—"God *damn*, but that was a short day!"

(*She throws back her head and laughs. Stella also makes an ineffectual effort to seem amused. Stanley pays no attention to the story but reaches way over the table to spear his fork into the remaining chop which he eats with his fingers.*)

BLANCHE: Apparently Mr. Kowalski was not amused.

STELLA: Mr. Kowalski is too busy making a pig of himself to think of anything else!

STANLEY: That's right, baby.

STELLA: Your face and your fingers are disgustingly greasy. Go and wash up and then help me clear the table.

(*He hurls a plate to the floor.*)

STANLEY: That's how I'll clear the table! (*He seizes her arm*) Don't ever talk that way to me! "Pig—Polack—disgusting—vulgar—greasy!"—them kind of words have been on your tongue and your sister's too much around here! What do you two think you are? A pair of queens? Remember what Huey Long said—"Every Man is a King!" And I am the king around here, so don't forget it! (*He hurls a cup and saucer to the floor*) My place is cleared! You want me to clear your places?

(*Stella begins to cry weakly. Stanley stalks out on the porch and lights a cigarette.*

(*The Negro entertainers around the corner are heard.*)

BLANCHE: What happened while I was bathing? What did he tell you, Stella?

STELLA: Nothing, nothing, nothing!

BLANCHE: I think he told you something about Mitch and me! You know why Mitch didn't come but you won't tell me! (*Stella shakes her head helplessly*) I'm going to call him!

STELLA: I wouldn't call him, Blanche.

BLANCHE: I am, I'm going to call him on the phone.

STELLA (*miserably*): I wish you wouldn't.

BLANCHE: I intend to be given some explanation from someone!

(*She rushes to the phone in the bedroom. Stella goes out on the porch and stares reproachfully at her husband. He grunts and turns away from her.*)

STELLA: I hope you're pleased with your doings. I never had so much trouble swallowing food in my life, looking at that girl's face and the empty chair! (*She cries quietly.*)

BLANCHE (*at the phone*): Hello. Mr. Mitchell, please. . . . Oh. . . . I would like to leave a number if I may. Magnolia 9047. And say it's important to call. . . . Yes, very important. . . . Thank you. (*She remains by the phone with a lost, frightened look.*)

(*Stanley turns slowly back toward his wife and takes her clumsily in his arms.*)

STANLEY: Stell, it's gonna be all right after she goes and after you've had the baby. It's gonna be all right again between you and me the way that it was. You remember that way that it was? Them nights we had together? God, honey, it's gonna be sweet when we can make noise in the night the way that we used to and get the colored lights going with nobody's sister behind the curtains to hear us!

(*Their upstairs neighbors are heard in bellowing laughter at something. Stanley chuckles.*)

Steve an' Eunice . . .

STELLA: Come on back in. (*She returns to the kitchen and starts lighting the candles on the white cake.*) Blanche?

BLANCHE: Yes. (*She returns from the bedroom to the table in the kitchen.*) Oh, those pretty, pretty little candles! Oh, don't burn them, Stella.

STELLA: I certainly will.

(*Stanley comes back in.*)

BLANCHE: You ought to save them for baby's birthdays. Oh, I hope candles are going to glow in his life and I hope that his eyes are going to be like candles, like two blue candles lighted in a white cake!

STANLEY (*sitting down*): What poetry!

BLANCHE: His Auntie knows candles aren't safe, that candles burn out in little boys' and girls' eyes, or wind blows them out and after that happens, electric light bulbs go on and you see too plainly . . . (*She pauses reflectively for a moment*) I shouldn't have called him.

STELLA: There's lots of things could have happened.

BLANCHE: There's no excuse for it, Stella. I don't have to put up with insults. I won't be taken for granted.

STANLEY: Goddamn, it's hot in here with the steam from the bathroom.

BLANCHE: I've said I was sorry three times. (*The piano fades out.*) I take hot baths for my nerves. Hydro-therapy, they call it. You healthy Polack, without a nerve in your body, of course you don't know what anxiety feels like!

STANLEY: I am not a Polack. People from Poland are Poles, not Polacks. But what I am is a one hundred percent American, born and raised in the greatest country on earth and proud as hell of it, so don't ever call me a Polack.

(*The phone rings. Blanche rises expectantly.*)

BLANCHE: Oh, that's for me, I'm sure.

STANLEY: *I'm* not sure. Keep your seat. (*He crosses leisurely to phone.*) H'lo. Aw, yeh, hello, Mac.

(*He leans against wall, staring insultingly in at Blanche. She sinks back in her chair with a frightened look. Stella leans over and touches her shoulder.*)

BLANCHE: Oh, keep your hands off me, Stella. What is the matter with you? Why do you look at me with that pitying look?

STANLEY (*bawling*): QUIET IN THERE!—We've got a noisy woman on the place.—Go on, Mac. At Riley's? No, I don't wanta bowl at Riley's. I had a little trouble with Riley last week. I'm the team-captain, ain't I? All right, then, we're not gonna bowl at Riley's, we're gonna bowl at the West Side or the Gala! All right, Mac. See you!

(*He hangs up and returns to the table. Blanche fiercely controls herself, drinking quickly from her tumbler of water. He doesn't look at her but reaches in a pocket. Then he speaks slowly and with false amiability.*)

Sister Blanche, I've got a little birthday remembrance for you.

BLANCHE: Oh, have you, Stanley? I wasn't expecting any, I—I don't know why Stella wants to observe my birthday! I'd much rather forget it—when you—reach twenty-seven! Well—age is a subject that you'd prefer to—ignore!

STANLEY: Twenty-seven?

BLANCHE (*quickly*): What is it? Is it for *me*?

(*He is holding a little envelope toward her.*)

STANLEY: Yes, I hope you like it!

BLANCHE: Why, why— Why, it's a—

STANLEY: Ticket! Back to Laurel! On the Greyhound! Tuesday!

(*The Varsouviana music steals in softly and continues playing. Stella rises abruptly and turns her back. Blanche tries to smile. Then she tries to laugh. Then she gives both up and springs from the table and runs into the next room. She clutches her throat and then runs into the bathroom. Coughing, gagging sounds are heard.*)

Well!

STELLA: You didn't need to do that.

STANLEY: Don't forget all that I took off her.

STELLA: You needn't have been so cruel to someone alone as she is.

STANLEY: Delicate piece she is.

STELLA: She is. She was. You didn't know Blanche as a girl. Nobody, nobody, was tender and trusting as she was. But people like you abused her, and forced her to change.

(*He crosses into the bedroom, ripping off his shirt, and changes into a brilliant silk bowling shirt. She follows him.*)

Do you think you're going bowling now?

STANLEY: Sure.

STELLA: You're not going bowling. (*She catches hold of his shirt*) Why did you do this to her?

STANLEY: I done nothing to no one. Let go of my shirt. You've torn it.

STELLA: I want to know why. Tell me why.

STANLEY: When we first met, me and you, you thought I was common. How right you was, baby. I was common as dirt. You showed me the snapshot of the place with the columns. I pulled you down off them columns and how you loved it, having them colored lights going! And wasn't we happy together, wasn't it all okay till she showed here?

(*Stella makes a slight movement. Her look goes suddenly inward as if some interior voice had called her name. She begins a slow, shuffling progress from the bedroom to the kitchen, leaning and resting on the back of the chair and then on the edge of a table with a blind look and listening expression. Stanley, finishing with his shirt, is unaware of her reaction.*)

And wasn't we happy together? Wasn't it all okay? Till she showed here. Hoity-toity, describing me as an ape. (*He suddenly notices the change in Stella*) Hey, what is it, Stel? (*He crosses to her.*)

STELLA (*quietly*): Take me to the hospital.

(*He is with her now, supporting her with his arm, murmuring indistinguishably as they go outside. The "Varsouviana" is heard, its music rising with sinister rapidity as the bathroom door opens slightly. Blanche comes out twisting a washcloth. She begins to whisper the words as the light fades slowly.*)

BLANCHE:

El pan de mais, el pan de mais,
El pan de mais sin sal.
El pan de mais, el pan de mais,
El pan de mais sin sal . . .

SCENE NINE

A while later that evening. Blanche is seated in a tense hunched position in a bedroom chair that she has recovered with diagonal green and white stripes. She has on her scarlet satin robe. On the table beside chair is a bottle of liquor and a glass. The rapid, feverish polka tune, the "Varsouviana," is heard. The music is in her mind; she is drinking to escape it and the sense of disaster closing in on her, and she seems to whisper the words of the song. An electric fan is turning back and forth across her.

Mitch comes around the corner in work clothes: blue denim shirt and pants. He is unshaven. He climbs the steps to the door and rings. Blanche is startled.

BLANCHE: Who is it, please?
MITCH (*hoarsely*): Me. Mitch.

(*The polka tune stops.*)

BLANCHE: Mitch!—Just a minute.

(*She rushes about frantically, hiding the bottle in a closet, crouching at the mirror and dabbing her face with cologne and powder. She is so excited that her breath is audible as she dashes about. At last she rushes to the door in the kitchen and lets him in.*)

Mitch!—Y'know, I really shouldn't let you in after the treatment I have received from you this evening! So utterly uncavalier! But hello, beautiful!

(*She offers him her lips. He ignores it and pushes past her into the flat. She looks fearfully after him as he stalks into the bedroom.*)

My, my, what a cold shoulder! And a face like a thunder-cloud! And such uncouth apparel! Why, you haven't even shaved! The unforgivable insult to a lady! But I forgive you. I forgive you because it's such a relief to see you. You've stopped that polka tune that I had caught in my head. Have you ever had anything caught in your head? Some words, a piece of music? That goes relentlessly on and on in your head? No, of course you haven't, you dumb angel-puss, you'd never get anything awful caught in your head!

(*He stares at her while she follows him while she talks. It is obvious that he has had a few drinks on the way over.*)

MITCH: Do we have to have that fan on?
BLANCHE: No!
MITCH: I don't like fans.
BLANCHE: Then let's turn it off, honey. I'm not partial to them!

(*She presses the switch and the fan nods slowly off. She clears her throat uneasily as Mitch plumps himself down on the bed in the bedroom and lights a cigarette.*)

I don't know what there is to drink. I—haven't investigated.

MITCH: I don't want Stan's liquor.

BLANCHE: It isn't Stan's. Everything here isn't Stan's. Some things on the premises are actually mine! How is your mother? Isn't your mother well?

MITCH: Why?

BLANCHE: Something's the matter tonight, but never mind. I won't cross-examine the witness. I'll just—(*She touches her forehead vaguely. The polka tune starts up again.*)—pretend I don't notice anything different about you! That—music again . . .

MITCH: What music?

BLANCHE: The "Varsouviana"! The polka tune they were playing when Allan— Wait!

(*A distant revolver shot is heard. Blanche seems relieved.*)

There now, the shot! It always stops after that.

(*The polka music dies out again.*)

Yes, now it's stopped.

MITCH: Are you boxed out of your mind?

BLANCHE: I'll go and see what I can find in the way of— (*She crosses into the closet, pretending to search for the bottle.*) Oh, by the way, excuse me for not being dressed. But I'd practically given you up! Had you forgotten your invitation to supper?

MITCH: I wasn't going to see you any more.

BLANCHE: Wait a minute. I can't hear what you're saying and you talk so little that when you do say something, I don't want to miss a single syllable of it. . . . What am I looking around here for? Oh, yes—liquor! We've had so much excitement around here this evening that I *am* boxed out of my mind! (*She pretends suddenly to find the bottle. He draws his foot up on the bed and stares at her contemptuously.*) Here's something. Southern Comfort! What is that, I wonder?

MITCH: If you don't know, it must belong to Stan.

BLANCHE: Take your foot off the bed. It has a light cover on it. Of course you boys don't notice things like that. I've done so much with this place since I've been here.

MITCH: I bet you have.

BLANCHE: You saw it before I came. Well, look at it now! This room is almost—dainty! I want to keep it that way. I wonder if this stuff ought to be mixed with something? Ummm, it's sweet, so sweet! It's terribly, terribly sweet! Why, it's a *liqueur*, I believe! Yes, that's what it *is*, a liqueur! (*Mitch grunts.*) I'm afraid you won't like it, but try it, and maybe you will.

MITCH: I told you already I don't want none of his liquor and I mean it. You ought to lay off his liquor. He says you been lapping it up all summer like a wild-cat!

BLANCHE: What a fantastic statement! Fantastic of him to say it, fantastic of you to repeat it! I won't descend to the level of such cheap accusations to answer them, even!

MITCH: Huh.

BLANCHE: What's in your mind? I see something in your eyes!

MITCH (*getting up*): It's dark in here.

BLANCHE: I like it dark. The dark is comforting to me.

MITCH: I don't think I ever seen you in the light. (*Blanche laughs breathlessly*) That's a fact!

BLANCHE: Is it?

MITCH: I've never seen you in the afternoon.

BLANCHE: Whose fault is that?

MITCH: You never want to go out in the afternoon.

BLANCHE: Why, Mitch, you're at the plant in the afternoon!

MITCH: Not Sunday afternoon. I've asked you to go out with me sometimes on Sundays but you always make an excuse. You never want to go out till after six and then it's always some place that's not lighted much.

BLANCHE: There is some obscure meaning in this but I fail to catch it.

MITCH: What it means is I've never had a real good look at you, Blanche.

BLANCHE: What are you leading up to?

MITCH: Let's turn the light on here.

BLANCHE (*fearfully*): Light? Which light? What for?

MITCH: This one with the paper thing on it. (*He tears the paper lantern off the light bulb. She utters a frightened gasp.*)

BLANCHE: What did you do that for?

MITCH: So I can take a look at you good and plain!

BLANCHE: Of course you don't really mean to be insulting!

MITCH: No, just realistic.

BLANCHE: I don't want realism.

MITCH: Naw, I guess not.

BLANCHE: I'll tell you what I want. Magic! (*Mitch laughs*) Yes, yes, magic! I try to give that to people. I misrepresent things to them. I don't tell truth, I tell what *ought* to be truth. And if that is sinful, then let me be damned for it!—*Don't turn the light on!*

(*Mitch crosses to the switch. He turns the light on and stares at her. She cries out and covers her face. He turns the light off again.*)

MITCH (*slowly and bitterly*): I don't mind you being older than what I thought. But all the rest of it—Christ! That pitch about your ideals being so old-fashioned and all the malarkey that you've dished out all summer. Oh, I knew you weren't sixteen any more. But I was a fool enough to believe you was straight.

BLANCHE: Who told you I wasn't—'straight'? My loving brother-in-law. And you believed him.

MITCH: I called him a liar at first. And then I checked on the story. First I asked our supply-man who travels through Laurel. And then I talked directly over long-distance to this merchant.

BLANCHE: Who is this merchant?

MITCH: Kiefaber.

BLANCHE: The merchant Kiefaber of Laurel! I know the man. He whistled at me. I put him in his place. So now for revenge he makes up stories about me.

MITCH: Three people, Kiefaber, Stanley and Shaw, swore to them!

BLANCHE: Rub-a-dub-dub, three men in a tub! And such a filthy tub!

MITCH: Didn't you stay at a hotel called The Flamingo?

BLANCHE: Flamingo? No! Tarantula was the name of it! I stayed at a hotel called The Tarantula Arms!

MITCH (*stupidly*): Tarantula?

BLANCHE: Yes, a big spider! That's where I brought my victims. (*She pours herself another drink*) Yes, I had many intimacies with strangers. After the death of Allan—intimacies with strangers was all I seemed able to fill my empty heart with. . . . I think it was panic, just panic, that drove me from one to another, hunting for some protection—here and there, in the most—unlikely places—even, at last, in a seventeen-year-old boy but—somebody wrote the superintendent about it—"This woman is morally unfit for her position!"

(*She throws back her head with convulsive, sobbing laughter. Then she repeats the statement, gasps, and drinks.*)

True? Yes, I suppose—unfit somehow—anyway. . . . So I came here. There was nowhere else I could go. I was played out. You know what played out is? My youth was suddenly gone up the water-spout, and—I met you. You said you needed somebody. Well, I needed somebody, too. I thanked God for you, because you seemed to be gentle—a cleft in the rock of the world that I could hide in! The poor man's Paradise—is a little peace. . . . But I guess I was asking, hoping—too much! Kiefaber, Stanley and Shaw have tied an old tin can to the tail of the kite.

(*There is a pause. Mitch stares at her dumbly.*)

MITCH: You lied to me, Blanche.
BLANCHE: Don't say I lied to you.
MITCH: Lies, lies, inside and out, all lies.
BLANCHE: Never inside, I didn't lie in my heart . . .

(*A Vendor comes around the corner. She is a blind Mexican woman in a dark shawl, carrying bunches of those gaudy tin flowers that lower class Mexicans display at funerals and other festive occasions. She is calling barely audibly. Her figure is only faintly visible outside the building.*)

MEXICAN WOMAN: *Flores. Flores. Flores para los muertos. Flores. Flores.*
BLANCHE: What? Oh! Somebody outside. . . . I—I lived in a house where dying old women remembered their dead men . . .
MEXICAN WOMAN: *Flores. Flores para los muertos . . .*

(*The polka tune fades in.*)

BLANCHE (*as if to herself*): Crumble and fade and—regrets—recriminations . . . 'If you'd done this, it wouldn't've cost me that!'

MEXICAN WOMAN: *Corones para los muertos. Corones . . .*

BLANCHE: Legacies! Huh. . . . And other things such as bloodstained pillow-slips—'Her linen needs changing'—'Yes Mother. But couldn't we get a colored girl to do it?' No, we couldn't of course. Everything gone but the—

MEXICAN WOMAN: *Flores.*

BLANCHE: Death—I used to sit here and she used to sit over there and death was as close as you are. . . . We didn't dare even admit we had ever heard of it!

MEXICAN WOMAN: *Flores para los muertos, flores—flores . . .*

BLANCHE: The opposite is desire. So do you wonder? How could you possibly wonder! Not far from Belle Reve, before we had lost Belle Reve, was a camp where they trained young soldiers. On Saturday nights they would go in town to get drunk—

MEXICAN WOMAN (*softly*): *Corones . . .*

BLANCHE: —and on the way back they would stagger onto my lawn and call—'Blanche! Blanche!'—The deaf old lady remaining suspected nothing. But sometimes I slipped outside to answer their calls. . . . Later the paddy-wagon would gather them up like daisies . . . the long way home . . .

(*The Mexican Woman turns slowly and drifts back off with her soft mournful cries. Blanche goes to the dresser and leans forward on it. After a moment, Mitch rises and follows her purposefully. The polka music fades away. He places his hands on her waist and tries to turn her about.*)

BLANCHE: What do you want?

MITCH (*fumbling to embrace her*): What I been missing all summer.

BLANCHE: Then marry me, Mitch!

MITCH: I don't think I want to marry you any more.

BLANCHE: No?

MITCH (*dropping his hands from her waist*): You're not clean enough to bring in the house with my mother.

BLANCHE: Go away, then. (*He stares at her*) Get out of here quick before I start screaming fire! (*Her throat is tightening with hysteria*) Get out of here quick before I start screaming fire.

(*He still remains staring. She suddenly rushes to the big window with its pale blue square of the soft summer light and cries wildly.*)

Fire! Fire! Fire!

(*With a startled gasp, Mitch turns and goes out the outer door, clatters awkwardly down the steps and around the corner of the building. Blanche staggers back from the window and falls to her knees. The distant piano is slow and blue.*)

SCENE TEN

It is a few hours later that night.

Blanche has been drinking fairly steadily since Mitch left. She has dragged her wardrobe trunk into the center of the bedroom. It hangs open with flowery dresses thrown across it. As the drinking and packing went on, a mood of hysterical exhilaration came into her and she has decked herself out in a somewhat soiled and crumpled white satin evening gown and a pair of scuffed silver slippers with brilliants set in their heels.

Now she is placing the rhinestone tiara on her head before the mirror of the dressing-table and murmuring excitedly as if to a group of spectral admirers.

BLANCHE: How about taking a swim, a moonlight swim at the old rock-quarry? If anyone's sober enough to drive a car! Ha-ha! Best way in the world to stop your head buzzing! Only you've got to be careful to dive where the deep pool is—if you hit a rock you don't come up till tomorrow . . .

(*Tremblingly she lifts the hand mirror for a closer inspection. She catches her breath and slams the mirror face down with such violence that the glass cracks. She moans a little and attempts to rise.*

(*Stanley appears around the corner of the building. He still has on the vivid green silk bowling shirt. As he rounds the corner the honky-tonk music is heard. It continues softly throughout the scene.*

(*He enters the kitchen, slamming the door. As he peers in at Blanche, he gives a low whistle. He has had a few drinks on the way and has brought some quart beer bottles home with him.*)

BLANCHE: How is my sister?

STANLEY: She is doing okay.

BLANCHE: And how is the baby?

STANLEY (*grinning amiably*): The baby won't come before morning so they told me to go home and get a little shut-eye.

BLANCHE: Does that mean we are to be alone in here?

STANLEY: Yep. Just me and you, Blanche. Unless you got somebody hid under the bed. What've you got on those fine feathers for?

BLANCHE: Oh, that's right. You left before my wire came.

STANLEY: You got a wire?

BLANCHE: I received a telegram from an old admirer of mine.

STANLEY: Anything good?

BLANCHE: I think so. An invitation.

STANLEY: What to? A fireman's ball?

BLANCHE (*throwing back her head*): A cruise of the Caribbean on a yacht!

STANLEY: Well, well. What do you know?

BLANCHE: I have never been so surprised in my life.

STANLEY: I guess not.

BLANCHE: It came like a bolt from the blue!

STANLEY: Who did you say it was from?

BLANCHE: An old beau of mine.

STANLEY: The one that give you the white fox-pieces?

BLANCHE: Mr. Shep Huntleigh. I wore his ATO pin my last year at college. I hadn't seen him again until last Christmas. I ran in to him on Biscayne Boulevard. Then—just now—this wire—inviting me on a cruise of the Caribbean! The problem is clothes. I tore into my trunk to see what I have that's suitable for the tropics!

STANLEY: And come up with that—gorgeous—diamond—tiara?

BLANCHE: This old relic? Ha-ha! It's only rhinestones.

STANLEY: Gosh. I thought it was Tiffany diamonds. (*He unbuttons his shirt.*)

BLANCHE: Well, anyhow, I shall be entertained in style.

STANLEY: Uh-huh. It goes to show, you never know what is coming.

BLANCHE: Just when I thought my luck had begun to fail me—

STANLEY: Into the picture pops this Miami millionaire.

BLANCHE: This man is not from Miami. This man is from Dallas.

STANLEY: This man is from Dallas?

BLANCHE: Yes, this man is from Dallas where gold spouts out of the ground!

STANLEY: Well, just so he's from somewhere! (*He starts removing his shirt.*)

BLANCHE: Close the curtains before you undress any further.

STANLEY (*amiably*): This is all I'm going to undress right now. (*He rips the sack off a quart beer-bottle*) Seen a bottle-opener?

(*She moves slowly toward the dresser, where she stands with her hands knotted together.*)

I used to have a cousin who could open a beer-bottle with his teeth. (*Pounding the bottle cap on the corner of table*) That was his only accomplishment, all he could do—he was just a human bottle-opener. And then one time, at a wedding party, he broke his front teeth off! After that he was so ashamed of himself he used t' sneak out of the house when company came . . .

(*The bottle cap pops off and a geyser of foam shoots up. Stanley laughs happily, holding up the bottle over his head.*)

Ha-ha! Rain from heaven! (*He extends the bottle toward her*) Shall we bury the hatchet and make it a loving-cup? Huh?

BLANCHE: No, thank you.

STANLEY: Well, it's a red letter night for us both. You having an oil-millionaire and me having a baby.

(*He goes to the bureau in the bedroom and crouches to remove something from the bottom drawer.*)

BLANCHE (*drawing back*): What are you doing in here?

STANLEY: Here's something I always break out on special occasions like this. The silk pyjamas I wore on my wedding night!

BLANCHE: Oh.

STANLEY: When the telephone rings and they say, "You've got a son!" I'll tear this off and wave it like a flag! (*He shakes out a brilliant pyjama coat*) I guess we are both entitled to put on the dog. (*He goes back to the kitchen with the coat over his arm.*)

BLANCHE: When I think of how divine it is going to be to have such a thing as privacy once more—I could weep with joy!

STANLEY: This millionaire from Dallas is not going to interfere with your privacy any?

BLANCHE: It won't be the sort of thing you have in mind. This man is a gentleman and he respects me. (*Improvising feverishly*) What he wants is my companionship. Having great wealth sometimes makes people lonely!

STANLEY: I wouldn't know about that.

BLANCHE: A cultivated woman, a woman of intelligence and breeding, can enrich a man's life—immeasurably! I have those things to offer, and this doesn't take them away. Physical beauty is passing. A transitory possession. But beauty of the mind and richness of the spirit and tenderness of the heart—and I have all of those things—aren't taken away, but grow! Increase with the years! How strange that I should be called a destitute woman! When I have all of these treasures locked in my heart. (*A choked sob comes from her*) I think of myself as a very, very rich woman! But I have been foolish—casting my pearls before swine!

STANLEY: Swine, huh?

BLANCHE: Yes, swine! Swine! And I'm thinking not only of you but of your friend, Mr. Mitchell. He came to see me tonight. He dared to come here in his work-clothes! And to repeat slander to me, vicious stories that he had gotten from you! I gave him his walking papers . . .

STANLEY: You did, huh?

BLANCHE: But then he came back. He returned with a box of roses to beg my forgiveness! He implored my forgiveness. But some things are not forgivable. Deliberate cruelty is not forgivable. It is the one unforgivable thing in my opinion and it is the one thing of which I have never, never been guilty. And so I told him, I said to him, "Thank you," but it was foolish of me to think that we could ever adapt ourselves to each other. Our ways of life are too different. Our attitudes and our backgrounds are incompatible. We have to be realistic about such things. So farewell, my friend! And let there be no hard feelings . . .

STANLEY: Was this before or after the telegram came from the Texas oil millionaire?

BLANCHE: What telegram? No! No, after! As a matter of fact, the wire came just as—

STANLEY: As a matter of fact there wasn't no wire at all!

BLANCHE: Oh, oh!

STANLEY: There isn't no millionaire! And Mitch didn't come back with roses 'cause I know where he is—

BLANCHE: Oh!

STANLEY: There isn't a goddam thing but imagination!

BLANCHE: Oh!

STANLEY: And lies and conceit and tricks!

BLANCHE: Oh!

STANLEY: And look at yourself! Take a look at yourself in that worn-out Mardi Gras outfit, rented for fifty cents from some rag-picker! And with the crazy crown on! What queen do you think you are?

BLANCHE: Oh—God . . .

STANLEY: I've been on to you from the start! Not once did you pull any wool over this boy's eyes! You come in here and sprinkle the place with powder and spray perfume and cover the light-bulb with a paper lantern, and lo and behold the place has turned into Egypt and you are the Queen of the Nile! Sitting on your throne and swilling down my liquor! I say—*Ha!—Ha!* Do you hear me? *Ha—ha—ha!* (*He walks into the bedroom.*)

BLANCHE: Don't come in here!

(*Lurid reflections appear on the walls around Blanche. The shadows are of a grotesque and menacing form. She catches her breath, crosses to the phone and jiggles the hook. Stanley goes into the bathroom and closes the door.*)

Operator, operator! Give me long-distance, please. . . . I want to get in touch with Mr. Shep Huntleigh of Dallas. He's so well-known he doesn't require any address. Just ask anybody who— Wait!!—No, I couldn't find it right now. . . . Please understand, I— No! No, wait! . . . One moment! Someone is— Nothing! Hold on, please!

(*She sets the phone down and crosses warily into the kitchen. The night is filled with inhuman voices like cries in a jungle.*

(*The shadows and lurid reflections move sinuously as flames along the wall spaces.*

(*Through the back wall of the rooms, which have become transparent, can be seen the sidewalk. A prostitute has rolled a drunkard. He pursues her along the walk, overtakes her and there is a struggle. A policeman's whistle breaks it up. The figures disappear.*

(*Some moments later the Negro Woman appears around the corner with a sequined bag which the prostitute had dropped on the walk. She is rooting excitedly through it.*

(*Blanche presses her knuckles to her lips and returns slowly to the phone. She speaks in a hoarse whisper.*)

BLANCHE: Operator! Operator! Never mind long-distance. Get Western Union. There isn't time to be— Western— Western Union!

(*She waits anxiously.*)

Western Union? Yes! I—want to—Take down this message! "In desperate, desperate circumstances! Help me! Caught in a trap. Caught in—" *Oh!*

(*The bathroom door is thrown open and Stanley comes out in the brilliant silk pyjamas. He grins at her as he knots the tasseled sash about his waist. She gasps and backs away from the phone. He stares at her for a count of ten. Then a clicking becomes audible from the telephone, steady and rasping.*)

STANLEY: You left th' phone off th' hook.

(*He crosses to it deliberately and sets it back on the hook. After he has replaced it, he stares at her again, his mouth slowly curving into a grin, as he waves between Blanche and the outer door.*

(*The barely audible "blue piano" begins to drum up louder. The sound of it turns into the roar of an approaching locomotive. Blanche crouches, pressing her fists to her ears until it has gone by.*)

BLANCHE (*finally straightening*): Let me—let me get by you!

STANLEY: Get by me? Sure. Go ahead. (*He moves back a pace in the doorway.*)

BLANCHE: You—you stand over there! (*She indicates a further position.*)

STANLEY (*grinning*): You got plenty of room to walk by me now.

BLANCHE: Not with you there! But I've got to get out somehow!

STANLEY: You think I'll interfere with you? Ha-ha!

(*The "blue piano" goes softly. She turns confusedly and makes a faint gesture. The inhuman jungle voices rise up. He takes a step toward her, biting his tongue which protrudes between his lips.*)

STANLEY (*softly*): Come to think of it—maybe you wouldn't be bad to—interfere with . . .

(*Blanche moves backward through the door into the bedroom.*)

BLANCHE: Stay back! Don't you come toward me another step or I'll—

STANLEY: What?

BLANCHE: Some awful thing will happen! It will!

STANLEY: What are you putting on now?

(*They are now both inside the bedroom.*)

BLANCHE: I warn you, don't, I'm in danger!

(*He takes another step. She smashes a bottle on the table and faces him, clutching the broken top.*)

STANLEY: What did you do that for?
BLANCHE: So I could twist the broken end in your face!
STANLEY: I bet you would do that!
BLANCHE: I would! I will if you—
STANLEY: Oh! So you want some rough-house! All right, let's have some rough-house!

(*He springs toward her, overturning the table. She cries out and strikes at him with the bottle top but he catches her wrist.*)

Tiger—tiger! Drop the bottle-top! Drop it! We've had this date with each other from the beginning!

(*She moans. The bottle-top falls. She sinks to her knees. He picks up her inert figure and carries her to the bed. The hot trumpet and drums from the Four Deuces sound loudly.*)

SCENE ELEVEN

It is some weeks later. Stella is packing Blanche's things. Sound of water can be heard running in the bathroom.

The portieres are partly open on the poker players—Stanley, Steve, Mitch and Pablo—who sit around the table in the kitchen. The atmosphere of the kitchen is now the same raw, lurid one of the disastrous poker night.

The building is framed by the sky of turquoise. Stella has been crying as she arranges the flowery dresses in the open trunk.

Eunice comes down the steps from her flat above and enters the kitchen. There is an outburst from the poker table.

STANLEY: Drew to an inside straight and made it, by God.
PABLO: *Maldita sea tu suerto!*
STANLEY: Put it in English, greaseball.
PABLO: I am cursing your rutting luck.
STANLEY (*prodigiously elated*): You know what luck is? Luck is believing you're lucky. Take at Salerno. I believed I was lucky. I figured that 4 out of 5 would not come through but I would . . . and I did. I put that down as a rule. To hold front position in this rat-race you've got to believe you are lucky.

MITCH: You . . . you . . . you. . . . Brag . . . brag . . . bull . . . bull.

(*Stella goes into the bedroom and starts folding a dress.*)

STANLEY: What's the matter with him?

EUNICE (*walking past the table*): I always did say that men are callous things with no feelings, but this does beat anything. Making pigs of yourselves. (*She comes through the portieres into the bedroom.*)

STANLEY: What's the matter with her?

STELLA: How is my baby?

EUNICE: Sleeping like a little angel. Brought you some grapes. (*She puts them on a stool and lowers her voice.*) Blanche?

STELLA: Bathing.

EUNICE: How is she?

STELLA: She wouldn't eat anything but asked for a drink.

EUNICE: What did you tell her?

STELLA: I—just told her that—we'd made arrangements for her to rest in the country. She's got it mixed in her mind with Shep Huntleigh.

(*Blanche opens the bathroom door slightly.*)

BLANCHE: Stella.

STELLA: Yes, Blanche?

BLANCHE: If anyone calls while I'm bathing take the number and tell them I'll call right back.

STELLA: Yes.

BLANCHE: That cool yellow silk—the bouclé. See if it's crushed. If it's not too crushed I'll wear it and on the lapel that silver and turquoise pin in the shape of a seahorse. You will find them in the heart-shaped box I keep my accessories in. And Stella . . . Try and locate a bunch of artificial violets in that box, too, to pin with the seahorse on the lapel of the jacket.

(*She closes the door. Stella turns to Eunice.*)

STELLA: I don't know if I did the right thing.

EUNICE: What else could you do?

STELLA: I couldn't believe her story and go on living with Stanley.

EUNICE: Don't ever believe it. Life has got to go on. No matter what happens, you've got to keep on going.

(*The bathroom door opens a little.*)

BLANCHE (*looking out*): Is the coast clear?
STELLA: Yes, Blanche. (*To Eunice*) Tell her how well she's looking.
BLANCHE: Please close the curtains before I come out.
STELLA: They're closed.
STANLEY: —How many for you?
PABLO: —Two.
STEVE: —Three.

(*Blanche appears in the amber light of the door. She has a tragic radiance in her red satin robe following the sculptural lines of her body. The "Varsouviana" rises audibly as Blanche enters the bedroom.*)

BLANCHE (*with faintly hysterical vivacity*): I have just washed my hair.
STELLA: Did you?
BLANCHE: I'm not sure I got the soap out.
EUNICE: Such fine hair!
BLANCHE: (*accepting the compliment*): It's a problem. Didn't I get a call?
STELLA: Who from, Blanche?
BLANCHE: Shep Huntleigh . . .
STELLA: Why, not yet, honey!
BLANCHE: How strange! I—

(*At the sound of Blanche's voice Mitch's arm supporting his cards has sagged and his gaze is dissolved into space. Stanley slaps him on the shoulder.*)

STANLEY: Hey, Mitch, come to!

(*The sound of this new voice shocks Blanche. She makes a shocked gesture, forming his name with her lips. Stella nods and looks quickly away. Blanche stands quite still for some moments—the silverbacked mirror in her hand and a look of sorrowful perplexity as though all human experience shows on her face. Blanche finally speaks but with sudden hysteria.*)

BLANCHE: What's going on here?

(*She turns from Stella to Eunice and back to Stella. Her rising voice penetrates the concentration of the game. Mitch ducks his head lower but Stanley shoves back his chair as if about to rise. Steve places a restraining hand on his arm.*)

BLANCHE (*continuing*): What's happened here? I want an explanation of what's happened here.

STELLA (*agonizingly*): Hush! Hush!

EUNICE: Hush! Hush! Honey.

STELLA: Please, Blanche.

BLANCHE: Why are you looking at me like that? Is something wrong with me?

EUNICE: You look wonderful, Blanche. Don't she look wonderful?

STELLA: Yes.

EUNICE: I understand you are going on a trip.

STELLA: Yes, Blanche *is*. She's going on a vacation.

EUNICE: I'm green with envy.

BLANCHE: Help me, help me get dressed!

STELLA (*handing her dress*): Is this what you—

BLANCHE: Yes, it will do! I'm anxious to get out of here—this place is a trap!

EUNICE: What a pretty blue jacket.

STELLA: It's lilac colored.

BLANCHE: You're both mistaken. It's Della Robbia blue. The blue of the robe in the old Madonna pictures. Are these grapes washed?

(*She fingers the bunch of grapes which Eunice had brought in.*)

EUNICE: Huh?

BLANCHE: Washed, I said. Are they washed?

EUNICE: They're from the French Market.

BLANCHE: That doesn't mean they've been washed. (*The cathedral bells chime*) Those cathedral bells—they're the only clean thing in the Quarter. Well, I'm going now. I'm ready to go.

EUNICE (*whispering*): She's going to walk out before they get here.

STELLA: Wait, Blanche.
BLANCHE: I don't want to pass in front of those men.
EUNICE: Then wait'll the game breaks up.
STELLA: Sit down and . . .

(*Blanche turns weakly, hesitantly about. She lets them push her into a chair.*)

BLANCHE: I can smell the sea air. The rest of my time I'm going to spend on the sea. And when I die, I'm going to die on the sea. You know what I shall die of? (*She plucks a grape*) I shall die of eating an unwashed grape one day out on the ocean. I will die—with my hand in the hand of some nice-looking ship's doctor, a very young one with a small blond mustache and a big silver watch. "Poor lady," they'll say, "the quinine did her no good. That unwashed grape has transported her soul to heaven." (*The cathedral chimes are heard*) And I'll be buried at sea sewn up in a clean white sack and dropped overboard—at noon—in the blaze of summer—and into an ocean as blue as (*Chimes again*) my first lover's eyes!

(*A Doctor and a Matron have appeared around the corner of the building and climbed the steps to the porch. The gravity of their profession is exaggerated—the unmistakable aura of the state institution with its cynical detachment. The Doctor rings the doorbell. The murmur of the game is interrupted.*)

EUNICE (*whispering to Stella*): That must be them.

(*Stella presses her fists to her lips.*)

BLANCHE (*rising slowly*): What is it?
EUNICE (*affectedly casual*): Excuse me while I see who's at the door.
STELLA: Yes.

(*Eunice goes into the kitchen.*)

BLANCHE (*tensely*): I wonder if it's for me.

(*A whispered colloquy takes place at the door.*)

EUNICE (*returning, brightly*): Someone is calling for Blanche.

BLANCHE: It *is* for me, then! (*She looks fearfully from one to the other and then to the portieres. The "Varsouviana" faintly plays*) Is it the gentleman I was expecting from Dallas?

EUNICE: I think it is, Blanche.

BLANCHE: I'm not quite ready.

STELLA: Ask him to wait outside.

BLANCHE: I . . .

(*Eunice goes back to the portieres. Drums sound very softly.*)

STELLA: Everything packed?

BLANCHE: My silver toilet articles are still out.

STELLA: Ah!

EUNICE (*returning*): They're waiting in front of the house.

BLANCHE: They! Who's "they"?

EUNICE: There's a lady with him.

BLANCHE: I cannot imagine who this "lady" could be! How is she dressed?

EUNICE: Just—just a sort of a—plain-tailored outfit.

BLANCHE: Possibly she's— (*Her voice dies out nervously.*)

STELLA: Shall we go, Blanche?

BLANCHE: Must we go through that room?

STELLA: I will go with you.

BLANCHE: How do I look?

STELLA: Lovely.

EUNICE (*echoing*): Lovely.

(*Blanche moves fearfully to the portieres. Eunice draws them open for her. Blanche goes into the kitchen.*)

BLANCHE (*to the men*): Please don't get up. I'm only passing through.

(*She crosses quickly to outside door. Stella and Eunice follow. The poker players stand awkwardly at the table—all except Mitch, who remains seated, looking down at the table. Blanche steps out on a small porch at the side of the door. She stops short and catches her breath.*)

DOCTOR: How do you do?

BLANCHE: You are not the gentleman I was expecting. (*She suddenly gasps and starts back up the steps. She stops by Stella, who stands just outside the door, and speaks in a frightening whisper*) That man isn't Shep Huntleigh.

(*The "Varsouviana" is playing distantly.*

(*Stella stares back at Blanche. Eunice is holding Stella's arm. There is a moment of silence—no sound but that of Stanley steadily shuffling the cards.*

(*Blanche catches her breath again and slips back into the flat. She enters the flat with a peculiar smile, her eyes wide and brilliant. As soon as her sister goes past her, Stella closes her eyes and clenches her hands. Eunice throws her arms comfortingly about her. Then she starts up to her flat. Blanche stops just inside the door. Mitch keeps staring down at his hands on the table, but the other men look at her curiously. At last she starts around the table toward the bedroom. As she does, Stanley suddenly pushes back his chair and rises as if to block her way. The Matron follows her into the flat.*)

STANLEY: Did you forget something?
BLANCHE (*shrilly*): Yes! Yes, I forgot something!

(*She rushes past him into the bedroom. Lurid reflections appear on the walls in odd, sinuous shapes. The "Varsouviana" is filtered into a weird distortion, accompanied by the cries and noises of the jungle. Blanche seizes the back of a chair as if to defend herself.*)

STANLEY: Doc, you better go in.
DOCTOR (*motioning to the Matron*): Nurse, bring her out.

(*The Matron advances on one side, Stanley on the other. Divested of all the softer properties of womanhood, the Matron is a peculiarly sinister figure in her severe dress. Her voice is bold and toneless as a firebell.*)

MATRON: Hello, Blanche.

(*The greeting is echoed and re-echoed by other mysterious voices behind the walls, as if reverberated through a canyon of rock.*)

STANLEY: She says that she forgot something.

(*The echo sounds in threatening whispers.*)

MATRON: That's all right.

STANLEY: What did you forget, Blanche?

BLANCHE: I— I—

MATRON: It don't matter. We can pick it up later.

STANLEY: Sure. We can send it along with the trunk.

BLANCHE (*retreating in panic*): I don't know you—I don't know you. I want to be—left alone—please!

MATRON: Now, Blanche!

ECHOES (*rising and falling*): Now, Blanche—now, Blanche—now, Blanche!

STANLEY: You left nothing here but spilt talcum and old empty perfume bottles—unless it's the paper lantern you want to take with you. You want the lantern?

(*He crosses to dressing table and seizes the paper lantern, tearing it off the light bulb, and extends it toward her. She cries out as if the lantern was herself. The Matron steps boldly toward her. She screams and tries to break past the Matron. All the men spring to their feet. Stella runs out to the porch, with Eunice following to comfort her, simultaneously with the confused voices of the men in the kitchen. Stella rushes into Eunice's embrace on the porch.*)

STELLA: Oh, my God, Eunice help me! Don't let them do that to her, don't let them hurt her! Oh, God, oh, please God, don't hurt her! What are they doing to her? What are they doing? (*She tries to break from Eunice's arms.*)

EUNICE: No, honey, no, no, honey. Stay here. Don't go back in there. Stay with me and don't look.

STELLA: What have I done to my sister? Oh, God, what have I done to my sister?

EUNICE: You done the right thing, the only thing you could do. She couldn't stay here; there wasn't no other place for her to go.

(*While Stella and Eunice are speaking on the porch the voices of the men in the kitchen overlap them.*)

STANLEY (*running in from the bedroom*): Hey! Hey! Doctor! Doctor, you better go in!

DOCTOR: Too bad, too bad. I always like to avoid it.

PABLO: This is a very bad thing.

STEVE: This is no way to do it. She should've been told.
PABLO: *Madre de Dios! Cosa mala, muy, muy mala!*

(*Mitch has started toward the bedroom. Stanley crosses to block him.*)

MITCH (*wildly*): You! You done this, all o' your God damn rutting with things you—
STANLEY: Quit the blubber! (*He pushes him aside.*)
MITCH: I'll kill you! (*He lunges and strikes at Stanley.*)
STANLEY: Hold this bone-headed cry-baby!
STEVE (*grasping Mitch*): Stop it, Mitch.
PABLO: Yeah, yeah, take it easy!

(*Mitch collapses at the table, sobbing.*

(*During the preceding scenes, the Matron catches hold of Blanche's arm and prevents her flight. Blanche turns wildly and scratches at the Matron. The heavy woman pinions her arms. Blanche cries out hoarsely and slips to her knees.*

MATRON: These fingernails have to be trimmed. (*The Doctor comes into the room and she looks at him.*) Jacket, Doctor?
DOCTOR: Not unless necessary.

(*He takes off his hat and now he becomes personalized. The unhuman quality goes. His voice is gentle and reassuring as he crosses to Blanche and crouches in front of her. As he speaks her name, her terror subsides a little. The lurid reflections fade from the walls, the inhuman cries and noises die out and her own hoarse crying is calmed.*)

DOCTOR: Miss DuBois.

(*She turns her face to him and stares at him with desperate pleading. He smiles; then he speaks to the Matron.*)

It won't be necessary.

BLANCHE (*faintly*): Ask her to let go of me.
DOCTOR (*to the Matron*): Let go.

(*The Matron releases her. Blanche extends her hands toward the Doctor. He draws her up gently and supports her with his arm and leads her through the portieres.*)

BLANCHE (*holding tight to his arm*): Whoever you are—I have always depended on the kindness of strangers.

(*The poker players stand back as Blanche and the Doctor cross the kitchen to the front door. She allows him to lead her as if she were blind. As they go out on the porch, Stella cries out her sister's name from where she is crouched a few steps up on the stairs.*)

STELLA: Blanche! Blanche, Blanche!

(*Blanche walks on without turning, followed by the Doctor and the Matron. They go around the corner of the building.*

(*Eunice descends to Stella and places the child in her arms. It is wrapped in a pale blue blanket. Stella accepts the child, sobbingly. Eunice continues downstairs and enters the kitchen where the men, except for Stanley, are returning silently to their places about the table. Stanley has gone out on the porch and stands at the foot of the steps looking at Stella.*)

STANLEY (*a bit uncertainly*): Stella?

(*She sobs with inhuman abandon. There is something luxurious in her complete surrender to crying now that her sister is gone.*)

STANLEY (*voluptuously, soothingly*): Now, honey. Now, love. Now, now, love. (*He kneels beside her and his fingers find the opening of her blouse*) Now, now, love. Now, love. . . .

(*The luxurious sobbing, the sensual murmur fade away under the swelling music of the "blue piano" and the muted trumpet.*)

STEVE: This game is seven-card stud.

Curtain

SUMMER AND SMOKE

Who, if I were to cry out, would hear me
among the angelic orders?

RILKE

FOR
CARSON McCULLERS

CHARACTERS

ALMA *as a child*
JOHN *as a child*
REV. WINEMILLER, *her father*
MRS. WINEMILLER, *her mother*
ALMA WINEMILLER
JOHN BUCHANAN, JR.
DR. BUCHANAN, *his father*
ROSA GONZALES
PAPA GONZALES, *her father*
NELLIE EWELL
MRS. BASSETT
ROGER DOREMUS
MR. KRAMER
ROSEMARY
VERNON
DUSTY

SCENES

PART ONE

A SUMMER

PROLOGUE:	The Fountain
SCENE 1	The same
SCENE 2	The Rectory Interior & Doctor's Office
SCENE 3	The Rectory Interior
SCENE 4	The Doctor's Office
SCENE 5	The Rectory Interior
SCENE 6	The Arbor

PART TWO

A WINTER

SCENE 7	The Rectory & Doctor's Office
SCENE 8	The Doctor's Office
SCENE 9	The Rectory & Doctor's Office
SCENE 10	The Fountain
SCENE 11	The Doctor's Office
SCENE 12	The Fountain

The entire action of the play takes place in Glorious Hill, Mississippi. The time is the turn of the Century through 1916.

AUTHOR'S PRODUCTION NOTES

As the concept of a design grows out of reading a play I will not do more than indicate what I think are the most essential points.

First of all—*The Sky.*

There must be a great expanse of sky so that the entire action of the play takes place against it. This is true of interior as well as exterior scenes. But in fact there are no really interior scenes, for the walls are omitted or just barely suggested by certain necessary fragments such as might be needed to hang a picture or to contain a door-frame.

During the day scenes the sky should be a pure and intense blue (like the sky of Italy as it is so faithfully represented in the religious paintings of the Renaissance) and costumes should be selected to form dramatic color contrasts to this intense blue which the figures stand against. (Color harmonies and other visual effects are tremendously important.)

In the night scenes, the more familiar constellations, such as Orion and the Great Bear and the Pleiades, are clearly projected on the night sky, and above them, splashed across the top of the cyclorama, is the nebulous radiance of the Milky Way. Fleecy cloud forms may also be projected on this cyclorama and made to drift across it.

So much for *The Sky.*

Now we descend to the so-called interior sets of the play. There are two of these "interior" sets, one being the parlor of an Episcopal Rectory and the other the home of a doctor next door to the Rectory. The architecture of these houses is barely suggested but is of an American Gothic design of the Victorian era. There are no actual doors or windows or walls. Doors and windows are represented by delicate frameworks of Gothic design. These frames have strings of ivy clinging to them, the leaves of emerald and amber. Sections of wall are used only where they are functionally required. There should be a fragment of wall in back of the Rectory sofa, supporting a romantic landscape in a gilt frame. In the doctor's house there should be a section of wall to support the chart of anatomy. Chirico has used fragmentary walls and interiors in a very evocative way in his painting called "Conversation among the Ruins." We will deal more specifically with these interiors as we come to them in the course of the play.

Now we come to the main exterior set which is a promontory in a park or public square in the town of Glorious Hill. Situated on this promontory is a fountain in the form of a stone angel, in a gracefully crouching position with wings lifted and her hands held together to form a cup from which water flows, a public drinking fountain. The stone angel of the fountain should probably be elevated so that it appears in the background of the interior scenes as a symbolic figure (Eternity) brooding over the course of the play. *This entire exterior set may be on an upper level, above that of the two fragmentary interiors.* I would like all three units to form an harmonious whole like one complete picture rather than three separate ones. An imaginative designer may solve these plastic problems in a variety of ways and should not feel bound by any of my specific suggestions.

There is one more set, a very small exterior representing an arbor, which we will describe when we reach it.

Everything possible should be done to give an unbroken fluid quality to the sequence of scenes.

There should be no curtain except for the intermission. The other divisions of the play should be accomplished by changes of lighting.

Finally, the matter of music. One basic theme should recur and the points of recurrence have been indicated here and there in the stage directions.

Rome, March, 1948.

PART ONE

A Summer

PROLOGUE

In the park near the angel of the fountain. At dusk of an evening in May, in the first few years of this Century.

Alma, as a child of ten, comes into the scene. She wears a middy blouse and has ribboned braids. She already has the dignity of an adult; there is a quality of extraordinary delicacy and tenderness or spirituality in her, which must set her distinctly apart from other children. She has a habit of holding her hands, one cupped under the other in a way similar to that of receiving the wafer at Holy Communion. This is a habit that will remain with her as an adult. She stands like that in front of the stone angel for a few moments; then bends to drink at the fountain.

While she is bent at the fountain, John, as a child, enters. He shoots a pea-shooter at Alma's bent-over back. She utters a startled cry and whirls about. He laughs.

JOHN: Hi, Preacher's daughter. (*He advances toward her.*) I been looking for you.

ALMA (*hopefully*): You have?

JOHN: Was it you that put them handkerchiefs on my desk? (*Alma smiles uncertainly.*) Answer up!

ALMA: I put a box of handkerchiefs on your desk.

JOHN: I figured it was you. What was the idea, Miss Priss?

ALMA: You needed them.

JOHN: Trying to make a fool of me?

ALMA: Oh, no!

JOHN: Then what was the idea?

ALMA: You have a bad cold and your nose has been running all week. It spoils your appearance.

JOHN: You don't have to look at me if you don't like my appearance.

ALMA: I like your appearance.

JOHN (*coming closer*): Is that why you look at me all the time?

ALMA: I—don't!

JOHN: Oh, yeh, you do. You been keeping your eyes on me all the time. Every time I look around I see them cat eyes of yours looking at me. That was the trouble today when Miss Blanchard asked you where the river Amazon was. She asked you twice and you still didn't answer because you w' lookin' at me. What's the idea? What've'y' got on y' mind anyhow? Answer up!

ALMA: I was only thinking how handsome you'd be if your face wasn't dirty. You know why your face is dirty? Because you don't use a handkerchief and you wipe your nose on the sleeve of that dirty old sweater.

JOHN (*indignantly*): Hah!

ALMA: That's why I put the handkerchiefs on your desk and I wrapped them up so nobody would know what they were. It isn't my fault that you opened the box in front of everybody!

JOHN: What did you think I'd do with a strange box on my desk? Just leave it there till it exploded or something? Sure I opened it up. I didn't expect to find no—*handkerchiefs!*—in it . . .

ALMA (*in a shy trembling voice*): I'm sorry that you were embarrassed. I honestly am awfully sorry that you were embarrassed. Because I wouldn't embarrass you for the world!

JOHN: Don't flatter yourself that I was embarrassed. I don't embarrass that easy.

ALMA: It was stupid and cruel of those girls to laugh.

JOHN: Hah!

ALMA: They should all realize that you don't have a mother to take care of such things for you. It was a pleasure to me to be able to do something for you, only I didn't want you to know it was me who did it.

JOHN: Hee-haw! Ho-hum! Take 'em back! (*He snatches out the box and thrusts it toward her.*)

ALMA: *Please* keep them.

JOHN: What do I want with them?

(*She stares at him helplessly. He tosses the box to the ground and goes up to the fountain and drinks. Something in her face mollifies him and he sits down at the base of the fountain with a manner that does not preclude a more friendly relation. The dusk gathers deeper.*)

ALMA: Do you know the name of the angel?

JOHN: Does she have a name?

ALMA: Yes, I found out she does. It's carved in the base, but it's all worn away so you can't make it out with your eyes.

JOHN: Then how do you know it?

ALMA: You have to read it with your fingers. I did and it gave me cold shivers! *You* read it and see if it doesn't give *you* cold shivers! Go on! Read it with your fingers!

JOHN: Why don't you tell me and save me the trouble?

ALMA: I'm not going to tell you.

(*John grins indulgently and turns to the pediment, crouching before it and running his fingers along the worn inscription.*)

JOHN: E?

ALMA: Yes, E is the first letter!

JOHN: T?

ALMA: Yes!

JOHN: E?

ALMA: E!

JOHN: K?

ALMA: No, no, not K!—*R!* (*He slowly straightens up.*)

JOHN: Eternity?

ALMA: *Eternity!*—Didn't it give you the cold shivers?

JOHN: Nahh.

ALMA: Well, it did me!

JOHN: Because you're a preacher's daughter. Eternity. What is eternity?

ALMA (*in a hushed wondering voice*): It's something that goes on and on when life and death and time and everything else is all through with.

JOHN: There's no such thing.

ALMA: There is. It's what people's souls live in when they have left their bodies. My name is Alma and Alma is Spanish for soul. Did you know that?

JOHN: Hee-haw! Ho-hum! Have you ever seen a dead person?

ALMA: No.

JOHN: I have. They made me go in the room when my mother was dying and she caught hold of my hand and wouldn't let me go—and so I screamed and hit her.

ALMA: Oh, you didn't do that.

JOHN (*somberly*): Uh-huh. She didn't look like my mother. Her face was all ugly and yellow and—terrible—bad-smelling! And so I hit her to make her let go of my hand. They told me that I was a devil!

ALMA: You didn't know what you were doing.

JOHN: My dad is a doctor.

ALMA: I know.

JOHN: He wants to send me to college to study to be a doctor but I wouldn't be a doctor for the world. And have to go in a room and watch people dying! . . . Jesus!

ALMA: You'll change your mind about that.

JOHN: Oh, no, I won't. I'd rather *be* a devil, like they called me and go to South America on a boat! . . . Give me one of them handkerchiefs. (*She brings them eagerly and humbly to the fountain. He takes one out and wets it at the fountain and scrubs his face with it.*) Is my face clean enough to suit you now?

ALMA: Yes!—Beautiful!

JOHN: *What!*

ALMA: I said "Beautiful"!

JOHN: Well—let's—kiss each other.

(Alma turns away.)

JOHN: Come on, let's just try it!

(He seizes her shoulders and gives her a quick rough kiss. She stands amazed with one hand cupping the other.

(*The voice of a child in the distance calls "Johnny! Johnny!"*

(*He suddenly snatches at her hair-ribbon, jerks it loose and then runs off with a mocking laugh.*

(*Hurt and bewildered, Alma turns back to the stone angel, for comfort. She crouches at the pediment and touches the inscription with her fingers. The scene dims out with music.*)

SCENE ONE

Before the curtain rises a band is heard playing a patriotic anthem, punctuated with the crackle of fireworks.

The scene is the same as for the Prologue. It is the evening of July 4th in a year shortly before the first World War. There is a band concert and a display of fireworks in the park. During the scene the light changes from faded sunlight to dusk. Sections of roof, steeples, weather-vanes, should have a metallic surface that catches the mellow light on the backdrop; when dusk has fallen the stars should be visible.

As the curtain rises, the Rev. and Mrs. Winemiller come in and sit on the bench near the fountain. Mrs. Winemiller was a spoiled and selfish girl who evaded the responsibilities of later life by slipping into a state of perverse childishness. She is known as Mr. Winemiller's "Cross."

MR. WINEMILLER (*suddenly rising*): There is Alma, getting on the bandstand! (*Mrs. Winemiller is dreamily munching popcorn.*)

AN ANNOUNCER'S VOICE (*at a distance*): The Glorious Hill Orchestra brings you Miss Alma Winemiller, The Nightingale of the Delta, singing . . . "La Golondrina."

MR. WINEMILLER (*sitting back down again*): This is going to provoke a lot of criticism.

(*The song commences. The voice is not particularly strong, but it has great purity and emotion. John Buchanan comes along. He is now a Promethean figure, brilliantly and restlessly alive in a stagnant society. The excess of his power has not yet found a channel. If it remains without one, it will burn him up. At present he is unmarked by the dissipations in which he relieves his demoniac unrest; he has the fresh and shining look of an epic hero. He walks leisurely before the Winemillers' bench, negligently touching the crown of his hat but not glancing at them; climbs the steps to the base of the fountain, then turns and looks in the direction of the singer. A look of interest touched with irony appears on his face. A couple, strolling in the park, pass behind the fountain.*)

THE GIRL: Look who's by the fountain!

THE MAN: Bright as a new silver dollar!

JOHN: Hi, Dusty! Hi, Pearl!

THE MAN: How'd you make out in that floating crap game?

JOHN: I floated with it as far as Vicksburg, then sank.

THE GIRL: Everybody's been calling: "Johnny, Johnny—where's Johnny?"

(*John's father, Dr. Buchanan, comes on from the right, as Rev. and Mrs. Winemiller move off the scene to the left, toward the band music. Dr. Buchanan is an elderly man whose age shows in his slow and stiff movements. He walks with a cane. John sees him coming, but pretends not to and starts to walk off.*)

DR. BUCHANAN: John!

JOHN (*slowly turning around, as the couple move off*): Oh! Hi, Dad. . . . (*They exchange a long look.*) I—uh—meant to wire you but I must've forgot. I got tied up in Vicksburg Friday night and just now got back to town. Haven't been to the house yet. Is everything . . . going okay? (*He takes a drink of water at the fountain.*)

DR. BUCHANAN (*slowly, in a voice hoarse with emotion*): There isn't any room in the medical profession for wasters, drunkards and lechers. And there isn't any room in my house for wasters—drunkards—lechers! (*A child is heard calling "I sp-yyyyyy!" in the distance.*) I married late in life. I brought over five hundred children into this world before I had one of my own. And by God it looks like I've given myself the rottenest one of the lot. . . . (*John laughs uncertainly.*) You will find your things at the Alhambra Hotel.

JOHN: Okay. If that's how you want it.

(*There is a pause. The singing comes through on the music. John tips his hat diffidently and starts away from the fountain. He goes a few feet and his father suddenly calls after him.*)

DR. BUCHANAN: John! (*John pauses and looks back.*) Come here.

JOHN: Yes, Sir? (*He walks back to his father and stands before him.*)

DR. BUCHANAN (*hoarsely*): Go to the Alhambra Hotel and pick up your things and—bring them back to the house.

JOHN (*gently*): Yes, Sir. If that's how you want it. (*He diffidently extends a hand to touch his father's shoulder.*)

DR. BUCHANAN (*brushing the hand roughly off*): You! . . . You infernal *whelp*, you!

(*Dr. Buchanan turns and goes hurriedly away. John looks after him with a faint, affectionate smile, then sits down on the steps with an air of relief, handkerchief to forehead, and a whistle of relief. Just then the singing at the bandstand ends and there is the sound of applause. Mrs. Winemiller comes in from the left, followed by her husband.*)

MRS. WINEMILLER: Where is the ice cream man?

MR. WINEMILLER: Mother, hush! (*He sees his daughter approaching.*) Here we are, Alma!

(*The song ends. There is applause. Then the band strikes up the Santiago Waltz.*

(*Alma Winemiller enters. Alma had an adult quality as a child and now, in her middle twenties, there is something prematurely spinsterish about her. An excessive propriety and self-consciousness is apparent in her nervous laughter; her voice and gestures belong to years of church entertainments, to the position of hostess in a rectory. People her own age regard her as rather quaintly and humorously affected. She has grown up mostly in the company of her elders. Her true nature is still hidden even from herself. She is dressed in pale yellow and carries a yellow silk parasol.*

(*As Alma passes in front of the fountain, John slaps his hands resoundingly together a few times. She catches her breath in a slight laughing sound, makes as if to retreat, with a startled "Oh!", but then goes quickly to her parents. The applause from the crowd continues.*)

MR. WINEMILLER: They seem to want to hear you sing again, Alma.

(*She turns nervously about, touching her throat and her chest. John grins, applauding by the fountain. When the applause dies out, Alma sinks faintly on the bench.*)

ALMA: Open my bag, Father. My fingers have frozen stiff! (*She draws a deep labored breath.*) I don't know what came over me—absolute panic! Never, never again, it isn't worth it—the tortures that I go through!

MR. WINEMILLER (*anxiously*): You're having one of your nervous attacks?

ALMA: My heart's beating so! It seemed to be in my *throat* the whole time I was singing! (*John laughs audibly from the fountain.*) Was it noticeable, Father?

MR. WINEMILLER: You sang extremely well, Alma. But you know how I feel about this, it was contrary to my wishes and I cannot imagine why you wanted to do it, especially since it seemed to upset you so.

ALMA: I don't see how anyone could object to my singing at a patriotic occasion. If I had just sung well! But I barely got through it. At one point I thought that I wouldn't. The words flew out of my mind. Did you notice the pause? Blind panic! They really never came back, but I went on singing—I think I must have been improvising the lyric! Whew! Is there a handkerchief in it?

MRS. WINEMILLER (*suddenly*): Where is the ice cream man?

ALMA (*rubbing her fingers together*): Circulation is slowly coming back . . .

MR. WINEMILLER: Sit back quietly and take a deep breath, Alma.

ALMA: Yes, my handkerchief—now . . .

MRS. WINEMILLER: Where is the ice cream man?

MR. WINEMILLER: Mother, there isn't any ice cream man.

ALMA: No, there isn't any ice cream man, Mother. But on the way home Mr. Doremus and I will stop by the drug store and pick up a pint of ice cream.

MR. WINEMILLER: Are you intending to stay here?

ALMA: Until the concert is over. I promised Roger I'd wait for him.

MR. WINEMILLER: I suppose you have noticed who is by the fountain?

ALMA: *Shhh!*

MR. WINEMILLER: Hadn't you better wait on a different bench?

ALMA: This is where Roger will meet me.

MR. WINEMILLER: Well, Mother, we'll run along now. (*Mrs. Winemiller has started vaguely toward the fountain, Mr.*

Winemiller firmly restraining her.) This way, this way, Mother! (*He takes her arm and leads her off.*)

MRS. WINEMILLER (*calling back, in a high, childish voice*): Strawberry, Alma. Chocolate, chocolate and strawberry mixed! Not vanilla!

ALMA (*faintly*): Yes, yes, Mother—vanilla . . .

MRS. WINEMILLER (*furiously*): I said *not* vanilla. (*shouting*) Strawberry!

MR. WINEMILLER (*fiercely*): Mother! We're attracting attention. (*He propels her forcibly away.*)

(*John laughs by the fountain. Alma moves her parasol so that it shields her face from him. She leans back closing her eyes. John notices a firecracker by the fountain. He leans over negligently to pick it up. He grins and lights it and tosses it toward Alma's bench. When it goes off she springs up with a shocked cry, letting the parasol drop.*)

JOHN (*jumping up as if outraged*): Hey! Hey, you! (*He looks off to the right. Alma sinks back weakly on the bench. John solicitously advances.*) Are you all right?

ALMA: I can't seem to—catch my breath! Who threw it?

JOHN: Some little rascal.

ALMA: Where?

JOHN: He ran away quick when I hollered!

ALMA: There ought to be an ordinance passed in this town forbidding firecrackers.

JOHN: Dad and I treated fifteen kids for burns the last couple of days. I think you need a little restorative, don't you? (*He takes out a flask.*) Here!

ALMA: What is it?

JOHN: Apple-jack brandy.

ALMA: No thank you.

JOHN: Liquid dynamite.

ALMA: I'm sure.

(*John laughs and returns it to his pocket. He remains looking down at her with one foot on the end of her bench. His steady, smiling look into her face is disconcerting her.*

(*In Alma's voice and manner there is a delicacy and elegance, a kind of "airiness," which is really natural to her as it is, in a less marked degree, to many Southern girls. Her gestures and mannerisms are a bit exaggerated but in a graceful way. It is understandable that she might be accused of "putting on airs" and of being "affected" by the other young people of the town. She seems to belong to a more elegant age, such as the Eighteenth Century in France. Out of nervousness and self-consciousness she has a habit of prefacing and concluding her remarks with a little breathless laugh. This will be indicated at points, but should be used more freely than indicated; however, the characterization must never be stressed to the point of making her at all ludicrous in a less than sympathetic way.*)

ALMA: You're—home for the summer? (*John gives an affirmative grunt.*) Summer is not the pleasantest time of year to renew an acquaintance with Glorious Hill—is it? (*John gives an indefinite grunt. Alma laughs airily.*) The Gulf wind has failed us this year, disappointed us dreadfully this summer. We used to be able to rely on the Gulf wind to cool the nights off for us, but this summer has been an exceptional season. (*He continues to grin disconcertingly down at her; she shows her discomfiture in flurried gestures.*)

JOHN (*slowly*): Are you—disturbed about something?

ALMA: That firecracker was a shock.

JOHN: You should be over that shock by now.

ALMA: I don't get over shocks quickly.

JOHN: I see you don't.

ALMA: You're planning to stay here and take over some of your father's medical practice?

JOHN: I haven't made up my mind about anything yet.

ALMA: I hope so, we all hope so. Your father was telling me that you have succeeded in isolating the germ of that fever epidemic that's broken out at Lyon.

JOHN: Finding something to kill it is more of a trick.

ALMA: You'll do that! He's so positive that you will. He says that you made a special study of bacter—bacter . . .

JOHN: Bacteriology!

ALMA: Yes! At Johns Hopkins! That's in Boston, isn't it?

JOHN: No. Baltimore.

ALMA: Oh, Baltimore. Baltimore, Maryland. Such a beautiful combination of names. And bacteriology—isn't that something you do with a microscope?

JOHN: Well—partly. . . .

ALMA: I've looked through a telescope, but never a microscope. What . . . what do you—see?

JOHN: A—universe, Miss Alma.

ALMA: What kind of a universe?

JOHN: Pretty much the same kind that you saw through the lens of a telescope—a mysterious one. . . .

ALMA: Oh, yes. . . .

JOHN: Part anarchy—and part order!

ALMA: The footprints of God!

JOHN: But not God.

ALMA (*ecstatically*): To be a doctor! And deal with these mysteries under the microscope lens . . . I think it is more religious than being a priest! There is so much suffering in the world it actually makes one sick to think about it, and most of us are so helpless to relieve it. . . . But a physician! Oh, my! With his magnificent gifts and training what a joy it must be to know that he is equipped and appointed to bring relief to all of this fearful suffering—and fear! And it's an expanding profession, it's a profession that is continually widening its horizons. So many diseases have already come under scientific control but the commencement is just—beginning! I mean there is so much more that is yet to be done, such as mental afflictions to be brought under control. . . . And with your father's example to inspire you! Oh, my!

JOHN: I didn't know you had so many ideas about the medical profession.

ALMA: Well, I am a great admirer of your father, as well as a patient. It's such a comfort knowing that he's right next door, within arm's reach as it were!

JOHN: Why? Do you have fits? . . .

ALMA: Fits? (*She throws back her head with a peal of gay laughter.*) Why no, but I do have attacks!—of nervous heart trouble. Which can be so alarming that I run straight to your father!

JOHN: At two or three in the morning?

ALMA: Yes, as late as that, even . . . occasionally. He's very patient with me.

JOHN: But does you no good?

ALMA: He always reassures me.

JOHN: Temporarily?

ALMA: Yes . . .

JOHN: Don't you want more than that?

ALMA: What?

JOHN: It's none of my business.

ALMA: What were you going to say?

JOHN: You're Dad's patient. But I have an idea . . .

ALMA: Please go on! (*John laughs a little.*) Now you have to go on! You can't leave me up in the air! What were you going to tell me?

JOHN: Only that I suspect you need something more than a little temporary reassurance.

ALMA: *Why?* Why? You think it's more serious than . . . ?

JOHN: You're swallowing air.

ALMA: I'm what?

JOHN: You're swallowing air, Miss Alma.

ALMA: I'm swallowing air?

JOHN: Yes, you swallow air when you laugh or talk. It's a little trick that hysterical women get into.

ALMA (*uncertainly*): Ha-ha . . . !

JOHN: You swallow air and it presses on your heart and gives you palpitations. That isn't serious in itself but it's a symptom of something that is. Shall I tell you frankly?

ALMA: Yes!

JOHN: Well, what I think you have is a *doppelganger*! You have a *doppelganger* and the *doppelganger* is badly irritated.

ALMA: Oh, my goodness! I have an irritated *doppelganger*! (*She tries to laugh, but is definitely uneasy.*) How awful that sounds! What exactly *is* it?

JOHN: It's none of *my* business. You are not *my* patient.

ALMA: But that's downright wicked of you! To tell me I have something awful-sounding as that, and then refuse to let me know what it is! (*She tries to laugh again, unsuccessfully.*)

JOHN: I shouldn't have said anything! I'm not your doctor. . . .

ALMA: Just how did you arrive at this—diagnosis of my case? (*She laughs.*) But of course you're teasing me. Aren't you? . . . There, the Gulf wind is stirring! He's actually moving the leaves of the palmetto! And listen to them complaining. . . .

(*As if brought in by this courier from the tropics, Rosa Gonzales enters and crosses to the fountain. Her indolent walk produces a sound and an atmosphere like the Gulf wind on the palmettos, a whispering of silk and a slight rattle of metallic ornaments. She is dressed in an almost outrageous finery, with lustrous feathers on her hat, greenish blue, a cascade of them, also diamond and emerald earrings.*)

JOHN (*sharply*): *Who is that?*

ALMA: I'm surprised that you don't know.

JOHN: I've been away quite a while.

ALMA: That's the Gonzales girl. . . . Her father's the owner of the gambling casino on Moon Lake. (*Rosa drinks at the fountain and wanders leisurely off.*) She smiled at you, didn't she?

JOHN: I thought she did.

ALMA: I hope that you have a strong character. (*He places a foot on the end of the bench.*)

JOHN: Solid rock.

ALMA (*nervously*): The pyrotechnical display is going to be brilliant.

JOHN: The what?

ALMA: The fireworks.

JOHN: Aw!

ALMA: I suppose you've lost touch with most of your *old* friends here.

JOHN (*laconically*): Yeah.

ALMA: You must make some *new* ones! I belong to a little group that meets every ten days. I think you'd enjoy them, too. They're young people with—intellectual and artistic interests. . . .

JOHN (*sadly*): Aw, I see . . . intellectual. . . .

ALMA: You must come!—sometime—I'm going to remind you of it. . . .

JOHN: Thanks. Do you mind if I sit down?

ALMA: Why, certainly not, there's room enough for two! Neither of us are—terribly large in diameter! (*She laughs shrilly.*)

(*A girl's voice is heard calling: "Goodbye, Nellie!" and another answers: "Goodbye!" Nellie Ewell enters—a girl of sixteen with a radiantly fresh healthy quality.*)

ALMA: Here comes someone much nicer! One of my adorable little vocal pupils, the youngest and prettiest one with the least gift for music.

JOHN: I know that one.

ALMA: Hello, there, Nellie dear!

NELLIE: Oh, Miss Alma, your singing was so beautiful it made me cry.

ALMA: It's sweet of you to fib so. I sang terribly.

NELLIE: You're just being modest, Miss Alma. Hello, Dr. John! Dr. John?

JOHN: Yeah?

NELLIE: That book you gave me is too full of long words.

JOHN: Look 'em up in the dictionary, Nellie.

NELLIE: I did, but you know how dictionaries are. You look up one long word and it gives you another and you look up that one and it gives you the long word you looked up in the first place. (*John laughs.*) I'm coming over tomorrow for you to explain it all to me. (*She laughs and goes off.*)

ALMA: What book is she talking about?

JOHN: A book I gave her about the facts of nature. She came over to the office and told me her mother wouldn't tell her anything and she had to know because she'd fallen in love.

ALMA: Why the precocious little—imp! (*She laughs.*)

JOHN: What sort of a mother has she?

ALMA: Mrs. Ewell's the merry widow of Glorious Hill. They say that she goes to the depot to meet every train in order to make the acquaintance of traveling salesmen. Of course she is ostracized by all but a few of her own type of women in town, which is terribly hard for Nellie. It isn't fair to the child. Father didn't want me to take her as a pupil because of her mother's reputation, but I feel that one has a duty to perform toward children in such—circumstances. . . . And I always say that life is such a mysteriously complicated thing that no one should really presume to judge and condemn the behavior of anyone else!

(*There is a faraway "puff" and a burst of golden light over their heads. Both look up. There is a long-drawn "Ahhh . . ." from the invisible crowd. This is an effect that will be repeated at intervals during the scene.*)

There goes the first sky-rocket! Oh, look at it burst into a million stars!

(*John leans way back to look up and allows his knees to spread wide apart so that one of them is in contact with Alma's. The effect upon her is curiously disturbing.*)

JOHN (*after a moment*): Do you have a chill?

ALMA: Why, no!—no. Why?

JOHN: You're shaking.

ALMA: Am I?

JOHN: Don't you feel it?

ALMA: I have a touch of malaria lingering on.

JOHN: You have malaria?

ALMA: Never severely, never really severely. I just have touches of it that come and go. (*She laughs airily.*)

JOHN (*with a gentle grin*): Why do you laugh that way?

ALMA: What way?

(*John imitates her laugh. Alma laughs again in embarrassment.*)

JOHN: Yeah. That way.

ALMA: I do declare, you haven't changed in the slightest. It used to delight you to embarrass me and it still does!

JOHN: I guess I shouldn't tell you this, but I heard an imitation of you at a party.

ALMA: Imitation? Of what?

JOHN: You.

ALMA: I?—I? Why, *what* did they imitate?

JOHN: You singing at a wedding.

ALMA: My voice?

JOHN: Your gestures and facial expression!

ALMA: How mystifying!

JOHN: No, I shouldn't have told you. You're upset about it.

ALMA: I'm not in the least upset, I am just mystified.

JOHN: Don't you know that you have a reputation for putting on airs a little—for gilding the lily a bit?

ALMA: I have no idea what you are talking about.

JOHN: Well, some people seem to have gotten the idea that you are just a little bit—affected!

ALMA: Well, well, well, well. (*She tries to conceal her hurt.*) That may be so, it may seem so to some people. But since I am innocent of any attempt at affectation, I really don't know what I can do about it.

JOHN: You have a rather fancy way of talking.

ALMA: Have I?

JOHN: Pyrotechnical display instead of fireworks, and that sort of thing.

ALMA: So?

JOHN: And how about that accent?

ALMA: Accent? This leaves me quite speechless! I have sometimes been accused of having a put-on accent by people who disapprove of good diction. My father was a Rhodes scholar at Oxford, and while over there he fell into the natural habit of using the long A where it is correct to use it. I suppose I must have picked it up from him, but it's entirely unconscious. Who gave this imitation at this party you spoke of?

JOHN (*grinning*): I don't think she'd want that told.

ALMA: Oh, it was a *she* then?

JOHN: You don't think a man could do it?

ALMA: No, and I don't think a lady would do it either!

JOHN: I didn't think it would have made you so mad, or I wouldn't have brought it up.

ALMA: Oh, I'm not mad. I'm just mystified and amazed as I always am by unprovoked malice in people. I don't understand it when it's directed at me and I don't understand it when it is directed at anybody else. I just don't understand it, and perhaps it is better not to understand it. These people who call me affected and give these unkind imitations of me—I wonder if they stop to think that I have had certain difficulties and disadvantages to cope with—which may be partly the cause of these peculiarities of mine—which they find so offensive!

JOHN: Now, Miss Alma, you're making a mountain out of a mole-hill!

ALMA: I wonder if they stop to think that my circumstances

are somewhat different from theirs? My father and I have a certain—cross—to bear!

JOHN: What cross?

ALMA: Living next door to us, you should know what cross.

JOHN: Mrs. Winemiller?

ALMA: She had her breakdown while I was still in high school. And from that time on I have had to manage the Rectory and take over the social and household duties that would ordinarily belong to a minister's wife, not his daughter. And that may have made me seem strange to some of my more critical contemporaries. In a way it may have—deprived me of—my youth. . . .

(*Another rocket goes up. Another "Ahhh . . ." from the crowd.*)

JOHN: You ought to go out with young people.

ALMA: I am not a recluse. I don't fly around here and there giving imitations of other people at parties. But I am not a recluse by any manner of means. Being a minister's daughter I have to be more selective than most girls about the—society I keep. But I do go out now and then. . . .

JOHN: I have seen you in the public library and the park, but only two or three times I have seen you out with a boy and it was always someone like this Roger Doremus.

ALMA: I'm afraid that you and I move in different circles. If I wished to be as outspoken as you are, which is sometimes just an excuse for being rude—I might say that I've yet to see you in the company of a—well, a—reputable young woman. You've heard unfavorable talk about me in your circle of acquaintances and I've heard equally unpleasant things about you in mine. And the pity of it is that you are preparing to be a doctor. You're intending to practice your father's profession here in Glorious Hill. (*She catches her breath in a sob.*) Most of us have no choice but to lead useless lives! But you have a gift for scientific research! You have a chance to serve humanity. Not just to go on enduring for the sake of endurance, but to serve a noble, humanitarian cause, to relieve human suffering. And what do you do about it? Everything that you can to alienate the confidence of nice people who love and respect your father.

While he is devoting himself to the fever at Lyon you drive your automobile at a reckless pace from one disorderly roadhouse to another! You say you have seen two things through the microscope, anarchy and order? Well, obviously *order* is not the thing that impressed you . . . conducting yourself like some overgrown schoolboy who wants to be known as the wildest fellow in town! And you—a gifted young doctor—*Magna cum Laude!* (*She turns aside, touching her eyelids with a handkerchief.*) You know what I call it? I call it a *desecration*! (*She sobs uncontrollably. Then she springs up from the bench. John catches her hand.*)

JOHN: You're not going to run off, are you?

ALMA: Singing in public always—always upsets me!—Let go of my hand. (*He holds on to it, grinning up at her in the deepening dusk. The stars are coming out in the cyclorama with its leisurely floating cloud-forms. In the distance the band is playing "La Golondrina."*) Please let go of my hand.

JOHN: Don't run off mad.

ALMA: Let's not make a spectacle of ourselves.

JOHN: Then sit back down.

(*A skyrocket goes up. The crowd "Ahhh . . . s."*)

ALMA: You threw that firecracker and started a conversation just in order to tease me as you did as a child. You came to this bench in order to embarrass me and to hurt my feelings with the report of that vicious—imitation! No, let go of my hand so I can leave, now. You've succeeded in your purpose. I *was* hurt, I *did* make a fool of myself as you intended! So let me go now!

JOHN: You're attracting attention! Don't you know that I really *like* you, Miss Alma?

ALMA: No, you don't.

(*Another skyrocket.*)

JOHN: Sure I do. A lot. Sometimes when I come home late at night I look over at the Rectory. I see something white at the window. Could that be you, Miss Alma? Or, is it your *doppelganger*, looking out of the window that faces my way?

ALMA: Enough about *doppelganger*—whatever that is!

JOHN: There goes a nice one, Roman candle they call it!

(*This time the explosion is in back of them. A Roman candle shoots up puffs of rainbow-colored light in back of the stone angel of the fountain. They turn in profile to watch it.*)

JOHN (*counting the puffs of light*): Four—five—six—that's all? No—seven! (*There is a pause. Alma sits down slowly.*)
ALMA (*vaguely*): Dear me . . . (*She fans herself.*)
JOHN: How about going riding?
ALMA (*too eagerly*): When . . . now?

(*Rosa Gonzales has wandered up to the fountain again. John's attention drifts steadily toward her and away from Alma.*)

JOHN (*too carelessly*): Oh . . . some afternoon.
ALMA: Would you observe the speed limit?
ALMA: Strictly with you, Miss Alma.
ALMA: Why then, I'd be glad to—John.

(*John has risen from the bench and crosses to the fountain.*)

JOHN: And wear a hat with a plume!
ALMA: I don't have a hat with a plume!
JOHN: Get one!

(*Another skyrocket goes up, and there is another long "Ahhh . . ." from the crowd. John saunters up to the fountain. Rosa has lingered beside it. As he passes her he whispers something. She laughs and moves leisurely off. John takes a quick drink at the fountain, then follows Rosa, calling back "Good night" to Alma. There is a sound of laughter in the distance. Alma sits motionless for a moment, then touches a small white handkerchief to her lips and nostrils. Mr. Doremus comes in, carrying a French horn case. He is a small man, somewhat like a sparrow.*)

ROGER: *Whew!* Golly! Moses!—Well, how did it go, Miss Alma?
ALMA: How did—what—go?
ROGER (*annoyed*): My solo on the French horn.
ALMA (*slowly, without thinking*): I paid no attention to it. (*She rises slowly and takes his arm.*) I'll have to hang on your arm—I'm feeling so dizzy!

(*The scene dims out. There is a final skyrocket and a last "Ahhh . . ." from the crowd in the distance. Music is heard, and there is light on the angel.*)

SCENE TWO

Inside the Rectory, which is lighted. Mrs. Winemiller comes in and makes her way stealthily to the love seat, where she seats herself. Opening her parasol, she takes out a fancy white-plumed hat which she had concealed there. Rising, she turns to the mirror on the wall over the love seat and tries on the hat. She draws a long, ecstatic breath as she places it squarely on her head. At that moment the telephone rings. Startled, she snatches off the hat, hides it behind the center table and quickly resumes her seat. The telephone goes on ringing. Alma comes in to answer it.

ALMA: Hello. . . . Yes, Mr. Gillam. . . . She did? . . . Are you sure? . . . How shocking! . . . (*Mrs. Winemiller now retrieves the hat, seats herself in front of Alma and puts the hat on.*) Thank you, Mr. Gillam . . . the hat is here.

(*Mr. Winemiller comes in. He is distracted.*)

MR. WINEMILLER: Alma! Alma, your mother . . . !

ALMA (*coming in*): I know, Father, Mr. Gillam just phoned. He told me she picked up a white plumed hat and he pretended not to notice in order to save you the embarrassment, so I—I told him to just charge it to us.

MR. WINEMILLER: That hat looks much too expensive.

ALMA: It's fourteen dollars. You pay six of it, Father, and I'll pay eight. (*She gives him the parasol.*)

MR. WINEMILLER: What an insufferable cross we have to bear. (*He retires despairingly from the room.*)

(*Alma goes over to her mother and seats her in a chair at the table.*)

ALMA: I have a thousand and one things to do before my club meeting tonight, so you work quietly on your picture puzzle or I shall take the hat back, plume and all.

MRS. WINEMILLER (*throwing a piece of the puzzle on the floor*): The pieces don't fit! (*Alma picks up the piece and puts it on the table.*) The pieces don't fit!

(*Alma stands for a moment in indecision. She reaches for the phone, then puts it down. Then she takes it up again, and gives a number. The telephone across the way in the doctor's office rings and that part of the scene lights up. John comes in.*)

JOHN (*answering the phone*): Hello?

ALMA: John! (*She fans herself rapidly with a palm leaf clutched in her free hand and puts on a brilliant, strained smile as if she were actually in his presence.*)

JOHN: Miss Alma?

ALMA: You recognized my voice?

JOHN: I recognized your laugh.

ALMA: Ha-ha! How are you, you stranger you?

JOHN: I'm pretty well, Miss Alma. How're you doing?

ALMA: Surviving, just surviving! Isn't it fearful?

JOHN: Uh-huh.

ALMA: You seem unusually laconic. Or perhaps I should say more than usually laconic.

JOHN: I had a big night and I'm just recovering from it.

ALMA: Well, sir, I have a bone to pick with you!

JOHN: What's that, Miss Alma? (*He drains a glass of bromo.*)

ALMA: The time of our last conversation on the Fourth of July, you said you were going to take me riding in your automobile.

JOHN: Aw. Did I say that?

ALMA: Yes indeed you did, sir! And all these hot afternoons I've been breathlessly waiting and hoping that you would remember that promise. But now I know how insincere you are. Ha-ha! Time and again the four-wheeled phenomenon flashes by the Rectory and I have yet to put my—my quaking foot in it!

(*Mrs. Winemiller begins to mock Alma's speech and laughter.*)

JOHN: What was that, Miss Alma? I didn't understand you.

ALMA: I was just reprimanding you, sir! Castigating you verbally! Ha-ha!

MRS. WINEMILLER (*grimacing*): Ha-ha.

JOHN: What about, Miss Alma? (*He leans back and puts his feet on table.*)

ALMA: Never mind. I know how busy you are! (*She whispers.*) Mother, *hush!*

JOHN: I'm afraid we have a bad connection.

ALMA: I hate telephones. I don't know why but they always make me laugh as if someone were poking me in the ribs! I swear to goodness they do!

JOHN: Why don't you just go to your window and I'll go to mine and we can holler across?

ALMA: The yard's so wide I'm afraid it would crack my voice! And I've got to sing at somebody's wedding tomorrow.

JOHN: You're going to sing at a wedding?

ALMA: Yes. "The Voice That Breathed O'er Eden!" And I'm as hoarse as a frog! (*Another gale of laughter almost shakes her off her feet.*)

JOHN: Better come over and let me give you a gargle.

ALMA: Nasty gargles—I hate them!

MRS. WINEMILLER (*mockingly*): Nasty gargles—I hate them!

ALMA: Mother, shhh!—please! As you no doubt have gathered, there is some interference at this end of the line! What I wanted to say is—you remember my mentioning that little club I belong to?

JOHN: Aw! Aw, yes! Those intellectual meetings!

ALMA: Oh, now, don't call it that. It's just a little informal gathering every Wednesday and we talk about the new books and read things out loud to each other!

JOHN: Serve any refreshments?

ALMA: Yes, we serve refreshments!

JOHN: Any liquid refreshments?

ALMA: Both liquid and solid refreshments.

JOHN: Is this an invitation?

ALMA: Didn't I promise I'd ask you? It's going to be tonight! —at eight at my house, at the Rectory, so all you'll have to do is cross the yard!

JOHN: I'll try to make it, Miss Alma.

ALMA: Don't say try as if it required some Herculean effort! All you have to do is . . .

JOHN: Cross the yard! Uh-huh—reserve me a seat by the punch bowl.

ALMA: That gives me an idea! We *will* have punch, fruit punch, with claret in it. Do you like claret?

JOHN: I just dote on claret.

ALMA: Now you're being sarcastic! Ha-ha-ha!

JOHN: Excuse me, Miss Alma, but Dad's got to use this phone.

ALMA: I won't hang up till you've said you'll come without fail!

JOHN: I'll be there, Miss Alma. You can count on it.

ALMA: Au revoir, then! Until eight.

JOHN: G'bye, Miss Alma.

(*John hangs up with an incredulous grin. Alma remains holding the phone with a dazed smile until the office interior has dimmed slowly out.*)

MRS. WINEMILLER: Alma's in love—in love. (*She waltzes mockingly.*)

ALMA (*sharply*): Mother, you are wearing out my patience! Now I am expecting another music pupil and I have to make preparations for the club meeting so I suggest that you . . . (*Nellie rings the bell.*) Will you go up to your room? (*Then she calls sweetly.*) Yes, Nellie, coming, Nellie. All right, stay down here then. But keep your attention on your picture puzzle or there will be no ice cream for you after supper!

(*She admits Nellie, who is wildly excited over something. This scene should be played lightly and quickly.*)

NELLIE: Oh, Miss Alma! (*She rushes past Alma in a distracted manner, throws herself on the sofa and hugs herself with excited glee.*)

ALMA: What is it, Nellie? Has something happened at home? (*Nellie continues her exhilaration.*) Oh, now, Nellie, stop that! Whatever it is, it can't be *that* important!

NELLIE (*blurting out suddenly*): Miss Alma, haven't you ever had—*crushes*?

ALMA: What?

NELLIE: Crushes?

ALMA: Yes—I suppose I have. (*She sits down.*)

NELLIE: Did you know that I used to have a crush on *you*, Miss Alma?

ALMA: No, Nellie.

NELLIE: Why do you think that I took singing lessons?

ALMA: I supposed it was because you wished to develop your voice.

NELLIE (*cutting in*): Oh, you know, and I know, I never had any voice. I had a crush on you though. Those were the days when I had crushes on girls. Those days are all over, and now I have crushes on boys. Oh, Miss Alma, you know about Mother, how I was brought up so nobody nice except you would have anything to do with us—Mother meeting the trains to pick up the traveling salesmen and bringing them home to drink and play poker—all of them acting like pigs, pigs, pigs!

MRS. WINEMILLER (*mimicking*): Pigs, pigs, pigs!

NELLIE: Well, I thought I'd always hate men. Loathe and despise them. But last night— Oh!

ALMA: Hadn't we better run over some scales until you are feeling calmer?

NELLIE (*cutting in*): I'd heard them downstairs for hours but didn't know who it was—I'd fallen asleep—when all of a sudden my door banged open. He'd thought it was the bathroom!

ALMA (*nervously*): Nellie, I'm not sure I want to hear any more of this story.

NELLIE (*interrupting*): Guess who it was?

ALMA: I couldn't possibly guess.

NELLIE: Someone you know. Someone I've seen you with.

ALMA: Who?

NELLIE: The wonderfullest person in all the big wide world! When he saw it was me he came and sat down on the bed and held my hand and we talked and talked until Mother came up to see what had happened to him. You should have heard him bawl her out. Oh, he laid the law down! He said she ought to send me off to a girl's school because she wasn't fit to bring up a daughter! Then she started to bawl him out. You're a fine one to talk, she said, you're not fit to call yourself a doctor. (*Alma rises abruptly.*)

ALMA: John Buchanan?

NELLIE: Yes, of course, Dr. Johnny.

ALMA: Was—with—your—mother?

NELLIE: Oh, he wasn't her beau! He had a girl with him, and Mother had somebody else!

ALMA: Who—did—he—have?

NELLIE: Oh, some loud tacky thing with a Z in her name!

ALMA: Gonzales? Rosa Gonzales?

NELLIE: Yes, that was it! (*Alma sits slowly back down.*) But him! Oh, Miss Alma! He's the *wonderfullest* person that I . . .

ALMA (*interrupting*): Your mother was right! He isn't fit to call himself a doctor! I hate to disillusion you, but this wonderfullest person is pitiably weak.

(*Someone calls "Johnny" outside.*)

NELLIE (*in hushed excitement*): Someone is calling him now!

ALMA: Yes, these people who shout his name in front of his house are of such a character that the old doctor cannot permit them to come inside the door. And when they have brought him home at night, left him sprawling on the front steps, sometimes at daybreak—it takes two people, his father and the old cook, one pushing and one pulling, to get him upstairs. (*She sits down.*) All the gifts of the gods were showered on him. . . . (*The call of "Johnny" is repeated.*) But all he cares about is indulging his senses! (*Another call of "Johnny."*)

NELLIE: Here he comes down the steps! (*Alma crosses toward the window.*) Look at him jump!

ALMA: Oh.

NELLIE: Over the banisters. Ha-ha!

ALMA: Nellie, don't lean out the window and have us caught spying.

MRS. WINEMILLER (*suddenly*): Show Nellie how *you* spy on him! Oh, she's a good one at spying. She stands behind the curtain and *peeks* around it, and . . .

ALMA (*frantically*): *Mother!*

MRS. WINEMILLER: She spies on him. Whenever he comes in at night she rushes downstairs to watch him out of this window!

ALMA (*interrupting her*): Be still!

MRS. WINEMILLER (*going right on*): She called him just now and had a fit on the telephone! (*The old lady cackles derisively.*

Alma snatches her cigarette from her and crushes it under her foot.) Alma's in love! Alma's in love!

ALMA (*interrupting*): Nellie, Nellie, please go.

NELLIE (*with a startled giggle*): All right, Miss Alma, I'm going. (*She crosses quickly to the door, looking back once with a grin.*) Good night, Mrs. Winemiller!

(*Nellie goes out gaily, leaving the door slightly open. Alma rushes to it and slams it shut. She returns swiftly to Mrs. Winemiller, her hands clenched with anger.*)

ALMA: If ever I hear you say such a thing again, if ever you dare to repeat such a thing in my presence or anybody else's—then it will be the last straw! You understand me? Yes, you understand me! You act like a child, but you have the devil in you. And God will punish you—yes! I'll punish you too. I'll take your cigarettes from you and give you no more. I'll give you no ice cream either. Because I'm tired of your malice. Yes, I'm tired of your malice and your self-indulgence. People wonder why I'm tied down here! They pity me—think of me as an old maid already! In spite of I'm young. Still young! It's you—it's you, you've taken my youth away from me! I wouldn't say that—I'd try not even to think it—if you were just kind, just simple! But I could spread my life out like a rug for you to step on and you'd step on it, and not even say "Thank you, Alma!" Which is what you've done always—and now you dare to tell a disgusting lie about me—in front of that girl!

MRS. WINEMILLER: Don't you think I hear you go to the window at night to watch him come in and . . .

ALMA: Give me that plumed hat, Mother! It goes back now, it goes back!

MRS. WINEMILLER: *Fight! Fight!*

(*Alma snatches at the plumed hat. Mrs. Winemiller snatches too. The hat is torn between them. Mrs. Winemiller retains the hat. The plume comes loose in Alma's hand. She stares at it a moment with a shocked expression.*)

ALMA (*sincerely*): Heaven have mercy upon us!

SCENE THREE

Inside the Rectory.

The meeting is in progress, having just opened with the reading of the minutes by Alma. She stands before the green plush sofa and the others. This group includes Mr. Doremus, Vernon, a willowy younger man with an open collar and Byronic locks, the widow Bassett, and a wistful older girl with a long neck and thick-lensed glasses.

ALMA (*reading*): Our last meeting which fell on July fourteenth . . .

MRS. BASSETT: Bastille Day!

ALMA: Pardon me?

MRS. BASSETT: It fell on Bastille Day! But, honey, that was the meeting before last.

ALMA: You're perfectly right. I seem to be on the wrong page. . . . (*She drops the papers.*)

MRS. BASSETT: Butterfingers!

ALMA: Here we are! July twenty-fifth! Correct?

MRS. BASSETT: Correct! (*A little ripple of laughter goes about the circle.*)

ALMA (*continuing*): It was debated whether or not we ought to suspend operations for the remainder of the summer as the departure of several members engaged in the teaching profession for their summer vacations . . .

MRS. BASSETT: Lucky people!

ALMA: . . . had substantially contracted our little circle.

MRS. BASSETT: Decimated our ranks! (*There is another ripple of laughter.*)

(*John appears outside the door-frame and rings the bell.*)

ALMA (*with agitation*): Is that—is that—the doorbell?

MRS. BASSETT: It sure did sound like it to me.

ALMA: Excuse me a moment. I think it may be . . .

(*She crosses to the door-frame and makes the gesture of opening the door. John steps in, immaculately groomed and shining, his white linen coat over his arm and a white Panama hat in his hand. He is a startling contrast to the other male *company, who seem to be outcasts of a state in which he is a prominent citizen.*)

ALMA (*shrilly*): Yes, it is—our guest of honor! Everybody, this is Dr. John Buchanan, Jr.

JOHN (*easily glancing about the assemblage*): Hello, everybody.

MRS. BASSETT: I never thought he'd show up. Congratulations, Miss Alma.

JOHN: Did I miss much?

ALMA: Not a thing! Just the minutes—I'll put you on the sofa. Next to me. (*She laughs breathlessly and makes an uncertain gesture. He settles gingerly on the sofa. They all stare at him with a curious sort of greediness.*) Well, now! we are completely assembled!

MRS. BASSETT (*eagerly*): Vernon has his verse play with him tonight!

ALMA (*uneasily*): Is that right, Vernon? (*Obviously, it is. Vernon has a pile of papers eight inches thick on his knees. He raises them timidly with downcast eyes.*)

ROGER (*quickly*): We decided to put that off till cooler weather. Miss Rosemary is supposed to read us a paper tonight on William Blake.

MRS. BASSETT: Those dead poets can keep!

(*John laughs.*)

ALMA (*excitedly jumping up*): Mrs. Bassett, everybody! This is the way I feel about the verse play. It's too important a thing to read under any but ideal circumstances. Not only atmospheric—on some cool evening with music planned to go with it!—but everyone present so that nobody will miss it! Why don't we . . .

ROGER: Why don't we take a standing vote on the matter?

ALMA: Good, good, perfect!

ROGER: All in favor of putting the verse play off till cooler weather, stand up!

(*Everybody rises but Rosemary and Mrs. Bassett. Rosemary starts vaguely to rise, but Mrs. Bassett jerks her arm.*)

ROSEMARY: Was this a vote?

ROGER: Now, Mrs. Bassett, no rough tactics, please!

ALMA: Has everybody got fans? John, you haven't got one!

(*She looks about for a fan for him. Not seeing one, she takes Roger's out of his hand and gives it to John. Roger is nonplussed. Rosemary gets up with her paper.*)

ROSEMARY: The poet—William Blake.

MRS. BASSETT: Insane, insane, that man was a mad fanatic! (*She squints her eyes tight shut and thrusts her thumbs into her ears. The reactions range from indignant to conciliatory.*)

ROGER: Now, Mrs. Bassett!

MRS. BASSETT: This is a free country. I can speak my opinion. And I have *read up* on him. Go on, Rosemary. I wasn't criticizing your paper. (*But Rosemary sits down, hurt.*)

ALMA: Mrs. Bassett is only joking, Rosemary.

ROSEMARY: No, I don't want to read it if she feels that strongly about it.

MRS. BASSETT: Not a bit, don't be silly! I just don't see why we should encourage the writings of people like that who have already gone into a drunkard's grave!

VARIOUS VOICES (*exclaiming*): Did he? I never heard that about him. Is that true?

ALMA: Mrs. Bassett is mistaken about that. Mrs. Bassett, you have confused Blake with someone else.

MRS. BASSETT (*positively*): Oh, no, don't tell me. I've read up on him and know what I'm talking about. He traveled around with that Frenchman who took a shot at him and landed them both in jail! Brussels, Brussels!

ROGER (*gaily*): Brussels sprouts!

MRS. BASSETT: That's where it happened, fired a gun at him in a drunken stupor, and later one of them died of T.B. in the gutter! All right. I'm finished. I won't say anything more. Go on with your paper, Rosemary. There's nothing like contact with culture!

(*Alma gets up.*)

ALMA: Before Rosemary reads her paper on Blake, I think it would be a good idea, since some of us aren't acquainted with his work, to preface the critical and biographical comments with a reading of one of his loveliest lyric poems.

ROSEMARY: I'm not going to read anything at all! Not I!

ALMA: Then let me read it then. (*She takes a paper from Rosemary.*) . . . This is called "Love's Secret."

(*She clears her throat and waits for a hush to settle. Rosemary looks stonily at the carpet. Mrs. Bassett looks at the ceiling. John coughs.*)

Never seek to tell thy love,
Love that never told can be,
For the gentle wind doth move
Silently, invisibly.
I told my love, I told my love,
I told him all my heart.
Trembling, cold in ghastly fear
Did my love depart.

No sooner had he gone from me
Than a stranger passing by,
Silently, invisibly,
Took him with a sigh!

(*There are various effusions and enthusiastic applause.*)

MRS. BASSETT: Honey, you're right. That isn't the man I meant. I was thinking about the one who wrote about "the bought red lips." Who was it that wrote about the "bought red lips"?

(*John has risen abruptly. He signals to Alma and points to his watch. He starts to leave.*)

ALMA (*springing up*): *John!*

JOHN (*calling back*): I have to call on a patient!

ALMA: Oh, John!

(*She calls after him so sharply that the group is startled into silence.*)

ROSEMARY (*interpreting this as a cue to read her paper*): "The poet, William Blake, was born in 1757 . . ."

(*Alma suddenly rushes to the door and goes out after John.*)

ROGER: Of poor but honest parents.

MRS. BASSETT: No supercilious comments out of you, sir. Go on Rosemary. (*She speaks loudly.*) She has such a beautiful *voice*!

(*Alma returns inside, looking stunned.*)

ALMA: Please excuse the interruption, Rosemary. Dr. Buchanan had to call on a patient.

MRS. BASSETT (*archly*): I bet I know who the patient was. Ha-ha! That Gonzales girl whose father owns Moon Lake Casino and goes everywhere with two pistols strapped on his belt. Johnny Buchanan will get himself shot in that crowd!

ALMA: Why, Mrs. Bassett, what gave you such an idea? I don't think that John even knows that Gonzales girl!

MRS. BASSETT: He knows her, all right. In the Biblical sense of the word, if you'll excuse me!

ALMA: No, I will not excuse you! A thing like that is inexcusable!

MRS. BASSETT: Have you fallen for him, Miss Alma? Miss Alma has fallen for the young doctor! They tell me he has lots of new lady patients!

ALMA: Stop it! (*She stamps her foot furiously and crushes the palm leaf fan between her clenched hands.*) I won't have malicious talk here! You drove him away from the meeting after I'd bragged so much about how bright and interesting you all were! You put your worst foot forward and simpered and chattered and carried on like idiots, idiots! What am I saying? I—I—please excuse me!

(*She rushes out the inner door.*)

ROGER: I move that the meeting adjourn.

MRS. BASSETT: I second the motion.

ROSEMARY: I don't understand. What happened?

MRS. BASSETT: Poor Miss Alma!

ROGER: She hasn't been herself lately. . . .

(*They all go out. After a moment Alma reenters with a tray of refreshments, looks about the deserted interior and bursts into hysterical laughter. The light dims out.*)

SCENE FOUR

In the doctor's office.

John has a wound on his arm which he is bandaging with Rosa's assistance.

JOHN: Hold that end. Wrap it around. Pull it tight.

(*There is a knock at the door. They look up silently. The knock is repeated.*)

I better answer before they wake up the old man.

(*He goes out. A few moments later he returns followed by Alma. He is rolling down his sleeve to conceal the bandage. Alma stops short at the sight of Rosa.*)

Wait outside, Rosa. In the hall. But be quiet!

(*Rosa gives Alma a challenging look as she withdraws from the lighted area. John explains about Rosa.*)

A little emergency case.

ALMA: The patient you had to call on. (*John grins.*) I want to see your father.

JOHN: He's asleep. Anything I can do?

ALMA: No, I think not. I have to see your father.

JOHN: It's 2 A.M., Miss Alma.

ALMA: I know, I'm afraid I'll have to see him.

JOHN: What's the trouble?

(*The voice of John's father is heard, calling from above.*)

DR. BUCHANAN: John! What's going on down there?

JOHN (*at the door*): Nothing much, Dad. Somebody got cut in a fight.

DR. BUCHANAN: I'm coming down.

JOHN: No. Don't! Stay in bed! (*He rolls up his sleeve to show Alma the bandaged wound. She gasps and touches her lips.*) I've patched him up, Dad. You sleep!

(*John executes the gesture of closing a door quietly on the hall.*)

ALMA: You've been in a brawl with that—woman! (*John nods and rolls the sleeve back down. Alma sinks faintly into a chair.*)

JOHN: Is your *doppelganger* cutting up again?

ALMA: It's your father I want to talk to.

JOHN: Be reasonable, Miss Alma. You're not that sick.

ALMA: Do you suppose I would come here at two o'clock in the morning if I were not seriously ill?

JOHN: It's no telling what you would do in a state of hysteria. (*He puts some powders in a glass of water.*) Toss that down, Miss Alma.

ALMA: What is it?

JOHN: A couple of little white tablets dissolved in water.

ALMA: What kind of tablets?

JOHN: You don't trust me?

ALMA: You are not in any condition to inspire much confidence. (*John laughs softly. She looks at him helplessly for a moment, then bursts into tears. He draws up a chair beside hers and puts his arm gently about her shoulders.*) I seem to be all to pieces.

JOHN: The intellectual meeting wore you out.

ALMA: You made a quick escape from it.

JOHN: I don't like meetings. The only meetings I like are between two people.

ALMA: Such as between yourself and the lady outside?

JOHN: Or between you and me.

ALMA (*nervously*): Where is the . . . ?

JOHN: Oh. You've decided to take it?

ALMA: Yes, if you . . .

(*She sips and chokes. He gives her his handkerchief. She touches her lips with it.*)

JOHN: Bitter?

ALMA: Awfully bitter.

JOHN: It'll make you sleepy.

ALMA: I do hope so. I wasn't able to sleep.

JOHN: And you felt panicky?

ALMA: Yes. I felt walled in.

JOHN: You started hearing your heart?

ALMA: Yes, like a drum!

JOHN: It scared you?

ALMA: It always does.

JOHN: Sure. I know.

ALMA: I don't think I will be able to get through the summer.

JOHN: You'll get through it, Miss Alma.

ALMA: How?

JOHN: One day will come after another and one night will come after another till sooner or later the summer will be all through with and then it will be fall, and you will be saying, I don't see how I'm going to get through the fall.

ALMA: Oh . . .

JOHN: That's right. Draw a deep breath!

ALMA: Ah . . .

JOHN: Good. Now draw another!

ALMA: Ah . . .

JOHN: Better? Better?

ALMA: A little.

JOHN: Soon you'll be much better. (*He takes out a big silver watch and holds her wrist.*) Did y' know that time is one side of the four-dimensional continuum we're caught in?

ALMA: What?

JOHN: Did you know space is curved, that it turns back onto itself like a soap-bubble, adrift in something that's even less than space. (*He laughs a little as he replaces the watch.*)

ROSA (*faintly from outside*): Johnny!

JOHN (*looking up as if the cry came from there*): Did you know that the Magellanic clouds are a hundred thousand light years away from the earth? No? (*Alma shakes her head slightly.*) That's something to think about when you worry over your heart, that little red fist that's got to keep knocking, knocking against the big black door.

ROSA (*more distinctly*): Johnny!

(*She opens the door a crack.*)

JOHN: Calla de la boca! (*The door closes and he speaks to Alma.*) There's nothing wrong with your heart but a little functional disturbance, like I told you before. You want me to check it? (*Alma nods mutely. John picks up his stethoscope.*)

ALMA: The lady outside, I hate to keep her waiting.

JOHN: Rosa doesn't mind waiting. Unbutton your blouse.

ALMA: Unbutton . . . ?

JOHN: The blouse.

ALMA: Hadn't I better—better come back in the morning, when your father will be able to . . . ?

JOHN: Just as you please, Miss Alma. (*She hesitates. Then begins to unbutton her blouse. Her fingers fumble.*) Fingers won't work?

ALMA (*breathlessly*): They are just as if frozen!

JOHN (*smiling*): Let me. (*He leans over her.*) Little pearl buttons . . .

ALMA: If your father discovered that woman in the house . . .

JOHN: He won't discover it.

ALMA: It would distress him terribly.

JOHN: Are you going to tell him?

ALMA: Certainly not! (*He laughs and applies the stethoscope to her chest.*)

JOHN: Breathe! . . . Out! . . . Breathe! . . . Out!

ALMA: Ah . . .

JOHN: Um-hmmm . . .

ALMA: What do you hear?

JOHN: Just a little voice saying—"Miss Alma is lonesome!" (*She rises and turns her back to him.*)

ALMA: If your idea of helping a patient is to ridicule and insult . . .

JOHN: My idea of helping you is to tell you the truth. (*Alma looks up at him. He lifts her hand from the chair arm.*) What is this stone?

ALMA: A topaz.

JOHN: Beautiful stone. . . . Fingers still frozen?

ALMA: A little. (*He lifts her hand to his mouth and blows his breath on her fingers.*)

JOHN: I'm a poor excuse for a doctor, I'm much too selfish. But let's try to think about you.

ALMA: Why should you bother about me? (*She sits down.*)

JOHN: You know I like you and I think you're worth a lot of consideration.

ALMA: Why?

JOHN: Because you have a lot of feeling in your heart, and that's a rare thing. It makes you too easily hurt. Did I hurt you tonight?

ALMA: You hurt me when you sprang up from the sofa and rushed from the Rectory in such—in such mad haste that you left your coat behind you!

JOHN: I'll pick up the coat sometime.

ALMA: The time of our last conversation you said you would take me riding in your automobile sometime, but you forgot to.

JOHN: I didn't forget. Many's the time I've looked across at the Rectory and wondered if it would be worth trying, you and me. . . .

ALMA: You decided it wasn't?

JOHN: I went there tonight, but it wasn't you and me. . . . Fingers warm now?

ALMA: Those tablets work quickly. I'm already feeling drowsy. (*She leans back with her eyes nearly shut.*) I'm beginning to feel almost like a water lily. A water lily on a Chinese lagoon.

(*A heavy iron bell strikes three.*)

ROSA: *Johnny?*

(*Alma starts to rise.*)

ALMA: I *must* go.

JOHN: I will call for you Saturday night at eight o'clock.

ALMA: What?

JOHN: I'll give you this box of tablets but watch how you take them. Never more than one or two at a time.

ALMA: Didn't you say something else a moment ago?

JOHN: I said I would call for you at the Rectory Saturday night.

ALMA: Oh . . .

JOHN: Is that all right? (*Alma nods speechlessly. She remains with the box resting in the palm of her hand as if not knowing it was there. John gently closes her fingers on the box.*)

ALMA: Oh! (*She laughs faintly.*)

ROSA (*outside*): *Johnny!*

JOHN: Do you think you can find your way home, Miss Alma?

(*Rosa steps back into the office with a challenging look. Alma catches her breath sharply and goes out the side door.*

(John reaches above him and turns out the light. He crosses to Rosa by the anatomy chart and takes her roughly in his arms. The light lingers on the chart as the interior dims out.)

SCENE FIVE

In the Rectory.

Before the light comes up a soprano voice is heard singing "From the Land of the Sky Blue Waters."

As the curtain rises, Alma gets up from the piano. Mr. and Mrs. Winemiller, also, are in the lighted room.

ALMA: What time is it, Father? (*He goes on writing. She raises her voice.*) What time is it, Father?

MR. WINEMILLER: Five of eight. I'm working on my sermon.

ALMA: Why don't you work in the study?

MR. WINEMILLER: The study is suffocating. So don't disturb me.

ALMA: Would there be any chance of getting Mother upstairs if someone should call?

MR. WINEMILLER: Are you expecting a caller?

ALMA: Not expecting. There is just a chance of it.

MR. WINEMILLER: Whom are you expecting?

ALMA: I said I wasn't expecting anyone, that there was just a possibility . . .

MR. WINEMILLER: Mr. Doremus? I thought that this was his evening with his mother?

ALMA: Yes, it is his evening with his mother.

MR. WINEMILLER: Then who is coming here, Alma?

ALMA: Probably no one. Probably no one at all.

MR. WINEMILLER: This is all very mysterious.

MRS. WINEMILLER: That tall boy next door is coming to see her, that's who's coming to see her.

ALMA: If you will go upstairs, Mother, I'll call the drug store and ask them to deliver a pint of fresh peach ice cream.

MRS. WINEMILLER: I'll go upstairs when I'm ready—good and ready, and you can put that in your pipe and smoke it, Miss Winemiller!

(*She lights a cigarette. Mr. Winemiller turns slowly away with a profound sigh.*)

ALMA: I may as well tell you who might call, so that if he calls there will not be any unpleasantness about it. Young Dr. John Buchanan said he might call.

MRS. WINEMILLER: See!

MR. WINEMILLER: You can't be serious.

MRS. WINEMILLER: Didn't I tell you?

ALMA: Well, I am.

MR. WINEMILLER: That young man might come here?

ALMA: He asked me if he might and I said, yes, if he wished to. But it is now after eight so it doesn't look like he's coming.

MR. WINEMILLER: If he does come you will go upstairs to your room and I will receive him.

ALMA: If he does come I'll do no such thing, Father.

MR. WINEMILLER: You must be out of your mind.

ALMA: I'll receive him myself. You may retire to your study and Mother upstairs. But if he comes I'll receive him. I don't judge people by the tongues of gossips. I happen to know that he has been grossly misjudged and misrepresented by old busybodies who're envious of his youth and brilliance and charm!

MR. WINEMILLER: If you're not out of your senses, then I'm out of mine.

ALMA: I daresay we're all a bit peculiar, Father. . . .

MR. WINEMILLER: Well, I have had one almost insufferable cross to bear and perhaps I can bear another. But if you think I'm retiring into my study when this young man comes, probably with a whiskey bottle in one hand and a pair of dice in the other, you have another think coming. I'll sit right here and look at him until he leaves. (*He turns back to his sermon.*)

(*A whistle is heard outside the open door.*)

ALMA (*speaking quickly*): As a matter of fact I think I'll walk down to the drug store and call for the ice cream myself. (*She crosses to the door, snatching up her hat, gloves and veil.*)

MRS. WINEMILLER: There she goes to him! Ha-ha! (*Alma rushes out.*)

MR. WINEMILLER (*looking up*): Alma! Alma!

MRS. WINEMILLER: Ha-ha-haaaaa!

MR. WINEMILLER: Where is Alma?—Alma! (*He rushes through the door.*) Alma!

MRS. WINEMILLER: Ha-ha! Who got fooled? Who got fooled! Ha-haaaa! Insufferable cross yourself, you old—windbag. . . .

(*The curtain comes down.*)

SCENE SIX

A delicately suggested arbor, enclosing a table and two chairs. Over the table is suspended a torn paper lantern. This tiny set may be placed way downstage in front of the two interiors, which should be darkened out, as in the fountain scenes. In the background, as it is throughout the play, the angel of the fountain is dimly visible.

Music from the nearby pavilion of the Casino can be used when suitable for background.

John's voice is audible before he and Alma enter.

JOHN (*from the darkness*): I don't understand why we can't go in the casino.

ALMA: You do understand. You're just pretending not to.

JOHN: Give me one reason.

ALMA (*coming into the arbor*): I am a minister's daughter.

JOHN: That's no reason. (*He follows her in. He wears a white linen suit, carrying the coat over his arm.*)

ALMA: You're a doctor. That's a better reason. You can't any more afford to be seen in such places than I can—less!

JOHN (*bellowing*): Dusty!

DUSTY (*from the darkness*): Coming!

JOHN: What are you fishing in that pocketbook for?

ALMA: Nothing.

JOHN: What have you got there?

ALMA: Let go!

JOHN: Those sleeping tablets I gave you?

ALMA: Yes.

JOHN: What for?

ALMA: I need one.

JOHN: *Now?*

ALMA: Yes.

JOHN: Why?

ALMA: Why? Because I nearly died of heart failure in your automobile. What possessed you to drive like that? A demon?

(*Dusty enters.*)

JOHN: A bottle of vino rosso.

DUSTY: Sure. (*He withdraws.*)

JOHN: Hey! Tell Shorty I want to hear the "Yellow Dog Blues."

ALMA: Please give me back my tablets.

JOHN: You want to turn into a dope-fiend taking this stuff? I said take one when you need one.

ALMA: I need one now.

JOHN: Sit down and stop swallowing air. (*Dusty returns with a tall wine bottle and two thin-stemmed glasses.*) When does the cock-fight start?

DUSTY: 'Bout ten o'clock, Dr. Johnny.

ALMA: When does *what start*?

JOHN: They have a cock-fight here every Saturday night. Ever seen one?

ALMA: Perhaps in some earlier incarnation of mine.

JOHN: When you wore a brass ring in your nose?

ALMA: Then maybe I went to exhibitions like that.

JOHN: You're going to see one tonight.

ALMA: Oh, no, I'm not.

JOHN: That's what we came here for.

ALMA: I didn't think such exhibitions were legal.

JOHN: This is Moon Lake Casino where anything goes.

ALMA: And you're a frequent patron?

JOHN: I'd say constant.

ALMA: Then I'm afraid you must be serious about giving up your medical career.

JOHN: You bet I am! A doctor's life is walled in by sickness and misery and death.

ALMA: May I be so presumptuous as to inquire what you'll do when you quit?

JOHN: You may be so presumptuous as to inquire.

ALMA: But you won't tell me?

JOHN: I haven't made up my mind, but I've been thinking of South America lately.

ALMA (*sadly*): Oh . . .

JOHN: I've heard that cantinas are lots more fun than saloons, and senoritas are caviar among females.

ALMA: Dorothy Sykes' brother went to South America and was never heard of again. It takes a strong character to survive in the tropics. Otherwise it's a quagmire.

JOHN: You think my character's weak?

ALMA: I think you're confused, just awfully, awfully confused, as confused as I am—but in a different way. . . .

JOHN (*stretching out his legs*): Hee-haw, ho-hum.

ALMA: You used to say that as a child—to signify your disgust!

JOHN (*grinning*): Did I?

ALMA (*sharply*): Don't sit like that!

JOHN: Why not?

ALMA: You look so indolent and worthless.

JOHN: Maybe I am.

ALMA: If you must go somewhere, why don't you choose a place with a bracing climate?

JOHN: Parts of South America are as cool as a cucumber.

ALMA: I never knew that.

JOHN: Well, now you do.

ALMA: Those Latins all dream in the sun—and indulge their senses.

JOHN: Well, it's yet to be proven that anyone on this earth is crowned with so much glory as the one that uses his senses to get all he can in the way of—satisfaction.

ALMA: Self-satisfaction?

JOHN: What other kind is there?

ALMA: I will answer that question by asking you one. Have you ever seen, or looked at a picture, of a Gothic cathedral?

JOHN: Gothic cathedrals? What about them?

ALMA: How everything reaches up, how everything seems to be straining for something out of the reach of stone—or human—fingers? . . . The immense stained windows, the great arched doors that are five or six times the height of the tallest man—the vaulted ceiling and all the delicate spires—all reaching up to something beyond attainment! To me—well, that is the secret, the principle back of existence—the everlasting struggle and aspiration for more than our human limits have placed in our reach. . . . Who was that said that—oh, so beautiful thing!—"All of us are in the gutter, but some of us are looking at the stars!"

JOHN: Mr. Oscar Wilde.

ALMA (*somewhat taken aback*): Well, regardless of who said it, it's still true. Some of us are looking at the stars! (*She looks up raptly and places her hand over his.*)

JOHN: It's no fun holding hands with gloves on, Miss Alma.

ALMA: That's easily remedied. I'll just take the gloves off. (*Music is heard.*)

JOHN: Christ! (*He rises abruptly and lights a cigarette.*) Rosa Gonzales is dancing in the Casino.

ALMA: You *are* unhappy. You hate me for depriving you of the company inside. Well, you'll escape by and by. You'll drive me home and come back out by yourself. . . . I've only gone out with three young men at all seriously, and with each one there was a desert between us.

JOHN: What do you mean by a desert?

ALMA: Oh—wide, wide stretches of uninhabitable ground.

JOHN: Maybe you made it that way by being stand-offish.

ALMA: I made quite an effort with one or two of them.

JOHN: What kind of an effort?

ALMA: Oh, I—tried to entertain them the first few times. I would play and sing for them in the Rectory parlor.

JOHN: With your father in the next room and the door half open?

ALMA: I don't think that was the trouble.

JOHN: What was the trouble?

ALMA: I—I didn't have my heart in it. (*She laughs uncertainly.*) A silence would fall between us. You know, a silence?

JOHN: Yes, I know a silence.

ALMA: I'd try to talk and he'd try to talk and neither would make a go of it.

JOHN: The silence would fall?

ALMA: Yes, the enormous silence.

JOHN: Then you'd go back to the piano?

ALMA: I'd twist my ring. Sometimes I twisted it so hard that the band cut my finger! He'd glance at his watch and we'd both know that the useless undertaking had come to a close. . . .

JOHN: You'd call it quits?

ALMA: Quits is—what we'd call it. . . . One or two times I was rather sorry about it.

JOHN: But you didn't have your heart in it?

ALMA: None of them really engaged my serious feelings.

JOHN: You do have serious feelings—of that kind?

ALMA: Doesn't everyone—sometimes?

JOHN: Some women are cold. Some women are what is called frigid.

ALMA: Do I give that impression?

JOHN: Under the surface you have a lot of excitement, a great deal more than any other woman I have met. So much that you have to carry these sleeping pills with you. The question is why? (*He leans over and lifts her veil.*)

ALMA: What are you doing that for?

JOHN: So that I won't get your veil in my mouth when I kiss you.

ALMA (*faintly*): Do you want to do that?

JOHN (*gently*): Miss Alma. (*He takes her arms and draws her to her feet.*) Oh, Miss Alma, Miss Alma! (*He kisses her.*)

ALMA (*in a low, shaken voice*): Not "Miss" any more. Just Alma.

JOHN (*grinning gently*): "Miss" suits you better, Miss Alma. (*He kisses her again. She hesitantly touches his shoulders, but not quite to push him away. John speaks softly to her.*) Is it so hard to forget you're a preacher's daughter?

ALMA: There is no reason for me to forget that I am a minister's daughter. A minister's daughter's no different from any other young lady who tries to remember that she *is* a lady.

JOHN: This lady stuff, is that so important?

ALMA: Not to the sort of girls that you may be used to bringing to Moon Lake Casino. But suppose that some day . . . (*She crosses out of the arbor and faces away from him.*) suppose that some day you—*married.* . . . The woman that you selected to be your wife, and not only your wife but—

the mother of your children! (*She catches her breath at the thought.*) Wouldn't you want that woman to be a lady? Wouldn't you want her to be somebody that you, as her husband, and they as her precious children—could look up to with very deep respect? (*There is a pause.*)

JOHN: There's other things between a man and a woman besides respect. Did you know that, Miss Alma?

ALMA: Yes. . . .

JOHN: There's such a thing as intimate relations.

ALMA: Thank you for telling me that. So plainly.

JOHN: It may strike you as unpleasant. But it does have a good deal to do with—connubial felicity, as you'd call it. There are some women that just give in to a man as a sort of obligation imposed on them by the—cruelty of nature! (*He finishes his glass and pours another.*) And there you are.

ALMA: There *I* am?

JOHN: I'm speaking generally.

ALMA: Oh.

(*Hoarse shouts go up from the Casino.*)

JOHN: The cock-fight has started!

ALMA: Since you have spoken so plainly, I'll speak plainly, too. There are some women who turn a possibly beautiful thing into something no better than the coupling of beasts!—but love is what you bring to it.

JOHN: You're right about that.

ALMA: Some people bring just their bodies. But there are some people, there are some women, John—who can bring their hearts to it, also—who can bring their souls to it!

JOHN (*derisively*): Souls again, huh?—those Gothic cathedrals you dream of!

(*There is another hoarse prolonged shout from the Casino.*)

Your name is Alma and Alma is Spanish for soul. Some time I'd like to show you a chart of the human anatomy that I have in the office. It shows what our insides are like, and maybe you can show me where the beautiful soul is located on the chart. (*He drains the wine bottle.*) Let's go watch the cock-fight.

ALMA: No! (*There is a pause.*)

JOHN: I know something else we could do. There are rooms above the Casino. . . .

ALMA (*her back stiffening*): I'd heard that you made suggestions like that to girls that you go out with, but I refused to believe such stories were true. What made you think I might be amenable to such a suggestion?

JOHN: I counted your pulse in the office the night you ran out because you weren't able to sleep.

ALMA: The night I was ill and went to your father for help.

JOHN: It was me you went to.

ALMA: It was your father, and you wouldn't call your father.

JOHN: Fingers frozen stiff when I . . .

ALMA (*rising*): Oh! I want to go home. But I won't go with you. I will go in a taxi! (*She wheels about hysterically.*) Boy! Boy! Call a taxi!

JOHN: I'll call one for you, Miss Alma.—Taxi! (*He goes out of the arbor.*)

ALMA (*wildly*): *You're not a gentleman!*

JOHN (*from the darkness*): Taxi!

ALMA: *You're not a gentleman!*

(*As he disappears she makes a sound in her throat like a hurt animal. The light fades out of the arbor and comes up more distinctly on the stone angel of the fountain.*)

PART TWO
A Winter

SCENE SEVEN

The sky and the southern constellations, almost imperceptibly moving with the earth's motion, appear on the great cyclorama.

The Rectory interior is lighted first, disclosing Alma and Roger Doremus seated on the green plush sofa under the romantic landscape in its heavy gilt frame. On a tiny table beside them is a cut glass pitcher of lemonade with cherries and orange slices in it, like a little aquarium of tropical fish. Roger is entertaining Alma with a collection of photographs and postcards, mementoes of his mother's trip to the Orient. He is enthusiastic about them and describes them in phrases his mother must have assimilated from a sedulous study of literature provided by Cook's Tours. Alma is less enthusiastic; she is preoccupied with the sounds of a wild party going on next door at the doctor's home. At present there is Mexican music with shouts and stamping.

Only the immediate area of the sofa is clearly lighted; the fountain is faintly etched in light and the night sky walls the interior.

ROGER: And this is Ceylon, The Pearl of the Orient!
ALMA: And who is this fat young lady?
ROGER: That is Mother in a hunting costume.
ALMA: The hunting costume makes her figure seem bulky. What was your mother hunting?
ROGER (*gaily*): Heaven knows what she was hunting! But she found Papa.
ALMA: Oh, she met your father on this Oriental tour?
ROGER: Ha-ha!—yes. . . . He was returning from India with dysentery and they met on the boat.
ALMA (*distastefully*): Oh . . .
ROGER: And here she is on top of a ruined temple!
ALMA: How did she get up there?
ROGER: Climbed up, I suppose.
ALMA: What an active woman.
ROGER: Oh, yes, active—is no word for it! Here she is on an elephant's back in Burma.
ALMA: Ah!
ROGER: You're looking at it upside down, Miss Alma!
ALMA: Deliberately—to tease you. (*The doorbell rings.*) Perhaps that's your mother coming to fetch you home.
ROGER: It's only ten-fifteen. I never leave till ten-thirty.

(*Mrs. Bassett comes in.*)

ALMA: Mrs. Bassett!
MRS. BASSETT: I was just wondering who I could turn to when I saw the Rectory light and I thought to myself, Grace Bassett, you trot yourself right over there and talk to Mr. Winemiller!
ALMA: Father has retired.

MRS. BASSETT: Oh, what a pity. (*She sees Roger.*) Hello, Roger! . . . I saw that fall your mother took this morning. I saw her come skipping out of the Delta Planters' Bank and I thought to myself, now isn't that remarkable, a woman of her age and weight so light on her feet? And just at that very moment—*down she went!* I swear to goodness I thought she had broken her hip! Was she bruised much?

ROGER: Just shaken up, Mrs. Bassett.

MRS. BASSETT: Oh, how lucky! She certainly must be made out of India rubber! (*She turns to Alma.*) Alma—Alma, if it is not too late for human intervention, your father's the one right person to call up old Dr. Buchanan at the fever clinic at Lyon and let him know!

ALMA: About—what?

MRS. BASSETT: You must be stone-deaf if you haven't noticed what's been going on next door since the old doctor left to fight the epidemic. One continual orgy! Well, not five minutes ago a friend of mine who works at the County Courthouse called to inform me that young Dr. John and Rosa Gonzales have taken a license out and are going to be married tomorrow!

ALMA: Are you—quite certain?

MRS. BASSETT: Certain? I'm always certain before I speak!

ALMA: Why would he—do such a thing?

MRS. BASSETT: August madness! They say it has something to do with the falling stars. Of course it might also have something to do with the fact that he lost two or three thousand dollars at the Casino which he can't pay except by giving himself to Gonzales' daughter. (*She turns to Alma.*) Alma, what are you doing with that picture puzzle?

ALMA (*with a faint, hysterical laugh*): The pieces don't fit!

MRS. BASSETT (*to Roger*): I shouldn't have opened my mouth.

ALMA: Will both of you please go!

(*Roger goes out.*)

MRS. BASSETT: I knew this was going to upset you. Good night, Alma. (*She leaves. Alma suddenly springs up and seizes the telephone.*)

ALMA: Long distance. . . . Please get me the fever clinic at Lyon. . . . I want to speak to Dr. Buchanan.

(*The light in the Rectory dims out and light comes on in the doctor's office. Rosa's voice is heard calling.*)

ROSA: *Johnny!*

(*The offstage calling of John's name is used throughout the play as a cue for theme music.*

(*John enters the office interior. He is dressed, as always, in a white linen suit. His face has a look of satiety and confusion. He throws himself down in a swivel chair at the desk.*

(*Rosa Gonzales comes in. She is dressed in a Flamenco costume and has been dancing. She crosses and stands before the anatomy chart and clicks her castanets to catch his attention, but he remains looking up at the roofless dark. She approaches him.*)

ROSA: You have blood on your face!

JOHN: You bit my ear.

ROSA: Ohhh . . . (*She approaches him with exaggerated concern.*)

JOHN: You never make love without scratching or biting or something. Whenever I leave you I have a little blood on me. Why is that?

ROSA: Because I know I can't hold you.

JOHN: I think you're doing a pretty good job of it. Better than anyone else. Tomorrow we leave here together and Father or somebody else can tell old Mrs. Arbuckle her eighty-five years are enough and she's got to go now on the wings of carcinoma. Dance, Rosa! (*Accordion music is heard. She performs a slow and joyless dance around his chair. John continues while she dances.*) Tomorrow we leave here together. We sail out of Galveston, don't we?

ROSA: You say it but I don't believe it.

JOHN: I have the tickets.

ROSA: Two pieces of paper that you can tear in two.

JOHN: We'll go all right, and live on fat remittances from your Papa! Ha-ha!

ROSA: Ha-ha-ha!

JOHN: Not long ago the idea would have disgusted me, but not now. (*He catches her by the wrist.*) Rosa! Rosa Gonzales! Did anyone ever slide downhill as fast as I have this summer? Ha-ha! Like a greased pig. And yet every evening I put on a clean white suit. I have a dozen. Six in the closet and six in the wash. And there isn't a sign of depravity in my face. And yet all summer I've sat around here like *this*, remembering last night, anticipating the next one! The trouble with me is, I should have been *castrated*! (*He flings his wine glass at the anatomy chart. She stops dancing.*) Dance, Rosa! Why don't you dance? (*Rosa shakes her head dumbly.*) What is the matter, Rosa? Why don't you go on dancing? (*The accordion continues; he thrusts her arm savagely over her head in the Flamenco position.*)

ROSA (*suddenly weeping*): *I can't dance any more!* (*She throws herself to the floor, pressing her weeping face to his knees. The voice of her father is heard, bellowing, in the next room.*)

GONZALES: *The sky is the limit!*

(*John is sobered.*)

JOHN: Why does your father want me for a son-in-law?

ROSA (*sobbing*): *I want you—I, I want you!*

JOHN (*raising her from the floor*): Why do you?

ROSA (*clinging to him*): Maybe because—I was born in Piedras Negras, and grew up in a one room house with a dirt floor, and all of us had to sleep in that one room, five Mexicans and three geese and a little game-cock named Pepe! Ha-ha! (*She laughs hysterically.*) Pepe was a good fighter! That's how Papa began to make money, winning bets on Pepe! Ha-ha! We all slept in the one room. And in the night, I would hear the love-making. Papa would grunt like a pig to show his passion. I thought to myself, how dirty it was, love-making, and how dirty it was to be Mexicans and all have to sleep in one room with a dirt floor and not smell good because there was not any bathtub! (*The accordion continues.*)

JOHN: What has that got to do with . . . ?

ROSA: Me wanting you? You're tall! You smell good! And, oh, I'm so glad that you never grunt like a pig to show your passion! (*She embraces him convulsively.*) Ah, but *quien sabe!* Something might happen tonight, and I'll wind up with some dark little friend of Papa's.

GONZALES (*imperiously*): Rosa! Rosa!

ROSA: Si, si, Papa, aqui estoy!

GONZALES (*entering unsteadily*): The gold beads . . . (*He fingers a necklace of gold beads that Rosa is wearing.*) Johnny . . . (*He staggers up to John and catches him in a drunken embrace.*) Listen! When my girl Rosa was little she see a string a gold bead and she want those gold bead so bad that she cry all night for it. I don' have money to buy a string a gold bead so next day I go for a ride up to Eagle Pass and I walk in a dry good store and I say to the man: "Please give me a string a gold bead." He say: "Show me the money," and I say: "Here is the money!" And I reach down to my belt and I pull out—not the money—but this! (*He pulls out a revolver.*) Now—now I have money, but I still have this! (*laughing*) She got the gold bead. Anything that she want I get for her with this (*He pulls out a roll of bills.*) or this! (*He waves the revolver.*)

JOHN (*pushing Gonzales away*): Keep your stinking breath out of my face, Gonzales!

ROSA: Dejalo, dejalo, Papa!

GONZALES (*moving unsteadily to the couch, with Rosa supporting him*): Le doy la tierra y si la tierra no basta—le doy el cielo! (*He collapses onto the couch.*) The sky is the limit!

ROSA (*to John*): Let him stay there. Come on back to the party.

(*Rosa leaves the room. John goes over to the window facing the Rectory and looks across. The light comes up in the Rectory living room as Alma enters, dressed in a robe. She goes to the window and looks across at the doctor's house. As Alma and John stand at the windows looking toward each other through the darkness music is heard. Slowly, as if drawn by the music, John walks out of his house and crosses over to the Rectory. Alma remains motionless at the window until John enters the room, behind her. The music dies away and there is a murmur of wind. She slowly turns to face John.*)

JOHN: I took the open door for an invitation. The Gulf wind is blowing tonight . . . cools things off a little. But my head's on fire. . . . (*Alma says nothing. John moves a few steps toward her.*) The silence? (*Alma sinks onto the love seat, closing her eyes.*) Yes, the enormous silence. (*He goes over to her.*) I will go in a minute, but first I want you to put your hands on my face. . . . (*He crouches beside her.*) Eternity and Miss Alma have such cool hands. (*He buries his face in her lap. The attitude suggests a stone* Pieta. *Alma's eyes remain closed.*)

(*On the other side of the stage Dr. Buchanan enters his house and the light builds a little as he looks around in the door of his office. The love theme music fades out and the Mexican music comes up strongly, with a definitely ominous quality, as Rosa enters the office from the other side.*)

ROSA: Johnny! (*She catches sight of Dr. Buchanan and checks herself in surprise.*) Oh! I thought you were Johnny! . . . But you are Johnny's father. . . . I'm Rosa Gonzales!

DR. BUCHANAN: I know who you are. What's going on in my house?

ROSA (*nervously*): John's giving a party because we're leaving tomorrow. (*defiantly*) Yes! Together! I hope you like the idea, but if you don't, it don't matter, because *we* like the idea and my father likes the idea.

GONZALES (*drunkenly, sitting up on the couch*): The sky is the limit!

(*Dr. Buchanan slowly raises his silver-headed cane in a threatening gesture.*)

DR. BUCHANAN: Get your—swine out of—my house! (*He strikes Gonzales with his cane.*)

GONZALES (*staggering up from the couch in pain and surprise*): Aieeeee!

ROSA (*breathlessly, backing against the chart of anatomy*): No! No, Papa!

DR. BUCHANAN (*striking at the chest of the bull-like man with his cane*): Get your swine out, I said! Get them out of my house!

(*He repeats the blow. The drunken Mexican roars with pain and surprise. He backs up and reaches under his coat.*)

ROSA (*wildly and despairingly*): No, no, no, no, no, no!

(*She covers her face against the chart of anatomy. A revolver is fired. There is a burst of light. The cane drops. The music *stops short. Everything dims out but a spot of light on Rosa standing against the chart of anatomy with closed eyes and her face twisted like that of a tragic mask.*)

ROSA (*senselessly*): Aaaaaahhhhhh . . . Aaaaaahhhhhh . . .

(*The theme music is started faintly and light disappears from everything but the wings of the stone angel.*)

SCENE EIGHT

The doctor's office.

The stone angel is dimly visible above.

John is seated in a hunched position at the table. Alma enters with a coffee tray. The sounds of a prayer come through the inner door.

JOHN: What is that mumbo-jumbo your father is spouting in there?

ALMA: A prayer.

JOHN: Tell him to quit. We don't want that worn-out magic.

ALMA: You may not want it, but it's not a question of what you want any more. I've made you some coffee.

JOHN: I don't want any.

ALMA: Lean back and let me wash your face off, John. (*She presses a towel to the red marks on his face.*) It's such a fine face, a fine and sensitive face, a face that has power in it that shouldn't be wasted.

JOHN: Never mind that. (*He pushes her hand away.*)

ALMA: You have to go in to see him.

JOHN: I couldn't. He wouldn't want me.

ALMA: This happened because of his devotion to you.

JOHN: It happened because some meddlesome Mattie called him back here tonight. Who was it did that?

ALMA: I did.

JOHN: It *was* you then!

ALMA: I phoned him at the fever clinic in Lyon as soon as I learned what you were planning to do. I wired him to come here and stop it.

JOHN: You brought him here to be shot.

ALMA: You can't put the blame on anything but your weakness.

JOHN: *You* call me weak?

ALMA: Sometimes it takes a tragedy like this to make a weak person strong.

JOHN: You—white-blooded spinster! You so right people, pious pompous mumblers, preachers and preacher's daughter, all muffled up in a lot of worn-out magic! And I was supposed to minister to your neurosis, give you tablets for sleeping and tonics to give you the strength to go on mumbling your worn-out mumbo-jumbo!

ALMA: Call me whatever you want, but don't let your father hear your drunken shouting. (*She tries to break away from him.*)

JOHN: Stay here! I want you to look at something. (*He turns her about.*) This chart of anatomy, look!

ALMA: I've seen it before. (*She turns away.*)

JOHN: You've never dared to look at it.

ALMA: Why should I?

JOHN: You're scared to.

ALMA: You must be out of your senses.

JOHN: You talk about weakness but can't even look at a picture of human insides.

ALMA: They're not important.

JOHN: That's your mistake. You think you're stuffed with rose-leaves. Turn around and look at it, it may do you good!

ALMA: How can you behave like this with your father dying and you so . . .

JOHN: Hold still!

ALMA: . . . so much to blame for it!

JOHN: No more than you are!

ALMA: At least for this little while . . .

JOHN: Look here!

ALMA: . . . you could feel some shame!

JOHN (*with crazy, grinning intensity*): Now listen here to the anatomy lecture! This upper story's the brain which is hungry for something called truth and doesn't get much but keeps on feeling hungry! This middle's the belly which is hungry for food. This part down here is the sex which is hungry for love because it is sometimes lonesome. I've fed all three, as much of all three as I could or as much as I wanted— You've fed none—nothing. Well—maybe your belly a little—watery subsistence— But love or truth, nothing but—nothing but hand-me-down notions!—attitudes! —poses! (*He releases her.*) Now you can go. The anatomy lecture is over.

ALMA: So that is your high conception of human desires. What you have here is not the anatomy of a beast, but a man. And I—I reject your opinion of where love is, and the kind of truth you believe the brain to be seeking!—There is something not shown on the chart.

JOHN: You mean the part that Alma is Spanish for, do you?

ALMA: Yes, that's not shown on the anatomy chart! But it's there, just the same, yes, there! Somewhere, not seen, but there. And it's *that* that I loved you with—that! Not what you mention!—Yes, did love you with, John, did nearly *die* of when you hurt me! (*He turns slowly to her and speaks gently.*)

JOHN: I wouldn't have made love to you.

ALMA (*uncomprehendingly*): What?

JOHN: The night at the Casino—I wouldn't have made love to you. Even if you had consented to go upstairs. I couldn't have made love to you. (*She stares at him as if anticipating some unbearable hurt.*) Yes, yes! Isn't that funny? I'm more afraid of your soul than you're afraid of my body. You'd have been as safe as the angel of the fountain—because I wouldn't feel *decent* enough to touch you. . . .

(*Mr. Winemiller comes in.*)

MR. WINEMILLER: He's resting more easily now.

ALMA: Oh . . . (*She nods her head. John reaches for his coffee cup.*) It's cold. I'll heat it.

JOHN: It's all right.

MR. WINEMILLER: Alma, Dr. John wants you.

ALMA: I . . .

MR. WINEMILLER: He asked if you would sing for him.

ALMA: I—couldn't—now.

JOHN: Go in and sing to him, Miss Alma!

(*Mr. Winemiller withdraws through the outer door. Alma looks back at John hunched over the coffee cup. He doesn't return her look. She passes into the blurred orange space beyond the inner door, leaving it slightly open. After a few minutes her voice rises softly within, singing. John suddenly rises. He crosses to the door, shoves it slowly open and enters.*)

JOHN (*softly and with deep tenderness*): Father?

(*The light dims out in the house, but lingers on the stone angel.*)

SCENE NINE

The cyclorama is the faint blue of a late afternoon in autumn. There is band-music—a Sousa march, in the distance. As it grows somewhat louder, Alma enters the Rectory interior in a dressing gown and with her hair hanging loose. She looks as if she had been through a long illness, the intensity drained, her pale face listless. She crosses to the window frame but the parade is not in sight so she returns weakly to the sofa and sits down closing her eyes with exhaustion.

The Rev. and Mrs. Winemiller enter the outer door frame of the Rectory, a grotesque-looking couple. Mrs. Winemiller has on her plumed hat, at a rakish angle, and a brilliant scarf about her throat. Her face wears a roguish smile that suggests a musical comedy pirate. One hand holds the minister's arm and with the other she is holding an ice cream cone.

MR. WINEMILLER: Now you may let go of my arm, if you please! She was on her worst behavior. Stopped in front of the White Star Pharmacy on Front Street and stood there like a mule; wouldn't budge till I bought her an ice cream cone. I had it wrapped in tissue paper because she had promised me that she wouldn't eat it until we got home. The moment I gave it to her she tore off the paper and walked home licking it every step of the way!—just—just to humiliate me! (*Mrs. Winemiller offers him the half-eaten cone, saying "Lick?"*)

MR. WINEMILLER: No, thank you!

ALMA: Now, now, children.

(*Mr. Winemiller's irritation shifts to Alma.*)

MR. WINEMILLER: Alma! Why don't you get dressed? It hurts me to see you sitting around like this, day in, day out, like an invalid when there is nothing particularly wrong with you. I can't read your mind. You may have had some kind of disappointment, but you must not make it an excuse for acting as if the world had come to an end.

ALMA: I have made the beds and washed the breakfast dishes and phoned the market and sent the laundry out and peeled the potatoes and shelled the peas and set the table for lunch. What more do you want?

MR. WINEMILLER (*sharply*): I want you to either get dressed or stay in your room. (*Alma rises indifferently, then her father speaks suddenly.*) At night you get dressed. Don't you? Yes, I heard you slipping out of the house at two in the morning. And that was not the first time.

ALMA: I don't sleep well. Sometimes I have to get up and walk for a while before I am able to sleep.

MR. WINEMILLER: What am I going to tell people who ask about you?

ALMA: Tell them I've changed and you're waiting to see in what way.

(*The band music becomes a little louder.*)

MR. WINEMILLER: Are you going to stay like this indefinitely?

ALMA: Not indefinitely, but you may wish that I had.

MR. WINEMILLER: Stop twisting that ring! Whenever I look at you you're twisting that ring. Give me that ring! I'm going to take that ring off your finger! (*He catches her wrist. She breaks roughly away from him.*)

MRS. WINEMILLER (*joyfully*): Fight! Fight!

MR. WINEMILLER: Oh, I give up!

ALMA: That's better. (*She suddenly crosses to the window as the band music gets louder.*) Is there a parade in town?

MRS. WINEMILLER: Ha-ha—yes! They met him at the station with a great big silver loving-cup!

ALMA: Who? Who did they . . . ?

MRS. WINEMILLER: That boy next door, the one you watched all the time!

ALMA: Is that true, Father?

MR. WINEMILLER (*unfolding his newspaper*): Haven't you looked at the papers?

ALMA: No, not lately.

MR. WINEMILLER (*wiping his eyeglasses*): These people are grasshoppers, just as likely to jump one way as another. He's finished the work his father started, stamped out the fever and gotten all of the glory. Well, that's how it is in this world. Years of devotion and sacrifice are overlooked an' forgotten while someone young an' lucky walks off with the honors!

(*Alma has crossed slowly to the window. The sun brightens and falls in a shaft through the frame.*)

ALMA (*suddenly crying out*): *There he is!* (*She staggers away from the window. There is a roll of drums and then silence. Alma now speaks faintly.*) What . . . happened? Something . . . struck me! (*Mr. Winemiller catches her arm to support her.*)

MR. WINEMILLER: Alma . . . I'll call a doctor.

ALMA: No, no, don't. Don't call anybody to help me. I want to die! (*She collapses on the sofa.*)

(*The band strikes up again and recedes down the street. The Rectory interior dims out. Then the light is brought up in the doctor's office. John enters, with his loving-cup. He is sprucely dressed and his whole manner suggests a new-found responsibility. While he is setting the award on the table, removing his coat and starched collar, Nellie Ewell appears in the door behind him. She stands by the anatomy chart and watches him until he discovers her presence. Nellie has abruptly grown up, and wears very adult clothes, but has lost none of her childish impudence and brightness. John gives a startled whistle as he sees her. Nellie giggles.*)

JOHN: High heels, feathers . . . and paint!

NELLIE: Not paint!

JOHN: Natural color?

NELLIE: Excitement.

JOHN: Over what?

NELLIE: Everything! You! You here! Didn't you see me at the depot? I shouted and waved my arm off! I'm home for Thanksgiving.

JOHN: From where?

NELLIE: Sophie Newcomb's. (*He remains staring at her, unbelieving. At last she draws a book from under her arm.*) Here is that nasty book you gave me last summer when I was pretending such ignorance of things!

JOHN: Only pretending?

NELLIE: Yes. (*He ignores the book. She tosses it on the table.*) . . . Well? (*John laughs uneasily and sits on the table.*) Shall I go now, or will you look at my tongue? (*She crosses to him, sticking out her tongue.*)

JOHN: Red as a berry!

NELLIE: Peppermint drops! Will you have one? (*She holds out a sack.*)

JOHN: Thanks. (*Nellie giggles as he takes one.*) What's the joke, Nellie?

NELLIE: They make your mouth so sweet!

JOHN: So?

NELLIE: I always take one when I hope to be kissed.

JOHN (*after a pause*): Suppose I took you up on that?

NELLIE: I'm not scared. Are you?

(*He gives her a quick kiss. She clings to him, raising her hand to press his head against her own. He breaks free after a moment and turns the light back on.*)

JOHN (*considerably impressed*): Where did you learn such tricks?

NELLIE: I've been away to school. But they didn't teach me to love.

JOHN: Who are you to be using that long word?

NELLIE: That isn't a long word!

JOHN: No? (*He turns away from her.*) Run along Nellie before we get into trouble.

NELLIE: Who's afraid of trouble, you or me?

JOHN: I am. Run along! Hear me?

NELLIE: Oh, I'll go. But I'll be back for Christmas!

(*She laughs and runs out. He whistles and wipes his forehead with a handkerchief.*)

SCENE TEN

An afternoon in December. At the fountain in the park. It is very windy.

Alma enters. She seems to move with an effort against the wind. She sinks down on the bench.

A widow with a flowing black veil passes across the stage and pauses by Alma's bench. It is Mrs. Bassett.

MRS. BASSETT: Hello Alma.

ALMA: Good afternoon, Mrs. Bassett.

MRS. BASSETT: Such wind, such wind!

ALMA: Yes, it nearly swept me off my feet. I had to sit down to catch my breath for a moment.

MRS. BASSETT: I wouldn't sit too long if I were you.

ALMA: No, not long.

MRS. BASSETT: It's good to see you out again after your illness.

ALMA: Thank you.

MRS. BASSETT: Our poor little group broke up after you dropped out.

ALMA (*insincerely*): What a pity.

MRS. BASSETT: You should have come to the last meeting.

ALMA: Why, what happened?

MRS. BASSETT: Vernon read his verse play!

ALMA: Ah, how was it received?

MRS. BASSETT: Maliciously, spitefully and vindictively torn to pieces, the way children tear the wings of butterflies. I think next Spring we might reorganize. (*She throws up her black-gloved hands in a deploring gesture.*)

(*Nellie Ewell appears. She is dressed very fashionably and carrying a fancy basket of Christmas packages.*)

NELLIE: Miss Alma!

MRS. BASSETT (*rushing off*): Goodbye!

NELLIE: Oh, there you are!

ALMA: Why Nellie . . . Nellie Ewell!

NELLIE: I was by the Rectory. Just popped in for a second; the holidays are so short that every minute is precious. They told me you'd gone to the park.

ALMA: This is the first walk I've taken in quite a while.

NELLIE: You've been ill!

ALMA: Not ill, just not very well. How you've grown up, Nellie.

NELLIE: It's just my clothes. Since I went off to Sophie Newcombe I've picked out my own clothes, Miss Alma. When Mother had jurisdiction over my wardrobe, she tried to keep me looking like a child!

ALMA: Your voice is grown-up, too.

NELLIE: They're teaching me diction, Miss Alma. I'm learning to talk like you, long A's and everything, such as "cahn't" and "bahth" and "lahf" instead of "laugh." Yesterday I slipped. I said I "lahfed and lahfed till I nearly died laughing." Johnny was so amused at me!

ALMA: Johnny?

NELLIE: Your nextdoor neighbor!

ALMA: Oh! I'm sure it must be a very fashionable school.

NELLIE: Oh yes, they're preparing us to be young ladies in society. What a pity there's no society here to be a young lady in . . . at least not for me, with Mother's reputation!

ALMA: You'll find other fields to conquer.

NELLIE: What's this I hear about *you*?

ALMA: I have no idea, Nellie.

NELLIE: That you've quit teaching singing and gone into retirement.

ALMA: Naturally I had to stop teaching while I was ill and as for retiring from the world . . . it's more a case of the world retiring from me.

NELLIE: I know somebody whose feelings you've hurt badly.

ALMA: Why, who could that be, Nellie?

NELLIE: Somebody who regards you as an angel!

ALMA: I can't think who might hold me in such esteem.

NELLIE: Somebody who says that you refused to see him.

ALMA: I saw nobody. For several months. The long summer wore me out so.

NELLIE: Well, anyhow, I'm going to give you your present. (*She hands her a small package from the basket.*)

ALMA: Nellie, you shouldn't have given me anything.

NELLIE: I'd like to know why not!

ALMA: I didn't expect it.

NELLIE: After the trouble you took with my horrible voice?

ALMA: It's very sweet of you, Nellie.

NELLIE: Open it!

ALMA: Now?

NELLIE: Why, sure.

ALMA: It's so prettily wrapped I hate to undo it.

NELLIE: I love to wrap presents and since it was for you, I did a specially dainty job of it.

ALMA (*winding the ribbon about her fingers*): I'm going to save this ribbon. I'm going to keep this lovely paper too, with the silver stars on it. And the sprig of holly . . .

NELLIE: Let me pin it on your jacket, Alma.

ALMA: Yes, do. I hardly realized that Christmas was coming. . . . (*She unfolds the paper, revealing a lace handkerchief and a card.*) What an exquisite handkerchief.

NELLIE: I hate to give people handkerchiefs, it's so unimaginative.

ALMA: I love to get them.

NELLIE: It comes from Maison Blanche!

ALMA: Oh, does it really?

NELLIE: Smell it!

ALMA: Sachet *Roses!* Well, I'm just more touched and pleased than I can possibly tell you!

NELLIE: The card!

ALMA: Card?

NELLIE: You dropped it. (*She snatches up the card and hands it to Alma.*)

ALMA: Oh, how clumsy of me! Thank you, Nellie. "Joyeux Noel . . . to Alma . . . from Nellie and . . . (*She looks up slowly.*) *John?*"

NELLIE: He helped me wrap presents last night and when we came to yours we started talking about you. Your ears must have burned!

(*The wind blows loudly. Alma bends stiffly forward.*)

ALMA: You mean you—spoke well of me?

NELLIE: "Well of"! We raved, simply raved! Oh, he told me the influence you'd had on him!

ALMA: Influence?

NELLIE: He told me about the wonderful talks he'd had with you last summer when he was so mixed up and how you inspired him and you more than anyone else was responsible for his pulling himself together, after his father was killed, and he told me about . . . (*Alma rises stiffly from the bench.*) Where are you going, Miss Alma?

ALMA: To drink at the fountain.

NELLIE: He told me about how you came in the house that night like an angel of mercy!

ALMA (*laughing harshly by the fountain*): This is the only angel in Glorious Hill. (*She bends to drink.*) Her body is stone and her blood is mineral water.

(*The wind is louder.*)

NELLIE: How penetrating the wind is!

ALMA: I'm going home, Nellie. You run along and deliver your presents now. . . . (*She starts away.*)

NELLIE: But wait till I've told you the wonderfullest thing I . . .

ALMA: I'm going home now. Goodbye.

NELLIE: Oh— Goodbye, Miss Alma.

(*She snatches up her festive basket and rushes in the other direction with a shrill giggle as the wind pulls at her skirts. The lights dim out.*)

SCENE ELEVEN

An hour later. In John's office.

The interior is framed by the traceries of Victorian architecture and there is one irregular section of wall supporting the anatomy chart. Otherwise the stage is open to the cyclorama.

In the background mellow golden light touches the vane of a steeple (a gilded weathercock). Also the wings of the stone angel. A singing wind rises and falls throughout scene.

John is seated at a white enameled table examining a slide through a microscope.

(*A bell tolls the hour of five as Alma comes hesitantly in. She wears a russet suit and a matching hat with a plume. The light changes, the sun disappearing behind a cloud, fading from the steeple and the stone angel till the bell stops tolling. Then it brightens again.*)

ALMA: No greetings? No greetings at all?

JOHN: Hello, Miss Alma.

ALMA (*speaking with animation to control her panic*): How white it is here, such glacial brilliance! (*She covers her eyes, laughing.*)

JOHN: New equipment.

ALMA: Everything new but the chart.

JOHN: The human anatomy's always the same old thing.

ALMA: And such a tiresome one! I've been plagued with sore throats.

JOHN: Everyone has here lately. These Southern homes are all improperly heated. Open grates aren't enough.

ALMA: They burn the front of you while your back is freezing!

JOHN: Then you go into another room and get chilled off.

ALMA: Yes, yes, chilled to the bone.

JOHN: But it never gets quite cold enough to convince the damn fools that a furnace is necessary so they go on building without them.

(*There is the sound of wind.*)

ALMA: Such a strange afternoon.

JOHN: Is it? I haven't been out.

ALMA: The Gulf wind is blowing big, white—what do they call them? cumulus?—clouds over! Ha-ha! It seemed determined to take the plume off my hat, like that fox terrier we had once named Jacob, snatched the plume off a hat and dashed around and around the back yard with it like a trophy!

JOHN: I remember Jacob. What happened to him?

ALMA: Oh, Jacob. Jacob was such a mischievous thief. We had to send him out to some friends in the country. Yes, he ended his days as—a country squire! The tales of his exploits . . .

JOHN: Sit down, Miss Alma.

ALMA: If I'm disturbing you . . . ?

JOHN: No—I called the Rectory when I heard you were sick. Your father told me you wouldn't see a doctor.

ALMA: I needed a rest, that was all. . . . You were out of town mostly. . . .

JOHN: I was mostly in Lyon, finishing up Dad's work in the fever clinic.

ALMA: Covering yourself with sudden glory!

JOHN: Redeeming myself with good works.

ALMA: It's rather late to tell you how happy I am, and also how proud. I almost feel as your father might have felt—if . . . And—are you—happy now, John?

JOHN (*uncomfortably, not looking at her*): I've settled with life on fairly acceptable terms. Isn't that all a reasonable person can ask for?

ALMA: He can ask for much more than that. He can ask for the coming true of his most improbable dreams.

JOHN: It's best not to ask for too much.

ALMA: I disagree with you. I say, ask for all, but be prepared to get nothing! (*She springs up and crosses to the window. She continues.*) No, I haven't been well. I've thought many times of something you told me last summer, that I have a *doppelganger.* I looked that up and I found that it means another person inside me, another self, and I don't know whether to thank you or not for making me conscious of it!—I haven't been well. . . . For a while I thought I was dying, that that was the change that was coming.

JOHN: When did you have that feeling?

ALMA: August. September. But now the Gulf wind has blown that feeling away like a cloud of smoke, and I know now I'm not dying, that it isn't going to turn out to be that simple. . . .

JOHN: Have you been anxious about your heart again? (*He retreats to a professional manner and takes out a silver watch, putting his fingers on her wrist.*)

ALMA: And now the stethoscope? (*He removes the stethoscope from the table and starts to loosen her jacket. She looks down at his bent head. Slowly, involuntarily, her gloved hands lift and descend on the crown of his head. He gets up awkwardly. She suddenly leans toward him and presses her mouth to his.*) Why don't you say something? Has the cat got your tongue?

JOHN: Miss Alma, what can I say?

ALMA: You've gone back to calling me "Miss Alma" again.

JOHN: We never really got past that point with each other.

ALMA: Oh, yes, we did. We were so close that we almost breathed together!

JOHN (*with embarrassment*): I didn't know that.

ALMA: No? Well, I did, I knew it. (*Her hand touches his face tenderly.*) You shave more carefully now? You don't have those little razor cuts on your chin that you dusted with gardenia talcum. . . .

JOHN: I shave more carefully now.

ALMA: So that explains it! (*Her fingers remain on his face, moving gently up and down it like a blind person reading Braille. He is intensely embarrassed and gently removes her hands from him.*) Is it—impossible now?

JOHN: I don't think I know what you mean.

ALMA: You know what I mean, all right! So be honest with me. One time I said "no" to something. You may remember the time, and all that demented howling from the cockfight? But now I have changed my mind, or the girl who said "no," she doesn't exist any more, she died last summer—suffocated in smoke from something on fire inside her. No, she doesn't live now, but she left me her ring—You see? This one you admired, the topaz ring set in pearls. . . . And she said to me when she slipped this ring on my finger—"Remember I died empty-handed, and so make sure that your hands have *something in them*!" (*She drops her gloves. She clasps his head again in her hands.*) I said, "But what about pride?"—She said, "Forget about pride whenever it stands between you and what you must have!" (*He takes hold of her wrists.*) And then I said, "But what if he doesn't want me?" I don't know what she said then. I'm not sure whether she said anything or not—her lips stopped moving—yes, I think she stopped breathing! (*He gently removes her craving hands from his face.*) No? (*He shakes his head in dumb suffering.*) Then the answer is "no"!

JOHN (*forcing himself to speak*): I have a respect for the truth, and I have a respect for you—so I'd better speak honestly if you want me to speak. (*Alma nods slightly.*) You've won the argument that we had between us.

ALMA: What—argument?

JOHN: The one about the chart.

ALMA: Oh—the chart!

(*She turns from him and wanders across to the chart. She gazes up at it with closed eyes, and her hands clasped in front of her.*)

JOHN: It shows that we're not a package of rose leaves, that every interior inch of us is taken up with something ugly and functional and no room seems to be left for anything else in there.

ALMA: No . . .

JOHN: But I've come around to your way of thinking, that something else is in there, an immaterial something—as thin as smoke—which all of those ugly machines combine to produce and that's their whole reason for being. It can't be seen so it can't be shown on the chart. But it's there, just the same, and knowing it's there—why, then the whole thing—this—this unfathomable experience of ours—takes on a new value, like some—some wildly romantic work in a laboratory! Don't you see?

(*The wind comes up very loud, almost like a choir of voices. Both of them turn slightly, Alma raising a hand to her plumed head as if she were outdoors.*)

ALMA: Yes, I see! Now that you no longer want it to be otherwise you're willing to believe that a spiritual bond can exist between us two!

JOHN: Can't you believe that I am sincere about it?

ALMA: Maybe you are. But I don't want to be talked to like some incurably sick patient you have to comfort. (*A harsh and strong note comes into her voice.*) Oh, I suppose I am sick, one of those weak and divided people who slip like shadows among you solid strong ones. But sometimes, out of necessity, we shadowy people take on a strength of our own. I have that now. You needn't try to deceive me.

JOHN: I wasn't.

ALMA: You needn't try to comfort me. I haven't come here on any but equal terms. You said, let's talk truthfully. Well, let's do! Unsparingly, truthfully, even shamelessly, then! It's no longer a secret that I love you. It never was. I loved you as long ago as the time I asked you to read the stone angel's name with your fingers. Yes, I remember the long afternoons of our childhood, when I had to stay indoors to practice my music—and heard your playmates calling you, "Johnny, Johnny!" How it went through me, just to hear your name called! And how I—rushed to the window to watch you jump the porch railing! I stood at a distance, halfway down the block, only to keep in sight of your torn red sweater, racing about the vacant lot you played in. Yes, it had begun that early, this affliction of love, and has never let go of me since, but kept on growing. I've lived next door to you all the days of my life, a weak and divided person who stood in adoring awe of your singleness, of your strength. And that is my story! Now I wish *you* would tell *me*—why didn't it happen between us? Why did I fail? Why did you come almost close enough—and no closer?

JOHN: Whenever we've gotten together, the three or four times that we have . . .

ALMA: As few as that?

JOHN: It's only been three or four times that we've—come face to face. And each of those times—we seemed to be trying to find something in each other without knowing what it was that we wanted to find. It wasn't a body hunger although—I acted as if I thought it might be the night I wasn't a gentleman—at the Casino—it wasn't the physical you that I really wanted!

ALMA: I know, you've already . . .

JOHN: You didn't have that to give me.

ALMA: Not at that time.

JOHN: You had something else to give.

ALMA: What did I have?

(*John strikes a match. Unconsciously he holds his curved palm over the flame of the match to warm it. It is a long kitchen match and it makes a good flame. They both stare at it with a sorrowful understanding that is still perplexed. It is about to burn his fingers. She leans forward and blows it out, then she puts on her gloves.*)

JOHN: You couldn't name it and I couldn't recognize it. I thought it was just a Puritanical ice that glittered like flame. But now I believe it *was* flame, mistaken for ice. I still don't understand it, but I know it was there, just as I know that your eyes and your voice are the two most beautiful things I've ever known—and also the warmest, although they don't seem to be set in your body at all. . . .

ALMA: You talk as if my body had ceased to exist for you, John, in spite of the fact that you've just counted my pulse. Yes, that's it! You tried to avoid it, but you've told me plainly. The tables have turned, yes, the tables have turned with a vengeance! You've come around to my old way of thinking and I to yours like two people exchanging a call on each other at the same time, and each one finding the other one gone out, the door locked against him and no one to answer the bell! (*She laughs.*) I came here to tell you that being a gentleman, doesn't seem so important to me any more, but you're telling me I've got to remain a lady. (*She laughs rather violently.*) The tables have turned with a vengeance!—The air in here smells of ether— It's making me dizzy . . .

JOHN: I'll open a window.

ALMA: Please.

JOHN: There now.

ALMA: Thank you, that's better. Do you remember those little white tablets you gave me? I've used them all up and I'd like to have some more.

JOHN: I'll write the prescription for you. (*He bends to write.*)

(*Nellie is in the waiting room. They hear her voice.*)

ALMA: Someone is waiting in the waiting room, John. One of my vocal pupils. The youngest and prettiest one with the least gift for music. The one that you helped wrap up this handkerchief for me. (*She takes it out and touches her eyes with it.*)

(*The door opens, first a crack. Nellie peers in and giggles. Then she throws the door wide open with a peal of merry laughter. She has holly pinned on her jacket. She rushes up to John and hugs him with childish squeals.*)

NELLIE: I've been all over town just shouting, shouting!

JOHN: Shouting what?

NELLIE: Glad tidings!

(*John looks at Alma over Nellie's shoulder.*)

JOHN: I thought we weren't going to tell anyone for a while.

NELLIE: I couldn't stop myself. (*She wheels about.*) Oh, Alma, has he told *you*?

ALMA (*quietly*): He didn't need to, Nellie. I guessed . . . from the Christmas card with your two names written on it!

(*Nellie rushes over to Alma and hugs her. Over Nellie's shoulder Alma looks at John. He makes a thwarted gesture as if he wanted to speak. She smiles desperately and shakes her head. She closes her eyes and bites her lips for a moment. Then she releases Nellie with a laugh of exaggerated gaiety.*)

NELLIE: So, Alma, you were really the first to know!

ALMA: I'm proud of that, Nellie.

NELLIE: See on my finger! This was the present I couldn't tell you about!

ALMA: Oh, what a lovely, lovely solitaire! But solitaire is such a wrong name for it. Solitaire means single and this means *two!* It's blinding, Nellie! Why it . . . hurts my eyes!

(*John catches Nellie's arm and pulls her to him. Almost violently Alma lifts her face; it is bathed in tears. She nods gratefully to John for releasing her from Nellie's attention. She picks up her gloves and purse.*)

JOHN: Excuse her, Miss Alma. Nellie's still such a child.

ALMA (*with a breathless laugh*): I've got to run along now.

JOHN: Don't leave your prescription.

ALMA: Oh, yes, where's my prescription?

JOHN: On the table.

ALMA: I'll take it to the drug store right away!

(*Nellie struggles to free herself from John's embrace which keeps her from turning to Alma.*)

NELLIE: Alma, don't go! Johnny, let go of me, Johnny! You're hugging me so tight I can't breathe!

ALMA: Goodbye.

NELLIE: Alma! Alma, you know you're going to sing at the wedding! The very first Sunday in Spring!—which will be Palm Sunday! "The Voice that Breathed o'er Eden."

(*Alma has closed the door. John shuts his eyes tight with a look of torment. He rains kisses on Nellie's forehead and throat and lips. The scene dims out with music.*)

SCENE TWELVE

In the park near the angel of the fountain. About dusk.

Alma enters the lighted area and goes slowly up to the fountain and bends to drink. Then she removes a small white package from her pocketbook and starts to unwrap it. While she is doing this, a Young Man comes along. He is dressed in a checked suit and a derby. He pauses by the bench. They glance at each other.

A train whistles in the distance. The Young Man clears his throat. The train whistle is repeated. The Young Man crosses toward the fountain, his eyes on Alma. She hesitates, with the unwrapped package in her hand. Then she crosses toward the bench and stands hesitantly in front of it. He stuffs his hands in his pockets and whistles. He glances with an effect of unconcern back over his shoulder.

Alma pushes her veil back with an uncertain gesture. His whistle dies out. He sways back and forth on his heels as the train whistles again. He suddenly turns to the fountain and bends to drink. Alma slips the package back into her purse. As the young man straightens up, she speaks in a barely audible voice.

ALMA: The water—is—cool.
THE YOUNG MAN (*eagerly*): Did you say something?
ALMA: I said, the water is cool.
THE YOUNG MAN: Yes, it sure is, it's nice and cool!
ALMA: It's always cool.
THE YOUNG MAN: Is it?
ALMA: Yes. Yes, even in summer. It comes from deep underground.
THE YOUNG MAN: That's what keeps it cool.
ALMA: Glorious Hill is famous for its artesian springs.
THE YOUNG MAN: I didn't know that.

(*The Young Man jerkily removes his hands from his pockets. She gathers confidence before the awkwardness of his youth.*)

ALMA: Are you a stranger in town?

THE YOUNG MAN: I'm a traveling salesman.

ALMA: Ah, you're a salesman who travels! (*She laughs gently.*) But you're younger than most of them are, and not so fat!

THE YOUNG MAN: I'm just starting out. I travel for Red Goose shoes.

ALMA: Ah! The Delt's your territory?

THE YOUNG MAN: From the Peabody Lobby to Cat-Fish Row in Vicksburg.

(*Alma leans back and looks at him under half-closed lids, perhaps a little suggestively.*)

ALMA: The life of a traveling salesman is interesting . . . but lonely.

THE YOUNG MAN: You're right about that. Hotel bedrooms are lonely.

(*There is a pause. Far away the train whistles again.*)

ALMA: All rooms are lonely where there is only one person. (*Her eyes fall shut.*)

THE YOUNG MAN (*gently*): You're tired, aren't you?

ALMA: I? Tired? (*She starts to deny it; then laughs faintly and confesses the truth.*) Yes . . . a little. . . . But I shall rest now. I've just now taken one of my sleeping tablets.

THE YOUNG MAN: So early?

ALMA: Oh, it won't put me to sleep. It will just quiet my nerves.

THE YOUNG MAN: What are you nervous about?

ALMA: I won an argument this afternoon.

THE YOUNG MAN: That's nothing to be nervous over. You ought to be nervous if you *lost* one.

ALMA: It wasn't the argument that I wanted to win. . . .

THE YOUNG MAN: Well, I'm nervous too.

ALMA: What over?

THE YOUNG MAN: It's my first job and I'm scared of not making good.

(*That mysteriously sudden intimacy that sometimes occurs between strangers more completely than old friends or lovers moves them both. Alma hands the package of tablets to him.*)

ALMA: Then you must take one of my tablets.

THE YOUNG MAN: Shall I?

ALMA: Please take one!

THE YOUNG MAN: Yes, I shall.

ALMA: You'll be surprised how infinitely merciful they are. The prescription number is 96814. I think of it as the telephone number of God! (*They both laugh. He places one of the tablets on his tongue and crosses to the fountain to wash it down.*)

THE YOUNG MAN (*to the stone figure*): Thanks, angel. (*He gives her a little salute, and crosses back to Alma.*)

ALMA: Life is full of little mercies like that, not *big* mercies but comfortable *little* mercies. And so we are able to keep on going. . . . (*She has leaned back with half-closed eyes.*)

THE YOUNG MAN (*returning*): You're falling asleep.

ALMA: Oh no, I'm not. I'm just closing my eyes. You know what I feel like now? I feel like a water-lily.

THE YOUNG MAN: A water-lily?

ALMA: Yes, I feel like a water-lily on a Chinese lagoon. Won't you sit down? (*The Young Man does.*) My name is Alma. Spanish for soul! What's yours?

THE YOUNG MAN: Ha-ha! Mine's Archie Kramer. Mucho gusto, as they say in Spain.

ALMA: Usted habla Espanol, senor?

THE YOUNG MAN: Un poquito! Usted habla Espanol, senorita?

ALMA: Me tambien. Un poquito!

THE YOUNG MAN (*delightedly*): Ha . . . ha . . . ha! Sometimes un poquito is plenty! (*Alma laughs . . . in a different way than she has ever laughed before, a little wearily, but quite naturally. The Young Man leans toward her confidentially.*) What's there to do in this town after dark?

ALMA: There's not much to do in this town after dark, but there are resorts on the lake that offer all kinds of after-dark entertainment. There's one called Moon Lake Casino. It's under new management, now, but I don't suppose its character has changed.

THE YOUNG MAN: What was its character?

ALMA: Gay, very gay, Mr. Kramer. . . .

THE YOUNG MAN: Then what in hell are we sitting here for? Vamonos!

ALMA: Como no, senor!

THE YOUNG MAN: Ha-ha-ha! (*He jumps up.*) I'll call a taxi. (*He goes off shouting "Taxi."*)

(*Alma rises from the bench. As she crosses to the fountain the grave mood of the play is reinstated with a phrase of music. She faces the stone angel and raises her gloved hand in a sort of valedictory salute. Then she turns slowly about toward the audience with her hand still raised in a gesture of wonder and finality as . . . the curtain falls.*)

THE ROSE TATTOO

TO FRANK

in return for Sicily

THE TIMELESS WORLD OF A PLAY

CARSON MCCULLERS concludes one of her lyric poems with the line: "Time, the endless idiot, runs screaming 'round the world." It is this continual rush of time, so violent that it appears to be screaming, that deprives our actual lives of so much dignity and meaning, and it is, perhaps more than anything else, the *arrest of time* which has taken place in a completed work of art that gives to certain plays their feeling of depth and significance. In the London notices of *Death of a Salesman* a certain notoriously skeptical critic made the remark that Willy Loman was the sort of man that almost any member of the audience would have kicked out of an office had he applied for a job or detained one for conversation about his troubles. The remark itself possibly holds some truth. But the implication that Willy Loman is consequently a character with whom we have no reason to concern ourselves in drama, reveals a strikingly false conception of what plays are. Contemplation is something that exists outside of time, and so is the tragic sense. Even in the actual world of commerce, there exists in some persons a sensibility to the unfortunate situations of others, a capacity for concern and compassion, surviving from a more tender period of life outside the present whirling wire-cage of business activity. Facing Willy Loman across an office desk, meeting his nervous glance and hearing his querulous voice, we would be very likely to glance at our wrist watch and our schedule of other appointments. We would not kick him out of the office, no, but we would certainly *ease* him out with more expedition than Willy had feebly hoped for. But suppose there had been no wrist watch or office clock and suppose there had *not* been the schedule of pressing appointments, and suppose that we were not actually facing Willy across a desk—and facing a person is *not* the best way to *see* him!—suppose, in other words, that the meeting with Willy Loman had somehow occurred in a world *outside* of time. Then I think we would receive him with concern and kindness and even with respect. If the world of a play did not offer us this occasion to view its characters under that special condition of a *world without time*, then, indeed, the characters and occurrences of drama would become equally pointless, equally trivial, as corresponding meetings and happenings in life.

The classic tragedies of Greece had tremendous nobility. The actors wore great masks, movements were formal, dance-like, and the speeches had an epic quality which doubtless were as removed from the normal conversation of their contemporary society as they seem today. Yet they did not seem false to the Greek audiences: the magnitude of the events and the passions aroused by them did not seem ridiculously out of proportion to common experience. And I wonder if this was not because the Greek audiences knew, instinctively or by training, that the created world of a play is removed from that element which makes people *little* and their emotions fairly inconsequential.

Great sculpture often follows the lines of the human body: yet the repose of great sculpture suddenly transmutes those human lines to something that has an absoluteness, a purity, a beauty, which would not be possible in a living mobile form.

A play may be violent, full of motion: yet it has that special kind of repose which allows contemplation and produces the climate in which tragic importance is a possible thing, provided that certain modern conditions are met.

In actual existence the moments of love are succeeded by the moments of satiety and sleep. The sincere remark is followed by a cynical distrust. Truth is fragmentary, at best: we love and betray each other not in quite the same breath but in two breaths that occur in fairly close sequence. But the fact that passion occurred in *passing*, that it then declined into a more familiar sense of indifference, should not be regarded as proof of its inconsequence. And this is the very truth that drama wishes to bring us . . .

Whether or not we admit it to ourselves, we are all haunted by a truly awful sense of impermanence. I have always had a particularly keen sense of this at New York cocktail parties, and perhaps that is why I drink the martinis almost as fast as I can snatch them from the tray. This sense is the febrile thing that hangs in the air. Horror of insincerity, of *not meaning*, overhangs these affairs like the cloud of cigarette smoke and the hectic chatter. This horror is the only thing, almost, that is left unsaid at such functions. All social functions involving a group of people not intimately known to each other are always under this shadow. They are almost always (in an unconscious way) like that last dinner of the condemned: where steak or turkey, whatever the doomed man wants, is served in his cell as a mockingly cruel reminder of what the great-big-little-transitory world had to offer.

In a play, time is arrested in the sense of being confined. By a sort of legerdemain, events are made to remain *events*, rather than being reduced so quickly to mere *occurrences*. The audience can sit back in a comforting dusk to watch a world which is flooded with light and in which emotion and action have a dimension and dignity that they would likewise have in real existence, if only the shattering intrusion of time could be locked out.

About their lives people ought to remember that when they are finished, everything in them will be contained in a marvelous state of repose which is the same as that which they unconsciously admired in drama. The rush is temporary. The great and only possible dignity of man lies in his power deliberately to choose certain moral values by which to live as steadfastly as if he, too, like a character in a play, were immured against the corrupting rush of time. Snatching the eternal out of the desperately fleeting is the great magic trick of human existence. As far as we know, as far as there exists any kind of empiric evidence, there is no way to beat the game of *being* against *non-being*, in which non-being is the predestined victor on realistic levels.

Yet plays in the tragic tradition offer us a view of certain moral values in violent juxtaposition. Because we do not participate, except as spectators, we can view them clearly, within the limits of our emotional equipment. These people on the stage do not return our looks. We do not have to answer their questions nor make any sign of being in company with them, nor do we have to compete with their virtues nor resist their offenses. All at once, for this reason, we are able to *see* them! Our hearts are wrung by recognition and pity, so that the dusky shell of the auditorium where we are gathered anonymously together is flooded with an almost liquid warmth of unchecked human sympathies, relieved of self-consciousness, allowed to function . . .

Men pity and love each other more deeply than they permit themselves to know. The moment after the phone has been hung up, the hand reaches for a scratch pad and scrawls a notation: "Funeral Tuesday at five, Church of the Holy Redeemer, don't forget flowers." And the same hand is only a little shakier than usual as it reaches, some minutes later, for a highball glass that will pour a stupefaction over the kindled nerves. Fear and evasion are the two little beasts that chase each other's tails in the revolving wire-cage of our nervous world. They distract us from feeling too much about things. Time rushes toward us with its hospital tray of infinitely varied narcotics, even while it is preparing us for its inevitably fatal operation . . .

So successfully have we disguised from ourselves the intensity of our own feelings, the sensibility of our own hearts, that plays in the tragic tradition have begun to seem untrue. For a couple of hours we may surrender ourselves to a world of fiercely illuminated values in conflict, but when the stage is covered and the auditorium lighted, almost immediately there is a recoil of disbelief. "Well, well!" we say as we shuffle back up the aisle, while the play dwindles behind us with the sudden perspective of an early Chirico painting. By the time we have arrived at Sardi's, if not as soon as we pass beneath the marquee, we have convinced ourselves once more that life has as little resemblance to the curiously stirring and meaningful occurrences on the stage as a jingle has to an elegy of Rilke.

This modern condition of his theater audience is something that an author must know in advance. The diminishing influence of life's destroyer, time, must be somehow worked into the context of his play. Perhaps it is a certain foolery, a certain distortion toward the grotesque, which will solve the problem for him. Perhaps it is only restraint, putting a mute on the strings that would like to break all bounds. But almost surely, unless he contrives in some way to relate the dimensions of his tragedy to the dimensions of a world in which time is *included*—he will be left among his magnificent debris on a dark stage, muttering to himself: "Those fools . . ."

And if they could hear him above the clatter of tongues, glasses, chinaware and silver, they would give him this answer: "But you have shown us a world not ravaged by time. We admire your innocence. But we have seen our photographs, past and present. Yesterday evening we passed our first wife on the street. We smiled as we spoke but we didn't really see her! It's too bad, but we know what is true and not true, and at 3 A.M. your disgrace will be in print!"

—*Tennessee Williams*

SCENES

ACT ONE

SCENE 1 Evening
SCENE 2 Almost morning, the next day
SCENE 3 Noon of that day
SCENE 4 A late spring morning, three years later
SCENE 5 Immediately following
SCENE 6 Two hours later that day

ACT TWO

SCENE 1 Two hours later that day

ACT THREE

SCENE 1 Evening of the same day
SCENE 2 Just before dawn of the next day
SCENE 3 Morning

AUTHOR'S PRODUCTION NOTES

The locale of the play is a village populated mostly by Sicilians somewhere along the Gulf Coast between New Orleans and Mobile. The time is the present.

As the curtain rises we hear a Sicilian folk-singer with a guitar. He is singing. At each major division of the play this song is resumed and it is completed at the final curtain.

The first lighting is extremely romantic. We see a frame cottage, in a rather poor state of repair, with a palm tree leaning dreamily over one end of it and a flimsy little entrance porch, with spindling pillars, sagging steps and broken rails, at the other end. The setting seems almost tropical, for, in addition to the palm trees, there are tall canes with feathery fronds and a fairly thick growth of pampas grass. These are growing on the slope of an embankment along which runs a highway, which is not visible, but the cars passing on it can occasionally be heard. The house has a rear door which cannot be seen. The facing wall of the cottage is either a transparency that lifts for the interior scenes, or is cut away to reveal the interior.

The romantic first lighting is that of late dusk, the sky a delicate blue with an opalescent shimmer more like water than air. Delicate points of light appear and disappear like lights reflected in a twilight harbor. The curtain rises well above the low tin roof of the cottage.

We see an interior that is as colorful as a booth at a carnival. There are many religious articles and pictures of ruby and gilt, the brass cage of a gaudy parrot, a large bowl of goldfish, cutglass decanters and vases, rose-patterned wallpaper and a rose-colored carpet; everything is exclamatory in its brightness like the projection of a woman's heart passionately in love. There is a small shrine against the wall between the rooms, consisting of a prie-dieu and a little statue of the Madonna in a starry blue robe and gold crown. Before this burns always a vigil light in its ruby glass cup. Our purpose is to show these gaudy, childlike mysteries with sentiment and humor in equal measure, without ridicule and with respect for the religious yearnings they symbolize.

An outdoor sign indicates that Serafina, whose home the cottage is, does "SEWING." *The interior furnishings give evidence of this vocation. The most salient feature is a collection of dressmaker's dummies. There are at least seven of these life-size mannequins, in various shapes and attitudes. (They will have to be made especially for the play as their purpose is not realistic. They have pliable joints so that their positions can be changed. Their arms terminate at the wrist. In all their attitudes there is an air of drama, somewhat like the poses of declamatory actresses of the old school.) Principal among them are a widow and a bride who face each other in violent attitudes, as though having a shrill argument, in the parlor. The widow's costume is complete from black-veiled hat to black slippers. The bride's featureless head wears a chaplet of orange blossoms from which is depended a flowing veil of white marquisette, and her net gown is trimmed in white satin—lustrous, immaculate.*

Most of the dummies and sewing equipment are confined to the dining room which is also Serafina's work room. In that room there is a tall cupboard on top of which are several dusty bottles of imported Sicilian Spumanti.

O slinger! crack the nut of my eye! my heart twittered with joy under the splendour of the quicklime, the bird sings O Senectus! . . . the streams are in their beds like the cries of women and this world has more beauty than a ram's skin painted red!

St. John Perse: *Anabasis*
T. S. ELIOT TRANSLATION

ACT ONE

It is the hour that the Italians call "prima sera," the beginning of dusk. Between the house and the palm tree burns the female star with an almost emerald lustre.

The mothers of the neighborhood are beginning to call their children home to supper, in voices near and distant, urgent and tender, like the variable notes of wind and water. There are three children: Bruno, Salvatore, and Vivi, ranged in front of the house, one with a red paper kite, one with a hoop, and the little girl with a doll dressed as a clown. They are in attitudes of momentary repose, all looking up at something—a bird or a plane passing over—as the mothers' voices call them.

BRUNO: The white flags are flying at the Coast Guard station.
SALVATORE: That means fair weather.
VIVI: I love fair weather.
GIUSEPPINA: Vivi! Vieni mangiare!
PEPPINA: Salvatore! Come home!
VIOLETTA: Bruno! Come home to supper!

(*The calls are repeated tenderly, musically.*

(*The interior of the house begins to be visible. Serafina delle Rose is seen on the parlor sofa, waiting for her husband Rosario's return. Between the curtains is a table set lovingly for supper; there is wine in a silver ice-bucket and a great bowl of roses.*

(*Serafina looks like a plump little Italian opera singer in the role of Madame Butterfly. Her black hair is done in a high pompadour that glitters like wet coal. A rose is held in place by glittering jet hairpins. Her voluptuous figure is sheathed in pale rose silk. On her feet are dainty slippers with glittering buckles and French heels. It is apparent from the way she sits, with such plump dignity, that she is wearing a tight girdle. She sits very erect, in an attitude of forced composure, her ankles daintily crossed and her plump little hands holding a yellow paper fan on which is painted a rose. Jewels gleam on her fingers, her wrists and her ears and about her throat. Expectancy shines in her eyes. For a few moments she seems to be posing for a picture.*

(*Rosa delle Rose appears at the side of the house, near the palm tree. Rosa, the daughter of the house, is a young girl of twelve. She is pretty and vivacious, and has about her a particular intensity in every gesture.*)

SERAFINA: Rosa, where are you?
ROSA: Here, Mama.
SERAFINA: What are you doing, cara?
ROSA: I've caught twelve lightning bugs.

(*The cracked voice of Assunta is heard, approaching.*)

SERAFINA: I hear Assunta! Assunta!

(*Assunta appears and goes into the house, Rosa following her in. Assunta is an old woman in a gray shawl, bearing a basket of herbs, for she is a fattuchiere, a woman who practises a simple sort of medicine. As she enters the children scatter.*)

ASSUNTA: Vengo, vengo. Buona sera. Buona sera. There is something wild in the air, no wind but everything's moving.
SERAFINA: I don't see nothing moving and neither do you.
ASSUNTA: Nothing is moving so you can see it moving, but everything is moving, and I can hear the star-noises. Hear them? Hear the star-noises?
SERAFINA: Naw, them ain't the star-noises. They're termites, eating the house up. What are you peddling, old woman, in those little white bags?
ASSUNTA: Powder, wonderful powder. You drop a pinch of it in your husband's coffee.
SERAFINA: What is it good for?
ASSUNTA: What is a husband good for! I make it out of the dry blood of a goat.
SERAFINA: Davero!
ASSUNTA: Wonderful stuff! But be sure you put it in his coffee at supper, not in his breakfast coffee.
SERAFINA: My husband don't need no powder!
ASSUNTA: Excuse me, Baronessa. Maybe he needs the opposite kind of a powder, I got that, too.
SERAFINA: Naw, naw, *no* kind of powder at all, old woman. (*She lifts her head with a proud smile.*)

(*Outside the sound of a truck is heard approaching up on the highway.*)

ROSA (*joyfully*): Papa's truck!

(*They stand listening for a moment, but the truck goes by without stopping.*)

SERAFINA (*to Assunta*): That wasn't him. It wasn't no 10-ton truck. It didn't rattle the shutters! Assunta, Assunta, undo a couple of hooks, the dress is tight on me!

ASSUNTA: Is it true what I told you?

SERAFINA: Yes, it is true, but nobody needed to tell me. Assunta, I'll tell you something which maybe you won't believe.

ASSUNTA: It is impossible to tell me anything that I don't believe.

SERAFINA: Va bene! Senti, Assunta!—I knew that I had conceived on the very night of conception! (*There is a phrase of music as she says this.*)

ASSUNTA: Ahhhh?

SERAFINA: Senti! That night I woke up with a burning pain on me, here, on my left breast! A pain like a needle, quick, quick, hot little stitches. I turned on the light, I uncovered my breast!—On it I saw the rose tattoo of my husband!

ASSUNTA: Rosario's tattoo?

SERAFINA: On me, on my breast, his tattoo! And when I saw it I knew that I had conceived . . .

(*Serafina throws her head back, smiling proudly, and opens her paper fan. Assunta stares at her gravely, then rises and hands her basket to Serafina.*)

ASSUNTA: Ecco! *You* sell the powders! (*She starts toward the door.*)

SERAFINA: You don't believe that I saw it?

ASSUNTA (*stopping*): Did Rosario see it?

SERAFINA: I screamed. But when he woke up, it was gone. It only lasted a moment. But I *did* see it, and I *did* know, when I seen it, that I had conceived, that in my body another rose was growing!

ASSUNTA: Did he believe that you saw it?

SERAFINA: No. He laughed.—He laughed and I cried . . .

ASSUNTA: And he took you into his arms, and you stopped crying!

SERAFINA: Si!

ASSUNTA: Serafina, for you everything has got to be different. A sign, a miracle, a wonder of some kind. You speak to Our Lady. You say that She answers your questions. She nods or shakes Her head at you. Look, Serafina, underneath Our Lady you have a candle. The wind through the shutters makes the candle flicker. The shadows move. Our Lady seems to be nodding!

SERAFINA: She gives me signs.

ASSUNTA: Only to you? Because you are more important? The wife of a barone? Serafina! In Sicily they called his uncle a baron, but in Sicily everybody's a baron that owns a piece of the land and a separate house for the goats!

SERAFINA: They said to his uncle "Voscenza!" and they kissed their hands to him! (*She kisses the back of her hand repeatedly, with vehemence.*)

ASSUNTA: His uncle in Sicily!—Si—But *here* what's he do? Drives a truck of bananas?

SERAFINA (*blurting out*): No! *Not* bananas!

ASSUNTA: Not bananas?

SERAFINA: Stai zitta! (*She makes a warning gesture.*)—No—Vieni qui, Assunta! (*She beckons her mysteriously. Assunta approaches.*)

ASSUNTA: Cosa dici?

SERAFINA: On top of the truck is bananas! But underneath—something else!

ASSUNTA: Che altre cose?

SERAFINA: Whatever it is that the Brothers Romano want hauled out of the state, he hauls it for them, underneath the bananas! (*She nods her head importantly.*) And money, he gets so much it spills from his pockets! Soon I don't have to make dresses!

ASSUNTA (*turning away*): Soon I think you will have to make a black veil!

SERAFINA: Tonight is the last time he does it! Tomorrow he quits hauling stuff for the Brothers Romano! He pays for the 10-ton truck and works for himself. We live with dignity in America, then! Own truck! Own house! And in the house will be everything electric! Stove—deep-freeze—*tutto!*—But tonight, stay with me . . . I can't swallow my heart!—Not till I hear the truck stop in front of the house and his key in the lock of the door!—When I call him, and him shouting back, *"Si, sono qui!"* In his hair, Assunta, he has—oil of roses. And when I wake up at night—the air, the dark room's—full of—roses . . . Each time is the first time with him. Time doesn't pass . . .

(*Assunta picks up a small clock on the cupboard and holds it to her ear.*)

ASSUNTA: Tick, tick, tick, tick.—You say the clock is a liar.

SERAFINA: No, the clock is a fool. I don't listen to it. My clock is my heart and my heart don't say tick-tick, it says love-love! And now I have two hearts in me, both of them saying love-love!

(*A truck is heard approaching, then passes. Serafina drops her fan. Assunta opens a bottle of spumanti with a loud pop. Serafina cries out.*)

ASSUNTA: Stai tranquilla! Calmati! (*She pours her a glass of wine.*) Drink this wine and before the glass is empty he'll be in your arms!

SERAFINA: I can't—swallow my heart!

ASSUNTA: A woman must not have a heart that is too big to swallow! (*She crosses to the door.*)

SERAFINA: Stay with me!

ASSUNTA: I have to visit a woman who drank rat poison because of a heart too big for her to swallow.

(*Assunta leaves. Serafina returns indolently to the sofa. She lifts her hands to her great swelling breasts and murmurs aloud:*)

SERAFINA: Oh, it's so wonderful, having *two* lives in the body, not *one* but two! (*Her hands slide down to her belly, luxuriously.*) I am heavy with life, I am big, big, big with life! (*She picks up a bowl of roses and goes into the back room.*)

(*Estelle Hohengarten appears in front of the house. She is a thin blonde woman in a dress of Egyptian design, and her blonde hair has an unnatural gloss in the clear, greenish dusk. Rosa appears from behind the house, calling out:*)

ROSA: Twenty lightning bugs, Mama!

ESTELLE: Little girl? Little girl?

ROSA (*resentfully*): Are you talking to me? (*There is a pause.*)

ESTELLE: Come here. (*She looks Rosa over curiously.*) You're a twig off the old rose-bush.—Is the lady that does the sewing in the house?

ROSA: Mama's at home.

ESTELLE: I'd like to see her.

ROSA: Mama?

SERAFINA: Dimi?

ROSA: There's a lady to see you.

SERAFINA: Oh. Tell her to wait in the parlor. (*Estelle enters and stares curiously about. She picks up a small framed picture on the cupboard. She is looking at it as Serafina enters with a bowl of roses. Serafina speaks sharply.*) That is my husband's picture.

ESTELLA: Oh!—I thought it was Valentino.—With a mustache.

SERAFINA (*putting the bowl down on the table*): You want something?

ESTELLE: Yes. I heard you do sewing.

SERAFINA: Yes, I do sewing.

ESTELLE: How fast can you make a shirt for me?

SERAFINA: That all depends. (*She takes the picture from Estelle and puts it back on the cupboard.*)

ESTELLE: I got the piece of silk with me. I want it made into a shirt for a man I'm in love with. Tomorrow's the anniversary of the day we met . . . (*She unwraps a piece of rose-colored silk which she holds up like a banner.*)

SERAFINA (*involuntarily*): Che bella stoffa!—Oh, that would be wonderful stuff for a lady's blouse or for a pair of pyjamas!

ESTELLE: I want a man's shirt made with it.

SERAFINA: Silk this color for a shirt for a *man*?

ESTELLE: This man is wild like a Gypsy.

SERAFINA: A woman should not encourage a man to be wild.

ESTELLE: A man that's wild is hard for a woman to hold, huh? But if he was tame—would the woman want to hold him? Huh?

SERAFINA: I am a married woman in business. I don't know nothing about wild men and wild women and I don't have much time—so . . .

ESTELLE: I'll pay you twice what you ask me.

(*Outside there is the sound of the goat bleating and the jingle of its harness; then the crash of wood splintering.*)

ROSA (*suddenly appearing at the door*): Mama, the black goat is loose! (*She runs down the steps and stands watching the goat. Serafina crosses to the door.*)

THE STREGA (*in the distance*): Hyeh, Billy, hyeh, hyeh, Billy!

ESTELLE: I'll pay you three times the price that you ask me for it.

SERAFINA (*shouting*): Watch the goat! Don't let him get in our yard! (*to Estelle*)—If I ask you five dollars?

ESTELLE: I will pay you fifteen. Make it twenty; money is not the object. But it's got to be ready tomorrow.

SERAFINA: Tomorrow?

ESTELLE: Twenty-five dollars! (*Serafina nods slowly with a stunned look. Estelle smiles.*) I've got the measurements with me.

SERAFINA: Pin the measurements and your name on the silk and the shirt will be ready tomorrow.

ESTELLE: My name is Estelle Hohengarten.

(*A little boy races excitedly into the yard.*)

THE BOY: Rosa, Rosa, the black goat's in your yard!

ROSA (*calling*): Mama, the goat's in the yard!

SERAFINA (*furiously, forgetting her visitor*): Il becco della strega!—Scusi! (*She runs out onto the porch.*) Catch him, catch him before he gets at the vines!

(*Rosa dances gleefully. The Strega runs into the yard. She has a mop of wild grey hair and is holding her black skirts up from her bare hairy legs. The sound of the goat's bleating and the jingling of his harness is heard in the windy blue dusk.*

(*Serafina descends the porch steps. The high-heeled slippers, the tight silk skirt and the dignity of a baronessa make the descent a little gingerly. Arrived in the yard, she directs the *goat-chase imperiously with her yellow paper fan, pointing this way and that, exclaiming in Italian.*

(*She fans herself rapidly and crosses back of the house. The goat evidently makes a sudden charge. Screaming, Serafina rushes back to the front of the house, all out of breath, the glittering pompadour beginning to tumble down over her forehead.*)

SERAFINA: Rosa! You go in the house! Don't look at the Strega!

(*Alone in the parlor, Estelle takes the picture of Rosario. Impetuously, she thrusts it in her purse and runs from the house, just as Serafina returns to the front yard.*)

ROSA (*refusing to move*): Why do you call her a witch?

(*Serafina seizes her daughter's arm and propels her into the house.*)

SERAFINA: She has a white eye and every finger is crooked. (*She pulls Rosa's arm.*)

ROSA: She has a cataract, Mama, and her fingers are crooked because she has rheumatism!

SERAFINA: Malocchio—the evil eye—*that's* what she's got! And her fingers are crooked because she shook hands with the devil. Go in the house and wash your face with salt water and throw the salt water away! *Go in! Quick!* She's coming!

(*The boy utters a cry of triumph.*

(*Serafina crosses abruptly to the porch. At the same moment the boy runs triumphantly around the house leading the captured goat by its bell harness. It is a middle-sized black goat with great yellow eyes. The Strega runs behind with the broken rope. As the grotesque little procession runs before her—the Strega, the goat and the children—Serafina cries out shrilly. She crouches over and covers her face. The Strega looks back at her with a derisive cackle.*)

SERAFINA: Malocchio! Malocchio!

(*Shielding her face with one hand, Serafina makes the sign of the horns with the other to ward off the evil eye. And the scene dims out.*)

SCENE TWO

It is just before dawn the next day. Father De Leo, a priest, and several black-shawled women, including Assunta, are standing outside the house. The interior of the house is very dim.

GIUSEPPINA: There is a light in the house.

PEPPINA: I hear the sewing machine!

VIOLETTA: There's Serafina! She's working. She's holding up a piece of rose-colored silk.

ASSUNTA: She hears our voices.

VIOLETTA: She's dropped the silk to the floor and she's . . .

GIUSEPPINA: Holding her throat! I think she . . .

PEPPINA: Who's going to tell her?

VIOLETTA: Father De Leo will tell her.

FATHER DE LEO: I think a woman should tell her. I think Assunta must tell her that Rosario is dead.

ASSUNTA: It will not be necessary to tell her. She will know when she sees us.

(*It grows lighter inside the house. Serafina is standing in a frozen attitude with her hand clutching her throat and her eyes staring fearfully toward the sound of voices.*)

ASSUNTA: I think she already knows what we have come to tell her!

FATHER DE LEO: Andiamo, Signore! We must go to the door.

(*They climb the porch steps. Assunta opens the door.*)

SERAFINA (*gasping*): Don't speak!

(*She retreats from the group, stumbling blindly backwards among the dressmaker's dummies. With a gasp she turns and runs out the back door. In a few moments we see her staggering about outside near the palm tree. She comes down in front of the house, and stares blindly off into the distance.*)

SERAFINA (*wildly*): Don't speak!

(*The voices of the women begin keening in the house. Assunta comes out and approaches Serafina with her arms extended. Serafina slumps to her knees, whispering hoarsely:* "Don't speak!" *Assunta envelopes her in the grey shawl of pity as the scene dims out.*)

SCENE THREE

It is noon of the same day. Assunta is removing a funeral wreath on the door of the house. A doctor and Father De Leo are on the porch.

THE DOCTOR: She's lost the baby. (*Assunta utters a low moan of pity and crosses herself.*) Serafina's a very strong woman and that won't kill her. But she is trying not to breathe. She's got to be watched and not allowed out of the bed. (*He removes a hypodermic and a small package from his bag and hands them to Assunta.*)—This is morphia. In the arm with the needle if she screams or struggles to get up again.

ASSUNTA: Capisco!

FATHER DE LEO: One thing I want to make plain. The body of Rosario must not be burned.

THE DOCTOR: Have you seen the "body of Rosario?"

FATHER DE LEO: Yes, I have seen his body.

THE DOCTOR: Wouldn't you say it was burned?

FATHER DE LEO: Of course the body was burned. When he was shot at the wheel of the truck, it crashed and caught fire. But deliberate cremation is not the same thing. It's an abomination in the sight of God.

THE DOCTOR: Abominations are something I don't know about.

FATHER DE LEO: The Church has set down certain laws.

THE DOCTOR: But the instructions of a widow have to be carried out.

FATHER DE LEO: Don't you know why she wants the body cremated? So she can keep the ashes here in the house.

THE DOCTOR: Well, why not, if that's any comfort to her?

FATHER DE LEO: Pagan idolatry is what I call it!

THE DOCTOR: Father De Leo, you love your people but you don't understand them. They find God in each other. And when they lose each other, they lose God and they're lost. And it's hard to help them.—Who is that woman?

(*Estelle Hohengarten has appeared before the house. She is black-veiled, and bearing a bouquet of roses.*)

ESTELLE: I am Estelle Hohengarten.

(*Instantly there is a great hubbub in the house. The women mourners flock out to the porch, whispering and gesticulating excitedly.*)

FATHER DE LEO: What have you come here for?

ESTELLE: To say good-bye to the body.

FATHER DE LEO: The casket is closed; the body cannot be seen. And you must never come here. The widow knows nothing about you. Nothing at all.

GIUSEPPINA: *We* know about you!

PEPPINA: Va via! Sporcacciona!

VIOLETTA: Puttana!

MARIELLA: Assassina!

TERESA: You sent him to the Romanos.

FATHER DE LEO: Shhh!

(*Suddenly the women swarm down the steps like a cloud of attacking birds, all crying out in Sicilian. Estelle crouches and bows her head defensively before their savage assault. The bouquet of roses is snatched from her black-gloved hands and she is flailed with them about the head and shoulders. The thorns catch her veil and tear it away from her head. She covers her white sobbing face with her hands.*)

FATHER DE LEO: Ferme! Ferme! Signore, fermate vi nel nome di Dio!—Have a little respect!

(*The women fall back from Estelle, who huddles weeping on the walk.*)

ESTELLE: See him, see him, just see him . . .

FATHER DE LEO: The body is crushed and burned. Nobody can see it. Now go away and don't ever come here again, Estelle Hohengarten!

THE WOMEN (*in both languages, wildly*): Va via, va via, go way.

(*Rosa comes around the house. Estelle turns and retreats. One of the mourners spits and kicks at the tangled veil and roses. Father De Leo leaves. The others return inside, except Rosa.*

(*After a few moments the child goes over to the roses. She picks them up and carefully untangles the veil from the thorns.*

(*She sits on the sagging steps and puts the black veil over her head. Then for the first time she begins to weep, wildly, histrionically. The little boy appears and gazes at her, momentarily impressed by her performance. Then he picks up a rubber ball and begins to bounce it.*

(*Rosa is outraged. She jumps up, tears off the veil and runs to the little boy, giving him a sound smack and snatching the ball away from him.*)

ROSA: Go home! My papa is dead!

(*The scene dims out, as the music is heard again.*)

SCENE FOUR

A June day, three years later. It is morning and the light is bright. A group of local mothers are storming Serafina's house, indignant over her delay in delivering the graduation dresses for their daughters. Most of the women are chattering continually in Sicilian, racing about the house and banging the doors and shutters. The scene moves swiftly and violently until the moment when Rosa finally comes out in her graduation dress.

GIUSEPPINA: Serafina! Serafina delle Rose!

PEPPINA: Maybe if you call her "Baronessa" she will answer the door. (*with a mocking laugh*) Call her "Baronessa" and kiss your hand to her when she opens the door.

GIUSEPPINA (*tauntingly*): Baronessa! (*She kisses her hand toward the door.*)

VIOLETTA: When did she promise your dress?

PEPPINA: All week she say, "Domani—domani—domani." But yestiddy I told her . . .

VIOLETTA: Yeah?

PEPPINA: Oh yeah. I says to her, "Serafina, domani's the high school graduation. I got to try the dress on my daughter *today*." "Domani," she says, "Sicuro! sicuro! sicuro!" So I start to go away. Then I hear a voice call, "Signora! Signora!" So I turn round and I see Serafina's daughter at the window.

VIOLETTA: Rosa?

PEPPINA: Yeah, Rosa. An' you know how?

VIOLETTA: How?

PEPPINA: *Naked!* Nuda, nuda! (*She crosses herself and repeats a prayer.*) In nominis padri et figlio et spiritus sancti. Aaahh!

VIOLETTA: What did she do?

PEPPINA: Do? She say, "Signora! Please, you call this numero and ask for Jack and tell Jack my clothes are lock up so I can't get out from the house." Then Serafina come and she grab-a the girl by the hair and she pull her way from the window and she slam the shutters right in my face!

GIUSEPPINA: Whatsa the matter the daughter?

VIOLETTA: Who is this boy? Where did she meet him?

PEPPINA: Boy! What boy? He's a sailor. (*At the word "sailor" the women say "Ahhh!"*) She met him at the high school dance and somebody tell Serafina. That's why she lock up the girl's clothes so she can't leave the house. She can't even go to the high school to take the examinations. Imagine!

VIOLETTA: Peppina, this time *you* go to the door, yeah?

PEPPINA: Oh yeah, I go. Now I'm getting nervous. (*The women all crowd to the door.*) Sera-feee-na!

VIOLETTA: Louder, louder!

PEPPINA: Apri la porta! Come on, come on!

THE WOMEN (*together*): Yeah, apri la porta! . . . Come on, hurry up! . . . Open up!

GIUSEPPINA: I go get-a police.

VIOLETTA: Whatsa matta? You want more trouble?

GIUSEPPINA: Listen, I pay in advance five dollars and get no dress. Now what she wear, my daughter, to graduate in? A couple of towels and a rose in the hair? (*There is a noise inside: a shout and running footsteps.*)

THE WOMEN: Something is going on in the house! I hear someone! Don't I? Don't you?

(*A scream and running footsteps are heard. The front door opens and Serafina staggers out onto the porch. She is wearing a soiled pink slip and her hair is wild.*)

SERAFINA: Aiuto! Aiuto! (*She plunges back into the house.*)

(*Miss Yorke, a spinsterish high school teacher, walks quickly up to the house. The Sicilian women, now all chattering at once like a cloud of birds, sweep about her as she approaches.*)

MISS YORKE: You ladies know I don't understand Italian! So, please . . .

(*She goes directly into the house. There are more outcries inside. The Strega comes and stands at the edge of the yard, cackling derisively.*)

THE STREGA (*calling back to someone*): The Wops are at it again!—She got the daughter lock up naked in there all week. Ho, ho, ho! She lock up all week—naked—shouting out the window tell people to call a number and give a message to Jack. Ho, ho, ho! I guess she's in trouble already, and only fifteen!—They ain't civilized, these Sicilians. In the old country they live in caves in the hills and the country's run by bandits. Ho, ho, ho! More of them coming over on the boats all the time. (*The door is thrown open again and Serafina reappears on the porch. She is acting wildly, as if demented.*)

SERAFINA (*gasping in a hoarse whisper*): She cut her wrist, my daughter, she cut her wrist! (*She runs out into the yard.*) Aiiii-eeee! Aiutatemi, aiutatemi! Call the dottore! (*Assunta rushes up to Serafina and supports her as she is about to fall to her knees in the yard.*) Get the knife away from her! Get the knife, please! Get the knife away from—she cut her wrist with—Madonna! Madonna mia . . .

ASSUNTA: Smettila, smettila, Serafina.

MISS YORKE (*coming out of the back room*): Mrs. Delle Rose, your daughter has not cut her wrist. Now come back into the house.

SERAFINA (*panting*): Che dice, che dice? Che cosa? Che cosa dice?

MISS YORKE: Your daughter's all right. Come back into the house. And you ladies please go away!

ASSUNTA: Vieni, Serafina. Andiamo a casa. (*She supports the heavy, sagging bulk of Serafina to the steps. As they climb the steps one of the Sicilian mothers advances from the whispering group.*)

GIUSEPPINA (*boldly*): Serafina, we don't go away until we get our dresses.

PEPPINA: The graduation begins and the girls ain't dressed.

(*Serafina's reply to this ill-timed request is a long, animal howl of misery as she is supported into the house. Miss Yorke follows and firmly closes the door upon the women, who then go around back of the house. The interior of the house is lighted up.*)

MISS YORKE (*to Serafina*): No, no, no, she's not bleeding. Rosa? Rosa, come here and show your mother that you are not bleeding to death.

(*Rosa appears silently and sullenly between the curtains that separate the two rooms. She has a small white handkerchief tied around one wrist. Serafina points at the wrist and cries out: "Aiieee!"*)

MISS YORKE (*severely*): Now *stop* that, Mrs. Delle Rose!

(*Serafina rushes to Rosa, who thrusts her roughly away.*)

ROSA: Lasciami stare, Mama!—I'm so ashamed I could die. This is the way she goes around all the time. She hasn't put on clothes since my father was killed. For three years she sits at the sewing machine and never puts a dress on or goes out of the house, and now she has locked my clothes up so *I* can't go out. She wants me to be like her, a freak of the neighborhood, the way she is! Next time, next time, I won't cut my wrist but my throat! I don't want to live locked up with a bottle of ashes! (*She points to the shrine.*)

ASSUNTA: Figlia, figlia, figlia, non devi parlare cosí!

MISS YORKE: Mrs. Delle Rose, please give me the key to the closet so that your daughter can dress for the graduation!

SERAFINA (*surrendering the key*): Ecco la—chiave . . . (*Rosa snatches the key and runs back through the curtains.*)

MISS YORKE: Now why did you lock her clothes up, Mrs. Delle Rose?

SERAFINA: The wrist is still bleeding!

MISS YORKE: No, the wrist is not bleeding. It's just a skin cut, a scratch. But the child is exhausted from all this excitement and hasn't eaten a thing in two or three days.

ROSA (*running into the dining room*): Four days! I only asked her one favor. Not to let me go out but to let Jack come to the house so she could meet him!—Then she locked my clothes up!

MISS YORKE: Your daughter missed her final examinations at the high school, but her grades have been so good that she will be allowed to graduate with her class and take the examinations later.—You understand me, Mrs. Delle Rose!

(*Rosa goes into the back of the house.*)

SERAFINA (*standing at the curtains*): See the way she looks at me? I've got a wild thing in the house, and her wrist is still bleeding!

MISS YORKE: Let's not have any more outbursts of emotion!

SERAFINA: Outbursts of—you make me sick! Sick! Sick at my stomach you make me! Your school, you make all this trouble! You give-a this dance where she gets mixed up with a sailor.

MISS YORKE: You are talking about the Hunter girl's brother, a sailor named Jack, who attended the dance with his sister?

SERAFINA: "Attended with sister!"—Attended with *sister!*—My daughter, she's nobody's sister!

(*Rosa comes out of the back room. She is radiantly beautiful in her graduation gown.*)

ROSA: Don't listen to her, don't pay any attention to her, Miss Yorke.—I'm ready to go to the high school.

SERAFINA (*stunned by her daughter's beauty, and speaking with a wheedling tone and gestures, as she crouches a little*): O tesoro, tesoro! Vieni qua, Rosa, cara!—Come here and kiss Mama one minute!—Don't go like that, now!

ROSA: Lasciami stare!

(*She rushes out on the porch. Serafina gazes after her with arms slowly drooping from their imploring gesture and jaw dropping open in a look of almost comic desolation.*)

SERAFINA: Ho solo te, solo te—in questo mondo!

MISS YORKE: Now, now, Mrs. Delle Rose, no more excitement, please!

SERAFINA (*suddenly plunging after them in a burst of fury*): Senti, senti, per favore!

ROSA: Don't you dare come out on the street like that!—*Mama!*

(*She crouches and covers her face in shame, as Serafina heedlessly plunges out into the front yard in her shocking deshabille, making wild gestures.*)

SERAFINA: You give this dance where she gets mixed up with a sailor. What do you think you want to do at this high school? (*In weeping despair, Rosa runs to the porch.*) How high is this high school? Listen, how high is this high school? Look, look, look, I will show you! It's high as that horse's dirt out there in the street! (*Serafina points violently out in front of the house.*) Si! 'Sta fetentissima scuola! Scuola maledetta!

(*Rosa cries out and rushes over to the palm tree, leaning against it, with tears of mortification.*)

MISS YORKE: Mrs. Delle Rose, you are talking and behaving extremely badly. I don't understand how a woman that acts like you could have such a sweet and refined young girl for a daughter!—You don't deserve it!—Really . . . (*She crosses to the palm tree.*)

SERAFINA: Oh, you want me to talk refined to you, do you? Then do me one thing! Stop ruining the girls at the high school! (*As Serafina paces about, she swings her hips in the exaggeratedly belligerent style of a parading matador.*)

ASSUNTA: Piantala, Serafina! Andiamo a casa!

SERAFINA: No, no, I ain't through talking to this here teacher!

ASSUNTA: Serafina, look at yourself, you're not dressed!

SERAFINA: I'm dressed okay; I'm not naked! (*She glares savagely at the teacher by the palm tree. The Sicilian mothers return to the front yard.*)

ASSUNTA: Serafina, cara? Andiamo a casa, adesso!—Basta! Basta!

SERAFINA: Aspetta!

ROSA: I'm so ashamed I could die, I'm so ashamed. Oh, you don't know, Miss Yorke, the way that we live. She never puts on a dress; she stays all the time in that dirty old pink slip!—And talks to my father's ashes like he was living.

SERAFINA: Teacher! Teacher, senti! What do you think you want to do at this high school? Sentite! per favore! You give this a dance! What kind of a spring dance is it? Answer this question, please, for me! What kind of a spring dance is it? She meet this boy there who don't even go to no high school. What kind of a boy? Guardate! *A sailor that wears a gold earring!* That kind of a boy is the kind of boy she meets there!—That's why I lock her clothes up so she can't go back to the high school! (*suddenly to Assunta*) She cut her wrist! It's still bleeding! (*She strikes her forehead three times with her fist.*)

ROSA: Mama, you look disgusting! (*She rushes away.*)

(*Miss Yorke rushes after her. Serafina shades her eyes with one hand to watch them departing down the street in the brilliant spring light.*)

SERAFINA: Did you hear what my daughter said to me?—"You look—disgusting."—She calls me . . .

ASSUNTA: Now, Serafina, we must go in the house. (*She leads her gently to the porch of the little house.*)

SERAFINA (*proudly*): How pretty she look, my daughter, in the white dress, like a bride! (*to all*) Excuse me! Excuse me, please! Go away! Get out of my yard!

GIUSEPPINA (*taking the bull by the horns*): No, we ain't going to go without the dresses!

ASSUNTA: Give the ladies the dresses so the girls can get dressed for the graduation.

SERAFINA: That one there, she only paid for the goods. I charge for the work.

GIUSEPPINA: Ecco! I got the money!

THE WOMEN: We *got* the money!

SERAFINA: The names are pinned on the dresses. Go in and get them. (*She turns to Assunta.*) Did you hear what my daughter called me? She called me "disgusting!"

(*Serafina enters the house, slamming the door. After a moment the mothers come out, cradling the white voile dresses tenderly in their arms, murmuring "carino!" and "bellissimo!"*

(*As they disappear the inside light is brought up and we see Serafina standing before a glazed mirror, looking at herself and repeating the daughter's word.*)

SERAFINA: Disgusting!

(*The music is briefly resumed to mark a division.*)

SCENE FIVE

Immediately following. Serafina's movements gather momentum. She snatches a long-neglected girdle out of a bureau drawer and holds it experimentally about her waist. She shakes her head doubtfully, drops the girdle and suddenly snatches the $8.98 hat off the millinery dummy and plants it on her head. She turns around distractedly, not remembering where the mirror is. She gasps with astonishment when she catches sight of herself, snatches the hat off and hastily restores it to the blank head of the dummy. She makes another confused revolution or two, then gasps with fresh inspiration and snatches a girlish frock off a dummy—an Alice blue gown with daisies crocheted on it. The dress sticks on the dummy. Serafina mutters savagely in Sicilian. She finally overcomes this difficulty but in her exasperation she knocks the dummy over. She throws off the robe and steps hopefully into the gown. But she discovers it won't fit over her hips. She seizes the girdle again; then hurls it angrily away. The parrot calls to her; she yells angrily back at the parrot: "Zitto!"

In the distance the high school band starts playing. Serafina gets panicky that she will miss the graduation ceremonies, and hammers her forehead with her fist, sobbing a little. She wriggles despairingly out of the blue dress and runs out back in her rayon slip just as Flora and Bessie appear outside the house. Flora and Bessie are two female clowns of middle years and juvenile temperament. Flora is tall and angular; Bessie is rather stubby. They are dressed for a gala. Flora runs up the steps and bangs at the cottage door.

BESSIE: I fail to understand why it's so important to pick up a polka-dot blouse when it's likely to make us miss the twelve o'clock train.

FLORA: Serafina! Serafina!

BESSIE: We only got fifteen minutes to get to the depot and I'll get faint on the train if I don't have m' coffee . . .

FLORA: Git a coke on th' train, Bessie.

BESSIE: Git nothing on the train if we don't git the train!

(*Serafina runs back out of the bedroom, quite breathless, in a purple silk dress. As she passes the millinery dummy she snatches the hat off again and plants it back on her head.*)

SERAFINA: Wrist-watch! Wrist-watch! Where'd I put th' wrist-watch? (*She hears Flora shouting and banging and rushes to the door.*)

BESSIE: Try the door if it ain't open.

FLORA (*pushing in*): Just tell me, is it ready or not?

SERAFINA: Oh! You. Don't bother me. I'm late for the graduation of my daughter and now I can't find her graduation present.

FLORA: You got plenty of time.

SERAFINA: Don't you hear the band playing?

FLORA: They're just warming up. Now, Serafina, where is my blouse?

SERAFINA: Blouse? Not ready! I had to make fourteen graduation dresses!

FLORA: A promise is a promise and an excuse is just an excuse!

SERAFINA: I got to get to the high school!

FLORA: I got to get to the depot in that blouse!

BESSIE: We're going to the American Legion parade in New Orleans.

FLORA: There, there, there, there it is! (*She grabs the blouse from the machine.*) Get started, woman, stitch them bandanas together! If you don't do it, I'm a-gonna report you to the Chamber of Commerce and git your license revoked!

SERAFINA (*anxiously*): What license you talking about? I got no license!

FLORA: You hear that, Bessie? *She hasn't got no license!*

BESSIE: *She ain't even got a license?*

SERAFINA (*crossing quickly to the machine*): I—I'll stitch them together! But if you make me late to my daughter's graduation, I'll make you sorry some way . . .

(*She works with furious rapidity. A train whistle is heard.*)

BESSIE (*wildly and striking at Flora with her purse*): Train's pullin' out! Oh, God, you made us miss it!

FLORA: Bessie, you know there's another at 12:45!

BESSIE: It's the selfish—principle of it that makes me sick! (*She walks rapidly up and down.*)

FLORA: Set down, Bessie. Don't wear out your feet before we git to th' city . . .

BESSIE: Molly tole me the town was full of excitement. They're dropping paper sacks full of water out of hotel windows.

FLORA: Which hotel are they dropping paper sacks out of?

BESSIE: What a fool question! The Monteleone Hotel.

FLORA: That's an old-fashioned hotel.

BESSIE: It might be old-fashioned but you'd be surprised at some of the modern, up-to-date things that go on there.

FLORA: I heard, I heard that the Legionnaires caught a girl on Canal Street! They tore the clothes off her and sent her home in a taxi!

BESSIE: I double dog dare anybody to try that on me!

FLORA: You?! Huh! You never need any assistance gittin' undressed!

SERAFINA (*ominously*): You two ladies watch how you talk in there. This here is a Catholic house. You are sitting in the same room with Our Lady and with the blessed ashes of my husband!

FLORA (*acidly*): Well, ex-cuse *me*! (*She whispers maliciously to Bessie.*) It sure is a pleasant surprise to see you wearing a dress, Serafina, but the surprise would be twice as pleasant if it was more the right size. (*to Bessie, loudly*) She used to have a sweet figure, a little bit plump but attractive, but setting there at that sewing machine for three years in a kimona and not stepping out of the house has naturally given her hips!

SERAFINA: If I didn't have hips I would be a very uncomfortable woman when I set down.

(*The parrot squawks. Serafina imitates its squawk.*)

FLORA: Polly want a cracker?

SERAFINA: No. He don't want a cracker! What is she doing over there at that window?

BESSIE: Some Legionnaires are on the highway!

FLORA: A Legionnaire? No kidding?

(*She springs up and joins her girl friend at the window. They both laugh fatuously, bobbing their heads out the window.*)

BESSIE: He's looking this way; yell something!

FLORA (*leaning out the window*): Mademoiselle from Armentieres, parley-voo!

BESSIE (*chiming in rapturously*): Mademoiselle from Armentieres, parley-voo!

A VOICE OUTSIDE (*gallantly returning the salute*): Mademoiselle from Armentieres, hadn't been kissed for forty years!

BOTH GIRLS (*together; very gaily*): Hinky-dinky parley-voooo!

(*They laugh and applaud at the window. The Legionnaires are heard laughing. A car horn is heard as the Legionnaires drive away. Serafina springs up and rushes over to the window, jerks them away from it and slams the shutters in their faces.*)

SERAFINA (*furiously*): I told you wimmen that you was not in a honky-tonk! Now take your blouse and git out! Get out on the streets where you kind a wimmen belong.—This is the house of Rosario delle Rose and those are his ashes in that marble urn and I won't have—unproper things going on here or dirty talk, neither!

FLORA: Who's talking dirty?

BESSIE: What a helluva nerve.

FLORA: I want you to listen!

SERAFINA: You are, you are, dirty talk, all the time men, men, men! You men-crazy things, you!

FLORA: Sour grapes—sour grapes is your trouble! You're wild with envy!

BESSIE: Isn't she green with jealousy? Huh!

SERAFINA (*suddenly and religiously*): When I think of men I think about my husband. My husband was a Sicilian. We had love together every night of the week, we never skipped one, from the night we was married till the night he was killed in his fruit truck on that road there! (*She catches her breath in a sob.*) And maybe that is the reason I'm not man-crazy and don't like hearing the talk of women that are. But I am interested, now, in the happiness of my daughter who's graduating this morning out of high school. And now I'm going to be late, the band is playing! And I have lost her wrist watch!—her graduation present! (*She whirls about distractedly.*)

BESSIE: Flora, let's go!—The hell with that goddam blouse!

FLORA: Oh, no, just wait a minute! I don't accept insults from no one!

SERAFINA: Go on, go on to New Orleans, you two man-crazy things, you! And pick up a man on Canal Street but not in my house, at my window, in front of my dead husband's ashes! (*The high school band is playing a martial air in the distance. Serafina's chest is heaving violently; she touches her heart and momentarily seems to forget that she must go.*) I am not at all interested, I am not interested in men getting fat and bald in soldier-boy play suits, tearing the clothes off girls on Canal Street and dropping paper sacks out of hotel windows. I'm just not interested in that sort of man-crazy business. I remember my husband with a body like a young boy and hair on his head as thick and black as mine is and skin on him smooth and sweet as a yellow rose petal.

FLORA: Oh, a *rose*, was he?

SERAFINA: Yes, yes, a rose, a rose!

FLORA: Yes, a rose of a Wop!—of a gangster!—shot smuggling dope under a load of bananas!

BESSIE: Flora, Flora, let's go!

SERAFINA: My folks was peasants, contadini, but he—he come from *land*-owners! *Signorile*, my husband!—At night I sit here and I'm satisfied to remember, because I had the best.—Not the third best and not the second best, but the *first* best, the *only* best!—So now I stay here and am satisfied now to remember, . . .

BESSIE: Come on, come out! To the depot!

FLORA: Just wait, I wanta hear this, it's too good to miss!

SERAFINA: I count up the nights I held him all night in my arms, and I can tell you how many. Each night for twelve years. Four thousand—three hundred—and eighty. The number of nights I held him all night in my arms. Sometimes I didn't sleep, just held him all night in my arms. And I am satisfied with it. I grieve for him. Yes, my pillow at night's never dry—but I'm satisfied to remember. And I would feel cheap and degraded and not fit to live with my daughter or under the roof with the urn of his blessed ashes, those—ashes of a rose—if after that memory, after knowing that man, I went to some other, some middle-aged man, not young, not full of young passion, but getting a pot belly on him and losing his hair and smelling of sweat and liquor—and trying to fool myself that *that* was love-making! I *know* what love-making was. And I'm satisfied just to remember . . . (*She is panting as though she had run upstairs.*) Go on, you do it, you go on the streets and let them drop their sacks of dirty water on you!—I'm satisfied to remember the love of a man that was mine—*only mine*! Never touched by the hand of *nobody*! *Nobody* but *me*!—Just me! (*She gasps and runs out to the porch. The sun floods her figure. It seems to astonish her. She finds herself sobbing. She digs in her purse for her handkerchief.*)

FLORA (*crossing to the open door*): Never touched by nobody?

SERAFINA (*with fierce pride*): Never nobody but me!

FLORA: *I* know somebody that could a tale unfold! And not so far from here neither. Not no further than the Square Roof is, that place on Esplanade!

BESSIE: Estelle Hohengarten!

FLORA: Estelle Hohengarten!—the blackjack dealer from Texas!

BESSIE: Get into your blouse and let's go!

FLORA: Everybody's known it but Serafina. I'm just telling the facts that come out at the inquest while she was in bed with her eyes shut tight and the sheet pulled over her head like a female ostrich! Tie this damn thing on me! It was a romance, not just a fly-by-night thing, but a steady affair that went on for more than a year.

(*Serafina has been standing on the porch with the door open behind her. She is in the full glare of the sun. She appears to have been struck senseless by the words shouted inside. She turns slowly about. We see that her dress is unfastened down the back, the pink slip showing. She reaches out gropingly with one hand and finds the porch column which she clings to while the terrible words strike constantly deeper. The high school band continues as a merciless counterpoint.*)

BESSIE: Leave her in ignorance. Ignorance is bliss.

FLORA: He had a rose tattoo on his chest, the stuck-up thing, and Estelle was so gone on him she went down to Bourbon Street and had one put on her. (*Serafina comes onto the porch and Flora turns to her, viciously.*) Yeah, a rose tattoo on her chest same as the Wop's!

SERAFINA (*very softly*): Liar . . . (*She comes inside; the word seems to give her strength.*)

BESSIE (*nervously*): Flora, let's go, let's go!

SERAFINA (*in a terrible voice*): Liar!—*Lie*-arrrrr!

(*She slams the wooden door shut with a violence that shakes the walls.*)

BESSIE (*shocked into terror*): Let's get outa here, Flora!

FLORA: Let her howl her head off. I don't care.

(*Serafina has snatched up a broom.*)

BESSIE: What's she up to?

FLORA: I don't care what she's up to!

BESSIE: I'm a-scared of these Wops.

FLORA: I'm not afraid of nobody!

BESSIE: She's gonna hit you.

FLORA: She'd better not hit me!

(*But both of the clowns are in retreat to the door. Serafina suddenly rushes at them with the broom. She flails Flora about the hips and shoulders. Bessie gets out. But Flora is trapped in a corner. A table is turned over. Bessie, outside, screams for the police and cries:* "Murder! Murder!" *The high school band is playing* The Stars and Stripes Forever. *Flora breaks wildly past the flailing broom and escapes out of the house. She also takes up the cry for help. Serafina follows them out. She is flailing the brilliant noon air with the broom. The two women run off, screaming.*)

FLORA (*calling back*): I'm going to have her arrested! Police, police! I'm going to have you arrested!

SERAFINA: *Have* me arrested, *have* me, you dirt, you devil, you *liar*! Li-i-arrrr!

(*She comes back inside the house and leans on the work table for a moment, panting heavily. Then she rushes back to the door, slams it and bolts it. Then she rushes to the windows, slams the shutters and fastens them. The house is now dark except for the vigil light in the ruby glass cup before the Madonna, and the delicate beams admitted through the shutter slats.*)

SERAFINA (*in a crazed manner*): Have me—have me—arrested—dirty slut—bitch—liar! (*She moves about helplessly, not knowing what to do with her big, stricken body. Panting for breath, she repeats the word "liar" monotonously and helplessly as she thrashes about. It is necessary for her, vitally necessary for her, to believe that the woman's story is a malicious invention. But the words of it stick in her mind and she mumbles them aloud as she thrashes crazily around the small confines of the parlor.*) Woman—Estelle— (*The sound of band music is heard.*) Band, band, already—started.—Going to miss—graduation. Oh! (*She retreats toward the Madonna.*) Estelle, Estelle Hohengarten?—"A shirt for a man I'm in love with! This man—is—wild like a gypsy."—Oh, oh, Lady—The—rose-colored—silk. (*She starts toward the dining room, then draws back in terror.*) No, no, no, no, no! I don't remember! It wasn't that name, I don't remember the name! (*The band music grows louder.*) High school—graduation—late! I'll be—late for it.—Oh, Lady, give me a—*sign*! (*She cocks her head toward the statue in a fearful listening attitude.*) Che? Che dice, Signora? *Oh, Lady! Give me a sign!*

(*The scene dims out.*)

SCENE SIX

It is two hours later. The interior of the house is in complete darkness except for the vigil light. With the shutters closed, the interior is so dark that we do not know Serafina is present. All that we see clearly is the starry blue robe of Our Lady above the flickering candle of the ruby glass cup. After a few moments we hear Serafina's voice, very softly, in the weak, breathless tone of a person near death.

SERAFINA (*very softly*): Oh, Lady, give me a sign . . .

(*Gay, laughing voices are heard outside the house. Rosa and Jack appear, bearing roses and gifts. They are shouting back to others in a car.*)

JACK: Where do we go for the picnic?

A GIRL'S VOICE (*from the highway*): We're going in three sailboats to Diamond Key.

A MAN'S VOICE: Be at Municipal Pier in half an hour.

ROSA: Pick us up here! (*She races up the steps.*) Oh, the door's locked! Mama's gone *out*! There's a key in that bird bath.

(*Jack opens the door. The parlor lights up faintly as they enter.*)

JACK: It's dark in here.

ROSA: Yes, Mama's gone out!

JACK: How do you know she's out?

ROSA: The door was locked and all the shutters are closed! Put down those roses.

JACK: Where shall I . . .

ROSA: Somewhere, anywhere!—Come here! (*He approaches her rather diffidently.*) I want to teach you a little Dago word. The word is "bacio."

JACK: What does this word mean?

ROSA: This and this and this! (*She rains kisses upon him till he forcibly removes her face from his.*) Just think. A week ago Friday—I didn't know boys existed!—Did you know girls existed before the dance?

JACK: Yes, I knew they existed . . .

ROSA (*holding him*): Do you remember what you said to me on the dance floor? "Honey, you're dancing too close?"

JACK: Well, it was—hot in the Gym and the—floor was crowded.

ROSA: When my girl friend was teaching me how to dance, I asked her, "How do you know which way the boy's going to move?" And she said, "You've got to feel how he's going to move with your body!" I said, "How do you feel with your body?" And she said, "By pressing up close!"—That's why I pressed up close! I didn't realize that I was—Ha, ha! Now you're blushing! Don't go *away*!—And a few minutes later you said to me, "Gee, you're beautiful!" I said, "Excuse me," and ran to the ladies' room. Do you know why? To look at myself in the mirror! And I saw that I was! For the first time in my life I was beautiful! You'd made me beautiful when you *said* that I was!

JACK (*humbly*): You *are* beautiful, Rosa! So much, I . . .

ROSA: *You've* changed, *too.* You've stopped laughing and joking. Why have you gotten so old and serious, Jack?

JACK: Well, honey, you're sort of . . .

ROSA: What am I "sort of?"

JACK (*finding the exact word*): *Wild!* (*She laughs. He seizes the bandaged wrist.*) I didn't know nothing like this was going to happen.

ROSA: Oh, that, that's nothing! I'll take the handkerchief off and you can forget it.

JACK: How could you do a thing like that over me? I'm—nothing!

ROSA: Everybody is nothing until you love them!

JACK: Give me that handkerchief. I want to show it to my shipmates. I'll say, "This is the blood of a beautiful girl who cut her wrist with a knife because she loved me!"

ROSA: Don't be so pleased with yourself. It's mostly Mercurochrome!

SERAFINA (*violently, from the dark room adjoining*): *Stai zitta!—Cretina!*

(*Rosa and Jack draw abruptly apart.*)

JACK (*fearfully*): I knew somebody was here!

ROSA (*sweetly and delicately*): Mama? Are you in there, Mama?

SERAFINA: No, no, no, I'm not, I'm dead and buried!

ROSA: Yes, Mama's in there!

JACK: Well, I—better go and—wait outside for a—while . . .

ROSA: You stay right here!—Mama?—Jack is with me.—Are you dressed up nicely? (*There is no response.*) Why's it so dark in here?—Jack, open the shutters!—I want to introduce you to my mother . . .

JACK: Hadn't I better go and . . .

ROSA: No. Open the shutters!

(*The shutters are opened and Rosa draws apart the curtains between the two rooms. Sunlight floods the scene. Serafina is revealed slumped in a chair at her work table in the dining room near the Singer sewing machine. She is grotesquely surrounded by the dummies, as though she had been holding a silent conference with them. Her appearance, in slovenly deshabille, is both comic and shocking.*)

ROSA (*terribly embarrassed*): Mama, Mama, you said you were dressed up pretty! Jack, stay out for a minute! What's happened, Mama?

(*Jack remains in the parlor. Rosa pulls the curtains, snatches a robe and flings it over Serafina. She brushes Serafina's hair back from her sweat-gleaming face, rubs her face with a handkerchief and dusts it with powder. Serafina submits to this cosmetic enterprise with a dazed look.*)

ROSA (*gesturing vertically*): Su, su, su, su, su, su, su, su, su!

(*Serafina sits up slightly in her chair, but she is still looking stupefied. Rosa returns to the parlor and opens the curtains again.*)

ROSA: Come in, Jack! Mama is ready to meet you!

(*Rosa trembles with eagerness as Jack advances nervously from the parlor. But before he enters Serafina collapses again into her slumped position, with a low moan.*)

ROSA (*violently*): Mama, Mama, su, Mama! (*Serafina sits half erect.*) She didn't sleep good last night.—Mama, this is Jack Hunter!

JACK: Hello, Mrs. Delle Rose. It sure is a pleasure to meet you.

(*There is a pause. Serafina stares indifferently at the boy.*)

ROSA: Mama, Mama, say something!

JACK: Maybe your Mama wants me to . . . (*He makes an awkward gesture toward the door.*)

ROSA: No, no, Mama's just tired. Mama makes dresses; she made a whole lot of dresses for the graduation! How many, Mama, how many graduation dresses did you have to make?

SERAFINA (*dully*): Fa niente . . .

JACK: I was hoping to see you at the graduation, Mrs. Delle Rose.

ROSA: I guess that Mama was too worn out to go.

SERAFINA: Rosa, shut the front door, shut it and lock it. There was a—policeman . . . (*There is a pause.*) What?—What?

JACK: My sister was graduating. My mother was there and my aunt was there—a whole bunch of cousins—I was hoping that you could—all—get together . . .

ROSA: Jack brought you some flowers.

JACK: I hope you are partial to roses as much as I am. (*He hands her the bouquet. She takes them absently.*)

ROSA: Mama, say something, say something simple like "Thanks."

SERAFINA: Thanks.

ROSA: Jack, tell Mama about the graduation; describe it to her.

JACK: My mother said it was just like fairyland.

ROSA: Tell her what the boys wore!

JACK: What did—what did they wear?

ROSA: Oh, you know what they wore. They wore blue coats and white pants and each one had a carnation! And there were three couples that did an old-fashioned dance, a minuet, Mother, to Mendelssohn's *Spring Song*! Wasn't it lovely, Jack? But one girl slipped; she wasn't used to long dresses! She slipped and fell on her—ho, ho! Wasn't it funny, Jack, wasn't it, wasn't it, Jack?

JACK (*worriedly*): I think that your Mama . . .

ROSA: Oh, my prize, my prize, I have forgotten my prize!

JACK: Where is it?

ROSA: You set them down by the sewing sign when you looked for the key.

JACK: Aw, excuse me, I'll get them. (*He goes out through the parlor. Rosa runs to her mother and kneels by her chair.*)

ROSA (*in a terrified whisper*): Mama, something has happened! What has happened, Mama? Can't you tell me, Mama? Is it because of this morning? Look. I took the bandage off, it was only a scratch! So, Mama, forget it! Think it was just a bad dream that never happened! Oh, Mama! (*She gives her several quick kisses on the forehead. Jack returns with two big books tied in white satin ribbon.*)

JACK: Here they are.

ROSA: Look what I got, Mama.

SERAFINA (*dully*): What?

ROSA: The Digest of Knowledge!

JACK: Everything's in them, from Abracadabra to Zoo! My sister was jealous. She just got a diploma!

SERAFINA (*rousing a bit*): Diploma, where is it? Didn't you get no diploma?

ROSA: Si, si, Mama! Eccolo! Guarda, guarda! (*She holds up the diploma tied in ribbon.*)

SERAFINA: Va bene.—Put it in the drawer with your father's clothes.

JACK: Mrs. Delle Rose, you should be very, very proud of your daughter. She stood in front of the crowd and recited a poem.

ROSA: Yes, I did. Oh, I was so excited!

JACK: And Mrs. Delle Rose, your daughter, Rosa, was so pretty when she walked on the stage—that people went "Oooooooooo!"—like that! Y'know what I mean? They all went—"Oooooooo!" Like a—like a—*wind* had—blown over! Because your daughter, Rosa, was so—*lovely* looking! (*He has crouched over to Serafina to deliver this description close to her face. Now he straightens up and smiles proudly at Rosa.*) How does it feel to be the mother of the prettiest girl in the world?

ROSA (*suddenly bursting into pure delight*): Ha, ha, ha, ha, ha, ha! (*She throws her head back in rapture.*)

SERAFINA (*rousing*): Hush!

ROSA: Ha, ha, ha, ha, ha, ha, ha, ha, ha, ha! (*She cannot control her ecstatic laughter. She presses her hand to her mouth but the laughter still bubbles out.*)

SERAFINA (*suddenly rising in anger*): Pazza, pazza, pazza! Finiscila! Basta, via! (*Rosa whirls around to hide her convulsions of joy. To Jack:*) Put the prize books in the parlor, and shut the front door; there was a policeman come here because of—some trouble . . . (*Jack takes the books.*)

ROSA: Mama, I've never seen you like this! What will Jack think, Mama?

SERAFINA: Why do I care what Jack thinks?—You wild, wild crazy thing, you—with the eyes of your—father . . .

JACK (*returning*): Yes, ma'am, Mrs. Delle Rose, you certainly got a right to be very proud of your daughter.

SERAFINA (*after a pause*): I am proud of the—memory of her—father.—He was a baron . . . (*Rosa takes Jack's arm.*) And who are *you*? What are you?—per piacere!

ROSA: Mama, I just introduced him; his name is Jack Hunter.

SERAFINA: Hunt-er?

JACK: Yes, ma'am, Hunter. Jack Hunter.

SERAFINA: What are you hunting?—Jack?

ROSA: Mama!

SERAFINA: What all of 'em are hunting? To have a good time, and the Devil cares who pays for it? I'm sick of men, I'm almost as sick of men as I am of wimmen.—Rosa, get out while I talk to this boy!

ROSA: I didn't bring Jack here to be insulted!

JACK: Go on, honey, and let your Mama talk to me. I think your Mama has just got a slight wrong—impression . . .

SERAFINA (*ominously*): Yes, I got an impression!

ROSA: I'll get dressed! Oh, Mama, don't spoil it for me!—the happiest day of my life! (*She goes into the back of the house.*)

JACK (*after an awkward pause*): Mrs. Delle Rose . . .

SERAFINA (*correcting his pronunciation*): Dell*e* Ros*e*!

JACK: Mrs. Delle Rose, I'm sorry about all this. Believe me, Mrs. Delle Rose, the last thing I had in mind was getting mixed up in a family situation. I come home after three months to sea, I docked at New Orleans, and come here to see my folks. My sister was going to a high school dance. She took me with her, and there I met your daughter.

SERAFINA: What did you do?

JACK: At the high school dance? We danced! My sister had told me that Rosa had a very strict mother and wasn't allowed to go on dates with boys so when it was over, I said, "I'm sorry you're not allowed to go out." And she said, "Oh! What gave you the idea I *wasn't!*" So then I thought my sister had made a mistake and I made a date with her for the next night.

SERAFINA: What did you do the next night?

JACK: The next night we went to the movies.

SERAFINA: And what did you do—that night?

JACK: At the movies? We ate a bag of popcorn and watched the movie!

SERAFINA: She come home at midnight and said she had been with a girl-friend studying "civics."

JACK: Whatever story she told you, it ain't my fault!

SERAFINA: And the night after that?

JACK: Last Tuesday? We went roller skating!

SERAFINA: And afterwards?

JACK: After the skating? We went to a drug store and had an ice cream soda!

SERAFINA: Alone?

JACK: At the drug store? No. It was crowded. And the skating rink was full of people skating!

SERAFINA: You mean that you haven't been alone with my Rosa?

JACK: Alone or not alone, what's the point of that question? I still don't see the point of it.

SERAFINA: We are Sicilians. We don't leave the girls with the boys they're not engaged to!

JACK: Mrs. Delle Rose, this is the United States.

SERAFINA: But we are Sicilians, and we are not cold-blooded. —My girl is a *virgin*! She *is*—or she *was*—I would like to know—*which*!

JACK: Mrs. Delle Rose! I got to tell you something. You might not believe it. It is a hard thing to say. But I am—*also* a—*virgin* . . .

SERAFINA: *What? No.* I do not believe it.

JACK: Well, it's true, though. This is the first time—I . . .

SERAFINA: First time you *what*?

JACK: The first time I really wanted to . . .

SERAFINA: Wanted to what?

JACK: Make—love . . .

SERAFINA: You? A sailor?

JACK (*sighing deeply*): Yes, ma'am. I had opportunities to!—But I—always thought of my mother . . . I always asked myself, would she or would she not—think—this or that person was—decent!

SERAFINA: But with my daughter, my Rosa, your mother tells you *okay*?—go ahead, son!

JACK: Mrs. Delle Rose! (*with embarrassment*)—Mrs. Delle Rose, I . . .

SERAFINA: Two weeks ago I was slapping her hands for scratching mosquito bites. She rode a bicycle to school. Now all at once—I've got a wild thing in the house. She says she's in love. And you? Do you say *you're* in love?

JACK (*solemnly*): Yes, ma'am, I do, I'm in love!—very much . . .

SERAFINA: Bambini, tutti due, bambini!

(*Rosa comes out, dressed for the picnic.*)

ROSA: I'm ready for Diamond Key!

SERAFINA: Go out on the porch. Diamond Key!

ROSA (*with a sarcastic curtsy*): Yes, Mama!

SERAFINA: What are you? Catholic?

JACK: Me? Yes, ma'am, Catholic.

SERAFINA: You don't look Catholic to me!

ROSA (*shouting, from the door*): Oh, God, Mama, how do Catholics look? How do they look different from anyone else?

SERAFINA: Stay out till I call you! (*Rosa crosses to the bird bath and prays. Serafina turns to Jack.*) Turn around, will you?

JACK: Do what, ma'am?

SERAFINA: I said, *turn around!* (*Jack awkwardly turns around.*) Why do they make them Navy pants so tight?

ROSA (*listening in the yard*): Oh, my God . . .

JACK (*flushing*): That's a question you'll have to ask the Navy, Mrs. Delle Rose.

SERAFINA: And that gold earring, what's the gold earring for?

ROSA (*yelling from the door*): For crossing the equator, Mama; he crossed it three times. He was initiated into the court of Neptune and gets to wear a gold earring! He's a shellback!

(*Serafina springs up and crosses to slam the porch door. Rosa runs despairingly around the side of the house and leans, exhausted with closed eyes, against the trunk of a palm tree. The Strega creeps into the yard, listening.*)

SERAFINA: You see what I got. A wild thing in the house!

JACK: Mrs. Delle Rose, I guess that Sicilians are very emotional people . . .

SERAFINA: I want nobody to take advantage of that!

JACK: You got the wrong idea about me, Mrs. Delle Rose.

SERAFINA: I know what men want—not to eat popcorn with girls or to slide on ice! And boys are the same, only younger.—Come here. Come here!

(*Rosa hears her mother's passionate voice. She rushes from the palm tree to the back door and pounds on it with both fists.*)

ROSA: Mama! Mama! Let me in the door, Jack!
JACK: Mrs. Delle Rose, your daughter is calling you.
SERAFINA: Let her call!—Come here. (*She crosses to the shrine of Our Lady.*) *Come here!*

(*Despairing of the back door, Rosa rushes around to the front. A few moments later she pushes open the shutters of the window in the wall and climbs half in. Jack crosses apprehensively to Serafina before the Madonna.*)

SERAFINA: You said you're Catholic, ain't you?
JACK: Yes, ma'am.
SERAFINA: Then kneel down in front of Our Lady!
JACK: Do—do what, did you say?
SERAFINA: I said to get down on your knees in front of Our Lady!

(*Rosa groans despairingly in the window. Jack kneels awkwardly upon the hassock.*)

ROSA: Mama, Mama, *now* what?!

(*Serafina rushes to the window, pushes Rosa out and slams the shutters.*)

SERAFINA (*returning to Jack*): Now say after me what I say!
JACK: Yes, ma'am.

(*Rosa pushes the shutters open again.*)

SERAFINA: I promise the Holy Mother that I will respect the innocence of the daughter of . . .
ROSA (*in anguish*): Ma-*maaa!*
SERAFINA: Get back out of that window!—Well? Are you gonna say it?
JACK: Yes, ma'am. What was it, again?
SERAFINA: I promise the Holy Mother . . .
JACK: I promise the Holy Mother . . .

SERAFINA: As I hope to be saved by the Blessed Blood of Jesus . . .

JACK: As I hope to be saved by the . . .

SERAFINA: Blessed Blood of . . .

JACK: Jesus . . .

SERAFINA: That I will respect the innocence of the daughter, Rosa, of Rosario delle Rose.

JACK: That I will respect the innocence—of—Rosa . . .

SERAFINA: Cross yourself! (*He crosses himself.*) Now get up, get up, get up! I am satisfied now . . .

(*Rosa jumps through the window and rushes to Serafina with arms outflung and wild cries of joy.*)

SERAFINA: Let me go, let me breathe! (*Outside the Strega cackles derisively.*)

ROSA: Oh, wonderful Mama, don't breathe! Oh, Jack! *Kiss* Mama! *Kiss Mama!* Mama, please kiss Jack!

SERAFINA: Kiss? Me? No, no, no, no!—Kiss my *hand* . . .

(*She offers her hand, shyly, and Jack kisses it with a loud smack. Rosa seizes the wine bottle.*)

ROSA: Mama, get some wine glasses!

(*Serafina goes for the glasses, and Rosa suddenly turns to Jack. Out of her mother's sight, she passionately grabs hold of his hand and presses it, first to her throat, then to her lips and finally to her breast. Jack snatches her hand away as Serafina returns with the glasses. Voices are heard calling from the highway.*)

VOICES OUTSIDE: Ro-osa!—Ro-osa!—Ro-osa!

(*A car horn is heard blowing.*)

SERAFINA: Oh, I forgot the graduation present.

(*She crouches down before the bureau and removes a fancily wrapped package from its bottom drawer. The car horn is honking, and the voices are calling.*)

ROSA: They're calling for us! *Coming!* Jack! (*She flies out the door, calling back to her mother.*) G'bye, Mama!

JACK (*following Rosa*): Good-bye, Mrs. Delle Rose!

SERAFINA (*vaguely*): It's a Bulova wrist watch with seventeen jewels in it . . . (*She realizes that she is alone.*) Rosa! (*She goes to the door, still holding out the present. Outside the car motor roars, and the voices shout as the car goes off. Serafina stumbles outside, shielding her eyes with one hand, extending the gift with the other.*) Rosa, Rosa, your present! Regalo, regalo—tesoro!

(*But the car has started off, with a medley of voices shouting farewells, which fade quickly out of hearing. Serafina turns about vaguely in the confusing sunlight and gropes for the door. There is a derisive cackle from the witch next door. Serafina absently opens the package and removes the little gold watch. She winds it and then holds it against her ear. She shakes it and holds it again to her ear. Then she holds it away from her and glares at it fiercely.*)

SERAFINA (*pounding her chest three times*): Tick—tick—tick! (*She goes to the Madonna and faces it.*) Speak to me, Lady! Oh, Lady, give me a sign!

(*The scene dims out.*)

ACT TWO

It is two hours later the same day.

Serafina comes out onto the porch, barefooted, wearing a rayon slip. Great shadows have appeared beneath her eyes; her face and throat gleam with sweat. There are dark stains of wine on the rayon slip. It is difficult for her to stand, yet she cannot sit still. She makes a sick moaning sound in her throat almost continually.

A hot wind rattles the cane-brake. Vivi, the little girl, comes up to the porch to stare at Serafina as at a strange beast in a cage. Vivi is chewing a licorice stick which stains her mouth and her fingers. She stands chewing and staring. Serafina evades her stare. She wearily drags a broken grey wicker chair down off the porch, all the way out in front of the house, and sags heavily into it. It sits awry on a broken leg.

Vivi sneaks toward her. Serafina lurches about to face her angrily. The child giggles and scampers back to the porch.

SERAFINA (*sinking back into the chair*): Oh, Lady, Lady, Lady, give me a—sign . . . (*She looks up at the white glare of the sky.*)

(*Father De Leo approaches the house. Serafina crouches low in the chair to escape his attention. He knocks at the door. Receiving no answer, he looks out into the yard, sees her, and approaches her chair. He comes close to address her with a gentle severity.*)

FATHER DE LEO: Buon giorno, Serafina.

SERAFINA (*faintly, with a sort of disgust*): Giorno . . .

FATHER DE LEO: I'm surprised to see you sitting outdoors like this. What is that thing you're wearing?—I think it's an undergarment!—It's hanging off one shoulder, and your head, Serafina, looks as if you had stuck it in a bucket of oil. Oh, I see now why the other ladies of the neighborhood aren't taking their afternoon naps! They find it more entertaining to sit on the porches and watch the spectacle you are putting on for them!—Are you listening to me?—I must tell you that the change in your appearance and behavior since Rosario's death is shocking—shocking! A woman can be dignified in her grief but when it's carried too far it becomes a sort of self-indulgence. Oh, I knew this was going to happen when you broke the Church law and had your husband cremated! (*Serafina lurches up from the chair and shuffles back to the porch. Father De Leo follows her.*)—Set up a little idolatrous shrine in your house and give worship to a bottle of ashes. (*She sinks down upon the steps.*)—Are you listening to me?

(*Two women have appeared on the embankment and descend toward the house. Serafina lurches heavily up to meet them, like a weary bull turning to face another attack.*)

SERAFINA: You ladies, what you want? I don't do sewing! Look, I quit doing sewing. (*She pulls down the* "SEWING" *sign and hurls it away.*) Now you got places to go, you ladies, go places! Don't hang around front of my house!

FATHER DE LEO: The ladies want to be friendly.

SERAFINA: Naw, they don't come to be friendly. They think they know something that Serafina don't know; they think

I got *these* on my head! (*She holds her fingers like horns at either side of her forehead.*) Well, I ain't got them! (*She goes padding back out in front of the house. Father De Leo follows.*)

FATHER DE LEO: You called me this morning in distress over something.

SERAFINA: I called you this morning but now it is afternoon.

FATHER DE LEO: I had to christen the grandson of the Mayor.

SERAFINA: The Mayor's important people, not Serafina!

FATHER DE LEO: You don't come to confession.

SERAFINA (*starting back toward the porch*): No, I don't come, I don't go, I—Ohhh! (*She pulls up one foot and hops on the other.*)

FATHER DE LEO: You stepped on something?

SERAFINA (*dropping down on the steps*): No, no, no, no, no, I don't step on—noth'n . . .

FATHER DE LEO: Come in the house. We'll wash it with antiseptic. (*She lurches up and limps back toward the house.*) Walking barefooted you will get it infected.

SERAFINA: Fa niente . . .

(*At the top of the embankment a little boy runs out with a red kite and flourishes it in the air with rigid gestures, as though he were giving a distant signal. Serafina shades her eyes with a palm to watch the kite, and then, as though its motions conveyed a shocking message, she utters a startled soft cry and staggers back to the porch. She leans against a pillar, running her hand rapidly and repeatedly through her hair. Father De Leo approaches her again, somewhat timidly.*)

FATHER DE LEO: Serafina?

SERAFINA: Che, che, che cosa vuole?

FATHER DE LEO: I am thirsty. Will you go in the house and get me some water?

SERAFINA: Go in. Get you some water. The faucet is working.—I can't go in the house.

FATHER DE LEO: Why can't you go in the house?

SERAFINA: The house has a tin roof on it. I got to breathe.

FATHER DE LEO: You can breathe in the house.

SERAFINA: No, I can't breathe in the house. The house has a tin roof on it and I . . .

(*The Strega has been creeping through the cane-brake pretending to search for a chicken.*)

THE STREGA: Chick, chick, chick, chick, chick? (*She crouches to peer under the house.*)

SERAFINA: What's that? Is that the . . . ? Yes, the Strega! (*She picks up a flower pot containing a dead plant and crosses the yard.*) Strega! Strega! (*The Strega looks up, retreating a little.*) Yes, you, I mean you! You ain't look for no chick! Getta hell out of my yard! (*The Strega retreats, viciously muttering, back into the cane-brake. Serafina makes the protective sign of the horns with her fingers. The goat bleats.*)

FATHER DE LEO: You have no friends, Serafina.

SERAFINA: I don't want friends.

FATHER DE LEO: You are still a young woman. Eligible for—loving and—bearing again! I remember you dressed in pale blue silk at Mass one Easter morning, yes, like a lady wearing a—piece of the—weather! Oh, how proudly you walked, *too* proudly!—But now you crouch and shuffle about barefooted; you live like a convict, dressed in the rags of a convict. You have no companions; women you don't mix with. You . . .

SERAFINA: No, I don't mix with them women. (*glaring at the women on the embankment*) The dummies I got in my house, I mix with them better because they don't make up no lies!—What kind of women are them? (*mimicking fiercely*) "Eee, Papa, eeee, baby, eee, me, me, me! At thirty years old they got no more use for the letto matrimoniale, no. The big bed goes to the basement! They get little beds from Sears Roebuck and sleep on their bellies!

FATHER DE LEO: Attenzione!

SERAFINA: They make the life without glory. Instead of the heart they got the deep-freeze in the house. The men, they don't feel no glory, not in the house with them women; they go to the bars, fight in them, get drunk, get fat, put horns on the women because the women don't give them the love which is glory.—I did, I give him the glory. To me the big bed was beautiful like a religion. Now I lie on it with dreams, with memories only! But it is still beautiful to me and I don't believe that the man in my heart gave me horns! (*The women whisper.*) What, what are they saying? Does ev'rybody know something that I don't know?—No, all I want is a sign, a sign from Our Lady, to tell me the lie is a lie! And then I . . . (*The women laugh on the embankment. Serafina starts fiercely toward them. They scatter.*) Squeak, squeak, squawk, squawk! Hens—like water thrown on them! (*There is the sound of mocking laughter.*)

FATHER DE LEO: People are laughing at you on all the porches.

SERAFINA: I'm laughing, too. Listen to me, I'm laughing! (*She breaks into loud, false laughter, first from the porch, then from the foot of the embankment, then crossing in front of the house.*) Ha, ha, ha, ha, ha, ha, ha! Now ev'rybody is laughing. Ha, ha, ha, ha, ha, ha!

FATHER DE LEO: Zitta ora!—Think of your daughter.

SERAFINA (*understanding the word "daughter"*): You, *you* think of my daughter! Today you give out the diplomas, today at the high school you give out the prizes, diplomas! You give to my daughter a set of books call the Digest of Knowledge! What does she know? How to be cheap already?—Oh, yes, that is what to learn, how to be cheap and to cheat!—You know what they do at this high school? They ruin the girls there! They give the spring dance because the girls are man-crazy. And there at that dance my daughter goes with a sailor that has in his ear a gold ring! And pants so tight that a woman ought not to look at him! This morning, this morning she cuts with a knife her wrist if I don't let her go!—Now all of them gone to some island, they call it a picnic, all of them, gone in a—boat!

FATHER DE LEO: There *was* a school picnic, chaperoned by the teachers.

SERAFINA: Oh, lo so, lo so! The man-crazy old-maid teachers! —They all run wild on the island!

FATHER DE LEO: Serafina delle Rose! (*He picks up the chair by the back and hauls it to the porch when she starts to resume her seat.*)—I *command* you to go in the house.

SERAFINA: Go in the house? I will. I will go in the house if you will answer one question.—Will you answer one question?

FATHER DE LEO: I will if I know the answer.

SERAFINA: Aw, you know the answer!—You used to hear the confessions of my husband. (*She turns to face the priest.*)

FATHER DE LEO: Yes, I heard his confessions . . .

SERAFINA (*with difficulty*): Did he ever speak to you of a *woman*?

(*A child cries out and races across in front of the house. Father De Leo picks up his panama hat. Serafina paces slowly toward him. He starts away from the house.*)

SERAFINA (*rushing after him*): Aspettate! Aspettate un momento!

FATHER DE LEO (*fearfully, not looking at her*): Che volete?

SERAFINA: Rispondetemi! (*She strikes her breast.*) Did he speak of a woman to you?

FATHER DE LEO: You know better than to ask me such a question. I don't break the Church laws. The secrets of the confessional are sacred to me. (*He walks away.*)

SERAFINA (*pursuing and clutching his arm*): I got to know. You could tell me.

FATHER DE LEO: Let go of me, Serafina!

SERAFINA: Not till you tell me, Father. Father, you tell me, please tell me! Or I will go mad! (*in a fierce whisper*) I will go back in the house and smash the urn with the ashes—if you don't tell me! I will go mad with the doubt in my heart and I will smash the urn and scatter the ashes—of my husband's body!

FATHER DE LEO: What could I tell you? If you would not believe the known facts about him . . .

SERAFINA: Known facts, who knows the known facts?

(*The neighbor women have heard the argument and begin to crowd around, muttering in shocked whispers at Serafina's lack of respect.*)

FATHER DE LEO (*frightened*): Lasciatemi, lasciatemi stare!—Oh, Serafina, I am too old for this—please!—Everybody is . . .

SERAFINA (*in a fierce, hissing whisper*): Nobody knew my rose of the world but me and now they can lie because the rose ain't living. They want the marble urn broken; they want me to smash it. They want the rose ashes scattered because

I had too much glory. They don't want glory like *that* in nobody's heart. They want—mouse-squeaking!—known facts.—Who knows the known facts? You—padres—wear black because of the fact that the facts are known by nobody!

FATHER DE LEO: Oh, Serafina! There are people watching!

SERAFINA: Let them watch something. That will be a change for them.—It's been a long time I wanted to break out like this and now I . . .

FATHER DE LEO: I am too old a man; I am not strong enough. I am sixty-seven years old! Must I call for help, now?

SERAFINA: Yes, call! Call for help, but I won't let you go till you tell me!

FATHER DE LEO: You're not a respectable woman.

SERAFINA: No, I'm not a respectable; I'm a woman.

FATHER DE LEO: No, you are not a woman. You are an animal!

SERAFINA: Si, si, animale! Sono animale! Animale. Tell them all, shout it all to them, up and down the whole block! The widow Delle Rose is not respectable, she is not even a woman, she is an animal! She is attacking the priest! She will tear the black suit off him unless he tells her the whores in this town are lying to her!

(*The neighbor women have been drawing closer as the argument progresses, and now they come to Father De Leo's rescue and assist him to get away from Serafina, who is on the point of attacking him bodily. He cries out, "Officer! Officer!" but the women drag Serafina from him and lead him away with comforting murmurs.*)

SERAFINA (*striking her wrists together*): Yes, it's me, it's me!! Lock me up, lock me, lock me up! Or I will—*smash!*—the marble . . . (*She throws her head far back and presses her fists to her eyes. Then she rushes crazily to the steps and falls across them.*)

ASSUNTA: Serafina! Figlia! Figlia! Andiamo a casa!

SERAFINA: Leave me alone, old woman.

(*She returns slowly to the porch steps and sinks down on them, sitting like a tired man, her knees spread apart and her head *cupped in her hands. The children steal back around the house. A little boy shoots a bean-shooter at her. She starts up with a cry. The children scatter, shrieking. She sinks back down on the steps, then leans back, staring up at the sky, her body rocking.*)

SERAFINA: Oh, Lady, Lady, Lady, give me a sign!

(*As if in mocking answer, a novelty salesman appears and approaches the porch. He is a fat man in a seersucker suit and a straw hat with a yellow, red and purple band. His face is beet-red and great moons of sweat have soaked through the armpits of his jacket. His shirt is lavender, and his tie, pale blue with great yellow polka dots, is a butterfly bow. His entrance is accompanied by a brief, satiric strain of music.*)

THE SALESMAN: Good afternoon, lady. (*She looks up slowly. The salesman talks sweetly, as if reciting a prayer.*) I got a little novelty here which I am offering to just a few lucky people at what we call an introductory price. Know what I mean? Not a regular price but a price which is less than what it costs to manufacture the article, a price we are making for the sake of introducing the product in the Gulf Coast territory. Lady, this thing here that I'm droppin' right in youah lap is bigger than television; it's going to revolutionize the domestic life of America.—Now I don't do house to house canvassing. I sell directly to merchants but when I stopped over there to have my car serviced, I seen you taking the air on the steps and I thought I would just drop over and . . .

(*There is the sound of a big truck stopping on the highway, and a man's voice, Alvaro's, is heard, shouting.*)

ALVARO: Hey! Hey, you road hog!

THE SALESMAN (*taking a sample out of his bag*): Now, lady, this little article has a deceptive appearance. First of all, I want you to notice how *compact* it is. It takes up no more space than . . .

(*Alvaro comes down from the embankment. He is about twenty-five years old, dark and very goodlooking. He is one of those Mediterranean types that resemble glossy young bulls. He is short in stature, has a massively sculptural torso and bluish-black curls. His face and manner are clownish; he has a charming awkwardness. There is a startling, improvised air about him; he frequently seems surprised at his own speeches and actions, as though he had not at all anticipated them. At the moment when we first hear his voice the sound of a timpani begins, at first very pianissimo, but building up as he approaches, till it reaches a vibrant climax with his appearance to Serafina beside the house.*)

ALVARO: Hey.

THE SALESMAN (*without glancing at him*): Hay is for horses! —Now, madam, you see what happens when I press this button?

(*The article explodes in Serafina's face. She slaps it away with an angry cry. At the same time Alvaro advances, trembling with rage, to the porch steps. He is sweating and stammering with pent-up fury at a world of frustrations which are temporarily localized in the gross figure of this salesman.*)

ALVARO: Hey, you! Come here! What the hell's the idea, back there at that curve? You make me drive off the highway!

THE SALESMAN (*to Serafina*): Excuse me for just one minute. (*He wheels menacingly about to face Alvaro.*) Is something giving you gas pains, Maccaroni?

ALVARO: My name is not Maccaroni.

THE SALESMAN: All right. Spaghetti.

ALVARO (*almost sobbing with passion*): I am not maccaroni. I am not spaghetti. I am a human being that drives a truck of bananas. I drive a truck of bananas for the Southern Fruit Company for a living, not to play cowboys and Indians on no highway with no rotten road hog. You got a 4-lane highway between Pass Christian and here. I give you the sign to pass me. You tail me and give me the horn. You yell "Wop" at me and "Dago." "Move over, Wop, move over, Dago." Then at the goddam curve, you go pass me and make me drive off the highway and yell back "Son of a bitch of a Dago!" I don't like that, no, no! And I am glad you stop here. Take the cigar from your mouth, take out the cigar!

THE SALESMAN: Take it out for me, greaseball.

ALVARO: If I take it out I will push it down your throat. I got three dependents! If I fight, I get fired, but I will fight and get fired. Take out the cigar!

(*Spectators begin to gather at the edge of the scene. Serafina stares at the truck driver, her eyes like a somnambule's. All at once she utters a low cry and seems about to fall.*)

ALVARO: Take out the cigar, take out, take out the cigar!

(*He snatches the cigar from the salesman's mouth and the salesman brings his knee up violently into Alvaro's groin. Bending double and retching with pain, Alvaro staggers over to the porch.*)

THE SALESMAN (*shouting, as he goes off*): I got your license number, Maccaroni! I know your boss!

ALVARO (*howling*): Drop dead! (*He suddenly staggers up the steps.*) Lady, lady, I got to go in the house!

(*As soon as he enters, he bursts into rending sobs, leaning against a wall and shaking convulsively. The spectators outside laugh as they scatter. Serafina slowly enters the house. The screen door rasps loudly on its rusty springs as she lets it swing gradually shut behind her, her eyes remaining fixed with a look of stupefied wonder upon the sobbing figure of the truck driver. We must understand her profound unconscious response to this sudden contact with distress as acute as her own. There is a long pause as the screen door makes its whining, catlike noise swinging shut by degrees.*)

SERAFINA: Somebody's—in my house? (*finally, in a hoarse, tremulous whisper*) What are you—doing in here? Why have you—come in my house?

ALVARO: Oh, lady—leave me alone!—Please—now!

SERAFINA: You—got no business—in here . . .

ALVARO: I got to cry after a fight. I'm sorry, lady. I . . . (*The sobs still shake him. He leans on a dummy.*)

SERAFINA: Don't lean on my dummy. Sit down if you can't stand up.—What is the matter with you?

ALVARO: I always cry after a fight. But I don't want people to see me. It's not like a man. (*There is a long pause; Serafina's attitude seems to warm toward the man.*)

SERAFINA: A man is not no different from no one else . . . (*All at once her face puckers up, and for the first time in the play Serafina begins to weep, at first soundlessly, then audibly. Soon she is sobbing as loudly as Alvaro. She speaks between sobs.*)—I always cry—when somebody else is crying . . .

ALVARO: No, no, lady, *don't* cry! Why should *you* cry? I will stop. I will stop in a minute. This is not like a man. I am ashame of myself. I will stop now; please, lady . . .

(*Still crouching a little with pain, a hand clasped to his abdomen, Alvaro turns away from the wall. He blows his nose between two fingers. Serafina picks up a scrap of white voile and gives it to him to wipe his fingers.*)

SERAFINA: Your jacket is torn.

ALVARO (*sobbing*): My company jacket is torn?

SERAFINA: Yes . . .

ALVARO: Where is it torn?

SERAFINA (*sobbing*): Down the—back.

ALVARO: Oh, Dio!

SERAFINA: Take it off. I will sew it up for you. I do—sewing.

ALVARO: Oh, Dio! (*sobbing*) I got three dependents! (*He holds up three fingers and shakes them violently at Serafina.*)

SERAFINA: Give me—give me your jacket.

ALVARO: He took down my license number!

SERAFINA: People are always taking down license numbers and telephone numbers and numbers that don't mean nothing—all them numbers . . .

ALVARO: Three, three dependents! Not citizens, even! No relief checks, no nothing! (*Serafina sobs.*) He is going to complain to the boss.

SERAFINA: I wanted to cry all day.

ALVARO: He said he would fire me if I don't stop fighting!

SERAFINA: Stop crying so I can stop crying.

ALVARO: I am a sissy. Excuse me. I am ashame.

SERAFINA: Don't be ashame of nothing, the world is too crazy for people to be ashame in it. I'm not ashame and I had two fights on the street and my daughter called me "disgusting." I got to sew this by hand; the machine is broke in a fight with two women.

ALVARO: That's what—they call a cat fight . . . (*He blows his nose.*)

SERAFINA: Open the shutters, please, for me. I can't see to work. (*She has crossed to her work table. He goes over to the window. As he opens the shutters, the light falls across his fine torso, the undershirt clinging wetly to his dark olive skin. Serafina is struck and murmurs: "Ohhh . . ." There is the sound of music.*)

ALVARO: What, lady?

SERAFINA (*in a strange voice*): The light on the body was like a man that lived here . . .

ALVARO: Che dice?

SERAFINA: Niente.—Ma com'è strano!—Lei è Napoletano? (*She is threading a needle.*)

ALVARO: Io sono Siciliano! (*Serafina sticks her finger with her needle and cries out.*) Che fa?

SERAFINA: I—stuck myself with the—needle!—You had—better wash up . . .

ALVARO: Dov'è il gabinetto?

SERAFINA (*almost inaudibly*): Dietro. (*She points vaguely back.*)

ALVARO: Con permesso! (*He moves past her. As he does so, she picks up a pair of broken spectacles on the work table. Holding them up by the single remaining side piece, like a lorgnette, she inspects his passing figure with an air of stupefaction. As he goes out, he says:*) A kick like that can have serious consequences! (*He goes into the back of the house.*)

SERAFINA (*after a pause*): Madonna Santa!—My *husband's body*, with the head of a *clown*! (*She crosses to the Madonna.*) O Lady, O Lady! (*She makes an imploring gesture.*) Speak to me!—What are you saying?—Please, Lady, I can't hear you! Is it a sign? Is it a sign of something? What does it mean? Oh, *speak to me*, Lady!—Everything is too strange!

(*She gives up the useless entreaty to the impassive statue. Then she rushes to the cupboard, clambers up on a chair and seizes a bottle of wine from the top shelf. But she finds it impossible to descend from the chair. Clasping the dusty bottle to her breast, she crouches there, helplessly whimpering like a child, as Alvaro comes back in.*)

ALVARO: Ciao!

SERAFINA: I can't get up.

ALVARO: You mean you can't get down?

SERAFINA: I mean I—can't get down . . .

ALVARO: Con permesso, Signora! (*He lifts her down from the chair.*)

SERAFINA: Grazie.

ALVARO: I am ashame of what happen. Crying is not like a man. Did anyone see me?

SERAFINA: Nobody saw you but me. To me it don't matter.

ALVARO: You are simpatica, molto!—It was not just the fight that makes me break down. I was like this all today! (*He shakes his clenched fists in the air.*)

SERAFINA: You and—me, too!—What was the trouble today?

ALVARO: My name is Mangiacavallo which means "Eat-a-horse." It's a comical name, I know. Maybe two thousand and seventy years ago one of my grandfathers got so hungry that he ate up a horse! That ain't my fault. Well, today at the Southern Fruit Company I find on the pay envelope not "Mangiacavallo" but "EAT A HORSE" in big print! Ha, ha, ha, very funny!—I open the pay envelope! In it I find a notice.—The wages have been *garnishee*! You know what garnishee is? (*Serafina nods gravely.*) Garnishee!—Eat a horse!—Road hog!—All in one day is too much! I go crazy, I boil, I cry, and I am ashame but I am not able to help it!—Even a Wop truck driver's a human being! And human beings must cry . . .

SERAFINA: Yes, they must cry. I couldn't cry all day but now I have cried and I am feeling much better.—I will sew up the jacket . . .

ALVARO (*licking his lips*): What is that in your hand? A bottle of vino?

SERAFINA: This is Spumanti. It comes from the house of the family of my husband. The Delle Rose! A very great family. I was a peasant, but I married a baron!—No, I still don't believe it! I married a baron when I didn't have shoes!

ALVARO: Excuse me for asking—but where is the Baron, now? (*Serafina points gravely to the marble urn.*) Where did you say?

SERAFINA: Them're his ashes in that marble urn.

ALVARO: Ma! Scusatemi! Scusatemi! (*crossing himself*)—I hope he is resting in peace.

SERAFINA: It's him you reminded me of—when you opened the shutters. Not the face but the body.—Please get me some ice from the icebox in the kitchen. I had a—very bad day . . .

ALVARO: Oh, ice! Yes—ice—I'll get some . . . (*As he goes out, she looks again through the broken spectacles at him.*)

SERAFINA: *Non posso crederlo!*—A clown of a face like that with my husband's body!

(*There is the sound of ice being chopped in the kitchen. She inserts a corkscrew in the bottle but her efforts to open it are clumsily unsuccessful. Alvaro returns with a little bowl of ice. He sets it down so hard on the table that a piece flies out. He scrambles after it, retrieves it and wipes it off on his sweaty undershirt.*)

SERAFINA: I think the floor would be cleaner!

ALVARO: Scusatemi!—I wash it again?

SERAFINA: Fa niente!

ALVARO: I am a—clean!—I . . .

SERAFINA: Fa niente, niente!—The bottle should be in the ice but the next best thing is to pour the wine over the bottle.

ALVARO: You mean over the ice?

SERAFINA: I mean over the . . .

ALVARO: Let me open the bottle. Your hands are not used to rough work. (*She surrenders the bottle to him and regards him through the broken spectacles again.*)

SERAFINA: These little bits of white voile on the floor are not from a snowstorm. I been making voile dresses for high school graduation.—One for my daughter and for thirteen other girls.—All of the work I'm not sure didn't kill me!

ALVARO: The wine will make you feel better.

(*There is a youthful cry from outside.*)

SERAFINA: There is a wild bunch of boys and girls in this town. In Sicily the boys would dance with the boys because a girl and a boy could not dance together unless they was going to be married. But here they run wild on islands!—boys, girls, man-crazy teachers . . .

ALVARO: Ecco! (*The cork comes off with a loud pop. Serafina cries out and staggers against the table. He laughs. She laughs with him, helplessly, unable to stop, unable to catch her breath.*)—I like a woman that laughs with all her heart.
SERAFINA: And a woman that cries with her heart?
ALVARO: I like everything that a woman does with her heart.

(*Both are suddenly embarrassed and their laughter dies out. Serafina smooths down her rayon slip. He hands her a glass of the sparkling wine with ice in it. She murmurs "Grazie."*)

(*Unconsciously the injured finger is lifted again to her lip and she wanders away from the table with the glass held shakily.*)

ALVARO (*continuing nervously*): I see you had a bad day.
SERAFINA: Sono così—stanca . . .
ALVARO (*suddenly springing to the window and shouting*): Hey, you kids, git down off that truck! Keep your hands off them bananas! (*At the words "truck" and "bananas" Serafina gasps again and spills some wine on her slip.*) Little buggers!—Scusatemi . . .
SERAFINA: You haul—you haul bananas?
ALVARO: Si, Signora.
SERAFINA: Is it a 10-ton truck?
ALVARO: An 8-ton truck.
SERAFINA: My husband hauled bananas in a 10-ton truck.
ALVARO: Well, he was a baron.
SERAFINA: Do you haul just bananas?
ALVARO: Just bananas. What else would I haul?
SERAFINA: My husband hauled bananas, but underneath the bananas was something else. He was—wild like a—Gypsy. —"Wild—like a—Gypsy?" Who said that?—I hate to start to remember, and then not remember . . .

(*The dialogue between them is full of odd hesitations, broken sentences and tentative gestures. Both are nervously exhausted after their respective ordeals. Their fumbling communication has a curious intimacy and sweetness, like the meeting of two lonely children for the first time. It is oddly luxurious to them both, luxurious as the first cool wind of evening after a scorching day. Serafina idly picks up a little Sicilian souvenir cart from a table.*)

SERAFINA: The priest was against it.

ALVARO: What was the priest against?

SERAFINA: Me keeping the ashes. It was against the Church law. But I had to have something and that was all I could have. (*She sets down the cart.*)

ALVARO: I don't see nothing wrong with it.

SERAFINA: You don't?

ALVARO: No! Niente!—The body would've decayed, but ashes always stay clean.

SERAFINA (*eagerly*): Si, si, bodies decay, but ashes always stay clean! Come here. I show you this picture—my wedding. (*She removes a picture tenderly from the wall.*) Here's me a bride of fourteen, and this—this—*this!* (*drumming the picture with her finger and turning her face to Alvaro with great lustrous eyes*) My *husband!* (*There is a pause. He takes the picture from her hand and holds it first close to his eyes, then far back, then again close with suspirations of appropriate awe.*) Annnh?—Annnnh?—Che dice!

ALVARO (*slowly, with great emphasis*): Che bell' uomo! Che bell' uomo!

SERAFINA (*replacing the picture*): A rose of a man. On his chest he had the tattoo of a rose. (*then, quite suddenly*)—Do you believe strange things, or do you doubt them?

ALVARO: If strange things didn't happen, I wouldn't be here. You wouldn't be here. We wouldn't be talking together.

SERAFINA: Davvero! I'll tell you something about the tattoo of my husband. My husband, he had this rose tattoo on his chest. One night I woke up with a burning pain on me here. I turn on the light. I look at my naked breast and on it I see the rose tattoo of my husband, on me, on *my* breast, *his* tattoo.

ALVARO: Strano!

SERAFINA: And that was the night that—I got to speak frankly to tell you . . .

ALVARO: Speak frankly! We're grown-up people.

SERAFINA: That was the night I conceived my son—the little boy that was lost when I lost my husband . . .

ALVARO: Che cosa—strana!—Would you be willing to show me the rose tattoo?

SERAFINA: Oh, it's gone now, it only lasted a moment. But I did see it. I saw it clearly.—Do you believe me?

ALVARO: Lo credo!

SERAFINA: I don't know why I told you. But I like what you said. That bodies decay but ashes always stay clean—immacolate!—But, you know, there are some people that want to make everything dirty. Two of them kind of people come in the house today and told me a terrible lie in front of the ashes.—So awful a lie that if I thought it was true—I would smash the urn—and throw the ashes away! (*She hurls her glass suddenly to the floor.*) Smash it, *smash it like that!*

ALVARO: Ma!—Baronessa!

(*Serafina seizes a broom and sweeps the fragments of glass away.*)

SERAFINA: And take this broom and sweep them out the back door like so much trash!

ALVARO (*impressed by her violence and a little awed*): What lie did they tell you?

SERAFINA: No, no, no! I don't want to talk about it! (*She throws down the broom.*) I just want to forget it; it wasn't true, it was false, false, false!—as the hearts of the bitches that told it . . .

ALVARO: Yes. I would forget anything that makes you unhappy.

SERAFINA: The memory of a love don't make you unhappy unless you believe a lie that makes it dirty. I don't believe in the lie. The ashes are clean. The memory of the rose in my heart is perfect!—Your glass is weeping . . .

ALVARO: *Your* glass is weeping too.

(*While she fills his glass, he moves about the room, looking here and there. She follows him. Each time he picks up an article for inspection she gently takes it from him and examines it herself with fresh interest.*)

ALVARO: Cozy little homelike place you got here.

SERAFINA: Oh, it's—molto modesto.—You got a nice place too?

ALVARO: I got a place with three dependents in it.

SERAFINA: What—dependents?

ALVARO (*counting them on his fingers*): One old maid sister, one feeble-minded grandmother, one lush of a pop that's not worth the powder it takes to blow him to hell.—They got the parchesi habit. They play the game of parchesi, morning, night, noon. Passing a bucket of beer around the table . . .

SERAFINA: They got the beer habit, too?

ALVARO: Oh, yes. And the numbers habit. This spring the old maid sister gets female trouble—mostly mental, I think—she turns the housekeeping over to the feeble-minded grandmother, a very sweet old lady who don't think it is necessary to pay the grocery bill so long as there's money to play the numbers. She plays the numbers. She has a perfect system except it don't ever work. And the grocery bill goes up, up, up, up, up!—so high you can't even see it!—Today the Ideal Grocery Company garnishees my wages . . . There, now! I've told you my life . . . (*The parrot squawks. He goes over to the cage.*) Hello, Polly, how's tricks?

SERAFINA: The name ain't Polly. It ain't a she; it's a he.

ALVARO: How can you tell with all them tail feathers? (*He sticks his finger in the cage, pokes at the parrot and gets bitten.*) Owww!

SERAFINA (*vicariously*): Ouuu . . . (*Alvaro sticks his injured finger in his mouth. Serafina puts her corresponding finger in her mouth. He crosses to the telephone.*) I told you watch out.—What are you calling, a doctor?

ALVARO: I am calling my boss in Biloxi to explain why I'm late.

SERAFINA: The call to Biloxi is a ten-cent call.

ALVARO: Don't worry about it.

SERAFINA: I'm not worried about it. You will pay it.

ALVARO: You got a sensible attitude toward life . . . Give me the Southern Fruit Company in Biloxi—seven-eight-seven!

SERAFINA: You are a bachelor. With three dependents? (*She glances below his belt.*)

ALVARO: I'll tell you my hopes and dreams!

SERAFINA: Who? Me?

ALVARO: I am hoping to meet some sensible older lady. Maybe a lady a little bit older than me.—I don't care if she's a little too plump or not such a stylish dresser! (*Serafina self-consciously pulls up a dangling strap.*) The important thing in a lady is understanding. Good sense. And I want her to have a well-furnished house and a profitable little business of some kind . . . (*He looks about him significantly.*)

SERAFINA: And such a lady, with a well-furnished house and business, what does she want with a man with three dependents with the parchesi and the beer habit, playing the numbers!

ALVARO: Love and affection!—in a world that is lonely—and cold!

SERAFINA: It might be lonely but I would not say "cold" on this particular day!

ALVARO: Love and affection is what I got to offer on hot or cold days in this lonely old world and is what I am looking for. I got nothing else. Mangiacavallo has nothing. In fact, he is the grandson of the village idiot of Ribera!

SERAFINA (*uneasily*): I see you like to make—jokes!

ALVARO: No, no joke!—Davvero!—He chased my grandmother in a flooded rice field. She slip on a wet rock.—Ecco! Here I am.

SERAFINA: You ought to be more respectful.

ALVARO: What have I got to respect? The rock my grandmother slips on?

SERAFINA: Yourself at least! Don't you work for a living?

ALVARO: If I *don't* work for a living I would respect myself *more.* Baronessa, I am a healthy young man, existing without no love life. I look at the magazine pictures. Them girls in the advertisement—you know what I mean? A little bitty thing here? A little bitty thing there?

(*He touches two portions of his anatomy. The latter portion embarrasses Serafina, who quietly announces:*)

SERAFINA: The call is ten cents for three minutes. Is the line busy?

ALVARO: Not the line, but the boss.

SERAFINA: And the charge for the call goes higher. That ain't the phone of a millionaire you're using!

ALVARO: I think you talk a poor mouth. (*He picks up the piggy bank and shakes it.*) This pig sounds well-fed to me.

SERAFINA: Dimes and quarters.

ALVARO: Dimes and quarters're better than nickels and dimes. (*Serafina rises severely and removes the piggy bank from his grasp.*) Ha, ha, ha! You think I'm a bank robber?

SERAFINA: I think you are maleducato! Just get your boss on the phone or hang the phone up.

ALVARO: What, what! Mr. Siccardi? How tricks at the Southern Fruit Comp'ny this hot afternoon? Ha, ha, ha!—Mangiacavallo!—What? You got the complaint already? Sentite, per favore! This road hog was—Mr. Siccardi? (*He jiggles the hook; then slowly hangs up.*) A man with three dependents!—out of a job . . . (*There is a pause.*)

SERAFINA: Well, you better ask the operator the charges.

ALVARO: Oofla! A man with three dependents—out of a job!

SERAFINA: I can't see to work no more. I got a suggestion to make. Open the bottom drawer of that there bureau and you will find a shirt in white tissue paper and you can wear that one while I am fixing this. And call for it later. (*He crosses to the bureau.*)—It was made for somebody that never called for it. (*He removes the package.*) Is there a name pinned to it?

ALVARO: Yes, it's . . .

SERAFINA (*fiercely, but with no physical movement*): Don't tell me the name! Throw it away, out the window!

ALVARO: Perchè?

SERAFINA: Throw it, throw it away!

ALVARO (*crumpling the paper and throwing it through the window*): Ecco fatto! (*There is a distant cry of children as he unwraps the package and holds up the rose silk shirt, exclaiming in Latin delight at the luxury of it.*) Colore di rose! Seta! Seta pura!—Oh, this shirt is too good for Mangiacavallo! Everything here is too good for Mangiacavallo!

SERAFINA: Nothing's too good for a man if the man is good.

ALVARO: The grandson of a village idiot is not that good.

SERAFINA: No matter whose grandson you are, put it on; you are welcome to wear it.

ALVARO (*slipping voluptuously into the shirt*): Sssssss!

SERAFINA: How does it feel, the silk, on you?

ALVARO: It feels like a girl's hands on me! (*There is a pause, while he shows her the whiteness of his teeth.*)

SERAFINA (*holding up her broken spectacles*): It will make you less trouble.

ALVARO: There is nothing more beautiful than a gift between people!—Now you are smiling!—You like me a little bit better?

SERAFINA (*slowly and tenderly*): You know what they should of done when you was a baby? They should of put tape on your ears to hold them back so when you grow up they wouldn't stick out like the wings of a little kewpie! (*She touches his ear, a very slight touch, betraying too much of her heart. Both laugh a little and she turns away, embarrassed.*)

(*Outside the goat bleats and there is the sound of splintering timber. One of the children races into the front yard, crying out.*)

SALVATORE: Mizz' Dell' Rose! The black goat's in your yard!

SERAFINA: Il becco della strega!

(*Serafina dashes to the window, throws the shutters violently open and leans way out. This time, she almost feels relief in this distraction. The interlude of the goat chase has a quality of crazed exaltation. Outside is heard the wild bleating of the goat and the jingling of his harness.*)

SERAFINA: Miei pomodori! Guarda i miei pomodori!

THE STREGA (*entering the front yard with a broken length of rope, calling out*): Heyeh, Billy! Heyeh. Heyeh, Billy!

SERAFINA (*making the sign of horns with her fingers*): There is the Strega! She lets the goat in my yard to eat my tomatoes! (*backing from the window*) She has the eye; she has the malocchio, and so does the goat! The goat has the evil eye, too. He got in my yard the night that I lost Rosario and my boy! Madonna, Madonna mia! Get that goat out of my yard! (*She retreats to the Madonna, making the sign of the horns with her fingers, while the goat chase continues outside.*)

ALVARO: Now take it easy! I will catch the black goat and give him a kick that he will never forget!

(*Alvaro runs out the front door and joins in the chase. The little boy is clapping together a pair of tin pan lids which sound like cymbals. The effect is weird and beautiful with the wild cries of the children and the goat's bleating. Serafina remains anxiously half way between the shutters and the protecting Madonna. She gives a furious imitation of the bleating goat, contorting her face with loathing. It is the fury of woman at the desire she suffers. At last the goat is captured.*)

BRUNO: Got him, got him, got him!
ALVARO: Vieni presto, Diavolo!

(*Alvaro appears around the side of the house with a tight hold on the broken rope around the goat's neck. The boy follows behind, gleefully clapping the tin lids together, and further back follows the Strega, holding her broken length of rope, her grey hair hanging into her face and her black skirts caught up in one hand, revealing bare feet and hairy legs. Serafina comes out on the porch as the grotesque little procession passes before it, and she raises her hand with the fingers making horns as the goat and the Strega pass her. Alvaro turns the goat over to the Strega and comes panting back to the house.*)

ALVARO: Niente paura!—I got to go now.—You have been troppo gentile, Mrs. . . .
SERAFINA: I am the widow of the Baron Delle Rose.—Excuse the way I'm—not dressed . . . (*He keeps hold of her hand as he stands on the porch steps. She continues very shyly, panting a little.*) I am not always like this.—Sometimes I fix myself up!—When my husband was living, when my husband comes home, when he was living—I had a clean dress on! And sometimes even, I—put a rose in my hair . . .
ALVARO: A rose in your hair would be pretty!
SERAFINA: But for a widow—it ain't the time of roses . . .

(*The sound of music is heard, of a mandolin playing.*)

ALVARO: Naw, you make a mistake! It's always for everybody the time of roses! The rose is the heart of the world like the heart is the—heart of the—body! But you, Baronessa—you know what I think you have done?
SERAFINA: What—what have I—done?
ALVARO: You have put your heart in the marble urn with the ashes. (*Now singing is heard along with the music, which continues to the end of the scene.*) And if in a storm some-

time, or sometime when a 10-ton truck goes down the highway—the marble urn was to *break!* (*He suddenly points up at the sky.*) Look! Look, Baronessa!

SERAFINA (*startled*): Look? Look? I don't see!

ALVARO: I was pointing at your heart, broken out of the urn and away from the ashes!—*Rondinella felice!* (*He makes an airy gesture toward the fading sky.*)

SERAFINA: Oh! (*He whistles like a bird and makes graceful winglike motions with his hands.*) Buffone, buffone—piantatela! I take you serious—then you make it a joke . . . (*She smiles involuntarily at his antics.*)

ALVARO: When can I bring the shirt back?

SERAFINA: When do you pass by again?

ALVARO: I will pass by tonight for supper. Volete?

SERAFINA: Then look at the window tonight. If the shutters are open and there is a light in the window, you can stop by for your—jacket—but if the shutters are closed, you better not stop because my Rosa will be home. Rosa's my daughter. She has gone to a picnic—maybe—home early—but you know how picnics are. They—wait for the moon to—start singing.—Not that there's nothing wrong in two grown-up people having a quiet conversation!—but Rosa's fifteen—I got to be careful to set her a perfect example.

ALVARO: I will look at the window.—I will look at the windooow! (*He imitates a bird flying off with gay whistles.*)

SERAFINA: Buffone!

ALVARO (*shouting from outside*): Hey, you little buggers, climb down off that truck! Lay offa them bananas!

(*His truck is heard starting and pulling away. Serafina stands motionless on the porch, searching the sky with her eyes.*)

SERAFINA: Rosario, forgive me! Forgive me for thinking the awful lie could be true!

(*The light in the house dims out. A little boy races into the yard holding triumphantly aloft a great golden bunch of bananas. A little girl pursues him with shrill cries. He eludes her. They dash around the house. The light fades and the curtain falls.*)

ACT THREE

It is the evening of the same day. The neighborhood children are playing games around the house. One of them is counting by fives to a hundred, calling out the numbers, as he leans against the palm tree.

Serafina is in the parlor, sitting on the sofa. She is seated stiffly and formally, wearing a gown that she has not worn since the death of her husband, and with a rose in her hair. It becomes obvious from her movements that she is wearing a girdle that constricts her unendurably.

(*There is the sound of a truck approaching up on the highway. Serafina rises to an odd, crouching position. But the truck passes by without stopping. The girdle is becoming quite intolerable to Serafina and she decides to take it off, going behind the sofa to do so. With much grunting, she has gotten it down as far as her knees, when there is the sound outside of another truck approaching. This time the truck stops up on the highway, with a sound of screeching brakes. She realizes that Alvaro is coming, and her efforts to get out of the girdle, which is now pinioning her legs, become frantic. She hobbles from behind the sofa as Alvaro appears in front of the house.*)

ALVARO (*gaily*): Rondinella felice! I will look at win-dooooo! Signora delle Rose!

(*Serafina's response to this salutation is a groan of anguish. She hobbles and totters desperately to the curtains between the rooms and reaches them just in time to hide herself as Alvaro comes into the parlor from the porch through the screen door. He is carrying a package and a candy box.*)

ALVARO: C'è nessuno?

SERAFINA (*at first inaudibly*): Si, si, sono qui. (*then loudly and hoarsely, as she finally gets the girdle off her legs*) Si, si, sono qui! (*To cover her embarrassment, she busies herself with fixing wine glasses on a tray.*)

ALVARO: I hear the rattle of glasses! Let me help you! (*He goes eagerly through the curtain but stops short, astonished.*)

SERAFINA: Is—something the—matter?

ALVARO: I didn't expect to see you looking so pretty! You are a *young* little widow!

SERAFINA: You are—fix yourself up . . .

ALVARO: I been to The Ideal Barber's! I got the whole works!

SERAFINA (*faintly, retreating from him a little*): You got—rose oil—in your hair . . .

ALVARO: Olio di rose! You like the smell of it? (*Outside there is a wild, distant cry of children, and inside a pause. Serafina shakes her head slowly with the infinite wound of a recollection.*)—You—*don't*—like—the smell of it? Oh, then I wash the smell *out*, I go and . . . (*He starts toward the back. She raises her hand to stop him.*)

SERAFINA: No, no, no, fa—niente.—I—*like* the smell of it . . .

(*A little boy races into the yard, ducks some invisible missile, sticks out his tongue and yells: "Yahhhhh!" Then he dashes behind the house.*)

SERAFINA: Shall we—set down in the parlor?

ALVARO: I guess that's better than standing up in the dining room. (*He enters formally.*)—Shall we set down on the sofa?

SERAFINA: You take the sofa. I will set down on this chair.

ALVARO (*disappointed*): You don't like to set on a sofa?

SERAFINA: I lean back too far on that sofa. I like a straight back behind me . . .

ALVARO: That chair looks not comfortable to me.

SERAFINA: This chair is a comfortable chair.

ALVARO: But it's more easy to talk with two on a sofa!

SERAFINA: I talk just as good on a chair as I talk on a sofa . . . (*There is a pause. Alvaro nervously hitches his shoulder.*) Why do you hitch your shoulders like that?

ALVARO: Oh, that!—That's a—nervous—habit . . .

SERAFINA: I thought maybe the suit don't fit you good . . .

ALVARO: I bought this suit to get married in four years ago.

SERAFINA: But didn't get married?

ALVARO: I give her, the girl, a zircon instead of a diamond. She had it examined. The door was slammed in my face.

SERAFINA: I think that maybe I'd do the same thing myself.

ALVARO: Buy the zircon?

SERAFINA: No, slam the door.

ALVARO: Her eyes were not sincere looking. You've got sincere looking eyes. Give me your hand so I can tell your fortune! (*She pushes her chair back from him.*) I see two men in your life. One very handsome. One not handsome. His ears are too big but not as big as his heart! He has three dependents.—In fact he has four dependents! Ha, ha, ha!

SERAFINA: What is the fourth dependent?

ALVARO: The one that every man's got, his biggest expense, worst troublemaker and chief liability! Ha, ha, ha!

SERAFINA: I hope you are not talking vulgar. (*She rises and turns her back to him. Then she discovers the candy box.*) What's that fancy red box?

ALVARO: A present I bought for a nervous but nice little lady!

SERAFINA: Chocolates? Grazie! Grazie! But I'm too fat.

ALVARO: You are not fat, you are just pleasing and plump. (*He reaches way over to pinch the creamy flesh of her upper arm.*)

SERAFINA: No, please. Don't make me nervous. If I get nervous again I will start to cry . . .

ALVARO: Let's talk about something to take your mind off your troubles. You say you got a young daughter?

SERAFINA (*in a choked voice*): Yes. I got a young daughter. Her name is Rosa.

ALVARO: Rosa, Rosa! She's pretty?

SERAFINA: She has the eyes of her father, and his wild, stubborn blood! Today was the day of her graduation from high school. She looked so pretty in a white voile dress with a great big bunch of—roses . . .

ALVARO: Not no prettier than her Mama, I bet—with that rose in your hair!

SERAFINA: She's only fifteen.

ALVARO: Fifteen?

SERAFINA (*smoothing her blue silk lap with a hesitant hand*): Yes, only fifteen . . .

ALVARO: But has a boyfriend, does she?

SERAFINA: She met a sailor.

ALVARO: Oh, Dio! No wonder you seem to be nervous.

SERAFINA: I didn't want to let her go out with this sailor. He had a gold ring in his ear.

ALVARO: Madonna Santa!

SERAFINA: This morning she cut her wrist—not much but enough to bleed—with a kitchen knife!

ALVARO: Tch, tch! A very wild girl!

SERAFINA: I had to give in and let her bring him to see me. He said he was Catholic. I made him kneel down in front of Our Lady there and give Her his promise that he would respect the innocence of my Rosa!—But how do I know that he was a Catholic, *really*?

ALVARO (*taking her hand*): Poor little worried lady! But you got to face facts. Sooner or later the innocence of your daughter cannot be respected.—Did he—have a—tattoo?

SERAFINA (*startled*): Did who have—what?

ALVARO: The sailor friend of your daughter, did he have a tattoo?

SERAFINA: Why do you ask me that?

ALVARO: Just because most sailors have a tattoo.

SERAFINA: How do I know if he had a tattoo or not!

ALVARO: *I* got a tattoo!

SERAFINA: *You* got a tattoo?

ALVARO: Si, si, veramente!

SERAFINA: What kind of tattoo you got?

ALVARO: What kind you think?

SERAFINA: Oh, I think—you have got—a South Sea girl without clothes on . . .

ALVARO: No South Sea girl.

SERAFINA: Well, maybe a big red heart with MAMA written across it.

ALVARO: Wrong again, Baronessa.

(*He takes off his tie and slowly unbuttons his shirt, gazing at her with an intensely warm smile. He divides the unbuttoned shirt, turning toward her his bare chest. She utters a gasp and rises.*)

SERAFINA: No, no, no!—*Not a rose!* (*She says it as if she were evading her feelings.*)

ALVARO: Si, si, una rosa!

SERAFINA: I—don't feel good! The air is . . .

ALVARO: Che fate, che fate, che dite?

SERAFINA: The house has a tin roof on it!—The air is—I got to go outside the house to breathe! Scu—scusatemi! (*She *goes out onto the porch and clings to one of the spindling porch columns for support, breathing hoarsely with a hand to her throat. He comes out slowly.*)

ALVARO (*gently*): I didn't mean to surprise you!—Mi dispiace molto!

SERAFINA (*with enforced calm*): Don't—talk about it! Anybody could have a rose tattoo.—It don't mean nothing.—You know how a tin roof is. It catches the heat all day and it don't cool off until—midnight . . .

ALVARO: No, no, not until midnight. (*She makes a faint laughing sound, is quite breathless and leans her forehead against the porch column. He places his fingers delicately against the small of her back.*) It makes it hot in the bedroom—so that you got to sleep without nothing on you . . .

SERAFINA: No, you—can't stand the covers . . .

ALVARO: You can't even stand a—*nightgown!* (*His fingers press her back.*)

SERAFINA: Please. There is a strega next door; she's always watching!

ALVARO: It's been so long since I felt the soft touch of a woman! (*She gasps loudly and turns to the door.*) Where are you going?

SERAFINA: I'm going back in the house! (*She enters the parlor again, still with forced calm.*)

ALVARO (*following her inside*): Now, now, what is the matter?

SERAFINA: I got a feeling like I have—forgotten something.

ALVARO: What?

SERAFINA: I can't remember.

ALVARO: It couldn't be nothing important if you can't remember. Let's open the chocolate box and have some candy.

SERAFINA (*eager for any distraction*): Yes! Yes, open the box!

(*Alvaro places a chocolate in her hand. She stares at it blankly.*)

ALVARO: Eat it, eat the chocolate. If you don't eat it, it will melt in your hand and make your fingers all gooey!

SERAFINA: Please, I . . .

ALVARO: Eat it!

SERAFINA (*weakly and gagging*): I can't, I can't, I would choke! Here, you eat it.

ALVARO: Put it in my mouth! (*She puts the chocolate in his mouth.*) Now, look. Your fingers are gooey!

SERAFINA: Oh!—I better go wash them! (*She rises unsteadily. He seizes her hands and licks her fingers.*)

ALVARO: Mmmm! Mmmmm! Good, very good!

SERAFINA: Stop that, stop that, stop that! That—ain't—nice . . .

ALVARO: I'll lick off the chocolate for you.

SERAFINA: No, no, no!—I am the mother of a fifteen-year-old girl!

ALVARO: You're as old as your arteries, Baronessa. Now set back down. The fingers are now white as snow!

SERAFINA: You don't—understand—how I feel . . .

ALVARO: You don't understand how *I* feel.

SERAFINA (*doubtfully*): How do you—feel? (*In answer, he stretches the palms of his hands out toward her as if she were a fireplace in a freezing-cold room.*)—What does—*that*—mean?

ALVARO: The night is warm but I feel like my hands are—freezing!

SERAFINA: Bad—circulation . . .

ALVARO: No, too *much* circulation! (*Alvaro becomes tremulously pleading, shuffling forward a little, slightly crouched like a beggar.*) Across the room I feel the sweet warmth of a lady!

SERAFINA (*retreating, doubtfully*): Oh, you talk a sweet mouth. I think you talk a sweet mouth to fool a woman.

ALVARO: No, no, I know—I know that's what warms the world, that is what makes it the summer! (*He seizes the hand she hold defensively before her and presses it to his own breast in a crushing grip.*) Without it, the rose—the rose would not grow on the bush; the fruit would not grow on the tree!

SERAFINA: I know, and the truck—the truck would not haul the bananas! But, Mr. Mangiacavallo, that is my hand, not a sponge. I got bones in it. Bones break!

ALVARO: Scusatemi, Baronessa! (*He returns her hand to her with a bow.*) For me it is winter, because I don't have in my life the sweet warmth of a lady. I live with my hands in my pockets! (*He stuffs his hands violently into his pants' pockets, then jerks them out again. A small cellophane-wrapped disk falls on the floor, escaping his notice, but not Serafina's.*)—You don't like the poetry!—How can a man talk to you?

SERAFINA (*ominously*): I like the poetry good. Is that a piece of the poetry that you dropped out of your pocket? (*He looks down.*)—No, no, right by your foot!

ALVARO (*aghast as he realizes what it is that she has seen*): Oh, that's—that's nothing! (*He kicks it under the sofa.*)

SERAFINA (*fiercely*): You talk a sweet mouth about women. Then drop such a thing from your pocket?—Va via, vigliacco! (*She marches grandly out of the room, pulling the curtains together behind her. He hangs his head despairingly between his hands. Then he approaches the curtains timidly.*)

ALVARO (*in a small voice*): Baronessa?

SERAFINA: Pick up what you dropped on the floor and go to the Square Roof with it. Buona notte!

ALVARO: Baronessa! (*He parts the curtains and peeks through them.*)

SERAFINA: I told you good night. Here is no casa privata. Io, non sono puttana!

ALVARO: Understanding is—very—necessary!

SERAFINA: I understand plenty. You think you got a good thing, a thing that is cheap!

ALVARO: You make a mistake, Baronessa! (*He comes in and drops to his knees beside her, pressing his cheek to her flank. He speaks rhapsodically.*) So soft is a lady! So, so, so, so, so *soft*—is a lady!

SERAFINA: Andate via, sporcaccione, andate a casa! Lasciatemi! Lasciatemi stare!

(*She springs up and runs into the parlor. He pursues. The chase is grotesquely violent and comic. A floor lamp is overturned. She seizes the chocolate box and threatens to slam it into his face if he continues toward her. He drops to his knees, crouched way over, and pounds the floor with his fists, sobbing.*)

ALVARO: Everything in my life turns out like this!

SERAFINA: Git up, git up, git up!—you village idiot's grandson! There is people watching you through that window, the—strega next door . . . (*He rises slowly.*) And where is the shirt that I loaned you? (*He shuffles abjectly across the room, then hands her a neatly wrapped package.*)

ALVARO: My sister wrapped it up for you.—My sister was very happy I met this *nice* lady!

SERAFINA: Maybe she thinks I will pay the grocery bill while she plays the numbers!

ALVARO: She don't think nothing like that. She is an old maid, my sister. She wants—nephews—nieces . . .

SERAFINA: You tell her for me I don't give nephews and nieces!

(*Alvaro hitches his shoulders violently in his embarrassment and shuffles over to where he had left his hat. He blows the dust off it and rubs the crown on his sleeve. Serafina presses a knuckle to her lips as she watches his awkward gestures. She is a little abashed by his humility. She speaks next with the great dignity of a widow whose respectability has stood the test.*)

SERAFINA: Now, Mr. Mangiacavallo, please tell me the truth about something. *When* did you get the tattoo put on your chest?

ALVARO (*shyly and sadly, looking down at his hat*): I got it tonight—after supper . . .

SERAFINA: That's what I thought. You had it put on because I told you about my husband's tattoo.

ALVARO: I wanted to be—close to you . . . to make you—happy . . .

SERAFINA: Tell it to the marines! (*He puts on his hat with an apologetic gesture.*) You got the tattoo and the chocolate box after supper, and then you come here to fool me!

ALVARO: I got the chocolate box a long time ago.

SERAFINA: How long ago? If that is not too much a personal question!

ALVARO: I got it the night the door was slammed in my face by the girl that I give—the zircon . . .

SERAFINA: Let that be a lesson. Don't try to fool women. You are not smart enough!—Now take the shirt back. You can keep it.

ALVARO: Huh?

SERAFINA: Keep it. I don't want it back.

ALVARO: You just now said that you did.

SERAFINA: It's a man's shirt, ain't it?

ALVARO: You just now accused me of trying to steal it off you.

SERAFINA: Well, you been making me nervous!

ALVARO: Is it my fault you been a widow too long?

SERAFINA: You make a mistake!

ALVARO: *You* make a mistake!

SERAFINA: Both of us make a mistake!

(*There is a pause. They both sigh profoundly.*)

ALVARO: We should of have been friends, but I think we meet the wrong day.—Suppose I go out and come in the door again and we start all over?

SERAFINA: No, I think it's no use. The day was wrong to begin with, because of two women. Two women, they told me today that my husband had put on my head the nanny-goat's horns!

ALVARO: How is it possible to put horns on a widow?

SERAFINA: That was before, before! They told me my husband was having a steady affair with a woman at the Square Roof. What was the name on the shirt, on the slip of paper? Do you remember the name?

ALVARO: You told me to . . .

SERAFINA: Tell me! Do you remember?

ALVARO: I remember the name because I know the woman. The name was Estelle Hohengarten.

SERAFINA: Take me there! Take me to the Square Roof!—Wait, wait!

(*She plunges into the dining room, snatches a knife out of the sideboard drawer and thrusts it in her purse. Then she rushes back, with the blade of the knife protruding from the purse.*)

ALVARO (*noticing the knife*): They—got a cover charge there . . .

SERAFINA: I will charge them a cover! Take me there now, this minute!

ALVARO: The fun don't start till midnight.

SERAFINA: I will start the fun sooner.

ALVARO: The floor show commences at midnight.

SERAFINA: I will commence it! (*She rushes to the phone.*) Yellow Cab, please, Yellow Cab. I want to go to the Square Roof out of my house! Yes, you come to my house and take me to the Square Roof right this minute! My number is—what is my number? Oh my God, what is my number?—64 is my number on Front Street! Subito, subito—quick!

(*The goat bleats outside.*)

ALVARO: Baronessa, the knife's sticking out of your purse. (*He grabs the purse.*) What do you want with this weapon?

SERAFINA: To cut the lying tongue out of a woman's mouth! Saying she has on her breast the tattoo of my husband because he had put on me the horns of a goat! I cut the heart out of that woman, she cut the heart out of me!

ALVARO: Nobody's going to cut the heart out of nobody!

(*A car is heard outside, and Serafina rushes to the porch.*)

SERAFINA (*shouting*): Hey, Yellow Cab, Yellow Cab, Yellow—Cab . . . (*The car passes by without stopping. With a sick moan she wanders into the yard. He follows her with a glass of wine.*)—Something hurts—in my heart . . .

ALVARO (*leading her gently back to the house*): Baronessa, drink this wine on the porch and keep your eyes on that star. (*He leads her to a porch pillar and places the glass in her trembling hand. She is now submissive.*) You know the name of that star? That star is Venus. She is the only female star in the sky. Who put her up there? Mr. Siccardi, the transportation manager of the Southern Fruit Company? No. She was put there by God. (*He enters the house and removes the knife from her purse.*) And yet there's some people that don't believe in nothing. (*He picks up the telephone.*) Esplanade 9-7-0.

SERAFINA: What are you doing?

ALVARO: Drink that wine and I'll settle this whole problem for you. (*on the telephone*) I want to speak to the blackjack dealer, please, Miss Estelle Hohengarten . . .

SERAFINA: Don't talk to that woman, she'll lie!

ALVARO: Not Estelle Hohengarten. She deals a straight game of cards.—Estelle? This is Mangiacavallo. I got a question to ask you which is a personal question. It has to do with a very goodlooking truckdriver, not living now but once on a time thought to have been a very well-known character at the Square Roof. His name was . . . (*He turns questioningly to the door where Serafina is standing.*) What was his name, Baronessa?

SERAFINA (*hardly breathing*): Rosario delle Rose!

ALVARO: Rosario delle Rose was the name. (*There is a pause.*) —È vero?—Mah! Che peccato . . .

(*Serafina drops her glass and springs into the parlor with a savage outcry. She snatches the phone from Alvaro and screams into it.*)

SERAFINA (*wildly*): This is the wife that's speaking! What do you know of my husband, what is the lie?

(*A strident voice sounds over the wire.*)

THE VOICE (*loud and clear*): Don't you remember? I brought you the rose-colored silk to make him a shirt. You said, "For a man?" and I said, "Yes, for a man that's wild like a Gypsy!" But if you think I'm a liar, come here and let me show you his rose tattooed on my chest!

(*Serafina holds the phone away from her as though it had burst into flame. Then, with a terrible cry, she hurls it to the floor. She staggers dizzily toward the Madonna. Alvaro seizes her arm and pushes her gently onto the sofa.*)

ALVARO: Piano, piano, Baronessa! This will be gone, this will pass in a moment. (*He puts a pillow behind her, then replaces the telephone.*)

SERAFINA (*staggering up from the sofa*): The room's—going round . . .

ALVARO: You ought to stay lying down a little while longer. I know, I know what you need! A towel with some ice in it to put on your forehead—Baronessa.—You stay right there while I fix it! (*He goes into the kitchen, and calls back.*) Torno subito, Baronessa!

(*The little boy runs into the yard. He leans against the bending trunk of the palm, counting loudly.*)

THE LITTLE BOY: Five, ten, fifteen, twenty, twenty-five, thirty . . .

(*There is the sound of ice being chopped in the kitchen.*)

SERAFINA: Dove siete, dove siete?

ALVARO: In cucina!—Ghiaccio . . .

SERAFINA: Venite qui!

ALVARO: Subito, subito . . .

SERAFINA (*turning to the shrine, with fists knotted*): Non voglio, non voglio farlo!

(*But she crosses slowly, compulsively toward the shrine, with a trembling arm stretched out.*)

THE LITTLE BOY: Seventy-five, eighty, eighty-five, ninety, ninety-five, one hundred! (*then, wildly*) *Ready or not you shall be caught!*

(*At this cry, Serafina seizes the marble urn and hurls it violently into the furthest corner of the room. Then, instantly, she covers her face. Outside the mothers are heard calling their children home. Their voices are tender as music, fading in and out. The children appear slowly at the side of the house, exhausted from their wild play.*)

GIUSEPPINA: Vivi! Vi-vi!

PEPINA: Salvatore!

VIOLETTA: Bruno! Come home, come home!

(*The children scatter. Alvaro comes in with the ice-pick.*)

ALVARO: I broke the point of the ice-pick.

SERAFINA (*removing her hands from her face*): I don't want ice . . . (*She looks about her, seeming to gather a fierce strength in her body. Her voice is hoarse, her body trembling with violence, eyes narrow and flashing, her fists clenched.*) Now I show you how wild and strong like a man a woman can be! (*She crosses to the screen door, opens it and shouts.*) Buona notte, Mr. Mangiacavallo!

ALVARO: You—you make me go *home*, now?

SERAFINA: No, no; senti, cretino! (*in a strident whisper*) You make out like you are going. You drive the truck out of sight where the witch can't see it. Then you come back and

I leave the back door open for you to come in. Now, tell me good-bye so all the neighbors can hear you! (*She shouts.*) Arrivederci!

ALVARO: Ha, ha! Capish! (*He shouts too.*) Arrivederci! (*He runs to the foot of the embankment steps.*)

SERAFINA (*still more loudly*): Buona notte!

ALVARO: Buona notte, Baronessa!

SERAFINA (*in a choked voice*): Give them my love; give everybody—my love . . . Arrivederci!

ALVARO: Ciao!

(*Alvaro scrambles on down the steps and goes off. Serafina comes down into the yard. The goat bleats. She mutters savagely to herself.*)

SERAFINA: Sono una bestia, una bestia feroce!

(*She crosses quickly around to the back of the house. As she disappears, the truck is heard driving off; the lights sweep across the house. Serafina comes in through the back door. She is moving with great violence, gasping and panting. She rushes up to the Madonna and addresses her passionately with explosive gestures, leaning over so that her face is level with the statue's.*)

SERAFINA: Ora, ascolta, Signora! You hold in the cup of your hand this little house and you smash it! You break this little house like the shell of a bird in your hand, because you have hate Serafina?—Serafina that *loved* you!—No, no, no, you don't speak! I don't believe in you, Lady! You're just a poor little doll with the paint peeling off, and now I blow out the light and I forget you the way you forget Serafina! (*She blows out the vigil light.*) *Ecco—fatto!*

(*But now she is suddenly frightened; the vehemence and boldness have run out. She gasps a little and backs away from the shrine, her eyes rolling apprehensively this way and that. The parrot squawks at her. The goat bleats. The night is full of sinister noises, harsh bird cries, the sudden flapping of wings in the cane-brake, a distant shriek of Negro laughter. Serafina retreats to the window and opens the shutters wider to admit the moonlight. She stands panting by the window with a fist pressed to her mouth. In the back of the house a door slams open. Serafina catches her breath and moves as though for protection behind the dummy of the bride. Alvaro enters through the back door, calling out softly and hoarsely, with great excitement.*)

ALVARO: Dove? Dove sei, cara?

SERAFINA (*faintly*): Sono qui . . .

ALVARO: You have turn out the light!

SERAFINA: The moon is enough . . . (*He advances toward her. His white teeth glitter as he grins. Serafina retreats a few steps from him. She speaks tremulously, making an awkward gesture toward the sofa.*) Now we can go on with our—conversation . . . (*She catches her breath sharply.*)

(*The curtain comes down.*)

SCENE TWO

It is just before daybreak of the next day. Rosa and Jack appear at the top of the embankment steps.

ROSA: I thought they would never leave. (*She comes down the steps and out in front of the house, then calls back to him.*) Let's go down there.

(*He obeys hesitatingly. Both are very grave. The scene is played as close as possible to the audience. She sits very straight. He stands behind her with his hands on her shoulders.*)

ROSA (*leaning her head back against him*): This was the happiest day of my life, and this is the saddest night . . . (*He crouches in front of her.*)

SERAFINA (*from inside the house*): Aaaaaahhhhhhhh!

JACK (*springing up, startled*): What's that?

ROSA (*resentfully*): Oh! That's Mama dreaming about my father.

JACK: I—feel like a—*heel!* I feel like a rotten heel!

ROSA: Why?

JACK: That promise I made your mother.

ROSA: I hate her for it.

JACK: Honey—Rosa, she—wanted to protect you.

(*There is a long-drawn cry from the back of the house: "Ohhhh—Rosario!"*)

ROSA: She wanted me not to have what she's dreaming about . . .

JACK: Naw, naw, honey, she—wanted to—protect you . . .

(*The cry from within is repeated softly.*)

ROSA: Listen to her making love in her sleep! Is that what she wants *me* to do, just—*dream* about it?

JACK (*humbly*): She knows that her Rosa *is* a rose. And she wants her rose to have someone—better than *me* . . .

ROSA: *Better* than—*you*! (*She speaks as if the possibility were too preposterous to think of.*)

JACK: You see me through—rose-colored—glasses . . .

ROSA: I see you with love!

JACK: Yes, but your Mama sees me with—common sense . . . (*Serafina cries out again.*) I got to be going! (*She keeps a tight hold on him. A rooster crows.*) Honey, it's so late the roosters are crowing!

ROSA: They're fools, they're fools, it's early!

JACK: Honey, on that island I almost forgot my promise. Almost, but not quite. Do you understand, honey?

ROSA: Forget the promise!

JACK: I made it on my knees in front of Our Lady. I've got to leave now, honey.

ROSA (*clasping him fiercely*): You'd have to break my arms to!

JACK: Rosa, Rosa! You want to drive me crazy?

ROSA: I want you not to remember.

JACK: You're a very young girl! Fifteen—fifteen is too young!

ROSA: Caro, caro, carissimo!

JACK: You got to save some of those feelings for when you're grown up!

ROSA: Carissimo!

JACK: Hold some of it back until you're grown!

ROSA: I have been grown for two years!

JACK: No, no, that ain't what I . . .

ROSA: Grown enough to be married, and have a—baby!

JACK (*springing up*): Oh, good—Lord! (*He circles around her, pounding his palm repeatedly with his fist and champing his teeth together with a grimace. Suddenly he speaks.*) I got to be going!

ROSA: You want me to scream? (*He groans and turns away from her to resume his desperate circle. Rosa is blocking the way with her body.*)—I know, I know! You don't want me! (*Jack groans through his gritting teeth.*) No, no, you don't want me . . .

JACK: Now you listen to me! You almost got into trouble today on that island! You almost did, but not quite!—But it didn't quite happen and no harm is done and you can just—forget it . . .

ROSA: It is the only thing in my life that I want to remember! —When are you going back to New Orleans?

JACK: Tomorrow.

ROSA: When does your—ship sail?

JACK: Tomorrow.

ROSA: Where to?

JACK: Guatemala.

SERAFINA (*from the house*): Aahh!

ROSA: Is that a long trip?

JACK: After Guatemala, Buenos Aires. After Buenos Aires, Rio. Then around the Straits of Magellan and back up the west coast of South America, putting in at three ports before we dock at San Francisco.

ROSA: I don't think I will—ever see you again . . .

JACK: The ship won't sink!

ROSA (*faintly and forlornly*): No, but—I think it could just happen once, and if it don't happen that time, it never can —later . . . (*A rooster crows. They face each other sadly and quietly.*) You don't need to be very old to understand how it works out. One time, one time, only once, it could be—God!—to remember.—Other times? Yes—they'd be something.—But only once, God—to remember . . . (*With a little sigh she crosses to pick up his white cap and hand it gravely to him.*)—I'm sorry to you it didn't—mean—that much . . .

JACK (*taking the cap and hurling it to the ground*): Look! Look at my knuckles! You see them scabs on my knuckles? You know how them scabs got there? They got there because I banged my knuckles that hard on the deck of the sailboat!

ROSA: Because it—didn't quite happen? (*Jack jerks his head up and down in grotesquely violent assent to her question. Rosa picks up his cap and returns it to him again.*)—Because of the promise to Mama! I'll never forgive her . . . (*There is a pause.*) What time in the afternoon must you be on the boat?

JACK: Why?

ROSA: Just tell me what time.

JACK: Five!—Why?

ROSA: What will you be doing till five?

JACK: Well, I could be a goddam liar and tell you I was going to—pick me a hatful of daisies in—Audubon Park.—Is that what you want me to tell you?

ROSA: No, tell me the truth.

JACK: All right, I'll tell you the truth. I'm going to check in at some flea-bag hotel on North Rampart Street. Then I'm going to get loaded! And then I'm going to get . . . (*He doesn't complete the sentence but she understands him. She places the hat more becomingly on his blond head.*)

ROSA: Do me a little favor. (*Her hand slides down to his cheek and then to his mouth.*) Before you get loaded and before you—before you—

JACK: Huh?

ROSA: Look in the waiting room at the Greyhound bus station, please. At twelve o'clock, noon!

JACK: Why?

ROSA: You might find me there, waiting for you . . .

JACK: What—what good would that do?

ROSA: I never been to a hotel but I know they have numbers on doors and sometimes—numbers are—lucky.—Aren't they?—Sometimes?—Lucky?

JACK: You want to buy me a ten-year stretch in the brig?

ROSA: I want you to give me that little gold ring on your ear to put on my finger.—I want to give you my heart to keep forever! And ever! And ever! (*Slowly and with a barely audible sigh she leans her face against him.*) Look for me! I will be there!

JACK (*breathlessly*): In all of my life, I never felt nothing so sweet as the feel of your little warm body in my arms . . .

(*He breaks away and runs toward the road. From the foot of the steps he glares fiercely back at her like a tiger through the *bars of a cage. She clings to the two porch pillars, her body leaning way out.*)

ROSA: Look for me! I will be there!

(*Jack runs away from the house. Rosa returns inside. Listlessly she removes her dress and falls on the couch in her slip, kicking off her shoes. Then she begins to cry, as one cries only once in a lifetime, and the scene dims out.*)

SCENE THREE

The time is three hours later.

We see first the exterior view of the small frame building against a night sky which is like the starry blue robe of Our Lady. It is growing slightly paler.

(*The faint light discloses Rosa asleep on the couch. The covers are thrown back for it has been a warm night, and on the concave surface of the white cloth, which is like the dimly lustrous hollow of a shell, is the body of the sleeping girl which is clad only in a sheer white slip.*

(*A cock crows. A gentle wind stirs the white curtains inward and the tendrils of vine at the windows, and the sky lightens enough to distinguish the purple trumpets of the morning glory against the very dim blue of the sky in which the planet Venus remains still undimmed.*

(*In the back of the cottage someone is heard coughing hoarsely and groaning in the way a man does who has drunk very heavily the night before. Bedsprings creak as a heavy figure rises. Light spills dimly through the curtains, now closed, between the two front rooms.*

(*There are heavy, padding footsteps and Alvaro comes stumbling rapidly into the dining room with the last bottle of Spumanti in the crook of an arm, his eyes barely open, legs rubbery, saying, "Wuh-wuh-wuh-wuh-wuh-wuh . . ." like the breathing of an old dog. The scene should be played with the pantomimic lightness, almost fantasy, of an early Chaplin comedy. He is wearing only his trousers and his chest is bare. As he enters he collides with the widow dummy, staggers back, pats her inflated bosom in a timid, apologetic way, remarking:*)

ALVARO: Scusami, Signora, I am the grandson of the village idiot of Ribera!

(*Alvaro backs into the table and is propelled by the impact all the way to the curtained entrance to the parlor. He draws the curtains apart and hangs onto them, peering into the room. Seeing the sleeping girl, he blinks several times, suddenly makes a snoring sound in his nostrils and waves one hand violently in front of his eyes as if to dispel a vision. Outside the goat utters a long "Baaaaaaaaaa!" As if in response, Alvaro whispers, in the same basso key, "Che bella!" The first vowel of "bella" is enormously prolonged like the "baaa" of the goat. On his rubbery legs he shuffles forward a few steps and leans over to peer more intently at the vision. The goat bleats again. Alvaro whispers more loudly: "Che* bel-*la!" He drains the Spumanti, then staggers to his knees, the empty bottle rolling over the floor. He crawls on his knees to the foot of the bed, then leans against it like a child peering into a candy shop window, repeating: "Che* bel-*la, che* bel-*la!" with antiphonal responses from the goat outside. Slowly, with tremendous effort, as if it were the sheer side of a precipice, he clambers upon the couch and crouches over the sleeping girl in a leap-frog position, saying "Che* bel-*la!" quite loudly, this time, in a tone of innocently joyous surprise. All at once Rosa wakens. She screams, even before she is quite awake, and springs from the couch so violently that Alvaro topples over to the floor.*

(*Serafina cries out almost instantly after Rosa. She lunges through the dining room in her torn and disordered nightgown. At the sight of the man crouched by the couch a momentary stupefaction turns into a burst of savage fury. She flies at him like a great bird, tearing and clawing at his stupefied figure. With one arm Alvaro wards off her blows, plunging to the floor and crawling into the dining room. She seizes a broom with which she flails him about the head, buttocks and shoulders while he scrambles awkwardly away. The assault is nearly wordless. Each time she strikes at him she hisses: "Sporcaccione!" He continually groans: "Dough, dough,*

dough!" At last he catches hold of the widow dummy which he holds as a shield before him while he entreats the two women.)

ALVARO: Senti, Baronessa! Signorina! I didn't know what I was doin', I was dreamin', I was just dreamin'! I got turn around in the house; I got all twisted! I thought that you was your Mama!—Sono ubriaco! Per favore!

ROSA (*seizing the broom*): That's enough, Mama!

SERAFINA (*rushing to the phone*): Police!

ROSA (*seizing the phone*): No, no, no, no, no, no!—You want everybody to know?

SERAFINA (*weakly*): Know?—Know *what*, cara?

ROSA: Just give him his clothes, now, Mama, and let him get out! (*She is clutching a bedsheet about herself.*)

ALVARO: Signorina—young lady! I swear I was *dreaming!*

SERAFINA: Don't speak to my daughter! (*then, turning to Rosa*)—Who is this man? How did this man get here?

ROSA (*coldly*): Mama, don't say any more. Just give him his clothes in the bedroom so he can get out!

ALVARO (*still crouching*): I am so sorry, so sorry! I don't remember a thing but that I was dreaming!

SERAFINA (*shoving him toward the back of the room with her broom*): Go on, go get your clothes on, you—idiot's grandson, you!—Svelto, svelto, più svelto! (*Alvaro continues his apologetic mumbling in the back room.*) Don't talk to me, don't say nothing! Or I will kill you!

(*A few moments later Alvaro rushes around the side of the house, his clothes half buttoned and his shirt-tails out.*)

ALVARO: But, Baronessa, I *love* you! (*A tea kettle sails over his head from behind the house. The Strega bursts into laughter. Despairingly Alvaro retreats, tucking his shirt-tails in and shaking his head.*) Baronessa, Baronessa, I love you!

(*As Alvaro runs off, the Strega is heard cackling:*)

THE STREGA'S VOICE: The Wops are at it again. Had a truckdriver in the house all night!

(*Rosa is feverishly dressing. From the bureau she has snatched a shimmering white satin slip, disappearing for a moment behind a screen to put it on as Serafina comes padding sheepishly back into the room, her nightgown now covered by a black *rayon kimona sprinkled with poppies, her voice tremulous with fear, shame and apology.*)

ROSA (*behind the screen*): Has the man gone?

SERAFINA: That—man?

ROSA: Yes, "that man!"

SERAFINA (*inventing desperately*): I don't know how he got in. Maybe the back door was open.

ROSA: Oh, yes, maybe it was!

SERAFINA: Maybe he—climbed in a window . . .

ROSA: Or fell down the chimney, maybe! (*She comes from behind the screen, wearing the white bridal slip.*)

SERAFINA: Why you put on the white things I save for your wedding?

ROSA: Because I want to. That's a good enough reason. (*She combs her hair savagely.*)

SERAFINA: I want you to understand about that man. That was a man that—that was—that was a man that . . .

ROSA: You can't think of a lie?

SERAFINA: He was a—truckdriver, cara. He got in a fight, he was chase by—policemen!

ROSA: They chased him into your bedroom?

SERAFINA: I took pity on him, I give him first aid, I let him sleep on the floor. He give me his promise—he . . .

ROSA: Did he kneel in front of Our Lady? Did he promise that he would respect your innocence?

SERAFINA: Oh, cara, cara! (*abandoning all pretense*) He was Sicilian; he had rose oil in his hair and the rose tattoo of your father. In the dark room I couldn't see his clown face. I closed my eyes and dreamed that he was your father! I closed my eyes! I dreamed that he was your father . . .

ROSA: Basta, basta, non voglio sentire più niente! The only thing worse than a liar is a liar that's also a hypocrite!

SERAFINA: Senti, per favore! (*Rosa wheels about from the mirror and fixes her mother with a long and withering stare. Serafina cringes before it.*) Don't look at me like that with the eyes of your father! (*She shields her face as from a terrible glare.*)

ROSA: Yes, I am looking at you with the eyes of my father. I see you the way *he* saw you. (*She runs to the table and seizes *the piggy bank.*) Like this, this *pig!* (*Serafina utters a long, shuddering cry like a cry of childbirth.*) I need five dollars. I'll take it out of this! (*Rosa smashes the piggy bank to the floor and rakes some coins into her purse. Serafina stoops to the floor. There is the sound of a train whistle. Rosa is now fully dressed, but she hesitates, a little ashamed of her cruelty—but only a little. Serafina cannot meet her daughter's eyes. At last the girl speaks.*)

SERAFINA: How beautiful—is my daughter! Go to the boy!

ROSA (*as if she might be about to apologize*): Mama? He didn't touch me—he just said—"Che bella!"

(*Serafina turns slowly, shamefully, to face her. She is like a peasant in the presence of a young princess. Rosa stares at her a moment longer, then suddenly catches her breath and runs out of the house. As the girl leaves, Serafina calls:*)

SERAFINA: Rosa, Rosa, the—wrist watch! (*Serafina snatches up the little gift box and runs out onto the porch with it. She starts to call her daughter again, holding the gift out toward her, but her breath fails her.*) Rosa, Rosa, the—wrist watch . . . (*Her arms fall to her side. She turns, the gift still ungiven. Senselessly, absently, she holds the watch to her ear again. She shakes it a little, then utters a faint, startled laugh.*)

(*Assunta appears beside the house and walks directly in, as though Serafina had called her.*)

SERAFINA: Assunta, the urn is broken. The ashes are spilt on the floor and I can't touch them.

(*Assunta stoops to pick up the pieces of the shattered urn. Serafina has crossed to the shrine and relights the candle before the Madonna.*)

ASSUNTA: There are no ashes.

SERAFINA: Where—where are they? Where have the ashes gone?

ASSUNTA (*crossing to the shrine*): The wind has blown them away.

(*Assunta places what remains of the broken urn in Serafina's hands. Serafina turns it tenderly in her hands and then replaces it on the top of the prie-dieu before the Madonna.*)

SERAFINA: A man, when he burns, leaves only a handful of ashes. No woman can hold him. The wind must blow him away.

(*Alvaro's voice is heard, calling from the top of the highway embankment.*)

ALVARO'S VOICE: Rondinella felice!

(*The neighborhood women hear Alvaro calling, and there is a burst of mocking laughter from some of them. Then they all converge on the house from different directions and gather before the porch.*)

PEPPINA: Serafina delle Rose!
GIUSEPPINA: Baronessa! Baronessa delle Rose!
PEPPINA: There is a man on the road without the shirt!
GIUSEPPINA (*with delight*): Si, si! Senza camicia!
PEPPINA: All he got on his chest is a rose tattoo! (*to the women*) She lock up his shirt so he can't go to the high school?

(*The women shriek with laughter. In the house Serafina snatches up the package containing the silk shirt, while Assunta closes the shutters of the parlor windows.*)

SERAFINA: Un momento! (*She tears the paper off the shirt and rushes out onto the porch, holding the shirt above her head defiantly.*) Ecco la camicia!

(*With a soft cry, Serafina drops the shirt, which is immediately snatched up by Peppina. At this point the music begins again, with a crash of percussion, and continues to the end of the play. Peppina flourishes the shirt in the air like a banner and tosses it to Giuseppina, who is now on the embankment. Giuseppina tosses it on to Mariella, and she in her turn to Violetta, who is above her, so that the brilliantly colored shirt moves in a zig-zag course through the pampas grass to the very top of the embankment, like a streak of flame shooting up a dry hill. The women call out as they pass the shirt along:*)

PEPPINA: Guardate questa camicia! Coloro di rose!
MARIELLA (*shouting up to Alvaro*): Corragio, signor!
GIUSEPPINA: Avanti, avanti, signor!

VIOLETTA (*at the top of the embankment, giving the shirt a final flourish above her*): Corragio, corragio! The Baronessa is waiting!

(*Bursts of laughter are mingled with the cries of the women. Then they sweep away like a flock of screaming birds, and Serafina is left upon the porch, her eyes closed, a hand clasped to her breast. In the meanwhile, inside the house, Assunta has poured out a glass of wine. Now she comes to the porch, offering the wine to Serafina and murmuring:*)

ASSUNTA: Stai tranquilla.

SERAFINA (*breathlessly*): Assunta, I'll tell you something that maybe you won't believe.

ASSUNTA (*with tender humor*): It is impossible to tell me anything that I don't believe.

SERAFINA: Just now I felt on my breast the burning again of the rose. I know what it means. It means that I have conceived! (*She lifts the glass to her lips for a moment and then returns it to Assunta.*) Two lives again in the body! Two, two lives again, two!

ALVARO'S VOICE (*nearer now, and sweetly urgent*): Rondinella felice!

(*Alvaro is not visible on the embankment but Serafina begins to move slowly toward his voice.*)

ASSUNTA: Dove vai, Serafina?

SERAFINA (*shouting now, to Alvaro*): Vengo, vengo, amore!

(*She starts up the embankment toward Alvaro and the curtain falls as the music rises with her in great glissandi of sound.*)

CAMINO REAL

"In the middle of the journey of our life I came to myself in a dark wood where the straight way was lost."

CANTO I, DANTE'S *Inferno*

FOR ELIA KAZAN

FOREWORD*

It is amazing and frightening how completely one's whole being becomes absorbed in the making of a play. It is almost as if you were frantically constructing another world while the world that you live in dissolves beneath your feet, and that your survival depends on completing this construction at least one second before the old habitation collapses.

More than any other work that I have done, this play has seemed to me like the construction of another world, a separate existence. Of course, it is nothing more nor less than my conception of the time and world that I live in, and its people are mostly archetypes of certain basic attitudes and qualities with those mutations that would occur if they had continued along the road to this hypothetical terminal point in it.

A convention of the play is existence outside of time in a place of no specific locality. If you regard it that way, I suppose it becomes an elaborate allegory, but in New Haven we opened directly across the street from a movie theatre that was showing *Peter Pan* in Technicolor and it did not seem altogether inappropriate to me. Fairy tales nearly always have some simple moral lesson of good and evil, but that is not the secret of their fascination any more, I hope, than the philosophical import that might be distilled from the fantasies of *Camino Real* is the principal element of its appeal.

To me the appeal of this work is its unusual degree of freedom. When it began to get under way I felt a new sensation of release, as if I could "ride out" like a tenor sax taking the breaks in a Dixieland combo or a piano in a bop session. You may call it self-indulgence, but I was not doing it merely for myself. I could not have felt a purely private thrill of release unless I had hope of sharing this experience with lots and lots of audiences to come.

My desire was to give these audiences my own sense of something wild and unrestricted that ran like water in the mountains, or clouds changing shape in a gale, or the con-

*Written prior to the Broadway premiere of *Camino Real* and published in the New York *Times* on Sunday, March 15, 1953.

tinually dissolving and transforming images of a dream. This sort of freedom is not chaos nor anarchy. On the contrary, it is the result of painstaking design, and in this work I have given more conscious attention to form and construction than I have in any work before. Freedom is not achieved simply by working freely.

Elia Kazan was attracted to this work mainly, I believe, for the same reason—its freedom and mobility of form. I know that we have kept saying the word "flight" to each other as if the play were merely an abstraction of the impulse to fly, and most of the work out of town, his in staging, mine in cutting and revising, has been with this impulse in mind: the achievement of a continual flow. Speech after speech and bit after bit that were nice in themselves have been remorselessly blasted out of the script and its staging wherever they seemed to obstruct or divert this flow.

There have been plenty of indications already that this play will exasperate and confuse a certain number of people which we hope is not so large as the number it is likely to please. At each performance a number of people have stamped out of the auditorium, with little regard for those whom they have had to crawl over, almost as if the building had caught on fire, and there have been sibilant noises on the way out and demands for money back if the cashier was foolish enough to remain in his box.

I am at a loss to explain this phenomenon, and if I am being facetious about one thing, I am being quite serious about another when I say that I had never for one minute supposed that the play would seem obscure and confusing to anyone who was willing to meet it even less than halfway. It was a costly production, and for this reason I had to read it aloud, together with a few of the actors on one occasion, before large groups of prospective backers, before the funds to produce it were in the till. It was only then that I came up against the disconcerting surprise that some people would think that the play needed clarification.

My attitude is intransigent. I still don't agree that it needs any explanation. Some poet has said that a poem should not mean but be. Of course, a play is not a poem, not even a poetic play has quite the same license as a poem. But to go to

Camino Real with the inflexible demands of a logician is unfair to both parties.

In Philadelphia a young man from a literary periodical saw the play and then cross-examined me about all its dream-like images. He had made a list of them while he watched the play, and afterward at my hotel he brought out the list and asked me to explain the meaning of each one. I can't deny that I use a lot of those things called symbols but being a self-defensive creature, I say that symbols are nothing but the natural speech of drama.

We all have in our conscious and unconscious minds a great vocabulary of images, and I think all human communication is based on these images as are our dreams; and a symbol in a play has only one legitimate purpose which is to say a thing more directly and simply and beautifully than it could be said in words.

I hate writing that is a parade of images for the sake of images; I hate it so much that I close a book in disgust when it keeps on saying one thing is like another; I even get disgusted with poems that make nothing but comparisons between one thing and another. But I repeat that symbols, when used respectfully, are the purest language of plays. Sometimes it would take page after tedious page of exposition to put across an idea that can be said with an object or a gesture on the lighted stage.

To take one case in point: the battered portmanteau of Jacques Casanova is hurled from the balcony of a luxury hotel when his remittance check fails to come through. While the portmanteau is still in the air, he shouts: "Careful, I have—"—and when it has crashed to the street he continues —"fragile—mementoes . . ." I suppose that is a symbol, at least it is an object used to express as directly and vividly as possible certain things which could be said in pages of dull talk.

As for those patrons who departed before the final scene, I offer myself this tentative bit of solace: that these theatregoers may be a little domesticated in their theatrical tastes. A cage represents security as well as confinement to a bird that has grown used to being in it; and when a theatrical work kicks over the traces with such apparent insouciance, security seems challenged and, instead of participating in its sense of freedom, one out of a certain number of playgoers will rush back out to the more accustomed implausibility of the street he lives on.

To modify this effect of complaisance I would like to admit to you quite frankly that I can't say with any personal conviction that I have written a good play, I only know that I have felt a release in this work which I wanted you to feel with me.

Tennessee Williams

AFTERWORD

ONCE in a while someone will say to me that he would rather wait for a play to come out as a book than see a live performance of it, where he would be distracted from its true values, if it has any, by so much that is mere spectacle and sensation and consequently must be meretricious and vulgar. There are plays meant for reading. I have read them. I have read the works of "thinking playwrights" as distinguished from us who are permitted only to feel, and probably read them earlier and appreciated them as much as those who invoke their names nowadays like the incantation of Aristophanes' frogs. But the incontinent blaze of a live theatre, a theatre meant for seeing and for feeling, has never been and never will be extinguished by a bucket brigade of critics, new or old, bearing vessels that range from cut-glass punch bowl to Haviland teacup. And in my dissident opinion, a play in a book is only the shadow of a play and not even a clear shadow of it. Those who did not like *Camino Real* on the stage will not be likely to form a higher opinion of it in print, for of all the works I have written, this one was meant most for the vulgarity of performance. The printed script of a play is hardly more than an architect's blueprint of a house not yet built or built and destroyed.

The color, the grace and levitation, the structural pattern in motion, the quick interplay of live beings, suspended like fitful lightning in a cloud, these things are the play, not words on paper, nor thoughts and ideas of an author, those shabby things snatched off basement counters at Gimbel's.

My own creed as a playwright is fairly close to that expressed by the painter in Shaw's play *The Doctor's Dilemma*: "I believe in Michelangelo, Velasquez and Rembrandt; in the might of design, the mystery of color, the redemption of all things by beauty everlasting and the message of art that has made these hands blessed. Amen."

How much art his hands were blessed with or how much mine are, I don't know, but that art is a blessing is certain and that it contains its message is also certain, and I feel, as the painter did, that the message lies in those abstract beauties of form and color and line, to which I would add light and motion.

In these following pages are only the formula by which a play could exist.

Dynamic is a word in disrepute at the moment, and so, I suppose, is the word *organic,* but those terms still define the dramatic values that I value most and which I value more as they are more deprecated by the ones self-appointed to save what they have never known.

Tennessee Williams
June 1, 1953

PROLOGUE

As the curtain rises, on an almost lightless stage, there is a loud singing of wind, accompanied by distant, measured reverberations like pounding surf or distant shellfire. Above the ancient wall that backs the set and the perimeter of mountains visible above the wall, are flickers of a white radiance as though daybreak were a white bird caught in a net and struggling to rise.

The plaza is seen fitfully by this light. It belongs to a tropical seaport that bears a confusing, but somehow harmonious, resemblance to such widely scattered ports as Tangiers, Havana, Vera Cruz, Casablanca, Shanghai, New Orleans.

On stage left is the luxury side of the street, containing the façade of the Siete Mares hotel and its low terrace on which are a number of glass-topped white iron tables and chairs. In the downstairs there is a great bay window in which are seen a pair of elegant "dummies," one seated, one standing behind, looking out into the plaza with painted smiles. Upstairs is a small balcony and behind it a large window exposing a wall on which is hung a phoenix painted on silk: this should be softly lighted now and then in the play, since resurrections are so much a part of its meaning.

Opposite the hotel is Skid Row which contains the Gypsy's gaudy stall, the Loan Shark's establishment with a window containing a variety of pawned articles, and the "Ritz Men Only" which is a flea-bag hotel or flophouse and which has a practical window above its downstairs entrance, in which a bum will appear from time to time to deliver appropriate or contrapuntal song titles.

Upstage is a great flight of stairs that mount the ancient wall to a sort of archway that leads out into "Terra Incognita," as it is called in the play, a wasteland between the walled town and the distant perimeter of snow-topped mountains.

Downstage right and left are a pair of arches which give entrance to dead-end streets.

Immediately after the curtain rises a shaft of blue light is thrown down a central aisle of the theatre, and in this light, advancing from the back of the house, appears Don Quixote de la Mancha, dressed like an old "desert rat." As he enters the aisle he shouts, "Hola!", in a cracked old voice which is still full of energy and is answered by another voice which is impatient and tired, that of his squire, Sancho Panza. Stumbling with a fatigue which is only physical, the old knight comes down the aisle, and Sancho follows a couple of yards behind him, loaded down with equipment that ranges from a medieval shield to a military canteen or Thermos bottle. Shouts are exchanged between them.

QUIXOTE (*ranting above the wind in a voice which is nearly as old*): Blue is the color of distance!

SANCHO (*wearily behind him*): Yes, distance is blue.

QUIXOTE: Blue is also the color of nobility.

SANCHO: Yes, nobility's blue.

QUIXOTE: Blue is the color of distance and nobility, and that's why an old knight should always have somewhere about him a bit of blue ribbon . . .

(*He jostles the elbow of an aisle-sitter as he staggers with fatigue; he mumbles an apology.*)

SANCHO: Yes, a bit of blue ribbon.

QUIXOTE: A bit of faded blue ribbon, tucked away in whatever remains of his armor, or borne on the tip of his lance, his—unconquerable lance! It serves to remind an old knight of distance that he has gone and distance he has yet to go . . .

(*Sancho mutters the Spanish word for excrement as several pieces of rusty armor fall into the aisle.*

(*Quixote has now arrived at the foot of the steps onto the forestage. He pauses there as if wandering out of or into a dream. Sancho draws up clanking behind him.*

(*Mr. Gutman, a lordly fat man wearing a linen suit and a pith helmet, appears dimly on the balcony of the Siete Mares, a white cockatoo on his wrist. The bird cries out harshly.*)

GUTMAN: Hush, Aurora.

QUIXOTE: It also reminds an old knight of that green country he lived in which was the youth of his heart, before such singing words as *Truth*!

SANCHO (*panting*): — Truth.

QUIXOTE: *Valor!*

SANCHO: —Valor.

QUIXOTE (*elevating his lance*): *Devoir!*

SANCHO: —Devoir . . .

QUIXOTE: —turned into the meaningless mumble of some old monk hunched over cold mutton at supper!

(*Gutman alerts a pair of Guards in the plaza, who cross with red lanterns to either side of the proscenium where they lower black and white striped barrier gates as if the proscenium marked a frontier. One of them, with a hand on his holster, advances toward the pair on the steps.*)

GUARD: Vien aquí.

(*Sancho hangs back but Quixote stalks up to the barrier gate. The Guard turns a flashlight on his long and exceedingly grave red face, "frisks" him casually for concealed weapons, examines a rusty old knife and tosses it contemptuously away.*)

Sus papeles! Sus documentos!

(*Quixote fumblingly produces some tattered old papers from the lining of his hat.*)

GUTMAN (*impatiently*): Who is it?

GUARD: An old desert rat named Quixote.

GUTMAN: Oh!—Expected!—Let him in.

(*The Guards raise the barrier gate and one sits down to smoke on the terrace. Sancho hangs back still. A dispute takes place on the forestage and steps into the aisle.*)

QUIXOTE: Forward!

SANCHO: Aw, naw. I know this place. (*He produces a crumpled parchment.*) Here it is on the chart. Look, it says here: "Continue until you come to the square of a walled town which is the end of the Ca*mi*no Re*al* and the beginning of the *Ca*mino *Re*al. Halt there," it says, "and turn back, Traveler, for the spring of humanity has gone dry in this place and—"

QUIXOTE (*He snatches the chart from him and reads the rest of the inscription.*): "—there are no birds in the country except wild birds that are tamed and kept in—" (*He holds the chart close to his nose.*) —*Cages!*

SANCHO (*urgently*): Let's go back to La Mancha!
QUIXOTE: Forward!
SANCHO: The time has come for retreat!
QUIXOTE: The time for retreat never comes!
SANCHO: *I'm* going back to *La Mancha!* (*He dumps the knightly equipment into the orchestra pit.*)
QUIXOTE: *Without me?*
SANCHO (*bustling up the aisle*): With you or without you, old tireless and tiresome master!
QUIXOTE (*imploringly*): *Saaaaaan-chooooooooo!*
SANCHO (*near the top of the aisle*): I'm going back to La *Maaaaaaaaan-chaaaaaaa* . . .

(*He disappears as the blue light in the aisle dims out. The Guard puts out his cigarette and wanders out of the plaza. The wind moans and Gutman laughs softly as the Ancient Knight enters the plaza with such a desolate air.*)

QUIXOTE (*looking about the plaza*): —Lonely . . .

(*To his surprise the word is echoed softly by almost unseen figures huddled below the stairs and against the wall of the town. Quixote leans upon his lance and observes with a wry smile—*)

—When so many are lonely as seem to be lonely, it would be inexcusably selfish to be lonely alone.

(*He shakes out a dusty blanket. Shadowy arms extend toward him and voices murmur.*)

VOICE: Sleep. Sleep. Sleep.
QUIXOTE (*arranging his blanket*): Yes, I'll sleep for a while, I'll sleep and dream for a while against the wall of this town . . .

(*A mandolin or guitar plays "The Nightingale of France."*)

—And my dream will be a pageant, a masque in which old meanings will be remembered and possibly new ones discovered, and when I wake from this sleep and this disturbing pageant of a dream, I'll choose one among its shadows to take along with me in the place of Sancho . . .

(*He blows his nose between his fingers and wipes them on his shirttail.*)

—For new companions are not as familiar as old ones but all the same—they're old ones with only slight differences of face and figure, which may or may not be improvements, and it would be selfish of me to be lonely alone . . .

(*He stumbles down the incline into the Pit below the stairs where most of the Street People huddle beneath awnings of open stalls.*

(*The white cockatoo squawks.*)

GUTMAN: Hush, Aurora.

QUIXOTE: And tomorrow at this same hour, which we call madrugada, the loveliest of all words, except the word alba, and that word also means daybreak—

—Yes, at daybreak tomorrow I will go on from here with a new companion and this old bit of blue ribbon to keep me in mind of distance that I have gone and distance I have yet to go, and also to keep me in mind of—

(*The cockatoo cries wildly.*

(*Quixote nods as if in agreement with the outcry and folds himself into his blanket below the great stairs.*)

GUTMAN (*stroking the cockatoo's crest*): Be still, Aurora. I know it's morning, Aurora.

(*Daylight turns the plaza silver and slowly gold. Vendors rise beneath white awnings of stalls. The Gypsy's stall opens. A tall, courtly figure, in his late middle years* [*Jacques Casanova*] *crosses from the Siete Mares to the Loan Shark's, removing a silver snuff box from his pocket as Gutman speaks. His costume, like that of all the legendary characters in the play* [*except perhaps Quixote*] *is generally "modern" but with vestigial touches of the period to which he was actually related. The cane and the snuff box and perhaps a brocaded vest may be sufficient to give this historical suggestion in Casanova's case. He bears his hawklike head with a sort of anxious pride on most occasions, a pride maintained under a steadily mounting pressure.*)

—It's morning and after morning. It's afternoon, ha ha! And now I must go downstairs to announce the beginning of that old wanderer's dream . . .

(*He withdraws from the balcony as old Prudence Duvernoy stumbles out of the hotel, as if not yet quite awake from an afternoon siesta. Chattering with beads and bracelets, she wanders vaguely down into the plaza, raising a faded green silk parasol, damp henna-streaked hair slipping under a monstrous hat of faded silk roses; she is searching for a lost poodle.*)

PRUDENCE: Trique? Trique?

(*Jacques comes out of the Loan Shark's replacing his case angrily in his pocket.*)

JACQUES: Why, I'd rather give it to a street beggar! This case is a Boucheron, I won it at faro at the summer palace, at Tsarskoe Selo in the winter of—

(*The Loan Shark slams the door. Jacques glares, then shrugs and starts across the plaza. Old Prudence is crouched over the filthy gray bundle of a dying mongrel by the fountain.*)

PRUDENCE: Trique, oh, Trique!

(*The Gypsy's son, Abdullah, watches, giggling.*)

JACQUES (*reproving*): It is a terrible thing for an old woman to outlive her dogs.

(*He crosses to Prudence and gently disengages the animal from her grasp.*)

Madam, that is not Trique.

PRUDENCE: —When I woke up she wasn't in her basket . . .

JACQUES: Sometimes we sleep too long in the afternoon and when we wake we find things changed, Signora.

PRUDENCE: Oh, you're Italian!

JACQUES: I am from Venice, Signora.

PRUDENCE: Ah, Venice, city of pearls! I saw you last night on the terrace dining with— Oh, I'm so worried about her! I'm an old friend of hers, perhaps she's mentioned me to you. Prudence Duvernoy? I was her best friend in the old days in Paris, but now she's forgotten so much . . .

I hope you have influence with her!

(*A waltz of Camille's time in Paris is heard.*)

I want you to give her a message from a certain wealthy old gentleman that she met at one of those watering places she used to go to for her health. She resembled his daughter who died of consumption and so he adored Camille, lavished everything on her! What did she do? Took a young lover who hadn't a couple of pennies to rub together, disinherited by his father because of *her!* Oh, you can't do that, not now, not any more, you've got to be realistic on the Camino Real!

(*Gutman has come out on the terrace: he announces quietly—*)

GUTMAN: Block One on the Camino Real.

BLOCK ONE

PRUDENCE (*continuing*): Yes, you've got to be practical on it! Well, give her this message, please, Sir. He wants her back on any terms whatsoever! (*Her speech gathers furious momentum.*) Her evenings will be free. He wants only her mornings, mornings are hard on old men because their hearts beat slowly, and he wants only her mornings! Well, that's how it should be! A sensible arrangement! Elderly gentlemen have to content themselves with a lady's spare time before supper! Isn't that so? Of course so! And so I told him! I told him, Camille isn't well! She requires delicate care! Has many debts, creditors storm her door! "How much does she owe?" he asked me, and, oh, did I do some lightning mathematics! Jewels in pawn, I told him, pearls, rings, necklaces, bracelets, diamond ear-drops are in pawn! Horses put up for sale at a public auction!

JACQUES (*appalled by this torrent*): Signora, Signora, all of these things are—

PRUDENCE: —What?

JACQUES: *Dreams!*

(*Gutman laughs. A woman sings at a distance.*)

PRUDENCE (*continuing with less assurance*): —You're not so young as I thought when I saw you last night on the terrace by candlelight on the— Oh, but— Ho ho!—I bet there is *one* old fountain in this plaza that hasn't gone dry!

(*She pokes him obscenely. He recoils. Gutman laughs. Jacques starts away but she seizes his arm again, and the torrent of speech continues.*)

PRUDENCE: Wait, wait, listen! Her candle is burning low. But how can you tell? She might have a lingering end, and charity hospitals? Why, you might as well take a flying leap into the Streetcleaners' barrel. Oh, I've told her and told her not to live in a dream! A dream is nothing to live in, why, it's gone like a—

Don't let her elegance fool you! That girl has done the Camino in carriages but she has also done it on foot! She knows every stone the Camino is paved with! So tell her this. You tell her, she won't listen to me!—Times and conditions have undergone certain changes since we were friends in Paris, and now we dismiss young lovers with skins of silk and eyes like a child's first prayer, we put them away as lightly as we put away white gloves meant only for summer, and pick up a pair of black ones, suitable for winter . . .

(*The singing voice rises: then subsides.*)

JACQUES: Excuse me, Madam.

(*He tears himself from her grasp and rushes into the Siete Mares.*)

PRUDENCE (*dazed, to Gutman*): —What block is this?
GUTMAN: Block One.
PRUDENCE: I didn't hear the announcement . . .
GUTMAN (*coldly*): Well, now you do.

(*Olympe comes out of the lobby with a pale orange silk parasol like a floating moon.*)

OLYMPE: Oh, there you are, I've looked for you high and low!—mostly low . . .

(*They float vaguely out into the dazzling plaza as though a capricious wind took them, finally drifting through the Moorish arch downstage right.*

(*The song dies out.*)

GUTMAN (*lighting a thin cigar*): Block Two on the Camino Real.

BLOCK TWO

After Gutman's announcement, a hoarse cry is heard. A figure in rags, skin blackened by the sun, tumbles crazily down the steep alley to the plaza. He turns about blindly, murmuring: "A donde la fuente?" He stumbles against the hideous old prostitute Rosita who grins horribly and whispers something to him, hitching up her ragged, filthy skirt. Then she gives him a jocular push toward the fountain. He falls upon his belly and thrusts his hands into the dried-up basin. Then he staggers to his feet with a despairing cry.

THE SURVIVOR: La fuente está seca!

(*Rosita laughs madly but the other Street People moan. A dry gourd rattles.*)

ROSITA: The fountain is dry, but there's plenty to drink in the Siete Mares!

(*She shoves him toward the hotel. The proprietor, Gutman, steps out, smoking a thin cigar, fanning himself with a palm leaf. As the Survivor advances, Gutman whistles. A man in military dress comes out upon the low terrace.*)

OFFICER: Go back!

(*The Survivor stumbles forward. The Officer fires at him. He lowers his hands to his stomach, turns slowly about with a lost expression, looking up at the sky, and stumbles toward the fountain. During the scene that follows, until the entrance of La Madrecita and her Son, the Survivor drags himself slowly about the concrete rim of the fountain, almost entirely ignored, *as a dying pariah dog in a starving country. Jacques Casanova comes out upon the terrace of the Siete Mares. Now he passes the hotel proprietor's impassive figure, descending a step beneath and a little in advance of him, and without looking at him.*)

JACQUES (*with infinite weariness and disgust*): What has happened?

GUTMAN (*serenely*): We have entered the second in a progress of sixteen blocks on the Camino Real. It's five o'clock. That angry old lion, the Sun, looked back once and growled and then went switching his tail toward the cool shade of the Sierras. Our guests have taken their afternoon siestas . . .

(*The Survivor has come out upon the forestage, now, not like a dying man but like a shy speaker who has forgotten the opening line of his speech. He is only a little crouched over with a hand obscuring the red stain over his belly. Two or three Street People wander about calling their wares: "Tacos, tacos, fritos . . ."—"Lotería, lotería"—Rosita shuffles around, calling "Love? Love?"—pulling down the filthy décolletage of her blouse to show more of her sagging bosom. The Survivor arrives at the top of the stairs descending into the orchestra of the theatre, and hangs onto it, looking out reflectively as a man over the rail of a boat coming into a somewhat disturbingly strange harbor.*)

GUTMAN (*continuing*): —They suffer from extreme fatigue, our guests at the Siete Mares, all of them have a degree or two of fever. Questions are passed amongst them like something illicit and shameful, like counterfeit money or drugs or indecent postcards—

(*He leans forward and whispers:*)

—"What is this place? Where are we? What is the meaning of—*Shhhh*!"—Ha ha . . .

THE SURVIVOR (*very softly to the audience*): I once had a pony named Peeto. He caught in his nostrils the scent of thunderstorms coming even before the clouds had crossed the Sierra . . .

VENDOR: Tacos, tacos, fritos . . .

ROSITA: Love? Love?

LADY MULLIGAN (*to waiter on terrace*): Are you sure no one called me? I was expecting a call . . .

GUTMAN (*smiling*): My guests are confused and exhausted but at this hour they pull themselves together, and drift downstairs on the wings of gin and the lift, they drift into the public rooms and exchange notes again on fashionable couturiers and custom tailors, restaurants, vintages of wine, hair-dressers, plastic surgeons, girls and young men susceptible to offers . . .

(*There is a hum of light conversation and laughter within.*)

—Hear them? They're exchanging notes . . .

JACQUES (*striking the terrace with his cane*): I asked you what has happened in the plaza!

GUTMAN: Oh, in the plaza, ha ha!—Happenings in the plaza don't concern us . . .

JACQUES: I heard shots fired.

GUTMAN: Shots were fired to remind you of your good fortune in staying here. The public fountains have gone dry, you know, but the Siete Mares was erected over the only perpetual never-dried-up spring in Tierra Caliente, and of course that advantage has to be—protected—sometimes by—martial law . . .

(*The guitar resumes.*)

THE SURVIVOR: When Peeto, my pony, was born—he stood on his four legs at once, and accepted the world!—He was wiser than I . . .

VENDOR: Fritos, fritos, tacos!

ROSITA: Love!

THE SURVIVOR: —When Peeto was one year old he was wiser than God!

(*A wind sings across the plaza; a dry gourd rattles.*)

"Peeto, Peeto!" the Indian boys call after him, trying to stop him—trying to stop the wind!

(*The Survivor's head sags forward. He sits down as slowly as an old man on a park bench. Jacques strikes the terrace again with his cane and starts toward the Survivor. The Guard seizes his elbow.*)

JACQUES: Don't put your hand on *me*!
GUARD: *Stay here.*
GUTMAN: Remain on the terrace, please, Signor Casanova.
JACQUES (*fiercely*):— *Cognac!*

(*The Waiter whispers to Gutman. Gutman chuckles.*)

GUTMAN: The Maître D' tells me that your credit has been discontinued in the restaurant and bar, he says that he has enough of your tabs to pave the terrace with!

JACQUES: What a piece of impertinence! I told the man that the letter that I'm expecting has been delayed in the mail. The postal service in this country is fantastically disorganized, and you know it! You also know that Mlle. Gautier will guarantee my tabs!

GUTMAN: Then let her pick them up at dinner tonight if you're hungry!

JACQUES: I'm not accustomed to this kind of treatment on the Ca*mi*no Re*al*!

GUTMAN: Oh, you'll be, you'll be, after a single night at the "Ritz Men Only." That's where you'll have to transfer your patronage if the letter containing the remittance check doesn't arrive tonight.

JACQUES: I assure you that I shall do nothing of the sort!—Tonight or ever!

GUTMAN: Watch out, old hawk, the wind is ruffling your feathers!

(*Jacques sinks trembling into a chair.*)

—Give him a thimble of brandy before he collapses . . . Fury is a luxury of the young, their veins are resilient, but his are brittle . . .

JACQUES: Here I sit, submitting to insult for a thimble of brandy—while directly in front of me—

(*The singer, La Madrecita, enters the plaza. She is a blind woman led by a ragged Young Man. The Waiter brings Jacques a brandy.*)

—a man in the plaza dies like a pariah dog!—I take the brandy! I sip it!—My heart is too tired to break, my heart is too tired to—break . . .

(*La Madrecita chants softly. She slowly raises her arm to point at the Survivor crouched on the steps from the plaza.*)

GUTMAN (*suddenly*): Give me the phone! Connect me with the Palace. Get me the Generalissimo, quick, quick, quick!

(*The Survivor rises feebly and shuffles very slowly toward the extended arms of "The Little Blind One."*)

Generalissimo? Gutman speaking! Hello, sweetheart. There has been a little incident in the plaza. You know that party of young explorers that attempted to cross the desert on foot? Well, one of them's come back. He was very thirsty. He found the fountain dry. He started toward the hotel. He was politely advised to advance no further. But he disregarded this advice. Action had to be taken. And now, and now—that old blind woman they call "La Madrecita"?—She's come into the plaza with the man called "The Dreamer" . . .

SURVIVOR: Donde?

THE DREAMER: Aquí!

GUTMAN (*continuing*): You remember those two! I once mentioned them to you. You said "They're harmless dreamers and they're loved by the people."—"What," I asked you, "is harmless about a dreamer, and what," I asked you, "is harmless about the love of the people?—Revolution only needs good dreamers who remember their dreams, and the love of the people belongs safely only to you—their Generalissimo!"—Yes, now the blind woman has recovered her sight and is extending her arms to the wounded Survivor, and the man with the guitar is leading him to her . . .

(*The described action is being enacted.*)

Wait one moment! There's a possibility that the forbidden word may be spoken! Yes! The forbidden word is about to be spoken!

(*The Dreamer places an arm about the blinded Survivor, and cries out:*)

THE DREAMER: *Hermano!*

(*The cry is repeated like springing fire and a loud murmur sweeps the crowd. They push forward with cupped hands extended and the gasping cries of starving people at the sight of bread. Two Military Guards herd them back under the colonnades with clubs and drawn revolvers. La Madrecita chants softly with her blind eyes lifted. A Guard starts toward her. The People shout "NO!"*)

LA MADRECITA (*chanting*): "Rojo está el sol! Rojo está el sol de sangre! Blanca está la luna! Blanca está la luna de miedo!"

(*The crowd makes a turning motion.*)

GUTMAN (*to the waiter*): *Put up the ropes!*

(*Velvet ropes are strung very quickly about the terrace of the Siete Mares. They are like the ropes on decks of steamers in rough waters. Gutman shouts into the phone again:*)

The word was spoken. The crowd is agitated. Hang on!

(*He lays down instrument.*)

JACQUES (*hoarsely, shaken*): He said "Hermano." That's the word for brother.

GUTMAN (*calmly*): Yes, the most dangerous word in any human tongue is the word for brother. It's inflammatory.—I don't suppose it can be struck out of the language altogether but it must be reserved for strictly private usage in back of soundproof walls. Otherwise it disturbs the population . . .

JACQUES: The people need the word. They're thirsty for it!

GUTMAN: What are these creatures? Mendicants. Prostitutes. Thieves and petty vendors in a bazaar where the human heart is a part of the bargain.

JACQUES: Because they need the word and the word is forbidden!

GUTMAN: The word is said in pulpits and at tables of council where its volatile essence can be contained. But on the lips of these creatures, what is it? A wanton incitement to riot, without understanding. For what is a brother to them but someone to get ahead of, to cheat, to lie to, to undersell in the market. Brother, you say to a man whose wife you sleep with!—But now, you see, the word has disturbed the people and made it necessary to invoke martial law!

(*Meanwhile the Dreamer has brought the Survivor to La Madrecita, who is seated on the cement rim of the fountain. She has cradled the dying man in her arms in the attitude of a* Pietà. *The Dreamer is crouched beside them, softly playing a guitar. Now he springs up with a harsh cry:*)

THE DREAMER: *Muerto!*

(*The Streetcleaners' piping commences at a distance. Gutman seizes the phone again.*)

GUTMAN (*into phone*): Generalissimo, the Survivor is no longer surviving. I think we'd better have some public diversion right away. Put the Gypsy on! Have her announce the Fiesta!

LOUDSPEAKER (*responding instantly*): Damas y Caballeros! The next voice you hear will be the voice of—the Gypsy!

GYPSY (*over loudspeaker*): Hoy! Noche de Fiesta! Tonight the moon will restore the virginity of my daughter!

GUTMAN: Bring on the Gypsy's daughter, Esmeralda. Show the virgin-to-be!

(*Esmeralda is led from the Gypsy's stall by a severe duenna, "Nursie," out upon the forestage. She is manacled by the wrist to the duenna. Her costume is vaguely Levantine.*

(*Guards are herding the crowd back again.*)

GUTMAN: Ha ha! Ho ho ho! Music!

(*There is gay music. Rosita dances.*)

Abdullah! You're on!

(*Abdullah skips into the plaza, shouting histrionically.*)

ABDULLAH: Tonight the moon will restore the virginity of my sister, Esmeralda!

GUTMAN: *Dance, boy!*

(*Esmeralda is led back into the stall. Throwing off his burnoose, Abdullah dances with Rosita. Behind their dance, armed Guards force La Madrecita and the Dreamer to retreat from the fountain, leaving the lifeless body of the survivor. All at once there is a discordant blast of brass instruments.*

(*Kilroy comes into the plaza. He is a young American vagrant, about twenty-seven. He wears dungarees and a skivvy shirt, the pants faded nearly white from long wear and much washing, fitting him as closely as the clothes of sculpture. He has a pair of golden boxing gloves slung about his neck and he carries a small duffle bag. His belt is ruby-and-emerald-studded with the word CHAMP in bold letters. He stops before a chalked inscription on a wall downstage which says: "Kilroy Is Coming!" He scratches out "Coming" and over it prints "Here!"*)

GUTMAN: Ho ho!—a clown! The Eternal Punchinella! That's exactly what's needed in a time of crisis!

Block Three on the Camino Real.

BLOCK THREE

KILROY (*genially, to all present*): Ha ha!

(*Then he walks up to the Officer by the terrace of the Siete Mares.*)

Buenas dias, señor.

(*He gets no response—barely even a glance.*)

Habla Inglesia? Usted?

OFFICER: What is it you want?

KILROY: Where is Western Union or Wells-Fargo? I got to send a wire to some friends in the States.

OFFICER: No hay Western Union, no hay Wells-Fargo.

KILROY: That is very peculiar. I never struck a town yet that didn't have one or the other. I just got off a boat. Lousiest frigging tub I ever shipped on, one continual hell it was, all the way up from Rio. And me sick, too. I picked up one of those tropical fevers. No sick-bay on that tub, no doctor, no medicine or nothing, not even one quinine pill, and I was burning up with Christ knows how much fever. I couldn't make them understand I was sick. I got a bad heart, too. I had to retire from the prize ring because of my heart. I was the light heavyweight champion of the West Coast, won these gloves!—before my ticker went bad.—Feel my chest! Go on, feel it! Feel it. I've got a heart in my chest as big as the head of a baby. Ha ha! They stood me in front of a screen that makes you transparent and that's what they seen inside me, a heart in my chest as big as the head of a baby! With something like that you don't need the Gypsy to tell you, "Time is short, Baby—get ready to hitch on wings!" The medics wouldn't okay me for no more fights. They said to give up liquor and smoking and sex!—To give up sex!—I used to believe a man couldn't live without sex—but he can—if he wants to! My real true woman, my wife, she would of stuck with me, but it was all spoiled with her being scared and me, too, that a real hard kiss would kill me!—So one night while she was sleeping I wrote her good-bye . . .

(*He notices a lack of attention in the Officer: he grins.*)

No comprendo the lingo?

OFFICER: What is it you want?

KILROY: Excuse my ignorance, but what place is this? What is this country and what is the name of this town? I know it seems funny of me to ask such a question. Loco! But I was so glad to get off that rotten tub that I didn't ask nothing of no one except my pay—and I got short-changed on that. I have trouble counting these pesos or Whatzit-you-call-'em.

(*He jerks out his wallet.*)

All-a-this-here. In the States that pile of lettuce would make you a plutocrat!—But I bet you this stuff don't add up to fifty dollars American coin. Ha ha!

OFFICER: Ha ha.

KILROY: Ha ha!

OFFICER (*making it sound like a death-rattle*): Ha-ha-ha-ha-ha.

(*He turns and starts into the cantina. Kilroy grabs his arm.*)

KILROY: Hey!

OFFICER: What is it you want?

KILROY: What is the name of this country and this town?

(*The Officer thrusts his elbow in Kilroy's stomach and twists his arm loose with a Spanish curse. He kicks the swinging doors open and enters the cantina.*)

Brass hats are the same everywhere.

(*As soon as the Officer goes, the Street People come forward and crowd about Kilroy with their wheedling cries.*)

STREET PEOPLE: Dulces, dulces! Lotería! Lotería! Pasteles, café con leche!

KILROY: No caree, no caree!

(*The Prostitute creeps up to him and grins.*)

ROSITA: Love? Love?

KILROY: What did you say?

ROSITA: *Love?*

KILROY: Sorry—I don't feature that. (*To audience*) I have ideals.

(*The Gypsy appears on the roof of her establishment with Esmeralda whom she secures by handcuffs to the iron railing.*)

GYPSY: Stay there while I give the pitch!

(*She then advances with a portable microphone.*)

Testing! One, two, three, four!

NURSIE (*from offstage*): You're on the air!

GYPSY'S LOUDSPEAKER: Are you perplexed by something? Are you tired out and confused? Do you have a fever?

(*Kilroy looks around for the source of the voice.*)

Do you feel yourself to be spiritually unprepared for the age of exploding atoms? Do you distrust the newspapers? Are you suspicious of governments? Have you arrived at a point on the Camino Real where the walls converge not in the distance but right in front of your nose? Does further progress appear impossible to you? Are you afraid of anything at all? Afraid of your heartbeat? Or the eyes of strangers! Afraid of breathing? Afraid of not breathing? Do you wish that things could be straight and simple again as they were in your childhood? Would you like to go back to Kindy Garten?

(*Rosita has crept up to Kilroy while he listens. She reaches out to him. At the same time a Pickpocket lifts his wallet.*)

KILROY (*catching the whore's wrist*): Keep y'r hands off me, y' dirty ole bag! No caree putas! No loteria, no dulces, nada— so get away! Vamoose! All of you! Quit picking at me!

(*He reaches in his pocket and jerks out a handful of small copper and silver coins which he flings disgustedly down the street. The grotesque people scramble after it with their inhuman cries. Kilroy goes on a few steps—then stops short—feeling the back pocket of his dungarees. Then he lets out a startled cry.*)

Robbed! My God, I've been robbed!

(*The Street People scatter to the walls.*)

Which of you got my wallet? *Which* of you dirty—? Shh—Uh!

(*They mumble with gestures of incomprehension. He marches back to the entrance to the hotel.*)

Hey! Officer! Official!—General!

(*The Officer finally lounges out of the hotel entrance and glances at Kilroy.*)

Tiende? One of them's got my wallet! Picked it out of my pocket while that old whore there was groping me! Don't you comprendo?

OFFICER: Nobody rob you. You don't have no pesos.

KILROY: Huh?

OFFICER: You just dreaming that you have money. You don't ever have money. Nunca! Nada!

(*He spits between his teeth.*)

Loco . . .

(*The Officer crosses to the fountain. Kilroy stares at him, then bawls out:*)

KILROY (*to the Street People*): We'll see what the American Embassy has to say about this! I'll go to the American Consul. Whichever of you rotten spivs lifted my wallet is going to jail—calaboose! I hope I have made myself plain. If not, I will make myself plainer!

(*There are scattered laughs among the crowd. He crosses to the fountain. He notices the body of the no longer Survivor, kneels beside it, shakes it, turns it over, springs up and shouts:*)

Hey! This guy is dead!

(*There is the sound of the Streetcleaners' piping. They trundle their white barrel into the plaza from one of the downstage arches. The appearance of these men undergoes a progressive alteration through the play. When they first appear they are almost like any such public servants in a tropical country; their white jackets are dirtier than the musicians' and some of the stains are red. They have on white caps with black visors. They are continually exchanging sly jokes and giggling unpleasantly together. Lord Mulligan has come out upon the terrace and as they pass him, they pause for a moment, point at him, snicker. He is extremely discomfited by this impertinence, touches his chest as if he felt a palpitation and turns back inside.*

(*Kilroy yells to the advancing Streetcleaners.*)

There's a dead man layin' here!

(*They giggle again. Briskly they lift the body and stuff it into the barrel; then trundle it off, looking back at Kilroy, giggling, whispering. They return under the downstage arch through which they entered. Kilroy, in a low, shocked voice:*)

What *is* this place? What kind of a hassle have I got myself into?

LOUDSPEAKER: If anyone on the Camino is bewildered, come to the Gypsy. A poco dinero will tickle the Gypsy's palm and give her visions!

ABDULLAH (*giving Kilroy a card*): If you got a question, ask my mama, the Gypsy!

KILROY: Man, whenever you see those three brass balls on a street, you don't have to look a long ways for a Gypsy. Now le' me think. I am faced with three problems. One: I'm hungry. Two: I'm lonely. Three: I'm in a place where I don't know what it is or how I got there! First action that's indicated is to—cash in on something—Well . . . let's see . . .

(*Honky-tonk music fades in at this point and the Skid Row façade begins to light up for the evening. There is the Gypsy's stall with its cabalistic devices, its sectional cranium and palm, three luminous brass balls overhanging the entrance to the Loan Shark and his window filled with a vast assortment of hocked articles for sale: trumpets, banjos, fur coats, tuxedos, a gown of scarlet sequins, loops of pearls and rhinestones. Dimly behind this display is a neon sign in three pastel colors, pink, green, and blue. It fades softly in and out and it says: "Magic Tricks Jokes." There is also the advertisement of a flea-bag hotel or flophouse called "Ritz Men Only." This sign is also pale neon or luminous paint, and only the entrance is on the street floor, the rooms are above the Loan Shark and Gypsy's stall. One of the windows of this upper story is practical. Figures appear in it sometimes, leaning out as if suffocating or to hawk and spit into the street below. This side of the street should have all the color and animation that are permitted by the resources of the production. There may be moments of dancelike action [a fight, a seduction, sale of narcotics, arrest, etc.].*)

KILROY (*to the audience from the apron*): What've I got to cash in on? My golden gloves? Never! I'll say that once more, never! The silver-framed photo of my One True Woman? Never! Repeat that! Never! What else have I got of a detachable and a negotiable nature? Oh! My ruby-and-emerald-studded belt with the word CHAMP on it.

(*He whips it off his pants.*)

This is not necessary to hold on my pants, but this is a precious reminder of the sweet used-to-be. Oh, well. Sometimes a man has got to hock his sweet used-to-be in order to finance his present situation . . .

(*He enters the Loan Shark's. A Drunken Bum leans out the practical window of the "Ritz Men Only" and shouts:*)

BUM: O Jack o' Diamonds, you robbed my pockets, you robbed my pockets of silver and gold!

(*He jerks the window shade down.*)

GUTMAN (*on the terrace*): Block Four on the Camino Real!

BLOCK FOUR

There is a phrase of light music as the Baron de Charlus, an elderly foppish sybarite in a light silk suit, a carnation in his lapel, crosses from the Siete Mares to the honky-tonk side of the street. On his trail is a wild-looking young man of startling beauty called Lobo. Charlus is aware of the follower and, during his conversation with A. Ratt, he takes out a pocket mirror to inspect him while pretending to comb his hair and point his moustache. As Charlus approaches, the Manager of the flea-bag puts up a vacancy sign and calls out:

A. RATT: Vacancy here! A bed at the "Ritz Men Only"! A little white ship to sail the dangerous night in . . .

THE BARON: Ah, bon soir, Mr. Ratt.

A. RATT: Cruising?

THE BARON: No, just—walking!

A. RATT: That's all you need to do.

THE BARON: I sometimes find it suffices. You have a vacancy, do you?

A. RATT: For you?

THE BARON: And a possible guest. You know the requirements. An iron bed with no mattress and a considerable length of stout knotted rope. No! Chains this evening, metal chains. I've been very bad, I have a lot to atone for . . .

A. RATT: Why don't you take these joy-rides at the Siete Mares?

THE BARON (*with the mirror focused on Lobo*): They don't have Ingreso Libero at the Siete Mares. Oh, I don't like places in the haute saison, the alta staggione, and yet if you go between the fashionable seasons, it's too hot or too damp or appallingly overrun by all the wrong sort of people who rap on the wall if canaries sing in your bed-springs after midnight. I don't know why such people don't stay at home. Surely a Kodak, a Brownie, or even a Leica works just as well in Milwaukee or Sioux City as it does in these places they do on their whirlwind summer tours, and don't look now, but I think I am being followed!

A. RATT: Yep, you've made a pickup!

THE BARON: Attractive?

A. RATT: That depends on who's driving the bicycle, Dad.

THE BARON: Ciao, Caro! Expect me at ten.

(*He crosses elegantly to the fountain.*)

A. RATT: Vacancy here! A little white ship to sail the dangerous night in!

(*The music changes. Kilroy backs out of the Loan Shark's, belt unsold, engaged in a violent dispute. The Loan Shark is haggling for his golden gloves. Charlus lingers, intrigued by the scene.*)

LOAN SHARK: I don't want no belt! I want the gloves! Eight-fifty!

KILROY: No dice.

LOAN SHARK: Nine, nine-fifty!

KILROY: Nah, nah, nah!

LOAN SHARK: Yah, yah, yah.

KILROY: I say nah.

LOAN SHARK: I say yah.

KILROY: The nahs have it.

LOAN SHARK: Don't be a fool. What can you do with a pair of golden gloves?

KILROY: I can remember the battles I fought to win them! I can remember that I used to be—CHAMP!

(*Fade in Band Music: "March of the Gladiators"—ghostly cheers, etc.*)

LOAN SHARK: You can remember that you *used to be*—Champ?

KILROY: Yes! I used to be—CHAMP!

THE BARON: Used to be is the past tense, meaning useless.

KILROY: Not to me, Mister. These are my gloves, these gloves are gold, and I fought a lot of hard fights to win 'em! I broke clean from the clinches. I never hit a low blow, the referee never told me to mix it up! And the fixers never got to me!

LOAN SHARK: In other words, a sucker!

KILROY: Yep, I'm a sucker that won the golden gloves!

LOAN SHARK: Congratulations. My final offer is a piece of green paper with Alexander Hamilton's picture on it. Take it or leave it.

KILROY: I leave it for you to *stuff* it! I'd hustle my heart on this street, I'd peddle my heart's true blood before I'd leave my golden gloves hung up in a loan shark's window between a rusted trombone and some poor lush's long ago mildewed tuxedo!

LOAN SHARK: So you say but I will see you later.

THE BARON: The name of the Camino is not unreal!

(*The Bum sticks his head out the window and shouts:*)

BUM: Pa dam, Pa dam, Pa dam!

THE BARON (*continuing the Bum's song*): Echoes the beat of my heart! Pa dam, Pa dam—*hello!*

(*He has crossed to Kilroy as he sings and extends his hand to him.*)

KILROY (*uncertainly*): Hey, mate. It's wonderful to see you.

THE BARON: Thanks, but why?

KILROY: A normal American. In a clean white suit.

THE BARON: My suit is pale yellow. My nationality is French, and my normality has been often subject to question.

KILROY: I still say your suit is clean.

THE BARON: Thanks. That's more than I can say for your apparel.

KILROY: Don't judge a book by the covers. I'd take a shower if I could locate the "Y."

THE BARON: What's the "Y"?

KILROY: Sort of a Protestant church with a swimmin' pool in it. Sometimes it also has an employment bureau. It does good in the community.

THE BARON: Nothing in this community does much good.

KILROY: I'm getting the same impression. This place is confusing to me. I think it must be the aftereffects of fever. Nothing seems real. Could you give me the scoop?

THE BARON: Serious questions are referred to the Gypsy. Once upon a time. Oh, once upon a time. I used to wonder. Now I simply wander. I stroll about the fountain and hope to be followed. Some people call it corruption. I call it—simplification . . .

BUM (*very softly at the window*): I wonder what's become of Sally, that old gal of mine?

(*He lowers the blind.*)

KILROY: Well, anyhow . . .

THE BARON: Well, anyhow?

KILROY: How about the hot-spots in this town?

THE BARON: Oh, the hot-spots, ho ho! There's the Pink Flamingo, the Yellow Pelican, the Blue Heron, and the Prothonotary Warbler! They call it the Bird Circuit. But I don't care for such places. They stand three-deep at the bar and look at themselves in the mirror and what they see is depressing. One sailor comes in—they faint! My own choice of resorts is the Bucket of Blood downstairs from the "Ritz Men Only."—How about a match?

KILROY: Where's your cigarette?

THE BARON (*gently and sweetly*): Oh, I don't smoke. I just wanted to see your eyes more clearly . . .

KILROY: Why?

THE BARON: The eyes are the windows of the soul, and yours are too gentle for someone who has as much as I have to atone for. (*He starts off.*) Au revoir . . .

KILROY: —A very unusual type character . . .

(*Casanova is on the steps leading to the arch, looking out at the desert beyond. Now he turns and descends a few steps, laughing with a note of tired incredulity. Kilroy crosses to him.*)

Gee, it's wonderful to see you, a normal American in a—

(*There is a strangulated outcry from the arch under which the Baron has disappeared.*)

Excuse me a minute!

(*He rushes toward the source of the outcry. Jacques crosses to the bench before the fountain. Rhubarb is heard through the arch. Jacques shrugs wearily as if it were just a noisy radio. Kilroy comes plummeting out backwards, all the way to Jacques.*)

I tried to interfere, but what's th' use?!
JACQUES: No use at all!

(*The Streetcleaners come through the arch with the Baron doubled up in their barrel. They pause and exchange sibilant whispers, pointing and snickering at Kilroy.*)

KILROY: Who are they pointing at? At me, Kilroy?

(*The Bum laughs from the window. A. Ratt laughs from his shadowy doorway. The Loan Shark laughs from his.*)

Kilroy is here and he's not about to be there!—If he can help it . . .

(*He snatches up a rock and throws it at the Streetcleaners. Everybody laughs louder and the laughter seems to reverberate from the mountains. The light changes, dims a little in the plaza.*)

Sons a whatever you're sons of! Don't look at me, I'm not about to take no ride in the barrel!

(*The Baron, his elegant white shoes protruding from the barrel, is wheeled up the Alleyway Out. Figures in the square resume their dazed attitudes and one or two Guests return to the terrace of the Siete Mares as—*)

GUTMAN: Block Five on the Camino Real!

(*He strolls off.*)

BLOCK FIVE

KILROY (*to Jacques*): Gee, the blocks go fast on this street!

JACQUES: Yes. The blocks go fast.

KILROY: My name's Kilroy. I'm here.

JACQUES: Mine is Casanova. I'm here, too.

KILROY: But you been here longer than me and maybe could brief me on it. For instance, what do they do with a stiff picked up in this town?

(*The Guard stares at them suspiciously from the terrace.*

(*Jacques whistles "La Golondrina" and crosses downstage. Kilroy follows.*)

Did I say something untactful?

JACQUES (*smiling into a sunset glow*): The exchange of serious questions and ideas, especially between persons from opposite sides of the plaza, is regarded unfavorably here. You'll notice I'm talking as if I had acute laryngitis. I'm gazing into the sunset. If I should start to whistle "La Golondrina" it means we're being overheard by the Guards on the terrace. Now you want to know what is done to a body from which the soul has departed on the Camino Real!—Its disposition depends on what the Streetcleaners happen to find in its pockets. If its pockets are empty as the unfortunate Baron's turned out to be, and as mine are at this moment—the "stiff" is wheeled straight off to the Laboratory. And there the individual becomes an undistinguished member of a collectivist state. His chemical components are separated and poured into vats containing the corresponding elements of countless others. If any of his vital organs or parts are at all unique in size or structure, they're placed on exhibition in bottles containing a very foul-smelling solution called formaldehyde. There is a charge of admission to this museum. The proceeds go to the maintenance of the military police.

(*He whistles "La Golondrina" till the Guard turns his back again. He moves toward the front of the stage.*)

KILROY (*following*): —I guess that's—sensible . . .

JACQUES: Yes, but not romantic. And romance is important. Don't you think?

KILROY: Nobody thinks romance is more important than me!

JACQUES: Except possibly me!

KILROY: Maybe that's why fate has brung us together! We're buddies under the skin!

JACQUES: Travelers born?

KILROY: Always looking for something!

JACQUES: Satisfied by nothing!

KILROY: Hopeful?

JACQUES: Always!

OFFICER: Keep moving!

(*They move apart till the Officer exits.*)

KILROY: And when a joker on the Camino gets fed up with one continual hassle—how does he get *off* it?

JACQUES: You see the narrow and very steep stairway that passes under what is described in the travel brochures as a "Magnificent Arch of Triumph"?—Well, that's the Way Out!

KILROY: That's the way out?

(*Kilroy without hesitation plunges right up to almost the top step; then pauses with a sound of squealing brakes. There is a sudden loud wind.*)

JACQUES (*shouting with hand cupped to mouth*): Well, how does the prospect please you, Traveler born?

KILROY (*shouting back in a tone of awe*): It's too unknown for my blood. Man, I seen nothing like it except through a telescope once on the pier on Coney Island. "Ten cents to see the craters and plains of the moon!"—And here's the same view in three dimensions for nothing!

(*The desert wind sings loudly: Kilroy mocks it.*)

JACQUES: Are you—ready to cross it?

KILROY: Maybe sometime with someone but not right now and alone! How about you?

JACQUES: I'm not alone.

KILROY: You're with a party?

JACQUES: No, but I'm sweetly encumbered with a—lady . . .

KILROY: It wouldn't do with a lady. I don't see nothing but nothing—and then more nothing. And then I see some mountains. But the mountains are covered with snow.

JACQUES: Snowshoes would be useful!

(*He observes Gutman approaching through the passage at upper left. He whistles "La Golondrina" for Kilroy's attention and points with his cane as he exits.*)

KILROY (*descending steps disconsolately*): Mush, mush.

(*The Bum comes to his window. A. Ratt enters his doorway. Gutman enters below Kilroy.*)

BUM: It's sleepy time down South!

GUTMAN (*warningly as Kilroy passes him*): Block Six in a progress of sixteen blocks on the Camino Real.

BLOCK SIX

KILROY (*from the stairs*): Man, I could use a bed now.—I'd like to make me a cool pad on this camino now and lie down and sleep and dream of being with someone—friendly . . .

(*He crosses to the "Ritz Men Only."*)

A. RATT (*softly and sleepily*): Vacancy here! I got a single bed at the "Ritz Men Only," a little white ship to sail the dangerous night in.

(*Kilroy crosses down to his doorway.*)

KILROY: —You got a vacancy here?

A. RATT: I got a vacancy here if you got the one-fifty there.

KILROY: Ha ha! I been in countries where money was not legal tender. I mean it was legal but it wasn't tender.

(*There is a loud groan from offstage above.*)

—Somebody dying on you or just drunk?

A. RATT: Who knows or cares in this pad, Dad?

KILROY: I heard once that a man can't die while he's drunk. Is that a fact or a fiction?

A. RATT: Strictly a fiction.

VOICE ABOVE: *Stiff in number seven! Call the Streetcleaners!*

A. RATT (*with absolutely no change in face or voice*): Number seven is vacant.

(*Streetcleaners' piping is heard.*
(*The Bum leaves the window.*)

KILROY: Thanks, but tonight I'm going to sleep under the stars.

(*A. Ratt gestures "Have it your way" and exits.*
(*Kilroy, left alone, starts downstage. He notices that La Madrecita is crouched near the fountain, holding something up, inconspicuously, in her hand. Coming to her he sees that it's a piece of food. He takes it, puts it in his mouth, tries to thank her but her head is down, muffled in her rebozo and there is no way for him to acknowledge the gift. He starts to cross. Street People raise up their heads in their Pit and motion him invitingly to come in with them. They call softly, "Sleep, sleep . . ."*)

GUTMAN (*from his chair on the terrace*): Hey, Joe.

(*The Street People duck immediately.*)

KILROY: Who? Me?
GUTMAN: Yes, you, Candy Man. Are you disocupado?
KILROY: —That means—unemployed, don't it?

(*He sees Officers converging from right.*)

GUTMAN: Jobless. On the bum. Carrying the banner!
KILROY: —Aw, no, aw, no, don't try to hang no vagrancy rap on me! I was robbed on this square and I got plenty of witnesses to prove it.
GUTMAN (*with ironic courtesy*): Oh?

(*He makes a gesture asking "Where?"*)

KILROY (*coming down to apron left and crossing to the right*): Witnesses! Witness! Witnesses!

(*He comes to La Madrecita.*)

You were a witness!

(*A gesture indicates that he realizes her blindness. Opposite the Gypsy's balcony he pauses for a second.*)

Hey, Gypsy's daughter!

(*The balcony is dark. He continues up to the Pit. The Street People duck as he calls down:*)

You were witnesses!

(*An Officer enters with a Patsy outfit. He hands it to Gutman.*)

GUTMAN: Here, Boy! Take these.

(*Gutman displays and then tosses on the ground at Kilroy's feet the Patsy outfit—the red fright wig, the big crimson nose that lights up and has horn rimmed glasses attached, a pair of clown pants that have a huge footprint on the seat.*)

KILROY: What is this outfit?
GUTMAN: The uniform of a Patsy.
KILROY: I know what a Patsy is—he's a clown in the circus who takes prat-falls but *I'm no Patsy!*
GUTMAN: Pick it up.
KILROY: Don't give me orders. Kilroy is a free agent—
GUTMAN (*smoothly*): But a Patsy isn't. Pick it up and put it on, Candy Man. You are now the Patsy.
KILROY: So you say but you are completely mistaken.

(*Four Officers press in on him.*)

And don't crowd me with your torpedoes! I'm a stranger here but I got a clean record in all the places I been, I'm not in the books for nothin' but vagrancy and once when I was hungry I walked by a truck-load of pineapples without picking one, because I was brought up good—

(*Then, with a pathetic attempt at making friends with the Officer to his right.*)

and there was a cop on the corner!
OFFICER: Ponga selo!
KILROY: What'd you say? (*Desperately to audience he asks:*) What did he say?
OFFICER: Ponga selo!
KILROY: What'd you say?

(*The Officer shoves him down roughly to the Patsy outfit. Kilroy picks up the pants, shakes them out carefully as if about to step into them and says very politely:*)

Why, surely. I'd be delighted. My fondest dreams have come true.

(*Suddenly he tosses the Patsy dress into Gutman's face and leaps into the aisle of the theatre.*)

GUTMAN: Stop him! Arrest that vagrant! Don't let him get away!

LOUDSPEAKER: Be on the lookout for a fugitive Patsy. The Patsy has escaped. Stop him, stop that Patsy!

(*A wild chase commences. The two Guards rush madly down either side to intercept him at the back of the house. Kilroy wheels about at the top of the center aisle, and runs back down it, panting, gasping out questions and entreaties to various persons occupying aisle seats, such as:*)

KILROY: How do I git out? Which way do I go, which way do I get out? Where's the Greyhound depot? Hey, do you know where the Greyhound bus depot is? What's the best way out, if there is any way out? I got to find one. I had enough of this place. I had too much of this place. I'm free. I'm a free man with equal rights in this world! You better believe it because that's news for you and you had better believe it! Kilroy's a free man with equal rights in this world! All right, now, help me, somebody, help me find a way out, I got to find one, I don't like this place! It's not for me and I am not buying any! Oh! Over there! I see a sign that says EXIT. That's a sweet word to me, man, that's a lovely word, EXIT! That's the entrance to paradise for Kilroy! Exit, I'm coming, Exit, I'm coming!

(*The Street People have gathered along the forestage to watch the chase. Esmeralda, barefooted, wearing only a slip, bursts out of the Gypsy's establishment like an animal broken out of a cage, darts among the Street People to the front of the Crowd which is shouting like the spectators at the climax of a corrida. Behind her, Nursie appears, a male actor, wigged and dressed austerely as a duenna, crying out in both languages.*)

NURSIE: Esmeralda! Esmeralda!
GYPSY: Police!
NURSIE: Come back here, Esmeralda!
GYPSY: Catch her, idiot!
NURSIE: Where is my lady bird, where is my precious treasure?
GYPSY: Idiot! I told you to keep her door locked!
NURSIE: She jimmied the lock, Esmeralda!

(*These shouts are mostly lost in the general rhubarb of the chase and the shouting Street People. Esmeralda crouches on the forestage, screaming encouragement in Spanish to the fugitive. Abdullah catches sight of her, seizes her wrist, shouting:*)

ABDULLAH: Here she is! I got her!

(*Esmeralda fights savagely. She nearly breaks loose, but Nursie and the Gypsy close upon her, too, and she is overwhelmed and dragged back, fighting all the way, toward the door from which she escaped.*

(*Meanwhile—timed with the above action—shots are fired in the air by Kilroy's Pursuers. He dashes, panting, into the boxes of the theatre, darting from one box to another, shouting incoherently, now, sobbing for breath, crying out:*)

KILROY: *Mary, help a Christian! Help a Christian, Mary!*
ESMERALDA: *Yankee! Yankee, jump!*

(*The Officers close upon him in the box nearest the stage. A dazzling spot of light is thrown on him. He lifts a little gilded chair to defend himself. The chair is torn from his grasp. He leaps upon the ledge of the box.*)

Jump! Jump, Yankee!

(*The Gypsy is dragging the girl back by her hair.*)

KILROY: *Watch out down there! Geronimo!*

(*He leaps onto the stage and crumples up with a twisted ankle. Esmeralda screams demoniacally, breaks from her mother's grasp and rushes to him, fighting off his pursuers who have leapt after him from the box. Abdullah, Nursie and the Gypsy seize her again, just as Kilroy is seized by his pursuers. The Officers beat him to his knees. Each time he is struck, Esmeralda screams as if she received the blow herself. As his cries subside into sobbing, so do hers, and at the end, when he is quite helpless, she is also overcome by her captors and as they drag her back to the Gypsy's she cries to him:*)

ESMERALDA: *They've got you! They've got me!*

(*Her mother slaps her fiercely.*)

Caught! Caught! We're caught!

(*She is dragged inside. The door is slammed shut on her continuing outcries. For a moment nothing is heard but Kilroy's hoarse panting and sobbing. Gutman takes command of the situation, thrusting his way through the crowd to face Kilroy who is pinioned by two Guards.*)

GUTMAN (*smiling serenely*): Well, well, how do you do! I understand that you're seeking employment here. We need a Patsy and the job is yours for the asking!

KILROY: I don't. Accept. This job. I been. Shanghied!

(*Kilroy dons Patsy outfit.*)

GUTMAN: Hush! The Patsy doesn't talk. He lights his nose, that's all!

GUARD: Press the little button at the end of the cord.

GUTMAN: That's right. Just press the little button at the end of the cord!

(*Kilroy lights his nose. Everybody laughs.*)

GUTMAN: Again, ha ha! Again, ha ha! Again!

(*The nose goes off and on like a firefly as the stage dims out.*
(*The curtain falls. There is a short intermission.*)

BLOCK SEVEN

The Dreamer is singing with mandolin, "Noche de Ronde." The Guests murmur, "cool—cool . . ." Gutman stands on the podiumlike elevation downstage right, smoking a long thin cigar, signing an occasional tab from the bar or café. He is standing in an amber spot. The rest of the stage is filled with blue dusk. At the signal the song fades to a whisper and Gutman speaks.

GUTMAN: Block Seven on the Camino Real— I like this hour.

(*He gives the audience a tender gold-toothed smile.*)

The fire's gone out of the day but the light of it lingers . . . In Rome the continual fountains are bathing stone heroes with silver, in Copenhagen the Tivoli gardens are lighted, they're selling the lottery on San Juan de Latrene . . .

(*The Dreamer advances a little, playing the mandolin softly.*)

LA MADRECITA (*holding up glass beads and shell necklaces*): Recuerdos, recuerdos?

GUTMAN: And these are the moments when we look into ourselves and ask with a wonder which never is lost altogether: "Can this be all? Is there nothing more? Is this what the glittering wheels of the heavens turn for?"

(*He leans forward as if conveying a secret.*)

—Ask the Gypsy! Un poco dinero will tickle the Gypsy's palm and give her visions!

(*Abdullah emerges with a silver tray, calling:*)

ABDULLAH: Letter for Signor Casanova, letter for Signor Casanova!

(*Jacques springs up but stands rigid.*)

GUTMAN: Casanova, you have received a letter. Perhaps it's the letter with the remittance check in it!

JACQUES (*in a hoarse, exalted voice*): Yes! It is! The letter! With the remittance check in it!

GUTMAN: Then why don't you take it so you can maintain your residence at the Siete Mares and so avoid the more somber attractions of the "Ritz Men Only"?

JACQUES: My hand is—

GUTMAN: Your hand is paralyzed? . . . By what? *Anxiety? Apprehension?* . . . Put the letter in Signor Casanova's pocket so he can open it when he recovers the use of his digital extremities. Then give him a shot of brandy on the house before he falls on his face!

(*Jacques has stepped down into the plaza. He looks down at Kilroy crouched to the right of him and wildly blinking his nose.*)

JACQUES: Yes. I know the Morse code.

(*Kilroy's nose again blinks on and off.*)

Thank you, brother.

(*This is said as if acknowledging a message.*)

I knew without asking the Gypsy that something of this sort would happen to you. You have a spark of anarchy in your spirit and that's not to be tolerated. Nothing wild or honest is tolerated here! It has to be extinguished or used only to light up your nose for Mr. Gutman's amusement . . .

(*Jacques saunters around Kilroy whistling "La Golondrina." Then satisfied that no one is suspicious of this encounter . . .*)

Before the final block we'll find some way out of here! Meanwhile, patience and courage, little brother!

(*Jacques feeling he's been there too long starts away giving Kilroy a reassuring pat on the shoulder and saying:*)

Patience! . . . Courage!

LADY MULLIGAN (*from the Mulligans' table*): Mr. Gutman!

GUTMAN: Lady Mulligan! And how are you this evening, Lord Mulligan?

LADY MULLIGAN (*interrupting Lord Mulligan's rumblings*): He's not at all well. This . . . climate is so enervating!

LORD MULLIGAN: I was so weak this morning . . . I couldn't screw the lid on my tooth paste!

LADY MULLIGAN: Raymond, tell Mr. Gutman about those two impertinent workmen in the square! . . . These two idiots pushing a white barrel! Pop up every time we step outside the hotel!

LORD MULLIGAN: —point and giggle at me!

LADY MULLIGAN: Can't they be discharged?

GUTMAN: They can't be discharged, disciplined nor bribed! All you can do is pretend to ignore them.

LADY MULLIGAN: I can't eat! . . . Raymond, stop stuffing!

LORD MULLIGAN: *Shut up!*

GUTMAN (*to the audience*): When the big wheels crack on this street it's like the fall of a capital city, the destruction of Carthage, the sack of Rome by the white-eyed giants from the North! I've seen them fall! I've seen the destruction of them! Adventurer suddenly frightened of a dark room! Gamblers unable to choose between odd and even! Con men and pitchmen and plume-hatted cavaliers turned baby-soft at one note of the Streetcleaners' pipes! When I observe this change, I say to myself: "Could it happen to ME?" —The answer is "YES!" And that's what curdles my blood like milk on the doorstep of someone gone for the summer!

(*A Hunchback Mummer somersaults through his hoop of silver bells, springs up and shakes it excitedly toward a downstage arch which begins to flicker with a diamond-blue radiance; this marks the advent of each legendary character in the play. The music follows: a waltz from the time of Camille in Paris.*)

GUTMAN (*downstage to the audience*): Ah, there's the music of another legend, one that everyone knows, the legend of the sentimental whore, the courtesan who made the mistake of love. But now you see her coming into this plaza not as she was when she burned with a fever that cast a thin light over Paris, but changed, yes, faded as lanterns and legends fade when they burn into day!

(*He turns and shouts:*)

Rosita, sell her a flower!

(*Marguerite has entered the plaza. A beautiful woman of indefinite age. The Street People cluster about her with wheedling cries, holding up glass beads, shell necklaces and so forth. She seems confused, lost, half-awake. Jacques has sprung up at her entrance but has difficulty making his way through the cluster of vendors. Rosita has snatched up a tray of flowers and cries out:*)

ROSITA: Camellias, camellias! Pink or white, whichever a lady finds suitable to the moon!

GUTMAN: That's the ticket!

MARGUERITE: Yes, I would like a camellia.

ROSITA (*in a bad French accent*): Rouge ou blanc ce soir?

MARGUERITE: It's always a white one, now . . . but there used to be five evenings out of the month when a pink camellia, instead of the usual white one, let my admirers know that the moon those nights was unfavorable to pleasure, and so they called me—Camille . . .

JACQUES: Mia cara!

(*Imperiously, very proud to be with her, he pushes the Street People aside with his cane.*)

Out of the way, make way, let us through, please!

MARGUERITE: Don't push them with your cane.

JACQUES: If they get close enough they'll snatch your purse.

(*Marguerite utters a low, shocked cry.*)

What is it?

MARGUERITE: *My purse is gone! It's lost! My papers were in it!*

JACQUES: Your passport was in it?

MARGUERITE: My passport and my permiso de residencia!

(*She leans faint against the arch during the following scene.*
(*Abdullah turns to run. Jacques catches him.*)

JACQUES (*seizing Abdullah's wrist*): Where did you take her?

ABDULLAH: Oww!—P'tit Zoco.

JACQUES: The Souks?

ABDULLAH: The Souks!

JACQUES: Which cafés did she go to?

ABDULLAH: Ahmed's, she went to—

JACQUES: Did she smoke at Ahmed's?

ABDULLAH: Two kif pipes!

JACQUES: Who was it took her purse? Was it *you*? We'll see!

(*He strips off the boy's burnoose. He crouches whimpering, shivering in a ragged slip.*)

MARGUERITE: Jacques, let the boy go, he didn't take it!

JACQUES: He doesn't have it on him but knows who does!

ABDULLAH: No, no, I don't know!

JACQUES: You little son of a Gypsy! Senta! . . . You know who I am? I am Jacques Casanova! I belong to the Secret Order of the Rose-colored Cross! . . . Run back to Ahmed's. Contact the spiv that took the lady's purse. Tell him to keep it but give her back her papers! There'll be a large reward.

(*He thumps his cane on the ground to release Abdullah from the spell. The boy dashes off. Jacques laughs and turns triumphantly to Marguerite.*)

LADY MULLIGAN: Waiter! That adventurer and his mistress must not be seated next to Lord Mulligan's table!

JACQUES (*loudly enough for Lady Mulligan to hear*): This hotel has become a mecca for black marketeers and their expensively kept women!

LADY MULLIGAN: Mr. Gutman!

MARGUERITE: Let's have dinner upstairs!

WAITER (*directing them to terrace table*): *This* way, M'sieur.

JACQUES: We'll take our usual table.

(*He indicates one.*)

MARGUERITE: Please!

WAITER (*overlapping Marguerite's "please!"*): This table is reserved for Lord Byron!

JACQUES (*masterfully*): This table is always our table.

MARGUERITE: I'm not hungry.

JACQUES: Hold out the lady's chair, cretino!

GUTMAN (*darting over to Marguerite's chair*): Permit me!

(*Jacques bows with mock gallantry to Lady Mulligan as he turns to his chair during seating of Marguerite.*)

LADY MULLIGAN: We'll move to *that* table!

JACQUES: —You must learn how to carry the banner of Bohemia into the enemy camp.

(*A screen is put up around them.*)

MARGUERITE: Bohemia has no banner. It survives by discretion.

JACQUES: I'm glad that you value discretion. *Wine list!* Was it discretion that led you through the bazaars this afternoon wearing your cabochon sapphire and diamond ear-drops? You were fortunate that you lost only your purse and papers!

MARGUERITE: Take the wine list.

JACQUES: Still or sparkling?

MARGUERITE: Sparkling.

GUTMAN: May I make a suggestion, Signor Casanova?

JACQUES: Please do.

GUTMAN: It's a very cold and dry wine from only ten metres below the snowline in the mountains. The name of the wine is Quando!—meaning when! Such as "When are remittances going to be received?" "When are accounts to be settled?" Ha ha ha! Bring Signor Casanova a bottle of Quando with the compliments of the house!

JACQUES: I'm sorry this had to happen in—your presence . . .

MARGUERITE: That doesn't matter, my dear. But why don't you *tell* me when you are short of money?

JACQUES: I thought the fact was apparent. It is to everyone else.

MARGUERITE: The letter you were expecting, it still hasn't come?

JACQUES (*removing it from his pocket*): It came this afternoon —Here it is!

MARGUERITE: You haven't opened the letter!

JACQUES: I haven't had the nerve to! I've had so many unpleasant surprises that I've lost faith in my luck.

MARGUERITE: Give the letter to me. Let me open it for you.

JACQUES: Later, a little bit later, after the—wine . . .

MARGUERITE: Old hawk, anxious old hawk!

(*She clasps his hand on the table: he leans toward her: she kisses her fingertips and places them on his lips.*)

JACQUES: Do you call that a kiss?

MARGUERITE: I call it the ghost of a kiss. It will have to do for now.

(*She leans back, her blue-tinted eyelids closed.*)

JACQUES: Are you tired? Are you tired, Marguerite? You know you should have rested this afternoon.

MARGUERITE: I looked at silver and rested.

JACQUES: You looked at silver at Ahmed's?

MARGUERITE: No, I rested at Ahmed's, and had mint-tea.

(*The Dreamer accompanies their speech with his guitar. The duologue should have the style of an antiphonal poem, the cues picked up so that there is scarcely a separation between the speeches, and the tempo quick and the voices edged.*)

JACQUES: You had mint-tea downstairs?

MARGUERITE: No, upstairs.

JACQUES: Upstairs where they burn the poppy?

MARGUERITE: Upstairs where it's cool and there's music and the haggling of the bazaar is soft as the murmur of pigeons.

JACQUES: That sounds restful. Reclining among silk pillows on a divan, in a curtained and perfumed alcove above the bazaar?

MARGUERITE: Forgetting for a while where I am, or that I don't know where I am . . .

JACQUES: Forgetting alone or forgetting with some young companion who plays the lute or the flute or who had silver to show you? Yes. That sounds very restful. And yet you do seem tired.

MARGUERITE: If I seem tired, it's your insulting solicitude that I'm tired of!

JACQUES: Is it insulting to feel concern for your safety in this place?

MARGUERITE: Yes, it is. The implication is.

JACQUES: What is the implication?

MARGUERITE: You know what it is: that I am one of those *aging—voluptuaries*—who used to be paid for pleasure but now have to pay!—Jacques, I won't be followed, I've gone too far to be followed!—*What is it?*

(*The Waiter has presented an envelope on a salver.*)

WAITER: A letter for the lady.

MARGUERITE: How strange to receive a letter in a place where nobody knows I'm staying! Will you open it for me?

(*The Waiter withdraws. Jacques takes the letter and opens it.*)

Well! What is it?

JACQUES: Nothing important. An illustrated brochure from some resort in the mountains.

MARGUERITE: What is it called?

JACQUES: Bide-a-While.

(*A chafing dish bursts into startling blue flame at the Mulligans' table. Lady Mulligan clasps her hands and exclaims with affected delight, the Waiter and Mr. Gutman *laugh agreeably. Marguerite springs up and moves out upon the forestage. Jacques goes to her.*)

Do you know this resort in the mountains?

MARGUERITE: Yes. I stayed there once. It's one of those places with open sleeping verandahs, surrounded by snowy pine woods. It has rows and rows of narrow white iron beds as regular as tombstones. The invalids smile at each other when axes flash across valleys, ring, flash, ring again! Young voices shout across valleys Hola! And mail is delivered. The friend that used to write you ten-page letters contents himself now with a postcard bluebird that tells you to "Get well Quick!"

(*Jacques throws the brochure away.*)

—And when the last bleeding comes, not much later nor earlier than expected, you're wheeled discreetly into a little tent of white gauze, and the last thing you know of this world, of which you've known so little and yet so much, is the smell of an empty ice box.

(*The blue flame expires in the chafing dish. Gutman picks up the brochure and hands it to the Waiter, whispering something.*)

JACQUES: You won't go back to that place.

(*The Waiter places the brochure on the salver again and approaches behind them.*)

MARGUERITE: I wasn't released. I left without permission. They sent me this to remind me.

WAITER (*presenting the salver*): You dropped this.

JACQUES: We threw it away!

WAITER: Excuse me.

JACQUES: Now, from now on, Marguerite, you must take better care of yourself. Do you hear me?

MARGUERITE: I hear you. No more distractions for me? No more entertainers in curtained and perfumed alcoves above the bazaar, no more young men that a pinch of white powder or a puff of gray smoke can almost turn to someone devoutly remembered?

JACQUES: No, from now on—

MARGUERITE: What "from now on," old hawk?

JACQUES: Rest. Peace.

MARGUERITE: Rest in peace is that final bit of advice they carve on gravestones, and I'm not ready for it! Are you? Are *you* ready for it?

(*She returns to the table. He follows her.*)

Oh, Jacques, when are we going to leave here, how are we going to leave here, you've got to tell me!

JACQUES: I've told you all I know.

MARGUERITE: Nothing, you've given up hope!

JACQUES: I haven't, that's not true.

(*Gutman has brought out the white cockatoo which he shows to Lady Mulligan at her table.*)

GUTMAN (*his voice rising above the murmurs*): Her name is Aurora.

LADY MULLIGAN: Why do you call her Aurora?

GUTMAN: She cries at daybreak.

LADY MULLIGAN: Only at daybreak?

GUTMAN: Yes, at daybreak only.

(*Their voices and laughter fade under.*)

MARGUERITE: How long is it since you've been to the travel agencies?

JACQUES: This morning I made the usual round of Cook's, American Express, Wagon-lits Universal, and it was the same story. There are no flights out of here till further orders from someone higher up.

MARGUERITE: Nothing, nothing at all?

JACQUES: Oh, there's a rumor of something called the Fugitivo, but—

MARGUERITE: The What!!!?

JACQUES: The Fugitivo. It's one of those non-scheduled things that—

MARGUERITE: When, when, when?

JACQUES: I told you it was non-scheduled. Non-scheduled means it comes and goes at no predictable—

MARGUERITE: Don't give me the dictionary! I want to know how does one get on it? Did you bribe them? Did you offer them money? No. Of course you didn't! And I know why! You really don't want to leave here. You *think* you don't want to go because you're brave as an old hawk. But the truth of the matter—the real not the royal truth—is that you're terrified of the Terra Incognita outside that wall.

JACQUES: You've hit upon the truth. I'm terrified of the unknown country inside or outside this wall or any place on earth without you with me! The only country, known or unknown that I can breathe in, or care to, is the country in which we breathe together, as we are now at this table. And later, a little while later, even closer than this, the sole inhabitants of a tiny world whose limits are those of the light from a rose-colored lamp—beside the sweetly, completely known country of your cool bed!

MARGUERITE: The little comfort of love?

JACQUES: Is that comfort so little?

MARGUERITE: Caged birds accept each other but flight is what they long for.

JACQUES: I want to stay here with you and love you and guard you until the time or way comes that we both can leave with honor.

MARGUERITE: "Leave with honor"? Your vocabulary is almost as out-of-date as your cape and your cane. How could anyone quit this field with honor, this place where there's nothing but the gradual wasting away of everything decent in us . . . the sort of desperation that comes after even desperation has been worn out through long wear! . . . Why have they put these screens around the table?

(*She springs up and knocks one of them over.*)

LADY MULLIGAN: There! You see? I don't understand why you let such people stay here.

GUTMAN: They pay the price of admission the same as you.

LADY MULLIGAN: What price is that?

GUTMAN: Desperation!—With cash here!

(*He indicates the Siete Mares.*)

Without cash there!

(*He indicates Skid Row.*)

Block Eight on the Camino Real!

BLOCK EIGHT

There is the sound of loud desert wind and a flamenco cry followed by a dramatic phrase of music.

A flickering diamond blue radiance floods the hotel entrance. The crouching, grimacing Hunchback shakes his hoop of bells which is the convention for the appearance of each legendary figure.

Lord Byron appears in the doorway readied for departure. Gutman raises his hand for silence.

GUTMAN: You're leaving us, Lord Byron?

BYRON: Yes, I'm leaving you, Mr. Gutman.

GUTMAN: What a pity! But this is a port of entry and departure. There are no permanent guests. Possibly you are getting a little restless?

BYRON: The luxuries of this place have made me soft. The metal point's gone from my pen, there's nothing left but the feather.

GUTMAN: That may be true. But what can you do about it?

BYRON: Make a departure!

GUTMAN: From yourself?

BYRON: From my present self to myself as I used to be!

GUTMAN: *That's* the *furthest* departure a man could make! I guess you're sailing to Athens? There's another war there and like all wars since the beginning of time it can be interpreted as a—struggle for *what*?

BYRON: —For *freedom!* You may laugh at it, but it still means something to *me*!

GUTMAN: Of course it does! I'm not laughing a bit, I'm beaming with admiration.

BYRON: I've allowed myself many distractions.

GUTMAN: Yes, indeed!

BYRON: But I've never altogether forgotten my old devotion to the—

GUTMAN: —To the *what*, Lord Byron?

(*Byron passes nervous fingers through his hair.*)

You can't remember the object of your one-time devotion?

(*There is a pause. Byron limps away from the terrace and goes toward the fountain.*)

BYRON: When Shelley's corpse was recovered from the sea . . .

(*Gutman beckons the Dreamer who approaches and accompanies Byron's speech.*)

—It was burned on the beach at Viareggio.—I watched the spectacle from my carriage because the stench was revolting . . . Then it—fascinated me! I got out of my carriage. Went nearer, holding a handkerchief to my nostrils! —I saw that the front of the skull had broken away in the flames, and there—

(*He advances out upon the stage apron, followed by Abdullah with the pine torch or lantern.*)

And there was the brain of Shelley, indistinguishable from a cooking stew!—*boiling, bubbling, hissing!*—in the *blackening—cracked—pot*—of his skull!

(*Marguerite rises abruptly. Jacques supports her.*)

—Trelawney, his friend, Trelawney, threw salt and oil and frankincense in the flames and finally the almost intolerable stench—

(*Abdullah giggles. Gutman slaps him.*)

—was *gone* and the burning was *pure*!—as a man's burning should be . . .

A man's burning *ought* to be pure!—*not* like mine—(a crepe suzette—burned in brandy . . .)

Shelley's burning was finally very *pure*!

But the body, the corpse, split open like a grilled pig!

(*Abdullah giggles irrepressibly again. Gutman grips the back of his neck and he stands up stiff and assumes an expression of exaggerated solemnity.*)

—And then Trelawney—as the ribs of the corpse unlocked —reached into them as a baker reaches quickly into an oven!

(*Abdullah almost goes into another convulsion.*)

—And snatched out—as a baker would a biscuit!—the *heart* of Shelley! Snatched the heart of Shelley out of the blistering corpse!—Out of the purifying—blue-flame . . .

(*Marguerite resumes her seat; Jacques his.*)

—And it was *over*!—I thought—

(*He turns slightly from the audience and crosses upstage from the apron. He faces Jacques and Marguerite.*)

—I thought it was a disgusting thing to do, to snatch a man's heart from his body! What can one man do with another man's heart?

(*Jacques rises and strikes the stage with his cane.*)

JACQUES (*passionately*): He can do this with it!

(*He seizes a loaf of bread on his table, and descends from the terrace.*)

He can twist it like this!

(*He twists the loaf.*)

He can tear it like this!

(*He tears the loaf in two.*)

He can crush it under his foot!

(*He drops the bread and stamps on it.*)

—And kick it away—like this!

(*He kicks the bread off the terrace. Lord Byron turns away from him and limps again out upon the stage apron and speaks to the audience.*)

BYRON: That's very true, Señor. But a poet's vocation, which used to be my vocation, is to influence the heart in a gentler fashion than you have made your mark on that loaf of bread. He ought to purify it and lift it above its ordinary level. For what is the heart but a sort of—

(*He makes a high, groping gesture in the air.*)

—A sort of—*instrument*!—that translates *noise* into *music*, chaos into—*order* . . .

(*Abdullah ducks almost to the earth in an effort to stifle his mirth. Gutman coughs to cover his own amusement.*)

—*a mysterious order!*

(*He raises his voice till it fills the plaza.*)

—That was my vocation once upon a time, before it was obscured by vulgar plaudits!—Little by little it was lost among gondolas and palazzos!—masked balls, glittering salons, huge shadowy courts and torch-lit entrances!—Baroque façades, canopies and carpets, candelabra and gold plate among snowy damask, ladies with throats as slender as flower-stems, bending and breathing toward me their fragrant breath—

—Exposing their breasts to me!

Whispering, half-smiling!—And everywhere marble, the visible grandeur of marble, pink and gray marble, veined and tinted as flayed corrupting flesh,—all these provided agreeable distractions from the rather frightening solitude of a poet. Oh, I wrote many cantos in Venice and Constantinople and in Ravenna and Rome, on all of those Latin and Levantine excursions that my twisted foot led me into—but I wonder about them a little. They seem to improve as the wine in the bottle—dwindles . . . *There is a passion for declivity in this world!*

And lately I've found myself listening to hired musicians behind a row of artificial palm trees—instead of the single —pure-stringed instrument of my heart . . .

Well, then, it's time to leave here!

(*He turns back to the stage.*)

—There is a time for departure even when there's no certain place to go!

I'm going to look for one, now. I'm sailing to Athens. At least I can look up at the Acropolis, I can stand at the foot of it and look up at broken columns on the crest of a hill—if not purity, at least its recollection . . .

I can sit quietly looking for a long, long time in absolute silence, and possibly, yes, *still* possibly—

The old pure music will come to me again. Of course on the other hand I may hear only the little noise of insects in the grass . . .

But I am sailing to Athens! *Make voyages!—Attempt them!* —there's nothing else . . .

MARGUERITE (*excitedly*): *Watch where he goes!*

(*Lord Byron limps across the plaza with his head bowed, making slight, apologetic gestures to the wheedling Beggars who shuffle about him. There is music. He crosses toward the steep Alleyway Out. The following is played with a quiet intensity so it will be in a lower key than the later Fugitivo Scene.*)

Watch him, watch him, see which way he goes. Maybe he knows of a way that we haven't found out.

JACQUES: Yes, I'm watching him, Cara.

(*Lord and Lady Mulligan half rise, staring anxiously through monocle and lorgnon.*)

MARGUERITE: Oh, my God, I believe he's going up that alley.

JACQUES: Yes, he is. He has.

LORD and LADY MULLIGAN: Oh, the fool, the idiot, he's going under the arch!

MARGUERITE: Jacques, run after him, warn him, tell him about the desert he has to cross.

JACQUES: I think he knows what he's doing.

MARGUERITE: I can't look!

(*She turns to the audience, throwing back her head and closing her eyes. The desert wind sings loudly as Byron climbs to the top of the steps.*)

BYRON (*to several porters carrying luggage—which is mainly caged birds*): THIS WAY!

(*He exits.*

(*Kilroy starts to follow. He stops at the steps, cringing and looking at Gutman. Gutman motions him to go ahead. Kilroy rushes up the stairs. He looks out, loses his nerve and sits—blinking his nose. Gutman laughs as he announces—*)

GUTMAN: Block Nine on the Camino Real!

(*He goes into the hotel.*)

BLOCK NINE

Abdullah runs back to the hotel with the billowing flambeau. A faint and far away humming sound becomes audible . . . Marguerite opens her eyes with a startled look. She searches the sky for something. A very low percussion begins with the humming sound, as if excited hearts are beating.

MARGUERITE: Jacques! I hear something in the sky!
JACQUES: I think what you hear is—
MARGUERITE (*with rising excitement*): —*No, it's a plane, a great one, I see the lights of it, now!*
JACQUES: Some kind of fireworks, Cara.
MARGUERITE: Hush! LISTEN!

(*She blows out the candle to see better above it. She rises, peering into the sky.*)

I see it! I see it! There! It's circling over us!
LADY MULLIGAN: Raymond, Raymond, sit down, your face is flushed!
HOTEL GUESTS (*overlapping*):
—What is it?
—The FUGITIVO!
—THE FUGITIVO! THE FUGITIVO!
—Quick, get my jewelry from the hotel safe!
—Cash a check!
—Throw some things in a bag! I'll wait here!
—Never mind luggage, we have our money and papers!
—Where is it now?
—There, there!
—It's turning to land!
—To go like this?
—Yes, go anyhow, just go anyhow, just go!
—Raymond! Please!
—Oh, it's rising again!

—Oh, it's—*SHH! MR. GUTMAN!*

(*Gutman appears in the doorway. He raises a hand in a commanding gesture.*)

GUTMAN: Signs in the sky should not be mistaken for wonders!

(*The Voices modulate quickly.*)

Ladies, gentlemen, please resume your seats!

(*Places are resumed at tables, and silver is shakily lifted. Glasses are raised to lips, but the noise of concerted panting of excitement fills the stage and a low percussion echoes frantic heart beats.*

(*Gutman descends to the plaza, shouting furiously to the Officer.*)

Why wasn't I told the Fugitivo was coming?

(*Everyone, almost as a man, rushes into the hotel and reappears almost at once with hastily collected possessions. Marguerite rises but appears stunned.*

(*There is a great whistling and screeching sound as the aerial transport halts somewhere close by, accompanied by rainbow splashes of light and cries like children's on a roller-coaster. Some incoming Passengers approach the stage down an aisle of the theatre, preceded by Redcaps with luggage.*)

PASSENGERS:
—What a heavenly trip!
—The scenery was thrilling!
—It's so quick!
—The only way to travel! Etc., etc.

(*A uniformed man, the Pilot, enters the plaza with a megaphone.*)

PILOT (*through the megaphone*): Fugitivo now loading for departure! Fugitivo loading immediately for departure! Northwest corner of the plaza!

MARGUERITE: Jacques, it's the Fugitivo, it's the non-scheduled thing you heard of this afternoon!

PILOT: All out-going passengers on the Fugitivo are requested to present their tickets and papers immediately at this station.

MARGUERITE: He said "out-going passengers"!

PILOT: Out-going passengers on the Fugitivo report immediately at this station for customs inspection.

MARGUERITE (*with a forced smile*): Why are you just standing there?

JACQUES (*with an Italian gesture*): Che cosa possa fare!

MARGUERITE: Move, move, do something!

JACQUES: *What!*

MARGUERITE: Go to them, ask, find out!

JACQUES: I have no idea what the damned thing is!

MARGUERITE: I do, I'll tell you! It's a way to escape from this abominable place!

JACQUES: Forse, forse, non so!

MARGUERITE: It's a way *out* and *I'm* not going to miss it!

PILOT: Ici la Douane! Customs inspection here!

MARGUERITE: Customs. That means luggage. Run to my room! Here! Key! Throw a few things in a bag, my jewels, my furs, but hurry! Vite, vite, vite! I don't believe there's much time! No, everybody is—

(*Outgoing Passengers storm the desk and table.*)

—Clamoring for tickets! There must be limited space! Why don't you do what I tell you?

(*She rushes to a man with a rubber stamp and a roll of tickets.*)

Monsieur! Señor! Pardonnez-moi! I'm going, I'm going out! I want my ticket!

PILOT (*coldly*): Name, please.

MARGUERITE: Mademoiselle—Gautier—but I—

PILOT: Gautier? Gautier? We have no Gautier listed.

MARGUERITE: I'm—*not* listed! I mean I'm—traveling under another name.

TRAVEL AGENT: What name are you traveling under?

(*Prudence and Olympe rush out of the hotel half dressed, dragging their furs. Meanwhile Kilroy is trying to make a fast buck or two as a Redcap. The scene gathers wild momen-*

tum, is punctuated by crashes of percussion. Grotesque mummers act as demon custom inspectors and immigration authorities, etc. Baggage is tossed about, ripped open, smuggled goods seized, arrests made, all amid the wildest importunities, protests, threats, bribes, entreaties; it is a scene for improvisation.)

PRUDENCE: Thank God I woke up!

OLYMPE: Thank God I wasn't asleep!

PRUDENCE: I knew it was non-scheduled but I *did* think they'd give you time to get in your girdle.

OLYMPE: Look who's trying to crash it! I know damned well *she* don't have a reservation!

PILOT (*to Marguerite*): What name did you say, Mademoiselle? Please! People are waiting, you're holding up the line!

MARGUERITE: I'm so confused! Jacques! What name did you make my reservation under?

OLYMPE: She has no reservation!

PRUDENCE: *I have, I got mine!*

OLYMPE: *I got mine!*

PRUDENCE: *I'm* next!

OLYMPE: Don't push *me*, you old bag!

MARGUERITE: I was here first! I was here before anybody! Jacques, quick! Get my money from the hotel safe!

(*Jacques exits.*)

AGENT: *Stay in line!*

(*There is a loud warning whistle.*)

PILOT: Five minutes. The Fugitivo leaves in five minutes. Five, five minutes only!

(*At this announcement the scene becomes riotous.*)

TRAVEL AGENT: *Four minutes! The Fugitivo leaves in four minutes!*

(*Prudence and Olympe are shrieking at him in French. The warning whistle blasts again.*)

Three minutes, the Fugitivo leaves in three minutes!

MARGUERITE (*topping the turmoil*): Monsieur! Please! I was here first, I was here before anybody! Look!

(*Jacques returns with her money.*)

I have thousands of francs! Take whatever you want! Take all of it, it's yours!

PILOT: Payment is only accepted in pounds sterling or dollars. Next, please.

MARGUERITE: You don't accept francs? They do at the hotel! They accept my francs at the Siete Mares!

PILOT: Lady, don't argue with me, I don't make the rules!

MARGUERITE (*beating her forehead with her fist*): Oh, God, Jacques! Take these back to the cashier!

(*She thrusts the bills at him.*)

Get them changed to dollars or—*Hurry! Tout de suite!* I'm—going to faint . . .

JACQUES: But Marguerite—

MARGUERITE: *Go! Go! Please!*

PILOT: Closing, we're closing now! The Fugitivo leaves in two minutes!

(*Lord and Lady Mulligan rush forward.*)

LADY MULLIGAN: Let Lord Mulligan through.

PILOT (*to Marguerite*): You're standing in the way.

(*Olympe screams as the Customs Inspector dumps her jewels on the ground. She and Prudence butt heads as they dive for the gems: the fight is renewed.*)

MARGUERITE (*detaining the Pilot*): Oh, look, Monsieur! Regardez ça! My diamond, a solitaire—two carats! Take that as security!

PILOT: Let me go. The Loan Shark's across the plaza!

(*There is another warning blast. Prudence and Olympe seize hat boxes and rush toward the whistle.*)

MARGUERITE (*clinging desperately to the Pilot*): You don't understand! Señor Casanova has gone to change money! He'll be here in a second. And I'll pay five, ten, twenty times the price of—*JACQUES! JACQUES! WHERE ARE YOU?*

VOICE (*back of auditorium*): We're closing the gate!

MARGUERITE: You can't close the gate!

PILOT: Move, Madame!

MARGUERITE: I won't move!

LADY MULLIGAN: I tell you, Lord Mulligan is the Iron & Steel man from Cobh! Raymond! They're closing the gate!

LORD MULLIGAN: I can't seem to get through!

GUTMAN: Hold the gate for Lord Mulligan!

PILOT (*to Marguerite*): Madame, stand back or I will have to use force!

MARGUERITE: Jacques! Jacques!

LADY MULLIGAN: Let us through! We're clear!

PILOT: Madame! Stand back and let these passengers through!

MARGUERITE: No, No! I'm first! I'm next!

LORD MULLIGAN: Get her out of our way! That woman's a whore!

LADY MULLIGAN: How dare you stand in our way?

PILOT: Officer, take this woman!

LADY MULLIGAN: Come on, Raymond!

MARGUERITE (*as the Officer pulls her away*): Jacques! Jacques! Jacques!

(*Jacques returns with changed money.*)

Here! Here is the money!

PILOT: All right, give me your papers.

MARGUERITE: —My papers? Did you say my papers?

PILOT: Hurry, hurry, your passport!

MARGUERITE: —Jacques! He wants my papers! Give him my papers, Jacques!

JACQUES: —The lady's papers are lost!

MARGUERITE (*wildly*): No, no, no, THAT IS NOT TRUE! HE WANTS TO KEEP ME HERE! HE'S LYING ABOUT IT!

JACQUES: Have you forgotten that your papers were stolen?

MARGUERITE: I gave you my papers, I gave you my papers to keep, you've got my papers.

(*Screaming, Lady Mulligan breaks past her and descends the stairs.*)

LADY MULLIGAN: Raymond! Hurry!

LORD MULLIGAN (*staggering on the top step*): I'm sick! I'm sick!

(*The Streetcleaners disguised as expensive morticians in swallowtail coats come rapidly up the aisle of the theatre and wait at the foot of the stairway for the tottering tycoon.*)

LADY MULLIGAN: You cannot be sick till we get on the Fugitivo!

LORD MULLIGAN: Forward all cables to Guaranty Trust in Paris.

LADY MULLIGAN: Place de la Concorde.

LORD MULLIGAN: Thank you! All purchases C.O.D. to Mulligan Iron & Steel Works in Cobh—Thank you!

LADY MULLIGAN: Raymond! Raymond! Who are these men?

LORD MULLIGAN: I know these men! I recognize their faces!

LADY MULLIGAN: Raymond! They're the Streetcleaners!

(*She screams and runs up the aisle screaming repeatedly, stopping half-way to look back. The Two Streetcleaners seize Lord Mulligan by either arm as he crumples.*)

Pack Lord Mulligan's body in dry ice! Ship Air Express to Cobh care of Mulligan Iron & Steel Works, in Cobh!

(*She runs sobbing out of the back of the auditorium as the whistle blows repeatedly and a Voice shouts.*)

I'm coming! I'm coming!

MARGUERITE: Jacques! Jacques! Oh, God!

PILOT: The Fugitivo is leaving, all aboard!

(*He starts toward the steps. Marguerite clutches his arm.*)

Let go of me!

MARGUERITE: You can't go without me!

PILOT: Officer, hold this woman!

JACQUES: Marguerite, let him go!

(*She releases the Pilot's arm and turns savagely on Jacques. She tears his coat open, seizes a large envelope of papers and rushes after the Pilot who has started down the steps over the orchestra pit and into a center aisle of the house. Timpani build up as she starts down the steps, screaming—*)

MARGUERITE: Here! I have them here! Wait! I have my papers now, I have my papers!

(The Pilot runs cursing up the center aisle as the Fugitivo whistle gives repeated short, shrill blasts; timpani and dissonant brass are heard.

(Outgoing Passengers burst into hysterical song, laughter, shouts of farewell. These can come over a loudspeaker at the back of the house.)

VOICE IN DISTANCE: Going! Going! Going!

MARGUERITE (*attempting as if half-paralyzed to descend the steps*): NOT WITHOUT ME, NO, NO, NOT WITHOUT ME!

(Her figure is caught in the dazzling glacial light of the follow-spot. It blinds her. She makes violent, crazed gestures, clinging to the railing of the steps; her breath is loud and hoarse as a dying person's, she holds a blood-stained handkerchief to her lips.

(There is a prolonged, gradually fading, rocketlike roar as the Fugitivo takes off. Shrill cries of joy from departing passengers; something radiant passes above the stage and streams of confetti and tinsel fall into the plaza. Then there is a great calm, the ship's receding roar diminished to the hum of an insect.)

GUTMAN (*somewhat compassionately*): Block Ten on the Camino Real.

BLOCK TEN

There is something about the desolation of the plaza that suggests a city devastated by bombardment. Reddish lights flicker here and there as if ruins were smoldering and wisps of smoke rise from them.

LA MADRECITA (*almost inaudibly*): Donde?

THE DREAMER: Aquí. Aquí, Madrecita.

MARGUERITE: Lost! Lost! Lost! Lost!

(She is still clinging brokenly to the railing of the steps. Jacques descends to her and helps her back up the steps.)

JACQUES: Lean against me, Cara. Breathe quietly, now.

MARGUERITE: Lost!

JACQUES: Breathe quietly, quietly, and look up at the sky.

MARGUERITE: Lost . . .

JACQUES: These tropical nights are so clear. There's the Southern Cross. Do you see the Southern Cross, Marguerite?

(*He points through the proscenium. They are now on the bench before the fountain; she is resting in his arms.*)

And there, over there, is Orion, like a fat, golden fish swimming North in the deep clear water, and we are together, breathing quietly together, leaning together, quietly, quietly together, completely, sweetly together, not frightened, now, not alone, but completely quietly together . . .

(*La Madrecita, led into the center of the plaza by her son, has begun to sing very softly; the reddish flares dim out and the smoke disappears.*)

All of us have a desperate bird in our hearts, a memory of—some distant mother with—wings . . .

MARGUERITE: I would have—left—without you . . .

JACQUES: I know, I know!

MARGUERITE: Then how can you—still—?

JACQUES: Hold you?

(*Marguerite nods slightly.*)

Because you've taught me that part of love which is tender. I never knew it before. Oh, I had—mistresses that circled me like moons! I scrambled from one bed-chamber to another bed-chamber with shirttails always aflame, from girl to girl, like buckets of coal-oil poured on a conflagration! But never loved until now with the part of love that's tender . . .

MARGUERITE: —We're used to each other. That's what you think is love . . . You'd better leave me now, you'd better go and let me go because there's a cold wind blowing out of the mountains and over the desert and into my heart, and if you stay with me now, I'll say cruel things, I'll wound your vanity, I'll taunt you with the decline of your male vigor!

JACQUES: Why does disappointment make people unkind to each other?

MARGUERITE: Each of us is very much alone.

JACQUES: Only if we distrust each other.

MARGUERITE: We have to distrust each other. It is our only defense against betrayal.

JACQUES: I think our defense is love.

MARGUERITE: Oh, Jacques, we're used to each other, we're a pair of captive hawks caught in the same cage, and so we've grown used to each other. That's what passes for love at this dim, shadowy end of the Camino Real . . .

What are we sure of? Not even of our existence, dear comforting friend! And whom can we ask the questions that torment us? "What is this place?" "Where are we?"—a fat old man who gives sly hints that only bewilder us more, a fake of a Gypsy squinting at cards and tea-leaves. What else are we offered? The never-broken procession of little events that assure us that we and strangers about us are still going on! Where? Why? and the perch that we hold is unstable! We're threatened with eviction, for this is a port of entry and departure, there are no permanent guests! And where else have we to go when we leave here? Bide-a-While? "Ritz Men Only"? Or under that ominous arch into Terra Incognita? We're lonely. We're frightened. We hear the Streetcleaners' piping not far away. So now and then, although we've wounded each other time and again—we stretch out hands to each other in the dark that we can't escape from—we huddle together for some dim-communal comfort—and that's what passes for love on this terminal stretch of the road that used to be royal. What is it, this feeling between us? When you feel my exhausted weight against your shoulder—when I clasp your anxious old hawk's head to my breast, what is it we feel in whatever is left of our hearts? Something, yes, something—delicate, unreal, bloodless! The sort of violets that could grow on the moon, or in the crevices of those far away mountains, fertilized by the droppings of carrion birds. Those birds are familiar to us. Their shadows inhabit the plaza. I've heard them flapping their wings like old charwomen beating worn-out carpets with gray brooms . . .

But tenderness, the violets in the mountains—can't break the rocks!

JACQUES: The violets in the mountains can break the rocks if you believe in them and allow them to grow!

(*The plaza has resumed its usual aspect. Abdullah enters through one of the downstage arches.*)

ABDULLAH: Get your carnival hats and noisemakers here! Tonight the moon will restore the virginity of my sister!

MARGUERITE (*almost tenderly touching his face*): Don't you know that tonight I am going to betray you?

JACQUES: —Why would you do that?

MARGUERITE: Because I've out-lived the tenderness of my heart. Abdullah, come here! I have an errand for you! Go to Ahmed's and deliver a message!

ABDULLAH: I'm working for Mama, making the Yankee dollar! Get your carnival hats and—

MARGUERITE: *Here, boy!*

(*She snatches a ring off her finger and offers it to him.*)

JACQUES: —Your cabochon sapphire?

MARGUERITE: Yes, my cabochon sapphire!

JACQUES: Are you mad?

MARGUERITE: Yes, I'm mad, or nearly! The specter of lunacy's at my heels tonight!

(*Jacques drives Abdullah back with his cane.*)

Catch, boy! The other side of the fountain! Quick!

(*The guitar is heard molto vivace. She tosses the ring across the fountain. Jacques attempts to hold the boy back with his cane. Abdullah dodges in and out like a little terrier, laughing. Marguerite shouts encouragement in French. When the boy is driven back from the ring, she snatches it up and tosses it to him again, shouting:*)

Catch, boy! Run to Ahmed's! Tell the charming young man that the French lady's bored with her company tonight! Say that the French lady missed the Fugitivo and wants to forget she missed it! Oh, and reserve a room with a balcony so

I can watch your sister appear on the roof when the moonrise makes her a virgin!

(*Abdullah skips shouting out of the plaza. Jacques strikes the stage with his cane. She says, without looking at him:*)

Time betrays us and we betray each other.

JACQUES: Wait, Marguerite.

MARGUERITE: No! I can't! The wind from the desert is sweeping me away!

(*A loud singing wind sweeps her toward the terrace, away from him. She looks back once or twice as if for some gesture of leave-taking but he only stares at her fiercely, striking the stage at intervals with his cane, like a death-march. Gutman watches, smiling, from the terrace, bows to Marguerite as she passes into the hotel. The drum of Jacques' cane is taken up by other percussive instruments, and almost unnoticeably at first, weird-looking celebrants or carnival mummers creep into the plaza, silently as spiders descending a wall.*

(*A sheet of scarlet and yellow rice paper bearing some cryptic device is lowered from the center of the plaza. The percussive effects become gradually louder. Jacques is oblivious to the scene behind him, standing in front of the plaza, his eyes closed.*)

GUTMAN: Block Eleven on the Camino Real.

BLOCK ELEVEN

GUTMAN: The Fiesta has started. The first event is the coronation of the King of Cuckolds.

(*Blinding shafts of light are suddenly cast upon Casanova on the forestage. He shields his face, startled, as the crowd closes about him. The blinding shafts of light seem to strike him like savage blows and he falls to his knees as—*

(*The Hunchback scuttles out of the Gypsy's stall with a crown of gilded antlers on a velvet pillow. He places it on Jacques' head. The celebrants form a circle about him chanting.*)

JACQUES: What is this?—a crown—

GUTMAN: A crown of horns!

CROWD: Cornudo! Cornudo! Cornudo! Cornudo! Cornudo!

GUTMAN: Hail, all hail, the King of Cuckolds on the Camino Real!

(*Jacques springs up, first striking out at them with his cane. Then all at once he abandons self-defense, throws off his cape, casts away his cane, and fills the plaza with a roar of defiance and self-derision.*)

JACQUES: Si, si, sono cornudo! Cornudo! Cornudo! Casanova is the King of Cuckolds on the Camino Real! Show me crowned to the world! Announce the honor! Tell the world of the honor bestowed on Casanova, Chevalier de Seingalt! Knight of the Golden Spur by the Grace of His Holiness the Pope . . . Famous adventurer! Con man Extraordinary! Gambler! Pitch-man par excellence! Shill! Pimp! Spiv! *And—great—lover . . .*

(*The Crowd howls with applause and laughter but his voice rises above them with sobbing intensity.*)

Yes, I said GREAT LOVER! The greatest lover wears the longest horns on the Camino! GREAT! LOVER!

GUTMAN: Attention! Silence! The moon is rising! The restoration is about to occur!

(*A white radiance is appearing over the ancient wall of the town. The mountains become luminous. There is music. Everyone, with breathless attention, faces the light.*

(*Kilroy crosses to Jacques and beckons him out behind the crowd. There he snatches off the antlers and returns him his fedora. Jacques reciprocates by removing Kilroy's fright wig and electric nose. They embrace as brothers. In a Chaplinesque dumb-play, Kilroy points to the wildly flickering three brass balls of the Loan Shark and to his golden gloves: then with a terrible grimace he removes the gloves from about his neck, smiles at Jacques and indicates that the two of them together will take flight over the wall. Jacques shakes his head sadly, pointing to his heart and then to the Siete Mares. Kilroy nods with regretful understanding of a human and manly folly. A Guard has been silently approaching them in a soft shoe dance. Jacques whistles "La Golondrina." Kilroy assumes a very nonchalant pose. The Guard picks up curiously the discarded fright wig and electric nose. Then glancing suspiciously at the pair, he advances. Kilroy makes a run for it. He does a baseball slide into the Loan Shark's welcoming doorway. The door slams. The Cop is about to crash it when a gong sounds and Gutman shouts:*)

GUTMAN: SILENCE! ATTENTION! THE GYPSY!

GYPSY (*appearing on the roof with a gong*): The moon has restored the virginity of my daughter Esmeralda!

(*The gong sounds.*)

STREET PEOPLE: Ahh!

GYPSY: The moon in its plenitude has made her a virgin!

(*The gong sounds.*)

STREET PEOPLE: Ahh!

GYPSY: Praise her, celebrate her, give her suitable homage!

(*The gong sounds.*)

STREET PEOPLE: Ahh!

GYPSY: Summon her to the roof!

(*She shouts:*)

ESMERALDA!

(*Dancers shout the name in rhythm.*)

RISE WITH THE MOON, MY DAUGHTER! CHOOSE THE HERO!

(*Esmeralda appears on the roof in dazzling light. She seems to be dressed in jewels. She raises her jeweled arms with a harsh flamenco cry.*)

ESMERALDA: OLE!

DANCERS: OLE!

(*The details of the Carnival are a problem for director and choreographer but it has already been indicated in the script that the Fiesta is a sort of serio-comic, grotesque-lyric "Rites of Fertility" with roots in various pagan cultures.*

(*It should not be over-elaborated or allowed to occupy much time. It should not be more than three minutes from the appearance of Esmeralda on the Gypsy's roof till the return of Kilroy from the Loan Shark's.*

(*Kilroy emerges from the Pawn Shop in grotesque disguise, a turban, dark glasses, a burnoose and an umbrella or sunshade.*)

KILROY (*to Jacques*): So long, pal, I wish you could come with me.

(*Jacques clasps his cross in Kilroy's hands.*)

ESMERALDA: Yankee!

KILROY (*to the audience*): So long, everybody. Good luck to you all on the Camino! I hocked my golden gloves to finance this expedition. I'm going. Hasta luega. I'm going. I'm gone!

ESMERALDA: Yankee!

(*He has no sooner entered the plaza than the riotous women strip off everything but the dungarees and skivvy which he first appeared in.*)

KILROY (*to the women*): Let me go. Let go of me! Watch out for my equipment!

ESMERALDA: Yankee! Yankee!

(*He breaks away from them and plunges up the stairs of the ancient wall. He is half-way up them when Gutman shouts out:*)

GUTMAN: Follow-spot on that gringo, light the stairs!

(*The light catches Kilroy. At the same instant Esmeralda cries out to him:*)

ESMERALDA: *Yankee! Yankee!*

GYPSY: What's goin' on down there?

(*She rushes into the plaza.*)

KILROY: Oh, no, I'm on my way out!

ESMERALDA: Espere un momento!

(*The Gypsy calls the police, but is ignored in the crowd.*)

KILROY: Don't tempt me, baby! I hocked my golden gloves to finance this expedition!

ESMERALDA: Querido!

KILROY: Querido means sweetheart, a word which is hard to resist but I must resist it.

ESMERALDA: Champ!

KILROY: I used to be Champ but why remind me of it?

ESMERALDA: Be champ again! Contend in the contest! Compete in the competition!

GYPSY (*shouting*): *Naw, naw, not eligible!*

ESMERALDA: *Pl-eeeeeeze!*

GYPSY: Slap her, Nursie, she's flippin'.

(*Esmeralda slaps Nursie instead.*)

ESMERALDA: Hero! Champ!

KILROY: I'm not in condition!

ESMERALDA: You're still the Champ, the undefeated Champ of the golden gloves!

KILROY: Nobody's called me that in a long, long time!

ESMERALDA: Champ!

KILROY: My resistance is crumbling!

ESMERALDA: Champ!

KILROY: It's crumbled!

ESMERALDA: Hero!

KILROY: GERONIMO!

(*He takes a flying leap from the stairs into the center of the plaza. He turns toward Esmeralda and cries:*)

DOLL!!

(*Kilroy surrounded by cheering Street People goes into a triumphant eccentric dance which reviews his history as fighter, traveler and lover.*

(*At finish of the dance, the music is cut off, as Kilroy lunges, arm uplifted towards Esmeralda, and cries:*)

KILROY: *Kilroy the Champ!*

ESMERALDA: *KILROY the Champ!*

(*She snatches a bunch of red roses from the stunned Nursie and tosses them to Kilroy.*)

CROWD (*sharply*): OLE!

(*The Gypsy, at the same instant, hurls her gong down, creating a resounding noise.*

(*Kilroy turns and comes down towards the audience, saying to them:*)

KILROY: *Y'see?*

(*Cheering Street People surge towards him and lift him in the air. The lights fade as the curtain descends.*)

CROWD (*in a sustained yell*): *OLE!*

(*The curtain falls. There is a short intermission.*)

BLOCK TWELVE

The stage is in darkness except for a spot light which picks out Esmeralda on the Gypsy's roof.

ESMERALDA: Mama, what happened?—Mama, the lights went out!—Mama, where are you? It's so dark I'm scared!—MAMA!

(*The lights are turned on displaying a deserted plaza. The Gypsy is seated at a small table before her stall.*)

GYPSY: Come on downstairs, Doll. The mischief is done. You've chosen your hero!

GUTMAN (*from the balcony of the Siete Mares*): Block Twelve on the Camino Real.

NURSIE (*at the fountain*): Gypsy, the fountain is still dry!

GYPSY: What d'yuh expect? There's nobody left to uphold the old traditions! You raise a girl. She watches television. Plays be-bop. Reads *Screen Secrets*. Comes the Big Fiesta. The moonrise makes her a virgin—which is the neatest trick of the week! And what does she do? Chooses a Fugitive Patsy for the Chosen Hero! Well, show him in! Admit the joker and get the virgin ready!

NURSIE: You're going through with it?

GYPSY: Look, Nursie! I'm operating a legitimate joint! This joker'll get the same treatment he'd get if he breezed down the Camino in a blizzard of G-notes! Trot, girl! Lubricate your means of locomotion!

(*Nursie goes into the Gypsy's stall. The Gypsy rubs her hands together and blows on the crystal ball, spits on it and gives it the old one-two with a "shammy" rag . . . She mutters "Crystal ball, tell me all . . . crystal ball tell me all" . . . as:*

(*Kilroy bounds into the plaza from her stall . . . a rose between his teeth.*)

GYPSY: Siente se, por favor.
KILROY: No comprendo the lingo.
GYPSY: Put it down!
NURSIE (*offstage*): Hey, Gypsy!
GYPSY: Address me as Madam!
NURSIE (*entering*): *Madam!* Winchell has scooped you!
GYPSY: In a pig's eye!
NURSIE: The Fugitivo has *"fftt . . ."*!
GYPSY: In Elizabeth, New Jersey . . . ten fifty seven P.M. . . . Eastern Standard Time—while you were putting them kiss-me-quicks in your hair-do! Furthermore, my second exclusive is that the solar system is drifting towards the constellation of Hercules: *Skiddoo!*

(*Nursie exits. Stamping is heard offstage.*)

Quiet, back there! God damn it!
NURSIE (*offstage*): She's out of control!
GYPSY: Give her a double-bromide!

(*To Kilroy:*)

Well, how does it feel to be the Chosen Hero?
KILROY: I better explain something to you.
GYPSY: Save your breath. You'll need it.
KILROY: I want to level with you. Can I level with you?
GYPSY (*rapidly stamping some papers*): How could you help but level with the Gypsy?
KILROY: I don't know what the hero is chosen for.

(*Esmeralda and Nursie shriek offstage.*)

GYPSY: Time will brief you . . . Aw, I hate paper work! . . . NURSEHH!

(*Nursie comes out and stands by the table.*)

This filing system is screwed up six ways from Next Sunday . . . File this crap under crap!—

(*To Kilroy:*)

The smoking lamp is lit. Have a stick on me!

(*She offers him a cigarette.*)

KILROY: No thanks.
GYPSY: Come on, indulge yourself. You got nothing to lose that won't be lost.
KILROY: If that's a professional opinion, I don't respect it.
GYPSY: Resume your seat and give me your full name.
KILROY: Kilroy.
GYPSY (*writing all this down*): Date of birth and place of that disaster?
KILROY: Both unknown.
GYPSY: Address?
KILROY: Traveler.
GYPSY: Parents?
KILROY: Anonymous.
GYPSY: Who brought you up?
KILROY: I was brought up and down by an eccentric old aunt in Dallas.
GYPSY: Raise both hands simultaneously and swear that you have not come here for the purpose of committing an immoral act.
ESMERALDA (*from offstage*): Hey, Chico!
GYPSY: *QUIET!* Childhood diseases?
KILROY: Whooping cough, measles and mumps.
GYPSY: Likes and dislikes?
KILROY: I like situations I can get out of. I don't like cops and—
GYPSY: Immaterial! Here! Signature on this!

(*She hands him a blank.*)

KILROY: What is it?
GYPSY: You always sign something, don't you?
KILROY: Not till I know what it is.

GYPSY: It's just a little formality to give a tone to the establishment and make an impression on our out-of-town trade. Roll up your sleeve.

KILROY: What for?

GYPSY: A shot of some kind.

KILROY: What kind?

GYPSY: Any kind. Don't they always give you some kind of a shot?

KILROY: "They"?

GYPSY: Brass-hats, Americanos!

(*She injects a hypo.*)

KILROY: I am no guinea pig!

GYPSY: Don't kid yourself. We're all of us guinea pigs in the laboratory of God. Humanity is just a work in progress.

KILROY: I don't make it out.

GYPSY: Who does? The Camino Real is a funny paper read backwards!

(*There is weird piping outside. Kilroy shifts on his seat. The Gypsy grins.*)

Tired? The altitude makes you sleepy?

KILROY: It makes me nervous.

GYPSY: I'll show you how to take a slug of tequila! It dilates the capillaries. First you sprinkle salt on the back of your hand. Then lick it off with your tongue. Now then you toss the shot down!

(*She demonstrates.*)

—And then you bite into the lemon. That way it goes down easy, but what a bang!—You're next.

KILROY: No, thanks, I'm on the wagon.

GYPSY: There's an old Chinese proverb that says, "When your goose is cooked you might as well have it cooked with plenty of gravy."

(*She laughs.*)

Get up, baby. Let's have a look at yuh!—You're not a bad-looking boy. Sometimes working for the Yankee dollar isn't a painful profession. Have you ever been attracted by older women?

KILROY: Frankly, no, ma'am.
GYPSY: Well, there's a first time for everything.
KILROY: That is a subject I cannot agree with you on.
GYPSY: You think I'm an old bag?

(*Kilroy laughs awkwardly. The Gypsy slaps his face.*)

Will you take the cards or the crystal?
KILROY: It's immaterial.
GYPSY: All right, we'll begin with the cards.

(*She shuffles and deals.*)

Ask me a question.
KILROY: Has my luck run out?
GYPSY: Baby, your luck ran out the day you were born. Another question.
KILROY: Ought I to leave this town?
GYPSY: It don't look to me like you've got much choice in the matter . . . Take a card.

(*Kilroy takes one.*)

GYPSY: Ace?
KILROY: Yes, ma'am.
GYPSY: What color?
KILROY: Black.
GYPSY: Oh, oh— That does it. How big is your heart?
KILROY: As big as the head of a baby.
GYPSY: It's going to break.
KILROY: That's what I was afraid of.
GYPSY: The Streetcleaners are waiting for you outside the door.
KILROY: Which door, the front one? I'll slip out the back!
GYPSY: Leave us face it frankly, your number is up! You must've known a long time that the name of Kilroy was on the Streetcleaners' list.
KILROY: Sure. But not on top of it!
GYPSY: It's always a bit of a shock. Wait a minute! Here's good news. The Queen of Hearts has turned up in proper position.
KILROY: What's that mean?
GYPSY: Love, Baby!

KILROY: Love?
GYPSY: The Booby Prize!—Esmeralda!

(*She rises and hits a gong. A divan is carried out. The Gypsy's Daughter is seated in a reclining position, like an odalisque, on this low divan. A spangled veil covers her face. From this veil to the girdle below her navel, that supports her diaphanous bifurcated skirt, she is nude except for a pair of glittering emerald snakes coiled over her breasts. Kilroy's head moves in a dizzy circle and a canary warbles inside it.*)

KILROY: WHAT'S—WHAT'S *HER* SPECIALTY?—Tea-leaves?

(*The Gypsy wags a finger.*)

GYPSY: You know what curiosity did to the tom cat!—Nursie, give me my glamour wig and my forty-five. I'm hitting the street! I gotta go down to Walgreen's for change.
KILROY: What change?
GYPSY: The change from that ten-spot you're about to give me.
NURSIE: Don't argue with her. She has a will of iron.
KILROY: I'm not arguing!

(*He reluctantly produces the money.*)

But let's be *fair* about this! I hocked my golden gloves for this saw-buck!
NURSIE: All of them Yankee bastids want something for nothing!
KILROY: I want a receipt for this bill.
NURSIE: No one is gypped at the Gypsy's!
KILROY: That's wonderful! How do I know it?
GYPSY: It's in the cards, it's in the crystal ball, it's in the tea-leaves! Absolutely no one is gypped at the Gypsy's!

(*She snatches the bill. The wind howls.*)

Such changeable weather! I'll slip on my summer furs! Nursie, break out my summer furs!
NURSIE (*leering grotesquely*): *Mink or sable?*
GYPSY: *Ha ha, that's a doll!* Here! Clock him!

(*Nursie tosses her a greasy blanket, and the Gypsy tosses Nursie an alarm clock. The Gypsy rushes through the beaded string curtains.*)

Adios! Ha ha!!

(*She is hardly offstage when two shots ring out. Kilroy starts.*)

ESMERALDA (*plaintively*): Mother has such an awful time on the street.

KILROY: You mean that she is insulted on the street?

ESMERALDA: By strangers.

KILROY (*to the audience*): I shouldn't think acquaintances would do it.

(*She curls up on the low divan. Kilroy licks his lips.*)

—You seem very different from—this afternoon . . .

ESMERALDA: This afternoon?

KILROY: Yes, in the plaza when I was being roughed up by them gorillas and you was being dragged in the house by your Mama!

(*Esmeralda stares at him blankly.*)

You don't remember?

ESMERALDA: I never remember what happened before the moonrise makes me a virgin.

KILROY: —That—comes as a shock to you, huh?

ESMERALDA: Yes. It comes as a shock.

KILROY (*smiling*): You have a little temporary amnesia they call it!

ESMERALDA: Yankee . . .

KILROY: Huh?

ESMERALDA: I'm glad I chose you. I'm glad that you were chosen.

(*Her voice trails off.*)

I'm glad. I'm very glad . . .

NURSIE: Doll!

ESMERALDA: —What is it, Nursie?

NURSIE: How are things progressing?

ESMERALDA: Slowly, Nursie—

(*Nursie comes lumbering in.*)

NURSIE: I want some light reading matter.
ESMERALDA: He's sitting on *Screen Secrets.*
KILROY (*jumping up*): Aw. Here.

(*He hands her the fan magazine. She lumbers back out, coyly.*)

—I—I feel——self-conscious . .

(*He suddenly jerks out a silver-framed photo.*)

—D'you—like pictures?
ESMERALDA: Moving pictures?
KILROY: No, a—motionless—snapshot!
ESMERALDA: Of you?
KILROY: Of my—real—true woman . . . She was a platinum blonde the same as Jean Harlow. Do you remember Jean Harlow? No, you wouldn't remember Jean Harlow. It shows you are getting old when you remember Jean Harlow.

(*He puts the snapshot away.*)

. . . They say that Jean Harlow's ashes are kept in a little private cathedral in Forest Lawn . . . Wouldn't it be wonderful if you could sprinkle them ashes over the ground like seeds, and out of each one would spring another Jean Harlow? And when spring comes you could just walk out and pick them off the bush! . . . You don't talk much.
ESMERALDA: You want me to *talk*?
KILROY: Well, that's the way we do things in the States. A little vino, some records on the victrola, some quiet conversation—and then if both parties are in a mood for romance . . . Romance—
ESMERALDA: Music!

(*She rises and pours some wine from a slender crystal decanter as music is heard.*)

They say that the monetary system has got to be stabilized all over the world.
KILROY (*taking the glass*): Repeat that, please. My radar was not wide open.

ESMERALDA: I said that *they* said that—uh, skip it! But we couldn't care less as long as we keep on getting the Yankee dollar . . . plus federal tax!

KILROY: That's for surely!

ESMERALDA: How do you feel about the class struggle? Do you take sides in that?

KILROY: Not that I—

ESMERALDA: Neither do we because of the dialectics.

KILROY: Who! Which?

ESMERALDA: Languages with accents, I suppose. But Mama don't care as long as they don't bring the Pope over here and put him in the White House.

KILROY: Who would do that?

ESMERALDA: Oh, the Bolsheviskies, those nasty old things with whiskers! *Whiskers scratch!* But little moustaches tickle . . .

(*She giggles.*)

KILROY: I always got a smooth shave . . .

ESMERALDA: And how do you feel about the Mumbo Jumbo? Do you think they've got the Old Man in the bag yet?

KILROY: The Old Man?

ESMERALDA: God. We don't think so. We think there has been so much of the Mumbo Jumbo it's put Him to sleep!

(*Kilroy jumps up impatiently.*)

KILROY: This is not what I mean by a quiet conversation. I mean this is no where! *No where!*

ESMERALDA: What sort of talk do you want?

KILROY: Something more—intimate sort of! You know, like—

ESMERALDA: —Where did you get those eyes?

KILROY: *PERSONAL! Yeah . . .*

ESMERALDA: Well,—where did you get those eyes?

KILROY: Out of a dead cod-fish!

NURSIE (*shouting offstage*): DOLL!

(*Kilroy springs up, pounding his left palm with his right fist.*)

ESMERALDA: What?

NURSIE: Fifteen minutes!

KILROY: I'm no hot-rod mechanic.

(*To the audience:*)

I bet she's out there holding a stop watch to see that I don't over-stay my time in this place!

ESMERALDA (*calling through the string curtains*): *Nursie, go to bed, Nursie!*

KILROY (*in a fierce whisper*): That's right, go to bed, Nursie!!

(*There is a loud crash offstage.*)

ESMERALDA: —Nursie has gone to bed . . .

(*She drops the string curtains and returns to the alcove.*)

KILROY (*with vast relief*): —Ahhhhhhhhhh . . .

ESMERALDA: What've you got your eyes on?

KILROY: Those green snakes on you—what do you wear them for?

ESMERALDA: Supposedly for protection, but really for fun.

(*He crosses to the divan.*)

What are you going to do?

KILROY: I'm about to establish a beach-head on that sofa.

(*He sits down.*)

How about—lifting your veil?

ESMERALDA: I can't lift it.

KILROY: Why not?

ESMERALDA: I promised Mother I wouldn't.

KILROY: I thought your mother was the broadminded type.

ESMERALDA: Oh, she is, but you know how mothers are. You can lift it for me, if you say pretty please.

KILROY: Aww——

ESMERALDA: Go on, say it! Say pretty please!

KILROY: No!!

ESMERALDA: Why not?

KILROY: It's silly.

ESMERALDA: Then you can't lift my veil!

KILROY: Oh, all right. Pretty please.

ESMERALDA: Say it again!

KILROY: Pretty please.

ESMERALDA: Now say it once more like you meant it.

(*He jumps up. She grabs his hand.*)

Don't go away.

KILROY: You're making a fool out of me.

ESMERALDA: I was just teasing a little. Because you're so cute. Sit down again, please—*pretty* please!

(*He falls on the couch.*)

KILROY: What is that wonderful perfume you've got on?

ESMERALDA: Guess!

KILROY: Chanel Number Five?

ESMERALDA: No.

KILROY: Tabu?

ESMERALDA: No.

KILROY: I give up.

ESMERALDA: It's *Noche en Acapulco*! I'm just dying to go to Acapulco. I wish that you would take me to Acapulco.

(*He sits up.*)

What's the matter?

KILROY: You gypsies' daughters are invariably reminded of something without which you cannot do—just when it looks like everything has been fixed.

ESMERALDA: That isn't nice at all. I'm not the gold-digger type. Some girls see themselves in silver foxes. I only see myself in Acapulco!

KILROY: At Todd's Place?

ESMERALDA: Oh, no, at the Mirador! Watching those pretty boys dive off the Quebrada!

KILROY: Look again, Baby. Maybe you'll see yourself in Paramount Pictures or having a Singapore Sling at a Statler bar!

ESMERALDA: You're being sarcastic?

KILROY: Nope. Just realistic. All of you gypsies' daughters have hearts of stone, and I'm not whistling "Dixie"! But just the same, the night before a man dies, he says, "Pretty please—will you let me lift your veil?"—while the Streetcleaners wait for him right outside the door!—Because to be warm for a little longer is life. And love?—that's a four-letter word which is sometimes no better than one you see printed on fences by kids playing hooky from school!—Oh, well—what's the use of complaining? You gypsies' daughters have ears that only catch sounds like the snap of a gold cigarette case! Or, pretty please, Baby,—we're going to Acapulco!

ESMERALDA: *Are* we?

KILROY: See what I mean?

(*To the audience:*)

Didn't I tell you?!

(*To Esmeralda:*)

Yes! In the morning!

ESMERALDA: Ohhhh! I'm dizzy with joy! My little heart is going pitty-pat!

KILROY: My big heart is going boom-boom! Can I lift your veil now?

ESMERALDA: If you will be gentle.

KILROY: I would not hurt a fly unless it had on leather mittens.

(*He touches a corner of her spangled veil.*)

ESMERALDA: Ohhh . . .

KILROY: What?

ESMERALDA: Ohhhhhh!!

KILROY: Why! What's the matter?

ESMERALDA: You are not being gentle!

KILROY: I *am* being gentle.

ESMERALDA: You are *not* being gentle.

KILROY: What was I being, then?

ESMERALDA: Rough!

KILROY: I am *not* being rough.

ESMERALDA: Yes, you *are* being rough. You have to be gentle with me because you're the first.

KILROY: Are you kidding?

ESMERALDA: No.

KILROY: How about all of those other fiestas you've been to?

ESMERALDA: Each one's the first one. That is the wonderful thing about gypsies' daughters!

KILROY: You can say that again!

ESMERALDA: I don't like you when you're like that.

KILROY: Like what?

ESMERALDA: Cynical and sarcastic.

KILROY: I am sincere.

ESMERALDA: Lots of boys aren't sincere.

KILROY: Maybe they aren't but I am.

ESMERALDA: Everyone says he's sincere, but everyone isn't sincere. If everyone was sincere who says he's sincere there wouldn't be half so many insincere ones in the world and there would be lots, lots, lots more really sincere ones!

KILROY: I think you have got something there. But how about gypsies' daughters?

ESMERALDA: Huh?

KILROY: Are they one hundred percent in the really sincere category?

ESMERALDA: Well, yes, and no, mostly no! But some of them are for a while if their sweethearts are gentle.

KILROY: Would you believe I am sincere and gentle?

ESMERALDA: I would believe that you believe that you are . . . For a while . . .

KILROY: Everything's for a while. For a while is the stuff that dreams are made of, Baby! Now?—Now?

ESMERALDA: Yes, now, but be gentle!—*gentle* . . .

(*He delicately lifts a corner of her veil. She utters a soft cry. He lifts it further. She cries out again. A bit further . . . He turns the spangled veil all the way up from her face.*)

KILROY: I am sincere.

ESMERALDA: I am sincere.

KILROY: I am sincere.

ESMERALDA: I am sincere.

KILROY: I am sincere.

ESMERALDA: I am sincere.

KILROY: I am sincere.

ESMERALDA: I am sincere.

(*Kilroy leans back, removing his hand from her veil. She opens her eyes.*)

Is that all?

KILROY: I am tired.

ESMERALDA: —Already?

(*He rises and goes down the steps from the alcove.*)

KILROY: I am tired, and full of regret . . .
ESMERALDA: Oh!
KILROY: It wasn't much to give my golden gloves for.
ESMERALDA: You pity yourself?
KILROY: That's right, I pity myself and everybody that goes to the Gypsy's daughter. I pity the world and I pity the God who made it.

(*He sits down.*)

ESMERALDA: It's always like that as soon as the veil is lifted. They're all so ashamed of having degraded themselves, and their hearts have more regret than a heart can hold!
KILROY: Even a heart that's as big as the head of a baby!
ESMERALDA: You don't even notice how pretty my face is, do you?
KILROY: You look like all gypsies' daughters, no better, no worse. But as long as you get to go to Acapulco, your cup runneth over with ordinary contentment.
ESMERALDA: —I've never been so insulted in all my life!
KILROY: Oh, yes, you have, Baby. And you'll be insulted worse if you stay in this racket. You'll be insulted so much that it will get to be like water off *a duck's back*!

(*The door slams. Curtains are drawn apart on the Gypsy. Esmeralda lowers her veil hastily. Kilroy pretends not to notice the Gypsy's entrance. She picks up a little bell and rings it over his head.*)

Okay, Mamacita! I am aware of your presence!
GYPSY: Ha-ha! I was followed three blocks by some awful man!
KILROY: Then you caught him.
GYPSY: Naw, he ducked into a subway! I waited fifteen minutes outside the men's room and he never came out!
KILROY: Then you went in?
GYPSY: No! I got myself a sailor!—The streets are brilliant! . . . Have you all been good children?

(*Esmeralda makes a whimpering sound.*)

The pussy will play while the old mother cat is away?
KILROY: Your sense of humor is wonderful, but how about my change, Mamacita?

GYPSY: What change are you talking about?

KILROY: Are you boxed out of your mind? The change from that ten-spot you trotted over to Walgreen's?

GYPSY: Ohhhhh—

KILROY: *Oh, what?*

GYPSY (*counting on her fingers*): Five for the works, one dollar luxury tax, two for the house percentage and two more pour la service!—makes ten! Didn't I tell you?

KILROY: —What kind of a deal is this?

GYPSY (*whipping out a revolver*): A rugged one, Baby!

ESMERALDA: Mama, don't be unkind!

GYPSY: Honey, the gentleman's friends are waiting outside the door and it wouldn't be nice to detain him! Come on— Get going— Vamoose!

KILROY: Okay, Mamacita! Me voy!

(*He crosses to the beaded string curtains: turns to look back at the Gypsy and her daughter. The piping of the Streetcleaners is heard outside.*)

Sincere?—Sure! That's the wonderful thing about gypsies' daughters!

(*He goes out. Esmeralda raises a wondering fingertip to one eye. Then she cries out:*)

ESMERALDA: Look, Mama! Look, Mama! A tear!

GYPSY: You have been watching television too much . . .

(*She gathers the cards and turns off the crystal ball as—*)
(*Light fades out on the phony paradise of the Gypsy's.*)

GUTMAN: Block Thirteen on the Camino Real.

(*He exits.*)

BLOCK THIRTEEN

In the blackout the Streetcleaners place a barrel in the center and then hide in the Pit.

Kilroy, who enters from the right, is followed by a spot light. He sees the barrel and the menacing Streetcleaners and then runs to the closed door of the Siete Mares and rings the bell. No one answers. He backs up so he can see the balcony and calls:

KILROY: Mr. Gutman! Just gimme a cot in the lobby. I'll do odd jobs in the morning. I'll be the Patsy again. I'll light my nose sixty times a minute. I'll take prat-falls and assume the position for anybody that drops a dime on the street . . . Have a heart! Have just a LITTLE heart. Please!

(*There is no response from Gutman's balcony. Jacques enters. He pounds his cane once on the pavement.*)

JACQUES: Gutman! Open the door!—*GUTMAN! GUTMAN!*

(*Eva, a beautiful woman, apparently nude, appears on the balcony.*)

GUTMAN (*from inside*): Eva darling, you're exposing yourself!

(*He appears on the balcony with a portmanteau.*)

JACQUES: What are you doing with my portmanteau?
GUTMAN: Haven't you come for your luggage?
JACQUES: Certainly not! I haven't checked out of here!
GUTMAN: Very few do . . . but residences are frequently terminated.
JACQUES: Open the door!
GUTMAN: Open the letter with the remittance check in it!
JACQUES: In the morning!
GUTMAN: Tonight!
JACQUES: Upstairs in my room!
GUTMAN: Downstairs at the entrance!
JACQUES: I won't be intimidated!
GUTMAN (*raising the portmanteau over his head*): What?!
JACQUES: Wait!—

(*He takes the letter out of his pocket.*)

Give me some light.

(*Kilroy strikes a match and holds it over Jacques' shoulder.*)

Thank you. What does it say?
GUTMAN: —Remittances?

KILROY (*reading the letter over Jacques' shoulder*): *—discontinued . . .*

(*Gutman raises the portmanteau again.*)

JACQUES: Careful, I have—

(*The portmanteau lands with a crash.*

(*The Bum comes to the window at the crash. A. Ratt comes out to his doorway at the same time.*)

—fragile—mementoes . . .

(*He crosses slowly down to the portmanteau and kneels as . . .*

(*Gutman laughs and slams the balcony door. Jacques turns to Kilroy. He smiles at the young adventurer.*)

—"And so at last it has come, the distinguished thing!"

(*A. Ratt speaks as Jacques touches the portmanteau.*)

A. RATT: Hey, Dad—Vacancy here! A bed at the "Ritz Men Only." A little white ship to sail the dangerous night in.
JACQUES: Single or double?
A. RATT: There's only singles in this pad.
JACQUES (*to Kilroy*): Match you for it.
KILROY: What the hell, we're buddies, we can sleep spoons! If we can't sleep, we'll push the wash stand against the door and sing old popular songs till the crack of dawn! . . . "Heart of my heart, I love that melody!" . . . You bet your life I do.

(*Jacques takes out a pocket handkerchief and starts to grasp the portmanteau handle.*)

—It looks to me like you could use a Redcap and my rates are non-union!

(*He picks up the portmanteau and starts to cross towards the "Ritz Men Only." He stops at right center.*)

Sorry, buddy. Can't make it! The altitude on this block has affected my ticker! And in the distance which is nearer than further, I hear—the Streetcleaners'—piping!

(*Piping is heard.*)

JACQUES: COME ALONG!

(*He lifts the portmanteau and starts on.*)

KILROY: NO. Tonight! I prefer! To sleep! Out! Under! The stars!

JACQUES (*gently*): I understand, Brother!

KILROY (*to Jacques as he continues toward the "Ritz Men Only"*): Bon Voyage! I hope that you sail the dangerous night to the sweet golden port of morning!

JACQUES (*exiting*): Thanks, Brother!

KILROY: Excuse the *corn*! I'm sincere!

BUM: Show me the way to go home! . . .

GUTMAN (*appearing on the balcony with white parakeet*): Block Fourteen on the Camino Real.

BLOCK FOURTEEN

At opening, the Bum is still at the window.

The Streetcleaners' piping continues a little louder. Kilroy climbs, breathing heavily, to the top of the stairs and stands looking out at Terra Incognita as . . .

Marguerite enters the plaza through alleyway at right. She is accompanied by a silent Young Man who wears a domino.

MARGUERITE: Don't come any further with me. I'll have to wake the night porter. Thank you for giving me safe conduct through the Medina.

(*She has offered her hand. He grips it with a tightness that makes her wince.*)

Ohhhh . . . I'm not sure which is more provocative in you, your ominous silence or your glittering smile or—

(*He's looking at her purse.*)

What do you want? . . . Oh!

(*She starts to open the purse. He snatches it. She gasps as he suddenly strips her cloak off her. Then he snatches off her pearl necklace. With each successive despoilment, she gasps and *retreats but makes no resistance. Her eyes are closed. He continues to smile. Finally, he rips her dress and runs his hands over her body as if to see if she had anything else of value concealed on her.*)

—What else do I have that you want?

THE YOUNG MAN (*contemptuously*): Nothing.

(*The Young Man exits through the cantina, examining his loot. The Bum leans out his window, draws a deep breath and says:*)

BUM: Lonely.

MARGUERITE (*to herself*): Lonely . . .

KILROY (*on the steps*): Lonely . . .

(*The Streetcleaners' piping is heard.*

(*Marguerite runs to the Siete Mares and rings the bell. Nobody answers. She crosses to the terrace. Kilroy, meanwhile, has descended the stairs.*)

MARGUERITE: Jacques!

(*Piping is heard.*)

KILROY: Lady?

MARGUERITE: What?

KILROY: —*I'm—safe* . . .

MARGUERITE: I wasn't expecting that music tonight, were you?

(*Piping.*)

KILROY: It's them Streetcleaners.

MARGUERITE: I know.

(*Piping.*)

KILROY: You better go on in, lady.

MARGUERITE: No.

KILROY: GO ON IN!

MARGUERITE: NO! I want to stay out here and I do what I want to do!

(*Kilroy looks at her for the first time.*)

Sit down with me please.

KILROY: They're coming for me. The Gypsy told me I'm on top of their list. Thanks for. Taking my. Hand.

(*Piping is heard.*)

MARGUERITE: Thanks for taking mine.

(*Piping.*)

KILROY: Do me one more favor. Take out of my pocket a picture. My fingers are. Stiff.
MARGUERITE: This one?
KILROY: My one. True. Woman.
MARGUERITE: A silver-framed photo! Was she really so fair?
KILROY: She was so fair and much fairer than they could tint that picture!
MARGUERITE: Then you have been on the street when the street was royal.
KILROY: Yeah . . . when the street was royal!

(*Piping is heard. Kilroy rises.*)

MARGUERITE: Don't get up, don't leave me!
KILROY: I want to be on my feet when the Streetcleaners come for me!
MARGUERITE: Sit back down again and tell me about your girl.

(*He sits.*)

KILROY: Y'know what it is you miss most? When you're separated. From someone. You lived. With. And loved? It's waking up in the night! With that—warmness beside you!
MARGUERITE: Yes, that *warmness* beside you!
KILROY: Once you get used to that. *Warmness!* It's a hell of a lonely feeling to wake up without it! Specially in some dollar-a-night hotel room on Skid! A hot-water bottle won't do. And a stranger. Won't do. It has to be some one you're used to. And that you. *KNOW LOVES* you!

(*Piping is heard.*)

Can you see them?
MARGUERITE: I see no one but you.
KILROY: I looked at my wife one night when she was sleeping and that was the night that the medics wouldn't okay me

for no more fights . . . Well . . . My wife was sleeping with a smile like a child's. I kissed her. She didn't wake up. I took a pencil and paper. I wrote her. Good-bye!

MARGUERITE: That was the night she would have loved you the most!

KILROY: Yeah, *that* night, but what about *after* that night? Oh, Lady . . . Why should a beautiful girl tie up with a broken-down champ?—The earth still turning and her obliged to turn with it, not out—of dark into light but out of light into dark? Naw, naw, naw, naw!—Washed up!—Finished!

(*Piping.*)

. . . that ain't a word that a man can't look at . . . There ain't no words in the language a man can't look at . . . and know just what they mean. and be. And act. And *go*!

(*He turns to the waiting Streetcleaners.*)

Come on! . . . Come on! . . . COME ON, YOU SONS OF BITCHES! KILROY IS HERE! HE'S READY!

(*A gong sounds.*

(*Kilroy swings at the Streetcleaners. They circle about him out of reach, turning him by each of their movements. The swings grow wilder like a boxer. He falls to his knees still swinging and finally collapses flat on his face.*

(*The Streetcleaners pounce but La Madrecita throws herself protectingly over the body and covers it with her shawl.*

(*Blackout.*)

MARGUERITE: Jacques!

GUTMAN (*on balcony*): Block Fifteen on the Camino Real.

BLOCK FIFTEEN

La Madrecita is seated: across her knees is the body of Kilroy. Up center, a low table on wheels bears a sheeted figure. Beside the table stands a Medical Instructor addressing Students and Nurses, all in white surgical outfits.

INSTRUCTOR: This is the body of an unidentified vagrant.

LA MADRECITA: This was thy son, America—and now mine.

INSTRUCTOR: He was found in an alley along the Camino Real.

LA MADRECITA: Think of him, now, as he was before his luck failed him. Remember his time of greatness, when he was not faded, not frightened.

INSTRUCTOR: More light, please!

LA MADRECITA: More light!

INSTRUCTOR: Can everyone see clearly!

LA MADRECITA: Everyone must see clearly!

INSTRUCTOR: There is no external evidence of disease.

LA MADRECITA: He had clear eyes and the body of a champion boxer.

INSTRUCTOR: There are no marks of violence on the body.

LA MADRECITA: He had the soft voice of the South and a pair of golden gloves.

INSTRUCTOR: His death was apparently due to natural causes.

(*The Students make notes. There are keening voices.*)

LA MADRECITA: Yes, blow wind where night thins! He had many admirers!

INSTRUCTOR: There are no legal claimants.

LA MADRECITA: He stood as a planet among the moons of their longing, haughty with youth, a champion of the prize-ring!

INSTRUCTOR: No friends or relatives having identified him—

LA MADRECITA: You should have seen the lovely monogrammed robe in which he strode the aisles of the Colosseums!

INSTRUCTOR: After the elapse of a certain number of days, his body becomes the property of the State—

LA MADRECITA: Yes, blow wind where night thins—for laurel is not everlasting . . .

INSTRUCTOR: And now is transferred to our hands for the nominal sum of five dollars.

LA MADRECITA: This was thy son,—and now mine . . .

INSTRUCTOR: We will now proceed with the dissection. Knife, please!

LA MADRECITA: Blow wind!

(*Keening is heard offstage.*)

Yes, blow wind where night thins! You are his passing bell and his lamentation.

(*More keening is heard.*)

Keen for him, all maimed creatures, deformed and mutilated—his homeless ghost is your own!

INSTRUCTOR: First we will open up the chest cavity and examine the heart for evidence of coronary occlusion.

LA MADRECITA: His heart was pure gold and as big as the head of a baby.

INSTRUCTOR: We will make an incision along the vertical line.

LA MADRECITA: Rise, ghost! Go! Go bird! "Humankind cannot bear very much reality."

(*At the touch of her flowers, Kilroy stirs and pushes himself up slowly from her lap. On his feet again, he rubs his eyes and looks around him.*)

VOICES (*crying offstage*): Olé! Olé! Olé!

KILROY: Hey! Hey, somebody! Where am I?

(*He notices the dissection room and approaches.*)

INSTRUCTOR (*removing a glittering sphere from a dummy corpse*): Look at this heart. It's as big as the head of a baby.

KILROY: My heart!

INSTRUCTOR: Wash it off so we can look for the pathological lesions.

KILROY: Yes, siree, that's my heart!

GUTMAN: Block Sixteen!

(*Kilroy pauses just outside the dissection area as a Student takes the heart and dips it into a basin on the stand beside the table. The Student suddenly cries out and holds aloft a glittering gold sphere.*)

INSTRUCTOR: Look! This heart's solid gold!

BLOCK SIXTEEN

KILROY (*rushing forward*): That's mine, you bastards!

(*He snatches the golden sphere from the Medical Instructor. The autopsy proceeds as if nothing had happened as the spot of light on the table fades out, but for Kilroy a ghostly chase commences, a dreamlike re-enactment of the chase that occurred at the end of Block Six. Gutman shouts from his balcony:*)

GUTMAN: Stop, thief, stop, corpse! That gold heart is the property of the State! Catch him, catch the golden-heart robber!

(*Kilroy dashes offstage into an aisle of the theatre. There is the wail of a siren: the air is filled with calls and whistles, roar of motors, screeching brakes, pistol-shots, thundering footsteps. The dimness of the auditorium is transected by searching rays of light—but there are no visible pursuers.*)

KILROY (*as he runs panting up the aisle*): This is my heart! It don't belong to no State, not even the U.S.A. Which way is out? Where's the Greyhound depot? Nobody's going to put my heart in a bottle in a museum and charge admission to support the rotten police! Where are they? Which way are they going? Or coming? Hey, somebody, help me get out of here! Which way do I—which way—which way do I—*go! go! go! go! go!*

(*He has now arrived in the balcony.*)

Gee, I'm lost! I don't know where I am! I'm all turned around, I'm *confused*, I don't understand—what's—happened, it's like a—*dream*, it's—just like a—dream . . . *Mary! Oh, Mary! Mary!*

(*He has entered the box from which he leapt in Act One.*
(*A clear shaft of light falls on him. He looks up into it, crying:*)

Mary, help a Christian!! Help a Christian, Mary!—It's like a dream . . .

(*Esmeralda appears in a childish nightgown beside her gauze-tented bed on the Gypsy's roof. Her Mother appears with a cup of some sedative drink, cooing . . .*)

GYPSY: Beddy-bye, beddy-bye, darling. It's sleepy-time down South and up North, too, and also East and West!

KILROY (*softly*): Yes, it's—like a—*dream* . . .

(*He leans panting over the ledge of the box, holding his heart like a football, watching Esmeralda.*)

GYPSY: Drink your Ovaltine, Ducks, and the sandman will come on tip-toe with a bag full of dreams . . .

ESMERALDA: I want to dream of the Chosen Hero, Mummy.

GYPSY: Which one, the one that's coming or the one that is gone?

ESMERALDA: The *only* one, *Kilroy! He* was *sincere!*

KILROY: That's *right! I was*, for a while!

GYPSY: How do you know that Kilroy was sincere?

ESMERALDA: He said so.

KILROY: That's the truth, I *was!*

GYPSY: When did he say that?

ESMERALDA: When he lifted my veil.

GYPSY: Baby, they're always sincere when they lift your veil; it's one of those natural reflexes that don't mean a thing.

KILROY (*aside*): What a cynical old bitch that Gypsy mama is!

GYPSY: And there's going to be lots of other fiestas for you, baby doll, and lots of other chosen heroes to lift your little veil when Mamacita and Nursie are out of the room.

ESMERALDA: No, Mummy, never, I mean it!

KILROY: I *believe* she means it!

GYPSY: Finish your Ovaltine and say your Now-I-Lay-Me.

(*Esmeralda sips the drink and hands her the cup.*)

KILROY (*with a catch in his voice*): I had one true woman, which I can't go back to, but now I've found another.

(*He leaps onto the stage from the box.*)

ESMERALDA (*dropping to her knees*): Now I lay me down to sleep, I pray the Lord my soul to keep. If I should die before I wake, I pray the Lord my soul to take.

GYPSY: God bless Mummy!

ESMERALDA: And the crystal ball and the tea-leaves.

KILROY: *Pssst!*

ESMERALDA: What's that?

GYPSY: A tom-cat in the plaza.

ESMERALDA: God bless all cats without pads in the plaza tonight.

KILROY: Amen!

(*He falls to his knees in the empty plaza.*)

ESMERALDA: God bless all con men and hustlers and pitchmen who hawk their hearts on the street, all two-time losers who're likely to lose once more, the courtesan who made the mistake of love, the greatest of lovers crowned with the longest horns, the poet who wandered far from his heart's green country and possibly will and possibly won't be able to find his way back, look down with a smile tonight on the last cavaliers, the ones with the rusty armor and soiled white plumes, and visit with understanding and something that's almost tender those fading legends that come and go in this plaza like songs not clearly remembered, oh, sometime and somewhere, let there be something to mean the word *honor* again!

QUIXOTE (*hoarsely and loudly, stirring slightly among his verminous rags*): Amen!

KILROY: Amen . . .

GYPSY (*disturbed*): —That will do, now.

ESMERALDA: *And, oh, God, let me dream tonight of the Chosen Hero!*

GYPSY: Now, sleep. Fly away on the magic carpet of dreams!

(*Esmeralda crawls into the gauze-tented cot. The Gypsy descends from the roof.*)

KILROY: *Esmeralda! My little Gypsy sweetheart!*

ESMERALDA (*sleepily*): Go away, cat.

(*The light behind the gauze is gradually dimming.*)

KILROY: This is no cat. This is the chosen hero of the big fiesta, Kilroy, the champion of the golden gloves with his gold heart cut from his chest and in his hands to give you!

ESMERALDA: Go away. Let me dream of the Chosen Hero.

KILROY: What a hassle! Mistook for a cat! What can I do to convince this doll I'm real?

(*Three brass balls wink brilliantly.*)

—Another transaction seems to be indicated!

(*He rushes to the Loan Shark's. The entrance immediately lights up.*)

My heart is gold! What will you give me for it?

(*Jewels, furs, sequined gowns, etc., are tossed to his feet. He throws his heart like a basketball to the Loan Shark, snatches up the loot and rushes back to the Gypsy's.*)

Doll! Behold this loot! I gave my golden heart for it!

ESMERALDA: Go away, cat . . .

(*She falls asleep. Kilroy bangs his forehead with his fist, then rushes to the Gypsy's door, pounds it with both fists. The door is thrown open and the sordid contents of a large jar are thrown at him. He falls back gasping, spluttering, retching. He retreats and finally assumes an exaggerated attitude of despair.*)

KILROY: Had for a button! Stewed, screwed and tattooed on the Camino Real! Baptized, finally, with the contents of a slop-jar!—Did anybody say the deal was rugged?!

(*Quixote stirs against the wall of Skid Row. He hawks and spits and staggers to his feet.*)

GUTMAN: Why, the old knight's awake, his dream is over!

QUIXOTE (*to Kilroy*): Hello! Is that a fountain?

KILROY: —Yeah, but—

QUIXOTE: I've got a mouthful of old chicken feathers . . .

(*He approaches the fountain. It begins to flow. Kilroy falls back in amazement as the Old Knight rinses his mouth and drinks and removes his jacket to bathe, handing the tattered garment to Kilroy.*)

QUIXOTE (*as he bathes*): Qué pasa, mi amigo?

KILROY: The deal is rugged. D'you know what I mean?

QUIXOTE: Who knows better than I what a rugged deal is!

(*He produces a tooth brush and brushes his teeth.*)

—Will you take some advice?

KILROY: Brother, at this point on the Camino I will take anything which is offered!

QUIXOTE: *Don't! Pity! Your! Self!*

(*He takes out a pocket mirror and grooms his beard and moustache.*)

The wounds of the vanity, the many offenses our egos have to endure, being housed in bodies that age and hearts that grow tired, are better accepted with a tolerant smile—like *this!*—You *see*?

(*He cracks his face in two with an enormous grin.*)

GUTMAN: Follow-spot on the face of the ancient knight!

QUIXOTE: Otherwise what you become is a bag full of curdled cream—*leche mala*, we call it!—attractive to nobody, least of all to yourself!

(*He passes the comb and pocket mirror to Kilroy.*)

Have you got any plans?

KILROY (*a bit uncertainly, wistfully*): Well, I was thinking of—going *on* from—*here!*

QUIXOTE: Good! Come with me.

KILROY (*to the audience*): Crazy old bastard.

(*Then to the Knight:*)

Donde?

QUIXOTE (*starting for the stairs*): Quien sabe!

(*The fountain is now flowing loudly and sweetly. The Street People are moving toward it with murmurs of wonder. Marguerite comes out upon the terrace.*)

KILROY: Hey, there's—!

QUIXOTE: Shhh! Listen!

(*They pause on the stairs.*)

MARGUERITE: Abdullah!

(*Gutman has descended to the terrace.*)

GUTMAN: Mademoiselle, allow me to deliver the message for you. It would be in bad form if I didn't take some final part in the pageant.

(*He crosses the plaza to the opposite façade and shouts "Casanova!" under the window of the "Ritz Men Only."*

(*Meanwhile Kilroy scratches out the verb "is" and prints the correction "was" in the inscription on the ancient wall.*)

Casanova! Great lover and King of Cuckolds on the Camino Real! The last of your ladies has guaranteed your tabs and is expecting you for breakfast on the terrace!

(*Casanova looks first out of the practical window of the flophouse, then emerges from its scabrous doorway, haggard, unshaven, crumpled in dress but bearing himself as erectly as ever. He blinks and glares fiercely into the brilliant morning light.*

(*Marguerite cannot return his look, she averts her face with a look for which anguish would not be too strong a term, but at the same time she extends a pleading hand toward him. After some hesitation, he begins to move toward her, striking the pavement in measured cadence with his cane, glancing once, as he crosses, out at the audience with a wry smile that makes admissions that would be embarrassing to a vainer man than Casanova now is. When he reaches Marguerite she gropes for his hand, seizes it with a low cry and presses it spasmodically to her lips while he draws her into his arms and looks above her sobbing, dyed-golden head with the serene, clouded gaze of someone mortally ill as the mercy of a narcotic laps over his pain.*

(*Quixote raises his lance in a formal gesture and cries out hoarsely, powerfully from the stairs:*)

QUIXOTE: *The violets in the mountains have broken the rocks!*

(*Quixote goes through the arch with Kilroy.*)

GUTMAN (*to the audience*): The Curtain Line has been spoken!

(*To the wings:*)

Bring it down!

(*He bows with a fat man's grace as—*

(*The curtain falls.*)

FROM

27 WAGONS FULL OF COTTON AND OTHER ONE-ACT PLAYS (1953)

"SOMETHING WILD . . ."

WHILE I was on the road with *Summer and Smoke* I was entertained one evening by the company of a successful community theater, one of the pioneer outfits of this kind and one of the few that operate on a profitable self-supporting basis. It had been 10 years since I had had a connection with a community theater. I was professionally spawned by one 10 years ago in St. Louis, but like most offspring, once I departed from the maternal shelter, I gave it scarcely a backward glance. Backward glances are a bit impractical, anyhow, in a theatrical career.

Now I felt considerable curiosity about the contact I was about to renew: but the moment I walked in the door I felt something wrong. Not so much something wrong as something missing. It seemed all so respectable. The men in their conservative business suits with their neat hair-cuts and highly polished shoes could have passed for corporation lawyers and the women, mostly their wives, were impeccably lady-like. There was no scratchy phonograph music, there were no dimly lit alcoves where dancing couples stood practically still, no sofas with ruptured upholstery, no garlands of colored crepe paper festooning the ceiling and collapsing onto the floor.

In my opinion art is a kind of anarchy, and the theater is a province of art. What was missing here, was something anarchistic in the air. I must modify that statement about art and anarchy. Art is only anarchy in juxtaposition with organized society. It runs counter to the sort of orderliness on which organized society apparently must be based. It is a benevolent anarchy: it must be that and if it is true art, it is. It is benevolent in the sense of constructing something which is missing, and what it constructs may be merely criticism of things as they exist. I felt in this group no criticism but rather an adaptation which was almost obsequious. And my mind shot back to the St. Louis group I have mentioned, a group called The Mummers.

The Mummers were sort of a long-haired outfit. Now there is no virtue, *per se*, in not going to the barber. And I don't suppose there is any particular virtue in girls having runs in their stockings. Yet one feels a kind of nostalgia for that sort of disorderliness now and then.

Somehow you associate it with things that have no logical connection with it. You associate it with really good times and with intense feelings and with convictions. Most of all with convictions! In the party I have mentioned there was a notable lack of convictions. Nobody was shouting for—or against—anything, there was just a lot of polite chit-chat going on among people who seemed to have known each other long enough to have exhausted all interest in each other's ideas.

While I stood there among them, the sense that something was missing clarified itself into a tremendous wave of longing for something that I had not been conscious of wanting until that moment. The open sky of my youth!—a peculiarly American youth which somehow seems to have slipped a little bit out of our grasp nowadays. . . .

The Mummers of St. Louis were my professional youth. They were the disorderly theater group of St. Louis, standing socially, if not also artistically, opposite to the usual Little Theater group. That opposite group need not be described. They were eminently respectable, predominantly middle-aged, and devoted mainly to the presentation of Broadway hits a season or two after Broadway. Their stage was narrow and notices usually mentioned how well they had overcome their spatial limitations, but it never seemed to me that they produced anything in a manner that needed to overcome limitations of space. The dynamism which is theater was as foreign to their philosophy as the tongue of Chinese.

Dynamism was what The Mummers had, and for about five years—roughly from about 1935 to 1940—they burned like one of Miss Millay's improvident little candles—and then expired. Yes, there was about them that kind of excessive romanticism which is youth and which is the best and purest part of life.

The first time I worked with them was in 1936, when I was a student at Washington University in St. Louis. They were, then, under the leadership of a man named Willard Holland, their organizer and their director. Holland always wore a blue suit which was not only baggy but shiny. He needed a haircut and he sometimes wore a scarf instead of a shirt. This was not what made him a great director, but a great director he was. Everything that he touched he charged with electricity. Was it my youth that made it seem that way? Possibly, but not probably. In fact not even possibly: you judge theater, really, by its effect on audiences, and Holland's work never failed to deliver, and when I say deliver I mean a sock!

The first thing I worked with them on was *Bury the Dead*, by Irwin Shaw. That play ran a little bit short of full length and they needed a curtain-raiser to fill out the program. Holland called me up. He did not have a prepossessing voice. It was high-pitched and nervous. He said I hear you go to college and I hear you can write. I admitted some justice in both of these charges. Then he asked me: How do you feel about compulsory military training? I then assured him that I had left the University of Missouri because I could not get a passing grade in the ROTC. Swell!, said Holland, you are just the guy I am looking for. How would you like to write something against militarism?

So I did.

Shaw's play, one of the greatest lyric plays America has produced, was a solid piece of flame. Actors and script, under Holland's dynamic hand, were one piece of vibrant living-tissue. Now St. Louis is not a town that is easily impressed. They love music, they are ardent devotees of the symphony concerts, but they preserve a fairly rigid decorum when they are confronted with anything off-beat which they are not used to. They certainly were not used to the sort of hot lead which the Mummers pumped into their bellies that night of Shaw's play. They were not used to it, but it paralyzed them. There wasn't a cough or creak in the house, and nobody left the Wednesday Club Auditorium (which the Mummers rented out for their performances) without a disturbing kink in their nerves or guts, and I doubt if any of them have forgotten it to this day.

It was The Mummers that I remembered at this polite supper party which I attended last month.

Now let me give you a picture of the Mummers! Most of them worked at other jobs besides theater. They had to, because The Mummers were not a paying proposition. There were laborers. There were clerks. There were waitresses. There were students. There were whores and tramps and there was even a post-debutante who was a member of the Junior League of St. Louis. Many of them were fine actors. Many of them were not. Some of them could not act at all, but what they lacked in ability, Holland inspired them with in the way of enthusiasm. I guess it was all run by a kind of beautiful witchcraft! It was like a definition of what I think theater is. Something wild, something exciting, something that you are not used to. Offbeat is the word.

They put on bad shows sometimes, but they never put on a show that didn't deliver a punch to the solar plexus, maybe not in the first act, maybe not in the second, but always at last a good hard punch was delivered, and it made a difference in the lives of the spectators that they had come to that place and seen that show.

The plays I gave them were bad. But the first of these plays was a smash hit. It even got rave notices out of all three papers, and there was a real demonstration on the opening night with shouts and cheers and stamping, and the pink-faced author took his first bow among the grey-faced coal-miners that he had created out of an imagination never stimulated by the sight of an actual coal-mine. The second play that I gave them, *Fugitive Kind*, was a flop. It got one rave notice out of the *Star-Times*, but the *Post-Dispatch* and the *Globe Democrat* gave it hell. Nevertheless it packed a considerable wallop and there are people in St. Louis who still remember it. Bad plays, both of them, amateurish and coarse and juvenile and talky. But Holland and his players put them across the footlights without apology and they put them across with the bang that is theater.

Oh, how long ago that was!

The Mummers lived only five years. Yes, they had something in common with lyric verse of a too romantic nature. From 1935 to 1940 they had their fierce little flame, and then they expired, and now there is not a visible trace of them. Where is Holland? In Hollywood, I think. And where are the players? God knows. . . .

I am here, remembering them wistfully.

Now I shall have to say something to give this recollection a meaning to you.

All right. This is it.

Today we are living in a world which is threatened by totalitarianism. The Fascist and the Communist states have thrown us into a panic of reaction. Reactionary opinion descends like a ton of bricks on the head of any artist who speaks out against the current of prescribed ideas. We are all under wraps of one kind or another, trembling before the spectre of investigating committees and even with Buchenwald in the back of our minds when we consider whether or not we dare to say we were for Henry Wallace. *Yes, it is as bad as that.*

And yet it isn't *really* as bad as that.

America is still America, democracy is still democracy.

In our history books are still the names of Jefferson and Lincoln and Tom Paine. The direction of the Democratic impulse, which is entirely and irresistibly away from the police state and away from any and all forms of controlled thought and feeling—which is entirely and irresistibly in the direction of that which is individual and humane and equitable and free—that direction can be confused but it cannot be lost.

I have a way of jumping from the particular to the abstract, for the particular is sometimes as much as we know of the abstract.

Now let me jump back again: where? To the subject of community theaters and their social function.

It seems to me, as it seems to many artists right now, that an effort is being made to put creative work and workers under wraps.

Nothing could be more dangerous to Democracy, for the irritating grain of sand which is creative work in a society must be kept inside the shell or the pearl of idealistic progress cannot be made. For God's sake let us defend ourselves against whatever is hostile to us without imitating the thing which we are afraid of!

Community theaters have a social function and it is to be that kind of an irritant in the shell of their community. Not to conform, not to wear the conservative business suit of their audience, but to let their hair grow long and even greasy, to make wild gestures, break glasses, fight, shout, and fall downstairs! When you see them acting like this—not respectably, not quite decently, even!—then you will know that something is going to happen in that outfit, something disturbing, something irregular, something brave and honest.

The biologist will tell you that progress is the result of mutations. Mutations are another word for freaks. For God's sake let's have a little more freakish behavior—not less.

Maybe 90 per cent of the freaks will be just freaks, ludicrous and pathetic and getting nowhere but into trouble.

Eliminate them, however—bully them into conformity—and nobody in America will ever be really young any more and we'll be left standing in the dead center of nowhere.

TALK TO ME LIKE THE RAIN AND LET ME LISTEN . . .

CHARACTERS

MAN

WOMAN

CHILD'S VOICE (off stage)

SCENE: *A furnished room west of Eighth Avenue in midtown Manhattan. On a folding bed lies a Man in crumpled underwear, struggling out of sleep with the sighs of a man who went to bed very drunk. A Woman sits in a straight chair at the room's single window, outlined dimly against a sky heavy with a rain that has not yet begun to fall. The Woman is holding a tumbler of water from which she takes small, jerky sips like a bird drinking. Both of them have ravaged young faces like the faces of children in a famished country. In their speech there is a sort of politeness, a sort of tender formality like that of two lonely children who want to be friends, and yet there is an impression that they have lived in this intimate situation for a long time and that the present scene between them is the repetition of one that has been repeated so often that its plausible emotional contents, such as reproach and contrition, have been completely worn out and there is nothing left but acceptance of something hopelessly inalterable between them.*

MAN: (*hoarsely*) What time is it? (*The Woman murmurs something inaudible.*) What, honey?

WOMAN: Sunday.

MAN: I know it's Sunday. You never wind the clock.

(*The Woman stretches a thin bare arm out of the ravelled pink rayon sleeve of her kimona and picks up the tumbler of water and the weight of it seems to pull her forward a little. The Man watches solemnly, tenderly from the bed as she sips the water. A thin music begins, hesitantly, repeating a phrase several times as if someone in a next room were trying to remember a song on a mandolin. Sometimes a phrase is sung in Spanish. The song could be* Estrellita.

(*Rain begins; it comes and goes during the play; there is a drumming flight of pigeons past the window and a child's voice chants outside—*)

CHILD'S VOICE: Rain, rain, go away!
Come again some other day!

(*The chant is echoed mockingly by another child farther away.*)

MAN: (*finally*) I wonder if I cashed my unemployment. (*The Woman leans forward with the weight of the glass seeming to pull her; sets it down on the window-sill with a small crash that seems to startle her. She laughs breathlessly for a moment. The Man continues, without much hope.*) I hope I didn't cash my unemployment. Where's my clothes? Look in my pockets and see if I got the cheque on me.

WOMAN: You came back while I was out looking for you and picked the cheque up and left a note on the bed that I couldn't make out.

MAN: You couldn't make out the note?

WOMAN: Only a telephone number. I called the number but there was so much noise I couldn't hear.

MAN: Noise? Here?

WOMAN: No, noise there.

MAN: Where was "there"?

WOMAN: I don't know. Somebody said come over and hung up and all I got afterwards was a busy signal . . .

MAN: When I woke up I was in a bathtub full of melting ice-cubes and Miller's High Life beer. My skin was blue. I was gasping for breath in a bathtub full of ice-cubes. It was near a river but I don't know if it was the East or the Hudson. People do terrible things to a person when he's unconscious in this city. I'm sore all over like I'd been kicked downstairs, not like I fell but was kicked. One time I remember all my hair was shaved off. Another time they stuffed me into a trash-can in the alley and I've come to with cuts and burns on my body. Vicious people abuse you when you're unconscious. When I woke up I was naked in a bathtub full of melting ice-cubes. I crawled out and went into the parlor and someone was going out of the other door as I came in and I opened the door and heard the door of an elevator shut and saw the doors of a corridor in a hotel. The TV was on and there was a record playing at the same time; the parlor was full of rolling tables loaded with stuff from Room Service, and whole hams, whole turkeys, three-decker sandwiches cold and turning stiff, and bottles and bottles and bottles of all kinds of liquors that hadn't even been opened and buckets of ice-cubes melting . . . Somebody closed a door as I came in . . . (*The Woman sips water.*) As I came in someone was going out. I heard a door shut and I went to the door and heard the door of an elevator shut . . . (*The Woman sets her glass down.*)—All over the floor of this pad near the river—articles—clothing—scattered . . . (*The Woman gasps as a flight of pigeons sweeps past the open window.*)—Bras!—Panties!—Shirts, ties, socks—and so forth . . .

WOMAN: (*faintly*) Clothes?

MAN: Yes, all kinds of personal belongings and broken glass and furniture turned over as if there'd been a free-for-all fight going on and the pad was—raided . . .

WOMAN: Oh.

MAN: Violence must have—broken out in the—place . . .

WOMAN: You were—?

MAN: —in the bathtub on—ice . . .

WOMAN: Oh . . .

MAN: And I remember picking up the phone to ask what hotel it was but I don't remember if they told me or not . . . Give me a drink of that water. (*Both of them rise and meet in the center of the room. The glass is passed gravely between them. He rinses his mouth, staring at her gravely, and crosses to spit out the window. Then he returns to the center of the room and hands the glass back to her. She takes a sip of the water. He places his fingers tenderly on her long throat.*) Now I've recited the litany of my sorrows! (*Pause: the mandolin is heard.*) And what have you got to tell me? Tell me a little something of what's going on behind your— (*His fingers trail across her forehead and eyes. She closes her eyes and lifts a hand in the air as if about to touch him. He takes the hand and examines it upside down and then he presses its fingers to his lips. When he releases her fingers she touches him with them. She touches his thin smooth chest which is smooth as a child's and then she touches his lips. He raises his hand and lets his fingers slide along her throat and into the opening of the kimona as the mandolin gathers assurance. She turns and leans against him, her throat curving over his shoulder, and he runs his fingers along the curve of her throat and says*—) It's been so long since we have been together except like a couple of strangers living together. Let's find each other and maybe we won't be lost. Talk to me! I've been lost!—I thought of you often but couldn't call you, honey. Thought of you all the time but couldn't call. What could I say if I called? Could I say, I'm lost? Lost in the city? Passed around like a dirty *post*card among people?—And then hang up . . . I am lost in this—city . . .

WOMAN: I've had nothing but water since you left! (*She says this almost gaily, laughing at the statement. The Man holds her tight to him with a soft, shocked cry.*)—Not a thing but instant coffee until it was used up, and water! (*She laughs convulsively.*)

MAN: Can you talk to me, honey? Can you talk to me, now?

WOMAN: Yes!

MAN: Well, talk to me like the rain and—let me listen, let me lie here and—listen . . . (*He falls back across the bed, rolls on his belly, one arm hanging over the side of the bed and occasionally drumming the floor with his knuckles. The mandolin continues.*) It's been too long a time since—we levelled with each other. Now tell me things. What have you been thinking in the silence?—While I've been passed around like a dirty postcard in this city . . . Tell me, talk to me! Talk to me like the rain and I will lie here and listen.

WOMAN: I—

MAN: You've got to, it's necessary! I've got to know, so talk to me like the rain and I will lie here and listen, I will lie here and—

WOMAN: I want to go away.

MAN: You do?

WOMAN: *I want to go away!*

MAN: How?

WOMAN: *Alone!* (*She returns to window.*)—I'll register under a made-up name at a little hotel on the coast . . .

MAN: What name?

WOMAN: Anna—Jones . . . The chambermaid will be a little old lady who has a grandson that she talks about . . . I'll sit in the chair while the old lady makes the bed, my arms will hang over the—sides, and—her voice will be—peaceful . . . She'll tell me what her grandson had for supper!—tapioca and—cream . . . (*The Woman sits by the window and sips the water.*)—The room will be shadowy, cool, and filled with the murmur of—

MAN: Rain?

WOMAN: Yes. Rain.

MAN: And—?

WOMAN: Anxiety will—pass—over!

MAN: Yes . . .

WOMAN: After a while the little old woman will say, Your bed is made up, Miss, and I'll say—Thank you . . . Take a dollar out of my pocketbook. The door will close. And I'll be alone again. The windows will be tall with long blue shutters and it will be a season of rain—rain—rain . . . My life will be like the room, cool—shadowy cool and—filled with the murmur of—

MAN: Rain . . .

WOMAN: I will receive a check in the mail every week that I can count on. The little old lady will cash the checks for me and get me books from a library and pick up—laundry . . . I'll always have clean things!—I'll dress in white. I'll never be very strong or have much energy left, but have enough after a while to walk on the—esplanade—to walk on the beach without effort . . . In the evening I'll walk on the esplanade along the beach. I'll have a certain beach where I go to sit, a little way from the pavillion where the band plays Victor Herbert selections while it gets dark . . . I'll have a big room with shutters on the windows. There will be a season of rain, rain, rain. And I will be so exhausted after my life in the city that I won't mind just listening to the rain. I'll be so quiet. The lines will disappear from my face. My eyes won't be inflamed at all any more. I'll have no friends. I'll have no acquaintances even. When I get sleepy,

I'll walk slowly back to the little hotel. The clerk will say, Good evening, Miss Jones, and I'll just barely smile and take my key. I won't ever look at a newspaper or hear a radio; I won't have any idea of what's going on in the world. I will not be conscious of time passing at all . . . One day I will look in the mirror and I will see that my hair is beginning to turn grey and for the first time I will realize that I have been living in this little hotel under a made-up name without any friends or acquaintances or any kind of connections for twenty-five years. It will surprise me a little but it won't bother me any. I will be glad that time has passed as easily as that. Once in a while I may go out to the movies. I will sit in the back row with all that darkness around me and figures sitting motionless on each side not conscious of me. Watching the screen. Imaginary people. People in stories. I will read long books and the journals of dead writers. I will feel closer to them than I ever felt to people I used to know before I withdrew from the world. It will be sweet and cool this friendship of mine with dead poets, for I won't have to touch them or answer their questions. They will talk to me and not expect me to answer. And I'll get sleepy listening to their voices explaining the mysteries to me. I'll fall asleep with the book still in my fingers, and it will rain. I'll wake up and hear the rain and go back to sleep. A season of rain, rain, rain . . . Then one day, when I have closed a book or come home alone from the movies at eleven o'clock at night—I will look in the mirror and see that my hair has turned white. White, absolutely white. As white as the foam on the waves. (*She gets up and moves about the room as she continues*—) I'll run my hands down my body and feel how amazingly light and thin I have grown. Oh, my, how thin I will be. Almost transparent. Not hardly real any more. Then I will realize, I will know, sort of dimly, that I have been staying on here in this little hotel, without any—social connections, responsibilities, anxieties or disturbances of any kind—for just about fifty years. Half a century. Practically a lifetime. I won't even remember the names of the people I knew before I came here nor how it feels to be someone waiting for someone that—may not come . . . Then I will know—

looking in the mirror—the first time has come for me to walk out alone once more on the esplanade with the strong wind beating on me, the white clean wind that blows from the edge of the world, from even further than that, from the cool outer edges of space, from even beyond whatever there is beyond the edges of space . . . (*She sits down again unsteadily by the window.*)—Then I'll go out and walk on the esplanade. I'll walk alone and be blown thinner and thinner.

MAN: Baby. Come back to bed.

WOMAN: And thinner and thinner and thinner and thinner and thinner! (*He crosses to her and raises her forcibly from the chair.*)—Till finally I won't have any body at all, and the wind picks me up in its cool white arms forever, and takes me away!

MAN: (*presses his mouth to her throat.*) Come on back to bed with me!

WOMAN: *I want to go away, I want to go away!* (*He releases her and she crosses to center of room sobbing uncontrollably. She sits down on the bed. He sighs and leans out the window, the light flickering beyond him, the rain coming down harder. The Woman shivers and crosses her arms against her breasts. Her sobbing dies out but she breathes with effort. Light flickers and wind whines coldly. The Man remains leaning out. At last she says to him softly—*) Come back to bed. Come on back to bed, baby . . . (*He turns his lost face to her as—*)

The Curtain Falls

SOMETHING UNSPOKEN

CHARACTERS

MISS CORNELIA SCOTT

MISS GRACE LANCASTER

SCENE: *Miss Cornelia Scott, 60, a wealthy southern spinster, is seated at a small mahogany table which is set for two. The other place, not yet occupied, has a single rose in a crystal vase before it. Miss Scott's position at the table is flanked by a cradle phone, a silver tray of mail, and an ornate silver coffee urn. An imperial touch is given by purple velvet drapes directly behind her figure at the table. A console phonograph is at the edge of lighted area.*

At rise of the curtain she is dialing a number on the phone.

CORNELIA: Is this Mrs. Horton Reid's residence? I am calling for Miss Cornelia Scott. Miss Scott is sorry that she will not be able to attend the meeting of the Confederate Daughters this afternoon as she woke up this morning with a sore throat and has to remain in bed, and will you kindly give her apologies to Mrs. Reid for not letting her know sooner. Thank you. Oh, wait a moment! I think Miss Scott has another message.

(*Grace Lancaster enters the lighted area. Cornelia raises her hand in a warning gesture.*)

—What is it, Miss Scott? (*There is a brief pause.*) Oh. Miss Scott would like to leave word for Miss Esmeralda Hawkins to call her as soon as she arrives. Thank you. Goodbye. (*She hangs up.*) You see I am having to impersonate my secretary this morning!

GRACE: The light was so dim it didn't wake me up.

(*Grace Lancaster is 40 or 45, faded but still pretty. Her blonde hair, greying slightly, her pale eyes, her thin figure, in a pink silk dressing-gown, give her an insubstantial quality in sharp contrast to Miss Scott's Roman grandeur. There is between the two women a mysterious tension, an atmosphere of something unspoken.*)

CORNELIA: I've already opened the mail.

GRACE: Anything of interest?

CORNELIA: A card from Thelma Peterson at Mayo's.

GRACE: Oh, how is Thelma?

CORNELIA: She says she's "progressing nicely," whatever that indicates.

GRACE: Didn't she have something removed?

CORNELIA: Several things, I believe.

GRACE: *Oh, here's the "Fortnightly Review of Current Letters!"*

CORNELIA: Much to my astonishment. I thought I had cancelled my subscription to that publication.

GRACE: Really, Cornelia?

CORNELIA: Surely you remember. I cancelled my subscription immediately after the issue came out with that scurrilous attack on my cousin Cecil Tutwiler Bates, the only dignified novelist the South has produced since Thomas Nelson Page.

GRACE: Oh, yes, I do remember. You wrote a furious letter of protest to the editor of the magazine and you received such a conciliatory reply from an associate editor named Caroline Something or Other that you were completely mollified and cancelled the cancellation!

CORNELIA: I have never been mollified by conciliatory replies, never completely and never even partially, and if I wrote to the editor-in-chief and was answered by an associate editor, my reaction to that piece of impertinence would hardly be what you call "mollified."

GRACE: (*She changes the subject.*) Oh, here's the new catalogue from the Gramophone Shoppe in Atlanta!

CORNELIA: (*She concedes a point.*) Yes, there it is.

GRACE: I see you've checked several items.

CORNELIA: I think we ought to build up our collection of Lieder.

GRACE: You've checked a Sibelius that we already have.

CORNELIA: It's getting a little bit scratchy. (*She inhales deeply and sighs, her look fastened upon the silent phone.*) You'll also notice that I've checked a few operatic selections.

GRACE: (*excitedly*) Where, which ones, I don't see them!

CORNELIA: Why are you so excited over the catalogue, dear?

GRACE: I adore phonograph records!

CORNELIA: I wish you adored them enough to put them back in their proper places in albums.

GRACE: Oh, here's the Vivaldi we wanted!

CORNELIA: Not "we" dear. Just you.

GRACE: Not *you*, Cornelia?

CORNELIA: I think Vivaldi's a very thin shadow of Bach.

GRACE: How strange that I should have the impression you—(*The phone rings.*)—Shall I answer?

CORNELIA: If you will be so kind.

GRACE: (*lifting receiver*) *Miss Scott's* residence! (*This announcement is made in a tone of reverence, as though mentioning a seat of holiness.*) Oh, no, no, this is Grace, but Cornelia is right by my side. (*She passes the phone.*) Esmeralda Hawkins.

CORNELIA: (*grimly*) I've been expecting her call. (*into phone*) Hello, Esmeralda, my dear. I've been expecting your call. Now where are you calling me from? Of course I know that you're calling me from the meeting, ça va sans dire, ma petite! Ha ha! But from which phone in the house, there's two, you know, the one in the downstairs hall and the one in the chatelaine's boudoir where the ladies will probably be removing their wraps. Oh. You're on the downstairs', are you? Well, by this time I presume that practically all the daughters have assembled. Now go upstairs and call me back from there so we can talk with a little more privacy, dear, as I want to make my position very clear before the meeting commences. Thank you, dear. (*She hangs up and looks grimly into space.*)

GRACE: The—Confederate Daughters?

CORNELIA: Yes! They're holding the Annual Election today.

GRACE: Oh, how exciting! Why aren't you at the meeting?

CORNELIA: I preferred not to go.

GRACE: You preferred *not* to go?

CORNELIA: Yes, I preferred not to *go* . . . (*She touches her chest breathing heavily as if she had run upstairs.*)

GRACE: But it's the annual election of officers!

CORNELIA: Yes! I told you it was! (*Grace drops the spoon. Cornelia cries out and jumps a little.*)

GRACE: I'm so sorry! (*She rings the bell for a servant.*)

CORNELIA: Intrigue, intrigue and duplicity, revolt me so that I wouldn't be able to breathe in the same atmosphere! (*Grace rings the bell louder.*) Why are you ringing that bell? You know Lucinda's not here!

GRACE: I'm so sorry. Where has Lucinda gone?

CORNELIA: (*in a hoarse whisper, barely audible*) There's a big colored funeral in town. (*She clears her throat violently and repeats the statement.*)

GRACE: Oh, dear. You have that nervous laryngitis.

CORNELIA: No sleep, no sleep last night.

(*The phone screams at her elbow. She cries out and thrusts it from her as if it were on fire.*)

GRACE: (*She picks up the phone.*) Miss Scott's residence. Oh. Just a moment, please.

CORNELIA: (*snatching phone*) Esmeralda, are you upstairs now?

GRACE: (*in a loud whisper*) It isn't Esmeralda, it's Mrs. C. C. Bright!

CORNELIA: One moment, one moment, one moment! (*She thrusts phone back at Grace with a glare of fury.*) How dare you put me on the line with that woman!

GRACE: Cornelia, I didn't, I was just going to ask you if you—

CORNELIA: *Hush!* (*She springs back from the table, glaring across it.*)—Now give me that phone. (*She takes it, and says coldly:*) What can I do for you, please? No. I'm afraid that my garden will not be open to the Pilgrims this spring. I think the cultivation of gardens is an esthetic hobby and not a competitive sport. Individual visitors will be welcome if they call in advance so that I can arrange for my gardener to show them around, but no bands of Pilgrims, not after the devastation my garden suffered last spring—Pilgrims coming with dogs—picking flowers and— You're entirely welcome, yes, goodbye! (*She returns the phone to Grace.*)

GRACE: I think the election would have been less of a strain if you'd gone to it, Cornelia.

CORNELIA: I don't know what you are talking about.

GRACE: Aren't you up for office?

CORNELIA: "Up for office"? What is "up for office"?

GRACE: Why, ha ha!—*running* for—something?

CORNELIA: Have you ever known me to *"run"* for anything, Grace? Whenever I've held an office in a society or club it's been at the *insistence* of the members because I really have an *aversion* to holding office. But this is a different thing, a different thing altogether. It's a test of something. You see I have known for some time, now, that there is a little group, a *clique*, in the Daughters, which is hostile to me!

GRACE: Oh, Cornelia, I'm sure you must be mistaken.

CORNELIA: No. There is a movement against me.

GRACE: A movement? A movement against you?

CORNELIA: An organized movement to keep me out of any important office.

GRACE: But haven't you always held some important office in the Chapter?

CORNELIA: I have never been *Regent* of it!

GRACE: Oh, you want to be *Regent*?

CORNELIA: No. You misunderstand me. I don't *"want"* to be Regent.

GRACE: Oh?

CORNELIA: I don't "want" to be anything whatsoever. I simply want to break up this movement against me and for that purpose I have rallied my forces.

GRACE: Your—*forces*? (*Her lips twitch slightly as if she had an hysterical impulse to smile.*)

CORNELIA: Yes. I still have some friends in the chapter who have resisted the movement.

GRACE: Oh?

CORNELIA: I have the solid support of all the older Board members.

GRACE: Why, then, I should think you'd have nothing to worry about!

CORNELIA: The Chapter has expanded too rapidly lately. Women have been admitted that couldn't get into a front pew at the Second Baptist Church! And that's the disgraceful truth . . .

GRACE: But since it's really a patriotic society . . .

CORNELIA: My dear Grace, there are two chapters of the Confederate Daughters in the city of Meridian. There is the Forrest chapter, which is for social riff-raff, and there is *this* chapter which was *supposed* to have a *little* bit of *distinction*! I'm not a snob. I'm nothing if not democratic. You know *that*! *But*—(*The phone rings. Cornelia reaches for it, then pushes it to Grace.*)

GRACE: Miss Scott's residence! Oh, yes, yes, just a moment! (*She passes phone to Cornelia.*) It's Esmeralda Hawkins.

CORNELIA: (*into phone*) Are you upstairs now, dear? Well, I wondered, it took you so long to call back. Oh, but I thought you said the luncheon was over. Well, I'm glad that you fortified yourself with a bite to eat. What did the buffet consist of? Chicken à la king! Wouldn't you know it! That is so characteristic of poor Amelia! With bits of pimiento and tiny mushrooms in it? What did the ladies counting their calories do! Nibbled around the edges? Oh, poor dears!—and afterwards I suppose there was lemon sherbet with lady-fingers? What, lime sherbet! And *no* lady-fingers? *What a departure!* What a *shocking* apostasy! I'm quite stunned! Ho ho ho . . . (*She reaches shakily for her cup.*) Now what's going on? Discussing the Civil Rights Program? Then they won't take the vote for at least half an hour!—Now Esmeralda, I *do* hope that you understand my position clearly. I don't wish to hold any office in the chapter unless it's by acclamation. You know what that means, don't you? It's a parliamentary term. It means when someone is desired for an office so unanimously that no vote has to be taken. In other words, elected automatically, simply by nomination, unopposed. Yes, my dear, it's just as simple as that. I have served as Treasurer for three terms, twice as Secretary, once as Chaplain—and what a dreary office that was with those long-drawn prayers for the Confederate dead!—Altogether I've served on the Board for, let's see, fourteen years!—Well, now, my dear, the point is simply this. If Daughters feel that I have demonstrated my capabilities and loyalty strongly enough that I should simply be named as Regent without a vote being taken—by unanimous acclamation!—why, then, of course I would feel obliged to accept . . . (*Her voice trembles with emotion.*) —But if, on the other hand, the—uh—*clique!*—and you know the ones I mean!—is bold enough to propose someone else for the office—Do you understand my position? In that eventuality, hard as it is to imagine,—I prefer to bow out of the picture entirely!—The moment another nomination is made and seconded, my own must be withdrawn, at once, unconditionally! Is that quite understood, Esmeralda? Then good! Go back downstairs to the meeting. Digest your chicken à la king, my dear, and call me again on the upstairs phone as soon as there's something to tell me. (*She hangs up and stares grimly into space. Grace lifts a section of grapefruit on a tiny silver fork.*)

GRACE: They haven't had it yet?

CORNELIA: Had what, dear?

GRACE: The election!

CORNELIA: No, not yet. It seems to be—imminent, though . . .

GRACE: Cornelia, why don't you think about something else until it's over!

CORNELIA: What makes you think that I am nervous about it?

GRACE: You're—you're *breathing* so fast!

CORNELIA: I didn't sleep well last night. You were prowling about the house with that stitch in your side.

GRACE: I *am* so sorry. You know it's nothing. A muscular contraction that comes from strain.

CORNELIA: What strain does it come from, Grace?

GRACE: What strain? (*She utters a faint, perplexed laugh.*) Why!—I don't know . . .

CORNELIA: The strain of *what*? Would you like *me* to tell you?

GRACE: —Excuse me, I—(*rising*)

CORNELIA: (*sharply*) Where are you going?

GRACE: Upstairs for a moment! I just remembered I should have taken my drops of belladonna!

CORNELIA: It does no good *after* eating.

GRACE: I suppose that's right. It doesn't.

CORNELIA: But you want to escape?

GRACE: Of course not . . .

CORNELIA: Several times lately you've rushed away from me as if I'd suddenly threatened you with a knife.

GRACE: Cornelia!—I've been—jumpy!

CORNELIA: It's always when something is almost—*spoken*—between us!

GRACE: I hate to see you so agitated over the outcome of a silly club-woman's election!

CORNELIA: I'm not talking about the Daughters. I'm not even thinking about them, I'm—

GRACE: I wish you'd dismiss it completely from your mind. Now would be a good time to play some records. Let me put a symphony on the machine!

CORNELIA: No.

GRACE: How about the Bach For Piano and Strings! The one we received for Christmas from Jessie and Gay?

CORNELIA: No, I said, No, I said, No!

GRACE: Something very light and quiet, then, the old French madrigals, maybe?

CORNELIA: Anything to avoid a talk between us? Anything to evade a conversation, especially when the servant is not in the house?

GRACE: Oh, here it is! This is just the thing! (*She has started the phonograph. Landowska is playing a harpsichord selection. The phonograph is at the edge of the lighted area or just outside it.*)

(*Cornelia stares grimly as Grace resumes her seat with an affectation of enchantment, clasping her hands and closing her eyes.*)

(*in an enchanted voice:*) Oh, how it smooths things over, how sweet, and gentle, and—pure . . .

CORNELIA: Yes! And completely dishonest!

GRACE: Music? Dishonest?

CORNELIA: Completely! It "smooths things over" instead of —speaking them out . . .

GRACE: "Music hath charms to soothe the savage breast."

CORNELIA: Yes, oh, yes, if the savage breast permits it.

GRACE: Oh, sublime—sublime . . .

CORNELIA: (*grudgingly*) Landowska is an artist of rare precision.

GRACE: (*ecstatically*) And such a noble face, a profile as fine and strong as Edith Sitwell's. After this we'll play Edith Sitwell's Façade. "Jane, Jane, tall as a crane, the morning light creaks down again . . ."

CORNELIA: Dearest, isn't there something you've failed to notice?

GRACE: Where?

CORNELIA: Right under your nose.

GRACE: Oh! You mean my flower?

CORNELIA: Yes! I mean your rose!

GRACE: Of course I noticed my rose, the moment I came in the room I saw it here!

CORNELIA: You made no allusion to it.

GRACE: I would have, but you were so concerned over the meeting.

CORNELIA: I'm not concerned over the meeting.

GRACE: Whom do I have to thank for this lovely rose? My gracious employer?

CORNELIA: You will find fourteen others on your desk in the library when you go in to take care of the correspondence.

GRACE: Fourteen other roses?

CORNELIA: A total of fifteen!

GRACE: How wonderful!—Why fifteen?

CORNELIA: How long have you been here, dearest? How long have you made this house a house of roses?

GRACE: What a nice way to put it! Why, of course! I've been your secretary for fifteen years!

CORNELIA: Fifteen years my companion! A rose for every year, a year for every rose!

GRACE: What a charming sort of a way to—observe the—occasion . . .

CORNELIA: First I thought "pearls" and then I thought, No, roses, but perhaps I should have given you something golden, ha ha!—Silence is golden they say!

GRACE: Oh, dear, that stupid machine is playing the same record over!

CORNELIA: Let it, let it, I like it!

GRACE: Just let me—

CORNELIA: Sit down!!—It was fifteen years ago this very morning, on the sixth day of November, that someone very sweet and gentle and silent!—a shy, little, quiet little widow!—arrived for the first time at Seven Edgewater Drive. The season was Autumn. I had been raking dead leaves over the rose-bushes to protect them from frost when I heard footsteps on the gravel, light, quick, delicate footsteps like Spring coming in the middle of Autumn, and looked up, and sure enough, there Spring was! A little person so thin that light shone through her as if she were made of the silk of a white parasol! (*Grace utters a short, startled laugh. Wounded, Cornelia says harshly:*) Why did you laugh? Why did you laugh like that?

GRACE: It sounded—ha ha!—it sounded like the first paragraph of a woman's magazine story.

CORNELIA: What a cutting remark!

GRACE: I didn't mean it that way, I—

CORNELIA: What other way could you mean it!

GRACE: Cornelia, you know how I am! I'm always a little embarrassed by sentiment, aren't I?

CORNELIA: Yes, frightened of anything that betrays some feeling!

GRACE: People who don't know you well, nearly all people we know, would be astounded to hear you, Cornelia Scott, that grave and dignified lady, expressing herself in such a lyrical manner!

CORNELIA: People who don't know me well are everybody! Yes, I think even *you*!

GRACE: Cornelia, you must admit that sentiment isn't like you!

CORNELIA: *Is nothing like me but silence?* (*The clock ticks loudly.*) *Am I sentenced to silence for a life-time?*

GRACE: It's just not like you to—

CORNELIA: Not like me, not like me, what do you know what's like me or not like me!

GRACE: You may deny it, Cornelia, as much as you please, but it's evident to me that you are completely unstrung by your anxieties over the Confederate Daughters' election!

CORNELIA: Another thinly veiled insult?

GRACE: Oh, Cornelia, please!

CORNELIA: (*imitating her gesture*) "Oh, Cornelia, please!!"

GRACE: If I've said anything wrong, I beg your pardon, I offer my very humble apologies for it.

CORNELIA: I don't want apologies from you. (*There is a strained silence. The clock ticks. Suddenly Grace reaches across to touch the veined jewelled hand of Miss Scott. Cornelia snatches her own hand away as though the touch had burned her.*)

GRACE: Thank you for the roses.

CORNELIA: I don't want thanks from you either. All that I want is a little return of affection, not much, but sometimes a little!

GRACE: You have that always, Cornelia.

CORNELIA: And one thing more: a little outspokenness, too.

GRACE: Outspokenness?

CORNELIA: Yes, outspokenness, if that's not too much to ask from such a proud young lady!

GRACE: (*rising from table*) I am not proud and I am not young, Cornelia.

CORNELIA: Sit down. Don't leave the table.

GRACE: Is that an order?

CORNELIA: I don't give orders to you, I make requests!

GRACE: Sometimes the requests of an employer are hard to distinguish from orders. (*She sits down.*)

CORNELIA: Please turn off the victrola. (*Grace rises and stops the machine.*) Grace!—Don't you feel there's—*something unspoken* between us?

GRACE: No. No, I don't.

CORNELIA: I do. I've felt for a long time something unspoken between us.

GRACE: Don't you think there is always something unspoken between two people?

CORNELIA: I see no reason for it.

GRACE: But don't a great many things exist without reason?

CORNELIA: Let's not turn this into a metaphysical discussion.

GRACE: All right. But you mystify me.

CORNELIA: It's very simple. It's just that I feel that there's something unspoken between us that ought to be spoken. . . . Why are you looking at me like that?

GRACE: How am I looking at you?

CORNELIA: With positive terror!

GRACE: Cornelia!

CORNELIA: You are, you are, but I'm not going to be shut up!

GRACE: Go on, continue, please, do!

CORNELIA: I'm going to, I will, I will, I— (*The phone rings and Grace reaches for it.*) No, no, no, let it ring! (*It goes on ringing.*) Take it off the hook!

GRACE: Do just let me—

CORNELIA: Off the hook, I told you! (*Grace takes the phone off the hook. A voice says: "Hello? Hello? Hello? Hello?"*)

GRACE: (*Suddenly she is sobbing.*) I can't stand it!

CORNELIA: *Be STILL! Someone can hear you!*

VOICE: Hello? Hello? Cornelia? Cornelia Scott? (*Cornelia seizes phone and slams it back into its cradle.*)

CORNELIA: Now stop that! Stop that silly little female trick!

GRACE: You say there's something unspoken. Maybe there is. I don't know. But I do know some things are better left unspoken. Also I know that when a silence between two people has gone on for a long time it's like a wall that's impenetrable between them! Maybe between us there is such a wall. One that's impenetrable. Or maybe *you* can break it. I know I can't. I can't even attempt to. You're the strong one of us two and surely you know it.—Both of us have turned grey!—But not the same kind of grey. In that velvet dressing-gown you look like the Emperor Tiberius!—In his imperial toga!—Your hair and your eyes are both the color of iron! Iron grey. Invincible looking! People nearby are all somewhat—frightened of you. They feel your force and they admire you for it. They come to you here for opinions on this or that. What plays are good on Broadway this season, what books are worth reading and what books are trash and what—what records are valuable and—what is the proper attitude toward—bills in Congress!—Oh, you're a fountain of wisdom!—And in addition to that, you have your—*wealth!* Yes, you have your—*fortune!*—All of your real-estate holdings, your blue-chip stocks, your—bonds, your—mansion on Edgewater Drive, your—shy little—secretary, your—fabulous gardens that Pilgrims cannot go into . . .

CORNELIA: Oh, yes, now you are speaking, now you are speaking at last! Go on, please go on speaking.

GRACE: I am—very—different!—Also turning grey but my grey is different. Not iron, like yours, not imperial, Cornelia, but grey, yes, grey, the—color of a . . . *cobweb* . . . (*She starts the record again, very softly.*)—Something white getting soiled, the grey of something forgotten. (*The phone rings again. Neither of them seems to notice it.*)—And that being the case, that being the difference between our two kinds of grey, yours and mine— You mustn't expect me to give bold answers to questions that make the house shake with silence! To speak out things that are fifteen years unspoken!—That long a time can make a silence a wall that nothing less than dynamite could break through and— (*She picks up the phone.*) I'm not strong enough, bold enough, I'm not—

CORNELIA: (*fiercely*) You're speaking into the phone!

GRACE: (*into phone*) Hello? Oh, yes, she's here. It's Esmeralda Hawkins. (*Cornelia snatches the phone.*)

CORNELIA: What is it, Esmeralda? What are you saying, is the room full of women? Such a babble of voices! What are you trying to tell me? Have they held the election already? What, what, what? Oh, this is maddening! I can't hear a word that you're saying, it sounds like the Fourth of July, a great celebration! Ha, ha, now try once more with your mouth closer to the phone! What, what? Would I be willing to what? You can't be serious! Are you out of your mind? (*She speaks to Grace in a panicky voice.*) She wants to know if I would be willing to serve as *vice*-Regent! (*into phone*) Esmeralda! Will you listen to me? What's going on? Are there some fresh defections? How does it look? Why did you call me again before the vote? Louder, please speak louder, and cup your mouth to the phone in case they're eavesdropping! Who asked if I would accept the vice-regency, dear? Oh, Mrs. Colby, of course!—that treacherous witch!—*Esmeralda!!* Listen! I—WILL ACCEPT—NO OFFICE—EXCEPT—THE HIGHEST! Did you understand that? I—WILL ACCEPT NO OFFICE EXCEPT—*ESMERALDA!* (*She drops phone into its cradle.*)

GRACE: Have they held the election?

CORNELIA: (*dazed*) What?—No, there's a five-minute recess before the election begins . . .

GRACE: Things are not going well?

CORNELIA: "Would you accept the vice-Regency," she asked me, "if for some reason they don't elect you Regent?"—Then she hung up as if somebody had snatched the phone away from her, or the house had—caught fire!

GRACE: You shouted so I think she must have been frightened.

CORNELIA: Whom can you trust in this world, whom can you ever rely on?

GRACE: I think perhaps you should have gone to the meeting.

CORNELIA: I think my not being there is much more pointed.

GRACE: (*rising again*) May I be excused, now?

CORNELIA: No! Stay here!

GRACE: If that is just a request, I—

CORNELIA: That's an order! (*Grace sits down and closes her eyes.*) When you first came to this house—do you know I didn't expect you?

GRACE: Oh, but, Cornelia, you'd invited me here.

CORNELIA: We hardly knew each other.

GRACE: We'd met the summer before when Ralph was—

CORNELIA: Living! Yes, we met at Sewanee where he was a summer instructor.

GRACE: He was already ill.

CORNELIA: I thought what a pity that lovely, delicate girl hasn't found someone she could lean on, who could protect her! And two months later I heard through Clarabelle Drake that he was dead . . .

GRACE: You wrote me such a sweet letter, saying how lonely you were since the loss of your mother and urging me to rest here till the shock was over. You seemed to understand how badly I needed to withdraw for a while from—old associations. I hesitated to come. I didn't until you wrote me a second letter . . .

CORNELIA: After I received yours. You wanted urging.

GRACE: I wanted to be quite sure I was really wanted! I only came intending to stay a few weeks. I was so afraid that I would outstay my welcome!

CORNELIA: How blind of you not to see how desperately I wanted to keep you here forever!

GRACE: Oh, I did see that you— (*The phone rings.*) Miss Scott's residence!—Yes, she's here.

CORNELIA: (*She snatches it up finally.*) Cornelia Scott speaking! Oh. It's you, Esmeralda! Well, how did it come out?—*I don't believe you! I simply don't believe you* . . . (*Grace sits down quietly at the table.*)—MRS. HORNSBY ELECTED? Well, there's a dark horse for you! Less than a year in the chapter . . . Did you—nominate—*me*?—Oh—I see! But I told you to withdraw my name if— No, no, no, don't explain, it doesn't matter, I have too much already. You know I am going into the Daughters of the Barons of Runymede! Yes, it's been established, I have a direct line to the Earl of— No, it's been straightened out, a clear line is established, and then of course I am also eligible for the Colonial Dames and for the Huguenot Society, and what with all my other activities and so forth, why, I couldn't *possibly* have taken it on if they'd—*wanted*. . . . Of course I'm going to resign from the local chapter! Oh, yes, I am! My secretary is sitting right here by me. She has her pencil, her notebook! I'm going to dictate my letter of resignation from the local chapter the moment that I hang up on this conversation. Oh, no, no, no, I'm not mad, not outraged, at all. I'm just a little—ha ha!—a little—amused . . . *MRS. HORNSBY*? Nothing succeeds like mediocrity, does it? Thanks and goodbye, Esmeralda. (*She hangs up, stunned. Grace rises.*)

GRACE: Notebook and pencil?

CORNELIA: Yes. Notebook and pencil . . . I have to—dictate a letter . . . (*Grace leaves the table. Just at the edge of the lighted area, she turns to glance at Cornelia's rigid shoulders and a slight, equivocal smile appears momentarily on her face; not quite malicious but not really sympathetic. Then she crosses out of the light. A moment later her voice comes from the outer dark.*)

GRACE: *What lovely roses! One for every year!*

Curtain

CAT ON A HOT TIN ROOF

And you, my father, there on the sad height,
Curse, bless, me now with your fierce tears, I pray.
Do not go gentle into that good night.
Rage, rage against the dying of the light!

DYLAN THOMAS

PERSON—TO—PERSON

OF COURSE it is a pity that so much of all creative work is so closely related to the personality of the one who does it.

It is sad and embarrassing and unattractive that those emotions that stir him deeply enough to demand expression, and to charge their expression with some measure of light and power, are nearly all rooted, however changed in their surface, in the particular and sometimes peculiar concerns of the artist himself, that special world, the passions and images of it that each of us weaves about him from birth to death, a web of monstrous complexity, spun forth at a speed that is incalculable to a length beyond measure, from the spider mouth of his own singular perceptions.

It is a lonely idea, a lonely condition, so terrifying to think of that we usually don't. And so we talk to each other, write and wire each other, call each other short and long distance across land and sea, clasp hands with each other at meeting and at parting, fight each other and even destroy each other because of this always somewhat thwarted effort to break through walls to each other. As a character in a play once said, "We're all of us sentenced to solitary confinement inside our own skins."

Personal lyricism is the outcry of prisoner to prisoner from the cell in solitary where each is confined for the duration of his life.

I once saw a group of little girls on a Mississippi sidewalk, all dolled up in their mothers' and sisters' castoff finery, old raggedy ball gowns and plumed hats and high-heeled slippers, enacting a meeting of ladies in a parlor with a perfect mimicry of polite Southern gush and simper. But one child was not satisfied with the attention paid her enraptured performance by the others, they were too involved in their own performances to suit her, so she stretched out her skinny arms and threw back her skinny neck and shrieked to the deaf heavens and her equally oblivious playmates, "Look at me, look at me, look at me!"

And then her mother's high-heeled slippers threw her off balance and she fell to the sidewalk in a great howling tangle of soiled white satin and torn pink net, and still nobody looked at her.

I wonder if she is not, now, a Southern writer.

Of course it is not only Southern writers, of lyrical bent, who engage in such histrionics and shout, "Look at me!" Perhaps it is a parable of all artists. And not always do we topple over and land in a tangle of trappings that don't fit us. However, it is well to be aware of that peril, and not to content yourself with a demand for attention, to know that out of your personal lyricism, your sidewalk histrionics, something has to be created that will not only attract observers but participants in the performance.

I try very hard to do that.

The fact that I want you to observe what I do for your possible pleasure and to give you knowledge of things that I feel I may know better than you, because my world is different from yours, as different as every man's world is from the world of others, is not enough excuse for a personal lyricism that has not yet mastered its necessary trick of rising above the singular to the plural concern, from personal to general import. But for years and years now, which may have passed like a dream because of this obsession, I have been trying to learn how to perform this trick and make it truthful, and sometimes I feel that I am able to do it. Sometimes, when the enraptured streetcorner performer in me cries out "Look at me!," I feel that my hazardous footwear and fantastic regalia may not quite throw me off balance. Then, suddenly, you fellow-performers in the sidewalk show may turn to give me your attention and allow me to hold it, at least for the interval between 8:40 and 11 something P.M.

Eleven years ago this month of March, when I was far closer than I knew, only nine months away from that long-delayed, but always expected, something that I lived for, the time when I would first catch and hold an audience's attention, I wrote my first preface to a long play. The final paragraph went like this:

"There is too much to say and not enough time to say it. Nor is there power enough. I am not a good writer. Sometimes I am a very bad writer indeed. There is hardly a successful writer in the field who cannot write circles around me . . . but I think of writing as something more organic than words, something closer to being and action. I want to work more and more with a more plastic theatre than the one I have (worked with) before. I have never for one moment doubted that there are people—millions!—to say things to. We come to each other, gradually, but with love. It is the short reach of my arms that hinders, not the length and multiplicity of theirs. With love and with honesty, the embrace is inevitable."

This characteristically emotional, if not rhetorical, statement of mine at that time seems to suggest that I thought of myself as having a highly personal, even intimate relationship with people who go to see plays. I did and I still do. A morbid shyness once prevented me from having much direct communication with people, and possibly that is why I began to write to them plays and stories. But even now when that tongue-locking, face-flushing, silent and crouching timidity has worn off with the passage of the troublesome youth that it sprang from, I still find it somehow easier to "level with" crowds of strangers in the hushed twilight of orchestra and balcony sections of theatres than with individuals across a table from me. Their being strangers somehow makes them more familiar and more approachable, easier to talk to.

Of course I know that I have sometimes presumed too much upon corresponding sympathies and interest in those to whom I talk boldly, and this has led to rejections that were painful and costly enough to inspire more prudence. But when I weigh one thing against another, an easy liking against a hard respect, the balance always tips the same way, and whatever the risk of being turned a cold shoulder, I still don't want to talk to people only about the surface aspects of their lives, the sort of things that acquaintances laugh and chatter about on ordinary social occasions.

I feel that they get plenty of that, and heaven knows so do I, before and after the little interval of time in which I have their attention and say what I have to say to them. The discretion of social conversation, even among friends, is exceeded only by the discretion of "the deep six," that grave wherein nothing is mentioned at all. Emily Dickinson, that lyrical spinster of Amherst, Massachusetts, who wore a strict and savage heart on a taffeta sleeve, commented wryly on that kind of posthumous discourse among friends in these lines:

I died for beauty, but was scarce
Adjusted in the tomb,
When one who died for truth was lain
In an adjoining room.

He questioned softly why I failed?
"For beauty," I replied.
"And I for truth,—the two are one;
We brethren are," he said.

And so, as kinsmen met a night,
We talked between the rooms,
Until the moss had reached our lips,
And covered up our names.

Meanwhile!—I want to go on talking to you as freely and intimately about what we live and die for as if I knew you better than anyone else whom you know.

Tennessee Williams

CHARACTERS OF THE PLAY

MARGARET

BRICK

MAE, sometimes called Sister Woman

BIG MAMA

DIXIE, a little girl

BIG DADDY

REVEREND TOOKER

GOOPER, sometimes called Brother Man

DOCTOR BAUGH, pronounced "Baw"

LACEY, a Negro servant

SOOKEY, another

Another little girl and two small boys

(The playing script of Act III also includes TRIXIE, another little girl, also DAISY, BRIGHTIE and SMALL, servants.)

NOTES FOR THE DESIGNER

The set is the bed-sitting-room of a plantation home in the Mississippi Delta. It is along an upstairs gallery which probably runs around the entire house; it has two pairs of very wide doors opening onto the gallery, showing white balustrades against a fair summer sky that fades into dusk and night during the course of the play, which occupies precisely the time of its performance, excepting, of course, the fifteen minutes of intermission.

Perhaps the style of the room is not what you would expect in the home of the Delta's biggest cotton-planter. It is Victorian with a touch of the Far East. It hasn't changed much since it was occupied by the original owners of the place, Jack Straw and Peter Ochello, a pair of old bachelors who shared this room all their lives together. In other words, the room must evoke some ghosts; it is gently and poetically haunted by a relationship that must have involved a tenderness which was uncommon. This may be irrelevant or unnecessary, but I once saw a reproduction of a faded photograph of the verandah of Robert Louis Stevenson's home on that Samoan Island where he spent his last years, and there was a quality of tender light on weathered wood, such as porch furniture made of bamboo and wicker, exposed to tropical suns and tropical rains, which came to mind when I thought about the set for this play, bringing also to mind the grace and comfort of light, the reassurance it gives, on a late and fair afternoon in summer, the way that no matter what, even dread of death, is gently touched and soothed by it. For the set is the background for a play that deals with human extremities of emotion, and it needs that softness behind it.

The bathroom door, showing only pale-blue tile and silver towel racks, is in one side wall; the hall door in the opposite wall. Two articles of furniture need mention: a big double bed which staging should make a functional part of the set as often as suitable, the surface of which should be slightly raked to make figures on it seen more easily; and against the wall space between the two huge double doors upstage: a monumental monstrosity peculiar to our times, a *huge* console combination of radio-phonograph (Hi-Fi with three speakers) TV set *and* liquor cabinet, bearing and containing many glasses and bottles, all in one piece, which is a composition of muted silver tones, and the opalescent tones of reflecting glass, a chromatic link, this thing, between the sepia (tawny gold) tones of the interior and the cool (white and blue) tones of the gallery and sky. This piece of furniture (?!), this monument, is a very complete and compact little shrine to virtually all the comforts and illusions behind which we hide from such things as the characters in the play are faced with. . . .

The set should be far less realistic than I have so far implied in this description of it. I think the walls below the ceiling should dissolve mysteriously into air; the set should be roofed by the sky; stars and moon suggested by traces of milky pallor, as if they were observed through a telescope lens out of focus.

Anything else I can think of? Oh, yes, fanlights (transoms shaped like an open glass fan) above all the doors in the set, with panes of blue and amber, and above all, the designer should take as many pains to give the actors room to move about freely (to show their restlessness, their passion for breaking out) as if it were a set for a ballet.

An evening in summer. The action is continuous, with two intermissions.

ACT ONE

At the rise of the curtain someone is taking a shower in the bathroom, the door of which is half open. A pretty young woman, with anxious lines in her face, enters the bedroom and crosses to the bathroom door.

MARGARET (*shouting above roar of water*): One of those no-neck monsters hit me with a hot buttered biscuit so I have t' change!

(*Margaret's voice is both rapid and drawling. In her long speeches she has the vocal tricks of a priest delivering a liturgical chant, the lines are almost sung, always continuing a little beyond her breath so she has to gasp for another. Sometimes she intersperses the lines with a little wordless singing, such as "Da-da-daaaa!"*

(*Water turns off and Brick calls out to her, but is still unseen. A tone of politely feigned interest, masking indifference, or worse, is characteristic of his speech with Margaret.*)

BRICK: Wha'd you say, Maggie? Water was on s' loud I couldn't hearya. . . .

MARGARET: Well, I!—just remarked that!—one of th' no-neck monsters messed up m' lovely lace dress so I got t'—cha-a-ange. . . .

(*She opens and kicks shut drawers of the dresser.*)

BRICK: Why d'ya call Gooper's kiddies no-neck monsters?

MARGARET: Because they've got no necks! Isn't that a good enough reason?

BRICK: Don't they have any necks?

MARGARET: None visible. Their fat little heads are set on their fat little bodies without a bit of connection.

BRICK: That's too bad.

MARGARET: Yes, it's too bad because you can't wring their necks if they've got no necks to wring! Isn't that right, honey?

(*She steps out of her dress, stands in a slip of ivory satin and lace.*)

Yep, they're no-neck monsters, all no-neck people are monsters . . .

(*Children shriek downstairs.*)

Hear them? Hear them screaming? I don't know where their voice-boxes are located since they don't have necks. I tell you I got so nervous at that table tonight I thought I would throw back my head and utter a scream you could hear across the Arkansas border an' parts of Louisiana an' Tennessee. I said to your charming sister-in-law, Mae, honey, couldn't you feed those precious little things at a separate table with an oilcloth cover? They make such a mess an' the lace cloth looks *so* pretty! She made enormous eyes at me and said, "Ohhh, noooooo! On Big Daddy's birthday? Why, he would never forgive me!" Well, I want you to know, Big Daddy hadn't been at the table two minutes with those five no-neck monsters slobbering and drooling over their food before he threw down his fork an' shouted, "Fo' God's sake, Gooper, why don't you put them pigs at a trough in th' kitchen?"—Well, I swear, I simply could have di-ieed!

Think of it, Brick, they've got five of them and number six is coming. They've brought the whole bunch down here like animals to display at a county fair. Why, they have those children doin' tricks all the time! "Junior, show Big Daddy how you do this, show Big Daddy how you do that, say your little piece fo' Big Daddy, Sister. Show your dimples, Sugar. Brother, show Big Daddy how you stand on your head!"—It goes on all the time, along with constant little remarks and innuendos about the fact that you and I have not produced any children, are totally childless and therefore totally useless!—Of course it's comical but it's also disgusting since it's so obvious what they're up to!

BRICK (*without interest*): What are they up to, Maggie?

MARGARET: Why, you know what they're up to!

BRICK (*appearing*): No, I don't know what they're up to.

(*He stands there in the bathroom doorway drying his hair with a towel and hanging onto the towel rack because one ankle is broken, plastered and bound. He is still slim and firm as a boy. His liquor hasn't started tearing him down outside.*

He has the additional charm of that cool air of detachment that people have who have given up the struggle. But now and then, when disturbed, something flashes behind it, like lightning in a fair sky, which shows that at some deeper level he is far from peaceful. Perhaps in a stronger light he would show some signs of deliquescence, but the fading, still warm, light from the gallery treats him gently.)

MARGARET: I'll tell you what they're up to, boy of mine!—They're up to cutting you out of your father's estate, and—

(*She freezes momentarily before her next remark. Her voice drops as if it were somehow a personally embarrassing admission.*)

—Now we know that Big Daddy's dyin' of—*cancer*. . . .

(*There are voices on the lawn below: long-drawn calls across distance. Margaret raises her lovely bare arms and powders her armpits with a light sigh.*

(*She adjusts the angle of a magnifying mirror to straighten an eyelash, then rises fretfully saying:*)

There's so much light in the room it—

BRICK (*softly but sharply*): Do we?

MARGARET: Do we what?

BRICK: Know Big Daddy's dyin' of cancer?

MARGARET: Got the report today.

BRICK: Oh . . .

MARGARET (*letting down bamboo blinds which cast long, gold-fretted shadows over the room*): Yep, got th' report just now . . . it didn't surprise me, Baby. . . .

(*Her voice has range, and music; sometimes it drops low as a boy's and you have a sudden image of her playing boy's games as a child.*)

I recognized the symptoms soon's we got here last spring and I'm willin' to bet you that Brother Man and his wife were pretty sure of it, too. That more than likely explains why their usual summer migration to the coolness of the Great Smokies was passed up this summer in favor of—hustlin' down here ev'ry whipstitch with their whole screamin' tribe! And why so many allusions have been made to Rainbow Hill lately. You know what Rainbow Hill is? Place that's famous for treatin' alcoholics an' dope fiends in the movies!

BRICK: I'm not in the movies.

MARGARET: No, and you don't take dope. Otherwise you're a perfect candidate for Rainbow Hill, Baby, and that's where they aim to ship you—over my dead body! Yep, over my dead body they'll ship you there, but nothing would please them better. Then Brother Man could get a-hold of the purse strings and dole out remittances to us, maybe get power-of-attorney and sign checks for us and cut off our credit wherever, whenever he wanted! Son-of-a-bitch!—How'd you like that, Baby?—Well, you've been doin' just about ev'rything in your power to bring it about, you've just been doin' ev'rything you can think of to aid and abet them in this scheme of theirs! Quittin' work, devoting yourself to the occupation of drinkin'!—Breakin' your ankle last night on the high school athletic field: doin' what? Jumpin' hurdles? At two or three in the morning? Just fantastic! Got in the paper. *Clarksdale Register* carried a nice little item about it, human interest story about a well-known former athlete stagin' a one-man track meet on the Glorious Hill High School athletic field last night, but was slightly out of condition and didn't clear the first hurdle! Brother Man Gooper claims he exercised his influence t' keep it from goin' out over AP or UP or every goddam "P."

But, Brick? You still have one big advantage!

(*During the above swift flood of words, Brick has reclined with contrapuntal leisure on the snowy surface of the bed and has rolled over carefully on his side or belly.*)

BRICK (*wryly*): Did you *say* something, Maggie?

MARGARET: Big Daddy dotes on you, honey. And he can't stand Brother Man and Brother Man's wife, that monster of fertility, Mae; she's downright odious to him! Know how I know? By little expressions that flicker over his face when that woman is holding fo'th on one of her choice topics such as—how she refused twilight sleep!—when the twins were delivered! Because she feels motherhood's an experience that a woman ought to experience fully!—in order to fully appreciate the wonder and beauty of it! HAH!

(*This loud "HAH!" is accompanied by a violent action such as slamming a drawer shut.*)

—and how she made Brother Man come in an' stand beside her in the delivery room so he would not miss out on the "wonder and beauty" of it either!—producin' those no-neck monsters. . . .

(*A speech of this kind would be antipathetic from almost anybody but Margaret; she makes it oddly funny, because her eyes constantly twinkle and her voice shakes with laughter which is basically indulgent.*)

—Big Daddy shares my attitude toward those two! As for me, well—I give him a laugh now and then and he tolerates me. In fact!—I sometimes suspect that Big Daddy harbors a little unconscious "lech" fo' me. . . .

BRICK: What makes you think that Big Daddy has a lech for you, Maggie?

MARGARET: Way he always drops his eyes down my body when I'm talkin' to him, drops his eyes to my boobs an' licks his old chops! Ha ha!

BRICK: That kind of talk is disgusting.

MARGARET: Did anyone ever tell you that you're an ass-aching Puritan, Brick?

I think it's mighty fine that that ole fellow, on the doorstep of death, still takes in my shape with what I think is deserved appreciation!

And you wanta know something else? Big Daddy didn't know how many little Maes and Goopers had been produced! "How many kids have you got?" he asked at the table, just like Brother Man and his wife were new acquaintances to him! Big Mama said he was jokin', but that ole boy wasn't jokin', Lord, no!

And when they infawmed him that they had five already and were turning out number six!—the news seemed to come as a sort of unpleasant surprise . . .

(*Children yell below.*)

Scream, monsters!

(*Turns to Brick with a sudden, gay, charming smile which fades as she notices that he is not looking at her but into fading gold space with a troubled expression.*

(*It is constant rejection that makes her humor "bitchy."*)

Yes, you should of been at that supper-table, Baby.

(*Whenever she calls him "baby" the word is a soft caress.*)

Y'know, Big Daddy, bless his ole sweet soul, he's the dearest ole thing in the world, but he does hunch over his food as if he preferred not to notice anything else. Well, Mae an' Gooper were side by side at the table, direckly across from Big Daddy, watchin' his face like hawks while they jawed an' jabbered about the cuteness an' brillance of th' no-neck monsters!

(*She giggles with a hand fluttering at her throat and her breast and her long throat arched.*

(*She comes downstage and recreates the scene with voice and gesture.*)

And the no-neck monsters were ranged around the table, some in high chairs and some on th' *Books of Knowledge*, all in fancy little paper caps in honor of Big Daddy's birthday, and all through dinner, well, I want you to know that Brother Man an' his partner never once, for one moment, stopped exchanging pokes an' pinches an' kicks an' signs an' signals!—Why, they were like a couple of cardsharps fleecing a sucker.—Even Big Mama, bless her ole sweet soul, she isn't th' quickest an' brightest thing in the world, she finally noticed, at last, an' said to Gooper, "Gooper, what are you an' Mae makin' all these signs at each other about?"—I swear t' goodness, I nearly choked on my chicken!

(*Margaret, back at the dressing-table, still doesn't see Brick. He is watching her with a look that is not quite definable.—Amused? shocked? contemptuous?—part of those and part of something else.*)

Y'know—your brother Gooper still cherishes the illusion he took a giant step up on the social ladder when he married Miss Mae Flynn of the Memphis Flynns.

(*Margaret moves about the room as she talks, stops before the mirror, moves on.*)

But I have a piece of Spanish news for Gooper. The Flynns never had a thing in this world but money and they lost that, they were nothing at all but fairly successful climbers. Of course, Mae Flynn came out in Memphis eight years before I made my debut in Nashville, but I had friends at Ward-Belmont who came from Memphis and they used to come to see me and I used to go to see them for Christmas and spring vacations, and so I know who rates an' who doesn't rate in Memphis society. Why, y'know ole Papa Flynn, he barely escaped doing time in the Federal pen for shady manipulations on th' stock market when his chain stores crashed, and as for Mae having been a cotton carnival queen, as they remind us so often, lest we forget, well, that's one honor that I don't envy her for!—Sit on a brass throne on a tacky float an' ride down Main Street, smilin', bowin', and blowin' kisses to all the trash on the street—

(*She picks out a pair of jeweled sandals and rushes to the dressing-table.*)

Why, year before last, when Susan McPheeters was singled out fo' that honor, y'know what happened to her? Y'know what happened to poor little Susie McPheeters?

BRICK (*absently*): No. What happened to little Susie McPheeters?

MARGARET: Somebody spit tobacco juice in her face.

BRICK (*dreamily*): Somebody spit tobacco juice in her face?

MARGARET: That's right, some old drunk leaned out of a window in the Hotel Gayoso and yelled, "Hey, Queen, hey, hey, there, Queenie!" Poor Susie looked up and flashed him a radiant smile and he shot out a squirt of tobacco juice right in poor Susie's face.

BRICK: Well, what d'you know about that.

MARGARET (*gaily*): What do I know about it? I was there, I saw it!

BRICK (*absently*): Must have been kind of funny.

MARGARET: Susie didn't think so. Had hysterics. Screamed like a banshee. They had to stop th' parade an' remove her from her throne an' go on with—

(*She catches sight of him in the mirror, gasps slightly, wheels about to face him. Count ten.*)

—Why are you looking at me like that?

BRICK (*whistling softly, now*): Like what, Maggie?

MARGARET (*intensely, fearfully*): The way y' were lookin' at me just now, befo' I caught your eye in the mirror and you started t' whistle! I don't know how t' describe it but it froze my blood!—I've caught you lookin' at me like that so often lately. What are you thinkin' of when you look at me like that?

BRICK: I wasn't conscious of lookin' at you, Maggie.

MARGARET: Well, I was conscious of it! What were you thinkin'?

BRICK: I don't remember thinking of anything, Maggie.

MARGARET: Don't you think I know that—? Don't you—? —Think I know that—?

BRICK (*coolly*): Know *what,* Maggie?

MARGARET (*struggling for expression*): That I've gone through this—*hideous!*—*transformation,* become—*hard! Frantic!*

(*Then she adds, almost tenderly:*)

—*cruel!!*

That's what you've been observing in me lately. How could y' help but observe it? That's all right. I'm not—thin-skinned any more, can't afford t' be thin-skinned any more.

(*She is now recovering her power.*)

—But Brick? Brick?

BRICK: Did you say something?

MARGARET: I was *goin'* t' say something: that I get—lonely. Very!

BRICK: Ev'rybody gets that . . .

MARGARET: Living with someone you love can be lonelier—than living entirely *alone!*—if the one that y' love doesn't love you. . . .

(*There is a pause. Brick hobbles downstage and asks, without looking at her:*)

BRICK: Would you like to live alone, Maggie?

(*Another pause: then—after she has caught a quick, hurt breath:*)

MARGARET: *No!—God!—I wouldn't!*

(*Another gasping breath. She forcibly controls what must have been an impulse to cry out. We see her deliberately, very forcibly, going all the way back to the world in which you can talk about ordinary matters.*)

Did you have a nice shower?

BRICK: Uh-huh.

MARGARET: Was the water cool?

BRICK: No.

MARGARET: But it made y' feel fresh, huh?

BRICK: Fresher. . . .

MARGARET: I know something would make y' feel *much* fresher!

BRICK: What?

MARGARET: An alcohol rub. Or cologne, a rub with cologne!

BRICK: That's good after a workout but I haven't been workin' out, Maggie.

MARGARET: You've kept in good shape, though.

BRICK (*indifferently*): You think so, Maggie?

MARGARET: I always thought drinkin' men lost their looks, but I was plainly mistaken.

BRICK (*wryly*): Why, thanks, Maggie.

MARGARET: You're the only drinkin' man I know that it never seems t' put fat on.

BRICK: I'm gettin' softer, Maggie.

MARGARET: Well, sooner or later it's bound to soften you up. It was just beginning to soften up Skipper when—

(*She stops short.*)

I'm sorry. I never could keep my fingers off a sore—I wish you *would* lose your looks. If you did it would make the martyrdom of Saint Maggie a little more bearable. But no such goddam luck. I actually believe you've gotten better looking since you've gone on the bottle. Yeah, a person who didn't know you would think you'd never had a tense nerve in your body or a strained muscle.

(*There are sounds of croquet on the lawn below: the click of mallets, light voices, near and distant.*)

Of course, you always had that detached quality as if you were playing a game without much concern over whether you won or lost, and now that you've lost the game, not lost but just quit playing, you have that rare sort of charm that usually only happens in very old or hopelessly sick people, the charm of the defeated.—You look so cool, so cool, so enviably cool.

(*Music is heard.*)

They're playing croquet. The moon has appeared and it's white, just beginning to turn a little bit yellow. . . .

You were a wonderful lover. . . .

Such a wonderful person to go to bed with, and I think mostly because you were really indifferent to it. Isn't that right? Never had any anxiety about it, did it naturally, easily, slowly, with absolute confidence and perfect calm, more like opening a door for a lady or seating her at a table than giving expression to any longing for her. Your indifference made you wonderful at lovemaking—*strange*?—but true. . . .

You know, if I thought you would never, never, *never* make love to me again—I would go downstairs to the kitchen and pick out the longest and sharpest knife I could find and stick it straight into my heart, I swear that I would!

But one thing I don't have is the charm of the defeated, my hat is still in the ring, and I am determined to win!

(*There is the sound of croquet mallets hitting croquet balls.*)

—What is the victory of a cat on a hot tin roof?—I wish I knew. . . .

Just staying on it, I guess, as long as she can. . . .

(*More croquet sounds.*)

Later tonight I'm going to tell you I love you an' maybe by that time you'll be drunk enough to believe me. Yes, they're playing croquet. . . .

Big Daddy is dying of cancer. . . .

What were you thinking of when I caught you looking at me like that? Were you thinking of Skipper?

(*Brick takes up his crutch, rises.*)

Oh, excuse me, forgive me, but laws of silence don't work! No, laws of silence don't work. . . .

(*Brick crosses to the bar, takes a quick drink, and rubs his head with a towel.*)

Laws of silence don't work. . . .

When something is festering in your memory or your imagination, laws of silence don't work, it's just like shutting a door and locking it on a house on fire in hope of forgetting that the house is burning. But not facing a fire doesn't put it out. Silence about a thing just magnifies it. It grows and festers in silence, becomes malignant. . . .

Get dressed, Brick.

(*He drops his crutch.*)

BRICK: I've dropped my crutch.

(*He has stopped rubbing his hair dry but still stands hanging onto the towel rack in a white towel-cloth robe.*)

MARGARET: Lean on me.

BRICK: No, just give me my crutch.

MARGARET: Lean on my shoulder.

BRICK: *I don't want to lean on your shoulder, I want my crutch!*

(*This is spoken like sudden lightning.*)

Are you going to give me my crutch or do I have to get down on my knees on the floor and—

MARGARET: *Here, here, take it, take it!*

(*She has thrust the crutch at him.*)

BRICK (*hobbling out*): Thanks . . .

MARGARET: We mustn't scream at each other, the walls in this house have ears. . . .

(*He hobbles directly to liquor cabinet to get a new drink.*)

—but that's the first time I've heard you raise your voice in a long time, Brick. A crack in the wall?—Of composure?

—I think that's a good sign. . . .

A sign of nerves in a player on the defensive!

(*Brick turns and smiles at her coolly over his fresh drink.*)

BRICK: It just hasn't happened yet, Maggie.

MARGARET: What?

BRICK: The click I get in my head when I've had enough of this stuff to make me peaceful. . . .

Will you do me a favor?

MARGARET: Maybe I will. What favor?

BRICK: Just, just keep your voice down!

MARGARET (*in a hoarse whisper*): I'll do you that favor, I'll speak in a whisper, if not shut up completely, if *you* will do *me* a favor and make that drink your last one till after the party.

BRICK: What party?

MARGARET: Big Daddy's birthday party.

BRICK: Is this Big Daddy's birthday?

MARGARET: You know this is Big Daddy's birthday!

BRICK: No, I don't, I forgot it.

MARGARET: Well, I remembered it for you. . . .

(*They are both speaking as breathlessly as a pair of kids after a fight, drawing deep exhausted breaths and looking at each other with faraway eyes, shaking and panting together as if they had broken apart from a violent struggle.*)

BRICK: Good for you, Maggie.

MARGARET: You just have to scribble a few lines on this card.

BRICK: You scribble something, Maggie.

MARGARET: It's got to be your handwriting; it's your present, I've given him my present; it's got to be your handwriting!

(*The tension between them is building again, the voices becoming shrill once more.*)

BRICK: I didn't get him a present.

MARGARET: I got one for you.

BRICK: All right. You write the card, then.

MARGARET: And have him know you didn't remember his birthday?

BRICK: I didn't remember his birthday.

MARGARET: You don't have to prove you didn't!

BRICK: I don't want to fool him about it.

MARGARET: Just write "Love, Brick!" for God's—

BRICK: No.

MARGARET: You've *got* to!

BRICK: I don't have to do anything I don't want to do. You keep forgetting the conditions on which I agreed to stay on living with you.

MARGARET (*out before she knows it*): I'm not living with you. We occupy the same cage.

BRICK: You've got to remember the conditions agreed on.

MARGARET: They're impossible conditions!

BRICK: Then why don't you—?

MARGARET: HUSH! Who is out there? Is somebody at the door?

(*There are footsteps in hall.*)

MAE (*outside*): May I enter a moment?

MARGARET: Oh, *you!* Sure. Come in, Mae.

(*Mae enters bearing aloft the bow of a young lady's archery set.*)

MAE: Brick, is this thing yours?

MARGARET: Why, Sister Woman—that's my Diana Trophy. Won it at the intercollegiate archery contest on the Ole Miss campus.

MAE: It's a mighty dangerous thing to leave exposed round a house full of nawmal rid-blooded children attracted t' weapons.

MARGARET: "Nawmal rid-blooded children attracted t' weapons" ought t' be taught to keep their hands off things that don't belong to them.

MAE: Maggie, honey, if you had children of your own you'd know how funny that is. Will you please lock this up and put the key out of reach?

MARGARET: Sister Woman, nobody is plotting the destruction of your kiddies.—Brick and I still have our special archers' license. We're goin' deer-huntin' on Moon Lake as soon as the season starts. I love to run with dogs through chilly woods, run, run leap over obstructions—

(*She goes into the closet carrying the bow.*)

MAE: How's the injured ankle, Brick?

BRICK: Doesn't hurt. Just itches.

MAE: Oh, my! Brick—Brick, you should've been downstairs after supper! Kiddies put on a show. Polly played the piano, Buster an' Sonny drums, an' then they turned out the lights an' Dixie an' Trixie puhfawmed a toe dance in fairy costume with *spahkluhs!* Big Daddy just beamed! He just beamed!

MARGARET (*from the closet with a sharp laugh*): Oh, I bet. It breaks my heart that we missed it!

(*She reenters.*)

But Mae? Why did y'give dawgs' names to all your kiddies?

MAE: *Dogs'* names?

(*Margaret has made this observation as she goes to raise the bamboo blinds, since the sunset glare has diminished. In crossing she winks at Brick.*)

MARGARET (*sweetly*): Dixie, Trixie, Buster, Sonny, Polly!—Sounds like four dogs and a parrot . . . animal act in a circus!

MAE: Maggie?

(*Margaret turns with a smile.*)

Why are you so catty?

MARGARET: Cause I'm a cat! But why can't *you* take a joke, Sister Woman?

MAE: Nothin' pleases me more than a joke that's funny. You know the real names of our kiddies. Buster's real name is Robert. Sonny's real name is Saunders. Trixie's real name is Marlene and Dixie's—

(*Someone downstairs calls for her. "Hey, Mae!"—She rushes to door, saying:*)

Intermission is over!

MARGARET (*as Mae closes door*): I wonder what Dixie's real name is?

BRICK: Maggie, being catty doesn't help things any . . .

MARGARET: I know! *WHY!*—Am I so catty?—Cause I'm consumed with envy an' eaten up with longing?—Brick, I've laid out your beautiful Shantung silk suit from Rome and one of your monogrammed silk shirts. I'll put your cuff-links in it, those lovely star sapphires I get you to wear so rarely. . . .

BRICK: I can't get trousers on over this plaster cast.

MARGARET: Yes, you can, I'll help you.

BRICK: I'm not going to get dressed, Maggie.

MARGARET: Will you just put on a pair of white silk pajamas?

BRICK: Yes, I'll do that, Maggie.

MARGARET: *Thank* you, thank you so *much!*

BRICK: Don't mention it.

MARGARET: *Oh, Brick!* How long does it have t' go on? This punishment? Haven't I done time enough, haven't I served my term, can't I apply for a—pardon?

BRICK: Maggie, you're spoiling my liquor. Lately your voice always sounds like you'd been running upstairs to warn somebody that the house was on fire!

MARGARET: Well, no wonder, no wonder. Y'know what I feel like, Brick?

(*Children's and grownups' voices are blended, below, in a loud but uncertain rendition of "My Wild Irish Rose."*)

I feel all the time like a cat on a hot tin roof!

BRICK: Then jump off the roof, jump off it, cats can jump off roofs and land on their four feet uninjured!

MARGARET: Oh, yes!

BRICK: Do it!—fo' God's sake, do it . . .

MARGARET: Do what?

BRICK: Take a lover!

MARGARET: I can't see a man but you! Even with my eyes closed, I just see you! Why don't you get ugly, Brick, why don't you please get fat or ugly or something so I could stand it?

(*She rushes to hall door, opens it, listens.*)

The concert is still going on! Bravo, no-necks, bravo!

(*She slams and locks door fiercely.*)

BRICK: What did you lock the door for?
MARGARET: To give us a little privacy for a while.
BRICK: You know better, Maggie.
MARGARET: No, I don't know better. . . .

(*She rushes to gallery doors, draws the rose-silk drapes across them.*)

BRICK: Don't make a fool of yourself.
MARGARET: I don't mind makin' a fool of myself over you!
BRICK: I mind, Maggie. I feel embarrassed for you.
MARGARET: Feel embarrassed! But don't continue my torture. I can't live on and on under these circumstances.
BRICK: You agreed to—
MARGARET: I know but—
BRICK: —Accept that condition!
MARGARET: *I CAN'T! CAN'T! CAN'T!*

(*She seizes his shoulder.*)

BRICK: Let go!

(*He breaks away from her and seizes the small boudoir chair and raises it like a lion-tamer facing a big circus cat.*

(*Count five. She stares at him with her fist pressed to her mouth, then bursts into shrill, almost hysterical laughter. He remains grave for a moment, then grins and puts the chair down.*

(*Big Mama calls through closed door.*)

BIG MAMA: Son? Son? Son?
BRICK: What is it, Big Mama?
BIG MAMA (*outside*): Oh, son! We got the most wonderful news about Big Daddy. I just had t' run up an' tell you right this—

(*She rattles the knob.*)

—What's this door doin', locked, faw? You all think there's robbers in the house?

MARGARET: Big Mama, Brick is dressin', he's not dressed yet.

BIG MAMA: That's all right, it won't be the first time I've seen Brick not dressed. Come on, open this door!

(*Margaret, with a grimace, goes to unlock and open the hall door, as Brick hobbles rapidly to the bathroom and kicks the door shut. Big Mama has disappeared from the hall.*)

MARGARET: Big Mama?

(*Big Mama appears through the opposite gallery doors behind Margaret, huffing and puffing like an old bulldog. She is a short, stout woman; her sixty years and 170 pounds have left her somewhat breathless most of the time; she's always tensed like a boxer, or rather, a Japanese wrestler. Her "family" was maybe a little superior to Big Daddy's, but not much. She wears a black or silver lace dress and at least half a million in flashy gems. She is very sincere.*)

BIG MAMA (*loudly, startling Margaret*): Here—I come through Gooper's and Mae's gall'ry door. Where's Brick? *Brick*—Hurry on out of there, son, I just have a second and want to give you the news about Big Daddy.—I hate locked doors in a house. . . .

MARGARET (*with affected lightness*): I've noticed you do, Big Mama, but people have got to have *some* moments of privacy, don't they?

BIG MAMA: No, ma'am, not in *my* house. (*Without pause*) Whacha took off you' dress faw? I thought that little lace dress was so sweet on yuh, honey.

MARGARET: I thought it looked sweet on me, too, but one of m' cute little table-partners used it for a napkin so—!

BIG MAMA (*picking up stockings on floor*): What?

MARGARET: You know, Big Mama, Mae and Gooper's so touchy about those children—thanks, Big Mama . . .

(*Big Mama has thrust the picked-up stockings in Margaret's hand with a grunt.*)

—that you just don't dare to suggest there's any room for improvement in their—

BIG MAMA: Brick, hurry out!—Shoot, Maggie, you just don't like children.

MARGARET: I do SO like children! Adore them!—well brought up!

BIG MAMA (*gentle—loving*): Well, why don't you have some and bring them up well, then, instead of all the time pickin' on Gooper's an' Mae's?

GOOPER (*shouting up the stairs*): Hey, hey, Big Mama, Betsy an' Hugh got to go, waitin' t' tell yuh g'by!

BIG MAMA: Tell 'em to hold their hawses, I'll be right down in a jiffy!

(*She turns to the bathroom door and calls out.*)

Son? Can you hear me in there?

(*There is a muffled answer.*)

We just got the full report from the laboratory at the Ochsner Clinic, completely negative, son, ev'rything negative, right on down the line! Nothin' a-tall's wrong with him but some little functional thing called a spastic colon. Can you hear me, son?

MARGARET: He can hear you, Big Mama.

BIG MAMA: Then why don't he say something? God Almighty, a piece of news like that should make him shout. It made *me* shout, I can tell you. I shouted and sobbed and fell right down on my knees!—Look!

(*She pulls up her skirt.*)

See the bruises where I hit my kneecaps? Took both doctors to haul me back on my feet!

(*She laughs—she always laughs like hell at herself.*)

Big Daddy was furious with me! But ain't that wonderful news?

(*Facing bathroom again, she continues:*)

After all the anxiety we been through to git a report like that on Big Daddy's birthday? Big Daddy tried to hide how much of a load that news took off his mind, but didn't fool *me*. He was mighty close to crying about it *himself!*

(*Goodbyes are shouted downstairs, and she rushes to door.*)

Hold those people down there, don't let them go!—Now, git dressed, we're all comin' up to this room fo' Big Daddy's birthday party because of your ankle.—How's his ankle, Maggie?

MARGARET: Well, he broke it, Big Mama.

BIG MAMA: I know he broke it.

(*A phone is ringing in hall. A Negro voice answers: "Mistuh Polly's res'dence."*)

I mean does it hurt him much still.

MARGARET: I'm afraid I can't give you that information, Big Mama. You'll have to ask Brick if it hurts much still or not.

SOOKEY (*in the hall*): It's Memphis, Mizz Polly, it's Miss Sally in Memphis.

BIG MAMA: Awright, Sookey.

(*Big Mama rushes into the hall and is heard shouting on the phone:*)

Hello, Miss Sally. How are you, Miss Sally?—Yes, well, I was just gonna call you about it. *Shoot!*—

(*She raises her voice to a bellow.*)

Miss Sally? Don't ever call me from the Gayoso Lobby, too much talk goes on in that hotel lobby, no wonder you can't hear me! Now listen, Miss Sally. They's nothin' serious wrong with Big Daddy. We got the report just now, they's nothin' wrong but a thing called a—spastic! *SPASTIC!*—colon . . .

(*She appears at the hall door and calls to Margaret.*)

—Maggie, come out here and talk to that fool on the phone. I'm shouted breathless!

MARGARET (*goes out and is heard sweetly at phone*): Miss Sally? This is Brick's wife, Maggie. So nice to hear your voice. Can you hear *mine*? Well, *good!*—Big Mama just wanted you to know that they've got the report from the Ochsner

Clinic and what Big Daddy has is a spastic colon. Yes. Spastic colon, Miss Sally. That's right, spastic colon. *G'bye, Miss Sally, hope I'll see you real soon!*

(*Hangs up a little before Miss Sally was probably ready to terminate the talk. She returns through the hall door.*)

She heard me perfectly. I've discovered with deaf people the thing to do is not shout at them but just enunciate clearly. My rich old Aunt Cornelia was deaf as the dead but I could make her hear me just by sayin' each word slowly, distinctly, close to her ear. I read her the *Commercial Appeal* ev'ry night, read her the classified ads in it, even, she never missed a word of it. But was she a mean ole thing! Know what I got when she died? Her unexpired subscriptions to five magazines and the Book-of-the-Month Club and a LIBRARY full of ev'ry dull book ever written! All else went to her hellcat of a sister . . . meaner than she was, even!

(*Big Mama has been straightening things up in the room during this speech.*)

BIG MAMA (*closing closet door on discarded clothes*): *Miss Sally sure is a case!* Big Daddy says she's always got her hand out fo' something. He's not mistaken. That poor ole thing always has her hand out fo' somethin'. I don't think Big Daddy gives her as much as he should.

(*Somebody shouts for her downstairs and she shouts:*)

I'm comin'!

(*She starts out. At the hall door, turns and jerks a forefinger, first toward the bathroom door, then toward the liquor cabinet, meaning: "Has Brick been drinking?" Margaret pretends not to understand, cocks her head and raises her brows as if the pantomimic performance was completely mystifying to her.*

(*Big Mama rushes back to Margaret:*)

Shoot! Stop playin' so dumb!—I mean has he been drinkin' that stuff much yet?

MARGARET (*with a little laugh*): Oh! I think he had a highball after supper.

BIG MAMA: Don't laugh about it!—Some single men stop drinkin' when they git married and others start! Brick never touched liquor before he—!

MARGARET (*crying out*): *THAT'S NOT FAIR!*

BIG MAMA: Fair or not fair I want to ask you a question, one question: D'you make Brick happy in bed?

MARGARET: Why don't you ask if he makes *me* happy in bed?

BIG MAMA: Because I know that—

MARGARET: *It works both ways!*

BIG MAMA: Something's not right! You're childless and my son drinks!

(*Someone has called her downstairs and she has rushed to the door on the line above. She turns at the door and points at the bed.*)

—When a marriage goes on the rocks, the rocks are *there*, right *there!*

MARGARET: *That's—*

(*Big Mama has swept out of the room and slammed the door.*)

—not—*fair* . . .

(*Margaret is alone, completely alone, and she feels it. She draws in, hunches her shoulders, raises her arms with fists clenched, shuts her eyes tight as a child about to be stabbed with a vaccination needle. When she opens her eyes again, what she sees is the long oval mirror and she rushes straight to it, stares into it with a grimace and says: "Who are you?"—Then she crouches a little and answers herself in a different voice which is high, thin, mocking: "I am Maggie the Cat!"—Straightens quickly as bathroom door opens a little and Brick calls out to her.*)

BRICK: Has Big Mama gone?

MARGARET: She's gone.

(*He opens the bathroom door and hobbles out, with his liquor glass now empty, straight to the liquor cabinet. He is whistling softly. Margaret's head pivots on her long, slender throat to watch him.*

(*She raises a hand uncertainly to the base of her throat, as if it was difficult for her to swallow, before she speaks:*)

You know, our sex life didn't just peter out in the usual way, it was cut off short, long before the natural time for it to, and it's going to revive again, just as sudden as that. I'm confident of it. That's what I'm keeping myself attractive for. For the time when you'll see me again like other men see me. Yes, like other men see me. They still see me, Brick, and they like what they see. Uh-huh. Some of them would give their—

Look, Brick!

(*She stands before the long oval mirror, touches her breast and then her hips with her two hands.*)

How high my body stays on me!—Nothing has fallen on me—not a fraction. . . .

(*Her voice is soft and trembling: a pleading child's. At this moment as he turns to glance at her—a look which is like a player passing a ball to another player, third down and goal to go—she has to capture the audience in a grip so tight that she can hold it till the first intermission without any lapse of attention.*)

Other men still want me. My face looks strained, sometimes, but I've kept my figure as well as you've kept yours, and men admire it. I still turn heads on the street. Why, last week in Memphis everywhere that I went men's eyes burned holes in my clothes, at the country club and in restaurants and department stores, there wasn't a man I met or walked by that didn't just eat me up with his eyes and turn around when I passed him and look back at me. Why, at Alice's party for her New York cousins, the best lookin' man in the crowd—followed me upstairs and tried to force his way in the powder room with me, followed me to the door and tried to force his way in!

BRICK: Why didn't you let him, Maggie?

MARGARET: Because I'm not that common, for one thing. Not that I wasn't almost tempted to. You like to know who it was? It was Sonny Boy Maxwell, that's who!

BRICK: Oh, yeah, Sonny Boy Maxwell, he was a good end-runner but had a little injury to his back and had to quit.

MARGARET: He has no injury now and has no wife and still has a lech for me!

BRICK: I see no reason to lock him out of a powder room in that case.

MARGARET: And have someone catch me at it? I'm not that stupid. Oh, I might sometime cheat on you with someone, since you're so insultingly eager to have me do it!—But if I do, you can be damned sure it will be in a place and a time where no one but me and the man could possibly know. Because I'm not going to give you any excuse to divorce me for being unfaithful or anything else. . . .

BRICK: Maggie, I wouldn't divorce you for being unfaithful or anything else. Don't you know that? Hell. I'd be relieved to know that you'd found yourself a lover.

MARGARET: Well, I'm taking no chances. No, I'd rather stay on this hot tin roof.

BRICK: A hot tin roof's 'n uncomfo'table place t' stay on. . . .

(*He starts to whistle softly.*)

MARGARET (*through his whistle*): Yeah, but I can stay on it just as long as I have to.

BRICK: You could leave me, Maggie.

(*He resumes whistle. She wheels about to glare at him.*)

MARGARET: *Don't want to and will not!* Besides if I did, you don't have a cent to pay for it but what you get from Big Daddy and he's dying of cancer!

(*For the first time a realization of Big Daddy's doom seems to penetrate to Brick's consciousness, visibly, and he looks at Margaret.*)

BRICK: Big Mama just said he *wasn't*, that the report was okay.

MARGARET: That's what she thinks because she got the same story that they gave Big Daddy. And was just as taken in by it as he was, poor ole things. . . .

But tonight they're going to tell her the truth about it. When Big Daddy goes to bed, they're going to tell her that he is dying of cancer.

(*She slams the dresser drawer.*)

—It's malignant and it's terminal.

BRICK: Does Big Daddy know it?

MARGARET: Hell, do they *ever* know it? Nobody says, "You're dying." You have to fool them. They have to fool *themselves.*

BRICK: Why?

MARGARET: *Why*? Because human beings dream of life everlasting, that's the reason! But most of them want it on earth and not in heaven.

(*He gives a short, hard laugh at her touch of humor.*)

Well. . . . (*She touches up her mascara.*) That's how it is, anyhow. . . . (*She looks about.*) Where did I put down my cigarette? Don't want to burn up the home-place, at least not with Mae and Gooper and their five monsters in it!

(*She has found it and sucks at it greedily. Blows out smoke and continues:*)

So this is Big Daddy's last birthday. And Mae and Gooper, they know it, oh, *they* know it, all right. They got the first information from the Ochsner Clinic. That's why they rushed down here with their no-neck monsters. Because. Do you know something? Big Daddy's made no will? Big Daddy's never made out any will in his life, and so this campaign's afoot to impress him, forcibly as possible, with the fact that you drink and I've borne no children!

(*He continues to stare at her a moment, then mutters something sharp but not audible and hobbles rather rapidly out onto the long gallery in the fading, much faded, gold light.*)

MARGARET (*continuing her liturgical chant*): Y'know, I'm *fond* of Big Daddy, I am genuinely fond of that old man, I really *am*, you know. . . .

BRICK (*faintly, vaguely*): Yes, I know you are. . . .

MARGARET: I've always sort of admired him in spite of his coarseness, his four-letter words and so forth. Because Big Daddy *is* what he *is*, and he makes no bones about it. He hasn't turned gentleman farmer, he's still a Mississippi red neck, as much of a red neck as he must have been when he was just overseer here on the old Jack Straw and Peter

Ochello place. But he got hold of it an' built it into th' biggest an' finest plantation in the Delta.—I've always *liked* Big Daddy. . . .

(*She crosses to the proscenium.*)

Well, this is Big Daddy's last birthday. I'm sorry about it. But I'm facing the facts. It takes money to take care of a drinker and that's the office that I've been elected to lately.

BRICK: You don't have to take care of me.

MARGARET: Yes, I do. Two people in the same boat have got to take care of each other. At least you want money to buy more Echo Spring when this supply is exhausted, or will you be satisfied with a ten-cent beer?

Mae an' Gooper are plannin' to freeze us out of Big Daddy's estate because you drink and I'm childless. But we can defeat that plan. We're *going* to defeat that plan!

Brick, y'know, I've been so God damn disgustingly poor all my life!—That's the *truth*, Brick!

BRICK: I'm not sayin' it isn't.

MARGARET: Always had to suck up to people I couldn't stand because they had money and I was poor as Job's turkey. You don't know what that's like. Well, I'll tell you, it's like you would feel a thousand miles away from Echo Spring!—And had to get back to it on that broken ankle . . . without a crutch!

That's how it feels to be as poor as Job's turkey and have to suck up to relatives that you hated because they had money and all you had was a bunch of hand-me-down clothes and a few old moldy three per cent government bonds. My daddy loved his liquor, he fell in love with his liquor the way you've fallen in love with Echo Spring!—And my poor Mama, having to maintain some semblance of social position, to keep appearances up, on an income of one hundred and fifty dollars a month on those old government bonds!

When I came out, the year that I made my debut, I had just two evening dresses! One Mother made me from a pattern in *Vogue*, the other a hand-me-down from a snotty rich cousin I hated!

—The dress that I married you in was my grandmother's weddin' gown. . . .

So that's why I'm like a cat on a hot tin roof!

(*Brick is still on the gallery. Someone below calls up to him in a warm Negro voice, "Hiya, Mistuh Brick, how yuh feelin'?" Brick raises his liquor glass as if that answered the question.*)

MARGARET: You can be young without money but you can't be old without it. You've got to be old *with* money because to be old without it is just too awful, you've got to be one or the other, either *young* or *with money,* you can't be old and *without* it.—That's the *truth,* Brick. . . .

(*Brick whistles softly, vaguely.*)

Well, now I'm dressed, I'm all dressed, there's nothing else for me to do.

(*Forlornly, almost fearfully.*)

I'm dressed, all dressed, nothing else for me to do. . . .

(*She moves about restlessly, aimlessly, and speaks, as if to herself.*)

I know when I made my mistake.—What am I—? Oh!—my bracelets. . . .

(*She starts working a collection of bracelets over her hands onto her wrists, about six on each, as she talks.*)

I've thought a whole lot about it and now I know when I made my mistake. Yes, I made my mistake when I told you the truth about that thing with Skipper. Never should have confessed it, a fatal error, tellin' you about that thing with Skipper.

BRICK: Maggie, shut up about Skipper. I mean it, Maggie; you got to shut up about Skipper.

MARGARET: You ought to understand that Skipper and I—

BRICK: You don't think I'm serious, Maggie? You're fooled by the fact that I am saying this quiet? Look, Maggie. What you're doing is a dangerous thing to do. You're—you're—you're—foolin' with something that—nobody ought to fool with.

MARGARET: This time I'm going to finish what I have to say to you. Skipper and I made love, if love you could call it, because it made both of us feel a little bit closer to you. You see, you son of a bitch, you asked too much of people, of me, of him, of all the unlucky poor damned sons of bitches that happen to love you, and there was a whole pack of them, yes, there was a pack of them besides me and Skipper, you asked too goddam much of people that loved you, you—superior creature!—you godlike being!—And so we made love to each other to dream it was you, both of us! Yes, yes, yes! Truth, truth! What's so awful about it? I like it, I think the truth is—yeah! I shouldn't have told you. . . .

BRICK (*holding his head unnaturally still and uptilted a bit*): It was Skipper that told me about it. Not you, Maggie.

MARGARET: I told you!

BRICK: After he told me!

MARGARET: What does it matter who—?

(*Brick turns suddenly out upon the gallery and calls:*)

BRICK: Little girl! Hey, little girl!

LITTLE GIRL (*at a distance*): What, Uncle Brick?

BRICK: Tell the folks to come up!—Bring everybody upstairs!

MARGARET: I can't stop myself! I'd go on telling you this in front of them all, if I had to!

BRICK: Little girl! Go on, go on, will you? Do what I told you, call them!

MARGARET: Because it's got to be told and you, you!—you never let me!

(*She sobs, then controls herself, and continues almost calmly.*)

It was one of those beautiful, ideal things they tell about in the Greek legends, it couldn't be anything else, you being you, and that's what made it so sad, that's what made it so awful, because it was love that never could be carried through to anything satisfying or even talked about plainly. Brick, I tell you, you got to believe me, Brick, I *do* understand all about it! I—I think it was—*noble!* Can't you tell I'm sincere when I say I respect it? My only point, the only point that I'm making, is life has got to be allowed to continue even after the *dream* of life is—all—over. . . .

(*Brick is without his crutch. Leaning on furniture, he crosses to pick it up as she continues as if possessed by a will outside herself:*)

Why I remember when we double-dated at college, Gladys Fitzgerald and I and you and Skipper, it was more like a date between you and Skipper. Gladys and I were just sort of tagging along as if it was necessary to chaperone you!—to make a good public impression—

BRICK (*turns to face her, half lifting his crutch*): Maggie, you want me to hit you with this crutch? Don't you know I could kill you with this crutch?

MARGARET: Good Lord, man, d' you think I'd care if you did?

BRICK: One man has one great good true thing in his life. One great good thing which is true!—I had friendship with Skipper.—You are naming it dirty!

MARGARET: I'm not naming it dirty! I am naming it clean.

BRICK: Not love with you, Maggie, but friendship with Skipper was that one great true thing, and you are naming it dirty!

MARGARET: Then you haven't been listenin', not understood what I'm saying! I'm naming it so damn clean that it killed poor Skipper!—You two had something that had to be kept on ice, yes, incorruptible, yes!—and death was the only icebox where you could keep it. . . .

BRICK: I married you, Maggie. Why would I marry you, Maggie, if I was—?

MARGARET: Brick, don't brain me yet, let me finish!—I know, believe me I know, that it was only Skipper that harbored even any *unconscious* desire for anything not perfectly pure between you two!—Now let me skip a little. You married me early that summer we graduated out of Ole Miss, and we were happy, weren't we, we were blissful, yes, hit heaven together ev'ry time that we loved! But that fall you an' Skipper turned down wonderful offers of jobs in order to keep on bein' football heroes—pro-football heroes. You organized the Dixie Stars that fall, so you could keep on bein' teammates forever! But somethin' was not right with it!—*Me included!*—between you. Skipper began hittin' the bottle . . .

you got a spinal injury—couldn't play the Thanksgivin' game in Chicago, watched it on TV from a traction bed in Toledo. I joined Skipper. The Dixie Stars lost because poor Skipper was drunk. We drank together that night all night in the bar of the Blackstone and when cold day was comin' up over the Lake an' we were comin' out drunk to take a dizzy look at it, I said, "SKIPPER! STOP LOVIN' MY HUSBAND OR TELL HIM HE'S GOT TO LET YOU ADMIT IT TO HIM!"—one way or another!

HE SLAPPED ME HARD ON THE MOUTH!—then turned and ran without stopping once, I am sure, all the way back into his room at the Blackstone. . . .

—When I came to his room that night, with a little scratch like a shy little mouse at his door, he made that pitiful, ineffectual little attempt to prove that what I had said wasn't true. . . .

(*Brick strikes at her with crutch, a blow that shatters the gem-like lamp on the table.*)

—In this way, I destroyed him, by telling him truth that he and his world which he was born and raised in, yours and his world, had told him could not be told?

—From then on Skipper was nothing at all but a receptacle for liquor and drugs. . . .

—*Who shot cock-robin? I with my—*

(*She throws back her head with tight shut eyes.*)

—*merciful arrow!*

(*Brick strikes at her; misses.*)

Missed me!—Sorry,—I'm not tryin' to whitewash my behavior, Christ, no! Brick, I'm not good. I don't know why people have to pretend to be good, nobody's good. The rich or the well-to-do can afford to respect moral patterns, conventional moral patterns, but I could never afford to, yeah, but—I'm honest! Give me credit for just that, will you *please*?—Born poor, raised poor, expect to die poor unless I manage to get us something out of what Big Daddy leaves when he dies of cancer! But Brick?!—*Skipper is dead! I'm alive!* Maggie the cat is—

(*Brick hops awkwardly forward and strikes at her again with his crutch.*)

—alive! I am alive, alive! I am . . .

(*He hurls the crutch at her, across the bed she took refuge behind, and pitches forward on the floor as she completes her speech.*)

—alive!

(*A little girl, Dixie, bursts into the room, wearing an Indian war bonnet and firing a cap pistol at Margaret and shouting: "Bang, bang, bang!"*

(*Laughter downstairs floats through the open hall door. Margaret had crouched gasping to bed at child's entrance. She now rises and says with cool fury:*)

Little girl, your mother or someone should teach you—(*Gasping*)—to knock at a door before you come into a room. Otherwise people might think that you—lack—good breeding. . . .

DIXIE: Yanh, yanh, yanh, what is Uncle Brick doin' on th' floor?

BRICK: I tried to kill your Aunt Maggie, but I failed—and I fell. Little girl, give me my crutch so I can get up off th' floor.

MARGARET: Yes, give your uncle his crutch, he's a cripple, honey, he broke his ankle last night jumping hurdles on the high school athletic field!

DIXIE: What were you jumping hurdles for, Uncle Brick?

BRICK: Because I used to jump them, and people like to do what they used to do, even after they've stopped being able to do it. . . .

MARGARET: That's right, that's your answer, now go away, little girl.

(*Dixie fires cap pistol at Margaret three times.*)

Stop, you stop that, monster! You little no-neck monster!

(*She seizes the cap pistol and hurls it through gallery doors.*)

DIXIE (*with a precocious instinct for the cruelest thing*): You're *jealous!*—You're just jealous because you can't have babies!

(*She sticks out her tongue at Margaret as she sashays past her with her stomach stuck out, to the gallery. Margaret slams the gallery doors and leans panting against them. There is a pause. Brick has replaced his spilt drink and sits, faraway, on the great four-poster bed.*)

MARGARET: You see?—they gloat over us being childless, even in front of their five little no-neck monsters!

(*Pause. Voices approach on the stairs.*)

Brick?—I've been to a doctor in Memphis, a—a gynecologist. . . .

I've been completely examined, and there is no reason why we can't have a child whenever we want one. And this is my time by the calendar to conceive. Are you listening to me? Are you? Are you LISTENING TO ME!

BRICK: Yes. I hear you, Maggie.

(*His attention returns to her inflamed face.*)

—But how in hell on earth do you imagine—that you're going to have a child by a man that can't stand you?

MARGARET: That's a problem that I will have to work out.

(*She wheels about to face the hall door.*)

Here they come!

(*The lights dim.*)

Curtain

ACT TWO

There is no lapse of time. Margaret and Brick are in the same positions they held at the end of Act I.

MARGARET (*at door*): *Here they come!*

(*Big Daddy appears first, a tall man with a fierce, anxious look, moving carefully not to betray his weakness even, or especially, to himself.*)

BIG DADDY: Well, Brick.
BRICK: Hello, Big Daddy.—Congratulations!
BIG DADDY: —Crap. . . .

(*Some of the people are approaching through the hall, others along the gallery: voices from both directions. Gooper and Reverend Tooker become visible outside gallery doors, and their voices come in clearly.*

(*They pause outside as Gooper lights a cigar.*)

REVEREND TOOKER (*vivaciously*): Oh, but St. Paul's in Grenada has three memorial windows, and the latest one is a Tiffany stained-glass window that cost twenty-five hundred dollars, a picture of Christ the Good Shepherd with a Lamb in His arms.

GOOPER: Who give that window, Preach?

REVEREND TOOKER: Clyde Fletcher's widow. Also presented St. Paul's with a baptismal font.

GOOPER: Y'know what somebody ought t' give your church is a *coolin'* system, Preach.

REVEREND TOOKER: Yes, siree, Bob! And y'know what Gus Hamma's family gave in his memory to the church at Two Rivers? A complete new stone parish-house with a basketball court in the basement and a—

BIG DADDY (*uttering a loud barking laugh which is far from truly mirthful*): Hey, Preach! What's all this talk about memorials, Preach? Y' think somebody's about t' kick off around here? 'S that it?

(*Startled by this interjection, Reverend Tooker decides to laugh at the question almost as loud as he can.*

(*How he would answer the question we'll never know, as he's spared that embarrassment by the voice of Gooper's wife, Mae, rising high and clear as she appears with "Doc" Baugh, the family doctor, through the hall door.*)

MAE (*almost religiously*): —Let's see now, they've had their *tyyy*-phoid shots, and their tetanus shots, their diphtheria shots and their hepatitis shots and their polio shots, they got *those* shots every month from May through September, and—Gooper? Hey! Gooper!—What all have the kiddies been shot faw?

MARGARET (*overlapping a bit*): Turn on the Hi-Fi, Brick! Let's have some music t' start off th' party with!

(*The talk becomes so general that the room sounds like a great aviary of chattering birds. Only Brick remains unengaged, leaning upon the liquor cabinet with his faraway smile, an ice cube in a paper napkin with which he now and then rubs his forehead. He doesn't respond to Margaret's command. She bounds forward and stoops over the instrument panel of the console.*)

GOOPER: We gave 'em that thing for a third anniversary present, got three speakers in it.

(*The room is suddenly blasted by the climax of a Wagnerian opera or a Beethoven symphony.*)

BIG DADDY: *Turn that damn thing off!*

(*Almost instant silence, almost instantly broken by the shouting charge of Big Mama, entering through hall door like a charging rhino.*)

BIG MAMA: *Wha's my Brick, wha's mah precious baby!!*
BIG DADDY: *Sorry! Turn it back on!*

(*Everyone laughs very loud. Big Daddy is famous for his jokes at Big Mama's expense, and nobody laughs louder at these jokes than Big Mama herself, though sometimes they're pretty cruel and Big Mama has to pick up or fuss with something to cover the hurt that the loud laugh doesn't quite cover.*

(*On this occasion, a happy occasion because the dread in her heart has also been lifted by the false report on Big Daddy's condition, she giggles, grotesquely, coyly, in Big Daddy's direction and bears down upon Brick, all very quick and alive.*)

BIG MAMA: Here he is, here's my precious baby! What's that you've got in your hand? You put that liquor down, son, your hand was made fo' holdin' somethin' better than that!
GOOPER: Look at Brick put it down!

(*Brick has obeyed Big Mama by draining the glass and handing it to her. Again everyone laughs, some high, some low.*)

BIG MAMA: Oh, you bad boy, you, you're my bad little boy. Give Big Mama a kiss, you bad boy, you!—Look at him shy away, will you? Brick never liked bein' kissed or made a fuss over, I guess because he's always had too much of it!

Son, you turn that thing off!

(*Brick has switched on the TV set.*)

I can't stand TV, radio was bad enough but TV has gone it one better, I mean—(*Plops wheezing in chair*)—one worse, ha ha! Now what'm I sittin' down here faw? I want t' sit next to my sweetheart on the sofa, hold hands with him and love him up a little!

(*Big Mama has on a black and white figured chiffon. The large irregular patterns, like the markings of some massive animal, the luster of her great diamonds and many pearls, the brilliants set in the silver frames of her glasses, her riotous voice, booming laugh, have dominated the room since she entered. Big Daddy has been regarding her with a steady grimace of chronic annoyance.*)

BIG MAMA (*still louder*): Preacher, Preacher, hey, Preach! Give me you' hand an' help me up from this chair!

REVEREND TOOKER: None of your tricks, Big Mama!

BIG MAMA: What tricks? You give me you' hand so I can get up an'—

(*Reverend Tooker extends her his hand. She grabs it and pulls him into her lap with a shrill laugh that spans an octave in two notes.*)

Ever seen a preacher in a fat lady's lap? Hey, hey, folks! Ever seen a preacher in a fat lady's lap?

(*Big Mama is notorious throughout the Delta for this sort of inelegant horseplay. Margaret looks on with indulgent humor, sipping Dubonnet "on the rocks" and watching Brick, but Mae and Gooper exchange signs of humorless anxiety over these antics, the sort of behavior which Mae thinks may account for their failure to quite get in with the smartest young married set in Memphis, despite all. One of the Negroes, Lacey or Sookey, peeks in, cackling. They are waiting for a sign to bring in the cake and champagne. But Big Daddy's not amused. He doesn't understand why, in spite of the infinite mental relief he's received from the doctor's report, he still has these same old fox teeth in his guts. "This spastic thing sure is something," he says to himself, but aloud he roars at Big Mama:*)

BIG DADDY: *BIG MAMA, WILL YOU QUIT HORSIN'?*— You're too old an' too fat fo' that sort of crazy kid stuff an' besides a woman with your blood-pressure—she had two hundred last spring!—is riskin' a stroke when you mess around like that. . . .

BIG MAMA: *Here comes Big Daddy's birthday!*

(*Negroes in white jackets enter with an enormous birthday cake ablaze with candles and carrying buckets of champagne with satin ribbons about the bottle necks.*

(*Mae and Gooper strike up song, and everybody, including the Negroes and Children, joins in. Only Brick remains aloof.*)

EVERYONE:

Happy birthday to you.
Happy birthday to you.
Happy birthday, Big Daddy—

(*Some sing: "Dear, Big Daddy!"*)

Happy birthday to you.

(*Some sing: "How old are you?"*)

(*Mae has come down center and is organizing her children like a chorus. She gives them a barely audible: "One, two, three!" and they are off in the new tune.*)

CHILDREN:

Skinamarinka—dinka—dink
Skinamarinka—do
We love you.
Skinamarinka—dinka—dink
Skinamarinka—do.

(*All together, they turn to Big Daddy.*)

Big Daddy, you!

(*They turn back front, like a musical comedy chorus.*)

We love you in the morning;
We love you in the night.
We love you when we're with you,
And we love you out of sight.
Skinamarinka—dinka—dink
Skinamarinka—do.

(*Mae turns to Big Mama.*)

Big Mama, too!

(*Big Mama bursts into tears. The Negroes leave.*)

BIG DADDY: Now Ida, what the hell is the matter with you?

MAE: She's just so happy.

BIG MAMA: I'm just so happy, Big Daddy, I have to cry or something.

(*Sudden and loud in the hush:*)

Brick, do you know the wonderful news that Doc Baugh got from the clinic about Big Daddy? Big Daddy's one hundred per cent!

MARGARET: Isn't that wonderful?

BIG MAMA: He's just one hundred per cent. Passed the examination with flying colors. Now that we know there's nothing wrong with Big Daddy but a spastic colon, I can tell you something. I was worried sick, half out of my mind, for fear that Big Daddy might have a thing like—

(*Margaret cuts through this speech, jumping up and exclaiming shrilly:*)

MARGARET: Brick, honey, aren't you going to give Big Daddy his birthday present?

(*Passing by him, she snatches his liquor glass from him.*
(*She picks up a fancily wrapped package.*)

Here it is, Big Daddy, this is from Brick!

BIG MAMA: This is the biggest birthday Big Daddy's ever had, a hundred presents and bushels of telegrams from—

MAE (*at same time*): What is it, Brick?

GOOPER: I bet 500 to 50 that Brick don't *know* what it is.

BIG MAMA: The fun of presents is not knowing what they are till you open the package. Open your present, Big Daddy.

BIG DADDY: Open it you'self. I want to ask Brick somethin! Come here, Brick.

MARGARET: Big Daddy's callin' you, Brick.

(*She is opening the package.*)

BRICK: Tell Big Daddy I'm crippled.

BIG DADDY: I see you're crippled. I want to know how you got crippled.

MARGARET (*making diversionary tactics*): *Oh, look, oh, look, why, it's a cashmere robe!*

(*She holds the robe up for all to see.*)

MAE: You sound surprised, Maggie.

MARGARET: I never saw one before.

MAE: That's funny.—*Hah!*

MARGARET (*turning on her fiercely, with a brilliant smile*): Why is it funny? All my family ever had was family—and luxuries such as cashmere robes still surprise me!

BIG DADDY (*ominously*): Quiet!

MAE (*heedless in her fury*): I don't see how you could be so surprised when you bought it yourself at Loewenstein's in Memphis last Saturday. You know how I know?

BIG DADDY: I said, Quiet!

MAE: —I know because the salesgirl that sold it to you waited on me and said, Oh, Mrs. Pollitt, your sister-in-law just bought a cashmere robe for your husband's father!

MARGARET: Sister Woman! Your talents are wasted as a housewife and mother, you really ought to be with the FBI or—

BIG DADDY: QUIET!

(*Reverend Tooker's reflexes are slower than the others'. He finishes a sentence after the bellow.*)

REVEREND TOOKER (*to Doc Baugh*): —the Stork and the Reaper are running neck and neck!

(*He starts to laugh gaily when he notices the silence and Big Daddy's glare. His laugh dies falsely.*)

BIG DADDY: Preacher, I hope I'm not butting in on more talk about memorial stained-glass windows, am I, Preacher?

(*Reverend Tooker laughs feebly, then coughs dryly in the embarrassed silence.*)

Preacher?

BIG MAMA: Now, Big Daddy, don't you pick on Preacher!

BIG DADDY (*raising his voice*): You ever hear that expression all hawk and no spit? You bring that expression to mind with that little dry cough of yours, all hawk an' no spit. . . .

(*The pause is broken only by a short startled laugh from Margaret, the only one there who is conscious of and amused by the grotesque.*)

MAE (*raising her arms and jangling her bracelets*): I wonder if the mosquitoes are active tonight?

BIG DADDY: What's that, Little Mama? Did you make some remark?

MAE: Yes, I said I wondered if the mosquitoes would eat us alive if we went out on the gallery for a while.

BIG DADDY: Well, if they do, I'll have your bones pulverized for fertilizer!

BIG MAMA (*quickly*): Last week we had an airplane spraying the place and I think it done some good, at least I haven't had a—

BIG DADDY (*cutting her speech*): Brick, they tell me, if what they tell me is true, that you done some jumping last night on the high school athletic field?

BIG MAMA: Brick, Big Daddy is talking to you, son.

BRICK (*smiling vaguely over his drink*): What was that, Big Daddy?

BIG DADDY: They said you done some jumping on the high school track field last night.

BRICK: That's what they told me, too.

BIG DADDY: Was it jumping or humping that you were doing out there? What were you doing out there at three A.M., layin' a woman on that cinder track?

BIG MAMA: Big Daddy, you are off the sick-list, now, and I'm not going to excuse you for talkin' so—

BIG DADDY: Quiet!

BIG MAMA: —*nasty* in front of Preacher and—

BIG DADDY: *QUIET!*—I ast you, Brick, if you was cuttin' you'self a piece o' poon-tang last night on that cinder track? I thought maybe you were chasin' poon-tang on that track an' tripped over something in the heat of the chase—'sthat it?

(*Gooper laughs, loud and false, others nervously following suit. Big Mama stamps her foot, and purses her lips, crossing to Mae and whispering something to her as Brick meets his father's hard, intent, grinning stare with a slow, vague smile that he offers all situations from behind the screen of his liquor.*)

BRICK: No, sir, I don't think so. . . .

MAE (*at the same time, sweetly*): Reverend Tooker, let's you and I take a stroll on the widow's walk.

(*She and the preacher go out on the gallery as Big Daddy says:*)

BIG DADDY: Then what the hell were you doing out there at three o'clock in the morning?

BRICK: Jumping the hurdles, Big Daddy, runnin' and jumpin' the hurdles, but those high hurdles have gotten too high for me, now.

BIG DADDY: Cause you was drunk?

BRICK (*his vague smile fading a little*): Sober I wouldn't have tried to jump the *low* ones. . . .

BIG MAMA (*quickly*): Big Daddy, blow out the candles on your birthday cake!

MARGARET (*at the same time*): I want to propose a toast to Big Daddy Pollitt on his sixty-fifth birthday, the biggest cotton-planter in—

BIG DADDY (*bellowing with fury and disgust*): *I told you to stop it, now stop it, quit this—!*

BIG MAMA (*coming in front of Big Daddy with the cake*): Big Daddy, I will not allow you to talk that way, not even on your birthday, I—

BIG DADDY: I'll talk like I want to on my birthday, Ida, or any other goddam day of the year and anybody here that don't like it knows what they can do!

BIG MAMA: You don't mean that!
BIG DADDY: What makes you think I don't mean it?

(*Meanwhile various discreet signals have been exchanged and Gooper has also gone out on the gallery.*)

BIG MAMA: I just know you don't mean it.
BIG DADDY: You don't know a goddam thing and you never did!
BIG MAMA: Big Daddy, you don't mean that.
BIG DADDY: Oh, yes, I do, oh, yes, I do, I mean it! I put up with a whole lot of crap around here because I thought I was dying. And you thought I was dying and you started taking over, well, you can stop taking over now, Ida, because I'm not gonna die, you can just stop now this business of taking over because you're not taking over because I'm not dying, I went through the laboratory and the goddam exploratory operation and there's nothing wrong with me but a spastic colon. And I'm not dying of cancer which you thought I was dying of. Ain't that so? Didn't you think that I was dying of cancer, Ida?

(*Almost everybody is out on the gallery but the two old people glaring at each other across the blazing cake.*

(*Big Mama's chest heaves and she presses a fat fist to her mouth.*

(*Big Daddy continues, hoarsely:*)

Ain't that so, Ida? Didn't you have an idea I was dying of cancer and now you could take control of this place and everything on it? I got that impression, I seemed to get that impression. Your loud voice everywhere, your fat old body butting in here and there!
BIG MAMA: Hush! The Preacher!
BIG DADDY: Rut the goddam preacher!

(*Big Mama gasps loudly and sits down on the sofa which is almost too small for her.*)

Did you hear what I said? I said rut the goddam preacher!

(*Somebody closes the gallery doors from outside just as there is a burst of fireworks and excited cries from the children.*)

BIG MAMA: I never seen you act like this before and I can't think what's got in you!

BIG DADDY: I went through all that laboratory and operation and all just so I would know if you or me was boss here! Well, now it turns out that I am and you ain't—and that's my birthday present—and my cake and champagne!—because for three years now you been gradually taking over. Bossing. Talking. Sashaying your fat old body around the place I made! I made this place! I was overseer on it! I was the overseer on the old Straw and Ochello plantation. I quit school at ten! I quit school at ten years old and went to work like a nigger in the fields. And I rose to be overseer of the Straw and Ochello plantation. And old Straw died and I was Ochello's partner and the place got bigger and bigger and bigger and bigger and bigger! I did all that myself with no goddam help from you, and now you think you're just about to take over. Well, I am just about to tell you that you are not just about to take over, you are not just about to take over a God damn thing. Is that clear to you, Ida? Is that very plain to you, now? Is that understood completely? I been through the laboratory from A to Z. I've had the goddam exploratory operation, and nothing is wrong with me but a spastic colon—made spastic, I guess, by *disgust!* By all the goddam lies and liars that I have had to put up with, and all the goddam hypocrisy that I lived with all these forty years that we been livin' together!

Hey! Ida! Blow out the candles on the birthday cake! Purse up your lips and draw a deep breath and blow out the goddam candles on the cake!

BIG MAMA: Oh, Big Daddy, oh, oh, oh, Big Daddy!

BIG DADDY: What's the matter with you?

BIG MAMA: *In all these years you never believed that I loved you??*

BIG DADDY: Huh?

BIG MAMA: *And I did, I did so much, I did love you!*—I even loved your hate and your hardness, Big Daddy!

(*She sobs and rushes awkwardly out onto the gallery.*)

BIG DADDY (*to himself*): *Wouldn't it be funny if that was true. . . .*

(*A pause is followed by a burst of light in the sky from the fireworks.*)

BRICK! HEY, BRICK!

(*He stands over his blazing birthday cake.*

(*After some moments, Brick hobbles in on his crutch, holding his glass.*

(*Margaret follows him with a bright, anxious smile.*)

I didn't call you, Maggie. I called Brick.

MARGARET: I'm just delivering him to you.

(*She kisses Brick on the mouth which he immediately wipes with the back of his hand. She flies girlishly back out. Brick and his father are alone.*)

BIG DADDY: Why did you do that?

BRICK: Do what, Big Daddy?

BIG DADDY: Wipe her kiss off your mouth like she'd spit on you.

BRICK: I don't know. I wasn't conscious of it.

BIG DADDY: That woman of yours has a better shape on her than Gooper's but somehow or other they got the same look about them.

BRICK: What sort of look is that, Big Daddy?

BIG DADDY: I don't know how to describe it but it's the same look.

BRICK: They don't look peaceful, do they?

BIG DADDY: No, they sure in hell don't.

BRICK: They look nervous as cats?

BIG DADDY: That's right, they look nervous as cats.

BRICK: Nervous as a couple of cats on a hot tin roof?

BIG DADDY: That's right, boy, they look like a couple of cats on a hot tin roof. It's funny that you and Gooper being so different would pick out the same type of woman.

BRICK: Both of us married into society, Big Daddy.

BIG DADDY: Crap . . . I wonder what gives them both that look?

BRICK: Well. They're sittin' in the middle of a big piece of land, Big Daddy, twenty-eight thousand acres is a pretty big piece of land and so they're squaring off on it, each determined to knock off a bigger piece of it than the other whenever you let it go.

BIG DADDY: I got a surprise for those women. I'm not gonna let it go for a long time yet if that's what they're waiting for.

BRICK: That's right, Big Daddy. You just sit tight and let them scratch each other's eyes out. . . .

BIG DADDY: You bet your life I'm going to sit tight on it and let those sons of bitches scratch their eyes out, ha ha ha. . . .

But Gooper's wife's a good breeder, you got to admit she's fertile. Hell, at supper tonight she had them all at the table and they had to put a couple of extra leafs in the table to make room for them, she's got five head of them, now, and another one's comin'.

BRICK: Yep, number six is comin'. . . .

BIG DADDY: Brick, you know, I swear to God, I don't know the way it happens?

BRICK: The way what happens, Big Daddy?

BIG DADDY: You git you a piece of land, by hook or crook, an' things start growin' on it, things accumulate on it, and the first thing you know it's completely out of hand, completely out of hand!

BRICK: Well, they say nature hates a vacuum, Big Daddy.

BIG DADDY: That's what they say, but sometimes I think that a vacuum is a hell of a lot better than some of the stuff that nature replaces it with.

Is someone out there by that door?

BRICK: Yep.

BIG DADDY: Who?

(*He has lowered his voice.*)

BRICK: Someone int'rested in what we say to each other.

BIG DADDY: Gooper?——*GOOPER!*

(*After a discreet pause, Mae appears in the gallery door.*)

MAE: Did you call Gooper, Big Daddy?

BIG DADDY: Aw, it was you.

MAE: Do you want Gooper, Big Daddy?

BIG DADDY: No, and I don't want you. I want some privacy here, while I'm having a confidential talk with my son

Brick. Now it's too hot in here to close them doors, but if I have to close those rutten doors in order to have a private talk with my son Brick, just let me know and I'll close 'em. Because I hate eavesdroppers, I don't like any kind of sneakin' an' spyin'.

MAE: Why, Big Daddy—

BIG DADDY: You stood on the wrong side of the moon, it threw your shadow!

MAE: I was just—

BIG DADDY: You was just nothing but *spyin'* an' you *know* it!

MAE (*begins to sniff and sob*): Oh, Big Daddy, you're so unkind for some reason to those that really love you!

BIG DADDY: Shut up, shut up, shut up! I'm going to move you and Gooper out of that room next to this! It's none of your goddam business what goes on in here at night between Brick an' Maggie. You listen at night like a couple of rutten peek-hole spies and go and give a report on what you hear to Big Mama an' she comes to me and says they say such and such and so and so about what they heard goin' on between Brick an' Maggie, and Jesus, it makes me sick. I'm goin' to move you an' Gooper out of that room, I can't stand sneakin' an' spyin', it makes me sick. . . .

(*Mae throws back her head and rolls her eyes heavenward and extends her arms as if invoking God's pity for this unjust martyrdom; then she presses a handkerchief to her nose and flies from the room with a loud swish of skirts.*)

BRICK (*now at the liquor cabinet*): They listen, do they?

BIG DADDY: Yeah. They listen and give reports to Big Mama on what goes on in here between you and Maggie. They say that—

(*He stops as if embarrassed.*)

—You won't sleep with her, that you sleep on the sofa. Is that true or not true? If you don't like Maggie, get rid of Maggie!—What are you doin' there now?

BRICK: Fresh'nin' up my drink.

BIG DADDY: Son, you know you got a real liquor problem?

BRICK: Yes, sir, yes, I know.

BIG DADDY: Is that why you quit sports-announcing, because of this liquor problem?

BRICK: Yes, sir, yes, sir, I guess so.

(*He smiles vaguely and amiably at his father across his replenished drink.*)

BIG DADDY: Son, don't guess about it, it's too important.

BRICK (*vaguely*): Yes, sir.

BIG DADDY: And listen to me, don't look at the damn chandelier. . . .

(*Pause. Big Daddy's voice is husky.*)

—Somethin' else we picked up at th' big fire sale in Europe.

(*Another pause.*)

Life is important. There's nothing else to hold onto. A man that drinks is throwing his life away. Don't do it, hold onto your life. There's nothing else to hold onto. . . .

Sit down over here so we don't have to raise our voices, the walls have ears in this place.

BRICK (*hobbling over to sit on the sofa beside him*): All right, Big Daddy.

BIG DADDY: Quit!—how'd that come about? Some disappointment?

BRICK: I don't know. Do you?

BIG DADDY: I'm askin' you, God damn it! How in hell would I know if you don't?

BRICK: I just got out there and found that I had a mouth full of cotton. I was always two or three beats behind what was goin' on on the field and so I—

BIG DADDY: Quit!

BRICK (*amiably*): Yes, quit.

BIG DADDY: Son?

BRICK: Huh?

BIG DADDY (*inhales loudly and deeply from his cigar; then bends suddenly a little forward, exhaling loudly and raising a hand to his forehead*): —Whew!—ha ha!—I took in too much smoke, it made me a little light-headed. . . .

(*The mantel clock chimes.*)

Why is it so damn hard for people to talk?

BRICK: Yeah. . . .

(*The clock goes on sweetly chiming till it has completed the stroke of ten.*)

—Nice peaceful-soundin' clock, I like to hear it all night. . . .

(*He slides low and comfortable on the sofa; Big Daddy sits up straight and rigid with some unspoken anxiety. All his gestures are tense and jerky as he talks. He wheezes and pants and sniffs through his nervous speech, glancing quickly, shyly, from time to time, at his son.*)

BIG DADDY: We got that clock the summer we wint to Europe, me an' Big Mama on that damn Cook's Tour, never had such an awful time in my life, I'm tellin' you, son, those gooks over there, they gouge your eyeballs out in their grand hotels. And Big Mama bought more stuff than you could haul in a couple of boxcars, that's no crap. Everywhere she wint on this whirlwind tour, she bought, bought, bought. Why, half that stuff she bought is still crated up in the cellar, under water last spring!

(*He laughs.*)

That Europe is nothin' on earth but a great big auction, that's all it is, that bunch of old worn-out places, it's just a big fire-sale, the whole rutten thing, an' Big Mama wint wild in it, why, you couldn't hold that woman with a mule's harness! Bought, bought, bought!—lucky I'm a rich man, yes siree, Bob, an' half that stuff is mildewin' in th' basement. It's lucky I'm a rich man, it sure is lucky, well, I'm a rich man, Brick, yep, I'm a mighty rich man.

(*His eyes light up for a moment.*)

Y'know how much I'm worth? Guess, Brick! Guess how much I'm worth!

(*Brick smiles vaguely over his drink.*)

Close on ten million in cash an' blue chip stocks, outside, mind you, of twenty-eight thousand acres of the richest land this side of the valley Nile!

(*A puff and crackle and the night sky blooms with an eerie greenish glow. Children shriek on the gallery.*)

But a man can't buy his life with it, he can't buy back his life with it when his life has been spent, that's one thing not offered in the Europe fire-sale or in the American markets or any markets on earth, a man can't buy his life with it, he can't buy back his life when his life is finished. . . .

That's a sobering thought, a very sobering thought, and that's a thought that I was turning over in my head, over and over and over—until today. . . .

I'm wiser and sadder, Brick, for this experience which I just gone through. They's one thing else that I remember in Europe.

BRICK: What is that, Big Daddy?

BIG DADDY: The hills around Barcelona in the country of Spain and the children running over those bare hills in their bare skins beggin' like starvin' dogs with howls and screeches, and how fat the priests are on the streets of Barcelona, so many of them and so fat and so pleasant, ha ha!—Y'know I could feed that country? I got money enough to feed that goddam country, but the human animal is a selfish beast and I don't reckon the money I passed out there to those howling children in the hills around Barcelona would more than upholster one of the chairs in this room, I mean pay to put a new cover on this chair!

Hell, I threw them money like you'd scatter feed corn for chickens, I threw money at them just to get rid of them long enough to climb back into th' car and—drive away. . . .

And then in Morocco, them Arabs, why, prostitution begins at four or five, that's no exaggeration, why, I remember one day in Marrakech, that old walled Arab city, I set on a broken-down wall to have a cigar, it was fearful hot there and this Arab woman stood in the road and looked at me till I was embarrassed, she stood stock still in the dusty hot road and looked at me till I was embarrassed. But listen to this. She had a naked child with her, a little naked girl with her, barely able to toddle, and after a while she set this child on the ground and give her a push and whispered something to her.

This child come toward me, barely able t' walk, come toddling up to me and—

Jesus, it makes you sick t' remember a thing like this! It stuck out its hand and tried to unbutton my trousers!

That child was not yet five! Can you believe me? Or do you think that I am making this up? I wint back to the hotel and said to Big Mama, Git packed! We're clearing out of this country. . . .

BRICK: Big Daddy, you're on a talkin' jag tonight.

BIG DADDY (*ignoring this remark*): Yes, sir, that's how it is, the human animal is a beast that dies but the fact that he's dying don't give him pity for others, no, sir, it—

—Did you say something?

BRICK: Yes.

BIG DADDY: What?

BRICK: Hand me over that crutch so I can get up.

BIG DADDY: Where you goin'?

BRICK: I'm takin' a little short trip to Echo Spring.

BIG DADDY: To where?

BRICK: Liquor cabinet. . . .

BIG DADDY: Yes, sir, boy—

(*He hands Brick the crutch.*)

—the human animal is a beast that dies and if he's got money he buys and buys and buys and I think the reason he buys everything he can buy is that in the back of his mind he has the crazy hope that one of his purchases will be life everlasting!—Which it never can be. . . . The human animal is a beast that—

BRICK (*at the liquor cabinet*): Big Daddy, you sure are shootin' th' breeze here tonight.

(*There is a pause and voices are heard outside.*)

BIG DADDY: I been quiet here lately, spoke not a word, just sat and stared into space. I had something heavy weighing on my mind but tonight that load was took off me. That's why I'm talking.—The sky looks diff'rent to me. . . .

BRICK: You know what I like to hear most?

BIG DADDY: What?

BRICK: Solid quiet. Perfect unbroken quiet.

BIG DADDY: Why?

BRICK: Because it's more peaceful.

BIG DADDY: Man, you'll hear a lot of that in the grave.

(*He chuckles agreeably.*)

BRICK: Are you through talkin' to me?

BIG DADDY: Why are you so anxious to shut me up?

BRICK: Well, sir, ever so often you say to me, Brick, I want to have a talk with you, but when we talk, it never materializes. Nothing is said. You sit in a chair and gas about this and that and I look like I listen. I try to look like I listen, but I don't listen, not much. Communication is—awful hard between people an'—somehow between you and me, it just don't—

BIG DADDY: Have you ever been scared? I mean have you ever felt downright terror of something?

(*He gets up.*)

Just one moment. I'm going to close these doors. . . .

(*He closes doors on gallery as if he were going to tell an important secret.*)

BRICK: What?

BIG DADDY: Brick?

BRICK: Huh?

BIG DADDY: Son, I thought I had it!

BRICK: Had what? Had what, Big Daddy?

BIG DADDY: Cancer!

BRICK: Oh . . .

BIG DADDY: I thought the old man made out of bones had laid his cold and heavy hand on my shoulder!

BRICK: Well, Big Daddy, you kept a tight mouth about it.

BIG DADDY: A pig squeals. A man keeps a tight mouth about it, in spite of a man not having a pig's advantage.

BRICK: What advantage is that?

BIG DADDY: Ignorance—of mortality—is a comfort. A man don't have that comfort, he's the only living thing that conceives of death, that knows what it is. The others go without knowing which is the way that anything living should go, go without knowing, without any knowledge of it, and yet a pig squeals, but a man sometimes, he can keep a tight mouth about it. Sometimes he—

(*There is a deep, smoldering ferocity in the old man.*)

—can keep a tight mouth about it. I wonder if—

BRICK: What, Big Daddy?

BIG DADDY: A whiskey highball would injure this spastic condition?

BRICK: No, sir, it might do it good.

BIG DADDY (*grins suddenly, wolfishly*): *Jesus, I can't tell you! The sky is open! Christ, it's open again! It's open, boy, it's open!*

(*Brick looks down at his drink.*)

BRICK: You feel better, Big Daddy?

BIG DADDY: Better? Hell! I can breathe!—All of my life I been like a doubled up fist. . . .

(*He pours a drink.*)

—Poundin', smashin', drivin'!—now I'm going to loosen these doubled up hands and touch things *easy* with them. . . .

(*He spreads his hands as if caressing the air.*)

You know what I'm contemplating?

BRICK (*vaguely*): No, sir. What are you contemplating?

BIG DADDY: Ha ha!—*Pleasure!*—pleasure with *women!*

(*Brick's smile fades a little but lingers.*)

Brick, this stuff burns me!—

—Yes, boy. I'll tell you something that you might not guess. I still have desire for women and this is my sixty-fifth birthday.

BRICK: I think that's mighty remarkable, Big Daddy.

BIG DADDY: Remarkable?

BRICK: *Admirable*, Big Daddy.

BIG DADDY: You're damn right it is, remarkable and admirable both. I realize now that I never had me enough. I let many chances slip by because of scruples about it, scruples, convention—crap. . . . All that stuff is bull, bull, bull!—It took the shadow of death to make me see it. Now that shadow's lifted, I'm going to cut loose and have, what is it they call it, have me a—ball!

BRICK: A ball, huh?

BIG DADDY: That's right, a ball, a ball! Hell!—I slept with Big Mama till, let's see, five years ago, till I was sixty and she was fifty-eight, and never even liked her, never did!

(*The phone has been ringing down the hall. Big Mama enters, exclaiming:*)

BIG MAMA: Don't you men hear that phone ring? I heard it way out on the gall'ry.

BIG DADDY: There's five rooms off this front gall'ry that you could go through. Why do you go through this one?

(*Big Mama makes a playful face as she bustles out the hall door.*)

Hunh!—Why, when Big Mama goes out of a room, I can't remember what that woman looks like, but when Big Mama comes back into the room, boy, then I see what she looks like, and I wish I didn't!

(*Bends over laughing at this joke till it hurts his guts and he straightens with a grimace. The laugh subsides to a chuckle as he puts the liquor glass a little distrustfully down on the table.*

(*Brick has risen and hobbled to the gallery doors.*)

Hey! Where you goin'?

BRICK: Out for a breather.

BIG DADDY: Not yet you ain't. Stay here till this talk is finished, young fellow.

BRICK: I thought it was finished, Big Daddy.

BIG DADDY: It ain't even begun.

BRICK: My mistake. Excuse me. I just wanted to feel that river breeze.

BIG DADDY: Turn on the ceiling fan and set back down in that chair.

(*Big Mama's voice rises, carrying down the hall.*)

BIG MAMA: Miss Sally, you're a case! You're a caution, Miss Sally. Why didn't you give me a chance to explain it to you?

BIG DADDY: Jesus, she's talking to my old maid sister again.

BIG MAMA: Well, goodbye, now, Miss Sally. You come down real soon, Big Daddy's dying to see you! Yaisss, goodbye, Miss Sally. . . .

(*She hangs up and bellows with mirth. Big Daddy groans and covers his ears as she approaches.*

(*Bursting in:*)

Big Daddy, that was Miss Sally callin' from Memphis again! You know what she done, Big Daddy? She called her doctor in Memphis to git him to tell her what that spastic thing is! Ha-*HAAAA!*—And called back to tell me how relieved she was that— Hey! Let me in!

(*Big Daddy has been holding the door half closed against her.*)

BIG DADDY: Naw I ain't. I told you not to come and go through this room. You just back out and go through those five other rooms.

BIG MAMA: Big Daddy? Big Daddy? Oh, big Daddy!—You didn't mean those things you said to me, did you?

(*He shuts door firmly against her but she still calls.*)

Sweetheart? Sweetheart? Big Daddy? You didn't mean those awful things you said to me?—I know you didn't. I know you didn't mean those things in your heart. . . .

(*The childlike voice fades with a sob and her heavy footsteps retreat down the hall. Brick has risen once more on his crutches and starts for the gallery again.*)

BIG DADDY: All I ask of that woman is that she leave me alone. But she can't admit to herself that she makes me sick. That comes of having slept with her too many years. Should of quit much sooner but that old woman she never got enough of it—and I was good in bed . . . I never should of wasted so much of it on her. . . . They say you got just so many and each one is numbered. Well, I got a few left in me, a few, and I'm going to pick me a good one to spend 'em on! I'm going to pick me a choice one, I don't care how much she costs, I'll smother her in—minks! Ha ha! I'll strip her naked and smother her in minks and choke her with diamonds! Ha ha! I'll strip her naked and choke her with diamonds and smother her with minks and hump her from hell to breakfast. *Ha aha ha ha ha!*

MAE (*gaily at door*): Who's that laughin' in there?

GOOPER: Is Big Daddy laughin' in there?

BIG DADDY: Crap!—them two—*drips.* . . .

(*He goes over and touches Brick's shoulder.*)

Yes, son. Brick, boy.—I'm—*happy!* I'm happy, son, I'm happy!

(*He chokes a little and bits his under lip, pressing his head quickly, shyly against his son's head and then, coughing with embarrassment, goes uncertainly back to the table where he set down the glass. He drinks and makes a grimace as it burns his guts. Brick sighs and rises with effort.*)

What makes you so restless? Have you got ants in your britches?

BRICK: Yes, sir . . .

BIG DADDY: Why?

BRICK: —Something—hasn't—happened. . . .

BIG DADDY: Yeah? What is that!

BRICK (*sadly*): —the click. . . .

BIG DADDY: Did you say click?

BRICK: Yes, click.

BIG DADDY: What click?

BRICK: A click that I get in my head that makes me peaceful.

BIG DADDY: I sure in hell don't know what you're talking about, but it disturbs me.

BRICK: It's just a mechanical thing.

BIG DADDY: What is a mechanical thing?

BRICK: This click that I get in my head that makes me peaceful. I got to drink till I get it. It's just a mechanical thing, something like a—like a—like a—

BIG DADDY: Like a—

BRICK: Switch clicking off in my head, turning the hot light off and the cool night on and—

(*He looks up, smiling sadly.*)

—all of a sudden there's—peace!

BIG DADDY (*whistles long and soft with astonishment; he goes back to Brick and clasps his son's two shoulders*): Jesus! I didn't know it had gotten that bad with you. Why, boy, you're—*alcoholic!*

BRICK: That's the truth, Big Daddy. I'm alcoholic.

BIG DADDY: This shows how I—let things go!

BRICK: I have to hear that little click in my head that makes me peaceful. Usually I hear it sooner than this, sometimes as early as—noon, but—

—Today it's—dilatory. . . .

—I just haven't got the right level of alcohol in my bloodstream yet!

(*This last statement is made with energy as he freshens his drink.*)

BIG DADDY: Uh—huh. Expecting death made me blind. I didn't have no idea that a son of mine was turning into a drunkard under my nose.

BRICK (*gently*): Well, now you do, Big Daddy, the news has penetrated.

BIG DADDY: UH-huh, yes, now I do, the news has—penetrated. . . .

BRICK: And so if you'll excuse me—

BIG DADDY: No, I won't excuse you.

BRICK: —I'd better sit by myself till I hear that click in my head, it's just a mechanical thing but it don't happen except when I'm alone or talking to no one. . . .

BIG DADDY: You got a long, long time to sit still, boy, and talk to no one, but now you're talkin' to me. At least I'm talking to you. And you set there and listen until I tell you the conversation is over!

BRICK: But this talk is like all the others we've ever had together in our lives! It's nowhere, nowhere!—it's—it's *painful*, Big Daddy. . . .

BIG DADDY: All right, then let it be painful, but don't you move from that chair!—I'm going to remove that crutch. . . .

(*He seizes the crutch and tosses it across room.*)

BRICK: I can hop on one foot, and if I fall, I can crawl!

BIG DADDY: If you ain't careful you're gonna crawl off this plantation and then, by Jesus, you'll have to hustle your drinks along Skid Row!

BRICK: That'll come, Big Daddy.

BIG DADDY: Naw, it won't. You're my son and I'm going to straighten you out; now that *I'm* straightened out, I'm going to straighten out you!

BRICK: Yeah?

BIG DADDY: Today the report come in from Ochsner Clinic. Y'know what they told me?

(*His face glows with triumph.*)

The only thing that they could detect with all the instruments of science in that great hospital is a little spastic condition of the colon! And nerves torn to pieces by all that worry about it.

(*A little girl bursts into room with a sparkler clutched in each fist, hops and shrieks like a monkey gone mad and rushes back out again as Big Daddy strikes at her.*

(*Silence. The two men stare at each other. A woman laughs gaily outside.*)

I want you to know I breathed a sigh of relief almost as powerful as the Vicksburg tornado!

BRICK: You weren't ready to go?

BIG DADDY: GO WHERE?—crap. . . .

—When you are gone from here, boy, you are long gone and no where! The human machine is not no different from the animal machine or the fish machine or the bird machine or the reptile machine or the insect machine! It's just a whole God damn lot more complicated and consequently more trouble to keep together. Yep. I thought I had it. The earth shook under my foot, the sky come down like the black lid of a kettle and I couldn't breathe!—

Today!!—that lid was lifted, I drew my first free breath in—how many years?—*God!—three.* . . .

(*There is laughter outside, running footsteps, the soft, plushy sound and light of exploding rockets.*

(*Brick stares at him soberly for a long moment; then makes a sort of startled sound in his nostrils and springs up on one foot and hops across the room to grab his crutch, swinging on the furniture for support. He gets the crutch and flees as if in horror for the gallery. His father seizes him by the sleeve of his white silk pajamas.*)

Stay here, you son of a bitch!—till I say go!

BRICK: I can't.

BIG DADDY: You sure in hell will, God damn it.

BRICK: No, I can't. We talk, you talk, in—circles! We get no where, no where! It's always the same, you say you want to talk to me and don't have a ruttin' thing to say to me!

BIG DADDY: Nothin' to say when I'm tellin' you I'm going to live when I thought I was dying?!

BRICK: Oh—*that!*—Is that what you have to say to me?

BIG DADDY: Why, you son of a bitch! Ain't that, ain't that—*important*?!

BRICK: Well, you said that, that's said, and now I—

BIG DADDY: Now you set back down.

BRICK: You're all balled up, you—

BIG DADDY: I ain't balled up!

BRICK: You are, you're all balled up!

BIG DADDY: Don't tell me what I am, you drunken whelp! I'm going to tear this coat sleeve off if you don't set down!

BRICK: Big Daddy—

BIG DADDY: Do what I tell you! I'm the boss here, now! I want you to know I'm back in the driver's seat now!

(*Big Mama rushes in, clutching her great heaving bosom.*)

What in hell do you want in here, Big Mama?

BIG MAMA: Oh, Big Daddy! Why are you shouting like that? I just cain't *stainnnnnnnd*—it. . . .

BIG DADDY (*raising the back of his hand above his head*): *GIT!* —outa here.

(*She rushes back out, sobbing.*)

BRICK (*softly, sadly*): *Christ. . . .*
BIG DADDY (*fiercely*): Yeah! Christ!—is right . . .

(*Brick breaks loose and hobbles toward the gallery.*
(*Big Daddy jerks his crutch from under Brick so he steps with the injured ankle. He utters a hissing cry of anguish, clutches a chair and pulls it over on top of him on the floor.*)

Son of a—tub of—hog fat. . . .
BRICK: Big Daddy! Give me my crutch.

(*Big Daddy throws the crutch out of reach.*)

Give me that crutch, Big Daddy.
BIG DADDY: Why do you drink?
BRICK: Don't know, give me my crutch!
BIG DADDY: You better think why you drink or give up drinking!
BRICK: Will you please give me my crutch so I can get up off this floor?
BIG DADDY: First you answer my question. Why do you drink? Why are you throwing your life away, boy, like somethin' disgusting you picked up on the street?
BRICK (*getting onto his knees*): Big Daddy, I'm in pain, I stepped on that foot.
BIG DADDY: Good! I'm glad you're not too numb with the liquor in you to feel some pain!
BRICK: You—spilled my—drink . . .
BIG DADDY: I'll make a bargain with you. You tell me why you drink and I'll hand you one. I'll pour you the liquor myself and hand it to you.
BRICK: Why do I drink?
BIG DADDY: Yea! Why?
BRICK: Give me a drink and I'll tell you.
BIG DADDY: Tell me first!
BRICK: I'll tell you in one word.
BIG DADDY: What word?
BRICK: DISGUST!

(*The clock chimes softly, sweetly. Big Daddy gives it a short, outraged glance.*)

Now how about that drink?

BIG DADDY: What are you disgusted with? You got to tell me that, first. Otherwise being disgusted don't make no sense!

BRICK: Give me my crutch.

BIG DADDY: You heard me, you got to tell me what I asked you first.

BRICK: I told you, I said to kill my disgust!

BIG DADDY: DISGUST WITH WHAT!

BRICK: You strike a hard bargain.

BIG DADDY: What are you disgusted with?—an' I'll pass you the liquor.

BRICK: I can hop on one foot, and if I fall, I can crawl.

BIG DADDY: You want liquor that bad?

BRICK (*dragging himself up, clinging to bedstead*): Yeah, I want it that bad.

BIG DADDY: If I give you a drink, will you tell me what it is you're disgusted with, Brick?

BRICK: Yes, sir, I will try to.

(*The old man pours him a drink and solemnly passes it to him.*

(*There is silence as Brick drinks.*)

Have you ever heard the word "mendacity"?

BIG DADDY: Sure. Mendacity is one of them five dollar words that cheap politicians throw back and forth at each other.

BRICK: You know what it means?

BIG DADDY: Don't it mean lying and liars?

BRICK: Yes, sir, lying and liars.

BIG DADDY: Has someone been lying to you?

CHILDREN (*chanting in chorus offstage*):

We want Big Dad-dee!
We want Big Dad-dee!

(*Gooper appears in the gallery door.*)

GOOPER: Big Daddy, the kiddies are shouting for you out there.

BIG DADDY (*fiercely*): Keep out, Gooper!

GOOPER: 'Scuse *me!*

(*Big Daddy slams the doors after Gooper.*)

BIG DADDY: Who's been lying to you, has Margaret been lying to you, has your wife been lying to you about something, Brick?

BRICK: Not her. That wouldn't matter.

BIG DADDY: Then who's been lying to you, and what about?

BRICK: No one single person and no one lie. . . .

BIG DADDY: Then what, what then, for Christ's sake?

BRICK: —The whole, the whole—thing. . . .

BIG DADDY: Why are you rubbing your head? You got a headache?

BRICK: No, I'm tryin' to—

BIG DADDY: —Concentrate, but you can't because your brain's all soaked with liquor, is that the trouble? Wet brain!

(*He snatches the glass from Brick's hand.*)

What do you know about this mendacity thing? Hell! I could write a book on it! Don't you know that? I could write a book on it and still not cover the subject? Well, I could, I could write a goddam book on it and still not cover the subject anywhere near enough!!—Think of all the lies I got to put up with!—Pretenses! Ain't that mendacity? Having to pretend stuff you don't think or feel or have any idea of? Having for instance to act like I care for Big Mama!—I haven't been able to stand the sight, sound, or smell of that woman for forty years now!—even when I *laid* her!—regular as a piston. . . .

Pretend to love that son of a bitch of a Gooper and his wife Mae and those five same screechers out there like parrots in a jungle? Jesus! Can't stand to look at 'em!

Church!—it bores the Bejesus out of me but I go!—I go an' sit there and listen to the fool preacher!

Clubs!—Elks! Masons! Rotary!—*crap!*

(*A spasm of pain makes him clutch his belly. He sinks into a chair and his voice is softer and hoarser.*)

You I *do* like for some reason, did always have some kind of real feeling for—affection—respect—yes, always. . . .

You and being a success as a planter is all I ever had any devotion to in my whole life!—and that's the truth. . . .

I don't know why, but it is!

I've lived with mendacity!—Why can't *you* live with it? Hell, you *got* to live with it, there's nothing *else* to *live* with except mendacity, is there?

BRICK: Yes, sir. Yes, sir there is something else that you can live with!

BIG DADDY: What?

BRICK (*lifting his glass*): This!—Liquor. . . .

BIG DADDY: That's not living, that's dodging away from life.

BRICK: I want to dodge away from it.

BIG DADDY: Then why don't you kill yourself, man?

BRICK: I like to drink. . . .

BIG DADDY: Oh, God, I can't talk to you. . . .

BRICK: I'm sorry, Big Daddy.

BIG DADDY: Not as sorry as I am. I'll tell you something. A little while back when I thought my number was up—

(*This speech should have torrential pace and fury.*)

—before I found out it was just this—spastic—colon. I thought about you. Should I or should I not, if the jig was up, give you this place when I go—since I hate Gooper an' Mae an' know that they hate me, and since all five same monkeys are little Maes an' Goopers.—And I thought, No!—Then I thought, Yes!—I couldn't make up my mind. I hate Gooper and his five same monkeys and that bitch Mae! Why should I turn over twenty-eight thousand acres of the richest land this side of the valley Nile to not my kind?—But why in hell, on the other hand, Brick—should I subsidize a goddam fool on the bottle?—Liked or not liked, well, maybe even—*loved!*—Why should I do that?—Subsidize worthless behavior? Rot? Corruption?

BRICK (*smiling*): I understand.

BIG DADDY: Well, if you do, you're smarter than I am, God damn it, because I don't understand. And this I will tell you frankly. I didn't make up my mind at all on that question and still to this day I ain't made out no will!—Well, now I don't *have* to. The pressure is gone. I can just wait and see if you pull yourself together or if you don't.

BRICK: That's right, Big Daddy.

BIG DADDY: You sound like you thought I was kidding.

BRICK (*rising*): No, sir, I know you're not kidding.

BIG DADDY: But you don't care—?

BRICK (*hobbling toward the gallery door*): No, sir, I don't care. . . .

Now how about taking a look at your birthday fireworks and getting some of that cool breeze off the river?

(*He stands in the gallery doorway as the night sky turns pink and green and gold with successive flashes of light.*)

BIG DADDY: *WAIT!*—Brick. . . .

(*His voice drops. Suddenly there is something shy, almost tender, in his restraining gesture.*)

Don't let's—leave it like this, like them other talks we've had, we've always—talked around things, we've—just talked around things for some rutten reason, I don't know what, it's always like something was left not spoken, something avoided because neither of us was honest enough with the—other. . . .

BRICK: I never lied to you, Big Daddy.

BIG DADDY: Did I ever to *you*?

BRICK: No, sir. . . .

BIG DADDY: Then there is at least two people that never lied to each other.

BRICK: But we've never *talked* to each other.

BIG DADDY: We can *now*.

BRICK: Big Daddy, there don't seem to be anything much to say.

BIG DADDY: You say that you drink to kill your disgust with lying.

BRICK: You said to give you a reason.

BIG DADDY: Is liquor the only thing that'll kill this disgust?

BRICK: Now. Yes.

BIG DADDY: But not once, huh?

BRICK: Not when I was still young an' believing. A drinking man's someone who wants to forget he isn't still young an' believing.

BIG DADDY: Believing what?

BRICK: Believing. . . .

BIG DADDY: Believing *what*?

BRICK (*stubbornly evasive*): Believing. . . .

BIG DADDY: I don't know what the hell you mean by believing and I don't think you know what you mean by believing, but if you still got sports in your blood, go back to sports announcing and—

BRICK: Sit in a glass box watching games I can't play? Describing what I can't do while players do it? Sweating out their disgust and confusion in contests I'm not fit for? Drinkin' a coke, half bourbon, so I can stand it? That's no goddam good any more, no help—time just outran me, Big Daddy—got there first . . .

BIG DADDY: I think you're passing the buck.

BRICK: You know many drinkin' men?

BIG DADDY (*with a slight, charming smile*): I have known a fair number of that species.

BRICK: Could any of them tell you why he drank?

BIG DADDY: Yep, you're passin' the buck to things like time and disgust with "mendacity" and—crap!—if you got to use that kind of language about a thing, it's ninety-proof bull, and I'm not buying any.

BRICK: I had to give you a reason to get a drink!

BIG DADDY: You started drinkin' when your friend Skipper died.

(*Silence for five beats. Then Brick makes a startled movement, reaching for his crutch.*)

BRICK: What are you suggesting?

BIG DADDY: I'm suggesting nothing.

(*The shuffle and clop of Brick's rapid hobble away from his father's steady, grave attention.*)

—But Gooper an' Mae suggested that there was something not right exactly in your—

BRICK (*stopping short downstage as if backed to a wall*): "Not right"?

BIG DADDY: Not, well, exactly *normal* in your friendship with—

BRICK: They suggested that, too? I thought that was Maggie's suggestion.

(Brick's detachment is at last broken through. His heart is accelerated; his forehead sweat-beaded; his breath becomes more rapid and his voice hoarse. The thing they're discussing, timidly and painfully on the side of Big Daddy, fiercely, violently on Brick's side, is the inadmissible thing that Skipper died to disavow between them. The fact that if it existed it had to be disavowed to "keep face" in the world they lived in, may be at the heart of the "mendacity" that Brick drinks to kill his disgust with. It may be the root of his collapse. Or maybe it is only a single manifestation of it, not even the most important. The bird that I hope to catch in the net of this play is not the solution of one man's psychological problem. I'm trying to catch the true quality of experience in a group of people, that cloudy, flickering, evanescent—fiercely charged!—interplay of live human beings in the thundercloud of a common crisis. Some mystery should be left in the revelation of character in a play, just as a great deal of mystery is always left in the revelation of character in life, even in one's own character to himself. This does not absolve the playwright of his duty to observe and probe as clearly and deeply as he legitimately *can: but it should steer him away from "pat" conclusions, facile definitions which make a play just a play, not a snare for the truth of human experience.*

(The following scene should be played with great concentration, with most of the power leashed but palpable in what is left unspoken.)

Who else's suggestion is it, is it *yours*? How many others thought that Skipper and I were—

BIG DADDY (*gently*): Now, hold on, hold on a minute, son.—I knocked around in my time.

BRICK: What's that got to do with—

BIG DADDY: I said 'Hold on!'—I bummed, I bummed this country till I was—

BRICK: Whose suggestion, who else's suggestion is it?

BIG DADDY: Slept in hobo jungles and railroad Y's and flophouses in all cities before I—

BRICK: Oh, *you* think so, too, you call me your son and a queer. Oh! Maybe that's why you put Maggie and me in this room that was Jack Straw's and Peter Ochello's, in which that pair of old sisters slept in a double bed where both of 'em died!

BIG DADDY: *Now just don't go throwing rocks at—*

(*Suddenly Reverend Tooker appears in the gallery doors, his head slightly, playfully, fatuously cocked, with a practised clergyman's smile, sincere as a bird-call blown on a hunter's whistle, the living embodiment of the pious, conventional lie.*

(*Big Daddy gasps a little at this perfectly timed, but incongruous, apparition.*)

—What're you lookin' for, Preacher?

REVEREND TOOKER: The gentleman's lavatory, ha ha!—heh, heh . . .

BIG DADDY (*with strained courtesy*): —Go back out and walk down to the other end of the gallery, Reverend Tooker, and use the bathroom connected with my bedroom, and if you can't find it, ask them where it is!

REVEREND TOOKER: Ah, thanks.

(*He goes out with a deprecatory chuckle.*)

BIG DADDY: It's hard to talk in this place . . .

BRICK: Son of a—!

BIG DADDY (*leaving a lot unspoken*): —I seen all things and understood a lot of them, till 1910. Christ, the year that— I had worn my shoes through, hocked my— I hopped off a yellow dog freight car half a mile down the road, slept in a wagon of cotton outside the gin— Jack Straw an' Peter Ochello took me in. Hired me to manage this place which grew into this one.—When Jack Straw died—why, old Peter Ochello quit eatin' like a dog does when its master's dead, and died, too!

BRICK: Christ!

BIG DADDY: I'm just saying I understand such—

BRICK (*violently*): Skipper is dead. I have not quit eating!

BIG DADDY: No, but you started drinking.

(*Brick wheels on his crutch and hurls his glass across the room shouting.*)

BRICK: YOU THINK SO, TOO?

BIG DADDY: *Shhh!*

(*Footsteps run on the gallery. There are women's calls.*
(*Big Daddy goes toward the door.*)

Go way!—Just broke a glass. . . .

(*Brick is transformed, as if a quiet mountain blew suddenly up in volcanic flame.*)

BRICK: You think so, too? You think so, too? You think me an' Skipper did, did, did!—*sodomy!*—together?
BIG DADDY: Hold—!
BRICK: That what you—
BIG DADDY: —*ON*—a minute!
BRICK: You think we did dirty things between us, Skipper an'—
BIG DADDY: Why are you shouting like that? Why are you—
BRICK: —Me, is that what you think of Skipper, is that—
BIG DADDY: —so excited? I don't think nothing. I don't know nothing. I'm simply telling you what—
BRICK: You think that Skipper and me were a pair of dirty old men?
BIG DADDY: Now that's—
BRICK: Straw? Ochello? A couple of—
BIG DADDY: Now just—
BRICK: —ducking sissies? Queers? Is that what you—
BIG DADDY: Shhh.
BRICK: —think?

(*He loses his balance and pitches to his knees without noticing the pain. He grabs the bed and drags himself up.*)

BIG DADDY: Jesus!—Whew. . . . Grab my hand!
BRICK: Naw, I don't want your hand. . . .
BIG DADDY: Well, I want yours. Git up!

(*He draws him up, keeps an arm about him with concern and affection.*)

You broken out in a sweat! You're panting like you'd run a race with—
BRICK (*freeing himself from his father's hold*): Big Daddy, you shock me, Big Daddy, you, you—*shock* me! Talkin' so—

(*He turns away from his father.*)

—casually!—about a—thing like that . . .

—Don't you know how people *feel* about things like that? How, how *disgusted* they are by things like that? Why, at Ole Miss when it was discovered a pledge to our fraternity, Skipper's and mine, did a, *attempted* to do a, unnatural thing with—

We not only dropped him like a hot rock!—We told him to git off the campus, and he did, he got!—All the way to—

(*He halts, breathless.*)

BIG DADDY: —Where?

BRICK: —North Africa, last I heard!

BIG DADDY: Well, I have come back from further away than that, I have just now returned from the other side of the moon, death's country, son, and I'm not easy to shock by anything here.

(*He comes downstage and faces out.*)

Always, anyhow, lived with too much space around me to be infected by ideas of other people. One thing you can grow on a big place more important than cotton!—is *tolerance!*—I grown it.

(*He returns toward Brick.*)

BRICK: Why can't exceptional friendship, *real, real, deep, deep friendship!* between two men be respected as something clean and decent without being thought of as—

BIG DADDY: It can, it is, for God's sake.

BRICK: —*Fairies.* . . .

(*In his utterance of this word, we gauge the wide and profound reach of the conventional mores he got from the world that crowned him with early laurel.*)

BIG DADDY: I told Mae an' Gooper—

BRICK: Frig Mae and Gooper, frig all dirty lies and liars!—Skipper and me had a clean, true thing between us!—had a clean friendship, practically all our lives, till Maggie got the idea you're talking about. Normal? No!—It was too rare to be normal, any true thing between two people is too rare to be normal. Oh, once in a while he put his hand on my shoulder or I'd put mine on his, oh, maybe even, when we were touring the country in pro-football an' shared hotel-rooms we'd reach across the space between the two beds and shake hands to say goodnight, yeah, one or two times we—

BIG DADDY: Brick, nobody thinks that that's not normal!

BRICK: Well, they're mistaken, it was! It was a pure an' true thing an' that's not normal.

(*They both stare straight at each other for a long moment. The tension breaks and both turn away as if tired.*)

BIG DADDY: Yeah, it's—hard t'—talk. . . .

BRICK: All right, then, let's—let it go. . . .

BIG DADDY: Why did Skipper crack up? Why have you?

(*Brick looks back at his father again. He has already decided, without knowing that he has made this decision, that he is going to tell his father that he is dying of cancer. Only this could even the score between them: one inadmissible thing in return for another.*)

BRICK (*ominously*): All right. You're asking for it, Big Daddy. We're finally going to have the real true talk you wanted. It's too late to stop it, now, we got to carry it through and cover every subject.

(*He hobbles back to the liquor cabinet.*)

Uh-huh.

(*He opens the ice bucket and picks up the silver tongs with slow admiration of their frosty brightness.*)

Maggie declares that Skipper and I went into pro-football after we left "Ole Miss" because we were scared to grow up . . .

(*He moves downstage with the shuffle and clop of a cripple on a crutch. As Margaret did when her speech became "recitative," he looks out into the house, commanding its attention by his direct, concentrated gaze—a broken, "tragically elegant" figure telling simply as much as he knows of "the Truth":*)

—Wanted to— keep on tossing—those long, long!—high, high!—passes that—couldn't be intercepted except by time, the aerial attack that made us famous! And so we did, we did, we kept it up for one season, that aerial attack, we held it high!—Yeah, but—

—that summer, Maggie, she laid the law down to me, said, Now or never, and so I married Maggie. . . .

BIG DADDY: How was Maggie in bed?

BRICK (*wryly*): Great! the greatest!

(*Big Daddy nods as if he thought so.*)

She went on the road that fall with the Dixie Stars. Oh, she made a great show of being the world's best sport. She wore a—wore a—tall bearskin cap! A shako, they call it, a dyed moleskin coat, a moleskin coat dyed red!—Cut up crazy! Rented hotel ballrooms for victory celebrations, wouldn't cancel them when it—turned out—defeat. . . .

MAGGIE THE CAT! Ha ha!

(*Big Daddy nods.*)

—But Skipper, he had some fever which came back on him which doctors couldn't explain and I got that injury—turned out to be just a shadow on the X-ray plate—and a touch of bursitis. . . .

I lay in a hospital bed, watched our games on TV, saw Maggie on the bench next to Skipper when he was hauled out of a game for stumbles, fumbles!—Burned me up the way she hung on his arm!—Y'know, I think that Maggie had always felt sort of left out because she and me never got any closer together than two people just get in bed, which is not much closer than two cats on a—fence humping. . . .

So! She took this time to work on poor dumb Skipper. He was a less than average student at Ole Miss, you know that, don't you?!—Poured in his mind the dirty, false idea that what we were, him and me, was a frustrated case of that ole pair of sisters that lived in this room, Jack Straw and Peter Ochello!—He, poor Skipper, went to bed with Maggie to prove it wasn't true, and when it didn't work out, he thought it *was* true!—Skipper broke in two like a rotten stick—nobody ever turned so fast to a lush—or died of it so quick. . . .

—Now are you satisfied?

(*Big Daddy has listened to this story, dividing the grain from the chaff. Now he looks at his son.*)

BIG DADDY: Are *you* satisfied?

BRICK: With what?

BIG DADDY: That half-ass story!

BRICK: What's half-ass about it?

BIG DADDY: Something's left out of that story. What did you leave out?

(*The phone has started ringing in the hall. As if it reminded him of something, Brick glances suddenly toward the sound and says:*)

BRICK: Yes!—I left out a long-distance call which I had from Skipper, in which he made a drunken confession to me and on which I hung up!—last time we spoke to each other in our lives. . . .

(*Muted ring stops as someone answers phone in a soft, indistinct voice in hall.*)

BIG DADDY: You hung up?

BRICK: Hung up. Jesus! Well—

BIG DADDY: Anyhow now!—we have tracked down the lie with which you're disgusted and which you are drinking to kill your disgust with, Brick. You been passing the buck. This disgust with mendacity is disgust with yourself.

You!—dug the grave of your friend and kicked him in it!—before you'd face truth with him!

BRICK: *His* truth, not *mine*!

BIG DADDY: His truth, okay! But you wouldn't face it with him!

BRICK: Who *can* face truth? Can *you*?

BIG DADDY: Now don't start passin' the rotten buck again, boy!

BRICK: *How about these birthday congratulations, these many, many happy returns of the day, when ev'rybody but you knows there won't be any!*

(*Whoever has answered the hall phone lets out a high, shrill laugh; the voice becomes audible saying: "no, no, you got it all wrong! Upside down! Are you crazy?"*)

(*Brick suddenly catches his breath as he realized that he has made a shocking disclosure. He hobbles a few paces, then freezes, and without looking at his father's shocked face, says:*)

Let's, let's—go out, now, and—

(*Big Daddy moves suddenly forward and grabs hold of the boy's crutch like it was a weapon for which they were fighting for possession.*)

BIG DADDY: Oh, no, no! No one's going out! What did you start to say?

BRICK: I don't remember.

BIG DADDY: "Many happy returns when they know there won't be any"?

BRICK: Aw, hell, Big Daddy, forget it. Come on out on the gallery and look at the fireworks they're shooting off for your birthday. . . .

BIG DADDY: First you finish that remark you were makin' before you cut off. "Many happy returns when they know there won't be any"?—Ain't that what you just said?

BRICK: Look, now. I can get around without that crutch if I have to but it would be a lot easier on the furniture an' glassware if I didn' have to go swinging along like Tarzan of th'—

BIG DADDY: FINISH! WHAT YOU WAS SAYIN'!

(*An eerie green glow shows in sky behind him.*)

BRICK (*sucking the ice in his glass, speech becoming thick*): Leave th' place to Gooper and Mae an' their five little same little monkeys. All I want is—

BIG DADDY: "LEAVE TH' PLACE," did you say?

BRICK (*vaguely*): All twenty-eight thousand acres of the richest land this side of the valley Nile.

BIG DADDY: Who said I was "leaving the place" to Gooper or anybody? This is my sixty-fifth birthday! I got fifteen years or twenty years left in me! I'll outlive *you*! I'll bury you an' have to pay for your coffin!

BRICK: Sure. Many happy returns. Now let's go watch the fireworks, come on, let's—

BIG DADDY: Lying, have they been lying? About the report from th'—clinic? Did they, did they—find something?—*Cancer.* Maybe?

BRICK: Mendacity is a system that we live in. Liquor is one way out an' death's the other. . . .

(*He takes the crutch from Big Daddy's loose grip and swings out on the gallery leaving the doors open.*

(*A song, "Pick a Bale of Cotton," is heard.*)

MAE (*appearing in door*): *Oh, Big Daddy, the field-hands are singin' fo' you!*

BIG DADDY (*shouting hoarsely*): BRICK! BRICK!

MAE: He's outside drinkin', Big Daddy.

BIG DADDY: *BRICK!*

(*Mae retreats, awed by the passion of his voice. Children call Brick in tones mocking Big Daddy. His face crumbles like broken yellow plaster about to fall into dust.*

(*There is a glow in the sky. Brick swings back through the doors, slowly, gravely, quite soberly.*)

BRICK: I'm sorry, Big Daddy. My head don't work any more and it's hard for me to understand how anybody could care if he lived or died or was dying or cared about anything but whether or not there was liquor left in the bottle and so I said what I said without thinking. In some ways I'm no better than the others, in some ways worse because I'm less alive. Maybe it's being alive that makes them lie, and being almost *not* alive makes me sort of accidentally truthful—I don't know but—anyway—we've been friends . . .

—And being friends is telling each other the truth. . . .

(*There is a pause.*)

You told *me*! I told *you*!

(*A child rushes into the room and grabs a fistful of firecrackers and runs out again.*)

CHILD (*screaming*): Bang, bang, bang, bang, bang, bang, bang, bang, bang!

BIG DADDY (*slowly and passionately*): CHRIST—DAMN—ALL—LYING SONS OF—LYING BITCHES!

(*He straightens at last and crosses to the inside door. At the door he turns and looks back as if he had some desperate question he couldn't put into words. Then he nods reflectively and says in a hoarse voice:*)

Yes, all liars, all liars, all lying dying liars!

(*This is said slowly, slowly, with a fierce revulsion. He goes on out.*)

—Lying! Dying! Liars!

(*His voice dies out. There is the sound of a child being slapped. It rushes, hideously bawling, through room and out the hall door.*

(*Brick remains motionless as the lights dim out and the curtain falls.*)

Curtain

ACT THREE

There is no lapse of time.
Mae enters with Reverend Tooker.

MAE: Where is Big Daddy! Big Daddy?

BIG MAMA (*entering*): Too much smell of burnt fireworks makes me feel a little bit sick at my stomach.—Where is Big Daddy?

MAE: That's what I want to know, where has Big Daddy gone?

BIG MAMA: He must have turned in, I reckon he went to baid. . . .

(*Gooper enters.*)

GOOPER: Where is Big Daddy?

MAE: We don't know where he is!

BIG MAMA: I reckon he's gone to baid.

GOOPER: Well, then, now we can talk.
BIG MAMA: What *is* this talk, *what* talk?

(*Margaret appears on gallery, talking to Dr. Baugh.*)

MARGARET (*musically*): My family freed their slaves ten years before abolition, my great-great grandfather gave his slaves their freedom five years before the war between the States started!
MAE: Oh, for God's sake! Maggie's climbed back up in her family tree!
MARGARET (*sweetly*): What, Mae?—Oh, where's Big Daddy?!

(*The pace must be very quick. Great Southern animation.*)

BIG MAMA (*addressing them all*): I think Big Daddy was just worn out. He loves his family, he loves to have them around him, but it's a strain on his nerves. He wasn't himself tonight, Big Daddy wasn't himself, I could tell he was all worked up.
REVEREND TOOKER: I think he's remarkable.
BIG MAMA: Yaisss! Just remarkable. Did you all notice the food he ate at that table? Did you all notice the supper he put away? Why, he ate like a hawss!
GOOPER: I hope he doesn't regret it.
BIG MAMA: Why, that man—ate a huge piece of cawn-bread with molasses on it! Helped himself twice to hoppin' john.
MARGARET: Big Daddy loves hoppin' john.—We had a real country dinner.
BIG MAMA (*overlapping Margaret*): Yais, he simply adores it! An' candied yams? That man put away enough food at that table to stuff a nigger *field*-hand!
GOOPER (*with grim relish*): I hope he don't have to pay for it later on. . . .
BIG MAMA (*fiercely*): What's *that*, Gooper?
MAE: Gooper says he hopes Big Daddy doesn't suffer tonight.
BIG MAMA: Oh, shoot, Gooper says, Gooper says! Why should Big Daddy suffer for satisfying a normal appetite? There's nothin' wrong with that man but nerves, he's sound as a dollar! And now he knows he is an' that's why he ate such a supper. He had a big load off his mind, knowin' he wasn't doomed t'—what he thought he was doomed to. . . .

MARGARET (*sadly and sweetly*): Bless his old sweet soul. . . .

BIG MAMA (*vaguely*): Yais, bless his heart, wher's Brick?

MAE: Outside.

GOOPER: —Drinkin' . . .

BIG MAMA: I know he's drinkin'. You all don't have to keep tellin' *me* Brick is drinkin'. Cain't I see he's drinkin' without you continually tellin' me that boy's drinkin'?

MARGARET: Good for you, Big Mama!

(*She applauds.*)

BIG MAMA: Other people *drink* and *have* drunk an' will *drink*, as long as they make that stuff an' put it in bottles.

MARGARET: That's the truth. I never trusted a man that didn't drink.

MAE: Gooper never drinks. Don't you trust Gooper?

MARGARET: Why, Gooper, don't you drink? If I'd known you didn't drink, I wouldn't of made that remark—

BIG MAMA: *Brick?*

MARGARET: —at least not in your presence.

(*She laughs sweetly.*)

BIG MAMA: *Brick!*

MARGARET: He's still on the gall'ry. I'll go bring him in so we can talk.

BIG MAMA (*worriedly*): I don't know what this mysterious family conference is about.

(*Awkward silence. Big Mama looks from face to face, then belches slightly and mutters, "Excuse me. . . ." She opens an ornamental fan suspended about her throat, a black lace fan to go with her black lace gown and fans her wilting corsage, sniffing nervously and looking from face to face in the uncomfortable silence as Margaret calls "Brick?" and Brick sings to the moon on the gallery.*)

I don't know what's wrong here, you all have such long faces! Open that door on the hall and let some air circulate through here, will you please, Gooper?

MAE: I think we'd better leave that door closed, Big Mama, till after the talk.

BIG MAMA: Reveren' Tooker, will *you* please open that door?!

REVEREND TOOKER: I sure will, Big Mama.

MAE: I just didn't think we ought t' take any chance of Big Daddy hearin' a word of this discussion.

BIG MAMA: *I swan!* Nothing's going to be said in Big Daddy's house that he cain't hear if he wants to!

GOOPER: Well, Big Mama, it's—

(*Mae gives him a quick, hard poke to shut him up. He glares at her fiercely as she circles before him like a burlesque ballerina, raising her skinny bare arms over her head, jangling her bracelets, exclaiming:*)

MAE: *A breeze! A breeze!*

REVEREND TOOKER: I think this house is the coolest house in the Delta.—Did you all know that Halsey Banks' widow put air-conditioning units in the church and rectory at Friar's Point in memory of Halsey?

(*General conversation has resumed; everybody is chatting so that the stage sounds like a big bird-cage.*)

GOOPER: Too bad nobody cools your church off for you. I bet you sweat in that pulpit these hot Sundays, Reverend Tooker.

REVEREND TOOKER: Yes, my vestments are drenched.

MAE (*at the same time to Dr. Baugh*): You think those vitamin B_{12} injections are what they're cracked up t' be, Doc Baugh?

DOCTOR BAUGH: Well, if you want to be stuck with something I guess they're as good to be stuck with as anything else.

BIG MAMA (*at gallery door*): *Maggie, Maggie, aren't you comin' with Brick?*

MAE (*suddenly and loudly, creating a silence*): *I have a strange feeling, I have a peculiar feeling!*

BIG MAMA (*turning from gallery*): What feeling?

MAE: That Brick said somethin' he shouldn't of said t' Big Daddy.

BIG MAMA: Now what on earth could Brick of said t' Big Daddy that he shouldn't say?

GOOPER: Big Mama, there's somethin'—

MAE: NOW, WAIT!

(*She rushes up to Big Mama and gives her a quick hug and kiss. Big Mama pushes her impatiently off as the Reverend Tooker's voice rises serenely in a little pocket of silence:*)

REVEREND TOOKER: Yes, last Sunday the gold in my chasuble faded into th' purple. . . .

GOOPER: Reveren' you must of been preachin' hell's fire last Sunday!

(*He guffaws at this witticism but the Reverend is not sincerely amused. At the same time Big Mama has crossed over to Dr. Baugh and is saying to him:*)

BIG MAMA (*her breathless voice rising high-pitched above the others*): In my day they had what they call the Keeley cure for heavy drinkers. But now I understand they just take some kind of tablets, they call them "Annie Bust" tablets. But *Brick* don't need to take *nothin'*.

(*Brick appears in gallery doors with Margaret behind him.*)

BIG MAMA (*unaware of his presence behind her*): That boy is just broken up over Skipper's death. You know how poor Skipper died. They gave him a big, big dose of that sodium amytal stuff at his home and then they called the ambulance and give him another big, big dose of it at the hospital and that and all of the alcohol in his system fo' months an' months an' months just proved too much for his heart. . . . I'm scared of needles! I'm more scared of a needle than the knife. . . . I think more people have been needled out of this world than—

(*She stops short and wheels about.*)

OH!—here's Brick! My precious baby—

(*She turns upon Brick with short, fat arms extended, at the same time uttering a loud, short sob, which is both comic and touching.*

(*Brick smiles and bows slightly, making a burlesque gesture of gallantry for Maggie to pass before him into the room. Then he hobbles on his crutch directly to the liquor cabinet and there is absolute silence, with everybody looking at Brick as everybody has always looked at Brick when he spoke or moved or *appeared. One by one he drops ice cubes in his glass, then suddenly, but not quickly, looks back over his shoulder with a wry, charming smile, and says:*)

BRICK: I'm sorry! Anyone else?

BIG MAMA (*sadly*): No, son. I *wish* you wouldn't!

BRICK: I wish I didn't have to, Big Mama, but I'm still waiting for that click in my head which makes it all smooth out!

BIG MAMA: Aw, Brick, you—BREAK MY HEART!

MARGARET (*at the same time*): *Brick, go sit with Big Mama!*

BIG MAMA: I just cain't *staiiiiiiiii-nnnnnd*—it. . . .

(*She sobs.*)

MAE: Now that we're all assembled—

GOOPER: We kin talk. . . .

BIG MAMA: Breaks my heart. . . .

MARGARET: Sit with Big Mama, Brick, and hold her hand.

(*Big Mama sniffs very loudly three times, almost like three drum beats in the pocket of silence.*)

BRICK: You do that, Maggie. I'm a restless cripple. I got to stay on my crutch.

(*Brick hobbles to the gallery door; leans there as if waiting.*

(*Mae sits beside Big Mama, while Gooper moves in front and sits on the end of the couch, facing her. Reverend Tooker moves nervously into the space between them; on the other side, Dr. Baugh stands looking at nothing in particular and lights a cigar. Margaret turns away.*)

BIG MAMA: Why're you all *surroundin'* me—like this? Why're you all starin' at me like this an' makin' signs at each other?

(*Reverend Tooker steps back startled.*)

MAE: Calm yourself, Big Mama.

BIG MAMA: Calm you'self, *you'self*, Sister Woman. How could I calm myself with everyone starin' at me as if big drops of blood had broken out on m'face? What's this all about, Annh! What?

(*Gooper coughs and takes a center position.*)

GOOPER: Now, Doc Baugh.

MAE: Doc Baugh?
BRICK (*suddenly*): SHHH!—

(*Then he grins and chuckles and shakes his head regretfully.*)

—Naw!—that wasn't th' click.

GOOPER: Brick, shut up or stay out there on the gallery with your liquor! We got to talk about a serious matter. Big Mama wants to know the complete truth about the report we got today from the Ochsner Clinic.

MAE (*eagerly*): —on Big Daddy's condition!

GOOPER: Yais, on Big Daddy's condition, we got to face it.

DOCTOR BAUGH: Well. . . .

BIG MAMA (*terrified, rising*): Is there? Something? Something that I? Don't—Know?

(*In these few words, this startled, very soft, question, Big Mama reviews the history of her forty-five years with Big Daddy, her great, almost embarrassingly true-hearted and simple-minded devotion to Big Daddy, who must have had something Brick has, who made himself loved so much by the "simple expedient" of not loving enough to disturb his charming detachment, also once coupled, like Brick's, with virile beauty.*

(*Big Mama has a dignity at this moment: she almost stops being fat.*)

DOCTOR BAUGH (*after a pause, uncomfortably*): Yes?—Well—

BIG MAMA: *I!!!*—want to—*knowwwwwww*. . . .

(*Immediately she thrusts her fist to her mouth as if to deny that statement.*

(*Then, for some curious reason, she snatches the withered corsage from her breast and hurls it on the floor and steps on it with her short, fat feet.*)

—*Somebody must be lyin'!—I want to know!*

MAE: Sit down, Big Mama, sit down on this sofa.

MARGARET (*quickly*): Brick, go sit with Big Mama.

BIG MAMA: *What is it, what is it?*

DOCTOR BAUGH: I never have seen a more thorough examination than Big Daddy Pollitt was given in all my experience with the Ochsner Clinic.

GOOPER: It's one of the best in the country.
MAE: It's *THE* best in the country—bar *none*!

(*For some reason she gives Gooper a violent poke as she goes past him. He slaps at her hand without removing his eyes from his mother's face.*)

DOCTOR BAUGH: Of course they were ninety-nine and nine-tenths percent sure before they even started.
BIG MAMA: Sure of what, sure of what, sure of—*what?—what!*

(*She catches her breath in a startled sob. Mae kisses her quickly. She thrusts Mae fiercely away from her, staring at the doctor.*)

MAE: Mommy, be a brave girl!
BRICK (*in the doorway, softly*):
"By the light, by the light,
Of the sil-ve-ry mo-ooo-n . . ."
GOOPER: Shut up!—Brick.
BRICK: —Sorry. . . .

(*He wanders out on the gallery.*)

DOCTOR BAUGH: But now, you see, Big Mama, they cut a piece off this growth, a specimen of the tissue and—
BIG MAMA: Growth? You told Big Daddy—
DOCTOR BAUGH: Now wait.
BIG MAMA (*fiercely*): You told me and Big Daddy there wasn't a thing wrong with him but—
MAE: Big Mama, they always—
GOOPER: Let Doc Baugh talk, will yuh?
BIG MAMA: —little spastic condition of—

(*Her breath gives out in a sob.*)

DOCTOR BAUGH: Yes, that's what we told Big Daddy. But we had this bit of tissue run through the laboratory and I'm sorry to say the test was positive on it. It's—well—malignant. . . .

(*Pause.*)

BIG MAMA: —Cancer?! Cancer?!

(*Dr. Baugh nods gravely.*
(*Big Mama gives a long gasping cry.*)

MAE and GOOPER: Now, now, now, Big Mama, you had to know. . . .

BIG MAMA: *WHY DIDN'T THEY CUT IT OUT OF HIM? HANH? HANH?*

DOCTOR BAUGH: Involved too much, Big Mama, too many organs affected.

MAE: Big Mama, the liver's affected and so's the kidneys, both! It's gone way past what they call a—

GOOPER: A surgical risk.

MAE: —Uh-huh. . . .

(*Big Mama draws a breath like a dying gasp.*)

REVEREND TOOKER: Tch, tch, tch, tch, tch!

DOCTOR BAUGH: Yes, it's gone past the knife.

MAE: That's why he's turned yellow, Mommy!

BIG MAMA: Git away from me, git away from me, Mae!

(*She rises abruptly.*)

I want Brick! Where's Brick? Where is my only son?

MAE: Mama! Did she say "*only* son"?

GOOPER: What does that make *me*?

MAE: A sober responsible man with five precious children!—*six!*

BIG MAMA: I want Brick to tell me! Brick! Brick!

MARGARET (*rising from her reflections in a corner*): Brick was so upset he went back out.

BIG MAMA: *Brick!*

MARGARET: Mama, let *me* tell you!

BIG MAMA: No, no, leave me alone, you're not my blood!

GOOPER: *Mama, I'm your son!* Listen to *me!*

MAE: Gooper's your son, Mama, he's your first-born!

BIG MAMA: Gooper never liked Daddy.

MAE (*as if terribly shocked*): *That's not TRUE!*

(*There is a pause. The minister coughs and rises.*)

REVEREND TOOKER (*to Mae*): I think I'd better slip away at this point.

MAE (*sweetly and sadly*): Yes, Doctor Tooker, you go.

REVEREND TOOKER (*discreetly*): Goodnight, goodnight, everybody, and God bless you all . . . on this place. . . .

(*He slips out.*)

DOCTOR BAUGH: That man is a good man but lacking in tact. Talking about people giving memorial windows—if he mentioned one memorial window, he must have spoke of a dozen, and saying how awful it was when somebody died intestate, the legal wrangles, and so forth.

(*Mae coughs, and points at Big Mama.*)

DOCTOR BAUGH: Well, Big Mama. . . .

(*He sighs.*)

BIG MAMA: It's all a mistake, I know it's just a bad dream.

DOCTOR BAUGH: We're gonna keep Big Daddy as comfortable as we can.

BIG MAMA: Yes, it's just a bad dream, that's all it is, it's just an awful dream.

GOOPER: In my opinion Big Daddy is having some pain but won't admit that he has it.

BIG MAMA: Just a dream, a bad dream.

DOCTOR BAUGH: That's what lots of them do, they think if they don't admit they're having the pain they can sort of escape the fact of it.

GOOPER (*with relish*): Yes, they get sly about it, they get real sly about it.

MAE: Gooper and I think—

GOOPER: Shut up, Mae!—Big Daddy ought to be started on morphine.

BIG MAMA: Nobody's going to give Big Daddy morphine.

DOCTOR BAUGH: Now, Big Mama, when that pain strikes it's going to strike mighty hard and Big Daddy's going to need the needle to bear it.

BIG MAMA: I tell you, nobody's going to give him morphine.

MAE: Big Mama, you don't want to see Big Daddy suffer, you know you—

(*Gooper standing beside her gives her a savage poke.*)

DOCTOR BAUGH (*placing a package on the table*): I'm leaving this stuff here, so if there's a sudden attack you all won't have to send out for it.

MAE: I know how to give a hypo.

GOOPER: Mae took a course in nursing during the war.

MARGARET: Somehow I don't think Big Daddy would want Mae to give him a hypo.

MAE: You think he'd want *you* to do it?

(*Dr. Baugh rises.*)

GOOPER: Doctor Baugh is goin'.

DOCTOR BAUGH: Yes, I got to be goin'. Well, keep your chin up, Big Mama.

GOOPER (*with jocularity*): She's gonna keep *both* chins up, aren't you Big Mama?

(*Big Mama sobs.*)

Now stop that, Big Mama.

MAE: Sit down with me, Big Mama.

GOOPER (*at door with Dr. Baugh*): Well, Doc, we sure do appreciate all you done. I'm telling you, we're surely obligated to you for—

(*Dr. Baugh has gone out without a glance at him.*)

GOOPER: —I guess that doctor has got a lot on his mind but it wouldn't hurt him to act a little more human. . . .

(*Big Mama sobs.*)

Now be a brave girl, Mommy.

BIG MAMA: It's not true, I know that it's just not true!

GOOPER: Mama, those tests are infallible!

BIG MAMA: Why are you so determined to see your father daid?

MAE: Big Mama!

MARGARET (*gently*): I know what Big Mama means.

MAE (*fiercely*): Oh, do you?

MARGARET (*quietly and very sadly*): Yes, I think I do.

MAE: For a newcomer in the family you sure do show a lot of understanding.

MARGARET: Understanding is needed on this place.

MAE: I guess you must have needed a lot of it in your family, Maggie, with your father's liquor problem and now you've got Brick with his!

MARGARET: Brick does not have a liquor problem at all. Brick is devoted to Big Daddy. This thing is a terrible strain on him.

BIG MAMA: Brick is Big Daddy's boy, but he drinks too much and it worries me and Big Daddy, and, Margaret, you've got to cooperate with us, you've got to cooperate with Big Daddy and me in getting Brick straightened out. Because it will break Big Daddy's heart if Brick don't pull himself together and take hold of things.

MAE: Take hold of *what* things, Big Mama?

BIG MAMA: The place.

(*There is a quick violent look between Mae and Gooper.*)

GOOPER: Big, Mama, you've had a shock.

MAE: Yais, we've all had a shock, but . . .

GOOPER: Let's be realistic—

MAE: —Big Daddy would never, would *never*, be foolish enough to—

GOOPER: —put this place in irresponsible hands!

BIG MAMA: Big Daddy ain't going to leave the place in anybody's hands; Big Daddy is *not* going to die. I want you to get that in your heads, all of you!

MAE: Mommy, Mommy, Big Mama, we're just as hopeful an' optimistic as you are about Big Daddy's prospects, we have faith in *prayer*—but nevertheless there are certain matters that have to be discussed an' dealt with, because otherwise—

GOOPER: Eventualities have to be considered and now's the time. . . . Mae, will you please get my briefcase out of our room?

MAE: Yes, honey.

(*She rises and goes out through the hall door.*)

GOOPER (*standing over Big Mama*): Now Big Mom. What you said just now was not at all true and you know it. I've always loved Big Daddy in my own quiet way. I never made a show of it, and I know that Big Daddy has always been fond of me in a quiet way, too, and he never made a show of it neither.

(*Mae returns with Gooper's briefcase.*)

MAE: Here's your briefcase, Gooper, honey.

GOOPER (*handing the briefcase back to her*): Thank you. . . . Of ca'use, my relationship with Big Daddy is different from Brick's.

MAE: You're eight years older'n Brick an' always had t'carry a bigger load of th' responsibilities than Brick ever had t'carry. He never carried a thing in his life but a football or a highball.

GOOPER: Mae, will y' let me talk, please?

MAE: Yes, honey.

GOOPER: Now, a twenty-eight thousand acre plantation's a mighty big thing t'run.

MAE: Almost singlehanded.

(*Margaret has gone out onto the gallery, and can be heard calling softly to Brick.*)

BIG MAMA: You never had to run this place! What are you talking about? As if Big Daddy was dead and in his grave, you had to run it? Why, you just helped him out with a few business details and had your law practice at the same time in Memphis!

MAE: Oh, Mommy, Mommy, Big Mommy! Let's be fair! Why, Gooper has given himself body and soul to keeping this place up for the past five years since Big Daddy's health started failing. Gooper won't say it, Gooper never thought of it as a duty, he just did it. And what did Brick do? Brick kept living in his past glory at college! Still a football player at twenty-seven!

MARGARET (*returning alone*): Who are you talking about, now? Brick? A football player? He isn't a football player and you know it. Brick is a sports announcer on TV and one of the best-known ones in the country!

MAE: I'm talking about what he was.

MARGARET: Well, I wish you would just stop talking about my husband.

GOOPER: I've got a right to discuss my brother with other members of MY OWN family which don't include *you.* Why don't you go out there and drink with Brick?

MARGARET: I've never seen such malice toward a brother.

GOOPER: How about his for me? Why, he can't stand to be in the same room with me!

MARGARET: This is a deliberate campaign of vilification for the most disgusting and sordid reason on earth, and I know what it is! It's *avarice, avarice, greed, greed!*

BIG MAMA: *Oh, I'll scream! I will scream in a moment unless this stops!*

(*Gooper has stalked up to Margaret with clenched fists at his sides as if he would strike her. Mae distorts her face again into a hideous grimace behind Margaret's back.*)

MARGARET: We only remain on the place because of Big Mom and Big Daddy. If it is true what they say about Big Daddy we are going to leave here just as soon as it's over. Not a moment later.

BIG MAMA (*sobs*): Margaret. Child. Come here. Sit next to Big Mama.

MARGARET: Precious Mommy. I'm sorry, I'm so sorry, I—!

(*She bends her long graceful neck to press her forehead to Big Mama's bulging shoulder under its black chiffon.*)

GOOPER: How beautiful, how touching, this display of devotion!

MAE: Do you know why she's childless? She's childless because that big beautiful athlete husband of hers won't go to bed with her!

GOOPER: You jest won't let me do this in a nice way, will yah? Aw right—Mae and I have five kids with another one coming! I don't give a goddam if Big Daddy likes me or don't like me or did or never did or will or will never! I'm just appealing to a sense of common decency and fair play. I'll tell you the truth. I've resented Big Daddy's partiality to Brick ever since Brick was born, and the way I've been treated like I was just barely good enough to spit on and sometimes not even good enough for that. Big Daddy is dying of cancer, and it's spread all through him and it's attacked all his vital organs including the kidneys and right now he is sinking into uremia, and you all know what uremia is, it's poisoning of the whole system due to the failure of the body to eliminate its poisons.

MARGARET (*to herself, downstage, hissingly*): *Poisons, poisons! Venomous thoughts and words! In hearts and minds!—That's poisons!*

GOOPER (*overlapping her*): I am asking for a square deal, and I expect to get one. But if I don't get one, if there's any peculiar shenanigans going on around here behind my back, or before me, well, I'm not a corporation lawyer for nothing, I know how to protect my own interests.—*OH! A late arrival!*

(*Brick enters from the gallery with a tranquil, blurred smile, carrying an empty glass with him.*)

MAE: Behold the conquering hero comes!

GOOPER: The fabulous Brick Pollitt! Remember him?—Who could forget him!

MAE: He looks like he's been injured in a game!

GOOPER: Yep, I'm afraid you'll have to warm the bench at the Sugar Bowl this year, Brick!

(*Mae laughs shrilly.*)

Or was it the Rose Bowl that he made that famous run in?

MAE: The punch bowl, honey. It was in the punch bowl, the cut-glass punch bowl!

GOOPER: Oh, that's right, I'm getting the bowls mixed up!

MARGARET: Why don't you stop venting your malice and envy on a sick boy?

BIG MAMA: *Now you two hush, I mean it, hush, all of you, hush!*

GOOPER: All right, Big Mama. A family crisis brings out the best and the worst in every member of it.

MAE: *That's* the truth.

MARGARET: *Amen!*

BIG MAMA: *I said, hush!* I won't tolerate any more catty talk in my house.

(*Mae gives Gooper a sign indicating briefcase.*

(*Brick's smile has grown both brighter and vaguer. As he prepares a drink, he sings softly:*)

BRICK:

Show me the way to go home,
I'm tired and I wanta go to bed.
I had a little drink about an hour ago—

GOOPER (*at the same time*): Big Mama, you know it's necessary for me t'go back to Memphis in th' mornin' t'represent the Parker estate in a lawsuit.

(*Mae sits on the bed and arranges papers she has taken from the briefcase.*)

BRICK (*continuing the song*):

Wherever I may roam,
On land or sea or foam.

BIG MAMA: Is it, Gooper?

MAE: Yaiss.

GOOPER: That's why I'm forced to—to bring up a problem that—

MAE: Somethin' that's too important t' be put off!

GOOPER: If Brick was sober, he ought to be in on this.

MARGARET: Brick is present; we're here.

GOOPER: Well, good. I will now give you this outline my partner, Tom Bullitt, an' me have drawn up—a sort of dummy—trusteeship.

MARGARET: Oh, that's it! You'll be in charge an' dole out remittances, will you?

GOOPER: This we did as soon as we got the report on Big Daddy from th' Ochsner Laboratories. We did this thing, I mean we drew up this dummy outline with the advice and assistance of the Chairman of the Boa'd of Directors of th' Southern Plantahs Bank and Trust Company in Memphis, C. C. Bellowes, a man who handles estates for all th' prominent fam'lies in West Tennessee and th' Delta.

BIG MAMA: Gooper?

GOOPER (*crouching in front of Big Mama*): Now this is not—not final, or anything like it. This is just a preliminary outline. But it does provide a basis—a design—a—possible, feasible—*plan!*

MARGARET: Yes, I'll bet.

MAE: It's a plan to protect the biggest estate in the Delta from irresponsibility an'—

BIG MAMA: Now you listen to me, all of you, you listen here! They's not goin' to be any more catty talk in my house! And Gooper, you put that away before I grab it out of your hand and tear it right up! I don't know what the hell's in it, and I don't want to know what the hell's in it. I'm talkin' in Big Daddy's language now; I'm his *wife*, not his *widow*, I'm still his *wife*! And I'm talkin' to you in his language an'—

GOOPER: Big Mama, what I have here is—

MAE: Gooper explained that it's just a plan. . . .

BIG MAMA: I don't care what you got there. Just put it back where it came from, an' don't let me see it again, not even the outside of the envelope of it! Is that understood? Basis! Plan! Preliminary! Design! I say—what is it Big Daddy always says when he's disgusted?

BRICK (*from the bar*): Big Daddy says "crap" when he's disgusted.

BIG MAMA (*rising*): That's right—*CRAP!* I say *CRAP* too, like Big Daddy!

MAE: Coarse language doesn't seem called for in this—

GOOPER: Somethin' in me is *deeply outraged* by hearin' you talk like this.

BIG MAMA: *Nobody's goin' to take nothin'!*—till Big Daddy lets go of it, and maybe, just possibly, not—not even then! No, not even then!

BRICK:

You can always hear me singin' this song,
Show me the way to go home.

BIG MAMA: Tonight Brick looks like he used to look when he was a little boy, just like he did when he played wild games and used to come home all sweaty and pink-cheeked and sleepy, with his—red curls shining. . . .

(*She comes over to him and runs her fat shaky hand through his hair. He draws aside as he does from all physical contact and continues the song in a whisper, opening the ice bucket and dropping in the ice cubes one by one as if he were mixing some important chemical formula.*)

BIG MAMA (*continuing*): Time goes by so fast. Nothin' can outrun it. Death commences too early—almost before you're half-acquainted with life—you meet with the other. . . .

Oh, you know we just got to love each other an' stay together, all of us, just as close as we can, especially now that such a *black* thing has come and moved into this place without invitation.

(*Awkwardly embracing Brick, she presses her head to his shoulder.*

(*Gooper has been returning papers to Mae who has restored them to briefcase with an air of severely tried patience.*)

GOOPER: Big Mama? Big Mama?

(*He stands behind her, tense with sibling envy.*)

BIG MAMA (*oblivious of Gooper*): Brick, you hear me, don't you?

MARGARET: Brick hears you, Big Mama, he understands what you're saying.

BIG MAMA: Oh, Brick, son of Big Daddy! Big Daddy does so love you! Y'know what would be his fondest dream come true? If before he passed on, if Big Daddy has to pass on, you gave him a child of yours, a grandson as much like his son as his son is like Big Daddy!

MAE (*zipping briefcase shut: an incongruous sound*): *Such a pity that Maggie an' Brick can't oblige!*

MARGARET (*suddenly and quietly but forcefully*): Everybody listen.

(*She crosses to the center of the room, holding her hands rigidly together.*)

MAE: Listen to what, Maggie?

MARGARET: I have an announcement to make.

GOOPER: A sports announcement, Maggie?

MARGARET: Brick and I are going to—*have a child!*

(*Big Mama catches her breath in a loud gasp.*)

(*Pause. Big Mama rises.*)

BIG MAMA: Maggie! Brick! This is too good to believe!

MAE: That's right, too good to believe.

BIG MAMA: Oh, my, my! This is Big Daddy's dream, his dream come true! I'm going to tell him right now before he—

MARGARET: We'll tell him in the morning. Don't disturb him now.

BIG MAMA: I want to tell him before he goes to sleep, I'm going to tell him his dream's come true this minute! And Brick! A child will make you pull yourself together and quit this drinking!

(*She seizes the glass from his hand.*)

The responsibilities of a father will—

(*Her face contorts and she makes an excited gesture; bursting into sobs, she rushes out, crying.*)

I'm going to tell Big Daddy right this minute!

(*Her voice fades out down the hall.*

(*Brick shrugs slightly and drops an ice cube into another glass. Margaret crosses quickly to his side, saying something under her breath, and she pours the liquor for him, staring up almost fiercely into his face.*)

BRICK (*coolly*): Thank you, Maggie, that's a nice big shot.

(*Mae has joined Gooper and she gives him a fierce poke, making a low hissing sound and a grimace of fury.*)

GOOPER (*pushing her aside*): Brick, could you possibly spare me one small shot of that liquor?

BRICK: Why, help yourself, Gooper boy.

GOOPER: I will.

MAE (*shrilly*): Of course we know that this is—

GOOPER: *Be still, Mae!*

MAE: I won't be still! I know she's made this up!

GOOPER: God damn it, I said to shut up!

MARGARET: Gracious! I didn't know that my little announcement was going to provoke such a storm!

MAE: *That* woman isn't *pregnant!*

GOOPER: Who said she was?

MAE: *She* did.

GOOPER: The doctor didn't. Doc Baugh didn't.
MARGARET: I haven't gone to Doc Baugh.
GOOPER: Then who'd you go to, Maggie?
MARGARET: One of the best gynecologists in the South.
GOOPER: Uh huh, uh huh!—I see. . . .

(*He takes out pencil and notebook.*)

—May we have his name, please?
MARGARET: No, you may not, Mister Prosecuting Attorney!
MAE: He doesn't have any name, he doesn't exist!
MARGARET: Oh, he exists all right, and so does my child, Brick's baby!
MAE: You can't conceive a child by a man that won't sleep with you unless you think you're—

(*Brick has turned on the phonograph. A scat song cuts Mae's speech.*)

GOOPER: *Turn that off!*
MAE: We know it's a lie because we hear you in here; he won't sleep with you, we hear you! So don't imagine you're going to put a trick over on us, to fool a dying man with a—

(*A long drawn cry of agony and rage fills the house. Margaret turns phonograph down to a whisper.*
(*The cry is repeated.*)

MAE (*awed*): Did you hear that, Gooper, did you hear that?
GOOPER: Sounds like the pain has struck.
MAE: Go see, Gooper!
GOOPER: Come along and leave these love birds together in their nest!

(*He goes out first. Mae follows but turns at the door, contorting her face and hissing at Margaret.*)

MAE: *Liar!*

(*She slams the door.*
(*Margaret exhales with relief and moves a little unsteadily to catch hold of Brick's arm.*)

MARGARET: Thank you for—keeping still . . .
BRICK: OK, Maggie.

MARGARET: It was gallant of you to save my face!
BRICK: —It hasn't happened yet.
MARGARET: What?
BRICK: The click. . . .
MARGARET: —the click in your head that makes you peaceful, honey?
BRICK: Uh-huh. It hasn't happened. . . . I've got to make it happen before I can sleep. . . .
MARGARET: —I—know what you—mean. . . .
BRICK: Give me that pillow in the big chair, Maggie.
MARGARET: I'll put it on the bed for you.
BRICK: No, put it on the sofa, where I sleep.
MARGARET: Not tonight, Brick.
BRICK: I want it on the sofa. That's where I sleep.

(*He has hobbled to the liquor cabinet. He now pours down three shots in quick succession and stands waiting, silent. All at once he turns with a smile and says:*)

There!
MARGARET: What?
BRICK: The *click*. . . .

(*His gratitude seems almost infinite as he hobbles out on the gallery with a drink. We hear his crutch as he swings out of sight. Then, at some distance, he begins singing to himself a peaceful song.*

(*Margaret holds the big pillow forlornly as if it were her only companion, for a few moments, then throws it on the bed. She rushes to the liquor cabinet, gathers all the bottles in her arms, turns about undecidedly, then runs out of the room with them, leaving the door ajar on the dim yellow hall. Brick is heard hobbling back along the gallery, singing his peaceful song. He comes back in, sees the pillow on the bed, laughs lightly, sadly, picks it up. He has it under his arm as Margaret returns to the room. Margaret softly shuts the door and leans against it, smiling softly at Brick.*)

MARGARET: Brick, I used to think that you were stronger than me and I didn't want to be overpowered by you. But now, since you've taken to liquor—you know what?—I guess it's bad, but now I'm stronger than you and I can love you more truly!

Don't move that pillow. I'll move it right back if you do! —Brick?

(*She turns out all the lamps but a single rose-silk-shaded one by the bed.*)

I really have been to a doctor and I know what to do and—Brick?—this is my time by the calendar to conceive!

BRICK: Yes, I understand, Maggie. But how are you going to conceive a child by a man in love with his liquor?

MARGARET: By locking his liquor up and making him satisfy my desire before I unlock it!

BRICK: Is that what you've done, Maggie?

MARGARET: Look and see. That cabinet's mighty empty compared to before!

BRICK: Well, I'll be a son of a—

(*He reaches for his crutch but she beats him to it and rushes out on the gallery, hurls the crutch over the rail and comes back in, panting.*

(*There are running footsteps. Big Mama bursts into the room, her face all awry, gasping, stammering.*)

BIG MAMA: Oh, my God, oh, my God, oh, my God, where is it?

MARGARET: Is this what you want, Big Mama?

(*Margaret hands her the package left by the doctor.*)

BIG MAMA: I can't bear it, oh, God! Oh, Brick! Brick, baby!

(*She rushes at him. He averts his face from her sobbing kisses. Margaret watches with a tight smile.*)

My son, Big Daddy's boy! Little Father!

(*The groaning cry is heard again. She runs out, sobbing.*)

MARGARET: And so tonight we're going to make the lie true, and when that's done, I'll bring the liquor back here and we'll get drunk together, here, tonight, in this place that death has come into. . . .

—What do you say?

BRICK: I don't say anything. I guess there's nothing to say.

MARGARET: Oh, you weak people, you weak, beautiful people! —who give up.—What you want is someone to—

(*She turns out the rose-silk lamp.*)

—take hold of you.—Gently, gently, with love! And—

(*The curtain begins to fall slowly.*)

I *do* love you, Brick, I *do*!

BRICK (*smiling with charming sadness*): Wouldn't it be funny if that was true?

The Curtain Comes Down

THE END

NOTE OF EXPLANATION

Some day when time permits I would like to write a piece about the influence, its dangers and its values, of a powerful and highly imaginative director upon the development of a play, before and during production. It does have dangers, but it has them only if the playwright is excessively malleable or submissive, or the director is excessively insistent on ideas or interpretations of his own. Elia Kazan and I have enjoyed the advantages and avoided the dangers of this highly explosive relationship because of the deepest mutual respect for each other's creative function: we have worked together three times with a phenomenal absence of friction between us and each occasion has increased the trust.

If you don't want a director's influence on your play, there are two ways to avoid it, and neither is good. One way is to arrive at an absolutely final draft of your play before you let your director see it, then hand it to him saying, Here it is, take it or leave it! The other way is to select a director who is content to put your play on the stage precisely as you conceived it with no ideas of his own. I said neither is a good way, and I meant it. No living playwright, that I can think of, hasn't something valuable to learn about his own work from a director so keenly perceptive as Elia Kazan. It so happened that in the case of *Streetcar*, Kazan was given a script that was completely finished. In the case of *Cat*, he was shown the first typed version of the play, and he was excited by it, but he had definite reservations about it which were concentrated in the third act. The gist of his reservations can be listed as three points: one, he felt that Big Daddy was too vivid and important a character to disappear from the play except as an offstage cry after the second act curtain; two, he felt that the character of Brick should undergo some apparent mutation as a result of the virtual vivisection that he undergoes in his interview with his father in Act Two. Three, he felt that the character of Margaret, while he understood that I sympathized with her and liked her myself, should be, if possible, more clearly sympathetic to an audience.

It was only the third of these suggestions that I embraced

wholeheartedly from the outset, because it so happened that Maggie the Cat had become steadily more charming to me as I worked on her characterization. I didn't want Big Daddy to reappear in Act Three and I felt that the moral paralysis of Brick was a root thing in his tragedy, and to show a dramatic progression would obscure the meaning of that tragedy in him and because I don't believe that a conversation, however revelatory, ever effects so immediate a change in the heart or even conduct of a person in Brick's state of spiritual disrepair.

However, I wanted Kazan to direct the play, and though these suggestions were not made in the form of an ultimatum, I was fearful that I would lose his interest if I didn't re-examine the script from his point of view. I did. And you will find included in this published script the new third act that resulted from his creative influence on the play. The reception of the playing-script has more than justified, in my opinion, the adjustments made to that influence. A failure reaches fewer people, and touches fewer, than does a play that succeeds.

It may be that *Cat* number one would have done just as well, or nearly, as *Cat* number two; it's an interesting question. At any rate, with the publication of both third acts in this volume, the reader can, if he wishes, make up his own mind about it.

Tennessee Williams

ACT THREE

AS PLAYED IN NEW YORK PRODUCTION

Big Daddy is seen leaving as at the end of Act II.

BIG DADDY (*shouts, as he goes out DR on gallery*): ALL—LYIN'—DYIN'—LIARS! LIARS! LIARS!

(*After Big Daddy has gone, Margaret enters from DR on gallery, into room through DS door. She X to Brick at LC.*)

MARGARET: Brick, what in the name of God was goin' on in this room?

(*Dixie and Trixie rush through the room from the hall, L to gallery R, brandishing cap pistols, which they fire repeatedly, as they shout: "Bang! Bang! Bang!"*

(*Mae appears from DR gallery entrance, and turns the children back UL, along gallery. At the same moment, Gooper, Reverend Tooker and Dr. Baugh enter from L in the hall.*)

MAE: Dixie! You quit that! Gooper, will y'please git these kiddies t'baid? Right now?

(*Gooper and Reverend Tooker X along upper gallery. Dr. Baugh holds, UC, near hall door. Reverend Tooker X to Mae near section of gallery just outside doors, R.*)

GOOPER (*urging the children along*): Mae—you seen Big Mama?
MAE: Not yet.

(*Dixie and Trixie vanish through hall, L.*)

REVEREND TOOKER (*to Mae*): Those kiddies are so full of vitality. I think I'll have to be startin' back to town.

(*Margaret turns to watch and listen.*)

MAE: Not yet, Preacher. You know we regard you as a member of this fam'ly, one of our closest an' dearest, so you just got t'be with us when Doc Baugh gives Big Mama th' actual truth about th' report from th' clinic.

(*Calls through door:*)

Has Big Daddy gone to bed, Brick?

(*Gooper has gone out DR at the beginning of the exchange between Mae and Reverend Tooker.*)

MARGARET (*replying to Mae*): Yes, he's gone to bed.

(*To Brick:*)

Why'd Big Daddy shout "liars"?

GOOPER (*off DR*): Mae!

(*Mae exits DR. Reverend Tooker drifts along upper gallery.*)

BRICK: I didn't lie to Big Daddy. I've lied to nobody, nobody but myself, just lied to myself. The time has come to put me in Rainbow Hill, put me in Rainbow Hill, Maggie, I ought to go there.

MARGARET: Over my dead body!

(*Brick starts R. She holds him.*)

Where do you think you're goin'?

(*Mae enters from DR on gallery, X to Reverend Tooker, who comes to meet her.*)

BRICK (*X below to C*): Out for some air, I want air—

GOOPER (*entering from DR to Mae, on gallery*): Now, where is that old lady?

MAE: Cantcha find her, Gooper?

(*Reverend Tooker goes out DR.*)

GOOPER (*X to Doc above hall door*): She's avoidin' this talk.

MAE: I think she senses somethin'.

GOOPER (*calls off L*): Sookey! Go find Big Mama an' tell her Doc Baugh an' the Preacher've got to go soon.

MAE: Don't let Big Daddy hear yuh!

(*Brings Dr. Baugh to R on gallery.*)

REVEREND TOOKER (*off DR, calls*): Big Mama.

SOOKEY and DAISY (*running from L to R in lawn, calling*): Miss Ida! Miss Ida!

(*They go out UR.*)

GOOPER (*calling off upper gallery*): Lacey, you look downstairs for Big Mama!

MARGARET: Brick, they're going to tell Big Mama the truth now, an' she needs you!

(*Reverend Tooker appears in lawn area, UR, X C.*)

DOCTOR BAUGH (*to Mae, on R gallery*): This is going to be painful.

MAE: Painful things can't always be avoided.

DOCTOR BAUGH: That's what I've noticed about 'em, Sister Woman.

REVEREND TOOKER (*on lawn, points off R*): I see Big Mama!

(*Hurries off L. and reappears shortly in hall.*)

GOOPER (*hurrying into hall*): She's gone round the gall'ry to Big Daddy's room. Hey, Mama!

(*Off:*)

Hey, Big Mama! Come here!

MAE (*calls*): Hush, Gooper! Don't holler, go to her!

(*Gooper and Reverend Tooker now appear together in hall. Big Mama runs in from DR, carrying a glass of milk. She X past Dr. Baugh to Mae, on R gallery. Dr. Baugh turns away.*)

BIG MAMA: Here I am! What d'you all want with me?

GOOPER (*steps toward Big Mama*): Big Mama, I told you we got to have this talk.

BIG MAMA: What talk you talkin' about? I saw the light go on in Big Daddy's bedroom an' took him his glass of milk, an' he just shut the shutters right in my face.

(*Steps into room through R door.*)

When old couples have been together as long as me an' Big Daddy, they, they get irritable with each other just from too much—devotion! Isn't that so?

(*X below wicker seat to RC area.*)

MARGARET (*X to Big Mama, embracing her*): Yes, of course it's so.

(*Brick starts out UC through hall, but sees Gooper and Reverend Tooker entering, so he hobbles through C out DS door and onto gallery.*)

BIG MAMA: I think Big Daddy was just worn out. He loves his fam'ly. He loves to have 'em around him, but it's a strain on his nerves. He wasn't himself tonight, Brick—

(*XC toward Brick. Brick passes her on his way out, DS.*)

Big Daddy wasn't himself, I could tell he was all worked up.

REVEREND TOOKER (*USC*): I think he's remarkable.

BIG MAMA: Yaiss! Just remarkable.

(*Faces US, turns, X to bar, puts down glass of milk.*)

Did you notice all the food he ate at that table?

(*XR a bit.*)

Why he ate like a hawss!

GOOPER (*USC*): I hope he don't regret it.

BIG MAMA (*turns US toward Gooper*): What! Why that man ate a huge piece of cawn bread with molassess on it! Helped himself twice to hoppin' john!

MARGARET (*X to Big Mama*): Big Daddy loves hoppin' john. We had a real country dinner.

BIG MAMA: Yais, he simply adores it! An' candied yams. Son—

(*X to DS door, looking out at Brick. Margaret X above Big Mama to her L.*)

That man put away enough food at that table to stuff a field-hand.

GOOPER: I hope he don't have to pay for it later on.

BIG MAMA (*turns US*): What's that, Gooper?

MAE: Gooper says he hopes Big Daddy doesn't suffer tonight.

BIG MAMA (*turns to Margaret, DC*): Oh, shoot, Gooper says, Gooper says! Why should Big Daddy suffer for satisfyin' a nawmal appetite? There's nothin' wrong with that man but nerves; he's sound as a dollar! An' now he knows he is, an' that's why he ate such a supper. He had a big load off his mind, knowin' he wasn't doomed to—what—he thought he was—doomed t'—

(*She wavers.*
(*Margaret puts her arms around Big Mama.*)

GOOPER (*urging Mae forward*): MAE!

(*Mae runs forward below wicker seat. She stands below Big Mama, Margaret above Big Mama. They help her to the wicker seat. Big Mama sits. Margaret sits above her. Mae stands behind her.*)

MARGARET: Bless his ole sweet soul.
BIG MAMA: Yes—bless his heart.
BRICK (*DS on gallery, looking out front*): Hello, moon, I envy you, you cool son of a bitch.
BIG MAMA: I want Brick!
MARGARET: He just stepped out for some fresh air.
BIG MAMA: Honey! I want Brick!
MAE: Bring li'l Brother in here so we cin talk.

(*Margaret rises, X through DS door to Brick on gallery.*)

BRICK (*to the moon*): I envy you—you cool son of a bitch.
MARGARET: Brick, what're you doin' out here on the gall'ry, baby?
BRICK: Admirin' an' complimentin' th' man in the moon.

(*Mae X to Dr. Baugh on R gallery. Reverend Tooker and Gooper move R UC, looking at Big Mama.*)

MARGARET (*to Brick*): Come in, baby. They're gettin' ready to tell Big Mama the truth.
BRICK: I can't witness that thing in there.
MAE: Doc Baugh, d'you think those vitamin B_{12} injections are all they're cracked up t'be?

(*Enters room to upper side, behind wicker seat.*)

DOCTOR BAUGH (*X to below wicker seat*): Well, I guess they're as good t'be stuck with as anything else.

(*Looks at watch; X through to LC.*)

MARGARET (*to Brick*): Big Mama needs you!
BRICK: I can't witness that thing in there!
BIG MAMA: What's wrong here? You all have such long faces, you sit here waitin' for somethin' like a bomb—to go off.

GOOPER: We're waitin' for Brick an' Maggie to come in for this talk.

MARGARET (*X above Brick, to his R*): Brother Man an' Mae have got a trick up their sleeves, an' if you don't go in there t'help Big Mama, y'know what I'm goin' to do—?

BIG MAMA: Talk. Whispers! Whispers!

(*Looks out DR.*)

Brick! . . .

MARGARET (*answering Big Mama's call*): Comin', Big Mama!

(*To Brick.*)

I'm goin' to take every dam' bottle on this place an' pitch it off th' levee into th' river!

BIG MAMA: Never had this sort of atmosphere here before.

MAE (*sits above Big Mama on wicker seat*): Before what, Big Mama?

BIG MAMA: This occasion. What's Brick an' Maggie doin' out there now?

GOOPER (*X DC, looks out*): They seem to be havin' some little altercation.

(*Brick X toward DS step. Maggie moves R above him to portal Dr. Reverend Tooker joins Dr. Baugh, LC.*)

BIG MAMA (*taking a pill from pill box on chain at her wrist*): Give me a little somethin' to wash this tablet down with. Smell of burnt fireworks always makes me sick.

(*Mae X to bar to pour glass of water. Dr. Baugh joins her. Gooper X to Reverend Tooker, LC.*)

BRICK (*to Maggie*): You're a live cat, aren't you?

MARGARET: You're dam' right I am!

BIG MAMA: Gooper, will y'please open that hall door—an' let some air circulate in this stiflin' room?

(*Gooper starts US, but is restrained by Mae who X through C with glass of water. Gooper turns to men DLC.*)

MAE (*X to Big Mama with water, sits above her*): Big Mama, I think we ought to keep that door closed till after we talk.

BIG MAMA: I swan!

(*Drinks water. Washes down pill.*)

MAE: I just don't think we ought to take any chance of Big Daddy hearin' a word of this discussion.

BIG MAMA (*hands glass to Mae*): What discussion of what? Maggie! Brick! Nothin' is goin' to be said in th' house of Big Daddy Pollitt that he can't hear if he wants to!

(*Mae rises, X to bar, puts down glass, joins Gooper and the two men, LC.*)

BRICK: How long are you goin' to stand behind me, Maggie?

MARGARET: Forever, if necessary.

(*Brick X US to R gallery door.*)

BIG MAMA: Brick!

(*Mae rises, looks out DS, sits.*)

GOOPER: That boy's gone t'pieces—he's just gone t'pieces.

DOCTOR BAUGH: Y'know, in my day they used to have somethin' they called the Keeley cure for drinkers.

BIG MAMA: Shoot!

DOCTOR BAUGH: But nowadays, I understand they take some kind of tablets that kill their taste for the stuff.

GOOPER (*turns to Dr. Baugh*): Call 'em anti-bust tablets.

BIG MAMA: Brick don't need to take nothin'. That boy is just broken up over Skipper's death. You know how poor Skipper died. They gave him a big, big dose of that sodium amytal stuff at his home an' then they called the ambulance an' give him another big, big dose of it at th' hospital an' that an' all the alcohol in his system fo' months an' months just proved too much for his heart an' his heart quit beatin'. I'm scared of needles! I'm more scared of a needle than th' knife—

(*Brick has entered the room to behind the wicker seat. He rests his hand on Big Mama's head. Gooper has moved a bit URC, facing Big Mama.*)

BIG MAMA: Oh! Here's Brick! My precious baby!

(*Dr. Baugh X to bar, puts down drink. Brick X below Big Mama through C to bar.*)

BRICK: Take it, Gooper!
MAE (*rising*): What?
BRICK: Gooper knows what. Take it, Gooper!

(*Mae turns to Gooper URC. Dr. Baugh X to Reverend Tooker. Margaret, who has followed Brick US on R gallery before he entered the room, now enters room, to behind wicker seat.*)

BIG MAMA (*to Brick*): You just break my heart.
BRICK (*at bar*): Sorry—anyone else?
MARGARET: Brick, sit with Big Mama an' hold her hand while we talk.
BRICK: You do that, Maggie. I'm a restless cripple. I got to stay on my crutch.

(*Mae sits above Big Mama. Gooper moves in front, below, and sits on couch, facing Big Mama. Reverend Tooker closes in to RC. Dr. Baugh XDC, faces upstage, smoking cigar. Margaret turns away to R doors.*)

BIG MAMA: Why're you all *surroundin'* me?—like this? Why're you all starin' at me like this an' makin' signs at each other?

(*Brick hobbles out hall door and X along R gallery.*)

I don't need nobody to hold my hand. Are you all crazy? Since when did Big Daddy or me need anybody—?

(*Reverend Tooker moves behind wicker seat.*)

MAE: Calm yourself, Big Mama.
BIG MAMA: Calm you'self *you'self*, Sister Woman! How could I calm myself with everyone starin' at me as if big drops of blood had broken out on m'face? What's this all about Annh! What?
GOOPER: Doc Baugh—

(*Mae rises.*)

Sit down, Mae—

(*Mae sits.*)

—Big Mama wants to know the complete truth about th' report we got today from the Ochsner Clinic!

(*Dr. Baugh buttons his coat, faces group at RC.*)

BIG MAMA: Is there somethin'—somethin' that I don't know?
DOCTOR BAUGH: Yes—well . . .
BIG MAMA (*rises*): I—want to—*knowwwww!*

(*X to Dr. Baugh.*)

Somebody must be lyin'! *I want to know!*

(*Mae, Gooper, Reverend Tooker surround Big Mama.*)

MAE: Sit down, Big Mama, sit down on this sofa!

(*Brick has passed Margaret Xing DR on gallery.*)

MARGARET: Brick! Brick!
BIG MAMA: *What is it, what is it?*

(*Big Mama drives Dr. Baugh a bit DLC. Others follow, surrounding Big Mama.*)

DOCTOR BAUGH: I never have seen a more thorough examination than Big Daddy Pollitt was given in all my experience at the Ochsner Clinic.
GOOPER: It's one of th' best in th' country.
MAE: It's *THE* best in th' country—bar none!
DOCTOR BAUGH: Of course they were ninety-nine and nine-tenths per cent certain before they even started.
BIG MAMA: Sure of what, sure of what, sure of what—*what*!?
MAE: Now, Mommy, be a brave girl!
BRICK (*on DR gallery, covers his ears, sings*): *"By the light, by the light, of the silvery moon!"*
GOOPER (*breaks DR. Calls out to Brick*): Shut up, Brick!

(*Returns to group LC.*)

BRICK: Sorry . . .

(*Continues singing.*)

DOCTOR BAUGH: But now, you see, Big Mama, they cut a piece off this growth, a specimen of the tissue, an'—
BIG MAMA: Growth? You told Big Daddy—
DOCTOR BAUGH: Now, wait—
BIG MAMA: You told me an' Big Daddy there wasn't a thing wrong with him but—

MAE: Big Mama, they always—
GOOPER: Let Doc Baugh talk, will yuh?
BIG MAMA: —little spastic condition of—
REVEREND TOOKER (*throughout all this*): *Shh! Shh! Shh!*

(*Big Mama breaks UC, they all follow.*)

DOCTOR BAUGH: Yes, that's what we told Big Daddy. But we had this bit of tissue run through the laboratory an' I'm sorry t'say the test was positive on it. It's malignant.

(*Pause.*)

BIG MAMA: *Cancer! Cancer!*
MAE: Now now, Mommy—
GOOPER (*at the same time*): You had to know, Big Mama.
BIG MAMA: *Why didn't they cut it out of him? Hanh? Hannh?*
DOCTOR BAUGH: Involved too much, Big Mama, too many organs affected.
MAE: Big Mama, the liver's affected, an' so's the kidneys, both. It's gone way past what they call a—
GOOPER: —a surgical risk.

(*Big Mama gasps.*)

REVEREND TOOKER: Tch, tch, tch.
DOCTOR BAUGH: Yes, it's gone past the knife.
MAE: That's why he's turned yellow!

(*Brick stops singing, turns away UR on gallery.*)

BIG MAMA (*pushes Mae DS*): Git away from me, git away from me, Mae!

(*XDSR*)

I want Brick! Where's Brick! *Where's my only son?*
MAE (*a step after Big Mama*): Mama! Did she say "only" son?
GOOPER (*following Big Mama*): What does that make me?
MAE (*above Gooper*): A sober responsible man with five precious children—*six*!
BIG MAMA: I want Brick! Brick! Brick!
MARGARET (*a step to Big Mama above couch*): Mama, let *me* tell you.

BIG MAMA (*pushing her aside*): No, no, leave me alone, you're not my blood!

(*She rushes onto the DS gallery.*)

GOOPER (*X to Big Mama on gallery*): Mama! I'm your son! Listen to me!

MAE: Gooper's your son, Mama, he's your first-born!

BIG MAMA: Gooper never liked Daddy!

MAE: That's not true!

REVEREND TOOKER (*UC*): I think I'd better slip away at this point. Goodnight, goodnight everybody, and God bless you all—on this place.

(*Goes out through hall.*)

DOCTOR BAUGH (*XDR to above DS door*): Well, Big Mama—

BIG MAMA (*leaning against Gooper, on lower gallery*): It's all a mistake, I know it's just a bad dream.

DOCTOR BAUGH: We're gonna keep Big Daddy as comfortable as we can.

BIG MAMA: Yes, it's just a bad dream, that's all it is, it's just an awful dream.

GOOPER: In my opinion Big Daddy is havin' some pain but won't admit that he has it.

BIG MAMA: Just a dream, a bad dream.

DOCTOR BAUGH: That's what lots of 'em do, they think if they don't admit they're havin' the pain they can sort of escape th' fact of it.

(*Brick X US on R gallery. Margaret watches him from R doors.*)

GOOPER: Yes, they get sly about it, get real sly about it.

MAE (*X to R of Dr. Baugh*): Gooper an' I think—

GOOPER: Shut up, Mae!—Big Mama, I really do think Big Daddy should be started on morphine.

BIG MAMA (*pulling away from Gooper*): Nobody's goin't to give Big Daddy morphine!

DOCTOR BAUGH: Now, Big Mama, when that pain strikes it's goin' to strike mighty hard an' Big Daddy's goin' t'need the needle to bear it.

BIG MAMA (*X to Dr. Baugh*): I tell you, nobody's goin' to give him morphine!

MAE: Big Mama, you don't want to see Big Daddy suffer, y'know y'—

DOCTOR BAUGH (*X to bar*): Well, I'm leavin' this stuff here

(*Puts packet of morphine, etc., on bar.*)

so if there's a sudden attack you won't have to send out for it.

(*Big Mama hurries to L side bar.*)

MAE (*X C, below Dr. Baugh*): I know how to give a hypo.

BIG MAMA: Nobody's goin' to give Big Daddy morphine!

GOOPER (*X C*): Mae took a course in nursin' durin' th' war.

MARGARET: Somehow I don't think Big Daddy would want Mae t'give him a hypo.

MAE (*to Margaret*): You think he'd want *you* to do it?

DOCTOR BAUGH: Well—

GOOPER: Well, Doc Baugh is goin'—

DOCTOR BAUGH: Yes, I got to be goin'. Well, keep your chin up, Big Mama.

(*X to hall.*)

GOOPER (*as he and Mae follow Dr. Baugh into the hall*): She's goin' to keep her ole chin up, aren't you, Big Mama?

(*They go out L.*)

Well, Doc, we sure do appreciate all you've done. I'm telling you, we're obligated—

BIG MAMA: Margaret!

(*XRC.*)

MARGARET (*meeting Big Mama in front of wicker seat*): I'm right here, Big Mama.

BIG MAMA: Margaret, you've got to cooperate with me an' Big Daddy to straighten Brick out now—

GOOPER (*off L, returning with Mae*): I guess that Doctor has got a lot on his mind, but it wouldn't hurt him to act a little more human—

BIG MAMA: —because it'll break Big Daddy's heart if Brick don't pull himself together an' take hold of things here.

(*Brick XDSR on gallery.*)

MAE (*UC, overhearing*): Take hold of what things, Big Mama?

BIG MAMA (*sits in wicker chair, Margaret standing behind chair*): The place.

GOOPER (*UC*): Big Mama, you've had a shock.

MAE (*X with Gooper to Big Mama*): Yais, we've all had a shock, but—

GOOPER: Let's be realistic—

MAE: Big Daddy would not, would *never*, be foolish enough to—

GOOPER: —put this place in irresponsible hands!

BIG MAMA: Big Daddy ain't goin' t'put th' place in anybody's hands, Big Daddy is *not* goin' t'die! I want you to git that into your haids, all of you!

(*Mae sits above Big Mama, Margaret turns R to door, Gooper X L C a bit.*)

MAE: Mommy, Mommy, Big Mama, we're just as hopeful an' optimistic as you are about Big Daddy's prospects, we have faith in prayer—but nevertheless there are certain matters that have to be discussed an' dealt with, because otherwise—

GOOPER: Mae, will y'please get my briefcase out of our room?

MAE: Yes, honey.

(*Rises, goes out through hall L.*)

MARGARET (*X to Brick on DS gallery*): Hear them in there?

(*X back to R gallery door.*)

GOOPER (*stands above Big Mama. Leaning over her*): Big Mama, what you said just now was not at all true, an' you know it. I've always loved Big Daddy in my own quiet way. I never made a show of it. I know that Big Daddy has always been fond of me in a quiet way, too.

(*Margaret drifts UR on gallery. Mae returns, X to Gooper's L with briefcase.*)

MAE: Here's your briefcase, Gooper, honey.

(*Hands it to him.*)

GOOPER (*hands briefcase back to Mae*): Thank you. Of ca'use, my relationship with Big Daddy is different from Brick's.

MAE: You're eight years older'n Brick an' always had t'carry a bigger load of th' responsibilities than Brick ever had t'carry; he never carried a thing in his life but a football or a highball.

GOOPER: Mae, will y'let me talk, please?

MAE: Yes, honey.

GOOPER: Now, a twenty-eight thousand acre plantation's a mighty big thing t'run.

MAE: Almost single-handed!

BIG MAMA: You never had t'run this place, Brother Man, what're you talkin' about, as if Big Daddy was dead an' in his grave, you had to run it? Why, you just had t'help him out with a few business details an' had your law practice at the same time in Memphis.

MAE: Oh, Mommy, Mommy, Mommy! Let's be fair! Why, Gooper has given himself body an' soul t'keepin' this place up fo' the past five years since Big Daddy's health started fallin'. Gooper won't say it, Gooper never thought of it as a duty, he just did it. An' what did Brick do? Brick kep' livin' in his past glory at college!

(*Gooper places a restraining hand on Mae's leg; Margaret drifts DS in gallery.*)

GOOPER: Still a football player at twenty-seven!

MARGARET (*bursts into UR door*): Who are you talkin' about now? Brick? A football player? He isn't a football player an' you know it! Brick is a sports announcer on TV an' one of the best-known ones in the country!

MAE (*breaks UC*): I'm talkin' about what he was!

MARGARET (*X to above lower gallery door*): Well, I wish you would just stop talkin' about my husband!

GOOPER (*X to above Margaret*): Listen, Margaret, I've got a right to discuss my own brother with other members of my own fam'ly, which don't include *you*!

(*Pokes finger at her; she slaps his finger away.*)

Now, why don't you go on out there an' drink with Brick?

MARGARET: I've never seen such malice toward a brother.

GOOPER: How about his for me? Why he can't stand to be in the same room with me!

BRICK (*on lower gallery*): That's the truth!

MARGARET: This is a deliberate campaign of vilification for the most disgusting and sordid reason on earth, and I know what it is! *It's avarice, avarice, greed, greed!*

BIG MAMA: Oh, I'll scream, I will scream in a moment unless this stops! Margaret, child, come here, sit next to Big Mama.

MARGARET (*X to Big Mama, sits above her*): Precious Mommy.

(*Gooper X to bar.*)

MAE: How beautiful, how touchin' this display of devotion! Do you know why she's childless? She's childless because that big, beautiful athlete husband of hers won't go to bed with her, that's why!

(*X to L of bed, looks at Gooper.*)

GOOPER: You jest won't let me do this the nice way, will yuh? Aw right—

(*X to above wicker seat.*)

I don't give a goddam if Big Daddy likes me or don't like me or did or never did or will or will never! I'm just appealin' to a sense of common decency an' fair play! I'm tellin' you th' truth—

(*X DS through lower door to Brick on DR gallery.*)

I've resented Big Daddy's partiality to Brick ever since th' goddam day you were born, son, an' th' way I've been treated, like I was just barely good enough to spit on, an' sometimes not even good enough for that.

(*X back through room to above wicker seat.*)

Big Daddy is dyin' of cancer an' it's spread all through him an' it's attacked all his vital organs includin' the kidneys an' right now he is sinkin' into uremia, an' you all know what uremia is, it's poisonin' of the whole system due to th' failure of th' body to eliminate its poisons.

MARGARET: Poisons, poisons, venomous thoughts and words! In hearts and minds! That's poisons!

GOOPER: I'm askin' for a square deal an' by God I expect to get one. But if I don't get one, if there's any peculiar shenanigans goin' on around here behind my back, well I'm not a corporation lawyer for nothin!

(*XDS toward lower gallery door, on apex.*)

I know how to protect my own interests.

(*Rumble of distant thunder.*)

BRICK (*entering the room through DS door*): Storm comin' up.

GOOPER: Oh, a late arrival!

MAE (*X through C to below bar, LCO*): Behold, the conquerin' hero comes!

GOOPER (*X through C to bar, following Brick, imitating his limp*): The fabulous Brick Pollitt! Remember him? Who could forget him?

MAE: He looks like he's been injured in a game!

GOOPER: Yep, I'm afraid you'll have to warm th' bench at the Sugar Bowl this year, Brick! Or was it the Rose Bowl that he made his famous run in.

(*Another rumble of thunder, sound of wind rising.*)

MAE (*X to L of Brick, who has reached the bar*): The punch bowl, honey, it was the punch bowl, the cut-glass punch bowl!

GOOPER: That's right! I'm always gettin' the boy's *bowls* mixed up!

(*Pats Brick on the butt.*)

MARGARET (*rushes at Gooper, striking him*): Stop that! You stop that!

(*Thunder.*

(*Mae X toward Margaret from L. of Gooper, flails at Margaret; Gooper keeps the women apart. Lacey runs through the US lawn area in a raincoat.*)

DAISY and SOOKEY (*off UL*): Storm! Storm comin! Storm! Storm!

LACEY (*running out UR*): Brightie, close them shutters!

GOOPER (*X onto R gallery, calls after Lacey*): Lacey, put the top up on my Cadillac, will yuh?

LACEY (*off R*): Yes, sur, Mistah Pollit!

GOOPER (*X to above Big Mama*): Big Mama, you know it's goin' to be necessary for me t'go back to Memphis in th' mornin' t'represent the Parker estate in a lawsuit.

(*Mae sits on L side bed, arranges papers she removes from briefcase.*)

BIG MAMA: Is it, Gooper?

MAE: Yaiss.

GOOPER: That's why I'm forced to—to bring up a problem that—

MAE: Somethin' that's too important t'be put off!

GOOPER: If Brick was sober, he ought to be in on this. I think he ought to be present when I present this plan.

MARGARET (*UC*): Brick is present, we're present!

GOOPER: Well, good. I will now give you this outline my partner, Tom Bullit, an' me have drawn up—a sort of dummy—trusteeship!

MARGARET: Oh, that's it! You'll be in charge an' dole out remittances, will you?

GOOPER: This we did as soon as we got the report on Big Daddy from th' Ochsner Laboratories. We did this thing, I mean we drew up this dummy outline with the advice and assistance of the Chairman of the Boa'd of Directors of th' Southern Plantuhs Bank and Trust Company in Memphis, C. C. Bellowes, a man who handles estates for all th' prominent fam'lies in West Tennessee and th' Delta!

BIG MAMA: Gooper?

GOOPER (*X behind seat to below Big Mama*): Now this is not—not final, or anything like it, this is just a preliminary outline. But it does provide a—basis—a design—a—possible, feasible—*plan!*

(*He waves papers Mae has thrust into his hand, US.*)

MARGARET (*XDL*): Yes, I'll bet it's a plan!

(*Thunder rolls. Interior lighting dims.*)

MAE: It's a plan to protect the biggest estate in the Delta from irresponsibility an'—

BIG MAMA: Now you listen to me, all of you, you listen here! They's not goin' to be no more catty talk in my house! And Gooper, you put that away before I grab it out of your hand and tear it right up! I don't know what the hell's in it, and I don't want to know what the hell's in it. I'm talkin' in Big Daddy's language now, I'm his *wife*, not his *widow*, I'm still his *wife*! And I'm talkin' to you in his language an'—

GOOPER: Big Mama, what I have here is—

MAE: Gooper explained that it's just a plan . . .

BIG MAMA: I don't care what you got there, just put it back where it come from an' don't let me see it again, not even the outside of the envelope of it! Is that understood? Basis! Plan! Preliminary! Design!—I say—what is it that Big Daddy always says when he's disgusted?

(*Storm clouds race across sky.*)

BRICK (*from bar*): Big Daddy says "crap" when he is disgusted.

BIG MAMA (*rising*): That's right—*CRAPPPP!* I say *CRAP* too, like Big Daddy!

(*Thunder rolls.*)

MAE: Coarse language don't seem called for in this—

GOOPER: Somethin' in me is *deeply outraged* by this.

BIG MAMA: *Nobody's goin' to do nothin'!* till Big Daddy lets go of it, and maybe just possibly not—not even then! No, not even then!

(*Thunder clap. Glass crash, off L.*

(*Off UR, children commence crying. Many storm sounds, L and R: barnyard animals in terror, papers crackling, shutters rattling. Sookey and Daisy hurry from L to R in lawn area. Inexplicably, Daisy hits together two leather pillows. They cry, "Storm! Storm!" Sookey waves a piece of wrapping paper to cover lawn furniture. Mae exits to hall and upper gallery. Strange man runs across lawn, R to L.*

(*Thunder rolls repeatedly.*)

MAE: Sookey, hurry up an' git that po'ch fu'niture covahed; want th' paint to come off?

(*Starts DR on gallery.*
(*Gooper runs through hall to R gallery.*)

GOOPER (*yells to Lacey, who appears from R*): Lacey, put mah car away!
LACEY: Cain't, Mistah Pollit, you got the keys!

(*Exit US.*)

GOOPER: Naw, you got 'em, man.

(*Exit DR. Reappears UR, calls to Mae:*)

Where th' keys to th' car, honey?

(*Runs C.*)

MAE (*DR on gallery*): You got 'em in your pocket!

(*Exit DR.*
(*Gooper exits UR. Dog howls. Daisy and Sookey sing off UR to comfort children. Mae is heard placating the children.*
(*Storm fades away.*
(*During the storm, Margaret X and sits on couch, DR. Big Mama X DC.*)

BIG MAMA: BRICK! Come here, Brick, I need you.

(*Thunder distantly.*
(*Children whimper, off L Mae consoles them. Brick X to R of Big Mama.*)

BIG MAMA: Tonight Brick looks like he used to look when he was a little boy just like he did when he played wild games in the orchard back of the house and used to come home when I hollered myself hoarse for him! all—sweaty—and pink-cheeked—an' sleepy with his curls shinin'—

(*Thunder distantly.*
(*Children whimper, off L. Mae consoles them. Dog howls, off.*)

Time goes by so fast. Nothin' can outrun it. Death commences too early—almost before you're half-acquainted with life—you meet with the other. Oh, you know we just got to love each other, an' stay together all of us just as close as we can, specially now that such a *black* thing has come and moved into this place without invitation.

(*Dog howls, off.*)

Oh, Brick, son of Big Daddy, Big Daddy does so love you. Y'know what would be his fondest dream come true? If before he passed on, if Big Daddy has to pass on . . .

(*Dog howls, off.*)

You give him a child of yours, a grandson as much like his son as his son is like Big Daddy. . . .

MARGARET: I know that's Big Daddy's dream.

BIG MAMA: That's his dream.

BIG DADDY (*off DR on gallery*): Looks like the wind was takin' liberties with this place.

(*Lacey appears UL, X to UC in lawn area; Brightie and Small appear UR on lawn. Big Daddy X onto the UR gallery.*)

LACEY: Evenin', Mr. Pollitt.

BRIGHTIE and SMALL: Evenin', Cap'n. Hello, Cap'n.

MARGARET (*X to R door*): Big Daddy's on the gall'ry.

BIG DADDY: Stawm crossed th' river, Lacey?

LACEY: Gone to Arkansas, Cap'n.

(*Big Mama has turned toward the hall door at the sound of Big Daddy's voice on the gallery. Now she X's DSR and out the DS door onto the gallery.*)

BIG MAMA: I can't stay here. He'll see somethin' in my eyes.

BIG DADDY (*on upper gallery, to the boys*): Stawm done any damage around here?

BRIGHTIE: Took the po'ch off ole Aunt Crawley's house.

BIG DADDY: Ole Aunt Crawley should of been settin' on it. It's time fo' th' wind to blow that ole girl away!

(*Field-hands laugh, exit, UR. Big Daddy enters room, UC, hall door.*)

Can I come in?

(*Puts his cigar in ash tray on bar.*

(*Mae and Gooper hurry along the upper gallery and stand behind Big Daddy in hall door.*)

MARGARET: Did the storm wake you up, Big Daddy?

BIG DADDY: Which stawm are you talkin' about—th' one outside or th' hullaballoo in here?

(*Gooper squeezes past Big Daddy.*)

GOOPER (*X toward bed, where legal papers are strewn*): 'Scuse me, sir . . .

(*Mae tries to squeeze past Big Daddy to join Gooper, but Big Daddy puts his arm firmly around her.*)

BIG DADDY: I heard some mighty loud talk. Sounded like somethin' important was bein' discussed. What was the powwow about?

MAE (*flustered*): Why—nothin', Big Daddy . . .

BIG DADDY (*XDLC, taking Mae with him*): What is that pregnant-lookin' envelope you're puttin' back in your briefcase, Gooper?

GOOPER (*at foot of bed, caught, as he stuffs papers into envelope*): That? Nothin', suh—nothin' much of anythin' at all . . .

BIG DADDY: Nothin'? It looks like a whole lot of nothing!

(*Turns US to group:*)

You all know th' story about th' young married couple—

GOOPER: Yes, sir!

BIG DADDY: Hello, Brick—

BRICK: Hello, Big Daddy.

(*The group is arranged in a semi-circle above Big Daddy, Margaret at the extreme R, then Mae and Gooper, then Big Mama, with Brick at L.*)

BIG DADDY: Young married couple took Junior out to th' zoo one Sunday, inspected all of God's creatures in their cages, with satisfaction.

GOOPER: Satisfaction.

BIG DADDY (*XUSC, face front*): This afternoon was a warm afternoon in spring an' that ole elephant had somethin' else on his mind which was bigger'n peanuts. You know this story, Brick?

(*Gooper nods.*)

BRICK: No, sir, I don't know it.

BIG DADDY: Y'see, in th' cage adjoinin' they was a young female elephant in heat!

BIG MAMA (*at Big Daddy's shoulder*): Oh, Big Daddy!

BIG DADDY: What's the matter, preacher's gone, ain't he? All right. That female elephant in the next cage was permeatin' the atmosphere about her with a powerful and excitin' odor of female fertility! Huh! Ain't that a nice way to put it, Brick?

BRICK: Yes, sir, nothin' wrong with it.

BIG DADDY: Brick says the's nothin' wrong with it!

BIG MAMA: Oh, Big Daddy!

BIG DADDY (*XDSC*): So this ole bull elephant still had a couple of fornications left in him. He reared back his trunk an' got a whiff of that elephant lady next door!—began to paw at the dirt in his cage an' butt his head against the separatin' partition and, first thing y'know, there was a conspicuous change in his *profile*—very *conspicuous*! Ain't I tellin' this story in decent language, Brick?

BRICK: Yes, sir, too ruttin' decent!

BIG DADDY: So, the little boy pointed at it and said, "What's that?" His Mam said, "Oh, that's—nothin'!"—His Papa said, "She's spoiled!"

(*Field-hands sing off R, featuring Sookey: "I Just Can't Stay Here by Myself," through following scene.*

(*Big Daddy X to Brick at L.*)

BIG DADDY: You didn't laugh at that story, Brick.

(*Big Mama X DRC crying. Margaret goes to her. Mae and Gooper hold URC.*)

BRICK: No, sir, I didn't laugh at that story.

(*On the lower gallery, Big Mama sobs. Big Daddy looks toward her.*)

BIG DADDY: What's wrong with that long, thin woman over there, loaded with diamonds? Hey, what's-your-name, what's the matter with you?

MARGARET (*X toward Big Daddy*): She had a slight dizzy spell, Big Daddy.

BIG DADDY (*ULC*): You better watch that, Big Mama. A stroke is a bad way to go.

MARGARET (*X to Big Daddy at C*): Oh, Brick, Big Daddy has on your birthday present to him, Brick, he has on your cashmere robe, the softest material I have ever felt.

BIG DADDY: Yeah, this is my soft birthday, Maggie. . . .

Not my gold or my silver birthday, but my soft birthday, everything's got to be soft for Big Daddy on this soft birthday.

(*Maggie kneels before Big Daddy C. As Gooper and Mae speak, Big Mama X USRC in front of them, hushing them with a gesture.*)

GOOPER: Maggie, I hate to make such a crude observation, but there is somethin' a little indecent about your—

MAE: Like a slow-motion football tackle—

MARGARET: Big Daddy's got on his Chinese slippers that I gave him, Brick. Big Daddy, I haven't given you my big present yet, but now I will, now's the time for me to present it to you! I have an announcement to make!

MAE: What? What kind of announcement?

GOOPER: A sports announcement, Maggie?

MARGARET: Announcement of life beginning! A child is coming, sired by Brick, and out of Maggie the Cat! I have Brick's child in my body, an' that's my birthday present to Big Daddy on this birthday!

(*Big Daddy looks at Brick who X behind Big Daddy to DS portal, L.*)

BIG DADDY: Get up, girl, get up off your knees, girl.

(*Big Daddy helps Margaret rise. He X above her, to her R, bites off the end of a fresh cigar, taken from his bathrobe pocket, as he studies Margaret.*)

Uh-huh, this girl has life in her body, that's no lie!
BIG MAMA: BIG DADDY'S DREAM COME TRUE!
BRICK: *JESUS!*
BIG DADDY (*X R below wicker seat*): Gooper, I want my lawyer in the mornin'.
BRICK: Where are you goin', Big Daddy?
BIG DADDY: Son, I'm goin' up on the roof to the belvedere on th' roof to look over my kingdom before I give up my kingdom—twenty-eight thousand acres of th' richest land this side of the Valley Nile!

(*Exit through R doors, and DR on gallery.*)

BIG MAMA (*following*): Sweetheart, sweetheart, sweetheart—can I come with you?

(*Exits DR.*
(*Margaret is DSC in mirror area.*)

GOOPER (*X to bar*): Brick, could you possibly spare me one small shot of that liquor?
BRICK (*DLC*): Why, help yourself, Gooper boy.
GOOPER: I will.
MAE (*X forward*): Of course we know that this is a lie!
GOOPER (*drinks*): Be still, Mae!
MAE (*X to Gooper at bar*): I won't be still! I know she's made this up!
GOOPER: God damn it, I said to shut up!
MAE: That woman isn't pregnant!
GOOPER: Who said she was?
MAE: She did!
GOOPER: The doctor didn't. Doc Baugh didn't.
MARGARET (*X R to above couch*): I haven't gone to Doc Baugh.
GOOPER (*X through to L of Margaret*): Then who'd you go to, Maggie?

(*Offstage song finishes.*)

MARGARET: One of the best gynecologists in the South.
GOOPER: Uh-huh, I see—

(*Foot on end of couch, trapping Margaret:*)

May we have his name please?

MARGARET: No, you may not, Mister—Prosecutin' Attorney!

MAE (*X to R of Margaret, above*): He doesn't have any name, he doesn't exist!

MARGARET: He does so exist, and so does my baby, Brick's baby!

MAE: You can't conceive a child by a man that won't sleep with you unless you think you're—

(*Forces Margaret onto couch, turns away C.*
(*Brick starts C for Mae.*)

He drinks all the time to be able to tolerate you! Sleeps on the sofa to keep out of contact with you!

GOOPER (*X above Margaret, who lies face down on couch*): Don't try to kid us, Margaret—

MAE (*X to bed, L side, rumpling pillows*): How can you conceive a child by a man that won't sleep with you? How can you conceive? How can you? How can you!

GOOPER (*sharply*): *MAE!*

BRICK (*X below Mae to her R, takes hold of her*): Mae, Sister Woman, how d'you know that I don't sleep with Maggie?

MAE: We occupy the next room an' th' wall between isn't soundproof.

BRICK: Oh . . .

MAE: We hear the nightly pleadin' and the nightly refusal. So don't imagine you're goin' t'put a trick over on us, to fool a dyin' man with—a—

BRICK: Mae, Sister Woman, not everybody makes much noise about love. Oh, I know some people are huffers an' puffers, but others are silent lovers.

GOOPER (*behind seat, R*): This talk is pointless, completely.

BRICK: How d'y'know that we're not silent lovers?

Even if y'got a peep-hole drilled in the wall, how can y'tell if sometime when Gooper's got business in Memphis an' you're playin' scrabble at the country club with other ex-queens of cotton, Maggie and I don't come to some temporary agreement? How do you know that—?

(*He X above wicker seat to above R end couch.*)

MAE: Brick, I never thought that you would stoop to her level, I just never dreamed that you would stoop to her level.

GOOPER: I don't think Brick will stoop to her level.

BRICK (*sits R of Margaret on couch*): What is your level? Tell me your level so I can sink or rise to it.

(*Rises.*)

You heard what Big Daddy said. This girl has life in her body.

MAE: That is a lie!

BRICK: No, truth is something desperate, an' she's got it. Believe me, it's somethin' desperate, an' she's got it.

(*X below seat to below bar.*)

An' now if you will stop actin' as if Brick Pollitt was dead an' buried, invisible, not heard, an' go on back to your peep-hole in the wall—I'm drunk, and sleepy—not as alive as Maggie, but still alive. . . .

(*Pours drink, drinks.*)

GOOPER (*picks up briefcase from R foot of bed*): Come on, Mae. We'll leave these love birds together in their nest.

MAE: Yeah, nest of lice! Liars!

GOOPER: Mae—Mae, you jes' go on back to our room—

MAE: Liars!

(*Exits through hall.*)

GOOPER (*DR above Margaret*): We're jest goin' to wait an' see. Time will tell.

(*X to R of bar.*)

Yes, sir, little brother, we're just goin' to wait an' see!

(*Exit, hall.*

(*The clock strikes twelve.*

(*Maggie and Brick exchange a look. He drinks deeply, puts his glass on the bar. Gradually, his expression changes. He utters a sharp exhalation.*

(*The exhalation is echoed by the singers, off UR, who commence vocalizing with "Gimme a Cool Drink of Water Fo' I Die," and continue till end of act.*)

MARGARET (*as she hears Brick's exhalation*): The click?

(*Brick looks toward the singers, happily, almost gratefully. He XR to bed, picks up his pillow, and starts toward head of couch, DR, Xing above wicker seat. Margaret seizes the pillow from his grasp, rises, stands facing C, holding the pillow close. Brick watches her with growing admiration. She moves quickly USC, throwing pillow onto bed. She X to bar. Brick counters below wicker seat, watching her. Margaret grabs all the bottles from the bar. She goes into hall, pitches the bottles, one after the other, off the platform into the UL lawn area. Bottles break, off L. Margaret re-enters the room, stands UC, facing Brick.*)

Echo Spring has gone dry, and no one but me could drive you to town for more.

BRICK: Lacey will get me—

MARGARET: Lacey's been told not to!

BRICK: I could drive—

MARGARET: And you lost your driver's license! I'd phone ahead and have you stopped on the highway before you got halfway to Ruby Lightfoot's gin mill. I told a lie to Big Daddy, but we can make that lie come true. And then I'll bring you liquor, and we'll get drunk together, here, tonight, in this place that death has come into! What do you say? What do you say, baby?

BRICK (*X to L side bed*): I admire you, Maggie.

(*Brick sits on edge of bed. He looks up at the overhead light, then at Margaret. She reaches for the light, turns it out; then she kneels quickly beside Brick at foot of bed.*)

MARGARET: Oh, you weak, beautiful people who give up with such grace. What you need is someone to take hold of you —gently, with love, and hand your life back to you, like something gold you let go of—and I can! I'm determined to do it—and nothing's more determined than a cat on a tin roof—is there? Is there, baby?

(*She touches his cheek, gently.*)

Curtain

CHRONOLOGY

NOTE ON THE TEXTS

NOTES

Chronology

1911 Born March 26 in Columbus, Mississippi, the second child of Edwina Estelle Dakin Williams and Cornelius Coffin Williams, and christened Thomas Lanier Williams III. (Grandfather Thomas Lanier Williams II was an unsuccessful candidate for governor of Tennessee who later served as state railroad commissioner. Father, born 1879 in Knoxville and known as "C.C.," served in the Spanish-American War, worked for a telephone company as a regional manager, and then became a traveling salesman for a Knoxville men's clothing company. Mother, born 1884 in Marysville, Ohio, moved between Ohio and Tennessee before her family settled in Mississippi in 1901. Parents married in 1907; their first child, Rose, was born in 1909.) Lives with mother, sister, and grandparents in the rectory of St. Paul's Church, where grandfather Walter Dakin, an Episcopal priest, serves as minister; father is usually away from home on business.

1913 Family moves to Nashville when grandfather becomes rector of the Church of the Advent.

1914 Father takes new job as traveling salesman for a St. Louis shoe company, and continues to be away from family most of the time.

1915 Family returns to Mississippi when grandfather becomes rector in Canton and then Clarksdale, town in the Mississippi Delta. Williams is read to by grandparents and mother and listens to animal stories told by "Ozzie," his African-American nurse.

1916 Develops diphtheria during summer, followed by Bright's disease, which leaves him confined to his house and unable to walk for a year and a half. Mother reads to him from Dickens and Shakespeare.

1918 Father moves family in July to St. Louis, where he has taken a job as a branch manager with the International

Shoe Company. Williams enters Eugene Field Elementary School in September. Intimidated by his father, who calls him "Miss Nancy" because of his sensitivity and shyness.

1919 Brother Walter Dakin Williams, called Dakin, born February 21. Tension increases between his parents.

1920 Williams is sent to Clarksdale to stay with his grandparents when his mother becomes ill.

1922 Father is promoted to sales manager and moves family into better apartment. Williams enters Stix School, where he becomes friends with Hazel Kramer.

1924 Family moves into another apartment. Williams enters Ben Blewett Junior High School and begins writing on a secondhand typewriter given to him by his mother. Short story "Isolated" is printed in the school newspaper in November.

1925 Poem "Demon Smoke" appears in school yearbook. Family spends August in Elkmont, Tennessee, in the Smoky Mountains, where Williams learns to swim. Father's drinking becomes chronic problem. Rose, growing increasingly disturbed and rebellious, is sent to All Saints College in Vicksburg, Mississippi. Friendship with Hazel Kramer continues.

1926 Mother has hysterectomy. Williams enters Soldan High School in January. Family moves in June to apartment in University City just west of St. Louis. Williams enters University City High School.

1927 Wins $5 as third prize from *Smart Set* for writing an answer to the question "Can a good wife be a good sport?" Wins a prize for reviewing the film *Stella Dallas.*

1928 Short story "The Vengeance of Nitocris" published in *Weird Tales.* Rose begins to show signs of a deepening depression. Williams goes with his grandfather Dakin to New York, where they see *Show Boat* on Broadway, then sails to Europe with grandfather and a church group from Mississippi for a tour of the Continent. Visits France, Italy, Switzerland, Germany, the Netherlands, and England.

1929 Graduates from high school and enters the University of Missouri at Columbia, intending to study journalism. Pledges Alpha Tau Omega fraternity at his father's insistence. Becomes good friends with Esmeralda Mayes, who is also a poet.

1930 Writes one-act play *Beauty Is the Word*, for a modern drama class he is auditing. Submits it to the Dramatic Arts Club contest and wins honorable mention, the first freshman to be so honored.

1931 Works as typist at International Shoe Company during the summer. Enrolls in the University of Missouri School of Journalism at Columbia.

1932 Completes third year of college, but because he has failed ROTC, father makes him leave school and work as a clerk at the shoe company. Votes for Socialist candidate Norman Thomas for president.

1933 Continues writing and has poems accepted for publication in various journals. Short story "Stella for Star" awarded first prize in the St. Louis Writers' Guild contest.

1935 Suffers collapse from exhaustion in January and is hospitalized. Father allows him to leave the shoe company and spend the summer in Memphis with his Dakin grandparents. Writes *Cairo! Shanghai! Bombay!*, which is produced by an amateur company in Memphis, Williams' first play to be staged. Begins reading the stories of Anton Chekhov. Returns to St. Louis in the fall and audits courses at Washington University.

1936 Admitted to Washington University and writes plays *The Magic Tower* and *Candles to the Sun* for the Mummers, a St. Louis drama group. Becomes friendly with a group of young poets, including Clark Mills McBurney, who introduces him to the work of Hart Crane. Publishes poetry in the university magazine. Deeply moved by seeing Alla Nazimova in a touring company of Ibsen's *Ghosts.*

1937 *Candles to the Sun* is performed by the Mummers in St. Louis in March. Rose is committed to a psychiatric ward in St. Louis, then moved to a Catholic convalescent home, where she is diagnosed as having dementia praecox (schizophrenia). In the summer she is transferred to the state hospital at Farmington, Missouri, and given insulin shock treatment. Supported by the Rev. and Mrs. Dakin, Williams studies playwriting at the University of Iowa under well-known professors E. C. Mabie and E. P. Conkle. Works on a "living newspaper" drama. *The Fugitive Kind* is produced by the Mummers. Completes a draft of *Spring Storm* late in the year.

1938 Submits *Spring Storm* in March to his playwriting class at the University of Iowa, but it is not well received. Awarded B.A. degree in English by the University of Iowa. Spends summer and fall in St. Louis and submits *Spring Storm* to the Mummers, but they do not produce it. Begins writing *Not About Nightingales* in September after reading newspaper account of inmates suffocated in a steam room in a Pennsylvania prison. The St. Louis Poets' Workshop, which McBurney and William Jay Smith had established, continues to meet in the Williams home. Uses name "Tennessee Williams" for the first time on entry form for Group Theatre play contest. Goes to New Orleans in late December for the first of many stays there and is shocked by the lifestyle in the French Quarter. Soon makes friends, and becomes accustomed to and embraces the free-wheeling attitude of Quarterites.

1939 Moves January 1 to 722 Toulouse in the French Quarter, where he remains several weeks, supporting himself briefly as a waiter. Meets artists and writers, including Lyle Saxon and Roark Bradford, and attempts to secure a position with the Federal Writers' Project. Submits *Fugitive Kind* to the Project and continues work on *Not About Nightingales.* Leaves for California on February 20 with James Parrott, a musician who becomes a close friend. Wins $100 from the Group Theatre in March for one-act play collection. Engages Audrey Wood as his agent after she contacts him; she places "The Field of Blue Children" with *Story* magazine, his first publication using the name "Tennessee." Visits Frieda Lawrence in New Mexico because of his devotion to D. H. Lawrence's work. Returns to St. Louis in December, where he learns that he has been awarded a $1,000 grant from the Rockefeller Foundation.

1940 Moves to New York and enrolls in John Gassner's modern drama course at the New School for Social Research. Becomes friends with Donald Windham and Gilbert Maxwell. Lives for a while in Provincetown, Massachusetts, where he meets and falls in love with Kip Kiernan, a dancer. The Theatre Guild opens *Battle of Angels*, directed by Margaret Webster, in Boston on December 30. Becomes friends with Paul Bigelow, who works for the Guild.

1941 *Battle of Angels* closes January 11. Receives draft deferment because of his poor eyesight. Stays briefly in St. Louis, Miami, and Key West, where he meets Marion Vaccaro, who will become one of his best friends. Receives $500 advance from the Theatre Guild to rewrite *Battle of Angels*. Returns to New York and submits the revised play, which is rejected by the Guild. Hume Cronyn takes an option on one-act plays. Spends part of the summer in Provincetown. Returns to New Orleans in September and in November goes to St. Louis, where his grandmother Dakin is ill. Takes a job as a cashier at a New Orleans restaurant in December. Completes draft of a long play, *Stairs to the Roof.*

1942 Stays with friends in New York in January, working on several plays and taking a variety of odd jobs. One-act plays anthologized in *American Scenes* and *Best One-Act Plays*. Collaborates with Donald Windham on a play, *You Touched Me!*, based on a D. H. Lawrence story. Spends part of the summer in Macon, Georgia, with Paul Bigelow, and in Jacksonville, Florida, where he operates a teletype for the U.S. Engineers Office. Returns to New York, where he stays with friends and continues work on *You Touched Me!* In Texas, meets Margo Jones, a leader in the regional theater movement. Meets James Laughlin, publisher of New Directions, in December; he becomes a close friend.

1943 Rose, still confined in a mental institution, undergoes a bilateral prefrontal lobotomy in January. Williams lives in a Brooklyn hotel, then moves to the YMCA. Works briefly as elevator operator, movie theater usher, and bellhop. Returns to St. Louis, where he works on a dramatic adaptation of his story "Portrait of a Girl in

Glass" called "The Gentleman Caller." In May, at the instigation of his agent Audrey Wood, goes to Hollywood to write for MGM at $250 a week. Works on a variety of scripts, including ones for Lana Turner and Margaret O'Brien, and his own "The Gentleman Caller," but is not successful as a screenwriter. *You Touched Me!* opens October 13 in Cleveland, Ohio, and is later staged in Pasadena, California.

1944 Grandmother Rose Dakin dies in January in St. Louis, where he is visiting. Kip Kiernan dies from brain tumor in March. Receives a $1,000 grant from Academy of Arts and Letters and goes to Provincetown, where he rewrites "The Gentleman Caller" as a stage play. In September James Laughlin publishes 26 of his poems in *Five Young American Poets* (from this point on, New Directions will publish most of Williams' books). During rehearsals for *The Glass Menagerie*, the new title of "The Gentleman Caller," returns to St. Louis and there is interviewed by a local drama critic, William Inge, an aspiring dramatist himself. *The Glass Menagerie* opens in Chicago on December 26, with Laurette Taylor as Amanda Wingfield. The play receives excellent reviews from drama critics Claudia Cassidy and Ashton Stevens, who write about it repeatedly and are instrumental in making it a hit in Chicago.

1945 *The Glass Menagerie* opens on Broadway on March 31 to generally favorable reviews. Critics have high praise for Laurette Taylor, but some, including George Jean Nathan, have reservations about the play. Two weeks after its opening, it wins the New York Drama Critics Circle Award. Success of the play relieves Williams from the financial troubles that have burdened him; he assigns half of the royalties to his mother. Following eye surgery, goes to Mexico to work on a play called "The Moth," then renamed "Blanche's Chair in the Moon," and later "The Poker Night." New Directions publishes *27 Wagons Full of Cotton and Other One-Act Plays.* Remains in Mexico until August, when he visits Margo Jones in Dallas, then goes to Boston for rehearsals of *You Touched Me!* It debuts in New York on September 25 to generally poor reviews, and closes after 109 performances.

1946 Settles in the French Quarter in New Orleans with Pancho Rodriguez y Gonzales, whom he had met in New Mexico. Writes *Ten Blocks on the Camino Real.* Travels with Rodriguez in May to Taos, where he suffers a severe attack of diverticulitis that requires surgery. Goes to Nantucket for the summer and writes an appreciative letter to Carson McCullers, who soon joins him on the island and shares a house with him and Rodriguez for the summer, beginning an enduring friendship. Meets dramatist Thornton Wilder on Nantucket. Moves in the fall to St. Peter Street in New Orleans and works on two plays, "The Poker Night" and "Chart of Anatomy." Learns of the death of Laurette Taylor. Grandfather Dakin comes to New Orleans to stay with Williams and Rodriguez.

1947 In January, Hume Cronyn produces three Williams plays, including *Portrait of a Madonna*, starring Jessica Tandy, in Los Angeles. Williams travels with Rodriguez and grandfather Dakin to Key West, where actress Miriam Hopkins has a party for them. Sends finished version of "The Poker Night," soon renamed *A Streetcar Named Desire*, to Audrey Wood in March. Meets Irene Selznick, who will produce the play, in Charleston, South Carolina. Settles with Rodriguez in Provincetown, where he meets Frank Merlo. Rodriguez is enraged and they soon end their often tempestuous relationship. Dallas production of "Chart of Anatomy," retitled *Summer and Smoke*, opens July 8. Goes to Los Angeles for a month and sees Jessica Tandy in *Portrait of a Madonna*; she is cast as Blanche in *Streetcar*. Goes to Dallas to see Margo Jones's production of *Summer and Smoke.* Marlon Brando comes to Provincetown in August to read and is cast as Stanley. *A Streetcar Named Desire*, directed by Elia Kazan and starring Tandy, Brando, and Kim Hunter, opens December 3 in New York. Williams leaves for Europe at the end of the year.

1948 Parents separate. *A Streetcar Named Desire* is awarded the Pulitzer Prize and the Drama Critics Circle Award. Williams stays in London, Paris, and Rome, where he meets Truman Capote and Gore Vidal and becomes involved with a young Italian named Salvatore. In England, visits Helen Hayes, who is in rehearsal for *The Glass Menagerie*; meets John Gielgud, Noël Coward, Laurence

Olivier, and Vivien Leigh. Becomes friends with Maria Britneva (later Lady Maria St. Just). Returns to Paris, where he meets Jean Cocteau, who wants to stage a French production of *Streetcar*. In July, his mother and brother come to London for the British opening of *The Glass Menagerie*. Returns to U.S. in September on the *Queen Mary* with Truman Capote. *One Arm and Other Stories* is published by New Directions. *Summer and Smoke*, directed by Margo Jones, opens in New York. In October Frank Merlo moves in with him, beginning the longest intimate relationship of his life. Starts work on a preliminary draft of *Sweet Bird of Youth*. Arranges for Rose to receive half the royalties from *Summer and Smoke*. Visits Paul and Jane Bowles in Tangier in December with Frank Merlo.

1949 Arranges for Rose to be transferred from the state hospital to a private sanitarium in Connecticut. Travels in January with Merlo to Italy, where they take an apartment, and later to Sicily, where they meet Merlo's family. Begins work on the novel *The Roman Spring of Mrs. Stone*. Starts to rely heavily on drugs. In March, travels with Merlo, Capote, and Jack Dunphy to Ischia. Argues frequently with Capote and others. Goes to London in April and visits with Laurence Olivier, director of the London production of *Streetcar*, and Vivien Leigh, who will star as Blanche. Returns with Merlo to New York in September, then goes to Hollywood to advise on the script of the film version of *The Glass Menagerie*. Moves with Merlo and grandfather Dakin to Key West in November. Begins work on *The Rose Tattoo*. New York production of *Streetcar* closes after two years, the longest run of any of his plays on Broadway.

1950 Goes to New York for the openings of Inge's *Come Back, Little Sheba* and Carson McCullers' stage adaptation of *The Member of the Wedding*. Returns to Key West and works on *The Rose Tattoo*, which he dedicates to Merlo. Attends a limited New York run of *Streetcar* starring Uta Hagen and Anthony Quinn and at the end of May sails with Merlo and Jane Smith to Europe. In Paris endeavors to persuade Anna Magnani to star in the stage production of *The Rose Tattoo* but she declines, feeling that she does not speak English well enough. With Merlo, again visits

Sicily, where he hopes to learn local dialect for use in *Tattoo*. They settle for a time in Rome, visit Vienna, then return to the U.S. Buys a house on Duncan Street in Key West that he had previously rented. *The Rose Tattoo* has its off-Broadway premiere in Chicago in December.

1951 *The Rose Tattoo*, starring Maureen Stapleton and Eli Wallach and produced by Cheryl Crawford, opens February 3 on Broadway and later wins Tony Award as best play. Transfers Rose to Stony Lodge, clinic near Ossining, New York, where she will spend most of the rest of her life; visits her often and on occasion takes her to visit Carson McCullers in Nyack or to shop in New York. Begins work on revision of *Battle of Angels* that will become *Orpheus Descending*. Travels with Merlo to England, Italy, Spain, Germany, and to Sweden and Denmark for the premieres of *The Rose Tattoo*. Grows increasingly dependent on alcohol and drugs. Goes to London for premiere of the play, then returns to the U.S. Elia Kazan's film of *A Streetcar Named Desire*, with Marlon Brando as Stanley and Vivien Leigh as Blanche, is released.

1952 Visits New Orleans, then goes to Key West, where he revises *Ten Blocks on the Camino Real* and a screenplay that will ultimately become *Baby Doll*. Goes to New York to see José Quintero's successful revival of *Summer and Smoke* in New York in April at Circle in the Square with Geraldine Page; is moved by the direction and acting. Elected to the National Institute of Arts and Letters. Spends summer in Europe with Merlo, with whom his relations are increasingly strained. Frequently sees Anna Magnani, Carson McCullers, and her husband, Reeves McCullers. Returns to Key West.

1953 *Camino Real* opens in New York March 19 after previews in New Haven and Philadelphia, and is not well received. Williams, depressed by the reviews and attacks from Walter Winchell and Ed Sullivan, returns to Key West to revise *Camino Real* for publication by New Directions. Works on *Cat on a Hot Tin Roof*. Directs Donald Windham's *The Starless Air* at the Playhouse Theatre in Houston. Argues with Windham about the play and their friendship is strained. Visits his grandfather at the Gayoso Hotel in Memphis, where the Reverend Dakin is living.

Travels extensively in Europe with Merlo and Paul Bowles in the summer. Begins work on a short story, "Man Bring This Up Road," that will ultimately become *The Milk Train Doesn't Stop Here Anymore*. Goes with Paul Bowles to Tangier in the fall. Returns to New York with Merlo in October, then goes to New Orleans, with grandfather Dakin, and spends the rest of the year there.

1954 Spends early months of the year in Key West working on *Cat on a Hot Tin Roof*. Continues work on screenplay, now called "Hide and Seek," that will become *Baby Doll*. Gives poetry reading with Carson McCullers in New York in May. Goes with Merlo a month later to Rome, where they join Maria Britneva and travel to Spain. Drinks heavily and takes increasing amounts of drugs. Returns to U.S. in September with Merlo and Anna Magnani for the filming of *The Rose Tattoo* in Key West. Continues work on revision of *Battle of Angels*. *Hard Candy*, his second collection of short stories, is published. Grandfather Dakin suffers a stroke in St. Louis.

1955 After some difficulty, Williams and agent Audrey Wood choose Elia Kazan to direct *Cat on a Hot Tin Roof*. Disagrees with Kazan on the ending of the play but eventually revises third act following Kazan's recommendation. Goes to New Orleans in mid-January to direct *27 Wagons Full of Cotton* and opera based on *Lord Byron's Love Letter* at Tulane University. Attends rehearsals of *Cat on a Hot Tin Roof* in New York. Grandfather Dakin dies February 14 in St. Louis at age 97. *Cat on a Hot Tin Roof*, starring Burl Ives, Barbara Bel Geddes, and Ben Gazzara, opens on Broadway March 24 with the revised third act and is a critical triumph. Subsequently wins the Drama Critics Circle award and the Pulitzer Prize. Film of *The Rose Tattoo* is released. Returns to Key West in April with Carson McCullers; they work together, then go to Havana briefly. In June goes again to Europe for the summer. Learns in July that Margo Jones has died. Suffering from writer's block, Williams continues to rely on drink and drugs. Attends Stockholm opening of the Swedish *Cat on a Hot Tin Roof* and visits his friend Lilla von Saher. Returns to New York to work on the screenplay of *Baby Doll*, and also works on "The Enemy: Time," which will become *Sweet Bird of Youth*.

1956 Goes with Maria Britneva and Marion Vaccaro to Miami, where Tallulah Bankhead is starring in a revival of *Streetcar*; his dissatisfaction with her performance is publicized and Williams apologizes to an angry Bankhead. *Sweet Bird of Youth*, directed by George Keathley, opens in Miami on April 16. Williams goes to Rome alone as the tension between him and Merlo increases. In November, *The Glass Menagerie* is revived in New York starring Helen Hayes as Amanda. The film *Baby Doll*, directed by Elia Kazan and starring Carroll Baker and Eli Wallach, is released; it is denounced by Cardinal Spellman, and condemned by the Catholic Legion of Decency and other groups. Goes to Key West with his mother. First collection of poetry, *In the Winter of Cities*, is published.

1957 Travels to New York for revisions and rehearsals of *Orpheus Descending*. Directed by Harold Clurman, the play opens on Broadway on March 21 and closes after two months; its negative reviews worsen Williams' depression. Father dies March 27, and Williams attends funeral in Knoxville with his brother Dakin. In June begins psychotherapy with Dr. Lawrence S. Kubie, a Freudian analyst, who, according to Williams, urges him to quit writing and to live as a heterosexual. Spends the summer in New York, visiting friends and often going to Stony Lodge to see Rose. Works on *Suddenly Last Summer*.

1958 On January 7 *Garden District*, consisting of *Suddenly Last Summer* and *Something Unspoken*, premieres Off Broadway in New York to favorable reviews. Returns to Key West to work on *Sweet Bird of Youth*. Ends his analysis with Dr. Kubie in March and leaves again for Europe. *Cat on a Hot Tin Roof* opens in London and in August the film version, directed by Richard Brooks and starring Elizabeth Taylor, Paul Newman, and Burl Ives, is released. Returns to Florida in the fall, and collaborates with Meade Roberts on script for film of *Orpheus Descending*, which is retitled *The Fugitive Kind*. Continues work on *Sweet Bird of Youth* and *Period of Adjustment*, which opens on December 29 for a brief run at the Coconut Grove Playhouse.

1959 Goes to New York in February for rehearsals of *Sweet Bird of Youth*. Directed by Elia Kazan and starring Geraldine

Page and Paul Newman, it opens on Broadway March 10. Depressed by critical response to the play, Williams leaves New York for Miami and then goes with Marion Vaccaro to Havana, where he meets Fidel Castro, an admirer of Williams' work. Returns with Vaccaro to Key West for a few weeks and in May flies with her to London for the English premiere of *Orpheus Descending*. Returns to New York in June for rehearsals of *The Fugitive Kind*. In July attends a Chicago production of *Suddenly Last Summer* with Diana Barrymore. After the play closes, returns to Havana with Vaccaro and Barrymore. Leaves in August on three-month around-the-world trip. Film of *Suddenly Last Summer*, directed by Joseph L. Mankiewicz and starring Katharine Hepburn, Elizabeth Taylor, and Montgomery Clift, is released.

1960 Settles with Merlo in Key West to work on *The Night of the Iguana* and *Period of Adjustment*. In June goes with his mother, brother Dakin, and Dakin's wife, Joyce, to Los Angeles, where they meet Elvis Presley and Mae West. Returns to Key West to work. Relations with Merlo, who shows signs of illness, are strained. *The Fugitive Kind*, film version of *Orpheus Descending*, directed by Sidney Lumet and starring Marlon Brando and Anna Magnani, is released. *The Night of the Iguana* is staged at Coconut Grove in August. *Period of Adjustment* opens on Broadway.

1961 Works in Key West on revisions of *The Night of the Iguana*. Goes with Vaccaro in January to Europe. In Rome they meet Donald Windham and Sandy Campbell, then settle in Taormina, Sicily, where he works on the play. Returns to Key West in the autumn, depressed by what he sees as his waning career and more and more dependent on liquor and pills. During previews in Detroit, Williams is hospitalized after his dog bites him. After previews in several other cities, *The Night of the Iguana*, starring Bette Davis, Margaret Leighton, and Patrick O'Neal, opens in New York on December 28.

1962 *The Night of the Iguana* wins Drama Critics Circle Award as best play. Buys a multi-story townhouse in the French Quarter in New Orleans, using income from film versions of his plays. Made lifetime member of the American Academy of Arts and Letters. Lucy Freeman collaborates with Williams' mother on her memoir, *Remember Me to Tom.* The Spoleto Festival of the Two Worlds in Italy premieres a version of *The Milk Train Doesn't Stop Here Anymore.* Poet Frederick Nicklaus, who has moved in with Williams and Merlo in Key West, accompanies him to Italy. Contacted in London by Audrey Wood, who informs him that Merlo is very ill, he flies back to the U.S.

1963 *Milk Train* moves to New York January 16 and runs for only two months. Merlo is diagnosed with lung cancer and goes to Key West, then back to New York to stay with Williams and Nicklaus. Williams begins revisions of *Milk Train* in preparation for a revival. Merlo dies in September. After the funeral, Williams and Nicklaus fly to Mexico where *Night of the Iguana* is being filmed by John Huston, with a cast including Ava Gardner, Deborah Kerr, and Richard Burton. Williams begins a period of depression and heavy dependence on drugs that he will call his "Stoned Age."

1964 Revival of *Milk Train*, starring Tallulah Bankhead, Tab Hunter, Ruth Ford, and Marion Seldes opens January 1 and closes after three days. Goes to Jamaica and then to Key West, where Nicklaus leaves him in March. Back in New York, he begins seeing a new analyst and becomes a patient of Dr. Max Jacobson, who provides him with amphetamines and barbiturates in pill and injection form. Writes *Slapstick Tragedy*, consisting of two short plays, *The Gnädiges Fräulein* and *The Mutilated.* Realizing that he should not be alone, given his reliance on alcohol and drugs, he hires the first of a series of paid companions, William Glavin, to move in with him and travel with him. Film of *The Night of the Iguana* released.

1965 *The Glass Menagerie* revived with Maureen Stapleton as Amanda. *Milk Train* is revived again in San Francisco and is positively received. Goes to St. Louis to visit his mother, who has begun to suffer from delusions. Continues work on *Slapstick Tragedy*, other plays, and short stories. *The Eccentricities of a Nightingale*, a revision of *Summer and Smoke*, is published.

1966 *Slapstick Tragedy*, starring Zoe Caldwell, Margaret Leighton, and Kate Reid opens in New York in January and runs for only four days. Williams issues a public statement condemning America's involvement in Vietnam. Reliance on drugs grows, abetted by Dr. Jacobson, and his mental state becomes progressively unstable. Works on the film script of *Milk Train*, then goes with Glavin and Lester Persky, who will produce it, to London. Film of *This Property Is Condemned*, loosely based on his one-act play, is released.

1967 Goes with Glavin to Virgin Islands where parts of "Goforth!" (soon retitled *Boom!*), based on *Milk Train*, are being filmed. Travels in the summer with Glavin to Europe, visiting Sardinia where *Boom!* is now being filmed by director Joseph Losey with a cast including Elizabeth Taylor, Richard Burton, and Noël Coward. Friends such as Audrey Wood and Elia Kazan are increasingly concerned by his dependence on drugs and his mental state. Carson McCullers dies September 29 following a massive stroke. *The Knightly Quest: A Novella and Four Short Stories* is published by New Directions. Attends the world premiere of *The Two-Character Play* in London in December with Audrey Wood.

1968 Production of *Kingdom of Earth* with Harry Guardino, Estelle Parsons, and Brian Bedford premieres in February in Philadelphia and then opens in New York on March 27 under the direction of José Quintero and retitled *The Seven Descents of Myrtle*. It runs only a month. *Boom!* is released to unfavorable reviews. Friend Lilla van Saher dies. Works on revision of *The Two-Character Play* and on a new play, *In the Bar of a Tokyo Hotel*. At the end of the year, suffering increasingly from paranoid symptoms exacerbated by drug use, goes with Glavin to Key West.

1969 Dakin, at Audrey Wood's suggestion, goes to Key West to check on Williams, who has grown confused and disoriented. Dakin arranges for him to be received into the Roman Catholic church on January 10, although Williams will later deny that the conversion was authentic. In the spring, assumes direction of the New York production of *In the Bar of a Tokyo Hotel*, which opens May 11 in New York and is widely condemned by critics.

Receives National Institute of Arts and Letters gold medal and an honorary doctorate from the University of Missouri at Columbia. In June, flies with actress Anne Meacham to Tokyo where they meet writer Yukio Mishima and see part of the Japanese production of *Streetcar*. Returns to Key West, where Glavin joins him, then goes to San Francisco again and to New Orleans to see Pancho Rodriguez. Becomes progressively more dependent on drugs and increasingly paranoid. In September Dakin convinces him to enter Barnes Hospital in St. Louis, where he is placed in the mental ward. Suffers seizures and two heart attacks related to withdrawal from drugs. Recovers sufficiently to return to Key West in December.

1970 Goes to New York in January for revival of *Camino Real*. Discusses his homosexuality in a television interview with David Frost. Marion Black Vaccaro dies in April. At the end of summer, travels with Oliver Evans to New Orleans and then to Hawaii, Hong Kong, Thailand, and Japan, where he meets with Yukio Mishima shortly before Mishima commits ritual suicide. *Dragon Country: A Book of Plays* is published.

1971 Attends rehearsals in Chicago of production of *Out Cry* (a revised version of *The Two-Character Play*), starring Donald Madden and Eileen Herlie. Resumes use of drugs and, in a fit of anger, dismisses his agent, Audrey Wood, who is replaced by Bill Barnes. Revises and expands *Confessional* into full-length play *Small Craft Warnings*. New Directions begins publication of the multi-volume set, *The Theatre of Tennessee Williams*. Speaks out against American involvement in the Vietnam War at a rally at the Cathedral of St. John the Divine in New York in December.

1972 Moves into an apartment in the New Orleans townhouse he had bought in 1962. *Small Craft Warnings* opens in Philadelphia in February and in New York in April. Awarded honorary degree by Purdue University. Appears in *Small Craft Warnings* as the character Doc in an attempt to boost ticket sales. Spends fall and winter in New York, Key West, and New Orleans. Completes first draft of *Memoirs*, using title "Flee, Flee This Sad Hotel." Attends the Venice Film Festival in August as a juror.

Robert Carroll becomes his companion-secretary and travels with him.

1973 *Out Cry*, with Michael York and Cara Duff-MacCormick, opens in New York March 1 and closes after twelve performances. Visits Los Angeles for a new staging of *Streetcar* and meets with Canadian television producer Harry Rasky, who has made a documentary film about him. Travels with Carroll to the Far East and then to Rome. In May Jane Bowles dies and in June William Inge commits suicide. Travels to Rome and then to Tangier to visit Paul Bowles. Works on *The Red Devil Battery Sign*. Saddened in September by the death of Anna Magnani. Awarded the first Centennial Medal of the Cathedral of St. John the Divine. Williams and Robert Carroll separate for a while.

1974 Travels extensively and visits Rose often. Works on *The Red Devil Battery Sign*. Goes to London in March for a revival of *Streetcar* with Claire Bloom. While in England, stays with Lady Maria St. Just (formerly Maria Britneva). In July *Cat on a Hot Tin Roof* is revived in New York with Elizabeth Ashley and Keir Dullea. Short story collection *Eight Mortal Ladies Possessed* is published.

1975 Receives National Arts Club's gold medal for literature in February and is given the key to the city of New York. Works on *This Is (An Entertainment)*. Second novel, *Moise and the World of Reason*, is published in May. In June, *The Red Devil Battery Sign* with Claire Bloom and Anthony Quinn opens in Boston and closes in 10 days. A successful revival of *Sweet Bird of Youth* opens in Boston and then moves to New York; there are also revivals of *Summer and Smoke* and of *The Glass Menagerie* in New York. *Memoirs* is published.

1976 *This Is (An Entertainment)* premieres in January in San Francisco, where Williams meets Lyle Leverich, whom he later selects as his biographer. Harry Rasky's documentary film *Tennessee Williams's South* appears on television. A series of young men alternate with Robert Carroll as paid companions. Returns in October to San Francisco for Leverich's production of *The Two-Character Play*. *The Eccentricities of a Nightingale* premieres in Buffalo, New

York, then moves to New York City November 23. *The Night of the Iguana* is revived in London. Inducted into the American Academy of Arts and Letters in December.

1977 *Vieux Carré* opens in May on Broadway and closes after only five performances. Goes to London in June for the premiere of *The Red Devil Battery Sign*. Second volume of poetry, *Androgyne, Mon Amour*, is published. Develops cataract on his right eye. Works on adapting the *Baby Doll* screenplay into a play, *Tiger Tail*, and writing the play *Creve Coeur*.

1978 *Tiger Tail* debuts in Atlanta but closes quickly. Returns to New Orleans for a public appearance in which he reads his poetry and fiction. The Spoleto Festival in Charleston, South Carolina, stages *Creve Coeur* (later retitled *A Lovely Sunday for Creve Coeur*). *Vieux Carré* is revived in London in August with Sylvia Miles. Mitch Douglas succeeds Bill Barnes as Williams' agent. Publishes collection of essays, *Where I Live*. Travels extensively before taking an apartment at Manhattan Plaza in New York. Brings Rose to New York for the holidays.

1979 *A Lovely Sunday for Creve Coeur* opens in New York on January 1 for a brief run. After his gardener in Key West is murdered, Williams discovers that the man had stolen manuscripts, other papers, and photographs. Works on revisions of *The Milk Train Doesn't Stop Here Anymore* and *Clothes for a Summer Hotel*. Brings Rose to Key West to live in a cottage near him, under the care of a cousin, but the arrangement proves unsatisfactory. *Kirche, Küchen, und Kinder* opens in New York in September. In December Williams receives Kennedy Center Honors from President Jimmy Carter.

1980 In January *Will Mr. Merriwether Return from Memphis?* premieres in Key West at the opening of the Tennessee Williams Performing Arts Center. *Clothes for a Summer Hotel*, directed by José Quintero and starring Geraldine Page and Kenneth Haigh, opens in Washington, then Chicago, and in New York on March 26, his birthday, which Mayor Ed Koch declares Tennessee Williams Day; it is to be his last play on Broadway during his lifetime. Mother dies on June 1 at age 95. Travels in Europe in

June and July with artist Henry Faulkner. Works at Goodman Theatre in Chicago on three one-act plays. Appointed Distinguished Writer in Residence at the University of British Columbia in Vancouver, but does not remain for the full term. The triad of short plays, collectively called *Tennessee Laughs*, is presented at the Goodman Theatre. Spends holiday season in Key West, where he arranges for Rose to be returned to the nursing home in Ossining, New York.

1981 Works on *A House Not Meant to Stand* at Goodman. The Goodman has a party to celebrate his seventieth birthday, after which *A House Not Meant to Stand* opens. In April, former agent Audrey Wood suffers a stroke that leaves her in a coma. In the summer, works on his version of Chekhov's *The Sea Gull*, which will become *The Notebook of Trigorin*, and on *Something Cloudy, Something Clear*. The latter opens August 24 for a limited run by the Jean Cocteau Repertory, the last of his plays to debut in New York during his lifetime. In the fall, two old friends, poet Oliver Evans and artist Henry Faulkner, die. Along with Harold Pinter, he is awarded the Common Wealth Award of $11,000. Luis Sanjurjo replaces Mitch Douglas as his agent.

1982 Works in Key West on a revision of *A House Not Meant to Stand*. Travels to New York in February to receive the city's medallion of honor. *Something Cloudy, Something Clear* is revived in February by the Jean Cocteau Repertory. Goes to Chicago to discuss staging of the revised and expanded *A House Not Meant to Stand*, which opens in April for a limited run. Receives an honorary doctorate from Harvard in June. Attends staging of several of his plays at the Williamstown Theater Festival in Williamstown, Massachusetts. Works in Key West on a screenplay, then travels with Jane Smith to London and Sicily, where he works on a new play, *The Lingering Hour*. Makes last public appearance in November at the 92nd Street Y in New York. Hospitalized in Key West in December suffering from drug toxicity.

1983 In January, visits Jane Smith in New York, returns to Key West, then goes to New Orleans to arrange the sale of his townhouse. Flies to Taormina in February for a final brief visit before returning to New York. Dies on February 24; the cause of death may have been the result of an overdose of Seconal or from asphyxia caused by choking on a plastic cap of the type used on bottles of nasal spray or eyedrops. Funeral services are held at the St. Louis Cathedral on March 5; Williams is buried next to his mother in the Calvary Cemetery in St. Louis.

Note on the Texts

This volume contains 19 plays written by Tennessee Williams between 1937 and 1955. The texts printed here are taken from the first editions of the plays in book form, with the exception of *Battle of Angels*, where the text is taken from its first periodical printing.

Because Williams habitually revised his works, most of his plays exist in multiple versions. Williams revised many of them after initial book publication for editions published by Dramatists Play Service (intended for use by actors and directors), for subsequent American and English book editions, and for the collected edition *The Theatre of Tennessee Williams*, published by New Directions. Williams also rewrote two of the plays included in the present volume, *Battle of Angels* and *Summer and Smoke*, and republished them as *Orpheus Descending* and *The Eccentricities of a Nightingale*, respectively.

The acting editions of the plays are meant chiefly to aid in staging; a statement by the publisher in the Dramatists Play Service version of *The Glass Menagerie* notes that it is "intended primarily for producing groups," and stage directions "have been drastically changed in order to guide the director and the actor." The acting editions also omit prefaces and commentary that are part of the texts of the book editions.

Williams revised several of his plays relatively soon after their first book publication. The second American edition of *A Streetcar Named Desire*, published in 1950, is a substantial revision of the 1947 first edition. The first English editions of *The Glass Menagerie* and *Summer and Smoke*, published within three years of their first American editions, are also revised versions of the American editions of these plays. Williams' changes, however, are not always retained in subsequent editions of the plays, which sometimes revert to the first editions. In certain instances, Williams' revisions cause inconsistencies within a play, and occasionally he deleted or altered potentially objectionable material.

In 1971, New Directions published the first three volumes of *The Theatre of Tennessee Williams*, a collected edition of Williams' plays. Three additional volumes of this eight-volume series were published during Williams' lifetime and incorporated substantial changes in several plays. For example, the version of *Battle of Angels* printed in *The Theatre of Tennessee Williams* incorporates scenes from Williams' 1957 play *Orpheus Descending*, and the concluding act of *Cat on a*

Hot Tin Roof combines passages from the two versions of the final act that were printed in the 1955 edition.

The texts of the first book editions have been chosen for inclusion here because they are the versions of the plays Williams published for general readers immediately following the plays' composition.

Williams completed "April Is the Cruelest Month," an early draft of the play that became *Spring Storm*, in the spring of 1937, while he was enrolled in the drama school at the University of Iowa. Hoping to get the play staged, he gave a copy of it to Willard Holland, the director of the Mummers, the St. Louis company that had produced Williams' play *Candles to the Sun* in March 1937. He continued to work on the play during the 1937–38 academic year at Iowa, and he read from it to Elsworth Conkle's class in April 1938 and to E. C. Mabie's class in August of the same year. Both Conkle and Mabie responded negatively to the play. Although the Mummers announced a production in May 1938, the play was never staged. Later that year, Williams submitted his typescript to a contest sponsored by the Group Theatre in New York, which rejected it. The same typescript was submitted to MGM in 1943 for possible adaptation as a film script. The play, neither performed nor published during Williams' lifetime, was first published by New Directions in 1999 in an edition, prepared by Dan Isaac, based on the typescript sent to the Group Theatre, now at the Harry Ransom Center at the University of Texas at Austin. Isaac's edition also incorporates a scene and several speeches from earlier drafts of *Spring Storm* and emends the text in several places where the play's internal chronology is inconsistent; these alterations are listed in the notes to the present volume. The 1999 New Directions edition of *Spring Storm* is the text printed here.

Williams began writing *Not About Nightingales* in September 1938, after reading a newspaper story about inmates suffocated in a steam room in a Pennsylvania prison. He worked steadily on the play during the fall of 1938, completing three drafts by the end of the year, and sent a typescript of the finished play in February 1939 to the Group Theatre, which rejected it. The play was neither staged nor published during Williams' lifetime. The typescript sent to the Group Theatre is in the collection of the Harry Ransom Center at the University of Texas at Austin. *Not About Nightingales* was first published by New Directions in 1998 in an edition prepared by Allean Hale, based on the typescript sent to the Group Theatre but with two scenes inserted from an earlier draft of the play entitled

Hell, An Expressionistic Drama. This volume prints the text of the Group Theatre typescript as it is presented in the 1998 New Directions edition; the two scenes taken from *Hell, An Expressionistic Drama* appear in the notes to this volume.

Shortly after arriving in New York City in September 1939, Williams completed the first draft of the play that would become *Battle of Angels*. On November 31 he sent a revised draft to his agent, Audrey Wood, who submitted the play to Harold Clurman of the Group Theatre. After it became clear that the Group Theatre would not stage it, Wood sent a newly revised version of the play to the producer Guthrie McClintic, who turned it down, and to the Theatre Guild in New York, which optioned it. *Battle of Angels* began its pre-Broadway trial run in Boston on December 30, 1940, and closed two weeks later. Lawrence Langner, its producer, told Williams that *Battle of Angels* would have to be revised before the Theatre Guild would stage it in New York; after receiving a new version from Williams in May, the Guild decided not to produce the play. Williams continued to work on Battle of Angels in the years that followed.

Battle of Angels was published in 1945 in the first two issues of *Pharos*, a magazine distributed by New Directions, Williams' publisher. Williams eventually rewrote *Battle of Angels* and published it as a new play, *Orpheus Descending*, in 1957. The first edition of *Orpheus Descending* included a version of *Battle of Angels* that does not contain "The History of a Play (with Parentheses)" but is otherwise not significantly different from the *Pharos* version. The version of *Battle of Angels* included in Volume 1 (1971) of *The Theatre of Tennessee Williams* combines passages from *Battle of Angels* and *Orpheus Descending*. The text printed here is taken from *Pharos* 1–2, Spring 1945.

In July 1939 Williams wrote to Audrey Wood that he wanted to write a play based on the life of D. H. Lawrence, and he discussed the idea with Frieda Lawrence in August 1939. He completed *I Rise in Flame, Cried the Phoenix* in 1941, but it was not published until New Directions brought out the play in a limited edition in 1951. The acting edition published by Dramatists Play Service in 1953 contains an altered ending, as well as other changes. These revisions were retained when the play was collected in *Dragon Country: A Book of Plays* (New York: New Directions, 1970). The text printed here is taken from the 1951 New Directions edition.

The seven one-act plays in this volume that were published in *27 Wagons Full of Cotton and Other One-Act Plays* in 1946 were written between 1939 and 1945. Four of these plays had previously appeared in anthologies: "This Property Is Condemned," as part of "Landscape with Figures (Two Mississippi Plays)" in *American Scenes*, edited by William Kozlenko (New York: John Day, 1941); "The Lady of Larkspur Lotion" in *The Best One-Act Plays of 1941*, edited by Margaret Mayorga (New York: Dodd, Mead & Company, 1942); "The Last of My Solid Gold Watches" in *The Best One-Act Plays of 1942*, edited by Margaret Mayorga (New York: Dodd, Mead & Company, 1943); "27 Wagons Full of Cotton" in *The Best One-Act Plays of 1944*, edited by Margaret Mayorga (New York: Dodd, Mead & Company, 1945). *27 Wagons Full of Cotton and Other One-Act Plays* was published by New Directions on January 14, 1946. Material from "27 Wagons Full of Cotton" was used by Williams in his screenplay *Baby Doll*, published by New Directions in 1956, which in turn was the basis for his 1978 play *Tiger Tail.* Williams did not revise any of the six other plays for publication after the 1946 New Directions *27 Wagons Full of Cotton and Other One-Act Plays.* An English edition of the book was published by John Lehmann in 1947. These plays were reprinted in Volume 6 of *The Theatre of Tennessee Williams.* The texts of "27 Wagons Full of Cotton," "The Lady of Larkspur Lotion," "The Last of My Solid Gold Watches," "Portrait of a Madonna," "Auto-da-Fé," "Lord Byron's Love Letter," and "This Property Is Condemned" printed here are taken from the 1946 New Directions edition.

Williams wrote several short stories in the late 1930's and early 1940's that are related to *The Glass Menagerie*, including "If You Breathe, It Breaks," "Daughter of Revolution," and "Portrait of a Girl in Glass," which was completed in 1943 and collected in *One Arm* (New York: New Directions, 1948). In July 1943 Williams sent Audrey Wood a scenario for a film based on "Portrait of a Girl in Glass," hoping that MGM would be interested in the project. After the scenario was rejected, Williams resumed work on a stage adaptation of the story, which used the working title "The Gentleman Caller." Williams completed a draft of "The Gentleman Caller" while living in Provincetown, Massachusetts, during the summer of 1944. In October, producer Eddie Dowling agreed to stage the play, now titled *The Glass Menagerie.* Williams continued to revise the play while it was in rehearsal. *The Glass Menagerie* premiered in Chicago on December 26, 1944, and opened in New York on March 31, 1945. The book version of the play was published by Random House on July 31, 1945.

Both the acting edition (New York: Dramatists Play Service, 1948) and the English edition of *The Glass Menagerie* (London: John

Lehmann, 1948) differ from the Random House edition, and there is also variation between the Dramatists Play Service edition and the Lehmann edition. Many of the speeches, particularly those of Amanda Wingfield, are revised and often expanded in the Lehmann and Dramatists Play Service editions. The Lehmann edition also includes a preface, "The Catastrophe of Success," which appears in the notes of the present volume. The version of *The Glass Menagerie* collected in Volume 1 (1971) of *The Theatre of Tennessee Williams* also includes this preface but otherwise follows the text of the first American edition. The text printed here is taken from the 1945 Random House edition.

In early 1945, while in Chicago for the first run of *The Glass Menagerie*, Williams began writing a play titled first "The Moth," then "Blanche's Chair in the Moon." He returned to the play while in Mexico during the summer of 1945 but then set it aside until the fall of 1946. He worked steadily on the play, using the working title "The Poker Night," during the fall and following winter, and he sent a draft to Audrey Wood in March 1947 for submission to producers. Irene Selznick agreed in early May to stage a production, with Elia Kazan as director. Williams then changed the title to *A Streetcar Named Desire* but did not make revisions during the rehearsals before its New York premiere on December 3, 1947. *A Streetcar Named Desire* was published by New Directions on December 22, 1947; an English edition, published by John Lehmann in 1949, did not include any revisions by Williams.

A second American edition, published by New Directions in 1950, incorporates changes made by Williams, including numerous cuts and alterations of dialogue and stage directions. The Dramatists Play Service edition, published in 1953, generally follows the 1950 edition for speeches and dialogue, though the stage directions are often different. The version that appears in Volume 1 (1971) of *The Theatre of Tennessee Williams* follows the 1950 New Directions text. The text printed here is taken from the 1947 New Directions edition of *A Streetcar Named Desire.*

In the fall of 1945, Williams began writing "Chart of Anatomy," a play that grew out of two of his stories, "Oriflamme" and the not yet completed "The Yellow Bird." After writing a few pages, he set aside "Chart of Anatomy" until the following summer, when he worked on the play fairly continuously. In October 1946 he submitted a draft to Audrey Wood, who sent the script to potential producers. Margo Jones agreed in March 1947 to stage the play, first in Dallas and then in New York. Williams continued to revise the play, now titled *Summer and Smoke*, while living in Provincetown during the summer of 1947. He did not go to Dallas while the play was in rehearsal or in production. In preparation for the New York production, Jones traveled to Europe in the spring of 1948 to meet with Williams and to discuss his most recent version of the play. Williams made further revisions while Jones' production was in rehearsal in New York. *Summer and Smoke* opened on October 6, 1948. The play was published by New Directions on November 17, 1948.

Williams revised *Summer and Smoke* for the 1950 Dramatists Play Service edition of the play, omitting the Prologue, adding a new scene between Scenes 1 and 2, and changing stage directions. The English edition of *Summer and Smoke* was published by John Lehmann in 1952; although this edition does not incorporate many of the changes Williams made for the Dramatists Play Service edition, it is different from the 1948 New Directions edition and contains revisions not included in the Dramatists Play Service edition. *Summer and Smoke* was rewritten and published in 1965 as *The Eccentricities of a Nightingale*. Volume 2 (1971) of *The Theatre of Tennessee Williams* reprints the text of the 1948 edition. The text of *Summer and Smoke* printed here is taken from the 1948 New Directions edition.

In December 1949 Williams completed a draft of "The Eclipse of May 29, 1919," one of several working titles he used for the play that would become *The Rose Tattoo*. He continued working on the play during the winter and following spring, when Cheryl Crawford announced that she would produce the play. Williams revised the play while in Sicily during the summer of 1950, then sent additional changes to Crawford in December while the play was in rehearsal for its Chicago premiere. After it opened on December 29, 1950, Williams went to Chicago to make further revisions while the play was in production. *The Rose Tattoo* opened in New York on February 2, 1951, and was published as a book by New Directions on March 30, 1951. "The Timeless World of a Play" was first published as "Concerning the Timeless World of a Play" in *The New York Times* on January 14, 1951. Williams did not revise *The Rose Tattoo* for its Dramatists Play Service edition, the English edition, or the version that appears in Volume 2 (1971) of *The Theatre of Tennessee Williams*. The text printed here is taken from the 1951 New Directions edition of the play.

Camino Real grew out of a one-act play, "Ten Blocks on the Camino Real," written in early 1946 and first printed in *American*

Blues, a pamphlet of one-act plays published by Dramatists Play Service in 1948. Williams finished a draft of a new, expanded version of the play in January 1952. Later that year Cheryl Crawford agreed to produce *Camino Real*, with Elia Kazan as director. After working on the play while in Europe during the summer of 1952, Williams met with Kazan in September to discuss the script. Following trial runs in New Haven and Philadelphia, the play opened on Broadway on March 19, 1953. Williams altered the script during the New Haven, Philadelphia, and New York productions, and the version published by New Directions in October 1953 incorporates further revisions made after *Camino Real* closed in New York. Williams did not revise *Camino Real* for the English edition published by Secker & Warburg in 1958 or for Volume 2 (1971) of *The Theatre of Tennessee Williams*. The text printed here is taken from the 1953 New Directions edition.

"Talk to Me Like the Rain and Let Me Listen" and "Something Unspoken" first appeared in an expanded edition of *27 Wagons Full of Cotton and Other One-Act Plays*, published by New Directions in 1953. Neither play was subsequently revised by Williams. "'Something Wild'" was first published as "On the Art of Being a True Non-Conformist" in the *New York Star*, November 7, 1948. It appeared as the introduction to the 1949 second edition of *27 Wagons Full of Cotton and Other One-Act Plays* and was reprinted without changes in all subsequent editions. The texts for "'Something Wild,'" "Talk to Me Like the Rain and Let Me Listen," and "Something Unspoken" are taken from the 1953 New Directions edition of *27 Wagons Full of Cotton and Other One-Act Plays*.

Cat on a Hot Tin Roof originated in the short story "Three Players of a Summer Game," first published in *The New Yorker* on November 1, 1952. Williams then adapted the story as a play. In late 1954, the Playwrights Company agreed to produce *Cat on a Hot Tin Roof* and named Elia Kazan as director. Williams came to New York to meet with Kazan, who suggested revisions in the script and asked Williams to rewrite the third act for the Broadway premiere. The play opened on March 25, 1955, with a revised third act; when published in book form by New Directions later that year, both Williams' original version of the third act and the version performed on Broadway were included, with a "Note of Explanation" discussing the circumstances of the revision. The Dramatists Play Service edition of the play prints the revised third act and does not include Williams' original version. The English edition, published by

Secker & Warburg in 1956, and the version that appears in Volume 3 (1971) of *The Theatre of Tennessee Williams* follow the 1955 New Directions edition. For a 1973 revival of *Cat on a Hot Tin Roof* Williams wrote still another version of the third act, combining passages from the two versions of the third act presented in the 1955 edition; he also made changes in the first two acts. This version was published in 1975 by New Directions. The text printed here is taken from the 1955 New Directions edition of *Cat on a Hot Tin Roof* and includes both versions of the third act.

This volume presents the texts of the original printings chosen for inclusion here, but it does not attempt to reproduce features of their typographic design. The texts are presented without change, except for the correction of typographical errors. Spelling, punctuation, and capitalization are often expressive features and are not altered, even when inconsistent or irregular. The following is a list of typographical errors corrected, cited by page and line number: 7.2, 'an; 12.11, Arthur's; 17.13, way?; 19.8, lets; 31.23, it's; 42.7, emotion; 44.12, embarrassment.; 44.26, No.; 62.6, me?; 64.15, sharecroppers; 64.33, you; 66.33, anymore; 91.1, thing; 94.11, Aunt; 95.7, Yes,; 99.5, "Yeah,; 175.25, somthing; 187.38, Jim,; 195.2, nickles; 200.11, Yes,; 202.21, SANDRAS; 205.13, boys; 210.4, would't; 214.27, youg; 220.10, wont; 225.11, Witche's; 226.2, 'listenin'; 229.10, *Is*; 232.16, easter; 247.21, dollor; 248.37, keds; 262.22, then; 272.34, thre; 273.16, Picture; 277.40, states; 278.32, thir; 284.9, appelation; 351.25, kindergardeners; 407.28, answer—while; 407.30, Oh!"; 509.20, face; 515.6, *Blanches*; 525.15, prevue; 531.20, till I; 540.11, *Blanches*; 542.18, unforgiveable; 558.21, STELLA: Yes; 639.12, So Alma you; 662.2, *Rose*; 664.16, crooked:; 664.19, because,; 688.29, Rose; 760.8, Maître 'D'; 815.33, for; 915.14, *dam*; 916.35, *Lacy*; 956.15, Gooper don't; 982.19, Bid; 984.11, going'; 1004.12, an. Corrections in second printing: 441.29, IS (LOA); 672.19, sister!—; 970.5, of our.

ACKNOWLEDGMENTS

The plays in this volume are published by arrangement with New Directions Publishing Corporation, New York, Publisher of the plays of Tennessee Williams, and with The University of the South, copyright proprietor of the works of Tennessee Williams.

Notes

In the notes below, the reference numbers denote page and line of this volume. No note is made for material included in standard desk-reference books such as Webster's *Collegiate*, *Biographical*, and *Geographical* dictionaries. Biblical quotations are keyed to the King James Version. Quotations from Shakespeare are keyed to *The Riverside Shakespeare*, ed. G. Blakemore Evans (Boston: Houghton Mifflin, 1974). Cast lists and production information are taken from the first book editions of the plays. For further biographical information than is contained in the Chronology, see Albert J. Devlin (ed.), *Conversations with Tennessee Williams* (Jackson: University Press of Mississippi, 1986); Ronald Hayman, *Tennessee Williams: Everyone Else Is an Audience* (New Haven: Yale University Press, 1993); Lyle Leverich, *Tom: The Unknown Tennessee Williams* (New York: W.W. Norton & Company, 1995); Harry Rasky, *Tennessee Williams: A Portrait in Laughter and Lamentation* (New York: Dodd, 1986); Donald Spoto, *The Kindness of Strangers: The Life of Tennessee Williams* (Boston: Little, Brown and Company, 1985); Dakin Williams and Shepherd Mead, *Tennessee Williams: An Intimate Biography* (New York: Arbor House, 1983); Edwina Dakin Williams as told to Lucy Freeman, *Remember Me to Tom* (New York: Putnam, 1963); Donald Windham (ed.), *Tennessee Williams' Letters to Donald Windham 1940–1965* (New York: Holt, Rinehart & Winston, 1977).

SPRING STORM

1.1 *Spring Storm*] *Spring Storm* was first performed publicly as a staged reading in New York City on October 26 and 27, 1996, as part of the Ensemble Studio Theatre's Octoberfest 96—Sixteenth Annual Festival of Member-Initiated Plays. Curt Demptster, Artistic Director; Jamie Richards, Executive Producer. The reading was directed by Dona D. Vaughn and initiated by Dan Isaac. The stage managers were Brian George and Sherry Stregack. The cast, in order of appearance, was as follows: DICK MILES: Tristan Fitch; HEAVENLY CRITCHFIELD: Melinda Hamilton; REVEREND HOOKER: Dan Isaac; AGNES PEABODY: Catherine Campbell; ETHEL ASBURY: Carolyn Marcell; SUSAN LAMPHREY: Ina Bass-Filip; MRS. LAMPHREY: Amy Coleman; ARTHUR SHANNON: Peter Sarsgaard; HERTHA NEILSON: Diana LaMar; LILA CRITCHFIELD: Celia Weston; ESMERELDA CRITCHFIELD: Dolores Sutton; OLIVER CRITCHFIELD: Peter Maloney; MRS. DOWD: Debbie Lee Jones; MRS. BUFORD: Amy Coleman; MRS. ADAMS: Kristin Griffith; HENRY ADAMS: Chris White; FANNY: Ina Bass-Filip; MRS. KRAMER: Debbie

Lee Jones; BIRDIE SCHLAGMANN: India Cooper; MABEL: Amy Coleman; RALPH: Brian George. STAGE DIRECTIONS: Mark Johannes. This version of *Spring Storm* also includes the following characters which were not part of the version prepared for the Ensemble Studio Theatre reading: RONALD ASBURY; OZZIE; JACKSON.

5.34–35 "Swear not by the inconstant—April!] Cf. Shakespeare, *Romeo and Juliet*, II.ii.109: "O, swear not by the moon, th' inconstant moon . . . ."

7.38 *The Sheik*] Novel (1921) by Edith Maude Hull.

8.27 Heavenly!] Williams' typescript reads "Helen!" Heavenly's character was named Helen in early drafts of the play.

9.10 *Satuhday's Children*?] *Saturday's Children*, play (1927) by Maxwell Anderson that depicts the marital problems of a young couple.

14.17 Sunday?] Williams' typescript reads "tomorrow?"

24.32 Agnes] Williams' typescript reads "Birdie".

27.17 Agnes Peabody] Williams' typescript reads "Birdie Schlagmann".

28.20–27 When . . . now!] "I Shall Not Care" (1915).

30.19 Sunday night.] These words were added in the 1999 New Directions edition.

30.33–34 "—But only . . . tree!"] Final line of Joyce Kilmer's "Trees" (1914).

31.27–28 Zella Armstrong's *Southern Families*] *Notable Southern Families*, published in six volumes, 1915–33.

36.24–25 the Havilland.] A type of porcelain.

50.1–52.6 SCENE . . . *Two*] This scene, which is part of a draft of *Spring Storm* but does not appear in Williams' finished typescript, is inserted here in the 1999 New Directions edition.

50.18–19 three o'clock in the morning?] Williams' draft reads "two in the morning?"

54.21 If it does rain,] The word "rain" is added in the 1999 New Directions edition.

65.14–19 She sits . . . me!] These lines, which are part of a draft of *Sping Storm* but do not appear in Williams' finished typescript, are inserted here in the 1999 New Directions edition.

69.1–3, 8–15, 18–23 What lips . . . more.] In his typescript of *Spring Storm*, Williams did not specify a poem to be read. The 1999 New Directions edition inserts this untitled sonnet (1923) by Edna St. Vincent Millay.

69.26–27 Alcott series.] Louisa May Alcott's novels for young readers included *Little Women* (1868–69), *An Old-Fashioned Girl* (1870), and *Little Men* (1871).

70.14 next Saturday night,] Williams' typescript reads "tomorrow,".

75.14 nine!] Williams' typescript reads "eleven!"

75.23 *nine*] Williams typescript reads "*eleven*".

80.20–27 (*suddenly . . . despair*)] These lines, which are part of a draft of *Sping Storm* but do not appear in Williams' finished typescript, are inserted here in the 1999 New Directions edition.

82.12–13 When . . . put.] This line was spoken by Heavenly in Williams' typescript but is given to Lila in the 1999 New Directions edition.

82.34–35 the Country Club] Williams' typescript reads "dinner".

83.6 your blue knitted suit.] Williams' typescript reads "her white organdy". The 1999 New Directions edition also omits Mrs. Critchfield's line, "I've simply worked miracles on that dress."

83.38 you what] Williams' typescript reads "you yesterday what".

88.28 *brilliance.*] The 1999 New Directions edition omits the line immediately following in Williams' typescript: "*In her white organdy dress with the orchid pinned to her shoulder she is a breathtaking vision.*"

88.32 the Country Club.] Williams' typescript reads "Lamphrey's."

NOT ABOUT NIGHTINGALES

97.1 *Not About Nightingales*] *Not About Nightingales* was given its world première on March 5, 1998, at the Royal National Theatre, London, England. It was directed by Trevor Nunn; set design was by Richard Hoover; costume design by Karyl Newman; lighting by Chris Parry, music arrangement by Steven Edis, and sound by Christopher Shutt. Production Manager was Jo Maund and Stage Manager, Courtney Bryant. The cast, in order of speaking, was as follows: THE VOICE OF THE LORELEI: Mark Heenehan; MRS. BRISTOL: Sandra Dickinson; EVA CRANE: Sherri Parker Lee; CANARY JIM: Finbar Lynch; BOSS WHALEN, *the Warden*: Corin Redgrave; SAILOR JACK: Richard Leaf; SCHULTZ, *a guard*: Richard Ziman; BUTCH O'FALLON: James Black; THE QUEEN: Juke Akuwudike; JOE: Alex Giannini; MCBURNEY, *a guard*: Craig Pinder; OLLIE: Dion Graham; SWIFTY: Mark Dexter; GOLDIE, *an apparition*: Sandra Dickinson; SHAPIRO: Joel Leffert; MEX: Chico Andrade; KRAUSE: Daniel Stewart; ALBERTS: Noble Shropshire; CHAPLAIN: Rom Hodgkins; REVEREND HOOKER: Noble Shropshire; GUARDS, CONVICTS, TROOPERS: Mark Heenehan, Richard Leaf, Daniel Stewart, Noble Shropshire.

130.38 *Blackout*] In the 1998 New Directions edition, the following scene from "Hell, An Expressionistic Drama," an early draft of *Not About Nightinglales*, is inserted here:

Announcer: "Butch Has A Dream."
Theme up: "Roses of Picardy." Fade.
GOLDIE: Hello, Butch.
BUTCH [*half-rising on his bunk*]: Goldie!
GOLDIE: Yes, it's me.
BUTCH: How didja get in here?
GOLDIE: Walls ain't thick enough to keep us apart always, Butch.
BUTCH: You mean you walked right through? They couldn't stop you?
GOLDIE: That's right, honey.
BUTCH: It's marvelous, marvelous!
GOLDIE: Sure. I never was an ordinary bim. There was always something unusual about me. You noticed that. How light I was on my feet and always laughing. A girl that danced like me, all night till they wrapped up the fiddles and covered the drums, that never got tired, that always wanted one more of whatever was offered, is something kind of special. You know that, Butch. You don't buy us two for a quarter at the corner drug.
BUTCH: Yeah, I know that, Goldie. I always had that special feeling about you, kid. Honey, I used to try to find words to tell yuh what you did to me nights when you opened your mouth against mine and give me your love . . .

Room twenty-three! That was yours. Six flights up the narrow stairs with brass tacks in an old red carpet and bulbs at the end of the hall. Fire-escape. We used to sit out there summer nights and drink iced beer till all we could do was giggle and then go to bed.

Day used to come so slow and easy through the long white blinds. Maybe a little wind making the curtains stir. The milk wagons rattled along, and out on the East River the fog horns blew. I never slept, I lay and watched you sleeping. Your face was like the face of a little girl then. A girl no man ever touched. I never told you about those times I watched you sleeping and how I felt toward you then. Because I wasn't good at making speeches. But I guess you knew.
GOLDIE: Of course I knew. I knew you loved me, Butch.
BUTCH: I wonder if your face still looks like that when you're sleeping.
GOLDIE: I haven't changed. You oughta know that, Butch.
BUTCH: You don't go out with other fellows, do you?
GOLDIE: No. You know I don't. I been as true as God to you, Butch.
BUTCH: But how do you live, how do you get along now, Goldie?
GOLDIE: As good as a girl can expect. I still work days over at the Imperial Dry Cleaners and nights I work at the Paradise, Butch.
BUTCH: I wanted you to quit the Paradise, Goldie.
GOLDIE: What for?
BUTCH: I don't like other guys dancin' witcha.

GOLDIE: They don't mean nothing. Just pasteboard tickets, that's all they are to me, Butch. I keep the stubs an' turn 'em in for cash. And that's as far as it goes.

BUTCH: But when they hold you close sometimes when the lights go out for the waltz–you don't ever close your eyes and blow your breath on their necks like you done for me, Goldie?

GOLDIE: No. Never.

BUTCH: You wouldn't lie to me, Goldie?

GOLDIE: Of course I wouldn't. Some of the girls say one man's as good as another. They're all the same. But I'm not made like that. I give myself, I give myself for *keeps.* And time don't change me none. I'm still the same.

BUTCH: The same old Goldie, huh?

GOLDIE: The same old kid. Running my dancing slippers down at the heels. But not forgetting your love. And going home nights alone. Sleeping alone in a big brass bed. Half of it empty, Butch. And waiting for you.

BUTCH: Waiting for me!

GOLDIE: Yes! Waiting for you! [*She begins to fade into the shadows.*]

BUTCH [*reaching toward her*]: Goldie!

GOLDIE: So long, Butch. So long . . .

BUTCH [*frantically*]: Goldie! Goldie! [*She has completely disappeared.*]

JOE [*sitting up on his bunk*]: What's the matter, Butch.

QUEEN: He's talkin' in his sleep again.

BUTCH [*slowly and with terrific emphasis*]: God—*damn*!

BLACKOUT

137.29 *Blackout*] In the 1998 New Directions edition, the following scene from "Hell, An Expressionistic Drama," an early draft of *Not About Nightingales*, is inserted here:

Announcer: "Hell—an Expressionistic Interlude."

The following scene takes place on a dark stage. The shuffling of feet is heard and continues for several moments. A whistle sounds.

VOICE: TAKE PLACES AT TABLES! [*More shuffling is heard.*] Set down! [*Now we hear the scrape of chairs or benches as the men sit.*]

VOICE: Start eating!

[*A low yammering commences.*]

VOICE: Start eating, I said! You heard me! Start eating!

[*Very softly, in a whisper, voices begin to be heard, transmitting a message from table to table with rising intensity.*]

VOICES: Quit eating—quit eating—quit eating—quit eating—don't eat no more a dis slop—trow it back in deir faces—quit eating—quit eating—we don't eat crap—we're human—quit eating—QUIT EATING—

[*The chorus grows louder, more hysterical, becomes like the roaring of animals. As the yammering swells there is a clatter of tin cups. The lights come up on Butch and others seated on benches at a table. Each has a tin cup and plate with which he beats time to the chorus of the Chant led by Ollie, who stands, stage forward, in the spotlight.*]

OLLIE: Devil come to meet us an' he rang on a bell,
Twenty-five men got a ticket to hell!

CHORUS: Turn on the heat, turn on the heat,
They're gonna give us hell when they turn on the heat.
Turn on the heat, turn on the heat,
They're gonna give us hell when they turn on the heat.

OLLIE: Down in Mizzoura where I was born
I worked all day in a field of corn,
Got pretty hot but at night it was nice
'Cause we kept our beer in a bucket of ice.

CHORUS: Turn on the heat, turn on the heat,
They're gonna give us hell when they turn on the heat.
Turn on the heat, turn on the heat,
They're gonna give us hell when they turn on the heat.

BUTCH: There's one rap that a connie can't beat
When the Warden says, Boys, we gonna turn on the heat!

CHORUS: Turn on the heat, turn on the heat,
They're gonna give us hell when they turn on the heat.

OLLIE: Devil come to meet us an' he rang on a bell,
Twenty-five men got a ticket to HELL!

CHORUS: Turn on the heat, turn on the heat,
They're gonna give us hell when they turn on the heat.
Turn on the heat, turn on the heat,
They're gonna give us hell when they turn on the heat.

[*The lights fade. There is a loud ringing of bells: a whistle sounds; then a sudden dead silence. The lights fade and come up on Schultz and the guards, entering cellblock. The prisoners are back in their cells.*]

SCHULTZ: Now you boys are gonna learn a good lesson about makin' disturbances in mess hall! Git one out of each cell! Keep 'em covered!

JOE [*to Butch*]: You started something all right.

QUEEN: Oh, Lord!

SCHULTZ: Ollie! Shapiro! Come on out, you're elected! Mex!

SHAPIRO: What for! Distoibance? I make no distoibance!

MEX: [*He protests volubly in Spanish.*]

OLLIE: What you want me fo', Mistuh Schultz?

SCHULTZ [*at the door of Butch's cell*]: Stand back there, Butch. [*He prods him with a gun.*] Who's in here with you? Joe? Queenie?

BUTCH: I started the noise.

SCHULTZ: I know you started the noise. But we're saving you, Butch. You're too good to waste on the Hole.

QUEEN: I didn't make any noise, Mr. Schultz. I was perfectly quiet the whole time.

SCHULTZ: Who's that on the bunk? Aw, the new boy. Playing Puss-in-the-Corner! Come on out.

QUEEN: He didn't make noise, Mr. Schultz.
SCHULTZ: Come out, boy!
SWIFTY [*shaking*]: I didn't make any noise. I was sick. I didn't want any supper. I've been sick ever since I come here.
SCHULTZ: Yes, I've heard you squawking! Git in line there.
SWIFTY: I wanta see the Warden. It makes me sick being shut up without exercise.
SCHULTZ: We'll exercise you! [*He blows a whistle.*]
SWIFTY [*wildly*]: The Hole? No! No!
SCHULTZ [*prodding him roughly with a billy*]: Git moving! Krause! Alberts! Awright, that's all!—Two weeks in the hole, bread an' water—maybe we'll finish off with a Turkish bath.—Step on it, Mex!
MEX: [*He swears in Spanish.*]
SHAPIRO: Distoibance? Not me. Naw.
SCHULTZ: Hep, hep, hep— [*A slow shuffling is heard as the lights begin to dim.*]
JOE: Christ!
QUEEN: Swifty won't make it! They'll kill him down there!
[*The whistle is heard, then the distant clang of steel.*]
BUTCH [*whistles a few bars then sings out*]:

They fly so high, nearly reach the sky
Then like my dreams they fade an' die!
Fawchun's always hiding—I looked ev'rywhere!

[*Theme up and dim out.*]
MEX: [*He protests in Spanish.*]
SCHULTZ: Fall in line! March! Hep, hep, hep— [*The voice diminishes as they move, heads bent, shoulders sagging, shuffling down the corridor.*]

BLACKOUT SLOWLY

164.4 *Jésus . . . pecados!*] Jesus—dead for our sins!
165.5–6 *Muerto . . . Sol!*] Dead—for our sins—red—with blood is—the sun!

BATTLE OF ANGELS

189.1 *Battle of Angels*] *Battle of Angels*, a play in 2 acts and 3 scenes, was presented by the Theatre Guild, Inc., at the Wilbur Theatre, Boston, for two weeks, starting December 30, 1940, and ending January 11, 1941. Margaret Webster directed, the scenery was by Cleon Throckmorton and the incidental music was by Colin McPhee, plus Negro spiritual recordings by H. F. Chalfin. No one is listed as lighting director in the program. *The Cast:* DOLLY BLAND: Dorothy Peterson; BEULAH CARTWRIGHT: Edith King; PEE WEE BLAND: Robert Emhardt; SHERIFF TALBOTT: Charles McClelland; CASSANDRA WHITESIDE: Doris Dudley; VEE TALBOTT: Katherine Raht; VALENTINE XAVIER: Wesley Addy; EVA TEMPLE: Hazel Hanna; BLANCH TEMPLE: Helen Carewe; MYRA TORRANCE: Miriam Hopkins; JOE: Clarence Washington; SMALL BOY: Bertram Holmes; BENNIE: Ican Lewis; JABE TORRANCE: Marshall Bradford.

229.15 *"Petty Girl"*] Popular pin-up images drawn by illustrator George Petty (1894–1975) that first appeared in *Esquire* magazine in 1933 and were later featured in advertisements, calendars, and film posters.

234.29 Peabody Roof!] Night club on the roof of the Peabody Hotel in Memphis.

246.21–22 hitting the sawdust trail.] The part of a revival meeting when audience members are invited to come forward as an affirmation of faith.

I RISE IN FLAME, CRIED THE PHŒNIX

289.15 *"Forest Lawn"*] A cemetery in Hollywood where many celebrities are buried.

292.6 Ja . . . dich.] Yes, it is for you.

295.27 Ja . . . Ewigkeit!] Of course! For all of eternity!

296.4 Wie du willst!] As you wish!

27 WAGONS FULL OF COTTON AND OTHER ONE-ACT PLAYS (1946)

307.3–5 *'Now* . . . SAPPHO] From Fragment 47.

312.24 dopes] Coca-Colas.

317.7 I'm not from Missouri!] Missouri is known as "the Show-Me State."

336.2–3 *Ce* . . . RIMBAUD] It can only be the end of the world, moving ahead: Arthur Rimbaud, *Les Illuminations* (1886), "Enfance," IV.

336.32 Sidney Greenstreet,] Sydney Greenstreet (1879–1954), character actor whose films included *The Maltese Falcon* (1941) and *Flamingo Road* (1949).

339.40 I.S.C.] International Shoe Company.

341.31–32 Some people . . . to *die.*] Reference to a tenet of the Jehovah's Witnesses.

360.31 John Abbott] English character actor (b. 1905) whose films included *The Shanghai Gesture* (1941) and *The Mask of Dimitrios* (1944).

381.19 *Canaille!*] Pig!

THE GLASS MENAGERIE

393.1 *The Glass Menagerie*] *The Glass Menagerie* was first produced by Eddie Dowling and Louis J. Singer at the Playhouse Theatre, New York City, on March 31, 1945, with the following cast: THE MOTHER: Laurette Taylor; HER SON: Eddie Dowling; HER DAUGHTER: Julie Haydon; THE GENTLEMAN

CALLER: Anthony Ross. SCENERY DESIGNED AND LIGHTED by Jo Mielziner; ORIGINAL MUSIC COMPOSED by Paul Bowles; STAGED by Eddie Dowling and Margo Jones.

Later editions of *The Glass Menagerie* include the following essay, "The Catastrophe of Success," written in 1948, as a preface:

The winter marked the third anniversary of the Chicago opening of "The Glass Menagerie," an event that terminated one part of my life and began another about as different in all external circumstances as could well be imagined. I was snatched out of virtual oblivion and thrust into sudden prominence, and from the precarious tenancy of furnished rooms about the country I was removed to a suite in a first-class Manhattan hotel. My experience was not unique. Success has often come that abruptly into the lives of Americans. The Cinderella story is our favorite national myth, the cornerstone of the film industry if not of the Democracy itself. I have seen it enacted on the screen so often that I was now inclined to yawn at it, not with disbelief but with an attitude of Who Cares! Anyone with such beautiful teeth and hair as the screen protagonist of such a story was bound to have a good time one way or another, and you could bet your bottom dollar and all the tea in China that that one would not be caught dead or alive at any meeting involving a social conscience.

No, my experience was not exceptional, but neither was it quite ordinary, and if you are willing to accept the somewhat eclectic proposition that I had not been writing with such an experience in mind—and many people are not willing to believe that a playwright is interested in anything but popular success—there may be some point in comparing the two estates.

The sort of life that I had had previous to this popular success was one that required endurance, a life of clawing and scratching along a sheer surface and holding on tight with raw fingers to every inch of rock higher than the one caught hold of before, but it was a good life because it was the sort of life for which the human organism is created.

I was not aware of how much vital energy had gone into this struggle until the struggle was removed. I was out on a level plateau with my arms still thrashing and my lungs still grabbing at air that no longer resisted. This was security at last.

I sat down and looked about me and was suddenly very depressed. I thought to myself, this is just a period of adjustment. Tomorrow morning I will wake up in this first-class hotel suite above the discreet hum of an East Side boulevard and I will appreciate its elegance and luxuriate in its comforts and know that I have arrived at our American plan of Olympus. Tomorrow morning when I look at the green satin sofa I will fall in love with it. It is only temporarily that the green satin looks like slime on stagnant water.

But in the morning the inoffensive little sofa looked more revolting than the night before and I was already getting too fat for the $125 suit which a fashionable acquaintance had selected for me. In the suite things began to break accidentally. An arm came off the sofa. Cigarette burns appeared on the polished surface of the furniture. Windows were left open and a rain storm flooded the suite. But the maid always put it straight and the patience of the management was inexhaustible. Late parties could not offend them seriously. Nothing short of a demolition bomb seemed to bother my neighbors.

I lived on room service. But in this, too, there was a disenchantment. Some time between the moment when I ordered dinner over the phone and when it was rolled into my living room like a corpse on a rubber-wheeled table, I lost all interest in it. Once I ordered a sirloin steak and a chocolate sundae, but everything was so cunningly disguised on the table that I mistook the chocolate sauce for gravy and poured it over the sirloin steak.

Of course all this was the more trivial aspect of a spiritual dislocation that began to manifest itself in far more disturbing ways. I soon found myself becoming indifferent to people. A well of cynicism rose in me. Conversations all sounded as if they had been recorded years ago and were being played back on a turntable. Sincerity and kindliness seemed to have gone out of my friends' voices. I suspected them of hypocrisy. I stopped calling them, stopped seeing them. I was impatient of what I took to be inane flattery.

I got so sick of hearing people say, "I loved your play!" that I could not say thank you any more. I choked on the words and turned rudely away from the usually sincere person. I no longer felt any pride in the play itself but began to dislike it, probably because I felt too lifeless inside ever to create another. I was walking around dead in my shoes and I knew it but there were no friends I knew or trusted sufficiently, at that time, to take them aside and tell them what was the matter.

This curious condition persisted about three months, till late spring, when I decided to have another eye operation mainly because of the excuse it gave me to withdraw from the world behind a gauze mask. It was my fourth eye operation, and perhaps I should explain that I had been afflicted for about five years with a cataract on my left eye which required a series of needling operations and finally an operation on the muscle of the eye. (The eye is still in my head. So much for that.)

Well, the gauze mask served a purpose. While I was resting in the hospital the friends whom I had neglected or affronted in one way or another began to call on me and now that I was in pain and darkness, their voices seemed to have changed, or rather that unpleasant mutation which I had suspected earlier in the season had now disappeared and they sounded now as they had used to sound in the lamented days of my obscurity. Once more they were sincere and kindly voices with the ring of truth in them and that quality of understanding for which I had originally sought them out.

As far as my physical vision was concerned, this last operation was only relatively successful (although it left me with an apparently clear black pupil in the right position, or nearly so) but in another, figurative way, it had served a much deeper purpose.

When the gauze mask was removed I found myself in a readjusted world. I checked out of the handsome suite at the first-class hotel, packed my papers and a few incidental belongings and left for Mexico, an elemental country where you can quickly forget the false dignities and conceits imposed by success, a country where vagrants innocent as children curl up to sleep on the pavements and human voices, especially when their language is not familiar to the ear, are soft as birds'. My public self, that artifice of mirrors, did not exist here and so my natural being was resumed.

Then, as a final act of restoration, I settled for a while at Chapala to work on a play called "The Poker Night," which later became "A Streetcar Named Desire." It is only in his work that an artist can find reality and satisfaction, for the actual world is less intense than the world of his invention and consequently his life, without recourse to violent disorder, does not seem very substantial. The right condition for him is that in which his work is not only convenient but unavoidable.

For me a convenient place to work is a remote place among strangers where there is good swimming. But life should require a certain minimal effort. You should not have too many people waiting on you, you should have to do most things for yourself. Hotel service is embarrassing. Maids, waiters, bellhops, porters and so forth are the most embarrassing people in the world for they continually remind you of inequities which we accept as the proper thing. The sight of an ancient woman, gasping and wheezing as she drags a heavy pail of water down a hotel corridor to mop up the mess of some drunken overprivileged guest, is one that sickens and weighs upon the heart and withers it with shame for this world in which it is not only tolerated but regarded as proof positive that the wheels of Democracy are functioning as they should without interference from above or below. Nobody should have to clean up anybody else's mess in this world. It is terribly bad for both parties, but probably worse for the one receiving the service.

I have been corrupted as much as anyone else by the vast number of menial services which our society has grown to expect and depend on. We should do for ourselves or let the machines do for us, the glorious technology that is supposed to be the new light of the world. We are like a man who has bought a great amount of equipment for a camping trip, who has the canoe and the tent and the fishing lines and the axe and the guns, the mackinaw and the blankets, but who now, when all the preparations and the provisions are piled expertly together, is suddenly too timid to set out on the journey but remains where he was yesterday and the day before and the day before that, looking suspiciously through white lace curtains at the clear sky he distrusts. Our great technology is a God-given chance for adventure and for progress which we are afraid to attempt. Our ideas and our ideals remain exactly what they were and where they were three centuries ago. No. I beg your pardon. It is no longer safe for a man even to declare them!

This is a long excursion from a small theme into a large one which I did not intend to make, so let me go back to what I was saying before.

This is an oversimplification. One does not escape that easily from the seduction of an effete way of life. You cannot arbitrarily say to yourself, I will now continue my life as it was before this thing, Success, happened to me. But once you fully apprehend the vacuity of a life without struggle you are equipped with the basic means of salvation. Once you know this is true, that the heart of man, his body and his brain, are forged in a white-hot furnace for the purpose of conflict (the struggle of creation) and that with the conflict removed, the man is a sword cutting daisies, that not privation but luxury is the wolf at the door and that the fangs of this wolf are all the little vanities and conceits and laxities that Success is heir to—why, then with this knowledge you are at least in a position of knowing where danger lies.

You know, then, that the public Somebody you are when you "have a name" is a fiction created with mirrors and that the only somebody worth being is the solitary and unseen you that existed from your first breath and which is the sum of your actions and so is constantly in a state of becoming under your own violation—and knowing these things, you can even survive the catastrophe of Success!

It is never altogether too late, unless you embrace the Bitch Goddess, as William James called her, with both arms and find in her smothering caresses exactly what the homesick little boy in you always wanted, absolute protection and utter effortlessness. Security is a kind of death, I think, and it can come to you in a storm of royalty checks beside a kidney-shaped pool in Beverly Hills or anywhere at all that is removed from the conditions that made you an artist, if that's what you are or were or intended to be. Ask anyone who has experienced the kind of success I am talking about— What good is it? Perhaps to get an honest answer you will have to give him a shot of truth serum but the word he will finally groan is unprintable in genteel publications.

Then what is good? The obsessive interest in human affairs plus a certain amount of compassion and moral conviction, that first made the experience of living something that must be translated into pigment or music or bodily movement or poetry or prose or anything that's dynamic and expressive—that's what's good for you if you're at all serious in your aims. William Saroyan wrote a great play on this theme, that purity of heart is the one success worth having. "In the time of your life—live!" That time is short and it doesn't return again. It is slipping away while I write this and while you read it, and the monosyllable of the clock is Loss, loss, loss, unless you devote your heart to its opposition.

393.2-3 *Nobody . . .* CUMMINGS] Final line of untitled poem beginning "somewhere I have never travelled, gladly beyond" (1931).

400.27 Guernica] Basque town bombed during the Spanish Civil War on April 26, 1937, by aircraft of the German Condor Legion, sent by Hitler to support the Nationalist forces led by General Francisco Franco. About 300 people were killed in the attack.

401.20 "OU SONT LES NEIGES."] Cf. François Villon, "Ballade des Dames du Temps Jadis": "Où sont les neiges d'antan" ("Where are the snows of yesteryear").

433.5 *"scattering poems in the sky"*] Cf. E. E. Cummings' untitled poem beginning "the hours rise up putting off stars and it is" (1922).

438.34 Dizzy Dean] Pitcher for the St. Louis Cardinals.

448.15–16 Century of Progress] Century of Progress Exposition in Chicago, 1933–34.

448.35–39 O blow, ye winds . . . away!] Cf. the chorus in Charles Edward Caryll's "Davy and the Goblin: A Nautical Ballad" (1886).

A STREETCAR NAMED DESIRE

467.1 *A Streetcar Named Desire*] *A Streetcar Named Desire* was presented at the Barrymore Theatre in New York on December 3, 1947, by Irene Selznick. It was directed by Elia Kazan, with the following cast: NEGRO WOMAN: Gee Gee James; EUNICE HUBBELL: Peg Hillias; STANLEY KOWALSKI: Marlon Brando; STELLA KOWALSKI: Kim Hunter; STEVE HUBBELL: Rudy Bond; HAROLD MITCHELL (MITCH): Karl Malden; MEXICAN WOMAN: Edna Thomas; TAMALE VENDOR: Richard Carlyle; BLANCHE DUBOIS: Jessica Tandy; PABLO GONZALES: Nick Dennis; A YOUNG COLLECTOR: Vito Christi; NURSE: Ann Dere; DOCTOR: Richard Garrick.

Scenery and lighting by Jo Meilziner, costumes by Lucinda Ballard. The action of the play takes place in the spring, summer, and early fall in New Orleans. It was performed with intermissions after Scene Four and Scene Six.

Assistant to the producer: Irving Schneider. Musical Advisor: Lehman Engel.

469.4 *The section*] The Faubourg Marigny, just outside the French Quarter.

471.16 street-car named Desire,] Desire, Cemeteries, and Elysian Fields were streetcar lines in and around the French Quarter until 1948. They did not connect in the manner described in the play.

474.25–27 Only . . . Weir!] Edgar Allan Poe, "Ulalame" (1847), line 9.

497.6 Xavier Cugat!] Popular Cuban orchestra leader of the 1940s.

498.9–11 "And . . . Browning!] Elizabeth Barrett Browning, *Sonnets from the Portuguese* (1850), sonnet 43, lines 13–14.

521.4 owl-car.] The last scheduled streetcar of the night.

537.17 Huey Long . . . King!"] Long often quoted this phrase from William Jennings Bryan's "Cross of Gold" speech delivered at the 1896 Democratic National Convention, and used it as the title of his autobiography.

546.31 *Flores para los muertos.*] Flowers for the dead.

SUMMER AND SMOKE

565.1 *Summer and Smoke*] *Summer and Smoke* was first produced by Margo Jones at her theater in Dallas, Texas. It was later produced and directed by Miss Jones in New York, opening at the Music Box Theater, October 6, 1948, with Margaret Phillips and Ted Andrews in the two leading roles; incidental music by Paul Bowles and scenery by Jo Mielziner.

565.2–4 *Who* . . . RILKE] The opening of Rainer Maria Rilke's *Duino Elegies.*

620.20–21 Le doy . . . cielo!] I give her the earth, and if the earth is not enough—I give her the sky.

630.3–4 Sophie Newcombe] Women's college in New Orleans.

641.8–9 From the Peabody . . . Vicksburg.] A popular description of the limits of the Mississippi Delta.

THE ROSE TATTOO

645.1 *The Rose Tattoo*] *The Rose Tattoo* was first produced by Cheryl Crawford at the Erlanger Theater in Chicago on December 29, 1950. It had its Broadway opening on February 3, 1951, at the Martin Beck Theater in New York City, with Daniel Mann as director, setting by Boris Aronson and music by David Diamond. Production Associate: Bea Lawrence. Assistant to Producer: Paul Bigelow. *Cast of the New York Production*: SALVATORE: Salvatore Mineo; VIVI: Judy Ratner; BRUNO: Salvatore Taormina; ASSUNTA: Ludmilla Toretzka; ROSA DELLE ROSE: Phyllis Love; SERAFINA DELLE ROSE: Maureen Stapleton; ESTRELLE HOHENGARTEN: Sonia Sorel; THE STREGA: Daisy Belmore; GIUSEPPINA: Rossana San Marco; PEPPINA: Augusta Merighi; VIOLETTA: Vivian Nathan; MARIELLA: Penny Santon; TERESA: Nancy Franklin; FATHER DE LEO: Robert Carricart; A DOCTOR: Andrew Duggan; MISS YORKE: Dorrit Kelton; FLORA: Jane Hoffman; BESSIE: Florence Sundstrom; JACK HUNTER: Don Murray; THE SALESMAN: Eddie Hyans; ALVARO MANGIACAVALLO: Eli Wallach; A MAN: David Stewart; ANOTHER MAN: Martin Balsam.

647.2–4 CARSON MCCULLERS . . . world."] "When We Are Lost," first published in *New Directions X* in 1948.

656.1–7 *O slinger!* . . . TRANSLATION] Saint-John Perse, *Anabase* (1924), translated by T. S. Eliot as *Anabasis* in 1930.

660.24–25 Stai zitta . . . Vieni qui] Be quiet. Come here.

660.30 Che altre cose?] What other thing?

661.20 Stai tranquilla! Calmati] Stay quiet! Be calm!

662.30 Che bella stoffa] What pretty material.

663.10 STREGA] Witch, sorceress.

663.27–28 Il becco della strega!] The witch's goat!

667.22–23 Ferme . . . di Dio!] Stop! Stop in the name of God!

668.29 Sicuro!] For sure!

669.21 Apri la porta!] Open the door!

669.35 Aiuto!] Help!

670.24 Smetilla,] Quit it.

671.15 Lasciami stare,] Leave me alone.

671.25 figlia . . . cosí!] Daughter, you should not talk like that!

671.28 Ecco la—chiave . . .] Here is the key.

672.33 Ho solo . . . questo mondo!] I have only you in this world!

673.12–13 'Sta fetentissima . . . maledetta!] It's the filthiest school! A cursed school!

673.25 Piantala,] Leave it.

673.32 Aspetta!] Wait!

674.6 Guardate!] Watch yourself!

685.33 Fa niente . . .] Doesn't matter.

687.30–31 Pazza . . . Finiscila!] Lunatic! Finish her.

688.3 per piacere!] If you please!

697.15 Zitta ora!] Quiet now!

704.13 Ma com'è . . . Napoletano?] But how strange! Are you from Naples?

704.19 Dov'è il gabinetto?] Where's the bathroom?

713.22 Miei . . . pomodori!] My tomatoes! Watch out for my tomatoes!

715.6 *Rondinella felice!*] Fortunate swallow!

716.29 C'è nessuno?] No one here?

726.34 Torno subito,] I'll be right back.

727.4 dove siete?] Where are you?

727.9 non voglio farlo!] I don't want to do it!

728.14 Sono . . . feroce!] I am a beast, a wild beast!

CAMINO REAL

741.1 *Camino Real*] *Camino Real* was first produced by Cheryl Crawford and Ethel Reiner, in association with Walter P. Chrysler, Jr., and following tryouts in New Haven and Philadelphia, it had its Broadway premiere on March 19, 1953, at the Martin Beck Theatre. The production was directed by Elia Kazan, with the assistance of Anna Sokolow; the scenery and costumes were designed by Lemuel Ayers; and incidental music was contributed by Bernardo Ségall. Production associate: Anderson Lawler. *Cast of the Broadway Production*: GUTMAN: Frank Silvera; SURVIVOR: Guy Thomajan; ROSITA: Aza Bard; FIRST OFFICER: Henry Silva; JACQUES CASANOVA: Joseph Anthony; LA MADRECITA DE LOS PERDIDOS: Vivian Nathan; HER SON: Rolando Valdez; KILROY: Eli Wallach; FIRST STREET CLEANER: Nehemiah Persoff; SECOND STREET CLEANER: Fred Sadoff; ABDULLAH: Ernesto Gonzalez; A BUM IN A WINDOW: Martin Balsam; A. RATT: Mike Gazzo; THE LOAN SHARK: Salem Ludwig; BARON DE CHARLUS: David J. Stewart; LOBO: Ronne Aul; SECOND OFFICER: William Lennard; A GROTESQUE MUMMER: Gluck Sandor; MARGUERITE GAUTIER: Jo Van Fleet; LADY MULLIGAN: Lucille Patton; WAITER: Page Johnson; LORD BYRON: Hurd Hatfield; NAVIGATOR OF THE FUGITIVO: Antony Vorno; PILOT OF THE FUGITIVO: Martin Balsam; MARKET WOMAN: Charlotte Jones; SECOND MARKET WOMAN: Joanna Vischer; STREET VENDOR: Ruth Volner; LORD MULLIGAN: Parker Wilson; THE GYPSY: Jennie Goldstein; HER DAUGHTER, ESMERALDA: Barbara Baxley; NURSIE: Salem Ludwig; EVA: Mary Grey; THE INSTRUCTOR: David J. Stewart; ASSISTANT INSTRUCTOR: Parker Wilson; MEDICAL STUDENT: Page Johnson; DON QUIXOTE: Hurd Hatfield; SANCHO PANZA, PRUDENCE DUVERNOY, OLYMPE: *Not in production*. Street Vendors: Aza Bard, Ernesto Gonzalez, Charlotte Jones, Gluck Sandor, Joanna Vische, Ruth Volner, Antony Vorno. Guests: Martin Balsam, Mary Grey, Lucille Patton, Joanna Vischer, Parker Wilson. Passengers: Mike Gazzo, Mary Grey, Page Johnson, Charlotte Jones, William Lennard, Salem Ludwig, Joanna Vischer, Ruth Volner. At the Fiesta: Ronne Aul, Martin Balsam, Aza Bard, Mike Gazzo, Ernesto Gonzalez, Mary Grey, Charlotte Jones, William Lennard, Nehemiah Persoff, Fred Sadoff, Gluck Sandor, Joanna Vischer, Antony Vorno, Parker Wilson.

744.38–39 Some poet . . . but be.] Archibald MacLeish, in the final lines of "Ars Poetica" (1926).

751.2 *Devoir!*] Duty!

751.16 Sus papeles! Sus documentos] Your papers! Your documents.

757.10–11 *A donde la fuente?*] Where is the fountain?

757.17 La fuente está seca!] The fountain is dry!

762.11–13 Rojo . . . de miedo!] The sun is red! The sun is red with blood! The moon is white! The moon is white with fear!

764.7 *Kilroy*] Graffiti scrawled on walls by American soldiers during World War II.

766.11 Dulces . . . con leche!] Sweets, sweets! Lottery! Lottery! Pastries, coffee with milk!

770.8 *Baron de Charlus,*] A character in Marcel Proust's *A la recherche du temps perdu (Remembrance of Things Past).*

770.33 Ingreso Libero] Free access.

773.18 the Bird Circuit.] Reference to several gay bars in New York in the 1940's and 1950's named after birds.

779.30 Ponga selo!] Put it on!

783.9 Recuerdos] Souvenirs.

786.32–33 Secret Order . . . Cross!] The Rosicrucians, an occultist secret society.

800.9 Che . . . fare!] What can you do?

800.16 Forse . . . so!] Perhaps, perhaps, I don't know!

821.18 Forest Lawn . . .] See note 289.15.

836.13–14 "Humankind . . . reality."] Cf. T. S. Eliot, *Murder in the Cathedral*, Part II.

27 WAGONS FULL OF COTTON AND OTHER ONE-ACT PLAYS (1953)

855.34 Victor Herbert] Irish-born American composer (1859–1924) of popular operettas such as *Naughty Marietta* (1910) and *Eileen* (1917).

859.5 Mayo's.] The Mayo Clinic in Rochester, Minnesota.

860.20–21 ça . . . petite!] That goes without saying, my little one!

CAT ON A HOT TIN ROOF

873.1 *Cat on a Hot Tin Roof*] *Cat on a Hot Tin Roof* was presented at the Morosco Theatre in New York on March 24, 1955, by The Playwrights' Company. It was directed by Elia Kazan; the scenery was designed by Jo Mielziner, and the costumes by Lucinda Ballard. The cast was as follows: LACEY: Maxwell Glanville; SOOKEY: Musa Williams; MARGARET: Barbara Bel Geddes; BRICK: Ben Gazzara; MAE: Madeleine Sherwood; GOOPER: Pat Hingle; BIG MAMA: Mildred Dunnock; DIXIE: Pauline Hahn; BUSTER: Darryl Richard; SONNY: Seth Edwards; TRIXIE: Janice Dunn; BIG DADDY: Burl Ives; REVEREND TOOKER: Fred Stewart; DOCTOR BAUGH: R. G.

Armstrong; DAISY: Eva Vaughan Smith; BRIGHTIE: Brownie McGhee; SMALL: Sonny Terry.

873.2–6 *And you* . . . THOMAS] "Do Not Go Gentle Into That Good Night," lines 16–19.

876.35 my first preface to a long play.] See pp. 275-86 in this volume.

955.23 hoppin' john.] A southern dish of black-eyed peas, rice, and seasoning.

Library of Congress Cataloging-in-Publication Data

Williams, Tennessee, 1911–1983.
[Plays. Selections]
Plays / Tennessee Williams.
p. cm. — (The Library of America 119–120)
Selection and notes by Mel Gussow and Kenneth Holditch.
Contents [v. 1] Plays 1937–1955: Spring storm. Not about nightingales. Battle of angels. I rise in flame, cried the phoenix. From 27 wagons full of cotton (1946). . . . The glass menagerie. A streetcar named Desire. Summer and smoke. The rose tattoo. Camino Real. From 27 Wagons full of cotton (1953). . . . Cat on a hot tin roof—[v. 2] Plays 1957–1980 : Orpheus descending. Suddenly last summer. Sweet bird of youth. Period of adjustment. The night of the iguana. The eccentricities of a nightingale. The milk train doesn't stop here anymore. The mutilated. Kingdom of earth (The seven descents of Myrtle). Small craft warnings. Out cry. Vieux Carré. A lovely Sunday for Creve Coeur.
ISBN 1–883011–86–8 (v. 1 : alk. paper)—ISBN 1–883011–87–6 (v. 2 : alk. paper)
I. Gussow, Mel. II. Holditch, Kenneth. III. Title. IV. Series.
PS3545.I5365 A6 2000
812'.54—dc21 00-030190

THE LIBRARY OF AMERICA SERIES

The Library of America fosters appreciation and pride in America's literary heritage by publishing, and keeping permanently in print, authoritative editions of America's best and most significant writing. An independent nonprofit organization, it was founded in 1979 with seed funding from the National Endowment for the Humanities and the Ford Foundation.

1. Herman Melville: *Typee, Omoo, Mardi*
2. Nathaniel Hawthorne: *Tales and Sketches*
3. Walt Whitman: *Poetry and Prose*
4. Harriet Beecher Stowe: *Three Novels*
5. Mark Twain: *Mississippi Writings*
6. Jack London: *Novels and Stories*
7. Jack London: *Novels and Social Writings*
8. William Dean Howells: *Novels 1875–1886*
9. Herman Melville: *Redburn, White-Jacket, Moby-Dick*
10. Nathaniel Hawthorne: *Collected Novels*
11. Francis Parkman: *France and England in North America*, vol. I
12. Francis Parkman: *France and England in North America*, vol. II
13. Henry James: *Novels 1871–1880*
14. Henry Adams: *Novels, Mont Saint Michel, The Education*
15. Ralph Waldo Emerson: *Essays and Lectures*
16. Washington Irving: *History, Tales and Sketches*
17. Thomas Jefferson: *Writings*
18. Stephen Crane: *Prose and Poetry*
19. Edgar Allan Poe: *Poetry and Tales*
20. Edgar Allan Poe: *Essays and Reviews*
21. Mark Twain: *The Innocents Abroad, Roughing It*
22. Henry James: *Literary Criticism: Essays, American & English Writers*
23. Henry James: *Literary Criticism: European Writers & The Prefaces*
24. Herman Melville: *Pierre, Israel Potter, The Confidence-Man, Tales & Billy Budd*
25. William Faulkner: *Novels 1930–1935*
26. James Fenimore Cooper: *The Leatherstocking Tales*, vol. I
27. James Fenimore Cooper: *The Leatherstocking Tales*, vol. II
28. Henry David Thoreau: *A Week, Walden, The Maine Woods, Cape Cod*
29. Henry James: *Novels 1881–1886*
30. Edith Wharton: *Novels*
31. Henry Adams: *History of the U.S. during the Administrations of Jefferson*
32. Henry Adams: *History of the U.S. during the Administrations of Madison*
33. Frank Norris: *Novels and Essays*
34. W.E.B. Du Bois: *Writings*
35. Willa Cather: *Early Novels and Stories*
36. Theodore Dreiser: *Sister Carrie, Jennie Gerhardt, Twelve Men*
37a. Benjamin Franklin: *Silence Dogood, The Busy-Body, & Early Writings*
37b. Benjamin Franklin: *Autobiography, Poor Richard, & Later Writings*
38. William James: *Writings 1902–1910*
39. Flannery O'Connor: *Collected Works*
40. Eugene O'Neill: *Complete Plays 1913–1920*
41. Eugene O'Neill: *Complete Plays 1920–1931*
42. Eugene O'Neill: *Complete Plays 1932–1943*
43. Henry James: *Novels 1886–1890*
44. William Dean Howells: *Novels 1886–1888*
45. Abraham Lincoln: *Speeches and Writings 1832–1858*
46. Abraham Lincoln: *Speeches and Writings 1859–1865*
47. Edith Wharton: *Novellas and Other Writings*
48. William Faulkner: *Novels 1936–1940*
49. Willa Cather: *Later Novels*
50. Ulysses S. Grant: *Memoirs and Selected Letters*
51. William Tecumseh Sherman: *Memoirs*
52. Washington Irving: *Bracebridge Hall, Tales of a Traveller, The Alhambra*
53. Francis Parkman: *The Oregon Trail, The Conspiracy of Pontiac*
54. James Fenimore Cooper: *Sea Tales: The Pilot, The Red Rover*
55. Richard Wright: *Early Works*
56. Richard Wright: *Later Works*
57. Willa Cather: *Stories, Poems, and Other Writings*
58. William James: *Writings 1878–1899*
59. Sinclair Lewis: *Main Street & Babbitt*
60. Mark Twain: *Collected Tales, Sketches, Speeches, & Essays 1852–1890*
61. Mark Twain: *Collected Tales, Sketches, Speeches, & Essays 1891–1910*
62. *The Debate on the Constitution: Part One*
63. *The Debate on the Constitution: Part Two*
64. Henry James: *Collected Travel Writings: Great Britain & America*
65. Henry James: *Collected Travel Writings: The Continent*

66. *American Poetry: The Nineteenth Century*, Vol. 1
67. *American Poetry: The Nineteenth Century*, Vol. 2
68. Frederick Douglass: *Autobiographies*
69. Sarah Orne Jewett: *Novels and Stories*
70. Ralph Waldo Emerson: *Collected Poems and Translations*
71. Mark Twain: *Historical Romances*
72. John Steinbeck: *Novels and Stories 1932–1937*
73. William Faulkner: *Novels 1942–1954*
74. Zora Neale Hurston: *Novels and Stories*
75. Zora Neale Hurston: *Folklore, Memoirs, and Other Writings*
76. Thomas Paine: *Collected Writings*
77. *Reporting World War II: American Journalism 1938–1944*
78. *Reporting World War II: American Journalism 1944–1946*
79. Raymond Chandler: *Stories and Early Novels*
80. Raymond Chandler: *Later Novels and Other Writings*
81. Robert Frost: *Collected Poems, Prose, & Plays*
82. Henry James: *Complete Stories 1892–1898*
83. Henry James: *Complete Stories 1898–1910*
84. William Bartram: *Travels and Other Writings*
85. John Dos Passos: *U.S.A.*
86. John Steinbeck: *The Grapes of Wrath and Other Writings 1936–1941*
87. Vladimir Nabokov: *Novels and Memoirs 1941–1951*
88. Vladimir Nabokov: *Novels 1955–1962*
89. Vladimir Nabokov: *Novels 1969–1974*
90. James Thurber: *Writings and Drawings*
91. George Washington: *Writings*
92. John Muir: *Nature Writings*
93. Nathanael West: *Novels and Other Writings*
94. *Crime Novels: American Noir of the 1930s and 40s*
95. *Crime Novels: American Noir of the 1950s*
96. Wallace Stevens: *Collected Poetry and Prose*
97. James Baldwin: *Early Novels and Stories*
98. James Baldwin: *Collected Essays*
99. Gertrude Stein: *Writings 1903–1932*
100. Gertrude Stein: *Writings 1932–1946*
101. Eudora Welty: *Complete Novels*
102. Eudora Welty: *Stories, Essays, & Memoir*
103. Charles Brockden Brown: *Three Gothic Novels*
104. *Reporting Vietnam: American Journalism 1959–1969*
105. *Reporting Vietnam: American Journalism 1969–1975*
106. Henry James: *Complete Stories 1874–1884*
107. Henry James: *Complete Stories 1884–1891*
108. *American Sermons: The Pilgrims to Martin Luther King Jr.*
109. James Madison: *Writings*
110. Dashiell Hammett: *Complete Novels*
111. Henry James: *Complete Stories 1864–1874*
112. William Faulkner: *Novels 1957–1962*
113. John James Audubon: *Writings & Drawings*
114. *Slave Narratives*
115. *American Poetry: The Twentieth Century*, Vol. 1
116. *American Poetry: The Twentieth Century*, Vol. 2
117. F. Scott Fitzgerald: *Novels and Stories 1920–1922*
118. Henry Wadsworth Longfellow: *Poems and Other Writings*
119. Tennessee Williams: *Plays 1937–1955*
120. Tennessee Williams: *Plays 1957–1980*
121. Edith Wharton: *Collected Stories 1891–1910*
122. Edith Wharton: *Collected Stories 1911–1937*
123. *The American Revolution: Writings from the War of Independence*
124. Henry David Thoreau: *Collected Essays and Poems*
125. Dashiell Hammett: *Crime Stories and Other Writings*
126. Dawn Powell: *Novels 1930–1942*
127. Dawn Powell: *Novels 1944–1962*
128. Carson McCullers: *Complete Novels*
129. Alexander Hamilton: *Writings*
130. Mark Twain: *The Gilded Age and Later Novels*
131. Charles W. Chesnutt: *Stories, Novels, and Essays*
132. John Steinbeck: *Novels 1942–1952*
133. Sinclair Lewis: *Arrowsmith, Elmer Gantry, Dodsworth*
134. Paul Bowles: *The Sheltering Sky, Let It Come Down, The Spider's House*
135. Paul Bowles: *Collected Stories & Later Writings*
136. Kate Chopin: *Complete Novels & Stories*
137. *Reporting Civil Rights: American Journalism 1941–1963*
138. *Reporting Civil Rights: American Journalism 1963–1973*
139. Henry James: *Novels 1896–1899*
140. Theodore Dreiser: *An American Tragedy*
141. Saul Bellow: *Novels 1944–1953*
142. John Dos Passos: *Novels 1920–1925*
143. John Dos Passos: *Travel Books and Other Writings*

144. Ezra Pound: *Poems and Translations*
145. James Weldon Johnson: *Writings*
146. Washington Irving: *Three Western Narratives*
147. Alexis de Tocqueville: *Democracy in America*
148. James T. Farrell: *Studs Lonigan: A Trilogy*
149. Isaac Bashevis Singer: *Collected Stories I*
150. Isaac Bashevis Singer: *Collected Stories II*
151. Isaac Bashevis Singer: *Collected Stories III*
152. Kaufman & Co.: *Broadway Comedies*
153. Theodore Roosevelt: *The Rough Riders, An Autobiography*
154. Theodore Roosevelt: *Letters and Speeches*
155. H. P. Lovecraft: *Tales*
156. Louisa May Alcott: *Little Women, Little Men, Jo's Boys*
157. Philip Roth: *Novels & Stories 1959–1962*
158. Philip Roth: *Novels 1967–1972*
159. James Agee: *Let Us Now Praise Famous Men, A Death in the Family*
160. James Agee: *Film Writing & Selected Journalism*
161. Richard Henry Dana, Jr.: *Two Years Before the Mast & Other Voyages*
162. Henry James: *Novels 1901–1902*
163. Arthur Miller: *Collected Plays 1944–1961*
164. William Faulkner: *Novels 1926–1929*
165. Philip Roth: *Novels 1973–1977*
166. *American Speeches: Part One*
167. *American Speeches: Part Two*
168. Hart Crane: *Complete Poems & Selected Letters*
169. Saul Bellow: *Novels 1956–1964*
170. John Steinbeck: *Travels with Charley and Later Novels*
171. Capt. John Smith: *Writings with Other Narratives*
172. Thornton Wilder: *Collected Plays & Writings on Theater*
173. Philip K. Dick: *Four Novels of the 1960s*
174. Jack Kerouac: *Road Novels 1957–1960*
175. Philip Roth: *Zuckerman Bound*
176. Edmund Wilson: *Literary Essays & Reviews of the 1920s & 30s*
177. Edmund Wilson: *Literary Essays & Reviews of the 1930s & 40s*
178. *American Poetry: The 17th & 18th Centuries*
179. William Maxwell: *Early Novels & Stories*
180. Elizabeth Bishop: *Poems, Prose, & Letters*
181. A. J. Liebling: *World War II Writings*
182s. *American Earth: Environmental Writing Since Thoreau*
183. Philip K. Dick: *Five Novels of the 1960s & 70s*
184. William Maxwell: *Later Novels & Stories*
185. Philip Roth: *Novels & Other Narratives 1986–1991*
186. Katherine Anne Porter: *Collected Stories & Other Writings*
187. John Ashbery: *Collected Poems 1956–1987*
188. John Cheever: *Collected Stories & Other Writings*
189. John Cheever: *Complete Novels*
190. Lafcadio Hearn: *American Writings*
191. A. J. Liebling: *The Sweet Science & Other Writings*
192s. *The Lincoln Anthology: Great Writers on His Life and Legacy from 1860 to Now*
193. Philip K. Dick: *VALIS & Later Novels*
194. Thornton Wilder: *The Bridge of San Luis Rey and Other Novels 1926–1948*
195. Raymond Carver: *Collected Stories*
196. *American Fantastic Tales: Terror and the Uncanny from Poe to the Pulps*
197. *American Fantastic Tales: Terror and the Uncanny from the 1940s to Now*
198. John Marshall: *Writings*
199s. *The Mark Twain Anthology: Great Writers on His Life and Works*
200. Mark Twain: *A Tramp Abroad, Following the Equator, Other Travels*
201. Ralph Waldo Emerson: *Selected Journals 1820–1842*
202. Ralph Waldo Emerson: *Selected Journals 1841–1877*
203. *The American Stage: Writing on Theater from Washington Irving to Tony Kushner*
204. Shirley Jackson: *Novels & Stories*
205. Philip Roth: *Novels 1993–1995*
206. H. L. Mencken: *Prejudices: First, Second, and Third Series*
207. H. L. Mencken: *Prejudices: Fourth, Fifth, and Sixth Series*
208. John Kenneth Galbraith: *The Affluent Society and Other Writings 1952–1967*
209. Saul Bellow: *Novels 1970–1982*
210. Lynd Ward: *Gods' Man, Madman's Drum, Wild Pilgrimage*
211. Lynd Ward: *Prelude to a Million Years, Song Without Words, Vertigo*
212. *The Civil War: The First Year Told by Those Who Lived It*
213. John Adams: *Revolutionary Writings 1755–1775*
214. John Adams: *Revolutionary Writings 1775–1783*
215. Henry James: *Novels 1903–1911*
216. Kurt Vonnegut: *Novels & Stories 1963–1973*
217. *Harlem Renaissance: Five Novels of the 1920s*

218. *Harlem Renaissance: Four Novels of the 1930s*
219. Ambrose Bierce: *The Devil's Dictionary, Tales, & Memoirs*
220. Philip Roth: *The American Trilogy 1997–2000*
221. *The Civil War: The Second Year Told by Those Who Lived It*
222. Barbara W. Tuchman: *The Guns of August & The Proud Tower*
223. Arthur Miller: *Collected Plays 1964–1982*
224. Thornton Wilder: *The Eighth Day, Theophilus North, Autobiographical Writings*
225. David Goodis: *Five Noir Novels of the 1940s & 50s*
226. Kurt Vonnegut: *Novels & Stories 1950–1962*
227. *American Science Fiction: Four Classic Novels 1953–1956*
228. *American Science Fiction: Five Classic Novels 1956–1958*
229. Laura Ingalls Wilder: *The Little House Books, Volume One*
230. Laura Ingalls Wilder: *The Little House Books, Volume Two*
231. Jack Kerouac: *Collected Poems*
232. *The War of 1812: Writings from America's Second War of Independence*
233. *American Antislavery Writings: Colonial Beginnings to Emancipation*
234. *The Civil War: The Third Year Told by Those Who Lived It*
235. Sherwood Anderson: *Collected Stories*
236. Philip Roth: *Novels 2001–2007*
237. Philip Roth: *Nemeses*
238. Aldo Leopold: *A Sand County Almanac & Other Writings on Ecology and Conservation*
239. May Swenson: *Collected Poems*
240. W. S. Merwin: *Collected Poems 1952–1993*
241. W. S. Merwin: *Collected Poems 1996–2011*

*This book is set in 10 point Linotron Galliard,
a face designed for photocomposition by Matthew Carter
and based on the sixteenth-century face Granjon. The paper
is acid-free lightweight opaque and meets the requirements
for permanence of the American National Standards Institute.
The binding material is Brillianta, a woven rayon cloth made
by Van Heek–Scholco Textielfabrieken, Holland. Composition
by The Clarinda Company. Printing and binding
by Edwards Brothers Malloy, Ann Arbor.
Designed by Bruce Campbell.*

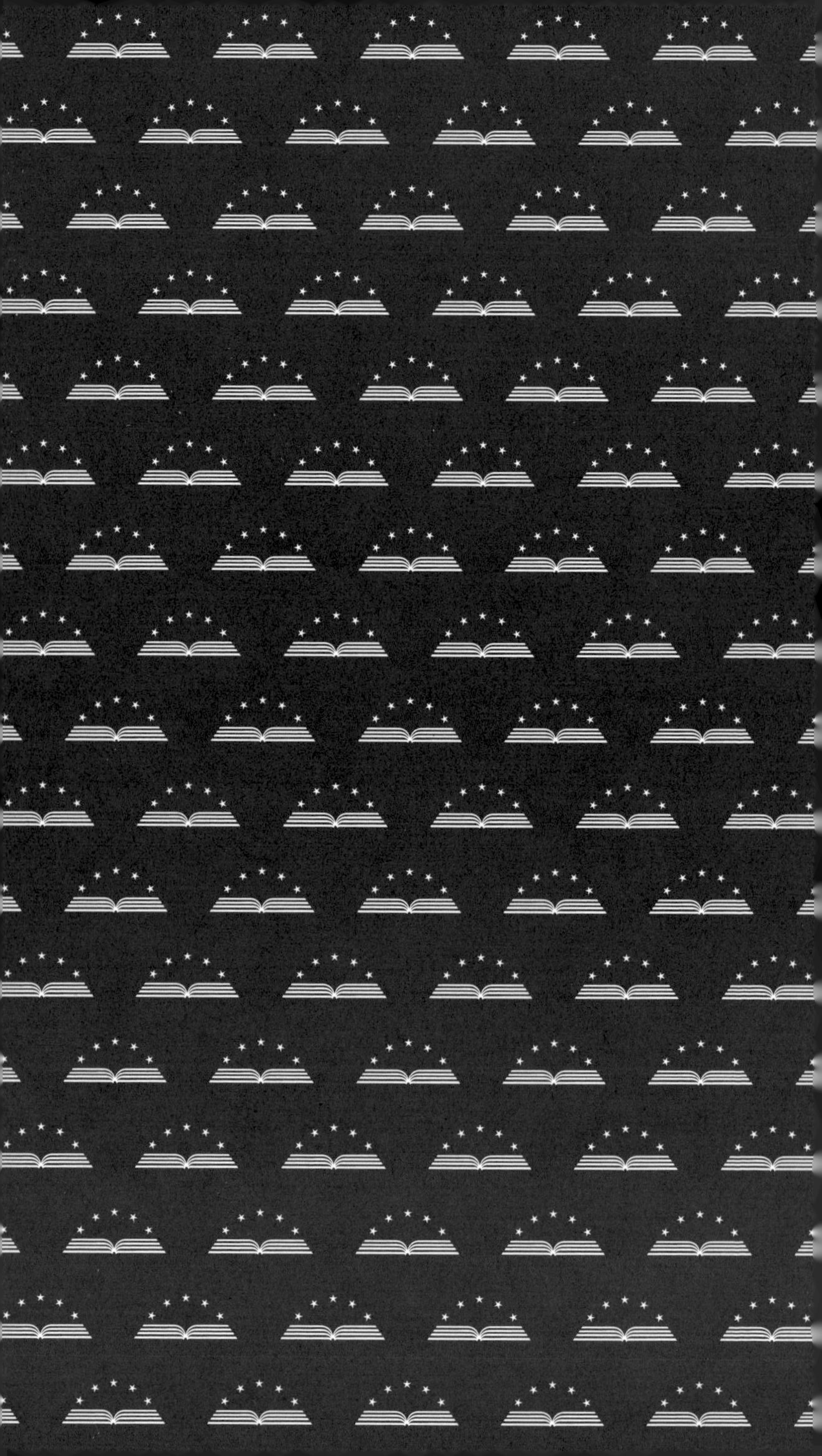